D0119385

WORDMASTER

J A Coleman

BROCKHAMPTON PRESS
LONDON

This book is dedicated to the memory of my father,
Humphrey James Coleman,
who also loved words.

First published in Great Britain 1994
by Eric Dobby Publishing Limited
12 Warnford Road
Orpington, Kent, BR6 6LW

This edition published 1998 by Brockhampton Press,
a member of Hodder Headline PLC Group
ISBN 1-86019-307-2

By the same author:
The Complete Guide to Cryptic Crosswords
Crossword Dictionary
Cluefinder – A Dictionary of Crossword Clues

Text typeset in Times New Roman by Kevin O'Connor, Poole
Printed and bound in Finland by WSOY

INTRODUCTION

To say that we use a dictionary to look up a word is only an approximation of the truth. Almost invariably we know the word exists and we turn to that word in the dictionary to find some information about it such as its correct pronunciation, meaning, derivation and so on. But what if we do not already know the word or - a familiar enough experience to most of us - know that we know it but cannot call it to mind? 'My brother is a ... what d'ya call it? He collects coins'. You knew it was 'numismatist' all along but you could not look up 'coin collector' or 'collector of coins' because standard dictionaries don't work that way. You need a dictionary that does work that way - from the definition to the word. You need a reverse dictionary.

Crossword enthusiasts need such a dictionary more than other people. The compiler has a marked advantage; he enters words in his grid asking only that they fit. Then he uses a standard dictionary to find meanings around which he can concoct his devious clues. The solver must work the other way round - from the definition in the clue to the word itself. For this he needs a reverse dictionary.

The standard type of dictionary has been with us for over 200 years. It was not until 1989 that the first reverse dictionary (published by Readers Digest) appeared. *Wordmaster* has its origins a little earlier. I had always felt the need for a dictionary of this sort when struggling with a crossword, such as *The Sunday Times* Mephisto, which regularly uses many words not found in the average solver's vocabulary and the lists appearing in the *Crossword Dictionary* published by Collins over my name constitute a form of reverse dictionary. Since that book contains, in addition to the lists, much material specifically related to crosswords, it was referred to as a Crossword Dictionary rather than a Reverse Dictionary. *Wordmaster* reproduces many of the lists from the Collins book but it has a far wider coverage in both the original subjects and in the range of subjects dealt with. The crossword-specific material has been omitted, leaving only the definition-leading-to-the-word format. Now, if you are stuck for the word for 'Sikh temple', you can turn to the headword Sikh, run down the list to find 'temple' and then across to GURDWARA. It's as simple as that. And if you choose to approach it from the 'temple' end rather than the 'Sikh' end, you will be referred to church buildings where there is a sub-section listing various types of 'temple', including the one you want.

So, if you want to know what Shakespeare called a footpad or which word Spenser might have used for a bull's-eye, you will find the answer here together with many, many more - about 80,000 more.

Many of the definitions are based on those used in the 1977 edition of the *Chambers 20th Century Dictionary* and I am grateful to the publishers for permission to use this material. Thanks are also due to Collins for their generosity in allowing the reproduction of some lists from the *Crossword Dictionary*.

James Coleman
Penkridge

James Coleman was born in 1920 in the Cotswolds. He entered local government after leaving school but found his professional studies interrupted by World War II. After 6 years with the Grenadier Guards (serving in North Africa and Italian campaigns) he took up his career again, qualifying as a chartered surveyor and becoming Engineer and Surveyor to the former Cannock RDC, a post from which he retired in 1974 to set up his own architectural and town-planning practice. He finally gave up work in 1986 to 'play about with words'; the results of this playing appear in *Wordmaster* and his earlier books, *The Complete Guide to Cryptic Crosswords* (soon to be republished by Eric Dobby Publications) and the large *Crossword Dictionary*, both originally published by Collins.

Index of headwords

Entries in the book are under main headwords and many are also cross-referenced. This Index provides a listing of those main headwords and their cross-references with some additional cross-referencing under general categories such as 'sport' or 'food'.

aborigine words   (*see* Australia)
absence of   (*see* without)
Abyssinian
acids
Adam
addiction to   (*see* love)
address
Afghan(istan)
African
Afrikaans   (*see* African)
agent
aircraft
airlines
airports
Albania
alchemy
Alderney
Algeria
alloys
alphabet
American
American football
amino-acid   (*see* acids)
anatomist   (*see* physician)
ancient words   (*see* old[1])
Andorra
Angola
animals   (*see* antelopes, bats, birds, butterfly,
    cats, cattle, deer, dogs, duck, fish, goats, goose,
    greyhound, hens, horse, insects, lizards,
    monkeys, ox, pigs, pigeon, rabbit, sheep,
    shellfish, snakes, whale)
anniversaries
antelopes
anthropology
Apostles
apparition   (*see* spirit)
apples
Arabia
archaeology
archaeologists   (*see* archaeology)
archaic words   (*see* old[1])

architects
architectural features
    (*see also* building construction)
architectural styles
Argentina
Armenia
armour
army
    (*see also* military, soldiers, weapon)
art
Asian
asteroids   (*see* astronomy)
astrology
astronomy
athletes
    (*see also* games)
atmosphere   (*see* meteorology)
Australia
Austria
authority of   (*see* power)
aversion to   (*see* fear)
bachelor
bacteriology   (*see* biology)
Bahamas
Bahrain
Balearic Islands
ballet
balsam   (*see* gum)
Bangladesh
Barbados
Barbary
baseball
Basque
bats
battles
bearing
    (*see also* having)
Bechuanaland
    (*see also* Botswana)
becoming
beginning
Belgium

Index of headwords

beliefs
   (*see also* worship)
Belize
Bengal
Benin
Biblical language   (*see* old[1])
biology
birds
   (*see also* duck, goose, hen, pigeon)
biscuits
blood   (*see* circulation)
boats
Bolivia
bone
books
botany   (*see* biology)
Botswana
bottle
bowls
boxing
brain
Brazil
bread
breeding   (*see* bearing)
bridge
British
Browning, Robert
Brunei
Buddhist
building construction
   (*see also* architectural features)
buildings   (*see* architects)
Bulgaria
bullfighting
Burkina Faso
Burma
Burns, Robert
   (*see also* Scottish)
Burundi
butterfly
Byzantine
cacti
cakes
Cambodia
camera   (*see* photography)
Cameroon
Canada
Canary Islands
Cape Verde Islands
capes
card games
carriages
carrying   (*see* bearing)
cart   (*see* carriages)
coach   (*see* carriages)
cats

cattle
   (*see also* ox)
cattle diseases
Celebes   (Sulawesi)
   (*see also* Indonesia, East Indies)
Celtic
   (*see also* Ireland, Scottish)
Central African Republic
Central America
   (*see also* South America)
cereal
   (*see also* grasses)
Ceylon
Chad
Chaldean
Channel Islands
cheese
cheese dishes
chemistry
chess
chief magistrate   (*see* magistrate)
Chile
china
China
church — building
church — personnel
church — terms
church — vestments
   (*see also* belief, garments, prayer, worship)
cinema
circulation
city
   (*see also* street, square)
classical Greek   (*see* Greece)
clergy   (*see* church—personnel)
climate   (*see* meteorology)
clothes
   (*see also* footwear, garments, headgear)
clouds   (*see* meteorology)
club
Cockney rhyming slang
cocktails
   (*see also* drinks, wine)
coffee
coins
collecting
collection of   (*see* group)
Colombia
colour
commander   (*see* leader)
complaint   (*see* diseases)
composers   (*see* musicians)
computing
concerning   (*see* pertaining)
condition   (*see* diseases)
Congo

constellations
    (*see also* astronomy)
cookery
Coptic
Costa Rica
counties
cricket
cross
    (*see also* decorations)
Cuba
cultivation   (*see* bearing)
cycling
Cyprus
Czechoslovakia
dance
decorations
deer
    (*see also* antelopes)
deficiency of   (*see* without)
demon   (*see* spirit)
Denmark
department
description of   (*see* write)
desert
dessert
detectives, fictional
dialects (English dialect words)
digestive system
dinosaur   (*see* lizards)
discoveries
    (*see also* first, inventor)
diseases
    (*see also* cattle diseases, horse diseases, plant
    diseases)
disorder   (*see* diseases)
divers   (*see* swimming)
divination
diving   (*see* swimming)
Doctors of
dogs
Dominica
Dominican Republic
dove   (*see* pigeon)
dramatists
    (*see also* Shakespeare)
drawing (of)   (*see* write)
drinks
drugs
duck
Dutch
dyes
ear
earth   (*see* geography)
earthquake
East Indian

eastern
    (*see also* Oriental)
eat
economics
Ecuador
egg
Egypt
eight
eighteen
eighth
eighty
El Salvador
electric
    (*see also* physics)
elements
    (*see also* physics)
eleven
embroidery   (*see* sewing)
engineers   (*see* architects)
English
engraving   (*see* write)
enzymes
equal
Eskimo
Ethiopia   (*see* Abyssinian)
Europe
excessive love for   (*see* love)
explorer
explosives
eyes
fabric
fabulous
    (*see also* monsters)
Faeroe Islands
failure of   (*see* without)
farewell
fastdays   (*see* holidays)
fastest
Fates
fear
feastdays   (*see* holidays)
feathers
feet
fences
fencing
ferns
festivals   (*see* holidays)
feudal   (*see* mediaeval)
fifty
figures of speech   (*see* rhetoric)
Fiji
films   (*see* cinema)
Finland
first
fish
fish dishes

Index of headwords

fishing
five
flags
flower
 (*see also* **plants**)
food   (*see* **apples, biscuits, bread, cakes, cereal, cheese, cheese dishes, cookery, dessert, egg, fish dishes, fruit, fungi, grape, herb, meat, meat dishes, menu, pasta, pasta dishes, pastry, poultry dishes, pulses, rice, sauce, sausage, shellfish, soup, spice, stew, sugar, tea, vegetable, vegetable dishes, vitamin**)
football
footwear
fortifications
forty
four
fourteen
fourth
France
French
fruit
fungi
 (*see also* **biology**)
fur
Furies
furniture
Gabon
Gaelic
 (*see also* **Ireland**)
Gambia
games[1]
games[2] (terms)
game (birds)   (*see* **poultry dishes**)
garments
gases
gazelles   (*see* **antelopes**)
gems
genetics   (*see* **biology**)
geography
 (*see also* **capes, counties, desert, earthquake, explorer, lakes, mountain, oceanography, rock, rivers, stone, swamp, volcano, waterfall, wind, zoological regions**)
geology   (*see* **geography**)
German
Ghana
ghost   (*see* **spirit**)
Gibraltar
girls
 (*see also* **woman**)
gland
glass
goats
gods
goddesses

golf
goose
government by   (*see* **power**)
governor
 (*see also* **leader, power**)
Graces
grammar   (*see* **rhetoric**)
grape
 (*see also* **wine**)
graph   (*see* **write**)
grass
 (*see also* **cereal**)
Greece
 (*see also* **mythology**)
Grenada
Grenadines
greyhound
group
Guatemala
Guernsey
gum
gun
Guyana
gymnastics
gypsy
hair
Haiti
harness   (*see* **horse**)
Harpies
hat   (*see* **headgear**)
hatred of   (*see* **fear**)
having
Hawaii
head
headgear
heart   (*see* **circulation**)
Hebrew
Hell
hens
Her
heraldic beasts   (*see* **monsters**)
heraldry
herb
heresies   (*see* **beliefs**)
hills   (*see* **mountain**)
Hindu
 (*see also* **Indian**)
His
historians
historical words   (*see* **old**[1])
holidays
Holland   (*see* **Dutch**)
holy
hominids   (*see* **anthropology**)
Honduras
Hong Kong

hormone
horse[1] (breeds)
horse[2] (terms and tackle)
horse diseases
horse racing
house
hundred
Hungary
hybrid
Iceland
illness   (*see* diseases)
India
        (*see also* Hindu, Sikh)
Indonesia
indoor sports   (*see* games[1])
insects[1]
insects[2] (terms)
institute/institution
instrument   (*see* instrument of torture,
        measuring instrument, musical instrument)
instrument of torture
international
inventors
        (*see also* discoveries, first)
Iran
        (*see also* Persia)
Iraq
Ireland
Islam   (*see* Moslem)
Isle of Man
Isle of Wight
Israel
        (*see also* Hebrew)
Italy
Ivory Coast
Jamaica
Japan
Javanese
Jersey
Jesus
jewellery
        (*see also* gems)
Jewish   (*see* Hebrew)
Jordan
judge   (*see* magistrate)
June
Kampuchea   (*see* Cambodia)
Kenya
kill
kings[1] (general)
kings[2] (British)
knife
knight
knot
knowledge of   (*see* study)
Korea

Kuala Lumpur
Kuwait
lack of   (*see* without)
lacking   (*see* without)
lake
Lamb (Charles)
language
        (*see also* rhetoric)
Laos
Latin
        (*see also* Roman)
law[1] (terms)
law[2] (describing, governing, stating that)
        (*see also* electric, physics)
leader
        (*see also* nobles, power)
leaf
leather
Lebanon
Lesotho
Liberia
library
Libya
        (*see also* Arab)
Licentiate
lichen   (*see* fungi)
Liechtenstein
life symbol
lifestyle
like   (*see* pertaining)
literature
lizards
logic
London
lord
        (*see also* leaders, nobles)
loss of   (*see* without)
Louis XIV
love
lover of   (*see* love)
low
Luxembourg
lymph   (*see* circulation)
Madagascar
magistrate
Malagasy   (*see* Madagascar)
Malawi
Malaya
Malaysia
Mali
Malta
mania for   (*see* love)
Manx
many
Maori   (*see* New Zealand)
martial arts   (*see* games)

Index of headwords

masonry   (*see* architectural features)
mass of   (*see* group)
master
material   (*see* fabrics)
mathematics
Mauritania
Mauritius
May
measures
measuring instrument
    (*see also* scientific instruments)
meat
 meat dishes
    (*see also* cookery, menu)
medal   (*see* decorations)
medi(a)eval
medical
    (*see also* diseases, physicians, surgery)
medical instruments   (*see* surgery)
medicines   (*see* drugs)
Mediterranean
member
menu
merchant
meteor   (*see* astronomy)
meteorology
metric weights   (*see* French)
Mexico
military
    (*see also* fortifications, soldier)
million
Milton, John
mineral
mineralogy   (*see* geography)
minus   (*see* without)
Miss
    (*see also* girl)
missile
    (*see also* space)
mites   (*see* insects[1])
Mongolia
monkeys
monsters
moons   (*see* astronomy)
Moor
    (*see also* Morocco)
Morocco
Moslem
moths
motor car
motorcycle
motor racing
motor rallying
mountain
mountaineers   (*see* mountain)
Mozambique

Mrs
muscle
Muses
mushroom   (*see* fungi)
music
musical instruments
musicals
musicians
Muslim   (*see* Moslem)
Myanmar   (*see* Burma)
mythical beasts   (*see* monsters)
mythology
    (*see also* gods, goddesses)
names
Namibia
national
naturalists   (*see* biology)
Navy
    (*see also* sailor)
needlepoint   (*see* sewing)
Nepal
nerve
Netherlands
    (*see also* Dutch)
New
New Zealand
newspaper
Nicaragua
nicknames
    (*see also* boxing, football)
Niger
Nigeria
nine
nineteenth
ninety
nobles
    (*see also* leader)
Norse
    (*see also* mythology, Scandinavia)
north
Norway
    (*see also* Norse, Scandinavia)
nose
Nova Scotia
nuclear reactors
numbers   (*see* mathematics)
nut
nymph(s)
observatory
obsession with   (*see* love)
obsolete words   (*see* old[1])
oceanography
of   (*see* pertaining)
of the nature of   (*see* pertaining)
old[1]
old[2] (former)

Olympians   (*see* gods, goddesses)
Oman
one
opera
operetta   (*see* musicals)
Order
    (*see also* decorations)
orders, religious   (*see* beliefs)
Ordinary
Ordnance
organ stops
Organisation
oriental
    (*see also* Eastern)
origins (of)   (*see* beginning)
ox
    (*see also* cattle)
pain   (*see* diseases)
painting
    (*see also* art)
Pakistan
palaeontology   (*see* archaeology)
Palestine
palm
Panama
Papal
Papua New Guinea
Paraguay
parliament
Parliamentary
particle
    (*see also* physics)
parts of the body   (*see* bone, brain, circulation,
    digestive system, ear, enzymes, eyes, feet, gland,
    hair, head, hormone, muscle, nerve, nose,
    respiratory system, teeth, toes)
pasta
pasta dishes
pastimes   (*see* games[1])
pastry
perfume
Persian
pertaining
Peru
Pharmaceutical Society
Pharmacopoeia Britannica
Philippines
Philological Society
philosophy
    (*see also* belief)
Philosophy, Politics and Economics
phobias   (*see* fear)
photograph (of)   (*see* write)
photography
physician
    (*see also* diseases, surgery)

physiologist   (*see* physician)
physics
pigs
pigeon
pigments   (*see* dyes)
pilot
pirate
Planck's constant
planets   (*see* astronomy)
plants
    (*see also* cacti, cereal, ferns, flower, fungi,
    grasses, palm, pulses, seaweed, shrubs, timber,
    trees)
plant diseases
plant pests   (*see* plant diseases)
playwrights   (*see* dramatists)
poetic
    (*see also* Burns, Milton, old, Scott, Shakespeare,
    Spenser)
poets
poison
Poland
police
Polynesian
porcelain   (*see* china)
Portugal
potato   (*see* vegetables)
potentate   (*see* leader)
poultry dishes
power
prayer
    (*see also* beliefs)
precious stones   (*see* gems, minerals)
presidents (US)
prime ministers (UK)
prince   (*see* leader)
printing
    (*see also* write)
producing   (*see* bearing)
proposer of   (*see* discoveries)
proteins
psychiatry   (*see* psychology)
psychology
public
Puerto Rico
pulses
Qatar
quarter
quasi-stellar object
Quebec
queen
rabbit
radio
railway
rearing
record (of)   (*see* write)

Index of headwords

Red Indian
relating to   (*see* pertaining)
religions   (*see* beliefs)
religious leader   (*see* church — personnel,
        leader)
reproduction (of)   (*see* beginning)
resident
resin   (*see* gum)
respiratory system
reverence for   (*see* worship)
rhetoric
        (*see also* language)
Rhodesia
        (*see also* Zimbabwe)
rice
rivers
rock
        (*see also* geography, mineral, stone)
rockets   (*see* missiles, space)
Roman
        (*see also* Latin)
Romania
room
rope
Royal
Royal Air Force
royal family   (*see* house)
Royal Marines
Royal Navy
rubber
rug
Rugby football
rule (by)   (*see* power)
ruler   (*see* leader)
Russia
Rwanda
sacred
sailor
        (*see also* Royal Navy)
St Lucia
St Vincent
saint's day   (*see* holidays)
salad   (*see* vegetables)
Sanskrit
        (*see also* Hindu, Indian)
Sao Tome
satellites, artificial   (*see* space)
satellites, natural   (*see* astronomy)
sauce
Saudi Arabia   (*see* Arabia)
sausage
Scandinavian
        (*see also* Norse)
science   (*see* acids, anthropology, archaeology,
        astronomy, biology, chemistry, computing,
        discoveries, economics, electric, elements,
enzymes, gases, geography, inventors, law[2],
        mathematics, measuring instrument,
        meteorology, nuclear reactors, observatory,
        oceanography, physics, psychology, radio,
        scientific instrument, space, surgery)
science of   (*see* study)
scientific instrument
        (*see also* measuring instruments)
Scotland
        (*see also* Scottish)
Scott, Sir Walter
Scottish
script   (*see* alphabet)
sculpture
seaweed
secret
semi-precious stones   (*see* gems)
Senegal
senior
sergeant
servant
seven
seventy
sewing
Seychelles
Shakespeare
Shakespeare's people
Shakespeare's plays(titles and characters)
shapes
sheep
shellfish
Shinto
        (*see also* Japanese)
ship[1] (types)
ship[2] (terms)
        (*see also* rope, boats, sailor)
shoes   (*see* footwear)
showjumping
shrubs
Siamese
Sierra Leone
Sikh
        (*see also* belief, Indian)
Singapore
six
sixteen
sixth
sixty
skating
skiing
snakes
snooker
soccer   (*see* football)
Society
soldier
solicitor

Somalia
son of
soup
South Africa
    (*see also* African)
South America
South Australia
South Island
South Pole
Soviet Union
    (*see also* Russia)
space
Spain
Spanish
special
speech   (*see* language, rhetoric)
Spenser, Edmund
spice
spiders   (*see* insects[1])
spirit
spectre   (*see* spirit)
sport   (*see* American football, athletes, baseball,
    boxing, bullfighting, chess, cricket, cycling,
    fencing, fishing, games, golf, gymnastics, motor
    racing, motor rallying, mountain, showjumping,
    skating, skiing, snooker, surfing, swimming,
    tennis, yachting)
square
Sri Lanka   (*see* Ceylon)
standard
stars
state[1]
state[2] (USA)
stew
stone
    (*see also* building construction, minerals, rocks)
street
student
study
    (*see also* pertaining, write)
Sudan
sugar
Sun   (*see* astronomy)
surfing
surgeon   (*see* physician)
surgery
surgical instruments   (*see* surgery)
Surinam(e)
swamp
Swaziland
Sweden
sweets
swimming
Swiss
Switzerland
sword

Syriac
Syrian
Taiwan
Tanganyika
tanks
Tanzania
tea
teeth
telescope   (*see* observatory)
temple   (*see* church—buildings)
ten
tennis
tenth
Thailand
    (*see also* Siamese)
theatre
theologian
    (*see also* church—personnel)
thirteen
thirty
thousand
three
Tibetan
timber
Titans   (*see* gods)
toasts
toes
Togo
Tonga
tools
Uganda
Ulster
united
universal
university
Uruguay
US(A)   (*see* America, states)
USSR
    (*see also* Russia)
Vanuatu
vegetable
vegetable dishes
vehicle
    (*see also* motor car)
veins   (*see* circulation)
Venetian
Venezuela
verse
vestments   (*see* church — garments)
Victoria
video
Vietnam
virtues
violin
vitamin
volcano

Index of headwords

volunteer
Wales
want of, etc   (*see* without)
water sports   (*see* games[1])
waterfall
weapon
weather   (*see* meteorology)
weight
Welsh
West Indian
Western Samoa
whale
which
wind
wine
winter sports   (*see* games[1]))
Wise Men
without
woman
   (*see also* girls)
words   (*see* rhetoric)
   (*see also* language)
world
worship
   (*see also* belief)
write
writers

Abyssinian

baboon	GELADA
capital	ADDIS ABABA
cereal	TOCUSSO
coin	BIRR, CENT, TALARI
grass	TEF(F)
insect	ZEBIB, ZIMB
king	NEGUS
language	AMHARIC, GEEZ, GIZ
measures	
—1 oz	OKET
—2 lb	NATR
—100 lb	KANTAR
parliament	SHENGO
patriarch	ABUNA
prince	RAS
self-governing towns	KABELE, KEBELE

acids

abscisic acid	ABSCISIN, DORMIN
acetic acid	ETHANOIC ACID
acetylsalicylic acid	ASPIRIN
acid linking chains	
in proteins	AMINO-ACID
amino-acetic acid	GLYCIN(E), GLYCOCOLL
amino-acid	ALANINE, ARGININE
	ASPARAGINE, ASPARTIC, CYSTEINE
	CYSTINE, GLUTAMIC, GLUTAMINE
	GLYCINE, HISTIDINE, ISO-LEUCINE
	LEUCINE, LYSINE, METHIONINE
	PHENYLALANINE, PROLINE, SERINE
	THREONINE, TYROSINE
	TRYPTOPHAN, VALINE
—in	
casein	METHIONINE
eggs	PHENYLALANINE
fish	HISTIDINE
milk	PHENYLALANINE
proteins	PROLINE
thyroid	THYROXIN(E)
wool	METHIONINE
amino-succinic acid	ASPARAGINIC ACID
	ASPARTIC ACID
aqua fortis	NITRIC ACID
aqueous sulphuric acid	AQ
ascorbic acid	CEVITAMIC ACID
	VITAMIN C
asparaginic acid	AMINOSUCCINIC ACID
	ASPARTIC ACID

aspartic acid	AMINOSUCCINIC ACID
	ASPARAGINIC ACID
aspirin	(ACETYL)SALICYLIC ACID
azoimide	HYDRAZOIC ACID
baking powder	TARTARIC
barbital	DIETHYLBARBITURIC ACID
	VERONAL
based on sulphur	THIO-ACID
	THIOCYANIC ACID
	THIOSULPHURIC ACID
bases forming amino-acid	TRIPLET
behenic acid	DOCOSANOIC ACID
benzoic acid	BENZENECARBOXYLIC ACID
boracic acid	(ORTHO)BORIC ACID
boric acid	BORACIC ACID
both acid and base	AMPHOTERIC
breaks down glucose	PYRUVIC ACID
butanedioic acid	SUCCINIC ACID
butanoic acid	BUTYRIC ACID
butenoic acid	CROTONIC ACID
cacodylic acid	DIMETHYL ARSINIC ACID
caproic acid	HEXANOIC ACID
carbolic acid	PHENOL
carbon dioxide and	
water	CARBONIC ACID
Caro's acid	PER(MONO)SULPHURIC ACID
cevitamic acid	ASCORBIC ACID, VITAMIN C
chain of	
—amino-acids	POLYPEPTIDE
—nucleotides	NUCLEIC ACID
chrysophanic acid	RHEIN
citric acid cycle	KREBS CYCLE
colourless solid	LACTIC ACID
	METAPHOSPHORIC ACID
compound of	
—tin	STANNIC ACID
—two amino-acids	PEPTIDE
—several amino-acids	POLYPEPTIDE
container for	CARBOY
containing carboxyl	
group(s)	(DI)CARBOXYLIC ACID
copper sulphate	BLUE VITRIOL
corrosive	AQUA FORTIS, AQUA REGIA
	HYDROCHLORIC, METHACRYLIC
	NITRIC, SELENIC, SULPHURIC
crotonic acid	BUTENOIC ACID
cyanuric acid	TRICYANIC ACID
description of acids	
based on valency	LEWIS ACID
diethylbarbituric acid	BARBITOL, VERONAL
dimethyl arsenic acid	CACODYLIC ACID
disinfectant	CARBOLIC ACID, PHENOL
docosanoic acid	BEHENIC ACID
dodecanoic acid	LAURIC ACID
dormin	ABSCISIC ACID, ABSCISIN
ethanedioic acid	OXALIC ACID

ethanoic acid	ACETIC ACID
excreted by primates, birds	
and reptiles	URIC ACID
fatty acid ERUCIC ACID, PROPANOIC ACID	
PROPIONIC ACID, PROSTAGLANDIN	
STEARIC ACID, TRIGLYCERIDE	
ferrous sulphate	GREEN VITRIOL
folic acid	PTEROYLGLUTAMIC ACID
formic acid	METHANOIC ACID
from/in	
—animal tissues	PANTOTHENIC ACID
—ants	FORMIC ACID
—apples	MALIC ACID
—argol	TARTARIC ACID
—bacterial metabolism	LACTIC ACID
—bile	GLYCOCHOLIC ACID
	TAUROCHOLIC ACID
—bran	PANTOTHENIC ACID
—breakdown of glucose	LACTIC ACID
—carbohydrates	LAEVULI(NI)C ACID
—castor oil	RICINOLEIC ACID
	SUBERIC ACID
—cells DEOXYRIBONUCLEIC ACID, DNA	
	RIBONUCLEIC ACID, RNA
—in DNA	NUCLEIC ACID
—electrolysis of	
brine	HYDROCHLORIC ACID
	MURIATIC ACID
	SPIRITS OF SALT
—ergot	LYSERGIC ACID
—fruit	CITRIC ACID
—fumitory	FUMARIC ACID
	HYDROXYSUCCINIC ACID
	MALIC ACID
—fungi	GIBBERELLIC ACID
—galactose	MUCIC ACID
—gallnuts	TANNIC ACID, TANNIN
—genes	DEOXYRIBONUCLEIC ACID
	DNA
—glucose	GLUCONIC ACID
—glycerides	OELIC ACID
—glycerol	GLYCERIC ACID
—gouty joints	URIC ACID
—grapes	TARTARIC ACID
—gum	MUCIC ACID
—hydrogen chloride	HYDROCHLORIC ACID
—malic acid	MALEIC ACID
—milk	LACTIC ACID
—mustard seed	ERUCIC ACID
—naphthalene	PHTHALIC ACID
—palm-oil	PALMITIC ACID
—peanut oil	ARACH(ID)IC ACID
—phosphorus	
pentoxide	PYROPHOSPHORIC ACID
—plants	FORMIC ACID
	PANTOTHENIC ACID
—rancid butter	BUTANOIC ACID
	BUTYRIC ACID
—rape seed	ERUCIC ACID
—rice	PANTOTHENIC ACID
—seaweed	ALGINIC ACID
—sugar beet	AMINOSUCCINIC ACID
	ASPARAGINIC ACID
	ASPARTIC ACID
—sumach	TANNIC ACID, TANNIN
—tea	TANNIC ACID
—thymus	THYMONUCLEIC ACID
—urine	URIC ACID
—vegetable oils	LINOLE(N)IC ACID
—vinegar	ACETIC
—wallflowers	ERUCIC ACID
—wood	PYROLIGNEOUS ACID
—wood sorrel	OXALIC ACID
fuming sulphuric acid	OLEUM
gallic acid TRIHYDROXYBENZOIC ACID	
gelatinous mixture	
from silicate	SILICIC ACID
glycin(e)	AMINOACETIC ACID
	AMINOETHANOIC ACID
	GLYCOCOLL
glycocoll	AMINOACETIC ACID
AMINOETHANOIC ACID, GLYCIN(E)	
growth	
—acid	OROTIC ACID, VITAMIN B
—regulator	GIBBERELLIC ACID
growth-inhibiting	
hormone in plants	ABSCISIC ACID
	ABSCISIN, DORMIN
having	
—one hydrogen atom	MONOBASIC ACID
—two hydrogen atoms	DIBASIC ACID
—three hydrogen atoms	TRIBASIC ACID
hexadecanoic acid	PALMITIC ACID
hexanoic acid	CAPROIC ACID
hydrated tungsten trioxide	TUNGSTIC ACID
hydrazoic acid	AZOIMIDE
hydrochloric acid	MURIATIC ACID
	SPIRITS OF SALT
—with nitric acid	AQUA REGIA
hydrocyanic acid	HYDROGEN CYANIDE
	PRUSSIC ACID
hydrogen	
—bromide dissolved	
in water	HYDROBROMIC ACID
—cyanide	HYDROCYANIC ACID
	PRUSSIC ACID
—fluoride dissolved	
in water	HYDROFLUORIC ACID
—iodide dissolved	
in water	HYDRIODIC ACID
hydroxypropanoic acid	LACTIC ACID
hydroxysuccinic acid	MALIC ACID

hygroscopic liquid	PERCHLORIC ACID
hypothetical	CHLORIC ACID
	CHLOROUS ACID, CHROMIC ACID
	ISOCYANIC ACID, MANGANIC ACID
	PERBORIC ACID, PERMANGANIC ACID
indicator of	LITMUS PAPER
iodine and nitric acid	IODIC ACID
isomer of maleic acid	FUMARIC ACID
lactic acid	HYDROXYPROPANOIC ACIC
lauric acid	DODECANOIC ACID
linole(n)ic acid	VITAMIN F
malic acid	HYDROXYSUCCINIC ACID
malonyl urea	BARBITURIC ACID
methanoic acid	FORMIC ACID
molecule containing	
genetic code	NUCLEIC ACID
muriatic acid	HYDROCHLORIC ACID
	SPIRITS OF SALT
neutraliser	ALKALI
niacin	NICOTINIC ACID, P-P FACTOR
nicotinic acid	NIACIN, P-P FACTOR
nitric acid	AQUA FORTIS
nonanoic acid	PELARGONIC ACID
nucleic acid with	
—protein	NUCLEO-PROTEIN
—ribose	RIBONUCLEIC ACID, RNA
octadecanoic acid	STEARIC ACID
oil of vitriol	SULPHURIC ACID
	VITRIOL
organic acids	FATTY ACIDS
orotic acid	VITAMIN B
orthoboric acid	BORACIC ACID
oxalic acid	ETHANEDIOIC ACID
palmitic acid	HEXADECANOIC ACID
pantothenic acid	VITAMIN B
pelargonic acid	NONANOIC ACID
pentanoic acid	VALERIC ACID
permonosulphic acid	CARO'S ACID
phenol	CARBOLIC ACID
picric acid	TRINITROPHENOL
poison	HYDROCYANIC, PRUSSIC
—gas	CYANIC ACID, CYANOGEN
P-P factor	NIACIN, NICOTINIC ACID
propanoic acid	PROPIONIC ACID
prussic acid	HYDROCYANIC ACID
	HYDROGEN CYANIDE
pteroylglutamic acid	FOLIC ACID
rhein	CHRYSOPHANIC ACID
smelling like	
—bitter almonds	HYDROCYANIC ACID
	HYDROGEN CYANIDE
	PRUSSIC ACID
—cheese	CAPROIC ACID
	HEXANOIC ACID
spirits of salt	HYDROCHLORIC ACID
	MURIATIC ACID

stearic acid	OCTADECANOIC ACID
	TRISTEARIN
succinic acid	BUTANEDIOIC ACID
sugar of lead	LEAD ACETATE
sulphur dioxide in water	SULPHUROUS ACID
sulphuric acid	(OIL OF) VITRIOL
tautomer of cyanic acid	ISOCYANIC ACID
tricyanic acid	CYANURIC CID
trihydroxybenzoic acid	GALLIC ACID
trinitrophenol	PICRIC ACID
tristearin	STEARIC ACID
universal solvent	ALCAHEST, ALKAHEST
unstable acids	PERIODIC ACIDS
used	
—as	
antiseptic	BORACIC ACID
	MANDELIC ACID
	(ORTHO)BORIC ACID
	SALICYLIC ACID
aspirin	SALICYLIC ACID
disinfectant	CARBOLIC ACID
	FLUOROSILICIC ACID
	HYDROFLUOROSILICIC ACID
	PHENOL
flavouring	BUTANOIC ACID
	BUTYRIC ACID, CAPROIC ACID
	GLUTAMIC ACID
	HEXANOIC ACID
food-preservative	BENZOIC ACID
oxidising agent	BROMIC ACID
	CARO'S ACID
	PER(MONO)SULPHURIC ACID
preservative	MALEIC ACID
reducing	
agent	HYPOPHOSPHOROUS ACID
rocket	
propellant	FUMING NITRIC ACID
solvent	PHENYL(ACETIC) ACID
stain in microscopy	OSMIC ACID
wart-remover	CHLOR(O)ACETIC ACID
weedkiller	CACODYLIC ACID
	DIMETHYL ARSINIC ACID
wood preservative	FLUOROSILICIC ACID
	HYDROFLUOROSILICIC ACID
—for	
cleaning metals	GLUCONIC ACID
flavouring	
drinks	ORTHOPHOSPHORIC ACID
glass-etching	HYDROFLUORIC ACID
	MORDANT
stimulating growth	
of plants	GIBBERELLIC ACID
treating	
—anaemia	FOLIC ACID
	PTEROYLGLUTAMIC ACID
	MORDANT

—burns	PICRIC ACID
—in	
acrylic resins	ACRYLIC ACID
baking powder	FUMARIC ACID
	TARTARIC ACID
barbiturates	MALONIC ACID
bleaching	HYPOCHLOROUS ACID
	OXALIC ACID
calico-printing	TARTARIC ACID
candles	STEARIC ACID
cosmetics	BEHENIC ACID
	DOCOSANOIC ACID
	DODECANOIC ACID
	LAURIC ACID, STEARIC ACID
detergents	DODECANOIC ACID
	LAURIC ACID
dyes	CACODYLIC ACID
	CARBOLIC ACID
	CHLOR(O)ACTIC ACID
	DIMETHYL ARSENIC ACID
	FORMIC ACID, LACTIC ACID
	MALEIC ACID, OXALIC ACID
	PHENOL, PICRIC ACID
	PHTHALIC ACID, SUCCINIC ACID
	SULPHANILIC ACID
	TARTARIC ACID
effervescent	
—drinks	TARTARIC ACID
—salts	CITRIC ACID
electroplating	FORMIC ACID
explosives	FUMING SULPHURIC ACID
	OLEUM, PICRIC ACID
fertilisers	ORTHOPHOSPHORIC ACID
histamines	HISTIDINE
hydrogen	
peroxide	PERDISULPHURIC ACID
ink	GALLIC ACID
	TRIHYDROXYBENZOIC ACID
	OXALIC ACID, TANNIC ACID
	TANNIN
lacquers	SUCCINIC ACID
lamp filaments	TUNGSTIC ACID
lead accumulators	SULPHURIC ACID
LSD	LYSERGIC ACID
lubricants	ARACH(ID)IC ACID
medicine	PHTHALIC ACID
metal polish	OXALIC ACID
nylon	ADIPIC ACID
organic synthesis	FUMING NITRIC ACID
perfume	CINNAMIC ACID
	PENTANOIC ACID
	VALERIC ACID
	PHTHALIC ACID
phosphites	PHOSPHOROUS ACID
plasticisers	ISOPHTHALIC ACID
	SEBACIC ACID

plastics	CARBOLIC ACID
	LAEVULI(NI)C ACID, PHENOL
	SUBERIC ACID
resins	FUMARIC ACID, MALEIC ACID
	SEBACIC ACID
	TEREPHTHALIC ACID
soap	DODECANOIC ACID, LAURIC ACID
	PALMITIC ACID, RICINOLEIC ACID
	STEARIC ACID
synthetic resins	ISOPHTHALIC ACID
synthesis	MUCIC ACID, TOLUIC ACID
—of	
barbiturates	BARBITURIC ACID
organic	
substances	BUTENOIC ACID
	CROTONIC ACID
	CYANURIC ACID
	TRICYANIC ACID
synthetic fibres	TEREPHTHALIC ACID
tanning	FORMIC ACID
	GALLIC ACID, LACTIC ACID
	TANNIC ACID, TANNIN
	TRIHYDROXYBENZOIC ACID
waxes	BEHENIC ACID
	DOCOSANOIC ACID
—to	
flavour drinks	ORTHOPHOSPHORIC ACID
stimulate plant	
growth	GIBBERELLIC ACID
treat anaemia	FOLIC ACID
	PTEROYLGLUTAMIC ACID
valeric acid	PENTANOIC ACID
veronal	BARBITAL
	DIETHYLBARBITURIC ACID
vinegar	ACETIC ACID, ETHANOIC ACID
vitamin A	RETINOIC ACID
B	FOLIC ACID
	OROTOIC ACID
	PANTOTHENIC ACID
	PTEROYLGLUTAMIC ACID
C	ASCORBIC ACID
F	LINOLE(N)IC ACID
M	FOLIC ACID
	PTEROYLGLUTAMIC ACID
vitriol	OIL OF VITRIOL
	SULPHURIC ACID
—blue	COPPER SULPHATE
—green	FERROUS SULPHATE
—white	ZINC SULPHATE
white	
—crystalline	MARONIC ACID
—vitriol	ZINC SULPHATE
yellow	
—crystal	PICRIC ACID, VANADIC ACID
—crystalline substance	MOLYBDIC ACID
—powder	IODIC ACID

zinc sulphate	WHITE VITRIOL
	(*see also* **chemistry** — salt of)
Adam	
Adam (and Eve)	BELIEVE
Adam's ale/wine	WATER
Adam's first wife	LILITH
Adam's apple	LARYNX
address	
mode of address for notables:	
ambassador	EXCELLENCY, HE
archbishop	GRACE
archdeacon	VEN(ERABLE)
baron	LORD
bishop	LORD
cardinal	EMINENCE
—old	MOST ILLUSTRIOUS
dean	VERY REV(EREND)
duke	GRACE
earl	LORD
judge	LORD
king	MAJESTY
knight	SIR
magistrate	HONOUR
marquess	LORD MARQUESS
mayor	WORSHIP
Member of Parliament	HON(OURABLE)
pope	HOLINESS
prince	HIGHNESS
Privy Councillor	RIGHT HON(OURABLE)
queen	MAJESTY
vicar	REV(EREND)
Afghan(istan)	AFG, PATHAN
capital	KABUL
clan	KHEL
coins	AFGHANI, AMANIA, PULS
greatcoat	POS(H)TEEN
language	PASHTO, PASHTU
	PAKHTO, PAKHTU
	PUSHTO(O), PUSHTU
native tribe	AFRIDI, KAFIR, PATHAN
sport	BUZ KASHI
African	
including: Afrikaans	
aardvark	ANT-BEAR, EARTH-HOG
	GROUND-HOG
aardwolf	EARTHWOLF
acacia	DOORN-BOOM
Afrikaans	TAAL
Afrikaner	BOER, BOOR, DUTCHMAN
airline	AIR AFRIQUE, SAA, ZAS
amaryllis	BELLADONNA
amulet	GREEGREE, GRI(S)GRI(S)
ant	
—bear	AARDVARK, EARTH-HOG
	GROUND-HOG
—eater	PANGOLIN

ape	CHIMPANZEE, GORILLA
aromatic seeds	GRAINS OF PARADISE
ass (extinct)	QUAGGA
assembly	RAAD
—of elders	KGLOTA
back of beyond	BUNDU
badger	RATEL
barbecue	BRAAIVLEIS
baobab	CREAM-OF-TARTAR TREE
	MONKEY-BREAD
bay	BAAI
beer	POMBE
begone!	VOETSAK
beryl	HELIODOR
bird	AASVOGEL, ADJUTANT-BIRD
	BALAENICEPS, BEEFEATER, BUPHAGA
	CAPE PIGEON, COUNCAL
	GUINEA-FOWL, HAMMERHEAD
	HAMMERKOP, HONEY-BIRD
	HONEY-GUIDE, LARK-HEELED CUCKOO
	MARABOU(T), MESSENGER, OSTRICH
	OX-PECKER, PRINIA, PLANTAIN-EATER
	SECRETARY-BIRD, SENEGAL, SHOE-BILL
	T(O)URACO, UMBER(-BIRD), UMBRETTE
	WHALE-HEAD, WHIDAH-BIRD
	WHYDAH-BIRD, WIDOW-BIRD
biscuit	SOETKOEKIE
biting spider	TARANTULA
blood-flower	HAEMANTHUS
body of warriors	IMPI
bracelet (money)	MANILLA
brandy	CAPE SMOKE, DOP
bread	KISRA
Briton	UITLANDER
bucket	EMMER
bugbear	MUMBO-JUMBO
bustard	DIKKOP, PAAUW, PAU
butter-tree	KANYA, KARITE, SHEA
camp	BOMA, LAAGER, LAER
cape	KAAP
Cape	
—Dutch	TAAL
—gooseberry	GOLDENBERRY, PHYSALIS
—hyrax	KLIPDAS, ROCK-BADGER
—Province	CP
carrier by wagon	TRANSPORT-RIDER
castle	CASBAH, KASBA(H)
cattle	ANKOLE
—disease	NAGANA
—pound	SCHUT
channel	SLOOT, SLUIT
charm	GREEGREE
	GRI(S)GRI(S), JU-JU
chief	CAID, KAID
civet	LINSANG, MEERCAT
	MEERKAT, NANDINE, SURICATE

cloak	JELLABA
	(*see also* **Arabia**)
clout	LAP(PIE), LAPJE
club	KERRIE, KIERIE, KIRI
	KNOBKERRIE
coin	(KRUGER)RAND, RD
—threepenny bit	TICK(E)Y
col	NEK
coney	DASSIE
coral	ZEETAK
—tree	KAFFIR-BOOM
cormorant	DUIKER, DUYKER
corral	KRAAL
cotton dress	KANGA
coucal	SWAMP PHEASANT
crown of rock on	
mountain top	KRANS, KRAN(T)Z
cup	BEKER
dead person still drawing	
wages as if alive	DIEMAN
deity of the python	ZOMBI(E)
delicious	LEKKER
deposit	LAY-BY(E)
desert plant	CAMEL'S THORN
detect by witchcraft	SMELL OUT
diseases	(*see* **disease**)
dish	COUSCOUS(OU), CUSCUS
	KHUSKHUS
ditch	SLOOT
dog	BASENJI
	RHODESIAN RIDGEBACK
domesticated animal	CAMEL
dove	NAMAQUA
dried	
—apricots	MEBOS
—meat	BILTONG
drink	POMBE, SKOKIAAN
	TOMBO
—after sunset	SUNDOWNER
drug	CAPE DAGGA
	RED DAGGA
durra	GUINEA-CORN
Dutch/English	KITCHEN DUTCH
eagle	BATELEUR, BERGHAAN
ear of maize	MEALIE
earth-wolf	AARDWOLF
edible	
—pods	OKRA
—tuber	ELEPHANT'S-FOOT
	HOTTENTOT BREAD
Englishman (soldier)	ROOINEK
esparto-grass	(H)ALFA
expedition	SAFARI, TREK
extinct wild ass	QUAGGA
farm cart	SCOTCH CART
fenced enclosure	BOMA

fetish	GREE-GREE
	GRI(S)GRI(S), JU-JU
fine	MOOI
fish	BARRACOUTA, DORAS
	KABELJOU(W), PANCHAX
	POLYPTERUS, SNOEK, SNOOK
	TILAPIA
florin	SCOTCHMAN
flowers	CHINCHERINCHEE
	CHINKERINCHEE
	CINERARIA, NEMESIA
	NERINE, STRELITZIA
fly	BROMMER, BRUMMER
	KIVU, TSETSE
folk-music	KWELA
ford	DRIFT
foreigner	UITLANDER
fort	CASBAH, KASBA(H), SCHANS
fox	FENNEC, ZERDA
freedom	UHURU
French soldier's hat	CHECHIA
frog	CAPE NIGHTINGALE
	PLATANNA
fruit	A(C)KEE, BITO, DIKA
	HOTTENTOT FIG, NAARTIE
	NAR(R)AS, NARTJIE
	SHEA-NUT, WILD MANGO
garden plot	ERF
garment	KANZU
gin	SQUARE-FACE
glass beads	AGGRI, AGGRY
go away!	VOETSEK
gorge	KLOOF
god	MUMBO-JUMBO
gold ore	BANKET
good	MOOI
goosefoot	AIZOON
government	SERKALI
grain	C(O)USC(O)S, FUNDI
grape	H(A)ANEPOOT, HONEYPOT
grass	FUNDI, GUINEA-GRASS
	MILLET PENNISETUM
—country	VELD(T)
green rock	VERDITE
greet	WISH
greeting	JAMBO
ground	FLOOR
guitar	SANCHO, SANKO
gully	DONGA
gum-resin	OLIBANUM
gun	ROER
hair ornament	HEAD-RING
headman	CABOCEER
hemp	IFE, SISAL
heron/stork	HAMMERKOP, UMBRETTE
high grassland	KAR(R)OO

hill	BERG, KOP(PIE), KOPJE		magistrate	FIELD-CORNET, LANDDROS(T)
hippopotamus	RIVER-HORSE, ZEEKOE		maize	MEALIES
honey-badger	RATEL		mango	DIKA
hooligan	TSOTSI		mantis	HOTTENTOT'S GOD
horse disease	NAGANA		master	BAAS, BWANA
horse's canter	TRIPPLE		—race theory	APARTHEID, BAASKAP
Hottentot			measures	
—fig	MESEMBRIANTHEMUM		—2 acres	MORGEN
	MESEMBRYANTHEMUM		—7½ gallons	ANKER
—god	PRAYING MANTIS		—31 gallons	AUM
hut	KRAAL, KYA, RONDAVEL		—3 bushels	MUID
hyena	TIGER-WOLF		—cloth	JACKTAN
hyrax	DASSIE		medicinal plant	BUCHU, BUCKU, CALUMBA
immature locust	VOETGANGER		millet	DARI, D(O)URA, D(H)URRA
Indian	GOAN		mixed race	BASTARD, BASTER
infantryman	VOETGANGER			(CAPE) COLOURED, GRIQUA
insect	GOGGA		mongoose	MEERCAT, MEERKAT
insectivore	ELEPHANT SHREW		Moslem	SENUSSI
	GOLDEN MOLE, OTTER-SHREW		mountain	BERG
iris	FREESIA		—pass	NEK, POORT
island(s)	EILAND(EN)		—range	GEBERGTE
it is not	AIKONA		mud hut	TEMBE
ivory	PANGANI		multi-coloured	BONT
jackal	DIEB		musical instrument	BALAFON, GORA(H)
jam	KONFYT			GOURA, KONA
javelin	ASSAGAI, ASSEGAI, ASSEGAY			KORA, HARP-LUTE, ZANZE
kaffir			narrow water-channel	SLUIT
—boom	ERYTHRINA		national independence	UHURU
—bread	PALM-PITH		native	
—English	KITCHEN KAFFIR		—hut	RONDAVEL
knife	PANGA		—soldiers	ASKARI, IMPI
lake	MEER, NYANZA		Negrito	NEGRILLO
language	AFRIKAANS, BANTU, BASUTO		no	AIKONA
	BASUTU, CAFFRE, CAPE DUTCH		nomadic race	TUAREG
	HERERO, HOTTENTOT, IBO, KABYLE		nothing at all	NIKS-NIE, NIX-NIE
	KAFFER, KAF(F)IR, MANDINGO		nut-tree	COLA, KOLA
	SWAHILI, TAAL, TSWANA, TUAREG		object of superstition	JU-JU
	TWI, (UNION) SHONA, X(H)OSA		open country	VELD(T)
	YORUBA, ZULU		open-sided bus	MAMMY-WAGON
	(see also races below)		one of	
	(see also separate entry)		—conservative views	VERKRAMPTE
legislative assembly	VOLKSRAAD		—liberal views	VERLIGTE
lemur	AGWANTIBO, POTTO		orange	NAARTJE, NARTJIE
leopard	TIGER		orchid	DISA
liberal	VERLIGTE		ostrich	STRUTHIO
lieutenant	FIELD-CORNET		ox-pecker	BEEF-EATER, BUPHAGA
lily of the Nile	PIG-LILY		palm	DOOM-PALM, D(O)UM-PALM
lizard	GECKO, (I)GUANA			PALMYRA
	MONITOR, SKINK			(see also separate entry)
locust before wings grow	VOETGANGER		—civet	NANDINE
look out	PAS OP		—wine	TOMBO
loose tunic	DASHIKI, KANZU		pangolin	MANIS
Lord's supper	NACHTMAAL, NAGMAAL		parliament	RAAD
low-lying ground	VLEI, VLY		pass	NEK, POORT
lynx	CARACAL		—book	REFERENCE BOOK
mackerel	ALBACORE, ALBICORE		peasant	KOPI

pedestrian	VOETGANGER
pedlar	SMOUCH, SMOUS(E)
	SMOUSER
perennial herb	LASERPICIUM
periwinkle	STROPHANTHUS
petrel	CAPE PIGEON
pheasant	FRANCOLIN
pioneer	VOORTREKKER
plain	VELD(T)
plant	GOA BEAN, GRAPPLE-PLANT
	ROSE OF JERICHO
	WELWITSCHIA
—extract	NIGER-OIL
plateau	PLATO
platform	STOEP
pole for crossing river	RIVER-HORSE
policeman	ASKARI
pool	VLEI, VLY
porch	STOEP
pounded maize	STAMP
preacher	PREDIKANT
precipice	KRANS, KRAN(T)Z
preserved fruit	KONFYT
prickly pear	JOINTED CACTUS
public house	CANTEEN
purslane tree	SPEKBOOM
pygmy	NEGRITO
pyrethrum	PELLITORY
race	BANTU, BASUTO, BASUTU, BEJA
	BERBER, BUSHMEN, CAFFRE
	GALLA, GRIQUA, HADENDOA
	HAMITE, HAUS(S)A, HERERO
	HOTTENTOT, IBO, KABYLE
	KAFFER, KAF(FIR), KIKUYU
	KROO, KRU, MASAI, MATABELE
	MANDINGO, SWANA
—theory	APARTHEID, BAASKAP
rag	LAP(PIE), LAPJE
rascal	SCHELM, SKELM
ratel	HONEY-BADGER
ravine	DONGA, KLOOF
rawhide	
—shoe	VELDSCHOEN, VEL(D)SKOEN
—string	RIEMPIE
—thong	REIM
remote country	BACK VELD(T), BUNDU
resin	SANDARIC
reward	BONSELLA
rhinoceros	KEITLOA
ridge overlooking valley	RAND
rifle-shooting competition	WAPINS(C)HAW
	WEAPON-S(C)HAW
	WA(P)PENS(C)HAW
river	RIVIER
	(see also rivers)
—fish	POLYPTERUS
—horse	HIPPOPOTAMUS
riverside plant	PALMIET
robe	KANZU
rock-badger	CAPE HYRAX, KLIPDAS
rue	HARMALA, HARMEL
rug	CAROSSE, KAROSS
Rugby player	SPRINGBOK
runner	CHEETAH, OSTRICH
sacrament	NACHTMAAL, NAGMAAL
sausage	BOEREWORS
scaly ant-eater	MANIS, PANGOLIN
scram!	VOETSEK
sea	MEER
secretary-bird	MESSENGER
segregation of races	APARTHEID
separate development	APARTHEID
series of strata	KAR(R)OO
sesame	BENNE
shea-tree	KARITE
sheriff	LANDDROS(T)
shrub	BUAZE, BUCHU, BUCKU, BWAZI
	PENTZIA, PROTEA
	SPEKBOOM, TEA-TREE
sir	BWANA
sitting up (courtship)	UPSITTING
skin blanket	CAROSSE, KAROSS
skunk	ZORILLA, ZORIL(LE)
small	
—garden	ERF
—gift	BONSELLA
—orange	NA(A)RTJE
—parrot	LOVE-BIRD
—piece of ground	ERF
snake	(see snakes)
snake-eating bird	SECRETARY-BIRD
soldier	ASKARI, SPAHI
soldiers	IMPI
sorghum	KAFFIR-CORN
spear	ASSAGAI, ASSEGAI, ASSEGAY
spell	GREEGREE, GRI(S)GRI(S), JU-JU
spider	BUTTON SPIDER
spotted hyena	NANDI BEAR
spring	BRON, FONTEIN
squatter	BIWONER, BYWONER
squirrel	XERUS
stinking flower	CARRION-FLOWER
stockade	BOMA
stork	MARABOU(T), SIMBIL
strawberry-tomato	CAPE GOOSEBERRY
tableland	KAR(R)OO
taffeta	ARIDAS
tallow	ROKA
Teddy boy	DUCKTAIL
thorn	DOORN
thorny plant	WAIT-A-BIT, WAIT-A-WHILE
	WAG-'N-BIETJIE

thug	TSOTSI
tick	TAMPAN
tiger-cat	BUSH-CAT, SERVAL
timber	(*see separate entry*)
tip	BONSELLA
toad	XENOPUS
trade as pedlar	SMOUCH, SMOUS(E)
transport	KURVEY
—rider	KURVEYOR
tree	ALOE, A(C)KEE, AMBATCH
	BAOBAB, BERG-CEDAR, BITO
	BOOM, BUBINGA, CAMWOOD, COLA
	DATE PALM, FUNTUMIA, GUMBO
	KOLA, LOTE, LOTOS, LOTUS
	MOLI, MONKEY-BREAD TREE
	MVULE, OBECHE, OKRA
	PITH-TREE, PROTEA, SHEA
	SILVER-TREE, SNEEZEWOOD
	SOUR-GOURD, TARFA, TEAK
	WA(GEN)BOOM, WILD MANGO
	(*see also* **timber**)
trek-wagon	BUCK-WAGON
tribal	
—conference	INDABA
—councillor	INDUNA
tribe	(*see* race *above*)
tuber	ELEPHANT'S FOOT
	HOTTENTOT BREAD, TANIA
tulip-tree	SPATHODEA
turaco	LORY
ultra-conservative	VERKRAMPTE
uncle	OOM
unknown animal	CATOBLEPAS
valley	DAL
vegetable	DOODY
vehicle	CAPE CART
verandah	STOEP
village	DORP, KRAAL
violet	SAINTPAULIA
viper	RIVER-JACK
vulture	AASVOGEL
wagon-trip	TREK
watercourse	SLOOT, SLUIT, SPRUIT
weaver-bird	GRENADIER, OX-BIRD
	QUELEA, TAHA, WHIDAH-BIRD
	WHYDAH-BIRD, WIDOW-BIRD
weight	OKA, ROTL
well of water	BRON
what's his name	DINGES, DINGUS
whip	(S)JAMBOK
white	
—rulers	SERKALI
—Teddy girl	SHEILA
wife purchase	LOBOLA
wild	
—cat	CHAUS, CIVET

—dog	HYENA-DOG
—hog	WART-HOG
—pig	RIVER-HOG
wine	CONSTANTIA
witch doctor	INYANGA, SANGOMA
woman's dress	KANGA
wooded veld	BUSHVELD(T), BOSCHVELD(T)
Zulu king	CETEWAYO, CHAL(K)A, CHAKA
	TCHAKA, INKOS, (I)NKOSI
agent	AGT, SPY
administering estate	TRUSTEE
acting in	
—court	ADVOCATE, ATTORNEY
	BARRISTER, PROCURATOR
	SOLICITOR
—spiritual court	PROCTOR
agent Orange	DEFOLIATOR
agent's fee	COMMISSION
American	G-MAN
dealing in property	ESTATE AGENT, REALTOR
document authorising	
agent	POWER OF ATTORNEY
deputy ruler	VICEGERENT, VICEREGENT
	VICEREINE, VICEROY
FBI	G-MAN
financial agent (Roman)	PROCURATOR
	QUAESTOR
go-between	INTERMEDIARY, PANDER(ER)
	PIMP, PROCURER
government agent	AMBASSADOR, EMISSARY
legal representative	
of company etc	SYNDIC
—at meetings	DELEGATE, PROXY
manager	
—for another	PROC(URA)TOR
—of estate	BAILIFF, REEVE, STEWARD
middleman	BROKER, FACTOR
representative of	
—Australian state or	
Canadian province	AGENT-GENERAL
—clergy	PROCTOR
—principal	ASSIGNEE, COMMISSARY
	DEPUTY, PROXY, VICAR
secret agent	DOUBLE AGENT, SPY
secretly representing another	DUMMY, FRONT
aircraft	
bombers/strike aircraft	
—American	BOSTON, BRONCO
	DAUNTLESS, FLYING FORTRESS
	HAVOC, HUDSON, HUSTLER, INTRUDER
	KEYSTONE, LIBERATOR, MITCHELL
	MUSTANG, PACKARD, SKYHAWK
	STANDARD, STEALTH
	STRATOFORTRESS, SUPERFORTRESS
	THOMAS MORSE, THUNDERBOLT
	THUNDERCHIEF, VIGILANTE

—British   AIRCO, AVRO, BATTLE
BLENHEIM, BUCCANEER, CANBERRA
CUCKOO, FOX, GUNBUS, HALIFAX
HANDLEY-PAGE, HARRIER, HAWK
LANCASTER, LINCOLN, MOSQUITO
STIRLING, SWORDFISH, VALIANT
VICTOR, VIMY, VULCAN
WELLESLEY, WELLINGTON
WIGHT
—European   EFA, TORNADO
—French   ALPHA JET, AMIOT, BLERIOT
BREGUET, CAUDRON, ETENDARD
FARMAN, MIRAGE, POTEZ
—German   AEG, DORNIER
FRIEDRICHSHAFEN, GOTHA
HEINKEL, JUNKERS, LVG, STUKA
STORMBIRD, STURMVOGEL, VAK
—Italian   ANSALDO, CAPRONI, POMILIO
SAVOIA, SIA
—Japanese   NAKAJIMA, VAL
—Russian   BACKFIRE, BADGER
BLACKJACK, BLINDER
BREWER, FIDDLER, FITTER
ILYA MOUROMETZ, ILYUSHIN
SUKHOI, TUPOLEV
—Spanish   HISPANO
—Yugoslav   GALEB, GULL
civil
—American   ARAVA, ATB
BEECH, BOEING, COMMUTER
CONVAIR, DAKOTA, DOUGLAS
ELECTRA, GULFSTREAM, JUMBO
LEARJET, MALLARD
MCDONNELL, MERLIN
METRO, STRATOLINER
(SUPER-)CONSTELLATION
TRISTAR, VEGA
—Australian   NOMAD
—Brazilian   BANDEIRANTE, BRASILIA
VECTOR
—British   AEROVAN, ALBATROSS
BRABAZON, BRITANNIA, CHALLENGER
(CANADA)DASH, CITATION, COMET
CONCORD, DOVE, ENSIGN
GEMINI, GULFSTREAM, HASTINGS
HERALD, HERMES, ISLANDER
JETSTREAM, ONE-ELEVEN, PHOENIX
RAPIDE, STATESMAN, TRIDENT
TRILANDER, TUDOR
VIKING, VISCOUNT
—Canadian   TWIN OTTER
—Czech   TURBOLET
—Dutch   FELLOWSHIP, FRIENDSHIP
—French   CARAVELLE, CONCORDE
CORVETTE, FALCON
FREGATE, MERCURE

—German   DORNIER, FOKKER
HANSA FAN JET, SKYSERVANT
—international   AIRBUS, AIRTECH
SAAB-FAIRCHILD
—Israeli   COMMODORE
—Russian   ANTONOV, BERIEV, CARELESS
CHARGER, CODLING, CONCORDSKI
FOXHOUND, ILYUSHIN
TUPOLEV, YAKOVLEV
—Spanish   AVIOCAR
early planes   ANTOINETTE, BLERIOT
DEMOISELLE, (GOLDEN) FLYER
JUNE BUG, PTERODACTYL, VOISIN
engine manufacturers
—American   GENERAL ELECTRIC
PRATT AND WHITNEY
—British   ROLLS-ROYCE
—French   SNECMA
—German   DAIMLER-BENZ
—Russian   SOLOVIEV
famous planes
—American president   AIR FORCE ONE
—dropped atom bomb   ENOLA GAY
—first
   commercial jetliner   COMET
   supersonic jetliner   CONCORD(E)
—Howard Hughes   SPRUCE GOOSE
—Jim Mollison   THE HEART'S CONTENT
—Kingsford Smith   SOUTHERN CROSS
—Lindbergh   SPIRIT OF ST LOUIS
—Lord Rothermere   BRITAIN FIRST
—solar-powered   SOLAR CHALLENGER
—Wiley Post   WINNIE MAY
—Wright brothers   FLYER
fighters/interceptors
—American   AIRABONITA, AIRACOBRA
AIRACOMET, AIRACUDA
BLACK WIDOW, BUFFALO
CORSAIR, CRUSADER
DELTA DART, EAGLE, FALCON
FREEDOM FIGHTER, HELLCAT
HORNET, KINGCOBRA, KITTYHAWK
LANCER, LUSAC, MOHAWK, MORSE
MUSTANG, PEASHOOTER, PHANTOM
SABRE, SHRIKE, STARFIGHTER
THUNDERBOLT, THUNDERCHIEF
TIGERCAT, TIGERSHARK, TOMCAT
WARHAWK, WILD WEASEL
—Argentinian   PUCARA
—Australian   BOOMERANG
—British   AIRCO, AVOCET, BAGSHOT
BEARDMORE, BEAUFIGHTER
BRISTOL BULLDOG, CAMEL
DEFIANT, DEMON, DESTROYER
DOLPHIN, FIREFLY, FURY, GAMECOCK
GAUNTLET, GLADIATOR, GREBE

HARRIER, HIPPO, HORNET, HOTSPUR
HUNTER, HURRICANE, KANGAROO
LIGHTNING, LINCOCK, MARTINSYDE
METEOR, NIGHTHAWK, PTERODACTYL
PUP, SALAMANDER, SCOUT, SE
SEA HAWK, SEA VIXEN, SEAFIRE
SISKIN, SNARK, SOPWITH, SNIPE
SPITFIRE, TEMPEST, TORNADO
TYPHOON, VAMPIRE, VENOM, WELKIN
WESTBURY, WHIRLWIND, WOODCOCK
—Czech   AVIA
—Dutch   KOOLHAVEN
—European   JAGUAR
—French   BEBE, BLOCH, CORSAIRE
DELANNE, HANRIOT, MILAN, MIRAGE
MORANE(-SAULNIER), NIEUPORT
PARASOL, RAFALE, SALMSON
(SUPER) ETENDARD
(SUPER) MIRAGE, SPAD SCOUT
VOISIN, WIBAULT
—German   ALBATROS(S), ARADO
ARROW, AVIATIK, BRANDENBERG
DFW, EINDEKKER, FALCON
FOCKE-WULF, FOKKER, HALBERSTADT
HANNOVER, KOMET, MESSERSCHMITT
MOSKITO, NATTER, OWL, PFALZ
PFIEL, PHONIX, ROLAND
RUMPLER, SALAMANDER
SCHWALBE, SIEMENS-(SCHUCKERT)
STARSTRUTTER, SWALLOW, TAUBE
UFAG, UHU, VIPER, VOLKSJAGER
—Italian   AMBROSINI, ANSALDO, CAPRONI
DARDO, FIAT, FALCO, FOLGORE
MERIDIONALI, PIAGGIO
REGGIANE, VIZZOLA
—Japanese   AURORA, BOLT OF LIGHT
DENKO, DRAGON KILLER, GALE
GEKKO, HAYABUSA, HAYATE, HIEN
HURRICANE, KIKKA, KYOKKO
MOONLIGHT, ORANGE BLOSSOM
PEREGRINE FALCON, RAIDEN
REPPU, SHIDEN(-KAI), SHUSUI
SWALLOW, SWINGING SWORD
THUNDERBOLT, TORYU
VIOLET LIGHTNING, ZERO(-SEN)
—South African   CHEETAH
—Swedish   DRAKEN, GRIPEN, VIGGEN
—Russian   ANADE, ANATRA, BEREZNIAK
FIDDLER, FIREBAR, FISHBED
FITTER, FLAGON, FLOGGER
FOXBAT, LAVOCHKIN
MIG, MIKOYAN
POLIKARPOV, SUKHOI
SHTURMOULK, YAK
—Yugoslav   IKARUS-ROGOZARSKI
HAWK, JASTREB

flying-boats
—American   BOEING, CATALINA
CURTISS, LARGE AMERICA
MALLARD, MARTIN
—British   EMPIRE, FELIXSTOWE
NORMAN THOMPSON
SUNDERLAND, WALRUS
—Canadian   CANADAIR
—German   DORNIER
—Japanese   SHIN MEIWA
—Russian   BERIEV, TCHAIKA
helicopters
—American   APACHE, BELL, BLACKHAWK
CHINOOK, COBRA
FAIRCHILD HILLER
HUGHES, HUEYCOBRA, IROQUOIS
JETRANGER, KAMAN SEASPRITE
MOJAVE, RANGER, SEABAT
SHAWNEE, SIKORSKY
SKYCRANE, TWIN TWO-TWELVE
VERTOL, WHIRLAWAY, WORK-HORSE
—Austrian   LOHNER
—British   AIRMARK WALLIS, AVRO
BELVEDERE, BRISTOL
CAMPBELL CRICKET
CIERVA ROTORCRAFT
DRAGONFLY, GYRODYNE
HELIPLANE, HOVERFLY, LYNX
ROTODYNE, SEAKING, SQUIRREL
SYCAMORE, WESTLAND
WHIRLWIND
—French   ALOUETTE, ARIEL
ASTAZOU, CHEETAH, DE MICHEN
DJINN, FRELON, GAZELLE
GYROPLANE, LAMA, PUMA, SPRITE
—German   BACHSTEIZE, DOBLHOFF
DRACHE, FLEITNER
FOCKE(-WULF)
—Russian   HIP, HIND, HOMER
HOODLUM, HOOK, HOPLITE
HORMONE, KAMOV
MIL, SWIDNIK, YAKOVLEV
—Spanish   AIR HORSE, CIERVA
PESCARA
light aircraft
—American   AEROSTAR, BEECHCRAFT
CESSNA, CITATION
GOLDEN EAGLE
LEARJET, MUSKETEER
PIPER NAVAJO, MERLIN
—Brazilian   IPANEMA
—British   FLYING FLEA, GIANT MOTH
GYPSY MOTH, ISLANDER
MEW GULL, NYMPH, PUSS MOTH
SILVER STREAK, TIGER MOTH
—Czech   TURBOLET, ZLIN

—French   DIPLOMATE, FALCON
                           RALLYE
—German   HANSA FAN JET
—Italian   BRAVO, MARCHETTI
                           OSCAR, PARTENAVIA
—New Zealand   AIRTOURER
—Romanian   IRMA
—Russian   SUKHOI
—Swedish   MFI
—Swiss   BRAVO
—very light and small   (HANG) GLIDER
                           MICROLIGHT

manufacturers
—American   BELL, BOEING, BREWSTER
         CONSOLIDATED, CONVAIR, CURTISS
         DOUGLAS, FAIRCHILD, FARMAN
         GATES, GENERAL DYNAMICS
         GOODYEAR, GRUMMAN, LOCKHEED
         MCDONNELL, MORSE
         NORTH AMERICAN, NORTHROP
         PACKARD, PIPER, REPUBLIC
         ROCKWELL, SEVERSKY, SIKORSKY
         SWEARINGEN, VOUGHT, WRIGHT
—Australian   GAF
—Brazilian   EMBRAER
—British   AIRMARK
         ARMSTRONG WHITWORTH
         AVRO, BEARDMORE, BLACKBURN
         BRISTOL, BRITTEN-NORMAN
         CAMPBELL, CIERVA, DE HAVILLAND
         FAIREY, FARNELL, GLOSTER
         HANDLEY-PAGE, HAWKER SIDDELEY
         PERCIVAL, SAGE, SAUNDERS-ROE
         SHORT, SOPWITH, SUPERMARINE
         VICKERS, WESTLAND
—Canadian   BOMBARDIER, CANADAIR
—Czech   LET
—French   AEROSPATIALE, BLERIOT
         BREGUET, BLOCH, DASSAULT
         DEWOITINE, NIEUPORT
         NORD, SALMSON
         SOCATA, SPAD
         SUD-AVIATION, SUD-EST
—German   BLOHM UND VOSS, DORNIER
         FOCKE-WULF, FOKKER, GOTHA
         HEINKEL, JUNKERS, MBB
         MESSERSCHMITT, PFALZ
—Indian   HAL
—Italian   AERMACCHI, FIAT
         REGGIANE, PARTENAVIA
         SAVOIA-MARCHETTI
—Japanese   AICHI, KAWANISHI
         KAWASAKI, KYUSHU
         MITSUBISHI, NAKAJIMA, NAMC
         SHIN MEIWA, TACHIKAW
         YOKOSUKA

—Russian   ANTONOV, ILYUSHIN
                     MIKOYAN, SIKORSKY
                     YAKOVLEV
—Spanish   HISPANO
—Swedish   SAAB, SVENSKA
—Yugoslav   SOKO
pilotless   DRONE
pilots
—American   BONG, BOYINGTON, BYRD
         CASTLE, CUNNINGHAM, EARHART
         GABRESKI, GENTILE, IACCACI
         JOHNSON, LAMBERT
         LEMAY, LEPPLA
         LINDBERGH, LUFBERY, LUKE
         MITCHELL, O'HARE, POST
         RICKENBACKER
         WRIGHT, YEAGER
commanders   CHENNAULT, MITCHELL
                         SPAATZ
—Australian   HINKLER
—Austro-Hungarian   ARIGI, BRUMOWSKI
         FIALA, LINKE-CRAWFORD
—Belgian   COPPENS, JACQUES
         MEULEMEESTER, THIEFFRY
—British   AARON, ALCOCK, BADER
         BALL, BEACHAMP-PROCTOR
         BEAMONT, BOOTHMAN, BROWN
         BULMAN, CARMICHAEL, CHESHIRE
         COBHAM, COLLISHAW, CUNNINGHAM
         DUKE, GIBSON, GREENWOOD
         HAWKER, JOHNSON
         KINGSFORD-SMITH
         MACLAREN, MANNOCK
         MCCUDDEN, MOLLISON, SAMSON
         SHORT, STAINFORTH, TRUBSHAW
         TUCK, WAGHORN
commanders   BARRATT
         BROOKE-POPHAM, DOWDING
         HARRIS, PARK, PORTAL
         SLESSOR, TEDDER, TRENCHARD
display team   RED ARROWS
—Canadian   BARKER, BISHOP, KENT
display team   SNOWBIRDS
—Finnish   LUUKKANEN
—French   BOYAU, CLOSTERMANN
         FARMAN, GARROS
         LE GLOAN, GUYNEMER
         MADON, NUNGESSER, PONCK
display team   PATROUILLE DE FRANCE
—German   BAR, BECKER, BERTHOLD
         BOELCKE, GALLAND, GOERING
         HARTMANN, HEINRICH, IMMELMANN
         LENT, LOERZER, LOWENHARDT
         MARSEILLE, MEYER, OSTERKAMP
         RICHTHOFEN, RUDEL, RUMEY
         SCHAUFER, TRATT, UDET, VOSS

commanders	GALLAND, GOERING
	LOHR, RICHTHOFEN
—Italian	BARACCA, BARRACHINI
	PICCIO, SCARONI
display team	TRICOLORI
—Japanese	FUCHIDA, IWAMOTO
	NISHIZAWA, SAKAI, SUGITA
—New Zealand	DEERE
—Polish	BRUMOWSKI
	LINK-CRAWFORD
—Portuguese display team	ASAS
—Russian	AVDYEYEV, D'ARGUEEFF
	KAZAKOV, SEVERSKY
	SMIRNOFF
—South African	MALAN, PATTLE
—Spanish display team	PATRULLA AGUILA
—Swiss	RUBENSDORFFER
display team	PATROUILLE SUISSE
pioneers	BLERIOT, BRABAZON
	CODY, FAIRCHILD, FARMAN
	GARROS, LILIENTHAL, NORTHROP
	SOPWITH, WRIGHT
reconnaissance planes	
—American	BLACKBIRD, HAWKEYE
	ORION, PROWLER, RAVEN
	SENTRY, VIGILANTE, VIKING
—British	BUCCANEER, HARRIER
	LYSANDER, NIMROD
	SHACKLETON
—French	ATLANTIC, BLERIOT
	CAUDRON, FARMAN
	LONGHORN, SHORTHORN
—German	AGO, BRANDENBERG, DFW
	HALBERSTADT, LOHNER, LVG
	RUMPLER, STEISLER
	STORCH, VAK
—Italian	SAML, SIA
—Russian	BLINDER, BREWER
	FIDDLER, TUPOLEV
seaplanes	
—American	BOEING
—British	CAMPANIA, SHORT
	SUPERMARINE, SWORDFISH
	WIGHT
—German	SABLATNIG
spy plane	BLACKBIRD, U2
terms	
—accident	PRANG
—advanced technology	
bomber	ATB, STEALTH
—air deflector	AIR-BRAKE, SPOILER
	WIND-BRAKE
—angle of wing	ANHEDRAL, DIHEDRAL
—baggage conveyor	CAROUSEL
—body	FUSELAGE
—bombing raid	MISSION

—cargo	PAYLOAD
—circular course	
over airfield	HOLDING PATTERN
—cockpit cover	CANOPY
—control	
stick	COLUMN, JOYSTICK
surface	AEROFOIL, ELEVATOR
	FLAP, RUDDER
—course	VECTOR
—curve of wing	CAMBER
—decrepit plane	CRATE
—ejecting cockpit	CAPSULE
—enemy aircraft	BANDITS
—engine housing	NACELLE
—experimental stealth	
technology	XST
—faster than sound	SST, SUPERSONIC
—fault (often inexplicable)	GREMLIN
—flight recorder	BLACK BOX
—fly across the wind	CRAB
in vertical circle	LOOP(-THE-LOOP)
low	HEDGE HOP
without power	GLIDE, VOLPLANE
—forecourt	APRON
—height recorder	ALTIMETER
—jet-assisted take-off	JATO
—land	TOUCH DOWN
beyond runway	OVERSHOOT
in the sea	DITCH
short of runway	UNDERSHOOT
—landing surface	RUNWAY, TARMAC
—lifting surface	AEROFOIL
—lose speed and fall	STALL
—mission	SORTIE
—move aircraft on land	TAXI
—navigation system	DECCA, TACAN
—operations centre	CONTROL TOWER
—passenger-carrying	
jet plane	JETLINER
—raid	SORTIE
—route	FLIGHT PATH
	FLIGHT PLAN
—shock wave	SONIC BOOM
—short take-off and landing	STOL
—speed recorder	MACHMETER
—start flight	TAKE OFF
—tail sections	EMPENNAGE
—take off quickly	SCRAMBLE
—testing chamber	WIND TUNNEL
—tilt sideways	BANK
—towed target	DROGUE
—training machine	SIMULATOR
—triangle-shaped	DELTA-WING
—vertical take-off and landing	VTOL
—visible trail in sky	CONTRAIL
	VAPOUR TRAIL

—waiting	
area	CONCOURSE
room	TRANSIT LOUNGE
—wheel cover	SPAT
—wind indicator	WIND CORE, WIND SLEEVE
	WINDSOCK
—wing	
or tailplane	AEROFOIL
storage attachment	POD
—with	
moveable wings	SWING-WING
	SWIVEL-WING
rotors on wings	TILT-ROTOR
training planes	
—British	AUSTER, AVRO, BULLDOG
	GNAT, HAWK, PROVOST
	STRIKEMASTER
—Canadian	TUTOR
—Czech	AERO, SKYDEVIL, ZLIN
—French	ALPHAJET, STAMPE
—Indian	MARUT
—Italian	AEROMACCHI, MARCHETTI
—Swedish	SAAB
—Swiss	BRAVO
—Yugoslav	GALEB
transport planes	
—American	CONSTELLATION, DAKOTA
	EXTENDER, GALAXY, HERCULES
	LOCKHEED, STARLIFTER
	STRATOCRUISER
—British	SKYVAN
—Canadian	BUFFALO, TWIN OTTER
—European	TRANSALL
—French	CARAVELLE
—Israeli	ARAVA
—Italian	FIAT
—Russian	ANTEI, ANTONOV
	ILYUSHIN, TUPOLEV
—Spanish	AVIOCAR
—Swiss	PILATUS PORTER
airlines	
Africa	AIR AFRIQUE, SAA
Alaska	WIEN AIR
America	AIR CAL, AMERICAN, APOLLO
	ARIZONA AIR, ARROW, BRANIFF
	CONTINENTAL, DELTA
	EAGLE, EASTERN
	FRONTIER, IMPERIAL, NORTHWEST
	OZARK, PANAM(ERICAN), PIEDMONT
	REPUBLIC, TRANSAIR, TRANSWORLD
	(TWA), UNITED, US AIRLINES
	WESTERN, WORLD AIRWAYS
Arabia	SAUDIA
Australia	QANTAS
Belgium	SABENA
Brazil	VARIG INTERNATIONAL

Britain	AIR EUROPE
	AIR UK, BA, BAC, BCAL, BEA
	BIRMINGHAM EUROPEAN
	BOAC, BRITISH CALEDONIAN
	BRITISH MIDLANDS, BRITANNIA
	BRYMON, DANAIR, FLEXAIR
	IMPERIAL AIRWAYS
	JERSEY EUROPEAN, LOGANAIR
	LONDON CITY AIRWAYS
	MANX AIRLINES, ORION
	PARAMOUNT, VIRGIN
Canada	AIR CANADA, AIR ONTARIO
	CP AIR, WARDAIR
Chile	LAN(CHILE)
China	CACC
Cuba	CUBANA DE AVIACION
Dominica	AEROMAR
Ecuador	ECUATORIANA
Egypt	ZAS
El Salvador	TACA
Finland	FINNAIR
France	AIR FRANCE, UTA
Germany	INTERFLUG, LUFTHANSA
Greece	OLYMPIC
Guatemala	AVIETECA
Gulf States	EMIRATES, GULF AIR
Hawaii	ALOHA, HAWAIIAN AIR
Honduras	AEREO (DE HONDURAS)
	SERVICEO
Hong Kong	CATHAY PACIFIC
India	AIR INDIA
Indonesia	GARUDA INDONESIA
Ireland	AER LINGUS, RYAN AIR
Israel	EL AL
Italy	ALITALIA
Japan	ALL NIPPON, ANA
	JAL, NAGASAKI
	NIHON KINKYOR, TOA
Jordan	ALIA, ARAB WING
	ROYAL JORDANIAN AIRLINES
Korea	KOREAN AIRLINES
Luxemburg	LUXAIR
Malaysia	MALAYSIAN AIR SERVICES
Mexico	AEROMEXICO
Netherlands	KLM, ROYAL DUTCH
New Zealand	AIR NEW ZEALAND
Pakistan	PAKISTAN INTERNATIONAL
Poland	LOT
Portugal	TAP
Romania	TAROM
Russia	AEROFLOT
Scandinavia	CONAIR
Singapore	SINGAPORE INTERNATIONAL
South Africa	SAA
Spain	IBERIA, SPANTAX
Sweden	LINJEFLYG

Switzerland	SWISSAIR
Thailand	THAI INTERNATIONAL
Venezuela	VIASA
Yugoslavia	JAT
airports	
America	
—Alaska	HARTFIELD INTERNATIONAL
—Boston	LOGAN INTERNATIONAL
—California	LOS ANGELES INTERNATIONAL
	SAN FRANCISCO INTERNATIONAL
—Chicago	O'HARE
—Dallas	DALLAS-FORT WORTH
	LOVE FIELD, REDBIRD
—Denver	STAPLETON INTERNATIONAL
—Florida	MIAMI INTERNATIONAL
—Hawaii	HONOLULU INTERNATIONAL
—New York	JOHN F KENNEDY
	LA GUARDIA, NEWARK
—St Louis	LAMBERT
—Texas	DALLAS/FORT WORTH REGIONAL
—Washington	WASHINGTON
	INTERNATIONAL
England	BIGGIN HILL, BIRMINGHAM
	EAST MIDLANDS, EXETER, GATWICK
	HEATHROW, HUMBERSIDE
	LEEDS/BRADFORD, LIVERPOOL
	LUTON, MANCHESTER, NEWCASTLE
	NORWICH, SOUTHAMPTON, SOUTHEND
	SPEKE, STANSTED
France	AEROPORT DE PARIS
	CHARLES DE GAULLE
	LE TOUQUET, ORLY
Canada	
—Toronto	PEARSON
Germany	
—Berlin	TEGEL, TEMPELHOF
—Frankfurt	FLUGHAFEN FRANKFURT MAIN
Holland	SCHIPHOL
Hong Kong	KAI TAK
Ireland	DUBLIN, COLLINS, SHANNON
Israel	BEN GURION
Italy	ROMA
Japan	
—Osaka	OSAKA INTERNATIONAL
—Tokyo	HAMEDA
	TOKYO INTERNATIONAL
Russia	SHEREMETEVA
Scotland	ABERDEEN, EDINBURGH
	GLASGOW, PRESTWICK
Singapore	AIRTROPOLIS, CHANGI
Albania	AL
brigand	KLEPHT
capital	TIRANA, TIRANE
cavalryman	SPAHI
coin	GROSH, LEK, QINDARKA
	QUINT(AR)

dialect	CHAM, TOSK
kilt	FUSTANELLA
mountaineer	ARNA(O)UT
ruler	MPRET
secret police	SIGURIMI
soldier	ARNA(O)UT, PALIKAR
alchemy	
alchemist	STAGYRIST
—Arabic	ALHAZEN, GEBER
	JABIR IBN-HAYYAN
—Dutch	VAN HELMONT
—Italian	DELLA PORTA
—Swiss	PARACELSUS
	VON HOHENHEIM
—Syrian	CALLINICUS
black(ish) compound	ETHIOPS
distilling flask	ALEMBIC
element involved in combustion	PHLOGISTON
furnace	ATHANOR
gold	SOL
mercury	AZOTH
—ammonal chloride	SAL ALEMBROTH
process in search of	
philosopher's stone	OLBATION, CIBAT
red	
—or black tincture	SERICON
—powder	COLCOTHAR
	CROCUS OF MARS
salt of wisdom	SAL ALEMBROTH
secret remedy	ARCANUM
silver	LUNA
solvent	MENSTRUUM
substance giving eternal life	ELIXIR
textbook	ALMAGEST
transmuting agent	ELIXIR, MAGISTERY
	PHILOSOPHER'S STONE
	SERICON
universal	
—remedy	ELIXIR, PANACEA
—solvent	ALCAHEST, ALKAHEST
vital principle	ARCH(A)EUS
Alderney	GBA
Algeria	ALG, DZ
capital	ALG(I)ERS, EL DJAZAIR
castle	CASBAH, KASBA(H)
cavalryman	SPAHEE, SPAHI
cheese	CAPRINO
coin	CENTIME, DINAR
dish	COUSCOUS(OU), CUSCUS
	KHUSKHUS
drink	AGRAS
fort	CASBAH, KASBA(H)
governor	DEY
infantryman	TURCO, ZOUAVE
measure	PIK
raid	ROZZIA

reedy grass	DISS
ship	XEBEC(K), ZEBEC(K)
shrub	BRIAR, BRIER
soldier	SOUAVE, TURCO, ZOUAVE
weight	ROTL
wine	PINARD
alloys	
aluminium	
—and	
brass	ALUMINIUM BRASS
copper	ALUMINIUM BRONZE
—zinc	AERO METAL
magnesium	MAGNALIUM
—hard	DURALUMIN(IUM)
anti-friction alloy	BABBIT(T'S) METAL
bismuth and	
—cadmium, lead, tin	WOOD'S METAL
	LIPOWITZ'S ALLOY
—lead, tin	FUSIBLE METAL
	ROSE'S METAL
brass	LATTEN, ORICHALC
—and manganese	MANGANESE BRONZE
Britannia metal	TUTANIA
bronze and tin	WHITE BRONZE
cast iron with nickel etc	NICROSILAL
ceramic and metal	CER(A)MET
cerium with iron	
and rare earths	MISCHMETAL
cobalt and	
—chromium, tungsten etc	STELLITE
—iron, nickel	KOVAR
commercial zinc	SPELTER
copper and	
—aluminium, zinc	DEVARDA'S ALLOY
—arsenic	TOMBAC, TOMBAK
—manganese, nickel	MANGANIN
—nickel	CONSTANTAN
	CUPRO-NICKEL
iron, etc	MONEL METAL
tungsten, zinc	PLATINOID
zinc	GERMAN SILVER
	NICKEL SILVER
—tin	BRONZE, GUN METAL
	SPECULUM METAL
phosphorus	PHOSPHOR BRONZE
zinc	GUN-METAL
	MOSAIC GOLD, MUNTZ METAL
	PINCHBECK, PRINCE'S METAL
	WHITE BRASS
—zinc	BRASS, DUTCH METAL
	MANGANESE BRASS
	MANGANESE BRONZE
	MOSAIC GOLD
	MUNTZ METAL, PINCHBECK
	PRINCE'S METAL, SIMILOR
	WHITE BRASS

etc	OREIDE, OROIDE
	ORMOLU, PLATINOID, POTIN
	TOMBAC, TOMBAK
	YELLOW-METAL
iron	DELTA METAL
nickel	GERMAN SILVER
tin	ORMULU
Egyptian	ASEM
emitting sparks	
when struck	PYROPHORIC ALLOY
for joining metals	SOLDER
gold and	
—brass	TALMI GOLD
—nickel	WHITE GOLD
—palladium	WHITE GOLD
—silver	ASEM, CARACOLY, EGYP
	ELECTRUM
gold-coloured	ORICHALC
imitating gold and silver	LEAF-METAL
imitation gold	PINCHBECK
iridium and osmium	IRIDOSMINE
	IRIDOSMIUM, OSMIRIDIUM
iron and	
—carbon	STEEL
—chromium, carbon	STAINLESS STEEL
—manganese and carbon	SPIEGEL(EISEN)
—nickel	PERMALLOY
carbon	INVAR
—other metal	FERRO-ALLOY
—with another metal	FERRO-ALLOY
kind of Britannia metal	TUTANIA
lead and	
—antimony, tin	TYPE METAL
—tin	CALIN, TERNE(-METAL)
copper, etc	PEWTER
light-coloured copper	WHITE COPPER
magnesium	
—alloy used as sheath	
for uranium rods	MAGNOX
—and aluminium	MAGNALIUM
magnetic alloys of	
copper, manganese,	
aluminium	HEUSLER'S ALLOYS
manganese and nitrogen	MEAN STEEL
mercury alloy	AMALGAM
misch metal and iron	AUER METAL
nickel	
—and	
chrome	NICHROME
copper	CONSTANTIN
iron, copper, manganese	MUMETAL
steel	INVAR
—based	MONEL METAL
non-ferrous	TULA
osmium and iridium etc	OSMIRIDIUM
pewter	BIDRI, TRIFLE

silver and	
—copper	SHIBIUCHI
etc	BILLON, VELLON
—nickel	ALFENIDE
silvery	OCCAMY
steel and	
—chromium	STAINLESS STEEL
—manganese	MANGANESE STEEL
—nickel	NICKEL STEEL
and chromium	ELINVAR
—silicon	STALLOY
tin	
—and	
copper, etc	BRITANNIA METAL
	BABBIT(T'S) METAL
	TUTANIA
lead, antimony	PEWTER
—based	WHITE METAL
tutania	BRITANNIA METAL
used in dentistry	AMALGAM
yellow	SIMILOR
zinc and	
—copper etc	TUTENAG
—lead etc	COMMERCIAL ZINC, SPELTER

alphabet

any based on syllables	SYLLABARY
Arabic	CUFIC, KUFIC
—script	NASK(H)I, NESK(H)I
Assyrian and Babylonian	CUNEIFORM
Bulgarian	CYRILLIC
Celtic	OG(H)AM
Chinese	HAN CHARACTERS
	IDEOGRAMS
	IDEOGRAPHY, PINYIN(ZIMU)
code words for letters	PHONETIC ALPHABET
Cretan	LINEAR A, LINEAR B
Egyptian	
—pictorial	HIEROGLYPHICS
—religious	HIERATIC
—secular	DEMOTIC
for the blind	BRAILLE, MOONTYPE
games	LEXICON, SCRABBLE
Greek	LINEAR B
	(*see also* **Greek**)
Hebrew	(*see* **Hebrew**)
Hindu	DEVANAGARI
Indian	DEVANAGARI
—group	NAGARI
international	IPA
Iranian	PAHLAVI, PEHLAVI
Irish	OG(H)AM
Italian (old)	CHALCIDIAN
Japanese	HIRAGANA, KANJI, KATAKANA
joined letters	CURSIVE
medieval	CAROLINGIAN, RUSTIC
	UNCIAL

old characters	EDH, ETH
	SCHARFES S, THORN, YOGH
Persian script	NASTALIK, NASTALIQ
	NASTAUK, NASTAUQ
phonetic	GLOSSIC, IPA, ROMIC
—signalling	ALPHA, BRAVO, CHARLIE
	DELTA, ECHO, FOXTROT, GOLF
	HOTEL, INDIA, JULIET, KILO
	LIMA, MIKE, NOVEMBER, OSCAR
	PAPA, QUEBEC, ROMEO, SIERRA
	TANGO, UNIFORM, VICTOR, WHISKY
	X-RAY, YANKEE, ZULU
pictorial	HIEROGLYPHICS, IDEOGRAMS
	PICTOGRAMS
Romany	ROMAJI
rounded script	UNCIAL
runic	FUTHARK, FUTHORC, FUTHORK
Russian	CYRILLIC
	(*see also* **Russian** — letters)
Sanskrit	(DEVA)NAGARI
Sicilian (old)	CHALCIDIAN
signaller's	MORSE CODE, SEMAPHORE
Sikh	GURMUKHI
Slavonic	GLAGOL(ITIC)
sloping script	ITALIC
standard	ROMAN
Sumerian	CUNEIFORM
Syriac	ESTRANG(H)ELO
teaching	ITA
upright script	ROMAN
wedge-shaped	CUNEIFORM

American

aboriginal	AMERIND, ESKIMO
	(RED) INDIAN, INUIT
accessories	FINDING
accustomed	WONTED
act as paid dance partner	HOSTESS
address of welcome	SALUTATORY
adherent of British	
government	ROYALIST
administrative district	TOWNSHIP
administrator of local	
school system	SUPERINTENDENT
admiring looks	EYE SERVICE
advertising leaflet	DODGER
advocate, council	MOUTHPIECE
affair	SHEBANG
agency	
—intelligence	CIA
—security	FBI
agitated	HET UP
agrimony	BONE-SET
air control	CAB
aircraft navigation system	VOR
airline	PAN AM, TWA
alert	HEADS-UP

all	
—clear	COPACETIC, COPESETTIC
—right	HUNKY(-DORY)
allowable	RULABLE
alluvial deposits	BOTTOM-LAND
almost	MOST
aloe	AGAVE, MAGUEY
alter	BUSHEL
ambassador	EMBASSADOR
Amelanchier	JUNEBERRY, SHADBUSH
anxious	ANTSY
American people	UNCLE SAM
animal	CRITTER, CRITTUR
anti	
—British Association	FENIAN
—cartel worker	TRUST-BUSTER
—fraud laws	BLUE SKY LAWS
antiquated	FOGRAM
anxious	ANTSY
any labiate plant	MINT
anything, something	
—dishonestly obtained	MAVERICK
—done for applause	HOKUM
—large	SCROUGER
—of little value	SMALL POTATOES
—rented or hired	RENTAL
—superfluous	BLITVIT
—very big	SLOCKDOLAGER
	SOC(K)DOLAGER, SOCDOLIGER
	SOCDOLOGER, SOGDOLAGER
	SOGDOLIGER, SOGDOLOGER
Apocynum	INDIAN HEMP
applaud	ROOT
apple	BALDWIN, JONATHAN
—brandy	APPLE-JACK
—pie or pudding	PANDOWDY
aquatic rodent	MUSK-RAT, MUSQUASH
area of	
—dark soil	BLACK-BELT
—negro population	BLACK BELT
armed right wing	
organisation	MINUTEMEN
army quartermaster	PAYMASTER GENERAL
arrest	BUST
arrogant	TOPPING
art gallery	MUSEUM
Artemisia	SAGEBRUSH
assistant purser	MUD-CLERK
astonished	BUG-EYED
Astragalus	LOCO(-PLANT)
	LOCO-WEED
asylum	BUG-HOUSE
at	
—any rate	LEASTWAYS, LEASTWISE
—odds	AT OUTS
—present	PRESENTLY

attend	
—class	AUDIT
—to	TEND OUT ON
audition	CATTLE CALL
autumn	FALL
aware of	KNOWING TO
awkward fellow	JAY
axolotl	MUD-PUPPY
baby's	
—dummy	PACIFIER
—nappy	DIAPER
backwoodsman	BUCKSKIN
back yard	DOOR-YARD
bad whiskey	TARANTULA JUICE
badge of naval rank	SHOULDER-MARK
badger	TAXEL
bag	
—from which gifts	
are drawn	GRAB-BAG
—net	FYKE
baggage to be laid down	
at a railway station	WAY-BAGGAGE
bait	HELLGRAM(M)ITE
baited line	TRAWL
bald eagle	WHITE-HEADED EAGLE
ball	FANDANGO
Baltimore oriole	FIRE-BIRD, HANGBIRD
	ICTERUS
bank	
—governor	PRESIDENT
—note	BILL
—rate	DISCOUNT RATE
Baptist sect	DUNKERS
barbecue	COOK-OUT
bar-room	EXCHANGE
bargaining	DICKER
baseball	(see separate entry)
bass	GROWLER
bat	MORMOPS
batter pudding	POPOVER
be	
—a school-teacher	TEACH SCHOOL
—furiously angry	STAMP
—in domestic service	LIVE OUT
—the guest of	VISIT WITH
bean	TEPARY
bear	CINNAMON-BEAR, GRIZZLY
	KODIAK, MUSQUAW
—berry	MANZANITA
beat	SHELL
beaten path	TRACE
beating the bounds	PROCESSIONING
bed	
—bug	CHINCH
—quilt	COMFORTABLE
	COMFORTER

—room over hall	HALL-BEDROOM
bedded oyster	PLANT
bee	
—hive	GUM
—line	AIRLINE
beer jug	GROWLER
beg	PANHANDLE
beggar	PANHANDLER, SCHNORRER
believe	GUESS
bird	APHRIZA, BALTIMORE (ORIOLE)
	BLACK-THROATED BUNTING
	BLUE-BIRD, BOBOLINK, BOBWHITE
	BUFFLEHEAD, BUSH-TIT
	CHAPARRAL COCK
	COW (BLACK-)BIRD
	DICKCISSEL, FIELD-LARK
	FIREBIRD, GOATSUCKER, GRA(CK)LE
	GREENLET, GROUND-ROBIN, HANGBIRD
	HANGNEST, MARSH-ROBIN
	MEADOW-LARK, MELOPSIZA
	MOCKING-THRUSH, PURPLE FINCH
	RAIL, REED-BIRD, RICE-BIRD
	ROAD-RUNNER, SCISSOR-TAIL
	SHARP-TAILED GROUSE, SKUNK-BIRD
	SNOW-GOOSE, SONG-SPARROW, SORA
	SPIRIT-DUCK, STONE-CURLEW, SURF-BIRD
	TATTLER, THRASHER, THRESHER
	TOWHEE, TURKEY-VULTURE
	TYRANT-BIRD, TYRANT-FLYCATCHER
	VEERY, VELVET SCOTER, VIREO
	WAV(E)Y, WHIP-POOR-WILL
	WHITEWING, WILLET, WOOD-THRUSH
	WOOD-WARBLER, WREN-TIT, ZOPILOTE
bird-catching spider	MYGALE
bison	BUFFALO
black	
—bass	GROWLER
—bird	GRA(C)KLE
—tailed deer	JUMPING DEER
—vulture	CARRION CROW
blackmail	STRIKE
bladder-campion	CAROLINA PINK, PINKROOT
bland	MICKEY
blarney	TAFFY
blind fish	AMBLYOPSIS
block of	
—buildings	SQUARE
—public land	TOWNSHIP
blockhead	MUTT
bloodroot	PUCCOON
blue-winged snow-goose	WHITEHEAD
board on which fish is cooked	PLANK
boat	DORY
bobolink	REED-BIRD, RICE-BIRD
	SKUNK-BIRD
bobwhite	QUAIL

boiled	
—flour dumpling	DOUGH-BOY
—maize	HOMINY
boiler-suit	COVERALL
bony pike	GARFISH
boo	BRONX CHEER
bookmaker's book of bets	HANDBOOK
boot of car	TRUNK
boring	
—old fool	FOGRAM
—person	SCHMO
boss	HONCHO
botch	FLUB, MUX
bottle of dark glass	JUNK-BOTTLE
bottom-drawer	HOPE-CHEST
bowfin	LAKE-LAWYER
Bowie knife	TOOTH-PICK
bowler hat	DERBY
bowls	TEN-PINS
box-wagon	BOX-CAR
Boxing Association	WBA
boy	BUB(BY)
braces	SUSPENDERS
branch post-office	STATION
brawl	ROUGH-HOUSE
brawn	HEADCHEESE
breach of river bank	CREVASSE
bread (maize)	CORN-BREAD
—root	PRAIRIE-TURNIP
breakdown truck	WRECKER
bribe	KICKBACK
bridesmaid	MAID OF HONOUR
bring up	FETCH UP
brisk run	BRUSH
brittle	BRASH
broad-brimmed hat	SUNDOWN
broadcasters	CBS, CNN, RCA
broken tree	RAMPICK, RAMPIKE
brook	CREEK, RILL
brother	BUD(DY)
brownish-yellow	CLAY-BANK
brown-paper patch	SHIN-PLASTER
brushwood thicket	CHAPARRAL
buckthorn	CEANOTHUS, WAHOO
buffalo-nut	OILNUT
buffalo/cow hybrid	BEEFALO
building	
—earning money to	
pay taxes	TAX-PAYER
—stone	BROWNSTONE, FIELDSTONE
bulge	BUG
bulrush	SCIRPUS, TULE
bumpkin	YAP
bunk	HOKUM
buoyed line with hooks	TRAWL
burbot	LAKE-LAWYER

burglar	YEGG(MAN)
burning bush	WAHOO
burrowing	
—animal	(POCKET-)GOPHER
—snake	GOPHER
bus with low fares	JITNEY
bush	CHAPARRAL
	CREOSOTE-PLANT
business	INC
bustle	RUSTLE
butter-nut	OILNUT
buzzard	RED-TAIL
by short cuts	ACROSS LOTS
bye-law	ORDINANCE
cabinet	OFFICIAL FAMILY
cake	CORN-CAKE, CORN-DODGER
	FRIEDCAKE, HOE-CAKE
	LOAF-CAKE, SHORTCAKE
Californian	
—buckthorn bark	CASCARA
—plant	FOUR-O'CLOCK
—shrub	CHAMISE, CHAMISO
—white oak	ROBLE
call on	GAM
camp	
--follower	BUMMER
—kettle	DIXIE
camping kit	DUFFEL, DUFFLE
Canadian	CANUCK, KANUCK
candlefish	EULACHON, OOLAKAN
	OULACHON, OULAKAN
candy floss	CANDY-COTTON
	COTTON CANDY
	FLUKUM, SPUN SUGAR
canvasser	SALESMAN, SOLICITOR
capital	WASHINGTON (DC)
car	AUTO(MOBILE)
—body (rear)	TONNEAU
—bonnet	HOOD
—boot	TRUNK
—park	PARKING LOT
—silencer	MUFFLER
—wing	FENDER
carbine	ESCOPETTE
card-game	EUCHRE
cardigan	WAM(M)US, WAMPUS
cargo ship	LIBERTY SHIP
caribou	REINDEER
Carolina	
--allspice	CALYCANTHUS
—jasmine	GELSEMIUM
carriage	BUCKBOARD, BUCKCART, BUGGY
	HERDIC, ROCKAWAY, SURREY
carry	TOTE
—on the hip	HIP
—out	FILL

cart	DEMOCRAT(-WAGON)
cast	MOLT
catapult	SLING-SHOT
catch	
—fish with seine-net	TRAWL
—of fish	MESS
caterpillar	WEBWORM
catfish	HORN(ED)-POUT
	MUD-CAT, SILURE
cattle-drover	PUNCHER
cause to fall	FALL
censorious	NEGATIVE
central reservation	PARKING
cereal	INDIAN CORN, MAIZE
	MEALIES
ceremony	EXERCISE
certainly	SURE
chairman of company	PRESIDENT
challenge to perform a feat	STUMP
change	
--over	TRANSFER
—in nature or politics	FLOP
changing hut	CABANA
chaos	SNAFU
chaotic	SNAFU
charivari	SHIVAREE
chat	VISIT
chat with	VISIT WITH
cheap	JITNEY
—cigar	LONG NINE
—hotel	FLOPHOUSE
checker-berry	PARTRIDGE-BERRY
cheeky	SASSY
cheer	ROOT
chemist	DRUGGIST
chemist's shop	DRUG-STORE
cheque	CHECK
cherry-laurel	MOCK-ORANGE
chest of drawers	DRESSER
chest-strap for carrying	TUMP-LINE
chevrotain	MOUSE-DEER
chewink	GROUND-ROBIN
child's	
—apron	TIER
—garment	PANTY-WAIST
chipmunk	GROUND-SQUIRREL
chiropodist	PODIATRIST
choice specimen	PEACHERINO
chopped bait	TOLL-BAIT
cicada	HARVEST-FLY
cigar(ette) end	SNIPE
circular saw	BUZZ-SAW
civil	
—law officer	MARSHAL
—War	WAR OF SECESSION
civilian	CITIZEN

clam	COHOG, QUAHOG, QUAHAUG
claptrap	HOKUM
class-room	RECITATION-ROOM
clear by felling trees	SLASH
clergyman	DOMINIE
clever	HEADS-UP
cliff-sided hill	BUTTE
climbing plant	GELSEMIUM
	CLUSIA, STAR-OF-THE-NIGHT
cloak-room	CHECK(ING)-ROOM
clot of dirt or colour	SPLATCH
clump of trees	MOT, MOTT(E)
clumsy person	SCHLEMIEL, SCHEMIHL
coalition	FUSION
cock's-foot grass	ORCHARD-GRASS
coffin	CASKET
coin	ROCK
—old (Spanish)	PISTAREEN, REAL
—cent	PENNY
—5 cents	JITNEY, NICKEL
—6½ cents (old)	PICAYUNE
—10 cents	DIME
—12 cents	BIT
—17 cents (silver)	PINE-TREE MONEY
—25 cents	QUARTER, TWO BITS
—50 cents	HALF-DOLLAR
—100 cents	DOLLAR
—dollar	BUCK, GREENBACK, WHEEL
—5 dollars	ABE'S CABE, FIN
—10-dollar bill	SAWBUCK, TENSPOT
—10 dollars	EAGLE
—20 dollars (gold)	DOUBLE EAGLE
—500 dollars	MONKEY
—proposed	MILL
—small	PICAYUNE
—unit	CENT
college	
—dance	PROMENADE
—lecturer	INSTRUCTOR
coloured nurse	MAMMY
comedy drama	DRAMEDY
comics in newspaper	FUNNIES
commercial traveller	DRUMMER
	SALESMAN
commotion	RUCKUS
company	CAHOOT, CORPORATION
—working together	OUTFIT
compass-plant	SILPHIUM
computer	ENIAC
concede	ALLOW
concerned with administration	PRUDENTIAL
conclusive argument	SLOCKDOLAGER
	SOCDOLIGER, SOCDOLOGER
	SOC(K)DOLAGER, SOGDOLAGER
	SOGDOLIGER, SOGDOLOGER
conduct in court, as a lawyer	TRY

conductor	LEADER
confectionery	CANDY
confederacy of Indian tribes	FIVE NATIONS
Confederated States	CFA
confer degree on	GRADUATE
confidence trick	BUNCO, BUNKO
confounded	BLAME(D)
confused	STREAKED
confused conflict	MUSS(LE)
congregation	PARISH
Congressman	SOLON
connecting-rod	PITMAN
conscription	DRAFT
conservative person	HUNKER
considerable	SMART
constituency	DISTRICT
constrain	OBLIGATE
con-trick	BUNCO, BUNKO
controller	HONCHO
convey rapidly	GIGGIT
conveyance	PROTOCOL
cook on a board	PLANK
coral-snake	ELAPS
corn	MAIZE
cornflour	CORNSTARCH
corny	MICKEY
cotton	
—cloth for shorts	MUSLIN
—stripping machine	LINTER
cougar	CATAMOUNT, PANTHER
	PUMA, PAINTER
courgette	ZUCCHINI
councillor	COUNCILMAN
country	
—dance	HOEDOWN, VIRGINIA REEL
—lout	JAKE
—music	STAR-SPANGLED BANNER
covered wagon	PRAIRIE-SCHOONER
cowardly man	PANTY-WAIST
cowboy	BUCKAROO, COWPOKE
	COWPUNCHER
—hat	STETSON, TEN-GALLON HAT
—leggings	CHAPS, SHAPS
cowcatcher	PILOT
coyote	PRAIRIE-WOLF
crack-shot	DEAD-EYE
crazy person	SCREWBALL
crib	HORSE, PONY, TROT
crime	HEIST
cripple confined to house	SHUT-IN
critical onlooker	KIBITZER
croquet	ROQUE
cross of twigs	GOD'S EYE
crossing with	
underpass	GRADE SEPARATION
crowd	RAFT

crushed	CHAWED UP
cuckoo	COW-BIRD
cure and brown	DUN
curtain	DRAPE
customs-officer	'NAVAL OFFICER
cycad	COONTIE, COONTY
cyclist	CYCLER
dabchick	DIPPER
dagga	MARIJUANA
dainty	CUNNING
dairy over stream	SPRING-HOUSE
damnation	(TAR)NATION
damned	BLAME(D)
dance	(*see* dance)
dandy	DUDE
dare	STUMP
dark sandstone	BROWNSTONE
dead	
—person	DECEDENT
—tree	RAMPICK, RAMPIKE
debris of trees	SLASH
debutante	BUD
decamp	ABSQUATULATE, DIG OUT
decayed tree	RAMPICK, RAMPIKE
decision of council	REBOUND
decisive blow	SLOCKDOLAGER
	SOCDOLIGER, SOCDOLOGER
	SOC(K)DOLAGER, SOGDOLAGER
	SOGDOLIGER, SOGDOLOGER
decoration for wounds	PURPLE HEART
decoy	TOLE, TOLL
deer	(*see* antelope)
deer-mouse	WHITE-FOOTED MOUSE
defeat	
—by small margin	EDGE
—totally	CHAW-UP, SKUNK
defeatist	NEGATIVE
deficiency	WANTAGE
denim trousers	CHINOS
denomination	PARISH
denominational	PAROCHIAL
dentist	DOCTOR
dentures	STORE TEETH
derail	DITCH
desert	BUG-OUT
destroy political influence of	SCALP
detective	FED, G-MAN
	JACK, SHAMUS
detectives	FBI
diagram	PLAT
difficulty	NINE HOLES
dinner-jacket	TUXEDO
disadvantage	OUT
disaster	PROVIDENCE
discharge from armed forces	MUSTER OUT
discompose	FAZE, PHASE

disconcert	DISCOMBOBERATE
	DISCOMBOBULATE
discontented person	SOREHEAD
discounter	NOTE-SHAVER
disgusting	SCUZZY
—person	SCUZZBALL
dismissal	BOUNCE
dissolute	BUM
distillery	STILL-HOUSE
district	SECTION
—juicy with bribes	TENDER-LOIN
disturbance	ROUGH-HOUSE, RUCKUS
diving duck	BUFFLEHEAD
do menial work	STRIKE
dock (plant)	CANAIGRE
docker	LONGSHOREMAN
doctor's consulting-room	OFFICE
dogbane	FLY-TRAP
	INDIAN HEMP
dollar	BUCK, WHEEL
—bill	SCRIP
dolt	CLUNK
domestication of animals	ZOOCULTURE
doss-house	FLOPHOUSE
double plough	LISTER
doughnut	CRULLER, OLYCOOK
	OLYKOEK, SINKER
downright	UP-AND-DOWN
drag	SCHLEP, TUMP
drawback	OUT
drawer (of chest)	DRAW
drawing-pin	THUMB-TACK
dress up	GUSSY UP, RAG
dressing	
—gown	BATH-ROBE
—table	DRESSER, LOW-BOY
drink	MINT-JULEP
drinking	
—bar	SALOON
—fountain on	
ship	SCUTTLEBUTT
—resort	DOGGERY
drive	
—cattle	PUNCH
—fast	BARREL
driving turnout	RIG
drought area	DUST-BOWL
druggist	DOCTOR
drunk	JAGGED
drunkard	SOUSE
duck	CANVAS-BACK
dull	
—person	FLAT TYRE
—town	BOHUNK, HICKSVILLE
dummy	PACIFIER
dumpling	CORN DODGER

dung-beetle	TUMBLE-BUG
	TUMBLE-DUNG
dust	
—bin	GARBAGE CAN, (TR)ASH-CAN
—coat	DUSTER
—man	GARBAGEMAN
Dutch rush	SCOURING-RUSH
dwarf	
—cherry	SAND-CHERRY
—chestnut	CHINCAPIN, CHINKAPIN
	CHINQUAPIN
early civilisation	ADENA, HOPEWELL
	MISSISSIPPIAN
eastern	
—Indian	MOUND-BUILDER
—New York	EAST SIDE
easy educational course	CAKE COURSE
eccentric	DIFFERENT DRUMMER
	SCREWBALL
eczema	SALT-RHEUM
edible berry	SAL(L)AL-BERRY
—bulb	CAMAS(S), CAMASH
	QUAMASH
—caterpillar	PUXI
—fungus	TUCKAHOE
—part of anything	MEAT
educational meeting	CHAUTAUQUA
effeminate man	PANTY-WAIST
elderly man	UNCLE
election	
—scrutiny	CANVASS
—with disputed	
result	CONTESTED ELECTION
elementary school	COMMON SCHOOL, GRADE
elk	MOOSE
elm	WAHOO
embezzle	KNOCK DOWN
encourage	ROOT
end of whiplash	SNAPPER
engine	
—driver	ENGINEER
—house with turntable	ROUND-HOUSE
enlist	MUSTER IN
—into military	INDUCT
enroll	MUSTER IN
entertain as guest	HOST
entrance	
—fee	INITIATION FEE
—hall	HALLWAY
enunciation	DICTION
equinoctial storm	LINE-STORM
estate agent	REALTOR
eternal	TARNAL
evangelist	RELIGIONIST
evening just past	OVERNIGHT
evening primrose	SUN-DROPS

evergreen	LIVE-OAK, MADRONA
	MADRONO, MOUNTAIN-TEA
ewer	PITCHER
ex-directory	UNLISTED
ex-serviceman	VET(ERAN)
excellent	COPACETIC, COPESETTIC
excessively enthusiastic	GUNG-HO
exchange courtesies with	GAM
exclusive social set	THE FOUR HUNDRED
exclusively fashionable	PINK
expert shot	DEAD-EYE
exploratory well	WILD-CAT
expression of	
—admiration	SOME POTATOES
—disgust	BLECH, BLEGH
—vexation	DOG ON IT, DOGGONE IT
expressway	THROUGHWAY, THRUWAY
exquisite	PINK
extinct bird	HEATH-HEN
	PASSENGER-PIGEON
exuberant	FEISTY
fail at	FLUB
false teeth	STORE TEETH
familiar	GAY
fancy dishes or adjuncts	DOINGS
fanlight	TRANSOM
farewell oration	VALEDICTORY
farm	BOWERY
—boundary fence	LINE-FENCE
fast car	HOT ROD
feign death	PLAY POSSUM
fellow	GUY, JACK
—lodger	ROOM-MATE
female night-club singer	CHANTEUSE
fence of pales	PICKET-FENCE
fight	MIX-IN
figure with	
—no sides parallel	TRAPEZIUM
—two sides parallel	TRAPEZOID
finch	CARDINAL-BIRD, CHEWINK
	GROUND-ROBIN, INDIGO BIRD
	PINE-FINCH, SNOW-BIRD
	TOWHEE
fine	SWELL
fireman's ladder	BIG STICK
firmness of character	SAND
first	
—Monday in September	LABOR DAY
—display of new	
season's goods	OPENING
fish	ALE-WIFE, BLACK BASS
	BLUE-FISH, BOWFIN, CAP(E)LIN
	CAVALLA, CAVALLY, CISCO, CONNER
	CUNNER, DARTER, DOLLY VARDEN
	GROUPER, HORNYHEAD, JEW-FISH
	LAKE-HERRING, MASKALONG

	MASKEL(L)ONGE, MASKINONGE
	MENHADEN, MISSISSIPPI STURGEON
	MUSKELLUNGE, PIG-FISH
	POMPANO, ROBALO, RONCADOR
	SCUP(PAUG), SEA-ROBIN
	SHEEP'S-HEAD, SHOVEL-HEAD
	SPECK, SQUETEAGUE, SUCKER
	SURF-FISH, TAUTOG, TILEFISH
	TOGUE, TORSK, TUNA, TUNNY
	WALL-EYE, WHITEBASS
	YELLOW-CAT
—bait	TOLL-BAIT
—split for cooking	SCROD
fit out	STAKE
fix	NINE HOLES
flag	OLD GLORY
	STARS AND STRIPES
—awarded for victory in games	PENNANT
—day	TAG-DAY
flapjack	SLAPJACK
flat	APARTMENT
—railway wagon	GONDOLA
—region	PLAT
flat-bottomed boat	MACKINAW
flat-sided	SLAB-SIDED
flattery	SOFT SAWDER, TAFFY
fliers	USAAF
flirt	CHIPPY
floating tree	SAWYER
floor behind theatre stalls	PARQUET CIRCLE
flounder	LIMANDA
flow	PUT
flower	COSMOS, INDIAN PIPE
	PENSTEMON, RUDBECKIA
	TARWEED, TRILLIUM, WAKE-ROBIN
fly	
—larvae used as bait	HELLGRAM(M)ITE
—catcher	KING-BIRD, SCISSOR-TAIL
—catching thrush	SOLITAIRE
folk concert	HOOTANANNY, HOOT(E)NANNY
	HOOTANANNIE, HOOT(E)NANNIE
fool	YAP
foolish	FOOL
football	(see separate entry)
fop	DUDE
forage grass	GAMA-GRASS
forbid	ENJOIN
forehead strap for carrying loads	TUMP-LINE
forest	
—clearing	SLASH
—land	TIMBER
formal proceeding	EXERCISE
forward	FORTH-PUTTING

fourth-year student	SENIOR
fowl	RHODE ISLAND RED
fox	VORCYRON
free admission	CUFFO
freeze	TAKE
French bean	STRING BEAN
fresh vegetables	TRUCK
freshwater	
—fish	ETHEOSTOMA, GOLDEYE
	LAKE-LAWYER, MOON-EYE
—mussel	DEER HORN
friction match	LOCOFOCO
fried	
—ball of dough	HUSH PUPPY
—cake	CRULLER
—chicken	BARNYARD PIMP
friend	BUD(DY), PAISANO, SIDEKICK
fringe	BANG
fruit	BLUEBERRY, CHOKEBERRY
	CRANBERRY, DEERBERRY
	HUCKLEBERRY, JUNEBERRY
	MARIONBERRY, MAY APPLE
	MIN(N)EOLA, SAL(L)AL-BERRY
	SASKATOON, SHADBERRY
—juice and vinegar	SHRUB
frying-pan	SKILLET
fudge	PENUCHE
full of	
—speed	NIP AND TUCK
—stumps	STUMPY
fun	MUSIC
funeral director	MORTICIAN
furnish	STAKE
furrow made with lister	LIST
galoshes	GUMSHOES
game	ROQUE
garden	
—party	LAWN-PARTY
—produce	TRUCK
gathering	
—for husking corn	HUSKING(-BEE)
—to help raise house-frame	RAISING-BEE
genuine	SURE-ENOUGH
German	DUTCH
get up (to horse)	HUDDUP
ghost	HAUNT
giant cactus	SAGUARO
girl	BABE, BROAD, DAME, QUAIL
give notice of mining claim	DENOUNCE
glance	SLANT
glassy (surface)	GLARE
goal or base in game	HUNK
goat/antelope	ROCKY MOUNTAIN GOAT
goatsucker	BULLBAT
gobstopper	JAWBREAKER

gold-seeker	FORTY-NINER	habituated	WONTED
good		hackberry	HAGBERRY
—condition	KELTER, KILTER	hackee	GROUND-SQUIRREL
—deal more	SOME	hagberry	HACKBERRY
—hand at cards	PAT	haggling	DICKER
—natured	CLEVER	hair grip	BOBBY PIN
goods		hairy creature (supposed)	BIGFOOT
—van or wagon	FREIGHT-CAR		SUSQUATCH
—wagon	FREIGHTER	hamlet	CROSSROAD
gooseberry	WORCESTER-BERRY	hand of welcome	GLAD HAND
gopher	CAMASS-RAT	handbag	CABA, POCKET-BOOK
gorge	BARRANCA, BARRANCO		PURSE
gossip	SCHMOOSE, SCHMOOZE	handbill freely distributed	THROW-AWAY
	SCUTTLEBUTT	handicraft article	BOONDOGGLE
got	GOTTEN	hard blow	SLOCKDOLAGER
government			SOC(K)DOLAGER, SOCDOLIGER
—certificate for acquisition of			SOCDOLOGER, SOGDOLGER
public land	LAND-SCRIP		SOGDOLIGER, SOGDOLOGER
—dockyard	NAVY YARD	hare	JACK-RABBIT
—exhortation to restrain wages	JAWBONE		SNOW-SHOE RABBIT
—money for improvements	PORK	herald	OLD SQUAW
—office as reward	PLUM	harmless snake	RING-SNAKE
—official who practises		harness horse	HITCH
outside office	SUNDOWNER	harvest-mite larva	CHIGGER, CHIGOE
grackle	BLACKBIRD		CHIGRE, JIGGER
graduand giving address	SALUTATORIAN	hat	STETSON
grain pest	JOINT-WORM	haul of fish	MESS
gramophone	PHONOGRAPH	have done	BE THROUGH
grape	CATAWBA, FOX-GRAPE	headmaster	PRINCIPAL
	SCUPPERNONG	head of	
grass	GRAMA, PASPALUM	—fire brigade	FIRE-MARSHAL
	SPIKE-GRASS, UNIOLA, XYRIS	—organisation	PRESIDENT
	YELLOW-EYED GRASS	—police or fire brigade	MARSHAL
grasshopper	KATYDID	hearing of prepared lesson	RECITATION
gratuity	LAGNIAPPE	heat anew	WARMED-OVER
great		heated	HET
—Bear	BIG DIPPER	hedge-tree	OSAGE ORANGE
—deal	SOME	height of room	STUD
grey wolf	TIMBER-WOLF	helicopter	CHOPPER, HOVER
griddle-cake	SLAPJACK	hellbender	MUD-PUPPY
groin	GROYNE	helping	ORDER
gromwell	PUCCOON	hemp-agrimony	MIST-FLOWER
ground		hen	PLYMOUTH ROCK
—cuckoo	CHAPARRAL-COCK		RHODE ISLAND RED
—floor	FIRST FLOOR	herd of saddle horses	REMUDA
—hog	MARMOT, WOODCHUCK	herdsman	WRANGLER
—squirrel	FLICKERTAIL, GOPHER	herdsmen's hut or village	RANCHERIA
grouse	PRAIRIE-CHICKEN	herring	MENHADEN
	SAGE-COCK, SAGE-GROUSE	hickory	PECAN(-TREE)
guard (railway)	CONDUCTOR	hiding-place	HIDY-HOLE
guard's van	CABOOSE	highwayman	ROAD-AGENT
guelder-bark	CRAMP-BARK	hill-country rustic	HILL-BILLY
guelder-rose	CRANBERRY-TREE	hillside terrace	OFF-SET
gully	GULCH	hilly upland region	COTEAU
gum tree	TUPELO	hire purchase	INSTALLMENT PLAN
gunman	GUNSEL	hired thug	GOON

hold	HOLT
holiday	LABOR DAY
hollo	HOLLER
home run	HOMER, TATER
homely philosophy	CRACKER-BARREL
hooligan	ROUGH-NECK
horse	
—breaker	WRANGLER
—chestnut	BUCKEYE
—Indian	CAYUSE
—piebald	PINTO
—poor	TACKY
—race	KENTUCKY DERBY
—riding	SADDLER
—sprinter	QUARTER-HORSE
—thin	RACKABONES
—wild	BRONC(H)O, MUSTANG
horsetail	SCOURING-RUSH
house	SHEBANG
—man	INTERN(E)
—of Congress	CAPITOL
—warming	INFARE
—with rooms to let	ROOMING-HOUSE
household goods	PLUNDER
however	LEASTWAYS, LEASTWISE
huckster	PITCHPERSON
humbug	GUM
Hungarian	BOHUNK, HUN(KY)
husband during wife's lying-in	GANDER-MOONER
husk	SHUCK
hut	SHEBANG
ice-cream counter	SODA-FOUNTAIN
icy surface	GLARE
idiot	AIRHEAD, APPLEHEAD
ill-conditioned person	TACKY
illegal Mexican immigrant	WETBACK
illicit liquor shop	SPEAK-EASY
immediately	LICKETY-SPLIT
impetuous	BRASH
impose on by talking	GAS
in	
—advantageous position	IN THE CATBIRD SEAT
—America	STATESIDE
—collusion	IN CAHOOTS
—good condition	THRIFTY
—good position	HUNKY(-DORY)
—less than	INSIDE OF
—partnership	IN CAHOOTS
—proper manner	ABOUT EAST
—the evening	EVENINGS
inclined or level stretch of road or railway	GRADE
inconclusive trial	MISTRIAL
increase	LIFT

Indian	AMERINO, RED INDIAN, REDSKIN
—corn meal	NOCAKE
—meal cake	HOE-CAKE
—Negro	GRIFF(E)
—poke	ITCHWEED
	(see also **Red Indian**)
indoor fair	KERMESS, KERMIS(S)
ineffectual person	LUNCH GUY
inefficient person	SLOUCH
inexperienced youth	GUNSEL
infant	CARPET-APE, RUG-APE RUG-RAT
infantryman	DOUGH-BOY
inferior	JAY, SCHLOCK
influence	DRAG
inform	CUE IN
informed of	KNOWING TO
informer	FINK
innkeeper	INNHOLDER
insect	GOLD-BEETLE, GOLD-BUG KATYDID
insectivorous plant	DIONAEA SARRACENIA SIDE-SADDLE FLOWER VENUS'S FLY-TRAP
insincere work	EYE SERVICE
inspecting policeman	ROUNDSMAN
intelligence	CIA
interjection	GEE, SON OF A GUN, ZOWIE
intermediate station	WAY-STATION
interpreter	LING(UI)STER, LINKSTER
into	
—confusion	GALLEY-WEST
—New England	DOWN EAST
—unconsciousness	GALLEY-WEST
intoxicating liquor	RUM, TANGLEFOOT
invalid confined to house	SHUT-IN
investigators	CIA, FBI
ivy	ANGELICA-TREE
jaguar	(AMERICAN) TIGER
jail	HOOS(E)GOW
jam tart	CUPID
Japanese immigrant	ISSEI, NISEI
jargon	BAFFLEGAB
jay	XANTH(O)URA
jubilee	SEMI-CENTENNIAL
jug	PITCHER
July 4th	INDEPENDENCE DAY
jumble	WUZZLE
June 14th	FLAG-DAY
Juneberry	AMELANCHIER, SHADBUSH
jury	
—man	VENIREMAN
—writ	VENIRE (FACIAS)
kaput	KABLOOEY, (KER)FLOOEY
Kentuckian	CORNCRACKER

key	HORSE, PONY, TROT	—or register of business	
keyless watch	STEMWINDER	to be transacted	DOCKET
kind	STRIPE	literal translation	TROT
king-bird	PETCHARY	litter-bin	TRASH-CAN
knitted jacket	WAM(M)US	little finger	PINKIE, PINKY
lake fish	MENOMINEE	lizard	UTA
land allotted to settler	HOMESTEAD	loaf	BUM
landsman	SHORESMAN	—around	SLOSH
larch	HACKMATACK	lobelia	INDIAN TOBACCO
	TAMARACK	—red	CARDINAL-FLOWER
larder over stream	SPRING-HOUSE	lobster fat	TOMALLEY
large		local councillor	SELECT-MAN
—estate	PLANTATION	lodge of Order of Patrons	
—fish	TARPON	of Husbandry	GRANGE
—quantity	SLATHER	lodge(r)	ROOM(ER)
—sandwich	HERO, SUBMARINE	lodging-house	ROOMING-HOUSE
larva of ant-lion	DOODLEBUG	long	
laurel	KALMIA	—jump	BROAD JUMP
lawless backwoodsman	ROWDY	—television programme	TELETHON
lawyer	COUNSELLOR	look	GANDER
	DA, JURIST	—out!	HEADS-UP
lax in law-enforcement	WIDE-OPEN	loose jacket	VAREUSE
leaf-nosed bat	MORMOPS	lorry	TRUCK
lean hog	LAND SHARK	Louisiana French or Spanish	CREOLE
leather support-strap		Louisianan of French descent	HABITANT
of carriage	THOROUGHBRACE	low	
leave		—public-house	GROGGERY
—hastily	BUG OUT	—sled	STONE-BOAT
—military	FURLOUGH	lower very slightly	SHADE
leaves round maize ear	CORN-HUSK	lucerne	ALFALFA
	CORN-SHUCK	luggage	
legislature	CONGRESS	—compartment of car	TRUNK
lending library	RENTAL LIBRARY	—room	CHECK(ING)-ROOM
leopard	OCELOT	—van	FREIGHT-CAR
lesson	RECITATION	lumberman	RAIL-SPLITTER
letter		lumberman's hook	PEAV(E)Y
—box	MAILBOX	lure	TOLE, TOLL
—for local delivery	DROP LETTER	lynx	BOBCAT, CATAMOUNT
level		mad	LOCO(ED)
—crossing	GRADE CROSSING	made to order	CUSTOM
—tract	BENCH	mafia	COSA NOSTRA
by river	INTERVALE	magnolia	CUCUMBER(-TREE)
licensing law	EXCISE LAW		SWEET-BAY
lift	ELEVATOR	main road	PIKE
light cart	BUCKBOARD	maize	CORN
lighter	GONDOLA	—bread	INDIAN BREAD
lights out	TAPS	—drink	CORN WHISKEY
lily	CAMAS(S), CAMASH	—dumpling	CORN-DODGER
	MEDEOLA, QUAMASH	—exchange mart	CORN-PIT
limitation of debate	CLOTURE	—loaf	CONE-PONE
linden tree	BEE-TREE	—plantation	CORN-BRAKE
liquor	RUM	majority over any other	PLURALITY
—law	EXCISE LAW	make	
—shop	GROCERY	—a plan of	PLAT
list		—up (prescription)	FILL
—of candidates	TICKET	—use of	IMPROVE

male		—HQ	PENTAGON
—homosexual	FRUIT	—policeman	SNOWDROP
—Indian	BUCK	militiaman	MINUTEMAN
—negro	BUCK	milkweed	PLEURISY-ROOT
malicious damage	MAYHEM	milkwort	SENEGA
man	BO, GUY, JACK	mink	VISON
—living apart from his wife	GANDER	miscellaneous lot	RAFT
marine	LEATHERNECK	Mississippi sturgeon	SHOVEL-HEAD
market		mock serenade	HORNING, SHIVAREE
—garden produce	TRUCK	mocking-bird	MIMUS
—gardener	TRUCK-FARMER	mole	STAR-NOSE
marmot	GROUND-HOG, WOODCHUCK	money	JACK, SCRIP, SPONDULICKS
	PRAIRIE-DOG	mongrel	MUTT
marsh-marigold	COWSLIP	monkey	MARMOSET
marshland creek	SLOUGH	month of lying-in	GANDER-MOON
marshy river or lake	BAYOU	more than	THE RISE OF
marsupial	(O)POSSUM	mosquito	GALLINIPPER, SKEETER
marten	BLACKCAT, BLACKFOX	mother-in-law	MADAM
	FISHER, PEKAN	motherless calf	DOGIE, DOGY
	WOODSHOCK	motor junk yard	POT LOT, IRON LOT
mass of floating waterfowl	RAFT	mottled	PINTO
matter	SHEBANG	mountain	
mean customer	DRAGGER	—bear	GRIZZLY
measures		—foothill region	PIEDMONT
—1¼ acres	ARPENT	—mocking-bird	SAGE-THRASHER
—¹/₁₆ pint	FLUID OUNCE	—valley	PARK
—6 fl. oz.	PINT	mountains	ROCKIES
—473-551cc	PINT	mounted policeman	TROOPER
meat closest to the bone	TENDER-LOIN	mouse	DEER-MOUSE
mechanic	GREASE-MONKEY	—deer	CHEVROTAIN
medicinal root	DRAGON-ROOT	move rapidly	GIGGIT
meeting of		mugger of women	MOLL BUZZER
—delegates	CAUCUS	municipal	
—voters	TOWN-MEETING	—division of county	TOWN
melon	CANTALOUP	—police	MP
member of		mush	SCHMALTZ
—Chinese secret society	HIGHBINDER	musk-rat	WATER-RAT
—gymnastic club	TURNER	musquash	ONDATRA
—incorporated company	INCORPORATOR	name-plate	SHINGLE
—Ku-Klux-Klan	NIGHT-RIDERS	nappy	DIAPER
—lynch party	NIGHT-RIDERS	narrow, rocky valley	GULCH
—People's Party	POPULIST	National	
—secret		—Broadcasting Company	NBC
fraternity	MOOSE	—Bureau of Standards	NBS
party	KNOW-NOTHING	—emblem	BALD EAGLE
memorial tablet	MARKER		WHITE-HEADED EAGLE
men's outfitter	HABERDASHER	—flag	OLD GLORY
mercenary soldier	HESSIAN		STARS AND STRIPES
merge	MELD	—Guard	MILITIA
merry-go-round	CAR(R)OUSEL	—holiday	FOURTH OF JULY
mess	JACKPOT, MUX		INDEPENDENCE DAY
messenger in Congress	PAGE		THANKSGIVING
Mexican	GREASER	native of	
middle	CENTER	—Illinois	SUCKER
military		—Nova Scotia	BLUENOSE
—decoration	PURPLE HEART	—Virginia	TUCKAHOE

naval	
—engineer	SEABEE
—petty-officer	QUARTER-GUNNER
—quartermaster	PAYMASTER GENERAL
—warrant officer	SAILING-MASTER
neck and neck	NIP AND TUCK
negative	NOPE
negro	MOKE
—in south-east	GULLAH
—patois in Louisiana	GUMBO
—song	SECULAR, SPIRITUAL
neighbouring	NEIGHBO(U)R
New York	BIG APPLE, GOTHAM
New Yorker	GOTHAMITE
	KNICKERBOCKER
news	
—agent	NEWS-DEALER
—boy	NEWSHAWK, NEWSY
night	
—hawk	BULLBAT
—jar	POORWILL
—train	OWL-TRAIN
—tram-car	OWL-CAR
—watchman of remuda	NIGHTHAWK
nincompoop	APPLEHEAD
Nissen hut	QUONSET HUT
non-venomous snake	GARTER-SNAKE
North Carolinian	TAR-HEEL
north-south strip	RANGE
northern sea-duck	OLD SQUAW
nose-bleed	YARROW
not	
—Mormon	GENTILE
—one	NARY
—surveyed or marked off	UNLOCATED
—trade union member	YELLOW DOG
note down for nomination	SLATE
notecase	BILLFOLD
noughts and crosses	TICK-TACK-TOE
now	PRESENTLY
numbers in lottery	POLICY
nut	HICKORY, PECAN
	PICHURIM BEAN, SASSAFRAS NUT
—tree	HICKORY, PECAN
oak	QUERCITRON
obtain	
—on credit	RUN ONE'S FACE
—right of pre-emption	ENTER
occupy	IMPROVE
occurring now and then	SEMI-OCCASIONAL
odd-job man	ROUSTABOUT
officer	
—who determines boundaries	PROCESSIONER
—of lowest rank	ENSIGN
oilskin	SLICKER

old	
—Democrat	LOCOFOCO
—fashioned	FOGRAM, SCHMALTZY
—man on a station	ROUSTABOUT
—negro	UNCLE TOM
—New York democrat	HUNKER
—political party	WHIG
olive tree	FRINGE TREE
on the same level	AT GRADE
one	
—from same area	PAISANO
—of Mexican descent	CHICANO
—out to make up to all and sundry	GLAD-HANDER
—prevented from winning	SHUTOUT
—who	
carries by pack	PACKER
conducts log rafts	RIVER-DRIVER
does	
—not conform	MAVERICK
—public work	ENGINEER
has been a JP	SQUIRE
plays hand as dealt	STAND-PATTER
serves ice-cream etc	SODA-JERKER
splits logs for fencing	RAIL-SPLITTER
open-air seating	BLEACHERS
opening with grille	WICKET
opossum	DIDELPHYS
optional	ELECTIVE
—subject of study	ELECTIVE
oral examination	QUIZ
ordinary	ORNERY
out	
—and-out	REGULAR, STRAIGHT-OUT
—of	
date	FOGRAM, LUNCHY
sorts	MEAN
outlying trading-station	FORT
outmoded	SCHMALTZY
outwit	EUCHRE
overhead railway	EL
overshoe	ARCTIC, RUBBER
owl	SAW-WHET, WAPACUT
pack saddle	KYACK
packed in jars	CANNED
paddle-steamer	STERN-WHEELER
page torn out for reference	TEAR-SHEET
pair of valves or transistors	FLIP-FLOP
pal	BUD(DY), SIDEKICK
paling	PICKET-FENCE
paltry	JITNEY
papa	POPPA, POPPER
paper money	SCRIP, SHIN-PLASTER
paraffin	KEROSENE
parched Indian corn	NOCAKE, PINOLE
parlour	SPARE ROOM

part of Corn Exchange floor	PIT		PHLOX, RAGWEED
particular sort	STRIPE		SEGO, SNEEZEWEED
partly burned tree	RAMPICK, RAMPIKE		SNOW-PLANT, WINTER-CLOVER
partner	PARD(NER)		WINTERGREEN
partnership	CAHOOT(S)	—fraudulent voters	COLONISE, COLONIZE
party	HOEDOWN	plateau	BARREN
—at which gifts are given	SHOWER	play	
pass over in favour of another	OVERSLAUGH	—hand as dealt	STAND PAT
passé	FOGRAM, LUNCHY	—pizzicato	PINCH
passenger	PAX	pleaded	PLED
path	TRACE	pliable	DOUGH-FACED
patriot	HUNDRED-PERCENTER	plot out	PLAT
paved road	PAVEMENT	plover	KILLDEE(R), STONE-SNIPE
pavement	FOOTWAY, PAVE, SIDEWALK	pluck	PINCH
payment	COMPENSATION	plum suitable for drying	PRUNE
penitent at revival meeting	MOURNER	pocket-gopher	POUCHED-RAT
perch-pike	SAUGER	pod	SHUCK
peregrine falcon	DUCK-HAWK	poison-oak	SUMAC(H)
period of slackening		poisoned by locoweed	LOCOED
business	ROLLING ADJUSTMENT	pokeweed	GARGET, PIGEON-BERRY
permission to go out	OUT	police	
personal		—patrol car	PROWL CAR
—announcement in newspaper	CARD	—station	STATION-HOUSE
—goods	PLUNDER	policeman	BULL
pertaining to woods	WOODSY	—on the beat	PATROLMAN
perturb	FAZE, PHASE	—without rank	PATROLMAN
petrol	COAL-OIL, GAS(OLENE)	policeman's	
	GASOLINE	—badge	SHIELD
pharmacist	DRUGGIST	—stick	NIGHT-STICK
philop(o)ena (game)	FILLIPEEN	policy involving spending	
Phytolacca	POKEBERRY, POKEWEED	on improvements	PORK-BARREL
pickerel-weed	PONTEDERIA	political	
picket fence	RAIL-FENCE	—conference	CONVENTION
picnic	CLAMBAKE	—division of county	TOWN
piebald horse	PINTO	—funds	BARREL
pie-plant	RHUBARB	—party machine	ORGANISATION
pig-sty	HOG-PEN	—party organisation	MACHINE
pigeon	GROUND-PIGEON	—speaker	STUMP-ORATOR
	GROUND-DOVE	—wire-puller	PIPE-LAYER
	MOURNING-DOVE	pond	TANK
—berry	GARGET, POKEWEED	Pontederia	PICKEREL-WEED
piggin	PIPKIN	poor	
pike	PICKEREL, SAUGER	—horse	CAYUSE, TACKY
pinafore	TIRE	—whisky	REDEYE
—dress	JUMPER	—white	CONCH, CORN-CRACKER
pine	LOBLOLLY(PINE)		LOW-DOWNER
pistol	DERRINGER, GAT, IRON, ROD	—whites	TRASH
pitcher-plant	DARLINGTONIA	porch	STOOP
plain	HOMELY, ORNERY	porter	RED-CAP
plan	PLAT	portion	GRIST, ORDER
plane-tree	BUTTON-WOOD, SYCAMORE	postal code	ZIP CODE
plant	CHECKERBERRY	postcard	MAILING-CARD, POSTAL(-CARD)
	EVENING-PRIMROSE	potassium bicarbonate	SALERATUS
	GODETIA, GOLDEN-SEAL	potato pest	COLORADO BEETLE
	JACK-IN-THE-PULPIT	pot-hole	THANK-YOU-MA'AM
	PARTRIDGE-BERRY	pouched-rat	(POCKET-)GOPHER

poultry	PLYMOUTH ROCK
	RHODE ISLAND RED
prairie	
—chicken	GROUSE
—dog	MARMOT, WISHTONWISH
—grass	BUFFALO GRASS
—oyster	RAW EGG
—schooner	COVERED WAGON
—turnip	BREADROOT
—wolf	COYOTE
president	PREXY
—of college	PREX
press-stud	SNAP FASTENER
pretty girl	DOLL, PEACHERINO, QUAIL
primrose	SUN-DROP
prison	BRIG, CALABOOSE, CAN
	HOOS(E)GOW, LOG-HOUSE
	PENITENTIARY
—cell	TANK
—enclosure	BULL-PEN
—van	PATROL-WAGON
private	
—compartment on train	DRAWING-ROOM
—detective	PINKERTON
probable customer	PROSPECT
professional killer	GUN(SEL)
Progne	SWALLOW
prohibit by injunction	ENJOIN
promiscuous woman	CHIPPY, HOOKER
promise to accept	
later invitation	RAIN-CHECK
promoter	PITCHPERSON
promptly	IN SHORT ORDER
prosecutor	DA
prosperous	THRIFTY
protection money	KICKBACK
provisions given for share in finds	GRUB-STAKE
public	
—auction sale	VENDUE
—lavatory	COMFORT STATION
—service	UTILITY
pucker	POCKET
puddle	LOBLOLLY
Pueblo Indian	ZUNI
pull	SCHLEP
puma	CATAMOUNT, COUGAR
	PAINTER, PANTHER, (RED)TIGER
pumpkin	CASHAW
pupil at kindergarten	KINDERGARTENER
pupil's mark	GRADE
puritanical person	BLUENOSE
purple medick	ALFALFA
purpose	CALCULATE
put in danger	JEOPARD
quail	BOB-WHITE, COLIN
	ODONTOPHORUS, ORTYX

quaintly pleasing	CLEVER
Quaker City	PHILADELPHIA
quantity	GRIST, MESS
quickly	LICKETY-SPLIT
quite	REAL
—as much as	RISING
rabbit	COTTONTAIL
rac(c)oon	COON, PROCYON
radio broadcast	DOPE
Radio Corporation	RCA
railway	AMTRAK, EL
	RAILROAD, ROAD
—buffer	BUMPER
—carriage	RAIL(ROAD)-CAR
—coach connection	VESTIBULE
—porter	RED-CAP
—saloon	PARLOUR-CAR
—signal	TARGET
—sleeper	TIE
—station	DEPOT
—van or truck	RAILROAD CAR
—worker	RAILROADER
ramify	SPRANGLE
rapid	SA(U)LT
rapids in a gorge	DALLE
rascal	SKEESICKS
raspberry	SALMON-BERRY
ravine	COULEE, FLUME, GULCH
	PURGATORY
raw egg	PRAIRIE-OYSTER
ray	STINGAREE
re-enlisted soldier	VETERAN
reactionary	BOURBON
real	SURE-ENOUGH
really	REAL
rear	FETCH UP
rebuke	SCORE
reckless	BRASH
—youth	HOT-RODDER
record of land transfer	PROTOCOL
recovery-vehicle	WRECKER
recurring spree	PERIODICAL
red squirrel	BOOMER, CHICKAREE
	S(E)WELLEL
red-breasted thrush	AMERICAN ROBIN
redtop (grass)	HERD('S) GRASS
reed-bird	BOBOLINK
refrigerator	COOLER
refuge	HOLT
refuse container	(TR)ASH-CAN
region	SECTION
register	LEDGER
registrar	REGISTER
reheated	WARMED-OVER
reindeer	CARIBOU
religious excitement	ROUSEMENT

Remembrance Day	DECORATION DAY	rustic	HICK, RUBE
	MEMORIAL DAY	saddle	
remove shell or husk	SHUCK	—girth	CINCH
remuneration	COMPENSATION	—horse	SADDLER
rented farm-land	MANOR	safe-breaker	YEGG(MAN)
repertory company	STOCK COMPANY	sailor in Navy	GOB
representing whole area	AT LARGE	salal	GAULTHERIA
reprimanded	CHAWED UP	salamander	HELL-BENDER, MENOPOME
request to accept			MUD-PUPPY
later invitation	RAIN-CHECK	saloon car	SEDAN
reservation	HOLD	sand	
residential part of town	UP TOWN	—bar	OVERSLAUGH
residing in college	PARIETAL	—piper/stint	SAND-PEEP
resolute	FLAT-FOOTED	sans-serif type	GOTHIC
return	ROUND-TRIP	saucy	SASSY
reverse charges call	COLLECT CALL	saunter	MOSEY
revolver	COLT, GAT, IRON, ROD	school	
rhododendron	RHODORA	—dance	PROMENADE
rhubarb	PIE-PLANT	—imposition	PENSUM
rice-bird	BOBOLINK	—mistress	SCHOOL-MA'AM
ridge or hollow in road	THANK-YOU-MA'AM	scion	CION
riding-horse	SADDLER	Scout's leather cord	BOONDOGGLE
rifle	WINCHESTER	scrutinise	CANVASS
right of state to oppose		sea	
federal government	INTERPOSITION	—board	TIDE-WATER
ringplover	KILLDEE(R)	—bream	PORGIE, PORGY
ringtail(-cat)	CACOMISTLE, CACOMIXL	—lavender	SEA-ROSEMARY
risen	RIZ	season ticket	COMMUTATION TICKET
river		seclusion	RETIRACY
—fish	GROWLER	second-year student	SOPHOMORE
—mussel	NIGGER-HEAD	secret organisation	KU-KLUX(KLAN)
—sides	UPLAND	Secretary of State	PREMIER
—water affected by tides	TIDE-WATER	sedge	CHUFA, NUT-GRASS
rivers	(see separate entry)		TIGER-NUT
riverside embankment	LEVEE	see-saw	TEETER(-BOARD)
robbery	HEIST	seize without right	MAVERICK
rocket fuel	HYDYNE	self	
Rocky Mountain sheep	BIGHORN	—appointed	
rodent	JUMPING-MOUSE	peace-keepers	LYNCH MOB
	KANGAROO-RAT, MARMOT		VIGILANCE COMMITTEE
	MOUNTAIN-BEAVER, POUCHED-MOUSE		VIGILANTES
	S(E)WELLEL, WOODCHUCK	—possession	COOL
rodeo performer	COWBOY	sell tickets at inflated prices	SCALP
roll	BAGEL	semibreve	WHOLE NOTE
room	SHEBANG	send (on passenger ticket)	CHECK
—attached to shop	PARLOUR	sentimentality	SCHMALTZ
rose	RIZ	sergeant-fish	COBIA, CRAB-EATER
—pest	ROSE-BUG	settle	LOCATE
rough country	BOONDOCKS	shadbush	AMELANCHIER, JUNEBERRY
roundabout	CAR(R)OUSEL		SASKATOON, SERVICE-BERRY
routine flight	MILK-RUN	shallow section of river	RIFFLE
rubber overshoe	GUM(SHOE)	sharp-tailed grouse	PRAIRIE-CHICKEN
ruffed grouse	PARTRIDGE	shebeen	SPEAK-EASY
rumour	SCUTTLEBUTT	shell	SHUCK
running on thin ice	KITTLY-BENDERS	shoe	TIE
rural area	STICKS	—lace	(SHOE-)STRING

shop	SHEBANG
—assistant	(SALES-)CLERK
—keeper	STOREKEEPER
short jacket	ROUNDABOUT
shortage	WANTAGE
shout	ROOT
show spirit	SPUNK
showy production	SCHMALTZ
shrewd	HEADS-UP
shrub	BUTTON-BUSH, BUFFALO-BERRY
	BUFFALO-NUT, CALICO-BUSH
	CANDLEBERRY-TREE, CORAL-BERRY
	FRANGIPANI, GREASEWOOD
	HAMAMELIS, HOP-TREE
	HUCKLEBERRY, KALMIA
	MOUNTAIN-LAUREL
	RED-JASMINE, SAL(L)AL
	SNOWBERRY, SPICE-BUSH
	STAFF-TREE, STRAWBERRY-TREE
	SYMPHORICARPUS, WAX-MYRTLE
	WINTER-BERRY, WITCH-ALDER
	WITCH-HAZEL, WITHE-ROD
	YA(U)PON, YUPON
side	
—in billiards	ENGLISH
—of valley	COTEAU
sightsee(r)	RUBBER-NECK(ER)
sign-board	SHINGLE
sign language	AMESIAN
simpleton	FLATHEAD
sir(rah)	SIRREE
six-mile width of town	RANGE
skipping	JUMP-ROPE
skittles	TEN-PINS
skunk	SEE-CAWK
—bird	BOBOLINK
Slav	BOHUNK
sloppy	SOZZLY
slops	SOZZLE
slush	SPOSH
small	
—college	FRESHWATER COLLEGE
—lizard	FENCE-LIZARD
—loaf (maize)	CORN-DODGER
—river	CREEK
—township	VILLAGE
smoker's haze	SMAZE
snack	LUNCH
snake	HOG-NOSE, PIT-VIPER
snipe	SHAD-BIRD, WILLET
snow	
—bird	JUNCO
—goose	WAV(E)Y
—up	STALL
social	SOCIABLE
—blunder	BREAK

—gathering	HOEDOWN
—intercourse	GAM
soda-fountain worker	SODA-JERK(ER)
sodium bicarbonate	SALERATUS
soft drink	SARSAPARILLA
soil, sticky when wet	GUMBO
soldier	DOUGH-BOY, GI, SAMMY
—of both world wars	RETREAD
solicit orders	DRUM
sound	COPACETIC
	COPESETTIC
source of patronage, etc	PIE-COUNTER
Southerner who co-operated	
with Republicans	SCAL(L)AWAG
	SCALLYWAG
Spanish-American	GREASER
—half-caste	MESTIZO
—speaking district	BARRIO
sparrow	SAVANNA-SPARROW
speaker of farewell	VALEDICTORIAN
special subject	MAJOR
specialise at college	MAJOR
spectacles	CHEATERS
speculative scheme	WILD-CAT
speculator	WILD-CAT
speedwell	NECK-WEED
spelling competition	SPELL-DOWN
spice-bush	BENJAMIN-TREE
spider	BLACK WIDOW
spies	CIA
spill	LAMP-LIGHTER
spindle-tree	BURNING BUSH
spiny	
—fish	SCULPIN
—lizard	HORNED TOAD
Spiraea	HARD-HACK
spiritless person	FLAT TYRE
spittoon	CUSPIDOR(E)
splash	SOZZLE
—of dirt or colour	SPLATCH
splotch	SPLATCH
spoil	MUX
sponge	BUM
sporting kit	DUFFEL, DUFFLE
spotted sandpiper	PEETWEET
sprawl	SPRANGLE
spree	BUM
sprinter (horse)	QUARTER-HORSE
spruce	HEMLOCK
spy	FINK
squalid	SCUZZY
squat	ABSQUATULATE
squirrel	CHIPMUCK, CHIPMUNK
	GROUND-SQUIRREL, HACKEE
	S(E)WELLEL
St John's-wort	ORANGE-GRASS

stag	
—beetle	HORNBUG
—party	STAG
stage-coach	THOROUGHBRACE
stalk	STILL-HUNT
starchy tuber	INDIAN TURNIP
start	JUMP-OFF
state	
—governor's deputy	LIEUTENANT-GENERAL
—militia	NATIONAL GUARD
states	(see separate entry)
—without slavery	FREE STATES
steal cattle	RUSTLE
stevedore	LONGSHOREMAN
stew	BURGOO
—of corn and beans	SUCCOTASH
stewed fruit	SAUCE
stock	
—of a commodity	INVENTORY
—farm	RANCH
stopping train	WAY-TRAIN
straggle	SPRANGLE
straight dress	SHIRTWAISTER
strawberry shrub	CALYCANTHUS
stray animal	MAVERICK
stream	CREEK, KILL
street	
—boy	TAD
—car	HORSECAR
—charges	STREETAGE
—ruffian	PLUG-UGLY
—vendor's barrow	PUSH-CART
strip	
—occupied by railway	
track or road	RIGHT-OF-WAY
—off	SHUCK
strong jacket	WAM(M)US, WAMPUS
struggle	SPRANGLE
student	SOPHOMORE
stunning girl	PEACHERINO
stupid	DUMB, JAY
—fellow, person	APPLEHEAD, BOB
	BUFFLEHEAD, DUMB-BELL, JAY
	KNUCKLE-DRUGGER, LUNKHEAD
	LUNCH GUY, SCHMO(CK)
	SCHMUCK, SCHNOOK
—youth	GUNSEL
sturdy fellow	HUSKY
sub-division of county	TOWNSHIP
submarine	PIG-BOAT
suburbs	BOONDOCKS
sulky	STUFFY
sumac	POISON-OAK
summer residence	COTTAGE
sunfish	CRAPPIE
supply	GRIST, STAKE

suppose	CALCULATE, GUESS
surmount	RISE
suspect	SUSPICION
swallow	PROGNE
—hole	SINK-HOLE
swamp	DISMAL, PURGATORY, VLEI, VLY
swan	TRUMPETER
swede	RUTABAGA
sweet	
—friedcake	CRULLER, WONDER
—popcorn	CORNBALL
—potato	YAM
—seller on train	BUTCHER
sweets	CANDIES
swerving throw at baseball	SCREWBALL
swift	CHIMNEY SWALLOW
swimming-pool	NATATORIUM
swindler's helper	BUNCO-STEERER
Swiss roll	JELLY ROLL
swot	POLER
symbol of luck	GOD'S EYE
take	
—a holiday	VACATION
—up residence	LOCATE
talk	
—bluntly	TALK TURKEY
—business	TALK TURKEY
—nonsense	BLATHER
talker of nonsense	BLATHERSKITE
tall hat	STOVEPIPE
tallboy	HIGHBOY
tap	FAUCET
teacher	SCHOOLMAN
teal	BLUE-WING
team gathering	HUDDLE
telephone	
—call-box	PAY-STATION
—circuit	TRUNK
television	VIDEO
—award	EMMY
temporary school	INSTITUTE
tender	PROPOSAL
tenderfoot	GREENHORN
—in Alaska	CHE(E)CHAKO
	CHEECHALKO, CHECHAQUO
term	SEMESTER
—of endearment	HONEY-CHILE
termite	WOOD-LOUSE
theatre stalls	PARQUET
theatrical award	TONY
theological student	THEOLOGUE
thick soup	BURGOO
thicket of canes	CANE-BRAKE
thin person or horse	RACKABONES
thingummy	HOOT(E)NANNY
	HOOTANANNY

think	CALCULATE, GUESS
third-year student	JUNIOR
thorn	
—apple	JIM(P)SON WEED
	JAMESTOWN WEED
—bush	MESQUITE
thorough	REGULAR
thoroughly	ALL TO PIECES
—acquainted with	NEXT TO
thousand	
—dollars	GRAND
—million	BILLION
—to	
fourth power	TRILLION
fifth power	QUADRILLION
sixth power	QUINTILLION
through and through	ALL TO PIECES
thrush	CAT-BIRD, VEERY
ticket given for future use	RAIN-CHECK
tidy up	PICK
tiger-nut	CHUFA
timber	LUMBER
	(*see also separate entry*)
—wolf	GREY WOLF
timothy (grass)	HERD('S) GRASS
tiny	TEENTY
titmouse	CHICKADEE
toady	BOOTLICK
tobacco	PERIQUE
toffee	TAFFY
toll for street facilities	STREETAGE
toll-free road	FREEWAY
top-hat	PLUG-HAT
tortoise	GOPHER, TERRAPIN
totalisator/tote	PARI MUTUEL
tough	ROUGH-NECK
towhee	GROUND-ROBIN
town	BURG
townsman	COCKNEY, DUDE
track	SIGN
trade union branch	LOCAL
trader with Indians	COMANCHERO
trader's jargon	CHINOOK
trail	SIGN
trailing plant	PARTRIDGE-BERRY
train with limited	
number of passengers	LIMITED EXPRESS
tram	STREET-CAR
—car	TROLLEY(-CAR)
—ticket	TRIP SLIP
tramp	HOBO
—light	SLUT LAMP
translation	HORSE, PONY, TROT
transport	HAUL
transportation of freight	
containers by ship or barge	FISHYBACK

transporting agent	FREIGHTER
travel bag	GRIP(SACK)
travelling trunk	SARATOGA(TRUNK)
tread softly	CATFOOT
tree	BLACK WALNUT, CATALPA
	DOUGLAS FIR, DYER'S OAK
	FRINGE-TREE, HALESIA
	HEADACHE TREE, HONEY-LOCUST
	JACK-PINE, JOJOBA, LIQUIDAMBAR
	LOBLOLLY(-PINE), OSAGE ORANGE
	PITCHPINE, QUERCITRON, SASSAFRAS
	SEQUOIA, SHAWNEE-WOOD, SILVER-BELL
	SLIPPERY ELM, SNOWDROP-TREE
	SUGAR-MAPLE, SUGAR-PINE
	SWAMP CYPRESS, TAXODIUM
	TULIP-TREE, WASHINGTONIA
	YELLOW-BARKED OAK
	YELLOW-WOOD
—allied to elm	HACKBERRY
—Gordonia	LOBLOLLY-BAY
—leathery-leaved	LOBLOLLY-TREE
—Tsuga	HEMLOCK
tree-frog	PEEPER
trilby	FEDORA
trite	MICKEY
trounce	SHELL
trouser turn-up	CUFF
trousers	HIP-HUGGERS, PANTS
trout	LAKER, TOGUE
truant	HOOKEY
truck-driver	TEAMSTER
truckling	DOUGH-FACED
truncheon	NIGHT-STICK
trunk	SARATOGA
—call	TOLL-CALL
tufted grouse	PHEASANT
tulip-tree	CUCUMBER-TREE, POPLAR
tumbleweed	WILD-INDIGO
turn-out	TEAM
turtle-dove	MOURNING-DOVE
tussock in swamp	NIGGER-HEAD
twilled cotton	CHINO
tyrant flycatcher	KING-BIRD, PETCHARY
ugly	HOMELY
unbranded animal	MAVERICK
uncomfortable	MEAN
underground railway	SUBWAY
undertaker	MORTICIAN
undue forwardness	FORTH-PUTTING
unduly familiar	GAY
unfounded story	MALARK(E)Y
uniform colour	OLIVE-DRAB
unit trusts	MUTUAL FUNDS
United States	UNCLE SAM
university calendar	CATALOG
unlucky person	S(C)HLIMAZEL

unmade road	DIRT-ROAD	—weed	ANACHARIS, ELODEA
unmanageable animal	OUTLAW	waxwing	CEDAR-BIRD
unmannerly lout	ROUGH-NECK	wayfaring-tree	HOBBLE-BUSH
unruly	TORN-DOWN	weasel	CARCAJOU, GLUTTON
unsaleable article	STOREKEEPER		WOLVERENE, WOLVERINE
unsound financial scheme	WILD-CAT	wedding gifts	SHOWER
until the end of	THROUGH	weed	SPANISH NEEDLES
unyielding	ROCK-RIBBED	weight	HEFT
up to and including	THROUGH	—25lb	QUARTER
upper		—100lb	CENTAL
—floor	LOFT		HUNDREDWEIGHT
—part of river-steamer	TEXAS	—750-1200lb (tobacco)	HOGSHEAD
unskilled worker	HUNKY	—2000lb	SHORT TON
usurer	NOTE-SHAVER	—2240lb	LONG TON
utterly	PLUMB	well off	FOREHANDED
valley side	COTEAU	wharf labourer	ROUSTABOUT
vegetable		wheat pest	HESSIAN FLY
—marrow	MARROW-SQUASH	whippoorwill	WISHTONWISH
—seller	SAUCEMAN	whisky	BOURBON, TANGLEFOOT
vegetables eaten with meat	SAUCE	—and soda	HIGHBALL
vehicle	SHEBANG, SURREY	white	
—for hire	HACK	—fish	ROUND-FISH
verandah	PIAZZA, PORCH, STOOP	—headed eagle	BALD EAGLE
veritably	REAL	—hellebore	INDIAN POKE
very much	SOME	—wash	SKUNK
—indeed	AND HOW	Whitsuntide	PINKSTER, PINXSTER
vice	VISE	whopper	SCROUGER, SLOCKDOLAGER
Virginian	TUCKAHOE		SOCDOLIGER, SOCDOLOGER
—fungus	INDIAN BREAD		SOC(K)DOLAGER, SOGDOLOGER
—quail	PARTRIDGE		SOGDOLAGER, SOGDOLIGER
visit at sea	GAM	wild	
vote illegally more		—cat	CATAMOUNT
than once	REPEAT	—horse	BRONC(H)O, MUSTANG
voters' meeting to		window	
nominate candidate	PRIMARY	—blind	SHADE
vow	VUM	—dressing	TRIM
vulture	TURKEY-BUZZARD	windscreen	WINDSHIELD
waistcoat	VEST	wine	CATAWBA, SCUPPERNONG
waiter	BUS-BOY, GOSSOON	wing	
waitress	BUS-GIRL	—making ell-shape	EL
walk	PASEAR	—or annex of house	EXTENSION
walking boundaries	PROCESSIONING	wintergreen	CHECKER-BERRY
wallet	BILLFOLD		GAULTHERIA
walnut	BUTTERNUT, CARYOCAR	wireless news bulletin	DOPE
warbler	REDSTART	witch	
warn not to pay or		—alder	FOTHERGILLA
give up goods	FACTORISE	—hazel	FOTHERGILLA, HAMAMELIS
warship	USS	with ice cream	A LA MODE
water		withhold support	BOLT
—cask	SCUTTLEBUTT	witness-box	CHAIR, STAND
—fall	SA(U)LT	witty thought after	
—lily	SPATTER-DOCK	the occasion	LATTER-WIT
leaf	PAD	woman	BROAD, DAME, DOLL(Y)
—proof	SLICKER		FRAIL, SKIRT
—shed	DIVIDE	women's	
—thrush	WAGTAIL	—academic society	SORORITY

—blouse	SHIRTWAIST
or bodice	WAIST
—club	SOROSIS
—widebrimmed hat	SUNDOWN
wonderful	BOFFO
wood	
—land	TIMBER
—louse	TERMITE
—shavings	EXCELSIOR
wooden bowl or pail	PIPKIN
woodpecker	FLICKER, YUCKER
work	LABOR
—basket	CABA
—of little value	BOONDOGGLE
worker in compressed air	SAND-HOG
workman's railcar	HANDCAR
workshop worker	SHOPMAN
worm-fence	SNAKE-FENCE
worry	FAZE, PHASE
worthless (fellow)	BUM
wrecking clause in document	JOKER
wrestle and throw	BULLDOG
wring evidence or	
confession from	SWEAT
writ issued by sheriff	VENIRE(FACIAS)
yard outside entrance	DOORYARD
yarrow	NOSE-BLEED
yearly stage in education	GRADE
yell to supplement a cheer	TIGER
yellow-wood	GOPHER
yes	YEP
—certainly	AND HOW
yodel	WARBLE
yokel	CORNBALL, HICK, JAKE, RUBE
young	
—man	GOSSOON
—townsman	MUCKER
zero score	GOOSE-EGG

American football

act of violence	PERSONAL FOUL
area behind goal-line	END ZONE
attempt to	
—progress	DOWN, PLAY
—sack quarterback	BLITZ, DOGGING
	PASS RUSH
catching quarterback in	
possession of ball	SACKING
distance a punted ball is	
carried after catching	PUNT RETURN
downfield kick	PUNT
dropping ball	FUMBLING
extra time	OVERTIME
famous players	ANDERSEN, BLANDA
	BROWN, CRAIG, DAVIS
DEMPSEY, ELWAY, HALAS, HIRSCH	
JAWORSKI, JOHNSON, JONES	

LARGENT, LOMBARDI, MARTIN	
MONTANA, NAMATH, NEALE	
PAYTON, PERRY, SIMPSON	
SINGH, SMITH, TAYLOR	
final match	SUPERBOWL
formations	
—attacking	I-FORMATION, MAN IN MOTION
SHORT YARDAGE, SHOTGUN, SPLIT	
	STANDARD PRO SET
	T-FORMATION, TWIN SET
—defending	BLITZ, DOG, FOUR-THREE
	SHORT YARDAGE
	THREE-FOUR
grouping to discuss tactics	HUDDLE
illegal	
—blocking	CLIPPING
—move in scrimmage	ENCROACHING
—throw to	
ground	INTENTIONAL GROUNDING
lateral running at	
scrimmage	IN MOTION
leagues	AMERICAN FOOTBALL
	CONFERENCE
NATIONAL FOOTBALL CONFERENCE	
line	ENDLINE, GOAL-LINE
	SIDELINE
—halfway mark	MIDFIELD STRIPE
—outside playing area	RESTRAINT LINE
—where ball is	
spotted	LINE OF SCRIMMAGE
—yard marker	HASH MARK
loss of (control of) ball	FUMBLING
movement to gain ground	PASSING
	RUSHING
obstruction	BLOCKING
officials	BACK JUDGE, FIELD JUDGE
HEAD LINESMAN, LINE JUDGE	
REFEREE, SIDE JUDGE, UMPIRE	
pass that is caught	COMPLETION
pitch	GRIDIRON
positions	CENTER, CORNER BACK
END, GUARD, LINEBACKER	
QUARTERBACK, RUNNING BACK	
SAFETY, WIDE RECEIVER	
progress towards goal	DRIVE
restart	
—after dropped ball	SCRIMMAGE
—between plays	SNAP
—out of bounds	SCRIMMAGE
scoring	
—1 point	CONVERSION, POINT AFTER
—2 points	SAFETY
—3 points	FIELD GOAL
—6 points	TOUCHDOWN
sign of foul	YELLOW FLAG
	YELLOW HANDKERCHIEF

space between teams		5 years	QUINQUENNIAL
at scrimmage	NEUTRAL ZONE	6 years	SEXENNIAL
start	KICK-OFF	7 years	SEPTENNIAL
stoppage	TIME-OUT	8 years	OCTENNIAL
—by referee	TWO-MINUTE WARNING	9 years	NOVENNIAL
supervisory		10 years	DECENNIAL
body	NATIONAL FOOTBALL LEAGUE, NFL	100 years	CENTENNIAL
team		200 years	BICENTENNIAL
—on field	ELEVEN	300 years	TERCENTENNIAL
—total	FORTY-FIVE		TRICENTENNIAL
teams		400 years	QUADRICENTENNIAL
—Atlanta	FALCONS		QUATERCENTENNIAL
—Buffalo	BILLS	500 years	QUINCENTENNIAL
—Chicago	BEARS	1000 years	MILLENNIUM
—Cincinnati	BENGALS	—wedding anniversary	
—Cleveland	BROWNS	1 year	COTTON
—Dallas	COWBOYS	2 years	PAPER
—Denver	BRONCOS	3 years	LEATHER
—Detroit	LIONS	4 years	FLOWER, FRUIT
—Houston	OILERS	5 years	WOOD
—Indianapolis	COLTS	6 years	IRON, SUGAR CANDY
—Kansas City	CHIEFS	7 years	WOOL
—Los Angeles	RAIDERS, RAMS	8 years	BRONZE
—Miami	DOLPHINS	9 years	COPPER, POTTERY
—Minnesota	VIKINGS	10 years	TIN
—New England	PATRIOTS	11 years	STEEL
—New York	GIANTS, JETS	12 years	LINEN, SILK
—Philadelphia	EAGLES	13 years	LACE
—Phoenix	CARDINALS	14 years	IVORY
—Pittsburgh	STEELERS	15 years	CRYSTAL
—San Diego	CHARGERS	20 years	CHINA
—San Francisco	FORTY-NINERS	25 years	SILVER
—Seattle	SEAHAWKS	30 years	PEARL
—Tampa Bay	BUCCANEERS	35 years	CORAL
—Washington	REDSKINS	40 years	RUBY
through-the-legs pass		45 years	SAPPHIRE
at start of play	SNAP	50 years	GOLD(EN)
time ball is in air after a punt	HANG TIME	55 years	EMERALD
transfer of possession of		60 years	DIAMOND
ball to opponents	TURNOVER	65 years	DIAMOND
trophy	AMERICAN BOWL	**antelopes**	
	LOMBARD TROPHY	including: deer	
	PRO-BOWL, SUPERBOWL TROPHY	gazelles	
unit of game	DOWN, PLAY	Abyssinia	MADOQUA
amino-acid	(*see* **acids**)	Alpine ibex	STEINBOCK
anatomist	(*see* **physician**)	Africa	ADDAX, ADMI, ARIEL, BISA
Andorra	AND		BLAUWBOK, BLESBOK, BLOUBOK
capital	ANDORRA LA VELLA		BLUE-BUCK, BONGO, BONTEBOK,
Angola			BOS(SH)BO, BOTIGO, BUBALIS
capital	LUANDA		BUSHBOK, BUSHBUCK, CAMA
coin	ANGOLAR, KWANZA, LWEI		CHEVROTAIN, COBA, DAMA, DIBITAG
sheep	ZUNA		DIK-DIK, DUIKER, DUYKER, ELAND
anniversaries			GEMSBOK, GNU, GRYSBOK, GUIB
2 years	BIENNIAL		HARNESSED ANTELOPE, HARTEBEEST
3 years	TRIENNIAL		IMPALA, IMPOPO, (I)NYALA, KAAMA
4 years	QUADR(I)ENNIAL		KLIPSPRINGER, KOB(O), KOODOO

KORIN, KUDO, LECHWE, MHORR, MOHR
NAGOR, NAKONG, ORIBI, ORYX, OUREBI
OX-ANTELOPE, PALA, PALEBUCK
PALLAH, POKU, POOKOO, PUKU
PYGARG, REEBOK
REITBOK, RHEBOK, RIETBOK, SABLE
SASSABY, SPRINGBOK, SPRINGBUCK
STEENBOK, STEINBOCK, STEMBOK
STEMBUCK, SUNI, TOPI, TORA
TSESSEBE, WATER-BUCK
WATER-DEER, WILDEBEEST

America	CABRIE, CABRIT, CARIACOU
	CARIBOU, CARCAJOU, ELK, MOOSE
	MULE-DEER, PRONGBUCK
	PRONGHORN
	ROCKY-MOUNTAIN GOAT
	VIRGINIAN DEER, WAPITI
Asia	AHU, ARIEL, AXIS, BARKING-DEER
	CHITAL, DZEREN, ELK, GAZEL(LE)
	HANGUL, KAKAR, MAHA, MUNTJAC
	MUNTJAK, MUSK-DEER, NAPU
	RATWA, RUSA, SAIGA, SAMBOO
	SAMBHUR, SAMB(O)UR
	SAMB(W)AR
Burma	THAMENG, THAMIN
China	MUSK-DEER, WATER-DEER
chamois	RUBICAPRA
East Indies	RUCERVUS
Europe	CHAMOIS, ELK, IBEX, IZZARD
female	DOE, ROE
Himalayas	GORAL, SEROW
India	AXIS, BLACKBUCK, CHI(N)KARA
	CHIRU, CHITAL, NILGAI, NYLG(H)AU
	RUSA, SAMBOO
	SAMBHUR, SAMB(O)UR
	SAMB(W)AR, SASIN, SEROW
Japan	SIKA
male	BUCK, STAG
Mongolia	DZEREN, DZERON
mouse-deer	CHEVROTAIN
puff-nosed	SAIGA
Pyrenees	IBEX, IZZARD
Russia	SAIGA
sable antelope	POTOQUANE
Senegal	NAGOR
South America	ALPACA, GUANACO
	HUANACO, LLAMA, PACO, PUDU
striped	HARNESSED-ANTELOPE
Tibet	GOA
white-bellied	LECHWE
young	FAWN

(*see also* deer)

anthropology
ages of human culture

—earliest	EOLITHIC
—Old Stone Age	PALAEOLITHIC
Early Palaeolithic	CHELLEAN
	OLDOWAN, ACHEULEAN
	ACHEULIAN, MOUSTERIAN
Upper Palaeolithic	AURIGNACIAN
	CHATEL PERONIAN
	PERIGORDIAN, GRAVETTIAN
	SOLUTREAN, SOLUTRIAN
	MAGDALENIAN
—Middle Stone Age	AZILIAN, MESOLITHIC
	EPIPALAEOLITHIC
—New Stone Age	NEOLITHIC
	ACERAMIC, CERAMIC
—transitional	AENOLITHIC
—Copper Age	CHALCOLITHIC
—later	BRONZE AGE
	HALLSTATT
	IRON AGE

anthropologists

—American	BENEDICT, GEERTZ
	HERSKOVITS, KROEBER
	LINTON, MALINOWSKI
	REDFIELD, VANTINA
	WARNER
—Belgian	VANTINA
—British	BATES, DALTON, GALTON
	LEAKEY, PERRY
	RADCLIFFE-BROWN, TYLOR
—French	LEVI-STRAUSS
	TEILHARD DE CHARDIN
—Polish	MALINOWSKI
—Spanish	BAROJA
biology of humans	ANTHROPOBIOLOGY

body types

—long, lean	ECTOMORPH
—muscular	MESOMORPH
—short	
rounded	ENDOMORPH
stocky	AMPLOSOME

civilisations

(earliest first)	EGYPTIAN
	SUMERIAN
	INDIC
	MAYAN
	MINOAN
	HITTITE
	CHINESE, SINIC
	BABYLONIAN
	GREEK, HELLENIC
	SYRIAC
	ESKIMO
	GREEK, SPARTAN
	POLYNESIAN
	ANDEAN
	KHMER
	JAPANESE, KOREAN
	WESTERN

	ORTHODOX CHRISTIAN	manlike	ANTHROPOID
	HINDU	measurement of	
	RUSSIAN CHRISTIAN	—body	ANTHROPOMETRY
	ARABIC	—head shape	CRANIOMETRY
	MEXICAN	primitive primate	ADAPID, OMOMYID
	OTTOMAN	races	AFRICAN, ASIATIC
	ISLAMIC		AMERINDIAN, AUSTRALOID
dawn man (hoax)	EOANTHROPUS		CAUCASOID, INDIC
	PILTDOWN MAN		MELANESIAN, MELANOCHROI
human ancestors			MICRONESIAN, MONGOLOID
(earliest first)	PRE-ADAMITE		NEGROID, POLYNESIAN
—Oligocene		study of	
Egypt	PROLIOPITHECUS	—ancient blood groups	PALAEOSEROLOGY
—Miocene		—distribution of	
East Africa	SIVAPITHECUS	mankind	ANTHROPO(GEO)GRAPHY
	LIMNOPITHECUS	—man	ANTHROPOLOGY
	PROCONSUL	—origins of man	ANTHROPOGENESIS
India	PALAEOSIMIA		ANTHROPOGENY
	SIVAPITHECUS		ANTHROPOGONY
Europe	PLIOPITHECUS	—remains of ancient	
India	DRYOPITHECUS	man	PALAEOPATHOLOGY
Africa	KENYAPITHECUS	transformation to shape	
India	RAMAPITHECUS	of human	ANTHROPOMORPHOSIS
—Pliocene		worship of man	ANTHROPOLATRY
Europe	OREOPITHECUS	**Apostles**	
	DRYOPITHECUS	Apostle of Northumbria	CUTHBERT
Asia	PLIOPITHECUS	Apostles of Christ	(*see* **twelve**)
Ethiopia	AUSTRALOPITHECUS	**apples**	ARTHUR TURNER
—Pleistocene			ASHMEAD'S KERNEL
Lower			BAKER'S DELICIOUS, BEAUTY OF BATH
—Africa	HOMO HABILIS		BESS POOL, BIFFIN, BLENHEIM (ORANGE)
	OLDUVAI MAN		BRAEBURN, BRAMLEY SEEDLING
	NUTCRACKER MAN		BRAEBURN, CHARLES ROSS
	ZINJANTHROPUS		CHIVER'S DELIGHT
	PLEISANTHROPUS		CLAYGATE PEARMAIN, CODLIN(G),
—Java	JAVA MAN, HOMO ERECTUS		COSTARD, COX'S ORANGE (PIPPIN)
	PITHECANTHROPUS		CRIMSON COSTARD, D'ARCY SPICE,
Middle			DEVONSHIRE QUARRENDON
—Africa	PARANTHROPUS		DISCOVERY, DUMELOW SEEDLING
	ATLANTHROPUS		EARLY VICTORIA, EGREMONT RUSSET
—China	PEKIN(G) MAN		ELLISON ORANGE, EMNETH EARLY
	HOMO ERECTUS		ENSTAR, FIESTA, FORGE, FORTUNE
	PITHECANTHROPUS		GEORGE CAVE, GOLDEN DELICIOUS
	SINANTHROPUS		GRANNY SMITH, GREENSLEEVES
—Europe	SWANSCOMBE MAN		GRENADIER, IDARED, INGRID
	STEINHEIM MAN		JAMES GRIEVE, JONATHAN
Upper			KATY, KING OF THE PIPPINS
—Europe	FONTECHEVADE		LADY SUDELEY, (LANE'S) PRINCE ALBERT
—Africa	SALDANHA		LAXTON'S FORTUNE, LAXTON'S SUPERB
—Israel	MOUNT CARMEL MAN		LITTLE HOG SNOUT, LORD BURGHLEY
—Europe	NEANDERTHAL MAN		LORD DERBY, LORD HINDLIP
—Java	SOLO MAN, HOMO SOLENSIS		LORD LAMBOURNE, MARIE
—Africa	BROKEN HILL MAN		MICHAELMAS STUBBARD
	RHODESIAN MAN		NEWTON WONDER, NORFOLK ROYAL
—Europe	CRO-MAGNON MAN		OLD FRED, PEASGOOD NONSUCH
—Holocene (Recent)	HOMO SAPIENS		PIG'S NOSE PIPPIN

	PITMASTON PINEAPPLE, QUEEN COX
	RED ELLISON, RIBSTON PIPPIN
	ROYAL GALA, RUSSET
	ST EDMUND'S PIPPIN, SPARTAN
	STAR OF DEVON, STAR KING
	STURMER PIPPIN, SUNSET
	SUNTAN, TIDEMAN'S LATE ORANGE
	TOM PUTT, WARNER'S KING
	WHITE MELROSE
	(WORCESTER) PEARMAIN
America	BALDWIN, JONAGOLD, JONATHAN
	WASHINGTON RED
Australia	COLANE
Canada	MACINTOSH RED, SPARTAN
France	GOLDEN DELICIOUS
	ORLEANS REINETTE, RED DESSERT
Germany	HOLSTEIN
green-skinned	GREENLING
Holland	BELLE DE BOSKOOP
Japan	CRISPIN
New Zealand	GALA, KIDD'S ORANGE RED
old	JENNETING, LEATHER-COATS
	POM(E)ROY, POMEWATER
	RENNET, SWEETING
Sweden	KATY
Arabia	UAR
anchorage	BANDAR, MARSA, MERSA
ancient people	HIMYARITE, SABA, SHEBA
ascetic	DERVISH
banker	SCHROFF
bay	BAHR, GHUBBAT
	KHALIG, KHALIJ
camel	DROMEDARY
—train	CAF(F)ILA, KAFILA
camp	D(O)UAR, DOWAR
canal	BAHR
cape	RAS
capital (Saudi)	AR RIYAD, RIYADH
chapter of Koran	SURA(H)
cherry	MAHALEB
chief	AMEER, AMIR, CAID, EMEER
	EMIR, KAID, RAIS, SA(Y)ID
	SAYYID, SCHIEK, SHEIK(H)
Christ's thorn	NABK, NEBBUK, NEBE(C)K
Christian	COPT
cistern	THAMAD
city	MADINAT
cloak	ABA, BERNOUS(E), BURNOUS(E)
	BURNOOSE, BOURK(H)A
	BURK(H)A, CAFTAN, (D)JIBBAH
	DJELLABA, GAL(L)ABEA(H), GALABIA
	GAL(L)ABI(Y)AH, GAL(L)ABI(Y)EH
	JUBBAH, KAFTAN, HAI(C)K
	HAIQUE, HYKE
coffee-cup without	
a handle	FINGAN, FINJAN

coins	BUCKSHA, DINAR, HALALAH
	QURSH, RIYAL, SAUDI
commando(s)	FEDAYEE(N)
courtyard	HOSH
cove	SHARM
cup-holder	ZARF, ZURF
dam	SADD
dancing-girl	ALMA(H), ALME(H)
demon	AFREET, AFRIT, MAHOUN(D)
depression	BAT(I)N, QA(RARAT)
dervish	SANTON
desert	BADIYAH, ERG
	NAFAD, SAHRA
—plant	CAMEL'S THORN
—rat	JERBOA
devil	SHAITAN
dish	COUSCOUS(OU), CUSCUS
	KHUSKHUS
dog	SALUKI
domed tomb	QUBBAH
domesticated animal	CAMEL
drink	BOSA, BOZA(H), LEBAN
	SHRAB
drug	BHANG, BENJ, HASHEESH
	HASHISH
dry river-bed	OUED, WADI, WADY
dune	NAFAD
dust-storm	SHAITAN
dynasty	ABBASSID, ALMORAVIDES
	AMMIAD, FATIMIDS, UMAYYAD
encampment	D(O)UAR, DOWAR
enclosed balcony	MOUCHARABY
estuary	MASABB
eye shadow	KOHL
fate	KISMET
father	ABU
fort	CASBAH, HISN, KASBAH
fortified camp	ZAREBA
girl	BINT
go away!	IMSHI, IMSHY
grain	TOMAND
gravel plain	JIDDAT, SAYH
gulf	KHALIG, KHALIJ
gum-resin	FRANKINCENSE, OLIBANUM
habit	(*see* cloak *below*)
harbour	BANDAR, MINA
head-dress	CHECHIA, FEZ, KAFFIYEH
	KEFFIYEH, TARBOOSH
	TARB(O)USH
—cord	AGAL
headman	MOCUDDUM, MOKADDAM
	MUQADDAM
hill	BARQA, CHEBKA, GARET, ILW, KEREB
	KULET, MINQAR, NASB, QARET, QOZ
	RIJM, RUJM, TEL(L), TILAT
	TALL(AT), TARAQ

41

hills	MANAQIR, QUR(AYYAT), QURUN
	TALL(AT), TARAQ, TULUL
holy	
—building (Mecca)	KAABA
—litter sent to Mecca	MAHMAL
in the name of Allah	BISMILLAH
jinni	MARID
language	ARABIC
look	SHUFTI
magistrate	CADI, CAID, KADI, KAID
	SHEREEF, SHERIF
market	SUQ, SOUK
marsh	CHOTT
measure	ARDEB, COVID(O), DEN
merchant	HOWADJI
millet grain	COUSCOUS(OU), CUSCUS
	KHUSKHUS
mosque	MASJED, MASJID, MESJID
mound	TEL(L)
mountain	(D)JEBEL, GEBEL, IDWET
	JABAL, J(E)BEL, HASHM, NASB
musical form	MAQAM
native quarter	MEDINA
nomad	BEDAWIN, BEDOUIN
	SARACEN, TUAREG
oasis	WAHAT
ornamental holder	ZARF, ZURF
pass	AQABAT, MAMARR, NAQB
	TENIET, TIZI
physician	HAKEEM, HAKIM
pilgrim	HADJI, HAJJI
pilgrimage	HADJ, HAJJ
plain	HADABAT, HAMMADAH
	HAMMADAT, SAHL, SUHUL
plateau	HAMADA, HAMEDET
	HAZM, TASSILI
poem	GAZEL, GHAZAL, GHAZEL
pool	BIRK-AT, BIRK-ET
race	BERBER
racing camel	DELOUL, MEHARI
raider	FEDAYEEN
rainpools	KHABARI
ravine	KHOR, WADI, WADY
reed pipe	ARGHOOL
religion	ISLAM, MOHAMMEDANISM
	MOSLEM, MUSLIM
religious	
—ceremony	DOSEH
—philosophy	AVERR(H)OISM
resurgence	BA'ATH
ridge	JAL, KEREB
river	NAHR, SHATT
—mouth	SHATT
rocky plateau	HAMMADAH, HAMMADAT
salt	
—flat	SABKHAT, SEBKRA
—lake	CHOTT
sand	
—dunes	IDHAN, GHARD, HADH(AT)
	IRQ, KATHI
—storm	HABOOB
sands	RAMLAT
script	CUFIC, KUFIC
	NASK(H)I, NESK(H)I
sea-captain	NOCADAH
shawl	KAFFIYEH, KEFFIYEH
ship	BAGGALA, D(H)OW
	FELUCCA, SAIC
shirt	CAMESE, CAMIS(E)
	CAMISO, KAMIS
shrine	CAABA, KAABA
shrub	K(H)AT, NABK
	NEBBUK, NEBE(C)K
sign of glottal stop	HAMZA(H)
skull-cap	CHECHIA
slave	MAMELUKE
smoking(hookah)	CHILLUM
Socialist party	BA'ATH
spirit	DJINNI, GENIE, GH(O)UL
	GINNI, JANN, JINNEE
	JINNI, MARID
spring	AIN, AYN
spur	RIJM, RUJM
state of bliss	KEF
stockade	ZARE(E)BA, ZEREBA
	ZERIBA
strait	BAB
stream	BAHR
street	SHARI
surrender	ISLAM
tariff	ZABETA
tea	K(H)AT, QAT
tent village	D(O)UAR, DOWAR
thorn hedge	ZARE(E)BA, ZEREBA
	ZERIBA
title	SIDI
tomb	MASTABET, QABR
town	MADINAT, MEDINA
tree	ALHAGI
trough in sands	KHABB, SHAQQAT
	SHIQAQ, SHUQQAT
unbeliever	CAFFRE, KAFIR
underground water	
channel	QANAT
uprising	INTIFADA
verse form	G(H)AZAL, GHAZEL
water	
—course	CHALB, FAJJ, FULAYJ
	GHADFAT, IRHZER
	SHAIB(AN), WADI
—hole	BID, KHABRAH, KHABRAT
—pipe	CHILLUM, HOOKA(H)

—skin	KIRBEH	—sediment layers	VARVE DATING
—wheel	SAKIA, SAKI(Y)EH	—tree rings	DENDROCHRONOLOGY
weak jinni	JANN	deposit under pile-	
weight	KELA, ROTL, ROT(T)OLO	dwelling (Italy)	TERRA MARA
well	AGUELT, AIN, ANOU, AYN	chamber in chalk	DENE-HOLE
	BIR, BIRK-AT, BIRK-ET	cold period of	
	GHADIR, GUELTA, HASSI, HASY	Pleistocene	GLACIAL PERIOD, ICE AGE
	IDD, KARIF, MASHASH, MATAN	double axe	LABRYS
	MISHASH, MUSHASH, OGLA, OGLET	embalmed body	MUMMY
	QALAMAT, QALIB, SANIYAT	exploration by measuring	
	THAMAD, UQLAT	sub-soil resistance	RESISTIVITY SURVEYING
whip	K(O)URBASH	flint tool	BURIN

archaeology

including: archaeologists		fortified island	CRANNOG
palaeontology		fossil	
ages of earth	(*see* **geography**)	—animal	PALAEOTHERIUM
archaeologists/palaeontologists			SIVATHERIUM
—American	GOULD, SEPKOSKI	—amphibians	LABYRINTHODONTIA
—British	BROOM, BURTON, CRAWFORD		STEGOCEPHALIA
	EVANS, KEITH, LAWRENCE	—arachnid	EURYPTERIDA
	LAYARD, LEAKEY, MARSHALL	—arthropod	TRILOBITE
	PETRIE, RAWLINSON, SMITH	—bird	(A)EPYORNIS, ARCHAEOPTERYX
	WHEELER, WOODWARD, WOOLLEY		ARCHAEORNIS, ICTHYORNIS
—Danish	STENNO, THOMSEN, WORSAAE		ODONTORNITHES, SAURURAE
—Dutch	DUBOIS, KOENIGSWALD	—bone	ODONTOLITE
—French	BOULE, BREUIL, CUVIER	—cephalopod	AMMONITE, BACULITE
	LARTET, NOUVEL, PERTHES	—dung	COPROLITE
	POIDEBARD	—fish	ACANTHODII, OSTEOLEPSIS
—German	SCHLIEMANN		PLACODERMI
Bronze Age		—fish-spine	ICTHYODORULITE
—axe	PALSTAFF, PALSTAVE		ICTHYODORYLITE
—building (Greek)	MEGARON	—fruit	LEPIDOSTROBUS
—cemetery	URNFIELD	—horse	HIPPARION
—ornament	LUNULA	—Hydrozoa	GRAPTOLITES
burial		—plant(s)	CALAMITE, PSILOPHYTALES
—mound	BARROW, TUMULUS		SPHENOPHYTALES
—place	BEEHIVE TOMB		PTERIDOSPERM(AE)
Celtic necklace	TORC, TORQUE	—reptiles	DINOSAURS
civilisations	(*see* **anthropology**)		ICTHYOSAURIA, ORNITHISCHIA
classification of artefacts	TYPOLOGY		SAURISCHIA, SAUROPTERYGIA
coffin (stone, lead, etc)	SARCOPHAGUS		THERAPSIDA, THERIODONTIA
dating by			THERIOMORPHA
—artefacts	TYPOLOGY		(*see also* **lizards**)
—astronomy	ORBITAL DATING	—resin	IXOLITE
—depth of strata	SEQUENCE DATING	—tooth	ODONTOLITE
	STRATIGRAPHY	—trees	GINKGOALES, LEPIDENDRON
—electrons	ELECTRON SPIN RESONANCE	—ungulate	UINTATHERIUM
	ESR	—whale	ZEUGODON(T)
—heating	THERMOLUMINESCENCE, TL	fragment of pottery	(POT)SHERD, SHARD
—magnetism	ARCHAEOMAGNETISM	hill-fort (Irish)	RATH
	MAGNETIC STRATIGRAPHY	Iron Age tower (Scot.)	BROCH, BRO(U)GH
—radioactivity	ARGON-ARGON DATING	lake-dwelling	CRANNOG, PALAFITTE
	CARBON(-14) DATING	mound	TEL(L)
	POTASSIUM-ARGON DATING	rubbish-heap	KITCHEN-MIDDEN
	RADIOCARBON DATING	seasonal deposit in still water	VARVE
	RADIOMETRIC DATING	shelter on piles	LAKE DWELLING
		spread of cultures	DIFFUSION

stone	
—circle	CROMLECH, HENGE
	PERISTALITH
—column	OBELISK
—implement (small)	MICROLITH
—large	MEGALITH
—monument	CROMLECH, DOLMEN
	MENHIR, NAVETA
Balearic Islands	TALAYOT, TAULA
—standing	MEGALITH, MENHIR
	MONOLITH
—table	DOLMEN
—tower (Scot.)	BROCH
—upright	
slab	STELA, STELE
stones with slab on top	DOLMEN
	TRILITH(ON)
Stone Age	
—axe	COUP DE POING
—tool (small)	MICROLITH
straight line between	
features of landscape etc	LEY (LINE)
study of	
—ancient inscriptions	EPIGRAPHY
—fossil animals	PALAEOZOOLOGY
—fossils	PALAEONTOLOGY
—human	
antiquities	ARCHAEOLOGY
blood groups	PALAEOSEROLOGY
remains	PALAEOPATHOLOGY
terrace in hillside	LINCH(ET), LYNCHET
tomb	
—earth-covered	BARROW, TUMULUS
—Egyptian	MASTABA, PYRAMID
—stone slabs	DOLMEN
vertical shaft	DENE-HOLE

architects
including: buildings
        engineers

American	FULLER, JENNEY, JOHNSON
	KIESLER, MEIER, PEI, RICHARDSON
	STEIN, SULLIVAN, WRIGHT
Austrian	ACHLEITNER, HOFFMANN
	KIESLER
Belgian	HORTA, VAN DE VELDE
Brazilian	NEIMEYER
British	BARRY, BRUNEL, BURLINGTON
	BURTON, CHAMBERS, CULLEN
	DANCE, DARBY, FARRELL
	FOSTER, GIBBERD
	GIBBS, HAWKSMOOR, INIGO JONES
	KENT, LASDUN, LUBETKIN
	LUTYENS, NASH, PETO
	PARRY, PAXTON, PENTY, PUGIN
	ROGERS, RUSKIN, SCOTT, SEIFERT
	SHAW, SMITHSON, SOANE, SPENCE

	STIRLING, STREET, TELFORD
	VANBRUGH, VENTRIS, VOYSEY
	WEBB, WILSON, WREN, WYATT
Chinese	PEI
Danish	SPRECKELSEN
designer of	
—Albert Dock, Liverpool	HARTLEY
—Albert Memorial, London	SCOTT
—Alton Towers, Staffs	PUGIN
—Arche de la Défense, Paris	SPRECKELSEN
—Ashmolean Museum, Oxford	COCKERELL
—Athenaeum, London	BURTON
—Balmoral	SMITH
—Bank of England	SOANE
—Banqueting Hall, Whitehall	JONES
—Bastille opera, Paris	OTT
—Battersea Power Station	SCOTT
—Blenheim Palace	VANBRUGH
—Brandenburg Gate, Berlin	LANGHANS
—Brighton Pavilion	NASH
—British Library	WILSON
—Castle Howard	VANBRUGH
—Centre Point, London	SEIFERT
—Charles de Gaulle airport	ANDREV
—Chatsworth, Derbyshire	PAXTON
—Clore Gallery, London	STIRLING
—Coventry Cathedral	SPENCE
—Crystal Palace, London	PAXTON
—Edinburgh University	ADAM
—Euston Arch, London	HARDWICK
—Foreign Office, London	SCOTT
—Free Trade Hall, Manchester	WALTER
—glass pyramids, Louvre	PEI
—Grand Hotel, Scarborough	BRODRICK
—Greenwich Hospital	WREN
—Guggenheim Museum, New York	WRIGHT
—Harrods, London	HUNT/STEVENS
—Holloway Prison	BUNNING
—Hong Kong and	
Shanghai Bank	FOSTER
—Houses of Parliament	BARRY, PETO
	PUGIN
—Irish National Gallery, Dublin	FOWKES
—iron bridge, Telford	DARBY
—Keddlestone Hall	ADAM
—King's Cross Station, London	CUBITT
—Law Courts, London	STREET
—Les Invalides	MANSART
—Liverpool Cathedral	
Anglican	SCOTT
Roman Catholic	GIBBERD
—Mansion House	DANCE
—Menai Bridge	STEPHENSON
—Mentmore Towers	PAXTON
—Midland Hotel, Manchester	TRUBSHAW
—Natural History Museum	WATERHOUSE

—Nelson's column, London	PETO
—Newgate gaol	DANCE
—New Scotland Yard	SHAW
—Osborne House, IoW	CUBITT
—Paddington Station	BRUNEL/WYATT
—Palm House, Kew	BURTON/TURNER
—Pompidou Centre, Paris	FOSTER
—Port Sunlight	OWEN
—Queen's House, Greenwich	JONES
—Radcliffe library	GIBBS
—Reform Club, London	BARRY
—Royal Crescent, Bath	WOOD
—Royal Infirmary, Edinburgh	BRYCE
—Royal Opera House, London	BARRY
—Royal Pavilion, Brighton	NASH
—St Martin-in-the-Fields	GIBBS
—St Pancras Station, London	BARLOW/ ORDISH/SCOTT
—St Paul's Cathedral	WREN
—St Peter's, Rome	BRAMANTE BRUNELLESCHI, MICHELANGELO
—Savoy Hotel, London	COLLCUTT/ MACKMURDO
—Scotland Yard	SHAW
—Scott Memorial, Edinburgh	KEMP
—Scottish National Gallery	PLAYFAIR
—Seagram Building, New York	MIES
—Somerset House	JONES, CHAMBERS
—Stuttgart Museum	STIRLING
—Suspension Bridge, Clifton	BRUNEL
—Sydney Opera House	UTZON
—Tower, Blackpool	MAXWELL/TUKE
—Tower Bridge, London	JONES/PARRY
—Town Hall	
Leeds	BRODRIC
Manchester	WATERHOUSE
Sheffield	MOUNTFIELD
—University of Glasgow	SCOTT
—Versailles	LE VAN, MANSART
—Viceroy's House, Delhi	LUTYENS
—Villa Savoie	CORBUSIER
—Westminster Abbey towers	HAWKSMOOR
—Westminster Cathedral	BENTLEY
—West Pier, Brighton	BIRCH
—Whitehall Court, London	ARCHER, GREEN
Dutch	DE VRIENDT, RIETVELD VAN EYCK, VAN NOORT VAN ZOYE
Finnish	AALTO, ENGEL, SAARINEN SONCK
French	BULLANT, DE L'ORME EIFFEL, FRIEDMAN, GUINARD LE CORBUSIER, LE VAU, LESCET MALLET-STEVENS, MANSART PERRET, ROUX-SPITZ, SEGUIN VIOLLET

German	BEHRENS, GROPIUS MEYER, MENDELSOHN MIES (VAN DER ROHE) MUTHESIUS, SCHINKEL SCHULTZE-NAUBURG, TAUT
—school	BAUHAUS
Greek	DOXIDIAS
Italian	ALBERTI, BERNINI BORROMINI, BRAMANTE BRUNELLESCHI, MADERNA MICHELANGELO, NERVI PALLADIO, SANSOVINO SANTELIA
Mexican	CANDELA
Russian	LUBETKIN
Scottish	ADAM, CAMPBELL GIBBS, MACKINTOSH
Spanish	BERRUGUETE, CANDELA DE HERRARA, GAUDI SORIA Y MATA
Swedish	MAILLART
Swiss	BILL, LE CORBUSIER, MEYER
Venetian	PALLADIO

architectural features

apex of building	FASTIGIUM
apse	CONCHA
arc of arch	HANCE, HAUNCH
arcade over aisle	TRIFORIUM
arch	
—across interior angle	SQUINCH
—linked to buttress	ARC BOUTANT FLYING BUTTRESS
—over gate	PORTAL
—springing from above capital	STILTED ARCH
—stone	VOUSSOIR
arched	
—roof	VAULT
—walkway	ARCADE
architrave	EPISTYLE
arm	BRACE
arrangement of small arcs and cusps	FEATHERING
astragal moulding	FUSAROL(E)
ball	
—on pillar	BALLOON
—shaped finial	POMMEL
band used with moulding	FILLET
base of pillar	DADO, PATTEN
bay	
—resting on brackets	ORIEL
—window	JUT-WINDOW
beam	
—at foot of —opening	SILL

—rafters	JOIST, WALL-PLATE
mid-point of rafters	COLLAR
or near foot of rafters	HAMMERBEAM
—forming ridge	RIDGE POLE
—over	
columns	ARCHITRAVE
door or window	LINTEL
—supporting	
joists, etc	BREASTSUMMER
BRESSUMMER, SUMMERBEAM	
rafters	PURLIN
belltower	CAMPANILE
board	
—at eaves	FA(S)CIA
—covering verge	BARGEBOARD
—under eaves	SOFFIT(E)
body of Corinthian capital	VASE
bottom stone of arch	SPRINGER
bracket under cornice	MODILLION
broad flat band	FASCIA
burial chamber	TOMB, VAULT
buttress supported	
by a corbel	HANGING BUTTRESS
cap of pier	CUSHION
capitals (Egypt)	(CLUSTERED) LOTUS BUDS
	HATHOR-HEADED
	INVERTED BELL, PALM
carved basket	CORBEIL
central stone of arch	KEYSTONE
chancel	ADYTUM
chapel	
—at west end of church	GALILEE
—of prothesis	PARABEMA
—within church	SACELLUM
chevron moulding	DANCETTE
choir-screen	REREDOS(SE)
	REREDORSE
church	(see separate entry)
clawlike ornament	GRIFF(E)
close-set columns	PYCNOSTYLE
colonnade	PORCH, PORTICO, STOA
column	
—base	PEDIMENT, PLINTH
—female figure	CARYATID
—fillet round column	ANNULET
—flat tablet on capital	ABACUS
—groove in shaft	FLUTE, FLUTING
—lower part of capital	NECK
—male figure(s)	ATLAS (ATLANTES)
	TELAMON(ES)
—moulding	
at base	TORUS
below abacus	ECHINUS
—section of shaft	DRUM, FRUSTRUM
—shaft	FUST, SCAPE, SCAPUS
	TIGE, TRUNK, VERGE

—spiral decoration	
on capital	HELIX, SCROLL, VOLUTE
—styles	COMPOSITE, CORINTHIAN
	DORIC, IONIC, TUSCAN
—top	CAPITAL
combination of	
—beams	TRABEATION
—truncated gable	
and lipped roof	JERKINHEAD
concave ceiling	CUPOLA
concave moulding	TROCHILUS
continuous	
—arch	BARREL VAULT
—pedestal	PODIUM
convex	
—projecting moulding	ECHINUS
—surface of arch	EXTRADOS
corner	
—of coping	SKEW-CORBEL
	SKEW-PUT, SKEW-TABLE
—stone	QUOIN
cornice above base of	
pedestal	SURBASE
covered	
—arcade	CLOISTER, LOGGIA
—colonnade	STOA
—entrance	PORTE COCHERE
—portico	XYST(OS), XYSTUS
—walkway	AMBULATORY, ARCADE
	PAWN
crescent-shaped space	LUNETTE
cresting	BRATTICING
	BRATTISHING
cross	
—beam	TRANSOM
—rib in vaulting	LIERNE
crossed fillets	STRAP-WORK
cupola	THOLOS, THOLUS
curve where	
—column merges	APOPHYGE
—vaults merge	GROIN
curved	
—timber roof support	CRUCK
—wall/ceiling junction	COVE
cylindrical part of dome	DRUM
cyma recta moulding	DOUCINE
decorated	
—band at top of wall	FRIEZE
—with leaves	FOLIATED
decoration in	
—moulding	LINEN-SCROLL
—panels	LINENFOLD
decorative scroll	CARTOUCHE
detached support	PILLAR
diagonal rib of vault	OGIVE
die of a pedestal	SOLIUM

disguised door	JIB-DOOR
dome	CUPOLA, THOLOS, THOLUS
doorway	PORTAL
—enclosure	PORCH
—surround	ARCHITRAVE
Doric order	MALE ORDER
dormer-window	LUCARNE
double-grooved ornament	DIGLYPH
dripstone	LABEL, LARMIER
droplike feature	GUTTA
dual-pitched roof	MANSARD(-ROOF)
east end of church	CHEVET
elliptical auditorium	SPHENDONE
enclosed space	CLOISTER
—of church	PARVIS(E)
enclosing wall of precinct	PERIBOLOS
	PERIBOLUS
entablature	TRABEATION
—highest part	CORNICE
—lowest part	ARCHITRAVE
—middle part	FRIEZE
—projecting part of cornice	CORONA
—underside	SOFFIT
entrance	PORTAL
—admitting carriage	PORTE-COCHERE
entresol	MEZZANINE
extension of church	
behind the altar	RETROCHOIR
external	
—curve of voussoir	EXTRADOS
—steps	PERRON
fascia	PLATBAND
female figure	
—used as column	CARYATID
—with basket	
on the head	CANEPHOR(A)
	CANEPHORE, CANEPHORUS
fillet	LIST
—above architrave	TAENIA
—below triglyph	REGULA
—between flutes	STRIA
finial	CROP
five-petalled feature	CINQUE-FOIL
flat	
—arch	PLATBAND
—fillet	BANDELET
—moulding	PLATBAND
—narrow moulding	REGLET
—on top floor	PENTHOUSE
—ornament	PATERA
floor	PLANCH
flower bud as ornament	KNOSP
flower-like ornament	FLEURON
four-lobed ornament	QUATREFOIL
	QUATREFEUILLE
French window fastener	ESPAGNOLETTE

front of building	FACADE
gable	FASTIGIUM
—coping stone	SKEW
gallery	PAWN
—over aisle	TRIFORIUM
garret	SOL(L)AR, SOL(L)ER
gate	PORTAL
—pillar	PIER
gateway	
—of Egyptian temple	PYLON
—to temple	PROPYLAEUM
	PROPYLON
glazed structure on roof	LANTERN
	ROOFLIGHT, SKYLIGHT
groove between neck of	
capital and shaft	HYPOTRACHELION
grooved border	SWAGE
grotesque ornamentation	BABERY
half-round moulding	ASTRAGAL
having	
—1 column	MONOSTYLE
—1 row of columns	PERIPTERAL
—2 columns	DISTYLE
—4 columns	TETRASTYLE
—5 columns	PENTASTYLE
—6 columns	HEXASTYLE
—8 columns	OCTASTYLE, OCTOSTYLE
—9 columns	ENNEASTYLE
—10 columns	DECASTYLE
—12 columns	DODECASTYLE
—many columns	POLYSTYLAR
—not more than four columns	PROSTYLE
head of column	
supporting arch	CHAPITER, CHAPTREL
hemispherical roof	CUPOLA, DOME
high narrow arch	LANCET ARCH
hollow moulding	CASEMENT, CAVETTO
	SCOTIA
horizontal	
—block	IMPOST
—division of window	TRANSOM
—member on wall	WALL-PLATE
inclined surface	SKEW-BACK
inner	
—chamber of temple	CELLA, NAOS
—fortified retreat	REDUIT
intercolumniation of	
—1½ diameters	PYCNOSTYLE
—2 diameters	SYSTYLE
—2¼ diameters	EUSTYLE
—3 diameters	DIASTYLE
—2-4 diameters	AR(A)EOSYSTYLE
—4 diameters	AR(A)EOSTYLE
internal part of dome	CUPOLA
internally splayed opening	EMBRASURE
	EMBRAZURE

intersection of vaults	GROIN
key	
—pattern	FRET
—stone	QUOIN, SAGITTA
lantern on dome	CUPOLA
level tablet	ABACUS
like silversmith's work	PLATERESQUE
lintel	PLATBAND, TRANSOM
—on corbels	SHOULDERED ARCH
little	
—chapel	SACELLUM
—round window	OEIL-DE-BOEUF
long lintel	BRESSUMMER
	(BREAST)SUMMER
longitudinal groove	FLUTE
low	
—side window	LYCHNOSCOPE
—spherical vault	CUL-DE-FOUR, CUPOLA
—storey between	
main storeys	ENTRESOL, MEZZANINE
—wall	STYLOBATE
lower part of	
—cupola or dome	DRUM
—internal wall surface	DADO, WAINSCOT
main body of church	NAVE
male figure(s) used	
as column(s)	ATLAS(ATLANTES)
	PERSIAN, TELAMON
mansard roof	GAMBREL ROOF
masonry	
—filled with rubble	EMPLECTON
	EMPLECTUM
—rough-faced	RUSTICATED
—smooth	ASHLAR
—uncoursed	(RANDOM) RUBBLE
—uniformly coursed	ISODOMON
	ISODOMUM
—with sunken joints	RUSTICATED
measure of proportion	MODULE
moulded border	SWAGE
moulding	
—above base of pedestal	SURBASE
—at	
base of column	TORUS
junction of	
shaft and capital	NECK-MOULDING
—hollow	CAVETTO
—ogee	CYMA, TALON
concave	CYMA RECTA
convex	CYMA REVERSA
—round door or wondow	ARCHITRAVE
—S-shaped	OGEE
narrow band	FILLET
neck of capital	HYPOTRACHELION
Norman moulding	DOG-TOOTH
notch in parapet	CRENEL

oblique opening	SQUINT
open	
—colonnade	XYST(OS), XYSTUS
—sided pavilion	BELVEDERE
opening for cannon	EMBRASURE
	EMBRAZURE
orders	CORINTHIAN, DORIC
	IONIC
ornament	
—in the form of	
basket	MODILLION
beads	PATERNOSTER
conventionalised leaf	ACANTHUS
curled leaf	CROCKET
festoon of flowers	SWAG
flower	CROCKET, FLEURON
—bud	KNOSP
—with	
3 petals	TREFOIL
4 petals	QUATREFEUILLE
	QUATREFOIL
5 petals	CINQUEFOIL
6 petals	SEXFOIL
garland	FESTOON
palm-leaf	PALMETTE
scroll	CARTOUCHE
waterlily	LOTE, LOTOS, LOTUS
—on	
capital	WATER-LEAF
gable	FINIAL
mouldings	EGG-AND-ANCHOR
	EGG-AND DART
pediment	ACROTER(ION)
	ACROTERIUM
pinnacle	CROCKET
—rose-shaped	ROSETTE
ornamental	
—bracket	MODILLION
—channel or fluting	GLYPH
—openwork	TRACERY
panelling	
—behind altar or seat	REREDORSE
	REREDOS(SE)
—on internal wall	DADO, WAINSCOT
part of jamb	SCONCHEON, SCUNCHEON
	SCONTION
partitioning	QUARTERING
pedestal	ACROTERION, ACROTERIUM
—base	DADO
pediment	ACROTER(ION)
	ACROTERIUM
pillar	
—between two	
openings	PIER, TRUMEAU
—supporting arch	PIER
—upper part	IMPOST

plain	
—face	
at base of wall	SOCLE
of plinth	SOCLE, ZOCCO(LO)
—plinth	SOCLE
plaster	
—cast in low relief	PRINT
—moulding	CORNICE, COVE
—wall coating	STUCCO
plate supporting end of beam	TASSEL, TORSEL
plinth at base of wall	SOCLE, ZOCCO(LO)
pointed dome	IMPERIAL
porch	STOA
—at west end of church	GALILEE
portico	PORCH
post placed against wall	PENDANT-POST
precinct	PERIBOLOS
	PERIBOLUS
privy behindmonastic	
dormitory	REREDORTER
projecting	
—arch stone	CROSSETTE
—band at bottom of wall	PLINTH
—carved spout	GARGOYLE
—course	STRING (COURSE)
—gallery	MACHICOLATION
—mould	HOOD-MOULD(ING)
—moulding	CORNICE
—part	JUTTY
—support pillar	BUTTRESS
—window	BAY, BOW, ORIEL
	SHOT-WINDOW
projection	CORBEL
—in carving	BOSS
—of cornice	CORONA
—on impost	CROSSETTE
raised area at entrance	PERRON
range of columns	COLONNADE
	PORTICO
—round building or	
square	PERISTYLE
recess	APSE, APSIS
recessed face of pediment	TYMPANUM
reinforcing pier	BUTTRESS
relief	RILIEVO
rib at intersection	GROIN
roof	
—arched	VAULT
—gutter	CULLIS
—supported by pillars	HYPOSTYLE
—tile	TEGULA
—with	
equal slopes	SPAN-ROOF
insulation above	
structure	INVERTED ROOF
one slope	MONOPITCH

steeply pitched glazing	NORTH-LIGHT
two slopes each side	MANSARD
roofed over	CL(E)ITHRAL
rose-window	CATHERINE-WHEEL, ROSACE
rosette	PATERA, ROSACE
round building	THOLOS, THOLUS
row of	
—arches	ARCADE
—corbels	CORBEL-TABLE
S-shaped moulding	OGEE
sacristy	DIACONICON, PARABEMA
screen behind altar	
or seat	REREDORSE, REREDOS(SE)
scroll ornament	CARTOUCHE
sculptured basket	PANNIER
secondary beam or joist	SOLIVE
semi-	
—circular recess	APSE, APSIS
—dome	CONCHA
—elliptical auditorium	SPHENDONE
sepulchral monument	CENOTAPH
shaft of column	FUST, SCAPE, SCAPUS
	TIGE, TRUNK, VERGE
shallow dome	SAUCER DOME
sharp-edged groove	QUIRK
shoulder in arch-stone	CROSSETTE
shrine for standards	SACELLUM
side of dormer	CHEEK
—surface of recess	REVEAL
six-lobed design	SEXFOIL
skirting	DADO
slab in frieze	METOPE
slope on top of moulding	WEATHERING
small column	COLUMEL
—fillet	ANNULET, LISTEL
—gable	GABLET
—low window	MEZZANINE
—moulding	BAGUETTE, REED
soffit	INTRADOS
space	
—between	
arch and moulding	SPANDREL, SPANDRIL
bed and wall	ROUELLE
columns	INTERCOLUMNIATION
corbels	MACHICOLATION
lintel and arch	TYMPANUM
pilasters	INTERPILASTER
pillars or windows	BAY
temple cell and pillars	PERIDROME
—for two triglyphs	DITRIGLYPH
—in Doric frieze	METOPE
spherical triangle formed	
by dome on square base	PENDENTIVE
spire	FLECHE
—or lantern formed by	
flying buttresses	CROWN

square	
—block	
at base of column	PLINTH
in moulding	DENTEL, DENTIL
—column against wall	PILASTER
—flat bracket	MUTULE
—pilaster	ANTA
—pilasters	ATTIC ORDER
stone	
—forming part of arch	HEADSTONE
	KEYSTONE, QUOIN
	VOUSSOIR
—pillar	OBELISK
storey over aisle	TRIFORIUM
sunken panel	COFFER, LACUNAR
stylobate	PODIUM
subordinate rib	TIERCERON
substructure of	
—dome	THOLOBATE
—row of columns	STYLOBATE
sunken panel	LACUNAR
support for	
—column	PEDESTAL
—inner part	
of wall	REAR-ARCH, RERE-ARCH
—roof	HAMMER BEAM, KING-POST
	PURLIN, QUEEN-POST
	RAFTER, SUMMER-BEAM, TRUSS
—wall	(FLYING) BUTTRESS
supporting	
—bracket	CORBEL
—pillar	BUTTRESS
swelling outline of column	ENTASIS
tall	
—building	POINT BLOCK, SKYSCRAPER
	TOWER BLOCK
—narrow	
pillar	OBELISK
window	LANCET WINDOW
temple gateway	PROPYLAEUM, PROPYLON
ten-column portico	DECASTYLE
three	
—grooved tablet	TRIGLYPH
—lobed tracery	TREFOIL
timber cladding	CLAPBOARD
	WEATHERBOARD
tomb	THOLOS, THOLUS
—as chapel	SACELLUM
toothlike ornament	CUSP
top of	
—column	CAPITAL
—entablature	CORNICE
tower	MINAR
—bell	CAMPANILE
—fort	MARTELLO
—mosque	MINARET

tracery on vault	FAN TRACERY
	FAN VAULTING
triangular	
—part of external wall	GABLE
—roof support	TRUSS
—structure over porch	PEDIMENT
twist in capital	HELIX
type of classical architecture	ORDER
under-curve of arch	ARCHIVOLT
underside of	
—arch	INTRADOS, SOFFIT
—eaves, stairs, etc	SOFFIT
uniformly coursed blocks	ISODOMON
	ISODOMUM
upper	
—lighted storey	CLEARSTORY
	CLERESTORY
—part of pillar	IMPOST
—room	SOL(L)AR, SOL(L)ER
upright	
—in roof truss	KING-POST, QUEEN-POST
—part of cupola	DRUM
ventilator	FEMERALL, FEMERELL
vertical member	MONTANT, MUNTIN
	STILE
voussoir	QUOIN
wall	
—between two openings	TRUMEAU
—panelling	DADO, WAINSCOT
weatherproof joint covering	FLASHING, SOAKER
wedge-shaped arch stone	VOUSSOIR
windows	
—bottom-hung	HOPPER
—centre-hung	PIVOT WINDOW
—circular	BULL'S-EYE
	CATHERINE WHEEL
	OEIL DE BOEUF
	PORTHOLE, ROSE
—curved head	EYEBROW WINDOW
—dormer	LUCARNE
—French	FENETRE
—full-length	
opening out	FRENCH WINDOW
sliding	PATIO DOOR
—high and shallow	CLERESTORY
—in	
roof	DORMER, LUCARNE
	ROOFLIGHT, SKYLIGHT
spire	LUCARNE
—opening at high level	FANLIGHT
—over door	FANLIGHT
—projecting	BAY, BOW, COMPASS
	JUT, ORIEL, SHOT
—side-hung	CASEMENT
—sliding	SASH
—small and low	MEZZANINE

—Spanish	VENTANA
—tall and pointed	LANCET
—wide	LANDSCAPE WINDOW
	PICTURE WINDOW
—with	
diamond-shaped panes	LATTICE
hinged shutter	SHOT-WINDOW
with flame-like tracery	FLAMBOYANT
wooden beam with steel tie	TRUSS-BEAM
zigzag moulding	DANCETTE

architectural styles (*see also* **building construction**)

5th c	BYZANTINE
pre 1066	PRE-CONQUEST, SAXON
11th c	NORMAN, ROMANESQUE
12th c	EARLY ENGLISH
12th-13th c	TRANSITIONAL
12th-16th c	GOTHIC
13th c	DECORATED
14th c	PERPENDICULAR
15th-16th c	RENAISSANCE, TUDOR
16th c	ELIZABETHAN, PALLADIAN
early 17th c	JACOBEAN
17th c	BAROQUE, CLASSICAL
early 18th c	QUEEN ANNE
18th c	GEORGIAN, NEO-CLASSIC(AL)
	PALLADIAN, ROCOCO
early 19th c	REGENCY
19th c	VICTORIAN
20th c	BRUTALIST, FUNCTIONALIST
	INTERNATIONAL, MODERNIST
	POSTMODERNIST
American	COLONIAL
—19th c	CHICAGO SCHOOL
classical architecture	
—Greek	CORINTHIAN, DORIC, IONIC
and Roman	CLASSICAL
—Roman	TUSCAN
formal based on classical styles	BEAUX ARTS
half-timbered	ELIZABETHAN, TUDOR
highly decorative style	BAROQUE, ROCOCO
of a particular place or time	VERNACULAR
with	
—pointed arches	GOTHIC
—semi-circular arches	ROMAN, NORMAN

Argentina	RA
barbecue	ASADO
capital	BUENOS AIRES
coin	AUSTRAL, CENTAVO, PESO
cowboy	GAUCHO
dance	TANGO
flower	PLATE
plain	CHACO, LLANO, PAMPA
tree	TALA
weight	GRANO, QUINTAL
Armenia	ARM, HAIKH
capital	(Y)EREVAN

armour	MAIL
air-hole	AVENTAIL(E)
breastplate	BYRNIE, CORS(E)LET
	CUIRASS, FELTRE
	PLACKET
—under hauberk	PLASTRON
buckler	PELTA, SHIELD
coat-of-mail	BRIGANDINE, BRIGANTINE
	HABERGEON, HAUBERK
contrivance on breastplate	REST
covering	
—arm	BRASSARD, BRASSART
	BRASSET, CORIUM
—body	BRIGANDINE, BRIGANTINE
	HAUBERK
—breast	BYRNIE, CORSELET
	CUIRASS, PECTORAL
	PLACKART, PLACKET
—chin and throat	MENTONNIERE
—crotch	FA(U)LD
—elbow	COP, COUDIERE
	COUTE(R), UBITIERE
—face	BEAVER, MESAIL, MEZAIL
	UMBREL, UMBR(I)ERE
	UMBRIL, VISOR, VIZOR
—foot	SABATON, SOLARET, SOLLERET
—forearm	LOWER CANNON
	VAMBRACE, VANTBRACE
—hand	GAUNTLET
—head	HELM(ET)
—hips	CULET(TE), FAULD
—horse's	
breast	PECTORAL, POITREL
head	CHAFFRON, CHAMFROM
	CHAMFRAIN
—joint	GUSSET
—knee	GENOUILLERE, POLEYN
—leg	CHAUSSES, GREAVE
	JAMB(E), JAMBEAU
—neck	BEVOR, HAUBERK
and shoulder	GORGET
—shoulder	AILETTE, BESADEUR
	GARDBRACE, PALLETTE
	PAULDRON, POULDRON, SPAUDIER
—stomach	PANSER
—thigh	CULET, TASSET
—throat	GORGET
—upper	
arm	MONION, REREBRACE
body	(PEASCOD-)CUIRASS
leg	CUISSE
crest of helmet	COMB
face-cover	VISOR, VIZOR
for	
—horse	BARBE, BARDCHANFRAN
	CRUPPER, HARNESS, SHANFRON

—man	BARD, HARNESS, MAIL
full suit of armour	PANOPLY
hand-shield on lance	VAMPLATE, VAMPLET
helmet	ARMET, BASINET, BURGANET
	BURGONET, CASK, CASQUE
	MORIAN, MOR(R)ION
	SALADE, SAL(L)ET
knee-piece	GENOUILLERE
leather	
—arm-piece	CORIUM
—coat	GAMBESON, JACK
—corselet	LORICA
—doublet with	
steel strips	PLACCATE, PLACKET
—Roman	LORICA
light headpiece	BASINET
long coat of chain-mail	HAUBERK
lozenge-shaped plate	MASCLE
mail-coat	BYRNIE
massive helmet	HEAUME
movable front	
of helmet	VENTAIL, VENTAYLE
open helmet	MOR(R)ION
overlapping piece	TACE, TASLET, TASSE(T)
padded	
—breast-shield	PLASTRON
—jacket	ACTON, GAMBESON
	HA(C)QUETON, (H)AKETON
part of skirt	TACE, TASLET, TASSE(T)
plate below tasses	TUILLE(TTE)
quilted coat	GAMBESON
set of armour	GARNITURE
shield	
—large	PAVIS(E)
—small	BUCKLER, PELTA
—worn on left gauntlet	GLOVE-SHIELD
shoulder-plate	AILETTE, PAULDRON
	POULDRON
skull-cap	CAPELINE
sleeveless mail-coat	HABERGEON
spear rest	FEWTER
splint armour	JAZERANT, JESSERANT
steel plates worn skirt-like	LAMBOYS
suit of mail	CATAPHRACT
thin metal plate	LAME
veil over helmet	LAMBREQUIN
visor/vizor	MESAIL, MEZAIL
	UMBREL, UMBRIL, VOLBR(I)ERE

army

chaplains	HCF, OCF
dentists	RADC
doctors	RAMC
paymasters	RAPC
ranks (lowest first)	
—other ranks	OR
	RECRUIT, ROOKIE

	(BANDSMAN, GUARDSMAN, GNR
	(GUNNER, PRIVATE, PTE
	(SAPPER, SIGNALMAN, TROOPER
—non-commissioned	
	LANCE-BOMBARDIER
	LANCE-CORPORAL
	BOMBARDIER, CORPORAL, CPL
	LANCE-SERGEANT, SERGEANT, SGT
—warrant officer I	STAFF SERGEANT
	COMPANY QUARTERMASTER-SERGEANT
	CQMS
	COMPANY SERGEANT-MAJOR, CSM
—warrant officer II	DRILL SERGEANT
	REGIMENTAL
	QUARTERMASTER-SERGEANT
	RQMS
	REGIMENTAL SERGEANT MAJOR, RSM
—commissioned rank	SECOND LIEUTENANT
	LT, LIEUTENANT
	CAPT, CAPTAIN
	MAJ, MAJOR
	LIEUTENANT-COLONEL, LT-COL
	COL, COLONEL
	BRIG, BRIGADIER
	MAJ-GEN, MAJOR-GENERAL
	LIEUTENANT-GENERAL, LT-GEN
	GEN, GENERAL
	FIELD MARSHAL, FM
teachers	RAEC
technicians	REME
vets	RAVC
(*see also* **military, soldiers**)	

art

amateur	DABBLER, DILETTANTE
art lover	AESTHETE
art movements	
—15th c Italian	QUATTROCENTO
—16th c Italian	MANNERISM
—17th/18th c	BAROQUE
—18th/19th c	NEO-CLASSICISM
	ROMANTICISM
—1848	PRE-RAPHAELITISM
—1890s	ART NOUVEAU
—19th c	REALISM
—19th c French	BARBIZON SCHOOL
	IMPRESSIONISM
—1920s and 1930s	ART DECO
—20th c	ABSTRACT EXPRESSIONISM
	CUBISM, DADAISM
	EXPRESSIONISM, FAUVISM
	OP ART, SURREALISM
British	VORTICISM
Dutch	DE STIJL, THE STYLE
German	BAUHAUS
Italian	FUTURISM
Russian	CONSTRUCTIVISM

—based on classical design	BEAUX ARTS
—characterised by	
depiction of life objectively	REALISM
depiction of machine	
age	FUTURISM
	VORTICISM
distortion of human figure	MANNERISM
dots of colour	POINTILLISM(E)
exploration of dreams and	
the unconscious	SURREALISM
expression of spiritual	
significance	NABIS, SYMBOLISM
extreme abstraction	DE STIJL
	THE STYLE
function dictating shape	BAUHAUS
geometric shapes	ART DECO
	CONSTRUCTIVISM
	CUBISM
	OP ART
immediate visual impact	
of the subject	IMPRESSIONISM
landscape	
for its own sake	BARBIZON SCHOOL
ornate shapes	BAROQUE
rejection of	
—classicism	ROMANTICISM
—impressionism	EXPRESSIONISM
—rationality	DADAISM
representation as two-	
dimensional decoration	FAUVISM
revival of classical	
proportions	NEO-CLASSICISM
style ahead of the times	AVANT GARDE
swirling shapes	ART NOUVEAU
use (in 19th c) of style	
of 15th c artists	PRE-RAPHAELITISM
visual illusion	OP ART
artists	(see **painting**)
artist's complete works	CORPUS, OEUVRE
—workroom	ATELIER, STUDIO
artistic circle	CLIQUE, COTERIE
—rebirth	RENAISSANCE
	RENASCENCE
artistically impressive object	OBJET 'DART
drawing showing exposed	
muscles	ECORCHE
exhibition covering many	
years of artist's work	RETROSPECTIVE
natural object displayed	
as a work of art	OBJET TROUVE
official exhibition	SALON
optical	
—aid	CAMERA LUCIDA
—illusion	TROMPE L'OEIL
ornamentation of metal by	
engraving etc	NIELLO

representation of human	
form	ANTHROPOMORPH
unconventional artist	BOHEMIAN
Asian	
anteater	PANGOLIN
bean(-plant)	SOJA, SOY(A)
bird	FROGMOUTH, MANDARIN DUCK
	MYNA(H), PEACOCK-PHEASANT
	PITTA, SIRGANG, TAILOR-BIRD
	TRAGOPAN
cattle	YAK, ZEBU, Z(H)O
	(see also **ox**)
cereal	JAPANESE MILLET
chief	CHAGAN, CHAM, KHAN
civet	PARADOXURE, ZIBET
climbing pepper	BETEL
day-lilies	FUNKIA
doctor/priest	SHAMAN
domesticated animal	CAMEL
desert plant	CAMEL'S THORN
durra	GUINEA-CORN
dziggetai	HEMIONE
evergreen shrub	CAMELLIA
falcon	LUGGER, SHAHIN
felt tent	KIBITKA
fibre	RAMIE
fish	PANCHAX
—hook money	LARI(N), LARREE
fowl	LANGSHAN
fox	ADIVE, CORSAC, CORSAK
fruit	BITO, WAMPEE
goat	JAGLA
hawk	SHIKRA
hemp	PUA
hornless deer	MUSK-DEER
horse	PRZEWALSKI'S HORSE
—disease	SURRA
kebabs	SATAY, SATE
kiang	HEMIONE
legume	COW-PEA
lizard	MONITOR
magician	SHAMAN
nut	PISTACHIO
orchestra	GAMELAN
orchid	DENDROBIUM
pangolin	MANIS
paradoxure	MUSANG
partridge	SEESEE
perennial herb	LASERPICIUM
periwinkle	STRIPHANTHUS
pheasant	TRAGOPAN
piping hare	PICA
plant	ABELMOSK, GOA BEAN
	HOSTA, LICORICE
	LIQUORICE
primitive heartland	ANGARALAND

prince	CHAGAN, CHAM, KHAN	—ruling at birth	HYLEG
pygmy negroid	NEGRITO		(*see also* **astronomy**)
religion	SHAMANISM	point on the ecliptic	
rodent	GERBIL	opposite to the ascendant	DESCENDANT
scaly ant-eater	MANIS	relative positioning of	
sheep	(*see separate entry*)	stars or planets	CONSTELLATION
shrub	PATCHOULI, PATCHOULY	—at	
	SKIMMIA, TCHE, TEA	72° apart	QUINTILE
snake	KING-COBRA	120° apart	TRINE
snow-leopard	OUNCE	moment of birth	HOROSCOPE
tailless hare	OCHOTONA, PICA	set of three signs	
tree	ACLE, AILANTO, ASAK, ASOK(A)	120° apart	TRIGON, TRIPLICITY
	BITO, CAL(L)IATOUR	signs of zodiac	(*see* **zodiac**)
	CAL(L)IATURE, DATE PALM	situation of one planet with	
	DIYA, LIQUIDAMBAR	respect to another	ASPECT
	PAPER-MULBERRY, RED SANDERS	trigon	
	(RED) SANDAL(-WOOD)	—1st: Cancer, Scorpio,	
	SAKSAUL, SAXAUL, SIRIS	Pisces	WATERY TRIGON
	TREE-OF-HEAVEN	—2nd: Taurus, Virgo,	
tribes	KALMUK, KIPCHAK, TA(R)TAR	Capricorn	EARTHLY TRIGON
trousers	SHERWAL, SHERRYVALLIES	—3rd: Gemini, Libra,	
wild		Aquarius	AIRY TRIGON
—ass	DZIGGETAI, HEMIONE	—4th: Aries, Leo,	
	KIANG, KYANG, ONAGER	Sagittarius	FIERY TRIGON
—dog	RAC(C)OON-DOG	**astronomy**	URANOLOGY
—goat	MARKHOR, SERPENT-EATER	age of Moon at start	
—horse	PRZEWALSKI'S HORSE	of calendar year	EPACT
asteroids	(*see* **astronomy**)	alignment of heavenly body	
astrology		with Sun and Earth	CONJUNCTION
apparent meeting of		angle between	
stars or planets	CONJUNCTION	—Earth and Sun as	
astrologers		seen from space	PHASE ANGLE
—Austrian	MESMER	—planet and its last	
—French	NOSTRODAMUS	perihelion	ANOMALY
benign	TRINE	angular distance from	
diagram of heavens at		celestial equator	DECLINATION
moment of one's birth	HOROSCOPE	pole	AZIMUTH
coincident influences	SYNASTRY	apparent	
comparison of horoscopes	SYNASTRY	—displacement of star	ABERRATION
division		—movement of body resulting	
--between signs of		from movement of observer	PARALLAX
the zodiac	CUSP	—path of Sun	ECLIPTIC
—of the zodiac	HOUSE, MANSION, SIGN	asteroids	ACHILLES, ABANDERADA
force from stars etc alleged			ADONIS, AMOR, APOLLO, ASTRAEA,
to affect actions	INFLUENCE		BAMBERGA, BETTINA, CAMILLA
forecast based on diagram			CERES, CHIRON, CYBELE
of heavens	HOROSCOPE, NATIVITY		DAVIDA, EGERIA, EKARD, EROS
horoscope	NATIVITY		EUGENIA, EUNOMIA, EUPHROSYNE
imaginary belt of			EUROPA, HALAWE, HAPAG, HERMES
the heavens	ZODIAC		HIDALGO, HYGEIA, ICARUS
overlapping of stars or planets	CONJUNCTION		INTEROMNIA, JUNO, LORELEI
part of the ecliptic just			MELPOMENE, NORC, PALLAS
risen above horizon	ASCENDANT		PATENTIA, PSYCHE, SYLVIA
planet			THEMIS, TORO, VESTA
—in conjunction with		astronomers	
or near the sun	COMBUST	—Alexandrian	PTOLEMY

—American	ADAMS, BAADE, BARNARD
	BOLTON, BOND, BOWEN, CHANDLER
	DOUGLAS, DUNHAM, DYCE, EDDY
	EWEN, GOLDSTEIN, GREENSTEIN, HALE
	HERBIG, HEWITT, HUBBLE, HUMASON
	JANSKY, KEELER, KOWAL, LANGLEY
	LEAVITT, LOWELL, MENZEL
	MINKOWSKI, MORGAN, MOULTON
	NINNINGER, PARKER
	PENZIAS, PICKERING, PURCELL, REBER
	RUSSEL, SAGAN, SANDAGE, SCHABERLE
	SCHMIDT, SEYFERT, SHAPLEY
	SHOEMAKER, SLIPHER
	TERRILE, TERRY, TOMBAUGH
	TRUMPLER, TUCKER, VAN DE KAMP
	WHIPPLE, WILDT, WILSON, ZWICKY
—Arabian	AL BATTANI, ARZACHEL
—Australian	CRAFORD, HAZARD
—Austrian	LITTROW
—Belgian	LEMAITRE, SWINGS, WENDELIN
—British	ABNEY, ADAMS, AIRY, BOND
	BONNOR, BRADLEY, DARWEN
	EDDINGTON, FLAMSTEED, GILL
	GOLD, GOODRICKE, HALLEY
	HENDERSON, HERSCHEL, HOOKE
	HOYLE, HUGGINS, HUSSEY, JEANS
	JEFFREYS, LOCKYER, LOVELL, MOORE
	NAPIER, NEWTON, PARSONS, POGSON
	RYLE, WREN, WOOLFSON
—Chinese	HONG-YEE CHIU
—Danish	BOK, BRAHE, HERTZSPRUNG
	KUIPER, ROEMER
—Dutch	DE SITTER, FABRICIUS
	HUYGENS, KAPTEYN, OORT
	SNEL VAN ROYEN, SNELLIUS
	VAN DE CAMP, VAN DE HULST
—Egyptian	SOSIGENES
—Estonian	OPIK
—French	CASSINI, FLAMMARION
	JANSSEN, LAPLACE, LE VERRIER
	LYOT, MESSIER, RICHER
—German	BAADE, BESSEL, BODE
	CLAVIUS, ENCKE, GALLE
	HARTMANN, HERSCHEL, KEPLER
	MARIUS, SCHWABE, SCHWARZCHILD
	VOGEL, VON STRUVE, WEIZSACKER
	WILDT, WITT, WURM
—Greek	ARISTARCHUS, ERATOSTHENES
	HIPPARCHUS, KAL(L)IPPOS
	METON, POSIDONIUS
—Indian	CHANDRASEKHAR
—Irish	OPIK
—Italian	BIANCHINI, GALILEO
	GRIMALDI, MAFFEI
	RICCIOLI, SCHIAPARELLI
	SECCHI

—Polish	COPERNICUS, HELVETIUS
—Russian	KARDASHEV, KOSYREV
	SAFFRONOV, SHKLOVSHY
	VON STRUVE
—Spanish	DE FERRER
—Sri Lankan	WICKRAMASINGHE
—Swedish	ALFVEN, ANGSTROM, CELSIUS
	LUNDMARK, SWEDENBORG
—Swiss	TRUMPLER, ZWICKY
—Uruguayan	FERNANDEZ
bands of darkness before	
and after solar eclipse	SHADOW BANDS
Big Bang theory	SUPERDENSE THEORY
blocking of light from	
one body by another	OCCULTATION
blue star with large	
red shift	BLUE STELLAR OBJECT, BSO
bright spots seen	
at total eclipse	BAILY'S BEADS
brightest star	SIRIUS
cascade shower	COSMIC RAY SHOWER
circle	
—of altitude	ALMACANTAR
—through poles	MERIDIAN
classification of stars	
by spectra	HARVARD CLASSIFICATION
	SPECTRAL CLASS, SPECTRAL TYPE
clockwork model of Solar System	ORRERY
cloud of gaseous matter	NEBULA
collapse of universe	BIG CRUNCH
coloured lights in	
sky over Poles	AURORA AUSTRALIS
	AURORA BOREALIS
comets	BENNETT, BIELA, BROOKS
	CHIRON, CHURIUMOV-GERASIMENKE
	CROMMELIN, D'ARREST
	DONATI, DUTOIT-HARTLEY
	ENCKE, FINLAY, GIACOBINNI-SINNER
	GREAT, HALLEY, HARTLEY
	HUMASON, LEVY, LEXELL'S, KOHOUTEK
	MRKOS, TEMPEL, TUTTLE
	WHIPPLE, WIRTANEN
conjunction (old)	SYNOD
constellations	(see separate entry)
cosmic ray shower	AUGER SHOWER
	CASCADE SHOWER
	PENETRATING SHOWER
	SOFT SHOWER
critical mass of star that	
can become a white	
dwarf	CHANDRASEKHAR'S LIMIT
cycle of moon phases	CAL(L)IPPIC CYCLE
	METONIC CYCLE
distance	
—Earth to Sun	ASTRONOMICAL UNIT
—parallax of 1 sec of arc	PARSEC

distant group of stars	NEBULA
extremity of major axis of orbit	APSIS
final stage of star	NEUTRON STAR
fluctuation of	
—Earth's movement	
round celestial pole	NUTATION
—equinoctial points along	
the ecliptic	PRECESSION(AL) MOTION
galaxy	
—extremely bright	SEYFERT GALAXY
—including Earth	MILKY WAY
—nearest	MAGELLANIC CLOUDS
—with arms in spiral form	SPIRAL GALAXY
	SPIRAL NEBULA
gas cloud	NEBULA
glare in sky	GEGENSCHEIN
	ZODIACAL LIGHT
graph of main sequence	
of stars	HERTZSPRUNG DIAGRAM
great circle	
—in the heavens	ECLIPTIC
—through poles	CELESTIAL MERIDIAN
group of stars	
—in recognised pattern	CONSTELLATION
—with common motion	OPEN CLUSTER
halo round	
—head of comet	COMA
—Sun or moon	CORONA
happening at sunrise	COSMIC(AL)
hazy patch in sky	NEBULA
highest point in heavens	VERTEX, ZENITH
horizontal bearing of	
celestial body	AZIMUTH
hypothetical one-	
dimensional warp	COSMIC STRING
imaginary sphere containing	
heavenly bodies	CELESTIAL SPHERE
instrument for	
—detecting radio frequencies	
of stars etc	RADIO TELESCOPE
—determining star's	
passage	ALMACANTAR
	ALMACANTUR
—following movement	
of stars etc	COELOSTAT
—measuring altitudes	ASTROLABE
—observing meridian	
passage	DIPLEIDOSCOPE
intense gravitational field	
preventing escape even	
of light	BLACK HOLE
intersection of plane of	
Equator with	
celestial sphere	CELESTIAL EQUATOR
interstellar	
—dust	COSMIC DUST

—gas clouds	COALSACK
—nebula	CRAB, HORSEHEAD NEBULA
large meteor	BOLIDE
laws governing movements	
of planets	KEPLER'S LAWS
light emitted by star	LUMINOSITY
line between	
—focus and	
point on orbit	RADIUS VECTOR
—light and dark	
areas of planet or moon	TERMINATOR
lining up of	
celestial bodies	CONJUNCTION
Earth between planet	
and Sun	OPPOSITION
luminous	
—patch	NEBULA
in	
—east at sunrise	ZODIACAL LIGHT
—west at sunset	ZODIACAL LIGHT
—ring round the Moon	BROCH, MACULA
magnitude of star	LUMINOSITY
measure of	
—elongation of	
ellipse	ECCENTRICITY
—star's brightness	MAGNITUDE
meteors	ANDROMEDID, AQUARID
	BIELID, GEMINID, LEONID
	LYRID, ORIONID, PERSEID
	QUADRANTID, TAURID, URSID
—large, bright	BOLIDE
—nickel-iron	SIDERITE
—stone	AEROLITE, AEROLITH
meteor craters	
—Africa	ASHANTI CRATER
	BOSUMTIBI, VREDEFORT RING
—America	BARRINGER CRATER
	COON BUTTE
	MANSON, SERPENT MOUND
	WELLS CREEK, WINSLOW
—Australia	GOSSES BLUFF
	WOLF'S CREEK
—Brazil	ARAGUAINHA DOME
—Canada	BRENT CRATER, CARSWELL
	CHARLEVOIX, CHUBB CRATER
	CLEARWATER LAKES
	DEEP BAY, HAUGHTON DOME
	HOLLEFORD, MANICOUAGAN
	MISTATIN, NEW QUEBEC
	STEEN RIVER, SUDBURY
—France	ROCHECHOUART
—Germany	(NORDLINGER) RIES
—Iraq	AL UMCHAIMIN
—Russia	KAMENSK, VLADIVOSTOK
—Siberia	TUNGUSKA
—Sweden	SILJAN

meteoric scar	ASTROBLEME
meteorite	AEROLITE, SIDER(OL)ITE
	THUNDERSTONE
—iron	AEROSIDERITE
—probable	AUSTRALITE, TEKTITE
—stony	CHONDRITE
Milky Way	WATLING STREET
minor planet	ASTEROID
moment when the Sun is	
—farthest	
north from the	
Equator	SUMMER SOLSTICE
south from the	
Equator	WINTER SOLSTICE
—overhead at the Equator	EQUINOX
Moon	LUNA, OLIVER
—area of high gravity	MASCON
—bays	ASTRONAUTS BAY
Bay of	
—Billows	SINUS AESTUUM
—Dew	SINUS RORIS
—Rainbows	SINUS IRIDUM
Central Bay	SINUS MEDII
—craters	ALPHONSUS, ARCHIMEDES
	ARISTARCHUS, ARISTOTELES
	ATLAS, BIANCHINI, COPERNICUS
	FLAMSTEED, GRIMALDI, HERCULES
	HIPPARCHUS, JOLIOT-CURIE
	LOMONOSOV, PLATO
	PTOLEMAEUS
—full moon	PLENILUNE
—inhabitant	LUNARIAN, SELENITE
—mock moon	PARASELENE
—mountains	ALTAI, CAUCASUS
	JURA, LEIBNITZ
—oscillation	LIBRATION
—period between	
new moons	LUNATION
	SYNODIC MONTH
—phases	NEW MOON
	FIRST QUARTER
	FULL MOON
	THIRD QUARTER
—seas	MOSCOW SEA
Ocean of Storms	OCEANUS
	PROCELLARUM
Sea of	
—Clouds	MARE NUBIUM
—Cold	MARE FRIGORIS
—Crises	MARE CRISIUM
—Fecundity	MARE FECUNDITATIS
—Humboldt	MARE HUMBOLDTIANUM
—Moisture	MARE HUMORUM
—Nectar	MARE NECTARIS
—Rains	MARE IMBRIUM
—Serenity	MARE SERENITATIS

—Tranquillity	MARE TRANQUILLITATIS
—Vapours	MARE VAPORUM
—sunlight reflected	
from Earth	EARTHSHINE
moons	
—Earth	LUNA, MOON
—Jupiter	ADASTREA, AMALTHEA
	ANANKE, CALLISTO, CARME
	ELARA, EUROPA
	GANYMEDE, HIMALIA, IO
	LEDA, LYSITHEA, METIS
	PASIPHAE, THEBE, SINOPE
—Mars	DEIMOS, PHOBOS
—Neptune	NEREID, TRITON
—Pluto	CHARON
—Saturn	ATLAS, CALYPSO, DIONE
	ENCELADUS, EPIMETHEUS
	HYPERION, IAPETUS, JANUS
	MIMAS, PHOEBE, RHEA, SPAHN
	SPONHOLZ, TELESTO, TETHYS
	TITAN
—Uranus	ARIEL, CORDELIA
	MIRANDA, OBERON, OPHELIA
	TITANIA, UMBRIEL
movement	
—across meridian	MERIDIAN PASSAGE
—from east to west	REGRESSION
—of	
equinoctial points	PRECESSION
lines on spectrum due to	
—approach of star	BLUE SHIFT
—recession of source	RED SHIFT
star across line	
of sight	PROPER MOTION
nearest star	PROXIMA CENTAURI
nebulous head of comet	CHEVELURE, COMA
non-distorting telescope	SCHMIDT CAMERA
Northern Lights	AURORA BOREALIS
	AURORA SEPTENTRIONALIS
observatory	(*see separate entry*)
occlusion of one body	
by another	ECLIPSE
optical representation of	
celestial bodies in dome	PLANETARIUM
orbit of planet round circle	EPICYCLE
oscillation of	
—axis of Earth	CHANDLER'S WOBBLE
—pole of Earth	NUTATION
—surface of Moon	LIBRATION
pair of stars	BINARY STAR
	DOUBLE STAR
path of one body round another	ORBIT
period	
—between successive	
conjunctions of a	
planet with sun	SYNODIC PERIOD

new moons	LUNATION
	SYNODIC MONTH
—of complete obliteration	
during an eclipse	ROTALITY
—of Earth's rotation	SIDEREAL DAY
planets	EARTH, JUPITER, MARS
	MERCURY, NEPTUNE, PLUTO
	SATURN, URANUS, VENUS
—blue planet	EARTH
—brightest	VENUS
—closer to Sun than Earth is	INFERIOR
—farther from Sun than	
Earth is	SUPERIOR
—largest	JUPITER
—minor	ASTEROID
	CERES, PALLAS, VESTA
—mythical (Hindu)	RAHU
—nearest	VENUS
—orbital point	
farthest from sun	PERIHELION
nearest to sun	APHELION
—red planet	MARS
—smallest	PLUTO
—Venus	(*see below*)
—watery planet	EARTH
point	
—directly above observer	VERTEX, ZENITH
—directly below observer	NADIR
—of	
conjunction or opposition	SYZYGY
infinite gravity	SINGULARITY
orbit	
—farthest from	
Earth	APOGEE
Moon	APOCYNTHION
Sun	APHELION
—nearest	
Earth	PERIGEE
Moon	PERICYNTHION
	PERILUNE
Sun	PERIHELION
—of very strong gravity	BLACK HOLE
—in heavens opposite	
nadir	VERTEX, ZENITH
zenith	NADIR
—where	
orbit intersects ecliptic	NODE
Sun crosses celestial	
equator	EQUINOX
position	
—at 90°	QUADRATURE
—of planet in orbit	ANOMALY
presumed site of collapsed	
star	BLACK HOLE
pulsating star	PULSAR
quartile aspect	SQUARE

quasar which is not a	
radio source	QUASI-STELLAR GALAXY
	QSG
quasi-stellar radio source	QUASAR
radiation from space	COSMIC RAYS
radio source	LACERTAE OBJECT
	QUASAR
rising with the Sun	COSMIC(AL)
rounded granule in meteorite, etc	CHONDRULE
search for other life in	
the universe	BIOASTRONOMY
shadow cast in eclipse	
—darker part	UMBRA
—lighter part	PENUMBRA
shape of	
—body between half and	
full phase	GIBBOUS
—Moon seen from Earth	PHASE
shower	
—extending over wide	
area	AUGER SHOWER
—of	
electrons etc	CASCADE SHOWER
	SOFT SHOWER
nucleons etc	PENETRATING SHOWER
situation of heavenly body	
—lined up with another	CONJUNCTION
—opposite another	OPPOSITION
skeleton sphere showing	
motions of stars etc	ARMILLARY SPHERE
small body	
—reaching Earth's surface	AEROLITE
	AEROLITH
	METEORITE
—travelling through space	ASTEROID
	COMET, METEOR
	SHOOTING-STAR
source of high radiation	QUASAR
Southern Lights	AURORA AUSTRALIS
space	(*see separate entry*)
space dust	COSMIC DUST
speed of	
—approach or recession	
of heavenly body	RADIAL VELOCITY
—light	C
—recession proportional	
to distance	HUBBLE'S LAW
star	(*see separate entry*)
study of	
—orbits and	
trajectories	CELESTIAL MECHANICS
—origins of universe	COSMOLOGY
Sun	
—absorption lines in	
spectrum	FRAUNHOFER LINES
—apparent path	ECLIPTIC

—appearance above horizon   DAWN
     SUNRISE
—bright area in
   chromosphere   SOLAR FLARE
   photosphere   FACULA
—dark area on surface   MACULA
     SUNSPOT
—disappearance
   below horizon   SUNSET
   during eclipse   TOTALITY
—fictitious, used in timekeeping   MEAN SUN
—halo   CORONA
—having Sun as centre   HELIOCENTRIC
—incandescent gas
   layer   CHROM(AT)OSPHERE
—intensity of radiation   SOLAR CONSTANT
—large flare of
   solar gas   (SOLAR) PROMINENCE
—light reflected by Earth
   to dark side of Moon   EARTHSHINE
—luminous envelope   PHOTOSPHERE
—mid-point on ecliptic
   between equinoxes   SOLSTICE
—mock sun   PARAHELION
—outbursts of high
   temperature   SOLAR FLARE
—stream of particles
   emitted by solar flares   SOLAR WIND
—study   HELIOLOGY
—time
   between successive
     returns of Sun to meridian   SOLAR DAY
   of greatest declination   SOLSTICE
—ultra-violet rays   ACTINIC RAYS
—visible at night in
   polar regions   MIDNIGHT SUN
—worship   HELIOLATRY
superdense theory   BIG BANG THEORY
system of galaxies   METAGALAXY
table of astronomical data   EPHEMERIS
telescopes   (*see* **observatory**)
theory of
—Earth as centre of
   Solar System   COPERNICAN THEORY
     GEOCENTRIC THEORY
—origin of universe   BIG BANG THEORY
     PULSATING UNIVERSE
     STEADY STATE THEORY
     SUPERDENSE THEORY
—planet formation   PLANETESIMAL
     HYPOTHESIS
     TIDAL HYPOTHESIS
—star formation   NEBULAR HYPOTHESIS
—Sun as centre of
   solar system   HELIOCENTRIC THEORY
     PTOLEMAIC THEORY

time
—difference between lunar
   and solar year   EPACT
—measured from movements
   of planets   EPHEMERIS TIME
twelfth of diameter of Moon
   or Sun   DIGIT
two stars with common
   centre of gravity   BINARY STARS
two-star system that can be
   resolved with optical
   telescope   VISUAL BINARY
universe as system of galaxies   METAGALAXY
value which determines
   elliptic orbit   ELEMENT
variation in
   —apparent motion
     of heavenly body   ABERRATION
   —orbit caused by mutual
     gravitational attraction   PERTURBATION
Venus
—as
   evening star   HESPERUS, VESPER
   morning star   LUCIFER
—mountainous region   BETA REGIO
—plain   GUINEVERE PLANITO
     ISHTAR TERRA
—volcano   THEIA MONTES
vertical angle of celestial body   ALTITUDE
Watling Street   MILKY WAY
zone containing orbits of Sun,
   Moon and planets   ZODIAC

athletes   (*see also* **games**)
(f) indicates women athletes
decathletes
—American   JENNER, JOHNSON
     MATHIAS, TOOMEY
—British   KRUGER, THOMPSON
     THORPE
—Canadian   SMITH
—Finnish   JARVINEN, YRJOLA
—German   EBERLE, HINGSEN
—Russian   AVILOV, KUTSENKO
     KUZNETSOV
—Swedish   LOMBERG, OHLSON
discus throwers
—American (m)   HOUSER, OERTER
     ROSE, WILKINS
     (f)   COPELAND
—British (f)   PICTON
—Bulgarian (f)   PETKOVA, VERGOVA
—Canadian   LAZDINS
—Czech (m)   BUGAR, DANEK
     (f)   FIKATOVA
—Dutch (f)   STALMAN
—French (f)   MAZEAS, OSTERMEYER

—German (m)	DANNENBERG, SCHMIDT
(f)	JAHL, SCHLAAK
—Polish (f)	WAJSOWNA
—Romanian (f)	MANOLIU, MENIS
—Russian (m)	BARTES, RASSOHUPKIN
(f)	MELNIK, PRESS
	ROMASHKOVA

hammer-throwers

—American	FLANAGAN, ROSE
—British	SMITH
—Finnish	TAIANEN
—Irish	O'CALLAGHAN
—Russian	BONDARCHUK, SEDYCH

heptathletes (f)

—American	JOYNER-KERSEE
—Australian	FLEMMING, NUNN
—British	HAGGER, SIMPSON
—German	BEHMER
—Russian	NIKITINA

high-jumpers

—American (m)	EWRY, FOSBURY, OSBORN
(f)	COACHMAN, DIDRIKSON
	MCDANIEL
—Australian (f)	STANTON
—British (m)	GRANT
(f)	LERWILL, TYLER
—Bulgarian (f)	KOSTADINOVA
—Canadian (m)	MCNAUGHTON, OTTEY
(f)	CATHERWOOD
—Cuban	SOTOMAYOR
—Czech (f)	REZKOVA
—German (m)	MOERGENBERG, WESSIG
(f)	ACKERMAN, MEYFARTH
—Hungarian (f)	CZAK
—Italian (f)	SIMEONI
—Romanian (f)	BALAS
—Russian	PAKLIN

hurdlers

—American (m)	CALHOUN, DAVIS
	DILLARD, KINGDOM
	KRAENZLEIN, MOSES
	NEHEMIAH, TEWKSBURY
(f)	DIDRIKSON
	FARMER-PATRICK
	FITZGERALD-BROWN
—Australian (f)	CAIRD
	FLINTHOFF-KING
	STRICKLAND
—British (m)	AKABUSI, BURGHLEY
	HEMERY, JACKSON
(f)	GUNNELL, MORLEY
—Bulgarian (f)	DONKOVA
—Canadian (m)	MCKOY
(f)	ROCHELEAU
—Dutch (f)	BLANKERS-KOEN
—French	CARISTON

—German (m)	SCHMIDT
(f)	BALZER, ERHART
	OSCHKENAT, SCHALLER
—Irish	BEATTIE
—Italian (f)	VALLA
—Monégasque (f)	MOUTAWAKEO
—Russian (f)	KOMISOVA, PRESS
	STEPANOVA

javelin-throwers

—American (m)	MILLER, OBERST, YOUNG
(f)	DIDRIKSON
—Austrian (f)	BAUMA
—British (m)	BACKLEY, BEVAN, OTLEY
(f)	SANDERSON, WHITBREAD
—Czech (m)	ZELEZNY
(f)	ZATOPKOVA
—Finnish	HAERFOENEN, JARVINEN
	MYRRA, RATY
—German (m)	TAFELMEIER
(f)	FELKE
—Hungarian (m)	NEMETH
(f)	NEMETH
—Japanese	MIZOGUCHI
—Romanian (f)	PENES
—Russian (m)	KULA, MAKAROV
(f)	OZOLINA, YAUNZEME
—Swedish	BODEN, LEMMING

long-jumpers

—American (m)	BEAMON, EWRY
	LEWIS, PRINSTEIN
(f)	WHITE
—Australian	HONEY
—British (m)	DAVIES
(f)	CAWLEY, MAY, RAND
—German (f)	DRESCHLER, ROSENDAHL
	VOIGT
—Hungarian (f)	GYARMATI
—New Zealand (f)	MOFFITT, WILLIAMS
—Polish (f)	KRZESINSKA, SZEWINSKA
—Romanian (f)	STANCUI
—Russian (m)	EMMIYAN
(f)	KOLPAKOVA, KREPKINA

marathon runners

—American (m)	COREY, HAYES, HICKS
(f)	BENOIT, LARRIEN-SMITH
	WIEDENBACH
—Australian (m)	DE CASTELLA, MARTIN
	MONEGHETTI
(f)	MARTIN
—British	DAVIES-HALE, FERRIS
	HARPER, HEATLEY, HUTTON
	JONES, MILOVSOROV, PETERS
	SPEDDING, THACKERY
—Chilean	PLAZA
—Chinese (f)	YOUFENG
—Czech	ZATOPEK

—Estonian	LOSSMAN
—Ethiopian	BIKILA, DENSIMO, WOLDE
—Finnish	KOLEHMAINEN, STENROOS
—French	EL OUAFI, MIMOUN, TEATRO
—Italian	BERTINI, BETTIOL
	BORDIN, PETRI
—Japanese	SON, TANIGUCHI
—Kenyan	WAKIIHURI
—New Zealand	RYAN
—Norwegian (f)	KRISTIANSEN, WAITZ
—Polish (f)	PANFIL
—Portuguese (m)	LOPES
(f)	MOTA
—Russian (m)	KOTOV, TOLSTIKOV
(f)	KLOCHKO
—Tanzanian	INKANGAA

middle-distance runners

—American (m)	CUNNINGHAM, EVANS
	LIGHTBODY, PETTIGREW
	REYNOLDS, SHEPPARD
	WHITFIELD, WHOTTLE
(f)	BABER, BRISCO-HOOKS
	MANNING
—Australian (m)	ELLIOTT, FLACK
	LANDY, CLARKE
(f)	FLINTHOFF-KING
—Belgian	MOENS, PUTTEMANS, RIEFF
—Brazilian	CRUZ, JUANTORENA
—British (m)	BANNISTER, BLACK, BILLY
	BUCKNER, CHATAWAY, COE, CRAM
	ELLIOT, FOSTER, HILL
	IBBOTSON, LOWE, MCKEAN
	MOORCROFT, OVETT, PIRIE
	REDMOND, SOLLY, WOODERSON
(f)	COOK, EDWARDS, HUNTER
	LYNCH, MCCOLGAN, MURRAY
	PACKER, WADE
—Canadian (m)	CUNNINGHAM
(f)	WILLIAMS
—Cuban (f)	QUIROT
—Czech (m)	ZATOPEK
(f)	KRATOCHVILOVA
—Dutch (f)	BLANKERS-KOEN
—Ethiopian	WOLDE, YIFTER
—Finnish	LARVA, NURMI, RITOLA
	VIREN, VIRTANEN
—French	MIMOUN
—German (m)	HOFFMEISTER
(f)	KOCH, ZINN
—Irish	DELANEY
—Italian (m)	MEI
(f)	CACCHI, DORIO
—Kenyan	BIWOTT, BOIT, ERENG, KEINO
	KIBET, KIBOR, KIROCHI
	KIPRIGUT, KONCHELLAH
	NGUGU, ONDIEKI, RONO, SIGEI

—Luxemburg	BARTHEL
—Moroccan	AOUITA
—New Zealand (m)	HALBERG, LOVELOCK
	QUAY, SNELL, WALKER
(f)	AUDAIN
—Nigerian	EGBUNIKE
—Norwegian (f)	KRISTIANSEN
—Romanian (f)	IVAN, MELINTE, PUICA
—Russian (m)	BOLOTNIKOV, KIROV, KUTS
(f)	AGLETDINOVA, BARGINA
	BOUDARENKO, KAZANKINA
	OLIZARENKO
—Somali	BILE
—South African (f)	BUDD
—Swedish	BACKMAN, WIDE
—Tunisian	GAMMOUDI

pentathletes

—American (m)	LEONARD, MAYO, THORPE
—British (f)	PETERS, RAND
—German (m)	HANDRICK, KAHL
(f)	BECKER, LASER
	ROSENTHAL, SIEGL
—Hungarian (m)	BALCZO, NAGY, NEMETH
(f)	KOVACS
—Russian (m)	LEDNEV, ONISHENKO
	STAROSTIN
(f)	PRESS, TKACHENKO
—Swedish (m)	DYRSSEN, HALL, LINDMAN

pole-vaulters

—American	HANSON, HOYT, RICHARDS
—Australian	ARKELL
—British	ASHURST
—French	QUINON
—German	NORDWIG
—Polish	KOSAKIEWICZ, SLUSARSKI
—Russian	BUBKA, GATAULLIN
	VOLKOV

shot-putters

—American	MATSON, O'BRIEN
	ROSE, WOODS
—Australian	MARTIN
—British	CAPES, COLE
—Bulgarian	CHRISTOVA
—French (f)	OSTERMEYER
—German (f)	BEYER, GUMMEL, KRIEGER
	LOSCH, SLUPIANEK, WERNER
—Italian	ANDRES
—Russian (m)	KISELYOV
(f)	PRESS, ZYBINA

sprinters

—American (m)	DILLARD, EVANS, HAHN
	HAYES, HINES, LEWIS
	MORROW, OWENS, SMITH
	TEWKSBURY, TOLAN
(f)	ASHFORD, CUTHBERT
	GRIFFITHS-JOYNER

	RUDOLF, SOWELL, TYUS	—hut	GOONDIE, GUNYA(H), HUMPY
	WALSH		MIAM(IA), MIMI, WURL(E)Y
—Australian (m)	FLINTHOFF	—woman	GIN, LUBRA
(f)	BOYLE, CUTHBERT	absurd story	FURPHY
	JACKSON, STRICKLAND	acacia	GIDGEE, GIDJEE
—Brazilian	DA SILVA		MULGA, MYALL
—British (m)	ABRAHAMS, BLACK		RASPBERRY-JAM TREE
	CHRISTIE, LIDDELL, MAFE		SALLEE, SALLY, WATTLE
	RADFORD, REGIS, WELLS	afternoon	ARVO
(f)	COOK, DOUGLAS	agricultural worker	STATION-HAND
	OAKES, PACKER, SIMPSON	air force	RAAF
—Bulgarian	PETROV	airline	QUANTAS
—Canadian (m)	ANDERSON, DWYER	alcoholic drink	GROG
	JOHNSON, MAHORN, WILLIAMS	amulet	CHURINGA
(f)	ISSAJENKO	angry	CROOK
—Dutch (f)	BLANKERS-KOEN	animal	KANGAROO, KOALA
—French (f)	BRESSON		(O)POSSUM, PLATYPUS
—German (m)	SCHMIDT		WALLABY, WOMBAT
(f)	DRESCHLER, ECKERT	—that has run wild	SCRUBBER
	GOEHR, KOCH, RICHTER	ant-eater	ECHIDNA, NUMBAT
	STECHER, WOCKEL, ZEHRT	apple	COLANE
—Italian	BERUTTI, ENNEA	aquatic rodents	HYDROMYS
—Jamaican (m)	MCKENLEY, MILLER	arboreal marsupial	KOALA, PHALANGER
	QUARRIE, STEWART, WINT	area outside towns	OUTSIDE COUNTRY
(f)	JACKSON, OTTEY	arm	WARDEN'S FARM
—Russian (m)	BORZOV, KRYLOV, MARKIN	assembly	ROLL-UP
(f)	KONDRATYEVA	Australian	AUSSIE, DIGGER, OZZIE
steeplechasers		—soldier	ANZAC, DIGGER
—American	ASHENFELTER, LIGHTBODY	back-country	OUTBACK
	MARSH	bad	ONCUS, ONKUS
—British	BRASHER, DALY, DISLEY	bag	DILLY
	HODGE	bandit	BUSHRANGER
—Canadian	FELL, ORTON	barbecue	BARBIE
—Finnish	NURMI	be itinerant	HUMP THE BLUEY
—German	METZER	bear	KOALA
—Kenyan	BIWOTT, JIPCHO	become involved in	BUY INTO
	KEINO, KORIR	beefwood	FOREST-OAK
—Polish	MALINOWSKI	beer	AMBER, FROSTY, GROG
—Russian	MALINOWSKI, SOKOLOV	—can	TUBE
—Swedish	GARDERUD, SJOSTRAND	—glass	MIDDY
—Tanzanian	BAYI	best thing or person	RINGER
triple jumpers		bird	ANT-THRUSH, BELL-BIRD
—American	EWRY, JOYNER, PRINSTEIN		BITTERN, BLACK SWAN
—Brazilian	DA SILVA		BLOOD-BIRD, BOWER-BIRD
—British	HERBERT		BROLGA, BUDGERIGAR
—Bulgarian	MARKOV		CASSOWARY, CAT-BIRD
—Japanese	ODA		COACHWHIP-BIRD, COOEE
—Polish	SZMIDT		COOEY, COUCAL, CURRAWONG
—Russian	SANEEV, UNDMAE		DRONGO, EM(E)U, EMU-WREN
atmosphere	(*see* **meteorology**)		FANTAIL, FROGMOUTH
Australia	AUS, DOWN UNDER, OZ		GALAH, HONEY-EATER
including aborigine words:			KOEL, KOOKABURRA
aborigine	ABO, BINGHI		LARK-HEELED CUCKOO
	BLACKFELLOW, MYALL		LEIPOA, LORIKEET, LORY
—dance	CORROBOREE		LYRE-BIRD, MOPEHAWK
—drum	UBAR		MOPOKE, MOREPORK

	MOUND-BIRD, QUARRIAN
	REGENT-BIRD, RHIPIDURA
	RIFLE(MAN)-BIRD
	SATIN-BIRD, SCRUB-BIRD
	SWALLOW-SHRIKE, THICKHEAD
	WATTLE-BIRD, WOOD-SWALLOW
	ZEBRA-PAR(R)AKEET
blanket bundle	BLUEY
blind mole	NOTOCYTES
boast	SKITE
boaster	GALAH
boiling-pan	BILLY(-CAN), BILLIE
boomerang	KARLI, KILIE, KYLEY
	KYLIE, TURRAMA
bottom drawer	GLORY BOX
boulder	GIBBER
bower-bird	REGENT-BIRD, SATIN-BIRD
bread	DAMPER
break for a smoke	SMOKE-HO, SMOKO
breakdown-lorry driver	TOWIE
brook	CREEK
buddy	COBBER
bullroarer	CHURINGA
	THUNDERSTICK
	TU(R)NDUN
bundle	BLUEY, DRUM, SWAG
burrowing marsupial	NOTOCYTES, WOMBAT
bush	
—country	MALLEE
—tramp	DRUMMER
—turkey	VULTURN
bushman's swag	MATILDA
cadge	HUM
can of beer	TUBE
capital	CANBERRA
—Territory	ACT
carpet shark	WOBBEGONG
carry on back	HUMP
cattleman	STOCKMAN
cheap covered seats	BLEACHERS
chestnut tree	CASTANOSPERMUM
chicken	CHOOK
child	ANKLE-BITER
children's cricket	KANGA CRICKET
chocolate-covered cake	LAMINGTON
clergyman	JOSSER
club	DOWAK, NULLA(-NULLA)
	WADDIE, WADDY
cockatoo	CORELLA, GALAH
coin	DOLLAR
—5cents	ZACK
—sixpence	ZACK
coin-tossing game	TWO-UP
cold beer	FROSTY
collie	KELPIE, KELPY
conversation	YABBER

cool-box for food, etc	COOLGARDIE SAFE
	ESKY
coucal	SWAMP PHEASANT
countryside	BACK BLOCKS, OUTBACK
courgette	ZUCCHINI
cowboy	WADDIE, WADDY
crane (bird)	BROLGA
crayfish	YABBY
creditor	ORNITHORHYNCUS
crowd	MOB
currant bread	BROWNIE
cut-off river loop	BILLABONG
cyclone	WILLY-WILLY
dairy farmer	COW-COCKY
dance festival	CORROBOREE
decrepit	WARBY
defeat	TOSS
delinquent youth	BODGIE
desert-pea	GLORY-PEA
detective	DEMON
dewpond	GHILGAI
diarrhoea	WOG GUT
difficult situation	(FAIR) COW
dingo	WARRAGAL, WARRIGAL
dip sheep's	
hindquarters	CRUTCH
dislike	DERRY
disordered	ONCUS, ONKUS
disreputable person	QUANDONG
dog	KELPIE, KELPY
dream time	ALCHERINGA
drive herds across country	OVERLAND
driver of team	PUNCHER
drunk	ON THE SHICKER
dwarf eucalyptus	MALLEE
ear	SHELL-LIKE
edible	
—drupe	NATIVE PEACH
—fern	NARDOO
—grubs	WITCHETTY
effeminate man	PUNCE
egg-laying	
mammal	DUCKBILL(ED PLATYPUS)
	DUCK-MOLE, ECHIDNA
enclosed field	PADDOCK
Englishman	POM
eucalyptus	COOLABAH, GUM, IRON-BARK
	MALLEE, SALLEE, SALLY
	TEWART, TOOART, TUART
excel	RING
expert (shearer)	RINGER
false report	FURPHY
fern	NARDOO
festive gathering	CORROBOREE
fibre	
—bag	DILLY BAG

—plant	HEMP-BUSH
fish	BARRAMUNDA, BARRAMUNDI
	CARANX, GROPER, JEW-FISH
	MORWONG, PAGROSOMUS, PEGASUS
	PIG-FISH, ROCK-COD, S(CH)NAPPER
	TREVALLY
—like sea-horse	PEGASUS
flashily dressed	LAIRED UP
—man	LAIR
fliers	RAAF
flock	MOB
fly-catcher	WAGTAIL
fodder grass	KANGAROO-GRASS
food	TUCKER
fool(ish)	DILL, DRONGO, GALAH, NONG
football	RULES
forest	BRUSH
forlorn hope	BUCKLEYS
free immigrant	SQUARE-HEAD
friar-bird	LEATHER-HEAD
friend	COBBER
frogmouth	MOPEHAWK, MOPOKE
	MOREPORK
fruit	NONDA, QUANDONG
gang of convicts	PUSH
genuine	DINKUM, DINKY-DI
germ	WOG
ginger-haired (person)	BLUEY
girl	SHELAH, SHEILA
glass of beer	MIDDY
glory-pea	(STURT'S) DESERT PEA
golden age	ALCHERINGA, DREAMTIME
good	BONZER, BUDGEREE
grass	BARCOO, SPINIFEX
—bag	DILLY BAG
—tree	BLACKBOY
Great Britain	OLD DART
gum tree	EUCALYPTUS, KARRI
	STRINGY-BARK, WANDOO
	YARRAH
half-beak	GARFISH
hard work	YACKER, YAKKA, YAKKER
head-frame for cows	BAIL, BAYLE
heath-like plant	EPACRIS
hen	AUSTRALORP
herd	MOB
herdsman	STOCKMAN
hibiscus	COTTON-TREE
hold-up	BAIL UP
honest	DINKUM, DINKY-DI
honey	
—eater	BLUE-EYE, FRIAR-BIRD
	WATTLE-BIRD
—mouse	TARSIPES
—possum	TAIT
hooligan	LAR(R)IKIN

hornless	POLEY
horse	WALER
—jump from all four legs	PIG-JUMP
hot places	BOOLIGAL, HAY-HELL
house on farm	HEAD-STATION
hut	(*see* aborigine *above*)
ice-lolly	ICEBLOCK
ill	CRONK, CROOK
illicit	SLY
immigrant from Britain	POM(MY)
impostor	BUNYIP
in funds	RIBBED UP
influenza	DOG'S DISEASE
informer	FIZ(Z)GIG
initiation rite	BORA
insect	LAAP, PERP, WITCHETTY
insignificant twerp	DRONGO
instrument	DIDGERIDOO
	WOBBLE BOARD
insulated box	COOLGARDIE SAFE, ESKY
interfering person	BOT
interior of station	BACK-BLOCKS
itinerant worker	SWAGMAN
jabber	YABBER
jackpot win	MOTSER, MOTZA
journey	WALKABOUT
jumping chicken	AUSTRALORP
kangaroo	BOOMER, ROO
—big	FORESTER
killjoy	WOWSER
kingfisher	KOOKABURRA
kitchen-midden	MIRRYONG
ladybird	VEDALIA
lager	AMBER, FROSTY
landowners	SQUATTOCRACY
language	STRINE
large	
—amount of money	MOTSER, MOTZA
—kangaroo	EURO, WALLAROO
—landowner	PASTORALIST, SQUATTER
laughing jackass	GOBURRA, KOOKABURRA
lavatory	DUNNY
learner	COLONIAL EXPERIENCE MAN
	JACKAROO, JACKEROO
leaves used for tea	MANUKA
liquor	NECK OIL
live monotonous life	VEG OUT
lizard	BLUE TONGUE, GO(H)ANNA
	MOLOCH, MONITOR
	PERENTIE, THORN-DEVIL
loafer	SUNDOWNER
look	CAPTAIN COOK
loop in river	ANABRANCH
lose one's temper	PERFORM
lottery agency	TATTERSALLS
lout	LAIR

lung-fish	BARRAMUNDA, BURNET SALMON, CERATODUS
lyre-bird	PHEASANT
mad	DILL, DRONGO, GALAH, NONG
magpie	PIPING CROW
marine animal	CUNJEVOI
marsupial	BANDICOOT, CUSCUS, DASYURE DENDROGALUS, EURO, KANGAROO KOALA, NUMBAT, PHALANGER QUOKKA, TAIT, TASMANIAN DEVIL TREE-KANGAROO, WALLABY WALLAROO, WOMBAT
marvellous	BEAUT
mate	COBBER
mean	HUNGRY
meeting	ROLL UP
midget kangaroo	QUOKKA
miner	HATTER
mining gleaner	FOSSICKER
mix	BOX
mixed collection	MOB
monkey-puzzle tree	BUNYA(-BUNYA)
monotreme	(DUCKBILLED-)PLATYPUS
monster	BUNYIP
most excellent thing or person	RINGER
moth	BOGONG, BUGONG
mound-bird	BRUSH TURKEY, LEIPOA MALLEE-BIRD, MALLEE-FOWL MALLEE-HEN, SCRUB-TURKEY
mountain	RANGE
mountainous	RANGY
mounted	
—herdsman	STOCK-RIDER
—policeman	TROOPER
native	
—dance/song	CORROBOREE
—dog	DINGO
—hut	GOONDIE, GUNYAH, HUMPY
Navy	RAN
nest	WURLEY
newcomer on sheep station	JACKAROO JACKEROO, JILLAROO
newly-arrived	YOUNG
New South Wales person	CORNSTALK
New Zealand(er)	ENZED(DER)
nitwit	DRONGO
no	
—chance at all	BUCKLEY'S (CHANCE)
—good	CROOK
north Queensland	NEVER-NEVER-LAND
nut	QUANDONG-NUT QUEENSLAND-NUT
objectionable person or thing	COW
odd-job man	KNOCKABOUT

old man on a station	ROUSEABOUT ROUSTABOUT
on the move	WALKABOUT
out of season	MURKEN
owl	BOOBOOK
owner of livestock	STOCKHOLDER
pack-animal	PACKER
parakeet	ROSELLA
parliamentary obstruction	STONEWALL
parrot	COCKATOO, COCKATEEL COCKATIEL, CORELLA LORIKEET, LORY
pest	BOT
petrel	TITI
phalanger	OPOSSUM, TAGUAN, TAIT TARSIPES, VULPINE OPOSSUM
pick-up truck	UTE
pigeon	BRONZE-WING WONGA(-WONGA)
pioneer	SAND-GROPER
plan	DART
plant	BANKSIA, BINDI-EYE BOTTLEBRUSH, CONJUVOI GRASS-TREE, HOYA, KANGAROO PAW LAPORTEA, LOGANIA, NETTLE-TREE PINK HEATH, SPIDER FLOWER SPIGELIA, STURT DESERT PEA WARATAN, WATTLE WAX-FLOWER
political union	ANZUS
pond	BILLABONG
poor quality	CRONK
porcupine-grass	SPINIFEX
posse	MUSTER-PARTY
potoroo	RAT-KANGAROO
prejudice	DERRY
prospect	FOSSICK
prude	WOWSER
Queensland hemp	SIDA
quickest sheep-shearer	RINGER
racket	RORT
rail serving as gate	SLIP-RAIL
rat-kangaroo	POTOROO
ray	STINGAREE
real	DINKUM, DINKY-DI
recent immigrant	NEW CHUM
regent-bird	BOWER-BIRD
relative	DISTANT COUSIN
reprove	ROUSE ON
right	APPLES
river	
—effluent	BILLABONG
—flowing full	BANKER
robber of diggings by night	NIGHT-FOSSICKER
rock hole in desert	GNAMMA HOLE

rodent	WATER-MOUSE
rough	LARRIKIN
round-up	MUSTER
Rugby player	WALLABY
rules	FOOTBALL
running bird	EM(E)U
rural area	OUTBACK
rush bag	DILLI, DILLY(-BAG)
savage	WARRAGAL, WARRIGAL
scheme	DART
scrounge	HUM
sea-berry	HALORAGIS
—bream	TARWHINE
—horse	SEA-DRAGON
search for profit	FOSSICK
shark	MAKO
shearwater	MUTTON-BIRD
shed	HUMPY
sheep	JUMBU(C)K, MONKEY
—dog	KELPIE
--shearer (quickest)	RINGER
shelter in the bush	GUNYAH
shield	HIELAMAN
shoulder	HUMP
shrub	BANKSIA, CLIANTUS
	LIGNUM(-SCRUB), PITURI
	PROTEA, SALT-BUSH
	TEA-TREE, TELOPEA, WARATAH
sick	CROOK
single-storey house	COTTAGE
site for town	TOWNSHIP
slice of chocolate cake	LAMINGTON
small	
—bottle	STUBBY
—farmer	COCKY
—kangaroo	WALLABY
—marsupial	HONEY-MOUSE
	POUCHED-MOUSE
—parrot	LORIKEET
—river	CREEK
—settlement	TOWNSHIP
soldier	ANZAC, DIGGER
—of both World Wars	RETREAD
something extremely good	PURLER
spear-thrower	WOOMERA
speech	STRINE, YABBER
spider	KATIPO, NIGHT STINGER
	TARANTULA
spinifex	PORCUPINE-GRASS
spit	WOG
spiv	RORTER
spoilsport	WOWSER
spore-case used as food	NARDOO
square	DINKUM, DINKY-DI
squatter	JACKEROO
stampede	BREAKAWAY

stampeding animal	BREAKAWAY
state/territory	AUSTRALIAN CAPITAL
	TERRITORY
	NEW SOUTH WALES
	NORTHERN TERRITORY
	QUEENSLAND
	SOUTH AUSTRALIA
	TASMANIA, VICTORIA
	WESTERN AUSTRALIA
—governor's deputy	LIEUTENANT-GENERAL
stick used in two-up	KIP
stingy	HUNGRY
stock	
—farm	STATION
—man	RINGER, STATION-HAND
stone polished by wind	GIBBER
stop suddenly (horse)	PROP
straight-haired	CURLY
strike with club or stick	WADDIE, WADDY
strong	
—drink	SHICKER
—tobacco	NAIL-ROD
stupid	DILL, DRONGO
	GALAH, NONG
submerged reef	BOMBORA
supplementary spouse	PIRRAURU
surfer	LEMONHEAD
surrender	BAIL UP
swag	MATILDA
sweepstake agency	TATTERSALLS
swimming costume	COSSIE
take up Crown land	FREE-SELECT
talk	YABBER
tall thin person	CORNSTALK
Tasmanian devil/wolf	DASYURE
tea	
—break	TEA-HO
—pot	BILLY(-CAN), BILLIE
—tree	TI
tease	CHYAK
tektite	AUSTRALITE
tend	TAIL
termite-eater	NUMBAT
thicket	DEAD-FINISH
	MALLEE-SCRUB
throwing-stick	BOOMERANG
	WO(O)MERA, WOOMERANG
thunderstick	(see bullroarer above)
till	PETER
timber-cart	JINKER
time of creation	ALCHERINGA, DREAMTIME
tramp	SWAGGER, SWAGMAN
tramp's bundle	BLUEY, SHIRALEE
	SWAG, SWAGGIE
travelling through	
the bush	ON THE WALLABY (TRACK)

tree	BEEF-WOOD, BELAH, BELAR, BILLA
	BOTTLE-TREE, CASUARINA
	CREAM-OF-TARTAR TREE, EUCALYPTUS
	FLINDERSIA, GEEBUNG, GIDYA
	HORSE-RADISH TREE, JARRAH
	KARRI, KURRAJONG, MANUKA
	MORETON BAY CHESTNUT, MULGA
	PENDA, PROTEA, QUANDONG
	QUEENSLAND-NUT, SHE-OAK
	SOUR-GOURD, SPEAR-WOOD
	SWAMP-OAK, TEWART
	TUART, TOOART, WADDYWOOD
	WHITE TEAK, WOODEN PEAR
—snake	DENDROPHIS
true	DINKUM, DINKY-DI
trunk for trousseau	GLORY BOX
try to deceive	COME THE RAW PRAWN
tulip	WARATAH
turkey	VULTURN
U-turn	UEY
unbranded animal	CLEAR-SKIN
uncultured man	OCKER
undermine another's	
claim	FOSSICK
unmanageable	ROP(E)ABLE
useless person	GALAH
vagrant	SWAGGER, SWAGMAN
very	
—angry	ROP(E)ABLE
—good	APPLES, BEAUT, BONZER
	BOSHTA, BOSHTER
	BOSKER, BUDGEREE
virus	WOG
vomit	CHUNDER, HURL
	LIQUID, LAUGH,
	TECHNICOLOUR YAWN
walk with swag	
on back	HUMP
	WALK MATILDA
	WALTZ MATILDA
walking-stick	WADDIE, WADDY
wallaby	BRUSH-KANGAROO
	PAD(D)YMELON, PADEMELON
wandering	WALKABOUT
war-club	WADDIE, WADDY
water-cart	FURPHY
waterproof coat	DRIZA BONE
wattle tree	BOREE, WAIT-A-WHILE

weapon	LILLIL, NULLANULLA
welsher	SHICER
West Australian	SAND-GROPER
white man	GUB(B)AH
—with aboriginal	
wife	COMBO
wild	ROP(E)ABLE
	WARRAGAL, WARRIGAL
—aboriginal	MYALL
—cat	DASYURE
—dog	DINGO, WARRAGAL
	WARRIGAL
—horse	BRUMBY, WARRAGAL
	WARRIGAL
—young bull	MICK(E)(Y)
win shearing competition	RING THE SHED
witch doctor	BOYLA
wool	BOTANY
work	
—alone	HAT
—over waste ore	FOSSICK
worn out	WARBY
wrasse	PIG-FISH
young	
—animal	JOEY
—kangaroo	JOEY
—pig	SLIP
zoological region	NOTOGAEA
Austria	A
capital	VIENNA, WIEN
coin	
—100 groschen	SCH, SCHILLING
—20 kreutzers	ZWANZIGER
—100 kreutzers	FLORIN
—100 heller	KRONE
—money of account	GULDEN
dance	WALTZ
dynasty	HABSBURG, HAPSBURG
flower	EDELWEISS
measure	FASS, MUTH
noble	HERTZOG
provinces	BURGENLAND,
	NIEDER OSTERREICH, KARNTEN
	OBER OSTERREICH, OST TIROL
	SALZBURG, STEIERMARK
	TIROL(TYROL), VORARLBERG
soldier	PANDOOR, PAND(O)UR
weight	UNZE

B

bachelor	B, BA, BACH
of	
—Arts	AB, BA
—Civil Law	BCL
—Commerce	BCOM(M)
—Dental Surgery	BDS
—Divinity	BD
—Education	BED, EDB
—Engineering	BAI, BE, BENG
—Law	BL, LLB
—Letters	BL
—Literature	BLITT
—Medicine	BM, MB
—Music	BMUSc
—Philosophy	PHB
—Science	BS, BSC, SCB
—Surgery	BCH, BS, CHB
bacteriology	(*see* **biology**)
Bahamas	
capital	NASSAU
coin	DOLLAR
Bahrain	BRN
capital	MANANA
coin	DOLLAR, FILS
Balearic Islands	E
ballet	
ballets	COPPELIA, DAPHNIS AND CHLOE
	FIREBIRD, GISELLE, LA BAYADERE
	LA FILLE MAL GARDEE, LA SYLPHIDE
	NUTCRACKER, ONDINE, PETRUSHKA
	ROMEO AND JULIET, LES SYLPHIDES
	SLEEPING BEAUTY, SWAN LAKE
characters	
—Coppelia	COPPELIUS, FRANZ
	SWANHILDA
—Giselle	ALBRECHT, BATHILDE
	GISELLE, HILARION
	LOYS, MYRTHA
—La Bayadère	GAMZATTI
	HIGH BRAHMIN
	NIKIYA, RAJAH, SOLOR
—La Fille mal Gardée	ALAIN, COLAS
	LISE, SIMONE, TOMAS
—La Sylphide	EFFIE, GURN, JAMES
	MADGE
—Nutcracker	CLARA
—Ondine	BERTA, ONDINE
	PALEMON, TIRRENIO

—Romeo and Juliet	FRAY LAWRENCE
	JULIET, ROMEO
—Sleeping Beauty	AURORA, CARABOSSE
	LILAC
—Swan Lake	ODETTE, ODILE
	SIEGFRIED
	VON ROTHBART
choreographers	ASHTON, BALANCHINE
	BEJART, CUNNINGHAM
	DE VALOIS, DIAGHILEV
	DOLIN, HELPMANN
	MACMILLAN
company	AMERICAN BALLET THEATRE
	BALLET JOOSS, BALLETS RUSSES
	BOLSHOI, BOROVANKSY, KIROV
	PARIS OPERA BALLET, RAMBERT
	ROYAL BALLET, SADLER'S WELLS
dancers	
—background dancer	FIGURANT(E)
—female	BARBIERI, BERIOSOVA
	DANILOVA, FONTEYN
	GUILLEM, JONES, KATRAK
	MAKAROVA, MARKOVA
	PAVLOVA, PENNEY
	SEYMOUR, SPIRA-CAPAB
	TUCKER, ULANOVA
	VAN PRAAGH
—in group	CORYPHEE
—male	ASHTON, BEJART, BLAIR
	DOLIN, DOWELL, HELPMANN
	LIEPA, MUKHAMEDOV
	NIJINKSY, NUREYEV, PRICE
	SCHAUFFUSS, RUZIMATOV
	WELCH
—supporting group	CORPS DE BALLET
direction of body	
—away from audience	(EN) ECARTE
	EN EFFACE
—bent	EN FONDU
—facing front	EN FACE
—leaning	PENCHEE
—legs crossed	EN CROISE
—turning	
inwards	EN DEDANS
outwards	EN DEHORS
movements	
—at slower tempo	SOUTENU
—basic	
jump	JETE, SAUT
step	PAS
—close to floor	A TERRE
—exercises	BATTEMENT, CAMBRE
	COUP DE PIED, DEMI PLIE
	DEVELOPPE, GRAND BATTEMENT
	GRAND PLIE, PENCHE, RELEVE
	RETIRE, ROND DE JAMBE

—leaps	ASSEMBLE, BALLON, BATTERIE
	BATTU, CABRIOLE, CAPRIOLE
	CHANGEMENT, ECHAPPE
	ENTRECHAT, GRAND JETE (EN AVANT)
	JETE (FOUTTE), (PAS) CISEAUX
	(PAS DE)BRAISE, REVOLTADE
	RIVOLTADE, SAUT, SOUBRESANT,
	TEMPS DE POISSON, TEMPS LEVE
	TOURS EN L'AIR
—move	
holding partner above	
head on one straight arm	STULCHAK
on floor	SPLITS
—positions	ARABESQUE, ATTITUDE
	BRAS BAS, CROISE, DEMI-BRAS
	DEMI-SECONDE, ECARTE
	EPAULEMENT, EFFACE, EN FACE
	PORT DE BRAS
—quickstep	PAS DE DOUBLE
—steps	ASSEMBLEE, GALOP, GLISSADE
	JETE, PAS BALIONE, PAS BRISE
	(PAS) CHASSE, PAS DE BOURREE
	PAS DE CHAT, PAS DE CHEVAL
	PAS DE CISEAUX, SISSONNES
—swaying	BALANCE DE COTE
—turns	FOUETTE, PIROUETTE
terms	
—ability to leap high	ELEVATION
—ankle	COU-DE-PIED
—bar	BARRE
—beaten	FRAPPE
—bow	REVERENCE
—classic costume	TUTU
—coach	REPETITEUR
—curtsey	REVERENCE
—dance for two	PAS DE DEUX
—director	REGISSEUR
—exercise rail	BARRE
—gliding	GLISSE
—interlude	DIVERTIMENTO
	DIVERTISSEMENT
—on toe	(SUR LES) POINTES
—practice dress	LEOTARD
—producer	REGISSEUR
—running steps together	ASSEMBLE
	ENCHAINEMENT
—scissors	CISEAUX
—senior dancer	CORYPHEE
—sliding	GLISSE
—solo dance	PAS DE SEUL
for male	VARIATION
—staccato	PIQUE
—stand on	
ball of foot	DEMI-POINTE
toe	POINTE
—step	PAS, POSE

—teaching of slow movements	ADAGE
Bangladesh	BD
capital	DACCA, DHAKA
coin	PAISA, TAKA
Barbados	BDS
Barbados pride	(RED)SANDALWOOD
capital	BRIDGETOWN
coin	CENT, DOLLAR
Barbary	MAGHREB
ape	MAGOT
privateer	CORSAIR
ship	SANDAL, SETTEE, XEBEC(K)
baseball	
abandoned game	CALLED GAME
aiming mark	PLATE
all bases full	BASES LOADED
ambidextrous batter	SWITCH-HITTER
area	
—between foul lines	FAIR TERRITORY
—inside four bases	INFIELD
—outside	
foul lines	FOUL TERRITORY
four bases	OUTFIELD
—over plate between knee	
and armpit	STRIKE ZONE
attempt to hit the ball	STRIKE
ball	
—hit into	
fair territory	FAIR BALL
foul territory	FOUL BALL
—skied from bat	FLY BALL
—thrower	PITCHER
bat	CLUB
batting	
—area	BATTER'S BOX
—position	PLATE
conceded out	SACRIFICE
corner of diamond	BASE
credit to fielder	ASSIST
deliberate pitching of	
four balls	INTENTIONAL WALK
dismiss	
—three men at once	TRIPLE PLAY
—two men at once	DOUBLE PLAY
dismissal	
—after three strikes	STRIKE OUT
—when two men occupy	
one base	FORCE PLAY
extra batter	DESIGNATED HITTER, DH
glove	MITT
hit	
—bringing four runs	GRAND SLAM
—over boundary fence	HOME RUN, HOMER
—resulting in run	BASE HIT, DOUBLE
	SINGLE, TATER, TRIPLE
leagues	AMERICAN, NATIONAL

number of balls or strikes	COUNT
old name	CHERMANY
pitch (ball)	CURVEBALL, FASTBALL
	FORKBALL, KNUCKLEBALL
	SCREWBALL, SCUFFBALL
	SLIDER, SPITBALL
—illegal	BALK
—in strike zone, not hit	STRIKE
—not stopped by catcher	PASSED BALL
—outside strike zone	BALL
—wide	WILD PITCH
players	
—batters	AARON, BANKS, BOONE
	CANESCO, COBB, DI MAGGIO
	DYKSTRA, GEHRIG, HORNSBY
	JACKSON, MANTLE, MATTHEWSON
	MAYS, PAIGE, REECE, ROBINSON
	ROSE, RUTH, RYAN, VALENZUELA
	WAGNER, YOUNT
—catchers	CARTER, FISK
—pitchers	BOUGH, CARLTON, CLEMENS
	FIDRYCH, GEDMAN, GOODEN
	MORRIS, NIERRO
	RYAN, SCOTT, YOUNG
playing	
—area	DIAMOND
—positions	CATCHER, CENTRE FIELD
	FIRST BASE, LEFT FIELD
	PITCHER, RIGHT FIELD
	SECOND BASE, SHORT STOP
	THIRD BASE
public seating	BLEACHERS
push ball with bat	BUNT
substitute batter	PINCH HITTER
team	NINE
teams	
—Atlanta	BRAVES
—Baltimore	ORIOLES
—Boston	RED SOX
—California	ANGELS
—Chicago	CUBS, WHITE SOX
—Cincinnati	REDS
—Cleveland	INDIANS
—Detroit	TIGERS
—Houston	ASTROS
—Kansas City	ROYALS
—Los Angeles	DODGERS
—Milwaukie	BREWERS
—Minnesota	TWINS
—Montreal	EXPOS
—New York	METS, YANKEES
—Oakland	ATHLETES
—Philadelphia	PHILLIES
—Pittsburgh	PIRATES
—St Louis	CARDINALS
—San Diego	PADRES

—San Francisco	GIANTS
—Seattle	MARINERS
—Texas	RANGERS
—Toronto	BLUE JAYS
touch player with ball	TAG
two games at one session	DOUBLE HEADER
umpire	HONCHO
—for	
major games	SIX
other games	FOUR
warm-up area	BULLPEN

Basque

dish	PIPERADE
game	PELOTA
language	EUSKARA
region	PYRENEES

bats HORSESHOE, NOCTULE
PIPISTRELLE, SEROTINE, VAMPIRE

battles

Abyssinia/Italy	ADOWA
Afghanistan/Britain	MAIWAND
America/Germany - WW1	BELLEAU WOOD
	CANTIGNY
/Japan	GUADALCANAL, IWO JIMA
	LEYTE, LUZON
	OKINAWA, TARAWA
—naval	BISMARCK SEA
	CAPE ESPERANCE, CORAL SEA
	JAVA SEA, LEYTE GULF
	MIDWAY, PEARL HARBOUR
	PHILIPPINE SEA
	SAN BERNARDINO STRAIT
	SANTA CRUZ, SURIGAO STRAIT
	TASSAFARONGA
American	
—civil war	BALL'S BLUFF

BELMONT, BULL RUN, CARRICK'S FORD
CEDAR MOUNTAIN, CHAMPION HILL
CHANCELLORSVILLE
CHICKAMAUGA VALLEY
CHICKASAW BLUFFS, CORINTH
CRAMPTON GAP, ELKHORN TAVERN
FAIROAKS, FOUR OAKS
FREDERICKSBURG, GETTYSBURG
IUKA, MANASSAS (JUNCTION)
MALVERN HILL, MARYE'S HEIGHTS
MILL SPRINGS, MISSIONARY RIDGE
MURPHREESBORO, PEA RIDGE
PETERSBURG, PRAIRIE GROVE
RICH MOUNTAIN, RICHMOND
SEVEN PINES, SHARPSBURG, SHILOH
SOUTH MOUNTAIN, STONE RIVER
THE ANTIETAM, TURNER'S GAP
VICKSBURG, WILLIAMSBURG
WILSON'S CREEK
WOGAN'S CROSS ROADS

—Indian war	LITTLE BIGHORN		HELIGOLAND BIGHT
	WOUNDED KNEE		JUTLAND
—Revolution	BEMIS'S HEIGHT	/Germany - WW2	ANZIO, ARDENNES
	BRANDYWINE, BUNKERS HILL		ARNHEM, CASSINO, EL ALAMEIN
	CHARLESTON, CHATTERTON HILL		FALAISE GAP, GAZALA, KASSERINE
	CONCORD, EUTAW SPRINGS		MEDENINE, MORTAIN, ST LO
	FREEMAN'S FARM, GERMANTOWN		SANGRO, SIDI REZEGH
	GREEN SPRING, GREENSBORO		THE BULGE, TOBRUK
	HANGING ROCK, HARLEM HEIGHTS	—air	BRITAIN
	KING'S MOUNTAIN, LEXINGTON	—naval	ATLANTIC
	LONG ISLAND, MONMOUTH, NEWTOWN		RIVER PLATE
	NINETY-SIX, ROCKY MOUNT	/Holland —naval	CAMPERDOWN
	SARATOGA, STILLWATER,	/India	ASSAYE, BUXAR
	TICONDEROGA, TRENTON, VINCENNES		CHILIANWALA, LASWARI
	WHITE PLAINS, YORKTOWN		MIANI, PANIPAT, PLASSEY
—naval	CHESAPEAKE BAY		SOBRAON
Arabs/Byzantium	YARMUK	/Italy - WW2	GAZALA, SIDI REZEGH
/French	POITIERS	—naval	CAPE MATAPAN
/Persians	KADESSIA, NEHAVEND	/Japan - WW2	IMPHAL, KOHIMA
	QADISIYA	/Russia	ALMA, BALACLAVA
/Spanish	NAVAS DA TOLOSA		INKERMAN
Athens/Sparta	ARGINUSAE, AEGOSPOTAMI	/South Africa	MAGERSFONTEIN
Austria/Britain	ALMANZA		MAJUBA HILL, SPION KOP
/Italy	ASIAGO, CAPORETTO, ISONZO		STORMBERG
	PIAVE RIVER, VITTORIO VENETO	/Spain - naval	CAPE PASSARO
/France	AUSTERLITZ		CAPE ST VINCENT
	HOHENLINDEN, MARENGO		ST JUAN DE ULLUA
	PAVIA, ULM, VALMY, WAGRAM	/Sudan	ABU KLEA, OMDURMAN
/Prussia	KOLIN, SADOWA	/Turks	CTESIPHON, GALLIPOLI
/Serbia	JADAR RIVER		GAZA, MEGIDDO, RAFA
	KOLUBRA RIVER		RAMADI, ROMANI, SHARQAT
/Swiss	MORGATEN	—naval	NAVARINO
/Turks	ZENTA		(see also England below)
Bavarians/Magyars	PRESSBURG	/Zulus	ISANDHLWANA
Belgium/Germany	LIEGE		RORKE'S DRIFT, ULUNDI
Britain/Denmark — naval	COPENHAGEN	Britons/Saxons	DYRHAM, MOUNT BADON
/France	ALBUERA, BADAJOZ	Byzantium/Arabs	YARMUK
	BAROSSA, BAYLEN, CORUNNA	/Persia	NINEVEH
	FONTENOY, HASTENBECK	/Turks	MANZIKERT, MELASGRID
	LAUFFELDT, MAIDA, MINDEN	Carthage/Rome	CANNAE, ZAMA
	SALAMANCA, TALAVERA	Christians/Moors	LAS NAVAS DE TOLOSA
	VIMIERA, VITTORIA	Denmark/Spain	LUTTER
	WANDEWASH, WATERLOO	/Sweden	LUND
—naval	ABOUKIR, LAGOS	Egypt/Hittites	QADESH
	LES SAINTES, QUIBERON BAY	/Romans - naval	ACTIUM
	THE NILE, TRAFALGAR, USHANT	/Syria	MEGIDDO
/Germany - WW1	AISNE, ARDENNES	England/Arabs	ACRE
	ARRAS, ARTOIS(-LOOS), CAMBRAI	/France	AGINCOURT, BAUGE
	FESTUBERT, FRONTIERS, LE CATEAU		BEACHY HEAD, BRIHUEGA
	LORRAINE, LOOS, MARNE, MESSINES		CASTILLON, COURTRAI, CRECY
	MONS, NEUVE CHAPELLE		DENAIN, LANDEN, LEIPZIG
	PASSCHENDAELE, SAMBRE, SOMME		MALPLAQUET, NAJERA, NAMUR
	VERDUN, VIMY RIDGE, YPRES		OUDENARDE, POITIERS
—naval	CORONEL		RAMILLIES, SPURS, STEENKIRK
	DOGGER BANK	-naval	LA HOGUE, MALAGA
	FALKLAND ISLANDS		SLUYS

/Ireland	AUGHRIM, BOYNE
	RATHMINES, YELLOW FORD
/Scotland	BANNOCKBURN
	BRANHAM MOOR, CHEVY CHASE
	CULLODEN, FLODDEN, GLENCOE
	HALIDON HILL, HARLAW
	HOMILDON HILL, KILLIECRANKIE
	NECTANSMERE, NEVILLE'S CROSS
	NORTHALLERTON, PINKIE
	PRESTON PANS, SOLWAY MOSS
/Spain - naval	AZORES
English civil war	ADWALTON MOOR
	BARNET, BENBERB, BOTHWELL BRIG
	BRADDOCK DOWN, CROPEDY
	DUNBAR, EDGEHILL, LANGPORT
	LOSECOAT, LOSTWITHIEL
	MARSTON MOOR, NASEBY
	NEWBURY, PRESTON
	SEDGEMOOOR, STRATTON
	WINCEBY, WORCESTER
English/Danes	ASHDOWN, ASHINGDON
	EDINGTON, MALDON
/Normans	HASTINGS
	TENCHEBRAI
/Norse	BRUNANBURH, FULFORD
	STAINMORE, STAMFORD BRIDGE
final battle, good/evil	ARMAGEDDON
	RAGNAROK
France/Austria	MAGENTA, SOLFERINO
/Germany	CHAMPAGNE, MULHOUSE
	SEDAN, VERDUN
/Italy	FORNOVO, RAVENNA
/Netherlands	BOUVINES
/Russia	EYLAU, FRIEDLAND
/Prussia	JENA, METZ, ROSSBACH
	SEDAN
/Spain	ST QUENTIN
/Switzerland	MARIGNANO
Franks/Huns	TROYES
/Visigoths	VOVILLE
Germans, Poles/Mongols	LEIGNITZ
Germans/Magyars	RIVER LECH
Germany/Italy	CAPORETTO
/Russia - WW1	GUMBINNEN, LODZ
	MASURIAN LAKES
	NAROCH LAKE
	STALLPONEN
	TANNENBERG
— WW2	BERLIN, KURSK
	STALINGRAD
/Sweden	LUTZEN
Greeks/Macedonia	CHAERONEA
/Persians	ISSUS, MARATHON
	PLATAEA
—naval	SALAMIS
/Romans	CYNOSCEPHALAE, PYDNA

Hungary/Russia	SEGESVAR
/Turks	NICOPOLIS
Irish/Norse	CLONTARF
Japan/Russia - naval	TSUSHIMA
Macedonia/Persians	ARBELA, GRANICUS
Mexico/Texas	ALAMO
Mongols/Turks	ANKARA
Poles/Teutonic Knights	TANNENBERG
Portugal/Spain	ALJUBAROTTA
Prussia/Sweden	FEHRBELLIN
Rome/Carthage	CANNAE, ZAMA
/Egypt - naval	ACTIUM
/Epirus	HERACLES
/Goths	ADRIANOPLE
/Huns	CATALAUNIAN FIELDS
/Persia	MAGNESIA
/Syria	MAGNESIA
Russia/Sweden	NARVA
/Turkey	ERZINCIAN, SARIKAMISH
	SINOPE
Serbia/Turks	KOSSOVO
Spain/Turks	LEPANTO
Sparta/Thebes	LEUCTRA
Wars of the Roses	BARNET, BLORE HEATH
	BOSWORTH, EDGECOTE
	HEDGELEY MOOR, HEXHAM
	LUDLOW, MORTIMER'S CROSS
	ST ALBANS, TEWKESBURY
	WAKEFIELD
with the gods	THEOMACHY

bearing

meaning: carrying
         producing

acorns	GLANDIFEROUS
all kinds	OMNIFEROUS
aluminium	ALUMINIFEROUS
apples	POMIFEROUS
arms	ARMIGEROUS
balsam	BALSAMIFEROUS
beans	LEGUMINOUS
berries	BACCIFEROUS
blood	SANGUIFEROUS
bones	OSSIFEROUS
bracts	GLUMIFEROUS
breasts	MAMMIFEROUS
bristles	CHAETIFEROUS
	CHAETOPHOROUS, STYLIFEROUS
catkins	AMENTIFEROUS
cells	CELLIFEROUS
claws	CHELIFEROUS
cloud	NUBIFEROUS, NUBIGINOUS
clubs	CLAVIGEROUS
coal	CARBONIFEROUS
copper	CUPRIFEROUS
coral	CORALLIFEROUS, CORALLIGENOUS
cross	CRUCIFEROUS

culm (coal)	CULMIFEROUS	partitions	SEPTIFEROUS
cupules	CUPULIFEROUS	pearl	MARGARITIFEROUS
death	LETHIFEROUS	pears	POMIFEROUS
diamonds	DIAMONDIFEROUS	peas	LEGUMINOUS
	DIAMANTIFEROUS	pests	PESTIFEROUS
disease	MORBIFEROUS	petrol	PETROLIFEROUS
drops	GUTTIFEROUS	platinum	PLATINIFEROUS
eggs	OVIFEROUS, OVIGEROUS	pods	LEGUMINOUS
excess hair	CHAETIFEROUS	pulses	LEGUMINOUS
	CHAETOPHOROUS	pupa case	PUPIGEROUS
fatty matter	SEBIFEROUS	pyrites	PYRITIFEROUS
feathers	PLUMIGEROUS	quartz	QUARTZIFEROUS
flame	FLAMMIFEROUS	salt	SALIFEROUS
flowers	FLORIFEROUS	seed	SEMINIFEROUS
forked appendage	FURCIFEROUS	shade	UMBRIFEROUS
fossils	FOSSILIFEROUS	shaft of column	SCAPIGEROUS
fossil reptiles	REPTILIFEROUS	shells	CONCHIFEROUS
fruit	FERACIOUS, FRUCTIFEROUS	silica	SILICIFEROUS
	FRUGIFEROUS, POMIFEROUS	silver	ARGENTIFEROUS
garnet	GARNETIFEROUS	sleep	SOMNIFIC, SOMNIFEROUS
glands	GLANDIFEROUS		SOPORIFEROUS, SOPORIFIC
glumes	GLUMIFEROUS	small	
god	DEIPAROUS	—cells	CELLULIFEROUS
gold	AURIFEROUS	—glands	GLANDULIFEROUS
good health	SALUTIFEROUS	—globes	GLOBULIFEROUS
granules	GRANULIFEROUS	—holes	FORAMINIFEROUS
grass stems	CULMIFEROUS	—nipples	PAPILLIFEROUS
guano	GUANIFEROUS	—round particles	GLOBULIFEROUS
gum	GUMMIFEROUS	—spines	SPINULIFEROUS
hair	CRINIGEROUS, PILIFEROUS	spines	SPINIFEROUS
honey	MELLIFEROUS		SPINIGEROUS
horn	KERATOGENOUS	spirally shaped parts	STROMBULIFEROUS
horns	CORNIGEROUS	spots	GUTTIFEROUS
hornstone	CORNIFEROUS	stars	STELLIFEROUS
incense	THURIFEROUS	stigmas	STIGMATIFEROUS
iron	FERRIFEROUS	style	STYLIFEROUS
keratin	KERATOGENOUS	suckers	STOLONIFEROUS
keys	CLAVIGEROUS	sweat	SUDORIFEROUS
lead	PLUMBIFEROUS	teeth	DENTIGEROUS
leaves	FRONDIFEROUS	thorns	SPINIFEROUS, SPINIGEROUS
lime	CALCIFEROUS, CALCIGEROUS	tin	STANNIFEROUS
light	LUCIFEROUS, LUMINIFEROUS	titanium	TITANIFEROUS
manganese	MANGANIFEROUS	tubers	TUBERIFEROUS
manna	MANNIFEROUS	urine	URINIFEROUS
metal	METALLIFEROUS	vines	VITIFEROUS
milk	GALACTOPHOROUS	well-being	SALUTIFEROUS
	LACTIFIC, LACTIFEROUS	whip	FLAGELLIFEROUS
monsters	TERATOGENIC		MASTIGOPHOROUS
mucus	MUCIFEROUS	wool	LANIFEROUS
musk	MOSCHIFEROUS	yolk	VITELLIGENOUS
nectar	NECTARIFEROUS	young	
nipple-like projections	PAPILLIFEROUS	—from eggs	OVIPAROUS
nuts	GLANDIFEROUS, NUCIFEROUS	inside body	OVOVIVIPAROUS
oil (as seeds)	OLEIFEROUS	—live	VIVIPAROUS
ovules	OVULIFEROUS	zinc	ZINKIFEROUS
oxide of yttrium	YTTRIFEROUS		(*see also* **having**)

Bechuanaland	(*see* Botswana)
becoming	
adult	ADOLESCENT
apparently cooler	DECALESCENT
atrophied	CONTABESCENT
better frame of mind	RESIPISCENT
big	TURGESCENT
bigger	ACCRESCENT
black	NIGRESCENT
born anew	RENASCENT
branched	DELIQUESCENT
bubbly	EFFERVESCENT
cooler	DEFERVESCENT
dark	NIGRESCENT
dry	ARESCENT
faded	EVANESCENT
flowers	FLORESCENT
glass	VITRESCENT
green	VIRIDESCENT, VIRESCENT
healthy	CONVALESCENT
hidden	DELITESCENT
hot	FERVESCENT
into being	NASCENT
latent	LATESCENT
leafy	FRONDESCENT
less	DECRESCENT
light	LUMINESCENT
liquid	(COL)LIQUESCENT
	DELIQUESCENT
luminous with heat	INCANDESCENT
male	VIRILESCENT
milk	LACTESCENT
milky	OPALESCENT
obsolete	OBSOLESCENT
old	SENESCENT
pale	PALLESCENT
quiet	QUIESCENT
rainbow-coloured	IRIDESCENT
red	ERUBESCENT, RUFESCENT
revived	REVIVESCENT, REVIVISCENT
rotten	PUTRESCENT
sexually mature	PUBESCENT
shrivelled	TABESCENT
sleepy	SOMNOLESCENT
stem-like	CAULESCENT
stone	LAPIDESCENT
swollen	(IN)TUMESCENT, TURGESCENT
together	COALESCENT, CONCRESCENT
tree-like	ARBORESCENT
warm	INCALESCENT
wasted	TABESCENT
white	ALBESCENT, CANESCENT
white-hot	(IN)CANDESCENT
withered	MARCESCENT
yellow	FLAVESCENT, LUTESCENT
youthful	JUVENESCENT

beginning	
meaning: origins (of)	
reproduction (of)	
according to laws of nature	NOMOGENY
all cells contributing to heredity	PANGENESIS
alternation	METAGENESIS
alternative	HETEROGENESIS
asexual	MONOGENESIS, MONOGONY
blood formation	HAEMATOGENESIS
bones	OSTEOGENESIS, OSTEOGENY
by	
—budding	BLASTOGENESIS
—fission	SCHIZOGENESIS
—radioactive disintegration	RADIOGENIC
cancer	CARCINOGENESIS
cartilage	CHONDROGENESIS
cells	CYTOGENESIS
continent-building	EPEIROGENESIS
cross-fertilisation	ALLOGAMY
crystals	CRYSTALLOGENESIS
cyclones	CYCLOGENESIS
determinate variation	ORTHOGENESIS
development of form	MORPHOGENESIS
different genes	ALLOGENESIS
differentiation	HISTOGENESIS
	HISTOGENY
disease	PATHOGENESIS, PATHOGENY
distinctive form	MORPHOGENESIS
doubling of parts	DIPLOGENESIS
eggs	OOGENESIS
evolutionary pedigree	PHYLOGENESIS
	PHYLOGENY
fission	SCHIZOGONY
from	
—like parents	HOMOGENESIS
—living things	BIOGENESIS
—male and female	SYNGENESIS
—non-living matter	ABIOGENESIS
	BIOPOIESIS
—nothing	ABIOGENESIS
	SPONTANEOUS GENERATION
—unfertilised ovum	PARTHENOGENESIS
gametes	GAMETOGENESIS
gods	THEOGONY
gradual production	EPIGENESIS
heat	THERMOGENESIS
human beings	ANTHROPOGENESIS
	ANTHROPOGENY
	ANTHROPOGONY
hypnotic state	HYPNOGENESIS
	HYPNOGENY
imperfect development	AGENESIS
in larval state	PAEDOGENESIS
individual development	ONTOGENESIS
involving all cells	PANGENESIS
like origins	ISOGENY

living	
—beings	ZOOGENY, ZOOGONY
—organisms	ORGANOGENESIS
many origins	POLYGENESIS, POLYGENY
mind	NOOGENESIS
	PSYCHOGENESIS
	PSYCHOGONY
minerals	PARAGENESIS
miraculous origin	THAUMATOGENY
mixed origins	MISCEGENATION
monsters	TERATOGENY
mountains	OROGENESIS
multiple origins	POLYGENESIS, POLYGENY
myths	MYTHOGENESIS
naturally	NOMOGENY
nervous activity	DYNAMOGENESIS
new birth	PALINGENESIS
	PALINGENESIA
	PALINGENESY
of parts	MEROGENESIS
organic evolution	BIOGENESIS
outside the body	ECTOGENESIS
ovum development	OOGENESIS, OOGENY
phantasms	PHANTASMOGENESIS
plants	PHYTOGENESIS, PHYTOGENY
rock from sediments	DIAGENESIS
segmentation	MEROGENESIS
self-fertilisation	AUTOGAMY
sexual reproduction	AMPHIMYXIS
	GAMOGENESIS
similar genes	ISOGENESIS, ISOGENY
	SYNGENESIS
soil	PEDOGENESIS
soul	PSYCHOGONY
species	SPECIATION
sperm	SPERMATOGENESIS
	SPERMATOGENY
spontaneous	ABIOGENESIS
	HETEROGENESIS
spores	SPOROGENESIS, SPOROGENY
systematic evolution	ORTHOGENESIS
teeth	ODONTOGENY
tissues	HISTOGENESIS, HISTOGENY
transmission of vibrations	PERIGENESIS
unlike parents	XENOGENESIS
virgin birth	PARTHENOGENESIS
weather front	FRONTOGENESIS
without fertilisation	APOMYXIS
Belgium	B, BELG
airline	SABENA
capital	BRUSSELS, BRUXELLES
coin	BELGA, CENTIME
	FRANC, MITE
language	FLEMISH, FRENCH
	WALLOON
races	FLEMISH, WALLOON

beliefs	
including: founders	
followers	
heresies	
orders	
religions	
1000 years of Christ's	
rule	CHILIASM, MILLENARIANISM
	MILLENIALISM
acceptance of complete	
divinity of Christ	APOLLINARIANISM
adult baptism	ANABAPTISTS
African Christian	DONATISM
—heretics	ABELITES, ABEL(OR)IANS
all gods	PANTHEISM
allegorical interpretation	ORIGENISM
Alpine Christian	VALDENSIAN, WALDENSIAN
American	AMISH, MORMONISM
—Assemblies of God	HOLY ROLLERS
	PENTECOSTAL CHURCH
—Quakers	SHAKERS
	UNITED SOCIETY OF BELIEVERS
Anabaptists	AMISH, HUTTERITES
	MENNONITES
Anglo-Catholics with leaning	
towards Rome	NEO-CATHOLICS
Arab	
—philosophy	AVERR(H)OISM
—religion	ISLAM, SHI'ISM
	SUFISM, SUNNISM, WAHABISM
Armenian sect	YEZIDEE, YEZ(I)DI
	ZEZIDEE
Arminian Methodism	WESLEYISM
ascribing	
—to God human	
feelings	ANTHROPOPATHISM
mind or	
soul	ANTHROPOPSYCHISM
nature	ANTHROPOPHUISM
—human characteristics	
to non-human	ANTHROPOMORPHISM
Asian	BUDDHISM, HINDUISM
	SHAMANISM
assertion of God's justice	THEODICY
attribution of soul	
to material objects	ANIMISM
Babylonia	MANDAEAN, MENDAITES
	NASOREAN, SABIANISM
	ZABIANIAM
baptism by immersion	BAPTISTS
baptist heretic	CATABAPTIST
	PEDOPABTIST, SE-BAPTIST
based on	
—Bible	BARTHIANISM
—Gospels	EVANGELICALISM
—spiritual healing	CHRISTIAN SCIENCE

bearing name of god	THEOPHORIC
beasts as gods	THERIOMORPHISM
belief in	
—Allah	ISLAM, MOHAMMEDANISM
	MOSLEM, MUSLIM
—Brahma	BRAHMANISM, BRAHMINISM
—Buddha	BUDDHISM
—god	DEISM, THEISM
—Jehovah	JUDAISM
—many gods	POLYTHEISM
—Mazda	ZOROASTRIANISM
—one god	MONOTHEISM
—two gods	DITHEISM
Benedictine	OLIVETAN, TIRONENSIAN
	TYRONENSIAN
birth and descent of gods	THEOGONY
Blackfriar	DOMINICAN
blending of religions	SYNCRETISM
Buddhism	
—Burma	MON
—China	CHAN, FOISM
—forms	HINAYANA, MAHAYANA
	THERAVADA, VAJRAYANA
—Japan	ZEN
—Tibet	GELUK PA, SAKYA PA, LAMAISM
	(see also **Buddhist**)
Bulgarian Moslem	POMAK
Burmese Buddhist	MON
Calixtin(e)	HUSSITE, UTRAQUIST
Calvinism	GENEVANISM
Canadian sect	D(O)UKHOBOR
Carmelite	WHITE FRIAR
Cathar(ist)	ALBIGENSIAN, MANICHAEAN
Catholic	
—Apostolic Church	IRVINGISM, IRVINGITES
—revival	OXFORDISM
	OXFORD MOVEMENT
	TRACTARIANISM
Children of God	SHAKERS
Chinese	CONFUCIANISM, FOISM, TAOISM
Christ	
—was a mere man	ARIANISM
	PSILANTHROPISM
—with one nature	COPTS
	MONOPHYSITES
	THEOPASCHITES
Christ's	
—body merged into Deity	
at Ascension	METAMORPHISTS
—divinity and humanity	
separate	NESTORIANISM
—second	
coming	(SEVENTH DAY) ADVENTISTS
Christianity as affected	
by war, etc	CRISIS THEOLOGY
	DIALECTICAL THEOLOGY

Church of	
—Christ	CHRISTIAN SCIENTISTS
—England	ANGLICANISM
Close Brethren	EXCLUSIVE BRETHREN
	PLYMOUTH BRETHREN
common ownership of	
property	SHAKERS
complete scepticism	PYRRHONISM
conditional mortality	CHRISTADELPHIANS
	THOMASITES
Darbyites	PLYMOUTH BRETHREN
denial of	
—Christ's divinity	ARIANISM
	PSILANTHROPISM
—existence of God	ANTITHEISM, ATHEISM
—marriage and priests	LIPOVANIANS
—original sin	PELAGIANISM
—predestination	ARMINIANISM
Devil worship	DEMONISM, SATANISM
devotion to	
—bishops	EPISCOPALIANISM
—Haile Selassie	RASTA(MAN)
	RASTAFARIAN
—priests	SACERDOTALISM
direct experience of the divine	MYSTICISM
discussion of	
Eucharist	EUCHARISTIC THEOLOGY
dissenter	RECUSANT
divine	
—abnegation	KENOSIS
—inspiration	THEOSOPHY
divinity made manifest	PANTHOS
doctrine	
—of	
last things	ESCHATOLOGY
life and work of Christ	CHRISTOLOGY
—that knowledge is from faith	FIDEISM
Dominican	BLACKFRIAR
Dutch Arminian	REMONSTRANT
early	
—Christian esoteric religion	GNOSTICISM
—heretic	CERINTHIAN
East European Catholic	UNIATE
Eastern	
—Orthodox sect	UNIATS
—sorcery	MAG(IAN)ISM
Egyptian Christian	COPT
English monks (13th c)	BETHLEHEMITES
ethico-dualistic philosophy	MARCIONITE
Evangelical Union	MORISONIANS
Exclusive Brethren	CLOSE BRETHREN
	PLYMOUTH BRETHREN
Father and Son of	
—of	
similar essence	HOMOIOUSIAN
the same essence	HOMOOUSIAN

—and Holy Ghost are one	SABELLIANISM
faith alone necessary	SOLIFIDIANISM
founded by	
—Annie Besant	THEOSOPHICAL SOCIETY
	THEOSOPHY
—anti-pope	NOVATIONISM
—Apollinaris	APOLLINARIANISM
—Aquinas	THOMISM
—Arius	ARIANISM
—Arminius	ARMIN(IAN)ISM
—Bab-ed-Sin	BABEEISM, BAHAI(I)SM
—Baha-Ullah	BAHAISM
—Bishop of Laodicea	APOLLINARIANISM
—Buddha	BUDDHISM
—Charles Russell	JEHOVAH'S WITNESSES
	RUSSELLITES
—Christ	CHRISTIANITY
—Cornelius Jansen	JANSENISM
—Emmanuel Swedenborg	NEW JERUSALEM
	CHURCH
	SWEDENBORGIANISM
—Erastus	ERASTIANISM
—Francis Barham	ALISM
—Gautama	BUDDHISM
—Georg Calixtus	CALIXTIN(E), SYNCRETISM
—George Fox	QUAKERISM
	SOCIETY OF FRIENDS
—George Rapp	RAPPISTS, RAPPITES
—Ghulam Ahmad	AHMADIYYA
—Ignatius Loyola	JESUITISM
	JESUITRY, JESUITS
	SOCIETY OF JESUS
—James Morison	MORISONIANISM
—J H Newman	OXFORDISM
	OXFORD MOVEMENT
	TRACTARIANISM
—J N Darby	DARBYITES
—John Calvin	CALVINISM, GENEVANISM
	PRESBYTERIANISM
	PURITANISM
—John Glas	GLASSITES
—John Hus	HUSSITES, MORAVIANS
—John Maron	MARONITE
—John Thomas	CHRISTADELPHIANS
	THOMASITES
—John Wesley	METHODISM
—John Wycliffe	LOLLARDISM
	LOLLARD(R)Y
—Joseph Smith	MORMONISM
—Kaspar v. Schwenkfeld	SCHWENKFELDERS
—Kong Qiu (Confucius)	CONFUCIANISM
—Lao-tzu	TAOISM
—Madame Blavatsky	THEOSOPHICAL SOCIETY
	THEOSOPHY

—Mahavira	JAINISM
—Mohammed (Mahomet)	ISLAM
	MOHAMMED(AN)ISM
	MOSLEM, MUSLIM
—Mani(chaeus)	MANICHAEANISM
—Marcion of Sinope	MARCIONITES
—Martin Luther	LUTHER(AN)ISM
	PROTESTANTISM
—Mary Baker Eddy	CHRISTIAN SCIENCE
—Melanchthon	SYNERGISM
—Menno Simons	MENNONITES
—Mo-zi	MOHISTS
—Nanak	SIKHISM
—Nestorius	NESTORIANISM
—Novaticinus	NOVATIONISM
—Peter Waldo	VALDENSES, WALDENSES
	WALDENSIANS
—Pyrrho of Elis	PYRRHONISM
—Richard Cameron	CAMERONIAN
—Robert Sandeman	SANDEMANIANS
—Ron Hubbard	SCIENTOLOGY
—Rudolf Steiner	ANTHROPOSOPHY
—Sabellius	MODALISM
—St Columba	COLUMBAN (CELTIC) CHURCH
—St Maron	MARONITE
—St Vincent de Paul	LAZARISM
—Sakyamuni	BUDDHISM
—Saraswati	ARYA SAMAJ
—Shirazi	BABISM, BAHAISM
—Søren Kierkegaard	CHRISTIAN
	EXISTENTIALISM
	EXISTENTIAL THEOLOGY
—Sun Myung Moon	MOONIES
	UNIFICATION CHURCH
—Thomas Erastus	ERASTIANISM
—Ulrich Zwingli	ZWINGLIANISM
—William Booth	SALVATION ARMY
—William J Seymour	PENTECOSTAL CHURCH
—Zarathustra	ZOROASTRIANISM
founded in	
—America	(SEVENTH DAY) ADVENTISTS
	MORMONISM
	RAPPISTS, RAPPITES
—Dublin	PLYMOUTH BRETHREN
	PLYMOUTHISM
—Geneva	CALVINISM
—India	THEOSOPHY
—Korea	MOONIES
	UNIFICATION CHURCH
—Pennsylvania	JEHOVAH'S WITNESSES
Franciscan	CAPUCHIN, CORDELIER
	GREYFRIAR, MINORITE
Free Presbyterian Church	WEE FREES
French	
—Gnosticism (13th c)	ALBIGENSIAN
	CATHARIST

—Protestant	CAMISARD, HUGUENOT
—Revolutionary	
creed	THEOPHILANTHROPY
fundamentalist	
Christians	JEHOVAH'S WITNESSES
	PENTECOSTALISTS, RUSSELLITES
fusion of religions	SYNCRETISM
Genevanism	CALVINISM
German	
—American Baptists	DUNKERS
—Jews	ASHKENAZIM
—Protestant	ANABAPTIST
	LUTHER(AN)ISM
gift of the Holy	
Spirit	CHARISMATIC MOVEMENT
	PENTECOSTAL CHURCH
Glassite	SANDEMANIAN
Gnostic creator	DEMIURGE
god	THEISM
—and devil	YEZIDEE, YEZ(I)DI
	ZEZIDEE
—as	
sole sovereign	THEOCRACY, THEISM
trinity	TRINITARIAN
unity	UNITARIAN
universe	PANTHEISM
—identified with cosmos	COSMOTHEISM
	PANTHEISM
—with	
one will	MONOTHELETISM
two wills	DITHELETISM
	(*see also* **gods**)
gospel-preaching	EVANGELICALISM
government by bishops	EPISCOPACY
	EPISCOPAL(IAN)ISM
Greek	
—Catholics in the Middle East	MELCHITES
—Christian Church	GREEK ORTHODOX
Greyfriar	FRANCISCAN
Harmonists	SECOND ADVENTISTS
Hebrew	JUDAISM
—asceticism	ESSENISM
	(*see also* **Hebrew**)
Hemerobaptist	MANDAEAN
High Church principles	PUSEYISM
Hindu	BRAHMANISM, S(H)IVAISM
	(*see also* **Hindu**)
host of heaven	SABAISM
Hussite	CALIXTIN(E), TABORITE
	UTRAQUIST
identifying one god	
as another	THEOCRASIA, THEOCRASY
idols	IDOLATRY
image	
—breaker	ICONOCLAST
—worshipper	ICONODULE

imminent end	
of the world	JEHOVAH'S WITNESSES
	RUSSELLITES
	(SEVENTH DAY) ADVENTISTS
in the likeness of a	
god	THEOMORPHIC
Indian	
—Moslems	COSSAS
—Parsees	ZOROASTRIANISM
—religions	BUDDHISM, HINDUISM
	ISLAM, JAINISM, SIKHISM
infallibility of Bible	FUNDAMENTALISM
inspired by god	THEOPNEUST(IC)
Iranian Guebres	ZOROASTRIANISM
Irvingism	CATHOLIC APOSTOLIC CHURCH
Islam	MOHAMMED(AN)ISM
	MOSLEM, MUSLIM
	(*see also* **Moslem**)
Italian	
—Gnosticism (13th c)	ALBIGENSIAN
	CATHARIST
—Unitarians	SOCINIANISM
Jamaican	RASTAFARIANISM
Japan	BUDDHISM, SHINTOISM
Japanese Buddhists	AMIDA, AMITA
	SOKA GAKKAI, ZEN
Jehovah	HEBREW, JEWISH, JUDAISM
Jesuits	SOCIETY OF JESUS
Jewish	
—Christian	NAZARENE
—formalist	PHARISEE
—sceptic	SADDUCEE
—sect	(C)HAS(S)ID(IC), ESSENE
performing daily	
ablutions	HEMEROBAPTISTS
last or final things	ESCHATOLOGY
Latter Day Saints	MORMONS
Lebanese	DRUSE, DRUZ(E)
	MARONITE
liberal	
—belief	LATITUDINARIANISM
—Catholic	NEO-CATHOLIC
literal truth of Bible	FUNDAMENTALISM
Logos in lieu of soul	APOLLINARIANISM
loss of belief	ANOMIE
Manichaean	CATHAR(IST), PATARIN(E)
manifestation of god	THEOPHANY
many gods	POLYTHEISM
—each supreme	KATHENOTHEISM
Maronite	UNIAT(E)
material good arriving with	
spirits of the dead	CARGO CULT
meditation	MYSTICISM
Middle Eastern Christian	
Church	EASTERN ORTHODOX
Milanese heretic	PATARIN(E)

missionary Protestants	MORAVIANS
	UNITED BRETHREN
mixture of religions	THEOCRASIA
	THEOCRASY
moderate Hussite	CALIXTIN(E), UTRAQUIST
Moonies	UNIFICATION CHURCH
Moravians	UNITED BRETHREN
Morisonians	EVANGELICAL UNION
Mormons	LATTER-DAY SAINTS
Moslem	
—mysticism	SOF(I)ISM, SUF(I)ISM
—sect	AHMADIYYA, IMAMITES
	ISMAILITES, KHARIJITES
	SHIA(H), SUNNI, WAHABEE
	WAHABI
—traditional teaching	SUNNA
mother of God	THEOTOKOS
	VIRGIN MARY
mystic religion	ALISM, SANTERIA
nature-worship	PAN(EN)THEISM
New Jerusalem Church	SWEDENBORGIANISM
non-belief	AGNOSTICISM, ATHEISM
	HEATHENISM, HUMANISM
	PAGANISM
non-believer	INFIDEL
non-Christian	PA(I)NIM, PAYNIM
one god	HENOTHEISM, MONOTHEISM
opposed to	
—marriage of priests	PATARIN(E)
—military service	DUNKERS
	D(O)UKHOBOR
order	
—founded at	
Camaldoli	CAMALDOLITES
Cassino	BENEDICTINE
Chartreuse	CARTHUSIAN
Citeaux	BENEDICTINE
	BERNARDINE
	CISTERCIAN
Cluny	BENEDICTINE, CLUNIAC
Monte Oliveto	OLIVETANS
Mount Carmel	CARMELITES
	WHITE FRIARS
Palestine	CARMELITE, WHITE FRIARS
Premontre	NORBERTINE
	PREMONSTRATENSIANS
	WHITE CANONS
T(h)iron	TIRONENSIANS
	TYRONENSIANS
—founded by	
Bernard of Clairvaux	BERNADINE
	CISTERCIAN
John Peter Caraffa	THEATINE
Pietro da Morrone	CELESTINE
St Augustine	AUGUSTINIAN
	AUSTIN FRIARS

St Bruno	CARTHUSIAN
St Dominic	BLACK FRIARS
	DOMINICAN
St Francis of Assisi	FRANCISCAN
	GREY FRIARS
St Francis of Paola	MINIMS
St Francis of Sales	SALESIANS, VISITANTS
St Ignatius of Loyola	JESUITS
St Norbert	NORBERTINE
	PREMONSTRATENSIANS
	WHITE CANONS
St Romuald	CAMALDOLITES
—wearing the sign	
of the Cross	CROSSED FRIARS
	CROUCHED FRIARS
	CRUTCHED FRIARS
orthodox	
—Jews	(C)HAS(S)ID(IC)
—Roman Catholic	TRIDENTINE
Oxford Movement	TRACTARIANISM
Papism	ROMAN CATHOLICISM
Parsee	ZOROASTRIAN
passionate belief	FUNDAMENTALISM
Pentecostalists	ASSEMBLIES OF GOD
	HOLY ROLLERS
Persian	BABEEISM, BAB(I)ISM
	BAHAISM, IMAMISM, MAGISM
	MANICH(A)EANISM, MAZDEISM
	MAZDAISM, MITHRAISM
	PARSEEISM, PARSIISM
	ZOROASTRIANISM
philosophical Taoism	TAO-CHIA
philosophy of God's justice	THEODICY
Plymouth Brethren	CLOSE BRETHREN
	DARBYITES
	EXCLUSIVE BRETHREN
Polish Jews	ASHKENAZIM
polytheism with each	
god supreme	KATHENOTHEISM
Portuguese Jews	SEPHARDIM
—converted to Christianity	MARRANOS
Protestant sect	MENNONITES
Protestantism	METHODISM
Quakers	SOCIETY OF FRIENDS
—sect	SHAKERS
reason, not authority	RATIONALISM
reasserting the influence	
of the Holy Ghost	CHARISMATICS
reconciling religion	
with science	PROCESS THEOLOGY
	SECULAR CHRISTIANITY
Reformed	
—Church	PROTESTANTISM
—Presbyterian Church	CAMERONIAN
regeneration is the work of	
the Holy Ghost	MONERGISM

reincarnation	THEOSOPHICAL SOCIETY
rejection of	
—Holy Trinity	CHRISTADELPHIANS
	D(O)UKHOBOR
—jurisdiction of bishops	ACEPHALITES
—religion	ATHEISM, HUMANISM
	SECULARISM
religion	
—in relation to	
ethics	MORAL THEOLOGY
science	PROCESS THEOLOGY
	SECULAR CHRISTIANITY
wars, etc	CRISIS THEOLOGY
—without a god	NON-THEISM
religious	
—emotion	THEOPATHY
—legalism	NOMISM
representation of God in	
human form	ANTHROPOMORPHISM
reverence for witch-doctors	SHAMANISM
Roman Catholic	JEBUSITE
	PAPISM, ROMANISM
rule of God	THEONOMY
Russian	
—Christian	UNIAT(E)
—Christian Church	EASTERN ORTHODOX
—sect	D(O)UKHOBOR, LIPOVANIANS
Salesian	VISITANT
salvation	
—by individual redeemer	MESSIANISM
—depends on faith alone	ANTINOMIAN
—doctrine	SOTEROLOGY
—through	
God's grace	CALVINIS
special knowledge of God	GNOSTICISM
Sandemanian	GLASSITE
Saudi Arabia	WAHABISM, ISLAM
scepticism	SADDUC(EE)ISM
Scottish	COLUMBAN CHURCH
—Free Church	WEE FREES
—monk (8th c)	CULDEE
—Presbyterian	CAMERONIAN
	WHIGGAMORE
Second Adventist	HARMONIST, HARMONITE
self	
—baptizing	SE-BAPTISTS
—subsistence of God	AUTOTHEISM
Siberian	SHAMANISM
sleep of soul after death	PYSCHEPANNYCHISM
snake-worship	OPHITISM
Society of	
—Friends	QUAKERS, SHAKERS
—Jesus	JESUITS
sole truth of the Bible	PLYMOUTH BRETHREN
Spanish	
—Jews	SEPHARDIM

converted to Christianity	MARRANOS
—sect	ILLUMINATI
	MOZARABS
speaking in	
tongues	CHARISMATIC MOVEMENT
spirit worship	SHAMANISM, VOODOOISM
spiritual marriage	AGAPEMONE
spiritualism	ANTHROPOSOPHY
State control of Church	ERASTIANISM
strange	
—beliefs	ESOTERISM
—gods	ALLOTHEISM
strict Catharists	PERFECTI
study of religion	THEOLOGY
Sunday as day of	
rest	LORD'S DAY OBSERVANCE SOCIETY
	SABBATARIANS
Supreme God and devil	YEZIDEE, YEZ(I)DI
	ZEZIDEE
Sweden(borgian)	NEW JERUSALEM CHURCH
Swedish	SWEDENBORGIANISM
Swiss Protestant sect	ZWINGLIANS
Syrian	DRUSE, DRUZ(E)
Taborite	HUSSITE
teetotallers	RECHABITES
that one is God	THEOMANIA
three gods	TRITHEISM
Tibetan	BUDDHISM, LAMAISM
Tractarianism	OXFORD MOVEMENT
transubstantiation	CAPERNAITE
tribal religions	PRIMITIVISM
Trinity as manifestations	
of one God	MODALISM
Turkish Muslim	KARMATHIAN, SALAR
two gods	DITHEISM
unbeliever	AGNOSTIC, ATHEIST
	HEATHEN
—Eastern	ZENDIK
Uniat(e)	MARONITE
Unification Church	MOONIES
United Brethren	MORAVIANS
unity of	
—churches	ECUMEN(ICAL)ISM
—God	ARIANISM
	UNITARIANISM
universal salvation	UNIVERSALISM
universe is the Logos	PANLOGISM
unorthodoxy	HERESY, HETERODOXY
Utraquist	CALIXTIN(E), HUSSITE
vision of God	THEOPHANY
Visitant	SALESIAN
war of the gods	THEOMACHY
West Indies	OBEAHISM, OBEISM
	OBIISM, VOODOOISM
	VOUDOUISM
White Friar	CARMELITE

will not free	DETERMINISM, FATALISM
	NECESSARIANISM
	PREDESTINATION
wisdom of	
—God	THEOSOPHY
—man	ANTHROPOSOPHY
	(see also **worship**)
Belize	BH
capital	BELMOPAN
coin	CENT, DOLLAR
former name	BRITISH HONDURAS
Bengal	
beggar	BAUL
bison	GAUR
boat	BATEL, BAULEA(H)
cotton cloth	BEZAN
measure	BEGA, CHATTACK, COTTA(H)
tree	BOLA
Benin	DY
capital	PORTO NOVO
coin	FRANC
biology	
including: bacteriology	
botany	
genetics	
abdominal	
—appendage	UROPOD
—cavity	PERITONEAL CAVITY
—segment	UROMERE
ability to	
—change colour	METACHROSIS
—resemble another animal	
or plant	MIMICRY
abnormal	
—elongation of axis	DIAPHYSIS
—growth	HYPERTROPHY
abrupt change	SALTATION
—in DNA of chromosomes	MUTATION
absence of pigments in skin,	
etc	ALBINISM
absorbing part of	
root	PILIFEROUS LAYER
acid linking chains	
in proteins	AMINO-ACID
actively dividing part of plant	MERISTEM
Adam's apple	LARYNX
adapted for walking	GRESSORIAL
additional calyx	EPICALYX
adjustments to focus	
of eye	ACCOMMODATION
aerophyte	EPIPHYTE
affecting more than one	
characteristic	PLE(I)OTROPIC
affinity of organism and	
its parts	HOMOLOGY
Agnatha	CYCLOSTOMATA

air	
—plant	EPIPHYTE
—sac in lung	ALVEOLUS
—tube	
large	BRONCHUS
small	BRONCHIOLE
alcohol compound in animals	
and plants	STEROL
algae	ANTHOPHYTA
BACILLARIOPHYTA, CHAROPHYTA	
CHLORELLA, CHLOROPHYTA	
CHRYPTOPHYTA, CRYSOPHYTA,	
EUGLENOPHYTA, PHAEOPHYTA	
PYRROPHYTA, RHODOPHYTA	
—and fungus in symbiosis	LICHEN
—bacteria and fungi	THALLOPHYTES
—blue-green CYANOPHYTA, MYXOPHYTA	
SCHIZOPHYCEAE	
—filamentous	CONFERVA
HETEROCONTAE	
—forming chain	DESMID
—living in sea	SEAWEED
	(see also **seaweed**)
—unicellular	DESMID
algal	
—cell in lichen	CHROMIDIUM
—part of lichen	PHYCOBIONT
alimentary canal	ENTERIC CANAL, GUT
alligators and crocodiles	CROCODILIA
alternation of	
—day and night	PHOTOPERIODISM
—methods of	
reproduction	HETEROGAMY
alternative forms of	
a gene	ALLEL(E), ALLELOMORPH
amino-acid	(see **acids**)
Amphibia	ANURA, APODA
GYMNOPHIONA, SALIENTIA	
URODELA	
anaerobic respiration	FERMENTATION
Angiospermae	DICOTYL(EDONE)AE
MONOCOTYL(EDONE)AE	
Angiosperms and	
Gymnosperms	PHANEROGAMIA
angle between leaf and stem	AXIL
animal(s)	
—attached to a surface	SESSILE
—cell undergoing meiosis	SPERMATOCYTE
—developing young	
in the uterus	DIDELPHIA
	MARSUPIALIA
	METATHERIA
—eating	
all foods	OMNIVORE
flesh	CARNIVORE
grass	HERBIVORE

—egg in shell	CLEIDOIC EGG
—feeding on others	CARNIVORE, PREDATOR
—forming part of colony	ZOOID
—kept by ants as guest	SYMPHILE
	SYNOECETE
—living	
on land or in water	AMPHIBIAN
under stones, etc	CRYPTOZOIC
—many-celled	METAZOA
—single-celled	AMOEBA(AMOEBAE)
	PROTOZOON(PROTOZOA)
—starch	GLYCOGEN
—suckling	
partly-developed young	MARSUPIAL
well-developed young	MAMMAL
—swallowing food for later	
digestion	RUMINANT
—with	
backbones	CHORDATA, VERTEBRATA
	VERTEBRATES
combined digestive and	
genital opening	MONOTREMATA
	MONOTREMES
	PROTOTHERIA
diploid nuclei	DIPLONT
four limbs	TETRAPODA, TETRAPODS
hoofs	UNGULATA, UNGULATES
many arms	HYDRANTH, POLYP(E)
padded feet	TYLOPODA
segmented bodies	ARTHROPODA
slender toes	LEPTODACTYL
solid hoofs	SOLIPED
two-part shell	BIVALVE
webbed feet	PALMIPED(E)
winged feet	ALIPED
—without	
backbones	INVERTEBRATA
	INVERTEBRATES
teeth	EDENTATA
—aardvarks	TUBULIDENTATA
—scaly anteaters	PHOLIDOTA
—sloths, etc	XENARTHRA
animalcules in moss etc	TARDIGRADA
animals and plants	
of sea-bottom	BENTHOS
Annelida	CHAETOPODA, GEPHYREA
	HIRUDINEA, LEECHES
	OLIGOCHAETA
Anthropoidea	PITHECOIDEA
antibody which catalyses	
target	ABZYME
apes, monkeys and man	ANTHROPOIDEA
	PITHECOIDEA
	PRIMATES
apoda	GYMNOPHIONA
appendage for cleaning antennae	STRIGIL

area	
—in which trees are grown	ARBORETUM
—of vegetation for study	QUADRAT
—retaining character in period	
of general change	REFUGIUM
arrangement of	
—folding in flower-bud	AESTIVATION
—organs to prevent self-	
fertilisation	HERCOGAMY
	HERKOGAMY
arrow-worms	CHAETOGNATHA
artery	(see circulation)
Arthropoda	ARACHNIDA, CHILOPODA
	CRUSTACEA, DIPLOPODA
	INSECTA, MYRIAPODA
	ONYCHOPHORA, SYMPHILA
	TRILOBITA
artificial insemination	AI
—gamete intra-fallopian	
transfer	GIFT
—zygote intra-fallopian	
transfer	ZIFT
artificially produced	
variety of plant	CULTIVAR
asexual	
—fungal spore	CONIDIUM
—reproduction	APOGAMY, APOMIXIS
	APOSPORY, BUDDING, FISSION
	GEMMATION, PARTHENOGENESIS
	VEGETATIVE REPRODUCTION
—reproductive unit	SPORE
—spore of algae etc	APLANOSPORE
asexually reproduced descendant	
of sexually produced individual	CLONE
association of	
—interdependent organisms	BIOCOENOSIS
—organisms for mutual	
benefit	SYMBIOSIS
atrophy	INVOLUTION
attachment of ovum to	
wall of womb	IMPLANTATION
axis	
—of	
compound leaf	R(H)ACIS
grass spike	RACHILLA
inflorescence	R(H)ACIS
—producing buds and leaves	STEM
back-plate of arthropod	TERGUM
bacteria	(see micro-organisms below)
bacterial disease of plants	BACTERIOSIS
bacterium	SCHIZOMYCOPHYTE
baleen	WHALEBONE
barnacles	CIRRIPEDIA
Barr body	SEX CHROMATIN
base(s)	
—forming amino-acid	TRIPLET

—of
DNA	ADENINE, CYTOSINE
	GUANINE, THYMINE
ovule	CHALAZA
RNA	ADENINE, CYTOSINE
	GUANINE, URACIL

based on similarity of
—evolution	PHYL(OGEN)ETIC
—individuals	PHENETIC

basic
—entity	PRION
—living matter	PROTOPLASM
batrachia	AMPHIBIA
bats	CHIROPTERA
bear-animalcules	TARDIGRADA

bee
—fertile female	QUEEN
—glue	PROPOLIS
—male	DRONE
—sterile female	WORKER
beginning of growth	GERMINATION
belly	ABDOMEN
belonging to the stem	CAULINARY, CAULINE
belt or saddle on worm	CLITELLUM
big toe	HALLUX
bile sac	GALL BLADDER
binomial nomenclature	LINNAEAN SYSTEM

biochemical reaction in
cells	CITRIC ACID CYCLE
	KREBS CYCLE
biogenous	PARASITIC
biological cycle	CIRCADIAN RHYTHM
	DIURNAL RHYTHM

biologists etc

—American   AVERY, BEADLE, BECKWITH
BITTNER, BORLANG, BURBANK
COHEN, COHN, CORBETT
CRAIG, DAVIS, DOBZHANSKY
DOISY, DUBOS, ELVEHJEM, ENDERS
EVANS, GRAFF, GREEN, HALBERG
HARARY, HARRISON, HERSHEY
HOLMES, HUBEL, KING, LEDERBERG
LETTVIN, LILLY, MAYER, MAYR
MCCOLLUM, MENDEL, MORGAN
MULLER, NATHAN, OCHOA,
RASMUSSEN, REED
RICKETTS, ROSE, SABIN, SALK
SCHOENHEIMER, SCOTT
SINSHEIMER, SMITH, SPALDING
STANLEY, STURTEVANT
SUTTON, TATUM, WALD, WATSON
WIESEL, WILLIAMS

—Argentinian	HOUSSAC
—Australian	BURNET, MILLER
—Austrian	BERTALANFFY, LORENZ
	MENDEL, PERUTZ, VON TSCHERMAK

—Belgian	BORDET, CLAUDE
	VAN BEDENEN
—Brazilian	MEDAWAR
—British	BALFOUR, BATESON, BAWDEN

BROWN, CHAIN, CRICK, DARWIN
DRUMMOND, ELFORD, FISHER
FLEMING, FLOREY, FORBES, GEDDES
GOSSE, GRIFFITH, HALDANE, HARDY
HODGKIN, HOPKINS, HUTTON
HUXLEY, ISAACS, LUBBOCK
MEDAWAR, MOORE, MORRIS
NEEDHAM, OWEN, PERUTZ, PETERS
PIRIE, ROSENHEIM, THOMPSON
THOMSON, TWORT, WADDINGTON,
WALLACE, WEBSTER, WELDON
WILLCOCK, WOODGER

—Canadian	AVERY, BERTALANFFY
	D'HERELLE
—Chilean	MATURANA
—Danish	DAM, GRAM, JOHANNSEN
	MULLER
—Dutch	BEIJERINCK, DE VRIES
	DONATH, JANSEN, KYLSTRA
	STAPEL, SWAMMERDAM
—Finnish	WILSKA
—French	CAREL, CUVIER, DE BUFFON
	DUBOS, DU POUY
	JACOB, LAMARCK, LAVERAN
	MILLER, MONOD, NICOLLE
	PASTEUR, RAMON, RUEL
—German	ASCHHEIM, BAER, BAUMANN

BENDA, BUETENANDT, CHAIN, COHN
CORRENS, DREISCH, FLEMMING
EHRLICH, HAECKEL, KOCH, LOFFLER
LOHMANN, KRUSE, MAYR
PFEFFER, SCHLEIDEN, SCHOENHEIMER
SCHWANN, SIEBOLD, SPEMANN
STENT, VIRCHOW, VON MAYER
VON MOHL, VON SACHS, WASSERMANN
WEISMANN, WILSTATTER, ZONDEK

—Greek	THEOPHRASTUS
—Hungarian	SZENT-GYORGI
—Italian	FRASCATORI, MARSIGLI
	SPALLANZANI, STELLUTI
—Japanese	OHDAKE, SHIMAMURA, SUZUKI
—New Zealand	WILKINS
—Norwegian	GUNNERA
—Polish	FUNK, REICHSTEIN, SABIN
—Russian	DOBZHANSKY, IVANOVSKI
	LYSENKO, METCHNIKOFF, OPARIN
	PALADE, PAVLOV, TSVETT, VAVILOV
—South African	THEILE
—Spanish	OCHOA
—Swedish	LINNAEUS, RUDBECK
—Swiss	AGASSIZ, BONNET, CANDOLLE
	MEISCHER, REICHSTEIN, VON NAGELI

birds	AVES
	(*see separate entry*)
—and reptiles	SAUROPSIDA
—mammals,reptiles	AMNIOTA
bisexual	HERMAPHRODITE
biting	
—pincers	CHELICERA(E)
—animal	GYNANDROMORPH
bivalves	LAMELLIBRANCHI(AT)A
	PELECYPODA
bladder near liver	GALL-BLADDER
blood	(*see* **circulation**)
blotched	CENTONATE
body and temperament type	SOMA(TO)TYPE
—muscular and aggressive	SOMATONIA
body	SOMA
—division(s)	TAGMA(TA)
—in cell	
carrying	
—chlorophyll	CHLOROPLAST
—food reserve	PLASTID
—genes	CHROMOSOME
—pigment	PLASTID
formed at mitosis	SPINDLE
forming starch	LEUCOPLAST(ID)
involved in secretion	GOLGI APPARATUS
	GOLGI BODY
	GOLGI MATERIAL
protoplasm	CENTROSOME
—in	
cytoplasm	CHONDRIOSOME
	MITOCHONDRIA
nucleus	
—containing RNA	NUCLEOLUS
—layers	ECTODERM, ENDODERM
	MESODERM
—of tapeworm	STROBILA
—segment	ARTHROMERE, MERO(SO)ME
	METAMERE, SOMITE
of insect	
—fore	PROTHORAX
—middle	THORAX
—rear	ABDOMEN
—substance to fight antigen	ANTIBODY
—which can separate and become	
new individual in	
plants	GEMMA
sponges	GEMMULE
bonding to parent	ATTACHMENT
bone	(*see separate entry*)
—marrow	MEDULLA
bottom(s) of hollow organ(s)	FUNDUS(FUNDI)
bract	
—enclosing	
grass	
—flower	LEMMA, PALEA

—spike	(STERILE) GLUME
spadix	SPATHE
—growing round inflorescence	PHYLLARY
brain	(*see separate entry*)
branch acting as leaf	CLADODE
	PHYLLOCLADE
branching part of neurone	DENDRITE
breaking into spores	SPORULATION
breaking down	
—and synthesis of organic	
compounds internally	METABOLISM
—by bacteria	BIODEGRADATION
	BIODESTRUCTION
	BIODETERIORATION
—in metabolism	CATABOLISM
	KATABOLISM
—of food by oxygen	RESPIRATION
	(*see also* decomposition *below*)
breathing	RESPIRATION
—organ of aquatic animal	GILL
—pore in	
animal	SPIRACLE
bark	LENTICEL
bringing forth of young	PARTURITION
bristle	
—of	
insect	SCOP(UL)A
invertebrate	SETA
—on	
grass, corn, etc	ARISTA, AWN
some worms	CHAETA
brittle-stars	OPHIUROIDEA
brood-pouch	OVISAC
Bryophyta	ANTHERCEROTAE, HEPATICAE
	LIVERWORTS, MUSCI
Bryozoa	POLYZOA
building up in metabolism	ANABOLISM
buoyancy organ in fish	SWIM-BLADDER
burning of leaves by sun	HELIOSIS
bursting open of pods	DEHISCENCE
cactus, house-leek, etc	SUCCULENT
calcium carbonate from	
marine skeletons	CORAL
calyx and corolla of flower	PERIANTH
camouflage in	
animals	CRYPTIC COLO(U)RATION
cancer-producing	CARCINOGENIC
	ONCOGENIC
capsule opening with circular	
detachable lid	PYXIDIUM
carbohydrate	
—in	
plant cell-walls	(HEMI)CELLULOSE
wood cells	LIGNIN
—sticky	MUCILAGE
—stored as food	STARCH

carbon-based	ORGANIC
carpels collectively	GYNAECEUM
	GYN(O)ECIUM
case	
—holding	
few spores	SPORANGIOLE
	SPORANGIOLUM
spermatia	SPERMAGONE
SPERMAGONIUM, SPERMOGENE	
	SPERMOGENIUM
spermatozoa	SPERMATOPHORE
spores	SPORANGIUM
—of protozoa, etc	LORICA
category within species	FORM
cats, dogs, lions, etc	CARNIVORES
causing abnormalities in embryo	TERATOGENIC
cavity	
—between intestines and	
wall of body	CELOM, COELOM(E)
—containing	
blood	HAEMOCOEL
digestive organs	ABDOMEN, BELLY
heart and lungs	CHEST, THORAX
—in protoplasm	VACUOLE
—of mouth	BUCCAL CAVITY
—serving as gut	COELENTERON
—where intestinal and urinary	
tracts discharge	CLOACA
cell(s)	CYTE(S), ENERGID
—body	PERICARYON, PERIKARYON
—containing pigment	CHROMATOPHORE
—cycle	G PHASE, M PHASE
MITOSIS, MITOTIC PHASE, S PHASE	
—division	MEIOSIS, MITOSIS
of diploid cells	MITOSIS
producing haploid cells	MEIOSIS
without mitosis	AMITOSIS
—formation	CYTOGENESIS
—forming	
fibrous tissue	FIBROBLAST, FIBROCYTE
stoma	GUARD-CELLS
structure of organism	SOMATIC CELL
tissues	HISTOBLAST
—found in connective	
tissue	FIBROBLAST, FIBROCYTE
—from	
fertilised egg	BLASTOMERE
which gamete is formed	GAMETOCYTE
—in	
fungus in which spores	
are produced	ASCUS
insect with symbiotic	
micro-organisms	MYCETOCYTE
pancreas secreting insulin	
and glucagon	ISLETS OF LANGERHANS
resting state	ARTHROSPORE

—layer responsible for	
leaf-fall	ABSCISS(ION) LAYER
—layers in body	ECTODERM, ENDODERM
	MESODERM
—movement in embryo	GASTRULATION
—multinucleate	SYNCYTIUM
—nucleus	
with membrane	EUCARYON
	EUKARYON
without membrane	PROCARYON
	PROKARYON
—particle	
reproducing like a gene	PLASMAGENE
which assembles protein	RIBOSOME
—prepared for examination	TISSUE CULTURE
—produced by division	
of single cell	DAUGHTER CELLS
	D NUCLEI
—producing	
spermatocytes	SPERMATOGONIUM
spermatozoa	SPERMATID
	SPERMATOCYTE
spores	ARCHESPORIUM
—wall envelope in bacteria	CAPSULE
—which	
can store foreign matter	ATHROCYTE
destroys bone	OSTEOCLAST
develops into an organ	BLASTEMA
forms	
—bone	OSTEOBLAST
—gametes	GAMETOCYTE
—ovum	OOCYTE
—with	
distinct form	IDIOBLAST
several nuclei	SYNCYTIUM
—of different	
genetic makeup	HETEROCARYON
	HETEROKARYON
—of same genetic	
makeup	HOMOCARYON
	HOMOKARYON
thick walls	SCLEREID(E)
centipedes	CHILOPODA
central	
—column of root or branch	STELE
	VASCULAR CYLINDER
—part of	
organ	MEDULLA
ovule	NUCELLUS
tree	HEARTWOOD
Cephalopoda	SIPHONOPODA
chaffy scale	RAMENTUM
chain of	
—amino-acids	POLYPEPTIDE
—nucleotides	NUCLEIC ACID
	POLYNUCLEOTIDE

—segments	STROBILA	—group(s)	TAXON(TAXA)
change from larva to adult	METAMORPHOSIS	—order of groups (smallest first)	SUB-SPECIES
changes in life-span of cell	CELL CYCLE		SPECIES
character due to mutated gene	MUTANT		GENUS
characteristics of organism	PHENOTYPE		TRIBE
chemical			SUB-FAMILY
—basis of			FAMILY
genes	(DEOXY)RIBONUCLEIC ACID		SUPER-FAMILY
	DNA, RNA		SUB-ORDER
—change in			ORDER
living organisms	METABOLISM		SUPER-ORDER
make-up of genes	MUTATION		COHORT
—inhibiting action of auxin	ANTIAUXIN		INFRA-CLASS
—involved in storage			SUB-CLASS
of light-energy	ADP		CLASS
	ADENINE DIPHOSPHATE		SUPER-CLASS
	ATP, ADENINE TRIPHOSPHATE		SUB-PHYLUM
—produced to evoke response			DIVISION, PHYLUM
from other animals	PHEROMONE		SUB-KINGDOM
—required by plants in			KINGDOM
large quantities	MACRONUTRIENT	—system	LINNAEAN SYSTEM
small quantities	MICRONUTRIENT		RAUNKIAER'S LIFE FORMS
—which kills		claw(s) of arthropod	CHELA(E)
algae	ALGICIDE	clear area in bacterial culture	PLAQUE
fungi	FUNGICIDE	climbing organ of plant	TENDRIL
insects	INSECTICIDE	climbing plant of the tropics	LIANA, LIANE
plants	HERBICIDE	cloning from minute	
rodents	RODENTICIDE	particles of bud	MICROCLONING
worms	ANTHELMINTHIC, VERMIFUGE	club mosses	LYCOPODIALES
	VERMICIDE	cnidoblast	THREAD CELL
chemistry of tissues	HISTOCHEMISTRY	coat of seed	INTEGUMENT
chemotaxis	CHEMOTROPISM	code of inherited characteristics	GENETIC CODE
chest	PLEURAL CAVITY, THORAX	Coelenterata	HYDROZOA
chin	MENTAL PROMINENCE	cold-bloodedness	POIKILOTHERMY
Choanata	AMPHIBIA, AVES	collagen band connecting	
	CHOANICHTHYES, MAMMALIA	bones at joint	LIGAMENT
	REPTILIA	collection of dried plants	HERBARIUM
chondriosomes	MITOCHONDRIA	colony of algae etc	COENOBIUM
chromosome		coloured	
—carrying genetic		—covering of some seeds	ARIL
instructions	SEX CHROMOSOME	—part of eye	IRIS
—of a species	GENOM(E)	colourless	
—other than sex chromosome	AUTOSOME	—algae	LEUCOPHYTE
chrysalis	PUPA	—plastid	LEUCOPLAST
Ciliophora	INFUSORIA, PROTOZOA	community of organisms and	
circle of nitrogen use		its environment	ECOSYSTEM
in nature	NITROGEN CYCLE	component part of	
circular laboratory dish	PETRI DISH	nucleic acid	NUCLEOTIDE
circulation of		compound	
—blood	(*see* **circulation**)	—making wood fibres rigid	LIGNIN
—carbon by living things	CARBON CYCLE	—of	
—protoplasm	CYCLOSIS	similar molecules	
citric acid cycle	KREBS CYCLE	but different atoms	ISOLOGUE
classification	TAXONOMY	sugar etc in cells	NUCLEOTIDE
—based on chromosome		—with amino and acidic	
characteristics	CYTOTAXONOMY	carboxyl groups	AMINO-ACID

concept of living things only from germ-cells	GERM THEORY
condition	
—in which	
different gametes are present	ANISOGAMY
similar gametes are present	ISOGAMY
unlike gametes reproduce	ANISOGAMY
	HETEROGAMY
—where male and female parts mature at the same time	HOMOGAMY
conditions determined by characteristics of the soil	EDAPHIC FACTORS
conduction of food etc in plant	TRANSLOCATION
conidium	ARTHROSPORE
conjugation	ZYGOSIS
—of similar gametes	ISOGAMY
connective tissue	ADIPOSE TISSUE
—attaching embryo to placenta	UMBILICAL CORD
	UMBILICUS
muscle to bone, etc	TENDON
—supporting an organ	CAPSULE
constituent of cell walls	CELLULOSE
container for	
—nectar	NECTARY
—pollen	POLLEN SAC
—seeds	OVARY
containing several antibodies	POLYVALENT
contraction	
—in tubular organs	PERISTALSIS
—of nucleus	PYCNOSIS, PYKNOSIS
control of functions by electronic monitoring	BIOFEEDBACK
conversion of	
—atmospheric nitrogen	NITROGEN-FIXATION
—glucose to lactic acid	GLYCOLYSIS
—plant food by light	PHOTOSYNTHESIS
—soil compounds to nitrates	NITRIFICATION
keratin	CORNIFICATION
coral with many pores	MILLEPORE
corals etc	ACTINOZOA
corium	DERMIS
cork	PHELLEM
—cambium	PERIDERM, PHELLEGEN
cotyledon of embryo of grass	SCUTELLUM
cover of gill-slits	OPERCULUM
covering	
—layer	INTEGUMENT
—of seed coat	TEGMEN

cows, goats, sheep, etc	ARTIODACTYLA
crabs, lobsters, etc	DECAPODA
creation (alleged) from non-living matter	BIOPOIESIS
creeping stem	
—that roots	FLAGELLUM, RUNNER
	STOLON
—underground	SOBOLE
criteria connecting illness to cause	KOCH'S POSTULATES
crop ploughed into soil	GREEN MANURE
cross	
—1st filial generation	F1 GENERATION
	F1 HYBRID
—2nd filial generation	F2 GENERATION
	F2 HYBRID
—between unlike parents	HYBRID
—fertilisation	ALLOGAMY
—of hybrid offspring with parent	BACKCROSS
crossing of	
—related individuals	INBREEDING
—unrelated individuals	OUTBREEDING
Crustacea	AMPHIPODA, CLADOCERA
	COPEPODA, DECAPODA
	ISOPODA, PHYLLOPODA
crustacean's organ of propulsion	SWIMMERET
Cryptogamia	BRYOPHYTA
	PTERIDOPHYTA, THALLOPHYTA
cultivation in water	HYDROPONICS
curving	
—at touch	HAPTOTROPIC
	THIGMOTROPIC
—of organ	
downward	EPINASTY
upward	HYPONASTY
cutting	
—back to trunk	POLLARDING
—grafted on to another plant	SCION
—trees to ground level	COPPICING
cycle of biological changes	BIORHYTHM
	CIRCADIAN RHYTHM
cyesis	PREGNANCY
cyst	
—of tapeworm larva	HYDATID (CYST)
—produced by sporulation	SPOROCYST
cytoplasm	
—containing centriole	CENTROSOME
—forming nerve-cell	CELL-BODY
	PERICARYON
	PERIKARYON
danger from living things	BIOHAZARD
dark phase of daily rhythm	SKOTOPHILE
dead tree cells	CORK, PHELLEM
death of part of plant or animal	NECROSIS

decomposition/destruction/ dissolution	
—by	
acid	ACIDOLYSIS
electricity	ELECTROLYSIS
enzymes	FERMENTATION
	ZYMOLYSIS
heat	PYROLYSIS
water	HYDROLYSIS
—of	
bacteria	BACTERIOLYSIS
cells	CYTOLYSIS, LYSIS
proteins	PROTEOLYSIS
substance catalysed by enzymes	ENZYMOLYSIS
tissues	HISTOLYSIS
—after death	AUTOLYSIS
decrease in size of organ	ATROPHY, INVOLUTION
defensive protein produced in response to an antigen	ANTIBODY
deglutition	SWALLOWING
dependence on organic foodstuffs	HETEROTROPHISM
destruction	(see decomposition above)
dermis	CORIUM
detachable joint in tapeworm	PROGLOTTIS
detached bud of water plant	TURION
depression where ducts etc enter organ	HILUM
deutoplasm	YOLK
development	
—from different kinds of cells	HETEROBLASTY
—of	
different characteristics from one gene	PLEIOTROPY
	PLEIOTROPISM
group of organisms	PHYLOGENESIS
	PHILOGENY
individual organism	ONTOGENESIS
	ONTOGENY
ovum without fertilisation	PARTHENOGENESIS
—towards specialised functions	DIFFERENTIATION
device for cutting very thin slices	MICROTOME
diagram of	
—parts of flower	FLORAL DIAGRAM
—resemblances of individuals in group	DENDOGRAM
diatom cell	FRUSTULE
diatoms	BACILLARIOPHYTA
dicotyledon (old)	EXOGEN

Didelphia	MARSUPIALIA
	METATHERIA
difference in	
—arrangement of mutations in chromosomes	CIS-TRANS EFFECT
—colour, etc	VARIEGATION
differentiation	VARIATION
diffusion of particles through membrane	OSMOSIS
digestive	
—fluid	BILE
—juice	SUCCUS ENTERICUS
—system	(see separate entry)
dilated part of oesophagus or gut used as food store	CROP
dioecious	UNISEXUAL
diploid number of chromosomes	ZYGOTIC NUMBER
directional growth in plant	TROPISM
disc producing styles	STYLOPODIUM
diseases of plants	(see **plant diseases**)
displacement of island species by mainland species	SETON'S LAW
dissolution	(see decomposition above)
distributed throughout	SYSTEMIC
division of	
—algae	BACILLARIOPHYTA
	CHAROPHYTA, CHLOROPHYTA
	CHRYSOPHYTA, CRYPTOPHYTA
	EUGLENOPHYTA, PYRROPHYTA
—birds and reptiles	SAUROPSIDA
—body	(METAMERIC) SEGMENTATION
—cell producing	
diploid daughter-cells	KARYOKINESIS
	MITOSIS
haploid daughter-cells	MEIOSIS
	REDUCTION DIVISION
—extinct reptiles	THERAPSIDA
—mammals	THEROPSIDA
—plant kingdom	BRYOPHYTA
—primitive plants	THALLOPHYTA
dizygotic twins	FRATERNAL TWINS
DNA	
—bases	ADENINE, CYTOSINE
	GUANINE, THYMINE
—purines	ADENINE, GUANINE
—pyrimidines	CYTOSINE, THYMINE
dormancy during	
—summer	AESTIVATION
—winter	HIBERNATION
doubling of chromosomes with cell-division	ENDOMITOSIS
drifting animals and plants	PLANKTON
dry	
—fruit with hard shell	NUT
—one-seeded fruit	ACH(A)ENIUM, ACHENE

duct	
—carrying ovum from ovary to uterus	FALLOPIAN TUBE UTERINE TUBE
—from	
coelom to exterior	COELOMODUCT
liver to intestine	BILE DUCT
ductless gland	ENDOCRINE GLAND
due to common ancestry	PATRISTIC
duplicate of specimen	ISOTYPE
earliest stage of plant or animal	EMBRYO
early stage of embryo	BLASTULA GASTRULA
ecdysis	MOULTING
Echinodermata	ASTEROIDEA CRINOIDEA, ECHINOIDEA HOLOTHUROIDEA, OPHIUROIDEA
ecology of	
—community	SYNECOLOGY
—species	AUTECOLOGY
ecosystem	
—in terms of crops per unit area	TROPHIC STRUCTURE
—of animals with same food chain	TROPHIC LEVEL
effect of osmosis on cell	PLASMOLYSIS
egg	
—capsule	NIDAMENTUM, OVISAC
—of louse	NIT
—producing organ	OVARY
—production	OVULATION
—requiring dormant period	RESTING EGG WINTER EGG
—shell	AMPHIONT
—tube in insect	OVIAROLE
—white	ALBUMEN
eight-armed creatures	OCTOPODA
electricity in living things	BIOELECTRICITY
elephants	PROBOSCIDEA
embryo	
—during cleavage stage	MORULA
—in mammal	FOETUS
—tapeworm	HEXACANTH ONCHOSPHERE
embryonic reproductive tract	
—female	MULLERIAN DUCT
—male	WOLFFIAN DUCT
Embryophyta	METAPHYTA
end of	
—axis carrying flower	RECEPTACLE
—stamen	ANTHER
endocrine gland	DUCTLESS GLAND
endogamy	INBREEDING
enteric canal	ALIMENTARY CANAL, GUT
enzyme	(see separate entry)
epiphytes	AEROPHYTES, PSILOTALES

essential organic substance in food	VITAMIN
evolution	
—by	
natural selection	DARWINISM
inherited characteristics	LAMARCKISM LYSENKOISM
several forms	ADAPTIVE RADIATION
—of	
group	PHYLOGENY
individual	ONTOGENY
—producing greater differences	DIVERGENCE
—producing greater similarity	CONVERGENCE
evolutionary pedigree	PHYLOGENY
excessive cell-growth	HYPERPLASIA
exchange of food in symbiosis	TROPHOBIOSIS TROPHOLLAXIS
excreting	
—urea	UREOTELIC
—uric acid	URICOTELIC
excretory organ	KIDNEY
existence in two forms	DIMORPHISM
exogamy	OUTBREEDING
explanation of biological phenomena in	
—physical terms	MECHANISTIC THEORY
—terms of vital force	VITALISTIC THEORY
explantation	TISSUE CULTURE
expression describing construction of a flower	FLORAL FORMULA
extension of	
—axis of flower between carpels	CARPOPHORE
—receptacle bearing carpels	GYNOPHORE
—stamen receptacle	ANDROPHORE
exudation of water drops by plant	GUTTATION
eye	(see separate entry)
factor controlling acceptance of foreign cells	HISTOCOMPATIBILITY
falling off early	CADUCOUS
Fallopian tube	UTERINE TUBE
false aril	CARUNCLE
fatty tissue	ADIPOSE TISSUE
—in whales, etc	BLUBBER
—secretion	SEBUM
—substance from animal decomposition	ADIPOCERE
feather	(see separate entry)
feeding	
—by filtering with thread-like lashes	CILIARY FEEDING

—like	
an animal	HOLOZOIC
a plant	HOLOPHYTIC
—on	
dead matter	SAPROBIOTIC
	SAPROPHAGOUS, SAPROZOIC
other animals	CARNIVOROUS
plants	HERBIVOROUS
various foods	OMNIVOROUS
feeler(s)	PALP, PALPUS(PALPI)
female	PISTILLATE
—gamete	MACROGAMETE
	MEGAGAMETE, OOCYTE
produced from oocyte	OVUM
—organs of flower	CARPEL, GYNAECEUM
	GYN(O)ECIUM, PISTIL
—sex organ	
algae and fungi	OOGONIUM
animals	OVARY, UTERUS
moss, etc	ARCHEGONIUM
seaweed	CARPOGONIUM, OOGONIUM
ferment	ZYME
fermentation	ZYMOSIS
fermentor	ZYMOGEN
ferns	FILICALES
—horsetails, clubmosses	PTERIDOPHYTA
fertilisation	
—by	
pollen	POLLINATION
two male	
gametes	DOUBLE FERTILISATION
—of large egg by	
small gamete	OOGENY
fertilised egg	AMPHIONT, SEED, ZYGOTE
fertilising microspores	POLLEN
fibres in larynx	
producing sound	VOCAL C(H)ORDS
filament in	
—algae	TRICHOME
—fungi	HYPHA
filtering through serous membrane	DIALYSIS
finger	DIGIT
fire algae	PYRROPHYTA
first	
—abdominal section	PROPODEON
—segment of insect	PROTHORAX
—stage of cell-division	PROPHASE
fishes	(*see separate entry*)
five-fingered limb	PENTADACTYL LIMB
fixed in position (animals)	SESSILE
flap of	
—cartilage at base of tongue	EPIGLOTTIS
—membranous tissue	LOMA
flask-shaped fungal	
fruit-body	PERITHECIUM
flesh-eating animals	CARNIVORES

flora and fauna	BIOTA
flower	
—receptacle	TORUS
—stalk	PEDICEL
—whorl	COROLLA
flowering	
—only once	MONOCARPIC
—plants	ANGIOSPERMS
	DICOTYL(EDON)AE
GYMNOSPERMS, MONOCOTYL(EDON)AE	
PHANEROGAMAE, PHANEROGAMIA	
SPERMA(TO)PHYTA, SPERMOPHYTA	
—shoot	INFLORESCENCE
flowerless plants	CRYPTOGAMIA
fluid	
—filled spaces	VASCULAR SYSTEM
—from	
animal tissues	LYMPH
gland	SUCCUS
—in	
brain and spine	
cavities	CEREBROSPINAL FLUID
joints	SYNOVA, SYNOVIAL FLUID
—secreted from	
endocrine glands	HORMONE
glands in mouth	SALIVA
skin glands	PERSPIRATION
	SEBUM, SWEAT
flukes (trematodes), cestodes	
and turbellarians	PLATYHELMINTHES
foetal envelope	CHORION
fold	
—in peritoneum	EPIPLOON, OMENTUM
—of skin producing shell	
in molluscs	MANTLE
food material	
—of plants	STARCH
—stored in seeds	ENDOSPERM
foot of hind leg	PES
forcing of liquid through tissues	PERFUSION
foreign substance in body	ANTIGEN
forewing	TEGMEN
form derived from	
—adaptation	ECAD
—mutation	MUTANT
—variation	SPORT, VARIANT
formation of	
—egg	OOGENESIS
—fruit without fertilisation	PARTHENOCARPY
—more than one embryo	
from one ovum	POLYEMBRYONY
—polymorphs	GRANULOPOIESIS
—species	SPECIATION
formative plant tissue	MERISTEM
four-footed animals	TETRAPODA
fraternal twins	DIZYGOTIC TWINS

free from micro-organisms	ASEPTIC
frequency of manifestation of dominant gene	PENETRANCE
fresh-water algae	CHLAMYDOMONAS
fringe round mouth of moss capsule	PERISTOME
frogs and toads	ANURA, SALIENTIA
front of tapeworm's head	ROSTELLUM
fruit	(*see separate entry*)
—body of fungus	APOTHECIUM ASCOCARP, CLEISTOCARP PERITHECIUM
—flies	DROSOPHILA
—of	
Compositae	CYPSELA
grasses	CARYOPSIS
fruiting	
—after cross-fertilisation	ALLOCARPY
—only once	MONOCARPIC
functional unit of animal or plant	ORGAN
fungi	(*see separate entry*)
fungus in symbiotic relationship with	
—alga	LICHEN
—roots of higher plant	MYCOR(R)HIZA
fused head and thorax	CEPHALOTHORAX
fusion of	
—cytoplasm	PLASMOGAMY
—flowers	SYNANTHY
—gametes	AMPHIMIXIS
—parts	SYMPHYSIS
—petals	COROLLA TUBE
gamete	GERM-CELL
—capable of movement	PLANOGAMETE
—non-motile	APLANOGAMETE
gametophyte in ferns, mosses, etc	OOPHYTE
gap in skull	FONTANELLE
gene	
—combination not present in parents	RECOMBINATION
—controlling	
actions of operon	REGULATOR GENE
biological rhythms	CLOCK GENE
single action at many points	POLYGENE
—not included in chromosome	PLASMAGENE
—over-ridden by dominant gene	RECESSIVE
—producing particular characteristic to the exclusion of others	DOMINANT
—suppression	EPISTASIS
—terminating life of bacteria	SUICIDE GENE

—which	
can reproduce without chromosome reproduction	EPISOME
has undergone change	MUTANT
genealogical history of	
—group	PHYLOGENESIS PHYLOGENY
—individual	ONTOGENESIS ONTOGENY
generation of living from non-living	BIOPOIESIS
genetic	
—element	EPISOME
in bacterial cell	
—autonomous	PLASMID
or integrated	EPISOME
—make-up of individual or group	GENOTYPE
genital passage in females	VAGINA
genus	
—of	
arthropods	PERIPATUS
diatoms	NAVICULA
Diptera	DROSOPHILA
Foraminifera	GLOBIGERINA
Protozoa	TRYPANOSOMA
—which includes man	HOMO
germ	
—cell	GAMETE, OVUM, SPERM(ATOZOON)
—layer	ECTODERM, ENDODERM MESODERM
—tube of fungus spore	PROMYCELIUM
germination	ECESIS
gizzard in insect	PROVENTRICULUS
gland	(*see separate entry*)
—in head of insect	CORPORATA ALLATA
—on leaf excreting water	HYDATHODE
—secreting nectar	NECTARY
globular bacterium	COCCUS
glycoprotein	MUCROPROTEIN
gnawing animal	RODENT
—hare, rabbit	LAGOMORPHA
—rat, squirrel	RODENTIA
golden-brown algae	CHRYSOPHYTA
gradation of form, etc	CLINE
graft	
—from	
another individual	ISOGRAFT
same individual	AUTOGRAFT HOMOGRAFT
same species	HOMOGRAFT
—with different genetic makeup	ALLOGRAFT
grafting of bud to stock	BUDDING
granule moving freely in statocyst	OTOLITH, STATOLITH
grazing animal	ARTIODACTYLA RUMINANT

green	
—algae	CHLOROPHYTA
—pigment converting light	CHLOROPHYLL
gristle	CARTILAGE
group	
—adapted to particular	
environment	ECODEME, ECOTYPE
—of	
animal kingdom	METAZOA, PARAZOA
	PROTOZOA
Anthropoidea	CATARRHINI
	PLATYRRHINI
antigens in blood-cells	
of some monkeys	RH(ESUS) FACTOR
cells	
—controlling rhythm of	
heart, etc	PACEMAKER
—from division of	
ovum	BLASTOSPHERE
	BLASTULA
closely related organisms	DEME
ecotypes	ECOSPECIES
fish	TELEOSTOMI
flowers on one stalk	INFLORESCENCE
fungi	ASCOMYCETES
	BASIDIOMYCETES
genes controlling	
synthesis of enzymes	OPERON
joined stamens	SYNANDRIUM
organisms with same	
characteristics	PHENOTYPE
Protozoa	FORAMINIFERA
sporangia	SORUS, SYNANGIUM
spores formed by meiosis	TETRAD
vertebrate classes	CHOANATA
—sharing same habitat	COMMUNITY
	TOPODEME
—which can interbreed	GAMODEME
	SPECIES
—with same genetic make-up	GENOTYPE
growing	
—by external additions	EXOGENOUS
—close to the ground	EPIG(A)EAL
—from root	RADICAL
—in sunlight	HELIOPHYTE
or shade	HELIOSCIOPHYTE
—just below the soil	HEMICRYPTOPHYTE
—on	
acid soil	CALCIFUGE
another plant	EPIPHYTE
chalky soil	CALCICOLE
dead matter	SAPROGENIC
	SAPROGENOUS, SAPROPHYTE
dry ground	GLARIAL
gravel	GLAREOUS
ice	CRYOPHYTE

rocks	LITHOPHYTE
	RUPICOLINE, RUPICOLOUS
salty soil	SALSIGINOUS
silica	SILICICOLOUS
snow	CRYOPHYTE
stem	CAULICOLOUS
top of	
—ovary	EPIGYNOUS
—petal	EPIPETALOUS
—sepal	EPISEPALOUS
—pale for lack of light	ETIOLATION
—point or root	
or stem	APICAL MERISTEM
—together of stems	FASCIATION
—towards the	
apex	ACROPETAL
base	BASIPETAL
—underground	HYPOG(A)EAL
gut	ALIMENTARY CANAL
	ENTERIC CANAL
—between	
mouth and oesophagus	PHARYNX
pharynx and stomach	(O)ESOPHAGUS
—breathing animal	ENTEROPNEUST
Gymnophiona	APODA
Gymnospermae	CONIFERALES, CYCADALES
	GINKGOALES, GNETALES
—extinct	CORDIATALES
	CYCADOFILICALES
gynaecium and androecium	
united	GYNOSTEMIUM
hair(s)	
—like appendages on	
bacteria cells	PILI
—used for propulsion	CILIUM(CILIA)
	FLAGELLUM(FLAGELLA)
hallux	BIG TOE
halves of frustule	EPITHECA, HYPOTHECA
hand	MANUS
hanging inflorescence	CATKIN
hard	
—layer of skin	SCLERODERM
—tissue resulting from wound	CALLUS
having	
—ability to form antibodies	IMMUNOGENIC
—anthers	
in form of tube	SYNANTHEROUS
	SYNGENESIOUS
maturing	
—after carpels	PROTOGYNOUS
—at different time	
from stigma	DICHOGAMOUS
—at same time as carpel	HOMOGAMOUS
—before carpels	PROTANDROUS
—all teeth the same	HOMODONT
—backbone	VERTEBRATE

—body with
   three layers of cells   TRIPLOBLASTIC
   two layers of cells   DIPLOBLASTIC
—bushy habit of growth   DUMOSE, DUMOUS
—claws   UNGUAL
   UNGUICULATE(D)
—cloven hoofs   BISULCATE
—cotyledons above ground   EPIG(A)EAL
—different
   areas of distribution   ALLOPATRIC
   forms   PLE(I)OMORPHIC
   POLYMORPHIC
   genes   HETEROZYGOUS
   kinds of teeth   HETERODONT
   set of genes   ALLOGEN(E)IC
—diploid number   ZYGOTIC
—downy covering   PUBESCENT
   TOMENTOSE
—eight times the normal
   number of chromosomes   OCTAPLOID
—embryos which develop
   in eggs   OVIPAROUS
   internally   VIVIPAROUS
   —in eggs   OVOVIPAROUS
—equal numbers of petals
   and sepals   ISOSTEMONOUS
—even number of toes   ARTIODACTYL(IC)
   ARTIODACTYLATE
   ARTIODACTYLOUS
—exact multiple of haploid
   number   EUPLOID
—eyes on stalks   PODOPHTHALMOUS
—female and hermaphrodite
   flowers on
   same plant   GYNODIOECIOUS
   separate plants   GYNOMONDECIOUS
—flower(s)
   parts
   —below gynaeceum   HYPOGYNOUS
   —enclosing gynaeceum   EPIGYNOUS
   —round gynaeceum   PERIGYNOUS
   which
   —do not open   CLEISTOGAMIC
   CLEISTOGAMOUS
   —open   CHASMOGAMIC
   CHASMOGAMOUS
—four
   long, two short stamens   TETRADYNAMOUS
   times haploid number of
   chromosomes   TETRAPLOID
—fringe of hairs   CILIATE
—full quota of chromosomes   DIPLOID
—fused
   anthers   SYNANTHEROUS
   SYNGENESIOUS
   carpels   SYNCARPOUS

   digits   SYNDACTYL(OUS)
   petals   GAMOPETALOUS
   sepals   GAMOSEPALOUS
   stamens   SYNANDROUS
—hard
   dry stem   SCLEROCAULY
   skin   SCLERODERMIC
   SCLERODERMOUS
   stiff leaves   SCLEROPHYLLOUS
   SCLEROPHYLLY
—hoofs   UNGULATE
—identical genes   HOMOZYGOUS
—lobes pointing backward   RUNCINATE
—male and female organs on
   different flowers   DECLINY
   DIOECIOUS
   same plant   HERMAPHRODITE
   MONOECIOUS
—male and hermaphrodite
   flowers on
   same plant   ANDROMONOECIOUS
   separate plants   ANDRODIOECIOUS
—many
   cells   MULTICELLULAR
   nuclei   MULTINUCLEATE
—more than
   normal number of digits   POLYDACTYLOUS
   twice haploid number
   of chromosomes   POLYPLOID
—no
   coelom   ACOELOMATE
   flowers or sepals   ACHLAMYDEOUS
   skull, brain etc   ACRANIAL
   stalk   SESSILE
   stamens   ANANDROUS
—odd number of toes   PERISSODACTYL(IC)
   PERISSODACTYLATE
   PERISSODACTYLOUS
—one
   bundle of stamens   MONADELPHOUS
   cell   UNICELLULAR
   chromosome
   instead of two   MONOSOME
   cotyledon   MONOCOTYLEDENOUS
   kind of spore   ISOSPOROUS
   perianth whorl   HAPLOCHLAMYDEOUS
   HOMOCHLAMYDEOUS
   MONOCHLAMYDEOUS
—open flowers   CHASMOGAMIC
—paired chromosomes
   in nucleus   DIPLOID
—parts in threes   TRIMEROUS
—perianth with
   one whorl   HAPLOCHLAMYDEOUS
   HOMOCHLAMYDEOUS
   MONOCHLAMYDEOUS

two whorls	DI(PLO)CHLAMYDEOUS
—pistils but no stamens	PISTILLATE
—same	
areas of distribution	SYMPATRIC
genes	ISOGEN(E)IC
	SYNGEN(E)IC
—separate	
carpels	APOCARPOUS
male and female	
individuals	DIOECIOUS, UNISEXUAL
petals	POLYPETALOUS
sepals	POLYSEPALOUS
—several stamen groups	POLYADELPHOUS
—sharp points	APICULATE
—single	
eye in centre	CYCLOPIA
set of chromosomes	HAPLOID
—stalk attached near	
centre of leaf	PELTATE
—stigma	STIGMAFEROUS
—spores of different kinds	HETEROSPOROUS
—stamens and carpels	BI-SEXUAL
	HERMAPHRODITE
in separate flowers	UNISEXUAL
—stamens in	
two groups	DIDELPHOUS
two alternating	
whorls	OBDIPLOSTEMONOUS
—sucker both ends	AMPHISTOMOUS
—sucking proboscis	HAUSTELLATE
	SUCTORIAL
—three	
chromosomes instead of two	TRISOME
or more times haploid	
number	POLYPLOID
parts	TRIMEROUS
times haploid number	TRIPLOID
—tubular flowers	TUBERLIFLOROUS
—two	
carpels	DICARPELLARY
cotyledons	DICOTYLEDENOUS
equal flagella	ISOKONT
or more	
—arrangements of	
reproductive parts	HETEROSTYLOUS
—leaf types	HETEROPHYLLOUS
pairs of stamens	DIDYNAMOUS
perianth whorls	HETEROCHLAMYDEOUS
—unbalanced number of	
chromosomes	ANEUPLOID
—uncloven hoofs	SOLIDUNGULATE
—unlike gametes	ANISOGAMY
—unpaired chromosomes	HAPLOID
head of tapeworm	SCOLEX
heart	(see circulation)
heart-urchins	SPANTANGUS

hedgehogs, moles, shrews, etc	INSECTIVORA
helmet-shaped part	GALEA
helminth	WORM
Hepaticae	LIVERWORTS
heredity factor	GENE
hermaphrodite	BISEXUAL
hermaphroditism	GYNANDRYISM
	GYNANDRY
heterosis	HYBRID VIGOUR
hind toe	HALLUX
Hirudinea	LEECHES
histiocyte	MACROPHAGE
holding palm	
—downward and	
backward	PRONATION
—forward and upward	SUPINATION
hollow	
—appendages in starfish etc	PODIA
	TUBE-FEET
—ball of cells	BLASTULA
holotype	TYPE SPECIMEN
hominid	(see separate entry)
homoiothermic	WARM-BLOODED
hoofed animals	UNGULATA, UNGULATES
hormone	(see separate entry)
hornworts	ANTHEROCEROTAE
horse	(see separate entry)
horses, etc	EQUIDAE, EQUUS
	PERISSODACTYLA
horsetails	EQUISETALES
human biology	ANTHROPOBIOLOGY
hybrid	
—from offspring of first	
filial generation	F2
	SECOND FILIAL GENERATION
starting generation	F1
	FIRST FILIAL GENERATION
—vigour	HETEROSIS
hypha-bearing	
sporangia	SPORANGIOPHORE
hypothetical	
—hereditary particle	GEMMULE
—unit of living matter	BIOGEN
	BIOPHORE, MICELLA
	MICELLE, MONAD
identical twins	MONOZYGOTIC TWINS
	UNIOVULAR TWINS
immature	
—flower	BUD
—form of animal	LARVA
—ovum	OOCYTE
impermeable area in	
some cells	CASPARIAN STRIP
inability	
—of hybrids to inter-	
breed	HYBRID STERILITY

—to
   regulate body
      temperature   POIKILOTHERMY
      self-fertilise   SELF-INCOMPATIBILITY
inbreeding   ENDOGAMY, HOMOGAMY
incomplete zygote   MEROZYGOTE
incorporation by digestion   ASSIMILATION
increased
   —diameter due to cell
      division   SECONDARY GROWTH
   —number of parts by
      branching   CHORISIS
   —numbers of plankton   BLOOM
   —size
      due to cell division   PRIMARY GROWTH
      of organ etc to
      compensate for other
      loss   COMPENSATORY HYPERTROPHY
   —vigour as result of
      crossing   HETEROSIS
         HYBRID VIGOUR
increasing thickness of cell walls   APPOSITION
individual
   —clone   RAMET
   —giving tissue for transfer   DONOR
   —intermediate between male
      and female   INTERSEX
inflorescence
   —types   BOSTRYX, CAPITULUM, CATKIN
         CINCINNUS, CORYMB, CYME
         DICHASIUM, HELICOID CYME
         MONOCHASIUM, PANICLE, RACEME
         RHIPIDIUM, SPADIX, SPIKE, STROBILUS
         UMBEL
   —definite   CYMOSE
   —highly condensed   VERTICILLASTER
   —indefinite   RACEMOSE
inflow of water by osmosis   ENDOSMOSIS
Infusoria   CILIOPHORA
ingrowth from another cell   T(H)YLOSIS
inhabited part of Earth
   and atmosphere   BIOSPHERE
inhabiting deep water   ABYSSAL
inhibition of bacterial growth   BACTERIOSTASIS
inimical relationship
   between organisms   ANTIBIOSIS
inner
   —digit   POLLEX
   —layer of
      bark   BAST, PHLOEM
      fruit wall   ENDOCARP
   —part of cytoplasm   ENDOPLASM
insects   (see separate entry)
insect-eaters   INSECTIVORES
integument   TUNIC
interbreeding   SYNGAMY

internal
   —opening of nasal cavity   CHOANA
         INTERNAL NARE
   —secretion having specific effect   HORMONE
intestine   (see digestion)
intolerant of
   —high temperature   STENOTHERMOUS
   —variable osmotic
      pressure   STENOHALINE
involution   ATROPHY
jaws and nose of animal   MUZZLE
jellyfish
   —corals etc   CNIDARIA, COELENTERATA
   —in polyp stage   SCYPHISTOMA
   —stinging organ   CNIDA, NEMATOCYST
junction between plates
   in insect   SUTURE
karyokinesis   MITOSIS
kidney filtering unit   MALPIGHIAN BODY
         MALPIGHIAN CORPUSCLE
kingdoms
   —many-celled animals   METAZOA
   —micro-organisms without
      nucleus   PROCARYOTA
   —microscopic protozoa   PROTISTA
   —single-celled animals   PROTOZOA
Krebs cycle   CITRIC ACID CYCLE
lachrymal gland   TEAR GLAND
lacking
   —coelom   ACOELOMATE
   —reproductive organs   NEUTER
lamp shells   BRACHIOPODA
lampreys, hagfish, etc   CYCLOSTOMATA
lancelet   AMPHIOXUS
large
   —ecological community   BIOME
   —molecule   MACROMOLECULE
      containing ribose   RIBONUCLEIC ACID
         RNA
larva of
   —butterfly, moth   CATERPILLAR
   —coelenterates, etc   PLANULA
   —crustacean   NAUPLIUS, ZOAEA
   —fluke   CERCARIA, REDIA
   —fly   MAGGOT
   —lamprey   AMMOCOETE
   —sea-urchin etc   PLUTEUS
   —tapeworm   BLADDER WORM
         CYSTICERCUS
last
   —segment of insect's body   METATHORAX
   —stage of cell-division   TELOPHASE
layer
   —of
      cells
      —below epidermis   HYPODERMIS

—in embryo	GERM-LAYER	
—lining cavities and covering surfaces of body	EPITHELIUM	
cortex formed by phellogen	PHELLODERM	
epidermis	MALPIGHIAN LAYER	
food cells round spore-cells	TAPETUM	
wood in tree laid down in one year	ANNUAL RING	
	GROWTH RING	
—on epidermis of plant	CUTICLE	
—which forms cork	PHELLOGEN	
produces skin	DERMATOGEN	
leaf	*(see separate entry)*	
—like structure	BRACT	
—of corolla	PETAL	
—stalk	PETIOLE	
leafless flower stem	SCAPE	
leeches	HIRUDINEA	
lid of capsule or egg	OPERCULUM	
life		
—begets life	BIOGENESIS	
—cycle of flower	ANTHESIS	
light-production by living organisms	BIOLUMINESCENCE	
line		
—of fusion of carpels	SUTURE	
—separating areas of Australian and Oriental animals	WALLACE'S LINE	
lining of		
—abdominal cavity	PERITONEUM	
—blood-vessel	INTIMA	
—chest cavity	PLEURA	
—uterus	ENDOMETRIUM	
linking of nucleic acid strands	BASE PAIRING	
Linnaean system	BINOMIAL NOMENCLATURE	
lip of plant or insect	LABIUM	
liquid carrying plant nutrients	SAP	
little beak	ROSTELLUM	
liver secretion	BILE	
liverworts	HEPATICAE	
living		
—above ground	EPIG(A)EAL	
—in mountains	MONTICOLOUS	
mud	LIMICOLOUS	
rocks	RUPICOLINE, RUPICOLOUS	
soil	TERRICOLOUS	
tubes	TUBICOLOUS	
—on land and in water	AMPHIBIOUS	
sea floor	DEMERSAL	
—under stones	LAPIDICOLOUS	

—without free oxygen	ANAEROBIC
lizards	LACERTILIA
—and snakes	SQUAMATA
	(see also separate entry)
local remains of wider distribution	RELIC(T) DISTRIBUTION
	RELIC(T) FAUNA, RELIC(T) FLORA
long	
—cells with thickened walls	COLLENCHYMA
—pod	SILIQUA
loss of	
—nitrogen from soil	DENITRIFICATION
—water through leaves, etc	TRANSPIRATION
lower	
—jaw of animal	MANDIBLE
—part of body	PERIN(A)EUM
—petals in orchid	LABELLUM
pea-flower	KEEL
lymph	*(see circulation)*
lymphoid tissue in pharynx	ADENOIDS, TONSILS
macrophage	HISTIOCYTE
main	
—habitat	METROPOLIS
—lymph vessel	THORACIC DUCT
—vertical root	TAP ROOT
maintenance of constant internal enviroment	HOMEOSTASIS
male	
—cell producing spermatozoa	SPERMATOCYTE
—component of flower	ANDROECIUM
—gamete	MICROGAMETE
	SPERM(MATOZOID)
	SPERMATOZOON
—reproductive organ	PENIS, TESTIS
—sex organ of algae etc	ANTHERIDIUM
flower	ANTHER, STAMEN
seaweed	SPERMATIUM
Mammalia	ARTIODACTYLA, CARNIVORA
	CETACEA, CH(E)IROPTERA
	EUTHERIA, MARSUPIALIA
	MONOTREMATA, PLACENTALIA
	THEROPSIDA
mammal-like reptiles	THEROPSIDA
mammary gland in animals	UDDER
manatees, sea-cows, etc	SIRENIA
mantis-shrimps	STOMATOPODA
manufacture of food from carbon dioxide and sunlight	PHOTOSYNTHESIS
marine	
—animals	ENTEROPNEUSTA
	HEMICHORDATA
with shells of lime	FORAMINIFERA

—burrowing worms	GEPHYREA	Metatheria	DIDELPHIA, MARSUPIALIA
—Protozoa with shells of silica	RADIOLARIA	micro-organism	GERM, MICROBE
mark on		—bacteria	SCHIZOMYCETES
—petal guiding insects to		diverse group	EUBACTERIA
nectaries	HONEY GUIDE	globular	COCCUS
—seed coat showing former		gram-positive	ACTINOMYCETE
attachment	HILUM	in soil	DENITRIFYING BACTERIA
marsupials	DIDELPHIA	ovoid	CLOSTRIDIUM
	METATHERIA	rod-shaped	BACILLUS
mass of			MYXOBACTERIUM
—amoeboid protoplasm	PLASMODIUM		RICKETTSIA, SHIGELLA
—hyphae in fungus	MYCELIUM	spindle-shaped	CLOSTRIDIUM
—pollen	POLLINIUM	spiral	SPIRILLUM, SPIROCHAETE
—tissue in			VIBRIO
one membrane	SYNCYTIUM	twisted chains	STREPTOCOCCI
ovule	NUCELLUS	—causing	
—twigs produced in		disease	PATHOGEN
response to		respiratory and	
fungal attack	WITCHES' BROOM	intestinal disease	ECHO VIRUS
maternal milk produced		—chemical pathogen which	
after childbirth	COLOSTRUM	multiplies in cells	VIRUS
mature insect	IMAGO	—converting	
maximum height of plant	DEFINITE GROWTH	ammonium to nitrites	NITROBACTERIA
meat-eating animal	CARNIVORE	carbohydrates to	
meatus	PASSAGE	lactic acid	LACTOBACILLUS
mechanism of		copper sulphide to	
evolution	NATURAL SELECTION	sulphate	
meiosis	REDUCTION DIVISION		THIOBACILLUS CUPRO-OXIDANS
membrane(s)	TUNIC	—floating in air	AEROPLANKTON
—between chest and abdomen	DIAPHRAGM	—like yeast	TORULA
—covering plant		—mature virus	VIRION
cells	PLASMA MEMBRANE	—not requiring oxygen	ANAEROBE
	PLASMALEMMA	—requiring oxygen	AEROBE
—enclosing embryo	AMNION	—unclassified	MYCOPLASMAS
—in egg	PUTAMEN	—virus	
—lining		cancer-forming	PAPOVAVIRUS
abdominal cavity	PERITONEUM	causing disease	PARVOVIRUS
chest cavity	PLEURA	outer shell	CAPSID
inside of body-wall	PARIETAL	parasitic on bacteria	PHAGE
tendons	SYNOVIAL MEMBRANE	—viruses and	
tubular cavity	MUCOUS MEMBRANE	rickettsias	MICROTATOBISTES
—mucous	MUCOSA(E)	microscopic organism	GERM, MICROBE
—nourishing foetus	PLACENTA		MICRO-ORGANISM
—round ovum	CHORION	middle	
	VITELLINE MEMBRANE	—layer of fruit wall	MESOCARP
	ZONA PELLUCIDA	—segment of thorax of insect	MESOTHORAX
metabolic regulator		mildew	MOULD
produced by		milk	
endocrine gland	HORMONE	—production	LACTATION
metabolism	METASTASIS	—secreting	
—of		animal	MAMMAL
complex substances		gland	MAMMARY GLAND
from simpler ones	ANABOLISM	milky fluid exuded by	
decomposition	CATABOLISM	cut surface of some plants	LATEX
	KATABOLISM	millipedes, etc	DIPLOPODA
Metaphyta	EMBRYOPHYTA	mitochondria	CHONDRIOSOMES

mitosis	KARYOKINESIS
mode of evolution	NATURAL SELECTION
	SEXUAL SELECTION
modified	
—hind-wing of fly	HALTERE
—inflorescence	TENDRIL
—leaf	BRACT
—wing(s) of beetle	ELYTRUM(ELYTRA)
moist lining membrane	MUCOUS MEMBRANE
molecule containing genetic	
code	NUCLEIC ACID
Mollusca	AMPHINEURA, CEPHALOPODA
	GASTROPODA
	LAMELLIBRANCHI(AT)A
	SCAPHOPODA, SIPHONOPODA
—with lungs	PULMONATA
monochlamydeous	HAPLOCHLAMYDEOUS
monozygotic twins	IDENTICAL TWINS
	UNIOVULAR TWINS
monthly cycle of ovum	
reproduction	MENSTRUAL CYCLE
mosses	MUSCI
mould	MILDEW
moulting	ECDYSIS
mouth-part	LABRUM, LABIUM
—of insect	MANDIBLE, MAXILLA
movement	
—curving	
downward	EPINASTY
upward	HYPONASTY
—in response to stimuli	(*see* response *below*)
—of population	MIGRATION
moving cell in blood of	
invertebrates	AMOEBOCYTE
mucroprotein	GLYCOPROTEIN
multicelled animals	METAZOA
multinucleate cell	SYNCYTIUM
Musci	MOSSES
muscle	(*see separate entry*)
mushroom	(*see* **fungus**)
mussels etc	MOLLUSCA
mutated gene	MUTANT
mutation	SPORT
Mycophyta	FUNGI
Myriapoda	CHILOPODA, DIPLOPODA
naked cell	MYXAMOEBA
name	
—which is the same	
in generic and	
specific forms	TAUTONYM
—without description	NOMEN NUDUM
naming system	BINOMIAL NOMENCLATURE
	LINNAEAN SYSTEM
narrow-mouthed	ANGIOSTOM(AT)OUS
navel	UMBILICUS
—string	UMBILICAL CORD

nematode	EELWORM, HOOKWORM
nerve	(*see separate entry*)
nest-building	NIDULATION
newts, salamanders	URODELA
non-cellular covering of	
animal or plant	CUTICLE
non-motile	
—gamete	APLANOGAMETE
—spore	APLANOSPORE
non-parasitic	
—animal living on another	EPIZOITE
—plant living on another	EPIPHYTE
nostrils	NARES
not	
—affected by environment	BIOSTABLE
—caused by genes	EXOGENETIC
—divided into cells	ACELLULAR
—splitting spontaneously	INDEHISCENT
nucleic acid	
—and protein compound	
in cell	NUCLEOPROTEIN
—containing ribose	RIBONUCLEIC ACID
	RNA
—deoxyribose	DEOXYRIBONUCLEIC ACID
	DNA
nucleolus	PLASMOSOME
nutritive tissue round	
embryo in plants	ENDOSPERM
obtaining energy	
—by	
chemical reactions	CHEMOTROPHIC
photosynthesis	PHOTOTROPHIC
—from	
external sources	HETEROTROPHIC
internal sources	AUTOTROPHIC
light	PHOTOTROPHIC
octopuses, squids, etc	CEPHALOPODA
	SIPHONOPODA
offspring of same parents	SIBLINGS, SIBS
one of two strands into	
which chromosome splits	CHROMATID
opening	
—in skull for spinal column	FORAMEN
—into pharynx	GLOTTIS
—to discharge seeds	DEHISCENT
organ	
—acting as kidney in	
invertebrates, etc	NEPHRIDIUM
—adapted for stimuli	RECEPTOR
—containing spores	
in mosses, etc	CAPSULE
—linking embryo to uterus	PLACENTA
—of	
balance in Crustacea etc	OTOCYST
hearing	EAR
sight	EYE, STATOCYST

smell	NOSE	virus	CAPSID
	OLFACTORY ORGAN	—covering of seed	TESTA
—producing		—envelope round embryo	CHORION
lymphocytes	SPLEEN	—layer of	CORTEX
secretions	GLAND	cells	EPIDERMIS
sex-cells	GONAD	cytoplasm	ECTOPLASM
silk	SPINNERET	flower	PERIANTH
organ(s) of abdomen	VISCUS(VISCERA)	fruit wall	EPICARP, EXOCARP
organic		meristem	CAMBIUM
—compound		ovule	PRIMINE
from distillation of alcohol and acid	ESTER	plant	PERIDERM
which hydrolyses into		root	EXODERM(IS)
amino acids	PROTEIN	tree	BARK
—material spread over soil	MULCH	wall of spore	EXOSPORE
—secretion of plant or insect	RESIN	xylem	SAPWOOD
organism		—part of	
—airborne	AEROPLANKTON	flower	CALYX
—bearing altered gene(s)	MUTANT	fruit	PERICARP
—in diploid stage	DIPLONT	limb of crustacean	EXOPOD(ITE)
—living		—wall of body	SOMATOPLEURE
in		outgrowth on	
—dirty water	SAPROBE	—fruit	ALA
—sea		—seeds	CARUNCLE, STROPHIOLE
floating	PLANKTON, SESTON	ovary	
swimming	NEKTON	—and stigma	CARPEL
on		—of plant (old)	GERM(EN), GERMIN
—sea-bottom	BENTHOS	—stigma and style	GYNAECEUM
—the			GYNOECIUM, PISTIL
inside of		ovum	GERM-CELL
another	ENDOPARASITE	paired chromosomes in meiosis	TETRAD
outside of another	ECTOPARASITE	pairing of parental	
—made of cells which can		chromosomes	SYNAPSIS, SYNDESIS
germinate	SPORIDESM	pancreas	SWEETBREAD
—which		parachute of wind-borne seed	PAPPUS
lives in symbiosis	SYMBIONT	parasite on	
occurs in different		—living organism	OBLIGATE PARASITE
forms	POLYMORPH	—living or dead	
seeks		host	FACULTATIVE PARASITE
—light	PHOTOPHIL(E)	parasitic	BIOGENOUS
—shade	SKOTOPHIL(E)	—on insects	ENTOMOGENOUS
tolerates heat and cold	EURYTHERM	—plant genus	VISCUM
—with		—Protozoa	SPOROZOA
chromosomes from two		part of	
different species	ALLOPOLYPLOID	—animal nearest to head	ANTERIOR
eight tentacles	ALCYONARIA	—animal's alimentary canal	GIZZARD
two or more genetically		—bird's stomach	PROVENTRICULUS
different tissues	CHIM(A)ERA	—body between chest	
orientation in response		and pelvis	ABDOMEN
to gravity	GEOTROPISM	—calyx	SEPAL
origin of parts of organisms	MORPHOGENESIS	—capsule after dehiscence	VALVE
	MORPHOGENY	—cell nucleus easily	
outbreeding	EXOGAMY	stained	CHROMATIN
outer			GOLGI BODY
—coat of		—embryonic digestive	
fruit body in fungi	PERIDIUM	system	STOMATADAEUM
seed	EPISPERM		STOMATOD(A)EUM

—egg undergoing division	BLASTODERM
—flower	BRACT, CARPEL, OVULE
	PETAL, RECEPTACLE, SEPAL
	STAMEN, STIGMA, STYLE
farthest from axis	ANTERIOR
—kidney	BOWMAN'S CAPSULE
—ovary bearing ovules	PLACENTA
—parasite attached to host	HAUSTORIUM
—perianth	TEPAL
—plant	
carrying	
—leaves, etc	STEM
—reproductive organs	RECEPTACLE
capable of growing into	
new individual	PROPAGULE
harbouring mites, etc	DOMATIUM
where differentiation occurs	HISTOGEN
—respiratory system	
in birds	AIR SAC
—seed which turns	
into root	RADICLE
—sperm head	ACROSOME
—style receiving pollen	STIGMA
partial sterilisation	PASTEURISATION
particle in cell	RIBOSOME
partition(s)	REPLUM(REPLA)
	SEPTUM(SEPTA)
passive stage between	
larva and adult	CHRYSALIS, PUPA
pathogenic agent requiring	
host cell for multiplication	VIRUS
pattern of	
—leaves in bud	VERNATION
—veins	VENATION
pertaining to the	
—body	SOMATIC
—effect of	
psychological factors	
on physiology	PSYCHOSOMATIC
period of pregnancy	GESTATION PERIOD
petals of flower	COROLLA
phellegen	CORK CAMBIUM
phellem	CORK
phosphorescent tunicates	PYROSOMA
photosynthetic pigment	CHLOROPHYLL
phylum	
—of	
animals	ANNELIDA, ARTHROPODA
	MOLLUSCA, VERTEBRATA
—with primitive spinal	
—column	CRANIATA
	(PROTO)CHORDATA
	VERTEBRATA
aquatic animals	CNIDARIA
	COELENTERATA
	ECHINODERMATA

physiological race	BIOTYPE
pincer(s)	CHELA(E)
pit of stomach	EPIGASTRIUM
pith	MEDULLA
placental mammals	EUTHERIA
plankton	
—animals	ZOOPLANKTON
—plants	PHYTOPLANKTON
plant	
—adapted to its environment	ECAD
—bud	GEMMA
—community over	
large area	FORMATION
—disease	(see separate entry)
—growing where not wanted	WEED
—hormone	AUXIN, PHYTAMIN
—living on dead matter	SAPROPHYTE
—of	
pea family	LEGUME
Gramineae family	CEREAL
—producing	
gametes	GAMETOPHYTE
zygospores	ZYGOPHYTE
—receiving graft	STOCK
—tissue giving	
mechanical support	SCLERENCHYMA
—which	
has adapted to its environment	ECAD
is tolerant of dry conditions	CACTUS
	SUCCULENT
reproduces by fission	SCHIZOPHYTE
stores water in	
its tissues	SUCCULENT
trails along the ground	PROCUMBENT
—with	
buds	
—above ground	PHANEROPHYTE
—below ground	CRYPTOPHYTE
diploid nucleus	DIPLONT
long life	PERENNIAL
net-veined leaves (old)	DICTYOGEN
one-year life-cycle	ANNUAL
radiating leaves	ROSETTE PLANT
recurring life-cycle	PERENNIAL
seeds not in ovary	GYMNOSPERM
stem, leaf and root	CORMOPHYTE
two-year life-cycle	BIENNIAL
—without chlorophyll	FUNGUS
plants	(see separate entry)
plastid storing oil	ELAIOPLAST
plate on insect	SCUTE, SCUT(ELL)UM
Platyhelminthes	CESTODA, FLUKES
	(TREMATODA) TURBELLARIA
podia	TUBE FEET
poikilothermic	COLD-BLOODED
point from which leaves develop	NODE

pointed outgrowth from epidermis	PRICKLE, THORN
poisonous to cells	CYTOTOXIC
pollen	
—brush in bees	SCOPA
—producing organ	STAMEN
pollex	THUMB
pollination by	
—birds	ORNITHOPHILY
—insects	ENTOMOPHILY
—pollen from same plant	SELF-POLLINATION
—snails	MALACOPHILY
—water	HYDROPHILY
—wind action	ANEMOPHILY
polyploid with all chromosomes from same species	AUTOPOLYPLOID
polysaccharide in food reserve in algae	CHRYSOLAMINARIN LEUCOSIN
Polyzoa	ECTOPROCTA
population of	
—animals	FAUNA
—plants	FLORA
pore(s)	SPIRACLE, STIGMA
—in plants	STOM(AT)A
—large	OSCULUM
—small	OSTIUM
pouch	
—containing testes	SCROTUM
—of marsupial	MARSUPIUM
pregnancy	CYESIS
prehensile claw(s)	CHELA(E)
premature flowering and seeding	BOLTING
preparation of micro-organisms used to stimulate immunity	VACCINE
pressure of sap, etc on cell walls	TURGOR
primitive	
—seed plants	CYCADALES
—spinal column	NOTOCHORD
—stele	PROTOSTELE
produced by	
—external stimuli	PARATONIC
—insertion of genes from one species to another	TRANSGENIC
producing	
—cells which form yolk	MEROISIC
—either male or female gametes	UNISEXUAL
—leaves	
after flowers	HISTERANTHOUS
and flowers together	SYNANTHOUS
—ova	OVULATION
—two offspring at a time	DITOKOUS

—young	
born alive	VIVIPAROUS
in eggs	OVIPAROUS
—hatched internally	OVOVIVIPAROUS
product of fusion of gametes	ZYGOTE
production of	
—chemicals by organisms	BIOSYNTHESIS
—enzymes by chemicals added to cell	INDUCTION
—fruit without fertilisation	PARTHENOCARPY
—milk	LACTATION
—new tissues by stimulus	INDUCTION
—small flowers that fail to open	CL(E)ISTOGAMY
—sound by insects	STRIDULATION
—spores by constricting stalk	ABSTRICTION
programmed cell death	APOPTOSIS
projection(s)	
—from root	ROOT-HAIR, ROOT-NODULE
—in intestine	VILLUS, (VILLI)
—of dermis	DERMAL PAPILLA(E)
—on	
body of fish	FIN
leaf	AURICLE
tongue containing taste-buds	TONGUE PAPILLA(E)
propagule	CUTTING, GEMMA SEED, SPORE
protective covering	
—of	
larvae etc	COCOON
plant embryo	SEED COAT, TESTA
—on growing point of root	ROOT-CAP
protein	(see separate entry)
—acting as catalyst	ENZYME
—and lipid in plant cell membrane	LIPOPROTEIN
—produced in the body to counter antigen	ANTIBODY
protoplasm	BIOPLASM
—from cell-division in fungi, etc	COENOCYTE
—in cell nucleus	CARYOPLASM KARYOPLASM
—of body cells	SOMATOPLASM
—outside nucleus of cell	CYTODE CYTOPLASM
—suggested as responsible for heredity	GERM-PLASM
—unit	ENERGID
Protozoa	FLAGELLATA MASTIGOPHORA RHIZOPODA, SARCODINA

Pteridophyta
—clubmosses   LYCOPODIALES
—epiphytes   PSILOTALES
—ferns   FILICALES
—horsetails   EQUISITALES
pupa   CHRYSALIS
pure culture   AXENIC
quantity of living material   BIOMASS
                               STANDING CROP
rabbits and hares   LAGOMORPHA
rasping organ in
  molluscs   ODONTOPHORE, RADULA
ratio of
  carbon dioxide
    expired to oxygen
    inspired   RESPIRATORY QUOTIENT
  male to female   SEX RATIO
rats, mice, squirrels, etc   RODENTIA
Raunkiaer's Life Forms
—woody plant with
    high buds   PHANEROPHYTE
    medium tree   MESOPHANEROPHYTE
    shrub   NANOPHANEROPHYTE
    small tree   MICROPHANEROPHYTE
    tall tree   MEGAPHANEROPHYTE
—woody plant with
    low buds   CHAMAEOPHYTE
—herb
    surviving winter as seed   THEROPHYTE
    with buds
      —at soil level   HEMICRYPTOPHYTE
      —below soil   GEOPHYTE
      —in
        mud   HELOPHYTE
        water   HYDROPHYTE
rear
—section of thorax of insect   METATHORAX
—segment of
    abdomen   TELSON
    arthropod   ABDOMEN
receptacle
—of flower   THALAMUS
—in fungus   PYCNIDIUM
receptor for taste   TASTE-BUD
recess   SINUS
recombination of genes
  on same chromosome   CROSSING OVER
region of active cells
  forming new tissue CAMBIUM, MERISTEM
regrowth of missing part   REGENERATION
—from remaining tissue   MORPHALLAXIS
relationship
—between sex and inherited
    characteristics   SEX LINKAGE
—of mutual benefit to
    organisms living together SYMBIOSIS

—where one organism is
    dependent upon another   PARASITISM
remains of organism
  found in rocks   FOSSIL
                               (*see* **archaeology**)
repeated splitting
  after fertilisation   CLEAVAGE
                               SEGMENTATION
reproduction
—by
    budding   BLASTOGENESIS
    fission   SCHIZOGENESIS
    grafting bud   BUDDING
    inserting part cut from
      one plant into
    —another   GRAFTING
    —soil   CUTTING
  part taken from parent
    plant   VEGETATIVE REPRODUCTION
  pegging down
    —growing stem   LAYERING
    —leaf   LEAF CUTTING
  splitting large plant   FRAGMENTATION
  transfer of pollen   CROSS-POLLINATION
  transmission of
    vibrations   PERIGENESIS
—from small part of ovum   MEROGONY
—in pre-adult form   PAEDOGENESIS
—of
    exact copies   CLONING, REPLICATION
    living young   VIVIPARITY
    —in plants   VIVIPARY
—without fertilisation   AGAMOSPERMY
                               APOMIXIS
                  ASEXUAL REPRODUCTION
                         PARTHENOGENESIS
reproductive
—asexual body   SPORE
—cell   GAMETE, GERM CELL
—cycle   OESTROUS CYCLE
—organ
  animal
    —female   OVARY, UTERUS, WOMB
    —male   PENIS, TESTES
  flowering plant
    —female   CARPEL, OVARY, STIGMA
    —male   ANTHER, STAMEN
  red algae
    —female   CARPOGONIUM
—sexual body   OVULE, OVUM
                      POLLEN, SPERM
—unit of Angiosperm   FLOWER
reptiles   REPTILIA
—crocodiles   CROCODILIA
—lizards   LACERTILIA
  and snakes   SQUAMATA

—snakes	ANGUIFAUNA, OPHIDIA
—tortoises and turtles	CHELONIA
—tuatara	RHYNCOCEPHALIA
respiration of	
—free oxygen	AEROBIC RESPIRATION
—plants in light	PHOTORESPIRATION
respiratory	
—organ in	
fish etc	GILL
mammals	LUNG
—root of plants growing	
in swamps	PNEUMATOPHORE
—tissue	ARENCHYMA
response to	
—alternation of day	
and night	NYCTINASTY
—chemical stimulus	CHEMOTAXIS
	TROPHOTROPISM
—directional stimulus	TAXIS
—food stimulus	TROPHOTAXIS
—general temperature	
change	THERMONASTY
—gravity	GEOTAXIS
	PLAGIOGEOTROPISM
at right angles	IAGEOTROPISM
—heat	THERMONASTY
—light	PHOTONASTY
	PHOTOTAXIS
—local contact	HAPTOTROPISM
—mechanical	
stimulus	THIGMORPHOGENESIS
—night	NYCTINASTY
	NYCTITROPISM
—non-directional light	PHOTONASTY
—shock	SEISMONASTY
—stimulus	AROUSAL, KINESIS
	TAXIS, (THIGMO)TROPISM
independent of	
direction	NASTIC MOVEMENT
	NASTY
—sunlight	HELIOTAXIS, HELIOTROPISM
resting stage of cell	INTERPHASE
retaining	
—larval features	
into adult stage	NEOTEINIA, NEOTENY
—leaves all year round	EVERGREEN
reversion to characteristics	
of ancestral type	ATAVISM
ridge on ovule	RAPHE
ring of	
—petals	PERIANTH
—similar parts of plant	WHORL
ripened ovary with seeds	FRUIT
ripening of male and	
female flowers at	
different times	DICHOGAMY

rise in respiration rate	CLIMACTERIC
RNA bases	ADENINE, CYTOSINE
	GUANINE, URACIL
rod-shaped	
—bacterium	BACILLUS
—body in cell producing	
spindle	CENTRIOLE
roof of mouth	PALATE, URANISCUS
root	RADICAL
—above ground	AERIAL ROOT
—as food store	TAP-ROOT
—from base of stem	SEMINAL ROOT
—like bulb	CORM
—of	
embryo	RADICLE
fungus	RHIZOMORPH
moss etc,	RHIZOID
—penetrating deep	TAP-ROOT
—small	RADICLE
—underground	
bud	BULB
stem	RHIZOME
—rooting at nodes	STOLON
—swollen	TUBER
—which pulls bulb into	
ground	CONTRACTILE ROOT
rudimentary	
—legs of caterpillar	PROLEGS
—organism	GERM
rule governing origin of	
living things from	
similar parents	PRINCIPLE OF BIOGENESIS
runner	SARMENTUM
rust fungi	URIDINALES
sac	
—for	
bile	GALL BLADDER
urine	BLADDER
—of secreting cells	
in gland duct	ALVEOLUS
saline solution used to sustain	
biological specimens	RINGER'S FLUID
scale(s)	SQUAMA(E), SQUAME
—chaffy	RAMENTUM
—on bird's foot	SCUTELLUM
scent organ on butterfly wing	PLUMULE
scientific naming	
of species	BINOMIAL NOMENCLATURE
	LINNAEAN SYSTEM
	TRINOMIAL SYSTEM
sea	
—anemones etc	ANTHOZOA (ACTINOZOA)
—butterflies	PTEROPODA
—gooseberries, etc	CTENOPHORA
—mats	BRYOZOA, ECTOPROCTA
	POLYZOA

—spiders	PYCNOGONIDA, PYKNOGONIDA
—squirts	TUNICATA, UROCHORDATA
—urchins, starfish, etc	ECHINODERMATA
—weed	(*see separate entry*)
seals, walruses, etc	PINNIPEDIA
seasonal variant	FORM
second stomach in bird	GIZZARD
secondary layer formed by phellogen	PHELLODERM
secreted fluid fed by pigeons to young	CROPMILK, PIGEON'S MILK
secretion of	
—endocrine gland	HORMONE
—gland	SUCCUS
—liver	BILE
—pancreas	PANCREATIC JUICE, PANCREATIN
—sebaceous gland	SEBUM
secretory organ	GLAND
section of DNA	
—between exons	INTRON
—controlling	
protein synthesis	EXON
structures in embryo	HOMEOBOX
sedentary (animals)	SESSILE
seed	SPERM
—coat	TESTA
—covering in sedge	PERIGONE
—leaf	COTYLEDON
—plant	
with ovary	ANGIOSPERM
without ovary	GYMNOSPERM
segmentation	MEROGENESIS
self	
—amputation	AUTOTOMY
—fertilisation in plants	AUTOGAMY
—pollination within unopened flower	CL(E)ISTOGAMY
sense organ	RECEPTOR
sensory	
—appendage	
at rear end of insect	CERCUS
of insects etc	ANTENNA, ANTENNULE
—hair of thread cell	CNIDOCIL
—system	SENSORIUM
sepals collectively	CALYX
sequence of	
—amino-acids and nucleotides	GENETIC CODE
—nucleotides determining amino-acid	CODON
sex	
—chromatin	BARR BODY
—chromosome	X, Y
sexual	
—impulse	OESTRUM, OESTRUS

—reproduction	AMPHIMIXIS
sharing of chromosomes	SEGREGATION
sharp-pointed	ACEROSE
sheath round	
—central cylinder of plant	ENDODERMIS
—grass	
plumule	COLEOPTILE
radicle	COLEORHIZA
shedding	
—leaves	ABSCISSION, DECIDUOUS
—outer skin	ECDYSIS
shell of	
—crabs, etc	CARAPACE
—insect's egg	CHORION
—slug	LIMACEL
ship-worm (a mollusc)	TEREDO
shoot	TENDRON
—from	
base of cut-back stem	TILLER
below ground	OFFSET, STOLON, SUCKER
—grafted on to another plant	SCION
—in embryo	PLUMULE
—pegged down to propagate	LAYER
showing recent origin from common stock	CLADISTIC
shrimps, etc	BRANCHIOPODA, CRUSTACEA
shrinkage of cell from osmosis	PLASMOLYSIS
Siamese twins	PARABIOTIC TWINS
side	
—petal (pea)	ALA
—sepal (milkwort)	ALA
—shoot of grasses	TILLER
—wall of thorax	PLEURON
single	
—breeding group	SPECIES
—celled	
animals	AMOEBA, PROTOZOA
fungi	YEASTS
micro-organism	BACTERIUM
organisms	CILIATA, CILIOPHORA, PROTISTA, SUCTORIA
plants	ALGAE, BACILLARIOPHYTA
skeleton	
—inside body	ENDOSKELETON
—outside body	EXOSKELETON
—small marine animals	CORAL
skin	CUTIS
—cell producing melanin	MELANOCYTE
—dead skin round nail	CUTICLE
—outer skin	CUTICLE
—pattern	DERMATOGLYPHIC
—true skin	DERM(A), DERMIS
slime moulds	ACRASIALES

slipper-animalcule	PARAMECIUM
slow-moving animals	TARDIGRADA
small	
—bract	BRACTEOLE
—bulb	BULBIL
—energy-producing body	
(bodies) in cytoplasm	MITOCHONDRION
	(MITOCHONDRIA)
—flower	FLORET
—fungus	MOULD
—gill-slit in fish	SPIRACLE
—particle in cytoplasm	MICROSOME
—portion of protoplasm	BIOPLAST
—sac	FOLLICLE
—scale(s)	SQUAMELLA(E)
—spore	SPORULE
smallest group in	
classification of plants	FORM
snakes	(see separate entry)
social hierarchy	PECKING ORDER
soft	
—corals, etc	ALCYONARIA
—plant tissue	PARENCHYMA
at centre	PITH
soil surrounding roots	RHIZOSPHERE
sound	
—producing organ in birds	SYRINX
—production in	
grasshoppers, etc	STRIDULATION
space between	
—lobes	SINUS
—viscera and	
body-wall	COELOM(E)
	PERIVISCERAL CAVITY
species that	
—can form fertile hybrids	COENSPECIES
—developed in isolation	VICAR
specimen used to	
describe new species	HOLOTYPE
	TYPE SPECIMEN
sperm	GERM-CELL
—duct	VAS DEFERENS
	VAS EFFERENS
—storing organ in	
insect	SPERMA(TO)THECA
spermatid	SPERMATOBLAST
spherical bacterium	COCCUS
spiders, etc	ARACHNIDAE
spindle-attachment	CENTROMERE
spinning organ	SPINNERET
sponges	PARAZOA, PORIFERA
spongy	
—animal tissue	PARENCHYMA
—tissue in skull	DIPLOE
spontaneous generation	ABIOGENESIS
	PARTHENOGENESIS

spore	
—bearing structure	SPOROPHORE
—case	SPORANGIUM
—formation	SPORULATION
—forming organ	SPOROCARP
—in red algae produced	
sexually	CARPOSPORE
—non-motile	APLANOSPORE
—not produced in a sporangium	CONIDIUM
—of rust-fungi	TELEUTOSPORE
—on promycelium	SPORIDIUM
—produced by abstriction	EXOSPORE
—produced by rust fungus	URED(INI)OSPORE
—produced in an ascus	ASCOSPORE
—producing bacterium	BACILLUS
—with thick wall	CHLAMYDOSPORE
sprout	TENDRON
squids, cuttlefish, etc	DECAPODA
stage of	
—cell-division	ANAPHASE
	DIPLOTENE, LEPTOTENE
	METAPHASE, ZYGOTENE
—development	
of embryo	BLASTULA, GASTRULA
stain for bacterial cultures	GRAM'S STAIN
staining	
—method of classifying	
bacteria	GRAM'S METHOD
—of tissue sections	FEULGEN METHOD
stalk(s)	SPIRE, STIPE(STIPITES)
—attaching ovule to placenta	FUNICLE
—carrying stigma	STYLE
—in mosses, etc	SETA
—looking and acting like a leaf	PHYLLODE
—of	
inflorescence	PEDUNCLE
leaf	PETIOLE
sedentary animal	PEDUNCLE
single flower	PEDUNCLE
—in inflorescence	PEDICEL
spore	STERIGMA
stalkless	SESSILE
stamens collectively	ANDROECIUM
start of growth	GERMINATION
state of paleness from	
lack of chlorophyll	ETIOLATION
stem	
—growing without being	
supplanted	MONOPODIUM
—leafless	SCAPE
—looking like and acting as leaf	CLADODE
	PHYLLOCLADE
—of	
plant	CAULIS
seedling between	
—cotyledon and leaf	EPICOTYL

—cotyledon and root	HYPOCOTYL
tree	CAUDEX
—rudimentary	CAULICLE
—secondary	CAULICULUS
—structures collectively	CAULOME
—with successive branches	
supporting main stem	SYMPODIUM
sterile stamen	STAMINODE
steroid promoting maleness	ANDROGEN
sterol in bloodstream	CHOLESTERIN
	CHOLESTEROL
stimulus-provoking	
instinctive reaction	RELEASER
stolon which forms	
new plant at	
growing tip	RUNNER, SARMENTUM
stomach in ruminants	
—first	PAUNCH, RUMEN
—second	BONNET, RETICULUM
—third	BIBLE, OMASUM
—fourth	ABOMASUM, ABOMASUS
	MAW
in calf	VELL
store of food in egg	YOLK
strand	
—from duplication	
of chromosome	CHROMATID
—of vascular tissue	VASCULAR BUNDLE
strap-shaped corolla	LIGULE
strengthening tissue in	
cells	COLLENCHYMA
string of albumen in egg	CHALAZA
structure	
—developed from	
fertilised ovule	SEED
ovum	EGG
zygote	EMBRYO
—of DNA	DOUBLE HELIX
—on cell surface to	
which chemicals attach	RECEPTOR
study of	
—cells	CYTOLOGY
—diseases of plants	PHYTOPATHOLOGY
—distribution of	
plants	PHYTOGEOGRAPHY
—form of organisms	MORPHOLOGY
—heredity	(CYTO)GENETICS
—light as affecting	
organisms	PHOTOBIOLOGY
—living things	BIOLOGY
—metabolism	BIOCHEMISTRY
—micro-organisms	BACTERIOLOGY
—organisms as affected	
by weather	PHENOLOGY
—plants	BOTANY
—viruses	VIROLOGY

sub-class of	
—Crustacea	BRANCHIOPODA
	CIRRIPEDIA, COPEPODA
—fish	TELEOSTEI
—Gasterododa	EUTHYNEURA
—Infusoria	CILIATA
—Mammalia	EUTHERIA
	PLACENTAL MAMMALS
	PLACENTALIA
sub-order of Polyzoa	CYCLOSTOMATA
sub-phylum of	
—Chordata	ACRANIA
	CEPHALOCHORDATA
	CRANIATA, VERTEBRATA
—Coelenterata	CNIDARIA, CTENOPHORA
substance	
—acting	
in conjunction with	
enzyme in catalysis	COENZYME
on embryonic cells to	
determine structure	MORPHOGEN
—causing	
cancer	CARCINOGEN
mutation	MUTAGEN
—controlling	
mitosis	CHALONE
plant growth	CYTOKININ
—forming	
cartilage	CHONDRIN
cuticle in plants	CUTIN
hard outer parts of insects etc	CHITIN
horn, etc	KERATIN
—found in cell-sap	TANNIN
—in cell aiding oxidation	CYTOCHROME
—inimical to body,	
stimulating formation	
of antibodies	ANTIGEN
—involved in metabolic	
process	METABOLITE
—of which living things	
are made	TISSUE
—on which enzymes act	SUBSTRATE
—produced by organisms	
which is inimical to	
other species	ANTIBIOTIC
—promoting plant growth	AUXIN
	PHYTAMIN
—released by animal affecting	
behaviour of others	PHEROMONE
—secreted by mucous	
membrane	MUCIGEN, MUCIN
	MUCUS
—which is foreign	
to the body	ANTIGEN
succession of communities	
of plants	SERE

—in	
dry spots	XEROSERE
water	HYDROSERE
—on rocks	LITHOSERE
sucking proboscis	HAUSTELLUM
sugary solution from plant	NECTAR
sun-animalcules	HELIOZOA
supposed force directing evolution	BATHISM
surface	
—farthest from spine	VENTRAL
—nearest to spine	DORSAL
—secreting mucus	MUCOUS MEMBRANE
survival from year	
to year	PERENNATION
suspended development	
in insects	DIAPAUSE
swallowing	DEGLUTITION
sweetbread	PANCREAS
swelling caused by	
—nitrogen-fixing	
bacteria	ROOT NODULE
—parasites	GALL
symmetrical about one	
plane (flowers)	ZYGOMORPHIC
	ZYGOMORPHOUS
synthesis	
—by chlorophyll using	
energy of light	PHOTOSYNTHESIS
—in metabolism	ANABOLISM
tactile organ on	
—head of worm	PALP
—mouth of mollusc	PALP
tail part of crustacean	TELSON
taking in of oxygen and	
expiration of CO_2	RESPIRATION
tapeworms	CESTODA
	(*see also* worms *below*)
tear-pit	LARMIER
technique of growing	
cells etc	EXPLANTATION
	TISSUE CULTURE
terminal bud	PLUMULE
termination of trachea	
in insect	TRACHEOLE
tetrapods	AMPHIBIA, ANIMALS
	BIRDS, MAMMALS
theory	
—of	
directed evolution	BATHISM
evolution by	
—natural selection	DARWINISM
—acquired	
characteristics	LAMARCKIS
in USSR	LYSENKOISM
gradual development of	
the embryo	EPIGENESIS

heredity	MENDELISM
reappearance of	
throwbacks	ATAVISM
—that life is due to some	
vital force	VITALISTIC THEORY
thorax of crustacean	PEREION
thread	
—cell	CNIDOBLAST
—like lash(es) on cell	CILIUM(CILIA)
—of protoplasm	PLASMODESM
—shaped body in cell	
nucleus carrying genetic	
instructions	CHROMOSOME
thumb	POLLEX
time between conception	
and birth	GESTATION (PERIOD)
tissue	
—between gill-slits	GILL-BAR
—cells	SOMA, SOMATIC CELLS
—culture	EXPLANTATION
—forming over wound	CALLUS
—of	
cells of aquatic plant roots	AERENCHYMA
plants	PARENCHYMA
thick-walled cells	SCLERENCHYMA
toad used in pregnancy	
testing	AFRICAN CLAWED TOAD
	XENOPUS
toe	DIGIT
tolerating variation of	
—osmotic pressure	EURYHALINE
—temperature	EURYTHERMOUS
tongue of gastropod mollusc	RADULA
tortoises and turtles	CHELONIA
touch receptors of bristle	VIBRISSAE
trace element	MICRONUTRIENT
transformation of	
—flower part to leaf-like structure	PHYLLODY
—tissue	METAPLASIA
translucent marine vertebrate	LANCELET
transmission of parental	
characteristics together	LINKAGE
treatment of plants to	
induce flowering	VERNALISATION
tree	
—retaining leaves	CONIFER, EVERGREEN
—shedding leaves	DECIDUOUS
	(*see also separate entry*)
tropical climber	LIANA, LIANE
true skin	CORIUM, DERMIS
trumpet-like part of flower	CORONA
tuatara	RHYNCOCEPHALIA
tube	
—connecting embryo	
and placenta	NAVEL-STRING
	UMBILICAL CORD

—feet	PODIA
—from throat to lungs	TRACHEA, WIND-PIPE
tunic	INTEGUMENT
	MEMBRANE
turning towards stimulus	TROPISM
twig	SARMENTUM
twin	
—from	
same ovum	MONOZYGOTIC TWIN
two ova	DIZYGOTIC TWIN
	FRATERNAL TWIN
—sterile female in cattle	FREE-MARTIN
type specimen	HOLOTYPE
typical species	GENOTYPE
underground	
—bud	BULB, TURION
—section of plant	ROOT
—stem	CORM, RHIZOME, SOBOLE
undifferentiated	
—perianth	PERIGONE
—plant-body	THALLUS
ungulates with	
—even number of toes	ARTIODACTYLA
—odd number of toes	PERISSODACTYLA
union of gametes	CONJUGATION
	FERTILISATION
	OOGAMY, SYNGAMY
unisexual	DIOECIOUS
unit	
—of	
corolla	PETAL
DNA in chromosome	GENE
	HEREDITY FACTOR
flower calyx	SEPAL
genetic information	CISTRON
living animal matter	CELL
—protoplasm	ENERAID, ENERGID
—in taxonomy	DEME
unopened flower-bud	KNOSP
urine	
—duct	
bladder to exterior	URETHRA
kidney to bladder	URETER
—sac	BLADDER
variant from normal	PARAMORPH, ROGUE
	SPORT
variation	DIFFERENTIATION
vascular	
—bundle in leaf	VEIN
—cylinder	STELE
—tissue in plant	WOOD, XYLEM
transporting nutrients	BAST, PHLOEM
veins	(*see* **circulation**)
vertebrate	
—adapted to land or water	AMPHIBIA
—birds	AVES

—groups	AMNIOTA, ANAMNIOTA
—with	
jaws	GNATHOSTOMATA
skull	CRANIATA
—without jaws	AGNATHA
verticil	WHORL
vesicle containing	
ovum	GRAAFIAN FOLLICLE
vessel conducting food	
etc in trees	TRACHEA
vibrating element in larynx	VOCAL C(H)ORD
virus	
—parasitic on	
bacteria	BACTERIOPHAGE
—used in studies	TOBACCO MOSAIC VIRUS
visceral arch	
in fish	BRANCHEAL ARCH
visual purple	RHODOPSIN
walking on	
—back of toes	DORSIGRADE
—soles of feet	PLANTIGRADE
—tips of hooves	UNGULIGRADE
—toes	DIGITIGRADE
wall of fruit	PERICARP
warm-blooded	IDIOTHERMIC
warning coloration	SYNAPOSEMATISM
waste product	DUNG, EXCREMENT, FAECES
	UREA, URIC ACID, URINE
wasting of	
—an organ	ATROPHY
—minerals from soil	LEACHING
water	
—absorbing layer	
on aerial root	VELAMEN
—conducting system	
in plants	VASCULAR SYSTEM
—fleas	CLADOCERA
—pressure in plants	ROOT PRESSURE
waxy sterol present in body	CHOLESTEROL
weak twig	SARMENTUM
web-forming organ in spider	SPINNERET
weight of all organisms	
in a system	BIOMASS
well supplied with	
nutrients	EUTROPHIC
whalebone	BALEEN
whales, porpoises, etc	CETACEA
wheel-animalcules	ROTIFERA
whip-like thread used	
for propulsion	FLAGELLUM
whorl round sex organs	
of mosses	PERICHAETIUM
wind-pipe	TRACHEA
winged	
—fruit	SAMARA
—growth on fruit	ALA

without	
—backbone	INVERTEBRATE
—leaves	APHYLLOUS
—petals	APETALOUS
—stalk	SESSILE
womb	UTERUS
wood	XYLEM
worm(s)	(*see separate entry*)
xylem	WOOD
yellow-green algae	XANTHOPHYTA
yolk	DEUTOPLASM
young	
—animal when parts are	
distinct	F(O)ETUS
—plant	SEEDLING
or animal after	
fertilisation	EMBRYO
—tree	SAPLING
youngest at	
—base, oldest at top	BASIPETAL
—top, oldest at base	ACROPETAL
zygote	AMPHIONT, SEED
birds	AVES, AVIFAUNA, ORNIS
including: alternative names	
classification	
group names	
able to leave nest at once	PRAECOCES
accentor	DUNNOCK
	HEDGE-SPARROW
—accentors	PRUNELLIDAE
Accipiter	SPARROW-HAWK
Alauda	(SKY)LARK
albatross	ALCATRAS, GOONEY(-BIRD)
—albatrosses	PROCELLARIIFORMES
Alca	SEA-AUKS
Alcatras	ALBATROSS, FRIGATE-BIRD
	GANNET, PELICAN
Alpine	SNOW-FINCH
Anas	GADWALL, TEAL, WI(D)GEON
annet	KITTIWAKE
Anous	NODDY
ant-thrush	PITTA
Antarctic	PENGUIN
Anthus	PIPIT
Arctic	SNOW-BUNTING, SNOW-GOOSE
Arenaria	STREPSILAS, TURNSTONE
ariel	PETREL, SWALLOW, TOUCAN
Astur	GOSHAWK
auk	DIVER, RAZOR-BILL
—auks	CHARADRIIFORMES
avocet	AVOSET
—avocets	CHARADRIIFORMES
	RECURVIROSTRIDAE
babbler	THRUSH
bald eagle	OSSIFRAGE
Baltimore oriole	HANGBIRD

bantam	DANDY-COCK, DANDY-HEN
bargoose	SHELDUCK
bar-tailed godwit	SCAMEL
barn owl	MADGE, SCREECH-OWL
barnacle goose	BARNACLE
	BERNICE-GOOSE, CLAIK
bats	(*see separate entry*)
bearded	
—tit(mouse)	REEDLING, REED-PHEASANT
—vulture	LAMMERGEIER
	LAMMERGEYER
bee-eater	MEROPIDIAN
bird of	
—paradise	STANDARD-WING
—prey	RAPTOR
bittern	ARDEA, BUTTER-BUMP
	MIRE-DRUM
—bitterns	ARDEIDAE
—group	SEDGE
black	
—backed gull	SWART-BACK
—bird	AMSEL, AMZEL, MERLE
	OUSEL(COCK), OUZEL
blackbirds	TURDIDAE
—cap	WARBLER
blackcaps	SYLVIIDAE
—cock	BLACK GROUSE
—grouse	BLACKCOCK, MOORCOCK
	MOORFOWL, HEATH BIRD
	HEATH FOWL
—guillemot	DOVEKIE, SEA-TURTLE
—headed gull (Scot.)	PICKMAW
blue penguin	KORORA
blue tit	BLUECAP, NUN, PINCHEM
	PINNOCK, TOMTIT, YAUP
Bombycilla	WAX-WING
bramblings	FRINGILLIDAE
brantail	REDSTART, RUTICULA
brent goose	BRANT-GOOSE
	BRENT-BARNACLE, QUINT GOOSE
brown owl	WOOD-OWL
Bucephala	GOLDENEYE
budgerigar	SHELL-PARAKEET
	SHELL-PARROT
	ZEBRA-PAR(R)AKEET
bullfinch	MONK, SHIRLEY
bunting	CIRL, ORTOLAN
—buntings	FRINGILLIDAE
bustard	OTIS
—bustards	GRUIFORMES
butcher-bird	SHRIKE
buzzard	PUTTOCK
—buzzards	FALCONIDAE
Calidris	KNOT
Cape pigeon	PINTADO
Capella	GALINAGO, SNIPE

capercaillie	CAPERCAILZIE, WOOD-GROUSE
—capercaillies	TETRAONIDAE
carrion	
—crow	GORCROW
—eater	VULTURE
cassowaries	CASUARIFORMES
Certhia	TREE-CREEPER
chaffinch	NAPPY, PINK, ROBINET
	SCOBBY, SPINK, WHEAT-BIRD
Charadrius	DOTTEREL, PLOVER
chats	SAXICOLA
chiff-chaff	WARBLER
Chinese	GOLDEN PHEASANT
	SILVER PHEASANT, SWAN-GOOSE
chough	CHEWET, SEA-CROW
—choughs	CORVIDAE
—group	CHATTERING
Ciconia	STORK
Circus	HARRIER
climbing	SCANSORES
coal-tit	COAL-MOUSE, COLE-MOUSE
	COLE-TIT
coastal bird	ROCK-PIPIT
Collocalia	SWIFTLET
common	
—eagle	GOLDEN EAGLE
—harrier	HEN-HARRIER
—kite (obs)	GLED(E)
—lark	SKYLARK
—swan	MUTE SWAN
—wild goose	GREY GOOSE, GREYLAG
coots	GRUIFORMES, RALLIDAE
—group	COVERT, RAFT
Coracias	ROLLER
cormorant	SEA-CROW, SEA-RAVEN, URILE
—cormorants	PHALACROCORACIDAE
	PELECANIFORMES
—Scottish	SCART(H), SKART(H)
corncrake	CRECK, CREX, LANDRAIL
	RAIL, RALLUS
—corncrakes	RALLIDAE
Corvus	CROW, JACKDAW, RAVEN, ROOK
covered with down	
at birth	PRAECOCES
crake	PORZANA
crane	DEMOISELLE
—cranes	GRUIDAE
—genus	GRUS
—group	HERD, SIEGE
creeper	CERTHIA
crest on head	COPPLE
crested	
—European bird	HOOPOE
—grebe	CARGOOSE
—heron	SQUACCO
—penguin	ROCK-HOPPER

—screamer	SERIEMA
Crex	CORNCRAKE, LANDRAIL
crocodile-bird	PLOVER, TROCHILUS
crossbill	LOXIA
—crossbills	FRINGILLIDAE
crow	CORVUS
—crows	CORVIDAE
—group	HOVER, MURDER
cuckoo	COUCAL
—cuckoos	CUCULIDAE, CUCULIFORMES
curlew	TITTEREL, (GREAT) WHAUP
—curlews	CHARADRIIFORMES
	SCOLOPACIDAE
Cuthbert's duck	EIDER DUCK
Cygnus	SWAN
Cypselus	APUS, SWIFT
dabchick	DIDAPPER, DIPCHICK
	DIPPER, DOBCHICK
	LITTLE GREBE
—dabchicks	PODICIPITIDAE
Dafila	PINTAIL
darcock	RALLUS, WATER-RAIL
darter	PLOTUS, SNAKE-BIRD
	WRYNECK
didapper	DOPPER
dipper	WATER-OUZEL
—dippers	CINCLIDAE
diseases	AVIAN TUBERCULOSIS
	COCCIDIOSIS, PARROT DISEASE
	PARROT FEVER, PSITTACOSIS
diver	GAVIA
—divers	GAVIIDAE, GAVIFORMES
diving bird	LOON
domestic duck	INDIAN RUNNER
dorbie	DUNLIN
dotterels	CHARADRIIDAE
dove	CULVER, PIGEON
—doves	COLUMBIDAE
—group	DOLE, DULE, FLIGHT
	PITYING, PRETTYING
duck	GARROT
—ducks	ANATIDAE, ANSERIFORMES
	TADORNA
—group	BADELYNGE, BAD(D)LING
	DOPPING, FLUSH, PLUMP, TEAM
	SMEATH, SMEE(TH)
dun-diver	MERGANSER
dunbird	POCHARD
dunlin	DORBIE, OX-BIRD, OX-PECKER
	PURRE, SEA-MOUSE
	SEA-PECK, STINT
—dunlins	SCOLOPACIDAE
dunnock	(HEDGE-)ACCENTOR
	HEDGE-SPARROW
eagle	ERNE
—eagles	FALCONIDAE

—group	CONVOCATION	—flycatchers	MUSCICAPIDAE
—owl	BUBO	flying reptiles	(*see* lizards)
Eastern dwarf goose	GOSLET	fork-tailed gulls	XEMA
edible-nest builder	COLLOCALIA	fossil	(*see* archaeology)
	SALANGANE, SWIFTLET	Fratercula	PUFFIN
eider duck	(ST)CUTHBERT'S DUCK	Fregata	FRIGATE-BIRD
	SOMATERIA	freshwater diver	GREBE
emus	CASUARIFORMES	friar-bird	FOUR O'CLOCK
erne	SEA-EAGLE	frigate-bird	ALCATRAS
European vulture	GRIFFON VULTURE		MAN-OF-WAR(BIRD)
eve-chur	NIGHTJAR	—frigate birds	FREGATIDAE
eve-jar	NIGHTJAR		PELECANIFORMES
excrement of sea-birds	GUANO	frogmouth	PODARGUS
extinct	DODO, MOA	—frogmouths	CAPRIMULGIFORMES
	PASSENGER PIGEON	fully-webbed	STEGANOPOD(ES)
fabulous	HARPY, HUMA, PHOENIX	fulmar	MALLEMUCK, MOLLYMAWK
	ROC, ROK, RUC, RUKH	—fulmars	PROCELLARIIDAE
	SIMORG, SIMURG(H), WHISTLER	gadwall	RADGE, RODGE
	(*see also* monsters)	Gallicrex	KORA, WATER-COCK
falcon	GERFALCON, HAWK, PEREGRINE	Gallinago	CAPELLA, SNIPE
	SACRE, SAKER(ET), STONE-HAWK	game bird	GROUSE, PARTRIDGE
	TASSEL-GENT(LE), TERCEL-GENTLE		PHEASANT, QUAIL
	TERCEL-JERKIN		WOODCOCK
—falcons	FALCONIDAE	—game birds	GALLIFORMES
—group	CAST	gannet	ALCANTRAS, BOOBY
Falkland Islands penguin	GENTOO		SOLAN(D)
female		—gannets	SULIDAE, PELECANIFORMES
—black grouse	HEATH-HEN	garden warbler	REELER
—blackcock	GREYHEN	garganey	ANAS
—falcon	LANNER	—garganeys	ANATIDAE
—grouse	GORHEN, GREY-HEN	Gavia	DIVER
—moorfowl	MOORHEN	Garrulus	JAY
—peregrine	FALCON-GENTIL	geese	
	FALCON-GENTLE	—flying group	SKEIN
—pochard	DUNBIRD	—geese	ANATIDAE, ANSERIFORMES
—ruff	REE(VE)	—group	FLOCK, GAGGLE, NIDE
—sandpiper	REEVE	giant fulmar	OSSIFRAGA
—swan	PEN	goat-owl	NIGHTJAR
fen-owl	NIGHTJAR	goatsucker	FROGMOUTH, MOTH-HUNTER
fern-owl	NIGHTJAR		NIGHT-HAWK
fieldfares	TURDIDAE	—goatsuckers	CAPRIMULGIDAE
fig-pecker	BECCAFICO		CAPRIMULGIFORMES
finch	BRAMBLING, BUNTING, CIRL	godwit	SCAMEL
	CITRIL, LINNET, SPINK	—godwits	SCOLOPACIDAE
—finches	FRINGILLIDAE	goldcrest	GOLDEN-CRESTED WREN
—group	TREMBLING, TRIMMING		KINGLET, REGULUS, ROITELET
firecrest	REGULUS	—goldcrests	REGULIDAE
flamingoes	CICONIIFORMES	golden	
fledgling	QUILLER	—crested wren	GOLDCREST, KINGLET
flightless			REGULUS, ROITELET
—bird	CASSOWARY, EM(E)U, KIWI	—eagle	AQUILA
	OSTRICH, PENGUIN, PINGUIN	—eye	BUCEPHALA
	RATITAE, RATITES, RHEA	goldeneyes	ANATIDAE
	STRUTHIONES	—oriole	LORIOT, WITWALL
—pigeon (old)	SOLITAIRE		WOODWALE, YELLOW-BIRD
flycatcher	MUSCICAPA		WOODWALL

goldfinch	GOLDSPINK, GOUDIE
	GOWDSPINK, RED-CAP
—group	CHARM, CHATTERING
	CHIRM, DRUM, TROUBLING
goosander	MERGANSER
—goosanders	ANATIDAE
goose	SADDLEBACK
gorcock	RED GROUSE
gorcrow	CARRION CROW
gorse-frequenting	WHINCHAT
grasshopper-warbler	REELER
great	
—auk	GAREFOWL, GAIRFOWL
—black-backed gull	SADDLEBACK
—northern diver	EMBER-GOOSE
—tit	OX-EYE
greater	
—shearwater	HACKBOLT, HAGBOLT
	HAGDEN, HAGDO(W)N
—spotted woodpecker	WITWALL
	WOODWALE, WOODWALL
grebe	DIVER
—grebes	PODICIPITIDAE
	PODICIPEDIFORMES
green	
—cormorant	SHAG
—finch	GREEN LINNET
—linnet	GREENFINCH
—shanks	SCOLOPACIDAE
—woodpecker	HICKWALL, WITWALL
	WOOD-SPITE, WOODWALE
	WOODWALL, YAFFLE
grey	
—duck	GADWALL, RADGE, RODGE
—lag	GOOSE
—parrot	PSITTACUS
grosbeak	HAWFINCH, PINE-FINCH
group of waterfowl	PLUMP
grouse	BLACKCOCK, BLACK GAME
	CAPERCAILLIE, CAPERCAILZIE
—female	GORHEN, GREY-HEN
—group	COVEY
—grouse	TETRAONIDAE
—male	GORCOCK
guillemot	MARROT, MURRE
	SEA-HEN, WILLOCK
—guillemots	ALCIDAE
guinea-fowl	GUINEA-HEN, PINTADO
gull	SCAURY, SEA-COB, (SEA-)MAW
	(SEA-)MEW, WAGGEL
—gulls	CHARADRIIFORMES, LARIDAE
—group	COLONY
haggard	HAWK
hareld	OLD WIFE
hatching	
—partly developed	NIDICOLOUS
—well developed	NIDIFUGOUS
having crossed	
mandibles	METAGNATHOUS
hawfinch	GROSBEAK
Hawaiian goose	NENE
hawk	BOWESS, GAVILAN
	HAGGARD, LANNER
	TARSEL, TASSEL(L)
	T(I)ERCEL(ET)
—group	CAST, LEASH
—hawks	FALCONIDAE
	FALCONIFORMES
—short-winged	GOSHAWK
heathcock	GROUSE
hedge-sparrow	DUNNOCK
	(HEDGE-)ACCENTOR
	PINNOCK, TITLING
—hedge sparrows	PRUNELLIDAE
hen	
—harrier	HEN-DRIVER
—like	GALLINACEOUS
heron	ARDEA, HERN
—group	SEDGE, SIEGE
—herons	ARDEIDAE, CICONIFORMES
—type	BOATBILL
hickwall	WOODPECKER
Himalayan pheasant	MONA(U)L
Himantopus	STILT(-PLOVER)
Hirundo	SWALLOW
hobbies	FALCONIDAE
honey	
—buzzard	PERN(IS)
—guide	INDICATOR
hooded	
—crow	HOODIE-CROW
	ROYSTON CROW
—pigeon	CAPUCHIN, JACOBIN
hoopoe	UPUPA
—hoopoes	CORACIIFORMES, UPUPIDAE
hornbills	CORACIIFORMES
humming-bird	RACKET-TAIL, COLIBRI
—group	CHARM, CHATTERING
	DRUM, TROUBLING
—humming birds	APODIFORMES
ibises	CICONIIFORMES
	PLATALEIDAE
Iceland falcon	ICELANDER
Icterus	TROOPIAL, TROUPIAL
imaginary (Liverpool)	LIVER(BIRD)
	(*see also* fabulous)
jacinth	PIGEON
jackdaw	JACK, KAE
—jackdaws	CORVIDAE
ja(e)ger	SKUA
jar-owl	NIGHTJAR
jay	GARRULUS

—group	BAND, PARTY
—jays	CORVIDAE
Jynx	WRYNECK
kestrel	STALLION, STANN(I)EL
	STAN(N)YEL
—kestrels	FALCONIDAE
kingfisher	ALCEDO, (H)ALCYON
—kingfishers	ALCEDINIDAE
	CORACIIFORMES
kinglet	FIRE-CREST(ED WREN)
—kinglets	REGULIDAE
kite	ELANET, FORK-TAIL
	MILVUS, PUTTOCK
—kites	FALCONIDAE
kittiwake	ANNET, HACKLET, HAGLET
—kittiwakes	LARIDAE
kiwis	APTERYGIFORMES
knot	CALIDRIS
—knots	SCOLOPACIDAE
kora	GALLICREX, WATER-COCK
Lagopus	PTARMIGAN
lammergeier	OSSIFRAGE
land-rail	CORNCRAKE, RALLUS
lapwing	PE(E)WIT, PIE-WIFE, PLOVER
	TIRWIT, TEW(H)IT
—group	DECEIT, DESERT
—lapwings	CHARADRIIDAE
—Scottish	PEASEWEEP, PEESWEEP
	PEEWEE, TEUCHAT
large	
—billed bird	PELICAN
—crow	RAVEN
—duck	GOOSANDER
—gull	BLACK-BACKED GULL
	HERRING-GULL
—running birds	STRUTHIONIDAE
	STRUTHIONIFORMES
—sea-bird	NELLY
—thrush	MISSEL
largest bird	OSTRICH
Laridae	GULLS
lark	GAVILAN, LAVEROCK
—group	BEVY, EXALTATION
—larks	ALAUDIDAE
leaving nest	
—immediately	NIDIFUGOUS
—later	NIDICOLOUS
Limosa	GODWIT
linnet	
—linnets	FRINGILLIDAE
—type	REDPOLL
litch-fowl	NIGHTJAR
little	
—auk	DOVEKIE, ICE-BIRD, ROCH
	ROTCH(E), SEA-DOVE
Scottish	DOVEKIE

—auks	ALCIDAE
—grebe	DABCHICK
living birds (except the	
flightless)	CARINATES
long	
—tailed duck	HARELD, OLD WIFE
—tailed tit	MAG
—winged seabird	TERN
loon	DIVER
loriot	(GOLDEN) ORIOLE
magpie	MADGE, MAG, PIE
—group	TIDING, TITTERING
male	
—black grouse	HEATHCOCK
—duck	DRAKE
—lanner	LANNERET
—peregrine	TERCEL-GENTLE
—red grouse	GORCOCK
—redstart	WHITECAP
—sandpiper	RUFF
—sparrow-hawk	MUSKET
—swan	COB
—thrush	THROSTLE-COCK
—turkey	STAG
mallard	
—group	FLUSH, PUDDLING, SORD, SUTE
—mallards	ANATIDAE
mallemuck	FULMAR, MOLLYMAWK
Mareca	WI(D)GEON
marsh	
—bird	BITTERN
—harrier	DUCK-HAWK, MOOR-BUZZARD
martin	MARTLET
—martins	HIRUNDINIDAE
mavis	(SONG-)THRUSH, THROSTLE
meadow-pipit	ANTHUS, TIT-LARK, TITLING
Meleagris	TURKEY
merganser	DUN-DIVER, SERULA
	SAW-BILL, SMEW
—mergansers	ANATIDAE
merlin	ROCK-HAWK
—merlins	FALCONIDAE
Milvus	KITE
missel-thrush	MISTLE-THRUSH
	SCREECH-THRUSH
	STORM-COCK, WOOD-THRUSH
moa	DIORNIS
mocking birds	MIMUS
mollymawk	FULMAR, MALLEMUCK
moor	
—buzzard	DUCK-HAWK
—fowl	GROUSE
—hen	WATER-HEN
moorhens	RALLIDAE
Motacillidae	WAGTAILS
mothhawk	NIGHTJAR

moth-hunter	GOATSUCKER
Mother Carey's chicken	STORM(Y) PETREL
mountain	
—dwelling grouse	PTARMIGAN
—linnet	TWITE
mousebirds	COLIIFORMES
Muscicapa	FLYCATCHER
myna	BOAT-TAIL, GRA(C)KLE
Nettapus	GOSLET
night-hawk	GOATSUCKER, NIGHTJAR
nightingale	PHILOMEL(A), PHILOMENE
	PROGNE
—group	WATCH
—nightingales	TURDIDAE
—type	BLUEBREAST, BLUETHROAT
nightjar	CHURN-OWL, DORHAWK
	EVE-CHUR, EVEJAR, FEN-OWL
	FERN-OWL, GOAT-OWL
	GOATSUCKER, JAR-OWL
	LITCH-FOWL, MOTHHAWK
	NIGHTHAWK, PICK(ERIDGE) BIRD
	SCREECH-HAWK, WHEELBIRD
—nightjars	CAPRIMULGIDAE
	CAPRIMULGIFORMES
northern	
—falcon	GERFALCON
	GYRFALCON, JERFALCON
—freshwater duck	GADWALL
—grouse	WILLOW-GROUSE
—sea-duck	EIDER(-DUCK), GOLDEN-EYE
	HARELD, OLD WIFE
	OEDEMIA, SCOTER
Nucifraga	NUTCRACKER
Numida	GUINEA-FOWL
nut	
—cracker	NUCIFRAGA
—hatch	SITTA
nuthatches	SITTIDAE
—jobber	SITTA
—pecker	SITTA
Oedemia	NORTHERN SEA-DUCK
	SCOTER
Oenanthe	WHEATEAR
oriole	LORIOT
—orioles	ORIOLIDAE
osprey	OSSIFRAGE, PANDION
	SEA-EAGLE, SEA-HAWK
—ospreys	FALCONIDAE
ossifrage	GIANT FULMAR, LAMMERGEIER
	OSPREY, BALD EAGLE
ostriches	STRUTHIONIFORMES
oven-tit	WILLOW-WARBLER
owl	JENNY, SCOPS, STRICK
—group	PARLIAMENT, STARE
—owls	STRIGES, STRIGIDAE
	STRIGIFORMES

ox	
—bird	DUNLIN, BEEFEATER
—pecker	DUNLIN, BUFFALO-BIRD
oyster-catcher	SEA-PIE
—oyster-catchers	CHARADRIIFORMES
	HAEMATOPODIDAE
Pandion	OSPREY
parakeet	BUDGERIGAR
parrots	PSITTACIFORMES
partridge	FRANCOLIN
—group	COVEY
—partridges	PHASIANIDAE
—quail cross	PERCOLIN
Parus	TITMOUSE
Passer	SPARROW
Pavo	PEACOCK
peacock	PAVO
—group	MUSTER, OSTENTATION
pecking birds	PICARIAE
—old	RASORES
peewit	LAPWING, PLOVER
pelican	ALCATRAS
—pelicans	PELECANIFORMES
	STEGANOPODES
penguin	
—group	COLONY, ROOKERY
—penguins	SPHENISCIFORMES
perching birds	PASSERIFORMES
—old	INSESSORES, PASSERES
	PASSERINES
Perdix	PARTRIDGE
peregrine	FALCON, GENTLE
pern	HONEY-BUZZARD
petrel	ARIEL, FULMAR, NELLY
	PINTADO, PROCELLARIA
	STORM-BIRD
—petrels	PROCELLARIIDAE
	PROCELLARIIFORMES
Petronia	ROCK-SPARROW
phalaropes	PHALAROPODIDAE
pheasants	
—group	BOUQUET, NYE
—pheasants	PHASIANIDAE
philip	SPARROW
Philomachus	RUFF, REE(VE)
Pica	MAGPIE
Picidae	WOODPECKERS
pick(eridge) bird	NIGHTJAR
pie	MAGPIE
pied wagtail	WATER-WAGTAIL
pigeon	(*see separate entry*)
pink	CHAFFINCH
—footed bird	GOOSE
pinnock	BLUE TIT, HEDGE-SPARROW
pintado	CAPE PIGEON, GUINEA-FOWL
	PETREL

pintail	DAFILA, SAND-GROUSE
	SMEATH, SMEE(TH)
—pintails	ANATIDAE
piping crow	FLUTE-BIRD
pipit	ANTHUS, TITLARK
—pipits	MOTACILLIDAE
Pitta	ANT-THRUSH
Plataleidae	SPOONBILL
plover	CHARADRIUS, DOTT(E)REL
	LAPWING, PEEWIT, SURF-BIRD
—group	CONGREGATION, LEASH, WING
—like	PRATINCOLE
—plovers	CHARADRIIDAE
	CHARADRIIFORMES
pochard	SCAUP-DUCK, SEA-DUCK
	SMEATH, SMEE(TH)
—pochards	ANATIDAE
Podargus	FROGMOUTH
Podiceps	GREBE
Porphyrio	PURPLE COOT
porzana	CRAKE, WATER-RAIL
prehistoric	(see archaeology)
Procellaria	PETREL
Progne	NIGHTINGALE, SWALLOW
Psittacus	(GREY) PARROT
ptarmigan	LAGOPUS, RYPE
	WILLOW-GROUSE
—ptarmigans	TETRAONIDAE
Pterocles	SAND-GROUSE
puffin	FRATERCULA, SEA-PARROT
	TOM NODDY
—puffins	ALCIDAE
—Scottish	TAMMIE NORIE
Puffinus	SHEARWATER
purple coot	PORPHYRIO, SULTAN
quail	
—group	BEVY, COVEY
—quails	PHASIANIDAE
Quaker-bird	SOOTY ALBATROSS
quint-goose	BRENT-GOOSE
racket-tail	HUMMING-BIRD
rafter-bird	SPOTTED FLYCATCHER
rails	GRUIFORMES, RALLIDAE
Rallus	CORNCRAKE
	(WATER-)RAIL
rapacious bird	KITE
rare bird	RARA AVIS
raven	
—group	UNKINDNESS
—ravens	CORVIDAE
razorbill	AUK, MURRE
—razorbills	ALCIDAE
red	
—backed sandpiper	DUNLIN
—breast	RADDOCK, ROBIN
	RUDDOCK, RUBECULA

—breasted merganser	HERALD(-DUCK)
—cap	GOLDFINCH
—grouse	MOORCOCK, MOORFOWL
male	GORCOCK
—headed duck	POCHARD, POCKARD
	POKER
—legged crow	CHOUGH
—polls	FRINGILLIDAE
—shank	GAMBET, SANDPIPER
	TAT(T)LER, TOTANUS
redshanks	SCOLOPACIDAE
—start	BRANTAIL, RUTICILLA
male	WHITECAP
redstarts	TURDIDAE
—wings	TURDIDAE
reed	
—bunting	JUNCO, REED-SPARROW
—pheasant	BEARDED TITMOUSE
—sparrow	REED-BUNTING
—thrush	REED-WARBLER
—warbler	REED-THRUSH, REED-WREN
—wren	REED-WARBLER
reedling	BEARDED-TIT
reeler	GRASSHOPPER-WARBLER
Regulus	FIRECREST, GOLDCREST
rheas	RHEIFORMES
Rhyncops	SKIMMER
ring	
—dove	CUSHAT
—ousels	TURDIDAE
robin	RADDOCK, REDBREAST
	RUBECULA, RUDDOCK
—robins	TURDIDAE
rock	
—bird	PUFFIN
—hopper	CRESTED PENGUIN
—lark	ROCK-PIPIT
—pipit	ROCK-LARK, SEA-LARK
—sparrow	PETRONIA
roller	CANARY, CORACIAS, PIGEON
rooks	
—group	BUILDING, PARLIAMENT
—rooks	CORVIDAE
rose-coloured starling	PASTOR
rotche	DOVEKIE
ruddock	REDBREAST, ROBIN
ruffed grouse	HAZEL GROUSE
—female	HAZEL HEN
ruffs	SCOLOPACIDAE
running	
—bird	EM(E)U, OSTRICH
	ROAD-RUNNER
—birds	CURSORES
rype	PTARMIGAN
St Cuthbert's duck	EIDER DUCK
saddleback	GOOSE, GULL

sand	
—grouse	PINTAIL
	PTEROCLES, SYRRHAPTES
—lark	SANDPIPER
—piper	DUNLIN, GREENSHANK, KNOT
	SAND-LARK, SANDERLING
	SEA-LARK, SEA-SNIPE
	SUMMER SNIPE, SURF-BIRD
	TAT(T)LER
female	REE(VE)
male	RUFF
sanderling	SANDPIPER
—sanderlings	CHARADRIIFORMES
	SCOLOPACIDAE
Saxicola	STONECHAT, WHEATEAR
	WHINCHAT
scaup(-duck)	POCHARD
scissor-bill	SKIMMER
Scolopax	WOODCOCK
Scops	OWL
scoter	NORTHERN SEA-DUCK
	OEDEMIA, SURF-DUCK, WHILK
—scoters	ANATIDAE
scraping birds	RASORES
scray(e)	TERN
screamers	ANSERIFORMES
screech	
—hawk	NIGHTJAR
—martin	SWIFT
—owl	BARN-OWL, LICH-OWL
	SHRIEK-OWL
—thrush	MISSEL-THRUSH
	MISTLE THRUSH
screecher	SWIFT
sea	
—auks	ALCA
—bar	TERN
—bird	TARROCK
—cob	SEAGULL
—crow	SKUA
—dotterel	TURNSTONE
—dove	ICE-BIRD, LITTLE AUK
—duck	POCHARD
—eagle	ERNE, OSPREY
—gull	SEA-COB, (SEA-)MAW
	(SEA-)MEW
—hawk	OSPREY, SKUA
—hen	GUILLEMOT
—lark	ROCK-PIPIT, SANDPIPER
—maw	GULL, SEA-MEW
—mew	GULL, SEA-MAW
—parrot	PUFFIN
—pie	OYSTER-CATCHER
—quail	TURNSTONE
—snipe	SANDPIPER
—swallow	STORM PETREL, TERN

—turtle	BLACK GUILLEMOT
secretary-bird	SERPENT-EATER
—secretary birds	FALCONIFORMES
sedge	
—bird	SEDGE-WARBLER, SEDGE-WREN
—warbler	REED-SPARROW
serin	CANARY
serpent-eater	SECRETARY-BIRD
shag	GREEN CORMORANT
—shags	PHALACROCORACIDAE
shearwater	HACKLET, HAGLET
	PUFFINUS
—shearwaters	PROCELLARIIDAE
	PROCELLARIIFORMES
shel(l)duck	BARGOOSE, TADORNA
sheldrake	BERGANDER, BURROW-DUCK
—group	DOPPING
shell-parrot	BUDGERIGAR
shoebills	CICONIIFORMES
shore bird	SAND-LARK
short-winged hawk	GOSHAWK
shovel(l)er	SPATULA
—shovelers	ANATIDAE
shrike	BUTCHER-BIRD, WOOD-CHAT
—shrikes	LANIIDAE
siskin	ABERDEVINE, TARIN
—siskins	FRINGILLIDAE
Sitta	NUTHATCH, NUTJOBBER
	NUTPECKER
skimmer	RHYNCOPS, SCAUP(-DUCK)
	SCISSOR-BILL
—skimmers	CHARADRIIFORMES
skua	BOATSWAIN, BONXIE, BOS(U)N
	JA(E)GER, SEA-CROW, SEA-HAWK
	STERCORARIUS
—skuas	CHARADRIIFORMES
	STERCORARIIDAE
skylark	ALAUDA
small	
—canary	SERIN
—crested heron	SQUACCO
—curlew	W(H)IMBREL
—falcon	HOBBY, KESTREL, MERLIN
—parrot	LOVE-BIRD, PAR(R)AKEET
—partridge	QUAIL
—sandpiper	DUNLIN, STINT
—sea-bird	MURRELET
—snipe	JACK SNIPE
smallest	FIRECREST, GOLDCREST
—web-footed	STORM(Y) PETREL
smew	MERGANSER, SMEATH
	SMEE(TH)
snake-bird	DARTER, WRYNECK
snipe	CAPELLA, GALINAGO
	JEDCOCK, MIRE-SNIPE
—group	WALK, WHISPER, WISP

—snipe	CHARADRIIFORMES
	SCOLOPACIDAE
—type	PAINTED SNIPE
snow	
—bunting	SNOWFLAKE, SNOWFLECK
	SNOWFLICK
—goose	WAV(E)Y
solan(d)	GANNET
Somateria	EIDER DUCK
song	
—birds	OSCINES
—thrush	MAVIS, THROSTLE
sooty	
—albatross	QUAKER-BIRD
—tern	EGG-BIRD
sparrow	PASSER, PHILIP, SP(R)UG
—group	HOST, QUARREL, TRIBE
—sparrows	PLOCEIDAE
sparrow-hawk	ACCIPITER
sparrow-like	HEDGE-WARBLER
Spatula	SHOVEL(L)ER
spoonbill	PLATALEIDAE
—spoonbills	CICONIIFORMES
	PLATALEIDAE
spotted flycatcher	RAFTER-BIRD
sprug	SPARROW
spug	SPARROW
squacco	CRESTED HERON
starling	STURNUS
—group	MURMURATION
—starlings	STURNIDAE
Stercorarius	SKUA
stilt(-plover)	HIMANTOPUS
—stilts	RECURVIROSTRIDAE
stint	DUNLIN
stone	
—chat	STONE-CHATTER
stonechats	TURDIDAE
—curlew	STONE-PLOVER
	THICK-KNEE
stone curlews	BURHINIDAE
—hawk	FALSON
stork	CICONIA
—storks	CICONIIFORMES
storm	
—bird	PETREL
—cock	MISSEL-THRUSH
—petrel	MOTHER CAREY'S CHICKEN
	MOTHER CAREY'S GOOSE
	SEA-SWALLOW
Strepsilas	ARENARIA, TURNSTONE
Streptopelia	TURTLE-DOVE, TURTUR
stupid	NODDY
Sturnus	STARLING
Sulidae	GANNETS
sultan	PURPLE COOT

summer	
—snipe	SANDPIPER
—teal	GARGANEY
—visitor	WHEATEAR
—warbler	YELLOW-BIRD
swallow	ARIEL, HIRUNDO, PROCNE
—swallows	HIRUNDINIDAE
swallow-like	MARTIN(ET)
swallow-tailed	KITE
swan	CYGNUS, MUTE, WHOOPER
	WHOOPING-SWAN
—female	PEN
—goose	CHINA GOOSE
—group	BANK, BEVY, GAME, HEAD
	SQUADRON, WEDGE, WHITENESS
—male	COB
—swans	ANATIDAE, ANSERIFORMES
—young	CYGNET
swart-back	BLACK-BACKED GULL
swift	APUS, CYPSELUS
	SCREECHER
	SCREECH-MARTIN, SENEX
—swifts	APODIDAE, APODIFORMES
swiftlet	COLLOCALIA
Sylvia	WARBLER
Syrrhaptes	SAND-GROUSE
Tadorna	SHEL(L)DUCK, SHIELDUCK
Tantalus	WOOD-IBIS
tat(t)ler	REDSHANK, SANDPIPER
	WOOD-SANDPIPER, TOTANUS
tawny owl	BROWN OWL, GREY OWL
teal	ANAS
—group	COIL, KNOB, RAFT, SPRING
—teal	ANATIDAE
tern	KIP(P), SCRAY(E), EGG-BIRD
	SEA-BAR, SEA-SWALLOW
—terns	CHARADRIIFORMES, LARIDAE
thick-knee	STONE-CURLEW
	STONE-PLOVER
throstle	MAVIS, (SONG-)THRUSH
thrush	BABBLER, MAVIS
	THROSTLE, TURDUS
—group	MUTATION
—thrushes	TURDIDAE
—type	FIELDFARE, REDWING
	RING OUSEL
tinamous	TINAMIFORMES
titlark	PIPIT
titling	HEDGE-SPARROW
	MEADOW-PIPIT
titmouse	PARUS
—titmice/tits	PARIDAE
Tom Noddy	PUFFIN
tomtit	BLUE-TIT, PINNOCK
Totanus	REDSHANK, SANDPIPER
	TAT(T)LER

toucan	ARIEL
—toucans	PICIFORMES
trained falcon	GENTLE
tree-creeper	CERTHIA
—tree-creepers	CERTHIDAE
Trochilus	CROCODILE-BIRD
Troglodytes	WREN
trogons	TROGONIFORMES
troopial	ICTERUS
tropic-bird	BOATSWAIN-BIRD
trumpeters	GRUIFORMES
tumbler pigeon	ROLLER
Turdus	BLACKBIRD, FIELDFARE
	RING OUSEL, THRUSH
turkey-buzzard	GALLINAZO
turkeys - group	DOLE, DULE, FLOCK
	RAFTER, RUFFLE
turnstone	ARENARIA, STREPSILAS
	SEA-DOTTEREL
—turnstones	CHARADRIIDAE
turtle-dove	STREPTOPELIA, TURTUR
Turtur	STREPTOPELIA, TURTLE-DOVE
twite	MOUNTAIN LINNET
—twites	FRINGILLIDAE
umbrella	DRAGOON-BIRD
unfledged	
—hawk	EYAS
—male hawk	EYAS-MUSKET
untamed hawk	HAGGARD
Upupa	HOOPOE
Uria	GUILLEMOT
variegated duck	HARLEQUIN DUCK
velvet-duck	VELVET-SCOTER
vulture	GRIPE
—bearded	LAMMERGEIER
	LAMMERGEYER
—European	GRIFFON VULTURE
—French	BOULDRAS
—North American	TURKEY-BUZZARD
—South American	CONDOR
—vultures	FALCONIFORMES
wading	
—bird	IBIS, KNOT, PHALAROPE
—birds	GRALLAE, GRALLATORES
	SCORPUS
wagtail	MOLLY, SEED-BIRD, TROTTY
—group	WALK
—wagtails	MOTACILLIDAE
warbler	FAUVETTE, PEGGY
	PETTICHAPS, PETTY-CHAPS
	SYLVIA
—warblers	SYLVIIDAE
water	
—bird	COOT, MOORHEN
—cock	GALLICREX, KORA
—hen	MOORHEN

—ousel	DIPPER
water ousels	CINCLIDAE
—rail	DARCOCK, PORZANA, RALLUS
—wagtail	PIED WAGTAIL
wax	
—bill	WEAVER-BIRD
—wing	BOMBYCILLA, CHATTERER
waxwings	BOMBYCILLIDAE
weaver-bird	BISHOP-BIRD, WAX-BILL
web-footed	PALMIPED(E)
whaup (Scot.)	CURLEW
wheat	
—bird	CHAFFINCH
—ear	OENANTHE
wheatears	TURDIDAE
wheelbird	NIGHTJAR
whimbrel	
—Scottish	LITTLE WHAUP
—whimbrels	SCOLOPACIDAE
whinchats	TURDIDAE
white	
—gerfalcon	ICELAND FALCON
—heron	EGRET
—owl	SNOWY OWL
—throat	BEARDIE, PEGGY
whitethroats	SYLVIIDAE
—throated thrush	RING-OUZEL
whooper	SWAN
wi(d)geon	ANAS, MARECA, SMEATH
	SMEE(TH), WHEWER
—group	BUNCH, COIL, COMPANY, KNOB
—wi(d)geons	ANATIDAE
wild	
—duck	BALDPATE, MALLARD
group	PLUMP
—pigeon	ROCK-DOVE, ROCK-PIGEON
willow	
—grouse	PTARMIGAN
—warbler	OVEN-TIT, WILLOW-WREN
	WOOD-WREN
—wren	WILLOW-WARBLER
wisp	SNIPE
witwall	WOODPECKER
wood	
—chat	SHRIKE, WOODPECKER
—cock	SCOLOPAX
group	CALL, FALL, PLUMP
woodcocks	SCOLOPACIDAE
—grouse	CAPERCAILLIE, CAPERCAILZIE
—ibis	TANTALUS
—owl	BROWN OWL
—pecker	AWL-BIRD, HICKWALL
	WHETTLE, WITWALL, WOODCHAT
	WOODWALE, WOODWALL, YAFFLE
woodpeckers	PICARIAE, PICIDAE
	PICIFORMES

—pigeon	CULVER, CUSHAT
	QUINCE(TY-COCK)
—sandpiper	TAT(T)LER
—spite	GREEN WOODPECKER
—thrush	MISSEL-THRUSH
—wale	(GREEN) WOODPECKER
—wren	WILLOW-WARBLER
	WOOD-WARBLER
wren	BUMBARREL, TROGLODYTES
—wrens	TROGLODYTIDAE
wryneck	DARTER, JYNX, SNAKE-BIRD
yaffle	GREEN WOODPECKER
yaup	BLUE TIT
yellow	
—bunting	YELLOW-HAMMER, YITE
—hammer	SCRIBBLING-SCHOOLMASTER
	YELDRIN, YELDROCK
	YELLOW-BUNTING, YELLOW-YITE
	YOLDRING, YORLING, YOWLEY
	ZIVOLA
—willow-warbler	WOOD-WARBLER
yellowish-green finch	SISKIN
yite	YELLOW BUNTING
young	BRANCHER, NESTLING, PEEPER
—black grouse	HEATH-POULT
—goose	GOSLING, GREEN GOOSE
—gull	SCAURY
—hawk	EYAS(-MUSKET)
—hen	PULLET
—heron	HERONSEW, HER(O)NSHAW
—owl	(H)OWLET
—partridge	FLAPPER
—wild duck	FLAPPER
zebra-par(r)akeet	BUDGERIGAR
zivola	YELLOW-HAMMER
biscuits	
almond-flavoured	MACAROON, RATAFIA
American	(BOSTON)BROWNIE
	COOKIE, COOKY
	CRACKER
bread baked crisp	RUSK
brittle	SHORTBREAD, SNAP
caraway	ABERNETHY
chocolate	
—flavoured	BOURBON
—nuts and fruit	FLORENTINE
circular semi-sweet	DIGESTIVE
coconut	MACAROON
coffee-flavoured	COFFEE KISSES
Cornish	CORNISH FAIRINGS
cracker	COSAQUE
—salted	SALTINE
—unsweetened	WATER BISCUIT
crisp	
—cheese biscuit	(CREAM) CRACKER
—salted	PRETZEL

—sweet	SHORTBREAD, SHORTCAKE
currant	GARIBALDI
dry, unsweetened	CRACKER, CRACKNEL
	CRISPBREAD
finger-shaped	LANGUE-DE-CHAT
ginger	
—cylindrical	BRANDY SNAP
—flat	(GRANTHAM)GINGERBREAD
	GINGERNUT, GINGERSNAP
hard	BROWN GEORGE
—unflavoured	HARDTACK
	SHIP('S) BISCUIT
Italian	AMARETTI
knot-shaped	PRETZEL
made with sour milk	SODA BISCUIT
marzipan	PETIT FOURS
nuts	FLORENTINES, NUT ROCK
oatmeal	
—Scottish	FARL(E), OATCAKE
—and syrup	FLAPJACK
plain	OSBORNE
ship's biscuit	HARDTACK, SEA BISCUIT
small, fancy	PETIT FOUR
South African	SOETKOEKIE
spiced (US)	HERMIT
sweet	NICE, SHORTBREAD
	SHORTCAKE
—US	GRAHAM CRACKER
thin crisp ring	JUMBLE, JUMBAL
unsweetened	BATH OLIVER
with printed motto	FORTUNE COOKIE
blood	(*see* **circulation**)
boats	
admiral's boat	BARGE
Annamese	GAY-YOU
barge	GABBARD, GABBART
bark-covered	CANOE
canal boat	BARGE, FLY(-BOAT)
	LONGBOAT, NARROWBOAT
Chinese	JUNK, SAMPAN, SANPAN
collapsible	BERTHON-BOAT
—rubber boat	DINGEY, DING(H)Y
coracle	GOPHER
Eskimo	KAYAK, UMIAK
Eton oarsman	WET BOB
fisherman's	COB(B)LE, CORACLE
flat-bottomed	MACKINAW, PUNT
fulcrum for oar	ROLLOCK, ROWLOCK
	RULLOCK
gopher	CORACLE
having	
—1 hull	MONOHULL
—2 banks of oars	BIREME
—2 hulls	CATAMARAN
—3 banks of oars	TRIREME
—3 hulls	TRIMARAN

—3 oars	RANDAN
—4 banks of oars	QUADRIREME
—5 banks of oars	QUINQUEREME
—5 oars	WHALER
—8 oars	PINNACE
—30 oars	TRIACONTER
—50 oars	PENTACONTER
hollowed tree-trunk	DUGOUT (CANOE)
	MONOXYLON
Indian	
—Ganges	PULWAR
—surf-boat	MASOOLAH, MASSOOLA
	MASULA
Irish	CURRACH, CURRAGH
Italian	BARCA, GONDOLA
light rowing-boat	GIG, SHELL, WHERRY
Malayan	COROCORE, COROCORO
	PRA(H)U, PROA
Maldives	DHONI
Maltese	DGHAJSA
motor-powered	POWERBOAT, SPEEDBOAT
motors	INBOARD, OUTBOARD
open rowing-boat	GALLEY
pin retaining oar	THOLE(-PIN), THOW(E)L
pointed at both ends	WHALER
propelled by	
—pedals	PEDALO
—pole	PUNT
punt pole	QUANT
race meeting	REGATTA
racing boat	OUTRIGGER, SHELL
Red Indian	(BIRCH-BARK) CANOE
rowing with odd	
number of oars	CUT-THROAT ROWING
Scottish	COB(B)LE
ship's boat	BARGE, CUTTER, JOLLYBOAT
	LAUNCH, WHALER
side plank	STRAKE, STRAIK
skiff of galley	CAIQUE
skin-covered	CANOE, CORACLE, CURRACH
	CURRAGH, KAYAK, UMIAK
small rowing-boat	DINGEY, DING(H)Y
	GIG, PINNACE, SCULL(ER)
	SHALLOP, SKIFF
South American	
dugout canoe	PERIAGUA, PIRAGUA
	PIROGUE
state barge	GALLEY-FOIST
Turkish skiff	CAIQUE
used	
—in loading etc	LIGHTER
—on the Bosporus	CAIQUE
—to bring fruit etc to ship	BUM-BOAT
Venetian	GONDOLA
warship's	
—second boat	BARGE

—tender	PINNACE
Welsh	CORACLE
with strakes	
—abutting	CARVEL-BUILT
—overlapping	CLINKER-BUILT
Bolivia	BOL
capital	LA PAZ
coins	
—unit	CENTAVO
—100 centavos	DOLLAR
measure	CELEMIN, LEAGUE
musical instrument	CHARANGA
ruminant	LLAMA, VICUNA
weight	LIBRA
bone	OS
abnormal outgrowth	OUTGROWTH
ankle	ASTRAGALUS, TALUS
back	
—bone	SPINAL COLUMN
	VERTEBRAL COLUMN
—of skull	OCCIPUT
basis of bone	OSSEIN
become bone	OSSIFY
beneath the tail (fish)	HYPURAL BONE
bone-destroying cell	OSTEOBLAST
bone-formation	OSTEOGENESIS
	OSTEOGENY
bone-forming	
—cell	OSTEOBLAST
—material	CARTILAGE
bone-marrow	MEDULLA
—cell	ERYTHROBLAST
bone(s) in	
—ankle	ASTRALAGUS, MALLEOLUS
	TALUS
—back	LUMBAR VERTEBRA(E)
—bottom of spine	COCCYX
—chest	(EPI)STERNUM
	(INTER)CLAVICLE
	MANUBRIUM, PECTORAL GIRDLE
	PRESTERNUM, RIBS, STERNUM
	THORACIC VERTEBRA(E)
	XIPHISTERNUM
—chin	MENTAL PROMINENCE
—ear	AUDITORY OSSICLE, INCUS
	MALLEUS, PERIOTIC, STAPES
birds, reptiles	COLUMELLA AURIS
—elbow	FUNNY BONE, OLECRANON
—embryo	DERMAL BONE
	MEMBRANE BONE
—foot	CALCANEUM, CUBOID
	CUNEIFORM, (META)TARSALS
	NAVICULAR, PHALANGES
	TALUS, TARSUS
—forearm	RADIUS, ULNA
—foreleg of horse	METACARPUS

—hand and wrist	CAPITATE, CARPUS	—skull bones	SINUS
	HAMATE, LUNAE, (META)CARPALS	for eye	ORBIT
	NAVICULAR, PHALANGES	cell	
	PISIFORM, RADIALE	—destroying bone	OSTEOCLAST
	SCAPHOID, TRAPEZIUM	—producing bone	OSTEOBLAST
	TRIQUETAL, ULNARE	changing to bone	OSSIFICATION
—head	BREGMA(TA), CHEEKBONE	channel in bone	HAVERSIAN CANAL
	CRANIUM, ETHMOID, FRONTAL	collarbone	CLAVICLE
	JUGAL, LACRIMAL, MALAR	connection of bones by	
	MANDIBLE, MASTOID PROCESS	—cartilage	SYNCHONDROSIS
	MAXILLA, OCCIPITAL	—ligaments	SYNDESMOSIS
	PALATINE, PARAQUADRATE	—muscle	SYSSARCOSIS
	(PARA)SPHENOID, PARIETAL	—tendons	SYNTENOSIS
	SKULL, SQUAMOSAL, TEMPORAL	container for bones	OSSUARY
	TRIQUETRUM, VOMER	cutting of bone	OSTEOTOMY
	WORMIAN, ZYGOMA(TIC)	cuttle bone	SEPIOST(AIRE), SEPIUM
	(see also skull below)	decay of bone	CARIES
—hip	HIP GIRDLE, ILIUM	dermal plate	OSTEODERM
	INOMINATE, ISCHIUM	description of bones	OSTEOGRAPHY
	PELVIC GIRDLE, PELVIS, PUBIS	diseases of bones	(see disease)
—hoof of horse	COFFIN BONE, PEDAL BONE	dorsal process of vertebra	DIAPOPHYSIS
—hyoid arch (fish)	HYOMANDIBULA	eating bones	OSSIVOROUS
—jaw	ARTICULAR, DENTARY	fibula	PERONE
	MANDIBLE, (PRE)MAXILLA	flat and winglike	ALA
	PTERYGOID, QUADRATE	fluid in joints	SINOVIA
—knee	KNEE-CAP, KNEE-PAN	forepart of skull	SINCIPUT
	PATELLA, ROTULA	formation of bone	OSSIFICATION
—lower leg	FIBULA, PERONE, TIBIA		OSTEOGENESIS, OSTEOGENY
—neck	CERVICAL VERTEBRA(E)	fracture	OSTEOCLASIS
—nose	ETHMOID, NASAL(CONCHAE)	—clean break	SIMPLE
	PINNA	—with bone(s)	
—pelvis	ILIUM, INNOMINATE BONE	crushed	COMMINUTED
	ISCHIUM, PUBIS, SACRUM	exposed	COMPOUND
—shoulder	CORACOID, SCAPULA	forced together	IMPACTED
—spine	VERTEBRA(E)	split	GREENSTICK
—tail of bird	PYGOSTYLE	funny bone	OLECRANON
—tendon	SESAMOID BONE	fusion of bones	SYMPHYSIS
—thigh	FEMUR		SYNOSTOSIS
—tongue (base)	HYOID	gap between bones	FONTANEL(LE)
—upper arm	HUMERUS	gill-cover bone (fish)	SUBOPERCULUM
—wing of bird	CARPOMETACARPUS	head of bone turning in socket	WHIRL-BONE
bone-store	OSSARIUM, OSSUARY	heel	CALCANEUS
bony		hip	
—fishes	OSTEICHTHYES	—girdle	PELVIC GIRDLE
	OSTEOGLOSSIDAE	—joint	COXA
—outgrowth	OSTEOPHYTE	—socket	ACETABULUM
—plate	OSTEODERM, PLACOID	holding teeth	ALVEOLAR ARCH
bottom of spine	COCCYX		DENTARY, (PRE)MAXILLA
breaking bone in surgery	OSTEOCLASIS	hole in bone	FORAMEN
breastbone	STERNUM	hollow in bone	ANTRUM, FOSSA
—of bird	WISHBONE		FOVEA
brittleness of bones	OSTEOPOROSIS	jawbone	
cartilage of ribs	TENDRON	—lower	MAXILLA
cartilaginous skull	CHONDROCRANIUM	—upper	MANDIBLE
cavity in		joint	
—jawbone	ALVEOLUS	—moving in one plane	GINGLYMUS

—with one bone in groove of another	SCHINDYLESIS
junction of bone	SUTURE
kneecap	PATELLA, WHIRL-BONE
knob on end of bone	CONDYLE
—in socket	WHIRL-BONE
little bone	OSSICLE
loss of calcium	OSTEOPOROSIS
lowest part of spine	COCCYX
manipulation of bones	CHIROPRACTIC
	OSTEOPATHY
membrane covering bone	PERIOSTEUM
movement of joint	ARTICULATION
neural arch (snakes)	ZYGANTRUM
	ZYGOSPHENE
part of	
—bone having its own ossification centre	EPIPHYSIS
—sternum	MANUBRIUM
—temporal bone	SQUAMOSAL
—vertebra	CENTRUM, DIAPHYSIS
	NEURAL ARCH
	NEURAL SPINE
plate for closing skull	OPERCULUM
projecting part	PROCESS
projection on	
—axis	ODONTOID PROCESS
—breastbone (birds)	CARINA, KEEL
—end of bone	CONDYLE
—hip girdle	PUBIS
—scapula	ACROMION, ACROMIUM
—skull	BULLA, OCCIPITAL CONDYLE
—thigh	TROCHANTER
—ulna	OLECRANON
—vertebra	PLEUROPOPHYSIS
rib	COSTA, PLEUROPOPHYSIS
segment(s) of	
—breastbone	STERNEBRA(E)
—spine	VERTEBRA(E)
shaft of long bone	DIAPHYSIS
shin	TIBIA
shoulder	
—blade	SCAPULA
—girdle	PECTORAL GIRDLE
—point	ACROMION
skeletal	
—bars (fish)	BRANCHIAL ARCH
	HYOID ARCH
	MANDIBULAR ARCH
	VISCERAL ARCH
—element	SCLERE
—plate	SCLERITE
—rod	NOTOCHORD
—tissue	CARTILAGE, SCLERENCHYMA
skeleton	
—external	EXOSKELETON

—internal	ENDOSKELETON
skull	
—brain and ear	NEUROCRANIUM
—cavity for eyeball	ORBIT
—enclosing ear	AUDITORY CAPSULE
—forepart	SINCIPUT
—in embryo	CHONDROCRANIUM
—jaws	SPLANCHNOCRANIUM
—knob at back	OCCIPITAL CONDYLE
—membrane bone	SQUAMOSAL
—plate for closing	OPERCULUM
—projecting part round ear	BULLA
—rear part	OCCIPUT
small bone	OSSICLE
—in sea-urchin	EPIPHYSIS
socket receiving head of	
—femur	GLENOID CAVITY
—humerus	ACETABULUM
soft tissue in bone cavity	MARROW
softening of bones	OSTEOMALACIA
spine	SPINAL COLUMN
	VERTEBRAL COLUMN
—bottom section	COCCYX
—section(s)	VERTEBRA(E)
spiny process of temporal bone	STYLOID
study of bones	OSTEOLOGY
surgery on bones	OSTEOPLASTY
	OSTEOTOMY
thin layer of bone	LAMELLA
tumour of bone	OSTEOMA
union of bones	SYNOSTOSIS
vertebra	SPONDYL
vertebrae	
—first	ATLAS
—second	AXIS
—situated in	
chest	THORACIC VERTEBRAE
hip region	SACRAL VERTEBRAE
neck	CERVICAL VERTEBRAE
waist region	LUMBAR VERTEBRAE
—supporting skull	ATLAS, AXIS
whalebone	BALEEN
wishbone	FOURCHETTE, FURCULA
with cartilage precursor	CARTILAGE BONE
	REPLACING BONE
without cartilage precursor	DERMAL BONE
wrist	CARPUS
yoke-piece of vertebra	ZYGAPOPHYSIS
books	
additional material	ADDENDUM
	APPENDIX
annual	ALMANAC(K)
author's early	JUVENILIA
bible	
—Chaldean	TARGUM

122

—Christian
earliest gospel
translation LINDISFARNE GOSPELS
first five books PENTATEUCH
first seven books HEPTATEUCH
in four versions TETRAPLA
versions AMERICAN STANDARD
AUTHORISED, BISHOP'S
BREECHES, COVERDALE'S
GENEVA, GOOD NEWS
GREAT, JERUSALEM
KING JAMES'S, MASSACHUSETTS
MATTHEW'S, NEW ENGLAND
REVISED, RHEIMS AND DOUAI
TAVERNER'S, TYNDALE'S
—Hebrew T(H)ORAH
—Latin translation VULGATE
—Moslem ALCORAN, (AL)KORAN
QORAN, QURAN
—Syrian PESHIT(T)A, PESHIT(T)O
blank leaf in book FLYLEAF
book
—binder BIBLIOPEGIST
—hater BIBLIOPHOBE
—lover BIBLIOMANIAC, BIBLIOPHILE
—seller BIBLIOPOLE
bookmaker's book of bets HANDBOOK
brief description BLURB
cased book HARDBACK
catalogue of books BIBLIOTHECA
censor's permission to publish NIHIL OBSTAT
cheap novel PAPERBACK, PULP
church rules PIE, PYE
collection of
— bible readings LEGEND
—church lessons LECTIONARY
—cuttings SCRAPBOOK
—formulae FORMULARY
—homilies POSTIL
—hymns HYMNAL
—learned papers FESTSCHRIFT
—lessons LECTIONARY
—maps ATLAS
—plants HERBAL
—prayers MASS BOOK
—precedents FORMULARY
—psalms PSALTER
—related subjects OMNIBUS
—rituals FORMULARY
—words DICTIONARY, GLOSSARY
LEXICON, THESAURUS
—writings ANTHOLOGY, OMNIBUS
complete condensed treatise COMPENDIUM
comprehensive book of
reference (EN)CYCLOPAEDIA
PANDECT

condensed treatise COMPENDIUM
correct use of language GRAMMAR
corrections CORRIGENDA, ERRATA
dates ALMANAC, CALENDAR
day-book DIARY, JOURNAL
dealing with
—earlier events PREQUEL
—later events SEQUEL
detective story ROMAN POLICIER
WHODUNNIT
diary JOURNAL INTIME
dictionary of
—derivations ETYMOLOGICON
—names ONOMASTICON
displaying photographs, etc ALBUM
drugs DISPENSATORY
FORMULARY, HERBAL
MIMS, PHARMACOPOEIA
early illustrated book BLOCK-BOOK
early printed book INCUNABULA
exercise book CAHIER
fiction NOVEL
financial JOURNAL, LEDGER
first textbook HORNBOOK, PRIMER
flowers CYBELE, FLORA
form of publication EDITION
formal study TREATISE
geographical index GAZETTEER
grammar DONAT, DONET
guide book BAEDEKER
handbook VADE MECUM
handwritten MANUSCRIPT
having sheets folded into
—8 leaves OCTAVO
—12 leaves DUODECIMO
—16 leaves SEXTODECIMO, SIXTEENMO
—18 leaves OCTODECIMO, EIGHTEENMO
heraldry ARMORIAL
illustration at front of
book FRONTISPIECE
Indian book of sayings SUTRA
introductory piece FOREWORD, PREFACE
large book TOME
left-hand page VERSO
licence to print or publish IMPRIMATUR
librarian BIBLIOTHECARY
library BIBLIOTHECA
list of
—baronets BARONETAGE
—books BIBLIOGRAPHY
BIBLIOTHECA
—clergy CROCKFORD'S
—goods CATALOGUE
—important people WHO'S WHO
—peers BURKE'S PEERAGE
—train times BRADSHAW

—words and meanings	DICTIONARY
	GLOSSARY, LEXICON
	THESAURUS
magazine	JOURNAL
manual	ENCH(E)IRIDION
	HANDBOOK, TEXTBOOK
manuscript volume	CODEX
medieval	
—before 1501	INCUNABLE, INCUNABULUM
—on	
alchemy	ALMAGEST
animals	BESTIARY
mixed fact and fiction	FACTION
navigator's manual	PORTOLANO
New Testament books	
—originally not accepted	ANTILOGOMENA
—taken as authentic	HOMOLOG(O)UMENA
notebook	COMMONPLACE BOOK
novel	
—about successive	
generations	ROMAN FLEUVE
—short	NOVELLA
—with	
a theme	ROMAN A THESE
disguised names	ROMAN A CLEF
number of copies at one printing	EDITION
Old Testament	HAGIOGRAPHA
—Greek	SEPTUAGINT
one of a series	VOLUME
page pasted to cover	END-PAPER
parliamentary	
—proceedings	HANSARD
—report	BLUE BOOK
part of book published in	
—instalments	HEFT
—volumes	LIVRAISON
periodical	JOURNAL, MAGAZINE
personal book	COMMONPLACE BOOK
	DIARY, JOURNAL, SCRAPBOOK
pocket companion	VADE MECUM
popular book or	
pamphlet	CHAPBOOK
prayer book	BREVIARY, EUCHOLOGION
	EUCHOLOGY, FORMULARY
	MISSAL, ORARIUM
—Hebrew	MA(C)HZOR, SIDDUR
primer	DONAT, DONE
printed by Caxton	CAXTON
promotional material	BLURB, FLYER
prophetic	SIBYLLINE
Psalms	PSALTER
quickly written book	POTBOILER
record of proceedings of	
—meetings	MINUTE(BOOK)
—parliament	HANSARD
records	ANNALS, JOURNAL

reference book	(EN)CYCLOPEDIA
	TEXTBOOK, TOME
	TREATISE, VADE MECUM
—on heraldry	ORDINARY
register	CARTULARY
religious instruction	CATECHISM
repository for books	BIBLIOTHECA
	LIBRARY
right-hand page of book	RECTO
Roman law digest	PANDECT
rule book	ORDINAND
scriptures	(*see* bible *above*)
section of book	
published separately	FASCIC(U)LE
	FASCICULUS
selections for beginners	CHRESTOMATHY
sequence of events	CHRONICLE
service-book	TE IGITUR
small book	BOOKLET, DUODECIMO
	MONOGRAPH, PAMPHLET
	SEXTODECIMO, SIXTEENMO
stamp book	ALBUM
study of books	BIBLIOGRAPHY
	BIBLIOLOGY
summary of contents	PRECIS, SYNOPSIS
surplus book	REMAINDER
text	
—of oper(ett)a	LIBRETTO
—with notes of editors	VARIORUM
travel guide	BAEDEKER
treatise	
—on ecclesiastical	
festivals	FESTILOGY, FESTOLOGY
—political or religious	TRACT
two pages of open book	SPREAD
typed	TYPESCRIPT
with	
—editorial annotations	VARIORUM
—soft covers	PAPERBACK
—stiff covers	HARDBACK
written in author's own hand	HOLOGRAPH
	(*see also* **literature**)
botany	(*see* **biology**)
Botswana	RB
capital	GABARONE
coin	
—unit	PULA
—100 pula	THEBE
former name	BECHUANALAND
bottle	
American - dark glass	JUNK-BOTTLE
Australian - small	STUBBY
eared bottle	COSTREL
empty	DEAD MAN
Franconian	BOCKSBEUTEL
Greek	AMPHORA, LEKYTHOS

Italian	FIASCO
large bottle	FLAGON, DEMIJOHN
	(*see also* **measures**-capacity)
leather	JACK
narrow-necked	LAGEN(A), LEKYTHOS
pilgrim's bottle	AMPULLA, COSTREL
quarter-bottle	SPLIT
Roman	AMPHORA, AMPULLA
small bottle	CRUSE, FLACON, PHIAL
	SPLIT, STUBBY, VIAL
	VINAIGRETTE
tear-bottle	LACRIMAL URN
	LACR(H)YMAL URN
used for growing plants	TERRARIUM
water bottle	CARAFE
whisky bottle	AULD KIRK
wine bottle	CARAFE
—with descending spout	PORRON
bowls	
area of green	RINK
captain	SKIP
part of team	RINK
players	
—Australian	PARELLA, SCHUBACK
—English (m)	ALLCOCK, BRYANT
	HEPPELL, SEKJER, SMITH
(f)	LINE
—Northern Irish	BAKER, CORKILL
(f)	JOHNSTON
—Scottish (m)	CORSIE, DICKINSON
	THOMSON, WOOD
(f)	MCCRONE
—Welsh (m)	PRICE, THOMAS, WEALE
(f)	ACKLAND
session of play	END
target	JACK
boxing	
arena	RING
attendant	SECOND
boundaries of ring	ROPES
boxers	
—American	ALI, ARMSTRONG, BAER
	BAKSI, BERBICK, BRADDOCK
	CHARLES, CLAY, CONN, CORBETT
	CURRY, DEMPSEY, DOKES, FOREMAN
	FOSTER, FRAZIER, FULLMER
	GRAZIANO, GREB, HAGLER
	HEARNS, HOLMES, JOHNSON, KETCHEL
	LA MOTTA, LEONARD, LESNEVICH
	LEVINSY, LEWIS, LISTON, LOUGHRAN
	LOUIS, MARCIANO, MAXIM, MOORE
	NORTON, NOVA, OLIN, PAGE
	PASTRANO, PATTERSON, PENDER
	PEP, QUARRY, ROBINSON, ROSENBLOOM
	SADLER, SAVOLD, SHARKEY, SMITH
	SPINKS, STRIBLING, SULLIVAN

	THOMAS, TUNNEY, TYSON, WALCOTT
	WEAVER, WILLARD, ZALE
—British	BECKETT, BERG, BODELL, BOON
	BRUNO, BUGNER, BYGRAVES
	COCKELL, CONTEH, COOPER
	CRAWLEY, DOWNES, DUNN, ERSKINE
	FITZSIMMONS, GAINS, GARDNER
	GREEN, HARVEY, HOOD
	JOHNSON, KANE, KAYLOR, LEWIS
	LONDON, MACAVOY, MILLS, MINTER
	NOTICE, PETERSEN, PHILLIPS
	PRESCOTT, SCOTT, SIBSON, STACEY
	TARLETON, TURPIN, WALKER
	WALSH, WOODCOCK
—Cuban	GAVILAN, LEGRA, PARET
—French	CARPENTIER, CERDAN, THIL
—German	NEUSEL, SCHMELLING
—Ghanaian	NELSON
—Irish	FINNEGAN, GILROY, KELLY
	MCGUIGAN, MONAGHAN
—Italian	CARNERA, MITRI
—Mexican	SALDIVAR
—Nicaraguan	ARGUELLO
—Panamanian	DURAN
—Scottish	BUCHANAN, LYNCH
	MCGOWAN, PATERSON
	WATT
—South African	COETZEE, FOORD
	MCCORKINGDALE
—Swedish	JOHANNSON
—Welsh	DOWER, DRISCOLL, FARR
	WELSH, WILDE, WINSTONE
floor of ring	CANVAS
governing body	WORLD BOXING ASSOCIATION
	WORLD BOXING COUNCIL
	WORLD BOXING FEDERATION
illegal blow	BELOW THE BELT
	KIDNEY PUNCH
	RABBIT PUNCH
knock down	PUT ON THE CANVAS
methods of winning	KNOCK-OUT, KO
	(ON) POINTS
	TECHNICAL KNOCK-OUT
mouth protector	GUM SHIELD
nicknames	
—Ali, Cassius Clay	LOUISVILLE LIP
—Baer	CLOWN PRINCE
—Corbett	GENTLEMAN JIM
—Dempsey	MANASSA MAULER
—Duran	MAN OF STONE, EL ANIMAL
—Hearns	HIT MAN
—Jake La Motta	RAGING BULL
—Louis	BROWN BOMBER
—Sullivan	STRONG BOY
—Tyson	IRON MIKE
—Wilde	MIGHTY ATOM

officials	JUDGE, REFEREE, TIME-KEEPER
punches	BOLO, CROSS, HOOK, LEFT
	RIGHT, STRAIGHT, SWING
	UPPERCUT
session of boxing	ROUND
venues	
—America	
Atlantic City	CONVENTION CENTRE
New York	MADISON SQUARE GARDENS
	POLO GROUNDS
	YANKEE STADIUM
—Britain	ALBERT HALL, WHITE CITY
weights	
< 108 lb	STRAW-WEIGHT
108	LIGHT-FLYWEIGHT
112	FLYWEIGHT
115	SUPER FLYWEIGHT
118	BANTAMWEIGHT
122	LIGHT-FEATHERWEIGHT
126	FEATHERWEIGHT
130	JUNIOR LIGHTWEIGHT
135	LIGHTWEIGHT
140	LIGHT-WELTERWEIGHT
147	WELTERWIGHT
153½	LIGHT-MIDDLEWEIGHT
160	MIDDLEWEIGHT
175	LIGHT-HEAVYWEIGHT
190	CRUISERWEIGHT
> 190	HEAVYWEIGHT
brain	ENCEPHALON
action of	CEREBRATION
active part	GREY MATTER
brain-shaped	CEREBRIFORM
brain-waves	ALPHA RHYTHM
	BETA WAVES
cavity	AQUEDUCT OF SILVIUS
	FORAMEN OF MONRO
	VENTRICLE
central lobe of cerebellum	VERMIS
connecting cortex and	
hypothalamus	LIMBIC SYSTEM
connective tissue	DURA MATER
disorders of brain	(*see* **disease**)
fibres joining hemispheres	PONS VAROLII
ganglion of forebrain	STRIATUM
grey matter	BASAL GANGLIA
	BASAL NUCLEI
H-shaped fissure	ZYGON
half of brain	HEMISPHERE
lobes of brain	AMYGDALA, INSULA
	OCCIPITAL, OLFACTORY
	OPTIC, PARIETAL
	(PRE-)FRONTAL, REIL'S ISLAND
	TEMPORAL, VERMIS
mass of cells related	
to a function	NUCLEUS

membrane(s)	ARACHNOID, DURA MATER
	MENINX(MENINGES)
	PIA MATER
—sheet of dura mater	TENTORIUM
nerve cell fibres	WHITE MATTER
old	HARN(ES)
olfactory lobe	RHINENCEPHALON
operations on brain	LEUCOTOMY
	LOBOTOMY
part controlling	
—appetite	HYPOTHALAMUS
—autonomic nervous	
system	HYPOTHALAMUS
—basic	
activities	VITAL CENTRE
emotions	LIMBIC SYSTEM
—blood flow	HYPOTHALAMUS
—co-ordination	NEOPALLIUM
	THALAMUS
—crude sensations	THALAMUS
—emotions	HYPOTHALAMUS
—endocrine glands	PITUITARY
—muscle action	BASAL GANGLIA
—reflex actions	CEREBELLUM
—response to	
stimuli	RETICULAR FORMATION
—sensation	CEREBRAL CORTEX
	SENSORIUM
—sight and hearing	MESENCEPHALON
—striped muscles	MOTOR CORTEX
—temperature	HYPOTHALAMUS
—thirst	HYPOTHALAMUS
—voluntary movement	CEREBRAL CORTEX
parts of	
—brain	
forebrain	CEREBRUM
	PROSENCEPHALON
glands	PINEAL, PITUITARY
hind-brain	CEREBELLUM
	EPENCEPHALON
	RHOMBENCEPHALON
joining hemispheres	CORPUS CALLOSUM
midbrain	MESENCEPHALON
where optic nerve	
emerges	OPTIC THALAMUS
—brainstem	PONS (VAROLII)
—cerebellum	VERMIS
—cerebrum	CAUDATE
	CEREBRAL CORTEX
	NEOCORTEX, (NEO-)PALLIUM
	PUTAMEN
half of	HEMISPHERE
—corpus callosum	SPLENIUM
—forebrain	DIENCEPHALON
—optic thalami	PINEAL BODY
—spinal cord	MEDULLA OBLONGATA

pituitary gland	HYPOPHYSIS
projection	
—into ventricle	CHOR(I)OID PLEXUS
—on optic thalamus	PULVINAR
raised curved trace in	
lateral ventricle	BIRD'S SPUR
	CALCAR AVIS
	HIPPOCAMPUS
ridge in surface	CONVOLUTION, GYRUS
supporting tissue	NEUROGLIA
ventricles	FOURTH, LATERAL, THIRD
Brazil	
ant	TUCANDERA
armadillo	TATOU, TATU
bird	CARACARA, GUAN, KAMICHI
biting-fly	MOTUCA, MUTUCA, PIUM
canoe-waterway	IGARAPE
capital	BRASILIA
club-moss	PILLIGAN
cocoa	GUARANA
coffee	BAHIA
coins	
—old coins	LEMPIRA, REIS
—1000 reis	MILREIS
—unit	CENTAVO
—100 centavos	CRUIZERO, CRUSADO
—1000 cruizeros	CONTO
dance	BATUQUE, BOSSA NOVA
	CARIOCA, MAXIXE, SAMBA
drink	ASSAI
drug	JABORANDI, PAREIRA
fish	PERAI, PIABA, PIRAL
	PIRAN(H)A, PIRAYA
flower	GLOXINIA, TREE-LILY
	VELLOZIA
flycatcher	YETAPA
grass	PARA-GRASS
—land	CAMPO
half-caste	MAMELUCO
hare	TAPETI
heron	SOCO
log canoe	MONTARIA
macaw	ARARA, MARACAN
monkey	SAI
negro	MINA
nut	COQUILLA, PARA-NUT
	SAPUCAIA
offspring of European	
and Indian	MAMELUCO
open forest	CAATINGA
opossum	SARIGUE
palm	(see separate entry)
parrot	ARA
piassava	PARA GRASS
plain	CAMPO, SAVANNAH
plant	IPECAC(UANHA), PIPI

pods used in tanning	PIPI
provinces	ACRE, AMAPA, AMAZONAS
	BAHIA, CEARA, GOIAS, MARANHAO
	MATO GROSSO, MATO GROSSO DO SUL
	MINAS GERAIS, PARA, PARAIBA
	PARANA, PERNAMBUCO, PIAVI
	RIO GRANDE DO SUL
	RIO GRANDE DO NORTE, RONDONIA
	RORAIMA, SANTA CATARINA
	SAO PAULO
rabbit	TAPETI
river	AMAZON
rodent	CAPIBARA, CAPYBARA
rosewood	PALISANDER
rubber	CAUCHO, (H)ULE, PARA
—tree	MANGABEIRA, SERINGA
sirenian	MANATEE, MANATI
snakes	(see separate entry)
soap-tree	TINGI, TINGUY
stork	JABIRU
timber	(see separate entry)
trade jargon	ERAL, LINGOA
tree	ANDA, APA, ARAROB, BARBATIMEO
	BRAUNA, DALI, GOMAEL, GUARABUA
	HERCULES CUB, LECYTHIS
	MACERANDUBA, MANGABEIRA
	MASSARANDUBA, MASSERANDUBA
	MUSTAIBA, PARANA PINE
	PRICKLY-ASH, SAPUCAIA, TINGUY
	TOOTHACHE-TREE, WALLABA
	XANTHOXYLUM
water-lily	VICTORIA
weight	
—1 lb	LIBRA
—32 lb	ARROBA
bread	
American	CORN PONE, JOHNNYCAKE
	QUICK BREAD
Australian	DAMPER
—currant bread	BROWNIE
browned by grilling	TOAST
casing with fruit	
filling	SUMMER PUDDING
coarse dark bread	BLACK BREAD
coated with egg and fried	FRENCH TOAST
containing baking powder	SODA BREAD
crescent-shaped	CROISSANT
crumbs from stale bread	RASPINGS
crumpet	PIKELET
date and sultana	TURKESTAN
desserts	BREAD (AND BUTTER) PUDDING
	SUMMER PUDDING
dough reserved as leaven	
for next batch	SOURDOUGH
dry, unsweetened biscuit	CRISPBREAD
finest bread	MANCHET

finger of hard dry toast	RUSK
flat	
—cake, unleavened	ROTI
—loaf	STOTY CAKE
for fillings	
—French	PISSALADIERE
—Italian	PIZZA
French	
—bread	PAIN
—long loaf	BAGUETTE, FICELLE
—roll	BRIOCHE, CROISSANT
German	
—bread	BROT
—crusty roll	BREZEL, PRE(T)ZEL
—rye bread	PUMPERNICKEL
—sweet bread	
toasted	ZWIEBACK
with fruit	STOLLEN
Greek	PIT(T)A
hard exterior of loaf	CRUST
Hebrew	
—rich	CHOLLA PLAIT
—ring	BAGEL
—unleavened	MATZA(H), MATZO(H)
	PASSOVER BREAD
—with poppy seeds	CHALLA(H)
Indian	CHAPAT(T)I, CHUPAT(T)I
	NA(A)N, PARAT(H)A
	PURI, ROTI
Irish	BARMBRACK, POTATO BREAD
	SCOFA, SODA BREAD
Italian	
—bread	PANE
sticks	GRISSINI
—flat loaf	FOCACCIA
—made with olive oil	CIABATTA
large	
—flat roll	BAP
—piece with savoury topping	CROUTE
—roll with filling	SUBMARINE
light soft loaf or roll	BRIOCHE
Lincolnshire	PLUM BREAD
loaf	
—offered in honour of	
the Virgin	PAN(H)AGIA
—shapes	BLOOMER, COTTAGE, ROLL
	SPLIT TIN, STICK, TIN
long	
—roll	HUFFER
—white loaf	FRENCH LOAF, FRENCH STICK
	OATIE BATON, VIENNA LOAF
with filling	HUFFER
made from	
—cornmeal	CORNBREAD
—finest flour	MANCHET
	WASTEL(-BREAD)
—maize	CORN PONE, JOHNNYCAKE
	SPOON BREAD, TORTILLA
—rye	RYEBREAD
—seaweed	LAVER BREAD
—unbleached flour	BROWN BREAD
—unsweetened rye	
or wheat	CRISPBREAD
—wholemeal flour	RAVEL(LED) BREAD
—whole wheat	GRANARY BREAD
	WHEATMEAL, WHOLEMEAL
Middle Eastern	PIT(T)A
New Zealand currant bread	BROWNIE
oat-bread	JANNOCK
open sandwich	SMORREBROD
outer part of loaf	CRUST
penny roll	TOMMY
poorest flour	RED-DOG
porous cake	CRUMPET
raised with sodium	
bicarbonate	SODA BREAD
round case for filling	PIZZA
sandwich with three	
slices	THREE-DECKER
Scottish flat bread	BANNOCK
ship's bread	HARD TACK
singed	TOAST
slice	ROUND
—baked crisp	RUSK
—browned by heat	TOAST
—on which food was placed	TRENCHER
slightly leavened	PITTA
small	
—cube crisply fried	CROUTON
—fragment	CRUMB
—piece	
as garnish	SIPPET
served with soup etc	CROUTON
with savoury topping	CANAPE
—portions in various	
shapes	ROLLS
-roll	FINGER ROLL, BRIDGE ROLL
soft	
—maize bread	SPOON BREAD
—roll	BARM CAKE
	DEVONSHIRE SPLIT
	OVEN BOTTOM
Spanish bread	PAN
stick(s)	GRISSINO (GRISSINI)
sweet	
—bread	SALLY LUNN, TEA BREAD
with currants	TEA CAKE
—roll	BRIOCHE
—sliced and toasted crisp	ZWIEBACK
thin loaf	FRENCH STICK
toasted	
—one side	FRENCH TOAST

—slice for savouries	CROUTE
—very thin	MELBA TOAST
two slices with filling	SANDWICH
unleavened bread	MATZA(H), MATZO(H)
	PASSOVER BREAD
used in Eucharist	HOST
Welsh	BARA BRITH
West Indian	COO-COO
wholemeal	PUMPERNICKEL
	RAVEL(LED) BREAD

bridge
built

—from stone slabs	CLAPPER BRIDGE
—with open girders	LATTICE BRIDGE
curved	ARCH BRIDGE
end support of bridge	ABUTMENT, PIER
famous bridges	
—Anglesey/	
Wales	MENAI SUSPENSION BRIDGE
—Avon	CLIFTON SUSPENSION BRIDGE
	SEVERN ESTUARY BRIDGE
—Australia	SYDNEY HARBOUR BRIDGE
—Bayonne, USA	KILL VAN KULL BRIDGE
—Berlin	GLIENICKER BRIDGE
—Budapest	ARPAD BRIDGE, CHAIN BRIDGE
—Cairo	AL GALA BRIDGE
	AL GAMMA BRIDGE
	SAYALA BRIDGE
	SIXTH OF JULY BRIDGE
	SIXTH OF OCTOBER BRIDGE
	TAHRIR BRIDGE
—Calcutta	HOWRAH BRIDGE
—Chester, USA	COMMODORE BARRY
	BRIDGE
—Czechoslovakia	ZDAKOV BRIDGE
—Denmark	LILLEBAELT BRIDGE
—Devon	TAMAR BRIDGE
—Dublin	O'CONNELL BRIDGE
—Fayetteville	NEW RIVER GORGE BRIDGE
—Florence	PONTE VECCHIO
—Humberside	HUMBER ESTUARY BRIDGE
—Ipswich	ORWELL BRIDGE
—Istanbul	ATATURK BRIDGE
	BOSPHORUS BRIDGE
	GALATA BRIDGE
—Japan	AKASHI-KAIKYO BRIDGE
	INNOSHIMA BRIDGE
	KAMMON STRAITS BRIDGE
	OHNARUTO BRIDGE
—Key West	SEVEN-MILE BRIDGE
—Lancashire	RUNCORN-WIDNES BRIDGE
—Le Havre	TANKARVILLE BRIDGE
—Lisbon	PONTE 25 ABRIL
—London	BATTERSEA BRIDGE
	BLACKFRIARS BRIDGE
	LONDON BRIDGE

	PUTNEY BRIDGE
	TOWER BRIDGE
	VAUXHALL BRIDGE
	WATERLOO BRIDGE
	WESTMINSTER BRIDGE
—Louisiana	BATON ROUGE BRIDGE
	GREATER NEW ORLEANS BRIDGE
—Madrid	PUENTE DE TOLEDO
—Maryland	BALTIMORE BRIDGE
—Michigan	MACKINAS STRAITS BRIDGE
—Moscow	MOSKVORETSKIY BRIDGE
—Nagasaki	SPECTACLES BRIDGE
—New Orleans	HUEY LONG BRIDGE
—New York	BRONX-WHITESTONE
	BRIDGE
	BROOKLYN BRIDGE
	GEORGE WASHINGTON BRIDGE
	MANHATTAN BRIDGE
	MARINE PARKWAY BRIDGE
	NYACK-TARRYTOWN BRIDGE
	QUEENSBORO BRIDGE
	TAPPAN-ZEE BRIDGE
	VERRAZANO NARROWS BRIDGE
	WILLIAMSBURG BRIDGE
—Newcastle	CLEVELAND BRIDGE
—Oregon	ASTORIA BRIDGE
	FREMONT BRIDGE
—Osaka	MINATO BRIDGE
—Panama	THATCHER FERRY BRIDGE
—Paris	PETIT PONT, PONT AU CHANGE
	PONT AU DOUBLE
	PONT D'ARCOLE
	PONT DE L'ARCHEVECHE
	PONT DE LA TOURNELLE
	PONT DE SULLY
	PONT LOUIS PHILIPPE
	PONT MARIE
	PONT NEUF, PONT NOTRE DAME
	PONT ST MICHEL
—Philadelphia	WALT WHITMAN BRIDGE
—Prague	CHARLES'S BRIDGE
	FIRST OF MAY BRIDGE
—Quebec	LAVIOLETTE BRIDGE
	PIERRE LAPORTE BRIDGE
	QUEBEC BRIDGE
—Rhodesia	BIRCHENOUGH BRIDGE
—Rio de Janeiro	PONTE RIO NITEROI
—Rome	PONTE CAVOUR
	PONTE GARIBALDI
	PONTE MARGHERITA
	PONTE MAZZINI
	PONTE PALATINO
	PONTE SISTO
	PONTE SUBLICIO
	PONTE VITTORIO EMMANUELE
—St Petersburg	KIROV BRIDGE

—San Francisco	CARQUINES STRAIT BRIDGE	company	BL
	GOLDEN GATE BRIDGE	Empire Medal	BEM
	OAKLAND BRIDGE	Home Stores	BHS
	SAN MATEO BRIDGE	Honduras	BH
	(TRANS)BAY BRIDGE	Institute of	
—Scotland	FORTH BRIDGE, TAY BRIDGE	—Management	BIM
—Shropshire	FREE BRIDGE	—Radiology	BIR
	IRON BRIDGE	Legion	BL
—Vancouver	LIONS GATE BRIDGE	Library	BL
	PORT MANN BRIDGE	Medical Journal	BMJ
	SECOND NARROWS BRIDGE	Museum	BM
—Venezuela	ANGOSTURA BRIDGE	—Library	BML
—Venice	RIALTO	Optical Association	BOA
—Vienna	ASPERN BRIDGE	Oxygen Company	BOC
	AUGARTEN BRIDGE	Pharmacopoeia	BP
	FRANZENS BRIDGE	Pharmaceutical Codex	BPC
	MARIEN BRIDGE	Petroleum	BP
	ROTUNDEN BRIDGE	Printing Corporation	BPC
	SCHWEDEN BRIDGE	Rail	BR
—Washington	LONGVIEW BRIDGE	Red Cross Society	BRCS
	TACOMA NARROWS BRIDGE	Road Services	BRS
—Wilmington	DELAWARE MEMORIAL	Shipbuilders	BS
	BRIDGE	Standards (Institution)	BS(I)
floating bridge	PONTOON	Steel (Corporation)	BS(C)
French	PONT	Sugar Corporation	BSC
German	BRUCKE	Summer Time	BST
hinged bridge	BASCULE, DRAWBRIDGE	Thermal Unit	BT(H)U
Italian	PONTE	**Browning**	
narrow with recesses	PACK BRIDGE	words used by:	
pivoting	SWING BRIDGE	bombast	AMPOLLOSITY
rail bridge	VIADUCT	dandruff	FURFAIR
rising	BASCULE BRIDGE	debate	DISCEPT
road bridge	FLYOVER, OVERPASS, VIADUCT	dispute	DISCEPT
Spanish	PUENTE	drive away	AROINT, AROYNT
steeply curved	HUMPBACKED BRIDGE	frighten away	AROINT, AROYNT
suspended from		greatest astrologer	ARCH-GENETHLIAC
—cables	SUSPENSION BRIDGE	horse's mane	ENCOLURE
—chains	CHAIN BRIDGE	instrument of torture	GADGE
temporary bridge	BAILEY BRIDGE	lucerne	LUZERN
types	ARCH, BAILEY, BASCULE	needed amount	EXIGENT
	CABLE STAY, CANTILEVER	play antics	ANTICISE
	PIVOT, PONTOON, SUSPENSION	spat upon	BESPATE
	SWING, TRANSPORTER, TRESTLE	turgidity	AMPOLLOSITY
	TRUSSED	**Brunei**	BRU
water bridge	AQUEDUCT	capital	BANDAR SERI BEGAWAN
with		coin	CENT, DOLLAR
—arms built out from piers	CANTILEVER	**Buddhist**	
—lifting arms	BASCULE	blissful state	NIBBANA, NIRVANA
—travelling carriage	TRANSPORTER	branches	(*see* **belief**)
British		Book of the Dead	BARDO THODOL
Academy	BA	canonical writings	TRIPITAKA
Airways	BA	Chinese sect	CHAN
Association	BA	circle	MANDALA
Broadcasting Corporation	BBC	column	LAT
capital	LONDON	compassion	KARUNA
Columbia	BC	concentration	SAMADHI

cross	SWASTIKA
demon	MARA
device	UPAYA
disciple	CHELA
discipline	VINAYA
discourse for laity	SUTRA
enlightenment	BODHI, NIBBANA, NIRVANA
ethical conduct	SHILA
evil spirit	MARA
faith	SHRADDHA
fate	KARMA
fertility spirit	YAKSHA, YAKSHI
finial of dagoba	TEE
form	RUPA
function	YUNG
future Buddha	BODHISATTVA
gateway	TORAN(A)
giving	DANA
highest	
—priest	DALAI LAMA
—state	NIRVANA
holy day	UPOSATHA
impermanence	ANICCA
inevitable consequence	KARMA
Japanese sect	AMIDA, AMITA
	SOKA GAKKAI, ZEN
law	DHARMA
—of effect	KARMA
liberation	NIBBANA, NIRVANA
means	UPAYA
meditation	BHAVANA
memorial shrine	STUPA, TOPE
—Sri Lanka	D(H)AGOBA
metaphysics	ABHIDHARMA
method	UPAYA
mind	CHITTA
monastery	LAMASERY, VIHARA
monk	AR(A)HAT, BO, BONZE
	LAMA, TALAPOIN
mound	STUPA, TOPE
—Sri Lanka	D(H)AGOBA
nativity	JATAKA
'no-self' doctrine	ANATTA
novice	CHELA
perfection	SIDDHA, SIDDHI
pillar	LAT
plane between life and death	BARDO
precinct	VIHARA
priest	BONZE, LAMA, PONGYI
reality	TATHATA
reincarnated person	TULKU
relic	STUPA
religious	
—book	PITAKA
—leader	DALAI LAMA, PANCHEN LAMA
—painting	TANKA

sacred	
—language	PALI
—lotus	PADMA
—mountain	OMEI
—text	SUTRA
—tree	BO, BODHI, PEEPUL
—verse	MANTRA
scripture	SUTRA, SUTTA, (TI)PITAKA
seed	BIJA
sermons of Buddha	SUTRA
shrine	DAGABA, DAGO(U)BA
	D(H)AGOBA, STUPA, TOPE
spiritual leader	DALAI LAMA
	PANCHEN LAMA
sudden enlightenment	SATORI
symbol	TRISUL(A)
—of the universe	MANDALA
teaching	SHASTRAS
temple	SANGHA, TERA, VIHARA
—hall	CHAITYA
three bodies of Buddha	TRIKAYA
throne	ASANA
Tibetan sect	GELUK PA, SAKYA PA
title	MAHATMA
tree nymph	YAKSHI
umbrella-shaped finial	TEE
unsatisfactoriness	DUKKHA
wheel of becoming	SAMSARA
wisdom	PRAJNA
world	LOKA
building construction	
arch	FLAT, SEGMENTAL
	SEMI-CIRCULAR
arrangement of bricks in wall	BOND
beam over opening	LINTEL
block materials	AERATED CONCRETE
	CLAY, CLINKER
	FOAMED CONCRETE
brick	
—cut to form arch	GAUGED BRICK
—laid	
flat	
—end showing	HEADER
—side showing	STRETCHER
on end, side showing	BRICK-ON-END
	SOLDIER COURSE
on side, end showing	BRICK-ON-EDGE
—part	BAT
cut diagonally	BEVELLED CLOSER
half, lengthwise	QUEEN CLOSER
with corner cut off	KING CLOSER
—shape having	
bevelled long edge	PLINTH BRICK
cavities	AIRBRICK
	CELLULAR BRICK
double rounded end	COWNOSE

grooved sides	KEYED
rounded end	BULLNOSE
various angles	SQUINT QUOIN
brick materials	CLAY, CONCRETE
	SAND-LIME
brickwork	
—bedding material	CEMENT(-LIME)MORTAR
	COMPO, MORTAR
—bonds	
all	
—headers	HEADER BOND
	HEADING BOND
—stretchers	STRETCHER BOND
	STRETCHING
alternate	
—courses of headers	
and stretchers	ENGLISH
—headers and	
stretchers in course	FLEMISH
one	
—stretcher course to	
several header	
courses	ENGLISH GARDEN WALL
—stretcher, several	
headers per	
course	FLEMISH GARDEN WALL
—joints	FLAT, FLUSH, KEYED
	RAKED, RECESSED
	TUCK(BASTARD), WEATHERED
horizontal	BED JOINTS
vertical	PERPENDS
cladding materials	ASBESTOS-CEMENT
	CONCRETE, FIBREGLASS
	GALVANISED IRON, PLASTIC
	SHEET STEEL, TIMBER
—fixed to frame	CURTAIN WALLING
concrete	PLAIN, REINFORCED
	PRESTRESSED
copper pipe joints	CAPILLARY, COMPRESSION
course of brick, stone,	
etc on top of wall	COPING
damp-proof	
—course	DPC
materials	BITUMEN FELT, COPPER
	LEAD, POLYTHENE, SLATE
—membrane	DPM
door types	FLUSH
	FRAMED, LEDGED AND BRACED
	LEDGED, LEDGED AND BRACED
	PANELLED, SLIDING
drainage	
—access points	INSPECTION CHAMBER
	MANHOLE, RODDING-EYE
—materials	ASBESTOS-CEMENT
	CAST-IRON, PITCH-FIBRE
	PLASTIC, SALT-GLAZED CLAY

—pipe	
horizontal	DRAIN, SEWER
preventing siphonage	ANTI-SIPHON PIPE
providing ventilation	VENT PIPE
taking	
—flow from sanitary	
fittings	FOUL DRAIN
—rain water	STORM(WATER) DRAIN
—waste water	
only	WASTE-PIPE
vertical	SOIL-PIPE
—tank	CESSPOOL, SEPTIC TANK
film on surface of concrete	LAITANCE
flue lining	PARGING
foundations	PILES, RAFT, STRIP
	TRENCHFILL
glass	
—fixing material	GLAZING BEAD
	PUTT, SPRIG
—type	ARMOURED, CAST, DIFFUSING
	FLOAT, GEORGIAN, LAMINATED
	OBSCURE, OPAQUE, PLAIN
	REEDED, ROLLED, SHEET
	TOUGHENED, WIRED
hot-water storage	CYLINDER
insulating materials	FIBREGLASS
	PERLITE, POLYSTYRENE
	VERMICULITE
lead joints	LEAD-BURNED, SPIGOT
	TAFT, WIPED
mortar	COMPO
—behind kerbs	HAUNCHING
—in	
angle	FILLET
manholes	HAUNCHING
—lining flue	PARGING
—round chimney pot	FLAUNCHING
—sealing tiles	PARGING
painting	
—coats	
first	PRIMER
intermediate	UNDERCOAT
final	FINISHING COAT
	GLOSS COAT, TOP COAT
—materials	BITUMEN PAINT
	CEMENT PAINT, DISTEMPER
	EGGSHELL, EMULSION
	EPOXIDE RESIN PAIN, FLAT PAINT
	GLOSS PAINT, MATT PAINT
	PLASTIC PAINT, PRIMER
	SILICATE PAINT, STONE PAINT
	THIXOTROPIC PAINT
	UNDERCOAT, VARNISH
—technique	BRUSH, ROLLER, SPRAY
piles	BEARING, BORED, DRIVEN
	FRICTION

plastering
— external   PEBBLE-DASH, RENDERING
ROUGHCAST
machine-applied   TYROLEAN
— layers
   first   RENDER(ING) COAT
   second   FLOATING COAT
   top   SETTING COAT
— materials   CEMENT, GYPSUM, LIME
SAND
— types   ANHYDRITE, ANHYDROUS
KEENE'S, PARIAN, PLASTER OF PARIS
RETARDED HEMIHYDRATE
rainwater fittings   GUTTER, DOWNPIPE
DROP OUTLET, STOPEND
reinforced concrete   FERROCONCRETE
roof
— covering materials   ASBESTOS-CEMENT
ASPHALT, BITUMINOUS FELT
BUTYL RUBBER, COPPER
GALVANISED IRON, LEAD
NURALITE, SLATE, TILES, ZINC
— edge
   bottom   EAVES
   side   VERGE
   top   RIDGE
— frame   TRUSS, TRUSSED RAFTER
— slate
   sizes: 12"x6"   SMALL
           13"x7"   DOUBLE
           16"x8"   LADY
           20"x10"   COUNTESS
           24"x12"   DUCHESS
           24"x14"   PRINCESS
           26"x16"   EMPRESS
   spacing   GAUGE, LAP
   types   COTSWOLD, CUMBERLAND
WELSH
— tiles
   materials   ASBESTOS-CEMENT
CLAY, CONCRETE, STONE
   spacing   GAUGE, LAP
   specials   ARRIS HIP TILES
BONNET HIP TILES, EAVES TILES
RIDGE TILES, VALLEY TILES
   types   INTERLOCKING, PLAIN
ROMAN, SPANISH
— types   COLLAR, COUPLE
COUPLE CLOSE, KING-POST
LEAN-TO, MANSARD
MONOPITCH, NORTH-LIGHT
PURLIN, QUEEN-POST
sanitary fittings   BATH
BIDET, LAVATORY BASIN
(SLOP-)SINK, SHOWER
URINAL, WATER-CLOSET

scaffolding parts   BRIDLE, CLIP, COUPLING
CROSS-BRACE, DIAGONAL BRACE
GUARD RAIL, LEDGER, STANDARD
TOE-BOARD, TRANSOM
sheet materials   ASBESTOS-CEMENT
BLOCKBOARD, CHIPBOARD
FIBREBOARD, HARDBOARD
LAMINBOARD, PEGBOARD
PLASTERBOARD
PLASTIC LAMINATE
PLYWOOD, SOFTBOARD
stairs
— diagonal step   WINDER
— parts   BALUSTER, BA(N)NISTER
CARRIAGE, HANDRAIL, NEWEL
NOSING, RISER, STRING, TREAD
— types   CIRCULAR, DOGLEG
GEOMETRICAL, HELICAL
OPEN WELL, SPIRAL, STRAIGHT
stone
— Cornwall   DE LANK, LAMORNA
— Derbyshire   BOLSOVER MOOR
DARLEYDALE, HOPTON WOOD
— Dorset   PORTLAND
PURBECK MARBLE
— Gloucestershire   PENNANT
— Kent   RAG
— Leicestershire   MOUNTSORREL
— Lincolnshire   ANCASTER, CLIPSHAM
— Nottinghamshire   MANSFIELD
— Scotland   CORRENNIE, CRETOWN
— Somerset   BATH
— Warwickshire   HORNTON
— Westmorland   SHAP
— Wiltshire   CHILLMARK
— without planes   FREESTONE
stone
— finishes   BOASTED, COMBED
DRAGGED, DROVED, FURROWED
HAMMER-DRESSED, MOULDED
PLAIN WORK, RETICULATED
RUBBED WORK, SCABBLED
SCAPPLED, SUNK WORK
TOOLED, VERMICULATED
— rubble   MOELLON
— walling
   rubble   COURSED RUBBLE, FLINT
KENTISH RAG
RANDOM RUBBLE (BUILT TO COURSES)
SNECKED RUBBLE, SQUARED RUBBLE
UNCOURSED RUBBLE
   dressed   ASHLAR, BLOCK IN COURSE
tie for
— brickwork   BUTTERFLY TIE, WALL-TIE
— stonework   ANCHOR BOLT, CRAMP
JOGGLE, TAILING IRON

timber		top	HEAD
curved roof support	CRUCK	—types	CASEMENT, DORMER
—for			FRENCH, HOPPER, ORIEL
concrete	FORMWORK		PATIO, PIVOT, SASH, SLIDING
trenches	POLING, PROP		SPRING BALANCE
	PUNCHEON, RUNNER, SOLDIER		(*see also* **architectural features**)
	STRETCHER, STRINGER	**Bulgaria**	BG, BULG
	STRUT, WALING	capital	SOFI(Y)A
—in		coins	LEV, LEY, STOTINKA
floor	JOIST, NOGGIN(G)	head of church	EXARCH
panelling		king	CZAR, TSAR, TZAR
—horizontal	STRETCHER	measure	KRINE, LEKHA
—vertical	MUNTIN		OKA, OKE
partitions	STUDDING	Moslem	POMAK
roof		national assembly	SOBRANJE, SOBRANYE
—at		revolutionary	COMITAJI, KOMITAJI
eaves	FA(S)CIA, SOFFIT	weight	OKA, OKE, TOVAR
verge	BARGE-BOARD	**bullfighting**	TAUROMACHY
—structural	BINDER, COLLAR	arena	PLAZA DE TOROS
	DRAGON-TIE, HANGER, JOIST	assistant bullfighter	
	KING-POST, PURLIN, QUEEN-POST	—Portugal	FORCADO
	RAFTER, TIE, WALLPLATE	—Spain	BANDERILLERO
—supporting tiles	BATTENS	bullfight	CORRIDA
—joints	BARE-FACED MORTICE	—France	COMBATS DE TAUREAUX
	CHASE MORTICE, COGGED, COMBED	—Portugal	CORRIDA DE TOUROS
	CORNER LOCKING, CROSS-TONGUE	—Spain	CORRIDA DE TOROS
	DOVETAIL, DOWELLED	bullfighter	ESPADA, MATADOR
	HALVED, HOUSED, MITRE		TOREADOR, TORERO
	MORTICE AND TENON	bullfighters	BAES, BIENVENIDA
	SCARF, STUB TENON, TUSK TENON		DOMINGUIN, EL CORDOBES
—round			EL LITRI, HIGGINS
door frames, etc	ARCHITRAVE		LAGARTIJO, MANOLETE
openings	LINING		MOLINA, PEREZ, ROMERO
walls		bullpen	TORIL
—door-head level	PICTURE RAIL	cape	MULETA
—floor level	SKIRTING	dart	BANDERILLA
—lower half	DADO	devotee	AFICIONADO
—waist level	CHAIR RAIL	fence round bullring	BURLADERO
—temporary support		flourish of cape	PASE, PASS, VERONICA
opening	NEEDLE	hat	MONTERA
overstressed walls	SHORE	kill	
—types	(*see separate entry*)	—final thrust	MOMENT OF TRUTH
walling materials	BRICK, CONCRETE	—man and bull moving	ZAL VOLAPIE
	FAIENCE, STONE	—torero standing still	RECIBIENDO
	TERRA-COTTA, TIMBER	mounted	
weatherproofing round		—bailiff	ALGUACILE
stack, etc	FLASHING, SOAKER	—fighters	
window		Portugal	CAVALEIRO
—materials	ALUMINIUM, IRON	Spain	PICADOR, TOREADOR
	PLASTIC, (STAINLESS)STEEL	part of session	TERCIO
	TIMBER	session	CORRIDA
—parts		troupe	CAUDRILLA
bottom	SILL	**Burkina Faso**	
horizontal member	TRANSOME	capital	OUAGADOUGOU
small dividing bar	GLAZING BAR	coin	FRANC
vertical member	MULLION	previous name	UPPER VOLTA

Burma	BUR
borderer	SHAN
Buddhist priest	PONGYI
capital	RANGOON, YANGON
civet	LINSANG
coin	KYAT, PYA
devil	NAT
garment	TAMEIN
girl	MINA
governor	WOON, WUN
guerrilla	CHINDIT
hill-dweller	LAI
knife	DA(H), DHAR, DOUT, DOW
language	KAREN, SHAN
measure	BYEE, DAIN, DHA
	LAN, PALGAT, TENG
modern name	MYANMAR
prostrate veneration	SHIKO
river	IRRAWADDY
robber	DACOIT, DAKOIT
robbery	DACOITAGE
	DACOITI, DACOITY
shrimp	NAPEE
state carriage	RATH
timber	(*see* **timber**)
tree	IRONWOOD, PADAUK
	PADOUK, PYENGADU
tribe	CHIN, KACHIN, KAREN(NI)
	LAI, MON, SHAN
violin	TURR
weight	KAIT, KYAT, MAT, TICUL, VIS(S)
Burns	
words used by:	
angle of wooden dish	LAGGEN, LAGGIN
beast not housed	OUTLER
bonny	BONIE
determine	LAW
dwarfish person	(K)NURL
fine linen	SEVENTEEN-HUNDER
get	FALL
highest character	ACE
hoop at bottom of wooden	
vessel	LAGGEN-GIRD
hot ashes	AIZLE, EASLE
one out of office	OUTLER
	(*see also* **Scots**)
	RU
Burundi	
capital	BUJUMBURA
coin	CENTIME, FRANC
language	KIRUNDI
butterfly	PSYCHE
black and scarlet	RED ADMIRAL

black-spotted	FRITILLARY
black with white spots	DINGY SKIPPER
	GRIZZLED SKIPPER
	WHITE ADMIRAL
blue	ADONIS, CHALKHILL BLUE
	COMMON BLUE, HOLLY BLUE
	LARGE BLUE, LONG-TAILED BLUE
	SHORT-TAILED BLUE, SMALL BLUE
brown	ARGUS, GATEKEEPER, GRAYLING
	HEATH, LULWORTH SKIPPER
	MEADOW BROWN
chocolate-brown with	
yellow edges	CAMBERWELL BEAUTY
copper	LARGE COPPER, SMALL COPPER
dark brown	ARGUS, RINGLET
groupings	LYCAENIDAE, NYMPHALIDAE
	PAPILIO, PIERIDAE
	RHOPALOCERA, SATYRIDAE
	THECLA, VANESSA
marbled	MARBLED WHITE
multi-coloured	SWALLOWTAIL
	TORTOISESHELL
purple	PURPLE EMPEROR
purplish-blue	MAZARINE BLUE
reddish-brown with	
'eyes'	PEACOCK
tawny-orange	CHEQUERED SKIPPER
	ESSEX SKIPPER
	LARGE SKIPPER, PAINTED LADY
	SILVER-SPOTTED SKIPPER
	SMALL SKIPPER
various colours	HAIRSTREAK
white	BATH WHITE
	BLACK-VEINED WHITE
	CABBAGE(-WHITE)
	GREEN-VEINED WHITE
	LARGE WHITE, SMALL WHITE
	WOOD WHITE
white-marked	COMMA, POLYGONIA
white with tipped wings	ORANGE-TIP
yellow	BRIMSTONE
	CLOUDED YELLOW
Byzantine	
capital	BYZANTIUM
	CONSTANTINOPLE
chancellor	LOGOTHETE
gold coin	BEZANT, BYZANT
	SOLIDUS
governor	CATAPAN, EXARCH
guard	PROTOSPATHARIUS
head of guard	ACOLOUTHOS
	AKOL(O)UTHOS

C

cacti
including: succulents
bishop's cap	ASTROPHYTUM
brain cactus	ECHINOFOSSULOCACTUS
bunny ears	OPUNTIA
burro's tail	SEDUM
candle plant	KLEINIA
Cape hart's tongue	GASTERIA
chain cactus	RHIPSALIS
Christmas cactus	SCHLUMBERGERA
	ZYGOCACTUS
cinnamon cactus	OPUNTIA
column cactus	CEREUS
Easter cactus	RHIPSALIDOPSIS
	SCHLUMBERGERA
fish hook cactus	FEROCACTUS
ghost plant	GRAPTOPETALUM
giant	SAGUARO
goat's horn	ASTROPHYTUM
golden barrel	ECHINOCACTUS
—lily	LOBIVIA
hen and chickens	SEMPERVIVUM
houseleek	SEMPERVIVUM
jelly bean plant	SEDUM
leaf cactus	PERESKIA
living stones	LITHOPS
Mexican sunball	REBUTIA
milk bush	EUPHORBIA
mistletoe cactus	RHIPSALIS
old man cactus	CEPHALOCEREUS
—of the Andes	OREOCEREUS
orchid cactus	EPIPHYLLUM
panda plant	KALANCHOE
peanut cactus	CHAMAECEREUS
pearl plant	HAWORTHIA
Peruvian old man	ESPOSTOA
pincushion cactus	MAMMILLARIA
rat's tail cactus	APOROCACTUS
silver torch cactus	CLEISTOCACTUS
South American	EASTER CACTUS
star window plant	HAWORTHIA
string of beads	SENECIO
sugar almond plant	PACHYPHYTUM
sunset cactus	LOBIVIA
tiger's jaws	FORCARIA
Tom Thumb cactus	PARODIA
Turkish temple	EUPHORBIA
velvet leaf	KALANCHOE

wart plant	HAWORTHIA

cakes
almond	ANGEL CAKE, FRANGIPANE
	FRANGIPANI, MACAROON
	MAID OF HONOUR, MANDELBROT
	RATAFIA, TRUFFLE CAKE
American	BROWNIE, CORN-CAKE
	CORN-DODGER, CRULLER, FRIEDCAKE
	GINGER MUFFIN, HOE-CAKE
	JELLY ROLL, JOHNNYCAKE
	LOAF-CAKE, MISSISSIPPI MUDCAKE
	OLYCOOK, OLYKOEK, SHORTCAKE
	SINKER
Austrian	(SACHER)TORTE
batter cake	GAUFFRE, WAFFLE
bread-like with currants	LARD(Y) CAKE
brittle, made of	
flour and butter	SHORTBREAD
	SHORTCAKE
cherries	GENOA CAKE
chocolate	DOBOZ TORTE, SACHERTORTE
—and	
cream	DEVIL'S FOOD CAKE
fruit	TORTE
nuts	BROWNIE, FLORENTINE
—Christmas roll	YULE LOG
—coated	LAMINGTON
coconut	COCONUT PYRAMID, MACAROON
—coated	MADELEINE
cream	(BLACK FOREST) GATEAU
	BRANDY SNAP, CHERUB CAKE
	CREAM HORN, CREAM PUFF
	ECLAIR, MERINGUE, PALMIER
—bun	CHOU
crumpet	PIKELET
currant	
—bun	BARMBRACK, CHELSEA BUN
	ROCK BUN, SINGIN(G) HINNY
—cake	BANBURY CAKE, ECCLES CAKE
	QUEEN CAKE
doughnut (US)	CRULLER, OLYCOOK
	OLYKOEK, SINKER
Easter	
—bun	HOT-CROSS BUN
—cake	SIMNEL CAKE
—Russian	PASHKA
egg-white and sugar	MERINGUE
fancy cake	GATEAU, TORTE
fatty	LARD(Y) CAKE
finger-shaped	LANGUE DE CHAT
flaky pastry	DANISH PASTRY
	MILLEFEUILLE(S)
	PALMIER, VANILLA SLICE
flat	DROP(PED) SCONE, FARL(E)
	GRIDDLE CAKE, PATTIE, PATTY
	SCOTCH PANCAKE, STOTTY CAKE

French	SAVARIN
fried in fat	DOUGHNUT
fruit baked with shell on top and served fruit side up	UPSIDE-DOWN CAKE
fruit cake	BANANA, CHERRY DUNDEE, FARMHOUSE GENOA, PARADISE, POUND CAKE TYROL, VINEGAR CAKE
gateau	TORTE
German	BLACK FOREST GATEAU KUCHEN, MOHNKUCHEN POPPYSEED CAKE SCHWARZWALDER KIRSCHTORTE STOLLEN
ginger	GINGERBREAD, PARKIN, PERKIN
Greek	FINIKIA
Hebrew	
—almond	MANDELBROT
—sponge	PLAVA
iced	FANCY CAKE
—bun	BELGIAN BUN JEFFERSON (BUN)
—cake	BIRTHDAY CAKE CHRISTMAS CAKE, NAPOLEON RUSSIAN, WEDDING CAKE
—pastry	VANILLA SLICE
—small	PETIT FOURS
Italian	PANETTONE
Japanese	MANJU
layers	
—cream and pastry	MILLE FEUILLE(S)
—meringue, cream, fruit	VACHERIN
—various mixes	LAYER CAKE
light sweet cake	ANGEL CAKE SPONGE (CAKE)
maize meal (US)	JOHNNY CAKE
marzipan	BATTENBERG CAKE PETIT FOURS
mottled	MARBLE CAKE
muffin	PIKELET, POPOVER
pancake	CARCAKE
—with wheat flour	WHEAT CAKE
pastry with	
—sweet filling	DANISH PASTRY
—spices	VIENNA PASTRY
plain	
—bun	ROCK BUN, SCONE
—cake	BATCH CAKE, SAND CAKE
—with raising agent	TEA BREAD
and currants	TEA CAKE
porous	MUFFIN
potato cake	GALETTE
rich cake	BROWNIE, CHRISTMAS CAKE DARIOLE, FUDGE, POUND CAKE SPICE CAKE
ring-shaped	DOUGHNUT, JUMBAL JUMBLE, SAVARIN
rum-flavoured	BABA AU RHUM (RUM) BABA
Russian	PASAHKA
sandwich with jam and jelly filling	WASHINGTON PIE
Scottish	BANNOCK, BLACK BUN BUTTER-BAKE, CARCAKE COOKIE, COOKY, FARL(E) FARTHEL, SCOTCH BUN
—Shrove Tuesday cake	CARCAKE
shell-shaped	MADELEINE
shortbread with cream, etc	SHORTCAKE
small	
—currant bun	ROCK BUN, ROCK CAKE
—plain cake with raising agent	SCONE
—sponge cake	MADELEINE
—sweet cake	MADELEINE, PETIT FOUR QUEEN CAKE, VIENNESE TART
Spanish	BRAZO DE GITANO
spicy	COBURG
sponge	CARIBBEAN, GENOESE
—cylindrical	SWISS ROLL
—lemon flavour	MADEIRA
—light	ANGEL-CAKE, ANGEL-FOOD
—roll with chocolate coating	YULE LOG
—with fat	VICTORIA SPONGE
sweet bun	BATH BUN, CHELSEA BUN SALLY LUNN
Swiss roll with jelly (jam)	JELLY ROLL
tea-cake	CRUMPET, MUFFIN PIKELET, SALLY LUNN
—Kent	HUFFKIN
thin	
—crisp sponge	SPONGE FINGER
—sweet cake	JUMBAL, JUMBLE
Twelfth Night cake	GALETTE
unsweetened griddlecake	CRUMPET
vegetable	CARROT CAKE GALETTE
wheat cake (Ind.)	PURI
Cambodia	K
capital	PHNOM-PENH
coin	RIEL
language	KHMER
modern name	KAMPUCHEA KHMER REPUBLIC
people	KHMER
camera	(see **photography**)
Cameroon	
capital	YAOUNDE
coin	FRANC
Canada	CDN
Air Force	RCAF
alewife (fish)	GASPEREAU

birds	HAIRY WOODPECKER
	SAW-WHET OWL
	SHARP-TAILED GROUSE
	STELLER'S JAY
bog	MUSKEG
Canadian	CANUCK, KANUCK
—of French descent	HABITANT
capital	OTTAWA
coin	CENT, DOLLAR
cut grain	SWATHE
dog	NEWFOUNDLAND
dried skin	PARFLECHE
fingers	BREAD HOOKS
fliers	RCAF
freeze	TAKE
half-caste	METIF
hare	SNOW-SHOE RABBIT
houseboat for loggers	WAN(I)GAN, WANGUN
Indian	
—language	ALGONKIN, ALGONQUIN
	MICMAC
—tribes	ALGONKIN, ALGONQUIN
	BEAVER, BEDTHUK, BLACKFOOT
	CARRIER, CREE, DOGRIB, ESKIMO
	HAIDA, HAN, HARE, INGALIK
	INNU, KASKA, KOYUKON
	KUTCHIN, KWAKIUTL, MANDAN
	MICMAC, MONTAGNAIS-NASKAPI
	SARCEE, SHUSWAP, TANANA
	TLINGIT, TSIMSHIAN, TUTCHONE
jay	WHISKY-JACK, WHISKY-JOHN
lumber-camp supply chest	WAN(I)GAN
	WANGUN
marsh	MUSKEG
mounted police	MOUNTIES, RCMP
national emblem	MAPLE LEAF
—Railway	CNR
navy	RCN
old-timer	SOURDOUGH
Pacific Railway	CPR
pay office	WAN(I)GAN, WANGUN
police force	MOUNTIES, RCMP
pondweed	WATER-THYME
porcupine	URSON
provinces/territories	
—Alberta	ALBA, ALTA
—British Columbia	BC
—Manitoba	MAN
—New Brunswick	NB
—Newfoundland	NF(D)
—Nova Scotia	NS
—Ontario	ONT
—Northwest Territories	NWT
—Prince Edward Island	PEI
—Quebec	PQ, Q, QUE
—Saskatchewan	SASK
—Yukon Territory	YT
ravine	COULEE
rice	INDIAN RICE
river	FRASER, NELSON
	ST LAWRENCE
Royal Academy	CRA
ruminant	MUSK-OX, MUSK-STEER
sailors	RCN
sea-bird	MURRELET
sledge	TRAIN
sluice-gate	ALBOLDEAU
soldiers	CEF
swamp	MUSKEG
tenderfoot	CHE(E)CHAKO
	CHEECHALKO, CHECHAQUO
timber	LUMBER
	(see also **timber**)
travel with dogs over snow	MUSH
waterweed	ELODEA
windproof garment	PARKA, PARKEE

Canary Islands	E
Cape Verde Islands	P

capes
including: cape
head
point
promontory
etc

Alaska	HALKETT, LISBURNE
	PRINCE OF WALES, ROMANZOF
Albania	GJUHEZES
Algeria	CARBON, DE FER, FIGALO
	MATIFOU, ROSA
Angola	DAS PALMAS, DAS SALINAS
	DE S BRAZ, DE STA MARTA
	DO DANDE
Arabia	AL HADD, AL QAIB, ASWAD
	FARTAK, HATIBA, JIBSH, KURKUMA
	MADRAKAH, SAJAR, SAWQIRAH
Argentina	BERMEJO, BLANCO
	BUEN TEMPO, CORRIENTES
	DE MOSTARDAS, DEL ESTE
	DELGADA, DOS BAHIAS, GUARDIAN
	LA PALOMA, LOBOS, MEDANOSA
	PASO, POLONZO, RASA
	SAN ANTONIO
	SAN FRANCISCO, STA MARIA
Australia	ARNHEM, BYRON
	CATASTROPHE
	D'ENTRECASTEAUX, DIRECTION
	DUIFREN, FLATTERY, GRENVILLE
	HAWKE, HOWE, KNOB, LEEUWIN
	LEVEQUE, LONDONDERRY
	MELVILLE, NATURALISTE
	NORTH-WEST, OTWAY, PAISLEY
	WILSON'S, YORK

Brazil	CACIPORE, CORUMBA
	DE ATALAIA, DE SAO ROQUE
	DO BALEIA, DO TOPAGE
	DOS PASTOS, MACEIO
	MAGUARINHO, MANGUES VERDES
	ORANGE, RASO, REDONDA
Burma	NEGRAIS
Canada	BATHURST, BRETON, CANSO
	CHARLES, CHIDLEY, ESKIMO
	GASPE, HATTON, HENRIETTA MARIA
	KELLET, M'CLURE, NORTH
	PRINCE ALBERT, RAGE, RAY
	ST LEWIS, SABLE, SCOTT
	WALSINGHAM, , WOLSTENHOLME
Chile	ALLENA, ANGAMOS, CARRANZA
	CARRIZAL, DE LOS LOBOS
	GORDA, GRUESTIA, LENGUA DE VACA
	MORRO, PILAR, PLATA, QUILAN
	SAN PEDRO, SAN VEDRA, TAITAO
	TETAS, TOPOCAIMA
Colombia	CHIRAMBIRA, CORRIENTES
	CRUCES, ESTRELLA, GALLINAS
	GUASCAMA, MANGLARES, MARZO
Crete	KRIOS, LITHINON, SIDHEROS
	SPATHA, STAVROS, TRIPTII
Cyprus	ARNAUTI, ASPRO, GATA
	GRECO, KORMAKITI, PLAKOTI
	POMOS, ST ANDREAS, , ZEVGHARI
Denmark	SKAGENS, THE SKAW
Ecuador	GALERA, LORENZO, PASADA
Egypt	ABU DARA, BENAS, EL KENAYIS
	KASAR, OLBA, RAWAI
England	BEACHY, DODMAN
	FLAMBOROUGH, FORMBY
	HARTLAND, LAND'S END
	LIZARD, NORTH FORELAND
	PORTLAND BILL, ST ALBAN'S
	ST BEES, SPURN, START, TINTAGEL
France	COURONNE, DE GRAVE
	DE LA COUBRE, DE LA HAGUE
	DE LA HEVE, DE L'AIGUILLE
	DE PENMARCH, GRIS NEZ
	ST GILDA'S
Gabon	LOPEZ, MATOUTT
	STE CATHERINE, TSHIBOBO
Ghana	THREE POINTS
Greece	AKRITAS, DORO, KAFIREUS
	KANASTRAION, KIMI, MALEA
	MASTIKHO, MATAPAN, MESTA
	PAPAC, SKILLAION, TAINARON
Guinea	VERGA
Hawaii	APUA, BARBER'S, KA LAE
	KAENA, KAUNA, KEEHOLE, KOKO
	KUHUKU, KUMUKAHI, LELEIWI
	MAKAPUU, PEPEEKEO, UPOLU
Hebrides	BARRA
Honduras	CAMERON, GRACIAS A DIOS
	HONDURAS
India	CALIMERE, CORMORIN
	MALAN, MONZE, NUH, PISHKAN
Iran	MAIDUNI
Ireland	BLOOD, CARNSORE, ERRIS
	FORELAND, MALIN
	OLD HEAD OF KINSALE
	ROSSAN, SLYNEHD, WICKLOW
Isle of Man	POINT OF AYRE
Isle of Wight	ST CATHERINE'S
Italy	CIRCEO, COLONNE, LICOSA
	RIZZUTO, S MARIA DI LEUCA
	S VITO, SPARTIVENTO, VATICANO
Liberia	PALMAS
Libya	MISURATA
Mauretania	BLANC
Mexico	ANGEL, CATOCHE, CORRIENTES
	DE HUATULCO, HERRERO
	S TELMO
Morocco	ALMINA, TRES FORCAS, YUBI
Mozambique	DA BURRA FALSA
Namibia	CROSS, DOLPHIN, ELIZABETH
	FRIO, PALGRAVE
New Guinea	D'URVILLE, DE JONG'S
	VALSCH
New Zealand	ABUT, BRETT, CAMPBELL
	CASCADE, COLVILLE, EGMONT
	FAREWELL, FOUL WIND, JACKSON
	KAHUTARA, KIDNAPPER'S, NORTH
	PALLISER, PROVIDENCE, PUYSEGUR
	ROCK, RUNAWAY, SOUTH-WEST
	TAUROA, TURNAGAIN
Nicaragua	GORDA
Norway	LINDESNES, NORDKAPP
	NORTH, THE NALE
Panama	MALA, MANZANILLO
	ARIATO, S BLAS
Peru	AGUJA, BLANCO, CHALA
	CHICHAMA, DE CHILCA, DE COLES
	PARINAS, PESCADORES, STA MARIA
	SALINAS
Philippines	BOJEADOR, ENGANO
	MAIRARIRA, NEGRA, TINACA
Russia	SARYCH
Scotland	BUCHAN, DUNCANSBY
	KINNAIRD, MULL OF GALLOWAY
	MULL OF KINTYRE, ST ABB'S
	WRATH
Senegal	VERDE, VERT
Sicily	CALAVA, S VITO
Sierra Leone	ST ANN, SIERRA LEONE
Somalia	GARDAFUI
South Africa	AGULHAS, CAPE POINT
	DANGER, GOOD HOPE, HANGKLIP
	ST FRANCIS, ST LUCIA, STONY

Spain	CALA BURRAS, CARVUEIRO
	DE CREUS, DE GATA, DE LA NAO
	DE LAS ENTINAS, DE PALOS
	DE SALOU, DE TORTOSA, ESPICHEL
	FINISTERRE, MACHICHACO
	MARROQUI, ORTEGAL, ROSA
	ST MARIA, ST VINCENT, SINES
	TINOSO, TORINANA, TRAFALGAR
Spanish Sahara	BARBAS, BOJADOR
Sri Lanka	DEVIL'S, DONDRA
	PAUL, PEDRO
Tanzania	DELGADO
Tasmania	GRIM, SOUTH-EAST
	SOUTH-WEST
Thailand	LIANT
Tierra del Fuego	SAN DIEGO, SAN JUAN
	SAN PABLO
Tunis	CAP BON
Turkey	BABA, KORAKA
USA	BANDA, BLANCO, CANAVERAL
	CHARLES, COD, COLNETT
	CONCEPTION, DISAPPOINTMENT
	EUGENIA, FALSO, FEAR, FLORIDA
	HATTERAS, LOOKOUT, MAY
	MENDOCINO, MONTAUK, S LAZARO
	S LUCAS, SABLE, SAN BLAS
Venezuela	BARIMA
Wales	BRAICH Y PWLL, GREAT ORME
	LITTLE ORME, NASH, ORMES
	ST BRIDE'S, ST DAVID'S
	ST GOWAN'S, STUMBLE, WORMS
Zaire	NOIRE, PADRAO
card games	ALL FOURS, BANK CRAPS
	BANKER, BEZIQUE, BLIND HOOKEY
	BRAG, CAS(S)INO, CATCH-THE-TEN
	CRIB(BAGE), GRAB, HEARTS
	KALABRIAS, KLABBERJASS
	KLOB(IOSH), LANTERLOO
	LONG WHIST, LOO, MATRIMONY
	NAP(OLEON), NEWMARKET
	NODDY, OLD FOURS
	ONE-AND-THIRTY, PAM
	PITCH, (PROGRESSIVE) WHIST
	RUFF (AND HONOURS)
	SANCHO-PEDRO, SETBACK
	SHORT WHIST, SLAM, SOLO WHIST
	SPECULATION, SPOIL-FIVE, TRUMP
32 cards	PICQUET
40 cards	COON CAN, MONTE, OMBRE
	QUADRILLE, SEVEN AND A HALF
	ZIGINETTE
45 cards	FARMER
48 cards	CRAP CARDS
ace of	
—clubs (quadrille)	BASTO
—trumps (gleek)	TIB

American game	EUCHRE, FARO
	PINOCHLE, POKER
bluff with four of same suit	FOUR FLUSH
bridge	AUCTION, CHICAGO
	CLUB, CONTRACT, FOUR-DEAL
card winning part of stakes	
for holder (old whist)	SWAB
children's game	BEGGAR-MY-NEIGHBOUR
	HAPPY FAMILIES
	MUGGINS, OLD MAID, SNAP
	SNIP-SNAP-SNORUM
declaration in bezique	MARRIAGE
European	KABARIATZ, KALIBRIZ
	(KLABER) JASS, SMOOSJASS
faro variants	BUCKING THE TIGER
	(CHINESE) FAN-TAN, FAROBANK
	JEWISH FARO, MONTE (BANK)
	PUT AND TAKE, RED DOG, SKIN
	STUSS, ZIGINETTE
fortune-telling	TAROK, TAROT
four aces etc in a hand	MOURNIVAL
French game	BACCARAT, BOUILLOTTE
	CHEMIN DE FER, ECARTE
	QUINZE, ROUGE-ET-NOIR
	TRENTE-ET-QUARANTE
	VINGT-ET-UN
hand	
—played with cards laid out	DUMMY
euchre	JAMBONE
solo whist	MISERE OUVERT
	OPEN MISERE
	ABONDANCE DECLAREE
	ABUNDANCE DECLARED
—with five highest	
cards (euchre)	JAMBOREE
—without trumps	CHICANE
highest card in loo	PAM
knave	JACK
—of clubs	KLABER JASS, PAM
like	
—bezique	PINOC(H)LE
—nap	PAM, PUT(T)
Mexican	THREE-CARD MONTE
old	BASSET, BINOCHLE, BRISCAN
	BRUSQUEMBILLE, CINQ CENTS
	FIVE HUNDRED, FLAKERNOBLE
	LANSQUENET, MARRIAGE, NODDY
	PRIMERO, REVERSIS
—Scottish	PENNEECH, PENNEECK
patience	KLONDIKE, KLONDYKE
	SOLITAIRE
pinochle variants	AEROPLANE, AUCTION
	CUTTHROAT, CHECK, CONTRACT
	FIREHOUSE, HARTFORD
	NEW ENGLAND
	(RADIO) PARTNERSHIP, TURN-UP

poker	DRAW, STUD
—variants	ACEY-DEUCY, ALBEMARLE
	ANACONDA, BASEBALL
	BASKETBALL, BEAT IT
	BEAT YOUR NEIGHBOUR
	BLAZER, BLIND ANTE
	BLIND OPENERS, BLUFF, BULL
	CANADIAN, CINCINNATI
	CONFUSION, CRAZY, CRISS CROSS
	DOUBLE BARTER, DOUBLE UP
	DR PEPPER, ENGLISH, FAIRVIEW
	FIVE BETS, FIVE-CARD
	FIVES AND TENS, FLIP
	FOLLOW MARY, FOLLOW THE KING
	FOLLOW THE QUEEN, FOOTBALL
	FOUR FORTY-FOUR, FREEZE-OUT
	HEINZ, HIGH-LOW, HOLD 'EM
	JACKPOT, KANAKEE, KLONDIKE (BOB)
	LAINO, LAME BRAIN (PETE)
	LEG, LOWBALL, MISTIGRIS
	MONTEREY, NEW YORK
	NIGHT BASEBALL, NO LOOKIE
	NO PEEKIE, OMAHA
	PASS THE GARBAGE
	PIG (IN A POKE), PROGRESSIVE
	PUT AND TAKE, ROCKLEIGH
	ROLL 'EM, ROLL OVER
	ROUND THE WORLD, RUM
	SCREW YOUR NEIGHBOUR
	SCREWY LOUIE, SHIFTING SANDS
	SHOWDOWN, SKARNEY, SKEETS
	SPANISH, SPIT IN THE OCEAN
	ST LOUIS, STORMY WEATHER
	THREE FORTY-FIVE, TIGER
	TURN-UP, TWIN BEDS, TWO-LEG
	WHISKY, WILD WIDOW, WOOLWORTH
pontoon	VINGT-ET-UN
—variants	ACE-DEUCE-JACK
	ACE LOW, BACCARAT (BANQUE)
	BANGO, BANKER AND BROKER
	BLACKJACK, CHEMIN-DE-FER
	CHEMMY, FARMER, FIFTEEN
	HORSE RACE, PONTOON
	QUINCE, SEVEN-AND-A-HALF
	SHIMMY, SLOGGER, THIRTY-FIVE
	TWENTY-ONE, VANJOHN
	VINGT-ET-UN, YOU CALL 'EM
rummy	GIN
—variants	BANKERS, BLOCK, BOAT HOUSE
	CALOOCHI, CANASTA, CAPTAINS
	CAROUSEL, CINCINNATI, COMBINATION
	CONTINENTAL, COON CAN, DIZZY
	ELIMINATION, FORTUNE, FREEZE OUT
	GIN, JAVA, JERSEY GIN
	INDIAN CRAPS, KALOOKI, KNOCK
	LIVERPOOL, MICHIGAN, MISSISSIPPI

	OKLAHOMA, OLD-FASHIONED, PAN
	PARTNERSHIP, PERSIAN, PIF-PAF
	PROGRESSIVE, QUEEN CITY, RAMINO
	ROUND ROBIN, ROUND-THE-CORNER
	SKARNEY, SKIP, STANDARD HOLLYWOOD
	SUPER GIN, TONK, TURN-UP
Russian game	VINT
second highest card	MANILLE
sequence of three cards	
of same suit	TIERCE
series of games (bridge)	RUBBER
sevenfold increase in	
stake at basset	SEPTLEVA
signal for trumps	PETER
silent game	MUMCHANCE
single-handed game	PATIENCE, SOLITAIRE
Spanish game	COON-CAN
stake at poker	ANTE
three-handed game	CUT-THROAT (BRIDGE)
	GLEEK, OMBRE
	SKAT, TRED(D)ILLE
tricks	
—no tricks (solo whist)	MISERE
with exposed hand	MISERE OUVERT
	OPEN MISERE
—5 tricks (solo whist)	SOLO
—12 tricks	
bridge	LITTLE SLAM
whist	SWAB
—13 tricks	
bridge	GRAND SLAM
solo whist	ABONDANCE
	ABUNDONCE
	BUNDLE
—with exposed	
hand	ABONDANCE DECLAREE
	ABUNDANCE DECLARED
unscientific whist	BUMBLE-PUPPY
Venetian game	BASSET
carriages	
including: cart	
coach	
2-wheeled	BANDY, BUGGY, CABRIOLET
	CHARIOT, CURRICLE, DENNET
	DOG-CART, DESOBLIGEANTE
	GIG, GOVERNESS CART
	GUINGUETTE, HANSOM CAB
	JAUNTING-CAR, JAUNTY
	(JIN)RICKSHAW, QUADRIGA
	SCOTCH CART, SCURRY
	STANHOPE, SULKY, TILBURY
	TONGA, TRAP
	TUMBREL, TUMBRIL
3-wheeled	
—pedal-car	TRISHAW
—for hire	PEDICAB

4-wheeled	BAROUCHE, BERLIN, BRAKE
	BREAK, BROUGHAM,
	BUCKBOARD, BUGGY
	CART, CHUCK-WAGON
	CLARENCE, COACH
	CONESTOGA WAGON
	COUPE, DILIGENCE
	DOS-A-DOS, DRAY, DROS(H)KY
	FIACRE, FLY, GROWLER
	HACKNEY CARRIAGE
	HACKNEY COACH, HERDIC
	PHAETON, PRAIRIE SCHOONER
	ROCKAWAY, SURREY
	VIS-A-VIS, WAG(G)ON, WAIN
—coach	FOUR-IN-HAND
—folding hood	CALASH, LANDAU
	VICTORIA
—(US)	BUGGY
	CHUCK-WAGON, HERDIC
	PRAIRIE SCHOONER
African	SCOTCH CART
agricultural	WAG(G)ON
baggage-wagon	FOURGON
bullock-cart (Indian)	BANDY
Burmese state carriage	RATH
cart	DRAY, WAG(G)ON, WAIN
Chinese	(JIN)RICKSHAW
coach	FOUR-IN-HAND
Continental stage-coach	DILIGENCE
closed	BROUGHAM
—covered	JINGLE, (HANSOM-)CAB
—military	TUMBREL, TUMBRIL
—US	HERDIC
dung-cart	TUMBREL, TUMBRIL
fast stagecoach	FLY
four-horse	FOUR-IN-HAND
French	DILIGENCE, FIACRE
	TUMBREL, TUMBRIL
gig	DENNET, GUINGETTE
	TILBURY, SPIDER
high-wheeled	
hired coach	HACKNEY-CARRIAGE
Indian	BANDY, BUGGY, EKKA
	GHARRI, GHARRY, TONGA
Irish	BIANCONI, GINGLE
	JAUNTING-CAR, JAUNTY
Italian	VETTURA
light	
—carriage	CHAISE(-CART), TRAP
—cart	SHANDRY(DAN)
—gig	(TIM-)WHISK(E)Y
long and open	DRAG
mail-coach	POST
old-fashioned chaise	SHANDRYDAN
one	
—horse	EKKA, FLY

—person	DESOBLIGEANTE, SULKY
—seater	STANHOPE
open carriage	WAGONETTE
passenger coach	STAGE-COACH
rickety vehicle	SHANDRYDAN
Roman	BIGA, CHARIOT, QUADRIGA
Russian	DROS(H)KY, TROIKA
—wagon	AR(A)BA, KIBITKA, TELEGA
small landau	LANDAULET(TE)
Spanish, covered	TARTANA
tip-cart	TUMBREL, TUMBRIL
wagonette	BRAKE, BREAK
with facing seats	VIS-A-VIS
cats	
American	MAINE COON
curly-coated	REX
disappearing cat	CHESHIRE
Eliot's book of	OLD POSSUM'S
fighting cat	KILKENNY
French cat	CHAT
German cat	KATZE
grinning cat	CHESHIRE
in Reynard the Fox	TIBERT
Italian	VETTURA
large	MAINE COON
long hair	ANGORA, BALINESE, BIRMAN
	MAINE COON, PERSIAN
	RAGDOLL, TURKISH
mythical	KELLAS CATS
Norwegian	SKOGCATT
old	GIB, GRIMALKIN
proverbial cat	KILKENNY
Samuel Johnson's cat	HODGE
Sancho Panza's cat	BAVIECA
Scottish cat	BAUDRONS
she-cat	TIB(CAT)
short hair	ABYSSINIAN, BOMBAY
	BURMESE, DEVON REX, EGYPTIAN
	EXOTIC, HAVANA, JAPANESE BOBTAIL
	KORAT, MANX, RUSSIAN BLUE
	SIAMESE, SINGAPURA, SNOWSHOE
	SOMALI, SPHYNX, TONKINESE
	WIREHAIR
slang	MOG(GIE), MOGGY
smiling cat	CHESHIRE
Spanish cat	GATA, GATO
swimming cat	TURKISH VAN
tailless	MANX
theatre cat	GUS, PUSS-IN-BOOTS
yellow and black	TORTOISE-SHELL
cattle	
African	AFRICANDER, ANKOLE, BAHEMI
	BAPEDI, BASHI, BORAN
	DRAKENSBERGER, KIGEZI, KURI
	LANDIM, N'DAMA
	NGUNI, WATUSI, WHITE FULANI

American	BEEFALO, BRAHMAN
	BRANGUS, HOLSTEIN-FRIESIAN
	SANTA GERTRUDIS
	TEXAS LONGHORN
Australian	DROUGHTMASTER
	MURRAY GREY
	TASMANIAN GREY
Austrian	PINZGAU(E)R
Belgian	BELGIAN BLUE
Canadian	HOLSTEIN-FRIESIAN
	RED AND WHITE FRIESIAN
castrated male	BULLOCK, OX, STEER
Channel Islands	ALDERNEY, GUERNSEY
	JERSEY
Danish	DANISH RED
dehorned	MUL(L)EY
English	BRITISH WHITE, DEVON
	GLOUCESTER, HEREFORD
	LINCOLN RED, LONGHORN
	RED AND WHITE FRIESIAN
	SHORTHORN, SOUTH DEVON
	SUSSEX, TEESWATER
	(WILD) WHITE PARK
Egyptian	BALADI, DAMIETTA
	MARYUTI, SAIDI
female	COW, HEIFER, OX
—sterile	FREE-MARTIN
Finnish	FINNCATTLE
	FINNISH AYRSHIRE
French	AUBRAC, BLONDE D'AQUITAINE
	CHAROL(L)AIS, GASCONNE
	LIMOUSIN, MAINE-ANJOU
	NORMANDY, PIE ROUGE DE L'EST
	SALERS, SIMMENTAL, TARENTAISE
German	ANGELN, FLECKVIEH
	GERMAN RED PIED
	GERMAN YELLOW, HOLSTEIN
heavy breed	FRI(E)SIAN
Hebrides	KYLOE
heifer (Scottish)	QUEY
hornless	REDPOLL
Indian	GIR KANKREJ KHILLARI
	RED SINDHI THARPARKAR
Irish	DEXTER, IRISH MOILED, KERRY
Italian	CHIANINA MARCHIGIANA
	PIE(D)MONTESE, ROMAGNOLA
male	BULL, BULLOCK, OX, STEER
Netherlandish	DUTCH FRIESIAN
	GRONINGEN
	MEUSE-RHINE-IJSSEL
Norwegian	BLACKSIDED TRONDHEIM
	TELEMARK
old	
—breed	BLUE ALBION
—terms	AVER, FEE, NEAT
Portuguese	BARROSA, GALEGA, MIRANDA

Russian	ALA TAU, KHOL MOGOR
	KOSTROMA, RED STEPPE
Scottish	ABERDEEN ANGUS, AYRSHIRE
	BELTED GALLOWAY, GALLOWAY
	HIGHLAND CATTLE, LUING
	SHETLAND, WEST HIGHLAND
	(see also **Scottish**)
short-horned	DURHAM
Spanish	ANDALUSIAN, FIGHTING BULL
	GALICIAN BLOND
Swiss	BROWN SWISS, SIMMENTAL
Texan	LONGHORN
Welsh	WELSH BLACK
West Country	DEVON
West Indian	JAMAICA HOPE
white-faced	HAWKEY, HAWKIE, HEREFORD
young	CALF, HEIFER, STEERLING
	STIRK
	(see also **ox**)
cattle diseases	ANTHRAX, BLACK QUARTER
	BLACKWATER, BLUE TONGUE
	BRUCELLOSIS, REDWATER
actinobacillosis	WOODY-TONGUE
actinomycosis	LUMPY JAW
bacterial	ANTHRAX, JOINT-ILL
	LEPTOSPIROSIS, NAVEL-ILL
	PLEURO-PNEUMONIA
	SALMONELLOSIS
	TUBERCULOSIS
bovine spongiform	
encephalitis	BST
cattle plague	RINDERPEST
	STEPPE MURRAIN
contagious abortion	BRUCELLOSIS
deficiency disease	ACETONAEMIA
	HYPOMAGNESAEMIA
	KETOSIS
eye disease	KERATOCONJUNCTIVITIS
	NEW FOREST EYE
foot	
—disease	FOOT AND MOUTH
	FOUL IN THE FOOT
	LAMINITIS
—and mouth disease	APHTHOUS FEVER
fungal	ACTINOMYCOSIS
	RINGWORM
gas in the stomach	BLOAT
grass staggers	HYPOMAGNESAEMIA
	TETANY
husk	LUNGWORM
hypocalcaemia	MILK FEVER
hypomagnesaemia	GRASS STAGGERS, TETANY
inflammation of	
—foot	LAMITIS
—throat	GARGET
—udder	GARGET, MAMMITIS

intestinal	JOHNES DISEASE
lumpy jaw	ACTINOMYCOSIS
mad cow disease	BSE
	BOVINE SPONGIFORM ENCEPHALITIS
milk fever	HYPOCALCAEMIA
parasitic	HUSK, LIVER FLUKE
	LUNGWORM, ROUNDWORM
	TAPEWORM, WARBLE-FLY
rinderpest	CATTLE PLAGUE
	STEPPE MURRAIN
steppe murrain	CATTLE PLAGUE
	RINDERPEST
tetany	GRASS STAGGERS
	HYPOMAGNESAEMIA
tuberculosis	PEARL DISEASE
udder disease	MASTITIS
viral	EBL, ENZOOTIC BOVINE LEUCOSIS
	IBR
	INFECTIOUS BOVINE RHINOTRACHETIS
woody tongue	ACTINOBACILLOSIS

Celebes (Sulawesi)

wild hog	BABIR(O)USA
	DEER HOG, HORNED HOG

Celtic

alphabet	OG(H)AM
festival	BELTANE
harp	CLAIRSCHACH, CLARSACH
high steward	MORMAOR
noble	TAOISEACH
sword	CLAYMORE, CLEDDYO

Central African Republic   CAR, RCA

capital	BANGUI
coin	FRANC

Central America

agave	SISAL
ant	KELEP
bird	MOTMOT, SAWBILL
coin	COLON
early civilisation	AZTEC, MAYA
	TOLTEC, ZAPOTEC
lapwing	TERU-TERO
Maya calendar cycle	
—1 day	KIN
—20 days	UINAL
—360 days	TUN
—7200 days	KATUN
—144,000 days	BAKTUN
measure	VARA
races	CORA, CUNA, GUAYMI, HUASTEC
	HUICHOL, LENCA, MISKITO, MIXTEC
	NAHUATL, NICARAO, PAYA, ZAPOTEC
rubber (tree)	(H)ULE
tree	AMATE, EBO(E),S(A)OUARI
	(*see also* **South America**)

cereal

African	MEALIE, TEFF(GRASS)

barley	
—shaped by grinding	PEARL BARLEY
—with husks removed	POT BARLEY
	SCOTCH BARLEY
boiled oatmeal	PORRIDGE
coarsely ground	GROATS, GROUT, MEAL
—maize	HOMINY(GRITS), SAMP
—oats	GRITS
ear of maize	CORNCOB
Eastern	JAPANESE MILLET
farina porridge	POLENTA
finely ground	FARINA, FLOUR
Indian	
—corn	MAIZE
—millet	RAGGEE, RAGGY, RAGI
inner husks	BRAN
Irish porridge	STIRABOUT
Italian porridge	POLENTA
lentil flour	ERVALENTA, REVALENTA
maize	INDIAN CORN, SWEETCORN
—Mexican dish	TAMAL(E), TOMALLEY
—porridge	MUSH
American	SAMP
mixed cereals	MASHLAM, MASHLIM
	MASHLIN, MASHLUM
	MASHLOCH, MASLIN
oatmeal and water	DRAMMACH, DRAMMOCH
oats, fruit, etc	MUESLI
other cereal dishes	BURGOO, CORNFLAKES
	CORN ON THE COB
	COUSCOUS, ENCHILADA
	KUSKUS, OATMEAL
	PEARL BARLEY, POT BARLEY
	SEMOLINA, SOWANS, SUCCOTASH
	TABBOULEH, TABBOULI, TAHINA
	TAHINI, TORTILLA
	(*see also* **rice**)
parched maize	NO-CAKE, PINOLE, POPCORN
products	CORNFLAKES, CORNFLOUR
	CORNMEAL, RICE CRISPIES
	SHREDDED WHEAT
Red Indian maize dish	SAMP, SUCCOTASH
	SUP(P)AWN
semolina porridge	POLENTA
South African maize	MEALIES
thin porridge	GRUEL
types	BARLEY, BUCKWHEAT, MAIZE
	MILLET, OATS, RICE, RYE
	SWEETCORN, TRITICALE, WHEAT
—buckwheat	SARRASIN, SARRAZIN
	TURKEY WHEAT
wheat	AMELCORN, EMMER
	TRITICOM
—boiled in milk, etc	FRUMENTY, FURMETY
—inferior	SPELT(Z)
—primitive	EINKORN

—rye hybrid	TRITICALE
—spring	DURUM
—wild	EMMER
young corn ears	GREEN CORN
Ceylon	SRI LANKA
aboriginal race	VEDDA(H)
bandicoot	PIG-RAT
Buddhist shrine	DAGOBA
capital	COLOMBO
coin	CENT
finial of dagoba	TEE
form of marriage	BEENAH
grass	CITRONELLA
language	PALI, SIN(G)HALESE, TAMIL
lemur	LORIS
milkweed	COW-PLANT
modern name	SRI LANKA
palm	CORYPHA, TALIPAT, TALIPOT
—leaf book	OCA
people	CINGALESE, SINHALA
	SIN(G)HALESE, TAMIL
pig-rat	BANDICOOT
spice	CINNAMON
timber	CALAMANDER, COROMANDEL
	(see also **timber***)*
umbrella-shaped finial	TEE
Chad	
capital	NDJAMENA
coin	FRANC
people	TUAREG
Chaldean	
bible	TARGUM
city	UR OF THE CHALDEES
Channel Islands	CI
islands	ALDERNEY, GUERNSEY
	HERM, JERSEY, SARK
coin	DOUBLE
cheese	
American	
—cottage	POT CHEESE
—processed	CLUB CHEESE
—soft	PHILADELPHIA
Ayrshire	DUNLOP
Belgian	LIMBURGER
Cornish	YARG
covered with grape	
seeds	TOME AU RAISIN
Cypriot	HALLOUMIS
Danish	BLUE CASTELLO, BOUCLET
	DANABLU, DANBO
	DANISH BLUE, ESROM, HARVARTI
	JUTLAND BLUE, LE MIDI
	ORANGE ROLL, SAMSOE, SATIA
	SVENBO, TOLKO, TYBO
Dorset	BLUE VINNEY
Dutch	EDAM, GOUDA

English	ADMIRAL'S, APPLEWOOD
	BEAMERDALE, BEL(L)SHIRE
	BLUE VINNEY, BOTTON, CHARNWOOD
	CHEDDAR, CHESHIRE, COTSWOLD
	COUNTY, CURD, DERBY
	DOUBLE GLOUCESTER, HUNTSMAN
	LANCASHIRE, LEICESTER
	LYMESWOLD, MORVEN, NUTWOOD
	PEPPERVALE, RUTLAND
	SAGE DERBY, SHERWOOD, SOMERTON
	SHROPSHIRE BLUE, STILTON
	WALGROVE, WALTON, WENSLEYDALE
	WHIRL, WINDSOR (RED)
French	BABYBEL, BANON, BEAUFORT
	BLANC DES CHAMPS, BLEU D'AUVERGNE
	BLEU DE BRESSE, BOMBEL
	BOULETTE, BOURSAULT
	BOURSIN, BREBIS DES PYRENEES
	BRIE(DE MEAUX), CABECOU
	CAMEMBERT, CANTAL, COULOMMIERS
	D'ANVESNES, DOUX DE MONTAGNE
	ETORKI, FOURME D'AMBERT
	FROMAGE (BLANC), FROMAGE FRAIS
	GERVAIS, GORMANDISE, IRATY
	LARUNS, LE ROULE, LIVAROT
	MEULE D'OR, MUNSTER, NEUCHATEL
	OSSAU, PETIT SUISSE, PIP CREM(E)
	PONT L'EVEQUE, PORT SALUT
	RAMBOL PEPPER, REBLOCHON
	RIGOTTE, RONDELLE, ROQUEFORT
	ST AGUR, ST CHEVRIER
	ST HECLAIRE, ST JULIEN
	ST MAURE, ST NECTAIRE
	ST PAULIN, TARTARE
	TERRES D'OR, TOMME DE CHANTAL
	VALBRESO, VALENCAY, VIEUX PANE
from	
—ewe's milk	BREBIS DES PYRENEES
	ETORKI, EWE-CHEESE, FETA
	HAL(O)UMI, IDIAZIBAL, IRATY
	LARUNS, MANCHEGO, OSSAU
	PARAMO DE GUSMAN, PECORINI
	ROQUEFORT, SERPA, SERRA
	VALBRESO
—goat's milk	CABECOU, CAW'S CARON
	CHEVRE, CHEVROTIN, FETA
	LOS BALACHARES, PANT-YS-GAWN
	PEN-Y-BONT, ST MAURE, VALENCAY
—soya bean milk	TOFU
garlic-flavoured	HRAMSA
German	ALLGAU, BLOU BAY
	BRUDER BASIL, CAMBOZOLA
	EMMENT(H)AL(ER)
	FRUHSTUCKSKASE, GRUNLAND
	HANDKASE, HARZ, LIMBURGER
	MAINZ, MIREE, MUNSTER, PIKADOR

	PILZKASE, QUARK, ROMADUR, RUPP
	SBRINZ, TILSIT(ER)
Greek	AGRAFA, FETA, KEFALOTYRI
high-fat	CREAM CHEESE
Indian	PANEER
indifferent	MOUSETRAP
Irish	CASHEL BLUE, GUBBEEN
	MILLEENS
Italian	BEL PAESE, CACIOCAVALLA
	DOLCELATTE, FONTINA
	GORGONZOLA, GRANO PADANO
	MASCARPONE, MASCHERPONE
	MOZZARELLA, PARMESAN
	PECORINO, PROVOLONE
	RICOTTO, ROBIOLA, ROMANO
	STRACCHINO, TALEGGIO
	TARTUFELLE
	TORTA SAN GAUDENZIO
	VENETO
lightly-salted	DEMI-SEL
low-fat	COTTAGE CHEESE
moulded by hand	HAND-CHEESE
Norwegian	JARL(E)SBERG, MYSOST
Portuguese	SERPA, SERRA
Scottish	CABOC, CROWDIE, DUNLOP
	KEBBOCK, KEBBUCK, ORKNEY
Somerset	CHEDDAR
Spanish	CABREALES, IDIAZABAL
	LOS BALACHARES, MAHON
	MANCHEGO, PARAMO DE GUSMAN
	TETILLA
Swiss	APPENZELL, EMMENT(H)AL(ER)
	GRUYERE, SAPSAGO, TILSIT
	TOGGENBURGER KASE
	VACHERIN
unripe soft cheese	COOK CHEESE
Welsh	ACORN, CAERPHILLY
	CARDIGAN, CAW'S CARON
	CAW'S CENARTH
	LLANBOIDY, MERLIN
	PANT-YS-GAWN, PENCAR(R)EG
	PEN-Y-BONT, SKIRRID, TEIFI

cheese dishes

—cheese and ham	
sandwich	CROQUE-MONSIEUR
—cooked	FONDUE
on toast	BUCK RABBIT
	WELSH RAREBIT, WELSH RABBIT
—individual	RAMAKIN, RAMEKIN
	RAMEQUIN
—melted (Swiss)	RACLETTE
—other	ALPINE EGG, CHEESE SOUFFLE
	CHEESECAKE, DUTCH OMELETTE
	FONDUE, PIZZA, ROMAN GNOCCHI
	ROQUEFORT QUICHE
	QUICHE LORRAINE

chemistry

absorption of	
—gas by solid	OCCLUSION
—water by solid	DELIQUESCENCE
acetylene	ETHYNE
acid	(*see separate entry*)
acting as acid to bases	
and vice versa	AMPHOTERIC
addition of	
—acetyl group	ACETYLATION
—halogen atoms	HALOGENTAION
—hydrogen	HYDROGENATION
	REDUCTION
—hydroxyls	HYDROXYLATION
—impurities to crystal	DOPING
—methyl	METHYLATION
—negative catalyst to	
prevent decomposition	STABILISATION
—nitro group	NITRATION
—oxygen	OXIDATION
—water	HYDRATION
alcohol	ETHANOL
	ETHYL ALCOHOL
alcoholic extract	TINCTURE
alkene	OLEFIN(E)
allotrope of oxygen	OZONE
alternative form	ALLOTOPE
aluminium oxide	CORUNDUM
ammonia and cupric	
hydroxide solution	SCHWEITZER'S REAGENT
amyl acetate	BANANA OIL
	PENTYL ACETATE
amylum	STARCH
analysis by	
—adsorption	CHROMATOGRAPHY
—use of reagents	TITRATION
anomalous water	POLYWATER
aromatic	
—hydrocarbon	TERPENE
—used as indicator	PHENOLPHTHALEIN
—with one or more	
hydroxyl groups	PHENOL
arrangement of elements	
by atomic weight	PERIODIC TABLE
arsenic	
—disulphide	REALGAR
—trioxide	WHITE ARSENIC
artificial water softener	ZEOLITE
atom with	
—free valency	RADICAL
—same	
atomic	
—mass as atom of	
another element	ISOBARE
—number and mass	
but different energy state	ISOMER

proton but different neutron number	ISOTOPE
—unpaired electrons	FREE RADICAL
—with added or missing electrons	ION
atomic weight of isotope	MASS NUMBER
average mass of atoms	ATOMIC WEIGHT
banana oil	AMYL ACETATE PENTYL ACETATE
base able to neutralise acid	ALKALI
benzene	PHENE
binary compound of	
—iodine	IODIDE
—oxygen	OXIDE
—sulphur	SULPHIDE
bond where	
—hydrogen atom is bonded to two electronegative atoms	HYDROGEN BOND
—two electrons are donated	SEMIPOLAR BOND
Brunswick green	COPPER OXIDE CHLORIDE
calamine	ZINC CARBONATE
calcium	
—carbonate	CHALK, LIMESTONE
—hydride	HYDROLITH
—hydroxide	LIME WATER, SLAKED LIME
—sulphate	GYPSUM
calomel	MERCUROUS CHLORIDE
carbamide	UREA
carbohydrate	
—in cell walls	CELLULOSE
—with	
5 carbon atoms	PENTOSE
6 carbon atoms	HEXOSE
carbon	
—based	ORGANIC
—dioxide	FIXED AIR
carbylamide	ISOCYANIDE, ISONITRILE
catalyst in polymerisation of ethylene and propylene	ZIEGLER CATALYST
caustic soda	SODIUM HYDROXIDE
chain of two or more amino-acids	PEPTIDE
change	
—caused by enzyme	FERMENTATION
—direct from solid to gas	SUBLIMATION
—in atomic nucleus	NUCLEAR TRANSITION
—of colour induced by light	PHOTOCHROMISM PHOTOTROPISM
—to stony structure	PETRIFACTION
chemical	
—analysis by current-voltage curves	POLAROGRAPHY

—attraction	AFFINITY
—bond	VALANCE, VALENCY
—formula showing arrangement of atoms	STRUCTURAL FORMULA
—influence	CATALYSIS
—reaction building compounds from simpler units	SYNTHESIS
chemically inactive	INERT
chemist	DRUGGIST, PHARMACIST
—American	ADAMS, ANFINSEN, ARNON
	AVERY, BAEKELAND, BENEDICT
	BERG, BIGELEISEN, BLOCH
	BRAND, BROWN, CALVIN
	CAROTHERS, CECH, CHARGAFF
	CHASE, CLEMENTI, COLLINS
	CORI, COREY
	CRAFTS, CRAM, DEBYE
	DOERING, FLORY, FOX, FRUTON
	GAIUQUE, GILBERT, HARKINS
	HAUPTMAN, HOAGLAND, HOFFMANN
	INGRAM, KAMEN, KARLE, KHORANA
	KOHMAN, LANGMUIR, LEVENE, LEWIS
	LIBBY, LIPMANN, LIPSCOMB
	MACLEOD, MATTHAE, MERRIFIELD
	MILLER, MIRSKY, MOORE, MCCARTHY
	MCCOY, MIDGLEY, MILLER
	MORLEY, MULLIKEN, NIRENBERG
	NORTHROP,, ONSAGER, ORO
	PALADE, PAULING, PEDERSEN
	RABINOWITCH, RICHARDS
	ROSE, ROSS, RUBEN, SAGER
	SCHAEFER, SEABORG, SHEMIN
	SILLIMAN, SPEDDING, STEIN
	SUMNER, TAUBE, UREY, VIGNEAUD
	WATSON, WHARTON, WILLIAMS
	WOLFGANG, WOODWARD
—Argentinian	LELOIR
—Australian	CORNFORTH, EDMAN
—Austrian	HARTECK, KUHN, PERUTZ
	PREGL, ZSIGMONDY
—Belgian	BAEKELAND, PRIGOGINE, STAS
—British	ABEL, ANDREWS, ASTBURY
	BARTLETT, BARTON, BLACK, BOYLE
	CORNFORTH, COUPER, CRICK, CROSS
	CULLEN, DALTON, DAVY, DEWAR
	GRAHAM, HODGKIN, HOWARTH, JOULE
	KEILIN, KENDREW, KIPPING, LOWRY
	MANN, MARTIN, MINSHELWOOD
	MITCHELL, NEWLANDS, NORRISH
	ORGELL, PARKES, PERKIN
	PERUTZ, PETERS, POLANYI
	POPE, PORTER, RAMSAY
	ROBINSON, RUTHERFORD, SANGER
	SODDY, SYNGE, TENNANT, TODD
	WESTALL, WILKINS, WILKINSON
	WOLLASTON

—Canadian	BAKER, BARTLETT
	HERTZBERG, HODSON
—Ceylonese	PONNAMPERUMA
—Croatian	RUZICKA
—Czech	HEYROVSKY
—Danish	BRONSTED
—Dutch	DEBYE, DE LA BOE, MULDER
	VAN HELMONT, VAN 'T HOFF
—Finnish	GADOLIN
—French	BERTHELOT, BOUCHARDAT
	BRACCONOT, BRANDENBERGER
	CAVENTON, CHARDONNET
	CHEVREUL, CLAUDE, CURIE
	DE BOISBAUDRAN, DUFAY, DUMAS
	FRIEDEL, GRIGNARD, HERAULT
	LAVOISIER, LE BEL, LEHN, MACQUER
	MOISSON, MORVEAU, PASTEUR
	PAYEN, PELLETIER, PEREY
	PERSOZ, PROUST, REGNAULT, SABATIER
	STAUDINGER, URBAIN, VILLARD
—German	ALDER, BAEYER, BERGMAN
	BLOCH, BOSCH, BRAND
	BUCHNER, BUNSEN, DIELS
	DOBEREINER, DOGMAGK
	EIGEN, EULER-HELPIN, FISCHER
	FRAENKEL-CONRAT, FUELGEN
	GRAEBE, HABER, HOFMANN
	HOPPE-SEYLER, INGRAM, KEKULE
	KILIANI, KIRCHHOFF
	KLAPROTH, KNOOP, KOLBE, KOSSEL
	KREBS, LIEBIG, LIPMANN, LUNGE
	LYNEN, MAYER, MEYER, MEYERHOF
	MORNER, NERNST, OSTWALD, PANETH
	STAHL, STAUDINGER, THIELE
	VON STRADONITZ, WALLACH
	WARBURG, WERNER
	WIELAND, WILLSTATER, WINDAUS
	WINKLER, WISLICENUS, WITTIG
	WOHLER, WOLFGANG, ZIEGLER
—Hungarian	HEVESY
—Indian	KHORANI
—Irish	ANDREWS, BOYLE
—Israeli	KATCHALSKI, WEIZMAN
—Italian	AVOGADRO, CANNIZZARO
	CLEMENTI, MENGHINI, NATTA
	SEGRE, SOBRERO
—Japanese	FUKUI, TAKAMINE, YAGI
—Norwegian	HASSEL
—Polish	ARNON, FRUTON
	SKLODOWSKA
—Russian	KIRCHHOFF, LEVENE
	LOMONOSOV, MENDELEEV
	OSTWALD, POPOV, RABINOWITCH
	SEMENOV
—South African	KLUG
—Spanish	OCHOA, ORO

—Swedish	ARRHENIUS, BERZELIUS
	CASPERSSON, EDMAN, GAHN
	MOSANDER, NILSON, SCHEELE
	SVEDBERG, TISELIUS
—Swiss	ABDERHALDEN, BOVET
	DE SAUSSURE, EULER-CHELPIN
	KARRER, MIESCHER, MULLER
	PRELOG, SCHONBEIN
—Yugoslav	PRELOG
chemistry of carbon	
compounds	ORGANIC CHEMISTRY
circulation of carbon	
by living things	CARBON CYCLE
citric acid cycle	KREBS CYCLE
coagulation of fine	
particles into larger	FLOCCULATION
colloid	
—in form of jelly	GEL
—of	
gel in water	HYDROGEL
one liquid in another	EMULSION
—particle	MICELLA, MICELLE
colloidal suspension	SOL
combination of	
—metals	ALLOY
—molecules of solvent and solute	SOLVATION
—oxygen	OXIDATION
—two or more polymers	COPOLYMER
	DIMER
combining	
—power of atom	VALENCY
—with	
hydrogen	HYDROGENATION
	REDUCTION
oxygen	OXIDATION
common salt	SODIUM CHLORIDE
compound	
—between alcohol and	
glycerine	GLYCOL
—containing	
carbon	ORGANIC COMPOUND
iron	FERRIC COMPOUND
	FERROUS COMPOUND
oxygen bound to two	
other atoms	EPOXY
water	HYDRATE
—formed from	
condensation	
of alcohol and an acid	ESTER
molecules of solvent and solute	SOLVATE
replacement of hydrogen	
in acid by a metal	SALT
union of molecules into	
larger molecules	POLYMER
—like alcohol but with two	
fewer hydrogen atoms	ALDEHYDE

—of
  amino-acids — PEPTIDE
  carbon
    —and hydrogen — HYDROCARBON
    ORGANIC COMPOUND
    —hydrogen and
      oxygen — CARBOHYDRATE
  cellulose, starch,sugar — CARBOHYDRATE
  mercury — AMALGAM
  metal with
    —halogen — HALIDE
    —nitrogen — NITRIDE
  nitrogen with
    —another element — NITRIDE
    —sugar — NUCLEOSIDE
  oxygen with
    —another element — OXIDE
    —two alkyl groups — ETHER
  sulphur with another
    element — SULPHIDE
  three elements — TERNARY COMPOUND
  two elements — BINARY COMPOUND
—which
  can form further
    compounds — UNSATURATEDCOMPOUND
  can give up proton
    to a base — ORGANIC ACID
  will not undergo further
    reaction — SATURATED COMPOUND
—with
  atoms linked with
    —one bond — SATURATED BOND
    —two or more
      bonds — UNSATURATED COMPOUND
  chains of molecules — POLYMER
  metallic ion bonded to
    two or more atoms — CHELATE
  molecules comprising three
    monomer molecules — TRIMER
  one component enclosed
    in cavities of another — CLATHRATE
  single molecules — MONOMER
concentration in solution — TITRE
constituents of air — CARBON DIOXIDE
  NITROGEN, OXYGEN
containing
  —bivalent tin — STANNOUS
  —hexavalent tellurium — TELLURIC
  —tetravalent
    tellurium — TELLUROUS
    tin — STANNIC
    titanium — TITANIC
    uranium — URANIC
  —trivalent
    thallium — THALLIC
    titanium — TITANOUS

    uranium — URANOUS
—univalent thallium — THALLOUS
conversion of
  —atmospheric nitrogen — NITROGEN FIXATION
  —liquid to vapour below
    boiling point — EVAPORATION
  —nitrogen by soil bacteria — NITRIFICATION
  —soil compounds to
    nitrates — NITRIFICATION
  —solid
    directly to vapour — SUBLIMATION
    or liquid to gas — GASIFICATION
  —vapour to liquid — CONDENSATION
convertible isomer — TAUTOMER
copper
  —carbonate — AZURITE, VERDIGRIS
  —oxide chloride — BRUNSWICK GREEN
  —sulphate — BORDEAUX MIXTURE
copperas — FERROUS SULPHATE
  GREEN VITRIOL
corundum — ALUMINIUM OXIDE
covalent bond — HOME-POLAR BOND
cracking — PYOLYSIS
crystal with
  —many branches — DENDRITE
  —regular lattice
    and no defects — IDEAL CRYSTAL
crystallisation by loss of
  water — EFFLORESENCE
dative bond — COORDINATE BOND
decomposition/dissolution
  —by
    acid — ACIDOLYSIS
    electricity — ELECTROLYSIS
    enzyme — FERMENTATION
    ZYMOLYSIS
    heat — ABLATION, CRACKING
    PYROLYSIS, THERMOLYSIS
    irradiation — RADIOLYSIS
    light — PHOTOLYSIS
    micro-organisms — FERMENTATION
    radiant energy — PHOTODISSOCIATION
    water — HYDROLYSIS
  —of
    substance catalysed
      by enzymes — ENZYMOLYSIS
    two compounds — DOUBLE DECOMPOSITION
    METATHESIS
derived lipid — STEROID, STEROL
description of process
  of electrolysis — IONIC HYPOTHESIS
deuterium — DIPLOGEN
  HEAVY HYDROGEN
  —oxide — HEAVY WATER
device for separating
  solid from liquid — FILTER

diagram of benzene ring	KEKULE FORMULA
diatomaceous earth	KIESELGUHR
dichlordiethyl sulphide	MUSTARD GAS
different form of element	ALLOTROPE
diffusion through porous membrane	OSMOSIS
dimethylbenzene	XYLENE, XYLOL
diplogen	DEUTERIUM
	HEAVY HYDROGEN
disorder of a system	ENTROPY
double	
—benzene ring	NAPHTHALENE
—decomposition	METATHESIS
easily melted	EUTECTIC
eau de Javelle	JAVELLE WATER
effect of catalyst on chemical reaction	CATALYSIS
electrically	
—charged particle	ELECTRON, ION, PROTON
—neutral particle	NEUTRON
electrode	
—negative	CATHODE
—positive	ANODE
electrons in outer shell	VALENCY ELECTRONS
electrovalent bond	(HETERO-)POLAR BOND
	IONIC BOND
element	
—of seventh group of periodic table	HALOGEN
—with atomic number above 92	TRANSURANIC ELEMENT
incomplete electron shell	TRANSITION ELEMENT
valency of	
—one	MONAD
—two	DYAD
—three	TRIAD
—four	TETRAD
ester of	
—fatty acids	LIPID
—gycerol	GLYCERIDE
ethanol	(ETHYL) ALCHOHOL
	SPIRITS OF WINE
	WOOD NAPHTHA
ethene	ETHYLENE
ethenyl	VYNIL
ether	DIETHYL ETHER
	DIETHYL OXIDE
ethyne	ACETYLENE
existence in	
—several forms	POLYMORPHISM
—two or more forms	ALLOTROPY
fats and oils	SIMPLE LIPIDS
ferrous sulphate	COPPERAS
	GREEN VITRIOL

fine particles suspended in air	AEROSOL
fixed air	CARBON DIOXIDE
fluid used in cooling systems	REFRIGERANT
force	
—acting between	
masses	GRAVITY
molecules	VAN DER WAAL'S BOND
nucleons	STRONG NUCLEAR FORCE
particles in atoms	ELECTRIC FORCE
	WEAK FORCE
—which binds atoms	AFFINITY
	CHEMICAL BOND
formation of	
—compounds	SYNTHESIS
—crystals by evaporation	EFFLORESCENCE
—ions	IONISATION
—soap	SAPONIFICATION
formula indicating structure of	
—composition of a molecule in a compound	MOLECULAR FORMULA
—molecule	STRUCTURAL FORMULA
—simple test of ratio between molecule's atoms	EMPIRICAL FORMULA
fractional distillation	RESTIFICATION
fusion by heat	SINTERING
gain of electrons by an atom	REDUCTION
gas	(see separate entry)
giving different colours when reacting with acid or base	AMPHICHRO(MAT)IC
Glauber's salts	SALTCAKE
	SODIUM SULPHATE
glycol	DIOL
grease remover	DETERGENT
green vitriol	COPPERAS
	FERROUS SULPHATE
group of atoms	
—forming molecular chain	MICELLA, MICELLE
stable entity	MOLECULE
—unchanged in various compounds	RADICAL, RADICLE
—VII elements	HALOGENS
halogen group	ASTATINE, BROMINE
	CHLORINE
	FLUORINE, IODINE
having	
—affinity for water	HYDROPHILIC
—different properties in different directions	AEOLOTROPIC
	ANISOTROPIC

structure but	
same composition	ALLOMORPHOUS
—isomerism resulting from	
different arrangement	
of atoms	STEREOISOMERISM
mirror-imaging	ENANTIOMERISM
—no affinity for water	HYDROPHOBIC
—same	
crystal structure	ISOMORPHOUS
form	ISOMER
—but different	
composition	HOMEOMORPHOUS
number of atoms	ISOTERIC
osmotic pressure	ISOTONIC
—similar structure but	
different composition	ALLOMERISM
—three atoms per molecule	TRIATOMIC
—two atoms per molecule	DIATOMIC
—valency of	
more than one	POLYVALENT
one	MONOVALENT
	UNIVALENT
two	BIVALENT, DIVALENT
three	TRIVALENT
four	TETRAVALENT
	QUADRIVALENT
five	PENTAVALENT
	QUINQUEVALENT
six	HEXAVALENT
	SEXIVALENT
seven	HEPTAVALENT
	SEPTIVALENT
heat	
—absorbed or released	
during change of state	LATENT HEAT
—content per unit mass	ENTHALPY
—required to raise unit mass	
through one degree	SPECIFIC HEAT
heavy	
—hydrogen	DEUTERIUM, DIPLOGEN
—water	DEUTERIUM OXIDE
hetero-polar bond	ELECTRO-VALENT BOND
homovalent bond	COVALENT BOND
horizontal series in	
periodic table	PERIOD
hydrated	
—ferric oxide	OCHRE
—silicate of calcium and	
aluminium	ZEOLITE
hydrocarbon	
—in essential oils	TERPENE
—series	PARAFFIN SERIES
—with	
closed carbon chain	AROMATIC
fluorine replacing	
hydrogen	FLUOROCARBON

one	
—double bond	ALKENE
—triple bond	ALKYNE
open carbon chain	ALIPHATIC
rings	NAPHTHENE
straight chains	ALKANE
	(*see also* organic *below*)
hydrogen	
—combined with another	
element	HYDRIDE
—isotopes	PROTIUM, DEUTERIUM
	TRITIUM
hydrolith	CALCIUM HYDRIDE
hydrolysis of an ester	SAPONIFICATION
indicator of pH value	LITMUS (PAPER)
inert gas	NOBLE GAS
insoluble substance	
deposited from solution	PRECIPITATE
introduction of	
—halogen atoms	HALOGENATION
—nitro group	NITRATION
ionic bond	ELECTROVALENT BOND
isomer	
—differing in position	
of attached atoms	EPIMER
—readily interchangeable	TAUTOMER
isonitrile	CARBYLAMIDE
	ISOCYANIDE
isotopes of radioactive sub-	
stances containing thorium	THORIDES
Javelle water	EAU DE JAVELLE
jelly-like colloid	GEL
law governing	
—atomic weights	PERIODIC LAW
—dissociation	OSTWALD'S DILUTION LAW
—heat produced in	
chemical reactions	HESS'S LAW
lead	
—antimoniate	NAPLES-YELLOW
—carbonate	WHITE LEAD
—monoxide	LITHARGE
letter(s) representing an	
atom of element	SYMBOL
lime water	CALCIUM HYDROXIDE
linkage by	
—one covalent and one	
electrovalent bond	SEMIPOLAR BOND
—shared electrons	COVALENT BOND
	HOMO-POLAR BOND
—transfer of	
electrons	ELECTRO-VALENT BOND
	HETERO-POLAR BOND
—two pairs of electrons	DOUBLE BOND
liquid	
—after	
elution	ELUATE

filtration	FILTRATE
—remaining after crystallisation	
of salt from brine	BITTERN
—used for elution	ELUANT
litharge	LEAD MONOXIDE
loss of electron(s)	OXIDATION
lowering of positive valency	REDUCTION
lunar caustic	SILVER NITRATE
material capable of resisting	
high temperature	REFRACTORY
measure of unsaturated fatty	
acid	IODINE VALUE
measurement of strength	
of a solution	TITRATION
mercaptan	THIOL
mercuric sulphide	VERMILION
mercurous chloride	CALOMEL
metathesis	DOUBLE DECOMPOSITION
methanol	METHYL ALCOHOL
	WOOD SPIRIT, WOOD NAPHTHA
methyl	
—alcohol	METHANOL
	WOOD SPIRIT
—benzene	TOLUENE, TOLUOL
minium	RED LEAD
mixture of	
—acid or alkali with salt	BUFFER
—calcium phosphate and	
sulphate	SUPERPHOSPHATE
—liquids or liquids	
and solids	SOLUTION
by random motion of particles	DIFFUSION
that	
—cannot be separated	
by distillation	AZEOTROPE
—freeze simultaneously	EUTECTIC
with	
—dense particles	SUSPENSION
—fine particles	COLLOID
molecular mixture of substances	SOLUTION
molecule	
—consisting of	
one atom	MONATOMIC MOLECULE
—large	MACROMOLECULE
—with	
free valency	RADICAL
lone electrons that can	
combine with proton	BASE
movement	
—caused by random motion	
of particles	DIFFUSION
—of	
amino group between	
compounds	TRANSAMINATION
liquid through	
semipermeable membrane	OSMOSIS

name that	
—conveys details	
of atomic structure	SYSTEMATIC NAME
—gives no details	
of atomic structure	TRIVIAL NAME
Naples-yellow	LEAD ANTIMONIATE
natural or synthetic polymer	RESIN
naturally occurring	
—hydrocarbons	CRUDE OIL
—polymer of glucose	STARCH
negatively charged	
—ion	ANION
—particle	ELECTRON
neither acid nor alkaline	NEUTRAL
nitre	POTASSIUM NITRATE
	SALTPETRE
nitrogen	AZOTE
—trichloride	AGENE
nitrogenous substance	PROTEIN
noble gas	ARGON, HELIUM, KRYPTON
	NEON, RADON, XENON
non-carbon compounds	INORGANIC
number of	
—hydrogen atoms with	
which an atom will combine	VALENCY
—particles in one	
mole	AVOGADRO'S NUMBER
—protons in nucleus	ATOMIC NUMBER
olefin(e)	ALKENE
organic compound	
—aliphatic hydrocarbon	ALKENE
—aromatic hydrocarbon	ARYL
—based on	
ammonia	AMIDE, AMINE
	AMINO-ACID
benzene ring	AROMATIC
sterol	CHOLESTEROL
—containing	
alkyd group attached to	
carboxyl group	FATTY ACID
carbon atoms in chains	ALIPHATIC
carboxyl group	CARBOXYLIC ACID
—and alkyd radicals	KETONE
chains of amino-acids	PROTEIN
oxygen, hydrogen, carbon	OXIME
sulphur and oxygen	MERCAPTAN
	THIOL
two	
—double bonds	DIENE
—ketone groups	DIKETONE
—derived from silicon	SILICONE
—hydroxyl groups and carbon	ALCOHOL
—in	
petroleum	ALKYL, ALKANE
plants	CHLOROPHYLL
—related to indigo	INDOL(E)

—which reduces surface
  tension   SURFACE ACTIVE AGENT
                             SURFACTANT
        (*see also* hydrocarbon *above*)
organic cyanide   NITRILE
oscillation of electrons
  between atoms   RESONANCE
oxidation state   VALENCY
oxide of iron   RUST
oxygen with three atoms per molecule   OZONE
paraffin series   ALKANES
  —gases   BUTANE, ETHANE
              METHANE, PROPANE
  —liquids   DECANE, HEPTANE, HEXANE
        NONANE, OCTANE, PENTANE
partial sterilisation   PASTEURISATION
particles   (*see separate entry*)
passage of gas through
  small apertures   ·   EFFUSION
pentyl acetate   AMYL ACETATE
                  BANANA OIL
percentage of iso-octane OCTANE NUMBER
phenylethylene   STYRENE
phospholipids etc   COMPOUND LIPIDS
plastic
  —hardening with heat   THERMOSETTING
  —softening with heat   THERMOPLASTIC
poison   (*see separate entry*)
polar bond   ELECTROVALENT BOND
polymeric siloxane   SILICONE
polymerised glucose   CELLULOSE
porcelain filter CHAMBERLAND CANDLE
positively charged
  —ion   CATION
  —particle   PROTON
potassium
  —bicarbonate   POTASH
  —ferric ferrocyanide PRUSSIAN BLUE
  —nitrate   NITRE, SALTPETRE
  —sodium tartrate   ROCHELLE SALT
power of atom to
  attract electron ELECTRONEGATIVITY
preparation of nitrogenous
  fertiliser   HABER PROCESS
pressure needed to prevent
  osmotic flow   OSMOTIC PRESSURE
process
  —by which atoms become
    attached to surface   ADSORPTION
  —for making
    salt   LEBLANC PROCESS
    washing soda   SOLVAY PROCESS
  —in which
    crystals are produced from
    solution
      (FRACTIONAL) CRYSTALLISATION

product of one reaction
  takes part in another   CHAIN REACTION
two molecules react to
  form one plus
  water   CONDENSATION REACTION
—not involving heat
  transfer   ADIABATIC
product of combustion
  —complete   CARBON DIOXIDE
  —incomplete CARBON MONOXIDE
  —of wood   CHARCOAL
production of chemicals
  by organisms   BIOSYNTHESIS
Prussian
  blue
    POTASSIUM FERRIC FERROCYANIDE
purification by
  distillation   RECTIFICATION
pyrimidines   CYTOSINE, THYMINE
                          URACIL
pyrolysis   CRACKING
racemic acid   TARTARIC ACID
radioactive chemicals   ACTINIDES
rare-earth elements   LANTHANIDES
ratio of mass to mass
  of carbon   MOLECULAR WEIGHT
re-freezing of ice after
  melting under pressure   REGELATION
reaction
  —in which
    carbon bonds are
    saturated   ADDITION REACTION
    heat is
    —absorbed   ENDOTHERMIC
    —produced   EXOTHERMIC
  —influenced by
    light   PHOTOCHEMICAL REACTION
  —requiring energy   ENDERGONIC
  —where one reagent
    is reduced and
    another oxidised REDOX (REACTION)
  —yielding energy   EXERGONIC
realgar   ARSENIC DISULPHIDE
red lead   MINIUM
reduction of viscosity by
  physical disturbance   THIXOTROPY
regular structure of crystal   LATTICE
relating to crystallisation
  with axes at right angles   ISOMETRIC
removal of
  —amino group   DEAMINATION
  —oxygen   REDUCTION
  —water   DEHYDRATION
rock salt   SODIUM CHLORIDE
rotating polarised
  light to the left   LAEVOROTATORY

rules describing formation of valency bonds	RULES OF FAJANS
rust	OXIDE OF IRON
salt of	
—alginic acid	ALGINATE
—aluminium hydroxide	ALUMINATE
—boric acid	BORATE
—bromic acid	BROMATE
—carbonic acid	CARBONATE
—chloric acid	CHLORATE
—chromic acid	CHROMATE
—cyanic acid	CYANATE
—fatty acid	SOAP
—ferric acid	FERRATE
—isocyanic acid	ISOCYANATE
—manganic acid	MANGANATE
—mucic acid	MUCATE
—nitric acid	NITRATE
—nitrous acid	NITRITE
—oxalic acid	OXALATE
—palmitic acid	PALMITATE
—permanganic acid	PERMANGANATE
—phenol	PHENOLATE
—phosphoric acid	PHOSPHATE
—phthalic acid	PHTHALATE
—propionic acid	PROPIONATE
—silicic acid	SILICATE
—stearic acid	STEARATE
—sulphuric acid	SULPHATE
—sulphurous acid	SULPHITE
—telluric acid	TELLURATE
saltcake	GLAUBER'S SALTS
	SODIUM SULPHATE
saltpetre	NITRE
	POTASSIUM NITRATE
seeding with small crystal	IMPING
separate part	PHASE
separation	
—by	
evaporation and recondensation	DISTILLATION
	FRACTIONATION
fractional distillation	RECTIFICATION
melting	LIQUATION
washing	ELUTION
—into constituent elements	ANALYSIS
—of	
colloids	DIALYSIS
liquid from a gel	SYN(A)ERESIS
series of elements in order of potential for oxidation	ELECTROCHEMICAL SERIES
shape of molecule resulting from position	CONFORMATION
silver nitrate	LUNAR CAUSTIC
similar compound	METAMER

simultaneous oxidation and reduction	REDOX
small particles in solution which cannot pass through a membrane	COLLOID
smallest particle showing characteristics of a substance	MOLECULE
sodium	
—carbonate	WASHING SODA
—chloride	(COMMON) SALT, ROCK SALT
—hydroxide	CAUSTIC SODA
—silicate	WATER GLASS
—sulphate	GLAUBER'S SALT
	SALTCAKE
solid	
—carbon dioxide	DRY ICE
—condensed from vapour of solid without liquid phase	SUBLIMATE
—mixture of several substances	SOLID SOLUTION
—particles in liquid medium	SUSPENSION
—with regular structural shape	CRYSTAL
solution	
—acting as electrical conductor	ELECTROLYTE
—holding maximum amount of solute	SATURATED SOLUTION
—in alcohol	TINCTURE
—maintaining pH level	BUFFER
—of	
hydrochloric acid	SPIRITS OF SALT
salt	BRINE
—used to test for	
ammonia	NESSLER'S SOLUTION
sugars	FEHLING'S SOLUTION
—with potassium hypochlorite	EAU DE JAVELLE
	JAVELLE WATER
space of missing electron	HOLE
spirits of wine	ETHANOL
	ETHYL ALCOHOL
spontaneous breaking up of compound	DISSOLUTION
starch	AMYLUM
—component with glucose chains	AMYLOPECTIN
	AMYLOSE
steroids	DERIVED LIPIDS
styrene	PHENYLETHYLENE
substance	
—acting in conjunction with enzyme in catalysis	COENZYME
opposite ways (acid/base, positive/negative)	AMPHIPROTIC
	AMPHOTERIC

—adding hydrogen to
  another   REDUCING AGENT
—affecting rate of chemical
  reaction   CATALYST
—assisting fusion of others   FLUX
—causing oxidation   OXIDIZING AGENT
—combining with base to
  form a salt   ACID
—composed entirely of
  similar atoms   ELEMENT
—deposited from solution
  or suspension   PRECIPITATE
—dissolved in a solvent   SOLUTE
—dissolving another   SOLVENT
—donating electrons
  to another   REDUCING AGENT
—existing in
  only one form   MONOTROPISM
  several forms   POLYMORPHISM
—fluorescing green   FLUORESCEIN
—forming lather with water   SAPONIN
—interfering with
  chemical reactions   INHIBITOR
—liberating hydrogen ions   ACID
—marking end of reaction
  by colour change   INDICATOR
—more active in
  reactions than in
  normal state   NASCENT ELEMENT
—produced by the action
  of pepsin on proteins   PEPTONE
—producing chemical reaction   REAGENT
—reacting with acid
  to form salt   BASE
—reducing surface tension   WETTING AGENT
—removing oxygen from
  another   REDUCING AGENT
—speeding chemical
  reaction   CATALYST
—supplying oxygen
  to a reaction   OXIDANT, OXYDANT
—taking part in
  chemical reaction   REACTANT
—transferring a proton to another   ACID
—turning vegetable blues red   ACID
—used
  in
    —chemical tests   REAGENT
    —dying   ALUM, ANILINE
    —paints, etc   ALKYD
    —papermaking   ALUM
  to
    —adulterate another to
      change its properties   DOPANT
    —seed clouds to
      produce rain   SILVER IODIDE

—show condition by
  colour change   INDICATOR
—signal end of titration   INDICATOR
—with
  atoms all of the
    same atomic number   ELEMENT
  elastic properties   ELASTOMER
  pH value
    —greater than 7   ALKALI
    —less than 7   ACID
  same
    —arrangement of atoms but
      different molecular
      weight   POLYMER(IDE)
    —atomic number but
      different mass number   ISOTOPE
    —molecular weight but
      different arrangement of atoms   ISOMER
sulphides of metals   PYRITES
surface-active agent for cleaning   DETERGENT
synthetic resin   ALKYD
table of elements   PERIODIC TABLE
tartaric acid   RACEMIC ACID
temperature
—at which
  element changes
    state   TRANSITION POINT
       TRANSITION TEMPERATURE
  ignition occurs   FLASH POINT
  substance can exist in all
    three states   TRIPLE POINT
—on Kelvin
  scale   ABSOLUTE TEMPERATURE
temporary, reversible
  decomposition   DISSOCIATION
test for
—acidity   LITMUS (PAPER)
—arsenic   MARSH'S TEST
—phenols   MILLON'S TEST
—proteins in solution   BIURET REACTION
thiol   MERCAPTAN
three covalent bonds   TRIPLE BOND
titanic oxide   TITANIA
     TITANIUM OXIDE
titanium oxide   ANATASE
toluene   METHYL BENZENE
     TOLUOL
treatment
—of illness with
  chemicals   CHEMOTHERAPEUTICS
     CHEMOTHERAPY
—with nitric acid   NITRIFICATION
trihydric alcohol   GLYCERIN(E)
     GLYCEROL
two or more elements
  combined   COMPOUND

unavailable energy in system	ENTROPY
urea	CARBAMIDE
use of micro-organisms to break down substance	FERMENTATION
valency of one covalent and one electrovalent bond	SEMIPOLAR BOND
vapour existing in equilibrium with the liquid form	SATURATED VAPOUR
verdigris	COPPER CARBONATE
vermilion	MERCURIC SULPHIDE
vertical column in periodic table	GROUP
vessel used for	
—cultures	PETRI DISH
—incineration	CRUCIBLE
washing	
—soda	SODIUM CARBONATE
—to effect separation	ELUTION
	LIXIVIATION
water	AQ, OXYGEN HYDRIDE
—glass	SODIUM SILICATE
weight of unit mass compared with water	SPECIFIC GRAVITY
white	
—arsenic	ARSENIC TRIOXIDE
—lead	LEAD CARBONATE
wood naphtha	ETHANOL, METHANOL
wood spirit	METHANOL
	METHYL ALCOHOL
xylene	DIMETHYLBENZENE
	XYLOL
zinc	
—carbonate	CALAMINE
—zinc oxide	ZINCITE
zincite	ZINC OXIDE
zirconia	ZIRCONIUM DIOXIDE

chess

alternating checks	SEE-SAW
attack	GREB'S
	NIMZOWITSCH-LARSEN
	RICHTER, TORRE
	TROMPOWSKY
—on two pieces	FORK, SKEWER
bishop hemmed in	BAD BISHOP
bishops on adjoining diagonals	HARROWITZ BISHOPS
blockaded position	TREBUCHET
	ZUGZWANG
check	
—by two pieces	DOUBLE CHECK
—from stationary piece	DISCOVERED CHECK
—in reply to check	CROSS-CHECK
controlling body	FIDE

defence	ALAPIN'S, ALEKHINE'S
	AMBUSH, BENONI, BERLIN
	BIRD'S, BOGOLJUBOW, CARO-KAUN
	CENTRE, CHIGORIN'S, CLASSICAL
	COONTER, COZIO'S, DAMIANO'S
	DORY'S, DUTCH, FIANCHETTO
	FRANCO-INDIAN, FRENCH, GRUNFELD
	HUNGARIAN, KERES, KING'S INDIAN
	MARSHALL'S, NIMIZOWITSCH
	NIMZO-INDIAN, OLD INDIAN
	ORTHODOX, PETROFF'S, PHILIDOR'S
	PIRC, POLISH, QUEEN'S INDIAN
	ROBATSCH, RUSSIAN, (SEMI-)SLAV
	SCHLIEMAN, SICILIAN, SMYSLOV'S
	STEINITZ, SYMMETRICAL, TARRASCH
	TWO KNIGHTS GAME, WESTPHALIA
ending with king not in check	STALEMATE
famous games	EVERGREEN, IMMORTAL
	POLISH IMMORTAL
file with no pawn	OPEN FILE
gambit/opening	ANDERSSEN'S, BENKO
	BIRD'S, BISHOP'S, BLACKMAR
	CATALAN, COLLE SYSTEM, DANISH
	ENGLISH, EVANS, FOUR KNIGHTS GAME
	GIUCO PIANO, GREB'S, KING'S
	KING'S FIANCHETTO, LATVIAN
	PONZIANI'S, QUEEN'S, RETI
	RUY LOPEZ, SARAGOSSA
	SCOTCH GAME, STAUNTON
	STONEWALL SYSTEM
	VAN'T KRUYS, VIENNA GAME
	VOLGA
games	CIRCE, COURIER, DOUBLE-MOVE
	FOUR-HANDED, KAMIKAZE
	KRIEGSPIEL, LOSING GAME
	MARSEILLES, MUST-CAPTURE
	NO-CAPTURE, PROGRESSIVE
	RANDOMISED, REFUSAL, RIFLE
	SCOTCH, THREE-DIMENSIONAL
—high speed	LIGHTNING CHESS
—using people as pieces	LIVING CHESS
immobilisation of piece	PIN
in danger of capture	EN PRISE
intermediate move	ZWISCHENZUG
knight's pawn early move	FIANCHETTO
machines	
—electronic	CHAOS-MASTER
	DEEP THOUGHT, FREEDOM
	HITECH, KAISSA
	MEPHISTO(-PORTOROSE)
	OSTRICH, PAPA, RABBIT, TELL
—mechanical	AJEEB, KEMPELEN'S TURK
	WIENER-SCHACHZEITUNG
mate of king surrounded by his own pieces	SMOTHERED MATE

move taking pawn which has moved two squares	EN PASSANT
moves taking in every square of board	KNIGHT'S TOUR
muse of chess	CAISSA
notation	ALGEBRAIC, DESCRIPTIVE FORSYTH
offered sacrifice in opening	GAMBIT
old names	
—Arabian	SHATRANJ
—Greek	ZATRIKION
—Indian	CHATRANGA
—Persian	CHATANG
pawn	
—not opposed	PASSED PAWN
—placed diagonally	PAWN CHAIN
piece	MAN
—in opponent's half supported by pawn	OUTPOST
pieces	BISHOP, CASTLE, KING KNIGHT, PAWN, QUEEN, ROOK
players	
—American	BROWNE, BENJAMIN CHRISTIANSEN, DE FIRMIAN DENHER, FINE, FISCHER, GULKO IVANOV, MARSHALL, MORPHY PILLSBURY, PINHUS, RESHEVSKY SEIRAWAN
—ancients	ALADDIN, AL-ADLI, ALFONSO AS-SULI, DAMIANO, LEONARDO
—Argentinian	NAJDORF, PANNO SANGUINETI
—Australian	KOSHNITSKY, PURDY
—Austrian	ALIGAIER, GRUNFELD ROBATSCH, SCHLECHER SPIELMAN, STEINITZ
—Belgian	COLLE, KOLTANOWSKI
—Brazilian	GERMAN, MECKING
—British	ABRAHAMS, ADAMS ALEXANDER, ATKINS, CHANDLER GOLOMBEK, GUNSBERG, HODGSON KEENE, KING, KOSTEL, MESTEL NORWOOD, NUNN, PENROSE, SHORT SPEELMAN, STAUNTON, SUBA WINTER, ZUKERTORT
—Bulgarian	BOBOTSOV, PADEVSKY RADULOV, TRINGOV
—Canadian	MORRISON, SPRAGGETT SUTTLES, YANOFSKY
—Colombian	CASTRO, ROJAS
—Cuban	CAPABLANCA, GARCIA
—Czech	DURAS, FLOHR, JANSA PACHMAN, RETI, RICHTER SMEJKAL
—Danish	ANDERSEN, LARSEN MORTENSEN
—Dutch	DONNER, EUWE, TIMMAN
—Estonian	KERES, MIKENAS
—Finnish	BOOK, YRIOLA
—French	DESCHAPELLES, JANOWSKI LA BOURDONNAIS, LAUTIER PHILIDOR, SAIT-AMANT TARTAKOWER
—German	AHUES, ANDERSSEN BOGOLJUBOW, HUBNER LASKER, UHLMANN, UNZICKER
—Hungarian	ADORJAN, BARCZA(Y) BREYER, GUNSBERG, POLGAR PORTISCH, RETI, SAX SZABO, TARRASCH
—Icelandic	HJARTARSON, OLAFSSON PETRURSSON, THORSTEINS
—Indian	AARON, SULTAN KHAN
—Iranian	HRANDI, SHARIF
—Irish	MCDONNELL, O'HANLON REILLY
—Israeli	OZERNIAK, PORATH
—Italian	MARIOTTI
—Latvian	BEHTING, MATTISON NI(E)MZOWITSCH PETROV, TAL
—Mexican	ARAIZA, TORRES
—New Zealand	SRAPU, SUTTON
—Norwegian	ADGESTEIN, BARDA DE LANGE, HOEN JOHANNESSEN, WIBE
—Peruvian	CANAL, QUINONES RODRIGUEZ
—Philippine	BALINAS, TORRE
—Polish	JANOWSKI, PERLIS RUBINSTEIN, SLIWA TARTAKOWER, WINAWER
—Portuguese	DA SILVA, DURAO
—Puerto Rican	KAPLAN
—Romanian	ALBIN, CIOCALTEA GEORGHIU, MARCO TROIANESCU
—Russian	ALBURT, ALEKHINE BOGOLJUBOW, BOTVINNIK CHIGORIN, DOLMATOV, DREEV EINGORN, GUREVICH, HALPRIN IVANCHUK, KARPOV, KASPAROV KORCHNOI, PETROSIAN, SMYSLOV SOKOLOV, SPASSKY, YUSUPOV
(f)	ALEXANDRIA GAPRINDASHVILI, MENCHIK
—Singaporean	TAN
—South African	FRIEDGOOD, HEIDENFELD KIRBY
—Spanish	ILLESCAS, LOPEZ
—Swedish	ANDERSSEN, HELLERS LUNDIN, STAHLBERG, STOLZ

—Syrian	STAMMA
—Tunisian	BELKADI, BOUAZIZ
—Turkish	ONAT, SUER
—Welsh	EVANS, HUTCHINGS
	WILLIAMS
—Yugoslav	NIKOLIC, PIRC
	UDOVCIC, VIDMAR
playing-strength rating	BCF SYSTEM
	ELO SCALE
	INGO(-HARNESS) SYSTEM
row of squares	
—across board	RANK
—up and down board	FILE
sacrifice of bishop	GREEK GIFT
threat to king	CHECK
three pawns in one file	TRIPLED PAWNS
tie-break system	BUCHHOLTZ SYSTEM
	SONNEBORN-BERGER'S SYSTEM
	SWISS SYSTEM
titles	GRAND MASTER
	INTERNATIONAL MASTER
	MASTER
trophy	BRILLIANCY TROPHY
	PIATIGORSKY CUP
two pawns in one file	DOUBLED PAWNS
unsupported pawn	HANGING PAWN
voluntary surrender	
of piece	SACRIFICE
winning move	(CHECK)MATE
Chile	RCH
capital	SANTIAGO
coin	CENTAVO, CONDOR
	DOBLON, PESO
flower	SCHIZANTHUS
fruit	LUCAMA
palm	COQUITO
saltpetre	CALICHE
shrub	MAQUI
tree	ALERCE
china	CERAMIC, PORCELAIN
	POTTERY
American	REDWARE
Austrian	VIENNA
Belgian	TOURNAI
black	
—background	FAMILLE NOIR
—unglazed pottery	BASALT WARE
brown terra-cotta	RUSTIC-WARE
Chinese	BLANC-DE-CHINE, CANTON
	CELADON, CHUN, HAN, JU(AN)
	KO, MING, NANKEEN, QING
	SUNG, TING, YUAN
clay	ARGIL, CHOAM, KAOLIN(E)
—mixing	
machine	BLUNGER
tool	BALLET

vessel	BLUNGER
coarse ware	SAXON STONE
	SEMI-PORCELAIN
	STONE CHINA
coloured pottery	SGRAFFITO
colourful glazed pottery	FAIENCE
crazed glaze	CRACKLE (WARE)
cream Wedgwood	QUEEN'S WARE
Danish	COPENHAGEN
decoration applied	
before firing	UNDERGLAZE
Dutch	DELF(T)
earthenware	CHOAM, FIGULINE
English	AYNSLEY, BOW, BRISTOL
	CHELSEA, COALPORT, COPELAND
	CROUCHWARE, (CROWN) DERBY
	DAVENTRY, DOULTON, LIVERPOOL
	LOWESTOFT, MOORCROFT, MINTON
	ROCKINGHAM, SPODE
	STAFFORDSHIRE, SUNDERLAND
	SWANSEA, WEDGWOOD
	WORCESTER
enamelled earthenware	MAJOLICA
—terra-cotta	DELLA-ROBBIA
felspar porcelain	PARIAN
fine	
—glaze	SMEAR
—pottery	PEBBLEWARE
fireclay case for firing	SAGGAR
French	CHANTILLY, LIMOGES
	MARSEILLES, PARIS, SEVRES
German	ANSBACH, DRESDEN
	FRANKFURT, MEISSEN
green pattern	FAMILLE VERTE
grey	
—blue glazed pottery	CLAIR DE LUNE
—green glazed pottery	CELADON WARE
hard	
—porcelain	JASPERWARE
—white pottery	IRONSTONE
heavy pottery	STONEWARE
Italian	CAPODIMONTE, FAENZA
	FAIENCE, MAIOLICA
	NAPLES, PESARO
Japanese	ARITA, HAMADA, IMARI
	KAKIEMON, SATSUMA, SHOJI
lead glaze	GLOST
liquid clay	SLIP
made of	
—clay or earthenware	CLOAM
—different coloured clays	PEBBLEWARE
	SCRODDLED
matt-surfaced stoneware	JASPERWARE
pebbleware on gold or	
blue	LAPIS LAZULI WARE
pink pattern	FAMILLE ROSE

Polynesian pottery	LAPITA WARE
refined earthenware	CREAMWARE
salt-glazed stoneware	CROUCH-WARE
scalloped edging	LAMBREQUIN
semi-translucent	BONE CHINA
sold at fairs	FAIRINGS
Switzerland	ZURICH
translucent	EGGSHELL
transparent with pictures	
showing through	LITHOPHANE
unglazed pottery	BISCUIT, BISQUE
	TERRACOTTA
very thin	EGGSHELL
white	
—china trinkets	
sold as mementos	GOSS
sold or given as prizes	
at fairs etc	FAIRINGS
—earthenware	IRONSTONE CHINA
—porcelain	PARIAN (WARE)
raised pattern	CAMEO WARE
	JASPER WARE
	PORCELAIN
with calcium phosphate	BONE-CHINA
yellow background	FAMILLE JAUNE
China	CATHAY, CH, CHIN
	MIDDLE KINGDOM
abacus	S(H)WANPAN
aborigines	LOLOS, MAIOTSE, MANS
	MANZU, YAO(-MIN)
agricultural worker	
with medical training	BAREFOOT DOCTOR
alphabetical system for	
translation	PINYIN, ZIMU
arch	PAILOU
archipelago	QUNDAO
assembly	HUI
association	TONG
bamboo stick	WHANGEE
barge carrying sewage	FOO-FOO BARGE
basin	PENDI
bay	AO, WAN
bean	ADZUKI, MUNG
best quality	FIRST CHOP
bird	SILVER-PHEASANT
	SWAN-GOOSE
boat	JUNK, SAMPAN
	SANPAN, TONGKANG
boat population	TANK(I)A
brand	CHOP
bridge	QIAO
bronze bowl	GUI
Buddha	FO(H)
Buddhist	
—paradise	CHINGTU
—priest	BONZE

—sect	CHAN
business	PIDGIN
cabbage	BOKCHOY, PAKCHOI
canal	YUNHE
cane	WHANGEE
cape (headland)	JIAO, ZUI
capital	BEIJING, PEKING
carriage	(JIN)RICKSHA(W)
chestnut	LING
Chinaman	CATAIAN, CAT(H)AYAN
	CHINK, CHOW
Chinese	CHIN, SERIC, SINAEAN
	SINIC, SINO
club (group)	TONG
coat	MANDARIN
coins	
—small coin	CASH, CHIAO, FEN
—unit	CHIAO
—10 chiao	YUAN
—silver bar	LIANG, SYCEE, TAEL
condiment	NAPEE
cooking pan	WOK
commune	GONGSHE
county	XIAN
crab	HA, MITTEN-CRAB
criminal society	TRIAD
cyclone	TYPHOON
dark principle	YIN
date-plum	KAKI
deities	(*see* **gods, goddesses**)
department	FOO
desert	SHAMO
dialect	CANTONESE, HAKKA
	MANDARIN
	PEKIN(G)ESE, WU
dish	CHOP-SUEY, CHOW-MEIN
	DIM SUM, WO MEIN, WONTON
divination system	I CHING
dress	CHEONG-SAM, SAMFOO
	SAMFU
drink	KAOLIANG, MAO-TAI
drug	GINSENG
duck	AP, MANDARIN
—eggs in brine	PIDAN
dynasty	CH'IN(G), CHOU
	HAN, MING, QIN(G), SHANG
	SUI, SUNG, TANG, XIA
	YIN, YUA, ZHOU
eating utensils	CHOP-STICKS
egg noodles	WO MEIN
exercise and mental	
training	QIGONG, TAI CHI(CHUAN)
fabulous	
—animal	KYLIN
—bird	FUM, FUNG
factory	HONG

feminine principle	YIN
fibre	CHINA-JUTE
fish	CARP, GOLDFISH
	PARADISE-FISH, TREPANG
foreign mercantile house	HONG
fried	
—noodles	CHOW MEIN
—rice	CHOW FAAHN
frying pan	WO(C)K
fruit	CUMQUAT, KUMQUAT
	LEECHEE, LITCHI, LYCHEE
	LONGAN, LOQUAT, WAMPEE
game	FAN-TAN, MAH-JONG(G), PUTZI
ginger	CURCCUMA, ZEDOARY
gorge	XIA
grass	RAMEE, RAMI(E), WHANGEE
grotesque figure	MAGOT
guild	HUI, TONG
harbour	GANG
hen	BRAHMA, LANGSHAN
herb	GINSENG
house-boat	TANKA-BOAT
idol	JOSS
incense	JOSS-STICK
instrument	KIN
island	DAO, HSU, TAO
jacket	MAKWA
jade	YU(-STONE)
jargon	PIDGIN ENGLISH
jigsaw	TANGRAM
jute	ABUTILON
labourer	COOLIE, COOLY
lacquered screen	COROMANDEL SCREEN
lake	HU
language	CANTONESE, KUO-YO
	MANCHOO, MANCHU
	MANDARIN
life-energy	QI
light principle	YANG
liquor	KAOLIANG
lobster	LUNG HA
magnolia	YULAN
mandarin's house	YAMEN, YAMUN
martial art	KUNG-FU
masculine principle	YANG
measures	
—1 inch	TSUN
—1 foot	CHIH
—12 feet	CHANG
—1/3 mile	LI
—15 galls	PARAH
military	
—district	COMMANDERY
—governor	TUCHUN
minister	AMBAN
mixed condiment	CHOW-CHOW
mountain	SHAN
—range	LING, SHANMAI
mouth organ	SANG
mustard relish	CHOW-CHOW
National People's Party	KUOMINTANG
negative principle	YIN
news agency	XINHUA
no good	NO CHOP
obeisance	COTTOW, KOWTOW
office	YAMEN, YAMUN
official	MANDARIN, TAO-TAI
	TAOYAN
oil	TUNG
old military race	MANCHOO, MANCHU
orange	TAEL
overseer	HOPPO
pagoda	TAA
pass	GUAN, SHANKOU
peak	FENG
Peking duck	KAO YA
peninsula	BANDAO
pheasant	TRAGOPAN
philosophy	CONFUCIANISM
pickled eggs	PIDAN
pillory	CANG(UE)
plain	PINGYUAN
poor quality	NO CHOP
porcelain	MING
pork	JU
positive principle	YANG
prefecture	FU
preserved fruits	CHOW-CHOW
promptly	CHOP-CHOP
prostration	KO(W)TOW
province	SHENG
provinces	ANHUI, FUJIAN, GANSU
	GUANGDON, GUANGXI, GUIZHOU
	HEBEI, HEILONGJIANG, HENAN
	HUNAN, JIANGSU, JIANGXI
	JILIN, LIAONING, NINGXIA
	QINGHAI, SHANDONG, SHA(A)NXI
	SICHUAN, XINJIAN
	YUNNAN, ZHEJIANG
puzzle	TANGRAM
quickly	CHOP-CHOP
raspberry	WINE-BERRY
rebel	TAIPING
reed instrument	CHENG
region	DIQU
religion	BUDDHISM, CONFUCIANISM
	TAOISM
resident official	AMBAN
rice spirit	SAMSHOO, SAMSHU
river	HE, JIANG
rodent	JUMPING-MOUSE

ruler MANCHOO, MANCHU
YAO(U), YAU
sauce SOY
sea HAI
seal (impression) CHOP
secret society BOXER, HOEY
TONG, TRIAD
self-defence system KUNG-FU
shark's fin soup YU TSI TANG
ship JUNK, SAMPAN, SANPAN
shop TOKO
silkworm AILANTHUS, SINA
TASAR, TUSSAH
silver PAKFONG, PAKTONG
sleeping platform KANG
snack DIM SUM
sorghum KAOLIANG
spring QUAN, YUAN
squid YO YI
statuette of seated figure MANDARIN
steamed dumplings DIM SUM
stir-fried vegetables CHOW CHOI
sugar cane SWEET SORGHUM
swivel-musket GINGAL(L), JINGAL
tax LIKIN
temple PAGOD(A), TAA
tip CUMSHAW
toy TANGRAM
trade intermediary COMPRADOR(E)
transit duty LIKIN
tree GINGKO, GINKGO, LITCHEE
LITCHI, LONGAN, LOQUAT
MAIDENHAIR-TREE, PAULOWNIA
TUNG-TREE, VARNISH-TREE
tuber KUDZOO, KUDZU
umbrella TEE
unarmed combat system KUNG-FU
vegetable dishes BAMBOO SHOOTS
BEAN SPROUTS
vehicle JINRICKISHA
(JIN)RICKSHA(W)
TRISHAW
village CUN
warehouse HONG
warlord TUCHUN
water
—chestnut MAH TAI
—jar KANG
wax insect TELA
weights
—1oz LIANG, TAEL
—1lb CATTY, CHIEN, KIN
—133lb PECUL, PICUL, PIKUL, TAN
well JING
wormwood MOXA
yellow dye WONGSHY
years (12-year cycle) BAT, OX, TIGER
HARE or RABBIT, DRAGON
SNAKE, HORSE, SHEEP or GOAT
MONKEY, ROOSTER, DOG, PIG
yoke CANG(UE)

church — building

abbey church MINSTER
aisle at east end AMBULATORY
apse in basilica BEMA
arcade in monastery CLOISTER
beam supporting cross ROOD BEAM
bell
—screen LOUVRE
—tower BELFRY, CAMPANILE
bishop's seat FALDISTORY, FALDSTOOL
—behind altar SYNTHRONUS
body of church NAVE
burial chamber TOMB, VAULT
canopy over throne, etc BALDACHIN
BALDACCHINO
BALDAQUIN
cathedral MINSTER
cells in hermitage LAURA
central part NAVE
chancel
—of church ADYTUM
—in basilica BEMA
chapel BETHEL, BETHESDA
EBENEZER
—at west end of church GALILEE
—Byzantine PARABEMA
—dedicated to Virgin LADY CHAPEL
—for eucharist table PROTHESIS
—in church LADY CHAPEL, SACELLUM
—of prothesis PARABEMA
choir SCHOLA CANTORUM
—screen REREDOS(E), REREDORSE
church
—attached to house CHAPEL
—with font DELUBRUM
clergyman's house MANSE, PARSONAGE
RECTORY, VICARAGE
colonnade ATRIUM
courtyard ATRIUM, PARVIS(E)
cross ROOD
(see also separate entry)
desk FALDSTOOL
detached from main church CHAPEL OF EASE
dissenters' church CHAPEL
division of nave AISLE
east end CHANCEL, CHEVET
CHOIR, PRESBYTERY
SACRARIUM, SANCTUARY
end space PARVIS(E)
extension beyond altar RETROCHOIR
finial FLECHE

gallery	TRIBUNE	—Greek	DIACONICON
—above rood-screen	ROOD-LOFT	sacred	
—over aisle	TRIFORIUM	—enclosure	SEKOS
gates of temple (Indian)	GOPURA(M)	—part of temple	ADYTUM
grotto-temple	SPEOS	sanctuary	DELUBRUM
inner chamber of temple	CELLA, NAOS	Scottish church	KIRK
intersection of nave		screen	ROOD SCREEN
and transept	CROSSING	—or panelling	
large church	BASILICA, CATHEDRAL	behind altar	REREDOS(E), REREDORSE
	MINSTER	seat	PEW
lavatory in monastery	LAVABO	seminary (RC)	THEOLOGATE
ledge on seat	MISERERE	shrine	DELUBRUM
	MISERICORD	south side	DECANAL, EPISTLE
little chapel	SACELLUM	steeple over rood-	
magnificent church	BASILICA	crossing	ROOD-STEEPLE
monastery	CLOISTER	storey over aisle	TRIFORIUM
	CONVENT, MINSTER	support for standing	MISERERE
—Tibetan	LAMASERY		MISERICORD(E)
narrow spire	FLECHE	surroundings	PRECINCT
nave	NEF	table	ALTAR
Nonconformist chapel	BETHEL, BETHESDA	—of eucharist	PROTHESIS
north side	CANTORIAL, GOSPEL	temple	DELUBRUM
northern apse	PROTHESIS	—Arabian	MASJED, MASJID, MESJID
nuncio's office	NUNCIATURE	—Babylonian	ZIGGURAT, ZIKKURAT
nunnery	CLOISTER, CONVENT	—Buddhist	CHAITYA, SANGHA
oratory	PROSEUCHE		TERA, VIHARA
part at right angles to nave	TRANSEPT	—Chinese	PAGOD(A), TAA
partition between nave		—dedicated to hero	HEROON
and choir	ROOD-SCREEN	—Eastern	PAGOD(A)
place of		—Greek	NAOS, NYMPHAEUM
—baptism	BAPTIST(E)RY	—Hindu	MANDIR(A)
—prayer	CHAPEL, ORATORY	—Indian	VIMANA
—worship	TABERNACLE	—Jain	MANDIR(A)
platform	TRIBUNE	—Jewish	SYNAGOGUE
pointed tower	SPIRE, STEEPLE	tent	TABERNACLE
porch	GALILEE, NARTHEX	—Mexican	TEOCALLI
portico	PARVIS(E)	—Moslem	KAABA, MOSQUE
prayer-stool	PRIE-DIEU	—Sikh	GURDWARA
preacher's gallery	PULPIT	temple-shaped tomb	HEROON
presbytery	CLASSIS	tower	SPIRE, STEEPLE
principal church of diocese	CATHEDRAL	—over church crossing	ROOD-TOWER
priory church	MINSTER	underground chamber	CRYPT
pulpit in mosque	MIMBAR		UNDERCROFT, VAULT
rail or screen	PARCLOSE	unroofed sanctuary	SACELLUM
reading desk	LECTERN, LECTURN	vestibule at front of	
	LETTERN	—church	NARTHEX
recess	APSE, APSIS, CHEVET	—temple	PRONAOS
—for vessels	ALMERY, A(U)MBRY	wall hanging	DOSSAL, DOSSEL, DOSSOL
robing room	VEST(IA)RY	washbasin	CANTHARUS
Roman Catholic church		water container	FONT, STOUP
with special privileges	BASILICA	waterspout	GARGOYLE
rood loft	JUBE	western portico	NARTHEX
room for sacred objects,		**church — personnel**	
vestments etc	SACRARIUM, SACRISTY	abbot (Greek)	ARCHIMANDRITE
	VEST(IA)RY		HEGUMEN
—Byzantine	PARABEMA	Abyssinian patriarch	ABUNA

arch-deacon (R.C.)	VICAR-GENERAL
archbishop	METROPOLITAN, PRIMATE
—Canterbury	CANTUAR
—German	ELECTOR
—York	EBOR
Armenian priest	VARTABAD
assistant	CURATE
—bishop	SUFFRAGAN
attached to military	CHAPLAIN, PADRE
attendant on cardinal	CONCLAVIST
bellringer	SEXTON
between bishop and deacon	PRESBYTER
	PRIOR
bishop	DIOCESAN
—Abyssinian	ABUNA
—Coptic	ABBA
—Eastern	ABBA
—of	
Portsmouth	CRISPIAN
Rome	POPE
—or cardinal	PRELATE
—over several dioceses	METROPOLITAN
—ranking above	
exarch	METROPOLITAN
metropolitan	PATRIARCH
—Scottish	PRIMUS
	TULCHAN-BISHOP
—Syriac	ABBA
bishop's deputy (R. C)	VICAR
bishops	EPISCOPACY, PRELACY
—itinerant	EPISCOPI VAGRANTES
Buddhist priest	BONZE
candidate for ordination	ORDINAND
canon	PREBENDARY
—other than canon regular	CANON SECULAR
—resident at cathedral	RESIDENTIARY
—who is not a member	
of cathedral chapter	MINOR CANON
—with no	
responsibilities	HONORARY CANON
caretaker	BEADLE, SEXTON
cathedral	
—administrator	DEAN
—church	MINSTER
chancellor of a diocese	VICAR-GENERAL
chief priest	PRELATE
—Roman (Syria)	SYRIARCH
clergy	CLOTH
clergyman	CAMISTER, MINISTER
	PARSON, PASTOR
	PRIEST, VICAR
—Australian	JESSER
—below priest (Episcopal)	DEACON
—in diocese	DIOCESAN
—of parish responsible	
for tithes	RECTOR

—over several parishes	RURAL DEAN
—receiving smaller tithes	
or salary	VICAR
—resident at	
cathedral	CANON RESIDENTIARY
—slang name	HOLY JOE, SKY PILOT
—who enjoys share	
of revenues	PREBENDARY
cleric who sings in	
cathedral choir	VICAR-CHORAL
Coptic bishop	ABBA
deputy	
—abbess	VICARESS
—bishop (France)	VIDAME
—church-warden	SIDESMAN
—head of abbey	PRIOR
diocesan administrator	ARCHDEACON
director of choral services	PRECENTOR
disciple	CHELA
Eastern monks	ACOEMETI
ecclesiastical	
successor (Irish)	CO(M)ARB
elder	PRESBYTER
elected representative of clergy	PROCTOR
Episcopal clergyman in	
USA or Scotland	RECTOR
exarch	METROPOLITAN
female in early Christian	
society	DEACONESS
French	
—Dominican monk	JACOBIN
—priest	ABBE, CURE
German prince-bishop	ELECTOR
gravedigger	SEXTON
head of	
—abbey	
female	ABBESS
male	ABBOT
—Abyssinian church	ABUNA
—Eastern church	PATRIARCH
—house of	
canons	PRIOR
friars	PRIOR
—priory of monks	PRIOR
—religious order	MINISTER
—Scottish church	MODERATOR
Hebrew religious teacher	RABBI
high	
—priest	PONTIFF
Roman	PONTIFEX
—ranking priest	PRELATE
itinerant	
—bishops	EPISCOPI VAGRANTES
—priest	BUCKLEBEGGAR
	HEDGE PARSON
	HEDGE PRIEST

layman who visits the sick	PARABOLANUS
leader of singers	
—female	PRECENTRESS
	PRECENTRIX
—male	PRECENTOR
legal officer	CHANCELLOR
member of an order between monks and secular clergy	CANON REGULAR
member of cathedral chapter	CANON
mendicant monk	FRIAR
metropolitan	EXARCH
minor orders	ABBE, ACOLYTE
	DOORKEEPER
	EXORCIST, LECTOR
	OSTIARY, PORTER
monk in a community	C(O)ENOBITE
next below arch-deacon	ACOLYTE, ACOLYTH
officer	
—advising pastor (Congregational)	DEACON
—dealing with secular matters (Presbyterian)	DEACON
—in charge of	
altar in convent	DEACONESS
lamps (Gr.)	LAMPADARY
robes, vessels, etc	SACRISTAN
	SEXTON
—inferior	ACOLYTE, ACOLYTH
—of	
church	BEADLE, VERGER
—Scottish	BEADLE, BED(E)RAL
ecclesiastical court	APPARITOR
—representing laity or church	CHURCH-WARDEN
—with pastoral duties (Protestant)	DEACONESS
officials of papal court	CURIA
one	
—just ordained	DEACON
—licensed to preach	PARSON
—living as	
monk without vows	BEGHARD
nun without vows	BEGUINE
—serving individual or institution	CHAPLAIN
—to whom the pope delegated a remote part of his jurisdiction	VICAR-APOSTOLIC
—using leavened bread in Holy Communion	ZYMITE
—who accepts the decrees of the Council of Trent	TRIDENTINE
—who prays for others	BEAD(S)MAN
	BEDE(S)MAN
order of bishops	EPISCOPATE

papal	
—ambassador	NUNCIO
—dignitary	MONSIGNOR
—officer	DATARY
pope	BISHOP OF ROME
	HOLY FATHER
	VICAR OF CHRIST
preacher in highly emotional sect	HOLY ROLLER
Presbyterian	ELDER, PRESBYTER
priest, religious teacher	HIEROPHANT
—Armenian	VARTABAD
—Buddhist	BONZE, LAMA
—Catholic Apostolic	PASTOR
—doing politically-committed work	LIBERATION-PRIEST
—Etruscan	HARUSPEX, LUCUMO
—French	ABBE, CURE
—Greek	PAPA
—gypsy term	PATERCOVE, PATRICO
—Hebrew	RABBI(N)
—Hindu	PUJARIA
—Italian	PRETE, SACERDOTE
—itinerant	BUCKLEBEGGAR
	HEDGE-PARSON
	HEDGE-PRIEST
—longwinded	SPINTEXT
—Moslem	AYATOLLAH, IMA(U)M
	MUEDDIN, MUEZZIN
—of Cybele	CORYBANT
—parish	PARSON, RECTOR, VICAR
—Roman	FLAMEN, PONTIFEX
Catholic	FATHER
—Scottish	MAS(S)JOHN, MES(S)JOHN
	MINISTER
with no parish	STICKIT MINISTER
—Spanish	CURA, PARROCO
	PRESTE, SACERDOTE
—Syrian (Roman)	SYRIARCH
—Tibetan	LAMA
prince of RC church	CARDINAL
priory church	MINSTER
rural dean	VICAR-FORANE
sacristan (Greek)	SCEUOPHYLAX
Scottish	
—bishop	PRIMUS, TULCHAN BISHOP
—priest	MAS(S)JOHN, MES(S)JOHN
	MINISTER
self-seeking cleric	ROME RUNNER
senior official of cathedral	PROVOST
Syriac bishop	ABBA
theologian	THEOLOGER, THEOLOGUE
—Alexandrian	ORIGEN
—American	MACKINTOSH, MATTHEWS
	RAUSCHENBURG, TILLICH
	WEIZMAN

—Austrian	BOLZANO, BUBER
—British	BEDE, CAMPBELL, INGE
	MAJOR, ROBINSON, SMITH
—Dutch	SPINOZA
—French	MALEBRANCHE
	TEILHARD DE CHARDIN
—German	BAVER, BULTMANNN
	BONHOFFER, OTTO
	SCHLEIERMACHER, SCHWEITZER
	TILLICH, TROELTSCH
—Irish	TYRELL, USSHER
—Italian	ANSELM, AQUINAS
—Swedish	SWEDENBORG
—Swiss	BARTH
title	
—given to	
certain prelates	MONSIGNOR
one in process	
of canonisation	VENERABLE
—of courtesy	ABBE
titular bishop	VICAR-APOSTOLIC
usher	BEADLE, VERGER
vicar of Chist	POPE
vicar's wife	VICARESS
Waldensian teacher	BARBE
would-be theologian	THEOLOGASTER
young deacon	ORDINEE

church — terms

administer last sacrament	ANELE
administrative	
—board	COLLEGIUM
—or legal department	CHANCERY
admission to the	
ministry by the	
laying on of hands	ORDINATION
altar-cloth	ANTEPENDIUM, FRONTAL
anointing	UNCTION
anthem	INTROIT
assembly	CONVENTICLE
	CONVOCATION, SYNOD
association of lay	
members	SODALITY
authorised doctrines	ORTHODOXY
bar sounded instead of bell	SEMANTRON
bell rung thrice daily	ANGELUS
Benedictine title	DOM
bishop's medallion of	
the Virgin	PAN(H)AGIA
bishopric	EPISCOPATE
blessing	BENEDICITE
body of cardinals	
to elect Pope	CONCLAVE
book of	
—Apocrypha	TOBIT
—hymns, prayers etc	BREVIARY
—lessons	LECTIONARY

—rules	PIE, PYE
books of the Bible	
—accepted by the Christian	
faith	CANON
—not accepted	APOCRYPHA
borderland of Hell	LIMBO, LIMBUS
calendar giving details	
of services for each	
day of the year	ORDO
canonical hours	
—dawn	MATINS
—after matins	LAUDS
—6 am	PRIME
—9 am	TIERCE
—noon	SEXT
—3 pm	NONES
—early evening	VESPERS
—late evening	COMPLINE
canopy carried	
over priest	BALDACHIN, BALDACCHINO
	BALDAQUIN
canticle of Zacharias	BENEDICTUS
Catholic title	DOM
ceremonial garments	VESTMENTS
Christ	CHR, X, XT
—appearance	CHRISTOPHANY
Christian	
—gospel	KERYGMA
—symbol	CHI RHO, FISH, ICHTHYS
code of law	CANON
	CODEX JURIS CANONICI
collection of bulls	BULLARY
college of cardinals	COLLEGIUM
confirmation	CHRIS(O)M
congregation charged	
with spreading	
the faith	PROPAGANDA (FIDE)
consecrated wafer	(EUCHARISTIC) HOST
container for	
—holy oil	CHRISMATORY
—host	MONSTRANCE, PYX
—incense	CENSER
—pyx	TABERNACLE
control by state	ERASTIANISM
court	CONSISTORY
—of papal see	CURIA
creed	APOSTLE'S, ATHANASIAN
	NICAEAN, NICENE
cross	(see separate entry)
—bearer	CRUCIFER
declaration by Pope	
—of sainthood	CANONISATION
—that a person is blessed	BEATIFICATION
degrees or grades	ORDERS
deification	APOTHEOSIS
deified ruler	THEOCRAT

deviation from authorised belief	HERESY
	HETERODOXY
devotions lasting nine days	NOVENA
digest of decrees etc	CANON LAW
discussion of the Eucharist	EUCHARISTIC THEOLOGY
divine	
—influence	GRACE
—intervention	THEURGY
doctrine	
—in which belief is obligatory	DE FIDE DOCTRINE
—of	
choice between right and wrong	TUTIORISM
infallibility	ULTRAMONTISM
last things	ESCHATOLOGY
the Holy Spirit	PNEUMATOLOGY
—that the bread and wine actually change into the body and blood of Christ	TRANSUBSTANTIATION
ecclesiastical	
—council	SYNOD
—court	CONSISTORY
—levy	ANNAT(ES)
edict of Pope under seal	BULL
endowment	BENEFICE
	PATRIMONY
eternal life	GRACE
Eucharist	HOLY COMMUNION, MASS
evening service	EVENSONG, VESPERS
exemption from ecclesiastical law	INDULGENCE
existence of Trinity each within the other	CIRCUMINCESSION
	CIRCUMINSESSION
feast of	
—Annunciation of the Virgin	LADY DAY
—birth of Christ	CHRISTMAS
—Exaltation of Cross	HOLYROOD DAY
	ROOD(MAS) DAY
—Invention of Cross	HOLYROOD DAY
	ROOD(MAS) DAY
—Resurrection	EASTER
—St Martin	MARTINMAS
—St Michael	MICHAELMAS
	(*see also* **holidays**)
feet-washing ceremony	MAUNDY, NIPTER
first	
—five books of Bible	PENTATEUCH
—seven books of Bible	HEPTATEUCH
give absolution	SHRIVE
gospel-preaching	EVANGELICALISM
governing body	CLASSIS

government by bishops	EPISCOPACY
	EPISCOPAL(IAN)ISM
grace	BENEDICITE
hand-washing ritual	LAVABO
holy	
—oil	CHRIS(O)M
—wine or vessel	AMA
home of souls of	
—those who died before the birth of Christ	LIMBUS PATRUM
—unbaptised babies	LIMBUS INFANTUM
hours set for prayers	CANONICAL HOURS
hymn	CANTICLE, CHORALE
—Holy, holy, holy	(TER)SANCTUS
—to the glory of God	DOXOLOGY
illustrated gospels	BOOK OF KELLS
	LINDISFARNE
income from benefice passed to Pope or Crown	ANNAT
indulgence given	
—for	
a	
—particular person	PERSONAL
—period	TEMPORAL
all sins	PLENARY
some sins	PARTIAL
—in a particular place	LOCAL
—until revoked	INDEFINITE
	PERPETUAL
inquisition	HOLY OFFICE
interpretation of Bible truths	HERMENEUTICS
introductory hymn etc	INTROIT
invocation of the Holy Spirit at mass	EPICLESIS
land	GLEBE
last book of the New Testament	APOCALYPSE
	REVELATIONS
Latin translation of the Bible	VULGATE
lesson	LECTION
—based on life of saint	SYNAXARION
—book	LECTIONARY
letter from	
—apostle	EPISTLE
—Pope to all bishops	ENCYCLICAL
list of	
—books banned by Church	INDEX (EXPURGATORIUS)
	INDEX LIBRORUM PROHIBITORUM
—saints	CANON
living	BENEFICE
manifestation	EPIPHANY
Mass	EUCHARIST
	HOLY COMMUNION
—for the dead	REQUIEM
--Latin	TRIDENTINE

—used from 16th c	TRIDENTINE MASS
—with music and incense	HIGH MASS
meeting	
—for worship	SYNAXIS
—of	
cardinals to elect Pope	CONCLAVE
Pope and cardinals	CONSISTORY
mercy of God	GRACE
miracle-making	THEURGY
modernisation	AGGIORNAMENTO
modernised	
Christianity	PROCESS THEOLOGY
	SECULAR CHRISTIANITY
	SOUTH BANK RELIGION
morning service	MATINS
movement involving the	
laity in worship	LITURGICAL MOVEMENT
narrative of Christ's life	GOSPEL
New Testament books	
—originally not accepted	ANTILOGOMENA
—taken as authentic	HOMOLOG(O)UMENA
non-metrical hymn	CANTICLE
office of	
—bishop	PRELACY
—deacon	DIACONATE
official	
—dress	CANONICALS
—statement by Pope	ENCYCLICAL
old hymn	(TER)SANCTUS
	TRISAGION
Old Testament (Greek)	SEPTUAGINT
origin and development of gods	THEOGONY
orthodox Roman Catholic	TRIDENTINE
papal	
—court	CURIA
—decree	BULL
settling point of	
canon law	DECRETAL
—seal	BULLA
pardonable sin	VENIAL SIN
part of	
—the Mass	CANON OF THE MASS
	DONA NOBIS
—service spoken	
in audible tones	ECPHONESIS
passage for reading	PERICOPE
place in which souls of	
the dead are purified	PURGATORY
portable shrine for relics	FERETORY
prayer	OR(A)ISON
—after a meal	GRACE
—before a meal	GRACE
--devotional	ANGELUS
—in	
ancient Greek	
church	KYRIE ELEISON

Latin church	CONFITEOR
ancient Greek in	
Latin mass	KYRIE ELEISON
—of	
belief	CREDO
confession	CONFITEOR
entreaty	LITANY
—short	COLLECT
—with responses	LITANY
prayer-book	EUCHOLOGY
	EUCHOLOGION
preliminary offering	PROTHESIS
Presbyterian church court	SYNOD
presbytery	CLASSIS
priest's handwarmer	POME
provincial synod	CONVOCATION
Psalm	CHORALE
—66	JUBILATE
—95	VENITE
—98	CANTATE
—100	JUBILATE
reading in Church	EPISTLE, GOSPEL
	LESSON
recognition as a saint	CANONISATION
release from vows	DISPENSATION
religion in relation	
to ethics	MORAL THEOLOGY
religious	
—festival	HOLY DAY
	SAINT'S DAY
—hypocrite	HOLY WILLIE
reliquary worn by Orthodox	
prelate	ENCOLPION
remission of temporal	
punishment	INDULGENCE
response	KYRIE ELEISON
revelation	EPIPHANY
rite	SACRAMENT
ritual	
—hand-washing	LAVABO
—service	LITURGY
Roman Catholic tribunal	DICASTERY
rule or custom	RUBRIC
—or law	CANON
ruling body	(GENERAL) SYNOD
—houses	BISHOPS, CLERGY, LAITY
sacrament	BAPTISM, CONFESSION
	CONFIRMATION, EXTREME UNCTION
	HOLY COMMUNION, LAST RITES
	MATRIMONY, ORDINATION
	RECONCILIATION
—at point of death	EXTREME UNCTION
	SACRAMENT OF THE SICK
	LAST RITES
—of the Lord's supper	EUCHARIST
	HOLY COMMUNION

salary	LIVING, PREBEND
	STIPEND
salvation	GRACE
saying(s) of Chist	AGRAPHON(AGRAPHA)
scriptures	HOLY WRIT
second	
—coming of Christ	PAROUSIA
—part of canon law	DECRETAL
serious sin	MORTAL SIN
service	LITURGY
short prayer	COLLECT
shrine carried in	
procession	FERETORY
song	ANTHEM, CANTICLE
	HYMN, PSALM
splitting of church	SCHISM
statement of	
—beliefs	CREED
—body of doctrines	DOGMATICS
	SYSTEMATIC THEOLOGY
study of	
—church forms	ECCLESIOLOGY
—religion	THEOLOGY
sudden insight	EPIPHANY
supreme ecclesiastical	
court	ROTA
take confessions	SHRIVE
teaching of Christ	GOSPEL
ten commandments	DECALOGUE
tenth share	TITHE
Trinity	FATHER, HOLY GHOST
	SON
tube for imbibing	
sacramental wine	FISTULA
Vatican department in	
charge of missionaries	PROPAGANDA (FIDE)
verse said by	
—congregation	RESPONSE
—leader	VERSICLE
vindication of God's	
justice	THEODICY
Virgin Mary's song	MAGNIFICAT
war against heresy or	
other religion	CRUSADE
	HOLY WAR, JIHAD
week before Easter	HOLY WEEK
church — vestments	
abbot's vestment	RO(T)CHET
alb (Greek)	STICHARION
archbishop's vestment	PALLIUM
bishop's	
—close-fitting surplice	RO(T)CHET
—cross	CROSIER, CROZIER
—hat	MITRE
—stockings	CALIGAE
—upper robe	CHIMER(E)

—vestment	CHIMER(E), DALMATIC
	RATIONAL(E), ROCHET
	TUNICLE
Eastern	OMOPHORION, SAKKOS
cape with hood	DOMINO
cassock	SLOP
—French	SOUTANE
—old	SUBUCULA
chorister's robe	CASSOCK
cloth covering bishop's lap	GREMIAL
deacon's robe	DALMATIC
Eastern	
—bishop's vestment	OMOPHORION
	SAKKOS
—vestment	PH(A)ELONION
ecclesiastical	
—cape	MOZETTA
—scarf	TIPPET
—skullcap	ZUCHETTO
French cassock	SOUTANE
friar's dress	HABIT
Greek alb	STICHARION
Jewish priest's surplice	EPHOD
long robe	CASSOCK
—Scottish	GENEVA GOWN
monk's	
—dress	HABIT
—hood	CAPUCHE, COWL
—sleeveless cloak	SCAPULAR
narrow shoulder vestment	STOLE
nun's	
—dress	HABIT
—kerchief	BARBE
—veil	W(H)IMPLE
official dress	CANONICALS
Pope's	
—headdress	TIARA
—short cape	FANON
—vestment	PALLIUM
preacher's gown	GENEVA GOWN
scarf	TIPPET
shawl worn on shoulders	HUMERAL VEIL
short silk	
vestment (Scot.)	CASSOCK
sleeveless	
—hooded vestment	COPE
—vestment	CHASUBLE
square cap	BIRETTA
—colour for	
bishop	PURPLE
cardinal	RED
priest	BLACK
stole	TIPPET
strip(s)	
—hanging from	
neck	GENEVA BANDS

shoulders	SCAPULAR, STOLE
—worn on	
left arm	FAN(I)ON
	FANNEL(L), MANIPLE
shoulder	AMICE, HUMERAL VEIL
sub-deacon's vestment	TUNICLE
surplice	EPHOD, COTTA
	STOLA, STOLE
—Scottish	SARK
tight-sleeved vestment	ALB
white linen vestment worn	
over cassock	SURPLICE

(see also **belief, garments***)*

cinema

actors

—American	ALLEN, ASTAIRE
	BARRYMORE, BEATTY, BOGART
	BRANDO, BRONSON, BRYNNER
	CAGNEY, CHANEY, CLIFT, COBB
	COBURN, COOPER, CROSBY, CURTIS
	DEAN, DOUGLAS, DREYFUSS
	EASTWOOD, FIELDS, FITZGERALD
	FONDA, GABLE, GOULD
	HACKMAN, HARDY, HESTON
	HOFFMAN, HOLDEN, JOLSON
	KEATON, LADD, LANCASTER
	LEMMON, LLOYD, MARCH, MARVIN
	MARX BROTHERS, MCCREA, MCQUEEN
	MITCHUM, MIX, MUNI, NEWMAN
	NICHOLSON, POWELL, POWER, QUINN
	REAGAN, REDFORD, REYNOLDS
	ROBINSON, SCOTT, SINATRA
	STALLONE, STEWART, TAYLOR, TONE
	TRACY, VALENTINO, VOIGT, WAGNER
	WALLACH, WAYNE, WEISSMULLER
	WELLES, WIDMARK
—Bahamian	POITIER
—British	ARLISS, ATTENBOROUGH
	BOGARDE, BURTON, CAINE, CHAPLIN
	COLMAN, CONNERY, CUSHING, DONAT
	FAIRBANKS, FINCH, GIELGUD
	GRAINGER, GRANT, GUINNESS
	HARDWICKE, HARRISON, HOPE
	HOWARD, KARLOFF
	LAUGHTON, LAUREL, LIVESEY, MASON
	MILLAND, MILLS, MOORE, NIVEN
	OLIVIER, PRICE, QUAYLE, REED
	RAINS, RICHARDSON, SANDERS
	SCOFIELD, SIM, SMITH
	TODD, USTINOV
—French	BARRAULT, BELMONDO, BOYR
	CHEVALIER, DELON, DEPARDIEU
	FERNANDEL, GABIN, MONTAND, TATI

(see also **theatre***)*

—German	JANNING, SCHELL
—Hungarian	LORRE, LUGOSI
—Irish	FLYNN, HARRIS
—Italian	FABRIZI, MASTROIANNI
—Tasmanian	FLYNN

actresses

—American	BACALL, BALL, BANCROFT
	BENNETT, COLBERT, CRAWFORD
	DAVIS, DE HAVILLAND, DUNAWAY
	FONDA, FONTAINE, GARDNER
	GARLAND, GAYNOR, GISH, GRABLE
	HAYES, HAYWOOD, HAYWORTH
	HEPBURN, HOLLIDAY, KELLY
	LAMARR, LAMOUR, LOMBARD
	MCGRAW, MINELLI, MONROE
	NEAL, OBERON, PICKFORD
	ROGERS, RUSSELL, SHEARER, SHIELDS
	STANWYCK, STREISAND, STREEP
	SWANSON, TEMPLE, TREVOR, WOOD
	WOODWARD, YOUNG
—British	ANDREWS, ASHCROFT
	COLLINS, DORS, HEPBURN, HOBSON
	JACKSON, KERR, LANSBURY, LEIGH
	LOCKWOOD, SHEARER, SIMS
	TAYLOR, TODD, WELCH
—French	BARDOT, CAPUCINE
	SEYRIG, SIGNORET
—German	DIETRICH, DRESSLER
—Greek	MERCOURI
—Hungarian	GABOR
—Italian	CARDINALE, LOREN
	LOLLOBRIGIDA, MAGNANI
—Swedish	GARBO, BERGMAN

(see also **theatre***)*

add a soundtrack	DUB
afternoon screening	MATINEE
assemblage of photographs	MONTAGE
board used to synchronise	
sound and picture	CLAPPERBOARD
biographical film	BIOPIC
brief appearance of well-	
known actor	CAMEO ROLE
cafeteria in film studio	COMMISSARY
comic	
—policeman	CLOUSEAU
—policemen	KEYSTONE COPS
	KEYSTONE KOPS
commentary by unseen	
speaker	VOICE-OVER
composite photograph	MONTAGE

directors

—American	ALLEN, ALTMAN, CAPRA
	COPPOLA, CUKOR, CURTIZ
	DE MILLE, DIETERLE, DISNEY
	FLAHERTY, FLEMING, FORD, FULLER
	GOLDWYN, GRIFFITH, HAWKS, HUSTON
	KAZAN, KUBRICK, LANG, LOSEY, LUCAS
	LUMET, LYNCH, MACK, MAMOULIAN

MANKIEWICZ, MAYSLES, POLANSKI
PORTER, PECKINPAH, PREMINGER, RAY
SENNETT, SPIELBERG, VIDOR, WELLES
WILDER, WYLER, ZINNEMAN
—Austrian STROHEIM
—British ASQUITH, ATTENBOROUGH
FORBES, GILLIATT, GRIERSON
HITCHCOCK, JORDAN, LEACOCK
LEAN, NEAME, POWELL
PRESSBURGER, PUTNAM, REED
SCHLESINGER, USTINOV
—Danish DREYER, SIRK
—French AUMONT-LARA, CARNE
CHABROL, CLAIR, COCTEAU
DUVIVIER, FERDUR, FRANK
GODARD, MALLE, MARKER
RENOIR, RESNAIS, RIVETTE
ROHMER, ROUCH, STRAUB
TATI, TRUFFAUT, VADIM, VIGO
—German FASSBINDER, HERZOG
LANG, LUBITSCH, OPHIUS
VON STERNBERG, WEINE
—Hungarian CURTIZ
—Indian RAY, ROY
—Italian ANTONIONI, BARBARO
BERTOLUCCI, DE SANTIS
DE SICA, FABRIZI, FELLINI
GUISEPPE, LEONE, LATTUADA
ROSSELLINI, VISCONTI, VITTORIO
—Japanese KUROSAWA, MIZOGUCHI
OSHIMA, OZU
—Polish POLANSKI
—Russian EISENSTEIN, KOZINTZEV
KULESHOV, TARKOVSKY
TRAUBERG, VERTOV
—Spanish BUNUEL
—Swedish BERGMAN
early BIOSCOPE, NICKELODEON
MUTOSCOPE, ZOECHROME
ZOETROPE, ZOOPRAXISCOPE
electrician GAFFER
film MOTION PICTURE
—library CINEMATHEQUE
—dealing with
earlier events PREQUEL
later events SEQUEL
—enthusiast CINEASTE
—featuring cowboys and
Indians HORSE OPERA
(SPAGHETTI) WESTERN
—making CINEMATOGRAPHY
—mixing fact and fiction FACTION
—representing life
realistically CINE VERITE
—using
animation CARTOON

some documentary
sequences COMPILATION FILM
nude actors SKINFLICK
filming
—sequence TAKE
—static drawings to
simulate movement ANIMATION
first unedited print of film RUSH
floodlight KLEIG LIGHT
KLIEG LIGHT
French movement of 1960's NEW WAVE
NOUVELLE VAGUE
gaffer's assistant BEST BOY
high-intensity lamp KLIEG LIGHT
holes on each side
of film SPROCKET HOLES
insert a shot CROSSCUT, INTERCUT
inserted shot CUT-IN
instrument simulating
movement with still
pictures PHENAKISTOSCOPE
joint in film SPLICE
lighting technician GAFFER
list of performers and
workers CREDITS
move camera to follow action TRACK
non-fictional DOCUMENTARY
DOCUDRAMA
one with artistic interest
in films CINEASTE
outdoor filming site LOCATION
pornographic film BLUE FILM
SKINFLICK
portion of film FOOTAGE
—discarded OUTTAKE
projection of film as
background for filming
other action BACK PROJECTION
quick change of image
size by use of special lens ZOOM(ING)
repeated single frame FREEZE FRAME
reversion to previous events FLASHBACK
scene change by
—abrupt transition JUMP CUT
—fading one scene
into another DISSOLVE
—gradual change FADE IN
FADE OUT
—line moving across
the screen WIPE
scenes depicting same
event in different ways MONTAGE
script
—describing camera
work and order of
filming SHOOTING SCRIPT

—giving full detailed
  version of the story   TREATMENT
—used for
  acting and camera
    directions   SCENARIO
                      SCREENPLAY
  ensuring consistency
    from scene to scene   CONTINUITY
sequence   FOOTAGE
single photograph
—in film   FRAME
—taken for publicity etc   STILL
small cinema   CINEMATHEQUE
studios   ELSTREE, HOLLYWOOD
superimposition of
  photographs   MONTAGE
swing camera to
  follow action   PAN
technique
—photographing at
    intervals to give
    speeded-up film   TIME-LAPSE
—using
    camera tricks   OPTICAL
               SPECIAL EFFECT
  two or more images
    on parts of one screen   SPLIT SCREEN
toy   ZOETROPE
trolley for moving camera   DOLLY
Western   HORSE OPERA
wide screen   CINEMASCOPE
                 CINEMIRACLE
           CINERAMA, IMAX
     TODD-AO, VISTAVISION

circulation
including: blood
         heart
         lymph
         veins
affecting contraction and
  dilation   VASOMOTOR
artificial regulator   PACEMAKER
artery
—blocking by
    clotted blood   THROMBOSIS
    solid fragment   EMBOLISM
—bulge in   ANEURYSM
—cutting of   ARTERIOTOMY
—deposit of cholesterol etc in   ATHEROMA
—from
  aorta to
    —abdomen   COELIAC, ILIAC
     MESENTERIC, RENAL
    —head   CAROTID
    —heart   CORONARY
    —leg   FEMORAL

—neck and arm   AXILLARY
      BRACHIAL, RADIAL
     SUBCLAVIAN, ULNAR
—upper right side   INOMINATE
heart to
—lungs   PULMONARY
—rest of body   AORTA
—hardening of   ARTERIOSCLEROSIS
—inflammation of   ARTERITIS
—narrowing of   STENOSIS
—small   ARTERIOLE
—swelling in carotid   CAROTID SINUS
  blockage   CLOT, EMBOLISM
     EMBOLUS, INFARCTION
blood   GORE, PINK
—agglutination
  common to
    man and monkey   RH(ESUS) FACTOR
  of cells in same
    group   ISOAGGLUTINATION
—anti-clotting agent   HEPARIN
—antibody
  causing clumping of
    bacteria   AGGLUTININ
  in globulin   IMMUNOGLOBULIN
—antigen in red cells   RH(ESUS) FACTOR
—bacteria-destroyer   BACTERIOPHAGE
          PHAGOCYTE
—bile in the blood   CHOLAEMIA
—bleeding   HAEMORRHAGE
—bloody   SANGUINARY
—blue pigment   HAEMOCYANIN
—breaking down of leucocytes LEUCOCYTOSIS
—bright red   ARTERIAL
—brown substance in dried
  blood   HAEMATIN
—cancer   LEUKAEMIA
—cavity containing blood   HAEMATOCELE
—cell   BLOOD CORPUSCLE
  fighting infection   LEUCOCYTE
     WHITE CORPUSCLE
  transporting oxygen   HAEMOCYTE
     RED CORPUSCLE
—checking bleeding   STYPTIC
—chemical peventing
  clotting   ANTICOAGULANT
—chloride of haematin   HAEMIN
—clotting
  agent   PLATELET, THROMBOCYTE
  enzyme   THROMBIN
—coagulating protein   FIBRIN, FIBROGEN
—cold-blooded   POIKILOTHERMIC
—colour   INCARNADINE
—compound formed by
  oxygen acting on
  haemoglobin   OXY-HAEMOGLOBIN

—constituent of haemoglobin	GLOBIN
—conversion of venous blood to arterial	HAEMATOSIS
—deficiency of	
blood sugar	HYPOGLYCAEMIA
red cells	(SP)ANAEMIA
—deprived of oxygen	VENOUS
—destruction of red cells	H(A)EMOLYSIS
—diffusion through membrane for purification	HAEMODIALYSIS
—dilation of blood vessel	ANEURISM
	ANEUYSM
—discharge of blood	HAEMORRHAGE
	STAXIS
—diseases of the blood	(*see* **disease**)
—dissolution of red corpuscles	HAEM(AT)OLYSIS
—dust	HAEMOCONIA
—excess of	
blood sugar	HYPERGLYCAEMIA
red cells	POLYCYTHAEMIA
—excessive bleeding	HAEMOPHILIA
—fatty	
acid in blood	TRIGLYCERIDE
deposit in vessels	ATHEROMA
	CHOLESTEROL
—fluid separated from coagulating blood	SERUM
—formation of	
blood	HAEMATOSIS
red cells	HAEM(AT)OPOIESIS
—granules in the blood	BLOOD-DUST
	HAEMOCONIA
—groups	A, B, AB, O
—haemoconia	BLOOD-DUST
—haemocyte	BLOOD CELL
	BLOOD CORPUSCLE
—haemoglobin in muscle fibre	MYOGLOBIN
—homoiothermic	WARM-BLOODED
—idiothermic	WARM-BLOODED
—immature red cell	RETICULOCYTE
—immune system cells	B-CELL, T-CELL
—immunising substance	PROPERDIN
—in combination	HAEMO-
—infection of blood	PYAEMIA
—infusion of blood from	
others	TRANSFUSION
self	AUTOLOGICAL TRANSFUSION
—in urine	H(A)EMATURIA
—large white cell	MONCYTE
—liquid constituent after removal of cells	PLASMA
—morbid state of blood	CACHAEMIA
—natural immuniser in blood	PROPERDIN

—nitrogen bubbles in blood	AEROEMBOLISM, BENDS
	CAISSON DISEASE
	DECOMPRESSION SICKNESS
—overproduction of white cells in response to infection	LEUCOCYTOSIS
—oxygenated haemoglobin	OXYHAEMOGLOBIN
—part of serum promoting phagocytosis	OPSONIN
—pigment	HAEM, HAEMOCYANIN
	HAEMOGLOBIN
—plasma without clotting agents	SERUM
—platelet	HAEMATOBLAST
	THROMBOCYTE
—poisoning	PYAEMIA, SEPTICAEMIA
	SUPRAEMIA, TOXAEMIA
—polypeptide in blood	KENIN
—pressure	BP, DISATOLIC
	RR, SYSTOLIC
high	HYPERTENSION
low	HYPOTENSION
measuring instrument	SPHYGMO(MANO)METER
—protective body	ALEXIN, ANTIBODY
	ANTIGEN
	GAMMA GLOBULIN
—protein	
clotting	FIBRIN
hormone	INSULIN
plasma	ALBUMEN, ALBUMIN
	FIBRINOGEN, GLOBULIN
protective	GAMMA GLOBULIN
red	HAEMOGLOBIN
—purification by machine	(HAEMO)DIALYSIS
—pus in blood	PYAEMIA
—red	
cell	ERYTHROCYTE
—with no	
corpuscle	ERYTHROCYTE
haemoglobin	RED CELL GHOST
pigment	HAEMOGLOBIN
—reduction of supply	ISCH(A)EMIA
—serum containing antibodies	ALS
	ANTI-LYMPHATIC SERUM
	GAMMA GLOBULIN
—smear on slide	BLOOD FILM
—spitting blood	EMPTYSIS
	HAEMOPTYSIS
—stimulating production of red cells	HAEMATINIC
—stoppage of bleeding	HAEMOSTASIS

—study of blood	HAEMATOLOGY
—substance	
preventing clotting	HEPARIN
stimulating production	
of agglutinin	AGGLUTINOGEN
—sugar	GLUCOSE
—swelling containing blood	HAEMATOMA
—vessels	ARTERIOLE, ARTERY
	CAPILLARY, VEIN, VENULE
—vomiting blood	HAEMATEMESIS
—warm-blooded	HOMOIOTHERMIC
	IDIOTHERMIC
	IDIOTHERMOUS
—white cell	BASOPHIL, EOSINOPHIL
	LEUCOCYTE, LEUKOCYTE
	LYMPHOCYTE, NEUTROPHIL
destroying bacteria etc	PHAGOCYTE
with granular cytoplasm	GRANULOCYTE
POLYMORPH(ONUCLEAR LEUCOCYTE)	
development of new	
blood vessels	NEOVASCULARISATION
dilation of arteries, etc	TELANGIECTASIS
expanding of blood vessel	VASODILATION
heart	
—abnormal sound	MURMUR
—cessation of	
heart-beat	CARDIAC ARREST
—chamber	ATRIUM, AURICLE
	VENTRICLE
in some animals	SINUS VENOSUS
—contraction	SYSTOLE
—dilatation	DIASTOLE
—fast-beating	TACHYCARDIA
—fluttering of heart muscle	FIBRILLATION
—inflammation of	CARDITIS
	(see also **disease**)
—irregular beat	ARRHYTHMIA
—lining membrane	ENDOTHELIUM
—muscle controlling	
heart-beat	PACEMAKER
—on right side of body	DEXTROCARDIA
—opening between	
auricles	FORAMEN OVALE
—recording instrument	CARDIOGRAPH
—rhythmic pressure to	
restart heart-beat	CARDIAC MASSAGE
—sac	PERICARDIUM
—slow-beating	BRADYCARDIA
—study of	CARDIOLOGY
—valves	AORTIC, MITRAL
	PULMONARY
	TRICUSPID
heart-burn	CARDALGIA, CARDALGY
heart-failure	CARDIAC FAILURE
heart-shaped	CARDIOID
lining of blood vessels	INTIMA

lymph	
—glands	ABDOMINAL, AXILLARY
	CERVICAL, INGUINAL
	MEDIASTINAL, POPLITEAL
	SUB-LINGUAL, SUB-MAXILLARY
—vessels	LACTEAL
	THORACIC DUCT
narrowing of blood	
vessel	VASOCONSTRICTION
small	
—artery	ARTERIOLE
—blood vessel	CAPILLARY
—vein	VENULE
space in tissue	SINUSOID
study of	
—ancient blood groups	PALAEOSEROLOGY
—blood	HAEMATOLOGY
—serums	SEROLOGY
veins	
—arrangement of	VENATION
—blockage of	EMBOLISM
	THROMBOSIS
—from	
abdomen	ILIAC
chest	(HEMI)AZYGOS
forelimbs	ANTERIOR VENA CAVA
head and neck	JUGULAR
iliac veins	INFERIOR VENA CAVA
inominate veins	SUPERIOR VENA CAVA
intestines to liver	PORTAL
jugular and subclavian	INNOMINATE
kidneys	RENAL
legs	FEMORAL
liver	HEPATIC
lungs	PULMONARY
rest of body	POSTERIOR VENA CAVA
—inflammation of	PHLEBITIS
—opening of	VENESECTION
—puncturing	VENEPUNCTURE
	VENIPUNCTURE
—small	VENULE
city	
Athens of the North	EDINBURGH
Auld Reekie	EDINBURGH
Big	
—A	ATLANTA
—Apple	NEW YORK
—Pretzel	PHILADELPHIA
Birmingham	SECOND CITY
Brighton of the North	NAIRN
Brummagem	BIRMINGHAM
Buenos Aires	BA
City of	
—100 towers	PAVIA
—angels	LOS ANGELES
—bells	BRUGES

—bridges	BRUGES
—canals	VENICE
—kings	LIMA
—masts	LONDON
—monuments	BALTIMORE
—palaces	ROME
—plains	SODOM, GOMORRAH
—prophet	MEDINA
—saints	SALT LAKE CITY
—seven hills	ROME
—three kings	COLOGNE
—victory	CAIRO
—violet crown	ATHENS
—West	GLASGOW
Crescent City	NEW ORLEANS
Edinburgh	AULD REEKIE
eternal city	ROME
Gotham	NEW YORK
granite city	ABERDEEN
Hollywood	TINSELTOWN
holy city	JERUSALEM, MEDINA
	MECCA, ROME
Hub of the Universe	BOSTON
Los Angeles	LA
New York	BIG APPLE, GOTHAM, NY
Philadelphia	BIG PRETZEL
Quaker City	PHILADELPHIA
Queen of the Riviera	NICE
Second City	BIRMINGHAM
Tinseltown	HOLLYWOOD
Venice of the north	BRUGES, LENINGRAD
Windy City	CHICAGO
clergy	(*see* **church—personnel**)
climate	(*see* **meteorology**)
clothes	DUDS, TOGS
academic clothing	SUBFUSC, SUBFUSK
baby's clothes	LAYETTE
bride's clothes	TROUSSEAU
civilian clothing	CIVVIES, MUFTI
clergy's clothing	HABIT, VESTMENTS
	(*see also* **church — vestments**)
clothes store	WARDROBE
clothing	HABERDASHERY
—in art	DRAPERY
—made to order	BESPOKE
—ready made	OFF THE PEG
—suitable for either sex	UNISEX
—worn by members of guild	LIVERY
designer of clothes	COUTURIER
designers	
—American	BEENE, BLASS, CASSINI
	DE LA RENTA, ELLIS, HALSTON
	JACOBS, KARAN, KELLY
	KORS, KLEIN, LAUREN, MACKIE
	MIZRAHI, NEVILLE, ZORAN
—Australian	TRYON

—British	AMIES, BLAIR, CONRAN
	COSTELLOE, EDELSTEIN
	EMMANUEL, FAHRI, GALLIANO
	HAMNETT, HARTNELL, HEMPEL
	JACKSON, MUIR, OLDFIELD, OSBEK
	POLLEN, QUANT, SASSOON
	TINLING, TRYON, WESTWOOD
—French	BOHAN, CAROCHE
	CHANEL, COURREGES, DIOR
	FATH, GAULTIER, GIVENCHY
	HECHTER, LACROIX
	LANVIN, ST LAURENT
—German	LAGERFELD
—Italian	ARMANI, BYBLOS, FABBRI
	FENDI, FERRAGAMO, FERRE
	GIGLI, MOSHINO
	SCHIAPARELLI, UNGARO
	TARLAZZI, VALENTINO
	VERSACE
—Japanese	KAWAKUBO, KENZO
	MIYAKE, YAMAMOTO, YUKI
—Russian	CASSINI, ZAITSEV
—South American	HERRERA
—Spanish	BALENCIAGA
—Tunisian	ALAIA
dressmaker (odd)	MANTUA-MAKER
expensive clothing	CAPARISON, FINERY
guild uniform	LIVERY
military clothes	FATIGUES, SD
	SERVICE DRESS, UNIFORM
model for clothes	DUMMY, MANNEQUIN
ornate clothing	FALLAL, FRIPPERY
	FROU-FROU
outfit	APPAREL, ATTIRE, ENSEMBLE
	GARB, HABILIMENTS, RAIMENT
plain clothes	MUFTI
servant's uniform	LIVERY
sports outfit	STRIP
	(*see also* **garments**)
clouds	(*see* **meteorology**)
club	CUDGEL
African	KERRIE, KIERIE, KIRI
	KNOBKERRIE
Australian	DOWAK, NULLA(-NULLA)
	WADDIE, WADDY
ceremonial	MACE
cudgel	ALPEEN
for killing fish	PRIEST
golf	(*see separate entry*)
Irish	ALPEEN, SHILLELA(G)H
	SHILLALY, TIPPERARY RIFLE
New Zealand	MERE, MERI
policeman's	TRUNCHEON
rubber	LIFE PRESERVER
short, heavy stick	BLUDGEON
spiked	ACLIDE, MACE

war-club	MAUL	tit willow	PILLOW
weighted	COSH, SAP	Tod (Sloan)	ALONE
clouds	(*see* **meteorology**)	**cocktails**	
Cockney rhyming slang		Advocaat and lemonade	SNOWBALL
Adam and Eve	BELIEVE	bourbon	
almond rocks	SOCKS	—absinthe, etc	SAZERAC
apple pie	SKY	—Amaretto di Saronno	
apples (and pears)	STAIRS	Drambuie	BARBERA
April showers	FLOWERS	brandy with	
army and navy	GRAVY	—Amaretto di Saronno	LEO
army rocks	SOCKS	rum	SCORPION
artful dodger	LODGER	—apricot brandy, lime	BACCHUS
bacon and eggs	LEGS	—Chartreuse	FRENCHMAN
Baden Powell	TROWEL	—cherry brandy	BRANDY FIX
bag of fruit	SUIT	—Cointreau	SIDECAR
baker's dozen	COUSIN	—crème de cacao	ALEXANDER
ball of chalk	WALK	—crème de menthe	STINGER
Band of Hope	SOAP	—dry vermouth, Calvados	KLONDIKE
Barnaby Rudge	JUDGE	—ginger ale	HORSE'S NECK
bath-bun	SON	—grenadine, lemon juice	BRANDY DAISY
blue moon	SPOON	—peach brandy, kirsch	ROYAL WEDDING
Bo-peep	SLEEP	—port, lemon juice	CREOLE PUNCH
butcher's (hook)	LOOK	—rum and	
Cain and Abel	TABLE	Amaretto	SCORPION
carving knife	WIFE	Cointreau	BETWEEN THE SHEETS
China (plate)	MATE	—soda water, mint	BRANDY SMASH
cut and carried	MARRIED	—van der Hum, fruit juice	SUNDOWNER
currant bun	SUN	Calvados	
Dicky Bird	WORD	—Benedictine	HONEYMOON
Dicky Dirt	SHIRT	—orange juice	HARVARD COOLER
dinky-doo	TWENTY-TWO	Campari, sweet vermouth	AMERICANO
Dutch (Duchess of Fife)	WIFE	champagne with	
four by two	JEW	—apricot brandy, Grand	
frog and toad	ROAD	Marnier	PALM BEACH FIZZ
half-inch	PINCH, STEAL	—brandy, bitters	CLASSIC
ham and eggs	LEGS	bitters, Curaçao	CHICAGO
Jack (Jones)	ALONE	—burgundy	COLD DUCK
Joanna	PIANO	—Calvados,	
King Dick	BRICK(LAYER), THICK	bitters	CHAMPAGNE NORMANDIE
loaf (of bread)	HEAD	—crème de cassis	KIR ROYALE
Mickey Mouse	HOUSE	—Curaçao	BLUE CHAMPAGNE
mince pies	EYES	—Galliano, orange juice	SECRET SMILE
Mutt and Jeff	DEAF	—gin, lemon juice	FRENCH 175
Ned Kelly	BELLY	—grenadine, peach juice	BELLINI
old Dutch	WIFE	—Guinness	BLACK VELVET
on one's Tod (Sloan)	ALONE	—orange juice	BUCK'S FIZZ
penny bun	SON, SUN	—Pernod	PERNOD FIZZ
pig's ear	BEER	—rum, crème de	
plates/platters (of meat)	FEET	banane	CARIBBEAN CHAMPAGNE
pride and joy	BOY	Cointreau, Galliano	GOLDEN LINING
Richard the Third	BIRD	crème de menthe	
Rosie/Rosy Lea/Lee	TEA	—crème de cacao	GRASSHOPPER
skin and blister	SISTER	—soda	BEACHCOMBER
sky rocket	POCKET	daiquiri with shaved ice	FROZEN DAIQUIRI
trouble (and strife)	WIFE	Drambuie	
tit for tat (titfer)	HAT	—orange juice	DRAMBUIE SHRUB

—peach schnapps, orange juice	FUZZY NAVEL
gin with	
—apricot brandy	
Calvados	ANGEL'S FACE
orange juice	PARADISE
—bitters	PINK GIN
lemon juice	GIN SLING
—brandy, lemonade, egg white	PINK LADY
—cherry brandy, Cointreau	SINGAPORE SLING
—Cointreau, lemon juice	WHITE LADY
—crème de menthe	GIN FIZZ
egg white	WHITE HORSES
—Dubonnet	DUBONNET
—dry vermouth	DRY MARTINI
cherry brandy	RED KISS
Cointreau	WOODSTOCK
fruit juice	BRONX
Kirsch	COLLINSON
Mandarine	STORMY WEATHER
onion	GIBSON
--Galliano, lemon juice	MILANO
—ginger ale	HORSE'S NECK
—grenadine, egg white	PINK LADY
—Kirsch, egg white	ETON BLAZER
—lemon or lime	GIN SOUR
	TOM COLLINS
—lime juice, soda water	RICKEY
—sweet vermouth	SWEET MARTINI
Chartreuse	BIJOU
—white vermouth, orange juice	ORANGE BLOSSOM
in sugar-coated glass	CRUSTA
Pernod, orange juice	ORANGE CLOUD
rum with	
—Advocaat, crème de cacao	ELDORADO
—Amaretto di Saronno	SERENADE
—apricot brandy, fruit juice	ZOMBIE
—Calvados	KICKER
—cherry brandy, soda	PINK TREASURE
—coca cola, lime juice	CUBRE LIBRE
—coconut milk, fruit juice	PINA COLADA
—crème de cacao, lime	TEMPO
—dry vermouth, apricot brandy	ROSALIE
—fruit juice	PLANTER'S COCKTAIL
	PLANTER'S PUNCH
egg white	MAI TAI
—Galliano, apricot brandy	JOLLY ROGER
—Irish Mist, pineapple juice	EDGEMOOR
—lime	DAQUIRI
—Malibu, fruit juice	BOMBAY SMASH
—Mandarine, orange juice	WATERLOO
—orange Nassau liqueur	SUMMERTIME
—soda water, fruit juice	FLORIDA SKIES

—tequila, vodka	COCO LOCO
sherry	
—soda water	SHERRY COBBLER
—vermouth	BAMBOO
Southern Comfort, Amaretto di Saronno	SICILIAN KISS
spirits with ice	SWIZZLE
tequila with	
—cherry brandy, Galliano	BROOKLYN BOMBER
—grenadine	TEQUILA SUNRISE
—Triple Sec, fruit juice	MARGARITA
vodka with	
—Benedictine, grapefruit juice	RUSSIAN SECRET
—Calvados, apple juice	NORMAN CONQUEROR
—coffee liqueur	BLACK RUSSIAN
—Cointreau, soda water	LE MANS
—consommé	BULLSHOT
—dry vermouth, onion	GIBSON
—Galliano Mandarine	BEHIND THE WALL
orange juice	HARVEY WALLBANGER
—ginger beer, lime	MOSCOW MULE
—Irish Mist, orange juice	ORANGE MIST
—orange juice	SCREWDRIVER
—Parfait Amour, maraschino	PERFECT LOVE
—sweet vermouth, tonic	HAIR RAISER
—tequila, Curaçao	BLUE MOON
—Tia Maria, milk	WHITE RUSSIAN
—tomato juice	BLOODY MARY
whisky with	
—Amaretto di Saronno	GODFATHER
—Angostura bitters	OLD-FASHIONED
—apricot brandy	CAPRICORN
—Benedictine, dry vermouth	BRAINSTORM
—Drambuie	RUSTY NAIL
Chartreuse	ROYAL SCOT
—dry vermouth	ROB ROY
—ginger wine	WHISKY MAC
lemon juice	SUPERMAC
—Grand Marnier	RITZ OLD-FASHIONED
—grenadine	CLUB
—lemon juice	WHISKY SOUR
—lime juice	NEW YORKER
—Pernod, grenadine	WHISKY DAISY
—soda water, mint	MINT JULEP
—sweet vermouth, bitters	MANHATTAN

coffee

beans	ARABICA, ROBUSTA
Brazilian	SANTOS
drinks	CAPPUCINO, EXPRESSO, MOCHA
flavouring	CHICORY
small cup	DEMI-TASSE

very sweet	TURKISH COFFEE
with	
—brandy	FRENCH
—Cointreau	MALORCAN
—liqueur	COFFEE ROYAL
—milk	CAFE AU LAIT
—rum	CARIBBEAN
—Scotch whisky	HIGHLAND
—Tia Maria	CALYPSO
—vodka	RUSSIAN
—whiskey and cream	GAELIC COFFEE
	IRISH COFFEE
without milk	CAFE NOIR

coins
(in ascending order)	
half-farthing	GROAT
two groats	FARTHING
farthing (old)	STICA, STYCA
½d	HA(LF)PENNY, MAG(PIE)
	MAIK, MAIL(E), MAKE
—old	OB(OLUM), OBOLUS
	PORTCULLIS
penny	COPPER, D, P
—old silver	STERLING
1½d	DANDIPRAT, DANDYPRAT
	THREE-HALFPENNY
3d	JOEY, THREEPENNY BIT
4d	GROAT, JOE(Y)
—silver	FOURPENNY
6d	SPRASI, TANNER
	TILBURY, TIZZY
—old	TESTER(N), TESTON, TESTRIL(L)
12d	SHILLING
shilling	DEANER, BOB, S
—old	TESTON, TESTER(N), TESTRIL(L)
1/6d-2/- (old)	GILDER
2 shillings	FLORIN
florin (gold)	FLORENCE
30d (old)	MANCUS
2/6d	HALF-CROWN
	SWORD-DOLLAR
5 shillings	CROWN
crown	THICKUN
6/8d	HALF-MARK, NOBLE
10 shillings	HALF-SOVEREIGN
—old	PISTOLET, RIAL, RYAL
10/6d	HALF-GUINEA
half-guinea	SMELT
13/4d (old)	MARK
15 shillings (gold)	SPUR-RIAL
	SPUR-R(O)YAL
20 shillings	POUND
—old	BROAD(-PIECE), UNITE
100p	POUND
pound	BRADBURY, NICKER, QUID
	SMACKER, SOVEREIGN

—old	CAROLUS, FLORENCE
	JACOBUS
sovereign	THICKUN
—poetic	SOVRAN
21 shillings	GEORDIE, GUINEA
22 shillings	UNITE
5 pounds	FIVER, HAWAII
10 pounds	BRITANNIA, JACK
	PLACIDO, TENNER,
25 pounds	BRITANNIA, PONY
50 pounds	BRITANNIA, HAWAII
100 pounds	BRITANNIA, TON
500 pounds	MONKEY
2,000 pounds	ARCHER
100,000 pounds	PLUM, SEYMOUR
coin issued in besieged places	SIEGE-PIECE
old gold coins	ANGEL, BRITANNIA
	ROSE NOBLE, RUDDOCK
	SCEATT, SPADE GUINEA
	SPANKER, YELLOW BOY
old silver coins	SCEATT
	THREE FARTHINGS
proposed coin	MIL(L)
small	DUMP, MAWPUS
	MOPUS, STIVER
—old silver	SILVERING

collecting
collecting	
—birthday cards	GENETHLIADELTIOLOGY
—cards	CARTOPHILY
with similar stamps	MAXIMAPHILY
—coins	NUMISMATICS
—comics	PANEOLOGY
—labels	PHILATELY
—matchboxes	PHILLUMENY
—medals	NUMISMATICS
—pig models, etc	PORCINOLOGY
—stamps	PHILATELY, TIMBROLOGY
	TIMBROMANIA
	TIMBROPHILY
—walking sticks	RHABDOPHILY
collector of trifles	EPHEMERIST

Colombia   CO
capital	BOGOTA
coins	
—unit	CENTAVO
—100 centavos	PESO

colour
amber	CHAMPAGNE
ashen	LIVID
black	ANTHRACITE, COAL, DWALE
	EBONY, JET, RAVEN, SABLE, SOOTY
—and	
blue	LIVID
brown	SKEWBALD
white	PIEBALD, PINTO

blackish/dark	FULIGINOUS, DUSKY	—two secondary colours	TERTIARY COLOUR
	SUBFUSC, SUBFUSK	mouse coloured	DUN
blood-red	SANGUINE	mulberry	MURREY
blue	AZURE, C(A)ERULEAN	multi-coloured	PRISMATIC
	COBALT, CYAN, GENTIAN	orange/brown	TENNE
	INDIGO, LAPIS LAZULI	orange/red	NACARAT
	NAVY BLUE, PERIWINKLE	pale blue or green paint	BICE
	ROYAL BLUE, SAPPHIRE	pink	SHRIMP
	SAXE BLUE, SAXON(Y)	primary colour	BLUE, RED, YELLOW
	SKY BLUE, SMALT	purple	HYACINTH, PORPHYROUS
	ULTRAMARINE, WATCHET		PUNIC
blue/green	LOVAT	purple/red	MULBERRY, MURREY
blue/grey	SLATE GREY	range of colours	PALETTE, SPECTRUM
blue/violet	AMETHYST, AUBERGINE	receding colour	BLUE
	HELIOTROPE	red	CARDINAL, CARMINE
brown	BAY, BEAVER, BISCUIT		CHERRY, CINNABAR
	(BURNT) UMBER		COCHINEAL, CRIMSON, LAKE
	CAFE AU LAIT, CAMEL		MADDER, MODENA, RUBY
	CARAMEL, CINNAMON		SCARLET, SOLFERINO
	COFFEE, DONKEY, DRAB, DUN		STAMMEL, VERMEIL(LE)
	HAZEL, MOCHA, NIGGER		VERMIL, VERMILION
	NUTMEG, SANDALWOOD	red/brown	BAY, BRICK, BURNT SIENNA
	SEPIA, TORTOISESHELL		CHESTNUT, COLCOTHAR
	VANDYKE, WALNUT		COROMANDEL, HENNA, MAHOGANY
brown/purple	PUCE		OXBLOOD, ROAN, RUBIGINOUS
brownish	BEIGE, FUSCOUS		RUSSET, RUST, SIENNA, SOAR(E), SORE
	TAN, TAUPE, TAWNY		SORREL, TERRACOTTA, TITIAN
buff	BEIGE, NANKEEN	red/purple	AMARANTH, BURGUNDY
	NANKIN		CERISE, FUSCHIA, MAGENTA
changing pattern of colour	KALEIDOSCOPE		MAROON, MAUVE, PUCE
cold colour	BLUE	red/yellow	AMBER, APRICOT, CORAL
colour scale	MUNSELL SCALE		FLAMINGO, ORANGE, PEACH
	OSTWALD SCALE		ROSE, SALMON, TANGERINE
dead leaves	FILEMOT	reddish	AUBURN, FERRUGINOUS
drab	QUAKER-COLOUR		GINGER, LAKE, PINK, PYRRHOUS
dull brown	DRAB		RUBI(GIN)OUS, RUDDY, RUFOUS
green	APPLE, CELADON, EAU DE NIL	saffron-coloured	CROCEATE, CROCEOUS
	EMERALD, JADE, KENDAL	sea-green	AQUAMARINE, C(A)ERULEAN
	LIME, LINCOLN, MOSS, NILE		GLAUCOUS
	SAGE, TEAL, TERRE-VERTE	shade	CAST, HUE, TINCTURE
	VIRIDIAN		TINGE, TINT
green/blue	AQUAMARINE, TURQUOISE	shimmering colour	IRIDESCENT
grey	BATTLESHIP, CHARCOAL		OPALESCENT
	CLERICAL, ELEPHANT, DOVE	study of colours	CHROMATICS
	DRAB, GUNMETAL, NUTRIA	variegated	MOTLEY, PARTI-COLOURED
grey/blue	GLAUCOUS, LOVAT		PIED, POLYCHROME
grey/brown	DUN		VARICOLOURED
greyish	BEIGE	violet	IANTHINE
greyish-beige	GRE(I)GE	visible light	
instrument for comparing	COLORIMETER	spectrum	VIOLET, INDIGO, BLUE
	TINTOMETER		GREEN, YELLOW, ORANGE, RED
lead coloured	LIVID		ROYGBIV, VIBGYOR
leek-green	PRASINE	warm colour	RED
light colour	PASTEL, TINT	white	ALABASTER, IVORY
mixture of		whitish	BISQUE, CREAM, ECRU
—two primary colours	SECONDARY COLOUR		EGGSHELL, OYSTER, PUTTY

yellow/brown	CHAMOIS, CHAMPAGNE
	CITRINE, CITRON
	DAFFODIL, FALLOW, FAWN
	FLAX, GAMBOGE, GOLD
	JONQUIL, MAIZE, MUSTARD
	NANKEEN, OCHRE, RAW SIENNA
	SAFFRON, TAN, TOPAZ
yellow/green	CHARTREUSE, RESEDA
	SAP-GREEN
yellow/grey	ECRU, ISABEL(LA)
	ISABELLINE
yellow/red	APRICOT, PEACH
yellowish	FULVOUS, LUTE(OL)OUS
	SALLOW
composers	*(see* **musicians***)*

computing

ability to intercommunicate	CONNECTIVITY
access another computer	LOG ON
adapt disk to a particular machine	FORMAT
add-on parts	PERIPHERALS
alter data in file	EDIT, UPDATE
amount of storage	CAPACITY
audio signal	EARCON
basic	
—circuit	AND-GATE, GATE
	NAND-GATE, NOR-GATE
	OR-GATE
—screen unit	PIXEL
binary	B
—digit	BIT
—language	MACHINE CODE
	MACHINE LANGUAGE
bits per second	BPS
block of data	PACKET, PAGE
botched job	KLUDGE
break down	CRASH, FALL OVER
	GO DOWN
broadcast information	CEEFAX, ORACLE
	PRESTEL, TELETEXT
calculate total of stored	
data	CHECKSUM
capacity for handling	
data	CHANNEL CAPACITY
character(s)	
—per second	CPS
—used to represent	
any other character	WILDCARD
chip	
—providing	
graded choices	FUZZY CHIP
CPU	MICRO-PROCESSOR
—using superconductivity	HYBRID CHIP
circle on storage disc	TRACK
circuit board	BREADBOARD
collection of	
—data in files	DATABASE

stored	
—one after the other	SEQUENTIAL FILE
—in no particular	
order	RAM
	RANDOM ACCESS FILE
—related data	RECORD
combine files in same order	MERGE
communications	COMMS
—net with additional	
services	VAD
	VALUE-ADDED DATA
compress data	PACK, SQUEEZE
computer	
—aided	
design	CAD
typesetting	CAT
—assisted	
instruction	CAI
learning	CAL
—club	BCS
—controller	OPERATOR
—integrated	
business	CIB
manufacturing	CIM
—hypothetical	TURING MACHINE
—language	
recorder	CLR
translator	CLT
—languages	ADA, ALGOL, BASIC, C
	COBOL, FOCUS, FORTH, FORTRAN
	LISP, LOGO, LUCID, MODUL, PASCAL
	PISTOL, POWERHOUSE, PROLOG
	REPORT PROGRAM GENERATOR, RPG
	SIMULA, SMART, SNOBOL
	UNIX, ZENIX
—managed instruction	CMI
—on a chip	TRANSPUTER
—oriented language	COL
—output microfilm	COM
—providing 'intelligent'	
choices	FUZZY COMPUTER
computers	ACER, ALCATEL, ALTOS
	AMDAHL, AMDEX, AMSTRAD, AMT
	APOLLO, APPLE, APRICOT, AST, ATARI
	ATT, BULL, BURROUGHS, BUSINESSLAND
	CANON, COMMODORE
	COMPAQ, COMPUTERLAND
	COMPUTERVISION, CONTROL DATA
	CONVEX, CORDATA, CRAY, DAP
	DATA GENERAL, DATAVUE, DEC, DELL
	DG, DIGITAL EQUIPMENT, ELONEX
	EPSON, ERICSON, ESPRIT, EVEREX
	FRANKLIN, GOULD, GRID, HARRIS
	HEWLETT-PACKARD, HITACHI
	HONEYWELL (BULL), HYUNDAI, IBM
	INTERGRAPH, KAYPRO, LEADING EDGE

MITAC, MITSUBISHI, NAS, NCR, NEC
NIXDORF, NOKIA DATA, NORSK DATA
OLIVETTI, OSBORNE, PRIME, SAMSUNG
SHARP, SIEMENS, SINCLAIR, SPERRY
SUN, TANDEM, TANDON, TANDY
TATUNG, TELEVIDEO
TEXAS INSTRUMENTS, TOSHIBA
TULIP, UNISYS, VICTOR
WANG, WYSE, XIOS, ZENITH

computerised	
—document store	FAXBOX
—scanner	CAT, CT
connection to other	
appliances	CHANNEL, INTERFACE
	MODEM
continuous repetition	RECURSION
control	
—program for microcomputers	CPM
—signal to move all bits	
one place	SHIFT REGISTER
correct fault	DEBUG
data	
—directly read by	
computer	MACHINE READABLE
—fed into computer	INPUT
—of variable quantities	ANALOG(UE)
—which has been processed	OUTPUT
database accessible from	
several routes	RELATIONAL DATABASE
delete stored data	CLEAR, ERASE, ZAP
designed for a particular	
purpose	DEDICATED
desk-top publishing	DTP
device(s)	
—attached to computer	PERIPHERAL
—controlled by another	SLAVE
—for	
converting one language	
to another	TRANSLATOR
drawing on screen	LIGHT PEN
giving instructions	
to computer	CONSOLE, JOYSTICK
	KEYBOARD, LIGHT-PEN
	MOUSE
handling music	MIDI
reading	
—data	READ HEAD
—and writing data	READ/WRITE HEAD
transcribing data from	
input source	READER, SCANNER
turning disks	DISK DRIVE
which work together	
without special	
adaptation	COMPATIBLE HARDWARE
writing data	WRITE HEAD
—linked to computer	PERIPHERAL

disk	
—circle	TRACK
—division	SECTOR
—location marker	ADDRESS MARK
—operating system	DOS
doodle at keyboard	NOODLE
easy to use	USER-FRIENDLY
eight bits	BYTE
electronic data-processing	EDP
enter command by mouse	CLICK
erasable program	
—keyed access	KEPROM
—read-only memory	EPROM
error(s)	BUG, VIRUS
extraction of data	OUTPUT, EXPUT
fail	CRASH, GO DOWN
	MALFUNCTION
fault	BUG, MALFUNCTION
floating-point calculations	
per second	FLOPS
garbage in, garbage out	GIGO
group of	
—bytes	BLOCK, PACKET
—characters	STRING
—interrelated units	
controlled by one CPU	SYSTEM
hand-held control	JOYSTICK
	LIGHT-PEN, MOUSE
hardware announced but	
not available for purchase	VAPOURWARE
heart of the computer	MICRO-PROCESSOR
hit keys at random	NOODLE
holding area	BUFFER
horizontal array of characters	ROW
IBM	BIG BLUE
in operation	UP
Industry Standard Architecture	ISA
information	
—entered	INPUT
—received	EXPUT, OUTPUT
input/output	
—device	TERMINAL
—point in system	(WORK)STATION
—system	BIOS
instruction	
—causing operation to be	
carried out	OPERAND
—in a program	CODE
—to a program	COMMAND
interaction between user and	
computer by	
visual prompts	GRAPHIC USER INTERFACE
	GUI
key	
—generating a function	CONTROL KEY
—to enter instructions	ENTER

kilobyte (1024 bytes)	K
language	
—immediately understood	
by computer	MACHINE CODE
	MACHINE LANGUAGE
—not requiring knowledge	
of machine	
code	HIGH LEVEL LANGUAGE
	PROGRAMMING LANGUAGE
	SOURCE PROGRAM
—symbolic	LOW-LEVEL LANGUAGE
laptop computer (US)	TRASH
large computer	MAINFRAME
	SUPERCOMPUTER
light-emitting diode	LED
liquid-crystal diode	LCD
list of program options	MENU
load program(me)	(RE-)BOOT
local area network	LAN
location and presentation	
of data	RETRIEVAL
machinery	HARDWARE
main memory	PRIMARY STORAGE UNIT
maximum throughput	RATED THROUGHPUT
measure of storage	
capacity	K, KILOBYTE
(see also **measures** —information)	
medium-sized computer	MINI-(COMPUTER)
memory used by two CPUs	SHARED MEMORY
micro	
—channel architecture	MCA
—processing unit	MPU
million	
—bits	MEGABIT
—instructions per second	MIPS
—million bits	TERABIT
miniaturised circuit	PCB
	PRINTED CIRCUIT BOARD
modulator-demodulator	MODEM
moveable pointer	CURSOR
move blocks of data	DUMP
moving screen display	SCROLLING
musical instrument digital interface	MIDI
neither letter nor	
number	SPECIAL SYMBOL
not working	DOWN
number of bits in	
smallest stored unit	WORD
numbering system	BINARY, OCTAL
	HEXADECIMAL
one who	
—controls computer	OPERATOR
—designs programs to	
solve problems	SYSTEMS ANALYST
—plans operating	
systems	PROGRAMMER

operating system	CPM, HELIOS, MS-DOS
	TRON, UNIX, VAX
operations on	
—data	DATA PROCESSING
—script	WORD PROCESSING
operator	LIVEWARE
optical character reader	OCR
output	EXPUT
—connecting point	PORT
—device	PRINTER, SCREEN
	TURTLE
—from printer	HARD COPY
—to screen	SOFT COPY
parallel processing in units	DATAFLOW
part of	
—screen running	
separate program	WINDOW
—store used for notes	SCRATCH-PAD
people as part of the system	HUMANWARE
pertaining to data in	
—numbers	DIGITAL
—variable quantities	ANALOG(UE)
pictorial information	GRAPHICS
point in system where	
—data is input	
or received	TERMINAL
	(WORK)STATION
—different	
parts are linked	INTERFACE
portable computer	LAPTOP
printed output	HARD COPY
processed information	OUTPUT
	READOUT
processing jobs in	
sequence	BATCH PROCESSING
processor	CPU
program	SOFTWARE
—controlling	
input/output, etc	OPERATING SYSTEM
—designed to	
counteract	
bogusware	ANTIVIRUS, VACCINE
—diagram	FLOWCHART
—of general application	PACKAGE
—supplied with	
computer	SYSTEM SOFTWARE
—which	
can be used on	
different	
machines	PORTABLE PROGRAM
damages or	
destroys others	BOGUSWARE
	LOGIC BOMB
	PHANTOM BUG
	TROJAN HORSE, VIRUS, WORM
	(see virus *below)*

prepares data for further processing	PREPROCESSOR
translates other languages to machine code	
—before use	COMPILER
—during use	ASSEMBLER
programmable read-only memory	PROM
random access memory	RAM
rate	
—at which data can be transmitted	THROUGHPUT
—of transmission	BAUD
read-only memory	ROM
re-arrange data	EDIT
recoding to reduce number of symbols	CHUNKING
reduced instruction set computer	RISC
refuse to respond to commands	LOCK UP
representation of one system by another	SIMULATION
rules	
—governing communication between computers	PROTOCOL
—of language	SYNTAX
screen	MONITOR, VDU
—display	SOFT COPY
—drawing instrument	LIGHT PEN, MOUSE
secret code for access	PASSWORD
section of	
—disk	SECTOR, TRACK
—operating system	SYSTEMS PROGRAM
—program	SUBPROGRAM (SUB)ROUTINE
—record	FIELD
set	
—of	
commands	PROGRAM(ME)
instructions	PROGRAM(ME)
—starting values	INITIALISE
simultaneous use of facilities	(NETWORK) RESOURCE SHARING
slot-in circuit board	CARD
small	
—computer	LAPTOP, MICRO(-COMPUTER) PC, PERSONAL COMPUTER WORKSTATION
—piece of silica with etched circuits	CHIP
software	
—announced but not available for purchase	VAPOURWARE
—for a particular application	VERTICAL SOFTWARE

sorting technique	BUBBLE SORT SHELL-METZNER SORT
spacing of pixels	DOT PITCH
speed	BPS
—computer	MIPS
—printer	CPS, PPM
start of	
—message	SOM
—text	STX
start-up program	BOOT(STRAP)
storage	MEMORY
—device	BUFFER, DISKETTE FLOPPY DISK, HARD DISK MAGNETIC DISK, MAGNETIC DRUM MAGNETIC TAPE WINCHESTER DRIVE
—immediately available	ONLINE STORAGE
store	
—accessed by keywords	ASSOCIATIVE STORE
—with ferrite rings	CORE STORE
stored program that cannot be altered	MICRO-PROGRAM
suitable for learners	ENTRY-LEVEL
symbol	
—that can be processed	CHARACTER
—on screen	ICON
system	
—capable of learning	NEURAL NET(WORK)
—for building identikit pictures from stored data	E-FIT
—of linked computer and terminals	NETWORK
—operator	SYSOP
—permitting changes without disturbing existing system	OPEN-ENDED SYSTEM
several users at once	TIME SHARING
—processing several items of data at once	NEURAL NET(WORK)
—requiring operator to make adjustments	OPEN LOOP
—which is easy to operate	USER-FRIENDLY
—with decision-making ability	EXPERT SYSTEM INTELLIGENT KNOWLEDGE-BASED SYSTEM IKBS
transmission	
—between computers	PACKET SWITCHING
—of data via telephone lines	EDI ELECTRONIC DATA INTERCHANGE

temporary store	BUFFER
terminal	
—distant from CPU	REMOTE TERMINAL
—in a network	NODE
time taken	
—for complete operation	THROUGHPUT
—to act on a command	RESPONSE TIME
transfer data from	
—computer to	
another system	PORT
storage device	WRITE
—memory to screen	READ
Transient Program Area	TPA
translate machine instructions	DECODE
unauthorised user	HACKER
under the control of the CPU	ONLINE
unerasable memory	FIRMWARE
unit of	
—information	BIT
(*see also* **measures** -information)	
—screen area	PIXEL
unobtainable software	
or hardware	VAPOURWARE
unprocessed information	RAW DATA
use of store	
—by use of keywords	KEYED ACCESS
—in	
any order	RANDOM ACCESS
sequence	SEQUENTIAL ACCESS
using same machine	
code	SOFTWARE COMPATIBLE
vertical array of characters	COLUMN
virus	ARMAGEDDON, CASCADE
	DARK AVENGER, DATACRIME
	FISH 6, FRODO, FU MANCHU
	ISRAEL DEFENCE FORCE
	JERUSALEM, JOKER, LIBERTY
	VACCINIA, VICTOR, WHALE
viruses, etc	BOGUSWARE
visual display unit	VDU
what you see is what you get	WYSIWYG
wide area network	WAN
write once, read many	WORM
Congo	RCB
capital	BRAZZAVILLE
coin	FRANC
constellations	
Northern hemisphere	
—Arrow	SAGITTA
—Berenice's Hair	COMA BERENICE
—Big Dipper	GREAT BEAR
—Bull	TAURUS
—Charioteer	AURIGA
—Charles's wain	GREAT BEAR, PLOUGH
	URSA MAJOR
—Colt	EQUULEUS

—Crab	CANCER
—Cynosure	URSA MINOR
—Dolphin	DELPHINUS
—Dragon	DRACO
—Eagle	AQUILA
—Fishes	PISCES
—Giraffe	CAMELOPARDALIS
—Great Bear	CHARLES'S WAIN
	PLOUGH
	URSA MAJOR
—Greater Dog	CANIS MAJOR
—Hercules	HERCULES
—Herdsman	BOOTES
—Hunter	ORION
—Hunting dog	CANES VENATICI
—Lesser	
Bear	LESSER WAIN
	URSA MINOR
	WAG(G)ON
Dog	CANIS MINOR
Lion	LEO MINOR
—Lion	LEO
—Lizard	LACERTA
—Lynx	LYNX
—Lyre	LYRA
—Milky Way	VIA LACTEA
—Northern Crown	CORONA BOREALIS
—Ox-driver	BOOTES
—Plough	CHARLE'S WAIN
	GREAT BEAR
	URSA MAJOR
—Ram	ARIES
—Serpent	SERPENS CAPUT
holder	OPHIUCHUS
—Seven Stars	ORION
—Sextant	SEXTANS
—Swan	CYGNUS
—Triangle	TRIANGULUM
—Twins	GEMINI
—Virgin	VIRGO
—Wag(g)on	LESSER BEAR
	LESSER WAIN
	URSA MINOR
—Wag(g)oner	AURIGA
—Water-monster	HYDRA
—Winged horse	PEGASUS
—others	ANDROMEDA, CASSIOPEIA
	CEPHEUS, CETUS
	MONOCEROS, VULPECULUS
Southern hemisphere	
—Archer	SAGITTARIUS
—Argo's stern	PUPPIS
—Balance	LIBRA
—Bird of Paradise	APUS
—Centaur	CENTAURUS
—Chameleon	CHAMAELEON

—Clock	HOROLOGIUM	—fat to dough	SHORTEN
—Crane	GRUS	—flavour	SEASON
—Crater	CRATER	—yeast	LEAVEN, RAISE
—Cross	CRUX	adding liquid to dry mixture	BINDING
—Crow	CORVUS	almond paste	MARZIPAN
—Dove	COLUMBA	appetiser	RELISH
—Eagle	AQUILA	appetisers	HORS D'OEUVRE
—Easel	PICTOR	—Greek	MEZE
—Fishes	PISCES	—Spanish	TAPAS
—Fly	MUSCA	arachis oil	PEANUT OIL
—Flying fish	VOLANS	aromatic seeds	ANISE(ED)
—four stars	SOUTHERN CROSS	artificial sweetener	SACCHARIN
	URSA (MAJOR)	bake eggs	SHIR(R)
—Goat	CAPRICORNUS	baked	
—Graving-tool	CAELUM	—in paper case	EN PAPILLOTE
—Hare	LEPUS	—souffle	FONDUE
—Hunter	ORION	baking pastry without	
—Indian	INDUS	filling	BAKING BLIND
—Keel	CARINA	ball of dough, boiled	DUMPLING
—Level	NORMA	batter pudding	YORKSHIRE PUDDING
—Lion	LEO	bean curd	TOFU
—Microscope	MICROSCOPIUM	beans, peas, etc	PULSES
—Net	RETICULUM		(*see* **pulses**)
—Peacock	PAVO	beat	WHIP, WHISK
—Pump	ANTLIA	—to a smooth consistency	CREAM
—Rule	NORMA	—together fat and sugar	CREAM
—Sail	VELA	—while cooking (eggs)	SCRAMBLE
—Scales	LIBRA	become clear	FINE
—Scorpion	SCORPIO, SCORPIUS	blend by gently turning in	FOLD
—Sculptor	SCULPTOR	boil	
—Serpent	SERPENS CAUDA	—down	DECOCT
—Seven Stars	ORION	—gently	SIMMER
—Shield	SCUTUM SOBIESKI	—slightly	BLANCH, CODDLE
—Southern			PARBOIL
Crown	CORONA AUSTRINA	boiled	
Fish	PISCIS AUSTRINUS	—fruit and sugar	CONSERVE, JAM
Triangle	TRIANGULUM AUSTRALE		PRESERVE, MARMALADE
—Swordfish	DORADO	—or stewed meat	BOUILLI
—Table	MENSA	braised and served in	
—Telescope	TELESCOPIUM	brown sauce	A LA MODE
—Triangle	TRIANGULUM	bread	(*see separate entry*)
—Veil	VELA	break	
—Virgin	VIRGO	—into crumbs	CRUMB
—Water		—up fat in milk	HOMOGENISE
carrier	AQUARIUS	brew tea	MASH
monster	HYDRA	brine solution	PICKLE
—Wolf	LUPUS	broil	GRILL
—others	ARA, ARGO, CETUS, ERIDANUS	—with seasoning	DEVIL
	FORNAX, HYDRUS, OCTANS	browning meat quickly	
	PHOENIX, PYXIS, SOUTHERN FISH	before grilling or roasting	SEARING

cookery

		bunch or sachet of herbs	BOUQUET GARNI
acid liquid from fermentation	VINEGAR		FAGGOT
add		buffet of various dishes	SMORGASBORD
—dash of brandy, etc	LACE, NEEDLE	butter substitute	MAGARINE
—decoration	GARNISH	cake	(*see separate entry*)
—dressing	DRESS	can	PRESERVE

candied stalks	ANGELICA
cassava starch	TAPIOCA
cheese dishes	(see separate entry)
cheese vat	CHESSEL
chickpea paste	MOUM(O)US, HUMMUS
chilled	FRAPPE
chip(ped potato)	FRENCH FRY
chips, hot dogs, etc	JUNK FOOD
chocolate	
—substitute	CAROB
—used for covering	COVERTURE
chop into	
—small pieces	MINCE
—very small pieces	HASH
chopped meats, eggs, etc	SALMAGUNDI
chopped-up food	HASH
clarified butter	GHEE, GHI
coat with	
—flour	FLOUR
—sugar	CANDY, CRYSTALLISE
coated with egg and breadcrumbs	A L'ANGLAISE
coating	
—inside of mould with jelly	MASKING
—meat etc with glaze	MASKING
cold	
—dish glazed with aspic	GALANTINE
—meats	CHARCUTERIE
—mixed vegetables	SALAD
colouring	COCHINEAL, SAFFRON TURMERIC
—for gravy	BROWNING
combining ingredients so that mixture retains lightness	FOLDING IN
concentrate by boiling	DECOCT
concentrated solution of sugar and water	SYRUP
condiment	MUSTARD, PEPPER SALT, VINEGAR
container for	
—cold liquid	COOLER
—hot or cold liquid	THERMOS FLASK
conversion of sugar to alcohol	FERMENTATION
cook	
—by	
direct heat	BROIL
frying	
—gently while stirring	SCRAMBLE
—in little fat	SAUTE
—rapidly while stirring	STIR-FRY
—till crisp	FRIZZLE
grilling or frying	DEVIL
light steaming	DUM
partly boiling	PARBOIL
radiant heat	GRILL
simmering	POACH
slow simmering	BRAISE, STEW
—in	
boiling water	BOIL
closed pan	BRAISE
fat or oil in a pan	(DEEP-)FRY
front of fire	ROAST
oven	BAKE, ROAST
pressurised vessel	PRESSURE-COOK
saucepan with fat	POT-ROAST
spicy sauce	BARBECUE
stewpan	CASSEROLE
syrup	CANDY
water below boiling	POACH, SIMMER
—over	
boiling water	STEAM
hot coals	BROIL
—in the open air	BARBECUE, BBQ
—partially	BLANCH, PARBOIL PRECOOK
—slowly in	
—fat	SWEAT
—heatproof dish	CASSEROLE
without boiling	CODDLE
cooked	
—flour and fat	ROUX
—in	
butter and herbs (fish)	MEUNIERE
oil, garlic and tomatoes	PROVENCALE
olive oil	A LA GRECQUE
onions	LYONNAISE
red wine	BOURGUIGNONNE
white wine (fish)	MARINIERE
—on a skewer	EN BROCHETTE
—with	
breadcrumbs or cheese	AU GRATIN GRATINE
brown sugar	BRULE
cider and cream	A LA NORMANDE
potatoes	PARMENTIER
tomatoes, etc	CACCIATORE
tomatoes, onions, etc	NICOISE
cooking	
—appliance	HOTPLATE (MICROWAVE) OVEN PRIMUS, RANGE, ROTISSERIE SPIT, STOVE
—fat	BUTTER, DRIPPING, LARD (OLEO)MARGARINE, SHEA BUTTER
Indian	GHEE, GHI, VANASPATI
—high quality	HAUTE CUISINE
—method (Indian)	TANDOORI
—oil	CORN OIL, COTTONSEED OIL OLIVE OIL, PALM OIL SUNFLOWER OIL, TRAIN OIL WHALE OIL

—particular style	CUISINE
—simple style	CUISINE MINCEUR
	LEAN CUISINE
	NOUVELLE CUISINE
—very high quality	CORDON BLEU
Cornish pasty	OGGY
course following fish course	ENTREE
cover with	
—crumbs	CRUMB
—icing	ICE
—sugar	FROST
covered with breadcrumbs	
or cheese	AU GRATIN
covering breast of poultry	
with pieces of bacon	BARDING
cream	
—separating pan	CREAMER
—thick	DOUBLE CEAM
—thickened by heating	CLOTTED CREAM
—thin	POURING CREAM
	SINGLE CREAM
—treated with lactic acid	(SOUR(ED)) CREAM
crisp	
—cooked skin of meat	CRACKLING
—residue of fat	CRACKLING
crumbs from stale bread	RASPINGS
crust of crumbs or cheese	GRATIN
cube of dried meat extract	BOUILLON CUBE
cup-shaped mould	TIMBALE
cure	
—by smoking	SMOKE
—with salt and smoke	KIPPER
curry with vinegar	VINDALOO
cut	
—into small cubes	CUBE, DICE
—into slices	FILLET
—surface into chequer pattern	CUBE
decorating	
—cake	ICING, PIPING
—edge of	
glass	FROSTING
pastry	CRIMPING, SCALLOPING
—for appearance	GARNISHING, GLAZING
—with egg white etc	GLAZING
dehydrate while frozen	DRY-FREEZE
delicacy	KICKSHAW
diced meat and vegetables	
in thick sauce	SALPICON
dietary requirements	CARBOHYDRATE
	FAT, FIBRE, MINERALS
	PROTEIN, SUGAR
	TRACE ELEMENTS, VITAMIN
dilute cooking juices	
with wine, etc	DEGLAZE
dip	
—into liquid	DUNK

—made from avocado	GUAC(H)AMOLE
dish of fried food	FRY(-UP)
	MIXED GRILL
distilling apparatus	STILL
dough with fat	PASTE, PASTRY
draw off liquid	DECANT
dress meat with fat	LARD
dressing	
—for salad	MAYONNAISE
	SALAD CREAM
	SALAD OIL
—with added pickle	RUSSIAN DRESSING
	(*see also* **sauces**)
dried	
—beans, peas, etc	PULSES
—breadcrumbs	RASPINGS
—seed(s)	BACCA(E)
dry rusk	BISCOTTE
drying tray	FLAKE
dumplings (China)	WANTAN, WONTON
	WUNTUN
dye for foodstuffs	COCHINEAL
earthenware casserole	
dish	TERRINE
edible	
—entrails	(M)UMBLES
—fat	SHORTENING
—lichen	ICELAND MOSS
—seaweed	CARRAGEEN, DULSE
	IRISH MOSS, LAVER
—snail	ESCARGOT, ROMAN SNAIL
egg dishes	(*see separate entry*)
emulsifying agent	AGAR(-AGAR)
encased in pastry	EN CROUTE
energy-value of food	(KILO)CALORIE
enzyme for curdling	
milk	RENNET, RENNIN
evaporate by boiling	DECOCT, REDUCE
extract	
—essence	DECOCT
—of juices, etc	ESSENCE
—used for curdling milk	RENNET
extracting	
—fat by melting	RENDERING
—flavour	INFUSING
fancy dish	CONFECTION, KICKSHAW
fast food	CONVENIENCE FOOD
	TAKEAWAY FOOD
fat	
—from	
cocoa beans	CACAO BUTTER
	COCOA BUTTER
pigs	LARD
roasting meat	DRIPPING
—liquid at room	
temperature	MONO-UNSATURATED

—liquid when refrigerated	POLY-UNSATURATED
—solid at room temperature	SATURATED
fermented milk	YOG(H)URT
	YOGHOURT
fermenting agent	FERMENT, YEAST
fine flour or meal	FARINA
finely ground	
—sugar	CASTER SUGAR
	ICING SUGAR
—wheat	FLOUR
fish dishes	(see separate entry)
flat metal	
—surface for cooking	GRIDDLE
—tray	BAKING TRAY
flavouring	CONDIMENT, ZEST
—additive	MONOSODIUM GLUTAMATE
—bitter	ALMOND, JUNIPER
—caffeine	COLA, KOLA
—coffee	MOCHA
—crocus	SAFFRON
—dried flowers	MELITOT
—for tea	JASMINE
—from	
American laurel	SASSAFRAS
Artemisia	TARRAGON
Mexican orchid	VANILLA
Sesamum indicum	SESAME
Smilax	SARSAPARILLA
Tonka beans	C(O)UMARIN
Trigonella	FENUGREEK
—ginger	JAMAICA GINGER
—lemon	LEMON THYME
—Mexican orchid	VANILLA
—mint	PENNYROYAL
—oil	ESSENTIAL OIL
—peppermint	PEPPERMINT OIL
—seeds	ANISEED, CARAWAY
—sweet	C(O)UMARIN, MELILOT
	(see also herbs, spices)
flour	
—and water paste	PASTA
—eggs, milk, etc	BATTER
—of cassava	MANDIOC(C)A, MANIHOC
	MANIHOT, MANIOC(A)
—with raising agent	SELF-RAISING FLOUR
—without raising agent	PLAIN FLOUR
food	
—cooked	
in	
—clay oven	TANDOORI
—cup-shaped mould	TIMBALE
—heatproof dish	CASSEROLE, TERRINE
on metal frame	GRILL

—dipped into liquid	SOP
—grilled on skewer	BROCHETTE, KEBAB
—prepared	CUISINE
by expert chef	CORDON BLEU
—ready for eating	DELICATESSEN
—reduced to a pulp	PUREE
—taken to work	SNAP
—tossed in shallow fat	SAUTE
—with low nutritional value	JUNK FOOD
force through nozzle	PIPE
forcemeat	FARCE
forcing cream etc through a nozzle	PIPING
form smooth layer	CREAM
firm to the teeth (pasta)	AL DENTE
fragrance	BOUQUET
freshly-chopped herbs	FINES HERBES
fried	
—batter with filling	FRITTER
—lightly	SAUTE
fruit	
—juice	SYRUP
—preserve	CONSERVE
fruits	(see separate entry)
game	(see poultry)
game stock	FUMET
garnish	DRESS
—for chicken dish	BONNE FEMME
—on surface	TOPPING
garnished with	
—crayfish	A LA NANTUA
—mushrooms etc	FORESTIERE
—onions, mushrooms, etc	BONNE FEMME
—potatoes	PARMENTIER
—vegetable strips	JULIENNE
—vegetables	JARDINIERE
—white grapes	VERONIQUE
giving body to gravy etc	THICKENING
glazed	GLACE
—with sugar	BRULE
golden syrup	TREACLE
goose liver	FOIE GRAS
—paste	PATE DE FOIE GRAS
gravy with ham juices	RED EYE GRAVY
greased paper wrapper	PAPILLOTE
grill	BROIL, DEVIL
grind very fine	FLOUR
gum used in confectionery	GUM ACACIA
	GUM ARABIC
hard	
—animal fat	SUET
—white icing	ROYAL ICING
heat	
—sugar into caramel	CARAMELISE
—to near boiling	SCALD

—with spices	MULL
heatproof dish	CASSEROLE
high	
—fibre food	ROUGHAGE
—standard cookery	HAUTE CUISINE
	CORDON BLEU
vegetarian	CORDON VERT
hors d'oeuvres	
—mixed	ANTIPASTO(MISTO)
—Russian	ZAKUSKI
hot	
—cake	PANCAKE
—curry	MADRAS, VINDALOO
—sandwich of cheese	
and ham	CROQUE-MONSIEUR
—seasoning	CURRY, MUSTARD
	PEPPER
ice a cake	FROST
icing	FROSTING
immerse briefly in	
boiling water	BLANCH
in pastry	EN CROUTE
Indian cooking	(*see* **Indian**)
individual Yorkshire	
pudding	POPOVER
inserting strips of fat into	
meat or poultry	LARDING
instructions for making dish	RECIPE
instrument for	
testing food	TENDEROMETER
insulated container	COOLER, HAYBOX
	THERMOS FLASK
introduce air	AERATE
jelly	GEL
—from	
cooked feet of	
—calves	CALF'S FOOT JELLY
—ox or cow	COW HEEL JELLY
cranberries	CRANBERRY JELLY
turtle	CALIPASH, CALIPEE
wild apples	CRAB APPLE JELLY
juice of	
—sugar cane	SYRUP
—unripe fruit	VERJUICE
kebab	SHASHLI(C)K
large	
—dish	TRENCHER
—prawn	KING PRAWN
—soup bowl	TUREEN
leg of cooked meat	GIGOT
liaison of flour and butter	BEURRE MANIE
light	
—dish with	
whipped cream, etc	MOUSSE
white of egg	SOUFFLE
—meal	COLLATION

liquor	
—from	
buttermaking	BUTTERMILK
meat, etc simmered in water	STOCK
thawing	DRIP
—in which meat etc	
has been cooked	STOCK
is steeped	MARINADE
—used to produce shiny coating	GLAZE
made	
—with hazel nuts	NOISETTE
—without	
meat	PAREVE
milk	PAREVE
make	
—butter by agitating milk	CHURN
—crisp	TOAST, FRIZZLE
—light	LEAVEN, RAISE
—tender by beating	TENDERISE
main dish	ENTREE
marchpane	MARZIPAN
meat	
—and vegetables cooked	
in liquid	STEW
—boiled	BOUILLI
—medium-cooked	A POINT
—set in aspic	CHAUDFROID
	GALANTINE
—underdone	AU BLEU, RARE
—well done	BIEN CUIT
	(*see also separate entry*)
meat dishes	(*see* **meat dishes**)
medium-cooked (meat)	A POINT
melted butter with	
seasoning	DRAWN BUTTER
metal frame for cooking on	GRID(IRON)
	GRILL
milk	
—dishes	CHERRICURDS, CUSTARD
	JUNKET, MACARONI PUDDING
	RICE PUDDING, SAGO PUDDING
	SEMOLINA PUDDING
—dried	POWDERED MILK
—fat content	CREAM
—fermented	YOG(H)URT, YOGHOURT
—heat-treated	PASTEURISED
	STERILISED
—partly concentrated	EVAPORATED
—powdered with malted	
cereal	MALTED MILK
—sour	CLABBER
—thick part	CURD
—thickened and sweetened	CONDENSED
—thin part	WHEY
—with little fat	SEMI-SKIMMED
—without fat	SKIMMED

minerals and trace elements	CALCIUM, COPPER FLUORINE, IODINE, IRON MAGNESIUM, MANGANESE PHOSPORUS, POTASSIUM SELENIUM, SODIUM, ZINC
mix	
—by tossing	TOSS
—to smooth texture	BLEND, CREAM
—with minimum liquid	BIND
mixed foods, fried	FRITTO MISTO MIXED GRILL
mixture of	
—cooked meat, etc used as filling	SALPICON
—flour and water	DOUGH
—fruits, brandy, etc	MINCEMEAT
—oil, vinegar etc for steeping	MARINADE
—vegetables	MIREPOIX
or fruit in jelly	MACEDOINE
moisten with fat during roasting	BASTE
mustard	
—hot	ENGLISH MUSTARD
—with vinegar	FRENCH MUSTARD
white wine	DIJON MUSTARD
oatmeal porridge	BROSE
outdoor meal	BARBECUE, PICNIC
oil from skin of citrus fruit	ZEST
open sandwich	SMORREBROD
over-brew tea	STEW
palm-tree shoots	PALM HEARTS
pancake	HOTCAKE, SLAPJACK
—mixture	BATTER
—thick	FLAPJACK
—with filling	FRENCH PANCAKE
parboil	BLANCH
partially	
—boil	BLANCH, PARBOIL
—cook	PRECOOK
—frozen	FRAPPE
—sterilise	PASTEURISE
pass through sieve	SIEVE, SIFT, STRAIN
pasta	(see separate entry)
paste	PATE, SPREAD
—from anchovies	ANCHOIADE
goose liver	PATE DE FOIE GRAS
peanuts	PEANUT BUTTER
pastry	(see separate entry)
peanut oil	ARACHIS OIL
peel of citrus fruit	ZEST
pertaining to	
—cooking	CULINARY

—kitchen	CULINARY
pickle	PRESERVE, SOUSE
pickled cucumber	DILL PICKLE
pickling liquid	BRAINE, SOUSE VINEGAR
picnic (US)	COOKOUT
piece of fruit etc cooked in batter	FRITTER
place fat or bacon on meat before cooking	BARD
plainly cooked	AU NATUREL
plunge in pickling liquid	SOUSE
poultry	(see separate entry)
pour	
—fat over meat while cooking	BASTE
—boiling water over to remove skin etc	SCALD
—water over food and leave to stand	STEEP
prepare food for cooking	DRESS
prepared or served with dressing of flaming liquor	FLAMBE
preserve	
—by cooling below 0°C	FREEZE
drying	CURE, DESICCATE
rapid freezing	QUICK-FREEZE
—in brine or salt	CORN, CURE, SALT
metal containers	CAN, TIN
strips	JERK
vinegar	PICKLE
—of fruit and sugar	CONSERVE, JAM JELLY, MARMALADE
preserved	
—cherry	MARAS(C)HINO
—onions etc	PICKLE
preserving liquid	PICKLE
press edged to seal	CRIMP
proteins	(see separate entry)
prunes on bacon, grilled	DEVILS ON HORSEBACK
pulp	PUREE
—by beating	MASH
passing through sieve or blender	PUREE
pure gelatine	ISINGLASS
purify	FINE
ragout of game etc	SALMI
raise	
—oven temperature before use	PREHEAT
—with yeast, etc	LEAVEN
raising agent	BAKING POWDER BICARBONATE OF SODA SALERATUS, YEAST

rare (meat)	AU BLEU
ready-prepared for consumption	CONVENIENCE FOOD
	FAST FOOD
	TAKEAWAY FOOD
real or artificial cream on food	CREME
reduce to	
—fluid consistency	LIQUIDISE
—pulp	PUREE
refined molasses	SYRUP, TREACLE
regional specialities	
—Abernethy	BISCUIT
—Aylesbury	DUCK
—Arbroath	SMOKIE
—Bakewell	TART
—Banbury	CAKE
—Bath	BUN, CHAP, OLIVER
—Cheddar	CHEESE
—Chelsea	BUN
—Cheshire	CHEESE
—Chorley	CAKE
—Cornish	CREAM, PASTY, FAIRINGS
—Cumberland	PIE
—Derby	BAKE
—Devonshire	CREAM, SPLIT
—Dundee	CAKE
—Eccles	CAKE
—Grantham	GINGERBREAD
—Irish	STEW
—Lancashire	HOTPOT
—Northumberland	SINGING HINNY
—Pontefract (Pomfret)	CAKES
—Scotch	BUN, EGG
	PANCAKE
—Shrewsbury	BISCUIT
—Welsh	RAREBIT
—Whitstable	OYSTERS
—Worcester	SAUCE
—Yorkshire	PUDDING, TEA-CAKE
re-heated food	RECHAUFFE
re-heating cooked vegetables after cooling with water	REFRESHING
remove	
—bones from	FILLET
—fat from surface of liquid	SKIM
—lumps	STRAIN
—pod, shell, etc	HULL, HUSK
	SHELL, SHUCK
—stalks, etc	TOP AND TAIL
—surface layer from liquid	SKIM
—water from	DEHYDRATE
rendered fat	DRIPPING, (LEAF)LARD
rice dishes	(see rice)
rich dish	CONFECTION

roast	
—in dry heat	PARCH
—whole	BARBECUE
roasting spit	BROACH
rod for holding meat over fire	SPIT
rolled slice of meat	ROULADE
round cake of meat or fish	RISSOLE
roughly chopped	CONCASSE
rub through sieve	PUREE
salad oil	OLIVE OIL, PEANUT OIL
salt	
—from evaporation	BAY SALT
	ROCK SALT
—solution	BRINE
—spices, etc	SEASONING
—used in baking powder	CREAM OF TARTAR
sandwich with	
—three slices of bread	CLUB SANDWICH
—two slices of bread	ROUND
sauce	DRESSING, RELISH
—for dipping	DIP
sauces	(see separate entry)
sausage in bread roll	HOT DOG
sausages	(see separate entry)
savoury	
—jelly	ASPIC
—on small piece of toast	CANAPE
—stuffing	FORCEMEAT
scald	BLANCH
score outside of meat	CRIMP
scrap of food	ORT
season highly	DEVIL
seasoned	
—filling mixture	DRESSING, STUFFING
—with sugar and lemon juice	SWEET-AND-SOUR
sedge roots	GALINGALE
sediment	GROUT, LEES
seeds of pea family	PULSES
segment of sausage chain	LINK
separate	
—fat from liquid	BREAK
—into flakes	FLAKE
—kernels from casing	HULL, HUSK, SHELL
serve on wooden board	PLANK
sesame	TIL
—seed paste	HOUM(O)US, HUMMUS
	TAHINA, TAHINI
setting agent	PECTIN
sift through fine mesh	BOLT
silver-coloured ball for decoration	DRAGEE
sherbet	SORBET
simmer eggs	CODDLE
skin of citrus fruit	ZEST

slash fish etc to allow heat to penetrate	CRIMP, SCORE
slice	
—finely	SHRED
—of bread	ROUND
small	
—bulb of garlic	CLOVE
—bunch of herbs	BOUQUET GARNI
—cake decorations	HUNDREDS AND THOUSANDS
—circular piece of fish or meat	MEDALLION
—cucumber	GHERKIN
—patty or pastry case	BOUCHE(E)
—pickled onion	PEARL ONION
—piece of food	CHIP, ORT
—crumbed and deep-fried	CROQUETTE
—for dipping	DUNK
meat	CALLOP, ESCALOPE
crisp pork fat	SCRATCHINGS
—(American)	CRACKNEL
raw vegetables	CRUDITES
—vol-au-vent	BOUCHEE
smear with lard	LARD
smooth preparation for spreading	PASTE, PATE, SPREAD
soak in blended liquid	MARINADE, MARINATE
soft	
—food	PAP, SOPS
—roe	MILT
soften in liquid	MACERATE
soldier's emergency food	IRON RATION
souffle served with bread crumbs	FONDUE
sour cream (Russia)	SMETANA, SMETANE
songbird used for food	BECCAFICO
soup	(see separate entry)
sour milk	CLABBER
spiced cassava juice	CASSAREEP
split open bird and cook	SPATCHCOCK
sprinkle with	SPARGE
—condiment, etc	PEPPER
—flour, sugar, etc	DREDGE
sprinkled with brandy and ignited	FLAMBE, FLAMED
squeeze juice from fruit	REAM
stack milk-curd slices	CHEFFAR
starch	FARINA
—for thickening	ARROWROOT
—from	
cassava	TAPIOCA
palm pith	SAGO
starchy root-stock	CASSAVA
steep in liquor	INFUSE, MACERATE
	MARINATE

stew	
—in a closed vessel	BRAISE
stock	FRICASSEE
—with seasoning	JUG(G)
stewed lentils	DA(H)L, DHAL
stews	(see separate entry)
stir	
—during cooking	SCRAMBLE
—or mix	SWIZZLE
stock	BOUILLON
stoneware cooking pot with heating element	CROCKPOT
store in freezer	DEEP-FREEZE
strain through fine cloth	TAMMY
strip of	
—fat for dressing	LARDO(O)N
laid over meat	BARD(E)
—icing	PIPIG
strong broth	BOUILLON
study of nutrition	DIETETICS
stuff	
—bird with forcemeat	FARCE
—with bacon or pork	LARD
stuffed	FARCI(E)
stuffing	FARCE, FORCEMEAT
style of cooking	CUISINE
substance	
—causing fermentation	FERMENT, LEAVEN
gelling	GEL(L)ANT
—used for increasing bulk of food	EXTENDER
raising bread, etc	LEAVEN
thickening	LIAISON
sugar	(see separate entry)
sweet	
—covering for cakes	ICING
—dish	DESSERT, PUDDING
	(see dessert)
—malt and water syrup	MALT EXTRACT
sweetened jelly	GELATIN(E)
sweetener	SACCHARIN, SUGAR, SYRUP
syrup from	
—cane sugar	GOLDEN SYRUP
—maize	CORN SYRUP
—used for sweetening	GLYCERINE
table with openings over boiling water	STEAM TABLE
tasteless liquid food	SLOP
tasty morsel	BONNE BOUCHE
test for fat content of milk	BABCOCK TEST
thick	
—cream	DOUBLE CREAM

—dip	FONDUE	—making pastry	PASTRY CUTTER
—pancake	FLAPJACK		ROLLING PIN
thicken		—mixer	BLENDER
—by boiling	DECOCT, REDUCE		FOOD PROCESSOR, WHISK
—like jelly	GEL	—oven used with	
thickening		pre-heated bricks	
—agent	LIAISON	or coals	DUTCH OVEN
—of fat and flour	ROUX	—ovenproof dish	CASSEROLE
—starch	TAPIOCA	—pot-stand	TRIVET
thin		—preparing vegetables	(POTATO) PEELER
—cream	POURING CREAM	—roasting-tin used in	
	SINGLE CREAM	front of open fire	DUTCH OVEN
—porridge	GRUEL	—rotating bar for roasting	BROACH, SPIT
—strip of food	ALUMETTE	—serving	FORK, KNIFE, SLICE
tie up (bird) for cooking	TRUSS		SPATULA, SPOON
treat with		—shell-shaped dish	COQUILLE
—boiling water or steam,	SCALD	—slicer for fruit and vegetables	MANDOLIN
—salt or brine	CURE, SALT	—small	
uncooked	AU NATUREL	baking-dish	RAMEKIN
underdone	RARE, SAIGNANT		RAMEQUIN
utensils		long-handled frying-pan	SKILLET
—baking dish		mould	DARIOLE
for one person	RAMAKIN, RAMEKIN	spit or skewer	BROCHETTE
	RAMEQUIN	—spit	BROACH
with close-fitting lid	CASSEROLE	—sprinkling	CASTER, DREDGER
—beater	BLENDER	—stewpan	CASSEROLE
	FOOD PROCESSOR	—straining	COLANDER, SALAD SHAKER
	MIXER, WHISK		SIEVE, STRAINER
—broad serving-knife	SLICE	—weighing	SCALES, (SPRING) BALANCE
—broiling frame	GRIDIRON, GRILL	vegetable	
—Chinese frying-pan	WO(C)K	—garnish	JARDINIERE
—cooking pot	SAUCEPAN	—salad in Russian dressing	RUSSIAN SALAD
—cup-shaped mould	TIMBALE	vinegar from	
—cutting tool	(CARVING) KNIFE	—ale	ALEGAR
	CLEAVER, MINCER	—cider	CIDER VINEGAR
	SCISSORS	—solution	PICKLE
—double saucepan	BAIN-MARIE	—wine	WINE VINEGAR
—earthenware pot	TERRENE	vitamins	(see separate entry)
—flat cooking surface	BAKING SHEET	warmed-up dish	RECHAUFFE
	GRIDDLE	water-ice	SORBET
—for		well done (meat)	BIEN CUIT, PERCOLT
cooking fish	FISH KETTLE	whalemeat	MUKTUK
deep frying in fat	FRYER	with wholemeal flour	
eating rice	CHOP STICKS	and sugar	SWEETMEAL
frying	FRYING PAN, SKILLET	without raising agent	UNLEAVENED
grating	GRATER, ZESTER	wooden dish	TRENCHER
grinding	MORTAR AND PESTLE	work dough	KNEAD, MOULD
	PEPPER MILL, SALT MILL	wrapped in pastry	EN CROUTE
holding meat together	SKEWER	yeast froth	BARM
icing	PIPING BAG	young	
making stock	STOCKPOT	—corn ears	GREEN CORN
popcorn roasting	POPPER	—duck	DUCKLING
steaming	STEAMER	—goose	GOSLING
—knife with flat blunt blade	PALETTE KNIFE	—hare	LEVERET
—large cooking pot	DUTCH OVEN	**Coptic**	COP(T)
—lifting tool	SLICE, TONGS	bishop	ABBA

chapel	HAIKAL
dialect	SAHIDIC
Costa Rica	CR
capital	SAN JOSE
coin	COLON
measure (11 bushels)	FANEGA

counties

England   AVON, BEDFORDSHIRE
BERKSHIRE, BUCKINGHAMSHIRE
CAMBRIDGESHIRE, CHESHIRE
CLEVELAND, CORNWALL, CUMBRIA
DERBYSHIRE, DEVON, DORSET
DURHAM, EAST SUSSEX, ESSEX
GLOUCESTERSHIRE, GREATER LONDON
GREATER MANCHESTER, HAMPSHIRE
HEREFORD AND WORCESTER
HERTFORDSHIRE, HUMBERSIDE
ISLE OF WIGHT, KENT, LANCASHIRE
LEICESTERSHIRE, LINCOLNSHIRE
MERSEYSIDE, NORFOLK
NORTHAMPTONSHIRE
NORTHUMBERLAND
NORTH YORKSHIRE
NOTTINGHAMSHIRE
OXFORDSHIRE, SHROPSHIRE
SOMERSET, SOUTH YORKSHIRE,
STAFFORDSHIRE, SUFFOLK, SURREY
TYNE AND WEAR, WARWICKSHIRE
WEST MIDLANDS, WEST SUSSEX
WEST YORKSHIRE, WILTSHIRE

—obsolete   CUMBERLAND
HUNTINGDONSHIRE
MIDDLESEX
RUTLAND, WESTMORLAND

Ireland   CARLOW, CAVAN, CLARE
CORK, DONEGAL, DUBLIN, GALWAY
LAOIS, LEITRIM, LIMERICK
LONGFORD, LOUTH, KERRY
KILDARE, KILKENNY, MAYO, MEATH
MONAGHAN, OFFALY, ROSCOMMON
SLIGO, TIPPERARY
WATERFORD, WESTMEATH
WEXFORD, WICKLOW

Northern Ireland   ANTRIM, ARMAGH, DOWN
FERMANAGH, LONDONDERRY
TYRONE

Scotland   BORDERS, CENTRAL SCOTLAND
DUMFRIES AND GALLOWAY, FIFE
GRAMPIAN REGION
HIGHLAND REGION
LOTHIAN, ORKNEY, SHETLAND
STRATHCLYDE, TAYSIDE
WESTERN ISLES

Wales   CLYWD, DYFED, GWENT
GWYNEDD, MID-GLAMORGAN
POWYS, WEST GLAMORGAN

cricket

3 wickets with consecutive balls	HAT-TRICK
8 consecutive balls	OVER
100 runs in an innings	CENTURY
1000 runs, 100 wickets	DOUBLE
apparent but not real catch	BUMP BALL
	SPECTATOR CATCH
appeal to umpire	HOW'S THAT, OWZAT

area
  —between stumps   PITCH, WICKET
  —within 30 yards of
   wickets   FIELDING CIRCLE

ball
  —bowled
   along the ground   GRUB
   at roughly head-height   BEAMER
   slowly and high   DONKEY-DROP
   underarm
    —fast   DAISY-CUTTER
    —slow   LOB
  —from which no score
   is made   DOT-BALL
  —out of batsman's reach   WIDE
  —that
   does not pitch between
    the wickets   FULL-PITCH
     FULL-TOSS
   is
    —short-pitched and
     easy to hit   DOLLY
     HALF-VOLLEY, LONG HOP
    —unlawfully
     delivered   NO-BALL
   keeps low   DAISY-CUTTER, SHOOTER
   moves in the air   INSWINGER
     OUTSWINGER

pitches
  —at batsman's feet   YORKER
  —in or near blockhole   YORKER

turns from
  —leg to off   LEG-BREAK, LEG-CUTTER
  —off to leg   OFF-BREAK
    OFF-CUTTER

batsman sent in to
  defend until close of play   NIGHTWATCHMAN

bowler who makes good
use of seam on ball   SEAM BOWLER

bowler's
  —action   OVERARM, ROUNDARM
    UNDERARM
  —aiming mark   STUMPS, WICKET
  —approach   RUN-UP

children's cricket   KANGA CRICKET
   KWIK CRICKET

close innings before
all wickets have fallen   DECLARE

continue with second innings immediately after first	FOLLOW ON
cross-pieces on stumps	BAILS
defend stubbornly	STONEWALL
derisory expression when easy catch is missed	BUTTER-FINGERS
dismissal of batsman	
—by ball striking pad	LBW
	LEG-BEFORE-WICKET
—caught out of his ground by wicketkeeper	STUMPED
—deflecting ball from bat to stumps	PLAYED-ON
—hitting ball twice	HIT BALL TWICE
—obstructing fielder	OBSTRUCTING THE FIELD
—running between wickets	RUN-OUT
—touching ball	HANDLED BALL
distance travelled by ball bowled before landing	LENGTH
easy catch	DOLLY (CATCH)
	SITTER
enforced start of second innings	FOLLOW-ON
fast	
—bowling directed at the batsman	BODYLINE
—short-pitched ball	BOUNCER, BUMPER
	THROAT BALL
fielder's throw that goes beyond the wicket	OVERTHROW
fielding positions	
—leg side	(BACKWARD) SHORT-LEG
	(DEEP) FINE LEG
	(DEEP) MID-WICKET
	(DEEP) SQUARE LEG
	FORWARD SHORT-LEG
	LEG SLIP, LONG-ON
	(SILLY) MID-ON
—off side	COVER POINT
	(DEEP) EXTRA COVER
	(DEEP) THIRD MAN, GULL(E)Y
	LONG-OFF, (SILLY) MID-OFF
	SHORT EXTRA COVER
	SHORT THIRD MAN
	(SILLY) POINT, SLIP
other	BAT-PAD, LONGSTOP
	WICKETKEEPER
grounds	
—Australia	
Adelaide	OVAL
Brisbane	WOOLLOONGABBA GROUND
Perth	CRICKET ASSOCIATION GROUND
Sydney	ALBERT GROUND

—England	
Cambridge University	FENNERS
Derbyshire	CHESTERFIELD
	QUEEN'S PARK
Essex	CHELMSFORD
Glamorgan	CARDIFF
	SOPHIA GARDENS
Gloucestershire	ASHLEY DOWN
	BRISTOL
Hampshire	HAMBLEDON
	SOUTHAMPTON
Kent	CANTERBURY
	ST LAWRENCE GROUND
Lancashire	MANCHESTER
	OLD TRAFFORD
MCC	LORDS
Middlesex	LORDS
Nottinghamshire	TRENT BRIDGE
Surrey	THE OVAL
	KENNINGTON
Sussex	EATON ROAD, HOVE
Warwickshire	EDGBASTON
Worcestershire	WORCESTER
Yorkshire	BRAMALL LANE
	HEADINGLEY
—India	
Bombay	BRABOURNE STADIUM
Calcutta	EDEN GARDENS
Delhi	FEROZ SHAH KOTLA GROUND
Karachi	NATIONAL STADIUM
Lahore	GADDAFI GROUND
Madras	CHIDAMBARAM GROUND
—New Zealand	
Auckland	EDEN PARK
Christchurch	LANCASTER PARK
Dunedin	CARISBROOK GROUND
Wellington	BASIN RESERVE
—South Africa	
Cape Town	NEWLANDS
Johannesburg	WANDERES GROUND
—West Indies	
Bridgetown, Barbados	KENSINGTON GROUND
Georgetown Guyana	BOURDA GROUND
Kingston, Jamaica	SABINA PARK
Port of Spain, Trinidad	QUEEN'S PARK OVAL
inadvertent stroke	SNICK, TOUCH
left-hand side (to r-h bat)	LEG, ON
leg protectors	PADS
maiden over in which a wicket is taken	WICKET-MAIDEN
mark made by batsman in front of stumps	BLOCKHOLE

move	
—ball in the air when bowling	SWING
—to position behind another fielder	BACK UP
—up the pitch in preparation for run	BACK UP
no score	DUCK
—in each innings	PAIR
obstruction of wicket with legs	LEG-BEFORE-WICKET
	LBW
off-break	
—bowled by left-handed bowler	CHINAMAN
—disguised as leg-break	GOOGLY
official	SCORER, UMPIRE
over from which no runs are scored	MAIDEN (OVER)
players	
—Australian	ARMSTRONG, BARNES
	BENAUD, BLACKHAM, BORDER
	BRADMAN, CHAPPELL, DAVIDSON
	FINGLETON, GREGORY, GRIMMETT
	HARVEY, HASSETT, IRONMONGER
	LAWRY, LILLIE, LINDWALL
	MARSH, MCCABE, MCDONALD
	MECKIFF, MILLER, OLDFIELD
	O'REILLY, PONSFORD, RITCHIE
	SIMPSON, SPOFFORTH, STODDART
	TALLON, TRUMPER, WALTERS
	WOODFULL
—English	ALLEN, AMES, BAILEY, BARNES
	BARRINGTON, BEDSER, BOTHAM
	BOWES, BOYCOTT, CHAPMAN, CLOSE
	COMPTON, COWDREY, DE FREITAS
	DEXTER, DILLEY, EDRICH, EMBUREY
	EVANS, FENDER, FOSTER, FREEMAN
	FRY, GATTING, GOOCH, GOWER, GRACE
	HAMMOND, HENDREN, HIRST, HOBBS
	HOLLIES, ILLINGWORTH, JESSOP, KNOTT
	LAKER, LAMB, LARWOOD, LEVER
	LEYLAND, LOCK, MAY, MACLAREN
	RHODES, SHEPPARD, SMALL
	SPOONER, SNOW, STATHAM
	SUTCLIFFE, TATE, TRUEMAN
	TYSON, UNDERWOOD, VERITY, VOCE
	WARDLE, WILLIS, WOOLLEY
	WRIGHT, WYATT
—Indian	AMARNATH, AZHARUDDIN
	BEDI, CHANDRASEKHAR
	CONTRACTOR, DEV
	DULEEPSINHJI, ENGINEER
	GAVASKAR, GUPTE, HANIF
	MANJREKAR, MANKAD, MERCHANT
	PRASANNA, RANJITSINHJI, SHASTRA
	TENDULKAR, UMRIGAR, VENGSARKAR

—New Zealand	COLLINGE, CONGDON
	COWIE, CROWE, DONNELLY
	DOWLING, HADLEE, LOWRY
	SUTCLIFFE, TURNER
—Pakistani	AKRAM, FAZAL, IMRAN
	IQBAL, JAVED, MOHSIN
	MUDASSAR, MUSHTAQ, QADIR
	QASIM, SADIQ, SARFRAZ
	WASIR, ZAHEER
—South African	BARLOW, BLAND
	CHEETHAM, FAULKNER
	NOURSE, POLLOCK, PROCTER
	RICHARDS, SCHWARTZ, TAYFIELD
	VOGLER
—Sri Lankan	MENDIS, RANATUNGA
	RANAYAKE, SILVA
	WETTIMUNY
—West Indian	BUTCHER, CONSTANTINE
	GARNER, GILCHRIST
	GREENIDGE, HALL, HAYNES
	HEADLEY, KALLICHARRAN
	KANHAI, LLOYD, MARSHALL
	RAMADHIN, RICHARDS, ROBERTS
	ROWE, SOBERS, SOLOMON
	VALENTINE, WALCOTT, WEEKES
	WORRELL
—Zimbabwean	HICK
point where bat rests on crease	BLOCKHOLE
position of	
—bat at rest	GUARD, LEG STUMP
	MIDDLE-AND-LEG
	MIDDLE-AND-OFF
	MIDDLE STUMP, OFF STUMP
—batsman	STANCE
practice area	NET(S)
right-hand side (to r-h bat)	OFF
rotation of ball by bowler's action	SPIN
run scored from	
—ball	
pitched wide of the crease	WIDE
that	
—is not hit	BYE
—strikes the batsman	LEG-BYE
unfairly delivered	NO-BALL
—bye, leg-bye, no-ball, wide	EXTRA
	SUNDRY
—throw that goes beyond the wicket	OVERTHROW
score	
—of 100 runs or more	CENTURY
—with prods and deflections	NURDLE
spare player	TWELFTH MAN
stop ball defensively with bat	BLOCK, STONEWALL

stroke	GLIDE, HOOK
	(LEG) GLANCE, OFF-DRIVE
	ON DRIVE, PULL
	(SQUARE-)CUT, SWEEP
trophy	THE ASHES
	(*see also separate entry*)
white	
—line on	
pitch	BATTING CREASE
	BOWLING CREASE
	FIELDING CIRCLE
edge of pitch	BOUNDARY
—panel set on boundary	SIGHT SCREEN
young player	COLT
cross	
archbishop's	CROSIER, CROZIER
as award	(*see* **decorations**)
Christ's cross	CRUCIFIX, ROOD(-TREE)
clerical	CARDINALS
	CONSTANTINIAN
	PASSION, ST PETER'S
crucifix	ROOD
English	ST GEORGE'S CROSS
forked	FOURCHE
having	
—arms	
bent clockwise at	
right angles	SVASTIKA
	SWASTIKA
of equal length	GREEK
with crutch heads	POTENT
—circle round point of	
intersection of limbs	CELTIC, CORNISH
	KILDALTON
—fleur-de-lis shape	FLEURY, FLORY
—pointed ends	FITCHE(E)
—three	
buds at each extremity	BOTONE, BOTTONY
	TREFLE(E), TREFLY
horizontal bars	PAPAL
—two horizontal bars	LORRAINE
	PATRIARCHAL
—two outward-curving	
branches on each limb	MOLINE
—two-pointed expanding	
limbs	MALTESE
in fretwork, as brooch etc	ROVEN CROSS
Latin cross on three steps	CALVARY
modified Greek	CAPITAL
orthodox prelate's cross	ENCOLPION
other	CROSSLET, FORME
	POMME, RUSSIAN
red on white ground	GENEVA CROSS
reverse swastika	FILFOT, FYLFOT
Scottish	ST ANDREW'S CROSS
square	QUADRATE

suspended from	
a heart	CROIX A LA JEANNETTE
swastika	GRAMMADION
	GRAMMATION
symbol of life	ANKH, ANSATE
T-shaped	ST ANTHONY'S, TAU
—with loop	ANKH, ANSATE
upright with lower limb	
the longest	LATIN
X-shaped	SALTIER, SALTIE
	ST ANDREW'S
Y-shaped	Y-CROSS
Cuba	C
capital	HAVANA
castle	MORRO
coin	CENTAVO, PESO
drum	BONGO, CONGA, ENKOMO
dance	CONGA, DANZA, DANZON
	GUAJIRA, GUARACHA
	HABANERA, HIP-HOP
	R(H)UMBA
knife	MACHETE
measure	TAREA
rattle	MARACA
secret police	PORRA
squall	BAYAMO
squash	ZAPALLO
tobacco field	VEGA
tree	CULLA, CUYA
weight	LIBRA, TERCIO
	(*see also* **West Indies**)
cycling	
leader's badge	
—Tour de France	YELLOW JERSEY
—Giro d'Italia	PINK JERSEY
races	
—Britain	MILK RACE
	TOUR OF BRITAIN
	WINCANTON CLASSIC
—France	PARIS-TOURS
	TOUR DE FRANCE
	TOUR DE PAYS BASQUE
—Germany	COLOGNE SIX DAYS
—Ireland	TOUR OF IRELAND
—Italy	GIRO D'ITALIA
	TOUR DE LOMBARDY
—Spain	TOUR DE CATALONIA
	VUELTA D'ESPANA
—types	CYCLE SPEEDWAY, PURSUIT
	SPRINT, TIME TRIAL
riders	
—American	HAMPSTEN, KNICKMAN
	LEMOND, SCHUTT
—Australian	ANDERSON, BISH, GRAY
	MOCKRIDGE, PATE, SUTTON
	VINNICOMBE, WOODS

—Belgian	CRIQUIELION, DE WILDE
	DHAENENS, HOOYDONCK
	LIBOTON, MAERTENS, MERCKX
	NOYELLE, PLANKAERT, POLLENTIER
	SERCU, STERKX, THEUNISSE
	THYS, VAARTEN
—British	ALEXANDER, BARRY
	BOARDMAN, BOOTY, CAMERON
	CAMMISH, COOK, CURRAN, DOYLE
	DREW, ELLIOTT, HARRIS, LODGE
	MCHUGH, MCLOUGHLIN, MILLAR
	PAULDING, REYNOLDS, SADLER
	SOUTHALL, STEPHENS, STURGESS
	WALLACE, WOOD, YATES
—Canadian	BAUER, SINGLETON, WALTON
—Colombian	FARFAN, PARRA
—Czech	DALER, FISERA, KUCHREK
	PENC, REHOUNEK, SIMUNTEK
	TRAK, VORBORIL
—Danish	FLACK, FREDBORG, FROST
	HANSEN, MARCUSSEN, OERSTED
—Dutch	BREUKINK, DE NIJS
	HERMANS, KUIPER, MINNEBOO
	PEETERS, ROOKS, TALEN
	THEUNISSE, VAN EGMOND, VAN IMPE
	VAN VLIET, VENIX, ZOETEMECK
—French	ANQUETIL, BAYAERT
	BEAUFRAND, BLANCHONNET
	BOBET, BONDUE, CHARPENTIER
	COLAS, DEPINE, DUPONT, FIGNON
	HINAULT, KILLY, MAGNE, MASSON
	MICHARD, MORELON, MOTTET
	REBILLARD, ROUSSEAU
	TAILLENDIER, TRENTIN
	VERNET, VIVIEN
—German	AMPLER, BRAUN, DROGAN
	GLUCKLICH, GREIL, GRUNKE
	HESSLICH, HUEBNER, KAPPES
	KLUGE, MACHA, MALCHOW
	MERKENS, PODLESCH, POEL
	RAAB, SCHEUTZ, SCHMIDTKE
	THALER, THOMS, WEBER
—Greek	KONSTANTINIDIS
—Irish	KELLY, ROCHE

—Italian	ARGENTIN, BALDINI
	BIANCHETTO, BUGNO
	CIPOLLINI, DI BASCO, DITANO
	DOTTI, FAGGIN, FONDRIEST
	GENTILI, GHELLA, GIARDONI
	GIOVANETTI, PAVESI, PETTENELLA
	SACCI, SARONNI, VIANELLI
	VICINO, ZATIN
—Japanese	HONDA, NAKANO, TAWARA
—New Zealand	BAMFORD, DAHLBERG
	RUSH
—Norwegian	KNUDSEN
—Polish	PIASECKI
—Portuguese	DA SILVA
—Russian	ECKIMOV, GANEEV
	KAPITONOV, KOPYLOV
	KOUROVTS, UMARAS
—Spanish	DELGADO, INDURAIN, OCANA
—Swedish	JOHANSSEN, STENQUIST
—Swiss	DILL-BUNDI, FREULER
	HURZELER, KURMANN
	ZIMMERMANN, ZWEIFEL
sprinter's badge	GREEN JERSEY
Cyprus	CY
capital	NICOSIA
coin	LIRA, POUND
scent	CHYPRE
Czechoslovakia	CS
capitals	PRAGUE, BRATISLAVA
castle	HRAD
coin	HALER, HELLER, KORUNA
countries	SLOVAKIA
	REPUBLIC OF CZECH STATES
	RCS
depression	KOTLINA, NIZINA
forest	LES
gate	BRANA
gymnastic club	SOKOL
measure	LATRO
mountain(s)	HORA
mountain range	HORY, POHORAI(E)
region	KRAJ
tableland	PLOSINA
town	MESTO

D

dance
acrobatic	BREAK DANCING
afternoon dance	THE DANSANT
Alpine	GAVOTTE
American	BARN DANCE, (BE)BOP
	BLACK BOTTOM, BOSTON (REEL)
	BREAK DANCE, BUNNY-HUG
	CAKEWALK, CHARLESTON
	ELECTRIC BOOGIE, GOGO, HOEDOWN
	JITTERBUG, JIVE, LINDY HOP
	PAUL JONES, RAG(TIME)
	ROCK 'N ROLL, TWIST
	TURKEY TROT, VOGUEING
Argentine	TANGO
art of dance	CHOREOGRAPHY
Austrian	LANDLER
back-to-back	DO-SI-DO
ballet	(see separate entry)
Basque	BOURREE
belly-dance (Egypt)	RAQS SARQI
Bohemian	POLKA, REDOWA
Brazilian	BATUQUE, BOSSA NOVA
	CARIOCA, LAMBADA
	MAXIXE, SAMBA
changing partners	PAUL JONES
Cockney	HOKEY-COKEY
	LAMBETH WALK
	KNEES-UP (MOTHER BROWN)
college	HOP, PROM
country	ALTHEA, AURESCA
	BARN DANCE, COTILL(I)ON
	DASHING WHITE SERGEANT
	ECOSSAISE, GAVOTTE
	HAY, HEY, HOEDOWN
	MORRIS(-DANCE), REEL
	ROUNDEL, (SIR) ROGER DE COVERLEY
	SQUARE DANCE
Cuban	CONGA, GUAJIRA
	GUARACHA, HABANERA
	HIP-HOP, R(H)UMBA
dance of death	DANSE MACABRE
disco dancing	GOGO
Dutch clog dance	MATELOT(E)
energetic	MOSHING
	SLAMDANCING
English regional dance	CLOG DANCE
	HORN DANCE
	MAYPOLE DANCE

erotic	BELLY-DANCE, DIRTY-DANCING
	HOOTCHIE-COOTCHIE
	LAMBADA, TOUCH-DANCING
fairy dance	RINGLET
fast fox-trot	QUICKSTEP
flapping arms	CHICKEN DANCING
folk-dance	(see country above)
for	
—four couples	QUADRILLE
—men only	STAG-DANCE
—opposing groups	CONTREDANSE
	COUNTERDANCE
—two persons	PAS DE DEUX, RIGADOON
fourth movement of	
quadrille	TRENISE
free-style exercise	EURYTHMICS
French	BOURREE, CANCAN, CHACONNE
	CORANTO, COURANTE, FARANDOLE
	GAVOTTE, GIGUE, RIGADOON
	RIGAUDON
—old	BRAN(S)LE, BRANTLE, BRAWL
frolicsome	CAPER
gavotte	CIBELL
German	ALLEMANDE, ALMAIN, LANDLER
gliding	COURANT(E), PALAIS GLIDE
	TWO-STEP, WALTZ
Greek	ROMAIKA, SIKINNIS
Hawaiian	HULA(-HULA)
Hebrew	HORA
hornpipe	MATELOTE
Hungarian	CSARDAS, CZARDAS
in	
—duple time	TWO-STEP
—ring	ROUND
Indian	BHANGRA, KATHAK
	NA(U)TCH
—hand movements	MUTRA
Irish	FADING, PLANXTY, REEL
	RINKAFADDA
Israeli	HORA
Italian	BERGAMASK, BERGOMASK, GIGA
	RIGOLETTO, SALTARELLO
	TARANTELLA, VOLTA
Jamaican	REGGAE
jumping	MOSHING, POGO, SLAM DANCING
leaping	ALLEMANDE, ALMAIN
like	
—minuet	PASPY, PASSEPIED
—polka	SCHOTTISCHE
lively	BOURREE, CORANTO, GALLIARD
	GALOP(ADE), GIG(UE), JIG
	RIGADOON, RIGAUDON, STOMP
—Shakespeare	CANARY, UPSPRING
Maori	HAKA
march	ONE-STEP
marching sequence	PROMENADE

Maytime	MORISCO, MORISK
	MORRIS(-DANCE)
Mexican	RASPA
modern	(BE)BOP, BODY-POPPING
	BOOGIE, BREAK-DANCE
	DISCO DANCING, FRUG, GOGO
	HIP-HOP, JITTERBUG, JIVE
	MOSHING, ROCK 'N' ROLL, SALSA
	SHUFFLE, SLAMDANCING
	TWIST, VOGUEING
	(see also American above)
Moorish	MORESCO
movement in quadrille	PANTALON
	PASTOURELLE
Neapolitan	TARANTELLA
Negro	BREAKDOWN, JUBA
	WALK-AROUND
New Zealand	HAKA
Norwegian	HALLING
obsolete (slow)	DUMP
old	BRAN(S)LE, BRANTLE
	BRAWL, CINQUE-PACE, GAILLARD
	GALLIARD, HAY-DE-GUISE
	HAY-DE-GUY(ES), HEY-DE-GUISE
	HEY-DE-GUY(ES), HUY-DE-GUY
	LAVOLT(A), LOURE, MINUET
	PASSY-MEASURE, PAVIN
	SINK-A-PACE, VOLTA
on	
—sanded surface	SAND-DANCE
—the same spot	POGO
orgiastic	SIKINNIS
originally Scottish	ECOSSAIS
Peruvian	CUECA
Polish	CRACOVIENNE, MAZURKA
	POLONAISE, VARSOVIENNE
Polynesian	HULA(-HULA), SIVA
Portuguese	FADO
Provencal	TAMBOURIN
public	RIDOTTO
quadrilles	LANCERS
quick	GALLOPADE, FOX-TROT
—movement of csardas	FRIS(KA)
—pavan(e)	PASSAMEZZO
	PASSE-MEASURE
	PASSY-MEASURE
—step	PAS REDOUBLE
ragtime	TURKEY-TROT
reel	CIRCASSIAN CIRCLE
	EIGHTSOME
ring-dance	RO(U)NDEL, ROUNDELAY
	ROUNDLE
Roman	TRIPUDIUM
round dance	ROUNDABOUT
Russian	GOPAK, KAZATZKA
	KOLO, ZIGANKA

sailor's	HORNPIPE
Scottish	ECOSSAISE, EIGHTSOME
	GAY GORDONS, HIGHLAND FLING
	HOOLACHAN, HULLACHAN
	PETRONELLA, REEL, STRATHSPEY
	SWORD-DANCE
Serbian	KOLO
shivering	SHIMMY(-SHAKE)
shuffling	FOX-TROT
Sicilian	SICILIANA, SICILIANO
	SICILIENNE
single file	CONGA
skipping	SALTARELLO
slow	CHACONNE
	(HESITATION-)WALTZ
	MINUET, PAVANE
—waltz	VALETA, VELETA
solo	VARIATION
Spanish	BOLERO, CACHUCHA, FANDANGO
	FARRUCA, FLAMENCO, JOTA
	MALAGUENA, PASO DOBLE
	PASSACAGLIA, PAVAN(E)
	PAVEN, PAVIN, SALTARELLO
	SARABAND(E), SARDANO
	SEGUIDILLA, ZAPATEADO
square	DOS-A-DOS, DO-SI-DO
	HOE-DOWN, QUADRILLE
stately	MINUET, PAVANE
under bar	LIMBO
Venetian	FORLANA, FURLANA
waltz	BOSTON, VALETA, VELETA
West Indian	BEGUINE, CHA-CHA(-CHA)
	LIMBO, MAMBO
with	
—fans	FAN-DANCE
—much jumping	LAVOLT(A)
—rigid limbs	ROBOTIC DANCING
writhing	MOSHING
decorations	
Crosses	AIR FORCE
	DISTINGUISHED FLYING
	DISTINGUISHED SERVICE
	GEORGE, MILITARY, VICTORIA
Medals	AIR FORCE MEDAL
	BURMA GALLANTRY
	CONSPICUOUS GALLANTRY
	DISTINGUISHED CONDUCT
	DISTINGUISHED FLYING
	DISTINGUISHED SERVICE
	GEORGE, MILITARY
Orders	DISTINGUISHED SERVICE
	IMPERIAL SERVICE ORDER
	INDIAN ORDER OF MERIT
	QUEEN'S SERVICE ORDER
—Order of	BATH, BRITISH EMPIRE
	BRITISH INDIA, BURMA

	COMPANION OF HONOUR
	CROWN OF INDIA, GARTER
	INDIAN EMPIRE, MERIT
	ST MICHAEL AND ST GEORGE
	STAR OF INDIA, THISTLE
—Royal	ROYAL RED CROSS ORDER
	ROYAL VICTORIAN
other	BRITISH EMPIRE MEDAL
	BRITISH EMPIRE SERVICE MEDAL
	CANADIAN FORCES DECORATION
	CANADIAN MEDAL
	COLONIAL POLICE MEDAL
	EFFICIENCY DECORATION
	EMERGENCY SERVICES DECORATION
	EMPIRE GALLANTRY MEDAL
	INDIAN DISTINGUISHED SERVICE MEDAL
	KING'S POLICE MEDAL
	MEDAL FOR MERITORIOUS SERVICE
	QUEEN'S GALLANTRY MEDAL
	QUEEN'S POLICE MEDAL
	SEA GALLANTRY MEDAL
	TERRITORIAL DECORATION
	VOLUNTEER OFFICERS DECORATION

deer

American	CARIACOU, CARIBOU, CARJACOU
	CHEVROTAIN, ELK, MOOSE
	MOUSE-DEER, VIRGINIAN DEER
Asian	MUNTJAC
European	FALLOW, RED DEER
female	DOE, HIND, ROE
knob on horn	CROCHE
male	BUCK
—in	
2nd year	BROCKETT
—(Shak.)	PRICKET
3rd year	SPAY(D), SPAD(E), SOR(R)EL
4th year (Shak.)	SOAR(E), SORE
—over	
4 years	BARE BUCK, STAG
5 years	HART
—with 12 points	ROYAL
rudimentary antler	BOSSET
small species	ROE DEER
tines	
—3rd	ROYAL
—over 3rd	SURROYAL
wax-secreting gland	CRUMEN, TEAR-PIT
	(*see also* **antelope**)

Denmark DK

bay	BREDNING, BUGT, VIG
beach	STRAND
bog	MOSE
bread and butter	SMOR(RE)BROD
cape	NAES, ODDE
capital	COPENHAGEN, KOBENHAVN
cheese	TYBO

cliff	KLINT
coin	KR, KRONE, ORE
dunes	KLIT
fiord	ISE, LIM
harbour	HAVN
hero	HOLGER, OGIER
hill	BJERG, HOJ
hors d'oeuvres	SMOR(RE)BROD
invader	JUTE
lake	SO
Lower House	FOLKETING
measure	ALEN, ESER, LANDMILL
	MORGEN, RODE, TOMME
national flag	DANNEBROG
order	DANNEBROG
parliament	RIGSDAG
sea monster	KRAKEN
strait	BAELT
Upper House	LANDST(H)ING
valley	DAL
weight	ESER, KVINT, PUND
	QUINT, TONDE

department DEPT, DPT

of	
—Economic Affairs	DEA
—Education and Science	DES
—Employment (and Productivity)	DE, DEP
—Health and Social Security	DHSS
—the Environment	DOE
—Trade (and Industry)	DOT, DTI

desert

Africa	LIBYAN, KALAHARI
	NAMIB, SAHARA, SOMALI, TEREVE
Arabia	AN NAFUD, ARRAB'AL KHALI
	EMPTY QUARTER, SYRIAN
Asia	GOBI, TAKLAMEN
Australia	ARUNTA, GIBSON, GREAT SANDY
	GREAT VICTORIAN, NULLARBOR PLAIN
	SIMPSON, STURT, WARBURTON
Chile	ATACAMA
China	TAKLA MAKAN, ORDOS
India	INDIAN, THAR
Iran	DASHT-E LUT, IRANIAN
Middle East	SYRIAN
North America	BLACKROCK, COLORADO
	GILA, GREAT SALT LAKE
	GREAT WESTERN, MOJAVE
	PAINTED, SONORAN
Peru	DESIERTO DE SECHURA
rocky	HAM(M)ADA
Russia	KARA KUM, KYZYL KUM
	TURKESTAN
sandy	ERG
South America	PATAGONIAN
stony	REG
Sudan	BAIYUDA, NUBIAN

dessert

almond-flavoured	BAKEWELL PUDDING
	BAKEWELL TART, FRANGIPANE
	MAID OF HONOUR, PRALINE
American	APPLE PIE, BLUEBERRY PIE
	PANDOWDY, PUMPKIN PIE
apple	
—pastry	APFELSTRUDEL
—sponge	EVE'S PUDDING
Austrian	APFELSTRUDEL
baked	
—apple and spices	BROWN BETTY
—fruit in dough	DUMPLING
batter	BATTER PUDDING
	YORKSHIRE PUDDING
blancmange	FLUMMERY
boiled pudding	DUFF, ROLY-POLY
	SPONGE, SUET PUDDING
—with currants	SPOTTED DICK
	SPOTTED DOG
bread	BREAD AND BUTTER PUDDING
	BREAD PUDDING
	OSBORNE PUDDING
	SUMMER PUDDING
—crumbs	CHARLOTTE
butter, milk, sugar, etc	FUDGE
candied chestnuts	MARRONS GLACES
caramelised nuts	PRALINE
chocolate	CHOC-AU-RHUM
choux pastry roll	PROFITEROLE
cold fruit purée with cream	FOOL
cone of refined sugar	SUGARLOAF
cream	CREME BRULEE
	CREME PATISSIERE
	CUSTARD CREAM, SYLLABUB
—and eggs	PARFAIT
—cake	GATEAU
—thickened by curdling	SYLLABUB
crushed fruit etc	FOOL
custard dishes	BAVAROIS, CREME BRULEE
	FLUMMERY, FOOL
	ZABA(GL)IONE
—and egg noodles (Heb.)	LOKSHEN
—with	
caramelised sugar	CREME BRULEE
	CREME CARAMEL
floating whipped	
egg white	FLOATING ISLAND
sponge cake, jelly, etc	TRIFLE
sponge fingers	CHARLOTTE RUSSE
diced fruit salad	MACEDOINE
egg and	
—chocolate	CHOC-AU-RHUM
—cream	SOUFFLE
sugar, etc	POSSET
—flour, spirits, etc	FLUMMERY

—lemon	LEMON CHIFFON
—sugar and wine	ZABAGLIONE
egg-white	
—sugar, etc	MERINGUE, SNOW
	SOUFFLE
—water-ice	SHERBE(R)T
flat	PANCAKE, CREPE SUZETTE
	WAFFLE
frothy confection	MOUSSE, SOUFFLE, WHIP
	ZABA(GL)IONE
frozen	
—cream, etc	ICE CREAM
—dishes	BAKED ALASKA
	BOMBE, NESSELRODE
	PARFAIT
—water, flavoured	WATER ICE
fruit	
—and	
cheese	CHEESECAKE
ice cream	COUPE
sponge layers	CHARLOTTE
—baked shell side up,	
served fruit side up	UPSIDEDOWN CAKE
—candied	SUCCADE
—fried in batter	FRITTER
—in syrup	COMPOTE, SUCCADE
—layered with	
ice cream, etc	PARFAIT
sugar	AMBROSIA
—mixed	SALAD
—mixture used in frozen	
sweets	NESSELRODE
—pudding	CHRISTMAS PUDDING
	DUCHESSE PUDDING
	LAFAYETTE PUDDING
	SCOTCH PUDDING, SPOTTED DICK
	SUMMER PUDDING
—purée and cream	RODGROD
—tart	CHARLOTTE, FLAN
—topped with flour, etc	CRUMBLE
—with	
cream and sugar	FOOL, MOUSSE
custard, cream, etc	TRIFLE
ice-cream	BANANA SPLIT
	PEACH MELBA
	PEAR BELLE HELENE, SUNDAE
	TUTTI-FRUTTI
rice pudding	CONDE
fudge with eggs, sugar, etc	DIVINITY
gelatine	JELLY
Greek	BACLAVA, BAKLAVA
heavy pudding	STICKJAW
Hebrew	CHOROSET
ice-cream dishes	BOMBE, COUPE
—flavoured frozen water	WATER-ICE
—in tall glasss	KNICKERBOCKER GLORY

—Indian	KULFI
—Italian	MELA STREGATA
	SEMI-FREDDO
—with	
bananas	BANANA SPLIT
coloured layers	NEAPOLITAN
fruit, etc	CASSATA, SUNDAE
mixed fruits	TUTTI-FRUTTI
nuts and rum	TORTONI
peaches	PEACH MELBA
pears	PEAR BELLE HELENE
sponge, served hot	BAKED ALASKA
Indian	GULAB YAM
Italian	GRANITA, TIRAMISU
	ZUPPA INGLESE
jam tart (US)	CUPID
jelly from oat-husks	FLUMMERY
	SOWANS, SOWENS
light pastry with filling	PUFF
like a cake	CABINET PUDDING
made in a small mould	DARIOLE
meringue	PAVLOVA
	QUEEN OF PUDDINGS
	VACHERIN
milk dishes	(BAKED) CUSTARD
	BLANCMANGE
	CARAMEL CREAM, CORNFLOUR
	JUNKET, MACARONI
	MILK PUDDING, RENNET
	RICE PUDDING, SAGO
	SEMOLINA, TAPIOCA
mixed fruits	TUTTI-FRUTTI
molasses on pastry crumble	SHOO-FLY PIE
pancake	
—filled	FRENCH PANCAKE
—flaming	CREPE SUZETTE
—Russian	BLIN(I)
—thin	BLINTZ(E)
pastry	
—case, filled	FLAN, PIE, TART
—topping	CRUMBLE
—with	
almond-flavoured	
filling	MAID OF HONOUR
fruit	MILLE-FEUILLES
soft filling	CHEESECAKE
	(*see also* **pastry**)
quinces and sugar	QUIDDANY
rice and milk, etc	MILK PUDDING
	RICE PUDDING
sandwich with jam and	
jelly filling	WASHINGTON PIE
Scottish	ATHOLL BROSE
sesame seeds and honey	HALVA(H)
shaved ice, flavoured	SNOWBALL
sliced fruit with ice cream	SPLOT

small	
—confection	KISS
—tart	TARTLET
soft, spongy confection	MARSHMALLOW
sponge cake, jelly,	
custard, etc	TRIFLE
sponge pudding	EVE'S PUDDING
	JAMAICA PUDDING
	MARBLED PUDDING
	STEAMED CASTLE PUDDING
—enclosing cream	CHARLOTTE RUSSE
steamed	CHRISTMAS PUDDING
	PLUM PUDDING, SPOTTED DICK
	SPOTTED DOG, TREACLE PUDDING
suet pudding with filling	ROLY-POLY
sugar, water and flavouring	FONDANT
sweet	
—batter	PANCAKE
filled	FRENCH PANCAKE
—pancake	CREPE
flaming	CREPE SUZETTE
tart	BAKEWELL, FRUIT PIE, MINCE PIE
thin pastry with	
fruit filling	STRUDEL
Turkish	HALVA(H), HALAVAH
water-ice	FRAPPE, GRANITA
	SHERBE(R)T, SORBET
with ice-cream (US)	A LA MODE
detectives	
in fiction:	
African	ZONDI
American	ARCHER, EDWARDS, HAMMER
	HELM, JOHNSON, JONES
	MARLOWE, QUEEN, ROME
	SPADE, SPENSER, URTH
	VAN DUSEN, WARSHAWSKI (f)
	WOLFE
Belgian	POIROT
British	APPLETON, BLAKE, BROWN
	CAMPION, COFFIN, DALGLEISH
	DALZIEL, FORTUNE, GETHRYN, HOLMES
	LOVE, MARPLE (f), MORSE, TRENT
	WIMSEY, WEXFORD
Chinese	CHAN
Dutch	VAN DER VALK
French	DUPIN, MAIGRET
Icelandic	HJERSON
Indian	GHOTE
Irish	MINOGUE
Japanese	IMANISHI, MOKO, OTANI
Navajo	LEAPHORN
Swedish	WAHLOO
Turkish	ISKIRLAK
dialects	
some dialect terms:	
abide	WON

about	AWAY
accusation (N)	THREAP, THREEP
ache	WORK
active (N)	WIMBLE
adit	STULM
advancing swiftly	RAKING
affected	
—person	MIMMICK, MINNOCK
	MINNOCK
—with fear	EERIE, EERY
—with sickness	WAMBLY
afternoon snack	FOUR(SES)
aftertaste	TWANG
agitate	WHEMMLE, WHOMBLE
	WHOMMLE, WHUMMLE
agitated	HET UP
alert	SPRACK, SPRAG
all (N)	A
allow to be believed	LET ON
almost	MOST
along	ALONGST
amount carried at one	
journey (N)	RAKE
anemone	ENEMY
angry word	MISWORD
annual holiday	WAKE
ant	EMMET
anything shrivelled	SCRUMP, SKRIMP
	SKRUMP
apart from	OUTSIDE OF
approaching	TOWARD
apt	TOWARD
area mined (Cornwall)	SET
arouse	YERK
arrogant	COBBY
as	
—if about	LIKE
—it were	LIKE
—much as	WHAT
ass (E. Anglia)	DICK(E)Y
assertion (N)	THREAP, THREEP
astride	STRIDE-WAYS
	STRIDLING
at	
—hand	TOWARD
—least	LEAST(A)WAYS
attention	GAUM, GORM
autumn	HARVEST
awkward	UNGAIN
—girl (E. Ang)	MAUTHER
	MAWTHER
awn-removing machine	HUMMELLER
bait with dogs	SLATE
baited line for catching birds	TEAGLE
baker's peel	PALE
bar (N)	RANCE

—in chimney (N)	RANDLE-BALK
	RANDLE-PERCH, RANDLE-TREE
	RANNEL-TREE, RANNLE-TREE
	RANTLE-TREE
barge(N)	GABBARD, GABBART
bark	WAFF
barter	COPE
basket	WISKET
batter	DIALECT
be	
—off work (N)	PLAY
—over-dainty	MIMMICK, MINNICK
	MINNOCK
—painful	WORK
—peevish (N)	NATTER
—sparing	STINT
—twisted or warped	WIND
—untidy or slovenly	SLATTER
bearer of coffin	UNDERBEARER
beat	JO(U)LE, JOLL, JOWL
	POLT, YERK
—violently	WHITHER, WUTHER
because	CAUSE
bed of fireclay	THILL
bed-time	DOWN-LYING
beetle	CLOCK
behave in affected	
manner	MIMMICK, MINNICK
	MINNOCK
belch	YESK, YEX
belly	WAME
—band of cart-horse	WANTY
bellyful	WAMEFUL
bend	TREND
beneath	NEATH
benumb (SW)	SCRAM
besmirch	SLUR
best (N)	WALE
bewitch	BESPEAK, WISH
big man	COB
bilberry	WINE-BERRY
bind	YERK
bindweed	WITH(Y)WIND
birch	BIRK
biscuit (N)	PARKIN
bite	SNACK
blame	WITE, WYTE
blanket	WHITTLE
blast	WHITHER, WUTHER
bleat	WHICKER
blink	WAPPER
blinking	WAPPER-EYED
blow	DA(U)D, WHITHER, WUTHER
—(W)	SCAT
blustering	BLUFF
bodily build	SET

boggy	SPEWY
bogle (N)	BOGGARD, BOGGART
	BOGGLE
boisterous	RANDIE, RANDY
booby	PATCH
botch	BODGE
	MUX
bottle (with ears)	COSTREL
bounce	BANG
bound	MERE
boundary	MERE
—ridge	LINCH(ET), LYNCHET
—stone	MERESTONE
branch	GRAIN, SHROUD
brawl	FRATCH
brawling	FRATCH(ET)Y
bread soaked in gravy	BREVIS
breastbone	HEART-SPOON
breccia (N)	BROCKRAM
bring forth young	YEAN
brisk	COBBY, KEDGE, KEDGY
	KIDGE, YARE
brood	TEAM
broil (N)	BRU(I)LZE
broth	BREVIS
brushwood	RICE
bugbear (N)	BOGGARD, BOGGART
	BOGGLE
bullroarer	HUMBUZZ
bumblebee	DUMBLEDORE
bump	JO(U)LE, JOLL, JOWL
bunch	BOB
bundle of hay	WAP
burn	SCALD
burning ember	GLEED
burrow	BURY
burst (N)	BRAST
buss	SMOUCH
bustle about	WHEW
buttermilk (N)	KIRN-MILK, WHIG
cairn (N)	RAISE
candle-snuffer	SNASTE
capsize	WHEMMLE, WHOMBLE
	WHOMMLE, WHUMMLE
careful	EYEFUL
carp	YERK
carrier	TRANTER
cart with last	
harvest load	HOCKCART
cartload	FOTHER, SEAM
cat-fish (N)	WOOF
catch with a bird-line	TEAGLE
cattle	
—dung	TATH
—shed	SHIPPEN, SHIPPON
caught	CATCHED, CATCHT

caul (N)	KELL
cause to stoop (SW)	STEEP
causing sickness	WAMBLY
cavity in rock (Cornwall)	VUG
celebration drink	BEVERAGE
chaffinch	SPINK
chain	TEAM
change one's clothes	SHIFT
changeable	WANKLE
chap	SPRAY, SPREATHE, SPREETHE
	SPREAZE, SPREEZE
chapped	SPRAID, SPRAYED
charm	COMETHER
chat	COSHER
chatter	MAG
cheat	FUGLE, MUMP
cheerful	CADGY
cheese-scoop	PALE
chide	BAN
children	CHILDER
chimney	CHIMLEY, CHUMLEY
chitterlings	CHIDLINGS, CHITLINGS
choice (N)	WALE
choose/choosing (N)	WALE
chubby	CHUFF, FUBBY, FUBSY
chum	BUTTY
churn (N)	KIRN
circus tumbler	JERRY-COME-TUMBLE
clamp	HOG
clean out (ditch)	FAY, FEY
clear (N)	REMBLE
climbing plant	WITH(Y)WIND
clip	DOD
clog	CLAM
closed handful	NIEVEFUL
clot	LOPPER
clover	SUCKLING
clown	JOSKIN
club-foot	POLTFOOT
clump	TUMP
clumsy	GAUMLESS, GORMLESS
	UNHEPPEN
—person (Cornwall)	LERRUP
cluster	BOB
coal-box	DAN
coarse grass	TATH
coax	CARN(E)Y
cockchafer	BUZZARD-CLOCK
	DUMBLEDORE
	HUMBUZZ
coddle	COSHER
collapse (W)	SCAT
comb	KEMB
combed	KEMPT
comely	GAINLY, LIKELY, TIDY
comfortable (N)	CANNY

commotion	FRAISE
comrade	BUTTY
conceal	HEAL, HEEL, HELE
conceited	CONCEITY
confoundedly	GALLOWS, MORTAL
confuse	MOIDER, MOITHER
confused sound	WHOOBUB
confusion	DUDDER, WHEMMLE
	WHOMBLE
	WHOMMLE, WHUMMLE
conical hill	PAP
connecting ridge	HALSE, HAUSE, HAWSE
consort	MAKE, SORT
conspire	COLLOGUE
contemptible	CRUDDY
contend strongly with	PINGLE
contract miners	BUTTY-COLLIER(S)
	BUTTY-GANG
contrary	CONTRAIR
convenient	GAIN
coolness	COOLTH
corn	
—marigold	GOLD
—spurrey	YARR
Cornish pasty	OGGY
cough	HOAST
country bumpkin	JOSKIN
courageous	WIGHT
cover	HEAL, HEEL, HELE
—with	
dish	WHEMMLE, WHOMBLE
	WHOMMLE, WHUMMLE
soil	HELE IN
cow	
—dung	SHARN
—dung and coal cake	SHARNY PEAT
—house	SHIPPEN, SHIPPON
cow's yield	MESS
crane-fly	JENNY-SPINNER
creak	FRATCH
creature	WIGHT
creek	WICK
crisp	CRUMPY
croak	CRAKE
crook	CROMB, CROME
cross	FRANZY
crouch	DARE
crow	CRAKE
crowberry	CRAKEBERRY
crowd	MONG
crumbly	NESH
cry-baby	MARDY
cunning	VARMENT, VARMINT
—mischief (N)	PAWK
cur (N)	TYKE
curd	CRUD
curdle	LOPPER, RUN, WHIG
	(Y)EARN
currant cake (N)	SINGING-HINNY
customer	CHAPMAN
cut the hair of	DOD
dace (N)	GRAINING
dally	PINGLE
damaged piece of cloth (N)	FENT
damnably	GALLOWS
dampness	CLAM
dangerous (N)	NO'CANNY
dash	DAD, DAUD
dashing	VARMENT, VARMINT
daze	GALLY
deaf	DUNNY
decent	GRADELY, GRAITHLY
decomposed rock (Cornwall)	GOSSAN
	GOZZAN
decoy	TOLE, TOLL
defective mentally	WANTING
defile	HALSE, HAUSE, HAWSE
defilement	MOIL
deformed person	URCHIN
degree	GRE(E)CE, GRECIAN
	GRE(E)SE, GREESING, GRESSING
	GRI(E)CE, GRISE, GRIZE
demure	MIM(-MOU'D)
depression in breast	HEART-SPOON
destructive	VENGEABLE
devour	SCOFF, SKOFF
die	SWELT
dig	GRAFT
diminutive person	NIFF-NAFF
dirt	CROCK
disease of horse's hoof	FRUSH
disgusting	MAWKISH
dismayed	DARE
dispense with	WANT
dispute (N)	THREAP, THREEP
dissolute	OUTWARD
distinctive flavour	TACK
ditch	GRAFT
—(SW)	REAN, REEN, RHINE
division of county (N)	WARD
do	
—anything briskly	LILT
—without	WANT
dog (N)	TYKE
donkey	CUDDIE, CUDDY
doorpost	DURN
doze	DARE
drain	SEW, SILE
drainage canal	EA(U)
draining-shaft	STULM
dram	TIFT
draw tight (stitches)	YERK

drawl	DRA(UN)T
dress up	BUCK
drink	TIFT
—money	BEVERAGE
drinker (N)	BIRLER
drone	DRA(U)NT
drop dung	TATH
drudge	MOIL
dwell	WON
earliest	RATHEST
early	
—fruit or vegetables	HASTINGS
—ripe (variety)	RATH(E)RIPE
earwig	FORIT-TAIL, FORKY-TAIL
easily handled	YARE
eat with feeble	
appetite	PINGLE
eerie	UNKED, UNKET, UNKID
egg	COCKNEY
either	OUTHER
elaborate flowerbed	KNOT
embankment (N)	STAITH(E)
embrace	HALSE, HAUSE, HAWSE
enclose	TINE
enclosed hollow part	WAME
end	SHANK
—of season	BACK-END
endearment	PIGSN(E)Y, PIGSNIE
endure	ABEAR
engage in with energy	YERK
ensnare	SNARL
equal	MAKE
escort (N)	SET
eve	E'EN, EVEN
everybody (N)	A'BODY
every way (N)	A'GATE
everywhere (N)	A'WHERE
ewe	YOW(E)
excavation	GRAFT
exceedingly	MAIN
except	NOBBUT, ONLY
	OUTSIDE OF, WITHOUT
exchange	COPE, TOLSEL
	TOLSEY, TOLZEY
excite loathing in	UG
exert oneself	PINGLE
exit (N)	OUTGATE
expert	SLY
express yearning	YAMMER
expression of	
—commendation	FAIR
—courtesy	FAIR
extremely	MORTAL
eye	WINKER
fade away	WALLOW
faggot	KNITCH

failure to understand	ANAN
fair	PLAYING
fairy (SW)	PISKY
faith	FAIX
falsehood	LEASING
fantastical	CONCEITED
farm	WICK
farthing	FARDEN, FARDING
fascinated	DARE
fast	
—horse	GANGER
—pace	RAKER
fastidious person	QUIDDLE(R)
fat clumsy woman	HORSE-GODMOTHER
favourable	TOWARD
feeble	WEARISH
feeling of nausea	WAMBLE
ferrule	VERREL
fertile	BATTLE
festival	PLAYING
fibre	VIVER
film (N)	KELL
finch	SPINK
fine	GRADELY, GRAITHLY
—Oxford	SCONCE
fireside ledge	STOCK
fish-pond	VIVER
fish-trap	WEEL
fist	NEIF, NEIVE, NIEF, NIEVE
fit	GRADELY, GRAITHLY
—of perversity	GEE
flap	FLACKER
flared	FLEW, FLUE
flat	FLEW, FLUE
—basket	TRUG
flattery	CARN(E)Y
flexible rod	WATTLE
flight of steps	GRE(E)CE, GRECIAN
	GRE(E)SE, GREESING
	GRESSING, GRI(E)CE
	GRISE, GRIZE
floor	PLANCH
—of coal-seam	THILL
flounder about	TOLTER
fluffy	PLUFFY
flutter	FLACKER
fly wide (hawk)	RAKE
fodder	FOTHER
follow scent (dog)	RAKE
fool	MUMCHANCE
foolish person	GUMP
foot-rot	HALT
forget	MISREMEMBER
fork	GRAIN
form into single file (N)	RAKE
forward	FORRAD

fowl	BIDDY
framework for corn-stack	HOVEL
freckle	FAIRNITIC(K)LE
	FERN(I)TIC(K)LE
	FERNYTIC(K)LE
friendly	CADGY
frightened	FRIT
frog of horse's hoof	FRUSH
frolic	GAMMOCK
frolicsome	CADGY
fuddle	FUZZLE
fuel (N)	ELDIN(G)
full cloth or yarn	WALK
fumes (SW)	SMEECH
fun	GAMMOCK, GIG
fungus for tinder	SPUNK
fuss	WORK
fusty	FROWSY, FROWZY
gable	GAVEL
gang (N)	RAKE
gap	SHARD, SHERD
garfish	HORNBEAK
gasp	CHINK
—(N)	KINK
gather windfalls	SCRUMP, SKRIMP, SKRUMP
geld	LIB
get	
—by begging	MUMP
—on well	GEE
—over	OVERGET
—together with an effort	SCAMBLE
getting on	TOWARD
ghost	GYTRASH
gid or sturdy in sheep	DUNT
gin and treacle	MAHOGANY
gird	YERK
girl	GAL
—East Anglia	MAUTHER, MAWTHER
give birth prematurely	WARP
glean	LEASE
glimpse	WHIFF
gluey material	LIME
go	GEE
—about	
idly	SAMP
noisily	CLUTTER
—astray	MISGO
—courting	WENCH
—easy (N)	CA'CANNY
—short	STINT
goad	BROD
goat (N)	GATE
goblin	
—in mine	KNOCKER
—(N)	BOGGARD, BOGGART
	BOGGLE

good	
—condition	KELTER, KILTER
—even	GOD-DEN
—number	THR(E)AVE
good-for-nothing	DONNAT, DONNOT
gooseberry	GOOSEGOG, WINE-BERRY
graceful	GAINLY
grandfather	GRANFER
grass (N)	HAVER
grating in river	HECK
grease on side of	
candle	WINDING-SHEET
great deal	MORT
greater spotted	
woodpecker	WITWALL
green woodpecker	HICKWALL, WITWALL
greyhound	GREW(HOUND)
grilse	PEAL, PEEL
grimace	MUMP
ground ivy	GILL
grumble	CHUNNER, CHUNTER
hair-net (N)	KELL
halter for hanging	WIDDY
hamper	PED
hand	DADDLE
handle	HANDFAST, STALE
	STEAL(E), STEEL
	STEIL, STELE
—on scythe shaft	NIB
handy	GEMMY, JEMMY
hanging clock (N)	WAG-AT-THE-WALL
	WAG-BY-THE-WALL
hangman's rope	WIDDY
happy chance	MERCY
harangue	SPEECH
harass	PINGLE
hard	
—blow	POLT
—work (Cornwall)	LOUSTER
hardened cutting edge	FIRE-EDGE
harmless (N)	CANNY
harsh word	MISWORD
harvest	
—home	HAWKEY, HOCKEY, HORKEY
—supper	HAWKEY, HOCKEY, HORKEY
have a mind to	MIND
having an eye	EYEFUL
hawker	TRANTER
he	A
head-pad	WASE
heap	TASS
heap (waste)	BING
heart of rotten tree	DADDOCK
hearty kiss	SMOUCH
heated	HET
heed	GAUM, GORM

help in need	BEETMISTER
helter-skelter	LIKE HEY-GO-MAD
hiccup	YESK, YEX
hidden	DE(A)RN
hide	HEAL, HEEL, HELE
hillcrest	KNAP
hillock	KNAP, TOFT, TUMP
him	UN
hither and thither	HITHER AND YON(D)
hobgoblin	BULLBEGGAR
hoist	TEAGLE
hold	HOLT
hollo	HOLLER
hollow enclosed part	WAME
homeward	UP ALONG
honey (N)	HINNY
honeysuckle	SUCKLING
hook	CROMB, CROME
hop about	LILT
horizontal mine-prop	STULL
horse	CUDDIE, CUDDY
	KEFFEL
—belly-band	WANTY
—block	JOSS-BLOCK
hot coal	GLEED
however	LEAST(A)WAYS
hubbub	WHOOBUB
hummocky	TUMPY
hunchback	URCHIN
hurdle	WATTLE
hurdy-gurdy	HUMSTRUM
hurt	NOY
husband	MASTER
hussy	HUZZY
I	A, CHE
—am	CHAM
—have	CHAVE
—will	CHILL
idler (N)	DONNAT, DONNOT
ill	QUEER
—natured person	PATCH
—tempered	STINGY
imbecile	INNOCENT
impending	TOWARD
improve	BEET, BETE
in	
—good	
condition or order	TIDY
spirits	PEART, PIERT
—order to	FOR TO
—poor health	INDIFFERENT
—the direction facing one	TOWARD
inclined	LIKE
inconvenient	UNGAIN
indict	TROUNCE
indirect	UNGAIN

infect(ion) (N)	SMIT
infectious (N)	SMITTLE
inferior asparagus (London)	SPRUE
inflate	BLAST
information	WITTING
infuse	MASH
inner door	HECK
innocent (N)	CANNY
insipid	MAWKISH
insist (N)	THREAP, THREEP
interjection of	
—excitement	HEY-GO-MAD
—surprise	LAWK(S)
inward	TOWARD
iris	GLADDON
it	A
itch(ing)	EWK, (Y)EUK, YOUK
	YUCK, YUKE
jack (bowls) (N)	KITTY
jail (N)	KITTY
jaw (N)	CHAFT
join	PIECEN
journey (N)	RAKE
jumping pole (E. Ang)	QUANT
keep from one year	
to next	OVERYEAR
keep scratching (W)	SCRATTLE
kick	WINCE, YERK
—(N)	PUNCH
kid	YEANLING
kindle	TIND
kiss	SMOUCH
knock	CON, JO(U)LE, JOLL, JOWL
—(N)	SCAT
knowledge	WITTING
known	BEKNOWN
labour	MOIL
ladder	STY
lamb	YEANLING
lame	GAMMY, MAIN
lament	YAMMER
lane between	
—houses	ENTRY
—walls or hedges	TWITTEN
lapwing	TEW(H)IT
larder	SPENCE
large beetle	CLOCKER
lark about	GAMMOCK
lash out with	YERK
last	YESTERN
late autumn	BACK-END
latter part	SHANK
lay eggs prematurely	WARP
lean from loin of pork	GRISKIN
leap(ed)	LEP
lease	SET

leash	TRASH
leave undisturbed	LET-A-BE
ledge	LINCH(ET), LYNCHET
leg	PESTLE
Lent boat races (Oxford)	TORPIDS
let	SET
letter z	IZZARD, IZZET
level a measure of grain	STRIKE
lie	LIG
—(N)	LIG(GE), LIGGEN
lies/lying	LEASING
lift	TEAGLE
light cart (N)	SHANDRY(DAN)
lightly cooked (eggs)	RARE
likely	LIKE
linger about	HANKER
liquid filth	ADDLE
litter	TEAM
little	LEET, LITE, LYTE
—pig	GRICE
—things	FEWTRILS
lively	COBBY, KEDGE
	KEDGY, KIDGE, PEART, PIERT
—(N)	KIPPER
load	FOTHER
—(N)	RAKE
loaf	MICHE
loathe	UG
loathly (N)	LAIDLY
loathsome	MAWKISH
loft (W)	TALLAT, TALLET, TALLOT
lonely	UNKED, UNKET, UNKID
long	SIDE
loose woman	MORT
lop(pings)	SHROUD
lore (N)	LARE
lounge about	HAWM
lout	LOBLOLLY
low	
—hill	HOW
—(N)	LAW
—stool	CRICKET
—whisper	PIG'S-WHISPER
lower part of door	HECK
luce	GED
lump	DAD, DAUD
	GOB, LUNCH
lunch	TIFT
lure	TOLE, TOLL
lurk	DARE
madam	MISTRESS
maggot(y)	MAWK(ISH)
maim	MAIN
maimed	GAMMY
maintain persistently (N)	THREAP
	THREEP

make	
—a	
harsh noise	FRATCH
mess of	BOSS
mound around	TUMP
sullen roaring	WHITHER, WUTHER
—an outcry	YAMMER
—progress by great effort	THRUTCH
—ready (Cornwall)	TEEL
—tea	WET
mall (N)	MELL
man	MUN
manageable	YARE
manner of doing (N)	GATE
manure	TATH
marble	MARL
marbled	MARLED, MARLY, MIRLY
mark	
—off	MERE
—with ruddle (N)	SMIT
marshy spot	SPEW, SPUE
maslin	MONGCORN, MUNGCORN
match	SPUNK
mate	MAKE
maudlin	MAWKISH
maul (N)	MELL
may (past tense)	MOUGHT
mean	FOOTY
mediator	STICKLER
mend	BEET, BETE
mentally	
—defective	WANTING
—normal	WISE
mess	MUX
mild explosion	PLUFF
militiaman	LUMP
milk-strainer	SYE
mine (Cornwall)	WHEAL
mining lease (Cornwall)	SET
mischievous	GALLOWS
missel thrush	THROSTLE-COCK
misshapen egg	COCKNEY
mixture	MONG
moderately warm	LUKE
mole	WANT
mop	MALKIN, MAWKIN
mope	MUMP
more forward	FORRADER
most convenient	EFTEST
mouch	MICHE
mould-board	PLAT
mouldy	FOUGHTY
mouthful	GOB
move	QUATCH, QUETCH
	QUITCH
—diagonally	CATER(CORNER)

—swiftly or with force	WHITHER, WUTHER
—tremulously	WAPPER
—unsteadily	WAMBLE
—with a jerk	YERK
mow	TASS
mowing	MATH
much	MORT
—(N)	MICKLE, MUCKLE
mud (N)	SLAKE
—flat (N)	SLAKE
mumble	MUMP
munch	MUMP
murderer	MURTHERER
musical instrument	HUMSTRUM
must	MAN, M(A)UN
musty	FOUGHTY
mutter	CHUNNER, CHUNTER
	MUMP
nag (horse)	KEFFEL
nail	BROD
nape of neck	NODDLE, SC(R)UFF, SCUFT
natty	VARMENT, VARMINT
near	GAIN
neat	GEMMY, JEMMY
neck	
—and spine of forequarter	RACK
—neck (N)	HALSE, HAUSE, HAWSE
neigh	WHICKER
neighbour	BOR
network (N)	KELL
never a ...	NARY
newt	ASK(ER)
next	NEIST
nighest	NEIST
nightjar	EVEJAR
nimble	WAN(D)LE, WANNEL, WIGHT
—(N)	WIMBLE
nipple	PAP
noise	CLUTTER
nonsense	FADDLE
normal mentally	WISE
not	
—dangerous (N)	CANNY
—one	NARY
—to be depended upon	WANKLE
—well	INDIFFERENT
notable man	COB
notice	GAUM, GORM, MIND
nourishing	BATTLE
now for	HEY FOR
nozzle	TEWEL
oak sapling	FLITTERN
oat-bread (N)	JANNOCK
oats (N)	HAVER
occasion	WHET

odd piece of cloth (N)	FENT
of	ON
—good omen	CANNY
—stone	STONERN
off we go	HEY FOR
offensive	FROWSY, FROWZY
on	
—acccount	LONG
of	ALONG
—hand	TOWARD
—the near or left side	TOWARD
one	UN
—who	
picks	PIKER
thrives	WELL-DOER
only	NOBBUT
ooze	SEW
open shed	LINHAY, LINNY
osier	
—pike-trap	KIPE
—rope	WIDDY
otter's den	HOLT
out-and-out	FAIR, TEETOTAL
outing	OUT
outlet (N)	OUTGATE
overcoat	JAMES, JEMMY
overcome	MOIDER, MOITHER
overthrow	WHEMMLE, WHOMBLE
	WHOMMLE, WHUMMLE
overturn	WHEMMLE, WHOMBLE
	WHOMMLE, WHUMBLE
oyster spawn	CUL(T)CH
pack-horse load	SEAM
pad on head	WASE
pamper	COSHER
pannier	PED
pantry	SPENCE
paralyse (SW)	SCRAM
parlour	KEEPING-ROOM
part of	
—leg of beef	MUSCLE
—spinning machine	HECK
parting gift	FOY
partition	TRAVIS, TREVIS(S)
partner	BUTTY
pass	HALSE, HAUSE, HAWSE
pasture	LEASE, LEAZE, LEASOW(E)
—(N)	RAKE
path (N)	GATE
pawky (N)	CANNY
pay attention to	GAUM, GORM
pedlar woodturner	BODGER
peel	PILL
peevish	FRANZY
peony	PINY
perch (E. Ang)	PERK

—(N)	PERK
period of work	YOLE
person	WIGHT
pet name (cow, etc)	MOG(GY)
petticoat	COAT
petulant child	MARDY
phosphorescence (sea)	BRIMING
physiognomy	VISNOMIE, VISNOMY
pick	PIKE
—(N)	WALE
pike	GED
pile (waste)	BING
pilfer	MICHE
pilferer	PIKER
pit of stomach	HEART-SPOON
pitch (N)	PICK
plank of oak	FLITTERN
plantain	WAYBREAD
play (N)	LAKE, LAIK
—the beggar	MUMP
—truant	MICHE
pleaded	PLED
pleasing	LIKELY
pliant	WAN(D)LE, WANNEL
plough	
—chain	TEAM
—handle	STILT
plump	TIDY
plunder	SCOFF, SKOFF
plunge in betting	RAKER
poke	PEG, POACH, POTE, PROKE
pole	PERCH
poll	DOD
pollard	DOD
pond	POUND
porridge-stick (N)	THIBLE, THIVEL
post	STOOP, STOUP
postman	POST
pot-bellied	KEDGE, KEDGY, KIDGE
potato	TATER
pour in a stream	HUSH
powder-puff	PLUFF
practise crystal-gazing	SCRY
praise	ROOSE
pre-breakfast snack	MORNING
prepared	YARE
preserve	PUT DOWN
press	THRUTCH
—eagerly (N)	THREAP, THREEP
pretend	LET ON
preternatural (N)	NO'CANNY
pretty drunk	FAIRISH
prick	BROD
prim	MIM(-MOU'D)
prize	GREE
probable	LIKE
proceed	RAKE
profitable occupation	THRIFT
projecting under-jaw	WAPPER-JAW
promptly	YARELY
prong	GRAIN
pronounce	TONGUE
prop (in mine)	STULL
—(N)	RANCE
proper(ly)	GRADELY, GRAITHLY
prostrate	FELL
protuberance	KNAP
protuberant part	WAME
public fountain (N)	PANT
puddle (N)	PANT
puff	PLUFF
puffed up	PLUFFY
pull	
—by the ears	SOOLE, SOWL(E)
—quickly or roughly	WAP
punch	POUNCE
punt mooring-pole	RIPECK, RY(E)PECK
punting pole (E. Ang.)	QUANT
puny	WEARY
—(SW)	SCRAM
puppet	PUPPY
purge	WORK
put in pickle	PUT DOWN
quake	WAMBLE
quantity	FOTHER
quarrel	FRATCH, OUTFALL, WHID
quarrelling	FRATCH(ET)Y
quick	YARE
quickly	YARELY
quill	TWILL
quilt	TWILT
quitch	QUICK(EN)
quite	FAIR
rack	
—and manger	HECK AND MANGER
—for fodder	HECK
ragged-Robin	WILD-WILLIAMS
raid orchards	SCRUMP, SKRIMP
	SKRUMP
rail	BAN
rain heavily	SILE
raised footpath	CLAPPER
ramify	SPRANGLE
range about	RAKE
rapid (SW)	STICKLE
rat	RATTON, ROTTAN, ROTTEN
raven	CRAKE
readiest	EFTEST
readily	GRADELY, GRAITHLY
ready	YARE
—to learn	TOWARD
rebuke (N)	THREAP, THREEP

recked (N)	RECKAN
recover from	OVERGET
red	
—apple (SW)	QUARANTINE
	QUARENDEN, QUAR(R)ENDER
	QUARRINGTON
—currant	WINE-BERRY
reed thicket (E. Ang.)	REED-RAND
	REED-ROND
refuge	HOLT
regard	GAUM, GORM
relating to yesterday	YESTERN
relieve	BEET, BETE
remind	REMEMBER
remnant (N)	FENT
remove (N)	REMBLE
—sprouts from	SPROUT
—stalk from (S)	STRIG
—to a distance	FAR
rend	RENT
reproach	WITE, WYTE
respectable	SPONSIBLE
responsible	SPONSIBLE
restrain	STINT
restraining hold	HANK
restraint	TRASH
rick in barn	GOAF
ricked (N)	RECKAN
ridge of land	STITCH
riot	WHOOBUB
rise	PLUFF
—with a jerk	YERK
river	EA(U)
roam	RAKE
rolling	
—in the stomach	WAMBLE
—movement	WAMBLE
roofing slab	SLAT
rootlet	VIVER
rope	WIDDY
—for securing hay	WANTY
rough	ROW
—bridge	CLAPPER
—mannered fellow (N)	TYKE
roughen	SPRAY, SPREATHE
	SPREETHE, SPREAZE, SPREEZE
roughened	SPRAID, SPRAYED
rouse	YERK
rowing-bench	THOFT
rubbish	CUL(T)CH
rump	NATCH
rung	SPELL
running water	EA(U)
rush	FEEZE, PHE(E)SE, PHEEZE
—basket	JUNKET
—of water	HUSH

sad	WO(E)
saddler	WHITTAW(ER)
sandwich	BUTTY
saucy	PEART, PIERT
scare	GALLY, SKEAR, SKEER
scarecrow	BOGGARD, BOGGART, BOGGLE
	GALLYBAGGER, GALLYBEGGAR
	MALKIN, MAWKIN
	GALLICROW, GALLYCROW
scatter	SCAMBLE
school	SCUL(L), SCULLE
scolding	HEARING
scope of choice (N)	WALE
scorch	SCALD, SCRAT
scratch	SCRAWM
screech	SHRITCH
scrimmage (Eton)	ROUGE
scuttle (W)	SCRATTLE
sea	
—bird of various kinds	TARROCK
—mist (E. coast)	HAAR
—weed	ORE, WARE
second boat or crew (Oxford)	TORPID
second-year salmon (N)	SPROD
secondary rainbow	WATER-GALL
secret	DE(A)RN
sedge	SEG
separate	SLEAVE
set	TILL
—on	SLATE
sewage	ADDLE
sewer	(COMMON-)SHORE
shaft	STALE, STEAL(E)
	STEEL, STEIL, STELE
—of vehicle	LIMBER
shake	DIDDER
shall (N)	SAL
shallot	SCALLION
shallow	FLEET, FLEW, FLUE
shamble	SCAMBLE
shank	STALE, STEAL(E)
	STEEL, STEIL, STELE
shape surface of mould	STRIKE
shapely	GAINLY, TIDY
sharp	VARMENT, VARMINT
—flavour	TWANG
she	A
sheaf of corn on end	GAIT
shed (N)	SHADE
ship's medicine	LOBLOLLY
shirt	SHIFT
shock of corn	STITCH
shoe sole	TAP
shoes	SHOON
shoot	CHIT, PLUFF
shore (N)	RANCE

short	
—and thick	PUNCH
—piece of cloth (N)	FENT
—rope	WANTY
shot	PLUFF
shove	THRUTCH
shovel	SHOOL
showy woman (N)	BOBBY DAZZLER
shrewd (N)	CANNY
shriek	SHRITCH
shrink	DARE
shrivel up	SCRUMP, SKRIMP
	SKRUMP
shrunk	WEARISH
shut	SHET, TINE
sick	QUEER
—at stomach	WAMBLE-CROPPED
sickly	MAWKISH
sieve	SYE
sigh	SITHE
sightly	EYEFUL
simpleton	GABY, ZANY
sip	TIFT
sit	SET
sitting-room	KEEPING-ROOM
skewer	SKIVER
skilful (N)	CANNY
skilfully	YARELY
skilled	
—amateur sportsman	VARMENT
	VARMINT
—in magic	WISE
skirt	COAT
skirting-board	WASH-BOARD
skulk	MICHE
slap	TWANK
slate	SLAT
slater	HELLIER
slatternly woman	BESOM
slice of meat	COLLOP
slight shower	SKIT
slime (N)	SLAKE
slimy material	LIME
slink	MICHE
slip	SLIVE
slipped	SLIVED, SLIVEN, SLOVE
slippery	GLIDDER
slop about	SLATTER
sloppy	SOZZLY
slops	SOZZLE
slow	LATE
slumber (N)	SLOOM
slush	LOPPER
slut	DRAZEL
sly (N)	CANNY
smack	SMOUCH, TACK, TWANG

small	
—branch	RICE
—enclosure (N)	PIGHTLE
—gate	HATCH
—landholder (N)	STATESMAN
—potato	CHAT
smart	GEMMY, JEMMY, SPIFF(Y)
smear	CLAM, SLUR
smoke	SMEECH
smooth	STRIKE
smothered laugh (N)	SNIRT
smut	CROCK
snack	BEVER, BUTTY
snail	DODMAN
snap	SNACK
snare	GRIN
—for fish	WEEL
snicker (N)	SNIRTLE
snigger	WHICKER
soak through	SIPE
soft	NESH
—and brittle	FROUGHY, FROWY
—sandstone (SE)	HASSOCK
soldier	SO(D)GER
something	SUMMAT
somewhat	SUMMAT
sorry	WO(E)
sound of	
—blow or blast	WHITHER, WUTHER
—rushing water	HUSH
sour	
—liquor	TIFT
—milk	WHIG
southern-wood	LAD'S LOVE
sown (N)	SAWN
spade (N)	PICK
sparing with money (N)	CANNY
spark	SPUNK
sparrow	SPUG
speaker of seditious words	LEASING-MAKER
speckled	SPRECKLED
spell (W)	SCAT
spider	ATTERCOP
spike	BROD
spill	SHED, SLATTER
—about	SWATTER
spirited person	SPUNK
spit	YESK, YEX
splash	FLOUSE, FLOUSH
	SLATTER, SOZZLE
—about	SWATTER
splayed	FLEW, FLUE
splinter	SPELL
spoil	MUX
spoilt child	MARDY
sponge	MUMP

sport	GIG	strip	UNSTRIP
—(N)	LAKE, LAIK	strive	PINGLE
spot	MOIL	stroke	JO(U)LE, JOLL, JOWL
spotted	GAY	strong	WIGHT
sprawl	SCAMBLE, SPRANGLE	strop	STRAP
sprightly	SPRACK, SPRAG	structure for	
springtime	WARE	shipping coal	STAITH(E)
sprout	CHIT	struggle	SPRANGLE
spruce	SPIFF(Y)	—with difficulties	PINGLE
squat	FUBBY, FUBSY	stubble field	AR(R)ISH
squatter	SWATTER	stubborn insistence (N)	THREAP, THREEP
squeamish	MAWKISH	stuffy	FROWSY, FROWZY
squeeze	SCRUZE	stupefy	MOIDER, MOITHER
squirrel	SKUG	stupid	GAUMLESS, GORMLESS
squirrel's nest	CAGE	—person	CUDDIE, CUDDY
staggering movement	WAMBLE	sudden shower (W)	SCAT
stain (N)	SMIT	suggestion	TWANG
stale liquor	TIFT	suit	GEE
stalk	STALE	sulk	MUMP
—(S)	STRIG	superiority	GREE
stall	TRAVIS, TREVIS(S)	supple	SOUPLE, WAN(D)LE
stare	DARE		WANNEL
statesman (N)	ESTATESMAN	supporting pillar	
steal	MAG	of coal	STOOP, STOUP
steep		surly	BLUFF
—narrow valley	GRIFF(E)	surveyor of boundaries	MERESMAN
—(SW)	STICKLE	suspect	SUSPICION
step	GRE(E)CE, GRECIAN, GRE(E)SE	sweet yellow gooseberry	HONEY-BLOB
	GREESING, GRESSING, GRI(E)CE	sweetmeats	SPICE
	GRISE, GRIZE	swell	BLAST, PLIM
stern	STARN	swift	WIGHT
stir	CLUTTER, QUATCH	taint (N)	SMIT
	QUETCH, QUITCH	tainted	FOUGHTY
—up	POACH	take the chill off	CHILL
stone or earthenware		tall awkward person	GAMMERSTANG
vessel	STEAN, STEEN	talon	TALENT
store vegetables in clamp	HOG	tap	TIT
stout	COBBY, STUGGY	tare	TINE
straddle	STRODDLE	tattle	TITTLE
straggle	SPRANGLE	tease	MAG
straggler	STRAG	tender	NESH
straight	GAIN	tepid	LUKE
straightforward	JANNOCK	terrace	LINCH(ET), LYNCHET
strain	SILE, SYE	territorial division (N)	WAPENTAKE
strainer	SILE(R)	test cheese	PALE
strange	UNKED, UNKET, UNKID	than	AS, NOR
stray	STRAG	that	YON
street (N)	GATE	—same	THILK
strenuous contest	PINGLE	(SW)	THICK
stretch		thatcher	HELLIER
—of work	YOKE	the (N)	T
—(N)	STREEK, STREAK	—one	TONE
strickle	STRIKE	—same	THILK
stride	STROAM	(SW)	THICK
strike	FRAP, YERK	—thing you know of	YON
string (N)	RAKE	they	A

thick	
—gruel	LOBLOLLY
—slice	LUNCH
thick-set	STUGGY
—man	PUNCH
thin	
—liquor	TIFT
—mud	SLUR
third finger of left hand	RINGMAN
thirty	THRETTY
this	THILK
—(SW)	THICK
those	YON
thou shalt (N)	THOUS
thrash	PAY
—(N)	RADDLE
throat	HALSE, HAUSE, HAWSE
throb	QUOP
throw	YERK
—against	DAD, DAUD
—into disorder	WHEMMLE, WHOMBLE
	WHOMMLE, WHUMMLE
—quickly or roughly	WAP
—violently	WHITHER, WUTHER
thrust	PEG, POACH, POTE
	THRUTCH, YERK
—(N)	PUT
thump	DAD, DAUD
tidy up	FETTLE
tie with a jerk	YERK
tiler	HELLIER
till next year	OVERYEAR
time	WHET
timid child	MARDY
timorous	EERIE, EERY
titter	WHICKER
to	
—bankruptcy (W)	SCAT
—some extent	LIKE
toil	MOIL
tolerate	ABEAR
toll	JO(U)LE, JOLL, JOWL
—booth	TOLSEL, TOLSEY, TOLZEY
top of hill	KNOLL
totter	DADDLE
touch-down in football (Eton)	ROUGE
towed barge	BUTTY
town	WICK
track (N)	RAKE
traditional belief (N)	THREAP, THREEP
trap	GRIN
—in knur and spell	SPELL
treat with setterwort root (N)	SETTER
tremble	WHITHER, WUTHER
trick	FUGLE
—(N)	PAWK

trifle	FADDLE, NIFF-NAFF
	PINGLE, QUIDDLE
trifles	FEWTRILS
trifling	FADDLE
trivet (Cornwall)	BRANDISAF
trouble	NOY, WORK
trouser braces	GALLUSES
trousers (N)	KECKS, KICKS
tub	DAN
tug	PUG
tun	COWL
turmoil	MOIL
turn	
—around	WAMBLE
—of string	WAP
—over and over	WAMBLE
—up to cover something	WHELM
—upside down	WAMBLE, WHEMMLE
	WHOMBLE, WHOMMLE
	WHUMMLE
turnip	TURMIT
tuyere	TEWEL
twelve-month (N)	TOWMON(D)
	TOWMONT
twig	WATTLE
twigs	RICE
twinge	TWANG
twist	WAMBLE
two	
—dozen	THR(E)AVE
stooks of sheaves	THR(E)AVE
—handled mug (Oxford)	SCONCE
uncomfortable	UNKED, UNKET, UNKID
uncouth	UNKED, UNKET, UNKID
undefiled	UNFILED
underclay	THILL
underhand throw	HAUNCH
underlip	FIPPLE, JIB
underneath	UNNEATH
undersized person	SCRUMP, SKRIMP
	SKRUMP
understanding	GAUM, GORM
unkempt	FROWSY, FROWZY
unless	WITHOUT
unpleasant	UNGAIN
unploughed strip	LINCH(ET), LYNCHET
unprepossessing	UNLIKELY
unreliable	WANKLE
unskilled	UNGAIN
unstable	WANKLE
unsteady	WAMBLY, WANKLE
—movement	WAMBLE
until (N)	WHILE
unwind	REAVE, REEVE
unyielding	STOUT
up the road	UP ALONG

uproar	WHOOBUB	wicked	WICK
urge (N)	THREAP, THREEP	widow	WIDDY
utter jerkily	YERK	widower	WIDOW-MAN
vagrant	STRAG, WALKER	wield	WELD, WIND
vegetable store	HOG	wife	WOMAN
vein of ore (N)	RAKE	wild	
veritable	FAIR	—orchis	PIONY
vermin	VARMENT, VARMINT	—vetch	TINE
very	GRADELY, GRAITHLY	will	WULL
	RIGHT	willow basket	WILL(E)Y
—much	PURELY	willowing-machine	WILL(E)Y
—small	TIDDLEY, TIDD(L)Y	wind (round, etc)	REAVE, REEVE
vexation	NOY	wisp of hay, straw etc	WASE
victory	GREE	withered	WEARISH
vigorous	SPRACK, SPRAG	—(SW)	SCRAM
village	WICK	without a mate	MAKELESS
villainous	GALLOWS	witless	GAUMLESS, GORMLESS
visit for purpose		woman	MORT, PIECE OF GOODS
of begging	MUMP	woman's head-dress	KELL
voice	STEVEN	womb	WAME
wail	YAMMER	wood	TIMBER
wait for	WAIT ON	—louse	SLATE
walk	TRAVEL	—pecker	WITWALL
—unsteadily	DADDLE	—pigeon	ZOO-ZOO
wander		woollen shawl	WHITTLE
—idly about	STROAM	word incorrectly	MISWORD
—in mind	MOIDER, MOITHER	work	
wanton	CADGY	—done at one stretch	YOKING
—girl	GAMMERSTANG	—hard	MOIDER, MOITHER
warrant	WARN	—ineffectually	PINGLE
wassail (Oxford)	SWIG	—mate	BUTTY
watch-hill (SW)	TOOT	—or roll (stomach)	WAMBLE
water-channel to mill	LEAT, LEET	worry	FRAB, PINGLE
watercourse (SW)	REAN, REEN, RHINE		WORRIT
watery-looking sky	WATER-GALL	worse (N)	WAR(RE), WAUR
wave	WAFFLE	worst (N)	WA(U)RST
way (N)	GATE	wrap (E. Anglia)	HAP
wearisome journey	JAUNCE, JAUNSE	wreck	WRACK
well		wrest (N)	WRAST
—disposed	TOWARD	wrestle (SW)	WRAXLE
—nigh	WELLY	wretched	WO(E)
wet	WEET	wriggle	WAMBLE, WIND
wharf (N)	STAITH(E)	wrinkle	FRUMPLE
whatsoever	WHATSOMEVER	writhe	WIND
wheedle	CARN(E)Y	yellow flower (N)	GOLLAN(D)
wheedling	COMETHER		GOWLAND
where are you going?	WHERE AWAY	yellow-hammer	YITE
whey	WHIG	yonder	YON
which	WHILK	young	
whine	YAMMER	—ewe	THEAVE
whisper	TITTLE	—oak	FLITTERN
wholemeal bread	RAVEL(LED) BREAD	—pig	SLIP
wholeness (N)	HALENESS	—sea-trout	PEAL, PEEL
whooping cough	CHINCOUGH	—sow	(Y)ELT
whore's baby	WOSBIRD	Yorkshireman	TYKE
wick	SNASTE	yours	YOURN

digestive system

cells in tongue	TASTE-BUD, TASTE-BULB
contractions of	
intestines propelling	
contents	PERISTALSIS
digestive fluid secreted	
—by	
liver	BILE
small intestine	SUCCIS ENTERICUS
—into mouth	SALIVA
diseases of	(see disease)
downward displacement	
of intestines	ENTEROPTOSIS
gland producing	
—bile etc	LIVER
—insulin etc	PANCREAS
—saliva	SALIVARY GLAND
gut	ENTERON
inflammation of	
—stomach	GASTRITIS
—intestines	ENTERITIS
internal	
—bulge(s) or pocket(s)	
in large	
intestine	DIVERTICULUM(DIVERTICULI)
—protrusion(s) in	
small intestine	VILLUS(VILLI)
intestines	
—in embryo	ARCHENTERON
—large	ASCENDING COLON
	CAECUM
	DESCENDING COLON
	TRANSVERSE COLON
	(VERMIFORM) APPENDIX
—small	DUODENUM
	JEJUNUM, ILEUM
lowest part of coelom	SPLANCHNOCELE
lymph vessels	LACTEALS
main digestive organ	STOMACH
membrane enclosing	PERITON(A)EUM
opening from	
—exterior to oesophagus	MOUTH
—stomach to intestines	PYLORUS
organ of taste	TONGUE
passage from	
—intestines to anus	RECTUM
—liver to small intestine	BILE DUCT
—mouth to	
anus	ALIMENTARY CANAL
	ENTERON
gullet	PHARYNX
stomach	GULLET
	(O)ESOPGHAGUS
—rectum to exterior	ANUS
poison causing food-	
poisoning	ENTEROTOXIN

protrusion of	
—intestine into	
top of thigh	ENTEROCELE
	HERNIA, RUPIURE
—stomach into chest	
cavity	DIAPHRAGM HERNIA
	HIATUS HERNIA
puncture of stomach	ENTEROCENTESIS
regurgitation of wind	BORBORYGMUS
	FLATULENCE
secondary digestive	
system	BOWELS, INTESTINES
slow-acting	BRADYPEPTIC
space between intestines	
and body-wall	COELOM
stomach	
—animals	MAW
—birds	
first	CRAW, CROP, MAW
second	GIZZARD
—ruminants	
first	PAUNCH, RUMEN
second	RETICULUM
third	MANYPLIES, OMASUM
	PSALTERIUM
fourth	ABOMASUM, MAW, RENNET
stone in stomach	ENTEROLITH
store for bile	GALL-BLADDER
surgical	
—formation of opening	COLOSTOMY
	ENTEROSTOMY
	GASTROTOMY
—incision of part	ENTEROTOMY
	GASTROTOMY
—removal of part	ENTERECTOMY
	GASTRECTOMY
upper throat	FAUCES
virus in intestines	ENTEROVIRUS
dinosaur	(see lizards)

discoveries

including: discoverer of
    proposer of

actinium	DEBIERNE
Aids virus	GALLO, MONTAGNIER
America	COLUMBUS, LEIF ERIKSON
anti	
—biotics	DUBOS
—histamines	BOVET, UNGAR
—matter	ANDERSON
—proton	LEE
—toxin	BEHRING
argon	RAMSAY, STRUTT
artificial	
radio-activity	JOLIOT-CURIE
astatine	CORSON, MACKENZIE
	SEGRE

asteroid	
—Bambega	PALISA
—Camilla	POGSON
—Ceres	PIAZZI
—Cybele	TEMPEL
—Davida	DUGAN
—Egeria	DE GASPARIS
—Eros	WITT
—Eugenia	GOLDSCHMIDT
—Eunomia	DE GASPARIS
—Euphrosyne	FERGUSON
—Europa	GOLDSCHMIDT
—Hidalgo	BAADE
—Hygeia	DE GASPARIS
—Icarus	BAADE
—Interamnia	CERULLI
—Juno	HARDING
—Lorelei	PETERS
—Pallas	OLBERS
—Patentia	CHARLOIS
—Psyche	DE GASPARIS
—Sylvia	POGSON
—Themis	DE GASPARIS
—Toro	HERRICK
—Vesta	OLBERS
atomic	
—mass	LAVOISIER
—theory	DALTON
atropine	BRANDES
aureomycin	DUGGAN
Australia	COOK
background radiation	PENZIAS, WILSON
bacteria	COHN, LEEUWENHOEK
benzene	FARADAY
blood	
—circulation	HARVEY
—groups	LANDSTEINER
brainwaves	BERGER
caffeine	CAVENTOU, PELLETIER
calcium	DAVY
capillaries	MALPIGHI
carbolic acid	LISTER
carbon	
—14	KAMEN, RUBEN
—dating	LIBBY
carborundum	ACHESON
cell	
—nucleus	BROWN
—theory	SCHLEIDEN
cephalosporins	BROTZU
charm(ed quark)	GLASHOW
chlorine	DAVY
chlorophyll	CAVENTOU, PELLETIER
chromatography	TSWETT
chromosomes	FLEMMING
city of Troy	SCHLIEMANN

colchicine	CAVENTOU, PELLETIER
cocaine formula	WOHLER
comet Chiron	KOWAL
conservation of energy	HELMHOLTZ
cosmic rays	HESS, MILLIKAN
cure for syphilis	EHRLICH
D° particle	GOLDHABER, PIERE
darkening of silver salts	SCHULTZE
DDT	MULLER
decipher	
—Rosetta stone	CHAMPOLLION
—Sumerian script	RAWLINSON
dendrochronology	DOUGLAS
deoxyribose	LEVENE
deuterium	UREY
diastase	PAYEN, PERSOZ
dimagnetism from	
superconductivity	MEISSNER
diseases caused by micro-organisms	PASTEUR
electricity in	
—muscles	GALVANI
—nerves	DU BOIS-REYMOND
electro	
—luminescence	DESTRIER
—magnetic radiation	MAXWELL
—magnetism	OERSTED
electron	THOMSON
exclusion principle	PAULI
francium	PEREY
gallium	DE BOISBAUDRAN
genetic (finger)printing	JEFFREYS
germanium	WINKLER
glycerol	SCHEELE
glycine	BRACONNOT
glycogen	BERNARD
gravity laws	NEWTON
group theory	GALOIS
hafnium	COSTER, HEVESY
helium	LOCKYER
hominids	
—Cro-Magnon man	LARTET
—Java man	DUBOIS
—Proconsul	LEAKEY
—Zinjanthropus	LEAKEY
hormones	BAYLISS, STARLING
hydrogen	
—in the sun	ANGSTROM
—radio waves	PURCELL
immunisation	PASTEUR
imprinting	LORENZ
infra-red light	HERSCHEL
inoculation against	
—anthrax	PASTEUR
—poliomyelitis	SABIN, SALK
—rabies	PASTEUR
—yellow-fever	THEILER

insulin	BANTING, BEST
interstellar gas	HARTMAN
iodine deficiency causes goitre	MARINE
isoprene	BOUCHARDAT
krypton	RAMSAY
language of bees	FRISCH
laughing gas	DAVY, PRIESTLEY
laws in inheritance	MENDEL
leucine	BRACCONOT
liposomes	BANGHAM
loss of magnetism with temperature	CURIE
LSD	HOFMAN
lutetium	URBAIN
magnesium	DAVY
magnetic induction	FARADAY
malaria carried by mosquitos	ROSS
Martian	
—canals	SCHIAPARELLI
—moons	HALL
mass of Earth	CAVENDISH
matrix mechanics	HEISENBERG
meson	YUKAWA
microsomes	CLAUDE
Minoan civilisation	EVANS
mitochondria	BENDA
morphine	SERTURNER
mutation by radiation	MULLER
Mycaenaean civilisation	SCHLIEMANN
neon	RAMSAY
Neptune	GALLE
nerves carry sensations	VON HALLER
neutrino	COWAN, REINES
neutron	CHADWICK
New Zealand	TASMAN
niridiazole	SCHMIDT
nitrogen	RUTHERFORD
nitroglycerine	SOBRERO
nitrous oxide	DAVY
North-west passage	FRANKLIN
nuclear fission	HAHN, STRASSMAN
nucleic acid	MEISCHER
—structure	CRICK, WATSON
ova in mammals	VON BAER
ovarian follicles	DE GRAAF, SCHWANN
oxygen	PRIESTLEY, SCHEELE
ozone	SCHONBEIN
ozonosphere	FABRY
penicillin	FLEMING
pepsin	SCHWANN
phenol	LISTER
photoelectric effect	LENARD
pi-meson (pion)	POWELL
piezo-electric effect	CURIE
polarised light rotated by crystals	BIOT
polio vaccine	SABIN, SALK
polonium	CURIE
positron	ANDERSON
promethium	CORYELL, GLENDENIN MARINSKY
proton	RUTHERFORD
protozoa	LEEUWENHOEK
pulsars	BELL, HEWISH
quantum mechanics	SCHRODINGER
quark (theory)	GELL-MANN
quasars	SCHMIDT
quinine	CAVENTOU, PELLETIER
radiation	
—belts in atmosphere	VAN ALLEN
—pressure	LEBEDEV
radio	
—activity	BECQUEREL
—emission of hydrogen	EWEN, PURCELL
—reflecting layers	APPLETON HEAVISIDE
—signals from space	JANSKY
—waves	HERTZ
in sun spots	HEY
radium	CURIE
radon	DORN
random movement of particles	BROWN
red blood corpuscles	SWAMMERDAM
rhenium	BERG, NODDACK TACKE
rh(hesus) factor	LANDSTEINER, WIENER
Rosetta stone	BOUSSARD
Saturn's moons	CASSINI
scandium	NILSON
sex hormones	ASCHEIM, ZONDEK
sickle-cell anaemia	HERRICK
silicones	KIPPING
solar	
—flares	CARRINGTON
—wind	PARKER
spermatozoa	HAM
spreading of ocean floor	VINE
static electricity	DUFAY
strangeness	GELL-MANN
streptomycin	WAKSMAN
structure of	
—atoms	RUTHERFORD
—DNA	CRICK, WATSON
—haemoglobin	PERUTZ
strychnine	CAVENTOU, PELLETIER
sulphapyridine	EVANS
superconductivity	KAMERLINGH-ONNES
Tasmania	TASMAN
technetium	LAWRENCE
tethecin	HOPPE-SEYLER
thermo-electricity	SEEBECK
thorium silicate	BREZELIUS
thyroid hormone	KENDALL

tomb of	
—Sethos	BELZONI
—Tutankhamun	CARTER
typhus carried by lice	NICOLLE
tyrosine	LIEBIG
ultra-violet light	RITTER
—as bactericide	FINSEN
uncertainty principle	HEISENBERG
vaccination	JENNER
variable star	FABRICIUS
variation in Moon's motion	TYCHO BRAHE
virus	BEIJERINCK
	IVANOVSKI
vitamins	FUNK
wave mechanics	SCHRODINGER
X-rays	RO(E)NTGEN
—from sun	FRIEDMAN
xenon	RAMSAY
yellow-fever carried by mosquitos	REED
Z particle	RUBBIA
zodiacal light	CASSINI
(*see also* **first, inventors**)	

diseases

including: complaint	
condition	
disorder	
illness	
pain	
abnormal	
—behaviour	PSYCHOACTIVE
	PSYCHOTROPIC
—cartilaginous growth	ENCHONDROMA
—childhood development	AUTISM
—contraction of pupil	MYOSIS
—development affecting	
language and communication	AUTISM
—enlargement	ANEURISM, ANEURYSM
	HYPERTROPHY
of breasts in male	GYNAECOMASTIA
	GYNAECOMASTY
—elation	EUPHORIA
—functioning of organ	DYSFUNCTION
—growth of spleen	SPLENOMEGALY
—rapidity of heart beat	TACHYCARDIA
—redness of skin	ROSACEA, RUBOR
—sensation	PARAESTHESIA
—sensitivity to	
pain	HYPERALGESIA
stimuli	HYPER(A)ESTHESIA
—sound from lungs	RALE, RHONCHUS
—thickness of skin	PACHYDERMIA
abnormally	
—high	
arches	PES CAVUS
blood pressure	HYPERTENSION
body temperature	HYPERPYREXIA

—low intestines	VISCEROPTOSIS
—swollen veins	VARICOSE VEINS
—tortuous vein	VARIX
abscess	BOIL, EMPYEMA
—round tonsil	QUINSY
absorption of rays	RADIATION SICKNESS
accumulation of fat	
on buttocks	STEATOPYGIA
actinomycosis	WOODEN-TONGUE
	WOODY-TONGUE
actinobacillosis	WOODEN-TONGUE
	WOODY-TONGUE
acute toxaemia	ECLAMPSIA
affecting behaviour	PSYCHOACTIVE
	PSYCHOTROPIC
air in pleural cavity	PNEUMOTHORAX
airman's disease	AEROEMBOLISM
	AREONEUROSIS
	FLIGHT FATIGUE
alastrim	SMALLPOX, VARIOLA MINOR
allergy	HAY-FEVER
alopecia	FOX-EVIL
alternating	
—laughter and tears	DACRYGELOSIS
—muscular spasm	CLONIC SPASM
amaurosis	BLINDNESS
amnesia	FUGUE
anaemia	CHLOROSIS, GREEN SICKNESS
anthrax	SANG, WOOLSORTER'S DISEASE
anxiety about health	HYPOCHONDRIA
apoplexy	STROKE
artificial sore	JIGGER
asbestos in lungs	ASBESTOSIS
athlete's foot	EPIDERMIPHYTOSIS
back-arching spasm	OPISTHOTONOS
back pain	LUMBAGO, SCIATICA
bacterial disease	LEPTOSPIROSIS
	LISTEROSIS
—infection	SEPSIS, SEPTICAEMIA
bad state of body	CACHEXIA, CACHEXY
Banti's disease	SPLENIC ANAEMIA
bedsore	DECUBITUS ULCER
bean poisoning	FAVISM
bejel	YAWS
bilharzia	SCHISTOSOMA
	SCHISTOSOMIASIS
birthmark	MOLE
Black Death	BUBONIC PLAGUE
blackhead	COMEDO
bleeding	HAEMORRHAGE
—disease	HAEMOPHILIA
—from nose	EPITAXIS
—into	
pleural cavity	HAEMOTHORAX
tissues	HAEMATOMA
urine	HAEMATURIA

—under skin	PURPURA
blind spot	SCOTOMA
blindness	AMAUROSIS
blister	VESICLE
blockage of artery	EMBOLISM
blood	
—disease	LEUCOCYTHAEMIA
	LEOCOCYTOPENIA, LEUCOCYTOSIS
	LEUC(H)AEMIA, LEUKAEMIA
	POLYCYTHAEMIA, PY(A)EMIA
	THALASS(A)EMIA
—poisoning	PYAEMIA, SEPTICAEMIA
	SUPRAEMIA, TOXAEMIA
—spitting	HAEMOPTYSIS
bloodlessness	ANAEMIA
blueness from lack	
of oxygen	CYANOSIS
boba	BUBA, BUTTON SCURVY
	FRAMBOESIA
	VERRUGA PERUVIANA, YAWS
bodily wasting	MARASMUS
boil	ABSCESS, FURUNCLE
—on eyelid	HORDEOLUM, STYE
bone	
—and cartilage	
erosion	OSTEO-ARTHRITIS
—deformation	PAGET'S DISEASE
	PERTHES' DISEASE
—disease	OSTEOPOROSIS
—injury	FRACTURE
—marrow disease	OSTEOMYELITIS
Bornholm disease	DEVIL'S GRIP
	PLEURODYNIA
botulism	FOOD POISONING
	SAUSAGE-POISONING
bow-leggedness	VALGUS
bowel disease	CONSTIPATION, DIARRHOEA
	DUODENAL ULCER, PEPTIC ULCER
	DYSENTERY, STEATORRHEA
brain	
—disorder	DELIRIUM (TREMENS)
	DISTONIA, ENCEPHALOPATHY
	EPILEPSY
—fever	ENCEPHALITIS, MENINGITIS
	PHRENESIS, PHRENITIS
breakbone fever	DANDY FEVER, DENGUE
breakdown of	
—immune system	AIDS
—red blood cells	HAEMOLYSIS
Bright's disease	NEPHRITIS
bronchial disease	ASTHMA, BRONCHITIS
brucellosis	MALTA FEVER
bruise	ECCHYMOSIS
buba	BOBA, BUTTON SCURVY
	FRAMBOESIA, VERRUGA PERUVIANA
	YAWS

bubonic plague	BLACK DEATH
bulging eyes	EXOPHTHALMIA
	EXOPHTHALMOS
	EXOPHTHALMUS
bursitis in	
—elbow	TENNIS ELBOW
—knee	HOUSE MAID'S KNEE
—lower back	WEAVER'S BOTTOM
—shoulder	DUSTMAN'S SHOULDER
button scurvy	BOBA, BUBA, FRAMBOESIA
	VERRUGA PERUVIANA, YAWS
calenture	SHIP FEVER
callosity	TYLOSIS
cancer	(see tumour below)
caused by	
—breathing	
rarefied air	MOUNTAIN-SICKNESS
	PUNA, SAROCHE
—flies or larvae	MYIASIS
—fungus	ATHLETE'S FOOT
	CANDIDIASIS, MONILIASIS
	MYCOSIS, THRUSH, TINEA
—mould	ASPERGILLOSIS
—tea-drinking	THEISM
—treatment	IATROGENIC ILLNESS
—vegetable parasite	PHYTOSIS
cerebro-spinal fever	MENINGITIS
cessation of breathing	APNOEA
chemical disorder of joint	GOUT
chest pain	ANGINA
chickenpox	VARICELLA
chilblain	PERNIO
chlorine poisoning	FLUOROSIS
chlorosis	GREEN SICKNESS
cholesterol deposits	XANTHOMA
chorea	ST VITUS'S DANCE
cirrhosis of liver	WHISKY-LIVER
clergyman's knee	BURSITIS
clot blocking artery	MBOLUS
clotting in blood	
vessel	THROMBOSIS
club-foot	KYLLOSIS, TALIPES
—in-turned	VARUS
—out-turned	VALGUS
coal-dust in lungs	ANTHRACOSIS
cold sore	HERPES (SIMPLEX)
colour-blindness	DALTONISM
	DICHROMATISM
	MONCHROMASY
comedo	BLACKHEAD
common cold	CORYZA
compression sickness	BENDS
compulsive pulling out	
of hair	TRICHOTILLOMAN(IA
congenital idiocy	DOWN'S SYNDROME
	MONGOLISM

congestion of blood	HYPERAEMIA
conjunctivitis	PINK-EYE
connective tissue disease	RHEUMATOID ARTHRITIS
constriction of blood vessels, pores, etc	STENOSIS
consumption	TB, TUBERCULOSIS
contagious disease	ZYMOSIS
contraction of pupil	MIOSIS, MYOSIS
convulsions	EPILEPSY, FIT PAROXYSM
—at end of pregnancy	ECLAMPSIA
corn on foot	HELOMA
cotton workers' disease	BYSSINOSIS
cough	TUSSIS
cowpox	VACCINIA
Crohn's disease	ENTERITIS
crop of boils	FURUNCULOSIS
curvature of spine	KYPHOSIS, LORDOSIS SCOLIOSIS
cyst	
—in gland under tongue	RANULA
—with porridge-like contents	ATHEROMA
cystic fibrosis	MUSCOVISCIDOSIS
dandruff	FURFUR
dandy fever	BREAKBONE FEVER, DENGUE
day blindness	HEMERALOPIA
death of part	NECROSIS
decay	GANGRENE
defect of	
—fibrin in blood	HYPINOSIS
—red blood cells	OLIGOCYTHAEMIA
defective	
—acid-alkali balance	ACIDOSIS ALKALOSIS
—bone growth	OSTEOCHONDRITIS OSTEOCHONDROSIS PERTHES' DISEASE, RICKETS SCHEUERMANN'S DISEASE SCHLATTER'S DISEASE
—interpretation of writing	PARALEXIA
—reasoning	PARALOGIA
—vision	ANOPIA
deficiency	
—disease	BERI-BERI PELLAGRA, SCURVY
—of	
alpha-galactosidase	ANDERSON-FABRY DISEASE
blood	ISCH(A)EMIA OLIGAEMIA
blood-clotting	HAEMOPHILIA
carbon dioxide	ACAPNIA
cartilage	ACHONDROPLASIA
enzyme	PHENYLKETONURIA

essential food	MALNUTRITION STARVATION
haemoglobin	ANAEMIA
hydrochloric acid	ACHLORHYDRIA
insulin	DIABETES
iron	SIDEROPENIA
oxygen	ANOXIA
red blood corpuscles	SPANAEMIA
selenium	KESHAN'S DISEASE
sugar in blood	HYPOGLYCAEMIA
thyroid hormone	CRETINISM
vitamins	AVITAMINOSIS
—B	ANAEMIA, BERI-BERI PELLAGRA
—C	SCURVY
—D	OSTEOMALACIA, RACHITIS RICKETS
white blood cells	AGRANULOCYTOSIS
deformation of	
—arms and legs	PHOCOMELIA
—ear	CAULIFLOWER EAR
—fingers	DUPUYTREN'S CONTRACTURE
—foetus	TERATOMA
—foot	CLUB-FOOT, TALIPES
—head	HYDROCEPHALY, MICROCEPHALY
—hip (splayed hip)	COXA VULGA
—joints	OSTEOARTHRITIS OSTEOARTHROSIS
—knee (knock-knee)	GENU VALGUM
—neck muscle	TORTICOLLIS WRYNECK
—toe-joint	HALLUX VALGUS
degeneration of kidney	ADDISON'S DISEASE NEPHROSIS
delirium	PHRENESIS, PHRENITIS
delusion	
—man as beast	ZOANTHROPY
—seeing animals	ZOOSCOPY
—self as another	APPERSONATION
dementia praecox	SCHIZOPHRENIA
dengue	BREAKBONE FEVER DANDY FEVER
deposit of melanin	MELANOSIS
depression	MELANCHOLIA MELANCHOLY
—in winter	SAD SEASONAL AFFECTIVE DISORDER
deranged nutrition	TROPHESY TROPHONEUROSIS
dermatitis	ECZEMA
destruction of kidneys	ADDISON'S DSSEASE
devil's grip	BORNHOLM DISEASE
diarrhoea	LIENTERY, WEANING-BRASH
—from Mexican food	MONTEZUMA'S REVENGE

—in Middle East	GIPPY TUMMY
	GYPPY TUMMY
difficulty in	
—breathing	DYSPNOEA
—focusing on	
near objects	PRESBYOPIA
—passing urine	DYSURIA, STRANGURY
—producing sound	DYSPHONIA
—swallowing	DYSPHAGIA
—understanding thought	DYSPHASIA
dilatation of	
—arteries	TELANGIECTASIS
—artery	ANEURISM, ANEURYSM
—blood vessels	HAEMORRHOIDS, PILES
—bronchi	BRONCHIECTASIS
—pupil	MYDRIASIS
—veins in anus	HAEMORRHOIDS, PILES
dimness of sight	CALIGO
discharge	
—from	
ear	OTORRHOEA
glands	SEBORRHOEA
nose	OZAENA
—of pus	PYORRHOEA
discoloration	
—due to extravasation	
of blood	ECCHYMOSIS
—of the skin	DYSCHRO(I)A
diseased feet	TRENCH-FEET
disintegration of blood cells	LYSIS
dislocation of joint	LUXATION
disordered	
—cell growth	CANCER, CARCINOMA
—condition of body	DYSCRASIA
—hearing	PARACUSIS
—speech	PARARTHRIA
displacement of	
—eye	PROTOPSIS
—intestines	ENTEROPTOSIS
—organ	HETEROTOPIA, PROLAPSE
forward	ANTEVERSION
—parts	ECTOPIA, ECTOPY
disseminated sclerosis	DS
	MULTIPLE SCLEROSIS
distension of	
—intestines	METEORISM
—lung	EMPHYSEMA
—stomach	FLATULENCE
distrophia	
DUCHENNE MUSCULAR DISTROPHY	
diver's affliction	BENDS
	CAISSON DISEASE
	COMPRESSED AIR SICKNESS
	DECOMPRESSION SICKNESS
dizziness	SCOTODINIA, SCOTOMA
double vision	DIPLOPIA

Down's syndrome	MONGOLISM
dracontiasis	GUINEA-WORM DISEASE
drooping of upper eyelid	PTOSIS
dropsy	(O)EDEMA, HYDROPSY
—in chest	HYDROTHORAX
—of	
abdomen	ASCITES
the brain	HYDROCEPHALUS
drowsiness	NARCOSIS
dryness of	
—conjunctiva	XEROMA
XEROPHTHALMIA, XEROSIS	
—hair	XERASIA
—mouth	XEROSTOMIA
—skin	ICTHYOSIS, XERODERM(I)A
dullness of sight	AMBLYOPIA
dumdum fever	KALA-AZAR
dust in lungs	PNEUMOCONIOSIS
PNEUMO(NO)KONIOSIS	
—asbestos dust	ASBESTOSIS
	MESOTHELIOMA
—carbon dust	ANTHRACOSIS
—cotton dust	BYSSINOSIS
—fungus	FARMER'S LUNG
—iron dust	SIDEROSIS
—silica dust	SILICOSIS
dustman's shoulder	BURSITIS
dwarfism	ATELEIOSIS
dyslexia	WORD BLINDNESS
dyspepsia	INDIGESTION
ear	
—ache	OTALGIA, OTALGY
—disorder	CHOLESTEATOMA
	OSTOSCLEROSIS
MENIERE'S DISEASE, TINNITUS	
early insanity	HEBEPHRENIA
East Coast fever	TICK FEVER
ecchymosis	BRUISE
eczema	DERMATITIS
elephantiasis	BARBADOS LEG
emaciation	TABES
encephalitis lethargica	SLEEPY-SICKNESS
enlargement of	
—baby's head	HYDROCEPHALIS
—bone	EXOSTOSIS
—kidney	HYDRONEPHROSIS
—male breasts	GYNAECOMASTIA
—prostate	PROSTATISM
—spleen	SPLENOMEGALY
—thyroid	GOITRE
enteric fever	GASTRIC FEVER, TYPHOID
epidemic disease	ZYMOSIS
epilepsy	FALLING SICKNESS, PETIT MAL
	PYKNOLEPSY
eruption on	
—nose	ROSE-DROP

—palms or soles	POMPHOLYX
eruptive disease	(SHEEP-)POX
erysipelas	ROSE, ST ANTHONY'S FIRE
excess of	
—body fat	ADIPOSITY, OBESITY
—calcium	HYPERCALC(A)EMIA
—gas in stomach	FLATULENCE
—red blood cells	POLYCYTHAEMIA
—salt in blood	HYPERNATRAEMIA
—sugar in blood	DIABETES
—urea in blood	URAEMIA
—water in tissue	(HY)DROPSY, OEDEMA
—white blood cells	MONONUCLEOSIS
excessive	
—activity of	
adrenal gland	HYPERADRENALISM
sebaceous gland	SEBORRHOEA
thyroid gland	THYROTOXICOSIS
—bleeding	HAEMOPHILIA
—chyle in urine	CHYLURIA
—deposit of fat in arteries	ATHEROMA
—discharge from	
fatty glands	SEBORRHOEA
nose	RHINORRHOEA
—excitement	HYPERSTHENIA
—fibrin in blood	HYPERINOSIS
—flow of	
mucus	CATARRH
saliva	PTYALISM
—formation of	
acetone or ketone	KETOSIS
urine	POLYURIA
—frequency of	
breathing	TACHYPNOEA
—growth	ACROMEGALY, GIGANTISM
of	
—brain supporting	
tissues	GLIOMATOSIS
—fat	LIPOMATOSIS
—papillae	PAPILLOMA
—tissue	HYPERPLASIA
	HYPERTROPHY
—nose-bleeding	RHINORRHAGIA
—number of	
breasts	POLYMASTIA
	POLYMASTISM, POLYMASTY
chromosomes	POLYSOMY
—secretion of	
hormones	CUSHING'S DISEASE
mucus	BLENNORRHOEA
—sensitivity to	
pain	HYPERALGESIA
stimuli	HYPERAESTHESIA
—sweating	HIDROSIS, HYPER(H)IDROSIS
—temperature	HYPERPYREXIA
—thirst	POLYDIPSIA

—vomiting	HYPEREMESIS
—vitamins	HYPERVITAMINOSIS
—wind	FLATULENCE
exophthalmic goitre	GRAVES DISEASE
expansion of blood	
vessels	VASODILATATION
eye disease	BLEPHARISM, BLEPHARITIS
	CATARACT, CERATITIS
	CONJUNCTIVITIS, CYCLOPLEGIA
	DETACHED RETINA, DIPLOPIA
	GLAUCOMA, HYPER(METR)OPIA
	KERATITIS, MYOPIA, NYSTAGMUS
	PANNUS, TRACHOMA
	TUNNEL VISION
failure	
—of	
brain growth	ANENCEPHALY
blood circulation	SHOCK
heart to empty itself	ASYSTOLE
—to	
assimilate	
—fats, etc	COELIAC DISEASE, SPRUE
—food	MALABSORPTION
co-ordinate movements	ATAXIA
secrete	
—milk	AGALACTIA
—urine	ANURIA
faint	SYNCOPE
false	
—joint	PSEUDARTHROSIS
—pregnancy	PSEUDOCYESIS
fatty	
—degeneration	STEATOSIS
—tumour	STEATOMA
faulty	
—alignment of	
eyes	SQUINT, STRABISM(US)
teeth	MALOCCLUSION
—healing of fracture	MALUNIO
fever	PLAGUE, PYREXIA
—recurring	
daily	QUOTIDIAN
every three days	TERTIAN
fifth disease	ERYTHEMA INFECTIOSUM
	SLAPPED CHEEK SYNDROME
fit	CONVULSION, EPILEPSY
	PAROXYSM, SEIZURE
fixed delusions	PARANOIA
flat foot	PES PLANUS
flatulence	BORBORYGMUS
flatulent distension	TYMPANITIES
flea-borne	PLAGUE, TYPHUS
floating kidney	NEPHROPTOSIS
fluid in knee-joint	WATER ON THE KNEE
food-poisoning	BOTULISM, LISTERIOSIS
	PTOMAINE, SALMONELLOSIS

framboesia	BOBA, BUBA
	BUTTON SCURVY, MORULA
	VERRUGA PERUVIANA, YAWS
freckle	LENTIGO
from	
—animals	ZOONOSIS
—birds	PARROT DISEASE
	PARROT FEVER
	PSITTACOSIS
—cattle	ACTINOMYCOSIS, BRUCELLOSIS
	COWPOX, UNDULANT FEVER
—dogs	LEPTOSPIROSIS
	TOXOCARIASIS
—farm animals	ANTHRAX, LEPTOSPIROSIS
—goats	MALTA FEVER
—rabbits	RABBIT-FEVER$
	TULAR(A)EMIA
—rats	LEPTOSPIROSIS
	RAT(BITE)-FEVER
—sheep	Q-FEVER
frozen shoulder	BURSITIS
functional derangement	NEUROSIS
fungal disease	ASPERGILLOSIS
	ATHLETE'S FOOT
	BLASTOMYCOSIS
	CRYPTOCOCCOSIS
	EPIDERMIPHYTOSIS
	FARMER'S LUNG, FAVUS
	MYCOSIS, TORULOSIS
furfur	DANDRUFF, SCURF
furuncle	BOIL
fusion of	
—bones	ANCHYLOSIS, ANKYLOSIS
—legs	MERMAID SYNDROME
	SIRENOMELIA
galactose in blood	GALACTOSAEMIA
gall-stones	CHOLELITHIASIS
gangrene	PHAGED(A)ENA, THANATOSIS
gaol fever	TYPHUS
genital	
—disease	GONORRHOEA, SYPHILIS
—ulceration	CHANCROID
German measles	ROSEOLA, RUBELLA
	RUBEOLA
giddiness	VERTIGO
glanders	FARCY
glandular	
—condition	ADENOSIS
—fever	MONONUCLEOSIS
glaucoma	WALL-EYE
goitre	STRUMA
gout	PODAGRA
—in	
all joints	HAMARTHRITIS
hand	PODAGRA
head	CEPHALAGRA

gouty deposit	TOPHUS
granular deposit	SABURRA
Graves' disease	EXOPHTHALMIC GOITRE
	THYROTOXICOSIS
green sickness	ANAEMIA, CHLOROSIS
gripes	TORMINA
growth	
—disorder	ACROMEGALY
—of fibrous tissue	FIBROSIS
Guinea-worm disease	DRACONTIASIS
gumboil	PARULIS
hair disease	TRICHOSIS
hard	
—swelling	SCIRRHUS
—tumour	SCLERIASIS
hardening	
—of	SCLEROMA, SCLEROSIS
arteries	ARTERIOSCLEROSIS
	ATHEROSCLEROSIS
skin	CALLOSITY, ICTHYOSIS
	SCLERODERM(I)A
tissue	SCLEREMA, SCLERIASIS
haemorrhage	STAXIS
haemorrhoids	PILES
having	
—high blood pressure	HYPERTENSION
—low blood pressure	HYPOTENSION
headache	MIGRAINE
heart	
—burn	CARDIALGY, CARDIALGIA
	PYROSIS, WATER-BRASH
—defects (congenital)	FALLOT'S TETRALOGY
—disease	ANGINA PECTORIS
	CORONARY THROMBOSIS
	ENDOCARDITIS, PERICARDITIS
in children	KAWASAKI DISEASE
—disorder	BRADYCARDIA
	TACHYCARDIA
	TOBACCO-HEART
hepatitis	FAVISM
hereditary	
—disease	CHOREA MAJOR
	CYSTIC FIBROSIS
	HAEMOPHILIA
	HUNTINGTON'S CHOREA
—tendency to disease	DIATHESIS
hernia	RUPTURE
—of bladder	CYSTOCELE
herpes	COLD SORE, DARTRE
	SHINGLES, ZOSTER
hiccuping	SINGULTUS
high blood pressure	HYPERPIESIA
	HYPERTENSION
hip-gout	SCIATICA
hives	LARYNGITIS, NETTLE RASH
	URTICARIA

Hodgkin's disease	LYMPHADENOMA
hordeolum	STYE
hospital gangrene	PHAGED(A)ENA
housemaid's knee	BURSITIS
hunchback	GIBBUS
hydatid disease	TAPEWORM
hydrocephalus	WATER ON THE BRAIN
hydrophobia	LYSSA, RABIES
	ST HUBERT'S DISEASE
hydropsy	DROPSY, OEDEMA
hyperthyroidism	EXOPHTHALMIC GOITRE
	GRAVES' DISEASE
	THYROTOXICOSIS
hysterical	
—mania	HYSTEROMANIA
—trance	CATALEPSY
icterus	JAUNDICE
imaginary illness	HYPOCHONDRIA
immersion foot	TRENCH FOOT
immovable joint	SYNARTHROSIS
immune system	
deficiency	AIDS
impairment of	
—function of organ	DYSFUNCTION
—reasoning power	PARALOGIA
—sensation	DYSAESTHESIA
imperfect development of	
—limb	DISMELIA
—organ or part	APLASIA
inability to	
—distinguish certain	
colours	COLOUR BLINDNESS
—perform	
intended motion	APRAXIA
purposive movements	PARAPHRAXIA
	PARAPHRAXIS
—swallow	HYDROPHOBIA
—write	DYSGRAPHIA
indigestion	DYSPEPSIA
infantile paralysis	POLIOMYELITIS
infection	
—after childbirth	MILK-FEVER
	PUERPERAL MANIA
—at childbirth	PUERPERAL FEVER
—by micro-organisms	TOXOPLASMOSIS
—following disease	SEQUELA
—of	
fifth cranial nerve	TIC DOLOUREUX
lungs	(LOBAR) PNEUMONIA
mucus membranes	CANDIDIASIS
	MONILIASIS, THRUSH
nervous system	TORULOSIS
part of lung	LOBAR PNEUMONIA
infectious	
—disease	ZYMOTIC
—mononucleosis	GLANDULAR FEVER

infestation with	
—lice	PEDICULOSIS
—parasites	PARASITOSIS
inflamed sore	FELON, MORMAL
inflammation of	
—all joints	PANARTHRITIS
—appendix	APPENDICITIS
—artery	ARTERITIS
—bladder	CYSTITIS
—blind-gut	TYPHLITIS
—blood vessels	VASCULITIS
in brain	CHOROIDITIS
—bone	OSTEO-MYELITIS, OSTEITIS
—brain	ENCEPHALITIS
	MENINGITIS
	PANOPHTHALMITIS
	PHRENESIS, PHRENITIS
—breast	CYSTIC DISEASE, MASTITIS
—bronchi	BRONCH(IOL)ITIS
—bursae	BURSITIS
—cerebrum	CEREBRITIS
—colon	COLITIS
—conjunctiva	CONJUNCTIVITIS
—connective tissue	SYNOVITIS
—cornea	CERATITIS, KERATITIS
—diverticula	DIVERTICULITIS
—duodenum	DUODENITIS
—ear	CONCHITIS, OTITIS
drum	MYRINGITIS
membrane	TYMPANITIS
—elbow joint	BURSITIS, TENNIS ELBOW
—eye	CONJUNCTIVITIS
	OPHTHALMIA
	OPHTHALMITIS
ball	SCLER(OT)ITIS
lid	BLEPHARITIS, TYLOSIS
—Fallopian tubes	SALPINGITIS
—fibrous tissue	BURSITIS, FIBROSITIS
—follicles	ACNE
—gall-bladder	CHOLECYSTITIS
—glands	ADENITIS
—gums	GINGIVITIS
—hair follicles	SYCOSIS
—head of optic nerve	PAPILLITIS
—heart	CARDITIS
sac	PERICARDITIS
valve	VALVULITIS
—heel	PLANTAR FASCIITIS
—ileum	CROHN'S DISEASE, ILEITIS
—inner ear	LABYRINTHITIS
—intestines	ENTERITIS
	PERITYPHLITIS
—iris	IRITIS, UVEITIS
—joints	(RHEUMATOID) ARTHRITIS
—kidneys	BRIGHT'S DISEASE
	(PYELO)NEPHRITIS, PYELITIS

—knee-joint	BURSITIS
	CLERGYMAN'S KNEE
	HOUSEMAID'S KNEE
—larynx	CROUP, LARYNGITIS
—lens of eye	CRYSTALLITIS
—lining of	
artery	ENDARTERITIS
heart	ENDOCARDITIS
node	RHINITIS
nose	RHINITIS
stomach	GASTRO-ENTERITIS
uterus	ENDOMETRITIS
—liver	HEPATITIS
—lymphatic glands	LYMPHANGITIS
—marrow	MYELITIS
—mastoid process	MASTOIDITIS
—mouth and throat	THRUSH
—mucous membrane of	
eyelids	TRACHOMA
mouth	STOMATITIS
nose	CATARRH, RHINITIS
—muscle	FIBROSITIS, MYOSITIS
—nail	ONYCHITIS
—nail-bed	ONYCHIA
—nerves	(POLY)NEURITIS
—nose and throat	RHINOPHARYNGITIS
—outside of stomach	PERIGASTRITIS
—ovary	OOPHORITIS, OVARITIS
—pancreas	PANCREATITIS
—parotid gland	PAROT(ID)ITIS
—part near blind-gut	PERITYPHLITIS
—pelvis of kidney	PYELITIS
—pericardium	PERICARDITIS
—peritoneum	PERITONITIS
of liver	PERIHEPATITIS
—pharynx	PHARYNGITIS
—pleura	EMPYEMA, PLEURITIS
	PLEURISY
—prostate	PROSTATITIS
—rectum	PROCTITIS
—retina	RETINITIS
—sinus	SINU(S)ITIS
—skin	DERMATITIS, INTERTRIGO
—spinal cord	(POLIO)MYELITIS
—spine	RACHITIS, SPONDYLITIS
—spleen	SPLENITIS
—stomach	GASTRITIS
and intestines	GASTRO-ENTERITIS
—subcutaneous	CELLULITIS
—tendon sheath	SYNOVITIS
—testicle	ORCHITIS
—throat	ANGINA
—tongue	GLOSSITIS
—tonsils	ANTIADITIS, TONSILLITIS
—thyroid gland	STRUMITIS, THYROIDITIS
—tongue	GLOSSITIS

—tonsils	TONSIL(L)ITIS
—trachea	TRACH(E)ITIS
—ureter	URETERITIS
—urethra	URETHRITIS
—uterus	HYSTERITIS
—uvula	STAPHYLITIS, UVULITIS
—vein	(THROMBO)PHLEBITIS
—vertebra	SPONDYLITIS
—whole eye	PANOPHTHALMIA
—womb	UTERITIS
inflammatory disease of	
the face	ERYSIPELAS
influencing brain	PSYCHOACTIVE
	PSYCHOTROPIC
influenza	GRIPPE
ingrowing toenail	ONYCHOCRYPTOSIS
insensibility	CARUS, COMA, LETHARGY
	SOPOR
intermittent fever	RELAPSING FEVER
intestinal	
—disease	CHOLERA
	C(O)ELIAC DISEASE, COLITIS
	DIARRHOEA, DIVERTICULITIS
	DUODENAL ULCER, DYSENTERY
	MEGACOLON
—displacement	ENTEROPTOSIS
intolerance of light	PHOTOPHOBIA
irregularity of heartbeat	ARRHYTHMIA
	EXTRASYSTOLE
itch	CACOETHES, PRURITIS
	PSORA, SCABIES
	SCOTCH FIDDLE
itching	PRURITIS
jail fever	TYPHUS
jaundice	ICTERUS
jelly-like tumour	MYXOMA
jet-lag	TIME-ZONE DISEASE
joint	
—disorder	GOUT, RHEUMATIC FEVER
	RHEUMATISM
—injury	FRACTURE, SPRAIN
kala-azar	DUMDUM FEVER
	LEISHMANIASIS
	LEISHMANIOSIS
kidney disease	ADDISON'S DISEASE
	BRIGHT'S DISEASE
	NEPHRITIS, NEPHROSIS
king's evil	SCROFULA, TUBERCULOSIS
knock-knees	VALGUS
kyllosis	CLUB-FOOT
lack of	
—food	MALNUTRITION, STARVATION
—hydrochloric acid	
in stomach	ACHLORHYDRIA
—muscular	
coordination	DISKINAESTH(A)ESIA

—pulsation	ACROTISM
—red cells in blood	(SP)ANAEMIA
—vitamins	AVITAMINOSIS
large boil	CARBUNCLE
laryngitis	HIVES
lateral spinal curvature	SCOLIOSIS
lead poisoning	MOLYBDOSIS
	PLUMBISM, SATURNISM
leakage of fluid	EXTRAVASATION
	EXUDATION
leprosy	LEONTIASIS
lice-borne disease	INTERMITTENT FEVER
	RELAPSING FEVER
	TRENCH-FEVER, TYPHUS
like	
—typhoid	PARATYPHOID
—typhus	TYPHOID
limited vision	TUNNEL VISION
limping	CLAUDICATION
Little's disease	CEREBRAL PALSY
	SPASTIC PARALYSIS
liver disease	CIRRHOSIS, HEPATITIS
	HODGKIN'S DISEASE
lock-jaw	TETANUS
long	
—sightedness	HYPER(METR)OPIA
—ulcer	FISTULA
looseness of bowels	DIARRH(O)EA
loss of	
—ability to	
focus eyes	PREBYOPIA
manipulate objects	APRAXIA
—all sensation	ANAESTHESIA
—appetite	ANOREXIA (NERVOSA)
	ANOREXY
—contact with reality	AUTISM
—hair	ALOPECIA, MADROSIS
	PSILOSIS
—hearing	DEAFNESS, PREBYACUSIS
—memory	AMNESIA
—menstruation	AMENORRHOEA
—mental powers	DEMENTIA
—movement in joint	ANKYLOSIS
—muscle control	PALSY
—power of	
motion	PARALYSIS
writing	AGRAPHIA
—sense of pain	ANALGESIA
—skin pigment	VITILIGO
—speech	ALALIA, APHEMIA
	DUMBNESS
—taste	AGEUSIA
—vision	AMBLYOPIA, BLINDNESS
—voice	APHONIA, APHONY
—weight	CACHEXIA
low blood pressure	HYPOTENSION

lung disease	ANTHRACOSIS, ASBESTOSIS
	BRONCHIECTASIS
	BRONCH(IOL)ITIS
	(BRONCHO)PNEUMONIA
	BYSSINOSIS, CONSUMPTION
	EMPHYSEMA, FARMER'S LUNG
	LEGIONNAIRES' DISEASE
	MESOTHELIOMA, MINER'S PHTHISIS
	PLEURISY, PNEUMONCONIOSIS
	PNEUMOTHORAX, SILICOSIS
	SIDEROSIS, TB, TUBERCULOSIS
lupus	TOUCH-ME-NOT
lymph node disease	HODGKIN'S DISEASE
	LYMPHANGITIS
lymphoid tumour	LYMPHOMA
Lyssa	HYDROPHOBIA, RABIES
maidism	PELLAGRA
malaria	MARSH-FEVER, PALUDISM
malarial fever (India)	TAP
Maltese fever	BRUCELLOSIS
matchmakers' disease	PHOSSY-JAW
measles	MORBILLI
melanin in blood	MELANAEMIA
memory disorder	PARAMNESIA
meningitis	CEREBRO-SPINAL FEVER
mental	
—derangement	PSYCHOPATHY
—disorder	ALZHEIMER'S DISEASE
	AMENTIA, AUTISM, DEMENTIA
	FOLIE A DEUX
	FRAGILE X SYNDROME
	HEBEPHRENIA, IDIOCY, IMBECILITY
	MANIA, MONGOLISM, PARANOIA
	PHOBIA, PSYCHASTHENIA
	(PSYCHO)NEUROSIS
	PSYCHOSIS, SCHIZOPHRENIA
metabolic	
—defect in	
excretion of pigment	PORPHYRIA
—disorder	PHENYLKETONURIA
mild smallpox	ALASTRIM
miner's	
—anaemia	ANCHYLOSTOMIASIS
	ANKYLOSTOMIASIS
—elbow	BURSITIS
—lung disease	PNEUMOCONIOSIS
	(*see also* dust *above*)
misshapen or incomplete	
limb	DYSMELIA
mongolism	DOWN'S SYNDROME
moniliasis	THRUSH
morbid	
—accummulation of	
bile in blood	CHOLAEMIA
—adhesion	SYNECHIA
—anxiety and despondency	DYSTHYMIA

—appetite for food	ACORIA
—condition resulting from	
anxiety about health	HYPOCHONDRIA
excess of tobacco	NICOTINISM
—contraction	STENOSIS
—enlargement of prostate	PROSTATISM
—growth of tissue	FIBROSIS
—habit of body	DYSTHESIA
—restlessness	DYSPHORIA
—state of blood	CACHAEMIA
morbilli	MEASLES
mortification	GANGRENE
morula	YAWS
mosquito-borne	FILARIASIS
	MALARIA, YELLOW FEVER
mountain sickness	PUNA, SOROCHE
mouth	
—gangrene	NOMA
—infection	APHTHA, CANDIDA
	MONILIASIS, THRUSH
	TRENCH MOUTH
	VINCENT'S DISEASE
multiple sclerosis	DS
	DISSEMINATED SCLEROSIS
mumps	PAROT(ID)ITIS
muscle	
—deterioration	MUSCULAR DYSTROPHY
—disease	MYASTHENIA
—pain	FIBROSITIS, MYALGIA
—spasm	CRAMP, OPISTHOTONOS
—tumour	MYOMA
muscular	
—atrophy	MYOPATHY
—debility	MYASTHENIA
—distrophy	MYOPATHY
—inflammation	MYOSITIS
—rheumatism	FIBROSITIS
—spasm	
contracting/relaxing	CLONIC, CLONUS
uniform	TONIC
—tension	MYOTONIA
—weakness	MYASTHENIA
	NARCOLEPSY
progressive	MYASTHENIA GRAVIS
myalgic encephalomyelitis	ME
	ROYAL FREE DISEASE
myopia	MOUSE-SIGHT
narrowing of	
—blood vessels	BUERGER'S DISEASE
	STENOSIS
	VASOCONSTRICTION
—organ	STENOSIS, STRICTURE
necrosis of jawbone	PHOSSY-JAW
	MATCHMAKER'S DISEASE
neoplasm	TUMOUR
nephritis	BRIGHT'S DISEASE

nerve pain	NEURALGIA
nervous	
—activity	NEUROSIS
—debility	NEURASTHENIA
—system	
disorder	DISSEMINATED SCLEROSIS
	EPILEPSY, LOCOMOTOR ATAXY
	MULTIPLE SCLEROSIS
	NEUROPATHY, NEUROSIS
nettle-rash	HIVES, URTICARIA
neuralgia	
—in face	FACE-ACHE, TIC DOULOUREUX
	TRIGEMINAL NEURALGIA
—of chest-wall	PLEURODYNIA
neuralgic pain in rectum	PROCTALGIA
neuritis of sciatic nerve	SCIATICA
nicotine poisoning	NICOTINISM
night-blindness	NYCTALOPIA
noise in ear	TINNITUS
nosebleed	EPITAXIS
numbness of legs	NIGHT-PALSY
nutritional disorder	TROPHESY
	TROPHONEUROSIS
obstruction of intestine	ILEAC PASSION
	ILIAC PASSION, ILEUS
oedema	(HY)DROPSY
onchocerciasis	RIVER BLINDNESS
one-eyed vision	MONOBLEPSIS
opacity of	
—cornea	LEUCOMA, ONYX
—lens	CATARACT
open sore	ULCER
ornithosis	PSITTACOSIS
over-	
—activity of thyroid	THYROTOXICOSIS
	HYPERTHYROIDISM
—excitability	HYPOMANIA
—growth of	AGROMEGALY
a part	HYPERPLASIA
skin of nose	RHINOPHYMA
—heating	HYPERTHERMIA
—nourishment	HYPERTROPHY
—production of mucus	
and fibrous tissue	CYSTIC FIBROSIS
pain in	
—foot	METATARSALGIA
—head	CEPHALALGIA
—hip	COXALGIA
—instep	TARSALGIA
—intercostal muscles	PLEURODYNIA
—joint	ARTHRALGIA
—kidneys	NEPHRALGIA, NEPHRALGY
—sciatic nerve	SCIATICA
—tongue	GLOSSODYNIA
—upper stomach	CARDIALGIA
	CARDIALGY

painful	
—bodily ailment	PASSION
—menstruation	DYSMENORRH(O)EA
palsy	PARALYSIS
paludism	MALARIA
papilloma	WART
paralysis	PALSY
—agitans	PARKINSONISM
—partial	PARESIS
paralysis of	
—arms and legs	QUADRAPLEGIA
	QUADRIPLEGIA
—both arms or both legs	DIPLEGIA
—eye muscles	OPHTHALMOPLEGIA
—facial nerve	BELL'S PALSY
—legs	LATHYRISM
—lower body	PARAPLEGIA
—one part	MONOPLEGIA
—part	PARESIS
—pupil	CYCLOPLEGIA
parasitic disease	BILHARZIA(SIS)
	BILHARZIOSIS
	CHAGASS DISEASE
	CRYPTOSPORIDIASIS
	HOOKWORM, KALA AZAR
	LEISHMANIASIS
	LEISHMANIOSIS, ONCHOCERCIASIS
	SCHISTOSOMIASIS
	SLEEPING SICKNESS, STRONGYLOSIS
	TOXOCARIASIS, TOXOPLASMOSIS
	TRICHINIASIS, TRICHINOSIS
	TRICHOMONIASIS, TRYPANOSOMIASIS
paronychia	WHITLOW
parotid gland infection	MUMPS
parot(id)itis	MUMPS
parrot-disease	PSITTACOSIS
partial	
—dislocation	SUBLUXATION
—paralysis	PARESIS
parulis	GUMBOIL
pathological	
—accumulation of fluid	
in tissue	DROPSY, (O)EDEMA
—conversion of cell walls	
to gum	GUMMOSIS
—softening	MALACIA
pellagra	MAIDISM
pernio	CHILBLAIN
Perthes' disease	OSTEOCHONDROSIS
pertussis	WHOOPING-COUGH
perverted appetite	MALACIA
pes planus	FLAT FOOT
pestilence	LUES
petit mal	EPILEPSY
piles	HAEMORRHOIDS
pimple	LENTIGO

pink	
—eye	CONJUNCTIVITIS
—rash	ROSEOLA
placental disease	HYDATIDIFORM MOLE
pleurisy with	
pneumonia	PLEURO-PNEUMONIA
pleurodynia	BORNHOLM DISEASE
plucking movements	CARPHOLOGY,
	FLOCCILATION
plumbism	LEAD-POISONING
poisoning by	
—acetone	KETOSIS
—antimony	STILBIALISM
—beans	FAVISM
—ergot	ERGOTISM, RAPHANIA
—ketone	KETOSIS
—lead	MOLYBDOSIS, PLUMBISM
	SATURNISM
—mercury	HATTER'S SHAKES
	MERCURIALISM
—tobacco	NICOTINISM
poliomyelitis	INFANTILE PARALYSIS
porous structure of bones	OSTEOPOROSIS
post-natal disease	MILK-LEG
	PUERPERAL FEVER, WHITE-LEG
premature	
—ageing	PROGERIA
—greying	POLIOSIS
—senility	ALZHEIMER'S DISEASE
presence of	
—diverticula	DIVERTICULOSIS
—endometrial material	
in other organ	ENDOMETRIOSIS
prickly heat	MILIARIA, SUDAMEN
primary disease	IDIOPATHY
protusion of	
—eyeballs	EXOPHTHALMIA
	EXOPHTHALMOS
—meninges	MENINGOCELE
—organ	HERNIA
—spinal cord	MYELOCELE
prunella	QUINSY, SORE THROAT
pruritis	ITCH
psittacosis	ORNITHOSIS
psora	ITCH, SCABIES
psychosis	MANIA
—with delusions	SCHIZOPHRENIA
pus in urine	PYURIA
putrefaction	SAPRAEMIA, SEPSIS
putrid fever	TYPHUS
pyrexia	FEVER
pyrosis	HEARTBURN, WATER-BRASH
quartan fever	MALARIA
quinsy	ANGINA, CYNANCHE
	PRUNELLA
rabbit-fever	TULAR(A)EMIA

rabies	HYDROPHOBIA, LYSSA
rachitis	RICKETS
rapid heart beat	TACHYCARDIA
rash	EXANTHEM
rat(bite)-fever	SODUKU, TULAR(A)EMIA
ravenous appetite	LIMOSIS
redness of skin	ERYTHEMA INFECTIOSUM
	FIFTH DISEASE, ROSACEA
	SLAPPED CHEEK SYNDROME
resembling typhoid	PARATYPHOID
respiratory	ASTHMA, CROUP, FLU
	INFLUENZA, PLEURISY
	PNEUMONIA
retention of	
—urine	HYDRONEPHROSIS
	STRANGURY
—waste in blood	UR(A)EMIA
rheumatism in lumbar region	LUMBAGO
rickets	RACHITIS
ringing in the ears	TINNITUS
ringworm	TINEA, TRICHOPHYTOSIS
river blindness	ONCHOCERCIASIS
Rock fever	UNDULANT FEVER
rose	ERYSIPELAS
—rash	ROSEOLA
roseola	GERMAN MEASLES
	ROSE-RASH
Royal Free disease	ME
	MYALGIC ENCEPHALOMYELITIS
rubella	GERMAN MEASLES
rubeola	(GERMAN) MEASLES
rupture	HERNIA, RHEXIS
sagging of organ	PTOSIS
sang	ANTHRAX
sausage-poisoning	BOTULISM
scabbiness	SCALL
scabies	ITCH, PSORA
	SCOTCH FIDDLE
scalp disease	FAVUS, PORRIGO
scaly scalp	DANDRUFF
scarlatina	SCARLET-FEVER
scarlet-fever	SCARLATINA
schistosomiasis	BILHARZIA
schizophrenia	DEMENTIA PRAECOX
sciatica	HIP-GOUT
scrofula	KING'S EVIL, STRUMA
	TUBERCULOSIS
scurf	FURFUR
sebaceous cyst	WEN
secretion of smelly	
sweat	OSMIDROSIS
seizure	EPILEPSY, STROKE
sensation	
—of ants on skin	FORMICATION
—without physical origin	HALLUCINATION
septic finger	FELON

severe	
—anaemia	CHLOROSIS
—anxiety neurosis	SHELL SHOCK
—depression	MELANCHOLIA
—schizophrenia	CATATONIA
shaking	TREMOR
—of brain	CONCUSSION
—palsy	PARKINSONISM
	PARKINSON'S DISEASE
shell-shock	WAR NEUROSIS
shingles	HERPES ZOSTER
ship-fever	CALENTURE, TYPHUS
shivering	AGUE, RIGOR
short-sightedness	MYOPIA
	PRESBYOPIA, PRESBYOPY
simulation of another	
disease	MIMESIS
single-minded madness	MONOMANIA
skin	
—crack	CHAP
—disease	ACNE, CHLOASMA
	CHLORACNE, DERMATITIS
	DERMATOSIS, ECZEMA
	ELEPHANTIASIS, ERYSIPELAS
	EXANTHEM(A), FAVUS, HERPES
	HIVES, ICHTHYOSIS, IMPETIGO
	INTERTRIGO, ITCH, LEPROSY
	MYXOEDEMA, NETTLE-RASH
	PEMPHIGUS, PITYRIASIS, PSORA
	PSORIASIS, ROSACEA, SCABIES
	SERPIGO, SHINGLES, THRUSH
	URTICARIA
fungal	ATHLETE'S FOOT
	CANDIDIASIS
	EPIDERMIPHYTOSIS
	MONILIASIS, RINGWORM, TINEA
old	SCALL
—eruption	EXANTHEM(A), PRURIGO
—ulcer	RUPIA
sleeping-sickness	TRYPANOSOMIASIS
sleepy-sickness	ENCEPHALITIS LETHARGICA
slow	
—digestion	BRADYPEPTIC
—heartbeat	BRADYCARDIA
small abscess	PUSTULE
smallpox	ALASTRIM, VARIOLA
soduku	RAT(BITE) FEVER
softening	MALACIA
—of bones	OSTEOMALACIA, RICKETS
sore throat	PRUNELLA
spasm	TIC
—of	
eyelids	BLEPHARISM
iris	HIPPUS
jaw muscles	TRISMUS
muscles	TETANY

spasmodic eye movement	NYSTAGMUS
speech disturbance	PARALALIA
spine	
—curvature	
backwards	KYPHOSIS
forward	LORDOSIS
sideways	SCOLIOSIS
—disease	POLIOMYELITIS
	RACHISCHISIS, RACHITIS
	SPINA BIFIDA, SPONDYLITIS
	SPONDYLOSIS, SYRINGOMELIA
spitting blood	HAEMOPTYSIS
spleen disease	HODGKIN'S DISEASE
splenic anaemia	BANTI'S DISEASE
spongy bone of ear	OTOSCLEROSIS
spontaneous bruising	PURPURA
spot on skin	PETECHIA
squint	STRABISM(US)
St Hubert's disease	HYDROPHOBIA
St Vitus's dance	CHOREA (MINOR)
stagnation of bile	CHOLESTASIS
stiff neck	MENINGISMUS
stomach	
—disease	GASTRIC ULCER
	GASTRITIS, PEPTIC ULCER
—pain	COLIC, GASTRALGIA
stone	
—gallstone	CALCULUS
—in	
body	LITHIASIS
gallbladder	CHOLELITHIASIS
kidney	NEPHROLITHIASIS
intestine	ENTEROLITH
urinary tract	UROLITH
—small stones	GRAVEL
stoppage of urine	ISCHURIA
streptococcal infection	RHEUMATIC FEVER
stroke	APOPLEXY, ICTUS
	SEIZURE
struma	GOITRE, SCROFULA
strychnine poisoning	STRYCH(NI)NISM
stye	HORDEOLUM
subnormal body	
temperature	HYPOTHERMIA
sugar in urine	GLUCOSURIA, GLYCOSURIA
summer flu	LYME DISEASE
sun-wart	ACTINIC KERATOSIS
superfluous mass	
of bone	EXOSTOSIS
suppuration in tooth	
socket	PYORRHOEA
suppurative tonsillitis	QUINSY
sweat blister	SUDAMEN
swelling	TUMOUR, TYMPANY
—composed of blood, etc	HAEMATOMA
—in nose	RHINOSCLEROMA

—of	
joints	GOUT
thyroid	GOITRE
swollen lymphatic gland	FARCY-BUD
—in groin	BUBO
syncope	FAINT
syphilis	LUES, POX
tabes dorsalis	LOCOMOTOR ATAXY
talipes	CLUB-FOOT
tapeworm	HYDATID DISEASE
tea-drunkenness	THEISM
teething rash	RED-GUM
temporary blindness	
with migraine	TEICHOPSIA
tennis elbow	BURSITIS
tetanic spasm of jaw	
muscles	TRISMUS
tetanus	LOCK-JAW
thanatosis	GANGRENE
thickening of	
—inner coat of	
arteries	ATHEROMA
—skin	ELEPHANTIASIS
thin concave fingernails	KOILONYCHIA
throat disease	CYNANCHE, DIPHTHERIA
	LARYNGITIS, PHARAYNGITIS
thrush	APHTHA, CANDIDA, MONILIASIS
thyroid	
—deficiency	MYXOEDEMA
—disease	EXOPHTHALMIC GOITRE
	GRAVES DISEASE
	THYROTOXICOSIS
thyrotoxicosis	GRAVES DISEASE
tick	
—borne disease	LYME DISEASE
	INTERMITTENT FEVER
	RELAPSING FEVER
	TYPHUS
—fever	EAST COAST FEVER
time-zone disease	JET-LAG
tinea	RINGWORM
tonsillitis	ANTIADITIS
toothache	DENTAGRA
tormina	GRIPES
torn skin beside nail	AGNAIL, HANGNAIL
torticollis	WRY-NECK
touch-me-not	LUPUS
transmitted by	
—birds	ORNITHOSIS, PSITTACOSIS
—cats	RABIES, TOXICARIASIS
	TOXOPLASMOSIS
—cattle	ACTINOBACILLOSIS
	ACTINOMYCOSIS, ANTHRAX
	BRUCELLOSIS
	FOOT AND MOUTH DISEASE
	KERATOCONJUNCTIVITIS

	LEPTOSPIROSIS, MALTA FEVER
	RINGWORM, SALMONELLOSIS
	TUBERCULOSIS
	UNDULANT FEVER
—chickens	CYTOMEGALOVIRUS, CMV
—dogs	TOXOCARIASIS
—flies	KALA-AZAR, SANDFLY FEVER
	SLEEPING SICKNESS
	TRYPANOSOMIASIS
—lice	INTERMITTENT FEVER
	RELAPSING FEVER
	TRENCH-FEVER, TYPHUS
	Q-FEVER
—mites	ACARIASIS, ITCH, SCABIES
	SCRUB-TYPHUS
—mosquitoes	DENGUE
	BREAKBONE FEVER
	DANDY FEVER
	ENCEPHALITIS, ELEPHANTIASIS
	MALARIA, YELLOW-FEVER
	YELLOW-JACK
—rabbits	CYTOMEGALOVIRUS, CMV
—rats	TULAR(A)EMIA
—rat fleas	PLAGUE
—ticks	INTERMITTENT FEVER
	LYME DISEASE
	RELAPSING FEVER
	ROCKY MOUNTAIN FEVER
	TYPHUS
trembling	TREMOR
trench	
—fever	TYPHUS
—foot	IMMERSION FOOT
—mouth	VINCENT'S ANGINA
trichophytosis	RING-WORM
trismus	LOCK-JAW
tropical diseases	
—complication of	
malaria	BLACKWATER FEVER
—dengue	BREAKBONE FEVER
	DANDY FEVER
—deficiency of	
protein	KWASHIORKOR
vitamin B	BERIBERI, PELLAGRA
—fly-borne	SLEEPING SICKNESS
	TRYPANOSOMIASIS
—fungal	MADURA FOOT
	MADUROMYCOSIS
—mouth infection	NOMA
—mosquito-borne	MALARIA
	YELLOW-FEVER
	YELLOW-JACK
—parasitic	BILHARZIA(SIS)
	BILHARZIOSIS, DELHI BOIL
	DUMDUM FEVER, FRAMBOESIA
	GUINEA WORM, HOOKWORM

	KALA-AZAR, LEISHMANIASIS
	LEISHMANIOSIS, LOA
	ONCHOCERCIASIS
	ORIENTAL SORE
	RIVER BLINDNESS
	YAWS
—rodent-borne	LASSA FEVER
—skin disease	BOBA, BUBA
	BUTTON SCURVY
	LEPROSY, FRAMBOESIA
	PINTA, VERRUGA PERUVIANA
	YAWS
—undernourishment	KWASHIORKOR
—viral	EBOLA DISEASE
	GREEN-MONKEY DISEASE
	MARBURG DISEASE
trypanosomiasis	SLEEPING-SICKNESS
tuberculosis of	
—lungs	CONSUMPTION, PHTHISIS
—lymph nodes	KING'S EVIL, SCROFULA
—skin	LUPUS (VULGARIS)
—vertebrae	POTT'S DISEASE
tuberculous lesion	TUBERCULOMA
tular(a)emia	RABBIT-FEVER
tumour	
—connected with teeth	ODONTOMA
—jelly-like	MYXOMA
—yellow	XANTHOMA
tumour of	
—blood	
cells	MYELOMA
vessels	AGIOMA, NAEVIS
—bone	OSTEO(CLASTO)MA, SARCOMA
marrow	MYELOMA
—connective tissue	SARCOMA
of brain	GLIOMA
—eyelid	STY(E)
—fat	LIPOMA
—fibrous tissue	FIBROMA
—glands	ADENOMA
—gums	EPULIS
—kidney	NEPHROBLASTOMA
—lungs	MESOTHELIOMA
—lymph glands	LYMPHOMA
—membrane	CARCINOMA
—mucous membrane	POLYP(E), POLYPUS
—muscle	MYOMA, SARCOMA
—nerve tissue	NEUROMA
—papilla	PAPILLOMA
—pigmented skin	MELANOMA
—sheath of tendon	GANGLION
—skin	RODENT ULCER
—supporting tissue of brain	GLIOMA
—testicle	SPERMATOCELE
—thymus	THYMOMA
—uterus	FIBROID

turning in of eyelashes	TRICHIASIS
twisted intestine	VOLVULUS
twitching of muscle fibre	FIBRILLATION
typhoid fever	ENTERIC FEVER
	GASTRIC FEVER
typhus	GAOL FEVER, JAIL FEVER
	PUTRID FEVER, SHIP-FEVER
	TRENCH FEVER
typist's	
—cramp	TENOSYNOVITIS
—disability	REPETITIVE STRAIN INJURY, RSI
ulceration	PHAGED(A)ENA
unconsciousness	COMA
undulant fever	BRUCELLOSIS
	MALTA FEVER
	MEDITERRANEAN FEVER
	NEAPOLITAN FEVER
	ROCK FEVER
uncontrollable sleepiness	NARCOLEPSY
uniform muscular spasm	TONIC SPASM
unnatural distension	
with air	EMPHYSEMA
unpigmented skin	LEUKODERMA, VITILIGO
unremembered automatic	
behaviour	FUGUE
urinary organ	
infection	UROSIS
urticaria	NETTLE-RASH, HIVES
vaccinia	COWPOX
varicella	CHICKENPOX, WATER-POX
variola	SMALLPOX
venereal disease	CHANCRE, GONORRHOEA
	SYPHILIS
verruca	PAPILLOMA, WART
verruga Peruviana	BOBA, BUBA
	BUTTON SCURVY
	FRAMBOESIA, YAWS
vertigo	GIDDINESS
vesicle	BLISTER
vesicular eruption	EMPHLYSIS
Vincent's angina	TRENCH MOUTH
viral disease	VIROSIS
vomiting blood	HAEMATEMESIS
vomito	YELLOW FEVER
wall-eye	GLAUCOMA
war neurosis	SHELL-SHOCK
wart	KERATOSIS, PAPILLOMA
	VERRUCA
wasting	
—away	ATROPHY, MARASMUS
—disease	HECTIC FEVER, PHTHISIS
	TABES
—of muscle tissue	DYSTROPHY
water	
—borne disease	CHOLERA
	CRYPTOSPORIDIOSIS

	LEGIONNAIRES' DISEASE
	TYPHOID
—brash	HEARTBURN, PYROSIS
—on the brain	HYDROCEPHALUS
—pox	VARICELLA
watery accumulation	(HY)DROPSY, OEDEMA
weakness of voice	PHONASTHENIA
weaning-brash	DIARRHOEA
Weil's disease	LEPTOSPIROSIS
whisky-liver	CIRRHOSIS
white	
—leg	PHLEGMASIA
—patches on	
skin	LEUKODERMA
membrane	LEUKOPLAKIS
whitlow	PANARITIUM, PARONYCHIA
whooping-cough	CHINCOUGH, PERTUSSIS
Wilm's tumour	NEPHROBLASTOMA
winter depression	SAD
	SEASONAL AFFECTIVE DISORDER
wolf-madness	LYCANTHROPY
wooden-tongue	ACTINOBACILLOSIS
woody-tongue	ACTINOBACILLOSIS
woolsorter's disease	ANTHRAX
word	
—blindness	DYSLEXIA
—substitution	PARAPHASIA
wound	TRAUMA
wrinkles caused by sun	PHOTO-AGEING
writer's cramp	SCRIVENER'S PALSY
wry-neck	TORTICOLLIS
yaws	BEJEL, BOBA, BUBA
	BUTTON SCURVY
	FRAMBOESIA, MORULA
	VERRUGA PERUVIANA
yellow	
—fever	VOMITO, YELLOW JACK
—tumour	XANTHOMA
yellowing	JAUNDICE
yuppie flu	ME
	MYALGIC ENCEPHALOMYELITIS
zoster	HERPES, SHINGLES
divination	SORTILEGE
by/from/with:	
arrows	BELINOMANCY
ashes	SPODOMANCY, TEPHROMANCY
atmospheric phenomena	AEROMANCY
augury	AURUSPICY
bible readings	BIBLIOMANCY
birds	ORNITHOMANCY
	ORNITHOSCOPY
books	BIBLIOMANCY
cards	CARTOMANCY
casting lots	SORTILEGE
Chinese book of diagrams	I CHING
crystal ball	SCRYING

divine inspiration	THEOMANCY
dreams	ONEIROMANCY
	ONEIROSCOPY
dropping of food scraps by birds	TRIPUDIUM
entrails of animals	HARUSPICATION
feet	PODOMANCY
figures on earth	GEOMANCY
fingernails	ONIMANCY
	ONYCHOMANCY
finger-rings	DACTYLIOMANCY
fire	PYROMANCY
flames	LAMPADOMANCY
flight of birds	AUGURY, AUSPICE
	ORNITHOMANCY
fortune-telling	DUKKERIPEN
ghosts	SCIOMANCY
hands	CH(E)IROMANCY
	PALMISTRY
hopping of birds while feeding	TRIPUDIUM
inspection of liver	HEPATOSCOPY
knots in umbilical cord	OMPHALOMANCY
large glasses	GASTROMANCY
lot	CIEROMANCY
lying behind waterfall on a hide	TAGHAIRM
meal strewed over victims of sacrifice	CRITHOMANCY
mirrors	CATOPTROMANCY
motions of axe	AXINOMANCY
movements of mice	MYOMANCY
numbers	NUMEROLOGY
objects used in sacrifice	HEIROMANCY
observation of animals	ZOOMANCY
oracles	THEOMANCY
patterns in dust	GEOMANCY
physical contact	PSYCHOMETRY
planets	ASTROLOGY, HOROSCOPE
plants	BOTANOMANCY
playing-cards	CARTOMANCY
rods	RHABDOMANCY
second sight	DEUTEROSCOPY
shoulder blades	SCAPULIMANCY
shoulders of beasts	ARMOMANCY
sieve and shears	COSCINOMANCY
sixth sense	ESP
	EXTRA-SENSORY PERCEPTION
smoke	CAPNOMANCY
soles of feet	PEDOMANCY
spirits of the dead	NECROMANCY
	NIGROMANCY
springs	PEGOMANCY
splits in burning shoulder-blades	OMOPLATOSCOPY
stars	ASTROMANCY

stomach noises	GASTROMANCY
stones	LITHOMANCY
transparent bodies	CRYSTALLOMANCY
visions	CLAIRVOYANCE
walking in a circle and falling from giddiness	GYROMANCY
water	HYDROMANCY
wax dropping into water	CEROMANCY
wine	OENOMANCY
Zodiac	ASTROLOGY, HOROSCOPE

Doctors of

—Canon and Civil Law	JUD, UJD
—Civil Law	DCL, JCD
—Dental Surgery	DDS
—Divinity	DD
—Education	DED
—Engineering	DENG, DING
—Law	LLD
—Letters	DLIT, LHD, LITD
—Literature	DLIT, LITD
—Medicine	MD
—Music	DMUS
—Philosophy	DPH, PHD
—Science	DSC, SCD
—Theology	DTH, THD

dogs

Abyssinian	KABERU
Afghan hound	BALKH HOUND
	BALUCHI HOUND
	BARUKZY HOUND
Afghanistan	AFGHAN HOUND
	AFGHAN SPANIEL
Africa	BAGANDA HUNTING DOG
	BASENJI, HAIRLESS DOG
	RHODESIAN RIDGEBACK
	SEALYDALE, SLUGHI
—wild	CAPE HUNTING DOG
aguara-guaza	MANED DOG, MANED WOLF
	RED WOLF
Airedale terrier	BINGLEY TERRIER
	WATERSIDE TERRIER
	WHARFEDALE TERRIER
Akita	JAPANESE DEERHOUND
	NIPPON INU
Alsatian	GERMAN SHEPHERD DOG
	SCHAFERHUND
America	AMERICAN COCKER SPANIEL
	AMERICAN (FOX)HOUND
	AMERICAN WATER SPANIEL
	CHESAPEAKE BAY RETRIEVER
	PLOTT HOUND, RACCOON DOG
	TIMBER WOLF DOG
Appenzell mountain dog	APPENZELL SENNENHUND
Arabia	SALUKI
Argentina	PILA

Arkwright pointer	BLACK POINTER
Australia	AUSTRALIAN TERRIER
	AUSTRALIAN CATTLE DOG
	BARB, KANGAROO DOG
	SIDNEY SILKY TERRIER
—Barb	BLACK KELPIE
—cattle dog	HEELER
—sheepdog	KELPIE, KELPY
—wild	DINGO
Austria	TYROLEAN SHEEPDOG
Azara's dog	AGUARACHAY, AZARA'S FOX
	BRAZILIAN DOG
Azores	FILA DA TERCEIRA
Aztec sacred dog	TEECHICHI
Balearic Islands	EIVISSENC
badgerhound	BASSET(HOUND)
	DACHSHUND
Barb	BLACK KELPIE
Barry's dog	NANA
Basenji	BELGIAN CONGO DOG
	CONGO BUSH DOG
	CONGO HUNTING TERRIER
basset	ARESIAN BASSET
	ARTOIS DOG
Bedlington terrier	NORTH COUNTIES TERRIER
	ROTHBURY TERRIER
Belgium	BICHON, BOUVIER DE FLANDRE
	BOUVIER DES ARDENNES
	BRABANCON, GRIFFON (BELGE)
	GROENENDAEL, KERTHALS GRIFFON
	LAEKENOIS, LEONBERGER
	MALINOIS, ST HUBERT HOUND
	TURVUEREN
Bergamaschi	CANE DE PASTOR BERGAMASCO
	ITALIAN BERGAMA SHEEPDOG
Bernese mountain	
dog	BERNESE SENNENHUND
	DURBACHLER
bird-dog	DROPPER
black and tan	
terrier	MANCHESTER TERRIER
bloodhound	LIME-HOUND, LYAM-HOUND
	LYME-HOUND, SLEUTH-HOUND
	SLOT HOUND
boarhound	GERMAN MASTIFF
	GREAT DANE
border terrier	REEDWATER TERRIER
borzoi	RUSSIAN GREYHOUND
	RUSSIAN WOLFHOUND
Boston terrier	ROUNDHEADED TERRIER
Bouvier	
—de Flandre	BELGIAN CATTLE DOG
—des Ardennes	ARDENNES CATTLE DOG
boxer	GERMN BULLDOG
Brabancon	SMOOTH-HAIRED GRIFFON
Branchiero	CANE DA MACELLAIO

Brazil	AZARA'S DOG
Breton spaniel	BRITTANY SPANIEL
	ESPAGNEUL BRETON
buckhound	DEERHOUND, STAGHOUND
bulldog	
—German	BOXER
—x mastiff	BULL MASTIFF
—x terrier	BOSTON TERRIER
	BULL TERRIER
bullfighter's dog	ALANO
Burns's dogs	CAESAR, LUATH
butterfly dog	PAPILLON
Cairn terrier	SHORT-HAIRED SKYE TERRIER
Canada	HARE INDIAN DOG, LANDSEER
	NEWFOUNDLAND
	NOOTKA DOG, TOGANEE
Cape hunting dog	HYENA DOG, WILDEHOND
Carisissi	BRAZILIAN FOX
	CRAB-EATING DOG
	SURINAM DOG
cartoon dog	DEPITY DAWG, LADY
	PLUTO, TRAMP
Catalan sheepdog	GOS D'ATURA
	PERRO DE PASTOR CATALAN
Chesapeake Bay	
retriever	AMERICAN DUCK RETRIEVER
	DUCKING DOG
chihuahua	MEXICAN DWARF DOG
	ORNAMENT DOG, PILLOW DOG
Chile	JUAN FERNANDEZ SHEEPDOG
China	ANHUI, CHINESE GREYHOUND
	CHOW-CHOW, COOLIE DOG
	HAIRLESS DOG, HAPPA DOG
	LO CHIANG, LOONG CHUA
	MANCHURIAN SNOW DOG
	MONGOLIAN MASTIFF
	PEKIN(G)ESE, PEN-LO, PUG
	SHANTUNG GREYHOUND
	SHAR PEI, SHIH TZU
—hairless dog	CRESTED DOG
chow-chow	CANTONESE BUTCHER DOG
	EDIBLE DOG, ORIENTAL SPITZ
	SHAN DOG
Clydesdale terrier	PAISLEY TERRIER
coach-dog	CARRIAGE-DOG
	DALMATIAN
coarse-haired terrier	GRIFF
cocker spaniel	COCKING SPANIEL
	WOODCOCK SPANIEL
colpeo	CHILE FOX, FOUR-TOED DOG
	MAGELLAN FOX
corgi	WELSH HEELER
coyote	NORTH AMERICAN WILD DOG
cross-bred	CUR, MONGREL, MUTT, POOCH
	TYKE, WOLF-DOG, YELLOW-DOG
Cuba	CUBAN BLOODHOUND

curly-tailed	TRENDLE-TAIL(ED)
	TRINDLE-TAIL(ED)
	TRUNDLE_TAIL(ED)
dachshund	BADGER DOG, TECKEL
Dalmatian	CARRIAGE DOG
	COACH DOG
	LESSER DANE
Dandie Dinmont	
terrier	CHARLIE'S HOPE TERRIER
	MUSTARD AND PEPPER TERRIER
Denmark	GREAT DANE
dingo	AUSTRALIAN NATIVE DOG
	AUSTRALIAN WILD DOG
	WARRIGAL
Dulux dog	OLD ENGLISH SHEEPDOG
Egypt	EGYPTIAN SHEEPDOG
	HAIRLESS DOG, MANBOUTOU
	SHILLUK DOG, TESEM
—sheepdog	ARMENT, ERMENTI, SABE
Eivissenc	BALEARIC HOUND
	CHARNEQUE, MALLORQUIN
	PODENCO IBICENCO
elkhound	GRAA DRYEHUND
	GRAHUND, GREY ELK DOG
Entlebuch mountain	
dog	ENTLEBUCHER SENNENHUND
Eskimo	HUSKY, MALAMUTE
	MALEMUTE
extinct	ANTARCTIC DOG
	BLUE PAUL, LOONG CHUA
	MANBOUTOU, NORFOLK SPANIEL
	SCOTTISH SPANIEL
	SOUTHERN HOUND, TALBOT
female	BITCH
fierce dog, tied up	BANDOG, BANN DOGE
fighting dog	BLUE PAUL
	PIT BULL TERRIER
	STAFFORDSHIRE BULL TERRIER
	TOSA
film star	LASSIE
Finland	FINNISH SPITZ, LAIKA
Finnish Spitz	BARKING BIRD DOG
	FINNISH COCK-EARED DOG
fox terrier	SMOOTH-HAIRED TERRIER
	WIRE-HAIRED TERRIER
France	CHIEN
	BEAUCERON, BOULDOGUE
	BRAQUE DE BOURBONNAIS
	BRAQUE ST GERMAIN
	BRETON SPANIEL, BRIARD
	CHIEN FAUVE DE BRETAGNE
	DOGUE DE BORDEAUX
	FRENCH BULLDOG, FRENCH POODLE
	PYRENEAN MOUNTAIN DOG
	PYRENEAN SHEEPDOG
	VENDEEN HOUND

Germany	HUND, AFFENPINSCHER
	ALSATIAN, BOXER, DACHSHUND
	DOBERMAN(N) (PINSCHER)
	HARLEQUIN PINSCHER
	JAGDTERRIER, MUNSTERLANDER
	POTSDAM GREYHOUND
	POMERANIAN (SHEEPDOG)
	POODLE, REISENSCHNAUZER
	ROTTWEILER, SCHNAUZER
	SPITZ, TECKEL, VORSTEHHUND
	WEIMARANER
Gordon setter	BLACK AND TAN SETTER
Great Dane	DANISH DOG
	(GERMAN) BOARHOUND
	TIGER DOG, ULMER MASTIFF
—coloured	HARLEQUIN
Greece	GREEK SHEEPDOG
Greenland	ANGMAGSSALIK HUSKY
greyhounds	BANJAR, CHINESE
	GRIG HOUND, HERHOUND
	ITALIAN, KANGAROO
	LEPORARIUS, LONG-DOG
	LONG-TAIL, NORTHWEST INDIAN
	PERSIAN, POTSDAM, RAMPUR
	SHANTUNG
—Afghan	BALKH
—hybrid	LURCHER
spaniel	WHIPPET
terrier	WHIPPET
—Irish	WOLFHOUND
—rough-coated	DEERHOUND
—Russian	BORZOI, TAZA
guard dogs	ALSATIAN, BANDOG
	BANN DOGE, BOXER
	BULL MASTIFF, BULL TERRIER
	CHOW-CHOW
	DOBERMAN(N) (PINSCHER)
	GREAT DANE, MALINOIS
	MASTIFF, PYRENEAN, ROTTWEILER
	STAFFORDSHIRE BULL TERRIER
—in Hades	CERBERUS
—of	
Hela	GARM
Helen	GARM
gun/sporting dogs	BRITTANY
	CHESAPEAKE BAY, CLUMBER
	COCKER, FIELD SPANIEL
	LABRADOR, POINTER
	MUNSTERLANDER
	RETRIEVER, SETTER, SPINNONE
	SPRINGER, WEIMARANER
Guyana	ARECUNA HUNTING DOG
hairless dog	NAKED DOG, PILA
Happa dog	CHINESE PUG, PEKING PUG
Hardy's dog	WESSEX
harrier	HARE HOUND

heavy-jawed dog	JOWLER
HMV dog	NIPPER
Holland	HERDERSHONDEN, KEESHOND
	SCHIPPERKE, SMOUSHOND
hounds	AFGHAN, AMERICAN, BALEARIC
	BALUCHI, BARUKHZY, BASSET
	BRITTANY, HARE
	JAPANESE BEAR, LIGHTNING RAG
	NORTH AFRICAN GAZELLE
	PLOTT, PYRENEAN, RAMPUR
	SLEUTH, SLOT, ST HUBERT
	SWEDISH, VENDEEN, WELSH
Hungary	KOMONDOR, KUVASZ
	PULI, PUMI, VIZSLA
hunting	
—dogs	AFGHAN, AKITA, ALAN(D)
	ALANT, ARECUNA, BASSET
	BEAGLE, BORZOI, BRACH,
	BRA(T)CHET, BUCKHOUND, COURSER
	DACHSHUND, DEERHOUND, EIVISSENC
	ELKHOUND, FOXHOUND, GREAT DANE
	GREYHOUND, HARRIER
	IBIZAN, IRISH WOLFHOUND
	KANGAROO DOG, KENNET, OTTERHOUND
	PHARAOH HOUND, POCKET BEAGLE
	PODENGO, POINTER
	RABBIT BEAGLE, RACCOON DOG
	RETRIEVER, RHODESIAN RIDGEBACK
	SALUKI, SETTER, SLUGHI, SPITZ
	STAGHOUND, WOLFHOUND
—by scent	RACHE, RATCH
husky	ANGMAGSSALIK HUSKY
	BAFFINLAND DOG, ESKIMO DOG
	MALAMUTE, MALEMUTE
	MACKENZIE RIVER DOG
	OSTIAK, SLED DOG
	TIMBER WOLF DOG, TOGANEE
Iceland	ICELANDIC SHEEPDOG
India	BANJARA, POLIGAR
	RAMPUR HOUND
—wild	DECCAN DOG, DHOLE
	KOLSUN, RAM-KUTTA
Ireland	GLEN OF IMAAL TERRIER
	IRISH SETTER, IRISH TERRIER
	IRISH WOLFHOUND, KERRY BEAGLE
	KERRY BLUE, WHEATEN TERRIER
	IRISH WATER SPANIEL
—setter	MODDER RHU, RED SETTER
	RED SPANIEL
—wolfhound	IRISH ELKHOUND
	IRISH GREYHOUND
Italy	CANE
	BERGAMASCHI, BOLOGNESE
	ITALIAN GREYHOUND
	MAREMMA, NEAPOLITAN MASTIFF
	SEGUGIO, SPINONE, VOLPINO
Isaac Newton's dog	DIAMOND
Japan	AKITA, CHIN (CHIN)
	INU NUS'TO
	SHIRA, SHISHI, TOSA
John Peel's dogs	BELLMAN, RANTER, TRUE
Kabyle dog	KABIL
	NORTH AFRICAN KABYLE
	OULED NAIL DOG
	SHAWIA DOG
kangaroo dog	KANGAROO GREYHOUND
Keeshond	DUTCH BARGE DOG
Kerry blue terrier	IRISH BLUE TERRIER
King Charles's Spaniel	CAVALIER
	COMFORTER
	ENGLISH TOY DOG
	SPANIEL GENTLE
kitchen dog	TURNSPIT, VERNEPATOR
kuri	MAORI DOG
	NEW ZEALAND WILD DOG
Lakeland terrier	FELL TERRIER
	PATTERDALE TERRIER
Lancashire	HEELER
lap dog	(see toy below)
large	GREAT DANE, MASTIFF
	NEWFOUNDLAND, ST BERNARD
lion-dog	LOWCHEN
long	
—bodied	BEDLINGTON (TERRIER)
	BLENHEIM, DACHSHUND
	TURNSPIT
—eared	BASSET, BEAGLE
	BLOODHOUND, SPANIEL
loose-skinned	SHAR PEI
Malaya	JENTERAH, SERIGALA
many-headed	CERBERUS
Maremma	ABRUZZI SHEEPDOG
	CANE DE PASTOR MAREMMANO
	MAREMMES SHEEPDOG
mastiff	ALAN, ALAUNT, BANDOGGE
	MOLLOSSUS, TIE-DOG
Mexico	CHIHUAHUA, HAIRLESS DOG
monkey terrier	AFFENPINSCHER
	MONKEY PINSCHER
mountain dogs	APPENZELL, BERNESE
	ENTELBUCH, ESTRELA
	PYRENEAN, ST BERNARD
New Zealand	KURI
Niam Niam	HAUTE-AGOOUE TERRIER
	NYAM NYAM TERRIER
Norway	ELKHOUND
Nottinghamshire	CLUMBER (SPANIEL)
old	LYM, SHOUGH, SHOWGHE
Odysseus's dog	ARGOS
Orient	PI(E)-DOG, PYE-DOG
	PARIAH
Owczarek	POLISH SHEEPDOG

Pekin(g)ese	DRAGON DOG, LION DOG
	PEKING PALACE DOG
Pen-lo	PA ERH
Perdigueiro	PORTUGUESE POINTER
performing tricks	TUMBLER
Persia	SALUKI
pet	LAP-DOG, TOY-DOG, POODLE
Philippines	PHILIPPINES EDIBLE DOG
	PHILLIPINES NATIVE DOG
poacher's dog	LURCHER
Podengo	PORTUGUESE RABBIT DOG
pointers	ARKWRIGHT, BLACK, BURGOS
	GERMAN, HUNGARIAN
	PORTUGUESE, SPANISH
	YELLOW
Poland	NIZINNY, OWCZAREK
	LOWLAND SHEEPDOG
Pomeranian	SPITZ
Portugal	PODENGO
	PORTUGUESE POINTER
	PORTUGUESE CATTLE DOG
	PORTUGUESE SHEEPDOG
	PORTUGUESE WATER DOG
—Podengo	PORTUGUESE RABBIT DOG
—cattle dog	CAO DE CASTRO LABOREIRO
—pointer	PERDIGUEIRO
—sheepdog	CAO SERRA DA ESTRELA
—water dog	CAO D'AGUA
	PORTUGUESE DIVING DOG
	PORTUGUESE FISHING DOG
pug	CARLIN, LO-SZE, MOPS
Punch's dog	TOBY
Pyrenean	
—mountain dog	GREAT PYRENEES
	PYRENEAN HOUND
—sheepdog	LABRI
raccoon dog	COONHOUND
racing dog	GREYHOUND, WHIPPET
Rampur	
hound	NORTHWEST INDIAN GREYHOUND
	RAMPUR GREYHOUND
retrievers	AMERICAN DUCK
	CHESAPEAKE BAY
	CURLY-COATED, FLAT-COATED
	GOLDEN, LABRADOR
	WAVY-COATED
Rhodesian ridgeback	RHODESIAN LION DOG
Romania	CARPATHIAN SHEEPDOG
Rottweiler	ROITWEIL DOG
	ROTTWEILER METZGERHUND
rough-coated greyhound	DEERHOUND
Russia	AFTCHARKA, BORZOI
	CAUCASIAN SHEEPDOG
	SAMOYED(E), TAZA
	UKRAINIAN SHEEPDOG
	WOLFHOUND

St Bernard	ALPINE MASTIFF
saluki	GAZELLE HOUND
	PERSIAN GREYHOUND
Scandinavia	ELKHOUND
Schipperke	BELGIAN BARGE DOG
Scotland	ABERDEEN TERRIER, BLUE PAUL
	CAIRN (TERRIER)
	CLYDESDALE TERRIER
	DANDIE DINMONT, GORDON SETTER
	SCOTCH TERRIER, SCOTCH COLLY DOG
	SCOTTISH SPANIEL, SCOTTISH TERRIER
	SHETLAND SHEEPDOG, SKYE TERRIER
	WEST HIGHLAND WHITE TERRIER
—lap-dog	MESSAN
—sheepdog	COLLIE
—terrier	SCOTTIE
setters	BLACK-AND-TAN, ENGLISH
	GORDON, IRISH
	LLEWELLIN, RED
shaggy dog	ICELAND DOG
	OLD ENGLISH SHEEPDOG
	SHOCK, SHOUGH
sheep/cattle dogs	ABRUZZI, AFTCHARKA
	ANATOLIAN, ARMENT
	AUSTRALIAN CATTLE DOG
	BEAUCERON, BELGIAN, BERGAMA
	BORDER, BOUVIER DE FLANDRE
	BOUVIER DES ARDENNES
	BRANCHIERO, BRIARD, BUGEILGI
	CAO SERRA DA ESTRELA
	CARPATHIAN, CATALAN, CAUCASIAN
	COLLIE, COLLY, CUMBERLAND
	DUTCH HERDER, EGYPTIAN, ENGLISH
	GERMAN SHEPHERD, GREEK
	GROENENDAEL, HUNGARIAN
	ICELANDIC, JUAN FERNANDEZ
	KABYLE DOG, KELPIE, KELPY
	KOMONDOR, MAREMMA, MALINOIS
	NOOTKA DOG, OLD ENGLISH
	OWCZAREK, OWTCHARKA
	POLISH LOWLAND, POMERANIAN
	PORTUGUESE, PUMI, PYRENEAN
	ROMANIAN, SERRA DA ESTRELA
	SHETLAND, SIBERIAN
	TOOROOCHAN, TYROLEAN
	UKRAINIAN, VALLHUND, WELSH
Shetland Islands	SHETLAND SHEEPDOG
	SHELTIE, SHELTY
—sheepdog	PEERIE DOG, TOONIE DOG
Shiba	JAPANESE TURF DOG, KAI DOG
Shih Tzu	TIBETAN LION DOG
Shishi	AINU DOG, CHOKEN
	JAPANESE BEAR HOUND
short	
—eared dog	ALAN(D), ALANT
	SCLATER'S DOG

—legged dog	AUSTRALIAN TERRIER
	CAIRN TERRIER, CORGI
	DANDIE DINMONT TERRIER
	BASSET, BEAGLE, BULLDOG
	DACHSHUND
	GLEN OF IMAAL TERRIER
	JACK RUSSELL TERRIER
	NORWICH TERRIER, SEALYHAM
	SIDNEY SILKY TERRIER
	SKYE TERRIER, TURNSPIT
	WEST HIGHLAND WHITE TERRIER
Siberia	LAIKA, OSTIAK
	SAMOYED(E)
	SIBERIAN WILD DOG
	TOOROOCHAN SHEEPDOG
Sicily	BRANCHIERO
silky-haired dog	MALTESE
	SIDNEY SILKY TERRIER
	YORKSHIRE TERRIER
sleeve dog	(*see* toy *below*)
Slughi	NORTH AFRICAN GAZELLE HOUND
small	
—hunting dog	JACK RUSSELL, KENNET
—poodle (old)	WATER-DOG
Smoushond	DUTCH SMOUS
snub-nosed dog	BULLDOG, PUG
South America	BUSH DOG, SCLATER'S DOG
	TARUMA HUNTING DOG
Spain	PERRO
	CATALAN SHEEPDOG
	PODENCO NAVARRO
	PYRENEAN MOUNTAIN DOG
	PYRENEAN SHEEPDOG
	SPANISH POINTER
—pointer	BURGOS POINTER
	SPANISH PEDIGUERO
spaniels	AFGHAN, AMERICAN COCKER
	AMERICAN WATER, BRETON
	BRITTANY, BROWN WATER
	BUTTERFLY, CAVALIER, CLUMBER
	COCKER, ENGLISH SPRINGER
	ENGLISH TOY, ENGLISH WATER
	FIELD, GENTLE, IRISH WATER
	KING CHARLES, NORFOLK, RED
	RED-AND-WHITE, SCOTTISH
	SPRINGER, SUSSEX, TIBETAN
	WELSH SPRINGER, WOODCOCK
Spitz	POMERANIAN
spotted dog	DALMATIAN
Springer spaniel	NORFOLK SPRINGER
staghound	BUCKHOUND, DEERHOUND
stray dog on race-course	DERBY DOG
Sudan	NIAM NIAM
Sumatra	BATAK
Sweden	SWEDISH FOXHOUND
	VALLHUND
Switzerland	APPENZELL MOUNTAIN DOG
	BERNESE SENNENHUND
	ENTLEBUCH MOUNTAIN DOG
	ST BERNARD, SWEDISH BEAGLE
tailless dog	SCHIPPERKE
Taruma hunting dog	WOYAWAI DOG
terriers	ABERDEEN, AIREDALE
	AUSTRALIAN
	BEDLINGON, BINGLEY
	BLACK AND TAN, BORDER
	BOSTON, BULL, CAIRN, CHARLIE'S HOPE
	CLYDESDALE, DANDY DINMONT
	DARJEELING, FELL, FOX
	GLEN OF IMAAL, HAUTE-AGOOUE
	IRISH (BLUE), KERRY BLUE
	LAKELAND, MANCHESTER
	MONKEY, MUSTARD AND PEPPER
	NORFOLK, NORTH COUNTIES
	NORWICH, PAISLEY
	(PARSON) JACK RUSSELL
	PATTERDALE, PIT BULL, POLTALLOCH
	REEDWATER, ROSENEATH, ROTHBURY
	ROUNDHEADED, SCOTTISH
	SEALYHAM, SILKY, SKYE
	SMOOTH FOX, STAFFORDSHIRE BULL
	TIBETAN, WATERSIDE
	WELSH, WEST HIGHLAND WHITE
	WHARFEDALE, WHEATEN
	WIRE FOX, YORKSHIRE
Tesem	EGYPTIAN HUNTING DOG
Tibet	LHASA APSO, SHIH TZU
	TIBETAN MASTIFF
	TIBETAN SPANIEL
	TIBETAN TERRIER
—spaniel	TIBETAN PRAYER DOG
—terrier	CHRYSANTHEMUM DOG
	DARJEELING TERRIER
Tosa	JAPANESE FIGHTING DOG
	JAPANESE MASTIFF
toy/lap/sleeve dogs	AFFENPINSCHER
	AUSTRALIAN SILKY TERRIER
	BICHON FRISE, BOLOGNESE
	BOSTON, BREVIPILIS
	BRUSSELS GRIFFON, CAVALIER
	CHIHUAHUA, CHIN-CHIN
	HAIRLESS DOG, HAVANA
	ITALIAN GREYHOUND
	KING CHARLES'S SPANIEL
	LHASA APSO, LOWCHEN, MALTESE
	MINIATURE PINSCHER
	MONKEY TERRIER, PAPILLON
	PEKIN(G)ESE, PEN-LO
	POMERANIAN, POODLE, PUG
	ROQUET, SHIH TZU
	TIBETAN SPANIEL
	YORKSHIRE TERRIER

tracker	BLOODHOUND, DRAGHOUND
Turkey	ANATOLIAN, HAIRLESS DOG
two-headed	ORTHOS
Vallhund	VASTGOTA SPITZ
Vizsla	HUNGARIAN POINTER
	YELLOW POINTER
Vorstehhund	GERMAN POINTER
Wales	CORGI, LLEWELLIN SETTER
	SEALYHAM, WELSH HOUND
	WELSH SHEEPDOG
	WELSH SPRINGER SPANIEL
	WELSH TERRIER
—corgi	CI SAWDL, WELSH HEELER
—hound	BYTHEUAD, WELSH FOXHOUND
—sheepdog	BUGEILGI, WELSH COLLIE
—Springer spaniel	RED-AND-WHITE SPANIEL
	STARTER, TARGI
—terrier	DAIARGI
watch-dog	(*see* guard dogs *above*)
West Highland White	
Terrier	POLTALLOCH TERRIER
	ROSENEATH TERRIER
West Indies	HAIRLESS DOG
whippet	LIGHTNING RAG HOUND
	SNAP DOG
wild	
—Abyssinia	KABERU
—Africa	SOMALI WILD DOG
	SOUTH AFRICAN WILD DOG
—America	COYOTE
—Australia	DINGO
—China	RACCOON-LIKE DOG
—India	BUANSUAH, DHOLE, PARIAH
	PI(E)-DOG, PYE-DOG
—Japan	RACCOON-LIKE DOG
—Malaya	JENTERAH, SERIGALA
—Orient	PI(E)-DOG, PYE-DOG
	PARIAH
—South America	AGUARA-GUAZA
	AZARA'S DOG, CARRISISSI
	COLPEO, ECUADOR BUSH DOG
	SANTA CATHARINA DOG
with flecked bluish	
fur	(BLUE) MERLE
worthless	CUR, HUNT-COUNTER
young dog	CUB, PUP(PY)
	SLEEVE-DOG, WHELP
young hound(s)	ENTRY
Yugoslavia	DALMATIAN
Dominica	
capital	ROSEAU
coin	CENT, DOLLAR
Dominican Republic	
capital	SAN DOMINGO
coin	CENTAVO, PESO

dramatists	
American	ALBEE, ANDERSON, ARENT
	BALDWIN, BROWN, BULLINS
	GELBER, HANSBERRY, JONES
	KOPIT, LOWELL, MCLEISH
	MILLER, ODETS, O'NEILL
	RICE, SAROYAN, WILLIAMS
Austrian	SCHNITZLER, WERFEL
Belgian	CROMMELYNCK, MAETERLINCK
British	ARDEN, AYCKBOURN, BENNETT
	BOLT, BOND, BRENTON, CLARK
	COWARD, DELANEY, DENNIS
	DRYDEN, EDGAR, ELIOT, FIELDING
	FRY, GALSWORTHY, GOLDSMITH
	GILBERT, GRANVILLE-BARKER
	GREENE, GRIFFITHS, HAMPTON
	HARE, KYD, LYLY, MARLOWE
	MCGRATH, MERCER, MIDDLETON
	MORTIMER, NICHOLLS, ORTON
	OSBORNE, PINERO, PINTER
	POLIAKOFF, POTTER, PRIESTLEY
	RATTIGAN, RUDKIN, SANDERS
	SHAFFER, SHAKESPEARE
	SHERIDAN, SIMPSON, SPENSER
	STOPPARD, STOREY, WELLAND
	WESKER, WHELAN, WHITEHEAD
	WILLIAMS, WOOD
Cuban	TRIANA
Czech	CAPEK, HAVEL
French	ANOUILH, ARRABAL, BATY
	BRIEUX, CLAUDEL, COCTEAU
	CORNEILLE, DUGARD, DURAS
	GIDE, IONESCU, JARRY
	MARTIN, MOLIERE, RACINE
	ROUSSEL, SALACROU, SARTRE
German	BALL, BRECHT, FRISCH
	GOETHE, GRASSE, HAUPTMANN
	HOCHHUTH, HOLZ, KALSER
	LARRONGE, SUDERMANN, TOLLER
	WEISS, ZUCKMEYER
Greek	AESCHYLUS, ARISTOPHANES
	EURIPIDES, SOPHOCLES
Hungarian	VON HORVATH
Irish	`BECKETT, BEHAN, GREGORY
	JOYCE, MAC LIAMMOIR, O'CASEY
	SHAW, SYNGE, WILDE, YEATS
Italian	PIRANDELLO, VERGA
Nigerian	SOYINKA
Norwegian	IBSEN
Romanian	IONESCU
Russian	ARBUZOBV, BULGAKOV
	CHEKHOV, DOSTO(Y)EVSKY
	GORKY, LUNTS, OSTROVSKY
	SUKOVO-KOBYLIN, TOLSTOY
	ZAMYATIN
South African	FUGARD

Spanish	ARRABAL, LORCA, PARMENO
	PINILLOS, SALINAS
Swedish	STRINDBERG, WEISS
Swiss	FRISCH
West Indian	HILL-JOHN, PHILLIPS
	WALCOTT, WHITE

drinks

acid drink	SOUR
African	SKOKIAAN, TOMBO
—beer	POMBE
after sunset	SUNDOWNER
aguardiente	BRANDY
alcohol flavoured or perfumed	LIQUEUR
alcoholic liquor (Scot.)	CREATURE
	THE CRATUR
ale	TIPPER
—and honey	BRAGGET
—cheap	TWOPENNY, FOUR-ALE
—new (Scots.)	SWATS
—Norfolk	NOG
—strong	MOROCCO, NAPPY
	NOG, OCTOBER
Sussex	TIPPER
—warmed and spiced	PURL
—with	
nutmeg	MACE ALE
pulped apples etc	LAMB'S-WOOL
roasted apples etc	WASSAIL
wormwood	PURL
Algerian	AGRAS
American	
—spirit, water, etc	SLING
—whisky	BOURBON, REDEYE, RYE
	TANGLEFOOT
—wine	CATAWBA, SCUPPERNONG
aniseed liqueur	OUZO
aperitif	ANIS, AMERPICON, BYRRH
	CAMPARI, CINZANO
	CREME DE CASSIS, DUBONNET
	KYR, LILLEY, MARTINI, OUZO
	PASTIS, PERNOD, PUNT E MES
	RICARD, ST RAPHAEL, SHERRY
	SUZE, VERMOUTH
bad	
—beer	SWIPES
—liquor	ROT-GUT
—whisky (US)	TARANTULA JUICE
beer	BITTER, BROWN ALE
	LIGHT ALE, MILD
	PALE ALE
—American	STEAM BEER
—Australian	AMBER, FROSTY, GROG
—Belgian	FARO
—black	GUINNESS, STOUT
—bottom-fermented	LAGER
—cheap	FOUR-ALE

—dark brown	PORTER
—drawn from cask	DRAUGHT, REALE ALE
—low in alcohol	SMALL BEER
—Egyptian	BO(U)SA, ZYTHUM
—exported	IPA, INDIA PALE ALE
—French	BIERE
—from wheat	WHEAT BEER
—German	BIER, BOCK, DORTMUNDER
	LAGER, MUNCHENER
	PILS(E)NER
—pale	BURTON
—poor (Scot.)	SWANK(E)Y
—Russian	KWASS, QUASS
—slang	GATTER, WALLOP
—stored under pressure	KEG BEER
—strong	STINGO
stout	BARLEYWINE
—top-fermented	ALE
—with	
gin	DOG'S-NOSE
ginger-beer	SHANDY(GAFF)
ground ivy	GILL-ALE, GILL BEER
lemonade	SHANDY(GAFF)
bingo	BRANDY
bitters	ANGOSTURA, FERNET BRANCA
	KHOOSH, ORANGE, PEACH
	UNDERBERG
blue ruin	GIN
bottled water	BADOIT, EVIAN, MALVERN
	PERRIER, RAMLOSA
	SPA, REINESPRING
brandy	AQUA VITAE, BINGO, EAU DE VIE
—and	
soda	PEG
water	BRANDYPAWNEE
	MAHOGANY
—Bulgarian	BRENDI
—distilled from	
cherries	KIRSCH
fruit juices (US)	MOBBIE, MOBBY
grape pomace	MARC
plums	SLIVOVITZ, TUICA
wine	FINE CHAMPAGNE
—French	ARMAGNAC, COGNAC
	EAU DE VIE, FINE
—Greek	METAXA
—Italian	GRAPPA
—Mediterranean	ROSOLIO
—obsolete	NANTZ
—Portuguese	AGUARDIENTE
—Romanian	TUICA
—South African	CAPE SMOKE
—Spanish	AGUARDIENTE
	FUNDADOR, SOBERANO
—Yugoslav	SLIVOVITZ, VINJAK
Brazilian	ASSAI

Bulgarian brandy	BRENDI
champagne	SILLERY, THE WIDOW
—and	
orange juice	BUCK'S FIZZ
stout	BLACK VELVET
—India	SIM(P)KIN
Chinese	KAOLIANG, MAO-TAI
cider	BLOODY BUTCHER
	HANDSOME MAUD
	SCRUMPY
cocktail	(see separate entry)
coffee and whiskey	IRISH COFFEE
cognac	BRANDY, FINE
cordial	PERSICO(T)
—after coffee	POUSSE-CAFE
—from	
anise	ANISETTE
berbs	LOVAGE
raisins	ROSO(G)LIO
sundew juice	ROSA-SOLIS
cups, punches, etc	APPLE POSSET
	BOATMAN'S CUP
	BUTTERED RUM
	CAIPIRINHA, CORPSE REVIVER
	EGG NOG, GLOGG, , GLUHWEIN
	HAIR OF THE DOG
	HONEYSUCKLE CUP
	HOT TODDY, MULLED ALE
	MULLED WINE
	POLISH HONEY DRINK
	PRAIRIE OYSTER, ROSE CUP
	SHERRY PUNCH, SUISSETTE
	SUMMER CUP, TEA TODDY
	WHITE WINE CUP
curdled	
—cream	SILLABUB, SYLLABUB
—milk	POSSET
demerara	RUM
different drink following	CHASER
distilled from wine	BRANDY
drink of the (Greek) gods	NECTAR
dry sherry	AMONTILLADO
	FINO, MANZANILLA
East Indies	NIPA
eastern	ARAK, ARRACK
effervescent	SHERBET
ethanol with approx	
50% alcohol	PROOF-SPIRIT
extra strong porter	STOUT
fermented	
—cow's milk	KEFIR, KEPHIR
—grape-juice	WINE
—mare's milk	K(O)UMISS
—palm juice	TODDY
—palm-sap	NIPA, SURA
—rice	RICE-BEER

fizzy	GINGER-ALE, GINGER-BEER
	LEMONADE, POP
	SHERBE(R)T, SODA-WATER
flavoured	
—milk	MILK-SHAKE
—schnapps (Tyrol)	ENZIAN
—with fruit kernels	RATAFIA
for	
—blending with spirits	MIXER
—doctoring port	GEROPIGA
—toats	WASSAIL
fortified wine	PORT
from	
—agave (Mex.)	PULQUE, TEQUIL(L)A
—almonds	ORGEAT
—anise	PERNOD
—apples	APPLEJACK, BATZI
	CALVADOS, CIDER
	EAU DE VIE DE CIDRE
	POMAGNE, TREBERN
—apricots	BARACK, PALINKA
—aromatic herbs	HERB-BEER, HERB-TEA
—barley	ORGEAT, PTISAN, TISANE
—cacao	CHOCOLATE, COCOA
—cactus	COCUI, PULQUE
—Coffea seeds	COFFEE
—cherries	KIRSCH, KIRSEBAELIKOER
—coconuts	AR(R)ACK
—corn	WHISKEY
—dandelions, sassafras	ROOT-BEER
—dates	AR(R)ACK, ZIBIB
—dough and sugar (US)	HOO(T)CH
—fruit-refuse	MARC(-BRANDY)
—ginger	GINGER WINE
—grain	AKVAVIT, AQUAVIT
	BOURBON, GENEVER
	GIN, CORN, SCHANPPS
	VODKA, WHISK(E)Y
—grape pomace	AGUARDIENTE
	BAGACEIRA
	GRAPPA, KOMOVICA
	MARC, TRESTERSCHNAPPS
—grapes	WINE
—herbs	BITTERS, LOVAGE
	PTISAN, TISANE
—honey (Welsh)	METHEGLIN
—maize	CHICHA
—milk	AWEIN, KOUMISS, SKHOU
—mint	PEPPERMINT
—molasses	AR(R)ACK, BASI, RAKEE
	RAKI, RUM
—orange flowers	ORGEAT
—Orchis	SALOOP
—palm trees	NIPA
—pears	BIRNGEIST, PERRY
	WILLIAMINE

—pepper plant	KAVA
—plums	MIRABELLE, QUETSCH
	SLIVOVITZ, TUICA
—pomegranates	GRENADINE
—potatoes	AKVAVIT, AQUAVIT
	SCHNAPPS, VODKA
—rice	AR(R)ACK, PANGASI, RAGI
	SAKE, SAKI, SHOCHU
—rose water	ZORGEAT
—spruce trees	SPRUCE BEER
—sassafras	SALOOP
—sugar cane	AGUARDIENTE, CANA
	RON, RUM
—tiger nuts	HORCHATA
—walnuts	NOCINO
—watermelons	KISLAV
fruit-juice	CRUSH, LEMONADE
	LIMEADE, ORANGEADE
	SHERBET, SQUASH
—and vinegar (Amer.)	SHRUB
fruit syrup	ROB, SUCCADE
German	
—beer	BIER, BOCK, DORTMUNDEN
	LAGER, MUNCHENER
	PILS(E)NER,
—gin	STEINHAGER
geneva	GIN
gin	BLUE RUIN, GENEVA,
	MAX, MOTHER'S RUIN
	OLD TOM, TWANKAY
—Dutch	HOLLAND, SCHNAP(P)S
	SCHIEDAM
—effervescent	GIN-FIZZ
—English	GORDON'S, LONDON DRY
	PLYMOUTH
—German	STEINHAGER
—illicit	BATHTUB(-GIN)
—with	
angostura	PINK GIN
treacle	MAHOGANY
vermouth	GIN AND IT
water	GIN-SLING
Goan	FENI, FENNY
good stuff	LIQUOR, WHISKY
grain and juniper berries	GENEVA
	GIN, HOLLANDS
grape juice	MUST
—with brandy, etc	GEROPIGA
Greek	
—spirit	MASTIKA, METAXA
	OUZO, RAKEE, RAKI
—strong drink	METHE
—wine	RETSINA, RESINATA
harsh whisky	CHAIN LIGHTNING
Hindu gods' drink	AMRITA
Holland gin	SCHNAP(P)S

honey and	
—mulberry juice	MORAT
—water	HYDROMEL, MEAD
hot	NEGUS, RUMFUSTIAN
	TODDY
—beer, spirits, etc	COBBLER'S PUNCH
—rum and eggs	TOM-AND-JERRY
—water, milk, sugar etc	CAMBRIC TEA
—wine and fruit	BISHOP, GLOGG
	GLUHWEIN
Hungarian wine	TOKAY
iced drink	COBBLER, COLLINS
	COOLER
illicit	
—gin	BATHTUB(-GEN)
—spirit (Aust., NZ)	SLY-GROG
—whisk(e)y	
America	BOOTLEG, MOONSHINE
Ireland	POT(H)EEN
imitation champagne	GOOSEBERRY(-WINE)
Indian	
—champagne	SIM(P)KIN
—spirit	SOMA
intoxicating liquor	BOOSE, BOOZE, BOUSE
—(Amer.)	TANGLEFOOT
invalid's drink	BEEF TEA, LUCOZADE
	WINCARNIS
Irish	GUINNESS
—illicit whiskey	POT(H)EEN
Italian	
—brandy	GRAPPA
—liqueur	NOCINO, SAMBUCA
—vermouth	IT
Japanese rice beer	SAKE, SAKI
late at night	NIGHTCAP
lemon juice with spirits	SHRUB
lettuce juice	THRIDACE
light beer	LAGER, PILS(E)NER
	TABLE-BEER
liqueur	
—after coffee	POUSSE-CAFE
—America	CORDIAL
	SOUTHERN COMFORT
—France	ABRICOTINE, ANISETTE
	BENEDICTINE, CHARTREUSE
	COINTREAU, GRAND MARNIER
	MANDARINE
—Germany	GOLDWASSER
—Greece	OUZO
—Holland	ADVOCAAT, KUMMEL
—Ireland	BAILEY'S IRISH CREAM
	IRISH MIST
—Italy	AMARO, AMARETTO DI SARONNO
	GALLIANO, MARASCHINO
	SAMBUCA, STREGA
—Jamaica	TIA MARIA

—made at Fécamp	BENEDICTINE
—made from	
almond or peach kernels	NOYAU
almonds	RATAFIA
Alpine plants	GENIPI
aniseed	
—France	ANISETTE
—Germany	GOLDWASSER
—Greece	OUZO
apples	CALVADOS
apricots	ABRICOTINE
	APRICOT BRANDY
blackberries	CREME DE MURE
blackcurrants	CREME DE CASSIS
brandy	ARMAGNAC, COGNAC
cherries	CHERRY BOUNCE
	CHERRY-BRANDY
	KIRSCH(WASSER)
	MARASCHINO
cumin and caraway	
seeds	KUMMEL
herbs	BENEDICTINE, CHARTREUSE
orange peel	CURACAO, CURACOA
oranges	COINTREAU, GRAND MARNIER
peaches	PEACH-BRANDY
peppermint	CREME DE MENTHE
plums	MIRABELLE, PRUNELLE
	SLIVOVITZ
rum and coffee	TIA MARIA
sloes	SLOE-GIN
tangerines	
—France	MANDARINE
—South Africa	VAN DER HUM
walnuts	NOCINO
whisk(e)y and	
—honey	DRAMBUIE, IRISH MIST
—peaches	SOUTHERN COMFORT
—Scotland	DRAMBUIE
—South Africa	VAN DER HUM
—Sweden	ARRACK PUNCH
—sweet	CREME
—West Indies	CREME DE CACAO
—with	
crushed ice	FRAPPE
rum, lime juice, etc	SHRUB
—Yugoslavia	MARASCHINO
liquor	GOOD STUFF, MALT, TIPPLE
—Scots	SKINK, STRUNT
liquorice (Scot.)	SUGARALLIE WATTER
Madeira	LONDON PARTICULAR
—dry	SERCIAL
—medium	
dry	VERDELHO
sweet	BUAL
—sweet	MALMSEY
Malay rum	TAFIA

malt liquor	JOHN BARLEYCORN, STINGO
Martinique spirit	EAU DE CREOLES
max	GIN
medicated ale	SCURVY-GRASS
medicinal	DILL WATER, PTISAN
	TISANE, SELTZER
Mediterranean spirit	RAKEE, RAKI
	ROSOLIO
Mexican	PEYOTE, PULQUE, TEQUIL(L)A
milk	
—and ice cream	MILK SHAKE
—curdled with wine etc	POSSET
—with rum or whisky	MILK-PUNCH
mineral water	BADOIT, EVIAN
	MALVERN, PERRIER, SELTZER
	VICHY(WATER), VITELLOISE
	VOLVIC
mixed drink	TWIST
mixer	BITTER LEMON, CANADA DRY
	GINGER ALE, IT
	SODA WATER, TONIC WATER
mixture added to	
weak beer	STUM
molasses and water	SWITCHEL
mother's ruin	GIN
muscatel	MUSCAT, MUSCADINE
narcotic drink	(K)AVA
negus	RUMFUSTIAN
new	
—ale (Scot.)	SWATS
—wine	STUM
Norwich strong ale	NOG
Old Tom	GIN
on horseback	STIRRUP-CUP
	STIRRUP-DRAM
orange juice and	
lemonade	HENRI, HENRY
palm wine	TOMBO
Paraguay tea	MATE
peach-flavoured	PECHER
Persian	BOSA, SHIRAZ
Philippines rice beer	PANGASI
plum brandy	QUETSCH, SLIVOVIC(A)
	SLIVOVITZ
Polynesian beer	(K)AVA
poor beer (Scot.)	SWANK(E)Y
Portuguese brandy	AGUARDIENTE
posset made with sack	SACK-POSSET
quince-juice and sugar	QUIDDANY
raisin wine	BASTARD
Red Indian whisky	HOO(T)CH
red wine and	
methylated spirit	RED BIDDY
residue from	
—brewing	DRAFF
—distilling	DUNDER

—whisky	POT ALE
—wine making	MARC
revived wine	STUM
rice spirit (China)	SAMSHOO, SAMSHU
Romanian plum brandy	TUICA
rum	DEMERARA, GROG
	NELSON'S BLOOD
—and water	GROG
—Malay	TAF(F)IA
—punch	RUMBO, TOM AND JERRY
—West Indies	TAF(F)IA
Russian	
—beer	KWASS, QUASS
—spirit	VODKA
Scandinavian spirit	AKVAVIT, AQUAVIT
Scottish	ATHOLL BROSE, HEATHER ALE
—poor beer	SWANK(E)Y
—sour, stale or thin liquor	TIFT
—spiced hot	PLOTTIE, PLOTTY
—whisky	MALT, SCOTCH
sherry with lemon, etc	SHERRY-COBBLER
sherry-type	MADEIRA
Sikh	AMRIT
small	
—beer	SWIPES
—measure	CHOTA-PEG, DRAM
	POUSSE-CAFE, SNIFTER
	SNORT(ER)
soft	BARLEY WATER, BITTER LEMON
	CREAM SODA, FLOAT, GINGER ALE
	GINGER BEER, GRENADINE
	HENRI, HENRY, JULEP
	LEMON SQUASH, LEMONADE
	LIMEADE, LUCOZADE, MILK SHAKE
	ORANGE SQUASH, ORANGEADE
	POP, PTISAN, SALOOP, SELTZER
	TISANE, TONIC WATER
—American	COCA-COLA, PEPSI-COLA
	SARSAPARILLA
sour liquor	TIFF
South African	SKOKIAAN
—beer	POMBE
—liqueur	VAN DER HUM
South American	ASSAI, AYAHUASCO
	CHICHA, DEMERARA, MATE
	PISCO, YERBA
Spanish	
—brandy	FUNDADOR, SOBERANO
—fortified wine	SHERRY
—liquor	AGUARDIENTE
—non-alcoholic	HORCHATA
—wine	ALICANT, MALAGA
	PETER-SEE-ME
	RIOJA, TARRAGONA
Shakespeare	BASTARD, SHERRIS-SACK
	(*see also separate entry*)

sparkling perry	BABYCHAM
spiced	
—ale	WASSAIL
—punch	TOM AND JERRY
—sherry etc	NEGUS
—sweetened wine	PIMENT
—wine	HIPPOCRAS, SANGAREE
	SANGRIA
spicy wine	MUSCADEL, MUSCATEL
spirit	
—cocktail	SWIZZLE
—from	
asclepiad	SOMA
blue plums	SLIVOVTZ
cashew nuts	FENI, FENNY
coconuts	FENI, FENNY
golden plums	MIRABELLE
pears	EAU DE VIE
purple plums	QUETSCH
raspberries	EAU DE VIE, FRAMBOISE
rice	SAMSHOO, SAMSHU
rye	RYE-WHISKY
sugar-cane	RUM
sweet-potatoes	MOBBIE, MOBBY
wormwood and aniseed	ABSINTHE
—Goan	FENI, FENNY
—Greek	MASTISKA, METAXA
	OUZO, RAKI
—Italian	CAMPARI
—Mediterranean	RAKI
—poor	ROTGUT
—Russian	VODKA
—Scandinavian	AKVAVIT, AQUAVIT
	SCHNAP(P)S
—sour or stale	TIFF
—with	
fruit juice, etc	SOUR
hot water, sugar	TODDY
water	
—and flavouring	SLING
—spice, etc	PUNCH
spoilt beer	SWIPES
spruce shoots and sugar	
or treacle	SPRUCE-BEER
stale liquor	TIFF
stimulant	BRACER
stout	GUINNESS, PORTER
strong	
—ale	MOROCCO, NAPPY, OCTOBER
Norwich	NOG
—beer	MARCH BEER, STINGO
—drink (Yiddish)	SHICKER
—liquor	HOGAN, HOGEN
Shakespeare	TICKLE-BRAIN
stum	MUST
stupefying drink	DWALE

sugar and water	
—Sikh	AMRIT
—with spices	GINGER WINE
Sussex strong ale	TIPPER
sweet wine	BARSAC, MALVESIE
	MALVOISIE, MALMSEY
	MALVASIA, SAUTERNES
sweetened	
—fruit juice	SHRUB
—gin	OLD TOM
—spirits (Amer.)	SLING
—water (Sikh)	AMRITA
—wine (W. Indies)	SANGAREE
syrup from	
—almonds, sugar, etc	ORGEAT
—aniseed	ANISETTE
—apples	POMME
—bananas	BANANE
—blackcurrants	CASSIS
—cherries	CERISE
—gooseberries	GROSEILLE
—grapes	RAISIN
—lemons	CITRON
—mint	MENTHE
—pineapple	ANANAS
—plums	PRUNE
—pomegranates	GRENADINE
—prunes	PRUNE
—pure sugar	GOMME
—raspberries	FRAMBOISE
—strawberries	FRAISE
taken (at)	
—after meal	DIGESTIF
—bedtime	NIGHTCAP
—before meal	APERITIF
—early evening	SUNDOWNER
—mid-morning	ELEVENSES
tasteless slop	WASH
tea	(*see separate entry*)
thin liquor	GROG, TIFF
treacle-beer	SWITCHEL
Turkish	AIRAN, BOZA
	MASTIC(H)
—fruit juice	PEKMEZ
unfermented	
—grape-juice	MUST, STUM
—malt and hops	WORT
vinegar and honey	OXYMEL
warm alcoholic drink	CUP, MULL, PUNCH
	TODDY
water containing salts	
or gases	MINERAL WATER
Welsh fermented liquor	METHEGLIN
West Indian	
—spirit	MOBBY, MOBBIE
—sweetened wine	SANGAREE

Westmorland ale	MOROCCO
wheatmalt beer	MUM
whisky	AQUA VITAE, AULD KIRK
	GOOD STUFF, HOO(T)CH
	MOUNTAIN-DEW, THE CRATUR
	USQUEBAUGH
—American	BOURBON, RYE, TANGLEFOOT
poor	REDEYE
—from maize	BOURBON, CORN WHISKEY
—harsh	CHAIN LIGHTNING
—Highland	PEAT-REEK
—illicit	
America	BOOTLEG, MOONSHINE
Ireland	POT(H)EEN
—with	
hot water, etc	WHISKY TODDY
lemon, etc	WHISK(E)Y SOUR
soda	HIGHBALL, STENGAH
	STINGER
white wine etc	FUSTIAN
—with wormwood	VERMOUTH
wine	(*see separate entry*)
with eggs added	FLIP
Yugoslav brandy	VINJAC
Zoroastrian ritual drink	HAOMA

drugs

including: drugs of abuse
        medicines

adulterated cocaine	CRACK
affecting the mind	PSYCHOTROPIC
aloes and canella bark	HICKERY-PICKERY
	HIERA-PICRA
	HIGRY-PIGRY
alpha-blocker	TOLAZOLINE
amphetamine	METHEDRINE
anabolic steroid	ANAPOLON, ANAVAR
	CYPIONATE, DECA DURABOLIN
	DIANABOL, NOLVADEX, PARABOLON
	STANAZOLOL
anaesthetic	BENZOCAINE, CHLOROFORM
	COCAINE, EPIDURAL
	ETHYL CHLORIDE, EUCAIN(E), EVIPAN
	HALOTHANE, LAUGHING-GAS
	LIGNOCAINE, NITROUS OXIDE
	NOVOCAINE, PROCAINE
	STOVAINE, THIOPENTONE
analgesic	(*see* painkiller *below*)
antibiotic	ACTINOMYCIN, AMOXYCILLIN
	AMPHOTERICIN, AMPICILLIN
	AUREOMYCIN, CEPHALORIDINE
	CEPHALOSPORIN, CHLORAMPHENICOL
	CYCLOSERINE, ERYTHROMYCIN
	GRAMICIDIN, GRISEOFULVIN
	IVERMECTIN, MAGAININ
	MITURAMYCIN, NYSTATIN
	OXYTETRACYCLINE, POLYMIXIN

	SEPTRIN, STREPTOMYCIN
	SULPHONAMIDE, SULPHONE
	TERRAMYCIN, TETRACYCLINE
	VIOMYCIN
anticoagulant	HEPARIN
antihistamine	CIMETEDINE, CLARITYN
	MEPYRAMINE, PRILAMINE
	TRILUDAN
anti-inflammatory	ARTRODAR, DIACERHEIN
antipyretic	ACETYSALICYLIC ACID
	ASPIRIN, FEBRIFUGE
	PHENACETIN, SALICIN
antiseptic	ACRIFLAVIN, CARBOLIC ACID
	MANDELIC ACID, PHENOL
arrow-poison	CURARE, CURARI
attacking nervous	
system	NEUROTOXIN
barbitol	DIETHYLBARBITURIC ACID
	VERONAL
barbitone	VERONAL
barbiturate	SECONAL
beta blocker	ATENOLOL, CELPROLOL
	DILEVOLOL, INDERAL
	SELECTOL, UNICARD
bhang	INDIAN HEMP
bile purgative	CHOLAGOGUE
bituminous	MUMMY
body-building	(ANABOLIC) STEROID
Brazilian	JABORANDI, PAREIRA
breaking down blood	
fibrin	FIBRINOLYSIN
calming	SEDATIVE
cannabis	BHANG, DAGGA
	(INDIAN) HEMP
	MARIJUANA, POT, PUFF
causing	
—dilation of pupil	MYDRIATIC
—flow of urine	DIURETIC
—vomiting	EMETIC
cocaine residue	BASUCO
constricting capillaries	PITRESSIN
coramine	NIKETHAMIDE
crack	FREEBASE, READY-WASH
	ROCK
dagga	BHANG, HASH, (INDIAN) HEMP
	LOVE-DRUG, MARIJUANA, POT
dilating pupil	MYDRIATIC
diuretic	ACETOZAMIDE, FRUSEMIDE
	MERSALYL, TROMETHAMINE
	TROMETHAMOL
East Indian	ZERUMBET
Ecstasy	E
emetic	APOMORPHINE, EMETINE
expectorant	APOMORPHINE
expelling waste matter	ECCRITIC, LAXATIVE
febrifuge	ANTIPYRETIC

for	
—contracting pupil	MIOTIC
	PILOCARPINE
—reducing	
bleeding	APROTININ
excitement	SEDATIVE
fever	ANTIPYRETIC
flatulence	CARMINATIVE
heart-rate	BETA-BLOCKER
pain	ANALGESIC
urine flow	PITRESSIN
temperature	ANTIPYRETIC, FEBRIFUGE
tension	TRANQUILLISER
—stimulating	
brain	NIKETHAMIDE
breathing	LOBELINE, PICROTOXIN
central nervous system	BEMEGRIDE
flow of urine	ACETOZOLAMIDE
	DIURETIC, MERSALYL
heart	CORAMINE, DIGITALIS
	NIKETHAMIDE
nervous system	ATROPINE, CAFFEINE
	STRYCHNINE
—treating	
abnormal cell growth	VINBLASTINE
	VINCRISTINE
Aids	ZIDOVUDINE
alcoholism	DISULFURAM
all ailments	PANACEA
allergies	ANTIHISTAMINE
	DIMOTANE
Alzheimer's	
disease	TETRAHYDROAMINO-ACRIDINE
	THA
amoebic dysentery	EMETINE
angina	ADALAT, AMYL NITRATE
	BETA BLOCKER, CARDIZEM
	VASODILATOR
anxiety	BETA BLOCKER, DIAZEPAM
	SEDATIVE, TRANQUILLISER
	VALERIAN, VALLIUM
arthritis	CORTISONE, FELDENE
	NAPROSYN, VOLTARENT
asthma	BRONCHODILATOR
	EPHEDRINE
	SALBUTAMOL, VENTOLIN
bacterial infections	ANTIBIOTIC
	ANTITOXIN
bilharzia	NIRIDAZOLE
blocked air passages	DECONGESTANT
	EXPECTORANT
blood clotting	ANTI-COAGULANT
	COUMARIN, HEPARIN
	PHENIDIONE
	TISSUE PLASMIN ACTIVATOR
	TPA, WARFARIN

burns	PICRIC ACID
cholesterol	SIMVASTIN, ZOCOR
colic	GRIPE WATER
constipation	CATHARTIC
	GLAUBER'S SALTS, LAXATIVE
	PURGATIVE
convulsions	PHENYTOIN
coughs	ANTITUSSIVE, CODEINE
depression	AMITRYPTILINE
	IMIPRAMINE, PHENELZINE
diabetes	INSULIN, TOLBUTAMIDE
diarrhoea	PAREGORIC, KAOLIN
dysentery	SULPHAGUANIDINE
epilepsy	ANTICONVULSANT
	PHENYTOIN, PRIMIDONE
fast heart-beat	PRACTOLOL
	PROPANOLOL
fever	ANTIPYRETIC
	FEBRIFUGE
fragile blood-vessels	RUTIN
fungal infections	AMPHOTERICIN
	NYSTATIN, TOLNAFTATE
glaucoma	PHYSOSTYGMINE
goitre	THIOURACIL
gout	ALLOPURINOL, CHINCHOPHEN
	COLCHICINE, PROBENECID
hay fever	CLARITYN, TRILUDAN
heart disease	CORAMINE, DIGITALIS
	DIGOXIN, EMINASE
	NIKETHAMIDE, SQUILL
herpes	ACYCLOVIR
	INOSINE, PRANOBEX
high blood	
—pressure	ANDROMEDOTOXIN
	ATENALOL, BETA BLOCKER
	CAPOTEN, CAPTOPRIL, DYAZIDE
	GUANETHEDINE, INDERAL
	METHYLDOPA, PINDOLOL
	PROPANALOL, RESERPINE
	SOTALOL, TENORMIN
	TIMOLOL, VASOTEC
—sugar level	TOLBUTAMIDE
infections	AMOXIL, CECLOR
	CLAFORAN, PRONTOSIL
	ROCEPHINT
inflammation	INDOMETHACIN
insomnia	CHLORAL HYDRATE
	HYPNOTIC, MOGADON
	NEMBUTAL, NITRAZEPAM,
	PENTOBARBITONE
	SEDATIVE, SOPORIFIC
	TRANQUILLISER
irregular heart beat	QUINIDINE
	SPARTEINE
jaundice	ICTERAL, ICTERIC
leprosy	DAPSONE
Lewis gas poisoning	BAL
	DIMERCAPROL
malaria	ARTEETHER, ATABRIN
	ATEBRIN, CHLOROQUINE
	MEPACRINE, PALUDRINE
	PRIMAQUINE, PYRIMETHAMINE
	QUINACRINE, QUININE
meningitis	CHLOROMYCETIN
	SULPHAPYRIDINE
migraine	ERGOTAMINE
mouth ulcers	DEMULCENT
muscular tension	TUBOCURARINE
nasal congestion	AMPHETAMINE
nausea	CYCLIZINE
nervous tension	NEUROLEPTIC
osteoarthritis	ARTRODAR
	DIACERHEIN
pancreatitis	APROTININ
parasitic infections	METRONIDAZOLE
	THIABENDAZOLE
Parkinson's disease	DEPRENYL
	ELDEPRYL, L-DOPA
	LEVODOPA
peptic ulcers	ATROPINE, BANTHINE
	SELEGILINE
phosphorus poisoning	PRALIDOXIME
pneumonia	SULPHAPYRIDINE
poliomyelitis	SALK VACCINE
protozoa	TRYPANOCIDE
psoriasis	CHRYSAROBIN
	DITHRANOL
rashes	ANTIHISTAMINE
respiratory problems	KEFRAL
rheumatism	CORTISONE
	IBRUPROFEN
river blindness	IVERMECTIN
schizophrenia	CLOZAPINE
	CLOZARIL
scurvy	ANTISCORBUTIC
shingles	ACYCLOVIR
shock	NORADRENALINE
skin infections	CALAMINE
	CORTISONE
	CRYSTAL VIOLET
	GENTIAN VIOLET
	METHOTREXAT
	NEOMYCIN
sleeping sickness	PENTAMIDINE
	TRYPARSAMIDE
staphylococci	SULPHATHIAZOLE
stomach disorders	ANTACID
syphilis	CALOMEL, SALVARSAN
tension	BETA BLOCKER, DIAZEPAM
	SEDATIVE, TRANQUILLISER
	VALERIAN, VALLIUM
tetanus	CURARE

travel sickness	CYCLIZINE
	DIMENHYDRINATE
	HYOSCINE
tuberculosis	CYCLOSERINE
	ETHAMBUTOL
	ISONIAZID(E), PAS
	STREPTOMYCIN
tumours	CYTOTOXIN
typhoid	CHLOROMYCETIN
ulcers	RANITIDINE, TAGAMET
	ZANTAC
virus infections	INTERFERON
water retention	DIURETIC
worms	ANTHELMITIC
	PIPERAZINE, QUASSIA
	SANTONIN, VERMIFUGE
freebase	CRACK
from	
—andromeda	ANDROMEDOTOXIN
—belladonna	ATROPINE
	HYOSC(YAM)INE
—broom	SPARTEINE
	SCOPOLAMINE
—cinchona	QUIN(ID)INE
—coal-tar	SAFFRANIN(E)
—coca leaves	COCAINE
—coffee	CAFFEINE
—cucumber	COLOCYNTH
—datura	STRAMONIUM
—ergot	ERGOMETRINE, ERGONOVINE
	ERGOTAMINE, ERGOTOXINE
	HISTAMINE, LSD
	LYSERGIC ACID
—foxgloves	DIGITALIS, DIGOXIN
—fungus	ERGOMETRINE, ERGOTAMINE
—henbane	HYOSC(YAM)INE
—jaborandi	PILOCARPINE
—lobelia	LOBELINE
—lupins	SPARTEINE
—meadow saffron	COLCHICINE
—morphine	CODEINE, HEROIN
—mould	PATULIN
—mushrooms	PSILOCYBIN
—nux vomica	STRYCHNINE
—opium	CODEINE, LAUDANUM
	MORPHIA, NARCOTINE, OPIATE
—Orchis	SALEP, SALOP
—periwinkle	VINBLASTINE, VINCRISTINE
—poppies	OPIUM, MORPHINE
	PAPAVERINE, RHOEADINE
—rauwolfia	RESERPINE
—strophanthus	OUABAIN, WABAIN
—tea	THEINE, THEOBROMINE
	THEOPHYLLINE
—thorn-apple	STRAMONIUM
—toads	BUFOTENIN
—tobacco	NICOTINE
—wood	OUABAIN
ganglion-blocker	MECAMYLAMINE
grass	MARIJUANA
hallucinatory	ACID, ANGEL-DUST
	BUFOTENIN, CANNABIS
	HALLUCINOGEN, LSD
	LYSERGIC ACID, MESCALIN(E)
	PEYOTE, PHENCYCLIDINE
	PSILOCYBIN, STP
hash(ish)	HASHEESH, INDIAN HEMP
heart stimulant	CORAMINE, NIKETHAMIDE
	NORADRENALIN
hemp	BHANG, MARIHUANA
	MARIJUANA, POT
heroin	HORSE
hormone-blocker	GOSERELIN
hypnotic	AMYTAL, BARBITOL
	BARBITONE, BARBITURATE
	DIETHYLBARBITURIC ACID
	HALCION, PARALDEHYDE
	PHENOBARBITONE, TERONAL
	VERONAL, ZIMOVANE
	ZOPICLORE
imaginary	SOMA
inactive	PLACEBO
increasing bodily activity	STIMULANT
Indian	BHANG, BIKH
inducing	
—removal of obstructions	ECPHRACTIC
—stopping of pores	EMPHRACTIC
—unconsciousness	ANAESTHETIC
—uterine contractions	ECBOLIC
killing cells	CYTOTOXIC
laxative	ECCOPROTIC, LIQUORICE
	SENNA
liquefies blood etc	VARIDASE
local anaesthetic	COCAINE, STOVAINE
lysergic acid	LSD
marijuana	BHANG, CANNABIS, DAGGA
	GRASS, HASH, INDIAN HEMP
	POT, SNOUT, TEA
mercurous chloride	CALOMEL
methylene	
dioxymethamphetamine	ADAM
	MDMA
Mexican	JALAP, MESCALIN(E)
mixture of drugs	CRACK, SPEED-BALL
muscle relaxant	CURARINE
	NARCEINE, SOMA
narcotic	MANDRAGORA, MANDRAKE
	OPIATE
—antidote	NALOXONE
opium	HOP
pain-killer	ANALGESIC, ASPIRIN
	CODEINE, INDOMETHACIN

	LIDOCAINE, MORPHIA, MORPHINE
	NUROFEN, OPIATE, PAMATEL
	PANADOL, PARACETAMOL
	PENTAZOCINE, PETHIDINE
	PHENACETIN, PHENAZONE
	PHENYLBUTAZONE, SALICIN, SOMA
phencyclidine	ANGEL-DUST
pot	BHANG, CANNABIS, DAGGA
	HASH, INDIAN HEMP
	MARIJUANA, TEA
powdered	
methamphetamine	CRYSTAL(METH)
preventing	
—blood-clotting	ANTICOAGULANT
—coughing	ANTITUSSIVE
—growth of micro-organisms	ANTSEPTIC
—itching	ANTIPRURITIC
—haemorrhage	ERGOMETRINE
	ERGONOVINE
—seizures	ANTICONVULSANT
—sickness	ANTINAUSEANT
producing	
—symptoms imitating	
mental illness	PSYCHOSOMIMETIC
	PSCYHOTOMIMETIC
—unconsciousness	ANAESTHETIC
puff	CANNABIS
purgative	CATHARTIC, HIERA-PICRA
	HICKERY-PICKERY
	HIGRY-PIGRY
quack remedy	NOSTRUM
reducing	
—inflammation	ANTIHISTAMINE
—mental activity	DEPRESSANT
relaxant	MEPROBAMATE
	MILTOWN
remedy for poison	ANTIDOTE
santonin	WORM-SEED
sedative	BARBITURATE, BETEL
	CODEINE, DESERPEDINE
	DOWNER, GOOFBALL, LAUDANUM
	MEPROBAMATE, MILTOWN
	NARCEINE, NEMBUTAL, OPIATE
	OPIUM, PENTOBARBITONE
	PHENOBARBITONE, TETRONAL
	THALIDOMIDE, THIOPENTONE
snout	MARIJUANA
sorrow-lulling	NEPENTHE
spinal anaesthetic	EPIDURAL
stimulant	ADAM, AMYL NITRATE, BENNY
	BLUE, COCA(AINE), CRACK
	CRYSTAL (METH), CUBEB
	DOLL, E, ECSTASY, MDM, POPPER
	PURPLE HEART, ROCK
	READY-WASH, SNOW
	SPEED(BALL), UPPER

stimulating	
—bowel movement	LAXATIVE, PURGATIVE
—central nervous system	AMPHETAMINE
	BENZEDRINE
—expulsion of mucus	EXPECTORANT
—heart	CORAMINE,
	NIKETHAMIDE
	(NOR)ADRENALIN(E), OUABAIN
—immune system	PIROXICAM
—ovulation	CLOMIPHENE
—uterus	ERGOTAMINE
	ERGOTOXINE
strengthening	ROBORANT
sulphonamide	PRONTOSIL
suppressing immune	
reaction	IMMUNOSUPPRESSIVE
synthetic	
—cortisone	HECOGENIN
—sex hormone	STILBOESTROL
—stimulant	AMPHETAMINE
	BENZEDRINE
	EPHEDRINE, METHADONE
	PENTAZOCINE, PETHIDINE
tea	(*see* marijuana *above*)
tincture of opium	LAUDANUM, PAREGORIC
tonic	ROBORANT
tranquilliser	CHLORDIAZEPOXIDE
	CHLORPROMAZINE, DIAZEPAM
	HALOPERIDOL, LARGACTIL
	LIBRIUM, MOGADON
	MEPROBAMATE, NITAZEPAM
	PHENOTHIAZINE, RESERPINE
	VALIUM
treating	
—depression	ANTIDEPRESSANT
—fast heart-beat	BETA-BLOCKER
—infections	ANTISERUM, ANTISEPTIC
	ANTITOXIN
—muscle spasms	ANTISPASMODIC
—respiratory problems	BRONCHIAL DILATOR
	DECONGESTANT
—snake bite	ANTIVENIN
—worms	ANTHELMINT(H)IC
truth-drug	HYOSCINE
	SCOPOLAMINE
universal antidote	MITHRIDATICUM
	PANACEA, PANPHARMICON
vegetable	ANDROMEDOTOXIN
	BOTANICAL
worm-seed	SANTONICA, SANTONIN
duck	
domestic	AYLESBURY, BARBARY
	CAMPBELL, INDIAN RUNNER
	MUSCOVY, PEKIN, PERUVIAN
	ROUEN, WELSH HARLEQUIN
	WHALESBURY

wild	BLACK, EIDER, FERRUGINOUS
	GADWALL, GARGANEY, GOLDENEYE
	GOOSANDER, HARLEQUIN
	LONG-TAILED, MALLARD
	MANDARIN, MERGANSER, PINTAIL
	POCHARD, RING-NECKED, RUDDY
	SCAUP, SCOTER, SHELDUCK, SHOVELER
	SMEW, TEAL
	TUFTED, WI(D)GEON

Dutch   DU

administrative centre	THE HAGUE
advocate	PENSIONARY
airline	KLM
bargain	KOOP
cape (headland)	HOEK
capital	AMSTERDAM
car	DAF
channel	DIEP
cheese	EDAM, GOUDA
chief magistrate	BURGEMEESTER
	BURGOMASTER
coins	DOIT, FLORIN
—½ farthing	DODKIN, DOIT(KIN)
—penny	STIVER
—florin	GLD, GULDEN, GUILDER
—gold coin	RIDER
—silver coin	STOOTER
obsolete	RIX-DOLLAR
county	AMT
cupboard	KAS
dog	KEESHOND, SCHIPPERKE
donkey	EZEL
drink	AKVAVIT, ACQUAVIT
	ADVOCAAT, HOLLANDS
	SCHIEDAM, SCHNAP(P)S
fair	KERMESS, KERMIS, KIRMESS
former name	HOLLAND
flower	TULIP
game	KORFBALL
half-caste	GRIQUA
head of state	STAD(T)HOLDER
horse	SCHIMMEL
housewife	FROW, WROUW
island(s)	EILAND(EN)
lake	MEER
legal adviser	PENSIONARY
lock/weir	SASSE
knife	SNEE
lace	LANGET
magistrate	AMMAN, AMTMAN, SCHEPEN
man	MYNHEER
meal	MAAL
measures	
—length	DUIM, VOET
—2 acres	MORGEN
—8 gallons	ANKER

—30-35 gallons	AAM
—cask	LEAGUER
mister	(MYN)HEER
modern name	THE NETHERLANDS
municipal officer	SCHOUT
my lord	MYNHEER
news agency	ANETA
night	NACHT
path	PAD
pottery	DELFT
president	GRAND PENSIONARY
privateer	APER
provincial governor	STAD(T)HOLDER
reclaimed land	POLDER
river	MAAS
saint	SINT
sandbank	PLAAT
sand-flat	WAD
sea	MEER, ZEE
seat of government	THE HAGUE
sir	MYNHEER
States General	HOGEN-MOGEN
stream	BEEK
uncle	EME, OOM
vagrant	LANDLOOPER
viceroy	STAD(T)HOLDER
village	DORP
wife/woman	FROW, VROUW

dyes

including: dyes	
pigments	
annatto	ROUCOU
bituminous pigment	MUMMY
coal-tar	SAFFRANIN(E)
colourless derivative	LEUCO-COMPOUND
colours	
—black	BLACK IRON OXIDE
	BONEBLACK, CARBON BLACK
	LAMPBLACK, NIGROSINE
—blue	(ANTHO)CYANIN(E), COBALT
	DYER'S WOAD, PRUSSIAN BLUE
	METHYLENE, MONASTRAL BLUE
	PHYCOCYAN(IN), ULTRAMARINE
	VERDITER
crushed glass	SMALT
—brown	BISTRE, BROWN OCHRE
	CACHOU, CATECHU, CUTCH
	(EN)MELANIN, PHYCOPHAEIN
	SEPIA, SIENNA, TANNIN, UMBER
—green	BRUNSWICK GREEN
	CHLOROCRUORIN, CHLOROPHYLL
	CHROME GREEN, CUPRIC ACETOARSENITE
	MONASTRAL GREEN, PARIS GREEN
	SCHEELE'S GREEN, SCHWEINFURT GREEN
	SUMAC(H), TERRE-VERTE
	VERDITER, VIRIDIAN

—ochre	TIVER
—orange	AN(N)ATTO, AN(N)OTTA
	ARNATTO, CAROTENE
	CAROTIN, KAMALA, KAMELA
	KAMILA, ROUCOU
—orange-red	HENNA, CHICA
—orange-yellow	SAFFRON
—purple	ANTHOCYANIN, CORKIR
	CUDBEAR, KORKIR
	LITMUS, ORCEIN
	PURPLE OF CASSIUS, TURNSOLE
	TYRIAN (PURPLE)
—purple-red	FUCHSINE, MAGENTA
—red	ALKANET, ANIL(INE)
	ANTHCYANIN, ARCHIL
	BRAZILIN, CARMINE, CAROTENE
	CHICA, CHROME RED, CINNABAR
	COCHINEAL, CONGO RED
	CORKIR, CROCEIN, CYANIN
	HAEM(ATOXYLIN), INDIAN RED
	KERMES, KORKIR, LAKE
	LOGWOOD, MADDER
	MERCURIC SULPHIDE, MINIUM
	ORCHEL(LA), ORCHIL(LA)
	ORSEILLE, PARA-RED
	PHYCOERYTHRIN, RADDLE
	RED LEAD, RED OCHRE, REDDLE
	RHODAMINE, ROSANILINE
	RUDDLE, SAFFLOWER
	TURKEY RED, TYRIAN, VERMILION
—red/yellow	CAROTENE, AROTIN
—red/violet	ANILINE VIOLET
	MAUVE, MAUV(E)IN(E)
—violet	ARCHIL, CUDBEAR
	GENTIAN (VIOLET)
	INDIGO, ORCHEL(LA)
	ORCHIL(LA), ORSEILLE
—violet-blue	ANIL, INDIGO(TIN)
—white	CHINESE WHITE
	LEAD CARBONATE
	TITANIUM WHITE
	WHITE LEAD, ZINC OXIDE
	ZINC WHITE
—yellow	ANTHIN, CADMIUM (YELLOW)
	CAROTENE, CAROTIN
	CHROME (YELLOW), CHRYSANILINE
	ETIOLIN, FLAVIN, FLAVONE, FUSTEC
	FUSTIC, GAMBOGE, INDIAN YELLOW
	LEAD ANTIMONIATE
	NAPLES YELLOW, PHYCOXANTHIN
	PICRIC ACID, UROCHROME
	YELLOW EARTH, YELLOW OCHRE
—yellow-brown	BISTE
dying technique	BATIK, KALAMKARI
	TIE-DYING
earths	OCHRE, SIENA, UMBER
eye-pigment	
—blue	IODOPSIN
—red	RHODOPSIN
found in	
—algae	FUCOXANTHIN
—blood	CHLOROCRUORIN, HAEM
	HAEMOCYANIN, HAEMOGLOBIN
—food	AMARANTH
—hair	MELANIN
—lichen	ARCHIL
—madder	TURKEY RED
—plants	
absorbing red light	PHYTOCHROME
green	CHLOROPHYLL
yellow	ANTHIN, FLAVONE
	XANTHOPHYLL
—safflower	CARTHAMINE
—seaweed	
blue	PHYCOCYAN(IN)
brown	PHYCOPHALEIN
red	PHYCOERYTHRIN
yellow	PHYCOXANTHIN
—skin	(EN)MELANIN
—trees	
Bixa	AN(N)ATTA, AN(N)ATTO
	ARNOTTO, ROUCOU
Haematoxylin	LOGWOOD
—urine	UROCHROME
roucou	AN(N)ATTA, AN(N)ATTO
	ARNOTTO
South American	CHICA, COBRES
types	ACID DYE, AZO DYE
	BASIC DYE, SYNTHETIC DYE
	VAT DYE

ear

bones	(*see separate entry*)
buzzing in ear	TINNITUS
cavities	CONCHA, SACCULE
	UTRICLE
ear disorders	(*see* **disease**)
eardrum	MYRINGA
	TYMPANIC MEMBRANE
external opening	(AUDITORY) MEATUS
fluid in ear	ENDOLYMPH, PERILYMPH
inner ear	MEMBRANOUS LABYRINTH
middle ear	TYMPANIC CAVITY
outer ear	PINNA
parts of ear	ANVIL, AURICLE, COCHLEA
	CONCHA, EUSTACHIAN TUBE
	FENESTRA OVALIS, HAMMER
	HELIX, INCUS, LOBE, LOBULE
	ORGAN OF CORTI, SALPINX
	STAPES, STIRRUP, TRAGUS
	TYMPANUM, UTRICLE, VESTIBULE
projection	(ANTI)TRAGUS
stone in ear	OTOLITH
testing machine	AUDIOGRAPH, AUDIOMETER
wax in ear	CERUMEN
earth	(*see* **geography**)
earthquake	SEISM
affected by same shock-waves	COSEISMAL
	COSEISMIC
at seabed	SEAQUAKE
line of equal earthquake shocks	COSEISMAL LINE
	HOMOSEISMAL LINE
	ISOSEISMAL LINE
location	EPICENTRE, EPICENTRUM
major earthquakes	AGADIR, ANCHORAGE
	ANDREANOL, ARMENIA, AVEZZANO
	BUCHAREST, CALCUTTA, EL ASNAM
	ERZINCAN, GANSU, GUATEMALA
	KAMCHATKA, KANSU, KWANTO PLAIN
	LEBU, LOS ANGELES, MESSINA
	NICARAGUA, NORTH YEMEN
	POTENZA, QUETTA, SAN FRANCISCO
	SHENSI, SKOPJE
	TABAS, TANGSHAN, TURKEY
recording instrument	SEISMOGRAPH
	SEISMOMETER
	TRONOMETER
record of	SEISOGRAM

scale of intensity	(GUTENBERG-)RICHTER SCALE
	KANAMORI SCALE
	MERCALLI SCALE
seismic	TERREMOTIVE
seismologist	
—American	GUTENBERG, RICHTER, REID
—British	OLDHAM
shock waves	
—after main earthquake	AFTERSHOCK
—before main earthquake	FORESHOCK
—bodily waves passing through Earth's core	P WAVE
	PRIMARY WAVE
stopped by Earth's core	S WAVE
	SECONDARY WAVE
—surface waves	
horizontal	LOVE WAVE
vertical	RAYLEIGH WAVE
—types	
following curve of earth	SURFACE WAVE
passing through earth	BODILY WAVE
slow movement of surface	BRADYSEISM
small	
—earthquake	TREMOR
—persistent tremor	MICROSEISM
study of earthquakes	SEISMOLOGY
subterranean origin	SEISMIC FOCUS
wave caused by earthquake	
—at sea	TSUNAMI
—in inland waters	SEICHE

East Indian

ape	ORANG(UTAN)
aromatic gum	BENZOIN, GUM BENJAMIN
	JEW'S FRANKINCENSE
—root	GALINGALE
aubergine	EGG-PLANT
berry	CUBEB
bird	CASSOWARY, JAVA SPARROW
	KORA, PADDY-BIRD, RICE-BIRD
	TAILOR-BIRD, WATER-COCK
breadfruit tree	JA(C)K (TREE)
brinjal	EGG-PLANT
civet	BINTURONG, LINSANG
	RASSE
climbing shrub	CUBEB, GAMBI(E)R
	ROSARY PEA
cloth	HUMHUM
coffee	
—flavoured plant	ABELMOST
—rat	MUSANG
coin	BONK, DUIT
condiment	CHUTNEY
currency	Y, YEN
drink	NIPA

drug	ZERUMBET
dying process	BATIK
edible fat	KOKUM BUTTER
egg-plant	AUBERGINE, BRINJAL
fern	BAROMETZ
fish	ANABAS, POMFRET
flying squirrel	TAGUAN
fruit	CARAMBOLA
	COROMANDEL GOOSEBERRY
	MANGO, MARKING-NUT
	ROSE-APPLE, TAMPOE
gamboge tree	TAMANU
ginger	CASSUMUNAR
ground pigeon	GOURA
gum-resin	TACAMAHAC
hat	MITRE
hibiscus	ROSELLE, ROZELLE
insectivore	SQUIRREL-SHREW
	TREE-SHREW
lemur	LORIS
mat	TAT
measures	
—dry	GANTANG
—yard	GUZ
—30-35 galls	AAM
native (New Guinea)	BOONG
orange dye	KAMALA, KAMELA
	KAMILA
palm	AT(T)AP, NIPA
parrot	LORY
plant yielding arrowroot	PIA
resting-frame	DUTCH WIFE
spice	NUTMEG
sqirrel-shrew	PENTAIL
tarsier	MALMAG
timber	BLOODWOOD, BRAZIL(-WOOD)
	JELUTONG
tree	ABROMA, AGALLOCH, AGILA, BILIAN
	B(I)LIMBI(NG), CARAMBOLA
	CUCUMBER-TREE, EAGLEWOOD
	EMBLIC(A), GARJAN, GURJUN, JELUTONG
	KAMALA, KAMELA, KAMILA, KUMBUK
	KOKUM, MANGO, MARGOSA, NUX VOMICA
	PONTIANAC, PONTIANAK
	POON, ROSE-APPLE, SANDAL(-WOOD)
	SAP(P)AN, TAMANU, UPAS, SACK-TREE
	SUNDARI, SUNDER, SUNDRA, SUNDRI
—lizard	DRAGON-LIZARD
—shrew	BANGSRING, BANXRING
tribe	D(A)YAK, IBAN
turkey	TALEGALLA
upas tree	SACK-TREE
weasel-cat	DELUNDUNG
weight (3½ cwts)	BAHAR
wild	
—hog	BABIR(O)USSA

—ox	(see **ox**)
weapon	TOMBOC
eastern	
acacia	BABLAH, BABUL
banker	SHROFF
bedcover	PALAMPORE, PALEMPORE
bird	ANT-THRUSH
bishop	ABBA
bishop's vestment	SAKKOS, OMOPHORION
bosun	SERANG
camel-hair fabric	ABA
chewing nut	BETEL(-NUT)
chieftain	AMEER, EMEER, EMIR
coasting vessel	GRAB
coffee-cup without handle	FINGAN, FINJAN
coin	CASH
couch	DIVAN
cymbal	ZEL
dervish	SANTON
disease	BERI-BERI
dish	BEAN CURD, PILAFF
	PIL(L)AU, PILAW, PILOW
dress	CHEONG-SAM
drink	ARAK, ARRACK
dulcimer	SANTIR, SANT(O)UR
dwarf goose	GOSLET
European Time	EET
eye-shadow	KOHL
fabulous bird	HUMA
folk dance	KOLO
fruit	SEBESTEN
gift	BA(C)KSHEESH, BA(C)KSHISH
	BAKHSHISH, BUCKSHISH
gold bar	TAEL
governor	MUDIR
governor's province	MUDIRIA, MUDIRIEH
guitar	TAMBOURA
gum	GALBANUM
guide	DRAGOMAN
headdress	TURBAN
inn	(CARAVAN)SERAI
	CARAVANSARY
	CHO(UL)TRY, KHAN
interpreter	DRAGOMAN
leader	E
magician	MAGE, MAGUS, ZENDIK
market	BAZA(A)R, SOUK
mendicant	FAKIR
money-changer/lender	SHROFF
musical instrument	PANDORA, PANDORE
	PANDURA
newcomer	GRIFFIN, GRIFFON
novice	GRIFFIN, GRIFFON
order of monks	ACOEMETI
ownerless dog	PARIAH
palm	PALMYRA

paymaster	BUCKSHEE, BUKSHI
pheasant	ARGUS
plane tree	CHENAR, CHINAR
porter	HAM(M)AL
printed cambric or muslin	PERSIENNE
punishment	BASTINADE
	BASTINADO
sailor	LASCAR
saint	SANTON
salutation	SALAAM
ship	JUNK
shrub	BITTER-KING
silk-satin	ATLAS
skirt	SARONG
slipper	BABOOSH, BAB(O)UCHE
tabor	TIMBREL
tambourine	TIMBREL
temple	PAGOD(A)
tip	BA(C)KSHEESH, BA(C)KSHISH
	BAKHSHISH, BUCKSHISH
title	AG(H)A, ALI, RAS
tree	LEBBEK, SEBESTEN
unbeliever	ZENDIK
vase	POTICHE
waterwheel	SAKIA, SAKI(Y)EH
vehicle	JINRIKSHA, (JIN)RICKSHAW
	TRISHAW
vestment	PH(A)ELONION
weight	ROTL
whip	K(O)URBASH
	(*see also* **Oriental**)

eat

including: eater of
eating

all things	OMNIVOROUS, PANTOPHAGY
animals	ZOOPHAGOUS
ants	MYRMECOPHAGOUS
bacteria	BACTERIOPHAGOUS
bees	APIVOROUS
berries	BACCIVOROUS
blood	SANGU(IN)IVOROUS
bones	OSSIVOROUS
books (avid reader)	BIBLIOPHAGE
carrion	NECROPHAGOUS
children	P(A)EDOPHAGOUS
dead bodies	NECROPHAGOUS
decaying matter	SAPROPHAGOUS
dung	COPROPHAGOUS
	SCATOPHAGOUS
earth	GEOPHAGY
family or tribe	ENDOPHAGY
fish	ICHTHYOPHAGOUS
	PISCIVOROUS
flesh	CARNIVOROUS
	CREOPHAGOUS
	SARCOPHAGOUS

—of strangers	EXOPHAGY
frogs	RANIVOROUS
fruit	CARPOPHAGOUS
	FRUGIVOROUS
fungus	MYCOPHAGOUS
god	THEOPHAGY
grain	GRANIVOROUS
grass	GRAMINIVOROUS
	HERBIVOROUS
honey	MELLIPHAGOUS, MELLIVOROUS
horses	EQUIVOROUS, HIPPOPHAGY
insects	ENTOMOPHAGOUS
	INSECTIVOROUS
large pieces of food	MACROPHAGOUS
leaves	PHYLLOPHGOUS
lotus eaters	LOTOPHAGI
man (cannibal)	ANTHROPOPHAGOUS
many different things	POLYPHAGIA
	POLYPHAGY
nails	ONYCHOPHAGY
nuts	NUCIVOROUS
nutmegs	MYRISTICIVOROUS
one kind of food	MONOPHAGOUS
oysters	OSTREOPHAGOUS
plants	PHYTOPHAGOUS
poisons	TOXI(CO)PHAGOUS
raw flesh	OMOPHAGIA
rice	ORYZIVOROUS
roots	RADICIVOROUS
	RHIZOPHAGOUS
seeds	GRANIVOROUS
self	AUTOPHAGOUS
small pieces of food	MICROPHAGOUS
snakes	OPHIOPHAGOUS
stone	LITHOPHAGOUS
thistles	CARDOPHAGOUS
toadstools	MYCOPHAGOUS
wood	LIGNIVOROUS
	XYLOPHAGOUS
wool	MALLOPHAGOUS
worms	VERMIVOROUS

economics

accounting period	FINANCIAL YEAR
	FISCAL YEAR
acquisition of company	
to sell its assets	ASSET STRIPPING
additional security for loan	COLLATERAL
adjustment of value of	
future income to current	
monetary value	DISCOUNTED CASH FLOW
agreement on tariffs	GATT
agricultural policy (EC)	CAP
alternate restriction and	
expansion of trade	STOP-GO
amalgamation of companies	
—by acquisition	TAKEOVER

—by agreement	CONSOLIDATION
	MERGER
analysis of	
—benefit from given	
expenditure	COST-BENEFIT ANALYSIS
—economic data	ECONOMETRICS
annual percentage rate	APR
annuity which increases	
as subscribers die	TONTINE
association of persons	
buying and selling	
stocks and shares	STOCK EXCHANGE
automatic increase in inland	
revenue from increased income	FISCAL DRAG
balance in favour of	
account-holder	CREDIT
band within which	
—EC currencies are	
allowed to float	(THE) SNAKE
—world currencies float	(THE) TUNNEL
bank	
—rate	
UK	MINIUMUM LENDING RATE, MLR
USA	DISCOUNT RATE
—taking deposits and	
making short-term	
loans, etc	COMMERCIAL BANK
	JOINT STOCK BANK
—trading in	
shares, etc	MERCHANT BANK
benefit derived from	
embezzlement	BEZZLE
benefits etc	
—at no cost to recipient	ZERO-PRICE
—linked to retail	
price index	INDEX-LINKED
—paid for by tax-payer	TAX-PRICE
bills for funding	
Government debt	TREASURY BILLS
block of shares etc	TRANCHE
bond in yen issued by non-	
Japanese company	SAMURAI BOND
Bretton Woods system	IMF
INTERNATIONAL MONETARY FUND	
	WORLD BANK
British Government	
stock	CONSOLIDATED STOCK
	CONSOLS
buildings, plant, etc	CAPITAL ASSETS
buying and selling	
—against the law	BLACK MARKET(EERING)
—international debts	FORFAITING
—shares	
in one company to	
inflate the price	WASH-TRADING
not yet quoted	GREY MARKET

calculation of income	
taking account	
of time	DISCOUNTED CASH-FLOW
capital	
—needed to run	
company	WORKING CAPITAL
—of company divisible	
into shares	STOCK
—sum paid to	
new employee	GOLDEN HELLO
redundant employee	
	GOLDEN HANDSHAKE
	PLATINUM HANDSHAKE
retiring employee	GOLDEN GOODBYE
—used for wages, etc	FLOATING CAPITAL
card authorizing	
purchases by	
deferred payment	CREDIT CARD
central bank	(*see* national banks *below*)
certificate entitling exporter	
to repayment of duty	DEBENTURE
changes in	
—financial resources	FUNDS-FLOW
—working capital	CASH-FLOW
charge for delay	
—of delivery	BACKWARDATION
—in discharge or	
loading of ship	DEMURRAGE
combination of firms	
—to control prices	CARTEL
—with like interests	CONSORTIUM
	SYNDICATE
company	
—in which shareholders	
are free to transfer	
shares	JOINT STOCK COMPANY
—trading in bills, etc	DISCOUNT HOUSE
comparison of costs based	
on actual expenditure	MARGINAL COSTING
compounded annual rate	CAR
computer fraud of	
small amounts	SALAMI TECHNIQUE
contour on chart showing	
—consumer's	
objectives	INDIFFERENCE CURVE
—production	ISOQUANT
contract based on cost plus	
a percentage	COST-PLUS
control of	
—currency fluctuations	ERM
EXCHANGE RATE MECHANISM	
—money in	
circulation	MONETARY POLICY
—taxation	FISCAL POLICY
—trade by	
one company	MONOPOLY

two companies	DUOPOLOY
several companies	OLIGOPOLY
convert net figure to gross	GROSS UP
corporation made up of companies with diverse interests	CONGLOMERATE
cost of action in a perfect market	OPPORTUNITY COST
currency	
—based on a strong economy	HARD CURRENCY
—note	TREASURY NOTE
whose exchange rate is determined by supply and demand	FLOATING CURRENCY
daily average price of shares	
—Japan	NIKKEI INDEX
—UK	FINANCIAL TIMES INDEX, FT INDEX
—USA	DOW JONES INDEX
debenture	BOND
debt	DEBIT
—owed by government	NATIONAL DEBT PUBLIC DEBT
deduction from normal price	DISCOUNT
depression	RECESSION, SLUMP
difference	
—between national imports and exports	BALANCE OF TRADE
receipts and payments	BALANCE OF PAYMENTS
—in price of stock and its par value	DISCOUNT
—income and expenditure	
positive	PROFIT
negative	LOSS
discount rate (US)	BANK RATE
doctrine of macroeconomics	KEYNESIANISM
ease of exchange	LIQUIDITY
econometrics applied to economic history	CLIOMETRICS
economist	
—American	ARROW, DEBREU, DOMAR DORFMAN, DE BREU, FRIEDMAN GALBRAITH, GERARD, ISARD LEONTIET, LEWIS, MARKOWITZ MARSHALL, MEANS, ROSTOW SAMUELSON, SCOTT, SOLOW, VEBLEN
—Austrian	HAYEK
—British	BAGEHOT, CLAPHAM, DOBB DOUGLAS, HARROD, HAWTHORNE HAYEK, HICKS, HOBSON, KEYNES MALTHUS, MILL, PHILLIPS RICARDO, , ROBBINS, SHOVE SMITH, STELLARS, WALTERS
—Canadian	JOHNSON
—French	DE NEMOURS, DEBREU GERARD, WALRAS
—German	MARX, MICHELS, MORGENSTERN
—Hungarian	KALDOR
—Irish	EDGEWORTH
—Italian	PARETO, VERRI
—Norwegian	FRISCH
—Polish	DORIAR, LANGE
—Russian	LEONTIET
economy based on	
—large businesses	CORPORATISM
—private enterprise	FREE ECONOMY FREE ENTERPRISE MARKET ECONOMY
—state	
control	SOCIALISM
intervention	DIRIGISME
electronic transfer of	
—funds (at point of sale)	EFT(POS)
—shares	TAURUS
employment of more workers than necessry	OVERMANNING
entry in account on	
—creditor side	CREDIT
—debtor side	DEBIT
excessive trading to increase commission etc	CHURNING
exchange of goods for other goods	BARTER COUNTERTRADE
expenditure on assets	CAPITAL EXPENDITURE
export of capital borrowed by a country for its own development	CAPITAL FLIGHT
extreme inflation	HYPERINFLATION
face value of security	NOMINAL VALUE PAR (VALUE)
fall in value of money	INFLATION
figure summarizing statistical trends	INDEX NUMBER
finance experts	NUMERATI
Financial Times/Stock Exchange 100 share index	FOOTSIE
fixed	
—exchange rate	BRETTON WOODS SYSTEM
—interest security	DEBENTURE, LOAN STOCK
fixing limits to fluctuation of share prices	CIRCUIT-BREAKING
free trade or protection	THE FISCAL QUESTION
fund made by uniting yield of various taxes	CONSOLIDATED FUND

goods	
—bought or sold for future delivery	FUTURES
—made for production rather than consumption	CAPITAL GOODS
government stock	GILT-EDGED SECURITIES GILTS
gradual surreptitious purchase of shares	CREEPING TAKEOVER FOOTHOLD BUYING
graph of	
—balance of payments following devaluation	J-CURVE
—unemployment and inflation	PHILLIPS CURVE
group of	
—currencies	BASKET
—nations applying common customs policy	CUSTOMS UNION
guaranteed IOU issued by the Treasury	TREASURY BILL
illegal transfer of money	LAUNDERING
impose limits on expenditure	CAP
income	
—from	
business etc	EARNED INCOME
investments	UNEARNED INCOME
services	INVISIBLE EARNINGS INVISIBLES
total economy	NATIONAL INCOME
—not reported for tax purposes	BLACK MONEY
increase in	
—amount of money available in relation to its buying power	INFLATION
—economic activity	BOOM, REFLATION
—official value of currency	REVALUATION
—prices	
due to excessive demand	OVERHEATING
to cover losses from shoplifting	BUNCING
—value	APPRECIATION
index of	
—share prices	
Japan	NIKKEI INDEX
UK	FINANCIAL TIMES INDEX
US	DOW-JONES INDEX
—statistical trends	FISHER INDEX LASPEYTRES INDEX PAASCHE INDEX
inflation	
—due to rise in cost of production	COST-PUSH

—in	
expanding economy	BOOMFLATION
recession	STAGFLATION
institution for buying and selling of stocks and shares	STOCK EXCHANGE
international trade without tariffs	FREE TRADE
intersection of graph lines for 75 and 200-day share movements	GOLDEN CROSS
investigation of	
—characteristics of customers	MARKET RESEARCH
—competitors' affairs	COMPETITOR ANALYSIS
investment	
—by bank of its own funds in takeovers, etc	MERCHANT BANKING
—trust that sells units in a combined portfolio	MUTUAL FUND UNIT TRUST
issue of	
—free shares	BONUS ISSUE SCRIP ISSUE
—new shares to existing shareholders	RIGHTS ISSUE
—notes not backed by gold, etc	FIDUCIARY ISSUE
lag between public expenditure and income	FISCAL DRAG
large-scale speculation by company	ZAITECH, ZAITEKU
law relating to	
—inferior currencies	GRESHAM'S LAW
—input/output ratio	LAW OF DIMINISHING RETURNS LAW OF VARIABLE PROPORTIONS
—supply and demand	SAY'S LAW
list of securities	PORTFOLIO
loan	
—to finance purchase of one asset before sale of another	BRIDGING LOAN
—with no fixed date for repayment	FUNDED DEBT
loss of value due to wear and tear	DEPRECIATION
making debt marketable	SECURITISATION
market for short-term loans	MONEY MARKET
measures to reduce inflation	DISINFLATION
mechanism for cutting guaranteed prices	STABILISER

monetary unit not corresponding to actual currency	MONEY OF ACCOUNT
	UNIT OF ACCOUNT
money	
—not permanently invested	FLOATING CAPITAL
—on high interest repayable after major loans have been paid off	MEZZANINE DEBT
—order	POSTAL ORDER
national banks	
—Germany	BUNDESBANK
—international	IMF
INTERNATIONAL MONETARY FUND	
	WORLD BANK
—UK	BANK OF ENGLAND
—USA	CENTRAL BANK
	FEDERAL RESERVE BANK
not susceptible to a takeover bid	BID-PROOF
one	
—called in to restore a failing company	COMPANY DOCTOR
—to whom a debt is due	CREDITOR
—who	
buys and sells stocks and shares	STOCKBROKER
exchanges notes, bills, etc at a discount	DISCOUNT BROKER
buys shares in threatened company	WHITE SQUIRE
guarantees to buy all shares left over	UNDERWRITER
holds	
—in trust	FIDUCIARY, TRUSTEE
—security for a loan	LOAN-HOLDER
—shares in	
private company	SHAREHOLDER
public company	STOCKHOLDER
practises insurance business	UNDERWRITER
rescues company threatened by closure or takeover	WHITE KNIGHT
risks his own capital	ENTREPRENEUR
studies the stock market	CHARTIST
trades in shares at a profit	MARKET-MAKER
opportunity for gain provided by tax structure	TAX BREAK
ordinary shares	COMMON STOCK
	EQUITIES
overseas sales of	
—goods	VISIBLE EXPORTS
—services	INVISIBLE EXPORTS
paper	
—for endorsement attached to bill of exchange	ALLONGE
—money	TREASURY BILL
payment	
—for insurance cover	PREMIUM
—to individual below income tax threshold	NEGATIVE INCOME-TAX
period of	
—increased economic activity	BOOM
—reduced economic activity	DEPRESSION
	RECESSION, SLUMP
policy based on	
—control of	
money supply	MONETARISM
taxes	FISCAL POLICY
wages, etc	INCOMES POLICY
—decontrol, etc	ROGERNOMICS
—restraint of trade	DISINFLATION
—tax reductions and deficit spending to increase productivity	REAGANOMICS
	SUPPLY-SIDE
postal order	MONEY ORDER
postpone payment of debt	RESCHEDULE
practice of acquiring company to sell off assets	ASSET-STRIPPING
price	
—assumed in maximisation exercise	SHADOW PRICE
—charged by vendor	SELLING PRICE
—fixing group	CARTEL
—paid by merchant	COST PRICE
profit	
—from sale of property, etc	CAPITAL GAIN
—sharing based on gains or savings	GAIN-SHARING
promise to repay a loan	IOU
	NOTE OF HAND
	PROMISSORY NOTE
progressive increase in prices	INFLATION
property income certificate	PINC
public funds	STOCKS
—office negotiating loans	LOAN-OFFICE
—purse	FISC, FISK
purchase	
—of	
majority holding	BUY-IN

securities   INVESTMENT
shares in companies
  which satisfy
  ethical
  standards   CONSCIENCE INVESTMENT
surplus produce for
  storing   INTERVENTION
—with money borrowed
  from vendor   BALLOON FINANCING
raise artificially the
  price of a commodity   VALORISE
rate
—at which banks
  can borrow   DISCOUNT RATE
—charged by central
  banks   BANK RATE
     MINIMUM LENDING RATE, MLR
ratio of borrowing
  to assets   GEARING
recession   DEPRESSION, SLUMP
reduced customs
  duty   PREFERENTIAL TARIFF
reduction
—caused by depletion   DRAW-DOWN
—in
  amount of money
  available in relation to
  its purchasing power   DEFLATION
  economic activity   DEPRESSION
     RECESSION, SLUMP
  official value of
  currency   DEVALUATION
  value   DEPRECIATION
risky security   JUNK-BOND
sale on trust   CREDIT
scheme of life annuity   TONTINE
school of economists   AUSTRIAN SCHOOL
sell shares one
  does not own   SHORT
selling
—additional services to
  existing customers   CROSS-MARKETING
     CROSS-SELLING
—overseas at reduced
  prices   DUMPING
—share futures in
  falling market   PORTFOLIO INSURANCE
sequence of boom and
  depression   TRADE CYCLE
share
—considered safe and
  profitable   BLUE CHIP
—on which dividends
  are paid before other
  types   PREFERENCE SHARE
—of public debt   STOCK

simultaneous trading in
  stocks and futures of
  those stocks   INDEX ARBITRAGE
slice of whole (money)   TRANCHE
slump   DEPRESSION
     RECESSION
speculative security   JUNK-BOND
speculator who
—buys
  in anticipation
  of rising prices   BULL
  to profit
  —by different prices
  in different markets   ARBITRAGEUR
  —on newly-issued shares   STAG
—sells
  for short-term gain   PROFIT-TAKER
  in anticipation of
  falling prices   BEAR
spending
—equal to tax income   BALANCED BUDGET
—in excess of tax
  receipts   DEFICIT SPENDING
split into separate
  companies   DEMERGE
starting a business   FLOTATION
state
—of the economy   CONJUNCTURE
—intervention   DIRIGISME
—treasury   FISC, FISK
statistical measure of
  prices etc   INDEX
—base-weighted   LASPEYRE'S INDEX
—current-weighted   PASSCHE INDEX
stock
—certificates, bonds etc   SECURITIES
—considered safe
  and profitable   GILT-EDGED SECURITIES
     GILTS
—held with others   JOINT STOCK
—used for business   CAPITAL
study of
—economics by
  statistical methods   ECONOMETRICS
—large-scale
  economics   MACROECONOMICS
sudden
—attempt to buy
  large shareholding   DAWN RAID
—collapse of share prices   FREE FALL
sum owing   DEB(I)T
summary of accounts   BALANCE SHEET
supplementary asset
  such as goodwill   INTANGIBLE
surreptitious dealing
  in goods   BLACK MARKET

system		—goods and services	
—based on supply and		produced in a country	
demand	MARKET ECONOMY	in one year	GNP
—fixing currency value			GROSS NATIONAL PRODUCT
in relation to gold	GOLD STANDARD	—property of	
—generating wealth		company	ASSETS
for individuals	CAPITALISM	deceased	ASSET
—of state intervention	COLBERTISM	traffic in buying	
	DIRIGISME	shares etc	ARBITRAGE
—vesting property, etc		transfer of funds from	
in the community	SOCIALISM	account in surplus	
in the state	COLLECTIVISM	to one in deficit	VIREMENT
	COMMUNISM	treating money as an	
taking excessive		article	COMMODIFICATION
interest on loan	USURY	unexpected profit	LUAU
tax		unfair trading	
—collected by		agreement	RESTRICTIVE PRACTICE
government agencies	DIRECT TAX	unfixed exchange	
traders	INDIRECT TAX	rate	FLOATING EXCHANGE RATE
—on		unfunded short-term	
alcohol,		loan	FLOATING DEBT
tobacco, etc	(EXCISE) DUTY	unofficial business	
capital	CAPITAL LEVY	evading the tax system	BLACK ECONOMY
companies	CORPORATION TAX	usurer	LOAN-SHARK
estate	DEATH DUTY	value of stock	
	INHERITANCE TAX	—equal to purchase price	PAR
gains	CAPITAL GAINS TAX	—over par	PREMIUM
gifts	CAPITAL TRANSFER TAX	—under par	DISCOUNT
imports	(CUSTOMS) DUTY	variable rate of exchange	FLOATING RATE
income	INCOME TAX, PAYE	warrant to buy	
	SUPERTAX	government securities	
increased value		at a fixed price	GILT WARRANT
of product	INPUT TAX, OUTPUT TAX	workforce	MANPOWER
	VALUE-ADDED TAX, VAT	written	
—policy	FISCAL POLICY	—acknowledgment of debt	DEBENTURE
—rebates instead of		—authorisation	
social benefits	NEGATIVE INCOME TAX	for credit	LETTER OF CREDIT
	REVERSE INCOME TAX	—IOU	NOTE OF HAND
temporary recovery			PROMISSORY NOTE
of share prices	DEAD-CAT BOUNCE	—obligation to pay	
theory		or perform contract	BOND
—of		yield from	
best strategies	NASH EQUILIBRIUM	—capital	INTEREST
development of		—shares, etc	DIVIDEND
the economy		**Ecuador**	EC
over time	TURNPIKE THEOREM	capital	QUITO
extending until marginal		coin	SUCRE
gains balance		**egg**	
marginal costs	MARGINAL PRINCIPLE	cooked	
—that trade cycles		—as light fluffy pancake	OMELETTE
result from bank		—in	
lending	CREDIT THEORY	baking dish	SHIRRED
total value of		fat	FRIED
—GNP less income from		—on one side	SUNNY SIDE UP
overseas investments	GDP	pan and stirred	SCRAMBLED
	GROSS DOMESTIC PRODUCT	water	BOILED

—lightly	CODDLED
without shell	POACHED
egg dishes	ALPINE EGG, CHILLI EGGS
	CROQUE MONSIEUR
	EGG A LA MORNAY, EGG BENEDICT
	EGG CUSTARD, EGG FLORENTINE
	EGG ROLL, FRAMED EGG
	MERINGUE, OMELETTE, PICKLED EGG
	PIPERADE, RAMAKIN, RAMEKIN
	RAMEQUIN, ZABAGLIONE
in sausage meat	SCOTCH EGG
omelette with vegetable	
filling	SPANISH OMELETTE
raw with seasoning	PRAIRIE OYSTER
scrambled egg on toast	
with anchovy paste	SCOTCH WOODCOCK
white of egg	ALBUMEN, GLAIR
—whisked till stiff	MERINGUE
yellow part of egg	YOLK

Egypt

administrative district	NOME
bean(s)	
—mashed	FALAFEL
—puree	BISSARA
—stew	FOUL MADAMES
beer	BO(U)SA, ZYTHUM
beetle	SCARAB
boat	BARIS
boulevard along Nile	CORNICHE
capital	CAIRO, EL QAHIRA
catfish	DOCMAC
characters	ET
Christian	COPT
coin	
—unit	MILLIEME
—100 milliemes	PIASTRE
—100 piastres	POUND
commander	SIRDAR
cotton	MACO, PIMO, SAK(EL)
cross	ANKH, TAU
crown	ATEF, PSCHENT
dance	GHAZIYA
dancing girl	ALMA(H), ALME(H)
deities	(see gods, goddesses)
department	NOME
double	KA
dynasty	HYKSOS, MAMELUKE
	PTOLEMAIC
embalming vase	CANOPUS
fish	OXYRHYNCUS, SAIDE
floating vegetable matter	SUDD
funeral effigy	USHABTI
granite	STENITE
guard	GHAF(F)IR
hat	FEZ
holy rattle	SISTRUM

jar	CANOPIC
king	PHARAOH
kings	AKHENATEN, AMASIS, AMENMESSE
	AMENEMHET, AMENHOTEP, AMOSIS
	CHEOPS, HOREMHEB, KHAFRE
	KHUFU, MENES, MENKAURE
	MERENPTAH, PEPI, RAMESES
	SESOSTRIS, SETI, SIPTAH
	TUTANKHAMUN, TUTANKHATEN
	TUTHMOSIS, ZOSER
lentils and rice	MEGADARA
life symbol	ANKH
measures	
—7½ miles	SCHENE
—100 sq. ft	AROURA
—209 sq. yds	QIRAT
—1 acre	FEDDAN
—½ bushel	KELA
—5 bushels	ARDEB
melon	ABDALAVI
military officer	BIMBASHI, BINBASHI
mongoose	ICHNEUMON
month	AHET, APAP
monument	OBELISK, PYRAMID, SPHINX
National Party	WAFD
pastry	BASBOUSA
peasant(s)	FELLAH(IN)
picture-writing	HIEROGLYPHICS
pike	MORMYRUS
potsherd	OSTRACON, OSTRAKON
precious alloy	ASEM
province	NOME
queens	CLEOPATRA, HATSHEPSUT
	NEFERTITI
region of the dead	AMENTI
religious ceremony	DOSEH
river	NILE
royal crown	PSCHENT
ruler	PHARAOH
ruling class	MAMELUKE
secret chamber	SERDAB
serpent emblem	URAEUS
ship	DAHABI(Y)EH
	DAHABBIYEH, DAHABEEAH
soda	TRONA
soldier-slave	MAMELUKE
soul	BA, KA, SAHJ
soup	MELOKHIA
sultan	MAMELUKE, SOLDAN
tambourine	RIKK
temporary dam	SUDD
tomb	MASTABA
underground chamber	SERDAB
vase (human-headed)	CANOPUS
viceroy	KHEDIVE
viceroy's wife	KHEDIVA

water	
—lift	SHADOOF, SHADUF
—lily	LOTE, LOTOS, LOTUS
weight	
—variable	ROTL
—$^1/_{30}$oz	K(H)AT
—1oz	ORIEH
—3lbs	OKA
—99lbs	CANTAR, KANTAR
	QUANTAR
white slave	MAMELUKE
wire rattle	SISTRUM
eight	
Biblical texts	OCTAPLA
Christmas presents	MILKMAIDS
cleft	OCTAFID
combining form	OCT-
figure of ...	SKATING
fold	OCTAPLOID, OCTOPLOID
	OCTUPL(ICAT)E
groups	EIGHTSOME, OCTAD
	OCTAVE, OCTET(T), OCTETTE
	OCTONARY, OCTUOR, OGDOAD
having eight	
—angles	OCTAGONAL
—arms	OCTOPOD
—columns	OCTOSTYLE
—eyes	OCTONOCULAR
—faces	OCTOHEDRAL
—feet	OCTONARIAN, OCTOPOD
—leaves per sheet	OCTAVO
—parts in eights	OCTAMEROUS
—petals	OCTOPETALOUS
—pistils	OCTOGYNIAN
	OCTOGYNOUS
—rows	OCTASTICHOUS
	OCTOSTICHOUS
—segments	OCTOFID
—sepals	OCTOSEPALOUS
—sides	OCTOGONAL
—stamens	OCTANDRIAN
	OCTRANDROUS
—styles	OCTOGYNIAN
	OCTOGYNOUS
—times normal number of	
chromosomes	OCTAPLOID
—tones	OCTACHORD
—year intervals	OCTENNIAL
hundred	O, OMEGA
hundred thousand	O, OMEGA
hundredth year	OCTINGEN(TEN)ARY
	OCTOCENTENARY
iron	NIBLICK
notes	OCTAVE
one over the ...	DRUNK
pieces of ...	COINS

yearly	OCTENNIAL
eighteen	MAJORITY
eighteen holes	GOLF COURSE
eighteen in team	AUSTRALIAN RULES
eighteen leaves per sheet	EIGHTEENMO
	OCTODECIMO
eighth	
note	QUAVER
part of circle	OCTANT
eighty	P, PI, R
eighty-eight	PIANO
eighty thousand	P, PI, R
eighty years old	OCTOGENARIAN
	OCTOGENARY
El Salvador	ES
capital	SAN SALVADOR
coin	CENTAVO, COLON
electric	
battery	CELL, VOLTAIC PILE
—terminal	ELECTRODE
cable tower	PYLON
channel for wires	CONDUIT, DUCT
circuit	
—for measuring resistance	METRE BRIDGE
	WHEATSTONE BRIDGE
—producing doubled	
DC voltage from AC	VOLTAGE DOUBLER
coil	
—acting as magnet	SOLENOID
—in dynamo or electric	
motor	ARMATURE
combination of	
two waves	AM, AMPLITUDE MODULATION
	FM, FREQUENCY MODULATION
component of impedance	REACTANCE
	RESISTANCE
condenser	CAPACITOR
conducting capacity of	
—circuit	CONDUCTANCE, G
—conductor	CONDUCTIVITY, K
conductor of current	ELECTRODE
connection point	SOCKET
connector for one or	
more plugs	ADAPTER
current	
—flowing in one	
direction	DC, DIRECT CURRENT
—that changes	
direction	AC, ALTERNATING CURRENT
—meter	AMMETER
—reversing commutator	RHEOTROPE
device	
—based on	
semiconductors	SOLID STATE
—changing voltage of	
alternating current	TRANSFORMER

—monitoring large current	AMPLIDYNE
	METADYNE
—producing	
alternating current	ALTERNATOR
	GENERATOR
direct current	DYNAMO
static	
electricity	WIMSHURST MACHINE
—reducing amount of	
current passing	SHUNT
—reversing direction	
of current	COMMUTATOR
—short-circuiting unwanted	
high voltages	VARISTOR
—transferring power	
between systems	TRANSDUCER
dialectric with permanent	
polarity	ELECTRET
difference in electrical	
states at two	
points	POTENTIAL (DIFFERENCE)
eddy current	INDUCED CURRENT
	FOUCAULT CURRENT
electricity	
—at rest	STATIC ELECTRICITY
—produced by	
friction	STATIC (ELECTRICITY)
	TRIBOELECTRICITY
heat	SEEBECK EFFECT
	THERMOELECTRICITY
heated crystal	PYROELECTRICITY
light	PHOTOELECTRIC EFFECT
	PHOTOVOLTAIC EFFECT
pressure	PIEZOELECTRICITY
	PIEZOELECTRIC EFFECT
temperature gradient	
in conductor	KELVIN EFFECT
	THOMSON EFFECT
water power	HYDROELECTRICITY
electro-	
—cardiogram	ECG
—convulsive therapy	ECT
—encephalogram	ECG
—magnetic unit	EMU
—motive force	EMF
—phoresis	CATAPHORESIS
—plated	EP
—static capacitor	LEYDEN JAR
—static unit	ESU
electron	
—tube connector	ELECTRODE
with two connectors	DIODE
with three connectors	TRIODE
—volt	EV
electronic	
—component	

built on silicon chip	MICROCHIP
changing voltage	TRANSFORMER
consisting of small	
circuits in single	
structure	INTEGRATED CIRCUIT
converting	
—AC to DC	COMMUTATOR, RECTIFIER
—DC to AC	INVERTER
focussing electron beam	
on fluorescent	
screen	CATHODE-RAY TUBE
opposing flow of	
current	RESISTOR, RHEOSTAT
reacting to humidity	HYGRISTOR
reversing flow of current	COMMUTATOR
storing charge	CAPACITOR
	CONDENSER
switch based on	
special glass	OVSHINSKY DEVICE
—data processing	EDP
failure of supply	OUTAGE
filter passing only	
selected frequencies	BAND-PASS FILTER
fixed voltage across valve	GRID BIAS
frame collecting current	
from overhead line	PANTOGRAPH
frequency x 2π	PULSATANCE
generation of force by	
change in current	INDUCTANCE, L
glow seen round ship's masts etc	CORPOSANT
	ST ELMO'S FIRE
having	
—no electric charge	NEUTRAL
—same	
number of electrons	ISOELECTRONIC
potential	ISOELECTRIC
heater in water tank	IMMERSION HEATER
in living things	BIOELECTRICITY
induced current	EDDY CURRENT
	FOUCAULT CURRENT
—due to change of	
current in another	
circuit	MUTUAL INDUCTION
instruments	(*see* **measuring instrument**)
	(*see* **scientific instrument**)
intermediate electrode	DYNODE
interrupter	RHEOTOME
lamp connector	BAYONET FIXING
law governing	
—strength of induced	
magnetic field	AMPERE'S LAW
—sum of electrical	
forces	KIRCHHOFF'S LAW
—voltage and current	OHM'S LAW
loudspeaker producing	
—high notes	TWEETER

—low notes	WOOFER
measures	(*see separate entry*)
metre bridge	WHEATSTONE BRIDGE
mutual conductance in	
thermionic valve	TRANSCONDUCTANCE
negative electrode	CATHODE
non-conductor	DIELECTRIC, INSULATOR
permanently polarised	
material	ELECTRET
point of connection	TERMINAL
positive electrode	ANODE
potential difference in	
conductor in magnetic field	HALL EFFECT
prevent transfer of current	INSULATE
producer of current	ALTERNATOR
	DYNAMO, GENERATOR
	POWER STATION
property of	
—having positive or	
negative charge	POLARITY
—inducing	
force by variation	
of current in circuit	INDUCTANCE
magnetism by proximity	INDUCTION
—opposition to current flow	IMPEDANCE
	REACTANCE
	RESISTANCE
—producing current by	
proximity	INDUCTION
—storing charge	CAPACITANCE
—transferring current	
in circuit	CONDUCTANCE
	CONDUCTIVITY
protective device	CIRCUIT BREAKER, FUSE
ratio of	
—changes in current	
and voltage in	
valve	MUTUAL CONDUCTANCE
	TRANSCONDUCTANCE
—displacement of field	
strength	PERMITTIVITY
—potential at ends of	
conductor	RESISTANCE
—power to voltage and	
current	POWER FACTOR
—two electrical quantities	
as logarithm	NEPER
reciprocal	
—of capacitance	ELASTANCE
—of conductivity	RESISTIVITY
relative permittivity	DIELECTRIC CONSTANT
resistor giving	
lowered voltage	POTENTIAL DIVIDER
	POTENTIOMETER
	VOLTAGE DIVIDER
rotor of electric motor	ARMATURE

screen used to insulate	
from interference	FARADAY CAGE
semiconductor	VARISTOR
solution that conducts electricity	ELECTROLYTE
specific	
—inductive	
capacity	DIELECTRIC CONSTANT
—resistance	RESISTIVITY
substance with	
—almost no	
resistance at very low	
temperature	SUPERCONDUCTOR
—conductivity at high	
temperature or when	
impure	SEMICONDUCTOR
—no conductivity at	
low temperature or	
when pure	SEMICONDUCTOR
sudden increase in current	SURGE
superimposition of waves	MODULATION
switch in electronic circuit	
based on special glass	OVSHINSKY DEVICE
system reducing	
unwanted sound	DOLBY (SYSTEM)
transformer producing	
high voltage current	TESLA COIL
valve	
—connector	ELECTRODE
—with heated	
electrodes	THERMIONIC VALVE
variable resistor	RHEOSTAT
vibrating part of	
loudspeaker etc	ARMATURE
voltage	ELECTROMOTIVE FORCE, EMF
—divider	POTENTIOMETER
Wheatstone bridge	METER BRIDGE
	(*see also* **physics**)

elements

ancient	EARTH, AIR, FIRE, WATER
imaginary	PHLOGISTON
modern listing (*alternative or unconfirmed names in*	
brackets)	
actinium	AC
alabamine	(*see* astatine)
alucinium	(*see* beryllium)
aluminium	AL
americium	AM
antimony (regulus)	SB, STIBIUM
argon	A
arsenic	AS
astatine (alabamine, helvetium)	AT
atomic number	
—57-71	LANTHANIDE, LANTHANON
	RARE, EARTH
—above 89	ACTINIDE, ACTINOID
barium	BA

berkelium	BK
beryllium (alucinium, glucinium)	BE
bismuth	BI
boron	B
bromine	BR
cadmium	CD
caesium	CS
calcium	CA
californium	CF
carbon	C
cassiopium	(*see* lutetium)
cerium	CE
chlorine	CL
chromium	CR
cobalt	CO
columbium (niobium)	CB
copper	CU, D, P
crypton	(*see* krypton)
curium	CM
didymium (supposed element)	
dysprosium	DY
einsteinium	ES
erbium	ER
europium	EU
fermium	FM
florentium	(*see* promethium)
fluorine	F
francium (virginium)	FR
gadolinium	GD
gallium	GA
germanium	GE
glucin(i)um (beryllium)	GL
gold	AU, BULL, OR
hafnium	HF
hahnium	HA
having incomplete inner shell	TRANSITION ELEMENT
helium	HE
helvetium	(*see* astatine)
holmium	HO
hydrogen (protium, deuterium, tritium)	H
illinium	(*see* promethium)
in 7th group	HALOGEN
indium	IN
iodine	I
iridium	IR
iron	FE
kalium	(*see* potassium)
krypton	KR
kurchatovium	(*see* rutherfordium)
lanthanum	LA
lawrencium	LR, LW
lead	PB
lithium	LI
lutetium (cassiopium)	LU

magnesium	MG
manganese	MN
masurium	(*see* technetium)
mendelevium	MD, MV
mercury	AZOTH, HG
molybdenum	MO
neodymium	ND
neon	NE
neoytterbium	(*see* ytterbium)
neptunium	NP
nickel	NI
niobium	(*see* columbium)
nitrogen	AZOTE, N
nobelium	NO
osmium	OS
oxygen	O
palladium	PD
phosphorus	P
platinum	PT
plutonium	PU
polonium	PO
potassium (kalium)	K
praseodymium	PR
promethium (florentium, illinium)	PM
pro(to)tactinium	PA
radium	RA
radon	RN
regulus (antimony)	SB, STIBIUM
rhenium	RE
rhodium	RH
rubidium	RB
ruthenium	RU
rutherfordium (kurchatovium)	RF
samarium	SM
scandium	SC
selenium	SE
silicon	SI
silver	AG, ARGENTUM
sodium	NA
strontium	SR
sulphur	S
tantalum	TA
technetium (masurium)	TC
tellurium	TE
terbium	TB
thallium	TL
thorium	TH
thulium	TM
tin	SN
titanium	TI
tungsten (wolfram)	W
uranium	U
vanadium	V
virginium	(*see* francium)
wolfram	(*see* tungsten)
xenon	XE

ytterbium (neoytterbium)	YB	—glucose	GLUCOKINASE
yttrium	Y	—glycogen into sugar	AMYLASE
zinc	ZN	—histamines	HISTAMINASE
zirconium	ZR	—hydrogen peroxide	CATALASE
eleven	SIDE, TEAM, XI	—lactose to glucose	LACTASE
Christmas presents	PIPERS	—maltose to glucose	MALTASE
having eleven		—nucleic acids	NUCLEASE
—leaves	HENDECAPHYLLOUS	—peptides	PEPTIDASE
—notes	HENDECACHORD	—phosphates	PHOSPHATASE
—pistils	HENDECAGYNIAN	—proteins	CATHEPSIN, EREPSIN
	HENDECAGYNOUS		PAPAIN, PEPSIN
—stamens	HENDECANDROUS		PROTE(IN)ASE
—styles	HENDECAGYNIAN		PROTEOLYTIC ENZYME
	HENDECAGYNOUS		TRYPSIN
—syllables	HENDECASYLLABIC	—rubonucleic acid	RUBONUCLEASE
hundred	MC	—starch	
engines of war	(*see* **weapons**)	to maltose	DIASTASE
English		to sugar	AMYLASE, PTYALIN
as a		—sugar to alcohol and	
—foreign language	EFL	carbon	ZYMASE
—second language	ESL	—trypsinogen to trypsin	ENTEROKINASE
battles	(*see separate entry*)		PEPTIDASE
capital	LONDON	—urea to ammonia and water	UREASE
Chamber Orchestra	ECO	catalyses oxidation	OXIDASE
Church Union	ECU	—of substrate	PERIOXIDASE
counties	(*see separate entry*)	—reduction	RESPIRATORY ENZYME
Dialect Society	EDS	catalyst in	
Golf Union	EGU	—hydrolysis	HYDROLASE
kings	(*see separate entry*)	—reduction	REDUCTASE
language teaching	ELT	coagulates milk proteins	RENNIN
national emblem	ROSE	co-enzyme	
patron saint	GEORGE	—acting as energy	
river	THAMES	source	ADENOSINE TRIPHOSPHATE
Speaking Union	ESU		ADT
enzymes		—cutting other molecules	
action of	ZYMOLYSIS	from RNA	RIBOZYME
activator	KINASE	—involved in energy	
adaptive enzyme	INDUCIBLE ENZYME	transfer	ADENOSINE DIPHOSPHATE
breaking down			ADP
—acetylcholine	CHOLINESTERASE	—reducing oxidation	DPN, FAD
—adrenaline	MONOAMINE OXIDASE	FLAVIN ADENINE DINUCLEOTIDE	
—amino-acids	PEPTIDASE	FLAVIN MONONUCLEOTIDE, NAD(P)	
—asparagine	ASPARAGINASE	digestive	(CHYMO)TRYPSIN, PAPAIN
—ATP	ATPASE		PEPSIN, RENNIN
—bacterial cells	LYSOZYME	early stage	ZYMOGEN
—cane-sugar to fructose		emulsin	SYNAPTASE
and glucose	INVERTASE, SUCRASE	fat-splitting	LIPOCLASTIC
—casein	EREPSIN	ferment	ZYME
—caseinogen to casein	RENNIN	fermentation	ZYMOSIS
—cells	LYSOZYME	fermentor	ZYMOGEN
—cellulose	CYTASE	formed in response to its	
—esters	ESTERASE	substrate	ADAPTIVE ENZYME
—fats to alcohol and acid	LIPASE		INDUCIBLE ENZYME
—fibrin	FIBRINOLYSIN	found in	
—fibrinogen to fibrin	THROMBIN	—all living tissues	PROTE(IN)ASE
—gelatine	EREPSIN	—almonds	EMULSIN, SYNAPTASE

—animal secretions	LYSOZYME
—blood	FIBRINOLYSIN
	THROMBIN
—cell nucleus	POLYMERASE
—digestive juices	LACTASE
—egg-white	LYSOZYME
—fatty tissue	ADIPSIN
—gastric juices	RENNIN
—germinating seeds	DIASTASE
—liver and kidneys	URICASE
—malt	DIASTASE
—pancreas	AMYLASE
	CHYMOTRYPSINOGEN
	RIBONUCLEASE, TRYPSIN
—pancreatic juices	DIASTASE
—papaw fruit	PAPAIN
—plants	LYSOZYME, PEROXIDASE
	(*see also* **biology**)
—prothrombin	THROMBIN
—RNA	RIBOZYME
—saliva	PTYALIN
—small intestine	ENTEROKINASE
	EREPSIN, PEPTIDASE
—stomach	PEPSIN, RENNIN
—yeast	MALTASE, ZYMASE
inactive	PROENZYME
inducible enzyme	ADAPTIVE ENZYME
inducing	
—fermentation	ZYMASE
—polymerisation of DNA	POLYMERASE
invertase	SUCRASE
inverts cane sugar	INVERTASE
no-protein part	COENZYME
not requiring inducement	
of substrate	CONSTITUTIVE ENZYME
producing	
—fructose	INULASE
—grape sugar	MALTASE
—luminosity	LUCIFERASE
—starch from sugar	DIASTASE
—sugar from starch	PTYALIN
promoting	
—alcoholic fermentation	ZYMASE
—oxidation	OXYDASE
protecting against bacteria	LYSOZYME
protein part	APOENZYME
proteolytic	CATHEPSIN
remaining inside living cell	ENDOENZYME
removes	
—amino group	DEAMINASE
—hydrogen	DEHYDROGENASE
repairs DNA	PHOTOLASE
secreted by skin	LYSOZYME
sucrase	INVERTASE
sugar-splitting	SUCROCLASTIC
synaptase	EMULSIN

used to soften meat	PAPAIN
variant type	ISO(EN)ZYME
equal	EQUI-, ISO-
agglutination of red	
cells within the same	
blood group	ISOAGGLUTINATION
antibody controlling	
isoagglutination	ISOAGGLUTININ
bilaterally symmetrical	ISOBILATERAL
day and night	EQUINOX
diagrams representing a	
particular number of instances	ISOTYPE
either of two atoms of identical mass	ISOBARE
having	
—all the teeth similar	ISODONT
—close similarity	
in crystalline form	ISOMORPHIC
—closed chain of like atoms	ISOCYCLIC
—equal	
angles	EQUIANGULAR, ISOGONIC
diameters	ISODIAMETRIC
differences	EQUIDIFFERENT
force	EQUIPOLLENT
hydrostatic equilibrium	ISOSTATIC
likelihood	EQUIPROBABLE
magnetic force	ISOMAGNETIC
meaning	EQUIVOCAL
number of electrons	ISOELECTRONIC
perimeters	ISOPERIMETRICAL
petals and stamens	ISOSTEMONOUS
political power	ISOCRACY
power	EQUIPOLLENT
	EQUIPOTENT, EQUIVALENT
pressure	ISOSTATIC
privileges	ISONOMY
rights	ISONOMY
sides	EQUILATERAL
strength	ISODYNAMIC
time units	ISORHYTHMIC
value	EQUIVALENT, EQUIVALUE
weight	EQUIPONDERANT
—gametes of equal size	ISOGAMY
—isomorphism between the	
two forms	ISODIMORPHISM
—laws	ISONOMY
—similar origins	ISOGENETIC
—spores of only one kind	ISOSPOROUS
—the same	
atomic number but different	
—energy	ISOMERIC
—mass number	ISOTOPIC
colour	ISOCHROMATIC
measure	ISOMETRIC
number of	
—atoms	ISOSTERIC
—neutrons	ISOTONE

osmotic pressure	ISOTONIC
potential	ISOELECTRIC
properties irrespective	
of direction	ISOTROPIC
tension	ISOTONIC
tone	ISOTONIC
—two	
equal sides	ISOSCELES
pairs of wings alike	ISOPTEROUS
—yolk distributed evenly	ISOLECITHAL
line	
—making equal angles	
with all meridians	LOXODROME
—of equal	
amounts of sunshine	ISOHEL
depths	ISOBATH
earthquake shock	ISOSEISMAL
frequency of auroral	
displays	ISOCHASM
magnetic dip	ISOCLINE
pressures	ISOBAR
rainfall	ISOHYET
temperatures	ISOTHERM
—in	
coldest time	ISOCRYME
summer time	ISOTHERE
—(mean winter)	ISOCHEIM, ISOCHIME
—underground	ISOGEOTHERM
time differences	ISOCHRONE
upheaval of land	ISOBASE
value with respect to	
—one variable	ISOGRAM
—two variables	ISOPLETH
—of simultaneous development	
of thunderstorms	ISOBRONT
—of variations of	
some quantity under	
conditions of	
constant volume	ISOCHOR(E)
pressure and temperature	
at constant volume	ISOMETRIC
—separating areas of	
different dialects	ISOGLOSS
masonry with courses of	
equal height	ISODOMON
multiplied by same number	EQUIMULTIPLE
performed in equal time	ISOCHRONAL
reciprocity of rights of	
citizenship	ISOPOLITY
Eskimo	HUSKY, IN(N)UIT
boat	OOMIA(C)K, UMIAK
	KAIAK, KAYAK
boot	MUCLUC, MUCKLUCK, MUCKLUK
clover	ALSIKE
conjurer	ANGEKKOK
dog	HUSKY, MALAMUTE, MALEMUTE

fur coat	ANARAK, ANORAK
house	IGLOO
language	HUSKY
skin tent	TUPAK, TUPIK
whale meat	MUKTUK
Ethiopia	ETH
	(*see* **Abyssinian**)
Europe	
articles	ELLA, LATHE, UNDER
Broadcasting Union	EBU
cherry	GEAN
clover	ALSIKE
Council	CE, EC
deer	ELK
Defence Community	EDC
Development Fund	EDF
dormouse	LEROT, LOIR
dwarf-cherry	GROUND-CHERRY
Economic	
—Commission	ECE
—Community	EEC
Exchange Rate Mechanism	ERM
extinct horse	TARPAN
fish (Danube)	ZINGEL
hawk	FALLER
inferior wheat	SPELT
kite	GLE(A)D, GLEDE
lily	GREEN DRAGON
Monetary Agreement	EMA
Payments Union	EPU
perennial herb	LASERPICIUM
plain	STEPPE
plant	GOLD-THREAD
Productivity Agreement	EPA
rabbit	CON(E)Y, LEPORID
rodent	ERD, LEMMING
shrub	DAPHNE, SPURGE-LAUREL
squirrel	SISEL
timber	SATIN-WOOD, ZANTE(-WOOD)
vulture	GALLINAZO, GRIFFON VULTURE,
	LAMMERGEIER, LAMMERGEYER
wildcat	CATAMOUNT
wine measure	ANKER
explorer	
American	PALMER, PEARY
Austrian	PAYER, WEYPRECHT
British	BAFFIN, BURTON, CABOT
	CONWAY, COOK, DAVIS
	GALTON, GILBERT, FITCH
	FRANKLIN, FROBISHER
	FUCHS, LIVINGSTONE, LUGARD
	MUNGO PARK, POWELL, ROSS
	SCOTT, SHACKLETON
	SMITH, SWAN, WEDDELL
Dutch	BARENTZ, TASMAN
French	CARTIER, COCTEAU

Greek	PYTHEAS	centre line	OPTIC AXIS
Italian	CABOT, COLUMBUS	coloured part of eye	IRIS
New Zealand	HILLARY	compound eye	OMMATEUM
Norwegian	AMUNDSEN, NANSEN	corner of eye	CANTHUS
Portuguese	VASCO DA GAMA	defect of lens	ASTIGMATISM
Russian	BERING	depression in retina	FOVEA CENTRALIS
Spanish	DE TORRES, MAGELLAN		MACULA
Swiss	PICCARD	dimness of vision	CALIGO
Venetian	MARCO POLO	duct from eye to nose	LAC(H)RYMAL DUCT

explosives

LACRIMAL DUCT

ammonium etc	AMATOL, AMMONAL	element(s) in	
	AMMONITE	compound eye	OMMATIDIUM(OMMATIDIA)
cellulose nitrate and		elementary eye	OCELLUS
nitroglycerine	CORDITE	eye disease	(*see* **disease**)
crystalline compound	TNB	fluid	
	TRINITORBENZENE	—in eyeball	VITREOUS HUMOUR
device used to fire		—round lens	AQEOUS HUMOUR
cartridges	PERCUSSION CAP	focussing body	(CRYSTALLINE) LENS
explosive filling in		fold of skin at corner	
bullets, shells, etc	PROPELLANT	of eye	EPICANTHUS
gas — methane and air	FIRE-DAMP	gland secreting tears	LAC(H)RYMAL GLAND
gun-cotton with			LACRIMAL GLAND
—barium nitrate	TONITE	inner lining of eyelid	CONJUNCTIVA
—nitroglycerin	BLASTING GELATIN	insect's eye	COMPOUND
liquid	AZOIMIDE	intersection of optic nerves	OPTIC CHIASM(A)
	HYDRAZOIC ACID	junction of optic nerve	
nitric acid on		and retina	BLIND SPOT
—cellulose	CELLULOSE NITRATE	layer of blood cells in retina	CHOROID
	GUN-COTTON	lens of compound eye	FACET
	NITROCELLULOSE	ligament supporting lens	ZONULE OF ZINN
—starch	PYROXYLE, XYLOIDINE	light-sensitive	
nitroglycerine		—layer at back of eye	RETINA
—cellulose nitrate, saltpetre etc	GELIGNITE	—spot in lower animals	EYE-SPOT
—in kieselguhr	DYNAMITE		STIGMA
—saltpetre, sawdust, etc	DUALIN	long sightedness	HYPER(METR)OPIA
petroleum jelly	NAPALM	membrane between sclera	
picric acid	MELINITE	and retina	CHOROID (COAT)
—nitrobenzene and vaseline	LYDDITE	nerve conveying	
plastic	SEMTEX	sensation from eye	OPTIC NERVE
potassium nitrate,		normal vision	EMMETROPIA
charcoal, and sulphur	GUNPOWDER	one-eyed	
smokeless	AMBERITE	—giant	CYCLOPS
used by Greeks in naval warfare	GREEK FIRE	—marine animal	CYCLOPS
yellow		opening admitting light	PUPIL
—crystalline solid	PICRIC ACID	outer	
—solid	TNT, TRINITROTOLUENE	—layer of cornea	CONJUNCTIVA

eyes

		—membrane of eyeball	SCLERA, SCLEROTIC
abnormal		part of iris	AREOLA
—dryness	XEROPHTHALMIA	pigmented layer	UVEA
—protusion	EXOPHTHALMIA	point of crossing of	
	EXOPHTHALMOS	optic nerves	OPTIC CHIASM(A)
	EXOPHTHALMUS	protrusion of eye	EXOPHTHALMIA
adjustable diaphragm	IRIS		EXOPHTHALMOS
angle between eyelids	CANTHUS		EXOPHTHALMUS
apple of the eye	PUPIL	reflecting layer in retina	TAPETUM
blindness	AMAUROSIS	refracting structure	CRYSTALLINE LENS

rudimentary third eye	MEDIAN EYE	stalk supporting eye	OMMATOPHORE
	PINEAL BODY	temporary blindness	TEICHOPSIA
sensory body in retina	CONE, ROD	thickened edge of choroid	CILIARY BODY
socket for eye	ORBIT	third eye	MEDIAN EYE
spasm of iris	HIPPUS		PINEAL BODY
spasmodic movements	NYSTAGMUS		
specialist	OCULIST	transparent front of eye	CORNEA
	OPHTHALM(OLOG)IST	vision in poor light	SCOTOPIA
	OPTICIAN, OPTOMETRIST	white	
		—patch in angle of cornea	LEUCOMA
spots before the eyes	MUSCAE VOLITANTES	—ring round cornea	ARCUS SENILIS
squint	STRABISMUS	—ring round eye	WALL-EYE
	WALL-EYE		

fabric

all-wool muslin	MOUSSELINE-DE-LAINE
aluminium thread	LUREX
American cloth	LEATHER-CLOTH
Angora goat's hair	MOHAIR
artificial silk	(CUPRAMMONIUM) RAYON
Asian silk	IKAT
bark (Pacific)	PAPER-CLOTH
black dress fabric	MOURNING-STUFF
blanket material	STROUDING
blue stuff	MAZARINE, PERSE, WATCHET
bold warp twill	WHIPCORD
book muslin	ORGANDIE
bookbinding fabric	SCRIM
bright green	LINCOLN-GREEN
brocade	BALDACHIN(O)
	BALDAQUIN, BAUDEKIN
buff coloured cotton	NANKEEN, NANKIN
cambric	LAWN
camel hair	AB(B)A, ABAYA
	BAR(R)ACAN, CAMELINE
	CAMELOT, CAMLET
canvas	BINCA, BURLAP
cashmere	CIRCASSIAN, CIRCASSIENNE
	KASHMIR
checked	
—cotton	GINGHAM, MADRAS
—woollen	TARTAN
closely woven	
—cotton	PERCALE
—French	PERCALE
—nylon, etc	GLORIA
—rayon	FAILLE
—silk	GLORIA, FAILLE, SATIN
—woollen	WORSTED
cloth	
—bearing imprint of face	
of Jesus	MANDILION, MANDYLIO
—of gold	CICLATO(U)N, GOLD-CLOTH
India	SONERI
or silver	LUPPA
coarse	
—calico (Indian)	DUNGAREE
—canvas	BURLAP
—cotton	BUCKRAM, CALICO
	CANVAS, DENIM, DUCK
	FROCKING, HUCKABUCK, JEAN
	MEXICAN, OSNABURG

East Indies	HUMHUM
—hemp	
jute	HARDS, HOPSACK, HURDS
cotton	CANVAS
—homespun cloth	HODDEN, RUSSET
—jean	FROCKING
—jute	BUCKRAM, GUNNY, HESSIAN
	HOPSACK, SACKCLOTH, SACKING
—linen	BUCKRAM, DOWLAS
	DRABBET(TE)DUCK, , HARDEN
	HARN, HOLLAND, HUCKABUCK
	LOCKRAM, OSNABURG
and wool	LINSEY-WOOLSEY
Brittany	DOWLAS
—muslin	MUSLINET
—Oriental	BAFT
—printed cotton	CALICO
—silk	DUPION, FILOSELLE
and mohair	GROGRAM
India	KINCOB, TASH
—twilled cotton	CORDUROY, DENIM
	FUSTIAN, MOLESKIN
	VELVETEEN
—waved or watered silk	TABBY
—woollen	BAIZE, KELT, KERSEY, RUG
black and white	HODDEN-GREY
blanket material	STROUDING
felted	DRUGGET
Orkney	WADMA(A)L, WADMOL(L)
russet	BURREL
undyed	HODDEN
combed wool	JERSEY
corded	REP(P), REPS
—cotton and wool	RUSSEL(-CORD)
—ribbed muslin	CORTELINE
—silk	GROSGRAIN, OTTOMAN
18th c	PADUASOY
and	
—wool or cotton	BENGALINE
—worsted	POPLIN
—woollen or cotton	MOREEN
cotton	
—and	
mohair	SICILIAN
rayon	BARATHEA
silk	VELVETEEN
wool	DOMETT, LUSTRE, WOOLSEY
	WINCEY, WINSEY
worsted	ORLEANS
—Bengal	BEZAN
—checked	GINGHAM
—crinkled	SEERSUCKER
—fibre sheet	BATT(ING)
—fine	LAWN
—glossy	PERCALINE
—heavy	MONK'S CLOTH

—imitation	POPLIN
flannel	FLANNELETTE
velvet	VELVETEEN
—knitted	BALBRIGGAN
—light	JACONET, MUSLIN, NAINSOOK
—like silk	SHANTUNG
—long-stapled	LISLE
—loosely-woven	CHEESECLOTH
—mattress-fabric	TICKING
—patterned	DIAPER
—piled-fabric	TERRY(TOWELLING)
—plain, raised both sides	WINCEYETTE
—printed	CRETONNE
—shaded	JASPE
—soft	MUSLIN
—strong	COUTIL(LE)
—tufted material	CANDLEWICK
—twilled	DRILL
—white	CAMBRIC, DIMITY
—with	
coloured stripe	GALATEA, GINGHAM
deep nap	LAMBSKIN
raised nap	WINCEYETTE
silk pile	VELVERET
woven pattern	DIAPER
crape-like	CREPE(-DE-CHINE)
	CREPOLIN, CREPON
crinkled linen or cotton	SEERSUCKER
curtain fabric	NET, SCRIM
dark	
—blue or bluish-grey fabric	PERSE
—grey woollen	OXFORD MIXTURE
delicate kind of tabby	TABBINET
double twilled fustian	MOLESKIN
dress material	TOILE
durable	
—cloth	DURANCE
—silk	FLORENCE, FLORENTINE
—woollen (old)	SEMPITERNUM
elasticated	STOCKINET(TE)
	STOCKINGETTE
embossed	CLOQUE, MATEL(L)ASSE
embroidered	
—damask	DAMASSIN
—silk (Indian)	KINCOB, TASH
embroidery	CREWELLERY
fawn-coloured silk	TASAR, TUSSER
	TUSSORE, TUSSAH, TUSSEH
fibre-cloth	TAP(P)A
figured	
—cotton	MOREEN
—linen	DAMASK
Belgian	DORNICK
—muslin	TANJIB, TANZIB
—silk	BROCADE
and linen	BROCATEL(LE)

—woollen	MOREEN, PAISLEY
fine	
—cloth	SINDON
—cotton	BATISTE, CAMBRIC
	LAWN, MADRAS, MUSLIN
	ORGANDIE, PONGEE
—dress fabric	MERINO
—lace	MIGNONETTE
—linen	BYSSUS, CAMBRIC
	LAWN, SENDAL
Dutch	HOLLAND
with cotton or wool	BATISTE
—muslin	ORGANDIE
—silk	PONGEE, TULLE
and wool	EOLIENNE
transparent	CHIFFON
—twilled woollen	CASSIMERE
	KEYSEYMERE
—white linen	CAMBRIC
—wool	BATISTE, BROADCLOTH
	CASSIMERE, CARMELITE
	FOULE, KERSEYMERE
	PUKE, WORCESTER, WORSTED
with cotton	MERINO
—worsted	CUBICA
firm	
—nylon cloth	BO(U)LTING CLOTH
—silk cloth	BO(U)LTING CLOTH
flag material	BEAUFORT
for	
—aprons	BAIZE
—billiard tables	BAIZE
—blankets	STROUDING
—bookbinding etc	SCRIM
—boot linings	WIGAN
—cloaks	MANTLING
—coat linings	SHALLOON
—curtains	BROCADE, MARQUISETTE
	NET, SCRIM
—dresses	FROCKING, RATINE
	RATTEEN
—forester's clothes	KENDAL-GREEN
—hatbands	GROSGRAIN
—linings	CUBICA
—loincloths (India)	D(H)OTI, LUNGI
—mattresses	COUTIL(LE), TICKING
—mosquito nets	MARQUISETTE
—overcoats	COVERT COATING
	MELTON, PETERSHAM
—ribbons	GROSGRAIN
—sacking	DUCK, HEMP, JUTE
—sails	CANVAS, DUCK
—Scots dress	PLAID
—shirts	SARKING
—skirts (Malay)	SARONG
—smock-frocks	DRABET(TE)

—stays	COUTIL(LE)
—suits	TWEED
—tablecloths	CHENILLE
—tents	CANVAS
—trousers	TROUSERING
—umbrellas	GLORIA
—upholstery	BROCADE, DRALON
	LAMPAS, MOQUETTE
—waistcoats	TOILINETTE
	WAISTCOATING
—wound dressings	CHARPIE
forester's cloth	KENDAL-GREEN
French	
—cambric	PERCALE
—coarse cloth	BURE, DRAP
—lace	ALENCON, CLUNY
	COLBERTINE, MOUSSELINE
	TORCHON, VALENCIENNES
—muslin	MOUSSELINE
—wool	DRAP-DE-BERRY
from	
—bark fibre	BARK CLOTH
	PAPER CLOTH
—lint or flax	LINEN
—llamas	LLAMA, VICUNA
—recycled rags	MONG(E), MUNGO
	SHODDY
—sheep, goats, etc	WOOL
—vicuña	VICUNA
—waste silk	SCHAPPE
—woody fibre	GRASS CLOTH, RAMIE
fulled	
—black woollen	BROADCLOTH
—cloth (Fr.)	FOULE
furnishing	MOQUETTE, TAPESTRY
galloon	CADDI, ORRIS
gauze	
—silk-like	TIFFANY
—wool	BAREGE
gimp	ORRIS
glazed	
—cloth	CIRE
—cotton	AMERICAN CLOTH
	CHINTZ, CIRE, SATEEN
—wool	TAMMY
—worsted	TAMIN(E)
glossy	
—cotton	PERCALINE, SATIN JEAN
—linen	SATEEN
—silk	LUSTRINE, LUSTRING
	LUTESTRING, (SILK)SATIN
	TAFFETA(S), TAFFETY
—wool	CALAMANCO
goat's hair	AB(B)A, ABAYA
	ANGORA, CASHMERE, KASHMIR
	MOHAIR, THIBET, TIBET CLOTH

—leather	CORDOVAN, CORDWAIN
	MAROQUIN
—underfleece	PASH(I)M, PASHMINA
gold	
—and silver embroidered	
damask	DAMASSIN
—embroidery	ORPHREY
—or silver lace	ORRIS
green	BAIZE, KENDAL-GREEN
	LINCOLN-GREEN
grain-surfaced material	MAROCAIN
grass-cloth	RAMIE
grey	DRAB, WIGAN
—woollen	OXFORD MIXTURE
gummed stiffening	FOUNDATION-MUSLIN
	FOUNDATION-NET
haircloth	CILICE
hand-knitted woollen	TRICOT
having loops of three threads	THREE-PILE
heavy	
—cotton cloth	MONK'S CLOTH
—goat's hair fabric	THIBET
—rayon	SHARKSKIN
—silk	SAMITE
—woollen	BEAVER, FRIEZE
hemp	
—and jute	HOP-SACK
—sail-cloth	RAVEN('S)-DUCK
homespun woollen	HODDEN
—black and white	HODDEN-GREY
horsehair and linen	CRINOLINE
imitation	
—buff leather	DURANT
—cotton	POPLIN
—flannel	FLANNELETTE
—lambswool	ASTRAKHAN
—leather	DURANT, LEATHER-CLOTH
	LEATHERETTE
—poplin	POPLINETTE
—velvet	VELVETEEN
Indian silk	CABECA, CABESSE, SURAH
Indonesian silk	IKAT
inferior cloth	SHODDY
—Flemish	MOCKADO
jaconet muslin	NAINSOOK
jute	
—cotton lining	BUCKRAM
—fabric	HESSIAN, HOPSACK
	SACKCLOTH, SACKING
knitted	JERSEY
—cotton	BALBRIGGAN
—woollen	TRICOT
knotted	
—into mesh	NET
—threadwork	MACRAME, MACRAMI
lace	GALLOON

—Belgian	MECHLIN
—French	ALENCON, CLUNY
	COLBERTINE, MOUSSELINE
	TORCHON, VALENCIENNES
—machine-made	BOBBIN(N)ET
—made of	
linen	CHANTILLY LACE
silk	BLOND(E)-LACE
	CHANTILLY LACE
—patterned	TROLL(E)Y
—peasant	TORCHON
—pillow	HONITON
Flemish	DUCHESSE LACE
—with no mesh	GUIPURE
—woven with bobbins	BONE-LACE
leather-cloth	AMERICAN CLOTH
	CORDOVAN, CORDWAIN
	MAROCAIN, MAROQUIN
	MOROCCO
light	
—cashmere	CIRCASSIAN
	CIRCASSIENNE
—cotton	JEANETTE
—dress material	CREPULINE, DELAINE
—jean	JEANETTE
—mixed dress stuff	BAREGE
—silk	CRAPE, CREPE(-DE-CHINE)
	CREPOLIN, CREPON
with cotton or wool	BENGALINE
—wool	BAREGE, CASHMERE
	CIRCASSIAN, CIRCASSIENNE
	KASHMIR, SHALLOON
and cotton	DELAINE
like	
—brocade	BROCHE
—damask	TABBINET
—leather	CORDOVAN, CORDWAIN
	MAROCAIN, MAROQUIN
	MOROCCO, SUEDE CLOTH
	SUEDETTE
—satin	SATEEN
—velvet	CHENILLE, PANNE
	VELVETEEN
—wool	ALPACA, ANGORA, VICUNA
linen	
—and wool, etc	WINCEY, WINSEY
—crinkled	SEERSUCKER
—patterned	DIAPER
—shredded for dressings	CHARPIE
—twilled	DRILL, SILESIA
—unbleached	ECRU
loosely woven	CHEESECLOTH
lustrous	CRYSTALLINE, SATARA
	SATEEN
machine-made lace	BOBBIN(N)ET
Madagascar	RABANNA

Malaysian silk	IKAT
Manila	JUSSI
man-made	(*see* synthetic *below*)
military drab	KHAKI
mixed	
—colours	MOTLEY
—fabric	GRENADINE
—twill for umbrellas	ZANELLA
modified satin	SATINET(TE)
mohair and cotton	ALEPINE
mosquito net	MARQUISETTE
moth fibre	SILK
muslin	JACONET, ORGANDIE
—French	MOUSSELINE
—Indian	GURRAH, JAMDANI
	MAMMODIS, NAINSOOK
	TANJIB, TANZIB
—open	TARLATAN
needlework with raised	
design	PIQUE WORK
nylon crepe	CREPON
old upholstery cloth	PARAGON
open	
—muslin	TARLATAN
—weave	
canvas	SCRIM
cotton	BUCKRAM, NET
jute	BUCKRAM
linen	BUCKRAM
openwork embroidery	BRODERIE ANGLAISE
orange-coloured	NACARAT
ornamental	TAPESTRY
orris	GALLOON, GIMP
pale blue material	WATCHET
patterned	
—cotton	DIAPER
—lace	TROLL(E)Y
with woven figures	FACONNE
—linen	DIAPER
—wool	PAISLEY
pile with	
—three loops	THREE-PILE
—uncut loops	TERRY
pillow lace	HONITON
—Flemish	DUCHESSE LACE
pineapple leaf fibre	PINA(-CLOTH)
plain cotton raised both	
sides	WINCEYETTE
point lace	NEEDLE-POINT
Polynesian	TAP(P)A
printed	
—cambric or muslin	PERSIENNE
—cotton	CHINTZ, CRETONNE
—East Indies	BAT(T)IK
raffia (Madagascar)	RABANNA
raised embroidery	STUMP-WORK

ramie	GRASS-CLOTH
rayon	
—heavy	SHARKSKIN
—like silk	SHANTUNG
—shaded	JASPE
rep of cotton and wool	RUSSEL-CORD
ribbed	
—cotton	CORDUROY
and wool	RUSSEL
—silk	SICILIENNE
—wool	DROGUET
Indian	SATARA
rich cloth	PALL
—piled	PLUSH
rough	
—dress fabric	RATINE, RATTEEN
—napped blue cloth	PETERSHAM
—silk	SHANTUNG
—wool	(HARRIS)TWEED
satin	
—soft	CHARMEUSE
—with matt finish	SLIPPER SATIN
—wool	CALAMANCO
Scottish	
—coarse grey cloth	MALDY
—shepherd's plaid	MAUD
semi-transparent	VOILE
shiny	SATEEN
shirt material	SARKING, SHIRTING
short-corded woollen	
or cotton	MOREEN
silk	TOBINE
—Asian	IKAT
—brocade	BALDACHIN(O)
	BALDAQUIN, BAUDERKIN
	BAWDKIN
—corded	GROSGRAIN
—crape	CREPE-DE-CHINE
	CREPOLIN, CREPON
—coarse	FILOSELLE
—Ghana	KENTE CLOTH
—glossy	TAFFETA(S), TAFFETY
—heavy	SAMITE
—Indian	CABECA, CABESSE
	SURAH
—Indonesian	IKAT
—lace	CHANTILLY LACE
—muslin	MOUSSELINE-DE-SOIE
—Malaysian	IKAT
—Philippines	HUSI
—satin	ATLAS
—Shakespeare	SAY
—soft	PONGEE, SURAH
—stiff	ARMOZEEN, ARMOZINE
	TAFFETA(S), TAFFETY
—textile	FLORENCE, FLORENTINE

—thin	CHIFFON, GEORGETTE
	GRENADINE, NINON, SARCENET
	SARS(E)NET, SENDAL, TULLE
—twilled	SURAH
—undyed	PONGEE
—untwilled	FOULARD
—voile	NINON
—wild	SHANTUNG, TUSSER, TUSSORE
—with	
cotton and wool	TOILINETTE
hair	FAR(R)ANDINE
	FERRANDINE
raised pattern	MATEL(L)ASSE
short pile	VELVET
two or more threads	ORGANZINE
wool	BARATHEA, CRYSTALLINE
	FAR(R)ANDINE, FERRANDINE
	LAMPAS
worsted	CHALLI(S), SHALLI
silk-like gauze	TIFFANY
smooth-surfaced	
woollen (French)	FOULE
soft	
—cotton	MUSLIN
—muslin	MULL, MULMUL(L)
—napped	VELVET-PILE
—satin	CHARMEUSE
—silk	FOULARD, PONGEE
and worsted	CHALLIS, SHALLI
—slightly-ribbed	TRICOT
—twilled silk	SURAH
—woollen	FLANNEL, NUN'S-VEILING
	ZIBEL(L)INE
—worsted	BARATHEA
stiff	
—canvas	PETERSHAM, SCRIM, WIGAN
—cotton	BUCKRAM, PIQUE
	FOUNDATION NET
	FOUNDATION MUSLIN
—jute	BUCKRAM, SCRIM
—linen	BUCKRAM, SCRIM
—silk	ARMOZEEN, ARMOZINE
	TAFFETA(S), TAFFETY
stout white cotton	DIMITY
striped	BAYADERE, DIMITY
	DO(O)REA, DORIA
	GALATEA, GINGHAM
	MADRAS, SUSI
stretchable	ELASTICATED, LYCRA
strong	
—coarse linen	CRASH
—cotton (mattress)	COUTIL(LE)
—jute	GUNNY
—silk	PRUNELLA, PRUNELLE
	PRUNELLO
—twilled cotton or linen	DRILL

—woollen	PRUNELLA, PRUNELLE PRUNELLO		—cotton and silk	SATIN-SHEETING
synthetic	ACETATE, ACRILAN ACRYLIC, COURTELLE CRIMPLENE, DACRON, DRALON DYNEL, LUREX, LYCRA, NYLON POLYESTER, RAYON, SARAN TERYLENE, VISCOSE		wool	GABARDINE, GABERDINE
			worsted	BOMBASINE, BOMBAZINE
			—linen	DRILL(ING), MARCELLA SILESIA
			—silk and worsted	BOMBASINE BOMBAZINE
Syrian	AB(B)A, ABAYA		—wool	PLAIDING, WHIPCORD
taffeta	ARMOZEEN, ARMOZINE		—worsted	SERGE, SHARKSKIN
—with pile	TUFF-TAFFETA TUFTAFFETY, TUFT-TAFFETA		and cotton	GAMBROON
tapestry			twisted warp	LENO
—Asian Minor	BERGAMA, BERGAMOT		unbleached	
—Belgian	BERGAMOT		—cotton	BALBRIGGAN
—of foliage	OUDENARDE		—linen	ECRU
tarred rags	HARDEN, HARDS HERDEN, HURDEN, HURDS		underfleece of goats	PASH(I)M PASHMINA
textile fabric (old)	WATERWORK		undyed	
thick			—silk	PONGEE
—coarse woollen	DUFFEL, DUFFLE		—woollen	BEIGE
—strong grey cloth	DRAB		untwilled silk	FOULARD
—woollen	WADMA(A)L WADMOL(L)		unwoven (wool etc)	FELT
			upholsterer's	
thin			—silk	TABARET
—cotton	CHEESECLOTH, LENO MUSLIN		—stiffening	BUCKRAM, SCRIM
			velvety	
—crinkly linen or cotton	SEERSUCKER		—cloth	CHENILLE
			—corded wool	VELOUTINE
—glossy silk-satin	TAFFETA(S) TAFFETY		—wool	VELOUR(S)
			vicuna-wool	VICUNA
—linen	SENDAL, SILESIA		wall-covering	TAPESTRY
and wool	LINSEY-WOOLSEY		watered	
—material	GAUZE, GOSSAMER		—ribbon	PAD
—muslin	CHEESECLOTH, LENO		—silk	MOIRE
—satin	SATINET(TE)		waterproof	MAC(K)INTOSH, OILSKIN
—silk	CHIFFON, GEORGETTE NINON, SARCENET SARS(E)NET, SENDAL, TULLE		—linen or hemp	TARPAULIN(G)
			—wool	LODEN
			waxed	WAX-CLOTH
or mixed fabric	GRENADINE		Welsh	FRAIZE
twisted	CRAPE		white	
—wool	TAMISE, ZEPHYR		—cotton	CALICO, DIMITY
—worsted	BUNTING, ZEPHYR		—woollen	BLANKET
and cotton or silk	COBURG		wild silk	SHANTUNG, TUSSER TUSSORE
transparent	GAUZE, TIFFANY		with	
—black fabric	CYPRESS, CYPRUS		—looped yarn	BOUCLE
—silk	GRENADINE, OIL-SILK ORGANZA		—metal threads	LAME, LUREX
			—soft nap	VELVET-PILE
trimming	GALLOON, GIMP, ORRIS		—stiff pile	MOQUETTE
tufted	CANDLEWICK		—woolly surface	NAP
twilled			wool	BEAVER, CHEVIOT DRAP DE BERRY, JAEGER LAMBSKIN, PAISLEY SAGATHY, WORCESTER
—cotton	CHINO, CORDUROY DENIM, DRILL(ING) FUSTIAN, JANE, JEAN MARCELLA, MOLESKIN VELVETEEN			
			—and cotton	LINSEY-WOOLSEY

goat's hair	C(H)AMLET, CAMELOT
	MOHAIR
silk	ALEPINE
—embroidery	ARRASENE
—clothing fabric	MARQUISETTE
—coloured	THIBET, TIBET-CLOTH
—dark grey	OXFORD MIXTURE
—dyed red	STAMMEL
—fine	CARMELITE
—for	
coat-linings	SHALLOON
waistcoats	TOILINETTE
—French	DRAP-DE-BERRY
—homespun (Scot.)	RAPLOCH
—like	
satin	SATEEN
serge	SAY
—lustred	SATARA
—Middle Ages	BURNET
—Orkney	WADMA(A)L, WADMOL(L)
—printed	THIBET, TIBET-CLOTH
—resembling satin	SATEEN
—roughly woven	HOPSACK
—short-piled	LODEN
—smooth	FOULE
—soft	FLANNEL, NUN'S VEILING
	ZIBEL(L)INE
—speckled	HEATHER MIXTURE
—thick	WADMA(A)L, WADMOL(L)
	(HARRIS) TWEED
—thin	TAMISE, ZEPHYR
worsted	
—and	
cotton	PAR(R)AMATTA
silk	BARATHEA
—old	INKLE
—ribbon	CADDIS
—soft	BARATHEA
—thin	BUNTING, ZEPHYR
woven	TEXTILE
—coarse wool	DRUGGET
—cotton, striped	GINGHAM
—hemp	WEBBING
—like brocade	BROCHE
—on card-controlled loom	JACQUARD
—with diagonal lines	TWILL

fabulous

beast	
—Chinese	KYLIN
—human in form of wolf	WER(E)WOLF
—Spenser	ANTILOPE
bird	
—Arabian	PHOENIX
—Chinese	FUM, FUNG
—elephant-carrying	ROC, ROK, RUC
	RUKH

—part bird, part woman	HARPY
—Persian	HUMA, SIMORG
	SIMURG(H)
—restless	HUMA
—Spenser	WHISTLER
fish (Spenser)	SCOLOPENDRA
person	WEREWOLF
robber	PROCRUSTES
tree	UPAS
	(see also **monsters***)*
Faeroe Islands	FR
capital	THORSHAVN

farewell

English	CHEERIO, GOODBYE
	SO LONG, TATA
French	ADIEU, AU REVOIR
German	AUF WIEDERSEHEN
Hawaian	ALOHA
Italian	ARRIVEDERCI, CIAO
Japanese	SAYONARA
Roman	VALE
Spanish	ADIOS, HASTA LA VISTA

fastest

animal	CHEETAH
bird	SWIFT
car	THRUST 2
liner	UNITED STATES
plane	X15
train	TGV

Fates

Greek	MOIRAE, MOIRAI
—spins thread of life	CLOTHO
—controls it	LACHESIS
—cuts it off	ATROPOS
Norse	NORNA, NORNS
—past	URD(A)
—present	VERDANDE, VERDANDI
—future	SKULD
Roman	PARCAE
	DECUMA, MORTA, NONA

fear   PHOBIA

including: aversion to
       fear of
      hatred of

aeroplanes	AEROPHOBIA
	PTEROPHOBIA
all things	PANTOPHOBIA
animals	ZOOPHOBIA
auroras	AUROROPHOBIA
bears	URSAPHOBIA
beards	POGONOPHOBIA
bees	API(O)PHOBIA, MELISOPHOBIA
being	
—alone	MONOPHOBIA
—buried alive	TAPHEPHOBIA
	TAPHOPHOBIA

—deformed	DISMORPHOPHOBIA	elves	ALFEAR
—looked at	SCOPOPHOBIA	emptiness	KENOPHOBIA
—soiled	RYPOPHOBIA	enclosed spaces	CLAUSTROPHOBIA
birds	ORNITHOPHOBIA	English	ANGLOPHOBIA
blood	HAEM(AT)OPHOBIA	environment	ECOPHOBIA
blushing	ERYTHROPHOBIA	everything	PANTOPHOBIA
books	BIBLIOPHOBIA	eyes	OMMATAPHOBIA
boys	ANDROPHOBIA	excrement	COPROPHOBIA
bridges	GEPHYROPHOBIA	falling from height	BATHOPHOBIA
cancer	CARCONOPHOBIA		HYPSOPHOBIA
cats	AIL(O)UROPHOBIA	familiar places	NOSTOPHOBIA
	GATOPHOBIA	fatigue	KOPOPHOBIA
cheerfulness	CHEROPHOBIA	fear	PHOBOPHOBIA
childbirth	TOCOPHOBIA	feathers	PTERONOPHOBIA
children	PAEDOPHOBIA	fire	PYROPHOBIA
Chinese	SINOPHOBIA	fishes	ICHTHYOPHOBIA
choking	PNIGOPHOBIA	flashes	SELAPHOBIA
clouds	NEPHOPHOBIA	flogging	MASTIGOPHOBIA
cold	CHEIM(AT)OPHOBIA	floods	ANTLOPHOBIA
	CRYOPHOBIA	flutes	AULOPHOBIA
	PSYCHROPHOBIA	flying	AEROPHOBIA, PTEROPHOBIA
colour	CHROMOPHOBIA	fog	HOMICHLOPHOBIA
computers	CYBERPHOBIA	food	SIT(I)OPHOBIA
confined spaces	CLAUSTROPHOBIA	foreign things	XENOPHOBIA, XENOPHOBY
	CLITHROPHOBIA		ZENOPHOBIA
contamination	MYSOPHOBIA	freedom	ELEUTHEROPHOBIA
corpses	NECROPHOBIA	French	GALLOPHOBIA
criticism	RHABDOPHOBIA	frogs	BATRACHOPHOBIA
crockery	CERAMOPHOBIA	fur	DORAPHOBIA
crossing streets	DROMOPHOBIA	germs	BACILLIPHOBIA
crowds	DEMOPHOBIA		MICROPHOBIA
	OCHLOPHOBIA		SPERM(AT)OPHOBIA
crystals	CRYSTALLOPHOBIA	Germans	GERMANOPHOBIA
dampness	HYGROPHOBIA	ghosts	PHASMOPHOBIA
darkness	ACHLUOPHOBIA, LYCOPHOBIA	girls	GYNOPHOBIA
	NYCTOPHOBIA, SCOTOPHOBIA	glass	NELOPHOBIA
dawn	EOSOPHOBIA	god	THEOPHOBIA
death	NECROPHOBIA	going to bed	CLINOPHOBIA
	THANATOPHOBIA	grandchildren	BABUSHKAPHOBIA
deep places	BATHOPHOBIA	gravity	BAROPHOBIA
deformity	DISMORPHOPHOBIA	(groundless fears)	PANOPHOBIA
demons	DEMONOPHOBIA	hair	CHAETOPHOBIA
deserts	XEROPHOBIA	heart disease	CARDIOPHOBIA
dirt	MOLYSOMOPHOBIA	heat	THERMOPHOBIA
	MYSOPHOBIA	heaven	OURANOPHOBIA
	RYPOPHOBIA	heights	ACROPHOBIA, ALTOPHOBIA
disease	NOSOPHOBIA, PATHOPHOBIA		CREMNOPHOBIA, HYPSOPHOBIA
dogs	CANOPHOBIA, CYNOPHOBIA	hell	HADEOPHOBIA, STYGIOPHOBIA
draughts	AEROPHOBIA	heredity	PATROIOPHOBIA
dreams	ONEIROPHOBIA	home	OIKOPHOBIA
drink	POTOPHOBIA	homosexuals	HOMOPHOBIA
drugs	PHARMACOPHOBIA	horses	HIPPOPHOBIA
drunkenness	DIPSOPHOBIA	humans	ANTHROPOPHOBIA
dry places	XEROPHOBIA	ideas	IDEOPHOBIA
dust	ANATHOPHOBIA, KONIPHOBIA	illness	NOSOPHOBIA, PATHOPHOBIA
electrity	ELEKTROPHOBIA	imperfections	ATELOPHOBIA

infinity	APEIROPHOBIA	punishment	POINEPHOBIA
influence of the stars	ASTROPHOBIA		RHABDOPHOBIA
injections	TRYPANOPHOBIA	rain	OMBROMOPHOBIA
injury	TRAUMATOPHOBIA	reference to self	AUTOPHOBY
insanity	LYSSOPHOBIA	reptiles	BATRACHOPHOBIA
	MANIAPHOBIA	responsibility	HYPEGIAPHOBIA
insects	INSECTOPHOBIA	returning	NOSTOPATHY
	ENTOMOPHOBIA	ridicule	KATAGELOPHOBIA
justice	DIKEPHOBIA	robbers	HARPAXOPHOBIA
lakes	LIMNOPHOBIA	ruin	ATEPHOBIA
languages	LINGUAPHOBIA	Russians	RUSSOPHOBIA
leaves	PYHLLOPHOBIA	Satan	SATANOPHOBIA
lice	PEDICULOPHOBIA	sea	THALASSOPHOBIA
light	PHOTOPHOBIA	sex	GENOPHOBIA
lightning	ASTRO(PO)PHOBIA	sharks	GALEOPHOBIA
	KERAUNOPHOBIA	shock	HORMEPHOBIA
loneliness	AUTOPHOBIA, EREMIOPHOBIA	sinning	PECCATOPHOBIA
	MONOPHOBIA	sitting	
machinery	MECHANOPHOBIA	—down	CATHISOPHOBIA
madness	LYSSOPHOBIA, MANIAPHOBIA	—idle	THAASOPHOBIA
marriage	GAMETOPHOBIA	skin	DERMATOPHOBIA
men	ANDROPHOBIA	sleep	HYPNOPHOBIA
metals	METALLOPHOBIA	slime	BLENNOPHOBIA, MYXOPHOBIA
meteors	METEOROPHOBIA	smells	OLFACTOPHOBIA
mice	MUSOPHOBIA	smothering	PNIGEROPHOBIA
mirrors	EISOPTROPHOBIA	snakes	OPH(ID)IOPHOBIA
moisture	HYGROPHOBIA	snow	CHIONOPHOBIA
money	CHROMETOPHOBIA	soiling	RYPOPHOBIA
monsters	TERATOPHOBIA	solitude	EREMITOPHOBIA
motion	KINESOPHOBIA	sound	AKOUSTICOPHOBIA
	KINETOPHOBIA	sourness	ACEROPHOBIA
(motorway madness)	AMAXOPHOBIA	speaking	GLOSSOPHOBIA
music	MUSICOPHOBIA	—aloud	PHONOPHOBIA
names	ONOMATOPHOBIA	speech	LALOPHOBIA
narrowness	ANGINOPHOBIA	speed	TACHOPHOBIA
needles	BELONEPHOBIA	spiders	ARACHNOPHOBIA
negroes	NEGROPHOBIA	standing	STASOPHOBIA
new things	NEOPHOBIA	stars	ASTROPHOBIA
night	NYCTOPHOBIA	stealing	KLEPTOPHOBIA
noise	PHONOPHOBIA	stings	CNIDOPHOBIA
nudity	GYMNOPHOBIA	stooping	KYPOPHOBIA
old age	GERASCOPHOBIA	strangers	XENOPHOBIA
one thing	MONOPHOBIA	streets	DROMOPHOBIA
open spaces	AGORAPHOBIA, KENOPHOBIA	string	LINONOPHOBIA
pain	ALGOPHOBIA, ODYNOPHOBIA	sun	HELIOPHOBIA
particular		surgery	ERGASIOPHOBIA
—place	TOPOPHOBIA		TOMOPHOBIA
—word	ONOMATOPHOBIA	swallowing	PHAGOPHOBIA
pins	ENETEPHOBIA	symmetry	SYMMETROPHOBIA
pleasure	HEDONOPHOBIA	syphilis	SYPHILOPHOBIA
points	AICHUROPHOBIA	taste	GEUMATOPHOBIA
poisons	IOPHOBIA, TOXI(CO)PHOBIA	teeth	ODONTOPHOBIA
pope	PAPAPHOBIA	thinking	PHRONEMOPHOBIA
poverty	PENIAPHOBIA	thirteen	TERDEKAPHOBIA
pregnancy	MAIEUSIOPHOBIA		TRISKAIDECAPHOBIA
public speaking	GLOSSOPHOBIA		TRISKAIDEKAPHOBIA

thunder	BRONTOPHOBIA
	KERAUNOPHOBIA
	TONITROPHOBIA
—and lightning	ASTRO(PO)PHOBIA
time	CHRONOPHOBIA
tiredness	KOPOPHOBIA
touch	HAPTOPHOBIA
touching	THIXOPHOBIA
trains	SIDERODROMOPHOBIA
travel	HODOPHOBIA
trees	DENDROPHOBIA
trembling	TREMOPHOBIA
venereal disease	SYPHILOPHOBIA
voids	KENOPHOBIA
walking	BATOPHOBIA
water	AQUAPHOBIA, HYDROPHOBIA
	HYGROPHOBIA
waves	CYMOPHOBIA
weakness	ASTHENOPHOBIA
wind	ANCRAOPHOBIA
	ANEMOPHOBIA
women	GYNOPHOBIA
words	LOGOPHOBIA
work	ERGOPHOBIA
worms	HELMINTHOPHOBIA
	SCOILECIPHOBIA
wounds	TRAUMATOPHOBIA
writing	GRAPHOPHOBIA
young people	PARTHENOPHOBIA
feast days	(*see* **holidays**)
feathers	
barb on shaft	VEXILLUM
bare patch on bird	APTERIUM
bastard-wing	ALULA
bird's crest	COPPLE
bunch of feathers	PLUME
—used in hawking	LURE
cause feathers to stand erect	RUFFLE
cleaning feathers	PREENING
covering quill bases	COVERTS, TECTRIX
depression holding	
feather	FEATHER FOLLICLE
develop feathers	FLEDGE
down-feather	PLUMULA, PLUMULE
expanded part of feather	VANE
eye-stripe	SUPERCILIUM
feathers	PLUMAGE
—used as plume	AIGRETTE
feather-seller	PLUMASSIER
filament	BARB
flight feather(s)	PINION
	REMEX(REMIGES)
hairlike	FILOPLUME
hollow part of feather	QUILL
large feather	PLUME, QUILL
like bristle(s) on beak	VIBRISSA(E)

mode of feathering	PTILOSIS
on back	MANTLE
—back of neck	HACKLES
—ears	AURICULAR
—neck	FRILL, RUFF
—rump of hawk	BRAIL
—shoulder	SCAPULAR
outer feathers	CONTOUR FEATHERS
plumage	PTILOSIS
projection on barb	BARBULE
shaft	RACHIS
shed feathers	MOULT
small	
—barbed projection	BARBICEL
—feather(s)	PLUMULA, PLUMULE
	TECTRIX(TECTRICES)
tail feather(s)	PENNA(E)
	RECTRIX (RECTRICES)
	SICKLE FEATHER
vane	PLUME
web	VANE
wing feather(s)	ALULA, BASTARD-WING
	PENNA(E), PRIMARY
	SECONDARY, TERTIAL
	TERTIARY
wingless	APTERAL, APTEROUS
feet	
animal with	
—2 feet	BIPED
—4 feet	QUADRUPED
—8 feet	OCTOPOD
—many feet	CENTIPEDE, MILLIPEDE
—modified feet	CEPHALOPOD
combining form	-PED(E), -PEDAL
footboard of piano	PEDAL-BOARD
	PEDAL-CLAVIER, PEDALIER
foot-operated	
—boat	PEDALO
—vehicle	MONOCYCLE, CYCLE
	PEDICAR, QUADRICYCLE
	TRICYCLE
having	
—1 foot	MONOPEDAL
—2 feet	BIPEDAL
—3 feet	TRIPEDAL
—4 feet	QUADRUPEDAL
	TETRAPODOUS
—8 feet	OCTOPODOUS
like a foot	PEDAL, PEDATE
object with	
—1 foot	MONOPOD
—2 feet	BIPOD
—3 feet	TRIPOD
—4 feet	TETRAPOD
one-footed man	MONOPODE
treatment	PEDICURE

fences

natural	HEDGE
sunken	HAHA
types	BARBED WIRE
	CHAIN-LINK, CHESTNUT PALE
	CLOSE-BOARDED, ELECTRIC
	INTERWOVEN, POST AND PANEL
	POST AND RAIL
	POST AND WIRE, RAZOR WIRE
	RING, RUSTIC

fencing

acknowledgment of hit	TOUCHE
attack after parry	RIPOSTE
backhanded stroke	REVERSO
body quilting	PLASTRON
deciding bout	BARRAGE
deflection of blade	PARADE, PARRY
downward stroke	STRAMACON
	STRAMAZON
exclamation on hit	HAY
false attack	FEINT
fencer (Shak.)	SCRIMURE
fencers	
—Belgian	ANSPACH, DELPORTE
—British (m)	CAMPBELL-GREY
(f)	SHEEN
—Cuban	DIAZ, FONST, TATHAM
—French (m)	ALIBERT, BUHAN, COSTE
	DE LA FALAISE, D'ORIOLA
	DUCRET, GAUDIN, GRAVELOTTE
	MASSARD
(f)	TRINQUET
—German (m)	HEHN, PUSCH
(f)	MEYER-SCHMID
—Greek	GEORGIADIS
—Hungarian (m)	FENYVESI, FUCHS
	KABOS, KARPATI, KOVACS
	KULCSAR, PEZSA
	PILLER, POSTA
(f)	ELEK, REJTO
—Italian (m)	CANTONE, DELFINO
	GAUDINI, MANGIAROTTI
	MARZI, NADI, PAVESE
	RICCARDI
(f)	CAMBER, LONZI
—Polish	FRANKE, WOYDA
—Romanian	DRIMBA
—Russian (m)	KORVOPUSHKOV, KRISS
	ROMANKOV, SIDIAK
	SMIRNOV, ZHDANOVICH
(f)	NOVIKOVA
—Swedish	HARMENBERG
fifth position	QUINTE
fighting area	PISTE
foot-stamping	APPEL
forward jump	BALESTA

fourth position	CARTE, QUART(E)
guard	COQUILLE
handle end of sword	FORTE
hit	HAY, VENEY
	VENEWE, VENUE
opposing movement	TRAVERSE
parry and riposte	TAC-AU-TAC
point end of sword	FOIBLE
practice	QUART(E) AND TIERCE
renewed attack	REMISE, REPRISE
running attack	FLECHE
second position	SECONDE
series of attacks	TAC-AU-TAC
sudden movement	VOLT
sword	EPEE, FOIL, SABRE
	(*see also separate entry*)
third position	TIERCE
thrust	BOTTE, FOIN, IMBROCCATA
	POTCH(E), STOCCADO, STOCCATA
	STOCK, STUCK
—into side	FLANCONADE
—with one foot forward	PASSADA
	PASSADO
upward blow	MONTANT
warning	EN GARDE
wound slightly	PINK

ferns

	ACROGEN, FILIC(AL)ES
	FILICINEAE
Adiantum	MAIDENHAIR FERN
aquatic	MARSILEA, MARSILIA
Asplenium	BIRD'S NEST FERN
	MOTHER SPLEENWORT
Athyrium	LADY FERN
bird's nest fern	ASPLENIUM
Boston fern	NEPHROLEPSIS
Botrychium	MOONWORT
bracken	PTERIDIUS, PTERIS
	TARA(-FERN)
button fern	PELLAEA
Christmas fern	POLYSTICHUM
cloak fern	DIDYMOCHLAENA
Cyathea	TREE-FERN
Cyrtomium	FISHTAIL FERN, HOLLY FERN
Davallia	RABBIT'S FOOT FERN
delta maidenhair	ADIANTUM
Didymochlaena	CLOAK FERN
Dryopteris	MALE FERN
feather fern	NEPHROLEPSIS
filmy fern	BRISTLE-FERN
fishtail fern	CYRTOMIUM
green brake fern	PELLAEA
hare's foot fern	PHLEBODIUM
hart's tongue fern	PHYLLITIS
holly fern	CYRTOMIUM
lace fern	NEPHROLEPIS
lady fern	ATHYRIUM

maidenhair fern	ADIANTUM
male fern	DRYOPTERIS
moonwort	BOTRYCHIUM
mother spleenwwort	ASPLENIUM
Nephrolepsis	BOSTON FERN
	FEATHER FERN
	LACE FERN, SWORD FERN
Osmunda	ROYAL FERN
peacock fern	SELAGINELLA
Pellaea	BUTTON FERN
	GREEN BRAKE FERN
Phlebodium	HARE'S FOOT FERN
Phyllitis	HART'S TONGUE FERN
Platycerium	STAG'S HORN FERN
Polystichum	CHRISTMAS FERN
	TSUSINA HOLLY FERN
Pteris	RIBBON FERN
	SILVER LACE FERN
	TABLE FERN, TREMBLING FERN
rabbit's foot fern	DAVALLIA
ribbon fern	PTERIS
rose maidenhair	ADIANTUM
royal fern	OSMUNDA
scale-fern	CETERACH
Selaginella	PEACOCK FERN
silver lace fern	PTERIS
stag's horn fern	PLATYCERIUM
sword fern	NEPHROLEPSIS
table fern	PTERIS
tara(-fern)	BRACKEN
tree-fern	CYATHEA
trembling fern	PTERIS
tropical genus	SCHIAEA
Tsusina holly fern	POLYSTICHUM
festivals	(see **holidays**)
feudal	(see **mediaeval**)
fifty	LA, L, N, NU, V
states	AMERICA, US(A)
thousand	L, N, NU, V
years old	QUINQUAGENARIAN
figures of speech	(see **rhetoric**)
Fiji	FJI
capital	SUVA
coin	CENT, DOLLAR
films	(see **cinema**)
Finland	SF
capital	HELSINGFORS, HELSINKI
coin	MARK, MARK(K)A
	MKK, PENNI
dialect	KAREL
dog	LAIKA
epic	KALEVALA
instrument	KANTELE
language	SUOMI
measure	KANNOR, TUNNA
underworld	TUONELA

first	
—first	
airship to fly round	
the world	GRAF ZEPPELIN
Astronomer Royal	FLAMSTEED
balloon to fly	
across Atlantic	DOUBLE EAGLE II
city	CATAL HUYUK
electronic computer	ENIAC
empire	AKKADIAN
English printer	CAXTON
jet airliner flight	TUPOLEV
—in service	COMET
manpowered aircraft	
to fly across the	
English Channel	GOSSAMER ALBATROSS
moving picture	BIRTH OF A NATION
non-stop flight	
round the world	
without refuelling	VOYAGER
novel written on	
a type-	
writer	THE ADVENTURES OF TOM SAWYER
postage stamp	PENNY BLACK
railway	STOCKTON-DARLINGTON
solar-powered plane to	
—fly	SOLAR CHALLENGER
over the English	
Channel	SOLAR CHALLENGER
steamboat	CHARLOTTE DUNDAS
steamship	PHOENIX
—to cross Atlantic	SAVANNAH
supersonic jet in service	CONCORD(E)
synthetic fibre	NYLON
talking picture	THE JAZZ SINGER
town	JERICHO
translation of	
gospels into	
English	LINDISFARNE GOSPELS
—first man or woman (f) to	
break sound barrier	YEAGER
build	
—computer	ECKERT
—radio telescope	REBER
—type foundry	GARAMOND
calculate mass of earth	CAVENDISH
circumnavigate the earth	MAGELLAN
—British	DRAKE
—non-stop	KNOX-JOHNSTON
—solo	SLOCUM
climb	
—Everest	HILARY, TENZING
—Matterhorn	WHYMPER
cross	
—Antarctic Circle	COOK
—Antarctica	FUCHS

crystallise	
—pepsin	NORTHROP
—urease	SUMNER
—virus	STANLEY
culture viruses	GOODPASTURE
decipher	
—Rosetta Stone	CHAMPOLLION
—Sumerian script	RAWLINSON
establish type-foundry	GARAMOND
fly	
—balloon over	
Atlantic	ABRUZZO, ANDERSON
	NEWMAN
Channel	BLANCHARD, JEFFRIES
—circumpolar route	LONG
—hang-glider over Channel	
(m)	MESSENGER
(f)	LEDEN
—in	
powered flight	WRIGHT
—in	
Europe	SANTOS-DUMONT
space	GAGARIN
—over	
Atlantic	READ
—non-stop	ALCOCK, BROWN
—solo (m)	LINDBERGH
(f)	EARHART
Channel	BLERIOT
—man-powered	ALLEN
—solar-powered	PTACEK
North Pole	BYRD
Pacific Ocean	KINGSFORD SMITH
	ULM
South Pole	BENNETT, BYRD
—round the world	WILEY POST
non-stop without	
refuelling	RUTAN, YAEGER
—supersonic	YEAGER
—to Australia	
solo (m)	HINKLER
(f)	JOHNSON
isolate	
—ACTH	OLLIP
—adrenalin	TAKAMINE
—anthrax bacillus	KOCH
—atropine	BRANDES
—aureomycin	DUGGAR
—chloramphenicol	BUCKHOLDER
—chlorophyll	BRANDENBERGER
—chlortetracycline	DUGGAR
—cholera bacterium	KOCH
—cocaine	NIEMAN
—colchichine	CAVENTON, PELLETIER
—diphtheria bacterium	KLEBS
—ergometrine	SPIRO, STOLL

—histamine	VOGT, WINDUS
—hydrogen	CAVENDISH
—insulin	BANTING, BEST
—oestrachol	MACORQUODALE
—oestrone	BUTENANDT, DOISY
—parathormone	CRAIG, RASMUSSEN
—progesterone	ALLEN, CORNER
—secretin	BAYLISS, STARLING
—testosterone	GALLAGHER, KOCH, MOORE
—tuberculosis bacillus	KOCH
—tubocurarine	KING
—uranium 235	DUNNING
—vitamin	
A	CORBET, HOLMES
B1	WILLIAMS
B2	KUHN
B12	FOLKERS, SMITH
C	SZENT-GYORGI
E	EVANS, SCOTT
K	DOISY
liquefy	
—helium	ONNES
—hydrogen	DEWAR
—oxygen	PICTET
measure parallax of star	BESSELL
orbit the earth	
—(m)	GAGARIN
—(f)	TERESHKOVA
produce	
—holograms	LEITH, UPATNIEKS
—photograph	NIEPCE
—photographic negative	FOX TALBOT
—star map	HIPPARCHUS
reach	
—Moon	ARMSTRONG
—North Pole	PEARY
—South Pole	AMUNDSEN
run four-minute mile	BANNISTER
see	
—cells through microscope	HOOKE
—Jupiter's red spot	
through telescope	HOOKE
swim Channel (m)	WEBB
(f)	EDERLE
synthesise	
—acetic acid	KOLBE
—adrenalin	STOLTZ
—alizarin	GRAEBE, PERKIN
—aniline dye	PERKIN
—chlorpromazine	CHARPENTIER
—cholesterol	WOODWARD
—cocaine	WILLSTATER
—cortisone	SARRETT
—ethyl alcohol	BERTHELOT
—glucose	KIRCHHOFF
—halothane	SUCKLING

—impramine	HAFLIGER	bass-like	
—indigo	BAEYER	—American	GROUPER
—magenta dye	PERKIN	—Australian	GROPER
—methane	BERTHELOT	bearded	BARBEL
—musk	RUSICKA, RUZICKA	bellows-fish	SNIPE-FISH, TRUMPET-FISH
—pethidine	EISLEB, SCHAUMANN	Belone	GARFISH, SEA-PIKE
—quinine	WOODWARD	bergylt	NORWAY HADDOCK, ROSE-FISH
—riboflavin	KARRER	bib	BLAIN, BRASSY
—strychnine	WOODWARD		(WHITING-)POUT
—urea	WOHLER	black goby	ROCK-FISH
—vitamin C	REICHSTEIN	blain	BIB, (WHITING-)POUT
translate Bible into English	WYCLIFFE	bleak	ABLET, BLAY, BLEY
transplant heart	BARNARD	blenny	BUTTERFLY FISH, EEL-POUT
use			SHANNY
—acriflavin	EHRLICH	blind fish (Kentucky)	AMBYLOPSIS
—aspirin	DRESSER	blue	
—ether	LONG, MORTON	—fish	SKIPJACK
—gas for illumination	MURDOCK	—roach	AZURINE
—nitrous oxide	WELLS	blueback salmon	SOCKEYE
—Novocain(e)	EINHORN	Bombay duck	BUM(M)ALO(TI)
—oxygen for treatment	HALDANE	bony	
—pethidine	HOECHST	—fish	ANABLEPS, COFFER-FISH
—phenytoin	MERRITT, PULMAN		OSTEICHTHYES
—procaine	EINHORN		OSTEOGLOSSIDAE, TELEOSTEI
—radioactive tracers	HEVESY, PANETH		TELEOSTOMI
—thyroid extract	MURRAY	—pike	LEPIDOSTEUS
—tracers	KNOOP	bottom-feeder	GROUNDLING
walk		bounce	MORGAY, SPOTTED DOGFISH
—in space	LEONOV	brassy	BIB, BLAIN
—to both Poles	SWAN		(WHITING-)POUT
(*see also* **discoveries, inventors**)		brill	TURBOT
fish[1]	PISCES	brisling	NORWEGIAN SPRAT
including: alternative names		bristled head	HOG-FISH
descriptions		Brosmius	CUSK, TORSK, TUSK
ablet	BLEAK	bull trout	SALMON-TROUT, SCURFF
Acipenser	STURGEON		SEA-TROUT
accompanies ships etc	PILOT-FISH	bullhead	MILLER'S-THUMB
adapted to see in air		bum(m)alo(ti)	BOMBAY-DUCK
and water	ANABLEPS	burbot	CUSK, EEL-POUT, TORSK
allis/allice	SHAD	burrowing fish	MUD-FISH
Anableps	FOUR-EYES	butter-fish	GUNNEL
angel-fish	MONK-FISH	Californian trout	RAINBOW-TROUT
angler	BRIABOT, DEVIL-FISH	candlefish	EULACHON, OOLAKAN
	FISHING-FROG, FROG-FISH		OULACHON, OULAKON
	GOOSE-EGG, PEDICULATI		ULIC(H)ON, ULIKON
archer-fish	DARTER	carp	CYPRINUS, ROUND-FISH
Argonaut	NAUTILUS	—type	BARBEL, BREAM
Atherine	SAND-SMELT, SILVERSIDES	cartilaginous	CHIM(A)ERA
Atlantic	ESCOLAR		CHONDRICHTHYES
Balistes	FILE-FISH	catfish	SEA-CAT, SILURE
ballan-wrasse	SEA-SWINE		WELS, WOLF-FISH
banny	MINNOW	—(N)	WOOF
barracouta	SNOEK, SNOOK	caught for sport	GAME FISH
basking-shark	SAIL-FISH, SUN-FISH	Cestracion	SHARK
bass	ROCCUS, SEA-DACE	char	RED-BELLY, SAIBLING
	SEA-PERCH	—Welsh	TORGOCH

Chinese fish	CARP, GOLDFISH
chub	CHAVENDER, CHEVEN, CHEVIN
classes	ACTINOPTERIGYII
	CHOANYCTHYES, CHONDRICHTHYES
	OSTEOICHTHYES, DIPNEUSTI
climbing fish	ANABAS
coal-fish	BLECK, COLEY, DORSE
	GLISSAUN, SAITH(E)
	SEA-SALMON, SILLOCK
—Scottish	SILLOCK, STENLOCK
cobia	SNOOK
Cobitidae	LOACH
cod	DORSE, GADUS
	MORRHUA, TORSK
—family	HADDOCK
—like	HAKE, ROCKLING
—small	CODLING
—type	CUSK, TORSK, TUSK
American	CROAKER, TOMCOD
coffer-fish	OSTRACION
coho(e)	PACIFIC SALMON
	SILVER SALMON
coley	COALFISH, SAITHE
conger	SEA-EEL
corkwing	GOLDFINNY, GOLDSINNY
covered with bony	
plates	PLACODERM
craig-fluke	WITCH
cramp-fish	ELECTRIC RAY, TORPEDO
crayfish	CRAWFISH, SPINY LOBSTER
cross-fish	ASTERIAS
cross-mouthed	PLAGIOSTOMATA
	PLAGIOSTOMI
cured cod	DUNFISH
cusk	BURBOT, TORSK, TUSK
cuttlefish	LOLIGO, SEA-SLEEVE, SEPIA
cyclostome	ROUND-MOUTH
dab	LIMANDA, LEMON-DAB
dace	DARE, DART, GRAINING
Danube fish	ZINGEL
dealfish	RIBBON-FISH
	TRACHYPTEROUS
deep-sea	GRENADIER
demoiselle	WRASSE
devilfish	ANGLER FISH, SEA-DEVIL
Diodon	GLOBE-FISH, SEA-PORCUPINE
dog	
—fish	GREY-FISH, HOUND-FISH
	HUSS, MORGAY, NURSE
	ROUSSETTE, SEA-DOG
	SEA-HOUND
—salmon	KETA
dolphin	CORYPHAENA, CORYPHENE
	DORADO
dolphin-fish	MAHI-MAHI
dorado	GOLDEN SALMON

dory	DOREE, JOHN DORY
	ST PETER'S FISH
dragonet	DRAGON-FISH, SCULPIN
	SEA-DRAGON
drumfish	SCIAENIDAE
eagle-ray	SEA-EAGLE
eel	ANGUILLA, CONGER, GRIG
	MORAY, MURRAY
	MURR(E)Y, MURAENA
—electric	GYMNOTUS
—larval	LEPTOCEPHALUS
—like	KINGKLIP
—pout	BLENY, BURBOT
—young	ELVER
elasmobranchs	CHONDROPTERYGII
electric	RAY, TORPEDO
—catfish	RAASH
—eel	GYMNOTUS
elleck	RED GURNET
Esox	PIKE
espada	SWORDFISH
European carp	ID(E)
father-lasher	BULLHEAD
	HARD-HEAD
file-fish	OLD WIFE
finnock	HERLING, HIRLING
flat fish	BUTT, FLOUNDER, HALIBUT
	HOLIBUT, PLAICE, PSETTA
	(DOVER) SOLE, LEMON SOLE
	TURBOT
—fishes	HETEROSOMATA
flounder	FLUKE
flying	PILOT-FISH, SEA-BAT
found in lakes	LAKER
fox-shark	SEA-FOX, THRESHER
freshwater	
—carp	GUDGEON, ROACH
—fishes	LEUCISCUS
garfish	FAAP, GREEN-BONE
	HORNBEAK, MACKEREL-GUIDE
	SNOOK
garpike	NEEDLE-FISH
ged	LUCE, PIKE
giant ray	DEVIL-FISH
globe-fish	DIODON, SEA-ORB
	SEA-PORCUPINE
	SEA-HEDGEHOG, TAMBOR
goatfish	RED MULLET
goby	DRAGONET, GOBIUS
	MUD-SKIPPER
goby-like	PERIOPHTHALMUS
gold-spotted on head	GILTHEAD
golden id	ORFE
golden-yellow	DOREE, (JOHN) DORY
goldfish with double	
tail-fins	FANTAIL

goldsinny	CONNER, CORKWING
	CUNNER
goramy	GO(U)RAMI
grayling	UMBER
green fish	DERBIO
grey gurnard	KNOUD
grundel	LOACH
gudgeon	WAPPER
gunnel	BUTTER-FISH
guppy	MILLIONS
gurnard	ELLECK, GURNET
	HARD-HEAD, SEA-COCK
	SEA-ROBIN, TUBFISH
gurnet	(*see* gurnard *above*)
Gymnotus	ELECTRIC EEL
haddock (Scot.)	HADDIE
hag-fish	MYXINE
hake	SEA-PIKE
hammerhead shark	SPHYRNA, ZYGAENIDAE
herring	CLUPEA, ELOPS
	SARDEL, SEA-RAT
—American	ALE-WIFE
—jocular	CAPON
—like	PILCHARD
—Mediterranean	ANCHOVY
—type	RABBIT-FISH, SHAD
	SPRAT, PILCHARD
—young	BRIT(T), WHITEBAIT
Hippocampus	SEA-HORSE
homelyn	SPOTTED RAY
hornyhead	JERKER
horse-mackerel	BOAR-FISH, SAUREL
	SCAD, SKIPJACK
humpback salmon	DOG-SALMON
huss	DOGFISH
inflating	BOTTLE-FISH
inkfish	SQUID
Irish trout	GILLAROO
jawless fishes	AGNATHA
jellyfish	ACALEPH(A), ACALEPHE
	ARVEL, CNIDA, MEDUSA
	QUARL, SARSIA, SCYPHOMEDUSAE
	SEA-BLUBBER, SEA-JELLY
	SEA-NETTLE
Japanese	CARP, GOLDFISH
Jew-fish	TARPON, TARPUM
kelt	LIGGER
keta	DOG-SALMON
king of herrings	RABBIT-FISH, SHAD
kingfish	MOLIDAE, OPAH, SUNFISH
Labrus	WRASSE
Lake Bala fish	GWINIAD, GWYNIAD
lamprey	CYCLOSTOME, HAG
	NINE-EYES, ROUND-MOUTH
	SAND-PRIDE, SAYNAY
Lampris	KINGFISH, OPAH, SUNFISH
langouste	(*see* shellfish)
large	
—headed	SCORPAENA
—mouthed	PELICAN-FISH
—ray	MANTA
launce	SAND-EEL
lemon-dab	SMEAR-DAB
lesser spotted dogfish	BOUNCE
ling	MOLVA
little trout	TROUTLET
	TROUTLING
lizard-fish	SAURUS
loach	GRUNDEL
lobster	(*see* shellfish)
Loch Lomond and	
Loch Eck fish	POWAN
Loligo	CUTTLEFISH, SQUID
long-tailed shark	FOX-SHARK
Lough Neagh fish	POLLAN
luce	GED, PIKE
lumpfish	LUMPSUCKER, SEA-OWL
lungfish	DIPNEUSTI, DIPNOI
	MUDFISH
—African	PROTOPTERUS
—Australian	EPICERATODUS
—South American	LEPIDOSIREN
Lutianidae	S(CH)NAPPERS
mackerel	CARANX, SCOMBER
—like	BREAM
—South Africa	ALBACORE
—type	DOREE, DORY
	JOHN DORY, WAHOO
maigre	BAR, MEAGRE, SCIAENA
Malay fish	GORAMY, GO(U)RAMI
male	MILTER
marine	
—perch	SEA-BASS
—stickleback	SEA-ADDER
Mediterranean	MEAGRE, MAIGRE
Megalops	TARPON
menhaden	HARD-HEAD, MOSSBUNKER
miller's	
—dog	PENNY-DOG
—thumb	BULLHEAD, LOGGE, POGGE
millions	GUPPY
minnow	BANNY, PINK, TIDDLER
Molidae	KINGFISH, OPAH, SUNFISH
monk-fish	ANGEL-FISH, SHARK
moonfish	OPAH
moray	MURAENA
mossbunker	MENHADEN
mud	
—fish	BOWFIN
—minnow	UMBRA
—skipper	GOBY
Mugil	MULLET

Mullis	MULLET	Prussian carp	GIBEL
mullet	ATHERINA, BOTARGO, MUGIL	Psetta	TURBOT
	MULLUS, MYXON, SARGINA	raash	CATFISH
—types	GREY, RED	rabbit-fish	KING OF THE HERRINGS
nautilus	ARGONAUT	rainbow-trout	CALIFORNIAN TROUT
needle-fish	GARPIKE, PIPE-FISH	ray	SAW-FISH, SKATE
oarfish	RIBBON-FISH		THORNBACK, TORPEDO
octopus	DEVIL-FISH	razor-fish	SOLEN
oily	MENHADEN	red	
old		—belly	CHAR
—wench	TRIGGERFISH	—eye	RUDD
—wife	TRIGGERFISH	—mullet	GOATFISH, SURMULLET
opah	KINGFISH, LAMPRIS	—northern sea fish	BERGYLT
	MOLIDAE, MOONFISH	ribbon-fish	BAND-FISH, DEALFISH
	SUNFISH		OAR-FISH, TRACHYPTEROUS
ornamental	BLACKMOOR, CARP	river	
	GOLDFISH, KOI, ORFE, RUDD	—fish	CHUB, DACE, LOACH
	SHUBUNKIN		TENCH, TROUT
Ostracion	COFFER-FISH	—lamprey	LAMPERN
oxyrhyncus	SACRED FISH	roach	ROCHET
Pacific salmon	KETA	robalo	SEA-PIKE, SNOEK, SNOOK
pandora-fish	BRAIZE	rock	
parrot-wrasse	SCAR(FISH), SCARUS	—eel	DOGFISH, ROCK SALMON
Pegasus	SEA-DRAGON	—fish	ROCK SALMON, WOLFFISH
pelican-fish	EURYPHARYNX	—goby	GRUNDEL
penny-dog	MILLER'S-DOG, TOPE	—perch	SCORPION-FISH
perch	BLACK FISH, BLACK RUFF	—salmon	DOGFISH, ROCK-EEL
	MARGOT, PERCA, ZINGEL		WOLFFISH
—like	BERYX	—turbot	WOLF-FISH
—pike	SANDER, ZANDER	rockling	MACKEREL-MIDGE
percoid	PIKE-PERCH		SEA-LOACH, WHISTLE-FISH
phosphorescent shrimps	KRILL	roker	RAY, THORNBACK
pike	ESOX, GED	rose-fish	BERGYLT
	GAR(FISH), LUCE		NORWAY HADDOCK
—perch	FOGASH	rough dab	SAND-SUCKER
—young	JACK	Royal fish	DOLPHIN, STURGEON, WHALE
pilot-fish	ROMERO, RUDDER-FISH	rudd	RED-EYE
pink	MINNOW, SAMLET	rudder-fish	PILOT-FISH
pipe		ruff(e)	POPE
—fish	NEEDLE-FISH, SEA-ADDER	Russian	GOLOMYNKA
	SUACOT	sacred fish	OXYRHYNCUS
—fishes	LOPHOBRANCH	sail	
	SYNGNATHIDAE	—fish	BASKING-SHARK, SPIKE-FISH
piranha	SERRASALMO		SWORD-FISH
plaice	PLEUONECTES	—fluke	WHIFF
Pleuronectes	PLAICE	saithe	COLEY
pogge	SEA-POACHER	Salmo	SALMON, TROUT
pollack	COAL-FISH, LYTHE	salmon	
	POLLOCK, SEA-SALMON	—1 year	BLUECAP
pope	RUFF(E)	—2 year	SPROD
porbeagle	MACKEREL-SHARK	—3 year	MORT
porgy	SCUP(PAUG)	—blueback	NERKA, SOCKEYE
Port Jackson shark	CESTRACION	—dog-salmon	KETA
pout	BIB, BLAIN, BRASSY	—female after spawning	KELT, SHEDDER
prehistoric	COELACANTH	—fry	ALEVIN
prickle-back	STICKLE-BACK	—grilse	PEAL, PEEL

—large	CHINOOK SALMON
	KING-SALMON, QUINNAT
—male after spawning	KIPPER
—old female	BAGGIT, BLACKFISH
—North Pacific	ONCORHYNCHUS
—Pacific	BLUEBACK, COHO(E), HUMP
	KETA, NERKA, SOCKEYE
—silver	COHO(E)
—sockeye	BLUEBACK, NERKA
—South America	DORADO
	GOLDEN SALMON
—spent	KELT, LIGGER
—trout	BULL-TROUT, SEA-TROUT
—type	SMELT
—young	ALEVIN, GRILSE, PAR(R)
	PINK, SALMONET, SAMLET
	SEWEN, SEWIN, SKEGGER
	SMOLT, SPRAG, SPROD
samlet	PINK
sand	
—eel	GRIG, LANCE
	LANT, (SAND) LAUNCE
—launce	SAND-EEL
—pride	LAMPREY
—sole	LEMON-SOLE
—sucker	ROUGH DAB
sander	PERCH-PIKE, ZANDER
sapphirine gurnard	TUB-FISH
sardine-type	SARDEL(LE)
Sargina	MULLET
saurel	GARANX, HORSE-MACKEREL
	SCAD, SKIPJACK
saury	SKIPPER
scad	CARANX, HORSE-MACKEREL
	SAUREL, SKIPJACK
scald-fish	MEGRIM
scaleless	EEL
scar(us)	PARROT-FISH
	PARROT-WRASSE
Sciaena	MAIGRE
Scomber	MACKEREL
scorpion-fish	ROCK-PERCH, CORPAENA
	SEA-SCORPION
sculpin	DRAGONET
	OLD WIFE, PORGY
Scyphomedusae	JELLYFISH
Scyphozoa	JELLYFISH
sea	
—adder	MARINE STICKLEBACK
	PIPEFISH
—ape	THRESHER SHARK
—bass	MARINE PERCH, ROCK-COD
—blubber	JELLYFISH
—bream	BRAISE, BRAIZE, GILT-HEAD
	PORGIE, PORGY, SAR(GO)
	SARGUS, SPARIDAE

—cat	CATFISH
—cock	GURNARD, GURNET
—dace	BASS
—devil	DEVILFISH
—dog	DOGFISH
—dragon	DRAGONET, PEGASUS
—eagle	EAGLE-RAY
—eel	CONGER
—fish with long fins	SEA-BAT
—fox	FOX-SHARK, THRESHER
—hedgehog	GLOBE-FISH
—horse	HIPPOCAMPUS
	LOPHOBRANCH
type	PIPE-FISH
—hound	DOGFISH
—jelly	JELLYFISH
—lawyer	SHARK
—loach	ROCKLING
—nettle	JELLYFISH
—owl	LUMPSUCKER
—perch	BASS(E), COMBER
	GAPER, SERRAN
—pike	BELONE, HAKE, ROBALO
—poacher	POGGE
—porcupine	DIODON, GLOBE-FISH
—robin	GURNARD
—salmon	COAL-FISH, POLLACK
—scorpion	ROCK PERCH
	SCORPAENA
	SCORPION-FISH
—sleeve	CUTTLEFISH
—snail	SNAIL-FISH
—surgeon	DOCTOR, SURGEON-FISH
—swine	BALLAN-WRASSE
—trout	BULL-TROUT, SALMOM-TROUT
young	FINNAC(K), FINNOCK
	HERLING, HIRLING, PEAL
	PEEL, PHINNOCK, PHINOC
	SEWEN, SEWIN, SMOLT
—wife	WRASSE
—wolf	WOLF-FISH
selachian	CHONDROPTERYGII, SHARK
self-inflating	GLOBE-FISH
sephen	STING-RAY
sepia	CUTTLEFISH
Serrasalmo	PIRANHA
shad	ALLIS, ALLICE
	KING OF THE HERRINGS
	TWAITE
shagreen ray	DUN-COW
shanny	SMOOTH BLENNY
shark	ANGEL-FISH, BEAGLE, CESTRACION
	GATA, HAMMERFISH, HAMMERHEAD
	MONK-FISH, MORGAY, NURSE
	PENNY-DOG, PORBEAGLE
	RHYN(E)ODON, SAW-FISH

	SEA-FOX, SEA-LAWYER, SELACHIAN
	THRESHER, TOPE
—sharks	ELASMOBRANCH, RHYNAE
	SELACHII, SPHYRNA
	ZYGAENIDAE
sharp-beaked	SAURY
sheat(h)-fish	CATFISH, SILURUS
shrimp	MYSIS
Silurus	SHEAT(H)-FISH
silver salmon	COHO(E)
skate	RAY
—skates	ELASMOBRANCH
skipjack	BLUEFISH, GARANX
	HORSE-MACKEREL, SAUREL
	SCAD
skipper	SAURY
sleeve-fish	SQUID
slimy fish	BLENNY
small	BITTERLING, CLIONE, FRY
	KRILL, MINNOW, NEKTON
	SPRAT, SHRIMP, STICKLEBACK
	TIDDLER, WHITEBAIT
—cod	CODLING, DORSE
—herring-type	SPRAT
—rockling	MACKEREL-MIDGE
—sardine-type	SARDEL(LE)
—sea-fish	WHITING
—shark	DOG-FISH
—sole	SLIP, SOLENETTE
—sturgeon	STERLET
smear-dab	SMOOTH DAB
smelt	ATHERINA
—Newfoundland	CAP(E)LIN
—Scottish	SPARLING, SPIRLING
smoked herring	BLOATER, BUCKLING
	KIPPER
smooth blenny	SHANNY
snail-fish	SEA-SNAIL
snake-fish	CEPOLA
snapper	GRUNTER
snappers	LUCIANIDAE
snipe-fish	BELLOWS-FISH, TRUMPET-FISH
snook	COBIA, BARRACOUTA
	GARFISH, ROBALO, SNOEK
sockeye	BLUEBACK SALMON
sole	MEGRIM
Solen	RAZOR-FISH
southern	ESCOLAR
Sparidae	SEA-BREAM
sparling	SMELT
spear-fish	SWORD-FISH, TETRAPTURUS
Sphyrna	HAMMER-HEADED SHARKS
spike-fish	SAIL-FISH
spinous loach	GROUNDLING
spiny	SCORPAENA, STICKLEBACK
spirling	SMELT

spotted	
—dogfish	BOUNCE, MORGAY
—ray	HOMELYN
sprat	BRISLING, CLUPEA
	GARVIE, GARVOCK
squid	LOLIGO, SLEEVE-FISH
star	
—fish	ASTER(O)ID, FIVE FINGERS
	SEA-PAD
—gazers	URANOSCOPUS
stenlock	COALFISH
stickleback	FLUTEMOUTH
	PRICKLE-BACK, TIDDLER
sting	
—fish	STING-BULL, TRACHINUS
	WEEVER
—ray	EAGLE-RAY, SEPHEN
	TRYGON
stockfish	LUBFISH
striped bass	ROCK-FISH
sturgeon	ACIPENSER, BELUGA
	CHONDROSTEI, HUSO
	OSSETER, STERLET
sucking-fish	LAMPREY, REMORA
sun-fish	BASKING-SHARK, OPAH
swine-fish	WOLF-FISH
sword-fish	ESPADA, GLADUS
	(H)ISTIOPHORUS, MARLIN
	SAIL-FISH, SPEAR-FISH
	XIPHIAS
Syngnathidae	PIPE-FISH
tarpon	ELOPS, MEGALOPS, STABALO
tench	TINEA
Tetrapturus	SPEAR-FISH
thornback	RAY, ROKER
thresher	FOX-SHARK, SEA-FOX
	SEA-APE, THRASHER
Thymallus	GRAYLING
tiddler	MINNOW, STICKLEBACK
tiger-shark	DEMOISELLE
Tinea	TENCH
tope	MILLER'S-DOG, PENNY-DOG
torgoch	CHAR
torpedo	(ELECTRIC) RAY
torsk	BROSMIUS
Trachinus	STING-BULL, STING-FISH
	WEEVER
Trachypterous	DEALFISH, RIBBON-FISH
tree-climbing fish	ANABAS
triggerfish	OLD WENCH, OLD WIFE
Trigla	GURNARD, GURNET
trout	FINNOCK, SCUFF
—American	LAKER, TOGUE
—Irish	GILLAROO
—young	WHITLING
trumpet-fish	BELLOWS-FISH, SNIPE-FISH

Trygon	STING-RAY
tubfish	GURNARD
tuna	TUNNY
tunny	ALBACORE, ALBICORE
	BONETTO, BONITO, TUNA
turbot	BRET, BRILL, PSETTA
—mouthed wrasse	ROCK-COOK
—type	SAIL-FLUKE, TOP-KNOT
	WHIFF
twaite	SHAD
Umbra	MUD-MINNOW
umber	GRAYLING
Uranoscopus	STAR-GAZER
various	LEATHER-JACKET
viviparous blenny	EEl-POUT, GREEN-BONE
weaver/weever	STING-BULL
	STING-FISH, TRACHINUS
Welsh	
—sea trout grilse	SEWEN, SEWIN
—whitefish (L. Bala)	GWINIAD, GWYNIAD
which jumps from the water	FLYING FISH
	SKIPJACK
whiff	SAIL-FLUKE
whistle-fish	ROCKLING
white fish	COREGONUS
—Lake District	VENDACE, VENDIS(S)
—Northern Ireland	POLLAN
—Scotland	VENDACE, VENDIS(S)
whiting	MIRLING
—pout	BIB, POUTING
whitish goldfish	SILVER-FISH
witch	CRAIG-FLUKE
with	
—bifocal eyes	ANABLEPS
—long under-jaw	HALF-BEAK
—lungs and gills	LUNG-FISH
—tufted gills	LOPHOBRANCH
—whiplike tail	HAIR-TAIL
wolf-fish	ROCK-TURBOT, SEA-WOLF
	SWINE-FISH
woof	CAT-FISH
wrasse	BALLAN, COMBER, CROWGER
	DEMOISELLE, GOLDFINNY
	GOLDSINNY, JULIS, LABRUS
	ROCK-FISH, SEA-WIFE
Xiphias	SWORD-FISH
young fish	BRIT
—coalfish	GREY-FISH
Scottish	PODLEY, SILLOCK
—cod	SCROD
—eel	ELVER
—herring	BRIT, SILD
—pike	JACK, PICKEREL
—pilchard	SARDINE
—salmon	(*see* salmon *above*)
—sea-trout	FINNAC(K), FINNOCK

	HERLING, HIRLING, PEAL
	PEEL, PHINNOCK, PHINOC
	SEWEN, SEWIN, SMOLT
—sprat	BRIT
—trout	WHITLING
zander	PIKE-PERCH, SANDER
Zygaenidae	HAMMER-HEADED SHARKS
	(*see also* **fishing**)
fish²	
includes: general terms	
air-sac	SWIM BLADDER
arrangement of scales	PHOLIDOSIS
ascending river to spawn	ANADROMOUS
buoyancy organ	SWIM-BLADDER
descending river to spawn	CATADROMOUS
description of fishes	ICHTHYOGRAPHY
eggs	OVA, ROE, SPAWN
fins	ANAL, CAUDAL, DORSAL
	MEDIAN, PECTORAL, PELVIC
fish	
—glue	ICHTHYOCOLLA
—dish	(*see separate entry*)
—pond	PISCINA
fish-eating	ICHTHYOPHAGOUS
	PISCIVOROUS
fish-shaped	PISCIFORM
fishing	(*see separate entry*)
flap(s) covering	
gill(s)	OPERCULUM(OPERCULA)
flies	COLLIE DOG, DRURY
	HAIRWING, TUBE
	WADDINGTON, WILLIE GUNN
fossil fish	ICHTHYODORULITE
	ICHTHYODORYLITE
rearing fish	PISCICULTURE
scales like teeth	DENTICLES
	PLACOID SCALES
sound detectors along	
each side	LATERAL LINE
spawn of shellfish	SPAT
sperm	MELT, MILT
stinging organ	CNIDA, NEMATOCYST
study of	ICHTHYOLOGY
with spine	
—running into upper	
lobe of tail	HETEROCERCAL
—not running into upper	
lobe of tail	HOMOCERCAL
	(*see also* **fishing**)
fish dishes	
angler fish, poached	CODA DI ROSPO
Bombay duck	BUM(M)ALO
cooked in vinegar	AU BLEU
deep-fried	GOUJON, SCAMPI, WHITEBAIT
dried	
—in open air	STOCKFISH

—salted cod	BACALAO
dumpling	QUENELLE
eels	STEWED EELS
—split and broiled	SPITCHCOCK
eggs	MILT, ROE
fishball	GEFILTE, GEFULLTE FISH
	QUENELLE, RISSOLE
French	BOUILLABAISSE, MATELOTE
Greek roe paste	TARAMASALATA
haddock	
—smoked	FINNAN
—(Scot.)	(ARBROATH) SMOKIE
herring	
—dried	KIPPER
—Dutch	MATIE, MATJE
—in vinegar	ROLLMOP
—partly dried	BLOATER
—pickled	ROLL-MOP, SOUSED
—salted and smoked	RED HERRING
—smoked	BUCKLING
in sauce with peas	WIGGLE
Indian	BOMBAY DUCK
	BUM(M)ALO, KEDGEREE
lobster	
—fat (US)	TOMALLEY
—in butter and Madeira	LOBSTER NEWBURG
—liver	TOMALLEY
Malay	OTAK OTAK
mussels	MOULES (A LA) MARINIERE
ovaries used in sauces	CORAL
oyster	
—cooked with cheese	AU GRATIN
—in the shell	AU NATUREL
paste	
—of mullet roe	TARAMASALATA
—Roman	GARUM
pie	FISHERMAN'S, RUSSIAN
	SEAMAN'S
prawns	SCAMPI
—in butter and Madeira	PRAWN NEWBURG
—with onions, peppers	PRAWN CREOLE
raw sliced fish (Jap.)	SASHIMI
relish made of roe	BOTARGO
roe of sturgeon, etc	CAVIAR(E)
Russian	COULIBIAC
salmon	SALMON TARTARE
scallops	COQUILLES
—with	
grated cheese	AU GRATIN
sauce	FRICASSEE
Scandinavian	GRAVADLAX
scored and grilled	CARBONADO
seafood and vegetables (Jap.)	TEMPURA
shark flesh	FLAKE
shellfish, etc	SEAFOOD
—stew	(CLAM) CHOWDER

slice of boneless fish	FIL(L)ET
smoked	
—haddock	FINNAN, FINDON
	SMOKIE, SMOKY
Scottish	ARBROATH SMOKIE
	FINNAN HADDIE
—herring	BLOATER, BUCKLING, KIPPER
—mackerel	BLOATER
—salmon	LOX
soft roe	MILT
sole	
—baked	
in	
—cider and cream	SOLE NORMANDIE
—herbs etc	SOLE VERONIQUE
—wine	SOLE BONNE FEMME
	SOLE DUGLERE
with	
—cheese sauce	SOLE MORNAY
—mussels etc	SOLE A LA NORMANDE
—deep-fried in	
breadcrumbs etc	SOLE COLBERT
—fried in butter	SOLE MEUNIERE
Spanish stew	ESQUEIXADA, PAELLA
split for cooking (US)	SCROD
squid	CALAMARI, CALAMARY
star	(*see separate entry*)
stew	(*see separate entry*)
stock	FUMET
strips of fish	GOUJONS
—breadcrumbed and fried	FISH FINGERS
	FISH STICKS
trout wih almonds	TRUITE AUX AMANDES
used for paté	ANCHOVY
with	
—mashed potatoes	FISH CAKE
—rice	KEDGEREE
fishing	
bait	LURE
—fixed in position	LEDGER BAIT
—thrown into water	GROUND BAIT
club for killing fish	PRIEST
compound hook	GANG-HOOK, JIG
concave lure	SPOON
connecting line	TRACE
dropping fly gently	
on surface	DAPPING
fish	
—pen	CRAWL
—tank	AQUARIUM
fisherman	ANGLER, PISCATOR
—female	PISCATRIX
fishing	
—basket	COOP, CREEL
—fly	FANCY FLY, HACKLE
—in fast-moving water	TROTTING

—with line behind a boat	TROLLING
flies	COLLIE DOG, DRURY
	HAIRWING, TUBE
	WADDINGTON, WILLIE GUNN
hand-fishing	GUDDLING, TICKLING
hooked pole	GAFF
instrument for removing	
hook	DISGORGER
line with shorter	
lines attached	PATERNOSTER
	SET LINE, TRAWL LINE
maggot	GENTLE, SQUATT
net	KEEP-NET, SEINE
	STAKE-NET, TRAMMEL
	TRAWL
ornament on fly	TAG
sea-fishing	SEINE-FISHING
	TRAWLING
skimming lure lightly	
over the water	SKITTERING
spinning bait	LURE, SPINNER
support for trace, hook etc	FLOAT
weight for line	CAPTA
weighted	
—hook	DRAIL
—line	LEDGER-TACKLE
winding back the bait	SPINNING

five

arrangement of five things	QUINCUNX
Articles	DOCTRINES
books of Old Testament	PENTATEUCH
bunch of fives	FIST
Christmas presents	GOLD RINGS
Cinque Ports	DOVER, HASTINGS
	HYTHE, ROMNEY, SANDWICH
cities	PENTAPOLIS
combining forms	PENT(A)-, QUINQU(E)-
daily interval	SEXTAN
days	PENTAD
event contest	PENTATHLON
fold	PENTAPLOID, QUINARY
	QUINQUEFARIOUS
	QUINTUPL(ICAT)E
groups	PENTAD, QUIN, QUINT
	QUINTET(T), QUINTETTE
	QUINTETTO, QUINTUPLET
having five	
—angles	PENTANGULAR
	QUINQUANGULAR
—atoms	PENTATOMIC
—bundles of stamens	PENTADELPHOUS
—electrodes	PENTODE
—faces	PENTAHEDRAL
—fingers	PENTADACTYL(E)
	PENTADACTYLIC
	PENTADACTYLOUS

—leaflets	QUINATE
	QUINQUEFOLIATE
—members	PENTAMEROUS
—parts	PENTAMEROUS
	QUINQUEPARTITE
	QUINTUPLE
—pistils	PENTAGYNIAN
	PENTAGYNOUS
—rays	PENTACT(INAL)
—rings	PENTACYCLIC
—rows	PENTASTICHOUS
	QUINQUEFARIOUS
—sets	QUINATE
—sides	PENTAGONAL
—stamens	PENTANDRIAN
	PENTANDROUS
—styles	PENTAGYNIAN
	PENTAGYNOUS
—times haploid number	PENTAPLOID
—toes	PENTADACTYL(E)
	PENTADACTYLIC
	PENTADACTYLOUS
—valencies	PENTAVALENT
—whorls	PENTACYCLIC
—xylem strands	PENTARCH
hundred	A, D
—years old	QUINCENTENARIAN
hundredth anniversary	QUINCENTENARY
	QUINGENTENARY
in	
—children's stories	FAMOUS
—government	PENTARCHY
iron	MASHIE
kings	PENTARCHY
Nations	RED INDIANS
one of five at birth	QUINTUPLET
Pentateuch	GENESIS, EXODUS
	LEVITICUS, NUMBERS
	DEUTERONOMY
Points	DOCTRINES
pound note	FIVER
rulers	PENTARCHY
senses	HEARING, SIGHT
	SMELL, TASTE, TOUCH
states	PENTARCHY
thousand	A, V
Towns	BURSLEM, HANLEY, LONGTON
	POTTERIES, STOKE, TUNSTALL
tricks	NAP
Ws	WHO, WHAT, WHERE, WHEN, WHY
years	LUSTRUM, PENTAD
	QUINQUENNIUM
—prison sentence	HANDFUL

flags

American flag	OLD GLORY
	STARS AND STRIPES

British flag	UNION JACK	cross-bred flower	HYBRID
cavalry flag	CORNET	cultivated flower	CULTIVAR
edge		cultivation of flowers	FLORICULTURE
—nearest flagpole	HOIST EDGE	drooping spike	AMENT, CATKIN
—furthest from pole	FLY EDGE	flower	
flag (flower)	IRIS, LIS	—liquid	NECTAR
flag officer	ADMIRAL, COMMODORE	—which	
flagbearer	ANCIENT, VEXILLARY	blooms continuously	PERPETUAL
flown		is pollinated by	
—on		—insects	ENTOMOPHILOUS
boats	BUNTING	—the wind	ANEMOPHILOUS
bow of ship	JACK	lives	
horizontal bar	GONFALON	—1 year	ANNUAL
mast of ship	BURGEE	—2 years	BIENNIAL
	SWALLOWTAIL	—3 years or more	PERENNIAL
—when leaving port	BLUE PETER	opens	
French flag	ORIFLAMME, TRICOLEUR	—during the day	DIURNAL
funeral flag	GUMPHION	—in the evening	VESPERINE
group of flags	HOIST	—without a stalk	SESSILE
hoisting rope	HALLIARD, HALYARD	head-dress of flowers	CHAPLET, CORONA
lance pennon	PAVON		CROWN, GARLAND
long, narrow flag	BANDEROL(E), BANDROL		WREATH
	BANNEROL, PENCEL	never-fading	AMARANTH, IMMORTELLE
	PENNANT, PENNON(CEL)	parts	ANTHER, BRACT, CALYX, CARPEL
	STREAMER		COROLLA, FILAMENT, GYNAECIUM
lower flag	STRIKE		NECTARY, OVARY, OVULE, PEDICEL
Merchant Navy flag	RED DUSTER		PERIANTH, PETAL, PISTIL
	RED ENSIGN		SEPAL, STALK, STAMEN, STIGMA
military flag	ANCIENT, BANNER		STYLE, TORUS, THALAMUS
	COLOUR, EAGLE, ENSIGN	ring of bracts	INVOLUCRE
	GUIDON, STANDARD	single flower in	
Naval Reserve flag	BLUE ENSIGN	inflorescence	FLORET
parade	TROOPING THE COLOUR	small flower	FLORET
pirate flag	JOLLY ROGER	stalk	CAULIS, PEDICEL
	SKULL AND CROSSBONES		PEDICLE, PEDUNCLE
quarantine flag	YELLOW JACK		PETIOLE
roll up flag	FURL	sun-facing flower	HELIOTROPE
Roman			(*see also* **plants**)
—standard	VEXILLIUM		
—standard-bearer	VEXILLARIUS	**football**	
	VEXILLARY	areas of pitch	CENTRE CIRCLE
Royal Navy flag	WHITE ENSIGN		GOAL AREA, PENALTY AREA
square flag	BANNER	attack opponent	TACKLE
study of flags	VEXILLOLOGY	Cup Final venue	WEMBLEY
flower		curving shot	BANANA SHOT
bell-shaped flower	CAMPANULA(TE)	grounds (British)	
bunch of flowers	BOUQUET, CORSAGE	—Aberdeen	PITTODALE
	GARLAND, LEI, NOSEGAY	—Arsenal	HIGHBURY
	POSY, SPRAY, WREATH	—Aston Villa	VILLA PARK
chain of flowers	FESTOON, GARLAND	—Birmingham	ST ANDREWS
	LEI, SWAG	—Blackburn	EWOOD PARK
cluster shapes	CAPITULUM, CORYMB	—Blackpool	BLOOMFIELD ROAD
	CYME, DICHASIUM, GLOMERULE	—Bournemouth	DEAN COURT
	INFLORESCENCE, MONOCHASIUM	—Brighton	GLADSTONE GROUND
	PANICLE, RACEME, SPADIX	—Bristol	ASHTON GATE
	SPIKE, THYRSUS, TRUSS, UMBEL	—Cambridge	ABBEY STADIUM
		—Charlton	THE VALLEY

—Chelsea	STAMFORD BRIDGE
—Coventry	HIGHFIELD ROAD
—Derby	BASEBALL GROUND
—Dundee	DENS PARK
—Everton	GOODISON PARK
—Gillingham	PRESTFIELD STADIUM
—Glasgow	
Celtic	PARKHEAD
Rangers	IBROX PARK
—Heart of Midlothian	TYNECASTLE PARK
—Hereford	EDGAR STREET
—Hibernian	EASTER ROAD
—Hull	BOOTHFERRY PARK
—Ipswich	PORTMAN ROAD
—Leeds	ELLAND ROAD
—Leicester	CUITY STADIUM
—Liverpool	ANFIELD
—Luton	KENILWORTH ROAD
—Manchester	
City	MAINE ROAD
United	OLD TRAFFORD
—Middlesborough	AYRESOME PARK
—Newcastle	ST JAMES PARK
—Norwich	CARROW LANE
—Notts County	COUNTY GROUND
—Oldham	BOUNDARY PARK
—Oxford	MANOR GROUND
—Portsmouth	FRATTON PARK
—Port Vale	VALE PARK
—Queens Park Rangers	LOFTUS ROAD
—Reading	ELM PARK
—St Mirren	LOVE STREET
—Sheffield	
United	BRAMALL LANE
Wednesday	HILLSBOROUGH
—Southampton	THE DELL
—Stoke	VICTORIA GROUND
—Sunderland	ROKER PARK
—Swansea	VETCH FIELD
—Tottenham	WHITE HART LANE
—Walsall	FELLOWS PARK
—Watford	VICARAGE ROAD
—West Bromwich	HAWTHORNS
—West Ham	UPTON PARK
—Wolverhampton	MOLINEUX
—Wrexham	RACECOURSE GROUND
illegal position	OFFSIDE
kick dropped ball	DROP-KICK, PUNT
lines on pitch	CENTRE CIRCLE
	CENTRE LINE, GOAL LINE
	TOUCH LINE
nicknames (British)	
—Aberdeen	DONS
—Arsenal	GUNNERS
—Aston Villa	VILLANS
—Birmingham City	BLUES

—Bournemouth	CHERRIES
—Bristol City	ROBINS
—Cardiff City	BLUEBIRDS
—Chelsea	PENSIONERS
—Coventry	SKY BLUES
—Crystal Palace	GLAZIERS
—Derby County	RAMS
—Everton	BLUES, TOFFEEMEN
—Glasgow	
Celtic	BHOYS, TIC
Rangers	BLUES, GERS
	TEDDY BEARS
—Heart of Midlothian	JAM TARTS
—Hibernian	HIBS
—Ipswich	TOWN
—Huddersfield Town	TERRIERS
—Hull City	TIGERS
—Leicester City	FILBERTS, FOXES
—Liverpool	POOL, REDS
—Manchester United	RED DEVILS
—Mansfield Town	STAGS
—Middlesbrough	BORO
—Newcastle United	MAGPIES
—Northampton	COBBLERS
—Norwich City	CANARIES
—Notts County	MAGPIES
—Peterborough United	POSH
—Portsmouth	POMPEY
—Sheffield	
United	BLADES
Wednesday	OWLS
—Southampton	SAINTS
—Stoke City	POTTERS
—Sunderland	ROKERITES
—Swindon	ROBINS
—Torquay United	GULLS
—Tottenham Hotspur	SPURS
—Walsall Town	SADDLERS
—West Bromwich Albion	BAGGIES
	THROSTLES
—West Ham	HAMMERS
—Wimbledon	DONS
—Wolverhampton Wanderers	WOLVES
officials	LINESMAN, REF(EREE)
old versions	
—Chinese	TSU-CHU
—Italian	CALCIO
pass ball between	
opponent's legs	NUTMEG
players	
—Argentinian	DI STEFANO, KEMPES
	MARADONA, STABILE
—Austrian	HERTZOG, KRANKL
	POLSTER, LINDENBERGER
—Belgian	CEULEMANS, DEGRYSE
	GERETS, VAN DER LINDEN

—Brazilian	BEBETO, BISMARK
	CARECA, CESAR, DIDI, EUSEBIO
	GARRINCHA, GERSON, GILMAN
	JAIRZINHO, LEONIDAS
	MOZER, PELE, RIVELINO
	ROMARIO, SANTOS, TAFFAREL
	TOSTAO, VAVA, ZICO
—Cameroon	BELL, BIYIK
—Colombian	HIGUITA, VALDERRAMA
—Czech	KOCIAN, NEJEDLY, KUIK
	STRAKA, ZIKAN
—Danish	LAUDRUP
—Dutch	CRUYFF, GULLITT, KOEMAN
	NEESKENS, RIJKAARD
	VAN BASTEN
—Egyptian	ABDEL-HAMID
	ABDEL-RASSOOL
	ABU-ZEID, EL KAS, HASSAN
—English	BALL, BANKS, BASTIN
	BLOOMER, BOWLES, BUCHAN
	CHANNON, CHARLTON, DEAN
	DOUGAN, DRAKE, FINNEY
	GREAVES, HAPGOOD, HAYNES
	HURST, JAMES, KEEGAN
	LAWTON, LINEKER, MANNION
	MATTHEWS, MILBURN, MOORE
	MORTENSEN, MORTON, ROBSON
	RUSH, SHILTON, STILES, SWIFT
	TRAUTMAN, WADDLE, WELSH
	WRIGHT
—French	FONTAINE, PLATINI
—German	BECKENBAUER, BONHOF
	HAESSLER, HOENESS, KLINSMANN
	KRAUT, MATTHAUS
	MU(E)LLER, OVERATH
	SEELER, VOLLER
—Hungarian	ALBERT, BOZSIK, CZIBOR
	GROSICS, KOCSIS, PUSKAS
	SAROSI, SZABO
—Irish	BEST, BLANCHFLOWER
	BRADY, DOHERTY, MCILROY
—Italian	BARESI, BERGOMI
	GENTO, MAZZOLA
	MEAZZA, RIVA, RIVERA
	ROSSI, VIALLI, ZOFF
—Polish	LATO
—Portuguese	COLUNA, EUSEBIO
—Romanian	BALINT, HAGI
	LACATUS, MATEUT
—Russian	ALEINIKOV, BLOKHIN
	DASAYEV, IVANOV, RATS
	YASHIN, ZAVAROV
—Scottish	BREMMER, DALGLEISH
	GALLACHER, JACKSON
	JOHNSTON, LAW, LORIMER
	MCCOIST, MCGRORY
—South Korean	SOON-HO
—Spanish	BAKERO, BUTRAGUENO
	DI STEFANO, MICHEL
	SUAREZ, VASQUEZ
—Swedish	EKSTROM, HYSEN
	MAGNUSSON
—Uruguayan	FRANCESCOLI, SOSA
—Welsh	ALLCHURCH, CHARLES
	JAMES, HUGHES
—Yugoslav	DZALJIC, JERKOVIC
	STOJKOVIC, VUJOVIC
playing positions	(CENTRE-)BACK
	CENTRE-HALF
	(CENTRE-)FORWARD, (FULL-)BACK
	GOAL-KEEPER, HALF-BACK
	INSIDE LEFT, INSIDE RIGHT
	LEFT-BACK, LEFT-HALF, LEFT WING
	RIGHT-BACK, RIGHT-HALF
	RIGHT WING, STRIKER, SWEEPER
	WINGER
result of	
—foul	FREE KICK
in penalty area	PENALTY (KICK)
—ball out of play	CORNER (KICK)
	GOAL KICK, THROW-IN
restart after	
—goal	KICK-OFF
—stoppage	DROPPED BALL
short lofted kick	CHIP
start of play	KICK-OFF
teams	
—Argentina	DEPORTIVO ESPANOL
	DEPORTIVO MANDIYA
	ESTUDIANTES DE LA PLATA
	FERRO CARRIL OESTE
	GIMNASIA ESGRIMA LA PLATA
	HURACAN, INDEPENDIENTE
	INSTITUTIO CORDOBA
	RACING CLUB, RACING CORDOBA
	RIVER PLATE, ROSARIO CENTRAL
	VELEZ SARSFIELD
—Austria	ADMIRA WACKER
	AUSTRIA SALZBURG
	AUSTRIA VIENNA, FCS TYROL
	FK AUSTRIA, GAK
	RAPID VIENNA, STURM GRAZ
	VORWAERTS STEYR
	WIENER SPORTS CLUB
—Belgium	CERCLE BRUGES
	ROYAL ANTWERP
	STANDARD LIEGE
—Brazil	FLAMENGO
—Britain	(*see* grounds, nicknames)
—Bulgaria	CSKA, LEVSKI, SLAVIA
—Colombia	ATLETICO NACIONAL
	MILLIONARIOS

—Czechoslovakia	BANIK OSTRAVA
	INTER BRATSILAVA
	SPARTA PRAGUE
—East Germany	CARL ZEISS JENA
	CHEMIE HALLE
	DYNAMO BERLIN
	DYNAMO DRESDEN
	ENERGIE COTTBUS
	HANSA ROSTOCK
	KARL MARX STADT
	LOKOMOTIV LEIPZIG
	ROTWEISS ERFURT
	STAHL BRANDENBERG
—Egypt	AL-AHLY, ZAMALEK
—France	PARIS ST GERMAIN
	OLYMPIQUE MARSEILLES
	RACING PARIS
—Greece	AEK, APOLLON, ARIS
	DOXA DRAMA, ETHNIKOS
	OFI CRETE, OLYMPIAKOS
	PANATHINAIKOS, PAOK
—Holland	AJAX AMSTERDAM
	FORTUNA SITTARD
	FV EINDHOVEN, WILLEM
—Hungary	BUDAPEST HONVED
	MTK VM, PECS MUNKAS
	RABO ETO GYOR
	UZPEST DOZSA
—Ireland	BOHEMIANS
—Italy	AC MILAN, ATALANTA
	INTER(NAZIONALE) MILAN
	JUVENTUS, LAZIO, NAPOLI
	ROMA, SAMPDORIA, TORINO
—Poland	GKS KATOWICE, GORNIK ZABRZE
	LECH POZNAN, LEGIA WARSZAWA
	JAGIELLONIA BIALYSTOK
	MOTOR LUBLIN, RUCH CHORZOW
	SLASK WROCLAW, STAL MIELIC
	WIDZEW LODZ, WISLA KRAKOW
	ZAGLEBIE LUBLIN
	ZAGLEBIE SOSNOWIEC
	ZAWISZA BYDGOSZCZ
—Portugal	BENFICA, GUIMARAES
	MARTITIMO
	NACIONAL, PORTO, SPORTING
—Romania	BIHOR ORADEA
	CORVINUL HUNEDOARA, CSKA
	DINAMO BUCHAREST
	FARUL CONSTANTA
	FLACARA MORENI
	INTER SIBIU, JIUL PETBOSANI
	PETROLUL PLOIESTI
	POLITEHNICA TIMISOARA
	SPORTUL STUDENTESC
	STEVA BUCHAREST, UNI CLUJ NAPOCA
	VICTORIA BUCHAREST

—Russia	DYNAMO KIEV
	MOSCOW DYNAMO
—Spain	ATLETICO BILBAO
	ATLETICO MADRID, BARCELONA
	REAL MADRID
	REAL MAJORCA, REAL SOCIEDAD
	REAL VALLECANO, REAL ZARAGOZA
	SPORTING GIJON
—Switzerland	GRASSHOPPER
	NEUCHATEL XAMAX
—Turkey	BESIKTAS, FENERBAHCE
	TRABZON
—West Germany	BAYER LEVERKUSEN
	BAYER URDINGEN
	BAYERN MUNICH
	BORUSSIA DORTMUND
	BORUSSIA MUNCHENGLADBACH
	EINTRACHT FRANKFURT
	FORTUNA DUSSELDORF
	KAISER LAUTERN
	WALDORF MANNHEIM
	WERDER BREMEN
—Yugoslavia	DINAMO, HAJDUK
	OLIMPIJA, RED STAR BELGRADE
	SPARTAK

footwear

army boots	AMMOS, AMMUNITION BOOTS
baseball boots	KICKERS
beach-wear	FLIP-FLOP
bi-coloured	CO-RESPONDENT'S SHOES
calf-length boots	RUSSIAN BOOTS
casual shoes	LOAFERS, MOCASSINS
	MOCCASINS
climber's boot	KLETTERSCHUHE
	SCARPETTO, VIBRAM
clumsy shoes	CLOD-HOPPERS
cobbler	CORDINER, CORDWAINER
	COSIER, COZIER, SNOB, SUTOR
—Scots	SOUTAR, SOUTER, SOWTAR
cobbler's paste	CLOBBER
crêpe soled shoes	BROTHEL-CREEPERS
dancing shoe	TAP-SHOE
Dutch	CLOG
elastic-sided boot	
—modern	CHELSEA BOOT
—old	JEMIMA
Elizabethan clog	HIGH CHOPIN(E)
embroidered sandal	
(Holy Roman Empire)	CALCEAMENTUM
Eskimo boot	MUC(K)LUC(K)
	MUKLUK
exercise shoes	BASEBALL BOOTS
	DAPS, GYMSHOES, KICKERS
	PLIMSOLLS, TRAINERS
felt-soled	KLETTERSCHUHE
French wooden shoe	SABOT

full-length waterproof	WADERS	—Eastern	BABOOSH, BAB(O)UCHE
half-boot	START-UP	—Scottish	PANTON
hemp-soled		soft-soled shoes	SNEAKERS
—boot or shoe	SCARPETTO	sole of shoe	TAP
—sandal	ALPARGATA	South African	VEL(D)SKOEN
high boot			VELDSCHOEN
—German	HESSIAN	spikes	CRAMPONS
—lumberman's	LARRIGANS	strong shoe	BROGAN, BROGUE
—old	BUSKIN, COTHURN(US)	suede ankle-boot	CHUKKA, DESERT BOOT
—Roman	PERO	—shoe	BROTHEL-CREEPER
high chopin	PANTABLE, PANTOF(F)LE	thick-soled boot	BUSKIN
	PANTOUFLE	—modern	DOC MARTENS
Indian sandal	CHAPPAL	—tragedian's	COTHURN(US)
insulated boots	MOON BOOTS	walking boot	BALMORAL
Japanese sandal	GETA	waterproof overshoes	GALAGES, GALOSHES
jogging shoes	TRAINERS		GOLOE-SHOES, GOLOSHES
kickers	BASEBALL BOOTS	—American	GUMSHOES, RUBBERS
laced boot	ALMORAL	white plimsolls	MUTTON-DUMMIES
Lancashire	CLOG	winged sandals	TALARIA
long boots	TOP-BOOTS	with	
lumberman's boot	LARRIGAN	—long pointed toe	POULAINE
made from deerskin	BUCKSKIN	—rubber sole	GUMSHOE
men's shoe	DERBY, OXFORD	—thick sole	PLATFORM SHOE
—14th c	POULAINE	without laces	SLIP-ON
Mercury's winged sandals	TALARIA	woman's	
metal shoe protectors	SEG, TAP, TRAMP	—heel-less slipper	MULE
Norwegian boots	FINN(E)SKO, FINSKO	—high-heeled shoe	STILETTO
Oriental heel-less slipper	BABOOSH	—plain shoe	COURT SHOE
	BAB(O)UCHE, PABOUCHE	—toeless shoe	PEEP-TOE
overshoe	PANTABLE, PANTOF(F)LE	—shoe with strap at rear	SLING-BANK
	PANTOUFLE	wooden shoe	CLOG
plastic sandals	FLIP-FLOPS	—French	SABOT
pointed		—Japanese	GETA
—boot	CRACOWE	—old	HIGH CHOPIN(E), PATTEN
—shoe	WINKLE-PICKER	Yorkshire	CLOG
rawhide shoe		**fortifications**	
—African	VELDSHOEN, VEL(D)SKOEN	area between moat	
—Scottish	RULLION	and castle	BERM
Red Indian shoe	MOCASSIN, MOCCASIN	basket filled with earth	CORBEIL
reindeerskin boots (Norway)	FINN(E)SKO	battlement	BARTISAN, BARTIZAN
	FINSKO	built by besiegers	CONTRAVALLATION
repairer	COBBLER, COSIER		SIEGEWORK
	COZIER, SNOB, SUTOR	bulwark	RAMPART
	(*see also* cobbler *above*)	central tower	DONJON, DUNGEON, KEEP
Roman boot	PERO	concrete bunker	BLOCKHOUSE, PILLBOX
rope-soled		covered passage	
—sandal	ALPARGATA	across ditch	CAPONIER(E)
—shoe	ESPADRILLE	defensive	
rubber boot	WELLIE, WELLINGTON, WELLY	—spike	CHEVAL-DE-FRISE
running shoes	SPIKES	—stakes	TROUS-DE-LOUP
Russian boots	COSSACK BOOTS	detached fieldwork	DEMI-LUNE, RAVELIN
sand-shoes	SNEAKERS	deviating from	
shoe (Amer)	TIE	general line	BRISURE
shoemaker	(*see* cobbler *above*)	dike of piles	ESTACADE
slipper	PANTABLE, PANTOF(F)LE	ditch	FOSSE, MOAT
	PANTOUFLE	earth bank	BULWARK, RAMPART, VALLUM

earthwork	
—chest-high	BREASTWORK
—protecting	AGGER
at rear	PARADOS
from front	PARAPET
embankment	ESCARPMENT, GLACIS
enclosed area of	
fortification	ENCEINTE
fieldwork enclosed on	
all sides	REDOUBT
firing-step	BANQUETTE, BARBETTE
flat open area	ESPLANADE
flat-topped mound	RAMPART
fortified	
—area	ENCEINTE
—gatehouse	BARBICAN
—house (Scot.)	BASTEL-HOUSE
—mound	DUN
—site of dwellings	RINGFORT
fortress	FORTALICE
—in city	CITADEL
French castle	CHATEAU
German castle	SCHLOSS
grille at entrance	PORTCULLIS
hastily-constructed	
earthwork	BREASTWORK
horizontal fence	FRISE
inner	
—court(yard)	INNER BAILEY, INNER WARD
—retreat	REDOUBT, REDUIT
—side of ditch	ESCARP
inward facing fieldwork	RE-ENTRANT
keeper of castle	CASTELLAN
	CHATELAIN(E)
	CONSTABLE
look-out post	SANGAR, SUNGAR
moat	FOSSE
mound	AGGER, DUN, MOTTE
moveable	
—shield	MANT(E)LET
—siege-tower	BASTILLE
opening	
—for passage of troops	DEBOUCHE
—in parapet	CRENELLE, EMBRASURE
outer	
—court(yard)	BAILEY, OUTER WARD
—side of ditch	COUNTERSCARP
—wall	BAILEY
outside main line or wall	OUTWORK
outward facing	
—projection	SALIENT
—wall or parapet	FLECHE
outwork	
—in front of curtain	TENAIL(LE)
—protecting drawbridge	BARBICAN
	BARTISAN, BARTIZAN

—to strengthen ravelin	TENAILLON
—with two embankments	RAVELIN
overhanging turret	BARTISAN, BARTIZAN
palisade	FRISE
parapet	BARTISAN, BARTIZAN
	BATTLEMENT, TRAVERSE
—between openings	MERLON
—forming salient	FLECHE
passage into fortifications	GORGE
projecting watch-tower	BARBICAN
protection from	
enfilading fire	DEFILADE
protective	
—bank	TRAVERSE
—mound	AGGER
—wall	REVETMENT
raised	
—mound and ditch	BERM
—portion of parapet	SURTOUT
rampart	BULWARK, VALLUM
—between bastions	CURTAIN
—made of	
earth and timber	AGGER
felled trees	ABAT(T)IS
—walk	RELAIS
rough stone breastwork	SANGAR, SUNGAR
salient angle	PIEND
short trench	FOXHOLE
side of ditch nearest	
—besiegers	COUNTERSCARP
—defenders	(E)SCARP(MENT)
slope	GLACIS
—at foot of wall	TALUS
small	
—fortress	FORT
—outwork	BONNET, FORTALICE
space behind parapet	TERREPLEIN
stake barrier	STOCKADE
strengthening work at	
side of ravelin	TENAILLON
stronghold	BASTION, DONJON
	DUNGEON, FASTNESS
	KEEP, REDOUBT
talus on inner side	
of rampart	TERREPLEIN
temporary	BARRICADE
top of rampart	TERREPLEIN
tower	
—at an angle to	
fortification	BASTION, LUNETTE
—for defending fortress	BASTILLE
trench inside	
outer walls	RETRENCHMENT
two faces forming	
a salient	REDAN
underground prison	DONJON, DUNGEON

—shelter	BUNKER
wall of	
—sods	VALLUM
—wooden stakes	PALISADE, STOCKADE
zigzag defensive line	CREMAILLERE
forty	F, M, MU, XL
days	QUADRAGESIMA
	QUARANTINE
Forty-five	JACOBITE REBELLION
forty-niner	GOLD-SEEKER, PROSPECTOR
in book	THIEVES
thousand	F, M, MU
winks	NAP
year old	QUADRAGENARIAN
four	IV
aces etc	QUATORZE
based	QUATERNARY
branches of mathematics	QUADRIVIUM
Christmas presents	COLLY BIRDS
	CALLING BIRDS
cleft	QUADRIFID
	QUADRIPARTITE
combining form	QUADR(I)-, QUADRU-
dramas	TETRALOGY
estates	CLERGY, COMMONS
	LORDS, PRESS
event contest	TETRATHLON
feet	ELL
fold	QUADRIFARIOUS, QUADRIFORM
	QUADRUPLEX, QUADRUPL(ICAT)E
	TETR(A)-
foot	ORGAN PIPE
fortresses	QUADRILATERAL
freedoms	FEAR, SPEECH, WANT
	WORSHIP
gills	PINT
gospels	JOHN, LUKE, MARK, MATTHEW
groups	QUAD, QUARTET(T), QUARTETTE
	QUARTETTO, QUATERNION
	QUATERNITY, TETRAD
having four	
—angles	QUADRANGULAR
	TETRAGONAL
—cells	QUADRILOCULAR
—columns	TETRASTYLE
—compartments	QUADRILOCULAR
—ethyl groups	TETRAETHYL
—electrodes	TETRODE
—faces	TETRAHEDRAL
—feet	QUADRUPED(AL)
	TETRAPODOUS
—fingers	TETRADACTYLOUS
—forms	QUADRIFORM, TETRAMORPHIC
—gills	TETRABRANCHIATE
—hands	QUADRUMANOUS
—languages	TESSARAGLOT

—leaflets	QUADRIFOLIATE
—leaves per sheet	QUARTO
—letters	QUADRILITERAL
	TETRAGRAM
—parts	QUADRIGEMINAL
	QUADRIGEMINATE
	QUADRIGEMINOUS
	QUADRIPARTITE
	TETRAMERAL, TETRAMEROUS
—petals	QUATREFOIL
—pistils	TETRAGYNIAN
	TETRAGYNOUS
—rays	TETRACT(INAL), TETRACTINE
—rings	TETRACYCLIC
—rows	QUADRIFARIOUS
—stamens	TETRADYNAMOUS
	TETRANDRIAN, TETRANDROUS
—styles	TETRAGYNIAN, TETRAGYNOUS
—syllables	QUADRISYLLABLE
	TETRASYLLABLE
—terms	QUADRINOMIAL
—times haploid number	TETRAPLOID
—toes	TETRADACTYLOUS
—valencies	QUADRIVALENT
	TETRAVALENT
—variables	QUATERNARY
—wheels	QUADRIROTAL
—whorls	TETRACYCLIC
—wings	TETRAPTERAN
	TETRAPTEROUS
—xylem strands	TETRARCH(ICAL)
hundred years	QUADRICENTENNIAL
hundredth anniversary	QUADRIGENARY
	QUATERCENTENARY
in-hand	COACH, NECKTIE
line poem	QUATRAIN
letter word	QUADRILITERAL, TETRAGRAM
men	QUADRUMVIRATE
one of four	QUADRUPLET
pence	GROAT
poster	BED
roads meeting	QUADRIVIUM
times a day	QID
towns	TETRAPOLIS
years	QUADRENNIUM
fourteen	
at piquet	QUATORZE
poem of fourteen lines	QUATORZAIN
	SONNET
pounds	STONE
fourth	QUARTER
dimension	TIME
man	SETH
part	QUARTER
—of circle	QUADRANT
power of a million	QUADRILLION

France	FR, RF
departments	
—Alsace	BAS-RHIN, HAUT-RHIN
—Aquitaine	DORDOGNE, GIRONDE
	LANDES, LOT-ET-GARONNE
	PYRENEES-ATLANTIQUE
—Auvergne	ALLIER, CANTAL
	HAUTE-LOIRE, PUY-DE-DOME
—Basse-Normandie	CALVADOS
	MANCHE, ORNE
—Bourgogne	COTE-D'OR, NIEVRE
	SAONE-ET-LOIRE, YONNE
—Bretagne	COTES-DU-NORD, FINISTERE
	ILLE-ET-VILAINE, MORBIHAN
—Centre	CHER, EURE-ET-LOIR
	INDRE, INDRE-ET-LOIRE
	LORET, LOIR-ET-CHER
—Champagne-Ardenne	ARDENNES, AUBE
	MARNE
—Corse	HAUT-CORSE, CORSE-DU-SUD
—Franche-Comté	DOUBS, HAUTE-SAONE
	JURA
	TERRITOIRE DE BELFORT
—Haute-Normandie	EURE, SEINE-MARITIME
—Ile-de-France	ESSONNE, PARIS
	SEINE-ET-MARNE
	VAL-D'OISE, YVELINES
—Languedoc-Roussillon	AUDE, GARD
	HERAULT, LOZERE
	PYRENEES-ORIENTALES
—Limousin	CORREZE, CREUZE
	HAUTE-VIENNE
—Lorraine	MEURTHE-ET-MOSELLE
	EURE, MOSELLE, VOSGES
—Midi-Pyrénées	ARIEGE, AVEYRON
	GERS, HAUTE-GARONNE
	HAUTES-PYRENEES, TARN
	TARN-ET-GARONNE
—Nord-Pas-de-Calais	NORD
	PAS-DE-CALAIS
—Pays de la Loire	LOIRE ATLANTIQUE
	MAINE-ET-LOIRE, SARTHE
	VENDEE
—Picardie	AINE, OISE, SEINE, SOMME
—Poitou-Charentes	CHARENTE
	CHARENTE-MARITIME
	DEUX-SEVRES, VIENNE
—Provence-Côte	
d'Azur	ALPES DE HAUTE PROVENCE
	ALPES-MARITIMES
	BOUCHES-DU-RHONE
	HAUTES-ALPES, VAR
	VAUCLUSE
—Rhône-Alpes	AIN, ARDECHE, DROME
	HAUTE-SAVOIE, ISERE
	LOIRE, RHONE, SAVOIE

regions	ALSACE, AQUITAINE
	AUVERGNE, BASSE-NORMANDIE
	BOURGOGNE, BRETAGNE, CENTRE
	CHAMPAGNE-ARDENNE, CORSE
	FRANCHE-COMTE, HAUTE-NORMANDIE
	ILE-DE-FRANCE
	LANGUEDOC-ROUSSILLON
	LIMOUSIN, LORRAINE, MIDI-PYRENEES
	NORD-PAS-DE-CALAIS
	PAYS DE LA LOIRE, PICARDIE
	POITOU-CHARENTES
	PROVENCE-COTE-D'AZUR, RHONE-ALPES

French

above	SUR
abridged	ABREGE
absent-minded	DISTRAIT(E)
about turn	VOLTE-FACE
Academician	IMMORTEL
accepted idea	IDEE RECUE
accomplished fact	FAIT ACCOMPLI
according to	A LA, AUX
—rule	DE REGLE, EN REGLE
—the menu	A LA CARTE
account rendered	COMPTE RENDU
acme	COMBLE
across	A TRAVERS
actor in farces	FARCEUR
added later	HORS SERIE
administration	REGIME
administrative	
—district	PREFECTURE
—head of department	PREFET
—law	DROIT ADMINISTRATIF
admission to Court	GRANDE ENTREE
adventurer	CHEVALIER D'INDUSTRIE
advice	CONSEIL
aeroplane	AVION
affected (artificial)	CHICHI, RECHERCHE
affecting (emotional)	FRAPPANT
after	APRES
aftertaste	ARRIERE-GOUT
again	ENCORE
against the grain	A REBOURS
agent	COMMIS
agreed	D'ACCORD
ahead of the times	AVANT-GARDE
air	ALLURE
alas	HELAS
Algerian infantryman	ZOUAVE
all	TOUT(E)
—the	
same	TOUT DE MEME
world	TOUT LE MONDE
—things considered	MALGRE TOUT
—together	EN MASSE
alluring	AGACANT(E)

aloud	A HAUTE VOIX	assumed name	NOM DE GUERRE
already seen	DEJA VU	astonishing event	COUP DE FOUDRE
alternate hot and cold	DOUCHE ECOSSAISE	at	
ambiguous	LOUCHE	—a fixed rate for board	EN PENSION
ambush	EMBUSQUE	—any	
amenities	AGREMENT(S)	cost	A TOUT PRIX
amongst the family	EN FAMILLE	risk	A TOUT HASARD
amusement after skiing	APRES-SKI	—bottom	AU FOND
ancient royal standard	ORIFLAMME	—ease	SANS GENE
andiron	CHENET	—great expense	A GRANDS FRAIS
angel	ANGE	—high speed	VENTRE A TERRE
annual income	RENTE	—home	CHEZ, EN FAMILLE
annulment of court decision	CESSATION	—once	TOUT DE SUITE
anthem	MARSEILLAISE	—one's ease	EN PANTOUFLES
April fool	POISSON D'AVRIL	—random	A TORT ET A TRAVERS
apparatus for testing		—room temperature	CHAMBRE(E)
strength of gunpowder	EPROUVETTE	—the	
applause	ECLAT, VIVE	forefront	AVANT GARDE
apple liqueur	CALVADOS	worst	AU PIS ALLER
apprentice chef	COMMIS	attitudiniser	POSEUR
approval	OUI	attractive woman	FEMME FATALE
apropos of nothing	A PROPOS DE RIEN	audacious	RISQUE
appropriate expression	MOT JUSTE	aunt	TANTE
appropriate(ly)	APROPOS	authorised transference of surplus	VIREMENT
arch	ESPIEGLE	avenue	ALLEE
aristocratic		away and hang them!	A LA LANTERNE
—man	GRAND SEIGNEUR	baby's complete outfit	LAYETTE
—lady	GRANDE DAME	background	FOND
arm(s) (body)	BRAS	back-to-back	DOS-A-DOS
armchair	FAUTEUIL	bad	MAL, MAUVAIS(E)
armed police force	GENDARMERIE	—form	MAUVAIS TON
arrogance	HAUTEUR	—luck	MAUVAISE CHANCE
arrow	FLECHE	—moment	MAUVAIS MOMENT
art of		—style	MAUVAIS TON
—make-up	MAQUILLAGE	—taste	MAUVAIS GOUT
—obtaining publicity	RECLAME	badly groomed	MAL SOIGNE(E)
artful	RUSE	baggage	
article	LE, LA, LES, UN, UNE	—of army	MATERIEL
—from magazine	TIRAGE A PART	—wagon	FOURGON
—made of esparto	SPARTERIE	bagpipe	CORNEMUSE, LOURE
—of artistic merit	OBJET D'ART		MUSETTE
artificially cooled	FRAPPE(E)	bailiff	HUISSIER
artistic		ballet	
—quarter of Paris	RIVE GAUCHE	—company	CORPS DE BALLET
	(LEFT BANK)	—dancer (f)	DANSEUSE
—skill	CHIC	—master	MAITRE
artless	NAIF, NAIVE	banteringly	EN BADINANT
as	COMME	barley	ORGE
—a friend	EN AMI	barracks	CASERNE
—a military man	EN MILITAIRE	base metal	BILLON
—a spectacle	EN SPECTACLE	bashfulness	MAUVAISE HONTE
—it should be	COMME IL FAUT	basic assumption	DONNEE
—one unit	EN BLOC	basis	FOND
ash-blond	CENDRE	bath	BAIN
assistant professor	ADJOINT	bay	ANSE, BAIE, GOLFE
associate	CONFRERE	beach	PLAGE

bean	FEVE, HARICOT	—girl	GAMINE
bearing	TENUE	brand	MARQUE
beaten track	PISTE	brandy	ARMAGNAC, COGNAC, FINE
beautiful	BEAU, BELLE	brawl	BAGARRE
bed	LIT	bread	PAIN
beef	BOEUF	—crumbs	PANURE
beer garden	BRASSERIE	—roll	PETIT PAIN
before	AVANT	breakfast	(PETIT) DEJEUNER
—this	CI-DEVANT	breeches	CULOTTE(S)
begone!	ALLEZ-VOUS-EN	bridgehead	TETE DE PONT
behind	DERRIERE, EN ARRIERE	brief outline	APERCU
being discussed	EN L'AIR	brother	FRERE
belly to the ground	VENTRE A TERRE	brotherhood	CONFRERIE
belt (clothing)	CEINTURE	brute	BETE
besides	AU RESTE	buckler	RONDACHE
best item	PIECE DE RESISTANCE	buffer zone	CORDON SANITAIRE
betrothal	FIANCAILLES	buffoon	FARCEUR
betrothed person	FIANCE(E)	bugbear	BETE NOIRE
betting-machine	PARI-MUTUEL	bulging	BOUFFANT
between		burning cloud	NUEE ARDENTE
—four	A QUATRE	business	METIER
—ourselves	ENTRE NOUS	—man	HOMME D'AFFAIRES
—two	A DEUX	butcher's shop	CHARCUTERIE
bewilderment	EGAREMENT	butler	SOMMELIER
bias	PARTI PRIS	butter	BEURRE
bill of exchange	LETTRE DE CHANGE	butterfly	PAPILLON
bitter-sweet	AIGRE-DOUX	buttocks	LE CUL
black beast	BETE NOIRE	button	BOUTON
blackmail	CHANTAGE	—hole	BOUTONNIERE
blandishments	AGREMENT(S)	by	PAR
blind alley	CUL-DE-SAC	—air	PAR AVION
blow	COUP	—all means	A TOUTE FORCE
blue		—force of arms	A MAIN ARMEE
—ribbon	CORDON BLEU	—halves	A DEMI, A MOITIE
—stocking	BASBLEU, FEMME SAVANTE	—mutual service	AU PAIR
bluish	BLEUATRE	—stealth	A LA DEROBEE
blunder	BEVUE, FAUX PAS	—the way	A PROPOS DE BOTTES
boarding-school	PENSIONNAT		EN PASSANT
boat	BATEAU	—way of ideal	PAR EXCELLENCE
bobbin lace	TORCHON(-LACE)	cab	FIACRE
boiled leather	CUIR-BOUILLI	cabaret performer	CHANSONNIER(E)
bond note	ASSIGNAT	cabbage	CHOU
bonfire	FEU DE JOIE	cabinet-maker	EBENISTE
bonnet	BONGRACE	cable-car	TELEFERIQUE
bookseller	LIBRAIRE	cafe	BISTRO
bookshop/book-trade	LIBRAIRIE	—with music	CAFE CHANTANT
bored	ENNUYE		CAFE CONCERT
boredom	ENNUI	cake	GATEAU
boring tool	AIGUILLE	calendar (Revolution)	
born	NE(E)	—January, rain	PLUVIOSE
both hands	A DEUX MAINS	—February, wind	VENTOSE
bottom of the matter	FIN MOT DE L'AFFAIRE	—March, seed	GERMINAL
bow	CONGE	—April, blossom	FLOREAL
box at theatre	LOGE	—May, pasture	PRAIRIAL
boxing with use of feet	SAVATE	—June, harvest	MESSIDOR
boyish	GAMIN(E)	—July, heat	THERMIDOR

—August, fruit	FRUCTIDOR	chic	CHICHI
—September, vintage	VENDEMIAIRE	chicken	POULE(T)
—October, fog	BRUMAIRE	chief	
—November, sleet	FRIMAIRE	—magistrate	AVOYER
—December, snow	NIVOSE	—point of interest	CLOU
call for surrender	CHAMADE	—prize	GRAND PRIX
calling	METIER	child	ENFANT
candour	FRANCHISE	—of	
cape		his times	ENFANT DE SON SIECLE
—garment	MANTILLE	the house	ENFANT DE LA MAISON
—headland	CAP, POINTE	chin	MENTON
capital	F, FONDS, PARIS	china	SEVRES
caprice	BOUTADE	Chinese objects	CHINOISERIE
captivated	EPRIS(E)	chocolate and cream cake	ECLAIR
carat	CARAT, METRIQUE	chop	COTELETTE
card game	BACCARAT, BOUILLOTTE	choreographer	MAITRE DE BALLET
	CHEMIN DE FER, OMBRE	churchmen	GENS D'EGLISE
carefully chosen	RECHERCHE	cinema enthusiast	CINEASTE
carriage	CARROSSE, FIACRE	circus	CIRQUE
	TENUE, VOITURE	civil	
—for one	DESOBLIGEANTE	—officer	ADJOINT
—with facing seats	VIS-A-VIS	—servant	FONCTIONNAIRE
carried away	ENLEVE	claret glass	MOUSSELINE
case	ETUI	classical age of France	GRAND SIECLE
cask	TONNEAU	clear soup	CONSOMME, JULIENNE
cassock	SOUTANE	clearing up	ECLAIRCISSEMENT
castle	CHATEAU	cleric's coif	CALOTTE
—governor	CHATELAIN(E)	cliff	ROCHER
—in Spain	CHATEAUX EN ESPAGNE	cloak	MANTEAU
casual combat	RENCONTRE	clog	SABOT
cats' concert	CHARIVARI	clog-wearer	SABOTIER
cattle	CHAROLLAIS, LIMOUSIN	close-fitting coat	JUPON
	(see also separate entry)	closure	CLOTURE
cauliflower	CHOU-FLEUR	clumsy(-iness)	GAUCHE(RIE)
cause	RAISON	coach	REPETITEUR
cavalier	CHEVALIER	—driver	VOITURIER
cavalryman	CHASSEUR	coarseness	GROSSIERETIE
ceiling	PLAFOND	coast	COTE
censer	CASSOLETTE	coastal plain	LANDE
challenger's loss at ombre	CODILLE	coffee	CAFE
chambermaid	FILLE DE CHAMBRE	—and rolls	PETIT DEJEUNER
chance meeting	RENCONTRE	—filtered	CAFE FILTRE
characteristic of the		—house	CAFE
ideas at end of century	FIN DE SIECLE	—with milk	CAFE AU LAIT
charm carried for luck	PORTE-BONHEUR	—without milk	CAFE NOIR
charmingly ugly	BELLE LAIDE	coin	
	JOLIE LAIDE	—unit	FRANC
charms	AGREMENT(S)	—farthing (old)	LIARD
chattering	BAVARDAGE	—halfpenny (old)	SOL
cheap	A BON MARCHE	—5 centimes	SOU
cheap(ly)	BON MARCHE	—10 centimes	DECIME
cheese	FROMAGE	—100 centimes	FRANC
	(see also separate entry)	—franc (old)	LIVRE
—sauce	FONDUE	—20 sols	LIVRE
chestnut	MARRON	—5 francs	ECU, SCUTE
chewed	MACHE	—20 franc piece	LOUIS(D'OR)

—20 francs (old)	NAPOLEON
—old	
copper coin	DENIER
gold coin	ANGELOT, LOUIS(D'OR)
silver coin	CARDECU(E)
	DENIER, ECU, SCUTE
cold blood	SANG-FROID
colleague	CONFRERE
collected tips	TRONC
collection of	
—jokes	SOTTISIER
—songs	CHANSONNIER
collector of objets-d'art	GRAND AMATEUR
collision	RENCONTRE
colourless	FADE
come	
—in	ENTREZ
—on	ALLONS
comet tail	CHEVELURE
comic opera	OPERA BOUFFE
committed to a point	ENGAGE
commons	TIERS-ETAT
communication trench	BOYAU
Communist	ROUGE
company (business)	CIE, COMPAGNIE, SA
competition	CONCOURS
—based on	
appearance	CONCOURS D'ELEGANCE
complete change (of views)	VOLTE-FACE
compromised	BRULE
conciliator	PRUD'HOMME
conclusive blow	COUP DE GRACE
concoction of old ideas	RECHAUFFE
concrete	BETON
confectioner	CONFISEUR
confectionery	CONFISERIE
confidential interview	TETE-A-TETE
confidentially	ENTRE NOUS
confused	DESORIENTE
confusion	EGAREMENT
conscription	LEVEE EN MASSE
contemptuously	DE HAUT EN BAS
contest	CONCOURS
contradiction	DEMENTI
contribution to paper	FEUILLETON
control by State	DIRIGISME
controversial public	
issue	CAUSE CELEBRE
conventional	
—art	ART POMPIER
—idea	IDEE RECUE
convict	FORCAT
cook	CHEF (DE CUISINE)
—shop	ROTISSERIE
cooked and served in	
—brown sugar	BRULE

—oiled paper envelope	EN PAPILLOTE
cookery	CUISINE
—staff	BOUCHE
cooking utensils	BATTERIE DE CUISINE
—vessel	BAIN-MARIE
cool walk	FRESCADE
coolness	APLOMB, FRAICHEUR
	SANG-FROID
coquetry	AGACERIE
corded silk fabric	GROS-GRAIN
cordial relations	RAPPROCHEMENT
corked	BOUCHE
Corpus Christi	FETE-DIEU
correct	COMME IL FAUT
cosmetics	MAQUILLAGE
council	CONSEIL
—of state	CONSEIL D'ETAT
counterblow	CONTRECOUP
country	PAYS
—house	BASTIDE, CHATEAU
courtesan	LORETTE
courtly love	AMOUR COURTOIS
covered	
—entrance	PORTE COCHERE
—walk	BERCEAU
—with crumbs or	
cheese	AU GRATIN
cradle	BERCEAU
—song	BERCEUSE
cream	CREME
—bun	CHOU
creative force	ELAN VITAL
credulous person	GOBE-MOUCHES
crescent roll	CROISSANT
crest of helmet	CIMIER
crime of passion	CRIME PASSIONEL
criminal	APACHE
—identification system	BERTILLONAGE
—investigation	
department	SURETE
critical examination	CRITIQUE
crop-payment system	METAYAGE
cross-stitch	GROS-GRAIN
crow	CORBEAU
cry from the heart	CRI DE COEUR
cunning	RUSE
—against cunning	RUSE CONTRE RUSE
cupboard	ARMOIRE
current affairs	ACTUALITES
curtain	VITRAGE
—raiser	LEVER DE RIDEAU
curvet	COURBETTE
custom-house	DOUANE
customs officer	DOUANIER
cutlet	COTELETTE
dainty (food)	FRIAND(E)

—served between courses	ENTREMETS
dais	HAUT PAS
daisy	MARGUERITE
damned soul	AME DAMNEE
dance	BOURREE, BRAWL, BRAN(S)LE
	BRANTLE, CAN-CAN
	CARMAGNOLE, CHACONNE
	CORANTO, COURANTE, GAVOTTE
—for two	PAS DE DEUX
—of death	DANSE MACABRE
—step	CHASSE-CROISE, CHASSEE
dandy	BEAU
dash	ELAN
daughter	FILLE
Dauphin	MONSEIGNEUR
day	JOUR
—dreamer	REVEUR, REVEUSE
—school	EXTERNAT
day's march	ETAPE
dazzling	FOUDROYANT
dead	MORT(E)
deadlock	IMPASSE
deal	DONNE
dealer in textiles	MERCIER
dear	CHER(E), CHOU,
death	MORT
debauchee	ROUE
decadent	FIN DE SIECLE
decanter	CARAFE
deception	RUSE
decision	PARTI
decorative trimming	PASSEMENT
decree	ARRET
deep red colour	SANG-DE-BOEUF
defence against cavalry	TROU-DE-LOUP
defensive	
—spike	CHEVAL DE FRISE
—stakes	TROUS-DE-LOUP
dejected	ABATTU, A LA MORT
deliberate	VOULU
delicate	FRIAND(E)
delicatessen	CHARCUTERIE
democrat	SANS-CULOTTE
denial	DEMENTI
department	
—administering monopoly	REGIE
—of	
crime detection	SURETE
Military Intelligence	DEUXIEME BUREAU
—officer	PREFET
depressed	ACCABLE
depression (emotion)	CAFARD
—about the state	
of the world	MAL DU SIECLE
deputy	COMMIS
descend rapidly	DEGRINGOLER

desk	BONHEUR DU JOUR
despatch	DEPECHE
desperate	ACHARNE
—course of action	PIS-ALLER
desperately	A CORPS PERDU
dessert	COUPE
developed	EVOLUE
diary	JOURNAL INTIME
different art	ART AUTRE
difficult	DIFFICILE
dike of piles	ESTACADE
diplomatic	DEMARCHE
—agent	CHARGE D'AFFAIRES
—Corps	CORPS DIPLOMATIQUE
—staff	CORPS DIPLOMATIQUE
disabled	HORS DE COMBAT
discomfort	MALAISE
dish	
—between main courses	ENTREE
—cloth	TORCHON
—from whipped cream	MOUSSE
—of	
fried food	FRITURE
the day	PLAT DU JOUR
	(see also cookery, menu)
disinfectant bleach	EAU DE JAVEL(LE)
dismal	MORNE
dismissal	CONGE
display of affection	MINAUDERIE
disposal of property of	
dead foreigner	AUBAINE
disposition	TALENT
distaste	DEGOUT
distinction	ECLAT
district recently included in city	FAUBOURG
ditty	CHANSONETTE
do-nothing	FAINEANT
dominant idea	CLOU
donkey	ANE
doorkeeper	HUISSIER
dormer-window	LUCARNE
dotted	CRIBLE
double meaning	DOUBLE ENTENDRE
	DOUBLE SENS
downwards	DE HAUT EN BAS
draught-horse	PERCHERON
drawing-room piece	MORCEAU DE SALON
drawing together	RAPPROCHEMENT
dream	REVE
dress	
—ball	BAL HABILLE
—maker	COUTURIER(E)
—making	COUTURE
dressing	
—case	NECESSAIRE
—gown	ROBE DE CHAMBRE

dried oranges	PETIT GRAIN
drop	GOUTTE
—by drop	GOUTTE-A-GOUTTE
drown	NOYER
drunkenness	IVRESSE
dry	BRUT, SEC
duck	CANARD
duckling	CANETON
due honour	BON ACCUEIL
duel	AFFAIRE D'HONNEUR
duenna	GOUVERNANTE
duke	DUC
dulled to pleasure	BLASE
dullness	FADEUR
dupe	BECASSE
duster	TORCHON
dynasty	BOURBON, CAPETIAN, VALOIS
early fruit	PRIMEUR
earnest man	HOMME SERIEUX
earth	TERRE
east	EST
easy	DEGAGE
eat	MANGER
eccentric person	MONSTRE SACRE
edible snail	ESCARGOT
educated savage	EVOLUE
educational quarter of Paris	LATIN QUARTER
	QUARTIER LATIN
eel	ANGUILLE
egg	OEUF
elder	AINE(E)
elegance	CHIC
elegant literature	BELLES-LETTRES
element	MILIEU
eleven	ONZE
Elysian Fields	CHAMPS-ELYSEES
embarrassing occurrence	CONTRETEMPS
embarrassment	GENE
—of	
choice	EMBARRAS DU CHOIX
wealth	EMBARRAS DE RICHESSES
emblem	FLEUR DE LIS
embroidered lace	FILET
embroidery	PETIT POINT
eminently	PAR EXCELLENCE
enamelled metalwork	CHAMPLEVER
encasement	EMBOITEMENT
encounter	RENCONTRE
end of	
—an era	FIN DE SIECLE
—the century	FIN DE SIECLE
endive	ESCAROLE
engaged person	FIANCE(E)
English Channel	LA MANCHE
enough	ASSEZ BIEN

entertain at a feast	FETE
enthusiasm	ENTRAINEMENT
entirely	TOUT (A FAIT)
entrance admitting carriages	PORTE-COCHERE
entry	ENTREE
environment	MILIEU
epic poem	CHANSON DE GESTE
epicure	BON VIVANT, BON VIVEUR
	FRIAND(E)
epilepsy	PETIT MAL
equal	PAREIL
equipment	MATERIEL
escapade	FREDAINE
establishment of ...	CHEZ
estuary	BOUCHE, EMBOUCHURE
estate	CHATEAU
evening party	SOIREE
event	DENOUEMENT
every	TOUT
—body	TOUT LE MONDE
—month	TOUS LES MOIS
exacting	EXIGEANT(E)
exaggerated	OUTRE
example	EXEMPLE
excellent cook(ing)	CORDON BLEU
excessive fondness	ENGOUEMENT
exchange	BOURSE
excluded from series	HORS SERIE
exotic	RECHERCHE
expected	EN L'AIR
experiment	COUP D'ESSAI
experimental balloon	BALLON D'ESSAI
explanation	ECLAIRCISSEMENT
	FIN MOT DE L'AFFAIRE
exposed to capture	EN PRISE
exposure	EXPOSE
extravagant admiration	FUREUR
face	FACADE, VISAGE
face-to-face	VIS-A-VIS
facing forward	EN FACE
faculty of knowing	SAVOIR-FAIRE
faded	PASSE(E)
fairy	FEE
—land	FEERIE
faker	TRUQUER
faking of works of art	TRUCAGE, TRUQUAGE
fall	CHUTE
false	
—modesty	MAUVAISE HONTE
—rumour	CANARD
—step	FAUX PAS
family	
—black (porcelain)	FAMILLE NOIRE
—consultation	CONSEIL DE FAMILLE
—green (porcelain)	FAMILLE VERTE
—pink (porcelain)	FAMILLE ROSE

—yellow (porcelain)	FAMILLE JAUNE
famous	
—make	GRANDE MARQUE
—trial	CAUSE CELEBRE
fancy	
—biscuit	PETIT FOUR
—cake	GATEAU
fantastic extremist	MERVEILLEUX
farewell	ADIEU
farmer who pays with crop	METAYEUR
fashionable	A LA MODE, CHIC
—dressmaking	HAUTE COUTURE
—society	BEAU MONDE
father	PERE
—in-law	BEAU PERE
fat liver	FOIS GRAS
favoured object	MAROTTE
favourite topic	CHEVAL DE BATAILLE
feast day	JOUR DE FETE
feat of strength or skill	TOUR DE FORCE
feeler	BALLON D'ESSAI
fellow member	CONFRERE
fellowship	CAMARADERIE
female	
—attendant in regiment	VIVANDIERE
—dancer	DANSEUSE
—friend	BELLE AMIE
—singer	CHANTEUSE
festival	FETE
fickle	VOLAGE
film	
—director	AUTEUR
—maker	CINEASTE
—style	NOUVELLE VAGUE
finally	ENFIN
fine	AMENDE
—arts	BEAUX-ARTS
—day	BEAU JOUR
—deportment	BEL AIR
—literature	BELLES-LETTRES
—period	BELLE EPOQUE
—prospect	BELLE VUE
finishing stroke	COUP DE GRACE
fipple-flute	FLUTE-A-BEC
fire	FEU
—works	FEUX D'ARTIFICE
first	
—attempt	COUP D'ESSAI
—floor	BEL ETAGE
—performance	PREMIERE
fish	POISSON
—chowder	BOUILLABAISSE
fixed	
—idea	IDEE FIXE
—price	PRIX FIXE
—price meal	TABLE D'HOTE
flaming torch	FLAMBEAU
flash	BLUETTE
flask	CARAFE
flat	MAISONNETTE
—bastion	MOINEAU
—cap	BERET
flatterer	PRONEUR
flayed	ECORCHE
fleece	TOISON
Flemish nationalist	FLAMINGANT
flighty	VOLAGE
floor	ETAGE
flower	FLEUR
fly-catcher	GOBE-MOUCHES
folly	FOLIE
fool	BECASSE
foolish	ETOURDI(E)
footpath	TROTTOIR
fop	PETIT MAITRE
for	POUR
—ever	A JAMAIS
—example	PAR EXEMPLE
—four hands	A QUATRE MAINS
—shame!	FI DONC
—want of better	FAUTE DE MIEUX
forage	ETAPE
forcemeat ball	QUENELLE
Foreign Office	QUAI D'ORSAY
foreigner	ETRANGER(E)
foremast	MISAINE
forerunner	AVANT-COURRIER
foresail	MISAINE
forest	BOIS, FORET
foretaste	AVANT-GOUT
forfeiture	DECHEANCE
forget	OUBLIER
forlorn hope	ENFANTS PERDUS
former(ly)	CI-DEVANT
forward	EN AVANT
foundation	FOND
—scholar	BOURSIER
foundling	ENFANT TROUVE
fountain	JET D'EAU
fragment	MORCEAU
frame	MONTURE
frankness	FRANCHISE
free	
—thinker	ESPRIT FORT
—verse	VERS LIBRE
freedom of	
—access	ENTREE
—action	CARTE BLANCHE
freshness	FRAICHEUR
friar	RELIGIEUX
fried	
—bread-slice	CROUTE

small piece	CROUTON
—lightly	SAUTE
—or toasted bread	CANAPE
friend	AMI(E)
—of the people	AMI DU PEUPLE
friendly agreement	ENTENTE(CORDIALE)
fringe of curls	FRISETTE
fritter	FRITURE
frogs' legs	CUISSES DE GRENOUILLES
frolicsome	ESPIEGLE
from	
—bad to worse	DE MAL EN PIS
—day to day	AU JOUR LE JOUR
—hand to mouth	AU JOUR LE JOUR
fulcrum	POINT D'APPUI
full dress	
—ladies' evening-dress	GRANDE TOILETTE
—military	GRANDE TENUE
fulled cloth	FOULE
fund	FONDS
—holder	RENTIER
fundamentally	A FOND
funeral procession	CORTEGE
furious	ACHARNE
furnishing material	MOQUETTE
fuss(y)	CHICHI
future	AVENIR
gait	ALLURE
gallant	CHEVALIER
gambling game	ROULETTE
game	JEU
—of bowls	BOULES, PETANQUE
garden	
—party	FETE CHAMPETRE
—path	ALLEE
garish	CRIANT
garlic	AIL
general	
—appearance	TOUT ENSEMBLE
—view	COUP D'OEIL
genius	BEL ESPRIT
gentleman	GENTILHOMME, M
gentlemen	MESSIEURS, MESSRS, MM
German	BOCHE
—beer	BOCK
gibe	BROCARD
giddy	VOLAGE
gift	CADEAU
gilded youth	JEUNESSE DOREE
girdle	CEINTURE
girl	FILLETTE, (JEUNE) FILLE
given	DONNE(E)
glance	OEILLADE
glass	
—dish	COUPE
—window	VITRAGE

glazed chestnuts	MARRONS GLACES
glimpse	APERCU
gloomy	MORNE
glory	GLOIRE
glued paper	PAPIER COLLE
God	DIEU
—and my right	DIEU ET MON DROIT
—with us	DIEU AVEC NOUS
godfather	COMPERE
gold	OR
golden fleece	TOISON D'OR
good	BEAU, BELLE, BON(NE)
—appearance	BONNE MINE
—bargain	BON MARCHE
—breeding	SAVOIR-VIVRE
—Christian	BON CHRETIEN
—comrade	BON CAMARADE
—day/morning	BONJOUR
—evening	BONSOIR
—faith	BONNE FOI
—friend	BON AMI
—grace	BONNE GRACE
—journey	BON VOYAGE
—luck	BONNE CHANCE
—man	HOMME DE BIEN
—nature	BONHOMIE
—reception	BON ACCEUIL
—society	BONNE COMPAGNIE
—taste	BON GOUT
—times	BEAU JOUR
goodbye	A BIENTOT, ADIEU
	AU REVOIR
good-for-nothing	VAURIEN
good-natured fellow	BON DIABLE
goose liver	FOIS GRAS
—paste	PATE DE FOIE GRAS
governess	GOUVERNANTE
	MADEMOISELLE
government	
—monopoly	REGIE
—securities	RENTE
gown	MANTEAU
gracious gesture	BEAU GESTE
grant	OCTROYER
gravy	JUS
great	GRAND(E)
—army	GRANDE ARMEE
—century	GRAND SIECLE
—luxury	GRAND LUXE
Greek	GREQUE
green earth	TERRE VERTE
grey gown	GRISETTE
grocer	EPICIER
gropingly	A TATONS
grossness	GROSSIERETE
ground	TERRE

group of		prostitute	GRANDE COCOTTE
—people	PARTI	—fashion	HAUT TON
—vineyards	CRU		HAUTE COUTURE
guerrillero	FRANC-TIREUR	—reaches of politics	HAUTE POLITIQUE
guild of clerks	BASOCHE	—relief	HAUT RELIEF
gulf	GOLFE	—society	BEAU MONDE
gully	COULOIR		GRAND MONDE, HAUT MONDE
hackney-coach	FIACRE	—spirits	JOIE DE VIVRE
hairdresser	FRISEUR	highest military officer	MARECHAL
hairpiece	CHIGNON	highness	ALTESSE
hake	COLIN	hill	COLLINE
half	DEMI	His Majesty	SA MAJESTE, SM
—dead	A LA MORT	hitch	CONTRETEMPS
—dressed	DESHABILLE	holder for crayon/pencil	PORTE-CRAYON
—light	DEMI-JOUR	holiday	FETE
hall	SALLE	holy water font	BENITIER
halting-place	ETAPE	homesickness	MAL DU PAYS
ham	JAMBON	honest people	GENS DE BIEN
hand	MAIN	honour with festivities	FETE
—kissing	BAISEMAIN	hopper	TREMIE
handkerchief	MOUCHOIR	horse	CHEVAL
handsome	BEAU	—race	GRAND PRIX DE PARIS
—man	BEAU GARCON	horse's	
—medium	JUSTE MILIEU	—actions	MANEGE
—woman	BELLE	—attempt to throw rider	ESTRAPADE
happy find	TROUVAILLE	horseman in armour	GENDARME
hard crayon	CONTE	hospital	HOTEL-DIEU
hardly perceptible quantity	SOUPCON	host's table	TABLE-D'HOTE
hash	HACHIS	hot lava gas	NUEE ARDENTE
hat	CHAPEAU	hotel-keeper	HOTELIER
haughtiness	HAUTEUR	house	MAISON
hauteur	MORGUE	—steward	MAITRE D'HOTEL
having shirred effect	PLISSE	household	MENAGE
hazel-nut	NOISETTE	—of three	MENAGE A TROIS
head	TETE	housekeeper	GOUVERNANTE
—of		hunter	CHASSEUR
finger-ring	CHATON	husband	MARI
hair	CHEVELURE	I	JE
—waiter	MAITRE D'HOTEL	—adjust (chess)	J'ADOUBE
head-to-tail	TETE-BECHE	—don't know what	JE NE SAIS QUOI
hearsay	ON-DI	ice cream	MOUSSE
heartbreak	CREVE-COEUR	—dessert	BOMBE
heartfelt entreaty	CRI DE COEUR	iced	FRAPPE(E)
heavenly voice	VOIX CELESTE	idea	IDEE
heedlessness	ETOURDERIE	identity card	CARTE-DE-VISITE
height of fashion	BON TON	idling	FLANERIE
help!	AU SECOURS	if you please	S'IL VOUS PLAIT
helpless giggling	FOU RIRE	ill	MALADE
Her Majesty	SA MAJESTE, SM	illustration inset	
herb mixture	FINES HERBES	separately into a book	HORS TEXTE
here	ICI	immediately	TOUT DE SUITE
here lies...	CI-GIT	immortal	IMMORTEL(LE)
high	HAUT(E)	impetuosity	ELAN
—class		impish	GAMIN(E)
cookery	HAUTE CUISINE	impishness	GAMINERIE
horsemanship	HAUTE ECOLE	impulsive act	ACTE GRATUIT

in	
—a body	EN MASSE
—abundance	A GOGO
—all seriousness	AU GRAND SERIEUX
	TRES AU SERIEUX
—any case	EN TOUT CAS
—bachelor style	EN GARCON
—broad daylight	EN PLEIN JOUR
—cavalier manner	EN CAVALIER
—clear	EN CLAIR
—close touch	EN RAPPORT
—connected series	EN SUITE
—direct relation	EN RAPPORT
—due order	EN REGLE
—emulation	A L'ENVIE
—effect	EN EFFET
—festivity	EN FETE
—flattering style	EN BEAUTE
—front	EN FACE
—full court	IN BANCO
dress	EN GRANDE TENUE
—good form	EN BON POINT
—great demand	RECHERCHE
—hand	A LA MAIN
—his mother's womb	
DANS LE VENTRE DE SA MERE	
—line	EN QUEUE
—male dress (woman)	EN TRAVESTI
—my opinion	A MON AVIS
—natural state	AU NATUREL
—outlawry	HORS LA LOI
—passing	EN PASSANT
—princely style	EN PRINCE
—principle	EN PRINCIPE
—progress	EN TRAIN
—relation to	VIS-A-VIS
—requital	EN REVANCHE
—retirement	EN RETRAITE
—return	EN REVANCHE
—shelter	A L'ABRI
—slippers	EN PANTOUFLES
—spite of (everything)	MALGRE (TOUT)
—succession	EN SUITE
—sympathy	EN RAPPORT
—the	
air	EN L'AIR
country	A LA CAMPAGNE
meantime	EN ATTENDANT
open air	A LA BELLE ETOILE
	EN PLEIN AIR
rear	EN ARRIERE
way	DE TROP
—town	EN VILLE
—truth	EN VERITE
—tune	D'ACCORD
incendiary	PETROLEUR

income from government	
securities	RENTE
indefinable something	JE NE SAIS QUOI
indelicate	RISQUE
infatuated	ENTETE(E)
infatuation	ENGOUEMENT
informal conference	POURPARLER
injured majesty	LESE-MAJESTE
inlay	MARQUETER
inn	AUBERGE
inner fortified retreat	REDUIT
innkeeper	AUBERGISTE
insanity	FOLIE
insectivorous plant	GOBE-MOUCHES
insipid	FADE
instrument of capital punishment	GUILLOTINE
insurgent Huguenot	CAMISARD
intense attachment	GRANDE PASSION
interest	CHALOIR
international	
—law	DROIT DES GENS
—motor race	GRAND PRIX
—pass for car	TRIPTYQUE
intimate conversation	TETE-A-TETE
irresistible beauty	BEAUTE DU DIABLE
irridescence	REFLET
irridescent	CHATOYANT
is it not so?	N'EST-CE PAS
island	I(S)LE
issue	DENOUEMENT
item	PIECE
jacket	CARMAGNOLE
jam	CONFITURE
janitor	CONCIERGE
jargon	BARAGOUIN
jellied sauce	CHAUD-FROID
jerking of reins	EBRILLADE
jet of water	JET D'EAU
jewel	BIJOU
—on forehead	FERRONNIERE
jewelled pendant	LAVALLIERE
jewellery	BIJOUTERIE
—setting	PAVE
joiner	MENUISIER
joint	PIECE DE RESISTANCE
—stock company	COMPAGNIE ANONYME
	SOCIETE ANONYM
joker	FARCEUR
joust	PAS D'ARMES
jovial companion	BON VIVANT, BON VIVEUR
joy of living	JOIE DE VIVRE
judge's bench	BANC
jugglery	LEGER DE MAIN
juggling	ESCAMOTAGE
junior	FILS
just mean	JUSTE MILIEU

juvenile lead	JEUNE PREMIER
keeping holiday	EN FETE
key	
—novel	ROMAN A CLEF
—chain	CHATELAINE
kidnapped	ENLEVE
kind (type)	SORTE
king	ROI, SM
—without power	ROI FAINEANT
king's	
—eldest	
son	DAUPHIN
son's wife	DAUPHINE
—throne	LIT DE JUSTICE
kitchen	CUISINE
knave	FRIPON
knavery	FRIPONNERIE
knick-knack	BIBELOT
knight	CHEVALIER
knob on top of deer's horn	CROCHE
know	CONNAITRE
knowledge of	
—polite usage	SAVOIR-VIVRE
—what to do	SAVOIR FAIRE
lace	ALENCON, CLUNY
	COLBERTINE, VALENCIENNES
—frill	JABOT
lack of taste	MAUVAIS GOUT
lady	DAME
lady's	
—maid	FEMME DE CHAMBRE
—room	BOUDOIR
lagoon	ETANG
lake	ETANG, LAC
lamb	AGNEAU
lampstand	TORCHERE
land	TERRE
—jointly shared	METAIRIE
landed property	FONDS
landslide	EBOULEMENT
langour	ENNUI
language	
—north	LANGUE D'OIL
—south	LANGUE D'OC
last	DERNIER
—resort	DERNIER RESSORT
—shift	PIS ALLER
—word	DERNIER CRI
latest fashion	DERNIER CRI
Latin quarter	QUARTIER LATIN
laundress	BLANCHISSEUSE
lawyer	AVOCAT, AVOUE
lawyers	GENS DE LOI
layered cake	MILLE FEUILLES
leader	CHEF
—of Republic	CONSUL

leading	
—actress, dancer etc	PREMIERE
—film or theatre star	GRANDE VEDETTE
learned woman	BAS BLEU
	FEMME SAVANTE
leather	CUIR
leave to depart	CONGE
lecturer	CONFERENCIER
left	GAUCHE
leg of mutton	GIGOT
legislative bill	PROJET DE LOI
lending	
—against landed property	CREDIT FONCIER
—moveable property	CREDIT MOBILIER
Lent	CAREME
let	
—do	LAISSER-FAIRE, LAISSEZ-FAIRE
—go	LAISSER-ALLER, LAISSEZ-ALLER
—pass	LAISSEZ-PASSER
—us go	ALLONS, EN ROUTE
letter	LETTRE
—of marque	LETTRE DE MARQUE
—under royal signet	LETTRE DE CACHET
liaison	AFFAIRE
light	
—infantryman	CHASSEUR
—fitting	LUMINAIRE
—minded	ETOURDI(E)
—o'-love	COCOTTE
—verse	VERS DE SOCIETE
lightly armed soldier	VOLTIGEUR
lightning	FOUDRE
like a	
—bachelor	EN GARCON
—great lord	EN GRAND SEIGNEUR
—tail	EN QUEUE
limited	BORNE
—liability	
company	SA, SOCIETE ANONYME
line	LIGNE
—of	
sentries	CORDON SANITAIRE
support	POINT D'APPUI
linen	LINGE
liqueur after coffee	POUSSE-CAFE
literally	AU PIED DE LA LETTRE
little	
—box	BIJOU
—song	CHANSONETTE
live	VIVRE
liveliness	ENTRAIN
lively	VIF, VIVE
—dance	GIGUE
liver paste	PATE DE FOIS GRAS
liveried attendant	CHASSEUR
living picture	TABLEAU VIVANT

loaf	BAGUETTE, FICELLE	manger	CRECHE
lobster	LANGOUSTE	manner of dress	TENUE
local (bar)	BISTRO	mannered	RECHERCHE
logically set out	RAISONNE	many thanks	GRAND MERCI
long live	VIVE	march	EN ROUTE
look sidelong	LORGNER	marchioness	MARQUISE
looked upon with distaste	MAL VU	marginal drawing	REMARQUE
looped yarn	BOUCLE	mark	MARQUE
loose		market-woman	DAME DE LA HALLE
—overcoat	PALETOT	marmoset	OUISTITI
—woman	COCOTTE	marriageable person	PARTI
loosely-tied bow	LAVALLIERE	marsh	MARAIS
lost		marshal	NEY
—children	ENFANTS PERDUS	marvellous	MERVEILLEUX
—one's bearings	DESORIENTE	masked ball	BAL MASQUE
—soul	AME PERDUE	masonry rubble	MOELLON
—wax	CIRE PERDUE	massive helmet	HEAUME
louvred screen	BRISE-SOLEIL	master	MAITRE
love	AMOUR	—key	PASSE-PARTOUT
—affair	AFFAIRE(D'AMOUR)	—of ceremonies	COMPERE
	AFFAIRE DE COEUR	—piece	CHEF D'OEUVRE
—at first sight	COUP DE FOUDRE	—stroke	COUP DE MAITRE
—letter	BILLET DOUX	material	MATERIEL
lover	BEAU, BELLE	matter	CHALOIR
	BON AMI	mattress	MATELAS
low	BAS	mayor	MAIRE
—minded person	AME DE BOUE	me	MOI
—vault	CUL-DE-FOUR	meal at a fixed price	TABLE D'HOTE
lower middle class	PETIT(E) BOURGEOIS(IE)	mean	MESQUIN(E)
loyalty to group	ESPRIT DE CORPS	meanness	MESQUINERIE
lunch	DEJEUNER	measure	DEMARCHE
luxurious	DE LUXE	—of watch movement	LIGNE
machine-gun	MITRAILLEUSE	measures	
madness	FOLIE	—small	MILLIMETRE
magistrate	BAILLI	—$1/3$ inch	CENTIMETRE
maid	BONNE	—$3\frac{1}{2}$ inches	DECIMETRE
—of honour	FILLE D'HONNEUR	—39 inches	METRE
	DAME D'HONNEUR	—33 feet	DECAMETRE
mail	POSTE	—2 metres	TOISE
maintain	MAINTENIR	—$5/8$ mile	KILOMETRE
major-domo	MAITRE D'HOTEL	—2.8 miles	LEAGUE
makeshift	PIS ALLER	—11 sq. ft.	CENTIARE
main fact	DONNEE	—12 sq. yds	DECIARE
male servant	GARCON	—120 sq. yds	ARE
malicious	NARQUOIS	—1200 sq. yds	DECARE
man	HOMME, M, MONSIEUR	—1-1½ acres (old)	ARPENT
—about town	BON VIVEUR	—2½ acres	HECTARE
—at-arms	GENDARME	—cubic metre	STERE
—in the street	HOMME MOYEN SENSUEL	—1/100 litre	CENTILITRE
—of		—1/10 litre	DECILITRE
fashion	HOMME DU MONDE	—1½ pints	LITRE
letters	HOMME DE LETTRES	—old	
wit	HOMME D'ESPRIT	capacity	MUID
worth	HOMME DE BIEN	pint	CHOPIN
management	MANEGE	—heat	THERMIE
manager of hotel	MAITRE D'HOTEL	—pressure	CENTIBAR

medal	
—civil	LEGION D'HONNEUR
—military	CROIX DE GUERRE
mediaeval	
—bishop's deputy	VIDAME
—poet	TROUVERE
medium	MILIEU
medley	MACEDOINE, MELANGE
melt	FONDRE
melted	FONDU(E)
member of	
—Académie	IMMORTEL
—literary brotherhood	FELIBRE
—majority	MAJORITAIRE
memorandum	BORDEREAU, CAHIER
men	MESSIEURS, MM
—of letters	GENS DE LETTRES
mental reservation	ARRIERE-PENSEE
menu	CARTE(DU JOUR)
merchant	MARCHAND
mere form of words	FACON DE PARLER
message	DEPECHE
metallic lustre	REFLET
method of voting	SCRUTIN-DE-LISTE
metrical tale(s)	FABLIAU(X)
middle	MILIEU
—class	BOURGEOISIE
mien	ALLURE
mild	DOUX, DOUCE
military	
—courier	ESTAFETTE
—man	HOMME D'EPEE
—men	GENS DE GUERRE
—policeman	GENDARME
—stratagem	RUSE DE GUERRE
mill	MOULIN
minor noble	VIDAME
mischievous goblin	ESPRIT FOLLET
misery	MISERE
Miss	MLLE, MADEMOISELLE
mistake	FAUX PAS
mister	MONSIEUR
mistress	BELLE AMIE, MAITRESSE
—of ceremonies	COMMERE
misunderstanding	MALENTENDU
mitten	MOUFFLE
mix	MELER
mixed face	BOIS-BRULE
mixture	MELANGE
—fruit, etc	MACEDOINE
mob	CANAILLE
mocking	NARQUOIS
mode of curling	FRISURE
model	EXEMPLE
—of sculpture	MAQUETTE
moderate Republican	GIRONDIN

moistened	MOUILLE
money	FONDS
—changing office	BUREAU DE CHANGE
monk	RELIGIEUX
monomania	IDEE FIXE
months	(see calendar above)
morale	ESPRIT DE CORPS
morsel	MORCEAU
mother	MERE
—in-law	BELLE-MERE
motionless scene by	
living persons	TABLEAU VIVANT
mottled	CHINE
mountebank	BALADIN(E), JONGLEUR
mountain	MONT
—range	CHAINE
mouth	BOUCHE
mounting	MONTURE
mournful	FUNEBRE
Mrs	MADAME
mule litter	CACOLET
museum	MUSEE
mushroom	CHAMPIGNON
musketeer	MOUSQUETAIRE
muslin	MOUSSELINE
mussels	MOULES
muzzle	MUSEROLLE
my	
—goodness!	MA FOI
—lord	MONSEIGNEUR
nail	CLOU
naive young woman	INGENUE
name	NOM
named	DIT
Napoleon's army	GRANDE ARMEE
narrow	
—braid	SOUTACHE
—entrance	GOULET
—minded	BORNE
natural	NAIF, NAIVE
naturalistic painting	BELLE PEINTURE
nave	NEF
near	PRES
nearly	A PEU PRES
neck bare	DECOLLETE
necklace of diamonds etc	RIVIERE
need	BESOIN
neglected	A L'ABANDON, NEGLIGE
neighbourhood	VOISINAGE
network	RESEAU
neutral buffer	
between states	CORDON SANITAIRE
nevertheless	MALGRE TOUT, QUAND MEME
new	NOUVEAU, NOUVELLE
—art	ART NOUVEAU
—Year's gift	ETRENNE(S)

newly rich	NOUVEAU RICHE
next friend	PROCHAIN AMI
nightclub	BOITE DE NUIT
nightmare	CAUCHEMAR
no	NON
—more bets	RIEN NE VA PLUS
—performance	RELACHE
nobility	NOBLESSE
noble	GRAND SEIGNEUR, VIDAME
—man	GENTILHOMME
non-interference	LAISSER-FAIRE
	LAISSEZ-FAIRE
nose	NEZ
nostalgia	MAL DU PAYS
not	
—at home	EN VILLE
—in	
cipher	EN CLAIR
competition	HORS-CONCOURS
notary	GREFFIER
notice	AFFICHE, AVIS (AU LECTEUR)
notoriety	ESCLANDRE, RECLAME
novel	
—about successive	
generations	ROMAN-FLEUVE
—with	
a message	ROMAN A THESE
disguised names	ROMAN A CLEF
novelty	PRIMEUR
nozzle	AJUTAGE
number	NOMBRE
—of book published in parts	LIVRAISON
nun	RELIGIEUSE
nursemaid	BONNE
nut	NOIX
object	OBJET
obligations of rank	NOBLESSE OBLIGE
obsession	IDEE FIXE
occasional verse	VERS D'OCCASION
of course	BIEN ENTENDU
off the peg	PRET-A-PORTER
officer in attendance	AIDE DE CAMP
official	FONCTIONNAIRE
offprint	TIRAGE A PART
often repeated	SANS NOMBRE
ogle	LORGNER
oil distilled from orange	PETIT GRAIN
old	
—democrat	MONTAGNARD
—game or joke	VIEUX JEU
—quilted doublet	POURPOINT
—stuff	DEJA VU
—supreme court	PARLEMENT
—fashioned	ARRIERE
nobility	ANCIENNE NOBLESSE
order	ANCIEN REGIME

on	SUR
—a	
level with	A L'HAUTEUR DE
pillion	EN CROUPE
skewer	EN BROCHETTE
—account	A COMPTE
—condition	BIEN ENTENDU
—every occasion	A TOUT PROPOS
—half-pay	EN RETRAITE
—my faith	MA FOI
—purpose	A DESSAIN
—the	
best of terms	AU MIEUX
carpet	SUR LE TAPIS
contrary	AU CONTRAIRE
crupper	EN CROUPE
first floor	AU PREMIER
road	EN ROUTE
second floor	AU SECOND
spot	SUR PLACE
one	UN(E)
—against whose decision	
there is no appeal	SANS-APPEL
—facing or opposite	VIS-A-VIS
—who	
avoids military service	EMBUSQUE
exercises power in	
the background	EMINENCE GRISE
lives on investment income	RENTIER
onion	OIGNON
open air	PLEIN AIR
opera with some spoken	
dialogue	OPERA COMIQUE
opinion-sounding	BALLON D'ESSAI
opinionative	ENTETE(E)
opposite	EN FACE
—number	VIS-A-VIS
orange colour	NACARAT
order	ORDONNER
ordinary	
—man	HOMME MOYEN SENSUEL
—rhyme	RIME SUFFISANTE
organ	ORGUE
ornamental	
—candlestick	TORCHERE
—design in book	CUL-DE-LAMPE
—stand	ETAGERE
orthodox	BIEN PENSANT
Our Lady	NOTRE DAME
out of	HORS
—action	HORS DE COMBAT
—date	PASSE(E)
—fashion	DEMODE
—season	HORS SAISON
outcast	CAGOT
outcome	DENOUEMENT

outlawed	HORS-LA-LOI	rank	GENS DE CONDITION
outline	CROQUIS, ESQUISSE	pepper	POIVRE
outside	HORS	perfect	PARFAIT
—shutter	JALOUSIE	perfectly	A MERVEILLE
outstanding feat	TOUR DE FORCE	performers of mystery plays	BASOCHE
over	SUR	perfume	MILLEFLEURS, PARFUM
overpowering attack	COUP DE MAIN	period of	
overthrow	BOULEVERSEMENT	—1795-99	DIRECTOIRE
—of government	COUP D'ETAT	—1880-1900	FIN DE SIECLE
ox		—1900-1914	BELLE EPOQUE
—blood	SANG-DE-BOEUF	—Louis XIV-XVI	HAUTE EPOQUE
—eye	OEIL-DE-BOEUF	permission to	
oysters	HUITRES	—elect	CONGE D'ELIRE
pain	MAL	—trade after quarantine	PRATIQUE
paint	PEINDRE	persecution of Prostestants	DRAGONNADE
painting		person who is deranged	DETRAQUE
—depicting figures in		pert girl	GAMINE
a pastoral setting	FETE GALANTE	pet	CHOU
—in dots	POINTILLISME	petrol	ESSENCE
pancake	CREPE	pewter	ETAIN
paper	PAPIER	pictorial representation	MISE-EN-SCENE
—trade	PAPETERIE	picture	TABLEAU
Parisian working-girl	MIDINETTE		VRAISEMBLANCE
parasol	EN TOUT CAS	piece of	
part of page used for serial story	FEUILLETON	—foil	PAILLON
particular district in town	QUARTIER	—music	MORCEAU
particularly choice	RECHERCHE	pigeon's wings	AILES DE PIGEON
parting	BOUDERIE	pithy saying	BON MOT
partition	CLOISON	placard	AFFICHE
pass		place	
—between hills	COL	—from which one cannot	
—document	LAISSEZ-PASSER	go forward	IMPASSE
passage	COULOIR	—setting	COUVERT
past one's best	PASSE(E)	—your bets!	FAITES VOS JEUX
paste	PATE	plain cooking	AU NATUREL
pastry		plainly	TOUT COURT
—case	CROUSTADE	play on words	JEU DE MOTS
—shop	PATISSERIE	pleasant	
patent	BREVET D'INVENTION	—looks	BONNE MINE
patented	BREVETE	—taste	BONNE BOUCHE
patron saint	DENIS	plebiscite	APPEL AU PEUPLE
patterned with dots	POINTILLE	plume	AIGRETTE
paved footway	TROTTOIR	pocket-book	PORTE-MONNAIE
pavement	PAVE	point of support	POINT D'APPUI
peak	AIGUILLE, CORNE	poison-pen letter writer	CORBEAU
	PIC, PUY, SOMMET	police	
pear	BLANQUET, POIRE	—man	FLIC
peas	POIS	—spy	MOUCHARD
peasant dance	BOURREE	policy reversal	VOLTE FACE
pen	PLUME	political moderate	POLITIQUE
penalty	AMENDE	popularisation of	
peninsula	PRESQU'ILE	scholarly subjects	HAUTE VULGARISATION
people	GENS	poppy	COQUELICOT
—of		popular uprising	EMEUTE
fashion	GENS DU MONDE	porcelain	SEVRES
humble condition	GENS DE PEU	pork	PORC

porter	CONCIERGE	pulped and sieved food	PUREE
potato	POMME DE TERRE	pun	JEU DE MOTS
poultry	VOLAILLE	punctured like a sieve	CRIBLE
pout	MOUE	pupil (school)	ELEVE
powdered side-curls	AILES DE PIGEON	pure	PUR
power in the background	EMINENCE GRISE	—blood	PUR SANG
practice of obtaining publicity	RECLAME	purpose of existence	RAISON D'ETRE
prank	FREDAINE	purr	CALEMBOUR
prattle	BAVARDAGE	purse	PORTE-MONNAIE
praying-desk	PRIE-DIEU	queen	REINE, SA MAJESTE, SM
precinct	BANLIEUE	quick return	A LA VOLEE
precious	CHICHI	quick(ly)	VITE
precocious		quickstep	PAS REDOUBLE
—boy	GAMIN	quite	TOUT
—child	ENFANT TERRIBLE	—at home	ENFANT DE LA MAISON
preconceived opinion	PARTI PRIS	—brief(ly)	TOUT COURT
preface	AVANT PROPOS	—the contrary	TOUT AU CONTRAIRE
pregnant	ENCEINTE	rabbit	LAPIN
prejudice	PARTI PRIS	rabble	CANAILLE
present	CADEAU	race	LE MANS (24 HEURES)
pretended	SOI-DISANT	ragout	BLANQUETTE
pretentious	CHICHI	railway	CHEMIN DE FER, METRO
pretty	JOLI(E)	—station	GARE
—well	ASSEZ BIEN	rainbow	ARC EN CIEL
—woman	BEAUX YEUX	raise	LEVER
priest	ABBE, CURE, PERE	raised	LEVE(E)
primogeniture	MAJORAT	—in relief	REPOUSSE
prisoner	DETENU	rake	ROUE
private		rammed earth or clay	PISE
—meeting	TETE-A-TETE	rank	ETAT
—soldier	PIOUPIOU, POILU	—imposes obligations	NOBLESSE OBLIGE
—staircase	ESCALIER DEROBE	rare	RECHERCHE
—talk	TETE-A-TETE	rations	ETAPE
procession	CORTEGE	raven	CORBEAU
procurator	PROCUREUR	ravishingly	A RAVIR
profession	METIER	raw	BRUT
professional male partner	GIGOLO	—sugar	CASSONADE
profligate	ROUE	ready	A LA MAIN
prolixity	LONGUEUR	—money	ARGENT COMPTANT
prop	POINT D'APPUI	—to wear	PRET-A-PORTER
proper	COMME IL FAUT	really	VRAIMENT
propriety	BIENSEANCE	rear	ARRIERE
prostitute	FILLE DE JOIE	—part of motor car	TONNEAU
protected	A COUVERT	reason	RAISON
Protestant	HUGUENOT	—for existence	RAISON D'ETRE
pseudonym	NOM DE GUERRE	rebellious youth	BLOUSON NOIR
public		recommended dish of day	PLAT DU JOUR
—confession	AMENDE HONORABLE	recurring theme in music	IDEE FIXE
—dancer	BALADIN(E)	red tape	CHICHI
—executioner	MONSIEUR DE PARIS	referring	RENVOI, RENVOY
—house	BISTRO	refugee	EMIGRE(E)
—nursery	CRECHE	refusal	NON
—prosecutor	PROCUREUR GENERAL	regimen	REGIME
—room off lobby	FOYER	registrar	GREFFIER
publicity	RECLAME	rehashed food	RECHAUFFE
puffed out	BOUFFANT	relaxation	DELASSEMENT, RELACHE

—of strained relations	DETENTE
relegation	RENVOI, RENVOY
reluctantly	A CONTRECOEUR
reminder	AIDE-MEMOIRE
remove	OTER
renewal of good relations	RAPPROCHEMENT
reply	REPONDEZ
report	COMPTE RENDU, CAHIER
reproach	CRI DE COEUR
Republic	REPUBLIQUE FRANCAISE
republican	SANS-CULOTTE
reputed	DIT
required by etiquette or fashion	DE RIGUEUR
resident's permit	PERMIS DE SEJOUR
respectable people	GENS DE BIEN
rest	REPOS
restaurant	BRASSERIE
reticent	BOUTONNE
reversal of policy	VOLTE-FACE
review	CRITIQUE
revolutionary	SANS-CULOTTE
—calendar	(see calendar above)
—fighters	NATIONAL GUARD
—hymn	MARSEILLAISE
—song	CARMAGNOLE
rhymed words	BOUTS RIMES
rice	RIZ
rich	
—rhyme	RIME RICHE
—soup	BISQUE
right	DROIT
—of superior	DROIT DE SEIGNEUR
—thinking	BIEN PENSANT
—to work	DROIT AU TRAVAIL
—word	MOT JUSTE
river	FLEUVE, RIVIERE
rivers	(see separate entry)
road	CHEMIN
—along cliff face	CORNICHE
—side cafe	BUVETTE
rock	ROCHE(R)
—angle	DIEDRE
—peak	AIGUILLE
—tripe	TRIPE DE ROCHE
rocky edge	ARETE
roguish	ESPIEGLE
roguishly	EN BADINANT
roll (bread)	BRIOCHE, CROISSANT
rope	
—for gun-carriage	PROLONGE
—ladder	ETRIER
—soled shoe	ESPADRILLE
rose-coloured	COULEUR DE ROSE
rough	
—draft	EBAUCHE
—music	CHARIVARI
—paper for painting	PAPIER TORCHON
—sketch	CROQUIS
royal warrant	LETTRE DE CACHET
rudeness	GROSSIERETE
ruin	BOULEVERSEMENT
rumour	ON-DIT
running	COURANT
rural festival	FETE CHAMPETRE
sacred monster	MONSTRE SACRE
sailor	MATELOT
Saint's day	(JOUR DE) FETE
salmon	SAUMON
salt	SEL
sandbank	BANC
sandy heath	LANDE
sauce	HOLLANDAISE
saucy	RISQUE
saunterer	FLANEUR
savouries before meal	HORS D'OEUVRES
say true/truth	VOIR DIRE
scamp	FRIPON
scatterbrain	TETE FOLLE
scent	
—bottle	FLACON
—of game when high	FUMET
school	ECOLE, LYCEE
scored against	TOUCHE
scraper	GRATTOIR, RACLOIR
scuffle	BAGARRE
sea	MER
—man	MATELOT
—sickness	MAL DE MER
seaport without duties	ENTREPOT
seat of member of French Academy	FAUTEUIL
second	SECONDE
secondary school	LYCEE
see	VOIR
—you again soon	A BIENTOT
seize	GRIPPER
select group	CORPS D'ELITE
self	
—criticism	AUTO-CRITIQUE
—esteem	AMOUR PROPRE
—possession	APLOMB, SANG-FROID
—seeker	ARRIVISTE
—styled	SOI-DISANT
sending back	RENVOI, RENVOY
senior	AINE(E)
sensation of having seen something before	DEJA VU
serious	
—love affair	GRANDE PASSION
—man	HOMME SERIEUX
seriously	AU SERIEUX
servant	BONNE, VALET
served with flaming liquor	FLAMBE(E)

set of ornaments	PARURE
setting	MILIEU, MONTURE
settled matter	CHOSE JUGEE
shady	LOUCHE
shaft	
—in glacier	MOULIN
—of a column	TIGE
sharp-shooter	TIRAILLEUR
sheath	ETUI
sheep	MOUTON
shirker	EMBUSQUE
shock troops	ENFANTS PERDUS
shooting contest	TIR
shop	BOUTIQUE
—keeper	BOURGEOIS
short	
—and stiff (hair)	EN BROSSE
—literary composition	MORCEAU
—story	CONTE, NOUVELLE
—sword	ESTOC
showy splendour	ECLAT
Shrove Tuesday	MARDI GRAS
shudder	FRISSON
sick	MALADE
sickness	MAL, MALAISE
silk	SOIE
silkworm disease	PEBRINE
silly saying	FADAISE
simply	TOUT COURT
singed	FLAMBE(E)
sir	MONSIEUR
siren	FEMME FATALE
sister	SOEUR
sketch	ESQUISSE
ski trail	PISTE
skirmish	ESCARMOUCHE
skirmisher	TIRAILLEUR, VOLTIGEUR
skull-cap	CALOTTE
skylight	ABAT-JOUR
slacker	EMBUSQUE
slang	ARGOT
sleeping	
—berth on train	COUCHETTE
—car	WAGON-LIT
sleeve	MANCHE
—less jacket	JUPON
sleight-of-hand	LEGER DE MAIN
slice(s) of	
—bread and butter	TARTINE(S)
—veal, larded	FRICANDEAU(X)
slope	COTE(AU)
small	PETIT(E)
—and	
cosy	INTIME
dainty	MIGNON(NE)
elegant	BIJOU

—cafe	ESTAMINET
—country house	COTTAGE ORNE
—dish	COCOTTE
—house	MAISON(NETTE)
—opening in wall etc	GUICHET
—pie	BOUCHE
—shot	MITRAILLE
smart	CHIC
smitten	EPRIS(E)
smooth	
—sauce	VELOUTE
—surfaced woollen	FOULE
snail	ESCARGOT
sniper	FRANC-TIREUR
so	
—called	SOI-DISANT
—much	TANT
the	
—better	TANT MIEUX
—worse	TANT PIS
society	SOCIETE
sofa for two, facing	TETE-A-TETE
soft	
—artificial fabric	SURAH
—pear	BEURRE
—rosette	CHOU
soldier	POILU
sombre	MORNE
something	
—composed for	
a special occasion	PIECE D'OCCASION
—disagreeable	DESAGREMENT
—found	OBJET TROUVE
—that deceives the eye	TROMPE L'OEIL
son	FILS
song	CHANSON
soul	AME
sound and light	SON ET LUMIERE
sounding-board	ABAT-VOIX
soup	
—bowl	ECUELLE
—without solid pieces	PUREE
south of France	MIDI
spade	PALETTE
spangle	PAILLETTE
spank	BLUETTE
special passport	LAISSEZ-PASSER
speculator	BOURSIER
spire	FLECHE
spirit	ENTRAIN, ESPRIT
spit	ROTISSERIE
splendid edition	EDITION DE LUXE
spoilt child	ENFANT GATE(E)
sponge cake	BRIOCHE
spray of jewels	AIGRETTE
spring	PRINTEMPS

squinting	LOUCHE
S-shaped couch	VIS-A-VIS
stable	ECURIE
staff of army, etc	ETAT-MAJOR
stag's trail	ABATURE
stage	ETAPE
—scene	MISE-EN-SCENE
stage-coach	DILIGENCE
stained glass	VITRAIL
staircase	ESCALIER
star	ETOILE
state	ETAT
—approval	AGREMENT
—pawnshop	MONT-DE-PIETE
—prison	BASTILLE
statesman	HOMME D'ETAT
stationery	PAPETERIE
steak	BIFTEK
—cut from ribs	ENTRECOTE
step	PAS, DEMARCHE
stew	CASSOULET, DAUBE, RAGOUT
stewed beef	BOUILLI
stirrup	ETRIER
stocking	BAS
Stone Age axe	COUP DE POING
stonecrop	ORPIN
stop thief!	AU VOLEUR
storehouse	ENTREPOT, ETAPE
storey	ETAGE
stout(ness)	EMBONPOINT
straight in the face	EN FACE
strange	ETRANGER(E)
stratagem of war	RUSE DE GUERRE
straw	PAILLE
strawberry	FRAISE
street	RUE
—Arab	GAMIN
striking	FRAPPANT
—effect	ECLAT
stroking massage	EFFLEURAGE
stroller	FLANEUR
strong	
—broth	BOUILLON
—punishment	PEINE FORTE ET DURE
students' quarter in Paris	QUARTIER LATIN
studied	VOULU
studio	ATELIER
stuffed	FARCI
stupid	
—blundering	ETOURDERIE
—person	BETE
stupidity	BETISE
style	CHIC
—of 1795-99	DIRECTOIRE
stylish	CHICHI
subdivision of a Department	ARONDISSEMENT
subdued light	DEMI-JOUR
subject	
—lacking novelty	VIEUX JEU
—of talk	SUR LE TAPIS
subscription	ABONNEMENT
substantial course	PIECE DE RESISTANCE
suburb	BANLIEUE
—beyond walls	FAUBOURG
subversive stroke	COUP D'ETAT
subway	METRO
success	SUCCES
—of approval	SUCCES D'ESTIME
—with wild enthusiasm	SUCCES FOU
successful	
—candidate	AGREGE
—stroke	GRAND COUP
sudden	
—and overwhelming	FOUDROYANT
—change (of views)	VOLTE-FACE
—descent	DEGRINGOLADE
—outburst	BOUTADE
—turn, as in play	COUP DE THEATRE
suddenly	A L'IMPROVISTE
sufficient rhyme	RIME SUFFISANTE
suggestive	RISQUE
sulking	BOUDERIE
summer	ETE
summit	CIME
sumptuous	DE LUXE
superfluous	DE TROP
superior	
—power	FORCE MAJEURE
—wine	VDQS
supplementary race	REPECHAGE
support	APPUI, APPUY
supporter of Bourbons	ROYALISTE
surfeited	BLASE
swaddling-clothes	MAILLOT
swamp	MARAIS
sweet	DOUX, DOUCE
sweetmeat	BONBON
—box	BONBONNIERE
system of drill	MARTINET
systematically arranged	RAISONNE
table	
—cloth	NAPPE
—wine	VIN ORDINAIRE
tact	SAVOIR-FAIRE
tactless(ness)	GAUCHE(RIE)
take	
—leave	CONGE
—one's bearings	S'ORIENTER
"talking drums"	ARMES PARLANTES
tart with tomatoes, etc	PISSALADIERE
tasty morsel	BONNE BOUCHE
tavern	BISTRO

tax on salt	GABELLE	title of rank	MONSEIGNEUR
tea with dancing	THE DANSANT	to	
team		—a	
—in sport	EQUIPE	certainty	A COUP SUR
—of cars	ECURIE	nicety	A POINT
technical college	GRANDE ECOLE	—arms!	AUX ARMES
tedious passage (in book)	LONGUEUR	—mere loss	EN PURE PERTE
teller of anecdotes	RACONTEUR	—no purpose	EN PURE PERTE
tempest	BOURRASQUE	—take leave	POUR PRENDRE CONGE, PPC
temporary lodging	PIED-A-TERRE	—the	
tender passion	BELLE PASSION	bitter end	A L'OUTRANCE
tenderloin	FILET	death	A L'OUTRANCE
territorial division	COMMUNE	highest degree	PAR EXCELLENCE
thanks to God	GRACE A DIEU	left	A GAUCHE
that		right	A DROITE
—is		very end	JUSQU'AU BOUT
all	VOILA TOUT	—your health!	A VOTRE SANTE
to say	C'EST A DIRE	tobacco sold by government	REGIE
—one	CELUI, CELLE	toilet-water	EAU DE COLOGNE
that's life!	C'EST LA VIE	tongue	LANGUE
the		too	
—blues	CAFARD	—late	APRES COUP
—buttocks	DERRIERE	—much	TROP
—Low Countries	LES PAYS-BAS	top	
theatre		—fashion-house	GRAND ATELIER
—box	BAIGNOIR	—to bottom	DE HAUT EN BAS
—stall	FAUTEUIL	total	PUR SANG
theatrical extravaganza	FEERIE	totalisator	PARI-MUTUEL
there is/there are	VOILA	touched	TOUCHE
thick		tourney	PAS D'ARMES
—end of undercut	FILET MIGNON	town	BOURG, VILLE
—foliage	BOCAGE	—hall	HOTEL DE VILLE
—grilled steak	CHATEAUBRIAND	—house	MAISON DE VILLE
—soup	POTAGE	toy reed-pipe	MIRLITON
thin glassware	MOUSSELINE	tradesman's stock	BOUTIQUE
thing already done	FAIT ACCOMPLI	traditional (art)	POMPIER
think	PENSER	traffic warden	PERVENCHE
third estate	TIERS-ETAT	train	MANEGE
this	CE, CET, CETTE	—of attendants	CORTEGE
thoroughbred	PUR SANG	tramp	CLOCHARD
thoroughly	A FOND	travelling	
thou	TOI, TU	companion	COMPAGNON DE VOYAGE
thoughtless	ETOURDI(E)	treachery	TRAHISON
thousand	MILLE	treason	TRAHISON
three-cornered hat	CHAPEAU BRAS	trench	CUNETTE, CUVETTE
	TRICORNE	triangular insertion in skirt	GODET
thrill	FRISSON	trickery	LEGER DE MAIN
through	A TRAVERS	triumphal arch	ARC DE TRIOMPHE
thrown	JETE	truly	VRAIMENT
thundering	FOUDROYANT	tun	TONNEAU
ticket-office window	GUICHET	turkey	DINDE, DINDON
tide-gate	ABOIDEAU, ABOITEAU	turmoil	TRACASSERIE
tilt	PAS D'ARMES	turned up	RETROUSSE
tip	POURBOIRE	turning round	VOLTE-FACE
—of toe	POINTE	tutor	REPETITEUR
titbit	BONNE BOUCHE	twaddle	FADAISE

twenty	VINGT
—one	VINGT-ET-UN
twilight	DEMI-JOUR
twin	JUMELLE
two men and two women	PARTIE CARREE
U-turn	VOLTE-FACE
unaffected	NAIF, NAIVE
unconstrained	EN PANTOUFLES
unconstraint	LAISSER-ALLER
	LAISSEZ-ALLER
uncoventional person	ENFANT TERRIBLE
under discussion	EN L'AIR, SUR LE TAPIS
undercut of beef	FILET
underground	
—chamber	SOUTERRAIN
—railway	METRO
understanding	ENTENTE
undertaker's parlour	CHAPELLE ARDENTE
undress (garment)	DESHABILLE
uneasiness	MALAISE
unembarrassed	DEGAGE
unexpectedly	A L'IMPROVISTE
unfit to fight	HORS DE COMBAT
uninspired (art)	POMPIER
unkempt	MAL SOIGNE(E)
unknown (person)	INCONNU(E)
unoriginal material	DEJA VU
unpleasant moment	MAUVAIS MOMENT
unpleasantness	ESCLANDRE
unravelling of plot	DENOUEMENT
unrestrained	DEGAGE
unsuccessful	MANQUE
unsuitable marriage	MESALLIANCE
unsweetened	BRUT
untrustworthy friend	AMI DE COUR
unwanted	DE TROP
unwilling	MALGRE
up to date	A LA PAGE
upon	SUR
upper middle class	HAUTE BOURGEOISIE
uproar	EMEUTE
upstart	NOUVEAU RICHE
	PARVENU
urchin	GAMIN
usher	HUISSIER
valiant knight	PREUX CHEVALIER
valley	VALLEE
varnishing	VERNISSAGE
vat of blended wine	CUVEE
veal	VEAU
verisimilitude	VRAISEMBLANCE
verse	VERS
very	TRES
—best	CREME DE LA CREME
—dear	AU POIDS DE L'OR
—small amount	SOUPCON

vine	
—grower	VIGNERON
—yard	CRU
violent epilepsy	GRAND MAL
visiting card	CARTE DE VISITE
visitor's permit	CARNET
vivacious young working-girl	GRISETTE
waiter	GARCON
walk	MARCHER
wall	MUR
wandering minstrel	JONGLEUR
want	BESOIN
war	GUERRE
—to the	
death	GUERRE A MORT
uttermost	GUERRE A L'OUTRANCE
warbler	FAUVETTE
warden	CONCIERGE
warehouse	ENTREPOT
warhorse	CHEVAL DE BATAILLE
warmed-up dish	RECHAUFFE
warmth of manner	EMPRESSEMENT
warning	EN GARDE
wartime guerrilla	MAQUISARD
—group	MAQUIS
watch-chain ornament	BRELOQUE
water	EAU
—bottle	CARAFE
—fall	CHUTE
—sprinkler	ASPERSOIR
wave (sea)	ONDE
way of speaking	FACON DE PARLER
weariness	ENNUI
weight	
—1 pound (old)	LIVRE
—1 cwt	QUINTAL
—small	MG, MILLIGRAMME
—10 milligrams	CENTIGRAMME, CG
—100 milligrams	DECIGRAMME, DG
—200 milligrams	(METRIC) CAR(R)AT
—10 grams	DECAGRAMME, DG
—100 grams	HECTOGRAMME, HG
—1000 grams	KG, KILOGRAMME
—1000 kilograms	MILLIER, T, TONNE
	TONNEAU
well	BIEN
—designed	BIEN ENTENDU
—done!	A LA BONNE HEURE
—groomed	SOIGNE(E)
—informed	AU COURANT, AU FAIT
—loved	BIEN-AIME
—mannered	BIEN ELEVE
—shod	BIEN CHAUSSE
—versed	BIEN ENTENDU
well-to-do classes	CLASSES AISEES
what	QUE

what's the good of it	A QUOI BON
whatever the consequences	QUAND MEME
while waiting	EN ATTENDANT
white	
—porcelain	BLANC DE CHINE
—wine	VIN BLANC
who	QUI
—goes there?	QUI VA LA
whole	TOUT
wholesale	EN BLOC
wholly yours	TOUT A VOUS
wide road	BOULEVARD
widow	VEUVE
wig	CHEVELURE, PERRUQUE
—maker	PERRUQUIER
wild laughter	FOU RIRE
William pear	BON CHRETIEN
willing	BON GRE
willy-nilly	MALGRE LUI, MALGRE MOI
wine	VIN
	(see separate entry)
—from famous vineyards	GRAND CRU
	LES GRANDS VINS
—waiter	SOMMELIER
wing	AILE
wink	OEILLADE
winter	HIVER
wiping aside of ink	RETROUSSAGE
wit	BEL ESPRIT
witticism	JEU D'ESPRIT
with	AVEC, PAR
—a giant stride	A PAS DE GEANT
—air of superiority	DE HAUT EN BAS
—cheese	AU FROMAGE
—child	ENCEINTE
—closed doors	A HUIS CLOS
—justice	A BON DROIT
—open arms	A BRAS OUVERTS
—pleasure	AVEC PLAISIR
—reference to	A PROPOS
—regard to	VIS-A-VIS
within range/reach	A PORTEE
without	SANS
—breeches	SANS CULOTTE
—care	SANS SOUCI
—ceremony	EN FAMILLE
	SANS CEREMONIE
—courtesy	SANS PHRASES
—phrases	SANS PHRASES
—preface	TOUT COURT
—reality	EN L'AIR
—restraint	SANS GENE
—serifs	SANSERIF
—worry	SANS SOUCI
witty saying	(BON) MOT
wolf-hole	TROU-DE-LOUP

woman	FEMME
—affecting over-refinement	PRECIEUSE
—greatly involved in love affairs	GRANDE AMOUREUSE
—of the world	FEMME DU MONDE
wonderfully	A MERVEILLE
woods	BOIS
wooden shoe	SABOT
woodland	BOCAGE
word	MOT
—fitting context	MOT JUSTE
work	
—applied or laid on	APPLIQUE
—box	NECESSAIRE
—of artist, etc	OEUVRE
—shop	ATELIER
worker	OUVRIER(E)
worn out	EPUISE(E)
worse and worse	DE PIS EN PIS
worst shift	PIS ALLER
worthless	MAUVAIS(E)
—fellow	MAUVAIS SUJET
would-be	SOI-DISANT
woven	BROCHE
writer of farces	FARCEUR
writing	
—book	CAHIER
—desk	ECRITOIRE
written statement	PROCES-VERBAL
yesterday	HIER
you	TOI, TU, VOUS
young	JEUNE
—love	JEUNE AMOUR
—man kept by an older woman	GIGOLO

fruit

Actinidia	CHINESE GOOSEBERRY
	KIWI FRUIT
African	A(C)KEE, BITO
	CAPE GOOSEBERRY, DATE
	DIKA, HOTTENTOT FIG
	LYCHEE, MIRACLE FRUIT
	NAARTJE, NAR(R)AS
	NARTJIE, PASSION FRUIT, SHEA NUT
	STRAWBERRY-TOMATO, WILD MANGO
aggregate fruit(s)	ACINUS(ACINI)
alligator-pear	AVOCADO
American	BLUEBERRY, CHOKEBERRY
	CRANBERRY, DEERBERRY
	JUNEBERRY, HUCKLEBERRY
	MARIONBERRY, MAYAPPLE
	MIN(N)EOLA, SAL(L)AL-BERRY
	SASKATOON, SHADBERRY
Ananas	PINEAPPLE
apple	POME
	(see also separate entry)

Arabian cherry	MAHALEB	cowberry	IDAEAN VINE
Arctic	CROWBERRY		RED WHORTLEBERRY
Asian	BITO, DATE	crushed apples	POMACE
aubergine	BRINJAL, EGG PLANT	custard-apple	CHERIMOYA, SOURSOP
	MAD APPLE	date-plum	PERSIMMON, SHARON FRUIT
Australian	GEEBUNG, NONDA	dewberry	BLACKBERRY, RUBUS
	NONDO, QUANDONG	dog-rose	HIP
avocado	ALLIGATOR-PEAR	dried grape	CURRANT, RAISIN, SULTANA
	AQUACATE	drupel	FRUITLET
azarole	MEDLAR	dry fruit	
Barberry fig	INDIAN FIG	—containing several seeds	LEGUME
	PRICKLY PEAR	—from two carpels	
bilberry	BLAEBERRY, WHINBERRY	long	SILIQUA, SILIQUE
	WHORT(LEBERRY)	short	SILICULA, SILIC(U)LE
bitter orange	SEVILLE ORANGE	—indehiscent	CARYOPSIS, NUT
black		—not splitting	INDEHISCENT
—berry	BLACK CURRANT	—one-seeded	ACHENE
	BRAMBLE-BERRY	—part of schizocarp	MERICARP
	DEWBERRY, RUBUS	—splitting	DEHISCENT
—currant	RIBES, QUINSY BERRY	along one line	FOLLICLE
—thorn	SLOE	into	
blaeberry	(see bilberry above)	—several parts	SCHIZOCARP
blueberry	HUCKLEBERRY	—two parts	CREMOCARP
bottle gourd	DUDI	—with hard shell	NUT
bramble	BLACKBERRY, DEWBERRY	dry-fruited	BARREN STRAWBERRY
brinjal	AUBERGINE	durian	JACKFRUIT
buckthorn	JUJUBE, RHEINBERRY	East Indian	CARAMBOLA
	RHINEBERRY		COROMANDEL GOOSEBERRY
cactus fruit	PRICKLY-PEAR, SAGUARO		EMBLIC (MYROBALAN)
candied chestnut	MARRON GLACE		MANGO, MARKING-NUT
Cape gooseberry	PHYSALIS		ROSE-APPLE, STAR FRUIT
	STRAWBERRY-TOMATO		TAMPOE
Channel Islands	BABACO	edible chestnut	MARRON
cherry		egg plant	AUBERGINE, BRINJAL
—bitter	MORELLO		MAD APPLE
—plum	MYROBALAN	Egyptian melon	ABDALAVI
—sweet	MAZ(Z)ARD	Eurasian	SOUR CHERRY
—wild	GEAN	fae-berry	FEA-BERRY, GOOSEBERRY
Chinese	KUMQUAT, LEECHEE	Ficus	FIG
	LICHEE, LI(T)CHI	fleshy fruit	POME, SARCOCARP, SOROSIS
	LONGAN, LOQUAT	foul-smelling	DURIAN, JACKFRUIT
	LUNGAN, LYCHEE	fragrant	
	MANDARIN(E), SATSUMA	—pear	MUSK-PEAR
	WAMPEE	—plum	MUSK-PLUM
—date	JUJUBE	from vines	GRAPE
—gooseberry	ACTINIDIA, CARAMBOLE	fruit-eating	CARPOPHAGOUS
	KIWI FRUIT		FRUGIVOROUS
—lantern	CAPE GOOSEBERRY	fruit-stone	PIT, PUTAMEN
	PHYSALIS	full of seeds	FIG, POMEGRANATE
—orange	MANDARIN(E), SATSUMA	gooseberry	FAE-BERRY, FEA-BERRY
—pear	TIENTSIN-YA		RIBES
citrus	BERGAMOT, CITRON	—US	WORCESTER-BERRY
	GRAPEFRUIT, LEMON	gourd	BABACO, CALABASH, SQUASH
	LIME, ORANGE	granadilla	GRENADILLO, PASSION-FRUIT
Colombia	TAMARILLO	grape	
compound	SYNCARP	—dried	RAISIN

—dried, seedless	CURRANT, SULTANA
hard	
—rinded	GOURD, POMEGRANATE
—water melon	CITRON
having	
—fruit in special casing	ANGIOCARPOUS
—leathery epicarp	HESPERIDIUM
—many	
lobules	AGGREGATE FRUIT
	COLLECTIVE FRUIT
	MULTIPLE FRUIT
seeds	BERRY, CAPSULE
—in hard epicarp	PEPO
—seeds in central capsule	POME
—single hard stone	DRUPE
—stone	
easily separated	
from the flesh	FREESTONE
not easily separated	
from the flesh	CLINGSTONE
hawthorn	HAW
hedgerow	ELDERBERRY, HAW, HIP
hindberry	RASPBERRY, RUBUS
huckleberry	BLUEBERRY
hybrid	
—blackberry	JOSTABERRY
x raspberry	BOYSENBERRY
	LOGANBERRY
x dewberry	YOUNGBERRY
—boysenberry x tayberry	HILDABERRY
—citron x orange	CITRANGE
—orange x tangerine	ORTANIQUE
—tangerine	
x grapefruit	UGLI (FRUIT)
x pomelo	TANGELO
Idaean vine	COWBERRY
	RED WHORTLEBERRY
Indian	B(A)EL, BENGAL QUINCE
	BHEL, CARAMBOLA, DURIAN
	MYROBALAN
—fig	BARBARY FIG, PRICKLY PEAR
Indonesian	AMBOINA BERRY
inner layer	ENDOCARP
Israel	KUMQUAT, SHARON FRUIT
jackfruit	DURIAN
Jamaican	HOG-PLUM, KIWANO
Japanese	LOQUAT, KAKI, NASHI
juice	SYRUP
jujube	CHINESE DATE
kiwi fruit	ACTINIDIA
	CHINESE GOOSEBERRY
large damson	DAMASCENE
	DAMSON-PLUM
like	
—apple	CRAB, MEDLAR
—banana	PLANTAIN

lime (Philippines)	CALAMANSI
little drupe	DRUPEL(ET)
locust tree	CAROB
love apple	TOMATO
Malayan	DURIAN, MANGOSTEEN
	RAMBUTAN
Malaysian	TAMARILLO
medlar	AZAROLE
melon	
—African	WATER-MELON
—American	WATER-MELON
—common melon	MUSK-MELON
—Egyptian	ABDALAVI
—French	CHARENTAIS
—hard water melon	CITRON
—horned	KIWANO
—Israel	GALIA
—like	NAR(R)AS
—musk melon	CANTALOUP(E)
—New Zealand	KIWANO
—oval	HONEYDEW
—segmented	CANTALOUP(E)
—small	CHARENTAIS, OGEN
—Spanish	FUTURA, GALIA
	PIEL DA SAPO, PIEL DE SAPO
—striped	TIGER MELON
—tree-melon	PAPAYA, PAW-PAW
—winter melon	CAS(S)ABA
—yellow winter	CASABA
moorland	BILBERRY, BLAEBERRY
	CRANBERRY, CROWBERRY
	WHINBERRY, WHORT(LEBERRY)
Morus	MULBERRY
mulberry	SYCAMINE
naseberry	NEESBERRY, NISBERRY
	SAPODILLA (PLUM)
Nephelium	LONGAN, LUNGAN
New Zealand	KIWANO, KIWI FRUIT
oil-producing	BERGAMOT, OLIVE
Olea	OLIVE
orange	
—bitter	SEVILLE
—Brazilian	NAVEL ORANGE
—Chinese	MANDARIN(E), SATSUMA
—Israeli	JAFFA, SHAMOUTI, TOPAZ
—large	JAFFA, SHADDOCK
—Maltese	BLOOD ORANGE
—mandarin	CLOVE ORANGE
	NOBLE ORANGE
—North African	TANGERINE
—oval	EGG ORANGE
—Portuguese	LISBON
—red-fleshed	BLOOD ORANGE
—small	CLEMENTINE, MANDARIN(E)
	SATSUMA, TANGERINE
—South African	NAARTJE, NARTJIE

—Spanish	CLAUSELLINA, SEVILLE
—type	HESPERIDIUM
—yielding oil	BERGAMOT
orange-coloured	AMBARELLA, APRICOT
Oriental	POMEGRANATE, POMELO
	SEBESTEN, SHADDOCK
outer layer	EPICARP, HULL, HUSK
	SHELL, ZEST
ovaries of several	
flowers on fleshy	
axis	COENOCARPIUM
papaw	PAPAYA, PAW-PAW
	TREE MELON
partition(s) in pod	REPLUM(REPLA)
passion-fruit	GRANADILLA
	GRENADILLO
peach	VICTORINE
—smooth-skinned	NECTARINE
peach-plum	PUPUNHA
pear	POME
—American	SECKLE, SHAKESPEAR
	RED-GLEEK
—Chinese	TIENTSIN-YA
—early	JARGONELLE
—Italian	PASSACRASSANA
—Japanese	NASHI
—old	CARMELITE, MALAKATOONE
	MELLICOTTON, MELOCOTO(O)N
	POPRIN, POPPERING
—soft	BEURRE
—varieties	ANSON, BARTLETT
	BERGAMOT, BOSC, CATILLAC
	CLAPP'S FAVOURITE
	COLMAR, CONCORDE, CONFERENCE
	(DOYENNE DU) COMICE
	GUYOT, JOSEPHINE, KIEFFER
	LAXTON'S FAVOURITE
	PACKMAN, PASSACRANA
	SECKEL, WILLIAMS
—winter	NELI(E)S
persimmon	DATE-PLUM, SHARON FRUIT
Peruvian	CHERIMOYA, CHERIMOYER
	CHIRIMOYA
Philippines	KALUMPIT
—lime	CALAMANSI
—plantain	ABACA
Physalis	CAPE GOOSEBERRY
	CHINESE LANTERN
pineapple	ANANA(S)
pink	RASPBERRY, STRAWBERRY
pips in fleshy container	SYCOMIUM
plantain (Philippines)	ABACA
plum	
—genus	ALMOND, APRICOT, PEACH
—green	GREENGAGE
—Oriental	SEBESTEN
—purple	DAMSON, VICTORIA
—red	FRIAR, ROYSON
—variety	MYROBALAN
pome	APPLE, PEAR
pomegranate	PUNIC APPLE
pomelo	GRAPEFRUIT, SHADDOCK
prickly pear	BARBARY FIG, INDIAN FIG
	TUNA
production without	
fertilisation	PARTHENOCARPY
Punic apple	POMEGRANATE
purple	MULBERRY
quandong	PEACH
quince	
—Cydonia	QUINCE
—Indian	B(A)EL, BENGAL QUINCE
	BHEL
—Japonica	JAPANESE QUINCE
quinsy-berry	BLACK CURRANT, RIBES
raspberry	HINDBERRY, RUBUS
red	
—currant	
American	SALMON-BERRY
Chinese	WINEBERRY
Scottish	RIZZAR(D), RIZZART
	RIZZER
—whortleberry	IDAEAN VINE, COWBERRY
Rheinberry/Rhineberry	BUCKTHORN
Ribes	BLACK CURRANT
	GOOSEBERRY
	RED CURRANT
	WHITE CURRANT
roebuck-berry	ROE-BLACKBERRY
	STONE BRAMBLE
rose	HIP
Rubus	BLACKBERRY, BRAMBLEBERRY
	DEWBERRY, RASPBERRY
salmon-berry (US)	RASPBERRY
sapodilla	SAPOTA
—plum	NASEBERRY
	NEESBERRY, NISBERRY
saskatoon	SERVICEBERRY
Scandinavian	CLOUDBERRY
serviceberry	SASKATOON
shadbush	JUNEBERRY
shaddock	POMELO
small fruit(s) in	
aggregate fruit	ACINUS(ACINI)
smooth-skinned peach	NECTARINE
soft fruit	BLACKBERRY
	BOYSENBERRY
	BRAMBLE, LOGANBERRY
	RASPBERRY, STRAWBERRY
	SUNBERRY, TAYBERRY
	TUMMELBERRY
South African	(*see* African *above*)

South American	ANANAS, BABACO
	CALABASH, CARAMBOLA
	GUAVA, LUCUMA
	PINEAPPLE, STAR FRUIT
	TAMARILLO
South Sea islands	BREADFRUIT
sour cherry	MORELLO
Spanish orange	CLAUSELLINA, SEVILLE
squash	(*see* **vegetables**)
star fruit	CARAMBOLA
stem	RHUBARB
stewed in sugar syrup	COMPOTE
stone	PIT, PUTAMEN
—bramble	ROE-BLACKBERRY
	ROEBUCK-BERRY
—fruit	APRICOT, CHERRY
	NECTARINE, PEACH
	PLUM
—in fruit	PUTAMEN
strawberry-tomato	CAPE GOOSEBERRY
sub-tropical	AVOCADO (PEAR)
	CHINESE GOOSEBERRY
	KIWI FRUIT
sweet cherry	MAZ(Z)ARD
Thai	ROSE APPLE
tomato	LOVE APPLE
tropical	ALLIGATOR-PEAR, ANANAS
	AVOCADO, BANANA, BREADNUT
	CRAB-NUT, GRANADILLA
	GRENADILLO, GUAVA, LIME
	MANGO(STEEN), PAPAYA, PA(W)PAW
	PASSION FRUIT, PINEAPPLE
	PINGUIN, SAPETILLO
	TAMARIND, TREE MELON
types	
—dry	
in pods	LEGUME, LOMENTUM
one-seeded	ACHENE, ACH(A)ENIUM
many-seeded	ETAERIO
—fleshy, from many flowers	SOROSIS
—succulent	
one-seeded	DRUPE
many-seeded	BERRY
Vaccinium	CRANBERRY
velvet-skinned	PEACH
wall of fruit	PERICARP
—inner layer	ENDOCARP
—outer layer	EPICARP, EXOCARP
West Indian	A(C)KEE, ANANA(S)
	ANCHOVY-PEAR
	BARBADOS GOOSEBERRY
	BREADFRUIT, BULLOCK'S HEART
	CHERIMOYA, COCOPLUM, CUSTARD APPLE
	GENIPAP, GOLDEN APPLE, GRENADILLA
	GUAVA, MAMMEE (APPLE), MANGO
	NASEBERRY, PASSION FRUIT, PAW-PAW

	PENGUIN, PINGUIN, SAPODILLA (PLUM)
	SAPOTA, SOURSOP, STAR APPLE
	SWEETSOP, UGLI
	(*see also* tropical *above*)
whinberry	(*see* bilberry *above*)
whort(leberry)	(*see* bilberry *above*)
wild	
—apple	CRAB
—cherry	GEAN
—damson	BULLACE
—fig	CAPRIFIG, GOAT FIG
—plum	BULLACE
winged	SAMARA
winter melon	CAS(S)ABA
Worcester-berry (US)	GOOSEBERRY
yellow	BANANA, PLANTAIN
fungi	MYCOPHYTA
including: lichen	
mushrooms	
algal part of lichen	PHYCOBIONT
American	TUCKAHOE
attacking	
—grasses	GIBBERELLA
—maple	RHYTISMA
—skin	DERMAPHYTE
—trees	HONEY FUNGUS
bacteria, fungi and algae	THALLOPHYTA
base of stem	VOLVA
black	DEAD MAN'S FINGERS
—and brown	BACHELOR'S BUTTONS
	POPE'S BUTTONS
bluish-grey to brown	OYSTER (MUSHROOM)
brown to brick-red	BOLETUS, CEPE, CEPS
causing disease in plants	BLIGHT
	MILDEW, RUST, SMUT
classes	ASCOMYCETES, BASIDIOMYCETES
	GASTEROMYCETES
	FUNGI IMPERFECTI, MYXOMYCETES
	PHYCOMYCETES, ZYGOMYCETES
covering of cap	SCALES
division	MYCOPHYTA
dry rot	MERULIUS
edible	BEEFSTEAK FUNGUS, BLEWITS
	BOLETUS, CEPE, CEPS, CHAMPIGNON
	CHANTERELLE, JEW'S EAR
	LAWYER'S WIG, MUSHROOM
	OYSTER, PARASOL, PENNY BUN
	PUFFBALL, STINKHORN, TRUFFLE
	TUCKAHOE, WOOD BLEWITS
—lichen	LECANORA
fairy-ring mushroom	SCOTCH BONNET
fungus in symbiotic	
relationship with	
—algae	LICHEN
—roots of higher plants	MICOR(R)HIZA
Geaster	EARTH-STAR

genus	AMANITA, PEZIZA
	SAPROLEGNIA
gill-fungi	AGARICACEAE
greyish to pale brown	BIRCH POLYPORE
	RAZORSTROP FUNGUS
growing on elder	JEW'S EAR
head	CAP, PILEUS
higher fungi	EUMYCETES
Hydnum	JUPITER'S BEARD
knob on cap	UMBO
lichen	CETRARIA, LECANORALES
—flat	FOLIOSE
—reproductive organ	SOREDIUM
—upright	FRUTICOSE
—used for dye	CROTAL, CROTTLE
manna lichen	LECANORA
membrane joining cap to stalk	VEIL, VELUM
mildews	ASCOMYCETES
moulds	ASCOMYCETES
mushroom	CHAMPIGNON
mushroom-like	TOADSTOOL
mushrooms	AGARICACEAE
orange	ORANGE CUP
plant producing	
zygospores	ZYGOPHYTE
poisonous	DEATH CAP, FLY AGARIC
	PANTHER CAP
	DESTROYING ANGEL
Puccinia	RUST
puffballs	LYCOPERDALES
	SCLERODERMATALES
red	
—or liver-coloured	BEEFSTEAK FUNGUS
—with white spots	FLY AGARIC
reddish brown	THE DECEIVER
resting stage	SCLEROTIUM
ring on stem	ANNULUS
roots	MYCELIUM
rust(s)	PUCCINIA, URIDINALES
sac fungi	ENDOMYCETALES
seed	SPORE
skin on cap	PELLICLE
slime fungi	MYXOMYCOPHYTA
	SLIME MOULDS
spore	
—bearing area	HYMENIUM
—from union of	
adjacent buds	ZYGOSPERM
	ZYGOSPORE
spreading root system	MYCELIUM
star-shaped	EARTH-STAR, GEASTER
stink-horns	PHALLALES
thallus of fungus	MYCELIUM
thread of mycelium	HYPHA
truffles	ASCOMYCETES
underground	TRUFFLE, TUCKAHOE

vanes on underside	GILLS, LAMELLAE
weeping	WEEPING WIDOW
whitish	COMMON EARTHBALL
	MUSHROOM, SLIMY BEECHCAP
	STINKHORN, WOOD WITCH
woolly growth	MOULD
yeasts	MYCOTA
yellow	COMMON YELLOW RUSSULA
	SULPHUR TUFT
yellow-green algae	CONFERVA, HETEROCONT
	HETEROKONT
	(*see also* **biology**)

fur

American marten	SKUNK
Arctic marten	SABLE
cloak	PILCH
coypu	NUTRIA
ermine (summer)	ROSELET
garment lined with fur	PELISSE
goat (underfleece)	PASH(I)M, PASHMINA
grey	CHINCHILLA, GRIS(E)
hat of fur	BEAVER, CASTOR
hood of fur	AMICE
lamb	
—Crimea	CRIMMER, KRIMMER
—curled	ASTRAKHAN
mercury treatment	SECRETAGE
mink	KOLINSKY
musk-rat	MUSQUASH
polecat	FITCHEW, KOLINSKY
rabbit	CHINCHILLA
sable	ZIBEL(L)INE
selectively bred	MUTATION MINK
skunk	ZORINO
squirrel	VAIR
stoat	ERMINE
tippet of fur	VICTORINE
weasel	MINK
wild llama	VICUNA
Furies	ERINYES, EUMENIDES
	ALECTO, MEGAERA
	TISIPHONE

furniture

artificially aged	DISTRESSED
bedroom furniture	BEDSTEAD
	CHEVAL GLASS
	CHEST OF DRAWERS
	DIVAN, DRESSING GLASS
	DRESSING TABLE, FOUR POSTER
	LOWBOY, TALLBOY
	MIRROR, WARDROBE
bishop's	
—chair	FALDSTOOL
—seat	THRONE
within the chancel	FALDISTORY
cabinet	ALMIRA(H)

canape	SOFA
cane furniture	RATTAN
chair	
—armchair	BERGERE, FAUTEUIL
—armless with low	
seat	FARTHINGALE CHAIR
—deep armchair	CLUB CHAIR
—dining chair with arms	CARVER
—folding	GLASTONBURY
—old	CAQUETOIRE
—other types	ABBOTSFORD CHAIR
	DERBYSHIRE CHAIR
	LAMBING CHAIR
	LANCASHIRE CHAIR
	MENDLESHAM CHAIR
	NORFOLK CHAIR
	SMOKERS' BOW (CHAIR)
	YORKSHIRE CHAIR
—small curved armchair	CABRIOLET
—sovereign's chair	THRONE
—with	
adjustable back	MORRIS CHAIR
chamberpot	COMMODE
curved runners	ROCKER
	ROCKING CHAIR
legs and back fixed	
into sockets	
in seat	WINDSOR CHAIR
semi-circular	
back	CAPTAIN'S CHAIR
church	
—desk	FALDSTOOL
—seat	PEW
—table	ALTAR
combined	BED-CHAIR, BED-SETTEE
coronation	
—chair	THRONE
—stool	FALDSTOOL
cupboard	ALM(E)RY, ALMIRA(H)
	A(U)MBRY
curved leg	CABRIOLE
cushion used as seat	BEAN-BAG, POUFFE
display furniture	CHIFFONIER
	(CHINA) CABINET, ETAGERE
	(WELSH) DRESSER
	WHATNOT
dresser	ALM(E)RY, A(U)MBRY
fabric trimming	GIMP, GUIMP(E)
	GUIPURE, PIPING
folding	
—bed	MURPHY BED, PUT-U-UP
—chair	GLASTONBURY
—stool	FALDSTOOL
—table	TRESTLE
furniture made from rough	
branches	RUSTIC

immoveable furniture	FITTINGS
inlay in wood	MARQUETRY
lamp-stand	TORCHERE
leg	
—curved	CABRIOLE
—square	MARLBOROUGH
long	
—bench	FORM, TRESTLE
with back	SETTLE
—upholstered seat	CHAISE LONGUE
	OTTOMAN, SOFA
mirror	
—on swivels	CHEVAL GLASS
	DRESSING GLASS
—tall and narrow	PIER GLASS
modern style	HI-TECH
moveable furniture	FITMENTS
music holder	CANTERBURY
ornamental candlestick	
or lampholder	TORCHERE
padded furniture	UPHOLSTERY
ready-made unit	MODULE
revolving	
—dessert stand	DUMB WAITER
—tray	LAZY SUSAN
scalloped edge	PIE-CRUST
seat	
—for one	BEAN-BAG, CHAIR
	CRICKET, MUSIC STOOL
	POUFFE, STOOL
—for two	DOS-A-DOS, LOVE SEAT
	TETE-A-TETE
shelves	
—for books	BOOK CASE
—for bric-a-brac	ETAGERE, WHATNOT
sideboard	CREDENCE, CREDENZA
	COMMODE
	(WELSH) DRESSER
sofa/couch	CANAPE, DAYBED
—backless	DIVAN, OTTOMAN
	POUFFE
—for two	LOVE SEAT
back-to-back	DOS-A-DOS
—large and padded	CHESTERFIELD
—on three sides of table	TRICLINIUM
—S-shaped	TETE-A-TETE
—used as bed at night	SOFA-BED
	BED-SETTEE
—with	
a back	SETTEE
one raised end	COUCH
stool	CRICKET, TABOURET
storage furniture	
—clothes	BACHELOR CHEST
	(CLOTHES) PRESS, LOWBOY
	TALLBOY, WARDROBE

—general	ARMOIRE
	BLANKET CHEST, CABINET
	CHEST (OF DRAWERS)
	(CLOSE) CUPBOARD, COMMODE
	COURT CUPBOARD, CREDENCE
	CREDENZA, MULE CHEST, PRESS
	SIDEBOARD, (WELSH) DRESSER
—outdoor clothes, etc	HALL STAND
	HAT STAND
	UMBRELLA STAND
—tea	CADDY, TEAPOY
styles	
—English (18th c)	ADAM, CHIPPENDALE
	HEPPLEWHITE
	QUEEN ANNE, SHERATON
—French	
17th c	BOUL(L)E, BUHL
	LOUIS-QUATORZE
18th c	LOUIS-QUINZE
19th c	SECOND EMPIRE
—German 19th c	BIEDERMEIER
support for standing	MISERICORD(E)
	MISERERE
swivelling wheel	CASTOR
table	
—beside altar	CREDENCE (TABLE)
	CREDENZA
—between windows	PIER TABLE
—circular	DRUM TABLE, LOO TABLE
—dining	REFECTORY
—extendible	DRAW(-TOP) TABLE

—for toilet	DRESSING TABLE
—on castors	DUMB WAITER, TROLLEY
—other	CARLTON HOUSE TABLE
	CRICKET TABLE
	HUTCH TABLE
	LIBRARY TABLE
	OCCASIONAL TABLE
	WORK TABLE
—small tea table	TEAPOY
—supported by brackets	CONSOLE TABLE
—with	
central support	MONOPODIUM
	WINE TABLE
baize top	CARD TABLE
flaps each end	GATE-LEG TABLE
	PEMBROKE TABLE
	SOFA-TABLE
	SUTHERLAND TABLE
folding legs	TRESTLE (TABLE)
three legs	TRIPOD
toilet	COMMODE, DRESSING TABLE
	TABLE, WASHSTAND
wardrobe	ALMIRA(H)ARMOIRE
writing and books	BONHEUR-DU-JOUR
	BOOKCASE
	BUREAU (ON STAND)
	CANTERBURY
	DAVENPORT, DESK (BOX)
	E(S)CRITOIRE (ON STAND)
	LIBRARY STEPS, LIBRARY TABLE
	SECRETAIRE

G

Gabon
capital   LIBREVILLE
coin   FRANC
Gaelic   ERSE, GAEL
poet   OSSIAN
  (*see also* **Ireland, Scottish**)
Gambia   WAG
capital   BANJUL, BATHURST
coin
 —unit   BUTUT
 —100 butut   DALASI
games[1]
including: indoor sports
  pastimes
  water sports
  winter sports
aerial   AEROBATICS, (HANG-)GLIDING
  PARACHUTING, PARAPENTE
  PARASCENDING
  PARASAILING, SKY-DIVING
American football   (*see separate entry*)
athletics   (*see separate entry*)
ball games   AMERICAN FOOTBALL
  ARENABALL
  (ASSOCIATION) FOOTBALL
  (AUSTRALIAN) RULES FOOTBALL
  BADMINTON, BALA LOCA, BANDY
  BASEBALL, BASKETBALL, BROOMBALL
  CAMOGIE, CRICKET, CROQUET
  ETON WALL GAME
  FAUSTBALL, FIVES, FLIPBALL
  (GAELIC) FOOTBALL, GOLF
  HANDBALL, HARDBALL, HOCKEY
  HORSEBALl, HURLEY, HURLING
  JAI ALAI, JAMBALL, KANGA CRICKET
  KORFBALL, KWIK CRICKET, LACROSSE
  (LAWN)TENNIS, NETBALL
  PELOTA (VASCA), POLO, PUSHBALL
  RACKETS, RACQUETS, REAL TENNIS
  ROLLERBALL, ROLLER HOCKEY
  ROUNDERS, ROYAL TENNIS
  RUGBY LEAGUE
  RUGBY UNION, SHINNY, SHINTY
  SHORT TENNIS, SOCCER, SOFTBALL
  SQUASH (RACKETS), STOOLBALL
  SUCKERBALL, TCHOUCK-BALL
  TRAP-BALL, WALLYBALL
  VOLLEYBALL

baseball   (*see separate entry*)
Basque   JAI ALIA, PELOTA (VASCA)
biathlon   SKIING, SHOOTING
bowling   BOCCIA, BOULES, BOWLS
  MARBLES, NINE HOLES
  PETANQUE, SKITTLES
  TEN-PIN BOWLING
  (*see also* **bowls**)
boxing   (*see separate entry*)
 —with use of feet   KICKBOXING, SAVATE
  THAI BOXING
card games   (*see separate entry*)
chess   (*see separate entry*)
children's
 —cricket   KANGA CRICKET
  KWIK CRICKET
 —cycling   BMX
 —games   BANDALORE, BLINDMAN'S BUFF
  CHARADES, COCKAL, CRAMBO
  DIABOLO, DIBS, HIDE-AND-SEEK
  HOOP BOWLING, HOPSCOTCH
  HOT COCKLE, HULA-HOOP
  HUNT-THE-SLIPPER
  JACKS, KNUCKLE-BONES, LEAP-FROG
  MURDER, MUSICAL CHAIRS
  PASS THE PARCEL, POGO STICK
  POSTMAN'S KNOCK, RING-O'-ROSES
  ROUNDERS, SCALECTRIX™
  SKATE-BOARDING, SKIPPING
  TIP-CAT, TOP-SPINNING, YOYO
 —races   EGG-AND-SPOON, SACK
  THREE-LEGGED, WHEELBARROW
 —tennis   SHORT TENNIS
Chinese   FAN-TAN, MAH-JONG(G), PUTZI
Christmas   LEVEL-COIL
cricket   (*see separate entry*)
cycling   (*see separate entry*)
decathlon   DISCUS
  FIFTEEN HUNDRED METRES
  FOUR HUNDRED METRES
  HIGH HUMP, HUNDRED METRES
  HURDLES, JAVELIN
  LONG JUMP, POLE VAULT
  SHOT(PUT)
dice games   CRAPS, PERUDO, POKER DICE
diving   BUNGEE ROPE DIVING
  HIGHBOARD, LAND DIVING
  SKYDIVING, SPRINGBOARD
  (*see also* **swimming**)
duathlon   CYCLING, RUNNING
Dutch   KORFBALL
equestrian   COACH-DRIVING, DRESSAGE
  EVENTING, HARNESS RACING
  PACING, POLO, RODEO
  SHOW JUMPING, TENT-PEGGING
  TROTTING

five events	PENTATHLON
fives varieties	ETON, RUGBY, WINCHESTER
football	(see separate entry)
four events	TETRATHLON
French	BOULES, PETANQUE, SAVATE
Gaelic	CAMOGIE, CURLING
	GAELIC FOOTBALL, HURLEY
	HURLING, SHINNY, SHINTY
golf	(see separate entry)
gymnastics	(see separate entry)
horse racing	(see separate entry)
hunting	BEAGLING, COURSING
	DEER HUNTING
	FOX HUNTING, OTTER HUNTING
indoor games	
—board games	BACKGAMMON, BINGO
	CHESS, CLUEDO
	CROWN AND ANCHOR
	DRAUGHTS, GO, GOBANG, GOMOKU
	HALMA, HOUSEY-HOUSEY, LEXICON
	LUDO, MAH-JONG, MONOPOLY
	PACHISI, SCRABBLE
	SNAKES AND LADDERS
	TRIC(K)-TRAC(K), TRIVIAL PURSUITS
African	MANCALA
Egyptian	SENET
Peruvian	PERUDO
—bowling	QUOITS, SKITTLES
	TEN-PIN BOWLING
—cards	(see separate entry)
—Chinese	FAN-TAN, MAH-JONG(G)
—Indian	PACHISI, PARCHEESI
—other	CHARADES, CONSEQUENCES
	DARTS, (DUMB) CRAMBO
	FORFEITS, HIDE AND SEEK
	HOUSEY-HOUSEY, JACK(STRAW)S
	JINGO-RING, KNUCKLEBONES
	LEVEL-COIL, MURDER
	SPILLIKINS, TOMBOLA
—table games	BAGATELLE
	BILLIARDS, BLOW FOOTBALL
	DICE, DOMINOES, NOVUM
	PINBALL, POOL, SHOVE HA(LF)PENNY
	SKITTLES, SNOOKER, SUBUTEO
	TABLE TENNIS, TIDDLEYWINKS
Irish	HURLING, HURLEY
Japanese	GO, GOBAN(G), GOMUKU, SHOGI
jumping	HIGH JUMP
	HOP, SKIP AND JUMP
	HURDLES, LONG JUMP
	STEEPLECHASE
	TRAMPOLINE, TRIPLE JUMP
—ancient Greek	HALMA
—long jump (US)	BROAD JUMP
karate styles	SHOTOKAN, WUKO
kung-fu styles	JEET-KUNE-DO, TAI CHI

martial arts	
—Chinese	KEMPO, KUNG-FU
	SHAOLIN BOXING, WU SHU
—Japanese	AIKIDO, AIKI-JITSU
	ESCRIMA, JI(U)JITSU
	JUDO(KWAN), JUJUTSA
	GOJO-RYU, KEMPO, KENDO
	KYOKUSHINKAI, NINJITSU
	SHITO-RYU, SHOTOKAI, SHOTOKAN
	TANG SOO DO, WADO-RYU
—Korean	HAPIKIDO, MU-GEN-DO
	SULKIDO, TAE KWON DO
	TANG SOO DO
—Okinawan	KARATE
—Thai	THAI BOXING
motor and motorcycle	
sports	AUTOCROSS
	CYCLO-CROSS, DRAG-RACING
	FORMULA ONE RACING
	(GO-)KARTING, GRAND PRIX RACING
	MOTOCROSS, RALLYING
	SCRAMBLING, SPEEDWAY RACING
	TOURIST TROPHY RACING
	(see also **motor-racing, motor-rallying**)
multi-discipline	
—2 events	BIATHLON
—3 events	TRIATHLON
—4 events	TETRATHLON
—5 events	PENTATHLON
—6 events	HEXATHLON
—7 events	HEPTATHLON
—10 events	DECATHLON
on ice	(see winter sports below)
on skates	
—blades	ICE HOCKEY
—wheels	ROLLERBALL, SUCKERBALL
outdoor activities	CAVING
	CROSS COUNTRY RUNNING
	JOGGING, MOUNTAINEERING
	ORIENTEERING, PAPER CHASE
	POT HOLING, ROCK CLIMBING
	WALKING
pentathlon	
—ancient	DISCUS THROWING, LEAPING
	RUNNING, SPEAR THROWING
	WRESTLING
—modern	
(m)	CROSS-COUNTRY RIDING
	CROSS-COUNTRY RUNNING
	FENCING, PISTOL SHOOTING
	SWIMMING
(f)	HIGH JUMP, HUNDRED METRES
	HURDLES, LONG JUMP, SHOT(PUT)
power-lifting	BENCH PRESS
	DEAD LIFT, SQUAT
	(see also weightlifting below)

pulling	TUG-O(F)-WAR
racket games	BADMINTON, BUMBLE-PUPPY
	FIVES, JAI-ALAI, LACROSSE
	SQUASH (RACKETS), TENNIS
Rugby football	(*see separate entry*)
running	CROSS COUNTRY
	FELL RUNNING
	HARE AND HOUNDS
	MARATHON, ORIENTEERING
	PAPER CHASE, RELAY
	SPARTATHLON, SPRINT
rustic game	FIVEPENNY MORRIS
	MAR(RE)LS, MEREL(L)S
	MERILS, MIRACLES, MORALS
	(NINEPENNY) MORRIS
sailing	(*see separate entry*)
'sailing' on land	LAND-SURFING
	LAND-YACHTING
	SAND-YACHTING
seven events	HEPTATHLON
shipboard	BULL, DECK QUOITS
	DECK TENNIS
shooting	
—bow and arrow	ARCHERY, TOXOPHILY
events	FIELD ARCHERY
	FLIGHT SHOOTING
	TARGET ARCHERY
—firearms	BIATHLON
	CLAY-PIGEON SHOOTING
	PISTOL, RIFLE, SKEET SHOOTING
	SMALL-BORE, TRAPSHOOTING
show-jumping	(*see separate entry*)
six events	HEXATHLON
skating	(*see separate entry*)
snooker	(*see separate entry*)
soccer	(*see* **football**)
Spanish	BALA LOCA
surfing	(*see separate entry*)
table tennis	PING-PONG
ten events	DECATHLON
terms	(*see* **games²**)
three events	TRIATHLON
throwing	CRICKET-BALL THROWING
	DARTS, HOOP-LA
	HAMMER-THROWING
	JAVELIN, QUOITS, SHOT(PUT)
	TOSSING THE CABER
trampoline	(*see* **gymnastics**)
triathlon	RUNNING, RIDING, SWIMMING
two events	BIATHLON, DUATHLON
war game	ARENABALL
water sports	NAUTICS
—ball game	WATER POLO
—boating/sailing	BOARD SAILING
	CANOEING, DINGHY SAILING
	EIGHTS, FOURS, JET SKIING
	KAYAK RACING, KNEE SKIING
	PAIRS, PEDALO, POWERBOAT RACING
	RAFTING, ROWING, SAIL BOARDING
	SCULLING, SURFING, WATER-SKIING
	WET-BIKING, WINDSURFING
	YACHTING
	(*see also* **sailing, surfing**)
—fishing	ANGLING, FLY-FISHING
—skis and paragliding	PARASAILING
—skiing without skis	BAREFOOTING
—swimming	(*see separate entry*)
—underwater	AQUAPUSH, DIVING
	SCUBA DIVING, SNORKELLING
	UNDERWATER HOCKEY
weightlifting	CLEAN AND JERK, PRESS
	SNATCH
	(*see also* powerlifting *above*)
winter sports	
—on	
ice	BANDY, BROOMBALL, CURLING
	ICE DANCING, ICE HOCKEY
	ICE POLO, ICE YACHTING
	SKATING
snow	BUMP-SKIING, DOWNHILL
	(GIANT) SLALOM
	HOT-DOGGING, LANGLAUF, LUGE
	PARAPENTE, SKI-BOB, SKIING
	SKIJORING, SKI-SURFING
	SLED-DOG RACING, SNOWBOARDING
	SNOWMOBILE, TOBOGGAN
—skiing	(*see separate entry*)
—skiing and shooting	BIATHLON
with	
—animals	BULLFIGHTING, CAMEL RACING
	CHARIOT RACING
	COACH DRIVING
	COURSING, FALCONRY, GRACING
	GREYHOUND RACING, HORSEBALL
	HORSE RACING, PIGEON RACING
	RIDE AND TIE, TRAP RACING
	TROTTING, WHIPPET RACING
—weapons	ARENABALL, JOUSTING
	FENCING
	(*see also* **fencing**)
wrestling	ALL-IN, ARM-WRESTLING
	CATCH-AS-CATCH-CAN
	CUMBERLAND STYLE
	FREESTYLE, GLIMA WRESTING
	GR(A)ECO-ROMAN STYLE
	LANCASHIRE, SAMBO, SUMO

games²

some sporting terms:

aiming mark	
—archery	BUTT, GOLD, TARGET
—baseball	PLATE
—bowls	JACK

—cricket	STUMPS, WICKET
—curling	TEE
—football	GOAL
—golf	HOLE, PIN
—hockey	GOAL
—shooting	BULL, BUTT, TARGET
aquapush	
—playing at one time	SIX
—team	TEN
Australian Rules	
—shape of pitch	OVAL
—team	EIGHTEEN
basketball	
—jumping and scoring	SLAM DUNK
—substitutes	SEVEN
—team	FIVE
billiards	
—balls	RED, WHITE
—cannon	CARAMBOLE, CAROM
—rebound	BRICOLE
—score	BREAK
—scoring shot	CANNON, IN-OFF, POT
	(*see also* **snooker**)
croquet	
—aiming mark	HOOP
—implement for striking	MALLET
curling	
—aiming mark	TEE
—cannon	INWICK
Gaelic football team	FIFTEEN
handball	
—modern team,	FIVE, SEVEN
—old team	ELEVEN
high-jumping styles	FOSBURY FLOP
	STRADDLE, WESTERN ROLL
hockey	
—start of play	BULLY OFF
—team	ELEVEN
hurley team	FIFTEEN
ice-hockey	
—'ball'	PUCK
—off-ice penalty box	SIN BIN
—team	SIX
judo	
—costume	JUDOGI
—expert	BLACK BELT
—level of proficiency	DAN
—participant	JUDOKA
korfball team	TWELVE
lacrosse	
—stick	CROSSE
—team	
men	TEN
women	TWELVE
netball team	SEVEN
pelota 'bat'	CHERISTA(K)

polo	
—session	CHUKKA
—team	FOUR
—venues	CIRENCESTER, COWDRAY PARK
	GUARDS'CLUB, KIRKLINGTON PARK
	RHINEFIELD, ROYAL BERKSHIRE
	SMITH'S LAWN
shinty	CAMANACHD
—stick	CAMAN
—team	TWELVE
shooting	
—target sections	BULL, INNER
	MAGPIE, OUTER
—venue	BISLEY
softball team	SEVEN
table tennis	PING-PONG
—early	GOSSIMA
Tchouckball team	NINE
trophy	(*see separate entry*)
volleyball	
—playing positions	BLOCKER, RECEIVER
	SERVER, SETTER, SPIKER
—team	SIX
wrestling	
—hold	ARMLOCK, FULL NELSON
	HALF NELSON, HEADLOCK
	SCISSORS
—school (old)	PALAESTRA
—throw	FLYING MARE
—winning move	FALL
garments	
African	KANZU, K(H)ANGA
alb (Greek)	STICHARION
Albanian kilt	FUSTANELLA
Alpine dress or skirt	DIRNDL
ankle-length robe	TALAR
anorak	CAGOUL(E), KAGOOL
	KAGOUL(E)
apron	BARM-CLOTH, PLACKET
Austrian leather trousers	LEDERHOSEN
baby's coat	MATINEE JACKET
baggy	
—knickerbockers	PLUS-FOURS
—sweater	SLOPPY JOE
—trousers	OXFORD BAGS
ballet	
—overall garment	LEOTARD
—skirt	TUTU
—tights	MAILLOT
band embroidered	
with Agnus Dei	SUCCINCTORIUM
	SUCCINCTORY
baptismal robe	CHRIS(T)OM
	CHRISOM-CLOTH
belted coat or gown	TUNIC
bikini	TANGA

bishop's	
—scarf	ORARIUM
—stole	EPITRACHELION
—vestment	CHIMER(E), PALLIUM
	RATIONAL(E), ROTCHET
black silk cloak	DOMINO
blanket with hole for head	PONCHO
blouse	SHIRT, SHIRTWAIST
	TUNIC
—American	WAIST
—fastened at waist	BLOUSON
—Indian	CHOLI
—loose	GARIBALDI
—short	BLOUSON
blue garment	MAZARINE
bodice	CHEMISETTE
—American	WAIST
—combined with skirt	PRINCESS
—extension	BASQUE
—loose fitting	BLOUSE
—of ballet dress	GILET
—Scottish	JIRKINET
—woman's (18thc)	PIERROT
boy's suit (19th c)	SKELETON SUIT
brassière padded with foam	GAY DECEIVER
breeches	TRUSSES
—buff-coloured cotton	NANKEENS
	NANKINS
—closefitting	HOSE, TREWS, TROUSE
—footman's	PLUSHES
—full (16th c)	TRUNK BREECHES
	TRUNK HOSE
—knee	SMALL CLOTHES
—long	TROUSERS
—loose	KNICKERBOCKERS
baggy	PLUS FOURS
—man's (17th c)	PETTICOAT-BREECHES
—wide	OXFORD BAGS, SLOPS
bride's outfit	TROUSSEAU
Burmese skirt	TAMEIN
bustle	DRESS-IMPROVER
cape	
—cyclist's	PONCHO
—knitted	SONTAG
—Mexican	SERAPE, ZARAPE
—short	MOZETTA
worn by Pope	FAN(I)ON
—shoulder	TIPPET
fur	VICTORINE
—triangular	FICHU
—with hood	DOMINO
Maltese	FALDETTA
—woman's	MANTEEL, PELERINE
caped riding hood	JOSEPH
cardigan (US)	WAM(M)US, WAMPUS
cassock	SLOP, SUBUCULA

—French	SOUTANE
casual jacket	SPORTS JACKET
chemise	SHIFT, SMOCK
—Scottish	SARK
chest-protector	PECTORAL
child's	
—apron (US)	TIER
—bodice and skirt (Scot.)	POLONAISE
—coat	PELISSE
—outer garment	PILCH
—pants and shirt (US)	PANTYWAIST
—undergarment	COM(B)S, COMBINATIONS
	LIBERTY BODICE
Chinese	CHEONG-SAM, SAMFOO
	SAMFU
christening	
—robe	CHRISOM(-CLOTH)
—veil	CHRISMAL
clerical	(see church—vestments)
cloak	AMICE, AMIS, MANTEAU
	MANTLE, PALL, WRAP
—African	JELLABA
	(see also African)
—Arab	BURNOUS(E)
	(see also Arabic)
—black silk	DOMINO
—coarse leather or woollen	PILCH
—fur	PILCH
trimmed	PELISSE
—Greek	CHLAMYS, HIMATION
—lady's	CARDINAL
—Levant	GREGO
—long	CAPOTE
—loose	GABARDENE, GABARDINE
	TALMA
—man's, short	ROQUELAURE
—Mexican	SERAPE, ZERAPE
—military	PELISSE
—Moslem women	BURK(H)A, BURQA
—old	RAIL
—Roman	ABOLLA, PAENULA, PALLIUM
	SAGUM, TOGA, TOGE
—Russian	SARAFAN
—Scottish	ROCKLAY, ROKELAY
—small	MANT(E)LET
—soldier's (old)	MANTEEL
—South American	PONCHO
—theatrical	TALMA
—with cape	INVERNESS
—woman's	DOLMAN
19th c	VISITE
French	ROQUELAURE
Roman	PALLA
Russian	SARAFAN
Scottish	ROCKLAY, ROKELAY
short	CARDINAL

close-fitting	JEISTIECOR
—ballet garment	LEOTARD
—breeches	HOSE, TREWS
	TROUSE
—coat	NEWMARKET, SURTOUT
	TRUSS
French	JUPON
—jacket	MONKEY JACKET
—legless pants	BRIEFS
—surplice	ROCHET
—upper garment	DOUBLET
French	POURPOINT
—waistcoat	JERKIN
clothes of rough woollen	TWEEDS
coarse	
—leather or woollen cloak	PILCH
—linen outer garment	SMOCK-FROCK
coat	
—baby's	MATINEE COAT
—belted	TUNIC
—close fitting	NEWMARKET, SURTOUT
	TRUSS
—double-breasted	FROCKCOAT, SURTOUT
—dress	SWALLOWTAIL
	TAIL-COAT
—herald's	TABARD
—Indian	ACHKAN
—informal	SMOKING-JACKET
—Japanese raincoat	MINO
—knight's	TABARD
—loose	DUFFEL COAT, SACK-COAT
	SWAGGER COAT, WRAP RASCAL
—military	BRITISH WARM, TRENCH COAT
	TUNIC
—of	
duffel	DUFFEL COAT
twilled cotton and wool	GABARDINE
	GABERDINE
—policeman's	TUNIC
—regimental	FROCK COAT
—riding	NEWMARKET
—short	JERKIN, JUMP
	MACKINAW, SHOOTING-JACKET
—sleeveless	CAPE, JERKIN, WAISTCOAT
—small	PETTICOAT
—soldier's	TUNIC
—waterproof	MACKINTOSH, RAINCOAT
	TRENCH COAT
American	SLICKER
—with	
curved sides	CUTAWAY
hood	DUFFEL COAT
	DUFFLE COAT, PARKA
	PARKEE, PARKI
collar	
—stand-up	PICCADILLY

—woman's (17th c)	WHISK
collarless undergarment	UNDERSHIRT
cotton	
—breeches	NANKEENS, NANKINS
—suit	SAFARI SUIT
cowboy riding trousers	CHAP(ERAJO)S
	CHAPEREJOS
	CHAPS, SHAPS
cravat	
—18th c	SOUBISE
—lace	STEENKIRK
crinoline, small	CRINOLETTE
cyclist's cape	PONCHO
deacon's stole (Greek)	ORARION
denim trousers	JEANS, LEVIS
dinner-jacket (US)	TUXEDO
divided skirt	CULOTTE(S)
	HAREM SKIRT
double-breasted coat	FROCK-COAT
doublet (French)	POURPOINT
drawers	HOSE
—frilled	FRILLIES, PANTALETS
—short	PANTIES
dress	FROCK, ROBE
—18th c	TROLLOPEE
—African	K(H)ANGA
—Alpine	DIRNDL
—coat	SWALLOW-TAIL
—for riding	RIDING HABIT
—full length	MOTHER HUBBARD
—Hawaiian	MUU-MUU
—homespun	RUSSET
—improver	BUSTLE
—Japanese	KIMONO
—made from	
flowered muslin	DOLLY VARDEN
Indian silk	TASAR, TUSSAH
	TUSSEH, TUSSER
	TUSSORE
—Moslem woman's	BURKA, BURQA
—rich	ROBE
—straight	SHIRT DRESS
	SHIRTWAISTER
—tight-fitting	SHEATH, TUBE DRESS
dressing-gown	PEIGNOIR, ROBE
—woman's	NEGLIGEE, PEIGNOIR
dressing-jacket	NIGHT-RAIL
Eastern bishop's	
vestment	OMOPHORION, SAKKOS
ecclesiastical	(*see* **church—vestments**)
farm-worker's garment	SMOCK-FROCK
fawn-skin worn by	
Bacchus	NEBRIS
flannel	
—scarf with sleeves	NIGHTINGALE
—undervest (Scot.)	WYLIE-COAT

flashy type of man's suit	ZOOT SUIT
flowered muslin dress	DOLLY VARDEN
flowing gown	MOTHER HUBBARD
footman's breeches	PLUSHES
for restraint	STRAIT-JACKET
	STRAIT-WAISTCOAT
foundation	
—for skirt	UNDERSKIRT
—garment	PANTY-GIRDLE
frilled drawers	PANTALETS
frock-coat	FROCK
—19th C	SURTOUT
front part of dress	GILET
full breeches (16th c)	TRUNK-BREECHES
	TRUNK-HOSE
fur	
—cloak	PILCH
—tippet	VICTORINE
—lined	PELISSE
gaudy clothes	TRAPPINGS
goats'-hair shawl	CASHMERE, KASHMIR
gown	SLOP, STOLE
—17-18th c	MANTEAU, MANTO, MANTUA
—belted	TUNIC
—loose	MOTHER HUBBARD
old	NEGLIGEE, SLAMMAKIN
	SLAMMERKIN
—morning	PEIGNOIR
—preaching	GENEVA GOWN
—Roman	STOLA
greatcoat	PETERSHAM
—Afghan	POS(H)TEEN
—caped	ULSTER
—loose (18th c)	WRAP RASCAL
Greek	
—deacon's stole	ORARION
—kilt	FUSTANELLA
—monk's habit	SCHEMA
—one-sleeved garment	EXOMIS
—veil	CALYPTRA, KALYPTRA
—woman's	
cloak	CHLAMYS, HIMATION
robe	PEPLOS, PEPLUM
	PEPLUS
Greenlander's jacket	ANARAK, ANORAK
handkerchief	BANDAN(N)A
hats	(see **headgear**)
Hawaiian dress	MUU-MUU
herald's coat	TABARD
high	
—collar (17th c)	PICCADILL(O)
	PICCADILLY, PIKADELL
—necked garment	TURTLE NECK
homespun dress	RUSSET
hood	
—old	SURTOUT

—riding	NITHSDALE, TROT-COSEY
	TROT-COZY
—Russian	BASHLYK
—woollen	CAPELINE
hooded	
—coat	DUFFELCOAT, DUFFLE COAT
	PARKA, PARKEE, PARKI
—jacket (Levant)	GREGO
hooped skirt	CRINOLINE, FARTHINGALE
house gown	
—informal	HOUSECOAT
—loose	TEA GOWN
Hussar's jacket	DOLMAN
Indian	
—coat	ACHKAN
—dress	BANIAN, BANYAN
	SAREE, SARI
—high-collared coat	SHERWANI
—shirt	K(H)URTA
—tunic	K(H)URTA
—woman's	
blouse	CHOLI
veil	CHAD(D)AR, CHADOR
	CHUDDAH, CHUDDAR
informal	
—gown	HOUSECOAT, NEGLIGEE
—jacket	SMOKING JACKET
—shirt	TEE-SHIRT, T-SHIRT
Inquisition victim's	
garment	SANBENITO
jacket	JERKIN
—American	
loose	VAREUSE
short	ROUNDABOUT
strong	WAM(M)US, WAMPUS
—boy's	ETON JACKET
—casual	SPORTS JACKET
—Chinese	MAKWA
trousers and jacket	SAMFOO, SAMFU
—close-fitting	MESS JACKET
	MONKEY JACKET
—dinner (US)	TUXEDO
—double-breasted	REEFER(-JACKET)
—Greenlander's	ANARAK, ANORAK
—hooded (Levant)	GREGO
—Hussar's	DOLMAN
—indoor	SMOKING-JACKET
—loose	LUMBER JACKET
	NORFOLK JACKET
—mediaeval peasant's	SAYON
—military undress	MESS JACKET
	SHELL JACKET
—padded, under armour	ACTON
	HA(C)QUETON
—riding	HACKING JACKET
	NEWMARKET

—sailor's	PEA-JACKET
—Scott	RAILLY
—sleeveless (Fr.)	JUPON
—with waistband	NORFOLK JACKET
—woman's	
16th-17th c	HALF-KIRTLE
19th c	POLKA
Scottish	SHORTGOWN
short	BOLERO
skirted	BASQUE, ZOUAVE
Japanese	
—dress	(KI)MONO
—raincoat	MINO
jester's garb	MOTLEY
Jewish	TALIS
—prayer-shawl	TALLITH
—priest's surplice	EPHOD
kilt (Albanian or Greek)	FUSTANELLA
knee-breeches	SMALL-CLOTHES
knickerbockers	PLUS FOURS
knight's coat	TABARD
knitted	
—blanket or shawl	AFGHAN
—jumper and cardigan	TWIN-SET
—upper garment	CARDIGAN
	GUERNSEY, JERSEY
	JUMPER, PULLOVER, SWEATER
lace cravat	STEENKIRK
large loose sweater	SLOPPY JOE
leather	
—or quilted coat	GAMBESON
—outer garment	PILCHER
—trousers (Austria)	LEDERHOSEN
leggings	GALLIGASKINS
	PUTTEES, SPAT(T)EES
light	
—dress (17th c)	CHIMER(E), CIMAR
	CYMAR
—indoor jacket	SMOKING-JACKET
—overcoat	ULSTERETTE
—waterproof coat	RAINCOAT
little tunic	TUNICLE
loin cloth	WAISTCLOTH
—Hindu	D(H)OTI
—Indian	LUNGI
long	
—breeches	TROUSERS
—cloak	CAPOTE, DOMINO
—covering whole body	BURK(H)A
	BURQA
—dress-like coat	HOUSE-COAT
—jacket suit	DRAPE SUIT
—overcoat	CHESTERFIELD, REDINGOTE
—robe	STOLE
loose	
—blouse	GARIBALDI

—breeches	KNICKERBOCKERS
—cloak	GABARDINE, GABERDINE
	TALMA
—coat	NORFOLK JACKET
	WRAP RASCAL
—dress	SHIFT
Hawaii	MUU-MUU
—fitting bodice	BLOUSE
—garment	SLOP
—gown	MOTHER HUBBARD
17th c	MANTEAU, MANTO
18th c	NEGLIGEE
old	SLAMMAKIN, SLAMMERKIN
over armour	MANDILION, MANDYLION
—greatcoat (18th c)	WRAP-RASCAL
—house-gown	TEA-GOWN
—jacket (US)	VAREUSE
—outer garment	BLOUSE, MANTLE
	MANTUA, ROBE
—overcoat	CHESTERFIELD, PALETOT
	ULSTER
—tunic	
African	DASHIKI, KANZU
Malayan	KABAYA
—undergarment (17th c)	CHIMER(E)
	CIMAR, CYMAR
—wrap	NIGHT-RAIL
low-necked blouse	PNEUMONIA BLOUSE
made from	
—coarse cotton	DUCKS
—corded silk	PADUASOY
—rough wool	TWEEDS
—silk with wool	
or hair	FAR(R)ANDINE
	FERRANDINE
—twilled cotton	JEANS, DENIMS
—wool with satin twill	CALAMANCO
Malayan	
—dress	SARONG
—tunic	KABAYA
man's	
—breeches (17th c)	PETTICOAT-BREECHES
—detachable shirt front	DICK(E)Y
—formal coat	TAIL-COAT
—loose coat	SACK-COAT
—neckwear	ASCOT, BOW, CRAVAT, TIE
—sash	CUMMERBUND
—short cloak (18th c)	ROQUELAURE
—suit (1940s)	ZOOT SUIT
—undergarment	BRIEFS, COMBINATIONS
	COM(B)S, JOCKEY SHORTS
	LONG JOHNS, PANTS, VEST
—undershirt (Roman)	SUBUCULA
maniple	FANON, FANNEL(L)
mantle	KIRTLE, PALL
—old	ROCHET, ROCQUET

—Roman	PALLIUM
woman's	PALLA
master's cape with hood	DOMINO
mediaeval	
—body garment	COTE HARDIE
—peasant's jacket	SAYON
Mexican cape	SERAPE, ZARAPE
military	
—cloak	PELISSE
—coat	BRITISH WARM
	TRENCH-COAT
—undress jacket	MESS JACKET
	SHELL JACKET
monk's	
—garment	FROCK, SCAPULAR
—habit (Gr.)	SCHEMA
—morning-gown	PEIGNOIR
Moslem	
—pilgrim's garb	IHRAM
—woman's	
dress	BURK(H)A, BURQA
veil	YASHMAK
narrow	
—skirt	HOBBLE SKIRT
—vestment	STOLE
neck covering	PARTLET, RUFF
neckerchief	BANDAN(N)A
—old	RAIL
—woman's	WHICK
nightclothes	(*see* sleepwear *below*)
officer's overcoat	(BRITISH) WARM
oilskin (US)	SLICKER
one-piece	
—ballet dress	LEOTARD
—bodice and skirt	POLONAISE
—outer garment	BOILER-SUIT
	CAT-SUIT, JUMP-SUIT
—swim-suit	MAILLOT
—undergarment	BODY STOCKING
	CAMIKNICKERS
	COMBINATIONS
	COMBS, TEDDY
one-sleeved garment (Gr.)	EXOMIS
outer	
—garment	PALL, STOLE, WRAP
coarse linen	SMOCK-FROCK
loose	MANTLE, ROBE
old	SURCOAT
—petticoat	KIRTLE
Basque	BASQUINE
over-jacket (old)	SPENCER
overall	APRON, JUMPER, PINAFORE
overalls	DUNGAREES
—American	COVERALL
overcoat	
—19th c	TAGLIONI

—dialect	JAMES, JEMMY
—German	LODEN
—heavy	GREATCOAT
—Italian	TAGLIONI
—Levantine	GREGO
—light	COVERT COAT, ULSTERETTE
—loose	CHESTERIELD, PALETOT
	ULSTER
—old	SURTOUT
—officer's	(BRITISH) WARM
—peasant's	TABARD
—sailor's	PEA-COAT, PEA-JACKET
—short	SPENCER
—with	
cape	INVERNESS
sleeves in one piece	
the shoulder	RAGLAN
overskirt	PEPLUM
peasant's overcoat	TABARD
penitent's robe	CILICE
petticoat	PLACKET, UNDERSKIRT
—figured woollen	BALMORAL
—French	JUPON
—Scottish	WYLIE-COAT
—stiffened	CRINOLINE
	FARTHINGALE
Philippines	MALO, PAREU
pinafore	OVERALL
—American	TIRE
—dress (US)	JUMPER
policeman's coat	TUNIC
Polynesian	
—skirt	LAVA-LAVA
—wrap	PAREU
Pope's	
—cape	FAN(I)ON
—vestment	PALLIUM
preaching gown	GENEVA GOWN
protective	APRON, COVERALL
	DUNGAREES, OVERALL
—military	FATIGUES, GASCAPE
	NODDY SUIT
pullover	
—sleeveless	TANK TOP
—woollen	GUERNSEY, JERSEY
	SWEATER
raincoat	BURBERRY, GABARDENE
	GABARDINE
—Japanese	MINO
ready-made clothing	PRET A PORTER
	REACH-ME-DOWNS
	SLOPS
religious vestment (Greek)	STICHARION
restraining	STRAITJACKET
	STRAIT-WAISTCOAT
rich dress	ROBE

riding		—small	TURNOVER
—breeches	JODHPURS	—triangular	FICHU
—coat	HACKING JACKET, NEWMARKET	—with shaped neck	TONNAG
—dress	RIDING-HABIT	—woollen	WHITTLE
—habit	RIDING-ROBE	sheepskin coat	AFGHAN
—hood	NITHSDALE, TROT-COSEY	—Spanish	ZAMARRA, ZAMARRO
	TROT-COZY	shepherd's plaid (Scot.)	MAUD
—neckerchief	STOCK	shift	CHEMISE, SHIRT, SMOCK
—trousers	CHAPAREJOS, CHAPEREJOS	shirt	
	CHAPS, SHAPS	—India	K(H)URTA
robe		—old	PARTLET
—Ghana	KENTE	—Scotland	SARK
—informal	HOUSECOAT, TEA-GOWN	shore clothes (Navy)	LONG-TOGS
—long	STOLE	short	
—old	PALLIAMENT, PARAMENT	—cape	MOZETTA
—penitent's	CILICE	worn by Pope	FANON
—reaching the ankles	TALAR	—coat	JERKIN, JUMP
—Roman	STOLA		SHOOTING-JACKET
Roman		—cloak (Gr.)	CHLAMYS
—cloak	TOGA, TOGE	—drawers	PANTIES
—gown	STOLA	—jacket	
—mantle	PALLIUM	boy's	ETON JACKET
woman's	PALLA	double-breasted	REEFER(-JACKET)
—military cloak	ABOLLA	military	MESS JACKET
	PALAUDAMENT(UM)		SHELL JACKET
	SAGUM	woman's	BASQUE, BOLERO
—robe	STOLA		ZOUAVE
—sleeveless garment	EXOMIS	—light overcoat	COVERT COAT
—travelling cloak	PAENULA	—loose coat	DUFFEL COAT
—undershirt	SUBUCULA		DUFFLE COAT, SACK COAT
ruff	PARTLET	—negligee	CAMISOLE
Russian		—overcoat	SPENCER
—hood	BASHLYK	—pleated skirt	RA-RA (SKIRT)
—peasant's cloak	SARAFAN	—sleeved garment (Shak.)	SEA-GOWN
sailor's		—sleeveless jacket	WAISTCOAT
—jersey	FROCK	—veil	KISS-ME
—overcoat	PEA-COAT, PEA-JACKET	at back of head	VOLET
—shore clothes	LONG-TOGS	—woollen coat	MACKINAW
—trousers	BELL-BOTTOMS	shoulder	
—upper garment	GUERNSEY	—cape	TIPPET
scarf	BANDAN(N)A	—covering	SHAWL
—bishop's	ORARIUM	shroud	WINDING-SHEET
—fur and feathers	BOA	skin-tight garment	LEOTARD
—man's	ASCOT, CRAVAT	skirt	
—rider's	STOCK	—Alpine	DIRNDL
—woman's	FICHU	—ballet	TUTU
Scottish		—Burmese	TAMEIN
—man's skirt	FILABEG, FIL(L)IBEG,	—divided	CULOTTE(S), HAREM SKIRT
	KILT, PHIL(L)ABEG	—hooped	CRINOLINE, FARTHINGALE
	PHIL(L)IBEG	small	CRINOLETTE
—nightshirt	SEMMIT	—hung from shoulders	PINAFORE DRESS
—shepherd's plaid	MAUD		PINAFORE SKIRT
—woman's jacket	SHORTGOWN	—long	MAXI
shawl	WRAP	—Malayan	SARONG
—Hebrew	TALLITH	—narrow	HOBBLE(-SKIRT)
—Scottish	MAUD	—Polynesian	PAREU

—padded at rear	BUSTLE	suit	
—short	MINI	—boy's (19th c)	SKELETON SUIT
pleated	RA-RA(SKIRT)	—cotton	SAFARI SUIT
puffy	BUBBLE SKIRT	—flashy (1940s)	ZOOT SUIT
—tight	TUBE SKIRT	—with long jacket	DRAPE SUIT
—trouser-like	CULOTTE(S)	supporting	
	DIVIDED SKIRT, HAREM SKIRT	undergarment	BRA(SSIERE), CORSET
sleepwear			CORSELET(TE), STAYS
—man's	NIGHT-SHIRT, PYJAMAS	surplice	COTTA, EPHOD, STOLA, STOLE
Scottish	SEMMIT	—Scotland	SARK
—woman's	NIGHT-DRESS, NIGHT-GOWN	swaddling cloth	PILCH
	PYJAMAS	swimsuit	
Scottish	WYLIE-COAT	—one-piece	MAILLOT
short	BABY-DOLL	—two-piece	BIKINI, TANGA
sleeveless		Syrian	AB(B)A, ABAYA
—child's garment	BARROW	tabard	CHIMER(E)
—cloak	MANTLE, PAENULA	tartan trousers	TREWS
—coat	CAPE, JERKIN, WAISTCOAT	three-cornered cape	FICHU
—dress	SUNDRESS	tights	
—jacket		—for ballet-dancer	MAILLOT
French	JUPON	—incorporating pants	PANTIHOSE
peasant's	SAYON	travelling cloak (Roman)	PAENULA
short	WAISTCOAT	triangular shawl	FICHU
—pullover	TANKTOP	trouser-like woman' garment	PANTALETS
—Roman robe	EXOMIS	trousers	BAGS, FLANNELS
—tabard	CHIMER(E)		PANTS, SLACKS
—tunic	TABARD	—Asian	SHERWAL, SHERRYVALLIES
—underbodice	CAMISOLE	—baggy	OXFORD BAGS, SLOPS
—vest	LIBERTY BODICE	—cricketer's	FLANNELS
small		—cut like skirt	CULOTTE(S)
—cloak	MANT(E)LET		DIVIDED SKIRT
—coat	PETTICOAT		HAREM SKIRT
—crinoline	CRINOLETTE	—ending	
—shawl	TURNOVER	above knee	SHORTS
—tunic	TUNICLE	below knee	BERMUDA SHORTS
smock	SHIFT, SLOP		KNEE-BREECHES
smock-frock	BLOUSE, FROCK		PLUS FOURS, PLUS TWOS
soldier's		—from the hips	HIP-HUGGERS,HIPSTERS
—cloak	MANTEEL	—made of	
—coat	TUNIC	denim	JEANS, LEVIS
—protective clothing	GASCAPE	double-twilled fustian	MOLESKINS
	NODDY SUIT	light wool	FLANNELS
—working clothes	FATIGUES	ribbed fustian	CORDUROYS
South American		—old	GALLIGASKINS
—apron	TAYO	—Pakistani	SHALWAR
—cloak	PONCHO	—Persian	SHULWAR
Spanish sheepskin coat	ZAMARRA	—tartan	TREWS
	ZAMARRO	—with	
stand-up collar	PICCADILLY	narrow	
stole	BOA	—bottoms	PEGTOPS
straight dress	SHIRT DRESS	—legs	DRAINPIPES
	SHIRTWAISTER	wide	
strip worn over shoulder		—bottoms	BELL-BOTTOMS
—by priest	SCAPULAR	—legs	OXFORD BAGS
—Scottish	PLAID	tunic	
sub-deacon's vestment	TUNICLE	—African	DASHIKI, KANZU

—Greek	CHITON
—Indian	K(H)URTA
—sleeveless	TABARD
—small	TUNICLE
Turkish robe	CAFTAN, DOLMAN, KAFTAN
underclothes	LINGERIE, SMALLS
	UNDIES
—17th c	CIMAR, CYMAR
undershirt (Roman)	SUBUCULA
underskirt	PETTICOAT
undertaker's cloak	MOURNING-CLOAK
undress	
—military jacket	MESS JACKET
	SHELL-JACKET
—regimental coat	FROCK
veil	
—christening	CHRISMAL
—covering head	MANTILLA
—draped round head etc	W(H)IMPLE
—short	KISS ME
vestments	(*see* church—vestments)
waistcoat	GILET
—American	VEST
—closefitting	JERKIN
waterproof	
—Australian	DRIZA-BONE
—coat	BARBOUR, BURBERRY
	RAINCOAT, TRENCH-COAT
US	SLICKER
—over-garment(s)	MAC(K)INTOSH
	OILSKIN(S)
waxed coat	BARBOUR
weatherproof anorak	CAGOUL(E), KAGOOL
	KAGOUL(E)
winding-sheet	SHROUD
windproof	ANARAK, ANORAK
	PARKA, PARKEE, PARKI
woman's	
—backless bodice	HALTER
—basque (18th c)	PIERROT
—blouse	SHIRT, SHIRTWAIST
or bodice (US)	WAIST
—cape	FICHU, MANTEEL, PELERINE
old	SURTOUT
—cloak	CARDINAL, DOLMAN
19th c	VISITE
Roman	PALLA
Russian	SARAFAN
Scottish	ROCKLAY, ROKELAY
—collar (17th c)	WHISK
—dress	FROCK, ROBE
18th c	TROLLOPEE
—dressing-gown	NEGLIGEE, PEIGNOIR
—garment with combined	
bodice and skirt	PRINCESS
India	SAREE, SARI

—informal gown	HOUSECOAT, TEA GOWN
—jacket	
16-17th c	HALF-KIRTLE
19th c	POLKA
short	BASQUE, BOLERO, ZOUAVE
—knitted cape	SONTAG
—long mantle	PELISSE
—loose jacket (Scot.)	SHORTGOWN
—morning gown	CAMISOLE, PEIGNOIR
—neckerchief (17th c)	WHISK
—outer garment	BODICE, STOLE
	TABARD
—riding	
coat	JOSEPH
hood (18th c)	NITHSDALE
—shift	SMOCK
—shirt	CHEMISE, SHIFT
—short	
cloak (Scot.)	ROK(E)LAY
jacket	BOLERO, BASQUE
	ZOUAVE
shorts	HOT-PANTS
undergarment	SPENCER
—sleeved jacket	CAMISOLE
—underclothing	LINGERIE, UNDIES
17th c	CIMAR, CYMAR
bust	BRA(SSIERE)
—and waist	BODICE, BUSTIER
	SPENCER, TEDDY
hips	GIRDLE
overall	BODYSHAPER, CAMIKNICKERS
	PETTICOAT, SLIP
pants	BLOOMERS, BRIEFS
	KNICKERS
—with stockings	PANTIHOSE, TIGHTS
stiffened	BODICE, CORSET
	CORSELET(TE)
supporting	
stockings	SUSPENDER BELT
woollen	
—coat, short	MACKINAW
—clothes, rough	TWEEDS
—knitted	(see knitted above)
—petticoat	BALMORAL
—shawl	WHITTLE
wrap	AMICE, AMIS, HAP
—loose	NIGHT-RAIL
gases	
acetylene	ETHYNE
after-damp	CHOKE-DAMP
anaesthetic	CHLOROFORM
	CYCLOPROPANE
	ETHER, NITROUS OXIDE
antimony hydride	STIBINE
argon	A
attacking nervous system	NERVE GAS

burning	MUSTARD
carbon	
—and water	WATER GAS
—dioxide	CARBONIC ACID GAS
	COO
and methane	BIOGAS
mixture	AFTER-DAMP
	BLACK DAMP, CHOKE DAMP
—monoxide	CO, WHITE DAMP
carbonyl chloride	PHOSGENE
carburetted hydrogen	ETHYLENE
causing deterioration of	
mental performance	PSYCHOCHEMICAL
	PSYCHOGAS
chlorine	CL
colourless	CARBON MONOXIDE
	ETHYLENE, HYDROGEN IODIDE
	KETEN, NITRIC OXIDE
combustible	BUTANE, FIRE-DAMP
	METHANE, PROPANE
corrosive	MUSTARD GAS, YPERITE
dichlordiethyl sulphide	MUSTARD GAS
ethyne	ACETYLENE
explosive gas	BLACK DAMP, CHOKE DAMP
	ELECTROLYTIC GAS
	EUCHLORINE
fire-damp	MARSH GAS, METHANE
fluorine	F
formed	
—by radioactive decay	EMANATION
	ACTINON, NITON
	RADON, THORON
—in incomplete	
combustion	CARBON MONOXIDE
found in coal gas	CARBON MONOXIDE
from	
—actinium	ACTINON
—boilers	FLUE GAS
—coal	COAL GAS
—coke	PRODUCER GAS, TOWN GAS
—decaying matter	EFFLUVIUM
—methanol	FORMALDEHYDE
—organic materials	BIOGAS
—steam on hot coke	WATER GAS
gas	
—burner	BUNSEN
—cooled reactor	AGR
greenish gas	EUCHLORINE, FLUORINE
helium	HE
heavy hydrogen	DEUTERIUM
hydrogen	H
—isotope	DEUTERIUM, TRITIUM
hypothetical gas	(A)ETHER
inert gas	NOBLE GAS, RARE GAS
	ARGON, HELIUM, KRYPTON
	NEON, RADON, XENON
inflammable	METHYLAMINE
irritant gas	BROMINE, CN, CS, TEAR GAS
krypton	KR
lachrymator	TEAR GAS
laughing-gas	NITROUS OXIDE
liquid	
—gas used in war	LEWISITE
—oxygen	LOX
—petroleum gas	LPG
liquefied gas	BUTANE, CALOR
marsh gas	FIRE-DAMP, METHANE
methane	FIRE-DAMP, MARSH GAS
—and carbon dioxide	BIOGAS
mustard gas	DICHLORODIETHYL SULPHIDE
	YPERITE
natural gas	FIRE DAMP, MARSH GAS
	METHANE
neon	NE
nerve gas	SARIN, TABUN
neutron	NU
niton	RADON
nitrogen	N
—and hydrogen	AMMONIA
olfiant	ETHYLENE
oxygen	O
pale yellow gas	HYDROGEN BROMIDE
phosgene	CARBONYL CHLORIDE
phosphuretted	
hydrogen	PHOSPHINE
poison gas	ANTIMONY HYDRIDE, ARSINE
	BROMINE, CARBON MONOXIDE
	CARBONYL CHLORIDE, CHLORINE
	CYANIC ACID, CYANOGEN
	MUSTARD GAS, PHOSGENE
	PHOSPHINE, PRUSSIC ACID
	STIBINE, YPERITE
propellant	FLUORINE
radon	NITON, RN
silicon hydride	SIL(IC)ANE
smelling of	
—almonds	CYANIC ACID GAS
	PRUSSIC ACID
—rotten eggs	HYDROGEN SULPHIDE
stibine	ANTIMONY HYDRIDE
tear gas	CS GAS, LACHRYMATOR
unstable oxygen	OZONE
used	
—as	
disinfectant	FORMALDEHYDE
fertiliser	AMMONIA
fuel	BUTANE, METHANE
	PROPANE
—for	
fluorescent lighting	HELIUM
	KRYPTON, NEON
illuminated signs	NEON

making
—aspirin KETEN
—plastics ETHYLENE
—synthetic rubber BUTADIENE, BUTANE
riot control CS GAS
welding ACETYLENE, ETHYNE
 OXYGEN

—in
aerosols CFC, CHLOROFLUOROCARBON
 PROPELLANT
fire extinguishers CARBON DIOXIDE
 CARBONIC ACID GAS
fizzy drinks CARBON DIOXIDE
lasers XENON
synthesis of organic
 compounds ETHANE
very hot gas PLASMA
war gas ARSINE, CHLORINE, LEWISITE
 MUSTARD GAS, NERVE GAS
 PHOSGENE, PSYCHOGAS
 PSYCHOCHEMICAL, SARIN
 TABUN, ZYKLON B
xenon XE

gems
including: semi-precious stones
agate SCOTCH PEBBLE
almandine PURPLE GARNET
amber-coloured AMBER, TOPAZ
artificial PASTE, RHINESTONE
 STRASS
associated with birth BIRTHSTONE
aventurine SUNSTONE
balas ruby SPINEL
banded AGATE, (SARD)ONYX)
beryllium compounds ALEXANDRITE
 AQUAMARINE, BERYL
 CHRYSOBERYL, CYMOPHANE
 EMERALD, GOSHENITE
 HELIDOR, MORGANITE
birthstones
—January GARNET
—February AMETHYST
—March AQUAMARINE, BLOODSTONE
—April DIAMOND
—May EMERALD
—June ALEXANDRINE, MOONSTONE
 PEARL
—July RUBY
—August PERIDOT, SARDONYX
—September SAPPHIRE
—October OPAL, TOURMALINE
—November TOPAZ
—December TURQUOISE, ZIRCON
black JAD(E)ITE, JET, MELANITE
 OBSIDIAN, RUTILE
 SCHORL, TOURMALINE

bloodstone GREEN CHALCEDONY
blue AMETHYST, AQUAMARINE, BERYL
 EMERALD, INDICOLITE
 LAPIS LAZULI
 LAZURITE, SODALITE
 SAPPHIRE, SPINEL, TOPAZ
 TURQUOISE, ZIRCON
blue-grey C(H)ALCEDONY, LABRADORITE
Bohemian ruby ROSE QUARTZ
Brazilian
—emerald TOURMALINE
—peridot TOURMALINE
brightness of gem LUSTRE, WATER
bronze speckled AVENTURINE, SUNSTONE
brown AGATE, AMBER, ANDRADITE
 CAIRNGORM, CAT'S-EYE
 CELONITE, JADE, JAD(E)ITE
 JASPER, MORGANITE
 SMOKY QUARTZ, TIGER'S-EYE
 TURQUOISE, SARDONYX
carbon DIAMOND
carnelian CORNELIAN, SARD
changeable CHATOYANT
cinnamon-stone (H)ESSONITE
 HYACINTH, JACINTH
colourless ALEXANDRITE, DIAMOND
 JARGO(O)N, ROCK CRYSTAL
 TOPAZ, ZIRCON
corundum RUBY, SAPPHIRE
cutter/polisher LAPIDARY
cutting styles BAGUETTE, BRILLIANT
 BRIOZETTE, CABOCHON
 CUSHION, MARQUISE
 NAVETTE, ROSE, STEP
 TABLE, TRAP
egeran GARNET
emerald SMARAGD(INE)
engraving on gems GLYPHOGRAPHY
 LITHOGLYPH
evening emerald PERIDOT
fabled stone from
 dragon's brain DRACONITES
fake DOUBLET, ICE
fel(d)spar AMAZONITE, AVENTURINE
 LABRADORITE, MOONSTONE
 SUNSTONE
fire-opal GIRASOL(E)
fossilised
—resin AMBER
—wood JET
garnet EGERAN, (H)ESSONITE
green ALEXANDRITE, AMAZONITE
 AQUAMARINE, BERYL, BLOODSTONE
 CHRYSOBERYL, CHRYSOPRASE
 CYMOPHANE, DELMANTOID
 GARNET, GROSSULARITE

	EMERALD, HELIOTROPE, JADE
	JAD(E)ITE, MALACHITE, NEPHRITE
	OBSIDIAN, OLIVINE, PERIDOT
	SPINEL, TOPAZ, TOURMALINE
	TURQUOISE, UVAROVITE
	VERDITE, ZIRCON
—chalcedony	BLOODSTONE
—corundum	ORIENTAL EMERALD
—fluorspar	FALSE EMERALD
—garnet	URALIAN EMERALD
—quartz	MOTHER OF EMERALD
—rock crystal	CITRINE
hydrated	
—copper carbonate	MALACHITE
—silica	OPAL
impure diamond	BOART
industrial diamond	BOART
jacinth	GARNET, QUARTZ
	TOPAZ, ZIRCON
jade	JAD(E)ITE, NEPHRITE
lignite	JET
lime-chrome garnet	UVAROVITE
Matura diamond	ZIRCON
magnesia-alumina	ALMANDINE, CARBUNCLE
	DELMANTOID, GARNET
	GROSSULARITE, MELANITE
	PYROPE, TOPAZITE
magnesium-iron silicate	OLIVINE, PERIDOT
milky-white	MOONSTONE, OPAL
multi-coloured	AGATE, (SARD)ONYX, OPAL
opal	
—flame-coloured	FIRE-OPAL, GIRASOL(E)
—milky	CACHALONG
—semi-transparent	HYDROPHANE
—transparent	HYALITE
opaque quartz	JASP(ER), JASPIS
orange	CARNELIAN, CHRYSOBERYL
	CITRINE, CORNELIAN, FIRE-OPAL
	GIRASOL(E), HESSONITE
	JACINTH, RUBICELLE
	SARD, TOPAZITE
oriental	
—emerald	GREEN CORUNDUM
—topaz	SAPPHIRE
pink	ALMANDINE, MORGANITE
	RHODOLITE, ROSE QUARTZ
pointed oval shape	MARQUISE, NAVETTE
polished uncut stone	CABOCHON
purple	ALMANDINE (SPINEL)
	AMETHYST, GARNET
	RHODOLITE
—garnet	ALMANDINE
pyrope	RED GARNET
quartz	
—opaque	JASP(ER), JASPIS
—rose	BOHEMIAN RUBY

red	ALEXANDRITE, BERYL
	CAIRNGORM, CARBUNCLE
	CARNELIAN, CORNELIAN
	FIRE-OPAL, GARNET
	GIRASOL(E), HYACINTH
	JACINTH, JAD(E)ITE, JASPER
	RUBASSE, RUBELLITE
	RUBY, RUTILE, SPINEL, ZIRCON
—garnet	PYROPE, PYROPUS
reddish-brown	(H)ESSONITE
rose quartz	BOHEMIAN RUBY
sapphire	TELESIA
sard	CARNELIAN, CORNELIAN
silica compounds	AGATE, AMETHYST
	CAIRNGORM (STONE)
	CARNELIAN, C(H)ALCEDONY
	CHRYSOPRASE, CITRINE
	CORNELIAN, JASPER
	ROCK CRYSTAL, ROSE QUARTZ
	SARD, (SARD)ONYX
	SMOKE QUARTZ
silicate of	
—aluminium and sodium	JAD(E)ITE
—calcium and magnesium	NEPHRITE
—fluorine and aluminium	TOPAZ
—sodium and iron	TIGER'S-EYE
—zirconium	JACINTH, JARGO(O)N
	ZIRCON
single stone	SOLITAIRE
smaragd(ine)	EMERALD
smoky	CAIRNGORM (STONE)
	SMOKE QUARTZ
spinel	BALAS RUBY
—blue	SPINEL SAPPHIRE
—brown	CELONITE
—crimson	SPINEL RUBY
—orange	RUBICELLE
—purple	ALMANDINE SPINEL
—rose-red	BALSAM RUBY
sulphide of iron	MARCASITE
sunstone	AVENTURINE
telesia	SAPPHIRE
tourmaline	
—colourless	ACHROITE
—black	SCHORL
—blue	INDICOLITE
—pink	RUBELLITE
—red	RUBELLITE
—violet	SIBERITE
transparency of gem	LUSTRE, WATER
transparent	
—opal	HYALITE
—zircon	JARGO(O)N
turquoise	TURKOIS
twinkling like a gem	CHATOYANT
unit of weight	CARAT

various colours	ZIRCON
varying composition	ACHROITE
	INDICOLITE, RUBELLITE
	SCHORL, TOURMALINE
violet	AMETHYST, SIBERITE
volcanic glass	OBSIDIAN
white	C(H)ALCEDONY
	GOSHENITE
	JAD(E)ITE, OPAL
with	
—incised design	INTAGLIO
—raised design	CAMEO
yellow	AMBER, BERYL
	CHRYSOBERYL, CITRINE
	FIRE-OPAL, GARNET
	GIRASOL(E), HELIODOR
	JASPER, TOPAZ(ITE)
	SAPPHIRE
—quartz	SCOTTISH TOPAZ
yellowish-brown	OBSIDIAN
zircon	
—brown	MALACON
—orange	HYACINTH, HYACYNTH
	JACINTH
—yellow	JARGO(O)N

geography

including: geology	
mineralogy	
abrupt turn in course	
of river	ELBOW CAPTURE
absorption of one river	
by another	ABSTRACTION
accumulation of rock	
fragments	DEBRIS, SCREE, TALUS
aclinic line	MAGNETIC EQUATOR
acquisition by one river	
or stream of another	BEHEADING
	RIVER CAPTURE
	RIVER PIRACY
action of	
—climate on rocks etc	WEATHERING
—ice	GLACIATION
ages of	
—earth	(*see* geological ages *below*)
—human culture	(*see* **anthropology**)
agricultural system in	
hill country	TERRACE CULTIVATION
alignment of features	GRAIN
alkaline marsh area	ALKALINE FLAT
alluvial	
—deposit at mouth of river	DELTA
Scotland	CARSE
traversed by many	
branches	BIRD'S FOOT DELTA
—plain	
alongside river	FLOOD PLAIN

America	BOTTOM
formed by distribution of	
moraine over wider	
area	OUTWASH PLAIN, SANDIR
—slope	BAHADA, BAHAJA
altitude above which	
trees do not grow	TIMBER LINE
ancient alluvium	GEEST
angle	
—between horizontal and	
direction of earth's	
magnetic field	DIP
—between true and magnetic	
north	(MAGNETIC) DECLINATION
	(MAGNETIC) VARIATION
—between vertical and	
a fault plane	HADE
—horizontal	AZIMUTH
—vertical	ALTITUDE
angular distance from	
—Equator	LATITUDE
—Greenwich meridian	LONGITUDE
animal life of region	FAUNA
approaching the end of a	
geological cycle	SENILE
area	
—adjoining sea	BEACH, COAST(AL PLAIN)
	FORESHORE, LITTORAL
	SEABOARD, SEASIDE
	(SEA) SHORE, SHORELINE
	STRAND, TIDEWATER
—almost surrounded by	
water	PENINSULA
—between	
low-water mark	
and edge of	
continental shelf	SUB-LITTORAL
tides	INTERTIDAL
tropics	INTERTROPICAL
—bounded by watersheds (US)	WATERSHED
—containing much soil	
moisture	WETLAND(S)
—covered by	
fresh water	BROAD, LAKE (BASIN)
	LOCH, LOUGH, MERE, TARN
ice on	
—land	ICE CAP, ICE FIELD
	ICE SHEET
—water	FLOE, ICE PACK
sand	DESERT
sand-dunes	ERG, LINKS
snow	SNOWFIELD
stones	REG
stunted trees or shrubs	SCRUB
trees	FOREST, JUNGLE
	PLANTATION, WOOD(LAND)

—drained by river	CATCHMENT AREA	unstable sand	QUICKSAND
	(RIVER) BASIN, VALLEY		RUNNING SAND
—encrusted with salt	SALT FLAT	untouched forest	
	SALT PAN	with undergrowth	BUSH
—eroded by wind	DUST-BOWL	—reclaimed from sea	POLDER
—falling to centre from		—subject to periodic	
all directions	BASIN	flooding	
—frequently covered by water	WASH	by river	FLOOD PLAIN
—in which particular		by sea	SALTING(S), SALTMARSH
rocks predominate	TERRANE	—surrounded by water	AIT, ATOLL, EYOT
—lying inland from coast	HINTERLAND		ISLAND
—of		—underlying glacier	SUBGLACIAL
active deformation of		—used for crops	TILLAGE
Earth's crust	MOBILE BELT	—where asphalt or bitumen	
arid, sandy soil	STEPPE	rises to surface	TAR PIT
calms	DOLDRUMS	—within polar circles	FRIGID ZONE
	HORSE LATITUDES	arid region of deep gullies	BAD LANDS
continent near sea		arrangement of	
plus the continental		—atoms in crystal	(SPACE) LATTICE
shelf	CONTINENTAL PLATFORM	—grooves	STRIATION
dense undergrowth	THICKET	—strata	STRATIFICATION
droughts and		artificial	
dust-storms	DUST BOWL	—chamber in chalk	DENE-HOLE
dwarf evergreen		—embankment	DIKE, DYKE
oaks (US)	CHAPARRAL	India	BUND
Earth		USA	LEVEE
—divided by Equator		—heap of stones	CAIRN
or meridian	HEMISPHERE	—lake	RESERVOIR
—covered by		—watercourse	CANAL, DIKE, DITCH
water	WATER HEMISPHERE		DYKE, RACE
—just outside		—watering system	IRRIGATION
Arctic Circle	SUBARCTIC	attraction of mass of bodies	GRAVITY
Antarctic Circle	SUBANTARCTIC	backwater (Austr.)	BILLABONG
fertile soil		bank of earth etc	DIKE, DYKE
—America	BLACK EARTH	—round area to be	
—India	BLACK COTTON EARTH	irrigated	LEVEE
—Russia	BLACK EARTH	bare hill	FELL
	CHERNOZEM	barren	
mud covered at		—area in North America	BADLANDS
high tide	MUDFLAT(S)	—land	DESERT
open water in sea ice	POLYNA	—region of Andes	PARAMOS
permanently frozen subsoil	TUNDRA	—upland plateau (Scand.)	FJELD
scrubland		base	
—Mediterranean	GAR(R)IGUE	—mark for levels	BENCH MARK
	MAQUIS		DATUM (LEVEL)
—North America	CHAPARRAL	—on which organisms live	SUBSTRATE
sea adjoining land		basin	
mass	CONTINENTAL SHELF	—filling with alluvial fans	BOLSON
shifting sand dunes	ERG, SAND-SEA	—forming lake after	
soft wet ground	BOG, CARR, FEN	heavy rain	PLAYA
	FLOW, MARSH, SWAMP	—shaped crater of	
strong westerly		volcanic origin	CALDERA
winds	ROARING FORTIES	beach	SANDS
	SCREAMING FIFTIES	belts of high pressure on	
uniform climate,		both sides of the Equator	HORSE LATITUDES
flora, etc	NATURAL REGION	bend in rock	FOLD

bending etc of Earth's surface	DIASTROPHISM
blind channel from river	BILLABONG
boggy area (Scot.)	SLACK
boulder transported and deposited by glacier	ERRATIC (BLOCK)
boundary between	
—drainage areas	WATERSHED
—land and sea	COAST(LINE) SHORE(LINE)
—layers of Earth	DISCONTINUITY MOHO MOHOROVICICIAN DISCONTINUITY
break	
—in sequence of sedimentary rocks	DISCONFORMITY
—up of ice in spring	DEBACLE
breaking off of iceberg from a glacier	CALVING
bronze lustre in minerals	SCHILLER
building	
—of	
continents	EPEIROGENESIS
mountains	OROGENESIS
—up of surface	AGGRADATION
calcium carbonate deposit	
—from hot springs	TRAVERTINE, TUFA
—in arid regions (USA)	CALICHE
canal taking ocean-going vessels	SHIP CANAL
can(y)on	GORGE, RAVINE
capes	(see separate entry)
cardinal points	NORTH, SOUTH EAST, WEST
carrying away of surface	ABLATION
cascade pool	LIN(N)
caused by	
—flooding	DILUVIAL
—rainfall	PLUVIAL
—rotation of Earth	GEOSTROPHIC
cave	ANTRE, CAVERN
—in limestone region	GROTTO
cavity containing mineral deposit	DRUSE, DRUSY CAVITY GEODE, POCKET
central	
—mountain mass	MASSIF
—ocean or land mass	CRATON
change in	
—different rocks to become similar	CONVERGENCE
—rocks involving chemical composition	METASOMATISM
—shape of rocks	DEFORMATION
due to	
—heat	THERMAL METAMORPHISM

—pressure	DYNAMIC METAMORPHISM
—shore lines	EUSTACY, EUSTASY
—water level in lake	SEICHE
channel	
—for running water	GULL(E)Y WATERCOURSE WATERWAY
—formed by running water	GULL(E)Y, STREAMBED
circle on earth's surface	
—midway between poles	EQUATOR
—of latitude	ALMACANTAR ALMACANTUR
—passing through centre	GREAT CIRCLE
clay	
—layer left by glacier	BOULDER CLAY
—red	BOLE
—sticky	GLEY
clearing	
—in forest	GLADE
—of forest areas	DEFORESTATION
cleft	
—between hills (Scot.)	SLACK
—in rock (Scot.)	RIVA
cliff	BLUFF
—projecting into sea	HEADLAND
climate	(see meteorology)
coastal outline	COAST(LINE) SHORE(LINE)
—cutting across main structural lines	DISCORDANT COAST(LINE)
—parallel to main structural lines	CONCORDANT COAST(LINE) LONGITUDINAL COAST(LINE) PACIFIC COAST(LINE)
cold areas	CRYOSPHERE
collection of gas over oil deposit	GAS CAP
column of earth with boulder on top	EARTH PILLAR
combination of arable and pastoral farming	MIXED FARMING
compass direction	POINT, QUARTER
condition of soil	TILTH
containing	
—carbon	CARBONACEOUS
—clay	ARGILLACEOUS
—diatom skeletons	DIATOMACEOUS
—grains	GRANULAR, GRANULOSE GRANULOUS
—graphite	PLUMBAGINOUS
—gravel	GLAREOUS
—little silica	(ULTRA)BASIC (ULTRA)MAFIC

—platelike crystals	TABULAR	creek (Scot.)	GEO, GIO, VOE
—sand	ARENACEOUS	—small	POW
—shell-like material	TESTACEOUS	creeping of saturated	
—silica	SILICEOUS	material down slope	SOLIFLUCTION
	SILICIOUS	crescent-shaped	
continent building	EPEIROGENESIS	sand-dune	BARCHAN(E)
	EPEIROGENY		BARK(H)AN
continents		crevasse at top	
—modern	AFRICA, ANTARCTICA	of glacier	BERGSCHRUND, RIMAYE
	ASIA, AUSTRALIA	crust of dyke or vein	SALBAND
	EUROPE, NORTH AMERICA	crystal	
	SOUTH AMERICA, OCEANIA	—having	
—old	BALTIC, EURAMERICA	2 angles at right angles	MONOCLINIC
	GONDWANA(LAND)	3 unequal angles	TRICLINIC
	LAURASIA	3 angles at right angles	ORTHORHOMBIC
—old supercontinents	AMAZONIA	3 angles at right	
	BAIKALIA, KENORA	angles, two equal	TETRAGONAL
	PANGAEA	two or more parts	TWIN CRYSTAL
conversion of		—examination by	
—limestone to marble	MARMAROSIS	X-ray	X-RAY DIFFRACTION
—loose material		—showing different	
to rock	CEMENTATION	colours from	
—sediment to rock	DIAGENESIS	different angles	PLEOCHROIC
copse in boggy ground	CARR	—visible only under a	
coral reef		microscope	MICROCRYSTAL
—detached from land	CORAL ISLAND	cultivation	(*see* farming *below*)
—enclosing lagoon	ATOLL	curved	
—parallel to shore	BARRIER REEF	—delta	ARCUATE DELTA
cotton growing area (US)	COTTON BELT	—sandbar	HOOK
county	SHIRE	cut to form vertical slope	SCARP
—division	HUNDRED, LATHE	cylindrical	
covering of a region		—body of ore	PIPE
by ice	GLACIATION	—hollow concretion	INCRETION
crack in		dam in watercourse	BARRAGE
—earth	CHASM	dark spot in crystal	MACLE
—glacier	CREVASSE	debris	
—horizontal limestone	GRIKE, GRYKE	—at foot of cliff	SCREE, TALUS
—rock	FISSURE	—deposited by running	
	RIFT, SLIP	water	WASH
narrow	CHIMNEY	—from glacier	
reverse fault with		along	
small angle	THRUST FAULT	—centre	MEDIAL MORAINE
Scottish	RIVA	—sides	LATERAL MORAINE
tapering	GULL	at foot	(TERMINAL) MORAINE
where		underneath	GROUND MORAINE
—movement		—produced by weathering	
has occurred	FAULT	of rock	ELUVIUM
is		decaying organic	
—occurring	ACTIVE FAULT	matter in soil	HUMUS, LEAF MOULD
—parallel to		deep	
—strike	STRIKE FAULT	—gulf	ABYSS
—hanging wall		—hollow	CHASM
has moved upwards	REVERSE FAULT	—part of	
with no movement	JOINT	harbour, river, etc	CHANNEL
cracking off of thin layers of rock	EXFOLIATION	old meander	ENTRENCHED MEANDER
	LAMINATION	—round hollow	CIRQUE, CORRIE

deformation of Earth's	
crust	DIASTROPHISM
dense	
—evergreen shrubs	SCRUB
—forest region of Amazon	SELVA(S)
—scrub (America)	CHAPARRAL
—tropical forest	JUNGLE
deposit	
—by action of wind	AEOLIAN DEPOSIT
	LO(E)SS, LIMON
—containing particles	
of gold etc	PLACER
—enriched by downward	
filtering materials	SUPERGENE
—from	
avalanche	AVALANCHE CONE
glacier	(GROUND) MORAINE
glacier stream	KAME
—confined to valley	VALLEY TRAIN
	(see also debris above)
—of	
calcium carbonate	
from hot springs	TRAVERTINE, TUFA
in arid regions (US)	CALICHE
gravel with sodium	
(Chile)	CALICHE
	CHILE SALTPETRE
minerals from upper	
layers by rainwater	ILLUVIATION
ore	LEAD, LEDGE
	LODE, MINE, REEF, VEIN
salts	STRASSFURT DEPOSIT
silt embankment	
in river	LEVEE
—originally derived	
from land	TERRIGENOUS DEPOSIT
—under prehistoric	
pile-dwelling (It.)	TERRAMARA
depression	
—caused by meteor strike	CRATER
—in	
America	DEATH VALLEY
	SALTON SINK
China	TURFAN
desert region	WADI, WADY
Earth's surface	BASIN, BOWL, VALLEY
Egypt	EL FAIYUM, QUATTARA
Ethiopia	DANAKIL
Israel	DEAD SEA
ocean floor	DEEP
top of volcano	CALDERA, CRATER
—where water collects	SINK (HOLE)
description of physical	
features of an area	TOPOGRAPHY
deserts	(see separate entry)
dictionary of place-names	GAZETTEER

difference	
—between latitude and 90°	COLATITUDE
—in altitude	RELIEF
direction	
—from one point	
to another	BEARING
—in which vein of ore lies	RUN
—of	
line at right	
angles to dip	STRIKE
stream flow	DOWNSTREAM
wind	LEE, DOWNWIND
—opposite to	
stream flow	UPSTREAM
wind	UPWIND
discontinuity in	
rock strata	UNCONFORMITY
disintegration of surface by	
—action of	
atmospheric phenomena	WEATHERING
—hot gases	PNEUMATOLYSIS
distance due	
—East	EASTING
—North	NORTHING
—South	SOUTHING
—West	WESTING
disturbance of magnetic	
field	MAGNETIC STORM
ditch	DIKE, DYKE, FOSSE
division of	
—biogeographic region	ZONE
—Carboniferous strata	
Lower	CARBONIFEROUS LIMESTONE
	MOUNTAIN LIMESTONE
Upper	COAL MEASURES
	CULM (MEASURES)
—continent	SUB-CONTINENT
—county	HUNDRED, LATHE
—Cretaceous (US)	COMANCHEAN
—Devonian	OLD RED SANDSTONE
—geological time	AGE, EPOCH
	ERA, PERIOD
—Lower Jurassic	LIAS(SIC)
	KIM(M)ERIDGEAN
—Mesozoic	TRIAS(SIC)
Africa	KAR(R)OO
Europe	BUNTER, KEUPER
	MUSCHELKALK
—Middle Jurassic	BATHONIAN, BAJOCIAN
—Palaeozoic (US)	MISSISSIPPIAN
	PENNSYLVANIAN
—Permian strata	
Germany	ZECHSTEIN
South Africa	KAR(R)OO
—rock formation	SERIES, SYSTEM
—Upper Jurassic	RHAETIC

drainage	
—basin (US)	WATERSHED
—downwards from peak	RADIAL DRAINAGE
—pattern	
in rectangles	TRELLIS DRAINAGE
like a tree	DENDRITIC DRAINAGE
drowned	
—river estuary	FIORD, FJORD
—valley	RIA
dry watercourse	
—Africa	DONGA
—Arab countries	KHORA, WADI, WADY
—Australia	BILLABONG
—India	NULLA(H)
—Mexico/Spain	ARROYO
dune	DENE
early form of coal	LIGNITE, PEAT
Earth	
—cold areas	CRYOSPHERE
—eastern hemisphere	OLD WORLD
—envelope of air	ATMOSPHERE
—inhabited part of surface	ECUMENE
—layers of atmosphere	
boundaries	
—magnetosphere	MAGNETOPAUSE
—mesosphere	MESOPAUSE
—stratosphere	STRATOPAUSE
—troposphere	TROPOPAUSE
defining magnetic	
field	MAGNETOSPHERE
in order of height	
—lowest	TROPOSPHERE
	STRATOSPHERE
	CHEMOSPHERE
	MESOSPHERE
	THERMOSPHERE
—outermost	EXOSPHERE
helium	HELIOSPHERE
hydrogen	PROTONOSPHERE
hypothetical	ATHENOSPHERE
ionised	APPLETON LAYER
	D LAYER, E LAYER
	F LAYER, IONOSPHERE
	KENNELLY-HEAVISIDE LAYER
radiation belt	VAN ALLEN BELT
where	
—ozone is formed	OZONE LAYER
	OZONOSPHERE
—water vapour is	
broken up	HYDROXYL LAYER
—layers of Earth	
core	
—liquid	MAGMA
—solid (nickel and iron)	NIFE
inner	BARYSPHERE
	CENTROSPHERE

—boundary	
	GUTENBERG DISCONTINUITY
middle	MANTLE
—boundary	MOHO
	MOHOROVICIC(IAN) DISCONTINUITY
outer	CRUST, LITHOSPHERE
—higher	GRANITIC
silica and alumina	SIAL
—lower	BASALTIC
silica and magnesia	SIMA
—model of	TERRELLA
—point at end of axis	(NORTH) POLE
	SOUTH POLE
—region of seas	
and oceans	HYDROSPACE
	HYDROSPHERE
—western hemisphere	NEW WORLD
earthquake	(*see separate entry*)
elevated area with	
deep valleys	DISSECTED PLATEAU
equilibrium between	
high and low	
land masses	ISOSTASY
	ISOSTATIC THEORY
erosion	(*see* wearing away *below*)
erosive action of	
ice or water	SCOUR
excrement of sea-birds	GUANO
exploration of caves	POT-HOLING
	SPELEOLOGY
extending across	
polar region	TRANSPOLAR
fall of earth,	
rocks, etc	AVALANCHE
	BERGFALL, LANDSLIDE
	LANDSLIP, MUD SLIDE
fan-shaped	
—area of alluvium	
at river mouth	ALLUVIAL FAN, DELTA
—deposit	APRON
farming	
—by	
alternate strips	STRIP CROPPING
continuous	
cropping	INTENSIVE CULTIVATION
succession of crops	ROTATION
—raising	
animals	PASTORAL
—and	
crops	MIXED
trees	AGROFORESTRY
—in confined	
areas	BATTERY FARMING
	INTENSIVE FARMING
crops	ARABLE
one crop	MONOCULTURE

—using drip irrigation with nutients	FERTIGATION	different angles	ASYMMETRIC FOLD
—without		—downfold	SYNCLINE
irrigation	DRY FARMING	—overturned anticline	OVERFOLD
soil	HYDROPONICS	—parallel to	
fast-flowing part		surrounding rock	RECUMBENT
of river	RAPID(S)	—pierced by underlying	
feature remaining		material	DIAPIR
after changes in		—upfold	ANTICLINE
surrounding area	RELICT	—which is not broken	COMPETENT
fertile		—with same dip each	
—area in desert	OASIS	side	ISOCLINE
—land		force caused by	
alongside river (Scot.)	CARSE	rotation of Earth	CORIOLIS FORCE
producing two crops		forest	
per year (Spain)	HUERTA	—adjoining tundra	TAIGA
—wooded area (US)	HAMMOCK	—alongside river	GALLERY FOREST
field of granular snow	FIRN, NEVE	subject to flooding	(I)GAPO
fill with eroded material	AGGRADE	—clearance	DEFORESTATION
final stage in development			SPARTAGE
of community	CLIMAX	—clearing	GLADE
fine		—hardwood	DECIDUOUS
—grained, plastic,		—hot evergreen	EQUATORIAL
moisture-retentive soil	CLAY		TROPICAL RAIN FOREST
—material deposited		—northern coniferous	TAIGA
by river, etc	SILT	—of thorny trees in	
—mineral particles	SILT, SAND, GRAVEL	arid area	THORN FOREST
finely ground		—open (Brazil)	CAATINGA
—matter produced by		—softwood	CONIFEROUS
action of glacier	ROCK FLOUR	—swampy (Russia)	URMAN
weathering	SILT	—tropical	EQUATORIAL FOREST
—quartz	SAND		JUNGLE
flat			MONSOON FOREST
—elevated land	TABLELAND, PLATEAU		RAIN FOREST
—land alongside river	HOLM	—wet (S. Amer.)	SELVA
which floods	FLOOD PLAIN	form of landscape	MORPHOLOGY
	RIVER TERRACE	formation of	
	WATER MEADOW	—continents	EPEIOGENESIS
—limestone block or ridge	CLINT		EPEIROGENY
—plane of breakage	CLEAVAGE (PLANE)	—minerals	PARAGENESIS
—stony desert (N. Africa)	REG	—mountains	OROGENESIS
—surrounded by slopes	AMPHITHEATRE	—soil	PEDOGENESIS
—topped mountain	MESA	formed	
—treeless area	PLAIN, PRAIRIE	—after enclosing rock	EPIGENETIC
—valley (Himalayas)	D(H)OON, D(H)UN	—at base of mountains	PIEDMONT
flattish region	PENEPLAIN	fracture in Earth's	
floating mass of		surface	FAULT
vegetable matter (Sudan)	SUDD	fragment(s) of rock	CLAST, DEBRIS
flood caused by			DETRITUS, RUBBLE
overflowing river	FRESHET		SCREE, TALUS
flooded forest	(I)GAPO	frequent movement	
flow of natural water		of tribes	NOMADISM
from the ground	BOURNE, SPA, SPRING	fruit growing area (US)	FRUIT BELT
fold in rock		gap in mountains	COL, PASS
—at		gas vent in surface	MOF(F)ETTE
		general slope of land	VERSANT
constant angle	MONOCLINE	gentle slope	GLACIS

geographers/geologists/ mineralogists		epochs	PALAEOCENE
			EOCENE
—American	ALVAREZ, BARGHOORN		OLIGOCENE
	BERKNER, BRIGGS, CHAMBERLAIN	Palaeocene, Eocene	
	DAVIS, DUTTON, EWING	and Oligocene	PALAEOGENE
	GILBERT, GUTENBERG, HESS		MIOCENE
	ISARD, WELLS		PLIOCENE
—Australian	DAVID	Miocene and Pliocene	NEOGENE
—Austrian	PENCK, SEUSS, WULFEN	period	QUATERNARY
—British	FAWCETT, HAGGETT	epochs	PLEISTOCENE
	HERBERTSON, LONSDALE		POST-GLACIAL
	LYELL, MACKINDER, MITCHELL		HOLOCENE, RECENT
	MURCHISON, ROHBY	—end of Mesozoic	
	SEDGWICK, SMAILES	to present day	NEOZOIC
—Croatian	MOHOROVICIC	geological	
—Dutch	SLICHER, VAN BATH	—deposit	HORIZON
—French	CHABOT, DAUBREE	—time divisions	(A)EON, AGE
	DE CHANCOURTOIS		EPOCH, ERA, PERIOD
	DEMANGEAU, GOTTMAN	geosyncline with highly	
	GUETTARD, MARTONNE, SIEGFRIED	folded limbs	SYNCLORIUM
	SION, VIDAL DE LA BLACKE	glacial	
—German	CHRISTALLER, FUCHS	—deposit	BOULDERCLAY, MORAINE
	LOSCH, MOHS, RATZEL	at	
	WEGENER, WERNER	—foot	TERMINAL MORAINE
—Italian	MERCALLI, MONTICELLI	—side	LATERAL MORAINE
—Swedish	HAGERSTRAND	during retreat of	
—Swiss	AGASSIZ, CHARPENTIER	ice	RECESSIONAL MORAINE
	VENETZ	in centre	MEDIAL MORAINE
geographical regions (*see* zoological regions *below*)		over an area	GROUND MORAINE
geological ages		—drift	TILL
(in date order)		—period	ICE AGE
—first moments		glaciation slope (Alps)	RISS
proton era	HADRONIC ERA	glacier	
electron era	LEPTONIC ERA	—at foot of mountain	PIEDMONT GLACIER
gamma ray era	RADIATION ERA	—in	
—earliest	HADEAN	a hollow	CIRQUE GLACIER
	ARCH(A)EAN		VALLEY GLACIER
—era	PRE-CAMBRIAN	Alaska	MALASPINA, NABESNA
periods	AZOIC	Alps	ALETSCHGLETSCHER
	ARCHAEOZOIC	Antarctica	BEARDMORE, DENMAN
	CRYPTOZOIC, PROTEROZOIC		LAMBERT-FISHER
	ALGONKIAN		NIMROD-LENNOL-KING
—era, ancient life	PRIMARY, PALAEOZOIC		RECOVERY, SLESSOR
periods	CAMBRIAN	Greenland	PETERMANS GLETSCHER
	ORDOVICIAN	Himalayas	FEDTSCHENKO
	SILURIAN		HISPAR-BIAFO
	DEVONIAN		KANCHENJUNGA
	CARBONIFEROUS		SIACHEN
—era, middle life	SECONDARY, MESOZOIC	Iceland	VATNAVOKULL
periods	TRIASSIC	New Zealand	TASMAN
	JURASSIC	Norway	JOSTEDALSERE
Lower Cretaceous	NEOCOMIAN	gold-bearing gravel	
	CRETACEOUS	deposit	LEAD
—era, modern life	CAINOZOIC, CENOZOIC	granular snow	FIRN, NEVE
	KAINOZOIC	grape growing	
period	TERTIARY	area (US)	GRAPE BELT

graph of height against area	HYPSOGRAPHIC CURVE
grassland	
—Brazil	CAMPO
—Hungary	PUSZTAS
—North America	PRAIRIE
—regularly grazed	PASTURE
mown	MEADOW
—Russia	STEPPES
—South Africa	KAR(R)OO, VELD(T)
—South America	LLANOS, PAMPAS
	SAVANNA(H)
gravel	
—deposit from glacier-stream	KAME, OUTWASH
—ridge	ESKAR, ESKER, KAME
	OS, TOMBOLO
grazing area (US)	RANGE
groove(s) in rockface	STRIA(E)
group of islands	ARCHIPELAGO
growing	(see also **rearing**)
—in Northern areas	BOREAL
—on	
dry ground	GLARIAL
gravel	GLAREOUS
silica	SILICICOLOUS
upland slopes below treeline	SUBALPINE
Guinea coast of West Africa	WHITE MAN'S GRAVE
gully (S. Afr.)	DONGA
hardness of minerals	MOHS SCALE
1	TALC
2	GYPSUM
3	CALCITE
4	FLUORITE
5	APATITE
6	ORTHOCLASE
7	QUARTZ
8	TOPAZ
9	CORUNDUM
10	DIAMOND
having same	
—folding	ISOCLINAL
—magnetic dip	ISOCLINAL
headland	(see projection below)
heap of stones as memorial or landmark	CAIRN
heath-covered plain (France)	LANDE
high	
—area between faults	HORST
—bleak part of Andes	PUNA
—flat land	PLATEAU, TABLELAND
—land of a region	UPLAND
—plateau (S. Amer.)	ALTIPLANO, PUNA
—point from which water flows off in different directions	DIVIDE
	WATER PARTING
	WATERSHED
—tidal wave in estuary	BORE
highest point of river reached by trading vessels	HEAD OF NAVIGATION
hill	
—Arab	TEL(L)
—bare	FELL
—cliff-sided	BUTTE
—flat-topped	MESA
—formed of debris carried by glacier	DRUMLIN
ejected magma	VOLCANO
—in permafrost	PINGO
—isolated (US)	MESA
—low	HOW
—North Africa	(D)JEBEL
—old	BARROW
—pointed	KIP(P)
—rising from plain in arid region	INSELBERG
—rocky	TOR(R)
—rounded	MAMELON, MORRO
Scottish	DOD, KNOWE
—Scottish	BRAE, LAW
—South Africa	BERG, KOP(JE), KOPPIE
—volcanic (France)	PUY
—Welsh	DUN
—with one steep face	CRAG AND TAIL
	CUESTA
pointed summit	PEAK
hillocks in a valley which has been glaciated	ROCHES MOUTONNEES
hillside (Scot.)	BRAE
hilly upland region (US)	COTEAU
hole	
—in solid rock	POT HOLE
—through which water and air are forced by tides	BLOW HOLE
hollow	
—at head of valley	CIRQUE
—formed by melting of ice block	GIANT'S KETTLE
	KETTLE(-HOLE)
—in Earth's crust	BASIN
glacier containing dust	DUST WELL

hillside	COMB(E), COOMB, CWM
karst region	POLJE
limestone	
—area	DOLINA, DOLINE
—dissolved by	
rainwater	GRIKE, GRYKE
mountainside	COVE
rock face	CAVE
—into which cold air	
sinks	FROST HOLLOW
—leading to undergound	
cavern	POTHOLE, SINKHOLE
	SWALLET, SWALLOW-HOLE
—small	DELL, DIMBLE, DINGLE
—where water collects	WATERHOLE
horizontal	
—line of rock stratum	STRIKE
—mine shaft	ADIT, DRIFT
	HEAD(ING)
—sheet of igneous rock	SILL
hot water from the	
ground	GEYSER, HOT SPRING
	THERMAL SPRING
ice	
—block(s) in steep	
glacier	ICE FALL, SERAC
—cap extending into sea	BARRIER
—floating	
blocks	DRIFT ICE, PACK ICE
mass	ICEBERG
sheet	ICE FLOE
thin fragments	PAN
—forming spicules in	
fast-flowing rivers	FRAZIL ICE
—from fresh inland water	LAND ICE
—glare from light	
reflected from ice	ICEBLINK
—hanging in tapering	
column	ICICLE
—large blocks floating	
together	PACK ICE
—large sheet of ice	ICE FIELD
—mass projecting into sea	ICE FOOT
—particles in atmosphere	ICE FOG
—pillar formed by	
breaking glacier	SERAC
—refreezing after	
melting under pressure	REGELATION
—river	GLACIER
—sheet formed by	
combined glaciers	PIEDMONT GLACIER
—small iceberg	CALF
—thin plates	PANCAKE ICE
—very large area	ICE CAP, ICE SHEET
igneous	PYROGENIC
increase in land area	ACCRETION

indentation in coastline	BAY, BIGHT
	COVE, GULF
inland sheet of water	LAKE
—small	MERE, POND, POOL, TARN
	(see also **lakes**)
inlet, long and narrow	RIA
instrument	
—indicating direction	COMPASS
—measuring	
areas on map	PLANIMETER
distances on map	OPISOMETER
firmness of soil	PENETROMETER
hardness of rocks	SCLEROMETER
magnetic	
—dip	INCLINOMETER
—intensity	MAGNETOMETER
percolation through	
soil	LYSIMETER
slope	(IN)CLINOMETER
—recording variations	
in magnetic field	MAGNETOGRAPH
intermittent	
—hot spring	GEYSER
—stream	(WINTER)BOURNE
irregularity of surface	ACCIDENT
irrigated land giving	
one crop per annum (Spain)	VEGA
island	
—coral	ATOLL
—in river	AIT, EYOT, HOLM
—low	CAY, KEY
—Scottish	INCH
isolated	
—dune	BARCHAN(E), BARK(H)AN
—mass of rock standing above	
softer rock surfaces	MONADNOCK
—rock mass	TOR
—rural area	
Australia	OUTBACK
USA	BOONDOCKS
jointing in coal	CLEAT
junction of	
watercourses	CONFLUENCE
	CONFLUENCY
jungle of mangrove	
trees in tropical	
coastal area	MANGROVE SWAMP
lacking	
—iron	NONFERROUS
—lime	NONCALCAREOUS
lagoon at river	
mouth (Baltic)	HAFF
lakes	(see separate entry)
land	
—belonging to the	
community	COMMON

—bordering sea	BEACH, (FORE)SHORE
—entirely surrounded by water	
—in river	AIT, EYOT
—in sea	ISLAND, ISLET
—fit or used for farming	ARABLE
—forming a lake only in heavy rains	PLAYA
—mass	CONTINENT
—used for	
cultivation	ARABLE
grazing	GRASSLAND, PASTURE
large	
—anticline	GEOANTICLINE
—bay	GULF
—crystal in porphyritic rock	PHENOCRYST
—hollow in karst region	POLJE
—land mass	MAINLAND (SUB-)CONTINENT
—mass of underground igneous rock	LACCOLITH
—particle	MACROAGGREGATE
—pothole	(GIANT'S) KETTLE
—sections of Earth's crust	TECTONIC PLATES
—syncline	GEOSYNCLINE
—unbroken expanse of land	FIELD
—watercourse	RIVER
latitude	
—0°	EQUATOR
—23° N	TROPIC OF CAPRICORN
—23° S	TROPIC OF CANCER
—66° N	ARCTIC CIRCLE
—66° S	ANTARCTIC CIRCLE
law relating to deflection due to Earth's rotation	FERREL'S LAW
layer(s)	STRATUM(STRATA)
—between others	INTERBEDDED
—in geological section	HORIZON
—of	
coal	SEAM
humus	MOR
minerals	SEAM
organic materials on forest floor	LITTER
rock	STRATUM
sediment (seasonal)	VARVE
soil	
—at surface	A-HORIZON, TOPSOIL
—below surface	B-HORIZON, SUBSOIL
—overlying	SUPERSTRATUM
—underlying	SUBSTRATUM
layering	STRATIFICATION
laying down of transported material	DEPOSITION

level	
—of underground water	LEVEL OF SATURATION WATER LEVEL, WATER TABLE
—tract	
bordering river	TERRACE
cut into hillside	TERRACE
of	
—high land	PLATEAU, TABLELAND
—low land	PLAIN
limestone	
—area drained underground	KARSTLAND KARST REGION
—depression	POLJE
—needle	
hanging from ceiling	STALACTITE
rising from floor	STALAGMITE
line	
—between poles	AXIS
—bounding view of earth from a particular spot	HORIZON
—joining	
points where magnetic needle remains horizontal	ACLINIC LINE MAGNETIC EQUATOR
waterfalls in different rivers	FALL LINE
—of	
latitude	PARALLEL
longitude	MERIDIAN
—where the date changes	INTERNATIONAL DATE LINE
zero magnetic declination	AGONIC LINE
—on	
Earth's surface	
—at constant angle to meridians	LOXODROME RHUMB LINE
—of plane through centre	GREAT CIRCLE, MERIDIAN
map showing equal	
—cloudiness	ISONEPH
—depth below sea-level	ISOBATH
—earthquake shock	COSEISMIC LINE HOMOSEISMAL LINE ISOSEISMAL LINE
—height	CONTOUR
—inclination to vertical	ISOCLINIC
—magnetic	
declination	ISOGONIC LINE
intensity	ISODYNAMIC LINE ISOMAGNETIC LINE
—rainfall	EQUIPLUVE, ISOHYET
—salinity	ISOHALINE
—sunshine	ISOHEL

—temperature	ISOTHERM
below ground	ISOGEOTHERM
in coldest times	ISOCRYME
summer mean	ISOTHERE
—time difference	ISOCHRONE
—upheaval of land	ISOBASE
—separating	
areas of different dialects	ISOGLOSS
Australian from	
Oriental biogeographic	
area	WALLACE'S LINE
drainage areas	WATERSHED
—showing profile of	
valley bottom	THALWEG
	VALLEY LINE
—value of various	
features	ISOGRAM, ISOLINE
	ISOMETRIC LINE
	ISOPLETH
wind speed	ISOTACH
—where land and	
sea meet	COAST(LINE)
	SHORE(LINE)
lines representing	
slopes on map	HACHURES
living in river	
or stream	FLUVIAL, FLUVIATILE
loamy deposit laid	
down by wind	LO(E)SS
long	
—mountain range with	
jagged peaks	SIERRA
—narrow	
ridge	HOGBACK, HOG'S BACK
sea inlet	FIORD, FJORD, FIRTH
—rounded rock mound	ROCHE MOUTONNEE
—stretch of land	
almost surrounded	
by water	PENINSULA
longitude 0°	GREENWICH MERIDIAN
	PRIME MERIDIAN
loop	
—in course of river	MEANDER
—of river cut off	
forming lake	OX BOW
loose	
—pebbles	SHINGLE
—rounded rock fragments	GRAVEL
loss of	
—snow , etc, by erosion	
evaporation, etc	ABLATION
—surface by erosion	ABRASION
—water by evaporation	
and transpiration	EVAPOTRANSPIRATION
low	
—ground between hills	DALE, VALLEY

—island	CAY, KEY
—land	LOWLAND(S)
adjoining sea	BEACH, COAST
	COASTAL PLAIN
	(FORE)SHORE, LITTORAL
between	
—faults	GRABEN, RIFT VALLEY
—hills	DALE
—moist area	SLADE
—pressure equatorial belt	DOLDRUMS
—reef	CAY, KEY
—wet land	BOG, CARR, FEN, MARSH
	MORASS, SWAMP, WASH
Canada	MUSKEG
lower limit of perpetual	
snow on high ground	SNOWLINE
lowest	
—level of stream-bed	BASE-LEVEL
—part of embankment etc	TOE
lying at foot of mountain	PIEDMONT
magnetic	
—Equator	ACLINIC LINE
—property of	
earth	TERRESTRIAL MAGNETISM
main compass points	CARDINAL POINTS
maize growing	
area (US)	CORN BELT
making new forest	AFFORESTATION
man-made	(see artificial above)
map	
—drawn in outline	CHART
—making	CARTOGRAPHY
—markings showing relief	HACHURES
—projections	AITOFF'S
	BARTHOLOMEW'S NORDIC
	BARTHOLOMEW'S REGIONAL
	BARTHOLEMEW'S TIMES
	BONNE'S, CONIC(AL)
	CYLINDRICAL, EQUAL AREA
	EQUIDISTANT, EQUIVALENT AZIMUTHAL
	GALL'S, GNOMIC
	GOODE'S INTERRUPTED HOMOLOSINE
	HAMMER(-AITOFF)HOMOLOGRAPHIC
	LAMBERT'S AZIMUTHAL EQUAL-AREA
	MERCATOR'S, MOLLWEIDE'S
	ORTHOGRAPHIC, ORTHOMORPHIC
	PETER'S, POLYCONIC
	SANSON-FLAMSTEED SINUSOIDAL
	STEREOGRAPHIC
	ZENITHAL EQUAL-AREA
	ZENITHAL EQUIDISTANT
—showing	
altitude pictorially	RELIEF MAP
relief	TOPOGRAPHIC MAP
land masses in	
accurate proportions	PETERS

small area in	
true shape	CONFORMAL
statistical information	
as diagrams	CARTOGRAM
mapping configuration	
of Earth's surface	TOPOGRAPHY
margin of body of water	WATERSIDE
marshy creek or river (US)	BAYOU
mass of	
—hard rock standing	
on neck of softer	
wind-eroded rock	ZEUGE(N)
—igneous rock formed by	
intrusion of magma	BATHOLITE
	BATHOLITH
	BATHYLITE, BATHYLITH
—minerals deposited	
from solution	CONCRETION
—ore left in to support	
mine roof	PILLAR
—sedimentary rock	
enclosing salt deposit	SALT DOME
—sliding snow	AVALANCHE
—stone round lake-margin	LAKE RAMPART
material	
—carried by river	LOAD
—deposited by	
glacier	MORAINE
ice	BOULDER CLAY
rain	ILLUVIUM
water	ALLUVIUM, SEDIMENT
wind	L(O)ESS
—water or ice	DRIFT
—enclosing crystals, etc	MATRIX
measure of hardness	
of minerals	MOHS SCALE
measurement of	
—angles in surveying	TRIANGULATION
—area	PLANIMETRY
—heights above sea-level	HYPSOMETRY
—land forms	MORPHOMETRY
—time by decay of radio-	
active materials	RADIOMETRICS
method of survey for	
map-making	TRIANGULATION
mineral	
—composition of rock	MODE
—valuable enough	
to be mined	ORE
—vein	LEDGE, LODE, REEF
	(see also **mineral***)*
mineralogists	*(see* geologists *above)*
mining from surface	OPENCAST (MINING)
	STRIP MINING
mixture of sulphides	MATTE
moat	FOSEE

molten rock	
—at centre of earth	MAGMA
—from volcano	LAVA
	(see also **volcano***)*
moorland pool (Scot.)	FLOW
mountain	*(see separate entry)*
mountainous land	HIGHLAND(S)
mouth of river	DEBOUCHEMENT
	ESTUARY
movement of	
—atmosphere	ATMOSPHERIC TIDE
—debris along shore	LONGSHORE DRIFT
—land masses	CONTINENTAL DRIFT
—rocks	
on either side of fault	SHIFT
producing fault	SLIP
—soil down slopes	SPOIL CREEP
	SOLIFLUCTION
—water or sand caused by wind	DRIFT
mud flat	SLOB
narrow	
—canyon	CANADA
—cleft in rock	CHIMNEY, CREVICE
—gorge	DEFILE, CLUSE
	WATER GAP
without water	WIND GAP
—headland	BILL
—ledge or shelf	BENCH
—neck of land	
between rivers	DOAB
joining land masses	ISTHMUS
—pass	DEFILE, GORGE
—passage	GUT
—sea	
inlet	FIORD, FIRTH, FJORD
passage	CHANNEL, GUT, KYLE
	SOUND, STRAIT
—shelf on rockface	LEDGE
—tongue of sand or	
gravel in sea	
attached to land	SPIT
connecting islands	TOMBOLO
not attached	BAR, SANDBANK
—valley	COMB(E), COOMB, CWM
	DEAN, DENE, DINGLE
	GLEN, GORGE
—water channel in rock	VEIN
natural	
—amphitheatre	CIRQUE, CORRIE
—features of Earth	LANDFORM
—home	HABITAT
navigable channel	WATERWAY
network of latitude	
and longitude lines	GRATICULE, GRID
north as	
—end of Earth's axis	TRUE NORTH

—indicated by compass	MAGNETIC NORTH
obstruction of stream forming lake	DAM
ocean	(*see* **oceanography**)
official	
—base for levels	NEWLYN DATUM
	ORDNANCE DATUM
—co-ordinates	NATIONAL GRID
—mapping authority (UK)	
	ORDNANCE SURVEY
old river affected by uplift of land	REJUVENATED RIVER
ooze	(*see* **oceanography**)
open	
—anchorage protected by reefs etc	ROADSTEAD
—area in woods	CLEARING, GLADE
—hilly land	DOWN
—uncultivated region	HEATH
—upland area	HEATH, MOOR
	PLATEAU, WOLD
in South Afica	KAR(R)OO
opening in ground emitting	
—carbon dioxide	MOFETTE
—gases	FUMAROLE
—hot water	GEYSER
—molten rock, etc	VOLCANO
optical illusion caused by heated layers of air	MIRAGE
ore deposit	LEAD, LEDGE, LODE
	MINE, VEIN, REEF
organic soil material	HUMUS
outcrop	BASSET
outwash plain	SANDR
overhang of snow	CORNICE
part of	
—country separated from the main part	ENCLAVE
—Earth including most of	
land areas	LAND HEMISPHERE
water areas	HYDROSPACE
	HYDROSPHERE
	WATER HEMISPHERE
partly-developed mine	PROSPECT
pass	GAP, GATE, COL
—Scottish	SLAP
—with a stream	WATER GAP
—without a stream	WIND GAP
passage	
—between land masses	INLET
—in mine	GALLERY, GANGWAY
	LEVEL
peak projecting from ice cap	NUNATAK

peat-bog	PETARY
peninsulas	ALASKA, ARABIA
	IBERIA, INDIA, LABRADOR
	SCANDINAVIA
period	
—between	
Ice Ages	INTERGLACIAL
tides	INTERTIDAL
—of	
equal night and day	EQUINOX
—in	
March	SPRING EQUINOX
September	AUTUMNAL EQUINOX
glaciation	ICE AGE
particular climatic conditions	SEASON
temporary retreat of ice	INTERSTADIAL
periodic movement of	
—Earth's crust	TIDE
—sea water	TIDE
permanent	
—area of frost	PERMAFROST
—mass of ice	GLACIER, ICECAP
	ICEFIELD
—snow	SNOWCAP, SNOWFIELD
pertaining to	
—centre of Earth	GEOCENTRIC
—Earth	CHTHONIAN, CHTHONIC
	TELLURAL, TELLURIAN
	TELLURIC, TERRENE
	TERRESTRIAL
—features of Earth	GEOMORPHIC
—form of rock masses	GEOTECTONIC
—glaciers	GLACIAL
—heat of Earth's interior	GEOTHERMAL
—Ice Ages	GLACIAL
—land	TERRENE, TERRESTRIAL
—magnetic remanence	THERMOREMANENT
—sediment on sea-floor from erosion of land	TERRIGENOUS
—soil conditions	EDAPHIC
—underground water supplies	PHREATIC
photographic representation of	
—Earth's surface	TOPOGRAPH
—model on map	PHOTO RELIEF MAP
physical features of an area	TERRAIN, TOPOGRAPHY
place showing evidence of mineral deposit	PROSPECT
places on opposite sides of Earth	ANTIPODES
plain	
—Arctic	TUNDRA

—Brazil	CAMPO
—India	MAIDAN
—North Africa	REG
—North America	PRAIRIE
—Persia	MAIDAN
—Russia	STEPPE
—South Africa	KAR(R)OO, VELD(T)
—South America	LLANO, PAMPAS
	PARAMO, SAVANNA(H)
plane	
—between strata	BEDDING PLANE
—of reverse fault	THRUST PLANE
plant	
—life of a region	FLORA
—remains	
from earlier age	FOSSIL
in coal	FUSAIN
planting of woodlands	REFORESTATION
plateau	
—Scandinavia	FJELD
—South Africa	KAR(R)OO
—Spain	MESETA
—with steep faces	TABLELAND
plates of Earth's crust	AFRICAN
	ANTARCTIC, ARABIAN
	AUSTRALIAN, CARIBBEAN
	EURASIAN, IRAN, NAZCA
	NORTH AMERICAN, PACIFIC
	PHILIPPINES, SOUTH AMERICAN
platform bordering river	RIVER TERRACE
point	
—at which slope of	
river changes	KNICK POINT
—of compass	RHUMB
pond	
—dry in summer (Ireland)	TURLOUGH
—fed by spring	WELL
—filled by condensation	DEWPOND
—formed by damming	
stream (India)	TANK
port	
—in China open to	
trade by treaty	TREATY PORT
—involved in import and	
export	ENTREPOT
precipice (S. Africa)	KRANS, KRAN(T)Z
principal compass	
points	CARDINAL POINTS
	N, NORTH, S, SOUTH
	E, EAST, W, WEST
process of deformation	
of Earth's crust	DIASTROPHISM
production of different	
rocks from common	
mother base	DIFFERENTIATION
profile of river bed	THALWEG

projecting layer of rock	LEDGE, SHELF
projection	
—from mountain or hill	OFFSET, SPUR
—into sea	BILL, CAPE
	HEADLAND, MORRO, MULL
	NAZE, NESS, POINT
	PENINSULA, PROMONTORY
	SCAW, SKAW, SPIT, TONGUE
protective barrier	
round harbour, etc	BREAKWATER, GROIN
	GROYNE, JETTY, MOLE
quicksand (Scot.)	FLOW
raised	
—area of seabed	BANK
—block between faults	HORST
—flat area(s)	PLATEAU(X)
	TABLELAND
—road or path over	
low-lying area	DIKE, DYKE, LEVEE
raising of Earth's	
surface	ELEVATION
rate of temperature	
change with altitude	LAPSE RATE
ravine	CAN(Y)ON, COULEE
	COULOIR, GAP, GORGE
	GULCH, KHOR, LIN(N)
—Scottish	CLEUCH, CLEUGH
	HEUCH, HEUGH
recession of water	DERELICTION
reclaimed land	POLDER, THWAITE
reef	CAY, KEY
reference level for altitudes	BENCHMARK
	DATUM (LEVEL)
region	
—between	
desert and temperate	
zone (Africa)	SAHELIAN
tropics and	
temperate	
region	SUB-TROPICAL REGION
tundra and cool	
temperate	
zone	COLD TEMPERATE REGION
	SUB-POLAR REGION
—inland of seaport	HINTERLAND
—of	
calms near tropics	CALMS OF CANCER
	CALMS OF CAPRICORN
intermediate rainfall	
and plant growth	GRASSLAND
seas and oceans	HYDROSPACE
	HYDROSPHERE
—south of Sahara desert	SAHELIAN
—where	
cereals are grown	
—North America	WHEAT BELT

—South America	WHEAT CRESCENT	not rejoining river	DISTRIBUTARY
life		rejoining	ANABRANCH
—exists	BIOSPHERE	sinking into ground	ANABRANCH
—is possible	ECOSPHERE	—branches uniting to	
remaining magnetism	REMANENCE	form network	ANASTOMOSIS
remains of plant or		—cutting through land	
animal from earlier age	FOSSIL	in its path	ANTECEDENT RIVER
remote country		—divided into network	
—Australia	OUTBACK	of channels	BRAIDED
—USA	BOONDOCKS	—draining land which	
removal of minerals etc		has been lifted	CONSEQUENT RIVER
from soil by rainwater	LEACHING	—flowing opposite to	
removing forest	DEFORESTATION	consequent river	OBSEQUENT RIVER
replacement of minerals		—flowing parallel	
by calcite and		to slope	SUBSEQUENT RIVER
dolomite	CALCIFICATION	—landing-place	LEVEE
replanting forest	REFORESTATION	—mouth affected by tides	ESTUARY, FIRTH
representation of Earth's		—or stream joining larger	BRANCH
curved surface on			TRIBUTARY
flat surface	MAP PROJECTION	—side	
resulting from deformation		embankment	LEVEE
of Earth's crust	TECTONIC	flat land	HOLM
ridge	DRUM		RIVER TERRACE
—carved in soft strata		forest	GALLERY FOREST
by wind	YARDANG	—subject to flooding	(I)GAPO
—in plain of softer rock	CUESTA	meadow	
—of		—Scottish	HAUGH, INCH
boulder clay	DRUMLIN	—subject to flooding	WATER MEADOW
gravel	AS, ESKAR, ESKER	plain (Scot.)	CARSE
	KAME	—tributary	
—at		of subsequent river	OBSEQUENT RIVER
foot of glacier	TERMINAL MORAINE	stream	AFFLUENT
side of glacier	LATERAL MORAINE	—valley	DALE
—connecting island to		—with tributaries	DRAINAGE SYSTEM
mainland or island	TOMBOLO		WATER SYSTEM
—in middle of		rock	(see also rocks)
glacier	MEDIAL MORAINE	—at sea-level	
hills (S. Africa)	RAND	composed of coral	ATOLL, BARRIER REEF
ice in glacier	SERAC		CORAL REEF
rocks near surface of sea	REEF		FRINGING REEF
sand	DUNE	—containing more than	
—across river mouth		one mineral	COMPOSITE
or harbour entrance	BAR	—exposed above Earth's	
—extending into sea	SPIT	surface	OUTCROP
—wall-like	RAMPART	—fissure containing	
—with sharp summit	HOG(S)BACK	mineral deposit	LODE, VEIN
rift valley	GRABEN	—formed by deposition	
rigid area of Earth's crust	CRATON	from water, etc	SEDIMENTARY
ripple on water	RIFFLE		SILTSTONE
river	(see separate entry)	—mass forming centre of	
—bank formed by deposit		continent	SHIELD
of silt	LEVEE	—on ice pedestal in glacier	GLACIER TABLE
—branch		—standing above ice	NUNATAK
joining		—through which vein of	
—river	TRIBUTARY	ore runs	WALL ROCK
—sea or lake	DISTRIBUTARY	rock-hole (Austr.)	GNAMMA HOLE

rocky	
—area in shallow water (US)	RIFFLE
—crust of Earth	LITHOSPHERE
—desert	HAM(M)ADA, REG
—edge of mountain	ARETE
—height	TOR(R)
—island	SKERRY, STACK
—mound (Scot.)	SCALP
—mountain top	KRANS, KRAN(T)Z
—peak	AIGUILLE
—place in stream (US)	RIFT
—recess	COVE
—uplands in desert region	HAM(M)ADA
—valley	RAVINE
America	GULCH
rounded	
—granule	CHONDRULE
—hillock (Scot.)	KNOWE
—hilltop (Scot.)	DOD
—lump	NODULE
formed by accretion	OOLITH
—pebbles	COBBLES, SHINGLE
route along which	
merchants regularly	
travel	TRADE ROUTE
rudaceous rock	SEDIMENTARY ROCK
rushing stream	TORRENT
salt	
—deposit left after	
evaporation of lake	SALINA, SALINE
	SALT PAN
—encrusted area	SALT-FLAT
—marsh	SALINA, SALINE
sand	
—bank formed by sea	DOLON
—dune	
crescent-shaped	BARCHAN
parallel to wind	SEIF
—hills (Scot.)	LINKS
sandy	
—desert (N. Africa)	ERG
—plains (France)	LANDES
—tract	DENE, DESERT
score marks made by	
glacial action	STRIAE
scrub	BRUSH
—Australia	MALLEE (SCRUB)
—dry, tropical	THORNBUSH
—eucalyptus	MALLEE (SCRUB)
—France	MAQUIS
—growing on poor land	GAR(R)IGUE
—Italy	MACCHIA
—Mediterranean	GAR(R)IGUE
sea	
—bed bordering	
land- mass	CONTINENTAL SHELF

—shore	BEACH, COAST
	LITTORAL
(*see also* **oceanography**)	
seasonal	
—layers of sediment	VARVE
—movement of livestock	TRANSHUMANCE
section showing slope	
of river bed	RIVER PROFILE
sedimentary	
—deposit	WARP
from river	ALLUVIAL CONE
	ALLUVIAL FAN
	ALLUVIAL PLAIN
	ALLUVIUM
—rock	RUDACEOUS ROCK
segment of Earth's	
crust	(TECTONIC) PLATE
semi-tundra (Andes)	PARAMOS
series of	
—strata	ZONE
—waterfalls	CASCADE, CATARACT
shaft in glacier	MOULIN
shallow	
—body of water	WASH
—channel worn by erosion	RILL
—lake in coastal sand dunes	ETANG
—marsh	EVERGLADE
—part of river that	
can be waded	FORD
—place in stream (US)	RIFT
—pond	
filled by dew	DEWPOND
filling with silt	ETANG
—soil over rock (US)	LITHASOL
—stretch of rough water	
in stream (US)	RIFFLE
sharp	
—point	AIGUILLE
—ridge	ARETE
sheet of	
—glacial deposit	GROUND MORAINE
—ice	
floating	(ICE) FLOE
on land	ICEFIELD
shifting sand dune area	ERG
shore raised by Earth	
movement	RAISED BEACH
showing correct	
directions from centre	ZENITHAL a
side	
—exposed to wind	UPWIND, WINDWARD
—of hill or mountain	SHOULDER
—sheltered from wind	DOWNWIND
	LEEWARD
sinkhole	SWALLET
	SWALLOW-HOLE

sinking of Earth's crust	SUBSIDENCE	—farm (Scot.)	CROFT
situated		—forest	WOOD
—below		—hill	HILLOCK, HUMMOCK
Earth's crust	SUBCRUSTAL		HUMP, MOUND
glacier	SUBGLACIAL	rounded	KNOLL
ground	SUBTERRANEAN	South African	KOPIE, KOPJE
—between low and high		—hollow	DELL, DIMBLE, DINGLE
tide marks	FORESHORE	—iceberg	CALF
—beyond mountains	TRAMONTANE	—island	AIT, EYOT, HOLM
	ULTRAMONTANE	—lake	MERE, POND, POOL
—just outside		in mountains	TARN
Antarctic Circle	SUBANTARCTIC	—prominence	MONTIC(U)LE
Arctic Circle	SUBARCTIC		MONTICULUS
—north of Alps	TRAMONTANE	—ridge in sand produced	
	TRANSALPINE	by wind or water	RIPPLE (MARK)
—on		—river	RIVULET
continent(al shelf)	EPICONTINENTAL	—rocky island	SKERRY
lower slopes of Alps	SUBALPINE	near coast	STACK
or near surface		—rounded glassy stone	AUSTRALITE
of Earth	SUBAERIAL		TEKTITE
—south of Alps	CISALPINE	—spring (US)	SEEP
—under		—stream	BROOK
ocean	SUBOCEANIC	Scottish	BURN
sea	SUBMARINE	—tributary	CREEK
slide	AVALANCHE, LANDSLIDE	—valley	DELL, DENE
	MUDSLIDE		DIMBLE, DINGLE, SLADE
slope	ESCARPMENT, GRADIENT, SCARP	—village	HAMLET
—ascending	ACCLIVITY	—watercourse	BOURN(E), BROOK
—covered with			FRESHET, PIRL, PURL
rock fragments	SCREE		RILL, RIVULET
scree	BAHADA, BAJADA		RUNNEL, STREAM
—descending	DECLIVITY	America	CREEK
—formed by accumulation		Scotland	BURN
of rock fragments	TALUS	temporary	(WINTER-)BOURNE
—from		—waterfall	CASCADE
base of eroded		—wood	COPPICE, COPSE, GROVE
sea-cliff	WAVE-CUT PLATFORM		SHAW, SPINN(E)Y
continental shelf			THICKET
to ocean bed	CONTINENTAL SLOPE	smooth surface produced	
land to sea	BEACH, SHORE	by rock movement	SLICKENSIDE
—in bedrock at foot of		soft moist clay, etc	SLIME
steeper slope	PEDIMENT	soil	
—leading up to mountains	PEDIMENT	—aggregate	PED
—of		—alkaline	PEDOCAL
mountain	VERSANT	—bound by grass, etc	TURF, SOD
rock stratum	DIP	—calcareous loam	MALM
—ascending	ACCLIVITY	—chalk, etc	RENDZINA
—descending	DECLIVITY	—clay	
sluggish tributary (US)	BAYOU	and	
small		—chalk	MALM
—cavity in rock	VESICLE, VUG(G), VUGH	—lime	MARL(ITE)
—coastal inlet	BAY, COVE, CREEK, INLET	friable	BOLE
—column of rock		sand and silt	LOAN
with grooves	STYLOLITE	sticky	GLEY
—creek (Scot.)	POW	—compacted clay	CLAYPAN, HARDPAN
—elevation	MONTIC(U)LE	—containing silica	CLAY

—covering mineral deposit	OVERBURDEN	South African —grassland	KAR(R)OO, VELDT
—crumbly limestone	MALM	—hill	KOP(J)E, KOPPIE
with humus	MULL	—mountain	BERG
—deposited by		—wooded grassland	BOSCHVELD(T)
water	ALLUVIUM, SILT		BUSHVELD
wind	LOESS, LIMON	spot where fluid oozes from ground	SEEP
—earthy clay	BOLE	spring	FOUNTAIN, SPA, WELL
—formation of	PEDOGENESIS	—as source of stream	FOUNTAINHEAD
—humus-rich	BLACK EARTH	—containing dissolved	
	CHERNOZEM	mineral matter	MINERAL SPRING
—lacking defined layers	AZONAL		SPA
—layer		—period of thaw (Siberia)	RASPUTITSA
A and B horizons	SOLUM	steep	
at surface	A-HORIZON, SOLUM	—crevasse	CHINE
	TOPSOIL	—drop in watercourse	SHOOT, WATERFALL
below surface	B-HORIZON, SUBSOIL	—headland	BLUFF
	SUBSTRATUM	—moorland area	FELL
	SUBSURFACE	—ravine	CHINE
weathered rock	C-HORIZON	—rock	CRAG
—leached by rainfall	PEDALFER	—rockface	CLIFF, LIN(N)
—marshy in spring,			PRECIPICE
frozen in winter	GLEI SOIL	—sheet of rock	DIKE, DYKE
—organic	LEAF MOULD, HUMUS	—sided hollow in	
—poor soil in		glacial deposit	GIANT'S KETTLE
arid or semi-arid			KETTLE(-HOLE)
region		—slope	ESCARPMENT, SCAR(P)
—dark	SOLONETZ	—spur cut off by	
—light	SIEROZEM	glacier	TRUNCATED SPUR
—pale	SOLONCHAK	stepped excavation	STOPE
sub-polar regions	PODSOL, PODZOL	stony desert	REG
—red		straight section of river	REACH
clayey	TERRA ROSSA	strata	
iron-bearing	LATERITE	—dipping	
tropical	LATOSOL	in the same	
—rich in mull	BROWN EARTH	direction	ISOCLINAL FOLDING
	BROWN FOREST SOIL	outwards in all	
—section showing		directions	PERICLINAL
layers	SOIL PROFILE		QUAQUAVERSAL
—sequence(s) in		—folded	
given area	CATENA(E)	downwards	SYNCLINE
—shallow over rock (US)	LITHASOL	upwards	ANTICLINE
—sticky		(see also division above)	
clay	GLEY	streaks in green rock	SCHLIEREN
when wet	GUMBO	stream that flows only	
—study of	PEDOLOGY, SOIL SCIENCE	after heavy rain	WINTERBOURNE
—with lime in		stretch of sea cut off	
surface layer	PEDOCAL	by strip of sand	LAGOON
solar radiation		study of	
on a given area	INSOLATION	—ancient organisms	PALAEONTOLOGY
solid matter transported		—area of Earth's surface	GEODESY
by river	RIVER LOAD	—bodies of water	HYDROLOGY
source of		—caves	SPELEOLOGY
—river	HEADSTREAM	—centres of spatial	
—spring or stream	WELLHEAD	distribution	CENTROGRAPHY

—crop production	AGRONOMY	—in arid region	
—deposits	SEDIMENTOLOGY	containing much salt	SALINA, SALINE
—distribution of			SALT-MARSH
animals	ZOOGEOGRAPHY	swampy pine forest	URMAN
—and plants	BIOGEOGRAPHY	swiftly flowing part of river	RAPIDS
human population	DEMOGRAPHY	system of mountain	
plants	PHYTOGEOGRAPHY	ranges	CORDILLERA
races	ETHNOLOGY	tableland	PLATEAU
—Earth		—South America	PUNA
measurement	GEODESY	temperate grassland	DOWNLAND, PAMPAS
sciences	GEOSCIENCE		PRAIRIE, STEPPE
	NATURAL HISTORY	temporary	
—Earth's		—lake	PLAYA
magnetism in past		—salt-lake (Algeria)	SHOTT
ages	PALAEOMAGNETISM	—stream	(WINTER-)BOURNE
surface	CHOROGRAPHY	terrace with steep	
	(PHYSICAL) GEOGRAPHY	slope on one side	MESA
	PHYSIOGRAPHY, TOPOGRAPHY	territorial division	COUNTY, HUNDRED
	TOPOLOGY		PROVINCE, REGION
—in past ages	PALAEOGEOGRAPHY		RIDING, STATE
—ecology in past ages	PALAEOECOLOGY	territory	
—economic		—enclosed by country	
activity	LOCATIONAL ANALYSIS	to which it does	
—effects of seasons on		not belong	ENCLAVE
flora and fauna	PHENOLOGY	—governed by League	
—features of earth	GEOMORPHOLOGY	of Nations	MANDATED TERRITORY
	PHYSIOGRAPHY	—jointly governed	CONDOMINIUM
—glaciers	GLACIOLOGY	—partly controlled by	
—influence of geography		another	PROTECTORATE
on politics	GEOPOLITICS	—ruled by state from	
—past ages from		which it is detached	DEPENDENCY
geological data	GEOCHRONOLOGY	—within which another	
—physical processes		state has freedom	
of Earth	GEOPHYSICS	of action	SPHERE OF INFLUENCE
—rock strata	STRATIGRAPHY	theory of	
—rocks	GEOLOGY, LIHOLOGY	—change by	
	PETROLOGY	existing	
—soil	PEDOLOGY, SOIL SCIENCE	processes	UNIFORMITARIANISM
—structure of		violent events	CATASTROPHISM
Earth's surface	(PLATE) TECTONICS	—continents formed	
—succession of rock		from large	
formation	STRATIGRAPHICAL GEOLOGY	land-mass	DISPLACEMENT THEORY
	STRATIGRAPHY	—distribution of	
—water in rivers, etc	HYDROLOGY	land masses	TETRAHEDRAL THEORY
submerged valley	RIA	—rock formation by	
subterranean		precipitation from sea	NEPTUNISM
—mass of solidified rock	PLUTON	subterranean heat	PLUTONISM
—passage	ADIT, TUNNEL		VULCANISM
summit of hill,		thicket	BRUSH(WOOD)
mountain, etc	CREST, CROWN	tidal wave in river	BORE, EAGRE
surface		time related to a	
—of slip in fault	FAULT PLANE	particular meridian	STANDARD TIME
—worn level by erosion	PENEPLAIN		ZONE TIME
	PENEPLANE	top of hill	BROW, CREST
swamp	BOG, FEN, MARSH, MORASS	tornado over the sea	WATERSPOUT
—Canada	MUSKEG	town with harbour	PORT

trading centre between countries	ENTREPOT
transformation of rock	METAMORPHISM
transportation of topsoil by rainwater	ELUVIATION
tree barrier	SHELTER BELT
treeless	
—plains of northern zones	STEPPES, TUNDRA
—upland	DOWN
tremor in Earth's crust	EARTHQUAKE
tributary	AFFLUENT
	CONFLUENT, INFLUENT
tropical coastal swamp	MANGROVE SWAMP
uncultivated	
—elevated land	MOOR(LAND)
—region	BUSH, DESERT
underground chamber	CAVE(RN)
unit of	
—ecological community	BIOME
—latitude or longitude	DEGREE
upland	
—meadow (Norway)	SAETER
—pastureland	DOWN
uplands	(see plateau above)
uplift of Earth's surface	UPTHRUST
upper	
—limit of growth in mountains	TREE LINE
—part of river	HEADWATERS
—strata pushed forward over lower	THRUST FAULT
	REVERSED FAULT
uppermost layer of forest	CANOPY
upward displacement of rock	UPTHROW
valley	VALE
—across a range	TRANSVERSE VALLEY
—American	ARROYO, CAN(Y)ON
	GULCH, RAVINE
—Arab	WADI, WADY
—between faults	GRABEN, RIFT VALLEY
—broad	STRATH
and level	VALE
—deep and narrow	GORGE, RAVINE
	GULCH
—drowned	RIA
—dry	DEAD VALLEY
—entering well above main river valley	HANGING VALLEY
—flooded as result of land subsidence	DROWNED VALLEY
	RIA, SUBMERGED VALLEY
—Indian	NULLA(H)

—long narrow	RAVINE
—narrow	COMB(E), COOMB, CWM
	DEAN, DELL, DENE, DINGLE
—parallel to range	LONGITUDINAL VALLEY
—round	CIRQUE, CORRIE
—Scottish	CLEUCH, CLEUGH
	CORRIE, GLEN, HEUCH
	HEUGH, STRATH
—side (US)	COTEAU
—small	DELL, DENE, DIMBLE
	DINGLE
—South African	DONGA
—Spanish	ARROYO
—steep	CHINE
—submerged	RIA
—transverse	CLUSE
—wide	DALE
—with	
lake in desert	BOLSON
watercourse	DALE
—without watercourse	DEAD VALLEY
	DRY VALLEY
—wooded	COMB(E), COOMB, CWM
	GHYLL
vertical	
—body of ore	SHOOT
—descent of water	WATERFALL
—displacement of fault	THROW
—distance between contours	CONTOUR INTERVAL
—height above sea level	ALTITUDE
—hole	POTHOLE
—opening to mine, etc	SHAFT
—rockface formed by erosion	RIMROCK
—shaft in	
earth	WELL
glacier	GLACIER MILL, MOULIN
rock	POTHOLE
violent	
—geological change	CATACLYSM
—stream of water	TORRENT
viscous mud	SLIME
vitrified sand fused by lightning	FULGURITE
volcano	(see separate entry)
wall of turf or stone	DIKE, DYKE
warming by trapped radiation	GREENHOUSE EFFECT
washing soil off bedrock	HUSH
water	
—bearing layer	AQUIFER
—existing below ground	GROUND WATER
	WATER TABLE

—from
　melting ice　　　　　　　MELTWATER
　the ground　　　　　　　SPA, SPRING
—hot from the ground　　　THERMAL SPRING
—in earth above
　water table　　　　　　　VADOSE
watercourses　　　　　BROOK, BURN, CANAL
　　　　　　　CHANNEL, DIKE, DITCH
　　　　　DYKE, RILL, RIVER, STREAM
—too small for valley
　in which it flows　　　　MISFIT RIVER
　　　　　　　　　　　MISFIT STREAM
—with no outlet to
　the sea　　　　　　INTERNAL DRAINAGE
　　　　　　　　　INTERIOR DRAINAGE
waterfall　　　　　　　FORCE, LIN(N)
—large　　　　　　　　　CATARACT
—series　CASCADE, CATARACT, RAPIDS
—small　　　　　　　　　CASCADE
　　　　　　　　(*see also* **waterfalls**)
wearing away of land
surface　　　　　　　　DENUDATION
—by
　breaking off of thin
　scales　　　　　　　　EXFOLIATION
　　　　　　　　ONION WEATHERING
　　　　SPHEROIDAL WEATHERING
　chemical action　　　　CORROSION
　climatic factors　　　　WEATHERING
　loose materials in
　transport　ABRASION, ATTRITION
　　　　CORROSION, DEGRADATION
　　　　　　　　　　　EROSION
　other than chemical
　action　MECHANICAL WEATHERING
　rainwater　　　　　ELUVIATION
　running water
　—in channel　　　GULLY EROSION
　—evenly　　　　SHEET EROSION
　wind　　　　　　　DEFLATION
—producing
　channel　　　　　　　FRETTING
　isolated
　elevation　CIRCUMDENUDATION
　smooth surface　　　　PLANATION
well bringing up water
by hydrostatic pressure　ARTESIAN WELL
wet
—forest (S. Amer.)　　　　　SELVA
—low-lying ground　　FEN, MARSH
　　　　　MORASS, (QUAKING) BOG
　　　　QUAGMIRE, SWAMP
—sand　　　　　　　QUICKSAND
winding course of stream
or river　　　　　　　MEANDER
wind-ridge in snow　SASTRUGA, ZASTRUGA

yield from ore sample　　　PROSPECT
zone
—based on altitude (S. Amer.)
　highest　　　　　　TIERRA FRIA
　middle　　　　TIERRA TEMPLADA
　lowest　　　　TIERRA CALIENTE
—between Capricorn
　and Cancer　　　　　　TROPICS
　　　　　　　　　TORRID ZONE
—between tropics and
　polar circles　TEMPERATE ZONES
—inside Arctic and
　Antarctic Circles　FRIGID ZONES
—not affected by
　frost (US)　　　THERMAL BELT
—using the same time　TIME ZONE
zoological regions
—Africa below Sahara　ETHIOPIAN
—Arctic　　　　　ARCTOGAEA
—Australasia　　　　NOTOGAEA
—Europe, North Africa
　North Asia (Old World)　PALAEARCTIC
—India, Indo-China　ORIENTAL
—Nearctic and Palaearctic　HOLOARCTIC
—Neotropical　　　　NEOGAEA
—North America, Greenland
　(New World)　　　NEARCTIC
—region of the bear　ARCTOGAEA
—South and Central America　NEOGAEA
　　　　　　　　NEOTROPICAL
—tropical America　　NEOGAEA
German　　　　　　　D, GER
about　　　　　　　　ETWA
aeroplane　DORNIER, FOKKER, HEINKEL
　　　　MESSERSCHMITT, STUKA
　　　　　　　　　　TAUBE
again　　　　　　　　UBER
after　　　　　　　　NACH
air
—force　　　　　　LUFTWAFFE
—line　　　　　　LUFTHANSA
alarm　　　　　　　STURM
Alsace-Lorraine　　REICHSLAND
amiable　　　　　　GEMUTLICH
ancient tribe　　　ALEMANNEN
and so forth　UND SO WEITER, USW
anxiety　　　　　　ANGST
apple　　　　　　　APFEL
—cake　　　　　　STRUDEL
approval　　　　　　JA
aristocrat　　　　　JUNKER
armed forces　　　WEHRMACHT
armoured corps　　PANZER
army
—reserve　　　　LANDWEHR
—surgeon　　　　FELDSCHER

arrangement	AUSGLEICH
art	
—school	BAUHAUS
—song	KUNSTLIED
article	DAS, DER, DIE, EIN, EINE
ass	ESEL
association	VEREIN
authentic	ECHT
bandmaster	CAPELLMEISTER
	KAPELLMEISTER
bar	BIERKELLER
baron(ess)	FREIHERR(IN)
basin	BECKEN
bay	BODDEN, BUCHT, HAFF
beach	STRAND
beef	RIND(FLEISCH)
beer	BIER, BOCK
—cellar	BIERKELLER
—mug	BIERKRUG, ENGHALSKRUG
	STEIN
biscuit rusk	ZWIEBACK
black-letter typeface	FRAKTUR
bless you!	GESUNDHEIT
blockade position (chess)	ZUGZWANG
blood	BLUT
—and	
earth	BLUT UND BODEN
honour	BLUT UD EHRE
iron	BLUT UND EISEN
—pudding	BLUTWURST
boat	BOOT
bog	MOOR, MOOS
border-crosser	GRENZGANGER
bread	BROT
broken	KAPUT(T)
brownie	KOBOLD
Brownshirts	STURMABTEILUNG
cabbage	KOHL
cake	KUCHEN
capitals	BERLIN, BONN
captain of cavalry	RITTMEISTER
carnival	FASCHING
carp	CRUCIAN, CRUSIAN
cartel	KARTELL
cast-iron	SPIEGELEISEN
castle	SCHLOSS
cattle-plague	RINDERPEST
cavalry soldier	REITER, U(H)LAN
Central European Time	MEZ
centre of diffusion of culture elements	KULTURKREIS
cheese	KASE
chicken	HAHN(CHEN), HUHN
chief	
—magistrate	BURGERMEISTER
	BURGOMASTER
—official	GAULEITER
child prodigy	WUNDERKIND
child(ren)	KIND(ER)
child's play	KINDERSPIEL
chocolate	SCHOKOLADE
choice	AUSLESE
civilisation	KULTUR
clamour	KATZENJAMMER
classical school	PROGYNMNASIUM
clavier	KLAVIER
cliff	WAND
climbing-boot(s)	KLETTERSCHUH(E)
clown hero	(H)OWLEGLASS, OWL-GLASS
	OWLSPIEGLE
coffee	KAFFEE
coin	
—small	PF, PFENNIG
—100 pfennigs	DEUTSCHEMARK, DM
	M, MARK
—10 marks	KRONE
—100 creutzers	FLORIN, GULDEN
—100 pfennings	GROSCHEN
—100 hellers	CROWN
—old coins	PFENNING, CROWN
	REUTZER, HELLER
	KR, KREUTZER, REICHSMARK
—gold	G(U)ILDER
—gold or silver	GULDEN
—silver	THALER
comfort	GEMUTLICHKEIT
comfortable	GEMUTLICH
commercial company	AG, GESELLSCHAFT
company	AG
complaint	MEASLES
co-ordination	GLEICHSCHALTUNG
copper	KUPFER
—ore	KUPFERSCHIEFER
count	(LAND)GRAF, LANDGRAVE
	MARGRAVE
countess	GRAFIN, LANDGRAVINE
court	HOF
courtly love	FRAUENDIENST
crevasse	BERGSCHRUND
cross-country skiing	LANGLAUF
culture	KULTUR
customs-union	ZOLLVEREIN
dachshund	TECKEL
dance	ALEMANDE, LANDLER
dance-tune	LANDLER
day	TAG
decoration	IRON CROSS
decree	DIKTAT
defector	GRENZGANGER
defence	WEHR
defile	KLAUSE
Democratic Republic	DDR, GDR

dialect	ALEMANNIC	fen	MARSCH
diatonite	KIESELGUHR	festival writing	FESTSCHRIFT
dipper	DUNKER	field-grey	FELDGRAU
direct perception	ANSCHAUUNG	field-marshal	FELDMARSCHALL
director of orchestra		fine for homicide etc	WERGILD
or choir	KAPELLMEISTER	flame-thrower	FLAMMENWERFER
dish	SAUERKRAUT	fish	FISCH
district	GAU, GEBIET, KREIS	folk	
ditch	GRABEN	—song	VOLKSLIED
dog	HUND	—tales	MARCHEN
	(see also **dogs**)	foot	FUSS
dominating principle	GEIST	for example	ZB, ZUM BEISPIEL
don't mention it	BITTE	Foreign Office	WILHELMSTRASSE
double(-goer)	DOPPEL-GANGER	foreigner	AUSLANDER
dove	TAUBE	forest	FORST, WALD
dramatic presentation	SINGSPIEL	—ranger	WALDGRAVE
drinking vessel	POKAL	form	GESTALT
dumpling	KNODEL	free thinkers (18th c)	ILLUMINATI
dynasty	CAROLINGIAN, CARLOVINGIAN	freshman	PENNAL
	FRANCONIAN, HANOVERIAN	friend	KAMERAD
	HOHENSTAUFEN, HOHENZOLLERN	frightful(ness)	SCHRECKLICH(KEIT)
	MEROVINGIAN, SALIAN	fruit cake	STOLLEN
	WITTELSBACH	German	HUN, TEDESCO, TEUTON(IC)
earth-spirit	ERDGEIST	gentleman	HERR
East Germany	DDR, GDR	genuine	ECHT
eastward thrust	DRANG NACH OSTEN	girl	FRAULEIN
edition	AUFLAGE	glacier	GLETSCHER
egg	EI	goblin	KOBOLD
elimination of all		goodbye	AUF WIEDERSEHEN
opposition	GLEICHSCHALTUNG	good luck	PROSIT
emergency		governor	BURGRAVE, GAULEITER
—force	LANDSTURM	governess	FRAULEIN
—levy	LANDSTURM	grand piano	FLUGEL
emotional distress	KATZENJAMMER	grease	SCHMALTZ
emperor	KAISER	ground	GRUND
empire	REICH	guest	
enamel	SCHMELZE	—house	GASTHAUS, GASTHOF
enlightenment	AUFKLARUNG	—worker	GASTARBEITER
eternity	EWIGKEIT	guide	FU(E)HRER
evening	ABEND	gulf	GOLF
evil spirit	RYE-WOLF	gypsy	ZIGEUNER
exclamation to avert		hail!	HEIL
ill-luck	UNBERUFEN	hall	SAAL
exclusion of political		ham	SCHINKEN
extremists from public		hangover	KATZENJAMMER
office	BERUFSVERBOT	harbour	HAFEN
experimental task	AUFGABE	having music	
fable(s)	MARCHEN	specially adapted	DURCHKOMPONI(E)RT
fagging system	PENNALISM(US)	head of university	RECTOR MAGNIFICUS
fake	ERSATZ	heath	HEIDE
Fatherland	VATERLAND	helmet	PICKELHAUBE
Federal		heroic race	VOLSUNGS
—armed forces	BUNDESWEHR	highway	AUTOBAHN
—German Republic	BRD, FRG	hill	HUGEL, KOPF
—lower house	BUNDESTAG	hilltop	KUPPE
Federation of Industry	BDI	history of civilisation	KULTURGESCHICHTE

Hitler's bodyguard	SCHUTZSTAFFEL, SS
Hitlerite	NAZI
homesickness	HEIMWEH
host of phantoms	WILD HUNT
hotel	GASTHAUS, GASTHOF
housewife	HAUSFRAU
how are you?	WIE GEHT'S
hunter	JA(E)GER
hunting-horn	FLUGEL-HORN, WALDHORN
I	
—beg your pardon	BITTE
—serve	ICH DIEN
ice	EIS
immigrant worker	GASTARBEITER
impact radiation	BREMSSTRAHLUNG
Imperial	
—Royal	KK
—territory	REICHSLAND
industrial standards	DIN
infant school	KINDERGARTEN
inlet	FORDE
inspiring principle	GEIST
instrument	KUH-HORN
	KRUM(M)HORN
interjection	DONNERWETTER
is it not true?	NICHT WAHR
island(s)	INSEL(N)
Jew baiting	JUDENHETZE
Jews	ASHKENAZIM
joint stock company	AG
journeymanship	WANDERJAHRE
junior school	PROGYMNASIUM
juvenile delinquent	HALBSTARKER
kindness	GEMUTLICHKEIT
knight	RITTER
knowall	BESSERWISSER
lagoon	HAFF
lake	MEER, SEE, WASSER
lamb	LAMM
lancer	U(H)LAN
land bailiff	LANDAMMAN(N)
large tankard	POKAL
leader	FU(E)HRER, LEITER
—of file	FLUGELMAN, FUGLEMAN
league	BUND(E)
leap	LAUF
leather trousers	LEDERHOSEN
legend	WILD HUNT
light beer	PILS(E)NER
lightning	BLITZ
limited liability company	GMBH
liqueur	KIRSCH(WASSER)
	KUMMEL
living space	LEBENSRAUM
local governor	GAULEITER
long	LANG

lord	HERR
love	LIEB(E)
lower house of parliament	REICHSTAG
lyric(s)	LIED(ER)
—poet (12-13th c)	MINNESINGER
magistrate	AM(T)MAN
man	MANN
manor	HOF
—house	SCHLOSS
mansion	SCHLOSS
many thanks	DANKE SCHON
master	HERR, MEISTER
—of horse	STALLMEISTER
—race	HERRENVOLK
marsh	MARSCH
meat	FLEISCH
medal	
—civil	FEDERAL CROSS
—military	IRON CROSS
mediaeval court	FEHM(GERICHT)
	VEHM(GERICHT)
mercenary	LANDSKNECHT
	LANZKNECHT
	LANSQUENET
mica	GLIMMER
migrant worker	GASTARBEITER
migration	VOLKERWANDERUNG
militia	LANDWEHR
milk	MILCH
mine	GRUBE
mister	HERR
mix	MISCHEN
monoplane	TAUBE
moor	HEIDE
morals	SITTLICHKEIT
Moravian	HERRNHUTER
morning-star	MORGENSTERN
motorway	AUTOBAHN
mountain	BERG, OROS
—flour	BERGMEHL
—imp	RUBESZAHL
Mrs	FRAU
mush	SCHMALTZ
mushrooms	PILZE
musician (14-16th c)	MEISTERSINGER
mutton	HAMMEL
National Socialist	NAZI
—official	GAULEITER
necessity	ANANKE
nettle	NESSEL
new	NEUE
noble	EDEL, HERZOG, JUNKER
	MARGRAVE, WALDGRAVE
noblewoman	LANDGRAVINE
	MARGRAVINE
noodle	NUDEL

not called for	UNBERUFEN	recurring theme	LEITMOTIF, LEITMOTIV
novel about early		refusal	NEIN
development of hero	BILDUNGSROMAN	region	GEBIET
	ERZIEHUNGSROMAN	relentless force	BLUT UND EISEN
now	NUN	religious	
oath	SAPPERMENT	—painter (19th c)	NAZARENE
old	ALT	—reformer (17th c)	PIETIST
—burgher poet	MEISTERSINGER	revolt	PUTSCH
—cornet	ZINKE	rice	REIS
—soldiers' organisation	STAHLHELM	ridge	GRAT, KAMM, RUCKEN
one	EIN	rifleman	JA(E)GER
—of United Brethren	HERRNHUTER	rift-valley	GRABEN
—who thinks he knows		river	FLUSS, RHEIN, RHINE
better	BESSERWISSER	rock	FELS
organised whole or unit	GESTALT	—fall	BERGFALL
other	ANDER	room to live	LEBENSRAUM
outlook on the world	WELTANSCHAUUNG	royal forester	WALDGRAVE
over	UBER	ruined	KAPUT(T)
palace	SCHLOSS	run	LAUF
parliament	BUNDESTAG, REICHSTAG	rye bread	PUMPERNICKEL
passion for miracles	WUNDERSUCHT	saint	SANKT
pastime	ZEITVERTREIB	salmon	LACHS
pattern	GESTALT	salted biscuit	PRETZEL
peak	GIPFEL, HORN, SPITZE	sauce	SASSE
peas	URBSEN	sausage	WURST
peninsula	HALBINSEL	score in music	PARTITUR
people	HERREN	sea	MEER
people's car	VOLKSWAGEN, VW	secondary school	GYMNASIUM
philosopher	KANT, NIETZSCHE	secret police	GESTAPO, STASI
pianoforte	HAMMERKLAVIER	selection	AUSLESE
pickled braised beef	SAUERBRATEN	sensation	EMPFINDUNG
pigeon	TAUBE	sentimental enthusiasm	SCHWARMEREI
pipe	STUMMEL	sentimentality	SCHMALTZ
pit	GRUBE	Serene Highness	DURCHLAUCHT
plain	PLATTE	settlement	AUSGLEICH
plateau	PLATTE	shape	GESTALT
please	BITTE	sharpshooter	JA(E)GER
pleasure in others'		shell (Great War)	PIPSQUEAK
misfortune	SCHADENFREUDE	Shrovetide carnival	FASCHING
polder	KOOG	silver	ALBATA
pork	SCHWEIN	sir	HERR
port	HAFEN	skiing	LANGLAUF
potato	KARTOFFEL	small smoked sausage	FRANKFURTER
powdery deposit	BERGMEHL	smashed	KAPUT(T)
power politics	MACHTPOLITIK	softly	LEISE
practical politics	REALPOLITIK	soldier	SOLDAT
pretentious art	KITSCH	song(s)	LIED(ER)
prince	ELECTOR	—without words	LIED OHNE WORTE
prisoner-of-war camp	OFLAG, STALAG	spa	BAD
province	LAND	—building	KURHAUS
Prussian aristocrat	JUNKER	space inhabited by living things	LEBENSRAUM
quick(ly)	SCHNELL	spirit	GEIST
race	LAUF	—of the	
rapid dance	WALTZ	age	ZEITGEIST
ravine	KLAMM	mines	KOBOLD
reception room	KURSAAL	spit	NEHRUNG

sprite	KOBOLD, NICKEL	town	STADT
squire	JUNKER	tramp about	PADDELN
star catalogue	DURCHMUSTERUNG	trash	KITSCH
state	REICH	trench	GRABEN
—bank	REICHSBANK	tribe	ANGLES, SAXONS
—legislature	LANDTAG	trombone	POSAUNE
steel	STAHL	trooper	REITER
stormtroopers	STURMABTEILUNG	trout	HUCK
stream	BACH	uncertain	MISCHEN
street	STRASSE	underground Nazi	WEREWOLF
stroke	SCHLAG	union	ANSCHLUSS, VEREIN
struggle	KAMPF	union of states	ZOLLVEREIN
student(s)	BURSCH(EN)	university	
—association	BURSCHENSCHAFT	—entrant	ARBITURIENT
—beerhouse	KNEIPE	—freshman	PENNAL
—bread	BROTSTUDIEN	—outsider	PHILISTER, PHILISTINE
—drinking party	KNEIPE	upper house	OBERHAUS
—duel	MENSUR	—of parliament	REICHSRAT(H)
—duelling sword	SCHLAGER	uproar	KATZENJAMMER
—society	CORPS	valley	GRUND, TAL, DORF
—song-book	KOMMERSBUCH	veal cutlet	(WIENER) SCHNITZEL
studies by which one		vegetables	GEMUSE
earns a living	BROTSTUDIEN	verse romance	ENGELHARD
substitute	ERSATZ	volume(s) of book	BAND(E)
superman	UBERMENSCH	war	KRIEG
superstition	ABERGLAUBE	—game	KRIEGSSPIEL
supplementary reserve	ERSATZ	—of culture	KULTURKAMPF
swarming	SCHWARMEREI	water	WASSER
swastika	HAKENKREUZ	—sprite	NIX
sweet		weight (cwt-50 kg)	CENTNER
—bread	STOLLEN	West Germany	FDR, FRG
—spiced bread toasted	ZWIEBACK	white horse	SCHIMMEL
sword	SCHLAGER	who is there?	WER DA
table	TISCH	wife	FRAU
—wine	TAFELWEIN	—of	
tank	PANZER	margrave	MARGRAVINE
tavern	KNEIPE	noble	WALDGRAVINE
teach	LEHREN	wine	(see separate entry)
teacher not member of		—cask	FUDER
salaried staff	PRIVAT DOCENT	wing	FLUGEL
	PRIVAT DOZENT	witches' revel	WALPURGIS(NACHT)
tendency	TENDENZ	with	MIT
terrier	PINSCHER	woman	FRAU
that		wooded hills	HARDT
—is to say	DAS HEISST, DH	world	WELT
—which is becoming	SITTLICHKEIT	—philosophy	WELTANSCHAUUNG
the day	DER TAG	—politics	WELTPOLITIK
thing in itself	DING AN SICH	—sorrow	WELTSCHMERZ
think	MEINEN	—spirit	WELTGEIST
thunder	DONNER	yard	HOF
—storm	DONNERWETTER	years of wandering	WANDERJAHRE
timbre	KLANGFARBE	yes	JA
title of nobility	WALDGRAVE	—indeed	JA WOHL
	WALDGRAVINE	young girl	BACKFISCH, FRAULEIN
toast	PROSIT	your health	GESUNDHEIT
tone colour	KLANGFARBE	Ghana	GH

capital	ACCRA
coin	
—unit	PESEWA
—100 pesewas	CEDI
former name	GOLD COAST
language	FANTEE, FANTI, TSHI, TWI
people	FANTEE, FANTI
robe	KENTE
silk cloth	KENTE CLOTH
ghosts	(*see* **spirits**)
Gibraltar	GBZ, GIB
girls	
from:	
America	BROAD, DAME
Australia	SHEILA
Egypt	BINT
France	FILLE(TTE)
Germany	FRAULEIN
Ireland	COLLEEN
Italy	RAGAZZA
Picardy	ROSE
Scotland	CUMMER, LASS
Spain	MUCHACHA, NINA
Tralee	ROSE
Troy	HELEN
Wales	MEGAN
Wessex	TESS
	(*see also* **woman**)
gland	
controlling growth	PITUITARY
discharging	
—internally	DUCTLESS GLAND
	ENDOCRINE GLAND
—through a duct	EXOCRINE GLAND
excretory gland in	
insects	MALPHIGIAN TUBULE
kidney	ADRENAL, APROCRINE
	SUPRARENAL
lymph purifying	LYMPH GLAND
	LYMPH NODE
salivary	PAROTID, PAROTIS
secreting	
—bile	LIVER
—digestive juices	PANCREAS
—disintegrated cells	HOLOCRINE
—fatty matter	SEBACEOUS
—fluid into mouth	SALIVARY
—hormone controlling	
calcium levels	PARATHYROID
metabolism and growth	THYROID
white blood cells	THYMUS
—insulin	PANCREAS
—internally	DUCTLESS
	ENDOCRINE
—milk	MAMMARY
—nectar in plants	NECTARY

—ova	OVARY
—perspiration	SWEAT GLAND
—sebum	SEBACEOUS
—seminal fluid	PROSTATE
—some disintegrated cells	APROCRINE
—sperm	SPERMARIUM
	SPERMARY
	TESTES
—tears	LACRIMAL
	LAC(H)RYMAL
—through duct	EXOCRINE
—urine	KIDNEY
—without disintegrating	MEROCRINE
situated in or near	
—abdomen	OVARY
—armpit	AXILLARY
—bladder	PROSTATE
—brain	EPIPHYSIS, HYPOPHYSIS
	PINEAL BODY, PINEAL GLAND,
	PITUITARY BODY
	PITUITARY GLAND
—chest	MEDIASTINAL, THYMUS
—eyelid	LACRIMAL, LAC(H)RYMAL
—groin	INGUINAL
—jaw	PAROTID, PAROTIS
	SUB-MAXILLARY
—kidneys	ADRENAL, SUPRARENAL
—mouth	ADENOID, TONSIL
—neck	CERVICAL, THYROID
—scrotum	TESTES
—skin	SEBACEOUS
—stomach	ABDOMINAL, PANCREAS
	PROSTATE
—thigh	POPLITEAL
—throat	(PARA)THYROID
tumour of a gland	ADENOMA
white-cell forming	LYMPH GLAND
	LYMPH NODE
glass	
blown disc	BOTTLE GLASS
	BULL'S-EYE
broken glass for re-use	CULLET
circular panes	CROWN GLASS
containing	
—alkali-lime	CROWN GLASS
—cobalt-oxide	SMALT
—lead silicate	FLINT GLASS
—sodium carbonate	SODA GLASS
convex mirror	CLAUDE LORRAINE GLASS
covering watchface	LUNETTE
dark	
—blue glass	SMALT
—spangled glass	AVANTURINE
	AVENTURINE
diamond-shaped pane	QUARREL(-PANE)
dish for cold dessert	COUPE

drinking glass	
—for	
beer	MUG, PONY, STEIN
	TANKARD
—Australian	MIDDY
champagne	BOAT, FLUTE
claret	MOUSSELINE
liqueur	PONY
rum	RUMMER
sherry	COPITA, SCHOONER
spirits	JIGGER
—large	BUMPER, STOUP, TUMBLER
sherry glass	SCHOONER
—small	PONY
—with handle	STEIN, TANKARD
flask	CARBOY, MATRASS
focussing glasses	FIELD GLASSES
	LENS, OPERA GLASSES
	PERISCOPE, TELESCOPE
fused coloured soda	MILLEFIORI
glass-fixer	GLAZIER
glasses (spectacles)	SPECS
—maker and seller	OPTICIAN
—single	MONOCLE
	QUIZZING GLASS
—with	
compound lens	BIFOCAL, TRIFOCAL
handle	LORGNETTE, LORGNON
	VARIFOCAL
—without	
frames	CONTACT LENSES, RIMLESS
side pieces	NOSE NIPPERS, PINCE-NEZ
glass-making tool	PUNTIL, PUNTY
hard glass	CROWN GLASS
	FLINT GLASS
	OPTICAL GLASS
heat resistant glass	PYREX, VITREOSIL
large tankard (German)	POKAL, STEIN
lump of glass before	
moulding	PARISON
manufacturers	
—English	BRIERLEY, STUART
	WEBB(-CORBETT)
—Irish	WATERFORD
—Scottish	EDINBURGH
multicoloured glass	AVENTURINE
	FAVRILE GLASS
	TIFFANY GLASS
	MURRHINE GLASS
ornamental	LALIQUE
potash for glass-making	POLVERINE
reacting to light	PHOTOCHROMIC
recycled glass	CULLET
reducing UV light	CROOKES GLASS
resistant to	
—chemicals	JENA GLASS

—heat	PYREX
safety glass	LAMINATED
strengthening process	ANNEALING
strong lens	MAGNIFYING GLASS
substitute for glass	PERSPEX
translucent glass	FROSTED GLASS
	OBSCURE GLASS
triangular block	PRISM
used	
—for fake jewels	PASTE, STRASS
—in decorative work	SCHMELZ
Venetian glass	AVANTURINE
	AVENTURINE
very thin glassware	MOUSSELINE
whitish glass	OPALESCENT
with bas-relief	LALIQUE
yellow-coloured	URANIUM GLASS
goats	
Anatolian	ANGOLA
Asian	MARKHOR
	SERPENT-EATER
Caucasian	ATCHI, TUR
female	CAPRA, NANNY
Himalayan	GOORAL, TAHR, TEHR
	THAR, SEROW
male	BILLY, BUTTER
Pyrenean	CHAMOIS, IBEX
	IZARD, ROCK-DOE
Tibetan	TAKIN
young	KID
gods	
African	
—Bushman's god	PRAYING MANTIS
—creator	NGAI
—Hottentot god	PRAYING MANTIS
—python god	ZOMBIE
—sky god	NGAI
American Indian	MANITO(U)
Anglo-Saxon	ING, SULIS
Aramaic	MAMMON
Assyrian	ASHUR
—earth	BEL
—sky	ANAT
—supreme	AS(S)HUR, AS(S)UR
—war	AS(S)HUR, AS(S)UR
Babylonian	BAAL, BEL
—atmosphere	ADDAD
—chief god	ENKI, (H)EA, MARDUK
—clouds	ADDAD
—Earth	BEL, ENLIL, KINGU
—harvest	(T)HAMMUZ
—messenger	MUMMUS
—sea	ANU
—sky	ANU
—Sun	T(H)AMMUZ
—tempest	ADDAD

—war	AS(S)HUR, AS(S)UR
	MARDUK, HERGAL
—water	APSU, (H)EA
—wisdom	MARDU, NABU, NEBO
Buddhist	BUDDHA
	GAUTAMA, SAKYAMUNI
Celtic	
—chief	DAGDA
—light	LUG(H)
—sea-god	LE(I)R
Central American rain-god	CHAC
Chaldean	NANNAR
Chinese	GOSS, JOSS, KUANYIN
	SHANGTI, SHEN-NUNG
	XANGTI
—Confucian	
supreme god	TIAN
creator of Universe	DEMIURGE
	DEMIURGUS
Egyptian	KNEPH
—air	SHU
—ape-headed	AANI
—art	THOTH
—artisans	PTAH
—artists	PTAH
—creator	KHNUM, PTAH
—darkness	SET
—dead	ANUBIS, OSIRIS
—Earth	GEB, KEB
—embalming	ANUBIS
—falcon-headed	HORUS
—fertility	AMEN, AM(M)ON
	AMUN, MIN
—harvest	OSIRIS
—hawk-headed	HORUS
—heaven	SEP
—ibis-headed	THOTH
—jackal-headed	ANUBIS
—learning	IMHOTEP
—life	AMEN, AM(M)ON, AMUN
—magic	THOTH
—medicine	IMHOTEP
—Moon	AAH, KHONS, YAH
—Nile	HAPI
—of Greeks in Egypt	SARAPIS, SERAPIS
—ram-headed	AMEN, AM(M)ON
	AMUN, BA, KHNUM
—science	THOTH
—son of Osiris	HORUS
—soul	BA
—star	SOTHIS
—Sun	HORUS, RA, RE
—supreme	AMEN, AM(M)ON
	AMUN, OSIRIS
—underworld	OSIRIS, SARAPIS
	SERAPIS, WEPWAWET

—war	SEPTU
—water	NUN
—wisdom	THOTH
—wolf-god	WEPWAWET
English war-god	TIU, TIW
Eskimo sky-god	SILA
Etruscan	MENRFA, TAGES
false	BAAL, IDOL
fish-god	EA
Germanic	(see Norse below)
Gnostic	ABRAXAS, DEMIURGE
	DEMIURGUS
Greek	
—attendant on Pan	PANISC, PANISK
—avenger	ANTEROS
—beauty	APOLLO, HELIOS
—creation	PROMETHEUS
—death	THANATOS
—destiny	NEMESIS
—divine justice	THEMIS
—dreams	MORPHEUS, ONEIROS
—earthquakes	EARTHSHAKER
	POSEIDON
—elder gods (Titans)	ATLAS, CRONUS
	HYPERION, KRONO
	IAPETUS, MNEMOSYNE
	OCEAN, PROMETHEUS
	TETHYS, THEMIS, URANUS
—fear	PHOBOS
—fire	HEPHAESTUS
—flocks	PAN
—healing	ASCLEPIOS, ASCLEPIUS
	ASKLEPIOS
—heavens	URANUS
—human justice	DIKE
—inferior	PANISC, PANISK
—light	APOLLO
—longing	HIMEROS
—love	EROS
—many-shaped	PROTEUS
—marriage	HYMEN
—medicine	APOLLO
—metal-working	HEPHAESTUS
	HEPHAISTOS
—mirth	COMUS
—mockery	MOMUS
—mountain	TMOLUS
—music	APOLLO
—north wind	BOREAS
—Olympians	APOLLO, ARES, HADES
	HEPHAESTUS, HERMES
	PLUTO, POSEIDON, ZEUS
—Poseidon	EARTHSHAKER
—rain	GANYMEDE
—re-birth	ADONIS
—reverence	AIDOS

—river	ACHELOUS, ALPHEUS
	ASOPUS, PENEUS
—sailors	CASTOR, PULLUX
—sea	GLAUCUS, NEREUS
	MELICERTES
	OCEANUS, PROTEUS
	POSEIDON, TRITON
—shepherds	PAN
—sky	ZEUS
—sleep	HYPNOS
—Sun	APOLLO, HELIOS, HYPERION
	PHOEBUS, TITAN
—supreme	CRONUS, KRONOS, ZEUS
—trade	HERMES
—travellers	HERMES
—truth	APOLLO
—tutelary god	PROMACHOS
—underworld	DIS, HADES
	PLUTO, PYTHON
—universe	URANUS
—vegetation	ADONIS, ATTIS
—vengeance	NEMESIS
—war	ARES
—wealth	PLUTUS
—wedding feasts	HYMEN
—west wind	ZEPHYRUS
—winds	(A)EOLUS
—wine	BACCHUS, DIONYSUS
—wisdom	HERMES
—woods	PAN, SILENUS, SATYR
Hebrew	ELOHIM, JAH(VEH), JAHWEH
	JEHOVAH, YAH(VEH), YAWE(H)
	YAHVIST, YAHWIST
Hindu	DEVA
—creator	BRAHMA
—demigod	GARUDA
—desire	KAMA
—destroyer	MAHADEVA, S(H)IVA
—Earth	KRISHNA
—elephant-headed	GANES(H)A
—fire	AGNI
—foresight	GANES(H)A
—good fortune	GANES(H)A
—heavens	INDRA, VARUNA
—intoxicating spirit and	
plant personified	SOMA
—love	CAMA, KAMA
	KAMADEVA
—monkey-god	HANUMAN
—Moon	SOMA
—preserver	KRISHNA, RAMA, VISHNU
—rain	INDRA
—reproducer	S(H)IVA
—storms	RUDRA
—Sun	SURYA
—supreme	BRAHMA, INDRA

—time	KALA
—war	INDRA, KARTTIKEYA
—warrior	AJUNA, BHISMA
—water	VARUNA
—wrath	MANYU
Italian (ancient)	
—son of Saturn	PICUS
—war god	QUIRINUS
Jain prophets revered	
as deities	TIRTHANKAR(A)
	TIRTHANKER
Japanese	KAMI
Knights Templar	BAPHOMET
Mexican rain god	TLALOC
Moabite	CHEMOSH
Moslem	ALLAH
mysterious infernal deity	DEMOGORGON
Norse	AS, ASA, AESIR, VANIR
—battle	TIWAZ
—blind god	HODER
—craftsmen	VOLUNDR, WAYLAND
	WE(I)LAND
—crops	THOR
—dragon-god	FAFNIR
—Earth	FREYR
—evil	LOKI
—fertility	FREYR
—fire	LOGI, LOKI
—founder-god	ING
—keeper of Bifrost	
(rainbow) bridge	HEIMDALL
—light	BALDER, BALDUR
—mischief	LOKI
—poetry	BRAGI
—sea	AEGIR, NJORD
—ships	NJORD
—sky	ALCIS
—son of Odin	BALDER, BALDUR
	HERMOD, HODER
—supreme	BALDER, BALDUR
	ODIN, WODEN, WOTAN
—thunder	DOWAR, THOR
—war	TYR
—wind	VAYU
—wisdom	KVASIR, MIMIR
Persian	(AHURA) MAZDA
	MITRA, MITHRAS(S)
	ORMAZD, ORMUZD
Philistine	DAGON
Phoenician	BAAL, BEELZEBUB
presiding deity	NUMEN
Polynesian	A'A
Red Indian	MANITO(U)
Roman	
—agriculture	LIBER PATER, MARS
	PICUS, SATURN

—boundaries	TERMINUS
—cattle	PALES
—dawn	JANUS
—dead	ORCUS
good	MANES
wicked	LARVAE, LEMURES
—doors	JANUS
—eloquence	MERCURY
—farming	SILVANUS
—fertility	LIBER PATER, LUPERCUS
	MARS, PICUS, PRIAPUS
—fire	MULCIBER, VOLCANUS
	VULCAN
—flocks	LUPERCUS
—food and drink	PENATES
—forests	SYLVANUS
—founder of Rome	QUIRINUS
—fruit trees	VERTUMNUS
—gardens	PRIAPUS, VERTUMNUS
—gateways	JANUS
—healing	AESCULAPIUS
—honesty	FIDES
—household	LAR(ES)
—husbands	PORTUNUS
—larder	PENATES
—light	APOLLO
—love	CUPID
—manuring	STERCULIUS
—merchants	MERCURY
—metalwork	MULCIBER, VOLCANUS
	VULCAN
—messenger	MERCURY
—Moon	JUPITER
—Olympians	APOLLO, JUPITER
	MARS, MERCURY, NEPTUNE
	PLUTO, VULCAN
—ploughmen	SYLVANUS
—protection	GENIUS
—rain	JUPITER
—ridicule	MOMUS
—sea	NEPTUNE
—shepherds	FAUN(US)
—sky	JUPITER
—sleep	SOMNUS
—sowing seed	CONSUS
—spirits of the dead	MANES
—Sun	APOLLO, JUPITER
—supreme	JOVE, JUPITER
—theft	MERCURY
—thunder	JUPITER
—thunderbolts	VULCAN
—travel	JANUS
—trees	SYLVANUS
—two-faced	JANUS
—underworld	DIS (PATER), PLUTO
—vines	SATURN

—war	MARS, QUIRINUS, ROMULUS
—wine	BACCHUS, LIBER
—wisdom	MERCURY
—woods	SILVAN, SYLVANUS
—working men	SATURN
—youth	JUVENTUS
Saxon	SULIS
Semitic	ASMODAY, ASMODEUS
	CAB(E)IRI
	MOLECH, MOLOCH
South American - creator	VIRACOCHA
Spanish love-god	AMADIS
Sri Lankan	KOHMBA
Syrian	RIMMON
Thracian	TRIBALLUS
West Indian snake god	ZOMBI(E)
wood-god	SILVAN
Yoruba	ESHU
Zoroastrian	HAOMA

goddesses

Australian	
mother-goddess	KADJERI, KUNAPIPI
	MUMINA
Babylon	
—chief	IS(H)TAR, NANAI, NINA
—death	GULA
—dragon-goddess	TIAMAT
—Earth	DAMKINA
Celtic	(D)ANA, (D)ANU
—fertility	BRIGIT
Chaldean	NINGAL
Egypt	
—cat-goddess	BASH(ET), BAST(ET)
—cow-goddess	HATHOR
—cobra-goddess	UDOT
—creation	HEKET
—destiny	SHAIT
—fertility	ISIS
—justice	MA(AT)
—lioness-headed	PASHT
—love	HATHOR
—maternity	APET
—Moon	ISIS
—queen of	
goddesses	SATI
heaven	ISIS
—right	MA
—sky	NUT
—tombs	PASHT
—truth	MA(AT)
—war	NEIT(H)
Eskimo seal-goddess	SEDNA
Greek	
—agriculture	ATHENA, DEMETER
—barley	ALPHITO
—beauty	APHRODITE, URANIA

—childbirth	ARTEMIS, EILEITHYIA
	ILITHYIA
—cities	ATHENA
—corn	DEMETER, PERSEPHONE
—darkness	HECATE
—dawn	EOS
—discord	ERIS
—divine justice	THEMIS
—Earth	CYBELE, GE, GAEA, GAIA
—female satyr	SATYRA, SATYRESS
—fertility	ARTEMIS
—fire	HESTIA
—foretelling the future	CAMENAE
—fountains	ARETHUSA
—good fortune	TYCHE
—handicrafts	ATHENA
—harvest	DEMETER
—health	CAMENAE, HYGEIA
—hearth	HESTIA
—hunting	ARTEMIS, CYNTHIA
—justice	ASTRAEA, DIKE
	THEMIS
—law	THEMIS
—love	APHRODITE, URANIA
—marriage	HERA
—memory	MNEMOSYNE
—mischief	ATE
—Moon	ARTEMIS, HECATE
	PHOEBE, SELENE
—nature	RHEA
—night	NOX, NYX
—Olympians	APHRODITE, ARTEMIS
	ATHENA, HERA, HESTIA
	JUNO
—persuasion	PEITHA
—punishment	POENA
—rainbow	IRIS
—retribution	ARA, NEMESIS
—sea	INO
—sky	HERA
—springs	ARETHUSA, CAMENAE
—underworld	PERSEPHONE
—vengeance	NEMESIS
—victory	NIKE
—war	ATHENA, ENYO
—wells	CAMENAE
—wisdom	ATHENA, ATHENE, PALLAS
—witchcraft	HECATE
—youth	HEBE
Hawaiian volcano	PELE
Hindu	
—dawn	US(H)AS
—destroyer	DURGA, KALI
—divinity	DEVI
—mother-goddess	KAN, SHAKTA, SHAKTI
—plenty	PURANDI
—rivers	SARAVATSI
—strength	DURGA, KALI
Japanese (Shinto)	AMATERASU
Norse	
—beauty	FREYA, IVERA
—dead	HEL(A)
—Earth	ERDA, NERTHUS
—fertility	FRIGG
—guarding golden apples	IDUNN
—handmaidens, Valhalla	VALKYRIE
—healing	EIR
—love	FRIGG, FRE(J)YA
	IVERA
—plenty	NEHALLENIA
—receiving dead virgins	GEFION
—sea	RAN
—underworld	GERDA, HEL(A)
—wife of	
Baldur	NANNA
Loki	SIGYN
Thor	SIF
—wisdom	FRIGGA
—youth	FRIGG, FRE(J)YA, IVERA
Peruvian	MAMA
Phrygian	CYBELE
Roman	
—beauty	VENUS
—cattle	BUBONA
—chance	FORTUNA
—chastity	DIAN(A)
—childbirth	EGERIA, JUNO, LUCINA
—corn	CERES
—craftsmen	MINERVA
—crops	AN(N)ONA
—dawn	AURORA
—Earth	TELLUS
—education	MINERVA
—fate	FORTUNA
—fertility	CYBELE, DIANA
	FAUNA, MAIA
—fields	BONA DEA, FAUNA
—fire	VESTA
—flocks	PALES
—flowers	FLORA
—fortune	FORTUNA
—fountains	EGRERIA
—fruit	POMONA
—fruitfulness	FLORA
—funerals	LIBITINA
—gardens	VENUS
—harvest	OPS
—hearth	VESTA
—herds	FAUNA
—horticulture	VACUNA
—horses	EPONA
—household	VESTA

—hunting	DIAN(A), LUCINA
—light	DIAN(A), JUNO
—love	VENUS
—marriage	JUNO, LUCINA
—Moon	DIAN(A)
—morning	MATUTA
—mother-goddess	CYBELE, MAGNA MATER
—nursing mothers	RUMINA
—Olympians	DIANA, JUNO, MINERVA
	VENUS, VESTA
—orchards	POMONA
—peace	IRENE
—persuasion	SUADELA
—pleasure	VOLUPTAS
—rumour	FAMA
—sea	MATER MATUTA
—spring flowers	FERONIA
—springs	CAMENAE, JUTURNA
	VENUS
—underworld	LIBITINA
—victory	VICTORIA
—war	BELLONA, MINERVA
—wealth	OPS
—wells	CAMENAE, VENUS
—wisdom	MINERVA

Saxon

—spring	EASTRE, EOSTRE

Semitic

—fertility	ASTARTE
	ASHTARETH, ASHTAROTH

Thracian   KOTYS, KOTYTTO

golf

courses

—America	AUGUSTA, DORAL, GLENVIEW
	GRAND CYPRESS, HARBOUR TOWN
	HILTON HEAD ISLAND, HOUSTON
	KEMPER LAKES, KIAWAH ISLAND
	LA COSTA, LAKE ORION, MEDINAH
	NEWPORT, OAK HILL
	OAKLAND HILLS, OAKMONT
	PALM BEACH, PALM SPRINGS
	PONTE VEDRA, SHINNECOCK HILLS
	WILLIAMSBURG, WOODLANDS
—Australia	KINGSTON HEATH
	ROYAL ADELAIDE
	ROYAL MELBOURNE
—Austria	GUT ALTENTANN
—Belgium	ROYAL WATERLOO
—Canada	GLEN ABBEY
—Channel Islands	LA MOYE
—England	AINSDALE, ASHDOWN FOREST
	BELFRY, BIRKDALE, BURNHAM
	CAMBERLEY HEATH, DEAL, FERNDOWN
	FLEMING PARK, FORMBY
	FRILFORD HEATH, HOYLAKE
	HUNSTANTON, HUNTERCOMBE

	KNOLE PARK, LITTLE ASTON
	LYTHAM, MID-SURREY, OLD THORN
	PATSHULL PARK, ST GEORGES
	ST MELLION, SANDWICH
	SAUNTON, SEAFORD, STENEDOC
	STOKE POGES, SUNNINGDALE
	THORNDEN PARK, THORPE WOOD
	WALTON HEATH, WENTWORTH
	WOBURN, WOODHALL SPA
—France	CHANTILLY, VERSAILLES
—Germany	WORTHSEE
—Holland	KENNEKAER
—Ireland	BALLYBUNION, NEWCASTLE
	PORTMARNOCK, PORTRUSH
—Jamaica	MONTEGO BAY
—Japan	TAKARAZUKA
—Monte Carlo	MONT AGEL
—Scotland	BALLATER, CARNOUSTIE
	GLENEAGLES, GLENROTHES
	MORAY, MUIRFIELD
	MUSSELBURGH, PRESTWICK
	ST ANDREWS, TROON
	TURNBERRY, WESTERN GAILES
—Spain	CLUB DE CAMPO, EL BOSQUE
	LA MANGA, PUERTO DI HIERRO
	TRAMONTANA, VALENCIA
—Sweden	DRITTNINGHOLM
—Wales	PORTHCAWL, ST DAVIDS
	ST PIERRE

players

—American (m)	ANDERSON, ARMOUR
	BARNES, CALCAVECCHIA
	CASPER, HAGEN, HOGAN
	HUTCHINSON, JONES, LEMA
	LITTLE, MILLER, NELSON
	NICKLAUS, PALMER, ROGERS
	SARAZEN, SHUTE, SNEAD
	TREVINO, WATSON, WEISKOPF
(f)	BAUGH, BERG, CONLEY
	DIDRIKSON, GEDDES, KING
	LOPEZ, MOON, SHEEHAN
	ZAHARIAS
—Argentinian	VINCENZO
—Australian (m)	DEVLIN, NAGLE, NORMAN
	OGLE, SENIOR, THOMSON
	VON NIDA
(f)	BELLOWIEN, DIBNAH
	JONES, LUNN
—Belgian (m)	VAN DONCK
(f)	DESCAMPE
—Canadian (m)	BALDING, KNUDSEN
(f)	KORTGAAZO
—English (m)	ALLIS, BONALLACK, BRAID
	BROWN, BURTON, COLES, COTTON
	DUNCAN, FALDO, FAULKNER
	HAVERS, HUNT, JACKLIN

	KING, OOSTERHUIS, PADGHAM	for	
	PERRY, RAY, TAYLOR, TORRANCE	—four	FOUR BALL, FOURSOME
	VARDON, WARD, WEETMAN	—two	TWOSOME
	WHITCOMBE	with prize money for	
(f)	BARTON, DAVIES	each hole	SKIN TOURNAMENT
	DOBSON, FISHWICK	—handicap of nil	SCRATCH
	NICHOLAS, IRVIN	—hit ball	
	STRUDWICK, WETHERED	to left	DRAW, HOOK, PULL
—French (f)	DE LORENZI	right	FADE, PUSH, SLICE
—German	LANGER	—lofted shot to green	PITCH
—Irish	DALY, O'CONNOR	—low approach shot	CHIP
	RAFFERTY	—nervous twitch when putting	YIPS
—Japanese	HOSOISHI, NAKAMURA	—obstruction of ball on the green	STYMIE
	OZAKI	—part of course	
—New Zealand (m)	CHARLES	between tee and	
(f)	ARNOLD	—green	FAIRWAY
—Peruvian (f)	DIBOS	—pin	HOLE
—Scottish (m)	GALLACHER, LYLE	not mown	ROUGH
(f)	WRIGHT	round green	APRON
— South African (m)	COLE, FROST	—porter	CADDIE
	LEGRANGE, LOCKE	—prepare to strike ball	ADDRESS
	PLAYER	—putting area	GREEN
(f)	MARITZ	—right to play first	HONOUR
— Spanish (m)	BALLESTEROS, MIGUEL	—score	
	OLAZABAL	1 over par	BOGEY
(f)	FIGUERAS-DOTTI	1 under par	BIRDIE
	WUNSCH-RUIZ	2 under par	EAGLE
—Swedish (f)	NEUMANN	3 under par	ALBATROSS
—Welsh	REES, WOOSNAM	where lead equals the	
terms		number of holes left	DORMIE, DORMY
—allowance		—scoring system	STABLEFORD
of strokes	HANDICAP	—seaside golf-course	LINKS
on putt for slope of green	BORROW	—shot	
—approach		bending	
shot	RUN-UP	—to left	DRAW, HOOK, PULL
to green	APRON	—to right	FADE, PUSH, SLICE
—bonus strokes	HANDICAP	from	
—built-in hazard	BUNKER	—fairway	APPROACH SHOT
—clod of earth cut out by club	DIVOT	—short distance to green	CHIP
—club		—tee	DRIVE
carrier	CADDIE, TROLLEY	that holes the ball	
names	BRASSIE, BRASSY, CLEEK	from a bunker	GOLDEN FERRET
	DRIVER, GOOSE, IRON	on green towards hole	PUTT
	MASHIE, NIBLICK, PUTTER	—slope on green	BORROW
	(SAND-)BLASTER, SPOON	—start the game	TEE-OFF
	WEDGE, WOOD	—starting point	TEE
numbers	ONE to NINE	—stroke	
— 5 iron	MASHIE	conceded as handicap	BISQUE
— 8 iron	NIBLICK	that misses the ball	AIR-SHOT
—distance	CARRY	—strokes allowed for a hole	PAR
—flag placed in hole	PIN	—types of game	FOUR BALL, FOURSOME
—game			MATCH PLAY, MEDAL PLAY
decided on number of			STROKE PLAY, TWOSOME
holes won	MATCH PLAY	—veer on drive	FADE
decided on number of		—vehicle used on course	BUGGY
strokes taken	STROKE PLAY	—warning	FORE

tournaments
—American	ATLANTIC CITY CLASSIC
	BOB HOPE CLASSIC
	DOUG SANDERS CELEBRITY CLASSIC
	HERITAGE CLASSIC
	LADY KEYSTONE OPEN
	MASTERS, OPEN
	PGA CHAMPIONSHIP
	PLAYERS' CHAMPIONSHIP
	QUAD CITIES' OPEN
	ST JUDE CLASSIC
	TRADITION, VARDON TROPHY
—American/British	CURTIS CUP
	RYDER CUP, WALKER CUP
—British	BRITISH MASTERS
	BRITISH OPEN, PGA TOURNAMENT
	VARDON TROPHY
—Dubai	DESERT CLASSIC
—international	WORLD MATCH PLAY
—Japanese	FOUR TOURS
—Spanish	CATALAN OPEN

goose
domestic	BRECON BUFF, CHINESE
	EM(B)DEN, ROMAN
	TOULOUSE
wild	BARNACLE, BEAN, BRENT
	CANADA, EGYPTIAN
	GREYLAG, HAWAIIAN
	LESSER WHITE-FRONTED
	PINK-FOOTED, RED-BREASTED
	SNOW, WHITE-FRONTED

government   (*see* **power**)

governor
acting sovereign	VICEROY
Algerian	DEY
Arab	MUDIR, SHEREEF, SHERIF
Brazilian	CATAPAN
Byzantine	CATAPAN, EXARCH
castle	CASTELLAN
Chinese	TUCHUN
district	WARDEN
Dutch	STAD(T)HOLDER
eastern	MUDIR
German	BURGRAVE
—Nazi	GAULEITER
Greek	
—district	TOPARCH
—modern	EPARCH
—of the people	ETHNARCH
—province	NOMARCH
Hungarian	BAN
Indian	HAKEEM, HAKIM
	NAIK, SUBA(H)DAR
Italian	PODESTA
mediaeval	ALDERMAN, EALDORMAN
Middle East	EMEER, EMIR

Moldavian	GOSPODAR, HOSPODAR
old	GREAVE, GRIEVE, RECTOR
Pakistan	HAKEEM, HAKIM
papal	LEGATE
Persian	CHAGAN, CHAM, KHAN
	SATRAP
provincial	SATRAP
Roman	PRO-CONSUL
Serbian	ZUPAN
Spanish	ADELANTADO, ALCA(I)DE
	ALCAYDE
Spartan	HARMOST
town	WARDEN
Turkish	BASHAW, BEG, BEGLERBEG
	BEY, CAIMAC(AM), KAIMAKAM
	PACHA, PASHA, VALI, WALI
Wallachian	GOSPODAR, HOSPODAR
Yugoslav	ZUPAN

Graces   CHARITES
good cheer	THALIA
mirth	EUPHROSYNE
splendour	AGLAIA

grape   UVA
American	CATAWBA, SCUPPERNONG
	SEYVAL, ZINFANDEL
Austrian	GRUNER VELTLINER
German	RIVANDER, SCHEUREBE
	SILVANER
Hungarian	FURMINT
Italian	MOSCATO, NIEBBOLO
	SANGIOVESE
	TREBBIANO
madeira	BUAL, MALMSEY
	VERDELHO
North African	CARIGNON
Sardinian	CANNONAU
sherry	LISTAN, PALOMINO
	PEDRO XIMENEZ
South African	STEEN
Spanish	CENCIBAL, TEMPRANILLO
Swiss	FENDANT
varieties	ALIGOTE, BACCHUS, BARBERA
	CABERNET, CARINENA
	CHARDONNAY, CHASSELAS, CHENIN
	DOLCETTO, GAMAY, GARGANEGA
	GARNACHA, GRACIANO, GRENACHE
	HUXELREBE, MALBEC, MALVASIA
	MARSANNE, MERLOT, MOSCATEL
	MULLER-THURGAU, MUSCADET
	MUSCAT, ORTEGA, MUSKAT
	NEBBIOLO, PALOMINO, PINOT
	RIESLING, ROMORONTiN, SAUVIGNON
	SEMILLON, SILVANER, SYLVANER
	SYRAH, TOKAY, TRAMINER
	UGNI, VERDOT, VIOGNIER, ZINFANDEL

(*see also* **wine**)

graph	(*see* **write**)
grass	GRAMINAE
African	(H)ALFA, PENNISETUM
	TEFF(GRASS)
agave fibre	SISAL(-GRASS)
Agrostis	BENT
Aira	HAIR-GRASS
Alopecurus	FOX-TAIL
American	PASPALUM
Ammophila	STAR(R)(-GRASS)
Anthoxanthum	VERNAL GRASS
anti-scorbutic	SCURVY-GRASS
aquatic grass	MANNA-GRASS
Australian	KANGAROO GRASS
	PORCUPINE GRASS, SPINIFEX
Avena	OAT
barley	SQUIRREL-TAIL
—type	SQUIRREL-TAIL
basket-grass	OPLISMENUS, PANICUM
bent	AGROSTIS
black salsify	VIPER'S GRASS
Bouteloua	MOSQUITO GRASS
Brazil	PARA-GRASS
Briza	QUAKING-GRASS
brome-grass	FESCUE, LOP(GRASS)
—bullrush	CAT'S-TAIL
butterwort	ROT-GRASS
canary-grass	PAINTED GRASS
cat's-tail	BULLRUSH, PHLEUM
	TIMOTHY
Ceylon grass	CITRONELLA
China grass	RAMEE, RAMI(E), RHEA
coarse grass	AIRA, AMMOPHILA
	HAIR-GRASS, LYME
	STAR(R)
cocksfoot	DACTYLIS, HARD-GRASS
cord-grass	RICE-GRASS
Cortaderia	PAMPAS-GRASS, GYNERIUM
cotton-grass	ERIOPHORUM
—Scottish	CANNA(CH)
	MOSS-CROP
couch-grass	DOG-GRASS, DOG-WHEAT
	QUICK(EN), QUITCH(-GRASS)
	(S)QUITCH, TWITCH
creeping	BUFFALO-GRASS
	CANARY-GRASS
—bent-grass	FIORIN
Cynosurus	DOG'S-TAIL GRASS
Dactylis	COCKSFOOT
darnel	LOLIUM
Digitaria	FINGER-GRASS
dog's-tail grass	CYNOSURUS
dry-stalk	BEN(N)ET
Dutch rush	SHAVE-GRASS
early-sprouting grass	VERNAL GRASS
eelgrass	GRASSWRACK, ZOSTER

esparto	(H)ALFA, SPANISH GRASS
	SPART
Falkland Islands grass	TUSSAC-GRASS
	TUSSOCK-GRASS
feather-grass	STIPA
fescue	FESTUCA, MELIC
Festuca	FESCUE, MELIC
float-grass	MANNA-GRASS
	MEADOW-GRASS
fodder-grass	RYE-GRASS
forage grass (US)	GAMA-GRASS
gardener's garters	PAINTED GRASS
	PHALARIS, RIBBON-GRASS
Gastridium	NIT-GRASS
glaucous	ELYMUS
Glyceria	FLOAT(ING)-GRASS
gold-edged	CAREX
goose-grass	CATCH-WEED, CLEAVERS
	CLIVERS
grasswrack	CLEAVERS, CLIVERS
	EELGRASS, ZOSTER
growth after hay-harvest	AFTERMATH
	FOG(GAGE)
Gynerium	CORTADERIA
	PAMPAS-GRASS
hair-grass	AIRA
Holcus	SOFT-GRASS
hybrid cereal	TRITICALE
Indian	BAJREE, DUR(R)A, JHOW
	KANS, LEMON GRASS
	RAGI, ROOSA, RUSA
Juncus	TOAD-GRASS
Kentucky	BLUE-GRASS
knot-grass	KNAWEL, PERSICARIA
	POLYGONUM, SCLERANTHUS
long-stalked varieties	WINDLESTRAW
Malayan	LALANG
manna-grass	MEADOW-GRASS
marram	MATGRASS, MATWEED
	SEA-REED
mat grass	NARDUS
meadow-grass	FLOAT(ING) GRASS, POA
mondo grass	OPHIOPOGON
moorland grass	BRIZA, MATGRASS
	MATWEED, QUAKING-GRASS
mosquito grass	BOUTELOUA
Nardus	MAT GRASS
New Zealand	TOI TOI
oat	AVENA
—type	BROME-GRASS
Ophiopogon	MONDO GRASS
Oplismenus	BASKET-GRASS, PANICUM
ornamental	PLUME-GRASS
painted grass	CANARY GRASS
	GARDENER'S GARTERS
pampas-grass	PASPALUM

Panicum	BASKET-GRASS
	OPLISMENUS, PANIC(-GRASS)
paper-reed	PAPYRUS
pasture grass	DOG'S-TAIL GRASS, RYE-GRASS
pennywort	ROT-GRASS
Persicaria	KNOT-GRASS
Phalaris	GARDENER'S GARTERS
Phleum	TIMOTHY
pinkfoot	WORMGRASS
Poa	MEADOW-GRASS, WIRE-GRASS
Polygonum	KNOT-GRASS
porcupine-grass	SPINIFEX
quitch-grass	SQUITCH
ramee/rami(e)	CHINA GRASS, RHEA
reed-mace	CAT'S-TAIL, ELEPHANT GRASS
rhea	RAMEE, RAMI(E), RHEA
ribbon-grass	GARDENER'S GARTERS
rice-grass	CORD-GRASS
rot-grass	BUTTERWORT, PENNYWORT
rush	JUNCUS
rye	DARNEL, LOLIUM, SECALE
rye-grass	LOLIUM
sand-binding	LYME-GRASS, MARRAM
	MARRUM
scurvy-grass	COCHLEARIA
sea-reed	MARRAM(-GRASS)
seaside grass	AMMOPHILA
	DOG'S-TOOTH GRASSTAR(R)
	MARRAM, MARRUM
Secale	RYE
second growth	AFTERMATH, EDDISH
	FOG(GAGE)
sedge	CAREX
sesame-grass	ZAMA GRASS
shave-grass	DUTCH RUSH
side shoot	TILLER
slow spreading	MISCANTHUS
smart-weed	WATERPEPPER
soft grass	ROT-GRASS
sorghum	SUDAN-GRASS
South American	PAMPAS GRASS
	PASPALUM, RESCUE GRASS
Spanish grass	ESPARTO, SPART
spart	ESPARTO
spartina	CORD-GRASS
stiff stalk	BENT
Stipa	FEATHER-GRASS
striped canary-grass	RIBBON-GRASS
—green/cream	MOLINIA
Sudan-grass	SORGHUM
sweet-smelling	HOLY GRASS
thin dry stalk	WINDLESTRAW
timothy	CAT'S-TAIL GRASS, PHLEUM
—America	HERD('S)GRASS
tropical	PASPALUM
Uniola	SPIKE-GRASS

variegated ribbon	GARDENER'S GARTERS
vernal grass	ANTHOXANTHUM
waterpepper	SMART-WEED
wheat/rye hybrid	TRITICALE
wire-grass	POA
woodland grass	MILLET-GRASS
wormgrass	PINKFOOT
worthless	SOFT-GRASS
Xyris (US)	YELLOW-EYED GRASS
yellow-eyed grass (US)	XYRIS
zama grass	SESAME-GRASS
Zoster	EELGRASS, GRASSWRACK
Greece	GR, HELLAS
including: classical terms	
modern words	
abbot	ARCHIMANDRITE
	HEGUMEN
abode of dead	ELYSIUM
above (music)	
—Aeolian	HYPERAEOLIAN
—Dorian	HYPERDORIAN
—Lydian	HYPERLYDIAN
—Phrygian	HYPERPHRYGIAN
account	LOGOS
—of saint's life	SYNAXARION
accuser	SYCOPHANT
ace	OINE
acorn	BALANOS
additional note	PROSLAMBANOMENOS
address by	
—chorus	PARABASIS
—coryphaeus	EPIRRHEMA
admiral	NAVARCH
advocate	SYNDIC
alb	STICHARION
alcove	ZOTHECA
all	PAN
alone	MONOS
alphabet	(*see* letters *below*)
among	META
anatomist	HEROPHILUS
ancient people	PELASGI(ANS)
and	
—so forth	KAI TA LEIPOMENA, KTL
—the rest	KAI TA LOIPA, KTL
angle	GONIA
annalist	LOGOGRAPHER
ant	MURMEX
antipodes	ANTICHTHON
ape	PITHECOS
apple	MELON
architect/artist etc	HIPPODAMUS
	ICTINUS, POLYGNOTUS
	PHIDIAS, PRAXITELES
	SCOPAS, ZEUXIS
arms	HOPLA

army	
—commander	TAXIARCH
—division	TAXIS
arrogance	HUBRIS
art	TECHNE
ass	ONOS
assembly	AGYRIS, ECCLESIA
astronomer	ARISTARCHUS, ERATOSTHENES
	HIPPARCHUS, POSIDONIUS
Athenian	
—aristocrat	EUPATRID
—colony	CLERUCHIACLERUCHY
—youth	EPHEBE
athletic contest	AGON
—auditor	LOGOTHETE(S)
away, Satan!	APAGE SATANAS
Bacchic rout	THIASUS
bachelorhood	AGAMIA
back	NOTON, NOTOS, PALIN
backward	OPISO
band of soldiers	ENOMOTY
banish by vote	OSTRACISE
barricade	PHRAXIS
base	HEDRA
bathing establishment	THERM
bay	ORMOS
—leaves	DAPHNI
beak	RHYNCHOS
bear	ARKTOS
beautiful, (the)	TO KALON
—place	TEMPE
becoming	TO PREPON
bed	KLINE
bee-eater	MEROPS
behind	OPISTHEN
below (music)	
—Aeolian	HYPOAEOLIAN
—Dorian	HYPODORIAN
—Lydian	HYPOLYDIAN
—Phrygian	HYPOPHRYGIAN
beside	META
bird	ORNIS, ORNITHOS, STROUTHION
birth	TOKOS
bishop	EXARCH
bishop's stole	EPITRACHELION
black	MELAS
bladder	KYSTIS
blade	PLATE
blind	ALAOS
blood	HAIMA
—sucking witch	LAMIA
bone	OSTEON
boundary marker	HERM
boy	PAEDOS, PAIDOS
bread	PSOMI
bride	NYMPHE
brigand	KLEPHT
bristle	CHAITE
brother	ADELPHOS
bud	BLASTOS
bulk	ONCOS
business	ERGON, PRAGMATA
cake	PIT(T)A
cakes	FINIKIA
canonical hours (lauds)	ORTHROS
cape (headland)	AKRA, AKROTIRION
	MITI
captain of guards	PROTOSPATHARIUS
capital city	ATHENS
case	THEKE
cave	SPEOS
cessation	PAUSIS
chamber	THALAMOS
champion	PROMACHOS
chariot	BIGA, TRIGA, QUADRIGA
chest	LARNAX
chief	
—magician	ARCHIMAGE
—tribal officer	PHYLARCH
child	PAEDOS, PAIDOS
choral odes	STASIMA
chorus leader	CHORAGUS, CHOREGUS
church stall	STASIDION
citadel	ACROPOLIS
city	POLIS
—badge	EPISEMON
—state	POLIS
claw	ONYX
cloak	HIMATION
cloud	NEPHELE, NEPHOS
coffin	LARNAX
coins	
—small	LEPTON
—100 lepta	DRACHMA
—1½ pence	OBOL(US)
—6 oboli	DRACHMA
—2 drachmas	DIDRACHMA
—4 drachmas	TETRADRACHM
—silver tetradrachm	STATER
—100 drachmas	MINA
—6000 drachmas	TALENT
collection of sermons	PANEGYRICON
colonist in	
—Asia Minor	AEOLIAN
—Italy	ITALIOT(E)
—Sicily	SICELIOT, SIKELIOT
colonnade	STOA, XYSTOS, XYSTUS
colonnaded market-hall	STOA
colour	CHROMA
commander of	
—10	DECADARCH
—1000	CHILIARCH

—cavalry	HIPPARCH, PHYLARCH	verse	PERIOD
—division	TAXIARCH	—of people	PHYLE
—sub-division	TETRARCH	dome	THOLOS, THOLUS
—trireme	TRIERARCH	Doric magistrate	EPHOR
common informer	SYCOPHANT	down	PAPPUS
company of worshippers	THIASUS	downbeat	THESIS
container	KYTOS	dowry	PHERNE
contemptible Greek	GREEKLING	dramatist/poet	AESCHYLUS,
copper	CHALKOS		ARISTOPHANES, EURIPIDES
corn	SITOS		HEGEMON, ION, MENANDER
corslet	THORAX		SOPHOCLES
council	BOULE	dream	ONEIROS
—chamber	BOULEUTERION	dressing-room (baths)	APODYTERIUM
—division	PRYTANY	drinking	
—representing all		—cup	COTYLE, CYLIX, HOLMOS
sections	PANHELLENION		KYLIX, RHYTON, SCYPHUS
	PANHELLENIUM	—song	DITHYRAMB, SKOLION
course	DROMOS	drug	PHARMAKON
court	AREOPAGUS	dwarf	NANOS
courtesan	ASPASIA, HETAIRA	dynasty (Syria)	SELEUCID
covered portico	XYST(OS), XYSTUS	ear	OTOS, OUS
covering	SHEUE	eating in public	SYSSITIA
credit	KUDOS	egg	OION
crowd	OCHLOS	egotism	ITACISM
cupola	THOLOS, THOLUS	elliptical auditorium	SPHENDONE
custom	NOMOS	embodiment of	
cut(ting)	TOME	—justice	ARISTIDES
dagger	PARAZONIUM	—self-discipline	ARISTIPPUS
dance	ROMAIKA	epic	
dancing-girl	HETAIRA	—poem	ODYSSEY
dawn	ORTHROS	—tale	ILIAD
day	HEMERA	eucharistic fan	RHIPIDION
deacon's stole	ORARION	explorer	PYTHEAS
dead (body)	NEKROS	eye	OMMA, OPHTHALMOS
decree of Athenian assembly	PSEPHISM	fabulous robber	PROCRUSTES
defender	PROMACHOS	fame	KUDOS
defilement	MYSOS	fan	RHIPIDIUM
deities	(see gods, goddesses)	fastening of woman's girdle	VIRGIN KNOT
delegate	SYNDIC	father	PAP(P)AS
—to council	AMPHICTYON	fawn-skin	NEBRIS
department	NOME, NOMOS	fear	PHOBOS
diadem	STEPHANE	female entertainer	HETAIRA
dialects	(A)EOLIC, ATTIC	festival	
	DORIC, IONIC, KOINE	—Apollo	THARGELIA
discarded letter	SAN	—Demeter	THESMOPHORIA
discourse	LOGOS	—Dionysius	ANTHESTERIA
dish	BAKLAVA, FASOLIA	—national	PANATHENAEA
	HOUMMOUS, KEBABS	few	OLIGOS
	MOUS(S)AKA	fibre	MITOS
	PILAFE, TARAMOSALATA	field	AGROS
	TSATSIKI, TZATZIKI	fillet	MITRA
divination	MANTEIA	fitting (that which is ...)	TO PREPON
divine voice	OMPHE	flabellum	RHIPIDIUM
division	DEME	flask	AMPHORA, LAGENA, OLPE
—in		flesh	KREAS
army	TAXIS	flower	ANTHEMON

fly	MYIA
folly	MORIA
fondness	PHILIA
food	OPSON(ION), SITOS, TROPHE
—plant	LASER, SILPHIUM
foot	PODOS
forehead	METOPON
form	MORPHE
formation	GENESIS
founder of drama	THESPIS
fountain (Mt. Helicon)	AGANIPPE
fourth part of province	TETRARCHATE
	TETRARCHY
fracture	KLASIS
frankincense	LIBANOS
front portico with not	
more than four columns	PROSTYLE
fruit	KARPOS
galley	BIREME, TRIREME
	QUADRIREME, QUINQUEREME
gem	OPALLIOS
generals	DIADOCHI
generation	GENESIS
gift	DORON
gills	BRANCHIA
glade	NEMOS
globular oil-flask	ARYBALLOS
glue	GLOIA, KOLLA
god	THEOS
golden mean	ARISTON METRON
good genius	AGATHODAIMON
governor	EPARCH, ETHNARCH, NOMARCH
	TOPARCH, TAXIARCH
grandfather	PAPPUS
granule	CHONDROS
great	MEGA
Greece	HELLAS
Greek	ATTIC, ARGIVE, GK, GR
—in ancient Italy	ITALIOT(E)
—people	ACHAEAN, ACHIAN, ARGIVE
	ATHENIAN, SPARTAN
grief	PENTHOS
grotto	NYPHAEUM
ground	PEDON
group of verses	SYSTEM
growth	PHYSIS
guest-house	TAVERNA
gulf	KOLPOS
gymnasium at Athens	LYCEUM
hair ornament (cicada)	TETTIX
half	HEMI
hat worn by Hermes	PETASOS, PETASUS
head	KEPHALE
—dress	STEPHANE
—fillet	MITRE
healing plant	PANAX

heath	HEIDE
heavily-armed soldier	HOPLITE
hero	ACHILLES, AENEAS
	AGAMEMNON, AJAX
	ALCIDES, CADMUS, HECTOR
	HERAKLES, HERCULES, JASON
	NESTOR, ODYSSEUS, PERSEUS
	PROMETHEUS, THESEUS, ULYSSES
highest lyre string	NETE
hilltop	KUPPE
historian	AMMIANUS, HERODOTUS
	PTOLEMY, THUCYDIDES
	XENOPHON
hole	TREMA
holy meteoric stone	BAETYL
home of oracle	DELPHI
honey	MELI
hook	ONKOS
hoop	TROCHOS, TROCHUS
horn	KERAS
house	MEGARON, OIKOS
hymns	HERMOI, HERMOS
—to Bacchus	DITHYRAMB
I have found	(H)EUREKA
imitator	MIMOS
impulse	OSMOS, OTHIMOS
incline	KLINEIN
infant	NEPIOS
infantry formation	PHALANX
infantryman	EVZONE
inhabitant of part	
of Constantinople	FANARIOT, PHANARIOT
inlet	FORDE
inn	TAVERNA
inner chamber of temple	CELLA, NAOS
instalment of epic	RHAPSODY
instrument	BOUZOUKI, CITHARA
	KITHARA, PHORMINX
intestines	ENTERON
introduction to a play	PROLOGUE
Ionian	TEIAN
—mode (mus.)	IASTIC
irregularly divided	ALLOIOSTROPHOS
island(s)	NESOS
islander	NESIOTES
jar	AMPHORA, STAMNOS
jaw	GNATHOS
joint	ARTHRON
judge	DICAST, DIKAST, SYNDIC
—of games	AGNOTHETES
judge's court	DICASTERY
jug	OLPE
juice	OPOS
junior archon	THESMOTHETE
keynote	MESE
kidney	NEPHROS

kilt	FUSTANELLA
know thyself	GNOTHI SEAUTON
knowing	GNOSIS
lagoon	LIMNOS
lake	LIMNOS
lamb	ARNOS
lament	THRENE
lamp attendant	LAMPADARY
land	GAIA
late	OPSE
law	NOMOS
—giver	NOMOTHETE(S)
	THESMOTHETE
lead	MOLYBDOS
leader	AGOGOS
—of	
chorus	CORYPHAEUS
worshippers	THIASARCH
learning	MATHE
legislator	DRACO, NOMOTHETES
length	MEKOS
lesson on life of a saint	SYNAXARION
letter	GRAMMA
—Y	PYTHAGOREAN LETTER
	SAMIAN LETTER
letters	ALPHA, BETA, CHI, DELTA
	EPSILON, ETA, GAMMA, IOTA
	KAPPA, LA(M)BDA, MU, NU
	OMEGA, OMICRON, PHI, PI
	PSI, RHO, SIGMA, TAU, THETA
	UPSILON, XI, ZETA
	(*see also* obsolete letters *below*)
life	BIOS
—saving reward	SOSTRUM
lightly-armed soldier	PELTAST
liking for	PHILIA
line	STICHOS
liqueur	OUZO
litany	SYNAPTE
little	MIKROS, OLIGOS
lizard	SAUROS
long-jump	HALMA
lord of men	ANAXANDRON
loss of rights as citizen	ATIMY
lowest	
—note but one	PARHYPATE
—string of lyre	HYPATE
lyre	CITHARA, KITHARA
madness	MANIA
magical	
—meteoric stone	BAETYL
—stone	PANTARBE
magistrate	ARCHON, EPHOR
magnet for gold	PANTARBE
main gate of Athens	DIPYLON
man	ANDROS, ANER, ANTHROPOS

manner of life	BIOSIS
marker	STELE
market-place	AGORA
marriage	GAMOS
marrow	MYELOS
mass	ONCOS
master of feast	
or conference	SYMPOSIARCH
mathematician	ARCHIMEDES, EUCLID
	PYTHAGORAS
measure(ment)	METRON
—600 feet	STADION
—1 quart (approx)	CH(O)ENIX
measuring cup (1½ pint)	CYATHUS
meat	
—balls	KEFTEDES
—casserole	STIFADO
medallion	PERIAMMA
medical	IATRIKOS
meeting	
—for worship	SYNAXIS
—place in Athens	AGORA, PNYX
—room	ANDRON
method of investigation	ORGANON
metre	METRON
metropolitan (church leader)	EXARCH
middle	MESE
—course	ARISTON METRON
—string of lyre	MESE
military	
—commander	POLEMARCH
—formation	PHALANX
—ruler	DIADOCHI
mill	MYLE, MYLON
mind	NOUS
mine	METALLON
misanthrope (Shak.)	TIMON
mist	NEPHELE
modern	
—coin	DRACHM(A)
—Greek	DEMOTIC, ROMAIC
modesty	AIDOS
monastery	MONI
monastic	
—habit	SCHEMA
—settlement	SCETE, SKETE
monk	CALOYER, MONASTES
monster	(*see separate entry*)
month	MEN
Moon	MENE, SELENE
morning service	ARTHROS
mother-city of colony	METROPOLIS
mountain	OROS
mouse	MYS
mouth	STOMA
mucus	MYXA

muscle	MYS
mushroom	MYKES
music hall	ODEON, ODEUM
musical	
—instrument	AULOS, BARBITOS
	BOUZOUKI, CITHARA, KITHARA
	LYRE, PHORMINX, SYRINX
—interval	DITONE
—modes	AEOLIAN, IONIAN, IASTIC
	(MIXO)LYDIAN, PHRYGIAN
—separation of	
chords	DIAZEUXIS
—tempo	AGOGE
mussel	MYAX
myth	MYTHOS
nail	ONYX
name	ONOMA
narrow-necked flask	LEKYTHOS
national festival	PANATHENAEA
	PYTHIAN GAMES
native of Zante	ZANTIOT(E)
nature	PHYSIS
navel	OMPHALOS
necessity	ANANKE
nerve	NEURON
new	KAINOS, NEOS
night	NYKTOS, NYX
northern	ARKTIKOS
nose	RHINOS, RHIS
note above hypate	PARHYPATE
now	NYN
numberless	MYRIOS
numbness	NARKE
numeral	SAMPI
nursing	TROPHEIA
obsolete letters	EPISEMON, DIGAMMA
	KOPPA, SAN, SAMPI, VAU
ode	STASIMON
office of	
—exarch	EXARCHATE
—harmost	HARMOSTY
official	POLEMARCH
on	EPI
Old Testament	SEPTUAGINT
olive tree	ELATA
olives	ELIES
one	
—of Greek official	
class	FANARIOT, PHANARIOT
—sleeved garment	EXOMIS
open-air auditorium	PNYX
opinion	DOXA
orator	DEMOSTHENES, GORGIAS
	LYSIAS, PERICLES
order of architecture	CORINTHIAN
	DORIC, IONIC

orchestra	KONISTRA
outer garment	HIMATION
over	HYPER
oyster	OSTREON
pain	ALGE, ALGOS, ODYNE
pale yellow	OCHROS
palm	PALAME
panacea	PANAX
paradise	ELYSIUM
parliament	BOULE
part of	MEROS
—Greek comedy	PARABASIS
—tetrachord	PYCNON
pass	STENON
peas	ARAKAS
penalty	POINE
peninsula	CHERSONESE, KHERSONISOS
people	DEMOS
perception	AISTHESIS
philosophers	ANAXAGORAS, ANAXIMANDER
	ANAXIMENES, ANTISTHENES
	ARISTIPPOS, ARISTOTLE
	DEMOCRITUS, DIOGENES
	EMPEDOCLES, EPICURUS
	HERACLIDES, HERACLITUS, HIPPIAS
	LEUCIPPUS, PARMENIDES, PLATO
	PLOTINUS, PRODICUS, PROTAGORAS
	PYRRHO, PYTHAGORAS, SOCRATES
	STAGIRITE, THALES
	THEOPHRASTUS, THRASYMACHUS
	XENOPHANES, ZENO
physician	ALCMAEON, ERASISTRATUS
	GALEN, HEROPHILUS
	HIPPOCRATES, PRAXAGORAS
pick-axe	ORYX
plant	PHYTON
play	
—first part	PROTASIS
—last part	APODOSIS
—main part	EPITASIS
poem about returning	NOSTOS
poet	(see writer below)
poetess	SAPPHO
poetic inspiration	AGANIPPE
point	AKME
political animal	ZOON POLITIKON
pollution	MIASMA
poor freeman	THETE
popular assembly	ECCLESIA
porch	STOA
portico	PTERON, STOA, XYSTOS, XYSTUS
potato	PATATA
place dedicated to a god	TEMENOS
potsherd	OSTRACON, OSTRAKON
pottery horn	RHYTON
poverty	PENIA

power	KRATOS	saint	AYIA, AYIOS
prayer-book	EUCHOLOGION	salad	HORIATIKI
	EUCHOLOGY, TRIODION	sanctuary	NYMPHAEUM, SEKOS
precinct	TEMENOS	sap	OPOS
preliminary oblation	PROTHESIS	saw	PRION
prestige	KUDOS	scale	CHROMA
pride	HUBRIS	school of philosophy	PAINTED PORCH
priest	PAPA		(see also philosophy)
priest's stole	EPITRACHELION	sculptor	PHIDIAS, PRAXITELES
principal hall	MEGARON		SCOPAS
professional orator	RHETOR	section of psalm-book	CATHISMA
prophet	MANTIS	sea	THALASSA, THALATTA
prostitute	HETAIRA	—nymph	NEREID
province	NOME, NOMOS	—perch	ORPHOS
—of		—sickness	NAUSIA
eparch	EPARCHATE, EPARCHY	—weed	PHYKOS
ephor	EPHORALTY	second of nine archons	KING-ARCHON
prudence	METIS	secret writing	SCYTALE
public		sect (14th c)	HESYCHAST
—disgrace	ATIMY	seed	SPERMA
—drinking-fountain	NYMPHAEUM	seemly	TO PREPON
—eating	SYSSITIA	seen	OPTOS
purchase of food	OPSONIA	sell	POLEEIN
purple cope	CHLAMYS	senate	BOULE
quill for string-plucking	PLECTRUM	serf	HELOT, PENEST, THETE
race course	DROMOS, STADION	service	
rabble	HOI POLLOI	—book	TRIODION
rain-storm	OBROMOS	—to the state	LITURGY
raw	OMOS	setting down	THESIS
rear-chamber in temple	OPISTHODOMOS	seven	
reason	LOGOS	—prayers	LYCHNAPSIA
renown	KUDOS	—tones	HEPTACHORD
restaurant	TAVERNA	severe critic	ARISTARCH
return	NOSTOS	shame	AIDOS
revolving prism in theatre	PERIAKTOS	shape	MORPHE
rice	RIZA	sharp	OXYS
—pudding	RIZOGALO	shell	OSTRAKON
right	ORTHOS	shield	AEGIS
river encircling world	OKEANOS	ship	ARGO, CAIQUE, HOLCAD, NAUS
rostrum	BEMA		SAIC, SAIK, SAIQUE
round building	THOLOS, THOLUS	—with 30 oars	TRIACONTER
row	STICHOS	—with 50 oars	PENTECOSTER
—of trees	ORCHATOS	shoot	BLASTOS
rule	ARCHE	short	
ruler of		—anthem	ISODICON
—district	TOPARCH	—cloak	CHLAMYS
—people	ETHNARCH	—hymn	CATHISMA, TROPARION
run	DROMOS	—sighted	MYOPS
sacred enclosure	SEKOS	shoulder	OMOS
sacristan	SCEUOPHYLAX	shrew	MYGALE
sacristy	DIACONICON, PARABEMA	shrine	TEMENOS
	SCEUOPHYLACIUM	shut	MYEIN
saddle of mountain	SELOMA	sickness	NOSOS
said (or written) once	HAPAX LEGOMENON	side	
sailor	NAUTES, NAUTILOS	—scene	PARASCENIUM
—in Argo	ARGONAUT	—wall of temple	PTEROMA

sight	OPSIS	temple	NAOS
single	MONOS	—of Athene	ATHENAEUM
skin	DERMA	—slave	HIERODULE
skull	KRANION	—with one ring of columns	MONOPTERON
slave	HELOT		MONOPTEROS
slime	MYXA	tempo	AGOGE
smallest subdivision	ENOMOTY	ten thousand	MYRIAS
smell	OSME	tend	KOMEEIN
snake	OPHIS	the	
snout	RHYNCUS	—many	HOI POLLOI
soda	NITRON	—vulgar	HOI POLLOI
soft	MALAKOS	theatre	ODEON, ODEUM
soldier	EVZONE, HOPLITE	thick	PACHYS
solitary	MONACHOS	third	
song	MELOS, OIDE	—actor	TRITAGONIST
—sung by chorus	STROPHE	—string of lyre	TRITE
soup	AVGOLEMONO	—tone of tetrachord	TRITE
sour	OXYS	thread	MITOS, NEMA
south	NOTOS	three-branched candlestick	TRICERION
southern hemisphere	ANTICHTHON	tile	OSTRAKON
space in temple	PERIDROME	time	CHRONOS
Spartan governor	HARMOST	tomato	DOMATA
speaking	PHRASIS	tomb	THOLOS, THOLUS
speech	LALIA	tone	
sphere	SPHAIRA	—above the mese	PARAMESE
spice	STORAX	—below the nete	PARANETE
spirit	DAIMON	tongue	GLOSSA
spit	OBELOS	tooth	ODOUS
sports-ground	STADION	torch-race	LAMPADEDROMY
squid	KALAMARAKIA		LAMPADEPHORIA
standing	STATOS	town	DEME
stanza	STROPHE	—hall	PYRTANEION, PRYTANEUM
stationary	STASIMON	—ship	DEME
statue	KOUROS, XOANON	toy	KLEIS, KLEIDOS
step	BEMA	track	ICHNOS
stink	OSME	traditional utterance of Christ	AGRAPHON
stone	LITHOS	translation of Hebrew bible	SEPTUAGINT
—at Delphi	OMPHALOS	tree-planted walk	XYST(OS), XYSTUS
—of the Sun	PANTARBE	tribe	PELASGI, PHYLE
story	MYTHOS	tripartite building	MEGARON
straight	ORTHOS	troop	
strait	STENON	—of worshippers	THIASUS
string struck with the forefinger	LICHANOS	—leader	PHYLARCH
stroke	PLEGE	trumpet	SALPINX
strong drink	METHE	tumour	ONCOS
stuffed olive leaves	DOLMADAKIA	tunic	CHITON, EXOMIUM, EXOMIS
	DOLMADES, DOLMATHES	turkey	GALAPOULA
sub-division	DEME	turn(ing)	TROPOS
Sun	HELIOS	tusk	CEROS
sweat	HIDROS	tutelary god	PROMACHOS
swelling	OIDEMA, ORGASMOS	two-handled vase	DIOTA
swimming	NEUSTOS	underground water channel	KATABOTHRON
talk	MYTHOS		KAVAVOTHRON
taper carrier	LAMPADARY	unguent	MYRON
teacher	PAIDEUTES	union	ENOSIS
—of rhetoric	RHETOR	unit	MONAS

unripe grape	OMPHAX
upright	ORTHOS
urn	STAMNOS
vase	DIOTA, PELIKE, PITHOS, RHYTON
veal	MOSHKARI
veil	CALYPTRA, KALYPTRA
verse style	ADONIC, ALCAIC
vespers	LYCHNIC
vessel	KYTOS
vestibule in front of temple	PRONAOS
vestment	SACCOS, SAKKOS
victory	NIKE
view	HORAMA
voice	OPS, PHONE
waist-belt	ZOSTER
war	
—cry	ALALAGMOS
—dance	PYRRHIS
watching	SKOPIA
water	HYDOR
—jar	HYDRIA, KALPIS
wax	KEROS
way	HODOS
weasel	GALEE
weight	DRACHMA
—3 pounds	OCQUE
—26-38kg (gold or silver)	TALENT
—money	MINA
well done!	EUGE
wheel	TROCHOS, TROCHUS
white	LEUKOS
—kilt for men	FUSTANELLA
wild	AGRIOS
—beast	THERION
—dance	SIKINNIS
wind	PARASCENIUM
wine	(see separate entry)
—jar	PITHOS
—throwing game	COTTABUS, KOTTABUS
wing	PTERON
—(theatre)	PARASCENIUM
wisdom	SOPHIA
with	META
woman	GYNE
woman's	
—head-band	SPHENDONE
—robe	PEPLOS, PEPLUM
womb	DELPHYS, HYSTERA
wood	HYLE
wooded pasture	NEMOS
wooden statue	ACROLITH
word	LEXIS
work	ERGON
world	KOSMOS
—city	COSMOPOLIS
worship	LATREIA

writer	AESCHYLUS, AESOP, ALCAEUS
	ANACREON, APOLLODORUS
	APOLLONIUS, ARISTOPHANES
	EURIPIDES, HERODOTUS, HESIOD
	HOMER, LUCIAN, PAUSANIAS
	PHERECRATES, PINDAR
	PLUTARCH, SIMONIDES, SOPHOCLES
	TERPANDER, TYRTAEUS
	(see also writers)
yes	OHI
young citizen	EPHEBE
youthful	NEANIKOS
	(see also mythology)
Grenada	WG
capital	ST GEORGES
coin	CENT, DOLLAR
Grenadines	WV
greyhound	
coursing event	WATERLOO CUP
famous greyhound	BEACH COMBER
	DULEEK DANDY
	GRAND CANAL, I'M SLIPPY
	JIMSUN, LACCA CHAMPION
	LAURIE'S PANTHER, LUCKY BOY
	PAGAN SWALLOW, PALME'S PRINTER
	PARKDOWN JET, TICO, TRIC-TRAC
	SARAH'S BUNNY, WHISPER WISHES
events	
—cross-country	COURSING
—track	GREYHOUND RACING
greyhound racing	GRACING, GREYCING
making a fast start	PINGING HIS LID
starting gate	TRAP
target	(ELECTRIC) HARE
venues	BIRMINGHAM, BRIGHTON
	CATFORD, EDINBURGH, OXFORD
	RAMSGATE, WALTHAMSTOW
	WEMBLEY, WIMBLEDON, WINDSOR
	WOLVERHAMPTON
group	CLASSIS
including: collection of	
group of	
mass of	
actors	CAST, COMPANY, TROUPE
ants	ARMY, COLONY
aeroplanes	FLIGHT, SQUADRON, WING
animals	FAMILY, GENUS, PHYLUM
	SPECIES
apes	SHREWDNESS
arms	STAND
artillery	BATTERY, PARK
artists	CENACLE, COTERIE
	MOVEMENT, SCHOOL
artistes	TROUPE
asses	DROVE, HERD, PACE

at cinema, theatre, etc	AUDIENCE	grass	TUFT
attendants	RETINUE, TRAIN	Greek citizens	PHYLE
badgers	CETE, COLONY	hares	DOWN, DROVE, LEASH
bards	GORSEDD		TRACE, TRIP
bears	SLOTH	harpists	MELODY
bees	HIVE, SWARM	having	
beggars	FIGHTING	—common interests	CLIQUE, COMMUNITY
beauties	BEVY, GALAXY		LOBBY, SOCIETY
birds	(see **bird**²)	—political aims	CABAL, CADRE
boars	HERD, SINGULAR, SOUNDER		CELL, JUNTA
boys	BLUSH	—same age and status	PEER GROUP
brotherhood	FELLOWSHIP, FRATERNITY	hay	BALE, TRUSS
	GUILD, SODALITY	hens	BROOD
business interests	CARTEL, CONSORTIUM	herrings	CRAN
	MONOPOLY, SYNDICATE	hermits	OBSERVANCE
butlers	DRAUGHT	hinds	PARCEL
cars	CONVOY, FLEET, MOTORCADE	horses	HARAS, HARRAS(E)
cards	HAND, SEQUENCE		HERD, REMUDA, STABLE
cats	CLOWDER, CLUSTER		TEAM, TROOP
cattle	DROVE, HERD	hounds	KENNEL, PACK
cavalrymen	TROOP	hunters	BLAST
church representatives	CONVOCATION	in	
clans	GATHERING	—Air Force	FLIGHT, SQUADRON, WING
cobblers	DRUNKENNESS	—Army	BATTALION, BRIGADE, COMPANY
	DRUNKENSHIP		CORPS, DIVISION, MESS, PLATOON
colts	RAG, RAKE		REGIMENT, SECTION
co-operating with			SQUAD(RON), TROOP
each other	ALLIANCE, ALIGNMENT	—Navy	CREW, FLEET, MESS
	BLOC, COALITION		SQUADRON, WATCH
	CONFEDERACY, FEDERATION	intellectuals	COTERIE, MOVEMENT
	LEAGUE	items	AGGREGATE, ASSEMBLAGE
corn	SHEAF		CONGERIES
cotton	HANK, SKEIN		CONGLOMERATION
cuckolds	INCREDIBILITY	jazz musicians	BAND, COMBO, GROUP
curs	COWARDICE	kangaroos	HERD, MOB, TROOP
dancers	CORPS DE BALLET, TROUPE	kine	DROVE
deer	HERD, LEASH	kittens	KINDLE, LITTER
directors	BOARD	knaves	RAYFUL
dogs	KENNEL, PACK	lawmen	POSSE
dolphins	POD	leopards	LEAP, LEPE
donkeys	DROVE, HERD, PACE	lions	PRIDE, TROOP
druids	GORSEDD	living in same area	COMMUNITY
eggs	CLUTCH	majors	MORBIDITY
elephants	HERD	machine-guns	NEST
elks	GANG	mares	STUD
famous people	GALAXY	martens	RICHESSE
ferrets	CAST, FESNYING	moles	COMPANY, LABOUR
firemen	BRIGADE, WATCH		MOVEMENT
fish	SHOAL	monkeys	CARTLOAD, TRIBE, TROOP
flower pots	CASTE	monopolising trade	CARTEL
foresters	STALK	Moslem theologians	ULEMA
foxes	LEAD, SKULK	mules	BARREN, PACK, RAKE, SPAN
friars	SKULK	musicians	BAND, COMBO, GROUP
frogs	ARMY, COLONY		OCTET, NONET, ORCHESTRA
funeral attendants	CORTEGE		QUARTET, QUINTET, SEPTET
goats	FLOCK, HERD, TRIBE		SEXTET, TRIO

nuns	SUPERFLUITY
officers	MESS
ornaments	GARNITURE, PARURE
otters	BEVY, FAMILY
oxen	SPAN, TEAM, YOKE
papers	BUDGET, QUIRE, REAM
pardoners	LYING
pearls	ROPE
pedlars	MALAPERTNESS
people	CONCOURSE, CONFLUENCE
	CROWD, DROVE, HORDE
	HOST, MOB, MULTITUDE
	PHALANX, RUCK, THRONG
performers	TROUPE
pigs	HERD, SOUNDER
piglets	FARROW, LITTER
pipers	POVERTY
players	CAST, SIDE, TEAM
playing	
—cricket	ELEVEN
—football	ELEVEN
—games	SIDE, TEAM
—Rugby League	THIRTEEN
—Rugby Union	FIFTEEN
polecats	CHINE
political	BLOC, CADRE, CAUCUS
	ENCLAVE, FACTION, PARTY
porpoises	SCHOOL
porters	SAFEGUARD
princes	STATE
puppies	LITTER
rabbits	BURY, COLONY
—young	NEST
raches	KENNEL
rats	COLONY
religious	CHURCH, FACTION, SECT
representatives	DELEGATION, DEPUTATION
rhinoceroses	CRASH
rifles	STAND
rowers	EIGHT, FOUR, PAIR
sailors	(*see* in Navy *above*)
saints	COMMUNITY
savages	HORDE, POSSE
schoolchildren	CLASS, FORM
seals	BOB, COLONY, CRASH
	HERD, POD, TEAM
secret intriguers	CABAL, JUNTA
sergeants	MESS, SUBTILNE
sharing property	COMMUNE
sheaves	STOOK
sheep	DROVE, FLOCK, FOLD, TRIP
ships	CONVOY, FLEET
	FLOTILLA, NAVY
	SQUADRON
silk	SKEIN

similar items	COMPENDIUM, ENSEMBLE
	SUITE
singers	CHOIR
small group	COVEY
snakes	DEN, NEST, PIT
soldiers	(*see* in Army *above*)
songs, plays, etc	REPERTOIRE
sportsmen	SIDE, TEAM
stars	CLUSTER, CONSTELLATION
	GALAXY
strawberries	PUNNET
subalterns	MESS, SIMPLICITY
swine	DROYLT, SOUNDER
tailors	DISGUISING
tame swine	DROYLT
teams	LEAGUE
thieves	GANG
thread	HANK
tigers	AMBUSH
tinkers	WANDERING
trees	CLUMP, COPPICE, COPSE, FOREST
	GROVE, SPINNEY, WOOD
turtles	DULE
undesirables	GALERE, ROGUES' GALLERY
vehicles	CONVOY
vigilantes	POSSE
voters	CONSTITUENCY
walruses	HERD, POD
whales	GAM, HERD, POD, SCHOOL
whelps	LITTER
wolves	HERD, PACK, ROUT
women	SORORITY
wool	BALL, HANK
workers	BEE, GUILD, UNION
worshippers	CONGREGATION
—Greek	THIASUS
writers	COTERIE
zebras	HERD
Guatemala	GCA
capital	GUATEMALA CITY
coin	CENTAVO, QUETZAL
Guernsey	GBG
gum	
including: balsam	
resin	
amber	SUCCINIE
balsam fir	CANADA BALSAM
British gum	DEXTRIN(E), STARCH GUM
colophony	ROSIN
ester gum	ROSIN ESTER
dark red	SHELLAC, SHELL-LAC
fossil resin	AMBER, SUCCINITE
from	
—acacia	GUM ACACIA, GUM ARABIC
—barberry	PODOPHYLLIN
—bullet (bully) tree	BALATA

—Canarium	ELEMI
—Commiphora tree	BDELLIUM
—fennel	AS(S)AF(O)ETIDA
—Garcinia	GAMBOGE
—hemp	CHARAS, CHURRUS
—lentisk	MASTIC(H)
—locust tree	ANIME, COURBARIL
—shrubs	TRAGACANTH
—trees	COPAL, DAMMAR, DAMMER
—turpentine	COLOPHONY, ROSIN
gamboge	CAMBOGIA GUM
Indian	DHOONA
liquid resin	BALSAM
Moroccan	SANDARAC(H)
natural resin from trees	COPAL
plum gum	CERASIN
South American	ANGICO, BALATA
	CARRANA, CARAUNA
synthetic	FURAN RESIN
	FURFURAL RESIN
thermosetting	UREA FORMALDEHYDE
tropical	CONIMA
used in	
—foam	URETHANE RESIN
—food	GUM ACACIA, GUM ARABIC
—lacquers	URETHANE RESIN
—metal coatings	FURAN RESIN
—varnish	COPAL, URETHANE RESIN
West Indian	ANIME, COURBARIL
yellow	GAMBOGE, MASTIC(A)
gun	
Afghan rifle	JEZAIL
air-gun	WIND-GUN
anti-aircraft	BOFORS, OERLIKON
	POMPOM
—submarine mortar	SQUID
—tank weapon	PIAT, BAZOOKA
arquebus	HACKBUT, HAGBUT
automatic	
—pistol	
American	AUTO-MAG, BROWNING, COLT
	DARDICK, GYROJET
	SMITH AND WESSON
Austrian	LAUMANN, MANNLICHER
	ROTH-STEYR, SCHONBERGER
Belgian	BROWNING
British	PAULSON-MARS
	WEBLEY(-FOSBERY)
German	BEHOLLA
	BERGMAN(-BAYARD)
	BORCHARDT, HECKLER AND KOCH
	LUGER, MANNLICHER, MAUSER
	WALTHER
Hungarian	FEGYVERGYAL
Italian	BERETTA, GLISENTI
Japanese	NAMBU

Russian	STECHKIN
—rifle	
American	ARMALITE, BANG, BAR
	BROWNING, COLT COMMANDO
	GARAND, M-16, PEDERSEN
Belgian	FAL, FN BROWNING
British	FARQUHAR-HILL
Danish	BANG
French	RSC, ST ETIENNE
German	STURMGEWEHR
Italian	CEI-RIGOTTI
Mexican	MONDRAGON
Russian	AK-47, FEDEROV
	KALASHNIKOV
bell-mouthed	BLUNDERBUSS
big gun	BIG BERTHA
camel-mounted	ZOMBORUK
	ZUMBOORU(C)K
cannon	FALCON
—9-10 pounder	DEMI-CULVERIN
—18 pounder	CULVERIN
—30-36 pounder	DEMI-CANNON
—dummy	QUAKER-GUN
—long	CULVERIN, LONG TOM
—modern naval	TURRET-GUN
—old	BASILISK, SERPENTINE
American	COLUMBIAD, DAHLGREN GUN
	SODA WATER BOTTLE
British	ARMSTRONG
—short	CARRONADE, HOWITZER
—small	CHAMBER, FALCONET
	MURDERER, MURDERING-PIECE
	SAKER
—stone-firing	PERRIER
—very large	BIG BERTHA, DUILLE GRETE
	HOCHDRUCKPUMPE
	MAD MARGARET
	MONS MEG, SCHLANKE EMMA
	SLENDER EMMA, SUPER GUN
carbine	ESCOPETTE
cowboy's	
—revolver	COLT (45)
—rifle	WINCHESTER
Dahlgren gun	SODA WATER BOTTLE
dummy cannon	QUAKER(GUN)
elephant gun	ROER
field-gun	FOUR-POUNDER
fired with spike	NEEDLE-GUN
firing stones, etc	PADERERO, PATERERO
	PED(E)RERO, PERRIER
flintlock	SNAPHA(U)NCE, SNAPHAUNCH
—British	BROWN BESS
—musket	FUSEE, FUSIL
for firing	
—salutes	PADERERO, PATERERO
	PED(E)RERO

—stones	PERRIER
fowling-piece	SHOTGUN
grenade-thrower	CO(E)HORN
hand-gun	GAT, IRON, PIECE
	PISTOL, REVOLVER
high angle	HOWITZER
	(TRENCH) MORTAR
horse-pistol	PETRONEL
large pistol	HORSE PISTOL
light	
—field-gun	AMUSETTE
—machine-gun	BREN, SUBMACHINE-GUN
—musket	CALIVER, CAR(A)BINE
—shotgun	FOWLING-PIECE
loaded from	
—front end	MUZZLE-LOADER
—rear end	BREECH-LOADER
long-barrelled	
—cannon	CULVERIN, LONG TOM
—revolver	BUNTLINE SPECIAL
machine gun	
—American	BENET-MERCIE, BROWNING
	GATLING, MARLIN
	MAXIM, VULCAN
—Austrian	SALVATOR-DORMUS, SKODA
	SCHWARZLOSE
—British	BETHEL-BURTON, BREN,
	DAVIS, ROBEY-PETERS
	LEWIS, VICKERS
—Czech	BREN
—Danish	MADSEN
—French	CHATELLERAULT, CHAUCHAT
	HOTCHKISS, MITRAILLEUSE
	ST ETIENNE, VICKERS-BETHIER
—German	BECKER, BERGMAN, DREYSE
	GAST, MACHINENGEWEHR
	PARABELLUM, RHEINMETALL
	SEMAG, SPANDAU, SZAKATS
—Italian	AGNELLI, BREDA, FIAT-REVELLI
—Russian	BERESIN, PULEMYOT MAXIMA
mortar	HOBIT
—anti-submarine	SQUID
—German (WW2)	MOANING MINNIE
	TOTENORGEL
—trench mortar	TOC EMMA
—types	ROCKET MORTAR
	SPIGOT MORTAR
	STOKES MORTAR
	TRENCH MORTAR
multi-barrelled	
—American	BILLINGHURST, GARDNER
	MARSTON PISTOL
	REFORM PISTOL
	REQUA BATTERY
	VANDENBURG, VOLLEY GUN
—Belgian	MARIETTE

—British	ALLEN, BOND, BUDDING
	KNOBLEY, NOCK, PROBIN
—cannon	MOB GUN, ORGAN
	ORGUE, POMPOM
—Danish	(ORGEL) ESPINGOLE
—French	MITRAILLEUSE
—German	MOANING MINNIE
	TOTENORGEL
—machine-gun	MAXIM, MITRAILLEUSE
—musket	RIBAULD(EQUIN)
—pistol	DUCKSFOOT, PEPPERPOT
—Russian	GORLOFF
—Swedish	NORFDENFELT
naval blunderbuss	MUSKETOON
old	
—cannon	BASILISK, SERPENTINE
—gun	RABINET
—mortar	CO(E)HORN
—musket	BISCAYAN, CALIVER, DOGLOCK
	DRAGOON, FLINTLOCK, FUSIL
	HACKBUT, HAKBUCHSE
	HACKENBUCHSE, (H)ARQUEBUS
	HARQUEBUSS, MATCHLOCK
	SNAPHAUNCE, WHEEL-LOCK
American	HUDSON'S BAY FUKE
	INDIAN MUSKET
	MACKINAW GUN
	NORTHWEST GUN
British	BROWN BESS
Chinese	GINGAL(L), JINGAL
French	CHARLEVILLE
German	SCHINKE
Indian	GINGAL(L), JINGAL
—pistol	DAG
cavalry	PETRONEL
German	PISTALA
—revolver	
American	ALLEN, (COLT) PEACEMAKER
	DERRINGER, LE MAT
	MANHATTAN, PATERSON
	READ, REMINGTON
	SCHOFIELD, WHEELER
British	(BEAUMONT-)ADAMS, COLLIER
	KERR, TRANTER, WEBLEY
Danish	RASMUSSEN
European	DREYSE
French	APACHE PISTOL, HOULLIER
	LEBEL, LEFAUCHEUX, MARCOU
	RAPHAEL, PERRIN
Italian	BODEO
long-barrelled	BUNTLINE SPECIAL
Russian	NAGANT
short-barrelled	BULLDOG, DERRINGER
Swedish	OFFRELL
—revolving gun	AGER, MAXIM, PUCKLE
—rifle	MINIE, MUZZLE-LOADER

American	CHAMBERS, HALL
	HARPER'S FERRY RIFLE, HAWKEN
	KENTUCKY RIFLE, KRAG-JORGENSEN
	LINDSAY, MAYNARD, PEABODY
	PLAINS RIFLE, REMINGTON
	SHARPS(-BORCHARDT), SPRINGFIELD
Austrian	WERDER
British	BAKER, (LEE-)ENFIELD
	FERGUSON, LANCASTER
	MARTINI(-HENRY), SNIDER
	WHITWORTH
Canadian	ROSS
Danish	KRAG-JORGENSEN
European	DREYSE, J(A)EGER
	NEEDLE-GUN
	SCHEUTZEN RIFLE
French	BERTHIER, CHASSEPOT
	LEBEL, PAULY
Israeli	GALIL
Japanese	ARISAKA
Russian	BERDAN, MOSIN-NAGANT
Scandinavian	SNAPLOCK RIFLE
short	CARBINE
slang	BANDOOK, BUNDOOK
Spanish	MIQUELET
Swiss	SCHMIDT-RUBIN
on	
—one side of ship	BROADSIDE
—pivot	SWIVEL-GUN
plastic	STEYR
queen's-arm	MUSKET
repeating rifle	
—American	CHAFFEE-REESE, HENRY
	PIM, SPENCER, VOLCANIC
	VOLITIONAL REPEATER
	WINCHESTER
—Austrian	FRUWIRTH, MANNLICHER
—British	COOKSON
—German	MAUSER
—Swiss	VETTERLI
revolver	GAT, HEATER, IRON, PIECE
	ROD, ROSCOE
	SHOOTING-IRON, SIX-SHOOTER
rifle	
—Afghan	JEZAIL
—African	ROER
—American	ARMALITE, GARAND
	WINCHESTER
—British	LEE-ENFIELD
—Davy Crockett's	OLD BETSY
—German	MANNLICHER, MAUSER
—Russian	KALASHNIKOV
—Sam's	MUSKET
set as a trap	SPRING-GUN
short	
—cannon	CARRONADE, HOWITZER

—gun	HOBIT
—musket	MUSQUETOON, MUSKETOON
—pistol	DAG
—revolver	BULLDOG
—rifle	CARBINE
shot-gun	CHOKE-BORE, SCATTER-GUN
siege-gun	HOWITZER
small	
—bore rifle	PEA-RIFLE
—cannon	CHAMBER, MURDERER
	MURDERING-PIECE
	FALCONET, SAKER
—hand-gun	DER(R)INGER, PISTOLET
—mortar	CO(E)HORN
smooth-bore	MUSKET, SHOTGUN
sporting	CHOKE BORE, FOWLING PIECE
	PUNT GUN, SHOT GUN
stone-firing cannon	PERRIER
sub-machine gun	
—American	THOMPSON, TOMMY GUN
—Australian	OWEN GUN
—British	LANCHESTER, STEN
	STERLING
—Czech	SKORPION
—fast-firing	BURP-GUN, ZIPGUN
—Finnish	LAHTI, SUOMI
—German	BERGMAN, SCHMEISSER
—Israeli	UZI
—Italian	BERETTA, VILLAR PEROSA
—Russian	STECHKIN
—Swiss	STEYR-SOLOTHURN
swivel	
—gun	LONG TOM
—musket	GINGAL(L), JINGAL
Tommy gun	CHICAGO PIANO
used in	
—police actions	RIOT GUN
—shooting gallery	SALOON-PISTOL
	SALOON-RIFLE
—war games	PAINTBALL GUN
wind-gun	AIR-GUN
Guyana	GUY
capital	GEORGETOWN
coin	CENT, DOLLAR
gymnastics	
asymmetric bar	
exercises	DISLOCATION CATCH
	HECHT DISMOUNT, HIP CIRCLE
	LONG HANG, MILL CIRCLE
	PIKED HANG, RADOCHLA SOMERSAULT
	SEAT CIRCLE, SOMERSAULT
	TUMBLE TURN, UNDERSWING
	UPSTART, WRAP
attendant	SPOTTER
backflip	FLIC-FLAC
backward body-arch	BRIDGE

beam exercises	BACKFLIP, CARTWHEEL
	(FREE)WALKOVER, JUMP, ROLL
	SCISSORS MOUNT
	SINGLE-LEG SQUAT
	SPLITS BRIDGE, SQUAT
	STRADDLE, TINSICA
extended legs raised	PIKE
floor exercises	BACKFLIP
	BACKWARD ROLL, CARTWHEEL
	FORWARD ROLL, FREEWHEEL
	HAND BALANCE, HANDSPRING
	HANDSTAND, HEADSPRING
	HEADSTAND, LEVER, NECKSPRING
	ROUND-OFF, SCALE, SOMERSAULT
	SUPPORT SEAT, TINSICA
	WALKOVER
full body extension	LAYOUT
gymnasts	
—American (m)	GLASS, HEIDA, HENNIG
	KORMANN, KRIZMERZ
(f)	DUNBAR
—British (m)	STUART, THOMAS
	WILD, WILSON
(f)	LENNOX, MUGRIDGE
	SLATER, WILLETT
—Czech (m)	PRAZAK, TABAK, VACHA
(f)	BOSAKOVA, CASLAVSKA
—French	BLONDIN, GRAVELET, LEOTARD
—German (m)	BRUCKNER, GIENGER
	KOESTE, SCHWARTZMANN
	WEINGARTNER
(f)	BURDA, GERSCHAU
	GITTA, GNAUCK, HELLMAN
	HINDORF, JANZ, KISCHE
	KRAKER, ZUCHOLD
—Hungarian (m)	MAGYAR, PELLE
(f)	CSASZAR, KELETI
	KORONDI
—Italian (m)	BRAGLIA, MENICHELLI
—Japanese (m)	ENDO, KAJIYAMA
	KASAMATSU, KENMOTSU
	NAKAYAMA, OKAMURA, ONO
	KATO, TAEKEMOTO
	TSUKAHARA, YAMASHITA
—Romanian (m)	GRECO
(f)	COMANECI, CONSTANTIN
	EDERLE, GABOR, TRUSCA
	UNGURREANU
—Russian (m)	ANDRIANOV, AZARIAN
	CHUKARIN, DETYATIN
	KLIMENKO, SHAKHLIN
	TITOV, VORONIN
(f)	ASTAKHOVA, FILATOVA
	GOROKHOVSKAYA, GROSDOVA
	KALINCHUK, KIM, KORBUT
	KOVAL, KUCHINSKAYA, LATYNIVA
	LAZAKOVITCH, SAADI
	T(O)URISCHEVA, VORONINA
—Swiss (m)	MACK, MIEZ, STALDER
horizontal bar	
exercises	BACK HIP CIRCLE, CIRCLE
	ENDO, FRONT HIP CIRCLE
	GIANT CIRCLE, GIANT SWING
	HALF GIANT SWING, SEAT CIRCLE
	SOLE CIRCLE, STALDER
	SWING, WHEEL
legs raised to chest	TUCK
one-legged pose	SCALE
parallel-bar	
exercises	CAST, DLOMIDOV
	HANDSTAND, HANG SWING
	KIP, ROLL, SHOULDER STAND
	STRELLI, STUTZE
	SUPPORT SWING, UPRISE
parts of vaulting horse	CROUP, NECK
	POMMEL, SADDLE
pommel-horse	
exercises	DOUBLE LEG CIRCLE
	FORWARD SCISSORS
	SINGLE LEG CIRCLE
	SINGLE LEG HALF-CIRCLE, TRAVEL
ring exercises	BACK LEVER, BODY CROSS
	CRUCIFIX, DISLOCATE
	HANDSTAND, KIP, L-SUPPORT
	(PIKED) HANG, PLANCHE
	STRADDLE LEVER, SWING
	UNDERSWING, UPRISE
routines	
—for men	FLOOR, HORIZONTAL BAR
	PARALLEL BARS, POMMEL HORSE
	RINGS, TRAMPOLINE, VAULT
—for women	ASYMMETRICAL BARS, BEAM
	FLOOR, TRAMPOLINE, VAULT
springboard	REUTHER BOARD, SKI RUN
tower of athletes	PYRAMID
trampoline exercises	BACK DROP
	BOUNCE, FACE DROP
	HALF TURNTABLE
	HALF TWIST DROP
	HALF TWIST JUMP
	HANDS AND KNEES DROP
	KNEE DROP, (PIKED) STRADDLE
	SEAT DROP, SWIVEL HIPS
	TWIST DROP, TWIST JUMP
vaults	FLANK, (GIANT) HECHT
	HANDSPRING, SQUAT, STOOP
	STRADDLE, THIEF, TSUKAHARA
	YAMASHITA
gypsy	CHAL, ROM
gentleman	RYE
priest	PATERCOVE, PATRICO
woman	CH(A)I

H

hair	PILUS
animal's hair	PELAGE
arrangement	COIFFURE
artificial hair	CHEVELURE, CHIGNON
	CREPE HAIR, DALMAHOY
	(PERI)WIG, PERUKE
	PERRUQUE, RUG
	SWITCH, TOUPEE
beard	BARBEL
—short pointed	VAN DYKE
—small triangular	CHARLEY, CHARLIE
—square	SPADE
bearded	BARBATED
braid	TRESS
—at back of head	PIGTAIL, QUEUE
braided queue	PLAIT
bristle	SETA, STRIGA
—on worm segment	CHAETA
bristling of hair on body	GOOSEFLESH
	HORRIPILATION
bushy wig (18th c)	DALMAHOY
clip (bar-shaped)	BARRETTE
coat of hair	PELAGE
coiffure (Scot.)	COCKERNONY
colour	ASH BLONDE, BROWN(ETTE)
	BRUNETTE, FLAXEN, REDHEAD
	(STRAWBERRY) BLONDE, TITIAN
comb (Scot.)	REDDING-COMB
	REDDING-KAME
court wig	TIE-WIG
curl on forehead	KISS-CURL
curly fringe	FRISETTE
downy hair of	
—beard	PAPPUS
—embryo	LANUGO
dress hair	COIF, SET
dressing	
—cleanser	SHAMPOO
—cream or oil	BRILLIANTINE
—gummy	BANDOLINE
—oil	(MACASSAR) OIL
—ointment	POMADE, POMATUM
dye	HENNA, PEROXIDE
embryonic hair	LANUGO
false hair	(*see* artificial *(above) and* wig *(below)*)
false hair piece	COCKERNONY
fillet of hair	COCKERNONY, SNOOD
goat's hair	MOHAIR

hairband	BANDEAU
hairdresser	BARBER, COIFFEUR
	COIFFEUSE, FRISEUR
	TONSOR
hairdressing	
establishment	SALON
hairless	GLABRATE, GLABROUS
hairlike	PILLARY
—process	VILLUS
—thread(s))	CILIUM(CILIA)
hairnet	CAUL, SNOOD
—Northern	KELL
hairpiece	CHIGNON, MERKIN
	SWITCH, TOUPEE
—Scottish	COCKERNONY
hairpowder	M(O)UST, MUIST
hairy	CRINIGEROUS, CRINITE
	CRINOUS, HIRSUTE, PILAR
	PILOSE, PILOUS
having	
—grey hair	GRIZZLED
—hair	CRINATE(D), CRINOSE
	CRINITE, HIRSUTE
	PILIFEROUS, PILOSE
	PILEOUS, VILLOUS
—hairy tufts	BARBATE
—short hair	CILIOLATE
—smooth hair	LISOTRICHOUS
—straight hair	LEIOTRICHOUS
—wavy hair	CYMOTRICHOUS
—woolly hair	LANATE, ULOTRICHOUS
head of hair	CHEVELURE, MANE
in nostrils	VIBRISSA(E)
light streak in hair	HIGHLIGHT
liquid for	
—colouring	BLEACH, TONER
—fixing	SETTING LOTION
—washing	SHAMPOO
lock across forehead	COWLICK
	LOVELOCK, QUIFF
long	
—curl	RINGLET
—flowing hair	TRESS(ES)
—hair	MANE
—lasting set	PERM(ANENT WAVE)
—lock	DREADLOCK
	RAT('S)-TAIL, TRESS
—soft hair	VILLUS
loss of hair	ALOPECIA, BALDNESS
	MADAROSIS, PSILOSIS
matted condition	PLICA (POLONICA)
method of curling	FRISURE
moustache	
—bushy	HANDLEBAR
—small	CHARLEY, CHARLIE
old slang	STRAMMEL, STRUMMEL

on	
—animal's neck	FRILL, HACKLES
	MANE, RUFF
—genital areas	PUBES
—horse's	
hoof	CRONET
neck	MANE
—man's	
cheek	SIDEBOARD, SIDEBURN
	(MUTTONCHOP)WHISKERS
chin	BEARD
upper lip	MOUSTACHE
ornament	POMPOON
—Greek	TETTIX
pad	TOQUE
periwig	CHEVELURE
pigment in hair	MELANIN
pigtail	QUEUE
plait	TRESS
powder for hair	M(O)UST, MUIST
protein in hair	KERATIN
removal of hair	(D)EPILATION
ringlet	LOCK
root sac of hair	FOLLICLE
shampooing	TRIPSIS
shaven head	TONSURE
shaving	POGONOTOMY
shed hair	MOULT
short soft hair	DOWN, LANUGO, PILE
single curl of hair	RINGLET
specialist	TRICHOLOGIST
stiff hair	BRISTLE, WHISKER
study of hair	TRICHOLOGY
style	COIFFURE, TONSURE
—men	BRUTUS, CREW CUT, DA
	DUCK'S-TAIL, EN BROSSE
African	AFRO
Red Indian	MOHICAN
West Indian	DREADLOCKS
—women	BANG, BEEHIVE, BOB
	BOUFFANT
	CRIMP, ETON CROP
	FRENCH PLEAT, FRENCH ROLL
	FRIZETTE, MARCEL WAVE
	PAGEBOY, PERM(ANENT WAVE)
	POMPADOUR, PONY-TAIL, POUFFE
	SHINGLE, URCHIN CUT
African	AFRO, CORN-ROWS
tactile hair(s)	VIBRISSA(E)
—in insects	SCOP(UL)A(E)
thick mass of hair	SHAG, SHOCK
tuft of hair	FEATHER, FLOCCUS, LOCK
—small	FLOCCULUS
used for propulsion	CILIUM(CILIA)
	FLAGELLUM(FLAGELLA)
wash with cleaning liquid	SHAMPOO

wave with hot iron	MARCEL (WAVE)
whiteness of hair	CANITIES
wig	BRUTUS, CAXON
	CHEVELURE
	DALMAHOY, JAS(E)Y, JAZY
	PERIWIG, PERUKE
	PERRUQUE, SPENCER
	TRANSFORMATION
—maker	PERRUQUIER
—partly covering head	SCRATCH(-WIG)
—Scottish	GIZZ, JIZ
Haiti	RH
capital	PORT AU PRINCE
coin	CENTIME, GOURDE
harness	(*see* horse)
Harpies	AELLO, CELAENO
	(or PODARGE), OCYPETE
hat	(*see* headgear)
having	
additional syllable	PERISSOSYLLABIC
alimentary canal	ENTERATE
all	
—knowledge	OMNISCIENT
—power	OMNIPOTENT
—sides equal	EQUILATERAL
—stamens united	MONADELPHOUS
alternation of	
generations	HETEROGONOUS
anthers formed into tube	SYNANTHEROUS
	SYNGENESIOUS
armoured plates or scales	LORICATE
backbone	VERTEBRATE(D)
backward-pointing lobes	RUNCINATE
bad breath	HALITOTIC
bag	UTRICULAR
base joined round stem	PERFOLIATE
barbs	BARBATE(D)
battlements	CASTELLATED
	CRENELLATED
beak	NASUTE
—and keel	ROSTROCARINATE
beams or lintels	TRABEATE(D)
beard	BARB(ELL)ATE
belts	ZONATE(D)
bilateral symmetry	ISOBILATERAL
bill curved downwards	CURVIROSTRAL
bladder	UTRICULAR
blisters	BULLATE
blood	SANGUINEOUS
bones of palate	
separate	SCHIZOGNATHOUS
bony scales	PLACOID
bracteoles	BRACTEOLATE
bracts	BRACTEATE
breasts	MAMMATE
	MAMMIFEROUS

bristles	STRIGATE, STRIGOSE
	STYLAR, STYLATE
—with barbs	BARBELLATE
broad	
—bill	LATIROSTRAL
—nose	PLATYRRHINE
—partition	LATISEPTATE
bulges	TOROSE
bulging eyeballs	EXOPHTHALMIC
bushy habit of growth	DUMOSE, DUMOUS
calyx and corolla	
different	HETEROCHLAMYDEOUS
carpels and stamens on	
same flower	ASEXUAL
	HERMAPHRODITE
case	THECATE
cavities	LACUNOSE
cell	UTRICULAR
central spot of	
another colour	PUPILLATE
chain of segments	STROBILACEOUS
chinks	FATISCENT
circumflex accent on last	
syllable	PERISPOMENON
claws	UNGUAL, UNGUICULATE(D)
closed chain of	
—different atoms	HOMOCYCLIC
—similar atoms	HETEROCYCLIC
cloven	
—feet	BISULCATE
—tongue	FISSILINGUAL
club-shaped antennae	CLAVICORN
column	SCAPIGEROUS
comb-like gills	PECTINIBRANCHIATE
conical beak	CONIROSTRAL
cracks	FATISCENT, RIMOUS
crescent-shaped ridges	
on teeth	SELENODONT
crest	CRISTATE
crooked tail	CURVICAUDATE
crossed mandibles	METAGNATHOUS
curved	
—leaves	CURVIFOLIATE
—ribs	CURVICOSTATE
curves	CURVATE(D), CURVILINEAL
	CURVILINEAR
cutting back teeth	SECODONT
daily rest	MONOPHASIC
deep grooves (round disc)	CONTORNIATE
definite shape	EFFIGURATE
depression	FOSSULATE
—like a navel	UMBILICATE
different	
—areas of distribution	ALLOPATRIC
—kinds of	
leaf	HETEROPHYLLOUS

spores	HETEROSPOROUS
—names	DISQUIPARANT
—numbers of parts	
in different whorls	HETEROCYCLIC
	HETEROMEROUS
—sets of teeth	HETERODONT
—types of mycelium	HETEROTHALLIC
divided ribs	FISSICOSTATE
double	
—beak	BIROSTRATE
—nature	TWO-NATURED
—womb	DIDELPHIC
down	PLUMULATE
downy covering	PUBESCENT, TOMENTOSE
drops	GUTTATE(D)
ears	AURATE
Earth as centre	GEOCENRIC
energy higher than that of	
thermal agitation	EPITHERMAL
equal	
—diameters	ISODIAMETRIC
—enthalpy	ISENTHALPIC
—entropy	ISENTROPIC
—power	EQUIPOLLENT
erect branches	FASTIGIATE
eyelike spots	OCELLATE(D)
eyes	OCULATE(D)
—meeting in front	HOLOPTIC
—on stalks	PODOPHTHALMUS
—without stalks	EDRIOPHTHALMIC
faces of crystalline form	IDIOMORPHIC
fat buttocks	STEATOPYGOUS
feathers	PENNATE, PINNATE(D)
—on	
feet	PLUMIPED
legs or feet	BRACCATE
shoulders	SCAPULATED
feet or legs used as oars	REMIPED
few parts	OLIGOMEROUS
fine	
—notches	CREN(UL)ATE(D)
—wrinkles	RUGULOSE
fins	PENNATE, PINNATE(D)
first and second toes	
turned backwards	HETERODACTYLOUS
fissure	SULCATE(D)
flat nose	CAMUS
flavour	SAPOROUS
flowers	
—in spathe	SPADICIFLORAL
—of both sexes	MONOECIOUS
foot	PEDATE
forms belonging to	
different declensions	HETEROCLITE
freckles	LENTIGINOSE
	LENTIGINOUS

fringe	FIMBRIATE
fruit enclosed in special casing	ANGIOCARPOUS
full powers	PLENIPOTENTIARY
furrow	SULCATE(D)
fused digits	SYNDACTYL(OUS)
gaping beak	FISSIROSTRAL
gaps	LACUNOSE
gills and lungs	DIPNOUS
glistening outer scales	GANOID
great	
—appetite	VETRIPOTENT
—diversity	MULTIFARIOUS
grey hair	GRIZZLED
groove	SULCATE(D)
groups of four spores	TETRASPORIC
	TETRASPOROUS
gynaecium with flower parts	
—around	PERIGYNOUS
—below	HYPOGYNOUS
—enclosing	EPIGYNOUS
hair	CILIATE(D), CRINATE(D)
	CRINITE, CRINOSE
	PILIGINOUS, VILLOUS
hairy	
—buttocks	DASYPYGAL
—leaves	DASYPHYLLOUS
—tufts	BARBATE
handle	ANSATE
hard	
—dry stem	SCLEROCAULY
—shell	LORICATE
—skeleton tissue	SCLERENCHYMATOUS
—skin	SCLERODERMIC
	SCLERODERMOUS
—tissue cells	SCLERENCHYMATOUS
heather-like leaves	ERICOID
hermaphrodite and female flowers	GYNOMONOECIOUS
hoof divided into more than two parts	MULTUNGULATE
hoofs	UNGULATE
hooks	HAMATE, HAMOSE
	HAMOUS, UNCATE
—at the end	UNCINATE(D)
horns	CORNICULATE
horny skeleton	KERATOSE
intercalary day	BISSEXTILE
itch	PSOR(AT)IC
keel	CARINATE
keelless breastbone	RATITE
knots	NODOSE, NODOUS
lacunae	LACUNOSE
large	
—buttocks	STEATOPYGOUS

—head	MACROCEPHALIC
	MEGACEPHALOUS
layers	STRATIFORM, STRATOSE
leaf-margin overlapping	INCUBOUS
leafless stem	NUDICAUL(OUS)
leaflets each side	PINNATE
lips	LABIATE
long	
—feathers	LONGIPENNATE
—fingers	MACRODACTYLOUS
—fins	MACROPTEROUS
—nose	LEPTORRHINE
—shoots	VIMINEOUS
—tail	LONGICAUDATE, MACRURAL
	MACRUROUS
—toes	MACRODACTYLOUS
—wings	LONGIPENNATE
	MACROPTEROUS
lower jaw projecting	HYPOGNATHOUS
lungs	PULMONARY
made a will	TESTATE
male	
—and female characteristics	ANDROGYNOUS
	HERMAPHRODITE
flowers	MONOECIOUS
reproductive organs near each other	PAROICOUS
—and hermaphrodite flowers	ANROMONOECIOUS
mane	JUBATE
mantle	CHLAMYDATE, PALLIATE
many...	(see separate entry)
medium-sized head	MESATICEPHALOUS
membrane	VELATE(D)
minute serrations	SERRATULATE
more than	
—one	
embryo	POLYEMBRYONATE
	POLYEMBRYONIC
spouse	POLYGAMOUS
—two	
dentitions	POLYPHYDONT
dimensions	MULTIDIMENSIONAL
cusps	MULTICUSPID(ATE)
terms	MULTINOMIAL
—three wheels	MULTICYCLE
—five foils	MULTIFOIL
—usual number of fingers or toes	POLYDACTYL
mouth-like opening	OSTIATE
multiple origins	POLYPHYLETIC
narrow	
—bill	ANGUSTIROSTRATE
—leaves	ANGUSTIFOLIATE
—mouth	ANGIOSTOM(AT)OUS

—nose	LEPTORRHINE	ruddy glow	RUTILANT
—opening	STENOPA(E)IC	runners	SARMENTOSE
neck	TRACHELATE		SARMENTOUS
needles	SPICULATE	S-shaped curves	OGEE
needle points	ACESOSE	same	
nipples	MAMILLATE(D), PAPILLATE(D)	—areas of distribution	SYMPATRIC
nodes	NODOSE	—colour	ISOCHROM(AT)IC
nodules	NODULATED, NODULOSE	—constituents throughout	HOMOGENEOUS
	NODULOUS	—curvature in all	
notched beak	DENTIROSTRAL	directions	SYNCLASTIC
notches	CRENATE(D)	—essence	HOMO(O)USIAN
nucleus	NUCLEOLATE	—form, different	
odd number of toes	PERISSODACTYL(ATE)	composition	HOMEOMORPHOUS
	PERISSODACTYLIC	—fundamental structure	HOMOTYPIC
	PERISSODACTYLOUS	—magnetic force	ISOMAGNETIC
opening	OSTIOLATE	—measures	ISOMETRIC
ossified septum	TICHORRINE	—number of	
other floral parts		atoms	ISOTERIC
below the ovary	HYPOGYNOUS	leaves	EUCYCLIC
overlapping scales	IMBRICATE	petals and stamens	ISOSTEMONOUS
paired		—potential	ISOELECTRIC
—chromosomes	DIPLOID	—tenor or tone	HOMOTONOUS
—gills	ZYGOBRANCHIATE	saw-bill	SERRATIROSTRAL
—leaves	JUGATE	scales	LEPIDATE, SQUAMATE
panicles	PANICLED, PANICULATE		SQUAMOSE, SQUAMOUS
partitions	SEPTIFEROUS, SEPTIFORM	scattered	
parts in eights	OCTAMEROUS	—hairs	PILOSE
pearly lustre	MARGAR(IT)IC	—perforations	TEREBRATE
perianth	CHLAMYDEOUS	schizophrenic characteristics	SCHIZOID
—leaves free	POLYPHYLLOUS	seal	SIGILLATE
petals united	SYMPETALOUS	separate	
phosphorescence	NOTILUCOUS	—carpels	APOCARPOUS
pistils	PISTILLATE	—digits	FISSIPED(E)
pits	FOSSULATE	—petals	POLYPETALOUS
plate-like scales	PLACOID	—sepals	POLYSEPALOUS
point	COSTATE	serrated	
pouch	SACCATE	—antennae	SERRICORN
power to		—beak	SERRATIROSTRAL
—strike	PERCUTIENT	—feet	SERRIPED
—combine with		several	
hydrogen atoms	(see valency below)	—alternating currents	POLYPHASE
prickles	ECHINATE(D)	—at one birth	POLYTOCOUS
proboscis	PROMUSCULATE	—axons	MULTIPOLAR
protecting plates	SCUTATE	—beats	POLYCROTIC
protective shell	LORICATE	—broods	MULTIVOLTINE
pupa-case	PUPIGEROUS	—bundles of stamens	POLYADELPHOUS
pupae within body of mother	PUPIPAROUS	—cells	POLYTHALAMOUS
rank smell	OLID	—chambers	POLYTHALAMOUS
reduced wings	MICROPTEROUS	—cotyledons	POLYCOTYLEDONOUS
resistance to disease	KLENDUSIC	—hydrogen atoms	POLYACID
retreating jaws	OPISTHOGNATHOUS	—hydroxyl groups	POLYHYDRIC
rhizoids	RADICULOSE	—mates	POLYANDROUS
rootlets	RADICULOSE	—meanings	POLYSEM(ANT)IC
rough scales	SQUARROSE	—musical keys	POLYTONAL
rows of leaflets	PINNATE(D)	—nuclei	MULTINUCLEAR
royal privileges	PALATINE		MULTINUCLEATE

—nucleoli	MULTINUCLEOLATE
—phases of activity	POLYPHASIC
—poles	MULTIPOLAR
—words	POLYONYMIC
	(*see also* **many**)
shaft	SCAPIGEROUS
shapely curves	CURVACEOUS
sharp points	ACEROSE, EPICULATE
	MURICATE(D), PUNGENT
sheath	THECATE
short	
—hairs	CILIOLATE
—wings	BREVIPENNATE
shoulder feathers	SCAPULATED
single chromosomes	HAPLOID
similar	
—calyx and corolla	HOMOCHLAMYDEOUS
—essence	HOMOIOUSIAN
—parts	HOM(O)EOMEROUS
	HOMOIOMEROUS
single	
—chromosomes	HAPLOID
—nucleus	MONONUCLEAR
—opening	MONOTREMATOUS
	MONOTREME
siphon	SIPHONATE
slender	
—bill	TENUIROSTRAL
—build	LEPTOSOM(AT)IC
—leaves	LEPTOPHYLLOUS
—nose	LEPTORRHINE
—tail	LEPTOCERCAL
—toes	LEPTODACTYLOUS
small	
—bags	UTRICULAR
—bladders	UTRICULAR
	VESICULATE(D)
	VESICULOSE
—blisters	VESICULATE(D)
	VESICULOSE
—branches	RAMULOSE, RAMULOUS
—bulges	TORULOSE
—cavities	VACUOLATE(D)
—compartments	LOCELLATE, LOCULATE
—feathers	PLUMULATE
—fibres	FIBRILLOSE
	FIBRILLOUS
—head	MICROCEPHALOUS
—holes	FORAMINATED
	FORAMINOUS
—hooks	HAMULATE
—projections	MONTICULATE
	MONTICULOUS
—sac	UTRICULAR
—scales	SQUAMULOSE
—scattered crystals	POIKILITIC

—spines	SPINULATE
	SPINULIFEROUS
	SPINULOSE, SPINULOUS
—swellings	TORULOSE
—wings	MICROPTEROUS
smell	OLENT
smooth hair	LISSOTRICHOUS
spaces	LACUNOSE
specific gravity greater	
than cerebro-spinal fluid	HYPERBARIC
spicules	SPICULATE
spike	SPICATE(D)
spines	SPINATE(D), SPINIFEROUS
spore-case	THECATE
spots	GUTTATE(D)
—eyes	OCULATE(D)
stalk	PEDICELLATE
	PEDICLED, PEDICULATE(D)
	PETIOLATE(D)
—near middle of leaf	PELTATE
stalkless eyes	EDRIOPHTHALMIC
stamens	STAMINATE
—fused with carpels	GYNANDROUS
—in two bundles	DIADELPHOUS
stem	CAULESCENT
stiff leaves	SCLEROPHYLLOUS
stipes	STIPITATE
straight	
—bill	RECTIROSTRAL
—hair	LEIOTRICHOUS
styles	STYLAR, STYLATE
—of different lengths	HETEROSTYLOUS
Sun as centre	HELIOCENTRIC
supernumary	
—breasts	POLYMASTIC
—chromosomes	POLYPLOID
swellings	NODOUS, TOROSE
—in middle	VENTRICOSE
	VENTRICOUS
sword-shaped leaves	XIPHOPHYLLOUS
tail	CAUDATE(D)
—used for propulsion	UROSTHENIC
taste	SAPOROUS
teeth	DENTATE(D)
—all alike	HOMODONT, ISODONT
—like comb	PECTINAL, PECTINATE(D)
—with	
crescent-shaped ridges	SELENODONT
paired cusps	ZYGODONT
transverse ridges	LOPHODONT
v-shaped ridges	ZALAMBDODONT
temperature of one's own	IDIOTHERMOUS
thick	
—digits	PACHYDACTYL(OUS)
—lips	LABROSE
—pericarp	PACHYCARPOUS

—skin	PACHYDERMIC
	PACHYDERM(AT)OUS
—woolly leaves	DASYPHYLLOUS
threads	FILAR
tongue attached	
in front	OPISTHOGLOSSAL
toothed	
—beak	RHYNCHODONT
—jaws	ODONTOSTOMATOUS
transverse	
—bars	TRABECULATE(D)
—lamellae on edge	
of bill	LAMELLIROSTRAL
triple form	TRIFORM(ED)
tubercles	TUBERCLED, TUBERCULAR
	TUBERCULATE(D)
tuberculosis	TUBERCULOSE(D)
	TUBERCULOUS
tubers	TUBEROSE, TUBEROUS
tufted gills	LOPHOBRANCHIATE
tufts	C(A)ESPITOSE
	PENICILLATE, SCOPATE
tunic	TUNICATE(D)
turrets	CASTELLATED
	TURRICULATED
twenty or more stamens	ICOSANDRIAN
	ICOSANDROUS
twigs	SARMENTOSE
	SARMENTOUS
uncloven hoofs	SOLIDUNGULATE
	SOLIPED(OUS)
undivided heart	MONOCARDIAN
unequal convex sides	GIBBOUS
unfeathered nostrils	GYMNORHINAL
united sepals	MONOSEPALOUS
unlimited power	OMNIPOTENT
unpaired chromosomes	HAPLOID
up-bent bill	RECURVIROSTRAL
upper and lower lobes	
of tail-fin alike	HOMOCERCAL
valency	
—above one	MULTIVALENT
—of	
one	UNIVALENT
two	DIVALENT
three	TERVALENT, TRIVALENT
four	QUADRIVALENT, TETRAVALENT
five	PENTAVALENT, QUINQUEVALENT
six	SEX(I)VALENT
valve	VALVATE, VALVULAR
variable blood-	
temperature	POIKILOTHERMIC
veil	VELATE(D)
veins	NERVATE, VENOSE
walls of carpels separate	
from septa	SEPTIFRAGAL

warts	VERRUCOSE, VERRUCOUS
water-storing tissue	PERICHYLOUS
waves	CRISPATE
wavy edges	CREN(UL)ATE(D)
	REPAND, SINUATE
webbed feet	PALMATE, PALMIPED(E)
	STEGANOPODOUS
whorls	VERTICILLATE(D)
wind-pipe	TRACHEATE(D)
winged feet	ALIPED
wings	ALARY, PENNATE
	PINNATE(D)
wires	FILAR
woody stem-base	SUFFRUTICOSE
woolly hair	LANATE, ULOTRICHOUS
wrinkles	RUGOSE, RUGOUS
zones	ZONATE(D)

Hawaii

acacia	KOA
dance	HULA(-HULA)
dish	POI
dolphin-fish	MAHI-MAHI
dress	MUU-MUU
drink	(K)AVA
fibre	PULU
garland	LEI
goddess	PELE
goose	NENE
greeting	ALOHA
group marriage	PUNALUA
ropy lava	PAHOEHOE
rough lava	AA
wreath	LEI

head

2-headed	BICEPS, BICIPITAL
	DICEPHALOUS
3-headed	TRICEPHALOUS, TRICEPS
4-headed	QUADRACEPS, QUADRICEPS
	QUADRICIPITAL
boat-shaped	SCAPHOCEPHALOUS
bony-plated	STEGOCEPHALOUS
flat-headed	PLATYCEPHALOUS
having	
—a head	CEPHALATE, CEPHALOUS
—own head	AUTOCEPHALOUS
large-headed	MACROCEPHALIC
	MACROCEPHALOUS
long-headed	DOLICOCEPHALOUS
man-headed	ANDROCEPHALOUS
many-headed	MULTICAPITATE
	MULTICIPITAL
medium-sized head	MESATICEPHALIC
	MESATICEPHALOUS
	MESOCEPHALIC
	MESOCEPHALOUS
pain in the head	CEPHALALGIA

pertaining to the head	CEPHALIC
ratio of length to breadth	CEPHALIC INDEX
short-headed	BRACHYCEPHALIC
	BRACHYCEPHALOUS
small-headed	MICROCEPHALIC
	MICROCEPHALOUS
headgear	COIF
academic	MORTARBOARD
	TRENCHER
African	TURBAN
—French soldier's	CHECHIA
American	
—bowler	DERBY
—cowboy's hat	STETSON
	TEN-GALLON (HAT)
—trilby	FEDORA
—woman's widebrimmed hat	SUNDOWN
Arab	CHECHIA, FEZ
	KAFFIYEH, KEFFIYEH
	KUFIAH, KUFIYA(H)
	TARBOOSH, TARB(O)USH
awarded to	
—champion	LAUREL WREATH
—sportsman	CAP
Basque hat	BER(R)ET
beaver fur hat	CASTOR
bishop's hat	MITRE
brimless	CAP
—fur	COSSACK HAT
bullfighter's hat	MONTERA
Canadian cap	TUQUE
cap	
—flat	BARRET(-CAP)
	SCOTCH BONNET
—military	CHEESE CUTTER, FORAGE CAP
—Roman	PILEUS
—Scottish	TAM-O'SHANTER, TAMMY
flat cap	BLUE BONNET
starched	COCKERNORY
woman's	MUTCH
—soft	BONNET
—with side flaps	HUMMEL BONNET, TOY
square peak	CHEESECUTTER
—worn inside coronet	BONNET
on Sundays	STATUTE CAP
ceremonial	CORONET, CROWN, TIARA
child's cap	BIGGIN
clergyman's hat	BIRETTA
college hood	AMICE
cord trimming	TORSADE
cover for head	CASQUE, COIF
	CURCH, HEADSCARF

—old	CASK
derby	BOWLER
Dervish's hat	TAJ
ecclesiastical skull-cap	ZUCHETTA
	ZUCHETTO
Egyptian	FEZ, TARBOOSH
	TARB(O)USH
Etonian cap	SCOG(GER)
fanciful (Shak.)	TIRE-VALIANT
felt	
—cap	
Roman	PILEUS
Turkish	CALPA(C)K, KALPAK
—used in hats	BAT(TING)
flat	
—cap	BARRET(-CAP), SCOTCH BONNET
	TAM-O'SHANTER, TAMMY
—round hat	BER(R)ET
for night-time wear	NIGHTCAP
fur	
—hat	BEAVER, CASTOR
—hood	AMICE
hair	
—band	BANDEAU
—net	KELL, SNOOD
hard round hat	BOWLER, CRASH HELMET
	SAFETY HELMET
hat	
—feather	COCKADE
—maker	MILLINER
hats for women	MILLINERY
headcloth	ROMAL, RUMAL
headdress	HEAD-TIRE, TIRE
—with flaps	LAPPET-HEAD
headscarf	CURCH, KERCHIEF
—Moslem	HIJAB
Hebrew	
—prayer cap	YARMULKA, YARMULKE
shawl	TALLITH
—priest's hat	TIARA
Hermes's hat	PETASUS
Holmes's hat	DEERSTALKER
hood	CAPUCHE, COWL
huntsman's hat	MONTERO
Indian	
—headcloth	ROMAL, RUMAL
—headdress	TAJ, TURBAN
—sun-hat	(*see* pith helmet *below*)
—turban	LUNGI, PAGRI, PUGG(A)REE
	PUGGERY, PUGRI
—ventilated hat	TERAI
indoor cap	MOB-CAP
jewelled	CIRCLET, CORONET
	CROWN, DIADEM, TIARA
light sunhat	PANAMA

man's hat (18th c)	RAMIL(L)IE(S)
Mexican	SOMBRERO
military headgear	
—cylindrical	SHAKO
—French	KEPI
—fur hat	BEARSKIN, BUSBY
—Guards	BEARSKIN
—helmet	
German	COALSCUTTLE
	PICKELHAUBE
modern	BATTLE BOWLER, TIN HAT
old	(see **armour**)
—Highland Regiment	HUMMEL BONNET
—Highlander's cap	GLENGARRY
—Hungarian	SHAKO
—hussars	BUSBY
—Polish	CHAPKA, CZAPKA
	SCHAPSKA
—undress cap	BERET, FORAGE-CAP
—woollen	STOCKING-CAP
monk's hood	CAPUCHE, COWL
motorcyclist's hat	CRASH HELMET
	SKID LID
narrow-brimmed felt hat	HOMBURG
nightcap	BIGGIN
nun's headdress	WIMPLE
official headgear	CAP
peaked cap, 15th c	BYCOKET
Persian	CIDARIS, TIARA
pilgrim's hat	COCKLE-HAT
pith-helmet	SOLA(R) HAT
	SOLA(R) HELMET, SOLAH HAT
	SOLAH HELMET
	TOPEE, TOPI
Polish peasant's cap	CHAPKA, CZAPKA
	SCHAPSKA
Pope's crown	TIARA
protective	HARD HAT, CRASH HELMET
Roman	
—felt cap	PILEUS
—God's headdress	MODIUS
—headband	VITTA
sailor's hat	TARPAULIN
Scottish	
—broad cap	KILMARNOCK
—flat cap	BLUE BONNET
	TAM-O'-SHANTER
	TAMMY
—Highlander's cap	GLENGARRY
—night cap	KILMARNOCK COWL
	PIRNIE
—with side flaps	HUMMEL BONNET, TOY
—woman's cap	MUTCH
serjeant-at-law's cap	COIF
slang	LID, TILE, TITFER
small bonnet	KISS ME QUICK

soft	
—broad-brimmed hat	SHOVEL
	SLOUCH (HAT), TRILBY
	WIDEAWAKE
—cap	BONNET
Spanish	
—horseman's	MONTERO(-CAP)
—lady's	MANTILLA
sportsman's hat	DEERSTALKER
square-peaked cap	CHEESE-CUTTER
squirrel-skin hat	SQUIRREL-TAIL
starched cap (Scot.)	COCKERNONY
straw hat	BALIBUNTAL, BOATER
	HIVE
sun-helmet	PITH HELMET, TERAI
	TOPI
symbolic head-dress	CAP
tall	
—17th/18th c	FONTANGE
—cylindrical hat	STOVEPIPE (HAT)
	TOP HAT
Tatar	CALPAC(K), KALPAK
top hat	OPERA HAT
—American	PLUG-HAT
three-cornered	CHAPEAU-BRAS
	TRICORN(E)
trimmed with flowers	DOLLY VARDEN
turban	LUNGI, PAGRI, PUGG(A)RE
	PUGGERY, PUGRI
Turkish	FEZ, MARTAGAN
—felt cap	CALPAC(K), KALPAK
two-cornered	BICORN
veil round head and neck	WIMPLE
ventilated sun-helmet	TERAI
waterproof	SOU'WESTER, TARPAULIN
with ear-flaps	DEERSTALKER
	HUMMEL BONNET, TOY
women's hats	
—16th c cap or turban	TOQUE
—bell-shaped	CLOCHE
—brimless hat	PAGE-BOY HAT
	PILL-BOX, TOQUE
—broad-brimmed	BONGRACE
—cap (Scot.)	MUTCH
with side pieces	TOY
—close-fitting	CLOCHE
—frilly indoor hat	MOB-CAP
—head cover	COIF
—headdress	KELL
—headwrap (fleecy)	NUBILIA
—hood	
and cape (Malta)	FALDETTA
with hoops	CALASH
—large	
hat trimmed with flowers	DOLLY VARDEN

high hat	COMMODE
—light head-dress	CAP
—soft broad-brimmed hat	SLOUCH (HAT)
—tall conical hat	CORNET
—very tall	FONTANGE
—with	
projecting front	POKE BONNET
strings	BONNET
heart	(*see* circulation)
Hebrew	HEB(R)
including: Israeli	
Jewish	
Yiddish	
acacia wood	SHITTIM(WOOD)
agricultural settlement	KIBBUTZ, MOSHAV
airline	EL AL
almond cake	MANDELBROT
alphabet	(*see* letters *below*)
ancient incense	ONYX
annual feast	PASSOVER
armies	SABAOTH
ascetic	ESSENE, NAZARITE, NAZIRITE
assassins (Biblical)	SICARII
assembly	SANHEDRIM, SANHEDRIN
—for worship	SYNAGOGUE
avenger	GOEL
beef sausage	VIENNA
beg(gar)	SCHNORR(ER)
Bible	TANAKH, T(H)ORAH
bitterness	MARAH
book of law	TALMUD, T(H)ORAH
bond	STARR
boring person	SCHMO(E)
bread	HALLAH, MATZO
—offering	SHEW-BREAD
cabbalistic method of	
interpreting Scriptures	GEMATRIA
candelabrum	MENORAH
cantor	CHAZAN
cape	ROSH
casserole	CHOLENT, TZIMMES
ceremonial meal	SEDER
cheek	CHUTZPAH
chicken-pea snack	FALAFEL
chief singer	CHAZAN
Christian	EBIONITE, GOY, MARRANO
circumciser	MOHEL
clean	KOSHER
cloak	GABARDINE, GABERDINE
clumsy person	KLUTZ, S(C)HLEMIEL
	SCHLEMIHL, SCHLEP
coins	
—small	GERAH
—10 gerahs	BEKA(H)
—12 gerahs	(GOLDEN) DADIC
—2 bekahs	SHEKEL

—50 shekels	MANEH, MINA
—3000 shekels	TALENT
—Israeli	AGORA, SHEKEL
—old	ZUZ
commandment	MITZVAH
commentaries on OT	AGADAH, HAGGADA(H)
	HALACHA(H), HALAKAH
	MIDRASHIM
commune	KIBBUTZ
complaint	KVETCH
compulsory marriage	LEVIRATE
container for Torah scrolls	ARK
council	SANHEDRIM, SANHEDRIN
	SYNEDRION, SYNEDRIUM
court	SANHEDRIM, SANHEDRIN
	SYNEDRION, SYNEDRIUM
crazy	MESHUG(G)A, MESHUGGE
—person	MESHUGGENAH
	MESSHUGENEH
critical OT notes	MASORA(H)
	MASORETH, MASSORAH
dagger	SICA
dance	HORA
devotional offering	CORBAN
dietary laws	KASHRUT(H), KOSHER
dirge	KINNAH
dish of bitter herbs	MAROR
dispersion	DIASPORA, GOLAH
divine presence	S(H)ECHINAH
	S(H)EKINAH
divorce	GET
doctor of law	RABBI, RABIN
dolt	GOLEM
drag	SCHLEP
drum	TOPH
dumpling filled with	
meat etc	KREPLACH
dunes	HOLOT
early Christian Jew	NAZARENE
Easter	PASCH
ecclesiastical court	BETH DIN
effrontery	CHUTZPAH
egg custard	LOKSHEN
eve of Sabbath	PARASCEVE
evening prayer	SHEMA
evil spirit	DYBBUK
exposition of OT	AGADAH, HAGGADA(H)
	HALACHA(H), HALAKAH
	MIDRASH
expounder of law	RABBI, RABIN
expounders of law	SOPHERIM
fallow year	SABBATICAL YEAR
feasts	HANUKAH, ISODIA, PASSOVER
	PURIM, YOM KIPPUR
	YOM TERUAH, YOM TOB, YOM TOV
	(*see* **holidays**)

field of blood	ACELDEMA	manna	GEN
fiftieth year festival	JUBILEE	marginal note	K'RI, KTHIBH
fish-balls	GEFILTE FISH	marriage	
fool	SCHLEP, SCHMO(E)	—broker	SHADCHEN
	SCHMOCK, SCHMUCK	—custom	LEVIRATE
	SCHNOOK	measures	
forceful woman	BERRIEH	—18 inches	CUBIT
formalist	PHARISEE	—52 inches	REED
Friday	PARASCEVE	—6 cubits	CANEH, KANEH
funeral prayer	KADDISH	—³/₄ pint	LOG
fuss	TZIMMES	—3 pints	CAB
garment	TALIS	—12 pints	HIN
Gentile	GOY	—14 pints	SEAH
German and Polish Jews	ASKENAZIM	—6 galls	BATH
giant	ANAK	—¹/₁₀ ephah	OMER
God	ELOHIM, JEHOVAH	—bushel	EPHA(H)
good deed	MITZVAH	—11 bushels	COR, HOMER
gossip	SCHMOOSE, SCHMOOZE	mercy seat	PROPITIATORY
harp	NEBEL	militia	HAGANAH
hellenising Jew	GREEK	miraculously provided food	GEN, MANNA
high priest's		months	
—breastplate	RATIONALE	Civil Ecclesiastic,	
—mitre	TIARA	1. Sep-Oct 7	ETHANIM, TIS(H)RI
Holocaust	SHOAH	2. Oct-Nov 8	BUL, (C)HES(H)VAN
homeland	ZION		MARCHES(H)VAN
human image	GOLEM	3. Nov-Dec 9	CHISLEV, KISLEU, KISLEV
idol	REMPHAN	4. Dec-Jan 10	TEBET(H), TEVET, THEBET
image(s)	TERAPH(IM)	5. Jan-Feb 11	S(H)EBAT, SHEVET
incompetent person	SCHLEP	6. Feb-Mar 12	ADAR
inferior priest	LEVITE	7. Mar-Apr 1	ABIB, NISAN
Jehovah	LORD OF HOSTS	7. Apr-May 2	(I)YAR, YAVAR, ZIF
Jew-baiting (German)	JUDENHETZE	9. May-Jun 3	SIVAN
Jewish quarter	GHETTO	10. Jun-Jul 4	TAMMUS, T(H)AMMUZ
knife	SICA	11. Jul-Aug 5	AB, AV
lake	YAM	12. Aug-Sep 6	ELIL, ELUL
land of rest	BEULAH	intercalary	ADAR SHENI, VEADAR
language	IVRIT, YIDDISH	morning prayer	SHEMA
law	T(H)ORAH	Moslem	DEUNME
lawyers	SOPHERIM	mountain	HAR, SHELUHAT
leader	H, MOSES	mush	SCHMALTZ
letters	AIN, ALEPH, AYIN	musical instrument	ASOR, SHOFAR
	BETH, CAPH, CHETH, DALETH		SHOPHAR, TIMBREL
	GIMEL, HE, HETH, JOD, KAPH		TOPH
	KOPH, LAMED, LOD, MEM, NUN	my great master	RABBONI
	PE, RESH, SAMECH, SAMEKH	native-born Israeli	SABRA
	SCHIN, SHIN, TAU, TETH, TZADDI	New Year	ROSH HASHANAH
	VAU, ZADE, ZAIN, ZAYIN	non-Jew	GENTILE, GOY
liquid myrrh	STACTE	—woman	SHIKSA
literary collection of laws		nose	SCHNOZZLE
and practices	TALMUD	not Kosher	TEREFA(H), TREF(A)
lord	ADONAI, ELOHIM	nothing	BUBKES
lost book	JASHAR, JASHER	of inferior quality	SCHLOCK
lyre	ASOR	old-fashioned	SCHMALTZY
mad	MESSHUG(G)A, MESSHUGGE	oral law	GEMARA, MISHA(H)
manhood ceremony	BAR MI(T)SVAH		MISHN(AY)OTH
	BAR MI(T)ZVAH	orthodox Jews	(C)HAS(S)IDIM

OT commentary	AGADAH, HAGGADA(H)
	HALACHA(H), HALAKAH
	MIDRASH, MASORA(H)
	MASSORA(H), MASORETH
pancake	BLINTZ(E)
—cheese	BLIN(I)
—potato	LATKES
parchment scroll	MEZUZA(H)
parliament	KENESET, KNES(S)ET
	SANHEDRM, SANHEDRIN
	SYNEDRION, SYNEDRIUM
part of	
—Midrash	AGADAH, HAGGAD(H)
	HALACHA(H), HALAKAH
—Talmud	GEMARA, MISHNA(H)
Passover ritual	HAGGADA, SEDER
pasta	FARFAL, FARFEL
pastry roll	FIGUELA
—filled	KNISHES
pause (in Psalms)	SELAH
peak	SHELUHAT
Pentateuch	T(H)ORAH
phylacteries containing	
sacred texts	TEFILLIN
place of	
—departed spirits	SHE'OL
—torment	TOPHET
—worship	SYNAGOGUE
plain	EMEQ
point	ROSH
Portuguese Jews	SEPHARDIM
potato pancake	LATKE
prayer	KADDISH, SHEMA
—book	MA(C)HZOR, SIDDUR, SUDDUR
—shawl	TALLIT(H)
priest	AARONITE, RABBI
	RABIN, SAGAN
priest's breastplate	PECTORAL
	RATIONAL(E)
Portuguese Jews	SEPHARDIM
—converted to	
Christianity	MARRANOS
pull	SCHLEP
pure	KOSHER
quarter	GHETTO
rabbinical commentator	HAKAM
ram's horn trumpet	SHOFAR, SHOPHAR
received tradition	QUBALLAH
religious	
—service	MINYAN
—symbol	STAR OF DAVID
ridge	REKHES
ritual	
—candlestick	MENORAH
—food preparation	KASHRUT(H), KOSHER
robot	GOLEM

roll (bread)	BAGEL
room for safe-keeping	
of documents	GENIZAH
ruins	HORVOT
Sabbath	SATURDAY, SHABBOS
—eve	PARAS(C)EVE
sacred objects	URIM
sage	HAKAM
Sanhedrin	SYNEDRION, THE SEVENTY
school for religious	
studies	YESHIVA
scribes	SOPHERIM
sea	YAM
secret lore	CAB(B)ALA, KAB(B)ALA
sect	(C)HAS(S)IDIM, ESSENE
	HEMEROBAPTIST, KARAITE
	MANDAEAN, MARONITE
seventh year	SABBATICAL YEAR
strip of parchment	
with passage from	
Scripture	PHYLACTERY
skullcap	YARMULKA, YARMULKE
something trivial	BUBKES
song	HAT(T)IKVAH
Spanish Jews	SEPHARDIM
—converted to	
Christianity	MARRANOS
spice	STACTE
spleen	MILTZ
sponge cake	PLAVA
sponger	SCHNORRER
star of David	MAGEN DAVID, MOGEN DAVID
stew	TZIMMES
strong drink	SHICKER
studies	YESHIVA
stupid person	SCHLEP, SCHMO(E)
	SCHMOCK, SCHMUCK
	SCHNOOK
sugary sentiment	SCHMALTZ
Supreme Council	SANHEDRIM, SANHEDRIN
	SYNEDRION, SYNEDRIUM
surplice	EPHOD
synagogue	S(C)HUL
teacher	RABBI, RABIN
temple	SYNAGOGUE, TABERNACLE
—servants	NETHINIM
thanksgiving	KADDISH
The Seventy	SANHEDRIN
theological college	YESHIVAH
title	RABBONI
town	QIRYAT
traditional oracle	URIM, THUMMIM
tree	SHITTAH
tribe	DAN, GAD, LEVITE
unclean	TEREFA(H)
unleavened bread	MATZA(H), MATZO(H)

unlucky person	S(C)HLIMAZEL
unquiet spirit	DYBBUK
veil	HUMERAL
village	KEFAR
vowel point	SCHWA, SEG(H)OL, SHEVA
wafer of bread	MATZA(H), MATZO(H)
weight	
—14 grams	SHEKEL
—20 gerahs	SHEKEL
well(s)	BE'ER(OT)
whine	KVETCH
wise man	HAKAM
womanhood ceremony	BAS MI(T)SVAH
	BAS MI(T)ZVAH
	BAT(H) MI(T)SVAH
	BAT(H) MI(T)ZVAH
Hell	ABADDON, AVERNUS
	DIS, EREBUS, HADES
	PIT, SHE'OL, TARTARUS
hens	ANDALUSIAN
	CUCKOO MARAN, DORKING
	GOLDEN SEABRIGHT
	MARENNES, MINORCA, LIGHT SUSSEX
	NORTH HOLLAND BLUE
	ORPINGTON, NEW HAMPSHIRE RED
	PARTRIDGE PEKIN, PLYMOUTH ROCK
	RHODE ISLAND RED, SPANISH
	SEBRIGHT BANTAM
	(SPECKLED)SUSSEX
	WHITE LEGHORN, WYANDOTTE
Australian	AUSTRALORP
Chinese	LANGSHAN
Indian	CHITTAGONG, MALAY
male	COCK(EREL), ROOSTER
small	BANTAM
tailless	RUMKIN
Turkish	SULTAN
Her	
Her (Britannic) Majesty	H(B)M
Her Catholic Majesty	HCM
Her Exalted Highness	HEH
Her Grace	HG
Her Imperial Highness	HIH
Her Imperial Majesty	HIM
Her Majesty's Customs	HMC
Her Majesty's Government	HMG
Her Majesty's Inspectorate	HMI
Herr Majesty's Service	HMS
Her Majesty's Ship	HMS
Her (Royal) Highness	H(R)H
Her Serene Highness	HSH
	(*see also* **His**)
heraldry	BLAZONRY, HER
about to take wing	RISING, ROUSANT
additional charge	AUGMENTATION
antelope	ARGASILL

antelope/horse	BAGWYN
antlers	ATTIRES
arched	ENARCHED, INVEXED
arms of deceased	HATCHMENT
arrowhead	PHEON
art of drawing coats-of-arms	(EM)BLAZONRY
back to back	ADDORSED
badge	COGNISANCE
ball of gold	MOUND
barbed head of arrow	PHEON
barrel-shaped metal	
cage	HERSE
barrulet	COTICE, COT(T)ISE
baton	BASTON, WARDER
bear quarterly	QUARTER
bearing	FLEUR-DE-LIS
	FLEUR-DE-LYS
—arms	ARMIGEROUS
—fruit	FRUCTED
—like a fish-trap	WEEL
—like a pallium	PALL
beasts	(*see* **monsters**)
beast's leg	GAMB, JAMB
bendlets interlaced	
with a mascle	FRET
bent	FLEXED
—round,striking side	PERCUSSANT
bird's leg cut off at thigh	A LA QUISE
black	DWALE, SABLE
blue	AZURE
border	
—near edge of shield	ORLE
—of shield	BORDURE
—with	
cotises	COT(T)IS
semi-circular indents	ENGRAIL
bowed	FLEXED
branch	SCROG
broad vertical stripe	PALE
broken	ROMPU
cadency mark of	
—eldest son	LABEL
—fourth son	MARTLET
—son	MULLET
cap	CHAPEAU
centre of escutcheon	FESSE-POINT
charge borne upon	
an ordinary	SUPERCHARGE
charged with	
—flowers etc	VERDOY
—squirrel fur	VERR(E)Y
—vair	VAIRE, VAIRY
charges used as border	ORLE
chequered	CHECKY
chief herald	GARTER KING-OF-ARMS
—of Scotland	(LORD)LYON

circular	
—shield (Scot.)	TARGE(T)
—symbol	ROUNDEL
—wreath	CHAPLET, GARLAND
clover-leaf	TREFOIL
coat of arms	BLAZON
colour	TINCTURE
—black	SA, SABLE
—blood red	SANGUINE
—blue	AZURE
—flesh colour	CARNATION
—gold	OR
—green	VT, VERT
—mulberry	MU, MURREY
—orange	TENNE
—purple	PURP, PURPURE
—scarlet	GU, GULES
—sky-blue	BLEU CELESTE
—tawny	TENNE
—yellow	OR
column with bifurcated	
capital and base	ZULE
combine palewise	IMPALE
coming	
—forth	NAISSANT
—up from another	ISSUANT
concave	CHAMPAGNE, CHAMPAINE
	INVEXED
—indentation	FLA(U)NCH
conventional figure	ORDINARY
conventionalised flower	PRIMROSE
cormorant	LIVER BIRD
cotice	BARRULET
covered with shells	ESCALLOPED
covering the field	SANS NOMBRE
crest	COGNISANCE, TIMBRE
cross	QUADRATE
—of filberts	AVELLANE
—with	
curved ends	MOLINE
three claw-like	
divisions	PATTE(E)
crutch-shaped	POTENT
curved backwards	REFLEXED
cushion tied at corners	WOOL PACK
cut off evenly	COUPE(D)
—to a point	FITCHE(E), FITCHY
death's head	MORTHEAD
depict	EMBLAZON
—in heraldic terms	BLAZON
device on a shield	CHARGE
devouring	VORANT
—prey	TRUSSING
diagonal cross	SALTIRE
diagonally	BENDWISE
diamond-shaped panel	HATCHMENT

diminish	REBATE
diminutive of	
—bend	COT(T)ISE
—bend sinister	SCARP
—fess	TRANGLE
—orle	TRESSURE
displaced	ROMPU
distinguishing arms of	
branch from main line	DIFFERENCE
divide quarterly	QUARTER
divided into	PARTY
—bends	BENDY
—quarters	QUARTERLY
—three	TIERCED, TRIPARTED
—vertically	PALY
diving	URINANT
division of	
—coat	QUARTERING
—shield for two coats	IMPALEMENT
double-bodied	BICORPORATE
drapery of coat-of-arms	MANTLING
drop	GOUTTE
eagle	AL(L)ERION
eight	
—leaved flower	EIGHTFOIL
—spoked charge	(ES)CARBUNCLE
elongated rhomboid	FUSIL
emblem	BEARING, CHARGE
	DEVICE
emerging from	
—behind	ISSUANT
—middle	NAISSANT
encircled	ENVIRONED, INVOLVED
—by sun's rays	EN SOLEIL
end-to-end	ABOUTE
entwined	ENVELOPED
escutcheon or shield	
—granted to commemorate	
a deed	ACHIEVEMENT
—hung over a tomb	ACHIEVEMENT
facing	
—each other	RESPECTANT
—the	
beholder	G(U)ARDANT
sinister	TRAVERSED
family shield	ESCUTCHEON
fan of feathers	PANACHE
fettered	SPANCELLED
field	CHAMP
figure surmounting helmet	CREST
fillet with pendants	LABEL
fire-bucket on pole	BEACON, CRESSET
five	
—petalled flower	CINQUEFOIL
—pointed star	MULLET
flame-shaped	RAYONNE

fleur-de-lis	LIS
floating in air or water	FLOTANT
flower with	
—four petals	QUATREFOIL
—five petals	CINQUEFOIL
—eight petals	OCTOFOIL
flying	
—horizontally	VOLANT
—tail down	CABRE
—upwards	SOARING
formed of crutch-heads	POTENT
full-face	CABOCHED, CABOSHED
fullness (of Moon)	COMPLEMENT
fully armed	CAP-A-PIE
funeral banner	GUMPHION
fur	ERMINE(S), ERMINOIS
	PEAN, TINCTURE, VAIR
gliding	GLISSANT
goat rampant	CLIMANT
gold	OR
—circle	BESA(U)NT, BEZANT
	TALENT
—or silver as tincture	METAL
green	VERT
grenade	PETARDIER
half a quarter	ESQUIRE, GYRON
halo	GLORY
hanging	PENDENT
having	
—a	
pommel	POMMELE
square opening	SQUARE-PIERCED
tongue	LANGUED
—another figure laid over	SURMOUNTED
—battlements	EMBATTLED
—border of convex curves	INVECTED
—branch stubs	RAGULY
—convex curvature	NOWY
—crown or coronet	
about the neck	GORGED
—empty centre	VOIDED
—endorse each side	ENDORSED
—ends entering mouth	
of animal	ENGOULED
—fesses	FESSE(E)-WISE
—fleurs de lis	FLEUR(ETT)Y
	FLOR(ETT)Y
—gyrons	GYRONNY
—head	
bowed	URINANT
facing up	HAURIENT
—horns etc a different	
colour from body	ENARMED
—inner part cut away	VOIDED
—narrow border	FIMBRIATE
—official headgear	ENSIGNED

—overlapping	
feathers	PLUMET(T)E, PLUMETTY
scales	PAPELLONE, PAPILLONE
—part displaced	FRACTED
—points	URDE(E), URDY
—raised wings	SEGREANT
—right foot raised	TRIPPANT
—small squares	CHECKY
—steps	GRIECED
—tail hanging down	DECLINANT
—trellis pattern	FRETTY
—wings	
expanded	DISPLAYED
folded	TRUSSED
joined	A VOL, IN LURE
open	OVERT
thrown back	ENDORSED
—water flowing through	TRANSFLUENT
hatchment	ACHIEVEMENT
hedgehog	HERISSON, HERIZON
	URCHIN
helmet	MANTLING
herald	BLAZONER
Herald of Arms	
—England	ARUNDEL, CHESTER
	NORFOLK, SOMERSET
	SURREY, YORK
—Scotland	ALBANY, DINGWALL
	MARMONT
	RICHMOND, SNOWDOUN
heraldic bearings	BLAZON
hollowed with narrow	
border	CLECHE
horizontal band	BAR, FESS(E)
horseman	CHEVALIER
in	
—sleeping posture	DORMANT
—the	
direction of	PER
manner of	PER
—upper part of shield	IN CHIEF
indentation in curved lines	ENGRAILMENT
indented	WAVED
interlaced	BRACED
inverted pyramidal	
figure	PILE
iron hat	CHAPEL-DE-FER
issuing from another	ISSUANT
jumping	SALIENT
King of Arms	
—England	CLARENC(I)EUX
	GARTER, NORROY AND ULSTER
—Scotland	LYON
knight	MILES
knotted	NOWED
—gold or silver cord	CORDELIERE

leaping	SALIENT	painted in	TRICK
left hand side from front	DEXTER	pair of bars	GEMMAL
less honourable		parrot	POPINJAY
armorial charge	SUBORDINARY	part of quartered shield	QUARTER
like		parted	PARTY
—a dragon in rear parts	DRAGONNE	pass through	ENFILE
—an arch	ENARCHED	passing in opposite	
—millstone rind	MOLINE	directions	COUNTER-PASSANT
lily	FLEUR-DE-LIS	personal flag on	
	FLEUR-DE-LYS	horizontal pole	GONFALLON
line	DOUBLE		GONFANNON
lines from edge of escutcheon		pierced	TRANSFIXED
to fesse-point	GIRON, GYRON	place bearing on	CHARGE
lion passant gardant	LEOPARD(ESS)	—quarterly	QUARTER
lizard	AMPHISBAENA	point	
long flag	STANDARD	—at centre of shield	FESSE-POINT
looking backward	REG(U)ARDANT	—below centre of	
lower part of shield	BASE	shield	NAVEL, NOMBRIL
lozenge	FUSIL	—just above fesse-	
—pierced with circle	RUSTRE	point	HONOUR-POINT
—shaped bearing	MASCLE	pointed	URDE(E), URDY
lying down		—at the foot	FITCHE(D), FITCHY
—head on paws	DORMANT	pole battle-axe	DOLOIRE, HALBERD
—head up	COUCHANT	potent	POTENCE
mark of dishonour	ABATEMENT	powdered	SEME(E)
—with badge or sign	ENSIGN	punning shield or	
mastiff	ALANT	emblem	ARMES PARLANTES
merman	NEPTUNE		CANTING ARMS
metal	ARGENT, OR, TINCTURE	Pursuivant	
monster	(see separate entry)	—English	FITZALAN, BLUE MANTLE
most ancient	PREMIER		PORTCULLIS, ROUGE CROIX
narrow			ROUGE DRAGON
—band of colour	FIMBRIATION	—Scottish	BUTE, CARRICK, KINTYRE
—bendlet	RIBAND		MARCH, ORMONDE
negro	BLACKAMOOR	rabbit	CONEY
of a cross with flower-		ragged	RAGULY
decorated ends	PATONCE	raguly	RAGGED
officer below herald	PURSUIVANT	raised on steps	MOUNTED
often repeated	SANS NOMBRE	rampant	
one of nine fixed		—goat	CLIMANT
positions	POINT	—griffin	SEGREANT
open lozenge	MASCLE	raven	CORBIE
orb of gold	MOUND	rearguard	ARRIERE-GARDE
ordinary		rearing	CABRE
—from		—horse	FORCENE
dexter chief to sinister base	BEND	red	GULES
sinister chief		reference book	ORDINARY
to dexter base	BEND SINISTER	relative status of sons	CADENCY
—horizontal	FESS(E)	represent half of	DIMIDIATE
—occupying		representation of two rafters	CHEVRON
fourth of shield	QUARTER	represented as flying	VOLANT
upper part of shield	CHIEF	right-hand side from front	SINISTER
—of shield	CANTON	ring	ANNULET
outline sketch	TRICK	rising	NAISSANT
overlaid	OPPRESSED, SUPPRESSED	—as	
overlying	JESSANT	a bird	ROUSANT

if to breathe	HAURIANT
	HAURIENT
—from the sea	ASSURGENT
rosette	COCKADE
roundel	
—azure	HURT
—black	GUNSTONE, OGRESS, PELLET
—blue	H(E)UT, HEURTE
—blue/silver	FOUNTAIN
—gold	BEZANT
—green	POMEIS, POMEY, POMME
—gules	TORTEAU
—murrey	MULBERRY
—purpure	GOLP(E)
—sable	GUNSTONE, OGRESS
	PELLET
—sanguine	GUZE
—silver	PLATE
—tenne	ORANGE
rows of squares of	
alternate tinctures	COMPONE
	COMPONY, GOBONY
ruling body	COLLEGE OF ARMS
—Scotland	COURT OF THE LORD LYON
running	COURANT
salient in opposite	
directions	COUNTER-SALIENT
scarf over helmet	LAMBREQUIN
science of coats-of-arms	BLAZON
Scottish	
—Herald	ALBANY
—King of Arms	(LORD) LYON
—pursuivant	UNICORN
scroll	ESCROL(L)
sea-horse	HIPPOCAMPUS
segment of circle	FLANCH
segmented cross	ARRONDEE
shackle for horse	FETTERLOCK
sheaf	GARB(E)
shedding drops of ...	DISTILLING
shield	BUCKLER
	(E)SCUTCHEON, SCOTCHEON
ship (Scot.)	LYMPHAD
shoulder guard	AILETTE
showing tincture	
of field	VOIDED
sign of illegitimacy	BAR-SINISTER
	BATON-SINISTER
silver	ARGENT
simple figure	ORDINARY
single shield borne	
as a charge	INESCUTCHEON
sitting	SEJANT
—on nest	EYRANT
six-rayed star	ESTOIL
skull	MORTHEAD

sleeve	MANCH(E), MAUNCH
small	
—banner	BANNERET, BANNEROLE
	BANNEROLL
—bend	BENDLET
—chevron	CHEVRONEL
—fesse	TRANGLE
—lion	LIONCEL
—pale	PALLET
—pennon	PENCELL, PENSELL
	PENNONCELLE
—shield at fesse	INESCUTCHEON
smeared	TRICK
spool of golden thread	TRUNDLE
spreading towards the ends	PATTE(E)
spur rowel	MOLET, MULLET
square	
—charge	CANTON
—sod	DELF, DELPH
squares of alternate	
tinctures	COMPONE, COMPONY
	GOBONY
squirrel fur	VAIR
St Andrew's cross	SALTIER, SALTIRE
standing	
—in profile	RAMPANT
—on four feet	STATANT
—shield for archer	PAVISE TALLEVAS
—still	POSE
star with wavy points	ESTOILE
stepped	GRIECED
stick with branch	
stubs	RAGGED STAFF
strawberry flower	FAISE
streamer	BANDEROLLE
strewn with small bearings	SEME(E)
subordinary	TRESSURE
sun with human face	SPLENDOUR
surcoat	CYCLAS
surface of shield	FIELD
surrounded by	ENVIRONED
	ENTOURED
swallow without feet	MARTLET
swimming horizontally	NAIANT
T-shaped mark	POTENCE
tail between the legs	COWARD
tearing prey	RAPING
tent	PAVILION, TABERNACLE
three-lobed	TREFOIL
tinctures	(see colour above)
—reversed	COUNTER-CHANGED
triangular	
—flag	PINSEL, PINSIL
—wedge	PILE
tripping	TRIPPANT
trumpet	CLARION

two parallel lines bounding an ordinary	BEND (SINISTER)
unde	OUNDY
upright rectangle	BILLET
variation of coat of arms	BRISURE
vertical band on shield	ENDORSE
vertically	PALEWISE
visit of herald	VISITATION
walking	AMBULANT
—stag	TRIPPANT
—to right	PASSANT
warhorse	DESTRIER
wavy	NEBULE, NEBULY, UNDE(E)
waxing (of Moon)	INCRESCENT
wheat-sheaf	GARBGERBE
wheel set with teeth	CATHERINE-WHEEL
whirlpool	GORGE, GURGES
white	ARGENT
wild boar	SANGLIER
wound	GOLPE, VULN
wreath	TORSE
Y-shaped ordinary	PALL
—with fringed bottom	PALLIUM
yellow circle	BEZANT
yoke on water-bags	BOUGET
zigzag or indented line	DANCETTE, DANCETTY RAGULY

herb

	SIMPLE
bennet	(WOOD-)AVENS
burnt in medical treatment	MOXA
Christopher	BANEBERRY
for seasoning	POTHERB
mixture of fresh herbs	FINES HERBES
of	
—grace	RUE
—repentance	RUE
others	AGRIMONY, ALOE, AMARACUS
	ANGELICA, ANISE, AVENS, BALM
	BANEBERRY, BASIL, BAY, BENNET
	BERGAMOT, BETONY, BLITE, BORAGE
	BURDOCK, CALAMINT, CAPER, CARAWAY
	CATMINT, CATNIP, C(H)AMOMILE, CHERVIL
	CHICORY, CLARY, COMFREY, CORIANDER
	CORNEL, COSTMARY, COVENS, CRESS
	DILL, DITTANY, ELECAMPANE, ENDIVE
	FENNEL, FENUGREEK, FINOC(C)HIO
	FINNOCHIO, GENTIAN, GINSENG
	HAMBURG PARSLEY, HELLEBORE
	HENBANE, HOREHOUND, HORSERADISH
	HYSSOP, ISATIS, LAD'S LOVE
	LADY'S MANTLE, LEMON BALM
	LEMON VERBENA, LICORICE, LIQUORICE
	LOVAGE, MARJORAM, MEDIC, MILFOIL
	MINT, MUGWORT, MUSTARD, MYRRH
	OREGANO, ORIGAN(E), ORIGANUM,

	ORPIN(E), PANICUM, PARSLEY
	PENNY ROYAL, PEPPERMINT
	PURSLANE, PURSLAIN, QUINOA
	RAMPION, ROSEMARY, RUE, SAFFRON
	SAGE, SALAD BURNET, SAMPHIRE
	SAVORY, SEDUM, SENNA, SESAME
	SORREL, SOUTHERNWOOD
	SPICKNEL, SUMMER SAVORY
	SUCCORY, SWEET CHERVIL
	SWEET CICELY, TANSY, TARRAGON
	TORMENTIL, THYME, VERVAIN
	WAYBREAD, WOAD, WOODRUFF
	WORMWOOD, YARROW
Paris	TRUE-LOVE
Peter	COWSLIP
Robert	STINKING CRANE'S-BILL
trinity	PANSY
wood sorrel	OXALIS

Hindu

Absolute	OM
adherent of Siva	S(H)AIVA
an age of the world	KALPA, KALIYUGA YUG(A)
ancient	
—language	SANSKRIT
—way of life	SANATAN-DHARMA
aphorism	SUTRA
Aryan way of life	ARYA-DHARMA
ascetic	SAD(D)HU, YOGI(N) GYMNOSOPH(IST), SIDDHU
aurora	USHAS
banker	SOUCAR
barge	BUDGERO(W)
bathing in Ganges	KUMBHA MELA
beauty spot	TIK(K)A
being	SAT
blackmail	CHOUT
bliss	ANANDA
book of	
—erotic love	KAMASUTRA
—ritual	SUTRA
Brahman beggar	SANNYASI(N)
caste	JATI, VARNA
(highest first)	
—priests	BRAHMANS, BRAHMINS
—barons/warriors	KSHATRIYAS
—commoners/merchants	VAISYAS
—artisans/labourers	SOODRA, S(H)UDRA
—untouchables	HARIJAN
—mark	TI(K)KA
chant	HARE KRISHNA
circle	MANDOLA
concentration	SAMADHI
convert to Islam	SHEIK(H)
cosmic age	YUGA
cycle of birth and death	SAMSARA

dancing-girl	BAYADERE
dark planet	RAHU
day (of Brahma)	CALPA, KALPA
deities	(*see* **gods, goddesses**)
demigod	GARUDA
demon that swallows the Sun and Moon at eclipses	RAHU
desire	KAMA
devotion	BHAKTI
devotional	
—offering	S(H)RADDHA
—song	BHAJAN
divine	
—in self	ATMAN
—power	MAYA
divinity	DEVA
dramatic performance of Ramayana	RAMLILA
drink of the gods	AMRITA
drug	BIKH
epic	BHAGAVADGITA MAHABHARATA RAMAYANA
errand boy	HURKARU
European	FARINGEE, FERINGHEE FERINGHI
evil spirit	RAKSHAS(A)
extortion	CHOUT
fairy	GLENDOVEER
fate	KARMA
female principle	S(H)AKTI
festival	DEWALI, DI(PI)VALI DIWALI, DURGA PUJA, HOLI KUMBHA MELA, NAVARATRA NAVARATRI, ONAM, PONGAL RSI-PANCAMI
first	
—mortal	YAMA
—of Vedas	RIGVEDA
forehead mark	TI(K)KA
gate tower	GOPURAM
gentleman	BABOO, BABU
gesture	MUDRA
ghost	BHUT
gnome	YAKSKA
god in three forms	TRIMURTI
gold ornament	TAHLI
good spirit	DEVA
heaven	SVARGA, SWARGA
hermitage	ASHRAM
hero	ARJUNA, RAMA
holy	
—book	VEDA
—man	SAD(D)HU
—writing	SHASTER, S(H)ASTRA

home of gods	MERU
idol	SWAMI
ignorance	AVIDYA
illusion	MAYA
immortality	AMRITATTVA
Indian Republic	BHARAT
incarnation	AVATAR
—of Vishnu	JAGANNATH, JUGGERNAUT KRISHNA, RAMA
instrument	SIT(T)AR
interpreter	DHOBASH
knowledge	GYAN, JNANA
land revenues	JAGHIRE
law of causation	KARMA
liberation (from circle of re-births)	MOKS(H)A
library	BHANDAR
life	
—cycle rites	SAMSKARAS
—principle	ATMAN, JIVA
loin-cloth	DHO(O)TI
love	KAMA
low caste	HARIJAN, UNTOUCHABLE
man/bird	GARUDA
manifestation	DARSHANA
material gain	ARTHA
mediaeval texts	PURANAS
mendicant	SAD(D)HU
merchant	BUN(N)IA
metal worker	KOFTGAR
moral order	RITA
musical form	RAGA
mythical planet	RAHU
mythological age	KALIYUGA
non-violence	AHIMSA
of high caste	TWICE-BORN
official script	DEVANAGARI
paradise	SVARGA, SWARGA
period (4320 million years)	CALPA, KALPA
philosopher	GYMNOSOPH(IST)
philosophical treatise	UPANIS(H)AD
philosophy	NYAYA, PURVA-MIMAMSA SAMKYHA, SANKHYA VAISESIKA, VEDANTA, YOGA
poison	BIKH
police officer	TANADAR
present age of the world	KALIYUGA
priest	PUJARI
priestly caste	BRAHMAN, BRAHMIN
Rajput prince	RANA
religious	
—commentary	VEDANGA
—instructor	GOOROO, GURU MAHARISHI, SWAMI

—instruction	SIDDHU
—retreat	ASHRAM
—school	ARYA SAMAJ
—treatise	UPANIS(H)AD
—writing	SMRITI, TANTRA, VEDA
righteousness	DHARMA
ritual	PUJA
—texts	BRAHMANAS
ruling class	RAJPOOT, RAJPUT
rural districts	MOFUSSIL
sacred	
—books	MANTRA(M), PURANA
	SHASTER, S(H)ASTRA
—snake	NAGA
—scriptures	SHRUTI
—text	MANTRA(M)
—writings	TANTRA, VEDA
sage	MUNI, RISHI
salvation	MOKSA
self-immolation by widow	SATI, SUTTEE
serpent-king	SESHA
short verse	SUTRA
Siva's trident	TRISUL(A)
slave	DASI
society	SOMAJ
soul	ATMAN
spirit	PURUSHA
spring festival	HOLI
statues of gods	MURTI
store	BHANDAR
strands	GUNAS
supreme	
—glorification	AVATAR
—principle of life	ATMAN
symbol of	
—Siva	LINGAM
—the universe	MANDALA
temple	MANDIR(A)
—attendant	PUJARI
theistic society	BRAHMA SAMAJ
	BRAHMO SOMAJ
title	MAHATMA, PANDIT, PUNDIT
trader	BANIAN, BANYAN
tradition	SRUTI
transmigration of soul	SAMSARA
trident of Siva	TRISULA
trinity of gods	TRIMURTI
truth	SAT
twice-born	DVIJA
untouchables	HARIJAN
usher	SOUCAR
Veda	ATHARVAVEDA, RIGVEDA
	SAMAVEDA, YAJURVEDA
—commentary	VEDANGA
Vedic	
—hymn	MANTRA(M)

—philosophical texts	UPANISHADS
veil	CHAD(D)AR, CHADOR
	CHUDDAH, CHUDDAR
Vishnu's consort	S(H)AIVA
vision	DARSHANA
wealth	ARTHA
wife of Siva	S(H)AKTI
wisdom	JNANA
wise man	MAHATMA, PANDIT
	PUNDIT
woman's garment	SAREE, SARI
worship	BHAKTI, POOJA(H), PUJA
worshipper	
—of Sakti	S(H)AKTA
—of Vishnu	VAISHNAVA
yoga	BHAKTI, HATHA, JNANA
	KARMA, KUNDALINI, LAYA
	MAHA, MANTRA, RAJA, SIDDHU
	(see also **Indian***)*

His

His (Britannic) Majesty	H(B)M
His Catholic Majesty	HCM
His Eminence	HE
His Exalted Highness	HEH
His Excellency	HE
His Grace	HG
His Imperial Highness	HIH
His Imperial Majesty	HIM
His Majesty's Customs	HMC
His Majesty's Government	HMG
His Majesty's Inspectorate	HMI
His Majesty's Service	HMS
His Majesty's Ship	HMS
His (Royal) Highness	H(R)H
His Serene Highness	HSH
	(see also **Her***)*

historians

American	FOGEL, KENNAN, SCHLESINGER
	TURNER, VANTINA, WITT,
Australian	CHILDE
British	ACTON, BRIGGS, BUTTERFIELD
	CLAPHAM, CLARENDON
	COHN, COLLINGWOOD
	GIBBON, HILL, HOBSBAWM
	HOLINSHED, KIER, MACAULAY
	MORRIS, NAPIER, NEEDHAM
	TAWNEY, TAYLOR
	TOYNBEE, TREVOR-ROPER
	SYME, (VENERABLE) BEDE
	WEDGWOOD, WOOLF
Dutch	HUIZINGA
French	BAIVILLE, BLOCH, BRAUDEL
	CHAUNU, DE TOCQUEVILLE
	GOUBERT, HALEVY, LADURIC
	LE FEBVRE, LE POPELINIERE
	LE ROY LADURIE

German	BAUER, FLECHTHEIM
	HARNACK, UHDE, WITTFOGEL
Greek	AMMIANUS, HERODOTUS
	PTOLEMY, THUCYDIDES
	XENOPHON
Indian	PANIKKAR
Roman	LIVY, TACITUS
Swiss	BLEULER

holidays
including: fast
        feast
        festival
        saint's day

American	
—July 4th	INDEPENDENCE DAY
—September	LABOR DAY
—October	COLUMBUS DAY
—November	THANKSGIVING (DAY)
Australian	
—April 25th	ANZAC DAY
Buddhist	
—July	BON, FEAST OF LANTERNS
—August	KUAN-YIN
—November	FESTIVAL OF LIGHTS
	KATHINA CEREMONY
Burmese	KATHINA CEREMONY
Canadian	
—July 1st	CANADA DAY, DOMINION DAY
—September	LABOR DAY
Chinese	
—Jan/Feb	NEW YEAR
—Feb/Mar	LANTERN FESTIVAL
—Mar/Apr	FESTIVAL OF BRIGHTNESS
—May/Jun	DRAGON-BOAT FESTIVAL
—Aug	ALL SOULS, KUAN-YIN
—Sep	MIDSUMMER
—Sep/Oct	DOUBLE NINTH FESTIVAL
—Nov/Dec	WINTER SOLSTICE
Christian	
—7 weeks before Easter	ASH WEDNESDAY
	SHROVE TUESDAY
—7th Sunday after Easter	PENTECOST
	WHITSUN(DAY)
—10-14 days after	
Pentecost	CORPUS CHRISTI
—40th day after Easter	ASCENSION DAY
--January 6th	EPIPHANY
	TWELFTH NIGHT
20th	ST AGNES'S EVE
—February 2nd	CANDLEMAS
	HYPAPANTE
—March 25th	LADY DAY
—March/April	EASTER, HOLY WEEK
	LENT
—May	ASCENSION DAY
—May/June	TRINITY SUNDAY

—June 11th	ST BARNABY'S DAY
23rd	ST JOHN'S EVE
—August 1st	LAMMAS
15th	ASSUMPTION DAY
—November 1st	ALL HALLOWS
	ALL SAINTS, HALLOWMAS
11th	MARTINMAS
—November/December	ADVENT
—December 24th	CHRISTMAS EVE
25th	CHRISTMAS (DAY)
27th	ST JOHN'S DAY
—All Hallows	HALLOWMAS
—All Saints	HALLOWMAS
—first fruits	LAMMAS
—Friday before Easter	BLACK FRIDAY
	GOLDEN FRIDAY
	GOOD FRIDAY
—harvest	HARVEST FESTIVAL
—love feast	AGAPE
—Resurrection	EASTER (DAY)
—Saturday before	
Easter	HOLY SATURDAY
—Sunday before Easter	PALM SUNDAY
—Thursday before	
Easter	MAUNDY THURSDAY
English	
—January 1st	NEW YEAR'S DAY
—February 14th	ST VALENTINE'S DAY
—April 23rd	ST GEORGE'S DAY
—July 15th	ST SWITHIN'S DAY
—September 29th	MICHAELMAS
—October 31st	HALLOWE'EN
25th	ST CRISPIN'S DAY
—Nov 5th	GUY FAWKES'S DAY
11th	ARMISTICE DAY
—December 26th	BOXING DAY
31st	NEW YEAR'S EVE
—beer festival	ALE
—shoemakers' festival	ST CRISPIN'S DAY
Epiphany	TWELFTH NIGHT
French	
—July 14th	BASTILLE DAY
—Shrove Tuesday	MARDI GRAS
German	
—April 30th	WALPURGISNACHT
	WALPURGIS NIGHT
—Shrovetide	FASCHING
Greek	
—festival of	
Adonis	ADONIA
Apollo	THARGELIA
Demeter	THESMOPHORIA
Dionysius	ANTHESTERIA
—national festival	PANATHENAEA
Hebrew	
—Jan/Feb	FESTIVAL OF LOTS, PURIM

—Feb/Mar	FAST OF ESTER	
	TAANIT ESTER	
—March 1st	FEAST OF LOTS, PURIM	
—Mar/Apr	FAST OF THE FIRSTBORN	
	TAANIT BEHORIM	
	PASSOVER, PESAC(H)	
	HOLOCAUST DAY	
	YOM HASHOAH	
—Apr/May	INDEPENDENCE DAY	
	YOM HAATZMAUT	
	JERUSALEM DAY	
	YOM YER SHALAYIM	
	REMEMBRANCE DAY	
	YOM HAZIKHARON	
—May/Jun	FESTIVAL OF THE WEEKS	
	PENTECOST, SHABUOTH	
—Sep/Oct	DAY OF ATONEMENT	
	SUCCOT(H), SUKKOT(H)	
	YOM KIPPUR	
	EIGHTH DAY OF CONCLUSION	
	SHEMINI ATZERET	
	FAST OF GEDALIAH	
	TSOM GEDALIAH	
	FEAST OF TABERNACLES	
	SUCCOTH, SUKKOT()H	
	REJOICING IN THE TORAH	
	SIMHAT TORAH	
—Sep 20th	ROSH HASHANAH	
—Nov/Dec	(C)HANUKKAH	
	FESTIVAL OF LIGHTS	
	HANUKAH	
—New Moon	ROSH HODESH	
—New Year	ROSH HASHANAH	
—other	YOM TERUAH	
	YOM TOB, YOM TOV	
—presentation of the virgin	ISODIA	
—sabbath	SHABAT	
Hindu		
—January	KUMBHA MELA, PONGALA	
—Feb/Mar	HOLI	
—Aug/Sep	KRISHNA JAYANTI, ONAM	
—Sep/Oct	DURGA PUJA	
—October	GANDHI JAYANTI	
—Oct/Nov	FESTIVAL OF LAMPS	
—Festival of Lamps	DEEPAVALI, DEWALI	
	DI(PI)VALI, DIWALI	
—other	NAVARATRA, NAVARATRI	
	PONGAL, RSI-PANCAMI	
—twelve-yearly	KUMBHA MELA	
—wife of Siva	DURGA PUJA	
Irish	FEIS(ANNA)	
—March 17th	ST PATRICK'S DAY	
—December 26th	ST STEPHEN'S DAY	
Jain	PAJJUSANA, PARYUSANA	
Japanese		
—November 3rd	ARTS AND CULTURE DAY	

23rd	LABOUR DAY	
Moslem		
—after Ramadan	BAIRAM, BAYRAM	
—Mar/Apr	RAMADAN	
—April 16th	ID-UL-FITR	
—June 23rd	ID-UL-ADHA	
—July 13th	NEW YEAR	
—Jul/Aug	MOHARRAM, MUHARRAM	
	MUHARREM	
—other	SAUM, SAWM	
New Orleans	MARDI GRAS	
New Zealand		
—February 6th	WAITANGI DAY	
—April 25th	ANZAC DAY	
Northern Ireland		
—July 12th	GLORIOUS TWELFTH	
	ORANGEMAN'S DAY	
pancake day	SHROVE TUESDAY	
Pentecost	WHITSUN(DAY)	
Peru	INTI RAYIMA	
Red Indian	POTLA(T)CH	
Roman		
—February 17th	QUIRINALIA	
—April 21st	PALILIA	
23rd	VINALIA	
—May 9-13th	LEMURIA	
—August 23rd	VULCANALIA	
—Bacchus	BACCHANALIA	
—boundaries	TERMINALIA	
—crops	AMBARVALIA	
—expiation	LUPERCALIA, QUIRINALIA	
—fertility	LUPERCALIA	
—flocks	PALILIA	
—shepherds	PALILIA	
—the dead	LEMURIA	
—Vulcan	VULCANALIA	
—wine	VINALIA	
Roman Catholic festival	CARNIVAL	
Scottish		
—January 25th	BURNS NIGHT	
—November 30th	ST ANDREW'S DAY	
—December 31st	HOGMANAY	
Shinto		
—Jan 1st	NEW YEAR'S DAY	
—equinoxes	IMPERIAL SPIRIT DAY	
—February 11th	EMPIRE FOUNDATION DAY	
—April 3rd	DEATH OF JIMMU	
—October 17th	PRESENTATION OF RICE	
—November 23rd	THANKSGIVING	
Sikh		
—Festival of Lamps	DEEPAVALI	
	DEWALI, DI(PI)VALI	
	DIWALI	
—Oct/Nov	FESTIVAL OF LAMPS	
South African		
—December 16th	DAY OF THE VOW	

Twelfth Night	EPIPHANY
Vietnamese New Year	TET
Whit Sunday	PENTECOST
Welsh	
—March 1st	ST DAVID'S DAY
Holland	(*see* **Dutch**)
holy	
Holy City	JERUSALEM, MECCA
	MEDINA, ROME
Holy Communion	EUCHARIST, HC
holy man	S, SAINT, ST
Holy Mother Mary	SMM
holy river	GANGES
Holy Roman Empire	SRI
Holy Virgin	HV
Holy Writ	BIBLE, NT, OT
hominids	(*see* **anthropology**)
Honduras	
capital	TEGUCIGALPA
coin	CENTAVO, LEMPIRA
Hong Kong	HK
hormone	AUTACOID
adrenaline	EPINEPHRINE
anti-diuretic	ADH, VASOPRESSIN
breaking glycogen down	
to glucose	GLUCAGON
causing moulting (insects)	ECDYSONE
controlling	
—adrenals	ACTH
—calcium in blood	(THYRO)CALCITONIN
—sugar metabolism	INSULIN
—synthesis of	
protein	INSULIN
female sex	(O)ESTRADIOL, (O)ESTRIOL
	(O)ESTROGEN, (O)ESTRONE
	PROGESTERONE, PROGESTOGEN
from	
—adrenal glands/kidneys	ACTH
	(AD)RENIN, ALDEROSTERONE
	CORTICOSTEROID
	CORTISOL, CORTISONE
	(NOR)ADRENALIN(E)
	(NOR)EPINEPHRINE
	ERYTHROPOIETIN
—pancreas	GLUCAGON, INSULIN
	PANCREATIN, SECRETIN
—parathyroid gland	CALCITONIN
	PARATHORMONE
—pineal gland	MELATONIN
—pituitary gland	ACTH
	ANTIDIURETIC HORMONE, ADCH
	CORTICOTROP(H)IN
	FOLLICLE-STIMULATING HORMONE, FSH
	GONADOTROP(H)IC HORMONE
	GONADOTROP(H)IN
	LACTOGENIC HORMONE, LTH

	LUTEOTROPIC HORMONE
	OXYTOCIN, OXYTONE
	PITUITRIN, PROLACTIN
	THYROTROP(H)IC HORMONE, TSH
	SOMATOTROP(H)IC HORMONE, STH
	VASOPRESSIN
—stomach	GASTRIN
—thyroid	CALCITONIN
	LUTEINIZING HORMONE
	THYROCALCITONIN
	THYROXIN
inducing sleep	MELATONIN
lactogenic	PROLACTIN
loosening pelvic ligaments	RELAXIN
male sex	ANDROGEN
	ANDROSTERONE
	TESTOSTERONE
plant	KINETIN, KININ
	PHYTAMIN
—affected by vernalisation	VERNALIN
—cytokinin	ZEATIN
—hypothetical	FLORIGEN
—inhibiting	
action of auxin	ANTIAUXIN
growth	ABSCISIC ACID
	ABSCISIN, DORMIN
—regulating growth	AUXIN
—stimulating	
cell division	CYTOKININ, PHYTOKININ
stem growth	GIBBERELLIN
preparing organs for	
pregnancy	PROGESTERONE
protects embryo	PROGESTERONE
reducing inflammation	CORTISONE
stimulating	
—growth	SOMATOTROPIC HORMONE
	STH
—production of	
milk	LACTOGENIC HORMONE, LTH
	LUTEOTROPIC HORMONE
	PROLACTIN
pancreatic juices	SECRETIN
progesterone	LACTOGENIC HORMONE
	LTH, LUTEOTROPIC HORMONE
	PROLACTIN
red blood cells	ERYTHROPOIETIN
sperm and	
ova	
	FOLLICLE-STIMULATING HORMONE
	FSH
—uterine contraction	OXYTOCIN
—sexual	
impulses	GONADOTROP(H)IC HORMONE
	GONADOTROPIN
—thyroid	
	THYROTROP(H)IC HORMONE, TSH

—water reabsorption	ANTIDIURETIC HORMONE
	ADH
synthetic oestrogen	STILB(O)ESTROL
horse[1]	CAPLE, CAPUL
including: breeds	
colours	
descriptions	
American	
—Indian	CAYUSE
—piebald	APPALOOSA, PINTO
—poor	TACKY
—riding	MORGAN
—wild	DUN, MUSTANG
Arabian	ARAB
Argentinian	FALABELLA
Asian	PRZEWALSKI'S HORSE
ass	BURRO, DONKEY
Australian	WALER
Austrian	HAFLINGER, LIPPIZ(Z)ANA
	LIP(P)IZ(Z)ANER
bay	BAYARD
black and white	PIEBALD
broken-winded horse	WHISTLER
Brunnhilde's horse	GRANE
burro	ASS, DONKEY
Caligula's horse	INCITATUS
carthorse	CLYDESDALE, SHIRE
chaser	HUNTER
circus	LIBERTY HORSE
colt	STAG
—Scottish	STAIG
competition horse	EVENTER
cowboy's mount	BRONC(H)O
dark-coloured horse	MOREL
Dick Turpin's horse	BLACK BESS
display horse	LIPPIZ(Z)ANA
	LIP(P)IZ(Z)ANER
docked	CURTAIL
—Shakespeare	CUT
donkey	ASS, BURRO
Don Quixote's horse	ROSINANTE
	ROZINANTE
draught-horse	PERCHERON, SHIRE
	SUFFOLK PUNCH
eight-legged	SLEIPNIR
El Cid's horse	BABIECA
entire	STALLION
extinct	
—breed	TARPAN
—type	EOHIPPUS
family	EQUIDAE
fast horse	DAISY-CUTTER
female	DAM, MARE
fine horse	BAYARD
first horse (myth)	ARION

fossil horse	HIPPARION
French	ARDENNES, PERCHERON
from Medusa's blood	CHRYSAOR
general use	HACK(NEY)
genus	EQUUS
golden coloured	PALOMINO
grey-brown	DUN
heavy horse	(see workhorse below)
highly bred	ARAB, THOROUGHBRED
Himalayan pony	GOONT
hybrid	(see separate entry)
Indian	TAT(TOO)
Irish	CONNEMARA
Jerusalem pony	ASS
loser	STUMER
light workhorse	HALF-LEG
male	COLT, GELDING, STALLION
	STEED, STUD
mare (Scot.)	YAUD
miniature	FALABELLA
mixed colour	ROAN
moderate racehorse	PLATER
Mohammed's flying horse	BORAK
mythological	
—horse	PEGASUS, UNICORN
—horse/man	(HIPPO)CENTAUR
Napoleon's horse	MARENGO
Odin's horse	SLEIPNIR
pacer	HOBBY
pack-horse	BATHORSE
pony	GRIFEN, GRIFFON
	GRIPE, GRYPHON
poor specimen	CROCK, HACK, JADE, PLUG
	NAG, RIP, ROSINANTE
	ROZINANTE, SCREW
racehorse	CHASER, PLATER
reddish-brown colour	SORREL
reliable horse	STAYER
riding-horse	NAG, HACK(NEY)
	ROUNCY
Rinaldo's horse	BAYARD
roan horse	SCHIMMEL
saddle horse	PALFREY
Scottish	CUDDIE, CUDDY
	GALLOWAY, SHELTIE
	SHETLAND
—mare	YAUD
—old	AVER, YAUD
—spirit horse	KELPIE
—stallion	STAIG
shaft-horse	FILLHORSE, THILLHORSE
short-legged breed	COB
slang name	PRAD
small horse	NAG, CANUCK, KANUCK
	GARRAN, GARRON, HOBBY
	PONY, SHETLAND

—Spanish	JENNET, GEN(N)ET
Spanish	ANDALUCIAN
	ANDALUSIAN
spirit horse (Scot.)	KELPIE
spirited horse	STEED
sprinter (US)	QUARTER-HORSE
stallion	ENTIRE, STAG
	STONE-HORSE
—Scottish	STAIG
—x she-ass	HINNY
Stevenson's donkey	MODESTINE
Suffolk	PUNCH
swift horse	BARB, CHARGER, COURSER
Swift horse	HOUYHNHNM
tan with white mane	PALOMINO
thoroughbred	BLOODSTOCK
trained horse	EVENTER
warhorse	DESTRIER
Wellington's horse	COPENHAGEN
white and	
—black	PIEBALD
—another colour	SKEWBALD
wild	
—ass	DZIGGETAI, HEMIONE, HULAN
	KIANG, K(O)ULAN, KYANG
	ONAGER
—horse	BRONC(H)O
	PRZEWALSKI'S HORSE, TARPAN
—ponies	DARTMOOR, NEW FOREST
	WELSH
workhorse	CARTHORSE, DOBBIN
	DRAYHORSE, MALT-HORSE
	PERCHERON, SHIRE(HORSE)
—Shakespeare	CUT
young	
—horse	FOAL
—mare	FILLY
—stallion	COLT
horse²	
including: tackle	
terms	
art of horsemanship	EQUITATION, MENAGE
attendant	GROOM, (H)OSTLER
	STABLEMAN
bitless bridle	HACKAMORE
bits	BRIDOON, DOUBLE-BRIDLE
	DOCTOR BRISTOL
	DOUBLE-JOINTED SNAFFLE
	EGGBUTT SNAFFLE
	FULMER SNAFFLE
	KIMBLEWICK, PELHAM
	SCRATCH, SNAFFLE
brush	COMB, CURRY, DANDY BRUSH
canine tooth	TUSH
caper	TITTUP
change of pace	TRANSITION

classical style of riding	HAUTE ECOLE
conveyance	HORSE-BOX
dealer	COPER
enclosure	CORRAL, LIVERY
	LOOSE-BOX, PADDOCK
	STABLE
exercises	RENVERS, TRAVERS
goad on heel of boot	SPUR
go lame	FOUNDER
harness	CAPARISON, TACK
	TRAPPINGS
—maker	
leather	SADDLER
metal	LORIMER, LORINER
spurs	SPURRIER
—parts	BARNACLE, BELLY BAND
	BLINDER, BLINKER
	BREECHING(LUG), BREECHING SEAT
	BRIDLE, BROW BAND, CHEEK BAND
	CHEEK PIECE, CINCH, COLLAR
	CROWN PIECE, CRUPPER, DRAGHOOK
	FRONT BAND, GIRTH-CINCH, HALTER
	HAME, HAME HASP, HAME TUG
	HIP STRAP, LOIN STRAP, MARTINGALE
	MUSROL, NOSEBAND, NOSE PIECE
	POMMEL, REIN, SADDLE
	SADDLE GIRTH, SADDLE PAD
	SHAFT TUG, SURCINGLE, TERRET
	THROAT STRAP, TRACE, WINKER
holding-rope	HACKAMORE, HALTER
horsemanship of the	
highest standard	HAUTE ECOLE
horse's actions and paces	MANEGE
horse-shoe	PANTON
horse show	GYMKHANA
jerking of rein	EBRILLADE
jumping competition	SHOW-JUMPING
—with very high jumps	PUISSANCE
long training rein	LUNGING REIN
measure of height (4")	HAND
meeting for equestrian	
sports	GYMKHANA
movements	
—in dressage	(see **show jumping**)
—responding to rider's	
indications	DRESSAGE
noseband	CAVESSON, GRACKLE
obstacle with hedge	
and rail	OXER
paces	CANTER, GALLOP, FOXTROT
	TROT, WALK
pad under saddle	NUMNAH, PANEL
parts	
—back	COUPLING
—foot	COFFIN, FROG, HOOF
—head	FORELOCK, FORETOP, POLL

—leg	CANNON, CASTOR, CHESTNUT
	FETLOCK, GAMBREL, GASKIN
	HOCK, PASTERN, STIFLE
—mane	ENCOLURE
—rear	CROUP(E), CROUPON
	CRUPPER, RUMP
—shoulders	WITHERS
performer on horseback	EQUESTRIAN
	EQUESTRIENNE
prance	TITTUP
racing	(*see separate entry*)
rail for training	CAVALETTO
rider	CAVALIER, EQUESTRIAN
	JOCKEY, POSTIL(L)ION
riding	
—for pleasure	HACKING
—school	MANEGE
saddle	
—blanket	PANEL
—cloth (military)	SHABRACK
shoer of horses	BLACKSMITH, FARRIER
show jumping	(*see separate entry*)
shy or refuse at a jump	BAULK, JIB
slaughterer	KNACKER
spur with one spike	PRICK-SPUR
stirrup-guard	TAPADERA
stud	HARAS, HARRAS(E)
training	
—of horses and riders	MANEGE
—in deportment	DRESSAGE
urine	STALE
wheel on spur	ROWEL
wound with spur	SPUR-GALL
horse diseases	
African	HORSE SICKNESS, NAGANA
Asian	SURRA
atrophy of shoulder muscles	SWEENY
blindness	GLASS-EYE
broken wind	HEAVES
contagious disease	DOURINE, STRANGLES
crack in hoof	SAND-CRACK
distemper	FIVES
eye diseases	MOON-EYE, PINK-EYE
farcy	GLANDERS
fever (Scot.)	WEED, WEID
foot disease	FRUSH, SEEDY-TOE
	WIRE-HEEL
glanders	FARCY
growth on leg	OSSELET, RAT(S)-TAIL
indigestion	GRASS-STAGGERS
	STOMACH-STAGGERS
inflammation of	
—bones	LAMINITIS
—brain	MAD STAGGERS
	SLEEPY STAGGERS
—frog	THRUSH

—hoof	FOUNDER, LAMINITIS
—scaphoid bone	NAVICULAR DISEASE
jaundice	YELLOWS
lameness	SPRING-HALT
leg tumour	GRAPE
lump in skin	SITFAST
lumpy jaw	ACTINOMYCOSIS
parasitic infection	DOURINE, NAGANA
respiratory	SCALMA
skin	
—disease of	
hock	SALLENDERS
pastern	SCRATCHES
—eruption	MAL(L)ANDER, MALLENDER
sore hoof	QUITTER, QUITTOR
spread by tsetse fly	NAGANA
study of horse diseases	HIPPIATRICS
swelling	GALL
—in mouth	LAMPAS(SE)
—on	
hock	BONE-SPAVIN
leg	CURB, GOURDINESS
pastern	CRATCHES
swollen	
—glands	VIVES
—hoof	QUITTER, QUITTOR
	TWITTER(BONE)
—vein on hock	BLOOD-SPAVIN
	BOG-SPAVIN
various diseases	STAGGERS
wart	ANBURY
wound in hind ankle	CREPANCE
horse racing	
be placed third or fourth	SHOW
bet	
—11 bets on four horses	YANKEE
—by bookmaker to divert	
attention from favourite	BLIND BET
—cumulative	ACCUMULATOR
	PARLAY
—first and second	EXACTA, FORECAST
	PERFECTA
—on	
win or place	EACH WAY
winners of two races	DOUBLE
—placed up to day	
before race	ANTEPOST BET
betting system in which	
all bets are pooled	PARI-MUTUEL
	TOTALISATOR, TOTE
bookmaker's system	
of hand-signals	TICKTACK
certain winner	CERT, NAP
Classics	DERBY, GRAND NATIONAL
	OAKS, THOUSAND GUINEAS
	TWO THOUSAND GUINEAS

cross-country race	POINT-TO-POINT
famous	
—fences	BECHER'S BROOK
	FOINAVON
	VALENTINE'S BROOK
—horses	
American	EASY GOER, SUNDAY SILENCE
British	ARKLE, BAHRAM
	DANCING BRAVE, DESERT ORCHID
	ECLIPSE, FREEBOOTER
	GOLDEN MILLER, HYPERION
	MARCH TOR, MILL REEF, NASHWAN
	NIJINSKY, NORTHERN DANCER
	OLD VIC, PHAR LAP
	RED RUM, REYNOLDSTOWN
	ROIMOND, SIR KEN, WINDSOR LAD
French	L'ESCARGOT, MA BICHE
	MIESQUE, RAVINELLA
Irish	DAWN RUN, PERSIAN WAR
	SEA PIGEON, SHERGAR
finishing position	PLACE
group of horses belonging	
to one owner	STRING
holding back by jockey	PULLING
horse entered under the	
name of another	RINGER
jockey's cap and shirt	SILKS
jockeys	
—American	ASMUSSEN, CAUTHEN
	CORDERO, LONGDEN, PINCAY
	SANTOS, SHOEMAKER
	VELASQUEZ
(f)	KRONE
—British	ARCHER, BRABAZON, CARSON
	CHAMPION, COCHRANE, EDDERY
	FRANCIS, FRANCOME, GILBERT
	MARSHALL, PIGGOTT, RICHARDS
	ROBERTS, SAUNDERS, SCUDAMORE
	SMIRKE, SWINBURN, WINTER
—Irish	MOLONY
—Italian	DETTORI
—French	ST MARTIN
—Peruvian	JACINTO
—Russian	NASIBOV
—South African	ROBERTS
jumping race	HURDLES, STEEPLECHASE
likely winner	FAVOURITE
odds offered	
—at start of race	SP, STARTING PRICE
—on	
likely winner	SHORT ODDS
unlikely winner	LONG ODDS
not subject to Jockey	
Club or National	
Hunt rules	FLAPPING
parade area	PADDOCK

place of bets to reduce	
possible losses	HEDGE, LAY OFF
race	
—for two-year olds	NURSERY STAKES
—in which	
extra weight is carried	
by some horses	HANDICAP
whole prize is awarded	
to the winner	SWEEPSTAKE
winner must be put	
up for sale	SELLING PLATE
	SELLING RACE
—with one starter	WALKOVER
races	
—America	ARLINGTON MILLION
	BELMONT STAKES
	BREEDER'S CUP MILE
	FLORIDA OAKS
	KENTUCKY DERBY
	PREAKNESS STAKES
—Australia	DALGETY CUP
	MACKINNON STAKES
	MELBOURNE CUP
	VICTORIA CUP
—England	CAMBRIDGESHIRE
	CESAREWITCH
	CHAMPAGNE STAKES
	CHAMPION STAKES
	CHELTENHAM GOLD CUP
	CORONATION STAKES, DERBY
	ECLIPSE STAKES, GIMCRACK STAKES
	GOLDEN MILE, GRAND NATIONAL
	GRAND SEFTON, KING GEORGE VI CHASE
	NASSAU STAKES, NELL GWYN STAKES
	OAKS, , PRINCESS OF WALES STAKES
	ST JAMES PALACE STAKES
	ST LEGER, STANLEY CHASE
	TOTE GOLD CUP
	(TWO) THOUSAND GUINEAS
	WHITBREAD GOLD CUP
—France	FRENCH DERBY, FRENCH OAKS
	FRENCH ST LEGER
	FRENCH (TWO) THOUSAND GUINEAS
	PRIX DE JACQUES LE MAROIS
	PRIX DE L'ARC DE TRIOMPHE
—Ireland	GALWAY HURDLE
	GALWAY PLATE, IRISH DERBY
	IRISH OAKS, IRISH GRAND NATIONAL
	IRISH ST LEGER
	IRISH (TWO) THOUSAND GUINEAS
	MILLION STAKES
—Italy	PALIO
—Japan	JAPAN CUP
—Scotland	AYR GOLD CUP
	SCOTTISH GRAND NATIONAL
racecourse official	STEWARD

racecourses
—America ARLINGTON, BELMONT PARK
CHURCHILL DOWNS
HOLLYWOOD PARK
TAMPA BAY DOWNS
—Australia (Sydney) WARDEN'S FARM
—Czechoslovakia VELKA PARDUBICKA
—England AINTREE, ASCOT, BATH
BEVERLEY, BRIGHTON, CARLISLE
CARTMEL, CATTERICK BRIDGE
CHELTENHAM, CHEPSTOW, CHESTER
DONCASTER, EPSOM, EXETER
FAKENHAM, FOLKESTONE
FONTWELL PARK
GOODWOOD, HAYDOCK, HEREFORD
HEXHAM, HOYLAKE, HUNTINGDON
KELSO, KEMPTON PARK, LEICESTER
LINGFIELD PARK, LIVERPOOL
LUDLOW, MARKET RASEN, NEWBURY
NEWCASTLE, NEWMARKET
NEWTON ABBOT, NOTTINGHAM
PLUMPTON, PONTEFRACT
REDCAR, RIPON, SALISBURY
SANDOWN PARK, SEDGEFIELD
SOUTHWELL, STRATFORD, TAUNTON
THIRSK, TOWCESTER, UTTOXETER
WARWICK, WETHERBY, WINCANTON
WINDSOR, WOLVERHAMPTON
WORCESTER, YARMOUTH, YORK
—France CHANTILLY, CLAREFONTAINE
DEAUVILLE, LA TOQUES
LONGCHAMPS
—Ireland FAIRYHOUSE
PHOENIX PARK, (THE) CURRAGH
—Japan TOKYO
—Scotland AYR, EDINBURGH
HAMILTON PARK, PERTH
—Wales BANGOR
racetrack HIPPODROME
ruling bodies JOCKEY CLUB
NATIONAL HUNT COMMITTEE
second, third or fourth PLACE
starting line GATE, STALLS
weight penalty HANDICAP, IMPOST
winning margin NOSE, LENGTH
(SHORT) HEAD

house
House of Keys HK
housemaid WENDY
housemaid's knee BURSITIS
Royal house ANJOU, BLOIS
BRUNSWICK-LUNEBERG, GOTHA
GREY, HANOVER, HABSBURG
LANCASTER, NORMANDY, ORANGE
PLANTAGENET, SAXE-COBURG
STUART, TUDOR, WINDSOR, YORK

hundred CENTURY, TON
100th anniversary CENTENARY
150th anniversary SESQUICENTENNIAL
hundred
—(number) C, CENTUM, CENTURY
P, R, RHO, TON
—(county division) CANTRED, CANTREF
CENTUM, CHILTERN
—and
one CI
four CIV
twenty GREAT HUNDRED
LONG HUNDRED
fifty CL, Y
sixty T
thousand LAC, LAKH, P, R, RHO
—pounds SEYMOUR
fifty thousand Y
sixty thousand T
hundredth CENTI-
Old Hundred PSALM
pounds
—sterling TON
—weight CENTAL
weight CWT
years CENTENARY
CENTENNIAL, CENTURY

Hungary H, HUNG
brigand HAIDUK, HEYDUCK
capital BUDAPEST
coin FILLER, FORINT
dance CSARDAS, CZARDAS
division BAN(N)AT, BANATE
dog VIZSLA
dynasty ARPAD
governor BAN
guerrilla HAIDUK, HEYDUCK
gypsy TZIGANE, TZIGANY
ZIGAN
Hungarian MAGYAR, TRANSLETHIAN
musical instrument CIMBALON, CIMBELON
pepper PAPRIKA
quick movement
of csardas FRIS(KA)
servant HAIDUK, HEWYDUCK
soldier PAND(O)UR
wine TOKAY

hybrid
American x Asian AMERASIAN
x Mexican CHICANO
American-Indian
x mulatto SAMBO
x Negro SAMBO
ass x mare MULE
canary x finch MULE
Caribbean CREOLE

cattle	
x bison	CAT(T)ALO
x zebu	CATEBU
cow	
x bison	BEEFALO
x yak	DHOMO, DSOBO, DSO(MO)
	(D)ZO, JOMO, Z(H)O
	ZHOMO, ZOBO, ZOBU
dog	MONGREL
	(*see also* **dogs**)
European	
x African	EURAFRICAN
x Asian	EURASIAN
x coloured	HALF-BREED
	HALF-CASTE
x half-caste	QUADROON
x Latin American	CRIOLLO
x mulatto	QUADROON
x Negro	MULATTO
x quadroon	MESTEE, METIF, MUSTEE
	OCTAROON, OCTOROON
x South American	
Indian	LADINO, MAMELUCO
French x American Negro	CREOLE
French-Canadian	CANUCK

x Indian	(BOIS-)BRULE
	METIS(SE)
fruit	(*see separate entry*)
half-caste	MESTINO, MESTIZO
—Negro redhead	BRIQUE
he-ass x mare	MULE
lion x tigress	LIGER
mixed race, southern USA	CREOLE
native but of mixed-blood	CREOLE
one with	
—eighth negro blood	OCTAROON
	OCTOROON
—quarter negro blood	QUADROON
partridge x quail	PERCOLIN
sheepxgoat	GEEP
South African	(CAPE) COLOURED
Spaniard x American	GREASER
x South American	
x Indian	MESTINO, MESTIZO
stallion x female ass	HINNY
x female zebra	ZEBRINNY
tiger x lioness	TIGON
wheat x rye	TRITICALE
zebra x female ass	ZEBRASS
x female horse	ZEBRULA, ZEBRULE
	(*see also* **monsters**)

I

Iceland	IS
bay	FLOI
beach	FJARA
cape (headland)	NES
capital	REYKJAVIK
cave	HELLIR
cliffs	HAMRAR
coin	AURA, EYRIR, KRONA
fiord	DJUP
glacier	JOKULL
hill	FELL, FJOLL, KULUR, NUPUR
island	DRANGAR, DRANGUR
lake	VATN
lava-field	HRAUN
lignite	SURTARBAND
	SURTURBAND
mountain	BUNGA, DYNGJA, FELL, FJOLL
	HAMAR, HOFOI, HRYGGUR
	HYRNA, KULUR
—range	FJALLGAROUR
peak	HORN, HYRNA
river	FLJOT
sandbank	EYRI
stream	FLJOT
valley	DALUR
waterfall	FOSS
India	BHARAT, IDN, IND
aconitine	BIKH
acrobat	NAT
adept	MAHATMA
adjutant stork	ARGALA
administrative	
—district	ZILA, ZILLAH
—service	IAS
affected speech	CHEE-CHEE
Afghan	PATHAN
agent	VAKEEL, VAKIL
agricultural society	SANTALS
allowance	BATTA
ancient	
—alphabet	BRAHMI
—language	SANSKRIT
—throne	PEACOCK-THRONE
antelope	ANTILOPE
	(*see also* **antelope**)
arboreal mammal	COLUGA
arched gateway	TORAN(A)
armed tribal force	LASHKAR
army officer	JAMADAR, JEMADAR
	JEMIDAR
arrangement	BANDOBAST, BUNDOBUST
ascetic	FAKEER, FAKIR
at once	EK DUM
attorney	VAKEEL, VAKIL
aubergine	BRINJAL
authority on law etc	PANDIT, PUNDIT
backgammon	PACHESI, PACHISI
bailiff	NAZIR
baking in clay oven	TANDOORI
balsam	GURJUN
Baluchi chief	TOMUNDAR
bamboo mat	TATTY
banana	PLANTAIN
bandicoot rat	PIG-RAT
bean	MUNG, URD
bear	BALOO, BALU
	HIMALAYAN BEAR
	SUN-BEAR
beast-fables	PANCHATANTRA
bedstead	CHARPOY
beggar	FAKEER, FAKIR
Bengal quince	BHEL
best quality	FIRST CHOP
betel	ARECA, PA(W)N, SIRI(H)
bird	AMADAVAT, AVADAVAT, BULBUL
	COUCAL, LARK-HEELED CUCKOO
	MINIVET, PRINIA, SHAMA
bitter gourd	KARELA
black	
—bear	SLOTH-BEAR
—mail	CHOUT
—soil	REGAR, REGUR
blessing (seeing or touching holy person)	DARSHAN
blouse	CHOLI
bo-tree	PEEPUL, PIPAL, PIPUL
board game	PACHISI
boat	BUDGERO(W), LANCHA
	PULWAR, PUTELI
book of aphorisms	SUTRA
bosun	SERANG
bottle	DUPPER
boycott	HARTAL, SWADESHI
braised meat	KORMA
brand	CHOP
brandy-and-water	BRANDY-PAWNEE
brass pot	LOTA(H)
bread	CHAPAT(T)I, CHAPATTY
	CHUPAT(T)I, NAN, PARATHA
	POP(P)ADOM, POP(P)ADUM
	PURI, ROTI
breakfast	(CHOTA-)HAZRI
bribe	DUSTOORY
British monarch	KAISAR-I-HIND

buffalo	ARNA, ARNEE, ARNI	—16 annas	R, RUPEE
	BUBALUS, WATER-BUFFALO	—100 new pice	R, RUPEE
bullock-cart	BANDY, HACKERY	—15 rupees	MOHUR
burial site (holy person)	DARGA	—100,000 rupees	LAC, LAKH
bum(m)alo	BOMBAY DUCK	—100 lac	CRORE
bustard	FLORICAN	—gold coin	PAGODA
butter	GHEE, GHI	—silver coin (Goa)	XERAFIN, XERAPHIN
—tree	MAHUA, MAHWA, MOW(R)A	collection of fables	HITOPADESA
calico	DUNGAREE	collectorate	TALUK
calling attention to		commander	SIRDAR
injustice etc	DHARNA	—of garrison	KILLADAR
camel	OONT	compliment	TASHRIF
camp		cooked	
—of soldiers	LASHKAR	—by steaming	DUM
—servant	BILDAR	—in	
cane sugar	GOOR, GUR	clay oven	TANDOORI
canopy	SHAMIANA(H)	curd etc	KHORMA
capital	DELHI	curry sauce	VINDALOO
captain	SUBA(H)DAR	copper pot	LOTA(H)
carpet fabric	D(H)URRIE	corporal	NAIK
carriage	BANDY, BUGGY	corruption	KHUTPUT
cart	G(H)ARRI, G(H)ARRY, TONGA	costus-root	PACHAK, PUTCHOCK
cattle food	BHOOSA		PUTCHUK
cavalry commander	RESSALDAR, RISALDAR	cotton cloth	BEZAN, SHALLI, SURAT
central shrine	VIMANA	coucal	SWAMP-PHEASANT
champagne	SIM(P)KIN	court	DURBAR
charging before		courthouse	CUTCHER(R)Y
magistrate	CHAL(L)AN		KACHAHRI, KACHERI
cheese	PANEER	crab's-eye plant	INDIAN LIQUORICE
chickpea flour	BESSAN	crane	SARUS
chief	SUDDER	cremation site	GHA(U)T
—minister of Mahrattas	PESWA	—of holy person	DARGA
	PEISHWA(H)	crocodile	MAGAR, MUGGER, NUGGAR
chintz	KALAMKARI		G(H)ARIAL, GAVIAL
cigarette	BEEDI	crop	KHARIF
civet	LINSANG, MONGOOSE	crown	RAJ
civil disobedience	SATYAGRAHA	cuckoo	BRAIN-FEVER BIRD, KOEL
Civil Service	CIS	cupboard	ALMIRA(H)
claret	LOLL-SHRAUB, LOLL-SHRUB	curry	
clay oven	TANDOOR	—dry	BHUNA
clerk	BABOO, BABU	—hot	MADRAS, VINDALOO
	CIRCAR, SIRCAR, SIRKAR	—lamb	ROGAN JOSH, ROGHAN GOSHT
cloak	CHUDDAH, CHUDDAR	—mild	DOPIAZI, DUPIAZI
cloth	KHADDAR, KHADI, SATARA	—rice and lentil	BIR(I)YANI
—of gold	SONERI	—with coconut milk	MOLEE
coarse		curtain to conceal women	PURDAH
—calico	DUNGAREE	cushion	GADI
—sugar	JAGGERY	cutlet	TIKKA
coat	ACHKAN	cymbals	DIN-DIN
coconut oilcake	POONAC	dagger	KUTTAR
coins		dal	PIGEON-PEA
—¹/₁₀₀ rupee	(NAYA)PAISA	dam	BAND(H), BUND
—¹/₄₀ rupee	DA(W)M	dance	KATHAK, NACH, NA(U)TCH
—¹/₁₂ anna	PIE	—drama	KATH(A)KALI
—3 pie	PICE	dancing	
—4 pice	ANNA	—girl	NA(U)TCH(-GIRL)

—hand movements	MUDRA
—performance	NACH, NA(U)TCH
development of vowel	SVARABHAKTI
dhak tree	PALAS
diamond mine	GOLCONDA
diet supplement	AMRIT KALASH
district	CIRCAR, SIRCAR, SIRKAR
division	TAHSIL
door-screen	CHI(C)K
dress	BANIAN, BANYAN, SAREE, SARI
dried	
—fish	BOMBAY DUCK
—mud	CUTCHA, KACH(CH)A, KUTCHA
drink	ARRACK, SOMA
—after sunset	SUNDOWNER
drug	BHANG, BENJ, CUBSHA
	GANJA, MAJOON, SOMA
drums	TABLA
dry curry	BHUNA
durra	GUINEA-CORN, JAWARI, JOWAR
dye tree	DHAK
dyeing process	KALAMKARI
dynasty	MOG(H)UL, MUGHAL
edible plant	SWORD-BEAN
elephant	
—driver	MAHOUT
—enclosure	KEDDAH, KHEDDA
—goad	ANKUS
embankment	BAND(H), BUND
embroidered fabric	KINGCOB
emperor	GREAT MOGUL, NAWAB
Englishman	QUI-HI, QUI-HYE
entertainment	TAMASHA
epic tale	MAHABHARATA
Eurasian	CHEE-CHEE
European	SAHIB, TOPI-WALLAH
—lady	MEMSAHIB, SAHIBA(H)
—(plural)	SAHIB-LOG
evil-doer	BADMASH, BUDMASH
exclamation of surprise	BOBBERY
extortion	CHOUT
eyeshadow	SURMA
factor	AMILDAR, AUMIL
factotum	CIRCAR, SIRCAR, SIRKAR
fan	PUNKA(H)
fasting on offender' doorstep	DHARMA
felt rug	NUMDAH
festival	POOJA(H), PUJA
fibre	CUSCUS, CUSKUS, DA, JUTE
	K(H)USK(H)US, MADRAS, OADAL
	SUNN (HEMP)
fiddle	SARANGI
fig	OPUNTIA
—tree	BANIAN, BANYAN, OPUNTIA
figured muslin	TANJIB, TANZIB
finance minister	DEWAN, DIWAN
—office of	DEWANI, DEWANNY
financier	BANIAN, BANYAN
fine flour	SOOJEE, S(O)UJEE
fish	BOMBAY DUCK, BUM(M)ALO
	DORAB, HILSAH, MAHSEER
	MAHSIR
flowers	BASTARD SAFFRON
	SAFFLOWER
fly-whisk	CHOWRY
foot-soldier	PEON
forced labourer	BEGAR
form for money payment	CHAL(L)AN
fort commander	KILLADAR
fortress	GURRY
fowl	CHITTAGONG
freebooter	PINDAR(EE), PINDARI
fried dough	PAPPADOM, POP(P)ADUM
fruit	BAEL(-FRUIT)
	BENGAL QUINCE
—tree	DURIAN, DURION
fuss	TAMASHA
game	PACHISI
gardener class	MALLEE, MALI
garland hung between	
two points	TORAN(A)
gentleman	PUKKA SAHIB
gift	NUZZER
ginger	CURCUMA, ZEDOARY
good	PAKKA, PUCKA, PUKKA
government	CIRCAR, SIRCAR, SIRKAR
governor	HAKEEM, HAKIM
	NAIK, SUBA(H)DAR
—of province	SUBA(H)DAR
grain harvest	RABI
grass	BAJREE, DUR(R)A, JHOW
	KANS, ROOSA, RAGA, RUSA
—mat	TATTY
groom	MEHTAR, S(A)ICE, SYCE
guide	DUBASH
guitar	SAROH
Gurkha knife	KUKRI
gypsy	BAZIGAR
handkerchief	BANDAN(N)A, ROMAL
	RUMAL
hat	TERAI, TOPEE, TOPI
head	
—cloth	ROMAL, RUMAL
—of state	RAJPRAMUKH
headdress	TAJ, TURBAN
heavy stick	LATHEE, LATHI
hemp	BHANG, DAGGA, KIF
—matting	TAT
—resin	CHARAS, CHURRUS
herb	PIA, REA, SESAME, SOLA
hermitage	ASHRAM(A)
high-collared coat	SHERWANI

Himalayan		—or dialect	PRAKRIT
—animal	PANDA, YETI	law officer	NAIB
—cedar	DEODAR	lawyer	MOOKTAR, MUKTAR
—pheasant	MONA(U)L	learned man	PANDIT, PUNDIT
Hindu	BABOO, BABU, GENTOO	lease	POTTAH
hired	TICCA	leggings	PUTTEE, PUTTIE
holder of a taluk	TALUKDAR	lentil	ARRAH, D(H)AL
holy leader	MAHATMA	—flour	BESAN
home rule	SWARAJ(I)	letter	DA(W)K
honey-badger	RATEL	light	
honorary title	NAWAB	—breakfast	CHOTA-HAZRI
horse from Australia	WALER	—meal	TIFFIN
hour	GHURRY	—scarf	PAGRI, PUGG(A)REE, PUGGERY
house for travellers	DAK(-BUNGALOW)	limestone	KUNKAR, KUNKUR
household attendant	CHAPRASSI	liquorice	JEQUIRTY
	CHUPRASSY	liquorice-tree seeds	
hundred thousand	LAC, LAKH	(prayer-beads)	CRABS-EYES
hunter	SHIKAREE, SHIKARI		CRAB-STONES
hunting	SHIKAR		JEQUIRITY (BEANS)
ice-cream	KULFI	litter	DHOOLIE, DHOOLY, DOOLIE
illusion	MAYA	loin-cloth	LUNGI
infantry regiment	PULTAN, PULTO(O)N	loom	TANTY
	PULTUN	low caste	PARIAH
inlaid metal	KOFTGARI, KOFTWORK	lunch	TIFFIN
—worker	KOFTGAR	Kashmiri	PUNCHI
interpreter	DOBHASH, MOONSHEE	magic	MAYA
	MUNSHI	magistrate	COTWAL, KOTWAL
intrigue	KHUTPUT	magistrate's office	CUTCHERY
irregular			KACHAHRI, KACHERI
—cavalryman	SILLADAR	Mahratta ruler	PE(I)SHWA(H)
—soldier	SEBUNDEE, SEBUNDY	mail	DA(W)K
isolated pillar	LAT	—carrier	DAK-RUNNER
jacket	BANIAN, BANYAN	makeshift	CUTCHA, KACH(CH)A
jaggery palm	KITTUL	malarial fever	TAP
judge	HAKEEM, HAKIM	mallow	URENA
labourer	COOLIE, COOLY	manager	AMILDAR, AUMIL
ladies's fingers	BHINDI, OKRA	manual of statecraft	ARTHSHASTRA
lake	SAGAR(A)	margosa	NIM
land		measures	
—division	PARGANA, PERGUNNAH	—1"	UNGUL
—owner	ZAMINDAR	—1¾ miles	COSS, KOS(S)
—revenue	JAG(H)IR, JAGHIRE	—5 miles	YOJAN(A)
holder of	JAGHIRDAR	—½ acre	BEEGAH, BIGHA
—tenure	RAIYATWARI, RYOTWARI	—1 acre	CAWNY
language	ASSAMESE, BENGALI	—24 minutes	GHURRY
	CANARESE, DRAVIDIAN	—hour	GHURRY
	GUJARAT(H)I, GUJERAT(H)I	meat-ball	KHEEMA, KOFFA
	GURKHALI, HINDEE, HINDI	messenger	PEON
	HINDOOSTANEE, HINDUSTANI	metal ware	BIDRI
	KANARESE, KANNADA	Melia	NIM
	KAS(H)MIRI, KOLARIAN	military head	SIRDAR
	MALAYALAM, MARATHI, MUNDA	millet	BAJRA, BAJREE, BAJRI
	ORIYA, PALI, PANJABI, PUNJABI		DARI, D(O)URA, D(H)URRA
	PUNJA(U)BEE, SANSKRIT		RAGGEE, RAGGY, RAGI
	SINDHI, TAMIL, TELEGU, URDU	Miss	KUMARI
—group	INDIC	money of account	FANAM

Mongol	MOGUL	paradoxure	MUSANG, PALM-CAT
mongoose	URVU		PALM-CIVET, TODDY-CAT
Moslem	COSSA	parcel	DA(W)K
—shrine	DURGAH	pariah-dog	PI(E)-DOG, PYE-DOG
mountain pass	GHA(U)T	parliament	
mounted attendant	SOWAR	—Lower House	LOK SABHA
murder	THAGI, THUGGEE	—Upper House	RAJYA SABHA
	THUGGERY	parrot	ZATI
murderer	THUG	partridge	CHIK(H)OR, CHUKAR
musical			CHUKOR
—form	RAGA	pass	CHAL(L)AN
—instrument	CHIKARA, SARANGI, SAROD	passive resistance	SATYAGRAHA
	SERINGHI, SITAR, TABLA	paymaster	BUKSHEE, BUKSHI
	TAMBOURA, VINA	pea	D(H)AL, DHOLL
—rhythm	TALA	peasant	KISAN, RAIYAT, RYOT
musk		percussion instrument	TABLA
—rat	SONDELI	perennial grass	LEMON-GRASS
—shrew	SONDELI	pheasant	IMPEYAN
musket	GINGAL(L), JINGAL	pigeon-pea	D(H)AL, DHOLL
muslin	GURRAH, JAMDANI	pig-rat	BANDICOOT
	MAMMODIS	pilaw	BIRYANI
nationalist movement	SWADESHI	pith-helmet	TOPEE, TOPI
nafive tribe	GOND	plain	MAIDAN
needlewoman	DIRZEE	planned effort against	
ne'er-do-well	BUDZAT	corruption	VIGILANCE
nim tree	MELIA	plant	AMIL, CHAY(A), DAL
no good	NO CHOP		DHOOP, GOA BEAN
noisy row	BOBBERY		HAT-PLANT, JUTE, MUDAR
non-violent campaign	SATYAGRAHA		RAMIE, SHAYA, SOLA
noodle	PHALUDA		SPONGEWOOD, SPIKENARD
nose flute	POOGYE		TELEGRAPH-PLANT
nursemaid	AMAH, AYAH	—extract (tannin)	CATECHU, CUTCH
nut	ILLIPE, ILLUPI	pleader	VAKEEL, VAKIL
office		pods (tanning)	BABLAH, BABUL
—boy	CHOKRA	poet	RISHI
—messenger	CHAPRASSI, CHUPRASSY	policeman	PEON, SEPOY, SIPAHI
official residence	STATION	police	
okra	BHINDI	—officer	JAMADAR, JEMADAR
	LADIES' FINGERS		JEMIDAR, TANNADAR
one-horse carriage	EKKA		T(H)ANADAR
open space	MAIDAN	—station	TANA, TANNA(H)
orchid	FAHAM		THANA(H), THANNA(H)
orderly	CHAPRASSI, CHUPRASSY	political prisoner	DETENU
ornamental		pond	TANK
metalwork	BENARES WARE	pony	TAT(TOO)
ox	BHYLE, BRAHMIN-BULL, GAUR	—Himalayan	GOONT
	G(A)YAL, MITHAN	poor quality	NO CHOP
	S(E)LADANG, ZEBU	prayer beads	INDIAN LIQUORICE
—cart	HACKERY	prince	NIZAM, (MAHA)RAJA(H)
pagan	GENTOO	princess	BEGUM, (MAHA)RANEE
palanquin	DHOOLIE, DHOOLY, DOOLIE		(MAHA)RANI
	PALKEE, PALKI	prison	CHOKEY
palm-cat	MUSANG, PALM-CIVET	product made in India	SWADESHI
	PARADOXURE, TODDY-CAT	province	CIRCAR, SIRCAR
panther	BAGHEERA		SIRKAR, SUBAH
parade ground	MAIDAN	provinces	MOFUSSIL

pulses	D(H)AL, DHOLL	savoury snack in batter	PAKORA
quince	BHEL	scarf	PAGRI, PUGG(A)REE
races	BHIL, CANARESE, GOORKHA		PUGGERY
	GURKHA, HINDOO, HINDU, KANARESE	scholar	INDIANIST
	LEPCHA, MAHRATTA, MARATHA	seal (impression)	CHOP
	MUNDA, PUNJABI, TELUGU, SIKH	seclusion of women	PURDAH
raft	ZAK	secretary	MOONSHEE, MUNSHI
Rajput chief	RANA	sect	JAIN(A), GHEBER, GHEBRE
representative	VAKEEL, VAKIL		GUEBER, GUEBRE, ORIYA
rat	BANDICOOT		PARSEE, PARSI, SIKH
ratel	HONEY-BADGER	sedan-chair	JAMPAN
ravine	KHUD, NAL(L)A	—bearer	JAMPANEE, JAMPANI
	NALLAH, NULLA(H)	self-government	SWARAJ(I)
rebel sepoy	PANDT	sergeant	HAVILDAR
reception	DURBAR	servant	MEHTAR, FERASH
red dye	CHAY(A)-ROOT	—of rajah	CHOBDAR
religious hostel	DHARMS(H)ALA	sesame (oil)	GINGELLY, GINGILI
reservoir	TANK		JINJILI, TEEL (OIL), TIL (OIL)
resin	DHOONA	settlement	BANDOBAST, BUNDOBUST
respect	TASHRIF		BUSTEE
revenue		shawl	CHUDDAH, CHUDDAR
—division	TAHSIL		ROMAL, RUMAL
—officer	TAHSILDAR	ship	PATAMAR
reverential observance		shirt	K(H)URTA
of festival	POOJA(H), PUJA	shooting platform	MACHAN
revolution	INQILAB	shot (plant)	CANNA
rhythmic pattern	TALA	show	TAMASHA
ribbed woollen cloth	SATARA	shrine	VIMANA
rice		side dish	SAMBUL, SUMBOL
—and lentil curry	BIR(I)YANI	silk	CABECA, CABESSE, SURAH
—dish	PILAFF, PIL(L)AU	—fabric	KINGCOB, TASH
	PILAW, PILOW, PULAO	small	
—water	CONGEE, CONJEE	—brass or copper pot	LOTA(H)
rich		—piece of meat	
—European	NABOB	for cooking	TIKKA
—soil	REGAR, REGUR	solar hat	TOPEE, TOPI
river	GANGES	soldier	JAWAN, PEON, SEPOY
robber	DACOIT, DAKOIT		SIKH, SIPAHI
robbery	DACOITAGE	sovereignty	RAJ
	DACOITY, DAKOITI	spinach	SAG
robe of honour	KELLAUT, KHALAT	spinning wheel	CHARKHA
	KHILAT, KILLUT	spirit of place	BONGA
rosewood	BITI	spiritual	
ruler of		—father	BAPU
—Baroda	GAEKWAR, GAIKWAR	—teacher	GOOROO, GURU
	GUICOWAR	spoken language	BAT
—Hyderabad	NIZAM	spotted wild-cat	LEOPARD-CAT
sabre	TULWAR	staff officers	OMLAH
sacking	GUNNY	starling	MINA, MYNA(H)
sacred		state	PRADESH
—book	PURANA	states	ANDHRA PRADESH, BIHAR
—lotus	PADMA		GUJARAT, HARYANA, HIMCHA
saddlecloth	NUMNAH		JAMMU, KARNATAKA, KASHMIR
sailor	CLASHEE, LASCAR		KERALIA, MADHYA PRADESH
salt efflorescence	REH		MAHARASHTRA, NORTHERN AREAS
sash	LUNGI		ORISSA, PUNJAB, RAJASTHAN

	TAMIL NADU, UTTAR PRADESH
	WEST BENGAL
steel	WOOTZ
steep in oil	TARKKA
stew	CURRY, CURRIE, DHANSAK
stoppage	BAND(H), BUND, HARTAL
stork	ADJUTANT, ARGALA
strangler	THUG
sub-division	
—of district	TALUK
—officer	TALUKDAR
sugar	RAAB
sun-blind	CHI(C)K
supreme court	SUDDER
surf-boat	MASOOLAH, MASSOOLA
	MASULA
sweet dish	BARFI, GULAB JAM
	JALEBIS, JELLABIES
table servant	K(H)IDMUTGAR
	K(H)ITMUTGAR
tailor	DARZI
tamarind	ABLI
tannin extract	CATECHU
tax collector	AMILDAR, AUMIL
	ZAMINDAR, ZEMINDAR
Telugu-speaker	GENTOO
temple gate	VIMANA
—tower	GOPURA(M)
ten million	CRORE
tent	SHAMIANA(H)
thicket	SHOLA
thin cotton fabric	SEERSUCKER
throne	GADI
timber	*(see separate entry)*
tip	BA(C)KSHEESH, BA(C)KSHISH
	BUCKSHISH, DUSTOORY
title of respect	BAHADUR, HUZOOR
	MIAN, SAHIB, S(H)RI
toll station	CHOKRY
tongue disease	AGROM
torch	MUSSAL
tract of land	TALUK
traditional theatre	TAMASHA
travelling	
—box for clothes	PETARA
—dealer (grain or salt)	BRINJARRY
tree	AMLI, AMPAC, BANYAN
	BASTARD TEAK, BHEL, BO, BUTEA
	CHAMPAC, CHAMPAK, CHAULMOOGRA
	CHAULMUGRA, COTTON-TREE
	DAR, DHAK, DITA, HYDNOCARPUS
	ILLIPE, ILLUPI, IVORY-TREE
	JAMBOOL, JAMBU(L)
	JAMBOLAN(A), JAROOL, JARUL, KHAIR,
	KOKRA, MARGOSA, MELIA
	MYROBALAN, NEEM, NIEPA, NIM

	PALAY, POON, SA(U)L, SIRIS, SISSOO
	TEAK, TIKUL, TOON
—snake	DENDROPHIS
trellis	TATTA, TATTIE
triangular pastry case	
filled and fried	SAMOSA
tribe	JAT, TAMIL, TELUGU
trooper	SOWAR
tunic	K(H)URTA
turban	LUNGI, PAGRI
	PUGG(A)REE, PUGGERY
two-wheeled vehicle	TONGA
umbrella	CHATTA(H)
usher	CHOBDAR
viceroy	NAWAB
village	BUSTEE
—chieftain	POLIGAR
—council	PANCHAYAT
washerman	DHOBI(E)
watchman	CHOKY, CHO(W)KIDAR
water	
—carrier	BHEESTIE, BHEESTY
	BHISTI(E)
—course	NULLA(H)
—lift	JANTU
—lily	LOTE, LOTOS, LOTUS, PADMA
—pot	CHATTY
waybill	CHAL(L)AN
weapon	PATA
weights	
—180 grains	TOLA
—2lbs	SEER
—3lbs	VISHAM
—25-80lbs	MAUND
—20 maunds	CANDIE, CANDY, KANDY
whisky and soda	STENGAH, STINGER
widow's suicide	SATI, SUTTEE
wild	
—cat	CHAUS, CIVET
—dog	DHOLE
—elephants	HATHI
wise man	GURU, MAHATMA
	PANDIT, RISHI
woman's	
—garment	SAREE, SARI
—quarters	ZENANA
wood for flutes	KOKRA
woollen rug	RABJIK
worship	POOJA(H), PUJA
young prince	UPPER ROGER
zinc alloy	TUTENAG
	(see also **Hindu, Sikh**)
Indonesia	RI
bay	TELUK
bread	ROTI
cape (headland)	TANJONG, UJUNG

capital	(D)JAKARTA
channel	SELAT
chicken	AJAM
coin	
—unit	SEN
—100 sen	RUPIAH
cooperation in work	ROJONG
curry	GULE
estuary	MUARA
fish	IKAN
—paste	BLACHAN, BLAKHAN
fried noodles	BAMI(E) GORENG
island	NUSA, PULAU
kebab	SATAY, SATE
lake	DANAO
lizard	KOMODO DRAGON
measure (1½m)	PAAL
meat	DAGING
mixed cooked vegetables	GADO-GADO
mountain	GUNUNG
—range	PEGUNUNGAN
omelette	DADAR
ox	ANOA, SAPI-(O)UTAN
rice	NASI
—dishes	RIJSTAF(F)EL
river	KALI, SUNGAI
sea	LAUT
strait	SELAT
stream	AIR, CI
village	KAMPUNG
witchdoctor	PAWANG
wood	SAPUR
insects[1]	HEXAPODA, INSECTA
including: mites	
spiders	
types	
ambrosia beetle	SCOLYTUS
ant	EMMET, PISMIRE
ants	FORMICIDAE
—male	ANER
—male/worker	ERGATANDROMORPH
—undeveloped female	ERGATE(S)
—wingless	ERGATOMORPH
female	ERGATOGYNE
male	ERGATANER
—worker	ERGATE(S)
aphis	GREENFLY, PLANT-LOUSE
	SMOTHER-FLY
apple pest	APPLE SAWFLY
	CODLIN(G)-MOTH
	RED SPIDER MITE
	ROSY APPLE APHID
	TORTRIX MOTH, WINTER MOTH
arachnids	SOLIFUGAE
Arctiidae	TIGER-MOTHS
Athalia	SAWFLY

bark-beetles	SCOLYTUS
bedbug	CIMEX, CINCH
bee-moth	WAX-MOTH
bees	
—bumble	BOMBIDAE
—hive	APIDAE
—homeless	NOMADIDAE
—humble	BOMBIDAE
—leafcutter	MEGACHILIDAE
—mining	ADRENIDAE
—potterflower	ANTHROPHORIDAE
beetle	BUPRESTIS, CHAFER
	CLAVICORNIA, WEEVIL
—with long antennae	LONGICORN
beetle	
—ambrosia beetle	SCOLYTUS
—rose beetle	CETONIA, ROSE CHAFER
—rove beetle	DEVIL'S COACH-HORSE
—sacred (Egyptian)	SCARAB
beetles	COLEOPTERA
	LAMELLIFORMES
—sub-orders	
carnivorous	ADEPHAGA
omnivorous	POLYPHAGA
—families	
bark beetles	SCOLYTIDAE
blister beetles	MELOIDAE
burying beetles	SILPHIDAE
cardinal beetles	PYROCHROIDAE
carrion beetles	SILPHIDAE
chafers	SCARABAEIDAE
click beetles	ELATERIDAE
dung beetles	SCARABAEIDAE
glow-worms	CANTHARIDAE
ladybirds	COCCINELLIDAE
leaf beetles	CHRYSOMELIDAE
longhorn beetles	CERAMBYCIDAE
nocturnal beetles	TENEBRIONIDAE
oil beetles	MELOIDAE
rove beetles	STAPHYLINIDAE
soldier beetles	CANTHARIDAE
stag beetles	LUCANIDAE
water scavengers	HYDROPHILIDAE
weevils	CURCULIONIDAE
bird	
—eating spider	AVICULARIA
—lice	MALLOPHAGA
biting	
—lice	MALLOPHAGA
—midge	SAND-FLY
black	
—aphis	DOLPHIN-FLY
—beetle	COCKROACH
—currant pest	BIG BUD MITE
blister-beetle	CANTHARID, SPANISH-FLY
blood-sucker	FLEA, LOUSE, TICK

blowfly	MEAT-FLY
Bombyx	SILKWORM
book	
—lice	CORRODENTIA, PSOCOPTERA
—scorpion	CHELIFER
boring flies	TRYPETA
bot-fly	BREESE, BREEZE, BRISE
	GAD-FLY, WARBLE-FLY
bristle-tail	THYSANURA
bumble-bee	HUMBLE-BEE
burnet-moth	ZYGAENA
burrowing	
—insect	DIGGER-WASP
	FEN-CRICKET, MOLE-CRICKET
	SAND-WASP
—mite	ITCH-MITE
burying-beetle	SEXTON(-BEETLE)
butterfly	(see separate entry)
cabbage pest	CABBAGE-APHID
	CABBAGE MOTH
	CABBAGE ROOT FLY
	TURNIP-FLEA
caddis-flies	TRICHOPTERA
caddis-fly	MAY-FLY, SEDGE-FLY
cantharid	BLISTER-BEETLE
	SPANISH-FLY
Carabidae	GROUND-BEETLES
carnivorous water-	
beetle	DYTI(S)CUS
carrot pest	CARROT FLY
caterpillar	CUT-WORM
cattle-fly	GAD-FLY, OX-WARBLE
centipede	THOUSAND-LEGS
centipedes	DIPLOPODA
—and millipedes	MYRIAPODA
cereal pest	HESSIAN FLY, WHEAT-FLY
	WHEAT-MIDGE, WHEAT-MOTH
Cetonia	ROSE-BEETLE, ROSE-CHAFER
cheese mite	TYROGLYPHID
cheese pest	CHEESE-HOPPER
	CHEESE-MITE
chigoe	JIGGER, SAND-FLEA
	SAND-HOPPER
cicada	TETTIX
Cicindelidae	TIGER-BEETLES
classification	
—class	INSECTA
—sub-classes	
wingless	AMETABOLA
	APTERYGOTA
winged forms	METABOLA
	PTERYGOTA
—divisions	
wings develop	
—externally	EXOPTERYGOTA
—internally	ENDOPTERYGOTA

—orders	
Apterygota	PROTURA
—bristletails	DIPLURA, THYSANURA
—springtails	COLLEMBOLA
Exopterygota	
—booklice	PSOCOPTERA
—bugs	HEMIPTERA
	RHYNCOTA
—cockroaches	ORTHOPTERA
—crickets	ORTHOPTERA
—demoiselle-flies	ODONATA
—dragonflies	ODONATA
—earwigs	DERMAPTERA
—grasshoppers	ORTHOPTERA
—lice	ANOPLURA
—mayflies	EPHEMEROPTERA
—stoneflies	PLECOPTERA
—thrips	THYSANOPTERA
Endopterygota	
—alderflies	NEUROPTERA
—ants	APOCRITA, HYMENOPETRA
—bees	HYMENOPTERA
—beetles	COLEOPTERA
—butterflies	LEPIDOPTERA
—caddis flies	TRICHOPTERA
—fleas	APHANIPTERA
	SIPHONAPTERA
—gall wasps	APOCRITA
	HYMENOPTERA
—horntails	HYMENOPTERA
	SYMPHYTA
—ichneumons	APOCRITA
	HYMENOPTERA
—lacewings	NEUROPTERA
—moths	LEPIDOPTERA
—sawflies	HYMENOPTERA
—scorpion-flies	MECOPTERA
—snakeflies	NEUROPTERA
—stylops	STREPSIPTERA
—termites	ISOPTERA
—thrips	THYSANOPTERA
—two-winged flies	DIPTERA
—wasps	APOCRITA
	HYMENOPTERA
—wood wasps	HYMENOPTERA
	SYMPHYTA
—white ants	ISOPTERA
click beetles	ELERATIDAE
clothes-moth	TINEA
Coccidae	WAX-BEETLES
cockchafer	BUZZARD-CLOCK
	MAY-BEETLE, MAY-BUG
coffee-tree pest	COFFEE-BUG
collector's name for	
some moths	MUSLIN, WAINSCOT
Collembola	SPRINGTAILS

crane-fly	(DADDY-)LONG-LEGS, TIPULA
—larva	LEATHER-JACKET
cricket	CICADA, CICALA
	GRASS-HOPPER, GRIG
cuckoo-fly	GOLD-WASP, RUBY-TAIL
Curculio	WEEVIL
cutworm-moth	DART-MOTH
daddy-long-legs	CRANE-FLY, TIPULA
death-watch beetle	ANOBIUM
destructive insect	LOCUST
devil's coach-horse	OCYPUS
	ROVE-BEETLE
dog-bee	DRONE
dor-beetle	DUNG-BEETLE
	SHARD-BEETLE
dragon-fly	DEMOISELLE, ODONATA
drone	DOG-BEE
Drosophila	FRUIT-FLY, POMACE-FLY
dung-beetle	COPROPHAGAN, SCARAB
earwig	FORFICULA
Egyptian scarab	SACRED BEETLE
Ephemera	DRAKE, MAY-FLY
flea	PULEX
fleas	SIPHONAPTERA
flesh-flies	SARCOPHAGA
flies	DIPTERA
—bat lice	NYCTERIBIDAE
—bee flies	BOMBYLIDAE
—bee lice	BRAULIDAE
—bluebottles	CALLIPHORIDAE
—blow-flies	CALLIPHORIDAE
—bot-flies	OESTRIDAE
—clegs	TABANIDAE
—crane-flies	TULIPIDAE
—Daddy-long-legs	TULIPIDAE
—forest flies	HIPPOBOSCIDAE
—fungus gnats	MYCETOPHILIDAE
—gad flies	TABANIDAE
—gall midges	CECIDOMYIDAE
—gnats	CULICIDAE
—green-bottles	CALLIPHORIDAE
—horse flies	ABANIDAE
—house flies	MUSCIDAE
—hover-flies	SYRPHIDAE
—midges	CHIRONOMIDAE
—mosquitoes	CULICIDAE
—parasitic flies	LARVAEVORIDAE
	TACHINIDAE
—robber flies	ASILIDAE
—sheep keds	HIPPOBOSCIDAE
—soldier flies	STRATIOMYIDAE
—stable flies	MUSCIDAE
—thick-headed flies	CONOPIDAE
—warble-flies	OESTRIDAE
flour mite	TYROGLYPHID
flying beetle	COCKCHAFER

forest	
—ant	WOOD-ANT
—fly	HORSEFLY
frog-hopper	FROTH-FLY
	FROTH-HOPPER
froth-fly	FROG-HOPPER
fruit pest	DROSOPHILA, POMACE-FLY
	RASPBERRY BEETLE
	RED SPIDER MITE
	VINEGAR-FLY
Fulgoridae	LANTERN-FLIES
gadfly	BREEZE, BREESE
	BRISE, TABANUS
gall	
—fly	RHODITES
—midge	CECIDOMYA
—wasp	CYNIPS
gallinipper	MOSQUITO
garden-spider	ARANEA, EPEIRA
Glossina	TSETSE
gnat	CULEX
gold-wasp	CUCKOO-FLY, RUBY-TAIL
golden-eye	LACE-WING
gooseberry moth	MAGPIE MOTH
gout fly	CORNFLY
grain pest	CORN-THRIP, CORN-WEEVIL
	CORN-WORM
grass-moth	VENEER-MOTH
grasshopper	CRICKET, CICADA
	CICALA, GRIG
greenfly	APHIS, PLANT-LOUSE
ground beetle	CARABUS
harvestmen	OPILIONES, PHALANGIDAE
hawk-moth	DEATH'S-HEAD MOTH, HAWK
	SPHINX
hive-bee	HONEY-BEE
hop pest	HOP-FLEA, HOP-FLY
horse-fly	FOREST-FLY
horse-pest	BOT-FLY, FOREST-FLY
	HORSE-FLY, WARBLE-FLY
hothouse pest	MEALY-BUG
house-fly	MUSCA
hunting-spider	LYCOSA
imagined to live in fire	PYRALIS
insect-eating fly	ROBBER-FLY
itch mites	SARCOPTES
Ixodidae	WOOD-TICKS
jigger	CHIGOE, SAND-FLEA
	SAND-HOPPER
jumping spiders	SALTIGRADE
ladybird	LADYBUG, LADYCOW
	LADYFLY, VEDDA
large	
—beetle	RHINOCEROS-BEETLE
—centipede	SCOLOPENDRA
—moths	SATURNIA, THRIPS

leaf pest	LEAF-HOPPER, RED SPIDER
leaf-insect	PHASMID, SPECTRE
	WALKING-LEAF
Lepisma	SILVER-FISH, SPRINGTAIL
library pest	BOOK SCORPION
like leaves	LEAF-INSECT
long-legged spider	HARVESTER
longicorn beetle	LONGHORN
lowest order	AMETABOLA
Lucilia	GREENBOTTLE
Lycosa	HUNTING-SPIDERS
	TARANTULA
	WOLF_SPIDER
Lymantriidae	TUSSOCK-MOTHS
magpie moth	GOOSEBERRY-MOTH
male	
—ant	ANER
—honey-bee	DRONE
may-flies	PLECTOPTERA
mayfly	GREEN-DRAKE, SEDGE-FLY
meal-worm	TENEBRIO
Mecoptera	SCORPION-FLY
Meloe	OIL-BEETLE
metallic-coloured	
—fly	BLUEBOTTLE
	GREENBOTTLE
—wasp	GOLD-WASP
midge	CHIRONOMID
millipede	PILL-WORM
	THOUSAND-LEGS
—millipedes	HILPODA
mite(s)	ACARID, ACARIDA(E)
	ACARUS(ACARI), (ACARINA)
	TYROGLYPHID
money-spider	MONEY-SPINNER
mosquito	AEDES, ANOPHELES
	STEGOMYIA
—America	GALLINIPPER
moth-like midge	SAND-FLY
moths	(*see separate entry*)
Ocypus	DEVIL'S COACH-HORSE
oil-beetle	MELOE
Oniscus	WOODLICE
owlet-moths	NOCTUID(AE)
parasitic insect	ICHNEUMON(-FLY)
	MALLOPHAGA
—on others	STREPSIPTERA
pear pest	CODLIN(G) MOTH
	PEAR SUCKER
	PEAR BEDSTRAW APHID
	TORTRIX MOTH
Perla	STONE-FLY
phalangid	HARVESTMAN
phasmid	LEAF-INSECT, STICK-INSECT
	SPECTRE
pill-bugs	ISOPODA

pine-beetle	PINE-CHAFER
plant pest	APHIS, CAPSID(-BUG)
	DOLPHIN-FLY, GALL-MIDGE
	GALL-WASP, GREENFLY
	LEAF-HOPPER
Podura	MYRIENTOMATA
potato pest	CLICK BEETLE
	COLORADO-BEETLE
	PEACH POTATO APHID
	WIREWORM
praying mantis	HOTTENTOT'S GOD
pubic louse	CRAB-LOUSE
Pulex	FLEA
puss-moth	SALLOW-KITTEN
rat pest	RAT-FLEA
red moth	CINNABAR
Rhaphidia	SNAKE-FLY
Rhopalocera	BUTTERFLIES
riverside insect	ALDER-FLY
rose	
—beetle	CETONIA, ROSE-CHAFER
—chafer	CETONIA, ROSE-BEETLE
—pest	RHODITES
rove-beetle	DEVIL'S COACH-HORSE
ruby	
—tail	CUCKOO-FLY, GOLD-WASP
—wasp	GOLD-WASP
sacred beetle	(EGYPTIAN) SCARAB
sand	
—flea	CHIGOE, JIGGER
	SAND-HOPPER, SAND-SKIPPER
—wasp	BEMBEX
sawfly	ATHALIA
scarab	DUNG-BEETLE
	SACRED BEETLE
Scolytus	AMBROSIA BEETLES
	BARK-BEETLES
scorpion	
—flies	MECOPTERA
—spider	WHIP-SCORPION
sea-spider	PYCNOGONID
sedge-fly	CADDIS FLY, MAYFLY
shard-beetle	DOR-BEETLE
sheep pest	SHEEP-LOUSE, SHEEP-KED
	SHEEP-TICK
short-lived insect	DRAGON-FLY
	EPHEMERA, MAY-FLY
silkworm	BOMBYX
silver-fish	LEPISMA, SPRINGTAIL
Sirex	WOOD-WASP
skipjack beetle	ELATER
skipper butterfly	HESPERID
small	
—fly	GNAT, SCIARID
—gnat	GNATLING
—gnat-like fly	MIDGE

—male ant	MICRANER
—puss-moth	KITTEN-MOTH
—spider	MONEY-SPIDER
smother-fly	APHIS
snake-fly	RAPHIDIA
snow-flea	SPRINGTAIL
soldier ant	WHITE ANT
Solifugae	ARACHNIDS
sow-bug	WOOD-LOUSE
Spanish-beetle	BLISTER-BEETLE
	CANTHARID
spectre	LEAF-INSECT, PHASMID
	STICK-INSECT
	WALKING-LEAF
	WALKING-STICK
	WALKING-STRAW
Sphinx	HAWK-MOTH
spider	ARACHNID, ARANEID
	EPEIRA
springtail	SILVER-FISH, SNOW-FLEA
—springtails	COLLEMBOLA, LEPISMA
	PODURA
stick-insect	LEAF-INSECT, PHASMID
	SPECTRE, WALKING-LEAF
	WALKING-STICK
	WALKING-STRAW
stinging insect	BEE, HORSE-FLY
	MOSQUITO, WASP
stone-fly	PERLA, PLECOPTERA
Stratiotes	WATER-SOLDIER
Strepsiptera	RHIPODOPTERA
	RHIPIPTERA
sugar pest	SUGAR-MITE
swallow-tailed	
butterfly	PAPILIO
Syrphus	HOVER-FLY
Tabanus	GAD-FLY
tarantula	HUNTING-SPIDER, LYCOSA
	WOLF-SPIDER
Tenebrio	MEAL-WORM
termite	WHITE ANT, WOOD-ANT
tettix	CICADA
Thrips	LEAF-HOPPER
Thysanura	BRISTLE-TAILS
tick	ACARID, ACARUS
	SHEEP-KED
tiger	
—beetles	CICINDELIDAE
—moths	ARCTIIDAE
tinea	CLOTHES-MOTH
Tipula	CRANE-FLY
	DADDY-LONG-LEGS
Tortrix	MOTH
tree pest	PINE-BEETLE, PINE-CHAFER
Tricoptera	CADDIS-FLIES
Troglyphid	CHEESE MITE, FLOUR MITE

Trombidium	HARVEST-BUG
	HARVEST-LOUSE
	HARVEST-MITE, HARVEST-TICK
Trypeta	BORING FLIES
tsetse flies	GLOSSINA
turnip pest	CUTWORM, TURNIP-FLEA
	TURNIP-FLY
tussock-moth	GYPSY MOTH, NUN
—tussock-moths	LYMANTRIIDAE
two-winged	DIPTERAN
Tyroglyphid	CHEESE MITE, FLOUR MITE
undergoing metamorphosis	METABOLA
various insects	SAW-FLY
vegetable pest	WHITE-FLY
veneer-moth	GRASS-MOTH
venomous spider	SOLPUGA
very small insect	MITE
Vespa	WASP
vine pest	GRAPE-LOUSE
	VINE-FRETTER
	PHYLLOXERA
vinegar-fly	FRUIT-FLY
warble fly	BOTFLY
wasp	SPHEX, VESPA
—digger	SPHECIDAE
—gall	CYNIPDAE
—ichneumon	BRACONIDAE
—mason	EUMENIDAE
—potter	EUMENIDAE
—solitary	EUMENIDAE
—spider	POMPILIDAE
wasps	VESPIDAE
wasp-like flies	SYRPHUS
water	
—beetle	GYRINUS, WHIRLIGIG
—boatman	NOTONECTA
—fleas	CLADOCERA
—insect	WATER-BEETLE
	WATER-BOATMAN
	WATER-BUG, WATER-FLEA
	WATER-FLY, WATER-STRIDER
—skaters	GYMNOCERATA
—soldier	STRATIOTES
wax	
—insects	COCCIDAE
—moth	BEE-MOTH
weevil	CURCULIO
wheat-pest	GOUTFLY
whip-scorpion	SCORPION-SPIDER
whirligig	GYRINUS, WATER-BEETLE
white	
—ant	SOLDIER, TERMITE
—moth	GHOST-MOTH
wingless	AMETABOLA, APTERYGOTA
—male ant	ERGATANER
—parasite	LOUSE

wolf-spider	LYCOSA, TARANTULA
wood	
—ant	TERMITE
—beetle	WOOD-ENGRAVER
—boring insect	DEATH-WATCH BEETLE
	FURNITURE BEETLE
	SIREX, WOOD-WASP
—eating insect	CARPENTER-BEE
—engraver	BEETLE
—lice	ONISCUS
—louse	MILLIPED(E)
	PILL-BUG, SOW-BUG
—ticks	IXODIDAE
—wasp	SIREX
worker ant	ERGATE(S)
yellow-fever fly	STEGOMYIA
Zygaena	BURNET-MOTH

insects[2]

including: terms	
air tube(s)	TRACHEA(E)
appendage on antenna	ARISTA
back-plate	TERGUM
—of rear section	PYGIDIUM
breathing hole(s)	SPIRACLE(S)
	STIGMA(TA)
edge of wing	COSTA
eyes	COMPOUND, SIMPLE
—simple eye(s)	OCELLUS (OCELLI)
feeler(s) on	
—head	ANTENNA(E)
—mouth	PALP, PALPUS (PALPI)
—rear	CERCUS (CERCI)
forewing(s)	TEGMEN (TEGMINA)
having larvae with biting	
jaws	METAGNATHOUS
insect-eater	INSECTIVORE
insecticides	CARBENDAZIM, DDT
	FENARIMOL, MALATHION
	PEMETHRIN
moult of larva	ECDYSIS
outer shell	EXOSKELETON
piercing instrument	STILET, STYLET
rear wings (rudimentary)	HALTERES
scale on wing	TEGULA
segment of	
—abdomen	VRITE
—body	ABDOMEN, HEAD, THORAX
—leg	COXA, TROCHANTER
—thorax	
front	PROTHORAX
middle	MESOTHORAX
rear	METATHORAX
sidewall of thorax	PLEURON
sound made by rubbing	STRIDULATION
stage	
—adult(s)	IMAGO (IMAGINES)

—between moults	INSTAR
—change	ECDYSIS
—early	CATERPILLAR, GENTLE
	GRUB, LARVA, MAGGOT
—immature adult	NYMPH
—passive	CHRYSALIS, PUPA
sucking proboscis	HAUSTELLUM
upper lip(s)	LABRUM(LABRA)
wax-producing tube	CORNICLE
	CORNICULUM
wingcase(s)	ELYTRUM(ELYTRA)

institute/institution

of:	
Actuaries	IA
Advanced Motorists	IAM
Bankers	IB
Building	IOB
Civil Engineers	ICE
Contemporary Artists	ICA
Journalists	IOJ
Linguists	IL
Mining and Metallurgy	IMM
Municipal Engineers	IMUNE
Physics	IP
Practitioners in Advertising	IPA

instrument	(*see* **instrument of torture,**
	measuring instrument,
	musical instrument)

instrument of torture

beating soles of feet	BASTINADE
	BASTINADO
body	
—crushing machine	
	SCAVENGER'S DAUGHTER
	SKEFFINGTON'S DAUGHTER
	SKEVINGTON'S DAUGHTER
—stretching machine	RACK
cucking-stool	TUMBREL, TUMBRIL
dropping from height tied	
to rope	STRAPPADO
finger-crushing instrument	PILLIWINKS
flogging	CAT-O'-NINE-TAILS
frame for	
—flogging	TRIANGLE
—head and hands	PILLORY
—head, hands and legs	STOCKS
iron	
—'coffin' with spikes	
internally	IRON MAIDEN
—ring round neck	JOUGS
pillory	TUMBREL, TUMBREL
—Scottish	JOUGS
stocks	CIPPUS
stool on which	
—scolds were tied	
and pelted	CUCKING-STOOL

—offenders were ducked in pond	DUCKING-STOOL
thumb-crushing instrument	THUMB-SCREW
torturing feet	SARPINES
yoke	DEVIL-ON-THE-NECK

international

bank	BIS
Development Association	IDA
Electrotechnical Commission	IEC
Finance Corporation	IFC
honour	CAP
Labour Organisation	ILO
Monetary Fund	IMF
Olympic Committee	IOC
organisation	UNO
Organisation for Standardisation	ISO
Phonetic Alphabet	IPA
Publishers' Association	IPA
Publishing Corporation	IPC
Rail Transport	TIF
Road Transport	TIR
Social Services	ISS
subscriber dialling	ISD
Telecommunications Union	ITU
Trade Organisation	ITO
unit	IU
Vehicle Registration	IVR

inventors

inventor of:

achromatic microscope	LISTER
actuarial tables	HALLEY
adding machine	PASCAL, SCHICKARD
aeroplane	WRIGHT
air-conditioning unit	CARRIER
airship	ZEPPELIN
—non-rigid	GIFFARD
alphabet for blind	BRAILLE
amplitude modulation	FESSENDEN
amusette	SAXE
anastigmatic lens	AIRY
antiseptic surgery	LISTER
artificial heart	JARVIK
artificial languages	
—Esperanto	ZAMENHOF
—Interglossa	HOGBEN
—Neo	ALFANDARI
—Novial	JESPERSON
—Volapük	SCHLEYER
bakelite	BAEKELAND
ball-point pen	BIRO, LOUD
bandore	ROSE
barbed wire	SMITH
barometer	TORRICELLI
bath glaze	BUICK
bathyscaphe	PICCARD

bathysphere	BEEBE
bicycle	MACMILLAN
—small-wheeled	MOULTON
bifocal lens	FRANKLIN
binary system	LIEBNITZ
blast furnace	BESSEMER
blind language	BRAILLE
bubble chamber	GLASER
bunsen burner	BUNSEN
burglar alarm	HOLMES
cable-suspended bridge	SEGUIN
calculating machine	LIEBNITZ
calculus	NEWTON
camera	
—folding	EASTMAN
—Leica	BERNAK
—pinhole	DELLA PORTA
—Polaroid	LAND
—roll-film	EASTMAN
—single-lens reflex	SUTTON
—twin-lens reflex	BECK
car	BENZ
carbon dating	LIBBY
carburettor	DAIMLER
carpet sweeper	BISSELL
cash register	RITTY, PARMALEE
cellophane	BRANDENBERGER
celluloid	HYATT, PARKES
cherista(k) (pelota)	CURUCHAGE
	DITHURBIDE
Christmas cracker	SMITH
chronometer	HARRISON
cinema	LUMIERE
Cinemascope	CHRETIEN
clinical thermometer	ALLBUTT
clock - pendulum	HUYGENS
Coca-Cola	PEMBERTON
collapsible boat	BERTHON
colour photography	LIPPMANN
compass	GIOIA
computer	ECKERT, MAUCHLY
	TURING
—language (Forth)	MOORE
computing machine	BABBAGE
concrete music	SCHAEFFER
cordite	ABEL, DEWAR
cotton gin	WHITNEY
cryostat	COLLINS
cybernetics	WIENER
cyclotron	LAWRENCE
dental plate (rubber)	GOODYEAR
dentures	PLANTSON
diesel engine	DIESEL
diffusion cloud chamber	LANGSDORF
diode valve	FLEMING
disc brakes	LANCHESTER

diving suit	SIEBE
double sleeve-valve engine	KNIGHT
dry photographic plates	EASTMAN
dynamite	NOBEL
dynamo	FARADAY, PIXII
electric	
—battery	TORRICELLI, VOLTA
—iron	SEELEY
—lamp	EDISON, SWAN
—motor	GRAMME, HENRY, TESLA
—razor	SCHICK
—telegraph	HENRY, MORSE
—welder	THOMSON
electrocardiograph	EINTHOVEN
electromagnet	STURGEON
electron microscope	KNOLL, RUSKA
electrophoresis	TISELIUS
electrostatic generator	VAN DE GRAAF
embossed letters for the blind	BRAILLE, MOON
Esperanto	ZAMENHOF
field ion microscope	MUELLER
film	
—moving	LE PRINCE
—musical	DE FOREST
—negative	FOX TALBOT
—talking	ENGL, MUSSOLLE, VOGT
folding bed	MURPHY
food processor	VERDUN
fountain pen	WATERMAN
four-stroke engine	OTTO
fuel cell	GROVE
Gaia hypothesis	LOVELOCK
galvanometer	AMPERE, SCHWEIGGER
game of life	CONWAY
gas lighting	MURDOCK
Glossic alphabet	ELLIS
governor	WATT
gramophone	EDISON
—disc	BERLINER
long-playing	GOLDMARK
guncotton	SCHONBEIN
gyroscope	FOUCAULT
gyroscopic compass	SPERRY
helicopter	OEHMICHEN
	SIKORSKY
hot-air balloon	MONTGOLFIER
hovercraft	COCKERELL
hydraulic lift	OTIS
iconoscope	ZWORYKIN
inflatable tyre	THOMSON
inoculation	PASTEUR
intelligence tests	BINET, SIMON
interferometer	MICHELSON
Interglossa	HOGBEN
internal combustion engine	LENOIR
invar	GUILLAUME

iris chart	JENSEN
italic type	MANUTIUS
jet engine	WHITTLE
katathermometer	HILL
laser	MAIMAN, TOWNES
—card	DREXLER
launderette	CANTRELL
lead/acid battery	PLANTE
Lego	CHRISTIANSEN
Leyden jar	VON KLEIST
lie detector	KEELER, LARSEN
lifeboat	GREATHEAD
	WOULDHAVE
light field gun	SAXE
lightning conductor	FRANKLIN
linoleum	WALTON
locomotive	TREVITHICK
logarithms	NAPIER
long-playing record	BACHMAN, GOLDMARK
loom	CARTWRIGHT
loudspeaker	SHORT
machine-gun	GATLING, PUCKLE
man-carrying glider	CAYLEY
map of magnetic	
declination	NORMAN
margarine	MEGE-MOURIES
mass	
—production	WHITNEY
—spectrograph	ASTON
matches	WALKER
method acting	STANISLAVSKI
microchip	KILBY, NOYCE
microphone	BELL
microscope	GALILEO, JANSSEN
	LEUUWENHOEK
miner's lamp	DAVY, STEPHENSON
minnonette (volleyball)	MORGAN
mobiles	CALDER
motion pictures	LE PRINCE
motor-cycle	DAIMLER
movable type	GUTENBERG
moving film equipment	EDISON
Neo	ALFANDARI
neon lamp	CLAUDE
nitro	
—cellulose	SCHONBEIN
—glycerine	SOBRERO
Novial	JESPERSON
nylon	CAROTHERS
open-hearth steel	SIEMENS
Oxford bags	ACTON
paper	CAI LUN, TS'AI LUN
—clip	VAALER
parachute	BLANCHARD, LENORMAND
parking meter	MAGEE
particle counter	GEIGER

pasteurisation	PASTEUR	self-starter	KETTERING
pendulum clock	HUYG(H)ENS	servo-mechanism	FARCOT
perforated card control		sewing-machine	THIMMONNIER
of machines	JACQUARD	silicon chip	KIRBY
period/luminosity curve		skyscraper	JENNY
for Cepheid variables	LEAVITT	slide rule	OUGHTRED
periodic table	MENDELEEV	smear test	PAPANICOLAOU
phonograph	EDISON	snooker	CHAMBERLAIN
photography		softball	HANCOCK
—calotype	FOX TAKBOT	sousaphone	SOUSA
—dry plate process	MADDOX	spark chamber	FUKUI, MIYAMOTO
—on		spectrohelioscope	HALE
film	CARBUTT	spectroscope	BUNSEN, KIRCHHOFF
metal	NIEPCE	sphygmo(mano)meter	RIVA-ROCCI
paper	FOX TALBOT	spinning	
—wet plate process	ARCHER	—frame	ARKWRIGHT
—with strobe lights	EDGERTON	—jenny	HARGREAVES
pig-iron boiling process	HALL	—mule	CROMPTON
pinhole camera	DELLA PORTA	staining bacteria	GRAM
plastic film	EASTMAN	stainless steel	BREARLEY
plastics	PARKS	standardisation of wine	GALL
pneumatic tyres	DUNLOP	steam	
Polaroid camera	LAND	—boat	FITCH
polygraph	KEELER, LARSEN	—car	CUGNOT
Portland cement	ASPDIN	—engine	SAVERY
pressure cooker	PAPIN	low-pressure	NEWCOMEN, WATT
printing		—hammer	NASMYTH
—machine (rotary)	HOE	—horseless carriage	MURDOCK
—press	GENSFLEISCH	—locomotive	STEPHENSON
	GUTENBERG	—ship	PERRIER
propellor (ship)	SMITH	—turbine	PARSONS
radar	TAYLOR, WATSON-WATT	steel process	BESSEMER
	YOUNG	stethoscope	LAENNAC
radio	MARCONI	strobe photography	EDGERTON
—astronomy	JANSKY	submarine	BUSHNELL
—telegraphy	LOOMIS	superheterodyne receiver	ARMSTRONG
transatlantic	MARCONI	tank	SWINTON
rayon	CHARDONNET, SWAN	tape recording	POULSEN
razor		telegraph	LAMMOND
—electric	SCHICK	—code	MORSE
—safety	GILLETTE	telephone	BELL, MEUCCI
refrigerator	HARRISON, TWINING	telescope	
revolver	COLT	—reflecting	GREGORY
rifling	BESSEMER	—refracting	LIPPERSHEIM
roller skating	MERLIN, PLIMPTON		LIPPERSHEY
rubber tyres	HANCOCK	television	
rubberised cloth	MACINTOSH	—electronic	FARNSWORTH
Rubik's cube	RUBIK	—mechanical	BAIRD
safety		television camera	ZWORYKIN
—lamp	DAVY, STEPHENSON	temporary bridge	BAILEY
—pin	HUNT	Terylene	DICKSON, WINFIELD
—razor	GILLETTE	test for diphtheria	SCHICK
sailboard	CHILVERS	thermometer	GALILEO
saxophone	SAX	thermostat	DREBBLE
Scotch tape	DREW	torsion balance	COULOMB, MICHELL
seismograph	PALMIERI	transformer	FARADAY

transistor	BARDEEN, BRATTEN
	SHOCKLEY
triode valve	DE FOREST
turbine	PARSONS
tutania	TUTIN
typewriter	TARRI
ultra-centrifuge	SVEDBERG
vaccination	JENNER
vacuum	
—cleaner	SPANGLER
—flask	DEWAR
Velcro	MESTRAL
viscose	CROSS
Volapük	SCHLEYER
volleyball	MORGAN
voltage multiplier	COCKCROFT, WALTON
vulcanising	GOODYEAR
watch	MANFREDI
water	
—closet	HARINGTON
—skiing	SAMUELSON
waterproof fabric	MACINTOSH
wax cylinder	TAINTER
wireless telegraphy	MARCONI
Xerography	CARSON
zip fastener	JUDSON
	(*see also* **discoveries, first**)
Iran	IR
	(*see also* **Persia**)
Iraq	IRQ
capital	BAGHDAD
coin	
—unit	FIL
—50 fils	DIRHAM
—4 dirhams	RIYAl
—5 riyals	DINAR
Ireland	EIRE, ERIN, EMERALD ISLE
	GREEN ISLE, IR, IR(E)L
accent	BROGUE
active person	STIR-ABOUT
again	AGIN
agrarian rebel	
—18th c	WHITEBOY
—19th c	MOONLIGHTER
alphabet	OG(H)AM
ancient	
—assembly(-blies)	FEIS(EANNA)
—people	TUATH
—soldier	FIANN
	GALLO(W)GLASS
—territorial division	TUATH
anti-British association	FENIAN
basket	SKEOUGH
black magic	PISHOGLE
blandish	SOOTHE
blood-fine	EIRIACH, ERIC

boat	CURRACH, CURRAGH
booth	BOTHAN
boy	GORSOON, GOSSOON
	SPALPEEN
bridge	FORD, WATERSPLASH
brownie	LEPRECHAUN, LEPRECHAWN
bustling person	STIR-ABOUT
cajoling talk	BLARNEY
capital	DUBLIN
carriage	BIANCONI, GINGLE
	JAUNTING-CAR, JAUNTY
Celtic noble	TAOISE(A)CH
chief's heir elect	TANIST
clan	SEPT
clay pipe	DUDEEN
clotted milk	BONNY-CLABBER
close-fitting breeches	TROUSE
club	SHILLALY
	SHILLELA(G)H
coins	
—counterfeit halfpenny	RAP
—old halfpenny	PATRICK
—pound	PUNT
compulsory billeting	COSHERY, SOREHON
corn	OATS
counterfeit coin	RAP
creature	CRATUR
cudgel	SHILLALY, SHILLELAGH
currant bun	BARMBRACK
dance	FADING, PLANXTY
	RINKAFADDA
Danish settlers	OSTMEN
darling	ACUSHLA, ASTHORE
	MAVOURNEEN
death omen	BANSHEE
deer (extinct)	IRISH ELK
deputy Prime Minister	TANAISTE
devotee	VOTEEN
dirge	CORONACH
dish	CHAMP, COLCANNON
district where the	
English had power	ENGLISH PALE
division of	
—county	BARONY
—tribe	SEPT
doctor	OLLAM(H), OLLAV
driver of carriage	JARVEY
drunk	STOTIOUS
Dublin Society	RDS
dynasty	O'NEILL
elf	LEPRECHAUN
	LEPRECHAWN
Elysium	TIR NAN-OG
emblem	SHAMROCK
evening of song and story	CEILIDH
expression of emotion	ARRAH

fairy	BANSHEE, BENSHI	judge	BREHON
favourite	WHITE-HEADED BOY	killed	KILT
female fairy	BANSHEE	labourer newly arrived	
festival	FEIS(EANNA)	in England	GRECIAN
field	PARK	lake	LOUGH
flatter	SOOTHE	—dwelling	CRANNOG
flattery	BLARNEY	land	
flowers	SHAMROCK	—of the young	TIR NAN-OG
fool	OMADHAUN	—reform association	LAND LEAGUE
foot soldier	KERN(E)	language	CELTIC, ERSE
fort	RATH		GAELIC, KELTIC
fortified island	CRANNOG	lament	ULLALOO
free accommodation		lane	BOREEN
of lord by tenant	SORREN	legislature	OIREACHTAS
Free State	IFS	limestone	CALP
funeral dirge	CORONACH	madman	OMADHAUN
Gael	GADHEL, GOIDEL	master	OLLAM(H), OLLAV
Gaelic	ERSE	measures	
game	HURLEY, HURLING, SHINTY	—2 feet	BANDLE
genealogist	SE(A)NNACHIE, SEANNACHY	—2240 feet	MILE
	SHANACHIE	—7840sq. yd (old)	ACRE
gentleman without money	STALKO	member of	
girl	COLLEEN	—Dail	TD, TEACHTA (DALA)
good		—peasant's	
—fellow	BROTH OF A BOY	association	WHITEBOY
—health!	SLAINTE	Methodist	SWADDLER
guard(s)	GARDA(I)	mischievous fellow	SPALPEEN
head		mocking ballad	LILLIBULLERO
—king	ARDRI(GH)	moderate party	FINE GAEL
—of family	CO(M)ARB	money-lender	GOMBEEN-MAN
heath	ST DABEOC'S HEATH	mud	CLABBER
hero	NAOISE	my	
hockey	HURLEY, HURLING	—child	ALANNAH
house	DAIL	—dear	MACHREE, MOCHREE
hut	BOTHAN	—love	MACHREE, MOCHREE
ill luck	BAD CESS	national emblem	SHAMROCK
illegal drinking-den	BOTHAN	never	SORRA
illicit		nickname	PAT, TEAGUE
—liquor-shop	SHEBEEN	no!	SORRA
—whiskey	POT(H)EEN	not	SORRA
indeed	AROO, ARU	oath	BEDAD, BEGORRA(H)
injure seriously	KILL		BEJABERS
interjection of		old	
—lament	O(C)HONE	—laws	BREHON LAWS
—surprise	MUSHA	—mayor	SOVRAN
invite a quarrel	TRAIL ONE'S COAT	—Protestants	PEEP-O'-DAY BOYS
Ireland forever	ERIN GO BRAGH	outlaw	WOODKERN
Irishman	BOG-TROTTER, GREEK	parliament	
	MICK(E)Y, PADDY, PAT	—lower house	DAIL (EIREANN)
Irish-speaking area	GAELTACHT	—upper house	SEANAD (EIREANN)
Jacobites who migrated		penniless gentleman	BUCKEEN
to the Continent	WILD-GEESE	people	TUATH
jaunting-car	INSIDE-CAR	pet	WHITE-HEADED BOY
	OUTSIDE-CAR	petty squire	SQUIREEN
—driver	JARVEY	plunderer	RAPPAREE
jocose	JOCOROUS	police	GARDA(I), RIC, RUC

—force	GARDA SIOCHANA
—man	GARDA
—men	GARDAI
political movement	SINN FEIN
politician	TD, TEACHTA (DALA)
pond dry in summer	TURLOUGH
poor Southerner	BUCKEEN
porridge	STIR-ABOUT
potato	MURPHY, PRATIE, PRATY
prehistoric fort	RATH
Prime Minister	TAOISEACH
Protestant	SWADDLER
rascal	SPALPEEN
rebel	CROPPY
region where Gaelic is spoken	GAELTACHT
Republican	
—Army	IRA
—Brotherhood	IRB
—Party	FIANNA FAIL
Republicans	SINN FEIN
river	LIFFEY, SHANNON
road	TOBY
robber	RAPPAREE, TORY
robbery on the road	TOBY
salt marsh	CORCASS
script	OG(H)AMIC, OGMIC
secret jargon	SHELTA
shale bed	CALP
shield of wickerwork	SKIATH
shinty	CAMANACHD
—stick	CAMAN
short clay pipe	DUDEEN
social gathering	CEILIDH
sod	SCRAW
sorcery	PISHOGUE
sorrow	SORRA
stew	COLCANNON
stream	STREEL
stringed instrument	TYMPAN
sublet	CO(R)NACRE
sub-tenant	WELDER
sweetheart	GRA
system of succession	TANISTRY
television service	RADIO TELEFIS EIREANN
	RTE
tenant	COTTIER
tenure	SOREHON, TANISTRY
term of abuse	SORRA
—to woman	STRAP
terrorists	IRA
tinker's jargon	SHELTA
trail	STREEL
transmitter of	
family lore	SE(A)NNACHIE, SEANNACHY
	SHANACHIE
transport organisation	CIE

tribal law	CINEL
Trinity College	TCD
trout	GILLAROO
turf	SCRAW
United Ireland	FINE GAEL
upper house	SEANAD
usurper	GOMBEEN-MAN
usury	GOMBEEN
vagrant's jargon	SHELTA
verse	RANN
wander	STREEL
water-plant	PIPEWORT
whiskey	POT(H)EEN, THE CRATUR
	USQUEBAUGH
witchcraft	PISHOGLE
young lad	BUCKO
Islam	(*see* **Moslem**)
Isle of Man	GBM, IOM
Isle of Wight	IOW, IW
Israel	
capital	JERUSALEM, YERUSHALAYIM
coin	
—unit	AGORA
—100 agorot	SHEKEL
	(*see also* **Hebrew**)
Italy	I
à la carte	AL CONTO
again	ANCORA
almond cakes	AMARETTI
anchovies	ALICI
ancient	ANTICO
—language	LATIN, OSCAN
	SAMNITE, UMBRIAN
—people	ACQUI, ETRUSCANS
	HERNICI, LATINS, OSCAN
	SABINES, SAMNITE, VOLSCI
applause	VIVA
approval	SI
aptly invented	BEN TROVATO
armed policeman	CARABINIERE
articles	IL, LA, LE, LO, UNA, UNO
artist's studio	BOTTEGA
aside	SOTTO VOCE
at	
—first sight	A PRIMA VISTA
—most	AL PIU
—pleasure	A PIACERE
bagpipes	PIFFERO, ZAMPOGNA
bakery	PANIFICIO
balcony	TERRAZZO
ball	PALLA
—game	PALLONE
barge	BARCA
bas relief	BASSO-RILIEVO
bay	GOLFO
bean purée	MACCO

beaten	BATTUTA
beef	MANZO
—casserole	STUFATO
beggar	BESOGNIO, LAZZARONE
bird	BECCAFICO
biscuits	AMARETTI
black	NERO
—pudding	SANGUINACCIO
boat	BARCA, GONDOLA
—song	BARCAROLA
borough	BORGO
boys	RAGAZZI
bound	LEGATO
brazier	SCALDINO
bread	PANE
—rolls	PANINAROS
brother	FRA(TELLO)
burial ground	CAMPO SANTO
butter	BURRO
by	
—fits and starts	A SALTI
—your leave	BENE PLACITO
cab	VETTURA
—driver	VETTURINO
camomile	MANZANILLA
cape (headland)	CAPO, PUNTA
capital	ROMA, ROME
car	VETTURA
carriage	VETTURA
—procession	CORSO
carved chest	CASSONE
cathedral	DUOMO
cheese	FORMAGGIO
	(see also separate entry)
chicken	POLLO
chief magistrate	GONFALONIERE
	PODESTA
child	BAMBINA, BAMBINO
circuit	CONTORNO
city	CITTA
clerk	SCRIVANO
coins	
—unit	CENTESIMO
—100 centesimi	L, LIRA
—Florentine	FLORIN
—silver	DUCAT, SCUDO
—old	AMBROSIN
	SOLDO, TESTOON
—old Papal	PAOLO
coloured glass or enamel	ZMALTO
comic opera	BURLETTA
	OPERA BUFFA
company	GIA, COMPAGNIA
comparative value of	
currency	VALUTA
confused mass	IMBROGLIO

congenial	SIMPATICO
connoisseur	COGNOSCENTO
contour	CONTORNA
contract	APPALTO
council meeting	CONSULTA
councillors	ANZIANI
country retirement	VILLEGGIATURA
courage!	CORAGGIO
courgette	ZUCCHINI
course	CORSO
criminal society	COSA NOSTRA, MAF(F)IA
cup	TAZZA
cured goat's meat	VIOLINI
dance	BERGAMASK, BERGOMASK
	RIGOLETTO, TARANTELLA
	VOLTA
dancing party	RIDOTTO
dash	BRAVURA
dear	CARA, CARO
device	IMPRESA
dictator	DUCE
discussion group	CONVERSAZIONE
dish	ANTIPASTO, GNOCCHI
	LASAGNE, OS(S)O BUCCO
	PASTA, PEPERONATA, PIZZA
	PROSCIUTTO, RAVIOLI
	RISOTTO, SALTIMBOCCA
	TOURNEDOS ROSSINI
	(see also **pasta***)*
do nothing	FAR NIENTE
doctor	MEDICO
dog	CANE, VOLPINO
double speed	DOPPIO MOVIMENTO
drinking song	BRINDISI
driver of carriage	VETTURINO
duck	ANITRA
duel	DUELLO
dumplings	GNOCCHI
dynasty	SAVOY
Earth	TERRA
Easter cake	PASTIERA
egg	UOVO
employer	PADRONE
enclosed courtyard	CORTILE
encore	ANCORA
enough	BASTA
enthusiasm	ESTRO, GUSTO
essence	ALMA
estuary	BOCCHE
evening	SERA
evil eye	JETTATURA
extra day off	PONTE
face to face	A QUATTR'OCHI
farm	PODERE
father	PADRONE
fencing thrust	IMBROCCATA

festival	FESTA
field	CAMPO
fifteenth century	QUATTROCENTO
fig-pecker	BECCAFICO
firm to the teeth	AL DENTE
first	PRIMA, PRIMO
fish	PESCE, TONETTO
—soup	BRODETTO
—stew	BRODETTO, BURIDDA
	CACCIUCCO
fixed rate	AL PASTO
fizzy	FRIZZANTE
flour	FARINA
—dough	PASTA
flowering	FIORITURA
flute	ZUF(F)OLO
folk-tales	PENTAMERON
follows	SEGUE
fool	CAPOCCHIA
football (old)	CALCIO
forward!	AVANTI
four hundred	QUATTROCENTO
fourteenth century	TRECENTO
franked	FRANCO
free	SCIOLTO
fresh	FRESCO
friar	FRATE
fried savouries	FRITTO MISTO
furious person	FURIOSO
gallant	CAVALIERE SERVENTE
game (old)	LONGUE PAUME, PALLONE
garden warbler	BECCAFICO
garlic	AGLIO
gentle blood	BEL SANGUE
girl	RAGAZZA
glazing by hand-rubbing	VELATURA
good	BENE
—bye	ADDIO, A(R)RIVEDERCI
	CIAO
—day	BUON GIORNO
—evening	BUONA SERA
—life	DOLCE VITA
—night	BUONA NOTTE
goose	OCA
government	QUIRINAL
governor	PODESTA
granite	MIAROLO
grape stalk	GRAPPA
great	GRAN
guide	CICERONE
guild comedy	COMMEDIA DELL'ARTE
gulf	GOLFO
gypsy (gipsies)	
—man	ZINGARO(ZINGARI)
—woman	ZINGARA(ZINGARE)
hand	MANO

harbour	PORTO
hare	LEPRE
headland	CAPO
headman	CAPITANO
hell	INFERNO
here is	ECCO
hero	GARIBALDI
high fashion	ALTA MODA
highness	ALTEZZA
hill	COLLINA
holiday	FESTA
hollow	CONCA
hors d'oeuvre	ANTIPASTO
house	CASA
ice cream	GELATO
image of child Jesus	BAMBINO
imitation stone	SCAGLIOLA
in	
—a low voice	SOTTO VOCE
—an undertone	SOTTO VOCE
—blank	IN BIANCO
—devotional manner	RELIGIOSO
—French style	ALLA FRANCA
—German style	ALLA TEDESCA
—marching style	ALLA MARCIA
—one's own mind	IN PETTO
—strict time	A BATTUTA
—the	
breast	IN PETTO
manner of fugue	FUGATO
—time	A TEMPO
—white	IN BIANCO
indifferent	POCOCURANTE
informal greeting	CIAO
inn	ALBERGO
—keeper	PADRONE
instrument	CHITARRONE
island(s)	ISOLA(ISOLE)
isolation hospital	LAZARET(TO)
Italian	AUSONIAN, EYETI(E), EYTIE
judge	PODESTA
king	RE
lady	DONNA, SIGNORA
lake	LAGO
lamb	AGNELLO
landlord	PADRONE
language	TUSCAN
large village	BORGHETTO
leader	DUCE
leading	
—dancer	PRIMA BALLERINA (ASSOLUTA)
—singer	PRIMA DONNA (ASSOLUTA)
liberation and unification	RISORGIMENTO
life of pleasure	LA DOLCE VITA
limestone	SCAGLIA

little	POCO	night	NOTTE
—by little	POCO A POCO	nonchalant	POCOCURANTE
liveliness	BRIO	not so quick	MENO MOSSE
look there	ECCO	official prosecutor	AVVOGADORE
Madam	DONNA, SIGNORA	open pie of tomatoes etc	PIZZA
madman	FURIOSO	or	O, OSSIA
mafia	COSA NOSTRA	orange	ARANCIA
magistrate	PODESTA	ornamental glass	MILLEFIORI
male		overcoat (19th c)	TAGLIONI
—exhibitionist	FUSTO	palace	PALAZZO
—soprano	CASTRATO	papal treasurer	CAMERLENGO
mansion	PALAZZO		CAMERLINGO
marchioness	MARCHESA	party (19th c)	IRREDENTISTS
mark	MARCARE	pass	COLLE, PASSO
marquis	MARCHESE	pasta	(see separate entry)
master	MAESTRO	peak	PIZZO
meal	PRANZO	peasant	CONTADINO
measure (cubit)	BRACCIO	peninsula	PENISOLA
meat	CARNE	pensive man	IL PENSEROSO
—balls	POLPETTE	perpetual motion	MOTO PERPETUO
—rolls	INVOLTINI	pheasant	FAGGIANO
medieval drama	LAUDA	pie	TORTA, PASTICCIO, PIZZA
medium relief	MEZZO-RILIEVO	pleasant idleness	DOLCE FAR NIENTE
melancholy	PENS(I)EROSO	poem	POEMA, POESIA
member of Florentine		poet	ARIOSTO, DANTE
Academia	DELLA-CRUSCAN		MARINI, TASSO
mendicant Franciscan	FRATE	poetic inspiration	ESTRO
mercenary leader	CONDOTTIERE	policeman	SBIRRO
merry cheerful man	L'ALLEGRO	porridge	POLENTA
middle	MEZZO	port	PORTO
Milanese opposed to		post-free	FRANCO
marriage of priests	PATARIN(E)	pottery	MAIOLICA, MAJOLICA
Miss	SIGNORINA	poultry	POLLAME
Mister	SIGNOR	prawns	SCAMPI
mixed dish of		proprietor of inn	PADRONE
fried food	FRITTO MISTO	puppets	FANTOCCINI
mizzen-sail	MEZZANA	quicker	PIU MOSSO
model sculpture	BOZETTO	quickly!	PRESTO
modernising	AGGIORNAMENTO	rabbit	CONIGLIO
monopoly	APPALTO	race	CORSO
more	PIU	rebirth	RISORGIMENTO
most illustrious	ILLUSTRISSIMO	recasting of literary	
mother	MADRE	or musical work	RIFACIMENTO
—of God	MADONNA	reef	SCOGLIO
motor-boat	MOTOSCAFO	refusal	NON
motorway	AUTOSTRADA	relief	RILIEVO
motto	IMPRESA	relish (roe)	BOTARGO
mountain	MONTE	restaurant	RISTORANTE, TRATTORIA
—troops	ALPINI	revival	RISORGIMENTO
mouth	BOCCA	rice	RISO
much	MOLTO	rifleman	BERSAGLIERE
mushrooms	FUNGHI	river	FIUME
nationalist	FASCIST(O)	—mouth	FOCE
Neapolitan		roast piglet	PORCHETTA
—dance	TARANTELLA	rock	SCOGLIO
—secret society	CAMORRA	run	CORSO

sad	MESTO
Saint's day	FESTA
score in music	PARTITURA
sea	MARE
second	SECONDO
secret society	CAMORRA
	CASA NOSTRA
	COMORRA, MAF(F)IA
serious opera	OPERA SERIA
sharpshooter	BERSAGLIERE
short verse-form	STORNELLO
simple	GONZO
singing style	BEL CANTO
sixteenth century	CINQUECENTO
skull-cap	ZUCHETTA, ZUCHETTO
sliding	GLISSANDO
slow	LENTO
small group	GRUPPETTO
snails	LUMACHE
soldier	BERSAGLIERE, SOLDATO
songbird	BECCAFICO
soul	ALMA, ANIMA, SPIRITO
soup	MINISTRE, MINESTRA
	MINESTRONE, ZUPPA
sour cherry	(A)MARASCA
spade	PALETTA
sparkling	FRIZZANTE
spiced sausage(s)	SALAME (SALAMI)
spirit	BRAVURA, BRIO
square	PIAZZA
squid	CALAMARI
standard of money	VALUTA
state pawnshop	MONTE DI PIETA
stew	OSSOBUCO
storm	BORASCO
strait	STRETTO
street	CALLE, STRADA, VIA
—where processions are held	CORSO
stringed instrument	PANDURA
sucking pig	PORCHETTA
summit	CIMA
supreme commander	GENERALISSIMO
sweet dish	ZABAGLIONE
taste	GUSTO
tangle	IMBROGLIO
tear	LACRIMA

terrace	TERRAZZO
there!	ECCO
thick laying on of paint	IMPASTO
three strings	TRE CORDE
thrusting	ALLA STOCCATA
time	TEMPO
tip	B(U)ONAMANA
title of rank	MONSIGNOR(E)
toast	BRINDISI
too much	TROPPO
touchstone	PARAGONE
touring car	GRAN TURISMO
town	CITTA
trade jargon	LINGUA FRANCA
trio	TERZETTO
turkey	TACCHINO
turn	VOLTA
type of carving	CAVO-RILIEVO
uninterested	POCOCURANTE
unknown	INCOGNITO
veal	VITELLO
vendetta	FAIDA
venison	CERVA
vermicelli	FEDELINI
vermouth	IT
verse form in triplets	TERZA-RIMA
very	MOLTO
—earnestly	CON AMORE
vivacity	BRIO
warbler	BECCAFICO
weight (variable)	ROTOLO
well	BENE
what	CHE
wine	VINO
	(*see also* wine)
with	CON
—fire	CON FUOCO
—grief	CON DOLORE
—love	CON AMORE
—movement	CON MOTO
—resolution	RISOLUTO
—spirit	SPIRITOSO
wood inlay	INTARSIA, INTARSIO
woodcock	BECCACCIA
workshop	BOTTEGA
zest	GUSTO
Ivory Coast	CI

Jamaica JA
  bark CARIBBEE BARK
  birthwort CONTRAYERVA
  capital KINGSTON
  cedar BARBADOS CEDAR
  coin CENT, DOLLAR
  drink RUM
  ebony COCUS-WOOD
  pepper ALLSPICE
  plum HOG-PLUM
Japan J, NIPPON
  abacus SOROBAN
  aboriginal race AINO, AINU
  acupressure SHIATSU
  administrative district PREFECTURE
  aeroplane ZERO
  airline JAL
  alcove TOKONOMA
  alphabet KATAKANA
  armorial device MON
  bamboo shoots TAKENOKO
  barehanded fighting J(I)-JITSU
  baron DAIMIO
  bay KAI, WAN
  bean ADZUKI
  beauty of age SHIBUI
  bed-roll FUTON
  beef GYUNIKU
  —dish SHABU-SHABU
  body-language HARAGEI
  box INRO
  boxing KEMPO
  bread PAN
  Buddhist sect SOKA GAKKAI, ZEN
  cake MANJU
  calligraphy SHODO
  cane WHANGEE
  cape (headland) BANA, MISAKI, ZAKI
  capital TOKYO
  carriage JINRICKISHA
  (JIN)RICKSHA(W)
  carved ornament NETSUKE
  cedar SUGI
  champion wrestler (sumo) OZEKI
  channel SETO, SUIDO
  cherry FUJI
  cherry-blossom time SAKURA
  chess SHOGI

chicken NIWATORI
chopsticks WARIBASHI
chrysanthemum badge KIKUMON
church TERA
cloisonné ware SHIPPO
code of chivalry BUSHIDO
coins
  —unit SEN
  —100 sen Y, YEN, YN
  —old gold coins COPANG
  KOBAN(G), OBANG
commander-in-chief SHOGUN(AL)
  TYCOON
conifer UMBRELLA-FIR
court DAIRO, DARI
current KUROSHIO
dancing girl GEISHA
deep-fried seafood or vegetables TEMPURA
deer SIKA
deities (see **gods, goddesses**)
demi-god KAMI
dish SUKIYAKI, SUSHI
  TEMPURA, TERIYAKI
drama KABUKI, NOGAKU, NO(H)
drink SAKE, SAKI
dumpling DANGO
dwarf tree BONSAI
early civilisation EDO
edible shoots (Aralia) UDO
elder statesmen GENRO
emigrant to US ISSEI
emperor MIKADO, TENNO
enamel ware SHIPPO
exalted gate MIKADO
fan OGI
fast food TONK-ATSU
fastener NETSUKE
female entertainer GEISHA
fencing IAIDO
firing process for
  porcelain RAKU
fish AYU, FUGU, CARP
  GOLDFISH
  —in batter TEMPURA
  —raw SASHIMI
    with vegetables CHIRINABE, NUTA
floor covering TATAMI
flower arranging IKEBANA
flowering tree CATALPA, CHERRY
forever BANZAI
fried pork TONK-ATSU
fruit LOQUAT, KAKI
game GO, GOBAN(G), GOMUKU
  SHOGI
garment (KI)MONO
gentle way JUDO

gentry	SHIZOKU	—ruler	SHOGUN
girdle	OBI	mountain	SEN, ZAN
girl	MOUSME(E)	mountain(s)	YAMA
god	KAMI	mushroom	KINOKO
gold foil work	KIRIKANE	musical	
goodbye	SAYONARA	—drama	KABUKI
grass	WHANGEE	—instrument	KOTO, S(H)AMISEN
grotesque figure	MAGOT	narrow print	HASHIRA
guest-house	MINSHUKU	noble	DAIMIO, KUGE
guitar	S(H)AMISEN	noodles	MENRUI
gulf	NADA	orange	SATSUMA
healing art	SHIATSU	ornament	NETSUKE
helmet	JINGASA	outcast	RONIN
horse-radish	WASABI	outsider	GAIJIN
image	ZO	painting style	UKIYO-E
informal feeling out	NEMAWASHI	palanquin	KAGO, NORIMON
inlay work	ZOGAN	paper	FUSAMI
inlet	GATA, KO	—folding art	ORIGAMI
island	JIMA, KO, SHIMA, TO	—screen	SHOJI
ivy	UDO	pass	TOGE
jacket	TANZEN	patina	SABI
jelly	KANTEN	peak	DAKE, TAKE
judo		peninsula	HANTO
—costume	JUDOGI	persimmon	KAKI
—expert	JUDOKA	pinball game	PACHINKO
kimono	YUKATA	plant	HOSTA, KUDZU
knife	KOZUKA	play	NO(H)
lacquer	URUSHI	plum	UMEBOSHI
—ware	NURIMONO	poem	HAIKAI, HAIKU, HOKKO
—work	KANAGAI	—with 5 lines	LINKED VERSE
lagoon	GATA		RENGA, TANKA
language	AINU	pork	BUTANIKU
laurel	AUCUBA JAPONICA	pottery	KYOTO, SATSUMA WARE
lord	KAMI	province	SATSUMA
low caste	ETA, HEIMIN	puppet theatre	BUNRAKU
martial art	AIKIDO, AIKI-JITSU	quince	CYDONIA JAPONICA
	JUDO, J(I)U-JITSU		PYRUS JAPONICA
	JUJUTSA, KARATE, KENDO	radish	DAIKON
mat	TATAMI	raincoat	MINO
measures		raspberry	WINE-BERRY
—1"	SUN	raw fish dish	SASHIMI
—12"	SHAKU	religion	BUDDHISM, SHINTO(ISM)
—2 yards	KEN	rice	GO-HAN, RAISU
—120 yards	CHO	—beer	SAKE, SAKI
—2½ miles	RI	river	GAWA, KAWA
—4sq. yds	TSUBO	robe	KIMONO
—¼ peck	SHO	root binding	NEMAWASHI
—5 bushels	KOKU	rose	KERRIA
—4 galls	TO	royal badge	KIKUMON, KIRIMON
—10,000 years	BANZAI	ruler	MIKADO
meat cooked in soy sauce	SUKIYAKI	salmon	MASU
medicine chest	INRO	salutation	BANZAI
medlar	LOQUAT	sash	OBI
Mikado's palace	DAIRI	script	KAKEMONO, KANA
military		scroll	MAKIMONO
—caste	SAMURAI	sea	KAI, NADA

—bream	TAI
—weed	KO(M)BU
secret society	YAKUZA
set meal	TEISHOKU
ship	MARO, MARU
shrub	KERRIA
sliding partition	SHOJI
sport	SUMO
strait	SETO, SUIDO
street	GINZA
sudden enlightenment	SATORI
suicide	HARAKARI, HARAKIRI
	SEPPUKU
—attack	KAMIKAZE
sword	
—fighting	KENDO
—hilt	TSUBA
syllabary	HIRAGANA, KATAKANA
tea	O-CHA
—ceremony	CHANOYU, SADO
temple gateway	TORII
tidal wave	TSUNAMI
title	KAMI
tree	GINGKO, GINKGO, HONOKI
	LOQUAT, MAIDENHAIR-TREE
	PAULOWNIA, RED-LAC, TSUGA
tuna	MAGURO
waitress	MOUSME(E)
wall-hanging	KAKEMONO
war-cry	BANZAI
warm current	KUROSHIO
warrior class	SAMURAI
weights	
—1oz	RIO
—1½lbs	CATTY, KIN
—8lbs	KWAN
wood block	YOKO
wooden	
—chopsticks	HASHI
—shoes	GETA
wrestling	SUMO
—champion	OZEKI
—tournament	SASHO
writing system	KANA
Javanese	JAV
badger	STINKARD, TELEDU
bird	JAVA SPARROW
capital	DJAKARTA
civet	RASSE
man	PITHECANTHROPUS
orchestra	GAMELAN(G), GAMELIN
plum	JAMBOLANA
tree	ANTIAR, UPAS
—shrew	BANGSRING, BANXRING
weapon	TOMBOC
weasel-cat	DELUNDUNG

Jersey	GBJ
Jesus	IHC, IHS, JC, JHC
jewellery	
assortment of small	
diamonds	MELEE
artificial	LOGIE, PASTE
—with glass under real	
jewels	DOUBLET
beetle-shaped	SCARAB
bone-shaped	SEVIGNE
brooch	FIBULA
—clasp	OUCH
—in hat	ENSEIGNE
cameo sewn to clothes	OUCH
cheap jewellery	BAUBLES
	BRUMMAGEN
	GEEGAWS, PASTE
	TRINKETS
clasp for cloak	FIBULA
clasped ornament	OUCH
close-fitting necklace	CHOKER
compartment in gold work	CLOISON
corsage	STOMACHER
cross suspended	
from a heart	CROIX A LA JEANNETTE
cut	
—4 facets	MAZARIN CUT, ROSE CUT
—11 facets	EMERALD CUT, STEP CUT
—56 facets	DIAMOND CUT
—chamfered	BAGUETTE
—domed	CABOCHON
—flat plane	FACET
—pointed oval	NAVETTE
decorative plaque	
on belt	CHATELAINE
delicate jewellery	BIJOUTERIE
ear	
—ornament	DROPPER, EAR-RING
temporary	SLEEPER
—ring	
cone hung from	
crescent	PELTA
long pendants	POISSOIDES
	FISHWIVES
enamelling	
—between wires	
soldered to plate	FILIGREE
—carved and enamelled	BASSE TAILLE
	CHAMPLEVE
—engraved and	
enamelled	TAILLE D'EPERGNE
—in	
cells	CLOISONNE
openwork	PLIQUE A JOUR
—modelled on surface	EN RONDE BOSSE
expert	LAPIDARIST

flange holding stone	BEZEL
Greek medallion	PERIAMMA
head	
—band	CIRCLET, CORONET
	CROWN, DIADEM, TIARA
—ornament	TRESSON
heart-shaped	CARDIACE
hinged case	LOCKET
imitation	
—diamonds	DIAMANTE, PASTE
—pearl	OLIVET
inlaid with hard stones	PIETRA-DURA
jewel-box	CASKET
lentil-shaped pendant	BULLA
lustre of pearl	ORIENT
matching set	
—2 or 3 pieces	DEMI-PARURE
—3 or more pieces	PARURE
matt gold	CANNETILLE
misshapen pearl	BAROQUE PEARL
mourning jewellery	MEMENTO MORI
neck ornament	GORGET, TORC
	TORQUE
necklace	
—or collar	CARCANET, TORQUE
—with several strands	RIVIERE
ornament worn	
—as charm	AMULET
—on	
ankle	ANKLET, SLAVE BRACELET
arm	BANGLE, BRACELET
chain	LAVALIERE, PENDANT
chest	PECTORAL
ear	DROPPER, EAR-RING
forehead	FERRON(N)IERE
head	TRESSON
lip	LABRET
pendant with	
—singly mounted stones	LAVALLIERE
	NEGLIGE
—smaller jewels attached	GIRANDOLE
perfume container	POMANDER
polished but uncut stone	CABOCHON

ring	
—cheap	GYPSY RING
—of metal holding stone	COLLET
—with	
interlocking loops	GIMMAL RING
	GIMMEL RING
monogram	SIGNET RING
single stone	SOLITAIRE
stones all round	ETERNITY RING
scroll-shaped	CARTOUCHE
setting with stones	
butted together	PAVE
sham	LOGIE, PASTE
sheen of	
—diamond	WATER
—moonstone	SCHILLER
—pearl	LUSTRE, ORIENT
—ruby	SILK
—sapphire	SILK
ship-shaped	NEF
socket for stone	OUCH
spray of feathers	AIGRETTE
stone	
—cutter	LAPIDARY
—used to test gold or	
silver	TOUCHSTONE
—with	
incised carving	INTAGLIO
relief carving	CAMEO
twisted necklace	TORC, TORQUE
used for religious	
purposes	VOTIVE JEWELS
worn to ward off evil	AMULET, TALISMAN
yellow-coloured diamond	CAPE
	(*see also* **gems**)
Jewish	(*see* **Hebrew**)
Jordan	HKJ
capital	AMMAN
coin	DINAR, FIL
June	
June 6th	D-DAY
June 25th	LONGEST DAY
	MIDSUMMER, SOLSTICE

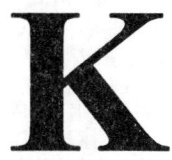

Kampuchea	(*see* **Cambodia**)
Kenya	EAK
capital	NAIROBI
coin	CENT, POUND, SHILLING
kill	
algae	ALGICIDE
babies	INFANTICIDE
bacteria	BACTERICIDE, GERMICIDE
bears	URSICIDE
birds	AVICIDE
brother	FRATRICIDE
children	FILICIDE, INFANTICIDE
	PROLICIDE
environment	ECOCIDE
father	PATRICIDE
f(o)etus	ABORTION, F(O)ETICIDE
fox	VULPICIDE
fungus	FUNGICIDE
giant	GIGANTICIDE
god	DEICIDE
human race	PROLICIDE
insects	INSECTICIDE
king	REGICIDE
larvae	LARVICIDE
living things	BIOCIDE
man	HOMICIDE
mind (brainwashing)	MENTICIDE
mites	ACARICIDE
mother	MATRICIDE
offspring	PROLICIDE
one's own children	FILICIDE
parasites	PARASITICIDE
parents	PARRICIDE
pest	PESTICIDE
plants	HERBICIDE
poet	VATICIDE
prophet	VATICIDE
protozoa	TRYPANOCIDE
race	ETHNOCIDE, GENOCIDE
rats	RODENTICIDE
reputation	FAMICIDE
rodents	RODENTICIDE
seaweed	ALGICIDE
self	SUICIDE
sheep	OVICIDE
sister	SORORICIDE
social group	ETHNOCIDE
sperm	SPERMICIDE

tyrant	TYRANNICIDE
vine	VITICIDE
virus	VIRICIDE
weeds	HERBICIDE, WEEDICIDE
wife	UXORICIDE
women	GYNOCIDE
worms	VERMICIDE
king	
including: general	
Cockney king	PEARLIE, PEARLY
King Charles	CR
King Edward	ER
king-emperor	RI
King George	GR
king of Basham	OG
king of France	ROI, SM
King William	WR
King's Bench	KB
King's College	KC
King's Counsel	KC
Sun King	LOUIS XIV
kings	
including: British	
pre-Conquest	ALFRED
	ATHELSTAN
	CANUTE, CNUT
	EDGAR ETHELING
	EDMUND IRONSIDE
	EDRED
	EDWARD THE CONFESSOR
	EDWARD THE ELDER
	EDWARD THE MARTYR
	EDWY
	ETHELRED
	EGBERT
	HAROLD GODWINSON
	HAROLD HAREFOOT
	HARTHACNUT
	SWEGN
English	CHARLES I-II
	EDWARD I-VIII
	GEORGE I-VI
	HENRY I-VIII
	JAMES I-II
	JOHN
	RICHARD I-III
	STEPHEN
	WILLIAM I-IV
Scottish	ALEXANDER I-III
	DAVID I-II
	DONALD
	DUNCAN I-II
	EDGAR
	JAMES I-VI
	JOHN
	LULACH

	MACBETH	—clasp knife	JOCKTELEG
	MALCOLM I-IV	Sikh	KIRPAN
	ROBERT I-III	slang	CHIV, SHIV
	WILLIAM	Spanish	CUCHILLO
knife		spring-loaded	FLICK KNIFE
African	PANGA		SWITCH-BLADE (KNIFE)
American	BOWIE KNIFE, TOOTH-PICK	surgical	BISTOURY, LANCET
Arab dagger	JAMBIA, KHANJAR		SCALPEL
artist's knife	PALETTE KNIFE	Turkish	ATAGHAN, HAN(D)JAR
Burmese	DA(H), DHAR, DOUT, DOW		YATAG(H)AN
carpenter's/cooper's		**knight**	K, KT, N, SIR
knife	DRAW(ING)-KNIFE	Knight Bachelor	KB
Cuban	MACHETE	Knight Commander of the	
dagger		—Bath	KCB
—curved	JAMBIYA(H)	—British Empire	KBE
—Greek	PARAZONIUM	Knight Grand Cross of	
—Hebrew	SICA	—Hanover	GCH
—narrow-bladed	MISERICORD(E)	—the	
	STILET(TO), STYLET	Bath	(K)GCB
—old	BAS(E)LARD, PUNCHEON	British Empire	GBE
—Roman	SICA	Knight of	
—short	AN(E)LACE	—Labour	KL
—small	BODKIN, DIRK, DUDGEON	—Malta	KM
	PONIARD, WHINGER	—the	
	WINIARD, WINYARD	Bath	KB
Dutch	SNEE	Legion of Honour	KLH
fighting knife	SNICKERSNEE	Order of the Garter	KG
folding knife	CLASP-KNIFE, JACK-KNIFE	Thistle	KT
—Scots	JOCKTELEG	**knot**	BLACKWALL HITCH, BOWLINE
French	COUTEAU		CARRICK BEND, CAT'S-PAW
general purpose knife	STANLEY KNIFE		CLOVE HITCH, COMMON BEND
	SWISS ARMY KNIFE		COW HITCH, GRANNY KNOT
German	MESSER		FIGURE-OF-EIGHT
glazier's tool	PUTTY KNIFE		FISHERMAN'S BEND
Gurkha	KUKRI		FISHERMAN'S KNOT
heavy knife	DA		HALF HITCH, JURY-MAST KNOT
Highland	DIRK		OVERHAND KNOT, REEF KNOT
Inca ceremonial knife	TUMI		ROLLING HITCH, SHEET BEND
Indian	KUTTAR		SHEEPSHANK, SLIP-KNOT
Italian	COLTELLO		SQUARE KNOT
Japanese	KOZUKA		STEVEDORE'S KNOT
large	CUTTO(E)		SWAB HITCH, THUMB KNOT
leatherworker's knife	MOON-KNIFE		TIMBER HITCH, TURK'S HEAD
Malay	CREASE, CREESE, KRIS	**Korea**	ROK
	KREESE, PARANG	airline	KAL
midshipman's knife	DIRK	capital	
Middle East	JAMBIYA(H)	—North	PYONGYANG
military knife	BAYONET	—South	S(E)OUL
	SWISS ARMY KNIFE	coin	CHON, HWAN, JEON
	TRENCH KNIFE		JUN, WON
painter's knife	PALETTE KNIFE	house	WON
Persian	HAN(D)JAR	martial art	HAPKIDO, TAEKWONDO
Philippines	BOLO		TANG SOO DO
Scottish	DIRK, GULLEY	trance	KUT
	SKEAN(DHU), SKENE(DHU)	**Kuala Lumpur**	KL
	SKEAN(OCCLE), SKENE(OCCLE)	**Kuwait**	KWT

lake

Africa	NYANZA
—lakes	ALBERT, BANGWEULU
	EDWARD, EYASI, KARIBA
	KIVU, MAI NDOMBE, MALAWI
	MOBUTU SESE SEKO, MWERU
	NYASA, RUDOLF, TANGANYIKA
	(T)CHAD, TURKANA, VICTORIA
America (N)	CHAMPLAIN LAKE
	GREAT LAKES
	GREAT SALT LAKE
	OKEECHOBEE, PEPIN
—Great Lakes	ERIE, HURON, MICHIGAN
	ONTARIO, SUPERIOR
artificial	RESERVOIR
Australia	AMADEUS, ERYE
	DISAPPOINTMENT, EVERARD
	FROME, GARDNER, MOORE
	TORRANCE, TORRENS
Bolivia	POOPO, TITICACA
Brazil	DOS PATOS, MIRIM
Cambodia	GREAT LAKE, TONLE SAP
Canada	ATHABASCA, GARRY
	GREAT BEAR LAKE
	GREAT SLAVE LAKE
	REINDEER LAKE, ST JOHN
	WINNIPEG, WINNEPEGOSIS
	(*see also* Great Lakes *above*)
China	BAGRASH KOL, LOP NOR
	KOKO NOR, POYANGHU, TAI HU
	TUNG TING HU
connecting with sea	SEA LOCH
dries up in hot conditions	PLAYA, SHOTT
England	BASSENTHWAITE LAKE
	BUTTERMERE, CONISTON
	CRUMMOCK WATER
	DERWENTWATER
	ENNERDALE WATER
	GRASMERE, HAWES WATER
	RYDAL WATER, THIRLMERE
	ULLSWATER, WASTWATER
	WINDERMERE
Estonia	LAKE PEIPUS
Ethiopia	LAKE TANA
Finland	INARI
formed by	
—blocking of valley	BARRIER LAKE
—meandering river	OXBOW, MORTLAKE

France	LAC
Germany	SEE
—lake	BODEN SEE
Guatemala	ATITLAN
having	
—deficiency of nutrients	OLIGOTROPHIC
—excess of nutrients	EUTROPHIC
Hungary	LAKE BALATON
	LAKE HEVIS
in	
—extinct volcano	CRATER LAKE
—mountains	TARN
Iran	LAKE URMIA
Ireland	LOUGH
—loughs	ALLEN, CONN, CORRIB, DERG
	ERNE, MASK, NEAGH, REE
Israel	LAKE TIBERIAS
Italy	LAGO
—lakes	BOLSENA, BRACCIANO, COMO
	ISEO, GARDA, MAGGIORE
	ORTA, TRASIMENO
Kashmir	DAL
made salty by evaporation	SALT LAKE
Mexico	LAKE CHAPALA
mountain lake	TARN
New Zealand	PUKAKI, TAUPO
	TE ANAU, TEKAPO
Nicaragua	LAGO DA NICARAGUA
North Africa - shallow lake	SHOTT
Peru	LAKE TITICACA
ridge of stones round margins	LAKE RAMPART
Russia	OZERO
—lakes	ALAK, BAIKAL, BALKHASH
	BAYKAL, HOVSGOL NOUR, ISSYK KUL
	KHANKA, KUYBYSHEVSKOYE
	LADOGA, LADOZHSKOYE
	ONEGA, ONEZHSKOYE, SEVAN
	STALINGRADSKOYE
	TENGIZ, ZAYSAN
salt	SALINA
Scotland	LOCH
—lochs	ARKAIG, AWE, FYNE, EARN
	ERICHT, LAGGAN, LINNHE
	LOCHY, LOMOND, LONG, MAREE
	MORAR, NEVIS, NESS
	RANNOCH, SHIEL, SHIN, TAY
—moorland pool	FLOW
sea-lake	FIORD
seasonal lake	PLAYA
shallow lake	
—in coastal sand dunes	ETANG
—large	EVERGLADE

—North Africa	SHOTT
small	MERE, TARN
Spain	LAGO
submerged river valley	RIA
Sweden	MALAR, VANERN
	VATTERN
Switzerland	LAC, SEE
—lakes	BODENSEE, BRIENZER SEE
	LAKE CONSTANCE, LAKE GENEVA
	HALLWILER SEE, LAC LEMAN
	LAC NEUCHATEL, SEMPACHER SEE
	THUNER SEE, URNER SEE
	VIERWALDSTATTER SEE
	WALENSEE, ZUGER SEE, ZURICH SEE
Turkey	AMIK, BATAKUK, BEYSEHID
	BURDUR, HOYRAN, IZNIK
	KUS, SUGLA, TUZ, ULLBAT, VAN
Uruguay	LAGO DA MANGUIERA
	LAKE MIRIM
valley	(see geology)
Venezuela	LAGO DE MARACAIBO
	LAGO VICTORIA
Wales	L(L)YN
—lakes	BALA LAKE, LAKE VYRNWY
	LYN CELIN, LYN TEGID
	TRAWSFYNYDD LAKE
water	
—higher level (warm)	HYPOLIMNIUM
—layer in between	THERMOCLINE
—lower level (cold)	EPILIMNIUM
—receiving sufficient	
sunlight for	
photosynthesis	PHOTIC ZONE
Yugoslavia	LAKE BOHINJ
Lamb (Charles)	ELIA
language	LINGO
1984 language	NEWSPEAK
ability to	
—read	LITERACY
—use	
language	ORACY
numbers	NUMERACY
Abyssinia	AMHARIC, GALLA, GEEZ
	GIZ, SOMALI
accent	BROGUE, DIALECT, TWANG
	(see also punctuation)
accidental omission	
of letters	LIPOGRAPHY
adage	PAROEMIA
addition	
—to word	EPITHESIS, PARAGOG(U)E
—of	
final r	NUNNATION
prefix	PROTHESIS
words to clarify	EPEXEGESIS
affected talk	CANT

Afghanistan	DARI, PAK(H)TO, PAK(H)TU
	PASHTO, PASHTU
	PUSHTO(O), PUSHTU
Afrasian	ARABIC
Africa	(see Africa)
Alfandari's language	NEO
Algeria	ARABIC, BERBER
	FRENCH
alteration of word from another	
language to fit familiar	
sound	FOLK ETYMOLOGY
	HOBSON-JOBSON
alternative form of phoneme	ALLOPHONE
alphabet	(see separate entry)
ambiguous	DOUBLETALK, NEWSPEAK
—phrase	AMPHIBOLOGY
American sign language	AMESLAN
Amerindian	MAYA, TUPI
analysis of	
—sentences	CONSTITUENT ANALYSIS
	PARSING
—sounds	PHONEMICISATION
—word	
meanings	COMPONENTIAL ANALYSIS
Andorra	CATALAN
Angola	BAKONGO, CHOKWE
	KIMBUNDU, OVIMBUNDU
apparently contradictory	
statement	PARADOX
appropriate word	MOT JUSTE
Aramaic dialect	SYRIAC
argument	LEMMA
arrangement of	
connections	PARATAXIS
articulated	
—weakly	LENIS
—strongly	FORTIS
artificial	INTERLINGUA, SPELIN
—by	
Alfandari	NEO
Hogben	INTERGLOSSA
Jesperson	NOVIAL
Schleyer	VOLAPUK
Zamenhof	ESPERANTO
—from Esperanto	IDO
as used	PAROLE
attack made verbally	INVECTIVE
Australia	STRINE
—aborigine	NYUNGAR
Austronesia	INDONESIAN, POLYNESIAN
	TAGALOG
Avestan	AVESTIC, ZEND
bad language	OBSCENITY, SWEARING
Bangaladesh	BENGALI
based on	
—analysis	DESCRIPTIVISM

—ideas of	
correctness	NORMATIVE GRAMMAR
	PRESCRIPTIVISM
—inflection	SYNTHETIC
—Latin	ROMANCE
—word order	ANALYTICAL, ISOLATING
basic unit	
—in lexicology	LEXEME
—of	
language	MORPHEME
meaning	GLOSSEME, SEMANTEME
	SEMEME
sound	PHONEME
Basque	EUSKARA
Belgium	FLEMISH, FRENCH, GERMAN
Bhutan	BUMTHANGKHA, DZONGKHA
	SARCHAPPKHA
blind language	BRAILLE
Bolivia	AMYARA, QUECHUA
bookmaker's sign language	TICK TACK
Botswana	SETSWANA
Brazil	PORTUGUESE
Breton dialect	ARMORIC
Brunei	MALAY
Buddhist sacred	
language	PALI
bureaucratic language	GOBBLEDEGOOK
	JARGON, OFFICIALESE
Burkina Faso	FRENCH, MOSSI
Burma	SHAN
Burundi	FRENCH, KIRUNDI
	KISWAHILI
Cape Verde Islands	CRIOULO, PORTUGUESE
Carthage	PUNIC
case (of noun)	
—direct object	ACCUSATIVE
—direction from, etc	ABLATIVE
—indirect object	DATIVE
—origin or possession	GENITIVE
—personal address	VOCATIVE
—subject	NOMINATIVE
Caucasus	ANDO, ARMENIAN, AVAR
	DAGESTANIAN, DARGWA, DIDO
	GEORGIAN, LAKK, LEZGIAN, NAKH
Celtic	BRETON, CORNISH, GAELIC
	GAULISH, IRISH, MANX, WELSH
Central African Republic	SANGHO
Chad	ARABIC, FRENCH
change	
—in	
form showing	
—function	CASE
—tense, gender	ACCIDENCE
	INFLECTION
sound of	
consonant	ASSIMILATION

internal letters	METATHESIS
vowel	ABLAUT, DIPHTHONG
	GRADATION, MUTATION
—to	
less favourable	
sense	DETERIORATION
	PEJORATION
more favourable	
sense	(A)MELIORATION
	ELEVATION
character representing	
sound	PHONOGRAM
characteristic	
expression	IDIOM
Chile	SPANISH
China	CANTONESE, KUO-YO
	MANCHOO, MANCHU
	MANDARIN, PEKIN(G)ESE
	SHAN
—dialect	AMOY, HAKKA, WU
Chinese Turkestan	TOCHARIAN
	TOCHARISH, TOKARIAN
	TOKARISH
choice of words	DICTION, PARLANCE
	PHRASEOLOGY
circumlocution	PERIPHRASIS
clarity of speech	ARTICULACY
	ARTICULATION, DICTION
	ELOCUTION, ENNUNCIATION
class of	
—nouns	DECLENSION,
—verbs	CONJUGATION
classroom with tape	
recorders, etc	LANGUAGE LABORATORY
clause	
—conditional	PROTASIS
—consequent	APODOSIS
—starting with	
(al)though	CONCESSIVE
if	CONDITIONAL
clever turn of phrase	CONCETTO
coincidence of vowels	ASSONANCE
collection of utterances	CORPUS
Colombia	SPANISH
colonial patois	CREOLE
combination and distortion	
of two languages into one	PIDGIN
Comoros	ARABIC, COMORAN
	SWAHILI
composition of	
unconnected pieces	CENTO
compound word where	
—each part has equal status	DVANDVA
—first part modifies the second	BAHUVRIHI
	TATPURUSHA
conditional clause	PROTASIS

confused language	BABBLE, BABEL	—Romance	FRIULIAN, LADIN(O)
	GALIMATIAS		RHAETO-ROMANIC
	GIBBERISH		ROMANSCH
confusion of meaning	SYNCHYSIS	—Scottish	LALLANS
Congo	BANTU, FRENCH	—which becomes common	
consequential clause	APODOSIS	language	CREOLE, KOINE
context			(see also dialect)
—bound	RESTRICTED CODE	difficulty in speaking	PHONASTHENIA
—free	ELABORATED CODE	dirty talk	COPROLALIA
Coptic dialect	SAHIDIC	distinguished by pitch	TONE LANGUAGE
core of word	STEM	Djibouti	AFAR, ARABIC
correct			FRENCH, SOMALI
—expression which ousts		Dominican Republic	SPANISH
wrong one	SUMPSIMUS	doubling for emphasis	EPIZEUXIS
—pronunciation	ORTHOEPY	Dravidian	CANARESE, KANARESE
—use of language	GRAMMAR		KANNADA, MALAYALA(A)M
correspondence in sound	ASSONANCE		TAMIL, TELUGU
Costa Rica	SPANISH	earliest known form	
Creolised English	GULLAH	of word	ETYMON
current use	USUS LOQUENDI	ease of conversation	EUTRAPELIA
Cyprus	GREEK, TURKISH		EUTRAPELY
deaf language	AMESLAN, SIGNING	East Iranian	AVESTAN, AVESTIC, ZEND
defect in		Ecuador	SPANISH
—articulation	PSELLISM(US)	effective speaking	ELOCUTION
—speech	IMPEDIMENT	Egypt	ARABIC
	STAMMER, STUTTER	El Salvador	SPANISH
definition relating		emphasis	ARSIS
words to objects	OSTENSIVE	Equatorial Guinea	BUBI, FANG, SPANISH
deliberately distorted	DOUBLETALK	error of mixing	
	NEWSPEAK	categories	CATEGORY ERROR
derivation of rules		Ethiopia	(see Abyssinia above)
of grammar	DISCOVERY PROCEDURE	evasive talk	CIRCUMLOCUTION
derived from Latin	ROMANCE	everyday speech	COLLOQUIAL, DEMOTIC
describe grammar of word	PARSE		VERNACULAR, VULGATE
description of		example of inflection	PARADIGM
—functional relationships	EMIC	exclusive to group	ARGOT, CANT, JARGON
—physical patterns	ETIC	expert	LINGUIST
development of		expressing negation	PRIVATIVE
—initial sound	PROTHESIS	expression	PHRASE
—vowel		familiar combination	
between consonants	ANAPTYXIS	of words	COLLOCATION
India	SVARABHAKTI	family	
dialect	IDIOM, LINGO	—European	INDO-EUROPEAN
—Aramaic	MANDAEAN, SYRIAC	—from Latin	ROMANCE
—Berber	KABYLE	fashionable word	BUZZ WORD
—Chinese	AMOY, HAKKU, WU	faulty vocabulary or spelling	CACOLOGY
—Coptic	SAHIDIC	feeling for correct use	SPRACHGEFUHL
—French	LANGUEDOC	figurative	TROPOLOGY
	LANGUE D'OUI	Fiji	FIJIAN, HINDI
—illiterate	PATOIS	final word sound	AUSLAUT
—London	COCKNEY	Finland	FINNISH, SWEDISH
—Liverpool	SCOUSE	Finno-Ugrian	
—Louisiana	GUMBO	—Permic	PERMIAN, PERMYAK
—Newcastle	GEORDIE		UDMURT-KOMI, VOYTAK
—Persian	DARI		ZYRYAN
—provincial	PATOIS	—Ugrian	MAGYAR, OSTIAK, VOGUL

flippant speech	BANTER, PERSIFLAGE
for the blind	BRAILLE
form(s) of	
—expression	IDIOM, USAGE
—language	IDIOM, DIALECT
—noun	CASE
—verb	CONJUGATION
	MOOD, VOICE
indicating	
—action turned back	
on the subject	REFLEXIVE
—mode of action	MOOD
—whether subject acts	
or is acted upon	VOICE
used in forming tenses or	
as an adjective	PARTICIPLE
France	BASQUE, PROVENCAL
	ROMANCE
—Brittany	BRETON
—Languedoc	OCCITAN
—North	LANGUE D'OUI
	LANGUE D'OIL
—South	LANGUE D'OC, PROVENCAL
French/Louisiana	CREOLE
Gabon	ESHIRA, FANG
	MBETE, FRENCH
Gambia	FULA, MANDIKA, WOLLOF
genuine or literal	
sense of a word	ETONYM
German Hebrew	YIDDISH
Germanic dialects	ANGLIAN, JUTISH
	SAXON
Ghana	ASANTI, DAGBANI
	EWE, FANTE, GA
gibberish	BABBLE, BABEL
	GALIMATIAS
glib speech	PATTER, SPIEL
graceful use of language	ELOQUENCE
gradation of linguistic	
features	CLINE
grammarians	
—American	CHOMSKY
—English	ORM, FOWLER
	PARTRIDGE
—Greek	ARISTARCHUS
grammatical	
—rules	RECTION
which can produce	
sentences	GENERATIVE GRAMMAR
—structure	SYNTAX
Greek dialect	(A)EOLIC, ATTIC
	DORIC, IONIC, KOINE
group of speech sounds	PHONEME
groups	AFRASIAN, ALENT
	ALTAIC, AMERINDIAN
	AUSTRALIAN ABORIGINE

	AUSTRONESIAN, CHINESE
	DRAVIDIAN, ESKIMO
	HAMITO-SEMITIC
	INDO-EUROPEAN, INDO-IRANIAN
	JAPANESE, KHOISAN, KOREAN
	MALAYO-POLYNESIAN, MON KHMER
	NIGER-CONGO, NILO-SAHARAN
	PALEO-SIBERIAN, SINO-TIBETAN
	TURKIC, URALIC
Guinea	FRENCH, FULANI
	MALINKE, PULAR, SUSU
Guinea-Bissau	BALANTE, FULANI
	MALINKE, PORTUGUESE
Guyana	HINDI, URDU
gypsy	
—jargon	ARGOT, CANT
—language	ROMANES, ROMANI
	ROMANY, SHELDRU
Haiti	CREOLE, FRENCH
Hamito-Semitic	ARABIC
having same syllable	
arrangement	TAUTOMETRIC(AL)
heading	LEMMA
Hebrew - modern	IVRIT
Holland	DUTCH
Honduras	SPANISH
Hungary	MAGYAR
hypothetical language	PROTOLANGUAGE
illiterate dialect	PATOIS
in the abstract	LANGUE
incorrect pronunciation	CACOEPY
increased vocal pitch	ARSIS
index of all words in text	CONCORDANCE
Indian	(see India)
individual speech habits	IDIOLECT
Indo-European languages	BENGALI
	(CLASSIC) GREEK
	CELTIC, ENGLISH, FRENCH
	GERMAN(IC), HINDUSTANI
	HITTITE, ITALIAN, JAPHETIC
	KELTIC, LATIN, MARATHI
	MYCAENEAN, POLISH, PORTUGUESE
	PUNJABI, ROMANCE, RUSSIAN
	SPANISH, UKRAINIAN, URDU
Indo-Iranian	DARD(IC), KAFIRI
	KASHMIRI, KHOWARI, PERSIAN
	PISAC(H)E, SANSKRIT, SHIHA
	VEDIC
Indonesia	BAHASI, BATAK, BUGIS
	JAVANESE, MACASSAR
	MADURESE, SUDANESE
inflections of	
—noun, pronoun or	
adjective	DECLENSION
—verb	CONJUGATION, MOOD
	VOICE

informal speech	COLLOQUIALISM
	DEMOTIC, SLANG
	VERNACULAR, VULGATE
ingenious use of words	CONCETTO
international at sea	SEASPEAK
interpreter (US)	LINGUISTER
insertion of extra sound	EPENTHESIS
invent a new word	COIN
Iran	ARABIC, AZERBAIJANI
	AZERBAIZHANI, DARI
	FARSI, KURDISH, IRANIAN
	PAHLAVI, PARSEE, PARSI
	PEHLEVI, ZEND
Iraq	ARABIC, KURDISH
	TURKOMAN
Ireland	ERSE, GAELIC
—accent	BROGUE
Israel	ARABIC, HEBREW
	IVRIT, YIDDISH
Italian	
—ancient	OSCAN, LATIN
	SAMNITE, UMBRIAN
—classical	TUSCAN
—dialect	LADIN(O)
Japan	AINU
jargon	BARAGOUIN, LINGO
—American Indian	
traders	CHINOOK
—Brazil	GERAL, LINGUA GERIL
—bureaucratic	GOBBLEDEGOOK
	OFFICIALESE
—combining English with	
another language	PIDGIN
—gypsy	ARGOT, CANT, SHELTA
—index	FOG INDEX
—Irish	SHELTA
—jazz	HIP, RAP, SCAT, VOUT
—lawyers	LEGALESE
—newspapers	JOURNALESE
—psychologists	PSYCHOBABBLE
—sect	CANT
—sociologists	SOCIOBABBLE
—Spanish Jews	LADINO
—technologists	TECHNOBABBLE
—thieves	ARGOT
—tinkers	SHELTA
—trade	
American Indian	CHINOOK
Brazil	LINGOA GERAL
English/Chinese	PIDGIN
Italy/Levant	LINGUA FRANCA
—vagrants	SHELTA
Jordan	ARABIC
Kampuchea	FRENCH, KHMER
Kenya	LUO, KIKUYU, SWAHILI
Kerala	MALAYALA(A)M

Khoisan	BUSHMAN
Kiribati	GILBERTESE, KIRIBATI
Kuwait	ARABIC
Laos	FRENCH, LAO
law governing	
—length of conjunct	
words	BEHAGEL'S LAW
—sound variations	
over a period	SOUND LAW
Lebanon	ARABIC, ARMENIAN
	FRENCH
lengthening of	
short syllables	ECTASIS
Lesotho	SETHOSO
letter with several	
sounds	POLYPHONE
Libya	ARABIC, BERBER
Liechtenstein	GERMAN
light-hearted style	BADINAGE, BANTER
	PERSIFLAGE, RAILLERY
limiting adjective	DETERMINER
line on language map	ISOGLOSS
linguists/philologists	
—American	BLOOMFIELD, CHOMSKY
	FILLMORE, HOCKETT, LAMB
	PIKE, SAPIR, WHORF
—British	BERNSTEIN, FIRTH
	HALLIDAY, HOGBEN
	LYONS, MULLER, OGDEN
—Danish	HJELMSLEV, JESPERSON
—French	LOISY
—German	AUERBACH, MULLER
	SCHLEYER
—Italian	ALFANDARI
—Polish	ZAMENHOF
—Russian	JAKOBSEN, TRUBETSKOY
—Swiss	SAUSSURE
linguistic	
—branches	BLOOMFIELDIANISM
	CASE GRAMMAR
	COMPUTATIONAL LINGUISTICS
—classification	CATEGORY
—unit	MORPHEME
literal translation of	
foreign expression	CALQUE
	LOAN TRANSLATION
literary or	
oratorical	RHETORIC, PERIODS
long-windedness	CIRCUMLOCUTION
	PERIPHRASIS, PROLIXITY
	SESQUIPEDALIANISM
Louisiana negro	
patois	GUMBO
Luxemburg	FRENCH, GERMAN
	LETZEBURGESCH
	LUXEMBOURGOIS

Madagascar	FRENCH, MALAGASY
make a vocal sound	PHONATE
Malawi	CHICHEWA
Malayo-Polynesian	BAHASA, INDONESIAN
	JAVANESE, MALAY
Malaysia	CHINESE, IBAN, MALAY
	TAMIL
Maldives	DHIVEHI, MALDIVIAN
Mali	BAMBARA, FULANI, FRENCH
Marrowsky	SPOONERISM
Mauritania	ARABIC, FRENCH
	HASSANIYA
Mauritius	BHOJPURI, CREOLE
	HINDI, URDU
meaning	
—by implication	CONNOTATION
—in normal use	ACCEPTATION
—on explicit reference	DENOTATION
meaningless	GIBBERISH
Melanesian/English	NEO-MELANESIAN
mental images of	
language forms	LANGUE
method of specifying	
meanings of	
words	COMPONENTIAL ANALYSIS
Mexico	MAYAN, SPANISH
Middle Persian	PAHLAVI, PEHLEVI
mixed, witty language	MACARONIC
mode of expression	IDIOM
modifying word	DETERMINER
Monaco	FRENCH
Mongolia	KHALKH, MONGOLIAN
Mon Khmer	KHMER, VIETNAMESE
mood (of verb)	
—calling for action	IMPERATIVE
—expressing	
condition or supposition	SUBJUNCTIVE
idea without	
number or person	INFINITIVE
query	INTERROGATIVE
—indicating matter	
of fact	INDICATIVE
Morocco	ARABIC, BERBER
Mozambique	PORTUGUESE
nasal speech	RHINOLALIA
needing other words to	
form a term	SYNCATEGOREMATIC
negro (south-east USA)	GULLAH
Nepal	NEPALI, METHIR
	TAMANG
Netherlands	DUTCH
new word or phrase	NEOLOGISM, NEOLOGY
New Zealand	ENGLISH, MAORI
Nicaragua	MISKITO, SPANISH
Niger	DIERMA, FULANI, FRENCH
	HAUSA, TUAREG

Nilo-Saharan	LUO
Norway	LANDSMA(A)L
	NEW NORSE, NYNORSK
noun	SUBSTANTIVE
—indeclinable	APTOTE
—with four cases	TETRAPTOTE
object of meaning	REFERENT
obscene speech	BAWDRY, COPROLALIA
	SMUT
obsolete word	FOSSIL
of	
—an idividual	IDIOLECT
—local area	DIALECT, VERNACULAR
Oman	ARABIC
omission of	
—conjunctions	ASYNDETON
—sound or syllable from	
middle of word	HAPLOLOGY
	SYNCOPATION, SYNCOPE
—word(s)	ELLIPSIS
one	
—clever with words	LOGODAEDALUS
—converting one language	
to another	
spoken	INTERPRETER
written	TRANSLATOR
origin of words	DERIVATION
	ETYMOLOGY
original	
—root of word	ETONYM
—speech	URSPRACHE
Orwell's language	NEWSPEAK
out of date	ARCHAISM
pair of words	DOUBLET
Paleo-Siberian	KET
Panama	SPANISH
Papua New Guinea	MORU, PIDGIN
Paraguay	GUARANI, SPANISH
part of	
—grammar dealing	
with inflections	ACCIDENCE
—sentence	PHRASE
which follows verb	
to complete predicate	COMPLEMENT
which says something	
about something	PREDICATE
participle that has	
no clear connection	
with the word	
it modifies	DANGLING PARTICIPLE
	MISRELATED PARTICIPLE
parts of speech	ADJECTIVE, ADVERB
	CONJUNCTION, INTERJECTION
	NOUN, PREPOSITION
	PRONOUN, VERB
peculiar talk	CANT

Persia	*(see* Iran *above)*	—vowels together	SYN(A)ERESIS
personal style	IDIOLECT, IDIOM	—words together	SLUR
	PARLANCE	Rwanda	KINYARWANDA, KISWAHILI
persuasive style	RHETORIC		FRENCH
pert speech	DICACITY	sacred language	PALI
Peru	AYMARA, QUECHUA	San Marino	ITALIAN
	QUICHUA, SPANISH	Sao Tome	PORTUGUESE
Philippines	AT(T)A, BIKOL, CHEBUANO	Scotland	GADHELIC, GAELIC, LALLANS
	FILIPINO, ILOCANO, MORO	script	*(see* **alphabet***)*
	TAGAL(OG), TINO	secret language	CIPHER, CODE
pictorial			CRYPTOLOGY
representation of		Semitic	ARAMAIC, ARABIC, HEBREW
—letter	PICTOGRAM	Senegal	FRENCH, FULANI, SERER
—object described	IDEOGRAM		TOUCOULEUR, WOLOF
—sound	PHONOGRAM	sentence	CLAUSE
—word	REBUS	Seychelles	CREOLE, FRENCH
pithy saying	ADAGE, APHORISM	short statement of a	
	APO(PH)THEGM, EPIGRAM	general truth	AXIOM, MAXIM
	GNOME, LACON(IC)ISM	single voice-sound	SYLLABLE
	MAXIM, PROVERB, SAW	Siberia	OSTIAK, OSTYAK
play on words	JEU DE MOTS, PUN	Sierra Leone	KRIO, MENDE, TEMNE
pleasant pronunciation	EUPHONY	sign	
pompous language	BOMBAST, EUPHUISM	—language	AMESLAN, SIGNING
	FUSTIAN, GRANDILOQUENCE		TICK TACK
	RHODOMONTADE	—representing	
popular phrase	CATCHPHRASE	diphthong	DIPHONE
	CATCHWORD	word	LOGOGRAM
possessive case	(SAXON) GENITIVE	—system	SEMIOLOGY, SEMIOTICS
primitive language	URSPRACHE		*(see also* pictorial *above)*
pronounce unclearly	SLUR	simple vowel sound	MONOPHTHONG
proverb	PAROEMIA	Singapore	MALAY, MANDARIN
provincial dialect	PATOIS		TAMIL, SINGLISH
Qatar	ARABIC	Sino-Tibetan	BEIFANGHUA, CANTONESE
raillery	DICACITY		CHINESE, FUKIEN, GUOYU
related to Sanskrit	PAKRIT		MANDARIN, MIN, WU
repetition of		slang	ARGOT, CANT
—initial letters	ALLITERATION		JARGON, LINGO
—'s' sound	SIGMATISM	sleep-talking	SOMNILOQUENCE
—sound	TAUTOPHONY	slurring of sounds	ELISION
—sounds	ASSONANCE	soft manner	
representation of sound	PHONETICISM	of speaking	DULCILOQUY
Romance		Somalia	ARABIC, ITALIAN, SOMALI
—dialects	FRIULIAN, LADIN(O)	sound	
	LANGUE D'OC, LANGUE D'OIL	—quality	ACOUSTICS, TIMBRE
	LANGUE D'OUI	—system	PHONEMICS, PHONETICS
	RHAETO-ROMANIC, ROMANSCH		PHONOLOGY
—languages	FRENCH, ITALIAN	sounding	
	PORTUGUESE, PROVENCAL	—of	
	ROMANIAN, ROMANSCH	final consonant	LIAISON
	SPANISH	'r' after vowel	RHOTACISM
rough 'r' sound	BUR(R)	—pleasant	EUPHONIOUS
roundabout speech	CIRCUMABAGES	—rich	RESONANT, SONOROUS
	CIRCUMLOCUTION	South Africa	AFRIKAANS, SEPEDI
running			SESOTHO, SESUTO, SETSWANA
—final vowel into			TSWANA, XHOSA, ZULU
next word	SYNALOEPHA	South American	TUPI

South Seas	BEACH-LA-MAR	charming but deceitful	BLARNEY
	BECHE-DE-MER	emotional	DECLAMATION
Spanish	BASQUE, CASTILIAN, CATALAN		ORATORY
	LADRINO, GALICIAN	empty of meaning	RHETORIC
speaking	DIALOGUE	ecstatic	GLOSSOLALIA
—between		hypocritical	CANT
three people	TRIALOGUE	long-winded	CIRCUMLOCUTION
two people	DUOLOGUE		PERIPHRASIS, PROLIXITY
—by one person	MONOLOGUE	pleasant in sound	EUPHONY
—in		pompous	BOMBAST, EUPHUISM
sleep	SOMNILOQUENCE		FUSTIAN, FLATULENCE
tongues	GLOSSOLALIA		GRANDILOQUENCE
—one language	MONOGLOT	ugly in sound	CACOPHONY
	MONOLINGUAL	splitting of word by	
—to oneself	SOLILOQUY	insertion of another	TMESIS
—together	COLLOQUY	spoken language	PAROLE
—two languages	BILINGUAL, DIGLOT	Spoonerism	MARROWSKY
—many languages	MULTILINGUAL	Sri Lanka	SINHALI, TAMIL
	POLYGLOT	string of clichés, etc	CENTO
speech		study of	
—longer than sentence	DISCOURSE	—comparative philology	GLOSSOLOGY
—of			GLOTTOLOGY
characters in story	DIALOGUE	—conversational pauses	CHRONEMICS
individual	IDIOLECT	—correct pronunciation	ORTHOEPY
particular		—derivation of words	ETYMOLOGY
—area	BROGUE, DIALECT, PATOIS	—form of words	MORPHOLOGY
	VERNACULAR	—grammar	SYNTAX
—group	ARGOT, CANT	—internal structure	
	JARGON, SLANG	of language	STRUCTURALISM
—sound	PHONE	—language	LINGUISTICS
—sounds			PHILOLOGY
breathy	ASPIRATE	at any one time	SYNCHRONIC
briefly blocking breath	PLOSIVE	in relation to	
explosive	PLOSIVE	—behaviour, etc	METALINGUISTICS
hissing	SIBILANT	—location	STYLISTICS
partially blocking		—thought	PSYCHOLINGUISTICS
breath	FRICATIVE	through historical	
	SPIRANT	development	DIACHRONIC
releasing breath	AFFRICATE	—local variations	DIALECTOLOGY
throaty	GUTTURAL, UVULAR	—mathematics of	
unstressed vowel	SCHWA	language	MATHEMATICAL LINGUISTICS
using		—meaning	SEMANTICS
—glottis	GLOTTAL STOP	as depending on user	PRAGMATICS
—gums	DENTAL	—neurological preconditions	
—lips	LABIAL	for development of	
and teeth	LABIODENTAL	language	NEUROLINGUISTICS
—teeth	DENTAL	—orthography of language	GRAPHOLOGY
—tip of tongue	APICAL	—pronunciation	PHONETICS
—tongue and teeth	DENTILINGUAL	—relationship of	
with tongue		basic units	STRUCTURAL LINGUISTICS
—behind teeth	ALVEOLAR	language patterns to	
—on soft palate	VELAR	psychological	
—which is		ideas	PSYCHOLINGUISTICS
capable of two		languages over	
explanations	AMBIGUITY	time	GLOTTOCHRONOLOGY
	EQUIVOCATION		LEXICOSTATISTICS

phonological shapes	MORPHOPHONEMICS
	MORPHO(PHO)NOLOGY
structure to meaning	
and gesture	METALINGUISTICS
—signs or signals	SEMIOLOGY, SEMIOTICS
—sound	PHONICS
in relation to words	PHONOTATICS
—speech sounds	PHONEMICS, PHONETICS
	PHONOLOGY
—spoken sounds	PHONICS
—use of	
language	GRAMMAR
words by a particular	
author	STYLOMETRY
—variations in language	STYLISTICS
style	
—appropriate to setting	REGISTER
—of expressing	DICTION
	PHRASEOLOGY
subtle argument	QUILLET
Sudan	ARABIC, NILOTIC
suppression of	
—sound	ECTHLIPSIS
—vowel or syllable	ELISION
Suriname	CREOLE, DUTCH
	HINDUSTANI, JAVANESE
Swaziland	SISWATI
Switzerland	FRENCH, GERMAN
	ITALIAN, ROMANSCH
syllable	
—character set	SYLLABARY
—writing (Jap.)	HIRAGANA, KATAKANA
symbol	CATCHWORD, WATCHWORD
	(*see* pictorial representation, sign *above*)
syntactic	SYNTAGMA
syntax	SYNESIS
Syria	ARABIC, ARAMAEAN, ARAMAIC
	ARMENIAN, CIRCASSIAN
	KURDISH, SYRIAC, TURKISH
Taiwan	AMOY, CHINESE
Tanzania	SWAHILI
teaching by formal	
grammar	DIRECT METHOD
tense (of verb)	AORIST, FUTURE (PERFECT)
	(HISTORIC) PAST
	IMPERFECT, INFINITIVE
	(PLU)PERFECT, PRESENT
	PRETERIT(E)(-PRESENT)
	PRETERITO-PRESENT(IAL)
Thailand	THAI, SHAN
theme	LEMMA
theory of language and	
mathematics	GLOSSEMATICS
thieves' jargon	ARGOT
three vowels in one syllable	TRIPHTHONG
tinkers' jargon	SHELTA

Tobago	FRENCH, HINDI, SPANISH
Togo	EWE, FRENCH, KABIYE
trade jargon	(*see* jargon *above*)
transposition of	
—initial letters	MARROWSKY
	SPOONERISM
—letters or sounds	METATHESIS
—words	HYPERBATON
Trinidad	HINDI, FRENCH, SPANISH
troubadours' language	LANGUE D'OC
trouvères' language	LANGUE D'OIL
	LANGUE D'OUI
Tunisia	ARABIC, FRENCH
Turanian	URAL-ALTAIC
Turkey	ARABIC, KURDISH
	TURKISH, ZAZA
Turkic	OGHUZ, TURKISH
two	
—letters printed as one	AESC
	DIPHTHONG
	LIGATURE
—nouns joined by 'and' to	
replace adjective and noun	HENDIADYS
—vowels in one syllable	DIPHTHONG
Uganda	ATESO, LUGANDA
	RUNYANKOGE
ugly sound	CACOPHONY, DISCORDANCE
	DISSONANCE
unaspirated consonant	TENUIS
uninflected verb	INFINITIVE
unintelligible	DOUBLE-DUTCH
	DOUBLE-TALK
—jargon	BARAGOUIN
—pronunciation	IDIOGLOSSIA
union of two vowels	SYN(A)ERESIS
	SYNECPHONESIS
	SYNIZESIS
Ural-Altaic	FINNO-UGRIAN, MANCHOO
	MANCHU, MONGOLIAN
	TUNGUS, TURKO-TATAR
Uralic	FINNO-UGRIC, HUNGARIAN
	SAMOYED
Uruguay	SPANISH
use of	
—complex words formed	
from component units	AGGLUTINATION
—descriptive words	
(time and place)	DEIXIS
—language to communicate	
feelings rather than ideas	PHASIS
—symbol	
for sound	PHONETIC SPELLING
to represent initial	
sound only	ACROPHONY
—words having same	
meaning	TAUTOLOGY

used	
—between speakers of different languages	LINGUA FRANCA
—to	
discuss another language	METALANGUAGE
establish relationships	PHATIC LANGUAGE
utter	
—childish sounds	PRATTLE
—meaningless sounds	GIBBER
Vanuatu	BISLAMA
variation of	
—tone carrying different meaning	PROSODIC FEATURE
—voice pitch	INTONATION
—word endings	INFLECTION
Venezuela	SPANISH
verb	
—accompanying main verb to indicate tense etc	AUXILIARY
—acting on the subject	REFLEXIVE
—expressing command	JUSSIVE
—that takes	
a direct object	TRANSITIVE
an indirect object	INTRANSITIVE
verbal	
—adjective	GERUNDIVE
—attack	INVECTIVE
—dexterity	LOGODAEDALY
—noun	GERUND
vocal sounds affecting tones of voice	PARALANGUAGE
voice (of verb)	ACTIVE, MIDDLE, PASSIVE
vowel-rhyme	ASSONANCE
witticism	BON MOT, JEU D'ESPRIT
word(s)	
—a, an or the	ARTICLE
—as expression of style	LOCUTION
—blindness	DYSLEXIA
—borrowed from another language	LOAN WORD
—coined for one occasion	NONCE WORD
—commonly used	COLLOQUIALISM
—comprising	
all letters of other word(s)	ANAGRAM TRANSPOSITION
first letters of other words	ACRONYM, ACROSTIC
syntactic unit	SYNTAGMA
—conveying a particular meaning	SEMANTEME SEMEME
—difficult for stutterers	JONAH WORD

—element used at	
either end	AFFIX
the beginning	PREFIX
the end	SUFFIX
—expressing emotion	INTERJECTION
—formed from supposed derivative	BACK FORMATION
—having	
opposite meaning	ANTONYM
same	
—meaning	SYNONYM
—pronunciation but different meaning	HOMOPHONE
with	
—same spelling	HOMOGRAPH
—perhaps the same spelling	HOMONYM
second meaning	DOUBLE ENTENDRE
two opposite meanings	ANTILOGY
—imitating sound	ONOMATOPOEIA
—indicating	
contrast	DISJUNCTIVE
equality	CONJUNCTIVE
increased size	AUGMENTATIVE
relationship	PREPOSITION
smallness	DIMINUTIVE
—list	DICTIONARY, GLOSSARY LEXICON, LEXIS VOCABULARY
—modifying,	
adjective, verb, etc	ADVERB
noun	ADJECTIVE
—newly invented	COINAGE, NEOLOGISM
—of action	VERB
—out of date	ARCHAISM
—overused	CLICHE
—placed before noun, etc	PREPOSITION
—regarded as a series of sounds	VOCABLE
—related in origin	COGNATE, PARONYM
—repeated in meditation	MANTRA
—standing for a noun	PRONOUN
—structure	MORPHOLOGY
—substituted for	
less offensive word	DYSPHEMISM
more offensive word	EUPHEMISM
noun	PRONOUN
—suggesting but evading promise	WEASEL WORD
—used	
as actor's cue	CATCHWORD
at top of page in dictionary, etc	CATCHWORD
for	
—description	ADJECTIVE

—identification	PASSWORD
	SHIBBOLETH, WATCHWORD
in headlines	CATCHWORD
	HEADWORD, LEMMA
incorrectly	BARBARISM, MALAPROPISM
	SOLECISM, SPOONERISM
to join phrases	CONJUNCTION
—using parts of two or	
more words	BLEND
	PORTMANTEAU WORD
—with	
circumflex accent on last	
—syllable	PERISPOMENON
—but one syllable	PROPERISPOMENON
acute accent on	
last	
—syllable	OXTYONE
—but one syllable	PAROXYTONE
—third last syllable	PROPAROXYTONE
—without accent	ENCLITIC
—worship	EPEOLATRY
word or phrase	
—serving as noun	SUBSTANTIVE
—with two meanings	DOUBLE ENTENDRE
word(-unit) that	
cannot be divided	MORPHEME
writing alternately from	
L to R and R to L	BOUSTROPHEDON
Yugoslavia	MACEDONIAN, SERBIAN
	SERBO-CROAT(IAN)
	SLOVENE, SLOVENIAN
Zaire	FRENCH, KIKONGO, KISWAHILI
	LINGALA, TSHILUBA
Zambia	BEMBA, LOZI, LUNDA
	LUVALE, NYANJA, TONGA
Zimbabwe	CHISHON, SINDEBELE
	(*see also* **rhetoric**)
Laos	LAO
capital	VIENGCHANE, VIENTIANE
coin	
—unit	AT
—100 at	KIP
Latin	
abandoned suit	NOLI PROSEQUI
about	CIRCA
absolute sovereignty	IMPERIUM
abyss	BARATHRUM
acceptable person	PERSONA GRATA
accidentally	EX ACCIDENTI
according to	SECUNDUM
—circumstances	PRO RE NATA
—one's prayer	EX VOTO
—the exigencies of the case	E(X) RE NATA
acquittance	QUIETUS
action	SUIT
—by informer	QUI TAM

actual	DE FACTO
administrative board	COLLEGIUM
adorn	ORNARE
after the manner	AD MODUM
—of our ancestors	MORE MAJORUM
against	CONTRA, V, VS, VERSUS
—the world	CONTRA MUNDUM
agreeable	GRATUM
alcohol	AQUA VITAE
all	OMNIS
—go out	EXEUNT OMNES
—that sort	HOC GENUS OMNE
—the more so	A FORTIORI
alternately	ALTERNIS VICIBUS
always	SEMPER
—faithful	SEMPER FIDELIS
—ready	SEMPER PARATUS
—the same	SEMPER IDEM
amateur musicians	COLLEGIUM MUSICUM
amazingly	MIRABILE DICTU
amicable arrangement	MODUS VIVENDI
among other	
—persons	INTER ALIOS
—things	INTER ALIA
amongst themselves	INTER SE
and	AC, ATQUE, ET
—all that sort of	
thing	ET HOC GENUS OMNE
—other	
people	ET AL, ET ALII
things	ET AL, ET ALIA
—so on	ETC, ET CETERA
—that which follows	ET SEQUENS
—the rest	ETC, ET CETERA
—those that follow	ET SEQUENTES
	ET SEQUENTIA
anew	DE NOVO
animal able to laugh	ANIMAL RISIBILE
annual average	COMMUNIBUS ANNIS
any	ULLUS
appealing to pity	AD MISERICORDIAM
appease	PACARE
applaud	PLAUDITE
apple	MALUM
argument	ARGUMENTUM
—for the sake of it	ARGUMENTI CAUSA
—from absurdity of	
the contrary	PER IMPOSSIBILE
—of the stick	AD BACULINUM
—to	
common sense	AD JUDICIUM
cupidity	AD CRUMENAM
opponent's	
—ignorance	AD IGNORANTIAM
—previous admissions	AD HOMINEM
prejudices	AD INVIDIAM

the point/purpose	AD REM
around	CIRCA
artificial memory	MEMORIA TECHNICA
as	QUA, UT
—a	
consequence	IPSO FACTO
favour	EX GRATIA
matter of form	PRO FORMA
poor man	IN FORMA PAUPERIS
present from	EX DONO
warning	IN TERROREM
whole	IN TOTO
—above	UT SUPRA
—an	
act of	
contumacy	IN CONTUMACIUM
grace	EX GRATIA
honour	HONORIS CAUSA
	HONORIS GRATIA
—below	UT INFRA
—far as	
concerns	
sacred matters	QUOAD SACRA
(this)	QUOAD (HOC)
—from the beginning	QUALIS AB INCEPTO
—if	QUASI
—it were	QUASI
—much	
as he deserved	QUANTUM MERUIT
more	ALTERUM TANTUM
—often as	TOTIES QUOTIES
—such	PER SE
—undivided	PRO INDIVISO
asses' bridge	PONS ASINORUM
at	
—a lucky moment	DEXTRO TEMPORE
—first sight	PRIMA FACIE
—full length	IN EXTENSO
—hand	AD MANUM
—my own risk	MEO PERICULO
—pleasure	AD LIB(ITUM)
—the	
last gasp	IN EXTREMIS
point of death	IN ARTICULO MORTIS
	IN EXTREMIS
—this time	HOC TEMPORE
Attic salt/wit	MERUM SAL, SAL ATTICUM
attendant	MINISTER
attested copy	VIDIMUS
author	AUCTOR
authoritatively	EX CATHEDRA
avowedly	EX PROFESSO
awnless	MUTICUS
back	DORSUM
bad	MALUS
badly	MALE

baggage	IMPEDIMENTA
bain-marie	BALNEUM MARIAE
bankruptcy process	CESSIO BONORUM
barley	HORDEUM
bastard	FILIUS NULLIUS
be	
—bent, not broken	FLECTI NON FRANGI
—born	NASCI
—silent!	TACE
beak	MUSUS
beaten path	VIA TRUTA
before	
—noon	ANTE MERIDIEM
—the	
light	ANTE LUCEM
war	ANTE BELLUM
begging the question	PETITIO PRINCIPII
behold the	
—man	ECCE HOMO
—proof	ECCE SIGNUM
—sign	ECCE SIGNUM
below	INFRA
—one's dignity	INFRA DIG(NITATEM)
benign mother	ALMA MATER
bereaved	ORBUS
besiege	OBSIDERE
best	OPTIMUS
better	MELIOR
between	
—parties	INTER PARTES
—themselves	INTER SE
beware	CAVE
—buyer	CAVEAT EMPTOR
—doer	CAVEAT ACTOR
—of the dog	CAVEAT CANEM
beyond	ULTRA
—measure	EXTRA MODUM
—one's power	ULTRA VIRES
—the walls	EXTRA MUROS
biographical sketch	CURRICULUM VITAE
bird	AVIS
bite	MORDERE, MORSUS
black	NIGER
blank tablet	TABULA RASA
bless you	BENEDICITE
blessed are the	
peace makers	BEATI PACIFICI
bold and cautious	AUDAX ET CAUTUS
bone	OS
book	LIBER
—plate	EX LIBRIS
bottom	FUNDUS
boxing glove	C(A)ESTUS
branch	RAMUS
brandy	AQUA VITAE
bravely	FORTITER

bread	PANIS	warrant	QUO WARRANTO
bread-basket	PANARIUM	—your leave	PACE TUA
breast	MAMMA, PECTUS	canonical hours	HORAE CANONICAE
breathe upon	INHALARE	case	
breathing	SPIRITUS	—already decided	RES JUDICATA
breeding animal	MATRIX	—of conscience	CASUS CONSCIENTIAE
breeze of popularity	AURA POPULARIS	cast	DRAMATIS PERSONAE
bride	NYMPHA	catch	MORSUS
bridge of asses	PONS ASINORUM	cattle	PECORA
bridle	FRENUM	cause	
bright	NITIDUS	—of war	CASUS BELLI
brine	MURIA	—to be done	FIERI FACIAS
bronze	AER	celebration of sacrament	OPUS OPERATUM
brother	FRATER	censor of morals	CENSOR MORUM
burden	ONUS	certain person	QUIDAM
butterfly	PAPILIO	chaff	PALEA
buttocks	NATES	chamber	CAMERA
by	PER	characters in play	DRAMATIS PERSONAE
—common consent	COMMUNI CONSENSU	charity	CARITAS
—courage and faith	ANIMO ET FIDE	chide	JUGARE
—divine law	JURE DIVINO	chief good	SUMMUM BONUM
—faith and		chin	MENTUM
confidence	FIDE ET FIDUCIA	church with a font	DELUBRUM
fortitude	FIDE ET FORTUDINE	circle	ORBIS
love	FIDE ET AMORE	—of lands	ORBIS TERRARUM
—faith, not arms	FIDE NON ARMIS	circumlocution	CIRCUITUS VERBORUM
—gift	EX DONO	civil	
—hand	MANU	—arm	BRACHIUM CIVILE
—head of population	PER CAPITA	—law	JUS CIVILE
—heart	MEMORITER	clamour of forum	FORENSIS STREPITUM
—himself	PER SE	clap your hands	PLAUDITE
—human law	JURE HUMANO	classical passage	LOCUS CLASSICUS
—labour and honour	LABORE ET HONORE	clean	MUNDUS
—law	JURE	cloak	PALLIUM
—leave of	PACE	closed sea	MARE CLAUSUM
—logical conversion	E CONVERSO	cloth	PANNUS
—my own fault	MEA CULPA	cloud	NUBES
—oral testimony	VIVA VOCE	collection of dried	
—reason of a vow	EX VOTO	plants	HORTUS SICCUS
—right	DE JURE	college of cardinals	COLLEGIUM
—that		combined with	CUM
fact	IPSO FACTO	comic power	VIS COMICA
name	EO NOMINE	command	IMPERIUM
—the		commander	IMPERATOR
grace of God	DEI GRATIA	common	COMMUNIS
living voice	VIVA VOCE	—good	COMMUNE BONUM
very fact	IPSO FACTO	—people	VULGUS
way	OBITER	commonly	VULGO
whole heavens	TOTO CAELO	completely	IN TOTO
—virtue of office	EX OFFICIO	compliance	OBSEQUIUM
	VIRTUTE OFFICII	compromise between	
—way of	VIA	people of different	
consequence	EX CONSEQUENTI	views	MODUS VIVENDI
example	EG, EXEMPLI GRATIA	compulsion from behind	VIS A TERGO
—what		conclusion	FINIS
right	QUO JURE	confidential	A LATERE

confidentially	SUB ROSA
conscript fathers	PATRES CONSCRIPTI
consider the end	FINEM RESPICE
contract	PACISCERE
contrariwise	E CONTRA
contrived solution	DEUS EX MACHINA
conversely	E CONTRA, E CONVERSO
council representing	
all sections of Greeks	PANHELLENIUM
country in town	RUS IN URBE
course of life	CURRICULUM VITAE, CV
created nature	NATURA NATURATA
creative nature	NATURA NATURANS
crime	NEFAS
—of forgery	FALSI CRIMEN
crucial test	EXPERIMENTUM CRUCIS
crumb	MICA
cup	CALYX
current usage of speech	USUS LOQUENDI
cursorily	OBITER
cursory remark	OBITER DICTUM
customs	MORES
darnel	LOLIUM
day	DIES
—of	
judgment	DIES IRAE
wrath	DIES IRAE
days	
—of	
festival	DIES FERIAE, DIES FESTI
wrath	DIES IRAE
—when	
judges do not sit	DIES NON
judgment could	
—be pronounced	DIES FASTI
—not be pronounced	DIES NEFASTI
dead force	VIS MORTUA
death	MORS
defender of the faith	FID DEF
	FIDEI DEFENSOR
deity	DEUS
deliver formally	SERVE
delusive idea	IGNIS-FATUUS
deputy	LOCUM(TENENS)
destination	TERMINUS AD QUEM
diametrically opposite	TOTO CAELO
disc-thrower	DISCOBOLUS
discharge	QUIETUS
disease	MORBUS
disgustingly	AD NAUSEAM
disinterested adviser	AMICUS CURIAE
dispersedly	PASSIM
disputed question	VEXATA QUAESTIO
distinguishing	
properties	DIFFERENTIA
divide and rule	DIVIDE ET IMPERA

divided	PARTITUS
divine right	JUS DIVINUM
divinity	NUMEN
do not	
—despair	NIL DESPERANDUM
—touch me	NOLI ME TANGERE
dogged labour	LABOR IMPROBUS
dogmatic pronouncement	IPSE DIXIT
dregs of the people	FAEX POPULI
dried dung	ALBUM GRAECUM
drink	
—up!	BIBITE
—distilled from	
spices and wine	AQUA MIRABILIS
drudge	MEDIASTINUS
dry wit	MERUM SAL, SAL ATTICUM
dumb	MUTUS
during life	DURANTE VITA
duty	OFFICIUM
dwelling	MANSIO
earnestly	EX ANIMO
earth	TERRA
easy first	FACILE PRINCEPS
eat and drink	EDITE BIBITE
egg	OVUM
eighth	OCTAVUS
either	UTER
emperor	IMPERATOR
emperor's decree	NOVELLA
empirical	A POSTERIORI
enclosing wall	PERIBOLUS
encumbrances	IMPEDIMENTA
end	FINIS, TERMINUS
enjoy the present	CARPE DIEM
enlightened	ILLUMINATI
enough	
—for the wise	SAT SAPIENTI
—of words	SATIS VERBORUM
enthusiasm	FUROR
entirely	IN TOTO
entity	ENS
—actually existing	ENS REALE
—existing	
as accident	ENS PAR SE
	ENS PER ACCIDENS
in the mind	ENS RATIONIS
equal	PAR
equally	EX AEQUO
equitably	EX AEQUO
essentially	PER SE
everywhere	PASSIM, UBIQUE
evil omen	MONSTRUM
examine orally	VIVA (VOCE)
example of all the rest	INSTAR OMNIUM
examples	EXEMPLA
except	NISI

excess	LUXUS
excitement	FUROR
existing condition	STATUS QUO
exploits	RES GESTAE
extinction	QUIETUS
extortioner	BARATHRUM
extracts	EXERPTA
extravagant	EXTRA MODUM
extreme perfection	NE PLUS ULTRA
exult	OVARE
eye	OCULUS
eyelid	PALPEBRA
facts relevant to case	RES GESTAE
fair reward	QUANTUM MERUIT
faith	FIDES
faithful and bold	FIDUS ET AUDAX
father	PATER
—of his country	PATER PATRIAE
favour	MERCES, OFFICIUM
—in return	QUID PRO QUO
fear	METUS
fearful	TIMIDUS
feather	PENNA
featherless animal	ANIMAL IMPLUME
fidelity and justice	FIDES ET JUSTITIA
field of Mars	CAMPUS MARTIUS
finger	DIGITUS
first	PRIMUS
—among equals	PRIMUS INTER PARES
fish's bladder	VESICA PISCIS
flame	FLAMMA
flax	LINUM
flourished	FLORUIT
fluency	COPIA VERBORUM
fly	MUSCA
focal chord	LATUS RECTUM
following	SECUNDUM
font	DELUBRUM
food	PABULUM
foot	PES
for	PRO
—a	
memorial	PRO MEMORIAM
pledge	IN DEPOSITO
special emergency	PRO RE NATA
—altars and	
firesides	PRO ARIS ET FOCIS
—instance	EG, EXEMPLI GRATIA
—making inquiry	AD INQUIRENDUM
—nothing	GRATIS
—one's country	PRO PATRIA
—so much	PRO TANTO
—special purposes	AD HOC
—the	
public good	PRO BONO PUBLICO
time being	PRO TEMPORE

—this turn or occasion	PRO HAC VICE
force	VIS
forename	PRAENOMEN
formal or solemn command	FIAT
former	QUONDAM
—pupil	ALUMNUS
formerly	FORMALITER
foster-son	ALUMNUS
freak of nature	LUSUS NATURAE
freely	AD LIB(ITUM)
French disease	MORBUS GALLICUS
frenzy	FUROR
from	EX
—cause to effect	A PRIORI
—effect to cause	A POSTERIORI
—excess caution	EX ABUNDANTI CAUTELA
—his own impulse	EX MERO MOTU
—inside	AB INTRO
—memory	MEMORITER
—office	AB OFFICIO
—one living person	INTER VIVOS
—one's own resources	EX PROPRIIS
—outside	AB EXTRA
—the	
beginning	AB INITIO, AB OVO
books	EX LIBRIS
chair of office	EX CATHEDRA
circumstances	E(X) RE NATA
converse	E(X) CONVERSO
depths	DE PROFUNDIS
first	AB ORIGINE
founding of the city	
(Rome)	AB URBE CONDITA
greater	A MAJORI
hypothesis	EX HYPOTHESI
less	A MINORI
mind	EX ANIMO
nature of things	A NATURA REI
	EX NATURA REI
	EX NATURA RERUM
side	A LATERE
—what	
has been conceded	EX CONCESSIS
is prior	A PRIORI
	EX CONCESSO
furrow	SULCUS
further on in book	INFRA
gain	LUCRUM
garden	HORTUS
gardener	(H)OLITOR, HORTULANUS
gem	OPALUS
generalisation	
from experience	AXIOMA MEDIUM
genuine	BONA FIDE(S)
gift of the king	REGIUM DONUM
girdle	C(A)ESTUS

—of Venus	CINGULUM VENERIS	—had it made	FF, FIERI FECIT
give us peace	DONA NOBIS PACEM	—hammered (this)	EXCUDIT
glove	MANICA	—has left well	BENE DECESSIT
glory	GLORIA	—invented (this)	INV(ENIT)
—(to God) on high	GLORIA IN EXCELSIS	—is ill	AEGROTAT
glowing language	ARDENTIA VERBA	—made (this)	F, FEC(IT)
go		—painted (this)	P, PINX(IT)
—in peace	VADE IN PACE	—printed (this)	EXCUDIT
—out	EXEUNT	—said (this)	IPSE DIXIT
—with me	VADE MECUM	—sculpted (this)	SCULP(SIT)
God	DEUS	—struck (this)	EXCUDIT
—be with you	DEUS VOBISCUM	head	CAPUT
—forbid	DEUS AVERTAT	—of family	PATERFAMILIAS
—grant	DEUS DET	heavenly voice	VOX ANGELICA
—out of the machine	DEUS EX MACHINA		VOX CAELESTIS
—willing	DEO VOLENTE	held of the Crown	IN CAPITE
	VOLENTE DEO	herbarium	HORTUS SICCUS
—wills it	DEUS VULT	herd of hirelings	GREX VENALIUM
goddess	DEA	here	
gold	AURUM	—and everywhere	HIC ET UBIQUE
golden	AUREUS	—buried	HIC SEPULTUS
—mean	AUREA MEDIOCRITAS	—lies	HIC JACET
good	BONUM	high Mass	MISSA SOLEMNIS
—faith	BONA FIDE(S)	highest	SUMMA
—health!	BENE VOBIS	his mere word	IPSE DIXIT
—manners	BONOS MORES	Holy	
goods	BONA	—of Holies	SANCTUM SANCTORUM
goose	ANSER	—water vessel	ASPERSORIUM
Graeco-Roman brickwork	OPUS LATERICUM	honey	MELL
grand		hoof	UNGULA
—father	AVUS	horn	CORNU
—son	NEPOS	hot bath	CALDARIUM
great work	MAGNUM OPUS	household gods	DI PENATES
greater gods	DI MAJORUM GENTIUM		LARES ET PENATES
grin	RISUS	humanities	LIT(T)ERAE HUMANIORES
grove	NEMUS	husband	MARITUS
hail and farewell	AVE ATQUE VALE	I	
halo of two circles	VESICA PISCIS	—am present	ADSUM
hammer	MALLEUS, MARCUS	—being judge	ME JUDICE
hand	MANUS	—distinguish	DISTINGUO
—book	VADE MECUM	—give that you may give	DO UT DES
—cuff	MANICA	—have spoken	DIXI
happily	FELICITER	if anybody (wants to	
harbour	PORTUS	know etc)	SI QUIS
harlot	MERETRIX	ignorant	NESCIUS
harvest	MESSIS	ignoring the point	IGNORATIO ELENCHI
hasten slowly	FESTINA LENTE	illegal compact	PACTUM ILLICITUM
have the body	HABEAS CORPUS	illogical conclusion	NON SEQUITUR
having		immediately	INSTANTER
—held an office	FUNCTUS OFFICIO	improvised	AD LIB(ITUM)
—legal right to act	SUI JURIS	in	
he		—a vacuum	IN VACUO
—cut (this)	INC(IDIT)	—absence	IN ABSENTIA
—devised (this)	INV(ENIT)	—accordance with the law	DE JURE
—executed (this)	F, FEC(IT)	—appearance	QUASI
—forged (this)	EXCUDIT	—bad faith	MALE FIDE

—capacity of	QUA	open air	SUB DIVO
—characteristic fashion	MORE SUO	order of nature	IN RERUM NATURAE
—chief	IN CAPITE	passage cited	LOC CIT
—deep despair	DE PROFUNDIS		LOCO CITATO
—desperate circumstances	IN EXTREMIS	place of a parent	IN LOCO PARENTIS
—English	ANGLICE	same place	IB, IBID(EM)
—equal quantities	ANA, AA, A	test-tube	IN VITRO
—express terms	EXPRESSIS VERBIS	time of	TEMPORE
—fact	DE FACTO	very act	FLAGRANTE DELICTO
—flocks	GREGATIM	work cited	OP CIT, OPERE CITATO
—former state	IN STATU QUO	—this	
—German	GERMANICE	place	HOC LOCO
—glass	IN VITRO	year	HOC ANNO
—his own way	MORE SUO	—of	
—ill condition	MALE HABITUS	Christ	ANNO CHRISTI
—itself	PER SE	foundation of	
—just so many words	TOTIDEM VERBIS	city (Rome)	AB URBE CONDITA
—living organism	IN VIVO		ANNO URBIS CONDITAE
—my opinion	ME JUDICE	our Lord	ANNO DOMINI
—nature	IN RERUM NATURA	redemption	ANNO SALUTIS
—order	SECUNDUM ORDINEM	the	
—original situation	IN SITU	—reign	ANNO REGNI
—part	PARTIM	—world	ANNO MUNDI
—passage	IN TRANSITU	—transit	IN TRANSITU
—peace	IN PACE	—unfavourable manner	IN MALAM PARTEM
—person	IN PROPRIA PERSONA	—wine is truth	IN VINO VERITAS
—place of parent	IN LOCO PARENTIS	incidental remark	OBITER DICTUM
—presence of		index of	
the king	CORAM DOMINO REGE	—authors	INDEX AUCTORUM
the people	CORAM POPULO	—places	INDEX LOCORUM
us	CORAM NOBIS	—things	INDEX RERUM
—private room	IN CAMERA	—words	INDEX VERBORUM
—proportion	AD VALOREM, PRO RATA	indispensable condition	SINE QUA NON
—reality	DE FACTO	ineffectual	BRUTUM
—respect of		ingenuity	INGENIUM
all things	QUOAD OMNIA	inhabit	COLERE
formal element	FORMALITER	injured majesty	LAESA MAJESTAS
—secret	IN CAMERA	inspection (accounts)	VIDIMUS
—self-defence	SE DEFENDENDO	intermediate object	TERTIUM QUID
—so far	QUA	into the midst of things	IN MEDIAS RES
—some respects only	SECUNDUM QUID	is silent	TACET
—the		it is	
absence of the		—denied	NEGATUR
accused	ABSENTE REO	—does not follow	NON SEQUITUR
abstract	IN ABSTRACTO	—not	
beginning	I PRINCIPIO	allowed	NON LICET
bosom	IN GREMIO	clear	NON LIQUET
father's lifetime	VITA PATRIS	Italian millet	PANICUM
first place	IMPRIMIS	itch for	
highest degree	IN EXCELSIS	—speaking	CACOETHES LOQUENDI
Lord	IN DOMINO	—writing	CACOETHES SCRIBENDI
manner	MORE	jar	OLLA
matter (of)	IN RE	joy of combat	GAUDIUM CERTAMINIS
meantime	AD INTERIM	journey	ITER
middle of things	IN MEDIAS RES	judge of taste	ARBITER ELEGANTARIUM
natural world	IN RERUM NATURAE	judicially	EX CATHEDRA

juice of grapes	MUSTUM	—from which	TERMINUS A QUO
just now	MODO	—to which	TERMINUS AD QUEM
keeper of the rolls	CUSTOS ROTULORUM	lion	LEO
kind reader	LECTOR BENEVOLE	list of prohibited	
kiss	OSCULUM	books	INDEX EXPURGATORIUS
knee	GENU	little	PARVUS, PAUL(L)US, PAUCUS
knotted	NODATUS	—mouth	OSCULUM
know thyself	NOSCE TEIPSUM	living	VIVUS
lamb of God	AGNUS DEI	—force	VIS VIVA
land	AGER	lobster	LOCUSTA
landed estate	LATIFUNDIUM	long	LONGUS
lantern	NOCTILUCA	—live	VIVAT
large	MAGNUS	look out!	CAVE
—pearl	UNIO	love of country	AMOR PATRIAE
larger	MAJOR	lower down the page	INFRA
last argument	ULTIMA RATIO	lowest species	INFIMA SPECIES
law of	JUS, LEX	lucky day	DIES FAUSTUS
—nations	JUS GENTIUM	male	MASCULUS
—nature	JUS NATURALE	man	ANIMAL BIPES, HOMO
—the talion	LEX TALIONIS	manner	MODUS
lawful days	DIES FASTI	manners	MORES
	DIES PROFESTI	marble	MARMOR
leader	DUX	mark	NOTA
leaf	FOLIUM	—well	NB, NOTA BENE
learned men	LITERATI	marks	INDICIA
leave		mass	MISSA, MOLES
—of absence	ABSIT	master	MAGISTER
—the stage	EXEUNT	Master of Arts	MAGISTER ARTIUM
—to appeal	AUDITA QUERELA	measure	MENSURARE
leaving certificate	BENE DECESSIT	measuring rod	GROMA
legal right	JUS	medical certificate	AEGROTAT
leisure	OTIUM	medicine (with gold)	AURUM POTABILE
less	MINOR	medlar	MESPILUS
let		men of letters	LITERATI
—him		mere assertion	GRATIS DICTUM
go out	EXEAT	merrymaking	GAUDEAMUS
not depart	NE EXEAT	mesh	MACULA
—it		messenger	NUNTIUS
be		metal	METALLUM
—done	FIAT	method of investigation	ORGANUM
—printed	IMPRIMATUR	middle	MEDIUS
flourish	FLOREAT	—coat	MEDIA TUNICA
—sleeping dogs lie	QUIETA NON MOVERE	—course	VIA MEDIA
—there be light	FIAT LUX	—letter	MEDIA LITTERA
—us		—vein	MEDIA NENA
be glad	GAUDEAMUS	midwife	OBSTETRIX
therefore rejoice	GAUDEAMUS IGITUR	mild	MITIS
letter	LIT(T)ERA	military service or force	MILITIA
—for letter	LIT(T)ERATIM	Milky Way	VIA LACTEA
life	VITA	mill	MOLA
—like	AD VIVUM	mind	ANIMUS, MENS
light	LUX	mine and thine	MEUM ET TUUM
—bringer	LUCIFER	mint	MONETA
—of the world	LUX MUNDI	mist	NEBULA
lily	LILIUM	mixed	MIXTUS
limit	TERMINUS	mnemonic device	MEMORIA TECHNICA

mob	FAEX POPULI	—offence	ABSIT INVIDIA
mode of operations	MODUS OPERANDI	nobody	NEMO
modillion	MUTULUS	nod to the wise	SAT SAPIENTI
money	MONETA	non-speaking character	PERSONA MUTA
monster	MONSTRUM	none	NULLUS
month	MENSIS	nose	NASUS
moon	LUNA, NOCTILUCA	nostrils	NARES
more	PLUS	not	NE, NON
—haste, less speed	FESTINA LENTE	—allowed	NON LICET
mosaic work	OPUS MOSIVUM	—any	NULLUS
moss	MUSCUS	—clear	NON LIQUET
mother	MATER	—hindering	NON OBSTANTE
—of family	MATERFAMILIAS	note	NOTARE
—stood	STABAT MATER	noteworthy sayings	NOTABILIA
mountain	MONS	nothing	NIHIL
mourn	LUGERE	—further	NE PLUS ULTRA
mouse	MUS	—to	
mouth	ORIS, OSTIUM	be despaired of	NIL DESPERANDUM
moveable goods	BONA MOBILIA	the point	NIHIL AD REM
much	MULTUS	notwithstanding	NON OBSTANTE
—in little	MULTUM IN PARVO	now	NUNC
—not many things	MULTUM NON MULTA	number	NUMERUS
mud	LUTUM	nut	NUX
mulberry	MORUM	nutlike	NUCALIS
murmur	MUTTUM	obviously pre-eminent	FACILE PRINCEPS
muscle	MUS	occupy	OBTINERE
musk	MUSCUS	of	
must be believed	DE FIDE	—blessed memory	BEATAE MEMORIAE
mutual consent	MUTUUS CONSENSUS	—himself,herself,itself	SUI
my fault	MEA CULPA	—his own accord	EX MERO MOTU
myth	MYTHUS		EX PROPRIO MOTU
naked	NUDUS		MOTU PROPRIO
name	NOMEN	—his/her age	AETATIS SUAE
—being changed	MUTATO NOMINE	—its own kind	SUI GENERIS
namely	SC, SCILICET	—one's own accord	SPONTE SUA
	VIDELICET, VIZ	—sound mind	COMPOS MENTIS
native soil	NATALE SOLUM	—the	
natural law	JUS NATURALE	morning	MATUTINUS
nature	NATURA	same kind	EJUSDEM GENERIS
necessity	SINE QUA NON	offered up	OBLATUS
necklace	MONILE	off-hand	BREVI MANU
neither	NEUTER		CURRENTE CALAMO
nest	NIDUS	oil	OLEUM
never say die	NIL DESPERANDUM	old	
new	DE INTEGRO, NOVUS	—boy	ALUMNUS
—wine	MUSTUM	—school	ALMA MATER
newsmonger	QUIDNUNC	—verse metre	SATURNIAN
night	NOX	on	
nine	NOVEM	—either side	EX UTRAQUE PARTE
ninety	NONAGINTA	—high	IN EXCELSIS
ninth	NONUS	—one side only	EX PARTE
nitric acid	AQUA-FORTIS	—that claim	EO NOMINE
—and hydrochloric	AQUA-REGIA	—the	
no		contrary	E CONTRARIO
—ill omen	ABSIT OMEN	face of it	PRIMA FACIE
—more beyond	NE PLUS ULTRA	first view	PRIMA FACIE

heights	IN EXCELSIS
threshold	IN LIMINE
one	UNUS
—of low birth	FILIUS TERRAE
onion	UNIO
only one of its kind	SUI GENERIS
opaque	OPACUS
open	PATERE
opportunity	OCCASIO
or	AUT
oral examination	VIVA (VOCE)
order	ORDINARE
original edition	EDITIO PRINCEPS
other	ALTER
—things being equal	CETERIS PARIBUS
out of	EX
—abundance	EX ABUNDANTIA
—court	EX CURIA
—goodness	EX GRATIA
—office	FUNCTUS OFFICIO
—the depths	DE PROFUNDIS
outside	EXTRA
oval window (ear)	FENESTRA OVALIS
over	SUPER
—one's cups	INTER POCULA
owing to a crime	EX DELICTO
ox	BOVIS
Oxford	
examination	LII(T)ERAE HUMANIORES
oyster	OSTREA
pact	PACTUM
—without consideration	PACTUM NUDUM
paint	PIGMENTUM
painted	PINXIT
pale	PALLIDUS
pan	PATELLA
pardon	VENIA
partial	EX PARTE
partially	PARTIM
passage	PORUS
passive resistance	VIS INERTIAE
patron	PATRONUS
peace	PAX
—be with you	PAX VOBISCUM
pending the suit	LITE PENDENTE
perishable goods	BONA PERITURA
perjury	CRIMEN FALSI
perpetual motion	PERPETUUM MOBILE
persistent labour	LABOR IMPROBUS
person	PERSONA
—not acceptable	PERSONA NON GRATA
—of humble birth	TERRAE FILIUS
personally	IN PROPRIA PERSONA
physician	MEDICUS
pious	PIA
—fraud	FRAUS PIA, PIA FRAUS

—regrets	PIA DESIDERIA
place	LOCUS
—for standing	LOCUS STANDI
plant	HERBA
plate	LANX
pledge	PIGNUS
plummet	LIBELLA
pocket-companion	VADE MECUM
poetic	
—frenzy	FUROR POETICUS
—licence	LICENTIA VATUM
polite letters	LIT(T)ERAE HUMANIORES
pot-herb	(H)OLUS
pouch	SACCUS
power of	VIS
—decision	ARBITRIUM
—inertia	VIS INERTIAE
powerful	POTENS
praise	LAUS
—to God	LAUS DEO
pray	ORARE
—and work	ORA ET LABORA
—for us	ORA PRO NOBIS
prayer for the dead	REQUIESCAT
precinct	PERIBOLUS
prejudiced	EX PARTE
present position	STATUS QUO
privately	SUB ROSA
professionally	SECUNDUM ARTEM
profound silence	ALTUM SILENTIUM
proof texts	DICTA PROBANTIA
property	BONA
Psalm	
—95	VENITE
—98	CANTATE
public opinion	VOX POPULI
Punic faith	FIDES PUNICA
	PUNICA FIDES
public intimation	SI QUIS
pure salt	MERUM SAL
puzzle for critics	CRUX CRITICORUM
question is asked	QUAERITUR
quickly	CITO
quite naked	IN PURIS NATURALIBUS
race	GENUS
rag	PANNUS
rage	FUROR
—for	
speaking	FUROR LOQUENDI
writing	FUROR SCRIBENDI
rain-water	AQUA CAELESTIS
rare bird, person or thing	RARA AVIS
razor	NOVACULA
reader	LECTOR
reasoning animal	ANIMAL RATIONALE
received text	TEXTUS RECEPTUS

refusal to accept	
responsible post	NOLO EPISCOPARI
refuse matter	EXCREMENTA
rejoicing	GAUDEAMUS
remains (on stage)	MANET, MANENT
reproach	PROBRUM
rest	
—in peace	REQUIESCAT IN PACE
	RIP
—is missing	CETERA DESUNT
résumé of career	CURRICULUM VITAE
retaliation	QUID PRO QUO
reticulated work	OPUS RETICULATUM
retrospective(ly)	EX POST FACTO
rib	COSTA
right	
—being saved	SALVO JURE
—of	
feudal superior	JUS PRIMAE NOCTIS
husband	JUS MARITI
—side	LATUS RECTUM
—to interfere	LOCUS STANDI
rightful	DE JURE
rise	ORIRI
road	VIA
roll	VOLVERE
room for penitence	LOCUS PAENITENTIAE
rotten	PUTER
rough breathing	SPIRITUS ASPER
round	ROTUNDUS
—window (ear)	FENESTRA ROTUNDA
rule	NORMA
ruler	IMPERATOR
sacred	SACER
safe	
—path	VIA TUTA
—through taking care	CAVENDO TUTUS
sailor	NAUTA, NAVITA
salmon	SALMO
same	IDEM
sanctuary	DELUBRUM
sane	COMPOS MENTIS
sardonic grin	RISUS SARDONICUS
satisfaction	POENA
saving the right	SALVO JURE
saw	SERRA
saying	DICTUM
scale of balance	LANX
sea	MARE
—carp	MERULA
—monster	ORCA
—nymph	NERINE
seat	SEDES
second	SECUMDUM
—to none	NULLI SECUNDUS
secret poison	AQUA TOFANA

secretly	SUB ROSA
secular arm	BRACHIUM SECULARE
see	VIDE
—above	VIDE SUPRA
—below	VIDE INFRA
selections	EXCERPTA
self-evident	A PRIORI
service	OFFICIUM
severe test for beginner	PONS ASINORUM
shadow	UMBRA
shape	FORMA
sheep	OVIS
shield	SCUTUM
shining	NITIDUS
ship	NAVIS
shore	ORA
shrine	DELUBRUM
sickness certificate	AEGROTAT
side	LATUS
siege	OBSIDIO
signs	INDICIA
silencing	QUIETUS
silently	EX TACITO
sinew	NERVUS
skilfully	SECUNDUM ARTEM
slanting	LIQUIS
slave-dealer	MANGO
sleeve	MANICA
slight fault	CULPA LEVIS
slip	LAPSUS
—of the	
memory	LAPSUS MEMORIAE
pen	LAPSUS CALAMI
tongue	LAPSUS LINGUAE
slippery	LUBRICUS
small	MINUTUS
smallest	MINIMUS
smallness	MINUTIA
smooth	
—breathing	SPIRITUS LENIS
—tablet	TABULA RASA
snow	NIX
so	SIC
—much the richer	TANTO UBERIOR
—throughout	SIC PASSIM
soft	MOLLIS
softening	MOLLITIES
soldier	MILES
some	ULLUS
somebody	QUIDAM
something	
—for something	QUID PRO QUO
—in addition	ETC, ET CETERA
—said	DICTUM
by the way	OBITER DICTUM
—sought for	QUAESITUM

son of		thee therefore	TE IGITUR
—nobody	FILIUS NULLIUS	there sat	SEDERUNT
—the		thereby	IPSO FACTO
people	FILIUS POPULI	thin plate	LAMELLA, LAMINA
soil	FILIUS TERRAE	thing	RES
	TERRAE FILIUS	things	
soul	ANIMA	—to be seen	VIDENDA
—of the world	ANIMA MUNDI	—worthy of notice	NOTABILIA
sounding the same	IDEM SONANS	third	TERTIUS
source and origin	FONS ET ORIGO	—person in triangle	TERTIUM QUID
spade	PALA	—something	TERTIUM QUID
spirit	SPIRITUS	this	HIC, HOC
—of the place	GENIUS LOCI	—do	HOC AGE
spit	OBELUS	thousand	MILLE
sport	LUSUS NATURAE	thread	FILUM
sports champion	VICTOR LUDORUM	threats	MINAE
spot	MACULA	throughout	A, AA, ANA, PASSIM
spring-water	AQUA FONTANA	thunderbolt	FULMEN
stake	PALUS	thus	SIC
star	STELLA	time	
starting-point	TERMINUS A QUO	—flies	TEMPUS FUGIT
state in which	STATUS QUO	—for penitence	LOCUS PAENITENTIAE
statute law	LEX SCRIPTA	to	
stem	CAULIS	—a nicety	AD UNGUEM
step	PASSUS	—be	ESSE
—mother	NOVERCA	further considered	AD REFERENDUM
stock quotation	LOCUS CLASSICUS	—each his own	SUUM CUIQUE
strong		—everyone	URBI ET ORBI
—defence	AES TRIPLEX	—for or with God	DEO
—smell	NIDOR	—infinity	AD INFINITUM
substance	QUID	—the	
substances used in		city and the world	URBI ET ORBI
medicine	MATERIA MEDICA	clergy	AD CLERUM
successfully	FELICITER	end	AD FINEM
sufficient quantity	QUANTUM SUFFICIT	greater	AD MAJUS
suicide	FELO DE SE	highest point	AD SUMMUM
Sun	SOL	less	AD MINUS
superior force	VIS MAJOR	man	AD HOMINEM
surveying pole	GROMA	nail	AD UNGUEM
sweet	DULCIS	point	AD REM
table	MENSA	—of disgust	AD NAUSEAM
tail	CAUDA	purpose	AD REM
take note	NB, NOTA BENE	purse	AD CRUMENAM
tear	LACRIMA	stars	AD ASTRA
temple	DELUBRUM	—this extent	QUOAD
test for beginner	PONS ASINORUM	—wit	SC, SCILICET, VIDELICET, VIZ
thanks to God	DEO GRATIAS	toga-wearing nation	GENS TOGATA
that		together	PARI PASSU
—is	ID EST, IE	token of respect	HONORIS CAUSA
—which a thing is	QUID		HONORIS GRATIA
the		tongue	LINGUA
—Fates oppose	FATA OBSTANT	tooth	DENS
—hour flies	HORA FUGIT	totally	IN TOTO
—King's Bench	IN BANCO REGIS	town	OPPIDUM
—same	ID, IDEM	traveller	VIATOR
—very words	IPSISSIMA VERBA	treacherously	MALA FIDE

treachery	FIDES PUNICA
tree	ARBOR
—of life	ARBOR VITAE
trifles	NUGAE
true value	QUAESITUM
turned against	OBVERSUS
turnip	NAPUS
twice	BIS
two-footed animal	ANIMAL BIPES
unacceptable person	PERSONA NON GRATA
unclaimed goods	BONA VACANTIA
under	
—consideration	SUB JUDICE
—penalty	SUB POENA
—that heading	SUB VOCE
—the	
appearance or aspect	SUB SPECIE
rose	SUB ROSA
sky	SUB DIVO
—this condition	HAC LEGE
unexpectedly	EX IMPROVISO
unformed mind	TABULA RASA
union	UNIO
unique	SUI GENERIS
university	ALMA MATER
unknown country	TERRA INCOGNITA
unlawful days	DIES NON
unless	NISI
unlucky days	DIES INFAUSTUS
unmixed	MERUS
unowned property	RES NULLUS
unspeakable	NEFANDUS
unusual person or	
thing	RARA AVIS
unwelcome person	PERSONA NON GRATA
unwritten law	LEX NON SCRIPTA
uprightly	RECTE
urn	OLLA
uttermost point	NE PLUS ULTRA
vacant see	SEDES VACANS
	SEDE VACANTE
valued possessions	LARES ET PENATES
various readings	VARIAE LECTIONES
vegetable	(H)OLUS
voice	VOX
—of	
God	VOX DEI
the people	VOX POPULI
votive (offering)	EX VOTO
wages	MERCES
wall	MURUS
war of	
extermination	BELLUM INTERNECINUM
was	ERAT
wash	LUERE
water	AQUA, LYMPHA

wave	UNDA
way	VIA
—of	
life	MODUS VIVENDI
the Cross	VIA DOLOROSA
working	MODUS OPERANDI
wayfarer	VIATOR
we	NOS
—command	MANDAMUS
—learn by	
teaching	DOCENDO DISCIMUS
weariness of life	TAEDIUM VITAE
weasel	MUSTELA
well-deserved	BENE MERENTIBUSHVX
what now?	QUID NUNC
wheel	ORBIS
—track	ORBITA
where	UBI
—are you going?	QUO VADIS
—mentioned above	UBI SUPRA
which	
—see	QUOD VIDE, QV
—was to be	
demonstrated	QED
	QUOD ERAT DEMONSTRANDUM
while	
—(she is) chaste	DUM CASTA
—war rages	FLAGRANTE BELLO
whisky	AQUA VITAE
whither	QUO
—goest thou?	QUO VADIS
who	QUI
—as much?	QUI TAM
—gains?	CUI BONO
whole world	ORBIS TERRARUM
why does he hinder?	QUARE IMPEDIT
wild animals	FERAE NATURAE
Will-o'-the wisp	IGNIS FATUUS
willy-nilly	NOLENS VOLENS
wing	PENNA
winner of the games	VICTOR LUDORUM
with	
—a grain of salt	CUM GRANUM SALIS
—distinction	MAXIMA CUM LAUDE
—easy mind	AEQUO ANIMO
—equal pace	PARI PASSU
—full authority	PLENO JURE
—God's favour	DEO FAVENTE
—greatest	
distinction	SUMMA CUM LAUDE
—many other things	CUM MULTIS ALIIS
—necessary changes	MUTATIS MUTANDIS
—notes of various	
(critics)	CUM NOTIS VARIORUM
—one	
mind	UNO ANIMO

voice	UNA VOCE	yoke	JUGUM
—praise	CUM LAUDE	you too	TU QUOQUE
—privilege	CUM PRIVILEGIO	you're another	TU QUOQUE
—proper			(*see also* **Roman**)
exceptions	EXCEPTIS EXCIPIENDIS	**law**[1]	
—running pen	CURRENTE CALAMO	some legal terms:	
—stronger reason	A FORTIORI	abandoned suit	NOLI PROSEQUI
—this law	HAC LEGE	abandonment of	
—thumb turned up	POLLICE VERSO	—claim	ABATEMENT
within	INTRA	—prosecution	NOLLE PROSEQUI
—legal powers	INTRA VIRES	absorption of estate	MERGER
—the		acknowledgment of justice	COGNOVIT
treaty	CASUS FOEDERIS	act backward	RETROACT
wall	INTRA MUROS	act of annulling	VACATUR
without	SINE	addition to will	CODICIL
—a day appointed	SINE DIE	against	V, VS, VERSUS
—changing letter	LITERATIM	alienate	DEVEST
—doubt	SINE DUBIO	annul	OVERRULE
—finishing the business	RE INFECTA	annulment	CASSATION
—issue	SINE PROLE	answer to charge	PLEA
—opposition	NEM CON	apply to the past	RETROACT
	NEMINE CONTRADICENTES	as near as possible	CY PRES
—payment or recompense	GRATIS	assize	OYER
—which not	SINE QUA NON	assumption from	
witness	TESTIS	known fact	PRESUMPTION
woe to the conquered	VAE VICTIS	at first sight	PRIMA FACIE
wolf	LUPUS	attested copy	VIDIMUS
womb	ALVUS, MATRIX, UTERUS	authority to act	
wonderful	MIRABILIS	for another	POWER OF ATTORNEY
—to		awareness of wrong act	MENS REA
see	MIRABILE VISU	be sustainable	LIE
tell	MIRABILE DICTU	being aware	SCIENTER
wonders	MIRABILIA	betray client by collusion	PREVARICATE
word		between parties	INTER PARTES
—for word	AD VERBUM, VERBATIM	beyond one's power	
—to the wise	VERB(UM) SAP(IENTES)	or authority	ULTRA VIRES
work	OPUS	bill of equity	INTERPLEADER
—is prayer	LABORARE EST ORARE	body of	
works	OPERA	—canon law	CORPUS JURIS CANONICI
workshop	OFFICINA	—civil law	CORPUS JURIS CIVILIS
world	MUNDUS	breach of	
worthwhile	TANTI	—civil law	TORT
worthless residue	CAPUT MORTUUM	—statute law	CRIME
wretched	MISER	bringing legal action	LITIGATION
writ			PROSECUTING, SUING
—in disputed		call for evidence	INVOCATION
presentation		cancel bequest	ADEEM
to benefice	QUARE IMPEDIT	case-law	PRACTIC
—requiring appearance	SCIRE FACIAS	claim	PLEA
—removing case		clause in deed defining	
to High Court	CERTIORARI	—tenure	TENENDUM
wrong	NEFAS	—terms	TESTATUM
yawn	OSCITARE	clearing from suspicion	PURGATION
year	ANNUS	codicil	LABEL
—of wonders	ANNUS MIRABILIS	come	
yellow	LUTEUS	—into effect	ENURE

—to a point or fact	ISSUE	equal law, rights, etc	ISONOMY
commit waste as tenant	ESTREPE	equality	OWELTY, PARAGE
compounding of		essential facts	
theft	THEFTBOOT, THEFTBOTE	of the crime	CORPUS DELICTI
conveyance of property	GRANT	establishing validity	
conditional release	PAROLE	of will	PROBATE
copy of legal writing	TRANSUMPT	exact copy of record	ESTREAT
corroboratory evidence	ADMINICLE	excessive	RANK
court		exchange of lands	EXCAMBION
—hearing	OYER		EXCAMBIUM
—sitting (Scot.)	SEDERUNT	excuse for not	
crime		appearing in court	ESSOIN, ESSOYNE
—minor	MISDEMEANOUR	exemption from penalties	
—serious	FELONY	or liabilities	INDEMNITY
criminal intent	MENS REA	fire-raising	ARSON
date back in application	RELATE	forbid	ENJOIN
decision of court	PLACITUM	forgery	FALSI CRIMEN
declare		formal document	DEED, WRIT
—heir (Scot.)	SERVE	fraud	STELLIONATE
—invalid	OVERRULE	—by mariners	BARRATRY
—will orally	NUNCIATE	free transfer of title	DONATION
deed		from	
—in hands of third		—another source	ALIUNDE
party	ESCROL(L), ESCROW	—one living person	
—under seal	SPECIALTY	to another	INTER VIVOS
defamation by spoken words	SLANDER	general pardon	AMNESTY
defendant's answer	REJOINDER	give	
definitely fixed	PEREMPTORY	—effect to	SERVE
delay	MORA	—up voluntarily	WAIVE
deliver formally	SERVE	handing over	TRADITION
denial of		hanging first, trying	
—part of allegation	SPECIAL ISSUE	afterwards	JEDDART JUSTICE
—whole of allegation	GENERAL ISSUE		JETHART JUSTICE
deprive of possession	DISSEISE		LYDFORD LAW, LYNCH LAW
	DISSEIZE	harsh	DRACONIAN
discuss adverse		having knowledge of	SCIENTER
claims	INTERPLEAD	hinder	ESTOP
dispossess	DISSEISE, DISSEIZE	holding what belongs	
dispossession	OUSTER	to another	DETAINER
distraint	NA(A)M, STRESS	illegal	
divine right	JUS DIVINUM	—bargain	CHAMPERTY
document	DEED	—deed	MALFEASANCE
—transferring		immovable property	REALTY
property	CONVEYANCE, DEED	in	
—certifying validity		—judge's chambers	IN CAMERA
of will	PROBATE	—secret	IN CAMERA
during litigation	PENDENTE LITE	—the act	IN FLAGRANTE DELICTO
ejection	OUSTER	incorrect union	MISJOINDER
emancipate from		information without oath	SUGGESTION
paternal authority	FORISFAMILIATE	infraction of law	OFFENCE
encroachment on		instigator of suit	PLAINTIFF
public property	PURPRESTURE	instructions to barrister	BRIEF
endow	VEST	intermediate	MESNE
enter		international law	JUS GENTIUM
—an action in court	LAY INFORMATION	interpose an action	INTERVENE
—unlawfully	TRESPASS	intrude on freehold	ABATE

issue for trial by		loss of rights after	
agreement of parties	FEIGNED ISSUE	conviction for treason	ATTAINDER
judge's		magistrate's warrant	PRECEPT
—commission	DEDIMUS	maker of conveyance	GRANTER, GRANTOR
—order or warrant	FIAT	malicious	
keep out by force	DEFORCE	—and defamatory	
kidnapping	PLAGIUM	publication	LIBEL
killing	HOMICIDE	statement	SLANDER
	MANSLAUGHTER	—damage	MAYHEM
	MURDER	married woman	FEME COVERT
	(*see also* kill)	material evidence	CORPUS DELICTI
know	WIT	misdemeanour	DELICT
land	REALTY	misspelt word accepted	IDEM SONANS
—tenure with only		mother	VENTER
religious obligations	FRANKALMOIGN	moveable effects	CHATTELS, FUNGIBLES
lapse	RESOLVE	nationality dependent on	
law-breaking		—country of birth	JUS SOLI
—civil	TORT	—parentage	JUS SANGUINIS
—statute	CRIME, FELONY	natural	
	MISDEMEANOUR	—justice	EQUITY
lawyer	ADVOCATE, BARRISTER	—law	JUS NATURALE
	SOLICITOR	negligence	LACHES
—American	ATTORNEY	not	
—as paid magistrate	STIPENDIARY	—admitting	NOLO CONTENDERE
—giving legal advice	COUNSEL	—enforced	DEAD LETTER
—government	ATTORNEY-GENERAL	—proceeded with	NOLLE PROSEQUI
	DIRECTOR OF PUBLIC PROSECUTIONS	—under bonds of	
	DPP, PUBLIC PROSECUTOR	matrimony	DISCOVERT
	SOLICITOR-GENERAL	note of transaction	MEMORANDUM
—in training	ARTICLED CLERK	number of words taken	
	BARRISTER, SOLICITOR	as length of document	FOLIO
—paltry	PETTIFOGGER	oath administered to	
—Scottish	LAW-AGENT	witness	VOIR DIRE
	(PROCURATOR-)FISCAL	obtain	
—using dubious methods	PETTIFOGGER	—a judgment	RECOVER
laws of natural justice	EQUITY	—other than by inheritance	PURCHASE
leasing on rent	LOCATION	offer to make oath	WAGE
legal		officer who filed writs	FILACER
—authorisation	POWER OF ATTORNEY		FILAZER
	PROCURATION	old distress warrant	DISTRINGAS
—case of great		on	
public interest	CAUSE CELEBRE	—behalf of	EX PARTE
—claim	DROIT	—one side only	EX PARTE
—document	DEED, WRIT	—the first view	PRIMA FACIE
—investigation	FORENSIC	one	
—means of redress	REMEDY	—acting as surety	MAINPERNOR
—philosophy	JURISPRUDENCE	—for whom another	
—right(s)	JUS(JURA)	becomes surety	PRINCIPAL
—usage	PRACTIC	—who	
legally		abets a crime	PRINCIPAL
—acceptable	ADMISSIBLE, VALID	commits a crime	PRINCIPAL
—qualified	COMPETENT, ELIGIBLE	employs another	PRINCIPAL
—required	LIABLE	holds property	
limitation of inheritance	TAIL	—at owner's	
—to male heirs	TAIL MALE	discretion	TENANT-AT-WILL
list of court rulings	DIGEST	—from sovereign	TENANT-IN-CHIEF

is sued	DEFENDANT	receiver of	
lays information	RELATOR	—conveyance	GRANTEE
receives property	ALIENEE	—wrecks	ABANDONEE
refuses to plead	MUTE	receiving	PERNANCY
sues	PLAINTIFF	reciprocal rights of	
transfers property	ALIENOR	citizenship	ISOPOLITY
oral defamation	SLANDER	recover good distrained	
order		upon	REPLEVY
—to keep the peace	BIND OVER	red-handed	IN FLAGRANTE DELICTO
—putting receiver		reduction of legacy	ABATEMENT
in possession	RECEIVING-ORDER	reference of a case	
—requiring person		to another	REMIT
not to pay another	GARNISH(EE)MENT	refusing to plead	MUTE (OF MALICE)
original document	SCRIPT	relevant facts	RES GESTAE
paper attached to will	LABEL	rendering void	DEFEASANCE
partial remission	RELAXATION	renounce title to a	
penalty	SANCTION	further share	FORISFAMILIATE
person		reply to defendant's	
—having interest	PRIVY	—rebuttal	SURREBUT(TAL)
—sued	DEFENDANT	—rejoinder	SURREJOIN(DER)
personal property	CHOSE, PERSONALTY	reserving clause	
pertaining to		in lease	REDDENDUM
—an agent or factor	INSTITORIAL	return an answer	REBUT
—fixed things	REAL	right(s)	DROIT, JUS(JURA), LIEN
—property	REAL	—of	
plea(ding)	PLACITUM	husband	JUS MARITI
—that facts do not		property	APPURTENANCE
support the case	DEMURRER	—over another's land	EASEMENT
poor lawyer	PETTIFOGGER	—to	
possession	SASINE, SEISIN	claim free lodgings	COR(R)ODY
postponed case	REMANET	cut	
preclude	ESTOP	—green trees	VERT
premeditation	MALICE AFORETHOUGHT	—wood	HAY-BOTE, HEDGE-BOTE
	MALICE PREPENSE	deal with thief	
privately	SUB ROSA	taken outside one's	
process	INSTANCE	jurisdiction	OUTFANGTHIEF
procuring advantage by		drop roof water	STILLICIDE
—concealing the truth	SUBREPTION	fish	PISCARY
—false statement	OBREPTION	fold sheep for manure	FALDAGE
produce for probate	PROPOUND	graze the aftermath	FOGGAGE
prohibit by injunction	ENJOIN	hold a court	LEET, SAC, SOC
proof of will	PROBATE	hunt game	WARREN
property	REALTY	keep game	WARREN
—acquired otherwise		necessaries allowed by law	ESTOVER
than by inheritance	PERQUISITE	resume earlier status	POSTLIMINY
—that can be passed		retain tenure on	
to an heir	HEREDITAMENT	reasonable terms	TENANT RIGHT
—right	APPURTENANCE	search for food in	
protection of intellectual		forest	PU(L)TURE
rights, etc	COPYRIGHT	seize property in war	ANGARY
public prosecutor	DPP	take peat	TURBARY
—Scotland	PROCURATOR FISCAL	unobstructed light	ANCIENT LIGHTS
put in possession	SEISE, VEST	use	
—of whole of		—another's property	USUFRUCT
father's land	FORISFAMILIATE	—something not	
putting an end to a right	EXTINGUISHMENT	one's own	EASEMENT

rights held in common	PRO INDIVISO
royal commission to determine criminal charges	OYER AND TERMINER
science of law	JURISPRUDENCE
	NOMOLOGY
second trial for same offence	DOUBLE JEOPARDY
secure	VEST
seize	DISTRAIN, EXTEND
seizure	DISTRAINT
	SEQUESTRATION
session of court	ASSIZES
settle	ENTAIL, VEST
settlement on series of heirs	ENTAILMENT
spinster	FEME SOLE
statement of grievance	PLAINT
sub-tenant	VALVASSOR
	VAVASOUR
submission	
—by one not party to a case	AMICUS BRIEF
—submission of dispute for decision	REFERENCE
suit	INSTANCE
summons	MONITION, SUBPOENA
	WRIT
supplement to will	CODICIL
surety	MAINPRISE
surrender of claim	REMISE
sworn statement	AFFADAVIT, DEPOSITION
taking	
—back	RECAPTION
—effect from a date in the past	EX POST FACTO
	RETROACTIVE
	RETROSPECTIVE
—possession	ENTRY
temporary suspension of law	RESPITE
theft	LARCENY
temporary owner	TERMOR
tenure by service	BURGAGE, SERGEANTRY
	SERJEANTRY, SOC(C)AGE
	SOKEMANRY
token of possession	SASINE, SEISIN
transfer of property to	
—a corporation	MORTMAIN
—another	ATTORN
transgression	DELICT, OFFENCE
under	
—consideration	SUB JUDICE
—legal age of maturity	INFANT
undertaking	RECOGNISANCE
undue delay	LACHES
union	JOINDER

unit of land	HIDE
unlawful	ILLEGAL, ILLEGITIMATE
	ILLICIT
unowned property	RES NULLIUS
unspecified fraud	STELLIONATE
use and profit	USUFRUCT
venue	VISNE
verdict giving right of recovery of debts	RECOVERY
void	INEPT
warrant of imprisonment	MITTIMUS
widow	FEME SOLE
wilfully	SCIENTER
withdrawal of action	NONSUIT
without consideration	NUDE
witness's oath	VOIR DIRE
woman	FEME
womb	VENTER
word of honour	PAROLE
writ	NOVERINT, PROCESS
—authorising	
arrest	CAPIAS
one other than a judge to act as judge	DEDIMUS
—commanding appearance	SUBPOENA
—for	
person in hiding	LATITAT
recovery of goods distrained upon	REPLEVIN
—moving case to	
county court	TOLT
High Court	CERTIORARI
—of	
distraint	DETINUE, DISTRINGAS
	FIERI FACIAS
execution	FIFA
higher court	MANDAMUS
Richard II	PRAEMUNIRE
—requiring	
appearance to show cause	SCIRE FACIAS
attendance at court	SUBPOENA
reasons for hindering presentation to benefice	QUARE IMPEDIT
—to	
produce prisoner	HABEAS CORPUS
seize property of debtor	EXTENT
show by what warrant one holds office	QUO WARRANTO
stay proceedings	INHIBITION
written	
—accusation	INDICTMENT, LIBEL
—declaration on oath	AFFADAVIT
	DEPOSITION

—defamation	LIBEL
—purpose	MENS REA
wrong	TORT
wrongful	
—act	DELICT, TORT
—detention of goods	DETINUE
—purpose	MENS REA

law²

law: describing
  governing
  stating that
anything that can go
  wrong will do so
	MURPHY'S LAW
	SOD'S LAW

bad money drives out good money	GRESHAM'S LAW
changes in stopped consonants	GRIMM'S LAW
displacement of island species	SETON'S LAW
effect of accent	VERNER'S LAW
expansion of work	PARKINSON'S LAW
flow of groundwater	DARCY'S LAW
help the less fortunate	CUTTER'S LAW
history of race repeated in individuals	BIOGENETIC LAW
inheritance	MENDEL'S LAWS
length of conjunct words	BEHAGHEL'S LAW
mathematical operations	ASSOCIATIVE LAW COMMUTATIVE LAW
movement of	
—planets	KEPLER'S LAWS
—winds	BUYS BALLOT'S LAW
only the impossible happens	MURPHY'S SECOND LAW
promotion	PETER PRINCIPLE
requisite variety	ASHBY'S LAW
supply creates demand	SAY'S LAW
	(see also **electric, physics**)

leader

including: commander
  potentate
  prince
  religious leader
  ruler	

general terms:	BELLWETHER GROUNDBREAKER, GUIDE INNOVATOR, PACEMAKER SCOUT, TRAILBREAKER TRENDSETTER, VANGUARD
acting sovereign	(VICE)REGENT, VICEROY
African	
—Ashanti chief	ASANTEHENE
—headman	CABOCEER

—ruler of Uganda	KABAKA
Albanian ruler	MPRET
American	PRESIDENT
—Indian	
North America	SACHEM, SAGAMORE
South America	CACIQUE
Arab	
—chief	AMEER, AMIR, CAID, EMEER EMIR, KAID, RAIS, SA(Y)ID SAYYID, SCHIEK, SHEIK(H)
—headman	MOCUDDUM, MOKADDAM MOQADDAM
Asian prince or chief	CHAM, KHAN
Austro-Hungarian emperor	KAISER
Baluchi chief	TOMUNDAR
borough	MAYOR
British	KING, QUEEN
—ancient chief	PENDRAGON
Chinese	
—military governor	TUCHUN
—senior official	MANDARIN
chorus	CORYPHAEUS
city council	LORD MAYOR
company	MANAGER MANAGING DIRECTOR
corporation	CHAIRMAN MANAGING DIRECTOR MAYOR
Cossack	ATAMAN, HETMAN
council	CHAIRMAN, MAYOR
deified ruler	THEOCRAT
Dutch viceroy	STAD(T)HOLDER
empire	EMPEROR, EMPRESS
English	KING, QUEEN
Egyptian	
—commander	SIRDAR
—ruler	PHARAOH
—sultan	MAMELUKE, SOLDAN
—viceroy	KHEDIVE
feudal lord	SEIGNEUR, SEIGNIOR SUZERAIN
French	PRESIDENT
—one of three heads of the Republic	CONSUL
German	LEITER
—archbishop	ELECTOR
—district official	GAULEITER
—emperor	KAISER
—leader in military drill	FUGELMAN, FUGLEMAN
—national leader	CHANCELLOR FU(E)HRER
—political leader	FUGELMAN, FUGLEMAN
—prince	ELECTOR
Greek	AGOGOS

—commamnder of	
10 men	DECADARCH
1000 men	CHILIARCH
division	TAXIARCH
subdivision	TETRARCH
trireme	TRIERARCH
—leader of worshippers	THIASARCH
—military rulers	DIADOCHI
—ruler of	
district	TOPARCH
the people	ETHNARCH
governor	(*see separate entry*)
head of Commonwealth	PROTECTOR
Holy Roman Emperor	KAISER
Indian	
—administrative officer	COLLECTOR
—British monarch	KAISAR-I-HIND
—chief	SUDDER
—head of state	RAJPRAMUKH
—Hindu	MAHATMA
—king	RAJAH
—military leader	SIRDAR
—Moslem prince	NAWAB
—potentate	HUZOOR
—prince	RAJAH
—Rajput chief	RANA
—ruler of	
Baroda	GAEKWAR, GAIKWAR
	GUICOWAR
Hyderabad	NIZAM
Sikkim	CHOGYAL
—viceroy of Mogul empire	NAWAB
—village chieftain	POLIGAR
Irish	
—head of family	CO(M)ARB
—king	(ARD)RI(GH)
—prime minister	TAOISEACH
Italian	
—chief official in	
Genoa and Venice	DOGE
—leader of mercenaries	CONDOTTIERE
—national leader	DUCE
Japanese	
—emperor	MIKADO, TENNO
—military commander	SHOGUN, TYCOON
Mafia leader	CAPO, DON
Malay chief	RAJAH
mediaeval lord	SUZERAIN
Moldavian prince	GOSPODAR, HOSPODAR
Moroccan prince	SHEREEF, SHERIF
Moslem	
—appearing in last days	MAHDI
—chief	DATTO
—high official	VEZIR, VISIER
	VIZI(E)R, WIZIER
—Ismaili leader	AGA KHAN

—prince	AMEER, AMIR, EMEER
	EMIR, NAWAB, SHEREEF
	SHERIF
—religious leader	AYATOLLAH, IMA(U)M
	MAHDI, MUFTI, SHEIK(H)
—revolutionary	MAHDI
—ruler	CALIF, CALIPH
	KHALIF(A)(H), SULTAN
—Shiite leader	AYATOLLAH
New Zealand	RANGATIRA
noble	(*see separate entry*)
Norse chieftain	JARL, YARL
North African prince	CHAM, KHAN
paramount ruler	SUZERAIN
Persian	
—ruler	CALIF, CALIPH, K(H)ALIF
	(PADI)SHAH, SOPHI, SOPHY
—viceroy	SATRAP
Red Indian chief	MUGWUMP, SACHEM
	SAGAMORE
republic	PRESIDENT
Roman	
—absolute ruler	CAESAR
—commander of	
10 soldiers	DECURION
100 soldiers	CENTURION
—emperor	CAESAR, IMPERATOR
—head of state	PRINCEPS POPULI
—leader	DUX
—lord	DOMINUS
—noble	PATRICIAN
—one of	
2	
—chief officials	CONSUL
—sharing power	DUUMVIR
3 sharing power	TRIUMVIR
—ruler of part of	
province	TETRARCH
ruler	DYNAST, PROTECTOR
	REGENT
—of the world	COSMOCRAT
—with absolute power	DESPOT, DICTATOR
	TYRANT
Russian	
—Cossack chief	ATAMAN, HETMAN
—emperor	CZAR, TSAR
Spanish	
—headman	CAPITANO
—leader	CAUDILLO, CID
subordinate prince	TETRARCH
supreme ruler	SUZERAIN
Tibetan Buddhists	
—deputy leader	PANCHEN LAMA
—leader	DALAI LAMA
Turkish	
—commander	AG(H)A, SERASKIER

—head of division	MUTESARRIF
—high official	(ATA)BEG, ATABEK
	BEY, VEZIR, VISIER
	VIZI(E)R, WIZIER
—military leader	BASHAW, DEY, PACHA
	PASHA, ZAIM
—prime minister	GRAND VIZIER
—religious	CALIF, CALIPH
	KHALIF(A)(H)
	PADISHAH, SULTAN
—ruler	ATABEG, ATABEK
	CALIPH, KHAN
	PADISHAH, SULTAN
visionary (leader)	GURU, MESSIANIC
Wallachian prince	GOSPODAR, HOSPODAR
West Indian chief	CACIQUE, CAZIQUE
	(*see also* **nobles, power**)

leaf　　　　　　　　　　　　　　　　　　　PHYLLOME

angle between leaf	
and stem,	AXIL
appendage at base of	
—leaf	STIPULE
—leaflet	STIPEL
arrangement of	
—leaves	PHYLLLOTAXIS
	PHYLLOTAXY, VERNATION
—veins	VENATION
axis of leaf	RACHIS
blade of leaf	LAMINA
branch acting like	
a leaf	CLADODE, PHYLLOCLADE
bud	GEMMA
cluster of leaves	FASCIC(U)LE
conversion of sunlight	
by leaves	PHOTOSYNTHESIS
division of	
—leaf	PINNA
—pinna	PINNULE
excessive leaf	
production	PHYLLOMANIA
extension along stem	ALA
fern leaf	FROND, STIPE
having	
—2 or more leaf types	HETEROPHYLLOUS
—3 leaflets	TREFOIL, TRIFOLIATE
—4 leaflets	QUADRIFOIL
	QUADRIFOLIATE
	QUATREFOIL
—5 leaflets	CINQUEFOIL
—branched vein system	MEGAPHYLL
—different structures	
on each side	DORSIVENTRAL
—flower in axil	BRACT
—leaves	
folded over	
succeeding leaves	EQUITANT

like heather	ERICOID
which fall each year	DECIDUOUS
—megasporangia	MACROSPOROPHYLL
	MEGASPOROPHYLL
—same structures on	
each side	ISOBILATERAL
—slender leaves	LEPTOPHYLLOUS
—sporangia	SPOROPHYLL
—stiff leaves	SCLEROPHYLLOUS
—unbranched vein system	MICROPHYLL
—woolly leaves	DASYPHYLLOUS
in carving	ACANTHUS
leaf	
—rosette	ROSULA
—scale	LIGULE
leaf-eating	PHYLLOPHAGOUS
leaflet	PINNA, PINNULE
leaflike	
—plant	STIPULE
—sheath	SPATHE
leaves	FOLIAGE
notch in edge of leaf	SINUS
overlapping	IMBRICATE
palm leaf	FROND
part of corolla	PETAL
petiole acting	
like a leaf	PHYLLODE
pigment in leaves	CHLOROPHYLL
pinnate	
—leaf	RACHIS
—without leaflet at the end	PARIPINNATE
pore	STOMA
projecting part of leaf	LOBE
projection on base	AURICLE
radiating leaves	WHORL
recess between lobes	SINUS
rib or vein	NERVURE
rudimentary leaf	CATAPHYLL
scale-like	AMPHIGASTRIUM
seed-leaf	COTYLEDON
shapes	
—arrowhead	SAGITTATE
—blade	SPATULATE
—circular	ORBICULAR
—feather	PINNATE, PINNATIFID
—finger	DIGITATE
—hand	PALMATE
—heart	CORDATE
—irregularly notched	EROSE
—kidney	RENIFORM
—lance	LANCEOLATE
—long and narrow	LINEAR
—lyre	LYRATE
—needle-pointed	ACEROSE, ACIFORM
—oval	ELLIPTIC, O(BO)VATE
—round-toothed	CRENATE

—saw-toothed	DENTATE
—scimitar	ACINACIFORM
—sharp-toothed	SERRATE
—shield	PELTATE
—shovel	SPATULATE
—sickle	FALC(UL)ATE
—spade	SPATULATE
—spear	HASTATE
—tapering to a point	ACUMINATE
	APICULATE, CUSPIDATE
—wavy-edged	CREN(UL)ATE, REPAND
	SINUATE
small leaf on	
flower-axis	BRACTEOLE, PROPHYLL
stalk	PETIOLE, STIPE(S)
stem acting as leaf	CLADODE
	PHYLLOCLADE
stiff leaf	SCLEROPHYLL
strip leaves	DEFOLIATE
swelling at base	PULVINULE, PULVINUS
transformation	
into leaves	PHYLLODY
vein	NERVURE
without a stalk	SESSILE
leather	
armour (Roman)	LORICA
bottle	JACK
calfskin, chrome tanned	BOX CALF
coat	GAMBESON, JACK
corslet(s)	LORICA(E)
doublet	PLACCAT(E), PLACKET
dress leather	DUB, CURRY, TAN, TAW
dresser	CURRIER
fawn-skin (Bacchus)	NEBRIS
flask (Greek)	OLPE
from	
—antelope	CHAMOIS
—buffalo	BUFF, PARFLECHE
—calves	BOX CALF(SKIN), SLINK
—deer	CHAMOIS
—elk	BUFF
—goat	CHEVEREL, CHEVERIL
	CHEVRETTE, CORDOVAN
	CORDWAIN, LEVANT
	MOCHA, MOROCCO
—kid	NAPPA, SUEDE
—lamb	NAPPA
—ox	BUFF
—reptiles	CROCODILE-SKIN
	SNAKESKIN
—sharks	SHAGREEN
—sheep	CABRETTA, CAPESKIN
	MOCHA, ROAN, SKIVER
—swine	HOGSKIN, PIGSKIN
—young ox or cow	KIPSKIN, KIP-LEATHER
glossy leather	GLACE (KID), PATENT

grained leather	ROAN
knife	MOON-KNIFE
leather-	
—dresser	CURRIER
—worker	CORDINER, CORDWAINER
morocco	LEVANT
outer garment	PILCHER
protective coat	JACK
rawhide	
—shoe (Scot.)	RULLION
—thong	RIEM
narrow	RIEMPIE
red-brown	RUSSIA LEATHER, YUFT
riding-leggings	CHAP(ARAJO)S
	CHAPAREJOS
Russia leather	YUFT
shavings from skins	MOSLINGS
shorts	LEDERHOSEN
sleeveless coat	JERKIN
stirrup guard	TAPADERA, TAPADERO
strap	BELT, STROP, TAWSE
	THONG
tanned with	
—chrome	CHROME-LEATHER
—sumach and dyed	SAFFIAN
treated for writing	PARCHMENT
trousers (Ger.)	LEDERHOSEN
undressed kid	SUEDE
untanned leather	RAWHIDE
water bottle	WATER-BOUGET
worker	LEATHERSMITH, SADDLER
yuft	RUSSIA LEATHER
Lebanon	
capital	BEIRUT
coin	
—unit	PIASTRE
—100 piastres	POUND
Lesotho	LS
capital	MASERU
coin	LISENTE, (MA)LOTI
language	SESOTHO
Liberia	LB
capital	MONROVIA
coin	DIRHAM, DINAR
library	
copyright libraries	BODLEIAN, OXFORD
	BRITISH NATIONAL
	CAMBRIDGE UNIVERSITY
	SCOTTISH NATIONAL
	TRINITY COLLEGE, DUBLIN
	WELSH NATIONAL
Libya	LAR
capital	TARABULUS, TRIPOLI
coin	DIRHAM, DINAR
newsagency	JANA
	(*see also* **Arab**)

Licentiate	
of	
—Apothecaries' Company	LAC
—College of Preceptors	LCP
—Society of Apothecaries	LSA
in	
—Dental Surgery	LDS
—Surgery	LCH
—Theology	LTH, THL
lichen	(*see* **fungus**)
Liechtenstein	FL
capital	VADUZ
coin	
—unit	CENTIME, RAPPEN
—100 rappen	FRANC
life symbol	ANKH
lifestyle	
affecting	
—a working-class image	MOCKNEY
—style of earlier	
generation	YOUNG FOGEY
black yuppie	BUPPIE, BUPPY
devoted to yacht-racing	CUPPIE, YOTTIE
double income, no kids	DINKY
drop-out	BEATNIK, HIPPIE
greying, leisured, affluent	
and married	GLAM
Japanese yuppie	JUPPIE, JUPPY
living in redeveloped	
docklands	DOCKN(E)Y
lots of money but a real	
dickhead	LOMBARD
no income, lots of kids	NILKY
old person	CRINKLY, CRUMBLY
	WRINKLY
person inheriting	
parents' property	PIPPIE, PIPPY
recently-acquired income	
deficiency syndrome	RAIDS
rich urban biker	RUB
success with peace of mind	SPOM
upper class, resident	
—in Sloane Square area	SLOANE RANGER
—near Sloane Square	SOANLY RANGER
wanting to be like someone else	WANNABEE
we have a nanny	WHANNY
well-off older person	WOOPIE
young	
—upwardly mobile	YUPPIE, YUPPY
—working-class male	PRINGLE
Youth International Party	YIPPIE
youthful, energetic,	
elderly person	YEEPIE
literature	LIT
addition	ADDENDUM
—at end	APPENDIX

affected style	GONGORISM
anonymous works	ADEPOTA
bombastic style	EUPHUISM
books	(*see separate entry*)
brief	
—account	ANECDOTE
—description	BLURB, PRECIS
	SUMMARY
category	GENRE
central idea	THEME
collected fragments	ANALECTA, ANALECTS
collection	ANTHOLOGY, CANON
composition	ESSAY
—of unconnected fragments	CENTO
controversial piece	POLEMIC
copies produced at one	
printing	EDITION
critical comment	ANNOTATION, GLOSS
delete offensive words etc	BOWDLERISE
	CENSOR
depicting	
—character's	
thoughts	INTERIOR MONOLOGUE
	STREAM OF CONSCIOUSNESS
—reality as	
representing	
underlying existence	SYMBOLISM
—section of society	SLICE OF LIFE
	TRANCHE DE VIE
double meaning	ALLEGORY
	DOUBLE ENTENDRE, PUN
dramatists	(*see separate entry*)
elegant	AUGUSTAN
excessively detailed	
description of trivia	CHOSISM
expression	PHRASE
extremism	ULTRAISM
factual	DOCUMENTARY
first part of work	PROLOGUE
florid style	EUPHUISM, GONGORISM
formal study	TREATISE
French movement (20th c)	LETTRISM
from the sublime to the	
ridiculous	BATHOS
fulsome comment	BLURB
German literary	
movement (18th c)	STURM UND DRANG
group of sentences	
on same subject	PARAGRAPH
handwritten	MANUSCRIPT
historians	(*see separate entry*)
homily	POSTIL
imaginative	FICTION
—set in the future	SCIENCE FICTION
imitation	
—based on ridicule	PARODY

—of another's style	PASTICHE
index of all words	CONCORDANCE
law protecting writers against plagiarism	COPYRIGHT
letter	EPISTLE
life-story by	
—others	BIOGRAPHY
—self	AUTOBIOGRAPHY
light-hearted work	JEU D'ESPRIT
list of	
—books	BIBLIOGRAPHY
	BIBLIOTHECA
—words	GLOSSARY
literary	
—characters	PERSONAE
—circle	BLOOMSBURY GROUP
	CLIQUE, COTERIE
	CENACLE
—essays	BELLES LETTRES
—theft	PLAGIARISM
literature as art	BELLES-LETTRES
long	
—essay	THESIS
—narrative	EPIC, SAGA
marginal note	POSTIL
materials for critical study of document	APPARATUS CRITICUS
novel	
—about wandering rogue	PICARESQUE NOVEL
—in form of letters	EPISTOLARY
—involving macabre incidents	GOTHIC NOVEL
—of	
early development of hero	BILDUNGSROMAN
family saga	ROMAN-FLEUVE
—representing real people	ROMAN A CLEF
—with no discernible plot	ANTI-NOVEL
one who	
—disputes authorship	CHORIZONT(IST)
—writes for another	GHOST WRITER
overused expression	CLICHE
part of sentence	PHRASE
pedantic style	EUPHUISM, GONGORISM
pen-name	NOM-DE-PLUME
	PSEUDONYM
persuasive style	RHETORIC
playwrights	(see dramatists)
poetry	(see verse)
poets	(see separate entry)
publishing another's work as one's own	PLAGIARISM
recasting	RIFACIMENTO

recurring theme	LEITMOTIF
rhetorical	
—style	EUPHUISM
—use of hypothetical works of another	MIMESIS
Russian literary	
—group	SERAPION BROTHERS
—movement	SOCIALIST REALISM
section of story	PASSUS
set of three works	TRILOGY
selection of works	ANTHOLOGY, ANALECTS
	CHRESTOMATHY, DIGEST
sentence	PHRASE
serious dramatic work	TRAGEDY
short	
—description	CAPTION
—introduction	FOREWORD
	PREFACE
—narrative with moral	FABLE
—novel	NOVELLA
—pithy saying	APHORISM
	APO(PH)THEGM
	EPIGRAM, WISECRACK
—statement of general truth	AXIOM, MAXIM
—summary	PRECIS
—version of book	ABBRIDGED EDITION
	DIGEST
showy style	INKHORN
Spanish movement	ULTRAISM(O)
spoken or written narrative	STORY, TALE, YARN
stock theme	TOPOS
story	NARRATIVE
—based on	
fact	FACTION
imagination	FICTION
ridicule	PARODY, SATIRE
—containing facts and myths	LEGEND
—fictional	NOVEL
—in verse	FABLIAU
—of superhuman or supernatural events	MYTH
—with double meaning	ALLEGORY
summary	PRECIS, SYNOPSIS
—at start of play, etc	EXPOSITION
symbolic reference	ALLEGORY
textural comments	ANNOTATION
trite expression	CLICHE
true-to-life style	NATURALISM
twentieth-century style of novel	ANTI-NOVEL
valediction to the dead	EPITAPH
	OBIT(UARY)
verse	(see separate entry)

word indicating	
literal quotation	SIC
words	
—in common use	COLLOQUIALISM
—of	
oper(ett)a	LIBRETTO
song	LYRICS
work published in	
author's real name	AUTONYM
writers	(*see separate entry*)
lizards	AGAMA, AGAMID(AE)
	GECKO(NES), LACERTA
African	GECKO, (I)GUANA
	MONITOR, SKINK
American	ANOLIS, FENCE-LIZARD
	GILA MONSTER, UTA
Asian	FRILLED LIZARD, MONITOR
Australian	BLUE TONGUE
	CHLAMYDOSAURUS
	FRILLED LIZARD, GO(H)ANNA
	MOLOCH, MONITOR, PERENTIE
	THORN-DEVIL
barking gecko	TOKAY
colour-changing	CHAM(A)ELEON
duck-billed	HADROSAUR
Egyptian	ADDA, WORRAL, WORREL
European	MAGYAROSAURUS
fish-like	ICHTHYOPTERYGIA
	ICHTHYOSAURUS
Indonesian	KOMODO DRAGON
	KOMODO LIZARD
monitor	VARANUS
Philippines	IBID, IBIT
prehistoric	ALLOSAURUS, ANATOSAURUS
	BRACHIOSAURUS, CARNOSAURUS
	CERATOSAURUS, COELUROSAURUS
	CORYTHOSAURUS, DEINOSAUR
	DINOSAUR, ELASMOSAURUS
	GORGOSAURUS, HYPSELOSAURUS
	HYPSILOPHODON(T), KRONOSAURUS
	LABYRINTHODONT, MELANOSAURUS
	MAMENCHISAURUS, MOSASAURUS
	ORNITHOSUCHUS, PANOPLOSAURUS
	PACHYCEPHALOSAURUS
	PARASAUROLOPHUS
	PELYCOSAURUS
	PLIOSAURUS, POLACANTHUS
	SAURIOPSIDA, SAURISCHIA
	STRETOSAURUS, THERAPODA
	TYLOSAURUS,
—Colorado/Wyoming	APATOSAURUS
	ATLANTOSAURUS
	BRONTOSAURUS
—Cretaceous	ANKYLOSAURUS
	HADROSAURUS
	IGUANODON, MEGALOSAURUS

	(PA)RHABDODON
	TITANOSAURUS, TRICERATOPS
	TYRANNOSAURUS (REX)
—flying	ARCHAEOPTERYX
	ORNITHOSAURUS
	PTERODACTYL(E)
	PTERANODON
	PTEROSAURUS, SAURURAE
—giant dinosaur	SAUROPOD, THERAPOD
—Jurassic	ATLANTOSAURUS
	CETEOSAURUS
	COMPSOGNATHUS
	DIPLODOCUS, EPANTERIAS
	IGUANADON, CETEOSAURUS
	STEGOSAURUS
—medium-sized dinosaur	LUFENGOSAURUS
	PROTOSAUROPOD
—Mesozoic	D(E)INOSAUR
	ICHTHYOSAURUS
	PLESIOSAURUS
—Tertiary	D(E)INOTHERIUM
South American	AMPHISBAENA, BASILISK
	(I)GUANA, TEGUEXIN
Varanus	MONITOR
venomous	GILA MONSTER
West Indian	GALLIWASP
logic	
apparently genuine but	
illogical argument	FALLACY
argument of probability	ENTHYMEME
based on	
—deductions	ARISTOTELIAN LOGIC
—mathematical	
relationships	BOOLEAN ALGEBRA
classification of	
propositions	MODAL LOGIC
	MODALITY
conclusion from premise	INFERENCE
converse of logical	
consequence	ENTAILMENT
deduction of body	
of laws	LOGICAL CALCULUS
diagram of	
relationships	VENN DIAGRAM
drawing	
—general from particular	INDUCTION
—particular from general	DEDUCTION
from	
—cause to effect	A PRIORI
—effect to cause	A POSTERIORI
illogical conclusion	NON SEQUITUR
imaginative rather	
than logical	
thinking	LATERAL THINKING
jump in argument	SALTUS
logical	RATIONAL

—argument in three	
propositions	SYLLOGISM
—disproof	REDUCTIO AD ABSURDUM
—element	CONSTRUCT
—error	FALLACY
—reasoning	DEDUCTION, SYNTHESIS
	RATIOCINATION
by inference	INDUCTION
logically	
—consistent	COHERENT
	LEGITIMATE, VALID
—inconsistent	INVALID, INCOMPATIBLE
—self-evident	APODITIC, TAUTOLOGOUS
meaning of expression	CONNOTATION
particular	SUBALTERN
preliminary proposition	LEMMA
premise taken for granted	LEMMA
proposition(s)	
—both of which	
are true	CONSISTENT
—stated or assumed	PREMISE, PREMISS
refutation	ELENCH(US)
relating to part of class	PARTICULAR
sophism	ELENCH(US)
sophistical puzzle	SORITES
species comprising lower genus	SUBALTERN
specious fallacy	SOPHISM
state as a property	PREDICATE
string of propositions	SORITES
study of	
—given truths	AXIOMATICS
—necessity	MODAL LOGIC
syllogism	
—confirmed by	
incidental proposition	EPICHEIREMA
—in which	
conclusion becomes	
major premise	PROSYLLOGISM
one premise is suppressed	ENTHYMEME
the minor premise	
is only probable	ABDUCTION
syllogistic argument	SORITES
technique for testing	
truth of a proposition	DECISION PROCEDURE
theory	
—about explanations	
of events	COVERING LAW THEORY
—referred to in	
expression	DENOTATION
(see also **mathematics, philosophy**)	
using symbols	MATHEMATICAL LOGIC
	SYMBOLIC LOGIC
word which	
—can be predicted of itself	AUTOLOGICAL
—cannot be predicted	
of itself	HETEROLOGICAL

London	
and North-Eastern Railway	LNER
County Council	LCC
Midland and Scottish	LMS
Missionary Society	LMS
Philharmonic Orchestra	LPO
School of Economics	LSE
Symphony Orchestra	LSO
lord	
Lord (Chief) Justice	L(C)J
Lord Provost	LP
lordship	LD, LP
(see also **leaders, nobles**)	
Louis XIV	SUN KING
love	
including: addiction to	
excessive love for	
love of	
lover of	
loving	
mania for	
obsession with	
alcohol	DIPSOMANIA, METHOMANIA
animals	ZOOPHILIA, ZOOPHILISM
	ZOOPHILY
archery	TOXOPHILY
ballet	BALLETOMANIA
birds	ORNITHOPHILY
bonds	SCRIPOPHILY
books	BIBLIOMANIA
	BIBLIOPHILY
bridges	GEPHYRMANIA
cats	AIL(O)UROPHILIA
Celts	CELTOMANIA
	KELTOMANIA
China	SINOPHILISM, SINOPHILY
cigarette-cards	CARTOPHILY
climbing buildings	STEGOPHILY
cold	PSYCHROPHILIA
combs	CTENOPHILY
corpses	NECROMANIA, NECROPHILIA
	NECROPHILISM, NECROPHILY
crowds	DEMOMANIA, OCHLOMANIA
Dante	DANTOPHILY
darkness	SCOTOPHILIA
	SKOTOPHILIA
death	THANATOMANIA
decaying matter	SAPROPHILIA
devils	DEMONOMANIA
dogs	CANOPHILIST, CYNOMANIA
dry conditions	XEROPHILY
drugs	NARCOMANIA
dung	COPROPHILIA
eating	PHAGOMANIA, SITOMANIA
English	ANGLOPHILY
ether	ETHEROMANIA

exaggerating	MYTHOMANIA
familiar places	NOSTOMANIA
ferns	PTERIDOMANIA
	PTERIDOPHILIA
filth	COPROPHILIA
fire	PYROMANIA
flowers	ANTHOMANIA
	ANTHOPHILOUS
foreign things	XENOMANIA
French	FRANCOPHILY
	GALLOMANIA, GALLOPHILY
Germans	GERMANOPHILY
god	THEOMANIA
—and man	THEOPHILANTHROPY
gold	CHRYSOPHILY
	GOLD FEVER
gramophone records	DISCOPHILY
Greece	PHILHELLENISM
heat	THERMOPHILY
horses	HIPPOMANIA, HIPPOPHILY
imitating Oriental	POTICHOMANIA
insects	ENTOMORPHILY
knowledge	PHILOSOPHY
lakes	LIMNOPHILOUS
language	LINGUAPHILY
leaf production	PHYLLOMANIA
learning	PHILOMATHY
light	PHOTOPHILY
low temperatures	PSYCHROPHILY
lying	MYTHOMANIA
mankind	PHILANTHROPY
moisture	HYGROPHILY
mushrooms	MYCOPHILIA
music	MELOMANIA, PHILHARMONY
negroes	NEGROPHIL(Y)
new things	NEOPHILIA
offspring	PHILOPROGENITIVENESS
oils	OLEOPHILIC
old people	GERONTOPHILY
personal cleanliness	ABLUTOMANIA
pictures	ICONOPHILIA
play-going	THEATROMANIA
pleasure	HEDONOMANIA
poisons	TOXICOMANIA
power	MEGALOMANIA
printing	TYPOMANIA

pulling out hair	TRICHOTILLOMANIA
rain	OMBROPHILE
religion	(EN)THEOMANIA
riches	CHREMATOMANIA
	PLUTOMANIA
Russians	RUSSOPHILE
salt	HALOPHILE
sand	AMMOPHILY
—(plants)	PSAMMOPHIL(Y)
seeds	SPERMOPHILY
self	EGOMANIA
sexual passion	EROTOMANIA
	NYMPHOMANIA
	SATYROMANIA
—pleasure	SCOP(T)OPHILIA
single idea	MONOMANIA
snakes	OPHIOPHILISM
special food	OPSOMANIA
stamps	TIMBROMANIA
	TIMBROPHILY
stealing	KLEPTOMANIA
stone	LITHOPHILY
sun	HELIOPHILY
surgery	TOMOMANIA
talking	LOGOMANIA, VERBOMANIA
travelling	DROMOMANIA, HODOMANIA
	PORIOMANIA
tulip-growing	TULIPOMANIA
Turks	TURCOPHILY
types in the Old	
Testament	YPOMANIA
washing	ABLUTOMANIA
water	HYDROPHILY
wine	OENOMANIA
	OENOPHILY
wisdom	PHILOSOPHY
women	PHILOGYNY
wood	XYLOPHILY
low	
low frequency	LF
Low German	LG
Low Latin	LL
low pressure	LP
low tension	LT
lower case	LC
Luxembourg	L

M

Madagascar	MALAGASH, MALAGASY, RM
bird	DRONGO-CUCKOO
brush turkey	TALEGALLA
capital	ANTANANARIVO, TANANARIVE
civet	FO(U)SSA
climbing plant	WAX-FLOWER
flower	STEPHANOTIS
hedgehog	TANREC, TENREC
insectivore	TENREC
language	MALAGASH, MALAGASY
lattice-leaf	WATER-YAM
lemur	MONGOOSE
poison	TANGHIN
race	HOVA
raffia fabric	RABANNA
snake	LANGAHA
tree	TANGHIN, TRAVELLER'S-TREE
water-plant	LATTICE-LEAF, OUVIRANDRA
wingless bird	AEPYORNIS
magistrate	JURAT, SYNDIC
including: chief magistrate	
judge	
English	
—old	REEVE
—paid	STIPENDIARY
—quarter-sessions	RECORDER
French	BAILLI
—chief	AVOYER
German	AM(T)MAN
Greek	ARCHON, EPHOR, SYNDIC
Indian	COLLECTOR, COTWAL, KOTWAL
Irish	BREHON
Italian	GIUDUCE, GONFALONIERE
	MAGISTRATO, PODESTA
—old	PRIOR
mediaeval	REEVE
Moslem	CADI, KADI, SHEREEF, SHERIF
Netherlands	AM(T)MAN, STAD(T)HOLDER
Orkney	FOUD
Pakistan	HAKEEM, HAKIM
Roman	AEDILE, CONSUL
Scandinavian	AM(T)MAN
Scottish	BAIL(L)IE, PROVOST
Shetland	FOUD
South African	FIELD-CORNET
	LANDDROS(T)
Spanish	ALCALDE, CORREGIDOR
Swiss	AM(T)MAN, LANDAMMAN(N)

Venetian	DOGE, PODESTA
Malagasy	(*see* **Madagascar**)
Malawi	MW
capital	LILONGWE
coin	
—unit	TAMBALE
—100 tambale	KWA(T)CHA
Malaya	
apple	OTAHEITE
aromatic oil	CAJEPUT, CAJUPUT
badger	TELEDU
bear	BRUANG, HONEY-BEAR
	SUN-BEAR
betel	ARECA, SIRI(H)
blow-pipe	SUMPIT(AN)
boat	COROCORE, COROCORO
	PRA(H)U, PROA
bosun	SERANG
cape (headland)	TANJONG
capital	KUALA LUMPUR
civet	HEMIGALE, PARADOXURE
courtyard	KAMPONG
dish	OTAK-OTAK
estuary	KUALA
field	PADANG
fish	GORAMY, GO(U)RAMI
fruit	RAMBUTAN
—bat	KALONG
—tree	DURIAN, DURION
garment	SARONG
grass	(L)ALANG(ALANG)
harbour	BANDAR, PELABOHAN
hill	BUKIT
inlet	BANDAR
island	PULAU
knife	CREASE, CREESE
	KREESE, KRIS, PARANG
lake	TASEK
language	SAKAI
lord	TUAN
mountain	GUNUNG
nut	ARECA-NUT, BETEL-NUT
petty-officer	TINDAL
phalanger	CUS-CUS
port	BANDAR
river	SUNGAI
sailor	LASCAR
rum	TAFIA
sir	TUAN
skirt	SARONG
timber	TEAK
title of respect	TUAN
tree	ILANG-ILANG, RAMBUTAN
	SAP(P)AN, TEAK
	YLANG-YLANG
tribe	SAKAI

tunic	KABAYA
verse form	PANTO(U)M
village	KAMPUNG, KAMPONG
whisky and soda	STENGAH, STINGER
Malaysia	MAL
capital	KUALA LUMPUR
chicken	AYAM
coin	
—unit	SEN
—100 sen	RINGGIT
curry	GULAI, GULE
fish	IKAN
kebab	SATAY, SATE
Maldives	
capital	MALE
coin	
—unit	LAARI
—100 laaris	RUFIYAA, RUPEE
Mali	RMM
capital	BANAKO
coin	FRANC
Malta	M
boat	DGHAJSA
capital	VALLETTA
coins	
—unit	MIL
—10 mils	CENT
—100 cents	LIRA
hood	FALDETTA
measure	CANNA, PIEDE
weight	ROTOLO
Manx	
parliament	TYNWALD
—lower house	HOUSE OF KEYS
many	
combining form	MULT(I)-, POLY-
having many	
—amino-acids	POLYPEPTIDE
—atoms	POLYATOMIC
—axes	POLYAXIAL, POLYAXON
—branches	MULTIRAMIFIED
—cells	MULTICAMERATE
	MULTICELLULAR
	POLYTHALAMOUS
—centres	MULTICENTRAL
—chambers	MULTICAMERATE
	MULTILOCULATE
	POLYTHALAMOUS
—circles	POLYCYCLIC
—coils	MULTISPIRAL
—colours	MULTICOLOURED
	POLYCHROM(AT)IC
—columns	POLYSTYLAR, POLYSTYLE
—components	MULTIPLE
—elements	MULTIPLE, POLYSYNTHETIC
—faces	MULTIFACED

—feet	MULTIPED
—fine teeth	MULTIDENTICULATE
—fingers	MULTIDIGITATE
—flowers	MULTIFLOROUS
—forms	PLEOMORPHIC
	POLYMORPHIC
—fruiting periods	POLYCARPIC
	POLYCARPOUS
—furrows	MULTISULCATE
—heads	MULTICAPITATE
	MULTICIPITAL
—husbands	POLYANDROUS
	POLYGAMOUS
—hydroxyl groups	POLYHYDRIC
—individuals in colony	POLYZOIC
—joints	MULT(I)ARTICULATE
—languages	MULTILINGUAL
—leaflets	MULTIFOLIOLATE
—leaves	MULTIFOLIATE
—lines	MULTILINEAL, MULTILINEAR
—lobes	MULTIFID(OUS)
	MULTILOBATE, MULTILOBED
—lobules	MULTILOBULAR
	MULTILOBULATE
—meanings	MULTIVOCAL
—names	POLYONYMOUS
—pairs of leaflets	MULTIJUGATE
	MULTIJUGOUS
—parents	POLYHYBRID
—partitions	MULTISEPTATE
—parts	MULTIPARTITE
	MULTI-STAGE
	POLYMEROUS
—pips	ACINACEOUS
—pistils	POLYGYNIAN
	POLYGYNOUS
—rays	POLYACT(INAL)
	POLYACTINE
—ribs	MULTICOSTATE
—rings	POLYCYCLIC
—sepals	POLYSEPALOUS
—shapes	MULTIFORM, POLYMORPHIC
—sides	MULTILATERAL
—small teeth	POLYPROTODONT
—sounds	MULTISONANT
—stems	MULTICAULINE
—styles	POLYGYNIAN, POLYGYNOUS
—syllables	POLYSYLLABIC
—teeth	MULTIDENTATE
—times normal number of chromosomes	POLYPLOID
—toes	POLYDACTYLOUS
—tones	POLYTONAL
—tubercles	MULTITUBERCULATE
—turns	POLYCYCLIC
—types	POLYTYPIC

—variables	MULTIVARIATE
—voices	POLYPHONIC
—ways	MULTIVIOUS
—whorls	POLYCYCLIC
—wives	POLYGYNOUS
—xylem strands	POLYARCH
—zones or belts	POLYZONAL
Maori	(*see* **New Zealand**)
martial arts	(*see* **games**)
masonry	(*see* **architectural features**)
master	
Master of	
—Arts	MA
—Dental Surgery	MDS
—Foxhounds	MOF
—Laws	LLM
—Science	MSC
—Surgery	MCH, MS, CHM, CM
—the Rolls	MR, CHAUFFEUR
—Theology	MTH
material	(*see* **fabrics**)
mathematics	
1 - cosine	VERSED SINE, VERSIN(E)
1 - sin	COSEC(ANT)
2,8,20,28,50,82,126	MAGIC NUMBERS
25% percentile	QUARTILE
50% percentile	MEDIAN
75% percentile	QUARTILE
addition	SUMMATION
aggregate	MANIFOLD
—of variables	(CO)DOMAIN
all elements	UNIVERSAL SET
analysis of	
mathematics	METAMATHEMATICS
analytical	
geometry	CO-ORDINATE GEOMETRY
angle	
—less than (<)90°	ACUTE
—90°	QUADRANT
	RIGHT ANGLE
—greater than (>)90°	OBTUSE
—180°	STRAIGHT ANGLE
—greater than (>)180°	REFLEX
—360°	PERIGON
	ROUND ANGLE
—and distance fixing	
position	POLAR COORDINATE
—between axis and vector	ARGUMENT
—measurement	DEGREE, MINUTE
	RADIAN, SECOND
—subtended by arc equal	
to radius	RADIAN
angles	
—on opposite sides of	
two intersecting	
lines	ALTERNATE ANGLES

—which total	
90°	COMPLEMENTARY ANGLES
180°	SUPPLEMENTARY ANGLES
apex of cone	VERTEX
Arabic notation	ALGORISM, ALGORITHM
area bounded by two	
concentric circles	ANNULUS
arithmetic average	MEAN
arrangement into	
—a possible order	COMBINATION
—every possible order	PERMUTATION
—groups	PERMUTATION
array of coefficients	
in a grid	MATRIX
assumption for proof of	
proposition in set	
theory	AXIOM OF CHOICE
	MULTIPLICATIVE AXIOM
at right angles	PERPENDICULAR
—to	
horizontal	PERPENDICULAR
vertical	HORIZONTAL
average	ARITHMETIC MEAN
—of	
number of errors	
or deviations	STANDARD DEVIATION
squares of	
deviation	VARIANCE
based on triangles	TRIGONOMETRY
branches	ALGEBRA, ARITHMETIC
	CALCULUS, GEOMETRY
	SETS, TOPOLOGY
	TRIGONOMETRY
—modern concepts	FRACTAL GEOMETRY
	MANDELBROT SET
	MENGER SPONGE
	STERPINSKI CARPET
	STRANGE ATTRACTORS
calculating device	ABACUS
	(ELECTRONIC) CALCULATOR
	NAPIER'S BONES, NAPIER'S RODS
	SLIDE RULE
calculation of continuously	
changing variables	CALCULUS
capable of coincident	
superimposition	CONGRUENT
chart giving values	
of variables	NOMOGRAM
	NOMOGRAPH
circular band	
incorporating	
180°twist	MOBIUS STRIP
class	SET
collection of	
defined elements	SET
co-ordinate geometry	ANALYTIC GEOMETRY

combination of
　—elements in set　　　　　　OPERATION
　—real and imaginary
　　numbers　　　　　　COMPLEX NUMBER
common fraction　　　　　VULGAR FRACTION
comparison of two
　similar quantities　　　　　　　　RATIO
cone with axis not
　perpendicular to base　　　　　SCALENE
conic section
　—not parallel to side　　　　HYPERBOLA
　—oblique to
　　axis　　　　　　　　　　ELLIPSE
　　base　　　　　　　　　　UNGULA
　—parallel to
　　base　　　　　　　　　　CIRCLE
　　side　　　　　　　　PARABOLA
consisting of
　—straight lines　　　　　RECTILINEAR
　—whole numbers　　　　　　INTEGRAL
constant
　—describing a conic section　　ECCENTRICITY
　—factor in conversion　　　　MODULUS
correspondence of
　—all points of image
　　with object in a
　　transformation　ROTATIONAL SYMMETRY
　—parts about an axis　　　　SYMMETRY
corresponding
　—ratios of two pairs
　　of quantities　　　　　PROPORTION
　—variables　　　　　　　　FUNCTION
counting frame　　　　　　　　ABACUS
corner of figure or solid　　　　　VERTEX
covering area with
　polygons to form
　regular pattern　　　　　TESSELLATION
curve
　—by which a curved figure
　　may be squared　　　　QUADRATRIX
　—conic section　　　　　HYPERBOLA
　　　　　　　　　　　　PARABOLA
　—drawn without retracing
　　any part of path　　　　UNICURSAL
　—expressed by
　　exponential
　　equation　　EXPONENTIAL CURVE
　—generated by
　　2 points for which the
　　difference of their
　　distances from two fixed
　　points is constant　　　HYPERBOLA
　　centres of curvature
　　of involute curve　　　　EVOLUTE
　　chain suspended at
　　each end　　　　　　CATENARY

intersection of
　plane and cone　　　CONIC SECTION
point
　—equidistant from a
　　fixed point and a
　　fixed straight line　　　PARABOLA
　—revolving about a
　　moving axis　　　　　　AXOID
$r = a \sin m\theta$　　　　　ROSETTE
sine wave　　　　　SINUSOID(AL)
string wound off or
　on to another curve　　　INVOLUTE
$y^2 = 4ax$　　　　　　PARABOLA
$y^n = px^m$　　　　　　PARABOLA
　　　　　(*see also* figure *below*)
　　　　　(*see also* solid *below*)
　—inward　　　　　　　CONCAVE
　—like shell　　　　　CONCHOID
　—of variable quantities
　　under fixed volume　　　ISOCHOR(E)
　—outward　　　　　　CONVEX
dealing with variable
　quantities　　DIFFERENTIAL CALCULUS
　　　　　　　INTEGRAL CALCULUS
decimal
　—fraction repeating
　　indefinitely　　RECURRING DECIMAL
　—portion of logarithm　　　MANTISSA
decision-making based
　on probabilities
　and odds　　　　　GAME THEORY
　　　　　　　　THEORY OF GAMES
definition of dimensions
　for intricate shapes　　MEASURE THEORY
derived function　　　　　DERIVATIVE
determinant derived from variables
　　　　　JACOBIAN (DETERMINANT)
determination of
　—intermediate values　　INTERPOLATION
　—length of curve　　　RECTIFICATION
　—values beyond range of
　　given data　　　　EXTRAPOLATION
deviation from mean　　　　VARIATION
diagram
　—for reckoning
　　probabilities　　PASCAL'S TRIANGLE
　—from which data
　　can be scaled　　　ABAC, ISOPLETH
　　　　　NOMOGRAM, NOMOGRAPH
　—of lines　　　　　　NETWORK
　—showing
　　information using a motif　PICTOGRAM
　　relationship
　　between sets　　ARROW DIAGRAM
　　of variables　　　　GRAPH
　—used in set theory　　VENN DIAGRAM

difference from the mean	DEVIATION
differential	
—coefficient	DERIVATIVE
—operator	LAPLACE OPERATOR
distance	
—across circle	
through centre	DIAMETER
—along	
x-axis	ABSCISSA
y-axis	ORDINATE
—from centre of circle	
to circumference	RADIUS
—round	
circle	CIRCUMFERENCE
sides of figure	PERIMETER
distribution of	
rare events	POISSON DISTRIBUTION
eight-sided figure	OCTAGON
eighth of circle	OCTANT
element of set	MEMBER
equal in all respects	CONGRUENT
equality of two ratios	PROPORTION
equation(s)	
—in which the variable	
occurs in the	
exponent	EXPONENTIAL
—having same solutions	SIMULTANEOUS
—involving derived	
functions	DIFFERENTIAL
—of	
first degree	LINEAR
second degree	QUADRATIC
—requiring integers	
as solution	DIOPHANTINE EQUATION
—showing connection	
between equalities	FORMULA
Euclidean space	HOMALOID
exact divisor	ALIQUOT PART
exponent	INDEX
expression	
—consisting of	
2 terms	BINOMIAL
3 terms	TRINOMIAL
several terms	POLYNOMIAL
—derived from another	TRANSFORMATION
external	
—edge of plane figure	PERIMETER
—surface of solid	PERIPHERY
factor	
—of a quantity which, taken	
a number of times, produces	
that quantity	ROOT
—which is a prime number	PRIME FACTOR
figure(s)	
—bounded by	
2 radii and an arc	SECTOR

chord and arc	SEGMENT
diameter and arc	SEMI-CIRCLE
straight lines	POLYGON
—derived from another	TRANSFORMATION
—generated by	
centre of circle rolling	
round another	EPICYCLE
conic section round	
a straight line	TORUS
point	
—on circle rotating	
inside larger circle	HYPOCYCLOID
—on circumference	
of revolving circle	CYCLOID
—rotating about	
another point	CIRCLE
rotating	
—ellipse	ELLIPSOID
—rectangle	CYLINDER
—having	
1 pair of sides parallel	TRAPEZIUM
2 dimensions	PIANE FIGURE
2 pairs of sides parallel	
—at right angles	RECTANGLE
—not at right angles	PARALLELOGRAM
3 dimensions	SOLID
3 sides	TRIANGLE
—all sides	
equal	EQUILATERAL
unequal	SCALENE
—two sides equal	ISOSCELES
4 sides	QUADRILATERAL
—all sides equal	
at right-angles	SQUARE
not at right angles	RHOMBUS
—2 pairs of sides equal	
at right angles	SQUARE
not at right	
angles	PARALLELOGRAM
all sides of equal	
length	EQUILATERAL FIGURE
no sides parallel	TRAPEZOID
several sides	POLYGON
—kite-shaped	DELTOID
—polygon	
with 1 reflex angle	RE-ENTRANT
with all sides and angles	
the same	REGULAR POLYGON
—representing a number	DIGIT
—which can be inscribed	
in a circle	CYCLIC FIGURE
	(*see also* **shape**)
find total value	INTEGRATE
finding a square equal to	
a given figure	QUADRATURE
fixed value	CONSTANT

flat surface	PLANE
formulae for faces	
etc of polyhedra	EULER'S FORMULAE
fraction(s)	
—expressed	
as negative power	
of ten	DECIMAL FRACTION
in binary	BICIMAL
—into which a fraction	
can be separated	PARTIAL FRACTIONS
—less than unity	PROPER FRACTION
—not less than unity	IMPROPER FRACTION
—that cancel to the	
same fraction	EQUIVALENT FRACTIONS
—with	
denominator of 100	PERCENTAGE
numerator greater	
than denominator	IMPROPER FRACTION
numerator less than	
denominator	PROPER FRACTION
—written with one number	
above and one below	
a line	COMMON FRACTION
	VULGAR FRACTION
fractional part of logarithm	MANTISSA
frequency distribution	
diagram	HISTOGRAM
function	OPERATOR
—analogous to	
trigonometrical	
ratios	HYPERBOLIC FUNCTION
—moving inversely	
against a variable	TRANSIENT
—obtained by	
fitting polynomials	
together	SPLINE FUNCTION
integration	INTEGRAL
—symbol	NABLA
—of function	FUNCTIONAL OPERATOR
geometry of	
—curved space	RIEMANNIAN GEOMETRY
—three-dimensional	
space	EUCLIDEAN GEOMETRY
graph	
—showing	
distribution of	
events	FREQUENCY CURVE
frequency by area	
of bars	HISTOGRAM
—using	
columns	BAR CHART
sectors of circle	PIE CHART
greater than any real	
quantity	INFINITY
group with at least one	
common characteristic	SET

half of	
—circle	SEMICIRCLE
—diameter of circle	RADIUS
—sphere	HEMISPHERE
—versine	HAVERSINE
having	
—1 dimension	LINEAR
—2	
intersecting planes	DIHEDRAL
terms	BINOMIAL
or more terms	MULTINOMIAL
	POLYNOMIAL
—equal	
diameters	ISODIAMETRIC
perimeters	ISOPERIMETER
—same	
centre	CONCENTRIC
shape	SIMILAR
—and size	CONGRUENT, IDENTICAL
higher arithmetic	NUMBER THEORY
highest	
—derivative in differential	
equation	ORDER
—value of a variable	MAXIMUM
horizontal	
—and vertical lines	
in graph	CARTESIAN COORDINATES
—measurement in graph	ABSCISSA
hyperbolic functions	COSECH, COSH
	COTH, SECH, SINH, TANH
in the same plane	COPLANAR
ideal proportions	GOLDEN MEAN
	GOLDEN SECTION
independent variable	ARGUMENT
indirect relationship	
of variables	IMPLICIT FUNCTION
intersection of curve	
and axis	VERTEX
invariable quantity	CONSTANT
inverse of	
—differentiation	INTEGRATION
—number	RECIPROCAL
—power	LOGARITHM
inverted delta symbol	NABLA
involving right angles	ORTHOGONAL
irrational quantity	SURD
largest number which is	
a factor of two other	
numbers	HIGHEST COMMON FACTOR
law	
—governing relationship	
of addition and	
multiplication	DISTRIBUTIVE
—stating irrelevance of	
order of operations	ASSOCIATIVE
	COMMUTATIVE

likelihood of happening	PROBABILITY
line(s)	
—at right angles to	
horizontal	VERTICAL
vertical	HORIZONTAL
—between two points	
on a curve	CHORD
—by reference to which a	
curve can be defined	DIRECTRIX
—cutting	
circle in half	DIAMETER
line, etc, in half	BISECTOR
off part of a circle	CHORD
—from centre	
to circumference	
of circle	RADIUS
perpendicular to side	
of polygon	APOTHEM
—from corner of triangle to	
centre of side opposite	MEDIAN
—in same plane which	
never meet	PARALLEL LINES
—joining	
corners of figure	DIAGONAL
two points on a curve	CHORD
—not parallel nor intersecting	SKEW
—on surface of sphere	
which cuts all meridians	
at the same angle	LOXODROME
—parallel to horizon	HORIZONTAL
—passing through centre	
of Earth	VERTICAL
—perpendicular to another	CATHETUS
—which	
approaches but never	
reaches curve	ASYMPTOTE
cuts a curve at two or	
more places	SECANT
touches a circle at	
a point	TANGENT
logarithm	
—to base 10	COMMON LOGARITHM
—to base *e*	NAPERIAN LOGARITHM
	NATURAL LOGARITHM
longer axis of ellipse	MAJOR AXIS
longest side in	
right-angled triangle	HYPOTENEUSE
lowest value of a variable	MINIMUM
mapping back from	
an image	INVERSE FUNCTION
	INVERSE MAPPING
mathematicians	
—Alexandrian	DIOPHANTOS, EUCLID
—American	BOWDITCH, CHURCH, DANZIG
	ELO, FULLER, GODEL
	MINSKY, MOULTON, SHANNON

	TARSKI, VON NEUMANN
	WHITEHEAD, WIENER
—Australian	BULLEN
—Austrian	EULER, HAHN, MENGER
—Belgian	LEMAITRE
—British	BABBAGE, BONDI
	BOULE, CLIFFORD, DE MORGAN
	FLETCHER, HAMILTON, HOYLE
	KEMP, MAXWELL, NAPIER
	NEWTON, POWELL, RUSSELL
	TURING, WHITEHEAD
—Czech	GOBEWL
—Dutch	SNEL VAN ROYEN, SNELLIUS
—French	CAUCHY, CLAIRAULT
	CORIOLIS, DESCARTES
	FERMAT, GALOIS, JORDAN
	LAPLACE, LISSAJOUS
	MERCENNE, PASCAL
	POINCARE
—German	BESSEL, CANTOR, FREGE
	GAUSS, HILBERT, KRONECKER
	LEIBNITZ, MINKOWSKI, OHM
	RIEMANN, WEIERSTRASS
	ZERMEL
—Greek	ARCHIMEDES, EUCLID
	PYTHAGORAS
—Hungarian	VON NEUMANN
—Irish	FITZGERALD, HAMILTON
—Italian	CARDANO, FIBONACCI
	GALILEO, LEONARDO
	PEANO, TARTAGLIA
—Paris group	BOURBAKI
—Polish	TARSKI
—Romanian	OBERTH
—Russian	CANTOR, KOLMOGOROV
	MARKOV, MINKOWSKI
—Swiss	BERNOULLI
matrix used in probability	
theory and binomial	
distribution	PASCAL'S TRIANGLE
measurement of	
—likelihood	PROBABILITY
—lines and figures	MENSURATION
measurements which fix a	
point in a frame of	
reference	COORDINATES
meeting point of	
straight lines	VERTEX
method of	
—dealing with continuously	
varying	
quantities	DIFFERENTIAL CALCULUS
—solving simultaneous	
equations	DETERMINANTS
—statistical	
reasoning	BAYESIAN STATISTICS

moment of inertia about axis	RADIUS OF GYRATION
most frequently occurring number in a set	MODE
movement by rotating, reflecting, translating or dilating an object	TRANSFORMATION
multiplier	
—½	HEMI-, SEMI-
—1	MONO-, UNI-
—1½	SESQUI-
—2	BI-, DI-
—3	TER-, TRI-
—4	QUADR(I)-, TETR(A)-
—5	CINQ-, PENT-, QUIN-
—6	HEX(A)-, SEX(I)-
—7	HEPTA-, SEPT(I)-
—8	OCTA-, OCTO-
—9	ENNEA-, NONA-
—10	DECA-
—11	UNDECA-
—12	DODECA-, DUODECI-
—of algebraic expression	COEFFICIENT
	FACTOR
—that results in unity	RECIPROCAL
nth root of product of n numbers	GEOMETRIC MEAN
number	
—0	CIPHER, NIL, NOUGHT
—above the line in a fraction	NUMERATOR
—added	ADDEND
—average	MAN
—below the line in a fraction	DENOMINATOR
—expressing	
cube root	SUBTRIPLICATE
irrational quantity	SURD
—from which another is subtracted	MINUEND
—giving power of another	EXPONENT
—greater than 0	POSITIVE NUMBER
—indicating	
power	EXPONENT, INDEX
quality	CARDINAL
sequence	ORDINAL
—involving square-root of negative number	IMAGINARY NUMBER
—large	ARMY, HOST
	MULTITUDE, MYRIAD
10^6	MEGA-, MILLION
—USA	BILLION
10^9	GIGA
10^{12}	BILLION, TERA-
10^{15}	PETA-

10^{18}	TRILLION
10^{24}	EXA-, QUADRILLION
10^{30}	QUINTILLION
10^{36}	SEXTILLION
10^{42}	SEPTILLION
10^{48}	OCTILLION
10^{54}	NONILLION
10^{60}	DECILLION
10^{100}	GOOGOL
10^{120}	VIGINTILLION
10^{140}	ASANKHYEYA
10^{600}	CENTILLION
10^{googol}	GOOGOLPLEX
$((((10^{10})^{10})^{10})^{10})^3$	SKEWES' NUMBER
Buddhist	ASANKHYEYA
hypothetical	MEGISTON
unspecified	ZILLION
—less than 0	FRACTION
	NEGATIVE NUMBER
—making a whole	COMPLEMENT
—most frequent in a list	MODE
—non-existent quantities	IMAGINARY NUMBERS
—not commensurable with natural number	IRRATIONAL NUMBER
expressible in rational numbers	SURD
—of	
arcs meeting at a node	ORDER
times a function has been differentiated	ORDER
—ratio of two integers	RATIONAL NUMBER
—rational or irrational	REAL NUMBER
—represented by a logarithm	ANTILOG(ARITHM)
—resulting from addition	SUM, TOTAL
—of real and imaginary numbers	COMPLEX NUMBER
division	QUOTIENT
—of sum of numbers in set by size of set	AVERAGE, MEAN
—into 1	INVERSE
	RECIPROCAL
multiplication	PRODUCT
—small	
10^{-6}	MICRO-
10^{-9}	NANO-
10^{-12}	PICO-
10^{-15}	FEMTO-
10^{-18}	ATTO-
—subtracted	SUBTRAHEND
—system based on 2	BINARY

8	OCTAL
10	DECIMAL
16	HEX(ADECIMAL)
—the square root of which is an integer	SQUARE NUMBER
—to be subtracted	SUBTRAHEND
—used as base of number system	RADIX
—which	
can be	
—divided by 2	EVEN NUMBER
exactly into another	ALIQUOT, FACTOR
—written as a fraction	RATIONAL NUMBER
cannot be	
—divided by 2	ODD NUMBER
—written as a fraction	IRRATIONAL NUMBER
contains an exact number of another	MULTIPLE
equals the sum of its factors	PERFECT NUMBER
has a negative square	IMAGINARY NUMBER
is	
—added to another	SUMMAND
—divided	
by another	DIVIDEND, NUMERATOR
into another	DIVISOR DENOMINATOR
—not a fraction	WHOLE NUMBER
—the sum of the two preceding numbers	FIBONACCI NUMBER
—multiplied by itself produces the number in question	SQUARE ROOT
—whole number (+ and —) and zero	INTEGER
with fraction	MIXED NUMBER
—with	
associated direction	VECTOR
equal number of numbers greater and less than itself	MEDIAN
no	
—associated direction	SCALAR
—factors	PRIME NUMBER
variable exponent	EXPONENTIAL FUNCTION
—written	DIGIT, FIGURE
above another	SUPERSCRIPT
below another	SUBSCRIPT
	(*see also* quantity *below*)

numbers	
—in which the order of a pair is significant	ORDERED PAIR
—intermediate between Hindu and Arabic	GOBAR NUMERALS
—used to	
count in different directions	DIRECTED NUMBERS
fix points	COORDINATES
—which have the same remainder when divided by a third number	CONGRUENT
numerical expression of factor in a term	COEFFICIENT
omission of some digits in decimal fraction	ROUNDING
one of equal factors	ROOT
operation of	
—combining functions	COMPOSITION
—converting vectors	QUATERNION
—deducting one number from another	SUBTRACTION
—splitting number into equal parts	DIVISION
operator	FUNCTION
parameter	COEFFICIENT
part of	
—circle bounded by	
chord and arc	SEGMENT
two radii and an arc	SECTOR
—circumference of circle	ARC
—whole number	FRACTION
partially ordered set	LATTICE
path generated by point in space	LOCUS
pattern of rays	
—reflected from curved surface	CATACAUSTIC
—refracted by curve	DIACAUSTIC
peculiarity of argument of some functions	SINGULARITY
perimeter of circle	CIRCUMFERENCE
perpendicular	NORMAL
—to side from centre	APOTHEM
pertaining to	
—cube roots	SUBTRIPLICATE
—square roots of cubes	SESQUIPLICATE
plane	HOMALOID
—dividing solid into two mirror images	PLANE OF SYMMETRY
—figure bounded by straight lines	POLYGON
—figures	(*see* **shape**)
—shape which folds to produce a solid	NET

point
—at which
  axes of graph cross — ORIGIN
  concave curve changes
  to convex — INFLEXION
—being transformed — OBJECT
—defining curve — FOCUS
—line or plane which
  generates a line,
  plane or solid — GENERATRIX
—of
  common tangent of
  two curves — TACNODE
  intersection — NODE, ORIGIN
  —of medians — CENTROID
—on curve with more than
  one tangent — NODE
—transformed — IMAGE
potency of point with
  respect to circle — POWER
power of number to given
  base — LOG(ARITHM)
preliminary proposition — LEMMA
procedure for solving
  problems — ALGORITHM, ALGORISM
process
—of determining
  differential
  coefficients — DIFFERENTIATION
—used in calculus — INTEGRATION
—using integration — INTEGRAL CALCULUS
—with some element
  of probability — STOCHASTIC PROCESS
product of
—a number
  and all numbers below it
    down to 1 — FACTORIAL
  of equal factors — POWER
properties of
—figures unchanged
  in deformation — TOPOLOGY
—lines, surfaces and
  solids — GEOMETRY
proportion where ratio of
  larger section to whole
  equals that of larger
  section to smaller — GOLDEN MEAN
                GOLDEN SECTION
proposition
—proved by negation
  of the opposite — INDIRECT PROOF
—without proof — AXIOM
putting calculated values
—between known values — INTERPOLATION
—on each side of
  known values — EXTRAPOLATION

quantity
—defined by magnitude
  alone — SCALAR QUANTITY
  and angle — VECTOR
—given by multiplying a
  number by itself — SQUARE
—on which
  a system of numeration
  is based — RADIX
  another depends — ARGUMENT
—relating
  face to effect — MODULUS
  force to effect — MODULUS
—used to transform systems
  of coordinates — TENSOR
—which
  can assume any value — VARIABLE
  cannot be expressed
  algebraically — TRANSCENDENTAL
  does not change when
  multiplied by itself — IDEMPOTENT
  gives specified number
  when raised to
  third power — CUBE ROOT
—with variable
  exponent — EXPONENTIAL FUNCTION
    (*see also* number *above*)
quarter of a circle — QUADRANT
quotient of two vectors — QUATERNION
ratio of
—angle and its sine — SINE CURVE
                SINUSOID(AL) CURVE
—circumference to
  diameter — PI
—sides of right-angled
  triangle — TRIGONOMETRICAL RATIO
  height to base — TAN(GENT)
  hypotenuse to
  —base — SECANT
  —side opposite given
    angle — COSEC(ANT)
  side
  —adjacent to side
    opposite — COT(ANGENT)
  —opposite given angle
    to hypotenuse — SIN(E)
—two whole numbers — RATIONAL NUMBER
—vertical to horizontal
  distance — GRADIENT
rational
—integral function of
  two or more variables — QUANTIC
—or irrational number — REAL NUMBER
rectangle between
  segments of chord
  or circle — POTENCY

rectangular	ORTHOGONAL
—arrangement of quantities	MATRIX
reference line	AXIS
regular	
—six-sided figure	CUBE
—solid	PLATONIC SOLID
relationship	
—between	
similar quantities	RATION
variables	FUNCTION
—in which each object has	
an image	MAPPING
resolve into factors	FACTORISE
result of	
—addition	SUM
—differentiation	DERIVED FUNCTION
	DERIVATIVE
—division	QUOTIENT
into 1	INVERSE, RECIPROCAL
—multiplication	PRODUCT
—transformation	IMAGE
root	
—number	RADIX
—which cannot be	
enumerated exactly	SURD
rule	
—for	
calculating irregular	
areas	SIMPSON'S RULE
	TRAPEZOIDAL RULE
solving problems	ALGORISM
	ALGORITHM
—of proportions	CHAIN-RULE
—relating sides and angles	
of triangle	SINE RULE
scalar quantity which changes	
sign in transition of	
co-ordinates	PSEUDO-SCALAR
scale	
—representing	
tenfold	
increase	LOGARITHMIC SCALE
—showing relative	
change	INDEX
scatter of numbers	
about their	
mean value	STANDARD DEVIATION
section of	
—circle	
between two radii	SECTOR
cut off by chord	SEGMENT
—solid cut off by plane	
parallel to the base	FRUSTUM
selection of specified	
number from larger	
number	COMBINATION

sequence of numbers	
—in general form	SERIES
—limited by zero	NULL SEQUENCE
—tending	
to move up and down	OSCILLATING
towards	
—infinity	DIVERGING
—given number	CONVERGING
series	
—based on	
constant increment	ARITHMETIC
constant multiplier	GEOMETRIC
powers	EXPONENTIAL
—of	
numbers each of	
which is the sum of	
the preceding	
two	FIBONACCI SEQUENCE
reciprocals in	
arithmetic	
progression	HARMONIC SERIES
—with	
constant common	
difference	
	ARITHMETICAL PROGRESSION
common multiplier	
	GEOMETRICAL PROGRESSION
set	CLASS
—of	
computational	
procedures	ALGORISM, ALGORITHM
elements	
—common to two sets	INTERSECTION
—on which binary	
operations can be	
carried out	FIELD
equations with	
common	
variables	SIMULTANEOUS EQUATIONS
four	QUATERNION
numbers mapped by a	
function	DOMAIN
real numbers	CONTINUUM
transformations	GROUP
—in every possible order	PERMUTATION
—selected without	
regard to order	COMBINATION
—which is part of	
larger set	SUB-SET
—with no elements	EMPTY SET
	NULL SET
shape	
—being transformed	OBJECT
—transformed to	IMAGE
—with all parts in	
one plane	PLANE FIGURE

three dimensions	SOLID
(*see* figure *above*)	
(*see also* **shape**)	
sheet	NAPPE
shorter axis of ellipse	MINOR AXIS
side	
—of polyhedron	FACE
—opposite right-angle	HYPOTENUSE
single numeral	DIGIT
size of	
—matrix	ORDER
—solid	VOLUME
—surface	AREA
slope of line or plane	GRADIENT
smaller than any real quantity	INFINITESIMAL
smallest number which	
contains two or more	
numbers	LCM
	LOWEST COMMON MULTIPLE
solid	
—angle	STERADIAN
enclosing surface area	
equal to square of	
radius of sphere	STERADIAN
—bounded by plane	
surfaces	POLYHEDRON
—catenary shape	CATENOID
—cut off by plane not	
parallel to base of cone	
or cylinder	UNGULA
—generated by	
line through a point	
moving round a circle	CONE
rotation of	
—circle on axis	SPHERE
—ellipse on axis	ELLIPSOID
	SPHEROID
—rectangle on axis	CYLINDER
—with	
equal square faces	CUBE
one polygonal face	
and several	
triangular faces	PYRAMID
polygonal faces	POLYHEDRON
rectangular faces	CUBOID
two congruent	
parallel faces	PRISM
(*see also* **shapes**)	
space	
—enclosed by surfaces	SOLID
—occupied by a body	VOLUME
speed in a given direction	VELOCITY
spiral	HELIX
square	
—of	
mean deviation	VARIANCE

natural number	SQUARE NUMBER
—inscribed in	
circle	CYCLIC QUADRILATERAL
statement	
—of equality between	
quantities	EQUATION, IDENTITY
—proved by logical	
deduction	THEOREM
—that one quantity is not	
equal to another	INEQUALITY
statistical	
—analysis of several	
types of	
measurement	MULTIVARIATE ANALYSIS
—procedure with	
random numbers	MONTE CARLO METHOD
—spread	VARIANCE
strip of paper twisted	
and formed into loop	MO(E)BIUS STRIP
study of	
—boundaries	HOMOLOGY (THEORY)
—natural numbers	NUMBER THEORY
—numerical data	STATISTICS
—shapes when	
stretched	HOMOTOPY (THEORY)
	TOPOLOGY
—triangles	TRIGONOMETRY
sum of	
—exponents of variables	DEGREE
—sequence of terms	SERIES
surface of sphere cut	
off by two parallel planes	ZONE OF SPHERE
symbol	
—representing	
negative	MINUS
nil	NOUGHT, ZERO
number	NUMERAL
positive	PLUS
—or negative	SIGN
value or relationship	EXPRESSION
zero	NOUGHT
—showing power to which	
a number is raised	EXPONENT
—which can take	
any value	VARIABLE
symbolic logic	BOOLEAN ALGEBRA
symmetry about axis	AXIAL SYMMETRY
system for finding values	
—for allocating variables	
to different	
sources	VARIANCE ANALYSIS
—for general	
expressions	DIOPHANTINE ANALYSIS
—involving random	
occurrences which	
are time-dependent	STOCHASTIC PROCESS

term subjected to integration	INTEGRAND
theorem	
—giving any power of a binomial	BINOMIAL THEOREM
value of number in terms of logarithm	EXPONENTIAL THEOREM
—of properties of right-angled triangle	PYTHAGORAS' THEOREM
theory of	
—conflict between two rational people	GAMES THEORY
—even numbers as sum of 2 prime numbers	GOLDBACH'S CONJECTURE
third power of number	CUBE
three-dimensional co-ordinates	SPHERICAL COORDINATES
transformation in which	
—all points coincide with the image	IDENTICAL TRANSFORMATION
slide parallel to a line or plane	SHEAR
turn through the same angle	ROTATION
—figure slides without turning	TRANSLATION
—lengths remain the same	ISOMETRY
treating	
—calculation by symbols	ALGEBRA
not representing arithmetical quantities	BOOLEAN ALGEBRA
—points, lines, surfaces, etc	GEOMETRY
—properties of figures which remain unchanged after distortion	TOPOLOGY
—triangles	TRIGONOMETRY
triangle on surface of sphere	SPHERICAL TRIANGLE
trigonometrical	
—ratio	COSECANT, COSINE COTANGENT, SECANT SINE, TANGENT
—series expanded from function or curve	FOURIER ANALYSIS
trigonometry of spherical triangles	SPHERICAL TRIGONOMETRY

unvarying quantity	CONSTANT
using symbols for numbers, etc	ALGEBRA
value of	
—angle and distance fixing position of a point	RADIUS VECTOR
vector fixing position of point	POLAR COORDINATE
—function of variable whose differential coefficient is known	INTEGRAL
—limiting specified percentage of large sample	PERCENTILE
—number given by one divided by that number	RECIPROCAL
—variable and associated probabilities	DISTRIBUTION
which satisfies an equation	ROOT
variable	PARAMETER
—defined in terms of another	EXPLICIT FUNCTION
—which produces change in another	FUNCTION
—within a given range of values	VARIATE
variation as result of error term affecting fixed values	REGRESSION
vector	
—operator symbol	NABLA
—quantity which changes sign in transition of coordinates	PSEUDO-VECTOR
—representing relationship of vectors	TENSOR
versed sine	SAGITTA
vertical measurement in graph	ORDINATE
vulgar fraction	COMMON FRACTION
weighted mean	EXPECTATION
whole number	INTEGER, NATURAL NUMBER RATIONAL NUMBER
—or fraction	RATIONAL NUMBER
whole-number	
—part of logarithm	CHARACTERISTIC INTEGRAL
—sets which fit Pythagoras' theorem	PYTHAGOREAN TRIPLES
written number	DIGIT, FIGURE
Mauritania	RIM

capital	NOUAKCHOTT	—¼ pint (beer)	NIP, SMALL
coin		—1⅓ pints	BOTTLE
—unit	KHOUM	—2 pints	QUART
—5 khoums	OUGUIYA	—2 pints (beer)	FLAGON
Mauritius	MS	—2½ pints	YARD OF ALE
extinct bird	DODO	—4 pints (wine)	MAGNUM
May		—⅓ bottle	DOP
May 8th	V-DAY	—2 bottles	MAGNUM
Mayday	SOS	—3 bottles	FLAGON, TREGNUM
measures		—4 bottles	JEROBOAM
angle		—6 bottles	REHOBOAM
—unit	SECOND	—8 bottles	IMPERIALE
—60 seconds	MINUTE		METHUSELAH
—60 minutes	DEGREE	—12 bottles	SALMANAZAR
—15 degrees	HOUR	—16 bottles	BALTHAZAR
—57.3 degrees	RADIAN	—20 bottles	NEBUCHADNEZZAR
—90 degrees	QUADRANT, RIGHT ANGLE	—1, 3 or 6 quarts (liquor)	TAPPIT
—360 degrees	CIRCLE, PERIGON	—2 quarts	POTTLE
	ROUND ANGLE	—4 quarts	GALLON
—⅛ circle	OCTANT	—½ gallon	STOUP
—⅙ circle	SEXTANT	—2 galls	PECK
—¼ circle	QUADRANT	—4½ galls	PIN
—¹/₁₀₀ right angle	GRADE	—8 galls	BUSHEL
—angular distance of 90°	QUADRATURE	—9 galls	FIRKIN
—division of		—10 gallons (beer)	ANKER
arc	SCRUPLE	—18 galls	KILDERKIN
compass	POINT	—36 galls	BARREL
—solid angle	STERADIAN	—42 galls	TIERCE
area		—46 gallons (petrol, USA)	BARREL
—272 sq. ft	ROD, PERCH, POLE	—46 galls (claret)	HOGSHEAD
—4840 sq. yds	ACRE	—52½ galls	HOGSHEAD
—¼ acre	ROOD	—54 galls (beer)	HOGSHEAD
—2.48 acres	HECTARE	—63 galls (wine)	HOGSHEAD
—13 acres	BOVATE, OXGATE, OXGANG	—70-120 galls	PUNCHEON
—26 acres	HUSBANDLAND	—108 galls (beer, sherry)	BUTT
—30 acres	YARDLAND, VIRGATE	—126 galls (wine)	BUTT
—100 acres	CARUCATE	—200 gallons (wine)	TONNEAU
—120 acres	HIDE	—216 galls (ale)	TUN
—circle	CIRCULAR MIL	—252 galls (wine)	TUN
—cross-section of nucleus	BARN	—9 pecks (apples)	SEAM
atmospheric pressure	BAR	—2 bushels	CO(O)MB
—1 mm of mercury	TORR	—4 bushels	CO(O)MB, COMBE
—1000 bars	KILOBAR	—6 bushels	BOLL
—low pressure unit	TORR	—8 bushels	QUARTER
—normal pressure	STANDARD ATMOSPHERE	—8 bushels (grain)	SEAM
capacity		—9 bushels	FAT
—577 cc	PINT	—40 bushels (corn or salt)	WEY
—277 cubic inches	GALLON	—96 bushels	CHALDER
—60 minims	FLUID DRACHM	—1 hogshead	MUID
—8 fluid drachms	FLUID OUNCE	—⅙ pipe	OCTAVE
—16 fluid ounces (US)	PINT	—3 tierces	PIPE
—20 fluid ounces	PINT	—2 hogsheads	PIPE
—¹/₃-¹/₆ gill (spirits)	TOT	—corn, etc	MUID
—1 gill (spirits)	NOGGIN	—mouthful (liquor)	SLUG
—4 gills	PINT	—small	MINIM
—¼ pint	GILL, NOGGIN, QUARTERN	handful or pinch	PUGIL

cloth	
—1½ yards	ELL
—20 hanks (linen yarn)	BUNDLE
—80 yards (worsted yarn)	LEA
—120 yards (cotton yarn)	LEA
—300 yards (linen yarn)	LEA
—180,000 yds (linen yarn)	BUNCH
distance	
—2.25 mm	LIGNE
—1⁻²³³²⁸cm	PLANCK LENGTH
—10⁻¹³ cm	FERMI
—¹/₁₀₀₀"	MIL
—¹/₇₂"	POINT
—¹/₁₆"	LINE
—¹/₃"	BARLEYCORN
—³/₄"	DIGIT
—2½"	NAIL
—3-4"	PALM
—4"	HAND
—8"	LINK
—9"	SPAN
—12"	FOOT, LAST
—18"-22"	CUBIT(US)
—30"	PACE
—33" (approx)	METRE
—36"	YARD
—37"	CLOTH-YARD
—45"	ELL
—58"	ROMAN PACE
—63,360"	MILE
—6 feet	FATHOM
—6,395 feet (Fr.)	TOISE
—20 feet	ROPE
—600 feet	CABLE
—600 feet (Greek)	STADION, STADIUM
—5280 feet	MILE
—6082 feet	KNOT, NAUTICAL MILE
—5½ yards	PERCH, POLE, ROD
—22 yards	CHAIN
—1760 yards	MILE
—1976 yards	SCOTIISH MILE
—2240 yards	IRISH MILE
—1000 double paces	ROMAN MILE
—10 chains	FURLONG
—8 furlongs	MILE
—1 minute of	
latitude	GEOGRAPHICAL MILE
—⁵/₈ mile (approx)	KILOMETRE
—1.4 miles	ROMAN MILE
—2.8 miles	FRENCH LEAGUE
—3 miles	LEAGUE
—4.2 miles	SPANISH LEAGUE
—60 miles	DEGREE
—93 million miles	ASTRONOMICAL UNIT, AU
—6 billion miles	LIGHT-YEAR
—19 billion miles	PARSEC

—fathom (old)	FEDDON
—handsbreadth	PALM
—length of forearm	CUBIT
—parallax of 1 second of arc	PARSEC
—small	BARLEYCORN
	EL, EM, EN, MM
—stretch of arms	FATHOM
—very small	ANGSTROM, FERMI
	MICROMILLIMETRE, MICRON
electrical	
—1000 electron-volts	KeV
—1,000,000 electron-volts	MeV
—96,500 coulombs	FARADAY
—amplitude	IMPEDANCE, Z
—capacitance	C, FARAD
—charge	COULOMB, Q
—charging unit	KILOWATT HOUR
—conductance	G, MHO, SIEMENS
—current	A, AMPERE, J
—dipole moment	DEBYE
—elastance	DARAF
—electrostatic charge	STATCOULOMB
—electromotive force	VOLT
—energy	ELECTRON-VOLT
	ELECTROMOTIVE FORCE
	EMF, VOLT
—impedance	Z
—inductance	HENRY
—power	WATT
—quantity	AMPERE-HOUR
—ratio of currents or voltages	NEPER
—reciprocal	
farad	DARAF
henry	YRNEH
ohm	MHO
—resistance	OHM
—signalling speed	BAUD
—transconductance	MHO, RECIPROCAL OHM
energy, work and heat	BTU, ERG, DYNAM
	DYNE, ERG
	JOULE, POUNDAL
—10⁷ ergs	JOULE
—10⁹ ergs	ERG-NINE
—100,000 BTUs	THERM
—746 watts	HORSEPOWER
—1000 lbs force	KIP
—1055 joules	HEAT UNIT
—1400 joules/second/square	
metre	SOLAR CONSTANT
—1,000,000 joules	MEGAJOULE
—British Thermal Unit	BT(H)U, HEAT UNIT
—energy content (food)	KCAL(ORIE)
	(LARGE)CALORIE
—force	DYNE, N, NEWTON, STHENE
—heat	BTU, CALORIE, JOULE, THERM
value	CALORIFIC VALUE

—kilowatt-hour	KELVIN, KWH
—large unit	MEGAWATT-DAY
—power	HORSEPOWER, WATT
—pressure	BARYE, PASCAL
—quantum of energy	PLANCK'S CONSTANT
—rate of flow	FLUX
—thermal efficiency	CARNOT
frequency	CYCLES PER SECOND
	HERTZ
—10^{12} hertz	FRESNEL
—transmission rate	BAUD
herrings	
—4 herrings	WARP
—33 warps	LONG-HUNDRED
—37½ gallons	CRAN
—5 long hundreds	MA(I)SE, MA(I)ZE, MEASE
information	
—binary digit	BIT
—1.44 bits	NEPIT, NIT
—4 bits	NIBBLE
—8 bits	BYTE
—2 bytes	WORD
—4 bytes	LONGWORD
—1024 bytes	K, KILOBYTE
—million instructions	
per second	MIPS
—transmission rate	BAUD
light	
—brightness	LAMBERT, STILB
of star	MAGNITUDE
—colour temperature	KELVIN, MIRED
—energy	LAMP-HOUR, TALBOT
—flux	LUMEN
—illumination	FOOT-CANDLE
	LUX, METRE-CANDLE
	PHOT, THORLAND
—light-bending power	REFRACTIVE INDEX
—low intensity	SKOT
—luminance	FOOT-LAMBERT, NIT
—luminous intensity	CANDELA
	(NEW) CANDLE
—reflectivity	ALBEDO
—refractive power	ABBE NUMBER
—wavelength	ANGSTROM (UNIT), AU
	NANOMETER
magnetism	
—10^{-8} webers	MAXWELL
—field strength	OERSTED
—flux	GAUSS, MAXWELL
	TESLA, WEBER
—magnetomotive force	AMPERE-TURN
	GILBERT, RELUCTANCE
—ratio of flux density to	
magnetising	
force	MAGNETIC PERMEABILITY
—reciprocal of reluctance	PERMEANCE

—strength	MAGNETIC POLE UNIT
metric	
—area	ARE
—capacity	LITRE
—length	METRE
—volume	STERE
—increments	
—million-million-millionth	ATTO-
—thousand-million-millionth	FEMTO-
—million-millionth	MICROMICR(O)-
	PICO-
—thousand-millionth	NANO-
—millionth	MICRO-
—thousandth	MILLI-
—hundredth	CENTI-
—tenth	DECI-
—ten	DECA-
—hundred	HECTO-
—thousand	KILO-
—million	MEGA-
—thousand million	GIGA-
—million million	TERA-
—thousand million million	PETA-
—million million million	EXA-
miscellaneous	
—$^{1}/_{12}$ of carbon 12	
atom	ATOMIC MASS UNIT
—12 items	DOZEN
—12 dozen	GROSS
—24 arrows	SHEAF
—20-26 tubs (coal)	SCORE
—100 cu. ft (ship)	TON
—100 runs	TON
—100 miles per hour	TON
—250 pulls (handpress work)	TOKEN
—1000 tons (explosives)	KILOTON
—acceleration	G, GAL
—area of nucleus	BARN
—bundle of hay	BOTTLE
—cloud cover $^{1}/_{8}$ of	
sky area	OKTA
—distance/velocity	
of galaxy	HUBBLE CONSTANT
—dried fruit in basket	CAROTEEL
—earthquakes	
	(GUTENBERG-)RICHTER SCALE
	KANAMORI SCALE
	MERCALLI SCALE
—flow of liquid in	
tube	REYNOLDS NUMBER
—fluidity	RHE
—fourth part of	FARDEL
circle	QUADRANT
hour	QUARTER
moon period	QUARTER
year	QUARTER

—genetic information	CISTRON	paper	
—gold	CAR(R)AT	—4 sheets	QUIRE
—gravitational unit	SLUG	—216 sheets	PRINTER'S REAM
—hardness	BRINELL NUMBER, MOH	—20 quires	REAM
—hotness of		—2 reams	BUNDLE
chillies	SCOVILLE HEAT UNIT	—10 reams	BALE
—ignition measurement	CETANE NUMBER	—leaves per sheet	
—insulation value	U-VALUE	2	FOLIO
of fabric	TOG	4	QUARTO
—lens power	DIOPTER, DIOPTRE	6	SEXTO
—mass	CRITH, GRAM	8	OCTAVO
	MOL(E), POUND, SLUG	12	DUODECIMO
of isotope	ATOMIC MASS UNIT	16	DECIMO-SEXTO
—metre/kilogram/second	MKS		SEXTODECIMO
—molecular			SIXTEENMO
volume	PARACHOR	18	EIGHTEENMO
weight of compound	MOL(E)		OCTODECIMO
—number of		—sizes (inches)	
atoms per mole	AVOGADRO'S CONSTANT	9" x 11½"	QUARTO
	AVOGADRO'S NUMBER, L, N	13½" x 17"	FOOLSCAP
molecules of gas		15" x 19"	POST
per cc	LOSCHMIDT'S CONSTANT	15" x 20"	CROWN
neutrons/second/sq cm	NEUTRON FLUX	16½" x 21"	LARGE POST
protons in nucleus	ATOMIC NUMBER	17½" x 22"	DEMY
—print measure	EL, EM, EN	18" x 23"	MEDIUM
—purchaser's allowance	TRET	20" x 25"	ROYAL
—rate of flow (liquid)	CUMIN, CUSEC	20" x 30"	DOUBLE CROWN
—ratio of circumference		22" x 30"	IMPERIAL
to diameter	PI	23" x 28"	ELEPHANT
—skins		26" x 34"	ATLAS
30 chamois skins	KIP	27" x 40"	DOUBLE ELEPHANT
50 goat skins	KIP	30" x 53"	ANTIQUARIAN
—sound	(DECI)BEL, PHON, SOME	36" x 45"	SADDLEBACK
—specific gravity	TWADDELL SCALE	48" x 72"	EMPEROR
—speed	KNOT, MPH	imperial	GRAND JESUS
of sound ratio	MACH (NUMBER)	larger than royal	JESUS, SUPER ROYAL
—strength of radio		precious stones	POINT
emission	JANSKY	—100 points	CARAT
—temperature	CELSIUS, CENTIGRADE	—200 grams	METRIC CARAT
	FAHRENHEIT, KELVIN	—205 grams	CARAT
	REAUMUR	radiation	
—tenth part	TITHE	—concentration of	
—turning force	TORQUE	strontium 90	STRONTIUM UNIT
—type ($^1/_{72}$")	POINT	—disintegration rate	CURIE
—unit of		—dosage	BECQUEREL, GRAY
meaning	SEMANTEME		RAD, REM, REP
sound	PHONEME		R(ONTGEN), SIEVERT
substance	GRAM-ATOM	—period over which	
	GRAM-EQUIVALENT	half the radioactive	
	GRAM-ION, GRAM-MOLECULE	atoms decay	HALF-LIFE
	MOL(E)	—radioactive decay	RD, RUTHERFORD
—viscosity	POISE, STOKES	—X-ray wavelength	XU, X UNIT
—watch movement	LIGNE	timber	
—water flow in 24 hours	MINER'S INCH	—35 cu. ft	STERE
—windspeed	BEAUFORT SCALE	—128 cu. ft	CORD
—wool (½ sack)	POCKET	—216 cu. ft	FATHOM

—100 sq. ft flooring	SQUARE
—round timber	HOPPUS (CUBIC) FOOT
time	
—10⁻⁴² second	PLANCK TIME
—60 seconds	MIN(UTE)
—60 minutes	H, HOUR, HR
—24 hours	D, DAY
—7 days	WK, WEEK
—14 days	FORTNIGHT
—27.32 days	PERIODIC MONTH
	SIDEREAL MONTH
	TROPICAL MONTH
	STELLAR MONTH
—27.55 days	ANOMALISTIC MONTH
—28-31 days	M, MONTH, MTH
—29.53 days	SYNODIC MONTH
—354 days	LUNAR YEAR
—364 days	EMBOLISMIC YEAR
—365 days	Y, YEAR, YR
—365 days 5h	ASTRONOMICAL YEAR
—365¼ days	JULIAN YEAR
—365 days 6h 9m	SIDEREAL YEAR
—365 days 6h 13m	ANOMALISTIC YEAR
—366 days	LEAP-YEAR
—6585 days	SAROS
—12/13 months	HEBREW YEAR
	LUNISOLAR YEAR
—5 years	LUSTRUM
—10 years	DECADE
—19 years	METONIC CYCLE
—76 years	CAL(L)IPPIC CYCLE
—100 years	CENTENARY, CENTENNIAL
	CENTURY
—400 years (Maya)	BAKTUN
—1000 years	MILLENARY, MILLENNIUM
—1460 years	SOTHIC CYCLE
	SOTHIC PERIOD
—3600 years	SAROS
—225 million years	COSMIC YEAR
—1000 million years	(A)EON
—4320 million years	
(Hindu)	KALPA
—accounting period	FINANCIAL YEAR
	FISCAL YEAR
—between successive	
returns of Sun	
to meridian	SOLAR DAY
—Canicular year	SOTHIC YEAR
—complete cycle of	
heavens	PLATONIC YEAR
—division of time	SCRUPLE
—in which	
half of radioactive	
atoms decay	HALF-LIFE
photon travels	
diameter of electron	CHRONON

—short period	MIN, MO, SEC, TICK
—Sothic year	CANICULAR YEAR
—very short period	MILLISECOND
	NANO-SECOND
	PICOSEC
volume	
—144 cu. in	CUBIC FOOT
—27 cu. ft	CUBIC YARD
—306 cu. ft	ROD
—occupied by	
mole	GRAM-MOLECULAR VOLUME
	(*for* metric measures *see* **French**)
measuring instrument	
for:	
air breathed	PNEUMATOMETER
alcohol in wine	VINOMETER
altitude	
—from boiling point	HYPSOMETER
—of heavenly bodies	ALTAZIMUTH
	ASTROLABE
angles	ALAIDAD(E), DIOPTER
	OCTANT, OPTICAL SQUARE
	QUADRANT, PLANE TABLE
	PROTRACTOR, SEXTANT
	TACHEOMETER, THEODOLITE
—of crystals	GONIOMETER
angular distance of Sun	HELIOMETER
area	PLANIMETER
atmospheric pressure	BAROGRAPH
	(FORTIN)BAROMETER
	SYMPIESOMETER
—and temperature	THERMOBAROGRAPH
atomic weights	MASS SPECTROGRAPH
bearing of heavenly	
bodies	ALMUCANTAR
	OCTANT, SEXTANT
blood pressure	SPHYGMO(MANO)METER
	TONOMETER
blueness of sky	CYANOMETER
bodily organs	ONCOMETER
boiling-points	EBULLIOSCOPE
	HYPSOMETER
brain waves	ELECTROENCEPHALOGRAPH
breathing movement	SPIROGRAPH
calculating	ABACUS, ARITHMOMETER
	CALCULATOR, COMPTOMETER
	COMPUTER, SLIDE RULE
changes in pressure	TASIMETER
chlorine	CHLORIMETER
	CHLOROMETER
circuit power	WATTMETER
cloud speed and	
direction	NEPHOSCOPE
cloudiness of liquids	NEPHELOMETER
colour concentration	COLORIMETER
colours	IRISCOPE

comparing	
—colour	
densities	(LOVIBOND) TINTOMETER
—wavelengths	SPECTROPHOTOMETER
compressibility	PIEZOMETER
consistency of soil	PENETROMETER
cooling power of air	KATATHERMOMETER
cornea	AUTOREFRACTOR
	KARATOMETER
	KERATOMETER
	PHOROPTER, RETINOSCOPE
counting paces	PEDOMETER
current of fluid	RHEOMETER
—pressure	SYMPIESOMETER
curvature	SPHEROMETER
density of	DENSIMETER
—air	AEROMETER
—gas	AEROMETER, DASYMETER
—liquid	HYDROMETER
	PYKNOMETER
—photographic	
image	DENSITOMETER
depth of water	BATHOMETER
	FATHOMETER
dew	DROSOMETER
diameter of	
—circular object	CAL(L)IPERS
	MICROMETER
—star	INTERFEROMETER
dichroism of crystals	DICHRO(O)SCOPE
diffracted X-rays	DIFFRACTOMETER
dip circle	INCLINOMETER
distance	DISTOMAT, (H)ODOMETER
	ODOGRAPH, TACHEOMETER
	TACHYMETER, TELEMETER
	TELLUROMETER, TROCHEAMETER
	TROCHOMETER
—between fluid levels	CATHETOMETER
—by	
vehicle	(H)ODOMETER, TACHOGRAPH
	TAXIMETER
wheel	CYCLOMETER, VIAMETER
—from size of image	ICONOMETER
—on maps	OPISOMETER
—using light beams	MEKOMETER
—walked	PEDOMETER
drops	STACTOMETER
dust in air	KONIMETER
earthquakes	SEISMOGRAPH, SEISMOMETER
elastic properties	
of wood	XYLOPHONE
elasticity	TENSIOMETER
electrical	
—charge	ELECTROSCOPE
	GALVANOMETER
—conductivity	DIAGOMETER, TASIMETER

—current	AMMETER
	ELECTRODYNAMOMETER
	ELECTROGRAPH, MILLIAMETER
	(TANGENT) GALVANOMETER
	VOLT(A)METER
—electrostatic	
voltage	ELECTROMETER
—inductance	INDUCTOMETER
	VARIOMETER
—potential	ELECTROMETER
	POTENTIOMETER
	VOLTMETER
—resistance	METRE BRIDGE, OHMMETER
	WHEATSTONE BRIDGE
electricity in body	ELECTROSCOPE
elements in sample	QUANTOMETER
endosmotic action	ENDOSMOMETER
energy distribution of	
radiation	(SCINTILLAION) SPECTROMETER
evaporation	EVAPORIMETER
exposure (film)	ACTINOMETER
eyes	AUTOREFRACTOR
	KARATOMETER, OPHTHALMOMETER
	OPTOMETER, PHOROPTER
	RETINOSCOPE
fare due	TAXIMETER
fermentation	ZYMO(SIM)METER
field of vision	PERIMETER
fluid	
—flow	FLOWMETER
—pressure	KYMOGRAPH
in eyeball	TONOMETER
fluorescence	FLUORIMETER
	FLUOROMETER
force	DYNAMOGRAPH
	DYNAMOMETER
—of breathing	PNEUMATOMETER
frequency of	
—radio waves	ONDOMETER
—tones	TONOMETER
gas	
—consumed	GAS-METER
—pressure	MANOMETER
gases	EUDIOMETER
gradient of magnetic	
field	GRADIOMETER
gradients	GRADIENTER
grain of film	DENSIMETER
gravitational field	GRAVIMETER
hardness of minerals	SCLEROMETER
hearing	AUDIOGRAPH
	AUDIOMETER
heart beats	ELECTROCARDIOGRAPH
heat	CALORIMETER
—based on electrical	
resistance	RESISTANCE THERMOMETER

—from Sun	PYRHELIOMETER
—of	
light	ACTINOMETER
radiation	BOLOMETER, RADIOMETER
	PYROSCOPE
reaction	BOMB CALORIMETER
	THERMOPILE
height	(RADIO) ALTIMETER
—above sea-level	HYPSOMETER
	OROMETER
—of	
cloud base	CEILOMETER
	CLOUD-BASE RECORDER
Nile	NILOMETER
water	WATER-GAUGE
high temperatures	PYROMETER
	RESISTANCE THERMOMETER
hours	CLOCK, CHRONOMETER
	HOROLOGE, SUNDIAL
humidity	GRAVIMETER, HYGRODEIK
	HYGROGRAPH, HYGROSCOPE
	HYGROMETER, PSYCHROMETER
	TENSIOMETER
intensity of	
—colour	SPECTROPHOTOMETER
—light	EXPOSURE METER
	LIGHT METER, PHOTOMETER
—radiated light	CROOKES RADIOMETER
—radiation	ACTINOMETER
—sunlight	HELIOGRAPH
light	PHOTO(-ELECTRIC) CELL
loudness	PHON(O)METER
low temperatures	CRYOMETER
luminous intensity	PHOTOMETER
lung capacity	SPIROMETER
magnetic	
—declination	DECLINATOR
	DECLINOMETER
—dip	INCLINOMETER
—field	MAGNETOMETER
—flux	FLUXMETER
density	GAUSSMETER
moment	BOHR MAGNETON
	NUCLEAR MAGNETON
—forces	VARIOMETER
—variations	MAGNETOGRAPH
magnitude of stars	ASTRO(PHANO)METER
meridian passage	DIPLEIDOSCOPE
metronome	RHYTHMOMETER
mileage, speed etc	TACHOGRAPH
molecular weight	
of gases	EFFUSIOMETER
movement of clouds	NEPHOGRAPH
	NEPHOSCOPE
muscular	
—contraction	ELECTROMYOGRAPH

—work	ERGOGRAPH, ERGOMETER
musical beat	METRONOME
	RHYTHMOMETER
nitrogen	NITROMETER
optical transmission	DENSITOMETER
osmotic pressure	OSMOMETER
oxygen in blood	OXIMETER
pelvis	PELVIMETER
percolation	LYSIMETER
permeability	PERMEAMETER
plane surfaces	PLANOMETER
plant growth	AUXANOMETER
porosity	POROSCOPE
power	DYNAMOGRAPH
	DYNAMOMETER
	WATTMETER
pressure	PIEZOMETER
—by electrical charges	TASIMETER
—in	
baby's skull	FONTANOMETER
eyeball	TONOMETER
—of	
current	SYMPIESOMETER
fluids	MANOMETER
pulse	PULSIMETER, SPHYMOGRAPH
radiant	
—energy	BOLOMETER, LIGHT-MILL
	RADIOMETER
—heat	PYROSCOPE
radiation	DOSIMETER, RADIOGRAPH
radio waves	RADIO TELESCOPE
radioactivity	GEIGER(-MULLER) COUNTER
	OBROMETER
	SCINTILLATION COUNTER
	SCINTILLATOR
	SCINTILLOMETER
	OBROMETER
rainfall	HYETOGRAPH, HYETOMETER
	HYETOMETROGRAPH, OBROMETER
	RAIN-GAUGE, PLUVIOMETER
	UDOMETER
rate of	
—climb or descent	VARIOMETER
—evaporaion	ATMOMETER
	EVAPORIMETER
—flow	PITOT TUBE, ROTAMETER
	VENTURI TUBE
—increase of speed	ACCELEROMETER
reaction times	PSYCHOMETER
recording over	
a distance	TELEMETER
reflected light	PHOTOMETER
reflective properties	DENSITOMETER
refraction of eye	OPTOMETER
refractive indices	REFRACTOMETER
	SPECTROMETER

relations of sounds	HARMONOMETER
relative	
—density of	
liquids	HYDROMETER
milk	LACTOSCOPE
—humidity	HYGRODEIK, HYGROMETER
	HYGROSCOPE
—number of	
particles	MASS SPECTROMETER
revolutions	TACHOMETER
richness of milk	LACTOSCOPE
rotation of plane of	
polarisation of light	POLARIMETER
saltness of water	SALI(NO)METER
sensitivity of film	SENSITOMETER
sight	OPSIOMETER
	OPTOMETER
size derived from image	ICONOMETER
sliding friction	TRIBOMETER
slopes	INCLINOMETER
small	
—angles	MICROMETER
—diameters	ERIOMETER
—differences in levels	
of liquids	CATHETOMETER
—distances	MICROMETER
—earthquakes	TRONOMETER
—forces	TORSION BALANCE
—sound intensities	AUDIOMETER
—strains	EXTENSOMETER
—temperature	
changes	AETHERIOSCOPE
	BECKMAN THERMOMETER
—thicknesses	PACHYMETER
	SPHEROMETER
—time intervals	CHRONOSCOPE
	CHRONOTRON
—variations in	
density of image	MICROPHOTOMETER
solar radiation	PYRHELIOMETER
solids	STEREOMETER
sound	
—pitch	TONOMETER
—vibration	PHONAUTOGRAPH
specific gravity	AR(A)EOMETER
	HYDROMETER, PYCNOMETER
	PYKNOMETER
—of	
milk	GALACTOMETER
solids	STEREOMETER
wood	XYLOMETER
speed	SPEEDOMETER
—in relation to sound	MACHMETER
—of	
celestial objects	NEPHOSCOPE
clouds	NEPHOSCOPE

rotation	TACHOGRAPH, TACHOMETER
wind	ANEMOMETER
squint	STRABOMETER
strains in structures	TASEOMETER
strength of	
—acid	ACIDIMETER
—wine	OENOMETER
subterranean	
temperature	GEOTHERMOMETER
sugar solution	SACCHARIMETER
	SACCHAROMETER
surface tension	STALAGMOMETER
	TENSIOMETER
surveying	TACHEOMETER, TACHYMETER
	THEODOLITE
swing of voting	SWINGOMETER
temperature	THERMO(METRO)GRAPH
	THERMOMETER
—bodily	CLINICAL THERMOMETER
—from	
bimetallic junction	THERMOCOUPLE
	THERMO-ELECTRIC
	THERMOMETER
electrical resistance	
	PLATINUM RESISTANCE
	THERMOMETER
light intensity	OPTICAL PYROMETER
pressure of gas	GAS THERMOMETER
—low	CRYOMETER
tensile strength	TENSIOMETER
testing food	TENDEROMETER
ticket-issuing	PASSIMETER
tides	MARIGRAPH
tilt of aeroplane	INCLINOMETER
time	CLOCK, CHRONOMETER
	SUN-DIAL, WATCH
—by	
sand	EGG-TIMER, HOUR-GLASS
water	HYDROSCOPE
transmitting measurements	TELEMETER
transparency	DENSIOMETER
trees	DENDROMETER
uptake of oxygen	WARBURG MANOMETER
vapour pressure	TONOMETER
variations in	
body size	PLETHYSMOGRAPH
vertical angles	ALIDAD(E), DIP CIRCLE
	(IN)CLINOMETER, OCTANT
	SEXTANT, TACHEOMETER
vibrations	VIBROGRAPH, VIBROMETER
—in rotating shaft	TORSIOGRAPH
viscosity	VISCOMETER
vision	OPTOMETER, OPSIOMETER
volume	
—changes in chemical	
reaction	EUDIOMETER

—expansion	DILATOMETER
—of	
gas	VOLUMETER
solid bodies	VOLUMOMETER
voting changes	SWINGOMETER
water	
—absorption by plant	POTOMETER
—in ship's hold	SOUNDING-ROD
wave-forms	OSCILLOSCOPE
wavelengths	ETALON, INTERFEROMETER
	SPECTROMETER, WAVEMETER
weight of air or gas	AEROMETER
windspeed	ANEMOMETER
X-ray	
—diffraction	DIFFRACTOMETER
—examination	FLUOROSCOPE
zenith distance	ZENITH-SECTOR
	(*see also* **scientific instruments**)

meat

bacon	
—cuts	BACK, BUTT, COLLAR
	(CORNER) GAMMON, GAMBREL
	GRISKIN, FLANK, FOREHOCK
	FORE SLIPPER, HOCK, MIDDLE CUT
	MIDDLE GAMMON, OYSTER BACK
	STREAKY
—side	FLITCH
—slice	RASHER
—uncured	GREEN BACON
braised	POT ROAST
brawn (US)	HEADCHEESE
calf	VEAL
—cuts	BREAST, CHOP, CUTLET
	ESCALOPE, FILLET, KNUCKLE
	LEG, LOIN, NECK, SCRAG
	SHIN, SHOULDER
—sweetbreads	RIS DE VEAU
cold meats	CHARCUTERIE
—set in jelly	GALANTINE
cooked, dried, salted	
or smoked meat	CHARCUTERIE
—cured	
ham	PARMA HAM, PROSCIUTTO
pig fat	FATBACK
—dried	
beef, sliced	CHIPPED BEEF
meat	BILTONG, CHARQUI
	JERKED MEAT, JERK(Y)
	PEM(M)ICAN
—salted	
beef	JUNK
pig	BACON
pork	SOWBELLY
sausage	SALAMI
—smoked	
beef	PASTRAMI

ham	VIRGINIA HAM
	WESTPHALIAN HAM, YORK HAM
pig	BACON
—tinned beef	BULLY BEEF, CORNED BEEF
cow	BEDPIECE, BEEF, STEAK
—cuts, beef	BARON, BLADE BONE, BRISKET
	CHUCK, CLOD, FLANK
	FLESHEND, FORERIB, GULLET
	LEG, LOIN, MOUSE, NECK, OXTAIL
	RIB, ROUND(END), SHIN, SHOULDER
	SKIRT, SILVERSIDE, SIRLOIN
	SLOAT, STICKING, TOPRIB
	TOPSIDE, VEIN, WING RIB
—cuts, steak	ENTRECOTE
	FILET MIGNON, FILLET
	PORTERHOUSE, RUMP, T-BONE
	TENDERLOIN, TOURNEDOS
	UNDERCUT
cube for grilling	KEBAB
cut	
—boneless	FIL(L)ET
—crossways for broiling	CARBONADO
—embedded in fat	EYE
—hindquarters	HAUNCH
—including	
both forequarters	FORESADDLE
the backbone	CHINE
—from neck	CUTLET
—front	
leg	FORELEG
—of pig	FOREHOCK
of side with leg	FOREQUARTER
—large piece for	
roasting	JOINT
—neck and spine	RACK
—rear of side with leg	HINDQUARTER
—small round piece	MEDALLION
	NOISETTE
—thin slice	ESCALOPE
—triangular thigh piece	EYE
—underpart of forequarter	PLATE
cutlet (Ind.)	TIKKA
crisply cooked skin	CRACKLING
deer meat	VENISON
edible	
—entrails	(M)UMBLES
cooked	CHITTERLING, TRIPE
—parts, not flesh (US)	VARIETY MEAT
forcemeat ball	QUENELLE
grilled on skewer	
—Greek	SOUVLAKIA
—Turkish	SHISH KEBAB
heart, liver and lungs	PLUCK
lamb	
—cuts	BEST END NECK, BREAST
	CHUMP, FILLET, LEG, LOIN

	MIDDLE NECK, NOISETTE
	RACK, SADDLE, SCRAG (END)
	SHOULDER
layer of fat lining	
abdomen	LEAF FAT, MESENTERY
leg	SHANK
lungs	LIGHTS
meat products	BEEFBURG(H)ER
	BLACK PUDDING, BRAWN
	CORNED BEEF, CROQUETTE
	FAGGOT, HAM, HAMBURGER, HASLET
	LUNCHEON MEAT, QUENELLE
	PATE, PASTE, RISSOLE, SAUSAGE
	SPAM, TONGUE, VIENNA STEAK
	(*see also* **sausage**)
meat substitute	KESP
	TEXTURED VEGETABLE PROTEIN
	TVP
meatball (Ind.)	KHEMA, KOFTA
minced meat	MINCE
offal	BRAIN, FEET, HEAD, KIDNEY
	LIVER, HEART, INTESTINES
	OXTAIL, STOMACH, SWEETBREAD
	TONGUE, TRIPE
pancreas	SWEETBREAD
pig	BACON, HAM, PIG-MEAT, PORK
—cuts	BARON, BATH CHAP, BELLY
	BLADE, BUFF, (CHUMP) CHOP
	COLLAR, FILLET, FLANK
	FOREHOCK, GAMMON, HAM
	HAND, HOCK, JOWL, KNUCKLE
	SLIPPER, SPARE RIB, SPRING
	TROTTER, (TENDER)LOIN
—feet	CRUBEENS, PETTITOES, TROTTERS
sheep	LAMB, MUTTON
—cuts	BREAST, CHOP, CROWN, CUTLET
	FILLET, GIGOT, KNUCKLE
	LEG, LOIN, NOISETTE, RIB
	SADDLE, SCRAG(-END)
	SHOULDER
sliced and rolled	ROULADE
small round piece	NOISETTE
strip of fat for dressing	LARDO(O)N
thin slice with	
savoury filling	PAUPIETTE, ROULADE
thymus gland	SWEETBREAD
unfit for food	CAGMAG
young goat	KID
	(*see also* **cookery, menu**)
meat dishes	
bacon	BACON-BURGER, BACON JACK
	(CARAMELLED) GAMMON
	DERBY BAKE
braised meat (Ind.)	KORMA
beef	BEEF OLIVE, BEEFBURGER
	BOURGUIGNONNNE, CARBON(N)ADE

	CORNED BEEF, DIANE
	EN CROUTE, EN DAUBE
	GOULASH, STIFADO, STROGANOFF
	STROGANOV, STUFATO
ham	CHARLOTTE, MONTMORENCY
—and veal in	
butter	SALTIMBOCA
lamb	BLANQUETTE D'AGNEAU
	CROWN OF LAMB, (DONER) KEBAB
	GIGOT, NAVARIN, NOISETTE
	YIOUVETSI
meatball	QUENELLE, RISSOLE
medallion	PICATA
mince	CHILLI CON CARNE
	COTTAGE PIE, CUMBERLAND PIE
	KROMESKY, MOUS(S)AKA
	SALMAGUNDI
	SCOTCH(ED) COLLOPS
	SHEPHERD'S PIE, TAMALE
—set in mould	SCRAPPLE
offal	CHITTERLING, HAGGIS, TRIPE
pies	BRIDIE, CORNISH PASTY
	FLORENCE, PORK PIE
	SAUSAGE ROLL, SQUAB PIE
pork	CROWN, FRIKADELLER
	NORMANDY, SPANISH
	SPARERIB, SWEET-AND-SOUR
several meats	MIXED GRILL
steak	DIANE, CARPETBAG
	CHATEAUBRIAND, HAMBURG(H)ER
	SAUTERNES, SWISS, TAGALOG
	TARTARE, TOURNEDOS (ROSSINI)
veal	ESCALOPE, FRICANDEAU
	OSSO BUC(C)O, VIENNA STEAK
	WIENER SCHNITZEL
white meat in sauce	BANQUETTE
medal	(*see* **decorations**)
medi(a)eval	
including feudal terms:	
acknowledgment of	
allegiance	HOMAGE
allegiance owed to	
feudal lord	FEALTY
amount of land adequate	
to support a household	HIDE
armour-bearer	ARMIGER
assembly	GEMOT, MOOT
attendant on knight	ARMIGER, (E)SQUIRE
	SCUTIGER
building for storage of	
grain paid as tithes	GRANGE
	TITHE-BARN
chief magistrate	REEVE
collector of tithes	TITHE-PROCTOR
copyholder	VILLEIN
council chamber	MOOT-HALL, MOOT-HOUSE

court	GEMOT, MOOT	major-domo	SENESCHAL
district under particular		meeting	GEMOT, MOOT
jurisdiction	SOKE(N)	militia	FYRD
division of county	CANTRED, CANTREF	mutual security of a	
	HUNDRED	tithing	FRANKPLEDGE
domestic slave	ESNE	noble	
eorl	EARL	—below eorl	THANE, THEGN
estate not subject to		—next below knight	(E)SQUIRE
feudal superior	AL(L)OD(IUM)	—of highest rank	ALDERMAN
feudal lord	LORD SUPERIOR		EALDORMAN
	SEIGNEUR, SEIGNIOR	—royal prince	A(E)THELING
	SUZERAIN	obligation to perform	
fine when tenant died	HERIOT	unpaid labour	CORVEE
forced loan or		officer dealing with	
contribution	BENEVOLENCE	—ceremonies etc	MARSHAL
foreign service due to		—domestic matters	SENESCHAL
overlord	FORINSEC	—military matters	CONSTABLE
free villager	VILLEIN	—offences within twelve	
freehold	FRANK-TENEMENT	miles of the	
freeholder	FRANKLIN	King's abode	KNIGHT-MARSHAL
freeman not of		one	
noble birth	CEORL, CHURL	—holding land from	
governor of a district	ALDERMAN	a tenant-in-chief	VALVASSOR
	EALDORMAN		VAVASO(U)R
group of ten householders		and owing allegiance	
bound by mutual		to a superior	VASSAL
responsibility for		—owing service to his	
good behaviour	TITHING	lord but not in bondage	VILLEIN
holding land by		—under feudal tenure	LIEGE
feudal tenure	FEODARY, FEUDA(TO)RY	peasant bound to land	SERF
house and land kept by		pig paid as tithe	TITHE-PIG
lord for his own use	DEMESNE	property that returns to	
king's		feudal lord for want of	
—companion	THANE, THEGN	heir or by forfeiture	ESCHEAT
—farrier	MARSHAL	pursuit of a felon	HUE AND CRY
land		rent	
—endowed to parish church	GLEBE	—based on number of	
—for which knight-		horned cattle	CORNAGE, HORNGELD
service was required	KNIGHT'S-FEE	—paid in lieu of services	QUITRENT
—held in return for		right	
military service	FEE, FEOFF	—of	
	FEUD, FIEF	feudal lord	
—tenanted with only		over vassals	DROIT DE SEIGNEUR
religious obligations	FRANKALMOIGN	to entertainment	CUDDY
landed proprietor	(E)SQUIRE	king to share of imported wine	PRISAGE
licensed seller of Papal		—to	
indulgences	PARDONER	claim free lodgings	COR(R)ODY
lord	LIEGE	cut green trees	VERT
—holding land from		cut peat	TURBARY
a superior	MESNE LORD	deal with thief taken	
—of manor	SEIGNEUR, SEIGNIOR	outside one's	
	SUZERAIN	jurisdiction	OUTFANGTHIEF
—to whom feudal		drop roof water	STILLICIDE
service is due	LIEGE (LORD)	fish	PISCARY
lowest (of tenant)_	PARAVAIL	fold tenant's sheep	
loyal vassal	LIEGE	for manure	FOLDAGE

hold local court	SOC
necessaries allowed	
by law	ESTOVER
pasture	
—on a common	COMMONAGE
—swine in forest	PANNAGE
use another's property	USUFRUCT
shield-bearer	(E)SQUIRE, SCUTIGER
steward	SENESCHAL
sub-division of cantred	
or hundred	COMMOT
superior	PARAMOUNT
supreme council	WITAN, WITENAGEMOT
tax	GELD
—for building and	
maintaining city walls	MURAGE
—in lieu of military	
service	SCUTAGE
—of one-tenth paid	
to church	TITHE
—on land	HIDAGE
tenant by socage	SOCAGER, SOCMAN
	SOKEMAN
tenure	
—by	
knight on condition	
of military service	KNIGHT-SERVICE
service	SOC(C)AGE
socage	SOKEMANRY
—in fee simple	FRANK-FEE
town-hall	MOOT-HALL, MOOT-HOUSE
vassal	LIEGE
vassals	MANRED
villein granted cottage	
in return for work	BORDAR, COTTAR
	COTTER

medical

medical instruments	(*see* **surgery**)
Medical Officer (of Health)	MO(H)
medical social worker	MSW
medicine	(*see* **drugs**)

Mediterranean   MED

artichoke	CARDOON
borage	ALKANET
buckthorn	CHRIST'S THORN
	JEW'S THORN
captain of ship	PATRON
edible gall	SAGE-APPLE
fever	BRUCELLOSIS
fish	ANCHOVY, BAND-FISH
	DENTEX, GILTHEAD, MEAGRE
	MAIGRE, PARROT-WRASSE
	PEACOCK-FISH
hen	ANCONA, ANDALUSIAN, MINORCA
Jew(s)	SEPHARDI(M)
lizard	STELLION, STELLIO LIZARD

mock privet	PHYLLYREA
plant	CUM(M)IN, ISATIS, LENTIL
	PLUMBAGO, RUE
	ROSEMARY, WOAD
salad-plant	ROCKET
scrubland	GAR(R)IGUE
shark	PORBEAGLE
ship	(*see separate entry*)
shrub	CHRIST'S THORN
	LAVENDER-COTTON
	NABK, NEBBUK, NEBE(C)K
	ANTOLINA
spirit	RAKE, RAKI
thicket	MAQUIS
tree	ALGARROBA, CAROB, LOCUST
	NUT-PINE, STONE-PINE
	TURKEY-OAK
wind	LEVANT(ER), GREGALE
wrasse	PEACOCK-FISH

member

Member of	
—Congress	MC
—Council	MC
—County Council	MCC
—House of Representatives	MHR
—Institute of Journalists	MJI
—Legislative	
Assembly	MLA
Council	MLC
—Order of the British Empire	MBE
—Parliament	MP
—Pharmaceutical Society	MPS
—Philological Society	MPS
—Royal Victorian Order	MVO

menu

additional charge	COVER CHARGE
	SERVICE CHARGE
appetiser	ENTREMES(SE), ENTREMETS
	HORS D'OEUVRES
bread, cheese,	
pickles, etc	PLOUGHMAN'S LUNCH
breakfast	
—cooked	ENGLISH BREAKFAST
—rolls and butter	FRENCH BREAKFAST
charge for drinks	
brought in	CORKAGE
chef	
—assistant	SOUS CHEF
—cold meats	GARDE-MANGER
set in jelly	GALANTINE
—deputy	COMMIS-CHEF
—pastry cook	PATISSIER
chilled	FRAPPE
choice of dishes	A LA CARTE
coated with	
—breadcumbs	AU GRATIN

—cheese	AU GRATIN, GRATINE
—egg and breadcrumbs	(A LA) MILANESE
	A L'ANGLAISE
cold dish glazed with aspic	GALANTINE
complete	
—leg (lamb)	GIGOT
—rib section (lamb, pork)	CROWN
—sirloin (beef)	BARON
	(see also **meat**)
cooked	
—at the table	NABE-MONO
—in	
brown sauce	A LA MODE
butter and	
—herbs (fish)	MEUNIERE
—parsley	MAITRE D'HOTEL
cider	NORMANDE
oil, garlic, tomatoes	PROVENCALE
olive oil	A LA GRECQUE
paper case	EN PAPILLOTE
pastry case	EN CROUTE
red wine	BOURGUIGNON
white wine (fish)	MARINIERE
—on a skewer	EN BROCHETTE
—slightly	AL DENTE
—with	
apples	NORMANDE
brown sugar	BRULE
cider and cream	A LA NORMANDE
garlic, tomatoes	NICOISE
potatoes	PARMENTIER
rice and tomatoes	CREOLE
spinach	FLORENTINE
dish of the day	PLAT DU JOUR
firm to the teeth	AL DENTE
first course	STARTER
fish in vinegar	AU BLEU
fixed	
—meal	TABLE D'HOTE
—price	AL PASTO, PRIX FIXE
flamed in brandy	FLAMBE
frogs	GRENOUILLES
garnished with	
—crayfish	A LA NANTUA
—mushrooms etc	FORESTIERE
—onions, mushrooms, etc	BONNE FEMME
—potatoes	PARMENTIER
—vegetable strips	JULIENNE
—vegetables	JARDINIERE
—white grapes	VERONIQUE
head waiter	MAITRE D'HOTEL
in cooking juices	AU JUS
including service charge	COMPRIS
fixed menu	TABLE D'HOTE
leg (of lamb)	GIGOT
main course	ENTREE

—served on platter	PLATE
—US	PLATE
meal	
—afternoon	TEA
—early	
evening	HIGH TEA
morning	BREAKFAST
—evening	DINNER
—late	
evening	SUPPER
morning	BRUNCH
—light	SNACK
—midday	LUNCH(EON)
—of the day	PLAT DU JOUR
medium cooked	A POINT
mixed herbs	FINES HERBES
partly frozen	FRAPPE
pastry cook	PATISSIER
place setting	COVER
plainly cooked	AU NATUREL
separately priced	A LA CARTE
set price	PRIX FIXE
small green peas	PETIT POIS
steak	
—centre of fillet	FILET MIGNON
	TOURNEDOS
—flambé	DIANE
—hindquarter	RUMP STEAK
—large fillet	CHATEAUBRIAND
—raw, minced	TARTARE
—sirloin	ENTRECOTE, T-BONE
large	PORTERHOUSE
—small	CLUB STEAK
—stuffed with oysters	CARPETBAG STEAK
—thin	MINUTE STEAK
—top of sirloin	CONTRE-FILET
	FAUX-FILET
stuffed	FARCI(E)
sweet course	DESSERT
underdone	EN BLEU, RARE
veal stuffed and roasted	FRICANDEAU
very thin toast	MELBA TOAST
well done	BIEN CUIT
wine waiter	SOMMELIER
with milk	AU LAIT
merchant	
Merchant Navy	MV
merchant vessel	MV
meteor	(see **astronomy**)
meteorology	AEROGRAPHY
	AEROLOGY
absolute humidity	VAPOUR CONCENTRATION
amount of water	
vapour in the	
atmosphere	ABSOLUTE HUMIDITY
analysis of clouds, etc	NEPHANALYSIS

anticlockwise movement of wind	BACKING
arc of colours	
—caused by sun on	
mist	SUNBOW
raindrops	RAINBOW
—seen in fog	FOG-BOW, (SEA-)DOG
area	
—between two areas	
of high or low pressure	COL
—of	
calms	DOLDRUMS
	HORSE LATITUDES
earth based on	
climate	CLIMATIC REGION
high atmospheric	
pressure	CYCLONE, HIGH, RIDGE
light rainfall in	
lee of high ground	RAIN SHADOW
low atmospheric	
pressure	CYCLONE
	DEPRESSION, LOW
warm air between	
fronts	WARM SECTOR
—permanently covered	
with snow	ICECAP, ICEFIELD
	SNOWFIELD
atmospheric	
—conditions	
averaged over long	
period	CLIMATE
over a period	WEATHER
—disturbance	ELECTRIC STORM
—layers	(*see* **geology**-Earth)
balloon carrying	
meteorological	
instruments	BALLON SONDE
	RAWINSONDE, RADIOSONDE
	SOUNDING BALLOON
bank of wind-blown snow	SNOWDRIFT
boundary	
—between	
air masses	DISCONTINUITY, FRONT
cold and warm air	POLAR FRONT
—of	
advancing	
—cold air	COLD FRONT
—warm air	WARM FRONT
air which is	
not moving	STATIONARY FRONT
brief flood after	
heavy rains	FLASH FLOOD
broad expanse of	
—ice	ICEFIELD
—snow	SNOWFIELD
caused by	
—action of hot water	HYDROTHERMAL

—floods	DILUVIAL
—rain	PLUVIAL
centre of cyclone	EYE
change(s)	
—caused by heat	
	THERMAL METAMORPHISM
—from	
liquid to vapour	EVAPORATION
vapour to liquid	CONDENSATION
—in	
atmospheric pressure	
over specified	
periods	PRESSURE TENDENCY
colour of moon from	
dust in atmosphere	BLUE MOON
temperature with	
height	LAPSE RATE
chart	(*see* map *below*)
clearness of atmosphere	VISIBILITY
climate	
—cooler than	
temperate	SUBTEMPERATE CLIMATE
—dependent upon	
altitude	MOUNTAIN CLIMATE
—hot	
and humid	EQUATORIAL, TROPICAL
dry season, cooler	
wet season	MONSOON CLIMATE
dry summer, mild	
winter	
	MEDITERRANEAN CLIMATE
—in	
cereal-growing	
areas	CORN BELT CLIMATE
cotton-growing	
area	COTTON BELT CLIMATE
equatorial region	EQUINOCTIAL
islands or coastal	
regions	INSULAR
large land masses	CONTINENTAL
polar regions	ICE-CAP CLIMATE
small habitat	MICROCLIMATE
warm temperate area	MEDITERRANEAN
—influenced by sea	MARITIME
—lacking regular	
rainfall	DESERT CLIMATE
—low rainfall	
hot days, cold	
nights	DESERT CLIMATE
very cold	POLAR CLIMATE
wide temperature	
variation	CONTINENTAL CLIMATE
—short summer, very	
cold winter	SUB-POLAR CLIMATE
—warm damp summer,	
mild wet winter	TEMPERATE CLIMATE

climatic zones	
—between	
pole and polar circle	FRIGID
polar circle and	
tropics	TEMPERATE
tropics	TORRID
clockwise movement of wind	VEERING
closing of cold front	
to warm front	OCCLUDED FRONT
	OCCLUSION
cloud	
—bearing	NUBIFEROUS
—born	NUBIGENOUS
—flying	RACK
—map	ISONETH
cloudiness	NUBECULA
clouds	
—anvil-like	CUMULONIMBUS
—at centre of tornado	
or waterspout	FUNNEL CLOUD
—bluish	NOCTILUCENT
—breaking off from top	
of cumulo-nimbus	FALSE CIRRUS
—cauliflower-like	CUMULUS
—charged with static	THUNDERCLOUD
—cirro-cumulus	WOOL-PACK
—cirrus	GOAT'S-HAIR
—covering	
high ground	HILL FOG
of alto- or cirro-	
cumulus clouds	MACKEREL SKY
—deep	CUMULONIMBUS
—delicate cirrus	CUMULOCIRRUS
—discharging showers	NIMBUS
—flying	RACK
—fragmented low cloud	SCUD
—globular masses	STRATOCUMULUS
—height of lowest	CEILING
—high	CIRRUS
detached	CIRRUS
fleecy	ALTOCIRRUS
sheet	CIRROSTRATUS
thin layer	CIRROSTRATUS
transparent veil	CIRROCUMULUS
—horizontal sheet	STRATUS
—lens shaped	LENTICULAR CLOUD
—loose wind-driven	
clouds	SCUD
—low	
narrow masses	MACKEREL SKY
rain	NIMBOSTRATUS
rounded masses	STRATOCUMULUS
—mackerel sky	CIRROCUMULUS
—middle	
grey	
—cloud layer	STRATUS

—sheet	ALTOSTRATUS
rain cloud	NIMBOSTRATUS
—mother-of-pearl	MACREOUS CLOUD
—on lee side of peak	ANNER CLOUD
—pertaining to	NUBIFORM
—rounded	
cumulus with	
horizontal base	WOOLPACK
heaps of cloud	CUMULUS
mass of cumulus	THUNDERHEAD
—small	
flakes or ripples	CIRROCUMULUS
rain cloud	WATER-DOG
—thin streaks of cirrus	MARE'S-TAILS
—very dark coloured	THUNDERCLOUD
—with rounded projection	CASTELLANUS
cloudy	NUBILOUS
cold sea-mist	HA(A)R
cooling factor combining	
wind and temperature	CHILL FACTOR
	WINDCHILL
covering of ice	
crystals	FROST, HOAR, RIME
current affecting climate in	
—Atlantic	GULF STREAM
—Pacific	EL NINO
cycle of climatic	
conditions	BRUCKNER CYCLE
cyclone in China Sea	TYPHOON
dark appearance of sky	
due to reflection	
from water	WATER SKY
descent of air mass	
towards earth's surface	SUBSIDENCE
description of atmosphere	AEROGRAPHY
development of	
—cyclone	CYCLOGENESIS
—weather front	FRONTOGENESIS
diagram of	
—weather data	TEPHIGRAM
—wind direction	WIND ROSE
difference between	
highest and lowest	
temperature	
—for each day	MEAN DIURNAL RANGE
—in given period	TEMPERATURE RANGE
distance at which	
objects can be seen	VISIBILITY
disturbance in magnetic	
field of earth	(GEO)MAGNETIC STORM
driving mist	RACK
drizzly mist	ROKE
—Scottish	DROW
dust etc causing reduced visibility	HAZE
electrical discharge	
—from cloud	LIGHTNING

—in	
northern region	AURORA BOREALIS
	NORTHERN LIGHTS
southern region	AURORA AUSTRALIS
—round masts, etc	ST ELMO'S FIRE
end of frost	THAW
envelope of air round the	
earth	ATMOSPHERE
	(*see also* **geography**)
extent of clouds	CLOUD COVER
faint light before dawn	
and after sunset	TWILIGHT
falling ice crystals	HAIL, SNOW
fine	
—dry snow	POWDER
—rain	DRIZZLE
fog	
—bow	SEA-DOG
—caused by	
damp air over cool	
surface	ADVECTION FOG
loss of heat radiated	
on clear night	RADIATION FOG
—with suspended dust, etc	SMOG
front formed when cold	
front overtakes	
warm front	OCCLUDED FRONT
	OCCLUSION
frost	
—from frozen	
dew	HOAR, RIME
fog	RIME
—smooth ice from	
frozen rain	GLAZED FROST
frozen	
—dew	HOAR FROST
—moisture	FROST
—rain	GRAUPEL, HAIL, SLEET, SNOW
—snowflakes	GRAUPEL
glow	(*see* light *below*)
graph of various types	
of climate	CLIMATOGRAPH
granular ice crystals	RIME FROST
	FROST FEATHERS
grass temperature of	
below 30°F	GROUND FROST
halo round tall objects	
caused by electrical	
discharge	ST ELMO'S FIRE
haze (Mediterranean)	CALINA
heating due to increase	
of carbon dioxide in	
atmosphere	GREENHOUSE EFFECT
heavy mists (W. Africa)	CACIMBO
high pressure area	ANTICYCLONE, HIGH
	RIDGE

ice-film on rock, etc	VERGLAS
illusion caused by	
heated air layers	MIRAGE
increase in temperature	
with altitude	INVERSION
instrument for	
—measuring	
atmospheric	
pressure	(ANEROID) BAROMETER
	WEATHER GLASS
height of cloud base	CEILOMETER
	CLOUDBASE RECORDER
moisture in soil	TENSIOMETER
rainfall	RAIN GAUGE
relative humidity	HYGROMETER
	PSYCHROMETER
snowfall	SNOW GAUGE
temperature	THERMOMETER
windspeed	ANEMOMETER
—observing clouds	NEPHOSCOPE
—recording	
atmospheric pressure	BAROGRAPH
clouds	NEPHOGRAPH
rainfall	HYETOGRAPH
relative humidity	HYGROGRAPH
temperature	THERMOGRAPH
—highest	MAXIMUM THERMOMETER
—lowest	MINIMUM THERMOMETER
windspeed	ANEMOGRAPH
—showing	
changes in humidity	HYGROSCOPE
direction of wind	WEATHER VANE
	WIND VANE
intermediate pressure	
area	COL
law relating to	
deflection due to	
Earth's rotation	FERREL'S LAW
light	
—above low Sun	SUN PILLAR
—in sky	
after twilight in	
east or before dawn	
in west	ZODIACAL LIGHT
caused by ice	
crystals	PARAHELIC CIRCLE
over	
—expanse of snow	SNOW-BLINK
—North Pole	AURORA BOREALIS
	NORTHERN LIGHTS
—South Pole	AURORA AUSTRALIS
after sunset in	
mountainous regions	AFTERGLOW
	ALPENGLOW
—over marsh	IGNIS FATUUS
	WILL-O'-THE-WISP

—round
  Brocken spectre — GLORY
  light source — CORONA
  masts, etc — ST ELMO'S FIRE
  Moon or Sun — HALO
—snowfall — FLURRY
lightning
—striking upward — FLACHENBLITZ
—types — BALL, CHAIN, FORKED
SHEET, THUNDERBOLT
line
—drawn through places
  with highest mean
  temperatures — THERMAL EQUATOR
—marking
  boundary between cold
  and warm air masses — FRONT
  simultaneous
  thunderstorms — ISOBRONT
—showing places of equal
  cloudiness — ISONEPH
  duration of sunshine — ISOHEL
  frequency of auroral
  phenomena — ISOCHASM
  pressure — ISOBAR
  —change — ISALLOBAR
  rainfall — EQUIPLUVE, ISOHYET
  sunshine — ISOHEL
  temperature — ISOTHERM
  —below ground — ISOGEOTHERM
  —in coldest time — ISOCHEIM
     ISOCRYME
  —summer mean — ISOTHERE
  value of specific
  climatic elements — ISOGRAM
  ISOLINE, ISOMETRIC LINE
     ISOPLETH
  variation from
  normal climatic
  standards — ISANOMALOUS LINE
  wind speed — ISOTACH
long
—area of
  high pressure — RIDGE, WEDGE
  low pressure — TROUGH
—period of
  drought — BIG DRY
  rain — BIG WET
longest day — SUMMER SOLSTICE
low-pressure area — CYCLONE, DEPRESSION
lower limit of perpetual
snow on high ground — SNOWLINE
luminous ring
opposite sun — ANTHELION
map showing
—clouds, etc — NEPHANALYSIS

—weather conditions
  for particular area — SYNOPTIC CHART
     WEATHER CHART
     WEATHER MAP
mass of condensed vapour
—at ground level — FOG, MIST
—in atmosphere — CLOUD
maximum humidity at a
  given temperature — SATURATION
measure of cloud cover — OKTA
measurement of
—atmospheric conditions — SOUNDING
—heat — TEMPERATURE
—moisture — HUMIDITY
melting of ice and snow — THAW
meteorologists
—British — CHAPMAN
—French — DE BORT
mirage with vertical
  distortion — FATA MORGANA
mixture of snow and rain — SLEET
moisture
—caused by condensation
  in atmosphere — FOG, MIST
  on the ground — DEW
—in atmosphere from
  cloud near ground — MIZZLE
     SCOTCH MIST
more than 6/10 covered — CLOUDY
morning and evening
  mists (Guinea) — SMOKES
movement
—caused by freezing of
  ground — FROST HEAVE
—of
  air — WIND
  atmosphere
  —downward — DOWNDRAUGHT
  —irregular — TURBULENCE
  —upward — UPDRAUGHT
  heat in atmosphere
  —horizontal — ADVECTION
  —vertical — CONVECTION
  high-pressure area — CLOCKWISE
  low-pressure area — ANTICLOCKWISE
  wind
  —anticlockwise — BACKING
  —clockwise — VEERING
partly
—frozen rain — SLEET
—melted snow — SLUSH
period of
—15 days
  with
  —little rain — DRY SPELL
  —some rain — RAINY SPELL, WET SPELL

without rain	ABSOLUTE DROUGHT
—29 days with little rain	PARTIAL DROUGHT
—dry weather	DROUGHT
—thaw (Siberia)	RASPUTITSA
—weather warm enough to melt ice and snow	THAW
phenomenon produced by moisture in atmosphere	HYDROMETEOR
photograph of cloud	NEPHOGRAM
place (in Siberia) which experiences excessively low temperatures	COLD POLE
powdery ice crystals	HOAR FROST
precipitation	
—liquid	DRIZZLE, RAIN
—semi-solid	SLEET
—solid	HAIL, SNOW
prehistoric climate (earliest first)	FEMIAN, SANGAMONIAN
	ST GERMAN
	PRE-BRORUP
	MOERSHOOFD
	HENGELO
	DENEKAMP
	OLDEST DRYAS
	BOLLING
	ALLEROD
	YOUNGER DRYAS
	PREBOREAL
	BOREAL
	ATLANTIC
	EARLY SUB-BOREAL
	LATE SUB-BOREAL
	SUBATLANTIC
	SCANDIC
	NEOATLANTIC
	PACIFIC
	LITTLE ICE AGE
	MODERN
pressure due to weight of air	ATMOSPHERIC PRESSURE
process of freezing	FROST
protective shelter for instruments	STEVENSON SCREEN
radiant heat from sun distributed over earth's surface	INSOLATION
rain	
—caused by cooling of rising air	CONVECTION RAIN
cyclonic conditions	CYCLONIC RAIN
moisture-laden air	
—filling low-pressure area over land mass	MONSOON

—rising over mountains	OROGRAPHIC RAIN
	RELIEF RAINFALL
—coloured red by desert sand	BLOOD-RAIN
—fine	DRIZZLE
Scotland	SMIR(R), SMUR
—frozen	HAIL, SNOW
—hail, sleet, snow	PRECIPITATION
—heavy downpour	CLOUDBURST
—measuring instrument	RAIN GAUGE
—short fall	SHOWER
—total on given area in given time	RAINFALL
—which eventually reaches streams	RUN-OFF
—with high acidity	ACID RAIN
snow	SLEET
thunder and lightning	THUNDERSTORM
rains	
—Australia	THE WET
—autumn (E. Africa)	MILLET RAINS
—periodic (India)	MONSOON
—spring (E. Afica)	MAIZE RAINS
(S. E. Asia)	BLOSSOM SHOWERS
	MANGO RAINS
—summer (Jap.)	BAI U, PLUM RAINS
rate of change of	
—atmospheric pressure	PRESSURE GRADIENT
—temperature	TEMPERATURE GRADIENT
ratio of actual to	
—maximum water vapour in air	RELATIVE HUMIDITY
—normal rainfall	PLUVIOMETRIC COEFFICIENT
record of	
—air temperature	THERMOGRAM
—relative humidity	HYGROGRAM
—vertical variation of atmospheric conditions	TEPHIGRAM
reduction of vision by	
—dust, etc	HAZE
—ice-particles	ICE-FOG
—moisture in atmosphere	FOG, MIST
—smoke and fog	SMOG
haze (US)	SMAZE
—snow	WHITEOUT
—wind-borne particles	DUST-STORM
	SAND-STORM
reversal of temperature gradient	INVERSION

ring of light round sun or moon	HALO
rising air current	CONVECTION CURRENT
	THERMAL
rocket carrying meteorological instruments	SOUNDING ROCKET
route of depressions crossing North America	NORTHERN CIRCUIT
	SOUTHERN CIRCUIT
satellite relaying meteorological data	WEATHER SATELLITE
sea	
—dog	FOGBOW
—fog	HAAR
—mist	FRET
shadow of observer on cloud or fog	BROCKEN SPECTRE
sheltered lee of mountain receiving little rain	RAIN SHADOW
ship making meteorological observations	WEATHER SHIP
short dry season (S. America)	VERANO
shortest day	WINTER SOLSTICE
small	
—area of low pressure associated with larger	SECONDARY DEPRESSION
—intense depression in tropics	TROPICAL CYCLONE
	TROPICAL REVOLVING STORM
snow	
—fine, dry	POWDER
—granular	FIRN
—soft	GRAUPEL
soft hail or snow	GRAUPEL
solar radiation on given area	INSOLATION
sound produced after lightning flash	THUNDER
spell of fine weather	
—in	
autumn	INDIAN SUMMER
October	ST LUKE'S SUMMER
November	ST MARTIN'S SUMMER
—very hot weather	HEAT WAVE
spring thaw (Siberia)	RASPUTITSA
squall (Scot.)	DROW
station making meteorological observations	WEATHER STATION

statistical description of velocity of molecules	
	MAXWELL-BOLTZMANN DISTRIBUTION LAW
storm with	
—snow	SNOWSTORM
and wind	BLIZZARD
—thunder and lightning	THUNDERSTORM
study of	
—atmosphere	AEROLOGY
—climate	CLIMATOLOGY
	METEOROLOGY
in	
—past ages	PALAEOMETEOROLOGY
—small systems	MICROCLIMATOLOGY
	MICROMETEOROLOGY
—clouds	NEPHOLOGY
—water in atmosphere	
	HYDROMETEOROLOGY
sudden	
—inrush of cold air from interior of land mass	COLD WAVE
—shower	SCAT
—storm	SQUALL
swirling dust column	DUST DEVIL
temperature	
—0°C or 32°F	FREEZING POINT, FROST
—100°C or 212°F	BOILING POINT
—at which moisture condenses	DEW-POINT
—change with altitude	LAPSE RATE
—increase caused by warm air from lower latitudes	WARM WAVE
—recorded by hygrometer	WET BULB TEMPERATURE
thick mist (Peru)	GARUA
thin transparent ice	BLACK ICE
	GLAZED FROST
treat clouds to produce rain	SEED
treatment of disease by climatic environment	CLIMATOTHERAPY
tropical storm	CYCLONE, HURRICANE
	MONSOON, TORNADO
	TYPHOON
turbulence in cloudless conditions	CLEAR AIR TURBULENCE
unit of atmospheric pressure	BAR, INCH OF MERCURY
	MILLIBAR, TORR
upper atmosphere as seen from Earth	SKY
variation in daily extremes of temperature, etc	DIURNAL RANGE

violent		floating garden	CHINAMPA
—rainstorm	CLOUDBURST	flower	BELLE-DE-NUIT
—snowstorm	BLIZZARD		MARVEL OF PERU
—thunderstorm	ELECTRIC STORM		TAGETES, TIGER-FLOWER
—wind	GALE, HURRICANE	grass	OTATE, TEOSINTE
	SQUALL	ground-cuckoo	CHAPARRAL-COCK
visible light from sun	SUNSHINE	hat	SOMBRERO
warm air between cold		hog	PECCARY
and warm fronts	WARM SECTOR	hors d'oeuvres	GUAC(H)AMOLE, TAPAS
warning of bad weather	STORM CONE	Indian market	TIAGUI
water		Indians	OMATIA, ZUNI
—droplets suspended		language	NAHUATL
in atmosphere	FOG, MIST	leaf fibre	HENEQUEN, HENEQUIN
—spout (US)	TWISTER		HENIQUIN
—vapour content of		leather riding leggings	CHAPARAJOS
atmosphere	HUMIDITY		CHAPAREJOS
given volume		maize	
of air	ABSOLUTE HUMIDITY	—cake	TORTILLA
watery snow	SLEET, SLUSH	—dish	TAMAL(E)
weather phenomenon	METEOR	minced-meat dish	TAMALE, TOMALLEY
—from 1-100Km	MESOSCALE	mushroom drug	PSILOCYBIN
wind-formed bank of snow	(SNOW)DRIFT	musical instrument	CLARIN
winds	(*see separate entry*)	pancake	ENCHILADA, TACO
Mexico	MEX		TORTILLA
agave	HENEQUEN, HENEQUIN	peasant	PEON
	HENIQUIN	peyote cactus	MESCAL
aloe	AGAVE, CENTURY PLANT	pepper sauce	TABASCO
	MAGUEY	persimmon	CHAPOTE
ancient		plums	ZAPOTE
—language	NAHUATL	pyramid temple	TEOCALLI
—race	AZTEC, MAYA, MIXTEC	rat	TUCAN, TUZA
	OLMEC, TOLTEC, ZAPOTEC	ranch	HACIENDA, RANCHO
avocado	CHININ, COYO	riding blanket	SERAPE, ZARAPE
Aztec emperor	MOCTEZUMA, MONTEZUMA	ringtail (cat)	CACOMISTLE, CACOMIXL
bean	FRIJOL(E)	river	RIO GRANDE
bird	CHAPARRAL-COCK	rodent	TUCAN
	ROAD-RUNNER	rubber-plant	GUYALE
blanket	SERAPE, ZARAPE	settlement	PUEBLO
brushwood thicket	CHAPARRAL	shirt	GUYAVERA
bulbous plant	JACOBEAN LILY	shrub	MESQUIT(E), JOJOBA
cactus	MESCAL, NOPAL, PEYOTE		POINSETTIA
capital	MEXICO CITY	spear-thrower	ATLATL
cape	SERAPE, ZARAPE	spiny tree	RETAMO
cherry	CAPULIN	spurge (wax)	CANDELILLA
coarse sugar	PANOCHA	stewed pork	CARNITAS
coin	DOLLAR, PESO	stirrup-guard	TAPADERA, TAPADERO
corn mush	ATOLE	street musicians	MARIACHI
cross of twigs	GOD'S EYE	sugar	PANOCHA
day-labourer	PEON	symbol of luck	GOD'S EYE
dog	CHIHUAHUA	tea	GOOSEFOOT
drink	MESCALI, PEYOTE	temple	TEOCALLI
	PULQUE, TEQUILA	timber	CANDLE-WOOD
drug	JALAP, MESCALINE	tortilla chip	FRITO
	PSILOCYBIN	town	PUEBLO, TULA
early civilisation	OLMEC, TOLTEC	trader with Indians	COMANCHERO
feathered serpent	QUETZALCOATL	tree	JOJOBA, MESQUITE

water gardens	CHALCHIHUITLICUE	—British	WAR OFFICE, WO
wild pig	PECCARY, TAJACU	express	ESTAFETTE
military		force into service	COMMANDEER
advance	ANABASIS		CONSCRIPT, CRIMP, DRAFT
assign accommodation	BILLET, CANTON		(IM)PRESS), LEVY
	QUARTER		PRESS(GANG)
attack or raid	INCURSION	formation	PHALANX, TESTUDO
auxiliary unit	RESERVE, PARAMILITARY	government by military	STRATOCRACY
	TA, TERRITORIALS	heavy concentration of	
bag on sword-belt	SABRETACHE	bombing or shelling	BARRAGE
barracks or quarters	CASERN		SATURATION, STONK
base or camp	INSTALLATION	join services	ENLIST, ENROLL
cane	SWAGGER-STICK	—of own free will	VOLUNTEER
canteen or shop	NAAFI	leaders	(*see separate entry*)
cartridge belt	BANDOLEER, BANDOLIER	leave	FURLOUGH
cleaning		lightning attack	BLITZKRIEG
—material	SOLDIER'S FRIEND	manoeuvre	
for		—attacking on both	
—buckles, etc	BRASSO	flanks	PINCER MOVEMENT
—rifle barrels	FOUR-BY-TWO	—drawing enemy away from	
—webbing	BLANCO	planned attack	DIVERSION
—tool for rifle-barrel	PULL-THROUGH	—using surprise	STRATAGEM
commission for higher rank	BREVET	medal	(*see* **decorations**)
cord on left shoulder	FOURRAGERE	menial work in barracks	FATIGUE
courier	ESTAFETTE	Military	
demand for supplies	REQUISITION	—Intelligence	MI
device used when		— Police	(R)MP
polishing brass		minor encounter	SKIRMISH
buttons, etc	BUTTON STICK	move forces to new area	REDEPLOY
department in charge of		mule litter	CACOLET
food supplies etc	COMMISSARIAT	official commendation	CITATION
detachment			MENTION IN DESPATCHES
—protecting		operation to achieve	
front	VANGUARD	—immediate objective	TACTIC
rear	REARGUARD	—long-term objective	STRATEGY
—sent in to support	REINFORCEMENTS	organisation and transport	
discharge		of men and equipment	LOGISTICS
—from service	DEMOB(ILISE)	persecution by military	DRAGONNADE
—with			DRAGOONING
dishonour	CASHIER, DRUM OUT	planning as an art	
illness or wounds	INVALID	or science	STRATEGY
disciplinarian	MARTINET	policy of destroying	
disorderly retreat	ROUT	anything useful to	
display outdoors	TATTOO	an enemy	SCORCHED-EARTH
dress	BATTLE DRESS, FATIGUES	position established	
	UNIFORM, SD, SERVICE DRESS	—in enemy	
drill		territory	BRIDGEHEAD, SALIENT
—on barrack-square	SQUARE-BASHING	—on enemy shore	BEACHHEAD
—sergeant's folding stick	PACE-STICK	post of soldiers	
emergency rations	C RATION, K RATION	stationed there	GARRISON
	IRON RATIONS	protective clothing	GAS CAPE
encampment	BIVOUAC		NODDY SUIT
engines of war	(*see* **weapons**)	punishment	DETENTION, FATIGUES
equipment	MATERIEL		JANKERS, PACK DRILL
establishment			REPRIMAND
—American	PENTAGON	ranks	(*see* **soldier**)

removal of	
—military presence	DEMILITARISATION
—weapons	DISARMAMENT
rifle-cleaning tool	PULL-THROUGH
ruling group of officers	JUNTA
saddle-cloth	SHABRACK
seize for military use	COMMANDEER
	REQUISITION
shop	
—American	POST EXCHANGE, PX
—British	NAAFI
sign up new members	ENLIST, ENROL
	RECRUIT
soldier	(see separate entry)
soldier's	
—belt	BALDRIC(K)
—equipment	ACOUTREMENTS
—mattress section	BISCUIT
straps, pack, etc	WEBBING
subdivision	ECHELON
tent	BIVOUAC
trial	COURT MARTIAL
unit	
—detached from main body	OUTPOST
—forming core of larger unit	CADRE
—of Army (in increasing	
size)	SECTION, PLATOON
	COMPANY, BATTALION
	REGIMENT, BRIGADE
	CORPS, ARMY, ARMY GROUP
—selected for	
special mission	DETACHMENT, PATROL
	STRIKE FORCE, TASK FORCE
—specialising in quick	
destructive raids	COMMANDO
	LONG RANGE DESERT GROUP
	SPECIAL BOAT FORCE
—within a military force	CONTINGENT
unofficial units	PARAMILITARY
volunteer for service	ENLIST, ENROL
weapons, ammunition etc	ORDNANCE
withdraw from action	DISENGAGE
	(see also soldier)
million	M, MEGA-
million cycles per second	MPS
million electron-volts	MEV
million joules	MJ
million to power of	
—two	BILLION
—three	TRILLION
—four	QUADRILLION
—five	QUINTILLION
—six	SEXTILLION
—seven	SEPTILLION
—eight	OCTILLION
—nine	NONILLION

—ten	DECILLION
—hundred	CENTILLION
thousand million	BILLION, GIGA-
	MILLIARD
million million	TERA-
million million million	EXA-
Milton	
some words found in	
Milton's works:	
able to speak	SPEAKABLE
abstruse	SUTTLE
act	
—as bishop	EPISCOPATE
—of planting	PLANTATION
adverse	PERVERSE
allow oneself	SPARE
amaurosis	DROP SERENE
archangel	HIERARCH
armour for forearm	VANTBRASS
arouse	UPRAISE
assail with din	PEAL
assembly	FREQUENCE
assuage	SWAGE
atmosphere	REGION
await	REMAIN
awakening	WAKEFUL
base wretch	RAKESHAME
battle	HOSTING
be	
—bent on	RAGE
—called	HEAR
—in excess	REDOUND
—subordinate	SUBSERVE
beat	SWINDGE
believe to exist	THINK
beloved	LIKING
beyond description	INEXPRESSIVE
blameless	UNREPROVED
blindness	DROP SERENE
blowing back	REBUFF
boisterous brawler	TURMAGANT
bottomless	UNFOUNDED
bragging	TONGUE-DOUGHTIE
bridesmaid	PARANYMPH
bridge(-work)	PONTIFICE
bring	
—back	
again	RECOLLECT
to better state	RECURE
—to perfection	SUM
bully	TURMAGANT
by the influence of heaven	HEAVENLY
call to witness	PROTEST
called	YCLEAP'D
canopy	STATE
capacity for receiving	RECEPTION

captive led in triumph	TRIUMPH	dye red	ENVERMEIL
cast	FUSIL(E)	early	RATHE
cause to degenerate	DEGENERATE	earn	ERN
chastise	SWINDGE	Earth's axis	HINGE
celebrate	REPEAT	easy to roll	VOLUBIL
claim	EXPOSTULATE	elusive	SUTTLE
close	STRAIT	encircle	WHEEL
compassionate feeling	REMORSE	encouraging	INCENTIVE
complete development of	SUM	ethereal	ETHEREOUS
concede to oneself	SPARE	even	EEV(E)N
confine	IMMANACLE	evening	EEVNING
confirm	STABLISH	evil	SHREWD
confusion	LURRY	exalted	HAUGHT, HAU(L)T
conjunction	INJUNCTION	exceed	EXCEL
constant	SAD	excessively exact	OVER-EXQUISITE
construct	FABRIC	excite	UPRAISE
contrive	PRACTISE	excommunication	EXCOMMUNION
coy	NICE	exhausted	FAINTED
crafty	SUTTLE	expand	INTEND
crash	RACK	expect	SUPPOSE
crowd	FREQUENCE	experience	TRY
cunning	SUTTLE	explode	DISPLODE
cure	RECURE	fabricate	FANGLE
defeat	DISCOMFIT	fallen	
delicate	SUTTLE	—angel	BELIAL
democracy	DEMOCRATY	—from heaven	HEAVEN-FALLEN
deprive of commission	DISCOMMISSION	false notion	IDOLISM
designate in print	PRINT	fancy	FANGLE
determine the value of	STATE	farmyard	VILLATIC
dethrone	DISENTHRONE	fatigued	SWINK'T
differentiated	DISTINCT	feed voraciously	ENGORGE
digression	EXTRAVAGANCE	female	FEMAL
dim-eyed	PALE-EYED	fetter	IMMANACLE
diminutive creature	MINIM	fiend	FEND
direct	INFORM	fine	QUAINT, SUTTLE
discharge	DISPLODE	fish route	SEA-PATH
discomposed	INCOMPOSED	flavoured by steam of	
disdain	SDAINE, SDAYN	melted ambergris	GRIS-AMBER-STEAM'D
	SDEIGNE, SDEIN	flourish	SWINDGE
disfavour	DISGUST	flow	FLOAT
disgrace	DISWORSHIP	flowed	FLOWN
dishonour	DISWORSHIP	flowering in spring	VERNANT
dispensation	DISPENSE	flowing forth	PROFLUENT
displeasure	DISGUST	fluency	FLUENCE
dissolute wretch	RAKESHAME	flying	FLIGHTED
distaste	DISGUST	forbid	RESTRAIN
distinguished	DISTINCT	foreign	FORREN
distracted	DISTRACT	form a sphere	INGLOBE
divided into groups		friar	FRIER
of four	QUATERNION'D	frightful	GREISLY
division of atmosphere	REGION	from	ON
Dog-star	SWART STAR	fulminate	FULMINE
double the darkness of	DOUBLE-SHADE	further	FURDER
drawn up again		fusible	FUSIL(E)
in battle	REIMBATTELL'D	gabbled formula	LURRY
dressed with flowers	FLOWERY-KIRTLED	gaping apart	INTERRUPT

ghastly	GREISLY
give	
—red colour to	ENVERMEIL
—way	RELENT, SWERVE
glassy transparent surface	HYALINE
grating	SCRANNEL
goal	GOLE
gory	GOARY
granary	GRANGE
great expanse	MAIN
grieve for	PINE, PYNE
grisly	GREISLY
groomsman	PARANYMPH
guide	LAND-PILOT
halt	ALT
hard-pressed	STRAIT
haughty	HAUGHT, HAU(L)T
having	
—forebodings	DIVINE
—perches	PERCHED
heal	RECURE
heathen(dom)	PANIM
held back	SUSPENS, SUSPENCE
hesitate	DEMUR
hideous	DEFORM
hold out	SUBSIST
holder of bishopric	EPISCOPANT
honesty	REALTIE
honeysuckle	EGLANTINE
hot-tempered	HOT-LIVERED
huddle	PESTER
hurtful	SHREWD
idolater	IDOLIST
igniting	INCENTIVE
ill-conditioned	SHREWD
ill-natured	SHREWD
immaterial	UNESSENTIAL
impalpable	SUTTLE
impervious to starlight	STAR-PROOF
impossible to	
—be formed	UNCONJUCTIVE
—undo	UNRECALLING
impregnable in virtue	VERTUE-PROOF
impregnate	IMPREGN
in due time	MATURE
inciting	INCENTIVE
inhabited world	INHABITATION
inlaid ornament	EMBLEM
innocent	OFFENCELESS
inordinate	DISORDINATE
inseparable	INDIVIDUAL
involve in mixture	IMMIX
jasmine	GESSAMINE
keep evenly outspread	WEIGH
kerchiefed	CHERCHEF'T
kindle	TINE

landing-place	STRAND
landscape	LANTSKIP
lash	SWINDGE
lay low	SUPPLANT
layer	LOFT
lewdness	SENSUALITY
libration of celestial	
sphere	TREPIDATION
like a devil	DEMONIAN
limit	MEASURE
look-out	PROSPECT
lost	UNOWNED
lustful	LUSTY
luxuriant	LUXURIOUS
make	
—a paradise of	IMPARADISE
—stable	STABLISH
mark out	REMARK
marked	DISTINCT
marry	SPOUSE
means of sustenance	SUSTAIN
mind	NOTION
mischievous	SHREWD
mix in	IMMIX
moisten	DIP
molestation	INFESTATION
molten	FUSIL(E)
monarch	SOVRAN
Moon not yet visible	SILENT
morning song	MATIN
motive power	PRINCIPLE
move nimbly	TROULE
moving	
—aslope	SLOPE
—slowly	LEADEN-STEPPING
murmuring	MUTTER
mutiny	MUTINE
named	YCLEAP'D
narrow	STRAIT
needy	STRAIT
nice	SUTTLE
non-Christian	PANIM
northern	SEPTENTRION(AL)
not	
—discordant	UNDISCORDING
—having skin	UNHIDEBOUND
—in liquor	UNLIQUORED
—subject to suspicion	UNSUSPECT
—suited to marriage	UNCONJUGAL
—to be recalled	UNRECALLING
object of favour	FAVOUR
obsequy	OBSEQUIE
opposition	RELUCTANCE
original elements	ORIGINS
outnumber	OVERMULTITUDE
overrefined	SUTTLE

pagan	PANIM
paltry	PITEOUS
partisan	SIDESMAN
paynim	PANIM
penetrating	SUTTLE
perfect	PERFET
permissible	VENIAL
persevere	INSIST
persuasion	INDUCEMENT
pertaining to numbness	NUMB
pestilence	MURREN
petty politician	POLITICASTER
pick out challengingly	SINGLE
pinion	PENNON
pity	REMORSE
place of rest	REPOSE
plant with magic properties	HAEMONY
planting	PLANTATION
pointing to stars	STAR-YPOINTING
precedent	PRESIDENT
preface	EPISTLE
preparedness	PROCINCT
prescient	DIVINE
president	PRESIDENT
prey	RAVEN, RAVIN(E)
private person	PRIVATE
product	PRODUCEMENT
prompt	PERNICIOUS
prune	REFORM
punishment	PENANCE
purpose	MIND
put	
—in	
a vial	VIOLD
chains	IMMANACLE
paradise	IMPARADISE
—into operation	ENURE
—under embargo	IMBAR
quash	REPEAL
quicksand	SYRTIS
raiment	WARDROP
rarefied	SUTTLE
ravishment	RAPINE
ready	PERNICIOUS
rebel	MUTINE
rebuild	REFORM
reck	WRECK
refusing indulgence	UNCONNIVING
remedy	RECURE
render	INFER
—unfamiliar	DISINURE
repress	REPEAL
resistance	RELUCTANCE
resort	SEEK
rest	ALT
restore	REFORM

revoke what has	
been predicted	UNPREDICT
revolving easily	VOLUBIL
rigorous	STRAIT
rise aloft	TOWER
river Oceanus	OCEAN-STREAM
rough	ROBUSTIOUS
round	GLOBY
rousing	WAKEFUL
route taken by fish	SEA-PATH
ruffled up	TO RUFFL'D
said	SED
sayest	SAIST
scaling-ladder	SCALE
scare	SCAR(RE)
scatter	SHATTER
scent	SENT
school	SCUL(L), SCULLE
scratchy	SCRANNEL
scythe	SITHE
second	VOUCH
seize	CEAZE, SEASE, SEAZE
sense	SENT
separable	DIVIDUAL
separate after bethrothal	DISESPOUSE
serenade	SERENATE
set	
—apart	EXEMPT
—as a plume	PLUME
—aside	REPEAL
—in	
a border	EMBORDER, IMBORDER
motion	WINNOW
—to words that smoothly	
fit the tune	SMOOTH-DITTIED
—up	STABLISH
shaft of light	RULE
shared in common	DIVIDUAL
sharpness	SHARP
showing fine discrimination	SUTTLE
shriek	SHREIK
shrink	SWERVE
sincerity	REALTIE
sluice	SLUSE
smell	SENT
snake	ELLOPS
snare	FRAUD
sober	UNLIQUORED
soft	DOUGH-KNEADED
soldier wearing armour	CATAPHRACT
source of motive power	PRINCIPLE
south-west wind	LIBECCHIO
sovereign	SOVRAN
span	OVERLAY
spareness	SPARE
sparing in giving	STRAIT

sphere	SPHEAR(E)	unknown insect	GRAYFLY
spot	FREAK	unless	LESS
spreading like a sail	SAIL-BROAD	unlike	UNCONFORM
sprouting in spring	VERNANT	unnaturally	UNKINDLY
square space	QUADRATURE	unobserved	UNSP'D
stand fast	SUBSIST	unoffending	OFFENCELESS
steadfast	SAD, STEDFAST	unshapely	DEFORM
steer	STEAR(E)	upper air	REGION
steerage	STEARAGE	vapid	FLASHY
steersman	STEARSMATE	variegate	FREAK
stir violently	TEMPEST	variegated	DISTINCT
stolen	STOLN	venture	VENTER
strait	STREIGHT	venturous	VENTROUS
streak	FREAK	verdict	VERDIT
strict	STRAIT	view-point	PROSPECT
strong	MAIN, ROBUSTIOUS	village	VILLATIC
struggling	RELUCTANT	voluble	VOLUBIL
studded with ice spangles	ICY-PEARLED	vouchsafe	VOUTSAFE
stupendous	STUPENDIOUS	wag the tongue	TROULE
stupidity	INSULSITY	want of distinct utterance	INFANCY
subjacent	SUBJECT	wardrobe	WARDROP
subtle	SUTTLE	watch	VIGILANCE
sublety	SUTTLETIE	western	PONENT
suffuse	DIP	wheel of night and day	RHOMB(US)
sung to the timbrel	TIMBREL'D	whirlpool	GURGE
superintendence	EPISCOPY	wild musical note	WOOD-NOTE
superintending	PRESIDENT	wing	PENNON
support	VOUCH	with	
supremely happy or blessed	HIGH-BLEST	—difficulty	SCARCE
surging	REDUNDANT	—hands joined	HANDED
survey	EPISCOPY	withholding the gospel	DISGOSPELLING
suspended	SUSPENS, SUSPENCE	without	
sward	SORD	—being	UNESSENTIAL
swashbuckler	SWIN(D)GE-BUCKLER	—bottom	UNFOUNDED
sway	SWINDGE	—knowing	UNWARE
swift	DISPATCHFUL, PERNICIOUS	—light	UNLIGHTSOME
tapestry	TAPSTRY	—origin or birth	UNORIGINAL
tenuous	SUTTLE	—pause	UNRESPITED
thin	SUTTLE	womb	SIDE
things stolen	STEALTH	worm injuring flocks	TAINT-WORM
time of shutting	SHUT	**mineral**	
toil-worn	SWINK'T	acid	
token of victory	TRIUMPH	—igneous rock	LIPARITE, RHYOLITE
transparent	TRANSPICIOUS	—magnesium silicate	TALC
transport	RAPINE	agate	MURRINESCOTCH PEBBLE
trick out	FANGLE	—with layers	ONYX
troop	TURME	albite feldspar	PERICLINE
turban	TURBANT		PERISTERITE
turf	TERF(E)	Alpine	
turquoise	TURKIS	—granite	PROTOGINE
ugly	OUGHLY-HEADED	—sandstone	FLYSCH
unchristianise	UNCHRISTEN	altered	
undergo	TRY	—andesite	PORPHYRITE, PROPYLITE
undeserving	IMMERITOUS	—basalt	MELAPHYRE
undistilled	UNFUME	—biotite	RUBELLAN
uninstructed	UNPRINCIPLED	—dolerite or basalt	DIABASE

—feldspar	SAUSSURITE
—mica	VERMICULITE
alum-stone	ALUNITE
alumina	ARGIL, CORUNDUM
aluminate of iron	HERCYNITE
aluminium	
—hydroxide	DIASPORE
—ore	B(E)AUXITE
—oxide	CORUNDUM
—phosphate	SPHAERITE, TURQUOISE
	VARISCITE
—silicate	CYANITE, FIBROLITE
	FULLER'S EARTH, HALLOYSITE
	KAOLINITE, KYANITE
	SILLIMANITE
—sodium silicate	NOSEAN
—magnesium silicate	SAPPHIRINE
alumino-silicate	ZEOLITE
amorphous silica	OPAL
anatase	OCTAHEDRITE
andalusite	CHIASTOLITE
antimonite	STIBNITE
antimony	
—oxysulphide	KERMES(ITE)
—trisulphide	STIBNITE
aquamarine	BERYL
aragonite	SATIN-SPAR
arborescent agate	DENDRACHATE
argentite	SILVER-GLANCE
argillaceous rock	MUDSTONE
arsenate of	
—cobalt	COBALT BLOOM, ERYTHRITE
—copper	ERINITE
arsenic	
—monosulphide	REALGAR, SANDARAC(H)
—trisulphide	ORPIMENT
arsenical pyrites	MISPICKEL
arsenide of	
—nickel	COPPER-NICKEL, NICCOLITE
—platinum	SPERRYLITE
asphalt	UINTA(H)ITE
augite	DIALLAGE
auriferous conglomerate	BANKET
autunite	TORBERNITE, URANITE
aventurine feldspar	SUNSTONE
banded	
—chalcedony	AGATE
—silica	CHALCEDONY
barium	
—carbonate	WITHERITE
—sulphate	BARITE, BARYTES
	CAULK
barytes with sulphur smell	HEPATITE
basalt	OCEANITE, WHIN(STONE)
—black	TACHYLITE, TACHYLYTE
	TOUCHSTONE

—lava	TOAD-STONE
—rich in aluminium	THOLEITE
—with nepheline	NEPHELINE-BASALT
basaltic rock	TEPHRITE
basic igneous rock	DOLERITE
beryllium	
—aluminate	CHRYSOBERYL
—aluminium silicate	EUCLASE
—silicate	PHENACITE
	PHENAKITE
between clay-slate and	
mica-schist	PHYLLITE
bituminous	ASPHALT(UM)
black	COAL
—basalt	TOUCHSTONE
—bitumen	ALBERTITE
—copper ore	MELACONITE, TENORITE
—diamond	CARBONADO
—garnet	MELANITE
—glassy igneous rock	TACHYLITE
	TACHYLYTE
—iron mineral	ILMENITE
—jasper	BASANITE
—lead	GRAPHITE
—marble	NERO-ANTICO, TOUCH
—mica	BIOTITE, LEPIDOMELANE
and plagiocite	KERSANITE
—spinel	HERCYNITE
—tourmaline	SCHORL
blackjack	ZINCBLENDE
bloodstone	HELIOTROPE
blue	
—asbestos	CROCIDOLIE
—cordierite	WATER-SAPPHIRE
—corundum	SAPPHIRE
—mineral like nosean	HAUYNE
—quartz	SAPPHIRE-QUARTZ
—stone	HYACINTH
—violet quartz	AMETHYST
boric acid	SASSOLITE
bornite	HORSEFLESH ORE
	PEACOCK-ORE
botryoidal graphite	PENCIL-ORE
brassy yellow	IRON PYRITE(S)
brick-earth	GAULT
bright non-metallic mineral	SPAR
brilliant pale zircon	JARGO(O)N
brown	
—coal	LIGNITE
—iron ore	LIMONITE
—or yellow quartz	CAIRNGORM-STONE
—tin dioxide	CASSITERITE
—with axe-shaped crystals	AXINITE
cadmium sulphide	GREENOCKITE
Cairngorm stone	SMOKY QUARTZ
calc-sinter	TUFA, TUFF

calcite-coloured	
ultramarine	LAPIS-LAZULI
calcium	
—aluminium	
silicate	ANORTHITE
	CHABAZITE, PREHNITE
magnesium	MELILITE
—carbonate	AR(R)AGONITE, CALCITE
	CALCSPAR, CARBONATITE
	ICELAND SPAR, LIMESTONE
—carbonate, etc	RENDZINA
—chloride	HYDROPHILITE
—fluoride	FLUORITE, FLUORSPAR
—in toothlike form	DOG-TOOTH SPAR
—magnesium	
amphibole	TREMOLITE
carbonate	DOLOMITE
pyroxene	DIOPSIDE
silicate	MONTICELLITE
—molybdate	POWELLITE
—oxalate	WHEWELLITE
—phosphate	
and fluoride	APATITE
etc	PHOSPHORITE
—potassium silicate	APOPHYLLITE
—salts in peat	DOPPLERITE
—silicate and titanate	SPHENE
	TITANITE
—sodium silicate	PECTOLITE
—sulphate	GYPSUM
anhydrous	ANHYDRITE
—tantalum, oxygen	MICROLITE
—titanium antimonate	LEWISITE
—tungstate	SCHEELITE
carbon	GRAPHITE
carbonaceous rock	COAL
carbonate of	
—calcium etc	ANKERITE
—copper	AZURITE, CHESSYLITE
	MOUNTAIN-BLUE
—iron	IRON-STONE
—nickel	ZARATITE
—sodium	NATRON, URAO
—strontium	STRONTIANITE
cassiterite	NEEDLE-TIN
cat's-eye	CHRYSOBERYL
	CYMOPHANE
cavity containing	
crystals	DRUSE, DRUSY CAVITY
	GEODE
cerium ore	CERITE
chalcedony	CHERT, MOSS AGATE
	SILICA
chalcopyrite	COPPER PYRITES
chalybite	SIDERITE
chiastolite	CROSS-STONE, MACLE

china-clay	KAOLIN, LITHOMARGE
chloride and phosphate of	
—lead	PYROMORPHITE
—potassium	CARNALLITE
chlorite with quartz	CHLORITE-SCHIST
chrome with iron oxide	CHROMITE
cinnamon-stone	(H)ESSONITE
	HYACINTH
clay	
—and	
alumina	B(E)AUXITE
sand	LOAM
—dark blue or grey	OXFORD CLAY
—formed by weathering	LATERITE
—from	
decomposed silicate	ILLITE
Lemnos	LEMNIAN EARTH
—ironstone	IRON-CLAY
	SPHAEROSIDERITE
—like kaolinite	NACRITE
—marble	(K)NICKER
—mineral	BENTONITE, FULLER'S EARTH
	JARGILLITE
	MONTMORILLIONITE
—rock	SHALE
—slate	OTTRELITE-SLATE
—splitting easily	
into layers	SHALE
—used for	
refractory bricks, etc	FIRE-CLAY
sun-dried bricks	ADOBE
—white	MEERSCHAUM, SEPIOLITE
—with little lime	FIRE-CLAY
—yellow	LONDON CLAY
clayey alum ore	ALUM-SHALE, ALUM-SLATE
	HALLOYSITE
clinkstone	PHONOLITE
clinochlore	RIPIDOLITE
coal	WALLSEND
—and iron	
carbonate	BLACK-BAND IRONSTONE
—early form	LIGNITE, PEAT
—from	
algae, etc	BOGHEAD COAL
sediment on	
sea bottom	SAPROPELITE
—glance	ANTHRACITE
coarse	
—grained igneous rock	GABBRO
	MONZONITE, PEGMATITE
	PERIDOTITE, SYENITE
—metamorphic rock	GNEISS
—nephaline syenite	LA(U)RDALITE
—oolite	PISOLITE
cobalt	
—arsenide	SKUTTERUDITE, SMALTITE

—carbonate	SPHAEROCOBALTITE
cockscomb pyrites	MARCASITE
coloured corundum	ORIENTAL AMETHYST
	ORIENTAL EMERALD
	ORIENTAL TOPAZ
	ORIENTAL RUBY
colourless	
—opal	HYALITE
—quartz	ROCK-CRYSTAL
common feldspar	ORTHOCLASE
compact flinty chalcedony	CHERT
compacted sand	SANDSTONE
composed of	
—pebbles	PSEPHITE
—sand-grains	PSAMMITE
concretion of silica	FLINT
conglomerate	PUDDINGSTONE
—of quartz	BANKET
containing	
—olivine	CIMINITE
—quartz	GRANODIORITE
copper	
—arsenate	OLIVENITE
—carbonate	MALACHITE
—glance	REDRUTHITE
—hydrogen arsenite	SCHEELE'S GREEN
—lead selenite	ZORGITE
—oxide	BORNITE
—pyrites	CHALCOPYRITE
	PEACOCK-COPPER
	PEACOCK-ORE
—silicate	DIOPTASE
—sulphide	CHALCOCITE
copperas	MELANTERITE
cordierite	DICHROITE, IOLITE
corundum	EMERY
cryoloite	ICE-STONE
crystal enclosed in a different mineral	ENDOMORPH
crystalline	SCHIST
—fibre in rock	SPHERULITE
—igneous rock	GABBRO
—limestone	MARBLE
—olivine	DUNITE
crystallised	
—calcite	NAIL-HEAD-SPAR
—haematite	OLIGIST
cubic	
—carbon	DIAMOND
—zeolite	ANALCIME, ANALCITE
cupreous oxide	CUPRITE
cupric sulphide	COVELLITE
dark blue or grey	
—clay	OXFORD CLAY
—fine-grained igneous rock	TRAP
—green silicates	CHLORITE

—porphyritic rock	MELAPHYRE
—tuff with crystals	PEPERINO
decomposed	
—basalt	WACKE
—ironstone	ROTTENSTONE
—rock	GOSSAN
devitrified igneous rock	FELSITE
diabase	OPHITE
diamond	
—coarse	BO(A)RT
—fragments or dust	BO(A)RT
—matrix	KIMBERITE
—ore	BLUEGROUND
—used as abrasive	CARBONADO
diatomite	KIESELGUHR, TRIPOLI
dichroite	CORDIERITE, IOLITE
dioptase	EMERALD-COPPER
diorite	DIABASE
—etc	GREENSTONE
—with quartz	GRANODIORITE
doggar	IRONSTONE
dolomite	BITTERSPAR, BROWNSPAR
—rock	MAGNESIAN LIMESTONE
dome of igneous rock	LACCOLITE
	LACCOLITH
double	
—carbonate of calcium and magnesium	DOLOMITE
—sulphate of aluminium and potassium	ALUM
dunite	OLIVINE
dyke rock	ELVAN
elastic bitumen	ELATERITE
electric calamine	HEMIMORPHITE
emerald	BERYL, SMARAGD
enclosed in another	ENDOMORPH
enclosing another	PERIMORPH
epidote and quartz	EPIDOSITE
erubescite	HORSEFLESH ORE
exfoliating clay	PYROPHYLLITE
feldspar	ANDESINE
—bluish	ANORTHOCLASE
—from Labrador	LABRADORITE
—greyish	ANORTHITE
—intermediate	BYTOWNITE
—opalescent	MOONSTONE
—reddish	ANORTHITE
—with	
aluminium silicate	ANDESINE
barium	HYALOPHONE
cleavage not at right angles	ANORTHITE
	PLAGIOCLASE
nepheline and aegirine	TINGUAITE
olivine	TROCTOLITE
	TROUTSTONE

potassium	TRACHYTE
feldspathic rock	PETUNTSE, PETUNTZE
feldspathoid	ULTRAMARINE
felstone	FELSITE
ferric	
—arsenite	SCORODITE
—oxide	GO(E)THITE, LIMONITE
—sedimentary rock	RED BED
ferro-magnesian mica	BIOTITE
ferrous	
—carbonate	CHALYBITE, SIDERITE
—phosphate	VIVIANITE
—sulphide	TROILITE
ferruginous red earth	TERRA-ROSSA
fibrolite	SILLIMANITE
fibrous	
—amphibole	ASBESTOS, CROCIDOLITE
	MOUNTAIN-LEATHER
—asbestos	AMIANT(H)US
—barytes	BOLOGNA STONE
—calcite	SATIN-SPAR
—serpentine	CHRYSOTILE
—sillimanite	FRIBROLITE
fiery red gem	PYROPE, PYROPUS
fine asbestos	AMIANT(H)US
fine-grained	
—basalt	TEPHRITE, TOUCHSTONE
—diorite	PORPHYRITE
—igneous rock	APHANITE
	KERATOPHYRE
	PHONOLITE, SPILITE
	TRACHYTE, TRAP
—lamprophyric rock	MONCHIQUITE
—metamorphic rock	SLATE
—quartz, etc	GAN(N)ISTER
—sedimentary	SHALE
—silicious rock	NOVACULITE
—syenitic rock	ORTHOPHYRE
finer portions of	
crushed ore	SCHLICH
fissile	
—greywacke	GREYWACKE-SLATE
—limestone	FOREST MARBLE
flinty	
—chalcedony	CHERT, HORNSTONE
—quartz	CHERT
fluoride of yttrium etc	YTTRO-CERITE
fluorspar	BLUE JOHN
formed of thin layers	FOLIACEOUS
	FOLIATED
found in Cornwall	REDRUTHITE
French	
—chalk	SOAPSTONE
	SPANISH CHALK
—limestone	CAEN-STONE
fuller's earth	CIMOLITE

gabbro	
—of hornblende and	
magnetite	GARNET-ROCK
—with pyroxene	NORITE
and	
—omphacite	ECLOGITE, EKLOGITE
—smaragdite	ECLOGITE, EKLOGITE
garnet with calcium	
and iron	ANDRADITE
geyserite	SINTER
glassy	
—lava	PUMICE
—orthoclase	ICE-SPAR
—stone	AUSTRALITE, TEKTITE
glimmer	MICA
gneiss	MIGMATITE
gneissose granite	PROTOGINE
gold ore	BANKET
gooseberry-stone	GROSSULAR(ITE)
granite, decomposed	CHIN-STONE
—with markings like	
Hebrew characters	GRAPHIC GRANITE
granular anhydrite	VULPINITE
graphic granite	PEGMATITE
graphite	PLUMBAGO
greasy nepheline	ELAEOLITE
green	
—amphibole	ACTINOLITE, PARGASITE
	SMARAGDITE
—banded marble	CIPOLLINO
—beryl	AQUAMARINE, EMERALD
—chalcedony	CHRYSOPRASE
—chlorite	CLINOCHLORE
—chromium mica	FUCHSITE
—chryso-beryl	ALEXANDRITE
—hornblende	AUGITE
—microcline	AMAZON-STONE
—mottled	OPHITE
—nickel magnesium silicate	GARNIERITE
—nickel-arsenate	ANNABERGITE
—porphyry	ORIENTAL VERD-ANTIQURE
—potassium, iron and	
aluminium silicate	GLAUCONITE
—pyroxene	AEGIRINE, AUGITE
	OMPHACITE
—quartz	PRASE
—spodumene	HIDDENITE
greenish beryllium	CHRYSOBERYL
Greenland spar	CRYOLITE
grey	
—igneous rock	GRANODIORITE
—or black mineral	
with metallic lustre	GLANCE
—sandstone	GREYWACKE
gypsum	ALABASTER, PLASTER-STONE
	SATIN-SPAR, SELENITE

haematite	SPECULAR IRON
halite	ROCK-SALT
halloysite	MOUNTAIN-SOAP
hard	
—chlorite	OTTRELITE
—coal	ANTHRACITE, SPLINT-COAL
—green stone	JADE
—quartz	FLINT
—sandstone	MILLSTONE-GRIT
	QUARTZITE
—siliceous stone	GAN(N)ISTER
—stone	RAG(G)
hardest mineral	DIAMOND
hardness	(*see* **geography**)
harmotome	CROSS-STONE
hatchettite	MOUNTAIN-TALLOW
having	
—crystal form of	
another mineral	PSEUDOMORPH
—crystals arranged like	
lettering	GRAPHIC
—metallic lustre	GLANCE
heavy spar	BARYTES
hemimorphite	ELECTRIC CALAMINE
hone-stone	NOVACULITE
horn-silver	CERARGYRITE
hornblende	SYNTAGMATITE
hyacinth	JACINTH
hydrogen calcium borate	PANDERMITE
hydrous	
—aluminium silicate	ALLOPHANE
—zinc silicate	HEMIMORPHITE
ice-stone	CRYOLITE
idocrase	VESUVIANITE
igneous rock	AMYGDALOID, BASALT
	BASANITE, BATHOLITE
—of labradorite etc,	GABBRO
—with feldspar	VARIOLITE
ilmenite	TITANIC IRON
impure	
—apatite	PHOSPHORITE
—talc or steatite	POTSTONE
—zinc	SPELTER
in Chinese porcelain	PETUNTSE
	PETUNTZE
intergrowth of albite	
and orthoclase	PERTHITE
intrusive quartz sheet	WHIN-SILL
—with black mica etc	LAMPROPHYRE
iolite	CORDIERITE
	DICHROITE
iridium and osmium	IRIDOSMINE
	IRIDOSMIUM, OSMIRIDIUM
iron	FERRITE
—arsenic and sulphur	ARSENO-PYRITES
	MISPICKEL

—disulphide	PYRITE(S)
—olivine	FAYALITE
—ore	BABINGTONITE, CHALYBITE
	HAEMATITE, SIDERITE
	TACONITE
with coal	BLACKBAND
—pyrites	FOOL'S GOLD, MUNDIC
—tantalate	TANTALITE
—titanium and oxygen	ILMENITE
ironstone	DOGGAR
jacinth	HYACINTH
jade	NEPHRITE, SPLEEN-STONE
	YU-STONE
kaolin	CHINA CLAY
kyanite	DISTHENE
lake deposit	SHELL-MARL
laminar lignite	PAPER-COAL
laminated	
—bituminous mineral	DYSODIL
	DYSODILE, DYSODYLE
—clay	SHALE
lead	
—antimony and sulphur	JAMESONITE
—arsenate	MIMETITE
—chromate	CROCOISITE
—glance	GALENA
—monoxide	LITHARGE
—sulphate	ANGLESITE
—sulphide	GALENA
—vanadate and chloride	VANADINITE
Lemnian earth	TERRA SIGILLATA
leucite	FEL(D)SPATHOID
lignite	COLOGNE-EARTH, JET
—Iceland	SURTARBAND, SURTURBAND
lime	
—alumina	
garnet	GROSSULAR(ITE)
mica	MARGARITE
—chrome garnet	UVAROVITE
—feldspar etc	EUCRITE
—silicate	HORNFELS
—zeolite	SCOLECITE
limestone	OOLITE
—composed of	
shells, etc	CHALK, COQUINA
—decomposed	ROTTENSTONE
—deposited from	
solution	TRAVERTIN(E)
—fetid	STINK-STONE
—used for coffins	SARCOPHAGUS
—white	CHALK, COQUINA
—with dendritic	
markings	LANDSCAPE-MARBLE
limonite	BOG-IRON, BOG-ORE
	PEA-IRON, STILPNOSIDERITE
limy clay	MARL

linite	WOOD-COAL	
liparite	RHYOLITE	
lithia mica	LEPIDOLITE	
lithium aluminium silicate	SPODUMENE	
loadstone	MAGNETITE	
loamy deposit	LO(E)SS	
loose rock at surface	MANTLE ROCK	
Lydian stone	TOUCHSTONE	
magnesia	PERICLASE	
—alumina garnet	PYROPE, PYROPUS	
—iron spinel	CEYLANITE, CEYLONITE	
	PLEONASTE	
—mica	PHLOGOPITE	
magnesian limestone	DOLOMITE	
magnesium		
—aluminate	SPINEL	
—and iron	MAFIC	
—borate and chloride	BORACITE	
—carbonate	DIALOGITE, MAGNESITE	
—hydroxide	BRUCITE	
—orthosilicate	HUMITE	
—oxide	BRAUNITE, PERICLASE	
—silicate	ENSTATITE, FORSTERITE	
	MEERSCHAUM, SERPENTINE	
	TALC	
—sulphate	KIESERITE, KAINITE	
magnetic		
—iron ore	MAGNETITE	
—oxide of iron and		
chromium	CHROMITE	
—pyrites	PYRRHOTITE	
manganese		
—alumina garnet	SPESSARTITE	
—aluminium arsenate	SYNADELPHITE	
—dioxide	PYROLUSITE	
—ore	WAD(D)	
—oxide	POLIANITE	
—silicate	RHODONITE	
—spar	RHODOCHROSITE	
—sulphide	ALABANDITE	
marble with green		
serpentine	OPHICALCITE	
marcasite	COCKSCOMB PYRITES	
	SPEAR PYRITES, WHITE PYRITES	
meerschaum	SEPIOLITE	
melaconite	TENORITE	
melanterite	COPPERAS	
mellite	HONEY-STONE	
mercuric		
—sulphate	QUEEN'S YELLOW	
	TURPETH MINERAL	
—sulphide	CINNABAR	
mercurous chloride	CALOMEL	
	HORN-MERCURY	
metamorphosed		
—diorite	EPIDIORITE	

—gabbroite	EPIDIORITE	
—sandstone	QUARTZITE	
mica	GLIMMER	
—and quartz	MICA-SCHIST, MICA-SLATE	
—ferro-magnesian	BIOTITE	
—peridotite	KIMBERLITE	
milky quartz or opal	CACHOLONG	
mineral		
—coal	STONE-COAL	
—pitch	MALTHA	
mispickel	ARSENICAL PYRITES	
	ARSENO-PYRITES	
molten rock	MAGMA	
molybdate of lead	WOLFENITE	
molybdenum disulphide	MOLYBDENITE	
moss agate	MOCHA STONE	
mostly hypersthene	HYPERSTHENITE	
mountain		
—soap	HALLOYSITE	
—tallow	HATCHETTITE	
muscovite granite	GRANITITE	
nepheline	FEL(D)SPATHOID	
—and pyroxene	NEPHELINITE	
—syenite	LA(U)RDALITE	
nephrite	GREENSTONE, JADE	
nickel		
—and iron	NIFE	
—arsenide	COPPER-NICKEL	
	KUPFERNICKEL, NICCOLITE	
niobate and titanate		
of yttrium etc	EUXENITE	
nodular rhyolite	PYROMERIDE	
nodule of oxide		
of iron	EAGLE-STONE	
novaculite	TURKEY HONE, TURKEY STONE	
oil-shale	TORBANITE	
olivine	CHRYSOLITE, DUNITE	
	PERIDOT(E)	
—and		
augite	LIMBURGITE, MONCHIQUITE	
iron oxides	MUGEARITE	
—with		
ferromagnesium	PICRITE	
pyroxenes	LHERZOLITE	
onyx		
—marble	ONYCHITE	
—with cornelian or sard	SARDONYX	
	ORIENTAL ALABASTER	
oolitic limestone	PORTLAND STONE	
opal	SILICA	
opalescent		
—chrysoberyl	CYMOPHANE	
—feldspar	MOONSTONE	
opaque		
—quartz	JASPER, JASPIS	
—white mineral	ALBIN	

orange-coloured spinel	RUBICELLE	porphyry with embedded	
orbicular diorite	NAPOLEONITE	crystals	GROUNDMASS
ore yielding profit	PAY DIRT	potash	
oriental alabaster	ONYX-MARBLE	—feldspar	MICROCLINE
orthoclase and			ORTHOCLASE, SANIDINE
—biotite	MINETTE	—mica	SERICITE
—hornblende	SYENITE	potassium chloride	SYLVINE
orthorhombic pyroxene	HYPERSTHENE	potstone	LAPIS OLLARIS
oxide of		potter's clay	ARGIL
—aluminium	ALUMINA	powdery constituent	
—lead and molybdenum	WULFENITE	of coal	FUSAIN
—lithium	LITHIA	precious spinel	RUBY-SPINEL
—manganese	MANGANITE		SPINEL-RUBY
	PSILOMELANE, WAD	pseudomorph of quartz	TIGER('S)-EYE
—sodium and boron	KERNITE	purple and white	
—tellurium	TELLURITE	—garnet	RHODOLITE
—tungsten	TUNGSTITE	—hard rock	PORPHYRY
—uranium	URANITE	pyromeride	RHYOLITE
—zinc	ZINCITE	pyrophyllite	PENCIL-STONE
pea		pyroxene	AEGRINE, AUGITE
—iron	LIMONITE		COCCOLITE, OMPHACITE
—stone	PISOLITE	pyrrhotite	MAGNETIC PYRITES
peacock-ore	BORNITE	quartz	SILICA
pearly		—and	
—lustred mineral	MARGARITE	feldspar	HALLEFLINTA
—zeolite	STILBITE		QUARTZ-PORPHYRY
peridotite	SAXONITE	mica, etc	GREISEN
philosopher's		orthoclase	ELVAN, FELSITE
stone	LAPIS PHILOSOPHICUS	—biotite diorite	TONALITE
phonolite	CLINKSTONE	—clear	ROCK CRYSTAL
phospate of		—containing topaz	GREISEN
—aluminium	LAZULITE	—crystal	BRISTOL-DIAMOND
	WAVELLITE	—feldspar	
—copper and uranium	TORBERNITE	and	
—thorium etc	MONAZITE	—mica	GRANITE, GNEISS
—uranium and calcium	AUTUNITE	—hypersthene	CHARNOCKITE
picolite	CHROME-SPINEL	etc	GRAYWACKE
pink			GREYWACKE
—garnet	RHODOLITE	with garnets	GRANULITE
—topaz	ROSE-TOPAZ	—flinty	CHERT
pinkish quartz	ROSE-QUARTZ	—leek-green	PRASE
pisolite	PEA-STONE	—like diorite	GRANDIORITE
pissasphalt	MINERAL TAR	—milky	CACHALONG
pitchblende	CLEVEITE	—opaque	JASP(ER), JASPIS
	URANINITE	—plagioclase	DACITE
plagioclase and		—porphyry	GRANOPHYRE
—augite	TESCHENITE	—rock	QUARTZITE
—hornblende	CAMPTONITE	—rough	BUHRSTONE, BURRSTONE
	DIORITE	—transparent	ROCK CRYSTAL
—feldspar	ANORTHITE	—with mica	AVANTURINE, AVENTURINE
—nepheline and augite	THERALITE	quartzite	ITACOLUMITE
pleochroic pyroxene	AEGIRINE	quicksand	SYRTIS
plumbago	GRAPHITE	realgar	SANDARAC(H)
plutonic rock	GRANITE, SYENITE	red	
porous rock	CALC-SINTER	—chalcedony	CARNELIAN, CORNELIAN
	TUFA, TUFF		SARD(IUS), SARDINE

—clay	BOLE	shelly limestone	PURBECK MARBLE
—copper ore	CUPRITE		PURBECK STONE
—corundum	RUBY	siderite	CHALYBITE
—garnet	ALABANDINE	silver-glance	ARGENTITE
	ALMANDINE	silica	CHALCEDONY, QUARTZ
—mercuric sulphide	CINNABAR	—and alumina	SIAL
—ochre from Lemnos	LEMNIAN RUDDLE	—in hexagonal scales	TRIDYMITE
—orthosilicate	GARNET	silicate minerals	AMPHIBOLES
—precious stone	CARBUNCLE	silicate of	
—spinel	BALAS(RUBY)	—alumina	CHLORITE
—tourmaline	RUBELLITE	—aluminium	ANDALUSITE, BENTONITE
—brown or yellow zircon	HYACINTH		CHIASTOLITE, CORDIERITE
redruthite	COPPER-GLANCE		DICHROITE, FULLER'S EARTH
repidolite	CLINOCHLORE		HAROMTOME, IDOCRASE
resembling spar	SPATHIC		IOLITE, JADEITE, LEUCITE
reworked china clay	BALL CLAY		MONTMORILLONITE, MUSCOVITE
rhodochrosite	MANGANESE SPAR		PENNINE, SCAPOLITE, SPODUMENE
rhodonite	MANGANESE SILICATE		STAUROLITE, TOPAZ, VESUVIANITE
rhyolite	LIPARITE	—beryllium	AQUAMARINE, BERYL
rock			EMERALD
—containing ores	GANG(UE), LODE	—boron and calcium	DATOLITE
—crystal	RHINESTONE	—calcium	TABULAR SPAR
—derived from clay or mud	PELITE		THAUMASITE, WOLLASTONITE
—forming	FEL(D)SPAR, MICA	and aluminium	ZOISITE
—of angular fragments	BRECCIA	etc	EPIDOTE, HORNBLENDE
—salt	HALITE		IDOCRASE, VESUVIANITE
	(see also **rock**)	—complex	TOURMALINE
rose-red pyroxene	RHODONITE	—copper	CHRYSOCOLLA
ruby	STAR-STONE	—iron	CHLORITE, FAYALITE
—copper	CUPRITE		GREEN EARTH
—silver	PROUSTITE, PYRARGYRITE	and magnesium	OLIVINE
sandarac(h)	REALGAR	—magnesia	CHLORITE
sandstone	HOLYSTONE	—magnesium and	
—formed from granite	ARKOSE	aluminium	SAPONITE
—grey	GREYWACKE	iron	HYPERSTHENE
—rough	GRIT(STONE)	—manganese	TEPHRITE
—with		—mineral	PYROXENE, PYROXENITE
feldspar	ARKOSE	—potassium etc	PHILLIPSITE
glauconite	GREENSAND	—sodium	
limonite	CARSTONE	and	
sandy shale	FA(I)KES	—aluminium	JADEITE
sapphire	STAR-STONE	—iron	CROCIDOLITE, RIEBECKITE
scapolite	MARIALITE, MEIONITE	etc	NEPHELINE NEPHELITE
	MIZZONITE	—thorium	THORITE
schistose quartzite	QUARTZ-SCHIST	—yttrium etc	GADOLINITE
schorl	TOURMALINE	—zirconium etc	EUDIALYTE
—and quartz	SCHORL-ROCK	silicon	
scoriaceous lava	SLAG	—and magnesium	SIMA
selenite	MOONSTONE, PHENGITE	—compound	SILICATE
sepiolite	MEERSCHAUM	—dioxide	CHALCEDONY, OPAL
serpentine			QUARTZ, SILICA
—and calcite	VERDE-ANTICO	sillimanite	FIBROLITE
	VERD-ANTIQUE	silver and	
—rock	OPHITE	—antimony	DYSCRASITE
shale (Scotland)	TORBANITE	—chloride	CERARGYRITE
sheet of rock	NAPPE	—glance	ARGENTITE

—iodide	IODYRITE	stibnite	ANTIMONITE
—mica	CAT-SILVER	stilbite	DESMINE
—ore	STEPHANITE	stilpnosiderite	LIMONOITE
red	PROUSTITE	stinkstone	SWINESTONE
silvery metal	ALUMINIUM	streaks in igneous rock	SCHLIEREN
sinter	GEYSERITE	streaky granular rock	MYLONITE
skeleton crystal	DENDRITE	stretching of rock into	
slaty diabase tuff	SCHALSTEIN	sausage shape	BONDINAGE
smaltite	SPEISS-COBALT	strontium sulphate	CELESTINE
smaragd	EMERALD	sulph-arsenide	
smoky quartz	CAIRNGORM (STONE)	of cobalt	COBALTITE
soapstone	FRENCH CHALK		COBALT GLANCE
	SPANISH CHALK, STEARITE	sulphate of	
soda		—aluminium	ALUNITE
—amphibole	ARFVEDSONITE	—iron	COQUIMBITE
—lime feldspar	ANORTHOSITE	and potassium	JAROSITE
	OLIGOCLASE	—magnesium etc	POLYHALITE
—mica	PARAGONITE	sulphide	
—syenite	LA(U)RVIKITE	—minerals	PYRITES
—trachyte	KERATOPHYRE	—of	
sodalite	FEL(D)SPATHOID	antimony	STIBNITE
sodium		arsenic	REALGAR, ZARNEC, ZARNICH
—aluminium		—and silver	PROUSTITE
fluoride	CRYOLITE	copper	
silicate	ANALCIME, ANALCITE	—and	
	LAZURITE, SODALITE	iron	COPPER PYRITES
zeolite	GMELINITE	antimony	TETRAHEDRITE
—calcium sulphate	GLAUBERITE	—etc	STANNITE
—carbonates	TRONA	iron	IRON PYRITES, MARCASITE
—chloride	(ROCK) SALT	—and nickel	PENTLANDITE
—nitrate	CHILE NITRE	lead	GALENA
	CHILE SALTPETRE	—and antimony	ZINKENITE
softest mineral	TALC	mercury	CINNABAR
South African quartz	CROCIDOLIE	silver	ARGENTITE
Spanish chalk	FRENCH CHALK	—and antimony	PYRARGYRITE
	SOAPSTONE	zinc	ZINCBLENDE
spear pyrites	MARCASITE	sulphur, arsenic etc	TENNANTITE
specular iron	HAEMATITE	sylvine and rock-salt	SYLVINITE
speiss-cobalt	SMALTITE	tabular spar	WOLLASTONITE
spelter	ZINC	tachylite	HYALOMELAN(E)
sphalerite	ZINC BLENDE	talc	
sphene	TITANITE	—soapy	FRENCH CHALK
spheroidal crystallite	GLOBULITE		SOAPSTONE, STEATITE
spinel containing iron etc	PICOTITE	—with other minerals	TALC-SCHIST
spleen-stone	JADE	tantalate of	
splitting into flakes	SPATHIC	yttrium etc	YTTRO-COLUMBITE
spotted			YTTRO-TANTALITE
—schist	KNOTENSCHIEFER	telluride of gold	
—slate	KNOTENSCHIEFER	or silver	SYLVANITE
	SPILOSITE	tennantite	FAHLERZ, FAHLORE
stalactitic calcite	DROP-STONE	tenorite	MELACONITE
star-stone	RUBY, SAPPHIRE	tetrahedrite	FAHLERZ, FAHLORE
staurolite	CROSS-STONE	titanic iron	ILMENITE
stearite	SOAPSTONE	thin-bedded sandstone	FA(I)KES
steatite	FRENCH CHALK, SOAPSTONE	thorium	
	VENICE TALC	—and uranium ore	CHERALITE

—silicate	THORITE
thulite	ZOISITE
tin	
—copper etc	STANNITE
—dioxide	CASSITERITE, TINSTONE
titanite	SPHENE
titanium oxide	ANATASE, BROOKITE
	RUTILE
toad-stone	BASALT LAVA, TUFF
topaz	PYCNITE
torbernite	AUTUNITE, URANITE
touchstone	LYDIAN STONE
tourmaline	SCHORL
—granite	LUXUL(L)IANITE
	LUXULYANITE
translucent opal	HYDROPHANE
transparent	
—calcite	ICELAND SPAR
—feldspar	ADULARIA
—gypsum	SELENITE
—mineral	SPECULAR STONE
—non-metallic	SPAR
—quartz	ROCK CRYSTAL
—silicate	TOURMALINE
—stone	PHENGITE
—zircon	JACINTH
travertine	CALC-SINTER, CALC-TUFF
	ONYX-MARBLE
treelike crystal	DENDRITE
tripoli	DIATOMITE
trisulphide of arsenic	ORPIMENT
troctolite	TROUTSTONE
troutstone	TROCTOLIE
tufa	CALC-SINTER, TUFF
tuff	CALC-SINTER
	TOAD-STONE, TUFA
tungstate of iron, etc	WOLFRAMITE
tungsten	WOLFRAM
Turkey stone	TURQUOISE
turquoise	TURKEY-STONE
under-clay	WARRANT
uraninite	PITCH-BLENDE
uranite	AUTUNITE, TORBERNITE
uranium	
—ore	COFFINITE, SAMARSKITE
—oxides	PITCHBLENDE
useless	GANGUE
vanadate of uranium	CORNOTITE
variety of garnet etc	JACINTH
veinstone	GANG(UE)
Venice talc	STEATITE
vesuvianite	IDOCRASE
vitreous lava	PALAGONITE
volcanic	
—dust	POZZ(U)OLANA, PUZZOLANA
—glass	PE(A)RLITE, PITCHSTONE

—rock	ANDESITE, OBSIDIAN
	PALAGONITE-TUFF
banded	EUTAXITE
—tuff	TARRAS, TERRAS, TRASS
	(*see also* **volcano**)
Wallsend	COAL
warrant	UNDER-CLAY
water-sapphire	CORDIERITE
waxy hydrocarbon	HATCHETTITE
	OZOCERITE, OZOKERITE
whin(stone)	BASALT
white	
—and grey chalcedony	CHALCEDONYX
—clay	KAOLIN(E)
	MEERSCHAUM, SEPIOLITE
—earthy mineral	TERRA ALBA
—feldspar	ALBITE
—lead ore etc	HEDYPHANE
—limestone	CHALK, COQUINA
—marble	PARIAN
—metal	ANTIMONY, NICKEL
	SILVER
—mica	MUSCOVITE
—pyrites	MARCASITE
Wollastonite	TABULAR SPAR
wood-coal	LIGNITE
worthless	GANGUE
yellow	
—beryl	HELIODOR
—clay	LONDON CLAY
—corundum	ORIENTAL TOPAZ
—garnet	TOPAZOLITE
—metal	COPPER, GOLD
—rock crystal	CITRINE
yellowish garnet	CINNAMON-STONE
yu(-stone)	JADE
zeolite	ANALCINE, ANALCITE
	CHABAZITE, HEULANDITE
	PHACOLITE, STILBITE
zinc	SPELTER
—blende	SPHALERITE
—carbonate	CALAMINE, HYDROZINCITE
	SMITHSONITE
—manganese spinel	FRANKLINITE
—oxide	ZINCITE
—silicate	HEMIMORPHITE
—spinel	GAHNITE
—sulphide	SPHALERITE
zirconium	
—dioxide	BADDELEYITE
—silicate	JACINTH, JARGOON, ZIRCON
—sulphate	GOSLARITE
zoisite	THULITE
Miss	
Atwell	MABEL (LUCY)
Austen	JANE

Barrett	ELIZABETH	—guenon	TALAPOIN
Bell	DAISY	—white-eyelid	MANGAB(E)Y
Brontë	CHARLOTTE, EMILY, ANN	American	MARMOSET, SPIDER MONKEY
Darling	GRACE	anthropoid ape	TROGLODYTE
Doone	LORNA	Assam gibbon	HOOLOCK
Durbeyfield	TESS	Ateles	SPIDER-MONKEY
Eyre	JANE	Barbary ape	INUUS, MAGOT, MACAQUE
Gabler	HEDDA	black	
Garbo	GRETA	—crested langur	SIMPAI
Gardner	AVA	—tailed marmoset	MICO
Hayworth	RITA	broad-nosed	PLATYRRHINE
Laurie	ANNIE	Borneo	PROBOSCIS MONKEY
Liddell	ALICE	Brazil	BELZEBUTH, GUARIBA
Lind	JENNY		MIKRIKI, SAI, TAMARIN
Lloyd	MARIE	Burma gibbon	HOOLOCK, LAR
Locket	LUCY	capuchin	CEBUS, SAI, SA(PA)JOU
MacDonald	FLORA, JEANETTE	Ceylon	
Monroe	MARILYN	—langur	WANDEROO
Oberon	MERLE	—lemur	LORIS
Piggy	GILT	—macaque	TOQUE
Scoley	AMELIA	chimpanzee	ANTHROPOPITHECUS
Spenlow	DORA	Cochin-China	DOUC
Tilley	VESTA	dog-ape	BABOON
Wickfield	AGNES	dog-faced baboon	CYNOCEPHALUS
Wilfer	(ISA)BELLA	East Indian	
Woodhouse	EMMA	—ape	ORANG(-UTAN)
missile			ORANG-OUTANG, GIBBON
American	ARROW, CRUISE, HAWK	—lemur	LORIS, MALMAG, TARSIER
	LANCE, MINUTEMAN	—tarsier	MALMAG
	PATRIOT, PERSHING, POLARIS	Ethiopian baboon	GELADA
	STINGER, TRIDENT	flying lemur	COLUGO, CYNOCEPHALUS
British	BLOWPIPE, BLUE STEEL		DERMOPTERA
	BLUESTREAK, LANCE, THOR		GALEOPITHECUS
German	V1, V2	gibbon	HYLOBATE
Indian	AGNI, PRITHVI	gorilla	PONGO
Israeli	JERICHO	Guinea baboon	SPHINX
Russian	SAM, SCUD	Indian	
South African	SKERPION	—bonnet monkey	MACAQUE, ZATI
	(*see also* **space**)	—lion-tailed	
		macaque	SILENUS, WANDEROO
Mongolia		—monkeys	BANDAR, BOONDER, LORIS
capital	ULAAN BAATAR, ULAN BATOR		RHESUS, TARSIER, TOGUE
coin		—sacred monkey	ENTELLUS
—unit	MONGO		HANUMAN, LANGUR,
—100 mongo	TUGRIK	Java gibbon	WOU-WOU, WOW-WOW
monkeys		lemur	HALFAPE, MACACO
African			MEERCAT, MEERKAT
—ape	CHIMPANZEE, GORILLA	macaque	TOQUE
—baboon	CHACMA, DRILL	Madagascar	
	MANDRILL	—lemur	AYE-AYE, BABACOOTE
—black and white	GUEREZA		BABAKOTO, INDRI(S)
—lemur	ANGWANTIBO, BUSH-BABY		MONGOOSE
	GALAGO, NIGHT-APE, POTTO	—monkey	VARI
—long-tailed	COLOBUS	Malay lemur	KUKANG
	CERCOPITHECUS	mangabey	WHITE-EYED MONKEY
	DIANA MONKEY, GRIVET	marmoset	MIDAS, WISTITI
	GUENON, MONA, VERVET		

New World	PLATYRRHINE		—mare	JUMART
(of pile-driver)	RAM		—with flames from	
Old World	CATAR(R)HINE		mouth	CARETYNE
orang-utan	PONGO, SATYR		bull-headed	BONNACON, MINOTAUR
Philippines - tarsier	MALMAG		Carroll	BANDERSNATCH
rhesus	MACAQUE			JABBERWOCK(Y)
Satan monkey	BLACK SAKI		cat with horns	CALYGREYHOUND
South American			camel/goat	YPOTRILL
—black saki	SATAN MONKEY		centaur	HIPPOCENTAUR
—broad-nosed	PLATYRRHINE		—with bow and arrow	SAGITTARIUS
—cowled monkey	CAPUCHIN			SAGITTARY
—golden	SQUIRREL-MONKEY		chaste-wife eater	CHICHEVACHE
—grey	GRISON		cock/serpent	COCKATRICE
—howler	MYCETES, MYCETIS		cockatrice/dragon	BASILISK
—long-tailed	SAKI, UAKARI		cow/stallion	JUMART
—marmoset	JACCHUS		Cretan	MINOTAUR
—monkeys	TEE-TEE, TITI		cruel	OGRE
	SAGOIN, SAG(O)UIN		decorative (China)	KYLIN
—night-ape	DOUROUCOULI, DURUKULI		dog	
—spider-monkey	COAITA, SAPAJOU		—2 headed	ORTHOS
—squirrel-monkey	SAIMIRI, TAMARIN		—3 headed	CERBERUS
spider-monkey	ATELES		—fish	HOUND MARINE, SEA-DOG
Sumatra			dragon	BASILISK
—gibbon	SIAMANG, WOU-WOU		—fish	SEA-DRAGON
	WOW-WOW		—Norse	FAFNIR, NIDHOGG
—langur	SIMPAI		—wingless	LINDWORM
proboscis genus	NASALIS		—with	
tarsier	MALMAG, SPECTRE-LEMUR		two legs	WIVERN, WYVERN
toque	MACAQUE		wings	GORGON
tufted monkey	MUSTAC		eagle with horns	TRAGOPAN
white-eyed monkey	MANGABEY		female	EURYALE, GORGON
with divided nostril	CATAR(R)HINE			MEDUSA, STHENO
monsters			firebreathing	CHIM(A)ERA, DRAGON
including: heraldic beasts			fish	SCOLOPENDRA
mythical beasts			fish-tailed, horselike	HIPPOCAMPUS
American	BIGFOOT, SUSQUATCH		fox/greyhound/wolf	ENFIELD
amphibious	WATER-BULL		Furies	(see separate entry)
antelope	ARGASILL, IBEX		giraffe	CAMELOPARD
—horse	BAGWYN		—with horns	CAMELOPARDEL
—with swivelling horns	YALE		goat/stag	HIRCOCERVUS, TRAGALEPH
Arab demon	AFREET		Greek	LAMIA, TYPHOEUS
Australian	BUNYIP		green-eyed	ENVY
Bantu	PALATYI		griffin-headed winged	
biblical	BEHEMOTH, LEVIATHAN		horse	HIPPOGRIFF
	LILITH			HIPPOGRYPH
bird	ROC, ROK, RUC, RUKH		hairy tyger	NEBEK
—Arabian	PHOENIX		Himalayas	ABOMINABLE SNOWMAN, YETI
—Persian	SIMORG, SIMURG(H)		Hindu	GARUDA
—restless	HUMA		horned beast (Spenser)	ANTELOPE
—rising from ashes/flames	PHOENIX		horse	
—whose whistle was fatal	WHISTLER		—cow	JUMART
bird/woman	HARPY		—fish	HIPPOCAMPUS
blood-sucking witch	LAMIA		—goat	SILENUS
bull			—griffin	HIPPOGRIFF, HIPPOGRYPH
—fish	BULL MARINE, SEA-BULL		—with	
—horse	BON(N)ACPON		single horn	UNICORN

tusks, horns, etc	YALE
wings	HIPPOGRIFF, HIPPOGRYPH
	PEGASUS
human wolf	WEREWOLF
hundred	
—handed	AEGEON, BRIARAEUS
	CENTIMANUS, COTTUS
	GY(G)ES, HECATONCHIRES
—headed	TYPHAEUS, TYPHON
Jewish	GOLEM
Lewis Carroll's	
invention	BANDERSNATCH
	JABBERWOCK(Y)
lion	
—dragon	OPINICUS
—eagle	BOREYNE, GRIFFIN, GRIFFON
	GRIPE, GRYPHON
—fish	SEA-LION
—goat	CHIM(A)ERA
—leopard/serpent	QUESTING BEAST
—scorpion	MANTICORE, MANTICORA
—with helmet	BOTRAGER
—wolf	TYGER
lizard	AMPHISBAENA
—in flames	SALAMANDER
man	
—ass	ONOCENTAUR
—bird	GARUDA
—bull	MINOTAUR
—covered with green hair	WODEHOUSE
—dragon	CECROPS
—eating	OGRE
—fish	MERMAN
—goat	FAUN, SATYR
—horse	(HIPPO)CENTAUR
	SAGITTARIIUS
	SAGITTARY, SILENII
—lion/antelope	SATYRAL
—lion/scorpion	MANTICORA
	MANTICORE, MANTYGRE
—with legs in form	
of serpents	GIGANTES
—wolf	WEREWOLF
man's head with ears	
of ass	MIDAS'S HEAD
many-headed	HYDRA, PEOPLE
	TYPHAEUS, TYPHON
mastiff/bloodhound	TALBOT
(monstrous regiment)	WOMEN
Norse	
—dragon	FAFNIR, NIDHOGG
—serpent	MIDGARD
Norwegian	KRAKEN
one-eyed	CYCLOPS
Persian bird	SIMORG, SIMURG(H)
prehistoric	DINOSAUR

reindeer with forward	
curving horns	TROGODICE
Rocky Mountains	BIGFOOT, SUSQUATCH
Roman	LAMIA, TYPHON
Scandinavian	TROLL
Scottish water-horse	KELPIE
sea	
—horse	HIPPOCAMPUS
—monster	LEVIATHAN, ORC
German	WASSERMAN
Norwegian	KRAKEN
man-shaped	WASSERMAN
scaly	PHOCA
—swallower	CHARYBDIS
six-headed	SCYLLA
snake-haired	EURYALE, GORGON
	MEDUSA, STHENO
Spenser	ANTELOPE, PHOCA
	ROSMARINE, SEASATYRE
	ZIFFIUS
stag/goat	HIRCOCERVUS, TRAGLEPH
star-spangled hind	PANTHEON
three	
—bodied	GERYON
—headed	CERBERUS
Tibetan	YETI
two	
—headed	JANICEPS
dog	ORTHOS
snake	AMPHISBAENA
—tailed mermaid	MELUSINE
under	
—Etna	TYPHOEUS
—rock	CHARYBDIS
unicorn/fish	SEA-UNICORN
water	
—demon	NICKER
—snake	HYDRA
whale-like	WHIRLPOOL
whirlpool	CHARYBDIS
wildcat	CAT-A-MOUNTAIN
winged	
—dragon	WIVERN, WYVERN
—female	GORGON
—horse	HIPPOGRIFF, HIPPOGRYPH
	PEGASUS
—serpent	PYTHON
wingless dragon	LINDWORM
with knotted tail	ALPHYN
wolf	
—cat/goat	CHATLOUP
—fish	SEA-WOLF
—fox/greyhound	ENFIELD
—with cloven feet	THEOW, THOS
woman	
—fish	MERMAID

—lioness	SPHINX	cloak	BURK(HA), BURQA
—seabird	SIREN		(D)JIBBAH, (D)JUBBAH
—serpent	ECHIDNA, LAMIA	cloth cover for Kaaba	KASWA
—vulture	HARPY	college	MADRAS(S)A(H)
moons	(*see* **astronomy**)		MEDRESSAH
Moor	SARACEN	confession of faith	SHAHADA
carpet	SOFRA, ZOFRA	convert (Hindu)	SHEIK(H)
dance	MORESCO	court official	HAJIB
dynasty (Spain)	NASRID	dancing fanatic	WHIRLING DERVISH
drum	ATABAL	date (after Hegira)	AH
pirate	SALLEE-MAN, SALLEE-MAN	demon	DJINN(I), GENIE, GINN
ship	GALLIVAY, XEBEC(K), ZEBEC(K)		JANN, JINN(EE), JINNI
violin	REBEC(K)	dervish	CALENDER, SADITE
	(*see also* **Morocco**)	dervish's cap	TAJ
		descendant of	
Morocco		—Fatima	FATIMID, SAID
capital	RABAT		SAY(Y)ID
chicken dish	DJEJ MATISHA	—Mohammed	EMIR, SEID
	DJEJ MQUALLI, MESLA		SHEREEF, SHERIF
coin	CENTIME, DERHAM, DIRHAM	disciple	MURID
	DIRHEM, FRANC	emblem	CRESCENT
dancer	CHIKHAT	empty litter in pilgrimage	
filled pancakes	BRIOUATES	to Mecca	MAHMAL
marzipan pastries	KAAB EL GHZAL	evil spirit	MAHOUN(D)
measure		examiner of the dead	NAKIR
—22 inches	DRAH	example of Mohammed	SUNNA
—bushel	MUDD	expert on law of Koran	MUFTI
pigeon pie	BISTEEYA	faith	CRESCENT
ruler	SULTAN	fallen angel	EBLIS, IBLIS
spice sauce	CHERMOULA	fanatic	ABDELS, GHAZI, MOOLA(H)
tree	ARAR, ARGAN		MOLLA(H), MULLA(H)
	SANDARAC(H), THYINE	fast	MOHARRAM, MUHARRAM
tribe	RIFF, MOOR		MUHARREM, RAMAD(H)AN
Moslem	MUSLIM, MUS(S)ULMAN		SAUM, SAWM
	SARACEN	festival	BAIRAM, BAYRAM
ablution	WUDU, WUZU	flight of Mohammed	HEJ(I)RA
alluring woman	HOURI		HEGIRA, HIJRA
almsgiving	ZAKAT	god	ALLAH
angel of death	AZRAEL	great leader	MAHDI
animal slaughter	HAL(L)AL	greeting	SALAAM
ascetic	DERVISH, FAKIR	headscarf	HIJAR
	FAQUIR	hermit	MARABOUT
ascribing partners		holy	
to God	SHIRK	—building in Mecca	KAABA(H)
become Moslem	TURN TURK	—city	MECCA, MEDINA
Bulgarian	POMAK	—man	IMA(U)M
caliphate	KHILIFAT	—state of pilgrim	IHRAM
call to prayer	ADAN, AZAN	—war	CRESCENTADE
canon law	SHARIA		JEHAD, JIHAD
chapter of Koran	SURA(H)	home of spirits	KAF
chief	AMEER, AMIR, DATTO	if God wills	INSHALLAH
	EMEER, EMIR	in India	COSSA
—magistrate	SHEREEF, SHERIF	infidel	GIAOUR, KAFIR
chieftain	AMIR, AMEER	interpretation of Koran	TAFSIR
	EMEER, EMIR	Jesus	NABI ISA
Christian turned Moslem	RENEGADE	knowledge of Koran	HAFIZ
	RENEGADO		

law	SHARIA(T), SHERIA(T)
lawyer	ALFAQUI, MOOLVEE, MOOLVI(E)
	MOOLWEE, MUFTI
leader	AG(H)A, IMA(U)M, MAHDI
legal decision	FATWA(H), FETWA
magistrate	CADI, KADI
member of dynasty	ABBASID(E)
mendicant	FAKIR, FAQUIR
minister	VEZIR, VISIER
	VIZI(ER), WAZIR, WIZIER
monk	DERVISH
months	
1	MOHARRAM, MUHARRAM
	MUHARREM
2	SAFAR
3	RABIA I
4	RABIA II
5	JUMADA I
6	JUMADA II
7	RAJAB
8	SHABA(A)N
9	RAMADAN
10	SHAWWAL
11	ZU'LKADAH
12	ZU'LHIJJAH
mosque	MASJED, MASJID
—school	MADRAS(S)A(H), MEDRESSEH
mystic	SOFI, SUFI
niche in mosque	
pointing to Mecca	KEBLAH, KIBLAB
	MIHRAB, QIBLA
North African	SENUSSI
nymph of paradise	HOURI
one who calls to prayer	MUEZZIN
orthodox Moslem	HANIF, SHAFI(ITE)
	SUNNI
pilgrim	HADJI, HAJ(J)I
—garb	IHRAM
pilgrimage	HADJ, HAJ(J)
prayer	KHOTBAH, KHOTBEH
	KHUTBAH, SALAT
preacher	AYATOLLAH, MOLLA(H)
	MOOLA(H), MULLA(H)
priest	IMA(U)M, MUEDDIN, MUEZZIN
prince	AMEER, AMIR, EMEER, EMIR
	SHEREEF, SHERIF
princess	BEGUM
prophet	MAHDI, MAHOMET
	MOHAMMED
public procession	MOHARRAM, MUHARRAM
	MUHARREM
pulpit in mosque	MIMBAR, MINBAR
purgatory	ARAF
religion	ISLAM, MOHAMMEDANISM
	MAMMETRY, MAUMETRY
	MAWMETRY, MOMMETRY

religious	
—leader	AYATOLLAH
—war	(*see* holy war *above*)
revealed law	SHARIA
rites	ABDEST, MADHAHIB
ritual animal	
slaughter	HAL(L)AL
ruler	CALIPH, SULTAN
Sabbath	JUMA
sacred	
—book	ALCORAN, (AL)KORAN
—fountain	ZEMZEM
—stone	BLACK STONE
saint's shrine	DURGAH
schoolmaster	MOLLA(H), MOOLA(H)
	MULLA(H)
scriptures	ALCORAN, (AL)KORAN
	QORAN, QURAN
sect	DRUSE, DRUZ(E)
	KHARIVISM, ISMAILI
	KARMATHIAN, MUTAZILAH
	SEN(O)USSI, SHIA(H), SHIITE, SOFI
	SUFI, SONNA, SONNI, SUNNI
	WAHABEE, WAH(H)ABI
Shiite	ISMAILI
shrine	MARABOUT, ZIARA
slab in mosque	MIHRAB
slave	DURGAH
spirit	GENIE, JINNEE, (D)JINNI
	GINN, DJINN
spiritual leader	CALIF, CALIPH
	KALIF(A)(H)
student	SOFTA
sultan's	
—lady	SULTANA
—standard bearer	ALEMBDAR
teacher	MOLLA(H), MOOLA(H)
	MOLLA(H), MULLA(H)
temple	KAABA, MOSQUE
theologians	ULEMA
title of respect	SIDI
tomb cloth	CHAD(D)AR, CHADOR
	CHUDDAH, CHUDDAR
towards Mecca	KEBLAH, KIBLAH
tower of mosque	MINARET
traditional lore	HADITH, SUNNA
tribune	DIKKAH
Turkish sect	KARMATHIAN
unbeliever	KAFIR
voluptuous woman	HOURI
warrior	GHAZI
what God wills	MASHALLAH
whole Moslem world	ISLAM
witness	SHAHADA
woman's	
—loose garment	BURK(H)A, BURQA

—headscarf	HIJAB		MAGPIE, MARCH, MOTTLED UMBER	
—veil	CHAD(D)AR, CHADOR		PALE TUSSOCK, PINE BEAUTY, PITH	
	CHUDDAH, CHUDDAR, YASHMAK			RASPBERRY
—wrap	IZAR		SMALL ERMINE, SWIFT, TORTRIX	
women's quarters	HARAM, HAREM, HARIM		TURNIP, VAPOURER, WINTER	
	SERAGLIO, SERAIL			WOOD LEOPARD
wonder-worker	FAKIR, FAQUIR			YELLOW UNDERWING
worship	SALAT	silkworm	BOMBYCID, PSYCHE	
moths	HETEROCERA	small moths	TENEIDAE	
Abraxas	GOOSEBERRY MOTH	tiger moths	BUFF ERMINE TIGER	
	MAGPIE MOTH			CREAM-SPOT TIGER
clothes moth	TENEID		GARDEN TIGER, RUBY TIGER	
Crethocampus	PROCESSIONARY MOTH			WHITE ERMINE TIGER
day-flying	CINNABAR			WOOD TIGER
	CURRANT CLEARWING, EMPEROR	**motor car**	GT, MINI, RR	
	FIVE-SPOT BURNET, FOX	air deflector	AIR-DAM, SPOILER	
	HORNET CLEARWING	automatically synchronised		
	KENTISH GLORY, OAK EGGAR	gears	SYNCHROMESH	
	ORANGE UNDERWING, SILVER-Y	axle		
	SIX-SPOT BURNET, VAPOURER	—containing revolving axle	LIVE AXLE	
Geometers	BEAUTY, CARPET, EMERALD	—dead with independent		
	MAGPIE, MOTTLED UMBER	half-shafts	DE DION	
	PALE BRINDLED BEAUTY	—not revolving	DEAD AXLE	
	PEPPERED, PUG, SWALLOWTAIL	—with		
	THORN, WINTER	half-shafts revolving with		
gooseberry moth	ABRAXAS	the wheels	FLOATING AXLE	
Hawk moths	BEE HAWK	pivoting axle casing	SWING AXLE	
	CONVOLVULUS HAWK	bar on front and rear	BUMPER	
	DEATH'S HEAD HAWK, EMPEROR	body	SHELL	
	EYED HAWK, HUMMING-BIRD HAWK	—in one piece	MONOCOQUE	
	LIME HAWK, PINE HAWK	booster	SUPERCHARGER	
	POPLAR HAWK		TURBOCHARGER	
	(SMALL) ELEPHANT HAWK	brake types	BAND, DISC, DRUM	
magpie moth	ABRAXAS	braking system		
night-flying	BUFF-TIP	—front	FWB	
	BULRUSH WAINSCOT	—self-correcting	ABS	
	BURNISHED BRASS	—using		
	COMMON SWIFT, DRINKER	cables or rods	MECHANICAL	
	GHOST SWIFT, GOAT	oil in pipes	HYDRAULIC	
	GOLDEN PLUSIA, GOLDEN-Y	car with enclosed rear		
	GOLD SPANGLE, GOLD SPOT	compartment	TOWN CAR	
	GOLD SWIFT, HERALD, KITTEN	clutch types	CONE, PLATE, SCROLL	
	LACKEY, LAPPET	computerised		
	LARGE YELLOW UNDERWING	suspension	(RE)ACTIVE SUSPENSION	
	LEOPARD, LOBSTER	cooling system	FAN, RADIATOR	
	MAP-WINGED SWIFT	decorative line	COACH-LINE	
	NOCTUID, NORTHERN SWIFT	designer		
	OLD LADY, ORANGE SWIFT, OWLET	—British	CHAPMAN, HELPERT	
	PUSS, RED-NECKED FOOTMAN		ISSIGONIS	
	RED UNDERWING, SHARK	—Italian	BERTONI, (PININ)FARINA	
	TUSSOCK		GANDINI, GHIA, GUIGIARO	
plant pests	ABRAXAS, BRINDLED BEAUTY	dilapidated	BANGER, BONE-SHAKER	
	BROWN-TAIL, BUFF-TIP		CRATE, HEAP	
	CABBAGE-WHITE, CLEAR-WING, CHERRY		JALOP(P)Y, RATTLETRAP	
	CODLING, DIAMOND BLACK, GOAT	direction indicator	TRAFFICATOR	
	GOOSEBERRY, LACKEY, LEAFROLLER	double overhead camshaft	DOHC	

drive-shaft/axle connection	DIFFERENTIAL (GEAR)
early car	VOITURETTE
eccentric revolving part	CAM
electrical system	ALTERNATOR
	BATTERY, COIL, DISTRIBUTOR
	DYNAMO, FUSE, GENERATOR
	MAGNETO, (SPARK(ING)) PLUG
	WIRING HARNESS
engine	
—cycle	OTTO CYCLE
—double sleeve-valve	KNIGHT ENGINE
—four-stroke	COMPRESSION, EXHAUST
	IGNITION, INDUCTION
—igniting fuel by compression	DIESEL
—types	AIR-COOLED, WATER COOLED
	FOUR-STROKE, TWO-STROKE
—with	
all cylinders cast in one piece	MONOBLOC
cylinders cast in blocks of two	PAIR-CAST
opposed cylinders	FLAT-FOUR
	FLAT-TWIN
overhead inlet and side outlet valves	F-HEAD
rotating piston	ROTARY, WANKEL
side valves	L-HEAD
—on each side	T-HEAD
two blocks of cylinders	BI-BLOCK
epicyclic gear	PLANETARY GEAR
film car	GENEVIEVE
folding rear seat	DICKEY SEAT
	RUMBLE SEAT
footboard	RUNNING BOARD
framework	CHASSIS
gear	
—types	AUTOMATIC
	CONTINUOUSLY VARIABLE
	CRYPTO, EPICYCLIC, MANUAL
	PLANETARY
—wheel	
used for final drive	BEVEL GEAR
	WORM DRIVE
with teeth on internal circumference	ANNULAR GEAR
gears etc	TRANSMISSION
having	
—2 doors	COUPE
—2 rows of seats	SALOON, SEDAN
—folding hood	CABRIOLET, CONVERTIBLE
	DROPHEAD COUPE,
	LANDAULET(TE), RAGTOP
	SOFT-TOP, SPYDER, TOURER
—removable top	HARDTOP

—sloping rear	FASTBACK
—upward opening rear door	ESTATE CAR
	HATCHBACK, STATION WAGON
high-speed car	DRAGSTER, GT
	GRAN TURISMO, HOT ROD
ignition system	ELECTRIC IGNITION
	HOT-TUBE IGNITION
indicator	TRAFFICATOR
inlet valve over exhaust valve	IOE
instruments	AMMETER
	(H)ODOMETER
	OIL PRESSURE GAUGE
	PETROL GAUGE
	REV(OLUTION) COUNTER
	SPEEDOMETER
	WATER TEMPERATURE GAUGE
interior light	COURTESY LIGHT
large car	TOURER, TOURING CAR
—American	GAS-GUZZLER
lubrication system	DRIP FEED, DRY SUMP
	SPLASH LUBRICATION
luxurious car	LIMO(USINE)
jointed shaft driving rear axles	CARDAN
joint in drive-shaft	UNIVERSAL JOINT
makes	
—American	AUBURN, BUICK, CADILLAC
	CHEVROLET, CHRYSLER, CORD
	DODGE, DUESENBERG, EDSEL, ESSEX
	FORD, GENERAL MOTORS, GM, HUDSON
	KAISER, LA SALLE, LENOX
	LINCOLN, MARMON, MCFARLAN
	MERCER, NASH, OAKLAND, OLDSMOBILE
	OVERLAND, PACKARD, PIERCE-ARROW
	PONTIAC, SIMPLEX, STUDEBAKER
	STUTZ, TUCKER, WELCH
—Austrian	STEYR-PUCH
—Australian	HOLDEN
—Belgian	MINERVA
—British	AC, ALLARD, ALVIS
	ARMSTRONG-SIDDELEY
	ASTON MARTIN
	AUSTIN(-HEALEY), BEAN, BENTLEY
	BOND, BRISTOL, CLYNO, CONNAUGHT
	CROSSLEY, DAIMLER, FORD
	FRAZER-NASH, GILBERN, GUY
	HEALEY, HILLMAN, HRG, HUMBER
	INVICTA, JAGUAR, JENSEN, JOWETT
	LAGONDA, LANCHESTER, LEA-FRANCIS
	LEYLAND, LOTUS, MARCOS, MG
	MINI(JEM), MORGAN, MORRIS
	PANTHER, PIPER, RELIANT, RILEY
	ROLLS-ROYCE, ROVER, SINGER
	STANDARD, SUNBEAM(-TALBOT),

	SWALLOW, TRIUMPH, TVR
	VANDEN PLAS, VAUXHALL
	WESTFIELD, WOLSELEY
—Czech	SKODA, TATRA
—Dutch	DAF
—French	AMILCAR, BEDELIA, BOLLEE
	BUGATTI, CITROEN, DE DIETRICH
	DE DION, DECAUVILLE, DELAGE
	DELAHAYE, DELAUNEY, FACEL VEGA
	HISPANO-SUIZA, HOTCHKISS
	PANHARD(-LEVASSOR), PEUGEOT
	RENAULT, SIMCA, TALBOT-LAGO
	VESPA, VOISIN
—German	AMPHICAR, AUDI, AUTO-UNION
	BMW, BORGWARD, DKW
	EUROCAR, GLAS, HEINKEL
	MAYBACH, MERCEDES(-BENZ)
	MESSERSCHMITT, NOBEL, NSU, OPEL
	PORSCHE, TRABANT, VOLKSWAGEN
	WARTBURG
—Italian	ABARTH, ALFA ROMEO
	CISITALIA, CIZETA MORODER
	DE TOMASO, ERMINA, FERRARI
	FIAT, ISO, ISOTTA-FRASCHINI
	ITALA, LAMBORGHINI, LANCIA
	MASERATI, SIATA
—Japanese	COLT, DAIHATSU, DATSUN
	HONDA, ISUZU, MAZDA
	MITSUBISHI, SUBARU, SUZUKI
	TOYOTA
—Korean	HYUNDAI
—Malaysian	PROTON
—Russian	GAZ, LADA, MOSKVITCH
	SPARTAK, TCHAIKA, VOLGA
	ZAPOROZHETS, ZAZ, ZIL, ZIM
—Spanish	HISPANO-SUIZA
	PEGASO, SEAT
—Swedish	SAAB, VOLVO
—Swiss	MONTEVERDI
—Yugoslav	SANA, YUGO
	(*see also* **motor racing**)
manufacturer's name	MARQUE
old	
—car	MODEL T (FORD)
	TIN LIZZIE
with	
—back-to-back seating	DOS-A-DOS
—face-to-face seating	VIS-A-VIS
—carburettor	SURFACE CARBURETTOR
—clutch	SCROLL CLUTCH
—ignition coil	TREMBLER COIL
—lubrication system	DRIP FEED
	SPLASH LUBRICATION
—open touring car	PHAETON
—tyred	CLINCHER
offset cylinder	DESAXE

open car	TOURER
panel housing instruments	CONSOLE
	DASHBOARD
pioneers	
—American	APPERSON, BRISCOE, BUICK
	CHADWICK, CHAPIN, CHRISTIE
	CHRYSLER, CORD, DOBLE
	DODGE, DUESENBERG, DURANT
	DURYEA, EARL, FLANDERS
	FORD, FRAZER, KETTERING, KING
	MAXWELL, METZ, NASH, OLDS
	PENNINGTON, PORTER, SLOAN
	STANLEY, STUTZ, THOMAS, WHITE
	WILLS, WILLYS, WINTON
—Austrian	LEDWINKA, MARKUS, PORSCHE
—Belgian	LENOIR
—British	AUSTIN, BENTLEY, CHAPMAN
	HAYNES, ISSIGONIS, LANCHESTER
	LAWSON, MORRIS, ROLLS, ROYCE
	SIMMS
—French	BOLLEE, CHARRON, CITROEN
	CLEMENT, COATALEN, DARRACQ
	DE DION, DELAGE, LAVASSOR
	PEUGEOT, RENAULT, SERPOLLET
	VOISIN
—German	BENZ, DAIMLER, HORSCH
—Italian	BUGATTI, FERRARI, JANO
—Swiss	BIRKIGT, CHEVROLET
	ROESCH
planetary gear	EPICYCLIC GEAR
police car	BLACK MARIA, PANDA
	PROWL CAR
power rating	ALAM RATING
	BHP, BRAKE HORSEPOWER
—French	CV, CHEVAL-VAPEUR
—German	PFERDE STARKE, PS
pre-1905	VETERAN
1905-1919	EDWARDIAN
1919-1930	VINTAGE
procession	MOTORCADE
rear of body	TONNEAU
revolutions per minute	REVS, RPM
ring sealing piston	JUNK RING
	PISTON RING
rod	

—carrying cams which
  operate (overhead)
  valves
	(OVERHEAD)CAMSHAFT

—connecting piston to crankshaft	CON(NECTING) ROD
—engine to rear wheels	TRANSMISSION SHAFT
—moving overhead valve	PUSHROD
—operating pushrod	ROCKER(-ARM)
—long rocker-arm	WALKING BEAM
—securing road wheels	KING-PIN

safety belt	SEAT BELT
—light	BRAKE LIGHT
	HAZARD WARNING LIGHT
saloon car (American)	SEDAN
small two-seater	RUNABOUT
specially made	CUSTOM-BUILT
sports car	ROADSTER
steam car	DOBLE, SERPOLLET
	STANLEY, WHITE
steering	STEERING COLUMN
	STEERING WHEEL, TRACK ROD
	WHEELS
strengthening bar	ROLL-BAR, ROLL-CAGE
suspension	
—independent	
front wheel	IFS
rear wheel	IRS
—system parts	SHOCK ABSORBER
	SPRING
supercharger	BLOWER
taxation class	RAC RATING
transmission	
—connection	UNIVERSAL (JOINT)
—disconnecting system	CLUTCH
—gears	CROWN WHEEL, PINION
—shaft	JACK SHAFT, HALF-SHAFT
	PROP(ELLOR) SHAFT
—system using	
leather or rubber	
belts	BELT DRIVE
petrol engine to drive	
a dynamo	PETROL-ELECTRIC
wheel rubbing on	
flywheel	FRICTION DRIVE
valve	
—chain-driven	ROTARY VALVE
—in four-stroke engine	POPPET VALVE
—opened and closed	
mechanically	DESMODROMIC VALVES
—overhead	OHV
—side	SV
—sliding	SLEEVE VALVE
wheel	
—maintaining momentum	FLYWHEEL
—with	
fine steel spokes	WIRE WHEEL
wooden or steel	
spokes	ARTILLERY WHEEL
wooden frame with steel	
plates	ARMOURED CHASSIS
motorcycle	
circuits	
—Australia	SYDNEY
—Austria	SALZBURG
—Belgium	SPA FRANCORCHAMPS
—Brazil	RIO DE JANEIRO

—Britain	BRANDS HATCH
	CADWELL PARK
	DONINGTON, DOUGLAS
	SILVERSTONE, SNETTERTON
—Czechoslovakia	BRNO
—Finland	KOUVOLA
—France	LE CASTELLE, LE MANS
	MONTL(H)ERY
—Germany	NURBURGRING
—Holland	ASSO
—Hungary	HUNGARORING
—Italy	MISANO ADRIATICO
—Japan	SUGO, SUZUKO
—Netherlands	ASSEN
—Portugal	VILA REAL
—Spain	JARAMA
—Sweden	ANDERSTOP
—USA	MONTEREY
—Yugoslavia	RIJEKA
luggage carrier	PANNIER
make	
—American	ACE, HARLEY-DAVIDSON
	HENDERSON, INDIAN
	PIERCE ARROW
—Belgian	FN, GILLET-HERSTAL
	MINERVA, SAROLEA
—British	ABC, AJS, ARIEL
	BROUGH (SUPERIOR), BSA
	CHATER-LEA, COTTON
	COVENTRY EAGLE, DOT, DOUGLAS
	EXCELSIOR, FRANCIS-BARNETT
	GRINDLEY-PEERLESS, HRD
	JAMES, MATCHLESS
	MONTGOMERY, NEW IMPERIAL
	NORTON, PANTHER, REX-ACME
	RALEIGH, ROYAL RUBY
	RUDGE-WHITWORTH, SCOTT
	SUNBEAM, TRIUMPH
	VAUXHALL, VELOCETTE
	VICTORIA, VINCENT, ZENITH
—Czech	CZ, JAWA
—Danish	NUMBUS
—Dutch	EYSINK
—French	DAX, PEUGEOT
	RATIER, SUBLIME
—German	ARDIE, BMW, DKW
	IMPERIA, MABECO, MAICO
	MZ, NSU, PATRIA
	SCHUTTOFF, SIMSON
	SPERBER, VICTORIA, ZUNDAPP
—Italian	AERMACCHI, APRILIA
	AZZARIA, BENELLI, BIANCHI
	DUCATI, GILERA, LAVERDI
	MORINO, MOTO GUZZI
	MV AGUSTA, PARILLA
	RONDINE

—Japanese	HONDA, KAWASAKI
	SUZUKI, YAMAHA
—Spanish	BULTACO, MONTESA
—Swedish	HUSQVARNA
—Swiss	CONDOR, MOTOSACOCHE
	UNIVERSAL
passenger	
—compartment	SIDECAR
—seat	PILLION
races	DIRT-TRACK, GRASS-TRACK
	ROAD, SPEEDWAY, TRACK
riders (motocross)	
—Australian	LEISK
—Belgian	GEBOERS
—British	THORPE
riders (track)	
—American	GARDNER, LAWSON
	MAMMOLA, RAINEY
	SCHWANTZ
—Australian	DOOHAN, MAGEE
	GARDNER, GODDARD
—Belgian	DE COSTER, ROBERT
—British	ARMSTRONG, DUKE
	FRITH, GUTHRIE, HAILWORTH
	HASLAM, KAVANAGH, MACKENZIE
	REDMAN, RYMER, SHEENE, SPENCER
	SURTEES, WALKINSHAW, WOODMAN
—Czech	FRIEDRICHS
—Dutch	SPANN
—French	RUGGIA, SARRON, VIEIRA
—German	PREIN, ROTH
—Irish	WOODS
—Italian	AGOSTINI, CALDALORA
	GIANOLA, GRESINI, LORENZETTI
	MASETTI, MILLANI
	PASOLINI, PROVINI
	REGGIANI, UBBIALI
—Japanese	KATOH, MIYAZAKI, OHSHIMA
—Spanish	JARRICA, MARTINEZ, PONS
—Swedish	ABERG, CORNU, LUNDIN
	NILSONN, TRIBBLIN
trophy	EUROLANTIC TROPHY
	ULSTER TOURIST TROPHY

motor racing

assembly area	PADDOCK
body shell	MONOCOQUE
cars	
—American	CHEVROLET, CUNNINGHAM
	DE SOTO, DUESENBERG, KISSEL
	MARMON, MILLER, THOMAS FLYER
—British	ALVIS, ARROWS, BENETTON
	BENTLEY, BRABHAM, BRM
	COOPER, ERA, FRAZER-NASH
	HESKETH, JAGUAR, LOLA, LOTUS
	MARCH, MCLAREN
	(TALBOT-)SUNBEAM

	THOMAS, TYRELL, VANWALL
	SHADOW, WILLIAMS
—French	BALLOT, BUGATTI, CHARRON
	DE DIETRICH, DELAGE, GORDINI
	HISPANO-SUIZA, LIGIER
	MATRA, MORS, RENAULT
	SALMSON, (TALBOT-)DARRACQ
	VOISIN
—German	AUTO-UNION, DAIMLER-BENZ
	MERCEDES, PORSCHE
	ZAKSPEED
—Italian	ALFA-ROMEO, FERRARI
	FIAT, ITALA, LANCIA, MASERATI
	MINARDI, OSELLA
—Japanese	HONDA
circuits	
—America	BROOKLYN, DETROIT
	INDIANAPOLIS
	LONG BEACH, MEADOWLANDS
	PEBBLE BEACH, PHOENIX
	RIVERSIDE, SEBRING
	WATKINS GLEN
—Argentina	BUENOS AIRES
—Australia	ADELAIDE
—Austria	OSTERREICHRING
—Belgium	SPA (FRANCORCHAMPS)
	ZOLDER
—Brazil	INTERLAGOS, JACAREPAGUA
	RIO DE JANEIRO, SAO PAULO
—Britain	AINTREE, BRANDS HATCH
	BROOKLANDS, DONINGTON
	MALLORY PARK, SANTA POD
	SILVERSTONE, THRUXTON
—Canada	MONTREAL, MOSSPORT
—France	CLERMONT-FERRAND
	DIJON, LE CASTELLET
	MONTLHERY, PAU, PAU
	RICARD, REIMS, ROUEN
—Germany	HOCKENHEIM
	NURBURGRING
—Holland	ZANDVOORT
—Hungary	BUDAPEST, HUNGARORING
—Ireland	DUNDROD
—Italy	MODENA, MONZA, PESCARA
—Japan	SUZUKA
—Mexico	MEXICO CITY
—Monaco	MONTE CARLO
—Morocco	CASABLANCA
—Portugal	OPORTO
—San Marino	IMOLA
—Sicily	SYRACUSE
—South Africa	KYALAMI
—Spain	BARCELONA, JARAMA
	JEREZ
—Sweden	ANDERSTORP
—Switzerland	BERNE

drivers			GRAND PRIX, INDIANAPOLIS
—American	ANDRETTI, CHEEVER		KAISERPREIS, LE MANS
	FOYT, GINTHER, JONES		MILLE MIGLIA, SEBRING
	MEARS, OLDFIELD, RAHAL		TARGA FLORIO
	RUTHERFORD, UNSER	safety barrier	ARMCO, STRAW BALE
—Argentinian	FANGIO, GONZALES	sharp bend	CHICANE
	REUTEMAN	smooth tyres	SLICKS
—Australian	BRABHAM, JONES	starting area	GRID
—Austrian	BERGER, LAUDA, RINDT	team	ECURIE
—Belgian	BOUTSEN, ICKX	trophy	(see separate entry)
—Brazilian	FITTIPALDI, PIQUET, SENNA	**motor rallying**	
—British	AMON, BARNATO, BIRKIN	drivers	
	BROOKS, BRUNDLE, CAMPBELL	—Belgian	ICKX, DELFERRIER, TARIN
	CLARK, COBB, COLLINS, DON	—British	ARTHUR, BROOKES, COWAN
	FAIRMAN, GERARD, HAWTHORN		HOPKIRK, LLEWELLIN, LOVELL
	HERBERT, HILL, HUNT, IRELAND		MCRAE, POND, SHORT, WILSON
	MANSELL, MOSS, SALVATORI	—Finnish	ALEN, ARIKKALA
	SEAMAN, SEAGRAVE, STEWART		KANK(K)UNEN, MIKKOLA
	THOMAS, TYRELL, WARWICK		SALONEN, SILANDER, VATANEN
	WATSON	—French	AURIOL, FONTENAY, LAFITTE
—Canadian	VILLENEUVE		MUSMARRA, SABY, TAMBAY
—Dutch	LUYENDYK, SPYKER		WAMBERGUE
—Finnish	ROSBERG	—German	SCHWARZ
—French	ARNOUX, BEHRA	—Italian	BIASSION, CERRATO
	CHIRON, LAFITTE, PROST	—Spanish	JUNCOSA, MOYA
	TAMBAY, TRINTIGNANT		PRIETO-PEREZ, REPO, SAINZ
—German	MASS, STUCK	—Swedish	BERGLUND, CARLSSON
	VON BRAUCHITSCH		CEDERBERG, EKLUND
—Italian	ALBORETO, ASCARI		ERIKSSON, PARMANDER
	CARACCIOLA, DE ANGELIS		SUNDSTROM, WALDEGAARD
	DE CESARIS, ETANCELIN	—New Zealand	MILLEN
	FARINA, NUVOLARI, PATRESE	rallies	
—Japanese	NAKAJIMO, SUZUKI	—Africa	EAST AFRICA SAFARI
—New Zealand	AMON, HULME, MCLAREN		IVORY COAST, KENYA SAFARI
—South African	SCHECKTER		PARIS-DAKAR
—Siamese	BIRA(BONGSE)	—America	PIKE'S PEAK
—Swedish	JOHANNSON, NILSSON	—Britain	(LOMBARD)RAC, SCOTTISH
	PETERSEN		ULSTER
—Swiss	REGAZZONI	—Corsica	TOUR OF CORSICA
end-of-race signal	CHEQUERED FLAG	—Europe	PIRELLI CLASSIC
famous cars		—Finland	THOUSAND LAKES
—Campbell	BLUEBIRD	—France	MONTE CARLO
—Eldridge	MEPHISTOPHELES	—Greece	ACROPOLIS
—Jenatzy	LA JAMAIS CONTENTE	—Ireland	CIRCUIT OF IRELAND
—Noble	THRUST 2	—Italy	SAN REMO
—Seagrave	GOLDEN ARROW	**mountain**	ALP, BEN, FELL, SIERRA, TOR
	SUNBEAM TIGER	including: equipment	
—Zborowski	CHITTY-CHITTY-BANG-BANG	mountaineers	
	HIGHAM SPECIAL	some hill ranges	
first at start	POLE POSITION	boots	KLETTERSCHUHE, VIBRAM
ground-hugging design	GROUND EFFECT	central mass	MASSIF
jet-powered	THRUST 2	climbing equipment	ALPENSTOCK
maintenance bay	PIT		CRAMPON, ETRIER
race	DAYTONA 24 HOURS		EVEREST PACK, ICE-AXE
	FORMULA 1,2,3,3000		JUMAR, KARABINER
	FORMULA FORD		PIOLET, PITON, ROPE

clip for rope	JUMAR, KARABINER
crack in	
—glacier	BERGSCHRUND, CREVASSE
—rock	CHIMNEY
descend by double ropes	ABSEIL, RAPPEL
description	OROGRAPHY
dividing ridge	DIVIDE, WATERSHED
facing	
—away from	
Equator	OPACO, SCHATTENSEITE
—towards	
Equator	ADRET(TO), SONNENSEITE
flat-topped	MESA
—in plain	BUTTE
formed by	
—cracking	MASSIF
—deposit on	
surface	MOUNTAIN OF ACCUMULATION
—earth movement	FOLDED MOUNTAIN
—erosion of surrounding	
rock	
	MOUNTAIN OF CIRCUMDENUDATION
	MOUNTAIN OF CIRCUMEROSION
	RELICT MOUNTAIN
—lowering of land around	HORST
—raising between faults	BLOCK
from which Moses	
—descended with	
the tablets	SINAI
—saw the Promised Land	PISGAH
group of mountain systems	CORDILLERA
high mountain	ALP
hill with one steep and	
one gentle slope	CRAG-AND-TAIL
—France	PUY
hills	
—England	BERKSHIRE DOWNS
	CHEVIOTS, CHILTERNS
	CLENT, CLEVELAND HILLS
	COTSWOLDS, DARTMOOR, EXMOOR
	GOG MAGOG HILLS, HAMPSHIRE DOWNS
	LINCOLN WOLDS, MALVERN, MENDIPS
	NORTH DOWNS, PURBECK DOWNS
	SOUTH DOWNS, THE WEALD
	WHITE HORSE HILLS
	YORKSHIRE MOORS
	YORKSHIRE WOLDS
—Scotland	CAMPSIE FELLS
	LAMMERMUIR, MOORFOOT
	OCHIL, PENTLAND
	SIDLAW, TWEEDSMUIR
ice-axe	PIOLET
in mythology	OSSA, PELION
metal peg	PITON
mountain	
—building	OROGENESIS, OROGENY

—dwelling	MONTICOLOUS
mountain in	
—Afghanistan	GUL KOH, NOSHAQ
—Africa	BERG
	BATIAN, DUWONI, EDWARD PEAK
	HAKANNSON, HUMPHREY'S PEAK
	IOLANDA PEAK, KARISIMBI
	KIBARA, KILIMANJARO, KULAL
	KUNDELUNGU, MARGHERITA PEAK
	MARUNGU, MOUNT BAKER
	MOUNT ELGON, MOUNT EMIN
	MOUNT GESSI, MOUNT KENYA
	MOUNT STANLEY, NGALIEMMA
	NYIRU, RUNGWE, RUWENZORI
	SELLA PEAK, TABLE MOUNTAIN
	THABANA NTLENYANA
	UHURU POINT, UMBEATO PEAK
—Alaska	BLACKBURN, BONA
	FAIRWEATHER, FORAKER
	LUCANIA, KING PEAK
	MCKINLEY, ST ELIAS, SANFORD
	SHISHALOIN, STEELE
—Albania	GRIBA, KORABI
—Algeria	ATAKOR
—Alps	EIGER, MATTERHORN
—Andorra	PLA DEL ESTANY
—Angola	SERRA VIGO
—Antarctica	ELIZABETH, EPPERLEY
	FALLA, FISHER, GARDNER
	GIOVINETTO, KAPLAN, KIRKPATRICK
	LISTER, LONG GABLES, MACKELLAR
	MARKHAM, MINTO, NANSEN
	OSTENSO, SHINN, SIDLEY
	TYREE, VINSON MASSIF, WADE
—Arabia	(D)JEBEL
	JEBEL HADHAR, JEBEL RAZIKH
—Argentina	ACONCAGUA, AMEGHINO
	ANTOFALLA, BONETE
	CERRO MANSO, EL MUERTO
	GONZALEZ, INCAHUASI
	LLULLAILLACO, MERCEDARIO
	NACIMIENTO, OJOS DE SALADO
	PISSIS, POQUIS, RAMADA
	TRES CRUCES, TUPUNGATO
—Assam	HKAKABO RAZI
—Australia	AUGUSTUS, BARRINGTON
	BARTLE FRERE, BEN LOMOND
	BLACK SUGARLOAF, BOGONG
	HEUGHLIN, KOSCIUSKO
	LINDESAY, MAGNET
	MOUNT MEHARRY, MOUNT ZIEL
	OXLEY'S PEAK, ROUND MOUNTAIN
—Austria	GROSSGLOCKNER
—Bahamas	MOUNT ALVERNIA
—Barbados	MOUNT HILLABY
—Belgium	BOTRANGE

—Belize	VICTORIA PEAK
—Bhutan	KHULA KANGRI
—Bolivia	ANCOHUMA, ILLAMPU
	ILLIMANI, NEVADA SAJAMA
	OLLAGUE, PALOMANI
	PUPAYA, SONEQUERA, SORATA
	TOCORPURI, TUNARI, UBINA
—Bulgaria	MUSALA, SYUTKYA
—Burkina Faso	MOUNT TEMA
—Burma	HKAKADO RAZI
	MOUNT VICTORIA
—Brazil	MOUNT RORAIMA
	PICO DE BANDIERA
—Cambodia	(*see* Kampuchea *below*)
—Cameroon	CAMEROON MOUNTAIN
—Canada	KEEL PEAK, ALBERTA
	ASSINIBOINE, CAMPBELL, CHRISTIE
	COLUMBIA, EDITH CAVELL
	EDUNI, FORBES, KING GEORGE
	LOGAN, LYELL, MITCHELL
	NELSON, ST ELIAS, SELOUS
	SIR DOUGLAS, RAINIER
	ROBSON, VANCOUVER, WOOD
—Canary Islands	MOUNT TEIDE
—Central African Republic	MOUNT GAOU
—Chad	EMI KOUSSI
—Chile	ARENALES, AZUFRE
	CAMPANARIO, CASTILLO, COPAHUE
	COPIAPO, CORCOVADO, CUMBRERA
	EL MUERTO, HORNIPIREN
	HUDSON, ILIAMA, ISLUGA
	LLULLAILLACO, LONGAVI, MACA
	MAINO, MELIMOYU, MERCADARIO
	O'HIGGINS, OJOS DE SALADO
	OSORNO, PETEROA, PIRAMIDE
	PISSIS, SAN LORENZO
	SILLAJHUAY, SOCAMPA
	TINGUIRIRICA, TRES CRUCES
	TRONADOR, TUPUNGATO
	VALENTIN, VILLARRICA
—China	AMNE MACHIN, DULAN KARA
	ILISU, KONGUR, MINYA KONKA
	MUNKU SARDYK, MUZTAGH ATA
	PEAK POPEDY, TUGADIR
	TURGEN ULA
—Colombo	COLON, HUILA
	PICO CRISTOBAL, SOTARA
	TOLIMA
—Comoros	MOUNT KARTALA
—Corsica	L'INCUDINE, MONTE CINTO
	MONTE ROTONDO
—Costa Rica	BLANCO, CHIRRIPO
—Crete	IDHI
—Cuba	PICO TURQUINO
—Cyprus	MOUNT OLYMPUS

—Dominica	IMRAY'S VIEW
—Dominican Republic	PICO DUARTE
	TRUJILLO
—East Indies	ENGGEA, IDENBERG TOP
	KERINTJE, KINABALU
	MOUNT BANGETA
	MOUNT ALBERT EDWARD
	MOUNT GILUWE, MOUNT HERBERT
	MOUNT HOGAN, MOUNT KINABALU
	MOUNT KUBOR
	MOUNT LEONARD DARWIN
	MOUNT SARAWAKET
	MOUNT VICTORIA
	MOUNT WILHELM, NGGA PULU
	PEAK JULIANA, PEAK MANDALA
	PEAK SUKARNO, PEAK TRICORA
	PEAK WILHELMINA
	PEAK WISNUMURTI
	PUNCAK JAYAKUSUMU
	SUNDAY PEAK
—Ecuador	ANTISANA, CHIMBORAZO
	COTOPAXI, PICHINCHA
	SANGAY
—Egypt	JEBEL KATHERINA
—England	BOWFELL, CONISTON OLD MAN
	COOMBE HILL, CROSS FELL
	DUNKERY BEACON, ESK PIKE
	FAIRFIELD, GARROWBY HILL
	GREAT GABLE, HELVELLYN
	LEITH HILL, PILLAR FELL
	PILOT HILL, SCAFELL(PIKE)
	SKIDDAW, THE CHEVIOT
	THE PEAK, THE WREKIN
	URRA MOOR, WALBURY HILL
—Equatorial Guinea	MOCA, MOKA
—Ethiopia	AMARA, AMEDAMIT
	BADDA, BIRHAN, DENDI
	GITCH, GARA GORFU
	GUNA, RAS DAJAN, RAS DASHAN
	SARENGA
—Europe/Asia	DYKH TAU, DZHANGI TAU
	EL BRUS, GESTOLA, JANGA
	JANGI TAU, KAZBEK, KATYJNH TAU
	KOSHTANTAU, KUNJUM MISHURGI
	MISHIRGI, PIK PUSHKIN
	PIK RUSTAVELI, SHKHARA, TETNULD
—Fiji	MOUNT TOMANIIVI
	MOUNT VICTORIA
—Finland	HALTIATUNTURI
—France	MONTAGNE
	AIGUILLE DU MIDI
	DENT DU GEANT, L'INDEX
	MONT BLANC, MONT VALLIER
	POINTE MONTCALM
	TETE BLANCHE, TOUR RONDE
—Gabon	MONT IBOUNDJI

—Germany	BERG
	FICHTELBERG, ZUGSPITZE
—Greece	ELIKON, ERIMANTHOS
	IMITTOS, LIKODHIMOS
	MAVROVOUNI, OITI, OXIA
	OLIMBOS, OLYMPUS
	PANAKHAIKON, PARNASSOS
	PARNASSUS, PARNIS
	PARNON, PERISTERI, PILION
	SMOLIKAS, TIMFRISTOS, TRINGIA
	TZOUMERKA, YERAKOVOUNI
—Guatemala	TAJUMULCO
—Guinea	MOUNT NIMBA
—Guyana	MOUNT RORAIMA
—Haiti	PIC LA SELLE
—Hawaii	MAUNA KEA, MAUNA LOA
—Himalayas	ANNAPURNA, CHANGTSE
	CHO OYU, CHOMO LONZO
	CHUMALHARI, DHAULAGIRI
	EVEREST, FANG, GOSAINTHAN
	GUARI SANKAR, GURLA MANDHATA
	GYACHUNG KANG, HIMALCHULI
	JANNU, K2, KAILAS, KAMET
	KANGBACHEN, KANCHENJUNGA
	KHINYANG, KULAKHANGRI, LANGPHU
	LHOTSE, MAKALU, MANASLU
	MOLAMENQING, NAMONA BARWA
	NANDA DEVI, NANGA PARBAT
	NGOJUMBA RI, NUPTSE
	PHOLA GANGCHEN, SAGARMATHA
	SHARTSE, SHISHMA PANGMA
	YALUNG KANG, ZEMU GAP
—Honduras	CERRO LAS MINAS
—Hungary	KEKES
—Iceland	HVANNADALSHNUKUR
—India	ANAI MADI, NANDA DEVI
—Indonesia	MOUNT SUKARNO
	NGGA PULA, PUNCAK JAYA
—Iran	GUH KUH, KUH-E-BUL
	KUH-E-HAZARAN, KUH-E-KHAIZ
	KUH-E-KONJ, KUHRAN
	MOUNT DEMAVENDZARD KHU
—Ireland	BAURTREGAUM, BEENKERAGH
	BRANDON, CAHER
	CARRANTUOHILL, CARRAUNTUAL
	ERRIGAL, GALTYMORE
	KIPPURE, LUGNAQUILLIA
	MULLACLEEVAUN, MWEELREA
	NEPHIN, SAWEL, SLIEVE DONARD
	TROSTRAN
—Isle of Man	SNAEFELL
—Italy	CORNO GRANDE, LA META
	MONTE ALBURNO, MONTE AMIATA
	MONTE BIANCO, MONTE CASSINO
	MONTE CATRIA, MONTE CERVATI
	MONTE CIMONE, MONTE CORNO

	MONTE EBRO, MONTE PAPA
	MONTE POLLINO, MONTE VELINO
—Ivory Coast	MONT TOUKUI
—Jamaica	BLUE MOUNTAIN
—Japan	FUJI(YAMA)
—Jordan	JABAL RAMM, HAR MERON
	MOUNT ATZMON
—Kampuchea	MOUNT KA KUP
—Kashmir/Nepal	BATURA MUZTAGH
	BILAPHOND, CHOGOLISA, DASPAR
	DIAMIR, , DISTEGHIL SAR
	GASHERBRUM, GOLDEN THRONE
	KANJUT SAR, KHULA KANGRI
	KUN, MAMOSTONG KANGRI
	MASHARBRUM, MOUNT SER
	MUZTAGH ATA, NANGA PARBAT
	NUN, QUNGUR, RAKAPOSHI
	SALTORO KANGRI, SASER KANGRI
	SHINGSHAL, SHISHPARE
	SKYANG KANGRI, TERAM KANGRI
	TIRICH MIR, TRIVOR
	ULUGH MUZTAGH, WHITE NEEDLE
	YUKSHIN GARDAS SAR, ZASKA
	(*see also* Himalayas *above*)
—Kenya	MOUNT KENYA
—Korea	HALLA SAN, PAITOUSHAN
	PEKTU SAN
—Laos	PHOU BIA, PHOU LEI LENG
	PHOU SAN
—Lebanon	ARUBA, JEBEL SANNIN
	QURNET ES SAUDA
—Lesotho	THABANA NTLENYANA
	THADENTSONYANE
—Liberia	MOUNT NIMBA
—Libya	PICO BETTE
—Liechtenstein	GRAUSPITZE
—Luxemburg	BOURGPLATZ
—Madagascar	ANKARATRA
	MAROMOKOTRO
—Malaysia	MOUNT KINABALU
—Malawi	MOUNT SAPITWA
—Mali	HOMBORI TONDO
—Mauritius	BLACK RIVER MOUNTAIN
—Mexico	CITLALTEPETL, COLIMA
	IXTACCIHUATL
	POPOCATEPETL, TANOITARO
	TOLUCA, YEOTEPEC
	ZEMPOALTEPEC
—Mongolia	MONH HAYRHAN
—Morocco	TOUBKAL
—Mozambique	MONTE BINGA
—Namibia	SPITZKOPPIE
—New Zealand	ASPIRING, COBB, COOK
	EGMONT, HECTOR, POLLUX
	RUAPEHU, SEFTON, TAPUAENUKU
	TASMAN, THE TWINS, TYNDALL

—Nicaragua	PICO MOGOTON
—Niger	MONT GREBOUN
—Nigeria	DIMLANG
—North Africa	(D)JEBEL
	DJEBEL TOUBKAL
—North America	ADAMS, BALDY, BAKER
	CHARLESTON, CLOUD, COWEN
	DELANO, ELBERT, FREMONT
	GANNET PEAK, GRAND TETON
	HARVARD, HOLY CROSS, HOOD
	LASSEN, LONGS PEAK, MANSFIELD
	MARCY, MEDICINE BOW PEAK
	MITCHELL, MONARCH, PIKES PEAK
	RAINIER, SIERRA BLANCA
	SAN FRANCISCO, SCOTT, SHASTA
	WASHAKIE NEEDLES, WHITNEY
	WIND RIVER, WYOMING
—Norway	GALDHOPIGGEN
—Oman	JEBEL ASH SHAM
—Pakistan	SAD ISTRAGH, TIRICH MIR
—Papua New Guinea	MOUNT WILHELM
—Paraguay	CERRO TATUG
—Peru	AUSANGATE, CHACHANI
	COROPUNA
	HUAMINA, HUASCARAN, MISTI
	PISCO, TOCLARRAJU, YERUPAJA
	YUCAMANI, WALLANARAJU SUR
—Philippines	MOUNT APO
—Poland	RYSY
—Romania	MOLDOVEANU
—Russia	BELUKHA, GORA BELUKHA
	GORA MAS KHAYA, GORA NARODNAYA
	KLYUCHEVSKAYA SOPKA
	PIK KOMMUNIZMA, PIK LENINA
	PIK POBEDA, STALINA PIK
—Rwanda	MOUNT KARISIMBA
—Sardinia	MONTE DEL GENNARGENTU
	MONTE DI SAN VITTORIA
	MONTE LINAS, MONTE RASU
—Scotland	BEN
	AN TEALLACH, AONACH BEAG
	AONACH MOR, BEINN A IBHUIRD
	BEN ALDER, BEN CRUACHAN
	BEN DEARG, BEN EIGHE, BEN HOPE
	BEN LAWERS, BEN LOYAL, BEN MACDHUI
	BEN MORE, BEN NEVIS, BEN VORLICH
	BEN-Y-GLOE, BRAERIACH
	BROAD LAW, CAIRN EIGE
	CAIRN GORM, CAIRN MOR DEARG
	CAIRN TOUL, CREAG MEAGAIDH
	GLAS MAOL, GREAT FELL, HART FELL
	LADHAR BHEINN, LIATHACH, LOCHNAGAR
	MERRICK, SGURR MOR
	SCHIEHALLION, SLIOCH
	THE STORR, SUILVEN
—Senegal	GOUNOU
—Sicily	ETNA, LE MADONIE
	MONTE LAURA
—Sierra Leone	BINTIMANII, KUNDUKONKO
—Somalia	MAKARAKOMBOU
—South Africa	INJASUTI
	TABLE MOUNTAIN
—Spain	MONTE PERDIDO
	MONTES MALDIDOS
	MULHACEN, POSETS
—Sri Lanka	ADAM'S PEAK
	PIDURUTALAGALA
—Sudan	MOUNT KINYETI
—Suriname	JULIANA TOP
—Swaziland	EMLEMBE
—Sweden	KEBNEKALSE
—Switzerland	BREITHORN, DOM
	DUFOURSPITZE, EGGINER
	EIGER, FINSTERAARHORN
	JAGIHORN, JUNGFRAU
	LA DENT BLANCHE, LA LUETTE
	LENZSPITZE, L'EVEQUE
	MATTERHORN, MONCH
	MONTE ROSA, NADELHORN
	POINTE KURTZ, TASCHHORN
	WELLENKUPPE
—Syria	JABAL ASH-SHAIKH
	MOUNT HERMON
—Tanzania	KILIMANJARO
—Tasmania	CRADLE MOUNTAIN
	LEGGES TOR
—Taiwan	MOUNT MORRISON, YU SHAN
—Thailand	DOI INTHANON
—Tibet	JOMA, MINYA KONKA
	NAMCHA BARWA
	(see also Himalayas *above)*
—Tonga	KAO
—Tunisia	DJEBEL CHAMBI
—Turkey	BOZ, BUYUK AGRIDAGA
—Uganda	MOUNT STANLEY
—Uruguay	CERRO DE LAS ANIMAS
—Venezuela	MOUNT RORAIMA
	PICO BOLIVAR
—Vietnam	FAN SI PAN
—Wales	ARAN FAWDDWY, CADER IDRIS
	CARNEDD DAFYDD
	CARNEDD LLEWELYN
	ELIDIR FAWR, FOEL TRAS
	GLYDER FACH, GLYDER FAWR
	MYNYDD, PLYNLIMON
	SNOWDON, TRYFAN, Y GARN
—Western Samoa	MAUGA SILISLI
—Yemen	JEBEL HADHAR
	QUARED AUDILLA
—Yugoslavia	DURMITOR, MAGANIK
	MAGLIC, RAVNO, TRIGLAV
—Zaire	MOUNT STANLEY, NGALIEMA

—Zimbabwe	INYANGANI
mountain over 3000 feet	MUNRO
mountaineers	
—Austrian	JOCHLER, TICHY
—British	BONINGTON, BROWN
	CROUCHER, HUNT, IRVINE
	MALLORY, MUMMERY
	SHIPTON, VENABLES
—Italian	COMPAGNON, LACEDELLI
—Nepali	TENZING
—New Zealand	HILLARY
—Swiss	EGGLER, EISELIN
	LUCHSINGER, REISS
—US	DYHRENFURTH, HOUSTON
overhang of snow	CORNICE
pass	COL
piolet	ICE-AXE
projecting part	BUTTRESS
pyramid-shaped	HORN
range	CORDILLERA, SIERRA
range in	
—Afghanistan	BAND-I-BABAO
	BAND-I-BAIAN, KOH-I-BABA
	HINDU KUSH, PAGHMAN
	PAROPAMBUS
—Africa	DRAKENSBERG, MITUMBA
	MUCHINGA
—Alaska	ALASKA RANGE
	ALEUTIAN RANGE
—Albania	ALPS
—Algeria	AHAGGAR, ATLAS, HOGGAR
	MASSIF DE L'OUARSENIS
—Andorra	PYRENEES
—Angola	BENGUELA PLATEAU, CHELA
	HUMPATO, RAND PLATEAU
—Antarctica	
	TRANS-ANTARCTIC MOUNTAINS
—Arabia	TIHAMAT ASH SHAM
—Argentina	CORDILLERA DE LOS ANDES
	SIERRA DE CORDOBA
—Asia	HIMALAYAS, HINDU KUSH
	KARAKORAM, PAMIR
	TIEN SHAN
—Australia	AUSTRALIAN ALPS
	BLUE MOUNTAINS,
DARLING RANGE, DAVENPORT RANGE	
FLINDERS RANGE, GAWLER RANGE	
	GREAT DIVIDING RANGE
	GREGORY RANGE, GREY RANGE
HAMERSLEY RANGE, KIRBY RANGE	
	LIVERPOOL RANGE
	MACDONNELL RANGES
MIDDLEBACK, MOUNT LOFTY RANGE	
	MUSGRAVE RANGES
	NEW ENGLAND RANGE
	PETERMAN RANGES

	TOMKINSON RANGE
TRUER RANGE, SELWYN RANGE	
STIRLING RANGE, SNOWY MOUNTAINS	
—Austria	ALPS, DOLOMITES
—Belgium	ARDENNES
—Belize	MAYA MOUNTAINS
—Bhutan	HIMALAYAS
—Bolivia	CORDILLERA DE LOS ANDES
	CORDILLERA CENTRAL
	CORDILLERA ORIENTAL
	CORDILLERA REAL
—Brazil	ATLANTIC COAST RANGE
	CORCOVADO
	SIERRA DE MANTIQUEIRA
SIERRA DO MAR, SIERRA GERAL	
	SIERRA GRANDE
	SIERRA TAGUANTINGA
—Bulgaria	STARA PLANINA
—Burma	ARAKAN YOMA, CHIN HILLS
	NAGA HILLS, PEGU YOMA
—Canada	CASCADES, CASSIAR, COAST
	COLUMBUS, DAWSON RANGE
	MACKENZIE, OGILVIE, PELLY
	ROCKIES, ROCKY MOUNTAINS
	SELWYN, ST ELIAS
—Central African	
Republic	CHAINE DE MONGOS
—Chad	ENNEDI, TIBESTI
—Chile	CORDILLERA DE LOS ANDES
—China	ASTIN TAGH, BAYAN KARA SHAN
	HIMALAYAS, KUNLUN SHAN
	NAIN SINGH RANGE
	NAN (LING) SHAN
	TANGLIA RANGE, TIEN SHAN
—Colombia	CORDILLERA CENTRAL
	CORDILLERA DE LOS ANDES
	CORDILLERA OCCIDENTAL
	CORDILLERA ORIENTAL
—Congo	SERRO DO CRYSTAL
—Costa	
Rica	CORDILLERA DEL GUANTACASTE
	CORDILLERA DE TALAMANCA
—Cuba	SIERRA MAESTRA
—Cyprus	KYRENIAN MOUNTAINS
	TROODOS
—Czechoslovakia	BOHEMIAN HIGHLANDS
	GIANT MOUNTAINS, KRKONOSE
	MORAVIAN HIGHLANDS, TATRAS
—Dominican	
Republic	CORDILLERA CENTRAL
—East Indies	CENTRAL BORNEO RANGE
	EAST SUMATRAN RANGE
	JAVANESE RANGE
—Ecuador	CORDILLERA DE LOS ANDES
—Egypt	EASTERN COASTAL RANGE
	SINAI

—England	CUMBRIAN MOUNTAINS	—Lebanon	ANTI-LEBANON
	PENNINES	—Lesotho	DRAKENSBERG
—Ethiopia	CHOKE, EASTERN HIGHLANDS	—Liberia	GUINEA HIGHLANDS
	ERITREAN HIGHLANDS	—Libya	AL ASWAD, AL KUFRAH
	ETHIOPIAN HIGHLANDS, MENDEBO		AL HARUN, JABAL ASSAWDA
	SEMIEN MOUNTAINS	—Liechtenstein	ALPS
	TIGRAY PLATEAU, TIGRE PLATEAU	—Luxemburg	ARDENNES
—Finland	MAANSELKA, SUOMENSELKA	—Madagascar	ANKARATRA
—France	ALPS, BLACK MOUNTAINS		MALAGASY RANGE
	CEVENNES, JURA		MASSIF DU TSARATANANA
	MASSIF CENTRAL	—Malaysia	TRENGGANU HIGHLANDS
	PYRENEES, VOSGES	—Mali	ADRAR DES IFORAS
—Germany	ALPS, BLACK FOREST		MANDIGUE PLATEAU
	ERZ GEBIRGE, SCHWARZWALD	—Mexico	SIERRA MADRE
	THURINGER WALD		SIERRA TARAHUMARE
—Ghana	AFADIATO	—Mongolia	ALTAI MOUNTAINS
—Greece	PINDUS		HANGAYN NURUU
—Guatemala	SIERRA DE CUACHUS	—Morocco	ANTI-ATLAS, ATLAS
	SIERRA DE LAS MINAS	—Mozambique	LEBOMBO RANGE
	SIERRA DE LOS CUCHUMANTANES	—Nepal	HIMALAYAS
	SIERRA MADRE		MAHABHARAT RANGE
—Guinea	FOUTA DJALON	—New Guinea	CENTRAL RANGE
—Guyana	KAMOA, KANUKU, PAKARAIMA		OWEN STANLEY RANGE
	SIERRA ACARAI	—New Zealand	CAMERON
—Haiti	MASSIF DE LA HOTTE		COROMANDEL RANGE, DUNSTAN
—Hungary	BAKONY, BUKK,		HUIARAU RANGE, KAIKOURA RANGE
	CSERHAT, MATRA		KAIMANAWA, KEPLER, LYELL RANGE
—India	ARAVALLI RANGE		MURCHISON, PUKETERAKI RANGE
	CHOTA NAGPUR, EASTERN GHATS		RAUKUMARA RANGE, RICHARDSON
	GRAVALLI, GRAVALTI		RICHMOND RANGE, SOUTHERN ALPS
	HAZARIBAGH RANGE		SPENSER, STUART, TARARUA RANGE
	HIMALAYAS, MAHADEO HILLS		YOUNG RANGE
	MAIKAL RANGE, SATPURA RANGE	—Nicaragua	CORDILLERA DE DARIEN
	WESTERN GHATS, VINDHYA RANGE		CORDILLERA ISABELLA
—Indonesia	BARISAN, BUKIT	—Niger	AIR, AZBINE
	PEQUNUNGAN JAYAWIJAYA		PLATEAU DU DJADO
—Iran	ELBURZ MOUNTAINS	—Nigeria	JOS PLATEAU
	KUHHA-YE-ZAGROS	—North Africa	ATLAS, DES KSOURS
—Iraq	KURDISTAN MOUNTAINS		NOULED NAIL
—Ireland	ANTRIM, CAHA, COMERAGH	—North America	ADIRONDACKS
	CONNEMARA, DONEGAL		ALLEGHENY
	GALTEE, KNOCKMEALDOWN		APPALACHIAN, BIGHORN
	MACGILLYCUDDYS REEKS		BLUE RIDGE, BOSTON
	MAYO, MOURNE, SILVERMINE		CASCADES, COAST RANGE
	SPERRIN, WICKLOW		NOTRE DAME, ROCKIES
—Italy	ALPS, APENNINES, DOLOMITES		ROCKY MOUNTAINS
—Ivory Coast	GUINEA HIGHLANDS		SAN BERNARDINO
	MAN MOUNTAINS		SANGRE DE CRISTO
—Jamaica	BLUE MOUNTAINS		SIERRA NEVADA, ST JUAN
—Japan	HIDA		WHITE, WIND RIVER RANGE
—Jordan	JUDEA MOUNTAINS	—Norway	LANGFJELLENE
—Kampuchea	CHAINE DES CARDAMOMES		SCANDINAVIAN RANGE
—Kashmir	KARAKORAM RANGE	—Oman	GREEN MOUNTAINS
—Kenya	ABERDARE		JABAL AKHDAS
—Korea	NAGNIM SANMAEK	—Pakistan	SALT RANGE
—Laos	ANNAMITIC RANGE		SULAIMAN RANGE

—Panama	SERRANIA DE SAN BLAS	—Wales	BERWYN, BLACK
	SERRANIA DE TABASARA		BRECON BEACONS
—Papua New Guinea	BISMARCK		CAMBRIAN
—Paraguay	CORDILLERA AMAMBAY	—Yemen	YEMEN HIGHLANDS
	SIERRA DE MARACAJU	—Yugoslavia	BALKAN MOUNTAINS
—Peru	CORDILLERA DE LOS ANDES		CARPATHIANS
—Philippines	CORDILLERA CENTRAL		RHODOPE RANGE
	DIUATA RANGE		SAR-PINDUS RANGE
—Poland	BESKIDS, CARPATHIANS		SLOVENE ALPS
	TATRA RANGE	—Zaire	MITUMBA, RUWENZORI
—Portugal	SIERRA DA ESTRELA	—Zambia	MUCHINGA MOUNTAINS
—Romania	CARPATHIANS	—Zimbabwe	ENYANGA, MELSETTER
—Russia	ALTAI, CAUCASUS	region above treeline,	
	KORYAKSKIY KREBET	below snowline	ALPINE
KREBET CHERSKOGO, KOLYMSKIY		—on east slope of Andes	MONTANA
	PAMIR, SREDINNIY KREBET	ridge of hills formed	
	TIEN SHAN, URALS	by erosion	CUESTA
	VERKHOYANSKIY KREBET	rope ladder	ETRIER
—Rwanda	CHAINE DE MITUMBA	rubble at foot of	
—Scotland	CUILLINS, GRAMPIANS, LIATH	—cliff	SCREE, TALUS
	NORTHWEST HIGHLANDS	—glacier	MORAINE
	SOUTHERN UPLANDS	sacred mountain	OMEI
	TROSSACHS	series of	
—Senegal	FOUTA DJALON	—parallel ranges	CORDILLERA
—Sierra Leone	LOMA	—ridges	RANGE
—Somalia	GUBAN	sharp	
—South Africa	DRAKENSBERG	—peak	AIGUILLE
—South		—ridge	ARRETE
America	(CORDILLERA DE LOS) ANDES	sickness	PUNA, SOROCHE
—Spain	CORDILLERA CANTABRICA	slope of	
	PICOS DE EUROPA	—loose stones	SCREE
	PYRENEES, SIERRA MORENA	—mountains	VERSANT
	SIERRA NEVADA	spiked staff	ALPENSTOCK
—Sudan	DARFUR HIGHLANDS	steep rock	CRAG
	NUBIAN MOUNTAINS	study of mountains	OROLOGY
—Suriname	KAYSER GEBERGTE	submarine mountain	GUYOT
	WILHEMINA GEBERGTE	system of	
—Swaziland	LUBOMBO	—parallel ranges	CHAIN
—Sweden	NORRLAND MOUNTAINS	—ranges	CORDILLERA
	SMALANH HIGHLANDS	top of mountain	PEAK
—Switzerland	ALPS	where Noah's ark landed	MOUNT ARARAT
—Syria	ANSARIYAH RANGE	with	
	JABAL AD DURUZ	—pointed summit	PIKE
	JABAL MALULA	—pyramidal peak	HORN
—Taiwan	CHU NYANG SHANMO	**Mozambique**	
—Tanzania	SOUTHERN HIGHLANDS	capital	LM, LOURENCO MARQUES
—Tasmania	HIGHLANDS		MAPUTO
—Tibet	ARKA TAGH, HIMALAYAS	coin	
	KARAKORAM RANGE	—unit	CENTAVO
—Turkey	ARMENIAN PLATEAU	—100 centavos	METICAL
	TAURUS MOUNTAINS	**Mrs**	
	TOROS DAGLARI	Boaz	RUTH
—Uganda	RUWENZORI	Copperfield	DORA
—Venezuela	CORDILLERA DO MERIDA	de Winter	REBECCA
	LA GRAN SABANA	Dombey	EDITH
	SIERRA DE PERIJA	Mopp	CHAR(WOMAN)

Partlett	HEN
Punch	JUDY
muscle	
albumin in muscle	MYOGEN
cell	
—developing from	
myoblast	MYOTUBE
—which produces muscle	MYOBLAST
circular	CONSTRICTOR
	SPHINCTER
contraction	CONVULSION
—of intestines	PERISTALSIS
—spontaneous	MYOGENIC
diseases affecting	
muscles	(*see* **disease**)
fibres attaching	
muscle to bone	TENDON
haemoglobin in muscle	MYOGLOBIN
having two adductor	
muscles	DIMYARIAN
in	
—buttock	GLUTEUS MAXIUMUS
	SUPINATOR
—chest	PECTORAL(IS MAJOR)
	SERRATUS ANTERIOR
—ear	STAPEDIUS
—eye	CILIARY, OBLIQUE, RECTUS
—forearm	EXTENSOR, FLEXOR
	PRONATOR
—head	ZYGOMATIC
—heart	MYOCARDIUM, PACEMAKER
—jaw	MASSETER, MYLOHYOID
—larynx	ARYT(A)ENDID
—loins	PSOAS
—lower leg	EXTENSOR, GASTROCNEMIUS
	SOLEUS
—neck	PLATSUMA, SPLENIUS
	STERNO-MASTOID
—pelvis	PSOAS
—shoulder	DELTOID, TRAPEZIUS
—spermatic cord	CREMASTER
—stomach	DIAPHRAGM
	RECTUS ABDOMINUS
—thigh	HAMSTRING, QUADRICEPS
	SARTORIUS, VASTUS
—thorax	SERRATUS
—upper arm	BICEPS, DELTOID
	TRICEPS
instrument recording	
contractions	MYOGRAPH
muscle sense	KINAESTHESIA
partial contraction	TONE
protein in muscle	MYOSIN
sheath	FASCIA, SARCOLEMMA
straight muscle	RECTUS
study of muscles	MYOLOGY

tissue binding muscles	PERIMYSIUM
tumour	MYOMA
twitching of muscle	FIBRILLATION
types	CARDIAC, SMOOTH
	STRIATED
—smooth	INVOLUNTARY, PLAIN
	VISCERAL
—striated	SKELETAL, STRIPED
	VOLUNTARY
which	
—cannot be	
consciously	
controlled	INVOLUNTARY MUSCLE
	REFLEX MUSCLE
—draws	
away	ABDUCTOR
down	DEPRESSOR
together	ADDUCTOR
—tightens	TENSOR
—turns hand	PRONATOR, SUPINATOR
Muses	PIERIDES
astronomy	URANIA
comedy	THALIA
dance	TERPSICHORE
erotic poetry	ERATO
epic poetry	CALLIOPE
festivals	THALIA
history	CLIO
lyric poetry	EUTERPE
music	EUTERPE
sacred song	POLY(HY)MNIA
tragedy	MELPOMENE
mushroom	(*see* **fungi**)
music	
above	SOPRA
accented	FORZATO, FZ
accidental	FLAT, NATURAL, SHARP
accompaniment	OBBLIGATO
additional bottom	
note	PROSLAMBANOMENOS
agitated	AGITATO
African	KWELA
all performers	TUTTI
allowing freedom of	
interpretation	ALEATORIC
	ALEATORY MUSIC
altered rhythm	SYNCOPATION
alternation of two notes	SHAKE, TRILL
alternative	OSSIA
always	SEMPRE
American	ARISTO-POP, BEACH MUSIC
	(BE)BOP, BLUES, (CHICAGO)HOUSE
	COUNTRY (AND WESTERN)
	COUNTRY ROCK, FUNK, GLAM ROCK
	GOSPEL, HEAVY METAL
	HILLBILLY, HIP-HOP, JAZZ

	POMP ROCK, POP, PSYCHOBILLY	4 notes	TETRACHORD
	PUNK (METAL), PUNK ROCK	5 notes	PENTACHORD
	RAG(TIME), RAP, ROCK (AND ROLL)	6 notes	HEXACHORD
	RHYTHM AND BLUES, SOUL	7 notes	HEPTACHORD
	SPEED METAL, THRASH(CORE)	8 notes	OCTACHORD
	TRASH METAL	church cantata	MOTET(T)
animatedly	ANIM(ATO)	clef	ALTO, BASS, C, F, G
answer in fugue	REPLY		SOPRANO, TENOR
anthem	MOTET(T)		TREBLE
Arabian	MAQAM	collection of songs	CANCIONERO
arrange	ORCHESTRATE	combined melodies	CHANSONNIER
augmented fourth	TRITONE		COUNTERPOINT
background music	MUSAK	complex tone	KLANG
	WALLPAPER MUSIC	composition	OPUS
bagpipe music	CEOL MOR, PIBROCH, PORT	—18th century	CASSATION
ballad	CANTILENA, SINGSONG	—for	
ballet interlude	DIVERTIMENTO	1	SOLO
	DIVERTISSEMENT	2	DUET, DUO
barely audible	SOTTO VOCE	3	TRIO
based on		4	QUARTET(T), QUARTETTE
—12 tone scale	DODECOPHONY		QUARTETTO
	SERIAL MUSIC	5	QUINTET(T), QUINTETTE
—set of notes rather			QUINTETTO
than a scale	SERIAL MUSIC	6	SESTET(T), SESTETTE
basic			SEXTET(T), SEXTETTE
—set of notes	TONE ROW	7	SEPTET(T), SEPTETTE
—tune or motif	THEME	8	OCTET(T), OCTETTE
bass octave	GREAT OCTAVE	9	NONET(TE), NONETTO
becoming		solo and orchestra	CONCERTO
—quicker	ACCELERANDO, STRINGENDO	voices and orchestra	ORATORIO
—slower	ALLARGANDO, CALANDO	—light symphony	SERENADE, SERENATA
	RALL(ENTANDO)	—polyphonic	FUGUE
—softer	DIM(INUENDO)	—using	
boating-song	BARCAROL(L)E	all notes equally	SERIAL MUSIC
bold style	DIASTALTIC	natural sounds	CONCRETE MUSIC
briskly	ALLEGRETTO		MUSIQUE CONCRETE
	ALLEGRO, CON MOTO	—with	
	VIVACE	much repetition	CANON, RONDO
broad and slow	LARGO		ROTA, ROUND
cacophonous music	CHARIVARI	several movements	SUITE
cadence	MODULATION		SYMPHONY
canon sung in unison	ROUND	concluding passage	CODA, POSTLUDE
cats' concert	CHARIVARI		VOLUNTARY
change key	TRANSPOSE	confusion	IMBROGLIO
cheerful song	LILT	continue	
choral		—in like manner	SIMILE
—composition	ANTHEM, CANON	—to next movement without	
	CANTATA, MOTET(T)	pause	SEGUE
	ORATORIO	continuous	
—ode(s)	STASIMUS(STASIMA)	—bass part	CONTINUO, THROUGH-BASS
chord	ITALIAN SIXTH	—glide	PORTAMENTO
	NEAPOLITAN SIXTH	country music	PASTORALE
—closing work or part	CADENCE	cradle song	BERCEUSE
—etc, on woodwind	BARTOLOZZI SOUNDS	crisply	STACCATO
—of		Cuban	SALSA
3 notes	TRIAD, TRICHORD	damped	SORDO

dance music	GAVOTTE, HORNPIPE, PASPY	eighth	OCTAVE
	PASSEPIED, RIGADOON	elaborate	
	TWO-STEP	—composition	ARABESQUE
—16/17th c	GAILLARD, GALLIARD	—fugue	RICERCAR(E), RICERCATA
—17th c	MINUET	embellishment	FIORITURA, MELISMA
—Argentinian	TANGO		ROULADE
—Bohemian	POLKA, REDOWA	end	FINE
—Brazilian	MAXIXE, SAMBA	ending	CODA
—French	CHACONNE	entr'acte	INTERMEZZO
—German	ALLEMANDE, LANDLER	essential part	OBBLIGATO
—hillbilly	HOE-DOWN	evening open-air performance	SERENADE
—Irish	PLANXTY		SERENATA
—Italian	SALTARELLO	excessively	TROPPO
—like polka	SCHOTTISCHE	exercise	
—Neapolitan	TARANTELLA	—in sol-fa	SOLFEGGIO
—Negro	WALK-AROUND	—piece	ETUDE, STUDY
—Norwegian	HALLING, SPRING	extended intervals	DIASTALTIC
—Polish	CRACOVIENNE, KRAKOWIAK	fading away	MANCANDO, MANCANTE
	MAZURKA, POLONAISE	falling volume	DECRESCENDO, DIMINUENDO
	VARSOVIENNE	fantasia	TOCCATA
—Provençal	TAMBOURIN	fast	PRESTO
—Scottish	REEL, SPRING, STRATHSPEY	fifth	QUINT
—slow	CHACONNE, WALTZ	—above tonic	DOMINANT
	PASSACAGLIA	figured bass	TASTO SOLO, TS
—Spanish	FLAMENCO, PASSACAGLIA	final theme	CODA
	PAVANE, SEGUIDILLA	first or principal part	PRIMO
—square	HOE-DOWN, QUADRILLE	five	
—West Indian	REGGAE	—lines on which music	
	(*see also* **dance**)	is written	STAVE
death of Christ	PASSION-MUSIC	—note octave	PENTATONIC SCALE
decrease in volume	DECRESC(ENDO)	florid	
decreasing	CAL(ANDO)	—embellisment	FIORITURA
depress soft pedal	UNA CORDA, UC	—in melody	MELISMATIC
detached	STACCATO	—treatment	FIGURATION
diapason	OCTAVE	—vocal passages	COLORATURA
difference in pitch	INTERVAL	flourish	CADENZA, FANFARE
direction to pianist	TRE CORDE	follow the	
dissonance in keyed		—singer	COLLA VOCE
instrument	WOLF(-NOTE)	—solo part	SUIVEZ
distorted rhythm	RUBATO	following	SEGUE
division of long work	MOVEMENT	for dancing in a ring	ROUND
double		forced	SF(Z), SFORZANDO
—speed	DOPPIO MOVIMENTO		SFORZATO
—tempo	ALLA BREVE	forerunner of fugue	RICERCAR(E)
dramatic oratorio	AZIONE(SACRA)		RICERCATA
draw out slightly	TEN(UTO)	form of first movement	SONATA FORM
drinking-song (Greek)	DITHYRAMB, SKOLION	four notes against three	SEQUITERTIA
dying away	MANCANDO, MANCANTE	fourth	QUART
	MORENDO, PERDENDO	—fifth or octave	PERFECT INTERVAL
each note		fraction of note	MICROTONE
—emphasised	MARC(ATO)	free	SCIOLTO
—shortened	STACCATO	—choice of time etc	AD LIB(ITUM)
early counterpoint	FA(UX)BURDEN	—style composition	CAPRICCIO
easy and flowing	CANTABILE		FANTASIA
eccentric piece	EXTRAVAGANZA	freedom of tempo	RUBATO
ecclesiastical melody	CANTUS	French Antilles	ZOUK

full range of	
—sound	DIAPASON
—voice	GAMUT
fundamental	
—and harmonics	KLANG
—note of chord	ROOT
funeral piece	CORONACH, DIRGE
	REQUIEM
Gaelic boating-song	JORRAM
gavotte trio	MUSETTE
gently	SORDAMENTE
German	
—song(s)	LIED(ER)
—style of opera	SINGSPIEL
grace note	ACCIACCATURA
	APPOGGIATURA
	MORDENT, NACHSCHLAG
	ORNAMENT, PRALLTRILLER
gracefully	GRAZIOSO
gradually	
—becoming	
quicker	ACCELERANDO, STRIGENDO
slower	CALANDO
—and softer	SMORZ(ANDO)
—decreasing speed	RIT(ARDANDO)
—fading	SMORZ(ANDO)
Gregorian cadence	EUOUAE, EVOVAE
ground-bass	OSTINATO
group of	
—2 notes	DUOLE, DUPLET
—3 notes	TRIAD, TRICHORD, TRIPLET
—4 notes	QUADRUPLET, TETRACHORD
—5 notes	PENTACHORD, QUINTUPLET
—6 notes	HEXACHORD, SEXTOLET
	SEXTUPLET
—7 notes	HEPTACHORD, SEPTIMOLE
	SEPTUPLET
—8 notes	OCTACHORD, OCTUPLET
—9 notes	NONUPLET
—10 notes	DECUPLET
—11 notes	UNDECIMOLE
—12 half-tones	OCTAVE
—notes played	
as one phrase	LIGATURE
at once	CHORD, TONE-CLUSTER
in different beat	TURLET
half staccato	SPICCATO
harmony in 3rds and 6ths	FAUXBOURDON
	FA(UX)BURDEN
hastening the time	STRINGENDO
having	
—5 notes	PENTATONIC
—7 notes	HEPTATONIC
—12 tones	DODECAPHONIC
—final in middle	PLAGAL
—several melodic lines	POLYPHONIC

heavy	PESANTE
height of note	PITCH
high soprano	COLORATURA
highest voice	SOPRANO, TREBLE
hold for full value	TEN(UTO)
humorous	
—medley of tunes	QUODLIBET
—piece	FANTASIA, HUMORESQUE
hymn	CANTICLE, CHORALE
idyllic opera	PASTORALE
immediately following	SEGUE
in	
—a	
marked manner	MARC(ATO)
melodious manner	ARIOSO
singing manner	CANTABILE
—declamatory style	PARLANDO
—devotional manner	RELIGIOSO
—free style	CAPRICCIOSO
—the	
manner of fugue	FUGATO
usual manner	SOLITO
increase volume	CRES(CENDO)
increasing in speed	ACCEL(ERANDO)
	STRINGENDO
Indian	BHANGRA, RAGA
—rhythmic pattern	TALA
informal evening	
of music (Gaelic)	CEILI(DH)
instantaneous	
composition	HEAD ARRANGEMENT
	IMPROVISATION
instrumental	
—composition	SONATA
—melody	CANTILENA
—passage in vocal	
work	RITORNEL(LO)
	RITORNELL(E)
	RITOURNELLE
—piece like a madrigal	CANZONE
—prelude	OVERTURE
intermediate	
—movement	INTERMEZZO
—part	MEAN
interpreting	
non-musical subject	TONE POEM
interval of	
—3 tones	TRITONE
—3rd	TIERCE
—4th	DIATESSARON
—5th	QUINT
—6th	SEXT
—7th	HEPTACHORD, SETTIMA
	SETTIMO
—8th	OCTAVE
—12th	DUODECIMO

—12 semitones	OCTAVE	medley of popular tunes	POTPOURRI
	SESQUITERTIA		QUODLIBET
—small	LIMMA	melodiously	ARIOSO
—with vibrations as		melody	
2 to 3	PERFECT FIFTH	—added to another	COUNTERPOINT
3 to 4	PERFECT FOURTH	—with no second part	CAVATINA
introduction	ENTREE, PRELUDE	mixing of two keys	BITONALITY
—to opera	OVERTURE	mock serenade	CHARIVARI
inverted mordent	PRALLTRILLER	moderate speed	ANDANTE, ANDANTINO
Irish	CEILI(DH)		MODERATO
irregular	RHAPSODY	moderately	
is silent	TACET	—loud	MEZZO-FORTE, MF
Italian folk song	RISPETTO	—slow	LARGHETTO
jazz	BEBOP, BLUES	—soft	MEZZO-PIANO, MP
	BOOGIE-WOOGIE, BOP, CHICAGO	modern	(see also American, jazz above)
	COOL, DIXIELAND, GUTBUCKET	modified rhythm	RUBATO
	HONKY-TONK, HOT MUSIC	modulation	CADENCE
	MAINSTREAM, RAGTIME, STRIDE	morning music	AUBADE
	SWING, TAILGATE, TRAD(ITIONAL)	most lively	VIVACISSIMO
	WEST COAST	mouth-music	PORT A BEUL
—type of folk-music	SKIFFLE	moving lightly and	
key	BASS, CLEF, MAJOR	rapidly	VOLANTE
	MINOR, TREBLE	much	MOLTO
—note	TONIC	music-loving	PHILHARMONIC
—of C major	PROPER CHANT	musical	
lament	DUMKA	—accompaniment to	
light		improvised poetry	RAP(PING)
—musical drama	OPERETTA	—drama	OPERA
—piece	DIVERTIMENTO	—instruments	(see separate entry)
	DIVERTISSEMENT	—shows	(see musicals)
little aria	ARIETTA	—stock-in-trade	REPERTOIRE
liturgical music	MASS, REQUIEM	—story, usually Biblical	ORATORIO
lively	SPIRITOSO, VIVACE	—training based on	
—dance tune	GIGUE	dancing	EURYTHMICS
—movement	SCHERZO	musicians	(see separate entry)
—tune	RANT	mute	SORDINO, SOURDINE
loud	F, FORTE	muted	SORDO
—as possible	FFF, FORTISSISSIMO	natural scale	DIATONIC
—then soft	FORTE-PIANO, FP	naturalism	VERISM(E)
love song	AMORET, TORCH-SONG	neither sharp nor flat	NATURAL
lovingly	AMOROSO	night music	NOCTURNE, SERENADE
low		non-stop piece	MOTO PERPETUO
—drum-beat	RUFF	normal range of voice	TESSITURA
—soprano	MEZZO-SOPRANO	not	
lower part of duet	SECONDO	—governed by rules	
lowest note of chord	FUNDAMENTAL	of form	FANTASIA
lyrical recitative	ARIOSO	—too much	NON TROPPO
madrigal	FA-LA	note(s)	BREVE, CROCHET
majestically	MAESTOSO		DEMI-SEMIQUAVER, MINIM
major third	PICARDY THIRD		QUAVER, SEMIBREVE
	TIERCE DE PICARDIE		SEMIQUAVER
march in procession	WALK-AROUND	—bass G	GAMUT
Martinique	ZOUK	—effecting smooth	
mass for dead	REQUIEM	transition	PASSING-NOTE
medium slow	ANDANTE	—forming unprepared	
	ANDANTINO	discord	PASSING-NOTE

—of	
chord played in	
rapid succession	ARPEGGIO
scale	DO(H), FA(H), LA(H)
	ME, MI, RE, SI, SO(H)
	SOL, TE, TI
—old	E-LA(-MI)
—played	
in progression	CHROMATIC
together	CHORD
—two octaves and a third	
above	TIERCE
obsolete ornament	BACKFALL
octave	DIAPASON
on the	
—bridge	SUL PONTICELLO
—key	SUL TASTO
one string	UNA CORDA, UC
opera	(*see separate entry*)
operatic air	CAVATINA
orchestral composition	SYMPHONY
original tempo	TEMPO PRIMO
ornament	ACCIACCATURA
	APPOGGIATURA
	GRACE NOTE, REL(L)ISH
—of four notes	TURN
out of tune	SCORDATO
overture	TOCCATA
part	
—in parallel motion	ORGANUM
—of	
aria	CABALETTA
fugue	STRETTO
larger work	MOVEMENT
—song	CATCH, GLEE
	MADRIGAL, ROUND
parts with independent	
melody	POLYPHONY
passage	
—for whole orchestra	TUTTI
—in quicker time	STRETTA, STRETTO
passionately	AFFETTUOSO
	APPASSIONATO
pastoral melody	MUSETTE
pause	FERMATA
percussion	TRIANGLE
perfect	
—fifth	HEMIOLIA, SESQUIALTERA
—fourth	SESQUITERTIA
Persian	DASTGAH
piano styles (jazz)	BOOGIE-WOOGIE
	HONKY-TONK, STRIDE
	WALKING BASS
piped music	MUSAK, MUZAK™
pitch standard	DIAPASON
plain	SECCO
—song	CANTO FERMO, CANTUS FERMUS
plaintively	LAGRIMOSO
play as desired	AD LIB(ITUM)
played by plucking	PIZZICATO
playful	PIACEVOLE
—piece	HUMORESQUE
playfully	SCHERZANDO
pleasant	PIACEVOLE
pluck the strings	PIZZ(ICATO)
polyphonic composition	FUGUE
preliminary passage	ENTREE
	PRAELUDIO, PRAELUDIUM
	PRAELUSION, PRELUDE
prelude	ENTREE, RITORNEL(LO)
	RITORNELL(E), RITOURNELLE
pretentious pop-music	POMP ROCK
progression of part	MOTION
quality of sound	KLANG, TIMBRE
quick	PRESTO
—dance	GALLOPADE
—staccato	SALTANDO, SALTATO
quicker	PIU MOSSO
quickly	PRESTO, VELOCE
quivering	TREMOLO, TREMOLANDO
rapidly	VELOCE
raising of a tone	ECBOLIC
random selection of notes	ALEATORIC MUSIC
rather loud	MEZZO-FORTE
recasting of composition	RIFACIMENTO
recurring theme	LEITMOTIV
refrain	EPISTROPHE, FA(UX)BURDEN
	RITORNEL(LO), RITORNELL(E)
	RITOURNELLE
recitative	PARLANDO
regular	GIUSTO
reinforced	RF(Z), RINF(ORZATO)
release soft pedal	TRE CORDE
religious story set to music	ORATORIO
remove mute	SENZA SORDINO
repeat	REPLICA
repeated figure	OSTINATO
—in jazz	RIFF
repetition	REPRISE
repetitions in higher tone	ROSALIA
resumption of first subject	REPRISE
retrained	RITENUTO
return to	
—pitch	LOCO
—sign	DAL SEGNO, DS
—the beginning	DA CAPO, DC
reverting to original speed	A TEM(PO)
rhythm	TEMPO
run	
—between two notes	TIRADE
—sung to one syllable	ROULADE
sad	MESTO

sadly	DOLOROSO		CONTRALTO, COUNTER-TENOR
sailors' song	CHANT(E)Y, CHANTIE		LYRIC SOPRANO
	SHANTY		MEZZO-SOPRANO, TENOR
score	PARTITUR(A)		TREBLE
scale	MAJOR, MINOR	singsong	BALLAD
—5 notes	PENTATONIC	sixth	SEXT
—5 whole, 2 semi-tones	DIATONIC	—above tonic	SUBMEDIANT
—6 hexachords	DITHYRAMB	sliding effect	GLISSANDO
—12 semitones	CHROMATIC	slow	ADAGIO, LENTO
—without sharps or flats	NATURAL	—and luxurious	LYDIAN
scene	SCENA	—beginning of trill	RIBATTUTA
school of music	CONSERVATOIRE	—movement	DUMKA
Scottish	CEILI(DH)	of csardas	LASSU
second movement	TRIO	—solemn dance style	PASSACAGLIA
semitone	FLAT, LIMMA, SHARP	—vocal composition	CHORALE
set of variations	PARTITA	—waltz	VALETA, VELETA
sharpening of a tone	ECBOLE	slowing	LENTANDO, RALLENTANDO
sharply	STACCATO		RITARDANDO
short			SLARGANDO(SI)
—aria	CAVATINA	slowly	LENTAMENTE
—cadence	TROPE	small interval	MICROTONE
—concerto	CONCERTINO	smoothly	LEG(ATO)
—fugue	FUGHETTA	soft	P, PIANO
—hymn or anthem	CATHISMA	—pedal	UNA CORDA
	ISODICON, TROPARION	softly	PIANO, SORDAMENTE
—instrumental piece	CAVATINA	—and sweetly	DOLCEMENTE
—opera or oratorio	CANTATA	solfeggio	CANTILENA
—rondo	RONDINO	solo narrative with music	CANTATA
—sonata	SONATINA	somewhat slow	LARGHETTO
—stressed note with		sonata movement	MINUET
longer note after	SCOTCH CATCH	song	CHANSON, LAY, MELISMA
	SCOTCH SNAP	—German	LIED
—toccata	TOCCATELLA, TOCCATINA	—in spoken style	RECITATIVE
show-piece	TOCCATA	—like a madrigal	CANZONE
sign		—little	CHANSONETTE
—at beginning or end		—of	
of repetitions	SEGNO	lamentation	THRENE, THRENODY
—of		praise	ANTHEM
change in pitch of note	NEUME	thanksgiving	P(A)EAN
pitch of		the dawn	AUBADE
—piece	CLEF, KEY SIGNATURE	—solo in opera, etc	ARIA
—note	ACCIDENTAL, FLAT	—unaccompanied	MADRIGAL, MOTET(T)
	NATURAL, SHARP	—West Indies	CALYPSO
tempo	TIME SIGNATURE	—with refrain	ROUNDELAY
silent	TACET	soprano	TREBLE
simple	SEMPLICE	Spanish	
simultaneous notes	DOUBLE STOP	—dance music	PASSCAGLIA
singing		—gypsy music or song	FLAMENCO
—exercise	CANTILENA, SOLFEGGIO	—serenade	RONDENA
—nonsense words (jazz)	SCAT(SINGING)	speed	TEMPO
—operatic style	BEL CANTO	spirited	SPIRITOSO
—unaccompanied	A(LLA) CAPPELLA	square dance	QUADRILLE
	ALLA BREVE	story set to music	OPERA
—voices	ALTO, BARITONE	—religious	ORATORIO
	BARYTON(E), BASS	strike strings with bow	COL LEGNO
	COLORATURA SOPRANO	strong tenor	HELDENTENOR

strongly accented	SFORZATO-PIANO, SFP
	SF(Z), SFORZANDO
	SFORZATO
study	ETUDE
—of properties of music	HARMONICS
succession of	
—chords at end	CADENZA
—notes sung to one	
syllable	NEUM(E)
sudden slowing	RITENUTO
suddenly accented	RF(Z), RINF(ORZATO)
suitable	GIUSTO
suite (18th c)	PARTITA
sung	
—common service	MASS
—mass for the dead	REQUIEM
—narrative	RECITATIVE
sunrise song	AUBADE
supplementary	RIPIENO
sustained	SOS(TENUTO), TENUTO
sweet	DOLCE
symphony	SINFONIA
syncopated music	JAZZ, RAG(TIME)
system of notation	SOLFEGGIO
	SOLMISATION
	TONIC SOL-FA
temporarily out of tune	SCORDATURA
temporary key signature	ACCIDENTAL
tender	AMOROSO
tenderly	AFFETTUOSO
tenor octave	SMALL OCTAVE
test piece	ETUDE
text of opera	LIBRETTO
third	
—above tonic	MEDIANT
—tone of tetrachord	TRITE
three	
—part structure	TERTIARY FORM
—strings	TRE CORDE
throbbing effect	VIBRATO
throughout	SEMPRE
timbre	KLANG
time	TEMPO, VOLTA
—division	BAR, BEAT, MODE
tone	
—colour	KLANG, TIMBRE
—one or more octaves	
from given tone	REPLICATE
too much	TROPPO
training piece	ETUDE
transformation of theme	VARIATION
treble	SOPRANO, TRIPLE
trembling	TREMANDO, TREMOLO
	TREMOLANDO
tremulous effect	TREMOLO
—on clavichord	BEBUNG

triplet	HEMIOLIA
trivial dance-tune	TOY
troubadour's lay	SIRVENTE
tune	MELISMA
turn	GRUPETTO, VOLTA
—over quickly	VOLTE SUBITO, VS
twelve semitones	OCTAVE
two	
—beats per bar	DUPLE
—crotchets per bar	TWO-FOUR
—or more tunes	
together	COUNTERPOINT
unaccompanied	A CAPELLA, ALLA BREVE
	SECCO
—song	GLEE, MOTET(T)
under the breath	SOTTO VOCE
undersong	FA(UX)BURDEN
unmeasured music	PLAINSONG
unpretentious composition	BAGATELLE
using several keys	POLYTONAL(ITY)
varying tempo	RUBATO
very	ASSAI, MOLTO
—loud	FF, FORTISSIMO
—quick	PRESTISSIMO
—slow(ly)	LENTISSIMO
—soft	PIANISSIMO, PP
vigorously	CON BRIO, VIGOROSO
violin strings	A. D. E. G
virtuoso passage	CADENZA
vocal	
—composition	CHORALE
—melody	CANTILENA
wallpaper music	MUSAK, MUZAK™
wavering of pitch	VIBRATO
weighty	PESANTE
West Indies	REGGAE, SKA
with	
—alternating subjects	RONDO
—bow close to	
bridge	SUL PONTICELLO
fingerboard	SUL TASTO
—dignity or majesty	MAESTOSO
—diminishing speed	RITARDANDO
—each note detached	STACCATO
—fervour	ZELOSO
—fire	CON FUOCO
—full time allowed for	
each note	SOS(TENUTO)
—fury	FURIOSO
—great rapidity	VELOCE
—hammering touch	MARTELLATO
—medium volume	MEZZA VOCE
—movement	CON MOTO
—mute	CON SORDINO
—parts each having	
separate melody	POLYPHONY

—rebounding bow	(ARCO)SALTANDO
	(ARCO)SALTATO
—spirit	CON SPIRITO, SPIRITOSO
—sudden	
accent	RINFORZANDO
emphasis	(S)FORZANDO, (S)FORZATO
—syncopation	(ALLO) ZOPPO
—the	
bow	(COLL')ARCO
voice	COLLA VOCE
wood	COL LEGNO
—tremulous effect	TREMOLANDO
without	SENZA
—a	
break	LEG(ATO)
mute	SENZA SORDINO
pause	SEGUE
—embellishments	SEMPLICE
write parts for	
instruments	ORCHESTRATE
musical instruments	
accordion	MELODEON
African	BALTON, HARP-LUTE
	GORA(H), GOURA, KONA
	KORA, ZANZE
—one-stringed	GURKEL
ancient	
—flute or pipe	TIBIA
—lute	DICHORD
Argentinian accordion	BANDOEON
Australian	DIDGERIDOO, WOBBLE BOARD
bagpipe	
—French	CORNEMUSE, MUSETTE
	SOURDELINE
—Italian	PIFFERO, ZAMPOGNA
—old	CHORUS
bandore	PANDORA, PANDORE
	PANDURA
barrel-organ for training	
song-birds	SERINETTE
bass	
—drum	TAMBOUR
—fiddle	(VIOLON)CELLO
—lute	THEORBO
—saxhorn	EUPHON(IUM)
—tuba	BOMBARDON
—viol	VIOLA DA GAMBA, VIOLONE
bassoon	FAGOTTO
bassoon-like (old)	RACKET(T)
bell and bars	GLOCKENSPIEL
bellows	ACCORDION, CONCERTINA
	MELODEON
bells	CARILLON
bird	
—call	QUAIL-CALL, QUAIL-PIPE
—shaped	OCARINA

boatswain's whistle	PIPE
Bolivian	CHARANGA
bombardon	BASS TUBA
brass	
—bass	BOMBARDON, HELICON, SAXHORN
	SOUSAPHONE, TUBA
—reed	SARRUSOPHONE
	SAXOPHONE, STRITCH
—slide	BAZOOKA, TROMBONE
—valved	CLARION, CORNET(-A-PISTONS)
	CORNOPEAN, ENGLISH HORN
	EUPHONIUM, FLUGEL-HORN
	FRENCH-HORN, MELLOPHONE
	OPHICLEIDE
	TRUMP(ET), (WAGNER) TUBA
—valveless	BUGLE
Bronze Age trumpet	LUR(E)
Burmese	TURR
Chinese	CHENG, KIN, SANG
cithern	GITTERN
—Shetland	LANGSP(I)EL
clavichord	CZLARICHORD, MONOCHORD
concertina	SQUEEZE-BOX, SQUIFFER
cornet-type (German)	ZINKE
crude oboe	PIFFERO
cymbal (Oriental)	ZEL
double	
—bass	VIOL
—necked lute	THEORBO
—reeded	BASSOON, COR ANGLAIS
	CRUMHORN, ENGLISH HORN
	KRUM(M)HORN, OBOE
	SHALM, SHAWM
drum	(see also percussion below)
dulcimer	CEMBALO, CIMBALON
	CIMBELON, ZIMBALOM
	PANTALEON
early	
—clarinet	CHALUMEAU
—piano	FORTEPIANO
Eastern	PANDORA, PANDORE, PANDURA
	SANTIR, SANT(O)UR
Egyptian tambourine	RIZZ
electronic	CLAVINOVA, MARTENOT
	MOOG, (ONDES) MARTINET
	MELLOTRON, SYNTHESISER
	THEREMIN
Elizabethan	BANDORE
English	
—flute	RECORDER
—horn	COR ANGLAIS, CORNO INGLESE
fiddle	
—Shetland	GJU, GU(E)
—Welsh	CROUTH, CROWD
—with strings in pairs	SULTANA
fife	PIFFERO

Finnish	KANTELE
fipple-flute	FLAGEOLET, FLUTE-A-BEC
	RECORDER
flageolet	FIPPLE-FLUTE
	PENNY-WHISTLE
French	
—bagpipe	CORNEMUSE, MUSETTE
	SOURDELINE
—horn	CORNO
without valves	WALDHORN
—viol	VIELLE
—woodwind	COUTAUT
German	
—trombone	POSAUNE
—woodwind	DULZIAN
glass harmonica	EUPHON
gong	TAM-TAM
gourd rattle	MARACA
graduated tuning forks	DULCITONE
grand piano	PIANO(FORTE)
Greek	AULOS, BARBITOS, BOUZOUKI
	CITHARA, KITHARA, LYRE
	PHORMINX, SALPINX, SYRINX
guitar	GITTERN
—Eastern	TAMBOURA
—Indian	SITAR
—Japanese	S(H)AMISEN
guitar-like	BANJO, MANDOLIN(E)
hand organ	HARMONICON, HURDY-GURDY
harmonica	MOUTH-ORGAN
	MUSICAL GLASSES
harmonium	REED-ORGAN
—early	PHYSHARMONICA
harp-like (old)	SACKBUT, SAMBUCA
	SAMBUKE
harpsichord	CLAVERIN
Hebrew	ASOR, SHOFAR, SHOPHAR
	TIMBREL, TOPH
—harp	NEBEL
highest-toned instrument	SOPRANINO
horn without valves	COACH HORN
	COR DE CHASSE, POST HORN
Hungarian	CIMBALON, CIMBELON
	ZIMBALOM
hunting-horn	FLUGEL-HORN, WALDHORN
hurdy-gurdy	VIELLE
Indian	CHIKARI, SAROD, SARANGI
	SERINGHI, SITAR, TABLA
	TAMBOURA
Irish	TYMPAN
Italian	CHITARRONE, FAGOTTO
Japanese	KOTO, S(H)AMISEN
Jew's harp	GUIMBARD, TRUMP
juke-box	NICKELODEON
kettledrum	NAKER, TIMBAL, TYMBAL
	TIMPANO, TYMPANO

key-bugle	FLUGEL-HORN, KENT-BUGLE
	OPHICLEIDE
keyboard	ACCORDION, BANDONEON
	CALLIOPE, CELESTA, CELESTE
	CLAVICEMBALO, CLAVECIN
	CLARICHORD, CLAVECIN
	CLAVICHORD, CLAVICYTHERIUM
	CLAVIER, DULCITONE
	HAMMOND ORGAN, HARMONICHORD
	HARMONIPHON(E), HARMONIUM
	HARPSICHORD, KLAVIER
	MELODEON, MELLOTRON
	(MOOG)SYNTHESISER
	(ONDES)MARTINET, ORGAN
	ORGANO, PIANO ACCORDION
	PIANOFORTE, (PLAYER) PIANO
	PORTATIVE ORGAN, REGAL
	SPINET(T), SPINETTE
	VIRGINAL, WURLITZER
—reed	SERAPHINE, VOCALION
—soundless	DUMB-PIAN
large	
—dulcimer (18th c)	PANTELEON
—lute	CHITARRONE, OPHARION
	OPHEOREON
—mandoline	MANDOLA, MANDORA
—serpent	ANACONDA
light-operated	LIGHT-ORGAN
like a lute	POLYPHONE
lute played by wheel	VIELLE
mechanical	GRAMOPHONE, JUKEBOX
	MUSIC BOX, MUSIC CENTRE
	PANHARMONICUM, PIANOLA
	PLAYER PIANO, POLYPHON
	RECORD PLAYER
mediaeval	CITOLE, ROTE
Mexican	CLARIN
mouth-organ	HARMONICA, HARMONICON
—Chinese	SANG
musical	
—box	POLYPHONE
—glasses	HARMONICA
Neapolitan	PANDURA
nickelodeon	JUKE-BOX
Northumberland bagpipes	SMALL-PIPES
oboe type	HECKELPHONE
old	
—fiddle	GJU, GU(E), SULTAN
—harplike	LYRE
—Scottish	STOCK-AND-HORN
—trumpet (Scand.)	LUR(E)
—viol	VIELLE
—viola	LYREA-VIOL
—zither-like	PSALTERY
orchestral	
—horn	FRENCH HORN

—kettledrum	TIMPANO
orchestrion	HARMONICON
panharmonicon	ORPHEUS HARMONICA
Pan('s) pipes	OATS, SYRINX
percussion	CYMBAL, DRUM, GONG
	IDIOPHONE, TAMBOURINE
	TRIANGLE, TUBULAR BELLS
—corrugated board	WASHBOARD
—Cuban	BONGO, CONGA, ENKOMO
—drum(s)	BASS DRUM, KETTLE DRUM
	PEDAL DRUM, SIDE DRUM
	SNARE DRUM, TABOR
	TAMBOUR, TAM-TAM
	TENOR DRUM, TIMBAL
	TOMTOM, TRAPS, TYMPAN
	TYMPANUM(TYMPANA)
	TYMPANY
—dulcimer	CEMBALO, CYMBALO
—Eastern	GAMELAN
—gourd	MARACA
—Indian	TABLA
—jazz	TRAP
—metal bars	DULCIMER, GLOCKENSPIEL
	TUBULAR BELLS
	VIBRAHARP, VIBRAPHONE
—Spanish	CASTANETS
—stones	LITHOPHONE
—wooden	
bars	MARIMBA, XYLOPHONE
block	CHINESE BLOCK
sticks	CLAVES
piano	PIANOFORTE
piano-like barrel-organ	PIANO-ORGAN
piccolo	OCTAVE-FLUTE
pipe made from reed	QUILL
player-piano	PIANOLA
pocket violin	KIT
portable organ	REGAL
practice instrument	DUMB-PIANO
primitive drum	TOM-TOM
rackett	SAUSAGE-BASSOON
recorder	FIPPLE-FLUTE
reed	
—organ	HARMONIUM, MELODEON
—pipes	OATS, PAN('S)-PIPES, SYRINX
Russian	BALALAIKA, DOMRA
	GUSLA, GUSLE, GUSLI
San Domingo	TUMBA
sausage-bassoon	RACKETT
Scottish	BAGPIPES, STOCK-AND-HORN
shallow drum	TAMBOURINE
shepherd's pipe	OAT
Shetland	GU(E), LANGSP(I)EL
small	
—bagpipe (French)	SORDELINE
—banjo	BANJULELE

—drum	TABO(U)R(IN), TABRET
—flute	FIFE, FLAGEOLET
	PICCOLO
—tabor	TABRET
sound-box and metal	
strips	HARMONICA
Spanish	CASTENETS, TENORA
	VIHUELA, ZAMBOMBA
squeeze-box	CONCERTINA, SQUIFFER
steam whistles with	
keyboard	CALLIOPE
straight trumpet (Roman)	TUBA
straw pipe	OAT
stringed	BASS FIDDLE, CELLO
	CONTRABASS(O), COUNTERBASS
	DOUBLE BASS, GUITAR, HARP
	MANDOLIN(E), UKELELE, UKULELE
	VIOLA, VIOLIN, VIOLONCELLO
—African	GURKEL, OUD
—Asian	OUD
—Celtic	CROUTH, CROWD
—early	CITHERN, GITTERN, LUTE
	PSALTERY, REBEC(K)
	REBIB(L)E, VIOL
—eastern	BANDORE, PANDORA
	PANDORE
—French	VIELLE
—Greek	BOUZOUKI, CITHARA
	KITHARA, LYRE
—Hawaiian	UKELELE, UKULELE
—Hungarian	CIMBALON
—Indian	SARANGI, SAROD, SITAR
—Irish	CLAIRSCHACH, TYMPAN
—Japanese	KOTO, S(H)AMISEN
—mediaeval	BANDORE, GITTERN
	ROTE
—Russian	BALALAIKA
	GUSLA, GUSLE, GUSLI
—Shetland	GJU, GU(E)
—Tirolese	CITHER(N), CITTERN
—viol	VIELLE
—Welsh	CROUTH, CROWD
—wind harp	AEOLIAN HARP
—with	
1 string	MONOCHORD
—African	GURKEL
—Balkan	GUSLA, GUSLE, GUSLI
3 strings	TRICHORD
4 strings	TETRACHORD
5 strings	BANJO, PENTACHORD
6 strings	GUITAR
7 strings	HEPTACHORD
8 strings	OCTACHORD
10 strings	TETRACHORD
29-42 strings	ZITHER(N)
Swiss	ALPENHORN

syrinx	PAN('S)PIPES
tabor (Eastern)	TIMBREL
tambourine (Eastern)	TIMBREL
tenor	
—fiddle	VIOLA
—oboe	TENOROON
—saxhorn	ALTHORN
—viol	VIOLA D'AMORE
	VIOLA DA BRACCIO
	VIOLA DA SPALLA
tin whistle	PENNY-WHISTLE
Tirolese zither	CITHER(N), CITTERN
toy	KAZOO, MUSICAL BOX
	OCARINA
—reed-pipe	MIRLITON
tromba marina	MONOCHORD, NUN'S-FIDDLE
	TRUMP MARINE
trombone (German)	POSAUNE
trumpet	CLARION
—Bronze Age	LUR(E)
—Greek	SALPINX
—Roman	TUBA
tuning forks	DULCITONE
Turkish	SAZ
upright	
—piano	PIANO(FORTE)
—spinet	CLAVICYTHERIUM
using flames	PYROPHONE
viol	
—medieval	REBEC(K)
—obsolete	TROMBA MARINA
—tenor	QUINT(E)
viola da gamba	GAMBA
violin	AMATI, CREMONA, FIDDLE,
	STRAD(IVARIUS)
Welsh	HORNPIPE, WELSH-HARP
—fiddle	CROUTH, CROWD
wind instrument	AEROPHONE
—like cornet (old)	ZINKE
—with	
loudspeaker	PIPELESS ORGAN
slide	SACKBUT, TROMBONE
woodwind	BASSET HORN, BASSOON
	CLARI(O)NET, CONTRABASSOON
	CONTRAFAGOTTO, COR ANGLAIS
	CORNO DI BASSETTO, CORNO INGLESE
	FIFE, FLAGEOLET, FLUTE
	HECKELPHONE, OBOE, PICCOLO
	RECORDER
—old	ANACONDA, BASS HORN
	CHALUMEAU
	CHORISTFAGOTT, CORNET(T)
	CREMONA, CREMORNE, CROMORNA
	CROMORNE, CRUMHORN
	CURTAL(L), COURTANT
	DULZIAN, FAGOTTO

	HAUTBOIS, HAUTBOY
	HOBOY, KRUM(M)HORN
	OBOE D'AMORE, OBOE DI CACCIA
	SERPENT, SHALM, SHAWM
xylophone	GAMELAN, MARIMBA
	METALLOPHONE
	STICCADO, STICCATO
zither-type	AUTOHARP
musicals	42ND STREET
	A CHORUS LINE, A LITTLE NIGHT MUSIC
	ANNIE GET YOUR GUN, ANYTHING GOES
	ASPECTS OF LOVE, BARNUM, BITTER SWEET
	BRIGADOON, BROADWAY MELODY
	CALL ME MADAM, CAMELOT
	CANCAN, CAROUSEL
	CATS, CHARLIE GIRL, COMPANY
	DESERT SONG, EVITA, FOLLIES
	GIGI, GUYS AND DOLLS, GYPSY, HAIR
	JESUS CHRIST SUPERSTAR
	KING'S RHAPSODY, KISS ME KATE
	LADY BE GOOD, LAND OF SMILES
	LAND OF SONG, MAID OF THE MOUNTAINS
	MAME, MISS SAIGON, MY FAIR LADY
	NAUGHTY MARIETTA
	NEW MOON, OKLAHOMA
	ON THE TOWN, ONE TOUCH OF VENUS
	PAINT YOUR WAGON, PAL JOEY
	PHANTOM OF THE OPERA
	PORGY AND BESS, PYJAMA GAME
	ROSE MARIE, SAIL AWAY
	SHOWBOAT, SINGING IN THE RAIN
	SOUTH PACIFIC, STARLIGHT EXPRESS
	SWINGTIME, THE BOHEMIAN GIRL
	THE BOY FRIEND, THE DANCING YEARS
	THE FIREBIRD, THE KING AND I
	THE VAGABOND KING
	THREEPENNY OPERA
	TOMMY, WEST SIDE STORY
D'Oyly Carte	BUNTHORNE'S BRIDE
	CASTLE ADAMANT, FALLEN FAIRIES
	HMS PINAFORE, IOLANTHE
	PATIENCE, PIRATES OF PENZANCE
	PRINCESS IDA, RUDDIGORE
	THE GODS GROW OLD
	THE GONDOLIERS, THE GRAND DUKE
	THE LASS THAT LOVED A SAILOR
	THE MIKADO, THE PEER AND THE PERI
	THE SLAVE OF DUTY, THE SORCERER
	THE TOWN OF TITIPU, THE WITCH'S CURSE
	THE YEOMEN OF THE GUARD, THESPIS
	TRIAL BY JURY, UTOPIA LTD,
musicians	
classical	
--composers	
American	BABBITT
	BERNSTEIN, CAGE, CARTER

	COPLAND, COWELL, GERSHWIN
	IVES, SONDHEIM
	VARESE, WEILL
Argentinian	KAGEL
Austrian	BERG, BRUCKNER, HAYDN
	MAHLER, SCHO(E)NBERG
	SCHUBERT, J. STRAUSS, SUPPE
	WEBERN, WELLESZ, WOLF
British	BAX, BYRD, BRITTEN
	CAGE, COWARD, DAVIES, DELIUS
	ELGAR, FRICKER, GIBBONS, GRAINGER
	HANDEL, HESELTINE, HOLST
	LLOYD-WEBBER, NOVELLO
	PARRY, PURCELL, RAWSTHORNE
	SEARLE, SMALLEY, SULLIVAN
	TIPPETT, WALTON, WARLOCK
	WILLIAMS
Canadian	ELSLER
Czech	DUSSEK, DVORAK, HABA
	JANACEK, SMETANA
Danish	NIELSEN
Dutch	ARCADELT, DE MONTE
	LASSUS, WILLAERT
Finnish	SIBELIUS
French	AURIC, BERLIOZ, BIZET
	BOULEZ, CHOPIN, COUPERIN
	DEBUSSY, DELIBES, DUPARC
	DUREY, FAURE, FRANCK
	GOUNOD, HALEVY, LULLY, MASSENET
	MESSIAEN, MILHAUD, POULENC
	POUPARD, POUSSEUR, RAMEAU
	RAVEL, SAINT-SAENS, SATIE
	SAUGES, SCHAEFFER, SPONTINI
	TAILLEFERRE, VARESE
German	BACH, BEETHOVEN, BRAHMS
	GLUCK, HANDEL, HENZE, HINDEMITH
	HOFFMAN, HUMMEL, MENDELSSOHN
	MEYERBEER, MOZART, PFIZNER
	REGER, SCHEIDT, SCHEIN
	SCHUMANN, SCHUTZ
	STOCKHAUSEN, R. STRAUSS
	WAGNER, WEBER, WEILL
Greek	XENAKIS
Hungarian	BARTOK, DOHNANYI
	KODALY, LISZT, SOLTI
Italian	ALBINONI, BELLINI
	BERIO, BOCCHERINI, BUSONI
	CASELLA, CAVALIERI, CAVALLI, CESTI
	CIMAROSO, CORELLI, DONIZETTI
	GABRIELLI, GEMINIANI
	MADERNA, MALIPIERO, MASCAGNI
	MONTEVERDI, PALESTRINA
	PRATELLA, PUCCINI, RESPIGHI
	ROSSINI, SCARLATTI, STRADELIA
	TORELLI, VERDI, VIVALDI
Japanese	TAKEMITSU

Norwegian	GRIEG
Polish	CHOPIN
Russian	BALAKIROFF, BORODIN
	GLINKA, MUSSORGSKY
	RIMSKY-KORSAKOV, SCRIABIN
	SHOSTAKOVITCH, STRAVINSKY
	TCHAIKOVSKY
Spanish	ALBENIZ, DE FALLA
	GRANADOS, TURINA, VICTORIA
Swedish	BLOMDAHL
Swiss	HONEGGER, MARTIN
—conductors	
American	BERNSTEIN, PREVIN
	STOKOWSKI
Austrian	BOHN, BRENDEL, MAHLER
	STRAUSS, WELSER-MOST
British	BARBIROLLI, BEECHAM
	BOULT, CAMERON
	DAVIS, LAMBERT, MACKERRAS
	PRITCHARD, RATTLE, SARGENT
	SOLTI, STOKOWSKI, WOOD
Dutch	HAITINK
Estonian	JARVI
French	BOULEZ
German	FURTWANGLER
	KNAPPERTSBUSCH, MASUR
	VON KARAJAN
	WALTER, WEINGARTEN
Hungarian	DOHNANYI, SOLTI
Indian	MEHTA
Italian	ABBADO, DE SABATA
	MUTI, TOSCANINI
Japanese	OZAWA
Latvian	JANSONS
Russian	ASHKENAZY, ROSTROPOVICH
—instrumentalists	
cello	CASALS, DU PRE, GENDRON
	HORNOY, MAISKY, OFFENBACH
	ROSTROPOVICH, TORTELIER
clarinet	BRYMER, DE PEYER, KELL
	THURSTON
flute	GALWAY
French horn	BRAIN, TUCKWELL
guitar	BREAM, SEGOVIA
oboe	GOOSENS
piano	ABBADO, ARRAU, ASHKENAZY
	BACKHAUS, BARENBOIM, BRENDEL
	BUSONI, CABEZON, CHOPIN, COWELL
	DOHNANYI, GIESEKING, HOROWITZ
	LIPATI, LISZT, LYMPANY, MEHTA
	MENDELSSOHN, MICHELANGELI, OGDON
	PADEREWSKI, PERAHIA, RICHTER
	RUBINSTEIN, SCHIFF, SCHNABEL
	ZIMMERMAN
trumpet	ANDRE
viola	BASHMET

violin	CHUNG, HEIFETZ, KREISLER	
	KYUNG-WHA, MENUHIN, MUTTER (f)	
	OISTRAKH, PAGANINI, PERLMAN	
	STERN, ZUKERMAN	

jazz
—composers   BERLIN, BLEY(f),
CARMICHAEL, CARTER, COREA
ELLINGTON, EVANS, GERSHWIN
HEFTI, HENDERSON, JARRETT
JOPLIN, LUNCEFORD, MERCER
MONK, POWELL, STRAYHORN
TAYLOR, WESTBROOK
—instrumentalists
bass   BLANTON, BRAUD, BROWN
CROSBY, HEATH, MINGUS
PAGE, PEDERSON
clarinet   BECHET, BIGARD, COE
DAVERN, DE FRANCO, DODDS,
GOODMAN, HAMILTON, HERMAN
HUCKO, LEWIS, MATLOCK
NOONE, RUSSELL, SHAW
WASHINGTON
drums   BLAKEY, CALLOWAY, CATLETT
CLARKE, COLE, HAMPTON, JONES
KRUPA, PARNELL, RICH, ROACH
TOUGH, WEBB
guitar   BENSON, BUNN, CHRISTIAN
CONDON, ELLIS, FARLOW
GAILLARD, GREEN, KESSEL
KING, LANG, MCLAUGHLIN
METHANY, MONTGOMERY
PASS, REINHARDT
WALKER, WATERS
piano   AMMONS, BASIE, BLAKE
BLEY(f), BRUBECK, COLE, COREA
CHARLES, ELLINGTON, EVANS
GARNER, HANCOCK, HINES, JARRETT
JOHNSON, KENTON, LEWIS, MONK
MORTON, MOTEN, PETERSON
POWELL, RUSSELL, SHEARING
SILVER, STRAYHORN, SUTTON
TATUM, TAYLOR, TRACY, TYNER
WALLER, WESTBROOK
WILLIAMS(f), WILSON
saxophone
—alto   ADDERLEY, CARTER
COLEMAN, DESMOND
DOLPHY, DORSEY, HODGES
JORDAN, KONITZ, MCLEAN
PARKER, PEPPER, STITT
WOODS
—tenor   AYLER, BARBIERI, BYAS, COE
COHN, COLEMAN, COLTRANE
DASH, DAVIS, FREEMAN, GETZ
GONSALVES, GORDON, GRAY
GRIFFIN, HAMILTON, HAWKINS

HAYES, JACQUET, KIRK
MILLER, PHILLIPS, PINE
QUEBEC, RIVERS, ROLLINS
RUSSELL, SANDERS, SCOTT
SHEPP, SHORTER, SIMS, STITT
STOBART(f), TATE, TURRENTINE
VENTURA, WASHINGTON
WEBSTER, YOUNG
—baritone   CARNEY, MULLIGAN
SURMAN, TEMPERLEY
—bass   ROLLINI
trumpet/cornet   ALLEN, ANDERSON
ARMSTRONG, BAKER
BEIDERBECKE
BERIGAN, BOLDEN, BRAFF
BROWN, CANDOLI, CARTER
CHERRY, CLAYTON, DAVIS
DAVISON, EDISON, ELDRIDGE
ELMAN, FAIRWEATHER, FERGUSON
GILLESPIE, GONELLA, HACKETT
HUBBARD, JAMES, JOHNSON
LITTLETON, MARSALIS
MASKELA, MCGHEE, MILEY
MORGAN, NAVARRO, OLIVER
PAGE, ROGERS, SHAVERS
SANDOVAL, SPANIER, STEWART
TERRY, WHEELER
trombone   BARBER, BROOKMEYER
DICKENSON, DORSEY, GRAY
GREEN, JOHNSON, LUSHER
MILLER, NANCE, NANTON, ORY
ROSSOLINI, TEAGARDEN, TIZOL
WELLS, WINDING
vibraphone   BURTON, HAMPTON
HUTCHERSON, JACKSON
NORVO
violin   GRAPELLI, JENKINS, NANCE
PONTY, SMITH, VENUTI
—leaders   ANTHONY, BARNET, BASIE
BROWN, CROSBY, DORSEY
ELLINGTON, GOODMAN, GRAY
HEATH, HEFTI, HENDERSON
HERMAN, KENTON, KIRK
LUNCEFORD, MILLER, SHAW
—singers
(f)   FITZGERALD, LAINE, HOLIDAY
LEE, MCCRAE, O'DAY
RAINEY, ROSS, SIMONE
SMITH, STAFFORD, VAUGHAN
WASHINGTON, WILSON
(m)   ARMSTRONG, CALLOWAY, COLE
GAILLARD, MELLY, RUSHING
TURNER, WALLER
WITHERSPOON
Muslim   (*see* **Moslem**)
Myanmar   (*see* **Burma**)

mythology		blinded	
—Greek and Roman		—Lycurgus	ZEUS
abandoned by		—Orion	OENOPION
—Aeneas	DIDO	—Polyphemus	ODYSSEUS
—Neoptolemus	ANDROMACHE	—Thamyris	MUSES
—Paris	OENONE	blinded by	
—Theseus	ARIADNE	—a dryad	RHOECUS
Achilles	AEACIDES	—himself	OEDIPUS
Aeacides	ACHILLES	—Muses	THAMYRIS
Aero	MEROPE	—Odysseus	POLYPHEMUS
Aesculapius	PAEAN	—Oenopion	ORION
Alcides	HERCULES	—Zeus	LYCURGUS
Alexander	PARIS	Bona Dea	MAIA
Aloadae	EPHIALTES, OTUS	breastplate of Zeus	AEGIS
Anadyomene	APHRODITE	brother of	
animal of		—Aegyptus	DANAUS
—Ares	DOG	—Agamemnon	MENELAUS
—Artemis	DEER	—Amphion	ZETHUS
—Hera	COW	—Antigone	ETEOCLES, POLYNEICES
Antiope	HIPPOLYTA	--Ares	HEPHAESTUS
Aphrodite	ANADYOMENE	—Artemis	APOLLO
	CYPRIAN, CYTHEREA	—Atlas	EPIMETHEUS, PROMETHEUS
Aphrodite's girdle	CESTUS	—Atreus	THYESTES
Apollo	DELIAN, PAEAN, PYTHIAN	—Biton	CLEOBIS
	SMINTHIAN	—Cleobis	BITON
Arges	CYCLOPS	—Danaus	AEGYPTUS
Argonauts	MINYAE	—Deiphobus	HECTOR, PARIS
armour-bearer to Hercules	HYLAS	—Dictys	POLYDECTES
Artemis	CYNTHIA, HECATE	—Dido	PYGMALION
	ORTHIA, PHOEBE	—Electra	ORESTES
	SELENE	—Ephialtes	OTUS
Ascanius	IULUS	—Epimetheus	ATLAS, PROMETHEUS
ate himself	ERYSICHTHON	—Eris	ARES
Bacchantes	MAENADS	—Eteocles	POLYNEICES
Bacchus	DIONYSIUS	—Europa	CADMUS
battles with		—Hebe	ARES, HEPHAESTUS
—Centaurs	LAPITHAE, THESEUS	—Hector	DEIPHOBUS, PARIS
—Lapithae	CENTAURS	—Helen	CASTOR, POLLUX
bearer of magic wand	HERMES	—Heliades	PHAETON
beautiful valley	TEMPE	—Helle	PHRIXUS
beekeeper	ARISTAEUS	—Hephaestus	ARES
betrayed Zeus's secret	SISYPHUS	—Hera	ZEUS
bird of		—Hestia	PLUTO, POSEIDON, ZEUS
—Aphrodite	DOVE, SPARROW, SWAN	—Iphigenia	ORESTES
—Apollo	RAVEN	—Ismene	ETEOCLES, POLYNEICES
—Ares	VULTURE	—Jocasta	CREON
—Athena	OWL	--Medea	APSYRTUS
—Hera	PEACOCK	—Menelaus	AGAMEMNON
—Zeus	EAGLE	—Neleus	PELIAS
birthplace of		—Niobe	PELOPS
—Aphrodite	CYTHERA	—Otus	EPHIALTES
—Apollo	DELOS	—Paris	DEIPHOBUS, HECTOR
—Artemis	DELOS	—Pelias	NELEUS
bitten by serpent and		—Philomena	ERECHTHEUS
abandoned	PHILOCTETES	—Pluto	POSEIDON, ZEUS
blind prophet	TEIRESIAS	—Polydectes	DICTYS

—Polyneices	ETEOCLES
—Poseidon	HADES, ZEUS
—Procne	ERECHTHEUS
—Prometheus	ATLAS, EPIMETHEUS
—Selene	HELIOS
—Thyestes	ATREUS
—Zethus	AMPHION
—Zeus	PLUTO, POSEIDON
brought	
—back	
bull from Crete	HERCULES
cattle of Geryon	HERCULES
Golden Apples	HERCULES
stag with golden horns	HERCULES
to life by	
—Aesculapius	HIPPOLYTUS
—Calypso	PROTESILAUS
—Cerberus from Hades	HERCULES
—from Hades by	
Hercules	CERBERUS, THESEUS
Hermes	PERSEPHONE
—Hippolytus back to life	AESCULAPIUS
—Persephone from underworld	HERMES
—Protesilaus from dead	CALYPSO
built	
—Argo	ARGUS
—labyrinth	DAEDALUS
—walls of Thebes	AMPHION, ZETHUS
captor of	
—Amazon	THESEUS
—boar on Mt Erymanthus	HERCULES
—Cerberus	HERCULES
—Odysseus	CALYPSO
—Proteus	MENELAUS
captured by	
—Greeks	ANDROMACHE
—Hercules	ANTIOPE, CERBERUS
	HIPPOLYTA
—Menelaus	PROTEUS
cared for	
—Aesculapius	CHIRON
—Zeus	IDA
—by	
Chiron	AESCULAPIUS
Ida	ZEUS
carried away by	
—Apollo	CREUSA
—Aurora	CEPHALUS
—Boreas	OREITHYIA
—bull	EUROPA
—Dionysius	SEMELE
—dragons	MEDEA
—eagle	GANYMEDE
—golden ram	HELLE, PHRIXUS
—Idas	MARPESSA
—Zeus	AEGINA

carried world on his shoulders	ATLAS
Castor and Pollux	DIOSCURI
centaur	CHIRON, NESSUS
—friend of Achilles	PHOLUS
challenged	
—Apollo at flute-playing	MARSYAS
—Minerva at weaving	ARACHNE
—Muses at poetry	THAMYRIS
changed	
—Actaeon into stag	ARTEMIS
—Callisto into bear	HERA
—Perdix into partridge	MINERVA
—Scylla into monster	CIRCE
—Tithonus into grasshopper	AURORA
changed into	
—bear by Hera	CALLISTO
—bird	ALCYONE, CEYX, SCYLLA
—cow	IO
—eagle	NISUS
—grasshopper by Aurora	TITHONUS
—hawk	TEREUS
—laurel tree	DAPHNE
—linden tree	BAUCIS
—monster by Circe	SCYLLA
—myrtle	MYRRHA
—nightingale	PROCNE
—oak tree	PHILEMON
—partridge	PERDIX
—poplar trees	HELIADES
—sea	
god	GLAUCUS, MELICERTES
goddess	INO
—spider	ARACHNE
—spring by Artemis	ARETHUSA
—stag by Artemis	ACTAEON
—stone	NIOBE
—sunflower	CLYTIE
—swallow	PHILOMENA
—tree	DRYOPE
—tuft of reeds	SYRINX
—wolf	LYCAON
changing shape at will	PROTEUS
charioteer	MYRTILUS
Charites	GRACES
	(*see also* **Graces**)
Clashing Rocks	SYMPLEGADES
cleaned Augean stables	HERCULES
cliff	SCYLLA
cloud-gatherer	ZEUS
conquered by	
—Atalanta	PELEUS
—Bellerophon	AMAZONS, SOLYMI
—Theseus	AMAAZONS
conqueror of	
—Amazons	BELLEROPHON, THESEUS
—Peleus	ATALANTA

—Solymi	BELLEROPHON
Corybantes	CURETES
cousin of	
—Hercules	THESEUS
—Orestes	PYLADES
—Pylades	ORESTES
—Theseus	HERCULES
created from ants	MYRMIDONS
creator of mankind	PROMETHEUS
Cronus	KRONUS
cup-bearer to gods	GANYMEDE, HEBE
Curetes	CORYBANTES
cut	
—down tree in Ceres' grove	ERYSICHTHON
—off Nisus's hair	SCYLLA
—out tongue of Philomena	TEREUS
—the Gordian knot	ALEXANDER
—to pieces by his daughters	PELIAS
Cyclops	ARGES, POLYPHEMUS STEROPES
Cynthia	ARTEMIS
Cyprian	APHRODITE
Cytherea	APHRODITE
Danaid	AMYMONE
daughter of	
—Acrisius	DANAE
—Aeolus	ALCYONE, ARNE
—Aesculapius	HYG(I)EIA, OCYRRHOE
—Aetes	MEDEA
—Agamemnon	CHRYSOTHEMIA ELECTRA, IPHIGENIA
—Alcinous	NAUSICAA
—Amata	LAVINIA
—Aphrodite	HARMONIA
—Apollo	HILARA
—Ares	AMAZONS, HARMONIA
—Arete	NAUSICAA
—Asopus	AEGINA
—Athamas	HELLE
—Atlas	HESPERIDES HYADES, MAIA
—Cadmus	AGAVE, AUTONOE INO, SEMELE
—Cassiopeia	ANDROMEDA
—Cecrops	AGLAUROS, HERSE PANDROSOS
—Cepheus	ANDROMEDA
—Clytemnestra	ELECTRA, IPHIGENIA
—Coeus	LETO
—Cronus	DEMETER, HESTIA
—Danaus	DANAIDS
—Demeter	PERSEPHONE
—Dione	APHRODITE
—Doris	NEREIDS
—Erectheus	CREUSA, ORITHYIA, PROCRIS
—Eurynome	AGLAIA, EUPHROSYNE GRACES, THALIA
—Eurystheus	ADMETA
—Eurytus	IOLE
—Graiae	EURYALE, MEDUSA, STHENO
—Harmonia	AGAVE, AUTONOE INO, SEMELE
—Harmony	AMAZONS
—Hecuba	POLYXENA
—Helen	HERMIONE
—Hera	HEBE, ILITHYIA
—Iasus	ATALANTA
—Icarius	PENELOPE
—Inachus	IO
—Jocasta	ANTIGONE, ISMENE
—king of	
Lemnos	HYPSIPYLE
Sidon	EUROPA
—Laomedon	HESIONE
—Latinus	LAVINIA
—Leda	CLYTEMNESTRA, HELEN
—Leto	ARTEMIS
—Leucippus	HILARA
—Lycaon	CALLISTO
—Menelaus	HERMIONE
—Minos	ARIADNE
—Nephele	HELLE
—Nereus	NEREIDS
—Nisus	SCYLLA
—Ocean	DORIS, EURYNOME OCEANIDS
—Oedipus	ANTIGONE, ISMENE
—Oenopion	AERO
—Pelias	ALCESTIS
—Phoebe	LETO
—Phorcys	GORGONS
—Priam	CASSANDRA
—Rhea	DEMETER, HESTIA
—Salmoneus	TYRO
—Schoeneus	ATALANTA
—Tantalus	NIOBE
—Themis	ASTRAEA
—Thestius	ALTHEA, LEDA
—Tyndareus	CLYTEMNESTRA TYNDARIS
—Zeus	AGLAIA, APHRODITE ARTEMIS, ASTREA, ATHENA EUPHROSYNE, GRACES, HEBE HELEN, MUSES, THALIA
death	
—Greek	THANATOS
—Roman	MORS
deified Romulus	QUIRINUS
Diomedes	TYDIDES
Dionysius	BACCHUS, IACCHUS
discoverers of iron	DACTYLA

divisions of underworld	EREBUS	—Ascanius	AENEAS
	TARTARUS	—Astraea	ZEUS
dog guarding entrance to		—Astyanax	HECTOR
Hades	CERBERUS	—Atalanta	IASUS, SCHOENIUS
drowned		—Athena	ZEUS
—by water nymph	HYLAS	—Atlas	IAPETUS
—in Hellespont	HELLE, LEANDER	—Atreus	PELOPS
Earth	GAEA	—Autonoe	CADMUS
earthshaker	POSEIDON	—Bellerophon	GLAUCUS, POSEIDON
east wind	EURUS	—Calais	BOREAS
eaten by his horses	GLAUCUS	—Callisto	LYCAON
Erechtheus	ERICTHONIUS	—Cassandra	PRIAM
Ericthonius	ERECHTHEUS	—Ceyx	LUCIFER
Erinyes	EUMENIDES, FURIES	—Chrysothemia	AGAMEMNON
Fate(s)		—Clytemnestra	TYNDAREUS
—Greek	MOIRA(E)	—Cresphontes	HERCULES
—Roman	PARCAE	—Creusa	ERECHTHEUS
	(see separate entry)	—Cronus	HEAVEN, URANUS
		—Danae	ACRISIUS
father of		—Daphne	PENEUS
—Abas	LYNCEUS	—dawn	HYPERION
—Achilles	PELEUS	—Deiphobus	PRIAM
—Admeta	EURYSTHEUS	—Demeter	CRONUS
—Adonis	CINYRAS	—Deucalion	PROMETHEUS
—Aeacus	ZEUS	—Diomedes	TYDEUS
—Aegina	ASOPUS	—Dionysius	ZEUS
—Aegisthus	THYESTES	—Doris	OCEAN
—Aeneas	ANCHISES	—Electra	AGAMEMNON
—Aeolus	HELLEN	—Electryon	PERSEUS
—Aepytus	CRESPHONTES	—Epaphus	ZEUS
—Aero	OENOPION	—Ephialtes	POSEIDON
—Aesculapius	APOLLO	—Epimetheus	IAPETUS
—Aetolus	ENDYMION	—Eteocles	OEDIPUS
—Agamemnon	ATREUS	—Euphrosyne	ZEUS
—Agave	CADMUS	—Eurynome	OCEAN
—Agenor	PRIAM	—Glaucus	SISYPHUS
—Aglaia	ZEUS	—Gorgons	PHORCYS
—Aglauros	CECROPS	—Graces	ZEUS
—Ajax	OILEUS, TELAMON	—Harmonia	ARES
—Alcestis	PELIAS	—Hebe	ZEUS
—Alcyone	AEOLUS	—Hector	PRIAM
—Althea	THESTIUS	—Helen	ZEUS
—Amazons	ARES	—Helle	ATHAMAS
—Amphion	ZEUS	—Hellen	DEUCALION
—Amphitryon	ALCAEUS	—Hercules	ZEUS
—Androgeus	MINOS	—Hermes	ZEUS
—Andromeda	CEPHEUS	—Hermione	MENELAUS
—Antigone	OEDIPUS	—Herse	CECROPS
—Antilochus	NESTOR	—Hesione	LAOMEDON
—Aphrodite	ZEUS	—Hesperides	ATLAS
—Apollo	ZEUS	—Hestia	CRONOS
—Apsyrtus	AETES	—Hilara	APOLLO, LEUCIPPUS
—Arcas	ZEUS	—Hippolytus	THESEUS
—Ares	ZEUS	—Hyades	ATLAS
—Aristaeus	APOLLO	—Icarus	DAEDALUS
—Arne	AEOLUS	—Icelus	HYPNOS
—Artemis	ZEUS		

—Ino	CADMUS	—Polydorus	CADMUS, PRIAM
—Io	INACHUS	—Polyneices	OEDIPUS
—Iole	EURYTUS	—Polyphemus	POSEIDON
—Ion	APOLLO	—Pontus	NEREUS
—Iphicles	AMPHITRYON	—Procris	ERECHTHEUS
—Iphigenia	AGAMEMNON	—Prometheus	IAPETUS
—Ismene	OEDIPUS	—Proteus	PSODEIDON
—Itys	TEREUS	—Pyrrha	EPIMETHEUS
—Jason	AESON	—Rhadamanthus	ZEUS
—Jupiter	SATURN	—Sarpedon	ZEUS
—Latinus	FAUNUS	—Scylla	NISUS
—Lausus	MEZENTIUS	—Semele	CADMUS
—Lavinia	LATINUS	—Silenus	PAN
—Leda	THESTIUS	—Sun	HYPERION
—Leto	COEUS	—Tantalus	ZEUS
—Linus	APOLLOA	—Telamon	AEACUS
—Machaon	AESCULAPIUS	—Telemachus	ODYSSEUS
—Maia	ATLAS	—Telephus	HERCULES
—Medea	AETES	—Tereus	ARES
—Meleager	OENEUS	—Teucer	SCAMANDER, TELAMON
—Memnon	TITHONUS	—Thalis	ZEUS
—Menelaus	ATREUS	—Theseus	AEGEUS
—Menoeceus	CREON	—Thyestes	PELOPS
—Midas	GORDUS	—Triton	POSEIDON
—Minos	ZEUS	—Troilus	PRIAM
—Moon	HYPERION	—Tydides	TYDEUS
—Morpheus	HYPNOS	—Tyndaris	TYNDAREUS
—Muses	ZEUS	—Tyro	SALMONEUS
—Nausicaa	ALCINOUS	—Zetes	BOREAS
—Neleus	POSEIDON	—Zethus	ZEUS
—Neoptolemus	ACHILLES	—Zeus	CRONOS
—Nereids	NEREUS	favourite	
—Nestor	NELEUS	—child of Zeus	ATHENA
—Niobe	TANTALUS	—Jupiter	MERCURY
—Oceanids	OCEAN	—Zeus	CYCLOPES
—Ocyrrhoe	AESCULAPIUS	ferryman	CHARON, NESSUS
—Odysseus	LAERTES	first	
—Oedipus	POLYBUS	—horse	ARION
—Orestes	AGAMEMNON	—man ashore at Troy	PROTESILAUS
—Orithyia	ERECHTHEUS	—woman	PANDORA
—Otus	POSEIDON	fisherman	DICTYS, GLAUCUS
—Pallas	EVANDER	flayed by Apollo	MARSYAS
—Pan	HERMES	flew too near the sun	ICARUS
—Pandrosos	CECROPS	flower of Adonis	ANEMONE, WINDFLOWER
—Paphos	PYGMALION	followers of	
—Paris	PRIAM	—Achilles	MYRMIDONS
—Parthenopaeus	MELANION	—Bacchus	BACCHANTES, MAENADS
—Pelias	POSEIDON		THYIADES
—Pelops	TANTALUS	foretelling the future	PROTEUS
—Penelope	ICARIUS	founder of	
—Perseus	ZEUS	—Carthage	DIDO
—Phaeton	HELIOS	—Rome	REMUS, ROMULUS
—Phantasus	HYPNOS	—Trojans	DARDANUS
—Philoctetes	POEAS	fountain (Parnassus)	CASTALIA
—Phrixus	ATHAMAS	freed by	
—Pollux	ZEUS	—Circe	ODYSSEUS

—Hercules	PROMETHEUS
—Hermes	ARES
friend of	
—Achilles	PATROCLUS
—Aeneas	ACHATES
Friendly Sea	EUXINE
Furies	ERINYES. EUMENIDES
	(*see also separate entry*)
gave	
—asses's ears to Midas	APOLLO
—golden apple to Aphrodite	PARIS
—necklace to Harmonia	APHRODITE
—shield to Perseus	ATHENA
giant	ANTAEUS, CACUS
	EPHIALTES, OTUS
	POLYBOTES, PORPHYRION
	RHOETUS, TITYUS
girdle of Amazons got by	HERCULES
given	
—ivory shoulder by gods	PELOPS
—necklace by Aphrodite	HARMONIA
—skin of Calydonian boar	ATALANTA
giver of	
—Golden Fleece to Aetes	PHRIXUS
—horse to mankind	POSEIDON
gnomes	CERCOPES
goat whose milk fed Zeus	AMALTHEA
Golden Fleece given by	
Phrixus to	AETES
good Centaur	CHIRON
Gorgons	EURYALE, MEDUSA, STHENO
Graces	CHARITES
	(*see separate entry*)
greatest musician	ORPHEUS
Greek equivalents	
—Aesculapius	ASKLEPIOS
—Ammon	ZEUS
—Bellona	ENYO
—Ceres	DEMETER
—Cupid	EROS
—Diana	ARTEMIS, LUCINA
—Dis	HADES, PLUTO
—Eileithyia	LUCINA
—Juno	HERA, LUCINA
—Jupiter	AMMON, ZEUS
—Latona	LETO
—Liber	BACCHUS, DIONYSIUS, LYAEUS
—Liberia	PERSEPHONE
—Lucina	DIANA, JUNO
—Maia	BONA DEA
—Mars	ARES
—Mater	
Matuta	AURORA, INO
Turrita	CYBELE, RHEA
—Mercury	HERMES
—Minerva	ATHENA

—Mors	THANATOS
—Mulciber	HEPHAESTUS
—Neptune	POSEIDON
—Proserpine	PERSEPHONE
—Saturn	CRONUS
—Sol	HELIOS
—Somnus	HYPNOS, HYPNUS
—Ulysses	ODYSSEUS
—Venus	APHRODITE
—Vesta	HESTIA
—Victoria	NIKE
—Vulcan	HEPHAESTUS
guardian(s) of	
—golden apples	HESPERIDES, LADON
—Hades	CERBERUS
—infant Zeus	CORYBANTES
	CURETES
—stream flowing with gold	GRIFFINS
guide of the dead	HERMES
Hades	PLUTO, POLYDECTES
hanged herself	ARACHNE
healer	APOLLO
Hecabe	HECUBA
Hecate	ARTEMIS, TRIVIA
Hecuba	HECABE
Helen	TYNDARIS
helped Theseus to escape	DAEDALUS
herald	HERMES
Hercules	ALCIDES
Hermes	PSYCHOPOMPUS
heroine of Troy	HELEN
Hesper	VESPER
Hesperia	ITALY
Hippolyta	ANTIOPE
Hippomenes	MELANION, MILANION
home of	
—the gods	OLYMPUS
—Hydra	LERNA, LERNE
—Titans	OTHRYS
horse from Medusa's blood	CHRYSAOR
hounds of Zeus	HARPIES
huntress	ARETHUSA, ARTEMIS
husband of	
—Aerope	ATREUS
—Aethra	AEGEUS
—Aglaia	HEPHAESTUS
—Alcestis	ADMETUS
—Amata	LATINUS
—Amphitrite	POSEIDON
—Andromache	HECTOR, HELENUS
—Andromeda	PERSEUS
—Anteia	PROETUS
—Aphrodite	HEPHAESTUS
—Arete	ALCINOUS
—Atalanta	MELANION
—Aurora	TITHONUS

—Baucis	PHILEMON
—Cassiopeia	CEPHEUS
—Clytemnestra	AGAMEMNON
—Creusa	XUTHUS
—Deianira	HERCULES
—Dido	SICHAEUS
—Dirce	LYCUS
—Doris	NEREUS
—Electra	PYLADES
—Eriphyle	ADRASTUS
—Eurydice	ORPHEUS
—Eurynome	GLAUCUS
—Evadne	CAPANEUS
—Gaea	URANUS
—Galatea	PYGMALION
—Harmonia	CADMUS
—Hebe	HERCULES
—Hecuba	PRIAM
—Helen	MENELAUS
—Hera	ZEUS
—Hermione	NEOPTOLEMUS
—Hesione	PROMETHEUS
—Hippodamia	PELOPS, PIRITHOUA
—Hippolyta	THESEUS
—Hypermnestra	LYNCEUS
—Ino	ATHAMAS
—Jocasta	LAIUS, OEDIPUS
—Laodamia	PROTESILAUS
—Lavinia	AENEAS
—Leda	TYNDAREUS
—Lybia	POSEIDON
—Maia	VULCAN
—Megara	HERCULES
—Merope	CRESPHONTES, POLYPHONTES
—Nephele	ATHAMAS
—Niobe	AMPHION
—Ops	SATURN
—Penelope	ODYSSEUS
—Persephone	HADES
—Phaedra	THESEUS
—Procne	TEREUS
—Procris	CEPHALUS
—Psyche	CUPID
—Pyrrha	DEUCALION
—Rhea	CRONOS
—Sidero	CRETHEUS
—Tethys	OCEAN
—Thetis	PELEUS
—Tyro	CRETHEUS
Hyades	NYSAEAN NYMPHS
Hypnos	HYPNUS
Iacchus	DIONYSIUS
immortal who grew older	TITHONUS
imprisoned	
—by	
Calypso	ODYSSEUS

Minos	DAEDALUS, ICARUS
—Daedalus	MINOS
—Icarus	MINOS
—in Labyrinth	DAEDALUS, ICARUS
inhabitant(s) of	
—Dodona	SELLI
—far bank of Ocean	CIMMERIANS
—Labyrinth	MINOTAUR
—north	HYPERBOREANS
—swamp at Lerna	HYDRA
Ino	LEUCOTHEA
inventor of	
—compass	PERDIX
—flute	ATHENA
—horse bridle	ATHENA
—lyre	HERMES
—saw	PERDIX
island sacred to Aphrodite	CYPRUS
Italy	HESPERIA
Iulus	ASCANIUS
judge in underworld	AEACUS, MINOS
	RHADAMANTHUS
kept snakes as pets	MELAMPUS
kidnapped by Theseus	HELEN
kidnapper of Helen	THESEUS
killed	
—and boiled	
by	
—Procne	ITYS
—his father	PELOPS
son	TANTALUS
—by	
Achilles	HECTOR, CHIRON
	MEMNON, PENTHESILEA
	TROILUS
Aegisthus	AGAMEMNON
Aeneas	TURNUS
Agave	PENTHEUS, CORONIS
	CYCLOPES, HYACINTH(US)
Apollo	TITYUS
Artemis	CORONIS, ORION
Bellerophon	CHIMAERA
boar	ADONIS
bull	ANDROGEUS
Cephalus	PROCRIS
Clytemnestra	AGAMEMNON
	CASSANDRA
Daedalus	PERDIX
Ephialtes	OTUS
Eteocles	POLYNEICES
Hercules	ANTAEUS, DIOMEDES
	EURYTUS, HYDRA, LAOMEDON
	LINUS, LITYERSES, MEGARA
	NEMEAN LION, NESSUS
Hermes	ARGUS
Idas	CASTOR

Ino	MELICERTES
Jason	APSYRTUS
Lycomides	THESEUS
Lycus	DIRCE
Maenads	ORPHEUS, PENTHEUS
Medea	APSYRTUS
Neoptolemus	PRIAM
Oedipus	LAIUS
Orestes	AEGISTHUS
	CLYTEMNESTRA, EPHIALTES
Paris	ACHILLES
Pelias	SIDERO
Pelops	MYRTILUS
Perseus	ACRISIUS, GORGONS
Philoctetes	PARIS
Polyneices	ETEOCLES
Polyphemus	ACIS
Theseus	MINOTAUR, PROCRUSTES
	SINIS, SCIRON
Zeus	ASKLEPIOS, SALMONEUS

killer of

—Achilles	PARIS
—Acis	POLYPHEMUS
—Acrisius	PERSEUS
—Aegisthus	ORESTES
—Agamemnon	AEGISTHUS
	CLYTEMNESTRA
—Antaeus	HERCULES
—Apsyrtus	JASON, MEDEA
—Argus	HERMES
—Asklepios	ZEUS
—Calydonian boar	MELEAGER
—Cassandra	CLYTEMNESTRA
—Castor	IDAS
—Chimaera	BELLEROPHON
—Chiron	ACHILLES
—Clytemnestra	ORESTES
—Cornis	ARTEMIS, APOLLO
—Cyclopes	APOLLO
—Diomedes	HERCULES
—Dirce	LYCUS
—dragon guarding spring	CADMUS
—eagle attacking Prometheus	HERCULES
—Ephialtes	OTUS
—Eteocles	POLYNEICES
—Eurytus	HERCULES
—Gorgons	PERSEUS
—Hector	ACHILLES
—Hyacinth(us)	APOLLO
—Hydra	HERCULES
—Itys	PROCNE
—Jason's bride	MEDEA
—Lalus	OEDIPUS
—Laomedon	HERCULES
—Linus	HERCULES
—Lityerses	HERCULES

—Megara	HERCULES
—Melicertes	INO
—Memnon	ACHILLES
—Minotaur	THESEUS
—Myrtilus	PELOPS
—Nemean lion	HERCULES
—Nessus	HERCULES
—Niobe's children	APOLLO, ARTEMIS
—Orion	ARTEMIS
—Orpheus	MAENADS
—Otus	EPHIALTES
—Paris	PHILOCTETES
—Penelope's suitors	ODYSSEUS
—Penthesilea	ACHILLES
—Pentheus	AGAVE, MAENADS
—Perdix	DAEDALUS
—Polyneices	ETEOCLES
—Priam	NEOPTOLEMUS
—Procris	CEPHALUS
—Salmoneus	ZEUS
—Sidero	PELIAS
—Stymphalian birds	HERCULES
—Theseus	LYCOMIDES
—Thespian Lion	HERCULES
—Tityus	APOLLO
—Troilus	ACHILLES
—Turnus	AENEAS

killers of husbands   DANAIDS

king of

—Aegina	AEACUS
—Alba Longa	AENEAS SYLVIUS
—Arcadia	LYCAON
—Argos	ACRISIUS, ADRASTUS
	PROETUS
—Athens	AEGEUS, ERECHTHEUS
—Attica	CECROPS
—Calydon	OENEUS, THESTIUS
—Chios	OENOPION
—Colchis	AEETES
—Corinth	GLAUCUS, POLYBUS
	SISYPHUS
—Crete	MINOS
—Greece	ATHAMAS
—Ithaca	ODYSSEUS
—Lapithae	PEIRITHEOS
—Latium	LATINUS
—Lydia	TANTALUS
—Megara	NISUS
—Mycenae	EURYSTHEUS
—Phaeacians	ALCINOUS
—Phocis	STROPHIUS
—Phrygia	MIDAS
—Rutulians	TURNUS
—Sparta	MENELAUS
—Thebes	CADMUS, LAIUS, LYCUS
	OEDIPUS, PENTHEUS

—Thessaly	ADMETUS, AEOLUS
	CEYX, MINYAS
—Thrace	DIOMEDES
—Troezen	PITTHEUS
—Troy	LAOMEDON, PRIAM
	TEUCER
—Tyre	PYGMALION
—winds	AEOLUS
Kora	PERSEPHONE
Kronus	CRONUS
lame god	HEPHAESTUS
land of oak trees	DODONA
leader of Cretans	IDOMENEUS
Leucothea	INO
liberator of	
—Ares	HERMES
—Odysseus	CIRCE
—Prometheus	HERCULES
loved by	
—Adonis	PERSEPHONE
—Aegisthus	CLYTEMNESTRA
—Anteia	BELLEROPHON
—Aphrodite	ADONIS
—Apollo	CORONIS, DAPHNE
	MARPESSA
—Ariadne	THESEUS
—Aurora	CEPHALUS, ORION
—Boreas	ORITHYIA
—Circe	GLAUCUS
—Clytemnestra	AEGISTHUS
—Dido	AENEAS
—Echo	NARCISSUS
—Ephialtes	ARTEMIS
—Eurydice	ORPHEUS
—Galatea	ACS
—Glaucus	SCYLLA
—Hades	PERSEPHONE
—Hercules	IOLE
—Hero	LEANDER
—Jason	MEDEA
—Leander	HERO
—Medea	JASON
—Meleager	ATALANTA
—Minos	SCYLLA
—Oenone	PARIS
—Orpheus	EURYDICE
—Orion	AERO, AURORA, MEROPE
—Paris	OENONE
—Pasiphae	BULL
—Persephone	ADONIS
—Phaedra	HIPPOLYTUS
—Polyphemus	GALATEA
—Pomona	VERTUMNUS
—Pyramus	THISBE
—Sappho	PHAON
—Scylla	MINOS

—Selene	ENDYMION
—Theseus	ARIADNE
—Thisbe	PYRAMUS
—Vertumnus	POMONA
—Zeus	AEGINA, CALLISTO
	IO, LETO, SEMELE
Lyaeus	BACCHUS
lyre given by Hermes to	APOLLO
made	
—Psyche immortal	JUPITER
—Tithonus immortal	ZEUS
Maenads	BACCHANTES
magic	
—herb given to Odysseus	MOLY
—wand of Hermes	CADUCEUS
magical beings of Lemnos	CABEIRI
maid of Tyro	SIDERO
maker of	
—Labyrinth	DAEDALUS
—lyre	CALYPSO
—reed pipe	PAN
—shepherd-pipe	CALYPSO
—Wooden Horse	EPEUS
Melanion	MILANION, HIPPOMENES
Melicertes	PALAEMON
Merope	AERO
messenger of Gods	CALYPSO, HERMES
	MERCURY
Minyae	ARGONAUTS
mother of	
—Abas	HYPERMNESTRA
—Achilles	THETIS
—Actaeon	AUTONOE
—Adonis	MYRRHA
—Aeacus	AEGINA
—Aeneas	APHRODITE
—Aepytus	MEROPE
—Aesculapius	ARSINOE, CORONIS
—Agamemnon	AEROPE
—Agave	HARMONIA
—Aglaia	EURYNOME
—Aloadae	IPHIMEDEA
—Amazons	HARMONY
—Amphion	ANTIOPE
—Andromeda	CASSIOPEIA
—Antigone	JOCASTA
—Aphrodite	DIONE
—Apollo	LETO
—Arcas	CALLISTO
—Ares	HERA
—Aristaeus	CYRENE
—Artemis	LETO
—Astraea	THEMIS
—Astyanax	ANDROMACHE
—Atreus	HIPPODAMIA
—Autonoe	HARMONIA

—Bellerophon	EURYNOME	—Parthenopaeus	ATALANTA
—Biton	CYDIPPE	—Pelias	TYRO
—Calais	ORITHYIA	—Pentheus	AGAVE
—Castor	LEDA	—Persephone	DEMETER
—Cerberus	ECHIDNA	—Perseus	DANAE
—Cleobis	CYDIPPE	—Phrixus	NEPHELE
—Clytemnestra	LEDA	—Pollux	LEDA
—Cupid	APHRODITE	—Polyxena	HECUBA
—Dardanus	ELECTRA	—Pontus	MOTHER EARTH
—Deiphobus	HECUBA	—Pyrrhus	DEIDAMIA
—Demeter	RHEA	—Rhadamanthus	EUROPA
—Dionysius	SEMELE	—Sarpedon	DEIDAMIA, EUROPA
—Electra	CLYTEMNESTRA	—Semele	HARMONIA
—Electryon	ANDROMEDA	—Telemachus	PENELOPE
—Epaphus	IO	—Thalia	EURYNOME
—Ephialtes	EPHIMEDIA	—Theseus	AETHRA
—Eros	APHRODITE	—Thyestes	HIPPODAMIA
—Euphrosyne	EURYNOME	—Triton	AMPHITRITE
—Graces	EURYNOME	—Xuthus	HELEN
—Harmonia	APHRODITE	—Zetes	ORITHYIA
—Hebe	HERA	—Zethus	ANTIOPE
—Hector	HECUBA	Moira(e)	FATE(S)
—Helen	LEDA	mountain of	
—Helle	NEPHELE	—Apollo	PARNASSUS
—Hellen	PYRRHA	—the	
—Hercules	ALCMENA	gods	OLYMPUS
—Hermes	MAIA	Muses	HELICON
—Hermione	HELEN	Muses	PIERIDES
—Hestia	RHEA		*(see also separate entry)*
—Hippolytus	HIPPOLYTA	musician of gods	APOLLO
—Hydra of Lerna	ECHIDNA	Neoptolemus	PYRRHUS
—Ilithyia	HERA	Nereid	AMPHITRITE, PANOPE
—Ino	HARMONIA		THETIS
—Ion	CREUSA	north wind	AQUILO, BOREAS
—Iphigenia	CLYTEMNESTRA	nursed by	
—Itys	PROCNE	—Adrastea	ZEUS
—Lavinia	AMATA	—Eurycleia	ODYSSEUS
—Leto	PHOEBE	—Hyades	BACCHUS
—Linus	PSAMATHE	nurse(s) of	
—Meleager	ALTHEA	—Bacchus	HYADES, NYSAEAN NYMPHS
—Melicertes	INO	—Odysseus	EURYCLEIA
—Memnon	AURORA	—Zeus	ADASTREA, IDA
—Minos	EUROPA	nymph	ADASTREA, IDA
—Minotaur	PASIPHAE		LOTI, SYRINX
—Muses	MNEMOSYNE	nymphs	*(see separate entry)*
—Nausicaa	ARETE	Nysaean Nymphs	HYADES
—Neleus	TYRO	obtained girdle of Hippolyta	HERCULES
—Nemean Lion	ECHIDNA	Old Man of the Sea	NEREUS
—Neoptolemus	DEIDAMIA	Olympians	*(see also* **gods, goddesses***)*
—Nereids	DORIS	one-eyed horseman	ARIMASPI
—Oceanids	TETHYS	oracle of	
—Orestes	CLYTEMNESTRA	—Apollo	DELPHI
—Otus	EPHIMEDIA	—Zeus	DODNA
—Palaemon	LEUCOTHEA	Orthia	ARTEMIS
—Paphos	GALATEA	outran Atalanta with	
—Paris	HECUBA	golden apples	MELANION

owner of	
—horn of plenty	AMALTHEA
—man-eating horses	DIOMEDES
Paean	AESCULAPIUS, APOLLO
painkilling drug given to Helen	NEPENTHE
Palaemon	MELICERTES
Paris	ALEXANDER
perpetually weeping	NIOBE
Persephone	KORA
Phoebe	ARTEMIS, SELENE
physician	AESCULAPIUS
—of the gods	PAEAN
—to Greek army at Troy	MACHAON
Pierides	MUSES
Pillars of Hercules	ABYLA, CALPE
Pleiades	ALCYONE, CELAENO
	ELECTRA, MAIA, MEROPE
	STEROPE, TAYGETE
Pluto	HADES
Polydectes	HADES
Polydeuces	POLLUX
priestess of	
—Aphrodite	HERO
—Hera	CYDIPPE
priests of Mars	SALII
prince of	
—Athens	THESEUS
—Ethiopia	MEMNON
princess of	
—Crete	ARIADNE
—Thebes	ANTIOPE, MEGARA, SEMELE
prophet	PHINEUS
—of Troy	HELENUS
protectress of youth	ARTEMIS
Psychopompus	HERMES
punished by	
—Hera	ECHO, IXION
—Olympians	TANTALUS
—Zeus	HERCULES, LYCAON
	SISYPHUS
pupil of	
—Athena	EURYNOME
—Chiron	ACHILLES, ACTAEON
	AESCULAPIUS
—Daedalus	PERDIX
purple-haired king	NISUS
pursued by Orion	PLEIADES
put eyes into peacock's tail	HERA
Pyrrhus	NEOPTOLEMUS
queen of	
—Amazons	HIPPOLYTA, PENTHESILEA
—Babylon	SEMIRAMIS
—Ethiopia	CASSIOPEIA
—Lydia	OMPHALE
—universe	RHEA

raised by	
—she-bear	ATALANTA
—she-wolf	REMUS, ROMULUS
received	
—asses's ears from Apollo	MIDAS
—golden apple from Paris	APHRODITE
—necklace from Aphrodite	MARMONIA
recovered	
—by Menelaus	HELEN
—Helen	MENELAUS
—sight at Lemnos	ORION
rescued by	
—Artemis	ARETHUSA, IPHIGENIA
—Athena	IPHIGENIA, ORESTES
	PYLADES
—Calypso	ODYSSEUS, PHRYXUS
—Castor and Pollux	HELEN
—Dionysius	ARIADNE
—Hercules	HESIONE
—Ino	ODYSSEUS
—Iris	HARPIES
—Nausicaa	ODYSSEUS
—Perseus	ANDROMEDA
—Poseidon	AMYMONE
—Zephyr	PSYCHE
—Zeus	ODYSSEUS
rescued from Hades by Hercules	ALCESTIS, THESEUS
rescuer of	
—Alcestis from Hades	HERCULES
—Amymone	POSEIDON
—Andromeda	PERSEUS
—Arethusa	ARTEMIS
—Ariadne	DIONYSIUS
—Harpies	IRIS
—Helen	CASTOR, POLLUX
—Hesione	HERCULES
—Iphigenia	ARTEMIS, ATHENA
—Odysseus	CALYPSO, INO
	NAUSICAA, ZEUS
—Orestes	ATHENA
—Phryxus	CALYPSO
—Prometheus	HERCULES
—Psyche	ZEPHYR
—Pylades	ATHENA
—Theseus from Hades	HERCULES
restored to life by gods	PELOPS
Rhea	CYBELE
rider of Pegasus	BELLEROPHON
river	
—encircling Earth	OCEAN
—in	
Delphi	CEPHISSUS
Hades	ACHERON, COCYTUS
	LETHE, PHLEGETHON, STYX
Phrygia	MEANDER

Tempe	PENEUS
Thrace	HEBRUS
—not seen by mortals	ERIDANUS
—of Troy	SCAMANDER, SIMOIS
	XANTHUS
Roman equivalents	
—Aphrodite	VENUS
—Ares	MARS
—Artemis	DIANA
—Asklepios	AESCULAPIUS
—Athena	MINERVA
—Aurora	MATER MATUTA
—Cronus	SATURN
—Demeter	CERES
—Dionysius	BACCHUS, LIBER, LYAEUS
—Enyo	BELLONA
—Eros	CUPID
—Hades	DIS
—Helios	SOL
—Hephaestus	MULCIBER, VULCAN
—Hera	JUNO
—Hermes	MERCURY
—Hestia	VESTA
—Hypnos	SOMNUS
—Ino	MATER MATUTA
—Leto	LATONA
—Eileithyia	JUNO, LUCINA
—Lyaeus	LIBER
—Nike	VICTORIA
—Odysseus	ULYSSES
—Persephone	LIBERIA, PROSERPINE
—Pluto	DIS
—Poseidon	NEPTUNE
—Thanatos	MORS
—Zeus	JOVE, JUPITER
ruler of Titans	CRONUS, EURYNOME
	OPHION
sacrificed before Troy	IPHIGENIA
satyr	FAUN, MARSYAS
saved	
—Amymone from satyr	POSEIDON
—Argonauts from Talus	MEDEA
—by	
Ariadne	THESEUS
dolphins	ARION
Medea from Talus	ARGONAUTS
Theseus	PIRITHOUS
Poseidon from satyr	AMYMONE
—Pirithous	THESEUS
—Theseus	ARIADNE
saviour of mankind	PROMETHEUS
sculptor	PYGMALION
sea nymph	DORIS, GALATEA
	HESIONE, THETIS
seer of Corinth	POLYIDUS
Selene	ARTEMIS, PHOEBE

serpent guarding golden apples	LADON
seven sisters	PLEIADES
shepherd	ENDYMION
—in Sicily	DAPHNIS
shield-carrier for Zeus	ATHENA
ship's pilot	ACETES, PALURINUS
shot Centaurs	ATALANTA
Sicily	TRINACRIA
Siren	PARTHENOPE
sister of	
—Agave	AUTONOE, INO, SEMELE
—Aglauros	HERSE, PANDROSUS
—Antigone	ISMENE
—Apollo	ARTEMIS
—Apsyrtus	MEDEA
—Ares	ERIS, HEBE
—Ariadne	PHAEDRA
—Autonoe	AGAVE, INO, SEMELE
—Cadmus	EUROPA
—Castor	HELEN
—Creon	JOCASTA
—Creusa	ORITHYIA, PROCRIS
—Doris	GALATEA
—Dryope	IOLE
—Erechtheus	PROCNE, PHILOMENA
—Eteocles	ANTIGONE, ISMENE
—Galatea	DORIS
—Gorgons	GRAIAE
—Graiae	GORGONS
—Helios	SELENE
—Herse	AGLAUROS, PANDROSUS
—Ino	AGAVE, AUTONOE, SEMELE
—Iole	DRYOPE
—Ismene	ANTIGONE
—Orestes	ELECTRA, IPHIGENIA
—Orithyia	CREUSA, PROCRIS
—Pandrosus	AGLAUROS, HERSE
—Pelops	NIOBE
—Phaedra	ARIADNE
—Phaeton	HELIADES
—Philomena	PROCNE
—Phrixus	HELLE
—Pluto	HESTIA
—Polyneices	ANTIGONE, ISMENE
—Poseidon	HESTIA
—Procne	PHILOMENA
—Procris	CREUSA, ORITHYIA
—Pygmalion	DIDO
—Semele	AGAVE, AUTONOE, INO
site of Orpheus' burial	LIBETHRA
slave of	
—Admetus	APOLLO
—Omphale	HERCULES
slept for 57 years	EPIMENIDES
Sminthian	APOLLO
snake-haired monsters	GORGONS

son of

—Achilles	NEOPTOLEMUS
—Aeacus	TELAMON
—Aegeus	THESEUS
—Aegina	AEACUS
—Aeneas	ASCANIUS
—Aerope	AGAMEMNON
—Aesculapius	MACHAON
—Aeson	JASON
—Aetes	APSYRTUS
—Aethra	THESEUS
—Agamemnon	ORESTES
—Agave	PENTHEUS
—Alcaeus	AMPHITRYON
—Alcmena	HERCULES, IPHICLES
—Althea	MELEAGER
—Amphitrite	TRITON
—Amphitryon	IPHICLES
—Anchises	AENEAS
—Andromache	ASTYANAX
—Andromeda	ELECTRYON
—Antiope	AMPHION, ZETHUS
—Aphrodite	AENEAS, CUPID, EROS
—Apollo	AESCULAPIUS, ARISTAEUS
	ION, LINUS
—Ares	TEREUS
—Arsinoe	AESCULAPIUS
—Atalanta	PARTHENOPAEUS
—Athamas	PHRIXUS
—Atreus	AGAMEMNON, MENELAUS
—Aurora	MEMNON
—Autonoe	ACTAEON
—Boreas	CALAIS, ZETES
—Cadmus	POLYDORUS
—Callisto	ARCAS
—Calypso	PAN, SILENUS
—Cinyras	ADONIS
—Clytemnestra	ORESTES
—Coronis	AESCULAPIUS
—Creon	MENOECEUS
—Cresphontes	AEPYTUS
—Creusa	ION
—Cronos	ZEUS
—Cydippe	BITON, CLEOBIS
—Cyrene	ARISTAEUS
—Daedalus	ICARUS
—Danae	PERSEUS
—Deucalion	HELLEN
—Electra	DARDANUS
—Endymion	AETOLUS
—Europa	MINOS, RHADAMANTHUS
	SARPEDON
—Eurynome	BELLEROPHON
—Evander	PALLAS
—Faunus	LATINUS
—Galatea	PAPHOS

—Glaucus	BELLEROPHON
—Gordus	MIDAS
—Heaven	CRONUS
—Hector	ASTYANAX
—Hecuba	DEIPHOBUS, HECTOR
	PARIS
—Helen	XUTHUS
—Hellen	AEOLUS
—Hera	ARES, HEPHAESTUS
—Hercules	CRESPHONTES, TELEPHUS
—Hermes	PAN
—Hippodamia	ATREUS, THYESTES
—Hypermnestra	ABAS
—Hypnos	ICELUS, MORPHEUS
	PHANTASUS
—Iapetus	ATLAS, PROMETHEUS
	EPIMETHEUS
—Ino	MELICERTES
—Io	EPAPHUS
—Iphimedia	EPHIALTES, OTUS
—Laertes	ODYSSEUS
—Leda	CASTOR, POLLUX
—Leto	APOLLO
—Lucifer	CEYX
—Lucothea	PALAEMON
—Lynceus	ABAS
—Maia	HERMES
—Merope	AEPYTUS
—Mezentius	LAUSUS
—Minos	ANDROGEUS
—Mother Earth	PONTUS
—Myrrha	ADONIS
—Neleus	NESTOR
—Nepele	PHRIXUS
—Nereus	PONTUS
—Nestor	ANTILOCHUS
—Odysseus	TELEMACHUS
—Oedipus	ETEOCLES, POLYNEICES
—Oeneus	MELEAGER
—Oileus	AJAX
—Orithyia	CALAIS, ZETES
—Pan	SILENUS
—Peleus	ACHILLES
—Pelops	ATREUS, THYESTES
—Penelope	TELEMACHUS
—Perseus	ELECTRYON
—Poeas	PHILOCTETES
—Polybus	OEDIPUS
—Poseidon	EPHIALTES, NELEUS, OTUS
	PELIAS, POLYPHEMUS
	PROTEUS, TRITON
—Priam	AGENOR, DEIPHOBUS, HECTOR
	PARIS, POLYDORUS, TROILUS
—Procne	ITYS
—Prometheus	DEUCALION
—Psamathe	LINUS

—Pygmalion	PAPHOS
—Pyrrha	HELLEN
—Saturn	JUPITER
—Scamander	TEUCER
—Semele	DIONYSIUS
—Sisyphus	GLAUCUS
—Sun	PHAETON
—Tantalus	PELOPS
—Telamon	AJAX, TEUCER
—Tereus	ITYS
—Theseus	HIPPOLYTUS
—Thetis	ACHILLES
—Thyestes	AEGISTHUS
—Tithonus	MEMNON
—Tydeus	DIOMEDES, TYDIDES
—Tyro	NELEUS, PELIAS
—Uranus	CRONUS
—Venus	AENEAS
—Zeus	AEACUS, AMPHION, APOLLO
	ARCAS, ARES, DIONYSIUS
	EPAPHUS, HEPHAESTUS, HERCULES
	HERMES, PERSEUS, POLLUX
	SARPEDON, TANTALUS, ZETHUS
soothsayer to Argonauts	MOPSUS
south wind	AUSTER, NOTUS
sowed dragon's teeth from which soldiers sprang	CADMUS
spear of Poseidon	TRIDENT
spirit in all things	GENIUS
spoke the language of animals	MELAMPUS
sprang from	
—foam of sea	APHRODITE
—head of Zeus	ATHENA
—Heaven's blood	GIANTS, ERINYES
	EUMENIDES, FURIES
spring	
—in	
Corinth	PIRENE
Delphi	CASTALIA
—on Mount Helicon	HIPPOCRENE
star-maiden	ASTRAEA
stole	
—Apollo's herds	HERMES
—cattle from Hercules	CACUS
—weapons from Hercules	CERCOPES
subdued Aetean bulls	JASON
suitor of Penelope	ANTINOUS
swallowed by Zeus	METIS
swam Hellespont nightly	LEANDER
swineherd	EUMAEUS
temple of Athena	PARTHENON
three women with one eye between them	GRAIAE
three-bodied monster	GERYON
thrown from walls of Troy	ASTYANAX

thunderer	ZEUS
tied to	
—bull by her hair	DIRCE
—wheel for ever	IXION
Titans	(*see* **gods**—Greek)
tongue cut out by Tereus	PROCNE
torn to pieces by his dogs	LINUS
tree of	
—Aphrodite	MYRTLE
—Artemis	CYPRESS
—Athena	OLIVE
—Zeus	OAK
Trinacria	SICILY
Trivia	HECATE
trumpeter of the sea	TRITON
turned	
—Anaraxete to stone	VENUS
—men into beasts	CIRCE
tutor of	
—Achilles	CHIRON
—Aesculapius	CHIRON
—Eurynome	ATHENA
—Perdix	DAEDALUS
twin brothers	AMPHION, ZETHUS
	CASTOR, POLLUX
	NELEUS, PELIAS
twins	APOLLO, ARTEMIS
Tydides	DIOMEDES
Tyndaris	CLYTEMNESTRA, HELEN
Typhoeus	TYPHON
Typhon	TYPHOEUS
ugly god	HEPHAESTUS
Unfriendly Sea	AXINE
usurper of Greek throne	PELIAS
valley in Thessaly	TEMPE
Vesper	HESPER
virgin goddess	ATHENA, ARTEMIS
	HESTIA
watchman with 100 eyes	ARGUS
wearer of winged	
—headgear	HERMES
—sandals	HERMES
weaver	ARACHNE
west wind	FAVONIUS, ZEPHYR
whirlpool	CHARYBDIS
winged horse	PEGASUS
witch	CIRCE
wife of	
—Admetus	ALCESTIS
—Adrastus	ERIPHYLE
—Aegeus	AETHRA
—Aeneas	LAVINIA
—Agamemnon	CLYTEMNESTRA
—Alcinous	ARETE
—Amphion	NIOBE
—Amphitryon	ALCMENA

—Athamas	INO, NEPHELE
—Atreus	AEROPE
—Cadmus	HARMONIA
—Capaneus	EVADNE
—Cephalus	PROCRIS
—Cepheus	CASSIOPEIA
—Ceyx	ALCYONE
—Cresphontes	MEROPE
—Cretheus	SIDERO, TYRO
—Cronus	RHEA
—Cupid	PSYCHE
—Deucalion	PYRRHA
—Glaucus	EURYNOME
—Hades	PERSEPHONE
—Hector	ANDROMACHE
—Helenus	ANDROMACHE
—Hephaestus	AGLAIA, APHRODITE
—Hercules	DEIANIRA, HEBE
	MEGARA
—King Tyndareus	LEDA
—Laius	JOCASTA
—Latinus	AMATA
—Lycus	DIRCE
—Lynceus	HYPERMNESTRA
—Melanion	ATALANTA
—Menelaus	HELEN
—Minos	PASIPHAE
—Neoptolemus	HERMIONE
—Nereus	DORIS
—Ocean	TETHYS
—Odysseus	PENELOPE
—Oedipus	JOCASTA
—Orpheus	EURYDICE
—Peleus	THETIS
—Pelops	HIPPODAMIA
—Perseus	ANDROMEDA
—Philemon	BAUCIS
—Pirithous	HIPPODAMIA
—Polyphontes	MEROPE
—Poseidon	AMPHITRITE, LYBIA
—Priam	HECUBA
—Proetus	ANTEIA
—Prometheus	HESIONE
—Protesilaus	LAODAMIA
—Pygmalion	GALATEA
—Pylades	ELECTRA
—Rhadamanthus	EUROPA
—Saturn	OPS
—Sichaeus	DIDO
—Tereus	PROCNE
—Theseus	PHAEDRA
	HIPPOLYTA
—Tithonus	AURORA
—Uranus	GAEA
—Xuthus	CREUSA
—Zeus	HERA

wounded by	
—Cronus	HEAVEN
—Diomedes	AENEAS
—Hercules	CHIRON, TELEPHUS
—Norse	
Asgarth	ASGARD
ash tree	YG(G)DRASIL(L)
Attila	ATLI
Balder	BALDUR
battlefield of gods' defeat	VIGRID
blind god	HODER, HODUR
boar	
—providing food in Valhalla	SERIMNIR
—pulling Freyr's car	GULLINBURSTI
—with golden pelt	GULLINBURSTI
brother of	
—Balder	HODER
—Fafnir	REGIN, OTTER
—Gudrun	GUNNAR
—Hoder	BALDER
—Otter	FAFNIR, REGIN
—Regin	FAFNIR, OTTER
—Signy	SIGMUND
bound with magic chain	FENRIS
bridge to Asgard	BIFROST
changed into dragon	FAFNIR
chasm before the creation	GINUNGAGAP
choosers of the slain	FREYA, VALKYRIES
city of giants	JOTUNHEIM
cow whose milk fed Ymir	AUDHUMBLA
daughter of	
—Angerbode	HELA
—Griemhild	GUDRUN
—Sigurd	SWANHILD
—Volsung	SIGNY
day of doom	RAGNAROK
died	
—in burning house	SIGNY
—of broken heart	NANNA
dog guarding Hela's gate	GARM
dragon	FAFNIR, NIDHOGG
dwarf	ANDVARI
enemies of gods	GIANTS
end of world	RAGNAROK
father of	
—Gunnar	GIUKI
—Odin	BOR
—Signy	VOLSUNG
—Sigurd	SIGMUND
—Sinfiotli	SIGMUND
—Swanhild	SIGURD
—Vidar	ODIN
fates	(*see separate entry*)
first	
—giant	YMIR
—man	ASK

—woman	EMBLA
follower(s) of Siegfried	NIBELUNG(EN)
gave up an eye for wisdom	ODIN
giant	FAFNER, FAFNIR
	FASOLT, JOTUM, MIMIR
	TAROLL, THRYM, YMER
	YMIR
giantess	GERDA, GROA, NATT
goblin	NIS, TROLL
gods	AESIR
guardian(s) of	
—treasure	NIBELUNG(EN)
—Urda's well	NORNA, NORNS
—Well of Knowledge	MIMIR
half-brother of	
—Gunnar	GUTTORM
—Guttorm	GUNNAR
hall	
—in Asgard	VALHALLA, WALHALLA
—for the slain	VALHALLA, WALHALLA
heaven	ASGARD, ASGARTH
	VALHALLA, WALHALLA
heroic race	VOLUSPA
holy well	URDA'S WELL
home of	
—elves	ELFHEIM
—goddesses	VINGOLF
—gods	ASGARD, ASGARTH
	VALHALLA, WALHALLA
horn of Heimdall	GIALLAR
horse of Odin	SLEIPNIR
husband of	
—Brynhild	GUNNAR
—Frigga	ODIN
—Gerda	FREYR
—Gudrun	ATLI, SIGURD
—Iduna	BRAGI
—Nanna	BALDER
—Signy	SIGGEIR
—Sigyn	LOKI
—Swanhild	JOMUNREK
inhabitants	
—of	
Jotunheim	FROST GIANTS
	MOUNTAIN GIANTS
Midgard	MANKIND
Utgard	GIANTS
—under Midgard	DWARFS
keeper of	
—apples of youth	IDUNA
—rainbow bridge	HEIMDALL
—flowers and streams	ELVES
killed by	
—Gudrun	ATLI
—Guttorm	SIGURD
—horses	SWANHILD

—Jomunrek	SWANHILD
—Loki	OTTER
—mistletoe bough	BALDER
—Odin	YMIR
—Sigurd	FAFNIR, REGIN
killer of	
—Atli	GUDRUN
—Fafnir	SIGURD
—Otter	LOKI
—Regin	SIGURD
—Sigurd	GUTTORM
—Swanhild	JOMUNREK
—Ymir	ODIN
king	ATU
—of Giukungs	GUNNAR
land of	
—fire	MUSPELHEIM
—giants	UTGARD
—mankind	MIDGARD
magic(al)	
—chain	GLEIPNIR
—inscriptions	RUNES
—ship	SKIDBLADNIR
maidens	VALKYRIE, WALKYRIE
man made from	ASH
memory	MUNIN
middle earth	MIDGARD
most loved god	BALDER
mother of	
—Balder	FRIGGA
—Fenris	ANGERBODE
—Gudrun	GRIEMHILD
—Gunnar	GRIEMHILD
—Hela	ANGERBODE
—Hermod	FRIGGA
—Midgard serpent	ANGERBODE
—Sinfiotli	SIGNY
Odin	WODEN
palace of	
—dead	VALHALLA, WALHALLA
—Frigga	FENSALIR
—Odin	GLADSHEIM
paradise	ASGARD, ASGARTH
	VALHALLA, WALHALLA
put to sleep by Odin	BRYNHILD
rainbow bridge	BIFROST
ravens of Odin	HUGIN, MUNIN
region of mist	NIFLHEIM
ruler of	
—Jotunheim	UTGARD-LOKI
—Muspelheim	SURTR
serpent	MITGARD
servant of	
—Freyr	SKIRNIR
—Loki	THIALFI
served by Thialfi	LOKI

ship built by dwarfs	SKIDBLADNIR	tied up in cavern	LOKI
sister of		trampled by horses	SWANHILD
—Gunnar	GUDRUN	underworld	NIFLHEIM
—Sigmund	SIGNY	Valkyrie	BRYNHILD
son of		wakens Brynhild	SIGURD
—Bor	ODIN	Walhalla	VALHALLA
—Frigga	BALDER, HERMOD	Woden	ODIN
	HODER, VIDAR	wife of	
—giant	LOKI	—Atli	GUDRUN
—Giuki	GUNNAR	—Balder	NANNA
—Griemhild	GUNNAR	—Bragi	IDUNA
—Odin	BALDER, HERMOD	—Freyr	GERDA
	HODER, VIDAR	—Gunnar	BRYNHILD
—Sigmund	SIGURD, SINFIOTLI	—Jomunrek	SWANHILD
—Signy	SINFIOTLI	—Loki	SIGYN
sprang from ice	BOR	—Odin	FRIGGA
stole Thor's hammer	THRYM	—Siggeir	SIGNY
supernatural		—Sigurd	GUDRUN
—dwarf	TROLL	wolf	FENRIS
—race	NIBELUNG(EN)	—of Odin	FREKI, GERI
swiftest of gods	HERMOD	world ash-tree	YG(G)DRASIL(L)
thought	HUGI(N)	Ymer	YMIR
threw mistletoe at Balder	HODER	*(see also* **gods, goddesses**)	

N

names
added name	AGNOMEN
assumed name	ALIAS, PSEUDONYM
code name	NOM DE GUERRE
distinguished name	EPONYM
false	ALIAS, ANONYM, PSEUDONYM
familiar name	COGNOMEN, NICKNAME
first name	CHRISTIAN NAME, FORENAME
giver of names	NOMENCLATOR
having	
—many names	MULTINOMIAL
	POLYNOMIAL
	POLYNOMIC
	POLYNYMOUS
—similar name	COGNOMINAL
last name (Roman)	COGNOMEN
name	
—taken from ancestor	PATRONYMIC
—with	
two words	BINOMIAL
three words	TRINOMIAL, TRIONYM
several words	POLYNYM
—without description	NOMEN NUDUM
nameless	ANONYMOUS
namesake	HOMONYM
naming	
—by	
2 attributes	BINOMIAL
3 attributes	TRINOMIAL
—parents from child	TEKNONYMY
—the subject	NOMINATIVE
nickname	COGNOMEN, SOBRIQUET
nicknames	(*see separate entry*)
one	
—named	NOMINEE
—whose name is used for	
some object	EPONYM
opposite	ANTONYM
pen name	NOM DE PLUME
	PSEUDONYM
pertaining to names	NOMINAL
place name	TOPONYM
propose by name	NOMINATE
pseudonym	TELONISM
real name (of author)	AUTONYM
rejected name in biology	HOMONYM
same name	HOMONYM, SYNONYM
second name (Roman)	NOMEN

surname	COGNOMEN
system of names	NOMENCLATURE
systematic name	SYNONYM
with author's name	ONYMOUS
written backwards	ANANYM
Namibia	SWAZA
capital	WINDHOEK

national
National Board for Prices and Incomes	PIB
National Book League	NBL
National Broadcasting Company	NBC
National Bureau of Standards	NBS
National Cash Register Company	NCR
National Coal Board	NCB
National Enterprise Board	NEB
National Exhibition Centre	NEC
National Farmers' Union	NFU
National Fire Service	NFS
National Front	NF
National Graphical Association	NGA
National Health	
—Insurance	NHI
—Service	NHS
National Incomes Commission	NIC, NICKY
National Insurance	NI
National Opinion Poll	NOP
National Physical Laboratory	NPL
National Portrait Gallery	NPG
National Rifle Association	NRA
National Trust (for Scotland)	NT(S)
National Union of	
—Journalists	NUJ
—Mineworkers	NUM
—Railwaymen	NUR
—Seamen	NUS
—Students	NUS
—Teachers	NUT
National University of Ireland	NUI
National Youth Orchestra	NYO
naturalists	(*see* **biology**)
Navy	RN
Naval Reserve Decoration	NRD
	(*see also* **sailor**)

Nepal
capital	KAT(H)MANDU
coin	
—unit	PAISA
—100 paisa	RUPEE

nerve
acting automatically	AUTONOMOUS
	REFLEX
all nerves except	
central nervous	
system	
	PERIPHERAL NERVOUS SYSTEM
axon of nerve-cell	NERVE-FIBRE

brain and spinal		dorsal root	POSTERIOR ROOT
cord	CENTRAL NERVOUS SYSTEM	external sheath	NEURILEMMA
	CNS		NEUROLEMMA
branching process	DENDRITE, DENDRON	fibre carrying impulse	AXON
bundle of		flat area of nerve	
—nerve fibres	TRACT	tissue	NEURAL PLATE
connecting centres	COMMISSURE	gap in nerve sheath	NODE OF RANVIER
—nerves	FASCIC(U)LE, FINICULUS	group of nerve cells	GANGLION
	GIANT FIBRE	in or controlling	
carrying		—arm	BRACHIAL, MEDIAN
—instructions for			RADIAL, ULNAR
movement	MOTOR	—arterioles	VASOMOTORA
—sensations		—back	COCCYGEAL, LUMBAR
from brain	DEFERENT, EFFERENT		SACRAL
to		—balance	VESTIBULAR
—brain	AFFERENT	—blood vessels	CONSTRICTOR, DILATOR
—central nervous		—breathing	PNEUMOGASTRIC, VAGUS
system	SENSORY	—calf	SURAL
cell	NEURON(E)	—chest	INTERCOSTAL, THORACIC
—body	CYTON	—digestive organs	PNEUMOGASTRIC
—connected with			VAGUS
receptor	SENSORY NERVE-CELL	—ear	AUDITORY, ACOUSTIC, OTIC
	SENSORY NEURON(E)	—eye	OPTIC, OPHTHALMIC
—connection	SYNAPSE	—eye muscles	ABDUCENT, OCULOMOTOR
—in retina	CONE, ROD		TROCHLEAR
—which		—face	(TRI)FACIAL, TRIGEMINAL
becomes nerve-cell	NEUROBLAST	—hearing	AUDITORY
sheathes nerve-fibres	SCHWANN CELL	—heart-beat	VAGUS
central nervous system	CNS	—jaw	MANDIBULAR, MAXILLARY
centre	GANGLION		TRIFACIAL, TRIGEMINAL
—controlling appetite	APPESTAT	—leg	FEMORAL, PERONEAL
channel holding spinal			SCIATIC, TIBIAL
cord	NEURAL CHANNEL	—lungs	PNEUMOGASTRIC, VAGUS
chemical messenger	NEUROTRANSMITTER	—neck	ACCESSORY, CERVICAL
	NEUROHUMOUR	—pharynx	GLOSSOPHARYNGEAL
connection	SYNAPSE	—shoulder	ACCESSORY
constriction in		—scalp	TRIFACIAL, TRIGEMINAL
nerve-fibre	NODE OF RANVIER	—skull	CRANIAL NERVE
core of nerve fibre	AXIS CYLINDER	—smell	OLFACTORY
cranial nerves		—spinal cord	SPINAL NERVE
—1. smell	OLFACTORY	—stomach	PNEUMOGASTRIC
—2. vision	OPTIC		SOLAR PLEXUS, VAGUS
—3. eye movements	OCULOMOTOR	—thigh	SCIATIC
—4. eye movements	TROCHLEAR	—tongue	HYPOGLOSSAL
—5. eye movements	ABDUCENT	inflammation	NEURITIS
—6. face and scalp, jaw	TRIFACIAL	intersection of nerves	CHIASM(A)
	TRIGEMINAL	large-diameter nerve	GIANT FIBRE
—7. face movements	FACIAL	mass of axons and dendrites	NEUROPIL
—8. acoustic		membranes covering	
balance	VESTIBULAR	central nervous system	
hearing	COCHLEAR		PIA-ARACHNOID MEMBRANES
—9. back of mouth	GLOSSOPHARYNGEAL	—inner	PIA MATER
—10. digestion, heart, etc	VAGUS	—outer	ARACHNOID
—11. neck and shoulder		motor	
muscles	ACCESSORY	—nerve root	ANTERIOR ROOT
—12. tongue	HYPOGLOSSAL		MOTOR ROOT, VENTRAL ROOT

—nerves to smooth muscles	AUTONOMIC NERVOUS SYSTEM
nerve-ending	EFFECTOR, RECEPTOR
nerve-fibre bundle uniting nerve centres	COMMISSURE
nervous	
—illnesses	NEURASTHENIA NEUROPATHY, NEUROSIS
—tissue in embryo	NEURAL TISSUE
network of cells	PLEXUS
neuro-transmitter	ACETYL CHOLINE
organ at end of motor nerve	MOTOR ENDPLATE
pain in nerve	NEURALGIA
part of system producing immediate response	REFLEX ARC
parts of nerve	AXON, DENDRITE DENDRON MEDULLARY SHEATH MYELIN, (NEUR)AXON NEURILEMMA, NODE SYNAPSE, TERMINAL
peripheral nerve	SENSORY NERVE
raised edge of neural plate	NEURAL FOLD
ridge in neural plate	NEURAL CREST
reacting to	
—coarse stimuli	PROTOPATHIC
—small stimuli	EPICRITIC
region with special function	NERVE CENTRE
root	
—animal	DORSAL, VENTRAL
—human	ANTERIOR, POSTERIOR
—in spinal cord	NERVE ROOT
—motor nerve	MOTOR ROOT
—with sensory fibres	SENSORY ROOT
secreting	
—adrenalin	ADRENERGIC
—acetylcholine	CHOLINERGIC
serving	
—automatic muscles	AUTONOMIC SYSTEM
—involuntary muscles	SYMPATHETIC SYSTEM
sheath round nerve fibres	MYELIN SHEATH
study of origins of nervous system	NEUROGENETICS
strand of nerve tissue	NERVE CORD
substance	
—forming nerve-sheaths	MYALIN
—secreted at nerve-ends	ACETYLCHOLINE, ACH ADRENALIN(E)
supporting tissue	(NEURO)GLIA

system	AUTONOMIC, CENTRAL (ORTHO)SYMPATHETIC PARASYMPATHETIC PERIPHERAL
—controlling movement	MOTARIUM
—in invertebrates	NERVE NET
—sensory	SENSORIUM
theory of discrete nerve-cells	NEURONE THEORY
tissue	
—binding nerves	PERINEURIUM
—carrying impulses	NERVE FIBRE
trifacial	TRIGEMINAL
tumour of nerve tissue	NEUROMA
vagus	PNEUMOGASTRIC NERVE
Netherlands	NL
Netherlands Antilles	NT
	(see also **Dutch***)*
New	
New Church	NC
New England	NE
New English	
—Bible	NEB
—Dictionary	NED
New Jersey	CALF, NJ
New Orleans	NO
New Providence	NP
New Smoking Material	NSM
New South Wales	NSW
New Testament	NT
New York	BIG APPLE, GOTHAM, NY
—City	NYC
district	BOWERY, BRONX HARLEM, MANHATTAN QUEENS
opera	MET
New Version	NV
New Zealand	NZ
including: Maori	
abalone	PAUA, PAWA
aborigine	MAORI
ancestral ornament	(HEI) TIKI
animal	TAEPO, TAIPO
basket	KIT(E)
biological region	ORNITHOGAEA
bird	APTERYX, BELL-BIRD, BUSH-WREN HONEY-BIRD, HUIA, KABOB, KIWI KOKAKO, MAKO, MAORI-HEN NOTORNIS, OWL-PARROT PARSON-BIRD, POAKA RIFLE(MAN)-BIRD TAKAHE(A), WEKA, WRY-BILL
blood-money	UTU
boy	TAMA
canoe	WAKA

capital	WELLINGTON
chief	RANGATIRA
cloth	PAR(R)AMATTA
club	MERE, MERI
currant bread	BROWNIE
dock labourer	SEAGULL
eel	TUNA
emblem	KOWHIA
extinct bird	MOA
feast	KAIKAI
fertility symbol	HEI TIKI
fish	HIKU, MORWONG
	PAGROSOMUS
	SNAPPER, TRUMPETER
flax	PHORMIUM
food	KAI(-KAI)
fort	PA(H)
funeral	TANGI
glory pea	KOWHAI, PARROT-BEAK
	PARROT-BILL, PARROT-JAW
good health!	KIA-ORA
grass	TOI TOI
hedge	KARO, KOHUHU
house	WHARE
husband	TANGATA
hut	WHARE
image	(HEI) TIKI
Indian corn	KANGA
laburnum	KOWHIA
Land of Long White Cloud	AOTEAROA
language	MAORI
lavatory	DUNNY
leaves used for tea	MANUKA
lily	PHORMIUM
lizard	HATTERIA, SPHENODON
	TUATARA, TUATERA
locust	WETA
man	TANGATA
Maori greeting	HONGI
measure of beer	HANDLE
meeting-place	MARAE
mourning	TANGI
mysterious power	MANA
native	MAORI
neck pendant	HEI TIKI
New Zealand	AOTEAROA
New Zealander	DIGGER, KIWI
noble	RANGATIRA
nose-rubbing as greeting	HONGI
original settler	SHAGROON
oven	HA(A)NGI
owl	MOPEHAWK, MOPOKE
	MOREPORK, PEHO, RURU
owl-parrot	KAKAPO, STRI(N)GOPS
palm	NIKAU
parrot	KAKA(-BEAK), KAKA-BILL, KEA

—bill	GLORY-PEA
parson-bird	POE(-BIRD)
	POY(-BIRD), TUI
penguin	KORORA
plant	FLAX-BUSH, FLAX-LILY
	VEGETABLE SHEEP
political union	ANZUS
requital	UTU
resin	KAURI-GUM
Rugby team	ALL BLACKS
settlement	PA(H)
settler	SHAGROON
shellfish	PAUA, PAWA
	TOHEROA
shrub	HOHERIA, KARO, KIEKIE
	KOWHAI, MANOAO
	PLAGIANTHUS, TUTU
soldier	ANZAC
spear	TAIAHA
spider	KATIPO, NIGHT-STINGER
stockade	PA(H)
stone figurine	(HEI) TIKI
storage pit	RUA
sweet potato	KUMARA
tattooing	MOKO
tea	MANUKA
thrush	TURNAGRA
thylacine	TIGER-WOLF
tree	HINAU, HINO, HINOU, KARAKA
	KAURI(-PINE), MANUKA, MAKOMAKO
	MIRO, NGAIO, PELU, RATA, RIMU, TAWA
	TITOKI, TOTARA, TUTU, WINE-BERRY
war-dance	HAKA
welcome!	HAERE MAI
white man	PAKEHA
wife	WAHINE
woman	WAHINE
work	MAHI
youth	TAMA
zoological realm	NOTOGAEA
newspaper	
Australia	THE AUSTRALIAN
	SUN NEWS HERALD
Canada	TORONTO GLOBE AND MAIL
China	PEOPLE'S DAILY
Egypt	AL NOOR, EL AKHBAR
France	LE FIGARO, LE MONDE
	LE PARISIEN, LIBERATION
Germany	BERLINER ZEITUNG
	BILD AM SONNTAG, BILD ZEITUNG
	DIE WELT
	FRANKFURTER ALLEGEMEINE ZEITUNG
Great Britain	
—national	DAILY EXPRESS, DAILY MAIL
	DAILY MIRROR, DAILY TELEGRAPH
	FINANCIAL TIMES, GUARDIAN

	INDEPENDENT, MORNING STAR
	SPORTING LIFE, STAR, SUN
	TIMES, TODAY
Sunday	INDEPENDENT ON SUNDAY
	MAIL ON SUNDAY
	MIRROR, NEWS OF THE WORLD
	OBSERVER, PEOPLE
	SUNDAY EXPRESS, SUNDAY SPORT
	SUNDAY TELEGRAPH
	SUNDAY TIMES
—provincial	BIRMINGHAM POST
	BIRMINGHAM EVENING MAIL
	DAILY POST, EAST ANGLIAN DAILY
	EASTERN DAILY PRESS
	EASTERN MORNING NEWS
	EVENING CHRONICLE
	EXPRESS AND STAR, LIVERPOOL ECHO
	LONDON EVENING STANDARD
	MANCHESTER EVENING NEWS
	NORTHERN ECHO, STAR
	THE JOURNAL
	WESTERN DAILY PRESS
	WESTERN MAIL, YORKSHIRE POST
Finland	ILTALEHTI
Germany	BERLINER ZEITUNG
	BILD AM SONNTAG, BILD ZEITUNG
	DIE WELT
	FRANKFURTER ALLGEMEINE ZEITUNG
India	TIMES OF INDIA
Iran	ABRAR
Iraq	BAGHDAD OBSERVER, EL QADISIYAH
Ireland	BELFAST TELEGRAPH
	IRISH NEWS, IRISH TIMES
Italy	CORRIERE DELLA SERA
	LA REPUBBLICA, LA STAMPA
Japan	ASAHI SHIMBUN
	MAINICHI SHIMBUN
	YOMIURI SHIMBUN
Pakistan	THE NATION
Russia	IZVESTIA, MOSCOW NEWS
	PRAVDA
Scotland	DAILY RECORD
	EVENING TIMES
	GLASGOW HERALD
	PRESS AND JOURNAL, SCOTSMAN
South Africa	BEEL, DAILY MAIL
Spain	EL PAIS
Syria	AL-THAWRA
Switzerland	DER BUND
USA	CHICAGO SUN-TIMES
	CHICAGO TRIBUNE, HERALD-TRIBUNE
	LOS ANGELES TIMES
	NEW YORK DAILY NEWS
	NEW YORK TIMES
	WALL STREET JOURNAL
	WASHINGTON POST

Nicaragua	NIC
capital	MANAGUA
coin	CENTAVO, CORDOBA
nickname	COGNOMEN, SOBRIQUET
Allen, G O	GUBBY
Armstrong, Louis	SATCHMO
Basie, William	COUNT, THE CHIEF
	THE KID FROM RED BANK
Bonaparte, Napoleon	BONEY, NAP
Cole, Nat(haniel)	KING
Cromwell, Oliver	NOLL
Durante, Jimmy	SCHNOZZLE
Eisenhower, Dwight	IKE
Elizabeth I	CYNTHIA, DARK LADY
	GLORIANA, GOOD QUEEN BESS
	VIRGIN QUEEN
Ellington, Edward K	DUKE
Gladstone, William	GOM, GRAND OLD MAN
Great Britain	JOHN BULL
	PERFIDIOUS ALBION
Hawkins, Coleman	THE BEAN, HAWK
Heseltine, Michael	TARZAN
Higgins, Alex	HURRICANE
Hines, Earl	FATHA
Holiday, Billie	LADY DAY
Howe, Sir Geoffrey	MOGADON MAN
IBM	BIG BLUE
Kinnock, Neil	WELSH WINDBAG
Laye, Evelyn	BOO
Lloyd George, David	WELSH WIZARD
Macmillan, Harold	SUPERMAC
McCartney, Paul	MACCA
McEnroe, John	SUPERBRAT
Morton, Ferdinand	JELLY ROLL
Nicklaus, Jack	GOLDEN BEAR
Nixon, Richard	TRICKY DICKY
Norman, Greg	GREAT WHITE SHARK
Parker, Charlie	BIRD
Skinner, Dennis	BEAST OF BOLSOVER
Smith, Willie	THE LION
Stalin	UNCLE JOE
Sutherland, Joan	LA STUPENDA
Thatcher, Mrs M	IRON LADY
Tormé, Mel	VELVET FOG
Trevino, Lee	SUPERMEX
United States	UNCLE SAM
Vaughan, Sarah	DIVINE SARAH, SASSY
Wellington, Duke of	IRON DUKE
Wilberforce, Samuel	SOAPY SAM
Wodehouse, P G	PLUM
	(*see also* **boxing, football**)
Niger	RN
capital	NIAMEY
coin	FRANC
Nigeria	WAN
capital	LAGOS

coin	
—unit	KOBO
—100 kobo	NAIRA
nine	IX, THETA
based	NONARY
Christmas presents	LADIES
combining form	ENNEA-, NON-
dancers	MORRIS MEN
days	ENNEATIC
—of devotion	NOVENA
days'...	WONDER
eyes	LAMPREY
groups	ENNEAD, NON-, NONET(TE)
	NONETTO, NONUPLET
	NOVENARY
having 9	
—angles	ENNEAGONAL, NONAGONAL
—columns	ENNEASTYLE
—faces	ENNEAHEDRON
—petals	ENNEAPETALOUS
—pistils	ENNEAGYNIAN
	ENNEAGYNOUS
—sides	ENNEAGONAL
	NONAGONAL
—stamens	ENNEANDRIAN
	ENNEANDROUS
—styles	ENNEAGYNIAN, ENNEAGYNOUS
hundred	CM, SAMPI
inches	SPAN
iron	NIBLICK
lives	CAT
magistrates of Athens	ARCHON
Muses	(see **Muses**)
ninth	ENNEATIC
orders of angels	ARCHANGELS, ANGELS
	CHERUBIM, DOMINIONS
	POWERS, PRINCIPALITIES
	SERAPHIM, THRONES, VIRTUES
pins	SKITTLES
points of ...	LAW
times	ENNEATIC
worthies	ALEXANDER, ARTHUR
	CHARLEMAGNE, DAVID
	GODFREY, HECTOR, JUDAS
	JULIUS, JOSHUA
yearly	NOVENNIAL
nineteenth	
hole	BAR, CLUBHOUSE
pertaining to nineteen	DECENNOVAL
ninety	N, Q, XC
having ninety faces	ENNEACONTAHEDRAL
ninetieth	NONAGESIMAL
ninety-nine	IC
—beautiful names	ALLAH
ninety thousand	N, Q
ninety years old	NONAGENARIAN

nobles	
Anglo-Saxon	A(E)THELING, ALDERMAN
	EALDORMAN, EORL
	(E)SQUIRE, THEGN, THANE
	VAVASOUR, VALVASOOR
Athenian	EUPATRID
Austrian	HERZOG
—count(ess)	GRAF(IN)
Celtic	TAOISEACH
continental	COUNT
count palatine	PALSGRAVE
eldest son of earl	LORD
English	BARON(ESS), BARONET
	COUNTESS, DUCHESS, DUKE, EARL
	KNIGHT, LORD, MARCHIONESS
	MARQUESS, MARQUIS
	VISCOUNT(ESS)
Etruscan prince	LUCOMO
French	
—dauphin's wife	DAUPHINE(SS)
—king's eldest son	DAUPHIN
—knight	CHEVALIER
—marchioness	MARQUISE
—mediaeval	VIDAME
feudal lord	SUZERAIN
German	BURGRAVE, BURGRAVINE
	EDEL, HERTZOG, (LAND)GRAF
	LANDGRAVE, LANDGRAVINE
	MARGRAVE, MARGRAVINE
—count(ess)	GRAF(IN)
—prince	ELECTOR
—young	JUNKER
Indian prince	GAEKWAR, (MAHA)RAJAH
	NAWAB, NIZAM
Irish	TAOISE(A)CH
Italian	
—marchioness	MARCHESA
—marquis	MARCHESE
Japanese	DAIMIO, KUGE
knight leading into	
battle	BANNERET
Moldavian prince	GOSPODAR, HOSPODAR
Moroccan prince	SHEREEF, SHERIF
Moslem	
—lord	OMRAH
—prince	AMEER, AMIR, EMEER
	EMIR, NAWAB
—princess	BEGUM
New Zealand	RANGATIRA
noble man	GALAHAD, KNIGHT
	MAGNATE
Norse	JARL
Persian prince	MIRZA
Polish	SAROSTA
Portuguese	FIDALGO, DOM
—prince	INFANTE

—princess	INFANTA
Prussian	JUNKER
Roman	PATRICIAN
Russian	BOYAR(D)
son of duke or	
marquis	LORD
Scottish	BARONETESS
Spanish	ADELANTADO, HIDALGA
	HIDALGO, DON, DONA
	GRANDEE
—prince	INFANTE
—princess	INFANTA
Swedish count(ess)	GRAF(IN)
Venetian	DOGE, MAGNIFICO
Wallachian prince	GOSPODAR, HOSPODAR
	VOIVODE
wife of	
—earl	COUNTESS
—marquis	MARQUISE, MARCHIONESS
	(*see also* **leader**)

Norse
chieftain	JARL, YARL
minstrel	SKALD
myths	EDDAS, VOLUSPAS
pirate	VIKING
ship	LONGSHIP
warrior	BERSERK(ER)
	(*see also* **mythology**)

north
	N
North Africa	MAGHREB, NA
	(*see also* **Africa**)
North America	NA, US, USA
	(*see also* **America**)
North British	NB
North Pole	NP
Northern French	NF
Northern Ireland	NI
Northern Territory	NT

Norway
	N
airline	NAL
bay	BOGEN, BUKT(EN)
	VAG, VIK
bread and butter	SMOR(RE)BORD
cape (headland)	KAPP, NES, ODDE
capital	OSLO
coins	KR, KRONE, ORE
country dance	HALLING
dance tune	SPRING
dog	ELKHOUND
forest cat	SKOGCATT
glacier	BRE(EN), FONN, JOKULEN
harbour	HAMN, HAVN
herring	SILD
hill	HAUG
hors d'oeuvres	SMOR(RE)BORD
hut	SAETER

island	HOLMEN
lake	S(J)O, VANN, VATN
language	LANDSMA(A)L, NORSE
	NYNORSK
measure (²/₃ acre)	MORGEN
mountain	BERG, FJELL(ET), VARRE
—hut	S(A)ETER
—pasture	S(A)ETER
parliament	STORT(H)ING
peak	HO
reindeer skin boots	FINN(E)SKO, FINSKO
river	ELV(A)
sea	
—loch	FIORD, FJORD
—monster	KRAKEN
toast	SKOAL
upland meadow	SAETER
Upper House	LAGT(H)ING
valley	DAL
waterfall	FOSS
whirlpool	MAELSTROM
wooden church	STAVE-CHURCH
	(*see also* **Norse, Scandinavian**)

nose
membrane	SCHNEIDERIAN MEMBRANE
parts of nose	ALA, DORSUM
	NARES, SEPTUM
passage to	
—mouth	INTERNAL NARES
—surface	EXTERNAL NARES
shape of nose	
—curved	AQUILINE
—high-bridged	ROMAN
—hooked	AQUILINE
—long and straight	GRECIAN
—short and flat	PUG (NOSE)
—turned up	RETROUSSE, SNUB
slang	CONK, HOOTER
	PROBOSCIS, SCHNOZZLE

Nova Scotia
	ACADIA, NS
capital	HALIFAX
island	CAPE BRETON

nuclear reactors
	ADVANCED GAS-COOLED
	AGR
	BOILING WATER, BWR
	GRAPHITE-MODERATED
	(FAST) BREEDER
	MAGNOX, POWER REACTOR
	PRESSURISED WATER
	PRODUCTION REACTOR
	PROPULSION REACTOR
	THERMAL REACTOR

numbers   (*see* **mathematics**)
nut
acajou	CASHEW
African	COLA, KOLA

American	PECAN	monkey-nut	PEA-NUT
—horse chestnut	BUCK-EYE	nicker	BONDUC, MOLUCCA BEAN
—tiger-nut	CHUFA	palm	BETEL, COCONUT, COHUNE-NUT
—white walnut	BUTTERNUT		COQUILLA, COROZO-NUT
Anacard	CASHEW		IVORY-NUT
Arachis	(*see* pea-nut *below*)	pea-nut	ARACHIS, MONKEY-NUT
areca	BETEL		EARTH-NUT, EARTH-PEA
Asiatic	PISTACHIO		PIG-NUT
Australian	QUANDONG-NUT	pecan	HICKORY
	QUEENSLAND-NUT	Philippines	PILI(-NUT)
beechnuts	MAST	sumach	PISTACHIO
betel	ARECA	tropical	BEN(-NUT), CARAP-NUT
bonduc	MOLUCCA BEAN, NICKER BEAN		CASHEW(-NUT), CRAB-NUT
Brazil	BERTHOLETTIA	true chestnut	SPANISH CHESTNUT
	BRAZIL-NUT, COQUILLA	used in game	PHILOPOENA, PHILIPPINA
	PARA-NUT, SAPUCAIA		PHILIPPINE
calthrop	WATER CHESTNUT	water chestnut	CALTHROP
cashew	ACAJOU, ANACARD	West Indian peanut	PINDA
Castanea	CHESTNUT	**nymph(s)**	
conker	HORSE-CHESTNUT	apple	MAELID
crab-nut	CAROB	ash	MELIC NYMPHS
cream-nut	BRAZIL	Buddhist	YAKSHI
double	COCO-DE-MER	Milton's	LIBERTY
earthnut (tuber)	ARNUT, PIGNUT	Mohammedan	HOURI
	EARTH CHESTNUT	mountain	EGERIA, OREAD(S)
earth-nut	(*see* pea-nut *below*)		OREAD(ES)
East Indian	KOKUM, MARKING-NUT	Nysaean	HYADES
European sedge root	CHUFA, TIGER-NUT	ocean	OCEANID(ES)
ground-nut	(*see* pea-nut *below*)	river	NAIAD(ES)
Guiana	BUTTERNUT, SOUARI	Russian (water)	RUSALKA
hard-shelled	ALMOND, BRAZIL	sea	AMPHITRITE, CALYPSO
hazel	COB, FILBERT		DORIS, GALATEA, HESIONE
hickory	PECAN		NEREID(S), SCYLLA, TETHYS, THETIS
Indian	ILLIPE, ILLUPI	spring	ARETHUSA
Juglans	WALNUT	water	ARETHUSA, CYRENE, HYDRIAD(ES)
large almond	JORDAN ALMOND		ONDINE, UNDINE(S)
	SPANISH ALMOND	wood	DRYAD(S)(ES), HAMADRYAD, LOTIS

observatory
including: optical telescopes
radio telescopes

lens
—nearest eye   EYEPIECE
—nearest object   OBJECTIVE
network of
—linked radio telescopes   MERLIN
—wires in eyepiece   GRATICULE
radio telescope   PARABOLIC REFLECTOR
     RADIO INTERFEROMETER
sites
—America   ALLEGHENY, FORT DAVIS
     GREENBANK, KITT PEAK
     LICK, MOUNT HOPKINS
  MOUNT PALOMAR, MOUNT WILSON
     NEW MEXICO, YERKES
—Australia   MOUNT STROMLO
     SIDING SPRINGS
—Canada   RICHMOND HILL
—Canary Islands   LA PALMA
—Chile   CERRO TOLOLO, LA CILLA
—England   CAMBRIDGE, HERSTMONCEUX
     JODRELL BANK, KEW
—France   HAUTE PROVENCE
     MEUDON, NICE
—Germany   POTSDAM
—Hawaii   MAUNA KEA
—in space   HUBBLE
—Puerto Rico   ARECIBO
—Russia   NAUCHNY
—Sweden   STJAERNEBERG
telescope
—radio   ARECIBO, CAMBRIDGE
—reflecting
100"   HOOKER
120"   LICK
158"   CERRO TOLOLO
200"   HALE
—refracting
33"   MEUDON
36"   LICK
40"   YERKES
—types   CASSEGRAIN(IAN)
     CATHETOMETER, COLLIMATOR
     COUDE SYSTEM, FINDER
     GALILEAN, GREGORIAN
  MAKSUTOV, NEW TECHNOLOGY, NTT
     NEWTONIAN, OPTICAL, RADIO
     REFLECTING, REFRACTING

oceanography
area of
—Earth covered by
oceans etc   HYDROSPACE, HYDROSPHERE
     WATER HEMISPHERE
—open water in ice   POLYNA
—sandbanks   SHOAL
—sea adjoining land
mass   CONTINENTAL SHELF
average level of sea
over a period   MEAN SEA LEVEL
backward flow of waves   BACKWASH
bay   BIGHT, COVE
—Africa   BIGHT OF BENIN
  BIGHT OF BIAFRA, FALSE BAY
  GULF OF ADEN, GULF OF GUINEA
—Alaska   BRISTOL BAY, COOK INLET
     GULF OF ALASKA
     NORTON SOUND
—Argentina   BAHIA BIANCA
     BAHIA GRANDE
     GULF OF SAN JORGE
     GULF OF SAN MATIAS
—Australia   EXMOUTH GULF
   GREAT AUSTRALIAN BIGHT
     GULF OF CARPENTARIA
     JOSEPH BONAPARTE GULF
   KING SOUND, MORETON BAY
   SHARK BAY, SPENCER GULF
  VAN DIEMEN GULF, VINCENT GULF
—Burma   GULF OF MARTABAN
—Canada   AMUNDSEN GULF
  BAY OF FUNDY, CHALEUR BAY
  CORONATION GULF, FOXE BASIN
     GULF OF BOOTHIA
     GULF OF ST LAWRENCE
  HAMILTON INLET, HUDSON BAY
  JAMES BAY, PLACENTIA BAY
     UNGAVA BAY
  VISCOUNT MELVILLE SOUND
—Central America   GULF OF CAMPECHE
     GULF OF HONDURAS
     GULF OF MEXICO
     GULF OF PANAMA
—Chile   GULF OF GUAFO
     GULF OF PENAS
—China   GULF OF TONKING
—Colombia   GULF OF DARIEN
—Ecuador   GULF OF GUAYAQUIL
—England   LYME BAY, THE WASH
—France/Spain   BAY OF BISCAY
—Greenland   BAFFIN BAY
—Indonesia   GULF OF CAMBAY
     GULF OF KUTCH

	GULF OF MANNAR
	GULF OF PAPUA
—Iran	PERSIAN GULF
—Ireland	BANTRY BAY, DONEGAL BAY
	DUNDALK BAY
—Libya	GULF OF SIRTE
—New Zealand	BAY OF PLENTY
	HAURAKI GULF
—North America	CHESAPEAKE BAY,
	GOLDEN GATE
	GULF OF CALIFORNIA
—Peru	BAY OF SECHURA
—Scandinavia	GULF OF BOTHNIA
	GULF OF FINLAND
—Siberia	GULF OF TARTARY
—Thailand	GULF OF SIAM
—Venezuela	GULF OF MARACAIBO
	GULF OF PARIA
	GULF OF VENEZUELA
—Wales	CARDIGAN BAY
between low-water mark and edge of continental shelf	SUBLITTORAL
bight	(see bay above)
broad sea inlet	SOUND
calcareous mud on bottom	GLOBIGERINA OOZE
calendar of tidal movements	TIDE TABLE
changes in coastline as a result of changes in sea-level	EUSTACY, EUSTASY
channel	
—Africa	MOCAMBIQUE CHANNEL
—Alaska	BERING STRAIT
	KOTZEBUE STRAIT
—Antarctica	DRAKE PASSAGE
—between reef and mainland	LAGOON
—Britain	BRISTOL CHANNEL
	ENGLISH CHANNEL, FIRTH OF CLYDE
	FIRTH OF FORTH, IRISH CHANNEL
	LITTLE MINCH, MORAY FIRTH
	NORTH CHANNEL, PENTLAND FIRTH
	ST GEORGE'S CHANNEL, SOLENT
	SOLWAY FIRTH, SOUTH MINCH
	SPITHEAD, STRAITS OF DOVER
—Canada	CUMBERLAND SOUND
	DIXON ENTRANCE, FOXE CHANNEL
	LANCASTER SOUND, HECATE STRAIT
	HUDSON STRAIT
	NORTHUMBERLAND CHANNEL
	PRINCE REGENT INLET
	STRAIT OF BELLE ISLE
	STRAIT OF GEORGIA
—Central America	YUCATAN CHANNEL

—Chile	STRAITS OF MAGELLAN
—China	STRAIT OF FORMOSA
—Falkland Islands	FALKLAND SOUND
—Greenland	DAVIS STRAIT
	DENMARK STRAIT
—in which tide runs	TIDEWAY
—India	EIGHT DEGREE CHANNEL
	NINE DEGREE CHANNEL
	PALK STRAIT
—Indonesia	TORRES STRAIT
—New Zealand	COOK STRAIT
	FOVEAUX STRAIT
—North America	FLORIDA STRAIT
	JUAN DE FUCA STRAIT
—Scandinavia	KATEGAT, SKAGERRAK
—Siberia	BERING STRAIT
—Spain	STRAITS OF GIBRALTAR
—Tasmania	BANKS STRAIT, BASS STRAIT
—Wales	MENAI STRAIT
—West Indies	WINDWARD PASSAGE
circular flow	EDDY, WHIRLPOOL
coal from sediment on bottom	SAPROPELITE
coastline	
—cutting across general structural features	DISCORDANT COAST(LINE)
—parallel to structural features	CONCORDANT COAST(LINE)
	LONGITUDINAL COAST(LINE)
	PACIFIC COAST(LINE)
cold sea-fog	HAAR
coral reef separated from land by lagoon	FRINGING REEF
current	
—equatorial	CROMWELL CURRENT
	EQUATORIAL COUNTER CURRENT
	INDIAN COUNTER CURRENT
	MONSOON DRIFT
	NORTH EQUATORIAL CURRENT
	SOUTH EQUATORIAL CURRENT
—flowing across another in opposite direction to	CROSSCURRENT
—another	COUNTERCURRENT
—surface current	EDDY, UNDERTOW
out from shore from return of waves	RIPTIDE
—in channel	TIDEWAY
—northern	ALASKA CURRENT
	CALIFORNIA CURRENT
	CANARIES CURRENT
	GULF STREAM, KURO SHIO
	LABRADOR CURRENT
	NORTH ATLANTIC DRIFT
	NORTH PACIFIC DRIFT
	OYA SHIO

—slow-moving	DRIFT
—southern	AGULHAS CURRENT
	BENGUELA CURRENT
	BRAZIL CURRENT
	CAPE HORN CURRENT
	EAST AUSTRALIAN CURRENT
	EL NINO, MOZAMBIQUE CURRENT
	PERU CURRENT
	WEST AUSTRALIAN CURRENT
	WEST WIND DRIFT
deep	
—channel in sea floor	TRENCH
—part of	
harbour, river, etc	CHANNEL
	ROADS(TEAD)
sea	ABYSS, GULF
—sea vehicles	(see undersea below)
deposits	
—inorganic	RED CLAY
—mud with	
iron	
—oxide	RED MUD
—sulphide	BLUE MUD
potassium	GREEN MUD, GREENSAND
—ooze	
shells	
—foraminifera	GLOBIGERINA OOZE
—molluscs	PTEROPOD OOZE
—radiolaria	RADIOLARIAN OOZE
—diatoms	DIATOMIC OOZE
—sediment	SAPROPEL
depression between waves	TROUGH
depth-sounder	SONAR
depths	SOUNDING
—highest level	LITTORAL
—intermediate	PELAGIC
—deepest	ABYSSAL
—less than 200m	NERITIC
—over 200m	OCEANIC
—200-1800m	BATHYAL
—below 6000m	HADAL
difference between	
high and low tides	TIDAL RANGE
direction of flow	SET
distance travelled by	
waves without	
obstruction	FETCH
drifting organisms	PLANKTON, SESTON
earthquake at sea-bed	SEAQUAKE
excrement of sea-birds	GUANO
fast tidal current	RACE
flat-topped submarine	
mountain	GUYOT
floating	
—block of ice	GROWLER, ICEBERG
—organisms	PLANKTON, SESTON

—sheet of ice	DRIFT ICE, FLOE
	PACK ICE
flora and fauna on	
sea bed	BENTHOS
formation of lake or bay	EMBAYMENT
frothing water	WHITE-WATER
gulf	(see bay)
having equal tide	
movements	COTIDAL
highest	
—level of tide	HIGH-WATER MARK
—tide	SPRING TIDE
hole through which tide	
forces air and water	BLOW-HOLE
ice	
—cap extending into sea	BARRIER
—floating	FLOE, GROWLER
	DRIFT ICE, ICEBERG
	PACK ICE
inflow of tide	FLOOD
instrument	
—measuring depth	ECHO-SOUNDER
	FATHOMETER, SONAR
—recording tides	MARIGRAPH
island	
—coral	ATOLL
—in river	AIT, AYOT
—low	CAY, KEY
—rocky	SKERRY
—Scottish	INCH
islet near coast	STACK
lagoon	HAFF
land adjoining sea	BEACH, COAST
	LITTORAL, SHORE
	STRAND
—US	TIDEWATER
large	
—bay	BIGHT, GULF
—surge of water	SWELL
layer(s) of	
—sediment with bands	
of clay or silt	VARVE
—water	STRATUM(STRATA)
lines on map of	
equal depth	ISOBATH
living	
—at moderate depths	PELAGIC
—near sea bottom	DEMERSAL
long	
—narrow trench in	
sea-floor	DEEP
—surge of water	SWELL
lowest	
—level of tides	LOW-WATER MARK
—tide	NEAP TIDE
mark left by highest tide	TIDEMARK

mean level between high and low tides	SEA LEVEL
measurement of depth	BATHYMETRY
	SOUNDING
mouth of river	ESTUARY
movement of	
—debris along coast by tidal action	LONGSHORE DRIFT
—surface water	(OCEAN) CURRENT
	SWELL, TIDE
caused by	
—earthquake	TSUNAMI
—ground tremor	GROUNDSWELL
—wind	GROUNDSWELL
mud-flat	SLOB
narrow	
—area with strong tides	EURIPUS
—bay (Orkney)	VOE
—channel in sandbank	SWASH (CHANNEL)
—neck of land	ISTHMUS
—passage of water	
between land areas	INLET
through pack-ice	LEAD
—sea	
inlet	CREEK, FIORD, FIRTH
	FJORD, GEO, VOE
passage	CHANNEL, GUT, KYLE
	SOUND, STRAIT
—tongue of sand or gravel	
attached to land	SPIT
connecting islands	TOMBOLO
not attached to land	BAR, SANDBANK
ocean floor (3500-5500m)	DEEP-SEA PLAIN
oceanographer	
—American	CROMWELL, EWING, HEEZEN
	HESS, MAURY, VOORHIS
—British	SWALLOW
oceans	
—modern	ARCTIC, ANTARCTIC
	NORTH ATLANTIC, NORTH PACIFIC
	SOUTH ATLANTIC, SOUTH PACIFIC
	INDIAN
—old	IAPETUS, TETHYS
open water in sea-ice	POLYNA
organisms in sea	
—floating	PLANKTON, SESTON
in Polar regions	PARMALES
—in reach of sunlight	PHOTOBENTHOS
—on the	
bottom	BENTHOS
surface	NEUSTON
—swimming	NEKTON
outflow of tide	EBB
passage	
—connecting two bodies of water	SOUND

—separating island from mainland	SOUND
period of no tidal movement	SLACK WATER
periodic rise and fall of sea	TIDE
pertaining to temperature and salinity	THERMOHALINE
pillar of rock in sea	STACK
plants living on sea-bottom	PHYTOBENTHOS
reclaimed land	POLDER
regular movement of sea surface	SWELL
ridge of	
—rocks	
just below the surface	LEDGE, SHELF, SHOAL
on seabed	REEF
—sand	
extending into sea	SPIT
in sea or river	SANDBANK, SANDBAR
rise and fall of sea	TIDE
rough sea caused by opposing tides or winds	RIPTIDE
rush of water up beach from breaking wave	SWASH
salt gradient	HALOCLINE
saltiness	SALINITY
sandbank formed by sea	DOWN
—under surface	BAR
sea	
—abounding in islands	ARCHIPELAGO
—adjoining coast (3 miles)	TERRITORIAL WATERS
—Africa	ARABIAN, RED
—Antarctic	ROSS, WEDDELL
—Arctic	BARENTS, BEAUFORT
	CHUKCHI, EAST SIBERIAN
	GREENLAND, KARA, LAPTEV
	LINCOLN, WHITE
—Asia	BERING, EAST CHINA
	SEA OF JAPAN, SEA OF OKHOTSK
	SOUTH CHINA, YELLOW
—Australia	TASMAN
—basin (Scot.)	FLOW
—deep	THALASSIC
—Europe	ADRIATIC, AEGEAN
	BALTIC, IONIAN, IRISH
	LIGURIAN, MEDITERRANEAN
	NORTH, NORWEGIAN
	SEA OF CRETE, TYRRHENIAN
—fog	HAAR
—Indonesia	ARAFULA, BANDA
	FLORES, CELEBES, CORAL
	SAVU, SOLOMOM, SULU, TIMOR

—inland	ARAL, BLACK, CASPIAN
	DEAD, SEA OF AZOV
	SEA OF GALILEE
	SEA OF MARMARA
—main body of water	PELAGIC
—Malaysia	ANDAMAN
—mist	FRET
—monsters	(*see* **monsters**)
—over Continental Shelf	NERITIC
—visible from shore	OFFING
—West Indies	CARIBBEAN
sediment	
—deposited by turbidity	
current	TURBIDITE
—on bottom	SAPROPEL
series of waves	SURGE
ships	CHALLENGER, METEOR
slope from continental	
shelf to ocean	
floor	CONTINENTAL SLOPE
small	
—bay	COVE
—iceberg	GROWLER, CALF
—inlet	CREEK
—plankton	SESTON
—ridge on sand produced	
by wind or wave	RIPPLE MARK
—wave	RIPPLE
US	RIFFLE
—whirlpool	EDDY
spread of sea over land	TRANSGRESSION
strait	SOUND
—connecting two	
bodies of water	NARROW(S)
—Scotland	KYLE
	(*see also* channel *above*)
structure built to	
protect coast	BREAKWATER, GROIN
	GROYNE, JETTY, MOLE
	PIER, SEAWALL
strong current	RACE, RIPTIDE
study of	
—bodies of water	HYDROGRAPHY
—distribution of water	HYDROLOGY
swimming organisms	NEKTON, NEUSTON
tidal	
—eddy	MAELSTROM
—estuary	CREEK
—flood	BORE, EAGRE
—movement affected by	
moon	LUNITIDAL
—race (Scot.)	ROOST, SWELCHIE
—wave	
caused by earthquake	TSUNAMI
in estuary	BORE, EAGRE
tornado at sea	WATERSPOUT

undercurrent	
—carrying sediment	TURBIDITY CURRENT
—of returning wave	UNDERTOW
undersea	
—area bordering land	
mass	CONTINENTAL SHELF
—craft	BATHYSCAPHE, BATHYSPHERE
	BARYSPHERE, BENTHOSCOPE
	CENTROSPHERE, DIVING BELL
	MESOSCAPHE, SUBMARINE
—deep points in sea floor	
Java Trench	PLANET DEEP
Mariana(s) Trench	CHALLENGER DEEP
Peru-Chile Trench	BARTHOLOMEW DEEP
Philippines Trench	GALATHEA DEEP
Puerto Rico Trench	MILWAUKEE DEEP
South Sandwich Trench	METEOR DEEP
Tonga-Kermadec Trench	VITYAZ
—explorer	BARTON, BEEBE
	COUSTEAU, PICCARD
—mountain	GUYOT, SEAMOUNT
—ridge or reef	LEDGE, SHELF, SKERRY
—ridges	ALBATROSS PLATEAU
	AZORES-CAPE ST VINCENT RIDGE
	BROMLEY PLATEAU, COCOS RIDGE
	FAEROE RISE
	GRAND NEWFOUNDLAND BANKS
	HAWAIIAN RIDGE
	INDIAN-ANTARCTIC RIDGE
	KERGUELEN-GAUSSBERG RIDGE
	LACCADIVE-CHAGOS RIDGE
	MACQUARIE-BALLENY RIDGE
	MID-ATLANTIC RIDGE
	MID-INDIAN RISE
	PACIFIC-ANTARCTIC RIDGE
	PRINCE EDWARD-CROZET RIDGE
	WALVIS RIDGE
	WYVILL-THOMPSON RIDGE
—valley	BASIN, DEEP, TRENCH
—valleys	AGULHAS BASIN
	ALEUTIAN TRENCH, ARGENTINE BASIN
	BANDA TRENCH, BRAZILIAN BASIN
	CAPE BASIN, CAPE VERDE BASIN
	CAYMAN TRENCH
	CENTRAL PACIFIC BASIN
	EAST PACIFIC BASIN
	GREAT GLOBAL RIFT
	GUATEMALA TRENCH, GUINEA BASIN
	IDZU-BONIN TRENCH
	JAVA TRENCH, JAPAN TRENCH
	KERMODEC TRENCH, KURIL TRENCH
	MARIANA(S) TRENCH
	NEW BRITAIN TRENCH
	NEW HEBRIDES TRENCH
	NANSEI-SHOTO TRENCH
	NORTH PACIFIC BASIN

	NORTH TRENCH
	NORTH-EASTERN ATLANTIC BASIN
	NORTH-WEST ATLANTIC BASIN
	PALAU TRENCH, PUERTO RICO TRENCH
	PERU-CHILE TRENCH
	PHILIPPINE TRENCH, ROMANCHE TRENCH
	RYUKYU TRENCH, SOLOMON TRENCH
	SOUTH SANDWICH TRENCH
	SOUTH-EASTERN ATLANTIC BASIN
	SOUTH-EASTERN PACIFIC BASIN
	SOUTH-WESTERN PACIFIC BASIN
	SUNDA TRENCH
	TONGA-KERMADEC TRENCH
	YAP TRENCH

water

—content of Earth	HYDROSPACE
	HYDROSPHERE
—overflowing on land	
at flood tide	TIDEWATER

wave

—broken on rock or shore	BREAKER
—following earthquake	TSUNAMI
—large	PURLER, SURGE
—long	
foaming	COMBER
heavy	ROLLER
—very high	TIDAL WAVE
in estuary	BORE, EAGRE
—white-topped	WHITE HORSE

whirlpool

—Scottish	ROOST, SWELCHIE
—small	EDDY
—strong	MAELSTROM
wide bay	BIGHT, GULF

old[1]

meaning: ancient
       archaic
       Biblical
       historical
       obsolete

'a' as a word	A-PER-SE
a little while ago	WHILE-ERE
abandon (stolen goods)	WAIVE
abate	VAIL
abdomen	WOMB
abide	WON
ability	ENGINE, INGINE
abjure	REN(A)Y, RENEY
able to	
—be seen	VISIVE
—see	VISIVE
abode	INN, MANSION, WON
abounding	ENORMOUS
about 9 a.m.	UNDERN
abrupt	SQUAB
abscess	IMPOST(H)UME

absolute	MERE
absolve	ASSOIL
abstruse	EXQUISITE
abundance	COPY
abut	CONFINE
abyss	ABYSM
accept	ALLOW
acceptable	PLAUSIBLE
acclaim	VOICE
accomplice	COMPLICE, FEDDARY
accost	ABORD
account	ACCOMPT, NOTE
—of daily transactions	EPHEMERIS
accumulate possessions	PURCHASE
accusation	TAX
accuse	ARGUE, REPROVE
accustom	OCCASION
ace of trumps in gleek	TIB
ache	AKE
achievement	CHEVISANCE
acid	EAGER
acknowledge	AGNISE, AGNIZE
	KNOWLEDGE
acknowledgment	
of mistake	JEOFAIL
acolyte	ACOLUTHITE
acquaintance	COAST
acquired by unjust methods	PURCHASED
acquisitiveness	COVETIVENESS
acquit	ACQUITE, ACQUIGHT
	ASSOIL
across	YOND
act	FACT, PRESENT
—as	
husband	HUSBAND
paid dance partner	HOSTESS
—carnally	CARNAL
—earlier than	PREVENT
—foolishly	FOLLY
—of	
guaranteeing	WARRANTISE
putting together	STRUCTURE
theft	MAINO(U)R, MANNER
touching	ATTAINT
—the master	MASTER
action at law	QUARREL
active	WIELDY
activity	FUNCTION
actor	STAGER
adapt	APPLY
adaptation	CONTEMPERATION
adapted for viewing	SPECULATORY
address in conciliatory tone	SPEAK FAIR
adduce	OBJECT
adjudge	AREAD, AREDE
	ARREEDE, ARET(T)

adjustment of dispute	MISE
administration of remedy	EXHIBITION
administrative division	GOVERNMENT
admiration	WONDER
adorn	BEDIGHT, BESEE
	ILLUSTRATE
adorn(ed)	DIGHT
adroit	PERT
adulterate	VITIATE
adulterer	AVOUTERER
adultery	AVOUTRY
advance	VAUNCE
—towards	COAST
advanced	FAR
adventure	AUNTER, AVENTURE
advice	REDE
advise	AVISE, AVIZE, AVYZE
	REDE, VISE
—against	DISSUADE
affability	FACILITY
affable	FACILE
affect	AMOVE
—coyness	COY
—with regret	RUE
affected by rheum	RHEUMATIC
affectedly fanciful	QUAINT
affection	AFFECT
affianced	ASSURED
affinity	AFFIANCE
afflict	VISIT
affliction	LANGUOR, TEEN(E), TENE
affray	EFFRAY
affright	DREAD, GRISE
afraid	EFFRAIDE, FEARED
afternoon	UNDERN
afterwards	EFT
again	AGEN, EFT
against the grain	AGAINST THE HAIR
agate	MURRINE
age	ELD
aged	WINTERED
aghast	AGAST
agree	FADGE, CONDESCEND
ailment supposed to be	
caused by a worm	WORM
alas	ALS, HARO, HARROW
albeit	AL(L)BE, ALBEE
alchemical	CHEMIC
alderman	EALDORMAN
ale	
—house	MUG-HOUSE
—sold at 4d per quart	FOUR-ALE
—with wormwood	PURL
alien	FORINSECAL
aligning	LIN(E)AGE
alive	QUICK

alkali	KALI
allay	ALAY
allayment	ALAIMENT
allegation	SURMISE
allege	ALLEDGE, PRETEND, TRUMP
allow to escape	LET
allowance	SIZE
—of food etc to servants	LIVERY
—to public officers	APPOINTMENT
allure	TRAIN, TROLL
alluring grace	VENUS
ally	COLLEAGUE
almond	AMYGDAL
almost	NIGHLY
—always	MOST AN END
alms	DEVOTION
aloes-wood	LIGN(-)ALOES
along	ALONGST, ENDLONG
always	ALGATE
ambassador	EMBASSADOR, LEAGUER
	LE(I)DGER, LEIGER, LIEGER
amber	LIGURE
ambergris	GRIS-AMBER
amends	MENDS
ammonia	VOLATILE ALKALI
among	EMONG(ES)
amongst	EMONG(E)ST
amorous	WANTON
—sport	TOY
amuse	PLAY, SPORT
ancestor	GRANDSIRE
ancestry	OFFSPRING
ancient	ANTIENT
and	AN
anew	OF NEW
anger	GRAM(E), TEEN(E), TENE
Anglican bishop	MAGPIE
angling fly	WATCHET
angry	CURST
aniline	CRYSTALLINE
animal with docked tail	CURTAL
ankle	ANCLE
—boot	HIGH-SHOE
—high shoe	HIGH-LOW
announce	DENOUNCE, MELD
annoy	HATTER
annul	VACUATE
anoint	ANELE
answer	RESOLVE
ant	EMMET
anthropoid ape	PIGMY, PYGMY
	TROGLODYTE
antic	ANTICK
anticipate	PREVENT
antiphon	ANTHEM
antique	ANTICKE

anxiety	CARK
anything	
—done	FACT
—hackneyed	HACK
—prepared after a recipe	RECEIPT
—that whirls	RHOMB(US)
apartment	MANSION
ape	JACKANAPES, PIGMY
	PYGMY, TROGLODYTE
aperture	OVERTURE
apology	SIR-REVERENCE
Apostle's Creed	THE BELIEF
apparatus	EQUIPAGE
apparel	TIRE
appeal to pity	FOR MERCY
appearance	FAVOUR, VISIBILITY
appease	ASLAKE
appendage to shoe	FORETOP
appertain	EFFEIR, EFFERE
apple	POME
application of kind	INTENTION
apply, as embroidery	LAY DOWN
appoint	VOICE
apprise	ASCERTAIN
approach	APPROPINQUATE
	APPROPINQUE, COAST
approaching	TOWARD
approbation	WELL-LIKING
apricot	ABRICOCK, APRICOCK
apron	BRAT, PLACARD
apt	TOWARD
arbitrator	STICKLER
arboretum	ARBORET
arch	EMBOW
archery target	GOAL
ardent desire	COVETISE
area near capital	INLAND
argue	WRANGLE
aristocratic ruffian	MOHOCK
arithmetic	ARSMETRICK
arm	ENARM
armed citizens	TRAIN-BAND
armistice	STILL-STAND
armour	WEED
—for man or horse	HARNESS
armoury	GARDEROBE
army	HOST, WAR
—clothing account	OFF-RECKONING
arrange	ADDRESS
arranged	ADDRESSED, ADDREST
—in harrow form	HERSED
array	BEDIGHT, RAY
arresting officer	SERGEANT, SERJEANT
arrive	BECOME
arrogance	SURQUEDY
arrogant	STOUT, WANTON

arsenic monosulphide	RESALGAR, ROSAKER
art	MISTERY, MYSTERY
—of	
engraving	ENGRAVERY
medicine	LEECHCRAFT
pastry-making	PASTRY
artful trick	SLIGHT
artifice	CRAFT, CROOK, REACH
artificial penis	DILDO
as	ALS
ascribe	APPLY
ash of saltwort	KALI
Ash Wednesday	PULVER WEDNESDAY
	PULVERING DAY
ask	
—back	REPEAT
—for	BID, YEARN
—price of	CHEAPEN
askance	ASCONCE
aspect	RESPECT, VISOR, VIZOR
aspirant to knighthood	DONZEL
aspire to	AFFECT
assail	INSULT
assailant	ONSETTER
assay	SAY
assayer	SAY-MASTER
assembly	GEMOT, MOOT, THING
assert	VOUCH
assess	CENSE
assign	ARET(T)
assigned place	ROOM
assistance	EASEMENT
assistant	
—clown or buffoon	ZANY
—minister	HELPER
assize	SIZE
assuage	ASSWAGE, LENIFY
assure	ASCERTAIN, RESOLVE
astonish	ASTONE, ASTONY, ASTUN
astonishment	MARVEL
asunder	ATWAIN
asylum	FRITHSOKEN, GIRTH
	GRITH
—for prostitutes	PENITENTIARY
at	
—a loss to know	SEEK
—hand	TOWARD
—home	WITHIN
—once	PRESENTLY, SWITH
	TIGHT, TIT, TITE(LY), TYTE
—present	PRESENTLY
—the	
door	ADOORS
same time that	WHILES
athletic contest	PRIZE
atone	ABY(E), ABIDE

atrocious	ENORMOUS
attached band or strip	LABEL
attack	ATTEMPT, BRASH
	STAND UPON
attaint	TAINT
attempt	FAND, FOND
attend	INTEND
attendant	VARLET, WAITING-VASSAL
attending servant	WAITER
attentive	ADVICEFUL, LISTFUL
	WHIST
attire	SUIT, TIRE
attired	READY
attribute importance to	FORCE
auction sale	OUTROOP
auctioneer	OUTROOPER
audacity	HARDIHEAD
augury	SOOTH
aunt	NAUNT
aurochs	URE
austere	STOOR, STOUR, STOWRE
	STURE
authorisation	WARRANTISE
autumn	HARVEST
avail	DOW, STEAD, VAIL
avenge	WREAK
average	MEDIUM
avert	FORFEND
avoid	VOID, WAIVE
await	BIDE, EXPECT, STAY, TARRY
award	ADEEM, ARET(T)
aware	KNOWING TO, WARE
away from	FROWARD(S)
awkward	UNGAIN
axiom	PETITION
axle	AXIS
babble	BRABBLE
back	RIDGE
—board	MONITOR
—bone	CHINE
—handed	AWKWARD
—of head	NODDLE
—side	BREECH
—to-back	DOS-A-DOS
—up	SOOTHE
backer	STICKLER
backgammon	GAMMON, TABLES
	VERQUERE
bad	LEWD, LITHER, NAUGHT
—lot	NAUGHTY PACK
—luck to	FOUL (BE)FALL
badger	GRAY, GREY
baffle	MATE
bag	COD
bagpipes	SYMPHONY
bail	REPLEVY

bailiff	HUNDREDER, REEVE
baker	BAXTER
balance	PEASE, PEAZE, PEISE
	PEIZE, PEYSE
—beam	BA(U)LK
baldmoney	SPICKNEL
bale in hide wrapper	SERO(O)N
ball	BOWL
ballast	POISE
band	FASCIA
—of musicians	MUSIC, NOISE
bandalore	QUIZ
bandy words	BA(U)LK
—in emulation	REVIE
bandying about	JACTITATION
banishment	EXPULSION
bank	CONTINENT, LINK
—of river	CONTINENT
banker	EXCHANGER
banquet	ENTERTAINMENT
bar	ESTOP
barded	BARD
bare	LEWD
—place	GALL
barefoot Highlander	GILLIE-WHITE-FOOT
	GILLIE-WET-FOOT
barely	SCRIMP
bargain	INDENT, PURCHASE
barred	BARD
barrel-organ	MUSIC-BOX
barter	PERMUTATION
base	HARLOTRY
basin	BASON
bass	BURTHEN
bath-house	BAGNIO
baton	BATOON
—of authority	WARDER
battalion	BATTLE
battle	
—array	HERSE
—axe	GISARME, SPARTH(E)
—field	PLACE
battlement	BARMKIN
bauble	GAUD
bay	REACH
—of library	CLASSIS
be	
—a	
claimant	PRETEND
schoolmaster	MASTER
—able	DOW
—anxious about	FEAR
—apprehensive	DOUBT
—associated and in concord	WALK
—aware of	WIT
—commonly stated	VOICE

—consequence of	IMPORT	—scant	SCANTLE
—defeated	GO BY THE WORST	—slack	FOR(E)SLACK
	GO WITH THE WORST	—surety	STIPULATE
—earlier than	PREVENT	—unveiled	UNVAIL(E)
—equal to	FILE WITH	—weak	FAINT
—extended at full length	LIE ALONG	becoming	HANDSOME
—false to	FALSE, FALSIFY	—stone	LAPIDECENT
—fitting	LONG	bed	DOWNY
—foolish	DOAT, DOTE, FON	bedaub	MOIL
—frivolous	FLUTTER	bedraggle	DAG
—good for a purpose	DOW	bedroom	DORMER
—impatient	BATE	been	BENE
—in		beer flavoured with	
attendance	INTEND	ground ivy	GILL(ALE), GILL BEER
expectation of	WAIT	befall	FORTUNE
motion	WALK	—unluckily	OSFALL
the habit	USE	befit	SORT
—intemperate	EXCEED	befool	ASSOT, BOB, FON, POOP, POUPE
—like	SEMBLE	before	OR, TOFORE
—likely	LIKE	befoul	BE(W)RAY
—off	VIA, WAG	befriend	FRIEND
—on watch	WAIT	beg	MAUND
—prominent	TOOT	began	GAN
—renewed	NEW	beget	KIND
—rife	WALK	begetting	GET
—rumoured	VOICE	beggar	MAUNDER, MUMPER
—spent (time)	WASTE	—hawking glass	GLASSMAN
—stupid	DOAT, DOTE	—posing as maimed	
—sulky	GLOUT	soldier	RUFFLER
—troublesome	IMPORTUNE	begging friar	MENDICANT
—whimsical	WHIM	begin	GIN, INCEPT, INCHOATE
become accustomed	WON	beginning	ENTRANCE, PRINCIPLE
beacon	FANAL		TO-FALL
beadle	BEDEL(L)	begone	AVAUNT
bear	EAN	begrime with coal dust	COLLY
beat	BOUNCE, FEEZE, PHE(E)SE	beguile	AMUSE, GLEEK
	PHEEZE, TUND	behave	USE
—back	REBUKE	—lewdly	PLAY THE WANTON
—down	FOIL	—riotously or noisily	ROAR
—everything	PASS	—towards	ENTREAT
—soundly	RIB-ROAST	—with boastful	
—to windward	LAVEER	insolence	INSULT
beaten	YBET	behaviour	CARRIAGE, GOVERNANCE
beautiful	BRIGHT, SMICKER, SPECIOUS	behead	HEAD
beautifully	FAIRISH, LOVELY	behove	IMPORT
beauty	FEATURE, FORM	belabour	SAUCE
beaver	BEVER	belching	RUCTATION
becalm	ENCALM	beleaguer	LEAGUER
because	FORWHY	believe	GUESS, TROW, WEEN
—of	IN RESPECT OF		WIS(H), WIST
become	BESIT, PROVE, WEAR	believer in medical	
—angry	WRATH	use of mercury	MERCURIALIST
—feeble	FAINT	bellows of organ	WIND-BAG
—hairless	PILL	belly	WEM(B), WEAMB
—husband	HUSBAND	belong	LONG
—neglectful	FOR(E)SLACK	beloved	L(I)EVE, LIEF

bend	EMBOW
benign	BENEDICT
bent	WRONG
benumb	DEAD
bereaved	ORB
bereavement	ORBITY
beset	IMPEACH, OBSESS
besiege	BESIT, OBSESS
besot	ASSOT
bestow part of	IMPART
bestrew	STROW
bet	HOLD
betray	BEWRAY
betrayer	TREACHER(ER), TREACHOUR
betroth	ENSURE, HANDFAST
	TROTH-PLIGHT
betrothal	HANDFAST(ING)
—by giving ring	
or gift	SUBARR(H)ATION
betrothed	AFFIED
bewilder(ment)	AMAZE
bewitch	BESPEAK, FASCINATE
	OVERLOOK
bicycle	BONESHAKER, VELOCIPEDE
bid	VIE
bier	HEARSE
bill	NOTE
bind	WAP
binding together	CONNEXIVE
bird's crest	COPPLE
birthmark	NAEVE
bishop's throne	SEE
bite	PINCH
—back	CROSSBITE
bitter	EAGER
black	
—bile	MELANCHOLY
—bird	OUSEL, OUZEL
—leg	SNOB
—marble	PARAGON, TOUCH
blame	WITE, WYTE
—for	GUILTY OF
blank panel	ORB
bleaching powder	CHEMIC
blended	(Y)BLENT
blending together	CONTEMPERATION
blessed	BENEDICT
blind	BLEND
—window	ORB
blinded	YBLENT
blindfold	MUFFLE
blinking	TWINKLING
blister	BLAD, MEASLES
blockhead	MOME
blow	BUFF, HUFF, PLAGUE
	WHERRET, WHIRRET

—into	INSPIRE
—on the	
neck	NECK-HERRING
ribs	RIB-ROASTER
blue	
—grey	GRISEOUS
—pigment	VERDITER
bluster(er)	HUFF
blustering	BULLY
board	COMMON
boast	AVAUNT, CRACK, GLORY
	YELP
boastful	THRASONICAL
—spirit	GLORY
bob	DOP, S, SHILLING
bobby	QUEACHY, QUEECHY
bodies	BODICE
body	BULK
—living or dead	LICH
—of	
forces	HEAD
soldiers in square	SQUADRON
vassals	MANRED
watchmen	WATCH
boggy	QUEACHY, QUEECHY
boiled	SODDEN
—vegetables	POTTAGE
bold	HAUGHTY
—faced person	FACER
boldness	HARDIHEAD
bombastic	GRANDILOQUOUS
bond	BAND
book	
—always in the	
same place	LEDGER, LIDGER
—of	
Bible readings	LEGEND
rules	ORDINAL
—seller	STATIONER
boon-companion	FRANION
boorish	SWAINISH
—fellow	JACK
booty	PURCHASE
border	COAST, CONFINE
—of false hair	TOUR
bore	BARE
boredom	SPLEEN
born a thrall	NATIVE
borne	YBORE
borough	BURGH, PORT
bosses of gold set with	
diamonds	OWCHES
bottom	GROUND
bought	BOUGHTEN
—provisions	ACATES
bound	BAND, HANDFAST

—by religious vows	VOWED
boundary	BOURN, GOAL, LIST, MARK
—fence	MOUND
bourdon	BURTHEN
bout	BRASH
bow	CROOK, LOUT, LOWT, MOVE
	MAKE ONE'S MANNERS
Bow Street officer	RUNNER
bowels	WOMB
box	BRUISE
boxer	PUGIL
boxing-glove	MUFFLE
boy	KINCHIN-COVE, GROOM
braggart	PUCKFIST
bragging	THRASONICAL
braid	BREDE
branch	BRAUNCH, GRAFT
brandish	WAG
brandy	NANTZ
—and water	MAHOGANY
brass	ALCHEMY, ALCHYMY
bravado	BRAVERY
brave person	VALIANT
bravo	BRAVE
brawl	BRABBLE
brawler	NICKER, ROARER
	ROARING-BOY
breach of law	UNLAW
bread	LOAF
—from finest flour	MANCHET
	WASTEL(-BREAD)
—soaked in gravy	BREWIS
break	
—in pieces	TO-BREAK
—up	REFORM, TO-BRUISE
breakfast	DEJEUNE
breaking of the sea	BREACH
breastplate	PLACARD
breath	SPIRIT
breathe into	INSPIRE
breed of sheep	HERDWICK
bribe	GIFT, GRATIFICATION
	TOUCH, VALES, VAILS, WAGE
bridesmaid	PARANYMPH
bright	NET(T), SHEER
—red	COCCINEOUS
brightly shining	SPLENDIDIOUS
bring	
—about	PURCHASE
—back	REDUCE
—forth young	YEAN
—forward	OBJECT
—in	INBRING, INDUCE
—success	SPEED
—to	
an end	DEFINE, SPEED

court	INBRING
finished state	SPEED
sorry plight	SPEED
—vessel close to wind	LOOF
bringing	
—back	REDUCTIVE
—intelligence	INTELLIGENT
—up	NOUR(R)ITURE
brisk	GAILLARD, GALLIARD, YARE
briskly	TIGHTLY
British soldier	LOBSTER
broach	BROCH
broiling-meat	CARBONADO
broke	BRAKE
broken	INFRACT
—pottery	POTSHARD
—tree	RAMPICK, RAMPIKE
brokerage	BROKERY
bronze	BRASS
brooch	BROCH
brood	TEAM
—(pheasants)	EYE
broth	BREVWS
brothel	BORDEL(L)O, CORINTH
	VAULTING-HOUSE
brought from a	
remote place	FAR-FETCHED
browned by sun	ADUST
bruise severely	TO-BRUISE
brushwood	BAVIN, RICE
bucket	SITULA, STOOP, STOUP
buffoon	ANTIC, INIQUITY
	JACK-PUDDING, MOME
build	EDIFY, TIMBER
building where salt	
is made	SALT-COTE
bulk	GREAT
bully	HUFF
bumper	ROUSE
bumpkin	PUT(T)
bunch of flowers	BOUGHPOT, BOWPOT
bundle	TROUSSEAU
burden	BURTHEN
burdensome	IMPORTUNATE, IMPORTUNE
burgess	PORTMAN
burial-place	CHARNEL
burly	BRAVE
burn	BREN(NE)
—in	INURE
burned	YBRENT
—in	INUST
burnet(-saxifrage)	PIMPERNEL
burning	UST(ULA)ION
—in	INUSTION
burnt	YBRENT
—up	ADUST

bury	EARTH, GRAVE	cart	
	INEARTH	—for removal of night-soil	NIGHT-CART
bus conductor	CAD	—load	SEAM
bustle	COIL	carve	ENTAIL, ENTAYLE
butt	PUSH		INSCULP
buttocks	CROUPON	—birds	DISMEMBER
buy and re-sell to		casque	CASK
raise price	REGRATE	cast	KEST, WARP
by	FORBY	—as obstruction	TRUMP
—day	ADAYS	—evil eye on	FASCINATE
—my faith!	PERFAY	—off clothes	FRIPPERY
—Our Lady(kin)	BYRLADY, BYRLAKIN	—spell on	ENCHARM
—way of love	PARAMOUR	castor	TRUCKLE
byword	NAY-WORD	casualty	CADUAC
cabbage	WORT	catalogue	CATELOG, RAGMAN
cake of soap	BALL		RAGMENT
calamity	BALE, RUTH	catamite	GANYMEDE, INGLE
calf	VEAL	catch	DEPREHEND, FANG
call	CLEEP, CLEPE, ENSTYLE	caterer	ACATER, ACATOUR, CATER
	HETE, HIGHT	cattle	AVER, FEE, NEAT
—back	REVOKE	—herder	HAYWARD
—in question	QUARREL	caught	IN BY THE WEEK
—out	PROVOKE	—at fault	TARDY
—to witness	ATTEST	cause	OCCASION
—to-arms	ALARM	—not to be	UNBE
called	HIGHT, HOTEN, NEMPT	—to	
	YCLEPED, YCLEPT	fall	FALL
camp	LEAGUER	fear	DREAD
campaign	JOURNEY	feel scruples	SCRUPLE
camphor	CAMPHIRE	glance	GLANCE
canal without locks	WATER-PLANE	know	KEN
cancerous growth	WOLF	sin	OFFEND
candied fruit	SUCKET	swear	ADJURE
cannon	BASILISK	causing	
—balls	GUN-STONES	—devastation	WASTEFUL
canopy	PAVILION	—uneasiness	IRKSOME
canto	FIT(T), FITTE, FYTTE	—wasting	WASTEFUL
cap	BIGGIN(G)	cauterisation	INUSTION, USTION
capable of	NOTABLE	caution	CAUTEL
—erring	ERRABLE	cautious	CAUTELOUS, WARE
—living	VITAL	Cavalier	MALIGNANT
capitalist	MONEYER	cavalry	
caprice	SPLEEN	—man	PLUNGER
capricious	HUMOUROUS, WANTON	fatigue cap	WATERING-CAP
captious arguing	CROCODILITE	—officer	CORNET
captivity	ENDURANCE	—standard	CORNET
care	CARK, FORCE, PASS	caviar	CAVIARIE
—for	KEEP, RECK	cavity	
career	CARIERE	—in the earth	MINE
careful	CHARY	—of a raised pie	COFFIN
carelessness	SECURITY	cease	STINT
carousal	ROUSE, UPSEE, UPS(E)Y	—from	RESPITE
carper	MOME	celebrate	MEMORISE, MEMORIZE
carry		—in song	BESING
—off	HENT, TRUSS	—Whitsun	SHROVE
—out the duties of	WAIT (UP)ON	celestial sphere	WHEEL

censure	TAXATION
centering	CENTRY
certain	SICCAR, SICKER
certainly	IWIS, YWIS
cessation	STINT
chafing-dish	CHAFER
chair	
—of sanctuary	FRITHSTOOL
—or canopy of state	ESTATE
chalaza	SPERM
challenge	APPEAL, CHAMPION
	DARRAIGN(E), DARRAIN(E)
	DARRAYN, DERAIGN
	DEFY, PROVOKE, VIE
challenger	APPELLANT
chambermaid	BOWERY WOMAN
champion	KEMP
chance	CHAUNCE, VENTURE
change	EXCHANGE, WEND
—colour	BRAID
—one's clothes	SHIFT
—the course of	WIND
changeable	HUMOROUS, VOLUBLE
chaplet	ROSARY
character	HAIR, PROPRIETY
—of a blackleg	LEGGISM
charcoal-burner	COLLIER
charge	QUARREL, TAX
chariot	WAG(G)ON, WAIN
charioteer	WAG(G)ONER
charm	ENCHARM, WEIRD
chase	CHACE
chaste	HONEST
chattel forfeited to Crown	DEODAND
cheap	GOOD-CHEAP
cheat	BAFFLE, BITE, CONY-CATCHER
	FOB, SLUR
—in return	CROSSBITE
check	BAFFLE, FOIL, REBUKE, SNEAP
—mated	MATE
cheek	WANG
cheer	ENCHEER
cheerful	LUSTICK
chemise	SMOCK
chemist	APOTHECARY, CHEMIC
chemistry	CHYMISTRY
cherish	REFOCILLATE
—with heat	FOMENT
chess board or piece	CHEQUER
chest	CAP-CASE
chicken	CHUCK
chided	CHOSE
chief	DUKE
—fifer	FIFE-MAJOR
—magistrate	(PORT)REEVE
—place in popular esteem	VOGUE

chignon	WATERFALL
child	WENCH
—left to be minded	MINDER
children	CHILDER
child's cap	BIGGIN
chimney-sweeper's boy	CHUMMY
chintz	PINTADO
chloride	MURIATE
choir	QUIRE
—stall with back	
to screen	HEADSTALL
choose	CHUSE
chorister	QUIRISTER
chough	CHEWET
Christ's cross	ROOD-TREE
christening robe	BEARING-CLOTH
Christmas game	LEVEL-COIL
church building	STEEPLE-HOUSE
churl	CARL
churlish	CARLISH
cider and water	BEVERAGE
cinnamon	CANELLA
circuitous movement	WINDLASS
circulate	TROLL, WALK
circumstanced	STATED
cite	ALLEGE
city	TROY, UR
clad	YCLAD, YCLED
—in satin	SATIN
claim	DARRAIGN(E), DARRAIN(E)
	DARRAYN, DERAIGN, PRETEND
—as one's own	OWN
—equality	MATE
claimant	TITLER
clamour	BRABBLE
clary	ORVAL
clash	HURTLE
clasp	SPANG, TACH(E)
class	SIEGE
—of	
inferior persons	VULGAR
thief	WASTER
claw	FANG, SERE
clean	EMUNGE, NEAT, NET(T)
—cut	TERSE
cleanse	GARBLE
clear	SHEER
—away	VOID
—space	HALL
—up	SALVE
cleared for action	PREDY
clever	ARTFUL, CONCEITED
	NOTABLE
climate	TEMPERAMENT
climb	STY
climbed	CLOMB

clip	DOD
cloak	CLOKE, PALLIATE
clock-weight	POISE
clod	GLEBE
cloddy	GLEBOUS, GLEBY
clog	PESTER
close	STRICT, CONSTIPATE
—fitting	JUST, SUCCINCT
breeches or drawers	HOSE
closed handful	NIEVEFUL
closely	NIGHLY, STRAIT
—united	CONTINUATE
cloth	
—covering Eucharist	CORPORAS
—of	
gold	CICLATO(U)N
mixed colours	MOTLEY
—pieced together	PANE
—separated by slashing	PANE
clothes	SHROUD, WEARING
clothing	WEED
clove-pink	SOPS-IN-WINE
clown	ANTIC
clownish	BOR(R)EL(L), CARLISH
club	BOURDON, HETAIRIA, POLT
clumsy	UNHANDSOME
co-exist	CONSIST
coal dealer	COLLIER
coarse	
—flour/meal	CRIBBLE
—woollen fabric	RUG
Orkney	WADMA(A)L, WADMALL
cobblestone	COPPLESTONE
coddled child	COCKNEY
codlin	QUODLIN
cohabit with	OCCUPY
coin	CROSS
	(see also coins)
coiner	MONEYER
cold in the head	RHEUM
collection of things said	RHAPSODY
colonial governor	PRESIDENT
colonist	INHABITOR
comb	KEMB
combed	KEMPT
come	VIA
—about	SORT
—forth	FORTHCOME
—near	LIKE
—to	
grief or ruin	SPILL
near an end	GROW TO WASTE
comfit	CONFIT
comfort	ENCHEER
coming from the eye	VISUAL
command	HETE, WILL

commemorate	REMEMBER
commendable	WELL-FOUND
comment	GLOZE
commercial	
—privilege	OCTROI, OCTROY
—traveller	RIDER
commit adultery	ADULTERATE
commodities	TRAFFIC
common	
—kite	GLED(E)
—land	MARK
—man	JACK
—topic	COMMONPLACE
commons	FOLK
commonwealth	(COMMON)WEAL
compact	COVIN, COVYNE, MATCH
companion	COPESMATE, FE(A)RE, FEER
	FIERE, PHEERE, MARROW
company	GING, SORT
—taking meal at	
fixed price	ORDINARY
compare	CONFER, PARAGON
	RESEMBLE
compartment in chest	TILL
compass	PRACTISE
compassionate	PITEOUS, REMORSEFUL
compel	COMPULSE
compelled	FAIN
competition	CONCURRENCE, GOAL
competitor	CONCURRENT
compiler	UNDERTAKER
complain	PLAIN
complaint	PLAIN, QUARREL
complaisance	PLEASANCE
complete	COMPLEAT
complexion	BLEE
compliment	DOUCEUR
comply	CONDESCEND
comport oneself	USE
compose	DITE, STICKLE
composition	DITE
—of drugs	CONFECTION
compound	ETHIOPS
compromise	TEMPERAMENT
compulsion	DISTRESS
conceal	VIZARD
concede	CONDESCEND
conceit	DEVICE
conceive	CONCEIT
concern	
—closely	NIP
—oneself with	MEDDLE
concerned with fate	WEIRD
concert of voices	CONCENT
conciliatory	COASTING
—words	FAIR WORDS

conclusion	FINE
concord	CONCENT
concubine	MADAM
condemn	CAST
condescend to	
—allow	VOUCHSAFE, VOUTSAFE
—grant	VOUCH(SAFE), VOUTSAFE
condition	CENSE, LIKING
condole with	MOAN
conduct	RULE
—on a journey	TRAVEL
confectioner	SUGAR-BAKER
confess	AGNISE, AGNIZE
confidential	INWARD
confine	STRAITEN
confinement	CONFINE
confirm	SOOTHE, STABLISH
—correctness of	RATIFY
conflict	CAMP
confound	MATE
confounded	POCKY
confront	CROSS
confused mass	FARRAGO
confusion	BAFFLE
confute	REDARGUE, REFEL
congratulate	GRATULATE, GREET
congratulatory	GRATULANT
conjectural	STOCHASTIC
connecting ridge	HALSE
conned	YCOND
conscience	INWIT
consecrate	HALLOW
consecration	SACRING
consent	CONDESCEND
conserve	CONFITURE
consider	ADVISE, CAST, VISE
considerable	NOTABLE
considered	CONSIDERATE
consort	LADY, MAKE, MATE
conspiracy	COVIN, COVYNE
conspire	COLLEAGUE, CONJURE
constable	BOW STREET RUNNER
	HARMAN(-BECK)
constable's district	CONSTABLEWICK
constant	UNREMOVABLE
constrain	OBLIGATE, PERSTRINGE
construe	CONSTER
consume	BEZZLE
consuming	WASTEFUL
contact	CONTINGENCY
contend	DEBATE
—with weapons	PLAY
content for want of	
something better	FAIN
contention	TOIL
contents of wardrobe	GARDEROBE

contest for prize	WAGE
continuance	DURANCE
continue	DURE, PERSEVERE
continuity of state	TENOUR
contradict	OUTFACE, UNDERSAY
contrary	CONTRAIR
contrivance	ENGINE
—for holding up	
skirt	PAGE
contrive	ENGINE, FRAME, WORK
control	WIND
controller	RECTOR
controlling fate	WEIRD
convenience	COMMODITY
convenient	HANDSOME, HEND
conversation	PARLANCE
convey to a distance	ELOI(G)N
	ESLOIN, ESLOYNE
conveying no idea	UNIDEAL
convict of	REPROVE
convince	RESOLVE
copious	FULSOME
copiousness	COPY
copper	AS, D, P
copse	SPRING
copy of legal writing	TRANSUMPT
copyholder	VILLEIN
cordial	ROSA-SOLIS
cornage	HORNGELD
corner	CANTON
corporate body	UNIVERSITY
correct	CHASTISE, CHASTIZE
—thing	CHEESE
correspondent	RESPONSIBLE
corroded	CANKERED
corrosive	CORSIVE
cosmetic	FUCUS
coupled	ME(I)NT, MENGED
	MEYNT, MINGED
couch	DAY-BED
could	COUTH
council	THING
counsel	ADVISEMENT, REDE
count	NICK
countable	COMPTIBLE
countenance	CHEER, FAVOUR
count(er)	COMPT(ER)
counter	COMPTER
counterbalance	POISE
counterfeit coin	SLIP
counterfeiter	FALSER
counterpoint	DESCANT, FA(UX)BURDEN
country	
—dweller	RURAL
—house	GRANGE
count(ship)	COUNTY

county division	WAPENTAKE
couple	MARROW, TWAIN
—up	MENG(E), MING
courageous	WIGHT
course	LOOSE, MESS, TRADE
court	MOOT, SUE, THING
—held in fairs and markets	COURT OF PIEPOWDERS
—messenger	BEADLE
—of	
guild	HALL-MOOT
lord of manor	HALL-MOOT
the manor	LEET
—official	CH(E)IROGRAPHER
	APPARITOR
courteous	HEND
courtesan	STALLION
courtesy	GENTILESSE, GENTLENESSE
cousin	COOSEN
coven	COVEN, COVYNE
cover	COUR, OVERCOME
—completely	WHELM
—dispersedly	STROW
—with	
earthwork	ENSCONCE
sconce	ENSCONCE
covering	TAPIS
covetousness	COVETISE
coward(ly)	HILDING, NITHING
cower	COURE
coxcomb	PRIG
cozen	COOSIN, POOP, POUPE
craft	MISTER(Y), MYSTERY
craftsman	ARTSMAN
crafty	SUBDOLOUS
—action	WINDLASS
cram	STOP
crate	SERO(O)N
create	
—at same time	CONCREATE
—with	CONCREATE
creature	WIGHT
creeping or crawling animal	WORM
crime committed	FACT
crimp with poting-stick	POTE
crimping	PRINT
—stick for ruffs	POTING-STICK
crimson	PURPLE
crippled	HALT
crisis	ACME, FIT
critic	OVERSEER
critical	NICE
—moment	ARTICLE
crooked	CRABBED, WRONG
Cross	WOOD
cross-grained	FRAMPOLD

crossed by streams	WATER-SHOT
crown	GARLAND
cruel	FELON
crupper	CROPPER
crush	OPPRESS
crutch	POTENT
crwth	CROWD
cry	
—at masque	A HALL, A HALL
—in fencing	HAY
—of	
impatience	CRIMINE
surprise	CRIMINE
—out	DISCLAIM
—up	SELL
cucking-stool	TUMBREL, TUMBRIL
cuckold	CORNUTE, CORNUTO
	ENGRAFT
—maker	HORNER
cuckoldise	GRAFT
cuckoldry	HORNWORK
cudgel	WASTER
cultivate	HUSBAND, MANURE
cultivated	SATIVE
cultivation	MANURANCE
cunning	QUAINT, SLIGHT
—rogue	GREEK
cunningly made	SLY
curb	REFRAIN
curd	CRUD
curdle	CRUDDLE, YEARN
cure	RECURE, REMEDY
curled	CRISP
curling	CRISP
currency	PASS
curse	BAN
cursory	CURSORARY
curt	SQUAB
curtsy	DOP, MAKE ONE'S MANNERS
curved	WRONG
custard	FLAM(M), FLAUNE, FLAWN
custody	HANDFAST
custom	WON
—house seal	COCKET
customer	CHAPMAN
customs officer	WAITER
cut	ENTAIL, ENTAYLE
—short	CURTAL
—the hair of	DOD
cutting	SARMENT
—back	RECISION
—off	RESCISSION
—short	SYNCOPE
cylindrical plait	QUILL
cymbal	SYMBOLE
cypress	GOPHER

dagger	BASELARD, PUNCHEON
dainties	CATES
dais	ESTATE
dally	TICK AND TOY
damage	WORST, WREAK
damned beforehand	FORE-DAMNED
dandy	FANTASTIC, JESSAMY
	MASHER, MUSCADIN
	PUSS-GENTLEMAN
dangerous	PERICULOUS
Danish underking	EORL
dark	WAN
—brown	BURNET
—colour	PUKE
—coloured horse	MOREL
darnel	TARE
dart	LANCE
dash	RASH
dastard	HILDING
dastardly	NITHING
daunt	AMATE, DANT, PALL, QUAIL
dawdle	DRAWL
dawn	DAW, SPRING
day	
—for begging	MUMPING-DAY
day's work or travel	JOURNEY
days of makeshift meals	SCAMBLING-DAYS
daze	AMAZE
dazzle	BLEND
dead tree	RAMPICK, RAMPIKE
deaden	DEAD
deaf	SURD
deal	ENTREAT
—with	TRANSACT
dealer	CHAPMAN, OCCUPIER
—in	
horses	HORSE-COURSER
second-hand goods	UPHOLDER
dealing	MERCHANDISE
dear	L(I)EVE, LIEF
death	EXPIRATION, MORT
debar	CONCLUDE
debased by commonness	PROSTITUTE
debate	WRANGLE
debauch	DEBOSH
decamp	SCAMPER
decay	FAINT, FORFAIR
decayed tree	RAMPICK, RAMPIKE
deceit	BARRAT, FORGERY
deceitfulness	FALLACY, FALSEHOOD
deceive	CHICANE, FALSE, TRUMP
—with smooth words	GLOZE
deceiver	TREACHER(ER)
	TREACHOUR
December 21st	MUMPING-DAY
deception	FALLACY, FUBBERY, GULLERY

decide	AREAD, AREDE, ARREEDE
	DARRAIGN(E), DARRAIN(E)
	DARRAYN, DERAIGN, DISCUSS
—against	CAST
decision of council	REBOUND
declare	AREAD, AREDE, ARREEDE
	MELD, VIE, VOUCH
—on oath	ALLEGE
—to be true	SOOTHE
decline	DEVALL, QUAIL, WELK
decoration	FLOURISH, PARAMENT
decorum	HONESTY
decoy for birds	STALE
decrease	WANZE
—in volume	WANE
dedicate to church	IMMOLATE
deduce	DEDUCT
deduct part of	DEFALLATE
deed	ASSURANCE, FACT
deeds	WORKINGS
—of prowess	VASSALAGE
deep metal plate	MAZARINE
deer's	
—entrails	QUARRY
—sweetbread	INCHPIN
defeat	PUT TO THE WORSE
defeated	PROFLIGATE
defenceless	SILLY
defend	WARRANT
—by flankers	FLANKER
defender	WARRANT
defiant protest	MARRY COME UP
deficient in interest	INCURIOUS
defile	HALSE, MOIL
defilement	CONSPURCATION, MOIL
deflect	WIND
deformed person	URCHIN
defraud	COG, LURCH
degree	GRE(E)CE, GRECIAN, GRE(E)SE
	GREE, GREESING, GRESSING
	GRI(E)CE, GRISE, GRIZE
dejected	AMORT
delay	FRIST, LET, TARRY
	TARRIANCE
—in action	RESPITE
deleterious	PREDATORY
deliberate	CONSIDERATE
deliberative	
assembly	MOOT
delicacy	CATE, TRINKET, JUNKET
delighting	RAPING
delineate	STELL
delirium	PHRENITIS
deliver	TAKE
—of a child	LAY
delivered of a child	LIGHT

delivery	LIVERY
demonstrate	REMONSTRATE
demonstration	MUSTER
deny	DENAY, REN(A)Y, RENEY
denial	DENAY
depart	AVAUNT, VADE, WALK, WEND
depict	DEVISE, RESEMBLE
depraved	FELONIOUS, GRACELESS
deprive	TWIN(E)
—of	
colour	STAIN
provisions	DISPURVEY
deputy to earl	VISCOUNT
derived	EXTRACT
describe	DESCRIVE, DEVISE, SPEAK
desert	DEMERIT
deserving of	GUILTY OF
—reproach	REPROACHFUL
design	MODEL
desirable	WISHFUL
desire	COURAGE, RECK
	RETCH, WILL
—strongly	EARN
desired	WISHFUL
despair	WANHOPE
despicable fellow	CULLION
despise	FORHOW
despite	DESPIGHT
destinate	DESTINE
destitute	VOID
—of	HELPLESS
destroy	FORDO, SPILL, UNBE
destructive	WASTEFUL
detached	DISCREET
detailed narration	ENARRATION
deteriorate	STARVE
determine	ASSOIL, PITCH
devastate	POPULATE
devastated	WASTE
devastation	WASTENESS
deviate	PREVARICATE
deviation from right way	ERROR
device	ENGINE
devoid	VAIN, VOID
dexterity	SLIGHT
dexterous	FEAT(E)OUS, FEATUOUS
	WIELDY
diagram	PLAT
dial of clock	WATCH
diamond	ADAMANT
dice	GOURDS
dictate	DITE
diction	PARLANCE
did	COUTH, GAN
die	GO UNDER, STERVE, SWELT
—impenitent	DIE HARD

—of hunger or thirst	FAMISH
difference	DIFFERENCY
	DIFFICILE
difficult	UNEASY, UNEATH
difficulty	HOBBLE
diffuse	LARGE
dig	GIRD, GRAVE
digest	ENDUE, INDUE
digest(ion)	DISGEST(ION)
dignity	WORSHIP
dilute	LOWER
dinner	DINE
—time	DINE, PUDDING-TIME
dip	MERGE
direct one's course	WEND
direction of mind	INTENTION
dirty drab	PUCELLE, PUZZLE
disadvantageous	DISADVANTAGEABLE
disaffected	MALIGNANT
disapprobation	MISLIKE
disapprove	DISPROVE, MISLIKE
disband	REFORM
disbanded soldier	REFORMADO
discard	DEFY
discern	WIT
discharge	ASSOIL
disclose	UNVAIL(E)
discomfit	SHEND
discontent	MISCONTENT
discourse	PARABLE, SPELL
discover	BEWRAY
discreet	WITTY
—man	PRUD'HOMME
discrete	DISCREET
discrimination	SKILL
disease of trees	MEASLES
disgrace	SCANDAL, SHEND
	VILLA(I)NY
—publicly	BAFFLE
—with inadequate	
praise	INDIGNIFY
disgraceful	INDIGN, OPPROBRIOUS
	REPROACHFUL
disguise	PALLIATE, VIZARD
dish	
—of food	MESS
cooked in cup-shaped	
mould	TIMBALE
—used in the Eucharist	PATINE
dishonest	UNHONEST
dishonourable	UNHONEST
dislike	DEFY, DISTASTE, MISLIKE
dismal	TRIST
dismay	AMATE
dismayed	MATED
dismiss	REFORM, VOID

dismissed soldier	REFORMADO	doff	AVAIL(E), AVALE, VAIL
disobliging	INOFFICIOUS	dole	DOOL(E), VALES, VAILS
disorder	MISTEMPER	doll	BABY
disown	REPROBATE	dolphin	MEERSWINE
dispel	ASSOIL	dolt	MOME
dispenser of hospitality	HOUSEKEEPER	domain	REAME, REIGN
disperse	SPERSE	domestic	DOMESTICAL
dispirited	SACKLESS	—slave	ESNE
display	MUSTER, SPLAY	don	ADDRESS
displease	MISLIKE	dormitory	DORMER, DORTER, DORTOUR
dispose	DISPONE	dot	PRICK
disposed	DIGHT	double Dutch	HIGH DUTCH
disproof	REPROOF	doubt	SCRUPLE
disprove	REFEL	doughty	TALL
dispute	REPROVE, WRANGLE	dovecote	LOUVER, LOUVRE
disregard	WAIVE	downward cut in	
disreputable fellow	SHAKE-RAG	fencing	STRAMACON, STRAMAZON
dissension	SQUARE	drag	RASH
dissolute behaviour	DISSOLUTION	dragon	WORM
distillate	ALCOHOL	drain out	EMULGE
distillery receiver	BOLT	dram-shop	GILL-HOUSE
distinctness	DISTINCTION	dramatic	
distinguished	EGREGIOUS, EXIMIOUS	—action	SCENERY
distort	WRITHE	—performance	PAGEANT
distortion	WRY	draw	LIMN
distracted	BESTRAUGHT	—along or on	TRAIN
distraint	NA(A)M	—together	ENTRAIN
distraught	BESTRAUGHT	drawer in chest	TILL
distress	MISEASE	dread	GASTINESSE
—warrant	DISTRINGAS	dreaded	YDRAD, YDRED
distressing	UNEATH	dream	SWEVEN
district of		dress	GUISE, RAY, TIFF
—court	SOKE	—distaff with flax	DIZEN
of lord	MANOR	—of puppets	PUPPETRY
—warden	WARDENRY	—ostentatiously	PRANK
disturb	BRASH	—up	DIZEN
disuse	INUSITATION	dressed	READY
divest oneself of	VOID	dressing	
divide	DEPART	—for the head	HEAD
—into chapters, etc	QUOTE	—gown	NIGHT-GOWN
divinely	HEAVENLY	—jacket	NIGHT-RAIL
division	CANTON	drink	
—of		—copiously	WASH ONE'S BRAINS
a song	FIT	—deeply	BOUSE
county	CANTRED, CANTREF	—hard	BEZZLE
the night	WATCH	drinking	
time or arc	SCRUPLE	—party	SYMPOSIUM
do	EXERT	—vessel	RUMKIN, STOOP, STOUP
—for	POOP, POUPE, SPEED	drive	DRAVE
—homage	VAIL	—off	FEEZE, PHE(E)SE, PHEEZE
—one's utmost	DO ONE'S ENDEAVOUR	—out	EXTERMINATE, WREAK
docked	CURTAL	drop	DRIB, GOUT
doctrine	LORE	dropped	KEST
document with		drove	DRAVE, DRIFT
pendant seals	RAGMAN, RAGMENT	drown	DRENH
doe	TEG(G)	druggist	APOTHECARY, DRUGGER

drum	SYMPHONY	—on	EDGE
drunk	CONCERNED, GROGGY	eglantine	EGLATERE
	OVERSEEN	egregious	PASSING
drying	AREFACTION	eightieth	FOUR-SCORTH
—room	HOT-FLUE	either	OUTHER
due	DEW, LOT	eject	EXPULSE
duenna	GRIFFIN, GRIFFON	elation	RUFF(E)
	GRIPE, GRYPHON	eldest daughter's right	
dull	DEAD, PERSTRINGE	of first choice	ESNECY
dumpy person	HODDY-DODDY	elect	VOICE
dung of deer, hare, etc	FEWMET(S)	elevation of gun	RANDOM
	FUMET(S)	elf	URCHIN
dunnage	FARDAGE	eloquence	ELOCUTION
dupe	PLOVER	elude	DELUDE
duped husband	HODDY-DODDY	embalm	BALM
durability	DURANCE	emblematic device	IMPRESA
durable		embrace	CLIP, COLL, COMPRESS
—cloth	DURANCE	embroidery frame	TENT
—woollen cloth	SEMPITERNUM	embryo	EMBRION
duration	ENDURANCE	emetic	PUKE
—of existence	DATE	eminence where	
duty	MISTERY, MYSTERY	idol stands	HIGH-PLACE
—of sentinel	WATCH	eminent	PASSING
dwell	STALL, WON	emit with force	UTTER
dwelling	MANSION, WONING	emollient	LENIENT
dye	TINCT	emotional activity	WORKING
each other	OTHER	employment of waiter	WAITERHOOD
eager	RATH(E)		WAITERING
—to	FAIN	empty	AVOID, VACUATE, VAIN
earl	COUNTY, EORL	encage	INCAGE
earliest	RATHEST	enchant	FASCINATE
early	RARE(LY), REAR, SOON	enchantment	GRAMMARY(E), MALEFICE
—evening	UNDERN	encircle	EMBAIL
—ripe	RARE-RIPE	enclose	EMBOWEL, ENCHASE
variety	RATH(E)RIPE	—in the bowels	EMBOWEL
earn	YEARN	—to prevent accidents	WARD
earnest	EAGER, FORWARD, WISTFUL	enclosed	
—desire	VOTE	—hollow part	WEM(B), WEAMB
earth	MOULD	—space	IMPALEMENT
easily		enclosure	HAW, TOWN
—handled	YARE	end	FINE, UPSHOT
—injured	NICE	—of existence	DATE
East	LEVANT	endanger	PERICLITATE
Easter	PASCH	endearment	PEAT, PIGGESNYE
easy	EATH, ETHE		PIGSN(E)Y, PIGSNIE
—to roll	VOLUBLE	endeavour	WORKING
ecclesiastical scarf	TIPPET	endorse	CONCLUDE
eclipse	DELIQUIUM	endue	ENDEW
eclogue	AEGLOGUE	endure	DURE, ENDEW
eddish	EADISH	enfold	PLIGHT
editor	OVERSEER, UNDERTAKER	enforced	NECESSARY
educate	INSTITUTE	engage in	VOUCHSAFE, VOUTSAFE
educational	INSTITUTIONARY	engine	GIMMAL
efficient action	EFFICIENCE	engraft	ENGRAFF, IMP
egg	COCKNEY	engulf	ENGULPH, INGULPH
—fried with bacon	COLLOP	enjoy	TASTE, WIELD

enjoyable	GUSTFUL	—being	SHREW
enjoyment	PLEASANCE, SUFFISANCE	—deed	MALEFICE, PRANK
ennoble	GENTLE	ewer	AQUAMANALE, AQUAMANILE
enormous	ENORM	exact transcript	TENOUR
enough	ENOW	exactitude	PRINT
—of that	VIA	examination by torture	QUESTION
enraged like a cuckold	HORN-MAD	example	ENSAMPLE
enshrine (in verse)	ENCHASE	—for warning	SAMPLE
ensign	ANCIENT, PAVILION	exceeding the normal	ENORMOUS
ensphere	EMBOW	exceedingly	EXCEEDING, HEAVENLY
entangle	ENGAGE		MONSTROUS, PASSING
enterprise	EMPRISE, VOYAGE	—great	STRANGE
entertainment for		excellent	EXIMIOUS, PURE
benefit of one		except	OUTTAKEN, WITHOUT
in need	FRIENDLY LEAD	exceptional	STRANGE
entice	ATTEMPT	excess	NIMIETY
entire	INTIRE	excessive	UNEQUAL
entirely	MERELY	excessively	WOUND(IL)Y
entomb	GRAVE	excite	URGE
entrance	INFARE	—loathing in	UG
entrap	CROSSBITE	excitement	RUFF(E)
entreating	ENTREATIVE	exclamation of	
entreaty	EXORATION	—astonishment	ZOUNDS
entremets	ENTREMES(SE)	—defiance	MARRY COME UP
epic poet	EPIC	—failure to understand	ANAN
epistolatory	LITERARY	—surprise	HOOKEY WALKER
epoch	EPOCHA		MARRY
equal	FE(A)RE, FEER, FIERE, PHEERE	exemplar	SAMPLER
	MAKE, MARROW, MATE	exercise	INURE
	PARAGON, PEREGAL	exertion of influence	LABOUR
equip	APPAREL, BEDIGHT	exhaust	FORDO
	DIGHT, EQUIPAGE	exhausted	FOREDONE
equipment	ORDINANCE, TIRE		FORFAUGHTEN
equipped	ADDRESSED, ADDREST	exile	WRETCH
—for fighting	WARLIKE	expect	HOPE, WEEN
ermine	ERMELIN	expeditate	LAW
errand-runner	CAD	expeditation	LAWING
error in pleading	JEOFAIL	expel forcibly	EXPULSE
erst	EARST	expend	DISPEND
escape	ESCAPADE	expenditure	GOINGS-OUT, MISE
especially	IN SPECIAL	experience	GUST, PROOF, RELISH
espial	SPIAL	experienced	WELL-SENN
espoused	HANDFAST	experiment	CONCLUSION, EXPERIENCE
establish	EDIFY, STABLISH	expert	SLY
estate	HAVING	—in gems	LAPIDARY
esteem	PASS	explain	AREAD, AREDE, ARREEDE
eternal	ETERNE		GLOZE, SALVE
eulogistic	EPAENETIC, EPAINETIC	—by hypothesis	SALVE
eulogy	LAUD	explanation	GLOZE
euphony	EUPHONIA	expose	DETECT
evade	SHIFT, WAIVE	exposed	OBNOXIOUS
eve	E'EN, EVEN	exposition	ENARRATION
—of Jewish Sabbath	PARASCEVE	expound	GLOZE, REDE
even	EEV(E)N	—scriptures	PROPHESY
evening	EEVNING	express	
evil	BALE, NAUGHT	—desire for	YEARN

—in words	LANGUAGE	—from choice	PROMISCUOUS
—joy at	GRATULATE	—through	THROUGHLY
expressing		farcical afterpiece	
—freely	LAXATIVE	or interlude	JIG
—love	ENDEARING	farcy (glanders)	FARCIN
expression of face	MIEN	farm	
exquisite	PINK	—worker	HIND
exterminate	EXTIRP	—yard	HOMESTALL
external appearance	GARB	farthing	FARDEN, FARDING
extinguish hope	QUENCH	fashion	FEIGN, ENTAIL, ENTAYLE
extol	ADVANCE	fashionable	FLASH
extract gently	SOLICIT	fast ship	ADVICE-BOAT
extraction	BROOD	fastening	TACH(E)
extraordinarily great	VENGEABLE	fastidiously exact	POINT-DEVICE
extremely	PARLOUS		POINT-DEVISE
extremity	EXIGENT	fate	EVENT, WEIRD
extricate oneself	WIND OUT	fathom	FEDDON
extrinsic	FORINSECAL	fatigue	FATIGATE
eye	LIGHT, PIGGESNYE	fatigued	SWINKED
	PIGSN(E)Y, PIGSNIE	fatten	BATTEN
eyelet	OILLET	fault	DEFAULT, GALL
eyes	EINE, EYNE	favourable	GRACIOUS, TOWARD(LY)
face	CHEER, FAVOUR	favoured advocate	PEAT
	VISOR, VIZOR	favourite	GRACIOSO
facetious	FACETE	fear	ADREAD, DOUBT, HOPE
fade	FAINT		REDOUBT
faded	BRAID, FADE	feat	POINT
failing to pass a test	REPROBATE	feathery structure	PLUME
fainting fit	SOUND, SWOUN	features	FAVOUR
fair where servants		feeble	SACKLESS
were hired	HIRING	feed	BATTLE
fairy	FAERIE, FAERY	—with fine food	PAMPER
fairyland	FAERIE, FAERY	feeding	PASTURE, RELIEF
faith	TROTH		CIBATION
falchion (sword)	FAULCHI(O)N	feel	
fall		—joy or sorrow	
—back	RECOIL	because of	RESENT
—short	FAULT	—vexation at	ENVY
falling of jaw	JAWFALL	feign	DISSEMBLE, FALSIFY
false		feigned	PERSONATE
—appearance	FALSEHOOD	fel(d)spar	FELSPATH
—representation	SUGGESTION	fellow	JACK, WAG
falsehood	FALSE	—Christian	EVEN-CHRISTIAN
falsification	ADULTERY	—lodger	INMATE
falsifier	FALSER	felsite	FELSTONE
familiar	PRIVY	female	
—acquaintance	HABITUDE	—camp-follower	LEAGUER-LADY
—friend	GOSSIP		LEAGUER-LASS
—to all	GENERAL	—child	MAID-CHILD
fan	FLABELLUM	—ruler	GOUVERNANTE
fanciful notion	REVERIE	fence	HAY
fancy	FANTASY, PHANTASY, WEEN	—in with stakes	IMPALE
fang	PHANG	ferment (liquid)	FRET
fantastic creation	WHIM	ferrule	VERREL
far		festival day	GAUDY
—fetched	FAR-FET	festivity	GAUD, TRIUMPH

fetch	FET(T)	—use	MAIDENHEAD
fetched	FET	firstly	ONCE
—from remote place	FAR-FETCHED	fish	
fetter	BILBOES	—carrier	RIPP(I)ER
feudal		—hook	ANGLE
—land division	VILL	—pond	VIVER
—right to dispose of		fist	NEIF, NEIVE, NIEF, NIEVE
vassal's heir in		fitness	PROPERTY
marriage	MARITAGE	fix	PITCH
—tax	TALLAGE	fixed	UNREMOVABLE
few	WHEEN	—payment	FARM
fictitious suit	FINE	—quantity	RATE
fiddle	GU(E)	flag	ANCIENT, PAVILION
fiddler	CROWDER	flat	
fidelity	TROTH	—part	PLAT
field	GLEBE	—thing	PLAT
—glass	PROSPECT	flatter	CLAW, GLOZE, STROKE
fierce	STOUT	flatterer	COURT-DRESSER
fiery	FRAMPOLD	flattery	COURT HOLY WATER
fight	CAMP	flavour	GUST
—for	DEBATE	flax fibre or seed	LINE
—with knives	SNICK AND SNEE	flay	UNCASE
	SNICK-A-SNEE, SNICKERSNEE	flee from	ESCHEW
	SNICK OR SNEE, STICK OR SNEE	fleet	FLIT(T)
fighter	GLADIATOR	fleeting	FLIT(T)
fighting spirit	GAME	flesh-colour	CARNATION
figure	IDOL	fleur-de-lis	FLOWER-DELICE
—planted in box	KNOT		FLOWER-DE-LUCE
filbert	FILBERD	flight of	
filch	DRIP, LURCH	—larks	EXALT
fill		—steps	GRE(E)CE, GRECIAN
—full	FULFIL		GRE(E)SE, GREESING
—up a deficiency in	SUPPLY		GRESSING, GRI(E)CE
—with people	EMPEOPLE		GRISE, GRIZE, SCALE
fillet	FASCIA	flighty girl	GIG
filling completely	FULFILLING	fling (oneself)	LANCE
film over the eye	WEB	flintlock	SHAPHA(U)NCE, SNAPHAUNCH
filth	GORE	flirt	MASH, PICKEER
final settlement	FINE	—with	COQUETTE
find fault with	PINCH	float	FLEET, WAVE
fine	ISSUE, PURE, UNLAW	flogging	WHIPPING-CHEER
—cloth	SINDON	floor	PLANCH
—paid		flout	FRUMP
by tenant's heir	RELIEFAF	flow	RAIL
on marriage of		flower-pot	BOUGHPOT, BOWPOT
daughter	MERCHET	flue	TEWEL
—woollen cloth	PUKE	fluoride	FLUATE
finger-bowl	WATER-GLASS	flush	GILD
fire		flute	TIBIA
—engine	WATER-ENGINE	flying about	VOLATIC
—work	WATERLOO CRACKER	foiled	NAUGHT
firm	SICCAR, SICKER	fold	PLIGHT, PRAN(C)K(E)
—grip	HANDFAST	follow	USE
first		—after	ENSUE
—born	PRIMOGENIT	followers	SEQUEL
—experience	MAIDENHEAD	fondness	WELL-LIKING

fool	ANTICK, FON, PATCH
	SOT, ZANY
foolish	FOND, PEEVISH
foolishly simple	NICE
football	CAMP
footing	TROD
fop	FANTASTIC, MUSCADIN
foppish	FALLAL, FANTASTIC(AL)
for	
—love's sake	PARAMOUR
—the time being	PRESENTLY
forage	PICKEER
forbid	DEFEND, DISCHARGE
	FOR(E)SAY, FOR(E)SPEAK, WARN
force	VIOLENT
—again	RENFORCE
—back	RECOIL
—open	SPORT
forcible	VIVE
forecourt	VESTIBULE
foreign	FORINSECAL
	OUTLANDISH
—coin bearing head	POLL
forenoon	UNDERN
foreshow	FIGUE
forestall	LURCH, PREVENT
forester	WALKER
forester's rights	PU(L)TURE
foretaste	ANTEPAST
foretokening	SOOTH
forfeit	CHEAT, FOR(E)GO
forgot	FORGAT
forgotten	FORGOT
fork of the body	TWIST
form	
—a scum	MANTLE
—by carving	INSCULP
—into	
community	EMPEOPLE
knot	KNIT
forming a thicket	QUEACHY, QUEECHY
formally set, crimped	
or plaited	IN PRINT
former	FORE
former(ly)	WHILE-ERE, WHILOM
formidable	STOOR, STOUR
	STOWRE, STURE
forming a thicket	QUEACHY, QUEECHY
forsake	DESTITUTE, FORLESE
	WAIVE
forsaken	LORN
forsooth	QUOTHA, MARRY
forswear	REN(A)Y, RENEY
forthwith	EFT
fortified	
—dwelling	PEEL-HOUSE, PEEL-TOWER

—town	PLACE
fortify	INSCONCE
fortress	PLACE
fortunate	SEELY
fortune	EVENT
forty	QUADRAGESIMAL
—days of Lent	QUADRAGESIMA
fought	FOUGHTEN
foul	HARLOTRY, PAW(PAW)
foulness	SOILINESS
founder (of colony)	OECIST, OIKIST
four branches of	
mathematics	QUADRIVIUM
fourth part	FARDEL, FARTHING
framework boarding	CONTIGNATION
frankpledge	FRITHBOHR
frantic	PHRENTICK
fraud	CONVEYANCE
fraudulent	COVINOUS
freckle	FERN(I)TIC(K)LE
	FAIRNITIC(K)LE
	FERNYTIC(K)LE
free	VINDICATE, VOID
—booter	SNAPHA(U)NCE
	SNAPHAUNCH
—from	
impediment	EXPEDITE
superfluous fat	ENSEAM
—passenger	CAD
—villager	VILLEIN
freeze	FRIZE
freight	FRAUGHT
freighted	FREIGHT
frenzical	PHRENSICAL
frenzy	PHRENITIS, PHRENSY
frequent	HABITUATE, PRACTISE
fret	VEX
—into anger or sorrow	GRATE
fretful	FRAMPOLD
friar licensed to beg	LIMITER
Friday	PARASCEVE
friend	INGLE
frieze	FRIZE
frightful	UGLY
frill	CHITTERLING
fringe	GUARD
frisk	FISK
frock-coat	SURTOUT
frog	PADDOCK
from	FRO
—the east	EOTHEN
front of top of head	FORETOP
froth on beer	YEAST
froward	AWKWARD
fruit	
—pip	PIPPIN

—preserved in syrup	SUCKET
fruits of own actions	BRINGINGS FORTH
frustration	FOIL
full	
—of moans	GROANFUL
—speed	RANDOM
fully equal	PEREGAL
funeral	
—pyre	BALE-FIRE
—undertaker	UPHOLDER
furnish	BEDIGHT, BESEE, PREPARE
—with a loft	LOFT
furniture	TIRE
further	FURDER
fuse	COLLIQUATE
fustet	FUSTIC, FUSTOC
gabble prayers	PATTER
gad	FISK
gadfly	BRIZE
gage	WAGE
gain	ESCHEAT, THRIFT, WIELD
—anew	REPRISE
gallery	ALURE
gallop	WALLOP
gallows	GALLUS, NUB
	NUBBING-CHEAT
game	NINE MEN'S MORRIS, PARTY
—with	
cherry stones	CHERRY-PIT
pins of wood	LOGGATS
gang	GING
garb	VESTIMENT
garden	ARBOUR
gargle	GARGARISE, GARGARISM
	GARGARIZE
garland	GIRLOND, SHROUD, WEED
garment	VESTIMENT
garrison	STUFF
gatekeeper	WARDEN
gauge	SCANTLING
gay	BONNY, BONNIE
—fellow	GAILLARD, GALLIARD
gaze at	WAIT (UP)ON
geld	GELT
general run or course	TENOUR
genius	ENGINE, INGINE
gentile	ETHNIC
gentle	MANSUETTE
gentleman-at-arms	PENSIONARY
gentlemanly	JA(UN)TEE
gentlemen	LORDINGS
gently	FAIRISH
genuine	ENTIRE
German	ALMAIN, DUTCH
get	FALL
—along somehow	SCAMBLE
—at	AREACH
—by heart	RECORD
—goods on credit	FINEER
—over	OVERGET
—the	
better of	WIN OF
start of	LURCH
—well	RECURE
getting	
—on	TOWARD
—out of bed	LEVEE
giant	ETEN, ETTIN, ROUNCEVAL
gibbet	POTENCE
gibe	GLEEK
gimbal	GIMMAL
gin	MAX
—and treacle	MAHOGANY
gipsy	EGYPT
girded up	SUCCINCT
girdle	WAIST
girl	GILL, JILL
	KINCHIN-MORT, PIGEON
give	TAKE
—a sharp blow to	WHERRET, WHIRRET
—an example of	ENSAMPLE
—as a remedy	EXHIBIT
—distinction or honour to	ILLUSTRATE
—form to	INFORM
—in	KNOCK UNDER
—one satisfaction	DO ONE REASON
—pleasure to	PLEASURE
—success	SPEED
—up	FORBEAR, RESPITE
—vogue to	VOGUE
giving freedom	LAXATIVE
glad	FAIN
glance	EY(E)LIAD, TWEER, TWIRE
glassy	GLAZEN
glazed	GLAZEN
gleam	SHEEN
—of light	LEAM, LEME
gliding	LAPSE
—movement in dancing	SLUR
glint	GLENT
glisten	GLISTER
glittering ornament	SPANG
gloomy	WAN
glorify	GLORY
gloss over	SOOTHE
glossy	POLITE
glow	LEAM, LEME
glum	GLUMPISH
glutton	LURCHER
go	BING, TRADE, WIND
—astray	MISGO

—away from	VOID	grant	CONDESCEND, PAY
—before	PREVENT	—of money to king	SUBSIDY
—down	VAIL	—religious liberty	INDULGE
—faster than	PREVENT	—time	FRIST
—forward	PRETEND	—to ministers	REGIUM DONUM
—little by little	DRIB	grantor's warranty	WARRANDICE
—on wooden shoes	PATTEN	grape	WINE-BERRY
—swiftly	STRIP	grasp	HENT
—to		grassy plot or seat	ARBOUR
law	LAW	gratification	EASEMENT, GUST
unfashionable part	MOB IT	gratuity to servants	
—wrong	MISS	or officers of court	GLOVE-MONEY
goat	GATE	gravel	GRIT
goblin	PUG	grazing ground	HERDWICK
God	GOG	grease	ENSEAM, SMEAR
—like	GODLILY	great	MUCH, STOOR, STOUR
—save	UDS		STOWRE, STURE
God's	UDS	—auk	PENGUIN, PINGUIN
—eyelid	'SLID	—bouncing woman	ROUNCEVAL
—heart	'SHEART	—quantity	MICKLE
—life	'SLIFE	—Roll of the Exchequer	PIPE ROLL
—light	'SLIGHT	—thanks	GRAMERCY
—nails	'SNAILS	greater part	HEFT
—wounds	'OONS, ZOUNDS	green pigment	VERDITER
gold	SOL	greenhorn	PUT(T)
golf	GOFF	greet	HALSE
good	RUM, SEELY	grey	GRIS(E), GRISEOUS
—bargain	GOOD-CHEAP	—fur	GRIS(E)
—condition	PLIGHT	grief	GRAM(E), TEEN(E), TENE
—evening	GOOD-DEN	grieve	RUE, VEX
—for nothing	NAUGHT	grim	GRISY
—fortune	SPEED	grin	SNEER
—luck to	FAIR (BE)FALL	grisly	GRISY
—many	WHEEN	grocer	PEPPERER
—morning	GOOD-MORROW	groom	COISTREL, COISTRIL
gossip	AUNT		COYSTREL, COYSTRIL
gourmand	GORMAND	groomsman	PARANYMPH
governed by humour	HUMOUROUS	grooved border	SWAGE
government	REGENCE	gross	
governor	GREAVE, GRIEVE, RECTOR	—in language	LIBERAL
—of		—overgrown person	FUSTILUGS
Papal province	LEGATE	ground-plan	PLATFORM
town or district	WARDEN	grounds	WALK
Moldavia	GOSPODAR, HOSPODAR	group	GLOBE, SORT
	VOIVODE	grow	
Wallachia	GOSPODAR, HOSPODAR	—in wealth	INCREASE
	VOIVODE	—rich	RICH
gracious	HANDSOME, HEND	—worse	WORST
graft	GRAFF, IMP	growing	
granary	GIRNEL	—beneath	SUBNASCENT
grand		—under water	DEMERSED
—father	GRANDSIRE	growl	GROIN
—mercy	GRAMERCY	grown	WAXEN
—ship	ARGOSY	grudge	ENVY, MALIGN
—son	NEPHEW	grumble	GROIN
—thanks	GRAMERCY	grunt	GROIN

guarantee	VOUCHSAFE, VOUTSAFE
	WARRANDICE, WARRANTISE
guard	WARD
guardianship	TUITION
guardship	ARMOUR
guess	AREAD, AREDE, ARREEDE
guile	DOLE
guileless	SACKLESS
guinea-fowl	TURKEY
—hen	TURKEY-HEN
gullet	WEAZAND
gullible person	CHIAUS, CHOUSE
gunner's assistant	MATROSS
gunwale	PORTLAST, PORTOISE
gush	RAIL
habit	WON
hackneyed	PROSTITUTE
hail from a distance	WHOA-HO-HO(A)
hair	STRAMMEL, STRUMMEL
—on horse's hoof	CRONET
—ornament	POMPOON
—pad	TOQUE
half	
—boot	START-UP
—guinea	SMELT
—penny	MAG, MAIK, MAKE
	MAGPIE, MAIL(E)
	PORTCULLIS
halter	WITHE
hamper	SERO(O)N
hand	HOND
handing over	LIVERY
handkerchief	MUCKENDER, ORARIUM
handle	HAND
—clumsily	GAUM, GORM
—of dagger	DUDGEON
handsome	FEAT(E)OUS, FEATUOUS
	FEATURELY
handy	HANDSOME
hang	HONG, JUSTIFY, KILT
	NUB, TRUSS
hanger	BASELARD
—on	CAD
hanging	TAPIS
hangman	NUBBING-COVE
hangman's rope	TIPPET
haphazard meal	SCAMBLING
happen	TIDE
happening	WEIRD
happy	SEELY
harangue	SPEECH
harass	TROUNCE
hard	
—drinking	CAROUSE
—plight	QUANDARY
hardihood	HARDIMENT

hardly	UNE(A)TH, UNEATHES
	UNNETHES
hardship	STRESS
hare	WAT
harlot	PUG, WAGTAIL
harm	BANE, WREAK
harmonise	ATONE, SALVE
harmony	CONCENT
—in thirds and sixths	FA(UX)BURDEN
harm physically	WRONG
harrow	HERSE
harsh	ASPER, STOOR, STOUR
	STOWRE, STURE
hart in third year	SPADE
	SPAY(AD), SPAYD
hasten	URGE
hasty and abridged Mass	HUNTING-MASS
hateful	LO(A)TH
haughtiness	HOGEN-MOGEN
haughty	SUPERB
haunch	HANCH
have	
—a liking for	AFFECT
—an inkling	SMOKE
—as essence	CONSIST-IN
—lustre	SHEEN
—sex with	KNOW
—traffickings	TRINKET
—underhand dealings	TRINKET
having	
—friends	FRIENDED
—good constitution	WELL-TEMPERED
—memory	MINDFUL
—natural ability	INGENIOUS
—seen many winters	WINTERED
—virtue or efficacy	VIRTUAL
hawk in first year	SOAR(E), SORE
hawk's	
—nostril	NARE
—quarry	MARK
hawker of	
broadsheets	SPEECH-CRIER
hawthorn	ALBESPINE, ALBESPYNE
hazard	VENTURE, WAGE
hazardous	NICE
—undertaking	EMPRISE
head	COSTARD
—and shoulders	
of a ling	POLL
—dress	HEAD, HEAD-TIRE, TIRE
with flaps	LAPPET-HEAD
—of frankpledge, tithing	
or decennary	HEADBOROUGH
—wind	DEAD WIND
headlong	PROCLIVE
—fall	PRECIPICE

heal	SAIN
health	HAIL, HEAL
healthy	SANE, WELL-DISPOSED
heap of slain	CARNAGE
hearse	HERSE
hearten	HEART
heartstricken	HEART-STROOK
heat	CALORIC, FLUSTER
heathen	ETHNIC, PA(I)NIM, PAYNIM
heathenism	HEATHENDOM, HEATHENESSE
	PA(I)NIM, PAYNIM
heavens	REGION
heavily armed soldier	GALLO(W)GLASS
heaving	HEFT
hedge	HAW, HAY, MOUND
heel	HEALD
—over suddenly	SEEL
height	HIGHT(H)
—of exaltation	RUFF(E)
heiress	FORTUNE
hele	HELL
heliotrope	GIRASOL(E)
hellenising Jew	GREEK
helm	STERN, TIMON
helmsman	TIMONEER
help	STEAD, SUPPLY
—in need	BEETMISTER
—to success	SPEED
helped	HOLP(EN)
hemp	NECK-WEED
henna	CAMPHIRE
herb	WORT
herdsman	HERD-GROOM
hereditary	SUCCESSIVE
hero	EORL
herring's head	COB
hest	COMMAND
hidden	ABSTRUSE, DE(A)RN
hide	PELL
hideous	LOATHLY
high	
—birth	GENEROSITY
—chopin	PANTOF(F)LE, PANTOUFLE
—Churchman	HIGH-FLIER, HIGH-FLYER
—Church Tory	TANTIVY
—minded	GENTLE
—official	REEVE
—pasture-ground	WALK
—spirits	HEYDAY, SPLEEN
—standing	WORSHIP
Highland chief's attendant	G(H)ILLIE
highway	
—man	HI(GH)JACKER, SCAMP
—robbery	LATROCINIUM, LATROCINY
hill	LOW
—crest	KNAP

hillock	KNAP
hinder	EMBAR, IMPEACH, LET
hindrance	LET
hinge	GEMMAL
hired	
—assassin	BRAVE
—drudge	HACKNEY
—thug	BULLY
hire for pay	WAGE
hit	HAY
—in tilting	TAINT
—it off	FADGE
hoard	HOORD, MUCKER, SPARE
hoax	FUN, GULL, SHAM
hobble for horse	PASTERN
hoist	HOISE
hoisted	HOISED, HOIST
hold	HOLT
—a late revel	WAKE
—together	CONSIST
holding of land	ROOM
hole in wall	
for light	DREAM-HOLE
holiness	HALIDON, SANCTIMONY
hollow enclosed part	WEM(B), WEAMB
holy	SANCTIMONIOUS
—place or thing	HALIDOM
homage	MANRED
homely	RUSSET
homespun	RUSSET
home-thrust	HAY
homestead	HOMESTALL, TOFT
homily	PRONE
honey	
—dew	MILDEW
—moon	HONEYMONTH
—suckle	CAPRIFOLE
hoot	WHOOT
hornbook	BATTLEDOOR, BATTLEDORE
horologe	HOROLOGIUM
horrible	GRISY, UGLY
horse	
—cloth	TRAP
—covering	FOOT-CLOTH
—doctor	HORSE-LEECH
—fly	BRIZE
horseman used for light work	HOBBLER
horse's pack strap	WANTY
hospital	SPITAL
	SPITTLE(-HOUSE)
hospitaller	HOSTEL(L)ER
host	HARBINGER
hostage	PLEDGE
hostel	ENTRY
—for travellers	HOSPITAL
hostess	LANDLADY

hostile	INFEST
hostility	ENVY
hot	WHOT
—bathing establishment	HOTHOUSE
hound	BRACH
hour	HOWRE
house for receipt of stolen goods	STALLING-KEN
household management	ECONOMICS
housewife	HUSSY, HUSWIFE
hover	WAVE
howsoever	HOWSO
hubbub	LEVEL-COIL
huge	HIDEOUS
humble	SILLY, PLUCK, DEMISSIVE
humbug	HOOKEY WALKER
humility	LOWLIHEAD
humorous	LUDICROUS
hunchback	URCHIN
hundred	CANTRED, CANTREF
—weight	QUINTAL
hung	HONG
hunter's horn-call	MOT
hunting-ground	WALK
hurdy-gurdy	SYMPHONY
hurricane	HURRICANO
hurt	GRIEVE, NOY, NUISANCE
hurtful	NAUGHT
husband	FEARE, FEER, FE(E)RE LORD, PHEERE
husbandman	CARL, HUSBAND
hush up	HUDDLE
hushed	WHIST
hussif	HUSSY
hustle out of sight	HUDDLE
hypnotism	BRAIDISM
hypochondria	HIP, HYP
hysteria	MOTHER
I am ready to go with you	HAVE WITH YOU
iatrochemical	CHEMIC
idiot	NATURAL, NIDGET
idle	
—fancy	FLAM
—report	TOY
—tale	TOY
idols	HIGH-PLACE
if	AN, GIF
ignorant	INGRAM, INGRUM, LEWD
—priest	HEDGE-PRIEST, LACK-LATIN
ilk	YLKE
ill	
—advised	OVERSEEN
—conduct	MISCARRIAGE
—humour	RHEUM, SPLEEN
—mannered fellow	JACK

—natured person	ATTERCOP
—will	ENVY, MAU(L)GRE
imagination	WIT
imagine falsely	FEIGN
imagined	FEIGNED
—substance	MAGNESIA
imbue	TINCT
immature	UNSIZ(E)ABLE
immediately	INCESSANTLY
immerse	DEMERSE
immoral	NAUGHT, UNHONEST
immure	ENCLOISTER
imp	URCHIN
impair	APPAIR, EMPERISH IMPEACH, WRONG
impart	IMPUTE
impassable	INVIOUS
impede	IMPEACH, PESTER
impending	TOWARD
imperceptibly	UNSENSIBLY
impetuous	STURDY
implement	LOOM
imply more than is said	EMPHASIS
import	CARRIAGE
importance	ESTIMATION
importunately	INSTANTLY
impose upon	SHAM
impostor	FAITOR, FAITOUR PHANTASM
impoverish	EMPOVERISH, WASTE
impregnated	IMPREGNANT
impression	DINT
imprison	LUMBER
improve	BEET, BETE
impudence	BRONZE
impudent person	SAUCE
impulse	SPLEEN
in	ON
—another way	OTHERGATES OTHERGUESS
—as much as	WHENAS
—company	IN FERE, YFERE
—comparison with	IN RESPECT OF
—dishabille	MOBBED
—exact order	IN PRINT
—extreme danger	PERDU(E)
—front	AFRONT
—good condition	TAUGHT, WELL-LIKING
—great excitement	IN HIGH LEG
—hardship	UNE(A)TH, UNEATHES UNNETHES
—inner room	WITHIN
—order to	FOR TO
—part	PARCEL
—particular	IN SPECIAL
—practice	PRACTIC

—ruins	RUINATE	inflict bodily pain on	GRIEVE
—short	AT A WORD, ONCE	inflow	INFLUENCE
—some degree	SOMEDEAL	infold	CLIP
—spite of	MALGRADO, MAU(L)GRE	inform	RESOLVE
—the		information	WIT(TING)
direction facing		informed of	KNOWING TO
one	TOWARD	informer	DISCOVERER
manner of	UPSEE, UPS(E)Y	ingenious	ARTIFICIAL, QUAINT, WITTY
—times past	OF YORE	ingenuity	ENGINE
—vain	IN WASTE	ingoing	INFARE
—want	PENURIOUS	ingot of gold or silver	WEDGE
inadequate	UNEQUAL	inhabit	HABIT
incapable of being		inhabitant	INHABITOR
fashioned	UNFASHIONABLE	—of	
incautious	WARELESS	garret	GARRETEER
incidence	TO-FALL	hundred	HUNDREDER
incidental occurrence	OBVENTION	inhere in	CONSIST IN
incite	WHET	inherence	INEXISTENCE
inclined	PROCLIVE	inheritance	FEE
include	CONCLUDE	injure	DE(A)RE, MISDO
incommode	DISCOMMODE	injury	BALE, DISGRACE, GRIEVANCE
inconvenience	DISCOMMODITY		NUISANCE, TEEN(E), TENE
inconvenient	UNGAIN, UNHANDSOME	injustice	UNREASON
increase	ENCREASE, IMPROVE	ink-holder	INK-HORN
—of wealth	THRIFT	inland	WITHIN LAND
incubus	EPHIALTES	inn	WATERING-HOUSE
incurable	RECURELESS	—keeper	ALE-DRAPER
indecent	UNHONEST	innate character	KIND
—matter	STUFF	innocent	SACKLESS
indecently opprobious	SCURRIL(E)	innovation	NOVITY
indeed	INSOOTH, IN GOOD TIME	inopportune	IMPORTUNATE
indeed!	MARRY	inordinately big	UNSIZ(E)ABLE
indicate	PRETEND	inscribed with book	
indict	(EN)DITE	titles	RUBRIC
indifferent actor	JAY	insect	
indignation	INDIGNANCE	—imagined to live in fire	PYRALIS
indirect	UNGAI	—pupa	NYMPH
—action	WINDLASS	—vermin	MOTH
indite	(EN)DITE	insert between	INTERSERT
individually	IN PARTICULAR	insignificant person	DANDIPRAT
induce	ENTREAT		DANDYPRAT
industrious	NOTABLE	insolent	WANTON
indwelling	INEXISTENT	inspect urine	CAST-WATER
inelegant	UNPOLITE	inspection	PERSPECTIVE, INSPECT
inexperienced	UNSEEN	installation	INSTALLMENT
inexpressible	INEXPRESSIVE	instantly	INSTANTIAL
infamous	OPPROBRIOUS	instrument	
—person	NITHING	—for winding spring	SPANNER
infantile thrush	SPRUE	—of	
infantry regiment	TERCIO	punishment	TUMBREL, TUMBRIL
infatuate	ASSOT	torture	ENGINE
infect with measles	MEASLES	insult	INJURY
inferior		insure	ENSURE
—assistant	CAD	insurrectionary force	HEAD
—Flemish cloth	MOCKADO	intellect	INTELLECTUAL
infest	PESTER	intended for use in war	WARLIKE

intensify	INTEND
intent	WISTFUL
intentness	INTENT
inter	EARTH, INEARTH
intercept	WAYLAY
intercepting	INTERCIPIENT
intercession	INTERPELLATION
intercessor	MEAN
interchange	ENTERCHAUNGE
intercourse	INTERDEAL
interest	USURY
—on money	USAGE, USE
interfere with	MAR
interjection	
—of	
dismissal	VIA
impatience	'SDEATH
surprise	MARRY
thanks or surprise	MERCY
—pledging health	TOPE
intermediate	MIDDLING
internal government	
of state	POLICE
interpose	STICKLE
interpret	AREAD, AREDE, ARREEDE
interpreter	TRUCHMAN
intimate	PRIVY, STRICT
intriguer	CHAMBERER, TRINETER
invention	WIT
inverted	AWKWARD
invite	BID
inviting	COASTING
involve	WIND(UP)
invulnerable	WOUNDLESS
inward	TOWARD
iris	FLOWER-DELICE
	FLOWER-DE-LUCE
Irish	
—labourer newly	
arrived	GRECIAN
—magistrate	RESIDENT MAGISTRATE, RM
irregular	HUMOUROUS
issue	PROOF
item	PARCEL
—of news	OCCURRENT
itinerant	PIEPOWDER
jack-maker	JACKSMITH
jackdaw	CHOUGH, DAW-COCK
jade	SPLEEN-STONE
jargon	PARLANCE
jasmine	JESSAMY
jealousy	YELLOWNESS
jemmy	BETTY
jerk	BRAID, YERK
jerking movement	JUT
jest	BOURD, JIG, TOY
jester	PATCH
jester's garb	MOTLEY
jetsam	JETSOM, JETSON
jettison	JETSAM
Jew	SMOUCH, SMOUS(E)
jewelled head ornament	CARCANET
jibe	BOB, GIRD
jingle	JIG
Joan of Arc	PUCELLE
job	SPOT
joining timber	CONTIGNATION
joint	ARTICLE
joke	GLEEK
journey	VOYAGE
jovial	WANTON
joy	LIST
judge	CENSURE, SCAN, STICKLER
jug	NEWGATE
juggle	PALTER
juggler	TREGETOUR
juggling trick	SLIGHT
jumping-jack	PANTINE
jury-writ	VENIRE(FACIAS)
justify	DARRAIGN(E), DARRAIN(E)
	DARRAYN, DERAIGN
jut	JET
keep	WARRANT
—away from	REFRAIN
—company	ASSORT
—in bondage or custody	WITHHOLD
—into later year	OVERYEAR
—out of the way	BE NAUGHT
—under observation	WAIT (UP)ON
—watch	WAKEN
keeper of a warren	WARRENER
kettledrum	TIMBAL, TYMBAL
key	KAIE
—of C major	PROPER CHANT
keynote	KEY
khan	CHAGAN, CHAM
kick	WINCE
—about the limbs	SPRAWL
kid	YEANLING
—glove	CHEV(E)RON
kidney	REIN
kill	QUELL, MISDO, MORTIFY
	SPILL, STRANGLE
kind treatment	CHEER
kindness	CANDOUR
king	COLE, LUD, OFFA, PRINCE
king's	
—bodyguard	HOUSE-CARL
—companion	THANE
kingdom	REAME, REIGN
kinship	SIB
knave	BOY, VARLET

—in cards	MAKER, PUR
knell	KNOLL
knew	COUTH
knife	CUTTLE
knob	POMMEL
know	CAN, WIS(H), WIST, WIT, WOT
knowledge	CUNNING, WITTING
known	BEKNOWN, COUTH
labour	MOIL
labours of thought	WORKINGS
lace	GUARD
—head-covering	SHADE
—up	TRUSS
laciniation	DAG
lackey	SKIP-KENNEL
ladder	SCALE, STY
lady	BURD
lady's	
—cape	MANTEEL
—hood	SURTOUT
—maid	TIRE-WOMAN
lamb	YEANLING
lament	PLAIN
lance-corporal	LANCE PESADE, PRISADE
	PRISADD, SPEISADE
land	MOULD
—holding	ROOM
—tax	TALLAGE
—tenure based on	
military service	KNIGHT SERVICE
—valued at a penny	
a year	PENNYLAND
languish	QUAIL
lap-dog	PUPPY
last	YESTERN
—night	TONIGHT
late	LOW
lately	ALATE, NOW OF LATE
later spring	MARTLEMAS
lavish	WASTEFUL
law-officer's coif	BIGGIN
lawsuit	PLEA
lay	
—aside	VOID
—blame on	WITE, WYTE
—down	SUBMIT
—hold of	LATCH
—out in trade	OCCUPY
—table	COVER
lazar-house	SPITAL, SPITTLE(-HOUSE)
laziness	IDLEHOOD
lazy	LITHER
—fellow	LUSK
lead astray	BEWILDER
leading idea	BURTHEN
leap	SA(U)LT

leather	
—doublet	PLACCATE, PLACARD
—water-bottle	WATER-BOUGET
leave out of	
consideration	WAIVE
leer	TWEER, TWIRE
leg armour	JAMBEAU, JAMB(I)ER
legging	START-UP
legislative assembly	MOOT
legislature	STATES
leisure	RESPITE
lengthen out	REACH
—in utterance	PROLATE
Lent	SCAMBLING-DAYS
leopard	LIBBARD, LUBBAR
leper	MEAZEL, MESEL
lesson memorised	LIRIPIPE, LIRIPOOP
let down	VAIL
level to the ground	SLIGHT
liable to censure	OBNOXIOUS
liberal	FRANK
libration of celestial	
sphere	TREPIDATION
lie	
—about	LUSK
—in ambush	WAIT
life	LIVELIHEAD, QUICK
lift one's hat	VAIL
light	
—blow	BOB
—evening meal	VOIDE
—meal	UNDERN
lighting up	ILLUSTRATION
lightly cooked (eggs)	RARE
like	MARROW
limit	COAST, STINT, MARK
lineage	PARAGE
lineal descendant	NEPHEW
liquid measure	WINE-MEASURE
listen	LIST
listening	ATTENT
literary composition	STYLE
litter	TEAM
little	LITE, LYTE, WHEEN
—ball	BULLET
—boat	NACELLE
—boy	DANDIPRAT, DANDYPRAT
—gentleman	FRANKLIN
—hut	CABINET
—star	STARNIE
livelihood	LIVELIHEAD
liveliness	LIVELIHEAD
lively	VIVE
liver, brain and heart	PERFECTIONS
living	
—flesh	QUICK

—form	LIVELIHEAD	lying in ambush	WATCH
load	BURTHEN	mace	MAUL
loaded	LOADEN	mad	LYMPHATIC
loaf from finest flour	MANCHET	madam	MISTRESS
loathe	UG	magic	GRAMMARY(E)
loathsome	LOATHLY	magnetic attraction	ADAMANTINE
lock	SASSE	magnify	MULTIPLY
lock-up	ROUND-HOUSE	maid (of Orleans)	PUCELLE
lodestone	MAGNES	maiden	BURD
lodge	BESTOW, KEEP	main body	CONTINENT
lodgings for debtors	SPUNGING-HOUSE	—body of army	BATTALIA
lofty	STEEP	make	
log-throwing game	LOGGAT	—a	
logic	REDECRAFT	difference	SKILL
lollipop	LULIBUB	lord	LORD
long	PROLIX	mouth	MOE
—ago	YORE	—angry	WRATH
—baby-clothes	LONG-COATS	—away with	RID
—for	EARN	—bold	BOLDEN
longer	LENGER	—bright	ILLUSTRATE
longest	LENGEST	—clear to the mind	ILLUSTRATE
look		—hairless	PILL
—at	VISE	—ready	ADDRESS, PRED
again	REVISE	—safe	SAFE
—to	BESEE	—scant	SCANTLE
lookout	SPECULATOR	—stable	POISE, STABLISH
—place	TOOT	—the sign of the	
loom	FRAME	cross over	SAIN
loose		—ugly	UGLY
—character	RIBALD	—up	
—cloak	GABARDINE	hastily	JUMP
—gown	SLAMMAKIN, SLAMMERKIN	with cosmetics	PRIME
—greatcoat	WRAP-RASCAL	—war upon	WARRAY, WARREY
—woman	MOB, NAUGHTY PACK	—wheel-shaped	WHEEL
—wrap	NIGHT-RAIL	—worse	WORST
lord	SIRE	male guinea-fowl	TURKEY-COCK
lose	GO BY THE WORST	malice	SPLEEN
	GO WITH THE WORST	maliciously	UNHAPPILY
—strength	PALL	manage	MANURE
—vitality	DEAD	manageable	YARE
lost	BEWILDERED, LORN	manganese	MAGNESIA, MAGNESIUM
lot	WEIRD	manner	WISE
lotion	LAVATORY	manor	VILL
louvre	LOVER	manorial holding	HUSBANDLAND
love	AFFECT	mantle	ROCHET, ROCQUET
—making	SWAINING	manual	MECHANICAL
lover	PARAMOUR, SWAIN	map of the world	MAPPEMOND
low-born		marked attention	PARTICULARITY
—character	RIBALD	market	VENT
—churchman	LOW-BOY	marriage	HYMEN
—fellow	LOON	married woman	WOMAN OF THE WORLD
lower	SUBMIT, VAIL	Martinmas	MARTLEMAS
luck	VENTURE	marvel	MARL(E)
lump	LOAF	marvellous	WOND(E)RED
lusty	RANK	mask	VIZARD
luxurious	WANTON	masked sword-dance(r)	MATACHIN

mass	MESS, SAL(A)MON
—of rock or stone	QUARRY
master	MAISTER, MAS(S)
	MES(S), SIRE
match	COPE, MARROW
	PARAGON, SAMPLE
mate	MAKE, MARROW
material	MASS
—universe	KIND
matter	MASS, SENTENCE, SKILL
—of discourse	PLACE
may	MOTE, MOUGHT
mayor	PORTREEVE
mead	MEATH(E)
meadow-sweet	MEAD-SWEET, MEADWORT
meal	MEAT, MESS
—time	MEAL-TIDE
mean	MEDIUM, MENE, SOUND
meaning	SENTENCE
measure	BE METE, MEED
meatless days	BANIAN-DAYS
medal	MODEL
mediate	STICKLE
mediator	MEAN
medical	PHYSIC
medicinal	PHYSICAL
meet	OCCUR
—in advance	PREVENT
—on the way	OBVIATE
melancholy	SPLEEN
melt	COLLIQUATE, RELENT
melting	COLLIQUABLE, COLLIQUANT
	COLLIQUATION
mend	BEET, BETE
menial of lowest grade	RIBALD
menstrual discharge	FLOWER
mental activity	WORKING
mention	MIND, REMEMBER
mercenary horse-soldier	RUTTER
merciless	WANTON
mercurial character	MERCURY
mere	MEER
merry	
—andrew	JACK-PUDDING
	PICKLE-HERRING
—mood	MERRY PIN
metal that is not	
malleable	SEMI-METAL
metaphor	TRANSUMPTION
Meum	SPICKNEL
mica	DAZE
middle	
—class revolutionary	MUSCADIN
—of day or night	WAIST
midwife	LUCINA
migraine	MEGRIM

military	
—engine	TREBUCHET
—expedition	VOYAGE
militia	FYRD
milk	MANSUETTE
mind	WIT
mineral dug from earth	FOSSIL
mirth	SPLEEN
misshapen egg	COCKNEY
mischief	BALE
misery	BALE
misfortune	CHANCE, DECAY, RUTH
misleading	SINISTER
missile	MISSIVE
missiles	ARTILLERY
mistaken	OVERSEEN
mistletoe	MISLETOE, MISSEL
mistress	WENCH
mitigate	ASLAKE
mix	(CO-)MEDDLE, , MENG(E)
	MING, MOULD
mixed	ME(I)NT, MENGED
	MEYNT, MINGED
mixing	CONTEMPERATION
mixture	MIXTION
—of liquids	BALDERDASH
mock orange	PIPE-TREE
mockery	MOCKAGE
mocking ballad	JIG
model	PRECEDENT
—of fashion	MODE
moderate	CHASTISE, CHASTIZE, MEAN
modest	PUDENT, PUDIC
moisture	HUMOUR
molar	WANG(-TOOTH)
moment	PUN(C)TO
monastery	MINSTER
money	CRAP, ROWDY
—grubber	MUCKER
monkey	JACKANAPES, MEERKAT
monstrosity	MONSTRUOSITY
monstrous	MONSTRUOUS
monumental stone	TOUCH
mope	PEAK
more	MO(E)
mortal	WORLDLING, WORLDLY
motto	MOT, POESY
moulded border	SWAGE
mound	MOT(T)E, MOTE-HILL
mount	STY
mountebank	ANTIC, SALTIMBANCO
mousetrap	SAMSON('S) POST
mouth	NEB
move	MEVE, MOOVE, QUATCH
	QUETCH, QUITCH, TROLL
—faster	PUT ON

—off	WALK
—on	WAG
moveable	
—shed for besiegers	SOW
—stage	PAGEANT
moving	MOTIVE
much	MICKLE, MUCHEL
muddy	LIMOUS
muffle	MOB(B)LE
—the head	MOB
muffler	MUFFETTEE
mugger	SCOWRER
mulberry-tree	SYCAMINE
mule	MOYL(E)
multitude	NUMBER
mummy	ANATOMY
municipal officer	VARLET
murder	MURTHER, QUELL
murderer	MURTHERER
muscatel	MUSCADINE
muscle	MOUSE
musical	
—composition	MUSIC
—instrument	ORGAN
—instruments	MUSIC
various	SYMPHONY
musicians at municipal	
ceremonies	WAITS
must	MOTE
mutiny	MUTINE
mutual dealings	INTERDEAL
nag	ROUNCY
name	CLEEP, CLEPE, HETE
	HIGHT, NEMN
—in a list or	
document	ENGROSS
named	BENEMPT, BYNEMPT, HIGHT
	NEMPT, YCLEPED, YCLEPT
narcissus	ROSE OF SHARON
narrate	RECORD
narrative	PROSE
narrow	STRAIT, STRICT
narrowing	REBATEMENT
narrowly	STRAIT
native-born	KINDLY
natural	KINDLY
naturally able	INGENIOUS
nature	KIND
naval camouflage	WAISTCLOTH
nave	NEF
navigation manual	PORTOLAN(O)(CHART)
near	FORBY, NIE
neat	FEAT(E)OUS, FEATUOUS
	NET(T)
neck	HALSE, SWIRE
—covering	PARTLET
—tie	WATERFALL
neckerchief	NECKATEE
needle	NEELD, NEELE
needy	WANTING
négligé	MOB
negotiation	PRACTICE
negotiations	INTERDEAL
negro	NIGER
neighbourhood	VOISINAGE
neighbouring	NEIGHBOUR
neither Christian nor Jew	HEATHEN
nevertheless	ALGATE
news	ADVERTISEMENT
newness	NOVITY
nick of time	ARTICLE
niggard	PUCKFIST
niggardly	NITHING
nigh	NY
night	
—cap	BIGGIN
—dress	NIGHT-SHIFT
—mare	EPHIALTES
nimble	FLIPPANT, WIGHT
nimbly	YARELY
no matter what	
may happen	FALL BACK, FALL EDGE
noble	GENEROUS, GENTLE, THANE
—youth	CHILD(E), CHYLDE
nobleman's bodyguard	HOUSE-CARL
noise	BRUIT
noisy	STREPENT
nominate	VOICE
non-Christian	SARACEN
noodle	DAW-COCK, HODDY-DODDY
normal	JUST
Norwich strong ale	NOG
nose	
—band for horse	MUSROL
—bleed	YARROW
nostril	NARE
nostrum	SECRET
not	NE
—bated	BATELESS
—burdened	UNBURTHENED
—customary	UNCUSTOMED
—described	NONDESCRIPT
—discovered with test	OCCULT
—easily	UNEATH
—exquisite	INCURIOUS
—facetious	INFECITE
—fastidious	INCURIOUS
—fitting	UNDECENT
—handsome	UNDECENT
—helped	UNHOLPEN
—improbably	LIGHTLY
—known	UNWIST

—made polished	UNFASHIONED
—provided with	UNPURVEYED
—to respect	DISRESPECT
—used up	INEXHAUSTED
—well up	UNSEEN
note	COMMON-PLACE
—G	GAMUT
—in written music	PRICK
notice	MIND
notion	NOTICE
notwithstanding	MAU(L)GRE
	NATH(E)LESS(E)
	NAYTHLES
now	PRESENTLY
number of people	CONSORT
nun	VOWESS
nuptials	HYMENALS
nurse	NOURICE
nurture	NOUR(R)ITURE
oaths	SBLOOD, SBODIKINS
	SBUDDIKINS, ZBUD
oatmeal porridge	POTTAGE
obedience	OBEISANCE
obedient	BUXOM
obeisance	OBEDIENCE
object	
—of	
taunts	TAUNT
terror	BUG
—to	QUARREL
objection	QUARREL
objectionable	PERT
obliging	OFFICIOUS
oblique	AWKWARD
obscene	PAW(PAW)
obscure	BLEND
obsequious person	WAGTAIL
observance	TRIUMPH
observation	SPIAL
observe	SMOKE, SPECULATE, USE
obstinate	STIFF-HEARTED
obstruct	WAYLAY
obstructed	LET
obstruction	LET, TRUMP
obverse of coin	CROSS
occupy	MANURE
—oneself	TRADE
occur to	REMEMBER
occurrence	OCCURRENT
octave of festival	UTAS
oddness	IMPARITY
oeillade	EY(E)LIAD
of	ON
—another kind	OTHERGATES
	OTHERGUESS
—good disposition	WELL-THEWED

—high social position	WORTHY
—no	
avail	UNAVAILABLE
effect	IN WASTE
—silver	LUNAR
—stone	STONERN
—things of the	
same species	UNIVOCAL
—whatever kind	WHATSO
offal	INCHPIN, QUARRY
offence	DEFAULT, DISTASTE
	INJURY
offend	DISTASTE
offer	PREFER, PRETEND
—as a pledge	WAGE
—for sale	UTTER
—greeting of	PRESENT
office	MISTERY, MYSTERY
—in Court of Exchequer	PIPE OFFICE
—of	
Chancellor	CHANCERY
warden	WARDENRY
officer	
—who rounded up	
stray pigs	HOG-REEVE
	HOG-CONSTABLE
—without command	REFORMADO
official	
—in lists	MARSHAL
—permit	PLACARD
—who clears the way	WHIFFLER
offspring	SPERM, STRAIN
old	
—clothes	ELD, YORE
dealer	FRIPPER(ER)
shop	FRIPPERY
trade	FRIPPERY
—person	ELD
—time	ELD, YORE
—woman	AUNT, GRANDAM, GRANNAM
omission	BA(U)LK
on	AN
—a	
desperate enterprise	PERDU(E)
forlorn hope	PERDU(E)
—account of	ALONG
—approval	ON LIKING
—hand	TOWARD
—purpose	NONCE
—the	
near or left side	TOWARD
table	ON THE TAPIS
—wheels	AWHEELS
once	WHILOM
one	
—acting as surety	MAINPERNOR

—after the other	A-ROW	oral	LIVELY
—apt to change	CHANGELING	orchard	ARBOUR, ORCHAT
—born under Mercury	MERCURIAL	order	INSTITUTE, WILL
—bound to keep horse		—of battle	BATTALIA
for military service	HOBBLER	orderless composition	RHAPSODY
—given to sensual		organ-bellows	WIND-BAG
enjoyment	EPICURE	organised for	
—granting indulgencies	QUESTOR	rapid movement	VOLANT
—in charge of fences	HAYWARD	ornamental rosary bead	GAUD
—of		ostentatious vulgarian	SNOB
a pair	MARROW	ostrich	ESTRICH, ESTRIDGE
low rank	SNOB	otter	WATER-DOG
the rabble	RASCAL	out	
worthless character	PACK	—of	
—sent before to		kindness	PARAMOUR
provide lodgings	HARBINGER	the way	GEASON
—who		—upon it	HARO, HARROW
barters	SCORSE	outcast	WRETCH
becomes surety	PLEDGE	outcome	PROOF
clears the table	VOIDER	—of toil	LABOUR
complains	PLAINANT	outdo	SUPERATE
constructs		outer	UTTER
—fortifications	ENGINEER	—garment	SURCOAT
—military engines	ENGINEER	outermost sphere	PRIMUM MOBILE
deposited money on		outflank	OVERWING
going abroad	PUTTER-OUT	outlast	OUTDURE
deserves hanging	WAGHALTER	outlaw a woman	WAIVE
dwells in fancied		outlawed	BROKEN
security	SECURITAN	outlay	MISE
haunts draper's shops	SILKWORM	output	GET
is		outrageous	ENORMOUS
—disliked	WARLING	outride	OVERRIDE
—fantastical	FANTASTIC	outstrip	COTE, STRIP
—good for nothing but		outward appearance	SPECIES
paying the bill	SHOT-CLOG	—of promise	UPCOME
leads astray	SEDUCTOR	outwit	CROSSBITE
plots	ENGINEER	over	ORE
practises	OCCUPIER	overbearing	SUPERCILIOUS
puts on a false show	FACER	overcoat	SURTOUT
sells short weight	LEGER	overcome	EVINCE, FORDO, SUPERATE
serves in war	SERVITOR	overflow	SURROUND
talks nonsense	TWADDLE	overflowing	REDUNDANT
with coat of arms	GENTLEMAN	overgarment	BRAT
within confines	CONFINER	overhang	OVERWHELM
onward rush	RACE	overhanging	INCUMBENT
open	(A)PERT	overpower	EVINCE
—space between woods	LAWN	overpowering lustre	GLARE
—to view	UNVAIL(E)	overreach	LURCH, OUTGO
opening	OVERTURE	overrun	OVERREN
operate	PLAY	overshoe	PANTOF(F)LE, PANTOUFLE
operation	URE	overspread	OVERCOME
oppress	OVERSET	overtake	OVERCATCH, OVERGET
oppressed with hunger	A(N)HUNG(E)RED		OVERRIDE
	(A)HUNGRY	overthrown	PROFLIGATE
oppressive	FAINT	owner	LORD
optical/optics	PERSPECTIVE	ownership	FEE, PROPRIETY

oxygen	VITAL AIR
pack	
—horse	SUMMER
—load	SEAM
—of cards	PAIR
packet-boat	POST
paeony	PION(E)Y
pah	PAW
pain	WO(E)
painful	BALE
pains	TEEN(E), TENE
paint	LIMN, PEINCT
—for face	FUCUS
painter	BRUSH, LIMNER
pair	TWAIN, TWIN
pale	PALL, WHITELY
—blue	WATCHET
—by comparison	STAIN
palisade	STACKET
palisaded enclosure	PEEL
paltry	BALD
pampered effeminate	
person	WANTON
pan	WORK
panacea	DIACATHOLICON
pancake	FLAM(M), FLAUNE, FLAWN
pander	BROKER
panegyric	ELOGE, ELOGY, ELOGIUM
panic	AMAZE
pansy	PA(U)NCE, PAWNCE
Papal province	LEGATION
paramour	FRANION, LEMAN
parcel	SORT
pardon	GRACE
parentage	BROOD
parish	TOWNSHIP
park	WALK
parliament	THING
parliamentary bill	PETITION
parsimony	PARCIMONY
part	PARTY, TWIN(E)
partake	PERTAKE
partition	TRAVIS, TREVIS(S)
partly	PARCEL
—burned tree	RAMPICK, RAMPIKE
partner	COMPANION
pass	HALSE, PACE
—round the table	TROLL
—the night	LIE
passage	ALURE, PACE
—in a book	PLACE
passionate person	FUME
password	WATCHWORD
past	FORBY
pastime	PASTANCE
patch up	JUMP

patchwork	MOTLEY
path	STY, TROD
pattern	SAMPLER, SPOT
pause	ALLOW
pawn	OPPIGNERATE, OPPIGNORATE
—broker	LUMBERER
—shop	LUMBER
pay	YIELD
—out	DISPEND
—retribution for	ABY
—wages to	WAGE
payment	
—for nurse	NOURICE-FEE
—in	
goods	TRUCK SYSTEM
lieu of military	
service	WARD-CORN
pea	
—plants	PEASON
—shooter	TRUNK
peace	FRITH
peach	MALAKATOONE
	MELICOTO(O)N, MELLICOTTON
pearl-grey	GRISEOUS
peas	PEASON
peasant	PESA(U)NT, PEZANT, SWAIN
peep-show	PERSPECTIVE
peevish	FRAMPOLD
pellucid	SHEER
pelt with stones	LAPIDATE
pen-case	PENNER
penalty	UNLAW
pendant	BOB
penned	PEND
penny	D
peony	PINY, PION(E)Y
people	FOLK, ICENI
peopled part of country	INLAND
perceiving together	CO-SENTIENT
perchance	PERCASE
perfect	PERFET
perform	EXERT, JUGGLE
performance	FUNCTION
—of music	LESSON
perhaps	BELIKE, PERCASE
periodical	
—gathering to check	
weaponry	WAPINS(C)HAW
	WEAPON-S(C)HAW
	WAP(P)ENS(C)HAW
—payment	PENSION
perish	FORFAIR, STARVE
perjured	MANSWORN
perquisite	VALES, VAILS
persistent attack	OBSESSION
person	WIGHT

—blindfolded in blindman's buff	HOODMAN
—used as tool	ENGINE
—with a tail	TAILARD
personal	
—appearance	CHARACTER
—attendant	GENTLEWOMAN
personate	PRESENT
pert	BRISK
—person	SAUCE, WAGTAIL
pertain	LONG
pertaining to	
—carrying in the womb	GESTATORIAL
	GESTATORY
—eggs	OVAL
—generation	GENIAL
—letters of the alphabet	LITERARY
—marriage	GENIAL
—sight	VISIVE
—whirlpool	VORAGINOUS
perturbation	DISTEMPERATURE
perverse	FROWARD
pestilence	MURRAIN
pet	PEAT
Peter's penny	ROME-PENNY, ROME-SCOT
petitioner	ORATOR
petticoat	PLACARD, PLACKET
petty	PELTING
phantom	FEATURE
philosopher's stone	TINCTURE
philtre from mare	HIPPOMANES
phraseology	PARLANCE
phrenetic	PHRENTICK
physical pain	WO(E)
physician	LEECH, MEDIC, MEDICINER
physiognomy	VISNOMIE, VISNOMY
pickpocket	FILE
pie	
—crust	COFFIN
—of meat and eggs	LUMBER-PIE
piece	PEECE
—of	
cloth	PANE
doggerel	JIG
excrement	SIR-REVERENCE
music	LESSON
needlework	SPOT
news	NOVEL
plunder	CHEAT
work	SPOT
—together	RHAPSODISE
	RHAPSODISE
pieces of old cordage	JUNK
pierce	ENGORE, RIVE
pike	PARTISAN
pilchard	PILCHER

piles	FIG
pile up	BALK
pilfer	NIM
pilfered	NAM, NIMMED
pilgrim's staff	BOURDON
pill	PEEL
pillage	PEEL
pillory	TUMBREL, TUMBRIL
pimp	BROKER, BULLY
pinafore	BRAT
pineapple	PINA, PINE-CONE
pink	POUNCE
pip	PEEP
pipe	TIBIA
pippin	PIP
piratical publisher	LAND-PIRATE
pistil	POINTEL
pitch reached by bird of prey	PLACE
pitched	(Y)PIGHT
pith of plants	MARROW
pity	PIETY
placcate	PLACARD
place	DO
—for	
hawking	RIVER
performance of penance	PENITENTIARY
—in favourable position	STATE
—of	
abode	LIBKEN
retirement	RETIRE
—underneath	SUPPOSE
placed	YPLAST
placket	PLACARD
plague-spot	TOKEN
plaintiff	PLAINANT
plait	PLIGHT
plan	MODEL, PLAT, PLATFORM
plane	
—figure or surface	PLATFORM
—tree	PLANTAIN
plank	PLANCH
plant	GRAFT
—resembling animal	ZOOPHYTE
platane	PLANTAIN
plate for tableware	NEF
platter	LANX
play	
—the	
epicure	EPICURISE, EPICURIZE
fool	FON
—trick on	GLEEK
—with	DELUDE
fingers	PADDLE
wooden sword	WASTER

playful	FLIPPANT
plead	PERSUADE
pleasant	AMENE, LUSTY, MERRY
—behaviour	PLEASANCE
—sound	EUPHONIA
—words	FAIR WORDS
pleasantness	PLEASANCE
please	AGGRATE, LIKE, LIST
pleasing	LIKING, LUSTY
pleasure	PLEASANCE
—of taste	GUST
—seeking	PLEASURABLE
pleat	PINCH, PRAN(C)K(E)
pledge	BORROW, ENGAGE, SECURE
	WAGE, WED
—oneself to	BETROTH
plentiful (yield)	FOISON
plight	LIKING, SECURE
plighted	YPLIGHT
plot	PLOD
—of ground	PLAT
plough	EAR, ERE
plucked	PLUMED
plump	WELL-LIKING
plunder	ESCHEAT, PEEL, PILL, RAPE
plunge	MERGE
pocket	PLACARD
pod (pea)	PEA(S)(E)COD
poem	DIT(T), POESY
poet	MAKER
—laureate	ARCH-POET
poetry	POESY
point	PIQUE, POYNT, PUN(C)TO
—at whist	CORNER
—of	
perfection	POINT-DEVICE
	POINT-DEVISE
weapon	ORD
pointed bar	GAD
poise	POYSE
poison	POYSON
poke	POTE
pole	PERCH
policeman	RUNNER
polished	POLITE
political	STATIST
poll	DOD
pollard	DOD
polluted	CANKERED
pomegranate	PUNIC APPLE
pomp	TRIUMPH
ponder	POISE
poniard	POI(G)NADO
pooh	PUGH, TUSH
poor	SEELY, WANTING
—author	GARRETEER

pope	PAPA
porpoise	MEERSWINE
port	LARBOARD
portable	
—inkwell	INK-HORN
—organ	PORTATIVE
portcullis	CATARACT
portent	PRODIGY
portion	MEED, PIECE
—of food and drink	SIZE
portrait	POURTRAICT
portray	PORTRAIT, POUTRAY
portrayed	POURTRAYD, PURTRAID
	PURTRAYD
position of honour	WORSHIP
positive	POZ(Z)
possess	WIELD
possession	FEE, HAVEOUR, HAVIOUR
possessions	AVER, WORTH
possibility of recovery	RECOVER
post for various	
exercises	QUINTAIN
postman	POST
postpone	FRIST, REFER
postponed	PROTRACTED
postulate	PETITION
posture	GESTURE
posy	POESY, TUZZI-MUZZY
potash	KALI
potsherd	POTSHARD
pottage	PORRIDGE
powder	POULDER, POULDRE, POUNCE
power	DANGER
—of	
explaining	INTERPRETATION
seeing	VISIBILITY
powerless	IMPUISSANT
practic	PRACTICK, PRACTIQUE
practice	URE
—of pastry-making	PASTRY
practise	USE
—crystal-gazing	SCRY
—extortion on	POLL
—with waster	WASTER
practising	PRACTIC
praise	LO(O)S
prank	ESCAPE, GAUD, REAK, REIK
pranks	REAKS, REX
pranky	FROLIC
pray	BID
—thee	PRITHEE, PRYTHEE
prayer	BEAD
preach	PROPHESY
precede	PREVENT
precious	CHARY
—metal	PLATE

—stone	JASPER	proceeds	AVAIL
preciousness	PRICE	proclamation	PLACARD
pre-eminence	PREHEMINENCE	procuress	AUNT, BROKER
pre-eminently	ONLY	procuring	BROK(ER)AGE
preen	PROIN(E), PROYN(E)	profession	FUNCTION, MISTER
	PROIGN, WHET	profile	PURFLE
preference	PRE-ELECTION	profit	(A)VAIL, UTILITY
—for	MARK ON	profitable	BEHOVEFUL, BEHOVELY
prefix	PREPOSITION	profitless	WASTEFUL
pregnant	GREAT, QUICK	profuse inflow	COLLIQUATIVE
prejudge	PREJUDICE	profusion	LAVISH, WASTE
prejudgment	PREJUDICE	progeny	IMP, INCREASE
preparation	ORDINANCE, PARASCEVE	prohibit	DEFEND
prepare	ADDRESS, INSTRUCT	projectile	FIREWORK
prepared	YARE, BOUND	projecting window	SHOT-WINDOW
presbytery	CLASSIS	projector	SCHEMATIST
prescription	LEECHDOM	prolong	PROROGUE
present	PREFER	prominent	EGREGIOUS
—to mind	OBJECT	promise	BANK, BEHIGHT, BEHOTE
preserve		promising	TOWARDLY
—in sugar	CONSERVE	prompt	EXPEDITE
—unhurt	SALVE	promptly	BELIVE, TIGHT(LY), TIT
press	STRIP		TITE(LY), TYTE, YARELY
—hard	OVERSET	prone	PROCLIVE
—together	CONSTIPATE	proof	PREEVE, PREIF(E)
pretended friend	BACK-FRIEND	property	FEE, PROPRIETY
pretext	SALVO	propitiation	PROPITIATORY
prevail	PERSUADE	propagate	TRADUCE
prevent	LET, SECURE	proposal	SUPPOSAL, PROPOSE
previous	FORE	propriety	PROPERTY
price	PURCHASE	prospect-glass	PROSPECT
prick with nail	ACCLOY	prosperity	THRIFT, WEALTH
priests	MAGI	prostitute	COCKATRICE, MUTTON
prince's friend	PRIVADO		PLOVER, PUBLIC WOMAN
princely stables	EQUERRY		PUNK, STEW, TRULL
principle extracted	TINCTURE	protect	WARRANT
printed	PRINT	—with	
prison	LUMBER, NEWGATE	earthwork	ENSCONCE
—chaplain	ORDINARY	sconce	ENSCONCE
privacy	PRIVITY	protective covering	BARD
private	INWARD	Protestant	RELIGIONER
—apartment	PARADISE	Protestantism	RELIGION
—end	SELF-END	protuberance	KNAP
—friend	PRIVADO	protuberant part	WEM(B), WEAMB
—marriage	HANDFASTING	proud	STIFF-RUMPT, STOUT, SUPERB
—parts	SHAME	prove	ASCERTAIN, DARRAIGN(E)
—property or right	PECULIAR		DARRAIN(E), DARRAYN
—room	CONCLAVE, GARDEROBE		DERAIGN, PREEVE
privy	GARDEROBE, PRIVATE, SIEGE	—to be true	SOOTHE
prize	PURCHASE	proved/proven	PREVE
probably	BELIKE	proverb	PARABLE
probationary marriage	HANDFASTING	provide	PREPARE
probe	TENT	—battlements	BATTLE
proceed	FAND, FOND, TRACE	—for	BESEE
proceeding from		in advance	PREVENT
divine favour	GRACIOUS	province	REAME

provision	STUFF	—in	
—of things for use		difficulty	STRAIT
in rotation	SHIFT	front of	OBJECT
provisions	BELLY-TIMBER	—off	FUB
—of the table	ENTERTAINMENT	in time	PROTRACT
prowess	VASSALAGE	—one's seal to	ENSEAL
prowl	PROLL	—or keep in loft	LOFT
prowler	PROLER	—out	UTTER
prudent	CONSIDERATIVE, WARE	of countenance	DOR
prune	PROIGN, PROIN(E)	—to	
	PROIN(E), PROYN(E)	shame	REBUKE, SHEND
	PRUINE, PREWYN, SHRED	trouble	PAIN
Prussia	(S)PRUCE	puzzle	PUSLE
pshaw	TUSH	quack	SALTIMBANCO
psychosis	DERANGE	quadrate	QUARTILE
public	APERT	qualify	CONDITIONATE
—report or rumour	FAME	quality	PROPRIETY
publication of book	EDITION	quarrel	SQUARE
publisher	STATIONER, UNDERTAKER	quarry	CURRIE, CURRY
puck	PUG	quay	KAY, KEY
puddle	FLUSH	queen	PRINCE
puff		—bee	KING
—of wind	HUFF	question	SCRUPLE
—up	HUFF	quick	EXPEDITE, RATH(E), YARE
pulley	TRICE	quickly	BELIVE, SWITH, YARELY
pulp of plants	MARROW	quiet	HUSH
pulpit	CHAIR	quinsy	SQUINANCY
pun	PUNDIGRION	quire	QUAIR
punctilio	PIQUE, PUN(C)TO	quit	QUITE, VOID
puncture	POUNCE	quiz	SMOKE
punish	JUSTIFY, SHEND	quoth	QUOD
	VISIT, WREAK	rabbit-hole	CLAPPER
punishment	PINE, PYNE, WAR(R)ISON	rabble	RASCAILLE, RASCAL
	WRACK, WREAK	race	GOAL, ROD
puny	PUISNE	—course	HIPPODROME
puppet show(man)	MOTION(-MAN)	rack	TOUSE, TOUZE, TOWSE, TOWZE
purchaser	CHAPMAN	rag	ROW
pure	MERE, NET(T)	rail	RAYLE
purely	MERELY	railway	GWR, LMS, LNER, SR
purgative electuary	DIACATHOLICON	rain	RAYNE
purify	CHASTISE, CHASTIZE	raised edge	LEDGE
purity	CANDOUR	rake	SWINGE-BUCKLER
purple	PUNIC	rally	REALLY, RELY
purplish/black	PUKE	ramble	TROLL
purport	TENOUR	rampart	RAMPIRE
purpose	CAST, PRETEND	range	RAUNGE
	PURPORT, SHAPE	rank	CENSE, GREE, SIEGE
purse	BUNG	—of captain	CAPTAINRY
purser	NIP-CHEESE	—with	FILE WITH
pursue	PERSUE	rant	TEAR A CAT, TEAR THE CAT
put	DO	rapine	RAPE
—an end to	WASTE	rarely	SELD
—away	WAIVE	rascal	RASCAILLE
—down	DO DOWN	rash	HASTY-WITTED
—forth	EXERT	rate	ROW
—forward	PREFER	—of tax	CENSE, CESS

rather	LIEFER, LIEVER	—from	OVERGET
rational	SOBER	recovery	RECOVER, RECURE
ravages	WASTES	red	
ravish	CONSTUPRATE, OPPRESS	—ochre	RUBRIC
	VITIATE	—pimple	BUBUKLE
—with delight	RAPE	reddish-brown	SOAR(E), SORE
raze	SLIGHT	redoubtable	REDOUBTED
reach	AREACH, HENT	reduce to hardship	STRAIT
—forward	PRETEND	reduction	BATEMENT
reached	RAUGHT, ROUGHT	reed	
read	REDE	—bunting	JUNCO
readily	YARELY	—grass	FLAG
reading	LECTURE	refinement	EXILITY
ready	YARE, BOUND	reflect	ADVISE
—for action	PREDY	reflection of self in eye	BABY
—to		reformed person	REFORMADO
learn	TOWARD	reformer	REFORMADO
make advances	COMING	refract	REFRINGE
take offence	MIFTY	refrain	BURTHEN, FA(UX)BURDEN
wither away	MIFTY		WITHHOLD
realgar	RESALGAR, ROSAKER	—of song	BOB
realm	REAME, REIGN	refresh	REFOCILLATE
rebellious	MALIGNANT	refreshment on journey	BAIT
rebound	RESULT	refuge	SUBTERFUGE
rebuked	SHENT	refutation	CONVINCEMENT, ELENCH
rebut	ELIDE	refute	CONVINCE, REDARGUE
recall	REVOKE		REFEL(L), REPROVE
—from banishment	REPEAL	regard with malice	MALIGN
recapture	REPRISE	regent	WARDEN
receive	ENTERTAIN, LATCH	registrar	REGISTER
	UNDERTAKE	regulate a contest	STICKLE
—a		reign	RAYNE
part of	PARTICIPATE	reinforce	RENFORCE, SUPPLY
person well or ill	RESENT	reinforcement	RECRUIT
recent (dates)	LOW	reject	CAST, WAIVE
receptacle	RESERVATORY	rejoicing	OVATION
reception		relate	REDE
—after childbirth	UPSITTING	relating to	
—of visitors while		—passions	PATHETIC
dressing	TOILET	—time	CHRONIC
reciter of romances	JESTER	—yesterday	YESTERN
reck	PASS, RETCH	relation	AFFINE, HABITUDE
—of	KEEP	release	ASSOIL
recked	RAUGHT	relic	RELICT
reckless	RECHLESS	relieve	BEET, BETE
reckon	IMPUTE, VOGUE	—by a pause	RESPITE
reckoning	NICK	religious	
recognise	ACKNOW, WIT	—direction	CAUTEL
—at a distance	KEN	—faith	LAY
recommend	WISH	—offerings	DEVOTION
recompense	GRATIFICATION	relish	GUST, TASTE
reconcile	ATONE	relishingly	SAVOURLY
record	MEMORISE, MEMORIZE	remain	
	MIND, REMEMBER	—awake	WAKEN
recount	REFER	—in expectation of	WAIT
recover	RECURE	remarkably	UNCOMMON

remedial	WHOLESOME
remedy	LEECHDOM, REMEAD
	REMEDE, REMEID
remember	PRESENT, RECONNOITRE
remind	MIND, REMEMBER
remorse	AYENBITE, HAD-I-WIST
remove	SUBLATE, VOID
—a veil from	UNVAIL(E)
—wrongfully	MISTAKE
rend	RENT
—in pieces	TO-REND
render as due or fitting	YIELD
renew efforts	RENFORCE
renounce	REN(A)Y, RENEY
rent	GAVEL, YRENT
repay	AP(P)AY, QUIT, YIELD
repeat the Lord's Prayer	PATTER
repentance	PENANCE
report with clamour	BRUIT
reprehend sharply	NIP
represent	PRESENT, REFER
—as bad	DEPRAVE
representative of King of Spain	VISITOR GENERAL
reprisals	MARQUE
reproach	SHEND
—with	EXPROBATE
reproduce	REFER
reproof	CORREPTION
republic	STATE
repulse	FOIL, REFEL
repulsive	LO(A)TH
reputation	LO(O)S, VOICE, WORSHIP
repute	SAVOUR, VOGUE
request	REQUIRE
require	WILL
requite	REQUIT
reservation	SALVO
reservoir	RESERVATORY
resident	LE(I)DGER, LEIGER, LIEGER
resign	WAIVE
resist	GAINSTRIVE
resolution	POINT
resort	FREQUENCY, USE
respect	WORSHIP
respectful	RESPECTIVE
respite	FRIST
rest	REQUIEM
resting-place	GITE
—on journey	MANSION
restive	RESTIFF, HOT-MOUTHED
restless	DISQUIET
restrain	CHASTISE, CHASTIZE, CONCLUDE
	REBUKE, REFRAIN, STINT
restrict	STINT

resulting from accident	OCCASIONAL
retain in service	ENTERTAIN
retreat	RECOIL, RETIRE
	RETRAI(C)T, RETRAITE
retrograde	REGREDE
return	RETIRE, REVOLVE
reveal	BEWRAY, UNVAIL(E)
reveller	ROARER, ROARING-BOY
reverse of coin	PILE
revert	RECOIL, RESORT
revile	MISSAY
revolving easily	VOLUBLE
reward	MEED, WAR(R)ISON, YIELD
rhetorical figure	SCHEME
rhinoceros	RHINOCEROT(E)
rhyme	RHIME, RHYTHM, RYTHME
ribaldry	RIBAUDRY
rich	
—cloth	PALL
—decoration	PARAMENT
rid	QUIT
riddle	CRIBBLE
ridge	BA(U)LK
ridicule	SMOKE
riding-horse	ROUNCY
right	
—moment	PUDDING-TIME
—to	
cut wood	HAY-BOTE, HEDGE-BOTE
food in forest	PU(L)TURE
hold court	LEET
hunt or keep game	WARREN
rigorously	STRAIT
rim	RYMME
rime	RHIME
ring-dance	CAROL
rioter	SWINGE-BUCKLER
rise	STY(E)
risk	PLIGHT
risque	RISK
rival	MATE, PARAGON
rive	RYVE
riven	YRIVD
river-mouth	OSTIUM
roast	ROST
roasting	USTULATION
robbed	RAFT
robe	PARAMENT
robustness	HARDIHEAD
rock dug from earth	FOSSIL
rod	GAD
rode	RID
rogue	LIMMER
roguish	ROGUY
—child or animal	WANTON
roll	TROLL, WALK

—back	REVOLVE
—in	
blood	WELTER
the grass	GREEN GOWN
—of parchment	PELL
rolling	VOLUTATION
—gait	WALLOW
Roman	ROMISH
romance	ROMAUNT
room	ROUM
—beside stage for	
musicians	MUSIC-ROOM
—mate	CHAMBER-FELLOW
root	WROOT
rote	ROATE
rough	ASPER, CRABBED, ROW, STURDY
round	ROWND
rout	HURRICANE
row of	
—stakes	ORGUE
—trees trained on stakes	ESPALIER
royal	REAL
Royalist	MALIGNANT
royalty	REALTY
rub	FEEZE, PHE(E)SE, PHEEZE
rudely jesting	INFECITE
ruff	PARTLET
ruffle	ROUSE
—feathers	FRILL
ruin	FORDO, HEAP
ruined	NAUGHT, RUINATE
ruinous	WASTE
rule	WIELD
—over	OVERRULE
ruler	RECTOR
rum	RUMBULLION
rumour	NOISE, SPEECH, TOY, VOICE
rump of horse	CROUPON
run	COURSE, RACE
—about	TROLL
—aground	GRAVEL
rush	LANCE, LOOSE, RANDOM, RASH
rustic	BOR(R)EL(L), RUSSET, SWAIN
	UPLANDISH, WOOLLEN
sack	BUDGET
—contents	BUDGET
sacrifice	SCARIFY
—of animal's shoulder	HEAVE-SHOULDER
sacrificial victim	HOST
sad	WO(E)
sadden	ATTRIST, CONTRIST
saddle	
—bow	ARSON
—cloth	PANEL
saddler	HORSE-MILLINER
sailor	SHIPMAN

saint	HALLOW
salad	SALLAD, SALLET
sale	VENT
salt	IODURET
—of uric acid	LITHATE
salutation in	
drinking	WASSAIL
salute	HALSE, MAKE ONE'S MANNERS
	MOVE, SALUE
—by raising hat	HAT
sanctuary	FRITH(SOKEN)
	GIRTH, GRITH
sane	SOBER
sarcasm	GIRD
sat	SATE
Satan	LEVIATHAN
satisfaction	CONTENTATION, SUFFISANCE
satisfied	PAID
satisfy	AP(P)AY, PAY
—in advance	PREVENT
saucepan	CHAFER
savage	SALVAGE
save	SA, SPARE
—from objection	SALVE
—your-reverence	SIR-REVERENCE
savings	THRIFT
savour	RESENT
savourless	WEARISH
savoury	GUSTFUL
say	
—in answer	UNDERSAY
—wrongly	MISSAY
saying	SPEECH
says	SAITH
scabbiness	SCALL
scantily	SCARCELY
scanty	PENURIOUS
scarcely	UNE(A)TH, UNEATHES
	UNNETHES
scarlet pimpernel	WINCOPIPE
scatter	STROW
scattered	BESPRENT
scent out	SMOKE
scheme	PLAT
scholar	ARTSMAN
school-teacher	SCHOOL-DOCTOR
scimitar	SEMITA(U)R, SYMITAR(E)
scion	IMP
scoff	DOR, GLEEK
scorched	ADUST
score	LAW
—for keeping account	NICK
Scottish	SCOTIAN
scout	SCURRIER, SCURRIOUR
	SPIAL
scrape	HOBBLE

scratch	SCRAT
screech	SHRITCH
screw	VICE, WREST
scribe	SCRIVENER
scrub	SHRUB
scrupulous	CURIOUS
scrupulousness	CURIOSITY
scum	MANTLE
sea	
—bird	PINK
—bottom	GROUND
—bred officer	TARPAULIN(G)
—monster	WASSERMAN
—serpent	ELLOPS
—wolf	SEA-ELEPHANT
seal up	ENSEAL
search	INQUEST
—out	INDIGATE
seasonable	TIDY
seasoning	SEASON
seat	ROOM, SEL(LE), SIEGE
—of	
authority	SEE
dignity	SEE, SIEGE
emotions	ENTRAILS
sanctuary	GRITH-STOOL
seclude oneself	SEQUESTER
second	STICKLER
secondary rainbow	WATER-GALL
secret	DE(A)RN
—arrangement	PACK
secure	RUG
security	BANK, WED
sedge	SEG
seduce	JAPE
seek	ENQUIRE, INQUIRE
—again	REPEAT
—by enquiry	HEARKEN
—to	
bring about	PURCHASE
induce	PERSUADE
seeking food	RELIEF
seem	BESEEM, SEMBLE
—likely	LIKE
segment	ARTICLE
seize	DEPREHEND, AREACH, LATCH
	REACH, SEIS, SURPRISE
—and carry off	RAPE
—upon	FANG
seized	HENT
seizure	PRIZE, PURCHASE, RAPE
seldom	SELD
select what serves	
one's purpose	GARBLE
self	
—congratulatory spirit	GLORY
—indulgent	WANTON
—seeking cleric	ROME-RUNNER
—willed	FROWARD
selfish end	SELF-END
seller of indulgences	PARDONER
semblance	LIKELIHOOD
send	
—away	VOID
—on a journey	TRAVEL
sense	SENTENCE
—of shame	PUDOR
senseless	SURD
sensible	WITTY
sentinel	CENTINEL(L), WAIT, WARDEN
sentry	CENTRY
separate	DISCREET, INTERVENE
	TWIN(E)
—and remove	ESLOIN, ESLOYNE
	ELOI(G)N
—from one another	DEPART
—lodging	MANSION
serf	HELOT, VILLEIN
serge	SURGE
sermon	SPELL
serpent	WORM
servant	FEEDER, (KITCHEN-)KNAVE
	SCULLION
serve	KA(E), STEAD
—as a soldier	MILITATE, TRAIL A PIKE
service	FEE, MISTERY
	MYSTERY, WAITERAGE
set	STEAD, TILL
—aside a veil	UNVAIL(E)
—forth	RECORD
—hand to	HAND
—in	
array	PITCH
front	PREFER
order	DISPONE, PRAN(C)K(E)
—of	
dice	BALE
persons eating together	MESS
—on edge	SURBED
—rolling off the tongue	TROLL
—up	ROUSE, STABLISH
—with stars	STELLIFY
setting	PRINT
settle	DISCUSS
—in	HABITUATE
settled	SPED
settler	INHABITOR
seven years	PROPHETIC WEEK
severally	IN PARTICULAR
sewer	(COMMON-)SHORE, SURE
sex	KIND, RACE
sexual intimacy	KNOWLEDGE

shake the feathers of	ROUSE
shaken	SHAKED, SHAKT, SHOOK
shameful	PUDENDOUS
shape	FEATURE
shaped	SHAPEN
shapely	FEAT(E)OUS, FEATUOUS
share	SNACK
—a dwelling	STALL
—of expense	LAW
—out	IMPART
sharpened	GROUNDEN
sharper	CONEY-CATCHER
shed light on	ENLIGHT(EN)
sheep	MUTTON
shelter from	WEATHER
shepherd	FEEDER
—boy	HERD-GROOM
sheriff	GREAVE, GRIEVE, VISCOUNT
shield worn on	
left arm	GLOVE-SHIELD
shine	LEAM, LEME, SHEEN
ship	ARGO, WOODEN HORSE
ship's decoration	WAISTCLOTH
shirt	PARTLET
shock	SCANDAL
shoes	SHOON
shoot	IMP, SPRNG
—arrow short or wide	DRIB
—out	LANCE
shore	CONTINENT, RIVAGE
short	
—burst of bird song	JERK
—musical phrase	POINT
—spear	DEMI-LANCE
—time ago	EVEN NOW
—veil at back of head	VOLET
shorten (sail)	SCANTLE
shortened	DAG
shortening in	
pronunciation	CORREPTION
shortly	AT A WORD
shot	SHOTTEN
—out into nooks	NOOK-SHOTTEN
shoulder-cloth while	
hair-dressing	TOILET
show	CON
—a (bold) face	FACADE
—forth	DETECT
—in favourable light	ILLUSTRATE
—place	VISIBILITY
showing care or nicety	CURIOUS
showy dress	BRAVERY
shrew	SHROW
shrewish	CURST
shrewd	SHROWD
shriek	SCRIKE, SHRITCH

shrivel	WELK
shrivelled	WRITHLED
shrubbery	ARBORET
shudder	GRISE
shuffle cards (dishonestly)	PACK
shut	SHET
—in	IMPALE
—the eyes	WINK
sickly	QUEACHY, QUEECHY
—smelling	FAINT
side	COAST, PLAT
sideboard	CREDENCE
siege	LEAGUER, OBSESSION
—engine	WAR-WOLF
sift	CRIBBLE, GARBLE
sigh	SITHE
sighed	SIGHT
sight	VISIBILITY
signify	BEMEAN, MAGNIFY, SKILL
silent	HUSH, WHIST
—game of cards	
or dice	MUMCHANCE
silly person	LIRIPIPE, LIRIPOOP
silver 1½d piece	DANDIPRAT, DANDYPRAT
similitude	LIKELIHOOD
simple	SILLY
simpleton	COKES, ROOK
	WOODCOCK, DAW
simulate belief	COLLOGUE
sin	FOLLY
since	SIN, SITHEN
sincerely	ENTIRE
sing	RECORD
singly	ONLY
sink	DEVALL
sip	DELIBATE
sir	LORDING
sit	SET
—well on	BESIT
sixpence	BENDER, TESTER(N)
skein	SKENE
ski	SNOW-SHOE
skilful	HEND, WELL-SEEN
skilfulness	WISDOM
skilfully	YARELY
skilled workman	PRUD'HOMME
skin	PELL
skirmish	ESCARMOUCHE
skirt	GORE
skulk	LUSK
slack	LASH
slake	ASLAKE
slander	MISSAY
slash	CARBONADO
slattern	SLAMMAKIN, SLAMMERKIN
slave	NATIVE, THEOW

sledge taking criminals to the gallows	HURDLE	sofa	DAY-BED
slenderness	EXILITY	softening	LENIENT
slid	SLIDED	spiked barrier	TURNPIKE
slighting	SLIGHT	soil	GLEBE
slimy	LIMOUS	sojourn	TARRY
slip glidingly	SLUR	soldier	CENTINEL(L), MAN-OF-WAR
slipper	SLIP-SHOE		MILITARY, SOULDIER
slippery	GLIB(BERY)	soldier's	
slogan	SLUGHORN(E)	—bastard	SON OF A GUN
slovenly-dressed woman	SLAMMAKIN	—cloak	MANTEEL
	SLAMMERKIN	sole of foot	PALM
slow	LASH	solicitude	CARK
sluggish	LENTOUS	solitary	DEARN
sluggishness	LENTOR	solve	ASSOIL
sluice	SASSE	something	
slut	PUCELLE, PUZZLE	—preparatory to	INDEX
small		—that surrounds	WAIST
—articles of wood	TREEN	somewhat	SOMEDEAL
—branch	RICE	son	SONNE
—bulb	CHIVE	song	FIT(T), FITTE, FYTTE
—freeholder	FRANKLIN	soothe	BALM, STROKE
—horse	PONEY	soothing	LENIENT
—hunting dog	KENNET	sophism	ELENCH
—quantity	DRIB	soreness of eyes	LIPPITUDE
—river	RIVERET	sorrel	SOAR(E), SORE
—silver coin	SILVERLING	sorrow	CONDOLEMENT, TEEN
—stone implement	MICROLITH	sorrowful	BALE, TRIST
smallness	EXILITY	sorry	WP(E)
smear with blood	GILD	sou	SOUS(E)
smile	SMOILE, SMOYLE	sound	SANE
smiling	BONNIE, BONNY	—in health	WHOLE
smock	SHIFT	sounding dreadfully	HORRISONOUS
smoke (tobacco)	DRINK	soundness	HEAL
smoker	TOBACCONIST	sour	EAGER
smooth	GLIB, SLIGHT, TERSE	source	OFFSPRING
smote	SMIT	—of	
smother	OPPRESS	hangman's rope	NECK-WEED
smuggle	OWL	motion	PRIMUM MOBILE
smuggler	OWLER	souse	SOUCE, SOWCE, SOWS(S)E
snake	ELLOPS, WORM	soused	SOUCT
snap	SNIP	spa	SPAW
snare	ENGINE	space	CANTON
snatch	REACH	Spanish broom	SPART
—away	HENT	sparing	SCARCE
sneaking	SHEEP-BITING	sparkle	GLISTER
snub	FRUMP	spawn	SPERM
snug	RUG	speak	BESPEAK
soaked in blood	BEWELTERED	—fair	PALP
sob	SINGULT	—of	VOICE
sociable	COMPANIABLE	—to or of	WORD
social party	HURRICANE	—wrongly	MISSAY
socially accessible	GENERAL	speaking	WORDING, PARLANCE
society	HETAIRIA	—freely	LAXATIVE
sod	SCRAW	spear	GAD(E), GAID, GLAIVE
			LA(U)NCEGAY(E)
		—rest	FEUTRE, FEWTER

spectacles	GLASS EYES	—performance	SCENE
speculation	WISDOM	—producer	UNDERTAKER
speculative imagination	PROJECT	stain	SMIT, SOILINESS, STAYNE
speech	PARLANCE, PARLE, SPELL	stair	STAYRE
spell	WEIRD	stake	PEEL, VIE
spend labour on	LABOUR	—higher	REVIE
spew	SPUE	stalemate	STALE
spiced sweetened wine	PIMENT	stall	TRAVIS, TREVIS(S)
spider	ATTERCOP	—keeper	STALLENGER, STALLINGER
spied	SPIDE	stalwart	PRETTY
spignel	SPICKNEL	standard bearer	ANCIENT
spiked portcullis	HERSE	standing out	EXTANT
spin	TROLL	stanza	STANCE
spine	CHINE	star	ASTER, STARN, STERN
spinner	SPINSTER	start	BRAID
spinning top	NUN	starting-post	GOAL
spiritless	AMORT, HILDING	starvation	FAMISHMENT
	SPRIGHTLESS	starve	STERVE
spiritual perception	WISDOM	state	ESTATE, REPUBLIC
spit on	BESPIT	state	
spite	MAU(L)GRE, SPLEEN	—barge	GALLEY-FOIST
splendent	SPLENDIDIOUS	—governor	PRESIDENT
splint	SPLINTER	—of being	
spoil	BRIBE, WRONG	awake	WATCH
spoilt child	WANTON	well	WEAL
spokesman	ORATOR	static	
sponge	SPUNGE	electricity	VITREOUS ELECTRICITY
sponsor	SUSCEPTOR, UNDERTAKER	statue	STATUA
—at baptism	GOSSIP	stay	MANSION
sport	BOURD	stayed	STAID
sportive	LUDICROUS	steadfast	STEDFAST
—child or animal	WANTON	steady	STEDDY, STEEDY
spot	GOUT, MOIL	steal	BRIBE, NIM
—of iron-mould	MOLE	steer	STEAR(E)
spotted as with plague	TOKENED	steerage	STEARAGE
spouse	COMPANION, FE(A)RE	steered	STEARD
	FEER, FIERE, PHEERE	steering-gear	STERN
spread	SPRED(D), SPREDDE(N)	steersman	PILOT, STEARSMATE
	STROW, WALK	steersman's place	STERN
—out	POUR	step	GREE, GRE(E)CE, GRECIAN
spring	LENT		GRE(E)SE, GREESING
—catch or trap	SNAPHA(U)NCE		GRESSIN, GRI(E)CE
	SNAPHAUNCH		GRISE, GRIZE
sprinkle	POUNCE	—mother	STEP-DAME
—with ornaments	SPANG	steward	REEVE
sprinkled	SPRENT	stick	GAD
—over	BESPRENT	stiff	STOOR, STOUR
spruce	BRISK		STOWRE, STURE
spy	SPIAL, WAIT	stimulate	URGE
squander	BEZZLE, LASH, SPORT	stint	SCANTLE
squire	DONZEL	stir	QUATCH, QUETCH, QUITCH
St Thomas's Day	MUMPING-DAY	—up	AMOVE
staff of authority	WARDER	stirring the emotions	WORKIN
stag's brow	RIGHTS	stocks	HARMANS
stage		stocking	NETHERSTOCK
—machine	PAGEANT	stole	NAM, NIMMED, STALE

stolen	STOLE
—article	CHEAT
—goods	PURCHASE
abandoned	WAIF
stomach	HEART, WOMB
stoop	LOUT, LOWT
stop	EMBAR, ESTOP, STAP, STINT
—contention	STICKLE
—for refreshment	BAIT
—up	CONSTIPATE
stout	TALL
—robber	ROBERDSMAN
	ROBERTSMAN
straddle	STRODDLE
straight	STRAIT
—on	ENDLONG
straightness	RECTITUDE
straightway	INCONTINENT
strain	FIT(T), FITTE, FYTTE
	INTEND, STREIGNE
straits	STRESS
strap for horse's load	WANTY
straw	STRAMMEL, STRUMMEL
—hat	HIVE
streaked in rings	RING-STRAKED
stream	LAKE
street	
—bully	SCOWRER
—cleaner	SCAVAGER
—refuse	SCAVAGE
—thief	BULKER
strength	HEAD
strengthen	COMFORT
stretch	REACH
stretched	INTENDED
strew	STRAW, STROW
strewed	STRAWED, STRAWN, STROWED
	STROWN, STRAWED, STRAWN
strife	BARGAIN, BARRAT
strike	
—to the heart	HEART-STRIKE
—with fear	AMAZE
string up	KILT, TRUSS
stringing together	
of poems	RHAPSODY
striped	GUARDED
strive	FORCE
—against	GAINSTRIVE
strode	STRID
stroke	BUFF, JERK, STRIKE
stroll	TROLL
strong	RANK, VALIANT, VALID
	WIGHT
—drink	BUB
—tobacco	MUNDUNGUS
strop	STRAP

struck	STRAKE, STOKE, STROOK(E)
	STRICKEN, STRO(O)KEN
	STRUCKEN
structure erected	
at conduit	STANDARD
struggle	CAMP
strumpet	BULKER, PUNK
	WAISTCOATEER
strut(ting movement)	JET
stubborn	STOUT
stumbling	OFFENCE
stun	AMAZE, STON(NE)
stung	STONG
stupendous	STUPENDIOUS
stupid person	WOODCOCK
sturdy beggar	ABRA(HA)M-MAN
style	ENSTYLE
subaqueous	DEMERSAL
sub-division of	
cantred or hundred	CAMMOT
subdue	DO DOWN, MATE, QUAIL
subject	
—for dissection	ANATOMY
—to	
authority	OBNOXIOUS
transmutation	TINCT
sublet	UNDERSET
submissive	SUBMISS, SUBORDINATE
submissively	SUBMISSLY
submit	PREFER
substance	SUBJECT
substitute fraudulently	SUPPOSE
subtenant	VALVASSOR
	VAVASOUR
subtle	SUBTIL(E)
succeed	FADGE
success	SPEED
successors	SEQUEL
sucker	GRAFT
sudden	
—heeling	SEEL
—inflow	ANCOME
—movement	BRAID
suddenly	UNWARES
sue	IMPLEAD
—for	PLEAD
suffer injustice	
or injury	HAVE WRONG
suffering	PASSIVE, PINE, PYNE
sufficiency	SUFFISANCE
sugar-refiner	SUGAR-BAKER
suit	EFFEIR, EFFERE, FADGE, HIT
suitable	HANDSOME
suite	SUIT
sulks	GLOUT, GLUMPS
sulky look	GLOUT

sullen	SOLEIN	swerve	WRY
sultan	SOLDAN	swift	WIGHT
sum and substance	CONTINENT	swim (head)	WHIM
summon	PROVOKE	swindle	BUNCKET
summons	INTERPELLATION	swindler	LEGER
sun	SONNE	swine	PORK
—dew	ROSA-SOLIS	swoon	DELIQUIUM
—flower	GIRASOL(E)	sword	FOX, GLADIUS, GLAIVE
sunk and dispirited	AMORT	swordplay	SPADROON
supercargo	MERCHANT	sycophant	PLACEBO
supercilious(ly)	OVERLY	symbolic meaning	MYTHOLOGY
superintend	INTEND	symbolise	BETOKEN, FIGURE
superior	OVERLY	syncopation	SYNCOPE
supernatural being	WIGHT	system of	
supine	BOLT UPRIGHT	—drill	MARTINET
supplement	MEND, SUPPLY	—principles	INSTITUTION
supply with husband	HUSBAND	table	
support	EASEMENT, SOOTHE	—implement	SUCKET-FORK
suppose	GUESS		SUCKET-SPOON
supposititious	SUPPOSED	—linen	NAPERY
supreme		—of contents	INDEX
—chief	PENDRAGON	tag	DAG
—council in Anglo-		tail of graduate's hood	LIRIPIPE
Saxon times	WITENAGEMOT		LIRIPOOP
sure	SICCAR, SICKER	take	HENT, LATCH
surety	BORROW, MAINPRISE		NIM, REACH
	UNDERTAKER	—a	
—for keeping the peace	FRITHBOHR	little	DRIB
surgeon	CHIRURGEON	roundabout course	WINDLASS
surgery	CHIRURGERY	—across	TRAJECT
surgical	CHIRURGICAL	—by surprise	OPPRESS
surliness	MELANCHOLY	—care of	BEWARE
surpass everything	PASS	—comfort	CHEER
surpassing	PASSING	—into stomach	ENDUE, INDUE
surplus	SUPERPLUS	—on (as servant)	ENTERTAIN
surprising by stealth	OBREPTION	—out	OUTTAKE
surrender	SURRENDRY	—pleasure in	PLEASURE
surveyor's staff	JACOB'S STAFF	—possession of	HENT
surviving trace	RELICT	—purses	PURSE
survivor	RELICT	—to the highway (as robber)	SCAMP
suspect	DOUBT, SMOKE	taken	TANE
suspicion	AIM	taking food	CIBATION
swagger	SQUARER	tale of fate	WEIRD
swaggerer	BRAVADO, ROARER	talk	DEVISE, PARLE, SPELL
	ROARING-BOY	talkative	DISCOURSIVE
sweat-bath	POWDERING-TUB	talker of twaddle	TWADDLE
sweating-sickness	STOOP-GALLANT	talon	FANG
sweep over	ENSWEEP	tame	MANSUETTE
sweet	DOUCE, SOOT(E)	tapestry	TAPIS
—food	SWEETMEAT	—frame	TENT
—heart	AMORET, JUNKET, LEMAN	tarnished	BRAID
—meat	MARCHPANE	tarragon	STARAGEN
tray	VOIDER	tarry	LENG
sweeten	EDULCORATE	tarrying	TARRIANCE
sweetness of manner	DOUCEUR	taste	ASSAY, GUST, RELISH
swell	HUFF	tasteless	WEARISH

taunt	GIRD
taut	TAUGHT
tavern open at night	NIGHT-HOUSE
tax	CESS, GELD, LOT
—farmer	UNDERTAKER
—on	
land	CARUCAGE, HIDAGE
wine	PRISAGE
teach	CON, LEAR(E), LEIR, LERE
teacher	DOCTOR
teaching	DOCTRINE, LORE
team	TEME
tear	RASH
tearful	MAUDLIN
tease out	TOUSE, TOUZE, TOWSE, TOWZE
technical	MECHANICAL
teeming	GREAT
telescope	OPTIC TUBE
	PROSPECT, TRUNK
tell falsehood	FABLE
temper	CONDITION, TAMPER
	TEMPERATE
tempering	TEMPERAMENT
temporal	TIMELY
tempt	ASSAY, ATTEMPT
temptation	TENTATION
tenant	
—by service	SOCAGER, SOCMAN
	SOKEMAN
—farmer	GEBUR
tend	SOUND
tenor	TENOUR
tense	TAUGHT
tenure	
—by service	SOC(C)AGE, SOKEMANRY
—in Kent	GAVELKIND
terce	UNDERN
terebinth-tree	TEIL
term of	
—abuse	SCARAB
—address to king	SIRE
—contempt	JACK, MECHANIC
	WHIPSTER
—endearment	FOOL, MOUSE
—exultation	VIA
—familiarity	BULLY
—opprobium	HARLOT
—reproach	TRUANT
terrace	TERRAS
terrify	FEAR
terrifying word	BUGWORD
territory	GOVERNMENT, MARK
—of lord	LORDSHIP
terror	BUG
test	EXPERIENCE, TASTE
—fatness	ASSAY

thane	THEGN
thank	REMERCY
—God	GOD-A-MERCY
that	
—may be	
applauded	PLAUSIBLE
shown	OSTENSIBLE
—which	
comes into contact	OCCURRENT
contains	CONTINENT
humbles gallants	STOOP-GALLANT
institutes	INSTITUTION
instructs	INSTITUTION
is	
—got	GET
—laid waste	WASTE
—preserved from loss	
in battle	PREY
—worn	WEARING
softens	LENIENT
—with which one	
is equipped	EQUIPAGE
the	YE
—one	TONE
theatre	
—dressing-room	TIRING-HOUSE
	TIRING-ROOM
—seat	ROOM
them	HEM
thick woollen cloth	WADMA(A)L
	WADMOL(L)
thicken	INCRASSATE
thicket	QUEACH
thief	LIMMER, WASTER
thieves' decoy	STALE
thieving	SHEEP-BITING
thing	RES
—doubtful or questioned	DOUBT
—stolen	MAINO(U)R, MANNER
—to lean on	LEAN
—which contains	CONTINENT
things of the	
intellect	INTELLECTUALS
think	CENSE, GUESS, WEEN
third	TIERCE
—finger of left hand	RINGMAN
—hour	UNDERN
thirst	THRIST
thirsty	ADRY
thong	LATCHET, LORE
thoroughly	THROUGHLY
thought	CONCEIT
thoughtful	CONSIDERATIVE
thrash	JERK, SMOKE, SWADDLE
thread	FILE
throat	HALSE, QUAIL-PIPE, WEAZAND

throb	QUOP
throne	SEE, STOOL
through	THOROUGH, YOND
throw	WARP
—away	ABJECT
—in or on	INJECT
—stones at	LAPIDATE
thrust	POTE, PUT, STOP
—out	ELIMINATE
thump	TUND
thunder	INTONATE
tie	
—the points of	TRUSS
—together	KNIT
tight	STRAIT
—gripping	HANDFAST
tighten	STRAIT(EN)
tightly	STRAIT
till	EAR
tilt	JOSTLE, JUSTLE
time	
—observer	TIMIST
—of	
currency	TENOUR
midday meal	UNDERNTIME
tinder	SPUNK
tinge	TAINT, TINCT
tinker	PRIG
tinner's poll-tax	WHITE-RENT
tint	TAINT, TINCT
tip	GRATIFICATION, VALES, VAILS
titled person	PERSON OF HONOUR
to	
—a great degree	OUT OF MEASURE
—an inner room	WITHIN
—ask a question	REQUIRE
—be	
brief	AT A WORD
pitied	SEELY, SILLY
—cause to burn with anger	EMBOIL
—conceive mentally	FANTASY, PHANTASY
—coop in	EMBAIL
—make famous	FAMOUS
—put under embargo	EMBAR
—sing for money	
at Whitsun	SHROVE
—the smallest detail	POINT-DEVICE
	POINT-DEVISE
—them	HEM
—windward	ALOOF
toad	PADDOCK
toadstool	PADDOCK-STOOL
toady	ZANY
toast	DRINK-HAIL, WASSAIL
tobacco-pipe	WOODCOCK'S-HEAD
toffee	TAFFY

together	IN COMMON, INFERE, YFERE
toil	SWINK
—worn	SWINKED
token	RECOGNISANCE
tomb	BURIAL
ton	TUN
too	
—drunk to whistle	WHISTLE(D)-DRUNK
—early	OVERTIMELY
—little	UNSIZ(E)ABLE
took	NAM, NIMMED
tool	LOOM
toothache	WORM
top	SUPERATE
—of anything	CROP
topic	PLACE
torch-bearer	LINKBOY, LINKMAN
tore	TARE
torment	PINE, PYNE
torture	PINE, PYNE
—with heat	FRY
torturer	TORMENTOR
Tory High Churchman	TANTIVY
toss	
—a coin	FLUTTER
—about	WALK
the limbs	SPRAWL
tossing about	JACTITATION
touch on	PERSTRINGE
touchwood	SPUNK
touchy	MIFTY
tournament	TOURNEY
—lists	BARRACE
tout	PLIER
town with market	
privileges	PORT
township	VILL
townsman	CIT
toy	BANDALORE
—dog	PUPPY
—with	FON
fingers	PADDLE
track	TROD
trackless	BEWILDERED, INVIOUS
tractable	TOWARDLY
trade	MISTER, MISTERY
	MYSTERY, OCCUPY
—guild	MISTERY, MYSTERY
trader	PLIER
trading voyage	TRAFFIC
traitor	NITHING, TREACHER(ER)
	TREACHOUR
trample with feet	FOIL
tranquillity	LEE
transcribe officially	TRANSUME
transcription	TRANSUMPTION

transept	CROSS-AISLE
transference	TRAJECT, TRANSUMPTION
transgression	ESCAPE
translate	TRADUCE
translator	INTERPRETER
transmission	TRAJECT
transmit	TRADUCE
transmuting element	TINCTURE
transport with delight	RAPE
trapped	IN BY THE WEEK
travail	TRAVEL
travel	TRAVAIL, VOYAGE
—on foot	WAYFARE
—with post-horses	POSTAGE
travelling	
—bag	MAIL
—case	CAP-CASE
tray for dirty dishes	VOIDER
treacherous person	TREACHER, TREACHOUR
tread	TRADE
—a measure	TRACE
treasure ships	PLATE-FLEET
treasurer	FISCAL
treat	BESEE, ENTERTAIN, ENTREAT
—with signs of honour	WORSHIP
treatise on gems	LAPIDARY
treatment	ENTREATMENT
tree	BEAM, WOOD
triad	TERN
trial	EXPERIENCE
tribe	ROD
tribute	GAVEL
trick	BANTER, CROOK, FOB FUN, GLEEK
—out	TIFF
trickery	SLIGHT
trickle	DRIB
tried	TRIDE
trifing	FALLAL
trifle	PADDLE
trim	NET(T)
trimmed	GUARDED
trimming on gown	ROBIN
trip	SPURN
tripod	TRIPOS
triumvirate	TRIUMVIRY
trivial	BALD
—dance-tune	TOY
trouble	BARRAT, GRAM(E) HATTER, NOY, VISIT
—taken	LABOUR
troublesome	INCOMMODIOUS, INFEST
trousers	TROSSERS, TROWSERS
truant	MICHER
truck	TRUNDLE

true	TREW
trump	TRIUMPH
trumpery	MOCKADO
trumpet of brass	ALCHEMY, ALCHYMY
trundle	TROLL
truss up	KILT
trust	AFFY, LET ALONE, TROW
truth	TROTH
try	FAND, FOND, TASTE, TRIE
tub	COWL
—for treatment of veneral disease	POWDERING-TUB
tuberculous excrescence	WOLF
tumulus	LOW, MOT(T)E, MOTE-HILL
tune	DUMP, NOTE
tunnel	TONNEL
turban	TULBAN, TULIPANT
tureen	TERREEN
turf	SCRAW
turfy	GLEBOUS, GLEBY
turkey	GUINEA-HEN
turmoil	MOIL
turn	CHAR(E)
turn	LOT, WEND
—about	CONVERT
—aside by caprice	WHIM
—from straight line	CROOK
what is right	CROOK
—of mind	ENGINE
—out	FADGE, SORT
well	PROVE
—over	VOLVE
—round (head)	WHIM
—the leaves of	TOSS
—to stone	LAPIDIFY
turned away	FROWARD
turning	VOLUTATION
—over in the mind	REVOLUTION
turnstile	TURNPIKE
turquoise	LIGURE, TURKIS
turret	GARRET
tutelage	TUTORAGE
tutor	GOVERNOR
twig	SARMENT, TWIST
twigs	RICE
twin	GEMMEL
twisted	WRONG
two	TWAIN
—tables of the law	TESTIMONY
type	HAIR, SAMPLER
tyrant	TYRAN(NE)
ugly	LO(A)TH, OUGHLY, OUGLIE
umbrella	OMBRELLA, UMBRELLO
unable	UNHABLE

—to	
take in	INCAPABLE
visit	UNVISITABLE
unaccustomed	UNCUSTOMED, UNWONT
	WONTLESS
unafraid	UNFEARED
unaware	WARELESS, UNWARES
unbending	STIFF-RUMPT
unborn child	BURDEN
unburdened	UNBURTHENED
uncanny	WEIRD
unchaste	LIGHT-HEELED
uncle	EME
unconnected composition	
or collection of things	RHAPSODY
uncover	DETECT
uncreated	INCREATE
uncritical	INCURIOUS
uncultivated	INCULT
under	
—consideration	ON THE TAPIS
—constable	THIRDBOROUGH
—iron for striking coins	PILE
—the control of	UNDERNEATH
underhand arrangement	PACK
—representation	SUGGESTION
undersong	FA(UX)BURDEN
understanding	WIT
undertake with intention	
of defeating	PREVARICATE
undisciplined	WANTON
undo	FOREDO, POOP, POUPE
undoing	DEFEASANCE
undress	MAKE UNREADY
unearthly	WEIRD
uneasiness	DISEASE, MISEASE
uneasy	DISQUIET
unencumbered	EXPEDITE
unexpected	INOPINATE, UNHOPED
unexpectedly	UNWARES
unfamiliar	UNCOUTH
unfitting	UNDECENT
unfledged	EYAS, NYAS
unfortunate	MISFORTUNED
unfriendliness	UNFRIENDSHIP
ungodly	WORLD
ungrateful	INGRATE
unhandsome	UNDECENT
unintelligent	INCAPABLE
union of neighbours	FRITHGILD
unite	ME(I)NT, MENG(E)
	MEYNT, MING
unite(d) in one body	CONCORPORATE
unjust	UNEQUAL
unknown	IGNORANT, UNCOUTH
—precious stone	LIGIURE
unless	EXCEPT, WITHOUT
unlucky days	DISMAL
unmanageable	WANTON
unmixed	MERE, NET(T)
unpleasant	DISPLEASANT, UNGAIN
—experience	DISTASTE
unpleasing	INGRATE
unpolished	UNPOLITE
unprepared	UNPURVEYED
unprepossessing	UNLIKELY
unproductive consumer	CATERPILLAR
unpromising	UNLIKELY
unprovided	UNPURVEYED
unquiet	DISQUIET
unreasonable	FROWARD
unrestrained	FRANK
unruly	WANTON
unseemly	UNHONEST
unsettled	UNDISCUSSED
unshaken	UNREMOVABLE
unskilful in action	UNHANDSOME
unskilled	UNGAIN, UNPERFECT
unstock	LAUNCH
unsuitable	UNLIKELY
—for	INCOMMODIOUS
until	WHILE
untimely	IMPORTUNE, OVERTIMELY
unwanted	INUSITATE
unwarily	UNWARELY
unworthiness	INDIGNITY
unworthy	INDIGN, WORTHLESS
unyielding	STOUT
up to	UP-TILL
upbraid	EXPROBATE
upholsterer	UPHOLDER
upholstery cloth	PARAGON
upper servant	PUG
upshot	PROOF
upside down	UP SO DOWN
upward curl of hat brim	PINCH
urate	LITHATE
urge on	EDGE
urgency	INSTANCE
urgent	INSTANT
urus	URE
use	INURE, URE
—tricks	CHICANE
used in oaths for God	DOG
useful	BEHOVEFUL, BEHOVELY
useless	WASTE
usual	WONTED
—fare	ORDINARY
utmost degree	UTTERANCE
—effort or force	UTTERANCE
utter	PEREMPTORY, WIELD
—fluently	TROLL

utterance	WORDING
utterly damned	FORE-DAMNED
vacate	WAIVE
vacillate	WAVE
vagabond	GADLING
vagrant	CURSITOR, TRUANT
vain	WASTE, WASTEFUL
—regret	HAD-I-WIST
valiant	PROW
valour	VIRTUE
—proved in war	WAR-PROOF
value	PRICE, VALOUR
vanish	FAINT
variable	FLUXIONARY
various musical	
instruments	SYMPHONY
vault	EMBOW, VAUT(E)
	VAWTE
vaunt	GAB
vegetable	WORT
veil	VAIL
velocipede	MULTICYCLE
veneer	FINEER
venery	VENUS
vengeance	WRACK, WREAK
venial offence	ESCAPE
venture	VENTER, VENTRE
venturous	VENTROUS
veranda(h)	VIRANDA, VIRANDO
verbal message	ERRAND
verbose	WORDISH
verdict	VARDY, VERDIT
verse of retraction	PALINODY
versed (in)	OVERSEEN
versify	MAKE
vertebra	RACK
very	RIGHT, UNCOMMON
—attentive	PARTICULAR
vestment	VESTIMENT
vexation	NOY
vexatious	PEEVISH
viands	CATES
vice	INIQUITY
view	ADVISE
—in a mirror	SPECULATE
viewing	SPECULATION
vigorous	RANK
vile	VILD(E)
vindicate	DARRAIGN(E), DARRAIN(E)
	DARRAYN, DERAIGN, SALVE
vinegar	EISEL(L), ESIL(E)
violate	VITIATE
violent	RANK, STURDY
violently	HEAD AND SHOULDERS
—angry	WRATH
violin	ROCTA

virgin	PUCELLE
virginal	SYMPHONY
virginity	PUCELAGE
virtue	VERTU(E)
virtuous	VIRTUAL
viscid	LENTOUS
viscidity	LENTOR
visible form	SPECIES
vision	SPECULATION
visit of herald	VISITATION
visiting-card	TICKET
visual	VISIVE
—image	SPECIES
vital	LIVELY
—power	NATURE
vitality	VIVACIOUSNESS
	VIVACITY, VIVENCY
vitiate	VICIATE
vivid	VIVE
vocabulary	NOMENCLATURE
voice	BREAST
voiceless	SHARP
void of shame	FRONTLESS
volunteer	VOLUNTARY
—serving as officer	REFORMADO
vomit	PARBREAK
voracious	VORAGINOUS
vouchsafe	VOUCH, VOUTSAFE
vow	BEHIGHT, BEHOTE
vulgar	SCURRIL(E)
vulture	GIER-EAGLE
wag the tongue	WALK
wage war	WARFARE
wager	WAGE, WED
wages	MEED
waggish	UNHAPPY
waist	GIRDLESTEAD, WAST
wait	EXPECT
—for	WATCH
waiting	TARRIANCE
wakeful	WATCHFUL
waldgrave	WILDGRAVE
walk	GO, TRACE
—behind battlements	ALURE
walking cane	WAND
wall	
—in	INTERMURE
—plant	HYSSOP
wallow in mud	MUDDLE
wallowing	VOLUTATION
wander	
—from right way	ERR
—till wearied	FORWANDER
wandering	EXTRAVAGANT
—course	ERROR
wane	WELK

want of	
—equity	INIQUITY
—fairness	INIQUITY
wanting in strength	FAINT
wanton	GIGLET, GIGLOT
—woman	JAY
war	
—club	MAUL
—equipment	WAR
—horse	DESTRIER
ward off	FORFEND
wardrobe	GARDEROBE
wariness	CAUTEL
warrant	WARRAN(D)
—safe	VOUCHSAFE, VOUTSAFE
warrior	EORL, WARMAN
wary	WARE
washed	WASHEN
waste	WAST
—away	WANZE
—place	WASTENESS
wasting	COLLIQUATION, COLLIQUATIVE
	COLLIQUABLE, COLLIQUANT
watch	AWAIT
—for	WAIT
—over	WARD
watchdog	HOUSEKEEPER
watchman	SPECULATOR
	WAIT(ER), WAKEMN
watchtower	GARRET, SENTRY-GO
watchful guardian	GRIPE, GRYPHON
	GRIFFIN, GRIFFON
watchman's cry	WATCH
water-channel	LAKE
water monster	NICKER
waterfall	OVERFALL
waterproof leggings	ANTIGROPILO(E)S
watery	
—looking sky	WATER-GALL
—place	FLUSH
wave	FLOTE
waver	WAVE
wax	WEX(E)
—candle	TAPER
—pale	APPAL
way	TRADE, VIA, WISE
wayfarer	DUSTY-FOOT, PIEPOWDER
wayside shrine	WEEPING-CROSS
weak	FADE
—in spirit	FAINT
—or effeminate man	DILDO
weaken	ENTENDER
	INTENDER, PALL
weald	WILD
wealth	WAR(R)ISON
weapon	WELSH-HOOK, VOU(L)GE

—with several barrels	ORGUE
wear before (others)	PREOCCUPY
wearer of	
—frock	FROCK
—silk	SILKWORM
weather	WELK
—conditions	WEATHERING
weave	PLIGHT
weaver	WEBSTER
wedding-feast	BRIDE-ALE
week	SENNIGHT
weigh	
—anchor	LOOSE
—down	POISE
—in the mind	POISE
weighed	WAID(E)
weight	BURTHEN, PEASE, PEAZE
	PEISE, PEIZE, PEYSE, POISE
welcome	GRATULATE
welfare	HEAL
well	
—being	WEALTH
—born	GENTLE
—disposed	TOWARD(LY)
	WELL-GIVEN
—judged liberality	MAGNIFICENCE
—made	FEAT(E)OUS, FEATUOUS
—mannered	WELL-THEWED
werewolf	TURNSKIN
wet	MOIL
whale-like sea-monster	WHIRLPOOL
what kind of	WHAT FOR A
whatever	WHATSO
—one can do for	
oneself	PURCHASE
whatsoever	WHATSO
when	WHENAS
where	WHEAR(E)
whereas	WHENAS
which	WHILK
while	THE WHILST
whim	FLAM
whimsical	
—person	WHIM
—tune or impromptu	MAGGOT
whip	
—out	BRAID
—top	GIG
whisper	ROUND
whist	WHISK
white	CANDID
—and viscous	GLA(I)REOUS
whiteness	CANDOUR
whitewash	WHITE-LIME
whiting	MIRLING
whitish	WHITELY

whitlow	ANCOME	without	WITHOUTEN
who	WHAT	—a mate	MAKELESS
whoever	WHATSO	—counsel or wisdom	REDELESS
whole body	CONTINENT	—favour	GRACELESS
whole(sale)	GREAT	—ideas	UNIDEAL
wholemeal bread	RAVEL(LED) BREAD	—mercy	GRACELESS
whore (verb)	WENCH	—modesty	FRONTLESS
why	FOR WHY	—self-control	IMPOTENT
wicked	FACINOROUS, FELON	—using flesh	MAIGRE
	FELONIOUS, GOAT	witty	CONCEITED
	SCELERAT(E), WICK	woe	BALE
—person	FELON	woman	FAIR, WOMANKIND
wickedness	NAUGHT	—fit for spinning-	
widow	RELICT	house	SPINSTER
widow's share of		—friend who comes	
husband's estate	WIDOW'S-BENCH	at a birth	GOSSIP
wield	WELD, WILD, WIND	—of fashion	GALLANT
wife	LADY	—who has taken vows	VOWESS
wig	MAJOR	woman's	
wile	ENGINE	—morning cap	MOB(-CAP)
will not	NILL	—shift	SMOCK
willing	VOLITIENT	—silk necktie	TAWDRY-LACE
willingly	L(I)EVE, LIEF	womb	MOTHER, WEM(B), WEAMB
wind up	SPAN	won	WAN
windfall	CADUAC	wonder at	ADMIRE, MARVEL
winding	MEANDRIAN	wonderful	GEASON
—course	ERROR	woo	ADDRESS
windlass	WINDAS	wooden	
window with hinged		—post	STUD
shutter	SHOT-WINDOW	—shoe	PATTEN
windpipe	WEAZAND	—sole on iron ring	PATTEN
wine		—sword	WASTER
—cup	PIECE	woodlouse	MULTIPED(E)
—mixing bowl	CRATER	woodruff	WOOD-ROOF
wink	EY(E)LIAD	woolsack	WOOL-PACK
winter	WINTER-TIDE	words of	
wipeout	NULL	—a villain	VILLA(I)NY
wise	WITTY	—song	DIT(T)
—man	WIZARD	wore	WARE
wish	WISE	work	
—for	WILL	—liquid	FRET
wit	WEET	—secretly against	UNDERWORK
witch	WEIRD	workaday	WORKY-DAY
witchery	GLAMOUR	workmanship	ARTIFICE
with		workshop	WORKING-HOUSE
—difficulty	UNE(A)TH	world	MAPPEMOND, MOULD
	UNEATHES, UNNETHES	—of fairies	FAERIE, FAERY
—exactitude	POINT-DEVICE	worship	SERVE
	POINT-DEVISE	worst	WORSE
—hardship	STRAIT	—state	PESSIMISM
—wool next to skin	WOOLWARD	worth	PRICE, VALOUR
withdraw	WALK	worthless	NAUGHT(Y), RACA, VOID
—from	VOID	—beast	HILDING
wither	BLAST	would be willing	HAD AS LIEF
withheld	WITHHAULT	would-be wit	HALF-WIT
within	ENTIRE	wound	ENGORE, PLAGUE

—by reproach	BITE
wrangle	BRANGLE, CAMPLE
wrap	WAP
wreaked	WROKE(N), WROKEN
wrestling school	PALAESTRA
wretched	WO(E)
wriggle	WIND
wrinkled	WRITHLED
writ	
—issued by sheriff	VENIRE (FACIAS)
—moving case to	
county court	TOLT
—of Richard II	PRAEMUNIRE
write	
—between	INTERSCRIBE
—out in musical notation	PRICK
writhe	WIND
writing	DITE, WRIT
written	WRATE, WRIT
wrong	UNRIGHT
wrongfully	UNDULY
wrote	WRIT, WROOT
yarrow	NOSE-BLEED
yearn	EARN
yeast	YEST
yellowish-green	GAUDY-GREEN
yeoman	GOODMAN
yew	EUGH
yewen	EUGHEN, EWGHEN
yield	KNOCK UNDER, VAIL
young	
—girl	DELL
—lady	DEMOISELLE
—man	IMP, SWAIN
—manservant	GROOM
—person	YONKER
your	THY
youth	YOUTHHOOD
—training for knighthood	PAGE
zealot	ZEAL
zealously	INSTANTLY
zedoary	CETYWALL, SETUALE
	SETWALL
	(*see also* **medi(a)eval**)

old²

including: former

old age pension(er)	OAP
old boy	ALUMNUS, OB
Old English	OE
old Dutch	WIFE
old Etonian	OE
Old French	OF(R)
old girl	ALUMNA, WIFE
Old Irish	OIR
old lady	WIFE
Old Measurement	OM

Old Norse	ON
Old Style	OS
Old Testment	OT
old woman	BETTER HALF
Olympians	(*see* **gods, goddesses**)
Oman	
capital	MASQAT, MUSCAT
coin	
—unit	BAIZA
—1000 baiza	RIAL
one	A, ACE, AN, MONAD, SINGELTON
	SINGULAR, SOLO, UNIT
and a half	SESQUI-
Christmas present	PARTRIDGE, PEAR-TREE
combining form	MON(O)-, UNI-
each	PER
having one	
—adductor muscle	MONOMYARIAN
—amino group	MONOAMINE
—ancestral group	MONOPHYLETIC
—atom	MONATOMIC
—axis	MONAXIAL, MONAXON(IC)
	UNIAXIAL
—brood per annum	UNIVOLTINE
—bundle of stamens	MONODELPHOUS
—buttock	HEMIPYGIC
—carpel	MONOCARPELLARY
—case	MONOTHECAL
—cavity	UNILOCULAR
—cell	MONOTHALAMOUS
	UNICAMERAL
	UNICELLULAR, UNILOCULAR
—centre	UNICENTRAL
—chamber	MONOTHALAMOUS
	UNICAMERAL
—colour	MONOCHRO(MAT)IC
	UNICOLORATE
	UNICOLOROUS, UNICOLOUR
—column	MONSTYLAR
—cotyledon	MONOCOTYLEDONOUS
—degree of freedom	UNIVARIANT
—dimension	LINEAR
—ear	MONAURAL, MONOPHONIC
—eye	MONOCULAR
—finger	MONODACTYLOUS
—flower	UNIFLOROUS
—foot	MONOPODE, MONOPOD(IAL)
	UNIPED
—fruiting period	MONOCARPIC
	MONOTOCOUS
—god	MONOTHEISTIC
—heart	MONOCARDIAN
—horn	MONOCEROUS, UNICORN
—husband	MONOGAMIC
	MONOGAMOUS
—hydrogen atom	MONACID, MONOBASIC

—hydroxyl group	MONOHYDRIC	—stamen	MONANDROUS
—key	MONOTONAL	—term	MONOMIAL
—leg	MONOPODE, MONPOD(IAL)	—thread	UNFILAR
	UNIPOD	—toe	MONODACTYLOUS
—language	MONOGLOT, MONOLINGUAL	—tone	MONOTONAL
	UNILINGUAL	—turn	MONOCYCLIC, UNICYCLIC
—leaf	UNIFOLIATE	—tusk	MONODONT
—letter	UNILITERAL	—type of mycelium	HOMOTHALLIC
—line	MONOSTICHOUS	—valency	MONATOMIC
—lip	UNILABIATE		MONOVALENT
—lobe	MONOTHECAL, UNILOBAR		UNIVALENT
	UNILOBED	—valve	UNIVALVE, UNIVALVULAR
—lobule	UNILOBULAR	—variant quantity	UNIVARIATE
—loculus	MONOTHECAL, UNILOCULAR	—wavelength	MONOCHROMATIC
—marriage	MONOGAMOUS	—wheel	MONOCYCLE, UNICYCLE
—meaning	UNIVOCAL	—whorl	MONOCYCLIC
—measure	MONOMETER	—whorled perianth	MONOCHLAMYDEOUS
—metal	MONOMETALLIC	—wife	MONOGAMIC
—nostril	MONORHINE, MONORHINAL		MONOGAMOUS
—nucleus	MONONUCLEAR, UNINUCLEAR		MONOGYNIAN
	UNINUCLEATE		MONOGYNOUS
—offspring at one birth	MONOTOCOUS	—wing	MONOPLANE
	UNIPAROUS	—word	MONOMIAL
—ovary	MONOCARPIC	xylem strand	MONARCH
	MONOCARPOUS	yearly occurrence	ANNUAL
—oxygen atom	MONOXIDE	thousand	IM, LAC
—part	UNIPARTITE	—pounds	GRAND
—perianth whorl	HAPLOCHLAMYDEOUS	under par	BIRDIE
	HOMOCHLAMYDEOUS		
	MONOCHLAMYDEOUS	**opera**	
—person ruling	DICTATORSHIP	operas	
	DESPOTISM, MONARCHY	—Balfe	THE BOHEMIAN GIRL
—petal	MONOPETALOUS	—Beethoven	FIDELIO
—phase	MONOPHASE, MONOPHASIC	—Bellini	NORMA, THE FOREIGNER
—plane of symmetry	MONOSYMMETRIC(AL)		THE PIRATE, THE PURITANS
—pole	UNIPOLAR		THE SLEEPWALKER
—rail	MONORAIL	—Berg	WOZZECK
—ray	MONACT(INAL), MONACTINE	—Berlioz	THE DAMNATION OF FAUST
—rib	UNICOSTATE	—Bizet	CARMEN
—ring	MONOCYCLIC		THE PEARL-FISHERS
of columns	MONOPTERAL	—Britten	ALBERT HERRING
—row	MONOSERIAL		BILLY BUDD, GLORIANA
	MONOSTICHOUS		MIDSUMMER NIGHT'S DREAM
	UNISERIAL, UNISERIATE		PETER GRIMES
—ruler	MONARCHY		THE RAPE OF LUCRETIA
—sac	MONOTHECAL		THE TURN OF THE SCREW
—sepal	MONOSEPALOUS	—Charpentier	LOUISE
—series	MONOSERIAL	—Cilea	THE ARLESIAN GIRL
—serrated edge	MONOPRIONIDIAN	—Debussy	PELLEAS AND MELISANDE
—set of		—Delibes	LAKME
chromosomes	HAPLOID	—Donizetti	DON PASQUALE
teeth	MONOPHYDONT		THE LOVE POTION
—sex	MONOECIOUS, UNISEX(UAL)		LUCIA DI LAMMERMOOR
—sheath	MONOTHECAL		LUCREZIA BORGIA
—side	UNILATERAL		THE DAUGHTER OF THE REGIMENT
developed	DIMIDIATE	—Flotow	MARTHA
		—Gershwin	PORGY AND BESS

—Giordano	ANDREA CHENIER, FEDORA
—Gluck	ORPHEUS AND EURYDICE
—Gounod	FAUST
—Handel	ACIS AND GALATEA
	BERENICE, XERXES
—Humperdinck	HANSEL AND GRETEL
—Leoncavallo	PAGLIACCI
—Mascagni	RUSTIC CHIVALRY
—Massenet	MANON, THAIS
—Menotti	AMAHL AND THE NIGHT
	VISITORS
—Meyerbeer	THE AFRICAN GIRL
	THE HUGUENOTS
—Mozart	COSI FAN TUTTE
	DON GIOVANNI
	THE MAGIC FLUTE
	THE MARRIAGE OF FIGARO
—Mussorgsky	BORIS GODUNOV
—Offenbach	BEAUTIFUL HELEN
	ORPHEUS IN THE UNDERWORLD
	THE TALES OF HOFFMAN
—Ponchielli	THE JOYFUL GIRL
—Puccini	GIANNI SCHICCHI
	LA BOHEME
	MADAME BUTTERFLY
	MANON LESCAUT, THE CLOAK
	THE GIRL OF THE GOLDEN WEST
	TOSCA, TURANDOT
—Rossini	SEMIRAMIDE
	THE BARBER OF SEVILLE
	THE ITALIAN GIRL IN ALGIERS
—Saint-Saëns	SAMSON AND DELILAH
—Smetana	THE BARTERED BRIDE
—Strauss	ELEKTRA, THE BAT
	THE KNIGHT OF THE ROSE
—Tchaikovsky	EUGENE ONEGIN
—Verdi	AIDA, DON CARLOS, ERNANI
	FALSTAFF,, LUISA MILLER
	MACBETH, A MASKED BALL
	NEBUCHADNEZZAR, OTHELLO
	RIGOLETTO, SIMON BOCCANEGRA
	THE FORCE OF DESTINY
	THE TROUBADOUR
	THE WAYWARD ONE
—Wagner	PARSIFAL
	SIEGFRIED, TANNHAUSER
	THE FLYING DUTCHMAN
	THE RHINE GOLD
	THE TWILIGHT OF THE GODS
	THE VALKYRIES
	TRISTAN AND ISOLDE
—Wolf-Ferrari	CINDERELLA
	THE JEWELS OF THE MADONNA

principal characters

—Aida	AIDA, AMNERIS, AMONASRO
	RADAMES, RAMFIS

—A Masked Ball	AMELIA
(Un Ballo in Maschera)	RICCARDO, SAM
	TOM, ULRICA
—Andrea Chenier	ANDREA, GERARD
	MADELEINE, ROUCHER
—Billy Budd	BILLY, CLAGGART, VERE
—Boris Godunov	BORIS, GRIGORY
	MISSAIL, PIMEN
	VARLAAM
—Carmen	CARMEN, DON JOSE
	ESCAMILLO, MICAELA
	ZUNIGA
—Cosí fan tutte	DON ALFONSO
	DORABELLA, FERRANDO
	FIORDILIGI, GUGLIELMO
—Don Carlos	PRINCESS EBOLI, RODRIGO
—Don Giovanni	DON GIOVANNI
	DONNA ANNA, ELVIRA
	LEPORELLO, MASETO
	ZERLINA
—Don Pasquale	DON PASQUALE
	ERNESTO, MALATESTA
	NORINA
—Elektra	CHRYSOTHEMIS, ELEKTRA
	KLYTEMNESTRA, OREST
—Ernani	DE SILVA, DON JUAN
	ELVIRA, ERNANI
—Eugene Onegin	LARINA, ONEGIN
	LENSKY, TATIANA
—Falstaff	ANNE, BARDOLPH
	FALSTAFF, FENTON, FORD
	PAGE, PISTOL, QUICKLY
—Faust	FAUST, MARGUERITE
	MEPHISTOPHELES
	SIEBEL, VALENTIN
—Fidelio	FLORESTAN, LEONORE
	MARZELLINE, PIZARRO, ROCCO
—Gianni Schicchi	LAURETTA
	RINUCCIO, SCHICCHI
—Hänsel und Gretel	GERTRUDE, GRETEL
	HANSEL, WITCH
—Rustic Chivalry	ALFIO, LOLA
(Cavalleria Rusticana)	SANTUZZA, TURIDDU
—La Bohème	ALCINDORO, MARCELLO
	MIMI, MUSETTA
	RODOLFO, SCHAUNARD
—Lakmé	GERALD, LAKME, NILAKANTHA
—Lohengrin	ELSA, KING HENRY
	HERALD, LOHENGRIN
	ORTRUD
—Louise	JULIEN, LOUISE
—Lucia di Lammermoor	ALICE, EDGAR
	HENRY, LUCY
	NORMAN
—Luisa Miller	FREDERICA, LUISA
	MILLER, RODOLFO, WURM

—Madame Butterfly	CIO-CIO-SAN, GORO
	KATE, PINKERTON
	SHARPLESS, SUZUKI
	YAMADORI
—Manon	DE BRETIGNY, DES GRIEUX
	LESCAUT, MANON
—Manon Lescaut	DES GRIEUX, GERONTE
	LESCAUT, MANON
—Martha	HARRIET, LIONEL, NANCY
	PLUNKETT, SHERIFF
	TRISTAN
—Nebuchadnezzar	ABIGAILLE
(Nabucco)	NABUCCO
—Norma	ADALGISA, CLOTILDA
	FLAVIO, NORMA
	OROVESO
—Othello	CASSIO, DESDEMONA
(Otello)	EMILIA, IAGO
	LODOVICO
	MONTANA, OTELLO
—Pagliacci	BEPPE, CANIO
	NEDDA, TONIO
—Parsifal	AMFORTAS, GURNEMANZ
	KLINGSOR, KUNDRY
	PARSIFAL
—Pelléas and Mélisande	KING ARKEL
(Pelléas et Mélisande)	GENEVIEVE,
	GOLAUD, MELISANDE
	PELLEAS, YNIOLD
—Peter Grimes	ELLEN, PETER
—Porgy and Bess	BESS, CROWN, PORGY
	SERENA, SPORTIN' LIFE
—Rigoletto	BORSA, DUKE, GILDA
	GIOVANNA, MADDALENA
	RIGOLETTO, SPARAFUCILE
—Siegfried	BRUNNHILDE, FAFNER
	MIME, SIEGFRIED
	WOTAN
—Simone Boccanegra	AMELIA
	BOCCANEGRA, FIESCO
	GABRIELE, MARIA
	PAOLO, PIETRO
—Tännhauser	ELISABETH, HERMANN
	TANNHAUSER, VENUS
	WOLFRAM
—Thaïs	ATHANAEL, THAIS
—The African Girl	INEZ, NELUSKO
(L'Africaine)	SELIKA
	VASCO DA GAMA
—The Barber of Seville	ALMAVIVA
(Il Barbiere di Siviglia)	BARTOLO
	DON ALONSO
	DON BASILIO, FIGARO
	LINDORO, ROSINA
—The Bartered Bride	JENIK, KECAL
	MARENKA, VASEK

—The Bat	ADELE, ALFRED, BLIN0D
(Die Fledermaus)	EISENSTEIN, FALKE
	FRANK, ORLOFSKY
	ROSALINDE
—The Bohemian Girl	ARLINE, ARNHEIM
	THADDEUS
—The Flying Dutchman	DALAND
(Der Fliegende Holländer)	ERIK, SENTA
—The Force of Destiny	CALATRAVA
(La Forza del Destino)	DON ALVARO
	DON CARLO
	GUARDIANO
	LEONORA
—The Girl of the Golden West	JOHNSON
(La Fanciulla del West)	MINNIE
	RANCE
—The Italian Girl in Algiers	ISABELLA
(L'Italiana in Algeri)	ELVIRA
	LINDORO
	MUSTAPHA
—The Jewels of the Madonna	GENNARO
(I Gioielli della Madonna)	MALIELLA
	RAFAELE
—The Joyful Girl	BADOERO, BARNABA
(La Giaconda)	GRIMALDI, LA CIECA
	LA GIACONDA, LAURA
—The Knight of the Rose	ANNINA
(Der Rosenkavalier)	FANINAL, OCTAVIAN
	PRINCESS, SOPHIE
	VALZACCHI
	VON LERCHENAU
—The Love Potion	BELCORE
(L'Elisir d'amore)	DULCAMARA
	NEMORINO
—The Magic Flute	MONOSTATOS
(Die Zauberflöte)	PAMINA, PAPAGENO
	QUEEN OF THE NIGHT
	SARASTRO, TAMINO
—The Marriage of Figaro	BARTOLO
(Le Nozze di Figaro)	CHERUBINO
	COUNT ALMAVIVA
	COUNTESS
	FIGARO, SUSANNA
—The Mastersingers	BECKMESSER
(Die Meistersinger)	DAVID, EVA
	KOTHNER, MAGDALENE
	POGNER, SACHS
	WALTHER
—The Pearlfishers	LEILA, NADIR
(Les Pêcheurs de Perles)	NOURABAD
	ZURKA
—The Puritans	ELVIRA, HENRIETTA
(I Puritani)	TALBOT, WALTON
—The Rape of Lucretia	COLLATINUS
	LUCRETIA
	TARQUINIUS

—The Rhinegold	ALBERICH, ERDA
(Das Rheingold)	FASOLT, FAFNER, FREIA
	FRICKA, HUNDING, LOGE
	SIEGLINDE, SIEGMUND
	WOTAN
—The Sleepwalker	AMINA, ELVINO
(La Sonnambula)	LISA, RODOLFO
—The Tales of Hoffman	ANDRES, ANTONIA
	COPPELIUS, CRESPEL
	DAPERTUTTO, GIULIETTA
	HOFFMAN, LINDORF
	NICKLAUSSE, SCHEMIL
	SPALANZANI, STELLA
—The Troubadour	AZUCENA, DI LUNA
(Il Trovatore)	INEZ, LEONORA
	MANRICO, RUIZ
—The Valkyries	BRUNNHILDE
(Die Walküre)	SIEGLINDE
	SIEGMUND, WOTAN
—The Wayward One	ALFREDO, FLORA
(La Traviata)	GIORGIO, VIOLETTA
—Tosca	ANGELOTTI, ATTAVANTI
	CAVARADOSSI, SCARPIA
	SPOLETTA, TOSCA
—Tristan and Isolde	ISOLDE
(Tristan und Isolde)	KING MARK
	KURWENAL, MELOT
	TRISTAN
—Turandot	CALAF, LIU, PANG
	PING, PONG, TIMUR
	TURANDOT
—Twilight of the Gods	BRUNNHILDE, HAGEN
(Götterdammerung)	GUNTHER
	GUTRUNE, NORNS
	SIEGFRIED, WALTRAUTE
—Wozzeck	ANDRES, DRUM MAJOR
	MARIE, WOZZECK

singers

—American (m)	MELCHIOR, MERRILL
	MILNES, TIBBETT
(f)	ANDERSON, DUNN, HORNE
	KIRSTEN, MILLO, NORMAN
	PONCELLE, PRYCE
	VAMNESS
—Australian (m)	DOWD
(f)	MELBA, SUTHERLAND
—Austrian (m)	TAUBER
(f)	LEHMANN
—Bulgarian (m)	CHIAUROV, CHRISTOFF
(f)	TORNOVA-SINTON
—Brazilian (f)	SUPERVIA
—Czech (m)	DVORSKY
(f)	DESTINN
—Danish (m)	MELCHIOR
—English (m)	NASH, PEARS, VICKERS
(f)	BAKER, BUTT, CROSS

	FERRIER, GERHARDT
	SHUARD, TEYTE, TURNER
—Finnish	TALVELA
—French (f)	PONS
—German (m)	ERB, FISCHER-DIESKAU
	HOTTER
(f)	BERGER, GERHARDT
	SCHUMANN, SCHWARZKOPF
—Greek (f)	CALLAS
—Irish	MCCORMACK
—Italian (m)	BATISTINI, BERGONZI
	CARUSO, CORELLI
	DE MONACO, DE STEFANO
	GIGLI, GOBBI
	MARTINELLI, PAVAROTTI
	PERTILE, PINZA, RUFFO
	SCHIPA, TAMAGNO
(f)	FRENI, GALLI-CURCI
	PATTI, PIRELLI, SCOTTO
	STIGNANI, TEBALDI
	TETRAZZINI
—New Zealand (f)	HAMMOND, TE KANAWA
—Norwegian (f)	FLAGSTAD, NILSSON
—Polish (m)	DE RESZKE
(f)	SEMBRICH
—Romanian (f)	COTRUBAS
—Russian (m)	CHALIAPIN
(f)	DIMITROVA, GRUBEROVA
	SLOBODSKAYA
	VISHNEVSHKAYA
—Spanish (m)	CARRERAS, DOMINGO
(f)	BERGANZA, CABALLE
	DE LOS ANGELES
—Swedish (m)	BJORLING
(f)	GULBRANSON, LIND
—Welsh (m)	EVANS, GLYNNE
(f)	JONES
—Yugoslav (m)	DERMOTA

song

| —in speaking voice | RECITATIVE |
| —solo | ARIA |

theatres

—Barcelona	GRAN TEATRO LICEU
—Bayreuth	FESTSPIELHAUS
—Berlin	DEUTSCHE OPER
	KOMISCHE OPER
	STAATSOPER
—Brussels	THEATRE DE LA MONNAIE
—Buenos Aires	TEATRO COLON
—Florence	TEATRO COMMUNALE
—Genoa	TEATRO CARLO FELICE
—Leningrad	KIROV THEATRE
—London	COVENT GARDEN
	DRURY LANE, LYCEUM THEATRE
	ROYAL FESTIVAL HALL
	SADLER'S WELLS THEATRE

—Manaus	TEATRO AMAZONAS
—Milan	LA SCALA
	TEATRO ALLA SCALA
—Monte Carlo	L'OPERA DE MONTE CARLO
—Moscow	BOLSHOY TEATR
—Munich	HOF-UND NAZIONALTHEATER
—Naples	TEATRO SAN CARLO
—New York	METROPOLITAN OPERA HOUSE
	PALMO'S OPERA HOUSE
—Paris	L'ACADEMIE DE MUSIQUE
	PARIS OPERA
	THEATRE DES CHAMPS-ELYSEES
	THEATRE-LYRIQUE
—Prague	CZECH THEATRE
	NARODNI DIVADLO
	NATIONAL THEATRE
—Rome	TEATRO APOLLO
	TEATRO DELL'OPERA
	TEATRO REALE
—Sydney	OPERA HOUSE
—Turin	TEATRO REGIO
	TEATRO VITTORIO EMANUELE
—Venice	TEATRO LA FENICE
	TEATRO SAN SAMUELE
—Vienna	BURGTHEATER
	STAATSOPER, VOLKSOPER
operetta	(*see* **musicals**)
Order	
Order of	
—British Empire	OBE
—Merit	OM
—St	
Augustine	OSA
Benedict	OSB
Francis	OSF
	(*see also* **decorations**)
Ordinary	
Ordinary National	
—Certificate	ONC
—Diploma	OND
ordinary seaman	OS
Ordnance	
Datum	OD
Survey	OS
organ stops	CLARABELLA
	CORNET, CORNO DI BASSETTO
	CROMORNA, CROMORNE, DOLCE
	DULCIANA, FLUTE, KRUM(M)HORN
	MUTATION-STOP, NASARD, OCTAVE
	PICCOLO, PRINCIPAL, PYRAMIDON
	QUINT, SALICET, SALICIONAL
	SESQUIALTERA, SEXT
	SUPEROCTAVE, TRUMPET

	TUBA, VOIX CELESTE, VOX HUMANA
	WALDFLUTE, WALHHORN
Organisation	
of	
—African Unity	OAU
—American States	OAS
oriental	
bathing establishment	HAMMAM
	HUMM(A)UM
bosun	SERANG
coin	DERHAM, DIRHAM
	DIRHEM
fruit	SHADDOCK
heel-less slipper	BABOOSH, BAB(O)UCHE
	PABOUCHE
javelin	JEREED, JERID
petty officer	TINDAL
plant	TURBITH, TURPETH
prison	BAGNIO
sailor	LASCAR
shrub	HENNA
tree	SEBESTEN
weight	DERHAM, DIRHAM, DIRHEM
	(*see also* **Eastern**)
ox	KINE, NEAT
Abyssinian	GALLA, SANGA
	SANGU, SUNGA
African	CAPE BUFFALO
	CONGO BUFFALO
	ZAMOUSE
American	BISON, BUFFALO
bison	BONAS(S)US
buffalo	BUBALUS
castrated	STEER
cattle/bison hybrid	CAT(T)ALO
cattle/zebu hybrid	CATTABU
Celebes (Sulawesi)	ANOA, SAPI-(O)UTAN
cow/yak	(*see* Himalayan *below*)
East Indian	BANTENG, BANTING
	TAMAROU
European	AUROCHS, BISON, URUS
extinct	AUROCHS
Himalayan	DSOMO, DSOBO, JOMO
	Z(H)O, ZHOMO, ZOBO, ZOBU
Indian	BHYLE, BRAHMIN BULL
	G(A)YAL, GAUR, MITHAN
	S(E)LADANG, ZEBU
Indonesian	DWARF BUFFALO
musk-ox	OVIBOS
old	ROTHER
Tibetan	SARLAC, SARLAK, YAK
wild ox	BUGLE, OWRE
young	CALF, STEERLING, STIRK

P

painting

abstract art	ABC ART, CONCRETE ART
	MINIMALISM
	NON-FIGURATIVE ART
	NON-REPRESENTATIONAL ART
actual colour uninfluenced by reflected colour	LOCAL COLOUR
aesthetic element in picture	SIGNIFICANT FORM
altar	
—frontal	ANTEPENDIUM, PALIOTTO
—piece	
two panels	DIPTYCH
three panels	TRIPTYCH
several panels	POLYPTYCH
apply monochrome base to detailed drawing	LAY-IN
appreciation of form in terms of light and shade	MALERISCH
areas of colour separated by blue or black lines	CLOISONNISME
arrangement	COMPOSITION
art of the real	MINIMALISM
austere and tragic quality	TERRIBILITA
backing plaster coat in fresco work	ARRICCI(AT)O
based on	
—antique exemplars	(NEO-)CLASSIC(AL)
—ink blobs	BLOT DRAWING
—light and movement	KINETIC ART
—living organisms	BIOMORPHIC ART
—passions	ROMANTIC
—use of the products of modern life	POP ART
binder for pigment	OIL, TEMPERA
black, red or brown chalk	CONTE
blot painting	TACHISM(E)
blue colours	COLD COLOUR
	COOL COLOUR
book of Claude drawings	LIBER VERITATIS
brown pigment	BISTRE, SEPIA
built up from various materials	COLLAGE
canvas prepared with dark brown earth and binder	BOLUS GROUND

carbon twigs	CHARCOAL
chalk on canvas	ABSORBENT GROUND
circular picture	TONDO
Cloisonnisme	SYMBOLISM, SYNTHETISM
collage	ASSEMBLAGE
	COMBINE-PAINTING
	TABLEAU-PIECE
colouring	PIGMENT
—blue	SMALT
—earths	BOLE, OCHRE, SIENA, UMBER
combination	
—into satisfactory visual whole	COMPOSITION
—of painting with objects	COLLAGE
combining human, animal and plant forms	GROTESQUE
contrasting light and shade	CHIAROSCURO
controlled by	
—subconscious mind	AUTOMATIC PAINTING
	AUTOMATISM
—unconscious mind	ACTION PAINTING
creating	
—three-dimensional effect	MODELLING
	PERSPECTIVE
	TROMPE L'OEIL
—visual illusions	OP(TICAL) ART
	TROMPE L'OEIL
critic	
—English	RUSKIN
—French	DIDEROT
dabs of primary colour	DIVISIONISM
dark brown or reddish earth	BOLE
depending on patterns of outlines	LINEAR COMPOSITION
depicting	
—a particular moment in a story	NARRATIVE PAINTING
—contemporary scene	SOCIAL REALISM
—the squalid and depressing	REALISM
—Virgin Mary with dead Christ	PIETA
design made by scratching through top layer	SGRAFFITO
detailed drawing for painting	CARTOON
doodling	AUTOMATIC PAINTING
	AUTOMATISM
dots of primary colours	POINTILLISM(E)
—in place of secondaries	OPTICAL MIXTURES
drying substance	SICCATIVE

dull finish	MAT, MATT(E)	ideal proportion	GOLDEN MEAN
easel painting inserted			GOLDEN SECTION
into ceiling		imaginary view	VEDUTA IDEATA
decoration	CARRIED PICTURE	imitation using motifs	
	QUADRO RIPORTATO	from several genuine	
elaborate ornament	GROTESQUE	works	PASTICCIO, PASTICHE
engraving		impression of the	
—technique	AQUATINT, CAMEO, CRAYON	open air	PLEIN AIR
	DRY-POINT, ETCHING	Impressionist views of	
	INTAGLIO, LINE, MEZZOTINT	everyday life	INTIMISME
	NIELLO, PLANAR, RELIEF	in	
	STIPPLE, SURFACE	—dots of colour	POINTILLISM(E)
—tool	BURIN, GRAVER	—one colour	MONOCHROME, GRISAILLE
—with punched dots	DOTTED PRINT	Japanese style	UKIYO-E
etching technique	AQUATINT, DRY-POINT	jelly-like paint	THIXOTROPIC
exaggerated		landscape	PAYSAGE
characterisation	CARICATURE	large altarpiece	ANCONA
exhibition (French)	SALON (D'APOLLON)	layer of paint not	
fantasy painting	CAPRICCIO	entirely covering	
figure or object in the		paint beneath	SCUMBLE
extreme foreground	REPOUSSOIR	Les Fauves	DERAIN, MANGUIN, MARQUET
figures and animals in			MATISSE, PUY, VALTAT
landscapes	STAFFAGE		VLAMINCK
film caused by aging	PATINA	lifelike flesh painting	MORBIDEZZA
first		line engraving	TAILLE-DOUCE
—coat	GESSO, GROUND	low-key painting	TENEBRISM
	PRIMER, PRIMING	made from fragments	COLLAGE
—print of engraving	PROOF	medium	ACRYLIC, DISTEMPER
Florentine engravings	BROAD MANNER		GOUACHE, INK, MAGILP
	FINE MANNER		MEGILP, OILS, PASTEL
flowing linear			TEMPERA, VEHICLE
decoration	ARABESQUE		WATER COLOUR
form showing through		mirror-image	
overpainting	PENTIMENTO	reproduction	COUNTERPROOF
frigid Neo-Classicism	L'ART POMPIER		OFFSET
front edge of imaginary		misty effect	SFUMATO
space in a picture	PICTURE PLANE	mixing-board	PALETTE
geometrical abstract		modelled by	
style	SUPREMATISM	—dots and flecks	STIPPLING
German school of design	BAUHAUS	—rubbing	STUMPED
glazing by rubbing		monochrome painting	GRISAILLE
by hand	VELATURA	naive art	PRIMITIVE ART
gradations of tone	VALUES	natural object as art	FOUND OBJECT
gradual transition			OBJET TROUVE
of colour	SFUMATO	network of small cracks	CRAQUELURE
ground	IMPRIMATURA	night-piece	NOCTURNE
gypsum or chalk used		not representing	
as ground	GESSO	any object	ABSTRACT
halo		of	
—enclosing whole figure	MANDORLA	—a	
—round heads	AUREOLE	detail	STUDY
	VESICA PISCIS	place	VEDUTA
hard glossy paint	ENAMEL	—angel	AMORINO, PUTTO
horizontal band	FRIEZE	—buildings	TOWNSCAPE
humorous or satirical		—Christ	
drawing	CARTOON	as child	BAMBINO

Mary and St John	DEESIS	—outside main tradition	PRIMITIVE
or saint on a panel	ICON	painter's	
standing in tomb	IMAGO PIETATIS	—hand-rest	MAHLSTICK, MAULSTICK
—Cupid	AMORINO, PUTTO	—studio	ATELIER, BOTTEGA
—everyday life	GENRE	painters	
—figures with heads on		—American	AUDUBON, BELLOWS, CASSATT
same level	ISOCEPHALY		COPLEY, DE KOONING, DEMUTH
—guard-room scenes	CORPS DE GARDE		DICKINSON, DINE, EAKINS
	KORTEGAARDJES		GORKY, GOTTLIEB, HENRI, HICKS
—inanimate objects	STILL LIFE		HOFFMANN, HOMER, JOHNS, KAPROW
—low-life and peasant			KELLY, KIENHOLZ, KLINE
subjects	BAMBOCCIATA		LICHTENSTEIN, LUKS, MACLUNUS
	GENRE		MAN RAY, MCLAUGHLIN, MOHOLY-NAGY
—Madonna and Child			MOSES, MOTHERWELL, NEWMAN
in rose garden	HORTUS CONCLUSUS		O'KEEFE, POLLOCK, RAUSCHENBERG
surrounded by angels	MAESTA		REINHARDT, RICHTER, ROTHKO
with saints	SACRA CONVERSAZIONE		SARGENT, SHEELER, SLOAN
—Mary mourning Jesus	PIETA		WARHOL, WEST, WHISTLER
—person	EFFIGY, PORTRAIT	—Argentinian	LE PARC
—rural		—Australian	DRYSDALE, NOLAN
life	PASTORAL, PAYSAGE	—Austrian	HAUSMANN, KLIMT, KOCH
setting (Fr.)	FETE CHAMPETRE		KOKOSCHKA, MOSER
	FETE GALANTE		SCHIELE
—saint	ICON, IKON	—Belgian/Flemish	ALECHINSKY, BREUGHEL
—sea	SEASCAPE		CORNEILLE, DELVAUX
—small boy	AMORINO, PUTTO		DOTREMONT, ENSOR, GOES
oil over tempera	MIXED METHOD		GOSSAERT, JORDAENS, LEMMEN
on			MAGRITTE, MEMLING, RUBENS
—circular panel	TONDO		TENIERS, VAN DER WEYDEN
—dry plaster	FRESCO SECCO		VAN DYCK, VAN EYCK
—fresh plaster	BUON FRESCO		VAN RYSSELBERGHE
—oval panel	MANDORLA	—British	AUERBACH, BACON
—wall or ceiling	FRESCO, MURAL		BELL, BEVAN
opaque watercolour	BODY COLOUR, GOUACHE		BLAKE, BONINGTON, BOMBERG
outdoor work	PLEIN AIR		BRATBY, BROWN, BURNE-JONES
outline forming			COLDSTREAM, CONSTABLE
boundary of shape	CONTOUR		COOPER, COTMAN, CROME, DEMUTH
over-sentimental			DOBSON, DRUMMOND, ETTY, FLINT
religious art	BONDIEUSERIE		FORBES, FREUD, FRY, FUSELI
paint			GAINSBOROUGH, GILLMAN
—containing rubber	LATEX PAINT		GIRTON, GORE, HAMILTON
—diluter	EXTENDER, LINSEED OIL		HEDLEY, HERRING, HILLIARD
	TURPENTINE, WHITE SPIRIT		HOCKNEY, HOGARTH, HUNT, JOHN
—thinned with			KNELLER, KNIGHT, LANDSEER
turpentine	LEAN PAINT		LELY, LEWIS
painted			LONG, MILLAIS, MORRIS, MUNNINGS
—crucifix	CHRISTUS PATIENS		NASH, NEVINSON, NICHOLSON
	CHRISTUS TRIUMPHANS		PALMER, PASMORE
—out of doors	PLEIN AIR		PIPER, PRITCHARD
—scroll	CARTELLINO		RATCLIFFE, REYNOLDS, RILEY(f)
painter			ROBERTS, ROMNEY, ROSSETTI
—before c 1500	PRIMITIVE		ROWLANDSON, SICKERT, SISLEY
—having completed			SMITH, SPENCER, STEER
apprenticeship	JOURNEYMAN		STUBBS, SUTHERLAND, TURNER
—naive and untrained	PRIMITIVE		WADSWORTH, WALTON, WATTS
—of devotional Madonnas	MADONNIERI		WILSON

—Czech	COUBINE, KUPKA
—Danish	JORN
—Dutch	APPEL, BOSCH, DE HOOCH, HALS
	KOONING, LEYDEN, MONDRIAN
	NEUWENHUYS, REMBRANDT
	RUISDAEL, VAN DOESBURG
	VAN DONGEN, VAN GOGH
	VERKADE, VERMEER
—French	ARMAN, ARNATT, ARP, BERNARD
	BONNARD, BOUCHER, BOUDIN
	BRAQUE, BRIANCHON, CAMOIN
	CASSANDRE, CEZANNE, CHAGALL
	CHANTREUIL, CHARDIN, CLAUDE
	COROT, COURBET, CROSS, DAUMIER
	DAVID, DEGAS, DELACROIX
	DELAUNAY, DENIS, DERAIN
	DE STAEL, DES VALLIERES, DUBUFFET
	DUCHAMP, DUFY, FANTIN-LATOUR
	FOUQUET, FRAGONARD, GAUGUIN
	GELLEE, GERICAULT, GLEIZES
	GREUZE, GRIS, GUILLAUMIN
	INGRES, KLEIN, KISLING
	KUPKA, LACOMBE, LAURENS, LATOUR
	LE FAUCONNIER, LE PAGE, LEGER
	LORRAIN, LUCE
	MANET, MANGUIN, MARQUET, MASSON
	MATISSE, METZINGER, MILLET, MIRO
	MONET, MOREAU, MORISOT (f), OZENFANT
	PASCIN, PEVSNER, PICABIA
	PISSARRO, POUSSIN, PUNI, PUY
	RAISSE, REDON, REDOUTE
	RENOIR, RIBOT, ROUAULT, ROUSSEAU
	SCHOFFER, SEURAT, SIGNAC
	SOUTINE, SURVAGE
	TANGUY, TOULOUSE-LAUTREC
	UTRILLO, VALADON(f), VALTAT
	VAN DONGEN, VASARELY, VLAMINCK
	VUILLARD, WATTEAU
—German	ALBERS, ALTDORFER, BECKMAN
	BEUYS, CAMPENDONK, CRANACH
	DIX, DURER, ENDE, ERBSLOH, ERNST
	FRIEDRICH, GROSZ, HEARTFIELD
	HECKEL, HOCH, HOFFMANN
	HOLBEIN, KIRCHNER, KNELLER
	KRANOLDT, MACKE, MARC, NOLDE
	NEUMANN, OVERBECK, PECHSTEIN
	RICHTER, SCHAD, SCHLEMMER
	SCHLICHTER, SCHWITTERS, VOGELER
	WEISS, ZEIGLER, ZIMMERMAN
—Greek	EL GRECO
—Hungarian	MOHOLY-NAGY, VASARELY
—Italian	AGOSTINO, BALLO, BELLINI
	BOCCIONI, BOTTICELLI, CARRA
	CARAVAGGIO, CASORATI,
	CHIRICO, DA MESSINA
	DEL CASTAGNO, DEL SARTO

	DUCCIO, FRA ANGELICO
	FRA FILIPPO LIPPI, FRANCESCA
	GENTILE, GIOTTO, GIOVANNI
	LEONARDO, LORENZETTI, LORENZO
	MANTEGNA, MARTINI, MASACCIO
	MICHELANGELO, MODIGLIANI
	MORANDI, ORCAGNA, PARMIGIANINO
	PERUGINO, PIERO, PREVIATI
	RAPHAEL, ROMANO, RUSSOLO
	SEGANTINI, SIGNORELLI
	TINTORETTO, UCCELLO
	(*see also* Venetian *below*)
—Japanese	FOUJITA, HIROSHIGE
	HOKUSAI, MOTONUBU
	UTAMARO
—Lithuanian	CIURLIONIS
—Mexican	OROZCO, RIVERA, SIQUEROS
—Norwegian	MUNCH
—Polish	KISLING, MULLER
—Russian	BURLIUK, CHAGALL
	DELAUNAY-TERK (f), EXTER, FALK
	GABO, GONCHAROVA(f), JAWLENSKY
	KANDINSKY, KONCHALOVSKY
	LARIONOV, LENTULOV, LISSITSKY
	MALEVICH, MASHKOV, NUSBERG
	PEVSNER, POPOVA(f), PUNI
	REPIN, RODCHENKO, SOUTINE
	STEPANOVA(f), SURVAGE
	TATLIN, UDALTSOVA(f)
—Scottish	CAMERON, CRAWHALL
	HORNEL, MACGREGOR, MELVILLE
	PATERSON, RAEBURN
	RAMSAY, WALTON
—Spanish	CANO, DALI, EL GRECO
	GOYA, GRIS, MASIP, MIRO
	MURILLO, PICASSO, RIBERA
	TAPIES, VELASQUEZ
—Swedish	DAHL, EGGLING, WEISS
—Swiss	BILL, DAW, ITTEN
	KAUFMANN, KLEE
—Venetian	BELLINI, CANALETTO
	CORREGGIO, GIORGIONE, GUARDI
	MONTAGNA, PIRANESI, TIEPOLO
	TINTORETTO, TITIAN, VERONESE
—West Indian	PISSARRO
painting	
—complete picture at	
one session	ALLA PRIMA
	AU PREMIER
—medium	BASE, VEHICLE
—miniatures	LIMNING
—on stone	LITHOCHROMATICS
	LITHOCHROMY
—surface	GROUND
—used for instruction	ACADEMY FIGURE
pair of paintings	DIPTYCH

paper	
—collage	PAPIER COLLE
—for water colours	TORCHON PAPER
patron saint	ST LUKE
pedigree of painting	PROVENANCE
pencil(ling) (18th c)	BRUSH(WORK)
perspective	
—obtained by	
overlapping features	COULISSE
—of single object	FORESHORTENING
pigment	
—brown	BISTRE
—reddish	BOLE
—with hot glue-size	SIZE COLOUR
	(*see also* **dye**)
pose with body twisted	CONTRAPPOSTO
preliminary	
—lay-in	UNDERPAINTING
—sketch	CARTOON, EBAUCHE
primacy of colour	
over form	ORPHIC CUBISM
	ORPHISM(E)
priming on	
—canvas or panel	IMPRIMATURA
—plaster	CLEARCOLLE
	GESSO, SIZE
print from	
—copper	
engraving	MEZZOTINT(O)
etching	AQUATINT
proof with annotated	
margins	REMARQUE PROOF
quasi-topographical	
subject	CAPRICCIO
quick-drying paint	ACRYLIC PAINT
range of colours	PALETTE
realism	VERISMO
red	
—colours	HOT COLOUR
	WARM COLSUR
—blue and yellow	PRIMARY COLOUR
reddish-brown	
—chalk	SANGUINE
—earth colour	SINOPIA
representing	
—mental concept	IDEAL ART
—objects	FIGURATIVE
roll of paper used to rub	
charcoal drawings	STUMP
rough sketch	BOZZETTO, MAQUETTE
rubbing technique	FROTTAGE
school	(*see* styles *below*)
scratched through	
surface to reveal	
colour	SGRAFFITO
sealing liquid	GESSO, SIZE

shading with parallel	
lines	HATCHING
silk-screen printing	SERIGRAPHY
single print	MONOTYPE
small	
—canvas used for	
portraits	KIT CAT, KITKAT
—easel painting	CABINET PICTURE
—painting	MINIATURE
—sketch for larger	
landscape	POCHADE
—version of larger	
picture	MODELL(ETT)O
smearing of ink on	
printing plate	RETROUSSAGE
Spanish kitchen scenes	BODEGON
stage of development	STATE
stand for painting	EASEL
still life	
—intimating brevity	
of life	VANITAS
—of solid subjects	RHYPAROGRAPHY
strip of paintings	
below altarpiece	PREDELLA
styles and schools	
—12th/13th c	GOTHIC
—14th c	INTERNATIONAL GOTHIC
—14th-15th c German	SOFT STYLE
—15th-16th c	
drawing technique	SILVERPOINT
—16th c	MANNERISM
French style	FONTAINEBLEAU
—17th c	
Dutch	UTRECHT SCHOOL
French movement	RUBENISME
painters	ITALIANISERS
—17th-18th c	BAROQUE
—17th-19th c Japanese	UKIYO-E
—18th c	NEO-CLASSICISM, ROCOCO
—18th-19th c	ROMANTICISM
—19th c	ART NOUVEAU
	ARTS AND CRAFTS MOVEMENT
	DIVISIONISM
	(NEO-)IMPRESSIONISM
	POINTILLISM
	POST-IMPRESSIONISM
	REALISM, ROMANTICISM
	SYMBOLISM
domestic scenes	INTIMISME
English	
painters	NEW ENGLISH ART CLUB
	PRB
	PRE-RAPHAELITE BROTHERHOOD
European	LES VINGT
French	
—Breton school	PONT-AVEN

—group	IMPRESSIONISTS
	LES NABIS
—landscape	
painters	BARBIZON SCHOOL
—symbolism	SYNTHETISM
German	
—movement	BAUHAUS, SEZESSIONEN
—religious school	BEURON SCHOOL
—style	BIEDERMEIERSTIL
Italian	
—group	I MACCHIAIOLI
—style	METAPHYSICAL PAINTING
	PITTURA METAFISICA
Scottish	GLASGOW SCHOOL
Viennese school	LUKASBRUDER
	NAZARENES
—19th/20th c	
American realist	ASHCAN SCHOOL
—20th c	ABC ART
	(ABSTRACT) EXPRESSIONISM
	ABSTRACT IMPRESSIONISM
	ACTION PAINTING, ART DECO
	ART OF THE REAL, BODY ART
	CONCEPTUAL ART, CUBISM, DADAISM
	EARTH ART, FIGURATIVE ART
	LAND ART, MINIMALISM
	NON-REPRESENTATIONAL ART
	SITUATIONISM, SURREALISM
American	NEW YORK SCHOOL
	PRECISIONISM
based on	
—everyday objects	POP ART
—movement	KINETIC ART
—optical effects	OP ART
Dresden painters	DIE BRUCKE
	THE BRIDGE
English	
—cubism	VORTICISM
—painters	BOROUGH GROUP
	CAMDEN TOWN GROUP
	EUSTON ROAD GROUP
	LONDON GROUP, NEWLYN SCHOOL
European group	COBRA
French	
—group	LES FAUVES
—movement	FAUVISM
	SCHOOL OF PARIS
German	
—group	FLUXUS
—movement	MAGIC REALISM
	MAGISCHER REALISMUS
	NEUE SACHLICHKEIT
	NEW OBJECTIVITY
—painters	BLUE FOUR
	DER BLAUE REITER
	THE BLUE RIDER

Italian movement	FUTURISM
	METAPHYSICAL PAINTING
	PITTURA METAFISICA
return to formal	
style of art	POST-IMPRESSIONISM
Russian movement	CONSTRUCTIVISM
	CUBO-FUTURISM
	RAYONISM, SUPREMATISM
suggestion implied in	
unfinished work	NONFINITO
sweetly sentimental	SOFT STYLE
system for representing	
three-dimensional space	PERSPECTIVE
technique using colour	
mixed with wax	ENCAUSTIC WAX
texture-rubbing	FROTTAGE
thickly applied paint	IMPASTO
thinner	WHITE SPIRIT
	TURPENTINE
three-dimensional	
—effect	MODELLING
	TROMPE-L'OEIL
—quality	PLASTICITY
three paintings	
created as unity	TRIPTYCH
top	
—layers of gesso	GESSO SOTTILE
—plaster coat in	
fresco work	INTONACO
total output of painter	OEUVRE
townscape	VEDUTA
traces of earlier	
painting showing	
through	PENTIMENTO
transparent layer of	
oil paint	GLAZE
travelling apprenticeship	WANDERJAHRE
two	
—or more portraits	
in one painting	CONVERSATION PIECE
—paintings created	
as a pair	DIPTYCH
—primary colours	
mixed	COMPLEMENTARY COLOUR
undercoat of gesso	GESSO GROSSO
unsophisticated painter	PRIMITIVE
using	
—abstract shape	
and primary colours	MINIMAL ART
—chalk or crayon	PASTEL
—dots	STIPPLING
of primary colours	POINTILLISM
—grey tones	GRISAILLE
—optical illusions	OP ART
	TROMPE L'OEIL
—several pictures	MONTAGE

—single colour	MONOCHROME
	MONOTINT
—transparent colours	AQUARELLE
—variety of materials	COLLAGE
	LAND ART
varnish sprayed on drawings	FIXATIVE
vehicle	MEDIUM
very small painting	MINIATURE
view of head that is turned away	PROFIL PERDU
visual	
—deception	ILLUSIONISM
	QUADRATURE, TROMPE-L'OEIL
—theme	MOTIF
voluptuous nude	ODALISQUE
wall-painting	FRESCO, MURAL
—method	FRESCO, SECCO
water	
—based paint	DISTEMPER, EMULSION
—colour with gum	GOUACHE
white	
—ground	GESSO
—line of canvas between areas of colour	ANTI-CERNE
wooden model	LAY FIGURE
Pakistan	PAK
airline	PIA
capital	ISLAMABAD
coins	PAISA, RUPEE
governor	HAKEEM, HAKIM
judge	HAKEEM, HAKIM
palaeontology	(*see* **archaeology**)
Palestine	PAL
Liberation Organisation	PLO
palm	EUTERPE
African	DATE-PALM, DOOM PALM
	D(O)UM PALM, PALMYRA
Arenga	GEMUTI, GEMUTO
Asian	DATE-PALM, PALMYRA
	TALIPAT, TALIPOT, TALIPUT
betel nut	ARECA
Borassus	WINE-PALM
Brazilian	ATTALEA, BABASSU
	CARNA(H)UBA, CHIQUICHIQUI
	COQUILLA, INAJA, LEOPOLDINIA
	PIASSABA, PIASSAVA, PAXIUBA
bussu	TROELIE, TROELY, TROOLIE
Californian	WASHINGTONIA
cane	CALAMUS
Ceylonese	CORYPHA, JAGGERY PALM
	KITTUL, TALIPAT
	TALIPOT, TALIPUT
Chilean	COQUITO
Chusan palm	TRACHYCARPUS
climbing	RAT(T)AN

Cordyline	GRASS PALM
corn palm	DRACAENA
cycad	ZAMIA
Dracaena	CORN PALM
East Indian	AT(T)AP, NIPA
Elaeus	OIL-PALM
European	CHAMAEROPS, PALMETTO
fan-palm	TALIPAT, TALIPOT, TALIPUT
	WASHINGTONIA
grass palm	CORDYLINE
Indian	JAGGERY PALM, KITTUL
Leopoldinia	PIASSABA, PIASSAVA
Malagasy	RAPHIA
Malay	GOMUTI, GOMUTO
Mexican	WASHINGTONIA
miriti	ITA, MORICHE
New Zealand	NIKAU
oil-palm	ELAEUS
palmetto	FAM-PALM, HEMP-PALM
	SABAL
peach-palm	PUPUHHA
Philippine	NIPA
piassava	CHIQUICHIQUI
producing	
—black fibre	GOMUTI, GOMUTO
—canes	CALAMUS
—edible pith	SAGO PALM
raphia	JUPATI, RAFFIA, WINE-PALM
royal palm	CABBAGE-PALM
sago-palm	ARENG, EJOO
	GOMUTI, GOMUTO
South American	ACCROCOMIA, ASSAI
	BURITI, BUSSO, COHUNE, COROZO
	GROO-GROO, GRU-GRU, JUPATI
	MACAHUBA, MACAW-TREE, MACOYA
	MIRITI, PEACH-PALM, PUPUNHA
	TUCUM, WAX-PALM
toddy palm	COCONUT PALM, PALMYRA
Trachycarpus	CHUSAN PALM
tropical seaside	COCO-PALM, COCO-TREE
	COCONUT-PALM
	DHANI, DUNNY
wine-palm	BORASSUS, RAPHIA
Panama	PA(N)
capital	PANAMA CITY
coin	BALBOA, CENTESIMO
Papal	
ambassador	NUNCIO
court	CURIA
delegate	EMISSARY, LEGATE
document	BULL
edict	DECRETAL
inability to err	INFALLIBILITY
letter	BULL
—of instructions	BRIEF
—to all bishops	ENCYCLICAL

licence	INDULT	—upper house	SENATE
officer who registers bulls	DATARY	Cornwall	STANNARY
representative	EMISSARY, LEGATE	Denmark	FOLKETING, RIGSDAG
treasurer	CAMERLENGO	—Upper House	LANDST(H)ING
	CAMERLINGO	Dominica	HOUSE OF ASSEMBLY
Papua New Guinea	PNG	Dominican Republic	
capital	PORT MORESBY	—lower house HOUSE OF REPRESENTATIVES	
coin		—upper house	SENATE
—unit	TOEA	Ethiopia	SHERGO
—100 toea	KINA	Fiji	
Paraguay	PY	—lower house HOUSE OF REPRESENTATIVES	
capital	ASUNCION	—upper house	SENATE
coin	CENTIMO, GUARANI	Finland	EDUSKUNTA
tea	YERBA, YERBA(DE)MATE	France	
parliament		—lower	NATIONAL ASSEMBLY
Abyssinian	SHENGO	—upper	SENATE
Andorra GENERAL COUNCIL OF THE VALLEY		Gambia	HOUSE OF REPRESENTATIVES
Anglo-Saxon	WITENAGEMOT	Germany	DEUTSCHES-BUNDESTAG
Antigua			REICHSTAG
—lower house HOUSE OF REPRESENTATIVES		—upper house	BUNDESRAT(H)
—upper house	SENATE		REICHSRAT(H)
Austria	BUNDESRAT	—State	LANDTAG
	BUNDESVERSAMMLUNG	Greece	VOULI
	FEDERAL ASSEMBLY	Greenland	LANDSTRAAD
	NATIONALRAT		NATIONAL CONGRESS
Australia		Holy Roman Empire	LANDTAG
—lower house HOUSE OF REPRESENTATIVES		Iceland	ALTHING
—upper house	SENATE	India	
Bahamas		—Lower House	LOK SABHA
—lower house HOUSE OF REPRESENTATIVES		—Upper House	RAJYA SABHA
—upper house	SENATE	Iran	MAJLIS, MEJLIS
Bangladesh	JATIYA SANGSAD	Ireland	OIREACHTAS
Barbados		—lower house	DAIL(EIREANN)
—lower house HOUSE OF REPRESENTATIVES		—upper house	SEANAD(EIREANN)
—upper house	SENATE	Isle of Man	TYNWALD(COURT)
Belize		—lower house	HOUSE OF KEYS
—lower house HOUSE OF REPRESENTATIVES		Israel	KENESET, KNES(S)ET
—upper house	SENATE	Italy	
Bohemia	LANDTAG	—lower house	HOUSE OF DEPUTIES
Bolivia		—upper house	SENATE
—lower house	HOUSE OF DEPUTIES	Jamaica	
—upper house	SENATE	—lower house HOUSE OF REPRESENTATIVES	
Brazil	NATIONAL CONGRESS	—upper house	SENATE
—lower house	HOUSE OF DEPUTIES	Japan	DIET, KOKKAI
—upper house	SENATE	—lower house	SHUGIIN
Bulgaria	NARODNA SUBRANIE	—upper house	SANGIIN
Canada	FEDERAL PARLIAMENT	Jordan	NATIONAL ASSEMBLY
—lower house	HOUSE OF COMMONS	—lower house	CHAMBER OF DEPUTIES
—upper house	SENATE	—upper house	CHAMBER OF NOTABLES
Channel Islands		Liechtenstein	DIET, LANDTAG
—Alderney	STATES OF ALDERNEY	Malaysia	
—Guernsey	STATES OF DELIBERATION	—lower house	DEWAN RAKYAT
—Jersey	STATES OF JERSEY	—upper house	DEWAN NEGARA
—Sark	COURT OF CHIEF PLEAS	Mexico	
Colombia		—lower house	HOUSE OF DEPUTIES
—lower house HOUSE OF REPRESENTATIVES		—upper house	SENATE

Mongolia	KHURAL
Moravia	LANDTAG
Morocco	CHAMBER OF REPRESENTATIVES
Nepal	NATIONAL PANCHAYAT
Netherlands	STATEN-GENERAAL
	STATES GENERAL
New Zealand	HOUSE OF REPRESENTATIVES
Norway	STORT(H)ING
—lower house	ODELST(H)ING
—upper house	LAGT(H)ING
Paraguay	NATIONAL CONGRESS
—lower house	HOUSE OF DEPUTIES
—upper house	SENATE
Persia	MAJLIS, MEJLIS
Portugal	CORTES
Russia	D(O)UMA
South Africa	HOUSE OF ASSEMBLY
	(VOLKS)RAAD
Spain	CORTES
—lower house	CONGRESS OF DEPUTIES
—upper house	SENATE
Sweden	RIKSDAG
—provincial	LANDST(H)ING
Switzerland	BUNDESVERSAMMLUNG
	COUNCIL OF STATES
	FEDERAL ASSEMBLY
United States	CONGRESS
—lower house	HOUSE OF REPRESENTATIVES
—upper house	SENATE
Venezuela	NATIONAL CONGRESS
—lower house	COUNCIL OF DEPUTIES
—upper house	SENATE
West Germany	DEUTSCHES-BUNDESTAG
Yugoslavia	SKUPSHTINA
Zambia	NATIONAL ASSEMBLY
Zimbabwe	
—lower house	HOUSE OF REPRESENTATIVES
—upper house	SENATE

Parliamentary

Labour Party	PLP
Private Secretary	PPS

particle

baryons	LAMBDA PARTICLE
	NEUTRON, NUCLEON
	OMEGA (MINUS) PARTICLE
	PROTON, SIGMA PARTICLE
	XI PARTICLE
—and mesons	HADRONS
basic particles	QUARKS
charged particle	ION
—negative	ANION, ANTI-PROTON
	ELECTRON, HYDROXYLION
—neutral	NEUTRON
—positive	CATION, POSITRON
	PROTON
and negative	ZWITTERION

circling nucleus	ELECTRON
curved path	BRACHISTOCHRONE
electrons, muons	
and neutrinos	LEPTONS
emitted by hot body	THERMION
force-carrying	
—colour force	GLUON
—electromagnetic force	PHOTON
—gravity	GRAVITON
—strong force	MESON
—weak force	W-MESON
gravity particle	GRAVITON
hadrons	BARYON, MESON
having spin	
—= ½	FERMION
—= 1	BOSON
heavy particle	BARYON, HYPERON, MESON
helium nucleus from	
radioactive source	ALPHA PARTICLE
	BETA PARTICLE
	GAMMA PARTICLE
hyperons	LAMBDA PARTICLE
	OMEGA PARTICLE
	SIGMA PARTICLE, XI PARTICLE
in nucleus	NEUTRON, PROTON
interacting	
—strongly	ELECTRON, LEPTON
	MUON, NEUTRINO, TAU
—weakly	BARYON, KAON, MESON
	NEUTRON, PION, PROTON
leptons	ELECTRON (NEUTRINO)
	MUON (NEUTRINO)
light particle	LEPTON
massless particle	GRAVITON, NEUTRINO
	PHOTON
meson	
μ-meson	LEPTON, MESOTRON, MUON
π-meson	PION
χ-meson	KAON
ψ-meson	PSION
mesons	CHARGED PION
	NEUTRAL PION
	NEUTRAL D PARTICLE
	NEUTRAL PSI PARTICLE
negative proton	ANTI-PROTON
nucleon	NEUTRON, PROTON
nucleus of heavy hydrogen	DEUT(ER)ON
	DIPLON
particle accelerator	(*see* **scientific instruments**)
positive electron	POSITRON
produced from nothing	VIRTUAL PARTICLE
properties of quarks	BEAUTY, BOTTOM
	CHARM, COLOUR
	SPIN, STRANGENESS
	TOP, TRUTH
protons and neutrons	BARYON

quantum of	
—gravity	GRAVITON
—light	PHOTON
quarks	CHARMED, DOWN
	STRANGE, UP
rules of spin	BOSE-EINSTEIN STATISTICS
	FERMI-DIRAC STATISTICS
study of charged	
particles	THERMIONICS
suggested particle	AXION, NUTRETTO
	PARTON, PREON
travelling	
—at speed of light	LUXON
—faster than light	TACHYON
—slower than light	TAROYON
uncharged particle	GRAVITON, NEUTRINO
	NEUTRON, PHOTON
unknown particle	GRAVIPHOTON
	GRAVISCALAR
	INTERMEDIATE BOSON
	W PARTICLE, Z PARTICLE
weakly-interactive	
massive particle	WIMP
pasta	
bows	FIOCHETTI
butterflies	FARFALLE
cartwheels	RUOTI
cocoons	BOZZOLI
coin-shaped	CORZETTI
corkscrews	FUSILLI
corrugated strips	MAFALDE
curls	CASARECCI
dumplings	GNOCCHI
elbows	TUBETTI LUNGHI
flat strips	LINGUINI
narrow strip	NOODLE
pipes	CANELLONI, MACARONI
quills	PENNE
ribbed tubes	RIGATONI
ribbons	FETTUCINI, TAGLIATELLE
rings	ANELLI
—small	ANELLINI
rods	SPAGHETTI
ruffled ribbons	LASAGNETTE
sheets	LASAGNE
shells	CONCHIGLIE
small	BUCATINI
—butterflies	FARFALLINI
—rings	ANELLINI
spinsters	ZITE
spirals	TROFIE
stars	STELLINE
strings	SPAGHETTI
thin	ANGEL'S HAIR, CAPELLINI
	VERMICELLI
—ribbons	TAGLIARINI

tubes	MANICOTTI, MILLERIGHI
—ridged	RIGATONI
twists	SPIRALE
wheels	ROUT(IN)E
pasta dishes	CANELLONI, FARFELLE
	LASAGNA, LASAGNE, MACARONI
	MACHERONI, TAGLIATELLE
	PANSOTTI, PAPARDELLE, RAVIOLI
	SPAGHETTI (BOLOGNESE)
	TORTELLI, TORTELLINI
—Hebrew	FARFAL, FARFEL
pastry	
boiled	
—ball of dough	DUMPLING
—pudding with	
bacon	BACON JACK
currants	SPOTTED DICK
	SPOTTED DOG
meat etc	STEAK AND
	KIDNEY PUDDING
choux pastry	
—filled with cream	PROFITEROLE
—with cheese	GOUGERE
Christmas confection	MINCE PIE
circle of pastry filled and	
folded in half	TURNOVER
covering for pie	PIECRUST
crisp pastry	SHORT(CRUST)
decoration from scraps of	
pastry	FLEURON
deep-fried	
—ball of	
choux	BEIGNET
dough (US)	HUSH PUPPY
—choux pastry	AIGRETTE
encased in pastry	EN CROUTE
flaky with apples	APFELSTRUDEL
Italian	PASTA
	(*see separate entry*)
light pastry	FLAKY, HUFF, PUFF
open case with filling	FLAN
pastry case filled with	
—almond paste	MAID OF HONOUR
—cream cheese	CHEESECAKE
—egg custard, etc	QUICHE (LORRAINE)
—meat	PATTIE, PATTY, PORK PIE
—mincemeat	MINCE PIE
—sausage meat	SAUSAGE ROLL
—sweet	
filling	FLAN, PASTRY, PIE, TART
or savoury filling	BOUCHE(E)
	PATTY, VOL-AU-VENT
—various fillings	QUICHE
Hebrew	KNISHES
Indian	SAMOSA
—vegetables	CORNISH PASTY

pastry cook	PATISSIER
shell	DARIOLE
short, with spices	VIENNA PASTRY
slices	VANILLA SLICES
small tart	TARTLET
strip with icing	ALLUMETTE
sweet pastry items	PATISSERIE
thin pastry	
—German	STRUDEL
—Greek	FILO
types of pastry	CHEESE, CHOUX, FILO
	FLAKY, FLAN, FORK-MIX
	HOT-WATER CRUST, QUICHE
	(ROUGH) PUFF, SHORT(CRUST)
	SUET CRUST, VIENNA
with fat	PASTE, SUET PASTRY
perfume	
from	
—Asian tree	PATCHOULI
—beaver	CASTOR
—citrus fruit	BERGAMOT
—flower petals	ATTAR
—iris	ORRIS
—tropical grass	CITRONELLA
—various animals	CIVET, MUSK
gum used in perfumes	MYRRH
mixed dried flower petals	POMANDER
	POTPOURRI
oil used in perfume	SAFROLE
perfumed	
—oil or cream	MACASSAR OIL
	POMADE, POMANDER
—smoke	INCENSE
—stick	JOSS STICK
—toilet water	EAU DE COLOGNE
Persian	
ancient people	ELAMITES, MEDES
bad principle	AHRIMAN
bosun	SERANG
bravo!	SHABASH
camel litter	KAJAWAH
canopy	SHAMIANA(H)
capital	TEH(E)RAN
carpet	KALI
chief ruler	PADISHA(H)
chintz	KALAMKARI
coins	
—unit	DINAR
—100 dinars	RIAL
—10,000 dinars	TOMA(U)N
—old	
copper	KRAN, SHAHI
gold	DINAR, MOHUR
—or silver	DARIC
council chamber	DIVAN
dagger	HAN(D)JAR

decree	FIRMAN
deities	(see gods, goddesses)
demi-god	YIMA
desert	DASHT
dog	SALUKI
drink	BOSA, SHIRAZ
dulcimer	SANTIR, SANTO(U)R
dyeing process	KALAMKARI
dynasty	ACHAEMENID, PAHLAVI
	QUAJAR, SAFAVID
	SASSANID, SELEUCID, ZAND
evil spirit	AHRIMAN, DEEV, DIV
excise duty	ABKARI
fabulous bird	SIMORG, SIMURG(H)
fairy	PERI
gateway	DAR
good principle	ORMAZD, ORMUZD
governor	CHAGAN, CHAM
	KHAN, SATRAP
gum-resin	OPOPANAX, SARCOCOLLA
hall	APADANA
harbour	BANDAR
headdress	CIDARIS, TIARA
headscarf	ROMAL, RUMAL
hookah	KALIAN, NARG(H)ILE
	NARGILEH, NARG(H)IL(L)Y
inn	CARAVANSARAI
	CARAVANSARY, CARAVANSERAI
	KHAN, SERAI
irrigation pipe	QANAT
lady	KHANUM
lake	DARYACHEH
language	FARSI, IRANIAN, PAHLAVI
	PARSEE, PARSI, PEHLEVI, ZEND
loincloth	LUNGI
lynx	CARACAL
king	CYRUS, SHAH, XERXES
magician	MAGE, MAGUS
measure (4 miles)	FARSANG, PARASANG
mineral	TURQUOISE
modern name	IRAN
Moslem fanatics	ABDALS
mountain	DAGH, KUH
—range	RESHTEH
musical form	DASTGAH
nightingale	BULBUL
open-vaulted hall	DIVAN
parade ground	MAIDAN
parliament	MAJLIS, MEJLIS
pass	GARDANEH, KUTAL, TANG
paymaster	BUCKSHEE, BUKSHI
philosophy	MAGISM, MAGIANISM
phoenix	HUMA
pickles	ACHAR
pleasure-ground	PARADISE
plain	MAIDAN

prayer-book	YASHT
priest	MAGE, MAGUS
prince	MIRZA
province	KHANATE, OSTAN, SATRAPY
religion	BAB(I)ISM, BABEEISM
	BAHAI(M), MITHRAISM, PARS(I)ISM
	PARSEEISM, ZOROASTRIANISM
river	AB, RUD(KHANEH)
robe	CAFTAN, KAFTAN
rug	HAMADAN, ISFAHN, KALI
	NAMMAD, SENNA
ruler	CALIF, CALIPH, K(H)ALIF
	SASSANID, SHAH, SOPHI, SOPHY
sailor	LASCAR
salt-desert	NAMAKZAR
sand	QUM
sash	LUNGI
script	NASTALIK, NASTALIQ
scriptures	(ZEND)-AVESTA
shawl	ROMAL, RUMAL
sovereign's seat	PEACOCK THRONE
stream	CHAI
tent	SHAMIANA(H)
throne	MUSNUD
tiara	CIDARIS
title	MIRZA
—of respect	(K)HODJA, KHOJA
tobacco	TUMBUK
torture	SCAPHISM
town	SHAHR
tribe	KURD
trousers	SHULWAR
turban	LUNGI
underground water channel	QANAT
verse	G(H)AZAL, GHAZEL
water	
—bag	MASHAQ
—pipe	HOOKA(H), KALIAN
—wheel	NORIA, SAKIA, SAKI(Y)EH
whip	CHABOUK
women's quarters	ZENANA
writing-case	KALAMDAN

pertaining

meaning: concerning	
like	
of	
of the nature of	
pertaining to	
relating to	
abdomen	COELIAC
abdominal organs	SPLANCHNIC, VISCERAL
abundance of moisture	HYDRIC
action	PRACTIC
—of heated water	HYDROTHERMAL
adjectives	EPITHETIC
adolescence	NEANIC

adult period	EPHEBIC
after-image	ACOL(O)UTHIC
agents	INSTITORIAL
ageing (period)	GERONTIC
agricultural	GEOPONIC, GEORGIC
air	PNEUMATIC
albumen	ALBUMINOID
alchemy	ALCHEMICAL, SPAGYRIC
algae	CONFERIOID
all-heal	VALERIANACEOUS
almonds	AMYGDALOID
almsgiving	ELEEMOSYNARY
amber	SUCCINIC
angels	HIERARCHAL, HIERARCHIC
animal	
—behaviour	EPIMELETIC, ETEPIMELETIC
—diseases	VETERINARY
—that lives on surface	
of another animal	EPIZOOTIC
animals	ZOIC
ankles	TARSAL
antelopes	ANTILOPINE
anthrax	ANTHRACOID
antimony	ANTIMONIAL, STIBIAL
ants	FORMIC, MYRMECOID
apes	PITHECOID, SIMIAL, SIMIAN
	SIMIOUS
apples	POMACEOUS
arches	FORNICATE
argument	ELENCTIC
armies	MILITARY
armpits	AXILLAR(Y)
arms	BRACHIAL
arrangement of five	
things	QUINCUNCIAL
arrows	SAGITTAL
artisans	BANAUSIC
asbestos	ASBESTIFORM, ASBESTOUS
ashes	CINERARY
athletic exercises	GYMNASTIC
atmospheric conditions	EPEDAPHIC
authors	AUCTORIAL
back	DORSAL, LUMBAR
—consonant	VELARIC
—of knee	POPLITEAL
—sides	PYGAL
badgers	MELINE, MUSTELINE
bags	UTRICULAR
ball of thumb	THENAR
baptism	CHRISMAL
Basques	EUSKARIAN
bathing/baths	BALNEAL
beans	FABACEOUS, LEGUMINOUS
bears	ARCTOID, URSINE
beasts	THERIOMORPHIC
	THERIOMORPHOUS, THEROID

beer	CERVISIAL
bees	APIAN
beetles	SCARABOID
belly	ALVINE, C(O)ELIAC
beans	LEGUMINOUS
berries	ACINACEOUS, ACINIFORM
biological cycle	CIRCADIAN
birds	AVIAN, AVINE, ORNITHIC
	ORNITHOID, VOLUCRINE
—of prey	RAP(TA)TORIAL
birth	NATAL
birthday	GENETHLIAC, NATALITIAL
birthmarks	NAEVOID
bishops	EPISCOPAL, PONTIFIC(AL)
bite	MORSAL
black tourmaline	SCHORLACEOUS
bladders	UTRICULAR, VESICAL
bladderwrack	FUCOID(AL)
blisters	VESICAL, VESIC(ULAR)
blood	HAEM(AT)IC, HAEMATOID
	SANGUINEOUS
—vessel	ANGIOID, VASCULAR
boars	PORCINE, SUIDIAN, SUILLINE
body	CORPOREAL, SOMATIC
body-segments	STROBILATE, STROBILIFORM
	STROBILINE, STROBILOID
bones	OSSEOUS, OSTEAL, OSTEOID
—marrow	MYELOID
—of forearm	RADIAL, ULNAR
boroughs	BURGHAL
bosom	GREMIAL
boundary	PERIMETRIC, PERIPHERAL
bowels	ENTERIC
bracelets	ARMILLARY
bracts	BRACTEAL, GLUMACEOUS
brain	CEREBRAL, CEREBRIC
—and spine	CEREBRO-SPINAL
bran	FURFURACEOUS, PITYROID
branch	RAM(E)AL, RAM(E)OUS
	RAMULAR
brass	ORICHALCEOUS
bread	PANARY
breaking up of red	
corpuscles	HAEMOLYTIC
bream	SPAROID
breast	MAM(M)ILLAR(Y), MAMMARY
	MASTOID, PECTORAL
—bone	STRENAL
breathing-holes	SPIRACULAR
	SPIRACULATE
bristles	STRIGATE, STRIGOSE
	STRIGOUS, STYLOID
brother	FRATERNAL
building	TECTONIC
bullheads	COTTOID
bulls	BOVINE, TAURIC, TAURINE
bunch of grapes	BOTRYOID, RACEMOSE
	STAPHYLINE
butter	BUTYRACEOUS
butterflies	PAPILIONACEOUS
	RHOPALOCERAL
	RHOPALOCEROUS
buttocks	PYGAL
calculation	LOGISTIC(AL)
calf	VITULAR, VITULINE
—of leg	SURAL
calling	VOCATIVE
calving	VITULAR
calyx	CALYCINAL, CALYCINE
	CALYCOIDEOUS
camel	CAMELOID
camp	CASTRAL
camphor	CAMPHORACEOUS
	CAMPHORIC
canal	CANALICULAR, MEATAL
cane	BACULINE, FERRULACEOUS
canton	CANTONAL
carbuncle	CARBUNCULAR
care of children by	
parents	EPIMELETIC
carp	CYPRINE, CYPRINOID
carriage in womb	GESTATORIAL
	GESTATORY
cartilage	CHONDROID
carving	GLYPTIC
case	THECAL
—expressing origin	GENITIVE
casting of nativities	GENETHLIAC
castor-oil	RICINOLEIC
cat	FELINE
—fishes	SILUROID
catechism	CATECHISMAL
	CATECHISTICAL
caterpillar	ERUCIFORM
catkins	AMENTAL, AMENTACEOUS
cattle	BOVINE, BUCOLIC
—tending	BUCOLIC
cave-dwellers	TROGLODYTIC(AL)
caves	SPELEOLOGICAL
cavities	LACUNARY, LACUNATE
cedars	CEDRINE
cell	CYTOID, UTRICULAR
centre of gravity	BARYCENTRIC
cereals	FARINACEOUS
chaff	PALEOUS
chain of segments	STROBILIFORM
	STROBILINE, STROBILOID
chains	CATENARY, CATENATE
chalk	CRETACEOUS
charity	ELEEMOSYNARY
chased metalwork	TOREUTIC
cheek	BUCCAL, MALAR

cheese	CASEOUS
chest	PECTORAL, THORACIC
chickenpox	VARICELLAR, VARICELLOID
chief	
—clerk of court	PROT(H)ONOTARIAL
—priests	PRELATIC
child	
—birth	PUERPERAL
—talk	HYPOCORISTIC(AL)
children	INFANTILE
	P(A)EDOMORPHIC, PUERILE
children's teeth	PAEDODONTIC
chin	GENIAL
China	SINAEAN, SINIC
choliamb	SCAZONTIC
church	ECCLESIASTIC(AL)
chrysalis	PUPAL
circle	CYCLOID
cirrus	CIRRATE
city	URBAN(E)
civet	VIVERRINE
civil matters	SECULAR
clauses	CLAUSULAR
claustrum	CLAUSTRAL
claws	UNGUAL
clay	ARGILLACEOUS, BOLAR
clergy	CLERICAL, PRELATIC
clothes	HABILATORY, SARTORIAL
	VESTIARY
cloud	NUBIFORM
clypeus	CLYPEAL
coast	ORARIAN
cobblers	CREPIDARIAN
cobbling	SUTORIAL, SUTORIAN
cobra	COBRIFORM
cobwebs	ARACHNOID, ARANEOSE
	ARANEOUS
coccyx	COCCYGEAL, COCCYGIAN
cochlea	COCHLEAR
cod	GADOID
coins	NUMISMATIC
	NUMM(UL)ARY
college	COLLEGIATE
colours	CHROMATIC
columns	COLUMNAL, COLUMNAR
comb	PECTIN(E)AL
common	
—people	PLEBEIAN, VULGAR
—rank	GREGARIAN
community	CIVIL
companionship	CONTUBERNAL
conducting vessels	VASCULAR
condyle	CONDYLAR, CONDYLOID
cone	CONOID(AL)
confirmation	CHRISMAL
conjunction	SYZYGIAL
connecting bars	ZYGAL
consent	CONSENSUAL
contraction	STENOTIC
controversy	ERISTIC
cooking	CULINARY
copper-rust	AERUGINOUS
coral	CORALLACEOUS
cords	FUNICULAR, FUNICULATE
	RESTIFORM
cork	PHELLOID, SUBEROSE
	SUBEROUS
corn	FRUMENTARIOUS
council	CONCILIAR(Y), CONSISTORIAL
	CONSITORIAN
count	COMITAL
country	RURAL
county	COMITAL
cows	BOVINE, BUCOLIC
	VACCINE
crabs	CANCRINE, CANCROID
cretin	CRETINOID
crickets	GRILLID
cross	CRUCIAL
—examination	ELENCTIC
—roads	COMPITAL
crow	CORVINE
crow's beak	CORONOID
crown	CORONAL, CORONARY
crustacean larvae	NAUPLOID
crypt	CRYPTAL
crystal	CRYSTALLOID
cultivation	MANURIAL
cups	CUPULAR, CUPULATE
curves in rays	
of light	DIACAUSTIC
cushion	PULVILLAR, PULVINAR
	PULVINATE
customs of city	CUSTUMAL
cutting edge	MORSAL
cuttlefish	SEPIARY
cyanogen	CYANIC
dancing	ORCHEST(R)IC
	TERPSICHOREAN
daughter	FILIAL
dauphin	DELPHIN
dawn	AURORAL, AUROREAN
day	DIURNAL, EOAN
deacons	DIACONAL
decree	DECRETAL
deep sea	BATHYAL, THALASSIC
deer	CERVINE, DAMINE
descent	PHYLETIC
desert	EREMIC
desire	EPITHYMETIC
devil	LUCIFER(I)AN, LUCIFERINE
dew	RORAL, RORIC, RORID, ROSCID

dialect	DIALECTIC
diaphragm	PHRENIC
digging	ORYCTIC
dinner	PRANDIAL
discourse	DIALECTIC
diseases of animals	VETERINARY
disputatious reasoning	ERISTIC
dissection	PROSECTORIAL
distribution of justice	JURIDICAL
divination	MANTIC
docks (weeds)	POLYGONACEOUS
Dog Star	CANICULAR
dogs	CANICULAR, CANINE
donkeys	ASININE
double womb	DIDELPHIC
doves	COLUMBINE
down	PAPPOSE, PAPPOUS
dragons	DRACONIC
dreams	ON(E)IRIC, SOMNIAL
dress	SARTORIAL
dressing	HABILATORY
dropsy	(O)EDEMATOUS
dross	SCORIAC(EOUS)
drum	TYMPANIC
dryness of skin	XERODERM(AT)IC
	XERODERMATOUS
duke	DUCAL
dung	STERCORACEOUS, STERCORAL
dyeing	TINCTORIAL
eagles	AQUILINE
ear	AURAL, AURICULAR, OTIC
—drum	TYMPANIC
earl	COMITAL
earliest times	PRISTINE
earth	CHTHONIAN, CHTHONIC
	TELLURAL, TELLURIAN
	TELLURIC, TERRENE
	TERRESTRIAL
earthquakes	SEISMAL, SEISMIC
	TERREMOTIVE
ecclesiastical council	CONCILIAR
echoes	PHONOCAMPTIC
edentates	EDENTAL
eels	ANGUILLIFORM
egg-yolk	VITELLARY
eggs (obsolete)	OVAL
Egyptian	
—king	PHARAONIC
—writing	HIERATIC
eight	OCTAL
electric current	GALVANIC, VOLTAIC
electricity and heat	ELECTROTHERMIC
elegy	EPICEDIAL, EPICEDIAN
elephant	ELEPHANTINE
	ELEPHANTOID
elf	ELFIN, ELFISH, ELVAN, ELVISH

ellipse	ELLIPTIC(AL)
elms	ULMACEOUS
embossed metalwork	TOREUTIC
embossing	EMPAESTIC
embryonic period	NEPIONIC
emeralds	SMARAGDINE
emotional forces	PSYCHODYNAMIC
emperor/empire	IMPERIAL
endosmosis	ENDOSMOTIC
enlarged veins	VARICOSE
entire Christian Church	ECUMENIC
episode	EPISODICAL
equinoxes	EQUINOCTIAL
erotic dreams	ON(E)IROTIC
examination of drugs	DOCIMASTIC
exchange	CATALLACTIC
excrement	EXCREMENTITIOUS
expenses	SUMPTUARY
experiment	PEIRASTIC
explanations	EXEGETIC(AL)
eye(s)	OCULAR, OPHTHALMIC
	OPTIC
—brows	SUPERCILIARY
—lids	PALPEBRAL
—like spots	OCELLAR
face	FACIAL
factor	INSTITORIAL
fairs	NUNDINAL
Fallopian tubes	SALPINGIAN
fat	ADIPOSE, LIPOID
	SEBACEOUS
father	PATERNAL
fathers of Church	PATRISTIC(AL)
fatty tumours	STEATOMATOUS
feast	FESTAL
feathered feet or legs	BRACCATE
feathers	PENNACEOUS
	PLUMOSE, PLUMOUS
federated state	STATAL
feet	PODAL(IC)
felony	FELONIOUS
felt	PANNOSE
fermentation	ZYMOGENIC, ZYMOID
	ZYM(OT)IC
ferns	CRYPTOGAMIAN, CRYPTOGAMIC
	CRYPTOGAMOUS
ferrets	MUSTELINE, VIVERRINE
fibrin	FIBRINOID, FIBRINOUS
fibrous structure	FIBRILLAR(Y)
	FIBRILLATE(D)
fibula	PERONEAL
field of vision	PERIMETRIC
fields	AGRESTIC, CAMPESTRAL
	CAMPESTRIAN
fifth degree	QUINTIC
fifty	QUINQUAGESIMAL

filament	FILAMENTARY
finches	FRINGILLACEOUS, FRINGILLINE
first	
—ages	PRIM(A)EVAL
—born	PRIMOGENITAL
	PRIMOGENITARY
	PRIMOGENITIVE
—fruits	PRIMITIAL
fish	ICHTHYOID(AL), PISCINE
—ascending rivers to spawn	ANADROMOUS
—descending rivers to spawn	CATADROMOUS
fishing	HALIEUTIC, PISCATORIAL
	PISCATORY
fissure	SULCAL
flags	IRIDEAL, VEXILLARY
flesh	CARNEOUS, CARNOSE
flour	FARINACEOUS
flowers	FLORAL
foam	SPUMOUS, SPUMY
f(o)etal envelope	CHOR(I)OID
f(o)etus	F(O)ETAL
foliage	FOLIACEOUS, FOLIAR, FOLIOSE
foot	PEDAL, PEDATE
—of two syllables	PYRRHIC
formation of earth	GEOGONIC
fowl	GALLINACEOUS
foxes	ALOPECOID, VULPINE
Franks	SALIAN
frogs	ANURAN, BATRACHIAN
	RANARIAN, RANIFORM
	RANINE, SALIENTIAN
froth	SPUMOUS, SPUMY
funeral	FERAL, FUNERARY
	FUNEREAL, FUNEBR(I)AL
fungus	FUNGOUS
furrow	SULCAL
gabbro	GABBROID
gall-nuts	ELLAGIC
Gal(lo)way	GALLOVIDIAN
	GAL(LO)WEGIAN
gallows	PATIBULARY
gametes	GAMETAL
gaps	LACUNARY, LACUNATE
garlic	ALLIACEOUS
garrison	PRESIDIAL
gas	PNEUMATIC
geese	ANSERINE
gem-carving	GLYPTIC
generation	GENITIVE
Gentile	ETHNIC
geometry of curved surfaces	GEODESIC
Germans	ALEMANNIC, TEUTONIC
germ-plasm	BLASTOGENIC

germs	GERMINAL
giant fennel	FERRULACEOUS
giants	CYCLOPEAN, CYCLOPIAN
	CYCLOPIC
gibbets	PATIBULARY
giddiness	DINIC
gills	BRANCHIAL, BRANCHIATE
ginger	ZINGIBERACEOUS
	ZINZIBERACEOUS
glacial rivers	FLUVIO-GLACIAL
gland	ADENOID, GLANDULAR
	GLANDULOUS
glass	HYALINE, VITREOUS
	VITRIFORM
glumes	GLUMACEOUS
gnats	CULICIFORM, CULICINE
gneiss	GNEISS(IT)IC, GNEISSOID
	GNEISSOSE
goats	CAPRIC, CAPRIFORM
	CAPRINE, HIRCINE
god	MERCURIAL
—of war	MARTIAL, MARTIAN
goitre	STRUMATIC, STRUMOSE
	STRUMOUS
gold	AURAL, AURIC
goldcrests	REGULINE
good digestion	EUPEPTIC
gorillas	GORILLINE
gourds	CUCURBITACEOUS
	CUCURBITAL
gout	PODAGRAL, PODRAGRIC(AL)
	PODAGROUS
government	POLITIC
—by elders	PRESBYTERIAN
priests	HIERARCHICAL, HIERARCHIC
	HIEROCRATIC
governors	GUBERNATORIAL
grain	CEREAL
grandfather	AVITAL
grandparents	AVAL
granite	GRANITIFORM
graphite	PLUMBAGINOUS
grass	GRAMIN(AC)EOUS
gravel	GLAREOUS
Greece	ACHAEAN, ACHIAN, HELLENIC
gripes	TORMINAL, TORMINOUS
grit	SABULOUS
groin	INGUINAL
groove	SULCAL
group or radical of different nature	PROSTHETIC
grove	NEMORAL
gull	LAROID
gullet	OESOPHAGEAL
gum	MUCILAGINOUS

gums	GINGIVAL
guts	ENTERAL, ENTERIC
	SPLANCHNIC
H-shaped fissure of	
brain	ZYGAL
hair	CAPILLACEOUS
	CRINAL, TRICHOID
—cutting	TONSORIAL
halls	AULARIAN
hammerheaded-sharks	ZYGAEN(O)ID
	ZYGAENINE
hands	CH(E)IRAL, MANUAL
	PODIAL
handle	MANUBRIAL
hard skin	SCLERODERMIC
	SCLERODERMOUS
hares	LEPORINE
harlotry	MERETRICIOUS
hawks	ACCIPITRINE
head	(EN)CEPHALIC
—of tree or comet	COMAL, COMATE
	COMOSE, COMOUS
healing	AESCULAPIAN
healthy nutrition	EUTROPHIC
heart	CARDIAC(AL)
—and blood vessels	CARDIOVASCULAR
—sac	PERICARDIAC
	PERICARDIAL
	PERICARDIAN
heat	THERMAL, THERMIC(AL)
	THERMOTIC(AL)
—of the earth	GEOTHERMAL
	GEOTHERMIC
heath	ERICACEOUS
heathen	ETHNIC
heavens	URANIAN
hedgehog	ECHINATE(D)
heightened state	
of perception	PSYCHEDELIC
	PSYCHODELIC
hemp	CANNABIC
hens	GALLINACEOUS
herald(ry)	HERALDIC
herbs	HERBACEOUS, HERBY
high	
—atmospheric pressure	HYPERBARIC
—priest	PONTIFIC(AL)
highest heaven	EMPYREAL, EMPYREAN
holidays	FERIAL, FESTAL
horn	KERATOID
horns	CORNUAL, CORNY
horse	CABALLINE, EQUINAL
	EQUINE, HIPPIC
horsemanship	EQUESTRIAN
hospital	NOSOCOMIAL
hospitality	XENIAL

hours	HORAL, HORARY
houses	DOMAL, DOMESTIC
hunting	CYNEGETIC, VENATIC(AL)
husband	MARITAL
hyacinth	HYACINTHINE
hyenas	THOOID
hypersthenia	HYPERSTHENIC
iambic trimeter	SCAZONTIC
icicles	STALACTIC(AL)
	STALACTICIOUS
ideas	NOTIONAL
ideology	IDEOLOGIC
idylls	IDYLLIAN, IDYLLIC
ileum	ILEAC, ILIAC
ill-health	VALETUDINARIAN
	VALETUDINARY
inch	UNCIAL
infants	INFANTILE
infectious disease	ZYMOTIC
inhabitants of Earth	TERRESTRIAL
insects	ENTOMIC
	INSECTIFORM, INSECTILE
interior of the ear	ENTOTIC
internal organs	SPLANCHNIC
interpretation	EXEGETIC(AL)
intestines	ENTERAL, ENTERIC
	SPLANCHNIC
introductions	ISAGOGIC, PROEMIAL
	PROLEGOMENARY
	PROLEGOMENOUS
—to discourse	EXORDIAL
introductory treatise	PRODROMAL
	PRODROMIC
irises	IRID(I)AL, IRIDIAN, IRIDIC
iron	FERREOUS
itching	PRURITIC
ivory	EBURNEAN
ivy	ARALIACEOUS, HEDERAL
jaundice	ICTERAL, ICTERIC
jaw	MAXILLARY
jawbone and hyoid	
bone	MYLOHYOID
jellyfish	MEDUSIFORM, MEDUSOID
Jews	JUDAIC
judge	JUDICIAL, JURIDICAL
judgements	JUDICIARY
kangaroos	MACROPINE
kidneys	NEPHRIC, NEPHRI)IC(AL)
	RENAL
kings	REGAL
kissing	OSCULAR, OSCULATORY
kitchen	CULINARY
—vegetables	OLITORY
knee	GENUAL
kneecap	PATELLAR
knot-grass	POLYGONACEOUS

knowledge of medicines	PHARMACEUTIC(AL)
labour	FABRILE
labyrinths	LABYRINTHAL, LABYRINTHINE
	LABYRINTHIAN
lacunae	LACUNARY, LACUNATE
ladders	SCALAR(IFORM)
lakes	LACUSTRINE
land	PR(A)EDIAL, TERRENE
	TERRESTRIAL
—and water	TERRAQUEOUS
—register	CADASTRAL
languages	LINGUISTIC(AL)
—spoken	PHONETIC
lap	GREMIAL
larch	LARCHEN
laughter	GELASTIC
law	EDICTAL, LEGAL
lay matters	SECULAR
lead	PLUMBAGINOUS
leaflets	FOLIOLATE, FOLIOLOSE
leather	CORI(ACE)OUS
leaves	FOLIACEOUS, FOLIAR
	FOLIATE, FOLIOSE
	FRONDESCENT, FRONDOSE
leeks	PRASINE
legal investigation	FORENSIC
legislation/legislators	LEGISLATORIAL
legs	CRURAL
lemurs	LIMURIAN, LIMURINE
	LIMUROID, TARSIOID
lenses	LENTICULAR, LENTOID
lentil-seed	LENTICELLATE
leopards	PARDINE
letters of alphabet	LITERAL, LITERARY
libido	LIBIDINAL
lice	PEDICULAR
life	ZOETIC
light	PHOTIC
lightning	FULGURAL, FULGUROUS
lilies	ARACEOUS, AROID
	LILIACEOUS
limbs	MEMBRAL
lime	CALCAREOUS
lines of verse	STICHIC
lips	LABIAL
lithium	LITHIC
liver	HEPATIC
liverworts	HEPATIC
living in slimy sediment	SAPROPELIC
lizards	AGAMOID, LACERT(IL)IAN
	LACERTINE
lobes	LOBAR
loins	ILIAC, LUMBAR
loss of hair	PSILOTIC

love	AMATORY
—of offspring	PHILOPROGENITIVE
low cloud	STRATOUS
lower leg	PERONEAL
lunch	CENAL
lungs	PNEUMONIC, PULMONARY
	PULMONIC
—and stomach	PNEUMO-GASTRIC
lymph	LYMPHATIC
—vessels	ANGIOID, LYMPHANGIAL
lynx	LYNCEAN
lyres	LYRICAL
mackerel	SCOMBROID
magic by good spirits	THEURGIC(AL)
magistrates	MAGISTERIAL
magnetic remanence	THERMOREMANENT
maigre (fish)	SCIAENOID
mail-service	POSTAL
mammals	THERIOMORPHOUS, THEROID
man	ANTHROPOID
	ANTHROPOMORPHOUS
manor	MANORIAL
mantles	PALLIAL
many arts or subjects	POLYTECHNIC(AL)
marble	MARMOREAL
markets	NUNDINAL
marks	STIGMATIC
marriage	CONNUBIAL, CONJUGAL
	HYMENAL, JUGAL, MARITAL
	MATRIMONIAL, NUPTIAL
	SPONSAL
—of unequals	MORGANATIC
marrow	MYELOID
Mars	MARTIAL, MARTIAN
marshes	PALUD(IN)AL, PALUDINE
	PALUDINOUS, PALUDOSE
	PALUDOUS, PALUSTRAL
	PALUSTRIAN, PALUSTRINE
martens	MELINE, MUSTELINE
master artist	MAGISTERIAL
meal	FARINACEOUS
meanings	SEMANTIC
measles	MORBILLIFORM, MORBILLOUS
measurement	MENSURAL, METRICAL
—by	
weight	GRAVIMETRIC
gas	GASOMETRIC
—of time	HOROMETRICAL
medical treatment of children	PAEDIATRIC
medicine	IATRIC(AL), OFFICINAL
	PHYSICKY
melody	CHROMATIC
membrane	MEMBRAN(AC)(E)OUS
meninx/meninges	MENINGEAL
mental forces	PSYCHODYNAMIC

merchants	MERCANTILE
messengers	INTERNUNCIAL
metalloid	METALLOIDAL
metals	METALLIC, METALLINE
metonymy	METALEPTIC(AL)
mice	MURINE
mid-brain	MESENCEPHALIC
midday	MERIDIAN
midline	MEDIAL
midwifery	OBSTETRIC
milk	LACTEAL, LACTIC
mill(er)s	MOLENDINAR(Y)
millet-seed	MILIARY
millions	MILLIONARY
mimicry	MIMETIC(AL)
mind	INTELLECTUAL, PSYCHIC
mining	ORYCTIC
minister/ministry	MINISTERIAL
mirrors	SPECULAR
mites	ACAROID
mitres	MITRAL
moderate water-supply	MESIC
modulus	MODULO
moles	TALPINE
monads	MONADIC(AL), MONADIFORM
monasteries	MONASTERIAL, MONASTIC
money	NUMISMATIC, PECUNIARY
mongooses	HERPESTINE
monkeys	SIMIAN
monks	MONASTERIAL, MONASTIC
months	MENSAL
Moon	LUNAR, SELENIAN
—and Sun	LUNISOLAR
morning	MATUTINAL, MATUTINE
mosses	SPHAGNOUS
mother	MATERNAL
—of-pearl	NACREOUS
motion	KINETIC
—of electricity	ELECTROMOTIVE
mountain-building	OROGEN(ET)IC
mouse	MURINE
mouth	BUCCAL, ORAL, OSTIAL
	STOMATIC
—and stomach	STOMATOGASTRIC
mucilage	MUCILAGINOUS
mucus	MUCOID, MUCOUS
	MUCULENT, PITUITARY
multiple origins	POLYPHYLETIC
muscles	MYOID
muses	AONIAN
mysteries	TELESTIC
names	ONOMASTIC
nasal partition	VOMERINE
—and cavity	VOMERONASAL
nations	ETHNIC
native land	PATRIAL

natural right	JURAL
navels	OMPHALOID, UMBILICATE
navigation	NAUTICAL
neck	CERVICAL, JUGULAR
nectar	NECTAREAL, NECTAREAN
	NECTAR(E)OUS
—gland	NECTARIAL
needles	SPICULAR
Negroes	NEGROID(AL)
Nero	NEROTIC
nerves	NERVAL, NEURAL
nests	NIDAL
nets	RETIARY, RETICULAR
	RETICULATE(D)
nettle	URTICACEOUS
network	RETIAL
newly born	NEONATAL
night	NOCTURNAL
night-shade	SOLANACEOUS
night-wandering	NOCTIVAGANT
Nile	NILOTIC
nine	NOVENARY
nineteen	DECENNOVAL
nipple	MASTOID
Noah	NOACHIAN
nodes	NODICAL, NODULAR
north	SEPTENTRIONAL
—wind	BOREAL
nose	NASAL, RHINAL
—and	
frontal bone	NASOFRONTAL
tears	NASOLACRYMAL
nostrils	NARIAL, NARINE
nucleus of cell	KARYOLOGICAL
nuns	MONASTERIAL, MONASTIC
nutrition	TROPHIC
nymphs	NYMPHAL
oak	QUERCINE
oats	AVENACEOUS
oblivion	LETHEAN
oceans	PELAGIC
octaves	OCTAVAL
ode of lamentation	THRENODIAL
	THRENODIC
	THRENETIC(AL)
old age	GERIATRIC
omens	OMINOUS
once in a lifetime	SECULAR
one	
—eye	MONOCULAR
—person	PRIVY
opals	OPALINE
opposition	SYZYGIAL
oracles	ORACULAR
order	ORDINAL
ordinary life	CIVIL

organic matter in soil	HUMIC, HUMOUS
origin	GENETIC
origins	FONTAL
orioles, etc	ICTERINE
oryx	ORYGINE
ostriches	STRUTHIOID, STROUTHIOUS
otters	LUTRINE, MUSTELINE
ounce	UNCIAL
ovary	OVARIAN
ovules	OVULAR
owls	STRIGIFORM, STRIGINE
own sex	HOMOSEXUAL
oxide of yttrium	YTTRIC, YTTRIOUS
oyster	OSTRACEAN, OSTRACEOUS
painters	PICTORIAL
palate	PALATINE
palm	
—(hand)	PALMAR, THENAR, VOLAR
—(tree)	PALMACEOUS
paper	CARTACEOUS
	PAPYRACEOUS
parabolas	PARABOLIC
parab(o)le	PARABOLIC
parasitic disease	TRICHINOTIC
	TRICHINOUS
parchment	PERGAMENEOUS
parish	PAROCHIAL
parrots	PSITTACINE
partition	SEPTIFORM
parturition	PARTURIENT
passage	MEATAL
pastors	PASTORAL
pastures	PASTORAL
peacocks	PAVONIAN, PAVONINE
pears	POMACEOUS
peas	LEGUMINOUS
pellagra	PELLAGROUS
penal settlement	PRESIDIAL
penance	PENITENTIARY
people	DEMOTIC, LAY, POPULAR
perch	PERCIFORM, PERCINE
	PERCOID
perching birds	PASSERINE
perineum	PERINEAL
pestilence	LUETIC
phalanx	PHALANG(E)AL
Pharisee	PHARISAIC(AL)
pharmacy	PHARMACEUTICAL
pharynx	PHARYNG(E)AL
phlegm	PITUITARY
phlox	POLEMONIACEOUS
phyla	PHYLETIC
physicians	IATRIC(AL)
pictures	PICTORIAL
	PICTURAL, PICTURESQUE
pigeons	PERISTERONIC

pigs	PORCINE, SUIDIAN
	SUILLINE
pile	VILLOSE, VILLOUS
pillars	STYLAR
pimple	PAPULOSE, PAPULOUS
pineal gland	CONARIAL
pineapples	BROMELIACEOUS
pitch	PICEOUS
plane-trees	PLATANACEOUS
planes	HOMALOIDAL
planet	JOVIAN, MARTIAL, MARTIAN
	MERCURIAL, NEPTUNIAN, PLUTONIAN
	SATURNIAN, URANIAN, VENUSIAN
planets	PLANETARY
planning of towns	URBANISTIC
plantain	PLANTAGINACEOUS
plants	BOTANICAL, HERBACEOUS
plates	PLACOID
plea(ding)s	PLACITORY
pleasure	APOLAUSTIC
ploughed land	ARVAL
plums	PLUMY
plunder	PREDATORY
polecats	MUSTELID, MUSTELINE
policy	POLITIC
pollen	POLLINIC
—baskets	CORBICULATE
polyp	POLYPOUS
polypus	POLYPOID
polyzoa	POLYZOOID
poor classes	LUMPEN
Pope	PONTIFIC(AL)
Pope's representative	INTERNUNCIAL
poppies	PAPAVEROUS
pores	POROSE
porphyry	PORPHYRITIC
position	STATIONAL
—in space	LOCAL
posterior	PYGAL
—part of iris	UVEAL
pot-herbs	OLERACEOUS
potassium	POTASSIC
potatoes	SOLANACEOUS
pouch	MARSUPIAL, SACCATE
	SACCIFORM, SACCULAR
practices	PRACTIC
preaching	HOMILETIC
preface	PREFATORY, PROEMIAL
prehistoric masonry	CYCLOPEAN
	CYCLOPIAN, CYCLOPIC
prelates	PRELATIC
preliminary deliberation	PROBOULEUTIC
preludes	PRELUDIAL, PRELUDIOUS
	PRELUSIVE, PROEMIAL
premonitions	PRODROMAL, PRODROMIC
present day	HODIERNAL

—world	SECULAR
presidents	PRESIDIAL
presidio	PRESIDIAL
priests	HIERATIC, SACERDOTAL
—of Mars	SALIAN
prisms	PRISMATIC(AL)
probability of recurrence of a particular state	ERGODIC
proboscis	PROMUSCULATE
processions in honour of Dionysos	ITHYPHALLIC
producing	GENITIVE
prophecy	VATIC
proverbs	PAROEMIAL
prudence	PRUDENTIAL
psyche	PSYCHIC
pubic bone	PECTINEAL
public	
—revenues	FISCAL
—treasury	FISCAL
pulse	SPHYGMOID
pulses (peas, etc)	LEGUMINOUS
punishment	PENAL
pyrites	PYRITIC(AL), PYRITOUS
quartz	QUARTOSE
quartzite	QUARTZITIC
questioning	PYSMATIC
rabbis	RABBINIC(AL)
rabbits	LEPORINE, ORYCTOLAGINE
race	ETHNIC
—course	CURSAL
—improvement	EUGENIC
racemes	RACEMOSE
radicles	RADICULAR
rain	HYETAL, PLUVIAL
—bow	IRID(I)AL, IRIDIAN
rattlesnakes	CROTALINE
ravens	CORVIVE
reasoning	LOGISTIC(AL)
receptors	SENSORY
red deer	ELAPHINE
reeds	ARUNDINACEOUS
	FERRULACEOUS
reflected light	CATOPTRIC
reflection and refraction	CATADIOPTRIC
refraction of sound	DIACOUSTIC
refutation	ELENCTIC
region beyond the moon	TRANSLUNAR
registers	MATRICULAR
registrar of court	PROT(H)ONOTARIAL
regular pattern	QUOTIDIAN
relations with guests	XENIAL
religious art	HIERATIC
reports	REPORTORIAL

reproduction	GENITAL
—in larval state	PAEDOGENETIC
reptiles	HERPETINE, HERPETOID
rhinoceroses	RHINOCEROTIC
rhombus	RHOMBIC, RHOMBOID(AL)
ribbon	TAENIATE, TAENIOID
ribs	COSTAL, COSTATE
river-banks	RIPARIAN
rivers	FLUVIAL, FLUVIATIC
	FLUVIATILE, POTAMIC
roads	VIATIC
rock masses	GEOTECTONIC
rodents	GLIRINEAL
rods	RHABDOID
Roman	
—dance	TRIPUDIARY
—heralds	FECIAL, FETIAL
—mile	MILIARY
—standards	VEXILLARY
roofs	TECTIFORM
rootlets	RADICULAR
roots	RADICAL, RADICIFORM
	RHIZOIDAL, RHIZOMATOUS
rope	FUNICULAR, FUNICULATE
roses	ROSACEOUS, ROSEAL
	ROSEATE
rotary motion	TROCHILIC
royal palaces	BASILICAN
ruby	RUBINEOUS
rudiments	GERMINAL
rump of animal	PYGAL
runners	SARMENTACEOUS
running	CURSORIAL
rural dean(ery)	RURIDECANAL
sable	ZIBEL(L)INE
sacs	THECAL
sacred writing	HIEROGRAPHIC(AL)
sacrum	SACRAL
sailors	NAUTICAL
saints	PATRONAL
saliva	SIALOID
saltwort	SALSOLACEOUS
salvation	SOTERIAL
sand	ARENACEOUS, SABULOUS
sandalwood	SANTALACEOUS
sapphires	SAPPHIRINE
Satan	LUCIFERAN
Saturday	SABBATINE
Saturn	SATURNIAN
scad	CARNGOID
scales	FURFURACEOUS
	SQUAMIFORM, SQUAMOSE
	SQUAMOUS
scallops	PECTINACEOUS
scapula	SCAPULAR
scarab	SCARABOID

scazon	SCAZONTIC
scissors	FORFICULATE
screw	HELICOID(AL)
scurf	FURFURACEOUS
scurvy	SCORBUTIC(AL)
sea	MARINE, MARITIME
	PELAGIC, THALASSIC
—lions	OTARINE
—sediment	TERRIGENOUS
—shore	LITTORAL
—trade	MARITIME
—urchin	ECHINOID
—weed	ALGOID, FUCOID
seals	
—(mammals)	PHOCID, PHOCINE
—(signets)	SIGILLARY, SPHRAGISTIC
second	
—skin	HYPODERMIC
—year student	SOPHOMORIC(AL)
sedge	CYPERACEOUS
sediment on sea floor	TERRIGENOUS
seed	SEMINAL
senescent period	GERONTIC
sensation after	
stimulus	ACOL(O)UTHIC
sense of smell	OLFACTORY
septum	SEPTIFORM, VOMERINE
serums (sera)	SEROUS
servants	MENIAL, SERVILE
servile work	MENIAL
seven	SEPTIMAL
seventy	SEPTUAGENARY
sewers	CLOACAL
sewing	SUTORIAL, SUTORIAN
sex organs	GENITAL
sexual	
—attraction towards	
opposite sex	HETEROSEXUAL
same sex	HOMOSEXUAL
—love	EROTIC
sheaths	THECAL
sheep	OVIFORM, OVINE, VERVECINE
shells	CONCHOIDAL
shepherds	PASTORAL
sheriff	SHRIEVAL
ships	NAUTICAL
shoemaker	CREPIDARIAN
shops	OFFICINAL
shoulder	HUMERAL
—blade	SCAPULAR
—and hyoid	OMOHYOID
side	LATERAL
—of cranium	TEMPORAL
sieges	OBSIDIONAL
sieves	CRIBRATE, CRIBRIFORM
	CRIBROSE, ETHMOID(AL)

sight	VISIVE, VISUAL
signature	ONOMASTIC
signets	SPHRAGISTIC
silica	SILICEOUS, SILICIOUS
silk	SERIC(EOUS)
silver	ARGENTINE
simultaneous	
sister	SORORAL
transmission of messages	
over same wire	DIPLEX
sine waves	SINUSOID(AL)
single eye	CYCLOPEAN, CYCLOPIAN
	CYCLOPIC
Sirius	CANICULAR
sixty	SEXAGESIMAL
skin	CUTANEOUS, DERMATIC
	DERMATOID
skinks	SCINCOID
skull	CRANIAL
skunks	MUSTELINE
slag	SCORIAC(EOUS)
slaves	SERVILE
sleep	HYPNIC, HYPNOID(AL)
slug	LIMACEOUS
small	
—bag, bladder	UTRICULAR, VESICULAR
—blisters	VESICULAR
—cavities	VACUOLAR
—cushions	PULVILLAR
—feathers	PLUMULACEOUS, PLUMULAR
—fibres	FIBRILLAR(Y), FIBRILLATE
	FIBRILLOUS
—hooks	HAMULAR
—matter	ATOMIC
—passage	POROSE
—sac	UTRICULAR, VESICULAR
—stars	STELLULAR, STELLULATE
—valves	VALVULAR
—worlds	MICROCOSMIC
smallpox	VARIOLOUS
smells	OLFACTORY
snakes	ANGUINE, COLUBRIFORM
	COLUBRINE, HERPETINE, HERPETOID
	OPHIDIAN, OPHIURAN
	OPHIUR(O)ID, SERPENTINE
snow	NIVEOUS
soap	SAPONACEOUS
soda	SODAIC
soft hair	VILLOSE, VILLOUS
soil	EDAPHIC
soldiers	MILITARY
sole (foot)	PLANTAR, THENAR
	VOLAR
son	FILIAL
song of mourning	THRENODIAL, THRENODIC
	THRENETIC(AL)

songbirds	OSC(IN)INE
sorcerer	MAGIAN
soul	PSYCHIC
sound	SONIC
—of speaking into bottle	AMPHORIC
—reproduction	ACOUSTIC
south of Sahara desert	SAHELIAN
space	LACUNARY, LACUNATE
	SPATIAL
spar	SPATHIC, SPATHOSE
speech sound	PHONETIC
spicule	SPICULAR
spinage	SPINACEOUS
spindles	CLOSTRIDIAL
spinster	SPINSTERIAL, SPINSTERIAN
spiral	HELICAL, HELICOID(AL)
spirit	ETHEREAL, ETHERIAL
spleen	LIENAL
splints	SPLENIAL
sponge	SPONGIFORM, SPONGOID
spore(s)	SPORIDIAL
—cases	THECAL
spring	VERNAL
squint	STRABISMAL, STRABISMIC(AL)
squirrels	SCIURINE, SCIUROID
stalactites	STALACTITAL
	STALACTIC(AL)
	STALACTIFORM
	STALACTITIOUS
stalagmites	STALAGMITIC
stalks	PEDUNCULAR, PETIOLAR
	STIPITATE
standing water	LENTIC
starlings	STURNINE, STURNOID
stars	ASTEROID, ASTRAL
	SIDEREAL, STELLAR
statue	STATUESQUE
stems	CAULINE, CAULINARY
stepmother	NOVERCAL
sticks	BACULINE
stimuli from movement	PROPRIOCEPTIVE
stomach	GASTRIC
stone	LAPIDARIAN, LAPIDARY
	LITHIC, LITHOID(AL)
	PETROSAL
—fruits	DRUPACEOUS
storms	ORAGIOUS
strap	LIGULATE, LORATE
straw	STRAMINEOUS
striking	PERCUTIENT
style	STYLIFORM, STYLOID
suffragan bishop	CHOREPISCOPAL
sugar	SACCHARINE
summer	AESTIVAL
Sun	HELIAC, SOLAR

surrounding region	PERIPHERAL
	PERIPHERIC
swallows	HIRUNDINE
sweat	HIDROTIC, SUDATORY
swimming	NATATORIAL, NATATORY
swine	PORCINE
swineherds	SYBOTIC
symptoms	SEM(E)IOTIC
syphilis	LUETIC
table	MENSAL
tailless amphibia	BATRACHIAN
tailors	SARTORIAL
tails	CAUDAL, CERCAL
tallow	SEBACEOUS
tapeworms	CESTOID, SCOLECIFORM
	TAENIATE, TAENIOID
taste	GUSTATIVE, GUSTATORY
taxation	FISCAL
teacher	MAGISTERIAL
teaching	DOCTRINAL
tears	LAC(H)RYMAL, LAC(H)RYMARY
	LAC(H)RYMATORY
	LACRIMAL, LACRIMA(TO)RY
teeth	DENTAL, ODONTIC
	ODONTOID
—with paired cusps	ZYGODONT
temperature and salinity	THERMOHALINE
tempered steel	CHALYBEOUS
temples	TEMPORAL
temporal bone	PETROSAL
tendon sheaths	SYNOVIAL
tendrils	CAPREOLATE
terminate variations	ORTHOGENETIC
testing minerals by flame	PYROGNOSTIC
thigh (bone)	FEMORAL
thin plate	LAMELLAR, LAMELLATE
	LAMELLIFORM, LAMELLOID
	LAMELLOSE, LAMINAR(Y)
things	
—not spiritual	SECULAR
—similar in form	HOM(O)EOMORPHIC
thorn	SPINIFORM
thought	DIANOETIC
thread	FILOSE
three	TERNAL
—parties	TRIPARTITE
—vowel sounds	TRIPHTHONGAL
throat	GUTTURAL
thrushes	TURDINE
thunder and lightning	FULMIN(E)OUS
tides controlled by moon	LUNITIDAL
tigers	TIGERY, TIGRINE, TIGROID
tin	STANNOUS

tissues	HIST(I)OID
—round teeth	PERIODONTAL
title	TITULAR
toads	BATRACHIAN, SALIENTIAN
tobacco	NICOTINA
tombs	SEPULCHRAL
tone	TONAL, TONEMIC, TONETIC
tongue	GLOTTAL, GLOTTIC, LINGUAL
tonsils	TONSILLAR
top	CACUMINAL
touch	HAPTIC
trachea	TRACHEAL
trade	MERCANTILE
travel(ling)	VIATIC
treatment of	
—disturbed children	ORTHOGENIC
—horse diseases	HIPPIATRIC
trees	ARBOREAL, ARBOREOUS
	DENDRITIC(AL)
	DENDRIFORM, DENDROID(AL)
Troy	ILIAC, ILIAN
trunk	TRUNCAL
trust	FIDUCIARY
tubers	TUBERACEOUS
tumours of teeth	ODONTOMATOUS
turf	C(A)ESPITOSE
twelve	DUODENARY
twenty	ICOSIAN
twigs	SARMENTACEOUS
twilight	CREPUSCULAR
	CREPUSCULOUS
two supreme gods	DITHEISTIC(AL)
tympanum	TYMPANIC, TYMPANAL
typhoid	TYPHOIDAL
typhus	TYPHOID, TYPHOUS
ulcer	HELCOID
unborn baby	F(O)ETAL
uncle	AVUNCULAR
underground water	
supplies	PHREATIC
underside of tongue	RANINE
underworld	CHTHONIAN, CHTHONIC
	HADEAN
undifferentiated	
plant body	THALLINE, THALLOID
upper	
—alimentary tract	STOMATOGASTRIC
—stomach	CARDIAC(AL)
urine	URETIC, URINARY, URINOUS
use in a country	ENCHORIAL
valve	VALVAL, VALVAR, VALVATE
varied learning	POLYHISTORIC
	POLYMATHIC
veal	VITULINE
vegetable matter	VEGANIC
vegetables	OLITORY

veins	VENOUS
verbs	RHEMATIC
verdigris	AERUGINOUS
vertigo	DINIC
vervain	VERBENACEOUS
very young	F(O)ETAL
vessels	VASCULAR
views	VISTAL
vintage	VINDEMIAL
viscera	SPLANCHNIC
visibility of objects	
within the eye	ENTOPTIC
vision	OCULAR
vital urge	LIBIDINAL
voice	PHONAL, PHONIC
—training	VOCICULTURAL
volcanoes	VOLCANIC, VULCANIC
	VULCANIAN
vultures	VULTURINE, VULTURISH
	VULTUROUS
wading birds	GRALLATORIAL
walking	PEDESTRIAN
walls	MURAL, MURIFORM, PARIETAL
walruses	ODOBENID, PHOCINE
war	MARTIAL
—dance	PYRRHIC
warfare	MILITARY
wart	VERRUCIFORM
washing	LAVATORIAL
water	
—cysts	HYDATIFORM
—ferns	SALVINIACEOUS
—rails	RALLINE
waves/waving	UNDULATORY
wax modelling	CEROPLASTIC
weasels	MUSTELINE
weddings	MATRIMONIAL, NUPTIAL
week	HEBDOMADAL
west wind	FAVONIAN
whales	CETACEAN
wheat	TRITICEOUS
wheel	TROCHAL, TROCHOID
whetstone	COTICULAR
whirlpool	VORAGINOUS
whirlwinds	TYPHONIC
whole world	MONDIAL
wife	UXORIAL
wild beasts	FERINE
wills	TESTAMENTAL, TESTAMENTARY
wind	AEOLIAN
wine	VINOUS
wings	ALARY, PENNATE
	PINNATE(D), PTERYGOID
winter	BRUMAL, BRUMOUS
	HIBERNAL, HIEMAL

wolves	LUPINE, THOOID
woman who has more than one child	MULTIPAROUS
	POLYTOKOUS
womb	UTERINE
women	GYNAECOID
wood	LIGNEOUS, NEMORAL
	XYLOID
woodcock	SCOLOPACEOUS
woodlice	ONISCOID
woodpeckers	PICARIAN
woods	SILVAN, SILVATIC
	SILVESTRIAN
wool	LANATE
words	RHEMATIC
worker	ERGATOID
working classes	PROLETARIAN
	PROLETARY
world	MONDIAL
worms	LUMBRICAL, VERMICULAR
wrasse	LABROID
wrist	CARPAL
writers	AUCTORIAL, AUTHORIAL
writing	LITERARY
—desk	ESCRITORIAL
wrong	TORTIOUS
wrongful injury	NOXAL
yesterday	HESTERNAL, PRIDIAN
yokes	JUGAL
yolk of egg	VITELLARY
young	F(O)ETAL
zebras	ZEBRINE, ZEBROID
zeolite	ZEOLITIC, ZEOLITIFORM
zone	ZONOID
Peru	PE
bark	CALISAYA, CINCHONA
bird	YUTA, YUTU
capital	LIMA
civilisation	CHAVIN, INCA
coins	
—unit	CENTIMO
—100 centimos	INTI
—old	LIBRA, SOL
counting device	QUIPO, QUIPU
dance	CUECA
dice game	PERUDO
dried beef	CHARQUI
emperor	INCA
fever	VERRUGA
fruit	CHERIMOYA, CHERIMOYER
	CHIRIMOYA
Indian	QUECHUA, QUICHUA, INCA
king	INCA
knotted cord	QUIPO, QUIPU
language	AYMARA, QUECHIA
	QUECHUA

pepper	MATICO
plant	INDIAN CRESS
shrub	COCA, MATICO, RATANY
skunk	ATOC, ATOK
Pharmaceutical Society	PS
Pharmacopoeia Britannica	PB
Philippines	
aborigines	AT(T)A, ITA, TAGAL
barge/lighter	CASCO
beef dish	STEAK TAGALOG
braised stew	ADOBO
candle-nut tree	LUMBANG
capital	MANILA
coin	PISO
dumpling soup	PANCIT MOLO
fibre (Manila hemp)	ABACA
fish	TANGUINGUE
knife	BOLO
language	AT(T)A, BIKOL, MORO
	TAGAL(OG), TINO
lime (fruit)	CALAMANSI
lizard	IBID, IBIT
measure	APATAN, CHUPA, GANTA
native	FILIPINO
nut	PILI(-NUT)
parrot	ABACAY, CAGIT, CALANGAY
peasant	TAO
plantain	ABACA, MANIL(L)A-HEMP
plum	DUHAT, LANSEH
public service vehicle	JEEPNEY
race	TAGALOG
rice beer	PANGASI
servant	ALILA
silk	HUSI
straw	BAKU
tree	DITA, ILANG-ILANG, KALUMPIT
	LIGAS, MABOLA, YLANG-YLANG
white man	CACHIL
Philological Society	PS
philosophy	
absolute authority of moral law	CATEGORICAL IMPERATIVE
abstract properties	UNIVERSALS
act performed by utterance	ILLOCUTION
actuality	ENTELECHY
all things determined by	
—causes	DETERMINISM
—exercise of choice	FREE-WILL
analysis	REDUCTIONISM
apparently ridiculous but logical statement	(LOGICAL)PARADOX
apriorism	RATIONALISM
argument	THESIS
assertion	
—based on aesthetics	VALUE-JUDGMENT

—of unsupported facts	DOGMATISM
atomic materialism	EPICUREANISM
attribution to	
—abstract things of	
real existence	HYPOSTATISATION
—objects of a soul	ANIMISM
based on first	
principle of	
—beauty	AESTHETICISM
—behaviour	BEHAVIOURISM
—chief good	HEDONISM
—pleasure	HEDONISM
—well-being of man	HUMANISM
basis of morality	
lies in utility	
of actions	UTILITARIANISM
being	ONTOLOGY
belief	
—governed by reason	RATIONALISM
—in	
concept of God	DEISM, THEISM
development of	
—discrete units	ATOMISM
—independent	
phenomena	EVOLUTIONISM
mind and matter	DUALISM
nothing	NIHILISM
ultimate reality beyond	
experience	TRANSCENDENTALISM
unconscious patterns	
of thought	STRUCTURALISM
—regulated by reason	RATIONALISM
—that	
all events are determined	
beforehand	FATALISM
	(PRE)DETERMINISM
	PREDESTINATION
the universe is	
—the	
best possible	OPTIMISM
worst possible	PESSIMISM
the world can be	
improved	MELIORISM
class of terms	CATEGORY
consequentialism	TELEOLOGY
creative evolution	BERGSONISM
denial of	
—absolute values	EXISTENTIALISM
—existence of abstract	
entities	NOMINALISM
—traditional values	NIHILISM
direct experience(s)	SENSE DATUM(DATA)
doctrine of	
—final causes	TELEOLOGY
—personal experiences	PHENOMENOLOGY
—pleasure	APOLAUSTIC

doctrine that	
—abstract entities	
do exist	PLATONISM
—all that exists is material	MATERIALISM
—faith and reason agree	THOMISM
—Gods are men writ large	EUHEMERISM
—highest good is	
happiness from	
—pleasure	HEDONISM
—reason	EUD(A)EMONISM
mankind's interests	HUMANISM
	NATURISM
pleasure	HEDONISM
practical consequences	PRAGMATISM
serving	
—others	ALTRUISM
—self	EGOTISM
the world of the	
spirit	ASCETICISM
—individuals have	
freedom and	
responsibility	EXISTENTIALISM
	PERSONALISM
—knowledge	
comes from direct	
perception	REPRESENTATIONALISM
depends on an	
individual	
viewpoint	PERSPECTIVISM
is relative	POSITIVISM
—mental states exist	SOLIPSISM
independently	MENTALISM
—moral truth is known	
directly	INTUITIONISM
—nothing can be known	
for certain	SCEPTICISM
—only	
matter exists	MATERIALISM
one (kind of) thing	
exists	MONISM
sensations are real	SENSATIONALISM
—phenomena	
are result of	
mechanical causes	MECHANISM
can be explained in	
physical terms	PHYSICALISM
	POSITIVISM
—pleasure is the highest good	HEDONISM
—soul is the vital principle	ANIMISM
—the world is a	
collection of	
experiences	NEUTRAL MONISM
—things perceived have	
a real existence	REALISM
—truth depends on time	
and the observer	RELATIVISM

—vital principle invests all living things	VITALISM
—we	
can know only phenomena	POSITIVISM
cannot know things outside experience	CRITICAL IDEALISM
do not know	AGNOSTICISM
doctrines of	
—Adam Smith	POLITICAL ECONOMY
—Alfred Ayer	LOGICAL POSITIVISM
—Alfred Whitehead	EVOLUTIONISM
—Arthur Schopenhauer	IDEALISM
—Aristippos	HEDONISM
—Aristotle	IDEALISM
—Auguste Comte	POSITIVISM
—Averroes	NEO-PLATONISM
—Benedetto Croce	REALISM
—Benedict de Spinoza	RATIONALISM
—Bertrand Russell	LOGICAL ATOMISM
	SCIENTISM
—Blaise Pascal	CRITICISM
—Boethius	NEO-PLATONISM
—Charles Pierce	PRAGMATISM
—David Hume	EMPIRICISM
—Edmund Husserl	PHENOMENOLOGY
—Emmanuel Mournier	PERSONALISM
—Emanuel Swedenborg	MYSTICISM
	SWEDENBORGIANISM
—Epicurus	ATOMISM, EPICUREANISM
	HEDONISM
—Erasmus	HUMANISM
—Erich Engels	DIALECTICAL MATERIALISM
—Francis Bacon	INDUCTIVE REASONING
—Friedrich Nietszche	EVOLUTIONISM
—Georg Hegel	ABSOLUTISM
—George Moore	IDEAL UTILITARIANISM
	LINGUISTIC PHILOSOPHY
—George Santayana	CRITICAL REALISM
—Georgy Plekhanov	DIALECTICAL MATERIALISM
—G E Stahl	ANIMISM
—Gottfried von Liebnitz	ABSOLUTISM
	IDEALISM, OPTIMISM
—Henri Bergson	EVOLUTIONISM
—Herbert Spencer	EVOLUTIONARY COSMOLOGY
—Immanuel Kant	CRITICAL PHILOSOPHY
—Jean-Paul Sartre	EXISTENTIALISM
—Jeremy Bentham	UTILITARIANISM
—Johann Fichte	ABSOLUTE IDEALISM
—John Dewey	INSTRUMENTALISM
	PRAGMATISM
—John Locke	DUALISM, EMPIRICISM
—John Stuart Mill	PHENOMENALISM
	UTILITARIANISM

—Karl Jaspers	EXISTENTIALISM
—Karl Marx	COMMUNISM
—Karl Popper	CRITICAL RATIONALISM
—Ludwig Wittgenstein	LINGUISTIC PHILOSOPHY
	LOGICAL ATOMISM
—Martin Heidegger	PHENOMENOLOGY
—mediaeval schoolmen	SCHOLASTICISM
—Nicolò Machiavelli	REALISM
—Parmenides	IDEALISM
—Peter Abelard	NOMINALISM
—Peter Ramus	RAMISM
—Plato	IDEALISM
—Plotinus	NEO-PLATONISM
—Protagoras	HUMANISM, RELATIVISM
—Pyrrho	SCEPTICISM
—Pythagoras	DUALISM
—René Descartes	DUALISM
—Roger Bacon	EMPIRICISM
—R W Emerson	TRANSCENDENTALISM
—St Anselm	REALISM
—St Augustine	ABSOLUTISM, OPTIMISM
—St Bonaventure	MYSTICAL ASCETICISM
—St Thomas Aquinas	THOMISM
—Socrates	IDEALISM
—Søren Kierkegaard	EXISTENTIALISM
—Thales	MONISM
—Thomas Hobbes	MATERIALISM
—Thomas More	UTOPIANISM
—Vienna Circle	LOGICAL POSITIVISM
	LOGICAL EMPIRICISM
—William James	PRAGMATISM
—William of Occam	NOMINALISM
—Zeno	EVOLUTIONISM
	PANTHEISM
	STOICISM
enquiry after truth	ZETETIC PHILOSOPHY
example of a concept	PARADIGM CASE
existence	ONTOLOGY
experiences of self	PHENOMENOLOGY
explanation of phenomena	
—by	
natural means	NATURALISM
reason alone	RATIONALISM
—requiring extra-material concept	NEO-VITALISM
—without reference to other things	ABSOLUTISM
fallacious argument	SOPHISTRY
fallacy	IDOLON, IDOLUM
fictitious school	RESISTENTIALISM
fine arts	AESTHETICS
forces of Empedocles	HATE, LOVE
from	
—cause to effect	A PRIORI
—effect to cause	A POSTERIORI

general terms have no reality	NOMINALISM
gradual introduction of Socialism	FABIANISM
hedonism	EPICUREANISM
ideas are not created by human minds alone	CONCEPTUALISM
indifference to pleasure or pain	STOICISM
indivisible constituents of all things	MONADS
inevitability	HISTORICISM
interpretation of philosophical problems in psychological terms	PSYCHOLOGISM
investigation of a priori knowledge	TRANSCENDENTALISM
knowledge	
—can only comprehend phenomena	PHENOMENALISM
—from	
direct perception	REPRESENTATIONALISM
experience	A POSTERIORI
induction	SCIENTISM
reason	A PRIORI
—lies between scepticism and dogmatism	CRITICISM
—of	
man's nature	ANTHROPOSOPHY
phenomena is relative	COMTISM
	(LOGICAL) POSITIVISM
—only	
from	
—experience and induction	EMPIRICISM
	RATIONALISM
—scientific method	SCIENTISM
of	
—phenomena	COMTISM
	(LOGICAL) POSITIVISM
—practical consquences	PRAGMATISM
law	JURISPRUDENCE
life ruled by reason	EUD(A)EMONIA
	EUD(A)EMONY
linguistic classification	CATEGORY
living each moment to the full	EXISTENTIALISM
meaning of	
—expression	CONNOTATION
—term	CONCEPT
mental sphere	NOOSPHERE
morals	ETHICS
necessitarianism	DETERMINISM

non-physical love	PLATONISM
nothingness	
—Heidegger	DAS NICHTS
—Sartre	LE NEANT
objects are really ideas	IDEALISM
only matter exists	MATERIALISM
outcome of opposing arguments	SYNTHESIS
perfect future	MILLENIARISM
phenomena are the only realities	PHENOMENALISM
philosophers	
—Arabic	AVICENNA
	MAIMONIDES
—American	BURKE, BURNHAM, CARNAP

CHOMSKY, CHURCH, DEWEY, EMERSON
FIEGL, JAMES, LEWIS, LOVEJOY
MARCUSE, PIERCE, QUINE, SANTAYANA
SCHUTZ, SCRIVEN, STEVENSON
WATTS, WHITEHEAD

—Australian	SMART
—Austrian	FIEGL, HAYEK, KELSEN

KLAGES, MACH, POPPER, SCHLICK
SCHUTZ, WAISMANN, WITTGENSTEIN

—Chinese	LAO-TSE, LAO-TZE, LAO-TZU
—Cretan	EPIMENIDES
—Danish	KIERKEGAARD
—Dutch	ERASMUS, SPINOZA
—English	ADAMSON, AYER, BACON

BENTHAM, BERLIN, BRADLEY
BUTLER, CHAMBERLAIN, CLIFFORD
COLERIDGE, COLLINGWOOD, GREEN
HARE, HICKS, HOBBES, HOBHOUSE
HULME, LOCKE, MCTAGGART, MILL
MOORE, MORE, OCCAM, OCKHAM
PEARSON, POLANYI, POPPER
RASHDALL, RUSSELL, RYLE
SCRIVEN, SMART, SPENCER
STRAWSON, WAISAMANN
WHITEHEAD

—French	ABELARD, ALTHUSSER

BACHELARD, BENDA, BERGSON
BONALD, BRENTANO, BRUNSCHVIG
COMTE, CONDORCET, DESCARTES
GASSENDI, MARRITAIN, MERLEAU-PONTY
MONTESQUIEU, PASCAL, POINCARE
RENOUVIER, ROUSSEAU, SARTRE
SOREL, TEILHARD DE CHARDIN
VOLTAIRE

—German	CARNAP, CASSIRER, COHEN

DILTHEY, ENGELS, FEVERBACH
FICHTE, FREGE, JASPERS, HEGEL
HEIDEGGER, HERBART, HORKHEIMER
HUSSERL, KANT, KLAGES, KRAFT-EBBING
KRAUSE, LANGE, LIEBNI(T)Z, MARCUSE
MARX, NATORP, NEURATH, NIETSZCHE

	REICHENBACH, RICKERT, SCHELER
	SCHELLING, SCHLEIERMACHER
	SCHOPENHAUER, TIEDEMAN
	TONNIES, TROELTSCH
—Greek	ANAXAGORAS, ANAXIMANDER
	ANAXIMENES, ANTISTHENES
	ARISTIPPOS, ARISTOTLE
	DEMOCRITUS, DIOGENES
EMPEDOCLES, EPICURUS, HERACLIDES
	HERACLITUS, HIPPIAS, LEUCIPPUS
	PARMENIDES, PLATO, PLOTINUS
	PRODICUS, PROTAGORAS, PYRRHO
	PYTHAGORAS, SOCRATES
STAGIRITE, THALES, THEOPHRASTUS
	THRASYMACHUS
	XENOPHANES, ZENO
—Hungarian	LUKACS
—Irish	BERKELEY, BURKE, TOLLAND
—Italian	·ANSELM, BRUNO, CROCE
JOHN OF FIDANZA, MACHIAVELLI
	ST BONAVENTURE
	ST THOMAS AQUINAS, SOFFICI
—Polish	ZAK
—Roman	AUGUSTINE, BOETHIUS
	LUCRETIUS, SENECA
—Russian	IVANOV, LAVROV
	TRUBETSKOY
—Scottish	ADAMSON, HUME, REID, SMITH
—Sicilian	EUHEMERUS
—Spanish	AVERROES
	MAIMONIDES, ORTEGA
	SANTAYANA
—Swedish	SWEDENBORG
Platonism with Oriental	
elements	NEO-PLATONISM
positivism	COMTISM
pragmatism	INSTRUMENTALISM
predestination	FATALISM
proof of truth	VERIFICATION
proposition which is	
—not necessarily true	CONTINGENT
—self-evident	AXIOM
rationalism	APRIORISM
real, not abstract	PARTICULAR
reality	
—has	
more than two	
components	PLURALISM
two components	DUALISM
—is	
beyond normal	
experience	
TRANSCENDENTAL METAPHYSICS
combination of	
—mental	
and physical	DUALISM

physical	
and essences	CRITICAL REALISM
direct contact	
with God	MYSTICISM
material and based on	
strife	DIALECTICAL MATERIALISM
neither physical	
nor spiritual	NEUTRAL MONISM
only appearance	PHENOMENALISM
psychical	IDEALISM
what we	
experience	IMMANENT METAPHYSICS
reasoning from	
—cause to effect	A PRIORISM
—thesis and antithesis	DIALECTIC
rejection of	
—a priori knowledge	EMPIRICISM
—absolute values	RELATIVISM
—conventional mores	ANTINOMIANISM
—existence of spirit	MATERIALISM
—God	ATHEISM
—idealism	REALISM
—objective universal	
values	EXISTENTIALISM
—orthodoxy	TRANSCENDENTALISM
—positivism	PHENOMENOLOGY
—realism	IDEALISM
—reality	NIHILISM
—supernatural	HUMANISM, MATERIALISM
	RATIONALISM
relationship of	
—bodily and mental	
events	EPIPHENOMENALISM
—cause and effect	CAUSALITY, CAUSATION
scepticism	PYRRHONISM
search for the best	IDEALISM
self	
—evident statement	AXIOM
—is the only certainty	SOLIPSISM
—origination	ASEITY
statements about good	
or evil merely prescribe	
moral attitudes	PRESCRIPTIVISM
study of	
—analysis and reason	LOGIC
—assessment of	
pleasure or pain	FELICIFIC CALCULUS
—conduct and morals	ETHICS
—duty	DEONTOLOGY
—ends	TELEOLOGY
—ethics	DEONTOLOGY
—feelings and sensations	AESTHETICS
—first principles	METAPHYSICS
	ONTOLOGY
—nature	
and reality	METAPHYSICS

of knowledge — EPISTEMOLOGY
—pure being — METAPHYSICS, ONTOLOGY
—purposes — TELEOLOGY
—reality — AXIOLOGY
—relationship of words
   to objects — SEMANTICS
—things — ONTOLOGY
—unconscious patterns
   of thought etc — STRUCTURALISM
—values — AXIOLOGY
system of logic — RAMISM
teleology — CONSEQUENTIALISM
terms have
—a corresponding reality — REALISM
—no corresponding reality — NOMINALISM
theory
—of
   all existence as
    an organism — ORGANICISM
   knowledge — EPISTEMOLOGY
—that essences exist — ESSENTIALISM
thing
—in itself — DING-AN-SICH, NOUMENON
—referred to in
   experience — DENOTATION
thought as
—basis of reality — IDEALISM
—instrument — INSTRUMENTALISM
truth
—from practical
   consequences — PRACTICALISM
      PRAGMATISM
—is
   found in consideration
    of ends — TELEOLOGY
   known by intuition — INTUITIONISM
   not absolute — RELATIVISM
underlying principles — METAPHYSICS
unit of discourse
—combined — PROPOSITION
—smallest — CONCEPT
unknowableness — ACATALEPSY
value-judgements are
—expressions of emotion — EMOTIVISM
—only personal — SUBJECTIVISM
wholes are greater
   than the sum of
   the parts — HOLISM, ORGANICISM
will is the determining
   factor — VOLUNTARISM
        (*see also* **belief**)

**Philosophy, Politics
 and Economics** — PPE
phobias — (*see* **fear**)
photography
 3-D camera — NIMSLO, STEREOSCOPE

abstract photograph with
   kaleidoscope — VORTOGRAPH
accessory holder — HOT SHOE
adjustable part of shutter — DIAPHRAGM
amount of light falling
   on film — EXPOSURE
aperture size — F NUMBER
      STOP (NUMBER)
automatic exposure system
—aperture
   automatic,
    speed manual — SHUTTER PRIORITY
   manual,
    speed automatic — APERTURE PRIORITY
auto-winder delay — INTERVALOMETER
back-lighting — CONTRE-JOUR
bar-code on film cassette — DX CODE
border effect — EBERHARD EFFECT
borders of image — FRAME
camera
—makes — ALPHA ROTO, ASAHI
   (BOX) BROWNIE, BRONICA
   CALUMET, CANON, CHINON
   CONTAX, CROWN GRAPHIC, DEARDORFF
   ERMANOX, FUJI, HANIMEX, HASSELBLAD
   HORSEMAN, HULCHER, JOS-PE,
   KI-MONOBAR, KODAK, KONICA, LEICA
   LEITZ, LINHOF, LUBITEL
   MAMIYA, MAREY, MARIONS, MINOLTA
   MINOX, NIKON, NIMSLO, OLYMPUS
   OMEGA, PENTAX, POLAROID
   PRAKTICA, PRAKTINA, RICOH
   ROBOT, ROLLEI(FLEX)
   SINAR, SOHO, SPEED GRAPHIC
   THORNTON-PICKARD
—types — 3D, BASEBOARD, BRIDGE, BOX
   CHRONOGRAPHIC, CINE,
   COMPACT, DETECTIVE, DISC
   DOLLY, FIELD, FLAT-BED
   HALF-FRAME, HALF-PLATE
   INSTAMATIC, MIRROR
   MONORAIL, NODARK, ONE-SHOT
   PANORAMIC, PERIPHERY, PINHOLE
   PLATE, POLAROID (LAND)
   QUARTER-PLATE, REFLEX
   SINGLE-LENS REFLEX, SLR
   STAND, STEREOSCOPIC, STUDIO
   (SUB-)MINIATURE, SWING, TECHNICAL
   TELEVISION, THREE DIMENSIONAL
   TLR, TWIN-LENS REFLEX
   TV, VIDEO, VIEW
colour classification — MUNSELL SYSTEM
      OSTWALD SYSTEM
—temperature scale — KELVIN, MIRED
coloured fringe
   round image — CHROMATIC ABERRATION

combination of photographs of different colours	CHROMOGRAM
composite photograph	MONTAGE, MOSAIC
defect in	
—flash photograph where subject looks at camera	RED-EYE
—lens	ASTIGMATISM CHROMATIC ABERRATION
delayed exposure	B, BULB, T, TIME, Z, ZEIT
deliberate under-exposure by using high film-speed number	PUSHING FILM
destruction of image by infra-red rays	HERSCHEL EFFECT
developing chemicals	
—groups	ACCELERATOR, ANTIOXIDANT BLIX, FIXER, MORDANT NEUTRALISER (PRE-)HARDENER, REDUCER RESTRAINER, STABILISER, TONER
—types	ACETIC ACID, ACETONE, ALUM AMIDOL, AMMONIA AMMONIUM CHLORIDE BICHROMATE, BORAX, CAUSTIC POTASH CHLORHYDROQUINONE, CHLORQUINOL CHROME ALUM, COPPER CHLORIDE COPPER SULPHATE, ELON FARMER'S REDUCER, FERRIC CHLORIDE HYDROCHLORIC ACID HYDROGEN PEROXIDE HYDROQUINONE, HYPO, IODINE LEAD ACETATE, MERCURIC CHLORIDE METOL, METOQUINONE, OXALIC ACID PHENIDONE, PINCRYPTOL POTASSIUM BROMIDE/CHLORIDE/CITRATE POTASSIUM DICHROMATE/FERROCYANIDE POTASSIUM HYDROXIDE/METABISULPHITE POTASSIUM PERMANGANATE/ THIOCYANATE POTASSIUM SULPHIDE, QUINOL QUININE, RODINAL SAL AMMONIAC, SILVER NITRATE SODIUM BICHROMATE/BISULPHITE SODIUM CARBONATE/CHLORIDE SODIUM HYPOSULPHITE/HYDROXIDE SODIUM METABISULPHITE/SULPHIDE SODIUM SULPHITE/THIOCYANATE SODIUM THIOSULPHATE SULPHURIC ACID, URANIUM NITRATE
developing, printing, etc	PROCESSING
device for	
—controlling exposure time	SHUTTER
—correcting chromatic aberration	TEINOSCOPE

—firing flash-gun	HOT-SHOE MICROPHOTOMETER
—increasing magnification	EXTENSION TUBE
—measuring light	EXPOSURE METER LIGHT METER
time-lapse photography	INTERVALOMETER
variations in reflectivity	DENSITOMETER
—transporting film automatically	AUTOWINDER MOTOR-DRIVE
—viewing negatives	VERTOSCOPE
discs of light	CIRCLES OF CONFUSION
distance from lens to focal point	FOCAL LENGTH
distortion caused by lens	SPHERICAL ABERRATION
existing light, natural or artificial	AVAILABLE LIGHT
exposure	
—calculator	ACTINOMETER
—value	EV, T STOP
extending development time to compensate for under-exposure	PUSH-PROCESSING
feature which adjusts amount of light admitted	AUTOMATIC EXPOSURE
film	
—container	CASSETTE
—for	
colour	
—prints	COLOUR NEGATIVE FILM
—slides	COLOUR REVERSAL FILM
sunlight or flash	DAYLIGHT FILM
—giving correct colour rendering	ISOCHROMATIC ORTHOCHROMATIC
—on iron plate	FERROTYPE
—sensitive to all colours	PANCHROMATIC
—sensitivity	SPEED
—speed scale	ANSI, ASA, BSI GOST, ISO, SCHEINER
filters	
—absorbing blue cast	SKYLIGHT
infra-red	HEAT FILTER
reflections	POLARISING, POLA-SCREEN
—colour conversion	CC
printing	CP
rendition	CORRECTION FILTER

—coloured sheet	GELATIN
—colourless	HAZE, ULTRA-VIOLET, UV
—grey	NEUTRAL DENSITY
—metallic-coated	DICHROIC
—monochrome	PANCHROMATIC VISION
—partly-coloured	GRADUATED
—primary colours	TRI-COLOUR
flash gun	
—control	THYRISTOR
—photography	SPARK PHOTOGRAPHY
—with daylight	SYNCHRO-SUN(LIGHT)
flexible lead to	
shutter	CABLE RELEASE
granular texture in	
photograph	GRAIN
hole in shutter	APERTURE, STOP
image	
—composed of many	
identical elements	MANDALA
—produced without	
a camera	PHOTOGRAM, RAYOGRAPH
	SCHADOGRAPH
intensification of	
latent image	LATENSIFICATION
interference rings	NEWTON'S RINGS
intrusive	
photographer(s)	PAPARAZZO(PAPARAZZI)
lamp attachment	BARN DOORS, DIFFUSER
	EVENLITE, HONEYCOMB
	KEYLITE, SLATS, SNOOT
	SOFTLITE,
lens	
—attachment	AFOCAL LENS, AUXILIARY
	EXTENSION TUBE
	LENS HOOD, LENS SHIELD
	MACRO, SUPPLEMENTARY
—distortion	ABERRATION
asymmetrical	COMA
causing	
curvature	PINCUSHION DISTORTION
due to	
—colour	CHROMATIC ABERRATION
—lens	BARREL DISTORTION
	SPHERICAL ABERRATION
of points	ASTIGMATISM
—treatment to	
cut out reflections	BLOOMING
	COATING
offset diffraction	APODISATION
—types	
1 element	SIMPLE
2 elements	DOUBLET
2 doublets	RAPID RECTILINEAR
2+ elements	COMPOUND
3 elements	TRIPLET
180°	FISHEYE, HILL CLOUD LENS

close-up	MACRO, SUPPLEMENTARY
compressing in one	
direction	ANAMORPHIC
concave/convex	MENISCUS
condenser with	
concentric rings	FRESNEL
continuously variable	ZOOM
converging	CONVEX, POSITIVE
diverging	CONVEX, NEGATIVE
double curvature	BI-SPHERICAL
highly corrected	PROCESS
increasing focal	
length	TELECONVERTER
	TELE-EXTENDER
long focal length	LONG TOM
	TELEPHOTO
moveable	SHIFT AND TILT
non-spherical	ASPHERICAL
non-symmetrical triplet	TESSAR
normal focal length	STANDARD
producing diffused	
image	SOFT FOCUS
protector	GOBO, LENS CAP
short focal	
length	INVERTED TELEPHOTO
	WIDE ANGLE
small aperture	SLOW
telephoto in short barrel	MIRROR
variable focus	ZOOM
wide	
—angle, curved field	PETZVAL
—wide aperture	FAST
with mirrors and lens	CATADIOPTRIC
without	
—astigmatism	ANASTIGMAT(IC)
—chromatic aberration	ACHROMATIC
—chromatic or spherical	
aberration	APOCHROMATIC
—spherical aberration	APLANAT(IC)
light	
—falling directly	
on subject	INCIDENT LIGHT
—line round dark area	MACKIE EFFECT
—outlining subject	
against a dark	
background	RIM LIGHTING
light-meter built	
into camera	THROUGH-THE-LENS METER
	TTL METER
light-sensitive	
layer of film	EMULSION
measure of	
—colour temperature	KELVIN, MIRED
—image sharpness	ACUTANCE
—light source	FLASH FACTOR
	GUIDE NUMBER

—refractive power	ABBE NUMBER
movement of parts of image in development	KOTINSKY EFFECT
opacity of negative	PHOTOGRAPHIC DENSITY
opening in front of lens	APERTURE
panoramic camera	PANTOSCOPE
paper	ALBUMEN, BROMIDE, CHLORIDE CHLOROBROMIDE, CHROMATYPE CONTACT, MULTI-GRADE PHOTOLINEN, PLATINUM, POP, RC RESIN-COATED, SELF-TONING
part positive, part negative effect	SABATTIER EFFECT
photograph	
—in natural colours	HELIOCHROME
—of manuscript	ROTOGRAPH
—produced without a camera	PHOTOGRAM PICTOGRAM RAYOGRAM
photographers	
—American	ARBUS, ANSEL ADAMS ARNOLD(f), AVEDON, FEININGER KLEIN, MAN RAY MAPPLETHORPE, PENN SHEELER, WINDGRAND
—Brazilian	SALGADO
—British	BAILEY, BEATON BOWN, BRANDT, CAMERON, FRESON HASKINS, IVES, LICHFIELD MCCULLIN, PARKINSON, RODGER SNOWDON
—Canadian	KARSH
—French	CARTIER-BRESSON DOISNEAU, LARTIGUE
—German	JACOBI(f), SCHAD
—Hungarian	CAPA
—intrusive (Italian)	PAPARAZZO
—Polish	SEYMOUR, SZYMIN
photography	
—by	
infra-red rays	THERMOGRAPHY
split laser beam	HOLOGRAPHY
X-rays	RADIOGRAPHY TOMOGRAPHY
—of	
cyclic movement	CHRONOCYCLOGRAPHY
moving objects	CHRONOPHOTOGRAPHY
small, inaccessible areas	ENDOSCOPY
—producing	
extreme close-ups	MACROPHOTOGRAPHY
larger-than-life images	PHOTOMICROGRAPHY
very small images	MICROPHOTOGRAPHY

—recording differences in refractive index	SCHLIEREN PHOTOGRAPHY
—three-dimensional	ANAGLYPH SYSTEM (FRAME SEQUENTIAL) STEREOSCOPY NIMSLO SYSTEM, NUOPTIC TACHISTOSCOPY, XOGRAPHY
pioneers	BARNACK, BAYARD BOLTON, BRADY, BREWSTER CAMERON, CAPA, CROS DAGUERRE, DAVY, DRIFFIELD DU HAURON, EASTMAN, ENGLAND FARMER, FENTON, FISHER FOX-TALBOT, GABOR, HERSCHEL HURTER, JOLY, KENNETT LANCHESTER, LAND, LIPPMAN LUMIERE, MADDOX, MAREY MAXWELL, MUYBRIDGE, NIEPCE READE, RUSSELL, SANGER, SAYCE STURM, VOGEL, WAINWRIGHT WEDGWOOD, WRATTEN, ZAHN, ZEISS
process	AGFACOLOUR, AMBROTYPE AMPHITYPE, ARISTOTYPE ARGENTOTYPE, AUTOCHROME BLUE PRINT, BROMETCHING BROMOIL, BROTYPE, CALOTYPE CARBRO, CIBACHROME CLICHE-VERRE, COLLAGE CYANOTYPE, DAGUERROTYPE DRY PLATE, DUFAY, EKTACHROME ELECTROPHOTOGRAPHY FERROTYPE, FINLAY, FUJI GALVANOGRAPHY, GELATIN SUGAR GUM BICHROMATE, GUM PLATINOTYPE HELIOTYPE, IVORYTYPE, JOLY JOS-PE, KALLITYPE, KODACHROME LIPPMAN, MONTAGE, OPALOTYPE OZOBROME, PAGET, PARAPHOTOGRAPHY PHOSPHOROPHOTOGRAPHY PHOTO-ENGRAVING, PHOTO-ETCHING PHOTOGRAVURE, PHOTOLITHOGRAPHY PHOTO SILK-SCREENING PLATINOTYPE, POSTERISATION SILK PRINT, SILK SCREEN SOLARISATION, STANNOTYPE TRICHROME CARBRO VIGNETTING, (WET) COLLODION WET PLATE, WOODBURYTYPE XEROGRAPHY
positive image viewed by transmitted light	DIAPOSITIVE, SLIDE TRANSPARENCY
rapid flash	STROBE STROBOSCOPIC FLASH
reflected light from flash-gun	BOUNCE FLASH

retouching	AIR BRUSHING, SPOTTING
reversal of tones	SOLARISATION
reversed image	ALBERT EFFECT
scattering of light in condenser	CALLIER EFFECT
shape and size of negative	FORMAT
shutter types	BETWEEN-THE-LENS, BTL
	CAPPING, COMPUR
	DIAPHRAGM, ELECTRONIC
	EVERSET, FARRADAY
	FOCAL PLANE
	KERR CELL, LEAF, SLIT
swing camera to follow subject	PAN
transparency	DIAPOSITIVE, SLIDE
unsharp image	BLUR
unwanted light on film	FLARE
wide-angle lens	PANTOSCOPE
zone of sharpness	DEPTH OF FIELD

physician

including: anatomist physiologist surgeon	
American	AXELROD, BAILEY, BALTIMORE
	BEADLE, BEAUMONT, BEIDLER
	BEKESY, BENACERRAF
	BEST, BLOCH, BLUMBERG
	BROWN, CANNON, CASTLE
	COOLEY, CROHN, CUSHING
	DE BAKEY, DELBRUCK
	DELGADO, DEMENT, EDELMAN
	ENDERS, ERLANGER, FRIDERICIA
	GAJDUSEK, GASSER, GOLDBERGER
	GOLDSTEIN, GOODPASTURE
	GOURNAND, GUILLEMIN, HALSTEAD
	HARARY, HARTZINE, HENCH, HERRICK
	HERSHEY, HOLLEY, HOLM, HOLMES
	HUBEL, HUGGINS, JARVIK, JENSEN
	KENDAL, KHORANA, KOLLER
	KORNBERG, LANDSTEINER
	LINDSLEY, LIPMANN
	LURIA, MARINE, MCCLINTOCK
	MINOT, MURPHY, NATHANS
	NIRENBERG, OCHOA, OLDS
	PAPANICOLAOU, PENFIELD
	REED, RICHARDS, ROBBINS
	ROUS, SABIN, SALK, SCHALLY
	SHUMWAY, SIMS, SMITH, SNELL
	SPERRY, STEINER, SUTHERLAND
	TAUSSIG(f), TEMIN, THEILER
	WAKSMAN, WALD, WATSON
	WEDERBERG, WELLER, WHIPPLE
	WIESEL, YALON
Argentinian	MILSTEIN
Australian	BURNET, ECCLES, SMITH
Austrian	ADLER, BREUER, GALL
	LANDSTEINER, LOEWI, LORENZ
	MESMER, SEMMELWEISS
	VON FRISCH
Belgian	DE DUVE, VESALIUS
British	ADDISON, ADRIAN, ANDERSON(f)
	ASHBY, BAYLISS, BELL
	BOWMAN, BRAID, BRIGHT, BUIST
	CHRISTISON, CORMACK, CRICK
	DALE, DART, DOWN, FINDLAY
	GARROD, GILBERT, HALDANE
	HALES, HALL, HARVEY
	HENSON, HILL, HODGKIN
	HOUNSFIELD, HUNTER, HUXLEY
	JACOUB, JENNER, JERNE, KATZ
	KEITH, KREBS, LIND, LISTER
	LISTON, MACINDOE, MCLEOD
	MEDAWAR, MILSTEIN
	MANSON, PAGET, PITT
	PORTER, POTTS, PROUT, RINGER
	ROSS, SHARPET-SCHAFER
	SHERRINGTON, SIMPSON, SMITH
	SNOW, STARLING, STENHOUSE
	STEVENS, SYDENHAM, TINBERGEN
	VANE, WALTER, WILKINS
	WILLIS
Canadian	BANTING, BEST
	HUGGINS, OSLER
Czech	PURKINJE
Danish	BANG, ELLERMAN
	FINSEN, GRAM, JERNE, WORM
Dutch	DE GRAAF, EIJKMAN
	EINTHOVEN, INGEN-HOUSZ
	ONNES, PEKELHARIN
	SWAMMERDAM
French	BABINSKI, BERNARD, BERT
	BICHAT, BORREL, BROCA
	CARREL, CHARGOT, CHRETIEN
	DAUSSET, DAVAINE, D'AZYR
	DUBOIS, DUCHENNE, DUPUYTREN
	DUTROCHET, FERNEL, FLOURENS
	GAUTIER, JACOB, LAENNAC
	LEJEUNE, LWOFF
	MAGENDIE, MONOD, OUDIN
	PARE, RICHET, TURPIN
German	BEHRING, BILLROTH
	DU BOIS-REYMOND
	EHRLICH, FORSSMANN, FRI(T)SCH
	HERING, HITZIG, KLEBS, KOCH
	KOHLER, KUHNE
	LANGERHANS, LOEWI, LORENZ
	LINEN, MINKOWSKI, MULLER
	SCHNEIDER, SCHULZE, SCHWANN
	SPEMANN, THAL, VIRCHOW, VON BAER
	VON MERING, VON WALDEYER
	WESTPHAL, WOLFF, WUNDT, ZINN

German/Swiss	PARACELSUS
	VON HOHENHEIM
Greek	ALCMAEON, ERASISTRATUS
	GALEN, HEROPHILUS
	HIPPOCRATES, PAPANICOLAOU
	PRAXAGORAS
Homeric	P(A)EAN
Hungarian	BEKESY
Irish	BENNETT, GRAVES
Italian	BOVET, CORTI, DE LUZZI, DULBECCO
	FABRICIUS, FABRIZZI
	FALLOPIO, FRASCATORO
	LEVI-MONTALCINI, MALPIGHI
	MONTESSOIR(f), REDI
Japanese	TONEGAWA
Mexican	CLAUDE, ROSENBLEUTH
of the Gods	P(A)EAN
Polish	LISTER
Portuguese	MONIZ
Roman	CELSUS, GALEN
Romanian	PALADE
Russian	PAVLOV
South African	BARNARD
Spanish	DELGADO, RAMON Y CAJAL
Swedish	BERGSTROM, HYDEN, RETZIUS
	EULER, GRANIT
	SAMUELSSON, THEGRELL
Swiss	ARBER, ERASTUS, HESS, KOCHER
	REICHSTEIN, RORSCHACH
	VON HALLER
	(*see also* **surgery**)

physics

ability	
—of lens system to	
separate small objects	RESOLVING POWER
—to transmit heat	DIATHERMANCY
absolute Fahrenheit	
scale	RANKINE SCALE
absorption	
—and re-emission of light	
using different	
wavelengths	FLUORESCENCE
—lines in Sun's	
spectrum	FRAUNHOFER LINES
—of neutron	PARASITE CAPTURE
accumulator	SECONDARY CELL
acting without gaining	
or losing heat	ADIABATIC
actinides (elements)	ACTINONS
	LANTHANIDES
action of forces	MECHANICS
—on body	
at rest	STATICS
in motion	DYNAMICS
addition of impurity	
to semiconductor	DOPING

aerial with two rods	DIPOLE
alternate speeding and	
slowing of electron	
stream	VELOCITY MODULATION
alternative form	
of element	ALLOTROPE
amount of	
—light	
emitted per	
second	LUMINOUS INTENSITY
passing through an area	
in one second	LUMINOUS FLUX
—material needed to start nuclear	
chain-reaction	CRITICAL MASS
analysis of mixtures by	
electrical conductivity	
of gases	GAS CHROMATOGRAPHY
angle	
—between	
Earth's magnetic field	
and horizontal	INCLINATION
	MAGNETIC DIP
geographical and magnetic	
north	MAGNETIC DECLINATION
	MAGNETIC VARIATION
vectors of	
quantities having the	
same frequency	PHASE ANGLE
—from geographical	
meridian	LONGITUDE
—subtended by radius of	
Earth at one astronomical	
unit	SOLAR PARALLAX
angular distance from	
Equator	LATITUDE
apparent	
—change in frequency	
due to motion	DOPPLER EFFECT
	DOPPLER SHIFT
—loss of weight of	
body in liquid	ARCHIMEDES PRINCIPLE
—movement of object	
resulting from movement	
of observer	PARALLAX
area	
—of high mass on Moon	MASCON
—within which a body	
exercises force	FIELD
arrangement of elements	
by atomic weight	PERIODIC TABLE
assembly used to study	
moderators in nuclear	
reactions	SIGMA PILE
atomic	
—energy	NUCLEAR ENERGY
—nucleus of isotope	NUCL(E)IDE

—number	PROTON NUMBER, Z
—pile	NUCLEAR REACTOR
—weight of	
element in grams	GRAM-ATOM
isotope	ISOPIC WEIGHT
	MASS NUMBER
atoms	
—of same element but	
different mass numbers	ISOTOPE
—with same number of	
neutrons but different	
atomic weights	ISOTONES
attraction	
—between	
bodies	GRAVITY
protons and neutrons in	
nucleus	NUCLEAR FORCE
—or repulsion due	
to magnetism	MAGNETIC FORCE
average	
—distance travelled by	
particle between	
collisions	MEAN FREE PATH
—time between two	
collisions of	
particle	MEAN FREE TIME
battery	(*see* cell *below*)
beat produced by	
superimposed waves	HETERODYNE
becoming liquid	DELIQUESCENT
bent tube which	
transfers liquids	
from high to low level	SIPHON
Big Bang theory	SUPERDENSE THEORY
blocking of light from	
one body by another	OCCULTATION
bluish light radiated	
by particles at	
high speed	C(H)ERENKOV RADIATION
body absorbing all	
radiation	BLACK BODY
brake radiation	BREMSSTRAHLUNG
break-up of nucleus	
into three parts	TERNARY FISSION
breakdown of	
—radioactive material	DECAY
—water molecules	
by uv radiation	PHOTO-DISSOCIATION
cable carrying signals	
as light	OPTICAL FIBRE
cadmium cell	WESTON CELL
cataphoresis	ELECTROPHORESIS
cathode ray tube with	
—four screens	CHROMATRON
	CHROMOSCOPE
—three electron guns	COLOURTRON

cell	
—producing energy	
from sunlight	SOLAR BATTERY
	SOLAR CELL
—secondary	GRAVITY CELL
(NICKEL-IRON) ACCUMULATOR	
—using photoconductive	
or photovoltaic	
effect	SELENIUM CELL
centre	
—line of lens	OPTICAL AXIS
—of	
atom	NUCLEUS
mass	BARYCENTRE
chamber with thermostatic	
control	INCUBATOR
change	
—in	
direction of light	
—bouncing off surface	REFLECTION
—passing through	
medium	REFRACTION
frequency of light passing	
through transparent	
medium	RAMAN EFFECT
optical rotation	MUTAROTATION
shape due to applied	
force	STRAIN
size due to	
magnetisation	MAGNETOSTRICTION
volume	DILAT(AT)ION
—from liquid to solid	FUSION
charge-to-mass ratio	
of a particle	SPECIFIC CHARGE
charged central part	
of atom	(ATOMIC) NUCLEUS
circle of plane through	
centre of sphere	GREAT CIRCLE
circuit	
—in	
single chip	
or package	INTEGRATED CIRCUIT
which there are	
several voltages	PHASE
—with several inputs	
and one output	GATE
circular laboratory dish	PETRI DISH
classification of	
particles by	
properties	UNITARY SYMMETRY
coagulation of fine	
particles into	
larger	FLOCCULATION
coherent beam of light	
of single wavelength	LASER
coil of electromagnet	FIELD COIL

cold flame	CHEMOLUMINESCENCE
combination of heavy atomic nuclei from lighter, releasing energy	NUCLEAR FUSION
communication by electro-magnetic radiation without wires	RADIO
composite photograph of particle track	MOSAIC
compressing metal particles into solid	SINTERING
concavo-convex lens	MENISCUS(LENS)
concentration of magnetic flux	FLUXOID
concept	
—of work done by magnetic force	MAGNETIC POTENTIAL
—that any situation should be reversible in time	TIME REFLECTION SYMMETRY
conductivity caused by	
—electrons	N-TYPE CONDUCTIVITY
—holes	P-TYPE CONDUCTIVITY
conductor	
—for microwaves	WAVE GUIDE
—where resistance varies inversely with temperature	SEMI-CONDUCTOR
constant	
—factor in conversion	MODULUS
—of proportionality of acceleration	MASS
—in gas equation $R=1,9858$ cal/°C/mole	GAS CONSTANT, R
—relating frequency to energy	PLANCK'S CONSTANT
to spectra similar to hydrogen	RYDBERG CONSTANT
constriction of	
—liquid conductor by large current	PINCH EFFECT
—plasma by strong magnetic field	PINCH EFFECT
containing bivalent iron	FERROUS
control of particles by magnetic field	PINCH EFFECT
controlled heating and cooling	ANNEALING
converse of particle with opposite charge	ANTI-PARTICLE
conversion of	
—alternating to direct current	RECTIFICATION
—kinetic energy to radiation	BRAKE RADIATION BREMSTRAHLUNG

—light to radiant heat	CALORESCENCE
—liquid to vapour	EVAPORATION
—metals to oxides by heat	CALCINATION
—vapour to liquid	CONDENSATION
cooling below freezing-point without freezing	SUPERCOOLING
cross-magnetism	DIAMAGNETISM
curved	
—path of particle	BRACHISTOCHRONE
—liquid surface	MENISCUS
cycles per unit of time	FREQUENCY
damping device	DASH-POT
dark lines in spectrum	ABSORPTION SPECTRUM FRAUNHOFER'S LINES
defect	
—caused by removal of atom from its normal lattice position	FRENKEL DEFECT
—of lens	ASTIGMATISM
deflection by fine particles	SCATTERING
delay between cause and effect	HYSTERESIS
demagnetisation	DEGAUSSING
descent in gravitational field	FREE-FALL
description of process of electrolysis	IONIC HYPOTHESIS
deuterium	HEAVY WATER
—oxide	HEAVY WATER
device	
—amplifying microwaves	MASER
—causing light beam to converge or diverge	LENS
—controlling large current by smaller	TRANSISTOR
—converging light rays	CONVEX LENS OPTICAL CONDENSER
—converting alternating to direct current	RECTIFIER
direct to alternating current	TRANSFORMER
electrical energy to mechanical	ELECTRIC MOTOR SOLENOID
mechanical work to electricity	DYNAMOGENERATOR
—correcting chromatic aberration	TEINOSCOPE
—detecting and measuring light	PHOTOCELL PHOTO-ELECTRIC CELL
radiation	GEIGER COUNTER

—extracting heat from
a fluid — HEAT PUMP
—firing electrons in
cathode ray tube — ELECTRON GUN
—in which
electrons flow from
heated cathode
to anode — THERMIONIC TUBE
THERMIONIC VALVE
heat measurements
can be made — CALORIMETER
—increasing signal
strength — AMPLIFIER
—measuring
radiation — IONISATION CHAMBER
—polarising light — NICOL PRISM
—producing
electricity from
chemical reaction — ACCUMULATOR
BATTERY, FUEL CELL
PRIMARY CELL
VOLTAIC CELL
enlarged image — MICROSCOPE
images on screen from
projected
electrons — CATHODE RAY TUBE, CRT
—selecting parts of
a wave — GATE
—splitting light into its
constituent colours — PRISM
—storing
electric charge — CAPACITOR
optical image electrically — MOSAIC
—transferring
heat from one fluid
to another — HEAT EXCHANGER
power from one system
to another — TRANSDUCER
—transforming one type
of signal to another — TRANSDUCER
—using magnetism to
contain plasma — MAGNETIC BOTTLE
—which
alters frequency
distribution — FILTER
amplifies
—light input to
intense narrow beam — LASER
—radiation by
velocity modulation — KLYSTRON
dewpoint — SATURATION POINT
diamagnetism as a
result of superconductivity — MEISSNER EFFECT
dielectric material with
some electrical
properties — FERROELECTRIC

difference between
—isotopic weight
and mass number — MASS DECREMENT
—mass of nucleus and
total mass of nucleons — MASS DEFECT
—number of neutrons
and protons — ISOTOPIC NUMBER
NEUTRON EXCESS
different elements with
same atomic number — ISOBARE
diffraction when light
source is at
—finite
distance — FRESNEL DIFFRACTION
—infinite
distance — FRAUNHOFER DIFFRACTION
diffusion through membrane — OSMOSIS
dimensional change of
dielectric in
electric field — ELECTROSTRICTION
direction of propagation
of light without double
refraction — OPTIC AXIS
directional aerial used
in TV and radio
astronomy — YAGI AERIAL
disappearing mass — MASS DEFECT
discharge of particles
from metal plate struck
by uv radiation — PHOTOELECTRIC EFFECT
displacement
—of atoms in crystal — DISORDERING
—towards red end
of spectrum — EINSTEIN SHIFT
RED SHIFT
distance between crests
in wave motion — WAVELENGTH
distillation at reduced
pressure — VACUUM DISTILLATION
distortion
—caused by lens — SPHERICAL ABERRATION
—of crystal lattice
by radiation — WIGNER EFFECT
distribution of
—electromagnetic radiation — SPECTRUM
—electrons in
shells — EXCLUSION PRINCIPLE
disturbance at
intersection of
waves of same length — INTERFERENCE
drift due to rotation
of earth — CORIOLIS EFFECT
efficiency of electric
circuit — GAIN
eight electrons in
outer shell of atom — OCTET

Einstein's theory	RELATIVITY
electrically	
—charged particle	ION
—induced distortion of	
lattice	PHONON
electricity	(*see* **electric**)
electrode in transistor	EMITTER
electromagnetic radiation	
(shortest first)	COSMIC RAYS
	GAMMA RAYS, X-RAYS
	ULTRA-VIOLET RAYS
	VISIBLE LIGHT, INFRARED RAYS
	HEAT, RADIO WAVES
—comes in packets	QUANTUM THEORY
electron	
—emission resulting from	
change to lower-energy	
state	AUGER EFFECT
—emitted by	
heated plate	
in valve	THERMIONIC EMISSION
radio-isotope	BETA PARTICLE
—in outer shell	VALENCE ELECTRON
	VALENCY ELECTRON
—revolving round	
atomic nucleus	ORBITAL ELECTRON
	PLANETARY ELECTRON
—shells	K-SHELL to P-SHELL
—stream escaping from	
valency band in	
magnetic field	ZENER CURRENT
electrovalent bond	IONIC BOND
element with some	
properties of both	
metals and non-metals	METALLOID
emanation of actinium	ACTINON
emission	
—by radioactive	
material	ALPHA RAY, BETA RAY
	GAMMA RAY
—of	
electrons caused by	
—electric field	FIELD EMISSION
—incident light	PHOTOEMISSION
flashes from incident	
radiation	SCINTILLATION
gamma rays by	
nuclei	MOSSBAUER EFFECT
light by crystals	
when crushed	TRIBOLUMINESCENCE
nuclear particles	
caused by incident	
particle	SPALLATION
particles from nucleus	DISINTEGRATION
wavelengths longer than	
incident waves	FLUORESCENCE

energy	
—absorbed or emitted	
during a reversible	
process	FREE ENERGY, G
	GIBBS FUNCTION
—as electromagnetic	
radiation	RADIANT ENERGY
—cycle	CARNOT CYCLE
—from	
conversion of mass	ATOMIC ENERGY
	NUCLEAR ENERGY
temperature difference	HEAT
—needed to move nucleon	
from nucleus	BINDING ENERGY
	SEPARATION ENERGY
—of	
motion	KINETIC ENERGY
neutrons expressed as	
temperature	NEUTRON TEMPERATURE
particles due to rotation	SPIN
substance at	
absolute zero	ZERO POINT ENERGY
—possessed by virtue	
of position	POTENTIAL ENERGY
—region round nucleus	NUCLEAR BARRIER
—released in nuclear	
reaction	Q-VALUE
—required to separate	
crystal ions	LATTICE ENERGY
—state of atom	SHELL
—stored in crystal	
after irradiation	WIGNER ENERGY
entrapment of charged	
particles in the	
atmosphere	CHRISTOFILOS EFFECT
equal	
—and opposite forces	COUPLE
—numbers of atoms and	
electrons	ISOSTERISM
—volumes of gas	
contain equal numbers of	
moles	AVOGADRO'S LAW
have equal number	
of particles	AVOGADRO'S PRINCIPLE
equation	
—governing	
distribution of	
molecules in	
gas	
MAXWELL-BOLTZMANN DISTRIBUTION	
flow of liquid	
through tube	POISEUILLE'S EQUATION
particles moving	
in a force	
field	
SCHRODINGER'S WAVE EQUATION	

—of
  physical laws for right-
  and left-hand
  systems   PARITY
  time and speed   KINEMATIC EQUATION
—relating space
  and time

       LORENTZ TRANSFORMATION
excitation in polar
  molecules   POLARON
excited state
  —in semiconductor   EXCITON
  —state of particle   METASTABLE STATE
existence in
  —one form   MONOTROPY
  —several forms   ALLOTROPY
              POLYMORPHISM
experiment to test directional
  speed of light

     MICHELSON-MORLEY EXPERIMENT
expression of strength
  of solution   MOLALITY, MOLARITY
factor
  —defining Earth's
    magnetic field   MAGNETIC ELEMENT
  —which measures
    specific property   COEFFICIENT
false line in spectrum   GHOST
faster than
  —Mach 1   SUPERSONIC
  —Mach 5   HYPERSONIC
figure representing
  —three forces
    acting at a point   TRIANGLE OF FORCES
  —velocities acting
    on a body   TRIANGLE OF VELOCITIES
fixed
  —part of electric
    generator or motor   STATOR
  —time curve   TAUTOCHRONE
flow of
  —electrons across gap   EDISON EFFECT
  —fluid over streamlined
    surface   LAMINAR FLOW
  —solids   CREEP
fluid
  —closest to surface
    below   BOUNDARY LAYER
  —used for cooling   COOLANT
  —which flows without
    friction   SUPERFLUID
force
  —acting
    between
      —atoms and
        molecules   VAN DER WAALS' FORCE

—basic particles   WEAK FORCE
—quarks   COLOUR FORCE
on
  —a surface   PRESSURE
  —all
    charged particles

       ELECTROMAGNETIC FORCE
    matter   GRAVITY
  —within the nucleus   STRONG FORCE
—field round magnet or
  electrical conductor   MAGNETIC FIELD
—including gravity and
  antigravity   SUPERGRAVITY
—of rotation   TORQUE
  towards
    —centre   CENTRIPETAL FORCE
    —rim   CENTRIFUGAL
—per unit area   PRESSURE, STRESS
—producing
  rotation   TORQUE
  same effect as several
  forces acting together   RESULTANT
formation of
  —closed ring of atoms   CHELATION
  —ions   IONISATION
formula
  —connecting pressure,
  volume, quantity and
  temperature
  of gas   GAS EQUATION
  —connecting pressure,
  volume, and temperature
  of gas   VAN DER WAALS' EQUATION
four
  —forces   ELECTROMAGNETIC
       GRAVITY, STRONG (NUCLEAR)
            WEAK (NUCLEAR)
  —states of matter   GAS, LIQUID
           PLASMA, SOLID
freezing   GELATION
frequencies in a group
  of emission spectra   SPECTRAL SERIES
frequency
  —at which light causes
  emission of electrons
  from metal   THRESHOLD FREQUENCY
  —of sound   PITCH
  —response   FIDELITY
gamma rays unaffected
  by nuclear recoil   MOSSBAUER EFFECT
gas
  —below critical temperature   VAPOUR
  —constant divided by
  Avogadro's
  constant   BOLTZMANN'S CONSTANT, K
  —ionised   PLASMA

gases	(*see separate entry*)
grand unified theory	GUT
gravitational attraction	
—determining inertial frames	MACH('S) PRINCIPLE
—of Earth on mass	WEIGHT
great circle through geographical poles	(TERRESTRIAL) MERIDIAN
grouping of spectral lines in magnetic field	ZEEMAN EFFECT
half-shadow	PENUMBRA
handedness	PARITY
hardness test	BRINELL TEST
having	
—all waves in same phase	COHERENT
—equal	
enthalpy	ISENTHALPIC
entropy	ISENTROPIC
osmotic pressure	ISOTONIC
—little or no reverberation	ANECHOIC
—no electric charge	NEUTRAL
—only one stable form	MONOTROPIC
—two axes at right-angles to third axis	MONOCLINIC
heat	
—content per unit	ENTHALPY, H
—required to raise unit mass 1 degree	SPECIFIC HEAT
—taken up or released in change of state	LATENT HEAT
—transference	
across intervening space	RADIATION
by movement of fluid	CONVECTION
through a solid	CONDUCTION
—waves longer than red light	INFRARED RAYS
heating	
—chamber	AUTOCLAVE, FURNACE
—vessel	CRUCIBLE
heavy	
—hydrogen	DEUTERIUM
—water	DEUTERIUM (OXIDE)
helium	
—making	NUCLEOSYNTHESIS
—nucleus	ALPHA PARTICLE
Helmholtz free energy	F, WORK FUNCTION
high-temperature zone where particle passes through a substance	THERMAL SPIKE
highest temperature at which liquid and vapour can exist together	CRITICAL TEMPERATURE

hot ionised gas	PLASMA
hotness of body	TEMPERATURE
hydrogen	
—atom spectrum theory	BOHR THEORY
—manufacturing process	SILICOL PROCESS
hydrolysis by an acid	ACIDOLYSIS
hydroxide of metal	ALKALI
hypothetical	
—force	SUPERGRAVITY
—one-dimensional constituent of matter	(SUPER)STRING
—particle	(*see* **particles**)
—two-dimensional constituent of matter	SUPERMEMBRANE
ignition measurement	CETANE NUMBER
image with coloured fringes	CHROMATIC ABERRATION
imperfection in semiconductor	ACCEPTOR, DONOR
increase in	
—conductivity due to absence of resistance at very low temperature	SUPERCONDUCTIVITY
increased light intensity	PHOTOCONDUCTIVE EFFECT
—energy of particle due to change of state	EXCITATION
—size due to heat	COEFFICIENT OF EXPANSION
—vibration caused by small vibration of same frequency	RESONANCE
indeterminancy principle	UNCERTAINTY PRINCIPLE
induction	
—due to change of current in another circuit	MUTUAL INDUCTION
—of	
magnetism by another magnetic field	MAGNETIC INDUCTION
radioactivity	ACTIVATION
interference	
—effect of lenses	NEWTON'S RINGS
—patterns due to wave motion of light	DIFFRACTION
insulator	DIELECTRIC
interval when ratio of frequencies is two to one	OCTAVE
invisible heat radiation	INFRARED RADIATION, RADIANT HEAT

ion having	
—negative charge	ANION
	HYDROXYL ION
—positive	
and negative	
charges	ZWITTERION
charge	CATION
ionic bond	ELECTROVALENT BOND
ionised layers of	
atmosphere	APPLETON
	HEAVISIDE(-KENNELLY)
ionising radiation	
—of	
high penetrating	
power	HARD RADIATION
low penetrating	
power	SOFT RADIATION
isobaric spin	ISOTOPIC SPIN, T
isotope of element	ISOBAR
isotopic	
—number	NEUTRON EXCESS
—spin	ISOBARIC SPIN, T
lagging of effect	
behind cause	HYSTERESIS
lanthanides (elements)	ACTINIDES
	ACTINONS
large	
—particles in solution	COLLOID
—vibration caused by	
smaller	RESONANCE
law governing	
—angle of polarisation	BREWSTER'S LAW
—atomic weights	PERIODIC LAW
—attraction between	
charged bodies	COULOMB'S LAW
—combination of	
gases	GAY-LUSSAC'S LAW
—conductivity of	
electrolyte	KOHLRAUSCH'S LAW
—deflection by rotation	
of Earth	FERRELL'S LAW
—diffusion of gases	GRAHAM'S LAW
—dissociation	OSTWALD'S DILUTION LAW
—dissolved gases	HENRY'S LAW
—electrolysis	FARADAY'S LAWS
—energy of gas	JOULE'S LAW
—equivalence of	
mass and energy	EINSTEIN'S LAW
—formation of valency	
bonds	RULES OF FAJANS
—frequency and	
energy	PLANCK'S LAW OF RADIATION
—gravitational	
attraction	NEWTON'S LAW
—heat produced by	
electric current	JOULE'S LAW

—magnetic susceptibility	CURIE'S LAW
—movement of planets	KEPLER'S LAWS
—number of molecules	
in quantity of gas	AVOGADRO'S LAW
	AVOGADRO'S HYPOTHESIS
—osmotic pressure	VAN'T HOFF'S LAW
—partial pressures	DALTON'S LAW
—periodic law	MENDELEEV'S LAW
of Newlands	LAW OF OCTAVES
—planetary motion	KEPLER'S LAWS
—pressure of	
fluid	PASCAL'S LAW
gas	BOYLE'S LAW, CHARLES' LAW
	MARIOTTE'S LAW
—quantum properties of	
electrons	
	PAULI EXCLUSION PRINCIPLE
—radiant heat from	
black body	STEFAN-BOLTZMANN LAW
	STEFAN'S LAW
—ratio of	
expansion coefficient	
to specific heat	GRUNEISEN'S LAW
latent heat to	
boiling point	TROUTON'S RULE
thermal to electrical	
conductivity	
	WIEDEMANN-FRANZ LAW
—reflected X-rays	BRAGG'S LAW
—refractive indices	SNELL'S LAW
—relationship of	
induced current to moving	
magnetic field	LENZ'S LAW
strain and stress	HOOKE'S LAW
—sines of angles of	
incidence and	
refraction	SNELL'S LAW
—sparking potential of	
electrodes	PASCHEN'S LAW
—speed of chemical	
change	MASS ACTION LAW
—strength of induced	
magnetic field	AMPERE'S LAW
—sum of electric	
forces	KIRCHHOFF'S LAW
—thermodynamics	NEWTON'S LAWS
—vapour pressure	
in solutions	RAOULT'S LAW
of solvent	BABO'S LAW
—velocity	
of air	
molecules	
	MAXWELL-BOLTZMANN LAW
in viscous media	STOKES' LAW
—voltage and current	OHM'S LAW
	(see also principle below)

layers of charged
 particles in
 atmosphere
    VAN ALLEN (RADIATION) BELTS
left-right symmetry   PARITY
lens
—causing
  parallel beam to
  —focus   CONVERGING LENS
  —spread   DIVERGING LENS
—nearest the object   OBJECTIVE
—types   BI-CONCAVE, BI-CONVEX
    CONCAVO-CONVEX, MENISCUS
    PLANO-CONCAVE, PLANO-CONVEX
—with no
  —chromatic aberration
    ACHROMATIC LENS
  —astigmatism   ANASTIGMATIC LENS
    (*see also* **photography**)
light
—caused by high
  temperature   INCANDESCENCE
—emission not caused
  by temperature   LUMINESCENCE
—emitted when
  charged particles pass
  through transparent
  medium
    C(H)ERENKOV RADIATION
  ultrasound passes
  through fluid   SONOLUMINESCENCE
—emitting property   LUMINOSITY
—from chemical
  reaction   CHEMOLUMINESCENCE
    COLD FLAME
—quantum   PHOTON
line
—defect in crystal   DISLOCATION
—giving relationship between
  pressure and temperature
  of liquid   ISOCHORE
—of
  equal
    —magnetic
     declination   ISOGONAL LINE
     dip   ISOCLINAL
     intensity   ISODYNAMIC LINE
    —pressure   ISOBAR
    —temperature ISOTHERM(AL LINE)
    magnetic declination   AGONIC LINE
    zero magnetic dip   ACLINIC LINE
    MAGNETIC EQUATOR
—on curved surface   GEODESIC (LINE)
—pattern of X-rays
  emitted by an
  element   X-RAY SPECTRUM

—showing temperature
  change with pressure   ISOMETRIC LINE
lines in visible
  spectrum of hydrogen   BALMER SERIES
link binding atoms
  in molecule   VALENCY BOND
linking of output
  to input   FEEDBACK
liquid of condensation   DISTILLATE
locating system using
  microwaves   RADAR
loss of
—electrical resistance at
  low temperatures SUPERCONDUCTIVITY
—energy of
  X-rays striking
  matter   COMPTON EFFECT
  light passing
  through medium   RAMAN EFFECT
low-temperature
  microwaves   BACKGROUND RADIATION
lowest
—freezing point of
  mixture of solids   EUTECTIC POINT
—possible temperature   ABSOLUTE ZERO
    ZERO KELVIN
—value producing
  specific effect   THRESHOLD
luminescence when emitted
  wavelength is different
  from that absorbed   FLUORESCENCE
    PHOSPORESCENCE
luminosity from
  electrical discharge
  through gas   GLOW DISCHARGE
luminous
—discharge round
  conductor   CORONA DISCHARGE
—intensity   LUMINANCE
—region near positive
  electrode   POSITIVE COLUMN
machine
—for producing electrical
  energy   ALTERNATOR, DYNAMO
    GENERATOR
—speed regulator   GOVERNOR
magnetic
—equator   ACLINIC LINE
—field focusing
  electron beam   ELECTRON LENS
—fields used to
  contain plasma   MAGNETIC BOTTLE
—flux
  density   B, MAGNETIC INDUCTION
  through unit area
    MAGNETIC FLUX DENSITY

—induction	B, MAGNETIC FLUX DENSITY
magnetism	
—across a force field	DIAMAGNETISM
—increases in steps	BARKHAUSEN EFFECT
—induced	
by electric coils	ELECTROMAGNETISM
in ceramics	FERRIMAGNETISM
—parallel to force	
field	PARAMAGNETISM
—strong	FERROMAGNETISM
	PARAMAGNETISM
maser using gas	
molecules	GAS MASER
mass	
—defect divided by	
mass number	PACKING FRACTION
—determined by	
gravitational	
attraction	GRAVITATIONAL MASS
momentum	INERTIAL MASS
—number	A, NUCLEON NUMBER
—of	
body	
—at speed	
approaching the	
speed of light	RELATIVISTIC MASS
—not in motion	REST MASS
isotope	ATOMIC MASS
unit volume	DENSITY
material which will return	
to original length after	
stretching	ELASTOMER
mathematical expression	
of wave motion	WAVE EQUATION
maximum	
—oscillation	AMPLITUDE
—velocity produced	
by given force	TERMINAL VELOCITY
measure of	
—capacity for work	E, ENERGY
—disorder	ENTROPY, S
—efficiency of fuel	
and oxidiser	SPECIFIC IMPULSE
—heat content	ENTROPY, S
—light absorbed by	
dissolved substance	
	EXTINCTION COEFFICIENT
—light-bending power	
of transparent	
medium	REFRACTIVE INDEX
—radiant energy related	
to solar energy	SOLAR CONSTANT
—radiation-reflecting	
capacity	REFLECTANCE
—radioactive decay	HALF-LIFE
—refraction	OPTICAL DENSITY

—resistance to	
shearing	RIGIDITY MODULUS
—rotating tendency	
of a force	MOMENT OF FORCE
—vibration in crystal	PHONON
measurement	
—of atmospheric	
humidity	PSYCHROMETRY
—system	CGS SYSTEM, FPS SYSTEM
	SI SYSTEM
mechanics of	
—liquids	FLUID MECHANICS
—motion	KINETICS
—very small	
systems	QUANTUM MECHANICS
	WAVE MECHANICS
metal which	
—corrodes	BASE METAL
—does not corrode	NOBLE METAL
metallic elements similar	
in properties and	
difficult to separate	RARE EARTHS
microscope with	
—one lens	SIMPLE MICROSCOPE
—two lenses	COMPOUND MICROSCOPE
—using electron	
beams instead	
of light	ELECTRON MICROSCOPE
microwave-producing	
valve	MAGNETRON
migration of particles	
in electric field	CATAPHORESIS
	ELECTROPHORESIS
minimum	
—distance for receipt	
of sky wave	SKIP DISTANCE
—quantity of radioactive	
material for chain	
reaction	CRITICAL MASS
mixture of	
—fluids due to movement	
of particles	DIFFUSION
—two	
primary colours	SECONDARY COLOUR
secondary colours	TERTIARY COLOUR
mnemonics for electric	
machines	FLEMING'S RULES
modulation types	AMPLITUDE
	FREQUENCY, PHASE
	VELOCITY
Mohs scale 1	TALC
2	GYPSUM
3	CALCITE
4	FLUORITE
5	APATITE
6	ORTHOCLASE

7	QUARTZ
8	TOPAZ
9	CORUNDUM
10	DIAMOND

molecular
weight — RELATIVE MOLECULAR MASS
molecule
—constituting electric
  dipole — POLAR MOLECULE
—weight of compound — GRAM-MOLECULE
  MOL(E)
moment of inertia — I
—about axis — RADIUS OF GYRATION
motion
—of fluids in
  parallel layers — LAMINAR FLOW
—round fixed point
  or axis — GYRATION
movement of
—liquid
  in narrow tube — CAPILLARITY
  CAPILLARY ACTION
  through semipermeable
  membrane — OSMOSIS
—particles in colloid
  BROWNIAN MOVEMENT
  PEDESIS
—polarised particles
  in electric field — DIELECTROPHORESIS
multiple of fundamental
frequency — HARMONIC
mutual conductance — TRANSCONDUCTANCE
narrow tube — CAPILLARY TUBE
natural course
  followed by fluid — STREAMLINE
negative
—acceleration — DECELERATION
  RETARDATION
—entropy — NEGENTROPY
—magnetism — DIAMAGNETISM
network of points
  in crystal — LATTICE
neutron
—excess — ISOTOPIC NUMBER
—number — N
nickel-iron
accumulator — EDISON ACCUMULATOR
no entropy change
  at absolute zero — NERNST HEAT THEOREM
noises produced during
  remagnetisation — BARKHAUSEN EFFECT
non-conductor — INSULATOR
—of electricity — DIELECTRIC
non-magnetic form of iron — GAMMA-IRON
normal energy state of atom — GROUND STATE
north-seeking pole — POSITIVE POLE

note of higher frequency
than the fundamental — OVERTONE
nuclear
—emission caused
  by photon — PHOTODISINTEGRATION
  PHOTODISSOCIATION
—energy — ATOMIC ENERGY
  change — Q-VALUE
—fission caused by
  photons — PHOTOFISSION
—heat of reaction — Q-VALUE
—reactor — ATOMIC PILE
nucleon number — A, MASS NUMBER
nucleus
—of
  deuterium atom — DEUTERON
  tritium atom — TRITON
—with
  odd number of protons
  —and neutrons — ODD-ODD NUCLEUS
  —even number of
    neutrons — ODD-EVEN NUCLEUS
nuclides with equal
—mass numbers — ISOBARES
—number of protons — ISOTOPES
number
—defining state of
  small system — QUANTUM NUMBER
—describing type of
  flow of liquid
  in tubes — REYNOLDS NUMBER
—of
  atoms in mole — AVOGADRO CONSTANT
  AVOGADRO NUMBER, L, N
  molecules of
  gas per cubic
  centimetre — LOSCHMIDT'S CONSTANT
  nucleons in nucleus — MASS NUMBER
  units of protons in
  nucleus — ATOMIC NUMBER
  waves per unit length — WAVE NUMBER
occurrence of mirror-
image cystalline
forms — ENANTIOMORPHISM
opacity to radiant heat — ATHERMANCY
opaque to radiation — RADIO-OPAQUE
opening admitting light — APERTURE
opposite
—ends of magnet — MAGNETIC POLES
—of centrifugal
  force — CENTRIPETAL FORCE
optical
—maser — LASER
—transistor — TRANSPHASOR
orbit of electrons
  round nucleus — ELECTRON SHELL

orbital electron	PLANETARY ELECTRON
oscillation caused by surge in voltage etc	TRANSIENT
outward force of rotation	CENTRIFUGAL FORCE
pairs of isobares with difference of one between atomic and neutron numbers	WIGNER NUCLIDES
partial sterilisation	PASTEURISATION
particle(s)	
—accelerator	(*see* **scientific instruments**)
—considered as waves	WAVE MECHANICS
—imagined to be exchanged by interacting bodies	VIRTUAL PARTICLE
—which cannot be sub-divided	ELEMENTARY PARTICLE
	(*see also* **particles**)
partly transparent to radiation	RADIOLUCENT
passage of electron energy barrier in semiconductor	TUNNEL EFFECT
path of	
—electron round nucleus	ORBIT
—projectile	TRAJECTORY
pattern	
—of scanning lines in cathode ray tube	RASTER
—showing wavelengths of electromagnetic radiation	SPECTRUM
periodic law	MENDELEEV'S LAW
—of Newlands	LAW OF OCTAVES
physicists	
—American	ALBURGER, ALVAREZ

ANDERSON, BAKER, BARDEEN
BETHE, BLOCH
BLOEMBERGEN, BRATTAIN
BRIDGMAN, CHAMBERLAIN, CHANCE
CHANDRASEKHAR, CHIU, CHRISTOFILOS
COBLENZ, COMPTON, COOPER, COTTON
COWAN, CREWE, CRONIN, DAVIS, DEUTSCH
DEMPSTER, DICKE, DUNNING, FERMI
FESSENDEN, FEYNMAN, FITCH, FOWLER
FRANK, FRANKLIN, FRIEDMAN, GAMOW
GELL-MANN, GEORGI, GIBBS, GIAEVER
GLASER, GLASHOW, GROEPPART-MAYER
HAFELE, HENRY, HEYL, HOLLOWAY
HOFSTADTER, HUGHES, KASPER
KEATING, KENNELLY, KERST, KUSCH
LAMB, LAND, LANGLEY, LAWRENCE, LEE
LYONS, MAIMON, MAYER, MCMILLAN
MICHELSON, MILLIKAN, MOTTELSON
MOULTON, NEUMANN, NEWELL

OPPENHEIMER, PARKER, PENZIAS
PLASS, PUNCELL, RABI, RAINWATER
REINES, RICHTER, ROWLAND, RUARK
RUMFORD, SCHLAWLOW, SCHRIEFFER
SCHRODINGER, SCHWINGER, SEGRE
SHOCKLEY, SZILARD, TELLER, THOMPSON
TING, TOWNES, VAN ALLEN
VAN DER GRAAF, VAN VLECK
WEINBERG, WIGNER, WILLIAMS
WILSON, YANGZINN

—Australian	BOWEN, ELWIN
—Austrian	BOLTZMANN, DEUTSCH
	DOPPLER, FRANK, HESS
	MACH, MEITNER, PAULI
	SCHRODINGER, STEFAN
—Belgian	NICOLET
—British	APPLETON, ASTBURY

BACON, BARKLA
BLACKETT, BOYLE, BRAGG, CANTON
CAVENDISH, CHADWICK, COCKCROFT
CRANSTON, CRICK, CROOKES, DALTON
DIRAC, EDDINGTON, FARADAY, FOWLER
GABOR, GALTON, GILBERT, GROVE
HAUKSBEE, HAWKING, HEAVISIDE
HEWISH, HOOKE, JEANS
JOSEPHSON, JOULE, KELVIN, KURTI
LODGE, LONDON, MAXWELL, MOSELEY
MOTT, NEWTON, NICOL, POWELL, RANKIN
RAYLEIGH, RICHARDSON, RUTHERFORD
RYLE, SODDY, STOKES, STRUTT
THOMSON, WALTON, WILSON
WATSON-WATT, WHEATSTONE
WYNN-WILLIAMS, YOUNG

—Canadian	DEMPSTER, PONTECORVO
	ZINN
-Chinese	CHIU, LEE, YANG
-Danish	BOHR, COSTER, MOTTELSON
	OERSTED, MOLLER
-Dutch	BLOEMBERGER, DEBYE, GOUDSMIT

HUYGHENS, KEESOM, LORENTZ
ONNES, UHLENBECK
VAN DER MEER, VAN DER WAALS
ZERNICKE

-French	AMONTONS, AMPERE, BABINET

BECQUEREL, BIOT, CARNOT
CHARLES, COULOMB, CURIE
DE BROGLIE, DE LATOUR, DEBIERNE
DESTRIER, FABRY, FIZEAU, FOUCAULT
FOURIER, GAY-LUSSAC, GUILLAUME
JOLIOT-CURIE, KASTLER, KOWARSKI
LAPLACE, LAVOISIER, LIPMAN
MALUS, NEEL, PASCAL, PERRIN
PLANTE, REAUMUR, WEISS

-German	ABBE, BALMER, BARKHAUSEN

BECKER, BEDNORZ, BERG, BETHE
BINNIG, BORN, BOTHE

BRILL, BYERMAN, CLAUSIUS, DORN
EINSTEIN, FAHRENHEIT, FRANCK
FRAUNHOFER, GEIGER, GOLDSTEIN
GUERICKE, HAHN, HEISENBERG
HELMHOLTZ, HERTZ, HERZOG, JENSEN
KIRCHER, KIRCHHOFF, KLITZING
LAVE, LENARD, LINDE, LONDON, MEITNER
MEYER, MICHELSON, MOSSBAUER
NERNST, NIEN, NODDACK, PLANCK
PENZIAS, RITTER, ROENTGEN, ROHRER
RUSKA, SCHWEIGGER, SEEBECK
STARKE, STERN, STRASSMAN
TACKE, VON LAUE, WUNDERLICH,

—Greek	CHRISTOFILOS
—Hungarian	GABOR, KURTI, NEUMANN
	NORDAU, SZILARD, TELLER
	WIGNER
—Indian	BOSE, RAMAN
—Iranian	JAVAN
—Irish	ANDREWS, FITZGERALD
	STONEY, TYNDALL, WALTON
—Israeli	NE'EMEN, PERKERIS
—Italian	FERMI, MARCONI, PALMIERI
	PONTECORVO, RUBBIA
	TORRICELLI, VIVIANI
—Japanese	ESAKI, TOMONAGA, YUKAWA
—Norwegian	BIRKELAND
—Pakistani	SALAM
—Polish	DANYSZ, PNIEWSKI
—Russian	AMBARTSUMIAN, ARTSIMOVICH
	BASOV, C(H)ERENKOV, DERYAGIN
	FLEROV, FRANK, GAMOW, KAPITZA
	LANDAU, LEBEDEV, PETRJAK
	POMERANCHUK, PROCHOROV
	SAKHAROV, TAMM, VEKSLER
—Serbian	MILANKOWICH
—Swedish	ALFVEN, ANGSTROM, KLEIN
	MULLER, SIEGBAHN, SIEVERT
—Swiss	BLOCH, GUILLAUME
	PICCARD, PICTET
—Yugoslav	MILANKOVICH
Planck's constant	H
planetary electron	ORBITAL ELECTRON

point
—at
  geometrical centre
   of lens   OPTICAL CENTRE
  which mass is
   concentrated   CENTRE OF MASS
—in lens system   NODAL POINT
—of
  convergence of rays   FOCUS
  zero wave displacement   NODE
—through which resultant
  force of gravity
  passes   CENTRE OF GRAVITY

positive
—charge on nucleus   NUCLEAR CHARGE
—ion   CATION
—particle   PROTON
potential
—gradient in conductor
  due to temperature
  gradient   KELVIN EFFECT
              THOMSON EFFECT
—produced by temperature
  gradient in magnetic
  field   NERNST EFFECT
practical application
 of hydrodynamics   HYDRAULICS
preparation of metals
 from oxides   GOLDSCHMIDT PROCESS
pressure
—applied to any part of fluid
  is transferred to
  all points   PASCAL'S PRINCIPLE
—needed to prevent
  osmotic flow   OSMOTIC PRESSURE
primary cell   BUNSEN CELL
        CADMIUM CELL, CLARK CELL
     DANIELL CELL, LECLANCHE CELL
     MERCURY CELL, VOLTAIC CELL
            WESTON CELL
—with constant voltage   STANDARD CELL
primary colours
—light   BLUE, GREEN, RED
—pigment   BLUE, RED, YELLOW
primordial matter   YLEM
principle governing
—identical quantum
  states
      PAULI'S EXCLUSION PRINCIPLE
—position and
  momentum UNCERTAINTY PRINCIPLE
—transfer of pressure
  in fluids   PASCAL'S PRINCIPLE
—weight of floating
  body   ARCHIMEDES' PRINCIPLE
probability of particle
 passing through
nuclear barrier   PENETRATION FACTOR
process
—for fixing atmospheric
  nitrogen   SERPEK PROCESS
—releasing heat EXOERGIC PROCESS
          EXOTHERMIC PROCESS
product of
—area and magnetic
  field strength   MAGNETIC FLUX
—area and vector   FLUX
—magnetic pole strength
  and length of magnet MAGNETIC MOMENT

—mass and velocity	MOMENTUM
production of	
—current in	
bimetallic circuit	
by heat	SEEBECK EFFECT
one circuit by	
current in another	INDUCTION
—electricity by electro-	
magnetic radiation	PHOTO-EMISSION
—electron and positron	
when particle interacts	
with nucleus	PAIR PRODUCTION
—heat at bimetallic	
junction	PELTIER EFFECT
property of	
—extreme	
stretchability	SUPERPLASTICITY
—liquid surface	SURFACE TENSION
proportion of solute	
to solvent	MOLALITY, MOLARITY
protons and neutrons	NUCLEONS
pull of gravity on	
a body	WEIGHT
pulse height analyser	KICKSORTER
quantity of	
—direction and magnitude	VECTOR
—matter	M, MASS
—substance	MOL(E)
quantum of	
—electromagnetic energy	PHOTON
—energy in vibrating	
crystal	PHONON
—gravity	GRAVITON
—radiation	PHOTON
radar screen	CATHODE RAY OSCILLOSCOPE
	CRO
radiation	
—from	
accelerating	
particle	BRAKING RADIATION
	BREMSSTRAHLUNG
Big Bang	BACKGROUND RADIATION
space	COSMIC RAYS
surroundings	BACKGROUND RADIATION
—of one wavelength	MONOCHROMATIC
—power loss	ATTENUATION
—spectrum (shortest first)	
	COSMIC RAYS
	GAMMA RAYS
	X-RAYS
	ULTRAVIOLET RAYS
	VISIBLE LIGHT
	INFRARED RAYS
	RADIO WAVES
—visible to human	
eye	VISIBLE SPECTRUM

radio wave(s)	HERTZIAN WAVES
—of constant amplitude	
and frequency	CARRIER WAVE
—received without	
reflection	DIRECT WAVES
	GROUND WAVES
radioactive	
—elements	ACTINIDES
—emissions	ALPHA RAY, BETA RAY
	GAMMA RAY
	KANALSTRAHLEN RAYS
	CHANNEL RAYS
—material from nuclear	
explosion	FALLOUT
random motion of	
small particles	BROWNIAN MOTION
	BROWNIAN MOVEMENT
range of energy states	
which can be occupied by	
valency electrons	VALENCY BAND
rare-earth metals	ACTINIDES
	LANTHANIDES
rate of	
—doing work	POWER
—heat transfer	THERMAL CONDUCTIVITY
—increase of speed	ACCELERATION
—loss of information	
due to noise	EQUIVOCATION
—motion	VELOCITY
ratio of	
—changes in current	
and voltage in	
valve	MUTUAL CONDUCTANCE
	TRANSCONDUCTANCE
—density of substance	
to that of water	RELATIVE DENSITY
	SPECIFIC GRAVITY, SG
—dimensions under stress	
to original dimensions	STRAIN
—energy output to input	EFFICIENCY
—intensity of beam after	
passing through medium	
to its original	
intensity	TRANSMISSION COEFFICIENT
—latent heat to	
boiling point	TROUTON'S RULE
—lateral and	
longitudinal	
strains	POISSON'S RATIO
—magnetomotive force	
to magnetic flux	RELUCTANCE
—magnetic flux density	
to external field	PERMEABILITY
—maximum load to	
sectional area	TENACITY
	ULTIMATE STRESS

—moles in substances in mixture	MOLE FRACTION
—potential difference to current	RESISTANCE
—sines of incident and refracted angles	REFRACTIVE INDEX
—size of image to object	MAGNIFICATION
	MAGNIFYING POWER
—stress to strain	ELASTIC MODULUS
	YOUNG'S MODULUS
—velocity of body to that of sound	MACH NUMBER
—viscosity to density	KINEMATIC VISCOSITY
—weight of atom of substance to that of oxygen	ATOMIC WEIGHT
substance to weight of water	SPECIFIC GRAVITY
rays from uranium compounds	BECQUEREL RAYS
reaction against stress	LE CHATELIER PRINCIPLE
reciprocal of	
—fluidity	VISCOCITY
—magnetic permeability	RELUCTIVITY
—poise	RHE
—rhe	POISE
—transmittance	OPACITY
—viscosity	FLUIDITY
—wavelength	WAVE NUMBER
reduction of energy when photon collides with electron	COMPTON EFFECT
refractive index - 1	REFRACTIVITY
region of gas where positive and negative ions are approximately equal	PLASMA
regular	
—array of atoms in crystal	LATTICE
—displacement either side of a mean	WAVE MOTION
relationship of	
—heat to other forms of energy	THERMODYNAMICS
—stress and strain	HOOKE'S LAW
—temperature to surface tension	PARACHOR
volume	CHARLES' LAW
—volume and pressure	BOYLE'S LAW
relative	
—atomic mass	ATOMIC WEIGHT
—density	SPECIFIC GRAVITY, SG
of gas or vapour	VAPOUR DENSITY
—molecular mass	MOLECULAR WEIGHT

—pressure of water vapour in atmosphere	RELATIVE HUMIDITY
remaining magnetism	REMANENCE
removal	
—by dissolving in liquid	ELUTION
—of	
moisture	DESICCATION
salt	DESALINATION
residual magnetism	REMANENCE
resistance	
—per unit length	RESISTIVITY
—to flow	VISCOSITY
restriction of vibration to single plane	POLARISATION
Röntgen	
—equivalent man	REM
—ray	X-RAY
rotating	
—part of machine	ROTOR
—polarised light to	
left	LAEVOROTATORY
right	DEXTROROTATORY
rotation of	
—atom caused by motion of electrons	LARMOR PRECESSION
—light related to wavelength	ROTARY DISPERSION
—particle on its axis	SPIN
—plane of polarisation by magnetism	FARADAY EFFECT
polarised light	OPTICAL ACTIVITY
	OPTICAL ROTATION
—polarised light by current	KERR EFFECT
rules	
—governing mass and length as affected by speed	LORENTZ-FITZGERALD EQUATIONS
—of spin of particles	BOSE-EINSTEIN STATISTICS
	FERMI-DIRAC STATISTICS
saturation point	DEWPOINT
scale of	
—hardness	MOHS SCALE
—specific gravity	BAUME SCALE
—temperature	CELSIUS, CENTIGRADE
	FAHRENHEIT, KELVIN
	RANKINE, REAUMUR
scattering of	
—light by particles	TYNDALL EFFECT
—photons by electrons	THOMSON SCATTERING
secondary cell	(see cell above)

semiconductor used for amplification, etc	TRANSISTOR
sensitive photo-electric cell	ELECTRON MULTIPLIER
	PHOTOMULTIPLIER
separately magnetised part of ferromagnetic substance	MAGNETIC DOMAIN
separating dish	CUPEL
separation of	
—gases	ATMOLYSIS
—insoluble matter from liquid by settlement	SEDIMENTATION
—isotopes	CASCADE PROCESS
—metals by hot-air process	CUPELLATION
—mixture into parts with different properties	FRACTIONATION
—particles by size by suspension	ELUTRIATION
—solids by melting	LIQUATION
sequence of energy transfer	CARNOT CYCLE
short focal lens with smaller lens in surface	FRESNEL LENS
short-wave electromagnetic radiation	MICROWAVES
shortening due to speed	FITZGERALD CONTRACTION
SI unit	
—distance	METRE, M
—electric current	AMPERE, A
—luminous intensity	CANDELA, CD
—mass	KILOGRAM, KG
—quantity	MOLE, MOL,
—temperature	KELVIN, K
—time	SECOND, S
slowing of atom vibrations by gravity	EINSTEIN SHIFT
small dynamo with spark-coil	MAGNETO
smallest portion retaining characteristics of the original substance	MOLECULE
solid carbon dioxide	DRY ICE
solution	
—carrying current which decomposes it	ELECTROLYTE
—from which substances have been crystallised	MOTHER-LIQUID
	MOTHER-LYE
south-seeking pole	NEGATIVE POLE
space	
—above inverted tube of mercury	TORRICELLIAN VACUUM
—within which one body attracts another	GRAVITATIONAL FIELD
—without matter	VACUUM
specific gravity	RELATIVE DENSITY
spectrum	
—lines in ultraviolet region	LYMAN SERIES
—of	
hydrogen	BALMER SERIES
increasing electric charge of ion beam	MASS SPECTRUM
—white light	VISIBLE SPECTRUM
	(*see also* radiation *above*)
speed	
—approaching the speed of light	RELATIVISTIC VELOCITY
—limit imposed by overheating	THERMAL BARRIER
—of	
light	C
sound	MACH NUMBER
spherical aberration in lens or mirror	COMA
spinning wheel maintaining position in space	GYROSCOPE
splitting of nucleus of atom, releasing energy	NUCLEAR FISSION
spontaneous disintegration of unstable nuclei	RADIOACTIVITY
spreading of light to produce spectrum	DISPERSION
state of particle imagined to be exchanged by interacting bodies	VIRTUAL STATE
statement of impossibility of determining both position and speed	INDETERMINANCY PRINCIPLE
	UNCERTAINTY PRINCIPLE
steam above normal boiling-point	SUPERHEATED STEAM
storage battery	ACCUMULATOR
strength of field through given area	FLUX
stress acting along the plane of a face	SHEAR
strong	
—heating	CALCINATION
—magnet reversing plasma flow	MAGNETIC MIRROR
strongly magnetic	FERROMAGNETIC
study of	
—charged particles	THERMIONICS
—deformation of matter	RHEOLOGY

—dynamics of gases   PNEUMATICS
—electricity   ELECTROLOGY
—electrodynamics of
  electrons in
  fluids   MAGNETOHYDRODYNAMICS
—fluids   HYDRAULICS
  in
    —equilibrium   HYDROSTATICS
    and in motion   HYDRODYNAMICS
    motion   HYDROKINETICS
—friction and lubrication   TRIBOLOGY
—heat and energy   THERMODYNAMICS
—ions in solution   POLAROGRAPHY
—jets of fluid in
  circuits   FLUID LOGIC, FLUIDICS
—light   OPTICS
—measurements   METROLOGY
—sound   ACOUSTICS, SONICS
  beyond human hearing   ULTRASONICS
—very low temperatures   CRYOGENICS
                   (*see also* **study**)
substance
—between conductor and
  insulator   SEMICONDUCTOR
—in gaseous state   VAPOUR
—producing luminescence   PHOSPHOR
—providing energy in
  nuclear reaction   NUCLEAR FUEL
—which
  loses plasticity when
   cooled after being
   heated   THERMOSETTING PLASTIC
  reduces surface
   tension   WETTING AGENT
  slows neutrons   MODERATOR
  softens with heat   THERMOPLASTIC
  turns litmus
    —blue   ALKALI
    —red   ACID
  varies its resistance with
   temperature change   THERMISTOR
—with atoms all of the
   same atomic number   ELEMENT
sum of atomic weights
  in ion   GRAM-ION
super-heavy hydrogen   TRITIUM
superdense theory   BIG BANG THEORY
supposed unit of
  magnetic charge   MAGNETIC MONOPOLE
suspended weight free
  to swing in all
  directions   FOUCAULT PENDULUM
system of
  measurement FOOT-POUND-SECOND SYSTEM
                           FPS SYSTEM
            CGS SYSTEM, SI UNITS

taking up moisture
  from the air   DELIQUESCENT
temperature
  —above which ferromagnets
   become paramagnetic   CURIE POINT
  —at which
   all three states are
   in equilibrium   TRIPLE POINT
   condensation occurs   DEWPOINT
                     SATURATION POINT
   element changes
   state   TRANSITION POINT
           TRANSITION TEMPERATURE
   enough inflammable
   vapour is produced to
   cause a flash   FLASH POINT
  ice and water are in
   equilibrium   ICE POINT
  liquid
   —and vapour are
   in equilibrium   STEAM POINT
   —changes to
    gas   BOILING POINT
    solid   FREEZING POINT
  magnetism is
   lost   CURIE TEMPERATURE
  saturation vapour pressure
   of liquid equals
   external pressure   BOILING POINT
  —calculated from
   light mission   OPTICAL TEMPERATURE
  —change from pressure
   differential   JOULE-KELVIN EFFECT
              JOULE-THOMSON EFFECT
  —scale   CELSIUS, CENTIGRADE,
            FAHRENHEIT, KELVIN
            RANKINE, REAUMUR
temporary magnet using
  electric current   ELECTROMAGNET
tendency to preserve existing
  state of rest or motion   INERTIA
theory
  —denying absolute
   motion   THEORY OF RELATIVITY
  —of
   combustion   PHLOGISTON THEORY
   energy as discrete
   units   QUANTUM THEORY
   light
    —as packets of
    energy   CORPUSCULAR THEORY
    —as waves   WAVE THEORY
  motion of particles
  based on quantum
   theory   QUANTUM MECHANICS
              WAVE MECHANICS

origin of	
universe	BIG BANG THEORY
	STEADY STATE THEORY
	SUPERDENSE THEORY
—to cover all four	
known forces	UNIFIED FIELD THEORY
thermal permeability	DIATHERMANCY
thermionic valve	VACUUM TUBE
time	
—between successive	
fissions in nuclear	
reaction	GENERATION TIME
—in which half the	
radioactive atoms decay	HALF-LIFE
—of one complete oscillation	PERIOD
toroidal container holding	
plasma in magnetic field	TOKAMAK
total pressure in	
liquid in tube	
is constant	BERNOULLI'S THEOREM
transconductance	MUTUAL CONDUCTANCE
transfer of	
—energy or matter by	
gas stream	ADVECTION
—heat	
by	
—air current	CONVECTION
—solid objects	CONDUCTION
through space	RADIATION
—light through fine	
glass rods	FIBRE OPTICS
transition from one	
energy level	
to another	QUANTUM LEAP
transparency to	
radiant heat	DIATHERMANCY
transparent cell with	
two electrodes	KERR CELL
travelling faster than	
—Mach 1	SUPERSONIC
—Mach 5	HYPERSONIC
triangular transparent	
prism	OPTICAL PRISM
turning effect	MOMENT, TORQUE
two equal but opposite	
charges	DIPOLE
ultra-violet from sun	ACTINIC RAYS
uncertainty	
principle	INDETERMINANCY PRINCIPLE
unit of	
—absorbed radiation	RAD
—energy	QUANTUM
—light	PHOTON
	(see also measures)
universal constant	
of energy	PLANCK'S CONSTANT

unoccupied site in	
crystal lattice	SCHOTTKY DEFECT
	VACANCY
unpredictable behaviour	
in systems	CHAOS
vacuum	
—in a barometer	TORRICELLIAN VACUUM
—tube	(THERMIONIC) VALVE
displaying cathode	
rays	CATHODE RAY TUBE, CRT
valve	
—carrying very high current	THYRATRON
—with	
2 electrodes	DIODE
3 electrodes	TRIODE
4 electrodes	TETRODE
5 electrodes	PENTODE
many electrodes	TROCHOTRON
vaporisation of liquid	
and condensation	
of vapour	DISTILLATION
vapour existing in	
equilibrium with	
the liquid form	SATURATED VAPOUR
variation of	
—carrier wave	AMPLITUDE MODULATION
	FREQUENCY MODULATION
—some characteristic	
of wave motion	MODULATION
—time shown by	
stationary and	
moving clocks	CLOCK PARADOX
—wavelength of	
radiation	DOPPLER-FIZEAU EFFECT
sound	DOPPLER EFFECT
velocity	
—of ion	ION MOBILITY
—required to	
overcome gravity	ESCAPE VELOCITY
sustain body in	
orbit	ORBITAL VELOCITY
very hot ionised gas	PLASMA
vibration at regular	
frequency	OSCILLATION
visible	
—display of colours	
in light	SPECTRUM
—electromagnetic waves	LIGHT
Voltaic pile	ELECTRIC BATTERY
voltage needed to cause	
spark to jump gap	SPARKING POTENTIAL
	SPARKING VOLTAGE
volume	
—of	
one mol	MOLECULAR VOLUME
unit mass	SPECIFIC VOLUME

—related to temperature   CHARLES' LAW
wave
  —form whose oscillation
     is represented by a
     sinusoidal curve   SINE WAVE
  —produced by two opposing
     waves   STANDING WAVE
           STATIONARY WAVE
  —which alternates between
     two values for equal
     times   SQUARE WAVE
  —with displacement
     across line of
       travel   TRANSVERSE WAVE
     in direction of
       travel   LONGITUDINAL WAVE
Weston cell   CADMIUM CELL
white heat   INCANDESCENCE
wireless waves   HERTZIAN WAVES
work
  —function   F, HELMHOLTZ FREE ENERGY
  —per unit of time   POWER
X-ray   ROENTGEN RAY
zone of wave differing from
  adjacent zone by half
  a period   FRESNEL ZONE
           HALF-PERIOD ZONE

pigs
Biblical   GADARENE SWINE
British   ESSEX, GLOUCESTER OLD SPOT
           HAMPSHIRE, LARGE BLACK
   LARGE WHITE, LONG WHITE LOP-EARED
           SADDLEBACK, TAMWORTH
           WELSH, WESSEX
Belgian   PIETRAIN
female   SOW
foot   TROTTER
herd of swine   SOUNDER
in novel   NAPOLEON, SNOWBALL
           SQUEALER
male   BOAR
smallest in litter   RECKLING, RUNT
           ST ANTHONY (PIG)
           TANTONY (PIG)
Swedish   LANDRACE
wild boar   SANGLIER
young   SHOAT, SHOTE, SHOT(T)
  —at one birth   FARROW, LITTER
  —boar   SOUNDER
  —sow   ELT, GILT

pigeon
including: dove
domestic   AFRICAN OWL
     AMERICAN DOMESTIC FLIGHT
     ARCHANGEL, BARRED STARLING
     BRUNETTE FRILL, CARRIER

     CHECKERED ICE, CRESTED HELMET
     DUN-FACED BLONDINETTE
     ENGLISH POUTER, FANTAIL
     FRANCONIAN, FRILLBACK
     FLYING POUTER, GAZZI
     GERMAN TOY, GIANT HOMER
     GIANT RUNT, GIMPEL, HELMET
     HIGHFLIER, ICE PIGEON, LARK
     LAHORE, MAGPIE, MALTESE
     MODENA, NORWICH CROPPER
     ORIENTAL FRILL, ORIENTAL ROLLER
     OWL PIGEON, PARLOUR TUMBLER
     PEKIN NASAL-TUFTED
     PIGMY POUTER, RACING HOMER
     ROLLER, SATINETTE FRILL
     SCANDAROON, SCHIETTI
     SCHOENEBERG TUMBLER
     SHIELD, SHOW HOMER, SHOW TIPPLER
     SHORT-FACED TUMBLER
     SILVERETTE FRILL, STARLING
     SWALLOW, SWING POUTER
     TIPPLER, TRUMPETER, TUMBLER
     VELVET-SHIELD, WHITE DANZIG
     WHITE KING
extinct (USA)   PASSENGER PIGEON
wild   BARBARY DOVE, COLLARED DOVE
     FERAL PIGEON, ROCK DOVE
     STOCK DOVE, TURTLE DOVE
     WOOD PIGEON

pilot
automatic pilot   GEORGE
Pilot-Officer   PO
     (*see also* **aircraft**)
pirate   BLACKBEARD, CORSAIR
     FLINT, MORGAN
     PRIVATEER, SILVER
pirate flag   JOLLY ROGER
     SKULL AND CROSSBONES

Planck's constant   H
planets   (*see* **astronomy**)
plants
Abrus   INDIAN LIQUORICE
     LIQUORICE-VINE
Acacia   MIMOSA
Acalypha   CHENILLE PLANT
     RED-HOT CATSTAIL
acanthus   BEAR'S-BREECH
     BRANKURSINE, RUELLIA
Aceras   MAN ORCHIS
Achimenes   CUPID'S BOWER
     HOT WATER PLANT
Achillea   MILFOIL, YARROW
Acidanthera   ETHIOPIAN GLADIOLUS
aconite   MONKSHOOD, WOLF'S-BANE
     WOLFSBANE
Acorus   SWEET-FLAG

Adam's	
—flannel	MULLEIN
—needle	CASSAVA, YUC(C)A
adder's-tongue	OPHIOGLOSSUM
adderweed	BISTORT
Adoxa	MOSCHATEL
Aechmea	URN PLANT, VASE PLANT
Aeschynanthus	LIPSTICK VINE
African	
—corn lily	IXIA
—lily	AGAPANTHUS
—marigold	TAGETES
—rue	HARMALA, HARMEL
—violet	SAINTPAULIA
Agapanthus	AFRICAN LILY
	LILY OF THE NILE
agave	SILK-GRASS
Alchemilla	LADY'S-MANTLE
ale-cost	COSTMARY
Alisma	WATER-PLANTAIN
all-heal	VALERIAN
Allium	ESCHALOT, GOLDEN GARLIC
	SHAL(L)OT
	GARLIC, LEEK
Alpine	
—flower	EDELWEISS, GENTIAN
—herb	CORNEL
—rose	RHODODENDRON
alsike	CLOVER
Alstro(e)meria	AMARYLLIS, HERB LILY
Althaea	HOLLYHOCK
	MARSH-MALLOW
aluminium plant	PILEA
Alyssum	GOLD DUST, MADWORT
Amaracus	MARJORAM
Amarant(h)us	LONDON PRIDE
	LOVE-LIES-BLEEDING, PIGWEED
	PRINCE'S FEATHER
Amaryllis	ALSTRO(E)MERIA
	BELLADONA LILY
	HIPPEASTRUM, LILY
	POLIANTHES
Ampelopsis	VIRGINIA CREEPER
ammoniac	OSHAC
Anacharis	CANADIAN PONDWEED
	WATER-WEED
Anagallis	BOG PIMPERNEL
Anana(s)	PINEAPPLE
	PAINTER'S PALETTE
Anatolian convolvulus	SCAMMONY
anemone	CORONARIA
	PASCHAL-FLOWER
	PASQUE-FLOWER, WIND-FLOWER
Angelica	AIT-SKEITER, OAT-SHOOTER
angel's wings	CALADIUM
anise	PIMPINELLA

Antennaria	EVERLASTING(-FLOWER)
Anthyllis	KIDNEY VETCH
Anthurium	FLAMINGO FLOWER
antirrhinum	FROG'S-MOUTH, SNAPDRAGON
Aphelandra	ZEBRA PLANT
aquatic plant	FONTINALIS, FROG-BIT
Aquilegia	COLUMBINE
Arabis	ROCK-CRESS, WALL-CRESS
Aralia	CASTOR-OIL PLANT
	FATSIA, PANAX
Ardisia	CORAL BERRY
Arenaria	SANDWORT
Argemone	PRICKLY-POPPY
Aristolochia	DUTCHMAN'S PIPE
	GOOSE-FLOWER, SNAKEROOT
Armeria	SEA-PINK, THRIFT
Arnoseris	SWINE'S-SUCCORY
aromatic plant	HYSSOP, PEPPERMINT
	SPEARMINT, SPIKENARD
arrow	
—head	SAGITTARIA
—root	MARANTA
—vine	SYNGONIUM
Artemisia	WORM-SEED, WORMWOOD
artillery plant	PILEA
arum	ACORUS, COLOCASIA
	ZANTEDESCHIA
Asclepias	MILK-WEED
asparagus	ASPIDISTRA
Asperugo	MADWORT
Asplenium	SPLEEN-WORT
aster	ALYCOMPAINE, ELECAMPANE
	STARWORT, STITCHWORT
Astilbe	GOAT'S BEARD, SPIRAEA
Astragalus	GOAT'S-THORN
	LIQUORICE-VETCH
	MILK VETCH
Astrantia	MASTERWORT
astrophel	PENTHIA, STARLIGHT
Aubrietia	BLUE ROCK CRESS
auricula	BEAR'S-EAR, DUSTY-MILLER
autumn-crocus	MEADOW-SAFFRON
avens	GEUM, HERB-BENNET
baby's tears	HELXINE
bacon and eggs	LINARIA, TOADFLAX
baldmoney	MEUM, SPICKNEL, SPIGNEL
balloon-vine	HEARTPEA, HEARTSEED
Ballota	BLACK HOREHOUND
	STINKING HOREHOUND
balsam	IMPATIENS, NOLI-ME-TANGERE
	TOUCH-ME-NOT
baneberry	BUGBANE, BUGWORT
	HERB-CHRISTOPHER
Barbarea	WINTER-CRESS
	YELLOW-ROCKET
barley	HORDEUM

basil(-thyme)	CALAMINT	Blechnum	HARD-FERN
bastard		bleeding-heart	DICENTRA, DIELYTRA
—pimpernel	CENTUNCULUS	—vine	CLERODENDRUM
—saffron	SAFFLOWER	blood	
bayberry	CANDLEBERRY	—leaf	IRESINE
bead plant	NERTERA	—lily	HAEMANTHUS
beans, peas, etc	PULSE	—root	POPPY
bearberry	FOXBERRY, UVA-URSI	blue	
bearded tongue	PENTSTEMON	—alpine flower	GENTIAN
bedwort	CROSSWORT	—bell	SCILLA, WOOD-HYACINTH
beefsteak plant	IRESINE		WILD HYACINTH
beet	GOOSEFOOT		WOOD HYACINTH
begonia	ANGEL'S WINGS	—bottle	CORNFLOWER
	ELEPHANT'S EARS	—rocket	LARKSPUR, MONKSHOOD
—vine	CISSUS	—veronica	GERMANDER SPEEDWELL
bell-flower	CAMPANULA, RAMPION	boat lily	RHOEO
Beloperone	SHRIMP PLANT	Bocconia	MACLEAYA, PLUME POPPY
Bengal fig	FICUS	bog	
benne	BEN(N)I, SESAME	—myrtle	MYRICA, SWEET-GALE
benth(e)	GROUND-IVY		SWEET-WILLOW
Bergamot	MONARDA	—pimpernel	ANAGALLIS
bilberry	BLAEBERRY, WHORTLEBERRY	—plant	BOG ASPHODEL, DROSERA
bindweed	BEARBINE, BELLBIND		SUNDEW, WATER-PURSLANE
	CONVOLVULUS	borage	BUGLOSS, COOL-TANKARD
bird of paradise	STRELITZIA		COMFREY, HELIOTROPE
bird's			HOUND'S-TONGUE, LITHOSPERMUM
—foot trefoil	LOTE, LOTOS, LOTUS		LUNGWORT, SYMPHYTUM
—nest	MONOTROPA	bottle	
bromeliad	NIDULARIUM	—brush	POTERIUM
birthwort	ASARABACCA	—plant	CALLISTEMON
Bishop's		Bougainvillea	PAPER FLOWER
—cap	SAXIFRAGE	Bouteloua	MOSQUITO GRASS
—weed	GOUTWEED, GOUTWORT	Bouvardia	JASMINE PLANT
—wort	BETONY, STACHYS	bowstring-hemp	SANSEVIERIA
bistort	ADDER('S-)WORT	bramble	LAWYER, RUBUS
	(PATIENCE-)DOCK	brassica	CABBAGE, KALE, TURNIP
	SNAKEROOT, SNAKEWEED	brassock	FIELD MUSTARD
bitter		brier	LAWYER
—herb	GERMANDER	brookweed	WATER PIMPERNEL
—vetch	ERS	broom	CYTISUS, HAG-WEED
bittersweet	DULCAMARA, SOLANUM	—parasite	BROOM-RAPE
	WOODY NIGHTSHADE	—rape	OROBRANCHE
black		Browallia	BUSH VIOLET
—cummin	FITCH	brown spiderwort	SIDERASIS
—currant	QUINSY-BERRY, RIBES	Brunella	SELF-HEAL
—hellebore	BEAR'S-FOOT, MELAMPODE	Brunnera	FORGET-ME-NOT
—medick	SHAMROCK	buck	
—salsify	SCORZONERA, VIPER'S GRASS	—bean	BOGBEAN
—saltwort	GLAUX	—thorn	RHAMNUS, RHEINBERRY
black-eyed Susan	THUNBERGIA		RHINEBERRY
bladder		—wheat	SARRASIN, SARRAZIN
—campion	CATCH-FLY, WHITE-BOTTLE	buck's-horn	
—senna	COLUTEA	plantain	STAR-OF-THE-EARTH
bladderwort	LENTIBULARIACEAE	Buddhist pine	PODOCARPUS
	UTRICULARIA	buff-coloured turnip	SWEDE
blanket flower	GAILLARDIA	bugle	AJUGA

bugloss	BORAGE	candytuft	IBERIS
bunch of keys	COWSLIP	Cannabis	HEMP
bur		Canterbury bell	CAMPANULA
—marigold	XANTHIUM		THROATWORT
—reed	SPARGANIUM	Cape	
—thistle	SPEAR THISTLE	—cowslip	LACHENALIA
—weed	BURDOCK, BUR-REED	—gooseberry	GROUND-CHERRY, PHYSALIS
burdock	CLOTBUR, XANTHIUM	—grape	RHOICISSUS
burnet	PIMPERNEL, PROTERIUM	—ivy	SENECIO
—rose	SCOTCH ROSE	—primrose	STREPTOCARPUS
—saxifrage	PIMPINELLA	Capsella	SHEPHERD'S PURSE
burning-bush	EUONYMUS, WAHOO	caraway	AJ(O)WAN
bush violet	BROWALLIA	Cardamine	CORAL-ROOT, TOOTHWORT
busy lizzie	IMPATIENS	carduus	MUSK-THISTLE
butcher's broom	JEW'S MYRTLE	Carex	SEDGE
	KNEE-HOLLY, RUSCUS	carnation	DIANTHUS
	SHEPHERD'S MYRTLE	Carolina	
Butomus	FLOWERING-RUSH	—jasmine	GELSEMIUM
buttercup	BACHELOR'S BUTTONS	—pink	SPIGELIA
	GIL(T)CUP, HELLEBORE	carrion-flower	STAPELIA
	KINGCUP, RANUNCULUS	cassava	ADAM'S NEEDLE, YUC(C)A
—type	MEADOW-RUE	Cassia	SENNA
butterfly flower	SCHIZANTHUS	Castilleja	PAINTED CUP
butterwort	LENTIBULARIACEAE	castor-oil plant	ARALIA, FATSIA
	PINGUICULA		PANAX, RICINUS
cabbage	BRASSICA, COLE(-WORT)	cat's	
	COLLARD, KALE	—ear	GROUND IVY
—rose	PROVINCIAL-ROSE		MOUNTAIN EVERLASTING
—tree	CORDYLINE	—foot	GROUND IVY
cactus	(see cacti)		MOUNTAIN-EVERLASTING
Cakile	SEA-ROCKET	—tail	REED-MACE
Caladium	ANGEL'S WINGS	catmint	CATNEP, CATNIP, NEP(ETA)
calamint	BASIL-THYME	Ceanothus	RED-ROOT
calceolaria	SLIPPER FLOWER	celery type	ALEXANDERS
	SLIPPERWORT	Celosia	COCKSCOMB, PLUME FLOWER
Calendula	MARIGOLD	Centaurea	STAR-THISTLE
Californian poppy	ESCHSCHOLTZIA	Centranthus	RED VALERIAN
calla lily	ZANTEDESCHIA		SPUR VALERIAN
Callistemon	BOTTLEBRUSH PLANT	Centunculus	BASTARD PIMPERNEL
Callistriche	WATER-STARWORT	Cerastium	MOUSE-EAR CHICKWEED
Calluna	HEATH(ER)	Cereus	CACTUS, TORCH-THISTLE
Caltha	KINGCUP	Cestrum	NIGHT JESSAMINE
Camelina	GOLD-OF-PLEASURE	cetywall	SETUALE, SETWALL, VALERIAN
camomile	ANTHEMIS, FEVERFEW	chalk plant	GYPSOPHILA
Campanula	BELLWORT	Chamaenerion	WILLOW-HERB
	CANTERBURY BELL	charlock	WILD MUSTARD
	(GIANT) BELLFLOWER	Cheiranthus	WALL (GILLY-)FLOWER
	NETTLE-LEAVED BELLFLOWER	Cheirinia	WALL (GILLY-)FLOWER
	STAR OF BETHLEHEM	chenille plant	ACALYPHA
	THROATWORT	Chenopodium	WORM-SEED
campion	CATCH-FLY, LICHNIS	chervil	CICELY, COW-CHERVIL
	FLOWER OF JOVE, LYCHNIS		COW-PARSLEY, COW-WEED
	RAGGED ROBIN	chestnut vine	TETRASTIGMA
Canada rice	ZIZANIA	chicken gizzard	IRESINE
Canadian pondweed	ANACHARIS	chick-pea	CHICH, CHICKLING VETCH
	WATER THYME		EGYPTIAN PEA, GRAM

chickweed	STELLARIA, STITCHWORT
—wintergreen	TRIENTALIS
chicory	ENDIVE, SUCCORY, WITLOOF
Chimaphila	WINTERGREEN
Chincherinchee	ORNITHOGALUM
Chinese	
—balloon flower	PLATYCODON
—lantern	PHYSALIS
Chionodoxa	GLORY OF THE SNOW
Chlorophytum	ST BERNARD'S LILY
	SPIDER PLANT
Christmas	
—pepper	CAPSICUM
—rose	BLACK HELLEBORE
cibol	WELSH ONION
Cicuta	WATER-HEMLOCK
cigar plant	CUPHEA
cinnamon	CANELLA
cinquefoil	FIVEFINGERS, MARSH-LOCKS
	POTENTILLA
	MINIATURE GRAPE IVY
Cirsium	CNICUS, SPEAR-THISTLE
Cissus	BEGONIA VINE, KANGAROO VINE
	MINIATURE GRAPE IVY
clary	ORVAL, SAGE
Claytonia	SPRING-BEAUTY
cleavers	GOOSE-GRASS
clematis	TRAVELLER'S-JOY
	VIRGIN'S-BOWER
Clerodendrum	BLEEDING HEART VINE
	GLORY BOWER
Clianthus	GLORY PEA
climbing	NASTURTIUM, PHILODENDRON
	WISTARIA, WISTERIA
—evergreen	IVY
—gourd	BRYONY
Clivia	KAFFIR LILY
clog plant	HYPOCYRTA
clotbur	SEA-BURDOCK, XANTHIUM
cloudberry	MOUNTAIN-BRAMBLE
clove	EUGENIA
—pink	SOPS-IN-WINE
clover	ALSIKE, HARE'S-FOOT(TREFOIL)
	TRIFOLIUM
club-moss	STAGHORN MOSS
club-rush	BULRUSH, SCIRPUS
Cnicus	CIRSIUM, (SPEAR-)THISTLE
coarse weed	HEMP-NETTLE
Cobaea	CUP AND SAUCER VINE
cock's-comb	CELOSIA, YELLOW RATTLE
cockle-bur	CLOTBUR
Codiaeum	CROTON, JOSEPH'S COAT
Colchicum	MEADOW SAFFRON
coleseed	NAVEW
Coleus	FLAME NETTLE
coltsfoot	HORSE-FOOT

columbine	AQUILEGIA
Columnea	GOLDFISH PLANT
Colutea	BLADDER SENNA
comfrey	BORAGE, SYMPHYTUM
common	
—arum	CUCKOO-PINT
	LORDS AND LADIES
—burnet	SALAD BURNET
—daisy	DOG-DAISY
—polypody	POLYPODIUM
—ragwort	YELLOW-WEED
condiment	DILL
coneflower	RUDBECKIA
Convallaria	LILY OF THE VALLEY
coral	
—berry	AECHMEA, ARDISIA
—root	CARDAMINE, TOOTHWORT
Cordatum	PHILODENDRON
Cordyline	CABBAGE TREE
	FLAMING DRAGON TREE
	GRASS PALM, TI PLANT
corn	
—bluebottle	BLAWORT, BLEWORT
—feverfew	MAYWEED
—flower	BLUEBOTTLE
—marigold	OX-EYE
—salad	LAMB'S-LETTUCE
—spurrey	YARR
corncockle	AGROSTEMMA
cornfield	
—plant	POPPY
—weed	KNAWEL
Coronaria	ANEMONE
Coronopus	SENEBIERA, SWINE'S-CRESS
Corrigiola	STRAPWORT
Cortaderia	PAMPAS GRASS
cotton thistle	SCOTCH THISTLE
cough remedy	HOARHOUND
	WHITE HOREHOUND
cow	
—bane	CICUTA
—berry	VACCINIUM
—parsley	LACE CURTAINS, KECK(S)
	KECKSY(E), KEDLOCK, KEX
—parsnip	PIGWEED
—pea	CHERRY-BEAN
cowslip	BUNCH OF KEYS
	CULVER-KEY, HERB-PETER
	PA(I)GLE
—x primrose	POLYANTHUS
cranberry	FEN-BERRY, VACCINIUM
cranesbill	DOVE'S-FOOT, GERANIUM
Crassula	ROCHEA
creeping	
—Jenny	LOOSESTRIFE, MONEYWORT
	PILEA

—moss	SELAGINELLA
Crepis	HAWKSBEARD
cress	CARDAMINE, CORAL-ROOT
Crithmum	SAMP(H)IRE
crocus	SAFFRON
Crossandra	FIRECRACKER FLOWER
Croton	CODIAEUM, JOSEPH'S COAT
crowberry	CRAKEBERRY
crowfoot	ANEMONE
crown of thorns	EUPHORBIA
Cryptanthus	EARTH STAR
	PHEASANT LEAF
	RAINBOW STAR, STARFISH PLANT
cuckoo	
—flower	CARDAMINE, LADY'S SMOCK
—pint	ARUM, WAKE-ROBIN
cucumber	COLOCYNTH, COLOQUINTIDA
Cucurbita	GOURD, SQUASH
cudweed	COTTON-WEED
cup and saucer vine	COBAEA
Cuphea	CIGAR PLANT
Cupid's bower	ACHIMENES
Cyanotis	TEDDY BEAR VINE
cyclamen	SOW-BREAD
Cynanchum	SWALLOW-WORT
Cyperus	UMBRELLA PLANT
daffodil	NARCISSUS
daisy	BELLIS
dame violet	HESPERIS, ROCKET
dandelion	TARAXACUM
Dane's blood	DANEWORT, DWARF ELDER
	WALLWORT
darnel	TARE
Datura	THORN-APPLE
day-lily	FUNKIA, HEMEROCALLIS
dead nettle	ARCHANGEL, DAY-NETTLE
deadly nightshade	ATROPA
	BELLADONNA, DWALE
deep-blue gentian	GENTIANELLA
Delphinium	LARKSPUR
desert privet	PEPEROMIA
devil's ivy	SCINDAPSUS
devil-in-a-bush	NIGELLA
(Devon and Cornwall)	ILLECEBRUM
Dianthus	(CHEDDAR-)PINK
	SWEET WILLIAM
Dicentra	DUTCHMAN'S BREECHES
Dieffenbachia	DUMB CANE, LEOPARD LILY
Digitalis	FOXGLOVE
dill	ANISE, FENNEL
dinner plate Aralia	POLYSCIAS
Dionaea	VENUS'S FLY-TRAP
Dipladenia	PINK ALLAMANDA
Diplotaxis	WALL-MUSTARD
	WALL-ROCKET
dittander	DITTANY, PEPPERWORT

dittany	BURNING BUSH
	SWEET HORSEMINT
Dizygotheca	FINGER ARALIA
dock	POLYGONUM, RUMEX
	SORREL
dog	
—bane	APOCYNUM, FLY-TRAP
—tooth violet	ERYTHRONIUM
—violet	VIOLA CANINA
—wood	HOUNDS-BERRY
dog's mercury	MERCURIALIS
Doronicum	LEOPARD'S-BANE
Dracaena	(MADAGASCAR) DRAGON TREE
	RIBBON PLANT
dragon	DRACONTIUM
—tree	DRACAENA
dragon's head	DRACOCEPHALUM
Drosera	SUNDEW
Dryopteris	MALE FERN
Duchesnea	INDIAN STRAWBERRY
duckweed	DUCK'S-MEAT, LEMNA
dumb cane	DIEFFENBACHIA
Dutch rush	SCOURING RUSH
Dutchman's	
—breeches	DICENTRA
—pipe	ARISTOLOCHIA
dwarf	
—elder	DANE'S BLOOD, DANEWORT
	WALLWORT
—marguerite	SHASTA DAISY
—poppy	ICELAND POPPY
dyer's rocket	MIGNONETTE, WELD
earth star	CRYPTANTHUS
Echinops	GLOBE-THISTLE
Echium	VIPER'S BUGLOSS
edible roots	(*see* **vegetables**)
eggplant	BRINJAL, BROWN JOLLY
Egyptian star cluster	PENTAS
Eichhornia	WATER-HYACINTH
Eleagnus	OLEASTER
elecampane	GOLDEN SAMPHIRE
elephant's	
—ear	PHILODENDRON
—foot	TORTOISE-PLANT
enchanter's nightshade	CIRCAEA
endive	ESCAROLE
Ephedra	SEA-GRAPE
Epilobium	WILLOW-HERB
Epipactis	HELLEBORINE
Episcia	FLAME VIOLET
	LACE FLOWER
Eranthis	WINTER ACONITE
Erica	HEATH, HEATHER
Erigeron	FLEA-BANE
Erodium	STORK'S-BILL
eryngo	SEA-HOLLY

Erysimum	TREACLE MUSTARD
	TREACLE WORM-SEED
Erythronium	DOG'S-TOOTH VIOLET
eschalot	ALLIUM, SHAL(L)OT
Ethiopian gladiolus	ACIDANTHERA
Eupatorium	HEMP-AGRIMONY
Euphorbia	(SUN-)SPURGE
euphrasy	EYE-BRIGHT
evening primrose	CLARKIA, GODETIA
	ENCHANTER'S NIGHTSHADE
	FUCHSIA, OENOTHERA
evergreen cherry	CHERRY-LAUREL
everlasting flower	IMMORTELLE
everlastings	XERANTHEMUM
evil-smelling	CARRION FLOWER
	DANE'S BLOOD, DANEWORT
	DWARF ELDER, FETID IRIS
	ROAST-BEEF PLANT
	SKUNK-CABBAGE, STAPELIA
	SYMPLOCARPUS, WALLWORT
Exacum	PERSIAN VIOLET
eye-bright	EUPHRASY
fat-headed Lizzie	FATSHEDERA
Fatshedera	FAT-HEADED LIZZIE
	IVY TREE
Fatsia	ARALIA, CASTOR-OIL PLANT
fennel-flower	LOVE-IN-A-MIST
ferns	(see separate entry)
Ferraria	TIGRIDIA
Ferula	GIANT FENNEL, LASERWORT
fetid iris	ROAST-BEEF PLANT
feverfew	BACHELOR'S BUTTONS
	PELLITORY, PYRETHRUM
Ficus	BENGAL FIG, FIDDLE LEAF FIG
	MISTLETOE FIG
	RUBBER PLANT, WEEPING FIG
fiddle	
—fig	FICUS
—leaf	PHILODENDRON
field mustard	BRASSOCK
figwort	ACANTHUS, MIMULUS
	NEMESIA, SCROPHULARIA
finger	
—aralia	DIZYGOTHECA
—nail plant	BLUSHING BROMELIAD
	NEOREGELIA
fingers and thumbs	GORSE
firecracker	
—flower	CROSSANDRA
—plant	MANETTIA
fire	
—thorn	PYRACANTH(A)
—weed	ROSE-BAY(WILLOW-HERB)
Fittonia	NERVE PLANT, MOSAIC PLANT
	PAINTED NET LEAF
	SILVER NET LEAF, SNAKESKIN PLANT

five-leaved clover	CINQUEFOIL
flagflower	IRIS
flame	
—nettle	COLEUS
—of the woods	IXORA
—violet	EPISCIA
flaming	
—dragon tree	CORDYLINE
—Katy	KALANCHOE
—sword	VRIESIA
flamingo flower	ANTHURIUM
flax	LINUM
flea-bane	ERIGERON
fleur-de-lis	IRIS
floating plant	BLADDERWORT
	UTRICULARIA
Florentine iris	ORRIS
flowering-rush	BUTOMUS
flowerless plant	CRYPTOGAM
	PTERIDOPHYTE
fodder-plant	SAIN(T)FOIN
fool's parsley	DOG-PARSLEY
forest lily	VELTHEIMIA
forget-me-not	BRUNNERA
	MOUSE-EAR
	MYOSOTIS
	SCORPION-GRASS
four-leaved clover	TRUE-LOVE GRASS
foxglove	DEADMEN'S BELLS
	DIGITALIS
	WITCHES'-THIMBLE
Fragaria	STRAWBERRY
Frankenia	SEA-HEATH
frankincense	LASER(WORT)
freckle face	HYPOESTES
French bean	HARICOT
friendship plant	PILEA
fritillary	CROWN-IMPERIAL
	SNAKE'S-HEAD
frogbit	HYDROCHARIS
fumitory	FUMARIA
Funkia	HOSTA, PLANTAIN LILY
furze	FINGERS AND THUMBS
	GORSE, ULEX, WHIN
Gaillardia	BLANKET FLOWER
Galanthus	SNOWDROP
Galucium	HORNED POPPY
garden	
—cress	LEPIDIUM
—daisy	HEN-AND-CHICKENS
gardener's garters	PHALARIS
garlic	ALLIUM
—mustard	JACK-BY-THE-HEDGE
garlic-like plant	ROCOMBOLE
Gaultheria	WINTERGREEN
gay feather	LIATRIS

genista	DYER'S-BROOM
	DYER'S-GREENWEED
	PETTY WHIN, GREENWEED
gentian	BALDMONEY, FELWORT
	YELLOW-CENTAURY
	YELLOW-WORT
geranium	PELARGONIUM
geum	AVENS
giant	
—bellflower	CAMPANULA, THROATWORT
—fennel	FERULA
gigantic mare's tail	GUNNERA
gillyflower	CLOVE-GILLYFLOWER
	STOCK-GILLYFLOWER
	WALLFLOWER
giving yellow dye	XANTHIUM
gladiolus	CORNFLAG
glasswort	KALI, MARSH SAMPHIRE
	MARSH-SAMPHIRE, SALICORNIA
Glaux	SEA-MILKWORT
globe thistle	ECHINOPS
Gloriosa	GLORY LILY
glory	
—bower	CLERODENDRUM
—lily	GLORIOSA
—of the snow	CHIONODOXA
—pea	CLIANTHUS
Gloxinia	SINNINGIA
goat's	
—beard	ASTILBE
	JACK-GO-TO-BED-AT-NOON
	SALSIFY
—weed	BISHOP('S) WEED
	GOUTWEED, GOUTWORT
Godetia	EVENING PRIMROSE
gold dust	ALYSSUM
golden	
—garlic	ALLIUM
—Pothos	SCINDAPSUS
—rod	AARON'S ROD
—samphire	ELECAMPANE
—seal	YELLOW-ROOT
goldfish plant	COLUMNEA
goose	
—flower	PELICAN-FLOWER
—foot	BLITE, FAT-HEN
	GOOD-KING-HENRY
	ORACH(E), PIGWEED
	SYNGONIUM
gorse	FINGERS AND THUMBS
	FURZE, ULEX, WHIN
gourd	CUCURBITA, SQUASH
goutweed	BISHOP('S) WEED, GOATWEED
grape	
—hyacinth	MUSCARI
	STARCH-HYACINTH

—ivy	RHOICISSUS
—vine	VITIS
grass	(see separate entry)
Gratiola	HEDGE-HYSSOP
great mullein	HAG-TAPER
	SHEPHERD'S CLUB
greater	
—celandine	SWALLOW-WORT
—knapweed	MAFELON
Greek valerian	JACOB'S LADDER
green	
—dragon	DRACUNCULUS
—weed	GENISTA
green-flowered orchid	LISTERA, TWAY-BLADE
Grevillea	SILK OAK
gromwell	SALFERN
ground ivy	BENTH(E)
groundsel	SENECIO
Guernsey lily	NERINE
Gypsophila	SOAP-ROOT
gypsywort	WATER HOREHOUND
Haemanthus	BLOOD LILY
hag	
—taper	(GREAT) MULLEIN
—weed	BROOM
hair-capped mosses	POLYTRICUM
harebell	BLAWORT, BLEWORT
	BLUEBELL, CAMPANULA
	HAIRBELL, HEATH BELL
	SCOTCH BLUEBELL
hare's ear	BUPLEVER
harlequin flower	SPARAXIS
hawksbeard	CREPIS
hawkweed	HIERACIUM
hazelwort	ASARABACCA
healing plant	PANACEA
heart's-ease	PANSY
heath	ANDROMEDA, BELL-HEATHER
	ERICA, GAULTHERIA
heather	CALLUNA, ERICA
—bell	HEATH BELL
hedge	
—hyssop	GRATIOLA
—mustard	FLIX-WEED
—plant	GARLIC MUSTARD
Hedera	IVY
Helenium	SNEEZEWEED
Helianthemum	ROCK-ROSE, SUN ROSE
Helianthus	SUNFLOWER
Helichrysum	EVERLASTING(-FLOWER)
Heliocharis	SPIKE-RUSH
Heliotrope	CHERRY-PIE
hellebore	CHRISTMAS FLOWER
	CHRISTMAS ROSE
Helxine	BABY'S TEARS
	MIND YOUR OWN BUSINESS

Hemerocallis	DAY-LILY
Hemigraphis	RED IVY
hemp-agrimony	EUPATORIUM
henbane	HYOSCYAMUS
Hepaticae	LIVERWORT
Heptapleurum	PARASOL PLANT
herb	(*see* **herbs**)
herb lily	ALSTRO(E)MERIA
Herniaria	RUPTUREWORT
herringbone plant	MARANTA
Hesperis	DAME VIOLET, ROCKET
Hieracium	HAWKWEED
high taper	MULLEIN
Hippeastrum	AMARYLLIS
hogweed	COW-PARSNIP
hollyhock	ALTHAEA, MALVA
	ROSE-MALLOW
honesty	BOTRYCHIUM, MOONWORT
hop-trefoil	SHAMROCK
horse-tail	BOTTLEBRUSH, DUTCH RUSH
	EQUISETINAE, EQUISETALES
	MARE'S-TAIL
Hortensia	HYDRANGEA
hosta	FUNKIA, PLANTAIN LILY
hot water plant	ACHIMENES
Hottonia	WATER-VIOLET
house	
—leek	JUPITER'S BEARD, SENGREEN
—lime	SPARMANNIA
Hoya	WAX PLANT
Humulus	HOP
husk tomato	GROUND-CHERRY
hybrid rose	NOISETTE
hydrangea	HORTENSIA
Hydrophyllum	WATER-LEAF
Hyoscyamus	HENBANE
Hypericum	AARON'S-BEARD
	ROSE OF SHARON
	ST JOHN'S WORT
	ST PETER'S WORT
Hypocyrta	CLOG PLANT
Hypoestes	FRECKLE FACE
	POLKA DOT PLANT
Iberis	CANDYTUFT
ice-plant	MESEMBRIANTHEMUM
Impatiens	BALSAM, BUSY LIZZIE
	JEWEL-WEED, NOLI-ME-TANGERE
	PATIENT LUCY, TOUCH-ME-NOT
Indian	
—corn	MAIZE, ZEA
—cress	LARK'S-HEEL, TROPAEOLUM
—pink	SPIGELIA
—pipe	MONATROPA
—poke	AMERICAN HELLEBORE
—rice	ZIZANIA
—strawberry	DUCHESNEA

indoor oak	NICODEMIA
insectivorous plant	BUTTERWORT
	DARLINGTONIA, DROSERA
	NEPENTHES, PITCHER-PLANT
	SARRACENIA, SUNDEW
Ipomoea	JALAP, MORNING-GLORY
Iresine	BEEFSTEAK PLANT
	BLOOD LEAF, CHICKEN GIZZARD
iris	GLADIOLE, GLADIOLUS
Irish heath	ST DABEOC'S HEATH
Isatis	WOAD
Ismene	PERUVIAN DAFFODIL
Isoetes	QUILLWORT
itchweed	FALSE HELLEBORE
	WHITE HELLEBORE
ivy	ARALIA, HEDERA
	LOVESTONE
—bush	TOD
—tree	FATSHEDERA
ivy-leaved speedwell	HEN-BIT
Ixia	AFRICAN CORN LILY
Ixora	FLAME OF THE WOODS
Jacob's ladder	GREEK VALERIAN
	POLEMONIUM
Jacobinia	KING'S CROWN
jalap	IPOMOEA
Japanese sedge	CAREX
jasmine	JESSAMINE
—plant	BOUVARDIA
Jasione	(SHEEP'S-BIT) SCABIOUS
	SHEEP'S-BIT
	SHEEP'S SCABIOUS
Jerusalem	
—artichoke	SUNFLOWER
—sage	PHLOMIS
jewel-weed	IMPATIENS
John-go-to-bed-at-noon	GOAT'S-BEARD
Joseph's coat	CODIAEUM, CROTON
Juncus	TOAD-GRASS, TOAD-RUSH
jute	CORCHORUS
Kaffir lily	CLIVIA, SCHIZOSTYLIS
Kalanchoe	FLAMING KATY
kale	BOECOLE
kalmia	MOUNTAIN-LAUREL
Karatus	SILKGRASS
kidney	
—bean	FLAGEOLET, FRENCH BEAN
	HARICOT, (SCARLET-)RUNNER
—vetch	ANTHYLLIS, CENTAUREA
	JUPITER'S BEARD
	LADIES'-FINGERS
	LADY'S-FINGERS
kingcup	CALTHA, MARSH-MARIGOLD
king's crown	JACOBINIA
knapweed	CENTAURY, HARD-HEAD
	ST BARNABY'S THISTLE

knawel	SCLERANTHUS
Kniphofia	RED-HOT POKER, TORCH-LILY
knot-grass	PERSICARIA, POLYGONUM
knotted	
—pearlwort	SAGINA
—spurrey	SAGINA
Labrador tea	LEDUM
lace curtains	COW PARSLEY
—flower	EPISCIA
Lachenalia	CAPE COWSLIP
lady's	
—fingers	KIDNEY-VETCH
—mantle	PARSLEY-P(I)ERT
—pincushion	THRIFT
—slipper	CYPRIPEDIUM
	MOCCASIN-FLOWER, ORCHID
—thistle	MILK-THISTLE
lake margin plants	LITORELLA
	SHORE-WEED
lamb's ear	STACHYS
larkspur	BLUE-ROCKET, DELPHINIUM
	LARK'S-HEEL, MONK'S HOOD
	STAVESACRE
Lathraea	TOOTHWORT
Lathyrus	SWEET-PEA, VETCHLING
laurel	LAURUS, SWEET-BAY
Lavatera	TREE-MALLOW
lavender	ASPIC, LAVANDULA
leafless parasite	DODDER
legume grown for forage	GUAR
lentils	PULSE
Leontodon	HAWKBIT
Leonurus	MOTHERWORT
leopard lily	DIEFFENBACHIA
Lepidium	PEPPER-GRASS
lesser yellow trefoil	SHAMROCK
Leucojum	SNOWFLAKE
levantine madder	ALIZARI
Liatris	GAY FEATHER
Ligusticum	LOVAGE
Ligustrum	PRIVET
like clover	MELILOT
lily	AMARYLLIS, ASPHODEL
	FRITILLARY
—of the	
Nile	AGAPANTHUS
valley	CONVALLARIA
—turf	OPHIOPOGON
—type	HYACINTH
Lima bean	SUGAR-BEAN
Limosella	MUDWORT
Linaria	BACON AND EGGS, TOADFLAX
Linum	FLAX
lipstick vine	AESCHYNANTHUS
Listera	TWAY-BLADE
Lithospermum	GROMWELL

Litorella	SHORE-WEED
liverwort	AGRIMONY, HEPATIC(A)
	MARCHANTIA, RICCIA
lollipop plant	PACHYSTACHYS
Lomeria	HARD-FERN
London pride	NANCY-PRETTY
	NONE-SO-PRETTY
	ST PATRICK'S CABBAGE
	SAXIFRAGA
Lonicera	HONEYSUCKLE
loosestrife	MONEYWORT
lousewort	PEDICULARIS
love	
—apple	TOMATO
—in-a-mist	DEVIL-IN-A-BUSH, NIGELLA
—lies-bleeding	AMARANT(H)US
lucerne	ALFALFA
lucky clover	OXALIS
Lunaria	HONESTY
Luzula	WOOD-RUSH
Lychnis	ROSE-CAMPION
Lycopus	GYPSY-WORT
Lysimachia	LOOSESTRIFE
Lythrum	PURPLE LOOSETRIFE
Macleaya	BOCCONIA, PLUME POPPY
Madagascar	
—dragon tree	DRACAENA
—jasmine	STEPHANOTIS
madder	GARDENIA, RUBIA
maize	INDIAN CORN
	SWEET-CORN, ZEA
Malcomia	VIRGINIA STOCK
mallow	ABUTILON, LAVATERA
	MALVA
mandrake	MANDRAGORA, SPRINGWORT
Manettia	FIRECRACKER PLANT
Maranta	HERRINGBONE PLANT
	NEVER NEVER PLANT
	PEACOCK PLANT, PRAYER PLANT
	RABBIT TRACKS
	RATTLESNAKE PLANT
	ZEBRA PLANT
mare's tail	BOTTLEBRUSH, HIPPURIS
marigold	CALENDULA
marjoram	AMARACUS, OREGANO
	ORIGAN(E), ORIGANUM
marsh	
—gentian	BUCKBEAN
—grass	REED
—lily	CALLA
—lousewort	RED-RATTLE
—mallow	ALTHAEA
—marigold	KINGCUP
—plant	MARE'S-TAIL, PENNY-WORT
	WATER-FERN
—samphire	GLASSWORT, SALICORNIA

martagon lily	TURK'S CAP
marvel of Peru	FOUR O'CLOCK, MIRABILIS
masterwort	ASTRANTIA
Matricaria	FEVERFEW
Matthiola	STOCK
matweed	NARD
mayweed	DOG'S-FENNEL
meadow	
—rue	THALICTRUM
—saffron	COLCHICUM, NAKED LADY
—sweet	QUEEN-OF-THE-MEADOW(S)
	SPIRAEA
Meconopsis	POPPY
medicinal plant	BETONY, BIRTHWORT
	CAR(R)AWAY
medick	MEDICAGO, SNAIL
melampode	BLACK HELLEBORE
melitot	FENUGREEK
Mentha	MINT, PENNYROYAL
	PEPPERMINT, SPEARMINT
Mercurialis	(DOG'S) MERCURY
mermaid vine	RHOICISSUS
Mertensia	OYSTER-PLANT
Mesembrianthemum	ICE-PLANT
Meum	BALDMONEY, SPIGNEL
	SPICKNEL
Michaelmas daisy	ASTER
mignonette	DYER'S ROCKET
	RESEDA, WELD
milfoil	ACHILLEA, YARROW
milk	
—root	POLYGAEA
—thistle	LADY'S-THISTLE
—vetch	ASTRAGALUS
	WILD LIQUORICE
—weed	ASCLEPIAS
—wort	POLYGALA, SNAKEROOT
Mimosa	TOUCH-ME-NOT
Mimulus	MONKEY-FLOWER
	MUSK-PLANT
mind-your-own-business	HELXINE
Ming Aralia	POLYSCIAS
miniature grape ivy	CISSUS
mint	CALAMINT, PENNYROYAL
Mirabilis	MARVEL OF PERU
mistletoe	VISCUM
—fig	FICUS
Mitella	BISHOP'S-CAP
mock privet	PHILLYREA
Monarda	BERGAMOT
moneywort	CREEPING JENNY
monk's	
—hood	ACONITE, BLUE-ROCKET
	LARKSPUR
—rhubarb	PATIENCE DOCK
monkey-flower	MIMULUS
Monstera	SPLIT LEAF PHILODENDRON
	SWISS CHEESE PLANT
Montbretia	TRITONIA
moon	
—seed	MENISPERMUM
—wort	BOTRYCHIUM, HONESTY
moorland plant	GRASS OF PARNASSUS
morning-glory	IPOMOEA, JALAP
mosaic plant	FITTONIA
moschatel	ADOXA
Moses in the cradle	RHOEO
moss	ACROGEN, CRYPTOGAM
mossy saxifrage	LADY'S-CUSHION
mother	
—in-law's tongue	SANSEVIERIA
—of thousands	STRAWBERRY GERANIUM
mountain	
—bramble	CLOUDBERRY
—laurel	KALMIA
—sorrel	OXYRIA, ROMAN SORREL
mourning-bride	SWEET SCABIOUS
mouse	
—ear chickweed	CERASTIUM
	SNOW-IN-SUMMER
—tail	MYOSURUS
mudwort	LIMOSELLA
mugwort	WORMWOOD
mulberry	MORUS
mullein	AARON'S ROD, ADAM'S FLANNEL
	HAG-TAPER, HIGH TAPER
	SHEPHERD'S CLUB, VERBASCUM
Muscari	GRAPE HYACINTH
	STARCH HYACINTH
musk	MIMULUS
—scented	MIMULUS, MUSK-MALLOW
—thistle	CARDUUS
mustard	SENVY
Myosotis	FORGET-ME-NOT
Myosurus	MOUSE-TAIL
Myriophyllum	WATER-MILFOIL
Myrrhis	SWEET-CICELY
myrtle	MYRTUS
naked lady	MEADOW-SAFFRON
Nancy-pretty	LONDON PRIDE
narcissus	JONQUIL, PHEASANT'S-EYE
nasturtium	INDIAN CRESS, LARK'S-HEEL
	TROPAEOLUM
Natal plum	CARISSA
navelwort	PENNYWORT
Neapolitan violet	PARMA VIOLET
needle-furze	PETTY WHIN
Nelumbium	LOTE, LOTOS, LOTUS
Nemesia	FIGWORT
nenuphar	WATER-LILY
Neoregelia	BLUSHING BROMELIAD
	FINGERNAIL PLANT

Nepenthe	PITCHER-PLANT	oxlip	FIVEFINGERS
Nepeta	CATMINT, GROUND-IVY	Oxalis	WOOD-SORREL
Nephthytis	SYNGONIUM	Oxyria	MOUNTAIN SORREL
Nerine	GUERNSEY LILY	oyster-plant	GROMWELL, MERTENSIA
Nertera	BEAD PLANT		SALSIFY
nerve plant	FITTONIA	Pachystachys	LOLLIPOP PLANT
nettle	URTICA	padma	SACRED LOTUS
—leaved bellflower	CAMPANULA	painted	
	THROATWORT	—cup	CASTILLEJA
—with female flowers	ROMAN NETTLE		PAINTED LADY
nettle-type	PELLITORY	—lady	PAINTED CUP
never-never plant	MARANTA	—net leaf	FITTONIA
New Zealand flax	PHORMIUM	—tongue	SALPIGLOSSIS
Nicodemia	INDOOR OAK	painter's palette	ANTHURIUM
Nicotiana	TOBACCO PLANT	pampas grass	CORTADERIA
Nidularium	BIRD'S NEST BROMELIAD	Panamiga	PILEA
Nigella	DEVIL-IN-A-BUSH	Panax	ARALIA
	FENNEL-FLOWER, FITCH	pansy	HERB-TRINITY
	LOVE-IN-A-MIST, RAGGED-LADY		LOVE-IN-IDLENESS, VIOLA
night		Papaver	POPPY
—jessamine	CESTRUM	paper	
—shade	HENBANE, MOREL, SOLANUM	—flower	BOUGAINVILLEA
none-so-pretty	LONDON PRIDE	—reed	PAPYRUS
northern fern	HARD-FERN	parasitic plant	MISTLETOE, VISCUM
nose-bleed	YARROW	parasol plant	HEPTAPLEURUM
Nuphar	WATER-LILY	Paris quadrifolia	HERB-PARIS
Nymphaea	LOTE, LOTOS	parkleaves	ST JOHN'S WORT, TUTSAN
	LOTUS, WATER-LILY	Paronychia	WHITLOW-GRASS
oat-shooter	ANGELICA, AIT-SKEITER		WHITLOW-WORT
Oenanthe	WATER-DROPWORT	parsley-fern	ROCK-BRAKE
	WATER-HEMLOCK	parsnip-type	MASTERWORT
Oenothera	EVENING PRIMROSE	parti-coloured	PAINTED LADY
offensive-smelling	DANE'S BLOOD	paschal-flower	ANEMONE, PULSATILLA
	DANEWORT, DWARF ELDER	pasque-flower	ANEMONE, PULSATILLA
	WALLWORT	Passiflora	LOVE-IN-A-MIST
oil-producing	RAPE		PASSION-FLOWER
old-fashioned rose	MOSS-ROSE		WATER-LEMON
oleander	NERIUM, RHODODAPHNE	patience-dock	MONK'S RHUBARB
	ROSE-BAY(LAUREL)	patient Lucy	IMPATIENS
	ROSE-LAUREL	peace lily	SPATHIPHYLLUM
oleaster	ELEAGNUS	peacock	
olive	OLEA	—fern	SELAGINELLA
Ononis	REST-HARROW	—plant	MARANTA
Ophiopogon	LILY TURF	pearlwort	SAGINA
Opuntia	PRICKLY-PEAR	Pedicularis	LOUSEWORT
orange-flowered lily	TIGER-LILY	Pelargonium	GERANIUM, STORK'S-BILL
orchid	CORAL-ROOT, FLY ORCHIS	pelican-flower	GOOSE-FLOWER
	LADY'S-SLIPPER	pellitory	FEVERFEW, YARROW
Ornithogalum	CHINCHERINCHEE		WALL-WORT
	STAR-OF-BETHLEHEM	pennywort	NAVELWORT
orpine	LIVELONG	Pentstemon	BEARDED TONGUE
orval	CLARY	Pentas	EGYPTIAN STAR CLUSTER
oshac	AMMONIAC	penthia	ASTROPHEL, STARLIGHT
ox		pepper-grass	LEPIDIUM
—eye daisy	MARGUERITE	pepperwort	DITTANDER, DITTANY
—tongue	PIERIS		SPANISH CRESS

perennial	
—herb	LASERPICIUM
—saxifrage	LONDON PRIDE
—weed	WILD(-)OAT
periwinkle	APOCYNUM, STROPHANTHUS
	VINCA
Persian violet	EXACUM
persicaria	KNOT-GRASS
Peruvian daffodil	ISMENE
petty whin	GENISTA, NEEDLE-FURZE
Phalaris	GARDENER'S GARTERS
pheasant leaf	CRYPTANTHUS
pheasant's eye	ADONIS, NARCISSUS
Phillyrea	MOCK PRIVET
Philodendron	CORDATUM
	ELEPHANT'S EAR, FIDDLE LEAF
	SWEETHEART PLANT
phlox	POLEMONIUM
Phormium	NEW ZEALAND FLAX
Physalis	CAPE GOOSEBERRY
	CHINESE LANTERN
	GROUND-CHERRY
	WINTER-CHERRY
Phytolacca	POKEWEED
pickling cabbage	RED CABBAGE
Pieris	OX-TONGUE
piggyback plant	TOLMIEA
pigweed	ARAMANTH, COW-PARSNIP
	GOOSEFOOT
Pilea	ALUMINIUM PLANT
	ARTILLERY PLANT
	CREEPING JENNY
	FRIENDSHIP PLANT, PANAMIGA
pilewort	CELANDINE, FIGWORT
pillwort	PILULARIA
Pilularia	PILLWORT
Pimpinella	ANISE, BURNET-SAXIFRAGE
pincushion	
flower	SCABIOUS
pineapple	ANANA(S), BROMELIA
—weed	(RAYLESS) MAYWEED
Pinguicula	BUTTERWORT
pink	CLOVE-GILLY-FLOWER
	CLOVE PINK, DIANTHUS
—Allamanda	DIPLADENIA
—root	WORM-GRASS
pipewort	ERIOCAULON
pitcher-plant	NEPENTHE
Plantago	RIBWORT(-PLAINTAIN)
plantain	RIBGRASS, WAYBREAD
—lily	FUNKIA, HOSTA
Platycerium	STAGHORN-FERN
Platycodon	CHINESE BALLOON FLOWER
Plectranthus	SWEDISH IVY
pleurisy-root	BUTTERFLY-WEED
Plumbago	SEA-LAVENDER, SEA-PINK

plume	
—flower	CELOSIA
—poppy	BOCCONIA, MACLEAYA
Podocarpus	BUDDHIST PINE
poisonous plants	CUCKOO PINT
	FOOL'S PARSLEY
	LORDS AND LADIES
	NIGHTSHADE
pokeweed	PHYTOLACCA
Polemonium	PHLOX
Polianthes	AMARYLLIS, TUBEROSE
polka dot plant	HYPOESTES
Polyanthus	PRIMULA
Polygala	MILKWORT
Polygonatum	SOLOMON'S SEAL
Polygonum	KNOT-GRASS, KNOTWEED
	PURPLE LOOSESTRIFE
	WILLOW-WEED
Polypodium	COMMON POLYPODY
Polyscias	DINNER PLATE ARALIA
	MING ARALIA
pomegranate	PUNICA
pond plant	ACORUS, SWEET-FLAG
pondweed	EELGRASS, FROG'S-LETTUCE
	GRASSWRACK
	HYDROCHARITACEAE
	PICKEREL-WEED
	POTAMOGETON, ZOSTER
poor man's	
—orchid	SCHIZANTHUS
—weather-glass	PIMPERNEL
poppy	MECONOPSIS, PAPAVER
Portulaca	PURSLANE
pot-herb	PURSLANE, PURSLAIN
potato	SOLANUM
Potentilla	CINQUEFOIL, SEPT-FOIL
	TORMENTIL, WILD STRAWBERRY
	BARREN STRAWBERRY
	SILVERWEED
Poterium	BOTTLE-BRUSH
prayer plant	MARANTA
prickly pear	INDIAN FIG, OPUNTIA
—poppy	ARGEMONE
—saltwort	KALI
—samphire	SALTWORT
primrose	BIRD'S-EYE, PRIMULA
Primula	OXLIP, PRIMROSE
prince's feathers	AMARANTHUS
	LONDON PRIDE
privet	LIGUSTRUM
producing red dye	MADDER
provincial-rose	CABBAGE-ROSE
Prunella	SELF-HEAL
Pulicaria	FLEA-BANE
Pulmonaria	LUNGWORT
Pulsatilla	PASQUE-FLOWER

pulse	CALAVANCE, CARAVANCE
	(*see separate entry*)
Punica	POMEGRANATE
purple	
—heart	SETCREASEA
—loosestrife	KNOTWEED
	WILLOW-WEED
	LONG-PURPLES, LYTHRUM
—medick	LUCERN(E)
—orchis	LONG-PURPLES
—passion vine	VYNURA
purslane	PORTULACA
Puschkinia	STRIPED SQUILL
pyracanth(a)	FIRETHORN
Pyrethrum	FEVERFEW
Pyrola	WINTERGREEN
queen-of-the-meadow(s)	MEADOW-SWEET
quillwort	ISOETES
quinsy-berry	BLACKCURRANT
rabbit tracks	MARANTA
radish	RAPHANUS
ragged	
—lady	NIGELLA
—robin	CAMPION, CUCKOO-FLOWER
	WILD-WILLIAMS
rag	
—weed	AMBROSIA, RAGWORT, SENECIO
—wort	AMROSIA, RAGWEED
	SENECIO, TANSY
rainbow star	CRYPTANTHUS
rampion	BELL-FLOWER
ramsons	WILD GARLIC
Ranunculus	BUTTERCUP, SPEARWORT
Rapa	SUGAR-BEET
rape	NAVEW
Raphanus	RADISH
rastibow	REST-HARROW
rattlesnake plant	MARANTA
rayless mayweed	PINEAPPLE-WEED
reate	WATER-CROWFOOT
Rechsteineria	CARDINAL FLOWER
red	
—currant	RIBES
—ivy	HEMIGRAPHIS
—rattle	MARSH LOUSEWORT
—root	CEANOTHUS
—valerian	CENTRANTHUS
	SPUR VALERIAN
red-hot	
—catstail	ACALYPHA
—hot poker	KNIPHOFIA, TORCH-LILY
	TRITOMA
reed-mace	BULRUSH, CAT'S-TAIL, TYPHA
Reseda	DYER'S-ROCKET, DYER'S-WELD
	DYER'S-YELLOWWEED
	MIGNONETTE

resinous plant	STYRAX
rest-harrow	LICORICE, LIQUORICE
	RASTIBOW
Resurrection plant	ROSE OF JERICHO
Retama	SPANISH BROOM
Rhamnus	BUCKTHORN
rhapontic	RHUBARB
Rheinberry/Rhineberry	BUCKTHORN
Rheum	RHUBARB
rhododaphne	OLEANDER
rhododendron	ALPINE ROSE, AZALEA
	ROSE-BAY
Rhoeo	BOAT LILY
	MOSES IN THE CRADLE
Rhoicissus	CAPE GRAPE, GRAPE IVY
	MERMAID VINE
rhubarb	RHAPONTIC, RHEUM
Rhus	SUMACH
ribbon plant	DRACAENA
Ribes	BLACK CURRANT, GOOSEBERRY
	RED CURRANT
ribgrass	PLANTAIN
ribwort(-plaintain)	PLANTAGO
Riccia	LIVERWORT
Richardia	LILY OF THE NILE
Ricinus	CASTOR-OIL PLANT
roadside weed	HEDGE-MUSTARD
	HEDGE-PARSLEY, SILVERWEED
roast-beef plant	FETID IRIS
Rochea	CRASSULA
rock	
—brake	PARSLEY-FERN
—cress	ARABIS, AUBRIET(I)A
	WALL-CRESS
—rose	CISTUS, HELIANTHEMUM
rocket	DAME VIOLET, HESPERIS
roe-blackberry	ROEBUCK-BERRY
	STONE-BRAMBLE
roebuck-berry	ROE-BLACKBERRY
	STONE-BRAMBLE
rose	
—campion	LYCHNIS
—laurel	OLEANDER
—mallow	HIBISCUS, HOLLYHOCK
—of	
Jericho	RESURRECTION PLANT
Sharon	HYPERICUM
—root	STONECROP
rosebay (laurel)	OLEANDER
	RHODODENDRON
—willow herb	SLINKWEED
Rubia	MADDER
rubber plant	FICUS
Rudbeckia	CONEFLOWER
rue	HERB-(OF)-GRACE
	HERB-OF-REPENTANCE

Ruellia	ACANTHUS, MANY-ROOT
Rumex	DOCK, SORREL
rupturewort	HERNIARIA
Ruscus	BUTCHER'S-BROOM
rutabaga	SWEDISH TURNIP
Saccharum	SUGAR-CANE
sacred lotus	NELUMBIUM, NELUMBO
	PADMA
safflower	BASTARD SAFFRON
saffron	CROCUS
sage	CLARY, SALVIA
Sagina	KNOTTED PEARLWORT
	KNOTTED SPURREY, PEARLWORT
Sagittaria	ARROW-HEAD
sainfoin	COCKSCOMB
Saint	
—Barbara's cress	YELLOW ROCKET
—Barnaby's thistle	KNAPWEED
—Bernard's lily	CHLOROPHYTUM
	SPIDER PLANT
—John's wort	AARON'S BEARD
	HYPERICUM, PARKLEAVES
	TUTSAN
—Patrick's cabbage	LONDON PRIDE
—Peter's wort	HYPERICUM
Saintpaulia	AFRICAN VIOLET
salad	
—herb	PURSLANE, PURSLAIN
—plant	CUCUMBER, LETTUCE, LOVAGE
	RADISH, ROCKET, WATER-CRESS
salfern	GROMWELL
Salicornia	GLASSWORT, MARSH-SAMPHIRE
	SALTWORT
saligot	WATER-CHESTNUT
sallow-thorn	SEA-BUCKTHORN
Salpiglossis	PAINTED TONGUE
salsify	GOAT'S-BEARD
	OYSTER-PLANT
Salsola	GLASSWORT, SALTWORT
salt	
—marsh plant	SEA-BLITE
	SEA-LAVENDER, STATICE
—wort	PRICKLY SAMPHIRE
	SALICORNIA, SALSOLA
Salvadora	MUSTARD-TREE
salvia	SAGE
Salvinia	WATER-FERN
samp(h)ire	CRITHMUM
sand	
—spurrey	SPERGULARIA
—wort	ARENARIA, SEA PURSLANE
Sansevieria	BOWSTRING-HEMP
	MOTHER-IN-LAW'S TONGUE
	SNAKE PLANT
Santolina	LAVENDER-COTTON
Sapindus	SOAP-BERRY

Sapium	TALLOW-TREE
Saponaria	SOAP-ROOT, SOAPWORT
Sarcostemma	SOMA
Sarracenia	SIDE-SADDLE FLOWER
sarrasin	BUCKWHEAT
Saussurea	SAW-WORT
Savoy	WINTER CABBAGE
saw-wort	SAUSSUREA, SERRATULA
saxifrage	AARON'S BEARD
	BISHOP'S CAP, STONE-BREAK
scabious	DEVIL'S-BIT
	PINCUSHION FLOWER
scammony	ANATOLIAN CONVOLVULUS
Scandix	SHEPHERD'S NEEDLE
	VENUS'S COMB
Scarborough lily	VALLOTA
scarlet	
—pimpernel	SHEPHERD'S GLASS
	WINK-O-PEEP
—runner	KIDNEY-BEAN
scentless mignonette	DYER'S-ROCKET
	WELD
Schefflera	UMBRELLA TREE
Schizanthus	BUTTERFLY FLOWER
	POOR MAN'S ORCHID
Schizostylis	KAFFIR LILY
Scilla	BLUEBELL, SQUILL
	WOOD-HYACINTH
Scindapsus	DEVIL'S IVY, GOLDEN POTHOS
	SILVER VINE
Scirpus	CLUB-RUSH
scorpion-grass	FORGET-ME-NOT
scorzonera	BLACK SALSIFY
Scotch	
—bluebell	HAREBELL
—rose	BURNET-ROSE
—thistle	COTTON THISTLE
scouring rush	DUTCH RUSH
Scrophularia	FIGWORT
scurvy-grass	HORSE-RADISH
Scutellaria	SKULLCAP
sea	
—buckthorn	SALLOW-THORN
—burdock	CLOTBUR, XANTHIUM
—gilliflower	THRIFT
—grape	EPHEDRA, GLASSWORT
	GULFWEED
—heath	FRANKENIA
—holly	ERINGO, ERYNGO
—lavender	PLUMBAGO, STATICE
—milkwort	GLAUX
—pink	ARMERIA
	LADY'S PINCUSHION
	PLUMBAGO, THRIFT
—purslane	SANDWORT
—rocket	CAKILE

seaside plants	CORRIGIOLA
	ENTEROMORPHA, FRANKENIA
	GLASSWRACK, MARRAM-GRASS
	SEA-COLEWORT, SEA-HEATH
	SEA-GILLIFLOWER, SEA-GRASS
	SEA-KALE, SEA-ORACH(E)
	SEA-REED, STRAPWORT, THRIFT
—shrubs	SEA-BUCKTHORN
	TAMARISK
sedge	CAREX, CLUB-RUSH, SPIKE-RUSH
—type	XYRIS
Sedum	STONECROP, WALL-PEPPER
Selaginella	CREEPING MOSS
	PEACOCK FERN
self-heal	BRUNELLA, PRUNELLA
Sempervivum	HOUSE-LEEK
Senebiera	CORONOPUS, SWINE'S-CRESS
Senecio	CAPE IVY, CINERARIA
	GROUNDSEL, RAGWEED
	RAGWORT
sengreen	HOUSE-LEEK
senna	CASSIA
senvy	MUSTARD
sept-foil	POTENTILLA, TORMENTIL
Serratula	SAW-WORT
sesame	BENNIE, BENN(I)
	TEEL, TIL
Seseli	MEADOW-SAXIFRAGE
Setcreasea	PURPLE HEART
setterwort	STINKING HELLEBORE
setwall	CETYWALL, SETUALE
	VALERIAN
shadbush	AMELANCHIER
shal(l)ot	ALLIUM, ESCHALOT
shamrock	LESSER YELLOW TREFOIL
Shasta daisy	(DWARF) MARGUERITE
sheep's	
—bit	JASIONE, SHEEP'S SCABIOUS
—scabious	JASIONE
shepherd's	
—club	HAG-TAPER, (GREAT) MULLEIN
—cress	TEESDALIA
—glass	SCARLET PIMPERNEL
—myrtle	BUTCHER'S BROOM
—needle	SCANDIX, VENUS'S COMB
—purse	CAPSELLA
—rod	SMALL TEASEL
Sherardia	FIELD MADDER
shield fern	ASPIDIUM
shore-weed	LITORELLA
showy flowers	SILENE, STRELITZIA
shrimp plant	BELOPERONE
shrubs	(see separate entry)
shrubby plant	HYDRANGEA
side-saddle flower	SARRACENIA
Siderasis	BROWN SPIDERWORT

silk	
—grass	AGAVE, KARATUS, YUCCA
—oak	GREVILLEA
silver	
—net leaf	FITTONIA
—vine	SCINDAPSUS
—weed	GOOSE-GRASS
	POTENTILLA, TANSY
single chrysanthemum	MARGUERITE
Sinningia	GLOXINIA
Sison	STONEWORT
Sium	SKIRRET, WATER-PARSNIP
skirret	SIUM, WATER-PARSNIP
skullcap	SCUTELLARIA
skunk-cabbage	SYMPLOCARPUS
slinkweed	ROSE-BAY WILLOW HERB
slipper	
—flower	CALCEOLARIA
—wort	CALCEOLARIA
sloe	BULLACE
small teasel	SHEPHERD'S ROD
smallage	WILD CELERY
smart-weed	WATERPEPPER
Smithiantha	TEMPLE BELLS
snail	MEDICK
snake	
—plant	SANSEVIERIA
—root	ARISTOLOCHIA
	BISTORT, MILKWORT
—skin plant	FITTONIA
—weed	ADDER('S) WORT, BISTORT
snake's-head	FRITILLARY
snapdragon	ANTIRRHINUM, FROG'S-MOUTH
sneeze	
—weed	HELENIUM
—wort	WHITE HELLEBORE, YARROW
snow	
—ball-tree	GUELDER-ROSE
—berry	SYMPHORICARPUS
—drop	GALANTHUS
—flake	LEUCOJUM
—in-summer	MOUSE-EAR CHICKWEED
soap	
—berry	SAPINDUS
—root	GYPSOPHILA, SAPONARIA
—wort	SAPONARIA
Solanum	BITTERSWEET, POTATO
	(WOODY) NIGHTSHADE
	WINTER CHERRY
Solidago	GOLDENROD
Solomon's seal	POLYGONATUM
soma	SARCOSTEMMA
Sonchus	SOW-THISTLE
sops-in-wine	CLOVE-PINK
sorrel	DOCK, RUMEX
southernwood	BOY'S LOVE

sow	
—bread	CYCLAMEN
—thistle	SONCHUS
Spanish	
—bayonet	YUCCA
—broom	RETAMA, SPART(IUM)
—cress	PEPPERWORT
Sparaxis	HARLEQUIN FLOWER
Sparganium	BUR-REED
Sparmannia	HOUSE LIME
spart(ium)	SPANISH BROOM
Spathiphyllum	PEACE LILY
spear	
—thistle	BUR-THISTLE
	CIRSIUM, CNICUS
—wort	RANUNCULUS
speckled carnation	PICOTEE
Specularia	VENUS'S LOOKING-GLASS
speedwell	BIRD'S-EYE
	FLUELLIN, VERONICA
Spergula	SPURREY
Spergularia	SANDWORT-SPURREY
sphagnum	BOG-MOSS
spider	
—plant	CHLOROPHYTUM
	ST BERNARD'S LILY
—wort	TRADESCANTIA
Spigelia	CAROLINA PINK
	INDIAN PINK
spignel	BALDMONEY, MEUM
	SPICKNEL
spike-rush	HELIOCHARIS
spikenard	NARD
spinach	SPINAGE
spinage	SPINACH
spineless thistle	KNAPWEED
spiny-leaved fern	HOLLY-FERN
Spiraea	DROP-WORT
	MEADOW-SWEET
spleenwort	ASPLENIUM, MAIDENHAIR
	WALL-RUE
split leaf Philodendron	MONSTERA
spotted orchis	WAKE-ROBIN
spring	
—beauty	CLAYTONIA
—start flower	TRITELIA
—wort	MANDRAKE
spur valerian	CENTRANTHUS
	RED VALERIAN
spurge	ALEURITES, EUPHORBIA
	POINSETTIA, WARTWEED
—laurel	DAPHNE
spurrey	SPERGULA
squash	CUCURBITA, GOURD
squill	SCILLA
squinancy-wort	QUINSY-WORT

Stachys	BETONY, BISHOP'S WORT
	LAMB'S EAR
staghorn	
—fern	PLATYCERIUM
—moss	CLUB-MOSS
Stapelia	CARRION-FLOWER
star	
—fish plant	CRYPTANTHUS
—light	ASTROPHEL, PENTHIA
—of Bethlehem	CAMPANULA
	ORNITHOGALUM
—of-the-earth	BUCK'S-HORN PLANTAIN
—thistle	CENTAUREA
—wort	ASTER, STITCHWORT
starch hyacinth	GRAPE HYACINTH
	MUSCARI
Statice	SEA-LAVENDER
stavesacre	DELPHINIUM, LARKSPUR
Stellaria	CHICKWEED
Stephanotis	MADAGASCAR JASMINE
stinking	
—camomile	MAYWEED
—crane's bill	HERB-ROBERT
—hellebore	SETTERWORT
stitchwort	ASTER, CHICKWEED
	STARWORT
stock	MATTHIOLA
Stoke's aster	STOKESIA
stone	
—bramble	ROEBUCK-BERRY
	ROE-BLACKBERRY
—break	SAXIFRAGE
—crop	ORPIN(E), ROSE-ROOT
	SEDUM, WALL-PEPPER
	WALL-WORT, WORM-GRASS
—wort	SISON
stork's-bill	ERODIUM, PELARGONIUM
strapwort	CORRIGIOLA
Stratiotes	WATER-SOLDIER
strawberry	FRAGARIA
—geranium	MOTHER OF THOUSANDS
—tomato	BLADDER-CHERRY
Strelitzia	BIRD OF PARADISE
Streptocarpus	CAPE PRIMROSE
striped squill	PUSCHKINIA
Strophanthus	PERIWINKLE
sub-Alpine	SPIGNEL
succory	CHICORY
sugar	
—bean	LIMA BEAN
—beet	RAPA
—cane	SACCHARUM
—grass	SWEET-SORGHUM
sumach	RHUS
sun	
—dew	DROSERA

—facing plant	TURNSOLE
—flower	HELIANTHUS
type	RUDBECKIA
—rose	HELIANTHEMUM
—spurge	EUPHORBIA
swallow-wort	ASCLEPIAS, CELANDINE
	CYNANCHUM
	GREATER CELANDINE
Swedish	
—ivy	PLECTRANTHUS
—turnip	RUTABAGA
sweet	
—bay	LAUREL, LAURUS
—brier	EGLANTINE
—Cicely	CHERVIL, MYRRHIS
—corn	MAIZE
—flag	ACORUS, CALAMUS
—gale	BOG-MYRTLE, MYRICA
	SWEET-WILLOW
—pea	LATHYRUS, VETCHLING
—scabious	MOURNING-BRIDE
—sorghum	SUGAR-GRASS
—William	DIANTHUS
—willow	BOG-MYRTLE, SWEET-GALE
sweetheart plant	PHILODENDRON
swine's	
—cress	CORONOPUS, SENEBIERA
	WART-CRESS
—succory	ARNOSERIS
Swiss cheese plant	MONSTERA
Symphoricarpus	SNOW-BERRY
Symphytum	BORAGE, COMFREY
Symplocarpus	SKUNK-CABBAGE
Syngonium	ARROWHEAD VINE
	GOOSEFOOT PLANT
	NEPHTHYTIS
Syrian rue	HARMALA, HARMEL
Tagetes	AFRICAN MARIGOLD
	FRENCH MARIGOLD
tallow-tree	SAPIUM
Tanacetum	TANSY
tansy	RAGWORT, SILVERWEED
	TANACETUM, YARROW
Taraxacum	DANDELION
tare	DARNEL, VETCH
taro	COLOCASIA
tarragon	STARAGEN
teasels	DIPSACUS
teddy bear vine	CYANOTIS
teel	SESAME, TIL
Teesdalia	SHEPHERD'S CRESS
telegraph-plant	DESMODIUM
temple bells	SMITHIANTHA
Tetrastigma	CHESTNUT VINE
Thalictrum	MEADOW-RUE
Thapsia	LASERWORT

thin-leaved ferns	FILMY FERNS
thistle	CARLINA, CNICUS
thorn-apple	DATURA
thrift	ARMERIA, SEA-GILLIFLOWER
	SEA-PINK
throatwort	CAMPANULA
Thunbergia	BLACK-EYED SUSAN
thyme	CALAMINT, THYMUS
Ti plant	CORDYLINE
tiger-flower	TIGRIDIA
Tigridia	FERRARIA
til	SESAME, TEEL
toad	
—flax	AARON'S BEARD
	BACON AND EGGS, FLUELLIN
	LINARIA, MOTHER OF MILLIONS
—grass	JUNCUS, TOAD-RUSH
tobacco	NICOTIANA
Tolmiea	PIGGYBACK PLANT
tomato	LOVE-APPLE, WOLF'S-PEACH
toothwort	CARDAMINE, CORAL-ROOT
	DENTARIA, LATHRAEA
torch	
—lily	KNIPHOFIA
	RED-HOT POKER, TRITOMA
—thistle	CACTUS, CEREUS
tormentil	POTENTILLA, SEPT-FOIL
tortoise-plant	ELEPHANT'S FOOT
touch-me-not	BALSAM, MIMOSA
Tradescantia	INCH PLANT
	SPIDERWORT, WANDERING JEW
tragacanth	ASTRAGALUS
traveller's joy	CLEMATIS
	OLD MAN'S BEARD
	VIRGIN'S-BOWER
treacle-mustard	ERYSIMUM
tree	
—mallow	LAVATERA, VELVET-LEAF
—peony	MOUTAN
trees	*(see separate entry)*
Treucrium	WOOD-GERMANDER
Trifolium	CLOVER
Trigonella	FENUGREEK
Tritelia	SPRING STAR FLOWERS
Triticum	WHEAT
Tritoma	KNIPHOFIA, RED-HOT POKER
	TORCH-LILY
Tritonia	MONTBRETIA
Trollius	GLOBE-FLOWER
Tropaeolum	NASTURTIUM
true-love	HERB-PARIS
trumpet flower	INCARVILLEA
tuberose	POLIANTHES
Turk's cap	MARTAGON LILY
tutsan	PARKLEAVES, ST JOHN'S WORT
tway-blade	LISTERA

two-flowered		
daffodil	PRIMROSE PEERLESS	
Typha	REED-MACE	
Ulex	GORSE	
umbrella		
—plant	CYPERUS	
—tree	SCHEFFLERA	
urn plant	AECHMEA	
Urtica	NETTLE	
Utricularia	BLADDERWORT	
uva-ursi	BEAR-BERRY	
Vaccinium	COWBERRY, CRANBERRY	
	WHORTLEBERRY	
valerian	ALL-HEAL, CENTRANTHUS	
	CETYWALL, SETUALE, SETWALL	
Vallota	SCARBOROUGH LILY	
variegated grass	GARDENER'S GARTERS	
vase plant	AECHMEA	
Veltheimia	FOREST LILY	
velvet plant	VYNURA	
Venus's		
—comb	SCANDIX, SHEPHERD'S NEEDLE	
—fly-trap	DIONAEA	
—looking-glass	SPECULARIA	
Veratrum	WHITE HELLEBORE	
Verbascum	MULLEIN	
Verbena	VERVAIN	
Veronica	SPEEDWELL	
vervain	LANTANA, VERBENA	
vetch	FITCH, TARE, VICIA	
vetchling	LATHYRUS, SWEET-PEA	
Viburnum	GUELDER-ROSE	
Vicia	VETCH	
Vinca	PERIWINKLE	
Viola	PANSY, VIOLET	
violet	VIOLA	
viper's		
—bugloss	BLUE WEED	
	BLUE THISTLE, ECHIUM	
—grass	BLACK SALSIFY	
virgin's bower	CLEMATIS	
	TRAVELLER'S-JOY	
Virginia		
—creeper	AMPELOPSIS, WOODBIND	
	WOODBINE	
—stock	MALCOMIA	
Viscum	MISTLETOE	
Vitis	GRAPE-VINE	
Vreisia	FLAMING SWORD	
Vynura	PURPLE PASSION VINE	
	VELVET PLANT	
wahoo	BURNING BUSH	
wake-robin	ARUM, CUCKOO-PINT	
	FRIAR'S COWL	
	LORDS AND LADIES	
	SPOTTED ORCHIS	

wall	
—cress	ARABIS, ROCK-CRESS
—flower	CHEIRANTHUS, CHEIRINIA
	GILLYFLOWER, JILLY-FLOWER
—mustard	DIPLOTAXIS, WALL-ROCKET
—pepper	SEDUM, STONECROP
	WALL-WORT
—plant	THALE-CRESS
—rocket	DIPLOTAXIS, WALL-MUSTARD
—rue	SPLEENWORT
—wort	DANE'S BLOOD, DANEWORT
	DWARF ELDER, PELLITORY
	STONE-CROP, WALL-PEPPER
wandering Jew	TRADESCANTIA, ZEBRINA
wart	
—cress	SWINE'S-CRESS
—weed	LICHEN, SPURGE, WARTWORT
water	
—chestnut	HORN-NUT, SALIGOT
—crowfoot	REATE
—dropwort	OENANTHE
—fern	PILLWORT, SALVINIA
—flag	YELLOW IRIS
—grass	REED
—hemlock	CICUTA, COWBANE
	OENANTHE
—hyacinth	EICHHORNIA
—leaf	HYDROPHYLLUM
—lemon	PASSION-FLOWER
—lily	CANDOCK, NELUMBIUM
	NELUMBO, NENUPHAR
	NUPHAR, NYMPHAEA
—milfoil	MYRIOPHYLLUM
—parsnip	SIUM, SKIRRET
—pepper	SMART-WEED
—pimpernel	BROOKWEED
—plant	ANACHARIS, HORN-WORT
	HYDROPHYTE, MYRIOPHYLLUM
	PIPEWORT
—plantain	ALISMA
—rice	ZIZANIA
—soldier	STRATIOTES
—speedwell	BROOKLIME
—starwort	CALLITRICHE
—thyme	CANADIAN PONDWEED
—violet	HOTTONIA
—weed	ANACHARIS
waterside plant	PURPLE LOOSESTRIFE
wax	
—myrtle	CANDLE-BERRY
—plant	HOYA
waybread	PLANTAIN
weeping fig	FICUS
weld	DYER'S ROCKET, MIGNONETTE
Welsh onion	CIBOL
wheat	TRITICUM

whin	FINGERS AND THUMBS
	FURZE, GORSE, ULEX
white	
—bottle	BLADDER CAMPION
—bryony	MANDRAKE
—clover	DUTCH CLOVER, SHAMROCK
—hellebore	SNEEZEWORT, VERATRUM
—lily	MADONNA-LILY
whitlow-grass	PARONYCHIA
	WHITLOW-WORT
whortleberry	BILBERRY, COWBERRY
	HUCKLEBERRY, HURTLEBERRY
	VACCINIUM
wild	
—aster	MICHAELMAS-DAISY
—celery	MARSHWORT, SMALLAGE
—chrysanthemum	CORN-MARIGOLD
	OX-EYE
—crab-apple	WILDING
—fig	CAPRIFIG, GOAT-FIG
—flax	LINUM, PURGING FLAX
—garlic	RAMSONS
—geranium	CRANESBILL
—hyacinth	CULVER-KEY
—marjoram	ORIGAN(E)
—mint	HORSEMINT
—mustard	CHARLOCK
—olive	OLEASTER
—pansy	KISS-ME
—pink	MAIDEN PINK
—rice	ZIZANIA
—rose	DOG-ROSE, EGLANTINE
	SWEET-BRIAR, SWEET-BRIER
—strawberry	POTENTILLA
—Swedish turnip	NAVEW
—Williams	RAGGED-ROBIN
willow	
—herb	CHAMAENERION, EPILOBIUM
	FIRE-WEED, ROSE-BAY
—weed	KNOTWEED
	PURPLE LOOSESTRIFE
wind-flower	(WOOOD-)ANEMONE
wink-o-peep	SCARLET PIMPERNEL
winter	
—aconite	ERANTHIS
	WINTER HELLEBORE
—cabbage	SAVOY
—cherry	CHINESE LANTERN PLANT
	PHYSALIS, SOLANUM
—cress	BARBAREA, YELLOW-ROCKET
—green	CHIMAPHILA, GAULTHERIA
	MONOTROPA, PYROLA
witches'-thimble	FOXGLOVE
with	
—long spikes	LUPIN(E)
—red bracts	POINSETTIA

—ribbed leaves	HOSTA, PLANTAIN
witloof	CHICORY
woad	ISATIS
wolf's	
—bane	ACONITE, FRIAR'S CAP
	MONKSHOOD
—peach	TOMATO
wood	
—anemone	WIND-FLOWER
—bind/woodbine	HONEYSUCKLE
	VIRGINIA CREEPER
—germander	TREUCRIUM
—hyacinth	BLUEBELL, SCILLA
—land plant	SANICLE
—loosestrife	YELLOW PIMPERNEL
—rush	LUZULA
—ruff	QUINSY-WORT
	SQUINANCY-WORT
—sorrel	OXALIS
woody-nightshade	BITTERSWEET, SOLANUM
worm-grass	PINKROOT, STONECROP
wormwood	ARTEMISIA, MUGWORT
	SOUTHERNWOOD
Xanthium	CLOTBUR, SEA-BURDOCK
Xeranthemum	EVERLASTINGS
yarr	CORN SPURREY
yarrow	ACHILLEA, MILFOIL
	NOSE-BLEED, PELLITORY
	SNEEZEWORT, TANSY
yellow	
—centaury	GENTIAN, YELLOW-WORT
—clover	HOP-TREFOIL
—flowered narcissus	DAFFODIL
—iris	WATER-FLAG
—jasmine	GELSEMIUM
—loosestrife	LYSIMACHIA
—pimpernel	(WOOD) LOOSESTRIFE
—poppy	WELSH POPPY
—rattle	COCKSCOMB
—rocket	BARBAREA
	ST BARBARA'S CRESS
	WINTER-CRESS
—root	GOLDEN-SEAL
—weed	COMMON RAGWORT, GROUNDSEL
—wort	GENTIAN, YELLOW CENTAURY
yuc(c)a	ADAM'S NEEDLE, CASSAVA
	SILK-GRASS, SPANISH BAYONET
	SPANISH DAGGER
Zantedeschia	ARUM-LILY, CALLA LILY
	LILY OF THE NILE
Zea	INDIAN CORN, MAIZE
zebra plant	AECHMEA, APHELANDRA
	MARANTA
Zebrina	INCH PLANT, WANDERING JEW
Zizania	CANADA RICE, INDIAN RICE
zoster	EELGRASS, GRASSWRACK

plant diseases

including: pests	
corky scab	OEDEMA
diseases	
—affecting	
apple trees	APPLE BLOSSOM WILT
	BROWN ROT, CANKER
	CORAL SPOT, LEAF SCORCH
	MILDEW, SCAB, WITHER TIP
beans	POD CANKER, RUST
cabbage	ANBURY, BLACK ROT
	CLUB ROOT
cereals	SMUT
citrus, etc	LEAF SPOT
currant bushes	BIG BUD, CORAL SPOT
	LEAF SPOT
cuttings	DAMPING OFF, DIE-BACK
fruit trees	AMERICAN BLIGHT
	CROWN GALL, DIE-BACK
	WOOLLY APHIS
onions	MILDEW, SMUT
peach trees	PEACH-LEAF BLISTER
	PEACH-LEAF CURL
palms, etc	ANTHRACNOSE
pear trees	PEAR LEAF BLISTER
	SCAB
plum trees	PLUM REE RUST, SCAB
	SILVER LEAF
potatoes	BLIGHT, (CORKY) SCAB,
	LEAF ROLL, POTATO MOSAIC
	POWDERY SCAB
	STORAGE DISEASE
	WART DISEASE
roses	BLACK SPOT, CROWN GALL
	DIE-BACK, MILDEW, RUST
rye	ERGOT
seedlings	DAMPING OFF, DIE-BACK
soft-leaved plants	BLACKLEG
	BOTRYTIS, RUST
trees	DUTCH ELM DISEASE
	HONEY FUNGUS
turnip	ANBURY, CLUB ROOT
various plants	BRAND, WILT
wheat	PUCCINIA, RUST
—oedema	CORKY SCAB
—producing	
anbury	SLIME FUNGUS
black	
—powder	SOOTY MOULD
—spots	ANTHRACNOSE
brown	
—spores	RUST
—spots	LEAF SPOT
cork-like growths	CORKY SCAB
	OEDEMA
grey mould	BOTRYTIS

rotten parts	BLACKLEG, CROWN ROT
	ROOT ROT, STEM ROT
	TUBER ROT
white powder	(POWDER)MILDEW
—rust fungus	UREDO
pests	
—affecting	
apple trees	APHIS
	APPLE BLOSSOM WEEVIL
	BARK BORER, CAPSID BUG
	CODLIN MOTH, LACKEY MOTH
	(OYSTER-SHELL)SCALE
	RED-FOOTED BEETLE, RED SPIDER
	SAWFLY, SMALL ERMINE MOTH
	SUCKER, TRUNK BORER
all plants	APHIS, CATERPILLAR
	EARWIG
asparagus	BEETLE FLY
beans	AMERICAN BEETLE, APHIS
	BEAN BEETLE, BEAN WEEVIL
	SPANISH BEETLE
	THRIP
bulbs	BULB MITE
cabbage	CABBAGE MOTH
	CABBAGE ROOT FLY
	CABBAGE WHITE BUTTERFLY
	DIAMOND-BLACK MOTH
carrots	CARROT FLY
celery	CELERY (STEM) FLY
	LEAF MINER
cherry trees	CHERRY MOTH SCAB
	CHERRY SAWFLY
	LACKEY MOTH, SLUGWORM
currant bushes	CURRANT MOTH
	MAGPIE MOTH, SAWFLY
	SCALE
cyclamen, etc	CYCLAMEN MITE
flowers	EARWIG, LEAF MINER
fruit trees	BROWN-TAIL MOTH
	CHAFER BEETLE
	GOAT MOTH
	LEAF-ROLLER MOTH
	LEAF TORTRIX
	SHOT-BORER BEETLE
	VAPOURER MOTH
	WINTER MOTH
	WOOD LEOPARD MOTH
gooseberry bushes	GOOSEBERRY MOTH
	MAGPIE MOTH
	SAWFLY
grape vines	BLACK WEEVIL
	MEALY BUG, VINE WEEVIL
greenfly	APHIS(APHIDES)
greenhouse plants	GHOST FLY
	WHITE FLY
nut trees	NUT SAWFLY

onions	ONION FLY	—noisily	OBSTREPERATE
parsnips	LEAF MINER	active	SPRINGE
pear trees	BARK BORER	accomplished	ARCH
	LACKEY MOTH, MIDGE	adopt native ways	GO FANTI
	(OYSTER-SHELL)SCALE	adorn	BEDIGHT
	PITH MOTH	affording redress	REDRESSIVE
	RED-FOOTED BEETLE	again	AGEN
	RED SPIDER, SAWFLY	against	GAINST
	SMALL ERMINE MOTH	alabaster	ALABLASTER
	SOCIAL PEAR MOTH	appeal	PROVOKE
	TRUNK BORER	are	ART
peas	PEA BEETLE, THRIP	array	BEDIGHT
pines	PINE BEAUTY (MOTH)	art of painting	PEINTURE
plum trees	BARK BORER	assembly	DIVAN
	LACKEY MOTH, MAGPIE MOTH	attack in the rear	REAR
	MOTTLED UMBER MOTH	attentive	INTENTIVE, LISTFUL
	(OYSTER-SHELL)SCALE	auxiliary power	UNDER-POWER
	SMALL ERMINE MOTH	avalanche	LAUWINE
	TRUNK BORER	avowed lover	PROTESTANT
potatoes	ROSY RUST MOTH	bank	RIVAGE
raspberries	CLAY-COLOURED WEEVIL	base	GROUNDLING
	RASPBERRY BEETLE	be	
	RASPBERRY MOTH	—flooded	FLOAT
	RASPBERRY SHOOT BORER	—languorous	SWOON
	RASPBERRY WEEVIL	—non-existent	UNBE
roots	EELWORM, FUNGUS	—soaked in blood	WELTER
	VINE WEEVIL	beautiful	SHEEN
roses	GALL-FLY, GOLDEN CHAFER	beneath	NEATH
	LEAF-CUTTER BEE	bestially	BEASTILY
	ROSE BEETLE	betray	CONFESS
	ROSE MAGGOT, ROSE TORTRIX	bevel-wheel	BEDEL
trees	GOAT MOTH, LACKEY MOTH	bird's love-song	VALENTINE
	LEAF-ROLLER MOTH	bittern	BITTO(U)R, BITTUR
	MARCH MOTH, SHOT-BORER BEETLE	black	SABLE
	SWIFT MOTH	—tincture	BUFO
	TORTRIX MOTH	blushing girl	BLUSHET
turnips	SAWFLY, TURNIP BEETLE	board	BO(O)RD, BORDE
	TURNIP FLY, TURNIP MOTH	body of	
	YELLOW UNDERWING MOTH	—knights-errant	KNIGHTHOOD ERRANT
various plants	CENTIPEDE, EARWIG	—water	WAVE
	LEATHER-JACKET, MILLIPEDE	boiled fat beef	GAG
	SLUG, SNAIL, SWIFT MOTH	boorish	SWAINISH
	WOODLOUSE	border	MARGENT
—aphis	GREENFLY	born under unpropitious	
—brown, disc-shaped	SCALE	star	EVIL-STARRED
—causing		bowstring	NERVE
fluffy patches	MEALY BUG	brainy	INTELLECTED
pale patches	VIRUS	break in pieces	TO-BREAK
—sap-sucker	APHIS, RED SPIDER MITE	bright	SHEEN
	WHITE FLY	capable of being clothed	HABILABLE
—small black flies	THRIPS	carry a message	MESSAGE
poetic		cease to be	UNBE
old words used by various poets		chariot	CAR
not covered elsewhere:		cicada	BALM-CRICKET
act		city urchin	TOWNSKIP
—like a fugleman	FUGLE	clad in purple	PORPORATE

close-fitting	SUCCINCT
clumsy	UNHEPPEN
collection of wagons	WAGONAGE
compelled	FAIN
complaining	MUTTERATION
content for want of better	FAIN
contrary of wealth or well-being	ILLTH
corpse	CORSE
cottage	COT
council	DIVAN
current	TIDE
curse	MALISON
daffodil	DAFFADOWNDILLY
	DAFFODILLY
dash	VIRETOT
day other than birthday	UNBIRTHDAY
dead-leaf colour	PHILOMOT
decoration of flowers	GARLANDAGE
den of iniquity	DOMDANIEL
denial of right to	
private property	ASPHETERISM
depict in pavement	IMPAVE
deprived of the appearance	
of a prince	DEPRINZED
desolate	WASTEFUL
despondency	DESPOND
detached	UNDIVESTED
did	GAN
discomfit	SHEND
disfavour	DISGUST
disgrace	SHEND
disorderly	RAGMATICAL
disorganise	UNMECHANISE
displeasure	DISGUST
distaste	DISGUST
divulge	UNCONFINE
domain	BOURN(E)
double limerick	TWINER
downcast	DOWN-LOOKED
dreamy	DREAMFUL
drummer	DRAKE
dullness	YAWN
dwelling	BOWER
eager to	FAIN
elicit	SWEEP
embroidered	SET-STITCH'D
empty region of air or water	WILD
emulate	EMULE
enchanted	FATED
enjoyment	PLEASANCE
equip	BEDIGHT
even	EEN
evening	EVE, EVEN
excellent	LUMMY
excess of formality	WIGGERY
face bravely	BIDE

fainting fit	SOUND, SWOUN
fancy	FANGLE
feathery	FLEDGY
field of battle	PLAIN
fiery red gem	PYROPUS
flash of fire or lightning	FIRE-FLAG
	FIRE-FLAUGHT
flourished	ARCH
flow in again	REINFUND
flushed	HECTIC
foaming	SPOOMING
follow	UPFOLLOW
forehead	FRONT
forgetfulness	OBLIVION
fortify	MUNITE
fount(ain)	FONT
fragment	FRUST
fray	FRIDGE
free from yoke	DISYOKE
frisky	WANTON
full of springs	FOUNTFUL
furnish	BEDIGHT
gad	VIRETOT
gay	WANTON
girded up	SUCCINCT
glad	FAIN
glance	ASPECT
gloomy	DARKSOME, DOWN-LOOKED
go native	GO FANTI
good news	EVANGEL
green woodpecker	YAFFINGALE
greet	DOLE
grotto	GROT
ground	MARL
growing luxuriously	WANTON
guardianship	WARDENRY
hall under sea	DOMDANIEL
halloo	HALLALOO
having	
—intellect	INTELLECTED
—the form of a tent	TENTING
heaven	SWERGA
heavenly spirit	GLENDOVEER
heed	HEARKEN
idleness	IDLESSE
illimitable	EXTERMINABLE
illumine	ILLUME
imaginary animal	WHANGAM
immaterial	UNESSENTIAL
impair	EMPERISH
impatient of	RESTLESS
imperfectly formed	UNDERSHAPEN
in	
—another way	ANOTHERGUESS
—strong words	IRON-WORDED
—the dark	DARKLINGS

India	IND	not	
industrious	WORKSOME	—burdensome	UNIMPOSING
inferior	UNDERRATE	—held back	UNWITHHOLDEN
—devil	PUG	—in agreement	UNCONSENTANEOUS
infernal cave	DOMDANIEL	—known	UNWIST
informal evening		—made noisy	UNBEDINNED
party	SMALL-AND-EARLY	obviate	MEET WITH
innkeeper	INNHOLDER	of	
inquiry	INQUIRATION	—another kind	ANOTHERGUESS
instrument		—the eye	VISUAL
—for bending		open	OPE
crossbow	WINDAC, WINDAS	—country	WEALD
—of torture	TRIP-HOOK	overcome by drowsiness	O'ER-DROWSED
intensify	INTENSATE	owl	GLIMMER-GOWK
interpretation	REDE	owlishness	OWLERY
interregnum	INTERREIGN	painted woman	PICT
it seems to me	MESEEMS	palmist	CH(E)IROGRAPHIST
it's	TIS	pamper	POMPEY
joyful	FAIN	paradise	SWERGA
joyous	FRABJOUS	pass tediously (time)	WEAR
kindle	TEEND	pay	SOLDE
knot	GORDIAN	—attention to	HEARKEN
last	DURE	peak	PIQUE
late mint	LATTER-MINT	peasant	SWAIN
level	STROW	perched aloft	UP-PERCHED
light	ILLUME	period of the night	WATCH
like prison	PRISONOUS	piercing	PERCEANT
listen	LIST	place as if in jelly	INJELLY
—to	HEARKEN	place one visits	VISIT
little god	GODLING	please	ARRIDE
look	ASPECT	pleasantness	PLEASANCE
lose colour	UNFLUSH	pleasure	PLEASANCE
love-making	SWAINING	poet	MINSTREL
lover	SWAIN	Poland	SARMATIA
lower sky	UNDERSKY	ponder beforehand	PREPONDERATE
make		postpone	WITHHOLD
—manifest	CONFESS	power of quelling	QUELL
—purring sound	CURR	prayer	BENE
maker of idols	GOD-SMITH	pre-eminence	SOVRANTY
margin	MARGENT	previous king	FOREKING
marked by deeds	DEEDFUL	prodigal	PROFUSER
meadow	MEAD	prow	PRORE
medical	MEDIC	punish	SHEND
melting away	DELIQUIM	pure	UNDROSSY
Milky Way	MILKEN-WAY	put	
moving		—in tune	STRING
—capriciously	WANTON	—to shame	SHEND
—freely	WANTON	rapacity	VULTURISM
mumbling speech	MUMBLEMENT	redeless	UNREADY
music	NOTE	reformed person	REFORMADO
musical instrument	SLUGHORN(E)	reformer	REFORMADO
named	NEMPT	remark following another	SUBJOINDER
nauseous mouthful	GAG	remuneration	SOLDE
necessity	NEEDYHOOD	reprisal	REPRISE
nimble	SPRINGE	reproach	SHEND
north country	NORLAN(D)	retrogression	REGREDIENCE

reveal	CONFESS	tear	RANCH
rich cake	ROUT-CAKE	tears	RHEUM
rind	RINE	that	YON
ring	CIRQUE	—which underlies	
riotous	RAGMATICAL	surface	UNDER-COUNTENANCE
riven	RAFT	the thing you know of	YON
river(-water)	TIDE	thirsty	ADRY
roll like the sea	WELTER	thorough-going	UNENDING
romantic setting	PLAIN	those	YON
rub	FRIDGE	tie-up	GORDIAN
rue	REW	tip-cat	TIP-CHEESE
rush	VIRETOT	trilled high	UPTRILLED
rustic	SWAIN	tuft	TUZZ
sail	SHEET	turquoise	TURKIS
savage	SALVAGE	unaccustomed	UNWONT
sceptred	SCEPTRY	undertaken	UNDERTA'EN
Scotland	SCOTIA	undutiful	UNDUTEOUS
scramble	SWERVE	unfortunate	EVIL-STARRED
sea	FOAM, WAVE	unfrequented	WASTEFUL
—serpent	ELLOPS	unfriendly	INIMICITIOUS
separate	UNCOMBINE	unhomelike	UNDOMESTIC
serenade	WAKE	uninhabited	WASTEFUL
sewing	SEAMSTRESSY	unrestrained	UNWITHHOLDEN
shady retreat	HERBAR	unwary	UNAWARE
sharp-edged	VORPAL	upriseth	UPRIST
shining	SHEEN	using archaic language	TUSHERY
shiny-pated	GLASSYHEADED	utter poetry	POESY
ship	PRORE	venturous	VENTROUS
shore	RIVAGE	village	VILL
—crab	OCHIDORE	visibility to the mind	VISUALITY
sly trick	UNDER-CRAFT	visitor's book	VISITING-BOOK
smooth	SOOTH	wagon	WAIN
smote	SMIT	warrior who cannot be	
soft	SOOTH	wounded with metals	WARLOCK
sorrow-lulling drink		winded	WIN'T
or drug	MANDRAGORA, NEPENTHE	windlass for crossbow	WINDAC, WINDAS
spend time	WEAR	window	WINDORE
spendthrift	PROFUSER	without being	UNESSENTIAL
spiritual	AERIE, AERY	wood-sorrel	SHAMROCK
state of floating	FLOAT	wooded country	WEALD
stately building	DOME	write bombastically	FUSTIANISE
staying in one place	LOCORESTIVE	yesterday evening	YESTREEN
steep	STEEPY	yonder	YON
stick of pipe-clay	PIPE	young man	SWAIN
stomach	LITTLE MARY	zealot	ZE(A)LANT
strengthen	MUNITE		
study of artillery	PYROBALLOGY		
subconscious thirst	UNDERTHIRST		

(see also **Burns, Milton, old, Scott, Shakespeare, Spenser**)

poets

subside	SWOON
summons to war	WAR-NOTE
supporter	UNDERSTANDER
surpassing	FRABJOUS
swarm	SWERVE
swell of the sea	WALLOW
sword	VORPAL
swung	SWANG

American AIKEN, BLACKMUR, BLY
BURROUGHS, CORMAN, CORSO
CRANE, CREELEY, CUMMINGS
DICKINSON(f), DOLITTLE
ELIOT, FERLINGHETTI
FROST, GINSBERG, HULSENBECK
KEROUAC, LINDSAY, LONGFELLOW
LOWELL, MACLEISH, MONROE(f)

MOORE(f), OLSEN, OPPEN, PLATH(f)
POE, POUND, RANSOM, REXBOTH
REZNIKOFF, ROBINSON, SANDBERG
SNYDER, STEVENS, TATE
WHITMAN, WHITTIER
WILLIAMS, WINTERS, ZUKOFSKY

Argentinian	BORGES
Australian	BRENNAN, GORDON, MURRAY
	PATTERSON, PORTER
Austrian	RILKE, TRAKL, WERFEL
Brazilian	XISTO
British	AE, AMIS, ARNOLD, AUDEN

BARNFIELD, BETJEMAN, BLAIR
BEARDSLEY, BEATTIE, BEERBOHM
BLAKE, BRETON, BRIDGES
BRONTE\:, BROOKE, BROWNING
BROWNING(f), BUNYAN
BYRON, CAMPION, CAREW
CHATTERTON, CHAUCER, CIBBER, CLARE
CLOUGH, CONQUEST, COLERIDGE
COLLINS, COWLEY, COWPER
CRABBE, CRASHAW, CRICHTON-SMITH
DAVIE, DAVIES, DE LA MARE
DONNE, DOWSON, DRYDEN, DUNNE
ELIOT, EMPSON, ENRIGHT, EUSDEN
FENTON, FLECKER, FLINT
FULLER, GASCOYNE
GOLDSMITH, GOWER, GRAVES
GRAY, GUNN, HARRISON, HEANEY
HENDRY, HENRI, HERBERT, HERRICK
HOBSBAUM, HODGSON, HOOD, HOPKINS
HUGHES, JAMES, JENNINGS(f)
JOHNSON, JONSON, KEATS
LANDOR, LANGLAND, LARKIN
LEAR, LEWIS, LOGIE, LOVELACE
LUCIE-SMITH, MACBETH
MACNEICE, MARSH
MARVELL, MASEFIELD, MCGOUGH
MEREDITH, MEYNELL(f)
MILTON, MONRO, MORGAN
MORRIS, NOYES, OWEN
PAMORE, PATTON, POPE, PYE
RAINE(f), RALEIGH, REDGROVE
RICHARDS, ROCHESTER, ROGERS
ROSENBERG, ROSSETTI, ROSSETTI(f)
ROWE, SASSOON, SHADWELL
SHAKESPEARE, SHELLEY, SITWELL
SKELTON, SMART, SOUTHEY
SPENDER, SPENSER, STEPHENS
SUCKLING, SURREY, SWIFT
SWINBURNE, SYDNEY, SYMONS
TATE, TENNYSON, THOMAS
THOMSON, TREECE, VAUGHAN
WAIN, WARTON, WATKINS
WHITEHEAD, WILMOT, WORDSWORTH
WYATT, YOUNG

Chilean	HUIDOBRO
Cuban	RODRIGUEZ
French	APOLLINAIRE, ARP
	BAUDELAIRE, CLAUDEL, ELUARD
	GARNIER, HUGO, ISOU, LAUTREAMONT
	LEMAITRE, MOREAS, NERVAL
	PREVERT, PONGE, RIMBAUD
	RONSARD, TZARA, VALERY
	VERLAINE, VILLON
Gaelic	OSSIAN
German	BALL, BENN, BRECHT
	CELAN, CELTES, CELTIS
	ENZENSBERGER, GERSHON(f)
	GOETHE, HEINE, HEYM, HOLZ
	HULSENBECK, NOVALIS, RILKE
	SCHLEGEL, SCHILLER, SCHWITTERS
	STEFAN, STAMM, TIECK
	VAN HARDENBERG
	ZUCKMEYER
Greek	HESIOD, HOMER, MOREAS
	PINDAR, RITSOS, SAPPHO(f)
Guatemalan	ASTURIAS
Hungarian	CELAN
Irish	AE, HEANEY, MOORE
	SYNGE, WILDE, YEATS
Indian	TAGORE
Italian	ARIOSTO, DANTE, GATTO
	LUZI, MARINETTI, MARINI
	MONTALE, ONOFRI, QUASIMODO
	SERENI, UNGARETTI
Japanese	SOSEKI
Lake School poet	LAKER, LAKIST
Martinique	CESAIPE
Mexican	PAZ
New Zealand	ADCOCK, BAXTER, CAMPBELL
Nicaraguan	DARIO
Nigerian	SOYINKA
one who writes doggerel	WATER-POET
Persian	HAFIZ, KHAYYAM
petty poet	POETASTER, POETICULE
Roman	CATULLUS, HORACE, JUVENAL
	MARTIAL, OVID
	TERENCE, STATIUS, VIRGIL
Romanian	CELAN, ISOU
Russian	AKHMATOVA(f), BELY, BLOK
	IVANOV, KHLEBNIKOV
	KRUCHENYKH, MANDELSHTAM
	MAYAKOVSKY, PASTERNAK
	POSNER, PUSHKIN
	RATUSHINSKAYA(f), TZARA
Scottish	BURNS, DOUGLAS, DUNBAR
	MACCAIG, MACDIARMID
	SCOTT
Senegalese	DIOP
Spanish	CERNUDA, LORCA
Swiss	CENDRARS

Uganda	P'BITEK
Welsh	MORGANWG, ORMOND, THOMAS
West Indian	BRAITHWAITE, BROWN
	JOHNSON, MORRIS, SCOTT
	WALCOTT
would-be poet	POETASTER, POETICULE
poison	TOXIN
antidote	ANTITOXIN, ANTIVENIN
	MITHRIDATE, SERUM
attacking	
—cells	CYTOTOXIN
—entire body	SYSTEMIC
—nervous system	NEUROTOXIN
bacterial	EXOTOXIN, PTOMAINE
buttercup	HELLEBORE
castor-oil bean	RICIN(E)
cereal fungus	ERGOT
conium	HEMLOCK
curare	CURARINE
deadly nightshade	ATROPOPINE
	BELLADONNA
dogbane	OUABAIN, WABAIN
element	ANTIMONY, ARSENIC
	STRONTIUM, THALLIUM
fly agaric	MUSCARINE
food poison	BOTULISM, LISTERIA
	PTOMAINE, SALMONELLA
	SALMONELLOSIS
fungus	AMANITIN, MUSCARINE
	PHALLOIDIN
hellebore	VERATRIN(E)
hemlock	CONIA, CONI(I)NE
henbane	HYOSC(YAM)INE
hydrocyanic acid	PRUSSIC ACID
immunity to poison	MITHRIDATISM
in stomach	ENTEROTOXIN
Java	UPAS
laburnum	CYSTISINE
lilies	HELLEBORE
Madagascar	TANGHIN
maize	AFLATOXIN
monkshood	ACONITE, ACONITUM
mushroom	MUSCARINE, PHALLIN
nux vomica	STRYCHNINE
opium	THEBAINE
peanuts	AFLATOXIN
periwinwkle	STROPHANTHIN
poppies	PAPAVERINE
putrefying flesh	NERINE, NUPINE
quick-acting	(HYDROGEN) CYANIDE
	HYDROCYANIC ACID
	PRUSSIC ACID
rat poison	WARFARIN
rye	ERGOT
sabadilla	VERATRIN(E)
snake	ECHIDNINE

South American	
—arrow poison	CURARA, CURARE, CURARI
—fish poison	SURINAM POISON
	TEPHROSIA, TIMBO
study of poisons	TOXICOLOGY
Tephrosia	SURINAM POISON
thorn-apple	DATURINE
tobacco	NICOTINE
weedkiller	DIOXIN, HERBICIDE
	PARAQUAT
wolfsbane	ACONITE, ACONITUM
wood	METHANOL, METHYL ALCOHOL
	WOOD SPIRIT
—sorrel	OXALIC ACID
Poland	PL, POL
cap	CHAPKA, CZAPKA, SCHAPSKA
capital	WARSAW
carriage	BRITSKA, BRITZ(S)KA
castle	GROD
coins	GROSZY, ZLOTY
dance	CRACOVIENNE, KRAKOWIAK
	MAZURKA, POLONAISE
dynasty	JAGELLON
forest	BOR
hill	GORKA
Jews	ASHKENAZIM
mountain	GORA
mountains	GORY
noble	SAROSTA
officer	HETMAN
reverse notation	RPN
town	GROD, MIASTO
police	CID, FORCE, FUZZ
	MET, THE BILL
police car	BLACK MARIA, PANDA
	PROWL CAR
Police Constable	PC
Police Corps	RMP
police district	MANOR
policeman	BIZZY, BLUEBOTTLE
	BOBBY, BOG(E)Y, BUSY
	COP(PER), MR PLOD, MP
	PC, ROZZER
Polynesian	
apple	KEVI
arrowroot	PIA
assembly	HUI
burial-place	AHU
chestnut	RATA
cloth	TAP(P)A
dance	HULA(-HULA), SIVA
demigod	AITU, MAUI
drink	(K)AVA
fern	TARA
garment	MALO, PAREU
labourer	KANAKA

paved court	MARAE	sandbank	BARRA
pepper	(K)AVA	sea	MAR
platform for statue	AHU	ship	LORCHA, MULETTE
pottery	LAPITA WARE	sir	DOM
skirt	LAVA-LAVA	Timor	P
sky	LANGI	title	DOM
tree	BELAH, TO(O)A, TI, TAMANU	town	VILA
wrap	PAREU	valley	VALE
porcelain	(*see* **china**)	water	
Portugal	LUSITANIA, P	—course	ARROIO
bay	BAIA, ZALEW	—fall	CACHOEIRA, SALTO
beach	PRAIA	weight (25lb)	ARROBA
cape (headland)	CABO	wine	(*see separate entry*)
capital	LISBON	wood	LAS
coins		**potato**	(*see* **vegetables**)
—unit	CENTAVO	**poultry dishes**	
—100 centavos	ESC, ESCUDO	including: game	
—1000 escudos	CONTO	animals	DEER, HARE, RABBIT
—old	PORTAGUE, PORTIGUE	bird split and cooked	SPATCHCOCK
	REE, REAL, REI(S), TESTOON	breastbone of bird	WISHBONE
—1000 reis	MILREIS	chicken dishes	A LA KIEV, A LA KING
—gold	CRUSADO, JO(H)ANNES		CHASSEUR, CHAUDFROID
	MOIDORE		COQ AU VIN, DEVILLED POUSSIN
country house	QUINTA		EVERGLADES, KORMA, MARENGO
dance	FADO		MARYLAND, PETTO DI POLLO
dam	REPRESA		SUPREME
depression	KOTLINA	cut into pieces and	
drowned valley	RIA	served in sauce	FRICASSEE
dynasty	AVIZ, BRAGANZA	deer meat	VENISON
epic poem	LUSIAD(S)	duck in orange	
folk song	FADO	sauce	CANARD A L'ORANGE
forest	LAS	duckling in cherry	
gentleman	FIDALGO	sauce	CANETON AUX CERISES
Guinea	P	edible organs	
harbour	PORTO	—birds	GIBLETS
island	ILHA	—deer	(H)UMBLES
Jews	SEPHARDIM	fat cockerel	CAPON
lady	DONA	game stew	SALM
lagoon	LAGAO	—Mexican	FAJITAS
lake	JEZIORO	hare	
man	DOM	—dish	CIVET DE LIEVRE
measure	MEIO, MOIO, PIPA		JUGGED HARE
mountain	MONTE	—stew (Greek)	STIFADO
—pasture	COXILHA	hens	(*see separate entry*)
—range	SERRA	game birds	BUSTARD, DUCK, GOOSE
mouth	BOCA		GROUSE, GUINEA-FOWL, MALLARD
no	NAO		PARTRIDGE, PHEASANT, PIGEON
parliament	CORTES		PLOVER, PTARMIGAN, QUAIL
plant	SERRADELLA, SERRADILLA		SNIPE, TEAL, TINAMOU, TURKEY
plateau	PLANALTO		WI(D)GEON, WOODCOCK
prince	INFANTE	—Europe	HAZEL HEN
princess	INFANTA	—USA	CANVASBACK
punishment of heretics	AUTO DA FE	large grouse	CAPERCAILLIE
river	RIBEIRAO, RIO	lower leg of bird	DRUMSTICK
—mouth	RIA	pheasant dish	A L'AMERICAINE
saint	SAN(TA), SANTO, SAO	pigeon pie	SQUAB PIE

prepare game	DRESS
quail dish	QUAILS IN ASPIC
red grouse	MOORFOWL
remove feathers	PLUCK
rump of bird	PARSON'S NOSE
	POPE'S NOSE
set in jelly	GALANTINE
turkey	CACCIATORA
young	
—chicken	BROILER, FRYER
	POUSSIN, SPRING CHICKEN
—duck	DUCKLING
—goose	GOSLING
—hare	LEVERET

power

meaning: authority of	
government by	
power of	
rule by	
1 person	AUTARCHY, AUTOCRACY
	DESPOTISM, DICTATORSHIP
	MONARCHY, MONOCRACY
2 persons	DIARCHY, DUUMVIRATE
3 persons	TRIARCHY, TRIUMVIRATE
4 persons	QUADRUMVIRATE
5 persons	PENTARCHY
6 persons	HEXARCHY
7 persons	HEPTARCHY, SEPTARCHY
8 persons	OCTARCHY
10 persons	DECADARCHY, DEKADARCHY
absolute power	AUTARCHY, IMPERIUM
actresses married to	
peers, etc	ACTRESSOCRACY
all people	PANTISOCRACY
army	STRATOCRACY
beggars	PTOCHOCRACHY
central and regional	FEDERALISM
cotton planting or manu-	
facturing interests	COTTONOCRACY
demons	DEMONOCRACY
dictatorship	ABSOLUTISM, DESPOTISM
	TOTALITARIANISM
divine rulers	THEARCHY, THEOCRACY
élite	MERITOCRACY
equal political powers	ISOCRACY
exclusive class	OLIGARCHY
experts	TECHNOCRACY
god	THEOCRACY, THEONOMY
holy persons	HAGIARCHY, HAGIOCRACY
joint sovereignty	SYNARCHY
land-owners	SQUATTOCRACY
	SQUIR(E)ACHY
law	NOMOCRACY
many	POLYARCHY
men	PATRIARCHY
military despot	STRATOCRACY

mill-owners	MILLOCRACY
mob	MOBOCRACY, OCHLOCRACY
money	DOLLAROCRACY
mothers	MATRIARCHY
natural order	PHYSIOCRACY
old people	GERONTOCRACY
one man	AUTOCRACY
paternal right	PATRIARCHY
paupers	PTOCHOCRACY
people	DEMOCRACY, ETHNARCHY
priests	HIERARCHY, HIEROCRACY
privileged class	ARISTOCRACY
prominent people	MERITOCRACY
property owners	TIMOCRACY
rich	PLUTOCRACY
	PLUTO-DEMOCRACY
saints	HAGIARCHY, HAGIOCRACY
scientists	TECHNOCRACY
self-governing state	DOMINION
self-government	AUTONOMY
slaves	D(O)ULOCRACY
small group	OLIGARCHY
sovereignty of the seas	THALASSOCRACY
	THALATTOCRACY
squires	SQUATTOCRACY
	SQUIR(E)ARCHY
teachers	PEDANTOCRACY
technical experts	TECHNOCRACY
wealth	CHRYSOCRACY
wealthy	PLUTOCRACY
	PLUTO-DEMOCRACY
Whigs	WHIGGARCHY
women	GYN(AEC)OCRACY
workers	ERGATOCRACY
world ruler	COSMOCRAT
worst	KAKISTOCRACY
worthy	MERITOCRACY
young people	YOUTHOCRACY

prayer

at specific times	
of day	CANONICAL HOURS
calling for	
transubstantiation	EPICLESIS
canonical hours	
—1st, dawn	MATINS
—2nd, 6am	PRIME
—3rd, 9am	TERCE
—4th, noon	SEXT
—5th, 3pm	NONES
—6th, early evening	VESPERS
—7th, late evening	COMPLINE
commemorating Annunciation	ANGELUS
confessing sins	CONFITEOR
during three days	
before Ascension	ROGATION
evening prayers	COMPLINE, VESPERS

for	
—God's help	INVOCATION
—souls of the dead	REQUIESCAT
Hail Mary	AVE MARIA
Islamic	FATIHA
Jewish	ALEINU, AMIDAH
	KADDISH, KOL NIDRE
	SHEMA
Lamb of God	AGNUS DEI
Lord have mercy	KYRIE ELEISON
Lord's prayer	PATERNOSTER
morning prayers	MATINS
of	
—praise	GLORIA
—supplication	ROGATION
on behalf of another	INTERCESSION
Our Father	PATERNOSTER
Roman Catholic	ANGELUS, AVE MARIA
	CANONICAL HOURS
	CONFITEOR
short prayer	COLLECT
three-part prayer	AGNUS DEI
with responses	LITANY
precious stones	(*see* **gems, minerals**)
presidents (US)	ADAMS, ARTHUR
	BUCHANAN, BUREN, BUSH
CARTER, CLEVELAND, CLINTON, COOLIDGE	
EISENHOWER, FILLMORE, FORD	
GARFIELD, GRANT, HARDING	
HARRISON, HAYES, HOOVER	
JACKSON, JEFFERSON, JOHNSON	
KENNEDY, LINCOLN, MADISON	
MCKINLEY, MONROE, NIXON, PIERCE	
POLK, REAGAN, ROOSEVELT	
TAFT, TAYLOR, TRUMAN, TYLER	
VAN BUREN, WASHINGTON	
	WILSON
prime ministers (UK)	ABERDEEN, ADDINGTON
ASQUITH, ATTLEE, BALFOUR	
BALDWIN, BATH, BEACONSFIELD	
BUTE, CALLAGHAN	
CAMPBELL-BANNERMAN	
CANNING, CHAMBERLAIN, CHATHAM	
CHURCHILL, DERBY, DEVONSHIRE	
DISRAELI, DOUGLAS-HOME, EDEN	
GLADSTONE, GODERICH, GRAFTON	
GRENVILLE, GREY, HEATH, LAW	
LIVERPOOL, LLOYD-GEORGE	
MACDONALD, MACMILLAN	
MAJOR, MELBOURNE	
NEWCASTLE, NORTH, PALMERSTON	
PEEL, PELHAM, PERCEVAL, PITT	
PORTLAND, ROCKINGHAM, ROSEBERY	
RUSSELL, SALISBURY, SHELBURNE	
THATCHER, WALDEGRAVE, WALPOLE	
WELLINGTON, WILMINGTON, WILSON	

printing	
adjustment of spacing	
between lines	CARDING, FEATHERING
accents	ACUTE, BOLLE, BREVE
	CARON, CEDILLA, DI(AER)ESIS
	DOT, DOUBLE ACUTE, DOUBLE GRAVE
	GRAVE, HACEK, HOOK, LATVIAN TAIL
	MACRON, OGONEK, STREG, STOKE
	TILDE, TREMA, UMLAUT, UPVEE
alignment of print	
on page	REGISTRATION
apprentice	DEVIL
arrangement of pages of	
type in a forme	IMPOSITION
blemish	MACKLE
brackets	ANGLE BRACKETS, BRACES
	PARENTHESES
	SQUARE BRACKETS
calculation of space that	
manuscript will occupy	
when set in type	CAST-OFF
capital letters	UPPER CASE
character with	
—2 letters making one sound	DIGRAPH
—2 or more letters joined	LIGATURE
—2 vowels joined	DIPHTHONG
—3 letters joined	TRIGRAPH
—3 vowels joined	TRIPHTHONG
copies of a book printed	
at one time	IMPRESSION
dots	
—indicating omission	
of words	ELLIPSES
	SUSPENSION POINTS
—or dashes linking	
separated words	LEADERS
double imprint on page	MACKLE
early printers	
—Antwerp	PLANTIN
—Basle	FROBEN
—Britain	CAXTON
—France	GARAMOND
—Germany	GUTENBERG
—Venice	ALDUS
embossed print for	
the blind	BRAILLE, MOON-TYPE
errand-boy	DEVIL
exclamation mark	GASPER, GASP MAR
	SCREAMER
frame holding type	CHASE
group of printed pages	
folded from one sheet	GATHER, SECTION
heavy print	BOLD, DOUBLE
imp of printing-house	RALPH
ink blot	MONK
inserted in space left in text	INCUT

insertion mark	CARET
inset from margin	INDENT
instruction to ignore	
correction	STET
left-hand page	VERSO
letter	
—or numeral at foot of page	SIGNATURE
—sloping	ITALIC
—upright	ROMAN
—written	
above the line	SUPERSCRIPT
below the line	SUBSCRIPT
lie flush at end	
of line	JUSTIFY, RANGE
line of cast type	SLUG
machine which sets a	
complete line of type	LINOTYPE
measure of	
—letter width	EL, EM, EN
—line length	ENNAGE
—print area	EM(M)AGE
misprint	LITERAL, TYPO
mould of papier-mâché	FLONG
old comma	VIRGULE
ornamental line on letter	SERIF
page number	FOLIO
paper	
—for newspapers	NEWSPRINT
—thick	BOND
—thin	BANK
papier-mâché sheet	FLONG
phonetic type	PHONOTYPE
photo-engraving	
—in intaglio	PHOTOGRAVURE
—using rotary press	ROTOGRAVURE
piece of type	
—bearing two or more	
characters	LOGOTYPE
—blank for spaces	QUAD(RAT)
—projecting	
beyond body or shank	KERN
plain letter	SANS SERIF
plate	
—cast from papier-	
mâché mould	CLICHE, STEROTYPE
—for casting type-faces	MATRIX
print	
—worker	COMPOSITOR, TYPESETTER
—union branch	CHAPEL
printed sheet from	
letterpress	IMPRESSION
printer's	
—marks	AMPERSAND, ARROW OUT
	ASTERISK, ASTERISM
	BACK-SLASH, BOX, BULLET
	CARET, CIRCLE DOT, CROSS

	DIAMOND, DIESIS, (DOUBLE) DAGGER
	(DOUBLE) GUILLEMOT, ELLIPSIS
	FILLED BOX, HASH, MARS
	OBELISK, OBELUS, OBLIQUE, ORDINAL
	PARAGRAPH MARK, PILCROW
	PRESA, SLASH, SOLIDUS, STAR
	SUSPENSION POINTS
	SWING DASH, TICK, VENUS, VIRGULE
	VIRGULE
—measure	DIDOT, EL, EM, EN, PT, POINT
—proof	GALLEY
—symbols	(*see* punctuation marks *below*)
printing	TYPOGRAPHY
—error	LITERAL, TYPO
—from stone	LITHOGRAPHY
—house imp	RALPH
—in several colours	STENOCHROMY
—left to right and right	
to left	BOUSTROPHEDON
—machine	BUBBLE JET, CYCLOSTYLE
	DAISY WHEEL, DOT MATRIX
	DUPLICATOR, FAX, FLATBED
	INKJET, LASER, LINE PRINTER
	MIMEOGRAPH, PHOTOCOPIER
	ROTARY, TELEPRINTER, TELEX
publisher's imprint	COLOPHON
punctuation marks	APOSTROPHE
	BRACKETS, COLON, COMMA
	DASH, EXCLAMATION MARK
	FULL-STOP, HYPHEN
	INVERTED COMMAS
	OPEN QUERY, OPEN SHRIEK
	POINT, QUESTION MARK
	QUOTATION MARKS, SEMI-COLON
	STIGME
right-hand page	RECTO
set of type characters	FO(U)NT
short last line at end of	
paragraph or top of	
column	ORPHAN, WIDOW
sloping print	ITALIC
small	
—letters	LOWER CASE
—tray in which type	
is set	COMPOSING STICK
spacing	
—between lines	LEADING
—of words to fill	
a column	JUSTIFICATION
tool	SHOOTING-STICK
technique of printing	
—from plate	
of which only parts	
accept ink	LITHOGRAPHY
with incised surface	GRAVURE
	INTAGLIO

with raised surfaces	LETTERPRESS
—from an inked cylinder	OFFSET
three stars	ASTERISM
title printed at head of every (alternate) page	RUNNING HEAD
tray holding set type	GALLEY
trial sheet of print	(GALLEY-)PROOF
trivia for filling odd spaces in newspaper	BALAAM
two pages of open book	SPREAD
type	
—10 letters per inch	PICA
—12 letters per inch	ELITE
—¹/₇₂ inch	POINT
—3½ point	MINIKIN
—4 point	BRILLIANT, MINION
—4½ point	DIAMOND
—5 point	PEARL
—5½ point	AGATE, RUBY
—6 point	NONPAREIL
—7 point	MINION
—8 point	BREVIER
—9 point	BOURGEOIS
—10 point	LONG PRIMER
—11 point	SMALL PICA
—12 point	PICA
—13 point	CICERO
—14 point	ENGLISH
—16 point	COLUMBIAN TWO-LINE BREVIER
—18 point	GREAT PRIMER
—20 point	PARAGON
—22 point	DOUBLE PICA
—24 point	TWO-LINE PICA
—28 point	TWO-LINE ENGLISH
—36 point	TWO-LINE GREAT PRIMER
—40 point	TWO-LINE PARAGON
—48 point	CANON, FOUR-LINE PICA
—60 point	FIVE-LINE PICA
—72 point	SIX-LINE PICA
—assembled in a chase	FORME
—black letter type	FRAKTUR, GOTHIC
—dark Gothic	TEXTURA
—heavy-faced	CLARENDON
—large	CANON
—rounded script	RONDE, UNCIAL
—sloping	ITALIC
—special type	ELZEVIR
—upright	ROMAN
—without serifs	SANSERIF
typesetters	PICA THUMPERS
typograph(y)	TYP(O)
wedge for locking type	QUOIN
white space between facing pages	GUTTER

word	
—indicating literal quotation	SIC
—printed at the top of page to indicate content	CATCHWORD
wrong font	WF
	(*see also* **write**)

proteins

acting as	
—catalyst	ENZYME
—gene inhibitor	HISTONE
affecting cells	INTERLEUKIN
anti-viral substance produced by infected cell	INTERFERON
basic protein	HISTONE
coagulating blood	FIBRIN, FIBROGEN
containing carbohydrate	GLUCOPROTEIN
	GLYCOPROTEIN
	MUCOPROTEIN
dissolved in blood	PLASMA PROTEIN
elastic fibre in connective tissue	ELASTIN
fibrous protein in surface coatings of animals	SCLEROPROTEIN
forming	
—fibrin	FIBRINOGEN
—gelatine	COLLAGEN
grains of protein stored in plants	ALEURONE GRAINS
group of soluble proteins	GLOBULIN
in	
—almonds	AMANDINE
—amniotic fluid	ALPHA-FETO PROTEIN
—barley	HORDEIN
—blood	FIBRIN(OGEN), GLOB(UL)IN
	HAEMOGLOBIN
	IMMUNOPROTEIN
—bones	GELATIN(E)
—cells	
after viral infection	INTERFERON
of living organisms	GLOBULIN
—cereal	GLUTEN
—chromosome	HISTONE
cell nucleus	CHROMATIN
—collagen	GELATIN(E)
—connective tissue	COLLAGEN
—egg	
white	(EGG-)ALBUMEN
yolk	VITELLIN
—eye	CRYSTALLIN
—fat	LIPOPROTEIN
—fibrous tissue	COLLAGEN, ELASTIN
—gluten	GLIADIN, PROLAMINE

—haemoglobin	GLOBIN
—hair, skin, etc	KERATIN
—Indian corn	ZEIN
—keratin, collagen, etc	SCLEROPROTEINS
—ligaments, etc	COLLAGEN
—liver and spleen	FERRITIN
—milk	CASEIN, LACTALBUMEN
	LACTOGLOBULIN
	LACTOPROTEIN
—mucus	MUCIN
—muscle	ACTIN, ACTOMYOSIN
	DYSTROPHIN, MYOGLOBIN
	MYOSIN
—nails	KERATIN
—saliva	MUCIN
—seeds	ALEURONE
—silk	FIBROIN
—skin	GELATIN(E), KERATIN
—sponges	SPONGIN
—thyroid gland	THYROGLOBULIN
—wheat flour	GLUTEN
—wool, hair, horn etc	KERATIN
including a lipid	LIPOPROTEIN
insoluble	FIBRIN
not denatured	NATIVE PROTEIN
nucleic acid with	
protein	NUCLEO-PROTEIN
part of enzyme	APOENZYME
plant protein acting	
as antibody	LECTIN
produced by action of	
virus in cell	INTERFERON
producing luminosity	LUCIFERIN
scleroprotein	COLLAGEN
	ELASTIN, KERATIN
simple protein	HISTONE
soluble in	
—alcohol	PROLAMIN(E)
—salt	GLOBULIN
—water	ALBUMIN
stopping gene activity	HISTONE
storing iron	FERRITIN
used	
—as protection	
against virus	INTERFERON
—in adhesives, foods, etc	GELATIN(E)
psychology	PNEUMATOLOGY
including: psychiatry	
absence of emotion	APATHY
act of will	VOLITION
adaptation to frequent	
stimuli	HABITUATION
Adler school	INDIVIDUAL PSYCHOLOGY
adoption of female	
dress and manners	
by male	EONISM, TRANSVESTISM

aggression	ANTAGONISTIC BEHAVIOUR
alternation between	
extreme	
moods	MANIC-DEPRESSIVE PSYCHOSIS
analysis of	
—differences between	
mental and	
physical	MIND-BODY PROBLEM
—social	
exchanges	TRANSACTIONAL ANALYSIS
arrangement of	
mental	
states and	
processes	STRUCTURAL PSYCHOLOGY
attachment to idea,	
person, etc	FIXATION
attempt to control	
behaviour	CONDITIONING
attribution of one's	
own feelings to others	PROJECTION
automatic behaviour	
not recalled	FUGUE
awareness of the future	PRECOGNITION
based on study	
—from	
parts to whole	ELEMENTARISM
whole to parts	
	ORGANISMIC PSYCHOLOGY
behaviour	
—establishing hierarchy	DOMINANCE
—inward-looking	INTROVERSION
—likely to	
satisfy some desire	APPETITIVE
elicit epimeletic	
response	ETEPIMELETIC
—outward-looking	EXTRAVERSION
—relating to care	
of young	EPIMELETIC
—reverting to earlier	
stage	REGRESSION
body	
—and temperament type	SOMATYPE
—muscular and aggressive	SOMATONIA
—types	
long and thin	ECTOMORPH
muscular	MESOMORPH
round	ENDOMORPH
bonding to parent	ATTACHMENT
character analysis	BIOENERGETICS
charge of mental energy	CATHEXIS
condition	
—of	
bodily rigidity	CATALEPSY
immobility emotionally	
caused	CATAPLEXY
schizophrenic stupor	CATATONIA

—where
  physical symptoms
  have mental
  origin   CONVERSION HYSTERIA
  relationships seem
  to be threatening   ENGULFMENT
connecting principle in
  coincidence   SYNCHRONICITY
conscious part of the
  personality   EGO
consideration of
  psychology   METAPSYCHOLOGY
control of behaviour by
  results of previous
  behaviour   INSTRUMENTAL CONDITIONING
     OPERANT CONDITIONING
death-wish   THANATOS
defence mechanism   IDENTIFICATION
     PROJECTION
     RATIONALISATION
     REGRESSION, REPRESSION
     SUBLIMATION
delusions of
  —grandeur   PARANOIA
  —self-importance   MEGALOMANIA
depression   MELANCHOLIA
device used for
  —communication with
  spirits   OUIJA BOARD
     PLANCHETTE
  —spirit-writing   PSYCHOGRAPH
disorder
  —affecting communication
  with others   AUTISM
  —caused by excessive
  wealth   AFFLUENZA
  —of mood with
  high spirits   ELATION
  low spirits   DEPRESSION
disruption of self-
  image   IDENTITY CRISIS
doctrine/theory
  —based on
  first year of life   KLEINIAN THEORY
  individual
  responsibility   EXISTENTIALISM
  response to
  environment   LEARNING THEORY
  —of
  Adler   PSYCHOANALYSIS
  Freud   DYNAMIC PSYCHOLOGY
  Galton   DIFFERENTIAL PSYCHOLOGY
     PSYCHOANALYSIS
  insanity as a
  social problem   RADICAL THERAPY
  Jung   PSYCHOANALYSIS

Maslow   HUMANISTIC PSYCHOLOGY
McDougall   HORMIC PSYCHOLOGY
     PURPOSIVISM
Skinner   BEHAVIOURISM
universal soul   PSYCHISM
—that
  man is responsible
  for his actions   PURPOSIVISM
  mental states exist
  independently   MENTALISM
  only minds exist   PANPSYCHISM
dreamlike state   FUGUE
estrangement from the
  real world   ALIENATION
exacted reaction   COMPENSATION
excessive
—fear   PHOBIA
     (*see also* **fear**)
—love of self   EGOMANIA, NARCISSISM
     (*see also* **love**)
—preoccupation with
  some subject   OBSESSION
expression of repressed
  feelings   CONVERSION
father-fixation in
  girl   ELECTRA COMPLEX
fear of
  —being destroyed   IMPLOSION
  —loss of ability to
  feel pleasure   APHANASIS
     (*see also* **fear**)
feeling of
  —inadequacy   INFERIORITY COMPLEX
  —unreality   DEPERSONALISATION
feminine side of male   ANIMA
fixed idea   DELUSION
flow of mental
  activity   STREAM OF CONSCIOUSNESS
formation of complete
  personality   INTEGRATION
Freudian school   PSYCHOANALYSIS
front shown to
  the world   PERSONA
goal-directed behaviour   HORME
highest moral
  example   CATEGORICAL IMPERATIVE
hypothesis basing
  natural science
  on psychology   PSYCHOLOGISM
hypothetical governing
  principle   PSYCHOID
idealised impression   IMAGO
illusion of movement   PHI-PHENOMENON
imagined illness   HYPOCHONDRIA(SIS)
inability to
  —decide   AB(O)ULIA

—experience pleasure	ANHEDONIA
—remember	AMNESIA
particular	
event	PSYCHOLOGICAL BLOCK
increased performance	
based on expectation	ROSENTHAL EFFECT
induction to rules	
of society	SOCIALISATION
inherited idea	ARCHETYPE
inkblot test	RORSCHACH TEST
insanity	
—starting in childhood	HEBEPHRENIA
—with loss of mental	
powers	DEMENTIA
interpretation of	
philosopical problems in	
psychological terms	PSYCHOLOGISM
investigation	
—into paranormal	PSYCHICAL RESEARCH
—of	
hidden motives	PSYCHOANALYSIS
personality	PSYCHODIAGNOSTICS
involuntary reaction	INSTINCT
IQ scale	BINET-SIMON SCALE
	STANFORD-BINET SCALE
irrational fear	ANXIETY, PHOBIA
Jungian school	ANALYTICAL PSYCHOLOGY
Laing's school	RADICAL THERAPY
learning	
—by rewards	OPERANT CONDITIONING
	INSTRUMENTAL LEARNING
—from	
entire patterns	GESTALT PSYCHOLOGY
stimuli	CLASSICAL CONDITIONING
	PAVLOVIAN CONDITIONING
life-force	ORGONE
loss of memory	ANMESIA
masculine side of	
female	ANIMUS
measure of	
intelligence	INTELLIGENCE QUOTIENT, IQ
mental	
—action directing	
physical	PSYCHOMOTOR
—and emotional energy	LIBIDO
—condition caused by	
withdrawal of all	
stimuli	SENSORY DEPRIVATION
—deficiency	AMENTIA
—derangement	PSYCHOPATHY
—disease without	
physical cause	PSYCHONEUROSIS
—disorder	NEUROSIS, PSYCHASTHENIA
	PSYCHOSIS
—illness	
affecting body	PSYCHOSOMATIC

alternate depression	
and elation	
	MANIC-DEPRESSIVE PSYCHOSIS
based on anxiety	HYSTERIA
following	
shock	TRAUMATIC NEUROSIS
with	
—delusions of	
greatness	MEGALOMANIA
persecution	PARANOIA
—euphoria, etc	MANIA
—inability to separate	
reality from	
delusion	SCHIZOPHRENIA
—reiteration of	
ideas, etc	OBSESSIONAL NEUROSIS
—processes with no	
connection	DISASSOCIATION
mild mania	HYPOMANIA
mind	PSYCHE
misinterpreted event	ILLUSION
morbid self-interest	EGOMANIA
mother-fixation	
in boy	OEDIPUS COMPLEX
movement of objects	
by paranormal force	PSYCHOKINESIS
natural response	INSTINCT
object as opposed	
to subject	NON-EGO
obsession	COMPLEX
one	
—interested in	
both himself and the	
external world	AMBIVERT
self only	INTROVERT
the external world	EXRAVERT
	EXTROVERT
—qualified in mind	
sciences	PSYCHIST
	PSYCHOLOGIST
—suffering from	
behavioural disorder	PSYCHOPATH
	SOCIOPTAH
—who	
trains the mind	PSYCHAGOGUE
shows pathological	
degree of instability	PSYCHOPATH
	SOCIOPATH
—treats mental illness	ALIENIST
	PSYCHIATRIST
—with power of	
divination by contact	PSYCHOMETER
part of mind	
—holding thoughts	
which cannot become	
conscious	UNCONSCIOUS

—outside awareness	SUBCONSCIOUS
partially unconscious	
part of personality	SUPEREGO
period of development	
between childhood	
and puberty	LATENCY PERIOD
persistent attachment	FIXATION
personality	
—test	RORSCHACH TEST
—types doing well in	
orthodox situations	CONVERGER
unorthodox situations	DIVERGER
physiological outcome	
of mental disturbance	ACTUAL NEUROSIS
pleasure	
—enhancing principle	ID
—from	
mental activity	CEREBROTONIA
pain to	
—others	SADISM
—self	MASOCHISM
and others	SADO-MASOCHISM
physical activity	SOMATOTONIA
sensation	VISCEROTONIA
potential thoughts	PRECONSCIOUS
power	
—of divination by	
contact	PSYCHOMETRY
—supposed to cause	
paranormal phenomena	PSYCHIC FORCE
problem solving by	
intense discussion	BRAINSTORMING
psychiatrist	PSYCHIATER
psychic energy	LIBIDO
psychical research	PARAPSYCHOLOGY
psychologists/psychiatrists	
—American	BANDURA, BERNE, BRUNER
	CATTELL, CLYNES, ERIKSON
	HORNEY, HULL, JAMES, JENSEN
	KANNER, KEELER, KOFFKA, KOHLER
	LARSEN, LEARY, LEWIN, LINDSLEY
	MASLOW, MAY, MEAD, MILLER
	MORENO, MURRAY, OLDS, REICH
	RHINE, ROGERS, ROSENTHAL
	SHELDON, SKINNER, SULLIVAN
	SZASZ, TERMAN, THORNDIKE
	THURSTONE, TITCHENER
	WATSON, WECHLER
	WOODWORTH
—Australian	MEAD
—Austrian	ADLER, BREUER, FREUD
	RANK, REICH, SAKEL
—British	BOWLBY, BURT, CLARKE
	DALTON, EYSENCK, GALTON
	MCDOUGALL, OGDEN, PEARMAN
	STRACHEY, WINNICOTT, WOOD

—Danish	LANGE
—French	BINET, COUE, JANET, LACON
	SARTRE, SIMON
—German	BERGER, ERIKSON, FECHNER
	FICHTE, FROMM, HERBART
	HERING, HORNEY, KOFFKA
	KOHLER, KRAEPELIN
	KRAFT-EBBING
	KRETSCHMER, TOLMAN
	WEITHEIMER, WINDT
—Italian	ASSAGIOLI
—Martinician	FANON
—Polish	LEWIN
—Russian	LURIA, PAVLOV
	VELIKOVSKY, VIGOTSKY
—Scottish	LANG
—Swiss	BLEULER, JUNG
	PIAGET, RORSCHACH
psychotic condition	PSYCHOPATHY
	SCHIZOPHRENIA
	SOCIOPATHY
purposive	
psychology	HORMIC PSYCHOLOGY
rapid conditioning	IMPRINTING
reaction to	
—conditioning	BEHAVIOURISM
—contrived stimuli	CONDITIONED REFLEX
	CONDITIONED RESPONSE
	PAVLOVIAN REFLEX
	PAVLOVIAN RESPONSE
redirection of feelings	DISPLACEMENT
relationship between	
—child and step-	
parent	PHAEDRA COMPLEX
—daughter and father	ELECTRA COMPLEX
—older man and young	
girl	LOLITA SYNDROME
—son and mother	OEDIPUS COMPLEX
release of repressed	
feelings	CATHARSIS
restraint of impulse	INHIBITION
reversion to earlier state	REGRESSION
reward for behaviour	REINFORCEMENT
Rogers's school	HUMANISTIC PSYCHOLOGY
Sartre school	EXISTENTIALISM
self	
—encouragement	AUTO-SUGGESTION
—interest	INTROVERSION
	NARCISSISM
—preservation instinct	EROS
sensation without	
physical cause	HALLUCINATION
set of unconscious ideas	COMPLEX
severe	
depression	INVOLUTIONAL MELANCHOLIA
	INVOLUTIONAL PSYCHOSIS

sex drive   LIBIDO
showing
—relationship between
  mind and body   PSYCHOSOMATIC
—tendency to
  schizophrenic
  behaviour   SCHIZOID
Skinner school   BEHAVIOURAL PSYCHOLOGY
social hierarchy   PECKING ORDER
soul   PSYCHE
specialist in mental
 illness   ALIENIST
spirit   PSYCHE
—writing   PSYCHOGRAM
                                 PSYCHOGRAPHY
spiritualist   PSYCHIC
—doctrine   ANTHROPOSOPHY
split personality   SCHIZOPHRENIA
statistical analysis
 of psychological
 data   MATHEMATICAL PSYCHOLOGY
strong attachment
 to object or idea   CATHEXIS
study of
—abnormal phenomena   METAPHYSICS
                                PARAPSYCHOLOGY
—bodily reflexes as
  affecting behaviour   REFLEXOLOGY
—body/mind
  relationship   PSYCHOBIOGRAPHY
                          PSYCHOBIOLOGY
—brain diseases as
  affecting behaviour NEUROPSYCHIATRY
—experiences and
  their effects   PHENOMENOLOGY
—extra-sensory
  perception   PARAPSYCHOLOGY
—human behaviour   CLINICAL PSYCHOLOGY
—measurable
  behaviour   BEHAVIOURISM
—mental
  illness   ALIENISM, PSYCHIATRY
  problems of the
  aged   PSYCHOGERIATRICS
—mind
  and behaviour   PSYCHICS
                             PSYCHOLOGY
  in its
  environment   PSYCHONOMICS
—motivation   DYNAMIC PSYCHOLOGY
—origins of mind   PSYCHOGENESIS
—physical psychology PSYCHOPHISIOLOGY
—private
  experiences
           INTROSPECTIVE PSYCHOLOGY
—psychic theories   METAPSYCHOLOGY

—psychology of
  abnormal states
  of mind   HUMANISTIC PSYCHOLOGY
                      PSYCHOPATHOLOGY
  individual DIFFERENTIAL PSYCHOLOGY
                       EGO PSYCHOLOGY
  measurable factors   PSYCHOMETRICS
                          PSYCHOMETRY
—relationship of mental
  to physical   PSYCHOPHYSICS
substitution of one
 activity for one
 less acceptable   SUBLIMATION
suppression of function   INHIBITION
temperament
—inclined to high and
  low spirits   CYCLOTHYMIA
—types
  ectomorph   CEREBROTONIC
  endomorph   VISCEROTONIC
  mesomorph   SOMATOTONIC
  optimistic   SANGUINE
  passionate   CHOLERIC
  pessimistic   MELANCHOLIC
  stolid   PHLEGMATIC
temporal displacement   UNCOUPLING
                            DECALAGE
test used as experiment   AUFGABE
theory
—emphasises the use
  of will   VOLUNTARISM
—of emotion   JAMES-LANGE THEORY
—that faculties
  are innate   NATIVISM
thinking part of personality   EGO
thought determined
 by motives   PSYCHIC DETERMINISM
total lack of response   STUPOR
transfer of emotion
 to another object   DISPLACEMENT
treatment
—by
  acting out problems   PSYCHODRAMA
  auto-suggestion   COUEISM
  exposing the
  subconscious   PSYCHONALYSIS
  hypnosis   PSYCHOTHERAPEUTICS
                      PSYCHOTHERAPY
  unpleasant
  stimuli   AVERSION THERAPY
—linking personality
  elements   PSYCHOSYNTHESIS
—of the whole
  person   GESTALT PSYCHOLOGY
                    CONFIGURATIONISM
                   (*see also* **treatment**)

true personality	ANIMA
unconscious	
—critical faculty	SUPEREGO
—movement of wishes etc	
from one person	
to another	TRANSFERENCE
—process to prevent	
thoughts becoming	
conscious	REPRESSION
—reaction to danger	DEFENCE MECHANISM
understanding of	
self	SELF-ACTUALISATION
public	
public address (system)	PA
public good	PB
pub(lic house)	INN, LOCAL, PH
public lending right	PLR
public library	PL
public record office	PRO
public relations (officer)	PR(O)
Public Service Vehicle	PSV
Public Services Authority	PSA
Puerto Rico	PR
capital	SAN JUAN
pulses	CALAVANCE, CARAVANCE
African	KENYA BEAN
American	BLACK-EYED PEAS, TEPARY
—green bean	SNAP BEAN
Asian	CHICKPEA, COWPEA
	MUNG BEAN, SOYA BEANS
bean curd	TOFU
black-eyed beans	COW-PEAS
broad bean	FAVA BEAN, FIELD BEAN
	HORSE BEAN
butter beans	LIMA BEANS
carob	ALGAR(R)OBA, ALGAR(R)OBO
	ST JOHN'S BREAD
cherry-bean	COWPEA
chick-pea	EGYPTIAN PEA
	GARBANZO PEA, GRAM
—flour	BESSAN
—Spanish	GARBANZOS
Chinese	MUNG
cow-pea	BLACK-EYED BEAN
	CHERRY BEAN
dried and halved	SPLIT PEAS

dry peas	MARROWFAT PEAS
eaten in pod	MANGE-TOUT
Egyptian pea	CHICK-PEA, GARBANZO PEA
field bean	BROAD BEAN, HORSE BEAN
French bean	FLAGEOLET, HARICOT
	WAX(POD) BEAN
Garbanzo pea	CHICK-PEA, EGYPTIAN PEA
great northern bean	HARICOT
green bean (US)	SNAP BEAN
Guiana seed	TONGA-BEAN, TONKA-BEAN
	TONQUIN-BEAN
haricot	FLAGEOLET, NAVY BEANS
	PINTO
horse bean	BROAD BEAN, FIELD BEAN
Indian	ARRAH, BLACK GRAM
	DA(H)L, DHAL, DHOLL
	MUNG, PALAS, PIGEON-PEA
	URD(-BEAN)
Italian	BORLOTTI, CANELLINI
Japanese	ADZUKI
kidney bean	CANELLINI, FLAGEOLET
lady's fingers	BHINDI, GUMBO, OKRA
large pea	MARROWFAT
Lima bean	BUTTER BEAN
Mediterranean	CAROB BEAN, LOCUST BEAN
Mexican	CHILLI
Middle East	FUL MESDAMES
mottled bean	PINTO BEAN
navy bean	HARICOT
other beans	BORLOTTI, BROAD BEANS
	BUTTER BEANS
	FIELD BEANS
parched Indian corn	ROKEAGE
red kidney bean	CHILLI BEAN
	MEXICAN BEAN
small	
—beans	HELIDA
—kidney bean	PEA BEAN
—seeded	SIEVA BEAN
snuff flavouring	TONGA-BEAN
	TONKA-BEAN
	TONQUIN-BEAN
South American	LIMA BEAN
Spanish	HELDA BEAN
sugar-pea	MANGETOUT
tropical bean	COW(H)AGE, COWITCH

Qatar
  capital   AD DAUHHAH, DOHA
  coin
    —unit   DIRHAM
    —100 dirhams   RIYAL
quarter   FRACTION, MERCY
     QR, QU(AR)
  Jew's quarter   GHETTO
  quartermaster(-general)   QM(G)
  quartermaster(-sergeant   QM(S)
  quarter-sessions   QS
quasi-stellar object   QSO, QUASAR
Quebec   Q, QUE
  inhabitant   QUEBECOIS
  measure (c. 1¼ acres)   ARPENT
queen   Q, QU, R
  Queen Anne   AR
  Queen Anne's Bounty   QAB
  queen city   CINCINATTI
  Queen Elizabeth   ER, ORIANA
    —Hall   QEH
  Queen Mary   MR
  Queen of
    —Carthage   DIDO

  —England   ANNE, ELIZABETH I & II
     JANE, MARY I & II
     MATILDA, VICTORIA
  —France   REINE
  —Germany   KONIGIN
  —heaven   ASHTORETH
  —Italy   REGINA
  —Navarre   MARGUERITE
  —Scotland   MARGARET, MARY
  —Sheba   AAZIZ, BALKIS
  —spades   BASTA
  —Spain   REINA
  —the
    dead   ERESHKIGOL, HEL
     PERSEPHONE, PROSERPINE
    fairies   MAB, TITANIA, UNA
    Nile   CLEO(PATRA)
  Queen Victoria   VIR, VR(I)
  Queen's Bench   QB
  queen's carriage   VICTORIA
  Queen's College   QC
  Queen's Counsel   QC
  Queensland   Q

R

rabbit

diseases	COCCIDIOSIS, MYXOMATOSIS
types	ALASKA, ANGORA, ARGENTE
	ASTREX, BEAVER KING, BELGIAN HARE
	BEVEREN, BLANC DE BUSCOT
	BLANC DE HOTOT, BRITISH GIANT
	CALIFORNIAN, CASTOR (REX)
	CHINCHILLA (GIGANTA)
	CHINESE SACRIFICIAL, DUTCH
	ENGLISH LOP, FLEMISH, FOX
	FRENCH DWARF, HARLEQUIN, HAVANA
	HIMALAYAN, LILAC
	LINCOLNSHIRE SPRIG, MARTEN SABLE
	NETHERLAND DWARF, NEW ZEALAND
	POLISH, REX, RHINELANDER, SATIN
	SIAMESE SABLE, SIBERIAN
	SILVER SPRIG, SMOKED PEARL
	TAN, THURINGER

radio

radiation protection adviser	RPA
radio	
—frequency	RF
—telephone	RT
radiological safety officer	RSO

railway RWY

railway	
—region	GWR, LMS, LNER, SR
—sorting office	RSO
—sub-office	RSO
Railway Traffic Officer	RTO
railwaymen	NUR

rearing

including: breeding cultivation	
animals	ZOOCULTURE
bees	APICULTURE
birds	AVICULTURE
fish	PISCICULTURE
flowers	FLORICULTURE
fruit	POMICULTURE
hair	CRINICULTURE
oysters	OSTREICULTURE
plants	HORTICULTURE
—stimulated by electricity	ELECTROCULTURE
sea animals and plants	MARICULTURE
silk worms	SERICULTIRE
single crop	MONOCULTURE
snails	HELICULTURE
trees	ARBORICULTURE
vines	VINICULTURE, VITICULTURE
voice training	VOCICULTURE
without soil	HYDROPONICS
woods	SILVICULTURE

Red Indian COPPERSKIN
MOUNDBUILDER
NATIVE AMERICAN, REDSKIN

arum root dish	TUCKAHOE
baby	PAPOOSE
bark canoe	WOOD-SKIN
beads from shells	WAMPUM(PEAG)
belt of shell-beads	WAMPUM-BELT
birch-bark box or basket	MOCOCK
blanket	MACKINAW
brave	SANNOP, SANNUP
carved pole	TOTEM (POLE)
chief	MUGWUMP, SACHEM
	SAGAMORE
child	PAPOOSE
communal house	LONG-HOUSE
confederacy of tribes	FIVE NATIONS
confer	POWWOW
conference	PAWAW, POWWOW
conjuror	PAWAW, POWWOW
currency	WAMPUM
dish	SUCCOTASH
drag	TRAVAIL, TRAVOIS
dried meat	PEM(M)ICAN
dwelling	HOGAN, HUT, LODGE, TEEPEE
	TENT, WICKIUP, WIGWAM
famous chiefs	BIG FOOT, COCHISE
	CRAZY HORSE, GERONIMO
	PONTIAC, SITTING BULL
	TECUMSEH
feast	PAWAW, POWWOW
Great Spirit	MANITO(U)
interjection	WAUGH
litter	TRAVAIL, TRAVOIS
liquor	HOO(T)CH
paradise	HAPPY HUNTING-GROUND
peace pipe	CALUMET
poetry	HIAWATHA
pole used in house-building	LODGE-POLE
pony	CAYUSE
porridge	HOMINY, SAMP, SUP(P)AWN
religious dance	CANTICOY, KANTIKOY
shaman	PAWAW, POW-WOW
shell money	PEAG, PEAK, WAMPUM(PEAG)
shoe	MOCCASIN, MOCASSIN
smoking mixture	KINNIKINICK
snakebite medicine	SENEGA
stew	SUCCOTASH
tent	TE(E)PEE, WIGWAM

tribes	ABENAKI, ALGONQUI(A)N
	ALGONKI(A)N
	APACHE, ARAPAHO, BANNOCK
	BLACKFOOT, BLOOD
	CADDO, CALUSA, CHEROKEE
	CHEYENNE, CHINOOK, CHIPPEWAY
	CHOCKTAW, CHUMASH, COCHIMI
	COMANCHE, CREE, CREEK, CROW
	DAKOTA, DELAWARE, ERIE
	FOX, HOPI, HUICHOL, HURON
	ILLINOIS, IROQUOIS, KAROK, KIOWA
	MANDAN, MASSACHUSET, MODOC
	MIAMI, MICMAC, MENOMINEE
	MOHAVE, MOHAWK, MOHEGAN
	MOHICAN, MOHOCK, MUSKOGE
	NARRAGANSET, NATCHEZ, NAVAHO
	NAVAJO, NEZ PERCES, NOOTKA
	OGLALA, OJIBWA(Y), OMAHA
	OSAGE, OTTOWA, PAIUTE, PAPAGO
	PAWNEE, PIMA, POMO, POTAWATOMI
	POWHATAN, PUEBLO, SAC, SARCEE
	SAUK, SENECA, SEMINOLE
	SHASTA, SHAWNEE, SHOSHONE
	SHOSHONI, SHUSWAP, SIOUX
	SIWASH, SNAKE, SUSQUEHANNOCK
	TARAHUMARA, TIMUCUA, UTE, WICHITA
	WINNEBAGO, YOKUTS, YUROK, ZUNI
	(*see also* **America, Canada**)
utensil used in war	
ceremony	WAR-KETTLE
village	PUEBLO
war	
—axe	TOMAHAWK
—cry	WHOOP
white man with Indian wife	SQUAW-MAN
wife	SQUAW
winter	
—feast	POTLA(T)CH
—festival	POTLATCH
woman	SQUAW
religion	(*see* **belief**)
resident	
Resident Medical Officer	RMO
Resident Surgical Officer	RSO
resident magistrate	RM
resin	(*see* **gum/resin**)
respiratory system	
branch(es) of windpipe	
—main	BRONCHUS(BRONCHI)
—small	BRONCHIA
—very small	BRONCHIOLE
breathing-hole	SPIRACLE
cavity at end of bronchiole	AIR-SAC
compartment(s) of	
air-sac	ALVEOLUS(ALVEOLI)
flap over gill	GILL-COVER

hair(s) in bronchi	CILIUM(CILIA)
membrane covering lung	PLEURA
opening for gill	GILL SLIT
respiratory organ	
—fish, etc	GILL
—spiders, etc	LUNG-BOOK
—vertebrates	LUNG
rudimentary gill slit	GILL POUCH
section of lung	LOBE
upper part of	
—gullet	PHARYNX
—trachea	LARYNX
windpipe	TRACHEA
rhetoric	
including: grammar	
speech	
words	
2 letters, 1 sound	DIGRAPH
2 vowel sounds as one	DIPHTHONG
3 letters, 1 sound	TRIGRAPH
3 vowel sounds as one	TRIPHTHONG
academic introduction	ISAGOGE
adage	PAROEMIA
added as finishing touch	EPIPHONEMA
addition	
—of words to	
clarify meaning	EPEXEGESIS
—to end of word	EPITHESIS
	PARAGOGE
adjective or verb	
applied to two nouns	ZEUGMA
affected style	EUPHUISM, GONGORISM
affirmation by	
—negation of contrary	ENANTIOSIS
	LITOTES
—substitution of	
contrary	ANTIPHRASIS
	ENANTIOSIS, IRONY
analyse	PARSE
anapaestic catalectic	PAROEMIA
anti-climax	BATHOS
anticipation	PROLEPSIS
apparent but not real	
absurdity	PARADOX
apposition	PARATHESIS
arch disparagement	DIASYRM
argument	
—of probability	ENTHYMEME
—to one point	DIALLAGE
arrangement in order of	
greater strength	CLIMAX
assigning human feelings	
to non-human objects	PATHETIC FALLACY
attack with words	INVECTIVE
attributive used as	
proper name	ANTONOMASIA

avoiding repetition	ANAPHORA
balancing of opposing ideas	ANTITHESIS
beginning	
—and ending sentence with same word	EPANADIPLOSIS
—successive sentences with the same word	(EP)ANAPHORA
boldness of speech	PARRHESIA
bombastic style	EUPHUISM
breach of syntax	SOLECISM
breaking of sentence	APOSIOPESIS
burlesque mixture of words	MACARONIC
change	
—in form of word to indicate tense, etc	INFLECTION
—of	
letter	PARAGRAM
relation of words in sentence	HYPALLAGE
—to an r-sound	RHOTACISE, RHOTACIZE
child-talk	GAMMACISM HYPOCORISM(A)
childish speech	LALLATION
circumlocution	PERIPHRASIS
clauses without connectives	PARATAXIS
combination of contradictory terms	OXYMORON
comparison of	
—unlike ideas or objects	SIMILE
—using transferred name	METAPHOR
compound words	TATPURUSHA
compounding of words	PARATAXIS
—without change	PARATHESIS
concession	SYNCHORESIS
concise	
—saying	EPIGRAM
—style	LACON(IC)ISM
concurrence of vowel sounds	HIATUS
condensed expression	BRACHYLOGY
conditional clause	PROTASIS
confusion of meaning	SYNCHYSIS
containing figures of speech	FIGURATIVE
contrast by parallelism in reversed order	CHIASMUS
correct expression displacing an incorrect one	SUMPSIMUS
corresponding in arrangement of syllables	TAUTOMETRICAL
coupling of opposites	SYNOECIOSIS
descent from sublime to ridiculous	ANTI-CLIMAX, BATHOS

description by	
—analogy	METAPHOR
—likening to something else	SIMILE
—negation	ENANTIOSIS
desultory talk	DISCURSION
development of vowel	ANAPTYXIS SVARABHAKTI
diacritical sign over	
letter n	TILDE
diaeresis	TREMA
digression in speech	APOSTROPHE ASIDE, ECBOLE, EXCURSION EXCURSUS, PARENTHESIS
direct address to one present or absent	APOSTROPHE
disingenuous	
—denial	APOPHASIS
—mention of a subject	METASTASIS
diversion	APOSTROPHE
downbeat	THESIS
drawing attention to a point by apparently ignoring it	PARAL(E)IPSIS
elision	ECTHLIPSIS
end of speech	PERORATION
ending of successive clauses with same word	EPISTROPHE
erroneous quotation	MISCITATION
exaggeration	HYPERBOLE
exclamation	ECPHONESIS, EPIPHONEMA
exhortation	ALLOCUTION PARAN(A)ESIS
explanatory note	SCHOLION, SCHOLIUM
explicit comparison	SIMILE
expression conveying opposite meaning	IRONY
faulty syllepsis	ZEUGMA
figurative	
—analogy	METAPHOR
—language	TROPOLOGY
—resemblance	SIMILE
figure of speech	TROPE
flattery of judge or audience	COMPROBATION
formal speech	ADDRESS, ALLOCUTION DISCOURSE, DISQUISITION LECTURE, ORATION
formation of new word by wrong derivation from an existing word	BACK FORMATION
freedom of speech	PARRHESIA
funeral oration	ELOGE
grammatical construction	SYNTAX
having	
—acute accent on penultimate syllable	PAROXYTONE

third last syllable	PROPAROXYTONE
—an additional syllable	PERISSOSYLLABIC
—circumflex accent on the penult	PROPERISPOMENON
—full number of syllables	ACATALECTIC
—one more syllable in cases other than nominative	IMPARISYLLABIC
high-flown expression	EUPHUISM
hinting at	INNUENDO
idiomatic expression	IDIOTISM
imitation of sound	ONOMATOPOEIA
	ONOMATOPO(I)ESIS
immediate repetition	EPIZEUXIS
important speech	KEYNOTE SPEECH
inconsistent comparison	MIXED METAPHOR
incorrect use of words	CATACHRESIS
	MALAPROPISM
indeclinable noun	APTOTE
insertion	PARENTHESIS
—of sound	EPENTHESIS
interchanged relation-ship of words	HYPALLAGE
	TRANSFERRED EPITHET
introduction	EXORDIUM, ISAGOGE
	PROLEGOMENON
inversion	ANASTROPHE
	HYSTERON-PROTERON
—of	
antithesis	ANTIMETATHESIS
meaning	ANTIPHRASIS
jumbling of words	SYNCHYSIS
lack of syntactical sequence	ANACOLUTHIA
	ANACOLUTHON
last but one syllable	PENULT(IMA)
lengthening of short syllable	ECTASIS
list of words to be avoided	ANTIBARBARUS
litotes	M(E)IOSIS
logical argument	SYLLOGISM
marrowsky	SPOONERISM
meiosis	LITOTES
melting of final vowel	SYNALOEPHA
metaphor	IMAGE, PARABOLE
metaphorical	FIGURATIVE
metonymy	METALEPSIS
milder term for unpleasant thing	EUPHEMISM
misapplication of words	CATACHRESIS
	MALAPROPISM
modification of sound caused by context	SANDHI
more than two words	POLYONYMIC

much talk with little to say	MACROLOGY
mutual interchange of relationships	HYPALLAGE
	TRANSFERRED EPITHET
narration of facts	DIEGESIS
non-literal expression	TROPE
noun	SUBSTANTIVE
obfuscation	SERMOCINATION
omission of	
—conjunctions	ASYNDETON
—first sound or syllable	APH(A)ERESIS
—last sound or syllable	APOCOPE
—sound or syllable from middle of word	HAPLOLOGY
	SYNCOPATION, SYNCOPE
—vowel at beginning of word	APHESIS
or syllable	ELISION
—word(s)	ELLIPSIS
oration	DIEGESIS
overstatement	HYPERBOLE
palatalised	MOUILLE
panegyric	ELOGE, ENCOMIUM
	EULOGY, EULOGIUM
perissology	PLEONASM, VERBIAGE
personification	PROSOPOEIA
pert speech	DICACITY
phrase found once only	HAPAX LEGOMENON
phrases describing different aspects of something	SYSTROPHE
pithy saying	ADAGE, APHORISM
APO(PH)THEGM, EPIGRAM, GNOME	
	LACON(IC)ISM, MAXIM
	PROVERB, SAW
play on words	PARAGRAM, PARONOMASIA
	PARONOMASY, PUN
pleasant pronunciation	EUPHONY
pleonasm	PERISSOLOGY
pompous language	BOMBAST, EUPHUISM
	FUSTIAN
	GRANDILOQUENCE
pretended neglect	PARAL(E)IPSIS
process by which word acquires	
—less favourable meaning	DETERIORATION
	PEJORATION
—more favourable meaning	AMELIORATION
	ELEVATION
professed doubt	APORIA
prolixity	MACROLOGY
pronounced in liquid manner	MOUILLE

pronouncing `r' as `l'	LALLATION
pronunciation with	
wide-open mouth	PLATEASM
proper name used	
as attributive	ANTONOMASIA
proverb	PAROEMA
question to oneself	HYPOPHORA
raillery	DICACITY
recapitulation	EPANADOS
redundant expression	PLEONASM
refined irony	ASTEISM
relationship of	
—two words side by side	
one explaining	
the other	APPOSITION
—word to other words	
in a sentence	CASE
repetition	
—at beginning and end	
of clauses	SYMPLOCE
—in reverse order	ANTIMETABOLE
—of	
connectives	POLYSYNDETON
important word or	
phrase	ANADIPLOSIS
occurrence of sounds	ASSONANCE
sound	TAUTOPHONY
word or clause	
for emphasis	PALLILOGY
—at the beginning	
of words	ALLITERATION
word	PALILLOGONY
—at	
begining	
and end of sentence	EPANADIPLOSIS
—of successive	
clauses	(EN)ANAPHORA
end of successive	
clauses	EPISTROPHE
—immmediately	EPIZEUXIS
—or clause	
after parenthetic text	EPANALEPSIS
at end of one clause	
and beginning	
of the next	ANADIPLOSIS
—useless	BATTOLOGY, TAUTOLOGY
reproachful accusation	INVECTIVE
responding alternately	AMOEBAEAN
resumption	EPANALEPSIS
retracting in order to	
correct or intensify	EPANORTHOSIS
reversion after a	
parenthesis	HYPOSTROPHE
rhetorical question	EROTEMA, EROTEME
	EROTESIS
riddle	LOGOGRIPH

ridicule	IRONY, SATIRE, SCORN
round-about expression	PERIPHRASE
	PERIPHRASIS
running together of vowels	SYN(A)ERESIS
—in separate words	SYNAL(O)EPHA
same	
—notion in two	
expressions	HENDIADYS
—relationship but	
different sense	SYLLEPSIS
sarcasm	INVECTIVE
satirical remark	SARCASM
self-evident truth	AXIOM, TRUISM
sentence	
—begins and ends	
with same word	EPANADIPLOSIS
—ending	CLAUSULA
separation of parts of	
compound words	TMESIS
series of syllogisms	POLYSYLLOGISM
setting down	THESIS
short clause at end	
of period	CLAUSULA
shortening of syllable	SYSTOLE
simile	IMAGE, PARABOLE
similitude	PARABOLE
solo speech	MONOLOGUE, SOLILOQUY
speech	
—of	
appeal	EXHORTATION, PLEA
denunciation	DIATRIBE, HARANGUE
	PHILIPPIC, TIRADE
emotion	EFFUSION
farewell	VALEDICTION, VALEDICTORY
lamentation	JEREMIAD
opening	INAUGURAL
praise	ENCOMIUM, EULOGY
	PANEGYRIC
—sound	PHONEME
—with	
enemies	PARLEY, POW-WOW
others	COLLUQUY, DIALOGUE
splitting of word by	
insertion of another	TMESIS
Spoonerism	MARROWSKY
study of verse	PROSODY
stuttering	GAMMACISM
suggestion wihout assertion	INNUENDO
suppression of	
—sound	ECTHLIPSIS
—vowel or syllable	ELISION
symbol with more than	
one phonetic value	POLYPHONE
syntax relating to meaning	SYNESIS
three letters, one sound	TRIGRAPH
time	TENSE

tirade	LAISSE
transference of	
—adjective	HYPALLAGE
—meaning	METALEPSIS, METONYMY
—name	METAPHOR
to related object	METALEPSIS
	METONYMY
transposition of	
—initial sounds	MARROWSKY
	SPOONERISM
—order	HYPERBATON
—sounds or letters	METATHESIS
trema	DIAERESIS
trite statement	TRUISM
turning away from	
main theme	APOSTROPHE
two	
—speaking	DUOLOGUE
—vowels pronounced	
as one	DIPHTHONG
understatement	LITOTES, M(E)IOSIS
ungrammatical	ASYNTACTIC
union of two vowels	SYNECPHONESIS
	SYNIZESIS
unprepared speech	AD LIB(ITUM)
	EXTEMPORISATION
	IMPROMPTU, IMPROVISATION
use of	
—adjective to apply to	
two words when appropriate	
only to one	ZEUGMA
—another's imagined words	MIMESIS
—I in excess	IOTACISM
—less offensive word	EUPHEMISM
—more offensive word	DYSPHEMISM
—personal name to	
refer to class	ANTONOMASIA
—redundant words	MACROLOGY
—synedoche	SYNEDOCHISM
—word	
in	
—place of another	
related to it	METONYMY
—anticipation	PROLEPSIS
—sense opposite to	
literal sense	ANTIPHRASIS
	ENANTIOSIS, LITOTES
	IRONY
to apply in different	
ways to two others	SYLLEPSIS
used in three cases	TRIPTOTE
useless repetition	BATTOLOGY
	TAUTOLOGY
using part for whole	
or whole for the part	SYNECDOCHE
valediction	APOPEMPTIC

variation of vowel	ABLAUT
verbiage	PERISSOLOGY
violent censure	INVECTIVE
vivid description	HYPOTYPOSIS
vocabulary of a dialect	IDIOTICON
vowel	
—pronunciation mark	DI(A)ERESIS
	UMLAUT
—sound	MONOPHTHONG
without	
—conjunctions	ASYNDETON
—the article	ANARTHROUS
word	
—containing more	
than 3 letters	PLURILITERAL
—expressing sentence	
or phrase	HOLOPHRASE
—found once only	HAPAX LEGOMENON
—having	
more than one meaning	POLYSEME
same	
—meaning	SYNONYM
—sound but	
different	
meaning	HOMONYM, HOMOPHONE
—spelling but	
different meaning	HETERONYM
	HOMOGRAPH
two constructions	SYLLEPSIS
—imitating sound	ONOMATOPOIEA
—of	
1 syllable	MONOSYLLABLE
2 syllables	DISYLLABLE
3 syllables	TRISYLLABLE
4 syllables	QUADRISYLLABLE
	TETRASYLLABLE
5 syllables	PENTASYLLABLE
6 syllables	HEXASYLLABLE
7 syllables	HEPTASYLLABLE
8 syllables	OCTOSYLLABLE
10 syllables	DECASYLLABLE
11 syllables	HENDECASYLLABLE
12 syllables	DODECASYLLABLE
many syllables	POLYSYLLABLE
—represented by single	
sound	GRAMMALOGUE
—riddle	LOGOGRIPH
—that reads alike	
backward and forward	PALINDROME
	(*see also* **language**)
Rhodesia	RSR
	(*see also* **Zimbabwe**)
rice	
dishes	
—East Indian	NASI GORENG
	RIJST(T)AFEL

—Indian	BIRIANI, BIRYANI
	PILAU, PULAO
—Italian	RISOTTO
—Japanese	SUSHI
—Middle East	PILAF(F), PILAU, PULAO
—rice and fish	KEDGEREE
—Spanish	PAELLA
types	
—American	CAROLINA
—Indian	BASMATI, PATNA
—Italian	ARBORIO
—long grain	PATNA
rivers	
Afghanistan	AB-I-PANJA, AMUDHRYA
	BANDIHALA, FARAH RUD
	HARI RUD, HELMAND, KOULM
	KUNDUZ, MURGHAB, OXUS
Alaska	YUKON
Albania	DRINI, SEMANI, VJOSA
Algeria	CHELIFF
Andorra	VALIRA
Angola	CUANDO, CUANZA, CUNENE
	KUANZA, KUNENE, KWANDO
Argentina	BERMEJO, CHICO, CHUBUT
	COLORADO, DE LA PLATO
	DULCE, LIMAY, NEGRO
	PARANA, PILCOMAYO
	PLATE, SALADO, URUGUAY
Australia	ASHBURTON, BARCOO, BARWAN
	BRISBANE, CULGOA, DALY
	DARLING, DAWSON, DE GREY
	DIAMANTINA, FINKE, FITZROY
	FLINDERS, FORTESCUE, GASCOYNE
	GEORGINA, GILBERT, HAY, LOCHLAN
	MITCHELL, MURCHISON
	MURRAY, MURRUMBIDGEE, ORD
	ROPER, SWAN, VICTORIA
	WARREGO, YARRA-YARRA
Austria	DANUBE, DONAU, INN, MUR
Bangladesh	GANGA, GANGES
	JAMUNA, JUMNA, MEGHNA
Belgium	ESCAUT, MEUSE, SAMBRE
	SCHELDT, YSER
Belize	HONDO, NEW
Bhutan	AMO-CHU, MACHU
	MANAS, WANG CHU
Bolivia	BENI, BENICTO, GUAPAY
	MADIDI, MAMORE
	PILCOMAYA, PARAGUAY
Botswana	CHOBE, SHASHI
Brazil	AMAZON, ARAGUAIU, DESEADO
	DOLCE, IRIRI, JAPURA
	JEQUITINHANHA
	JURUA, MADEIRA, NEGRO
PARAGUAY, PARANA, PARAPANEMA	
	PARNAIBA, PURUS

	SAO FRANCISCO, SOLIMOES
	TAPAJOS, TOCANTINS
	TROMBETAS
Brunei	BRUNEI
Bulgaria	DANUBE, DUNAN, ISKAR
	ISKUR, MARITZA, TUNDZHA
Burkina Faso	VOLTA BLANCHE
	VOLTA NOIRE, VOLTA ROUGE
Burma	CHINDWIN, IRRAWADDY
	MEKONG, NU CHIANG
	SALWEEN, SITTANG
Burundi	KAGERA, RUZIZI
Cambodia	MEKONG
Cameroon	NYONG, SANAGA
Canada	ALBANY, ASSINIBOINE
	ATHABASCA, CHURCHILL
	COLUMBIA, FRASER, MACKENZIE
	MOOSE, NELSON, PEACE, RED
	ST LAWRENCE, SASKATCHEWAN
	SEVERN, SLAVE, SNAKE
	TESLIN, YUKON
Central African Republic	KOTTO
	OUBANGUI
Ceylon	KELANI GANGA
	MAHAWELI GANGA
Chad	BAHR, CHARI, KEITA, LAGONE
Chile	BIO-BIO, LAO, MAULE, VALDIVA
China	ARGUN, CHANJIANG
	CHANG KIANG
	HAN KIANG, HUANGHE
	HUNGSHUI HO, HWANG HO
	IRRAWADDY, KHOTAN
	KIALING KIANG, MEKONG
	SALWEEN, SI KIANG, SIANG KIANG
	TARIM, TATU HO, TSANGPO, WEI HO
	YALUNG KIANG, YANGTZE KIANG
	YARKAND, YELLOW RIVER
Colombia	AMAZON, CAUCA, CAQUETA
	GUAVIARE, MAGDALENA
	META, NEGRO
Costa Rica	RIO GRANDE
Cuba	CAUTO
Cyprus	PEDIEAS, SERANHIS
Czechoslovakia	DANUBE, DUNAJ, ELBE
	HRON, LABE, MORAVA
	NITRA, VAH
Denmark	GUDENA
Dominica	LAYOU
Dominican Republic	YAQUE DEL NORTE
Ecuador	CURARAY, DAULE
	NAPO, PASTAZA
Egypt	NILE
El Salvador	LEMPA
encircling	
—earth (myth)	OCEAN
—Hela's domain (myth)	GYOLT

England	AIRE, ARUN, AVON, CAM
	CHERWELL, DEE, DOVE, EDEN, EXE
	ISIS, KENNET, LEA, LUNE, MERSEY
	NENE, OUSE, PARRETT, RIBBLE
	ROTHER, SEVERN, SOW, STOUR
	SWALE, TAMAR, TAME, TARE, TAW
	TEES, TEST, THAMES, TRENT, TYNE
	USK, WEAR, WELLAND, WEY, WHARFE
	WITHAM, WYE
Equatorial Guinea	BENITO, CAMPO, MUNI
Ethiopia	ABBAY, AWASH, JUBA
	OMO, SAGAN, TEKEZE
	WEBBE SHIBELI, WEBI SHEBELE
Fiji	BA, NADI, NAVUA
	RIWA, SIGATOKA
Finland	KEMIJOKI, LEVOJOKI
	KORKIMAENJOKI
	PAATSJOKI, TORNIOJOKI
France	RIVIERE, DORDOGNE
	GARONNE, GIRONDE, LOIRE
	MARNE, MOSELLE, OISE
	RHINE, RHONE
	SAONE, SEINE, SOMME
Gabon	OGOOUE, OZOUE
Gambia	GAMBIA
Germany	FLUSS
	DANUBE, DONAU, ELBE
	EMS, HAVEL, MOSEL, ODER
	RHEIN, RHINE, WESER
Ghana	OTI, VOLTA
Guatemala	MOTAGUA, USUMACINTA
Guinea	BAFING, KOGON
	KONKOURE, NIGER
Guinea-Bissau	CACHEU, CORUBEL
	GEBA, MANSOA
Guyana	BERBICE, COURANTYNE
	DEMERARA, ESSEQUIBO
	MAZARUNI
Hades (myth)	
—fire	PHLEGETHON
—forgetfulness	LETHE
—lamentation	COCYTUS
—oath of gods	STYX
—woe	ACHERON
Haiti	ARTIBONITE
Honduras	PATUCA, ULUA
Hungary	DANUBE, DRAVA, DUNA
	RBA, TISZA
Iceland	SKJALFANDAFLJOT, THJORSA
India	BHADRA, BHIMA, BOLAN
	BRAHMAPUTRA, CAUVERY, CHAMBAL
	GANGA, GANGES, GHAGHARA
	GODAVARI, HUGLI, JUMNA, KISTNA
	KRISHNA, MAHANADI, NARBADA
	NARMEDA, PENNER, SON, SUTLEJ
	TAPTITUNGA, YAMUNA

Indonesia	BARITOS, DIGUL, HARI
	KAJAN, KAPUAS, MAHAKAM
Iran	ATRAK, KARKHEH, KARUN
	SAFID, SEFID RUD
	ZAYANDEH
Iraq	EUPHRATES, TIGRIS
Ireland	ALLEN, BANN, BARROW
	BLACKWATER, BOYNE, ERNE
	LAGANLEE, LIFFEY, SHANNON
	SLANEY, SUIR
Israel	JORDAN, QISHON
Italy	FIUME, ADIGE, AGRI, ARNO
	BALTEA, BIFERNO, BORMIDA
	BRADANO, BRENTA, DORA
	GARIGLIANO, ISONZA, LIRI, MAIRA
	METAURO, OMBRONE, PANARO
	PIAVE, PO, RENO, SANGRO
	SECCHIO, SELE, SERCHIO, SESIA
	STURA, TAGLIAMENTO, TANARO
	TARO, TEVERE, TIBER, TICINO
	TREBBIO, TRONTO
	VALDI-FIEMME, VOLTURNO
Ivory Coast	BANDAMA, KOMOE
	SASSANDRA
Jamaica	BLACK
Japan	ISHIKARE, KITAKAMI
	SHINANO, TONE
Java	SOLO
Jordan	JORDAN
Kenya	ATHI, MATHIOYA, TANA, UMBA
Korea	CHONGCHON, HAN, IMJIN
	KUM, NAKTONG, NAM
	SOMJIN, YALU, YONGSAN
Laos	MEKONG
Lebanon	JORDAN, LEONTES
legendary (Hebrew)	SAMBATION
	SANBATION
Lesotho	CALEDON, ORANGE
Liberia	CESS, ST JOHN, ST PAUL
Libya	WADI EL-FARIGH
Liechtenstein	RHEIN, RHINE, SAMINA
Luxembourg	ALZETTE, MOSEL(LE)
	OUR, SURE
Madagascar	IKOPO, MANGOKY, MANIA
Malawi	SHIRE
Malaya	KELANTAN, PAHANG
Mali	FALEME, NIGER, SENEGAL
Mauritania	SENEGAL
Mexico	BALSAS, BRAVO, CONCHOS
	FUERTE, GRANDE, GRIJALVA
	PANUCO, SONORA
Mongolia	HERELENG, KERULEN, KHODASIN
	NUN, OB, ORHON, SELENGA
	SELENGE, SUNGARI, URUNGU
Morocco	OUED DRA, OUED MOULOUYA
	OUED OUM-ER-RBIA, SEBOU

Mozambique	LIMPOPO, LUGENDA, RUVUMA
	SAVE, SHIRE, ZAMBEZI
Namibia	CUNENE, OKAVANGO
Nepal	KARNALI, KOSI, NARYANI
Netherlands	IJSSEL, MAAS, MEUSE
	RHINE, WAAL
New Zealand	AWATERE, BULLER
	CLARENCE, CLUTHA, HOKITIKA
	HURUNUI, MANAWATU, MOKAU
	MOTUEKA, ORETI, RAKAIA
	RANGITAIKI, RANGITATA
	RUNGITIKEI, TAIERI, THAMES
	WAIAPU, WAIHOU, WAIKATO
	WAINOA, WAIRAU, WAITAKI
	WANGANUI, WHAKATANE
Nicaragua	COCO, ESCONDIDO, GRANDE
	SAN JUAN, SEGOVIA
Niger	DILLIA, NIGER
Nigeria	ANGERMA, BENUE, CROSS
	INDALS, NIGER
North America	ALABAMA, ALLEGHENY
	ARKANSAS, BRAZOS, CHEYENNE
	COLORADO, COLUMBIA, GILA
	HUDSON, MISSISSIPPI, MISSOURI
	NORTH PLATTE, OHIO, POTOMAC
	PECOS, RED, RIO GRANDE
	SACRAMENTO, SAN JOAQUIM, SNAKE
	SOUTH PLATTE, ST JOHN, ST JUAN
	SUSQUEHANNA, YELLOWSTONE
Norway	GLAMA, GLOMMA, LAGEN
	TANAELV, UME
oblivion	LETHE
Pakistan	BEAS, CHENAB, DASHT
	GANGES, INDUS, JHELUM
	RAVI, SOAN, SUTLEJ
Panama	BAYANO, CHUCUNAQUE
	SANTA MARIA, TUIRA
Papua New Guinea	FLY, SEPIK
	STRICKLAND
Paraguay	HONDO, PARAGUAY
	PARANA, PILCOMAYO, SALGADO
Peru	AMAZON(AS), PURUS, TAMBORYACU
	UCAYALI, URUMBAMBA
Philippines	ABRA, AGNO, AGUSAN
	CAGAYAN, LAOANG, MAGAT
	PAMPANGA
Phrygia	MEANDER
Poland	NAREW, ODER, ODRA
	VISTULA, WISLA
Portugal	LIMA, TAGUS, TEJO
Romania	DANUBE, DUNAREA, MURES, PRUT
Russia	ALDAN, AMGUN, AMUR, ANADYR
	ANGARA, ANYUY, ARRAKS, BARGUZIN
	BIRYUSA, BOLSHAYA, CHUNA
	DNEIPER, DON, DVINA, EMBA, ILIM
	IRTYSH, ISHIM, KAZYM, KHROMA

	KIRENGA, KOLYMA, KORKODON
	KOTUY, KURA, KUREYKA, LENA
	MAYA, NADYM, OLEKMA, OLENEK
	OLOY, OKA, OMOLON, PECHORA
	PRIPYAT, SUGAI, TAZ, TOBOL
	TUNGUSKA, UNZHA, URAL, VETLUGA
	VITIM, VOLGA, YANA, YENISEY
	YUDOMA, ZEYA
Rwanda	LUVIRONZA
Scotland	CLYDE, DEE, DON, FORTH
	NITH, SPEY, TAY, TEVIOT
	TWEED
Senegal	CASAMANCE, GAMBIA
	GAMBIE, SENEGAL
Sierra Leone	JONG, ROKEL, SIWA
Somalia	GIUBA, JUBA
	SHEBELE, SHEBELI
South Africa	ORANGE, VAAL
Spain	RIO
	DOURO, DUERO, EBRO
	GUADALQUIVIR, GUADIANA
	TAGUS, TAJO
Sudan	ATBARA, LOL, NILE
Suriname	COMMEWIJNE, COPPENAME
	CORANTIJN, MARONI
	MAROWIJNE, NICKERIE
	SARAMACCA, SURINAME
Swaziland	INGWAVUMA, KEMATI
	UMBULZI, USUTU
Sweden	ANGERMAN, DAL, KLARALVEN
	MJOSA, TORNE, UME
Switzerland	AARE, INN, RHEIN
	RHINE, TICINO
Syria	ASI, EL FURM, ORONTES
Taiwan	CHOSHUI CHI, HSIA-TAN-SHUI
	TANSHUI, WU CHI
Tanzania	PANGANI, RUAHA, RUFIJI
	RUVU, RUVUMA
Tasmania	DERWENT, GORDON, TAMAR
Tempe (myth)	PENEUS
Thailand	CHAD PYHA, MEKONG
	PING, YOM
Trinidad	CORONI, OROPUCHE, ORTOIRE
Tunisia	MEDJERDA
Turkey	DICLE, EUPHRATES, FIRAT
	HALYS, IRMAK, KIZILIRMAK
	MURAT, SAKARYA, TIGRIS
Uganda	NILE, SEMLIKI
Uruguay	URUGUAY
Venezuela	APURE, META, ORINOCO
Vietnam	BLACK RIVER, MA, MEKONG
	RED RIVER, SONG BO
	SONG KOI
Wales	CLEDDAU, CLWYD, DYFI
	TAFF, TAW, TEIFI, TOWY
	USK, VYRNWY, YSTWITH

Yugoslavia	DANUBE, DRAVA, DUNAU
	MORAVA, SAVA, VARDAR
Zaire	CASSAI, CONGO, KASAI, KWA
	KWILU, LUALABA, LUBILASH
	LUKENIE, LUKUGA, LULUA
	LUVUA, SANGA, SANKURU
	TSHUPA, UBANGUI, UELE, ZAIRE
Zambia	LUANGWA, LUAPULA, KAFUE
	ZAMBESI, ZAMBEZI
Zimbabwe	LIMPOPO, LUNDI, NUANETSI
	ODZI, SABI, SHANGANI
	UMNIATA, UMZINGWANI
	ZAMBESI, ZAMBEZI

rock

above fault-plane	HANGING WALL
aggregate of loosened	
fragments	DETRITUS
angle in rock-face	DIEDRE
balanced on another	LOG(G)AN(-STONE)
	LOGGING-STONE
banded	GNEISS
below fault-plane	FOOT WALL
body of rock enclosing	
an intrusion	COUNTRY ROCK
boulder transported by glacier	ERRATIC
calcium carbonate as	
stalagmite or stalactite	DRIPSTONE
cave-dweller	TROGLODYTE
cavity	
—containing crystals	DRUSE
	DRUSY CAVITY, GEODE
—in rock	CAVE, GEODE, VESICLE
Cornwall	VUG
change in shape	DEFORMATION
	METAMORPHISM
—due to	
pressure	DYNAMIC METAMORPHISM
reaction with	
enclosing rock	ENDOMORPHISM
—involving chemical	
composition	METASOMATISM
character of rock	LITHOLOGY
clay rock	SHALE
column with grooves	STYLOLITE
composed of	
—angular fragments	AGGLOMERATE
	BRECCIA
—calcium-containing	
minerals	TESTACEOUS
—fragments	CLASTIC
—lime silicates	HORNFELS
—mixed minerals	AGGREGATE
—pebbles	PSEPHITE
—rock	RUPESTRIAN
—rounded fragments	CONGLOMERATE
	PUDDING STONE

—separable fragments	AGGREGATE
—sand grains	PSAMMITE
—volcanic fragments	AGGLOMERATE, TUFF
containing	
—carbon	CARBONACEOUS
—crystalline and	
glassy material	HEMICRYSTALLINE
—diatom skeletons	DIATOMACEOUS
—grains	GRANULAR
	GRANULOSE
	GRANULOUS
—graphite	PLUMBAGINOUS
—gravel	GLAREOUS
—less than 10% silica	INTERMEDIATE
—little silica	BASIC
—more than	
10% silica	ACID ROCK
one material	COMPOSITE
—ore	GANGUE, LODE
—plate-like crystals	TABULAR
—sand	ARENACEOUS
—shell-like material	TESTACEOUS
—silica	SILICEOUS, SILICIOUS
—steam cavities	AMYGDALOID
conversion of	
—loose material to rock	CEMENTATION
—sediment to rock	DIGENESIS
Cornish	ELVAN
crack in	
—horizontal limestone	GRIKE, GRYKE
—rock	CHIMNEY, CREVICE
	FAULT, FISSURE
	JOINT, RIFT
crest of fold	ANTICLINE
debris	
—at	
foot of	
—glacier	MORAINE
—slope	SCREE, TALUS
side of glacier	LATERAL MORAINE
—produced by	
weathering of rock	ELUVIUM
decomposed rock at outcrop	GOSSAN
	GOZZAN
deposited by	
—hot springs	CALC-TUFF
	SINTER, TRAVERTINE
—water	SEDIMENTARY
description of rocks	PETROGRAPHY
displaced by folding	NAPPE
distinguishing features	FACIES
division of rock	
formation	SERIES, SYSTEM
easily split into lamina	SCHIST, SLATE
exposed on surface	OUTCROP
extrusive rock	BASALT

fall of rock	BERGFALL	—round hot springs	GEYSERITE
flat limestone block	CLINT	fragment(s) of rock	CLAST, DEBRIS
flowing			DETRITUS, RUBBLE
—into cracks	INTRUSIVE	—angular	GRAVEL
—out at surface	EXTRUSIVE	—at base of cliff	SCREE, TALUS
fold		—embedded in another	XENOLITH
—at constant angle	MONOLINE	—rounded	COBBLE, PEBBLE
—dipping outward in			SHINGLE
all directions	PERICLINAL	—small	GRIT
	QUAQUAVERSAL	frothy lava	PUMICE
—downward	SYNCLINE	greywether	SARSEN
large	GEOSYNCLINE	hard broken rock	RAG
—highly folded		having	
geoanticline	ANTICLINORIUM	—crystalline structure	AUTOMORPHIC
geosyncline	SYNCLINORIUM	—no	
—overturned anticline	OVERFOLD	crystalline structure	ANHEDRAL
—parallel to surrounding		regular arrangement	AMORPHOUS
rocks	RECUMBENT	hole (Australia)	GNAMMA HOLE
—upward	ANTICLINE	igneous	PYROGENIC
large	GEOANTICLINE	—fine-grained	VULCANITE
—with almost parallel		—in	
sides	ISOCLINE	horizontal sheet	SILL, TRAP
formation		mound below surface	LACCOLITE
—exposed at Earth's			LACCOLITH
surface	OUTCROP	vertical sheet	DIKE, DYKE
—from fragments	LITHIFICATION	—injected into fissure	DIKE(-WALL)
formed			DYKE(-WALL)
—at depths below		—intrusive mass	BATHOLITE, BATHOLITH
the surface	HYPOGENE		BATHYLITE, BATHYLITH
—after enclosing rock	EPIGENETIC	—lens-shaped mass	PHACOLITH
—by			SADDLE-REEF
accretion	OOLITH	—not reaching surface	HYPABYSSAL
alteration of limestone	DOLOMITE	—rocks	AMYGDALOID, BASALT
altered composition due			BASANITE, BATHOLITE
to high temperature			DOLERITE, GABBRO, GRANITE
and pressure	METAMORPHIC		MONZONITE, PERMATITE
change of molecular			PERIDOTITE, PHONOLITE
structure	PARAMORPH		PORPHYRY, RHYOLITE
compression of clay	SLATE		SPILITE, TRACHYTE
cooling of lava			VARIOLITE, WHINSTONE
or magma	EXTRUSIVE	isolated rock	
	IGNEOUS	—pillar in sea	STACK
deposit of calcium etc		—standing above	
from moving water	FLOWSTONE	ice	NUNATAK
deposition	SEDIMENTARY	its surroundings	MONADNOCK
evaporation of sea-water	EVAPORITE	large rounded lump of rock	BOULDER
hardening of silt	SILTSTONE	layer(s) of rock	STRATUM (STRATA)
outpouring of lava	EFFUSIVE	lens-shaped mass of	
subterranean heat	ABYSSAL	igneous rock	PHACOLITH
	PLUTONIC		SADDLE-REEF
—in volcanoes	(see volcano)	limestone	
—from		—coarse	PISOLITE
clay or mud	PELITE	—crystalline	MARBLE
organic material	BIOLITH	—decomposed	ROTTENSTONE
—of thin layers	FOLIACEOUS	—deposited from	
	FOLIATED	solution	TRAVERTIN(E)

—Dorset	PURBECK MARBLE
	PURBECK STONE
—granular	OOLITE
—India	KUNKAR, KUNKUR
—needle	
growing upward	STALAGMITE
hanging down	STALACTITE
—patterned	LANDSCAPE MARBLE
—soft and crumbly	MALM
living in rocks	LITHODOMOUS
	RUPICOLINE, RUPICOLOUS
long rounded rock	ROCHE MOUTONNEE
looking like another	
which it has replaced	PSEUDOMORPH
loose rock at	
—foot of cliff	SCREE, TALUS
—surface	MANTLEROCK, REGOLITH
magnetic rock	LOADSTONE, LODESTONE
mantle rock	REGOLITH
mass of	
—igneous rock	
formed by intrusion	
of magma	BATHOLITE, BATHOLITH
	BATHYLITE, BATHYLITH
lens-shaped	PHACOLITH, SADDLE-REEF
—plutonic rock	PLUTON
—rock balanced on slender	
neck	PEDESTAL ROCK
—carried away by	
natural phenomena	BOULDER, ERRATIC
—sandstone	
in Alps	FATSCH
left after erosion	
of layer	GREYWETHER, SARSEN
—wall rock	
interrupting lode	HORSE
—with convex sides	LENS
mechanical breakup	CATACLASIS
metamorphic rocks	GNEISS, MYLONITE
	PORPHYROID, SCHIST
	SLATE
mineral composition	
of rock	MODE
mining from surface	OPENCAST
—US	STRIP MINING
molten rock	MAGMA
moved by glacier	ERRATIC
new rock surrounded	
by older	OUTLIER
non-crystalline rock	AMORPHOUS
old rock surrounded	
by newer	INLIER
on	
—ice in glacier	GLACIER TABLE
—or near surface	EPIGENE ROCK
outcrop	BASSET

overlying rock	OVERBURDEN
painting or inscription	
on rock	PETROGLYPH
paramorphic change	METASTASIS
partially decomposed	SAPROLITE
particle	GRAIN, GRANULE
peak	CRAG
permitting passage	
of water	PERMEABLE ROCK
	PERVIOUS ROCK
pile of rock	CAIRN, TOR
pillar of limestone	
—hanging	STALACTITE
—standing	STALAGMITE
plateau	MASSIF
plutonic rock	GRANITE, SYENITE
pointed mass of rock	AIGUILLE, CRAG
porous	TUFA, TUFF, PUMICE
preventing passage	
of water	IMPERMEABLE ROCK
	IMPERVIOUS ROCK
production of different	
rocks from common	
mother base	DIFFERENTIATION
radioactive rock	AUTONITE, CARMENITE
	PITCH-BLENDE, RADIUM
	TORBANITE, URANIUM
ridge running into sea	PROMONTORY
rock	
—boring	LITHOPHAGOUS
—building	LITHOGENOUS
—dwelling	RUPICOLINE, RUPICOLOUS
—guano	SOMBRERITE
—oil	PETROLEUM
rocky	
—crust of Earth	LITHOSPHERE
—desert	HAM(M)ADA, REG
—edge of mountain	ARETE
—height	TOR(R)
—island	SKERRY, STACK
—mound (Scot.)	SCALP
—recess	COVE
—valley	GULCH, RAVINE
rudaceous rock	SEDIMENTARY
sandy	
—ironstone	DOGGER
—shale	FA(I)KES
sarsen	GREYWETHER
sedimentary rocks	BRECCIA, CHACK, CLAY
	COAL, GRIT, IRONSTONE
	LIMESTONE, MUDSTONE
	QUARTZITE, SANDSTONE
	SHALE, SLATE
series of rocks	FORMATION
shaly sandstone	FA(I)KES
sheet of rock	NAPPE

sloping		tribes	COMITIA TRIBUTA
—area of scree	TALUS	assembly	FORUM
—bedrock at foot of		auxiliary soldier	FOEDERATUS
steeper slope	PEDIMENT	awning	VELARIA
small lump of rock	NODULE	axe	DOLABRA
splitting into layers	CLEAVAGE	barrack-room	CONTUBERNIA
	LAMINATION	barracks	CAN(N)ABA
standing above ice	NUNATAK	bathing establishment	THERM
steep rock(-face)	CRAG, CLIFF	block of buildings	INSULA
stone polished by wind	VENTIFACT	blood-sucking witch	LAMIA
streaks in igneous rock	SCHLIEREN	body of soldiers	LEGION
stretching of rock into		boring engine	TEREBRA
sausage shape	BOUDINAGE	boundary	LIMES
study of		brickwork	OPUS LATERICUM
—rocks	GEOLOGY, LITHOLOGY	bridge builder	PONTIFEX
	PETROLOGY	building	INSULA
—rock strata	STRATIGRAPHY	—where senate met	CURIA
subterranean mass of		bundle of rods	FASCES
solidified rock	PLUTON	calendar	FASTI
thin layer(s) of rock	LAMINA(E)	camp gate	PR(A)ETORIAN GATE
through which vein of		cap of free slave	PHRYGIAN CAP
ore runs	WALL ROCK	capital	ROME
transported from original		catapult	BAL(L)ISTA
site by glacier	ERRATIC	Catholic	RC
under sea	LEDGE, REEF	centurion's badge	VINE ROD
underlying		chair	CURULE
—rock	BEDROCK	chariot	BIGA, QUADRIGA
—surface	BEDDING PLANE	chief	
—stratified rocks	BASEMENT (COMPLEX)	—magistrate	CONSUL
useless	GANGUE	—priest (Syria)	SYRIARCH
vertical face formed		—secretary of chancery	PROT(H)ONOTARY
by erosion	RIMROCK	children's ornament	BULLA
volcanic rock	(see volcano)	church	
water-bearing	AQUIFER	—basin	CANTHARUS
without crystalline		—office	NONES
structure	GLASS	circus barrier	SPINA
worthless	GANGUE	citizen	QUIRITES
(see also geography, mineral, stone)		clan	GENS
rockets	(see missiles, space)	cloak	TOGA, TOGE
Roman	ROM	—for travelling	PAENULA
acquisition by occupation	USUCAPTION	—military	ABOLLA
actor	ROSCIUS	—of manhood	TOGA VIRIUS
—in dumb show	PANTOMINE	—woman's	PALLA
actor's mask	PERSONA	coin metal	POTIN
additional name	AGNOMEN	coins	
administrative building	BASILICA	—copper	AS, SEMUNCIA
administrator	PROCURATOR	—1/6 as	SEXTANS
agate	MURR(H)A	—1/4 as	KODRANTES, QUADRANS
amphitheatre	COLOSSEUM, COLISEUM	—1/2 as	SEMIS
ancient kingdom	PONTUS	—2 asses	DUPONDIUS
apartment house	INSULA	—2½ asses	SESTERCE
assemblies		—10 asses (silver)	DENARIUS
—for laws	COMITIA	—2 denarii	ANTONINIANUS
—of		—12 denarii (silver)	SOLIDUS
centuries	COMITIA CENTURIATA	—1000 sesterces	SESTERTIUM
patricians	COMITIA CURITA	—old	DUPONDIUS

—gold	AUREUS, SOLIDUS
college of heralds	FETIALES
colonial governor	PRO-CONSUL
comedy	PALLIATA
commander of	
—10 soldiers	DECURION
—100 soldiers	CENTURION
commoner	PLEB
company of soldiers	MANIPLE
	VEXILLIUM
conquered ally	FOEDERATUS
consul's robe	TRABEA
cooling room	FRIGIDARIUM
couch	TRICLINUM
councillor	DECURION
country house	VILLA
court	CURIA
—official	LICTOR
—(yard)	AULA
cross	TEN, X
curved tile	IMBREX
cushioned seat	PULVINAR
dagger	SICA
dance	TRIPUDIUM
daring conspirator	CATALINE
dates	
—1st of each month	CALENDS
—9th before ides	NONES
—13th/15th	IDES
days	
—Monday	DIES LUNAE
—Tuesday	DIES MARTIS
—Wednesday	DIES MERCURII
—Thursday	DIES JOVIS
—Friday	DIES VENERIS
—Saturday	DIES SATURNI
—Sunday	DIES SOLIS
—when business	
legal	FASTI
not legal	NEFASTI
decree of senate	SC
	SENATUS CONSULT(UM)
deities	(*see* **gods, goddesses**)
descendant of original	
Roman people	PATRICIAN
digest of law	PANDECT
dining-room	TRICLINUM
dish	PATERA
ditch round amphitheatre	EURIPUS
diviner	AUGUR, AUSPEX
	HARUSPEX
division of tribe	CURIA
divorce	DIFFAREATION
dominion governor	PRO-CONSUL
drinking cup	CANTHARUS
dual officials	DUUMVIR

early Roman empire	PRINCIPATE
earth mound	AGGER
earthenware jar	DOLIUM
election canvass official	NOMENCLATOR
emperor's	
—bodyguard	PR(A)ETORIAN GUARD
—decree	INDICTION, NOVELLA
engine of war	TORMENTUM
entrance hall	ATRIUM
epic poem	AENEID
exit door	VOMITORIUM
family name	COGNOMEN
farmstead	VILLA
fastening of woman's sash	VIRGIN KNOT
favourite food	MUR(A)ENA
felt cap	PILEUS
festival of	
—boundaries	TERMINALIA
—cornfields	AMBARVALIA
—exorcism	LEMURIA
—fertility	LUPERCALIA
—Pales	PALILIA
—Saturn	SATURNALIA
—Vulcan	VULCANIA
—wine	VINALIA
fifteen-year cycle	INDICTION
financial agent	PROCURATOR
fish sauce	GARUM
flask	AMPHORA, AMPULLA
flat dish	PATERA
forename	PRAENOMEN
former master of slave	PATRON
forming friendship	
by dividing stone	CONTESSERATION
fort	CASTELLUM
freeman	AERARIAN
galley	BIREME, TRIREME
	QUADRIREME, QUINQUEREME
games	SECULAR GAMES
general's	
—cloak	PALUDAMENT(UM)
—quarters	PRINCIPIUM
—tent	PR(A)ETORIUM
ghost(s) of the dead	LEMUR(ES)
gift	CONGIARY
gladiator	SAMNITE
—armed with net	RETIARIUS
god	DEUS
god's head-dress	MODIUS
governor's residence	PR(A)ETORIUM
grappling hook	CORVUS
hall	ATRIUM, AULA
headband	VITTA
headquarters	PR(A)ETORIUM
	PRINCIPIA
heavy javelin	PILUM

heraldic	FECIAL, FETIAL
Hermes's rod	CADUCEUS
hill of Rome	QUIRINAL
himation	PALLIUM
historian	LIVY, TACITUS
hospital	VALETUDINARIUM
household gods	LARES AND PENATES
imperial	
—official	COUNT
—standard	LABARUM
internal quadrangle	COMPLUVIUM
jar	AMPHORA, DOLIUM, OLLA
javelin	PILE
judge	CENTUMVIR, QU(A)ESTOR
kill every tenth man	DECIMATE
knight	EQUES
land tax	INDICTION
lapsing (law)	CADUCOUS
large hall	BASILICA
law	LEX
—digest	PANDECT
leader	DUX
leather armour	LORICA
legal transfer	MANCIPATION
legion	COHORT
low-class citizen	PROLETARIUS
magistrate	(A)EDILE, (PRO)PR(A)ETOR
	PRO-CONSUL, QU(A)ESTOR
	TRIBUNE
—whose ancestors had	
never held office	NOVUS HOMO
magistrate's	
—attendant	LICTOR
—badge	FASCES
—chair	CURULE
man	VIR
man's undergarment	SUBUCULA
mantle	PALLIUM, TOGA, TOGE
manuscript style	RUSTICA
market	
—day	NUNDINE
—place	FORUM
marriage	CONFAR(R)EATION
mausoleum	MOLE
measures	
—58 inches	PACE
—1000 double paces	MILE
—1.4 miles	LEAGUE
—1 gallon	CONGIUS
—1 peck	MODIUS
milestone	MILIARY
military	
—cloak	ABOLLA, PALUDAMENT(UM)
	SAGUM
—earthwork	AGGER
—shelter formed by shields	TESTUDO

—standard	LABARUM
—wheeled shelter	TESTUDO
missile-thrower	TORMENTUM
monarch	CAESAR
monster	LAMIA, TYPHON
moray	MUR(A)ENA
mortuary	SPOLIARY
mound	AGGER
name	NOMEN
—without description	NOMEN NUDUM
noble	PATRICIAN
oak wreath	CIVIC CROWN
officer's cloak	PALUDAMENT(UM)
official	LICTOR
—scrivener	TABELLION
one of	
—board of	
two men	DUUMVIR
three men	TRIUMVIR
four men	QUADRUMVIR
five men	QINQUEVIR
six men	SEXTUMVIR
seven men	SEPTEMVIR
ten men	DECEMVIR
—two divisions of	
Roman people	PLEBS
open area in middle of	
house	COMPLUVIUM
orator	CICERO
patrician	PATRON
—marriage	CONFARREATION
—virgin	VESTA
perpetual right in land	EMPHYTEUSIS
platter	LANX
pledge in lawsuit	SACRAMENT
poet	(*see* writer *below*)
porridge	PULS
pound	LIBRA
precious metal	MURR(H)A
precluding debate	PEREMPTORY
	PLAUTUS, PLINY
priest	FLAMEN, PONTIFEX
—foretelling future	AUGUR, AUSPEX
	HARUSPEX
—of field deities	ARVAL BRETHREN
privy council (chamber)	CONSISTORY
prize to first to mount	
wall of besieged city	MURAL CROWN
procession in honour	
of victorious general	TRIUMPH
prosecutor	QU(A)ESTOR
province (ancient)	PONTUS
provincial governor	PROPRAETOR
public	
—baths	THERMAE
—hall or court	BASILICA

—square	FORUM	stool	CURULE
purification ceremony	LUSTRE, LUSTRUM	straight trumpet	TUBA
rain-water receptacle	IMPLUVIUM	stripe on senator's tunic	LATICLAVE
rampart	VALLUM	surplice	STOLA
ramps	ASCENSI	surveying instrument	GROMA
reclining couch	TRICLINUM	swimming-pool	PISCINA
register	ALBUM	sword	GLADIUS, SPATHA
religious		symbol of authority	FASCES
—ceremony	LECTISTERNIUM	tax-collector	PUBLICAN
—dance	TRIPUDIUM	temple of	
—festival	LUPERCAL(IA)	—all gods	PANTHEON
	QUIRINAL(IA)	—Jupiter	CAPITOL
—head-band	INFULA	tenth part of	
—offerings	INFERIAE	—legion	COHORT
repository for Penates	SACRARIUM	—tribe	CURIA
richest booty	SPOLIA OPTIMA	third (family) name	COGNOMEN
road	VIA	three-pronged weapon	TRIDENT
Roman people	PR	tile	TEGULA
royal palace	BASILICA	training ground	CAMPUS MARTIUS
ruler	CAESAR	travelling-cloak	PAENULA
ruling body	SENATE	tribe	GENS
rural deity	FAUN	triple officials	TRIUMVIR
sacrifice	INFERIAE	trumpet	BUCCINA
—of animals	SUOVETAURALIA	underfloor space	
satirist	JUVENAL(IS)	for heating	HYPOCAUST
score	DOUBLECROSS	undergarment	SUBUCULA, TUNIC
scroll	STEMMA	veteran	VEXILLARY
sea-fight	NAUMACHIA, NAUMACHY	wall decoration	TOPIA
second name	NOMEN	warm room in baths	TEPIDARIUM
senate	CURIA	weights	
senators	CONSCRIPT FATHERS	—½ ounce	SEMUNCIA
	PATRES CONSCRIPTI	—12 ounces	AS
shallow pan	PATINA	—pound	AS, LIBRA
shield	SCUTUM	white tablet	ALBUM
—from heaven	ANCILE	wine	
sleeveless garment	EXOMIS, PAENULA	—festival	VINALIA
soldier(s)		—jar	DOLIUM
—company	MANIPLE, VEXILLATION	woman's	
of		—mantle	PALLA
—10	DECURIA, DECURY	—robe	STOLA
—100	CENTURY	workshop	FABRICIA
—300-600	COHORT	writer	APULEIUS, CATULLUS, HORACE
—3000-6000	LEGION		JUVENAL, LUCRETIUS, OVID
—in charge of			PLAUTUS, PLINY, TERENCE, VIRGIL
10 men	DECURION		(see also **Latin, mythology**)
100 men	CENTURION	**Romania**	R(O)
—lightly-armed	VELITE	capital	BUCHAREST, BUCURESTI
—tenth of legion	COHORT	coins	BANI, LEU
soldier's oath	SACRAMENT	newsagency	AGERPRES
soothsayer	AUGUR, AUSPEX	secret police	SECURITATE
	HARUSPEX	stew	TOCANA
spear	PILUM	**room**	
spirits of the dead	MANES	alcove for private study	CARREL(L)
staircases	ASCENSI	artist's room	STUDIO
standard	LABARUM, VEXILLUM	bedchamber (Fr.)	ROUELLE
—bearer	VEXILLARY	behind stage	GREEN ROOM

circular	ROTUNDA
council chamber	DIVAN
court of justice	DIVAN
dining room	
—in college etc	REFECTORY
—Roman	TRICLINIUM
dungeon with opening	
only in the top	OUBLIETTE
entrance	ANTECHAMBER, ANTEROOM
	HALL, LOBBY, VESTIBULE
	FOYER
—college etc	(PORTER'S) LODGE
—Roman	ATRIUM
for	
—conversation	LOCUTORY
—domestic work	KITCHEN, SCULLERY
	UTILITY, WASH-HOUSE
—manoeuvre	LATITUDE, LEEWAY
	PLAY, SCOPE
—meals	DINER, DINETTE
	DINING ROOM, REFECTORY
—parties (Amer.)	RUMPUS ROOM
—prayer	ORATORY, PROSEUCHE
—private use	DEN, SANCTUM
	SNUG, STUDY
—sleeping	BEDROOM, DORMITORY
garret	SOL(L)AR, SOL(L)ER
hot-room	
—Roman	SUDATORIUM
—Swedish	SAUNA
in	
—roof	ATTIC, GARRET
—synagogue	GENIZAH
ladies' private room	BOUDOIR, BOWER
library	ATHENAEUM
living room	LOUNGE
	PARLOUR, SITTING ROOM
	(WITH)DRAWING ROOM
meeting room	HALL
—of coterie	CENACLE
open, central room	ATRIUM
photographer's room	DARK ROOM, STUDIO
reception room	(WITH)DRAWING ROOM
	PRESENCE CHAMBER, SALON
reading room	ATHENAEUM, LIBRARY
retiring-room	(WITH)DRAWING ROOM
—in theatre	GREEN ROOM
room on	
—ship	CABIN, CUDDY
	STATEROOM
—train	COMPARTMENT
rooms linked together	SUITE
sitting-room (military)	ANTEROOM
small	
—compartment	CUBICLE
—room	CAMARILLA

—storeroom	BOXROOM, CUBBY HOLE
	GLORY HOLE
smoking-room	DIVAN
staffroom	COMMON ROOM
store for	
—bones	CHARNEL HOUSE, OSSUARY
—books	ARCHIVE, LIBRARY
—clothes	DRESSING-ROOM
	GARDEROBE, WARDROBE
—documents	ARCHIVE
—medicines etc	DISPENSARY
—provisions	BUTTERY, PANTRY
	LARDER, STILL-ROOM
—vestments	SACRISTY, VESTRY
sun-room	SOLARIUM
supper room	CENACLE
upper room	SOL(L)AR, SOL(L)ER
where	
—cardinals meet to	
select Pope	CONCLAVE
—privy council of Roman	
Empire met	CONSISTORY
writing room	LIBRARY, SCRIPTORIUM

rope

circus rope	JEFF
coil	HANK
cowboy's rope	LARIAT, LASSO
	REATA, RIATA
fastener	TOGGLE
groove between strands	CANTLINE
—clockwise	Z-LAID
—counter-clockwise	S-LAID
halter for horse-breaking	HACKAMORE
handrail on ship	MANROPE
hanging noose	HALTER
hoisting sling	PARBUCKLE
joint in rope	SPLICE
knotted rope for	
calculating (Peru)	QUIPO, QUIPU
ladder	ETRIER, JACOB'S LADDER
lashing round	
bowsprit	GAMMON
loop	CAT'S-PAW, BIGHT, HANK
neck-cord	LANIARD, LANYARD
picket-rope	HOBBLE, LARIAT
rigging	CORDAGE, TACKLE
—below	
bowsprit	BOBSTAY
yard	FOOTROPE
—for	
fastening	
—bowline to sail	BRIDLE
—furled sail to yard	GASKET
furling square sails	CLEW-LINE
	CLEW-GARNET
hoisting	GANTLINE

raising sail or flag	HALLIARD	
	HALYARD	
setting yards	BRACE	
—from		
boom to deck	KICKING-STRAP	
	VANG	
lower corner of sail	SHEET	
	TACK	
sail to bow	BOWLINE	
—guy rope for gaff	VANG	
—on reef-band for furling	REEF-POINT	
—round edge of sail	BOLT-ROPE	
—step in shrouds	RATLIN(E)	
	RATTLIN(E), RATTLING	
—supporting		
awning	CROWFOOT	
masts	SHROUD, STAY	
—to prevent bellying		
of sail	BUNTLINE	
rope-making material	COIR, HEMP	
	MANILA, NYLON	
	JUTE, SISAL	
rope-soled shoe	ESPADRILLE	
rope's-end (navy)	COLT	
running noose	LASSO	
securing gun to ship	BREECHING	
short rope		
—for fastening	LANIARD, LANYARD	
—with metal ring inside	CRINGLE	
small cable	HAWSER	
strong rope	CABLE	
tent-rope	GUY, STAY	
trailing from balloon	DRAGROPE	
used for		
—leading animal	HALTER	
—mooring boat	PAINTER	
—mooring ship	CABLE, HAWSER, WARP	
—towing ship	CABLE, TOWROPE	
	HAWSER	
—tying		
animal	HOBBLE, TETHER	
or binding	CORD, LASHING	
	MARLIN(E), STRING	
	WHIPPING	
weighted rope (S. Amer.)	BOLAS	

Royal

Academician/Academy	RA
Academy of Music	RAM
Air Force	(*see separate entry*)
Artillery	RA
Australian Navy	RAN
Automobile Club	RAC
Arch Charter	RAC
Armoured Corps	RAC
Asiatic Society	RAS
Astronomical Society	RAS

Canadian Academy	RCA
College of	
—Art	RC, RCA
—Music	RCM
—Organists	RCO
—Physicians	RCP
—Preceptors	RCP
—Science	RCS
—Sculptors	RCS
Corps of	
—Signals	RCS
—Transport	RCT
Dublin Society	RDS
Engineers	RE
Exchange	RE
Flying Corps	RFC
Geographical Society	RGS
Grenadier Guards	RGG
Highness	RH
Horse Artillery	RHA
Hibernian Academy	RHA
Highland	
—Fusiliers	RHF
—Show	RHS
Historical Society	RHS
Horse Guards	RHG
Horticultural Society	RHS
Humane Society	RHS
Institute	RI
—of Chemistry	RIC
Institution of Painters	RI
Irish	
—Academy	RIA
—Constabulary	RIC
Mail	RM
—Steamer	RMS
Marines	(*see separate entry*)
Microscopical Society	RMS
Military	
—Academy	RMA
—Police	RMP
National Lifeboat Institution	RNLI
Naval Reserve	RNR
Navy	(*see separate entry*)
Observer Corps	ROC
Order of Victoria and Albert	VA
Philharmonic Orchestra	RPO
Photographic Society	RPS
Radar Establishment	RRE
School of Music	RSM
Scottish	
—Academician/Academy	RSA
—Water Colour Society	RSW
Society	
—for Prevention of	
Accidents	ROSPA

Cruelty to Animals	RSPCA	—commissioned	SECOND LIEUTENANT
—of			ACTING LIEUTENANT
Antiquaries	RSA		LT, LIEUTENANT
Arts			CAPT, CAPTAIN
British			MAJ, MAJOR
—Artists	RBA		LT-COL, LIEUTENANT-COLONEL
—Sculptors	RBS		COL, COLONEL
Edinburgh	RSE		BRIG, BRIGADIER
Etchers and Engravers	RE		MAJ-GEN, MAJOR-GENERAL
Literature	RSL		LT-GEN, LIEUTENANT-GENERAL
Medicine	RSM		GEN, GENERAL
Painters in Water Colours	RWS	**Royal Navy**	RN
Portrait Painters	RP	common names	
Statistical Society	RSS	—air engineer	GRUBBER
Ulster Constabulary	RUC	—first mate	NUMBER ONE
Yacht Squadron	RYS	—leading seaman	KILLICK
Yachting Association	RYA	—master-at-arms	JAUNTY
Zoological Society	RZS	—midshipman	SNOTTY
Royal Air Force	RAF	ranks (lowest first)	
common names		—other ranks	(ORDINARY RATING
—aircraftman	ERK		(ORDINARY SEAMAN
—rear gunner	TAIL-END CHARLIE		AB, ABLE RATING, ABLE SEAMAN
ranks (lowest first)			LEADING RATING
—non-commissioned	AC, AIRCRAFTMAN		LEADING SEAMAN
	LAC, LEADING AIRCRAFTMAN	—non-commissioned	PETTY OFFICER, PO
	SAC, SENIOR AIRCRAFTMAN		CHIEF PETTY OFFICER, CPO
	JUNIOR TECHNICIAN		FLEET CHIEF PETTY OFFICER
	CORPORAL		MIDDY, MIDSHIPMAN
	SERGEANT	—commissioned	ACTING SUB-LIEUTENANT
	CHIEF TECHNICIAN		SUB-LIEUTENANT
	FLIGHT SERGEANT		LT, LIEUTENANT
	WARRANT OFFICER		LIEUTENANT-COMMANDER
—commissioned	PILOT OFFICER, PO		COMMANDER
	FLYING OFFICER, FO		CAPT, CAPTAIN
	FLIGHT LIEUTENANT		COMMODORE
	SQUADRON LEADER		REAR-ADMIRAL
	WING COMMANDER		VICE-ADMIRAL
	GROUP CAPTAIN		ADM, ADMIRAL
	AIR COMMODORE		ADMIRAL OF THE FLEET
	AIR VICE-MARSHAL	**rubber**	
	AIR MARSHAL	Central American rubber	(H)ULE
	AIR CHIEF MARSHAL	latex	
	MARSHAL OF THE RAF	—from rubber trees	CAOUTCHOUC
royal family	(*see* **house**)		GUM ELASTIC, INDIA RUBBER
Royal Marines	RM	—producing dandelion	KOK-SAGHYZ
common name - marine	JOLLY	natural	GUTTA PERCHA, (H)ULE
ranks (lowest first)			JELUTONG, PONTIANAC
—other ranks	MARINE I		PONTIANAK
	MARINE II	rubber-like polymer	THIOKOL
—non-commissioned	CORPORAL, CPL	rubber-producing fluid	LATEX
	SERGEANT, SGT	synthetic	BUTYL RUBBER, NEOPRENE
—warrant officer	COLOUR-SERGEANT		NITRILE RUBBER
	WARRANT OFFICER II		SILICONE RUBBER
	REGIMENTAL SERGEANT-MAJOR		STEREO-REGULAR RUBBER
	RSM		STYRENE-BUTADIENE RUBBER, SBR
	WARRANT OFFICER I		TRANS-POLYCHLOROPRENE

with sulphur	VULCANISED RUBBER
	VULCANITE
rug	BAKU, BERGAMA, BERGAMOT
	BOKHARA, BUKHARA, CHICHI
	DAGESTAN, DERBENT, HAMADAN
	HEREKE RABJIK, KABISTAN, KALI
	KASHAN, KILIM, KIRMAN
	LEZGIAN, NUMBAH, PANEDERMA
	RABJIK, TABRIZ
British	AXMINSTER, WILTON
Chinese	TIENTSIN
French	AUBUSSON
Greek	FLOKATIS
Indian	RABJIK
Pakistani	BOKHARA, BUKHARA
Spanish	CORDOBA
Rugby football	
area between scrum	
and touchline	BLIND SIDE
deflection of tackle	HAND-OFF
famous players	
—Australian	BURGESS, CAMPESE
	CATCHPOLE, CUTLER, ELLA
	GOULD, HIPWELL, POIDEVIN
	SLACK
—English	BEAUMONT, BENNETT
	COTTON, DALTO, DUCKHAM
	GREGORY, HANLEY, HARE
	HELME, HILL, HILLER, IRO
	IRVING, LOCHORE, LYDON
	MOORE, OBOLENSKY, ROGERS
	SHARP, TEAGUE, UNDERWOOD
	UTTLEY, WHEELER, WOODWARD
originator	ELLIS
—French	BERRANNE, BLANCO, DAUGA
	FOUROUX, PAPAREMBORDE
	RIVES, SPANGHERO
	VILLEPREUX
—Irish	CAMBELL, GIBSON
	KIERNAN, MACBRIDE, MCGANN
	SLATTERY, WARD
—New Zealand	DAVIS, FITZGERALD
	FRASER, GOING, HADEN
	HEWSON, KIRKPATRICK, LAIDLAW
	LOVERIDGE, MEADS, MOURIE
	NORTON, REID, ROBERTSON
	SHELFORD, WILLIAMS, WILSON
—Scottish	BROWN, CALDER
	CARMICHAEL
	MCLAUCHLAN, MOURIE
—South African	BOTHA, DE VILLIERS
	DU PREEZ, GERBER
	PLESSIS, VISAGTE
—Welsh	DAVIES, DAWES, EDWARDS
	HOLMES, JOHN, PRICE
	RICHARDS, WILLIAMS

famous teams	BARBARIANS, HARLEQUINS
	SARACENS, WASPS
high kick downfield	GARRYOWEN
kick dropped ball	DROP-KICK, PUNT
lines on field	GOAL LINE, TOUCH LINE
	TWENTY-FIVE YARD LINE
mass of forwards around	
the ball on the ground	SCRUM
national teams	
—Australian	WALLABIES
—Argentine	PUMAS
—British	LIONS
—New Zealand	ALL BLACKS
—South African	SPRINGBOKS
playing positions	(BLINDSIDE) FLANKER
	CENTRE, FLY-HALF, FORWARD
	FULL-BACK, HOOKER
	LEFT CENTRE, LEFT WING
	LOCK, NO 8, PROP, RIGHT CENTRE
	RIGHT WING, SCRUM-HALF
	STAND-OFF (HALF), WING
restart of play	DROP-OUT
result of	
—ball out	
of play	LINE-OUT, SCRUM
—foul	PENALTY (KICK)
score	CONVERSION, DROP GOAL
	PENALTY, TRY
seize an opponent	TACKLE
teams	
—Rugby League	THIRTEEN
—Rugby Union	FIFTEEN
venues	
—England	TWICKENHAM
—Ireland	LANSDOWNE ROAD, DUBLIN
—Scotland	MURRAYFIELD
—Wales	CARDIFF ARMS PARK
rule	(*see* **power**)
Russia	SU, USSR
includes: former USSR	
administrative division	GUBERNIYA
	OBLAST
agreement	DA
airline	AEROFLOT
alphabet	CYRILLIC
approval	DA
aristocrat	BOYAR
association	COMINTERN
	KOMINTERN
bay	BUKTA, GUBA, ZALIV
beef	GOVYADINA
bleached sand soil	PODSOL, PODZOL
blizzard	BURAN
bog	BOLOTO
bureaucrat	APPARATCHIK
	CHINOVNIK

cabbage	KAPUSHTA	drink	KVASS, QUASS, VODKA
—soup	SHTCHI, SHCHI	dog	BORZOI, SAMOYED(E)
cakes	TORTI		WOLF-HOUND
canal	KANAL	duck	UTKA
cape (headland)	MYS	dynasty	ROMANOV, VARANGIAN
capital	MOSCOW	Easter cake	KULICHPASHKA
card game	VINT	edict	UKASE
carriage	DROS(H)KY, TROIKA	eggs	YAITZA
cart	TELEGA	emperor	CZAR, TSAR, TZAR
castle	GRAD	emperor's	
cathedral	SOBOR	—daughter	CZAREVNA, TSAREVNA
cavalry	COSSACKS	—eldest son	CESAREVI(T)CH
caviar	IKRA		CESAREWI(T)CH
channel	PROTOKA, VOROTA		TSESAREVI(T)CH
cheese	SYR	—son	CZAREVI(T)CH
chicken	KURITSA		TSAREVI(T)CH
Christian	UNIAT	—wife	CZARINA, TSARINA
citadel	KREMLIN		CZARITSA, TSARITSA
cloth	SERGE	estuary	USTYE
coins		exploiter	KULAK
—unit	COPEC(K), KOPEC(K), KOPEK	extinct horse	TARPAN
—100 kopeks	R(O)UBLE	extreme Socialist	BOLSHEVIK
collective farm	KOLKHOZ	farmer	KULAK
Committee for State		fellow-traveller	POPUTCHIK
Security	KGB	fermented milk	K(O)UMISS
Commonwealth of		fertile soil	CHERNOZEM
Independent States	CIS	fish	RYBA
—members	AZERBAIJAN, BELARUS	—L Baikal	GOLOMYNKA
	GEORGIA, KAZAKHSTAN	—soup	UKKA
	KYRGYZIA TADJIKISTAN	forced labour camp	GULAG
	TURKMENISTAN, UKRAINE	forest	LES
Communist party		former USSR states	ARMENIA, AZERBAIJAN
machine	APPARAT		BELARUS, ESTONIA
comrade	TOVARI(S)CH		GEORGIA, KAZAKHSTAN
concierge	DVORNIK		KYRGYZIA, LATVIA, LITHUANIA
Cossack			MOLDOVA, TADJIKISTAN
—headman	ATAMAN, HETMAN		TURKMENISTAN, UKRAINE
—troop	SOTNIA	fox	KARAGAN
council	D(O)UMA, SOVIET	gallery	HERMITAGE
country-house	DACHA	glacier	LEDNIK
covered cart or sled	KIBITKA	government department	
croquette fried in		head	COMMISSAR
bacon or calf's udder	KROMESKY	grandmother	BABUSHKA
dance	GOPAK, KOLO	ground squirrel	S(O)USLIK
	ZIGANKA	gulf	LIMAN
dandelion	KOK-SAGYZ	gypsy woman	TSYGANKA
Decembrist	DEKABRIST	head-scarf	BABUSHKA
decree	UKASE	hemp	RHYNE
department store	GUM	highlands	NAGORYE
depression	KOTLOVINA, VPADINA	hill	SOPKA, UVAL
desert	PESKI, TUNDRA	hollow wooden dolls	MATRIOSHKA
dish	BLINI, KASHA, KNISH	holy man	STARETS, STARETZ
	KROMESKY, PELMENY	hood	BASHLYK
dissident	RASKOLNIK, REFUSENIK	hors d'oeuvres	ZAKUSKI
district	OKRUG, RAYON	house	DACHA, ISBA, IZBA
—assembly	ZEMSTVO	hut	ISBA, IZBA

illicit vodka	SAMOGON	oil fuel	ASTATKI
information bureau	COMINFORM	one refused permission	
	KOMINFORM	to emigrate	REFUSENIK
insectivore	DESMAN	openness	GLASNOST
isinglass	CARLOCK	outstanding worker	STAKHANOVITE
island(s)	OSTROV(A)	pancake	BLINI, BLINY
Jewish area	JEWISH PALE	parliament	D(O)UMA
kebab	SHASHLYK	partly-trained doctor	FELDSHER
lake	KUL, OZERO	party executive	POLITBUREAU
lamb	BARASHEK		POLITBURO
launching site for		pass	PEREVAL
spacecraft	COSMODROME	peace	MIR
leather	YUFT	peak	PIK
legislature	D(O)UMA, PR(A)ESIDIUM	peasant	M(O)UJIK, MUZHIK
	SUPREME SOVIET	—cloak	SARAFAN
letters	AS, BUKI, DOBRO, FERT	peninsula	POLUOSTROV
	GLAGOL, ISHE (BREVE), KAKO	pheasant	FAZAN
	KHERR, LIUDI, MUISLETE, NASH	plain	RAVNINA, RAZLIVY
	ON, POKOI, RTSUI, SHA, SHTSHA		STEPPE
	SLOVO, TSHERV, TSUI, TVERDO	plateau	PLATO, PLOSKOGORYE
	YA, YER, YERUI, YEST, YU	poem	BYLINA
	ZEMLA, ZHIVETE	pole-cat	KOLINKSY
little pies	PIROSHKI, PIROSHKI	poor soil	PODSOL, PODZOL
local		pork	SVININA
—council	ZEMSTVO	porridge	KASHA
—government division	VOLOST	porter	DVORNIK
marsh	BOLOTO	principality of Moscow	MUSCOVY
marshy forest	TAIGA, URMAN	Protestant	STUNDIST
massacre	POGROM	province	OBLAST
measures		provincial council	ZEMSTVO
—28 inches	ARSHEEN, ARSHIN(E)	race	COSSACK, SAMOYED(E)
—7 feet	SAGENE, SAJEN(E), SAZHEN	rapids	POROGI, SHIVERA
—²/₃ mile	VERST	reconstruction	PERESTROIKA
—2.7 acres	DESSIATINE, DESSYATIN(E)	refusal	NIET, NYET
—quart	S(H)TOFF	region	KRAY
—3 galls	VEDRO	religious	
meat	MYASA	—dissenter	RASKOLNIK
—pie	PIROG, PIROSHKI	—teacher	STARETS, STARETZ
	PIROZHKI, PIROZHOK	republics	AMUR, BAROVSK
minister	COMMISSAR		BASHKORKTOSTAN, BURYAT
mink	KOLINSKY		CHECHENYA, CHUVASH, DAGESTAN
moderate			KABARDINO-BALKAR, KALMYK
—liberal	OCTOBRIST		KAMCHATKA, KARELIA, KOMI
—Socialist	MENSHEVIK		LITVA, MAGADAN, MARI
mole-like amphibian	DESMAN		MORDOVIA, NORTH OSSETIA
mountain	GORA, TAU		RUSSIA, SAKHA, TATARSTAN
—range	KHREBET		TUVA, UDMURT, YAKUTSK
mountains	GORY	rice	RIS
mushroom	GRIBI	rich peasant	KULAK
Muscovite guard	STRELITZ	ridge	GREBEN, GRYADA, KRYAZH
musical instrument	BALALAIKA, DOMRA	rock	KAMEN
	GUSLA, GUSLE, GUSLI	ruling committee	POLITBURO
musk-shrew	DESMAN	rye beer	KVASS, QUASS
news		sable	SOBOL
—agency	NOVESTI, TASS	salt-lake	SOLONCHAK
—paper	ISVESTIA, PRAVDA	sandpiper	TEREK

Russia		Rwanda	
sandy desert	KUM	tomb	KURGAN
satellite	SPUTNIK	travelling companion	SPUTNIK
sea	MORE	underground printing	SAMIZDAT
secret		union of states	SOVIET UNION, SU
—police	GRU, KGB, MVD, NKV	UNION OF SOVIET SOCIALIST REPUBLICS	
	OGPU, (T)CHEKA		USSR
—printing	SAMIZDAT	vehicle	DROS(H)KY
sect	D(O)UKHOBOR		TARANTAS(S)
settlement	POSELOK		TROIKA
shore	BEREG	village	
sledge	KIBITKA	—community	MIR
small pie or pastry	PIROG, PIROZHOK	—headman	STAROSTA
snack	ZAKUSKA	violent revolutionary	BOLSHEVIK
snow-ridge	SASTRUGA, ZASTRUGA	wagon	AR(A)BA, KIBITKA
soldier	STRELITZ		TELEGA
soup	BORSCH(T), BORTSCH(T)	water-nymph	RUSALKA
sour cream	SMETANA	weight	ZOLOTNIK
soviet of rural district	VOLOST	—1 pound	FUNT
special troops	SPETSNA(T)Z	—36 pounds	POOD, PO(U)D
spermophile	S(O)USLIK	wheat meal	SASHA
	SPERMOPHILUS	whip	KNOUT
spider	KARAKUT	wild ass	K(O)ULAN
spirit	VODKA	wind storm	BURAN
spring of water	BULAK, KUDUK	woman's cloak	SARAFAN
standing committee	PR(A)ESIDIUM	worker	STAKHANOVITE
state		workers' guild	ARTEL
—farm	SOVKHOZ	world	MIR
—store	GUM	youth organization	COMOSOOL
stew	RAGU		KOMOSOL
strait	PROLIV, VOROTA	zizel	S(O)USLIK
sturgeon	BELUGA	**Rwanda**	RWA
tea urn	SAMOVAR	capital	KIGALI
team of three (horses)	TROIKA	coin	CENTIME, FRANC
title of respect to foreign men	GOSPODIN		

S

sacred

book	
—Christian	BIBLE
—Hebrew	(T)HORAH
—Hindu	MANTRA(M), PURANA
	SHASTER, S(H)ASTRA
—Moslem	ALCORAN, KORAN
	QORAN, QURAN
bull (Egypt)	APIS
character	HIEROGLYPH(IC)
drink	
—Sikh	AMRIT
—Zoroastrian	HAOMA
enclosure in temple	SEKOS
fish	OXYRHYNCUS
flower	LOTUS
fountain	ZEMZEM
language	PALI
law (Islam)	SHARIA
lotus	PADMA
monkey	HANUMAN
mountain	OMEI
part of temple	ADYTON
person	SHAMAN
river	ALPH
scriptures	SHRUTI
snakes	NAGA
stone	BLACK STONE
syllable	OM
symbol	HIEROGRAM, HIEROGRAPH
text	
—Buddhist	SUTRA
—Hindu	AVESTA, MANTRA(M), PURANA
	SHASTER, S(H)ASTRA
	TANTRA, VEDA
—Jain	KALPA-SUTRA
—Zoroastrian	AVESTA
tree	BO, BODHI, PEEPUL
verse	MANTRA
word	OM

sailor — AB, BLUEJACKET, SALT, TAR

bed	HAMMOCK
biscuit	HARDTACK
—softened in water and baked	DUNDERFUNK
boiled oatmeal, etc	BURGOO
captain	OLD MAN, SKIPPER

carousing	MALLEMAROKING
carving in whalebone etc	SCRIMSHAW
chapel	BETHEL
clothing and bedding	SLOPS
dance	HORNPIPE
experienced	WATER-DOG
famous sailors	
—American	
WW1	BENSON, SIMS
WW2	DOORMAN, FLETCHER, HALSEY
	HART, KIMMEL, KING, LEAHY
	MITSCHER, NIMITZ, OLDENDORFF
	POWNALL, SPRAGGE, SPRUANCE
—Austria/Hungary	
WW1	HAUS, HORTHY
—British	
American revolution	GRAVES, HOOD
Elizabethan	DRAKE, GRENVILLE
Napoleonic wars	NELSON
WW1	BACON, BEATTY, CARDEN
	CRADOCK, DE ROBECK, FISHER
	JACKSON, JELLICOE, KEYES
	MADDEN, MILNE, MOUNTBATTEN
	OLIVER, STURDEE, TROUBRIDGE
	TYRWHITT, WEMYSS
WW2	CUNNINGHAM, MOUNTBATTEN
	PHILLIPS, RAMSAY
—Dutch	DE RUYTER, VAN TROMP(E)
—French	
Napoleonic wars	DE BARRAS
	DE GRASSE, VILLENEUVE
WW1	DARTIGE, GAUCHET, LACAZE
	RONARCH
WW2	DARLAN
—German	
WW1	ARNAUD, BACHMAN, BULOW
	HIPPER, HOLTZEDORFF, REUTER
	SCHEER, SOUCHON, SPEE
	TIRPITZ, TROTHA
WW2	DO(E)NITZ, RAEDER
—Italian	
WW1	ABRUZZI, THAON DI REVEL
—Japanese	
WW2	KOGA, KURITA
	NAGUMO, NISHIMURA, NOMURA
	OZAWA, SHIMA, SUZUKI, TAKAGI
	TOGO, YAMAMOTO
—Russian	
WW1	EBERHARDT, ESSEN
	GRIGOROVICH, KOLCHAK
	(*see also* **explorers**)
—Spanish	GRAVINA
first mate	NUMBER ONE
force or trick	
into service	CRIMP, COMMANDEER
	(IM)PRESS, PRESS-GANG, SHANGHAI

goods	
—found floating	FLOTSAM
—thrown overboard	JETSAM
grave	DAVY JONES'S LOCKER
gruel	LOBLOLLY
Indian	CLASHEE, LASCAR
inexperienced	LANDLUBBER
lascar	
—bosun	SERANG
—petty officer	TINDAL
master-at-arms	JA(U)NTIE
	JA(U)NTY, JONTY
meat and biscuit stew	LOBSCOUSE
midshipman	REEFER, SNOTTY
old sailor	SHELLBACK
officers	UPPER DECK
ordinary sailor(s)	DECKHAND, LOWER DECK
Oriental	
—bosun	SERANG
—petty officer	TINDAL
—sailor	LASCAR
plug leak with canvas etc	FOTHER
punishment	FLOGGING, KEELHAULING
	WALKING THE PLANK
rope's end	COLT
sailors	CREW, NUS, RN
salt beef	JUNK
sea-bred officer	TARPAULIN
song	SHANTY
stew	LOBSCOUSE, LOB'S COURSE
trousers	BELL BOTTOMS
Turkish	GALIONGEE
waterproof hat	SOU'WESTER, TARPAULIN
	(see also **Royal Navy***)*
St Lucia	WL
St Vincent	WV
Saint's day	*(see* **holidays***)*
salad	*(see* **vegetables***)*
Sanskrit	SANS
book of fables	PANCHATANTRA
law	DHARMA
righteousness	DHARMA
sacred text	PURANA
script	NAGARI
unrighteousness	ADHARMA
	(see also **Hindu, Indian***)*
Sao Tome	P
capital	SAO TOME
coin	CENTAVO, DOBRA
satellites	
artificial	*(see* **space***)*
natural	*(see* **astronomy***)*
sauce	
bechamel and	
—aspic	CHAUDFROID
—cheese	MORNAY

—eggs	TARTARE
—tomato paste	AURORE
berries, fruit	APPLE, CHESTNUT
	CRANBERRY, GOOSEBERRY
breadcrumbs	BREAD SAUCE
—and stock	PANADA
brown sugar, brandy, etc	BRANDY BUTTER
butter and	
—sugar	BUTTERSCOTCH
with flavouring	HARD SAUCE
capers, vinegar, etc	CAPER SAUCE
cheese and	
—mustard	CHEESE SAUCE
—wine	FONDUE
Chinese	HOISIN
cocoa	CHOCOLATE SAUCE
curry	DANSAK, KORMA, MADRAS
	ROGAN JOSH, VINDALOO
demi-glaze and	
—truffles	PERIGEUX
—Madeira wine	MADEIRA
—Marsala wine	MARSALA
—mushrooms	MUSHROOM SAUCE
—port	PORT WINE SAUCE
eggs and	
—cream, butter, sherry	NEWBURG(H)
—herbs	REMOULADE
—mayonnaise	TARTARE
—sugar	SABAYON
—vinegar	HOLLANDAISE
	MAYONNAISE
—white sauce	EGG SAUCE
espagnole and	
—aspic jelly	CHAUDFROID
—gravy	DEMI-GLAZE
—onions	ROBERT
—orange peel	BIGARADE
—redcurrants	REFORME
—stock	PEPPER
fish (Roman)	GARUM
garlic mayonnaise	AIOLI
German	GREEN SAUCE, GRUNE SOSSE
herb	HORSERADISH, MINT
	PARSLEY, SALSA VERDE
hollandaise with cream	MOUSSELINE
hot	HORSERADISH, HP
	PICCALILLI, WORCESTER
jam, arrowroot, etc	JAM SAUCE
Japanese	TAMARI
mayonnaise with tomato	
puré	ROUILLE
mushrooms, peppercorns, etc	VELOUTE
oil and vinegar	FRENCH DRESSING
	VINAIGRETTE
olive oil and lemon	
juice	SALMORIGLIO

onions and	
—bacon, etc	ESPAGNOLE
—breadcrumbs	BREAD SAUCE
—butter, etc	BECHAMEL
—coconut	SAMBAL
—curry powder	CURRY SAUCE
—eggs, etc	BEARNAISE
—mushrooms	CHASSEUR
orange and	
—cornflour	ORANGE SAUCE
—lemon	CUMBERLAND
parsley, butter, etc	MAITRE D'HOTEL
	MEUNIERE
peanuts, etc	SATAY
peppers	TABASCO
raspberries	MELBA
redcurrants	OXFORD
roux and stock	BROWN SAUCE, VELOUTE
salad dressing	(FOAM) MAYONNAISE
	FRENCH, GOLDEN
	OLIVE OIL, RUSSIAN DRESSING
	SOUR CREAM
	THOUSAND ISLANDS
	VINEGAR, VINAIGRETTE
seaweed	LAVER
shallots	PIQUANT
—and wine	BERCY, BORDELAISE
	BOURGUIGNONNE
shrimps, lemon peel	SHRIMP SAUCE
Sicilian	SALMORIGLIO
sour cream	GRADVALAK, GRADVALAX
soya beans	SOY SAUCE
—Japanese	TAMARI
spicy	CURRY SAUCE, HOISIN
thickened meat juices	GRAVY
tomatoes, etc	CATCHUP, CATSUP
	KETCHUP, TOMATO SAUCE
velouta with	
—eggs and cream	ALLEMANDE
—vinegar	RAVIGOTE
Welsh	LAVER
white sauce and	
—anchovies	ANCHOVY SAUCE
—cream	SUPREME
—eggs	EGG SAUCE
—lemons	LEMON SAUCE
—onions	ONION SAUCE, SOUBISE
—parsley	PARSLEY SAUCE
Saudi Arabia	(*see* **Arabia**)
sausage	
Australian	SNAG
blood sausage	BLACK PUDDING
—German	BLUTWURST
British	BANGER, BLACK PUDDING
	CUMBERLAND
Frankfurter	WIENER

—short	VIENNA SAUSAGE
French	
—large	TOULOUSE SAUSAGE
pork	ANDOUILLE(TTE)
—salami	SAUCISSON
German	BIERWURST, BLUTWURST
	BOCKWURST, BRATWURST
	CERVELATWURST
	FRANKFURTER, HAMBURG(H)ER
	(KNACK)WURST, LEBERWURST
	SCHINKENWURST, WIENER(WURST)
	ZUNGERWURST
—boiled	KOCHWURST
—preserved	BOHWURST
—scalded	BRUHWURST
Greek	KOKORETSI, LUKANIKA
Hebrew	VIENNA SAUSAGE
highly-seasoned	CHORIZO, SALAMI
	SAVELOY
in	
—bread roll	HOT DOG
—pastry case	SAUSAGE ROLL
—Yorkshire pudding	TOAD-IN-THE-HOLE
Italian	BOLOGNA, CERVELLATA
	MORTADELLA, PEPPERONI
	POLONY, SALAMI
large sausage	CUMBERLAND
	HAMBURG(H)ER, TOULOUSE
liver (Ger.)	LEBERWURST
long thin sausage	CABANO, KABANO
partly cooked	POLONY
Polish	KIELBASA, KRAKAUER
	KRAKOWSKA, ZYWIECKA
pork meat and fat	WHITE SAUSAGE
pre-cooked	FRANKFURTER, SALAMI
	SAVELOY
salted	SALAMI
sausage sandwich	HOT DOG
small sausage	CHIPOLATA
	COCKTAIL SAUSAGE
smoked	
—German	CERVELATWURST
	FRANKFURTER
—Italian	SALAMI
—pork	CERVELAT
South African	BOEREWORS
Spanish	CHORIZO, SALCHICA
Scandinavian	
ancient	NORSE
casserole	NORRLANDS PUDDING
dynasty	VARANGIAN
fish dish	GRAVADLAX
frost giant	YMIR
goblin	NIS
hors d'oeuvres	SMORGASBORD
magistrate	AMMAN, AMTMAN

old coin	SKILLING
open sandwich	SMOR(RE)BROD
parliament	THING
pirate	VIKING
soup	LAPSKAUS
spirit	AKVAVIT, AQUAVIT
stew	LABSKAUS
toast	SKO(A)L

scientific instruments

absorption of light	ABSORPTIOMETER
accurate	
—clock	CHRONOMETER
—recording clock	CHRONOGRAPH
amplifying	
—microwaves	PARAMETRIC AMPLIFIER
—small sounds	PHONENDOSCOPE
analysing spectra	SPECTROSCOPE
apparatus for gas	
analysis	EUDIOMETER
atom-smasher	(*see* particle accelerator *below*)
automatically replying	
to received signal	TRANSPONDER
balloon carrying	
instruments measuring	
—electrical data	ELECTROSONDE
—meteorological data	RADIOSONDE
calculating ruler	SLIDE RULE
carrying sound	PHONOP(H)ORE
cathode-ray tube with	
four screens	CHROMATRON
	CHROMOSCOPE
chamber	
—controlled at very low	
temperature	CRYOSTAT
—for heating under	
pressure	AUTOCLAVE
changing voltage of	
alternating current	TRANSFORMER
combining coloured images	CHROMOSCOPE
comparing	
—series of astronomical	
photographs	BLINK COMPARATOR
	BLINK MICROSCOPE
—structure of	
spectral lines	INTERFEROMETER
compass based on	
spinning wheel	GYRO-COMPASS
	GYROSCOPIC COMPASS
concave reflector	DISH AERIAL
	PARABOLIC REFLECTOR
	PARABOLOID REFLECTOR
condenser	DEPHLEGMATOR, RECTIFIER
—in microscope	ABBE CONDENSER
—to collect components	
boiled off at different	
temperatures	FRACTIONATING COLUMN

controlling	
—electrical resistance	RHEOSTAT
—current flowing in one	
circuit by current	
in another circuit	RELAY
converting	
—alternating current to	
direct current	CONVERTER
—direct to alternating	
current	INVERTER
—electrical	
impulses to sound	(LOUD)SPEAKER
to mechanical energy	SOLENOID
—frequency modulation to	
amplitude modulation	DISCRIMINATOR
—optical image to	
electrical signal	ICONOSCOPE
—sound to electrical	
impulses	MICROPHONE
—vapour to liquid	(LIEBIG) CONDENSER
—X-rays to	
visual image	IMAGE CONVERTER
correcting chromatic	
aberration	TEINOSCOPE
counting	
—alpha particles	SPINTHARISCOPE
—drops	STACTOMETER
—flashes from	
scintillator	SCINTILLATION COUNTER
—ionised	
particles	GEIGER(-MULLER) COUNTER
—neutrons	BORON COUNTER TUBE
cup for melting	
substances	CRUCIBLE
cuts very thin slices	MICROTOME
detecting	
—air pressure changes	STATOSCOPE
—electric currents	ELECTROSCOPE
	GALVANOSCOPE
—electric waves by	
reduced resistance	COHERER
—radio frequencies of	
celestial bodies	RADIO TELESCOPE
—temperature changes	THERMISTOR
	THERMOSCOPE
—underwater sound	HYDROPHONE
—water	HYDROSTAT
determining	
—amount of flue gases	ORSAT APPARATUS
—decrease in temperature	
due to evaporation	CRYOPHORUS
—freezing points	CRYOSCOPE
—mass of atoms	MASS SPECTROGRAPH
	OMEGATRON
dialysis machine	DIALYSER
diffracting lens	FRESNEL LENS

displaying polarised light phenomena	POLARISCOPE
distilling	
—apparatus	RECTIFIER, STILL
fractional	COFFEY STILL
—flask	RETORT
(old)	ALEMBIC
drying chamber	DESICCATOR
dual prism	NICOL PRISM
electron-tube in which beam is modified	KLYSTRON
electrostatic accelerator	TANDEM GENERATOR
emission tube with ten cathodes	DEKATRON
estimating temperature of furnace	SEGER CONE
eye-piece with two plano-convex lens	RAMSDEN EYEPIECE
filtering by suction	BUCHNER FUNNEL
flask	RETORT
—flat-bottomed, conical	KERLENMEYER FLASK
—for estimation of nitrogen	KJELDAHL FLASK
focusing light into parallel beams	COLLIMATOR
gas burner	BUNSEN BURNER
glass	
—container with two or more necks	WASH BOTTLE WOULFE BOTTLE
—cover	BELL JAR
—graduated tube	PIPETTE
with tap	BURETTE
—vessel with narrow neck	RETORT
high	
—speed separator	CENTRIFUGE
—temperature thermostat	PYROSTAT
interferometer	ETALON
ionisation chamber	BORON CHAMBER
isotope separator	ISOTRON
jar lined with tinfoil	LEYDEN JAR
locating objects by reflected	
—radio waves	RADAR
—sound waves	SONAR
liquefying gas	CASCADE LIQUEFIER
maintaining	
—electric resistance	RHEOSTAT
—humidity	HYGROSTAT, HUMIDISTAT
—low temperature	CRYOSTAT
—pressure	BAROSTAT
—temperature	THERMOSTAT
measuring	(*see* **measuring instruments**)
microscope using	
—electron beam	ELECTRON MICROSCOPE

—reflected and transmitted light	PHASE CONTRAST MICROSCOPE
—ultraviolet light	ULTRAVIOLET MICROSCOPE
microwave amplifier	PARAMETRIC AMPLIFIER
observing star passage	ALMACANTAR ALMACANTUR
optical projector	EPIDIASCOPE
—double	STEREOPTICON
particle	
—accelerator	BETATRON, BEVATRON COSMOTRON, CYCLOTRON ELECTRON-POSITRON COLLIDER ELECTRON SYNCHROTRON LARGE ELECTRON-POSITRON COLLIDER LEP, LINAC, LINEAR ACCELERATOR PHASOTRON, SUPERCOLLIDER SYNCHROCYCLOTRON ZETA
—counter	SPINTHARISCOPE
—detector	BUBBLE CHAMBER (DIFFUSION) CLOUD CHAMBER HODOSCOPE, SPARK CHAMBER STREAMER CHAMBER
passing light in one plane	NICOL PRISM
photographing	
—spectra	SPECTROGRAPH
—sun	(SPECTRO)HELIOGRAPH
porcelain filter cup with small holes	GOOCH CRUCIBLE
producing	
—alternating current	ALTERNATOR
—direct current	DYNAMO, GENERATOR
—electricity from heat	THERMOPILE
junction of dissimilar metals	THERMOCOUPLE
—gas from action of liquid on solids	KIPP'S APPARATUS
—high-voltage oscillation	TESLA COIL
—image of electrical quantities	OSCILLOSCOPE
—interference in light patterns	INTERFEROMETER
—nuclear fusion	TORUS TOROIDA KAMERA MAGNETIC TOKAMOK, STELLERATOR SCYLLAC
—output after a specified number of inputs	SCALER SCALING CIRCUIT

—polarised light	ROCHON PRISM
	WOLLASTON PRISM
—reactance in a circuit	REACTOR
—reducing amount of	
current passing	SHUNT
—resistance	
in a circuit	RESISTOR
varying with	
temperature	THERMISTOR
—sound waves	OSCILLATOR
—spectrum of beam	
of ions	MASS SPECTROMETER
—static electricity	ELECTROPHORUS
	VAN DER GRAAF GENERATOR
	WIMSHURST MACHINE
quartz prism	WOLLASTON PRISM
radar screen	CATHODE RAY OSCILLOSCOPE
	CRO
rapidly flashing	
light source	STROBE, STROBOSCOPE
recording	
—atmospheric pressure	BAROGRAPH
—cloud patterns	NEPHOGRAPH
—earthquakes	SEWISMOGRAPH
—electric currents	OSCILLOGRAPH
—electrical action	
in muscles	ELECTROMYOGRAPH
—enlarged or reduced	
image	PANTOGRAPH
—humidity	HYGROGRAPH
—intensity of sun	HELIOGRAPH
—over a distance	TELEMETER
—particle tracks	BUBBLE CHAMBER
—pressure	BAROGRAPH
—short time interval	CHRONOGRAPH
—sound vibrations	PHONAUTOGRAPH
—speed and time of use	
of vehicles	TACHOGRAPH
—temperature	THERMO(METRO)GRAPH
	(*see also* **write**)
reducing current in	
circuit	(ELECTRICAL) SHUNT
reflecting sun in	
constant direction	HELIOSTAT
restoring coherer	DECOHERER
semiconductor with	
negative resistance	
in part of range	TUNNEL DIODE
separating substances by	
rotation	CENTRIFUGE
shallow glass dish	PETRI DISH
showing effects of	
electrical discharge	
through gases	GEISSLER TUBE
signalling by reflected	
sunlight	HELIOGRAPH

small sighting telescope	COLLIMATOR
steriliser	AUTOCLAVE
storage bottle	WINCHESTER (QUART)
sub-dividing measuring	
scale	VERNIER
suction filter	BUCHNER FUNNEL
switch based on	
superconductivity	CRYOTRON
television screen	CATHODE RAY TUBE
	CRT
testing	
—lenses and prisms	INTERFEROMETER
—vacuums	TESLA COIL
thermionic valve used	
as switch	THYRATRON
tracking charged	
particles	BUBBLE CHAMBER
	CLOUD CHAMBER
	HODOSCOPE
transferring power	
between systems	TRANSDUCER
transmitting data	TELEMETER
	TRANSPONDER
—from balloon	RADIOMETEOROGRAPH
	RADIOSONDE
tube	
—condenser	LIEBIG CONDENSER
—used to centrifuge	
blood	HAEMATOCRIT
used in switching	
circuits	TUNNEL DIODE
vacuum	
—flask	DEWAR FLASK
—pump	CONDENSATION PUMP
	DIFFUSION PUMP
—tube	
displaying cathode	
rays	CATHODE RAY TUBE, CRT
with electrodes	CROOKES TUBE
	GEISSLER TUBE
variable resistor	RHEOSTAT
viewing	
—crystal structure	STAUROSCOPE
—distant objects	TELESCOPE
—electric current	OSCILLOSCOPE
—fast movement	STROBE, STROBOSCOPE
—fermentation	ZYMOSCOPE
—heavens	TELESCOPE
—high-energy particles	BUBBLE CHAMBER
	HODOSCOPE
—meridian passage	DIPLEIDOSCOPE
—objects	
above eye-level	PERISCOPE
under water	HYDROSCOPE
—optical spectra	SPECTROSCOPE
—short-lived images	TACHISTOSCOPE

—small objects	(ELECTRON) MICROSCOPE
—sun	HELIOSCOPE
—temperature at	
remote distance	TELETHERMOSCOPE
—tissues	
on fluorescent screen	FLUOROSCOPE
in 3-dimensions	STEREO-FLUOROSCOPE
—two-dimensional	
photographs in	
three dimensions	STEREOSCOPE
—radar signals	RADARSCOPE
—X-ray images	FLUOROSCOPE
	(*see also* **astronomy**)
weighing very small	
amounts	TORSION BALANCE
wire rheostat	RHEOCHORD
	(*see also* **measuring instruments**)

Scotland   CALEDONIA, SCOTIA
                               (*see also* **Scottish**)

Scott
  words found in his writings:

ace of trumps	TIB
akin	SIBB
arrogance	SURQUEDY
astute	ASTUCIOUS
backgammon	VERQUIRE
bad luck	WANION
bag-piping	SACK-DOUDLING
bank-notes	SNUFF(-PAPER)
blood relation	SIBB
bough used as torch	ROUGHIE
brandish	WAMPISH
brisket	BREASKIT
brother or sister	SIBB
brown bread roll	SOUTER'S CLOD
byrlawman	BIRLIEMAN
cajole	BEFLUM
club	TRUNNION
commotion	STEERY
coward	VILLAGIO
cross-grained	FRAMPAL
cudgel	SOUPLE
curse	WANION
cut out	SNECK
dash	VIRETOT
dilapidated house	HURLEY-HOUSE
dry bough	ROUGHIE
eldin	YEALDON
enchanter/enchantress	REIM-KENNAR
endearment	YARTO
excited by moon	MOON-RAISED
falcon	TERCEL-GENTLE
favouritism	PEATSHIP
fierce warrior	WAR-WOLF
fiery	FRAMPAL
fish-roe	RAUN, RAWN

flighty	WEATHER-HEADED
flourish	WAMPISH
fool	BEFLUM
fortified site	KAME, KAIM
four of trumps at gleek	TIDDY
friar with short frock	CURTAL-FRIAR
fuel	YEALDON
gad	VIRETOT
give landlord information	
leading to raising of rent	WHISTLE
half-guinea	SMELT
hawk's turn	CANCELEER, CANCELIER
heart	YARTO
help in need	BEETMASTER
horn-blast	PRYSE
hypochrondriac	PHRENESIAC
infantry regiment	TERTIA
interjection of derision	QUEP
irascible	TOUSTIE
jacket	RAILLY
kinship	SIBB
knob	NOOP
law	LAUCH
literary style	BOW-WOW
loop	LOUP
low collar	RABATINE
Lowlander	SASSENACH
maddened by moon	MOON-RAISED
make a display	PROPALE
Moon	MACFARLANE'S BUAT
nick	SNECK
not	
—bruised or crushed	UNBRIZZED
—to be molested	SACLESS
note of assault	WAR(R)ISON
official who searched	
for stolen goods	RANZELLAAR
old card-game	PENNEECH, PENNEECK
overweening	OUTRECUIDANCE
pardoner	QUAESTIONARY
pear	QUEEZ-MADDAM
peaty	TURBINACIOUS
pedlar	PEDDER-COFFE
peevish	FRAMPAL
pigment	PIMENT
pinnacle	PINNET
plate	VASSAIL, VESSAIL
presumption	OUTRECUIDANCE
private	SINGLE SOLDIER
probationer	STIBBLER
prophetess	VOLUSPA
proportion of malt	STRAIK
pursuit of moss-troopers	HOT TROD
rabble	RASCAILLE
racked	RECKAN
rascal	RASCAILLE

ransack	RANSHA(C)KLE	—parts of plant	SHAW
ricked	RECKAN	absconding from justice	FUGITATION
riding-hood	TROT-COSEY, TROT-COZY	absolve	ASSOILZIE
rush	VIRETOT	abundance	FOUTH, FOWTH, ROUTH
scoundrelly	HOUNDS-FOOT		ROWTH, SONCE, SONSE
scree	SCRAE		STOUTH AND ROUTH
search	RANSHA(C)KLE	abundant	ROUTHIE, ROWTHIE
shawl from goat hair	TOZIE	abuse	SNASK
sibyl	VOLUSPA	abusive language	SNASH
slash	SCORCH	accusation	THREAP, THREEP
small curiosity	GABION	accused person(s)	PANEL
snick	SNECK	accustom oneself	USE
snip	SNECK	acquisition	CONQUEST
spiced, sweetened wine	PIGMENT	acrobat	SPEELER
stay as guest	GUESTEN	across	YONT
state official	BARON-OFFICER	act of dragging	HARL
steal	CONDIDDLE, MAG	action to	
stick	TRUNNION	—declare false or forged	IMPROBATION
subordinate spy	UNDER-ESPIAL	—prove witness perjured	
subterranean prison	MASSYMORE	or biased	REPROBATOR
sulky	GUMPLE-FOISTED	active	BIRKIE, YA(U)LD, YANKNG
sun-dried	TILED	—fellow	SWANK(E)Y
supporter of popish prelates	PAPAPRELATIST	addition	EIK
tall raw-boned woman	RANDLE-TREE	adept	DEACON
talon	TALENT	adjust	SORT
tarred rags	HARDS, HURDS	advancing	ONCOMING
tern	PICTARNIE	adze	EATCHE
tip (of elbow)	NOOP	affair	EFFEIR, EFFERE
tithes	PARSONAGE	affected person	PRICK-ME-DAINTY
trace of a fact	REMNANT	afflicted	WAESOME
trinket	TRANKUM	afoot	AGAIT
trouserless	BARE-BREACHED	afraid	FEARED, RAD
twist about	WELK	afternoon refreshment	FOUR-HOURS
unchallengeable	SACLESS	afterwards	SYNE
unguarded	LIPPEN	against	ANENT
unsaluted	UNHALSED	aggressively outspoken	RANDIE, RANDY
vengeance	WANION	agile	SWANK
vessels	VASSAIL, VESSAIL	agitation	CARFUFFLE, CERFUFFLE
wave about	WAMPISH		KEFUFFLE
wench	GOUGE	—of water	JABBLE
wheel-barrow	MONOTROCH	ago	SYNE
worn out	OVERSCUTCHED	agony of death	DEAD THRAW
young gull	SCOURIE, SCOWRIE	agree	GREE, SORT
Scottish	SCOT	agreement	AYE
including: legal terms		ague	EXIES
a	ANE	aim	ETTLE, MINT, VISIE, VIZY, VIZZIE
—moment ago	ENOW	air	LIFT
abandon	FORHOO(IE), FORHOW	ajar	AGEE, AJEE, JEE
—proceedings	DESERT THE DIET	akin	SIB
abate	FAIK	alarm	GLIFF, GLIFT
abbacy	ABTHANE	alas	EWHOW, WAESUCKS, WALY
ablaze	ALOW(E)	alderman	BAIL(L)IE
able	FERE	ale	YILL
above	ABUNE	—brewing (Islands)	BUMMOCK
above-ground		—house	CHANGE-HOUSE
—part of potato	TATTIE-SHAW	alert	GLEG

alive	TO THE FORE
alley-way	VENNEL
allodial (Islands)	UDAL
allowance to mill servants	SEQUEL
alms	ALMOUS, AWMOUS
alone	HIMSELF, HIS LANE
	MY LANE
along	ENDLANG
aloof	ABEIGH, SKEIGH
also	ALS
alternately	TIME ABOUT
amber	LAMMER
amiable	COUTHIE
ample	WAL(L)Y
amuse	PLAY
amusing	
—person or thing	DIVERT
—story	BA(U)R, BAWR
an	ANE
ancestor	FOR(E)BEAR
ancient	AULD-WARLD
—castle	BROCH, BR(O)UGH
—race	PICT
ankle	COOT, CUIT, CUTE, QUEET
annat	ANN
annoy(ance)	FASH
annual payment under feu	FEU-DUTY
annul	REDUCE
any	ARY
anything	
—beaked	KIP(P)
—built	BIGGIN
—eaten as relish	KITCHEN
—frightful	WIRRICOW
	WORRICOW, WORRYCOW
—small	PINK
—stunted	SCRUNT
apiece	THE PIECE
apology	OFFCOME
apothecary	POTTINGAR
apparatus	GRAITH
apparition	TAIS(C)H
appeal	RECLAIM
appear	CAST UP
—above ground	BRAIRD, BREER
—and disappear	COOK, KOOK
—ignorant	MISKEN
—in court	COMPEAR
appearance	EFFEIR, EFFERE, SHAW
appendage	POFFLE
appetising	GUSTY
applaud/applause	RUFF
appliance for winding yarn	WINNLE
appointed deputy	DEPUTE
apprentice	SERVITOR

approach(ing)	ONCOMING
April Fool	GOUK, GOWK
apt	GLEG
—to feel chilly	CAULD-RIFE
arbiter	BYRLAWMAN, ODDSMAN
arch	COOM
area of operation	SUCKEN
armpit	OXTER
argue snappishly	NYAFF
arranged	RED(D)ED
array	EFFEIR, EFFERE
arts student	MAGISTRAND
as soon as	WHENE(V)ER
ascent	UPGANG
ash bucket	BACKET
ashes	AIZLE, EASLE
ask	SPEER, SPEIR
askew	AGLEE, AGLEY, SKIVIE
aslant	ASKLENT
aspire	ETTLE, MINT
assault	STOUND, STOWND
—in own house	HAMESUCKEN
assertion	THREAP, THREEP
assess	MODIFY
assess(ment)	STENT
assistant	SERVITOR
associate with women	WINCH
assuage	MEASE
assume	HECHT
assuming	UPSETTING
astir	AGAIT
astray	WILL, WULL
astride	STRIDE-LEGS
	STRIDE-LEGGED
at	
—a loss	WILL, WULL
—all	AVA, OUGHTLINGS
—present	PRESENTLY
—the big house	UPBY(E)
—times	WHILES
attack	ONFALL
attempt	MINT
attend to	SORT, TENT
attercop (spider)	ETHERCAP, ETTERCAP
auction	ROUP
avail	DOW
availed	DOCHT, DOUGHT
avaricious	GRIPPY
awake	WAKEN
award	MODIFY
away	AWA
awkward	BLATE
—person	BUCKIE
awl	BROG, ELS(H)IN, STOB
awnless	HUMBLE, HUMMEL
awry	AGLEE, AGLEY

back	
—of	
knee-joint	HOUGH
shoulder	BACK-SPAUL(D)
—passage	DUNNY
backward and forward	BUT AND BEN
bad luck	WANION
bag	POCK
—pudding	POCK-PUDDING
bagged	BAGGIT
bagpipe music	LUTHA, PIBROCH, URLAR
bail	CAUTION
bailiff (Islands)	FOUD
bailiff's jurisdiction	FOUDRIE
baker's grater	RISP
balk	HEN
ball	BA
ballad	BALLA(N)T, BALLET
bamboozle	BUMBAZE
bank	BINK, SUNK
bankrupt(cy)	DYVOUR(Y)
bankruptcy	SEQUESTRATION
—process	CESSIO BONORUM
banter	TROCK, TROKE
bar	RANCE, SPAR
—across condemned cell	GAD
—in chimney	RANDLE-TREE
	RANDLE-BALK
	RANDLE-PERCH, RANNEL-TREE
	RANNLE-TREE, RANTLE-TREE
—of grate	RIB
barefoot Highlander	GILLIE-WHITE-FOOT
	GILLIE-WET-FOOT
bargain	WANWORTH
barge	GABBARD, GABBART
bark like snarling dog	YAFF
barley	BERE, BIGG
barrel projection	LAGGEN, LAGGIN
barren	HI(R)STIE, YELD
barrister	ADVOCATE
barter	COUP, NIFFER, TROCK, TROKE
basement	DUNNY
bashful	BLATE
basket	MURLA(I)N, MURLIN
bathe	DOOK
baulk	REEST, REIST
bawdy talk	SCULDUDD(E)RY
	SKULDUDDERY
bay (Islands)	VOE
be	
—able	CAN, DOW
—active or excited	STEER
—frightened	FLAY, FLEY
—gaudy	SKYRE
—good for a purpose	DOW
—half asleep	DOVE

—hanged	STRING, WALLOP IN A TOW
	WALLOP IN A TETHER
—ignorant	MISKEN
—in training	BREED
—out of bed	STEER
—perverse	THRAW
—restive	FLISK
—smoke-dried	REAST, REEST, REIST
—stupefied	DOVE
—tamely submissive	SNOOL
—undecided	SWITHER
—vexed	FASH
beacon-fire	BALE-FIRE
beam	TREST
—of a balance	WEIGH-BANK
bear	BERE, BIGG, DREE
beat	DUNT, FIRK, LOUNDER
	PHEASE, TOUK
beating	LOUNDERING, PAIK
—the bounds	COMMON-RIDING
beautiful	WALY
become	SET
bed	
—of mussels	MUSSEL-SCAUP
—valance	PAND
bedaub	SLAISTER
bedraggle	TRAUCHLE
bee's nest	BINK
beetle	CLOCK
befit	SET
befool	BEGUNK
before bedtime	FORENIGHT
beg	FLEECH, THIG
beggar's pouch	GABERLUNZIE
begged	THIGGIT
begging	FLEECHING, FLEECHMENT
—for eggs	PACE-EGGING
begin to move	STEER
behave riotously	GIL(L)RAVAGE
	GIL(L)RAVITCH, GALRAVAGE
	GALRAVITCH
behaviour	HAVING
beheading machine	MAIDEN
behind	AHIND, AHINT
being facile	FACILITY
bell-rope	TOW
bellow	BULLER
belly	KITE, KYTE, WAME
beloved one	JO(E)
bench	BINK
beneath	ANEATH
benefit society	MENAGE
bent	
—double	TWAFALD
—spade	CASCHROM, CAS CROM
bequeath to charity	MORTIFY

bequest to charity	MORTIFICATION	—Islands	YARFA, YARPHA
beside	ASIDE	boggy	
besides	BY, FORBY	—place	SLACK
besom	COW, KOW	—water-channel	LATCH
bespatter	JAUP	boisterous	GOUSTROUS
best	WALE	—girl or boy	GILP(E)Y
bestir oneself	JEE ONE'S GINGER	boldly	CROUSE
	JOW ONE'S GINGER	boorish vulgarian	KEELIE
bewildered	MOIDERT, WILL, WULL	booth	BOTHAN
bewitch	FOR(E)SPEAK	—for selling	CRAME
beyond	AYONT, OUTWITH	booty	CREACH, CREAGH
—the bounds of	FURTH OF	border	ROON
bid	BODE	borough	BROGH, BURGH
big knife	GULL(E)Y	botch	CLATCH
bilberry	BLAEBERRY	—up	CLAMPER
bind with thread or cord	OOP, OUP	botched work	CLATCH
birch	BIRK	bother	FASH
biscuit	BAKE	bottom upward	TAPSALTEERIE
bishop	PRIMUS	bought	COFT
—who transmitted		bounce	STOT(TER)
revenues	TULCHAN BISHOP	bound	SCOUP, SCOWP, SPANG
bit of doggerel	RAT-RHYME		STEN(D)
biting	TOOTHY	—along	SKELP
bittern	BULL-OF-THE-BOG	boundary	MEITH
	MOSSBLUITER	—mark	DOOL
black		—stone	HARE-STANE
—berry	BRAMBLE	bow	JOUK
—clothes	BLACKS	box	BUIST
—eye	KEEKER	boy	LOON(IE)
—headed gull	PICKMAW	brain-pan	HARN-PAN
—smith	BURN-THE-WIND	brains	HARNS
blackish	BLAE	brand	BUIST
blame	WITE, WYTE	—new	SPLIT-NEW
blast	SCAITH, SKAITH, WAP	brandish	WAMPISH
blaze	LOW(E), LUNT	brat	GYTE
bleak	BLAE	brawl	FLITE, FLYTE
bleeding nose	JEELY NOSE		TUILYE, TUILZIE
blemish	TASH	breach	SLAP
blight	SCOUTHER, SCOWDER	—of chastity	SCULDUDD(E)RY
block	DIT		SKULDUDDERY
—head	TUMPHY	bread	LOAF
—of tenements	LAND	breakfast	DISJUNE
blood	BLUDE, BLUID	—roll	BAP
blow	CLA(U)TLOUNDER, PAIK	breathing space	BARLEY
	WHAMPLE, YANK	breeches	BREEKS
—on the head	CRUNT	brewing	BROWST
blue	BLAE	bridesmaid	BESTMAID
—bell	HAREBELL	bridge	BRIG
—gown	GABERLUNZIE	—centering	COOM
board	BROD	bridle	BRANKS
bob	HOD	brigand	CATERAN
bobbin	PIRN	brimming	REAMING
bodice	JIRKINET	bringing misery or calamity	WAESOME
body	BOUK, BUIK, BUKE	brisk	CANT
—of vassals	MANRENT	bristle	BIRSE
bog	MOSS	bristly	BIRSY

brittle	BRICKLE, BRUCKLE, FRUSH
broad	BRAID
—Scots	LALLANS
—valley	STRATH
broil	BRU(I)LZIE, STRAMASH
broken	
—branch	SCROG
—ground in bog	HAG(G)
brood	CLOCK, CLECKING
—of children	BAIRN-TEAM, BAIRN-TIME
brooding hen	CLOCKER
brook	BURN
—lime	WATER-PURPIE
brother	BILLIE, BILLY
—in-law	GUDE-BROTHER
brow	BROO
browse	MOOP
brushwood	HAG(G)
budge	JEE
buffet	YANK
build	BIG
building-site	STANCE
bulk	BOUK, BUIK, BUKE
bumble bee	BUM-BEE
bump	CLOUR, DUNCH, DUNSH
bun	COOKIE
bunch of twigs	COW, KOW
bundle	DORLACH
bung	DOOK
bungle	BAUCHLE, BLUNK
	MIS(H)GUGGLE
burden of a song	O'ERCOME
	O'ERWORD, OWREWORD
burial fee	GR(O)UND MAIL
burly	BUIRDLY
burn	SCOUTHER, SCOWDER
burrow	HOWE, HOWK
burst	LOUPEN, LOUPIT, LOWP
—of anger	FUFF
bushy place	SCROG
busy	EIDENT
butt	DUNCH, DUNSH
buttermilk and water	
(Islands)	BLAND
buttocks	DOUP, FUD, HINDER-END
	HINDERLAN(D)S, HURDIES
buxom	GAUCY, GAWSY, SONCIE
	SONCY, SONSIE, SONSY
buy	COFF
by	
—my faith	HAITH
—stealth	STOW(N)LINS
—the time of	GIN
cabbage	
—broth	KALE, KAIL
—patch (Islands)	PLANTIE-CRUIVE

—seller	KAILWIFE
—stock	CASTOCK, CUSTOCK
cackle	KECKLE
cajole	CUITTLE
cake	BANNOCK, BUTTER-BAKE
	FARL(E), FARTHEL
—Shrove Tuesday	CARCAKE
call	CA
—by an ill name	MISCA(LL)
—to	
cows	PROO, PRUH
horse	HIE, HIGH
calm	LOUN(D), LOWN(D)
cannot	CANNA
—be bothered	DOWNA
cap	KILMARNOCK
—Highland Regiment	HUMMEL BONNET
capacity	BIND
caper	SCOUP, SCOWP
—about	FLISK
capital	AULD REEKIE, EDINBURGH
capricious	CAPERNOITED, CAPERNOITIE
	CAP(P)ERNOITY
caraway	CARVY
card	FLAUGHT
care	K(I)AUGH, SUSSY
careful look	VISIE, VIZY, VIZZIE
carefully	HOOLY
careless	UNTENTY
carouse	BIRL(E)
carriage	HURLY-HACKET
carrion	KET
—crow	HOODIE
case-law	PRACTIC
cast an eye around	GLEDGE
castle-goblin	RED-CAP, RED-COWL
casual	ORRA
casual(ly)	OVERLY
cat	BAUDRONS
catch	CLAUGHT, KEP, TACK
—fish with seine-net	TRAWL
—word	O'ERWORD
catechism	CARRITCH
catgut	THAIRM
cattle	BESTIAL, KY(E), NOUT, NOWT
—disease	MOOR-ILL
—Islands	KYLOES, LUING CATTLE
—farm	STORE-FARM
—lifting	SPREAGHERY, SPRECHERY
—theft	HERSHIP
caught	KEPPIT
cause to	
—bounce	STOT(TER)
—flee	FLAY, FLEY
cause(d)	GAR(T)
cease	DEVALL

Celt	GADHEL
certain	SICCAR, SICKER
certainly	CERTES, CERTIE, CERTY
cesspool	JAWHOLE
chaffinch	SNABBY
chairman	PR(A)ESES
challenge to act of daring	HEN(NER)
change one's	
—abode	FLIT
—mind	TAKE THE RUE
charge	DITTAY
charlock	RUNCH
charm	WEIRD
chat	CRACK
chatter	CHITTER, CLASH, GABNASH,
	NASHGAB, YATTER
cheat	JINK
cheerful	CANT(Y)
cheerfully	
—complacent	JOCO
—confident	CROUSE
cheese	CABOC, KEBBOCK, KEBBUCK
chemise	SARK
chest	BUNK, KIST
—for holding meal	MEAL-ARK
chide	QUARREL
chief	
—herald	(LORD) LYON
—magistrate	PROVOST
cities	LORD PROVOST
chief's	
—barge (Islands)	BIRLINN
—heir elect	TANIST
child	BAIRN, CHIEL(D)
	GAIT, GEITA, GYTE
	LITTLEANE, LITTLIN, SMOUT
	SMOWT, WEAN
—beginning to walk	GANGREL
child's garment	POLONAISE
children's	
—entitlement	BAIRN'S-PART, LEGITIM
—game	NIEVIE-NICK-NACK
chill	OORIE, OURIE, OWRIE
chilling	CAULD-RIFE
chimney	LUM
—cap	OLD WIFE
—corner	LUG
—top	LUM(-HEAD)
chip	SPALE
choice	WALE
choke	WORRY
choose/choosing	WALE
chore	TROCK, TROKE
church	KIRK
—court	KIRK-SESSION
—government system	PRESBYTERIANISM

—of Scotland	AULD KIRK
—officer	BEADLE, BED(E)RAL
—yard	KIRK-YA(I)RD
churl	BODACH
cibol	SYBOE, SYBO(W)
circle of hunters	TINCHEL
circular stone tower	BROCH
cite	SIST
cithern (Islands)	LANGSP(I)EL
claim	CRAVE
clamber	SPRAICKLE, SPRAUCHLE
clamour	RAIRD, REIRD
clasp-knife	JOCKTELEG
clatter	HOTTER
clause in charter specifying	
vassal's service	REDDENDO
claw	CLA(U)T
clean out of money	RUMP
clear up	RED(D)
cleavage	SLOT
cleft	CLOFF
—between hills	SLACK
—in rock (Islands)	RIVA
clerical function	DIET
clever	GLEG, SOUPLE
cleverness	CLEVERALITY
cliff	CRAIG
climb	SCLIM, SKLIM, SPEEL
climbing-iron	SPEELER
clock	KNOCK
—wise	DEASIL
clods	MOOLS, MOULS
clog	CLAG
close	
—fitting garment	JEISTIECOR
—look	VISIE, VIZY, VIZZIE
closed	LUCKEN
clot	LAPPER
—of dirt or colour	SPLATCH
cloth	CLOOT
clothes	CLAES, TROGGS
—horse	SCREEN
cloud-drift	CARRY
cloven-hoof	CLOOT
club-moss	BURR
cluck	CLOCK
clumsy	
—girl	TAUPIE, TAWPIE
—person	BAUCHLE
clutch	CLAUCHT, CLAUGHT
	GLAUM
coal	
—bin	BUNK
—bucket	BACKET
—fish	SAITH(E), SILLOCK
	STENLOCK

coaly fireclay	TUMPHY
coarse	RUDAS
—cloth	KELT
—file	RISP
—grained	CURN(E)Y
—woollen (Orkney)	WADMA(A)L
	WAFDMALL
coarsely outspoken	RANDIE, RANDY
coax	CUITTLE, FLEECH
coaxing	FLEECHING, FLEECHMENT
cobbler	SOUTAR, SOUTER, SOWTER
cock	
—crow	SKREIGH OF DAY
—that will not fight	FUGIE
cocker	CUITER
codfish	KEELING
coffin	KIST
coiffure	COCKERNONY
coil	FANK
coins	
—small copper (old)	PLACK
—¹/₆ penny	BOD(D)LE
—farthing (old)	TURNER
—halfpenny	BAUBEE, BAWBEE
—3d bit (old)	BAUBEE, BAWBEE
—2p (old)	QUADRUPLE
—1³/₄d	MERK
—18/-	UNICORN
—£1	PISTOLE
—74/-	LION
—£12 (old)	PISTOLE
—eighth of mark (Islands)	URE
—gold coin (old)	BONNET-PIECE
—silver coin (old)	SWORD-DOLLAR
cold	FRAIM, FREMD, FREMIT
	WEED, WEID
colic	BATTS
collar-bone	HAUSE-BANE
collect (parcel)	UPLIFT
collection	
—of small things	SMYT(E)RIE
—plate	BROD
colt	STAIG
comb	KAME, KAIM, RED(D)
come	
—across	MEET IN WI(TH)
—to light	SPUNK OUT
comely	SONSIE, SONSY
comfortable	BEIN, BIEN, CANNY
	COUTHIE, TOSH
—looking	SONSIE, SONSY
coming on	ONCOME
common sense	RUMGUMPTION
	RUM(M)EL-GUMPTION
	RUM(M)LE-GUMPTION
	RUMBLE-GUMPTION

commotion	CARFUFFLE, CURFUFFLE
	KEFUFFLE, HOTTER
	TIRRIVEE, TIRRIVIE
communion service	OCCASION
companion-in-arms	BILLIE, BILLY
compel	GAR
compel(led)	GAR(T)
complain peevishly	GIRN, WHEENGE
	WHINGE
complete	
—set	STAND
—sum	SOLIDUM
completely	STOOP AND ROOP
comply with	OBTEMPER
concerned with fate	WEIRD
concerning that matter	THEREANENT
concurrence	CONCOURSE
condition	FID, PLISKIE, PLISKY
	PLY
conduct sheep into fold	WEAR
conductor of	
festival (Islands)	SCUDDALER, SCUDLER
	SKUDLER
cone of damp gunpowder	PEEOY, PIOY(E)
confidential	PACK
confirmation by	
subsequent act	HOMOLOGATION
confound	BUMBAZE
confuse	MOIDER
confused	
—disturbance	BRU(I)LZIE
—jumble	MIXTER-MAXTER
	MIXTIE-MAXTIE
	MIX(T)Y-MAX(T)Y
confusedly mixed	THROUGH-OTHER
confute	REDARGUE
connecting ridge	HAUSE, HAWSE
connivance at adultery	LENOCINIUM
considerable	GAY, GEY
—number	HANTLE
considerably	GAY, GEY
conspicuous	KENSPECKLE
contemptible fellow	SMAIK
contend strongly with	PINGLE
contention	STURT
continue to wait	WAIT ON
contradict	THREAP, THREEP
contrary to course	
of sun	WID(D)ERSHINS
	WITHERSHINS
controlling fate	WEIRD
conundrum	GUESS
convey in wheeled vehicle	HURL
cool	CALLER
cormorant	SCART(H), SKART(H)
corn	OATS

—dolly	KIRN-BABY, KIRN-DOLLIE
—maiden	MAIDEN
corporation of royal burgh	GUILDRY
corpse	LIKE
cosy	COSH
cottage	BOTHIE, BOTHY
—room	END
cottager	MAILER
cottar's-house	COT-HOUSE
cottars	COT-FOLK
cotton-grass	CANNA(CH), MOSS-CROP
cough loudly	KINK
counter for casting lots	CAVEL
country	
—dance	PETRONELLA
—lass	JENNY
—talk	CLASH
court	
—judgement	DECREET
—official	DEMPSTER, DOOMSTER
—sitting	SEDERUNT
—usher	MACER
Covenanter	WHIGGAMORE
Covenanters	HILLFOLK, HILLMEN
cover	
—by drifting (snow)	WREATH
—of pot	PAT-LID
cow	
—dung	SHA(I)RN
—house	BYRE
—man	BYREMAN
	NOWT-HERD
—or ox killed and	
salted	MART
cow's yield	MELTITH
coward	FUGIE
cower down	CROODLE
cows	KY(E), NOUT, NOWT
coy	SKEIGH
crab	PARTAN
—apple	SCROG
crabbed	CAPERNOITED, CAPERNOITIE
	CAP(P)ERNOITY, CRABBIT
crafty	LOOPY
—person	SNECK-DRAWER
—twist	W(H)IMPLE
crag	HEUCH, HEUGH
cram	CRAP, PANG, STAP
crammed	PANG
crane-fly	JENNY-LONG-LEGS
cranky	FIFISH
crash	FRUSH
cravat	OVERLAY
crazy	DOILED, DOILT, DOTTLE(D)
	GYTE, WOWF
cream	REAM

crease	LIRK
creature	CRATUR
credit	MENSE
creek (Islands)	GEO, GIO, VOE
creep (of the flesh)	GREW, GRUE
crested	TAPPIT
criminal intention	DOLE
cringe	SNOOL
cripple	LAMETER, LAMITER
crisp	CRUMP
crook-handled	
walking-stick	KEBBIE
crooked	CAMSHO(CH), CAMSHEUGH
	THRAWARD, THRAWART
crop	CRAP, STOW
cross	THRAW
—examine	TARGE
—grained	ILL-HAIRED, THRAWN
—question	BACKSPEER, BACKSPEIR
crow steps	CORBIE-STEPS
crowd of children	SMYRTIE
crowded	PANG
crown of head or causeway	CANTLE
crumb	NIRL
crumble	MURL
crupper	CURPEL
crush	CHACK, CHECK
cry	GLEET, GOWL, SPRAICH
—fretfully	WHEENGE, WHINGE
cupboard	AWMRIE, AWMRY
cuckoo	GOUK, GOWK
cudgel	KEBBIE
cuff	GOWF
cunning mischief	PAWK
cup	QUAICH, QUAIGH, TASSIE
cur	MESSAN
curdle	LAPPER
—(of blood)	GREW, GRUE
curdled milk	LAPPER(ED)-MILK
cure with smoke	REAST, REEST, REIST
curlew	(GREAT)WHAUP
curry favour	CUITTLE
curse	WEARY, WINZE
—of Scotland	QUEEN OF DIAMONDS
curtailed	CUTTY
cushion	COD
cut	
—and dry peat	CAST
—on something	INSCULP
—turf	FLAUGHTER
cutter on plough	CO(U)LTER
cutting of last sheaf	KERN, KIRN
dabble in	
—liquid	PLOTTER, PLOUTER
	PLOWTER
—miry matter	CLATCH

dabbling	PLOTTER, PLOUTER, PLOWTER	—sea fishing ground	
dagger	DIRK, SKEAN, SKENE	(Islands)	HAF
	WHINGER, WHINIARD	defamation	SLANDER
	WHINYARD	defeat	WA(U)RST
dainty	GENTY, SUNKET	defile	FILE, HAUSE, HAWSE
dally	PINGLE	deformed	ILL-FAURD
dam	STANK	delay	SIST
—in stream	CAULD	delicate	DORTY
damage	SCAITH, SKAITH	deliveryman	POSTIE
damson	PLUMDAMAS	dell	DARGLE, HOWE
dance	BOB, HIGHLAND FLING	demure	MIM(-MOU'D), PRIMSIE
	LOWP, PETRONELLA, REEL	departing	WAY-GOING
	STRATHSPEY	depend	LIPPEN
—tune	SPRING	dependent interest	RIDING-INTEREST
dandle	DOODLE	deplorable	WAESOME
dangerous	MISCHANCY, NO'CANNY	deprive	TWIN(E)
	UNCHANCY, WANCHANCIE	deranged	SKIVIE
	WANCHANCY	derisive gesture	GECK
dangle after	TRAIK AFTER	derived	EXTRACT
dapple-grey	LIART, LYART	desert	FORHOO(IE), FORHOW
dare	DAUR	desolate	GOUSTY
dark blue	BLAE	despicable fellow	FOOTRA, FOUTRA
dart		destine	WEIRD
—obliquely	SKITE, SKYTE	devastated place	WASTAGE
—of pain	STEN(D)	Development	
dash	JABBLE, SPANG	—Agency	SDA
—of pen	SCART	—Department	SDD
daub	CLATCH, SLAKE	devil	AULD MIS(C)HANTER
daunt	DANTON		CLOOT(IE), CLOOTS, DEIL
day's work	DARG		HORNIE, NICKIE-BEN
daybreak	SKREIGH OF DAY		WIRRICOW
days of merriment			WORRICOW, WORRYCOW
(New Year)	DAFT DAYS	devour ravenously	WORRY
dazzling	GLAIK	dialect of islands	NORN
dead	DEED, DEID	dib-stones	CHUCKIE-STANES, CHUCKS
deafen	DEAVE	die	DEE
deal out sparingly	TAPE	died	DEED
dealer	COUPER	difference	DIFFER
dealings	TROCK, TROKE	dig	HOWK
dean's warrant	JEDGE	diligent	EIDENT
death	DEID	din	RAIRD, REEL, REIRD
—throe	DEID-THRAW		STOUND, STOWND
debt under £20	SMALL-DEBTS	dingy	OORIE, OURIE, OWRIE
deceive	MISLIPPEN	dinner	KALE, KAIL
decent	WISE-LIKE	dip in hot water	PLOT
decisive movement	UPCOME	direction	AIRT
deck out	DAIKER	dirge	CORANACH, CORONACH
declare		dirt	GUTTERS
—heir	SERVE	disappoint	MISLIPPEN
—to be an idiot	COGNOSCE	disarray	TASH
decline in health	TRAIK	disaster	MIS(C)HANTER
decorous	MENSEFUL	disciplinarian	
decree	DECERN, MODIFY	in University	HEBDOMADAR
deed of qualification	BACK-BOND		HEBDOMADER
deep		disease coming without	
—draught	WILLIEWAUGHT	known cause	INCOME

disentangle	RED(D)	—oneself	HARL
disfigure	BLA(U)D, TASH	draggle	TRACHLE, TROLLOP
disgust	SCOMFISH, SCUNNER	drain	POUR, SHEUCH, SHEUGH
dish	ASHET, BRO(U)GH, HAGGIS		SIVER, SYVER
	HOWTOWDIE, (PEASE-)BROSE	draining-board	BUNK
dismal	DOWIE	dram	TIFT
disorder	CARFUFFLE, CURFUFFLE	drank	DRUCKEN
	KEFUFFLE	draught	WAUCHT, WAUGHT
dispatch unceremoniously	SHANK	—animal	AVER
disperse	SCALE, SCAIL, SKAIL	—board	DAMBOARD, DAMBROD
dispirited	SACKLESS	—man	DAM
displacement	JEE	draw (money)	UPLIFT
dispute	THREAP, THREEP	dreary	DREICH, GOUSTY
disputed	THREAPIT, THREEPIT		OORIE, OURIE, OWRIE
distort	THRAW	drench	DROOK, DROUK
distorted	THRAWN	drenched	DROOKIT, DROUKIT
distrain	POIND	dress	BOUN, GRAITH
distraint	POINDER, POINDING	—neatly	DINK
distress	PUT ABOUT	dresser	AUMRIE, AWMRIE, AWMRY
distressed	ILL	dried	
district thirled to mill	SUCKEN	—heath	ROUGHIE
distrust	MISLIPPEN	—meat (Islands)	VIFDA, VIVDA
disturb	JEE, STEER	drily humorous	PAWKY
disturbance	COLLIESHANGIE	drink	ATHOLL BROSE
	STRAMASH, STURT		HEATHER ALE, TIFT
disturbed	MISTRYSTED	—cup out	BEND THE BICKER
ditch	SHEUCH, SHEUGH, SIKE, STANK	—hard at	BEND
divination	TAGHAIRM	—in large draughts	WAUCHT, WAUGHT
divine	SPAE	drinking	
diviner	SPAER, SPAEMAN	—bout	BEND
division of county	WARD	—cup	QUAICH, QUAIGH
dizziness	MIRLIGOES	drive	CA
do	DIV	driver of horses at plough	GADSMAN
document produced in court	PRODUCTION	drizzle	SCOUTHER, SCOWDER
dodge	JINK, JOUK		SMIR(R), SMUR
doggerel	RAT-RHYME	drizzling mist	DROW
dolphin	CA(A)ING-WHALE	drone or play, as bagpipe	DOODLE
dominate	O'ERGANG	drooping	OORIE, OURIE, OWRIE
donkey	CUDDIE, CUDDY	drub(bing)	PAIK
doom	WEIRD	drudge	SCOGIE
door	YETT	drudgery	SLAISTERY
—catch	SNETCH	drunk	FOU, STOTIOUS
—knocker	RISP	drunkard	SAND-BED
dotard	DOTTLE	drunken	FOU, WAT
double		drunken(ness)	DRUCKEN(NESS)
—feu-duty	DUPLICAND	dry	EILD, HI(R)STIE
—handful	GOWPEN		REEST, REIST
dove	DOO	—in the	
—cote	DOOCOT, DOOKET	sun	RIZZAR, RIZZER, RIZZOR
dower	TOCHER	wind	WIN
down-and out	FORFAIRN	—stone	
down-at-heel	SHAUCHLE	wall	DRY-STANE DIKE
dowry	TOCHER	waller	COWAN
doze	DOVER	—with smoke	REAST, REEST, REIST
drag		duck	JOOK, JOUK
—along ground	HARL	dull	DOWF, DOWIE

—witted	DONNERD, DONNERED	elude	JINK
	DONNERT, FOZY	emaciated	WANTHRIVEN
dunce	SUMPH	emblem	THISTLE
dunderhead	GOMERAL, GOMERIL	embrace	HAUSE, HAWSE
dung-fork	GRAIP	emerge	CAST UP
dupe	GECK	empty	BOSS, GOUSTY, TOOM
dust	STOOR, STOUR, STOWRE	enable to last	WEAR
dusty	STOURY	enclosure	HAINING
dwarf	DROICH	end of eggshell	DOUP
dwell	STAY	ends of ribbon	FATTRELS
dynasty	STEWART, STUART	endearment	BURD(IE), LEEZE ME
each	ILK(A)	—Island	JARTA, YARTA
—other	OTHER	endure	DREE, THOLE, WEAR
eager	FRACK, FRECK	English	SOUTHRO(U)N
ear of corn	ICKER	—man	POCK-PUDDING, SASSENACH
Earl Marshal	EARL MARISCHAL	enough	ENOW, SAIRING
early dram	MORNING	entail	TAILLIE, TAILYE, TAILZIE
earnest of bargain	ARLES	entangle	FANKLE, TAIGLE
	ARLE(S) PENNY	entreat	PRIG
earth	(Y)EARD, YERD, YIRD	equipment	GRAITH
—house	PICTS' HOUSE	escapade	SPLORE
—hunger	(Y)EARD)-HUNGER	essential virtue	FIZZEN, FUSHION
	YERD-HUNGER	established church	AULD KIRK
	YIRD-HUNGER	estranged	FRAIM, FREMD, FREMIT
earthenware (crock)	PIG	Evangelical	HIGH-FLIER, HIGH-FLYER
earwig	HORNIE-GOLOCH	even if	SUPPOSE
easily		evening	FORENIGHT
—recognised	KENSPECKLE	—party	ROCKING
—tickled	KITTLY	every day (but Sunday)	ILKADAY
Easter-egg	PACE-EGG	everything	HALE HYPOTHEC
easterly	EASSEL(GATE), EASSIL(GATE)	ewe	YOW(E)
	EASTLIN(G)	—after lambing	KEB
eastwards	EASSEL, EASSIL	exacting person	FIKE, FYKE
easy enough	GEY AND EASY	examine	COGNOSCE
eat with		exclamation	TOOTS, TUTS
—a spoon	SUP	excavation	HEUCH, HEUGH
—feeble appetite	PINGLE	excel	WA(U)RST
eatables	VIVERS, VIVRES	excellent	WAL(L)Y
eccentric	SHKITE, SKTE	excessive	NIMIOUS
ecclesiastical function	DIET	exchange	EXCAMB, NIFFER
ecstasy	EXIES		SCORSE, TROCK, TROKE
edge sheep into fold	WEAR	—of	
edible		goods	TROCK, TROKE
—crab	PARTAN	lands	ESCAMBIUM, EXCAMBION
—seaweed	BADDERLOCK	excite loathing in	SCUNNER
Education		excuse	FAIK
—Certificate	SCE	exempt	EXEEM, EXEME
—Department	SED	exert oneself	PINGLE
Educational Institute	EIS	exhausted	FORFAIRN
effeminate man	JENNY, JESSIE		FORFEUCHEN
efficacy	FECK		FORFOUGHEN
eke	ECHE, EIK	—from travelling	WAYGONE
elder	PRESBYTER	expect	LIPPEN
—tree	BOUNTREE, BOURTREE	expenses for catching	
elderly woman	LUCKIE, LUCKY	rogues	ROGUE-MONEY
elegant	JIMP(Y), JINTY	experience a pang	STOUND, STOWND

experienced	USED
expert	SKEELY, SKILLY, USED
expiry	ISH
extinguish	SLO(C)KEN
extract	HOWK
extraordinary	BY-ORDINAR, BYOUS
eye	EE, KEEKER
eyebrow	BREE
eyes	EEN, EYNE
face	GIZZ
fail	MISGIVE
—in health	DWALM, DWAUM
—to	
keep appointment	MISTRYST
recognise	MISKEN, TARTLE
faint	DWAMY, SWERVE
fairly	GAY, GEY
faithful	AEFA(U)LD, AFA(W)LD
fall	FA
—of snow	STORM
false hair piece	COCKERNONY
familiar jog-trot	HEICH-HOW
famous	NAMELY
fantastic	
—ornamentation	WHIGMALEERIE
	WHIGMALERY
—round ornament	CURLIEWURLIE
farm	
—cottage	BOTHIE, BOTHY
—in joint tenancy	TOWNSHIP
—overseer	GRIEVE
—song	CORN-KISTER
—stead	FARM-TOUN, FERMTOUN
	ONSTEAD, TOWN
—worker	HIND
fasten	STEEK
fastened	SNECKED
fat	FOZY
fate	WEIRD
father-in-law	GUDE-FATHER
faulty state	VICIOSITY, VITIOSITY
favoured	FA'ARD, FAURD
fearless	RAUCLE
fearsome	UNCO
feathered legs	COOTIE
feeble	FIZZENLESS, FUSHIONLESS
	SACKLESS, SHILPIT
	SOBER, WERSH
—person or animal	WALLYDRAG
	WALLYDRAIGLE
feebleness in intelligence	WANT
feed with corn	CORN
female	
—auctioneer	ROUPING-WIFE
—fish	RAUN, RAWN
—outworker	BONDAGER

ferrule	VIRL
feudal service	ARRIAGE
few	WHEEN
fibre	TAIT, TATE
fictitious dwarf	PICT
fiddle	ITCH
—(Islands)	GJO, GJU, GU(E), GOU
fidget	FIDGE, FIKE, FYKE
—with eagerness	HOTCH
field	PAIRK
fierce	WUD
fiery person	SPUNKIE
fight	TUILYE, TUILZIE, WAP
—in heat of passion	CHAUD-MELLE
fight(er)	FECHT(ER)
filled full	PANGFU(LL)
find by skilful means	EXPISCATE
fine	GRASSUM, UNLAW
—misty rain	SMIR(R), SMUR
—powder	SMEDDUM
finely dressed	BRAW
finger-hole of wind	
instrument	LILL
finical	PERJINK(ETY), PREJINK
fire-screen	HALLAN
fireside disputation	KILFUD-YOKING
firm	SICCAR, SICKER
	STEEVE, STIEVE
—place in bog	HAG(G)
first	
—attendance of magistrate	
after election	KIRKIN(G)
—church attendance after	
marriage	KIRKIN(G)
—furrow	FEERING
—shoots of crop	BRAIRD, BREER
fish	
—roe	RAUN, RAWN
—spawn	REDD
—trap	CRU(I)VE
—with the hands	GUDDLE, GUMP
fit of	
—hysterics	EXIES
—passion	TIRRIVEE, TIRRIVIE
—perversity	THRAW
—stubbornness	REEST, REIST
—the sulks	TOUT, TOWT
fitting	WISE-LIKE
flagstones	PLAINSTANES
flake	FLAUGHT
flame	LOW(E)
flannel undervest	WYLIE-COAT
flap	FLACK, FLAFF(ER), WAP
—about	WALLOP
flapping	FLAUGHT
—rag	WALLOP

flash	FLAUGHT, GLAIK
flat	
—bonnet	BALMORAL
—cake	BANNOCK
—fish	CRAIGFLUKE
—moist land	FLOW
flatter	FLEECH, PHRASE
flattering	FLEECHING, FLEECHMENT
flaunt	SKYRE
flax (seed)	LINT (SEED)
fled	LOUPEN, LOUPIT
flee	LOWP
fleece	KET, PLOT
flicker	FLAUGHTER
flicking with thumbnail	SPANG-COCKLE
flight	FLAUGHT
flighty	HELLICAT
	LOUP-THE-DYKE
flock of sheep	HIRSEL
flourish	WAMPISH
flow lumpily	SLUMP
fluff	OOZE
fluffy	PLUFFY
flurry	SWITHER
flutter	FLAUGHTER, FLICHTER
—of wings	FLAFF
fluttering motion	FLAUGHTER
flying shower	SCOUTHER, SCOWDER
fold	LIRK
—back	FLIPE
food	BROSE, SCAFF, VIVERS
	VIVRES
—scraps	BROCK
fool	DOTTLE, GOUK, GOWK
foolish	DOILED, DOILT, DOTTLE(D)
	FOOL, GLAIKIT
—fellow	GOMERAL, GOMERIL
—person	HAVEREL
—talk	HAVER(ING)S
foot-stamping	RUFF
football game	BA'ING, BA'SPIEL
footballers	SFA
footless stocking	HOGGER, MOGGAN
for	ON
—the express purpose	ONCE ERRAND
	ANCE ERRAND
	YINCE ERRAND
foray	CREACH, CREAGH, SPREAGH
forcible	VIVE
ford	LIRK, RACK
foreign	FRAIM, FREMD, FREMIT
foreman	TOPSMAN
forenoon	FOREDAY
foretell	SPAE
forewarn	WEIRD
form of Scots	LALLAN

formerly	UMQUHILE
foreseeing the future	FAY, FEY, FIE
forth	FURTH
fortified	
—house	BASTEL-HOUSE
—island	CRANNOG
forward	FORRIT, THRAWARD
	THRAWART
—girl	YIP
foster-child	DA(U)LT
foul-mouthed old woman	RUDAS
found	FAND
fourth part	FORPET, FORPIT
fowl	BRISSEL-COCK
—house manure	HEN-PEN
fox	LOWRIE(-TOD)
	TOD-LOWRIE, TOD
fragment	BLA(U)D
freckle	FAIRNYTIC(K)LE
free	
—defendant of charge	ASSOILZIE
—hold estate	BARONY
Islands	UDAL
—of claim	ASSOILZIE
—range	SCOUTH, SCOWTH
freebooter	CATERAN
freeholder (Islands)	UDALLER
Free Church of Scotland	WEE FREES
frequency	COMMONALTY
fresh	CALLER
—man	BAJAN(T), BEJAN(T)
friable	CRUMP
fried dish	SKIRL-IN-THE-PAN
friendly	COUTHIE, TOSH
fright	FLEG, GLIFF, GLIFT
frighten	FLEG, FLAY, FLAY
	FRICHT, SCAUR
frivolous excuse	WHITTIE-WHATTIE
frog	PADDOCk
—spawn	REDD
frolic	SPLORE
from	FRAE, THRAE
froth	REAM
fuddled	TA(I)VERT
fuel	EILDING
fulfilment	IMPLEMENT
full	FOU, SKELPING
funeral banner	GUMPHION
furious	WUD
furnace cinders	DANDER
furnish	PLENISH
furniture	INSIGHT, PLENISHING
	STOUTH(E)RIE
furrow	FUR(R), SHEUCH, SHEUGH
further on or up	UPBY(E)
fuss	FIKERY, FYKERY

fussy	FIKISH, FIKY, FYKISH, FYKY
—talk	PHRASE
gable	GAVEL
gad	TRAIK
Gael	GAHDEL, GOIDEL
Gaelic-speaking	
districts of Scotland	GAIDHEALTACHD
gag	BRANKS
gaiter	COOTIKIN, CU(I)TIKIN
	QUEET
gallows	DULE-TREE, WOODIE
game	SHINNY, SHINTY
gamekeeper	GILLY, G(H)ILLIE
gap in fence	SLAP
garb	THRATCH
garish	ROARIE, ROARY
garret	ROOST
gasp for breath	KINK
gate	YATE, YET(T)
—crash	SORN
gave	GAE, GIED
genealogist	SEANNACHIE, SEANNACHY
	SENNACHIE, SHANACHIE
generous	MENSEFUL
gentle	CANNY
get	
—by	
begging	THIG
groping	POWTER
—lost	TRAIK
—over	OVERCAST
gey and...	GEYAN
ghastliness	GASHLINESS
ghastly	GASH(FUL), GASHLY
ghost	CHAPPIE, WAFF
giddy	GLAIKIT
—headed	HELLICAT
gift	PROPINE
—given on last day of year	HOGMANAY
—of escheat	SUBREPTION
gig	HURLY-HACKET
girdle	GRIDDLE
girl	CUMMER, CUTTY, KIMMER
	LASSIE, QUEAN, QUEYN(IE)
	QUIN(I)E
give	GID, GIE
—and take	GIFF-GAFF
—judgement on	COGNOSCE
—security for another	CAUTIONRY
—up the charge	DESERT THE DIET
given	GIEN
giving possession	SASINE
glance	GLEY
glancing blow	SKITE, SKYTE
gleam	SHEEN
—of sunshine	SUN-BLINK

glen	HOWE
glide	SCRIEVE, SKITE, SKYTE
—obliquely	SKITE, SKYTE
glimmer	STIME, STYME
glimpse	GLEDGE, GLIFF, GLIFT
	GLIM, GLISK, GLIST
	STIME, STYME, WAFF
globe-flower	LUCKENGOWAN
gloom	DOOL
gloomy	DRUMLY
glower	GLAUR
gluttonous	GUTSY
go	GAE, GANG
—about or forth	STEER
—arm-in-arm	CLEEK
—counter	THRAW
—easy	CA'CANNY
—on crutches	STILP
—slowly	WEAR
—to sleep	FALL OVER
—wearily	TRAIK
go-by	GANG-BY
goal	DOOL, DULE
—(in games)	HAIL
gob	GAB
goblin	BODACH, BROWNIE
	RED-CAP, RED-COWL
godmother	CUMMER, KIMMER
going	GAUN
gold	GOOL, GULE, GOWD
—finch	GOUDIE, GOWDIE, GOWDSPINK
golf	GOWF
—ball	GOWF-BA
gone	GANE
good	GUID, GUDE
—condition	PLY
—deal	HANTLE
—fortune	SEIL
—health!	SLAINTE
—looking	WEEL-FAIRED, WEEL-FA(U)R'D
	WEEL-FA(U)RT
—luck	SONCE, SONSE
—manners	HAVING
—many	HANTLE
	SONSY
—turn	CAST
good-for-nothing	NE'ER-DO-WEEL
goodly	FAIR-FARAND
good-natured	SONCIE, SONCY, SONSIE
goodness!	(MY) CONSCIENCE
gooseberry	GROSER(T), GROSET, GROSSART
gore	GAIR
gossip	CLASH, CLATTER, CLAVER
	CLISH-CLASH, CLISHMACLAVER
	CUMMER, JAUNDER, KIMMER
got	GOTTEN

—off lightly with	CHEAP OF	guess	ETTLE
grace	MENSE	guide	
graceful	GENTY	—in certain direction	W(E)ISE, WEIZE
graceless	MENSELESS	—sheep into fold	WEAR
gracious	MENSEFUL	guileless	SACKLESS
grain	CURN	guillemot	LUNGIE
—chest	CORN-KIST	gull	SCAURY, SCOURIE
—crops, cut or ready	VICTUAL		SCOWRIE, SEA-MAW
—due to miller's servant	KNAVESHIP	gully (Islands)	GEO, GIO
—measure	WECHT	gulp	SUILK
—of corn	PICKLE	gun-sight	VISIE, VIZY, VIZZIE
granary	GIRNEL	gurgle	BULLER, RUCKLE
grand		gurgling sound	GOLLAR
—child	OE, OY(E)	gust	FLAUGHT
—father	GUDESIRE, GUTCHER	gutsiness	GREEDINESS
	LUCKIE-DAD	gutter	STRAND
—mother	GUDE-DAME	guttural bawl	GOLLAR
grantor's warranty	WARRANDICE	gypsy	CAIRD, TINK(LER)
granular	CURN(E)Y	habitual saying	O'ERWORD, OWREWORD
grasp	CLA(U)T, GLAUM	habituate	USE
grass field	PARK	hack	HAG
grate	CHIRK, RISP	haddock	HADDIE, SPELD(R)IN(G)
grating over drain	SIVER, SYVER	hag	RUDAS
gratuity	MAG(G)S	haggle	NIFFER, PRIG
grave	GRAFF	hair	
—digger	BEADLE, BED(E)RAL	—comb	REDDING-COMB
gravel	CHANNEL		REDDING-KAME
grazing blow or		—piece	COCKERNONY
movement	SKIFF	—powder	M(O)UST, MUIST
grease	CREESH	halberd	LOCHABER-AXE
great	FELL, UNCO	hale	FRACK, FRECK, RAUCLE
—stride	STEN(D)	half	HALFLIN(G)S
greedy	GARE	—a silver penny	HALFLIN(G)
gridiron	BRANDER	—grown person	HALFLIN(G)
grief	VEX	hall	HA
grim	DOUR, GURLY	ham	HOUGH
grimace	MURGEON	hand over to as one's fate	WEIRD
grin	GIRN	handful	GOWPEN, LOOFFUL
groove in masonry	RAGGLE		RIP(P)
grope	GRAPE, RIPE	handkerchief	NAPKIN
gross amount	SLUMP	handsome	BRAW
ground		hang	STRAP
—floor house	MAINDOOR	hanging clock	WAG-AT-THE-WALL
—for one grave	LAIR		WAG-BY-THE-WALL
ground-rent	GROUND ANNUAL	hangman	LOCKMAN
group of		hangman's rope	TOW
—cot-houses	COT-TOWN	happening	WEIRD
—houses	TOWN	happiness	SEIL
growl	GURL	harass	PINGLE
gruel	BROCHAN, CROWDY	harbour	RESET
grumble	GIRN	—due	SHORE-DUE
grunt	GRUMPH	harbouring of criminal	RESET
guarantee	WARRANDICE	hard blow	DEV(V)EL
guarantor	OBLIGANT	hardened clay	BLAE
guard	WEAR	hardly	JIMPLY
guardian of minor	TUTOR	hare	BAUDRONS, MALKIN, MAWKIN

—bell	BLAWORT
hare's tail	FUD
harm	SCAITH
—physically	WRONG
harmless	CANNY
harry	HERRY
harvest	HAIRST
—field	HAIRST-RIG
—home	KERN, KIRN
hasp	HESP
hatch eggs	CLECK
haughty	PAUGHTY
haul	RUG
haunch	HAINCH
haunt	HOUFF, HOWFF
have	HAE
—a holiday	PLAY
—dealings	INTROMIT
—done	BE THROUGH
—lustre	SHEEN
having a certain	
appearance or manner	FAR(R)AND
	FARRANT
hawk	KEELIE
hawker	YAGGER
hazard	NIFFER
hazy	URY
head	POW
—of hair	POW
—to foot	HEADS AND THRAWS
headland in field	HEAD-RIG
headlong	RAMSTAM
health	HEAL
heap of mortar	BINK
heard	HARD
heart (Islands)	JARTA, YARTA
heave up	HEEZE
heavens	LIFT
heavy	DOWF
—blow	LOUNDER
—impact	DUSH
heed	TENT
heifer	QUEY
held	HADDEN, HUDDEN
helmet	KNAPSCAL, KNAPSCULL
	KNAPSKULL
hemp-nettle	DAE-NETTLE, DAY-NETTLE
herald	UNICORN
hesitate	TARROW
hew	HAG
hide	FLAUGHT
hideous	GASH(FUL), GASHLY
hideousness	GASHLINESS
hiding place	HIDLING(S), HIDLINS
	HIDY-HOLE
higgledy-piggledy	THROUGH-OTHER

high tea	TOUSY TEA
Highland	HIELAND
—dancer's shout	HOOCH
—dagger	DIRK
—festival	MOD
—gentleman of	
inferior rank	DUN(N)I(E)WASSAL
—whisky	PEAT-REEK
Highlander	NAINSEL(L), PLAIDMAN
Highlander's cap	GLENGARRY
hill	LAW, BRAE
—pass	SLAP
hinder	TAIGLE
hint	MINT
hire	FEE
hired mourner	SALLIE, SALUIE, SAULIE
hitch	HOTCH
hoar frost	CRANREUCH
hoarse	ROOPIT, ROOPY, ROUPIT
hoarseness	ROOP, ROUP
hoary old stone	HARE-STANE
hoax	GEGG
hob nail	TACKET
hobble	HILCH
hobgoblin	WIRRICOW, WORRICOW
	WORRYCOW
hobnail	TACKET
hock	HOUGH
hoe	CLA(U)T
hog's lard	SAIM
hoist	HEEZE
hold	CLAUCHT, CLAUGHT
	HAD, HAU(L)D
holder of	
—document	HAVER
—land under feu	FEUAR
—small feu	PORTIONER
—underlease	SUBTACKSMAN
holding	HADDIN
holiday	PLAYING
hollow	BOSS, CORRIE, HOWE
—of two hands	GOWPEN
homage	MANRENT
home	HAME
—farm	MAINS
—made firework	PEEOY, PIOY(E)
—spun	RAPLOCH
homeward	HAMEWITH
honey	HINNY
hoof	CLOOT
hoop	GIRD, GIRR
hooped dish	LUGGIE
hop-scotch	PEEVERS
horizontal tombstone	THROUGH-STANE
hornless	
—cow	DODDY, HUMLIE

—(stag)	HUMBLE, HUMMEL
horse	CUDDIE, CUDDY, GALLOWAY
—backband	RIGWIDDIE, RIGWOODIE
—collar	BRECHAM
—dealer	HORSE-COUPER
—disease	WEED, WEID
—feeding on stubble	STIBBLER
—fever	WEED, WEID
—fly	CLEG
—old	AVER, YAUD
—shoe	PANTON-SHOE
hot	HET
—pursuit	HOT-TROD
—water bottle	PIP
house	BIGGIN
—agent	HOUSE-FACTOR
—leek	FOUAT, FOUET
—of turf	BLACKHOUSE
—one room deep	SINGLE HOUSE
—the harvest	LEAD IN
—warming	INFARE
household goods	INSIGHT
hovel	CRU(I)VE
howl	GOWL
huff	STRUNT
hug	OXTER
hum softly	SOWF(F), SOWTH
hungry	YAUP
hurl	BUM
hurry off	WHIRRY
hurt	MIS(C)HANTER
	SCAITH, SKAITH
husband	GUIDMAN
hush!	WHEESHT
hussy	LIMMER
hut	BOTHAN, BOTHIE, BOTHY
	SHEAL(ING), SHEEL(ING)
	SHEIL(ING), SHIEL(ING)
—Islands	SKEO, SKIO
hysterics	EXIES
I shall	ISE
ice-cream between wafers	SLIDER
idiot	TUMPSHIEHEID
idle	
—about	DAIDLE
—talk	CLAVER
if	GIF, GIN
ignorant of	UNACQUAINT
ignore	MISKEN
ill	
—conditioned	MISLEARED
—favoured	ILL-FAURD
—grown	WANTHRIVEN
—looking	ILL-FAURD
—natured person	ETHERCAP, ETTERCAP
—omened	UNCHANCY

—tempered	GIRNIE
—treat	DEMEAN, MISGUIDE
illegal drinking-place	BOTHAN
impediment in speech	HALT
impervious clay	TILL
impetuosity	BIRR
importune	PRIG
impound	POIND
improvised sledge	HURLY-HACKET
impudent	BARDY
in	INTIL
—arrear	BACK-GANGING
—being	TO THE FORE
—confusion	HIRDY-GIRDY
—contrary direction	WID(D)ERSHINS
	WITHERSHINS
—dotage	DOITED, DOITIT
—indiscriminate	
mixture	THROUGH-OTHER
—the country	LANDWARD(S)
—turns	TIME ABOUT
into	INTIL
incipient movement	MINT
incline to think	DOUBT
inclined to	
—avarice	GRIPPY
—shiver or shudder	OORIE, OURIE, OWRIE
increase in stipend	AUGMENTATION
indecision	SWITHER
indeed	ATWEEL, DEED
indictment	DITTAY
indoors	THEREIN
indulge	PETTLE
inert	THOWLESS
infield	INTOWN
infuse	MASK
inhabitant	RESIDENTER
injure	SCAITH, SKAITH
injury	MIS(C)HANTER
	SCAITH, SKAITH
inn-keeper	STABLER
inner room	BEN, SPENCE
innocent	SACKLESS
inquire	SPEER, SPEIR
insignificant person	SCOOT
insinuating person	SNECK-DRAWER
insist	THREAP, THREEP
insisted	THREAPIT, THREEPIT
insolence	SNASH
insolent	BARDY
inspector of coal	KEEKER
inspiration	TAGHAIRM
instalment selling	MENAGE
instant	WHIP
instrument for winnowing	WECHT
instrumental tune	PORT

intent	ETTLE	—private consideration	AVISANDUM
intercourse	TROCK, TROKE		AVIZANDUM
interdict	INJUNCTION	judicious	WISE-LIKE
interfere	INTROMIT	jumble	JABBLE
interjection	OCH	jurisdiction	FOUDRIE, SUCKEN
—deploring	AICH WOW	jury	ASSIZE
	(EH) WHOW, EWHOW	keen	GLEG, SNELL
—of		keep in subjection	SNOOL
concession	OU, OW	kestrel	KEELIE
irritation	HOOT, HOOT(S)-TOOT(S)	kick strongly	BLOOTER
	HOUT, HOUT(S)-TOUT(S)	kill in fit of passion	CHAUD-MELLE
lamentation	O(C)HONE	kilt	FILABEG, FIL(L)IBEG
surprise	HECH		PHIL(L)ABEG, PHIL(L)IBEG
interpose	INTERPONE	kind	ROUTHIE
intestine	THAIRM	kindle	LUNT
intimate	CHIEF, PACK, TOSH	kindly	COUTHIE
—friend	FAR BEN	kine	KY(E)
intractable	KITTLE	King's evil	CRUEL(L)S, CREWELS
intricate	TIRLIE-WIRLIE	kiss	PREE
invest with heritable		kitchen	BUT
property	INFEFT	—boy	GALOPIN
inwards	INBY(E)	—garden	KAILYARD
Irish stew	STOVIES	(Islands)	PLANTIE-CRUIVE
iron	AIRN	knave	JOCK
—mould	IRON-MAIL	knick-knack	WHIGMALEERIE
irregular Highland troops	WATCH		WHIGMALERY
island	INCH	knife	GULLEY
issue	ISH	knob of hair	TOORIE
it does not matter	IT MAKSNA	knock	CA, CLOUR, DAUD, DAWD
jabber	YAB, YATTER	—at door	CHAP
Jack	JOCK	—down	DING DOUN
jackdaw	KA(E)	—off work	LOWZE
jade	LIMMER	knocked off work	LOWSIT
jaded	DISJASKIT	knotty	NIRLIE, NIRLY
jam sandwich	JEELY PIECE	know	KEN
jape	BEGUNK	—not	KENNO
jaw	CHAFT	knowing	CANNY
jelly	JEELY	—look	GLEDGE
jest	BA(U)R, BAWR	lace	PEARLIN(G)
Jew's harp	TRUMP	lack of spirit	FOZINESS
jog	DUNCH, DUNSH, HOD, HOTCH	lacking freshness	FOZY
—along	WHIG	lad	CALLANT
join	OOP, OUP	ladder to loft	TRAP
joint-heiress	HEIR-PORTIONER	laid aside in store	PAST
joint on hind leg	HOUGH	lake	LOCH
jollification	SPLORE	—dwelling	CRANNOG
jolly	GAUCIE, GAUCY, GAWCY	lament	GLEET
	GAWSY	lamp	CRU(I)SIE, CRUSY
jolt	HOTTER	—lighter	LEERIE
jostle with shoulder	HOG-SHOUTHER	land	(Y)EARD, YERD, YIRD
journey in wheeled vehicle	HURL	—holder	F(E)UAR
joust	GIOUST	—owner	LAIRD
judge	DECERN	—paying feu-duty	
—of Court of Sessions	LAW-LORD	(Islands)	URE
judge's		—tenure	RUNDALE, RUNRIG
—decree	INTERLOCUTION	landed proprietor	LAIRD

landholder liable to public burdens	HERITOR	lease	SET, TACK
landmark	MEITH	leased tenement	TACK
lane	LOAN(ING), VENNEL, WYND	ledge	SCARCEMENT
language	GADHELIC, GAELIC	left	
	LALLANS, SCOTS	—handed	FISTY
languid	DWAMY	—over	ORRA
lank	SCRANKY	—thumbhole in bagpipe	BACK-LILL
lantern	BOWAT, BOWET, BUAT	legal	
lap-dog	MESSAN	—practitioner	WRITER
lapwing	PEASEWEEP, PEESWEEP	—restriction	BURDEN
	PEEWEE, TEUCHAT	—usage	PRACTIC
large		lengthwise	ENDLANG
—beetle	CLOCKER	lessee	TACKSMAN
—cravat	O'ERLAY	let	LITTEN, LOOT(EN)
—draught	WAUCHT, WAUGHT		LUIT(EN), LUTTEN
—hook	CLEEK	letters in the sovereign's name requiring payment	LETTERS OF HORNING
last		levity	GLAIKITNESS
—clause of deed	TESTING CLAUSE	levy	STENT
—day of year	HOGMANAY	liar	LEEAR
—night	YESTREEN	liberty of going out	ISH
—of		licensed beggar	BEAD(S)MAN
cow's milk	JIBBINGS		BEDE(S)MAN
family	BIRD-ALANE	lichen (dye)	CORKIR, KORKIR
	BURD-ALANE	lick	SLAKE
—three days of March	BORROWING-DAYS	lie	LEE, WHID, YANKER
latch	SNECK	lief is me	LEEZE ME
latched	SNECKED	lien on goods for debt	HYPOTHEC
late	UMQUHILE	lifeless	CAULD-RIFE
later	SYNE	lift	HEEZE, HEEZIE
Latin prose	VERSION	light	LICHT
latter end	HINDER-END	—and soft	FUFFY
laugh	LAUCH	limb	SPALL, SPAUL, SPA(U)LD
laughed	LEUCH(EN), LEUGH(EN)	limp	HILCH
laughing-stock	OUTSPECKLE	limping gait	HIRPLE
lawsuit	PLEA	line	LING
lawyer's clerk	SERVITOR	linen	LIARN
lay		linger	TAIGLE
—blame on	WITE, WYTE	linnet	LINTIE, LINTWHITE
—eggs in out-of-the-way places	LAY AWAY	liquor	SKINK
—out (corpse)	STRAUCHT, STRAUGHT	—from boiling	BROO
	STREEK, STREAK	liquorice	SUGAR-ALLIE, SUGAR-ALLY
lazy	SWEER, SWEIR	list	ROON, RUND
lead pencil	KEELIVINE, KEELYVINE	—of	
leader of mummers (Islands)	SCUDLER, SCUDDALER	candidates	LEET
	SKUDLER	court cases	SUMMAR ROLL
leaky	GIZZEN	nobles pledged to Edward I	RAGMAN ROLLS
lean and tough	RIGWIDDIE, RIGWOODIE	persons for trial	PORTEOUS ROLL
leap	LOWP	poor litigants	POOR'S-ROLL
—over	OWERLOUP	listless	THOWLESS, UPSITTING
leaped/leapt	LAP, LOUPEN		WAFF
	LOUPIT, LUPPEN	listlessness	UPSITTING
leaping-pole	KENT	little	
learning	LEAR(E), LEIR, LERE	—amount	CURN

—auk	DOVEKIE	—born person	GUTTERBLOOD
—bit	BITTOCK, KENNING	—lying (land)	LAIGH
—drop	DRAPPIE, DRAPPY	—lying meadow	INCH
—finger	PINKIE, PINKY	—price	WANWORTH
—hat	HATTOCK	—spirited	DOWIE
—lamb	LAMBIE	lowering	GURLY
—star	STARNIE	lowland	LALLAN, LAWLAND
—way over	O(W)ERBY	luck	SONCE, SONSE
live on alms	THIG	—bringing	SONSIE, SONSY
lively	CANT(Y), CROUSE, VIVE	lucky	CANNY, SONCIE, SONCY
livid	BLAE		SONSIE, SONSY
load	LADE, LAID	lumbering thing	CLATCH
loaf made in pan	PAN-LOAF	lump	CLA(U)T, NIRL, SLUMP
loan	LEN(D)	—sum paid on lease	GRASSUM
loathing	SCUNNER	lumpsucker	PADDLE, PA(I)DLE
loathly	LAIDLY	—female	HEN-PAIDLE
local jurisprudence	BOURLAW, BYRLAW	—male	COCK-PAIDLE
lock of hair	TAIT, TATE	lunch	DISJUNE, TIFT
lodging and entertainment	UP-PUTTING	lurch	STOIT
loft	ROOST	lurk	SNOWK
—ladder	TRAP	lurking with	
lofty	BRENT	treacherous purpose	FELL-LURKING
log transporter	JANKER	lusty	FRACK, SKELPING
loin	LUNGIE, LUNYIE	mad	DOILED, DOILT, GYTE
loiter	TAIGLE		WOWF, WUD
lone	LANE	magician	WARLOCK
long	DEE, GREEN, GREIN, LANG	magistrate	BAIL(L)IE
—ago	(AULD) LANG SYNE	magpie	PIET, PYAT, PYET, PYOT
—drawn out	DREICH	maid-servant	LASS
—for	WEARY	maintain persistently	THREAP, THREEP
—frost	STORM	maintained persistently	THREAPIT
—handled spade	PATTLE, PETTLE		THREEPIT
—since	LANG SYNE	make	MA(C)K, MAIK
look cunningly	GLEDGE	—a	
looking-glass	KEEKING-GLASS	grating sound	RISP
loose	LOWZE	groove in masonry	RAGGLE
—heap	RICKLE	hoarse sound	ROOP
—young woman	GILLET, JILLET	long-drawn-out cry	WHEEPLE
loosed	LOWSIT	low sound	CHIRL
lord	LOSH	scratchy sound	SCRAICH, SCRAIGH
lore	LAIR	squawk	SCRAUCH, SCRAUGH
lose	TINE, TYNE	—afraid	FRICHT
—courage or resolution	HEN	—faces at	MURGEON
loss	TINSEL	—known	KITHE, KYTHE
—(of sheep)	TRAIK	—one's way quietly	SLIP ONE'S WAYS
lost	AMISSING, TINT	—over to another	DISPONE
lot	CAVEL, KAVEL, WEIRD	—palatable	KITCHEN
loth	LAITH, SWEER(ED)	—ready	GRAITH
	SWEERT, SWEIR(T)	—tidy	RED(D)
loud rattling	REEL	—to last	KITCHEN
lounge	DA(C)KER, DAIKER	—trial of	PREE
lout	COOF, CUIF, GOMERIL, KEELIE	—void	IRRITATE
love	LEAR(E), LEIR, LERE	maker	WRIGHT
	LO'E, LOO	male sheep	DINMONT
lover	LAD	man	CHIEL(D), MAN-BODY
low	LAW		MON

—covered in seaweed (Orkney)	TANGIE	meatless broth	MUSLIN-KALE
man's skirt	KILT	meeting-point in front of mansion	COVIN-TREE
manifestation of loathing	SCUNNER	mentally weak	FACILE
manner of doing	GATE	merry	VOGIE
many	MONY	messenger	SEND
mar	MIS(H)GUGGLE	—returning late or not at all	CORBIE-MESSENGER
marble	BOWL	metal knitting-needle	WIRE
mare	YAUD	mettle	SMEDDUM
mark with ruddle	KEEL	mettlesome	METTLE
market	MERCAT	—person	SPUNKIE
—for hiring farm-servants	FEEING-MARKET	mickle	MUCKLE
—place	TRON(E)	midday dram or nap	MEDRIDAN
marriage settlement	DOWN-SITTING	midwife	HOWDIE, HOWDY
marry	WAD		WISE WOMAN
marshal	MARISCHAL	mighty	FELL
Martinmas	REMOVAL TERM	mild explosion	PLUFF
masonry groove	RAGGLE	milk	
master	MAISTER	—can	PITCHER
—of company	DEACON	—cheese	CROWDIE
mat	TAUT, TAWT	—closely	JIB
matted	TATTY, TAUTIT, TAWTIE	—strainer	MILSEY
—wool	KET	milking-pail	LEGLAN, LEGLEN
matter	MAKE		LEGLIN, SKEEL
May 28th	REMOVAL TERM	mill	
meal	MELTITH	—district	SUCKEN
—and water mixed	DRAMMACH	—race or tail-race	MILLDAM
	DRUMMOCK	—servant's quantity of meal	LOCK
	DRUMMOCK, WATER-BROSE	—stream	LADE
—chest	GIRNEL	miller	MULLER
—time	MELTITH	minced meat	MINCED COLLOPS
sponger	SCAMBLER	mine own	MINE AIN
means of		minimum (of vision)	STIME, STYME
—compelling	COMPULSITOR	minister	PRESBYTER
—ignition	LUNT	minister's house	MANSE
measures		mire	GLAUR, LAIR, LATCH
—37 inches	ELL	mirror	KEEKING-GLASS
—1976 yards	MILE	mischievous	ILL-DEEDY, SCATHY
—6150 sq. yds (old)	ACRE	—boy	NICKUM
—variable land area	PLOUGHGATE	—girl/woman	CUTTY
—¼ pint (Scottish)	MUTCHKIN	—trick	PLISKIE, PLISKY
—³/₄ pint (imperial)	MUTCHKIN	miser	SCRUNT
—1 quart	CHOPIN	miserly	GARE, HOODOCK
—3 pints	(SCOTTISH) PINT	misfortune	MIS(C)HANTER
—½ gallon	LIPPIE, LIPPY	mishap	MIS(C)HANTER
—¼ peck	LIPPIE, LIPPY	missing	AWANTING
—1 bushel	FOU	mistaught	MISLEARED
—¼ boll	FIRLOT	mistress of house	HERSELF
—2-6 bushels	BOLL	mitigate	MEASE
—16 bolls	CHALDER	mixed	
—40 bottles of hay or straw	KEMPLE	—confusedly	THROUGH-OTHER
meat		—grain	MASHLIN, MASHLOCH
—pie	BRIDIE		MASHLUM, MASHLAM
—plate	ASHET		MASHLIM
—turnover	BRIDIE		

mixture of foods	POWSOWDIE
	POWSOWDY
mobbing of curates	RABBLING
mock with grimaces	MURGEON
mocking deception	GLAIK
moisten	SLO(C)KEN
mole	MOUDI(E)WART
	MOUDI(E)WORT
	MODIWORT, MOULDWARP
moment	GLIFF(ING), GLIFT
monastic territory	ABTHANE
money	SILLER
—box	PENNY-PIG
—to be paid by vassal	REDDENDO
mongrel	MESSIN
monkey	PUGGY
mood	FID
moor	MUIR
moorland pool	FLOW
morass	FLOW
more	MAE
morning	FORENOON
mortgage	HERITABLE SECURITY
	WADSET(T)
mortgagee	WADSETTER
moss	FOG
mostly	FECKLY
mother-in-law	GUDE-MOTHER
mouldy	MOOL, MOUL
mountain over 3000ft	MUNRO
mounting-stone	LOUPING-ON-STANE
mouth	GAM, MOU
—music	PORT A BEUL
move	STEER
—along briskly	SKELP
—around or to activity	STEER
—nimbly	LINK
—quickly	WHID, WHIRRY
—slowly	WEAR
—with whizzing sound	WHEESHT
much	MUCKLE
mud	DUBS, GUTTERS
muddle	FANKLE
muddled	MOIDERT, TA(I)VERT
muddy	DRUMLY, SLASHY
mule	MUIL
multitude	HIRSEL
multure	MOUTER
murmur like a dove	CROODLE
musical instrument	BAGPIPES
	STOCK-AND-HORN
	THAIRM
musk	M(O)UST, MUIST
must	MAUN
—not	MAUNNA
mutter	WHITTIE-WHATTIE

mutton from sheep that died	
from disease or accident	TRAIK
nag	YAFF
named	HECHT
nap	OOZE
napkin round infant's hips	HIPPING
narrow	
—alley	WYND
—strait	KYLE
national	
—emblem	THISTLE
—Orchestra	SNO
—Party	SNP
native of the town	TOWN'S BAIRN
natural death in bed	STRAE-DEATH
nauseate	SCOMFISH, SCUNNER
ne'er-do-well	SKELLUM
near	EWEST, INBY(E)
—the	
farmhouse	INTOWN
house	INBY(E)
nearly	FECKLY, NEAR-HAND
neat	DINK, DONSIE, GENTY
	JIMP(Y), NOUT, SNOD, TOSH
necessity	MISTER
neck	CRAIG, HAUSE, HAWSE
—ring	JOUGS
need	MISTER
neglect	MISLIPPEN
neglected	WAIF
neigh	NICHER, NICKER
neither one thing	
nor the other	NEITHER HUP NOR WIND
nest of bees/wasps	BIKE, BYKE
nevertheless	STILL AND ON
new	
—ale	SWATS
—pupil in Edinburgh	GAIT, GEIT, GYTE
news	SPEERINGS, SPEIRINGS
New Year gift	NE'ERDAY
New Year's Day	NE'ERDAY
next	STANCHEL, SYNE
nibble	MOOP
nicety	PERJINKITY
nickname for Scotsman	SAWN(E)Y
niggard	CARL, SCRUNT
niggardly	NEAR-(BE)GAUN
	NIRLIE, NIRLY
nightcap	KILMARNOCK COWL, PIRNIE
nightdress	WYLIE-COAT
nimble	SWACK, YA(U)LD
no	NA(E)
—laughing matter	NAE MOWS
nobody	NAEBODY
noddle	CAPERNOITIE
	CAP(P)ERNOITY

noise of frying	SKIRL-IN-THE-PAN	odour	WAFF
noisy	ROARIE, ROARY	of good omen	CANNY
—frolic	GALRAVAGE, GALRAVITCH	offer	BODE, PROPINE, SHORE
	GIL(L)RAVAGE	—and acceptance	MISSIVES
	GIL(L)RAVITCH, RANT	offspring	BURD
—musician	RANTER	old	AULD
—quarrel	BRULYIE, BRULZIE	—fashioned	AULD-FARAND
—wrangling	COLLIESHANGIE	—horse	AVER, YAUD
none	NAE	—man	BODACH
nonsense	CLAMJAMPHRIE	—rusty sword	SHABBLE
	CLANJAMFRAY, HAVER	—woman	CAILL(E)ACH, CAILLIACH
noonday meal	TWALHOURS		CARLINE, LUCKIE
noose	FANK	—world	AULD-WARLD
north country	NORLAN(D)	omen	FREET, FREIT
not	NA, NO	on one's feet	UPSTANDING
—akin	FRAIM, FREMD, FREMIT	once	ANCE, ENE, YINCE
—altogether absurd	NO SAE HIELANT	one	AE, ANE, YIN
—dangerous	CANNY	—in nervous state	HEN ON A HOT GIRDLE
—frosty	FRESH	—licensed to preach	PROBATIONER
—giving milk	YELD	—nominated to benefice	POSTULATE
—matched	ORRA	—of a pair	NEIGHBOUR
—of gentle birth	SEMPLE	—receiving lands	
—so bad as might be	NO SAE HIELANT	escheated to the	
—subject to feudal		Crown	DONATORY
superior (Islands)	UDAL	—roomed dwelling	SINGLE-END
—to mention	LET BE	—sent to fetch a bride	SEND
—yielding milk	EILD	—to whom feu-duty is paid	SUPERIOR
notch edges of	LIP, MUSH	—who	
nothing	NAETHING	cuts the corn left	
notice	TENT	by the reaper	STIBBLER
notorious	NOTOUR	lets go	LETTER-GAE
—rumour about minister	FAMA CLAMOSA	lifts the latch	SNECK-DRAWER
November 28th	REMOVAL TERM	presents graduates	PROMOTOR
now	PRESENTLY	submits tamely to	
nozzle	STROUP	wrong	SNOOL
nudge	DUNCH, DUNSH	talks nonsense	BLETHER(AN)SKATE
number	FECK	onion	FOUAT, FOUET, INGAN
O yes	OU AY	only	ANERLY
oak	AIK	onset of disease	ONCOME, ONFALL
oat	AIT	onslaught	ONFALL
—cake	BANNOCK, FARLE	onward rush	RACE
—meal	GRITS	ooze	GLEET
dish	BROWSE, CROWDIE	open	
	FLUMMERY, SOWANS, SOWANS	—stitching	OPEN-STEEK
object of		—weather	FRESH
—loathing	SCUNNER	opponent of Protester	REMONSTRANT
—scorn	GECK	opportune time	SEIL
obligation to		opportunity of reading	READ
entertain (Islands)	WATTLE	opposite to	FORNENT
observant	TENTIE	ordinary	ORDINAR
obstinate	DOUR, THRAWART	—plain bread	LOAF-BREAD
obtrude oneself	SORN	organ	KIST O' WHISTLES
occasional	DAIMEN, ORRA	ornament	MENSE
odd	ORRA	other than heritable	MOVABLE
—job man	ORRA-MAN	ounce	UNCE
—looking	ODD-LIKE	ousting of curates	RABBLING

out of doors	OUTBY(E), THEREOUT	—of	
outdoor possessions	OUTSIGHT	carcase of beef	SEY
outlaw	BROKEN-MAN, HORN	flail	SOUPLE
—by three blasts of		—the hair	SHADE
the horn	PUT TO THE HORN	partially	HALFLIN(G)S
outside	FURTH OF	particle	CURN
—of	FURTH, OUTWITH	parting cup	DEOCH-AN-DORUIS
—stair	FORE-STAIR	partition	HALLAN
—wc	CLUDGIE	partridge	PAITRICK
outward appearance		Pasch	PACE
of promise	UPCOME	pass	HAUSE, HAWSE
outward	OUTWITH	—judgement	DECERN
oven	OON	passage	
over	O'ER, OUT-OWRE, OWER	—in salmon cruive	SLAP
	OWRE	—left between fields	
—bearing assumption	UPSETTING	of corn	LOAN(ING)
—flow	REAM	Passover	PACE
—hanging bank	HAG(G)	pasture (for one cow)	SOUM, SOWM
—heat	SCOUTHER, SCOWDER	pasty thing	CLATCH
—look	MISLIPPEN	pat	CLAP
—plus	O'ERCOME	path	GATE
—precise	PRICK-ME-DAINTY	patron	STOOP, STOUP
—turn	COUP, COWP	—saint	ANDREW
own	AIN, NAIN	paunch	KITE, KYTE
—self	NAINSEL(L)	pavement	PLAINSTANES
owner of estate	HERSELF	pawky	CANNY
owner's mark	BUIST	pawn	WADSET(T)
ox-eye daisy	(HORSE-)GOWAN	pay penalty	PAY THE CAIN
oxen	OWSEN	payment	MAIL
pact	PACTION	—in goods	TROCK, TROKE
pad	SUNK	—to miller by those	
paddling	PLOTTER, PLOUTER	compelled to have	
	PLOWTER	grain ground	INTOWN MULTURE
paddock	PARK	peaceable	DOUCE
pains	FASH	peacock	PAWN, POW(I)N
pair of scales	WEIGH-BANKS	peasant	BLUEBONNET, COTTAR
pale	WHITELY		COTTER
—blaes	CA(L)M, CAUM	peat	VAG
palm of hand	LOOF	—hole	HAG(G)
paltry	WAESOME, WAFF	—spade (Islands)	TUSKAR, TUSKER
pamper	CUITER		TWISCAR
panel	BOX	peaty soil (Islands)	YARFA, YARPHA
pang	STOUND, STOWND, THRAW	pedlar	PEDDER, PETHER, YAGGER
pant	FLACK, FLAFF, PECH, PEGH	peep	COOK, KEEK, KOOK, PEEK
pantry	AWMRIE, AWMRY	peewit	PEASEWEEP, PEESWEEP
parched grain	GRADDAN		PEEWEE, TEUCHAT
pare	FLAUGHT	peg-top	PEERIE
paring of turf	FLAUGHTER	pellicle of ice	GREW, GRUE
parish	PARISCHAN(E), PARISHEN	pen	CRU(I)VE
	PAROCHIN(E)	penalty	UNLAW
—minister	MAS(S)-JOHN	—drink	KELTIE, KELTY
	MES(S)-JOHN	pendant	POFFLE
park	PAIRK	pendicle	POFFLE
parlour	SPENCE	penny (sterling)	TWALPENNY
paroxysm	THRAW	peppermint sweet	PAN-DROP
part	TWIN(E)	perhaps	A(I)BLINS, YIBBLES

periodical gathering to check weaponry	WAP(P)ENS(C)HAW
	WAPINS(C)HAW
	WEAPON-S(C)HAW
pernickety person	FIKE, FYKE
peroration	PIRLICUE, PURLICUE
perplex	FICKLE
persevere	STICK IN
person	WYE
—first nominated as heir	INSTITUTE
—in disguise	GUISARD, GUISER
—sued or accused	DEFENDER
pert	CROUSE
—chatterer	GABNASH, NASHGAB
—girl	YIP
pertaining to	
—a sucken	INSUCKEN
—will	TESTAMENTAR
perverse	CAMSTAIRY, CAMSTEARY
	CAMSTEERIE, DONSIE
	THRAWN
pet	DAUT(IE), DAWT(IE)
	MAKE OF, PETTLE, TOUT, TOWT
petticoat	WYLIE-COAT
pettish	DORTY
petty possessions	SPREAGHERY, SPRECHERY
petulant	TOUTIE
pick	WALE
Pict	PECH(T), PEGH(T)
philosopher	HUME
piece of	
—news	UNCO
—property	SUBJECT
—slate	SCLATE-STANE
pierce	SLAP, STEEK
pigswill	BROCK
pile up	BIG
pilfering	PICKERY
pillory	JOUGS
pillow	COD
pimple	PLOOK
pin	PREEN
—of door-latch	TIRLING-PIN
pinch	CHACK, POOK, POUK
	TATE, TAIT
—of snuff	SNEESH(AN), SNEESHIN(G)
—with cold	NIRL
pinched	POOKIT, POUKIT
pink	CLOW-GILLIEFLOWER
pinnacle	PINNET
pipe-clay	CA(LM), CAUM
pit in a bog	MOSS-HAG(G)
pitch-dark	PIT-MIRK
pithless	THOWLESS
pitiful	WAEFU(L), WAESOME

place	
—for milking cows	LOAN(ING)
—of punishment	TRON(E)
plaid	MAUD
plain needlework	WHITE-SEAM
plaintiff	PURSUER
plant	
—refuse	ROSS
—temporarily	SHEUCH, SHEUGH
plantation	PLANTING
plaster	CLATCH, PLAISTER
plate-rack	BINK
play	
—fool	DAFF
—marbles	BOWL
—truant	KIP
playing card	CARTE
pleaded	PLED
pleasure-grounds round mansion	POLICY
pledge	WAD
—in drinking	PROPINE
plentiful	FOUTH, FOWTH, ROUTH
	ROWTH
plenty	SCOUTH, SCOWTH
	STOUTH AND ROUTH
pliant	SWACK, SWANK
plight	PLISKIE
plough	PLEUCH, PLEUGH
—cleaning tool	PATTLE, PETTLE
—up	RIVE
pluck	POOK, POUK
plucked	POOKIT, POUKIT
plug (of tobacco)	DOTTLE
plump	BONNIE, BONNY, SONCIE
	SONCY, SONSIE, SONSY
plunder	HERSHIP, REAVE, REIVE
	SPREAGH(ERY), SPRECHERY
	SPU(I)LZIE, SPULY(I)E
ply with drink	BIRL(E)
pochard	SCAUP-DUCK
pocket in end of plaid	PLAID-NEUK
poet	MAKAR
pointed hill	KIP(P)
poke	POCK, POWTER
pole	CABER, KENT
poll	POW
pollack	LYTHE
polled cow	HUMLIE
pollute	FILE
pond	LOCHAN, POUND
pool	STANK
—of foul water	DUB
—or hole in bog	HAG(G)
poor	PUIR, SOBER
—thin beer	SWANK(E)Y

popgun	BOURTREE-GUN
—made of quill	PEN-GUN
population thirled	
to mill	SUCKEN
porpoise	PELLACH, PELLACK
	PELLOCK
porridge	BROCHAN, CROWDIE
	PARRITCH
—stick	SPURTLE
portly	GAUCIE, GAUCY, GAWCY
	GAWSY
portmanteau	POCKMANKY, POCKMANTIE
possession	SASINE
post	STELL
posthumous stipend	ANN, ANNAT
potato	TATTIE
—fork	GRAIP
—haulms	TATTIE-SHAW
—soup	TATTIE-CLAW
potatoes served in	
their jackets	PEEL-AND-EAT
potsherd	PIG
potter	DA(C)KER, DAIDLE, DAIKER
	PLOTTER, PLOUTER, PLOWTER
pouch	SPORRAN
poult	POOT, POUT
pour	TOUT, TOWT
—out	BIRL(E)
—unsteadily	JIRBLE
powder	M(O)UST, MUIST, POUTHER
—puff	PLUFF
power of pump-suction	FANG
powerlessness	DOWNA-DO
praise	ROOSE
prattle	GABNASH, NASHGAB
precentor	LETTER-GAE
precise	PRECEESE
precocious	AULD-FARAND
prejudice	SCUNNER
preliminary examination	
of witnesses	PRECOGNITION
premature birth of lamb	KEB
premium	GRASSUM
prepare	BOUN
Presbyterian	WHIGGAMORE
—transgressor	DIKE-LOUPER
present	PROPINE
presently	ENOW
preserve	HAIN
president	PR(A)ESES
presiding bishop	PRIMUS
press eagerly	THREAP, THREEP
pressed eagerly	THREAPIT, THREEPIT
presumption	UPSETTING
pretentious display	PARAF(F)LE
preternatural	NO'CANNY

pretext	OFFCOME
pretty	BONNIE, BONNY
prey	SPREAGH
price of grain	FIARS
prick	BROG, JAG
priest with no parish	STICKIT MINISTER
prim	MIM(-MOU'D)
	PERJINK(ETY)
	PREJINK, PRIMSIE
private agreement among	
creditors	SUPERSEDERE
proceedings in criminal libel	DIET
proclaim banns	CRY
procure	SORT
prodigality	WAST(E)RY
progeny	BURD
projection of building	OUTSHOT
promise	HECHT
promontory	MULL
prompt	FRACK
promptly	BELIVE
proof	PRIEF(E)
prop	RANCE
propel	CA
property	
—given as dowry	TOCHER-GOOD
—which may be bequeathed	DEAD-PART
proportion of sheep	
or cattle suitable	
for pasture	SOUM, SOWM
propose	PROPONE
propound	PROPONE
propriety	MENSE
prosecute	PURSUE
prosecuting solicitor	CROWN AGENT
prosecutor	(PROCURATOR-)FISCAL
prosperous	WELL-TO-LIVE
protection	BEELD, BIELD
Protestor	REMONSTRANT
prove	PREE, PRIEF(E)
proved/proven	PREE
provide	PLENISH, SORT
provision	STOUTH(E)RIE
prowl about	SNOWK
pshaw!	OCH
public	
—knowledge	HABIT AND REPUTE
—notice	PROGRAMME
—weighing-machine	TRON(E)
puddle	DUB
puff	FLAFF, FUFF, PLUFF, SKIFF
puffed up	PLUFFY
puffin	TAMMIE NORIE
puffy	PLUFFY
pull roughly	RUG
punch	KNEVELL, NEVEL

pungency	NIPPING
pungent	FELL
punt(ing pole)	KENT
purblind person	STIMIE, STIMY, STYMIE
purport	FECK
purpose	ETTLE, MINT
purse	SPLEUCHAN
purslane	PURPIE, PURPY
pursuer's reply	TRIPLY
put	PAT, PIT, PITTEN, PUTTEN
—before a court	PROPONE
—forward	PROPONE
—in order	RED(D)
—into goal	HAIL
—out	MISTRYSTED, SMORE
of humour	MISSET
of shape	SHAUCHLE
—to	
flight	FLEME
rights	SORT
puzzle	FICKLE, KITTLE
—game	GLAIK
quaint	AULD-FARAND
quantity of liquid	JABBLE
quarrel	CAST OUT, OUTCAST
	WAP, WHID
quarry-face	HEUCH, HEUGH
quarter	AIRT
—days	BELTANE, CANDLEMAS
	HALLOWMAS, LAMMAS
—evil	SPAULD-ILL
—of round cake of	
flour or oatmeal	FARL(E)FARTHEL
queer	FIFISH
—person	SKITE, SKYTE
quench	SLO(C)KEN
quick turn	JINK
quickly	BELIVE
quiet	LOUN(D), LOWN(D), SACKLESS
quite	REAL
—alone	LEE(SOME)-LANE
quiver	DIRL, TIRL
quoth	CO, QUO
rabbit's tail	FUD
rabble	CLAMJAMPHRIE
	CLANJAMFRAY
race at wedding	BROOSE, BROUZE
rail	SPAR
rain suddenly	PLUMP
rainy	SODDEN
—blast	BLATTER
raise a bump	CLOUR
rake	CLA(U)T
rampage	RAMPAUGE
ramshackle structure	
or collection	RICKLE

randy	RUDAS
range	
—of cattle pasture	GANG
—over	SCUR, SKER, SKIRR
	SQUIRR
ransack	RIPE
rap	YANKER
rapid noiseless movement	WHID
rascal	SMAIK
rasp	RISP
rather	GAY, GEY, LOOR
ratification of executor	CONFIRMATION
rattle	TIRL
—in throat	RUCKLE
raucous squawk	SCRAUCH, SCRAUGH
rave	TA(I)VER
ravine	CLEUCH, CLOUGH, HEUCH
	HEUGH
raw (weather)	WERSH
—hide shoe	RULLION
ray	STIME, STYME
reach	RAX, RYKE
—out	RAX
real property	HERITABLE PROPERTY
really	REAL
reap with sickle	SHEAR
reaping contest	KEMP
rear premises	BACKSIDE
rebound	STOT(TER)
rebuke	THREAP, THREEP
rebuked	THREAPIT, THREEPIT
receive knowing to	
be stolen	RESET
receptacle	LOOM
recess	BOLE
—in wall of room	OUTSHOT
reckless	RAMSTAM
reclaimed wastelands	NOVALIA
Records Office	REGISTER HOUSE
recover	OVERCAST
red	
—currant	RIZZAR(D), RIZZART, RIZZER
—ochre	KEEL
rede	RED(D)
redeem	LOWZE
redeemed	LOWSIT
reel	PIRN
refrain	O'ERWORD
refusal	NAE, REEST, REIST
refuse	RED(D)
—to	
move (horse)	REEST, REIST
recognise	MISKEN
refute	REDARGUE
rehabilitate	REPONE
reign	RING

reinstatement	REPOSITION
relapse	WEED, WEID
related by common descent	SIB
relating to Argyll	ARGATHELIAN
relative	FRIEND
—on mother's side	COGNATE
release	EXEEM, EXEME
—from outlawry	RELAXATION
religion	PRESBYTERIANISM
relish	SA(I)R
reluct	TARROW
reluctant	SWEER, SWEIR
rely	LIPPEN
remainder	LAVE
remarkable (thing)	UNCO
remarkably	UNCO
remedy	REMEAD, REMEDE, REMEID
remember	MIND
remind	MIND
rendering void	IRRITANT
rent	MAIL(ING)
—in	
kind	CAIN, KAIN
money	PENNY MAIL
rented farm	MAILING
repentance fine	BUTTOCK-MAIL
replication	REPLY
reply to a	
—duply	TRIPLY
—triply	QUADRUPLY
reprimand	TARGE
reproach	UPCAST
reproof	SLOAN
residence	HADDIN
resist law officer	DEFORCE
resort	HOUFF, HOWFF
resourceful	FENDY
respectable	MENSEFUL
restive	FLISKY
restless	WANRESTFUL
restlessness	FIKE, FYKE
restore to office	
or status	REPONE
restrain	COMPESCE, HEFT
resume in conclusion	PIRLICUE
	PURLICUE
retain (milk or urine)	HEFT
return	RETOUR
—of the feu	RECOGNIZANCE
revival of an action	WAKENING
Reynard	TOD-LOWRIE
rickety structure or	
collection	RICKLE
riddle	GUESS
ridge of land for oats	CORN-RIG
riding hood	TROTCOSY, TROTCOZY

right	
—opposite	FOREANENT, FORNEN(S)T
—to	
cut sods	FEAL AND DIVOT
use for life	LIFE-RENT
rigmarole	RAGMAN, RAGMENT
rigorous in morals	UNCO GUID
rill	SIKE
rim	ROON
ring	JOW
—dove	CUSHAT
ringing in	JOWING IN
rinse	SIND, SYND
riotous merrymaking	GALRAVAGE
	GALRAVITCH
	GIL(L)RAVAGE
	GIL(L)RAVITCH
rippling	JABBLE
rise	PLUFF
rived	RAVE
river	CLYDE, FORTH, TWEED
—horse	KELPIE, KELPY
	WATER-HORSE
riverside	
—meadow or flat	HAUGH
—plain	CARSE
rivulet	STRAND
road	RAID
—junction	TOLL
rob	REAVE, REIVE, RUB
robbed	RUBBET, RUBBIT, RAFT, REFT
robber	CATERAN, REAVER, REIVER
rock	JOW
rode	RADE, RAID
Rogation Days	GANG DAYS
rogue	HEMPY
roguery	JOOKERY, JOUKERY
	JOUKERY-PAWKERY
roll	ROW
—the eyes	WAUL, WAWL
rolling pace eggs	PACE-EGGING
roof	
—gutter	ROAN, R(H)ONE
—of loft or garret	ROOST
rope	TOW
rose	RA(I)SE
rosin	ROSET, ROSIT, ROZET, ROZIT
rough	GURLY, RAMGUNSHOCH
	RAUCLE
—justice	JEDDART
roughcast	HARL
roughened bar	RISP
round	
—flat stone	PENNY-STANE
—hillock	KNOWE
rounded hill-top	DOD

rouse	FIRK, STEER
routine	HEICH-HOW
row	SPLORE
rowan	RODDIN
royal steward	MAORMAR
rubbish	BROCK, CLAMJAMPHRIE
	RED(D), TROCK, TROKE
	CLANJAMFRAY
—tip	TOOM
ruddle	KEEL
rude	GOUSTROUS
Rugby Union	SRU
ruined place	WASTAGE
rummage	POWTER
rump	RUMPLE
run	RACE, RIN, SCOUP
—as if lame	HIRPLE
—jauntily	LAMP
—wild	LAMP
runaway	FUGIE, LOUP-THE-DYKE
rush	RASH, THRESH
rustle	FISSLE
rusty sword	SHABBLE
sackless	SAIKLESS
sad	DOWIE
sadness	WAENESS
safe	AWMRIE, AWMRY
sagacious	AULD-FARAND
sailor	TARRY-BREEKS
saint	SAUNT
sale by auction	ROUP
salmon-curing house	CORF-HOUSE
salmon spear	LEISTER, WASTER
salt	SAUT
salutation	BECK
salute by raising hat	HAT
salve	SAW
same	AE, SAMEN
sample	SWATCH
sand-lark	SANDY-LAVEROCK
sandstone	KINGLE
sated	STAWED
satisfy	SAIR
saucepan	GOBLET, KAIL-PAT
saucy	NEBBY
saunter	DA(C)KER, DAIKER
	DA(U)NDAR, DAUNER, DAWNER
save	HAIN
savour	SAIR
savoury	GUSTY
Saxon	SASSENACH
say	
—be quiet!	WHEESHT
—nothing of	LET BE
scald	SCAUD
—and pluck	PLOT

scales	WEIGHT
scallop edges	MUSH
scalp	SCAUP
scamp	SKELLUM
scamper	LAMP, SCAUP, SCOUP, SCOWP
scant	JIMP(Y), JINTY
scare	GLIFF, GLIFT, SCAR(RE), SCAUR
scarecrow	TATTIE-BOGLE
scatter	SCALE, SCAIL, SKAIL
scavenger	SCAFFIE
scholarship	BURSARY
school fight	BICKER
schoolmaster	DOMINIE
scold	FLITE, FLYTE, RAGE, YAFF
scolding	DIRDUM, DURDUM
	THROUGH-GAUN
	KAILWIFE, SCAUD
—match	FLYTE, FLYTING
scold's bridle	BRANKS
scope	SCOUTH, SCOWTH
—of choice	WALE
scorch	BIRSLE, SCOUTHER, SCOWDER
score	RIT(T)
—(goal)	HAIL
scorn	GECK, SCOUTHER
scour	SCUR, SKER, SKIRR, SQUIRR
scowl	GLOOM
scramble	SPRATTLE
scrap	GLIM
scrape	SCART, SNAPPER, SPLORE
scraping of anything	HARL
scratch	CLA(U)T, RIT(T), SCART
screech	SCRAICH, SCRAIGH, SCREICH
	SCREIGH, SKRIECH, SKREIGH
screen between door	
and fireplace	HALLAN
scrofula	CRUEL(L)S, CREWELS
scrubby wood	SCRODG
scruff	CUFF
scuff	CUFF
scuffle	TUILYE, TUILZIE
sea basin or sound	FLOW
seahorse (Orkney)	TANGIE
seal	SEALCH, SEALGH, SELKIE
	SILKIE, SILKY
search	RIPE, SCUR, SKER
	SKIRR, SQUIRR
—for stolen goods	
(Islands)	RANCEL, RANZEL
searching of gutters	STRAND-SCOURING
season	SEIL
seaweed	WARE
second	
—reply in law case	DUPLY
—sight	TAIS(C)H
—year student	SEMI-BAJAN

secrecy	HIDLING(S), HIDLINS	—shelter	SHEAL(ING)
secret	HIDLING(S), HIDLINS		SHEIL(ING), STELL
—hoard	POSE	shelf	BINK
sect (extinct)	BEREAN	shellfish	BUCKIE
security	CAUTION, WAD	shelter	BEELD, BIELD, SCO(O)G
—on goods in respect			SCOUG, SHEAL(ING)
of a debt	HYPOTHEC		SHIEL(ING)
sedate	DOUCE	sheltered	LOUN(D), LOWN(D)
seed-time (Islands)	VOAR	shepherd's	
seek	SIK	—crook	KEBBIE
seer	SPAEMAN, SPAER	—own sheep	PACK
	SPAEWIFE	—plaid	MAUD
seethe	BULLER	sheriff	SHIRRA
seisin	SASINE	sheriff's messenger	SHELLYCOAT
select list of candidates	SHORT-LEET	shilling	TWALPENNY
selection of verse	BLA(U)D	shilly-shally	WHITTIE-WHATTIE
self	SEL(L)	shin-bone soup	SKINK
selvage	ROON, RUND	shine	SHEEN, SKYRE
sensible	WISE-LIKE	shinty-stick	CAMAN
sensitive	KITTLY	ship	LYMPHAD
sentence of outlawry	FUGITATION	shirt	SARK
sentimental story		shiver	CHITTER, GREW, GRUE
writers	KAILYARD SCHOOL	shock	STOUND, STOWND
separate	RED(D), TWIN(E)	shoemaker	SOUTAR, SOUTER, SOWTER
separation of churches	DISRUPTION	shoemaker's thread	LINGEL, LINGLE
serve	SAIR	shoot	PLUFF
—as relish	KITCHEN	—like a pang	STOUND, STOWND
served right	CHEAP OF	shore	RANCE
service to be rendered		short	CUTTY
by a vassal	REDDENDO	—clay pipe	CUTTY
serving-dish	ASHET	—connecting-pipe	HOGGER
session	DOWN-SITTING	—distance	WEE
set	STELL	—dumpy girl	CUTTY
—in		—shift	CUTTY-SARK
motion	STEER	—time	WEE
order	SNOD	—winded	PURFLED
—off	MENSE	shot	PLUFF
—on one side	JEE	shoulder	SHOUTHER, SPALL, SPAUL
—things in order	RED(D)		SPA(U)LD, SPEAL, SPULE
—to work	YOKE	—blade	SPULEBANE
setting in order	REDDING-UP	—of hill	DOD
severe	ILL, SNELL	shovel	SHOOL
shabby	OORIE, OURIE, OWRIE	show	EFFEIR, EFFERE, SHAW
shadow	SCO(O)G, SCOUG	—perturbation	JEE ONE'S GINGER
shake	WAP		JOW ONE'S GINGER
shaky	COGGLY	shower	SCOWTHER
shallow ford	RACK	showy	BRANKY, BRAW
shamble	BAUCHLE	shred	TA(I)VER
share	RUG	shrewd	CANNY
sharp	GLEG, SNELL	shriek	SCRAICH, SCREICH, SCREIGH
shavings	RISPINGS		SKIRL, SKREICH, SKREIGH
sheaf	DORLACH		SKRIECH, SKRIEGH, SPRAICH
shed (Islands)	SKEO, SKIO	shrill cry	SKIRL(ING)
sheep		shrink	CRINE, NIRL
—disease	BRAXY, LOUPING-ILL	—from dryness	GIZZEN
—fold	FANK	shrivel	NIRL

shrivelled	GIZZEN	sledging	HURLY-HACKET
Shrove Tuesday	BROSE AND BANNOCK DAY	sleek	SNOD
	FASTE(R)N('S)-E'EN	sleepy	SLEEP(E)RY
shudder	GREW, GRUE	slender	JIMP(Y), JINTY, SWANK
shuffle	SHAUCHLE	slice of	
shut	STEEK	—beef	RUNNER
shy	BLATE, SKEIGH	—bread	SHIVE
	WILLYARD, WILLYART	slid	SLADE, SLAID
sickly	DONSIE, DWAMY, WERSH	slide	HIRSLE
—looking	SHILPIT	slight	LICHTLY
side		—attack of illness	BRASH
—by side	HEADS AND THRAWS	—fit of ill-humour	DOD
—glance	GLEDGE	—shower	SCOUTHER, SCOWDER
sieve	SILE, SYLE	—slap	SCLAFF
sift	SEARCE	—touch	SKIFF
signal	WAFF	slip	SKITE, SKYTE
silence!	WHEESHT	—in conduct	SNAPPER
silly person	DOTTLE	—suddenly	SCOOT
silver	SILLER	slipper	MUIL, PANTON
simple	AFA(W)LD, AEFA(U)LD	slippery	GLID(DERY)
	SACKLESS, SEMPLE	slit	RIT(T)
simpleton	GOMERAL, GOMERIL	slobbery mess	SLAISTER
since	SIN(E), SYN(E)	sloe	SLAE
—that time	SINSYNE	sloping-ceilinged	COOMCEILED
sing shrilly	SKIRL	sloppy	
singe	SCOUTHER, SCOWDER	—drink	SWANK(E)Y
single	AFA(W)LD, AEFA(U)LD	—thing	CLATCH
sink	JAWBOX	slops	CLATS, SLAISTERY
sinner	DIKE-LOUPER	slothful	SWEER(ED), SWEERT, SWEIR(T)
sip	SOWP, TIFT	slough in a bog	MOSS-HAG(G)
sir	STIR	sloven	HACHEL
sirloin	(BACK-)SEY	slovenly	
sirrah	STIRRA(H)	—person	WALLYDRAG, WALLYDRAIGLE
sister	TITTY	—work	SLAISTER
—in-law	GUDE-SISTER	slow	
sit	CLOCK	—match	LUNT
sitting	DOWN-SITTING	—moving stream	POW
six	SAX	sluggish stream	LANE
sketch	SKIFF	slush	LAPPER
skilful	CANNY, SKEELY	slut	CLATCH
skilled	SKEELY, SKILLY	sly	CANNY, SLEE
skim	REAM, SKIFF	—person	TOD
skimming	SKIFF	slyly	PAWKILY
skin	FLAUGHT	smacking	SKELPING
skip about	FLISK	small	PINKIE, PINKY
skittish	SKEIGH	—amount of bread	PIECE
—young woman	GILLET, JILLET	—cake	NABKET
skua (Islands)	BONXIE	—creek	POW
sky	LIFT	—cup	TASSIE
slabbery daub	SLAKE	—drawer	SHOTTLE, SHUTTLE
slake	SLO(C)KEN	—drink	SOWP
slant	SKLENT	—drop	DRAPPIE, DRAPPY
slap	CLATCH, SCUD, SKELP	—goods	TROCK, TROKE
slate	SCLATE, SKLATE	—heap	TOORIE
—pencil	CA(L)M, CAUM	—inn	CHANGE-HOUSE
slatternly woman	BESOM	—job	TROCK, TROKE

—landowner	BONNET LAIRD	somehow	SOMEGATE
—person	NYAFF, SMOUT, SMOWT	something	
—portion	KENNING, TATE, TAIT	—of slender importance	SHEEP-SHANK
—quantity	CURN, HARL, PICKLE, WHEEN	—pledged or pawned	WADSET(T)
—thing	NYAFF	somewhere	SOMEGATE
—tree	SCROG	son of	MAC
—wage	PENNY-FEE	song	SANG
—wares	TROCK, TROKE	soon	BLIVE, ENOW
smash	STRAMASH	sore	SAIR
smear	SLAKE	sorrel	SOUROCK
smell about	SNOWK	sorrow	DOOL, TEAN
smelt	SPARLING, SPIRLING	sorrowful	WAE(SOME)
smithy	SMIDDY	soul	SAUL
smoke	SMEEK, SMEIK, SMEKE	sound	FERE
	SMOOR	—of liquid from bottle	
—tobacco	LUNT	or cork drawn	CLUNK
smoky	REEKIE	sound of slap	SCLAFF
smolt	SMOUT, SMOWT	soundness	HEAL
smooth	BRENT, SLEEKIT, SNOD	soup	COCKALEEKIE, COCKIELEEKIE
—tongued	SLEEKIT		COCKILEEKY
smother	SMORE	—ladle	DIVIDER
smothered laugh	SNIRT	sour liquor	TIFT
snack	CHACK	southern	SOUTHRO(U)N
snap	CHACK, SNACK	southernwood	APPLERINGIE
—at	HANCH	sow	SAW
snare	GIRN	sowens	FLUMMERY
snarl	GIRN	space	
snatch	CLAUCHT, CLAUGHT	—before kiln fire	LOGIE
snicker	SNIRTLE	—in front of kiln	KILLOGIE
snigger	SNICHER, SNICKER	spare	HAIN
snipe	HEATHER-BLEAT(ER)	sparing (with money)	CANNY
	HEATHER-BLUITER	spark	FLAUGHT, SPUNK
	HEATHER-BLUTTER	sparrow	SPRUG
sniveller	SNOOL	spasm	THRAW
snob	SNAB	spatter	JA(U)P
snooze	DOVER	spawning-place	REDD
snub	SLOAN, SNIB, SNOOL	spear with leister	LEISTER
snuff	NABKET	specify	CONDESCEND
	SNEESH(AN), SNEESHIN(G)	specious	FAIR-FARAND
—about	SNOWK	spectacle	OUTSPECKLE
—box	MILL, MULL, SNEESHIN-MULL	spell	TACK, WEIRD
snug	COSH, COUTHIE, SNOD	spend	BIRL, MOIDER, WARE
snuggle	CROODLE	—thriftlessly	WASTER
so	SAE	spiced hot drink	PLOTTIE, PLOTTY
soap suds	SAPPLES	spider	ETHERCAP, ETTERCAP
sob	SAB	spill	SCALE, SCAIL, SKAIL
sober	DOUCE	spin	BIRL
sock	HUSHION	spinning party	ROCKING
sod	FAIL	spirit	SMEDDUM
—for roofing	DIVOT	spiritless(ness)	DOWF(NESS)
soft, sheepish fellow	SUMPH	spirituous liquor	STRUNT
softly	HOOLY	spitting of cat	FUFF
softness	FOZINESS	splash	BLASH, JABBLE, JA(U)P
soil	TASH	—of dirt or colour	SPLATCH
solely	ALLENARLY	splashing sound	CLATCH
solicitor	LAW-AGENT	splinter	FRUSH, SPALE

split and	
—dried fish	SPELD(R)IN(G)
—lay open	SPELD(ER)
splotch	SPLATCH
spoil	BAUCHLE, BLUNK
	SPUILZIE, SPULYE
spoliation	HERRIMENT, HERRYMENT
	REIF, SPU(I)LZIE, SPULY(I)E
spongy	FOZY
spool	PIRN
spoonful	SOWP
spot (of iron-mould)	MAIL
spout	STROUP
sprain	STAVE, WREST
sprat	GARVIE, GARVOCK
spread open	SPELD(ER)
spree	SKITE, SKYTE, SPLORE
spring	
—in a marsh	WELL-HEAD
—(Islands)	VOAR
—time	WARE
sprinkle	STRINKLE
—of snow	SCOUTHERING, SCOWDERING
sprout	BREER, BRERE
spruce	SPRUSH
spur-leather	SPUR-WHANG
squall	DROW
squat	SQUATTLE
squint	GLEDGE, GLEE, GLEY, SKELLY
—eyed	GLEED, GLEYED
squirt	SCOOT
stable-keeper	STABLER
stagger	DAIDLE, WINTLE
	STOITER, WINTLE
stake	STOB
stale liquor	TIFT
stallion	COOSER, CU(I)SER, STAIG
stalwart	BUIRDLY, PRETTY
stamp	STRAMP
stanchion	STANCHEL, STANCHER
standing	
—place	STANCE
—stone	HARE-STANE
star	STARN, STERN
starched cap	COCKERNONY
stark mad	RED-WOOD, RED-WUD
start with fear	STURT
state	
—of anger or displeasure	KIPPAGE
—the object	CONCLUDE
statement of case	CONDESCENDENCE
station	STANCE
stay	STAW, SIST
—as guest	GUESTAN, GUESTEN
steelyard (Islands)	BISMAR
steep	BRENT, MASK, STEY

—in hot water	PLOT
—sided valley	HEUCH, HEUGH
stew	STOVE
stewardship	STEWARTRY
stewed potatoes	STOVIES
sticky and dirty	CLARTY
stiff	STEEVE, STIEVE
—clay	TILL
stiffly	STEEVELY
stifle	SCOMFISH
still	ALWAY
stir	JEE, STEER
stirrup-cup	DEOCH-AN-DORUIS
stitch	STEEK
stock	PLENISH
—and goods in lease	STEELBOW
—farm	STORE-FORM
stocking-shaped net	HOSE-NET
stoke	TOUK
stole	STAW, STEALED, STEALT
stolen	STOWN, STEALED, STEALT
stomach	GEBBIE
stone hammer	KNAPPING-HAMMER
stood	STOODEN, STUDDEN
stool	BUFFET, SUNKIE, TREST
—of repentance	CREEPIE, CUTTY-STOOL
stop	DEVALL, DIT, SIST
storm	WAP
stout	STUFFY
straight	STRAICHT, STRAUCHT, STRAUGHT
—on	ENDLANG
—staircase	SCALE-STAIR(CASE)
strain	RAX, SEIL, SILE, SYLE
strainer	SEIL, SILE(R)
strait	KYLE
strange	FRAIM, FREMD, FREMIT, UNCO
—folk	FRAIM, FREMD, FREMIT
stranger	FRAIM, FREMD, FREMIT, UNCO
strangle	THRAPPLE
strap	TAWS(E)
straw	STRAE
stray	TRAIK, WAFF
streaked	HAWKIT
stream	BURN
streamer	PINNET
street	GATE
—fight	BICKER
—leading to water	WATER-GATE
—sweepings	POLICE-MANURE
—swindler	MAGSMAN
strength	FIZZEN, FUSHION
strenuous contest	PINGLE
stress (pronunciation)	BIRR
stretch	RAX, STRAUCHT
	STRAUGHT
strict examination	EXPISCATION

stride	
—along	LAMP
—vigorously	STEN(D)
strife	BICKER
strike	BLA(U)D, GOWF
—(clock)	CHAP
—heavily against	DUSH
striking part of flail	SUPPLE
string round leg	
below knee	NICKY-TAM
strip	JIB, TIRL, TIRR
—of thread or cloth	ROON, RUND
—off	TIRR
—worn over shoulder	PLAID
striped	PIRNIE, PIRNIT
—woollen nightcap	PIRNIE
strive	BARGAIN, PINGLE
stroke	STOUND, STOWND, STRAIK
—of	
bell	JOW
pen	SCART
—received in trying to	
separate fighters	REDDING-STRAIK
stroll	DA(U)NDER
	DAUNER, DAWNER
strolling beggar	GABERLUNZIE
strong	YA(U)LD
struck	STRA(C)K
struggle	TUILYE, TUILZIE
—with difficulties	PINGLE
strut	STRUNT
stub	STOB
stubble	STIBBLE
stubborn	RIGWIDDIE, RIGWOODIE
—insistence	THREAP, THREEP
stuck	STACK, STICKIT
stuff	CRAP, PANG, STAP
stuffed	PANG
—haddock's head	CRAPPIT-HEAD
	CRAPPIT-HEID
stumble	SNAPPER, STOIT
stump	STOB
—and rump	STOOP AND ROOP
stumpy	NIRLIE, NIRLY
stun with a blow	DEV(V)EL
stunned	DONNERD, DONNERT
stunt	NIRL
stunted	WANTHRIVEN
—bush	SCROG(-BUSS)
—child	URF
—person	NIRL
—tree	SCRUNT
stupefy	DOZEN
stupid	TA(I(VERT
—fellow	HASH
—person	CUDDIE, CUDDY

sturdy	STEEVE, STIEVE, STUFFY
—beggar	HALLAN-SHAKER
stutter	HABBLE
sty	CRU(I)VE
subdue	DANTON
subject to pangs	THRAW
submerge	TAKE
substance	FECK
substitution of one	
obligation for another	INNOVATION
subterfuge	OFF-COME
subterranean dwelling	WEEM
such	SICCAN
sudden	
—blow	SPANG, WHAMPLE
—fall of rain	PLUMP
—flame	LUNT
—illness	TOUT, TOWT, WEED, WEID
—movement	SPANG
—sickness	DWALM, DWAUM
—storm	ONCOME, ONFALL
suddenness	SUDDENTY
sue	PURSUE
—for	PLEAD
suet pudding	CLOOTIE DUMPLING
suffer pangs	THRAW
suffocate	SMORE
suit of clothes or armour	STAND
sulk	DORT
sulks	DORTS, STRUNTS
sulky	STUNKARD
sullen	DOUR, STUNKARD
—look	GLOOM
summary	SUMMAR
summer pasture	SHEALING, SHIELING
summon	SIST
sunken	LAIGH
sunrise	DEASI(U)L, DEASOIL
	DEIS(H)EAL
supernumary	ORRA
superstition	FREET, FRIET
superstitious	FREETY, FREITY
supervise strictly	TARGE
supplement	EIK
support under arm	OXTER
supporter	STOOP, STOUP
sure	SICCAR, SICKER
surety	CAUTIONER, VADIUM
surfeit	STAW
surge of liquid	JAW
surly	GURLY
surpass	DING
surplice	SARK
suspect	J(E)ALOUSE, MISLIPPEN
swaggerer	BIRKIE
swarm	BIKE, BYKE, HOTTER

swarming	HOTTER
sway	SWEE, THRAW
sweated	SWAT
sweep	SOOP
sweetheart	JO(E)
swell	HOVE
swelling	CLOUR
swig of liquor	SCOUR
swim	SOOM
swine	GRUMPHIE
swing	SWEE
swingle	SUPPLE
swipple	SOUPLE, SUPPLE
swoon	DWALM, DWAUM
sword	CLAYMORE, SPURTLE(-BLADE)
—blade	ANDREA FERRARA
ANDREW FERRARA, ANDRO FERRARA	
—rusty	SHABBLE
symbolical occupation	INFEFTMENT
system of	
—succession	TANISTRY
—weights	TRON(E)
table linen	NAPERY
tailor	PRICK-(THE-)LOUSE
take	TA(C)K
—a loathing to	SCUNNER
—copy of	EXTRACT
—heed	TENT
—no trouble in	
the matter	NEVER FASH YOUR THUMB
—pains	FASH
—trouble	FASH
—under the arm	OXTER
—up for burial	LIFT
taking of evidence by judge	PROOF
tale of fate	WEIRD
talk	
—frivolously	NYAFF
—impudently	SNASH
—nonsense	BLETHER, HAVER
talkative	GASH
talker of nonsense	BLETHER(AN)SKATE
tall hat	LUM(-HAT)
tangle	FANK(LE), TAUT, TAWT
tangled	TATTY, TAUTIT, TAWTIE
tantrum	TIRRIVEE, TIRRIVIE
tap	TOUK
tar barrel	CLAVIE
task	DARG
taste	PREE
tasteless	SAURLESS, WERSH
tattle	GASH
tavern reckoning	LAW
tax	STENT
—assessor	STENTO(U)R, STENTMASTER
(Islands)	WATTLE

tea-urn	KITCHEN
teach	LEAR(E), LEIR, LERE
tear	TIRR
tease	TEAN
tedious	DREICH, EDI(OU)SOME
television	STV
tell tales	CLIPE, CLYPE
temples	HAFFET, HAFFIT
tenant	SUCKENER
—bound by thirlage	SUCKENER
—of	
crown	THANE
same stock as landlord	
or whose family has held	
land in succession	KINDLY TENANT
tenure	FEU, HOLDING, TACK
—watching	BURGAGE
term-day (11th November)	MARTINMAS
territorial jurisdiction	REGALITY
Text Society	STS
than	BY, NOR
thank God!	BE THANKIT, BETHANKIT
thatch	THACK, THEEK
thaw	FRESH
the	
—bulk	FECK
—one	TA(N)E
—sulks	THE DODS
theft	STOUTH(E)(RIE)
—with violence	STOUTHRIEF
them	THAIM
then	SIN(E), SYN(E)
theological college	DIVINITY HALL
these	THIR
thick	
—bawling noise	GOLLAR
—witted Highlander	TEUCHTER
—woollen (Islands)	WA(AD)MAL
	WADMOL(L)
thin	SKINKING
—broth	MUSLIN-KALE
—liquor	TIFT
—porridge	WATER-BROSE
third reply in law case	TRIPLY
thistle	THRISSEL, THRISTLE
thorn	STUG
thorough-going	THROUGH-GANGING
those	THAE
thrash	TARGE
thrashing	LICKS
threaten	SHORE
—by movement	MINT
—rain or snow	SCOUTHER, SCOWDER
threatening	SHORE
—gesture	MINT
threw	THRAWN

thrifty	FENDY
thrill	DINDLE, DINNLE, DIRL
throat	CRAIG, HAUSE, HAWSE, THRAPPLE
throe	THRAW
throng	THRANG
thropple	THRAPPLE
throttle	THRAPPLE
through	YONT
—passage	TRANCE, TRANSE
throw	CLOD, THRAW
—down	DING DOUN, DUSH
—into a lump	SLUMP
thrust	STAP
—onward	STAVE
thump	DAUD, DAWD, DUNT
	LOUNDER, PAIK
thwart	THRAW
tickle	KITTLE
—trout	GUDDLE
ticklish	KITTLE
tidal race (Islands)	ROOST, SWELCHIE
tidied	REDDED
tidy up	RED(D)
tight	ANG
timber transporter	JANKER
time	STOUND, STOWND
—long past	LANG SYNE
—of	
day	SEIL
trial	HOUR OF CAUSE
trouble	STOUND, STOWND
timid	BLATE
tingle	DINDLE, DINGLE, DIRL, TIRL
tingling after a blow	DIRL
tinker	CAIRD, TINK(LER)
tiny	WEE
tip	MAG(G)S, PROPINE
—up	COUP, COWP
tired out	FORJASKIT, FORJESKIT
tiresome	DREICH
—chatter	YATTER
tirl	RISP
tithe	TEIND
titlark	MOSS-CHEEPER
to	ON, TAE
—be lost	TINE, TYNE
—debar the unworthy	
from communion	FENCE THE TABLES
toad	PADDOCK
toadstool	PADDOCK-STOOL
toast	BIRSLE
—slightly	SCOUTHER, SCOWDER
tobacco	
—pipe stem	PIPE-STAPPLE
	PIPE-STOPPLE
—pouch	SPLEUCHAN

toe	TAE
together	THEGITHER
toil	MOIDER
told	TAULD, TELD, TELL'D, TELT
toll	JOW
tomboy	GILP(E)Y
tomorrow	THE MORN
—morning	THE MORN'S MORN
—night	THE MORN'S NICHT
too	TAE
—bright	ROARIE, ROARY
tooth	GAM
top	TAP
—of chimney	LUM-HEAD
toper	SAND-BED
topsy-turvy	REEL-RALL
	TAPSALTERIE, TAPSIETEERIE
torrent of words	BLATTER
toss	BUM
—coin	BIRL
totter	HOTTER
tough	TEUCH, TEUGH
towards	ANENT
—the	
coal face	INBY(E)
interior	INBY(E)
town (burgh)	BURROWSTOWN
tractable	TAWIE
trade	TREAD
traditional	
—belief	THREAP, THREEP
—dish	HAGGIS
trample	STRAMP
tranquil	LOWN
transient experience	GLIFF, GLIFT
transmitter of	
family lore	SEANNACHIE, SEANNACHY
	SENNACHIE, SHANACHIE
trash	TRASHTRIE
tread	TRAMP
—in a tub, washing	
clothes	TRAMP
treason	PURDELLION
treat in return	ARCHILOWE
tree-trunk	CABER
tremble	HOTTER
trench	SHEUCH, SHEUGH
trews	SKILTS
trial	
—at instance of	
Lord Advocate	INDICTMENT
—without jury	PROOF
tribute	CAIN, KAIN
trick	BEGUNK, CANTRIP, GEGG
	GLAIK, PAWK, SHAVIE
	SKITE, SKYTE

trickery	JOCKERY, JOUKERY
	JOUKERY-PAWKERY
trifle	DAIDLE, PINGLE
trim	DINK, DONSIE, SNOD
	TOSH
trinket	WHIGMALEERIE
	WHIGMALERY
trip along briskly	LINK
troll for fish	HARL
—Islands	DROW, TROW
troth	TROGGS
trouble	FASH, K(I)AUGH, STURT
troublesome	BRICKLE, FASHIOUS
trouser braces	GALLUSES
trousers	BREEKS, TREWS
truce	BARLEY
truck	TROCK, TROKE
trudge	TAIGLE
truss	DORLACH
trust	LIPPEN
try to beat down price	PRIG DOWN
tub	SKEEL
tuft	TATE, TAIT
—on a bonnet	TOORIE
tug	RUG, TIT
tumult	HIRDY-GIRDY
	STRAMASH, STRAMASH
turbid	DRUMLY
turbulence in water	BULLER
turf	FAIL, FLAUGHT
—seat	SUNK
—wall	FAIL-DIKE
turkey-cock	BUBBLY-JOCK
turn	THRAW, TIRL
—down a bed	MAKE DOWN
—edge of	LIP
—to left	HIE, HIGH
—up	CAST UP
turnip	TUMPSHIE, NEEP
turnstile	TIRL
tusk	GAM
tut	OCH, TOOT(S), TUTS
tutor	DOMINIE
twelve	TWAL
—month	TOWMON(D), TOWMONT
twill	TWEEL
twirl(ed)	TIRLIE-WIRLIE
twist	THRAW, TWISTLE
twisted	THRAWN
twitch	TIT, TWIRK
two	TWA(E), TWA(Y)
—fold	TWAFALD
—roomed house	A BUT AND BEN
—some	TWASOME
—storied	TWA-LOFTED
—wheeled barrow	HURLY

—year old animal	TWINTER
—years old	TWINTER
ugly	ILL-FAURD
umpire	BYRLAWMAN, ODDSMAN
	OVERSMAN
umwhile (formerly)	UMQUHILE
unacquainted	UNACQUAINT
uncanny	ELDRITCH, WANCHANCIE
	WANCHANCY, WEIRD
uncared for	UNTENTED
uncivil	MENSELESS
uncommon	UNCO
under a liability	PASSIVE
undergo one's	
destiny	DREE ONE'S WEIRD
underground	
—dweller	PICT
—dwelling	WEEM
underlease	SUBTACK
undershirt	SEMMIT
unearthly	WEIRD
unevenly wrought	PIRNIE
unfriendly	FRAIM, FREMD, FREMIT
ungainly person	CLATCH
unheeded	UNTENTED
unite closely	WAD
unlucky	DONSIE, MISCHANCY
	UNCHANCY, WANCHANCIE
	WANCHANCY
—chance	MIS(C)HANTER
unmanageable	NEITHER HUP NOR WIND
unmannerly	MISLEARED
unmusical	TIMBER
unnecessary outcry	HUMDUDGEON
unpleasantly severe	UNCANNY
unproductive	YELD
unqualified mason	COWAN
unruly	CAMSTEARY
	CAMSTEERIE
	CAMSTAIRY
unsafe	UNCANNY
unsalted	WERSH
unstable	BRUCKLE
untilled patch to	
avert Devil's	
malice	GOODMAN'S CROFT
unto	INTIL
unusual	UNCO
unworthy	WANWORDY
unyoke (horses)	LOWZE
unyoked	LOWSIT
up	
—the way	UPBY(E)
—there	UPBY(E)
—to	UP-TILL
uphold	UPHAUD

upright beam	STANCHEL, STANCHER
uproar	COLLIESHANGIE, RAIRD, REIRD
	DIRDUM, DURDUM
upset	UPCAST, WHEMMLE
—plans	COUP (THE CRAN), COWP
upside down	HEELS O'ER GOWDY
urchin	HURCHEON
urge	THREAP, THREEP
—forward	WHIG
urged	THREAPIT, THREEPIT
use	
—sparingly	KITCHEN, TAPE
—thriftlessly	WASTER
useful	WAKERIFE
useless person	BAUCHLE
usher in court	MACER
utter volubly	BLATTER
vacated	RED(D)
vagabond	RINTHEROUT, WAIF
vagrant	CAIRD, RINABOUT
	GANGREL, GANG-THERE-OUT
	RINTHEROUT, TINK(LER)
vague language	WHITTIE-WHATTIE
vain	VOGIE
valance	PAND
valise	DORLACH, WALISE
valley	CLEUCH, CLOUGH, CORRIE
	GLEN, STRATH
valuation	STENT
value	APPRIZE
variegated	BROCKED, BROCKIT
vault	COOM
vaulted passage	PEND
venture	MINT
veritably	REAL
very	AE, UNCO
—big	SKELPING
—hard rock	KINGLE
—much	FELL
vessel with spout	POURIE
vex	FASH, TEAN
vexatious	FASHIOUS
—detail in work	FIKE, FYKE
vibrate	DIRL, TIRL, HOTTER
vibration	DIRL, HOTTER
victuals	VIVERS
vigilant	WAKERIFE
vigorous	RAUCLE
village	CLACHAN
—with parish church	KIRKTO(W)N
violent push	BIRR
violin (Islands)	GJO, GJU, GU(E), GOU
virago	RUDAS
viscera	HARIGAL(D)S
vitality	FIZZEN, FUSHION
vivid	VIVE

voice of one about	
to die	TAIS(CH)
voracious hunger	(Y)EARD-HUNGER
	YERD-HUNGER
	YIRD-HUNGER
vow	HECHT
waddle	DAIDLE
wag	LICK
wainscot	BOX
wait	BIDE
—at appointed place	BIDE TRYST
wakeful	WAKERIFE
waking	WAKEN
walk as if lame	HIRPLE
walker	GANGER
wall	DIKE, WA
—opening	BOLE
—plug	DOOK
wander	STRAVAIG, TRAIK, TA(I)VER
wandering	WAFF
want of spirit	FOZINESS
wanting	AMISSING
wanton girl	GILLFLIRT, JILLFLIRT
warble	CHIRL
ward off	WEAR
warn	SHORE
warning cry	GARDELOO, JORDELOO
warrant to	
—apprehend fugitive	
debtor	FUGIE-WARRANT
—arrest debtor	CAPTION
—produce witnesses etc	DILIGENCE
was	
—able	DOCHT, DOUGHT
—good for a purpose	DOCHT, DOUGHT
washy	SHILPIT
wasps' nest	BINK
waste away	DWINE
wasteful	WASTERIFE
wasteland	REESK
watch over dead	LIKEWAKE, LIKEWALK
	LYKEWAKE
water	
—bailiff	WATER-BAILIE
—goblin	SHELLYCOAT
—plant (Islands)	PIPEWORT
—spirit (Orkney)	TANGIE
—sprite	KELPIE, KELPY
	RIVER-HORSE
watery	SKINKING
—bog	MOSS-FLOW
—stuff	BLASH
wave	WAFF
waxed thread	LINGEL, LINGLE
way	GATE
wayward	LOUP-THE-DYKE

weak	BRICKLE, FIZZENLESS	whisper	HARK, WHEESHT
	FUSHIONLESS		WHITTIE-WHATTIE
wean	SPANE, SPAIN, SPEAN	whistle	FISSLE, SOWTH
wearer of		—feebly	WHEEPLE
—kilt	KILTIE, KILTY	—softly	SOWF(F), SOWTH
—short shift	CUTTY SARK	whit	HAET, HAIT
weary with drudgery	TRAUCHLE	white	
weasel	WHIT(T)RET	—faced	HAWKIT
	WHITTERICK	—pudding	WHITE-HASS, WHITE-HAWSE
weaver	WABSTER	whitening-stone	CAMSTA(U)NE, CAMSTONE
wed	WAD	whitish	WHITELY
week	OU(L)K	Whitsuntide	REMOVAL TERM
weep	GLEET, GREET	whiz	WHIDDER
weighing machine	TRON	whole	HALE
weight		—affair	HALE HYPOTHEC
—12-34lbs (Islands)	LISP(O)UND	wholesome	HEALSOME
—80 stone	SERPLATH	whooping-cough	KINK-H(O)AST
weir	CAULD	whortleberry	BLAEBERRY
weird	ELDRITCH	why yes	OU AY
weld	WALD	wicked creature	HELLICAT
welfare	HEAL	widow's right to a third	TERCE
well	A(T)WEEL, WEEL	wife	GUIDWIFE
—favoured	WEEL-FA(U)R'D	wig	GIZZ, JIZ
—known	NOTOUR	wild	
—off	BEIN, BIEN, WELL-TO-LIVE	—daisy	GOWAN
—wishing	GOOD-WILLY	—radish	RUNCH
went	GAED	wilful	WILLYARD, WILLYART
wept	GRAT, GRUTTEN	will not	WINNA
western	WESTLIN	Will-o'-the-wisp	SPUNKIE
wet	WAT	willow	SAUCH, SAUGH
—slovenly work	SLAISTER	wind (clock)	ROLL
what!	SICCAN	winding stair	TURNPIKE(STAIR)
—does it matter?	WHAT RECK	window	WINDOCK, WINNOCK
—kind of?	WHATEN, WHATNA	—seat	BUNK
wheedle	CUITER, PHRASE	windpipe	THRAPPLE
wheel	HURL	winter sport	CURLING
—barrow	HURL-BARROW	wipe	DICHT
wheeze	WHAISLE, WHAIZLE	wish	WISS
where	WHAUR	witch	CARLINE, GYRE-CARLIN, WEIRD
which	QUHILK, WHILK	witch's spell	CANTRIP
whilom	UMQUHILE	wither	GIZZEN, SCAITH, SKAITH
whim	FLISK, WHIGMALEERIE	within	BEN, INWITH
	WHIGMALERY	without	
whimbrel	LITTLE WHAUP	—dowry	UNTOCHERED
whimper	PEENGE	—feudal superior	
whine	PEENGE, WHEENGE	(Islands)	UDAL
	WHINGE	—injury	SCAITHLESS, SKAITHLESS
whinstone	WHUNSTANE	—intermission	EVEN ON
whip	FIRK	—orderliness	THROUGH-OTHER
whirl	BIRL, TIRL	—scratches	SCART-FREE
whirlpool (Islands)	SWELCHIE	woe	DOOL(E), DULE, WAE
whirring sound	BIRR	woeful	DOLENT, WAEFU(L), WAESOME
whisk	WHID	woman	CUTTY, CUMMER, KIMMER
whisky	AULD KIRK, THE CRATUR		WOMAN-BODY
	USQUEBAUGH	—(contemptuously)	GIMMER
—bottle	AULD KIRK	—keeping ale-house	LUCKIE, LUCKY

—practising witchcraft	WITCH-WIFE	—assertion	TESTIFICATE
—who buys at auction	ROUPING-WIFE	wrong way	WID(D)ERSHINS, WITHERSHINS
woman's		wry	THRAWN
—cap	MUTCH	yap	NYAFF
with side flaps	TOY	yarn-winding appliance	WINNLE
—loose jacket	SHORTGOWN	yawn	GA(U)NT
—short cloak	ROCKLAY, ROKELAY	yearn	GREEN, GREIN
womanish man	JENNY, JESSIE	yell	SKELLOCH, YELLOCH
wonder	FERLY	yelp	NYAFF
wood	WUD	yeoman	COCKLAIRD
wooden		yes	AYE
—bowl	COG, COG(G)IE	—(Islands)	JOKOL, YOKUL
—drinking-cup	CA(U)P	yesterday evening	YESTREEN
—in tone	TIMBER	yon(der)	THON(DER)
—leg	PIN-LEG	young	YOUTHY
—peg-top	PEERIE, PEERY	—animal	BURD
—vessel	COG(UE)	—bird	BURD
wool	OO	—coalfish	PODLEY
—of sheep's neck	HAUSE-LOCK	—ewe	GIMMER
word	WHID	—gull (Islands)	SCAURY
—of reproach	RIGWIDDIE, RIGWOODIE	—hen	EIRACK
work	WARK	—onion	SYBOE, SYBO(W)
—contest	KEMP	youngest of family	WALLYDRAG
—house	POOR'S-HOUSE		WALLYDRAIGLE
	PUIR'S-HOOSE	youth	HALFLIN(G)
—ineffectually	PINGLE	script	(see alphabet)
—into miry matter	CLATCH	sculpture	
—into paste	CLATCH	bas relief gemstone	CAMEO
worker's free allowance	MAG(G)S	broad chisel	BOASTER, BOLSTER
worn out	DISJASKIT	bronze-casting	
	FORFAIRN, TRAIKIT	technique	CIRE PERDUE
—shoe	BAUCHLE		LOST-WAX PROCESS
worry	DEAVE, FASH, PHEESE, PINGLE	bust	
worse	WAR(RE), WAUR	—and pedestal in one	
worst	WA(U)RST	piece	TERM
worthless	ORRA, WAFF, WANWORDY	—on square base	HERM(A)
—fellow	FOOTRA, FOUTRA	carving	
—person	NYAFF, WALLYDRAG	—of basket of fruit	CORBEIL
	WALLYDRAIGLE	—in	
—thing	NYAFF	bas relief	ANAGLYPH
wot	WAT	intaglio	DIAGLYPH
wound	DUNT	—not free-standing	RELIEF
wrack and ruin	PIGS AND WHISTLES	chip from stone	SPALL
wrap	HAP	clay mould	MANTLE
wreck	STRAMASH	curved file	RIFFLER
wrench	THRAW, TWISTLE	decorated with gold	
wrest	THRAW	and ivory	CHRYSELEPHANTINE
wrestle	WARSLE	form a rough shape	BOAST
wretched	WAESOME	incised stone	INTAGLIO
wriggle	HIRSLE	later impression from mould	RESTRIKE
wring	THRAW	metal skeleton	ARMATURE
wrinkle	LIRK	moving sculpture	KINETIC SCULPTURE
writ requiring security			MOBILE
against doing violence	LAW-BURROWS	plaster/glue mixture	GESSO
writhe	THRAW, WINTLE	pointed hammer	BOUCHARDE
written	WRATE	pose with torso twisted	CONTRAPPOSTO

raised carving	BAS RELIEF	—Spanish	CANO, GONZALEZ
	BASSO-RELIEVO	—Swedish	MILLES, OLDENBURG
	BASSO RILIEVO	—Swiss	BILL, GIACOMETTI, ITTEN
	(LOW) RELIEF		POERRI, TINGUELY
rough model	BOZETTO, MAQUETTE	stationary sculpture	STABILE
sculptors		statue	
—American	CALDER, KIENHOLZ, KIESLER	—as column	
	LEWITT, LIPCHITZ, MORRIS	female figure	CARYATID
	OLDENBURG	male figure(s)	ATLAS(ATLANTES)
—Austrian	DONNER, KIESLER	—cherub	PUTTO
—British	ADY(E), ARCHER, BANKS	—crucifixion	CALVARY
	BUTLER, CARO, CHANTREY	—Cupid	AMORINO
	CHADWICK, CHERE, EPSTEIN	—Greek	
	FLAXMAN, GAUDIER-BRZESKA	female	KORE
	GIBBONS, GIBSON	male	KOUROS
	GILBERT, GILL, HEPWORTH	—Mary and Jesus	PIETA
	HEWETSON, JOSEPH, MOORE	support frame for model	ARMATURE
	PAOLOZZI, SMITH, WILTON	workbench	BANKER
—Danish	THORWALDSEN	**seaweed**	ALGA, (BLADDER)WRACK
—Dutch	DE VRIES		OARWEED, ORE(WEED)
—Flemish	DELVAUX, NOLLEKENS		SEA-TANG(LE), SEA-WARE, TANGLE
	RYSBRACK, SHEEMAKERS	Ascophyllum	SEA-WHISTLE
	SLUTER	bladderwrack	FUCUS, ROCK-WEED
—French	ADAM, ARP, BONHEUR		SEA-BOTTLE
	BOURDELLE, BRANCUSI	blue-green	NOSTOC
	DAVID, DEGAS, FALCONET	brown	KELP, KILP, LAMINARIA
	GAUDIER-BRZESKA, LACOMBE		PHAEOPHYCEAE
	LAURENS, LE MARCHAN		SEA-FURBELOW, WRACK
	MAILLOL, PEVSNER, PIGALLE	carrag(h)een	SEA-MOSS
	RODIN, ROUBILIAC	cast ashore	WRACK
—German	BARLACH, GUNTER	Channel Islands	VRAIC
	HECKEL, HOELZEL	Chorda(ria)	WHIPCORD
	MACKENSON, MODERSOHN	coarse seaweed	TANG(LE)
—Greek	GLYCON, PHIDIAS	coralline	NULLIPORE
	PRAXITELES, SCOPAS	dialect	ORE, WARE
—Hungarian	FLEISCHMAN	edible	DULSE, LAMINARIA, LAVER
—Italian	ALGARDI, AMMANATI		PORPHYRA, TANGLE
	BANDINELLI, BARISANUS	Fucaceae	WRACK
	BERNINI, BOCCIONI	grasswrack	EELGRASS, EELWRACK
	BRUNELLESCHI, BUGATTI	green	CHLOROPHYCEAE
	CANOVA, CELLINI, DANTI		ENTEROMORPHA
	DELLA ROBBIA, DESIDERIO		GREEN ALGAE, IKODONT
	DONATELLO, GHIBERTI	growing on shore	WRACK
	GIAMBOLOGNA	gulf-weed	SARGASSO, SARGASSUM
	GUELFI, LEONARDO		SEA-GRAPE, SEA-LENTIL
	MASTROIANNI, MICHELANGELO	kelp	VAREC(H)
	MUNARI, PISANO	Laminaria	SEA-GIRDLE, TANGLE
	SANSOVINO, VITTORIA	laver	PORPHYRA
—Latvian	LIPCHITZ	olive-brown	GULF-WEED
—Nigerian	ENENWEOUN	pink	CORALLINE
—Norwegian	VIGELAND	Porphyra	(PURPLE) LAVER
—Romanian	BRANCUSI	purple	CARRAG(H)EEN, IRISH MOSS
—Russian	ARCHIPENKO, GABO		LAVER, PORPHYRA
	GONCHAROV, PEVSNER	red	CHONDRUS, FLORIDEAE, LAVER
	ZADKINE		PORPHYRA, RHODOPHYCEAE
—Scottish	PAOLOZZI		RHODYMENIA

ribbon-weed	SUGAR-WRACK	sergeant-at-law	SL
rock-weed	BLADDERWRACK	sergeant-major	SM
Sargassum	GULFWEED, SEA-GRAPE	**servant**	
sea-		acolyte (old)	ACOLOUTHITE
—girdle	LAMINARIA, TANGLE	agent	BAILIFF, COMMIS, FACTOR
—grape	GULFWEED, SARGASSUM		REEVE, STEWARD
—lentil	GULFWEED	American	
—lettuce	GREEN LAVER, ULVA	—hotel page or porter	BELL-HOP
—moss	CARRAG(H)EEN	—messenger (Congress)	PAGE
—whistle	ASCOPHYLLUM	—railway porter	REDCAP
sugar-wrack	RIBBON-WEED	apprentice chef, waiter	
tangle	LAMINARIA, SEA-GIRDLE	or steward	COMMIS
translucent	BLADDERWRACK, SEA-BOTTLE	assistant	ACOLYTE, ACOLYTH
Ulva	GREEN LAVER, SEA-LETTUCE	—to official	YEOMAN
varec(h)	KELP, WRACK	attendant	ACOLTE, ACOLYTH
whipcord	CHORDA, CHORDARIA		FAMULUS, VARLET
wrack	FUCACEAE, VAREC(H)		WAITING-VASSAL
secret		—armed (Turkey)	CAVASS, KAVASS
Secret Intelligence Service	MI, SIS	—at races	STEWARD
secret jargon of vagrants	SHELTA	—for horses	GROOM, OSTLER
secret police			STABLE-BOY, STABLE-LAD
—East Germany	STASI	—on	
—Nazi Germany	GESTAPO	aeroplane	STEWARD(ESS)
—Romania	SECURITATE	Highland chief	G(H)ILLIE, GILLY
—Russia	(T)CHEKA, GRU, KGB, MVD		GILLIE-WETFOOT
	NKVD, OGPU		GILLIE-WHITEFOOT
—South Africa	BOSS	knight	ARMIGER, (E)SQUIRE
—Sweden	SAPO		SCUTIGER, VARLET
secret printing	SAMIZDAT	ship	STEWARD
secret script (Greek)	SCYTALE	boy attendant	BUTTONS, PAGE
secret society	FRATERNITY	carrier	BEARER, PORTER
—Algerian French	OAS	Chinese labourer	COOLIE
—American	KU-KLUX KLAN	cook	CHEF
mafia	BLACK HAND, COSA NOSTRA	doing all kinds	
—Chinese	BOXER, HOEY, TONG	of work	FACTOTUM
	TRIAD		GIRL FRIDAY, HOUSEKEEPER
—claiming mystical			MAN FRIDAY
knowledge	ROSICRUCIANS	door-keeper	CONCIERGE, PORTER
—French	MAQUIS	driver	CHAUFFEUR, CHAUFFEUSE
—German (18th c)	ILLUMINATI	Eastern	
—international	(FREE)MASONS	—harem servant	EUNUCH
—Italian		—(nurse)maid	AMAH
Calabrian	NDRANGHETA	factor	CHAMBERLAIN, SENESCHAL
Neapolitan	CAMORRA	factotum	CIRCAR, FAMULUS
Sicilian	MAFIA		SIRCAR, SIRKAR
republican	CARBONARI	family servant	RETAINER
—Japanese	YAKUZA	female servant	HANDMAID(EN)
—Kenyan	MAU MAU	—suckling child for mother	WET-NURSE
—Muslim	ASSASSINS	—working for board and	
—South African	BROEDERBOND	lodgings	AU PAIR
Senegal	SN	foreman	STEWARD
senior	SENR, SR	footman	FLUNKEY, LACKEY, LACQUEY
senior common room	SCR	French	
Senior Deacon	SD	—doorkeeper	CONCIERGE
Senior Medical Officer	SMO	—maid	BONNE
sergeant	NCO, SERG(T), SGT	gatekeeper	CONCIERGE, PORTER

general steward	MAJOR DOMO, SENESCHAL	secretary	AMANUENSIS, FAMULUS
group of servants	RETINUE, TRAIN	shoe cleaner	BOOTBLACK
hotel or inn		slave	BOND(S)MAN, HELOT
—bootblack	BOOTS		VASSAL
—page	BELL-BOY, BUTTONS	South African (nurse)maid	AYAH
—pulling off guests'		Spanish governess	DUENNA
boots	BOOT-CATCHER	steward	CHAMBERLAIN
—serving drinks	BARMAN		SENESCHAL
	POT-BOY, POT-MAN	university servant	BEDDER, FAG, GYP
house servant	DOMESTIC		SCOUT, SKIP
Hungarian	HAIDUK, HEYDUCK	valet	LACKEY, LACQUEY
Indian		warden	CONCIERGE
—domestic	WALLAH	witch's servant	FAMILIAR
—groom	SYCE	**seven**	VII, S
—hotel servant	BEARER	against Thebes	ADRASTUS, AMPHIARAUS
—household servant	BEARER		CAPANEUS, HIPPOMEDON
—maid	AYAH		PARTHENOPAEUS
—nursemaid	AYAH		POLYNICES, TYDEUS
—personal servant	BEARER	based	SEPTENARY, SEPTIMAL
—porter	SHERPA	books of OT	HEPTATEUCH
—rajah's servant	CHOBAR	champions	ST ANDREW, ST ANTHONY
—waiter	K(H)IDMUTGAR		ST DAVID, ST DENIS
	K(H)ITMUTGAR		ST GEORGE, ST, JAMES
Irish boy-servant	GORSOON, GOSSOON		ST PATRICK
janitor	CONCIERGE	Christmas presents	SWANS
Jewish temple servants	NETHININ	cleft	SEPTEMFID
ladies' maid	ABIGAIL, SOUBRETTE	combining forms	HEPTA-, SEPT(I)-
	TIRE-WOMAN, TIRING-WOMAN		SEPTEM-
land steward	BAILIFF	creations	ANIMALS, EARTH, FIRE, HUMANS
liveried servant	FLUNKEY		PLANTS, SKY, WATER
maidservant	SOUBRETTE	daughters of Atlas	PLEIADES
manservant		days	HEBDOMAD, WEEK
—attending to clothes etc	VALET	Deadly Sins	ANGER, COVETOUSNESS
—in charge of food			ENVY, GLUTTONY, LUST
and drink etc	BUTLER, PANTLER		PRIDE, SLOTH
—liveried	FOOTMAN	Dwarfs	BASHFUL, DOC, DOPEY
—serving at table	SEWER, WAITER		GRUMPY, HAPPY
menial servant	DOGSBODY, DRUDGE		SLEEPY, SNEEZY
	MINION, SCULLION	fold	SEPTIFORM, SEPTUPLE
	SKIVVY, SLAVE(Y)	groups	HEBDOMAD, HEP, HEPTAD
messenger	BEARER		SEPTENARY, SEPTET(T
military servant	BATMAN		SEPTETTE, SEPTUOR
native	BEARER	having seven	
officer of court (old)	APPARITOR	—angles	HEPTAGONAL, SEPTANGULAR
one in charge of		—cusps	SEPT-FOIL
building	CONCIERGE	—faces	HEPTAHEDRONAL
	JANITOR, SUPERINTENDENT	—feet	HEPTAPODIC, SEPTEMPEDAL
overseer	STEWARD		SEPTIPEDAL
page	BELL-BOY, BELL-HOP	—languages	HEPTAGLOT
	BUTTONS	—leaflets	SEPTEMFOLIATE
personal assistant	PA	—measures	HEPTAMETER
porter	CONCIERGE, BELL-BOY	—parts	HEPTAMEROUS
Scottish			SEPTEMPARTITE
—barefoot messenger	GILLE-WETFOOT	—sides	HEPTAGONAL, SEPTILATERAL
	GILLIE-WHITEFOOT	—stamens	HEPTANDRIAN, HEPTANDROUS
—guide	G(H)ILLIE, GILLY	—styles	HEPTAGYNIAN, HEPTAGYNOUS

—syllables	HEPTASYLLABIC
Heptateuch	**Pentateuch** *plus*
	JOSHUA, JUDGES
hills of Rome	AVENTINE, CAELIAN
	CAPITOLINE, ESQUILINE
	PALATINE, QUIRINAL, VIMINAL
hundred	PSI
hundredth anniversary	SEPTINGENTENARY
hundred thousand	PSI
in government	HEPTARCHY
	SEPTEMVIRATE
Magnificent	FILM
notes	SEPTIMOLE, SEPTUPLET
one of seven	
—at one birth	SEPTUPLET
—men	SEPTEMVIR
Sages	BIAS, CHILON, CLEOBOLUS
	PERIANDER, PITTACUS
	SOLON, THALES
Seas	ANTARCTIC, ARCTIC
	N & S ATLANTIC, INDIAN
	N & S PACIFIC
senses	*as* **five** *plus* SPEECH
	UNDERSTANDING
sevens	RUGBY
Sisters	ROCKS
sleepers	CHRISTIAN YOUTHS
Stars (of Pleiades)	GREAT BEAR, PLOUGH
	SEPTENTRION(ES)
	TRIONES, PLOUGH
stories told in 7 days	HEPTAMERON
thousand	Z
times as much added to stake	SEPTLEVA
tones	HEPTACHORD
virtues	CHARITY, FAITH
	FORTITUDE, HOPE, JUSTICE
	PRUDENCE, TEMPERANCE
Wonders of World	COLOSSUS
	HANGING GARDENS
	MAUSOLEUM, PHAROS
	PYRAMIDS, STATUE OF ZEUS
	TEMPLE OF ARTEMIS
works	SPIRITUAL MERCY
year ...	ITCH
years	PROPHETIC WEEK
	SEPTENATE, SEPTENNIUM
seventy	O, OMICRON, S
seventy-eight	DISC, RECORD
The Seventy	JEWISH COUNCIL
	SANHEDRIN
thousand	O, OMICRON, S
year old	SEPTUAGENARIAN
sewing	
including: embroidery	
needlepoint	
applied decoration	APPLIQUE

blunt needle	BODKIN
border on clerical vestment	ORPHREY
diagonal line	BIAS
edging	PURL
embroider on edge	PURFLE
embroidery	
—frame	TAMBOUR
—needle	CREWEL
—with padding	QUILTING, TRAPUNTO
gathering	SHIRRING, SMOCKING
knotted threadwork	MACRAME, MACRAMI
narrow braid	SOUTACHE
non-fraying edge	SELVAGE, SELVEDGE
open pattern	BRODERIE ANGLAISE
overlapping seam	MONK'S SEAM
patterns stitched	
on fabric	EMBROIDERY
	NEEDLEPOINT
	TAPESTRY
perforated shapes	BRODERIE ANGLAISE
pre-shrunk	MERCERISED
raised	
—strip	RIB(BING)
—surface	NAP
round strip	PIPING
seam stitched on both sides	FRENCH SEAM
slit in garment	PLACKET
spool	BOBBIN
stitches	BARGELLO, BLANKET
	BUTTONHOLE
	CABLE, CHAIN, CLOUD FILLING
	CRETAN FLY, CROSS, DARNING
	FEATHER, FISHBONE, HERRINGBONE
	HOLBEIN, JAPANESE, LAZY-DAISY
	MOSS, RAISED, RUNNING, SQUARE
	VANDYKE, WAVE, WEAVING
	WHIPPED WEB, WOVEN
stitching	
—diagonally	TENTWORK
—heavy thread	COUCHING
—over weft	TRAMMING
—with two threads	COUCHING
superimposed materials	APPLIQUE
tapestry stretcher	BLOCKING BOARD
temporary stitching	BASTING, TACKING
triangular insert	GORE, GUSSET
trimming	GIMP
wavy	
—braid	RICKRACK
—edge	LETTUCE EDGE
weft in embroidery	TRAM(MING)
woven edge	SELVEDGE
zigzag needlepoint	BARGELLO
Seychelles	SY
capital	(PORT) VICTORIA
coin	CENT, RUPEE

Shakespeare
words found in his works:

a thing discovered	DESCRY
abate	PLUCK OFF
abhorred	HELL-HATED
abide	REMAIN
able to perform wonders	WOND(E)RED
abode	BEING, REMAIN
abominable	EXSUFFLICATE
abounding in rooks	ROOKY
about	SOON AT
abreast	AFRONT
absence	REMOVE
—of restraint	LET-ALONE
abstain from	REFRAIN
absurd medley	GALLIMAUFRY
abundance	TALLENT
abundant of produce	INCREASEFUL
abuse with violence	LANDDAMNE
abusive language	ROPE TRICKS
acceptance	ADMITTANCE
accident	UPCAST
accompanied by a woman	WOMAN'D
accompany	ASSOCIATE, ASSIST
	SERVE
accomplice	FEDAR(AR)IE, FEDERARY
	FOEDARIE, FOEDAIRE
accomplishment	COMPLIMENT, EXERCISE
accord	CONGREE
accost	ASSAY, BOARD
account	RENDER
accountant	ONEYER
accusation	CAUSE
accuse	APPEACH, APPEAL
	DETECT, PEACH
accustomed	TAME
accruing	GROWING
accumulation	ENGROSSMENT
accuse	APPEAL
achieve by kneeling	KNEE
acid	AYGRE, EAGER
acquit	UNCHARGE
act	ISSUE
—according to one's	
nature	DO ONE'S KIND
—as	
a boy	BOY
regent for	PROTECT
—lazily and stupidly	DRUMBLE
—of	
aiming	LEVEL
devising	FRAME
extending	EXTENT
seizing	PREY
standing	STATION
—up	EVEN

—upon	SALUTE
acting as a procurer	PANDERLY
actions	EFFECTS
active	FACTIOUS, QUIVER
—youth	LEAPING-TIME
actor's profession	QUALITY
actual	BODILY
adapt measures	ORDER
add up	PARCEL
addicted	FREQUENT
—to looking in a mirror	GLASS-GAZING
addition	VANTAGE
additional title or	
designation	SURADDITION
address	BOARD, SUPERSCRIPT
adjudge to one side	
or the other	SIDE
adjustment in ratio	PROPORTION
admission to office	ENTERTAINMENT
admonition	ADVERTISEMENT
adorn with a brooch	BROOCH
adorned	CROWNED
adroit	QUAINTLY
adulterate	CARD
—wine with lime	LIME
adulterer	BED-SWERVER
advantage	COMMODITY, EMINENCE
	PRISE, PROCEEDING
—yielded	PRIVILEGE
advent	INCOME
adventurous	DAREFUL
adverse	AWKWARD
advisement	VIZAMENT
affair	CAUSE
affect	SALUTE
affectation	AFFECTION
affirmed before	FOREVOUCHED
afflict with apoplexy	APOPLEX
afflictions at sea	SEA-SORROW
affright	GHAST
afraid	AF(F)EARD
against proper feeling	UNKINDLY
aggressive person	SQUARER
agitate	BETOSS, JUMP
agree	ATONE, CONGRUE, CONVENT
	GREE, HIT
—to	CONGREE, UNDERWRITE
agreement	COMART
alarm	TIRRIT
alas!	WELLANEAR
alchemist's elixir	TINCT
alembic	LIMBEC(K)
Algiers	ARGIER
all	
—destroying	NONE-SPARING
—night drinkers	CANDLE-WASTERS

—round	FULL-FRAUGHT
allege	LEGE
allot	SORT
allotment	DOLE, LOTTERY
allow	BETEEM(E)
allowed three-suits p. a.	THREE-SUITED
allusion	POLLUTION
always opening	UNSISTING
amazed	AGAZED
Amazon	HIPPOLYTA, PENTHESILEA
ambitious	EMULATE
amorous	LOVELY
amount	SUBSTANCE
amulet	PERIAPT
ancient	FANS
anger	INCENSEMENT
animal's	
—bed	CABINET
—entrails	CHAWDRON
animated	AUDACIOUS
—by lust	LUST-BREATHED
annoyance	NOYANCE
annul with a kiss	UNKISS
anoint	BALM
answer	REIN
antagonism	OPPUGNANCY
antecedent happening	PREMISE, PREMISS
anticipating	FOREHAND
antipodes	UNDER-GENERATION
any odds	LOTS TO BLANKS
anything	
—calculated to arouse	HUNT'S-UP
—displayed for show	FLAUNT
—engraved	SCULPTURE
—of value	WORTHY
—human	CIVIL
—protuberant and	
hanging loosely	WALLET
—that dashes hopes	COOLING-CARD
—very small	HALFPENNY
anyway	ALL-THING
apparently true	TRUE-SEEMING
apparitor	PARITOR
appear	EYE, LOOK OUT
appearance	OSTENT, PORT
—of life	LIVELIHOOD
appendages	ASSIGNS
appendix to bill	SCEDULE
apple	LEATHER-COATS
	POMEWATER, SWEETING
apply mouths	MOUTH
appoint	LIMIT, SCEDULE
—a time for	SET DOWN
—by writing	PAPER
appointment	MATCH
apposite	PREGNANT

appraisal	PRISE
appraise	PRAISE
approach	COST(E)
approaching the sky	SKYISH
approbation	ALLOWANCE, APPROOF
appropriate	PROPERTY
apt to learn	SPACKT, SPRAG
arbitration	COMPROMISE
ardour	WRATH
arithmetician	COUNTER-CASTER
armour for arm	BRACE
army	BATTLE
aromatic herb	NOSE-HERB
arrange	SCEDULE
arrest	REST
arrogance	OPINION
arrow	BIRD-BOLT
art of fencing	DEFENCE
artful	ARTIFICIAL
	CAUTELOUS, FINE
as it may happen	HEREBY
ashamed	SHENT
ask for writ	
delivering	
freehold to heir	SUE ONE'S LIVERY
askance	ASCONCE
aspire to	SPEAK TO
assail	ASSAY
—with	
rattling	RATTLE
words	TONGUE
assailant	OFFERING
assault	ASSAY
assay	SAY
assayer	SAY-MASTER
assemble	CONDUCE
assembled	DREW
assembly	DISSEMBLY
assign	SORT
—to one side	SIDE
—value to	PRAISE
assistant tapster	UNDERSKINKER
associate	COMPETITOR, COMPLICE
assume	UNDERTAKE
assurance	SURANCE
assure	PASS, SECURE
assured	THOUGHTEN
assuredly	PARDIE, PARDY, PERDIE
	PERDY
astonishment	ADMIRATION
astride	COLOSSUS-WISE
at	
—an end	EXPIATE
—any rate	AT ANY HAND
—night	ANIGHT
—peace	WHIST

—the	
beginning	AT HAND
present time	THE WHILE
—this very time	INSTANTLY
—variance	ODD
atmosphere	REGION
atone	ABIDE, ABY(E)
atrociously wicked	FACINERIOUS
attack	BOARD, EXTENT
attend	TEND
—as servant	STAY
attend to	RECK
attendants	TENDANCE
attentive	ADVERTISING, ATTENT
attraction	FAVOUR
auburn	ABRAM
augment	ECH(E), EECH, ICH
auspicious	FAIR-BODING
avarice	MISERY
avaricious	CHUFF
avenge	VENGE
avenging	REVENGE
averse to conversation	UNQUESTIONABLE
avoid	EVITATE
avowed	BARE-FACED
awry	CAM, KAM(ME)
back up	VERIFY
backbiting	BACK-WOUNDING
backward fall	TAILOR
bad luck	WANION
badge of dignity	GUARD
badly tempered	ILL-TEMPERED
bailiff	BUM-BAYLIE
	SHOULDER-CLAPPER
bait	STALE
balance	PEASE, PEAZE, PEISE
	PEIZE, PEYSE
—evenly	WEIGH
—of an account	REMAINDER
ball of thread	BOTTOM
balsamic liquor	MUMMY
baneful	BATEFUL
banish	ABANDON
bank	RIVAGE
—of river	WHARF
banker	ONEYER
bankrupt	TRADE-FALNE
bar	MAKE
—tailed godwit	SCAMEL
bargain	COMPOSITION
barrel	BOMBARD, BUMBARD
base	CULLIONLY
—tyke	HUNT-COUNTER
basket	MAUND
baste	ENLARD
bathed	BALKED

batter by violence	
of weather	OVERWEATHER
battle	WAGE
baubles with fool's head	FOOLS ZANIES
bawd	GREEK
bawl	GAPE
be	BIN
—a	
guest	HOST
pattern for	PATTERN
widow	WIDOW
wooer	SUE
—amends for	PURCHASE
—an accessory	BE OF CONSENT
—conciliatory	MAKE FAIR WEATHER
—consistent	ADHERE
—daunted	DISMAY
—deluded with hopes	EAT THE AIR
—dilatory	FORESLOW
—distasteful	DISTASTE
to	RESIST
—equal in value	WAGE
—equivalent to	REANSWER
—imprisoned	LIE
—in	
fashion	WEAR
service	DEPEND
waiting	TEND
—inconstant	BLENCH
—intent	TIRE
—intimately mixed	LARD
—lodged	LIE AT HOST
—married	GO TO THE WORLD
—over-punctilious	STRAIN COURTESY
—perverse	BE OPPOSITE WITH
—security for	SURETY
—silent	PEACE
—sluggish	DRUMBLE
—suitable	CONVENT
—surety for	UNDERTAKE
—the better	AVAIL
—transacted	PROCEED
been	BIN
bear	
—in mind	REMEMBER
—like a crest	UNDERCREST
beard	EXCREMENT
beardless	UNRUFFE
bearing	CONCERNANCY
bearing	PORTANCE
beast of the chase	VENISON
beat	COMB, FIRK, PAY, PRAT
	SWINDGE, SWITS
beater	SWITS
beauty	FAIR
because	THAT

beckoning	WAFTURE	bird's nest	CABINET
become	BESORT	biting in tongue	WASP-STUNG
—an informer	PEACH		WASP-TONGUE
—lank	LANK	bitter	AYGRE, EAGER
—mouldy	HOAR	—end	UTTERANCE
bedcover	COUNTERPOINT	black	COLLIED, ROOKY
bedraggle	BEMOIL	—as hell	HELL-BLACK
beetle for clothes	BATLET, BATLER	—bird	WOOSEL(L)
befall	BEFORTUNE	—jack	BOMBARD
befit	BESORT	blandishment	SOOTH
befooled	POUPT	blast	STRIKE, TAKE
before	TOFORE	—by lightning	THUNDER-STROKE
beforehand	FORMER	blasted	DEROGATE
beggar	BEZONIAN	bleacher of linen	WHITSTER
begging bowl	CLACK-DISH	bleaching-time	WHITING-TIME
begone	AROINT, AROYNT	blight	BLASTMENT, STRIKE
behaving like a fop	FASHION-MONGING	blind	BEESOME, BISSON
behaviour	GESTURE, PORTANCE		C(O)URB, WINKING
beholden	BEHOLDING	—fold	W(H)IMPLE
being in a passion	PASSIONING	—man's buff	HOODMAN-BLIND
belated	LATED	blinding	BISSON, SEELING
beldame	TROT	blinking	PINK
believe	WIS(T)	blockhead	CLOTPOLL, SNIPE
belladonna	INSANE ROOT	bloodhound	LYM
beloved	TENDER	blooming	PRIMY
belt	CENTER	blow	PASH
bend	COMPASS, CURB	—in fencing	MONTANTO
—one's course	SWAY	blundering word	NON-COME
beneficiary	BENEFIT	blunt	DISEDGE
bent	CRISP	—arrow	BIRD-BOLT
—upon prey	PREYFUL	blusterer	RUDESBY, SWASHER
benumb	PROROGUE	boarded	PLANCHED
beset	LAY	boasting	MAGNIFICENT
beshrew	SHREW	—of	REPUTING
best	DEAR, WHIP	bodge	BUDGE
bestially drunk	SWINE-DRUNK	bodily	
bet	LAY	—constitution	COMPLEXION
bethink	REMEMBER	—pain	GRIEF
betide	BETIME	—quality	THEW
betray	PEACH	body	
betroth	ASSURE, TROTH	—of people owing allegiance	SUBJECT
betrothal	ASSURANCE	—servant	GENTLEMAN
betrothed	COMBINATE	boggled	BODGED
	TROTH-PLIGHT	boiling pot	STEW
between sand-blind		boldness	DARE
and stone-blind	HIGH-GRAVEL-BLIND	bookish man	INKHORN-MATE
bewitchment	TAKING	boredom	SPLEEN
beyond description	UNEXPRESSIVE	born	
bias	PARTIALISE	—in dung	SHARD-BORNE
Bible	TEXT	—to a procuress	BAUD-BORN
biliousness	CHOLER	borne by scaly wings	SHARD-BORNE
bind	COMBINE	bosky	BUSKY
—as in gratitude	ENDEAR	bosom friend	CATER-COUSIN
—in fetters	ENFETTER	botcher	COSIER, COZIER
—weed	WOODBIND, WOODBINE	bout	VENEW
bird of ill-omen	NIGHT-CROW	bowl-beating	BOLD-BEATING

bowsprit	BEAK		by	
boy	CRACK, JACK-A-LENT		—all means	OF ALL LOVES
	KNAVE		—common report	REPORTINGLY
brabble	PRABBLE		—God!	BEGAD, BEGAR
brain	PIA MATER		—scent of the foot	DRY-FOOT
—sick	BRAINISH		—starts	STARTINGLY
brand	WIPE		—word of mouth	VERBATIM
—with infamy	INFAMONISE		bystander	STANDER-BY
bravery	HARDIMENT		byword	AYWORD
bravest	BEST		Caesar	KEISAR
brawl	BRABBLE, PRAWLE		cake	BAKE
breach of amity	FRACTION		calamity	BALE
break	FRACT, FRUSH		call	
bred in heat of passion	MAD-BRED		—a whore	BEWHORE
brevity	FEWNESS		—to account	TAKE-UP
bright red	WAX-RED		calling	
brimming with tears	WATER-STANDING		—for haste	RASH
bring	PROCURE		—in question	IMPEACH
—back to better state	RECURE		camp follower	BOY
—forth young	EAN, KINDLE		candlestick	CANSTICK
—into plot	PACK		cane	SWITS
—on	INFER		cannot be	
—safely	SAFE		—cloyed	CLOYLESS
—to			—wounded	INTRENCHANT
an end	FINE		canon	SQUIER, SQUIRE
me	DUCDAME		canto	CANTON
broach	STRIKE		cap worn on Sundays	STATUTE-CAP
broad linen tape	INKLE		capable	DELIGHTED
broken with care	CARE-CRAZED		—of taking oath	OATHABLE
brood	KINDLE		capacious	CAPTIOUSWOMBY
—in nest	AERIE, AERY, AYRIE		caparisoned	BARBED
	EYRIE, EIRY		caprice	SPLEEN
brothel	HOTHOUSE, LEAPING-HOUSE		captiousness	CURIOSITY
bruise	FRUSH		card	TOAZE
bruised	PASHED		care	TENDER
brushing blow	SWITS		careful of	OBSEQUIOUS
bubonic plague	RED-MURRAIN, RED-PLAGUE		carefully chosen	CHOICE-DRAWN
buck of fourth year	SOAR(E), SORE		caress	COY
bucket	STO(O)PE		carpenter's square	SQUIER, SQUIRE
budge	BOUGE		carriage	PORTANCE
bully	CUTTLE		carried by itself	SELF-BORNE
bullying	SWASHING		carry	
bumblebee	DRUMBLEDOR		—away in spirit	
burden	CARRIAGE		or with joy	RAP
—of a song	FADING, HOLDING		—foolish appearance	FACE
	WHEEL		—off	TRANSPORT
burdensome	CHARGEFUL		carted	SCUTCHED
burdock	HARDOKE, HORDOCK		carve(d)	INSCULP(T)
burnt torches used			case	SHALE
as blacking	LINK		cast	
bury	INHEARSE, INHERCE		—a	
but slightly	SMALL		light	REFLECT
butt of the company			spell	TAKE
at table	TABLE-SPORT		—down	DEJECT
buy too dear	OVERBUY		—of the eye	ELIAD, ILLIAD, OEILIAD
buzzard	PUTTOCK		—off	CASTED

castrate	GLIB
cataract	PIN AND WEB, WEB AND PIN
catch	FANG, GYVE, PHANG
—in	
a lapse	LAPSE
the act	WATCH
—of the voice	SNATCH
catchword	NAYWORD
catgut string	CATLING
casually dropped	SCATTERED
cause to	
—act	COMMAND
—be remembered	MEMORISE, MEMORIZE
—contract or wrinkle	WARP
—mourn	YEARN
—start	FIT
—tremble	QUAKE
caused by soreness	
of heart	HEART-SORE
causing	
—drowsiness or sleep	YAWNING
—numbness	NUMB
cautious	ADVISED
—in speech	CLOSE-TONGUED
—person	ACHITOPHEL, AHITHOPHEL
cave	ANTAR
cease to exist	DETERMINE
censure	APPEACH
centre	CENTRY
certain	PERFECT
cesspool	DRAUGHT
chaffering	BARGAIN
chain	CARKANET
challenge	ASSAY
chamber	LONDON
—pot	JORDAN
chance	UPCAST
change to a worse state	DISTASTE
changeover	SWITS
character	COMPOSURE, OPINION
—of fox	FOXSHIP
charm worn round neck	PERIAPT
chaste	GRACED
chastise	FIRK, SWINDGE
chastity	HONESTY
chatterer	CHEWET
cheat	BOB, COLT, CONY-CATCH
	GULL-CATCHER, HARLOT
check	TRASH
cheese-rind	CHEESE-PARING
cherub	CHERUBIN
chided	ACOLD
chief	ARCH
child	BA(I)RN, COLLOP
	CRACK, EYAS-MUSKET, KIND
children	IMAGES

children's game	PU PIN
chin	SHINNE
chlorosis	WHITE DEATH
chop (logic)	BA(U)LK
church service	MASS
churl	CARLOT
cincture	CENTER
circle	OE, RONDURE, ROUNDER
circlet	RIGOL(L)
cite	CONVENT
civilised	INLAND
clad in armour	IRON
claim	PLEA
clamour	UTIS
clandestine visiting	TRUNK-WORK
clasp	TASSEL
claw	CLOYE
clever	QUAINTLY
close	SEAM
—connection	IMMEDIACY
—covering	MODEL
—in approach	UPON
closed	WINKING
closely interwoven	THICK-PLEACHED
cloth made in Wales	FRIZE
clothed	SUITED
clothes	
—hung round ship	
to hide crew	FIGHTS
—washing implement	BATLER, BATLET
clouded	NIGHTED
clover-stalk	HONEY-STALK
clown	CARL, LOWT, NORTHERN MAN
club	BAT
coarse	UNBOLTED
—beef	BULL-BEEVES
cobbler	COSIER, COZIER
cockboat	COCK
cockchafer	DRUMBLEDOR
coign	COIN
coin	G(U)ILDER, STAMP
colour	LEER
comb	PHEEZE
combat	OPPOSITION
combination	QUILL
combustible	COMBUSTIOUS
come	
—down the scale	PLUCK OFF
—to a head	HEADED
—with me	DUCDAME
comedy	COMMONTY
coming	
—close upon	THICK-COMING
—in	INCOME
command	CHECK, IMPOSE
commanding battalion	HYE-BATTEL'D

commit adultery	ADULTERATE
common	MODERN, UNPROPER
—sewer	FILTH
—woman	CUSTOMER
commonalty	COMMON
commonness	COMMUNITY
commonplace	MODERN
commotion	GARBOILS, ROMAGE
communicative	INTELLIGENT
companion	COMATE, COPES-MATE
	SKAINES MATE
—devil	YOKE-DEVIL
—in study	BOOK-MATE
	INKHORN-MATE
companionable	FELLOWLY
company	HAUNT, HEAP
—arriving	ARRIVANCY
compare	LIKE
compartment	SQUARE
compassionate feeling	REMORSE
complain	MEAN(E), MEIN, MENE
complaint	PLAINING
complete	PARCEL, REPLENISHED
completely	HOME
—contented	PERFECT
complexion	HAIR, LEER
complimentary	BREATHING
composed of ribaldry	RIBAUDRED
composition	COMPOSTURE
compost	COMPOSTURE
compound	TAKE UP
compounded	CREATE
comprehensive	CAPABLE
compulsory	COMPULSATIVE
conceal	OVERGREEN
conceit	OPINION
conceited fellow	PRINCOX
conceive	ENWOMB
—of	BRAIN
conception	HENT
concern	CERNE, TENDER
concerted music	BROKEN MUSIC
conclude	CROWN, INCLUDE
concordancy	COMPOSITION
concupiscence	CONCUPY
condescend	YIELD
condescended unwillingly	COYED
conduce	SHAPE
conduct	GOVERNMENT, ORDER, PASS
—itself	CONDUCE
confederate	COMPETITOR, FEDAR(AR)IE
	FEDARARY, FOEDARIE
	FOEDAIRE
confederates	QUALITY
confession	EXERCISE, RENDER
	SUBMISSION

confessional	SHRIFT
confidence	INWARDNESS
confine	BALE
—as in hoop	INHOOP
confinement	PRISONMENT
confirm	AFFEAR, AFFEER
	COMPACT, STABLISH, TIE
confirmation	APPROBATION
confirmed	AFFEARD
—possession	STABLISHMENT
—state of manhood	PROOF
confoundedly	PLAGUY
confused sound	WHOOBUB
confutation	REPROOF
confute	CONTROL, PUT DOWN
conjecture	CONJECT, ESTIMATION
conjoin	COJOIN
connected consistency	DEPENDENCY
connecting link	COMMA
conquer	HARROW
conscious of	WITTOL
consciousness	CONSCIENCE
consent	GRANT
consequence	COLLECTION
considerate	RESPECTIVE
consideration	CONSIDERANCE
constant	STILL
consume	CONFOUND
consummate	MADE UP, REPLENISHED
contemplation	BEHOLDING
contemptible	EXSUFFLICATE
	PELTING
—person	SNIPE
contend	WAGE
contention	BATE
contents	ARGUMENT
—of bag or satchel	SCRIPPAGE
continue chaste	VIRGIN
continuously	AN-END
contradict	TAKE-UP, FORESPEAK
contrariety	ADVERSITY
contrary	RETROGRADE
control	CHECK, DANGER
controversy	DEBATEMENT
convene	CONVENT
convent	COVENT
conversation	QUESTION
converse	DIALOGUE, PROPOSE
	QUESTION, REASON
conveyance	ASSURANCE
	TRANSPORTANCE
convict	APPROVE, CONVINCE
	INDITE
convinced	PERFECT
cool	KEEL, RESPECTIVE
cope with	TAKE UP

copy	TAKE OUT	—artful device	DAWBRY
corner	COIGNE	cruel through holiness	HOLY-CRUEL
—stone	COIN	crush	PASH
corollary	COLLECTION	crust of a pie	CUSTARD-COFFIN
coroner	CROWNER	cry triumph over	ORECROWE
corporal	NYM	cuckold-maker	HORN-MAKER
corpulent	GORBELLIED	cudgel	BALLOW, BAT(TERO)
corrected	ATTASKED, ATTASKT	cunning	FOXSHIP, SKILL
	CORRIGIBLE		SUBTILE-WITTED
corroded	CORROBORATE	Cupid	BOW-BOY
corrupt	CORROBORATE, DISTASTE	cur	CURTAIL, TYKE
Cotswold	COTSALE	curdle	POSSET
cough	TISICK	cure	RECURE
countenance	PATRONAGE	curry	PHEEZE
counterpane	COUNTERPOINT	curse	VENGEANCE, WANION
course	STERNAGE	cursory	CURSELARIE, CURSENARY
—of events	OCCASION	curtail	ABATE
courtesan	BONA-ROBA, GUINEA-HEN	curtains	CHAMBER-HANGINGS
courtesy	GENTRY	curve	COMPASS
cover		cut	SLISH
—ground	RID WAY	—notches in	NICK
—to real purpose	STALE	—slightly	SCOTCH
—up	HOODWINK	—to pieces	MAMMOCK
—with red colour	OVERRED	cutpurse	BUNG
covered with		cutting	SECT
—high growth	HIGH-GROWN	cynic	CRITIC
—wickerwork	TWIGGEN	dabchick	DIVE-DAPPER
cow	ROTHER(-BEAST)	daily	JOURNAL
—dung	SHARD	dainties	CATES
coward	VILIACO, VILLIAGO	dairymaid	DAY-WOMAN
—cock	COSTREL, CONSTRIL	dance	CINQUE-PACE, SINKE-A-PACE
	COYSTRIL	—tune	LIGHT-O'-LOVE
cowardice	COWARDSHIP	—with much leaping	LAVOLT(A)
cowardly	COWISH, MEACOCK	Dane	DANSHER
	MILK-LIVERED	dark	
coxcomb	PRINCOX	—as night	NIGHTLY
coyness	NICETY	—complexioned person	WOOSEL(L)
cozened	POUPT	—spot on horse's face	CLOUD
crabbed	CURST	darken	COLLY
crack	WHIP	darkened	NIGHTED
cradle	LULLABY	darling	SWEETING
craft	CAUTEL	dart in	ENDART
craftiness	FOXSHIP	dash	PASH
crafty	BRAID(E)	dastardly creature	MEACOCK
cram	FRANK	daubed with blood	BLOOD-BOLTERED
crazy	WOOD	daubing	DAWBRY
creative	FORGETIVE	Dauphin	DOLPHIN
crewel	INKLE	day for settling disputes	LOVE-DAY
crime	MALEFACTION	daze	ASTONISH, DARE
critic	CARREN	dead	
crone	TROT	—body	GHOST
crooked	CAM, KAM(ME)	—dog	DITCH-DOG
crowd	VARLETRY	deaden	PROROGUE
crowfoot	CROW-FLOWER	deal with a pimp	BROKE
crown	PALE	dealing	MERCHANDISE
crude	CRUDY	dear	CHARITABLE

—to the heart	HEART-DEAR
dearest	LIEFEST
death	DEFUNCTION, FUNERAL
	LETHEE
decay	BRUSH
deceitful	BRAIDE, DECEPTIOUS
	PROPER-FALSE
deceive	BLEAR, MISUSE
decency	GOVERNMENT
decide	MAKE UP, PASS
—to go to a place	RESOLVE ON
decipher	CIPHER, CYPHER
decisive	EFFECTUAL
defend by bars	SPERR(E)
declare	DISCUSS
decorations	FURNITURE
deed	ISSUE
deer	VENISON
—out of condition	RASCAL
defame	INFAMONISE
defect	DECIPHER
defence	PROPUGNATION
defend	ENGUARD
—from the weather	WEATHER-FEND
defer	REJOURN
defile	ENSEAM, FILE, RAY
deft	FEAT
deftest	EFTEST
degenerate	DEROGATE, RECOIL
degraded	DEROGATE
degrees about court	MESSES
deify	GOD
deign	DAINE
delay	FOR(E)SLOW, FORSLOE
	INDURANCE
delegation	SUBSTITUTION
delicacy	CATE
delicate	INCONIE, INCONY
	KONY
delightful	DELIGHTED
delineated	STEELD
deliver back	RELIVER
demeaned	BORE
demolish	RUINATE
demure	PRENZIE
den	ANTRE
dentist	TOOTH-DRAWER
departure	DEPART
depending on negotiation	LITIGIOUS
depict	IMPAINT
depravity	FOLLY
depress	ABATE
deprive	UNPROVIDE
—of	
all chance	LURCH
beauty	UNFAIR

edge	DISEDGE
horse	UNCOLT
life	UNLIVE
possession	DISPROPERTY
state or dignity	UNSTATE
wits	UNWIT
deprived of orb	DISORBED
deputation	ATTORNEY
deranged	BRAIN-SICKLY
description	ADDITION, DEFINEMENT
design	INTENDMENT, PRETENCE
	SKILL
desire	AFFECTION, BOSOM
—strongly	EARN
despatch	EXPEDIENCE
destination	LIST
destitute of kindness	KINDLESS
destroy	CONFOUND, LANDDAMNE
	QUELL, RUINATE, SPOIL
	STROY, UNLACE
destruction	DEFEAT
detachment	DISTRACTION
detail	SEVERAL
—item by item	PARCEL
determine	DETERMINATE
determined	FAST
—person	RESOLUBLE
detractor	SUBTRACTOR
detrition	BRUSH
device	IMPRESS, PLATFORM
	PRETENCE
devil	GOODYEAR, SETEBOS
devolve	SUCCEED
devotion	DEVOTEMENT
devouring	MOUSING
dexterously	FEATLY
diadem	CIRCUIT
dice game	NOVUM, TRAY-TRIP
didapper	DIVE-DAPPER
die	CEASE, GO OFF
difficulty	STRAIN
dignified	CROWNED
dilate	DELATE
dilatory	PROLIXIOUS
dim-sighted	THICK-SIGHTED
diminutive figure	AGLET BABIE
	AGLET BABY
din	UTIS
direct	REFLEX
—one's course	INTEND
direction	
—by mute signs	ACTION
—of the eye	BEND
dirty	RAY
—drab	PUSSEL
—woman	MALKIN, MAWKIN

disarmed of his senses	UNQUALITIED	diurnal	JOURNAL
disavow	DISVOUCH	divert	SWITS
disburse	DISPURSE	divided	DIVIDABLE
discandying	DISCANDERING	dividing	MEER'ED
discoloured by smoke	RE(E)CHIE, REECHY	divinitary agitation	MOTION
discharge		division of atmosphere	REGION
—as if with rending	RIVE	do	
—from		—battle	DARRAIGN(E), DARRAIN(E)
a sponge	DISPUNGE		DARRAYN, DERAIGN
nose	SALT-RHEUM	—homage	VAIL
disclosure	OVERTURE	—it	DICH
discontent	DISEASE	—up	DUP
discourse	ENTREATMENT, PROPOSE	—without	MISS
	REASON	doctor	BODY-CURER
discourteousness	KILL-COURTESY	dog	LYM, SHOUGH
discover	SMOKE		SHOWGHE, TYKE
discovered by fire-light	UMBERED	—rose	CANKER
discovery	DENOTEMENT	doing	OCCASION
discuss	EXPOSTULATE, QUESTION	domestic office	STRACHY
discussion	QUESTION	domestics	MEINIE, MEIN(E)Y
discussed too much	OVERHANDLED	dominion	EMPERY
disdain	COY	done	SPED
disdainful	DISDAINED	—for	POUPT
	ORGILLOUS, ORGULOUS	dotard	DOTANT
disfigure	DEFEAT	doubt	STRAIN
disfigurement	DEFEATURE	down in a feather	DOWL(E)
disgrace	REPROOF	down(y)	DOWLNE(Y)
disguise	DAUB, IMMASK	dragged by the head	HEAD-LUGGED
disguised	SELF-COVERED	draught of merriment	ROUSE
dishearten	UNHEART	draw	
dishonest	LOZEL(L)	—advantage	AVAIL
—practice	INDIRECTION	—in	INSHELL
dismal	TRISTFUL	—out	EXHALE, TOAZE
dismiss	CAST, DAFF	drawn	
dismissal	AVAUNT	—by doves	DOVE-DRAWN
dismissed from the		—in a just cause	RIGHT-DRAWN
world in peace	PEACE-PARTED	—out of bogs	FEN-SUCKED
disorder	DEFUSE, GARBOIL	dread	GASTNESS(E)
disordered	BETUMBLED	—of evil to come	MISDREAD
disparage	DISVALUE	dreadful	DE(A)RN
dispel	RESOLVE	—event	STRATAGEM
dispersal	SEGREGATION	dreamy fellow	JOHN-A-DREAMS
dispirited	PALE-HEARTED	dregs of the people	LEGGE
display to view	IMBARE	dress	TRICKING
dispose	SORT	—of	
disposed	PREGNANT	knights on horseback	BASE
disposition	AFFECTION, INTENDMENT	new-born child	SWATH
disregard	OMIT	dressed	SUITED
dissembling	BRAIDE	drift	HULL, RACK
disseminate	SCALE	drinking	
dissolution	CRACK	—between meals	BY-DRINKING
dissolve	RESOLVE	—cry	RIVO
—from candy	DISCANDIE, DISCANDY	—vessel	STO(O)PE
distempered	ILL-TEMPERED	drive	RACK
distinction	DISTINGUISHMENT	—away	OVERBLOW
distinguishable	DIVIDANT	from habitation	DISHABIT

—by fits	FIT
—mad	MAD
—out of roost	UNROOST
droop	LOB
drown the voice of	OUTVOICE
drub with bloodshed	DRYBEAT
drudge	DRUG
drunk	FAP, PAID
drunken fellow	COYSTRIL
dry up	ENSEAR
due	FITMENT
—performance	PROPERTY
dull	BARREN, BLUNT-WITTED
	DISEDGE, FAT
	ILLUSTRIOUS, MULL
dung	SIEGE
dutiful	OFFICIOUS
dwarfish person	AGATE
dwell	REMAIN
dying young	TENDER-DYING
eager	AYGRE, PRONE, WATERY
—to rival	EMULATE
eagerness of desire	INTENTION
earnest	DEAR
earnestly	WISTLY
easily	LIGHTLY
easy work	BEDWORK
eat one's words	EAT THE LEEK
echo	CHIDE, REPLICATION
	RESPEAK, REWORD
edict	PROCESS
efface	DISLIMN
effeminate	MEACOCK
—person	CARPET-MONGER
effusion	EFFUSE
eggs	PULLET-SPERM
eke out	ECH(E), EECH, ICH
elicit	TOAZE
emanate	VANISH
emasculated	NICKED
embark	INSHIP
embassy	EMBASSADE
embed in sand or ooze	DOCK
emblem	IMPRESS(E)
embrace	CHAIN, EMBRASURE
	INCLIP
emergence from egg	DISCLOSE
emotion	GIRD
empiricutic	EMPIRICKQUTIQUE
employ	EXECUTE
employment of exercise	EXECUTION
empty	CAST
enactment	ENACT
encamp	SET DOWN
encamped	FIELDED
encircle	ENWHEEL, PALE

enclose	EMBOSS, EMBOUND
	RIB, WOMB
—as in hearse	INHEARSE, INHERCE
enclosing wall	EMURE
encounter	CLOSE, COPE
encouragement	AIM
encroach	JET
end	LOOSE, SPOIL, UTMOST
—and purpose of coming	PROFESSION
—of all	EXIGENT
endanger	DANGER
endearing	CHARITABLE
endless	FINELESS
endow with widow's rights	WIDOW
endowed with	FULL-FRAUGHT
—grace	GRACED
—parts	PARTED
endowments	BELONGINGS
endue	DUE
endurable	PORTABLE
endure	ABROOKE, PERDURE
enduring	UNDERGOING
enema syringe	CLYSTER-PIPE
enemy of mankind	PREGNANT ENEMY
enfold	INCLIP
engage in fight	MEDDLE
engineer	ENGENER
engrave(d)	INSCULP(T)
engraving	SCULPTURE
enigma	EGMA
enjoy carnally	TASTE
enjoyment	SUFFIGANCE
enormously wicked	HIGH-VICED
enough	BASTA
enrich	RICH
enriched	MADE
enseam	INSEEM
enshelled	ENSHIELD
entangle	ENROOT
—hair	ELF
enter into articles	ARTICULATE
entered upon manhood	MAN-ENTERED
enterprise	DESIGNMENT
	EXPEDIENCE
entertainment	ENTERTAIN
entice(ment)	TICE
entire	MEERED
entrails	CHAUDRON
entrance	INDUCTION
entreaty	BESEECH, TREATY
entry on probation	APPROBATION
epithet(on)	APATHATON
equal	COMPEER, EGAL
—rank	RIVALITY
equality	RIVALITY

equipment	FURNITURE, TIRE
equipped	FULL-FRAUGHT
erect	STRAIGHT-PIGHT
ergo	ARGAL
escort	TEND
essential detail	PROPERTY
establish	APPROVE, STABLISH
estimated amount or value	RATE
estimation	RATE
evade by trick or lie	FUB OFF
evening just past	OVERNIGHT
evenness of temper	GOVERNMENT
evens	MEET
event	LOOSE, SPEED
—foretold	OMEN
events	OCCASION
everlasting	PERDURABLE
everyday	MODERN
evidence	ARGUMENT, AVOUCH
	INSTANCE
evident	PREGNANT
evil	SHREWD
—usage or behaviour	MISUSE
exact	COMMAND
exactly	JUMP
exaggerate	RACK
exale	VANISH
exalted	HAUGHT, HAU(L)T
examine	QUOTE
—on oath	DEPOSE
example for imitation	SAMPLE
exceed in	
—addiction to	
mistresses	OUT-PARAMOUR
—beauty	OUTBRAG
—boldness	OUTBRAVE
—clamour	OUTVOICE
—cunning	OUTCRAFTY
—estimation	OUTPRIZE
—poisonousness	OUTVENOM
—splendour	OUTBRAG, OUTBRAVE
—value	OUTWORTH
—villainy	OUTVILLAIN
exceedingly	VENGEANCE
excel	OUTPEER
excellence	WORTHY
excelling	PASSED
except	ABATE
excess	VANTAGE
excessively	OUT OF ALL CESSE
exchange	COUNTERCHANGE
excite	ACCITE, SOLICIT, TARRE
execute	OVERSEE
executioner	EXECUTOR
exercise	
—of power	FACULTY

—office over	O'REOFFICE
—one's craft	CRAFT
exhausted	EMBOWELLED
exhibited in articles	ARTICULATED
exhilaration preceding	
death	LIGHTNING
exhortation	EXERCISE
existent	ESSENTIAL
expectation	EXPECT, SUPPOSE
expediency	COMMODITY
expeditious	EXPEDIENT
expend	CONFOUND
expensive	CHARGEFUL
experience	ASSAY
expired	EXPIATE
explain	UNBOLT
exploit	TOUCH
express	
—in writing	PRINT
—purpose	NONCE
expression	EXPRESSURE
—of contempt	COBBY
exquisite	PICk
exterminate	EXTERMINE, EXTIRP
	KILL-UP
external appearance	OUTWALL, OUTWARD
extinguished	EXTICTED
extracted	EXTRAUGHT
extractor of teeth	TOOTH-DRAWER
extravagant	DIFFUSED, FANATICAL
extremely	VENGEANCE
extremity	UTTERANCE
eye	
—disease	PIN AND WEB
	WEB AND PIN
—lids	WINDOWS
face	PROPOSE
—down	OUTLOOK
—in profile	HALF-CHEEK
—out with scorn	OUTSCORN
facinorous (wicked)	FACINERIOUS
fade	VADE
fail to check	UNCHECK
faint	SWELT
fair	PROPER FALSE
fairy	OUPH(E)
—ring	ORB
faith	FAY
faithful	HOLY
falcon	TASSEL-GENTLE
falconer	ASTRINGER
fall	
—headlong	PRECIPITATE
—short of	SHORT
falling	CADENT
fallow deer, second year	PRICKET

false	
—friend	MOUTH-FRIEND
—hood	DAUBERY, DAWBRY
—in religion	IRRELIGIOUS
—pretence	DAWBRY
—step	MISTREADING
falsify	COG
falsifying	FALSING
familiarity	INWARDNESS
fanciful head-dress	TIRE-VALIANT
fancy	LOVE, TOY
fanfare	SENNET
fang	PHANG
fantastic	FANTASTICO
—person	PHANTASIM(E)
far from observing	WIDE OF
far-fetched	EXQUISITE
farcin/ farcy	FASHIONS
fashion	FEAT
fasten	LATCH
—by rein	REIN
—talons on	TIRE
fastening	TASSEL
fastidious	CHARY
fat	
—bellied	GOR-BELLIED
—of ox or cow	TALLOW KEECH
father	MALE
fatigued	WAPPEND
fatten	ENGROSS, FRANK
faucet-seller	FOSSET-SELLER
favour done	LOVE
favoured	GRACED
favouring	SECOND
favours	ENTREATMENT
fawn on	SPANIEL
fawned on	PANELLED, SMOOTHED
feast together	CONVIVE
feather	DOWLE
feature	LEER, TOUCHE
features	FAVOUR
fed to repletion with	
empty promises	PROMISE-CRAMMED
feeble old man	PANTALOON
feed	REPAST
—greedily	TIRE
—one's thoughts or desires	TIRE
feel tenderness for	TENDER
feign	TAKE UPON ONESELF
feigned	SUPPOSED
fellow	COMPANION, COMPETITOR
	RIVAL, SEMBLABLE
felt	APPROVED
female	
—child	MAID-CHILD
—fox	FIXEN

—infant	CHILD
—messenger	WOMAN-POST
—offender	OFFENDRESS
feminine	EFFEMINATE
fencer	SCRIMER, SCRIMURE
fencing	
—term	HAY
—thrust	PASSADO, STUCK
ferry	TRANECT
fervent	PRONE
festivity	CARPET CONSIDERATION
fetched from a depth	DEEP-FET
few	PAUCAS
—words	FEWNESS
fickle person	CHANGING-PIECE
fickleness	CHANGE
fiend	OBIDICUT
fierce	WALL-EYED, WOOD
fig	FICO, FIGO, FOOTRA, FOUTRA
fight	STRIKE
—against	REPUGN
fighting person	SQUARER
figure and rank	SORT AND SUIT
fill with	
—horror	ABHOR
—lies	BELIE
filthy	SCALD
final throw at bowls	UPCAST
fine	INCONIE, INCONY, KONY
—collector	CHEATER
—fellow	BAWCOCK
—filament	SLEAVE
—velvet	THREE-PILE
finger	
—as on a virginal	VIRGINAL
—hole	VENTIGE
—nails	TEN COMMANDMENTS
finical	NEAT
—delicacy	CURIOSITY
fire for trying or proving	TRIAL-FIRE
firm in belief	THOUGHTEN
firmly	FASTLY
firmness	FIXTURE
first	
—act of military	
service	FLESHMENT
—in procession	WHIFFLER
—of women	PRINCIPALITY
—part	VAUNT
fish on land	LAND-FISH
fist	NEAF(F)E
fit	FADGE, RAPTURE
—of lunacy	LUNE
—to be shaved	RAZORABLE
fits of bad temper	LINES
fitting	LIABLE

five-spotted	CINQUE-SPOTTED
fix firmly	CONFIX
fixed	PIGHT, STEELED
flake	FLAW
flap wings impatiently	BATE
flash	FLAKE
flat	
—buttock	QUATCH-BUTTOCK
—pancake	FLAPJACK
flatter	MAKE FAIR WEATHER, WORD
fleece	FETCH OFF
flesh-eating	CARNAL
fleshing	FLESHMENT
flew	FLEWED
flexible twig	SWITS
flighty person	MINUTE-JACK
float	HULL
flock bed	QUILT
flood	RAGE
florid	TAFFETA(S), TAFFETY
flourish	SWINDGE
—on a trumpet	TUCKET
flout	LOUT
flow	RECOURSE
flowed	FLOWN
fluke	UPCAST
flushed	ROSED
flutter	BEAT
—like a hawk	BATE
fly	
—off	BLENCH
—over	OREPEARCH
—up and perch on	OREPEARCH
flying cloud	RACK
foam on water	YEAST
fodder	STOVER
fold	PLEACH
folding of tops of boots	RUFF
follow like a spaniel	SPANIEL
followed as by spaniel	PANELLED
follower	SEQUENT
food	REPASTURE
fool	ASINICO, CHIPOCHIA
	COLT, GECK, LACK-BRAIN
	PIED NINNY, SNIPE
fool's word	IMPETICOS
foolhardy	DARING-HARDY
foolish person	BAUBLE
foolishly	SHALLOWLY
footing	FEET
footpad	FOOT-LAND-RAKER, STRIKER
fop	BARBER-MONGER
foppish	FANGLED
—megalomaniac	MONARCHO
for	
—any sake	OF ALL LOVES

—shooting point-blank	FOREHAND
forbear compliance	STAND OFF
force	
—back against the current	RESTEM
—from	OUTFACE
forefront	VAWARD
forehead	FRONTIER
foreign	STRANGE
foremost	FORMER
forenamed	PRENOMINATE
forerunner	PRECURRER
forfend	SHIELD
form	
—of particulars	SCEDULE
—the freight of a vessel	FRAUGHT
formed	FEATED
—into	
ridges	ENRIDGED
stars	STEELED
formulate	PROPOSE
forsaken	
—by mistress	LASS-LORN
—person	FORLORN
fortune	HAVING
foul	REEKY
found	STAY
four inches wide	FOUR-INCHED
fowl	BIDDY
fragment	FLAW, QUANTITY
frame of mind	TEMPERALITIE
frantic	WOOD
free	LARGE
—from domestic cares	UNHOUSED
—school	CHARGE-HOUSE
freedom	LET-ALONE
French disease	GOOD-JER
	GOODYEAR
frenzy	LUNES
frequent	OLD
frequenter of theatre pit	GROUNDLING
freshness	YOUTH
friend	LOVER
friendliness	FRIENDING
fright	TIRRIT
frighten	DARE, GALLOW, GAST
frightened at oneself	SELF-AFFRIGHTED
fringed with a beard	VALANCED
frolicsome person	GAMESTER
from	ON
—time to time	STILL AND END
front	FOREWARD, VAWARD
fruitful	CONCEPTIOUS
fruiting	CHILDING
fuddled	FAP
fulfil in substitution	STEED UP
fulfilment	ENACTURE

full	
—of	
daring	DAREFUL
faults or crimes	FAULTFUL
honest zeal	TRUE-DEVOTED
obstructions	BAR(RE)FUL
small openings	LOOPED
—speed	RANDON
—to the brim	TOPFULL
—with acorns	FULL-ACORNED
fully	BY WEIGHT, IN WEIGHT
	WITH WEIGHT
—completed	EXPIATE
fully-charged	FULL-FRAUGHT
fumitory	FEMETARY, FEMITER
	FENITAR, FUMITER
furious	BRAINISH, WOOD
furnish	STUFF
—supper for	SUP
furniture	TIRE
gain	
—advantage over	RECOVER (THE WIND)
—money	COIN
gallant	CHAMBERER
gallantry	GAME
gallants	GALLANTRY
gallery of theatre	SCAFFOL(D)AGE
galligaskins	GASKINS
gallows	GALLOWSES
gallows-bird	HEMP-SEED
game	
—killed in hunt	HUNT
—like bagatelle	TROLL-MY-DAME
	TROU-MADAME
—running figure	
of eight	QUAINT-MAZES
—with dice	TRAY-TRIP
gamester	CHEATER
gaming	DIE
gaoler	ADAM
gap in fence	MUSET, MUSIT
gape with astonishment	YAWN
gash	SCOTCH
gay fellow	CAVALERO
gelded	UNPAVED
genuflection	KNEE
get married	GO INTO THE WORLD
ghostly	SPRIGHTLY
gibberish	LINSEY-WOOLSEY
gibe	GLEEK, GLIKE
gift of no value	NOTHING-GIFT
gild	ENGILD
gillyflower	GILLYVOR
gimmal	GIMMOR
gimmalled	JYMOLD
ginger rootstock	RACE

gipsy	TURLEYGOOD, TURLUPIN
give	BETEEM(E)
—a share of	PARTAKE
—away	LEAVE
—freedom to	ENFREEDOM
—new life to	REQUICKEN
—place	BACCARE, BACKARE
—up by signing	SUBSCRIBE
given due consideration	WELL-RESPECTED
giving	
—attention	ATTENT
—no help	HELPLESS
—offence	OFFENCE-FUL
glade	LAUND
glance	ELIAD, ILLIAD, OEILIAD
glaring	WALL-EYED
glittering	CLINQUANT
glorying	MAGNIFICENT
glutted with prey	RAVINED
go	PATH
—hang	SNECK UP, SNICK UP
—on	CONDUCE
—to the deuce	GO WHISTLE
—between	RING-CARRIER
in romantic affairs	LOVE-BROKER
goblin	OUPH
God's	
—foot	'SFOOT
—pity	OD'S-PITIKINS
gold-thread made in Venice	VENICE GOLD
golden	
—money	GILD
—russet	LEATHER-COAT
—tresses	TALLENT
gone	
—by	BY-PAST
—equal distance with	FILED
good	
—manners	GENTRY
—sense	MATTER
gorged	RAVIN'D
gorgeously variegated	PROUD-PIED
gorging	MOUSING
gorse	GOSSE
grace	DUE, FAVOUR
graduation on a dial	PRICK
grant	BETEEM(E)
grasping	LARGE-HANDED
grassy place	LAUND
gratification	SUPPLIANCE
gratify with a sixpence	TESTERN
gratifying	GRATULATE
gratuity	GRATILLITY
grave	CIVIL
—digger	GRAVE-MAKER
—import	STATE

grease	ENLARD, SEAM(E)	hat fringed with thrums	THRUMMED-HAT
greasy	RE(E)CHIE, REECHY	hatch	DISCLOSE
great		hated as hell	HELL-HATED
—event	STRATAGEM	haughty	HAUGHT, HAU(L)T
—expanse	MAIN		SURLY
—gun	CHAMBER	haul out	EXHALE
greet (again)	REGREET	haunt	SPRIGHT
greeting	COMMEND	have	
greetings	REGREET	—a holiday	PLAY
grieve	CONDOLE, TAKE THOUGHT	—engagement	BE PROMISED
grievous	DEAR(E), DERE	—done	BE THROUGH
grimace	MOE	—ill-will towards	BEAR HARD
grip	FANG, VICE	—in the womb	ENWOMB
gross	SALT-BUTTER	—value	WEIGH
grossly	GREASILY	having	
—covered	MABLED, MOBLED	—a	
grotesque		child	CHILDED
—endearment	PRINCOX	lover	LOVERED
—pageant	ANTIC	—abilities	PARTED
grow cold	QUENCH	—chaps of a hound	FLEWED
guarantee legal		—curly hair	CURLED-PATE
possession	VOUCH	—died at a natural time	TIMELY-PARTED
guard	ENGUARD, FORTRESS	—dislocated shoulder	SHOULDER-SHOTTEN
guess	AIM	—ejected spawn	SHOTTEN
guilt	FACT	—fewer customers	CUSTOM-SHRUNK
guilty	GUILTY-LIKE	—fiery eyes	FIRE-EYED
guinea(-hen)	GYNN(E)Y	—literary knowledge	LITERATURED
gull	ZANY	—mind of	
gun (30lb)	DEMI-CANNON	a puppy	PUPPY-HEADED
habit of frequenting	HAUNT	mixed contents	MOTLEY-MINDED
hale	EXHALE	—nailed soles	CLOUTED
half		—performed wonders	WOND(E)RED
—gallon drinking-pot	POTTLE-POT	—power to do many things	MULTIPOTENT
—wolf	DEMI-WOLF	—protuberances	WHELKED
halloo	SO-HO	—right to	CAPABLE
hamstring	HOX	—skin eruptions	TETTEROUS
hand	PICKER	hawk-keeper	ASTRINGER
handkerchief	HANDKERCHER	hawklike	HAWKING
handsome	GOOD-FACED	hazard	JUMP
handsome and deceitful	PROPER-FALSE	he-ass	ASSINEGO
hanging		head	COCKSCOMB, MAZ(Z)ARD
—in rags	TOTT'RING		NOLE, NOWL, PASH
—like fetters	DOWN-GYVED	—dress shaped like	
hangman's noose	HEMPEN CAUDLE	soup-dish	PORRENGER
happen	PROCEED		PORRINGER
—to	BEFORTUNE	heal	RECURE
happening once a minute	MINUTELY	healthy	LUSTICK, LUSTIQUE
hard-hearted	FLINT-HEART(ED)		WHOLESOME
harden by cold	BAKE	heap up	UPHOORD
hardship	DISGRACE	hear over again	OVERHEAR
hare	BAUD	hearken	TEND
harlot	HIREN	heart	BOWER
harm	VENGEANCE	—in medical astrology	TAURUS
harsh	AYGRE, EAGER	heartily	AGOOD
haste	EXPEDIENCE, POST	heart's desire	BOSOM
hasty	FESTINATE	hearty eater	TRENCHER-MAN

heaving	HEFT
heavy galley	GALLEASS
Hecate	HECAT
hedged in with poles	POLE-CLIPT
height	BROW
—of mockery	ARCH-MOCK
heir	
—apparent	APPARENT
—to much wealth	RICH-LEFT
held	HILD
hell	TARTAR
helm	STERN
helpful	SECOND
hemlock	INSANE ROOT
henbane	HEBENON, HEBONA
	INSANE ROOT
hen-pecked	WOMAN-TIRED
hesitate	MAMMER
hiccough	WAXEN, YEXEN
hide	ENCAVE, HOODWINK
high	
—crowned	COPATAINE
—spirits	SPLEEN
highly accomplished	ABSOLUTE
hill where grain is	
winnowed by the wind	SHEALING-HILL
	SHEELING-HILL
	SHIELING-HILL
	SHILLING-HILL
hinged	JYMOLD
hiss	HIZZ
hist	PEACE
hit	PAY
—in fencing	VENEWE, VENEY
ho!	WHOOP
hoard	UPHOORD
hold up as example	PARAGON
holiday	PLAYING
hollow	COVERED, WOMBY
holy-water vessel	STO(O)PE
homely	FOUL
homicidal (error)	HON(E)Y-SUCKLE
homicide (error)	HON(E)Y-SEED
honest fellow	TRUEPENNY
hope	ESPERANCE
honorary ornaments	CEREMONIES
hook fastening clothes	POINT
horn-call to assemble	
hounds	RECHATE, RECHEAT
horned	FORKED
horoscope	FIGURE
horse	CUT
horse's	
—canine tooth	TUSH
—disease	FIVES
horseback journey	RODE

hot	
—and passing like	
a summer	SUMMER-SEEMING
—headed	BRAINISH
	WASPISH-HEADED
—spiced	
gingerbread	PEPPER-GINGERBREAD
hour-point on a clock	PRICK
house made gloomy	
by discontent	DARK HOUSE
how does it happen that?	HOW CHANCE
howl at	BEHOWL
hubbub	WHOOBUB
human	
—creature	CIVIL
—feet	PETTITOES
humbled	PLUME-PLUCKT
humid	HUMOROUS
humour	COMPLEXION
humorous	CAPRICIOUS
hunchback	CROOKBACK
hungry	HUNGERLY, SHARP
hungrily	HUNGERLY
hurried	FESTINATE
hurry away with whizzing	
sound	WHIR(R)
hurtful	SHREWD
husk	SHALE, SHEAL, SHEEL
	SHIEL, SHILL
husky	CORKY
hyena	HYEN
hypocrisy	COUNTENANCE
I	CHE
—tell fortunes	DUCDAME
idle chatter	BIBBLE-BABBLE
ignoble	UNNOBLE
ignominy	IGNOMY
ignorant	UNCONFIRMED
ill	
—conditioned	SHREWD
—mixed	ILL-TEMPERED
—natured	SHREWD
—regulated	INCORRECT
illumine	OVERSHINE
image	MODULE, SHRINE
imaginary	AIR-DRAWN
imagination	AFFECTION
imaginative	FORGETIVE
imagine	PROPOSE
—expectantly	WEEN
imbued with properties	PROPERTIED
immature	PUPPY-HEADED
—peascod	SQUASH
immoderately	OUT OF ALL CESSE
immodest woman	TOMBOY
immortal	EVER-LIVING

immure	EMURE	inclination	CARE
impact	POISE	incline	PROPEND
impart	PARTAKE	incomprehensible	UNCOMPREHENSIVE
impatient of question	UNQUESTIONABLE	inconsiderable	EASY, PELTING, WEAK
impeach	APPEACH	inconsiderate	UNWEIGHING
impede	RUB	inconsistent medley	GALLIMAUFRY
impending evil	IMMINENCE	inconstant	GIGLET, GIGLOT
importunacy	IMPORTANCE	incontinent	UNSTANCHED, WAPPEND
importunate	IMPORTANT	incorporate	INCORPSE
importunity	IMPORTANCE	—one's own share	PIECE UP
imposition	DAUBERY, DAWBRY	increasing	CRESSIVE
impossible to undo	UNRECALLING	incredible	INCREDULOUS
imprecation	GOODYEAR	incurable	UNRECURING
impregnated with		incursion	RODE
bitumen	BITUMED	indecent	UNACCUSTOMED
impresa	IMPRESS(E)	indebted	DEBTED
impression	CHARACTERY, CICATRICE	indeed	GOOD-DEED
	(IM)PRESSURE	indicate	DESIGN
imprint	SET	indication	DENOTEMENT
imprisonment	PRISONMENT	indifferent to	WIDE OF
improve	PROFIT	indignation	MOTIONS
imprudent fellow	JACK SAUCE	indirect course	INDIRECTION
impulse	SPLEEN	individual person	SEVERAL
in		individuality	PROPERTY, PROPRIETY
—a		indivisible	INDIVIDABLE
body	IN SORT, IN THE QUILL		INTRENCHANT
derogatory manner	DEROGATELY	induce to come	PROCURE
moment	UPON A THOUGHT	indulge	ALLOW
	WITH A THOUGHT	indulged in	EMBRACED
—any case	IN ANY HAND	ineffective	UNPREGNANT
—concert	IN THE QUILL	inevitable	UNSHUN'D, UNAVOIDED
—custody	FORTHCOMING	inexorable	INEXECRABLE
—consequence of that	THEREUPON	inexperienced	PUNY, UNEXPERIENT
—full		inexpressible	TERMLESS
bloom	FLUSH	infant	EYAS MUSKET
extent	HOME	infection	ATTAINT
—good earnest	A-GOOD	inference	COLLECTION
—like manner	SEMBLABLY	inferior	IMPAIR
—most thought	CONSCIENCE	infested by thieves	THIEVISH
—my name	IN MY VOICE	infix strongly	CHARACTER
—one's		inflammable	COMBUSTIOUS
prime	PRIMY	—as tinder	TINDER-LIKE
right mind	WELL-ADVISED	inflated	BOMBAST
—rapid motion	RACKING	—as with pride	HIGH-BLOWN
—readiness	ALL POINTS	inflict pain on	SUFFER
—state of just		inform	RECOMMEND, YIELD
proportion	WEAL-BALANCED	—against	PEACH
—succession	SUCCESSANTLY	ingoing	ENTER
—the		inhabitant	CONFINER
field of battle	FIELDED	initiated	WELL-ENTERED
least	IN THE SMALLEST	initiating excitement	FLESHMENT
meantime	THE WHILE	initiation	ELEMENT
night	ANIGHT	injunction	IMPOSE
inattentive	UNRESPECTIVE	inquiry	ENQUIRE, INQUIRE
incapable of retaining	INTENIBLE	insanity	INFAMIE, INSANIE
incite to fight	TARRE	inscrutable	INVIS'D

insensible	BLUNT, IRON-WITTED
—to shame	SHAME-PROOF
insert in a schedule	ENSCHEDULE
inshelled	COCKLED, ENSHIELD
inside	INWARD
insidious	CAUTELOUS
—purpose	CAUTEL
insignificant	PICKING, PUISNY
—person	QUAT, WATER-FLY
insincere	MOUTH-MADE
insincerity	MOUTH-HONOUR
insinuate	SUGGEST
insist	CONSIST
—upon	STRAIN
insisting	UNSISTING
inspection	OVERVIEW
instigator	PUTTER-ON
instruct	STUDY
—in Gospel	GOSPEL
instructed	WELL-ENTERED
insult	INSULTMENT
—by gesture	FIG
intangible	UNFELT
intensive	AND TWENTY
intention	DESIGNMENT, HENT
	INTENDMENT, REGARD
—of going	PURPOSE
interchange	CONVERSE
interest	MEANS
interjection	CAESE, CEAS(E)
	HANDY-DANDY
	SESE(Y), SESSA
—boisterous	HOO
—imitating arrow sound	HEWGH
—of	
impatience	TILLY-FALLY
	TILLY-VALLY
surprise	GEMINI, GEMINY
	GEMONY, JIMINY
—to call a person	WHY
interest	USANCE, USE
interested	INTEREST
interpret	SCAN
intertwine	IMPLEACH
interval	BETWEEN
interwoven	ENTERTISSUED
intimacy	INWARDNESS
intimate friend	INWARD
intoxication	DISTEMPER
intricate	INTRINCE, INTRINSE
	INTRINSICATE
introduction	INDEX
inured by practice	BREATHED
inventive	FORGETIVE
inventory	SCEDULE
invested with power of destiny	FATED

invigoration by resting	REST
invisible	SIGHTLESS
invite	INDITE
inviting	COASTING
invoke	SWEAR
involved	PLIGHTED
involving trust	TRUSTY
ironical endearment	PRINCOX
irregular	DIFFUSED
irresistible	OPPOSELESS
irretentive	INTENIBLE
irritated	RAG'D, RAGDE
is of no importance	SKILLS NOT
jack	
—at bowls	MISTRESS
jack-in-office	JACK GUARDANT
jade	NAG
jagged	RAG'D, RAGDE
jaunt	JAUNCE, JAUNSE
jealous of higher authority	EMULOUS
jerk	PECKE, SWITS
jest	GLEEK, GLIKE
jester	MOTLEY, PIED NINNY
jilt	HUSWIFE
jocular endearment	PRINCOX
jog-trot	RANKE
join	INJOINT, SPLINTER
—as partner	PARTNER
—together	INTERJOIN
joined as with sinews	INSINEW
joining again	REIOYNDURE
joint	
—bargain	CO-MART
—in mechanism	GIMMOR
jointed	JYMOLD
jolly	
—cock	BAWCOCK
—companion	EPHESIAN
journey	GEST
Jove	THUNDER-BEARER
	THUNDER-DARTER
	THUNDER-MASTER
judge by evidence	TESTIMONY
judgement	DIRECTION
juicy	MOIST
just	JUMP, TRUE-DISPOSING
justify	APPROVE
keen	HAWKING, PARLOUS
keenly	SHREWD
keep	
—a hawk from sleep	WATCH
—busy with scruples	TASK
—from exertion	PROROGUE
—good watch or	
order	KEEP GOOD QUARTER
—head to wind	TRY

—in suspense	PEIZE
—off	EXPEL, OVERBLOW
keeping	
—back knowledge	IGNORANT
—off the sun	SUN-EXPELLING
kestrel	STALLION, STANYEL
kettle-drum	KETTLE
key on musical instrument	CHIP, JACK
kindness	LOVE
kindred	KINDLY
kite	PUTTOCK
—of infernal breed	HELL-KITE
knack	QUIRK
knave	COISTREL, COISTRIL
	COYSTREL, COYSTRIL
knavery	PATCHERY
kneel	KNEE
knight's stall	INSTALLMENT
know	WEET(E), WIS(T), WOT
—how to behave	UNDERSTAND
knowing	ACKNOWNE, WITTOL
knowledge	KNOW
known by heart	RECOLLECTED TERMS
knurled	GNARLED
lace tag	AGLET BABIE
ladykin	LAKIN
laid	
—by the wind	LODGED
—waste	BARE
lame	MAIN
lament	MEAN(E), MEIN, MENE
large	WIDE-STRETCHED
lark-song	TIRRA-LIRRA, TIRRA-LYRA
lascivious	CAPRICIOUS, SAUCY
lash	SWINDGE, SWITS
—made of wire	WIRE
last	LATTER
—night	TONIGHT
—purpose	CROWNET
—strait	EXIGENT
latrine	BENCH-HOLE
latter part	POSTERIOR
lattice-work on stomacher	WINDOW-BARNE
laugh	LOFFE
lawless	IRREGULOUS
lawn	LAUND
lay	
—bare	SCALE
—claim to	SPEAK TO
—man	TERRESTRIAL
—open	IMBARE
—under water	ENSTEEP
lazy fellow	BED PRESSER
league	COMPACT
leaky	UNSTANCHED
lean person	BARE-BONE

learned	AUTHENTIC, LITERATURED
leave	AVOID, LET, PART
—off	OMIT
lecherous	CODDING
lecture	EXERCISE
led in divisions	WING-LED
left	BESTOWED
legend	LEGION
legitimate	LOYAL
lending at interest	USANCE
lens of the eye	EYE-GLASS
leopard	LUBBAR
leprosy	MEAZEL, MESEL
let	
—go	OMIT
—me understand	TAKE ME WITH YOU
—slip	DELAY
letter	CAPON
levy	TAKE-UP
lewd	
—person	GAMESTER
—woman	CALLET, MALKIN
	MAWKIN
liable to schoolboy	
punishment	BREECHING
licentious	IRREGULOUS, LIBERAL
	LARGE, UNMASTERED
lick over	LATCH, LETCH
lie	COG
—to	TRY
life of pleasure	PRIMROSE PATH
	PRIMROSE WAY
life-blood	LETHEE
lift up	DUP, RELIEVE
light	
—giver	TORCHER
—on a beacon	CREDIT
like	SEMBLABLE
—a	
contented cuckold	WITTOLLY
surgeon	CHIRURGEONLY
vault	VAULTY
—the sky	SKYISH
liken	LIKE
limb by limb	LIMBMEAL
line of trees	LINE-GROVE
lineage	DESCENDING
liquor jug	BOMBARD
list	FILE, SCEDULE
—of actors and parts	SCRIPT
litigious	ACTION-TAKING
litter	KINDLE
little	PRETTY
—by little	BY SMALL AND SMALL
—gentleman	FRANKLIN
—heart	HEARTIKIN

—smile	SMILET
lively dance	UPSPRING
liver, brain and heart	PERFECTIONS
load	BALLAST
loading	FRAUTAGE
lodestone	MAGNESSTONE
lodge	HOST
lofty	HIGH-STOMACHED, SKYISH
loiter	FORESLOW
lonely	DEARN
long	LONGLY, SIDE
—continued	PERDURABLE
—delayed end	LAG-END
—distance arrow	FLIGHT
—for	EARN
longingly	WISTLY
look	
—demurely	DEMURE
—of one destined to hang	GALLOWS
looking upwards	HIGH-SIGHTED
loop in sword-belt	CARRIAGE
loose	
—and frivolous person	HOBBY-HORSE
—part of a coat	FORESKIRT
—vicious person	PAGAN
loosen	TOAZE
lose	LEESE
lost	LORE, LORN
lot	SORT
love	FANCY
—of	
oneself	SELF-CHARITY
youthful pleasures	COLT'S TOOTH
—sick	FANCY-SICK
	SICK-THOUGHTED
lovelock	LOCK
lover of malted liquor	MALT-WORM
loving	BELOVING, LOVELY
low-born	
—fellow	LOWNE
—prostitute	STALE
—servant	JACK SLAVE
—wretch	VASSAL
luck	ISSUE
lug out	EXHALE
lump of	
—fat	KEECH
—tallow	TALLOW-CATCH
lunacy	LUNES
lurking thief	MICHER
lustful	LUXURIOUS, RANK
lustreless	PALE-DEAD
lusty	LUSTICK, LUSTIQUE
lute-string of catgut	CATLING
mad	FOOLBEGGED, WOOD
—house	DARK-HOUSE

made	
—neat	FEATED
—of	
brands	PLANCHED
ropes	TACKLED
straw	SHEAVED
thread	THREADEN
wickerwork	TWIGGEN
—pensive	PENSIV'D
—up of	COMPACT
madness	ECSTASY
magpie	MAG(G)OT-PIE
maiden's funeral garland	CRANTS
maim	MAIN
maintain	ESCOT
maintenance	KEEPING
make	
—a	
fool of	BOB(B)
head	CAPITULATE
pattern	PATTERN
whore of	BEWHORE
—amorous advances	CARVE
—an agreement	CLAP HANDS
—away with	FETCH OFF
—believe	TAKE UPON ONESELF
—childless	UNCHILD
—clear	SCALE
—common cause	PARTAKE
—difficulties	MAKE IT STRANGE
—dishonest	
arrangement with	PACK CARDS WITH
—drunk	CUP
—faces	MOO
—fair	FLOURISH
—feat	FEAT
—grotesque	ANTIC
—happy	HAPPY
—haste	DESPATCH, DISPATCH
—heir	INHERIT
—hoary	HOAR
—known	DISCUSS
—lank	LANK
—lazy	SLUG
—much of	MAKE ON
—neat	FEAT
—pay dear	SAUCE
—plain	PLAIN
—progress	PROFIT, RID WAY
—rents in	WINDOW
—secret arrangement	PACK
—stable	STABLISH
—terms	DISPOSE
—to	
fail	SHORT
pass quickly	FLEET

—unlike	DISLIKEN	meddle	TEMPER
—up into total	PARCEL	medicinal virtue	FACULTY
maker of sport	GAMESTER	meditation	COMMENT
making		meet	COPE
—maps	MAPPERY	melancholy	ALLICHOLY, ALLYCHOLY
—no exception	EXCEPTLESS		SPLEEN, THOUGHT
male puppet	MOTION GENERATIVE	—strain	DUMP
malignant		memoranda	TABLES
—composition	HELL-BROTH	mercenary	COSTER-MONGER
—influence	TAKING	merchant	MARCATANT, MERCATANTE
Malvolio	BIDDY	mermaid	SEA-MAID
man		merry	
—killer	MAN-QUELLER	—and impetuous	HURTLING
—like	MANKIND	—festival	UTIS
—of the world	TERRESTRIAL	—meeting	ALE
—who busies himself		messenger	MISSIVE
with woman's affairs	COT-QUEAN	middle-age	MID-AGE
mandrake	MANDRAGORA	mien	MINE
mangle	MAMMOCK	mighty	MIGHTFUL
mangy	ROYNISH	mild	SARCENET, SARS(E)NET
manner	QUALITY	military pioneer	PIONER, PYONER
—of meeting	ENCOUNTER	milksop	COCKNEY, MEACOCK
many	MUCH	mind	MINE, NOTION
mark	CICATRICE	mine	MINERAL
marriage contract	CONTRACTION	—uncle	NUNCLE
marzipan	MARCHPANE	minute's time	MINUTE-WHILE
mask	CARACT, IMMASK	mirror	STONE
mast-head	HIGH-TOP	misanthrope	MISANTHROPOS
match	BESORT, MEET	miscellaneous gathering	GALLIMAUFRY
	PATTERN	mischief	MALICHO, MALLECHO
matchmaker	BROKER		VENGEANCE
mate	COMATE	mischievous	SHREWD
matted hair	ELFLOCKS	misdeed	MISTREADING
matter	CAUSE	misfortune	WRO(A)TH
—of		misgiving	GAINGIVING
conscience	REMORSE	mistake	MISTAKING
responsibility	OCCASION	mistaken	VICIOUS
matterful	MATERIAL	mistress	DOXY
mature	FLUSH	mitigation	REMORSE
may it		mix	CARD
—do	DICH	mixed	BLENT
—profit you	PROFACE	—badly	MISTEMPERED
meal of fish	FISH MEAL	mixture	COMPOSTURE
mean	CULLIONLY, FOXSHIP	moan	MEAN(E), MEIN, MENE
	ROYNISH, SCALL	model	MODULE
—fellow	COYSTRIL	moderation	MODESTY
meanest persons	LAG	modesty	PUDENCY
meaning	INTELLECT, INTENDMENT	moment	POIZE
meanly	COSTER-MONGER	moist	HUMOUROUS
—pretty	MODERN	moisten	BEWET, LATCH, MOIST
means	MEASURE	moment	POIZE
measure	CESS, HOOP, WHOOPING	momentum	SWAY
—½ gall.	STOUP	money	CHINKS, GILT
—of corn	MOY	moon's influence	
measured by sand	SANDY	on plants	PLANTAGE
mechanic	MECHANICAL	Moorish pike	MORRIS-PIKE

moral	L'ENVOY	necessary	NEEDY
more	MOE	negative side	NAYWARD
—execrable	INEXECRABLE	necklace	CARKANET
—fish than man	LAND-FISH	negligence	NEGLECTION
—quickly	RATHER	Negro	THICK-LIPS
—serious	SLOWER	neighbouring	SISTERING
—than enough	OLD	neither one thing	
morning	MATIN	nor another	ODD-EVEN
most		new-born lamb	EANLING
—beloved	ALDER-LIEFEST	never at rest	UNSISTING
—efficacious part	VIRTUE	newly	
—rascally	RASCALLIEST	—introduced	UPSTRING
—valuable part	HEART	—baptised child	CHRISOM-CHILD
motion of		nibble all over	OVEREAT
—contempt	FICO, FIGO	nightmare	CACOD(A)EMON, MARE
—horse	CAREIRES	nimble	QUIVER
motionless	STONE-STILL	—witted	VOLABLE
motto	IMPRESS(E)	nipping	SNEAPING
mould	MODEL	no alternative	NO REASON BUT
mournful elegy	DUMP	noise of clock pendulum	JAR
mouser	MOUSE-HUNT	noisy	BLUSTROUS, SWASHING
moustache	EXCREMENT	north	SEPTENTRION
movable rail	SWITS	—wind	AQUILON
move in zigzag course	INDENT	Norwegian	NORWEYAN
moving part of body	MOTIVE	not	
much		—adorned with holes	UNPINKT
—good may it do you	PROFACE	—artificial or counterfeit	UNCOYNED
—sought after	WELL-ADMIRED	—blown	UNBLOWED
muffled	MOBLED	—brought into action	UNEXECUTED
murderer	MAN-QUELLER	—bruised or crushed	UNBRUSED
murderous	CARNAL	—contradicted	UNCHECKED
murky	ROOKY	—controlled	UNSWAI'D
muscle	THEW	—dealt with	UNTRIDE
music	NOISE	—despised	UNCONTEMNED
musket	CALIVER	—dressed	UNREADY
muster-roll	MUSTER-FILE	—exercised	UNBREATHED
mutation	REVOLUTION	—having	
mutineer	MUTINE	a body	INCORPORAL
mutiny	MUTINE	bloomed	UNBLOWED
my lady	MADONNA	received sacrament	UNHOUSLED
name			UNHOUZZLED
—before	FORE-RECITED	—in	
—beforehand	PRENOMINATE	common use	UNTRACED
—of plant	CUCKOO-BUD	the secret	OUTWARD
nameless	TITLELESS	—marked off as paid	UNCROSSED
narrative	PROCESS	—noticed	UNTRIDE
native		—one's own	UNPROPER
—born	SELF-BORNE	—pinked	UNPINKT
—goodness	SELF-BOUNTY	—practised	UNBREATHED
—of Denmark	DANSKER	—produced by ordinary	
natural	UNCOYNED	generation	UNGENITURED
—spirit	SELF-METTLE	—quickened by lively	
nature of a child	CHILDNESS	sense	UNPREGNANT
navel	NAVE	—regulated	INCORRECT
neat(ly)	FEAT(LY)	—restrained in movement	FREE-FOOTED
necessarily	NEEDLY	—rustic	INLAND

—strongly timbered	UNTIMBERED	omission	OMITTANCE
—swung	UNSWAI'D	omit	LET
—to be		on	
blunted	BATELESS	—account	LONG
recalled	UNRECALLING	—purpose	NONCE
—ventured upon	UNTRIDE	—the spur of the moment	UPON THE GAD
—wielded	UNSWAI'D	—what grounds	WHEREUPON
—willed	UNWILLING	one	
—yet born	UNBRED	—administering	
notify	FRUTIFY	correction	CORRECTIONER
notion	PROJECT, SUPPOSAL	—and the same	ONE SELF
number of		—bound by the same vow	VOW-FELLOW
—fish together	SCUL(L), SCULLE	—deformed	STIGMATIC
—individuals	POLL	—deserving hanging	CRACK-HEMP
nun	CLOISTRESS		CRACK-ROPE
nursing	NURSERY, SICK-SERVICE		CRACK-HALTER
oaf	OUPH(E)	—in charge of provisions	PANT(L)ER
oath	BY COCK AND PIE	—making progress	PROFICIENT
—on the Bible	BOOK-OATH	—on a quest	QUESTANT, QUESTER
obedient	BUXOM		QUESTRIST
object for flouting	FLOUTINGSTOCK	—only	ONE SELF
obliged	DEBTED	—partly a bawd	PARCEL-BAWD
obliterate	DISLIMN	—who	
obscure		affects wit	WIT-SNAPPER
—dungeon in prison	HELL	breaks engagements	CRACK-TRYST
—word	AN HEIRES, BRAKE	can keep secrets	COUNSEL-KEEPER
obseqious		concerns himself	
—attendant	OBSERVANT	with love	FANCY-MONGER
—bowing	FLEXURE	deserves gallows	GALLOWS
observed	COTED	draws with	
observer	SPECULATION	confederate	COACH-FELLOW
obstinacy	OPINION	entreats	IMPLORATOR
obstinate	HIGH-STOMACHED	foments argument	BREED-BATE
	OBSTACLE	hunts counter	HUNT-COUNTER
obtain on credit	TAKE UP	incurs punishment	FORFEITER
occupy oneself	TIRE	is	
occurrences	CURRENTS	—ill	SICKMAN
oeillade (glance)	ELIAD, ILLIAD	—suntanned	TANLING
of		rides in front	FORE-SPURRER
—a jovial turn	GOOD-LIFE	seeks for another	QUESTRIST
—anticipation	FOREHAND	sells taps	FOSSET-SELLER
—good stock	WELL-DERIVED	settles business of	PHEAZAR
—great importance	OF GREAT ARTICLE	takes on another's	
—necessity	NO REMEDY	quarrel	UNDERTAKER
—no value	IMMOMENT	travels post	POSTER
—partiality	PARTIAL	with pasty face	TALLOW-FACE
—the air	REGION	one's own utterances	SELF-BREATH
offence	MALEFACTION	open	DUP, RAZE
offer	PROPOSITION	—mouthed	WIDE-CHAPPED
office	FACULTY	opening	PORTAGE
officer of		—up	OVERTURE
—(bishop's) court	PARITOR	operating suddenly	RASH
—the Exchequer	HEATER	opinion	DEEM
officious	SUPERSERVICEABLE	opportunity	HENT, VANTAGE
—fellow	PLEASEMAN	oppose	REPUGN
oil of consecration	BALM	opposition	REPUGNANCY

oppress by bulk	OVERBULK	—fellow	HILDING
oppressive supervisor	SHEEP-BITER	pamper	ENGROSS
orange-seller	ORANGE-WIFE	pampered by lust	LUST-DIETED
ordain	FOR(E)SAY	pander	GREEK
ordaining	ORDINANT	pang	THROW(E)
ordinary experience	USE	paper of conditions	BOOK
orifice	ORIFEX	parallel	PATTERN
original of a copy	PRECEDENT	parasite	TRENCHER-FRIEND
ornament	FLOURISH, GARLAND		TRENCHER-KNIGHT
	GUARD	parcel	COMMODITY
—for the neck	RABATO	paroxysm	THROW(E)
—with puffs	BLISTER	parson	SOUL-CURER
ostentation	OSTENT	part	SQUARE
ostentatiously dressed	CURLED	—of an army, camp, etc	QUARTER
out of breath	OUTBREATH'D	partake	PERTAKE, UNDERGO
outdo	LURCH	particular	SEVERAL
outer garment of leather	PILCHER	—nature	PROPRIETY
outgrowth	EXCREMENT	—purpose	NONCE
outlying sentinel	PERDU(E)	parting	DEPART
outshine	OUTLUSTRE, OVERSHINE	partner	RIVAL
outside garb	CASE	pass	
outstare	ORE-STARE	—by	COTE
outward	WITHOUT-DOOR	—in succession	SUCCEED
outweigh completely	WEIGH TO THE BEAM	—over on knees	KNEE
outwork	FRONTIER	—time	ENTREAT
over		passionate	WASPISH-HEADED
—dainty	SUPERDAINTY	passive	PRONE
	TAFFETA(S), TAFFETY	patched	CLOUTED
—come	CONVINCE	patronise	EMPATRON
by jesting	OUTJEST	pattern	SPOTTE
—grown with wild		pawn	FINE
orchises	PIONED	pay	
—power	CONVINCE, THRONG	—for	ESCOT
—reached	OE'R-RAUGHT	—of an army	ENTERTAINMENT
	ORE-RAUGHT	—ready-money	PITCH AND PAY
	ORE-WROUGHT	—up	COME OFF
—ridden	SUR-REYN'D	peace	
—subtle	SUPERSUBT(I)LE	—maker	MAKE-PEACE
—take	COTE	—officer	FARBOROUGH
—value	OVERHOLD		THARBOROUGH
—worked	SUR-REINED, SUR-REYNED	peacock	PAIOCK(E), PAJOCK(E)
—worn	OVERSCHUTCH	pearl	UNION
—wrested	ORE-RESTED	peasant	CARLOT
own affairs	SELF-AFFAIRS	peculiar sorrow	FEE-GRIEF
ox	ROTHER(-BEAST)	pedant	PEDASCULE
pace	RANK	peep under	UNDERPEEP
pain	MEAN	peer	SQUINNY, TWEER, TWIRE
painful	PANGING	people	MEINIE, MEIN(E)Y
paint	IMPAINT	perceive	SURVEY
—face	GAUD, GAWD	perform	
painted in	TRICK	—by proxy	ATTORN
pair (eyes)	GEMINI, GEMINY	—sleight of hand	CONVEY
	GEMONY, JIMINY	performance of promise	DEED OF SAYING
pale-faced	PALE-VISAGED	peril	APPERIL
—like a sick girl	MAID-PALE	perjured person	PERJURE
paltry	BARE, PELTING	perjury	OATH-BREAKING

perky	PERT	plague	GOODYEAR
petty	PELTING	—spot	DEATH-TOKEN
persistent	PERSISTIVE	—spots	THE LORD'S TOKENS
person with a tail	TAILOR	plan	SCEDULE
personal		—of action	PLATFORM
—identity	PROPERTY	planning	MAPPERY
—relation	PARTICULAR	plants in general	PLANTAGE
personality	CHARACT	plausible	PLAUSIVE, PROBALL
persuasion	INDUCEMENT	play	
pert		—part in a mask	JEST
—boy	CRACK	—trick on	GLEEK, GLIKE
—woman	FLIRT-GILL	plebeian	PLEBEAN
pertaining to the dead	DEFUNCTIVE	pleasant	LUSTICK
perverse	PEEVISH	please	FREET
perversity	ADVERSITY	pleasing	PLAUSIVE
pestilence	MURREN, MURRION	pleasure	LUST
petard	PETAR	pledge	FINE
petty	PUISNY	plenty	FUL(L)NESS
phrase	COMMA	plot	PRACTISE
—appropriated to		pluck	RASE, TO(A)ZE
pilgrims	WOOLWARD	plume	PRANK
—in combat	UTTERANCE	pluming oneself	REPUTING
physician	MEDICINE	plump	PLUMPIE, PLUMPY
physiognomy	FISNOMIE	pocket	POAKE
piano key	JACK	point in tennis	CHASE
picked	RECOLLECTED TERMS	poison	BANE, MINERAL
pickthank	PLEASEMAN	poke	POAKE
picture giving		Pole/Polish	POLACK
fantastic effect	PERSPECTIVE	pole for carrying baskets	COWL-STAFF
piddling	PICKING	polished	INLAND
pie-crust on		politeness	COMPLEMENT
custard-pie	CUSTARD-COFFIN	pollute	FILE
piece	SPLINTER	poltroon	POULTROONE
—of		pomander	POUNCET
cow-dung	SHARD	pooh	POWWAW, PUH
fluff	DOWL(E)	poor	SCALD, SINGLE
money	MOY	popular	WELL-GRACED
needlework	SPOTTE	porcupine	PORPENTINE
pierced with grief	GRIEF-SHOT	portent	AUGUR
pig-sty	FRANK	portholes	PORTAGE
pilchard	PILCHER	portion	COMMODITY, SCANTLE
pile-driver	THREE-MAN-BEETLE	position	FIXTURE
pious	ZEALOUS	—for being observed	PROSPECT
pip	PEEP(E)	post-horse	POST
pirate	WATER-THIEF	postpone	PROLONG, PROROGUE
pish!	PUSH		REJOURN
pitch	PECKE, SET DOWN	pot-thumping	BOLD-BEATING
pity	BOWEL, REMORSE	potentate	POTENT
place	BIDING	pound	PUN
—in		pour	INFUSE
order	ENRANK	—out	BETEEM
the sky	ENSKY	power of overcoming	PREVAILMENT
—noted for brothels	PICKT-HATCH	powerful	MIGHTFUL
—on lee side	BELEE	practice arrow	BUTT-SHAFT
—where pastry is made	PASTRY	practised	TRADED
placed in a window	WINDOWED	praise	COMMEND

—excessively	SUPERPRAISE	proof	ASSAY, INSTANCE
prance	JAUNCE, JAUNSE	propensity	PROPENSION
precedent	PRESIDENT	propitious	WHOLESOME
precipice	PRECEPIT	proportion	QUANTITY
precipitate	STEEP(E)-DOWN(E)	prosperous	WELL TO LIVE
	STEEP(E)-UP	prostitute	CUSTOMER, GUINEA-HEN
precisely	BY THE SQUIRE		LACED MUTTON, POLECAT
precondition	PREMISE, PREMISS		QUAIL, RODE, STALE
preface	INDEX		VENTURE
pregnant	GREAT-BELLIED	protect plant from cold	WINTER-GROUND
premature	TIMELESS	protected against	
preparation	APPOINTMENT, INDUCTION	floods by plaited	
	PREPARE	osiers	TWILLED
prepare	ADDRESS	protract	LINGER
presage	ABODE	proud	ORGILLOUS, ORGULOUS
present with sixpence	TESTERN	—in the highest degree	TOP-PROUD
preserve from decay	SEASON	—spirited	HIGH-STOMACHED
press		prove	CITE
—for	STRAIN	—by	
—hard	THRONG	evidence	TESTIMONY
pressure	OPPRESSION	testing	TRY
pretend	INTEND	provender	PROVAND, PROVEND
pretty	INCONIE, INCONY		PROVIANT
prevail over	CARRY	provocation	PROVOKEMENT
prevent	UNDO	provoke	TARRE
previous practice	ELEMENT	proxy	SUBSTITUTE
prey to mournful			PREWYN, PROIN(E), PROYN(E)
sensations	PASSIONATE		PRUINE, SWITS
price	ESTIMATE	public	GENERAL
prim	PRENZIE	pudding with many	
primer	ABSEY BOOK	ingredients	HODGE-PUDDING
primogeniture	PRIMOGENIT	puff in scorn	BLURT
prince	HAMLET, POTENT	puffed	
princely	PRENZIE	—out	EXSUFFLICATE
principal	ARCH, CAP	—sleeve	TRUNK-SLEEVE
prison	CONFINE	puffy	EMBOSSED
private	REMOVED	pull	TOZE
—grief	FEE-GRIEF	—by the ears	SOLE, SOWL
—person	PRIVATE	pulse	PULSIDGE
—room	BY-ROOM	punctilious	PICK
privilege	COMMODITY, PRISE	puny	PUISNY
privy	AJAX, JAKES, DRAUGHT	puppet	MOTION
prize	PRICE, PRISE, REPRISAL	—thrown at in Lent	JACK-A-LENT
problem	CONCLUSION	purblind	BEESOME, BISSOM
proceed	SWAY	purport	PURPOSE
proclaim	PROTEST	purpose	DESIGNMENT, MIND
procrastination	INDURANCE	purposeless	SHAPELESS
produced in heaven	HEAVEN-BRED	put	
profit	COMMODITY	—an end to	PERIOD
prognostication	PRECURSE	—aside	DAFF, DOFF
programme	SCEDULE	—forward repeatedly	VIE
project	REFLEX	—in	
—beyond	JUTTY	gaol	ENGAOL
prologue	INDEX	pocket	IMPETICOS
prolong	LINGER, RESPITE	shelter	ENSHELTER
prompt	PRIME	splint	SPLINTER

the stocks	STOCK-PUNISHT	—at hand	AT AN INCH
—off	FUB OFF	—for tears	WEEPING-RIPE
by	DAFF	—to sink	SINKING-RIPE
with contempt	SLIGHT OFF	real	BODILY, ESSENTIAL
—on oath	DEPOSE		UNCOINED, UNCOYNED
—to death	TRANSPORT	rear	CATASTROPHE, HAUNCH
putting under embargo	EMBARQUEMENT	reason	SKILL
pygmy	ATOMY	reasonable	WHOLESOME
quadrangular space		reassemble	RE-ENFORCE
on hand	TABLE	rebel	MUTINE, REVOLT
qualify	ABLE	rebuke	SAUCE
quality	AFFECTION, ASSAY	rebuked	SHENT
qualm	CALM	recall of pursuers	RETREAT
quarreller	QUARREL	receiving ball	EMBALLING
quarrelsome	QUARRELOUS	recently made sad	NEW-SAD
—person	CHIDER, SQUARER	receptacle for	
quarrelsomeness	QUARREL	—meal	BOLTING-HATCH
question propounded	PROPOSITION	—tallow	TALLOW-CATCH
quibble	SNATCH	recipient	CAPTIOUS
quick!	YARE	reciprocation	COUNTERCHANGE
—minded	BAVIN-WITS	recital	RECOUNTMENT
—to understand	APPREHENSIVE	recited before	FORE-RECITED
quickest	RATHEREST	reck	WREAK(K)
quit	AVOID, PART	reckon up	PARCEL
quite		reckoning	ICK, WHOOPING
—alone	HIGH-LONE	reckoner	COUNTER-CASTER
—new	FRE NEW	recoil	REQUOYLE
quits	MEET	recollect	ADVISE
quoin	COIN	recompense	REGUERDON
quote	COAT(E), COTE	red	CAIN-COLOURED
rabble	VARLETRY	reduce to	
race	RAZE	—poverty	RUINATE
rage	VIOLENT	—subjugation	ASSUBJUGATE
raged	RAG'D, RAGDE	re-echo	REWORD
ragged	RAG'D, RAGDE	refer	PUT OVER
raid	RODE	refined	INLAND, PICK
raise	ADVANCE	reflecting the	
—from the dead	ARAISE, ARAYSE	sentiments of another	GLASS-FACED
raising of a siege	REMOVE	reflection	REGARD
rally	RE-ENFORCE	refresh	REPAIR
rank	ORDINANCE	refuse-basket	SIEVE
rarely shown	SELDSHOWN	regale in the cook-room	KITCHEN
rascal	COMPANION, FAITO(U)R	regard	COTE, TENDER
rashness	GUST	regarded without awe	AWELESS
ravening	RAVEN, RAVIN(E)	regardful	RESPECTIVE
ravished	YRAVISHED	region	CLIMAT(UR)E
reach	DANGER, MEASURE	register of soldiers	
read	SCAN	or sailors	MUSTER-BOOK
readiest	EFTEST	reinforcing	SUPPLIANT
read(ing) over	SUPERVISE	reins halfway up side-	
readily	LIGHTLY	piece of bit	HALF-CHECKED
—inclined	PROMPT	reject	ABHOR
ready	ADDRESSED, ADDREST	rejoining	REIOYNDURE
	FEAT, PREGNANT	relation in detail	RECOUNTMENT
	PREST, PRONE	relevance	CONCERNANCY
—apprehension	RECEIVING	religious recluse	ANCHORET

relinquish	GIVE OUT	revengeful	VENGEABLE, VINDICATIVE
relish	SAY	reverberation	REPLICATION
rely	STAY	revival preceding death	LIGHTNING
remain in a certain place	CLIMATE	revivify	REPAIR
remark	REASON	revocation	REVOKEMENT
remedial	REMEDIATE	revoke by contrary shout	UNSHOOT
remedy	RECURE	revolution	INNOVATION
remit a debt or offence	FORGIVE	revulsion	REVOLT
remoteness	REMOTION	reward	REGUERDON
removal	REMOTION	—with sixpence	TESTERN
remove a covering	DISCASE	rheum	RUME
render		rich	CHUFF
—destitute	DISFURNISH	riches	TAL(L)ENT
—dumb	DUMB	riddle	CONCLUSION
—spiritless	CRAVEN	ride	RODE
—trivial	TRIFLE	—hastily	SKIRR
repairing	STILL-PEERING	riding-whip	SWITS
	STILL-PIECING	right of sanctuary	PRIVILEGE
repeat	REWORD	riot	RUFFLE, WHOOBUB
repetition of same rhyme	RANKE	ripe	FLUSH
replenishment	SUPPLYMENT	—for tears	WEEPING-RIPE
repletion	PLURISIE, PLURISY	rising on high	MOUNTANT
report	NOISE, QUEST, YIELD	risk	JUMP
—the words of	REDELIVER	river-bank	WHARF
reporting	REPORT	road	RODE
reposing	REPOSALL, REPOSURE	roam	WHEEL
reprehended	ATTASKED, ATTASKT	roar	RORE
represent anew	REFIGURE	robe	PALLIAMENT
representation	EXPRESSURE	robed in fire	FIRE-ROBED
representative	IMAGE	rod	SWITS
reprieve	REPREEVE	roguery	PATCHERY
reproach	AYWORD, BRAID	roll	FILE
reproachfully	INVECTIVELY	Roman robe	PALLIAMENT
reprobation	REPROBANCE	rondure	CIRCLE
reproduce	REFIGURE	root	RAZE
reprove	TAKE UP	rope-torture	STRAPPADO
reputation	ESTEEM, OPINION, PASS	rose tree	ROSIERE
requital	QUITTAL	rotation	SWAY
requited	REQUIT(TED)	rote	ROATE
resembling	SEMBLABLE, SEMBLATIVE	rough	
residence	BIDING, MASONRY	—coated apple	LEATHER-COAT
resist	REPUGN	—mannered fellow	TYKE
resolved	PIGHT	round	COMPASSED
resort	HAUNT, TRADE	—off	PARCEL
resorting to law	ACTION-TAKING	roundure	RONDURE
restlessly	DISQUIETLY	rousingly defiant	ROISTING, ROYSTING
restore	REPAiR	rowdy gang	TRIBULATION
restrict	COMBINE	rub with oil or grease	LIQUOR
retain	CONTAIN	ruck	ROOK
retard	TARDY	ruddock	RADDOCKE
retching	HEFT	rudiment	GERMAIN(E)
retinue	MEIN(E)Y, MEINIE	ruin	RUINATE
retrace	UNTREAD	ruined	SHENT
return	REGUERDON, REPAIR	rule	SQUIER, SQUIRE
reveal	DECIPHER	ruled with difficulty	HARD-RULED
revel at night	NIGHT-RULE	rummage	ROMAGE

rumour	MURMUR	scurvy	ROYNISH, SCALL
run		—woman	RONYON, RUNNION
—through from first		scythe	SIETH, SITHE
to last	DECLINE	sea bird	SCAMEL, SEA-MELL
—over as in race	HEAT	seal with others	COUNTERSEAL
rush	RANDON	seam	LARD
rustic	BACON	search-party	SEARCH
—game	(PRISON-)BASE	season	BESPICE
said	FAINE, SAINE	seat	
sailor	CANVAS-CLIMBER	—in church porch	CHURCH-BENCH
sailor's private venture	PORTAGE	—of dignity	STATE
salacious	SALT	secret	INWARD
salt hake	POOR JOHN	—council	CHAMBER-COUNCIL
salutation	REGREET	—going or passage	STEALTH
salute mutually	CONGREET	—message	PRIVATE
salutiferous	VIRTUOUS	secretary	CHANCELLOR
sanctities	SONTIES	seeming	SEMBLATIVE
sane	FORMAL	seen	SAWN
sanity	WISDOM	seigneur	SIGNIEUR
sated	RAVIN'D	seize	CEAZE, EXTEND, SEASE, SEAZE
satiety	CLOYMENT	—upon	PHANG
satire	TAXATION	seizure	EXTENT, SEYSURE
satisfaction	SUFFIGANCE	self	
satyr	SALTIER	—confidence	OPINION
savage	SALVAGE	—deception	SELF-ABUSE
—practices	FELL-FEATS	semblance	ASSEMBLY
savouring of the		senior	SIGNEUR
ale-house	RED-LATTICE	seniority	SIGNEURIE
scabby	ROYNISH	sense	SENT
—fellow	SCROYLE	sensible	WHOLESOME
scaffolding	SCAFFOLAGE	sensitive	COUNTABLE
scapegrace	SKAIN(E)S MATE	sent before due time	PREMISED
scar	WIPE	sentence	CENSURE
scare	GALLOW, SCAR(RE)	sententious saying	REASON
scarecrow	CROWKEEPER	sentry-box	WATCH-CASE
scattering silver	SILVER-SHEDDING	separable	DIVIDANT
scent	SENT	separate	DISTRACT
schedule	SCEDULE	—body	DISTRACTION
scheme	PLATFORM	sequence	SEQUEL
school	CHARGE-HOUSE, SCUL(L)	serge	SURGE
	SCULLE	serious	OBSEQUIOUS
—fellow	BOOK-MATE, INKHORN-MATE	serpigo	SAPEGO, SUPPEAGO
—master	PEDANT	serve	CONVENT
scion	S(E)YEN, SIEN	serviceable	COMMODIOUS
scissors	CIZERS	set	
scoff	GALL	—aside	REPEAL
scold	CALLET	with contempt	SLIGHT OFF
Scotsman	BLUECAP	—astray	STRAY
scour	SKIRR	—at defiance	BEARD
scout	DISCOVERER	—before the mind	PROJECT
scramble	MUSS(LE)	—crosswise	TRAVERSED
—for	SCAMBLE	—forth	PROJECT
scrap	QUANTITY	—free	ENFREE
scrawl	MARTIAL-HAND	—in	
screech-owl	SCHREECH-OWL	battle array	DARRAIGN(E), DARRAIN(E)
scurry	SCUR, SKER, SKIRR, SQUIRR		DARRAYN, DERRAIGN

tender frame	TENDER-HEFTED	—reluctance	MAKE IT STRANGE
—mark of folly on	NICK	shower	ASPERSE, ASPERSION
—of		showing	
anchors	ANCHORAGE	—marks of travel	TRAVEL-TAINTED
four	MESS	—part of face	HALF-FACED
—on	TARRE	shrew	SHROW
—squatting	ROOK	shrewd	PARLOUS, SHROWD
—up	STABLISH	shrewdly	UNHAPPILY
setting	VAIL	shrewish	SHREWD, WASP-STUNG
settle	TAKE UP		WASP-TONGUE
—a dispute	TAKE UP A QUARREL	shriek	SHREEK, SHRIKE
—the business of	FEEZE	shrill in throat	SHRILL-GORGED
	PHE(E)SE, PHEEZE	shuffle	PALTER
severe	WEIGHTY	shut	MAKE
—in manner	OVEREARNEST	—up	SPERR
sewer	COMMON-SHORE	in sty	FRANK
shaft	FIL(L)	shy	CHARY
—horse	P(H)ILHORSE	sick with the thought	THOUGHT-SICK
shaggy	RAG'D, RAGDE	sidesman	STICKLER
—lapdog	SHOWGHE	sigh	HEAVE
shame	REPROOF	sight	BEHOLDING
shamefacedness	PUDENCY	sign	CARACT, DENOTEMENT
shameless	UNBASHFUL	—of ale-house	RED LATTICE
shape	PROJECT	silence	CLAMOUR
shapeless	UNFASHIONABLE	silent	LANGUAGELESS
share	COMMON	silk	SAY
sharing	IMPARTMENT	silver coin	PLATE
sharp	AYGRE, EAGER	similar	SEMBLABLE
—pointed buttock	PIN-BUTTOCK	simply	SHALLOWLY
shaven	PIEL'D	simulative	SEMBLATIVE
she		since	SITH(ENS), SITHENCE
—cat	TIB-CAT	sincerely beloved	HEART-DEAR
—physician	MEDICINE	sing in chorus	CHOIR
sheathed	BREACHED	singing a simple theme	PLAINSONG
shed in small drops	DRIZZLE	singular	UNTRACED
shedding	EFFUSE	sink down	SWAGG
sheer drop	PRECIPITATION	sixpence	TESTRIL(L)
shekel	SICKLE	Sium	CYME
shell	SHALE, SHEAL, SHEEL	skeleton	ATOMY
	SHIEL, SHILL	skewer	PRICK
shelter	WEATHER-FEND	skilful	QUAINT
sheltered under dung	SHARDED	skill	DIRECTION, DOCTRINE
sheriff's officer	YEOMAN		MISTERY, MYSTERY
sherry	SHERRIS	skin disease	SAPEGO, SUPPEAGO
shine upon	OVERSHIRE	—eruption	TETTER
shining through	TRANSPARENT	skull	MAZ(Z)ARD
shiplike head-dress	SHIP-TIRE	sky-blue	WELKIN
shoal	SCHOOLE	slacken	QUAIL
shock	SHOUGH	slaked	YSLAKED
—headed	RUG-HEADED	slanderous	VENOM'D-MOUTH'D
shoot	GERMAIN(E)	slash	RACE, SCORCH
—up	SPIRT	slaying	QUELL
short-sleeved garment	SEA-GOWN	sleaved	SLE(I)DED
show	CITE, LOOK OUT	sleeping house	LULLABY
	OSTENT, PORT	slice	SCANTLE
—in glory	TRIUMPH	slight	EASY, SINGLE

—salute	HALF-CAP	sounding	SONUANCE
slink about	PEAK	sour	AYGRE, EAGER
slow		sourness	RANCOUR
—dance	PAVAN(E), PAVEN, PAVIN	souse	SOUCE, SOWS(S)E
	PADUAN	soused	SOUCT
—flying	FLY-SLOW	sovereign command	EMPERY
—witted	UNPREGNANT	sowing	SEEDNESS
sluggish	RESTY	sown	SAWN
small	PINK, SINGLE	space under gable	BAY
—box for perfumes	POUNCET-BOX	Spanish wine	BASTARD, SHERRIS-SACK
—cannon	CHAMBER	sparrow	PHILIP
—coin	SOLIDARE	spasm	THROW(E)
—freeholder	FRANKLIN	speak	
—French coin	DENIER	—against	FOR(E)SPEAK
—gratuity	GRATILLITY	—ill of	MISREPORT, MISUSE
—herb	HERBELET	—louder than	OUTTONGUE
—hole	VENTIGE	speaker	DISCOURSER
—shade of colour	EYE	specify	FRUTIFY, LIMIT
—share	MOIETY	specious nobleman	COUNT CONFECT
—stream of water	FRESH	speechless	LANGUAGELESS
—tusk	TUSH	speedy	SOON
smeared	TRICK	spend time	ENTREAT, CONTRIVE
smell	SENT	spent by time	TIME-BEWASTED
smile	SMOILE, SMOYLE	spermaceti	PARMACITIE
smutted with coal	COLLIED	sphere	SPHEAR(E)
snap	SNATCH	spinner	SPINSTER
snatch	RASE, RUFFLE	spirited	SPRIGHTFUL
sneak about	PEAK	spiritless	MUDDY-METTLED
snort	BLURT	spite	SPIGHT
so let it be!	WHY, SO	splendid phraseology	FESTIVAL TERM
social class or order	ORDINANCE	splinter	FLAW
soft	LITHER	spoil taste of	DISTASTE
soften	TEMPER	spoilt child	PRINCOX
soldier	MILITARIST	sport beyond the limits	OUTSPORT
sole	MEER'ED	spots (plague)	DEATH-TOKENS
solicitation	INSUIT	spotted	MEAL'D
solicitous	CURIOUS	sprang	SPRONG
solid		spray	ASPERSE, ASPERSION
—lump or mass	KEECH	spread	SCALE
—thing	SOLIDITY	spring	WHITING-TIME
something		sprinkle	DISPUNGE
—fitted to an end	FITMENT	sprinkling	ASPERSION
—needed	NEEDMENT	sprite	SPRIGHT
—savoury	SALAD	sprout	SPIRT
—showing anger	INDIGNATION	spume	YEAST
—to fill up time	SUPPLIANCE	spy	SURVEY
—waved	WAFTURE	square	SQUIER, SQUIRE
—with poisonous juice	HEBONA	squat	
sometimes	SOME	—buttock	QUATCH-BUTTOCK
—humble	PRONE	—down	ROOK
sooner	RATHER	squatting position	TAILOR
soonest	RATHEREST	squint	SQUINNY
soothe	COY	stab	BORE
sorrowful	TRISTFUL	stability	FIXTURE
sound	CHIDING	stage	GEST
—to call back dogs	RECH(E)ATE, RECHEAT	—fanfare	SENNET

stagger along	REEL	strictness	STRICTURE
stained	MEAL'D	strife	BATE
—with neighbour's		strike	PASH
blood	NEIGHBOUR-STAINED	—aghast	GHAST
stake	IMPONE	—off the roll	UNROLL
stalking-horse	STALE	—with	
stamp	PRESSURE	switch	SWITS
stand		violence	PASH
—as godfather	GOSSIP	strip	DISFURNISH, UNCASE
—back	BACCARE, BACKARE	—naked	CASE
—erect (hair)	ROUSE	stripped of plumes	PLUME-PLUCKT
—muttering	MAMMER	strive	PURCHASE
—under	UNDERSTAND	stroke	COY
—upon	CONSIST	—of lightning	THUNDER-STROKE
standstill	STILL-STAND	—with claw	CLOYE
stank more than	ORE-STUNCK	strong	BONNIE, BONNY
stanza	STANZE, STANZO	—liquor	TICKLE-BRAIN
start		stubborn	IMPERSEVERANT
—aside	BLENCH	—foe	WRANGLER
—off	BLENCH	studied	RECOLLECTED TERMS
state	PORT	stuffing for cooked	
—beforehand	PRENOMINATE	carcase	PUDDING
—of defence	BRACE	stumble	PECKE
statesman	WEALSMAN	strumpet	BONA-ROBA, TIB
stay	REMAIN	stun	ASTONISH
—beyond	OUTDWELL	stunted	SCRUBBED
stead	STEED	stupefy	MULL
steadfast	STEDFAST	stupid	BARRED, CLAY-BRAINED
steep	ENSTEEP		CONCEITLESS
steerage	STERNAGE	sty	FRANK
steering-gear	STERN	subdue	ABATE, CONVINCE, HARROW
steersman's place	STERN	subject	LIABLE
sterile	HUNGRY	—by need	NECESSITIED
stiff collar	RABATO, REBATER, REBATO	—to	
stigmatise	SEAR	pangs	THROW(E)
stimulate	TARRE	whipping	BREECHING
stir	COIL, GARBOILS	submission	SUBSCRIPTION
stock of children	AERIE, AERY	submissive	COMPTIBLE
	AYRIE, EYRIE, EYRY	submissiveness	DEPENDACIE
stocking	BOOT-HOSE	submit	SUBSCRIBE
stolen goods	EQUIPAGE, PURCHASE	subside in passion	QUENCH
stool	SIEGE	substance of the thing	MATERIAL
stoop to supplicate	C(O)URB	substitutions	SUPPOSES
stop		subtitles	QUIDDITS
—in a machine	STICKING-PLACE	success in conclusion	ISSUE
—ringing of	CLAMOUR	sucking rabbit	RABBIT-SUCKER
store	STUFF	suffer	BETEEM
stout	BONNIE, BONNY	—pangs	THROW(E)
stoutness	HARDIMENT	sufficiency	SUFFIGANCE
straight	STRAIGHT-PIGHT	suffusion	EYE
—path	FORTHRIGHT	suggest	INCENSE
strand	STROND	suggestion	PROMPTURE
strange	MUCH	suitable	LIABLE
strength	THEW	—company	BESORT
strengthen	FORSE	summer-house	GARDEN-HOUSE
strewings	STREWMENT	summon	CONVENT

superabundance	PLURISIE, PLURISY
supercilious	HIGH-SIGHTED
superscription	SUPERSCRIPT
superstitious	CEREMONIOUS
supplementary	SUPPLIANT
—document	SCEDULE
supplementing	SUPPLYMENT
supply	IMP
supplying	SUPPLIANCE
support	KEEPING, SUPPORTANCE
—for ruff	RABATO, REBATER, REBATO
suppose	PROPOSE
suppositions	SUPPOSES
surface	BREAST
surfeit	CLOYMENT
surpass	COME OVER, OUTPEER
	PARAGON
—in work	OUTWORK
surrender	SUBSCRIBE
surround	ENROUND
sustain	UNDERBEAR
swaddling-clothes	SWATHLING-CLOTHES
	SWOTHLING-CLOTHES
swaggerer	RUDESBY, SQUARER
swallow	GULF
swashbuckler	SWINDGE-BUCKLER
swashing	WASHING
sway	SWINDGE
swayed	WAID(E)
sweet	HONEYED
—juicy apple	POM(E)WATER
—wine	CHARNECO
sweetness	SOOTH
swell out	FARCE
swift	FLIGHTY
swiftly fierce	TIGER-FOOTED
swinge	SWINDGE
switch	SWITS
swollen	BOLLEN, EMBOSSED, RANK
table	SCEDULE
—cloth	CARPET
tailor	COSIER, COZIER
take	
—by cheating	BOB
—counsel	RESOLVE
—in	
hand	UNDERGO
security	ARREST
—shape or form	INFORM
—to highway	HACK
taken	TANE
—possession of	PROPERTIED
tale-bearer	CARRY-TALE
	MUMBLE-NEWS
talk	PROPOSE
—endearingly	HONEY

talon	TALENT
tame	ENTAME
—a hawk	MAN
—spirited	SOFTLY-SPRIGHTED
tamper	TEMPER
tape	INKLE
tapestries	CHAMBER-HANGINGS
tapster	UNDER-SKINKER
tattered	TOTTERED
tax	TASK
tear	EYE-DROP
—and tug	TIRE
—away	RASE
—off	RASE
—to pieces	MAMMOCK
tease	PHEEZE
—out	TOAZE
teeming	CHILDING
temper	CO-MEDDLE, TEMPERALITIE
temperament	COMPOSURE
tempered	
—badly	MISTEMPERED
—for evil	MISTEMPERED
tempt	SUGGEST
temptation	PROMPTURE
ten at cards	SINGLE TEN
tenderness	BOWEL
tending	
—in sickness	SICK-SERVICE
—sheep	SHEEP-WHISTLING
tenor	TENURE
—of a discourse	SAW
tenth or tithe	DISME
tenure at fixed rent	FEE-FARM
term	
—in	
fencing	HAY, VENEWE, VENEY
tennis	CHACE
the manege	HOLLA
—of	
abuse	CUT, FUSTILARIAN
	FUSTIL(L)IRIAN, PILCHER
	RAMPALLION
contempt	CASTILIANO VULGO
	COBLOAF, COBBY, DRIBBLING
	NIT, RAG, SCALD, SPRAT
	TILLY-FALLY, TILLY-VALL(E)Y
	TWANGLING
contemptuous dismissal	AVAUNT
disdain	MUCH
endearment	CHUCK
highest reproach	COLLIER
opprobium	CASTILIAN
reproach	BEZONIAN, GIB-CAT
	PATCH, RONYON, RUNNION
	SCALL, SKAINES-MATE

terrify	GAST
test	APPROVE
—by evidence	TESTIMONY
testimony	ATTEST, REPORT
tetter	SAPEGO, SERPIGO
	SUPPEAGO
than	AND
thank with ill-will	GRUDGE A THOUGHT
thanks	THANKINGS
that which	
—cannot be cut	INTRENCHANT
—crowns or accomplishes	CROWNET
—is	
characterised	CHARACTERY
distilled	DISTILMENT
loaned	LENDER
—stares fatally	MORTAL-STARING
thatch	STOVER
theft	CONVEYANCE, STEALTH
theme	COPY
thence	SITHENCE
thereafter	UPON
thickly interwoven	THICK-PLEACHED
thief	LIFTER, NUTHOOK, PRIG
	TROJAN
thieving	PUGGING
thigh-armour	CUSH
thill	FIL(L)
—horse	P(H)IL-HORSE
thin	
—as a lath	LATTEN
—faced	PAPER-FACED
thing	
—imported	IMPORTANCE
—seen	REGARD
think ill of	MISTHINK
third	TRIPLE
thistle	CARDUUS
thoughtless	UNWEIGHING
thrash	PAY
threatened with death	DEATH-PRACTISED
three-cornered	THREE-NOOKED
threnody	THRENOS
throat	GULF
throe	THROW(E)
throw	
—at bowls	UPCAST
—into uproar or confusion	UPROAR
—open	WIDEN
thrown from its sphere	DISORBED
thrust	HAVE-AT-HIM, POTCH(E)
—in fencing	FOIN, STOCK
—with quick motion	YERK
thunderbolt	THUNDER-STONE
tick	JAR
ticklish	SUBTLE

tie by rein	REIN
tight	STRAIT, STRICT
tighten	RESTRAIN
till this time	HERETO
time	
—fixed for stay in place	GEST
—for	
confession	SHRIVING-TIME
giving rings	RING-TIME
—of	
beginning	SPRING
midday meal	UNDERTIME
silence	SILENT
—server	MINUTE-JACK, TIME-PLEASER
—table	SCEDULE
timorous	MEACOCK
tincture	SMATCH
tinge	EYE
tinselly	CLINQUANT
tiny	TINE, TYNE
tipple	POT
tippler	MALT-WORM
tired	WAPPEND
—as a dog	DOG-WEARY
—by day's work	DAY-WEARIED
—of life	LIFE-WEARY
title	ADDITION
to	
—be heir	INHERIT
—condescend to take	DEIGN
—go over to enemy	FALL OVER
—make aghast	GAST
—put into dialogue	DIALOGUE
—the smallest detail	TO POINT
—too great an extent	OVERFAR
—what	WHEREUNTIL
token	PRECEDENT
tokens of respect	CEREMONIES
told before	FOREVOUCHED
tom-cat	GIB-CAT
tonsured	PIEL'D
toothless	BROKEN
top	UPWARD
—of head	NOLE
toper	EPHESIAN
toss	
—contemptuously	SLIGHT
—in blanket or canvas	CANVASS
touching the	
—clouds	CLOUD-KISSING
—sky	HEAVEN-KISSING
toy	GAUD
trace	TRACT
track	TRACT
traffic	MART, PASSAGE
—in	MERCHANDISE, MERCHANDIZE

traitor	FAITOR
transcendent in glory	TRIUMPHANT
transfixed	BROACHED
transform	TRANSPOSE, TRANS-SHAPE
transformed person	TRANSFORMATION
transport	TRANSPORTANCE
travel	
—stained	TRAVEL-TAINTED
—worn	SEASICK
tread back	UNTREAD
treat	
—as property	PROPERTY
—tenderly	TENDER
—with	
contempt	JADE, LOUT, LOWT
scant courtesy	STRAIN COURTESY
treatment by fasting	
and sweating	TUBFAST
trenched	PIONED
tress	SWITS
trick	BOBB, COLT, GLEEK
	GLIKE, PASS, QUIRK
—deserving the gallows	ROPE-TRICK
tricky	SUBTLE
tried	TOUCHED, TRIDE
trifles befitting a lady	LADY-TRIFLES
trifling	BAUBLING
trim	GUARD
triple time	TRIPLEX
trite	MODERN
triumphal	TRIUMPHANT
triumvirate	TRIUMPHERY
Trojan	TROYAN
troublesome person	WATER-FLY
trousers	STROSSERS
truckle	CURB
trull	CALLET
try to have restored	
to favour	REPEAL
tuft	TUFFE
tumult	ROMAGE, RORE
tune to arouse hunters	HUNT'S-UP
turban	TURBAND, TURBOND
turbulent	COMBUSTIOUS
turn	INTEND, SWITS, WAFT
—aside	ASKANCE, ASKANT, DAFF
—round	RETURN
—to stone	STONE
turned awry	TORTIVE
turquoise	TURKIES
tusk	TUSH
tutor	SCHOOLMASTER
twenty paces	SCORE
twilight	COCKSHUT
twisted	WEALK'D, WELKT
type of apple	BITTERSWEET
typical woman's name	TIB
ugly	FOUL
unaching	UNAKING
unadapted	UNSQUARED
unadorned	UNCOINED, UNCOYNED
unassisting	UNSISTING
unbearded	UNROUGH, UNRUFFE
unbecoming	ILL-SEEMING
unblunted	UNBATED
unbounded	UNCONFINABLE
unbroken	CONTINUATE
uncertain	INCERTAIN
uncharitable	INCHARITABLE
unchaste	WAPPEND
uncivil	INCIVIL
unconciliating	UNTEMPERING
unconsidered	UNSKAN'D
under-butler	BREAD-CHIPPER
under command	BUXOM
under-constable	THIRDBOROUGH
underpraise	UNDERPRISE
understanding	CONCEIT
undertaken	UNDERTA'EN
undervalue	DISABLE
undeserving	UNMERITABLE
undiscriminating	UNRESPECTIVE
undo	DEFEAT, DUP, UNLACE
undone	POUPT
undress	DEVEST, DISCASE, UNCASE
undressed	UNREADY
uneasily	DISQUIETLY
unexpected	UNWARIE
unfaded	UNBRAIDED
unfavourably	UNHAPPILY
unfeeling	IRON-WITTED
unfit	IMPAIR
unfledged bird	GULL
unfortunate	MISADVENTURED
unfurnish	UNPROVIDE
unhackneyed	UNTRADED
uninfluenced	UNSWAI'D
unintentional	UNWILLING
unknowingly	UNWARES
unknown word	HACK, SCARRE
unlawfully	FORBIDDENLY
—begotten	MISBEGOT(TEN)
unlikely	UNLIKE
unlikeness	DISLIKENESS
unlimited	CONFINEIESS
unlucky	WICKED
unnatural	KINDLESS
unobtrusive going	
or passage	STEALTH
unowned	UNOWED
unpolished person	HOMESPUN
unprepared	DISAPPOINTED

unprolific	HUNGRY	vast	WASTE
unready	REDELESS, UNDRESSED	veiled	MABLED, MOBLED
	UNPREGNANT	velvet	VELURE
unrefined	UNCOINED	—trimmings	VELVET-GUARDS
unreliable person	BREAK-VOW	vend	MART
	BREAK-PROMISE	vengeance	WAN(N)ION
unresisting	UNSISTING	venture	JUMP
unresting	UNSISTING	venue	VENEWE, VENEY
unrestrained	UNYOKED	verbal intercourse	ENTREATMENT
unripe peascod	SQUASH	verbose	VERBAL
unruly	RAG'D, RAGDE	verse	STANZE, STANZO
unsated	UNSTANCHED	versed	TRADED
unsearchable	UNTENTED	very	
unseasonable	UNSEASONED	—durable	PERDURABLE
unseasonably pregnant	CHILDING	—famous	WELL-FAMED
unseeing	IMPERSEVERANT	—rude or uncivil	GIANT-RUDE
unseemly	UNACCUSTOMED	—small person	MINIMUS
unseen	INVIS'D	viands	CATES
unshaven	UNBARBED	vigorous	LUSTICK, LUSTIQUE
unsightly	SIGHTLESS	vile	VILD(E)
unstable person	MINUTE-JACK	village people	VILLAGREE
unsuccessful in trade	TRADE-FALNE	villages	VILLAGREE
unsuitable	IMPAIR	villainy	PATCHERY
unthinking	UNRESPECTIVE	vindictive	VINDICATIVE
unthinkingly	LIGHTLY	viola da gamba	VIOL-DE-GAMBOYS
until	WHILE(S)	violate	FRACT
untilled	UNEARED	violation of promise	PROMISE-BREACH
untrimmed	UNBARBED	violence	EXTENT
unused in any action	UNDEEDED	—beyond measure	OUTRAGE
unwounded	UNGORD	violent	ROBUSTIOUS
upheaval	ROMAGE	viragoish	MANKIND
uphold	ABLE	virtuous	GRACED
upper		visor	SIGHT
—air	REGION	vives	FIVES
—hand	EMINENCE	vixenish	SHREWD
—part of shoe	OVERLEATHER	vizier	PHEAZAR
upright	AN END	void of guile	SINGLE
uproar	GARBOIL(S), WHOOBUB	voluntarily	BY MY WILL
uproot	SUPPLANT	vote	TONGUE
upshot	LOOSE	vow	PROTEST
upstart	START-UP	voyage	SHIPPING
urge	PERSUADE, STRAIN	vulgar	GENERAL
urine	CHAMBER-LYE	—fellow	JACK-SLAVE
use		wafting	WAFTURE
—ceremony	COMPLY	wager	IMPONE
—roughly	HARRY	wait	STAY
usury	EXCESS	walking so that legs	
utmost degree of any passion	BENT	interfere	NEAR-LEGGED
utter ringingly	TANG	wall	MORALL, MURAL, MURE
vagrancy	EXTRAVAGANCY	—in	CIRCUMMURE
vagrant	VAGROM	wander	WHEEL
valuation	PRISE, PRIZE	wandering	WINDRING
value	PRAISE, PRICE	want of respect	NON-REGARDANCE
—a thing	RESPECT	wanting	
vanguard	VA(U)NT, VAWARD	—linen	LACK-LINEN
varlet	VARLETTO	—spontaneity	RECOLLECTED TERMS

wanton	GAMSTER, NICE, RIGGISH	wholly decayed	DIRT-ROTTEN
—woman	FLIRT-GILL	whore	QUAIL
wantonness	LUXURY	—monger	FLE MONGER
wappered	WAPPEND	—son	HORSON
warble	REL(L)ISH	whoring	DRAB
wardship	GUARDAGE	wicked	FACINERIOUS, NAUGHTY
warn	VOR		SPOTTED
warrant	WARN	wickered	TWIGGED, TWIGGING
waste time	BURN DAYLIGHT	wide-mouthed	STRETCH-MOUTH'D
wasted	CONFOUNDED	widow's right	WIDOWHOOD
watchful	OPEN-EYED	wife	KICKIE-WICKIE
—heed	OBSERVANCE		KICKSY-WICKSY
watchword	NAYWORD	wild mustard	HARLOCKS
water		willing	WILFUL
—colours	WATER-WORK	wilt	WO(O)T
—parsnip	CYME	win	LURCH
watering	WATERY	wind	BOTTLE
waterspout	HURRICANO	winding	WINDRING
waving	WAFTURE	wink	ELIAD, ILLIAD
way	QUIRK	winter	HIEMS
—worn	JOURNEY-BATED	wintry	HIEMAL
weak	FOND, SINGLE	wise	WINNOWED
wealth	FUL(L)NESS, TALLENT	—in folly, foolish	
wear out	CONTRIVE	in wisdom	FOOLISH-WITTY
wearing a toga	TOGED	wish	BOSOM
weasel	MOUSE-HUNT	—not to be	UNWISH
weigh down	PEASE, PEAZE	wit	WEET(E)
	PEISE, PEIZE, PEYSE	witch-goddess	HECAT
weight	POIZE	with	
weird	WEY(W)ARD	—a	
well		face like tripe	TRIPE-VISAG'D
—balanced	WEAL-BALANCED	sense of loss	MISSINGLY
—off	WELL TO LIVE	slant	ASCAUNT, ASLANT
—proportioned	CLEAN-TIMBERED	sweep of the stakes	SOOPSTAKE
wencher	CORINTHIAN		SWOOP-STAKE-LIKE
wet	BEWET	vengeance	WITH A WITNESS
what		—downcast eyes	PRONE
—if	WHAT AN IF	—eyes shut	WINKING
—the devil	WHAT A PLAGUE	—moral right	UPRIGHTEOUSLY
—though	WHAT AN IF	—promise of success	SUCCESSFULLY
—went before	VAUNT	—the speed of thought	UPON A THOUGHT
when times are getting			WITH A THOUGHT
better	TIME-BETTERING	—well-nourished rump	RUMP-FED
whereunto	WHEREUNTIL	—wide strong wings	FULL-WINGED
whip	FIRK	—young	IN KINDLE
whipped at cart tail	OVERSCHUTCH	withdraw	INSHELL
whippersnapper	WHIPSTER	withered	CORKY
whisk	SWITS	without	
whispered	EAR-BUSSING	—bounds	CONFINELESS
	EAR-KISSING	—consequence	IMPORTLESS
whisperer	BUZZER	—good repute	REPUTELESS
whit	FICO, FIGO	—means of generation	UNSEMINAR(IE)D
Whitsun	WHEESON		UNGENITURED
whoever	WHAT	—possessions	UNPOSSESSING
whole weight	SWAY	—shrubs	UNSHRUBD
wholesome	PHYSIC	—sinews	UNSINNOWED

—superior	TOPLESS	youth	JUVENAL
witness	ATTEST		LEAPING-TIME
woman	PLACCAT, PLACKET		SALAD DAYS
—of bad character	CALLET	youthful freshness	MAY-MORN(ING)
womanish	FEMALE	**Shakespeare's people**	
womb	VENTRICLE	abbess of Ephesus	AEMILIA
wonder	ADMIRATION	agent for Silvia	EGLAMOUR
—struck	WONDER-WOUNDED	ambassador	EUPHRONIUS
wonderful	MIRABLE, MUCH	—Charles V	CAPUCIUS
wonted	TAME	—France	CHATILLON
woo	SUE	ancient	IAGO, PISTOL
wooded	BUSKY	archbishop	
wooden funnel	TUN-DISH	—Canterbury	BOURCHIER, CRANMER
word of any meaning	HUMOUR	—York	ROTHERHAM, SCROOP
worked secretly against	UNDERWROUGHT	armourer	HORNER
working-horse	CUT	attendant to	
worn	CONFOUNDED	—Antipholus	DROMIO
—in winter	WINTERED	—Cleopatra	ALEXAS, CHARMIAN
—with armour	ARMGAUNT		DIOMEDES, IRAS, MARDIAN
worsted	INKLE		SELEUCUS
—ribbon	CADDYSS	—Duke of Illyria	CURIO, VALENTINE
worthless	JADED, LOZEL	—exiled Duke	AMIENS, JAQUES
—dog	HUNT-COUNTER	—Hero	MARGARET, URSULA
—person	TRASH	—Horner	PETER
worthy of respect	RESPECTIVE	—Imogen	HELEN
wound	BATTERY, BORE	—Katharine	ALICE
—with spur	SPUR-GALL	—King of Navarre	BIRON, DUMAIN
wrap up	MAIL		LONGAVILLE
wrench	FIT	—Olivia	MARIA
wretch	MISER, SCROYLE	—Princess of France	BOYET, MARIA
wristband	SLEEVEHAND		KATHARINE, MERCADE
write	CHARACTER		ROSALINE
—down	PAPER	—Queen Katharine	PATIENCE
—on scroll	INSCROLL		
writing	CHARACTERY	bawd	DOLL TEARSHEET
written			MRS OVERDONE
—music	PRICK-SONG	bellowsmender	FLUTE
—securities	PAPER	betrothed to Angelo	MARIANA
wrong-doing	MISS	bishop	
wry face	MOO	—Ely	MORTON
yearn	EARN	—Winchester	BEAUFORT, GARDINER
yellow	CAIN-COLOURED, SANDED	brother of	
yet in the bud	UNBLOWED	—Agamemnon	MENELAUS
yew	EUGH	—Brabantio	OTHELLO
yewen	EUGHEN, EWGHEN	—Don Pedro	DON JOHN
yield	COME, SUBSCRIBE	—Edward IV	CLARENCE
yielding	LITHER	—exiled duke	FERDINAND
—up life	LIFE-RENDERING	—Henry	GLOSTER
yoke	BOW	—Henry V	BEDFORD, GLOSTER
—of garment	SQUARE	—Isabella	CLAUDIO
Yorkshireman	TYKE	—King	
young		John	ARTHUR
—fox	KID-FOX	of Naples	SEBASTIAN
—lamb	EANLING	—Lady Grey	RIVERS
—thoughtless person	SKIPPER	—Leonato	ANTONIO
younger	LATTER-BORN	—Marcus	TITUS

—Menelaus	AGAMEMNON
—Othello	BRABANTIO
—Saturninus	BASSANIUS
—Titus	MARCUS ANDRONICUS
—Viola	SEBASTIAN
butler	STEPHANO
carpenter	QUINCE
chamberlain to	
King John	DE BURGH
clown	COSTARD, TOUCHSTONE
—Greek	ACHILLES, AJAX
	DIOMEDES, NESTOR
	PATROCLUS, ULYSSES
—Trojan	AENEAS, ANTENOR
conjurer	BOLINGBROKE, PINCH
conspirator	
—English	CAMBRIDGE, GREY
	SCROOP
—Roman	CASCA, CASSIUS, CIMBER
	CINNA, DECIUS BRUTUS
	LIGARIUS, MARCUS BRUTUS
	TREBONIUS
constable	DULL, ELBOW
corporal	NYM
councillor of Naples	GONZALO
count-Rousillon	BERTRAM
countess	OLIVIA
country fellow	WILLIAM
courtier	CORNELIUS, CURAN
	GUILDENSTERN, LE BEAU
	OSRIC, ROSENKRANTZ
	VOLTIMAND
cousin of	
—Henry V	YORK
—Justice Shallow	SLENDER
creature	BAGOT, BUSHY, GREEN
curate	NATHANIEL
daughter of	
—Baptista	BIANCA, KATHARINA
—Calchas	CRESSIDA
—Capulet	JULIET
—Charles VI	KATHARINE
—Cymbeline	IMOGEN
—Duke of Milan	SILVIA
—Egeus	HERMIA
—exiled duke	ROSALIND
—Frederick	CELIA
—Glendower	LADY MORTIMER
—Hermione	PERDITA
—King Lear	CORDELIA, GONERIL, REGAN
—Leonato	HERO
—Pericles	MARINA
—Polonius	OPHELIA
—Prospero	MIRANDA
—Reignier	MARGARET
—Shylock	JESSICA

—Simonides	THAISA
—Titus	LAVINIA
—widow	DIANA
dauphin	CHARLES, LOUIS
deputy to Duke of Vienna	ANGELO
duchess of Gloster	ELEANOR
duke of	
—Anjou	REIGNIER
—Athens	THESEUS
—Clarence	GEORGE
—Ephesus	SOLINUS
—Exeter	BEAUFORT
—Gloster	HUMPHREY, RICHARD
—Illyria	ORSINO
—Lancaster	JOHN OF GAUNT
—Milan	ANTONIO, PROSPERO
—Norfolk	BIGOT, MOWBRAY
—Vienna	VICENTIO
—York	EDMUND, PLANTAGENET
	RICHARD
earl of	
—Douglas	ARCHIBALD
—Essex	FITZ-PETER
—March	MORTIMER
—Norfolk	BIGOT
—Northumberland	PERCY, SIWARD
—Pembroke	MARESHALL
—Richmond	HENRY
—Rutland	EDMUND
—Salisbury	LONGSWORD
—Somerset	BEAUFORT
—Worcester	PERCY
emperor-Rome	SATURNINUS
executioner	ABHORSON
fairy	COBWEB, MOTH
	MUSTARDSEED
	PEASBLOSSOM, PUCK
fantastic	LUCIO
—Spaniard	DON ADRIANO
father of	
—Arviragus	CYMBELINE
—Cordelia	LEAR
—Fleance	BANQUO
—Florizel	POLIXENES
—Goneril	LEAR
—Guiderius	CYMBELINE
—Hector	PRIAM
—Helenus	PRIAM
—Hermia	EGEUS
—Hero	LEONATO
—Imogen	CYMBELINE
—Jaques	DE BOIS
—Jessica	SHYLOCK
—Juliet	CAPULET
—Lady Mortimer	GLENDOWER
—Laertes	POLONIUS

—Lavinia	TITUS
—Lucentio	VINCENTIO
—Mamillius	LEONTES
—Marcius	CORIOLANUS
—Margarelon	PRIAM
—Margaret	REIGNIER
—Marina	PERICLES
—Martius	TITUS
—Miranda	PROSPERO
—Mutius	TITUS
—Oliver	DE BOIS
—Ophelia	POLONIUS
—Orlando	DE BOIS
—Paris	PRIAM
—Proteus	ANTONIO
—Publius	MARCUS
—Quintus	TITUS
—Regan	LEAR
—Richard	PLANTAGENET
—Romeo	MONTAGUE
—Thaisa	SIMONIDES
—Troilus	PRIAM
follower of	
—Bertram	PAROLLES
—Cade	DICK, GEORGE, JOHN
	MICHAEL, SMITH
—Don John	BORACHIO, CONRADE
—Falstaff	BARDOLPH, GADSHILL
	NYM, PETO, PISTOL, POINS
Franciscan	JOHN, LAWRENCE
friar	JOHN, LAWRENCE
	PETER, THOMAS
friend of	
—Antonio	BASSANIO, GRATIANO
	LORENZO, SALANIO, SALARINO
—Antony	DEMETRIUS, DERCETAS
	ENOBARBUS, EROS
	PHILO, POMPEIUS
	SCARUS, VENTIDIUS
—archbishop of York	MICHAEL
—Bassanio	GRATIANO, LORENZO
	SALANIO, SALARINO
—Brutus	CATO, LUCILIUS, MESSALA
	TITINIUS, VOLUMNIUS
—Caesar	AGRIPPA, DOLABELLA
	GALLUS, MAECENAS
	PROCULIEUS, THYREUS
—Cassius	CATO, LUCILIUS
	MESSALA, TITINIUS
	VOLUMNIUS
—Coriolanus	AGRIPPA
—Cymbeline	POSTHUMUS
—Demetrius	HELENA
—duke of Illyria	VIOLA
—Hamlet	HORATIO
—Henry IV	BLUNT, WESTMORELAND

—Hermione	DEMETRIUS, LYSANDER
—Philario	IACHIMO
—Pompey	MENAS, MENECRATES
	VARRIUS
—Posthumus	CYMBELINE
—Romeo	MERCUTIO
—Shylock	TUBAL
—Virgilia	VALERIA
general	
—Antony	CANIDIUS
—Athenian	ALCIBIADES
—fighting	
Goths	TITUS
Volscians	CORIOLANUS
—Caesar	TAURUS
—Greek	AGAMEMNON
—Roman	ANTONY, CAIUS
	CORIOLANUS, COMINIUS
	JULIUS CAESAR
	TITUS ANDRONICUS
—Scottish	BANQUO, MACDUFF
—Volscian	AUFIDIUS
gentleman (of)	
—foolish	FROTH
—Kent	IDEN
—Padua	BAPTISTA
—Pisa	VICENTIO
—Sicilian	ROGERO
—Venetian	RODERIGO
—Verona	PETRUCHIO, PROTEUS
	VALENTINE
—Windsor	FORD, PAGE
—young	CLAUDIO, FENTON
gentlewoman	HELENA
goldsmith	ANGELO
governor of	
—Cyprus	MONTANO, OTHELLO
—Messina	LEONATO
—Mitylene	LYSIMACHUS
—Tower	SCALES
Greek - deformed	THERSITES
heiress	PORTIA
herald - French	MOUNTJOY
hostess of tavern	DAME QUICKLY
husband of	
—Emilia	IAGO
—Helen	MENELAUS
—Imogen	POSTHUMUS LEONATUS
—Mrs Quickly	PISTOL
—Octavia	ANTONY
—Paulina	ANTIGONUS
—Portia	BRUTUS
—Virgilia	CORIOLANUS
imposter	SIMPCOX
jester	TRINCULO
Jew	SHYLOCK, TUBAL

joiner	SNUG
justice	SHALLOW, SILENCE
king of	
—Antioch	ANTIOCHUS
—Bohemia	POLIXENES
—Britain	CYMBELINE, LEAR
—Denmark	CLAUDIUS
—fairies	OBERON
—France	CHARLES VI, LOUIS XI
	PHILIP
—Henry IV	BOLINGBROKE
—Naples	ALONSO
—Navarre	FERDINAND
—Pentapolis	SIMONIDES
—Scotland	DUNCAN, MACBETH
—Sicilia	LEONTES
—Troy	PRIAM
kinsman of Brabantio	LODOVICO
lady	EMILIA
—of Verona	JULIA
legate - Pope	PANDULPH
lieutenant of the Tower	BRAKENBURY
	WOODVILLE
lord (of)	
—Antioch	THALIARD
—banished	BELARIUS
—Bohemian	ARCHIDAMUS
—chamberlain	POLONIUS
—Ephesus	CERIMON
—flatterer of Timon	LUCIUS, SEMPRONIUS
—Florentine	CLAUDIO
—French	GRANDPRE, MELUN
	RAMBURES
—Naples	ADRIAN, FRANCISCO
—old	LAFEU
—Padua	BENEDICK
—Sicilian	ANTIGONUS, CAMILLO, DION
—Tyre	ESCANES, HELICANUS
—Vienna	ESCALUS
lover - Jessica	LORENZO
master of the revels	PHILOSTRATE
merchant	BALTHASAR
—Syracuse	AEGEON
—Venice	ANTONIO
messenger - from Venice	SALERIO
mistress	
—Alcibiades	PHRYNIA, TIMANDRA
—Cassio	BIANCA
Moor	AARON, OTHELLO
mother of	
—Arthur	CONSTANCE
—Coriolanus	VOLUMNIS
—King John	ELINOR
—Perdita	HERMIONE
neighbour to widow of Florence	MARIANA, VIOLENTA

nephew of Capulet	TYBALT
niece of	
—King John	BLANCH
—Leonato	BEATRICE
—Pandarus	CRESSIDA
—Toby Belch	OLIVIA
noble	
—Athenian	TIMON
—Roman	AEMILIUS, CORIOLANUS
—Scottish	ANGUS, CAITHNESS
	LENNOX, MACDUFF
	MENTEITH, ROSS
—young	PARIS
nun	FRANCISCA
nurse-Marina	LYCHORIDA
officer	BERNARDO
—attending Macbeth	SEYTON
—foolish	DOGBERRY, VERGES
—in army	ERPINGHAM, FLUELLEN
	GOWER, JAMY, MACMORRIS
	MARCELLUS
—in Ventidius's army	SILIUS
page to	
—Armado	MOTH
—Falstaff	ROBIN
parson - Welsh	EVANS
philosopher	APEMANTUS
physician	CORNELIUS
—French	CAIUS
—Henry VIII	BUTTS
poet	CINNA
predecessor - Othello	MONTANO
priest	HUME, SOUTHWELL
	URSWICK
—Trojan	CALCHAS
prince of	
—Arragon	DON PEDRO
—Denmark	HAMLET
—Gloster	HUMPHREY
—Lancaster	JOHN
—Norway	FORTINBRAS
—Tyre	PERICLES
—Verona	ESCALUS
—Wales	EDWARD
prisoner	BARNARDINE
prophet	PETER
prophetess	CASSANDRA
protector	GLOSTER
queen of	
—Amazons	HIPPOLYTA
—Denmark	GERTRUDE
—Edward IV	ELIZABETH
	LADY GREY
—England	ANNE
—fairies	TITANIA
—France	ISABEL

Shakespeare's people

—Goths	TAMORA
—Henry VI	MARGARET
—Sicilia	HERMIONE
rebel	CADE
recruit	BULLCALF, FEEBLE
	MOULDY, SHADOW, WART
regent of France	BEDFORD
rival of Valentine	THURIO
rogue	AUTOLYCUS
schoolmaster	HOLOFERNES, PINCH
sea captain	ANTONIO
senator - Roman	BRABANTIO, CICERO
	LENA, PUBLIUS
servant (of)	BOULT, CAPHIS
	HORTENSIUS, PHILOTUS
—Antonio	PANTHINO
—Bassanio	LEONARDO
—Brutus	CLAUDIUS, DARDANIUS
	LUCIUS, STRATO, VARRO
—Capulet	CHAPMAN, GREGORY
—Cassius	PINDARUS
—clownish	SPEED
—Cressida	ALEXANDER
—Dionyza	LEONINE
—Don Pedro	BALTHAZAR
—Dr Caius	MRS QUICKLY, RUGBY
—duke of Vienna	VARRIUS
—Lady Faulconbridge	GURNEY
—Leonato	IMOGEN
—Lucentio	BIONDELLO, TRANIO
—Luciana	LUCE
—Montague	ABRAHAM
—Mrs Overdone	CLOWN
—Northumberland	MORTON, TRAVERS
—Oliver	ADAM, DENNIS
—Olivia	CLOWN, FABIAN
—Petruchio	CURTIS, GRUMIO
—Polonius	REYNALDO
—Portia	BALTHAZAR, STEPHANO
—Posthumus Leonato	PISANIO
—Proteus	LAUNCE
—Romeo	BALTHAZAR
—Shallow	DAVY
—Shylock	GOBBO
—Slender	SIMPLE
—Timon	FLAMINIUS, LUCILIUS
	LUCIUS
—Wolsey	CROMWELL
shepherd	CORIN, SILVIUS
shepherdess	DORCAS, MOPSA, PHEBE
sheriff's officer	FANG, SNARE
shrew	KATHARINE
sister of	
—Adriana	LUCIANA
—Claudio	ISABELLA
—Katharine	BIANCA

—Luciana	ADRIANA
—Queen of France	BONA
—Sebastian	VIOLA
slave	CALIBAN
soldier	BARDOLPH, BATES
	CASSIO, COURT, FRANCISCO
	IAGO, NYM, PISTOL, WILLIAMS
son of	
—Aegeon	ANTIPHOLUS
—Banquo	FLEANCE
—Coriolanus	MARCIUS
—Cymbeline	ARVIRAGUS, GUIDERIUS
—De Bois	JAQUES, OLIVER, ORLANDO
—Duke of York	AUMERLE
—Duncan	DONALBAIN
—Edward IV	RICHARD, YORK
—Gloster	EDMUND, EGDGAR
—Henry IV	CLARENCE, THOMAS
	HUMPHREY, JOHN
	THOMAS
—Henry VI	EDWARD
—King	
Duncan	MALCOLM
John	HENRY
of Naples	FERDINAND
—Lady	
Faulconbridge	PHILIP, ROBERT
Grey	DORSET
—Leontes	MAMILLIUS
—Marcus	PUBLIUS
—Montague	ROMEO
—Northumberland	HOTSPUR, PERCY
—Plantagenet	EDWARD, RICHARD
—Polixenes	FLORIZEL
—Polonius	LAERTES
—Priam	DEIPHOBUS, HECTOR
	HELENUS, MARGARELON
	PARIS, TROILUS
—Richard I	FAULCONBRIDGE
—Tamora	ALARBUS, CHIRON
	DEMETRIUS
—Titus	MARTIUS, MUTIUS
	QUINTUS
—Vincentio	LUCENTIO
—Volumnia	CORIOLANUS
sophist	ARTEMIDORUS
spirit	ARIEL, CERES, IRIS, JUNO
steward to	
—Goneril	OSWALD
—Olivia	MALVOLIO
—Timon	FLAVIUS
suitor	
—Bianca	GREMIO, HORTENSIO
—Katharine	PETRUCHIO
—Portia	PRINCE OF ARRAGON
	PRINCE OF MOROCCO

Shakespeare's people

tailor	STARVELING
tinker	SLY, SNOUT
tribune	FLAVIUS, JUNIUS BRUTUS
	MARCUS ANDRONICUS
	MARULLUS, SICINIUS, VELUTUS
triumvir	AEMILIUS LEPIDUS
	ANTONIUS LEPIDUS
	MARK ANTONY, OCTAVIUS
uncle of	
—Cressida	PANDARUS
—Duke of York	MORTIMER
—Henry V	EXETER
—Henry VI	GLOSTER
—Olivia	BELCH
—Richard II	LANCASTER, YORK
—Tybalt	CAPULET
usher to Queen Katharine	GRIFFITH
vicar	MARTEXT
waiting-maid to Portia	NERISSA
weaver	BOTTOM, SMITH
wench	AUDREY, JAQUENETTA
widow	
—Henry VI	MARGARET
—Prince of Wales	ANNE
wife of	
—Antigonus	PAULINA
—Antipholus	ADRIANA
—Antony	OCTAVIA
—Brutus	PORTIA
—Caesar	CALPURNIA
—Cleon	DIONYZA
—Coriolanus	VIRGILIA
—Hector	ANDROMACHE
—Henry VIII	KATHARINE
—Hotspur	LADY PERCY
—Iago	EMILIA
—Leonatus	IMOGEN
—Menelaus	HELEN
—Othello	DESDEMONA
—Pistol	MRS QUICKLY
—Posthumus	IMOGEN
witch	HECATE, JOURDAIN
wrestler	CHARLES
youth	HENRY

Shakespeare's plays

titles and characters:

A Midsummer Night's	
Dream	BOTTOM, COBWEB, DEMETRIUS
	EGEUS, FLUTE, HELENA, HERMIA
	HIPPOLYTA, LYSANDER, LION
	MOONSHINE, MOTH, MUSTARDSEED
	OBERON, PEASBOTTOM, PHILOSTRATE
	PUCK, PYRAMUS, QUINCE
	ROBIN GOODFELLOW, SNOUT
	SNUG, STARVELING, THESEUS
	THISBE, TITANIA, WALL

Shakespeare's plays

All's Well That	
Ends Well	BERTRAM, COUNTESS
	DIANA, DUKE, HELENA, KING
	LAFEU, MARIANA, PAROLLES
	VIOLENTA
Antony and	
Cleopatra	AGRIPPA, ALEXAS, ANTONY
	CANIDIUS, CHARMIAN, CLEOPATRA
	DEMETRIUS, DERCETAS, DIOMEDES
	DOLABELLA, ENOBARBUS, EROS
	EUPHRONIUS, GALLUS, IRAS
	LEPIDUS, MARDIAN, MECAENAS
	MENAS, MENECRATES, OCTAVIA
	OCTAVIUS, PROCULEIUS, POMPEIUS
	PHILO, SCARUS, SELEUCUS
	SILIUS, TAURUS, THYREUS
	VARRIUS, VENTIDIUS
As You Like It	ADAM, AMIENS, AUDREY
	CELIA, CHARLES, CORIN, DENNIS
	DUKE, FREDERICK, HYMEN, JAQUES
	LE BEAU, MARTEXT, OLIVER
	ORLANDO, PHOEBE, ROSALIND
	SILVIUS, TOUCHSTONE
	WILLIAM
Coriolanus	AGRIPPA, AUFIDIUS
	BRUTUS, COMINIUS, CORIOLANUS
	LARTIUS, MARCIUS, VALERIA
	VELUTUS, VIRGILIA, VOLUMNIA
Cymbeline	ARVIRAGUS, BELARIUS
	CLOTEN, CORNELIUS, CYMBELINE
	GUIDERIUS, HELEN, IACHIMO
	IMOGEN, LEONATUS, LUCIUS
	PHILARIO, PISANIO, QUEEN
Hamlet, Prince	
of Denmark	BERNARDO, CLAUDIUS
	CORNELIUS, FORTINBRAS
	FRANCISCO, GERTRUDE
	GUILDENSTERN, HAMLET
	HORATIO, LAERTES
	MARCELLUS, OPHELIA, OSRIC
	POLONIUS, REYNALDO
	ROSENCRANTZ, VOLTIMAND
Julius Caesar	ANTONIUS, ARTEMIDORUS
	CALPURNIA, CASCA, CASSIUS
	CATO, CICERO, CIMBER, CINNA
	CLAUDIUS, CLITUS, DARDANIUS
	DECIUS BRUTUS, FLAVIUS
	JULIUS CAESAR, LENA, LEPIDUS
	LIGARIUS, LUCILIUS, LUCIUS
	MARCUS BRUTUS, MARULLUS
	MESSALA, OCTAVIUS, PINDARUS
	PORTIA, PUBLIUS, STRATO
	TREBONIUS, VARRO, VOLUMNIUS
King Henry IV	
(Part I)	ARCHIBALD, BARDOLPH
	BLUNT, FALSTAFF, GADSHILL

GLENDOWER, HOTSPUR, KING HENRY
MICHAEL, MORTIMER, PERCY
NORTHUMBERLAND, PETO, POINS
PRINCE JOHN, PRINCE OF WALES
QUICKLY, SCROOP, VERNON
WESTMORELAND, WORCESTER
(Part II)   BARDOLPH, BULLCALF
COLEVILLE, DAVY, FALSTAFF
FANG, FEEBLE, GOWER, HARCOURT
HASTINGS, KING HENRY, MORTON
MOULDY, MOWBRAY, NORTHUMBERLAND
PAGE, PETO, PISTOL, POINS
PRINCE HUMPHREY, PRINCE JOHN
PRINCE OF WALES, QUICKLY
SCROOP, SHADOW, SHALLOW
SILENCE, SNARE, SURREY
TEARSHEET, THOMAS, TRAVERS
WART, WARWICK, WESTMORELAND
King Henry V   ALICE, ARCHBISHOP
BARDOLPH, BATES, BEDFORD
BOURBON, BURGUNDY, CAMBRIDGE
COURT, ELY, ERPINGHAM, EXETER
FALSTAFF, FLUELLEN, GLOSTER
GOWER, GRANDPRE, GREY
ISABEL, JAMY, KATHARINE
KING CHARLES, KING HENRY
LOUIS, MACMORRIS, MONTJOY
NYM, ORLEANS, PISTOL
QUICKLY, RAMBURES, SALISBURY
SCROOP, WARWICK, WESTMORELAND
WILLIAMS, YORK
King Henry VI
(Part I)   ALENCON, BASSET
BEAUFORT, BEDFORD, BURGUNDY
CHARLES, COUNTESS OF AUVERGNE,
EXETER, FASTOLFE, GARGRAVE
GLANSDALE, GLOSTER, JOAN OF ARC
KING HENRY, LUCY, MARGARET
MORTIMER, ORLEANS, PLANTAGENET
REIGNIER, SALISBURY, SOMERSET
SUFFOLK, TALBOT, VERNON
WARWICK, WOODVILLE
(Part II)   BEAUFORT, BOLINGBROKE
BUCKINGHAM, CADE, CLIFFORD
DICK, EDWARD, ELEANOR, GEORGE
HORNER, HUME, HUMPHREY, IDEN
JOHN, JOURDAIN, KING HENRY
MARGARET, MICHAEL, MORTIMER
PETER, PLANTAGENET, RICHARD
SALISBURY, SAY, SCALES
SIMPCOX, SMITH, SOMERSET
SOUTHWELL, STANLEY, STAFFORD
SUFFOLK, VAUX, WARWICK
WHITMORE
(Part III)   BONA, CLIFFORD
EDWARD, EXETER, GEORGE

HASTINGS, HENRY, KING HENRY
LADY GREY, LOUIS XI, MARGARET
MONTAGUE, MONTGOMERY, MORTIMER
NORFOLK, NORTHUMBERLAND, OXFORD
PEMBROKE, PLANTAGENET, RICHARD
RIVERS, RUTLAND, SOMERSET
SOMERVILLE, STAFFORD, STANLEY
WARWICK, WESTMORELAND
King Henry VIII   ABERGAVENNY, ANNE
BRANDON, BUCKINGHAM, BUTTS
CAMPEIUS, CAPUCIUS, CRANMER
CROMWELL, DENNY, GARDINER
GRIFFITH, GUILDFORD, KATHARINE
KING HENRY, LINCOLN, LOVELL
NORFOLK, PATIENCE, SANDS
SUFFOLK, SURREY, VAUX, WOLSEY
King John   ARCHDUKE, ARTHUR
BIGOT, BLANCH, CHATILLON
CONSTANCE, DE BURGH, ELINOR
FAULCONBRIDGE, FITZ-PETER
GURNEY, KING JOHN, LONGSWORD
LOUIS, MARESHALL, MELUN
PANDULPH, PETER, PHILIP
PRINCE HENRY
King Lear   ALBANY, BURGUNDY, CORDELIA
CORNWALL, CURAN, EDGAR
EDMUND, GLOSTER, GONERIL, KENT
KING LEAR, KING OF FRANCE
OSWALD, REGAN
King Richard II   AUMERLE, BAGOT
BERKLEY, BOLINGBROKE, BUSHY
CARLISLE, DUCHESS OF GLOSTER
DUCHESS OF YORK, FITZWATER
GAUNT, GREEN, KING RICHARD
LANGLEY, MOWBRAY
NORTHUMBERLAND
PIERCE, PERCY, QUEEN, ROSS
SALISBURY, SCROOP, SURREY
WILLOUGHBY, WESTMINSTER
King Richard III   ANNE, BOURCHIER
BRACKENBURY, BUCKINGHAM
BLOUNT, CATESBY, CLARENCE
DORSET, DUCHESS OF YORK
ELIZABETH, GLOSTER, GREY
HASTINGS, HERBERT, KING EDWARD
LOVEL, MARGARET, MORTON, NORFOLK
OXFORD, PRINCE OF WALES
RATCLIFFE, RICHMOND, RIVERS
ROTHERHAM, STANLEY, SURREY
TYRREL, URSWICK, VAUGHAN
YORK
Love's Labour's
Lost   BIRON, BOYET, COSTARD
DON ADRIANO, DULL, DUMAIN
FERDINAND, HOLOFERNES
JAQUENETTA, KATHARINE

LONGAVILLE, MARIA, MERCADE
MOTH, NATHANIEL, PRINCESS
ROSALINE,

Macbeth   ANGUS, BANQUO, CAITHNESS
DONALBAIN, DUNCAN, FLEANCE
HECATE, LENNOX, MACBETH
MACDUFF, MALCOLM, MENTEITH
NORTHUMBERLAND, ROSS
SEYTON, SIWARD

Measure for
Measure   ABHORSON, ANGELO
BARNARDINE, CLAUDIO, CLOWN
ELBOW, ESCALUS, FRANCISCA
FROTH, ISABELLA, JULIET
LUCIO, MARIANA, OVERDONE
PETER, THOMAS, VARRIUS
VICENTIO

Merry Wives of
Windsor   BARDOLPH, CAIUS, EVANS
FALSTAFF, FENTON, FORD
NYM, PAGE, PISTOL, QUICKLY
ROBIN, RUGBY, SHALLOW
SIMPLE, SLENDER

Much Ado About
Nothing   ANTONIO, BALTHAZAR
BEATRICE, BENEDICK, BORACHIO
CLAUDIO, CONRADE, DOGBERRY
DON JOHN, DON PEDRO
HERO, LEONATO, MARGARET
URSULA, VERGES

Othello, The Moor
of Venice   BIANCA, BRABANTIO
CASSIO, DESDEMONA, DUKE
EMILIA, GRATIANO, IAGO
LODOVICO, MONTANO
OTHELLO, RODERIGO

Pericles, Prince
of Tyre   ANTIOCHUS, BOULT
CERIMON, CLEON, DIANA
DIONYZA, ESCANES, GOWER
HELICANUS, LEONINE
LYCHORIDA, LYSIMACHUS
MARINA, PHILEMON, PERICLES
SIMONIDES, THAISA
THALIARD

Romeo and Juliet   ABRAHAM, BALTHASAR
BENVOLIO, CAPULET, ESCALUS
GREGORY, JOHN, JULIET, LAWRENCE
MERCUTIO, MONTAGUE, PARIS
PETER, ROMEO, SAMPSON, TYBALT

The Comedy
of Errors   ADRIANA, AEGEON, AEMILIA
ANGELO, ANTIPHOLUS
BALTHAZAR, DROMIO
LUCIANA, LUCE
PINCH, SOLINUS

The Merchant of
Venice   ANTONIO, BALTHAZAR
BASSANIO, GOBBO, GRATIANO
JESSICA, LAUNCELOT, LEONARDO
LORENZO, NERISSA, PORTIA
PRINCE OF ARRAGON
PRINCE OF MOROCCO
SALANIO, SALARINO
SALERIO, SHYLOCK
STEPHANO, TUBAL, VENICE

The Taming of
The Shrew   BAPTISTA, BIANCA
BIONDELLO, CURTIS, GREMIO
GRUMIO, HORTENSIO, KATHARINA
LUCENTIO, PETRUCHIO, SLY
VINCENTIO

The Tempest   ADRIAN, ALONSO, ANTONIO
ARIEL, CALIBAN, CERES
FERDINAND, FRANCISCO, GONZALO
IRIS, JUNO, , MIRANDA, PROSPERO
SEBASTIAN, STEPHANO, TRINCULO

The Winter's
Tale   ANTIGONUS, ARCHIDAMUS
AUTOLYCUS, CAMILLO, CLEOMENES
DION, DORCAS, EMILIA, FLORIZEL
HERMIONE, LEONTES, MAMILLIUS
MOPSA, PAULINA, PERDITA
POLIXENES

Timon of Athens   ALCIBIADES, APEMANTUS
CAPHIS, FLAMINIUS, FLAVIUS
HORTENSIUS, LUCILIUS, LUCIUS
LUCULLUS, PHILOTUS, PHRYNIA
SEMPRONIUS, SERVILIUS, TIMANDRA
TIMON, TITUS, VENTIDIUS

Titus Andronicus   AARON, AEMILIUS
ALARBUS, BASSIANUS, CHIRON
DEMETRIUS, LAVINIA, LUCIUS
MARCUS, MARTIUS, MUTIUS
PUBLIUS, QUINTUS, SATURNINUS
TAMORA, TITUS

Troilus and Cressida   ACHILLES, AENEAS
AGAMEMNON, AJAX
ALEXANDER, ANDROMACHE
ANTENOR, CALCHAS, CASSANDRA
CRESSIDA, DEIPHOBUS, DIOMEDES
HECTOR, HELEN, HELENUS
MARGARELON, MENELAUS, NESTOR
PANDARUS, PARIS, PATROCLUS
PRIAM, THERSITES, TROILUS
ULYSSES

Twelfth Night
or What You Will   AGUECHEEK, ANTONIO
BELCH, CURIO, FABIAN
MALVOLIO, MARIA, OLIVIA
ORSINO, SEBASTIAN
VALENTINE, VIOLA

| Two Gentlemen of Verona | ANTONIO, DUKE, EGLAMOUR, JULIA, LAUNCE, LUCETTA, PANTHINO, PROTEUS, SILVIA, SPEED, THURIO, VALENTINE |

shapes

all shapes	OMNIFORM
almond	AMYGDALOID
almost circular	PENANNULAR
anchor ring	TORIC, TOROID)AL)
appearing to be halved	DIMIDIATE
approximately circular	ORBICULAR
arch	ARCUATE, FORNICATE
arrow	SAGITTAL
—head	SAGITTIFORM, SAGITTATE
awl	SUBULATE
axe	SECURIFORM
bacillus	BACILLAR(Y), BACILLIFORM
bag	CYSTIFORM
ball	ORB, SPHERE
basin	PELVIFORM
bell	CAMPANIFORM
berry	BACCIFORM
bilaterally symmetrical	ZYGOPLEURAL
bird	AVIFORM
bladder	CYSTIFORM
boat	SCAPHOID
bow	ARCUATE
brain	CEREBRIFORM
breast	MAMMIFORM
bristle	STYLIFORM
—tail	CAMPODEIFORM
brush	PENICILLATE, PENICILLIFORM
buckler	CLYPEATE, CLYPEIFORM, PELTATE, SCUTATE, SCUTIFORM
bull	TAURIFORM, TAUROMORPHOUS
buttocks	NATIFORM
C-shaped	SIGMOID
cake	PLACENTIFORM
calyx	CALYCIFORM
cap	PILEATE(D)
capital lambda	LAMBDOID(AL)
caterpillar	ERUCIFORM
chisel	SCALPRIFORM
circular	
—pyramid	CONE
—rod	CYLINDER
cirrus	CIRRIFORM
claw	UNGUIFORM
cleaver	DOLABRIFORM
cloud	NUBIFORM
club	CLAVATE, CLAVIFORM, ROPALIC
—somewhat	CLAVULATE
coin	NUMMULAR
comb	CTENIFORM, CTENOID

shapes

cone	CONIFORM
constant intercept of tangent and fixed line	TRACTRIX
coral	CORALLIFORM, CORALLOID(AL)
cord	RESTIFORM
—hanging between two points	CATENARY
corolla	COROLLIFORM, COROLLINE
cowl	CUCULLATE
crab	CANCRIFORM, CANCROID
crescent	CRESCENTIC, LUNATE(D), LUNULAR, LUN(UL)ATE
crest	CRISTIFORM
cross	CRUCIATE, CRUCIFORM
crow's beak	CORACOID
crustacean larva	NAUPLIFORM
cube	CUBIFORM
cumulus	CUMULIFORM, CUMULOSE
cup	CRATERIFORM, COTYLOID, CUPULAR, CUPULATE, CYATHIFORM, POCULIFORM, SCYPHIFORM
—in front	PROCOELOUS
curve	CURVIFORM
cushion	PULVILLIFORM
cylindrical and smooth	TERETE
cyst	CYSTIFORM
diamond	LOZENGE, RHOMBOID(AL)
disc	COTYLIFORM, DISCOID(AL)
doughnut	TORIC, TOROID(AL)
drop(let)	GLOBULAR, GUTTATE, STILLIFORM
drum	TYMPANIFORM
eagle's beak	AQUILINE
ear	AURIFORM, AURICULATE
eel	ANGUILLIFORM
egg	OBOVATE, OBOVOID, OOIDAL, OVATE, OVIFORM, OVOID(AL)
fan	FLABELLATE, RHIPIDATE
feather	PENNIFORM, PINNATE
fiddle	PANDURATE(D), PANDURIFORM
figure of eight	LEMNISCATE
finch	FRINGILLIFORM
finger	DIGITATE, DIGITIFORM
fish	PISCIFORM
flask	LAGENIFORM, VASIFORM
flattened circle	ELLIPSE, OVAL (see also egg above)
flattened sphere	OBLATE
flower	ANTHOID, FLORIFORM
foot	PEDIFORM
fork	FURCATE(D), FURCULAR

funnel	INFUNDIBULAR
	INFUNDIBULATE
	INFUNDIBULIFORM
globe	GLOBATE(D), GLOBED, GLOBOID
	GLOBOSE, GLOBOUS, GLOBULAR
gnat	CULICIFORM
goat	CAPRIFORM
granule	GRANULIFORM
hair	PILIFORM, VILLIFORM
half	
—arrowhead	SEMI-SAGITTATE
—cylinder	SEMITERETE
—moon	SEMI-LUNAR, SEMI-LUNATE
—sphere	HEMISPHEROID
halved	DIMIDIATE
hammer	MALLEIFORM
hand	MANIFORM, PALMATE
hatchet	DOLABRIFORM
having	
—1 form	MONOMORPHIC
	MONOMORPHOUS
—2	
faces	DI(H)EDRAL, JANIFORM
	JANUFORM
—hollow each side	BICONCAVE
—convex each side	BICONVEX
feet	BIPEDAL
forms	DIMORPHIC, DIMORPHOUS
sides	BILATERAL
—equal	ISOSCELES
—3	
angles	TRIANGLE
faces	TRIGONAL, TRIHEDRAL
feet	TRIPEDAL
forms	TRIMORPHIC, TRIMORPHOUS
lines	TRIGRAM
prongs	TRINACRIAN
radiating curves	TRISKELE
	TRISKELION
sides	TRIANGLE, TRIGON
	TRILATERAL
—4	
angles	QUADRANGLE
faces	PYRAMID, TETRAHEDRON
forms	QUADRIFORM, TETRAMORPHIC
lines	TETRAGRAM
sides	DIAMOND, LOZENGE
	PARALLELOGRAM
	QUADRANGLE, QUADRILATERAL
	RECTANGLE, RHOMB(US), SQUARE
	TRAPEZIUM, TRAPEZOID
—5	
angles	PENTAGON, PENTANGLE
	QUINQUANGLE
faces	PYRAMID
lines	PENTAGRAM
points	PENTACLE, PENTAGON
	PENTAGRAM, PENTALPHA
sides	PENTAGON
—6	
angles	HEXAGON
faces	HEXAHEDRON
	PARALLELEPIPED
—rhombi	RHOMBOHEDRON
lines	HEXAGRAM
points	HEXAGON, HEXAGRAM
sides	HEXAGON
—7	
angles	HEPTAGON, SEPTANGLE
faces	HEPTAHEDRON
ranges of six	
faces	HEPTAHEXAHEDRON
sides	HEPTAGON, SEPTILATERAL
—8	
angles	OCTAGON
faces	OCTAHEDRON
sides	EIGHT-SQUARE, OCTAGON
—9	
angles	ENNEAGON
faces	ENNEAHEDRON
sides	ENNEAGON, NONAGON
—10	
angles	DECAGON
faces	DECAHEDRON
sides	DECAGON
—11 sides	(H)ENDECAGON
—12	
faces	DODECAHEDRON
sides	DODECAGON
—18 faces	TETRAKISHEXAHEDRON
—20 faces	ICOSAHEDRON
—24 faces	ICOSITETRAHEDRON
	TRIAKISOCTAHEDRON
	TRISOCTAHEDRON
—90 faces	ENNEACONTAHEDRON
—1000	
faces	CHILIAHEDRON
sides	CHILIAGON
—full number of faces	HOLOHEDRON
—many	
faces	POLYHEDRON
—like trapezoids	TRAPEZOHEDRON
forms	POLYMORPHIC
	POLYMORPHOUS
sides	POLYGON
—various forms	VARIFORM
—varying forms	VERSIFORM
head	CAPITATE
heap	CUMULIFORM
helmet	GALEATE(D)
heart	CARDIOID, CORDATE
	CORDIFORM

honeycomb	FAVEOLATE, FAVOSE	pentagonal	PYRITOHEDRON
hood	CUCULLATE	pine-cone	PINEAL
hook	UNCIATE(D), UNCIFORM		STROBILIFORM, STROBILOID
—beak	RHAMPHOID	pitcher	ARYT(A)ENOID
horn	CORNICULATE, CORNIFORM		URCEOLATE
horse-shoe	HIPPOCREPIAN	pointed	ACULEATE(D), FASTIGIATE
hump-back	GIBBOUS	potato	SOLANOID
indented	CRENELLATE(D)	pouch	BURSIFORM, SACCATE
intersection of cone			SACCIFORM
and plane		prism	PRISMOID
—parallel to side	PARABOLA	pyramid	PYRAMIDAL, PYRAMIDIC(AL)
—cutting both branches		rectangle	QUADRATE
of cone	HYPERBOLA	relationship of angle	
irregularly notched	EROSE	to its sine	SINE CURVE
jellyfish	MEDUSIFORM	rhombus	LOZENGE, RHOMBOID
keel	CARINATE		SECURIFORM
kidney	NEPHROID, RENIFORM	ribbon	CESTOID, T(A)ENIATE
kite	DELTOID		T(A)ENIOID
knife	CULTRATE, CULTRIFORM	ring	ANNULAR, CIRCINATE, CRICOID
ladder	SCALARIFORM		TOROID
lance	LANCEOLATE, LANCIFORM	rod	BACILLAR(Y), BACILLIFORM
lance-head	LANCEOLATE		VIRGATE, VIRGULATE
larvae	LARVIFORM	roof	TECTIFORM
lattice	CLATHRATE	root	RADICIFORM
leaf	(see leaf²)	rounded teeth	CRENATE(D)
lens	LENTICULAR, LENTIFORM	—finely crenate	CRENULATE(D)
	PHACOID(AL)	S-shaped	OGEE, SIGMOID
lentil	LENTICULAR, PHACOID(AL)	saddle	HYPERBOLIC PARABALOID
letter		saucer	PATELLATE, PATELLIFORM
—C	SIGMATE, SIGMOID(AL)	saw tooth	RUNCINATE, SERRATE
—H	ZYGAL	scale	SQUAMIFORM
—S	OGEE, SIGMATE, SIGMOID(AL)	scalpel	SCALPELLIFORM
—upsilon	HYOID	scimitar	ACINACIFORM
—ypsilon	YPSILIFORM, YPSILOID	screw	HELICOID(AL)
lily	CRINOID(AL)	sesame seed	SESAMOID
limpet	PATELLATE, PATELLIFORM	shell	CONCHATE, CONCHIFORM
long			CONCHOID
—and narrow	LINEAR	shield	CLYPEATE, CLYPEIFORM, PELTATE
—spiral	TURRICULATED		SCUTATE, SCUTIFORM
lozenge	RETICULATE(D), RHOMB(US)		THYR(E)OID
lyre	LYRATE(D)	shovel	SPATULATE
mitre	MITRIFORM	sickle	FALC(UL)ATE, FALCIFORM
mushroom	FUNGIFORM	sieve	COLIFORM, CRIBIFORM
needle	ACEROSE, ACICULAR, ACIFORM	slipper	CALCEOLATE
net	RETIFORM	sloping to point	FASTIGIATE
nipple	MAMILLAR(Y), MAMMILATE(D)	slug	LIMACIFORM
	PAPILLIFORM	small fragments	LAPILLIFORM
obelisk	OBELISCAL, OBELISCOID	snail shell	COCHLEATE
olive	OLIVARY	snake	ANGUIFORM, SERPENTIFORM
orange	OBLATE	socket	GLENAL, GLENOID
oval	VULVIFORM	solid	
	(see also egg above)	—catenary form	CATENOID
palm	PALMATE(D)	—parabola	PARABOLOID
partition	SEPTIFORM	spade	SPATULATE
pea	PISIFORM	spear	HASTATE(D)
pear	PYRIFORM	spike	SPICATE(D)

spindle	CLOSTRIDIAL, FUSIFORM
spine	SPINIFORM
spiral	COCHLEATE(D), HELIX
	HELICAL, TURBINAL
	TURBINATE, VOLUTE(D)
spoon	COCHLEAR(IFORM)
	COCHLEATE(D)
spur	CALCARATE, CALCARIFORM
	CALCARINE
stalactite	STALACTIFORM
star	STELLAR, STELLATE(D)
	STELLIFORM
stem	CAULIFORM
strainer	COLIFORM
strap	LIGULATE
style	STYLIFORM
suspended chain	CATENARY
sword	ENSATE, ENSIFORM
	GLADIATE, XIPHOID
tapering to a point	ACUMINATE
	APICULATE, CUSPIDATE
tapeworm	CESTOID
thin plate	LAMELLIFORM
thorn	SPINIFORM
tongue	LINGUIFORM, LINGULATE
tooth	DENTIFORM, DENTOID
top	STROMBULIFORM
torus	TORIC, TOROID(AL)
trapezium	TRAPEZIFORM
tree	DENDRIFORM, DENDROID
triangle	DELTOID, TRIANGULAR
tube	TUBIFORM, TUBULAR, VASIFORM
tuber	TUBERIFORM
turnip	NAPIFORM
twig	VIRGATE
umbrella	UMBRACULIFORM
undifferentiated into	
root, stem and leaves	THALLIFORM
urn	URCEOLATE
vase	VASCULIFORM
violin	PANDURATE(D), PANDURIFORM
wand	VIRGATE
watch-glass	MENISCOID
wavy-edged	CRENULATE, REPAND
	SINUATE
wedge	CUNEAL, CUNEATE
	CUNEIFORM, SECURIFORM
	SPHENIC, SPHENOID
wheel	ROTATE, TROCHAL, TROCHATE
whip	FLAGELLATE, FLAGELLIFORM
wing	ALARY, ALARIFORM
woman	GYNAECOMORPHOUS
worm	HELMINTHOID, LUMBRICIFORM
	LUMBRICOID, VERMICULAR
	VERMIFORM
yoke	ZYGOMORPHIC, ZYGOMORPHOUS

sheep

Angolan	ZUNA
Asian	AMMON, ARGALI
	CARACUL, KARAKUL
Australian	JUMBU(C)K
British	BORDER LEICESTER
	CANNOCK GREYFACE
	CANNOCK HEATH
	CHEVIOT, COTSWOLD
	HERDWICK, ROMNEY
	SHROPSHIRE DOWN, WENSLEYDALE
Corsican	MUS(I)MON, M(O)UF(F)LON
diseases	GID, SCRAPIE, STURDY
	WATERBRAIN
female	EWE, KEB, TEG(G)
flock-leader	BELLWETHER
hand-reared	COSSET
Himalayan	BHARAL, BLUE SHEEP
	BURREL(L), BUR(R)HEL
	NAHOOR, NAHOUR
	OORIAL, URIAL
horned	JACOB (SHEEP)
Lake District	HERDWICK
male	DINMONT, RAM, TUP, WETHER
North African	AOUDAD
	BARBARY SHEEP
old ewe	CROCK
second-year	HOG(-SHEEP), TEG(G)
short-legged	ANCON
South American	ALPACA, GUANACO
	HUANACO, LLAMA, PACO
Spanish	LATXA, MERINO
Tibetan	SHAPO, SHAHPU
woolly-faced	MUG
yearling	HOG(G), HOGGEREL, HOGGET
young	LAMB, YEANLING
—ewe	GIMMER, THEAVE

shellfish

abalone	EAR-SHELL, ORMER, SEA-EAR
—New Zealand	PAUA, PAWA
American clam	BUTTER CLAM, COHOG
	QUAHOG, QUAHAUG
	ROUND CLAM
arthropod with	
hard shell	CRUSTACEAN
Australian	PIPI
bivalves	CLAM, COCKLE, LAMELLIBRANCH
	MUSSEL, OYSTER, RAZOR CLAM
	RAZOR SHELL, SCALLOP
clam	SCALLOP(-SHELL)
clinging to ships, rocks etc	BARNACLE
crab	PARTON
Crangon	SHRIMP
crawfish	CRAYFISH, LANGOUSTE
	NORWAY LOBSTER, ROCK LOBSTER
	SPINY LOBSTER

decapod crustacean	BRACHYURA, CRAB
edible	
—crustacean	LOBSTER, SHRIMP
—gasteropod	(PERI)WINKLE
French	
—mussel	MOULE
—winkle	VIGNETTE
freshwater decapod	CRAYFISH
highest class of molluscs	CEPHALOPOD
Homarus	LOBSTER
langoustine	DUBLIN BAY PRAWN
	KING PRAWN
large oyster	CHAMA
like small lobster	CRAYFISH, LANGOUSTE
	LANGOUSTINE, PRAWN, SHRIMP
marie snail	(PERI)WINKLE, WHELK
New Zealand	PAUA, PIPI
Norway lobster	LANGOUSTINE, SCAMPI
ormer	ABALONE, EAR-SHELL
	SEA-EAR
oysters on toast	ANGELS ON HORSEBACK
Pacific Ocean	COCONUT CRAB
pearl producing	OYSTER
Pecten	SCALLOP(-SHELL)
sea-ear	ABALONE
segmented	ARTHROPOD
single-shelled	UNIVALVE
small	
—clam	COQUINA
—shrimps	KRILL
Solen	RAZOR-CLAM, RAZOR-FISH
spiny lobster	LANGOUSTE, ROCK LOBSTER
squid-like	CUTTLEFISH
ten-legged	CRAB, CRAWFISH, CRAYFISH
	LOBSTER, SHRIMP
unsegmented	
invertebrate	MOLLUSC, MOLLUSK
Venus mollusc	COHOG, QUAHOG
	QUAHAUG, ROUND CLAM
West Indies	CONCH
whalefood	KRILL
with	
—broad foot	GAST(E)ROPOD
—ear-shaped shell	ABALONE, ORMER
—fan-shaped shell	SCALLOP
—hinged shells	BIVALVE
—spiral shell	NAUTILUS, (PERI)WINKLE
	WHELK

Shinto

ancient texts	KOJIKI
code of moral principles	BUSHIDO
domestic shrine	KAMI-DANA
goddess	AMATERASU
gods and their powers	KAMI
holy	
—object in temple	SHINTAI
—part of temple	HONDON
outer shrine of temple	HAIDEN
purification	HARAI
ritual prayers	NORITO
truthfulness	MAKOTO
underworld	YOMI
	(see also **Japanese***)*

ship[1]

includes: types	
1 hull	MONOHULL
2 hulls	CATAMARAN
3 hulls	TRIMARAN
American	DORY, SHOWBOAT
	STERNWHEELER
Annamese	GAY-YOU
ancient galley	BIREME, TRIREME
	QUADRIREME, QUINQUEREME
—oars and sails	GALLEAS, GALLEY
Arab	*(see* Egyptian *below)*
argosy	CAR(R)ACK, CARRACT
	CARRECT
armed merchantman	Q-SHIP
Baltic	
—1-masted	COG
—2-masted	NEF
—3-masted	CHEBECK, SHEBECK
barge	GABBARD, GABBART
	WHERRY
British	
—coal lighter	KEEL
—coal-vessel	CAT
—flat-bottomed	KEEL
—small yacht	KNOCKABOUT
cargo	COASTER, FREIGHTER, TRAMP
cargo-warship	CAR(R)ACK, CARRACT
	CARRECT
carrying	
—cargo	FREIGHTER, TRAMP
in crates	CONTAINER SHIP
—coal	COLLIER, GEORDIE, KEEL
—oil	OILER, TANKER
—passengers	CRUISE SHIP, LINER
—vehicles and passengers	FERRY, RORO
Chinese	JUNK, SAMPAN, SANPAN
corvette	SLOOP
cut-down	RAZEE
despatch boat (Spanish)	AVISO
disguised warship	Q-SHIP
dismantled	HULK
dredger	PETER-BOAT
Dutch	BESANT, BEZANT, KOFF
	PINK(IE), PINKY
—1-masted	HOY
—2-masted	BILANDER, BYLANDER
	BUSS, DOGGER
	HOOKER, HOWKER, KOFF

—3-masted	FLUYT
—cargo	GAL(L)IOT
—flat-bottomed	
lighter	PRA(A)M
	SCOW, SCHUIT, SCHUTT
—privateer	CAPER
Eastern coaster	GRAB
Egyptian	DAHABEEAH
	DAHABIYAH, DAHABIYEH
	FELUCCA, NUGGAR, SAMBOOK
	SAMBUC(C)O, SAMBUK, ZARUG
escort	CORVETTE
excavator	DREDGER
European	
—1-masted	BILLY-BOY, COG, CUTTER
	DANDY, SHALLOP, SLOOP, YAWL
—2-masted	BRIG(ANTINE)
	KETCH, LUGGER
	PINNACE, SNOW
—2-6 masted	SCHOONER
—3-masted	CLIPPER, CORVETTE
	FRIGATE
—3-4 masted	BARK(ENTINE)
	BARQUE(NTINE)
—4-masted	JACKASS-BARK
—trading	CAR(A)VEL, CAR(R)ACK
	CARRACT, CARRECT, CRARE
	CRAYER, GALLEON, LUGGER
famous ships	
—American battleships	DELAWARE
	NEVADA, OKLAHOMA
	NEW JERSEY
—Amundsen	FRAM
—Anson	CENTURION
—balsa raft	KON TIKI
—Beatles	YELLOW SUBMARINE
—British battleships	ARK ROYAL, BROKE
	DREADNOUGHT
	DUKE OF YORK
	HOOD, INVINCIBLE, IRON DUKE
	ORION, PRINCE OF WALES
	QUEEN ELIZABETH, RENOWN
	REPULSE, RODNEY
	ROYAL SOVEREIGN
—Captain	
Bligh	BOUNTY
Cook	ENDEAVOUR
Nemo	NAUTILUS
Scott	DISCOVERY
—Chichester's yacht	GIPSY MOTH
—clipper	ARIEL, CUTTY SARK
	SERICA, TAIPING
—Columbus	SANTA MARIA
—crewless	MARIE CELESTE
—Darwin	BEAGLE
—Drake	GOLDEN HIND

—first nuclear-powered	
cruiser	LONG BEACH
merchant ship	SAVANNAH
oil-fired battleship	ROSTISLAV
submarine	NAUTILUS
—French battleships	BRETAGNE, COURBET
	LORRAINE, PROVENCE
—German battleships	BISMARCK, BLUCHER
	DEUTSCHLAND, EMDEN
	GOEBEN, GNEISENAU
	GRAF SPEE, HIPPER
	SCHARNHORST
—Gilbert and Sullivan	HMS PINAFORE
—Greenpeace	RAINBOW WARRIOR
—Heyerdahl	KON TIKI, RA, TIGRIS
—Italian battleship	ANDREA DORIA
—Japanese fishing-boat	
contaminated by first	
atomic explosion	LUCKY DRAGON
—leather boat	BRENDAN
—liner sunk by iceberg	TITANIC
—Longfellow's schooner	HESPERUS
—Magellan	VITTORIA
—Mountbatten	KELLY
—mystery ship	MARIE CELESTE
—Nelson	VICTORY
—oceanographic	CHALLENGER
—paddle steamer	COTTON BLOSSOM
—Pilgrim Fathers	MAYFLOWER
—reed boat	RA, TIGRIS
—royal yacht	BRITANNIA, OSBORNE
—Russian battleship	POTEMKIN
—salvaged woodenwall	MARY ROSE
—Shackleton	QUEST
—Showboat	COTTON BLOSSOM
—Slocum's yacht	SPRAY
—Sopwith's yacht	ENDEAVOUR
—spectral	FLYING DUTCHMAN
—Tudor battleship	MARY ROSE
	ROYAL SOVEREIGN
—Weddell	JANE
fast sailer	CUTTER, SLOOP
	(TEA-)CLIPPER
fishing-boat	BANKER, DOGGER, DRIFTER
	(HERRING-)BUSS, LUGGER,
	PETER-BOAT, SMACK, TRAWLER
flat-bottomed	KEEL
Flemish sloop	BOYER
French carrack	NEF
galleon	GALLOON
galley	
—beaked	DRAKE
—Greek	(see Greek below)
—heavy	GALLEAS
—old	(see ancient above)
—Scottish	LYMPHAD

—small	GAL(L)IOT
Greek	
—30 oars	TRIACONTER
—50 oars	PENTECONTER
guard-boat	VEDETTE
heavy galley	GALLEAS
Indian	BUDGERO(W), LANCHA
	PATAMAR, PUTELI, SAMBOK
	SAMBUC(C)O, SAMBUK
jointed ship	CONNECTOR
Italian merchant	ARGOSY
Japanese	MARO, MARU
largest	SEAWISE GIANT
Levantine ketch	SAIC(K), SAIQUE
Malay	COROCORE, COROCORO
	GALLIVAT
	PRA(H)U, PROA
Mediterranean	SANDAL, SET(T)EE
	TARTAN(E)
—2-masted	CAR(A)VEL, FELUCCA
—3-masted	CAR(A)VEL, CHEBEC(K)
	SHEBEC(K), XEBEC(K), ZEBEC(K)
	POLACRE, POLACCA
—coaster	MISTICO
—warship	DROMON(D)
Newfoundland	BANKER
non-fighting naval ship	AUXILIARY
Norse	
—magic ship	SKIDBLADNIR
—merchant ship	KNORR
—Viking ship	LONGSHIP
old ship fitted as place	
of worship	BETHEL
passenger	CRUISER, LINER
plying across rivers, etc	FERRY
Portuguese	CAR(A)VEL, LORCHA
	MULETTE
prefabricated	LIBERTY SHIP
	VICTORY SHIP
prison-ship	BRIG, HULK
privateer	CORSAIR, CRUISER
refuelling ship	OILER
river-boat	PADDLEBOAT, PADDLER
	SHOWBOAT, STERNWHEELER
Scottish	
—barge	BIRLINN
—flat-bottomed	COB(B)LE
—galley	LYMPHAD
shallow, fast	WHERRY
small	LUGGER, PINK, PINNACE
—galley	GAL(L)IOT
Spanish	CAR(A)VEL, GALLEASS
	GALLEON, ZABRA
spectral	FLYING DUTCHMAN
state barge	GALLEY-FOIST
supply	MAILBOAT, PACKET, TENDER

supported on	
—air cushion	HOVERCRAFT
—runners	HYDROFOIL
Thames fishing	BAWLEY, BORLEY
Tigris ferry	GUFA
trader	INDIAMAN
Turkish	CAIC, CAIQUE
underwater	SUBMARINE
unwieldy	HULK
Venetian	ARGOSY, FRIGATOON
	VAPORETTO
warship	AIRCRAFT CARRIER, CORVETTE
	CRUISER, DESTROYER, DREADNOUGHT
	FRIGATE, IRONSIDE, MAN-O(F)-WAR
	MINELAYER, MINESWEEPER
	MONITOR, Q-SHIP
	(MOTOR)TORPEDO BOAT, MTB
	SLOOP, SUBMARINE
—old	SHIP OF THE LINE
	WOODENWALL
—used in harbour defence	BLOCK-SHIP
West Indian coaster	DROG(H)ER
yacht	(see yachting)

ship²

includes: terms	
access panel	HATCH
across the ship	(A)THWARTSHIPS
adjust sails to catch	
the wind	TRIM
adjustable stay for mast	(LEE) RUNNER
	WEATHER RUNNER
after part of	
—bow	LOOF, LUFF
—ship	POOP, STERN
anchor	KILLICK, KILLOCK
—at bow	BEST BOWER, SMALL BOWER
—rope	MESSENGER
apparatus for determining	
speed of ship	LOG
arms for raising and	
lowering lifeboats	DAVITS
beam for raising anchor	CATHEAD
beat to windward	LAVEER
body of ship	HULL
bottom member of hull	KEEL
bracket carrying rowlock	OUTRIGGER
break over stern (waves)	POOP
bring ship to standstill	HEAVE-TO
built with	
—flush planking	CARVEL-BUILT
—overlapping planking	CLINKER-BUILT
call to exertion	HEAVE-HO
capstan bar	NORMAN
cargo space	HOLD
carousing on icebound	
ship	MALLEMAROKING

cast the log into the water	HEAVE THE LOG
change course	
—by swinging sail to other side	JIBE, GYBE
—close to another boat	SLAM DUFF
clean ship's bottom	BREAM
close-hauled to the wind	FULL AND BYE
coastal trading	CABOTAGE
cover over opening in deck	(COMPANION-)HATCH
	SCUTTLE
deck	
—high at rear	POOP
—housing main armament	GUN DECK
—lowest	ORLOP
deviate temporarily from a straight course	YAW
distance between tacks	REACH
doctor	SURGEON
examine ship's papers	JERK, JERQUE
eyelet in sail	CRINGLE
fasten sail securely	FRAP, LASH
fix a mast	STEP
front of	
—keel	FOREFOOT
—ship	BOW, CUTWATER, FOC'S'LE
	FORECASTLE, STEM
fulcrum for oar	ROLLOCK, ROWLOCK
	RULLOCK
galley	CABOOSE
haul	TRICE
high deck at stern	POOP
hijack a ship	SEAJACK, SHIPJACK
hole	
—in	
bows for cable	HAWSE-HOLE
stern for cable	CAT-HOLE
—to drain deck	SCUPPER
immersion while hanging over side	TEABAGGING
in a vertical position (anchor)	ATRIP
inferior sailor	GREENHAND
inner keel	KE(E)LSON
inward slope of ship's side	TUMBLEHOME
kitchen	CABOOSE, GALLEY
lashing round bowsprit	GAMMON
launching ramp	SLIPWAY
let the wind out of sail	SPILL
loading mark	PLIMSOLL LINE
lower sail, flag, etc	STRIKE
lowest deck	ORLOP
movable keel	CENTREBOARD
on duty	ON WATCH

opening in deck	HATCHWAY, SCUTTLE
part of	
—boat between thwarts and stern or bow	SHEETS
—bows	HAWSE
—deck abaft the mainmast	QUARTER-DECK
—sail (that can be) rolled up	REEF
pig-iron ballast	KENTLEDGE
pin	
—for keeping oar in place	THOLE(-PIN), THOW(E)L
—for securing rope	BELAYING PIN
plate taking strain of rigging	CHAIN-PLATE
platform on mainmast	MAINTOP
pole supporting sail	SPAR, YARD(ARM)
props supporting ship before launch	DOGSHORES
projecting float	OUTRIGGER
race meeting	REGATTA
raised and secured (anchor)	CATTED AND FISHED
rail round table etc	FIDDLE
rear part of	
—deck	TRANSOM
—ship	STERN
record of voyage, etc	LOG
rig	
—chief sails square	SQUARE-RIGGED
—mainsail on one side, foresail on the other	GOOSE-WINGED
—mixed rig	HERMAPHRODITE RIG
—one large fore-and-aft sail	CAT-RIGGED
square sail	LUG(GER)-RIGGED
—three or more masts	FULL-RIGGED
—triangular mainsail	BERMUDA RIG
	GENOA RIG
	MARCONI RIG
rigging	(*see* **rope**)
roll up part of sail	FURL, REEF
rope	(*see separate entry*)
rower's bench	THWART
run before the wind	SCUD, SPOON
sail	
—close to the wind	LUFF
—hoisted ready for trimming	ATRIP
—into wind	BEAT
on zigzag course	TACK
—slightly sideways to offset drift	CRAB
—with wind from behind	RUN
one side	REACH

sailing rhumb lines	LOXODROMY
sailor	(*see separate entry*)
sails	
—above	
lower topsail	UPPER TOPSAIL
mainsail	LOWER TOPSAIL
royal	SKYSAIL
skysail	MOONSAIL
topgallant	ROYAL
upper topsail	TOPGALLANT
—asymmetric spinnaker	GENNAKER
	GENNIKER
—attached to another	BONNET
—at end of yard	STUNSAIL
—between	
foremast and bowsprit	FLYING JIB
	FORESTAYSAIL
	INNER JIB, OUTER JIB
masts	STAYSAIL
—corner of sail	CLEW, TACK
—extended by a sprit	SPRIT-SAIL
—four-sided sail on	
diagonal spar	LUG(SAIL)
—front edge of sail	LEADING EDGE
	LUFF
—headsail	YANKEE
—lower corners of mainsail	
or foresail	GOOSE-WING
—lowest on mast	COURSE, MAINSAIL
—mid-section of sail	BAG, BUNT
—on	
foremast	SPENCER
mainmast	SPENCER
mizzen mast	CRO(SS)JACK
	DRIVER, SPANKER
—rigged along line	
of vessel	FORE-AND-AFT
—side edge of sail	LEECH
—small sail set high on mast	KITE
—storm sail	HULLOCK
—strengthening strip	REEF-BAND
—triangular mainsail	
slung from diagonal	
spar	LATEEN (SAIL)
used on racing	
vessels	BERMUDA, GENNAKER
	GENNIKER, GENOA
	MARCONI, SPINNAKER
scrub deck with sandstone	HOLYSTONE
search ship	JERK, JERQUE
seat set across boat	THWART
sheltered side of ship	LEE
ship over the stern	POOP
short spell of duty	DOGWATCH
side of ship	
—above deck	BULWARK

—facing wind	WEATHER SIDE
—sheltered from wind	LEE (SIDE)
socket receiving mast	TABERNACLE
spar	
—of fore-and-aft sail at	
foot	BOOM
head	GAFF
—for extended sails	OUTRIGGER
—projecting from	
bows	BOWSPRIT
mast	CROSSTREE, YARD(ARM)
—set diagonally to	
extend sail	SPRIT
—under bowsprit	MARTINGALE, SNOTTER
speed recorder	LOG
staircase	COMPANION-WAY
steering mechanism	RUDDER, TILLER
storage compartment	HOLD
strap for fastening	
furled sails to yard	GASKET
swing sail to other side	JIBE, GYBE
take soundings	HEAVE THE LEAD
temporary mast, etc	JURY RIG
tie up sails to yards	CLEW (UP)
tilt when sailing into wind	HEEL
to the rear of	ABAFT
top plank of bulwark	GUNNEL, GUNWALE
tube for anchor-chain	HAWSE-PIPE
turn	
—into the wind	BROACH, LUFF
—vessel on its side	
for repair, etc	CAREEN
upper part of	
—side	GUNELL, GUNWALE
—stern	TAFFEREL
	TAFFRAIL
watches	
—midnight-4am	MIDDLE WATCH
—4am-8am	MORNING WATCH
—8am-noon	FORENOON WATCH
—noon-4pm	AFTERNOON WATCH
—4pm-6pm	FIRST DOG WATCH
—6pm-8pm	LAST DOG WATCH
	SECOND DOG WATCH
—8pm-midnight	FIRST WATCH
windward side of ship	LUFF
wooden block	
—for lanyard	DEADEYE
—holding lines of crowfoot	(E)UPHROE
written record of events	LOG
shoes	(*see* **footwear**)
showjumping	
dressage movements	
—backward	REINBACK
—balancing on hind legs	LEVADE
—curvet	FALCADE

—diagonal	CANTER-HALF-PASS		LENG, LORISTON-CLARKE
—fast showy walking	RACK, SINGLE-FOOT		MCIRVINE, MAC, MASON
—half turn	CARACOLE		PRIOR-PALMER
—high-stepping trot	PASSAGE		THOMSON, WINTER
—leap with rear legs		—Canadian (m)	GREENOUGH
under-belly	CROUPADE	(f)	MILLER
—low prancing jump	CURVET, GAMBADO	—Dutch (m)	LANSINK, MORTANGES
—sideways walk	PASSAGE	—French (m)	DOLLAND, DURAND
tracing circle	VOLTE		GODIGNON, JOUSSEAUME
—slow trot	PIAFFE		MARLON, ORIOLA,ROZIER, TOPS
—standing on hind legs	PESADE	(f)	BOST, CREPIN, D'ESME
—turn on haunches	PIROUETTE	—German (m)	BECKER, BEERBAUM
—upward jump	CAPRIOLE		HAFEMEISTER, KIMKE, MOHLE
famous horses	BARBERRY, BENTON		ROTHENBERGER, SCHOCKE
	BOOMERANG, CHAGALL		SLOOTHAACK, TEBBEL
	CHARISMA, DEISTER		WINKLER, THIEDEMANN
	FOXHUNTER, GRANAT	(f)	LISENHOFF, UPHOFF
	HALLA, METEOR, MILTON	—Irish (m)	DARAGH, MACKEN, MULLINS
	PINOCCHIO, RYAN'S SON	—Italian	CHECCOLI, ROMAN
	WAYFARER	—New Zealand (m)	TAIT, TODD
high-jumping event	PUISSANCE	(f)	LATTA
no faults	CLEAR ROUND	—Russian	FILTOV, KILATOV, MENKOVA
penalties		—Swedish	ST CYR, SANDSTROM
—exceeding time	1/4 FAULT PER SECOND		MORNER, NORLANDER
—failing to finish	ELIMINATION	—Swiss (m)	GALBA THULER
—fall	8 FAULTS	venues	
second	ELIMINATION	—Britain	BADMINTON
—foot in water	4 FAULTS		GATCOMBE PARK
—knocking down fence	4 FAULTS		HICKSTEAD, OLYMPIA
—landing on tape marker	4 FAULTS		WHITE CITY
—omitting an obstacle	ELIMINATION	—France	DINARD
—refusal	3 FAULTS	—Germany	AACHEN, BERLIN, DORTMUND
second	6 FAULTS	—Ireland	DUBLIN
third	ELIMINATION	—Luxemburg	MONDORF LES BAINS
—starting too soon	ELIMINATION	—Netherlands	GEESTERN
penalty point	FAULT		'S HERTOGENBOSCH
raised poles for jumping	CAVALLETTI	—Sweden	FALSTERBO
riders		—USA	MADISON SQUARE GARDEN
—American (m)	COFFIN, DAVIDSON, MATZ	**shrubs**	
	STEINKRAUS, THOMPSON	acacia	MIMOSA
	TUTTLE	Actinidia	CHINESE GOOSEBERRY
(f)	STIVES	Alexandrian laurel	DANAE
—Australian (m)	MCVEAN	Aloysia	LIPPIA
(f)	LEONE, ROYCROFT	Ampelopsis	PARTHENOCISSUS
—Austrian (m)	FRUHMANN, SIMON		VIRGINIA CREEPER
	VANGEENBERGHE	Andromeda	PIERIS
—Belgian (m)	HAEGEMAN, PHILIPPAERTS	Aristolochia	DUTCHMAN'S PIPE
	VAN DEN BROECK	azalea	WINTER-BLOOM
—Brazilian (m)	PESSOA	barberry	BERBERIS, PODOPHYLLUM
—British (m)	BROOME, EVANS, HEFFER	beauty bush	KOLKWITZIA
	HUNT, LLEWELLYN, MEADE	berberis	BARBERRY, PODOPHYLLUM
	ROBESON, SKELTON	Berberidopsis	CORAL PLANT
	SMITH, STARK, TODD, TURI	Bignonia	CAMPSIS, TRUMPET VINE
	WELDON, WHITAKER	blackberry	DEWBERRY, RUBUS
(f)	BRADLEY, CARRUTHERS	—x raspberry	BOYSENBERRY
	GREEN, HOLGATE, HUNT		LOGANBERRY

bladder	
—nut	STAPHYLEA
—senna	COLUTEA
box	BUXUS
bramble	RUBUS
broom	CYTISUS, GENISTA
Buddleia	BUTTERFLY BUSH
burning bush	EUONYMUS, WAHOO
butcher's broom	RUSCUS
buttercup shrub	POTENTILLA
butterfly bush	BUDDLEIA
Buxus	BOX
Californian lilac	CEANONTHUS
Calluna	HEATHER
Campsis	BIGNONIA, TRUMPET VINE
Cape jasmine	GARDENIA
castor oil plant	FATSIA
Ceanothus	CALIFORNIAN LILAC
Ceratostigma	PLUMBAGO
Chaenomeles	CYDONIA
	FLOWERING QUINCE
	JAPONICA
Chilean firebush	EMBOTHRIUM
Chimonanthus	WINTER SWEET
Chinese	
—gooseberry	ACTINIDIA
—hawthorn	PHOTINIA
—sacred bamboo	NANDINA
Choisya	MEXICAN ORANGE BLOSSOM
Cistus	ROCK ROSE
clammy azalea	SWAMP AZALEA
	WHITE HONEYSUCKLE
Clerodendron	GLORY TREE
Clianthus	LOBSTER-CLAW PLANT
	PARROT'S BILL
Cneorum	DAPHNE (MEZEREUM)
	MEZEREON, WIDOW-WAIL
Colutea	BLADDER SENNA
coral plant	BERBERIDOPSIS
Cornus	DOGWOOD
Cotinus	SMOKE TREE
cranberry	FEN-BERRY, VACCINIUM
Cydonia	CHAENOMELES
Cytisus	BROOM
Daboecia	IRISH HEATH
daisy bush	OLEARIA
Danae	ALEXANDRIAN LAUREL
daphne	SPURGE-LAUREL
—mezereum	CNEORUM, MEZEREON
	WIDOW-WAIL
Diervilla	WEIGELA
dogwood	CORNUS
double-flowered gorse	ULEX
Dutchman's pipe	ARISTOLOCHIA
Easter rose	JEW'S MALLOW, KERRIA
elder	SAMBUCUS
Embothrium	CHILEAN FIREBUSH
Erica	HEATHER
Exochorda	PEARL BUSH
Fatsia	CASTOR OIL PLANT
firethorn	PYRACANTHA
flowering	
—currant	RIBES
—nutmeg	LEYCESTERIA
—quince	CHAENOMELES
forsythia	GOLDEN BELL BUSH
gardenia	CAPE JASMINE
Genista	BROOM, SPANISH GORSE
glory tree	CLERODENDRON
golden bell bush	FORSYTHIA
guelder rose	GELDER('S)-ROSE
	ROSE-ELDER, VIBURNUM
Halesia	SNOWDROP TREE
Hamamelis	WITCH HAZEL
heather	CALLUNA, DABOECIA, ERICA
Hebe	VERONICA
Hedera	IVY
Hibiscus	ROSE-MALLOW, ROSE OF CHINA
	TREE HOLLYHOCK
holly	ILEX
—leafed Berberis	MAHONIA
honeysuckle	CAPRIFOLE, LONICERA
	WOODBIND, WOODBINE
Hypericum	ST JOHN'S WORT
Ilex	HOLLY
Irish heath	DABOECIA
ivy	HEDERA
Japanese	
—bitter orange	PONCIRUS
—spurge	PACHYSANDRA
japonica	CHAENOMELES
Jerusalem sage	PHLOMIS
Jew's mallow	KERRIA
Kerria	EASTER ROSE
	JEW'S MALLOW
Kolkwitzia	BEAUTY BUSH
Lantana	SHRUB VERBENA
Laurus	SWEET BAY
Laurustinus	VIBURNUM
lavender	LAVANDULA
lemon-scented verbena	LIPPIA
Leycesteria	FLOWERING NUTMEG
Ligustrum	PRIVET
lilac	SYRINGA
Lippia	ALOYSIA
	LEMON-SCENTED VERBENA
lobster-claw plant	CLIANTHUS
	PARROT'S BILL
Lonicera	HONEYSUCKLE
magnolia	TULIP TREE
Mahonia	HOLLY-LEAVED BERBERIS
Mexican orange blossom	CHOISYA

mezereon	CNEORUM	shrubby germander	TEUCRIUM
	DAPHNE (MEZEREUM)	silver lace	POLYGONUM
	WIDOW-WAIL		MILE-A-MINUTE VINE
mile-a-minute vine	POLYGONUM	smoke tree	COTINUS, RHUS
	SILVER LACE	snowball tree	VIBURNUM, WHITSUN ROSE
mimosa	ACACIA	snowberry	SYMPHORICARPUS
mock orange	PHILADELPHUS, SYRINGA	snowdrop tree	HALESIA
Myrica	TAMARISK	Spanish	
myrtle	MYRTUS	—broom	SPARTIUM
Nandina	CHINESE SACRED BAMBOO	—gorse	GENISTA
naseberry	NEESBERRY, SAPODILLA PLUM	Spartium	SPANISH BROOM
Nerium	OLEANDER	Staphylea	BLADDER NUT
Oleander	NERIUM	swamp azalea	CLAMMY AZALEA
Olearia	DAISY BUSH		WHITE HONEYSUCKLE
Pachysandra	JAPANESE SPURGE	sweet bay	LAURUS
parrot's bill	CLIANTHUS	Symphoricarpus	SNOWBERRY
	LOBSTER-CLAW PLANT	syringa	LILAC, MOCK ORANGE
Parthenocissus	AMPELOPSIS		PHILADELPHUS
	VIRGINIA CREEPER	tamarisk	MYRICA
pearl bush	EXOCHORDA	Teucrium	SHRUBBY GERMANDER
periwinkle	VINCA	Trachycarpus	CHUSAN PALM
Perovskia	RUSSIAN SAGE	tree hollyhock	HIBISCUS
Philadelphus	MOCK ORANGE, SYRINGA	Tropaeolum	SCOTCH CREEPER
Phlomis	JERUSALEM SAGE	trumpet vine	BIGNONIA, CAMPSIS
Photinia	CHINESE HAWTHORN	tulip tree	MAGNOLIA
Pieris	ANDROMEDA	Ulex	DOUBLE-FLOWERED GORSE
plumbago	CERATOSTIGMA	veronica	HEBE
Polygonum	MILE-A-MINUTE VINE	Viburnum	LAURUSTINUS
	SILVER LACE	Virginia creeper	AMPELOPSIS
Podophyllum	BARBERRY, BERBERIS		PARTHENOCISSUS
	RACCOON-BERRY	Weigela	DIERVILLA
pomegranate	PUNICA	white honeysuckle	CLAMMY AZALEA
Poncirus	JAPANESE BITTER ORANGE		SWAMP AZALEA
Potentilla	BUTTERCUP SHRUB	Whitsun rose	SNOWBALL TREE
privet	LIGUSTRUM		VIBURNUM
Punica	POMEGRANATE	widow-wail	CNEORUM
Pyracantha	FIRETHORN		DAPHNE (MEZEREUM)
raccoon-berry	PODOPHYLLUM		MEZEREON
raspberry	RUBUS	winter	
Rhus	SMOKE TREE	—bloom	AZALEA, WITCH HAZEL
Ribes	FLOWERING CURRANT	—sweet	CHIMONANTHUS
rock rose	CISTUS	witch hazel	HAMAMELIS, WINTER-BLOOM
rose-elder	GUELDER-ROSE	**Siamese**	
rose of China	HIBISCUS	bay	AO
rosemary	ROSEMARINUS	canal	KLONG
Rubus	BLACKBERRY, BRAMBLE	cape (headland)	LAEM
	RASPBERRY	capital	BANGKOK
Ruscus	BUTCHER'S BROOM	coin	BAHT, SATANG, TICAL
Russian sage	PEROVSKIA	creek	KLONG
sage	SALVIA	dynasty	CHAKKRI
St John's wort	HYPERICUM	island	KO
Sambucus	ELDER	language	THAI
Sapodilla plum	NASEBERRY, NEESBERRY	measure	
Scotch creeper	TROPAEOLUM	—1"	NIU
sea buckthorn	HIPPOPHAE	—20"	SAWK
shrub verbena	LANTANA	—80"	WAH

—44 yards	SEN
—⅓ acre	RAI
mountain	DONG
river	(MAE) NAM
town	NAKHON
twins	PARBIOTIC
weight (3 lb)	CHANG
Sierra Leone	WAL
capital	FREETOWN
coin	CENT, LEONE
Sikh	
baptism ceremony	AMRIT
fanatic	AKALI
holy	
—book	GRANTH (SAHIB)
—person	SANT
knife	KIRPAN
law of causality	KARMA
nectar	AMRIT
organiser of worship	GRANTHI
script	GURMUKHI
sugar-and-water drink	AMRIT
temple	GURDWARA
	(*see also* **belief, Indian**)
Singapore	SGP
six	
at dice	SICE, SIZE
balls	OVER
books of OT	HEXATEUCH
Christmas presents	GEESE
cleft	SEXFID
combining forms	HEX(A)-, SEXA-
counties (of Northern	
Ireland)	ANTRIM, ARMAGH
	FERMANAGH, DOWN
	(LONDON)DERRY, TYRONE
daily	SEXTAN
day fever	SEXTAN
days of creation	HEXAEMERON
fold	SEXTUPLE(X), SEXTUPLICATE
groups	HEXAD, SENARY, SESTET(T)
	SESTETTE, SEXTET(T)
	SEXTETTE, SEXTUOR
having six	
—angles	HEXAGONAL, SEXAGONAL
—columns	HEXASTYLE
—compartments	SEXLOCULAR
—feet	HEXAPODAL
—fingers	HEXADACTYLIC
	HEXADACTYLOUS
	SEXIDIGITAL
	SEXIDIGITATE(D)
—languages	HEXAGLOT
—leaves	SEXFOIL
—lines	HEXASTICH(AL)
—lobes	SEXFOIL

—metrical feet	HEXAMETER
	HEXAMETRIC(AL)
—notes	HEXACHORD
—parts	HEXAMEROUS
	HEXPARTITE
—pistils	HEXAGYNIAN, HEXAGYNOUS
—plane faces	HEXAHEDRON
—rays	HEXACT(INAL)
—sides	HEXAGONAL
—stamens	HEXANDRIAN, HEXANDROUS
—styles	HEXAGYNIAN, HEXAGYNOUS
—times normal number	
of chromosomes	HEXAPLOID
—toes	HEXADACTYLIC
	HEXADACTYLOUS, SEXIDIGITAL
	SEXIDIGITATE(D)
—valencies	SEX(I)VALENT
—vascular strands	HEXARCH
—versions	HEXAPLAR(IC)
	HEXAPLARIAN
headed monster	SCYLLA
hours	QUARTER-DAY
hundred	BALACLAVA, DC
	LIGHT BRIGADE, VIC
—years	SEXCENTENARY
notes	SEXTOLET
nymphs	HYADES
on die	CISE, SICE, SISE
one of six at a birth	SEXTUPLET
pence	SICE, TANNER
six-footer	ANT, BEE, INSECT
yearly	SEXENNIAL
sixteen	
sixteen leaves per sheet	SEXTODECIMO
	SIXTEENMO
sixteenth note	SEMIQUAVER
verse of sixteen lines	SIXTEENER
sixth	
sixth (music)	SEXT
sixth of circle	SEXTANT
sixth-sense	ESP
sixty	LX
sixty grains	DRAM
sixty-year-old	SEXAGENARIAN
	SEXAGENARY
sixtieth	SEXAGESIMAL
skating	
arena	RINK
events	COMPULSORY FIGURES
	FIGURE SKATING, FREE STYLE
	ICE DANCING, SPEED SKATNG
movements	AXEL, CAMEL-SPIN, CHOCTAW
	LUTZ, MOHAWK, SALCHOW
	TOE-LOOP
on	
—blades	ICE SKATING

—boards with wheel	BOARDSKATING	—German	THOMA
	SKATEBOARDING	—Norwegian	HUGSTEAD, RUUD
—wheels	ROLLER SKATING	leaning foward on skis	VORLAGE
skaters		marked slopes	PISTE
—American (m)	BUTTON, JENKINS	most direct line	FALL-LINE
(f)	ALBRIGHT, FLEMING	mound of compacted snow	BOSSE, MOGUL
	HAMILL	off-piste skiing	RANDONNEE
	HEISS, TRENARY	paragliding with skis	PARAPENTE
	YAMAGUCHI, YOUNG	ski suit	SALOPETTE
—Austrian (m)	BOCKL, SCHAFER	skiers	
	SCHWARTZ	—American (f)	ROFFE
(f)	SCHUBA	—Austrian (m)	AAS, HOEFLEHNER
—British (m)	COUSINS, CURRY, DEAN		KLAMMER, MADER, NIERLICH
(f)	ALTWEGG, TORVIL		OSTREIN, SAILER, TRITSCHER
—Canadian (m)	BROWNING, PAUL, STOKJO	(f)	BUDER, HECHER
(f)	SCOTT, WAGNER		KRONBERGER
—Czech (m)	DIVIN, NEPELA		STANGASSINGER, WACHTER
—Dutch (m)	SCHENK, VERKERK	—British	BELL
(f)	BORCKINK, DIJKSTRA	—Canadian	VILLIARD
	SCHUT	—Finnish (m)	HAKULINEN, MANTYRANTA
—Finnish(m)	THUNBERG, SKUTNABB	—French (m)	ALPHAND, KILLY
	VASENIUS		PICCARD, REY
(f)	MUSTONEN	(f)	CHAUVET, GOITSCHEL
—French (m)	BRUNET		MASNADA, MERLE
(f)	BRUNET	—German (m)	BITTNER, KRAUSS, ROTH
—German (m)	FALK, KELLER		SCHICK, STUFFER, WASMEIER
	SCHNELLDORFER	(f)	GERG, MITTERMAIER
(f)	BECKER, FALK		WEHLING
	POTZSCH, WITT	—Italian (m)	GEROSA, GHEDINA, MAIR
—Norwegian (m)	BALLANGRID, MAIER		POLIG, RUNGGALDIER
(f)	HENIE, JENSEN		THOENI, TOMBA
—Russian (m)	GRISHIN, PETRENKO	—Japanese	OKABE
	PROTOPOPOV, ULANOV	—Luxemburg	GIRARDELLI
	ZAITSEV	—Norwegian (m)	BRENDEN, FURUSETH
(f)	AVERINA, BELOVSOVA		GRONNINGEN, HAUG
	LEBEDEVA, RODNINA		SKAARDAL, THORSEN
	SKOBLIKOVA	(f)	KNUTSEN
—Swedish (m)	GRAFSTROM, SALCHOW	—Russian (m)	BAJUKOV, VEDENIN
skiing		(f)	BOYARSKIKH, KULAKOVA
Alpine ski touring	RANDONNEE		SMETANINA, ZELENSKAJA
bicycle on skis	SKIBOB	—Swedish (m)	ERIKSSON, HENNING
climbing with skis			STENMARK
pointing outward	HERRINGBONING	(f)	ANDERSSON, JERNBERG
cross-country events	NORDIC (SKIING)		NILSSON, WIBERG
—skiing	LANGLAUF	—Swiss (m)	BESSE, MAHRER
downhill			ZURBRIGGEN
—fast run	SCHUSS	(f)	FIGINI, NADIG
—run with skis parallel	WEDELN		SCHNEIDER, WALLISER
—slalom racing	ALPINE	—Yugoslav (f)	BOKAL, BENEDIK, SVET
—zigzag	(GIANT) SLALOM, SUPER G	skiing	
freestyle skiing	HOT-DOGGING	—and shooting competition	BIATHLON
hardest run	BLACK	—behind horse or vehicle	SKIJORING
jump in downhill run	GELANDESPRUNG	—diagonally across slope	TRAVERSE
jumpers		—disciplines	AERIALS, BALLET, MOGULS
—Austrian	VETTORI	—on single ski	SKI-SURFING
—Finnish	NYKA(E)NEN		SNOW BOARDING

—over rough ground	BUMP-SKIIING
slowing by turning	
skis inwards	SNOW-PLOUGHING
slope prepared for aerials	KICKER
stationary turn	KICK-TURN
turn	
—by pushing out	
heel of ski(s)	STEM TURN
—high speed	SWING
—jump-turn	QUERSPRUNG
—medium-fast	CHRISTIANIA
	CHRISTIANSEN
	CHRISTIE, CHRISTY
—on outer ski	TELEMARK
—short zigzag	WEDELN
—stationary	KICK-TURN
unmarked slopes	OFF-PISTE
venues	
—Australia	THREDBO
—Austria	HAUS, HINTERSTODER
	INNSBRUCK, KITZBUHEL
	LECH, MINTER GLEMM, ST ANTON
	ST CHRISTOPH, SALBACH
	SCHLADMING, STUBEN, ZURS
—Britain	AVIEMORE
—Canada	BLACKCOMB, CALGARY
	LAKE LOUISE, MOUNT ST ANNE
	NORQUEY, SUNSHINE PEAK
	WHISTLER MOUNTAIN
—Czechoslovakia	JASNA
—France	ARGENTIERE, CHAMONIX
	GRENOBLE, LES ARCS
	MARIBEL
—Germany	BADWEISSEE
	BORSCHTESGADEN
	GARMISCH-PARTENKIRCHEN
	LENGGRIES, PFRONTEN
—Italy	CORTINA D'AMPEZZO
	COURMEYEUR
	MADONNA DI CAMPIGLIO
	IANCAVALLO, SESTRIERE
—Japan	SAPPORO
—North America	
California	HEAVENLY VALLEY
	MAMMOTH
	SQUAW VALLEY
Colorado	ARAPAHOE BASIN, ASPEN
	BEAVER CREEK
	BRECKENRIDGE
	COPPER MOUNTAIN, CRESTED BUTTE
	KEYSTONE, TELLURIDE
	STEAMBOAT SPRINGS, VAIL
Nevada	MOUNT ROSE
	SLIDE MOUNTAIN
New Mexico	TAOS VALLEY
New York	LAKE PLACID

Utah	ALTA, BRIGHTON
	DEER VALLEY, PARK CITY
	SNOWBIRD, SOLITUDE
Vermont	KILLINGTON
Wyoming	GRAND TRAGHEE
	JACKSON HOLE
—Norway	GEILO, HEMSEDAL
	OSLO, STRANDA, TROMSO
—Romania	POIANA BRASOV
—Sweden	ARE, KLOVSJO, SALEN
	VEMDALEN
—Switzerland	ADELBODEN, ANDERMATT
	BRIGELS, HINTERTUXM LAAX
	MURREN, ST MORITZ
	VAL D'ISERE, VAL GARDENA
	VAL THORENS, VERBIER
	WENGEN, ZERMATT
—Yugoslavia	KRANJSKA GORA
	MARIBAR, SARAJEVO
snakes	ANGUIFAUNA, OPHIDIA
adder	VIPER
Africa	BERG-ADDER, COBRA
	MAMBA
—garter-snake	ELAPS, HOMORELAPS
—horned-viper	CERASTES
—tree-snake	BOOMSLANG
—viper	RIVER JACK
America	BLACK-SNAKE, BULLSNAKE
	COPPERHEAD
—coral-snake	ELAPS, MICRURUS
—non-venomous	GARTER-SNAKE
	GREEN SNAKE, RING-SNAKE
—rattlesnake	PIT-VIPER
—viper	RATTLER, RATTLESNAKE
—venomous	MOCASSIN, MOCCASIN
—water-moccasin	COTTONMOUTH
Asiatic	KING-COBRA
Australia	BLACK-SNAKE
	CARPET-SNAKE
	DEATH-ADDER
	TAIPAN, TIGER-SNAKE
Britain	ADDER, GRASS SNAKE
	RING(ED) SNAKE, VIPER
coach-whip snake	MASTICOPHIS
coral-snake	SCYTALE
East Indies	BOIGA
Egypt	
—juggler's snake	NAGA, NAIA, NAJA
Eryx	SAND-SNAKE
fabulous snake	AMPHISBAENA
fer-de-lance	YELLOW VIPER
flying	CHRYSOPELEA, COLOBRIDAE
green	BOIOBI
Hydrophidae	SEA-SNAKE
India	BONGAR, HAMADRYAD
—boa	JIBOYA

—cobra	COBRA DA CAPELLO
	NAGA, NAIA, NAJA
—rock-snake	KAA, K(A)RAIT, PYTHON
krait	ROCK-SNAKE
legless lizard	GLASS-SNAKE
Madagascar	LANGAHA
Masticophis	COACH-WHIP SNAKE
non-venomous	COLUBER, DIPSAS
	HOOP-SNAKE
puff-adder	CLOTHO
python	ROCK-SNAKE
rattlesnake	CROTALUS, CROTALIDAE
sand snake	ERYX
sea-snakes	HYDROPHIDAE
serpent	ASP, BOYUNA
short-tailed	SAND-SNAKE
snakes	OPHIDIA
South America	
—anaconda	SUCURUJA
—bushmaster	SURUCUCU
—python	(A)BOMA, BOA
—venomous	BUSHMASTER
	EYELASH VIPER
	FER-DE-LANCE, JARARACA
	JARARAKA, LACHESIS
	SURUCUCU
—water-boa	ANACONDA, SUCURUJU
spitting cobra	RINCHAL
tree-snake	DENDROPHIS
two-headed (myth)	AMPHISBAENA
venomous	ASP, ASPIC(K), KOKOB, SEPS
viper	ADDER
West Indies	FER-DE-LANCE
yellow viper	FER-DE-LANCE
snooker	
balls	BLACK, BLUE, BROWN
	GREEN, PINK, RED
	WHITE, YELLOW
cue ball	WHITE
game	FRAME
line across table	BAULK LINE
obstruction by another	
ball	SNOOKER
opening in cushions	POCKET
padded edge of table	CUSHION
players	
—Canadian	CHAPERON, DOLNALDSON
	ROBIDOUX, THORBURN
	WERBINUK
—English	CORR (f), DAVIS, FISHER (f)
	JAMES, PARROTT
	PULMAN, TAYLOR, WHITE
—Irish	HIGGINS
—Scottish	HENDRY
—Thai	WATTANA
—Welsh	GRIFFITHS, MOUNTJOY

rod for striking ball	CUE
score made in one turn	
at the table	BREAK
start of play	BREAK OFF
stroke with cue held in	
vertical position	MASSE
venues	
—County Kildare	GOFFS
—Derby	ASSEMBLY ROOMS
—Preston	GUILD HALL
—Reading	THE HEXAGON
—Sheffield	THE CRUCIBLE
—Stoke-on-Trent	JOLLEES
soccer	(*see* **football**)
Society	
for Psychical Research	SPR
of	
—Antiquaries	SA
—Arts	SA
—Engineers	SE
—Incorporated Accountants	SAA
—Jesus	SJ
—the Holy Cross	SSC
soldier	
Albanian	ARNA(O)UT, PALIKAR
African	
—infantryman	VOETGANGER
—native warriors	IMPI
—soldier	ASKARI
Algerian	
—cavalry	SPAHEE, SPAHI
—infantry	GOUM, TURCO, ZOUAVE
American	
—commanders	
Civil War	
—Confederate	BEAUREGARD, BRAGG
	EARLY, HOOD, JACKSON
	JOHNSON, JOHNSTON, LEE
	LONGSTREET, PICKETT
—Federal	GRANT, HALLECK, MEADE
	LEE, MCCLELLAN, SCOTT
	SHERIDAN, SHERMAN
Indian Wars	CUSTER
Mexican War	HOUSTON
Revolution	ALLEN, ARNOLD, CLARK
	GATES, GREEN, HERKIMER, HOWE
	LAFAYETTE, LEE, LINCOLN
	MARION, MONTGOMERY, MOULTRIE
	MORGAN, PHILLIPS, PICKENS
	ST CLAIR, SCHUYLER, SULLIVAN
	SUMTER, WASHINGTON
WW1	BLISS, BULLARD, LIGGETT
	MARCH, PERSHING
WW2	BEDELL-SMITH, BRADLEY
	BUCKNER, CLARK, COLLINS
	DEVERS, EAKER, EISENHOWER

	GAVIN, HODGES, KENNY, KING
	KRUEGER, LEMAY, LUCAS
	MACARTHUS, MARSHALL, PATCH
	PATTON, STILWELL, SULTAN
	TRUSCOTT, WEDEMEYER
—civil war soldier	ZOUAVE
—Confederate	GREY-COAT
—ex-serviceman	VET(ERAN)
—militiaman	MINUTEMAN
—of both World Wars	RETREAD
—soldier	DOUGHBOY, GI, JOE
	SAMMY
Arab commando(s)	FEDAYEE(N)
armed with short rifle	CARABINEER
artilleryman	GUNNER
—old	BOMBARDIER
assistant to	
commanding officer	ADJUTANT
Australian	ANZAC, DIGGER
—commander - WW1	MONASH
Austrian	PANDOOR, PAND(O)UR
Austro-Hungarian	
—commanders - WW1	BOHM-ERMOLLI
	BOROEVIC, CONRAD
	DANKL, EUGEN
	JOSEPH, KOVESS
Belgian commander - WW1	LEMAN
bomb-thrower (old)	GRENADIER
British	LOBSTER, REDCOAT
	TOMMY
—commanders	
American Revolution	BURGOYNE
	CARLETON, CLINTON
	CORNWALLIS, GAGE
	HAMILTON, HOUSE
	PARKER, RAWDON
Canada	WOLFE
India	CLIVE, WELLESLEY
Napoleonic wars	WELLESLEY
	WELLINGTON
old	BOADICEA (f)
	BOUDICCA (f)
Spanish Succession	MARLBOROUGH
WW1	ALLENBY, BYNG
	CRADDOCK, FRENCH, FULLER
	GOUGH, HAIG
	HAMILTON, KIGGELL, KITCHENER
	MARSHALL, MAUDE, MILNE
	MONRO, MURRAY, NIXON, PLUMER
	RAWLINSON, ROBERTSON
	SMITH-DORRIEN, TOWNSHEND
	WILSON
WW2	ALEXANDER, AUCHINLECK
	BROOKE, CUNNINGHAM, DILL
	GORT, HARDING, IRONSIDE
	ISMAY, LEESE, MONTGOMERY

	PLATT, RITCHIE, SLIM
	WAVELL, WILSON, WINGATE
Carthaginian	HANNIBAL
cavalryman	TROOPER, YEOMAN
—Cromwellian	IRONSIDE
—French	CHASSEUR
—French-Algerian	SPAHEE, SPAHI
—heavy	DRAGOON
—light	HUSSAR, LANCER, H(H)LAN
—officer	CORNET
—Turkish	SPAHEE, SPAHI
Circassian slave	MAMELUKE
Croat in Austrian service	PANDOOR
	PAND(O)UR
commando(s)	GREEN BERETS
—Arab	FEDAYEE(N)
—in	
boats	SBS, SPECIAL BOAT SERVICE
Burma	CHINDIT
desert	LONG RANGE DESERT GROUP
	LRDG
planes	PARATROOPS, SAS
	SPECIAL AIR SERVICE
Cromwellian	ROUNDHEAD
—cavalryman	IRONSIDE
Czech commander	SVOBODA
East African	ASKARI
Egyptian	
—commander	SIRDAR
—officer	BIMBASHI, BINBASHI
—soldier/slave	MAMELUKE
Eighth Army	DESERT RAT
élite troops	COMMANDOS, SAS
	SPECIAL AIR SERVICE
engineer	SAPPER
enrolled compulsorily	CONSCRIPT
European mercenary	CONDOTTIERE
fighting for	
—money	MERCENARY
—the Holy Land	CRUSADER
	KNIGHT TEMPLAR
foot soldiers	INFANTRY, YEOMANRY
force men to serve	COMMANDEER
	CONSCRIPT, DRAFT
	LEVY, IMPRESS
	PRESS(GANG)
French	SOLDAT
—cavalryman	CHASSEUR
Algerian	SPAHEE, SPAHI
—commanders	
18th-19th c	NAPOLEON
WW1	ANTHOINE, BERTHOLET
	CASTELNAU, DE GAULLE, DUBAIL
	FAYOLLE, FOCH, GALLIENI, GOURAUD
	GUILLAUMAT, JOFFRE, LANREZAC
	MAISTRE, MANGIN, MAUNOURY

	MICHELER, NIVELLE, PAL, PETAIN
	ROQUE, SARRAIL, WEYGAND
WW2	BILOTTE, CORAP, DE GAULLE
	DENTZ, DOUMENC, GAMELIN
	GEORGES, GIRAUD, GUINGAND
	FOCH, HUNTZINGER, JOFFRE
	JUIN, LATTRE DE TASSIGNY
	LECLERC, NEY, PETAIN
	RUBY, WEYGAND
—guerrilla	FRANC-TIREUR
—light infantryman	CHASSEUR
	VOLTIGEUR
—in North Africa	LEGIONNAIRE
—infantryman	POILU
—private (slang)	PIOU-PIOU
—rifleman	TIRAILLEUR
—sniper	FRANC-TIREUR
German	SOLDAT
—army reserve	LANDWEHR
—commanders	
WW1	ARZ, AUFFENBERG, BOTHMAN
	BULOW, EICHHORN, EINEM
	FALKENHAIN, GOLTZ, GROENER
	HINDENBURG, HOFFMAN, HUTIER
	GLUCK, KRAFT, LEOPOLD, LIMAN
	LINSINGEN, LOSSBERG, LUDENDORFF
	MACKENSEN, MARWITZ, MOLTKE
	PRITTWITZ, SEECKT
WW2	ARNIM, BALCK, BAYERLEIN
	BOCK, BLOMBERG, BLUMENTRITT
	BRAUCHITSCH, BUSCH, CHOLTITZ
	DIETL, DIETRICH, DOLLMAN
	EBERBACH, FALKENHORST, FRANK
	FRIEDBURG, FROMM, GOERING
	GUDERIAN, HALDER, HARPE
	HAUSSER, HINDENBURG, HOEPNER
	HOTH, JODL, KEITEL, KESSELRING
	KLEIST, KLUGE, KREBS, KUCHLER
	LEEB, LIST, LOSSOW, LUDENDORFF
	MANSTEIN, MARCKS, MILCH, MODEL
	NEHRING, PAULUS, REICHENAU
	REINHARDT, ROMMEL, SCHLIEBEN
	SCHWIFFEN, SCHORNER, SPEIDEL
	SPERRLE, STUDENT, VIETINGHOFF
	WELCHS, WEIDLING, WENCK
	WESTHAL, WIESE, WOLFF
	ZANGEN, ZEITZLER
—emergency force	LANDSTURM
—Hitler's bodyguard	SCHUTZSTAFFEL, SS
—lancer	U(H)LAN
—mercenary	HESSIAN, LANDSKNECHT
	LANZNECHT, LANSQUENET
—rifleman	JA(E)GER
Greek	
—at siege of Troy	MYRMIDON
—captain of guards	PROTOPATHARIUS

—commander of	
10	DECADARCH
1000	CHILIARCH
10000	MYRIARCH
cavalry	HIPPARCH, PHYLARCH
division	TAXIARCH
sub-division	TETRARCH
—commanders	
old	ALEXANDER
modern	METAXAS, PAPAGOS
	TSOLAKOGLU
—heavily armed	HOPLITE
—lightly armed	PELTAST
—military commander	POLEMARCH
—soldier	EVZONE
group of soldiers	DETACHMENT, DETAIL
	PATROL, SQUAD
—in increasing size	SECTION, TROOP
	PLATOON, BATTERY
	COMPANY, SQUADRON
	BATTALION, COMMANDO
	REGIMENT
	BRIGADE
	CORPS
	ARMY
	ARMY GROUP
guards	
—cavalry	HORSE GUARDS
	HOUSEHOLD CAVALRY
	LIFE GUARDS, THE BLUES
—infantry	COLDSTREAM, GRENADIER
	IRISH, SCOTS, WELSH
home-based troops	HOME GUARD, MILITIA
horse soldiers	CAVALRY
Hungarian	
—cavalryman	HUSSAR
—guerrilla	HAIDUK, HEYDUCK
in	
—full suit of armour	CATAPHRACT
—leather armour	JACKMAN
Indian	JAWAN, SIKH
—captain	SUBA(H)DAR
—cavalry commander	RESSALDAR
	RISALDAR
—corporal	NAIK
—foot-soldier	JAWAN
—in British service	SEPAHI, SEPOY
—irregular	SEBUNDEE, SEBUNDY
cavalryman	SILLADAR
—mercenary	PINDAREE, PINDARI
—military leader	SIRDAR
—mounted	SOWAR
—officer	JAMADAR, JEMADAR
	JEMIDAR
—Nepalese	GURKHA
—sergeant	HAVILDAR

—staff officers	OMLAH	—of	
—troop of armed tribesmen	LASHKAR	high rank	BRASS-HAT
—trooper	SOWAR	Yeomen of the Guard	EXON
infantryman	BROWN JOB, PRIVATE	—on duty	ORDERLY OFFICER
	(PERCY) PONGO, SQUADDIE	—responsible for	
	SQUADDY, TOMMY (ATKINS)	planning strategy	GENERAL STAFF
—armed with		—responsible for	
axe-like weapon	HALBERDIER	provisions	QUARTERMASTER
bow	ARCHER, BOWMAN	old	
spear	PIKEMAN	—names	CENTINEL(L), MAN-OF-WAR
irregular soldier	GUERRILLA, PARTISAN		MILITARY, SOULDIER
Irish		—soldier	RETREAD, SWEAT, VET(ERAN)
—ancient	FIANN, GALLO(W)GLASS	on	
—expatriate	WILD GEESE	—guard duty	SENTRY
—foot soldier	KERN(E)	—ship	MARINE
—freebooter	RAPPAREE	Oriental	LASCAR
Italian	SOLDATO	Parachute Regiment	RED DEVILS
—commanders		part-time troops	MILITIA
WW1	CADORNA, CAPELLO, DIAZ		TERRITORIALS
WW2	BADOGLIO, BERGONZOLI	persecution by soldiers	DRAGONNADE
	GRAZIANI		DRAGOONING
—mercenary leader	CONDOTTIERE	police	REDCAPS, (R)MP
—mountain troops	ALPINI	Polish commander	SKORZENY
—rifleman	BERSAGLIERE	private	SQUADDIE, SQUADDY
	CARABINIERE		SWAD(DY)
Japanese		professional	REGULAR
—commander		quarters	BARRACKS, BILLET
WW1	KAMIO		CANTONMENT, CASERN(E)
WW2	ADACHI, HOMMA, IIDA	ranks	
	IMAMURA, MATSUI, MUTAGUCHI	—private	FUSILIER, GUARDSMAN
	USHIJIMA, YAMASHITA		GUNNER, RIFLEMAN
Knights of St John of			TRAINED SOLDIER, TROOPER
Jerusalem		—non-commissioned officer	NCO
—commander	TUCOPOLIER		BOMBARDIER
—soldier	TURCOPOLE		(LANCE) CORPORAL
loyalist	CAVALIER		(LANCE) SERGEANT
mercenary (16th c)	LANDSKNECHT	—warrant officer	WO
mounted			COMPANY QUARTERMASTER-SERGEANT
—sentry	VEDETTE, VIDETTE		CQMS
—soldiers	CAVALRY, DRAGOONS		COMPANY SERGEANT-MAJOR, CSM
	HUSSARS		DRILL SERGEANT
Muscovite guard(s)	STRELITZ(STRELZI)		STAFF SERGEANT
Muslim	GHAZI		REGIMENTAL QUARTERMASTER-
Nepalese in British army	GURKHA		SERGEANT
New Zealand			RQMS
—commander	FREYBERG		REGIMENTAL SERGEANT-MAJOR, RSM
—soldier	ANZAC, KIWI	—officer	CORNET, ENSIGN
newly enlisted	RECRUIT, ROOKIE		SECOND LIEUTENANT
Norse	BERSERKER		LIEUTENANT
officer			CAPTAIN, MAJOR
—acting as administrative			LIEUTENANT-COLONEL
assistant	ADC, ADJUTANT		COLONEL
	AIDE (DE CAMP)		BRIGADIER
—below captain	SUBALTERN		MAJOR-GENERAL
—commanding	COMMANDANT		LIEUTENANT-GENERAL
—in training	CADET		GENERAL, FIELD MARSHAL

recruit	NIG-NOG, ROOKIE, ROOKY
rifleman (old)	FUSILIER, MUSKETEER
Roman	
—auxiliary	FOEDERATUS
—company	VEXILLATION
—emperor's	
bodyguard	PR(A)ETORIAN GUARD
—infantry	
company	MANIPLE
regiment	TERCIO
—lightly-armed	VELITES
—officer in charge of	
10	DECURION
100	CENTURION
—soldier	LEGIONARY
—squad of	
$^{1}/_{10}$ legion	COHORT
10	DECURIA, DECURY
100	CENTURY
—standard-bearer	VEXILLARY
Royalist	CAVALIER
Russian	
—commanders	
WW1	ALEKSEEV, BRUSILOV
	DANILOV, EVERT, GURKO
	IVANOV, KORNILOV, KUROPATKIN
	PLEHVE, RENNENKAMPF, RUZSKI
	SAMSONOV, SHCHERBACHEV
	SUKHOMLINOV, YANUSHKEVICH
	YUDENICH, ZHILINSKY
WW2	ANTONOV, BUDENNY, CHUIKOV
	GOLIKOV, KIRPONOS, KONIEV
	LELYOSHENKO, MALINOVSKY
	POPOV, ROKOSSOVSKY, ROMANENKO
	SHTEMENKO, SOKOLOVSKY
	TIMOSHENKO, TOLBUKHIN
	TUKHACHEVSKY, VATUTIN, VLASOV
	VORONOV, VOROSHILOV, YEREMENKO
	ZHUKOV
—guard(s)	STRELITZ(STRELZI)
Serbian nationalist	CHETNIK
servant	BATMAN, ORDERLY
serving	
—at sea	MARINE
—for money	MERCENARY
—with another nation	AUXILIARY
sharpshooter	SNIPER, TIRAILLEUR
slang name	BROWN JOB, GALOOT
	PONGO, TOMMY
small mounted group	COSSACK POST
South African	
—commanders	BOTHA, SMUTS
—soldier	VOETGANGER
Spanish	SOLDADO
—commanders	CORTES, CORTEZ
	PIZARRO

—in Mexico or Peru	CONQUISTADOR
—infantry regiment	TERCIO
special	
forces	(*see* commando(s) *above*)
standing in front of	
squad drilling	FUGLEMAN, MARKER
trained to drop	
from aircraft	PARA, PARATROOP(ER)S
Turkish	NIZAM
—armed attendant	CAVASS, KAVASS
—army officer	BIMBASHI, BINBASHI
	SPAHEE, SPAHI
—cavalryman	SPAHEE, SPAHI
—commander	AG(H)A
Crusades	SALADIN
-in-chief	SERASKIER
WW1	ABDUL KERIM, DJEMEL PASHA
	ENVER PASHA, IZZET PASHA
—footguard	JANISSARY, JANIZARY
—irregular	BASHIBAZOUK
—militiaman	TIMARIOT
—palace guard	BOSTANGI
using heavy guns	ARTILLERY
volunteer serving	
as officer	REFORMADO
solicitor	SOL(R)
Solicitor at Law	SL
solicitor before superior court	SSC
Solicitor General	SG
Somalia	
capital	MOGADISCIO, MOGADISHU
coin	CENTESIMO, SHILLING
son of	
a	
—bitch	SOB
—Scot	MAC
—Welshman	AP
an Englishman	FITZ
soup	
African - okra pod soup	GUMBO
American - shellfish	CHOWDER
Asian	BIRD'S-NEST SOUP
barley and vegetables	SCOTCH BROTH
beef broth	BREWIS
beetroot	BORSCHT, BOR(T)SCH
bread and tomato	POPPO AL POMODORO
brown	WINDSOR SOUP
calf's head	MOCK TURTLE
chicken/leek	COCK-A-LEEKIE
chilled cream soup	VICHYSSOISE
clear soup	CONSOMME, JULIENNE
crayfish	BISK, BISQUE
cream	VICHYSOISSE
curry-soup	MULLIGATAWNY
East Indian	MULLIGATAWNY
egg-Spanish	TONILLO

Egyptian	MELOKHIA
fish	BISQUE, BOUILLABAISSE
	CHOWDER, TURTLE
—Russian	UKKA
Florentine	RIBOLLITA
French	BISQUE, CREME DUBARRY
	MADRILENE
German	LEBERKNODELSUPPE
Greek	AVGOLEMONO
—fish	BARASOUPA, KAKAVIA
Hungarian	GOULASH, GULYASLEVES
Indian	MULLIGATAWNY
Italian	MINESTRE IN BRODO
	MINESTRONE
	POPPO AL POMODORO
leeks, potatoes, etc	VICHYSSOISE
lobster	BISQUE DE HOMARD
meat with	
—curry	MILLIGATAWNY
—dumplings (US)	PEPPER POT
mutton	SCOTCH BROTH
New Zealand	TOHEROA
oatmeal gruel	BURGOO
Philippines dumpling soup	TANCIT MOLO
Polish	ZUPA
Russian	
—beetroot	BORSCHT, BOR(T)SCH
—cabbage	SHCHEE, SH(T)CHI
—fish	UKKA
Scandinavian	LAPSKAUS
Scottish	COCKALEEKIE, PUNCHNEP
	MUSLIN-KALE
shark's fin	YU TSI TANG
shellfish	BISQUE, TURTLE
Spanish	GALICIAN
—cold	BOURRISE, GAZPACHO
—egg	TONILLO
—fish	CALDO DE PESCADO
strong broth	BOUILLON, CULLIS
thick soup	POT(T)AGE, SCOTCH BROTH
thin soup	BOUILLON, BROTH
	CONSOMME, GRUEL, SKILLY
tomato-flavoured	MADRILENE
Turkish yoghurt	YAYLA CORBASI
various meats and vegetables	STOCKPOT
without solid pieces	PUREE
with pasta	MINESTRE IN BRODO
South Africa	RSA, SA, ZA
capitals	CAPE TOWN, PRETORIA
coin	CENT, RAND, RD
homelands	BOPHUTHATSWANA
	CISKEI, TRANSKEI, VENDA
provinces	CAPE PROVINCE, NATAL
	ORANGE FREE STATE
	TRANSVAAL
	(see also **African**)

South America	SA
alligator	CAIMAN, CAYMAN
ant	SAUBA-ANT, UMBRELLA-ANT
—bear	TAMANOIR
—eater	ARMADILLO, TAMANDUA
—thrush	ANT-BIRD
armadillo	PEBA, TATOU
aromatic kernel	PICHURIM BEAN
arrow-poison	CURARA, CURARE
balsam	COPAIBA, COPIAYA
bat	DESMODUS
beetle	HERCULES BEETLE
beetles	PYROPHORUS
bird	AGAMI, ANT-THRUSH, ARAPUNGA
	BELL-BIRD, CAMPANERO
	COCK-OF-THE-ROCK, CONDOR, COTINGA
	CURASSOW, , HOA(C)TZIN, JABIRU
	JACAMAR, MANAKIN, MOTMOT
	MUSK-DUCK, OVEN-BIRD
	PUFF-BIRD, QUETZAL, RHEA, SERIEMA
	STINK-BIRD, SUN-BITTERN, TAPACOLO
	TAPACULO, TERU-TERO, TOPAZ
	TOUCAN(ET), TROGON, TRUMPETER
	TURCO, UMBRELLA-BIRD, URUBU
	YNAMBU, ZOPILOTE
—catching spider	TARANTULA
birthwort	ARISTOLOCHIA
brome-grass	RESCUE-GRASS
burrowing armadillo	PICHICIAGO
butterfly	MORPHO
butternut	S(A)OUARI(-NUT)
cactus	CHRISTMAS CACTUS
canoe	PERIAGUA, PIRAGUA
	PIROGUE
Cape gooseberry	STRAWBERRY-TOMATO
capybara	RIVER-HOG
carica	PA(W)PAW, PAPAYA
catfish	HASSAR
cattle	
—farm	ESTANCIA
—farmer	ESTANCIERO
cavy	GUINEA-PIG
cereal	QUINOA
chain	ANDES
climbing plant	AYAHUASCO
	CANARY CREEPER
	INDIAN CRESS, MARCGRAVIA
	PASSION-FLOWER, PHILODENDRON
	SMILAX, SARSAPARILLA, TIMBO
	TROPAEOLUM, WAX-FLOWER
cloak	PONCHO
coin	PESO
coral-flowered plant	EASTER CACTUS
corkwood	BALSA
cowboy	GAUCHO, VAQUERO
crab-tree	CARAPA

—fruit	CARAP-NUT
crested screamer	CHAUNA, , CARIAMA
	SERIEMA
crocodile	CAIMAN, CAYMAN
dance	PAVANE, ZAPATEO
dorado	GOLDEN SALMON
dormouse	ECHIMYD
drink	ASSAI, AYAHUASCO, CHICHA
	MATE, YERBA (DE MATE)
drug	PAREIRA BRAVA
early civilisation	HUARI, TIAHUANACO
edentate	SLOTH
edible	
—grub	GROO-GROO, GRU-GRU
—tuber	ARRACACHA, OCA
eel	CARAPO
epiphyte	TILLANDSIA
estate	HACIENDA
establishment	HACIENDA
factory	HACIENDA
finch	TANAGER
fireflies	PYROPHORUS
fish	ANGEL-FISH, ARAPAIMA
	CARIBE, CHICHLID, PERAI, PIRAI
	PIRANHA, PIRARUCU, PIRAYA
	SWORD-TAIL
—poison	SURINAM POISON, TIMBO
flea	CHIGGER, CHIGOE
	CHIGRE, JIGGER
flooded forest	(I)GAPO
flowers	ALSTROEMERIA, ANTHURIUM
	GLOXINIA, TAGETES
fox	ZORRO
fruit	A(C)KEE, ASSAI, CASHEW-APPLE
	CASHEW-NUT, GUAVA, LUCUMA
	SOUR-SOP, SUGAR-APPLE
	SWEET-SOP
game bird	GUAN
garment	TAYO
golden	
—breasted trumpeter	AGAMI
—salmon	DORADO
goosefoot	QUINOA
gourd	CACOON
grass	PASPALUM
gum	ANGICO, CONIMA
hare-lipped bat	NOCTILIO
hawk	CARACARA
hoatzin	STINK-BIRD
holly	MATE
Honduras bark	CASCARA
horned screamer	PALAMEDEA
horseman	GAUCHO, LLANERO
humming-bird	SWORD-BILL, SYLPH
hut	TOLDO

Indians	GUARANI, TUPI
indigo	COBRES
jacaranda	PALISANDER
kinkajou	HONEY-BEAR, POTTO
landmark	SENAL
language	CARIB, GURANI, TUPI
lapwing	TERU-TERO
large eagle	(HARPY) EAGLE
laurel tree	PICHURIM
leaf-carrying ant	SAUBA
leopard	JAGUAR
liquor	CHICA
lizard	AMPHISBAENA, BASILISK
	(I)GUANA, TEGUEXIN
lion	COUG(U)AR, PUMA
maize drink	CHICHA
marmalade-tree	MAMMEE-SAPOTA
marmoset	JACCHUS
measure (33"-43")	VARA, VARE
missile	BOLAS
mortgage	CEDULA
moth	OWL-MOTH
mountain-sickness	PUNA
mud-fish	LEPIDOSIREN
mulberry tree	CONTRAYERVA, CRECOPIA
nest-building	
catfish	HASSAR
night-ape	DOUROUCOULI, DURUKULI
non-Spaniard	GRINGO
oil-bird	GUACHARO, GUACHERO
opossum	MARMOSE
orchid	ONCIDIUM
ostrich	NANDOO, NANDU, RHEA
pack animal	ALPACA, PACO
	GUANACO, HUANACO, LLAMA
palisander	JACARANDA
palms	(*see* **palms**)
papaya	CARICA, PA(W)PAW, PAPAYA
parrot	AMAZON, MACAW
pineapple	TILLANDSIA
Pithecolobium	RAIN-TREE
plain	CAMPOS, LLANO, PAMPA(S)
	PARAMO, SAVANNA(H)
—dweller	LLANERO
plant	ARTILLERY-PLANT, BIXA
	DUMB-CANE, FURCRAEA
	PAREIRA, PETUNIA
—yielding	
curare	(O)URALI, (O)URARI
	WOORALI, WOURALI
snakebite antidote	GUACO
poison	CURARA, CURARE
pouch-toad	NOTOTREMA
purgative nut	PHYSIC-NUT
quail	TINAMOU
rabbit-squirrel	CHINCHA

racoon	COATI(MONDI)
	COATI(MUNDI), KINKAJOU
rail	COURLAN
rain forest	SELVA
ranch	HACIENDA
red jasmine	FRANGIPANI
rescue-grass	BROME-GRASS
resin	CARANNA, CARAUNA
riding-whip	QUIRT
river	AMAZON
—hog	CAPYBARA
rodent	ACOUCHY, AG(O)UTI
	AG(O)UTY, BISCACHA
	CAPYBARA, CAVY
	CHINCH(ILL)A, COYP(O)U, PACA
	DILOCHOTIS, GUINEA-PIG, MARA
	PATAGONIAN HARE, TUCOTUCO
	TUCUTUCO, TUKUTUKU
	VISCACHA. VIZCACHA
—colony	VISCACHERA
rosewood	PALISANDER
rubber substitute	BALATA
screamer	KAMICHI
settlement	PUEBLO
shrub	ESCALLONIA, JABORANDI
	PILOCARPUS, RHATANY
	SIMARUBA, TREE-0TOMATO
skunk	ATOC, ATOK, ZORILLO
sloth	AI, UNAU
spiny fish	DORAS
spirit	DEMERARA
strainer for juice	TIPITI
tableland	MESETA, PUNA
three-toed sloth	AI
tiger-cat	MARGAY
timber	*(see separate entry)*
tinamous	PARTRIDGE
town	PUEBLO
tree	ACACIO, ACAJOU, A(C)KEE, ANGICO
	BEBEERU, BOMBAX, CACAO, CALABASH
	CANDLE-TREE, CANNONBALL-TREE
	CASHEW, CHINA(CHINA), COW-TREE
	DALI, FIDDLEWOOD, FUSTIC, FUSTOC
	GRAPETREE, GREENHEART, GUAIACUM
	GUAVA, JACARANDA, KINA(KINA)
	LEOPARD-WOOD, LETTER-WOOD
	LIMA-WOOD, LOGWOOD, LUCUMA
	MAHOGANY, MASSARANDUBA
	MILK-TREE, MISSEL-TREE, OITICICA
	OMBU, PAPAYA, PALISANDER
	QUASSIA, QUEBRACH, RAIN-TREE
	S(A)OUARI, SAVANNA-WATTLE
	SNAKEWOOD, SOAP-BARK, SOUR-SOP
	SUGAR-APPLE, SWEET-SOP
	SWEETWOOD, TRUMPET-TREE
	WALLABA, XYLOPIA

—frog	NOTOTREMA
—yielding quinine	CHINA(CHINA)
	CINCHONA, KINA(KINA)
	QUINA(QUINA)
	QUINQU(INA
turtle	MATAMATA
two-toed sloth	UNAU
ungulate	TAPIR
uplands	CUCHILLA
village	PUEBLO
vine	AYAHUASCO
vulture	CONDOR, URUBU
walking fish	DORAS
water-opossum	YAPO(C)K
weasel	GRISON, TAIRA, TAYRA
weevil	DIAMOND-BEETLE
wet forest	SELVA
wild	
—cat	EYRA, JAGUAR(ONDI)
	JAGUARUNDI
	MARGAY, OCELOT
	PUMA
—llama	GUANACO, HUANACO
	VICUNA
—pig	PECCARY, TAPIR
—turkey	CRAX, CURASSOW
	PENELOPE
wood-sorrel	OCA
Yankee	GRINGO
South Australia	SA
South Island	SI
South Pole	SP
Soviet Union	*(see* **Russia**)
space	
capsule	
—USA	APOLLO, AURORA, FAITH
	FREEDOM, FRIENDSHIP
	GEMINI, LIBERTY
	MERCURY
	SIGMA, SKYLAB
—USSR	SOYUZ, VOSHKOV
	VOSTOK, ZOND
probe	
—Halley's comet	GIOTTO
—Jupiter	GALILEO, PIONEER
	VOYAGER
—Mars	MARINER, ORBITER
	VIKING
—Mercury	MARINER
—Moon	LUNA, LUNIK, ORBITER
	RANGER, SURVEYOR
	ZOND
—Neptune	VOYAGER
—Saturn	VOYAGER
—Sun	HELIOS
—Uranus	VOYAGER

—Venus	MAGELLAN, MARINER	—Russian	BURAN, ENERGIA
	VENERA	station	FREEDOM, MIR, VOSTOK
rocket		traveller	ASTRONAUT, COSMONAUT
—fuel	HYDYNE, LIQUID OXYGEN	velocity required	
	LOX	to overcome gravity	ESCAPE VELOCITY
—launching site			(see also astronomy)
American	CAPE CANAVERAL	**Spain**	E
French	KOUROU, GUIANA	**Spanish**	HISPANO-, IBERIAN, SP
Japanese	KAGOSHIMA	act	AUTO
Russian	BAIKANOUR, COSMODROME	agreement	SI
—pioneers		almond	ALMENDRA
American	GODDARD	American half-caste	MESTIZO
German	OBERTH, VON BRAUN	anchovy paste	ANCHOIADE
Russian	MOLCHANOFF, TSIOLKOVSKY	apple	MANZANA
—range	WOOMERA	articles	EL, LA, LAS, LOS
—small rocket controlling		baby	NENE
direction, etc	VERNIER ENGINE	barracks	CASERNA
	VERNIER MOTOR	Basque	
	THRUSTER	—ball game	PELOTA
—types		—separatists	ETA
American	ARROW, ALAS, CRUISE	bar	CANTINA
	DELTA, HAWK, LANCE	bay	BAHIA, GOLFO
	MINUTEMAN, PEGASUS, PERSHING	bazaar	ALCAICERIA
	POLARIS, REDSTONE, SATURN	beach	PLAYA
	STINGER, TRIDENT	beer	CERVEZA
	WAC CORPORAL	black	NEGRO
British	BLOWPIPE, BLUE STEEL	—pudding	MONDONGO
	BLUESTREAK, LANCE, THOR	blanket	MANTA
Chinese	LONG MARCH	blusterer	CACAFOGO, CACAFUEGO
French	ARIANCE	boundary-house	POSADO
German	V1, V2	boy	MUCHACHO
Indian	AGNI, PRITHVI		NINO
Israeli	JERICHO	brazier	BRASERO
Russian	AMOS, ARCHER, ATOLL	bread	PAN
	SAM	bridge	PUENTE
South African	SKERPION	brother	HERMANO
satellite	ARABSAT, ASIASAT, AST	—hood	HERMANDAD
	ASTERIX, ASTRA	bullfighting	(see separate entry)
	BSB, CHINA, COBE, COSMOS	cabal	JUNTA, JUNTO
	DELTA STAR, EARLY BIRD	cabinet	VARGUENO
	EINSTEIN OBSERVATORY	canape	TAPA
	EXPLORER, EUTELSAT, EXOSAT	canyon	CANON
	GORIZONT, HIPPARCHUS	cape	CAPA, MANTILLA
	INTELSAT, IRAS, LANDSAT, LACROSSE	—(headland)	CABO, PUNTA
	MARCO POLO, METEOR, METEOSAT	capital	MADRID
	MUSES-A, NIMBUS, NOAA	cask	BARRICA
	OLYMPUS, OPEK, OSUMI	chalk	SOAPSTONE
	PALAPA, PEGASUS, PROSPERO, RADUGA	chamber	CAMARA
	ROHINI, RORSAT, SKYLAB	champion	CAMPEADOR, CID
	SOLAR MAX, SPOT 2, SPUTNIK	chaperone	DUENNA
	SYNCOM, TELECOM, TELSTAR	cheer	OLE
	TIROS, TRANSIT, VANGUARD	cheese	QUESO
	VELA, WESTAR, ZIRCON	chicken	POLLO
shuttle		chickpeas	GARBANZOS
—American	ATLANTIS, CHALLENGER	chief	CID
	COLUMBIA, DISCOVERY	—magistrate	CORREGIDOR

child	NINO	fan	AFICIONADO
Christian	MOZARAB	fascist	FALANGE, PHALANGE
city	CIUDAD	father	PADRE
cloak	CAPA, CAPOTE, MANTA	favoured	GRACIOSO
clown	GRACIOSO	festival	FIESTA
cliff	PENA	few words	POCAS PALABRAS
coast	COSTA	fish	PESCADO
code of law	FUEROA	—soup	CALDO DE PESCADO
coins		—stew	ZARZUELA DE PESCADO
—unit	PESO, PESETA	fleet	ARMADA, FLOTA
—½ peseta	REAL, RIAL, RYAL	fly	BLISTER-BEETLE, CANTHARID
—2 reals	PISTAREEN	folk-dance	SARDANA
—8 reals	PIECE OF EIGHT	forest	SELVA
—5 pesetas	DURO, PESO	fortress	ALCAZAR
—dollar	PIECE OF EIGHT	gap	PORTILLO
—old		garlic	AJO
2 pistoles	DOUBLOON	—mayonnaise	AIOLI
copper coin	MARAVEDI, VELLON	gentleman	CABALLERO, DON, HIDALGO
gold coin	PISTOLE	girl	NINA
silver coin	COB	glazed tile	AZULEJO
cold soup	GAZPACHO	good	
collection of songs	CANCIONERO	—afternoon	BUENAS TARDES
commander	ENCOMENDERO	—day/morning	BUENOS DIAS
commandery	ENCOMIENDA	—night	BUENAS NOCHES
conqueror	CONQUISTADOR	goodbye	ADIOS
constitution	FUERO	gorge	CANADON, CAN(Y)ON
council	JUNTA	governor	ADELANTADO
—meeting	CONSULTA		ALCA(I)DE, ALCAYDE
country house	QUINTA	governess	DUENNA
courtyard	PATIO	grandee	ADELANTADO, GRANDE
covered wagon	TARTANA		HIDALGO, PROCER
cress	PEPPERWORT	grape	UVA
dance	BALLE	grass	ESPARTO
dances	BOLERO, CACHUCHA, FANDANGO	gulf	GOLFO
	FARRUCA, FLAMENCO, JOTA	gypsy	
	PASO DOBLE, PASSACAGLIA	—man	ZINCALO
	SARABAND, SEGUIDILLA	—song	FLAMENCO
	ZAPATEADO	—woman	ZINCALA
danger warning on chart	VIGIA	gypsies	ZINCALI
deep valley	CUENCA	ham	JAMON
desert plateau	PUNA	hamlet	ALDEA
desk	VARGUENO	harbour	PORTO, PUERTO
despatch boat	AVISO	hare	LIEBRE
dialect	CASTILIAN, CATALAN	head	
	LADRINO	—covering	MANTILLA
dish	PAELLA, SALPICON	—of state	CAUDILLO
district	BARRIO	headman	CAPITANO
doctor	MEDICO	hero	(EL) CID
donkey	BURRO	highness	ALTEZA
drama	AUTO	highway	CAMINO REAL
drunken fellow	BORACHIO	highwayman	BANDOLERO
dynasty	BOURBON	hill	CERRO, COLLADO, LOMA
—Moorish	NASRID	holiday	FIESTA
egg	HUEVO	horseman's cap	MONTERO
—soup	TONILLO	hostel	PARADOR
estuary	ESTERO	hotel	PARADOR, POSADA

hunter	MONTERO	naked	EN CUEROS
I kiss your hands	BESO LAS MANOS	nap	SIESTA
ice cream	HELADO	narrow	
icing	ALCORZA	—canyon	CANADA
in close-fitting dress	EN CUERPO	—pass	PUERTA
infantry regiment	TERCIO	narrows	ANGOSTURA
inlet	ESTERO	noble	DON, GRANDEE
inn	POSADA	notary	ESCRIBANO
insectivore	DESMAN	nothing	NADA
intriguers	CARARILLA	oil	ACEITE
interjection of annoyance	CARAMBA	olive paste	OLIVADE
island	ISLA	on	
jar	OLLA, TINAJA	—horseback	EN CABALLO
Jews	SEPHARDIM	—the contrary	AL CONTRARIO
judge	ALCALDE	open area in town	PLAZA
kebab	PINCHO	orange	NARANJA
kidney bean	FRIJOL(E)	otter	NUTRIA
knife	CUCHILLO	palace	ALHAMBRA, ALCAZAR
lady	DON(Y)A, HIDALGA	parliament	CORTES
lake	LAGO, LAGUNA	partridge	PERDIZE
language	BASQUE, CATALAN	pass	PASO, PORTILLO
	CASTILIAN, LADINO	peak	CERRO, CORNO
large			PICACHO, PIC(O)
—cigar	PERFECTO	peas	GUISANTES
—jar	TINAJA	penal settlement	PRESIDIO
leader	CAUDILLO, (EL) CID	pheasant	FAISAN
liquor	AGUARDIENTE	plain	LLANO, PLANA, PLANICIE
little	POCO	police	GUARDIA CIVIL
madam	DONA, SENORA		RURALES
man	HOMBRE, SENOR	—officer	ALGUACIL, ALGUAZIL
manifesto	PRONUNCIAMENTO	political boss	CACIQUE, CAZIQUE
mantle	MANTILLA	port	PORTO, PUERTO
market-place	PLAZA	potato omelette	TORTILLA
marsh	BANADO	pot	OLLA
matador	ESPADA	poultry	AVES
mayor	ALCALDE	prairie	LLANO
measure		priest	CURA, PADRE
—yard	METRO	prince	INFANTE
—4.2 miles	LEAGUE	princess	INFANTA
—2¼ pints	LITRO	proclamation	PRONUNCIAMENTO
meat and fish pie	EMPANADILLA	province	ANDALUSIA
military post	PRESIDIO	public	
milk and egg pudding	CREMA CATALANA	—square	PLAZA
miracle-worker	SALUTER	—walk	ALAMEDA
miss	SENORITA	punishment of heretics	AUTO DA FE
mister	DON, SENOR, SR	rabbit	CONEJO
mixed stew	OLLA-PODRIDA	race	BASQUE
Moslem lawyer	ALFAQUI	rapids	TORRENTE
mounted bullfighter	PICADOR	ravine	ARROYO, CANADA
mountain	MONTE	reservoir	EMBALSE
—range	CORDILLERA, CUCHILLAS	restaurant	HOSTERIA
	SIERRA	reward (for good news)	ALBRICIAS
muleteer	ARRIERO	river	RIO
municipal council	AYUNTAMIENTO	—mouth	RIA
musical instrument	TENORA, VIHUELA	road-house	PARADOR
	ZAMBOMBA	robber	LADRON

rock	CAYO, PENA	—fish	ESPADA
rotten	PRODRIDA	tableland	MES(ET)A
royal road	CAMINO REAL	talk	PALABRA
saddle	COLLADO	tavern	FONDO
saddlebag	ALFORGA	telephone company	TELEFONICA
saint	SAN(TA), SANTO	title	DON
saint's day	FIESTA	tomorrow	MANAN(Y)A
salad	ENSALADA	town	CIUDAD
saloon	CANTINA	treaty	AS(S)IENTO
salt		trooper	GINETE
—lake	SALADA	turkey-buzzard	GALLINAZO
—pan	SALAR, SALINA	until we meet again	HASTA LA VISTA
sandal	ALPARGATA	urn	OLLA
sandbank	BANCO	valley	VAL(L)
sauce	SALSA	vaudeville	ZARZUELA
sausage	CHORIZA, SALCHICA	veal	TERNERA
sea	MAR	vegetable soup	GAZPACHO
see you		vehicle	VOLANTE
—later	HASTA LUEGO	village	ALDEA, PUEBLO
—tomorrow	HASTA MANANA	volcano	VOLCAN
serenade	RONDENA	waiter	MOZO
shawl	MANTILLA, MANTON	walk	PASEO
sheep	MERINO	war	GUERRA
—skin coat	ZAMARRA, ZAMARRO	—to the knife	GUERRA AL CUCHILLO
sherry	AMONTILLADO, JEREZ	watch-tower	ATALAYA
shop	TIENDA	water	
shore	COSTA	—cooler	ALCARRAZA
shrub	CNEORUM, WIDOW-WAIL	—course	ARROYO
sir	DON, SENOR, SR	—fall	CATARATA, SALTO
slaughtering and freezing		well	FUENTE
establishment	FRIGORIFICO	weight	
sleep	SIESTA	—gram	GRAMO
small		—25lb	ARROBA
—fumarole	HORNITO	who knows?	QUIEN SABE?
—room	CAMARILLA	wild marjoram	OREGANO
smoked pilchard	FUMADO	window	VENTANA
snack	TAPA	wine	VINO
soldier	SOLDADO		(*see also separate entry*)
song	CANCION	—shop	BODEGA, CANTINA
soup	BOURRIDE	—skin	BORACHIO
source	FUENTE	woman	MUJER, SENORA
spitfire	CACAFOGO, CACAFUEGO	wood	SELVA
sponge roll	BRAZO DE GITANO	word	PALABRA
square	PLAZA	**special**	
squid	CALAMAR	Special Air Service	SAS
standard bearer	ALFEREZ	Special Constable	SC
steak	BISTEC	special drawing right(s)	SDR
stew	OLLA-PODRIDA	special order	SO
strait	ESTRECHO, PASO	**speech**	(*see* **language, rhetoric**)
strangulation	GAR(R)OTTE	**Spenser**	
street	CALLE, PASEO	words used in his works:	
sun-dried brick	ADOBE	abandon	ABAND
swamp	ESTERO	abash	QUELL
sweetmeat	ALCORZA	abate	APPAL, QUELL, RELENT
sword	BILBO, ESPADA, ESTOQUE	abiding place	GRANGE
—blade	TOLEDO	able	HABLE

abounding	RANK	appeal	PEAL
absolve	QUIGHT, QUYTE	appearance	HEW
accomplish	COMPLISH	appease	DEFRAY
accusation	CRIME	approach	CO(A)ST, COST(E), SUCCEED
accuse	APPEAL	—death	FIT
acquit	QUIGHT, QUYTE	arbour	HERBAR
act		arm	EMBATTLE
—amiss	MISDONNE	arrange	ENRAUNGE
—of seizing	PREY	arranged	COMPACT
active	WIMBLE	array	ATTRAP, PLIGHT
adjudge	BEHIGHT, BEHOTE	arrear	AREAR, ARERE
adjudicator	DAYES-MAN	arrogance	SURQUEDRY
adjust	CONCENT	arrowhead	FORKHEAD
admiration	ADMIRA(U)NCE	art	FEAT
adorn	ADORE, ATTRAP, DITE	artifice	GIN
adorned	DITE	as	
advance	AVAUNT	—conveying an impression	PURPORT
—in hostility	SWAY	—soon	ALSOON(E)
advancing	VAUNCING	assail	ASSAY
advantage	VAUNTAGE	assault	ASSAY, STOUND, STOWND
advise	AVISE, AVIZE, AVYSE, REED(E)	assay	SAY
affect	ASSAY	assayer	SAY-MASTER
—disagreeably	UNSEASON	assembled	ACCOYLD
affectedly nice or prim	QUAINT	assembly	ASSEMBLA(U)NCE
afflict	ASSAY	assuredly	PARDIE, PARDY, PERDIE
affliction	TINE, TYNE		PERDY
afraid	ADRAD, ADRED	astound	STOUND
aged	SHOT	astounded condition	STOUND
ago	YGO(E)	astray	ABORD
agreed upon	COMPACT	astronomy	STAR-READ
aim	UPSHOT	Astrophel	PENTHIA, STARLIGHT
air	DEMAINE, DEMAYNE	at a distance	WIDE
	DEMEANE	athletic contest	PRISE
akin	SYBBE	atone	ATTONE
alembic	LIMBEC(K)	attack	BODRAG, BORDRAGING
alike	YLIKE	attain	SEISE
allegiance	FOY	attempted	FOND
alleviate	AL(L)EGGE	attendance at court	COURTING
alleviation	AL(L)EGGAUNCE	attention	ATTENT
allot	TEENE	attentive consideration	INTENDIMENT
allow	BETEEM(E)	augury	SOOTHE
almost	UNE(A)TH, UNEATHES	avenger	VENGER
	UNNETHES	avowal	AVOURE
altogether	ALGATE	await	REMAIN
amaze	AWHAPE	award	ADDOOM, ADWARD
ambush	AWAIT	away	AWAYES
amerced	AMERST	axis	HENGE
amice	AMIS	back	CHINE
amount	MOUNTENA(U)NCE	—up	ABET
anew	OF NEW	bait	BAYT
anger	TINE, TYNE	balance	LAUNCE, PEASE, PEAZE
animated	EMPASSIONED		PEISE, PEIZE, PEYSE, POUND
annoy	NOY	baldric(k)	BAUDRICKE
annoyance	NOYANCE	ban	BAND
antagonist	PEER	banderol	BANNERALL
anvil	ANDVILE	bandy	CHAFFER

banish	BAND, FOR(E)SAY	besprinkle	SHED
bar	SPARRE, SPERRE	bestow part of	EMPART
barren	BLUNT	betroth	SPOUSE
basket	FLASKET	between whiles	ATWEEN
bate	BAYT	bid	BED
bathe	BAY(E), EMBAY	bight	BOUGHT
battle	BATTIL	bind	EMBRACE
be		bistort	POLYGONY
—a guest	HOST	bit	WHAT
—abashed	BASH	bite	REMORSE
—active or excited	STIRE, STYRE	bitten	GRYPT
—filled	REDOUND	bittern	BITT(O)UR
—flooded	FLOAT	bitterness	FELL
—it how it may	HOWBE	black hellebore	MELAMPODE
—necessary	MISTER	blameless	UNREPROVED
—on		blast	SCATH
guard	WAITE	blatant	BLATTANT
the side next	SIDE	blemish	BLEMISHMENT
—out of bed	STIRE, STYRE	blockhead	MOME
—painful	TINE, TYNE	blood	
—sorry for	FORTHINK	—relation	SYBBE
—spoken of	HEAR	—relationship	KINDRED
—stopped by	STAY	blossom	BLOOSME
beak	BECKE	blow	PEASE, PEAZE, PEISE
bear	BIER		PEIZE, PEYSE
bearing AMENAUNCE, DEMAINE, DEMAYNE		blue	BLEW
DEMEANE, DEMAINE, DEMAYNE		boast	CRAKE
DEMEANE, PORTANCE		body	SOYLE
—towards another	DEMEASNURE	boiling pot	STEW
beaten by cold	WINTER-BEATEN	bolt	SPERRE
beautiful and good woman	BELLIBONE	—for cross-bow	QUAR'LE
because	BY MEANS	bonny lass	BON(N)ILASSE
becoming	BESITTING	border	BOARD, FRONTIER
bed	BID	borrowed	STRAUNGE
bedyed	BEDIDE	bought provisions	ACHETES
befit	BEFALL	bound up	UPBOUND(EN)
beforehand	PARAVA(U)NT	boundaries	OUTBOUNDS
begin to move	STIRE, STYRE	boundary water	SHARD, SHERD
begot	KYNDED	brace	EMBRACE
beguile	GUILE	braid	EMBRAID
behaviour COMPORTANCE, DEMEASNURE		brandish	BLESS, HURTLE
HAVEOUR, HAVIOUR		breaded	BREDE
beheaded	TRUNKED	break	CESURE
behest	HEAST(E)	—mail from	DISMAYL
belabour	LAY ON LOAD	bright	SHERE
believe wrongly to be	MISTAKE	bring	
bellow in return	REBELLOW	—back	RELATE, REVERSE
beloved	BEL(L)AMOURE	to better state	RECURE
bend	BOUGHT	—discredit on	BLAME
benefit	VANTAGE	—down	EMBACE
bent	CORBE	—into being	REAR
beseech	BESEEKE	—on	INFER
beset	EMPEACH	—reproach on	UPBRAY
—by	BESTAD(D)E	—to	
besides	FOREBY	an end	EXPIRE
besiege	ASIEGE	bear	SERVE

mind	MIND	—to whirl or roll	REEL
—together	COMPILE, UPKNIT	cave	DELVE
—up	NOUSELL, NOU(R)SLE	cease	BLIN, CESSE, LIN
	NUZZLE	—to	
—urgently	COMPEL	occupy	QUIGHT, QUYTE
brittle	BRICKLE	put forward	DISADVANCE
broken		ceiled	SIELD
—pottery	POTSHARE	ceiling	SEELING
—up	TO-BRUSD	centre of target	MARK-WHITE
brother	SYBBE	certainly	SICCAR, SICKER
brought down	EMBASTE	chafe	CHAUFE, CHAUFF
bruise	INTUSE	champion	DOUCEPERE, DOUZEPER
—with walking	SURBATE	chapiter	CHAPTER
bruised severely	TO-BRUSD	charge with	
—with walking	SURBATED, SURBET	overwhelming force	SURCHARGE
bubble	ROWNDELL	charged with	ENFOULDERED
budget	BOUGET	—passion	EMPASSIONED
burden	BEARE	chariot	CHARET
burdensome	CHARGEFUL	chase	SCORSE
burning	SEARE	chastise	DISPLE, REFORM
—within	INBURNING	check	REVOKE
burst	BRUST, DISTRAIN	cheer	CHERRY
bush	TODDE	chest for records	SCRINE, SCRYNE
—of hair over eyes	GLIB	chief magician	ARCHIMAGO
busy in traffic	TRADEFUL	choice	TRYE
by	FOREBY	choicest	PRIMROSE
call	CLAME, ENQUERE, ENQUIRE	choke	ACCLOY
	INQUERE, INQUIRE	circumstances	STEAD
—by an ill name	MISCALL	cite	CONVENT
called	HOTE, NEMPT	claim	CLAME
camlet	CHAMELOT	clamour	OUTRAGE
canal superintendent	ZANJERO	clamorous	BLATTANT
cannot be helped	HELPLESS	clear	CLEAN, NEAT
canon	SQUIER, SQUIRE	—of blame	QUIGHT, QUYTE
canto	CANTICLE	—off	QUIGHT, QUYTE
cap	CALL	clemency	CLEMENCE
captain	CAPITAYN	climb	STIE, STYE
captive	CAITIVE	climbed	CLAMBE, SCAND
captivity	CAPTIVA(U)NCE	clog	ACCLOY
career	CARIERE	close	STRAIT
careful	HEEDY	—fight	GRAPLEMENT
carpenter's square	SQUIER, SQUIRE	cloth covering	DRAPET
carriage	PORTANCE	clothe	EMBOSS
carve	KERVE	—again	REVEST
case	STEAD	clown	PATCHC(H)OCKE
cast about	THROW ABOUT	coach	COCH
castaway	WEFT(E)	coast	BOARD, COST(E)
casually dropped	SCATTERED	coil	BOUGHT
caterwaul	WRAWL	cold	FRENNE
caught	KEIGHT	colour	HEW
caul	CALL	coltsfoot	COLTSWOOD
cauldron	CAUDRON	combatant	BATTEILANT
cause	ENCHEASON, GARRE	come	
—of		—forth alone	SINGLE
grief	HEART-SORE	—to grief	MISWEND
wrongdoing	CRIME	comedown	AVALE, AVAIL(E)

comer	COMMER	cuirass	CURAT, CURIET
command	HEAST(E)	cunning	PRACTIC
—a view of	SURVEW	cup of maple wood	MAZER
commit	ARRET(T)	cur	KURRE
companying	COMPANING	curdle	CRUDDLE
comparison	PARAGON	curdy	CRUDDY
compassionate feeling	REMORSE	cure	RECURE
compel	GARRE	curse upon	MA(U)LGRE
competition	PARAGON	curtal-axe	CURTAXE
complain	MEAN(E), MEIN, MENE	custody	BAIL
completeness	COMPLEMENT	cut	
compose	COMILE	—asunder	DISCIDE
conceal	HEAL, HEEL, HELE	—into	ENTRENCH, INTRENCH
concealing	COVERT	chines	CHYND
conceive	CONTRIVE	—off	SHARE
conclude	UPKNIT	cutting	TRENCHAND
condition	HOOD, STEAD	daily	ADAYS
conference	EMPARLAUNCE	dairy	DAYR-HOUSE
confound	AWHAPE	damage	EMPEACH, SCATH
congratulate	GREET	danger	DOUBT
conned	COND	dare	DARRE
consent	AFFOORD	dark/darken/darkly	DIRK(E)
constant	SAD	darling	DEARLING
consummateness	COMPLEMENT	dastard	HYLDING
contemptuous	DESPITEOUS	daunted	QUAYD
contradict	UNDERSAYE	day of ill omen	DISMAL DAY
contrivance	GIN	daze	DARE
controversy	DEBATEMENT	dealt mercifully with	MERCIFIDE
convene	CONVENT	dearth	DERTH
conversation	BOARD	death	FUNERAL
conversation(al speech)	PURPOSE	debase	EMBACE
converse	COMMON	debased	EMBASTE
convey	REPORT	deceit	MALENGINE
corbel	CORBE	deceiver	FALSER, TREACHETOUR
coronation	CARNATION	decline	WELKE
could not	NOTE	decorate	EMBRAVE
counsel	AREAD, AREDE, ARREEDE	decrease	DECREW
	READ, REED(E)	decree	SAW
counterfeit	IDOL	deemed	DEMPT
counterplot	COUNTERCAST	defaced	DEFAST(E)
courageous	STOMACHOUS	defame	DEFACE
course	FARE, TRACE	defence	MUNIFIENCE
cover	HEAL, HEEL, HELE	deformed	DISMAYD
covered	COURD	degenerate	DEGENDER
—over	OVERDIGHT	degrade	EMBACE
—with sweat	FORSWATT	degraded	EMBASTE
coward	COWHE(A)RD	deify	GOD
coward(ly)	HYLDING	delay	FOR(E)SLOW, FORSLOE
cowardice	COWARDREE	delight in	FAIN
coyness	NICETY	dense	RANK
crew together	CONCREW	depart	QUIGHT, QUYTE
crimson	CREM(O)SIN	—from	QUIGHT, QUYTE
cross-bow bolt	QUAR'LE	departure	DEPART, PARTURE
cry		depression	DELVE
—like a cat	WRAWL	deprive of armour	DISMAYL
—triumph over	OVERCRAW	deserving	CONDIGN

design	DESINE, DESYNE, SLEIGHT	divide	DEPART, DISCIDE
designate	INTEND	do	DOEN, DONE, DONNE
desire	FAIN	—amiss	MIS
—strongly	EARN	—battle	DARRAIGN(E), DARRAINE
desk	DESSE		DARRAYN, DERRAIGN
despairing	DESPAIRFUL	—service	SUE
despised	CONTEMPT	—wrongly	MISDONNE
detention	DETAIN	doff	UNDIGHT
determine	HIGHT	doing daring deeds	DER-DOING
dethrone	DISTHRONISE	domain	REAME
detriment	EMPEACH	doom	DOME
device	SLEIGHT	doubtless	DREADLESS
devour	ENGORGE	drag	TRAYNE
dew	DEAW	draw	
dewy	DEAWIE, DEWAY	—back	DISADVANCE
dexterously	FEATEOUSLY	—over	OVERHA(I)LE
dialect	LEDDEN	drawn	
die	QUELL, STERVE	—aside	DISTRAUGHT
difficult to wield or move	UNWELDY	—away	MISTRAYNED
dig beneath	UNDERMINDE	dread(ed)	DRAD
digest mentally	ENDEW, INDEW	dreariness	DRE(A)RE, DRERYHOOD
dilute	DELAY		DRERYMENT
diminish	BAYT	dreary	GASTFULL
din	DEEN, STOUND, STOWND	dress	AGUISE, AGUIZE, ATTRAP
direct	AVENTRE, HIGHT	drifter	DROVER
disapprove	DISPROOVE	drive	
discern	SCERNE	—improperly	WREST
discharge	QUIGHT, QUYTE	—with thunderbolts	THUNDER-DRIVE
discipline	DISPLE	drove	DRIVE
disclose	UNHEAL, UNHELE	drowned	DRENT, DROWNDED
disclosed	DISCLOST	drowsiness	DROWSIHE(A)D
discomfit	YSHEND	drum	DROOME
discouraging onslaught	DISMAY	due	DEWFULL
discourse	PURPOSE	dwelling-place	HABITAUNCE
discourteous	DISCOURTEISE	dye	HEW
discover	DISCOURE, DISCURE	earlier	RATHER
disdain	SDAINE, SDAYN, SDEIGNE	earn	ERNE
	SDEIN	easily	EATH(E), EATHLY, ETHE
dishearten	DISPARAGE	easy	EATH(E), ETHE
dishonourable	DISLEAL	ebony	HEBON
disinherit	DISHERIT	echo back a loud noise	REBELLOW
disloyal	DISLEAL	efts	EWFTES
dismal	GASTFULL	elegant	DAINT(Y), DAYNT
dispense	DISPENCE, SHED	embrace	BRACE
dispersed	SPERST	embraced	HAULST
displeasure	DISPLEASANCE	embraid	EMBREAD
disposed	DISPOST, DITE	emerald	EMERAUDE
dispute	CONTROVERSE	emulate	AEMULE
dissemble	FEIGN	emulation	PARAGON
dissuade	DISCOUNSEL	encircle	STEMME
distance	MOUNTENA(U)NCE	encircled	EMBAYLD
distract	FORHAILE	enclose	EMBOSS
distracting	DIVERSE	encompass	BRACE
distress	DISMAY	encounter	COUNTER
disturb	STIRE, STYRE	encourage	ACCO(U)RAGE
ditty	DIT	encouraged	UPCHEARD

encumber	ACCLOY	exterminate	EXTIRP
endeavour	ENDEAVOURMENT	extolled	EXTOLD
endow	ENDEW	extort	OUTWREST, RACK
endue	ENDEW, INDEW	extraction	EXTREAT
enduring	DUREFUL	fabulous	
enflame	ENFIRE	—beast	ANTELOPE
enfold	IMPLY	—bird	WHISTLER
enlarge	ENLARGEN	—fish	SCOLOPENDRA
enquire	ENQUERE	faced	FAST
enrage	ENRANCKLE	fail	MIS
enrolled	ENTROLD, INTROLD	failure to value	MESPRISE, MESPRIZE
enslave	BETHRALL		MISPRIZE
ensue	ENSEW	faint	STANCK, SWELT
entangle	ENSNARL	fainting fit	SOWND, SWOUND
entanglement	ENTRAIL	falcon	TASSELL-GENT
entertain	ACCOURT	fall back	RECOYLE, RECU(I)LE
—guest	HOST	fallen unluckily	MISFALNE
entertainment	ENTERTAIN	false	
entrails	ENTRALLES	—appearance	MISSEEMING
entrance	INGATE	—religious belief	MISCREAUNCE
entrap	UNDERFONG	familiar friend	GOSSIB
entreat	INTREAT	familiarly	COMMONLY
entreating	ENTREATFULL	far	FAR-FORTH
entreaty	IMPLORE	fasten	EMBRACE
entrust	ARRET(T)	—with a spar	SPERRE
entwine	ENTRAIL	favour	GREE
enviable	ENVIOUS	fear	AFFRAY
enwrap	ENROL(L)	feign	FAIN(E), FAYNE
equality	EQUAL	fell	FELONOUS
equip	AGUISE, AGUIZE, DITE	female	
equipment	PURVEYANCE	—animal	SHIDDER
erase	RACE	—dolphin	DOLPHINET
error	MESPRIZE	—poet	POETRESSE
establish	STABLISH	festivity	JOYANCE
esteem	PRISE, STEEM, WAY	feud	FOOD
estranged	FRENNE	fewter	ENCHASE
everywhere	OVERALL	fiat	FIAUNT
evil device	MALENGINE	fickle	CHOICEFUL
exalted	HAUGHT, HAU(L)T	fierce	BREEM, BREME, STOUT
examine	APPOSE	figure	AUMAIL
example for imitation	SAMPLE	find	INVENT
excellently	GOODLY	fine	QUAINT
excess	OUTRAGE	first	PARAVA(U)NT
exchange	CHAFFER, SCORSE	—fruits	PRIMITIAS
excite	EMMOVE, ENMOVE	—year's revenue	PRIMITIAS
excuse	ESSOIN, ESSOYNE	fish-basket	HASK
exile	EXUL	fishing boat	DROVER
exit	OUTGATE	fit	CONCENT, DEWFULL, DUEFUL
expectation	TENDANCE		QUEME, CONCENT
expensive	CHARGEFUL	—for war	WARHABLE
experience	ENTERTAIN, EXPERT	fling headlong	RUINATE
—a pang	STOUND, STOWND	flitted	FLITT
explain	UPKNIT	flock of birds	FLUSH
expound	COMMENT, REED(E)	flow	FLEET, RAILE, RAYLE
extended	DISTENT	foam	FRY
extension in time	PROTENSE	foes	FOEN, FONE

foil	FOYLE
foin	FOYNE
fold	PLIGHT
food	PASTURE
foolhardiness	FOOLHARDISE
	FOOLHARDIZE
footing	TROAD(E), TRODE
for	
—a long time in the past	LONG SIN
—that	FORTHY
foray	FORRAY
force	
—away	WREST
—back	RECOYLE, RECU(I)LE
forced again	RENFORST
foreign	FRENNE, STRAUNGE
forester	FOSTER
foretokening	SOOTHE
forgery	COUNTERFEASAUNCE
form	
—anew	REALLIE
—into roll	ENROL(L)
forsaken	FORLORE
fortalice (fortress)	FORTILAGE
for the most part	MOSTWHAT
fortification	MUNIFIENCE
foster	NOUSELL, NOU(R)SLE
	NUZZLE
foul person	DREVILL
found	FOND
fountain-basin	LAVER
free	QUIGHT, QUYTE
freedom	RANDON
frigate	FRIGOT
frighten	AFEAR, AFFEAR(E), DARE
frightful	GRIESLY, GRISELY, GRYESLY
frisk	COLT
from being fordone	FROM FORDONNE
frosty	FRORY
frozen	FRORY
fulfil a term	EXPIRE
full	
—of	
air or fragrance	BREATHFUL
devices	DEVICEFUL
life	LIFULL, LYFULL
moans	GRONEFUL
—speed	RANDON
fulminate	FULMINE
funeral service	HERSE
furious	YOND
—onset	AFFRET
furnish with	
buildings	EDIFY
furnishing	FURNIMENT, PURVEYANCE
fury	DREAD

futility	VAINESSE
gaiety	JOYANCE
gain	EXCHEAT
—anew	REPRIZE
gained	WAN
gall	FELL
gape	GERNE
garb	VESTIMENT
garment	VESTIMENT
gate	YATE
gear	GEARE, GERE
Genoese coin	JANE
gentle	GENT
get	COMPARE
—back	RECURE
—out of	OUTWIN
—the better of	CONVINCE
ghastly	GREISLY, GRIESLY
	GRISELY, GRYESLY
gibbet	CROOK
gilded	GILDEN, GUILT, GYLDEN
—leather	CHECKLATON
gillyflower	GELLIFLOWRE
gilt	GELT, GUILT
girl	GERLE
give	
—excuses for	CAUSEN
—out as if on hire	OUTHYRE
—over	LIN, OVERGIVE
—up	FORGIVE, OVERGIVE
—vent to	DISCLOSE
—way	RELENT
given	YEVEN
giving attention	ATTENT
glad	GLADFUL
gladly	FAIN
glanced	YGLAUNST
glided	GLODE
glittering	GLITTERAND
gloom	DRE(A)RE
glory	GARLAND
go	GOE, YEAD, YEDE, YEED
—about or forth	STIRE, STYRE
—astray	MISWEND
—back	RECOURSE
—over in one's mind	RECORD
—up	AMOUNT
goat	GATE
gold	GOOLD
gondola	GONDELAY
gone	GOE, YGO(E)
good	
—and fair maid	BON(N)IBELL
—day	GOD DAY
—for the heart	HARTIE-HALE
—for-nothing	LORRELL, LOZEL

—friend	BELAMY	hard-pressed	STRAIT
—health or fortune	WELL	harden	ENDURE
—reception	BEL-ACCOYLE	harnessed in a team	TE(E)MED
goodness	GOODLIHEAD	harsh	RIGOROUS
	GOODLYHEAD	hastened	HIDE
goodwill	GREE	haughty	HAUGHT, HAU(L)T
gore	ENGORE		STOMACHOUS
got at	ARRAUGHT	have	
government	GOVERNALL	—need	MISTER
graced	GRASTE	—(plural)	HAN
graciously	GOODLY	—wrong opinion	MISWEEN
grant	BETEEM(E)	having	
granted beforehand	FOR(E)LENT	—many layers	MANY-FOLDED
grapple	CRAPPLE, GRAPLE	—power	VERTUOUS
grasp	ENGRASP, HEND	hazard	HAZARDIZE
grasping	GRIPLE	heal	G(U)ARIS, RECURE
gravel	GRAILE, GRAYLE	healthy	HARTIE-HALE
great knight	DOUCEPERE, DOUZEPER	heap up	COMPILE, UPHOORD
greedy	GRIPLE	heaped	HEPT
greeted	SALUED, SALVE'D	heard	HARD
grey	BLONCKET, GRIESIE, GRYSESY	hearse	HERSE
grief	TINE, TYNE, WAYMENT	heart(en)	HART(EN)
grieve	ENGRIEVE, WAYMENT	heartily	HARTELY
grievous	CAREFUL, DEAR(E), NOYOUS	heartless	HARTLESSE
grin	GERNE, GIRN, GREN	heat	BEATH
grinned	GRIND	heaved	HEFT(E)
griped	GRYPT	heavily awkward	UNWELDY
griping	GRIPLE	heed	RESPECT
gripped	GRYPT	heedful	HEEDY
grisly	GREISLY, GRIESLY	height	LOFT
ground tackle	GROUND-HOLD	held	HILD
growl	ROYNE	hell	TARTAR(E), TARTARIE, TARTARY
grudge	GRUTCH	herd	HEARD
guard	SAVEGARD	hest	HEAST(E)
guess	DEVISE, GESSE, GHESSE	hide	HEAL, HEEL, HELE
guild	GYELD	hie	HYE
guile	GUYLE	high	HAUGHTY, HYE
guise	GUYSE, PURPORT	hind	HYNDE
gullet	WEASAND-PIPE	hinder	EMPEACH
gush	RAILE, RAYLE	hindrance	IMPEACH
gypsy	GIPSEN	hither(ward)	HETHER(WARD)
hacking	HEW	having shoulders that	
haggling	CHAFFER	displace the sea	SEA-SHOULD'RING
hailed	SALUED, SALVE'D	hoar	HORE
hair	HEARE	hoard	UPHOORD
hairy	HEARIE	hold	
hale	HAYLE	—down	SUPPRESS
half	HALFEN(DEALE)	—together	COMPRISE
halloo	BLEW	hole	DELL, DELVE
hammer	MARTEL	hollow	DELVE
handle	STEAL(E), STEEL, STEIL	holly	HOLM
	STELE	home	HAEME
hang in clusters	SHAG	honeysuckle	CAPRIFOIL
happen		hood	CAPUCCIO
—ill	MISHAPPEN	hooped in	EMBAYLD
—to	BEHAPPEN	hot	WHOT

hover	HO(O)VE
however	HOWBE
hue	HEW
humble	AFFLICTED, DEMISS
humbleness	HUMBLESSE
hurt	NOY, SCATH
hush	WHIST
husk	PILL
hyacinth (stone)	HYACINE
idea	CONCEIT
ignoble	UNNOBLE
ignorant person	IGNARO
ill	
—arranged	MISDIGHT
—gotten	MISGOTTEN
—shaped	MISHAPT
—tempered	GIRNIE
—treat	DEMEAN
—will	MALTATENT
illumine	ENLUMINE
imagined character	PERSONAGE
imbrue	EMBREWE
imbue	EMBAY
imp	YMP
impair	EMPA(I)RE, EMPAYRE
	EMPERISH
impairment	EMPEACH
impeach	EMPEACH
imped	YMPT
impede	EMPEACH
implant	ENRACE
improper feeding	MISDIET
in	
—a row	AREW
—averse direction	FROWARD
—complete confusion	UPSIDEOWNE
—front	PARAVA(U)NT
—some degree	SOMEDELE
—sorry plight	MISDIGHT
—time	TIMELY
inadvertent	UNADVISED
inasmuch	IN SORT
inattention	MISREGARD
incisive	TRENCHAND
increase	ACCREW
incursion	RODE
indecorous	SEEM(E)LESS(E)
indeed	SOOTHLICH
Ind(ia)	YND
indicate	DESIGN
indue	INDEW
ineffectual	RESTY
infamy	DEFAME
infatuated	ASSOTT(ED)
inflamed	FLAMED
inform	ENFORM, PARTAKE

infusion	INFUSE
inglorious	IRRENOWNED
ingots	INGO(W)ES
ingress	INGATE
inhabitant	INHOLDER
inhabiting woods	WOODY
inhospitable	HOSTLESSE
injure	SCATH
injured by cold	WINTER-BEATEN
injurious	NOYOUS
injury	BLAME, EMPEACH, SCATH
	TINE, TYNE, TORT
—to oneself	SELFE-DESPIGHT
inner	ENTIRE
innermost thoughts	PRIVITY
innocent	SEELY
inoperative	RESTY
inquire	ENQUERE, INQUERE
Irish chieftaincy	CHEVERYE
inscribe	ENDOSS
instruction	DOCUMENT
instrument of torture	GIN
insult	REPRIEFE
integument	PILL
intend	HIGHT
intention	ATTENDEMENT
intercourse	ENTERDEALE
interest in property	STATE
interlace	ENTRAIL
interpretation	READ
interruption	CESURE
intimately	COMMONLY
intrigue against	UNDERMINDE
inward	ENTIRE
irresistible	INSUPPORTABLE
irrigating canal	ZANJA
is not	NIS, NYS
ivy-bush	TODDE
jasper	JASP
jaw	CHAW
jealous	GEALOUS
jealousy	GEALOUSY, GELOSY
jeer	GEARE
jellied	GELLY
journey	WAY, WENT
joust	GIOUST
joyousness	JOYANCE, JOVYSAUNCE
	JOUISANCE, JOUYSAUNCE
judge wrongly	MISWEEN
judged wrongly	MISDEMPT
junket	JUNCATE
jurisdiction	BAIL
keen	BREEM, BREME
keep	
—head to wind	TRIE
—in subjection	UNDERKEEP

—watch	WAITE	letter of introduction	BENEFICIAL
keeping time	TIMELY	levy	LEAVE
keyhole	CLINK	liar	FALSER
kick	RECOYLE, RECU(ILE)	lie	LIG(GE), LIGGEN
killed	KILD, KILT	—down	SEAT
kind	KYND(E)	—in folds	W(H)IMPLE
—look	BELGARD	—out of the way	BA(U)LK
kindled	TIND, TYND(E)	—to	TRIE
kindly	GOODLY	lift up	EXTOL
kine	KYNE	light	LITE
kingdom	REAME	like	LICH
kinship	SYBBE	—a Centaur	HALF-HORSY
kite	KIGHT	—lightning	ENFOULDERED
knew	KOND	likeness	LIKELINESS
knob	SNUBBE	limb	SPALLE
know	CON(NE), KON, WEET(E)	limiter	LYMETER
	WEETEN, WOT	lineage	LIGNAGE, LYNAGE
knowest	KYDST	linen	LYNE
ladder	STIE, STYE	linger	HO(O)VE
laid before	FORELAY	list(en)	LEST
lair	LARE	listless	LUSTLESS
lame	ACCLOY	lithe	LYTHE
lament	MEAN(E), MEIN, MENE	little bush	BUSKET
	WAYMENT	livelihood	LIVELO(O)D
lamentation	WAYMENT	living thing	QUICK
lance	LAUNCE	load	TODDE
lancing	LA(U)NCH	loam	LOME
language	LEDDEN	loathsome	LOTH(E)FULL
lasting	DUREFUL	lodge	BOWER, HOST
latch	CLINK	lodging	BRAME, FERM, HOSTRY
launch forth	OUTLAUNCE	loiter	HO(O)VE
lawless	RULESSE	loll (the tongue)	LILL
lay		long	LENG, SIDELONG
—about one	THROW	—for	EARN
—in a cradle	ENCRADLE	longer	LENGER
—on	POUND	longest	LENGEST
lazy	LAESIE	look over	SURVEW
leak	LEKE	loop	LOUP
lean	LEANY	loose	LOAST, LOSE(N)
leaped/leapt	LEPPED, LOPE	—(hair)	UNDIGHT
learn	CON(NE), KON, LEAR(E)	—robe	CAMIS, CAMUS
	LEIR, LERE	—woman	FRANION
lease	FARM	lose	LEESE
leave off	QUIGHT, QUYTE	lost	LOAST, LOS'TE
lecher	LEACHOUR	lout	LOORD
leech	LEACH	lovingly	LOVELY
left	LORE, LORN, OTHER	lower	AVALE, AVAIL(E), EMBACE
leg armour	GAIMBEUX	lowered	EMBASTE
leisure	LEASURE	lumpish	LOMPISH
lest	LEAST	mad	YOND
—by chance	ENAUNTER	made footsore	SURBATED, SURBET
let		madman	GELT
—forth as from entrails	DISENTRAIL	mail	MALE
	DISENTRAYLE	make	
—go	QUIGHT, QUYTE	—a show of	COUNTENANCE
—out for pay	WAGE	—amends	DISPENSE

—busy	EMBUSY	misshapen	DISMAYD, MISSHAPT
—divine	DIVINE	misused	MISUST
—feeble	FEEBLE	moan	MEAN(E), MEIN, MENE
—fierce	EFFIERCE, ENFELON, ENFIERCE	moderate	RELENT
—footsore	SURBATE	moiety	MOYITY
—fortunate	FORTUNIZE	moil	MOYLE
—happy	FORTUNIZE	momentum	POISE
—known	READ	monster	ROSMARINE, SEASATYRE
by display	VAUNT		ZIFFIUS
—little or less	MINISH	month	MONETH
—pregnant	ENWOMB	mostly	MOSTWHAT
—showy	EMBRAVE	mount	STIE, STYE
—thick	ENGROSS	movable front of	
—uneasy	DISEASE	helmet	VENTAILE
mannered	THEWED		VENTAYLE
many-coloured	DISCOLOURED	move	EMMOVE, ENMOVE, MIEVE
marked	DISTINCT		QUICH, QUINCHE
—with spots	EYE-SPOTTED	—around or to	
marred	MARD	activity	STIRE, STYRE
massive	TIMBERED	much	MOCHELL, MUCHELL
master	MAISTERDOME, MAYSTER	—worn	FORWORN
mastering	MAISTRING	muscle	BOWR
match	AMATE, PRISE	must	MOT(E)
mate	PARAGON	muster	HOSTING
may	MOT(E)	musty	FROUGHY, FROWIE, FROWY
—(past tense)	MOUGHT	mutter	ROYNE
meadow-sweet	MEDAEWORT	mutual dealings	ENTERDEALE
mean person	HYLDING	name	BEHIGHT, BEHOTE, READ
meaning	INTENDIMENT	named	HOT(E), NEMPT
means of living	LIVELO(O)D	narrow	STRAIT
meantime	MEAN	narwhal	MONOCEROS
meet	ENTERTAIN	nathless	NETHELESS
meeting place of guild	GYELD	near	FOREBY
melted	YMOLT	nearer	NARRE
mention	HIGHT	neatly	FEATEOUSLY
mercenary soldier	WAR-MONGER	needy	STRAIT
merciful	MERCIABLE	negotiations	ENTERDEALE
mere	MEARE	never the more	NATHEMO(RE)
mered	MEAR'D	new thing	NEWELL
merriment	JOLLIMENT	newly weaned child	
merrymaking	MERIAMKE	or animal	WEANEL
meted	MOTT	nimble	WIMBLE
mews	MEAWES	nobility	NOBILESSE
middle(most)	IDDEST	noble	DOUCEPERE, DOUZEPER
military expedition	HOSTING		GENT
misbecome	MISSEEM	—youth	INFANT
misbegotten	MISGOTTEN	noise	NOYES
miscarry	MISWEND	not	
misconception	MISCONCEIT	—akin	FRENNE
misfortune	MISFARE	—braced	UNBRASTE
mishap	DISAVENTURE, DRE(A)RE	—challenged	UNDEFIDE
misled	MISTRAYNED	—civilised	UNCIVIL
mislike	MISLEEKE	—clear in the head	ILL-HEDDED
mismade	DISMAYD	—defied	UNDEFIDE
mismanagement	MISGOVERNAUNCE	—dressed	UNDIGHT
misshaped	MISSHAPT	—favouring	FAVOURLESS

—known	UNWIST
—lamented	UNPLAINED
—marred	UNMARD
—matching	MATCHLESS
—prayed for	UNBID
—provided with	UNPURVAIDE
—the more	NATHEMO(RE)
—to be appeased	IMPACABLE
notwithstanding	HOWBE
object gazed at	GAZEMENT
oblique	OBLIQUID
occasion	ENCHEASON
occupy	EMBUSY
—oneself with	ENTREAT
ochre	OAKER
of	
—a tree	TREEN
—straw	STRAWEN
—the same	
province	COMPROVINCIAL
time of day	TIMELY
offer up	APPEAL
omen	SOOTHSAY
one who proclaims	BLAZER
only	ONELY
onset	SALIAUNCE
open place	OVERTURE
orbit	SPHERE
ordain	BEHIGHT, BEHOTE
ore	OWRE
originate	REAR
ornament	GARLAND
ostrich	OSTRIGE
out of condition	RAW
outcry	STEVEN
outlet	OUTGATE
outward appearance	FORESIDE, PURPOST
overcast	OVERKEST
overcome	CONVINCE, UNDERFONG
—by wrestling	OVERWRESTLE
overflow	REDOUND
overlay	SPILL
overspread	OVERDIGHT
overtake	OVERHENT
overtaken	OVERCAUGHT, OVERHENT
overtook	FORHENT
overworked	FORSWONCK
ownerless property	WAIFT, WEFT
ox	STEARE
painful experience	FIT
pains	TINE, TYNE
paint	DEPAINT
painted	IMPICTURED
paltry fellow	SQUIB
panacea	PANACHAEA
pang	STOUND, STOWND, THROW(E)

pansy	PA(U)NCE, PAWNCE
parleying	EMPARLAUNCE
paroxysm	THROW(E)
partake	PERTAKE
pass	
—away	VADE
—like a fever	SWELT
passage	FARE
passion	BRAME
past	FOREBY
pasture	LARE
path	STIE, STYE, TROAD(E)
	TRODE, WENT
pattern	SLEIGHT
pay	QUIGHT, QUYTE, SOLD
—for	PRYSE
—the price of	PRICE
payment	HAN(D)SEL
peacock	PAVONE
peal	PELE
pease	POUSSE
pebble	PUMY(STONE)
peep	TOOT
peer	PEARE
—about	TOOT
peised	PAYSD
pen	PENNE
penal retribution	VENGEMENT
penalty	HAN(D)SEL
penetrate	SEIZE
penny	PENI(E)
penthia	ASTROPHEL, STARLIGHT
perceive	UNDERTAKE
perch (of land)	LUG
performance	CHEVISANCE
perilous	PERLOUS
perish	QUELL, TINE, TYNE
perplex	DISTROUBLE
personality of beast	BEASTLY-HEAD
pestilence	MURRIN
phantom	PHANTOSME
piece of tapestry	TAPET
pierce	EMP(I)ERCE, LA(U)NCH
	PEARCE, PERCE, PERSE
pierced	GRYPT, PEARST, PIERST
piercing	THRILLANT
pinion	PENNE
pinioned	PINNOED
pioneer work	PYONINGS
pitch	PRICK
pitched	PIGHT
pitied	MERCIFIDE
pity	REMORSE
placed	PLAST(E)
—above	OVERPLAST
plant (unknown)	TETRA

plash	PLESH
playing games of hazard	HAZARDRY
pleaded	PLED
please	QUEME
pleasure	LUST
pledge	BANK
plight	TAKING
pluck	RACE
plunder	BEROB, EXCHEAT, HERRIMENT
	HERRYMENT, PREY
plundering	SPOYLEFULL
plunge	EMPLONGE, PLONG(E)
plunged	PLONGD
poetess	POETRESSE
poignant	POYNANT
point	PRICK
—out	PRESAGE
poise	PEASE, PEAZE, PEISE
	PEIZE, PEYSE
poised	PAYSD
poisonous plant	SAMNITIS
policy	POLLICIE, POLLICY
politeness	COMPLEMENT
pollute	BLEND
pompous	STATE
pool	PLESH
poplar	ASPINE
porpoise	PORCPISCE
portable breviary	PORTAS, PORTESS(E)
	PORT(E)OUS, PORTHORS
	PORTHOS, PORTHOUSE
portion	WHAT
portrait(ure)	RETRAITT, RETRATE
portrayed	POURTRAHED
possessing virtue	VERTUOUS
postpone	PROLONG
pot	CREWE
potsherd	POTSHARE
pour	POWRE
praise	HERRY, HERY(E)
prance	PRAUNCE
precarious	T(R)ICKLE
precedent	PRESIDENT
precepts	SCHOOLERY
precisely	BY THE SQUIRE
predicted	FORESHEWED
pre-eminently	PARAVA(U)NT
preferred	PREFARD
preparation in advance	PURVEYANCE
press	PEASE, PEAZE, PEISE
	PEIZE, PEYSE
	PREACE
—down	SUPPRESS
pressure	STRAINT
pretended	COUNTERFECT
prey	PRAY, RAVEN, RAVIN(E), SOYLE

price	PRISE
prick	ACCLOY
private counsels	PRIVITY
prize	PRISE
proceed	YEAD, YEDE, YEED
proceeded	FOND, YOD(E)
process of combat	DISCOURSE
profit	VANTAGE
prognostication	PREJUDIZE
promise	BEHIGHT, BEHOTE
promptly	B(Y)LIVE
proof	ASSAY
proper	DEWFULL, DUEFUL
proportion	REASON
prosper	THEE
protect	SAVEGARD
protection	PATRONAGE
prove	TRIE
provide	COMPARE
province	REAME
pry	TOOT
puddle	PLESH
pull apart	DISTRAIN
punching	POUNCING
punish	YSHEND
purified	TRYE
purpose	DEVISE, PROPOUND
purse	CRUMENAL
purslane	PERSELINE
pursue	POURSEW, POURSUE, PURSEW
pursuit	POURSUIT(T), SUIT
put	
—at a distance	DISLOIGN
—down	UNDERLAY
—far apart	DISLOIGN
—forth as shoot or fruit	SPIRE
—into	
action	SERVE
operation	ENURE
—on	INVEST
—out of countenance	DEFACE
—to shame	YSHEND
—together	COMPILE
putting to death	DEAD-DOING
quagmire	WAGMOIRE
quaint	QUEINT
quaked	QUOOKE
quality	ASSAY
quarrel	QUAR'LE
quarrelsome	DEBATEFULL
quarter	QUART
quash	REPEAL
quenched	QUEINT
question	APPOSE
quickly	B(Y)LIVE
quickness	NIMBLESSE

quince	QUEENE-APPLE
quit	QUIGHT, QUYTE
quite	QUIGHT
race	RAUNCH
raced	RAST
raid	BODRAG, BORDRAGING
rail	SPARRE
raise	LEAVE
—in front	FORELIFT
rancid	FROUGHY, FROWIE, FROWY
rang	RONG
range about	DISPACE
rapt	YRAPT
rapture	ENRAGEMENT
rare	GEASON, SE(E)LD
rashness	HAZARDRY
ravish	SUPPRESS
ray	RAYON
raze	RACE
reach	SEISE
read	RAD, RED(D)
ready	PREST
realm	REAME
reason	ENCHEASON
rebound	RECOYLE, RECU(I)LE
rebuild	RE-EDIFY
recapture	REPRIZE
receive	ENTERTAKE
reck	REKE, WREAK(E)
recognised character	PERSONAGE
recoil	REBUT, RECOYLE,
	RECU(I)LE
reconcile	UPKNIT
reconciled	AFFRENDED
recover	RECOURE, RECOWER, RECURE
rede	REED(E)
reduce	DEDUCT, MINISH
refreshment of sleep	REPAST
refund	REDISBURSE
refuse	NILL
—to agree	DISACCORD
refused	NILLED, NOULD(E)
regard as holy	HERRY, HERY(E)
region	QUART, REAME
regret	FORTHINK, RELENT
rehearsal	HERSALL
reign	RAIN(E)
—to the end of	OUTRAIGNE
reinforced	RENFORST
reinstate	RESEIZE
rejoined	RELIDE
relate	REED(E)
relax	RELENT
relaxed	UNBRASTE
release	
—from obligation	QUIGHT, QUYTE

—on payment by	
instalment	STAL'D
relied	RELIDE
remedy	RECURE
remembrance	SOVENA(U)NCE
remit	QUIGHT, QUYTE
remove	DISLOIGN
—wrongly	MISTAKE
removed	REMOUD
—from hearse	UNHERST
remuneration	SOLD
renewed efforts	RENFORST
renounce	FOR(E)SAY
rent (cuddy)	CUDDEEHIH
repay	QUIGHT, QUYTE
repeat from memory	RECORD
repent	RELENT
repentance	REPENT
reprehend	SPOT
represented beforehand	FORESHEWED
repress	REPEAL
reprieve	REPRIVE, REPRYVE
reproach	REPRIEFE, YSHEND
reproof	REPRIEFE
reprove	REPRIEVE
require	REQUERE
requite	QUIGHT, QUYTE, REQUIGHT
requited	REQUIGHT, REQUIT
rescue	RESKEW
resentful	STOMACHOUS
resigned beforehand	FOR(E)LENT
resistless	IMPORTUNE
response	RESPONDENCE
rest one's weight	UPLEAN
restitution	RESTORE
restore to its position	REPAIR
restrain	ABSTAIN, BEHOLD
rethink	FORTHINK
retrace	REMEASURE
retreat	RECOYLE, RECU(I)LE
	RETRATE
return	RECOURSE, REVERSE
reveal	DESCRY, PRESAGE
reversed	RENVERST
revert	RECOYLE, RECU(I)LE
—in the mind	RECOURSE
revive	RELIVE
ribald	RIBAUD, RYBAULD
ribaldry	RYBAUDRYE
rid	QUIGHT, QUYTE
rife	RYFE
rightly	ARIGHTS
rigorous	STRAIT
rind	RINE
rise	HOVE, STIE, STYE
—one above another	REDOUND

riven	RIFTE
—fragment	RIFT
river	LEE
road	RODE
roar	ROYNE
rod (of land)	LUG
rode	RAD
roll about wallowing	ENWALLOW
root out	OUTWEED
rounded	COMPAST
rouse	ABRAY, AMO(O)VE
	STIRE, STYRE
rove over	ENRAUNGE
ruby	RUBIN(E)
ruff	RUFFIN
ruffle	RUFF
rule	SQUIER, SQUIRE
ruleless	RULESSE
run	RENNE, RONNE
running	RONNING
runt	RONT(E)
rush	RANDON
rustic	HOBBINOLL
sacramental	HOUSLING
saddle	SEL(LE)
safeguard	SAUFGARD
sage	SAULGE
salience	SALIAUNCE
saluted	SALEWD, SALUED
sate	ACCLOY
satisfy	DEFRAY
savage	SALVAGE
save	SAFE
say	SAINE, SAYNE
—in answer	UNDERSAYE
sayest	SAIST
saying	READ
scale	SCAND
scaly sea-monster	PHOCA
scanned	SCAND
scarified	SCARIFIDE
scent	SENT
scheme	GIN
scimitar	CEMITARE
scion	SIENT
scorch	SCATH
scorn	MESPRISE, MESPRIZE, MISPRIZE
screech-owl	SHRIECH-OWL, STRICH
screen	SCRIENE, SKREENE
scuffle	CUFFLE
scutcheon	SCUCHI(O)N
scythe	SITHE
sea	
—horse	HIPPODAME
—monster	ROSMARINE
	SEA-SATYRE, ZIFFIUS

secret proceeding	COVERTURE
seemliness	SEEMLYHED
seize	HEND, SEASE, SEAZE, CEAZE
seized	ARRAUGHT, FORHENT
sell	CHAFFER
send downstream	POUR
sense	SENT
sentinel	CENTONEL(L)
set	PIGHT
—about by	BESTAD(D)E
—in	
battle array	DARRAI(G)N(E)
	DARRAYN, DERRAIGN
motion	STIRE, STYRE
—on fire	ENFIRE
—spear in rest	ENCHASE
—up	ADDRESSED, ADDREST
	FEUTRE, FEWTER
settle downward	PEASE, PEAZE
	PEISE, PEIZE, PEYSE
shade	OVERCAST
shadow forth	SHADE
shaft	STEAL(E), STEEL
	STEIL, STELE
shaken off	OFF-SHAKT
shallow pool	PLESH
shame	REPRIEFE, YSHEND
shank	STEAL(E), STEEL
	STEIL, STELE
shaped	SHOPE
share	CO-PORTION
—out	EMPART
shared	SHARD
sheer	SHERE
shining	NEAT
—obscurely	GLOOMING
shiver in pieces	DISSHIVER
shock	STOUND, STOWND
shoot like a pang	STOUND, STOWND
shoulder	SPALLE
shout	CLAME
showed beforehand	FORESHEWED
shower	POUND
showing	
—much white (eye)	WHALLY
—through the skin	RAW
shriek	SCRIKE, SHREEK
	SHRIECH, SHRIGHT, SHRIKE
shrine	SCRINE, SCRYNE
shrink from	RECOYLE, RECU(I)LE
shrive	SHRIEVE
shy	LOFT
sic	SIKE
silence	WHIST
similar	LIKELY
simple	SEELY

simplicity	SIMPLESSE	spur	SPURNE
since	SENS, SITHENS, SITHENCE	spy	SPYAL
sing in measure	MEASURE	squeeze	SCRUZE
singe	SWINGE	stagger back	RECOYLE, RECU(I)LE
sister	SYBBE	stain	STAYNE
sit down	SEAT	stair	STAYRE
skill	FEAT	stand	STANDEN, STOND
skilled	PRACTIC	standing on end	UPSTART
skirmish	SCARMOGE	start	
skirt worn by knight	BASE	—back	RECOYLE, RECU(I)LE
skull	PANNIKELL	—up	ASTART
sky-blue	CAERULE	startled bird	FLUSH
slacken (pace)	RELENT	starvation	PINE, PYNE
slant	RASH	starve	STERVE
sleep	SWOON	stayed	STAID
sleepiness	DRWOSIHE(A)D	stead	STED(D), STED(D)E
slight	MESPRISE, MESPRIZE	steadfast	SAD
	MISPRIZE	steam	STEEM
slow down	RELENT	steep	EMBAY
small boat	COTT	steer	STEAR(E), STIRE
smeared in blood	BEGORED	steerage	STEARAGE
smell	SENT	steered	STEARD
smite	SMIGHT	stir	STIRE, STYRE, QUICH
snag	SNUBBE		QUINCHE
snarl	GIRN, SNAR	stone	PUMY(STONE)
snatch	RACE	—or earthenware vessel	STEANE
snub	SNIB	stop for	STAY
solve	LOOSE	stoppage	BLIN
something	WHAT	stoutly	STATE
—taught	SCHOOLERY	straight	STREIGHT
somewhat	SOMEDELE	strain	STRENE
song	CANTION, CHARM	strait	STREIGHT
soot	SOUT	strand	STROND
soothe	ACCOY	strange	FRENNE, SELCOUTH
sorrow	REPENT		STRAUNGE
sorrowful	CAREFUL	stray far	FORWANDER
sorry scamp	LORRELL, LOZEL	strayed	
souse	SOUCE, SOWS(S)E	—animal	WAIFT, WEFT
soused	SOUCT	—over	MISWANDRED
space of time	STEAD	strengthening band	BEND
spared	SPARD	stretch forth	INTEND
sparing in giving	STRAIT	—or in front	PRETEND
sparingly	NIGHLY	strict	STRAIT
spasm	THROW(E)	strife	CONTECK
spawn	BLOT	strifeful	STRYFULL
speak to	BEHIGHT, BEHOTE	strike	AFFRAY
speech	LEDDEN	stripe	STAKE, STRAIK
spire	SPYRE	strive	ENFORCE
spirited	STOMACHOUS	stroke	STOUND, STOWND
spiritless	HYLDING	—in return	COUNTERSTROKE
spite	SPIGHT	struck	
spot (of iron-mould)	MOLD	—by thunderbolt	YTHUNDERED
spray of water	WATER-SPRINKLE	—with downward	
spread	SPRAD	blow	OVERSTROOKE
—out below	SUBJECT	stub	SNUBBE
sprite	SPRIGHT	stun	STOUN, STOUND

stunned	STOUND
—condition	STOUND
stupid	DOTED
stupidity	BRUTENESS
subdue	ADAW, SUBDEW
subject	CAITIVE
—to pangs	THROW(E)
submerge	EMPLONGE
subside	QUELL
successively	BY-AND-BY
such	SICH, SIKE
suddenly	UNWARELY
sue	SEW
suffer pangs	THROW(E)
suing	SEWING
suit	QUEME
sullen	SOLEIN
sum up	UPKNIT
summon	CONVENT
support	LIVELO(O)D
suppose	DEVISE
surely	SICCAR, SICKER, YKER
surge	REDOUND
surly	SYRLYE
surpass	UNDERLAY
surround with border	EMPALE
survey	SURVEW
surview	SERUEWE, SERVEWE
suspected	MISDEMPT
swaddling-band	SWEATH-BAND
sweated	SWAT
sweating-sickness	STOOPE-GALLAUNT
sweetly	SOOT(E)
sword	BRONDYRON, SWEARD
swordfish	MONOCEROS
tabor player	TABRERE
take	
—away	REAR
—in	ENDEW, INDEW
—off	UNDIGHT
taken	TANE
tale	SCORE
talon	TALA(U)NT
tambourine	TAMBURIN
tame	AMENAGE
tar	TARRE
teamed	TE(E)MED
tear	
—away	RACE
—off	RACE
teen	TINE, TYNE
temper	DELAY
tender	FRAIL
terrace	TERRAS
terrify	AGRISE, AGRIZE, AGRYZE
territory	RIGHT

that which humbles	
gallants	STOOPE-GALLAUNT
thatch	THETCH
theft	STEALTH
then	THO
therefore	FORTHY
thicket	GRE(A)VE
thing aimed at	LEVEL
thirst	THRIST, THRUST
those	THO
thou art	THOUS
thought wrongly	MISDEMPT
thoughtful	CONCEITFUL
thread	RID
thrive	THEE
throat	WEASAND-PIPE
throe	THROW(E)
throw off	DISCUSS
thrust	AVENTURE
—in the bowels	EMBOWEL
thunder	FOULDER
ticklish	T(R)ICKLE
tied	TIDE, TIGHT, TYDE
tier of guns	TIRE
time	SITH(E), SYTHE
	STOUND, STOWND
—of trouble	STOUND, STOWND
tinged	TINCT
tingle	TICKLE
tint	HEW
tired animal	TYRELING JADE
titmouse	TITMOSE
to	
—be at discord	DISACCORD
—burn with anger	EMBOIL
—carve	CARVEN
—catch	CATCHEN, KETCH
—pierce	PERCEN
—the smallest detail	TO POINT
—toss	TOSSEN
together	SAM, YSAME
told	TELD
tomb	FUNERAL
took	WAN
top of head	NOULE
torch	TEAD(E)
torn	ENRIVEN
—to pieces	TO-RENT
tossed	YTOST
total number	SCORE
trace	TRACT
track	CHALLENGE, TRACT, TRADE
	TROAD(E), TRODE
—of blood	PERSUE
trail	TRADE, TRAYNE
train	TIRE

traitor	TREACHETOUR
transferred	TRANSFARD
transform	DISCLOSE
transmute	TRANSMEW, TRANSMOVE
traverse	WEAR
treading	TRADE
treat	DEMEAN
—insultingly	INDIGNIFY
treatment	DEMAINE, DEMAYNE
	DEMEANE
tree used for carving	CARVER
tree-trunk	STUD
trenching	PYONINGS
trick	COUNTERCAST
	COUNTERPOINT
tried	FOND, TRIDE
trod	TROAD(E), TRODE
Trojan	TROYAN
trouble greatly	DISTROUBLE
troublesome	BRICKLE
truce	TREAGUE
truly	SOOTHLICH
truncated	TRUNKED
try expedients	THROW ABOUT
turban	TURRIBANT
turn	
—aside	DIVERSE, REVERSE
—back	RETURN
—out	TRIE
twain	TWAY
twist	BOUGHT
twisting	ENTRAIL
twit	TWIGHT
ugly-faced	ILL-FASTE
umpire	DAYES-MAN
unaccustomed	UNWONT
unbecoming	MISSEEMING
—a knight	KNIGHTLESS
uncommon	SE(E)LD
uncontrolled state	RANDON
uncounted	UNRED
uncover	UNHEAL, UNHELE
uncurdled	UNCRUDDED
undergrowth	SPRING
underlying	SUBJECT
understand	CONTRIVE
understanding	INTENDIMENT
undertake	UNDERFONG
undertaken	UNDERTANE
undo	UNDIGHT
undoing	DEFEATURE
undress	DISATTIRE
undue divergence from mean	OUTRAGE
unequal match	DISPARAGE
unexpectedly	UNWARELY
unfledged	EYAS

unformed	INFORMED
unfriendly	FRENNE
ungovernable	IMPOTENT
unguarded state	RANDON
unidentified plant	ASTROFELL
	ASTROPHEL
unjustly held	WRONGFUL
unknowing	UNWIST
unlaced	UNLAST(E)
unlikly	UNLIKE
unmanageable	UNWELDY, WEELDLESSE
unobserved	UNSPIDE
unpierceable	IMPERCEABLE
unprepared	UNPURVAIDE
unprovided	UNPURVAIDE
unread	UNRED
unruliness	UNRULIMENT
unruly	RULESSE
unseemly	SEEM(E)LESS(E)
unshed	UNPARTED
unstable	UNSTAYED
unsweet	UNSOOTE
unthriftiness	UNTHRIFTYHE(A)D
untired	ENTIRE
untold	UNRED
unusual	UNACQUAINTED
unweave	UNREAVE
upbraid(ing)	UPBRAY
upheld	UPHILD
upper region	LOFT
upriseth	UPRYST
upset	RENVERST
upside down	UPSIDEOWNE
urge earnestly	PROCURE
urgent	IMPORTUNE
utter in measure	MEASURE
utterly	RANK
vagrant	SCATTERLING
valuation	PRIZE
vanity	VAINESSE
variegate	AUMAIL
variegated	DISTINCT
veil	VEALE, VELE
velvet	VELLET
vengeance	VENGEMENT
venturous	VENTROUS
verdict	VERDIT
vervain	VERVEN
vestment	VESTIMENT
vex	NOY
vexatious	NOYOUS
view	ADVEW
vile	VILD(E)
villeinage	VELLENAGE
violent	RIGOROUS
violently	RANK

visor	UMBREL, UMBR(I)ERE, UMBRIL	withdraw	REVOKE
vitiate	BLEND	wither	SCATH
vulgar	BLATTANT	without	
wafted	WEFT	—knowing	UNWARE
waif	WAIFT, WEFT(E)	—luxury	BARE
waist-belt	TAWDRY-LACE	—possibility of escape	UNREDREST
wait	WAITE	—redress	UNREDREST
waived	WEFT(E)	—rules	RULESSE
walk about	SPACE	woe	WAE
wall-eyed	WHALLY	won	WAN, WOON
walrus	ROSMARINE	wont	FAIN
wane	WELKE	woo	WOW
want	PINE, PYNE	worn out	TO-WORNE
wariness	WARIMENT	worse	WAR(RE)
warlike	BATALIOUS	worthless	
warn	AWARN	—beast	HYLDING
was		—fellow	JAVEL
—accustomed	DID WON	—scamp	LORRELL, LOZEL
—called	HOT(E)	worthy	CONDIGN
waste		wot not	NOTE
—away	FORPINE	would not	NOULDE
—utterly	FORWASTE	wound	ENTRENCH, INTRENCH
watch	AWAIT	wrap	EMBOSS
watchful	AVIZEFULL	wreaked	(Y)WROKE, YWRAKE
wax faint	APPAL	wreathe	WRETHE
waxed	WOX(EN)	wretch	MISER
way	TRACE	wrinkled	WRIZLED
—in	INGATE	wrong	TORT
weak	BRiCKLE	—doing	MISFARING
weaken	DEDUCT, DELAY	wrongful challenge	MISCHALLENGE
—gradually	UNDERMINDE	yearn	EARN, ERNE
weapon	SPARKE	yet	HOWBE
weary out	FORWEARY	yew	EUGH
weave	WIND	yewen	EUGHEN, EWGHEN
weep	GREET	young	YOUTHLY
weigh	WAY	—female sheep	SHIDDER
weight of		—gentleman	YOUNKER
—blows	LOAD	—knight	YOUNKER
—wool	TODDE	—male sheep	HIDDER
welfare	HAYLE	youth	SPRING, YOUNGTH
well-knit	PIGHT	youthful	YOUNGTHLY, YOUTHLY
went	YOD(E)	**spice**	
while	THROW	allspice	PIMENTO
whole(some)	HOLE(SOME)	amaracus	MARJORAM
wick	WEEKE	aniseed-flavoured	DILL
wicker	SALE	Artemisia	TARRAGON
wide as a basin	BASEN-WIDE	black berries	JUNIPER, PEPPER
wield	SOWND	cardamon	AMOMUM
wifehood	WIVEHOOD	Carum	CARAWAY
will	WULL	cayenne pepper	PIM(I)ENTO
—not	NILL	chilli	
windpipe	WEASAND-PIPE	—dried	ANCHO, CHERRY-TYPE
wit	WEET(E), WEETEN, WOT		CHIPOTLE, RAT-DROPPINGS
with			SANNAM
—clothing unfastened	UNBRASTE	—green	ANAHEIM, LION
—tension relaxed (drum)	UNBRASTE		JALAPENO, SHISHI-TO

—large	ANAHEIM, CAYENNE	zingiber	GINGER
	PEPPERONCINI	**spirit**	MONAD
—red	WESTLANDSE LANGE	including: apparition	
coarse cinnamon	CASSIA	demon	
condiment	MUSTARD, PEPPER, SALT	ghost	
	VINEGAR	spectre	
curcuma	TURMERIC	African	ZOMBI(E)
curry		appearance of ghost	APPARITION
—mixture	GARAM MASALA		MATERIALIZATION
—spices	CORIANDER, CUMIN		VISITATION
	TURMERIC	apparition	EIDOLON, FETCH, PHANTASM
decorative	POPPY SEED		WRAITH
from		Arab	AFREET, AFRIT
—Africa	FRESNO CHILLI, MALAGUETTA	(*see also* Moslem *below*)	
—capsicum	CAYENNE PEPPER	between man and god	D(A)EMON
	CHILE, CHIL(L)I	bog(e)y	BOGLE, GOBLIN
	PAPRIKA, PIM(I)ENTO	brownie	HOB
—China	CHERRY-TYPE CHILLI	Buddhist	
—climbing orchid	VANILLA	—fertility	YAKSHA, YAKSHI
—crocus	SAFFRON	—tree	YAKSHA, YAKSHI
—East Indies	CASSUMUNAR, NUTMEG	Caribbean	DUPPY
—Europe	CORIANDER	causing mechanical trouble	GREMLIN
—Holland	WESTLANDSE LANGE	devil	DEMON, INCUBUS
—Hungary	PAPRIKA		SCRAT(CH)
—India	SANNAM CHILLI	—Scottish	(*see* **Scottish**)
—Indonesia	GALANGAL(L), GALENGALE	disembodied soul	SHADE, SPIRIT
	GALINAGLE	dog-like goblin	BARGAIST, BARG(H)EST
—Japan	LION CHILLI	domestic goblin	BROWNIE
	SHISHI-TO CHILLI	double	ALTER EGO, DOPPELGANGER
—Mediterranean	CAPER, CUM(M)IN		FETCH
—Mexico	VANILLA	Eastern demon	GH(O)UL
—Moluccas	CLOVE, CORIANDER	emanation	ECTOPLASM
—Sri Lanka	CINNAMON	evil spirit	DEMON, INCUBUS
—Thailand	BIRD('S EYE) CHILLI	fairy	HOB
—West Indies	ALLSPICE	—Irish	LEPRECHAUN
	JAMAICAN PEPPER, PIMENTO	—malignant	ELF
	SCOTCH BONNET CHILLI	female attacking	
ginger	AMOMUM, CARDAMON	sleeping men	SUCCUBA, SUCCUBUS
	CASSUMUNAR, TURMERIC	frightful apparition	(HOB)
	ZINGIBER	German	
Grains of Paradise	AMOMUM	—domestic brownie	KOBOLD
	MALAGUETTA	—king of the elves	ERL-KING
Hebrew	STACTE, STORAX	—mountain	BERGGEIST
Jamaican pepper	PIM(I)ENTO	imp	RUBESZAHL
liquorice	ANISEED	—spirit of the mines	KOBOLD
malaguetta	GRAINS OF PARADISE	—water-spirit	NIX
marjoram	AMARACUS	—wraith	DOPPEL-GANGER
mild	CORIANDER	ghost	APPARITION, BOGEY, BOGLE
mixture	GARAM MASALA, TAMARA		GYTRASH, LARVA, PHANTASM
nutmeg	MACE		PHANTOM, REVENANT, SHADE
pimento	ALLSPICE		SPECTRE, SPIRIT, SPOOK
piper nigrum	PEPPER		WRAITH
red pepper	CAYENNE, PAPRIKA	gnome	GOBLIN, SPRITE
Sinapis	MUSTARD	goblin	BOG(E)Y, BOGLE, GNOME
Spanish paprika	PIMIENTO		PUCK, SPRITE
turmeric	CURCUMA	—in mine	KNOCKER

good spirit	D(A)EMON
Greek	DAIMON
guardian	ANGEL
Hebrew evil spirit	DYBBUK
Hindu	PURUSHA
Indian	PURUSHA
—evil	RAKSHAS(A)
—good	DEVA
—spirit of place	BONGA
Irish	BANSHEE, LEPRECHAUN
malignant fairy	ELF
mischievous	
—fairy	ELF, HOBGOBLIN
—spirit	POLTERGEIST
—sprite	PUCK
Moslem spirit	(D)JINNI, GENIE
	JINNEE
—(plural)	GINN, (D)JINN
—jinni	
less powerful	JANN
powerful	MARID
nocturnal (Shak.)	PONK
Norse goblin	NIS, TROLL
nymph	(*see separate entry*)
one returned from the dead	REVENANT
Persian	AHRIMAN, DEEV, DIV
phantom	EIDOLON
presiding spirit	GENIUS
Red Indian	MANITO(U)
Roman	
—ghost(s) of the dead	LEMUR(ES)
—spirit investing	
everything	GENIUS
—spirits of the dead	MANES
Scandinavian goblin	NIS, TROLL
Scottish	
—apparition	TAIS(C)H
—goblin	BODACH, BODRACK,
BROWNIE, RED-CAP, RED-COWL	
—water	
goblin	SHELLYCOAT
spirit	TANGIE
sprite	KELPIE, KELPY, RIVERHORSE
Shakespeare	
—nocturnal	PONK
—spirits	ARIEL, CERES
	IRIS, JUNO
soul	PNEUMA, PSYCHE
spectre	(*see ghost above*)
spirit	PNEUMA, PSYCHE
—attending at call	FAMILIAR
—dwelling in all things	ARCH(A)EUS
—matter	ECTOPLASM
—of the	
air	ARIEL, SYLPH
woods	FAUN, SATYR

sprite	GOBLIN, GNOME
supernatural visitor	VISITANT
voodoo spirit	ZOMBI(E)
water	
—demon	NICKER
—spirit	ARIEL
West Indies	DUPPY, JUM,BIE
	JUMBY, ZOMBI(E)
wicked	IMP
wraith of living person	FETCH
sport	(*see* **games**)
square	
Berlin	ALEXANDERPLATZ
	MARX-ENGELS PLATZ
	POTSDAMERPLATZ
Brussels	GRANDE PLACE
Bucharest	PALACE SQUARE
	UNIVERSITY SQUARE
Cairo	ARABA SQUARE
	REPUBLIC SQUARE
	TAHRIR SQUARE
France	PLACE
Germany	PLATZ
Italy	PIAZZA
London	BERKELEY SQUARE
	GROSVENOR SQUARE
	OXFORD CIRCUS
	PICCADILLY CIRCUS
	RUSSELL SQUARE
	TRAFALGAR SQUARE
Madrid	PLAZA DE CASTELAR
	PLAZA DE CASTILLA
	PLAZA DE ROMA
	PLAZA DE TOROS
	PLAZA MAYOR
Milan	PIAZZA DEL DUOMO
Moscow	DZERZHINSKY SQUARE
	RED SQUARE
	PUSHKIN SQUARE
New York	TIMES SQUARE
	WASHINGTON SQUARE
Paris	PLACE DE LA BASTILLE
	PLACE DE LA CONCORDE
	PLACE DE LA NATION
	PLACE DE LA REPUBLIQUE
	PLACE DE L'ETOILE
	PLACE D'ITALIE
Peking	TIANANMEN SQUARE
Prague	WENCESLAS SQUARE
Rome	PIAZZA COLONNA
	PIAZZA DEL POPOLO
	PIAZZA DI PORTA CAPENA
	PIAZZA SANTA PIETRA
	PIAZZA VENEZIA
Siena	PIAZZA DEL CAMPO
Spain	PLAZA

Venice	PIAZZA SAN MARCO	red	
	ST MARK'S SQUARE	—dwarf	BARNARD'S STAR, ERIDANI
Vienna	HELDEN PLATZ		PROXIMA CENTAURI, ROSS
	KARLS PLATZ	—giant	ANTARES, BETELGEUSE
	MESSE PLATZ		BETELGEUX, BETELGEUZ, CRUCIS
	MORZIN PLATZ		MIRA, RAS ALGETHI, SCHEAT
	OTTO WAGNER PLATZ	seven stars	PLEIAD(E)S
	SCHWARZENBERG PLATZ	—Plough	SEPTENTRION(E)S
Sri Lanka	CL	shooting star	METEOR(ITE)
	(see **Ceylon**)	star in	
standard	STD	—Andromeda	ALMACH, ALPHERATZ
Standard Book Number	SBN		MIRACH
standard deviation	SD	—Aquila	ALTAIR
Standard Serial Number	SSN	—Aries	HAMAL
standard temperature and		—Argo	CANOPUS
pressure	STP	—Auriga	CAPELLA
Standard Wire Gauge	SWG	—Boötes	ARCTURUS, IZAR
stars		—Cancer	ALTARF
always visible	CIRCUMPOLAR STAR	—Canis Major	ADHARA, SIRIUS
brightest star	SIRIUS	—Capricornus	ALGEDI
brightness	MAGNITUDE	—Carina	AVIOR, MIAPLACIOUS
classification	HARVARD CLASSIFICATION	—Cassiopeia	RUCHBAH
	SPECTRAL CLASS	—Centaur	ALPHA CENTAURI, RIGIL
	SPECTRAL TYPE		HADAR-KENT, MENKENT
constellations	(see separate entry)	—Cetus	DIPHDA, MENKAR, MIRIA
Day Star	VENUS	—Columba	PHAET
developing from interstellar			HADAR-KENT, MENKENT
matter	PROTOSTAR	—Cetus	DIPHDA, MENKAR
Dog Star	CANICULA, SIRIUS	—Corvus	ALGORAB, ALKES, GIENAH
Evening Star	HESPER(US)	—Crux	ACRUX, BECRUX, GACRUX
	VENUS, VESPER	—Cygnus	DENEB
exploding star	NOVA	—Delphinus	ROTANEV
	PLANETARY NEBULA	—Draco	ELTANIN, THUBAN
	SUPERNOVA	—Eridanus	ACAMAR, ACHERNA(R)
five stars	HYADES	—Gemini	CASTOR, POLLUX
flaring star	NOVA	—Grus	AL NAIR
group of stars	ASTERISM, GALAXY	—Hydra	ALPHARD
	CONSTELLATION	—Leo	DENEBOLA, REGULUS
halo	CORONA	—Lesser Dog	PROCYON
high red luminosity	RED GIANT	—Libra	ZUBENELGENUBI
large red star	RED GIANT	—Lyrae	VEGA
largest star	ALPHA HERCULIS	—Mensa	NUBECULA MAJOR
lode star	NORTH STAR, POLARIS	—Ophiuchus	RASALHAGUE
low			SABIK, YED
—luminosity	WHITE DWARF	—Orion	ALNILAM, BELATRIX
—red luminosity	RED DWARF		BETELGEUSE
Morning Star	DAYSTAR, LUCIFER		BETELGEUZE, RIGEL
	PHOSPHORUS, VENUS	—Pavo	PEACOCK
most massive	PLASKETT'S STAR	—Pegasus	ENIF, MARKAB, SHEAT
nearest star	PROXIMA CENTAURI	—Perseus	MIRFAK
North Star	TYRIAN CYNOSURE	—Phoenix	ANKAA
pair of stars	BINARY STAR	—Piscis Austrinus	FORMALHAUT
Pole Star	LOADSTAR, LODESTAR	—Plough	MIZAR, SEPTRION(E)S
	NORTH STAR, POLARIS		TRIONES
pulsating star	PULSAR	—Pleiades	MAIA
quasi-stellar object	QUASAR	—Puppis	NAOS

—Sagittarius	KAUS AUSTRALIS, NUNKI	Michigan	MICH
—Scorpio	ANTARES, SHAULA	Minnesota	MINN
—Southern Fish	FOMALHAUT	Mississippi	MI, MISS
—Taurus	ELNATH, HYADES	Missouri	MO
	PLEIADES	Montana	MONT
—Toucan	NUBECULA MINOR	Nebraska	NEB(R)
—Triangulum Australe	ATRIA	Nevada	NEV
—Ursa Major	ALIOTH, ALKAID	New Hampshire	NH
	DUBHE, MERAK	New Jersey	NJ
	MIZAR, PHECDA	New Mexico	NM(EX)
—Ursa Minor	KOCHAB	New York	NY
—Vela	SUHAIL	North Carolina	NC
—Virgo	SPICA	North Dakota	ND(AK)
Star of David	MAGEN DAVID	Ohio	O
	MOGEN DAVID	Oklahoma	OKLA
symbol	ASTERISK	Oregon	OR(E), OREG
system	CONSTELLATION, GALAXY	Pennsylvania	PA, PENN
types	BINARY, BROWN DWARF	Rhode Island	RI
	(CEPHEID) VARIABLE	South Carolina	SC
	FLARE, NEUTRON, NOVA, PULSAR	South Dakota	SD, S DAK
	QUASAR, RED DWARF	Tennessee	TEN(N)
	RED (SUPER-)GIANT	Texas	TEX
	SUB-GIANT, SUPERNOVA	Utah	U(T)
	WHITE DWARF, X-RAY	Vermont	VT
variable star	MIRA, VIRGINIS STAR	Virginia	VA
white dwarf	PROCYON, THE PUP	Washington	WASH
	VAN MAANEN'S STAR	West Virginia	WVA
		Wisconsin	WIS

state[1]

State Certificated Midwife	SCM	Wyoming	WY(O)
State Enrolled Nurse	SEN	unofficial names:	
State Registered Nurse	SRN	Aloha State	HAWAII

state[2] (USA)

official names and abbreviations:

		Apache State	ARIZONA
		Badger State	WISCONSIN
Alabama	AL, ALA	Baked Bean State	MASSACHUSETTS
Alaska	ALAS	Bay State	MASSACHUSETTS
Arizona	ARIZ	Bayou State	LOUISIANA
Arkansas	ARK	Battle born State	NEVADA
California	CAL	Beef State	NEBRASKA
Colorado	COL(O)	Bear State	ARKANSAS
Columbia (District)	DC	Beaver State	OREGON
Connecticut	CT	Beehive State	UTAH
Delaware	DEL	Blue Grass State	KENTUCKY
(District of Columbia)	DC	Buckeye State	OHIO
Florida	FLA	Cavalier State	VIRGINIA
Georgia	GA	Centennial State	COLORADO
Hawaii	HAWAII	Chinook State	WASHINGTON
Idaho	ID, IDA	Constitution State	CONNECTICUT
Illinois	ILL	Cornhusker State	NEBRASKA
Indiana	IND	Cotton State	ALABAMA
Iowa	IA	Coyote State	SOUTH DAKOTA
Kansas	KAN, KS	Creole State	LOUISIANA
Kentucky	KEN, KY	Diamond State	DELAWARE
Louisiana	LA	Elephant State	WASHINGTON
Maine	ME	Empire State	NEW YORK
Maryland	MD	—of the south	GEORGIA
Massachusetts	MASS	Equality State	WYOMING

Evergreen State	WASHINGTON	American	BURGOO, SUCCOTASH
First State	DELAWARE	beans and meat	CASSOULET
Flickertail State	NORTH DAKOTA	beef with	
Free State	MARYLAND	—beer	CARBON(N)ADE
Garden State	NEW JERSEY	—red beans	CHILLI CON CARNE
Gem State	IDAHO	—vegetables	POT-AU-FEU
Golden State	CALIFORNIA	bread (Portugal)	ACORDA
Gopher State	MINNESOTA	East Indian	MULLIGATAWNY
Grand Canyon State	ARIZONA	Egyptian	FOUL MEDAMES
Granite State	NEW HAMPSHIRE	fish and vegetables	CHOWDER
Green Mountain State	VERMONT		MATELOT(T)E
Hawkeye State	INDIANA		MULLIGAN
Heart of Dixie	ALABAMA	—French	BOUILLABAISSE
Hoosier State	INDIANA	—Swedish	GRAVADLAX
Jayhawk State	KANSAS	French	BOUILLABAISSE, DAUBE
Keystone State	PENNSYLVANIA		NAVARIN, POT-AU-FEU
Land of			RATATOUILLE
—Enchantment	NEW MEXICO	game	SALMI(S)
—Opportunity	ARKANSAS	Greek	STIFADO
—the Midnight Sun	ALASKA	Hebrew	
Last Frontier	ALASKA	—brisket and vegetables	CHOLENT
Little Rhody	RHODE ISLAND	—vegetables and	
Lone Star State	TEXAS	dried fruit	TZIMMES
Magnolia State	MISSISSIPPI	highly seasoned	RAGOUT
Mountain State	WEST VIRGINIA	Hungarian	GOULASH, PORKOLT
North Star State	MINNESOTA	Italian	BRODETTO, BURIDDA
Nutmeg State	CONNECTICUT		CACCIUCCO
Old		lamb and vegetables	LANCASHIRE HOTPOT
—Colony State	MASSACHUSETTS	—French	NAVARIN (PRINTANIER)
—Dominion	VIRGINIA	meat	
—Line State	MARYLAND	—highly seasoned	GOULASH
—North State	NORTH CAROLINA	—in	
Palmetto State	SOUTH CAROLINA	red wine (French)	DAUBE
Panhandle State	WEST VIRGINIA	stock	FRICASSEE
Peach State	GEORGIA	—with	
Pelican State	LOUISIANA	beer	CARBONADE
Peninsula State	FLORIDA	biscuit	LOBSCOUSE
Pine Tree State	MAINE	potatoes, etc	HOTPOT, IRISH STEW
Prairie State	ILLINOIS	vegetables	HASH, MULLIGAN
Sagebrush State	NEVADA		RAGOUT
Show Me State	MISSOURI	—French	POT-AU-FEU
Silver State	NEVADA	—Indian	DHANSAK
Sioux State	NORTH DAKOTA	—Spanish	OLIO, OLLA PODRIDA
Sooner State	OKLAHOMA	Mexican	CHILLI CON CARNE
Sugar State	LOUISIANA	mutton and vegetables	IRISH STEW
Sunflower State	KANSAS	rabbit	HASENPFEFFER
Sunshine State	FLORIDA, NEW MEXICO	ragout in cream sauce	BLANQUETTE
	SOUTH DAKOTA	Romanian	TOCANA
Tar Heel State	NORTH CAROLINA	Russian	RAGU
Treasure State	MONTANA	sailor's	(LOB)SCOUSE
Tree Planter's State	NEBRASKA	Scandinavian	LABSKAUS
Volunteer State	TENNESSEE	seafood	(CLAM) CHOWDER
Wolverine State	MICHIGAN	shellfish	CLAM CHOWDER
Wonder State	ARKANSAS	ship's	
Yellowhammer State	ALABAMA	—gruel	LOBLOLLY
stew	HOTPOT, RAGOUT	—stew	LOB'S COURSE, LOBSCOUSE

Spanish
—beans and sausage   FABADA ASTURIANA
—chicken, rice, etc   PAELLA
—lentils   COCHIDA DE LENTEJA
—meat and vegetables   OLLA-PODRIDA
Swedish fish stew   GRAVADLAX
tomatoes, aubergines etc   RATATOUILLE
thick   BURGOO
tinned meat and vegetables   MACONOCHIE
two meats and vegetables   BRUNSWICK
vegetables and biscuits   LOB'S COURSE
                                  (LOB)SCOUSE
West Indian   PEPPERPOT
white meat in sauce   BLANQUETTE

stone
amulet (Australia)   CHURINGA
artificial   RECONSTRUCTED STONE
                                        TABBY
at Delphi   OMPHALOS
balanced on another   LOG(G)AN(-STONE)
                              LOGGING-STONE
band of stone   CORDON, STRING-COURSE
bare rock projecting
above ground   GREY-WEATHER
                           SARACEN'S-STONE
            SARS(D)EN, SARSEN-STONE
becoming stone   LAPIDESCENT
building stone   BATH, FLINT, GRANITE
                   IRONSTONE, LIMESTONE
                    MARBLE, PORTLAND
               RAG, SANDSTONE, YORK
—American   BROWNSTONE
centre stone of arch   KEYSTONE
change to stone   PETRIFICATION
circle of standing
stones   CROMLECH, CYCLOLITH
                   HENGE, PERISTALITH
coffin made of stone   SARCOPHAGUS
column   OBELISK
corner stone   QUOIN
crushing (in body)   LITHOLAPAXY
cutter   LAPIDARY
cutting   LITHOTOMY
                               STEREOTOMY
dressed stone   MASONRY
—lining opening   RYBAT
drystone waller   COWAN
engraving on stone   LITHOGLYPH
fastener for stonework   AGRAFFE, GUDGEON
four-sided pillar   OBELISK
fragment of stone   SPALL
gall-stone   CHOLELITH
having
—magical properties   ELIXIR
                        PHILOSOPHER'S STONE
—magnetic properties   LODESTONE

imitation stone
—limestone chips and cement   SCAGLIOLA
—stone dust
cement   RECONSTRUCTED STONE
in
—animal cell   LITHITE
—body   CALCULUS
—ear   OTOLITH
—gall-bladder   GALL-STONE
—kidney   KIDNEY-STONE
—intestines   ENTEROLITH
—nose   RHINOLITH
—protozoa   RHABDOLITH
—stomach (goats, etc)   BEZOAR
—urinary tract   UROLITH
inscribed with Egyptian
hieroglyphics   ROSETTA STONE
irregular stone   RUBBLE
Italian limestone   SCAGLIA
jetty   MOLE
large stone   MEGALITH
like marble   MARMOREAL
lintel   SUMMER(BEAM)
living in
—rocks   LITHODROMOUS
—stones   LAPIDICOLOUS
Lydian stone   TOUCHSTONE
marble
—Dorset   PURBECK MARBLE
                             PURBECK STONE
—Italy   CARRARA
megalith
—England   AVEBURY, STONEHENGE
—France   CARNAC
memorial
—heap   CAIRN
—stone   EBENEZER
meteoric stone   AEROLITE, AEROLITH
                                   ASTROLITH
mound of stones   CAIRN
of the sun (Greek)   PANTARBE
old stone implement   EOLITH
on top of wall   CAPSTONE, COPESTONE
                             COPING STONE
paving slab   FLAG(STONE)
painting on stone   LITHOCHROMATICS
polished by the wind   VENTIFACT
prehistoric monument   CROMLECH, DOLMEN
                     MEGALITH, MENHIR
—Balearic Islands   NAVETA
                         TALAYOT, TAULA
ring of stone pillars   CROMLECH, HENGE
rocking stone   LOG(G)AN(-STONE)
                             LOGGING-STONE
rounded stone   BOULDER, COBBLE
                                     PEBBLE

rubble in masonry	MOELLON	New York	BROADWAY
sacred stone (Mecca)	BLACK STONE		FIFTH AVENUE
	KAABA		PARK AVENUE
slab	LEDGER		WALL STREET
small fragments	AGGREGATE, GRAVEL	Naples	VIA CHIARA
spout	GARGOYLE	New Orleans	SOUTH RAMPART STREET
standing stone	MEGALITH, MENHIR	Oxford	BROAD STREET
	MONOLITH		CARFAX
Stone Age			HIGH STREET
—Old	PALAEOLITHIC	Paris	AVENUE VICTOR HUGO
—Middle	MESOLITHIC		CHAMPS ELYSEES
—New	NEOLITHIC		RUE DE RIVOLI
stone-eating	LITHOPHAGOUS		RUE LAFAYETTE
stony	LAPIDEOUS	Rome	CORSO VITTORIO EMMANUELE
—organism	LITHOPHYTE		VIA DEI FORI IMPERIALI
—sponge	LITHISTID		VIA DEL CORSO
through a wall	PARPANE, PARPEN(D)		VIA DEL QUIRINALE
	PARPENT, PARPOINT		VIA NATIONALE
	PERPEND, PERPENT		VIALE TRASTEVERE
throw stones at	LAPIDATE	Spain	CALLE
tomb in form of chest	CIST	Washington	ARLINGTON BOULEVARD
tool	NEOLITH		PENNSYLVANIA AVENUE
—small	MICROLITH		THE MALL
touchstone	LYDIAN STONE	**student**	L
transparent	PHENGITE	Student Christian Movement	SCM
turn to stone	LAPIDIFY, PETRIFY	Student of Civil Law	SCL
undressed stone	RUBBLE	Student Representative Council	SRC
upright stone	ORTHOSTAT	student's union	NUS
—slab	STELA, STELE	**study**	
—with crossbeam	DOLMEN, TRILITH(ON)	including: knowledge of	
wedge-shaped (in arch)	VOUSSOIR	science of	
worker in stone	MASON, SCULPTOR	study of	
	(*see also* **building construction**)	abnormal	
	(*see also* **minerals, rock**)	—growths	TERATOLOGY
		—working of the mind	PSYCHOLOGY
street			PSYCHOPATHOLOGY
Berlin	KURFURSTENDAMM	action of	
	UNTER DEN LINDEN	—forces	MECHANICS
	WILHELMSTRASSE	—ice	GLACIOLOGY
Dublin	O'CONNELL STREET	adages	PAROEMIOLOGY
Edinburgh	PRINCES STREET	adaptation of machinery	
France	RUE	to suit humans	ERGONOMICS
Germany	STRASSE		BIOTECHNOLOGY
Italy	STRADA, VIA(LE)	aerial navigation	AERONAUTICS
London	BOND STREET	aerolites	AEROLITHOLOGY
	DOWNING STREET	ageing	GERONTOLOGY
	FLEET STREET	agricultural pests	PESTOLOGY
	OLD KENT ROAD	agriculture	GEOPONICS
	OXFORD STREET	airborne organisms	AEROBIOLOGY
	PARK LANE	alchemy	HERMETICS
	REGENT STREET	algae	ALGOLOGY, PHYCOLOGY
	THE MALL	amphibia	HERPETOLOGY
	THE STRAND	anatomy of fleshy parts	SARCOLOGY
Los Angeles	SUNSET BOULEVARD	ancestry	GENEALOGY
Madrid	CALLE MAYOR	ancient	
	PASEO DE LA CASTELLANA	—blood groups	PALAEOSEROLOGY
Moscow	GORKY STREET		

—customs	FOLK-LORE
—environment	PALAEOECOLOGY
—geography	PALAEOGEOGRAPHY
—human remains	PALAEOPATHOLOGY
—Italians	ETRUSCOLOGY
—magnetism in rocks	PALAEOMAGNETISM
—man	PALAEOETHNOLOGY
—papyri	PAPYROLOGY
—soils	PALAEOPEDOLOGY
—things	HIEROLOGY
—weather	PALAEOCLIMATOLOGY
—writing	PALAEOGRAPHY
animal	
—behaviour	ETHOLOGY
—diseases	ZOOPATHOLOGY
—life	ZOOLOGY
—pathology	ZOOPATHY
—tissues	HISTOLOGY
animals	THEROLOGY
	ZOOGRAPHY
—resembling plants	ZOOPHYTOLOGY
antibiotics	SEROLOGY
ants	MYRMECOLOGY
apples and pears	POMOLOGY
applied	
—nuclear physics	NUCLEONICS
—thermodynamics	HYDRAULICS
—sciences	TECHNOLOGY
aquatic animals	CETOLOGY
aqueous vapour	ATMOLOGY
arrangement of atoms	STEREOCHEMISTRY
artillery	PYROBALLOGY
assaying	DOCIMOLOGY
assisting memory	MNEMONICS
	MNEMOTECHNICS
astronomical measurement	URANOMETRY
astronomy	URANOLOGY
atmosphere	AEROLOGY
atomic nuclei	ATOMIC PHYSICS
bacteria	BACTERIOLOGY
ballet	CHOREOLOGY
bathing	BALNEOLOGY
beasts	THEROLOGY
behaviour of	
—genes	MENDELISM
—radioactive substances in living tissues	RADIOBIOLOGY
being	METAPHYSICS
bells	CAMPANOLOGY
biological	
—effects caused by light	PHOTOBIOLOGY
—forms	MORPHOLOGY
—rhythms	CHRONOBIOLOGY
biology by cine film	CINEBIOLOGY
bionomics	ETHOLOGY
birds	ORNITHOLOGY
birds'	
—eggs	OOLOGY
—nests	CALIOLOGY
blood	HAEMATOLOGY
bodies affected by forces	DYNAMICS
body	
—and mind relationship	PSYCHOBIOGRAPHY
	PSYCHOBIOLOGY
—movement conveying information	KINESICS
mechanics of	KINESIOLOGY
—reflexes	REFLEXOLOGY
bones	OSTEOLOGY
books	BIBLIOLOGY
	BIBLIOGRAPHY
botany	PHYTOLOGY
brain	
—disorders as affecting human behaviour, etc	NEUROPSYCHIATRY
	NEUROPSYCHOLOGY
—functions	NEUROPHYSIOLOGY
brambles	BATOLOGY
breeding	
—animals	ZOOTECHNY
—domestic animals	THREMMATOLOGY
brewing	ZYMURGY
building	ARCHITECTURE
	ARCHITECTONICS
—as an art	TECTONICS
bumps on head	PHRENOLOGY
butterflies	LEPIDOPTEROLOGY
calculation	LOGISTICS
cancers	ONCOLOGY
casting nativities	GENETHLIALOGY
causation	AETIOLOGY
causes at work in development	EPIGENETICS
caves	SPELEOLOGY
cells	CYTOLOGY
—nuclei	KARYOLOGY
—shed from internal body surfaces	EXFOLIATIVE CYTOLOGY
centres of spatial distribution	CENTROGRAPHY
changes associated with chemical reactions	PHYSICAL CHEMISTRY
chaos	CHAOLOGY
character	ETHOLOGY
—from face	METOPOSCOPY
charged particles	THERMIONICS
charters, diplomas, etc	DIPLOMATOLOGY
chemical	
—composition of Earth's crust	GEOCHEMISTRY

—methods applied to radioactive materials	RADIOCHEMISTRY	communities	DEMOLOGY
—reactions caused by light	PHOTOCHEMISTRY	—of plants and animals	SYN(O)ECOLOGY
chemistry		comparative	
—applied to		—measurements of parts of animals	ZOOMETRY
agricultural products	CHEMURGY	—philology	GLOSSOLOGY
medical theory	IATROCHEMISTRY		GLOTTOLOGY
—dealing with very small quantities	MICROCHEMISTRY	composition of substances	STOICHIOMETRY
—of		conditions in towns	URBANOLOGY
carbon compounds	ORGANIC CHEMISTRY	congenital abnormalities	TERATOLOGY
living things	BIOCHEMISTRY	conservation of energy	THERMODYNAMICS
radioactivity	RADIOCHEMISTRY	constitution of universe	COSMOGRAPHY
substances under high pressure	PIEZO-CHEMISTRY	control mechanisms	CYBERNETICS
		cooking	GASTROLOGY
the		correct pronunciation	ORTHOEPY
—body	ZOOCHEMISTRY	cosmetics	COSMETOLOGY
—Earth	GEOCHEMISTRY	crime	CRIMINOLOGY
tissues	HISTOCHEMISTRY	crustaceans	CARCINOLOGY
children	P(A)EDOLOGY	crystals	CRYSTALLOGRAPHY
children's		—using X-rays	X-RAY CRYSTALLOGRAPHY
—development and growth	P(A)EDOLOGY	cultivation using mineral solutions	HYDROPONICS
—diseases	PAEDIATRICS	cyphers	CRYPTOLOGY
—teeth	PAEDODONTICS	data obtained by touch	HAPTICS
China	SINOLOGY	dates	CHRONOLOGY
Christ	CHRISTOLOGY	—from growth-rings	DENDROCHRONOLOGY
chromosomes and genetics	CYTOGENETICS	death	ESCHATOLOGY
church forms and practices	ECCLESIOLOGY		THANATOLOGY
ciphers	CRYPTOLOGY	deformation and flow of matter	RHEOLOGY
citizenship	CIVICS	demons	DEMONOLOGY
classification	TYPOLOGY	dentistry concerned with gum diseases	PERIODONTICS
—laws	BIOSYSTEMATICS		PERIODONTOLOGY
—of		deposits	SEDIMENTOLOGY
animals	ZOOTAXY	derivation of words	ETYMOLOGY
diseases	NOSOLOGY	descent of families	GENEALOGY
organisms	CLADISTICS	descriptive	
plants and animals	TAXONOMY	—astronomy	URANOGRAPHY
climate	AEROGRAPHY	—botany	PHYTOGRAPHY
	CLIMATOLOGY	determination of chemical equivalents	STOICHIOMETRY
	METEOROLOGY	development of	
—in relation to life	BIOCLIMATOLOGY	Earth's crust	GEOLOGY
—of restricted areas	MICROCLIMATOLOGY	devil-lore	DIABOLOLOGY
clocks	HOROGRAPHY, HOROLOGY	diagnosis	DIAGNOSTICS
clouds	NEPHOLOGY	dialects	DIALECTOLOGY
cockroaches etc	ORTHEROPTOLOGY	dictionaries	LEXICOLOGY
codes	CRYPTOLOGY	dietetics	SIT(I)OLOGY
coins	NUMISMATICS	dining	ARISTOLOGY
	NUMISMATOLOGY	diseases	NOSOLOGY
collective biographies	PROSOPOGRAPHY		PATHOLOGY
colour	CHROMATICS	—as influenced by environment	GEOMEDICINE
—change	PHOTOCHROMICS	—classification of	NOSOLOGY
communications in man and machine	CYBERNETICS		

—of	
man	ANDROLOGY
mind	PSYCHIATRY
plants	PHYTOPATHOLOGY
rectum	PROTOLOGY
women	GYNAECOLOGY
—widespread	EPEDEMIOLOGY
disorder	CHAOLOGY
distilling	ZYMORGY
distribution of	
—animals	ZOOGEOGRAPHY
and plants	BIOGEOGRAPHY
—chemicals in tissues	HISTOCHEMISTRY
—currents	ELECTROKINETICS
—human groups	GEOANTHROPOLOGY
—ice	GLACIOLOGY
—living things	BIOGEOGRAPHY
—mankind	ANTHROPO(GEO)GRAPHY
—plants	PHYTOGEOGRAPHY
—population	DEMOGRAPHY
—races	ETHNOLOGY
dogma	DOGMATOLOGY
domestication of animals	ZOOTECHNY
dosage	POSOLOGY
dreams	ONEIROLOGY
drugs	PHARMACOLOGY
ductless glands	ENDOCRINOLOGY
dust in air	KONIOLOGY
duty	DEONTOLOGY
dynamic forces within	
the Earth	GEODYNAMICS
dynamics of gases	AERODYNAMICS
ear	OTOLOGY
—nose and	
throat	OTORHINOLARYNGOLOGY
early history	PREHISTORY
	PROTOHISTORY
Earth	CHOROLOGY, GEOSCIENCE
—measurement	GEODESY
—quakes	SEISMOGRAPHY
	SEISMOLOGY
—sciences	NATURAL HISTORY
Earth's	
—atmosphere	AERONOMY
—surface	CHOROGRAPHY, GEOGRAPHY
	PHYSICAL GEOGRAPHY
	PHYSIOGRAPHY, TOPOGRAPHY
echoes	PHONOCAMPTICS
ecology of	
—groups	SYN(O)ECOLOGY
—individual organisms	AUTOECOLOGY
econometrics in history	CLIOMETRICS
economic data	ECONOMETRICS
effects of	
—disease on body	
tissues	HISTOPATHOLOGY

—dissolved substances	
on freezing points	CYROSCOPY
—drugs on	
behaviour	PSYCHOPHARMACOLOGY
—radiation on	
living tissue	RADIOBIOLOGY
—space travel on	
organisms	BIO-ASTRONAUTICS
eggs	OOLOGY
Egypt	EGYPTOLOGY
election results	PSEPHOANALYSIS
	PSEPHOLOGY
electric	
—charges in motion	ELECTRODYNAMICS
	ELECTROKINETICS
—technology	ELECTROTECHNICS
electrical	
—circuits	ELECTRONICS
—measurements	ELECTROMETRY
—phenomena in living	
organisms	ELECTROBIOLOGY
	ELECTROPHYSIOLOGY
electricity	ELECTROLOGY
—and	
chemical change	ELECTROCHEMISTRY
electromagnetic	
radiation	PHOTO-ELECTRONICS
heat	ELECTROTHERMICS
	ELECTROTHERMY
magnetism	ELECTROMAGNETISM
—at rest	ELECTROSTATICS
—generated by	
plasma flow in	
magneticfield	
	MAGNETOTHERMODYNAMICS
—in	
ore separation	
	ELECTROMETALLURGY
motion	ELECTRODYNAMICS
	ELECTROKINETICS
electronic	
communication	INFORMATION TECHNOLOGY
	IT
electronics in aviation	AVIONICS
electrons emitted from	
heated substance	THERMIONICS
elements	
—and their	
compounds	INORGANIC CHEMISTRY
—of animal tissue	STOECHIOLOGY
	STOICH(E)IOLOGY
embryos	EMBRYOLOGY
emotional forces	PSYCHODYNAMICS
endemic diseases	ENDEMIOLOGY
energy	
—laws	ENERGETICS

—using spectroscope	SPECTROSCOPY
engraved gems	DACTYLIOGRAPHY
	DACTILIOLOGY
environment	(O)ECOLOGY
environmental pollution	ECOTOXICOLOGY
enzymes	ENZYMOLOGY
epidemic animal diseases	EPIZOOTICS
epidemics	EPEDEMIOLOGY
esoteric science	HERMETICS
ethics	DEONTOLOGY
—of medical research	BIOETHICS
evolution	GENETICS
exercise	PHYSIOTHERAPEUTICS
excrement	SCATOLOGY
experimental psychology	PSYCHOPHYSIOLOGY
extraterrestrial life	BIO-ASTRONOMY
	EXOBIOLOGY
eyes	OPHTHALMOLOGY
eyesight	OPTOLOGY
fathers	PATRISTICS, PATROLOGY
faulty pronunciation or vocabulary	CACOLOGY
features of limited area	TOPOGRAPHY
feet	PODOLOGY
fermentation	(EN)ZYMOLOGY
	ZYMURGY
ferns	PTERIDOLOGY
fevers	PYRETOLOGY
figures	GEOMETRY
final	
—causes	TELEOLOGY
—things	ESCHATOLOGY
finger	
—prints	DACTYLOGRAPHY
	DACTYLOLOGY
—rings	DACTYLIOGRAPHY
	DACTYLIOLOGY
—talking	DACTYLOGRAPHY
	DACTYLOLOGY
fireworks	PYROTECHNICS
first principles	METAPHYSICS
fishes	ICHTHYOLOGY
fishing	HALIEUTICS
flags	VEXILLOLOGY
fleshy parts	SARCOLOGY
floras	FLORISTICS
flow	
—and change of shape of matter	RHEOLOGY
—of fluids	FLUIDICS
flowers	ANTHOECOLOGY
	FLORISTICS
folk-lore	STORIOLOGY
food and nutrition	BROMATOLOGY
footprints	ICHNOLOGY

forecasting	FUTUROLOGY
force producing motion	KINETICS
form	MORPHOLOGY
—of land	GEOMORPHOLOGY
formation of Earth	GEOGENY, GEOGONY
fossil(s)	ORYCTOLOGY
	PALAEONTOLOGY
—animals	PALAEOZOOLOGY
—fishes	PALAEOICHTHYOLOGY
—plants	PALAEOBOTANY
	PALAEOPHYTOLOGY
freshwater life	LIMNOLOGY
friction	TRIBOLOGY
fruit	CARPOLOGY, POMOLOGY
—growing	POMOLOGY
functioning of living organisms	PHYSIOLOGY
fungi	MYC(ET)OLOGY
future developments	FUTUROLOGY
gases	AEROMETRY, AEROSTATICS
	PNEUMATICS, PNEUMATOLOGY
	PNEUMODYNAMICS
gem-engraving	GLYPTICS
general structure of Earth	GEOGNOSY
genetic	
—basis of nervous system	NEUROGENETICS
—control	EUGENICS
genetics in relation to cells	CYTOGENETICS
geological	
—distribution	CHOROLOGY
—time	GEOCHRONOLOGY
geology	
—from air photographs	PHOTOGEOLOGY
—of Moon etc	ASTROGEOLOGY
geometry of changing shapes	TOPOLOGY
germ-free animals	GNOTOBIOTICS
gesture	CH(E)IROLOGY
ghosts	SPETROLOGY
giants	GIGANTOLOGY
glaciers	GLACIOLOGY
glands	ENDOCRINOLOGY
god	THEOLOGY
good eating	GASTROLOGY
	GASTRONOMY
government	ARCHOLOGY
	POLITICAL SCIENCE
gramophone records	DISCOGRAPHY
grasses	AGROSTOLOGY
ground plans	ICHNOGRAPHY
growing plants in water	HYDROPONICS
growth	
—and development of children	P(A)EDOLOGY

—of embryos	EMBRYOLOGY
—rings in trees	DENDROCHRONOLOGY
guns	BALLISTICS
hair	TRICHOLOGY
hand	CH(E)IROLOGY
—writing	GRAPHOLOGY
hearing	AUDIOLOGY
heart	CARDIOLOGY
heat	THERMOLOGY
	THERMOTICS
—as mechanical agent	THERMODYNAMICS
—in chemical reactions	THERMOCHEMISTRY
heavenly bodies	ASTROLOGY, ASTRONOMY
	COSMOGONY, URANOLOGY
heredity	(CYTO)GENETICS, MENDELISM
heresies	HERESIOLOGY
high-frequency pressure waves	SUPERSONICS
	ULTRASONICS
history	HISTORIOLOGY
—from psychological viewpoint	PSYCHOHISTORY
—of	
languages	GLOTTOCHRONOLOGY
proper names	ONOMASTICS
words	LEXICOLOGY
horse diseases	HIPPIATRICS
horses	HIPPOLOGY
human	
—antiquity	ARCHAEOLOGY
—biology	ANTHROPOBIOLOGY
—body	SOMATOLOGY
—muscles	KINESIOLOGY
—population	DEMOGRAPHY
—settlements	EKISTICS
—society	SOCIOLOGY
humour	HUMOROLOGY
hydrodynamics	HYDRAULICS
	HYDROMECHANICS
hymns	HYMNOLOGY
hypnotism	NEUR(OH)YPNOLOGY
hypothetical creatures	CRYPTOZOOLOGY
ice movements	GLACIOLOGY
icons	ICONOLOGY
ideas	IDEOLOGY
illness diagnosed from marks on iris	IRIDOLOGY
images in art	ICONOGRAPHY
immunity	IMMUNOLOGY
improvement in living standards	EUTHENICS
industrial chemical processes	CHEMURGY
influence of the stars	ASTROLOGY
inheritance	GENETICS, MENDELISM

inland water	LIMNOLOGY
insects	ENTOMOLOGY
	INSECTOLOGY
instruction	PEDAGOGY
integrated circuits	SOLID STATE PHYSICS
interconversion of chemical and electrical energy	ELECTROCHEMISTRY
interpretation of	
—Scripture	HERMENEUTICS
—text	EXEGETICS
interrelationship of environment and organisms	BIONOMICS, ECOLOGY
ions in solution	POLAROGRAPHY
iris	IRIDOLOGY
jets of fluids to perform tasks	FLUID LOGIC, FLUIDICS
kidneys	NEPHROLOGY
knowledge	EPISTEMICS, EPISTEMOLOGY
labels	PHILATELY
lakes	LIMNOLOGY
land management	AGRONOMICS
language	LINGUISTICS, PHILOLOGY
—detail	MICROLINGUISTICS
—in relation to	
culture	ETHNOLINGUISTICS
gesture	METALINGUISTICS
literature	STYLISTICS
locality	DIALECTOLOGY
meaning	METALINGUISTICS
other features of behaviour	META-LINGUISTICS
society	SOCIO
larynx	LARYNGOLOGY
last or final things	ESCHATOLOGY
law	JURISPRUDENCE, NOMOLOGY
laws of energy	ENERGETICS
life	
—and work of Christ	CHRISTOLOGY
—processes	PHYSIOLOGY
—without germs	GNOTOBIOTICS
light	OPTICS
—as affecting	
chemical reactions	PHOTOCHEMISTRY
organisms	PHOTOBIOLOGY
limits in sets	TOPOLOGY
liquids	HYDRAULICS
—at rest	HYDROSTATICS
—in motion	HYDRODYNAMICS
liver	HEPATOLOGY
liverworts	HEPATICOLOGY
living	
—things	BIOLOGY, BIOMETRY
	BIOMETRICS, BIOSCIENCE

in relation to	
chemistry	BIOGEOCHEMISTRY
—tissues	HISTOLOGY
logic of reasoning	DIALECTICS
low temperatures	CRYOGENICS
	CRYOPHYSICS
lubrication	TRIBOLOGY
lying	PSEUDOLOGY
lymph vessels	ANGIOLOGY
magnetism	
—and electricity	ELECTROMAGNETISM
—of ancient rocks	PALAEOMAGNETISM
malaria	MALARIOLOGY
malformations	TERATOLOGY
man	ANTHROPOLOGY
managing fermentation	ZYMO-TECHNICS
manoeuvring	TACTICS
maps	CARTOLOGY
mathematical drawing	GRAPHICS
matter	
—in solid state	SOLID STATE PHYSICS
—using spectroscope	SPECTROSCOPY
—with motion	KINETICS
—without motion	STATICS
Maya people	MAYOLOGY
meaning	SIGNIFICS
—of words	LEXICOLOGY
meanings	SEMANTICS
	SEMASIOLOGY
measurable psychological	
factors	PSYCHOMETRICS
	PSYCHOMETRY
measurement	
—and recording of stars	ASTROMETRY
—of	
height above Earth's	
surface	HYPSOMETRY
social phenomena	SOCIOMETRY
time	HOROLOGY
very small things	NANOTECHNOLOGY
measurements	METRICS, METROLOGY
mechanics of the	
electric circuit	ELECTROMECHANICS
medals	NUMISMATICS
	NUMISMATOLOGY
mediaeval chemistry in	
medicine	IATROCHEMISTRY
medical problems of	
old people	GERIATRICS
medicines	PHARMACEUTICS
mental	
—attributes of historical	
figures	PSYCHOHISTORY
—disorders	PSCYHOPATHOLOGY
—faculties	PHRENOLOGY
—forces	PSYCHODYNAMICS

—illness	ALIENISM, PSYCHIATRY
—problems of the	
aged	PSYCHOGERIATRICS
—states quantified	PSYCHOMETRICS
meteor stones	AEROLITHOLOGY
	ASTROLITHOLOGY
meteors	METEORITICS
metrical theory	STICHOLOGY
metals	METALLURGY
	METALLOGRAPHY
metaphysics	IDEOLOGY
methods and rules	METHODOLOGY
micro-organisms	BACTERIOLOGY
	MICROBIOLOGY, VIROLOGY
microscopically	
small things	NANOTECHNOLOGY
midwifery	OBSTETRICS
mind	NOOLOGY
—and behaviour	PSYCHICS, PSYCHOLOGY
—in its environment	PSYCHONOMICS
—measurement	NOOMETRY
mineral	
—fossils	ORYCTOLOGY
—springs	BALNEOLOGY
minerals	MINERALOGY
missiles	BALLISTICS
mites	ACAROLOGY
moisture content of	
the atmosphere	HYDROMETEOROLOGY
molecules in living	
organisms	MOLECULAR BIOLOGY
molluscs	CONCHOLOGY
	MALACOLOGY
monads	MONADOLOGY
Moon	SELENOGRAPHY
	SELENOLOGY
—surface	SELENOMORPHOLOGY
morals	DEONTOLGY, ETHICS
mosses	BRYOLOGY, MUSCOLOGY
	SPHAGNOLOGY
moths	LEPIDOPTEROLOGY
motion	
—involving force	KINETICS
—not involving force	KINEMATICS
—of	
air or other gases	AERODYNAMICS
bodies in	
—air	AERODYNAMICS
—space	ASTRODYNAMICS
fluids	HYDRAULICS
	HYDRODYNAMICS
	HYDROKINETICS
mountains	OR(E)OLOGY
mouth (disorders)	STOMATOLOGY
movement	
—and supply of troops	LOGISTICS

—of	
humans	KINESIOLOGY
living creatures	BIOMECHANICS
mud	PELOLOGY
muscles	MYOLOGY
museums	MUSEOLOGY
music	HARMONICS, MUSICOLOGY
—of primitive	
peoples	ETHNOMUSICOLOGY
myths	MYTHOLOGY
natural	
—agents in shaping	
the Earth's crust	DYNAMICAL GEOLOGY
—science	PHYSICS
nature	PHYSIOGRAPHY
—and essence	ONTOLOGY
navigation	NAUTICS
nervous system	NEUROLOGY
neurological	
—disorders	NEURO(PATHO)LOGY
—factors in language	
development	NEUROLINGUISTICS
nose	RHINOLOGY
nuclear physics	NUCLEONICS
numbers	NUMEROLOGY
numerical	
—data	STATISTICS
—proportions in which	
substances react	STOICH(E)IOMETRY
nutrition	TROPHOLOGY
obstetrics	TOCOLOGY, TOKOLOGY
old age	GERONTOLOGY
ontology	METAPHYSICS
optics	PHOTICS
—and electronics	OPTOELECTRONICS
orbits and	
trajectories	CELESTIAL MECHANICS
organic molecules	MOLECULAR BIOLOGY
organised whole	GESTALT PSYCHOLOGY
organisms	BACTERIOLOGY
—as affected by climate	PH(A)ENOLOGY
origins of	
—man	ANTHROPOGENY
	ANTHROPOGONY
—proper names	ONOMASTICS
—things	ARCHOLOGY
—universe	COSMOGONY
—words	ETYMOLOGY
parasites	PARASITOLOGY
particular place	TOPOLOGY
pathology of nervous	
system	NEUROPATHOLOGY
pauses, etc in	
conversation	CHRONEMICS
pears	POMOLOGY
peat-mosses	SPHAGNOLOGY
pecuniary management	ECONOMICS
personal	
—appearance	PROSOPOGRAPHY
—interrelationships	SOCIOMETRY
personality traits	CHARACTEROLOGY
phenomena	PHENOMENOLOGY
phonological shapes	MORPHO(PHO)NEMICS
	MORPHO(PHO)NOLOGY
physical	
—condition of	
heavenly bodies	PHYSICAL ASTRONOMY
—features of	
an area	TOPOGRAPHY
Earth	PHYSIOGRAPHY
—geography	PHYSIOGRAPHY
—properties of	
chemicals	PHYSICAL CHEMISTRY
—state of Earth and	
atmosphere	GEOPHYSICS
physics	NATURAL PHILOSOPHY
—of	
heavenly bodies	ASTROPHYSICS
living things	BIOPHYSICS
the Earth	GEOPHYSICS
physiological	
psychology	PSYCHOPHYSIOLOGY
pigs	PORCINOLOGY
place-names	TOPONYMICS, TOPONYMY
plant	
—anatomy	PHYTOTOMY
—communities	SYNOECOLOGY
—diseases	PHYTOPATHOLOGY
—distribution	PHYTOGEOGRAPHY
—nutrition	AGROBIOLOGY
plant(s)	BOTANY, PHYTOLOGY
—and	
animals in relation	
to environment	ECOLOGY
geography	GEOBOTANY
—population and	
habitats	GENECOLOGY
—sociology	PHYTOSOCIOLOGY
—tissues	HISTOLOGY
plastic surgery	COSMETOLOGY
plays	DRAMATICS
pleasure	HEDONICS
poisons	TOXICOLOGY
political	
—economy	PLUTOLOGY, PLUTONOMY
—science	ECONOMICS
pollen grains	PALYNOLOGY
pollutants	ECOTOXICOLOGY
population	DEMOGRAPHY, LARITHMICS
portraits	ICONOGRAPHY
postcards	DELTIOLOGY
pottery	CERAMOGRAPHY

practical application of science	TECHNOLOGY
preaching	HOMILETICS
precious stones	GEMMOLOGY
prediction	HOROSCOPY
pressure of gases	AEROSTATICS
primitive customs	AGRIOLOGY
prison management	P(O)ENOLOGY
probability	STATISTICS
problems of states	GEOPOLITICS
processes leading to invention	SYNECTICS
production of wealth	POLITICAL ECONOMY
prognosis	FUTUROLOGY
prolonging life	MACROBIOTICS
pronunciation	PHONETICS, PHONOLOGY
proper names	ONOMASTICS
properties of	
—angles	TRIGONOMETRY
—figures unchanged by deformation	TOPOLOGY
—heavenly bodies	ASTROPHYSICS
—large masses of particles	STATISTICAL MECHANICS
—lines, surfaces and solids	GEOMETRY
—matter	PHYSICS, SOMATOLOGY
protozoa	PROTOZOOLOGY
proverbs	PAROEMIOLOGY
psychic phenomena	
—extraordinary	METAPHYSICS
—theorising	METAPSYCHOLOGY
psychical research	PARAPSYCHOLOGY
psychological factors affecting physiology	PSYCHOSOMATIC MEDICINE
psychology	PSYCHICS
—of	
abnormal mental states	PSYCHOPATHOLOGY
animals	ZOOPSYCHOLOGY
—measurable factors	PSYCHOMETRICS
public institutions	ESTABLISHMENTOLOGY
punishment	PENOLOGY
pure being	ONTOLOGY
purposelessness	DYSTELEOLOGY
quantity	POSOLOGY
race	
—deterioration	CACOGENICS
—improvement	EUGENICS
races	ETHNOGRAPHY, ETHNOLOGY
radiation on tissues	RADIOBIOLOGY
radioactivity	RADIOLOGY
rainfall	HYETOLOGY

reaction of matter to forces	MECHANICS
reality	AXIOLOGY
reasoning	LOGIC
reflected light	CATOPTRICS
reflection and refraction of light	GEOMETRICAL OPTICS
reflexes	REFLEXOLOGY
refracted sounds	DIACOUSTICS
refraction	DIOPTRICS
refuse collection and disposal	GARBOLOGY
relationship of	
—electrical and mechanical forces	ELECTRODYNAMICS
—languages	GLOTTOCHRONOLOGY
—living things	BIOSYSTEMATICS
to their surroundings	BIONOMICS, ECOLOGY, ETHOLOGY
—mental to physical	PSYCHOPHYSICS
—perceived and actual characteristics of stimuli	PSYCHOPHYSICS
—workers to their environment	ERGONOMICS
religion	DIVINITY, THEOLOGY
religious feasts	HEORTOLOGY
replication of animal movements by machine	BIONICS
reptiles	HERPETOLOGY
rhythm	RHYTHMICS
rhythmic movement	EURHYTHMICS
rivers	LIMNOLOGY, POTAMOLOGY
rock masses	STRUCTURAL GEOLOGY
rocks	LITHOLOGY, PETROGRAPHY, MINERALOGY, ORYCTOLOGY, PETROLOGY
—layering	STRATIGRAPHICAL GEOLOGY, STRATIGRAPHY
rural economy	AGRONOMY
Russian politics	KREMLINOLOGY
sacred things	HIEROLOGY
sailing on rhumb lines	LOXODROMICS, LOXODROMY
saints' lives	HAGIOLOGY
salvation	SOTERIOLOGY
sanitary principles	HYGIENICS
seals	SPHRAGISTICS
seas	HYDROGRAPHY, OCEANOLOGY, THALASSOGRAPHY
seasons	PH(A)ENOLOGY
seaweeds	ALGOLOGY, PHYCOLOGY
secret writing	CRYPTOLOGY
secretions	ECCRINOLOGY
seeds	CARPOLOGY

self	AUTOLOGY
—regulating systems	AUTONOMICS
semantics	SEMASIOLOGY
semiconductors	SOLID STATE PHYSICS
senility	NOSTOLOGY
serums	SEROLOGY
sexual behaviour	SEXOLOGY
shape	MORPHOLOGY
shaping metals by electrical means	ELECTROMETALLURGY
shells	CONCHOLOGY
signets and seals	SPHRAGISTICS
significance of	
—terms	SIGNIFICS
—values	AXIOLOGY
signs and signals	SEM(E)IOLOGY
—in language	SEMIOTICS
skin	DERMATOLOGY
—patterns	DERMATOGLYPHICS
skull	CRANIOLOGY, PHRENOLOGY
small	
—electronic systems	MICROELECTRONICS
—objects	MICROLOGY
—organisms	MICROBIOLOGY
—quantities of chemicals	MICROCHEMISTRY
—scale weather systems	MICROMETEOROLOGY
—worlds	MICROCOSMOGRAPHY
smell	OLFACTOLOGY
snakes	HERPETOLOGY, OPHIOLOGY
social	
—anthropology	ETHNOLOGY
—behaviour	SOCIOBIOLOGY
	SOCIOMETRY
—groups	SOCIOLOGY
—types	TYPOLOGY
Socratic art	MAIEUTICS
soil	AGROLOGY, EDAPHOLOGY
	PEDOLOGY
—yields	AGROBIOLOGY
sound	ACOUSTICS, PHONICS
—applications	SONICS
—beyond human hearing	ULTRASONICS
—echoes	CATACOUSTICS
	CATAPHONICS
space travel	ASTRONAUTICS
spectra	SPECTROSCOPY
speech	
—sound in writing	GRAPHEMICS
—sounds	PHONEMICS
	PHONETICS, PHONOLOGY
spiders	ARACHNOLOGY
spiritual beings	PNEUMATOLOGY
spoken sounds	PHONICS
sponges	SPONGOLOGY

spores	PALYNOLOGY
spread of disease	EPIDEMIOLOGY
stamps	PHILATELY, TIMBROLOGY
standing water	HYDROSTATICS
stars	ASTRONOMY
static electricity	ELECTROSTATICS
statics of rigid bodies	GEOSTATICS
statistical	
—analysis of economic data	ECONOMETRICS
—biology	BIOMETRY
stomach and intestines	GASTRO-ENTEROLOGY
stones (in body)	LITHOLOGY
strata	STRATIGRAPHY
structural geology	(GEO)TECTONICS
structure of	
—metals and alloys	METALLOGRAPHY
—organisms	MORPHOLOGY
—soil, etc	AGROLOGY
	MICROMORPHOLOGY
—tissues	HISTOLOGY
subatomic particles	MICROPHYSICS
	NUCLEAR PHYSICS
sugars	GLYCOBIOLOGY
Sun	HELIOLOGY
—dials	HOROGRAPHY
surface	
—features of Earth	GEOMORPHOLOGY
—tension	STALAGMOMETRY
surfaces	TOPOLOGY
—in contact	TRIBOLOGY
symbols	SYMBOL(OL)OGY
symptoms	SEM(E)IOLOGY, SEM(E)IOTICS
	SYMPTOMATOLOGY
systems	SYSTEMATOLOGY
teaching	PEDAGOGY
technology of metals	METALLURGY
teeth	ODONTOLOGY
terrestrial magnetism	GEOMAGNETISM
theological explanations	ISAGOGICS
theory of knowledge	EPISTEMOLOGY
thermionic valves	THERMIONICS
three-dimensional vision	STEREOSCOPY
	STEREOPTICS
ticks	ACAROLOGY
time	CHRONOLOGY
—by sundial	GNOMONICS
—pieces	HOROGRAPHY, HOROLOGY
tissues	HISTOLOGY
—in relation to disease	HISTOPATHOLOGY
—round teeth	PERIDONTIA
	PERIDONTICS
	PERIDONTOLOGY
—using chemical reactions	HISTOCHEMISTRY

trajectory of missiles	BALLISTICS
transmitting messages	TELEGRAPHY
treatment of	
—diseases	THERAPEUTICS, THERAPY
—prisoners	PENOLOGY
—the aged	GERONTOTHERAPEUTICS
tree-rings	DENDROCHRONOLOGY
trees	DENDROLOGY, FORESTRY
triangles	TRIGONOMETRY
tumours	ONCOLOGY
Turin shroud	SINDONOLOGY
types	TYPOLOGY
ultimate nature	AXIOLOGY
unchanging properties	
of figures	TOPOLOGY
unclean things	COPROLOGY
unidentified flying objects	UFOLOGY
universal benevolent	
interference	PANTOPRAGMATICS
universe	COSMOLOGY
unpredictable behaviour	
in systems	CHAOLOGY
urine	UR(IN)OLOGY
variations in language	STYLISTICS
variety of humans	ETHNOLOGY
venereal disease	SYPHILOLOGY
	VENEREOLOGY
versification	PROSODY
veterinary surgery	ZOIATRICS
vines	VINOLOGY
viruses	VIROLOGY
visibility	ENTOPTICS
vision	OPTOLOGY, OPTOMETRY
volcanoes	VULCANOLOGY
wars	POLEMOLOGY
wasps	VESPOLOGY
water	
—bodies	HYDROGRAPHY
—inland	LIMNOLOGY
—resources	HYDROLOGY
wealth	CHREMATISTICS
weapons	HOPLOLOGY
wear in machinery from	
iron in lubricants	FERROGRAPHY
weather	AEROGRAPHY
	METEOROLOGY
weights and measures	METROLOGY
whales	CETOLOGY
wind	ANEMOLOGY
wine-making	ZYMURGY
wines	OENOLOGY
wisdom	PHILOSOPHY
with microscope	MICROGRAPHY
women's diseases	GYNAECOLOGY
wood	XYLOLOGY
woodlands	FORESTRY

word origins	ETYMOLOGY
working of things	BIONICS
worms	HELMINTHOLOGY
writing hymns	HYMNOGRAPHY
X-rays and gamma rays	RADIOLOGY
	ROENTGENOLOGY
	(*see also* **pertaining, write**)

Sudan

capital	EL KHARTUM, KHARTOUM
coin	
—unit	MILLIEME
—10 milliemes	PIASTRE
—100 piastres	POUND

sugar

aldehyde	ALDOSE
arabinose	PECTINOSE
artificial sweetener	SACCHARIN
beet sugar	SUCROSE
blood-sugar deficiency	HYPOGLYCAEMIA
brown crystallised	
sugar	DEMERARA
cane sugar	SUCROSE, SACCHAROSE
—residue	BAGASSE
coarse	
—Indian	GOOR, GUR, JAGGERY
—Mexican	PANOCHA, PANOCHE
common sugar	BEET SUGAR, CANE SUGAR
	SUCROSE, SACCHAROSE
compound	
—from which sugar can be	
derived	GLYCOSIDE
—with one hydrogen	
atom replaced	GLUCOSIDE
containing several	
simple sugars	POLYSACCHARIDE
converted cane-sugar	INVERT SUGAR
dextrose	GLUCOSE
disaccharide	LACTOSE, MALTOSE
	SUCROSE
excess of blood-sugar	HYPERGLYCAEMIA
finely-ground sugar	CASTER SUGAR
	CASTOR SUGAR
from	
—aldehyde	ALDOSE
—arabin	ARABINOSE
—beet	BEET SUGAR
—cane	CANE SUGAR
—cells	(DEOXY)RIBOSE
—cereals	MALTOSE
—fruit	FRUCTOSE, LAEVULOSE
—glucose	ARABINOSE, PECTINOSE
—gum	ARABINOSE, PECTINOSE
—honey	FRUCTOSE, LAEVULOSE
—lactose	GALACTOSE
—maple	MAPLE SUGAR
—nectar of flowers	FRUCTOSE, LAEVULOSE

—ribonucleic acid	RIBOSE
—starch	DEXTROSE, GLUCOSE
	MALTOSE
—various plants	DULCOSE
fructose and glucose	
mixed	INVERT SUGAR
fruit sugar	FRUCTOSE, L(A)EVULOSE
grape-sugar	DEXTROSE, GLUCOSE
	GLYCOSE
having	
—five carbon atoms	PENTOSE
—molecules with	
more than one	
monsaccharide	POLYSACCHARIDE
two monosaccharides	DISACCHARIDE
three	
monosaccharides	TRISACCHARIDE
—six carbon atoms	HEXOSE
hexose	DEXTROSE, GALACTOSE
	GLUCOSE
malt sugar	MALTOBIOSE, MALTOSE
milk sugar	LACTOSE
monosaccharide	FRUCTOSE, GALACTOSE
	GLOCUSE, HEXOSE, KETOSE
	PENTOSE, SIMPLE SUGAR
palm sugar	JAGGERY
pectinose	ARABINOSE
pentose	RIBOSE
polysaccharide	GLYCOGEN
—in	
fruit	PECTIN
insect cuticle	CHITIN
plants	PECTIN
—plants	XYLAN
—stored as food in	
algae	(CHRYSO)LAMINARIN
	LEUCOSIN
plants	INULIN
powdered	ICING SUGAR
pressed into lumps	CUBE SUGAR
refined in cigar shape	LOAF SUGAR
residue of cane sugar	BAGASSE
simple sugar	(MONO)SACCHARIDE
study of sugars	GLYCOBIOLOGY
substitute	ACESULFAME POTASSIUM
	ASPARTAME, CYCLAMATE
	GLUCOSE SYRUP, ISOMALT
	MALTITIOL, SACCHARIN(E)
	SORBITOL, THAUMATIN
	XYLITOL
—proprietary	CANDEREL, HERMESETAS
	NUTRASWEET, SWEETEX
sugar-coated	CRYSTALLISED, GLACE
sugar-regulating	
hormone	INSULIN
sugar-splitting	SUCROCLASTIC

syrup	MOLASSES, TREACLE
trisaccharide	RAFFINOSE
used for culture medium	ARABINOSE
	PECTINOSE
unrefined	BROWN SUGAR, CASSONADE
	GOOR, GUR, MUSCOVADO
wood sugar	XYLOSE
Sun	(*see* **astronomy**)
surfing	
crest of wave	LIP
cylinder formed by	
curling wave	TUBE
froth of foam	SOUP
moving from back of	
board to front	BOARDWALKING
put toes over edge	
of board	HANG FIVE, HANG TEN
reverse direction	CUTBACK
ride	
—down breaking wave	FLOATER
	GO OVER THE FALLS
—over edge of wave	AERIAL
shoot off top of wave	OFF-THE-LIP
surfers	
—Australian	ELKERTON, HORAN
	MACAULAY
—British	HARDMAN, LYNCH, POTTER
	WILLIAMS
—Hawaiian	BURNS, DAVID, GARCIA
	HO, OCEAN PACIFIC PRO
tournaments	BILLABONG, MARUI MASTERS
turn full circle	THREE-SIXTY
venues	
—Britain	CORNWALL
—California	BIG SUR
	HUNTINGTON BEACH
—France	BIARRITZ, COTE SAUVAGE
	LACANAU, LA SAUZAIE
	LE ROZEL, LES CAVALIERS
	SEIGNOSSE, SIOUVILLE
—Hawaii	NORTH SHORE, PIPELINE
	SUNSET BEACH, WAIMEA BAY
—Portugal	COXOS, MACHO LESTE
	RIBIERA D'ILHAS
—South Africa	BAY OF PLENTY
—Spain	LOS LOCOS, MUNDACO
surgery	
including: medical instruments	
surgical instruments	
atomiser	NEBULISER
brain surgery	PSYCHOSURGERY
crushing of bladder stone	LASERTRIPTY
	LITHOLAPAXY
cutting into	
—2 parts	BISECTION, DICHOTOMY
—3 parts	TRISECTION, TRICHOTOMY

—4 parts	QUADRISECTION	—windpipe	TRACHEO(S)TOMY	
	TETRACHOTOMY	—womb	HYSTEROTOMY, UTEROTOMY	
—abdominal wall	LAPAROTOMY	cutting out		
—animals	ZOOTOMY	—adenoids	ADENOIDECTOMY	
—artery	ARTERIOTOMY	—appendix	APPEND(IC)ECTOMY	
—beard	POGONOTOMY	—bladder	CYSTECTOMY	
—bladder	CYSTOTOMY	—bone	OSTECTOMY	
—bodies of animals	ZOOTOMY	of middle ear	STAPEDECTOMY	
—bone	OSTEOTOMY	—bony plate	LAMINECTOMY	
—bowel	ENTERO(S)TOMY	—bowel	ENTERECTOMY	
—brain	ENCEPHALOTOMY, LEUCOTOMY	—breast	MASTECTOMY	
	LOBOTOMY	—cerebral cortex	TOPECTOMY	
—chest cavity	THORACTOMY	—duodenum	DUODENECTOMY	
—colon	COLOTOMY	—Fallopian tubes	SALPINGECTOMY	
—cornea	KERATOTOMY		TUBECTOMY	
—ear-drum	MYRINGOTOMY	—gall-bladder	CHOLECYSTECTOMY	
—front of brain	LEUCOTOMY, LEUKOTOMY	—gland	ADENECTOMY	
	LOBOTOMY	—gums	GINGIVECTOMY	
—gall-bladder	CHOLECYSTO(S)TOMY	—intestines	ENTERECTOMY	
—head	CEPHALOTOMY	—iris	IRIDECTOMY	
of foetus	CRANIOTOMY	—kidney	NEPHRECTOMY	
—human anatomy	ANTHROPOTOMY	—larynx	LARYNGECTOMY	
—inner ear	FENESTRATION	—liver	HEPATECTOMY	
—iris	IRIDOTOMY	—lobe (of lung)	LOBECTOMY	
—intestine	ENTERO(S)TOMY	—lump in breast	LUMPECTOMY	
—kidney	NEPHROTOMY		TYLECTOMY	
—larynx	LARYNGOTOMY	—lung	PNEUMONECTOMY	
—living animal	VIVISECTION	—nerve	SYMPATHECTOMY	
—lobe of organ	LOBOTOMY	—organ	ABLATION, EXCISION	
—lung tissue	PNEUMONECTOMY		EXTIRPATION	
—nerve	NEUROTOMY	—ovaries	OOPHORECTOMY	
fibres in neck	CORDOTOMY		OVARIECTOMY	
roots	RHIZOTOMY	—part of body	ABLATION, AMPUTATION	
—ovary	OVARIOTOMY		EXCISION, EXTIRPATION	
—perin(a)eum	EPISIOTOMY	—pituitary body	HYPOPHYSECTOMY	
—pharynx	PHARYNGOTOMY	—prostate gland	PROSTATECTOMY	
—plant	PHYTOTOMY	—root of tooth	APICECTOMY	
—pleura	PLEUROTOMY	—specimen	BIOPSY	
—pubic junction	SYMPHYSEOTOMY	—sperm duct	VASECTOMY	
	SYMPHESIOTOMY	—spleen	SPLENECTOMY	
—skull	CRANIOTOMY	—stomach	GASTRECTOMY	
—solids	STEREOTOMY	—sympathetic nerve	SYMPATHECTOMY	
—spine	CORDOTOMY	—testicle	ORCHIDECTOMY	
—stomach	GASTROTOMY	—tongue	GLOSSECTOMY	
—tendon	TENOTOMY	—tonsils	TONSIL(L)ECTOMY	
—thorax	THORACOTOMY	—uterus	HYSTERECTOMY	
—to			UTERECTOMY	
cure squinting	STRABOTOMY	—wrinkles	RHYTIDECTOMY	
make opening	SYRINGOTOMY	delivery of foetus		
remove stones	LITHOTOMY	surgically	CAESARIAN SECTION	
—tonsils	TOLSIL(L)OTOMY	destruction of		
—trachea	TRACHEO(S)TOMY	—brain tissue using		
—tumour	ONCOTOMY	electricity	STEREOTAXIA	
—uterus	HYSTEROTOMY, UTEROTOMY	—tissues by burning	CAUTERY	
—vagina	EPISOTOMY	drainage of fluid		
—vein	PHLEBOTOMY, VENESECTION	from eye	GONIOPUNCTURE	

facelift	RHYTIDECTOMY	field of vision	PERIMETER
forming		oxygen in blood	PULSE OXIMETER
—artificial anus	COLOSTOMY	sharpness of hearing	AUDIOMETER
—opening	SYRINGOTOMY	—opening a body	
fracture of bone	OSTEOCLASIS	passage	SPECULUM
instrument for		—percussion	PLESSOR, PLEXOR
—artificial respiration	IRON LUNG		PLESSIMETER, PLEXIMETER
—auscultation	STETHOSCOPE	—piercing	TROCAR
—breaking bones	OSTEOCLAST	—pressing down	DEPRESSOR
—collecting cells from		—recording	
cervix	CYTOBRUSH	brain	
—cutting	BISTOURY, ECRASEUR	activity	ELECTROENCEPHALOGRAPH
	FLEAM, LANCET, SCALPEL	changes in heartbeat,	
bone	OSTEOTOME	breathing and blood	
brain tissue	LEUCOTOME	pressure	POLYGRAPH
discs of bone		heartbeats	ELECTROCARDIOGRAPH
from skull	TREPAN, TREPHINE	muscle activity	ELECTROMYOGRAPH
skin for grafting	DERMATOME	variations in blood	
stones	LITHOTOME	pressure	KYMOGRAPH
—crushing stones in body	LITHOCLAST	—removing	
	LITHO(N)TRI(P)TOR	liquids from	
	LITHOTRITE	body cavity	ASPIRATOR, CATHETER
—delivery of babies	FORCEPS, RONGEUR	obstruction in	
—destruction of tissues		—bronchi	BRONCHOSCOPE
by burning	CAUTER(Y)	—throat	PROBANG
—dilating	BOUGIE	stones from bladder	GORGET
—draining or injecting fluid	CANNULA	tumours	ECRASEUR, SNARE
—examination of		—resuscitation	DEFIBRILLATOR
bladder	CYSTOSCOPE	—scraping	CURETTE
bronchi	BRONCHOSCOPE	bones	RASPATORY, XYSTER
ear	OTOSCOPE	uterus	RESECTOSCOPE
eardrum	MYRINGOSCOPE	—stretching canals	BOUGIE
eye	OPHTHALMOSCOPE	—three-dimensional	
	RETINOSCOPE	X-ray photographs	CAT SCANNER
interior of stomach	GASTROSCOPE		(*see also* **X-ray**)
internal		listening (to lungs etc)	AUSCULTATION
—cavities	ENDOSCOPE	opening artifically made	FISTULA
—organs	LAPAROSCOPE	piercing	PARACENTESIS
—parts	FLUOROSCOPE	—intestine	ENTEROCENTESIS
joints	ARTHROSCOPE	—uterus	AMNIOCENTESIS
lower colon	SIGMOIDOSCOPE	—vein	VENEPUNCTURE
lungs	STETHOSCOPE		VENIPUNCTURE
neck of uterus	COLPOSCOPE	plastic surgery	(*see* repair *below*)
nose	RHINOSCOPE	reflex separation	AUTOTOMY
tissues and organs	FIBRESCOPE	removing	
—examination using		—dead tissue	DEBRIDEMENT
ultra-sound	SOMASCOPE		NECROTOMY
—fracturing bone	OSTEOCLAST	—gall stones	CHOLELITHOTOMY
—holding open incisions	RETRACTOR	—kidney stones	LITHONEPHROTOMY
—incision	LANCET, SCALPEL	—stones in the body	LITHOTOMY
—injecting	CANNULA, CATHETER	repairing or reshaping	
	HYPODERMIC NEEDLE	—artery	ARTERIOPLASTY
—lifting and holding		—bone	OSTEOPLASTY
blood vessels	TENACULUM	—breast	MAMMOPLASTY
—measuring		—chest wall	THORACOPLASTY
blood pressure	SPHYGMO(MANO)METER	—cornea	KEROTOPLASTY

—damaged tissue	ALLOGRAFT	coin	
	AUTOGRAFT	—unit	ORE
	AUTOPLASTY, HOMOGRAFT	—100 øre	KR, KRONA
	HOMOPLASTY	complaints officer	OMBUDSMAN
—ear	OTOPLASTY	farm	TORP
—mouth	STOMATOPLASTY	harbour	HAMN
—nose	RHINOPLASTY	hors d'oeuvres	SMORGASBORD
—roof of mouth	URANOPLASTY	manual training	SLOID, SLOYD
removal of tissue for		measure (2/3 acre)	MORGEN
examination	BIOPSY	moor	MYR
scraping	CURETTAGE	mountain	BERG, FJALL
self-amputation	AUTOTOMY	parliament	RIKSDAG
separation after fracture		province	LAN
or wound	ABDUCTION	provincial council	LANDST(H)ING
sew up wound	SUTURE	river	ALV(EN)
spray	NEBULISER	saint	SANKT
sterilisation		secret police	SAPO
—female	TUBAL LIGATION	strait	SUND
—male	CASTRATION, VASECTOMY	swamp	MYR
stitch in wound	SUTURE	toast	SKOAL
surgeon	VET	turnip	RUTABAGA
surgeons	RCS	valley	DAL
	(*see also* **physician**)	wild turnip	NAVEW
surgical thread	LIGATURE	**sweets**	
tapping (fluids)	PARACENTESIS	almond	
	(*see also* piercing *above*)	—flavoured	MACAROON
Surinam(e)		—paste	MARZIPAN
capital	PARAMARIBO	aromatic	COUGH DROP, LOZENGE
coin	CENT, GULDEN		PASTIL(LE), PEPPERMINT
	GUILDER, FLORIN	chewy	BUBBLE GUM, CHEWING GUM
swamp	BOG, FEN, MARSH, MORASS		NOUGAT, TOFFEE
	(QUAG)MIRE, SLOUGH	chocolate	
	SWALE, WASH	—coated	BONBON
American	BAYOU, EVERGLADES	—disc	CHOCOLATE DROP
	VLEI, VLY	covered with coloured	
Canadian	MUSKEG	sugar balls	NONPAREIL
exhalation from marsh	MIASM(A)	—drop	DRAGEE
light hanging		coconut and sugar	COCONUT ICE
over marsh	FRIAR'S LANTERN	crystallised sugar	CANDY
	IGNIS FATUUS	flat	
	JACK-O'-LANTERN	—boiled sweet	LOLLIPOP, LOLLYPOP
	WILL-O'-THE-WISP	—liquorice	POMFRET CAKE
marsh-gas	METHANE		PONTEFRACT CAKE
South African	VLEI, VLY	flavoured boiled sweet	SUGARPLUM
Swaziland	SZD	frozen	ICE CREAM
capital	MBABANE	—between biscuit layers	WAFER
coin	CENT, LILANGENI	—covered in chocolate	CHOC-ICE
Sweden	S	—in conical biscuit	CORNET
aeroplane	SAAB	—on a stick	ICE LOLLY
airline	SAS	hard	BOILED SWEET
bay	BUKT(EN)	ice-cream	(*see* **desserts**)
beach	STRAND	jelly cubes, dusted	
cape (headland)	UDDEN	with sugar	LOK(O)UM
capital	STOCKHOLM		TURKISH DELIGHT
chief magistrate	LANDAMMAN(N)	large round sweet	BULLSEYE, GOBSTOPPER
clover	ALSIKE		JAWBREAKER

liquorice	
—sweet	POMFRET CAKE
	PONTEFRACT CAKE
mixture	LIQUORICE ALLSORTS
lozenge	CACHOU
medicated	COUGH SWEET, LOZENGE
	PASTIL(LE)
mixed sweets	DOLLY MIXTURE
nougat (Italian)	TORRONE
nuts	
—fruit, etc, in sugar	SWEETMEAT
—in	
boiled sugar	BRITTLE
sugar paste	NOUGAT
on a stick	TOFFEE APPLE
scented	CACHOU
silvered ball	DRAGEE
small	HUNDREDS AND THOUSANDS
soft and spongy	MARSHMALLOW
spun sugar	CANDY FLOSS
stick of boiled sugar	ROCK
—America	ROCK CANDY
stickjaw	TOFFEE
sticky	CARAMEL, TOFFEE
sugar-coated nut	COMFIT, DRAGEE
	PRALINE, PRAWLIN
	SUGARED ALMOND
sweetened cocoa block	CHOCOLATE
toffee	STICKJAW, TOM-TROT
—butter	BUTTERSCOTCH
—chewy	CARAMEL
thin piece of	
chocolate	LANGUE-DE-CHAT
tom-trot	TOFFEE
Turkish delight	LOK(O)UM
swimming	
including: divers	
diving	
divers	
—American (m)	DESJARDINS, GALITZEN
	LOUGHANIS, LEE, PINKSTON
	TOBIAN, WEBSTER, WHITE
(f)	BECKER, COLEMAN
	MCCORMICK, POYNTON-HILL
	RIGGIN
—British (m)	PHELPS
(f)	FERRIS
—Canadian (f)	BERNIER
—Chinese (f)	JIHONG
—Czech (f)	DUCHKOVA
—German (f)	ENGEL-KRAMER
—Italian (m)	DIBIASI
—Japanese (m)	OHTSUBO
—Mexican (m)	CAPILLA, PEREZ
—Russian (m)	PORTNOV, VASIN
(f)	KALININA

diving	
—events	HIGH BOARD, SPRINGBOARD
—movements	PIKE, SOMERSAULT
	TUCK, TWIST
strokes	BACKSTROKE, BREAST STROKE
	BUTTERFLY, CRAWL, FREESTYLE
swimmers	
—American (m)	BURTON, GAINES
	GOODELL, HENCKEN, HICKOK
	KAHANAMOKU, KEALOHA
	NABER, SCHOLLANDER
	SPITZ, LUNDQUIST
	WEISSMULLER
(f)	ANDREWS, BABASHOFF
	CAULKINS, COHEN, HOGSHEAD
	KOLB, LUNDQUIST, MCFARLANE
	MEAGHER, MEYER, NORELIUS
	ROTHHAMMER, STEINSEIFER
	WAITE
—Australian (m)	BAILDON, ROSE, SIEBEN
	THIELE, WENDEN
(f)	CRAPP, FORD
	FRASER, GOLD
—British (m)	GOODHEW, HOLMAN
	JARVIS, MOORHOUSE
	ROBINSON, TAYLOR, WILKIE
(f)	BROWNSDON, COOMBES
	DAVIES, FOOT, GRINHAM
	LONSBOROUGH
	SCARBOROUGH
—Canadian (m)	BAUMANN, DAVIS
	DRAXINGER, KELLY
	TEWKSBURY
(f)	DUGGAN, GIGWERE
	OTTENBRITE
—Chinese (m)	JIANGIANG
—Cuban (m)	HERNANDEZ
—Danish (m)	JENSEN, JACOBSEN
—Dutch (m)	ELZERMANN
(f)	DE ROVER, MASTENBROEK
	MUIS, NORD
—German (m)	AROSS, HACKMAN
	HASE, HERMANN
	HOFFMEISTER, MATTHES
	PYTTER, SITT, WARNECKE
	WEBER, WOITHE
(f)	ENDER, FRIETSCHE
	JAHNICHEN, KRAUSE
	ORTWIG, OSYGUS, REINECH
	RICHTER, STEVENS
	STRAUSS, THURMER
—Italian (m)	LAMBERTI
(f)	DALLAVALLE
—Japanese (m)	KIYOKAWA, SUZUKI
	TAGUCHI, TAKASE
	TSURUTA, YAMANAKA

(f)	NATSUME, SHITO	curved sword	SABRE, S(C)IMITAR
	TANAKA, TSURUTA	Damascene	DAMASCUS BLADE
—Norwegian (f)	DALBY	Doge's bodyguard's	
—Russian (m)	FESENKO, KOPLIAKOV	sword	SCHIAVONE
	SALNIKOV, VOLKOV, ZULPA	duelling-sword	SHARP, SMALL-SWORD
(f)	KASKUSHITE, KOSHEVAIA	engraved	DAMASCE(E)NE, DAMASKEEN
—Swedish (m)	ARVIDSSON, BORG		DAMASKIN, DAMASQUIN
	HENNING, HOLMERTZ	—sword	DAMASCUS BLADE
	LARSSON	fencing weapon	EPEE, FOIL, SMALL-SWORD
(f)	CEDERQUIST	fighting sword	ESPADRON, SPADROON
team		fight with swords	DIGLADIATE
—game	AQUAPUSH	German	SCHLAGER
	UNDERWATER HOCKEY	Indian	TULWAR
	WATER POLO	Lewis Carroll's sword	VORPAL
—swimming	SYNCHRONISED SWIMMING	long slender sword	RAPIER
underwater swimming	SCUBA DIVING	King Edward's	
	SNORKELLING	sword	(*see* sword of mercy *below*)
Swiss	HELVETIAN	knob on hilt	POMMEL
alpenhorn melody	RANZ-DES-VACHES	naval sword	CUTLASS
cabin	CHALET	—short	HANGER
cantons	AARGAU, BASELLAND, BERN(E)	Norse myth	BALMUNG, GRAM
	FRIBOURG, GLARUS, GRABUNDEN	obsolete	FOX
	JURA, NEUCHATEL, NIDWALDEN	old sword	GLAIVE
	ST GALLEN, SCHAFFHAUSEN, SCHWYZ	part of	
	SOLOTHURN, THURGAU, TICINO	—guard	KNUCKLE-BOW
	UNTERWALDEN, URI, VAUD	—rapier blade	RICASSO
	WAADT, WALLIS, ZURICH	Persian	S(C)IMITAR
capital	BERN(E)	rapier	BILBO
coin	FRANC, RAPPEN	—(Shak.)	TUCK
dish	BERNERPLATTE, MUESLI	rare	GLADIUS
division	CANTON	Roland's sword	CO(U)RTAIN
dried potatoes	RO(E)STI	Roman	GLADIUS, SPATHA
herdsman's song	RANZ-DES-VACHES	St George's sword	ASCALON, ASKELON
hero	TELL	Saxon	SEAX
magistrate	AM(T)MAN	Scots	CLAYMORE
measure (small)	LIGNE		SPURTLE-BLADE
sled	LUGE	—rusty	SHABBLE
Switzerland	CH	short sword	ESTOC
sword	BRAND, GLAIVE	—curved	FALCHION, FAULCHI(O)N
	WHITE ARM	—naval	HANGER
arm of cross-guard	QUILLON	Siegfried's sword	BALMUNG
Arthur's sword	CALIBURN, EXCALIBAR	Siegmund's sword	GRAM, NOTHUNG
	EXCALIBUR	Sir Bevis's sword	MORGLAY
blunted sword	CURTANA, CURTA(E)	small sword	SHARP
	CURTEIN(E), CURTEYNE	Spanish	BILBO, ESPADA
broad-bladed	BACKSWORD		ESPADIN, ESTOQUE
	BROADSWORD	suspended	SWORD OF DAMOCLES
—curved sword	SEAX	sword of mercy	CURTANA, CURTAN(E)
—sword (short)	CURTAL-AX		CURTEIN(E), CURTEYNE
bullfighter's sword	ESTOQUE	sword-bearer	BALDRIC(K), SELICTAR
cavalry sword	SABRE	swordsman	SPADASSIN
Celtic	CLAYMORE, CLEDDYO	Turkish	SCIMITAR
ceremonial sword	CURTEIN	two-edged sword	PATA
Charlemagne's sword	FLAMBERGE	wooden sword	WASTER
concealed	JACOB'S-STAFF	**Syriac**	
	SWORD-CANE, SWORD-STICK	alphabet	ESTRANG(H)ELO

bishop	ABBA	—100 piastres	POUND
testament	PESHITTA, PESHIT(T)O	dynasty	SELEUCID
Syrian	SYR	garment	AB(B)A, ABAYA
abbess	AMMA	hyrax	DAMAN
Aramaic dialect	SYRIAC	newspaper	AL-THAWRA
bishop	ABBA	nomad	SARACEN
capital	DAMASCUS, DIMASHQ	plant	ROSE OF JERICHO
chief priest (Roman)	SYRIARCH	pot-herb	JEW'S MALLOW
cloth	AB(B)A, ABAYA	rue	HARMALA, HARMEL
coin		sect	DRUSE, DRUZ(E)
—unit	PIASTRE	society	REMOBOTH
		tobacco	LATAKIA

T

Taiwan	RC
capital	TEIPEI
coin	CENT, DOLLAR
Tanganyika	EAK
tanks	
American	ABRAMS, BULLDOG
	CALLIOPE, CHAFFEE
	CHRISTIE, GRANT, LEE, PERSHING
	PRIEST, SHERMAN, WALKER, WHIZBANG
British	ARTHUR, BIG WILLIE
	CARDEN-LLOYD, CENTAUR, CENTURION
	CHALLENGER, CHIEFTAIN
	CHURCHILL, COMET, CONQUEROR
	COVENANTER, CROMWELL, CRUSADER
	FIREFLY, HONEY, INDEPENDENT
	INTERNATIONAL, LIBERTY, MATILDA
	MORRIS-MARTEL, MOTHER, SCORPION
	VALENTINE, VICKERS, WARRIOR
—with 6-pdr gun	MALE
—with machine-guns only	FEMALE
French	CHAR D'ASSAUT
	CHAR ST CHAMOND, RENAULT
	SCHNEIDER
German	ELEFANT, FERDINAND
	KOENIGSTIGER, LEOPARD
	(JAGD) PANTHER
	PANZERBEFEHLSWAGEN
	PANZERJAGER, PANZERKAMPWAGEN
	ROYAL TIGER, STURMMORSER
	STURMPANZER, STURMTIGER
	(JAGD) TIGER, (KING) TIGER,
Tanzania	EAT, EAZ
capital	DODOMA
coin	CENT, SHILLING
tea	
black	CAPER-TEA, OOTAK
China	BOHEA, CAPER-TEA, CONGO(U)
	DIMBULA, GUNPOWDER
	HYSON, JASMINE, KEEMUN
	LAPSANG SOUCHONG, LYCHEE
	NUWARA ELIYA, OOLONG, OULONG
	PADRA, PEKOE, POUCHONG
	TWANKAY, YUNNA, UVA
flavoured	
—bergamot	EARL GREY
—lemon	LEMON TEA
—rose petals	ROSE PUCHONG
green	HYSON, TWANKAY

herbal	CAMOMILE, PEPPERMINT
	ROSE-HIP
hot water, milk, etc	CAMBRIC TEA
India	ASSAM, DARJEELING
	NILGIRI
Labrador	LEDUM
Mexico	CHIA
Paraguay	MATE
purgative	SENNA
small leaves	DUST, FANNINGS
South America	YERBA (DE MATE)
Sri Lanka	CEYLON, DIMBULA, URA
teeth	CHOPPERS
artificial teeth	CAP, CROWN
	DENTURES, FALSE TEETH
bone holding teeth	DENTARY
	PREMAXILLA
broken tooth	SNAGGLETOOTH
care of teeth	DENTISTRY
cavity	
—in tooth	PULP CAVITY
—into which tooth fits	ALVEOLUS
cell forming dentine	ODONTOBLAST
cleaning materials	DENTAL FLOSS
	DENTIFRICE, TOOTH PASTE
	TOOTH POWDER
corrective wiring	BRACE
crushing tooth	MOLAR
—with deciduous	
predecessor	PREMOLAR
cusp of molar	METACONE
cutting	
—of teeth	DENTITION, ODONTIASIS
—tooth	INCISOR
decay	(DENTAL) CARIES
dental x-rays	BITE-WING, PANORAMIC
	PERIAPICAL
dentist	ODONTIST
description	ODONTOGRAPHY
diagram of arrangement	
of teeth	DENTAL FORMULA
false teeth	DENTURES
film of bacteria etc on teeth	PLAQUE
first set of teeth	DECIDUOUS TEETH
	MILK TEETH
fossil tooth	ODONTOLITE
gum disease	GINGIVITIS, PYORRHOEA
hard film	SCALE
having	
—crescent-shaped ridges	
in teeth	SELENODONT
—cutting back teeth	SECODONT
—more than two dentitions	POLYPHYDONT
—nodules on teeth	BUNODONT
—rounded teeth	CRENATE
—teeth	DENTIGEROUS

all the same	HOMODONT
like a shrew	SORICIDENT
of different kinds	HETERODONT
on inside of jawbone	PLEURODONT
—toothed jaws	ODONTOSTOMATOUS
—transverse ridges on teeth	LIPHODONT
horse's canine	TUSH
in pharynx of wheel-animalcules	TROPHI
long pointed tooth	CANINE, DOG-TOOTH
	EYE-TOOTH, FANG
	TUSH, TUSK
molar	MOLENDINAR, WANG(-TOOTH)
origin of teeth	ODONTOGENY
premolar	BICUSPID
projection on tooth	CUSP
repair	BRACE, BRIDGE, FILLING
scissor-tooth in carnivore	CARNASSIAL TOOTH
second set of teeth	PERMANENT TEETH
small	
—toothlike structure	DENTEL
	DENTICLE, DENTIL
—tusk	TUSH
socket	ALVEOLUS
space between teeth	DIASTEMA
sprouting of teeth	DENTITION
sticky film	PLAQUE
study	ODONTOLOGY
substance	
—covering teeth	ENAMEL
—of which teeth are made	DENTIN(E)
third molar	WISDOM TOOTH
tooth	CRENA
—ache	DENTAGRA
	ODONTALGIA, ODONTALGY
toothed whale	ODONTOCETE
toothlike	
—decoration	DENTELLE
—projection	DENTATION
treatment of	
—teeth	DENTISTRY
—tissues round teeth	PERIDONTIA
	PERIDONTICS
	PERIDONTOLOGY
tumour	ODONTOMA
types	CANINE, EYETOOTH, INCISOR
	(PRE-)MOLAR, WISDOM
upper	
—canine	EYE-TOOTH
—tooth (fish)	VOMERINE TOOTH
telescope	(*see* **observatory**)
temple	(*see* **church—buildings**)
ten	
based	DECIMAL, DENARY
cents	DIME

combining form	DECA-
groups	DECAD, DECADE, DENARY
having 10	
—arms	DECAPODAL, DECAPODAN
	DECAPODOUS
—columns	DECASTYLE
—faces	DECAHEDRON
—feet	DECAPODAL, DECAPODAN
	DECAPODOUS
—lines (poem)	DECASTICH
—parts	DECAMEROUS
—pistils	DECAGYNIAN, DECAGYNOUS
—sides	DECAGON
—stamens	DECANDRIAN, DECANDROUS
—syllables	DECASYLLABLE
Christmas presents	LORDS
Commandments	DECALOGUE, FINGERNAILS
dollar bill	SAWBUCK, TENSPOT
events	DECATHLON
fold	DECUPLE
gallon hat	SOMBRERO
gram(me)s	DECAGRAM(ME)
Green...	BOTTLES
litres	DECALITRE
Little...	NIGGERS
Lost Tribes	ASHER, EPHRAIM, DAN, GAD
	ISSACHAR, MANNASEH
	NAPHTALI, REUBEN
	SIMEON, ZEBULUN
men (Roman)	DECEMVIR
metres	DECAMETRE
steres	DECASTERE
thousand	MYRIAD, TOMAN, X
years	DECADE, DECENNARY
	DECENNIUM

tennis

area within which served ball must land	SERVICE-COURT
ball served and	
—landing outside service area	FAULT
—striking net but landing in service court	LET, NET
championship of Australia, France, UK and USA	GRAND SLAM
courts	CLAY, GRASS, HARD
	INDOOR
first stroke	SERVICE
four major championships	GRAND SLAM
group of	
—games	SET
—sets	MATCH
line at	
—end of court	BASELINE
	SERVICE-LINE
—side of court	SIDELINE, TRAMLINE

officials	LINE-JUDGE, REFEREE
	UMPIRE
put ball into play	SERVE
players	
—American (m)	AGASSI, AUSTIN, CHANG
	CONNORS, FALKENBURG, FLACH
	FLEMING, GERULAITAS, GILBERT
	GONZALES, GOTTFRIED, KRAMER
	MCENROE, MAYER, MCKINLEY
	MULLOY, OLMEDO, PARKER
	PATTY, RALSTON, REISSEN
	SAVITT, SCHROEDER, SEGUSO
	SEIXAS, SMITH, TILDEN
	TRABERT
(f)	ARTH, AUSTIN, BROUGH
	CAPRIATI, CASALS, CONNOLLY
	EVERT, FRY, GIBSON, HARD, HART
	JORDAN, KING, KIYOMURA, LLOYD
	MICHEL, MOFFITT, RICHEY
	RUSSELL, SHRIVER, SMITH
	SUSMAN, TODD
—Argentinian (m)	MANICINI
(f)	SABATINI
—Australian (m)	BROMWICH, CASE, CASH
	COOPER, DAVIDSON, EMERSON
	FLETCHER, FRASER, HARTWIG
	HEWITT, HOAD, HOWE, LAVER
	MASTERS, MCGREGOR, MCNAMARA
	MCNAMEE, NEWCOMBE, QUIST
	ROCHE, ROSE, ROSEWALL
	SEDGMAN, STONE
(f)	CAWLEY, COGHLAN, COURT
	GOOLAGONG, REID, SMITH
	SMYLIE, TEGART, TURNBULL
	TURNER
—Brazilian (m)	BUENO
—British (m)	BATES, LLOYD, PERRY
(f)	BUXTON, DURIE, JONES
	MOODY, MORTIMER, SCRIVEN
	SHILCOCK, WADE
—Bulgarian	MALEEVA
—Czech (m)	DROBNY, KODES
	LENDL, MECIR
(f)	MANDLIKOVA, NAVRATILOVA
	SUKOVA
—Dutch (m)	SCHAPERS
(f)	STOVE
—Ecuadorian	GOMEZ
—French (m)	BOROTRA, NOAH, LECONTE
	PARADIS, PETRA
(f)	DURR, LENGLEN
—German (m)	BECKER, VON CRAMM
(f)	GRAFF, KOHDE-KILSH
—Hungarian (m)	TAROCZY
—Japanese (f)	SAWAMATSU
—Mexican (m)	OSUNA, PALAFOX, RAMIREZ

—Romanian	NASTASE
—South African (m)	CURREN, HEWITT
	MCMILLAN, STURGESS
(f)	STEVENS, SUMMERS
—Spanish (m)	SANCHEZ, SANTANA
(f)	MARTINEZ
—Swedish (m)	BORG, EDBERG
	GUNNARSSON, JARRYD
	NYSTROM, WILANDER
—Swiss	GUNTHARD
—Yugoslav (f)	SELES
playing area	COURT
rebound	BRICOLE
scores	
—nil	LOVE
—first point	FIFTEEN
—second point	THIRTY
—third point	FORTY
—three points each	DEUCE
—point after deuce	ADVANTAGE
—final point	GAME
scoring unit	POINT
service with foot in front	
of baseline	FOOT FAULT
short game to decide winner	
of tied game	TIE-BREAK
strokes	BACKHAND, FOREHAND
	HALF-VOLLEY, LOB, SERVICE
	SMASH, (STOP-)VOLLEY
venues	
—America	BOSTON, FLUSHING MEADOW
	KEY BISCAYNE, INDIAN WELLS
	MADISON SQUARE GARDEN
	NEWPORT, PHILADELPHIA
—Australia	MELBOURNE
—Britain	BECKENHAM, BRIGHTON
	DEVONSHIRE PARK
	EASTBOURNE, EDGBASTON
	QUEEN'S CLUB, TELFORD
	WEMBLEY, WEST KIRBY
	WIMBLEDON
—France	ROLAND GARROS STADIUM
	PARIS
—Germany	DUSSELDORF, FRANKFURT
	HAMBURG, STUTTGART
—Monaco	MONTE CARLO
—Switzerland	GSTAAD
tenth	
tenth in methane series	DECANE
tenth of	
—are	DECIARE
—bel	DECIBEL
—franc	DECIME
—gram(me)	DECIGRAM(ME)
—litre	DECILITRE
—metre	DECIMETRE

—normal concentration	DECINORMAL
—stere	DECISTERE
Thailand	T
	(*see also* **Siamese**)
theatre	
accommodation for	
prompter	PROMPT BOX
acting	
—production or study	
of plays	DRAMATICS
—style identifying	
with character	METHOD (ACTING)
actor(actress)	
—delivering	
closing speech	EPILOGUE
opening speech	PROLOGUE
—in	
comedy	COMEDIAN(-ENNE)
folk drama	MUMMER
tragedy	TRAGEDIAN(-ENNE)
actors	
—American	STRASBERG
—British	BARKWORTH, BUCHANAN
CHARLESON, CONTI, COWARD, COWEN	
DENNISON, DEVINE, DU MAURIER	
FINLAY, GODFREY, GUINNESS, HARRIS	
HARRISON, HORDERN, IRVING	
JOHNS, KEMBLE, MCCOWAN	
MCKELLAN, MILLER, MILLS	
NEVILLE, OLIVIER, QUAYLE	
QUILLEY, SCOFIELD, SUTHERLAND	
TREE, USTINOV, VAN GYSEGHEM	
WOLFIT	
—French	ARTAUD, BARRAULT
COREAU, DASTE, DULLIN	
JOUVET, GERARD, PITOEFF	
TALMA	
—German	HILPERT
—Irish	HARRIS, MAC LIAMMOIR
—Roman	ROSCIUS
—Russian	MEYERHOLD, OKHLOPKOV
PITOEFF, STANISLAVSKY	
VAKTANGOV	
(*see also* **cinema**)	
actors' trade union	EQUITY
actresses	
—American	HAYES, MALINA
—British	ASHCROFT, ASHER
BENNETT, CAMPBELL	
COURTNEIGE, DENCH, EVANS	
GRAY, HIRD	
JACKSON, KENDAL, LANGTRY	
LAYE, LEIGH, MILES, PLOWRIGHT	
SCALES, SEYLER, SMITH, THORNDIKE	
TUTIN, TEMPEST, WORTH	
—Canadian	LILLIE

—French	BERNHARDT, FEUILLERE
	SIGNORET
—German	MALINA, WEIGEL
—Greek	MERCOURI
—New Zealand	PORTER
	(*see also* **cinema**)
allegorical play	MORALITY PLAY
American repertory	
company	STOCK COMPANY
ancient farcical play	MIME
astonishing piece of	
stagecraft	COUP DE THEATRE
back-stage rest-room	GREEN ROOM
climax or unravelling	CATASTROPHE
	DENOUEMENT
characters in play	CAST
	DRAMATIS PERSONAE
	ENSEMBLE
chief actor	LEADING MAN
	PROTAGONIST
—actress	LEADING LADY
comedy of hopelessness	BLACK COMEDY
	PIECE NOIRE
contrived solution	DEUS EX MACHINA
copy of script used	
by prompter	PROMPT-BOOK
	PROMPT-COPY
courtly spectacle	MASQUE
curtain drawn upward	
and outward	TABLEAU CURTAIN
—hiding scene changes	DROP CURTAIN
	DROP SCENE
—to contain fire	SAFETY CURTAIN
curved backcloth	CLYCLORAMA
deliberate effect of	
reducing audience	
involvement	A-EFFECT
	ALIENATION EFFECT
dialogue in alternate	
lines	STICHOMYTHIA
dramatists	(*see separate entry*)
entertainment between	
acts	DIVERTISSEMENT
	ENTR'ACTE, INTERLUDE
first part of play	PROTASIS
forget one's lines	
on stage	DRY (UP)
German theatre	
association	PEOPLE'S STAGE
	VOLKESBUHNE
god brought in by	
mechanical device	DEUS EX MACHINA
Greek theatre	ODEON
group of	
—3 related dramas	TRILOGY
—4 related dramas	TETRALOGY

—actors chanting comment	CHORUS
—supporting actors	ENSEMBLE
guild comedy of Italian	
Renaissance	COMMEDIA DELL'ARTE
height of drama	CATASTATIS
humorous play	COMEDY
horror play	GRAND GUIGNOL
imitation blood	KENSINGTON GORE
incidental actions	
by actor	BUSINESS
Japanese play	KABUKI
	NOGAKU, NO(H)
laugh on stage at	
inappropriate time	CORPSE
lights	
—at front of stage	FLOATS
	FOOTLIGHTS
—overhead	FLOODS, SPOTS
living picture	TABLEAU (VIVANT)
London theatre group	THEATRE WORKSHOP
	UNITY THEATRE
main action of Greek	
drama	EPITASIS
method acting	STANISLAVSKY METHOD
monologue by character	
to himself	SOLILOQUY
motionless	
representation	TABLEAU (VIVANT)
movement of chorus	
to one side	STROPHE
narrative style	EPIC THEATRE
one	
—in charge of	
costumes	DRESSER
furniture, etc	PROPERTY MANAGER
	PROPS
set, etc	STAGE MANAGER
—reminding forgetful	
players	PROMPT(ER)
outdoor theatre	AMPHITHEATRE
part	
—before entry of chorus	PROLOGUE
—played by female	
in male dress	BREECHES PART
piece of scenery	FLAT
—in wings	TORMENTOR
play	
—based on	
humour and terror	THEATRE OF PANIC
improvisation and	
aggression	LIVING THEATRE
pain and	
suffering	THEATRE OF CRUELTY
threats as comedy	COMEDY OF MENACE
use of lights,	
movement, etc	TOTAL THEATRE

—dealing with	
dreadful events	BLACK COMEDY
	PIECE NOIRE
events in the Bible	
or lives of saints	MIRACLE PLAY
	MYSTERY PLAY
sordid domestic	
life	KITCHEN-SINK DRAMA
the faults of	
society	COMEDY OF MANNERS
—emphasising futility	
of modern life	THEATRE OF THE ABSURD
—with	
gestures but no speech	MIME
musical accompaniment	
(old)	MELODRAMA
no artistic	
merit	BOULEVARD THEATRE
one speaking part	MONOLOGUE
sad ending	TRAGEDY
two speaking parts	DUOLOGUE
playwrights	(see dramatists)
purification of emotions	CATHARSIS
reappearance of actor(s)	
on stage at end of play	CURTAIN CALL
recognition leading to	
dénouement	ANAGNORISIS
retiring room	GREEN ROOM
returning dance	
of chorus	ANTISTROPHE
revolving prism giving	
scene changes	PERIAKTOS
Roman theatre	ODEUM
romantic and sensational	
drama	MELODRAMA
room	
—behind stage	GREEN ROOM
—below stage	MEZZANINE
—for resting actors	GREEN ROOM
seating area	AUDITORIUM
—balcony	LOGGIA
—box	LOGE
—high	BALCONY, GALLERY, GODS
—low	FAUTEUILS, PIT, STALLS
serious drama	LEGITIMATE (THEATRE)
short comic piece	COMEDIETTA
situation where irony is	
apparent to audience	
but not to characters	DRAMATIC IRONY
sound-effect devices	THUNDERSHEET
	WIND MACHINE
speech	
—at end of play	EPILOGUE
—introducing the action	PROLOGUE
stage	
—3 sided set	BOX SET

—arch framing stage	PROSCENIUM (ARCH)
—area	
above stage	FLIES
at side of stage	COULISSE, WINGS
behind proscenium	
arch	PICTURE-FRAME STAGE
in front of curtains	APRON STAGE
	FORESTAGE
over proscenium	LOGUM
used by chorus	ORCHESTRA
—back of stage	UPSTAGE
—front of stage	DOWNSTAGE
	PROSCENIUM
—left side of stage	OPPOSITE PROMPT
—open	
front of set	FOURTH WALL
on all sides	OPEN STAGE
	THEATRE IN THE ROUND
—right side of stage	PROMPT SIDE
—room under stage	MEZZANINE
—scenery	DECOR, SET
—slide	COULISSE
—slope of stage	RAKE
—surrounded by	
audience	ARENA THEATRE
	THEATRE-IN-THE-ROUND
—trapdoor	SCRUTO
—wings	COULISSES
—with audience on	
three sides	PLATFORM STAGE
stock of pieces that a	
company can perform	REPERTOIRE
	REPERTORY
storage building	SKENE
story of life and action	DRAMA
sudden	
—change of fortune	PERIPET(E)IA
—turn of events	COUP DE THEATRE
theatre company with	
stock of plays	REPERTORY (COMPANY)
three canons of	
classical drama	
(action, time, place)	UNITIES
tragedian's boot	BUSKIN, COTHURN(US)
young	
—actor	JUVENILE
—actress	INGENUE
theologian	BD, DD
	(see also **church—personnel**)
thirteen	BAKER'S DOZEN, DEVIL'S DOZEN
	LONG DOZEN, RL TEAM
	UNLUCKY NUMBER
thirteen witches	COVEN
thirteenth loaf	MAKEWEIGHT
thirty	L, LA(M)BDA
thirty requiem masses	TRENTAL

thirty-three	DISC, LP, RECORD
thirty-nine	
—Books	OLD TESTAMENT, OT
—in	
novel	STEPS
religious belief	ARTICLES
thirty thousand	L, LA(M)BDA
thousand	CHILIAD, G, K, M, X
combining form	KILO-
group	CHILIAD
thousand and one	MI
thousand million	BILLION, MILLIARD
thousand years	MILLENARY, MILLENNIUM
thousandth	MILLESIMAL
—anniversary	MILLENARY, MILLENNIUM
three	CROWD, GAMMA
B's	BACH, BEETHOVEN, BRAHMS
canons of classical	
drama	UNITIES
cards	P(AI)RIAL, PAIR-ROYAL
choices	TRILEMMA
Christmas presents	FRENCH HENS
cleft	TRIFID, TRIPARTITE
combining form	TER-, TRI-
cornered hat	TRICORN(E)
days	TRIDIUM
Estates of the Realm	COMMONS
	LORDS SPIRITUAL
	LORDS TEMPORAL
F's	FAIR RENT, FAIR SALE
	FAIR TENURE
Fates	(see separate entry)
feet	YARD
fold	TRI(N)AL, TRIPLEX, TRIPLICATE
Furies	(see separate entry)
Graces	(see separate entry)
grooved tablet	TRIGLYPH
groups	P(AI)RIAL, PAIR-ROYAL
	TERN(ION), TERZETTO
	TRIAD, TRILOGY, TRINE
	TRINITY, TRIO, TRIPLE
Harpies	(see separate entry)
having three	
—apses	TRIAPS(ID)AL
—atoms	TRIATOMIC
—axes	TRIAXIAL, TRIAXONIC
—beats	TRICOTIC, TRICOTOUS
—bodies	TRICORPORATE
—branches	TRICHOTOMOUS
	TRIFURCATE(D), TRIGEMINAL
	TRISULCATE
—bundles of stamens	TRIADELPHOUS
—carpels	TRICARPELLARY
—cells	TRILOCULAR
—colours	TRICHRO(MAT)IC
	TRICOLOUR(ED)

—consonants	TRICONSONANTAL
—corners	TRICORN(E)
—cusps	TRICUSPID, TRITUBERCULAR
—days	TRIDUUM
—dimensions	TRIDIMENSIONAL
—electrodes	TRIODE
—ethyl groups	TRIETHYL
—extremities	TRINACRIAN
	TRINACRIFORM
—faces	TRIFACIAL, TRIHEDRAL
—feet	TRIPEDAL
—fingers	TRIDACTYLOUS
—focal lengths	TRIFOCAL
—forks	TRIFURCATE(D)
—forms	TRIFORM(ED)
	TRIMORPHIC, TRIMORPHOUS
—furrows	TRISULCATE
—heads	TRICEPHALOUS, TRICEPS
—horns	TRICERATOPS, TRICORN(E)
—hydrogen atoms	TRIACID, TRIBASIC
—hydroxyl groups	TRIHYDRIC
—interlaced arcs	TRIQUETRA
—languages	TRIGLOT, TRILINGUAL
—leaflets	TERNATE, TRIFOLIATE
—leaves	TRIFOLIATE, TRIPHYLLOUS
—legs	TRIPOD(AL)
—letters	TRILITERAL
—lines	TRIGRAM, TRILINEAR
—lobes	TREFOIL, TRILOBATE(D)
	TRILOBE(D)
—marriages	TRIGAMOUS
—measures	TRIMETER, TRIMETRIC
—methyl radicals	TRIMETHYL
—oxygen atoms	TRIOXIDE
—parts	TRIMEROUS, TRIPARTITE
—petals	TRIPETALOUS
—phenyl groups	TRIPHENYL
—pistils	TRIGYNIAN, TRYGYNOUS
—points	TRICUSPID(ATE)
	TRINACRIAN, TRINACRIFORM
—prongs	TRIDENT(AL), TRIDENTATE
	TRIDENTED, TRINACRIAN
	TRINACRIFORM
—rays	TRIACT(INAL), TRIACTINE
	TRIRADIAL, TRIRADIATE
—ribs	TRICOSTATE
—rings	TRICYCLIC
—rows	TRIFARIOUS, TRISTICHOUS
—sides	TRILATERAL
—stamens	TRIANDRIAN, TRIANDROUS
—strings	TRICHORD
—styles	TRIGYNIAN, TRIGYNOUS
—sulphur atoms	TRISULPHIDE
	TRITHIONIC
—teeth	TRIDENTATE, TRIDENTED
—terms	TRINOMIAL, TRIONYM

—times	
haploid number	
of chromosomes	TRIPLOID
molecular mass	TRIMERIC
—toes	TRIDACTYL(OUS)
—tubercles	TRITUBERCULAR
—unequal axes	TRICLINIC
—use of 3 elements	TRIPHIBIOUS
—valencies	TERVALENT, TRIATOMIC
	TRIVALENT
—valves	TRIVALVE(D)
	TRIVALVULAR
—ways	TRIFARIOUS
—whorls	TRICYCLIC
—wings	TRIPLANE, TRIPTEROUS
—wives	TRIGAMOUS, TRIGAMY
	TRIGYNIAN, TRIGYNOUS
—words	TRINOMIAL, TRIONYM(AL)
—xylem strands	TRIARCH
—yearly occurrences	TRIENNIAL
hulled boat	TRIMARAN
hundred	B
—years	TERCENTENARY
in	
—one	TRINITY, TRIUNE
—the fountain	COINS
Jerome characters	MEN IN A BOAT
Jewels	RIGHT CONDUCT
	RIGHT FAITH
	RIGHT KNOWLEDGE
legged race	MANX
letter word	TRILITERAL
lines	TERCET, TERZETTA
lobed fossil	TRILOBITE
men in office	TRIUMVIRATE
monthly	TRIMONTHLY
months	TRIMESTER
Musketeers	ARAMIS, ATHOS
	PORTHOS
one of three at birth	TRIPLET
people	CROWD
	ETERNAL TRIANGLE
persons	
—ruling	TRIARCHY
—speaking	TRIALOGUE
pipped card or domino	TREY
pronged spear	TRIDENT
tablets	TRIPTYCH
thousand	B
times	TREBLE, TRIPLE
—a day	TID
tragedies	TRILOGY
under par	ALBATROSS
wheeled vehicle	TRICAR, TRICYCLE
	TRISHAW
winged aeroplane	TRIPLANE

Wise Men (Magi)	BALTHAZAR
	GASPAR(CASPAR), MELCHIOR
yearly	TRIENNIAL

Tibetan

abominable snowman	YETI
animal	(GIANT) PANDA
antelope	GOA
barley dish	TSAMBA
Buddhist sect	GELUK PA, SAKYA PA
capital	LHASA
cloth	KATA
dog	LHASA APSO, SHIH TZU
goat	TAKIN
hybrid cattle	DSO(MO), DZO, JOMO, Z(H)O
	ZHOMO, ZOBO, ZOBU
language	PALI
leader	LAMA
mysterious beast	YETI
monastery	LAMASERY
monument	STUPA
ox	SARLAC, SARLAK
	YAK, Z(H)O
—pannier	YAKHDAN
pony	TANGUN
porch	TORAN
priest	LAMA
religious leader	DALAI LAMA
	PANCHEN LAMA
scarf	KATA
sheep	SHAHPU, SHAPO
tribe	SHERPA
wild ass	KIANG, KYANG

timber

from	
—conifers	SOFTWOOD
—deciduous trees	HARDWOOD
hardwood	
—Andaman Islands	BOMBWAY
	BULLET-WOOD
	CANARIUM, CHUGLAM, HOKKO
	MARBLEWOOD, PADAUK, PADOUK
	PAPITA, PYINMA, RED DHUP
	THINGAN
—Angola	AVODIRE, COPALWOOD
	MUNINGA
—Argentina	QUEBRACHO
—Asia	BOXWOOD, MAPLE
	PAULOWNIA, WALNUT
—Asia Minor	BOXWOOD, HORNBEAM
—Australia	ALPINE ASH, BLACK BEAN
	BLACKBUTT, BLACKWOOD, BLUE GUM
	BRUSH BOX, CEDAR, COACHWOOD
	IRONBARK, JARRAH, KARRI
	MULGA, NEGRO-HEAD BEECH
	QUEENSLAND MAPLE, (RED) SATINAY
	ROSE GUM, ROSE MAHOGANY

	SALIGNA GUM, SHE-OAK
	SILKY OAK, SILVERTOP ASH
	SPOTTED GUM, TALLOWWOOD
	TASMANIAN MYRTLE, TASMANIAN OAK
	TURPENTINE, WALNUT, WANDOO
	WHITE ASH, WHITE OAK
	YELLOW STRINGBARK
	YELLOW WALNUT
—Borneo	KAPUR, LAUAN, MENGKULANG
	MERANTI, MERBAU, SEPETIR
	SELANGAN(BATU), SERAYA
—Botswana	MUGONGO
—Brazil	ARARACANGA, BASRALOCUS
	BICUIBA, BRAZILWOOD, CANELLA
	CURUPAY, EMBUIA, FREIJO, IMBUYA
	IPE, JEQUITIBA, KABUKALLI, KINGWOOD
	LOURO, MAHO, MAHOGANY, MANDIO
	PALISANDER, PEROBA, QUARUBA
	QUEBRACHO, RED LOURO, ROSEWOOD
	SUCUPIRA, TULIPWOOD, VINHATICO
	ZEBRAWOOD
—Burma	ANAN, CEDAR, CHICKRASSY
	ENG, GURJUN, GMELINA
	HALDU, HOKKO, IRONWOOD
	KATON, KAUNGHMU, KERUING
	LAUREL, MERSAWA, PADAUK
	PADOUK, PAPITA, PYINMA
	PYINKADO, TEAK, THINGAN
	THITKA, TULIPWOOD, YON
—Canada	ASPEN, BEECH
	BALSAM POPLAR, BASSWOOD, BIRCH
	BUTTERNUT, CHERRY, COTTONWOOD
	HICKORY, HORNBEAM
	PACIFIC MAPLE, PAPER BIRCH
	RED OAK, ROCK ELM, ROCK MAPLE
	SOFT MAPLE, WALNUT, WHITE ASH
	WHITE ELM, WHITE OAK
	WHITEWOOD, YELLOW BIRCH
—Celebes (Sulawesi)	EBONY
—Central and	
tropical Africa	AFZELIA, ALBIZZIA
	ALSTONIA, ANTIARIS, BOMANGA
	DITSHIPI, ERIMANDO, GABOON
	MISSANDA, MUGONGO, MUKANGU
	MUKULUNU, MUSIZI, M(U)TONDO
	MUGONGO, MUTOBO, OLON
	WAIKA CHEWSTICK
—Central and	
tropical America	ALCANTOR, ANGELIN
	BALSA, BANAK, BITTERWOOD
	BLACK CABBAGE-BARK, CAOBA
	CATIVO, CEIBA, CEDAR
	(CEDRO) COLORADO, CELTIS
	COCOBOLO, COURBARIL, DALLI
	DEGAME, EBONY, ESPAVEL, FUSTIC
	FUTUI, GLASSY WOOD, HOGPLUM

HURA, JIGUA, LAPACHO, LETTERWOOD
LIGNUM VITAE, LONGUI ROUGE
LOURO PRETO, MAHOE, MAHOGANY
MANGLE, MASTIC, MAYFLOWER, PILON
PARTRIDGE-WOOD, PRIMAVERA
PURPLEHEART, SALMWOOD
SANTA MARIA, SAPAN DE PALOMA
SAPODILLA, SATINE, SIMARUBA
SNAKEWOOD, WAIKA CHEWSTICK
—Chile   COIGUE BEECH, LAUREL
LINGUE, OLIVILLO, RAULI BEECH
ROBLE BEECH, TEPA, ULMO
—China   KATSURA
—Colombia   KABUKALLI
—Congo   MUTENYE, TCHITOLA, WENGE
—Cuba   COCUS WOOD, DEGAME
MAHOE, MAHOGANY, SABICU
—East Africa   BLACKWOOD, CANARIUM
CANDELABRA-WOOD, CELTIS
DAHOMA, ELGON OLIVE, EBONY
GEDU, GREENHEART, IROKO, MAFU
LOLIONDO, MAHOGANY, MECODZE
MOBURA, MSANDARUSSI, MTONDO
MUERI, MUHUHU, MUKALI, , MUKEO
MUKUMARI, MUSINE, MUTOBO
M(U)TONDO, MVULE, NKUNYA, NOHOR
OTU, PANGA, PILLARWOOD
RAPANEA, SILKY OAK, WALNUT
—East Indies   BELIAN, MERBAU, MERANTI
ROSEWOOD, SEPETIR, SERAYA
—Ecuador   ALCANTOR, FERNAN SANCHEZ
—Ethiopia   OLIVE
—Europe   ALDER, APPLE, ASH
ASPEN, BEECH, BIRCH
BLACK POPLAR, BOXWOOD
CHERRY, CHESTNUT, ELM
HOLM OAK, HORNBEAM, LIME
MAPLE, OAK, PEAR, PLANE
ROBINIA, ROWAN, SWEET CHESTNUT
SPINDLEWOOD, SYCAMORE
TURKEY OAK, WALNUT
WHITEBEAM
—Ghana   AFRORMOSIA, ANOPYXIS
AVODIRE, MAKORE, WHIMAWHE
—Guatemala   GUANACASTE, NARANGO
—Guyana   BAROMALLI, BASRALOCUS
GREENHEART, HIARIBALLI
(ITURI)WALLABA, KABUKALLI
KUROKAI, MAHO, MANDIO
(MORA)BUKEA, RED LOURO
VIROLA, WAIKA CHEWSTICK
WARAMA, YARURU
—Honduras   CRAMANTEE, MAHOGANY
NARGUSTA, ROSEWOOD, YEMERI
—India   ANAN, APITONG, AXLEWOOD
BENTEAK, BIJASAL, CALAMANDER

CEDAR, CHICKRASSY, COROMANDEL
EBONY, ELM, GARDENIA, GMELINA
GURJUN, HALDU, HOKKO, KERUING
KINDAL, KUMBAR, KUMBUK, LAUREL
PALO, POON, PISSUR, PYINMA
ROSEWOOD, SAL, SANDALWOOD
SATINWOOD, SISSOO, TEAK
THINGAN, YANG, YON
—Indonesia   JELUTONG, NYATOH
PUNAH, PYINMA
—Iran   OAK
—Ivory Coast   AVODIRE
—Jamaica   COCUS WOOD, HOGPLUM
—Japan   ASH, BEECH, ELM
HORSE CHESTNUT, KATSURA
MAPLE, OAK, SEN, WALNUT
—Java   ROSEWOOD
—Kenya   CAMPHORWOOD, OLIVE
—Malaya   APITONG, GURJUN
JELUTONG, KAPUR, KERUING
LAUAN, MACHANG, MELAWIS
MENGKULANG, MERANTI, MESUA
NEMESU, RAMIN, TEAK, YANG
—Malaysia   ANAN, BALAU, BINTANGOR
CANARIUM, GERONGGANG, GURJUN
JELUTONG, KAUNGHMU, KEMPAS
KERENTAI, KERUING, KUNGKUR
MATA ULAT, MERBAO, MERANTI
MERAWAN, MERSAWA, NYATOH
PUNAH, SATIN ASH, SELANGAN
SEPETIR, SERAYA, TEAK
TERENTANG
—Mexico   PRIMAVERA
—Mozambique   AFZELIA, BANGA WANGA
BEKUNGU, KNOBTHORN
MECRUSSE, MUNINGA
MZIMBE, PAU FERRO
—New Guinea   PALDAO
—New Zealand HARD BEECH, RED BEECH
SOUTHLAND BEECH, TAWA
—Nigeria   AFZELIA, CEIBO, CORDIA
HOMALIUM, OMO, OPEPE, TEAK
—North America   ALDER, APPLE, ASH
ASPEN, BALSAM POPLAR
BASSWOOD, BEECH, BIRCH
BLACK WILLOW, BUCKEYE
BUTTERNUT, BUTTONWOOD
CELTIS, CHERRY, CHESTNUT
COFFEETREE, COTTONWOOD
DOGWOOD, ELM, GREEN ASH
GUM, HACKBERRY, HICKORY, HOLLY
HONEYLOCUST, HORNBEAM, KOA
MAGNOLIA, MANGROVE, MAPLE, MYRTLE
OAK, PACIFIC MAPLE, PAPER BIRCH
PECAN, PERSIMMON, PLANE, RED OAK
RED GUM, RED OAK, ROBINIA

ROCK ELM, ROCK MAPLE, SOFT MAPLE
SYCAMORE, TUPELO, WALNUT
WHITE ASH, WHITE ELM
WHITE OAK, WHITEWOOD
YELLOW BIRCH
—Pakistan   CHICKRASSY, SISSOO
—Peru   MAHOGANY
—Philippines   APITONG, GURJUN, LAUAN
KERUING, PALDAO
PALOSAPIS, SERAYA, YANG
—Sabah BINUANG, GAGIL, KAPUR(MERAH)
KEMBANG, RANGGU
SELANGAN BATU, SERAYA
—Sarawak   JONGKONG, RAMIN
MELAWIS, MENGKULANG
—Sierra Leone   TOFEE
—Siam   (see Thailand below)
—South Africa   BOXWOOD, CAPE BEECH
COPALWOOD, KAMASSI, MULGA
MUNINGA, WHITE ELS
—South America   AMARILLO, ANDIROBA
BALSA, BASRALOCUS, BITTERWOOD
CANGERANA, CEDAR, CIRUELILLO
CRABWOOD, DALLI, DEGARLE
FREIJO, GREENHEART, IMBUYA
LANCEWOOD, LETTERWOOD, LOURO
MAHOGANY, PADDLEWOOD
PARTRIDGE-WOOD, PAU MARFIM
PURPLEHEART, QUEBRACHO
ROSEWOOD, SANTA MARIA
SNAKEWOOD, TINEO, VERA WOOD
ZEBRA-WOOD
—South-east Asia   BALAU, GERONGGANG
KAPUR, KERUING APITONG
LAUAN, MENBAU, MENGKULANG
MERANTI, NYATOH
SERAYA, SEPETIR
—Sri Lanka CALAMANDER, COROMANDEL
EBONY, HORA, KATABODA
KUMBUK, LUNUMIDELLA
PALU, SATINWOOD
—Sudan   HARAZ, HEGLIG, NEEM
SEYAL, SUNT
—Sumatra   KAPUR(MERAH)
—Tanzania   BUSSEI, CAMPHORWOOD
MAHOGANY, MCHENGA, MEGUZA
MFUNE, MGONGO, MJOMBO
—Thailand   ANAN, APITONG
CHUMPRAK, ENG
GURJUN, HALDU, KAPONG, KATON
KAUNGHMU, KERUING, MAIDU
MERSAWA, PADAUK, PADOUK
TEAK, TASUA, THINGAN
PYINMA, YANG, YOM HIN, YON
—Trinidad   NARGUSTA, SERRETE
—Uganda   MUCHENCHE, MUHIMBI

—United Kingdom   APPLE, ASH, ASPEN
BEECH, BLACK POPLAR, BOXWOOD
CHERRY, CRACK WILLOW
CRICKET-BAT WILLOW, DUTCH ELM
EUROPEAN ELM, EUROPEAN OAK
GREY POPLAR, HAZEL, HOLLY
HOLM OAK, HORNBEAM, LABURNUM
LIME, LUCOMBE OAK, PEAR
PLANE, RED OAK, ROBINIA
ROWAN, SMOOTH-LEAVED ELM
SWEET CHESTNUT, SYCAMORE
TURKEY OAK, WALNUT
WHITEBEAM, WHITE POPLAR
WHITE WILLOW, WYCH ELM
—Venezuela   MAHOGANY, MARACAIBO
PATRIDGE-WOOD, SUCUPIRA
—West Africa   ABURA, ADJOUOBA, AFARA
AFINA, AFRORMOSIA, AFZELIA
AGBA, AKAK, APOME, AVODIRE, AYAN
AZOBE, BERLINIA, BOMBAX, BUBINGA
CAMWOOD, CANARIUM, CASSINE
CELTIS, COUL ATTAI, DAHOMA
DANTA, DIFOU, DOUKA, DOUSSIE
EBIARA, EBONY, EDINAM, EKKI
EKOP, ESSIA, GEDU, GUAREA, IDIGBO
IROKO, LANDA, LIMBA, MOBURA
MAHOGANY, MAKORE, MANSONIA
MOABI, NIA(N)GON, NIOVE, NOHOR
NYANKOM, OBECHE, ODOKO, ODUDU
OLON, OKAN, OKWEN, OMU, OPEPE
OSOL, OTU, PADAUK, PADOUK, POGA
PTERYGOTA, PYCNANTHUS, RIBI
RIKIO, SAPELE, SIBO, SOUGUE
STERCULIA, TENDRE, UTILE
WALNUT, ZEBRANO
—West Indies   ANGELIN, BALSA
CANDLE-WOOD, CATIVO, CEDAR
COCO(A)-WOOD, COCUS-WOOD
COURBARIL, CRABWOOD, FUSTIC
HURA, JAMAICA EBONY, KOKRA-WOOD
LANA, LANCEWOOD, LIGNUM VITAE
MAHOGANY, MAYFLOWER, PILON
SABICU, SALMWOOD, SANTA MARIA
SAPAN DE PALOMA, SATINWOOD
YACCA
—Zambia   MUGONGO, MUNINGA, TEAK
—Zimbabwe   COPALWOOD, MUGONGO
MUNINGA, TEAK
softwood
—Argentina   PARANA PINE
—Asia Minor   CEDAR
—Australia   BUNYA PINE
CELERY TOP PINE, HOOP PINE
HUON PINE, KAURI PINE
KING WILLIAM PINE
RADIATA PINE

—Borneo	SEMPILOR
—Brazil	PARANA PINE
—Canada	ALPINE FIR, AMABILIS FIR
	BALSAM FIR, BLACK SPRUCE
	DOUGLAS FIR, ENGELMANN SPRUCE
	GRAND FIR, HEMLOCK, INCENSE CEDAR
	JACK PINE, LODGEPOLE PINE
	PONDEROSA PINE, RED PINE
	RED SPRUCE, TAMARACK LARCH
	WESTERN LARCH, WESTERN RED CEDAR
	WHITE CEDAR, WHITE PINE
	WHITE SPRUCE, YELLOW PINE
—Central America	PITCH PINE
—Chile	ALERCE PINE, MANIO
—China	JAPANESE CEDAR
—Cuba	PITCH PINE
—Cyprus	ALEPPO PINE
—East Africa	CEDAR, CYPRESS
	MANIO, PODO
—East Indies	KAURI
—Europe	AUSTRIAN PINE, CEDAR
	CORSICAN PINE, LARCH
	MARITIME PINE, REDWOOD
	SCOTS PINE, SILVER FIR
	(SITKA) SPRUCE, WHITEWOOD
—Fiji	KAURI PINE
—Guatemala	CYPRESS
—Honduras	YELLOWWOOD
—India	BLUE PINE, CEDAR
	HIMALAYAN SPRUCE
	SILVER FIR
—Japan	LARCH, CEDAR
—Kenya	PODO, YELLOWWOOD
—Malta	THUYA
—Manchuria	SIBERIAN PINE
—New Guinea	HOOP PINE
—New Zealand	KAURI PINE, KEWAKA
	MATAI, MIRO, RIMU
	SILVER PINE, TOTARA
	WHITE PINE
—North Africa	THUYA
—North America	ALPINE FIR
	AMABILIS FIR, BALSAM FIR
	BLACK SPRUCE, CYPRESS
	DOUGLAS FIR, ENGELMANN SPRUCE
	GRAND FIR, HEMLOCK
	INCENSE CEDAR, JACK PINE
	LODGEPOLE PINE, NOBLE FIR
	PITCH PINE, PONDEROSA PINE
	PORT ORFORD CEDAR, RADIATA PINE
	RED PINE, RED SPRUCE, SEQUOIA
	SITKA SPRUCE, SUGAR PINE
	TAMARACK LARCH, WESTERN LARCH
	WESTERN RED CEDAR, WHITE CEDAR
	WHITE PINE, WHITE SPRUCE
	YELLOW CEDAR, YELLOW PINE

—Russia	SIBERIAN LARCH
—Sarawak	SEMPILOR
—Siberia	LARCH, SCOTS PINE
	SIBERIAN PINE
—South Africa	RADIATA PINE
—Tanzania	PODO, YELLOWWOOD
—Uganda	PODO, YELLOWWOOD
—United Kingdom	AUSTRIAN PINE
	CEDAR, CORSICAN PINE
	DUNKELD LARCH, EUROPEAN LARCH
	EUROPEAN SPRUCE, JAPANESE LARCH
	LEYLAND CYPRESS, NOBLE FIR
	SCOTS PINE, SILVER FIR
	SITKA SPRUCE, WELLINGTONIA
	YEW
Titans	(*see* **gods**)
toasts	
Austrian	PROST
Chinese	GUN-BEI
Danish	SKAL
Dutch	PROOST, SANTJES
English	BOTTOMS UP, CHEERS
	CHIN-CHIN, GOOD HEALTH
	MUD IN YOUR EYE
Finnish	KIPPIS, SKAL
French	A VOTRE SANTE
	BONNE SANTE
German	GESUNDHEIT, PROS(I)T
Irish	SLAINTE
Israeli	L'CHAIM
Italian	CIAO, SALUTE
Japanese	KAMPAI
naval	SANDY BOTTOMS
Norwegian	SKOAL
Portuguese	SAUDE
Roman	BENE VOBIS
Scottish	SLAINTE MHATH
South African	GELUK, GESONDHEID
Spanish	SALUD
Swedish	SKAL
Welsh	IECHYD DA
toes	
1-toed	MONDACTYLOUS
2-toed	DIDACTYLOUS
3-toed	TRIDACTYLOUS
4-toed	TETRADACTYLOUS
5-toed	PENTADACTYLOUS
6-toed	HEXADACTYLOUS
even-toed	ARTIODACTYLOUS
many-toed	POLYDACTYLOUS
Togo	TG
Tonga	
capital	NUKU'ALOFA
coin	
—unit	SENITI
—100 seniti	PA'ANGA

tools

blacksmith's tools	ANVIL, DUFT, FILE
	FLATTER, FULLER, HARDY
	LEAF HAMMER, MANDREL
	PINCERS, RASP, SETT HAMMER
	SWAGE, TONGS
bricklayer's tools	BOASTER, BOLSTER
	HAWK, HOD, PLUMB-LINE
	POINTING TOOL, SPIRIT LEVEL
	TROWEL
butcher's tools	CLEAVER, KNIFE
	STEEL, SAW
carpenter's tools	ADZE, BRACE (AND BIT)
	BROACH, CHISEL, CLAMP
	FILE, GAUGE, GIMLET, GOUGE
	HAMMER, HAMMER-DRILL
	MALLET, MITRE-BOX
	PINC(H)ERS, PLANE, PLIERS
	PROTRACTOR, PUNCH
	QUANNET, RASP, REAMER, RIMER
	ROUTER, RULE(R), SAW, SCORPER
	SCRAPER, SCREWDRIVER, SCRIBER
	SET SQUARE, SHAPER
	SHOOTING BOARD
	SPIRIT LEVEL, SPOKESHAVE
	T-SQUARE
chisels	COLD CHISEL, FIRMER CHISEL
	GOUGE, MORTICE CHISEL
	MORTISE CHISEL, SCORPER
concretor	MIXER, TAMPING BOARD
	TREMIE, TROWEL
	VIBRATOR
contractor's plant	BACKHOE
	CONCRETE MIXER, DIGGER
	DRAGLINE, DUMPER
	EXCAVATOR, HIMAC
	JACK HAMMER
	JCB, PILEDRIVER, ROAD DRILL
	ROLLER, SCAFFOLD(ING)
	(TOWER-)CRANE, TREMIE
	VIBRATOR
cultivating	(CHAIN) HARROW
	DISC HARROW
	MUCKSPREADER, PLOUGH
	ROTAVATOR, ROTOVATOR
	SCUFFLER, SEED-DRILL
digging	CROW-BAR, FORK, LOY
	MATTOCK, PICKAXE
	SPADE, TROWEL
drilling	AUGER, (BRAD-)AWL
	BRACE AND BIT, BROACH
	COUNTERSINK BIT, GIMLET
	REAMER, SHELL DRILL
	TWIST DRILL, WIMBLE
engraving tool	BURIN
enlarging tool	FRAISE, REAMER, RIMER

excavator	BONING ROD
	JACK HAMMER, PICK(-AXE)
	PNEUMATIC DRILL, SHOVEL
	SIGHT RAIL, SPADE
file	
—mounted like a plane	QUANNET
—with curved ends	RIFFLER
garden tools	BESOM, DIBBER, DIBBLE
	DRAW HOE, DUTCH HOE, EDGING TOOL
	FORK, PRUNER, RAKE, SECATEURS
	SHEARS, SPADE, TROWEL
glazier	(*see* painter *below*)
gouging chisel	SCORPER
grass-cutting	CLIPPERS
	(CYLINDER-)MOWER, (EDGINS-)SHEARS
	FLAIL-MOWER, FLYMO, GANG-MOWER
	HOVER MOWER, ROTARY MOWER
	SCYTHE, SICKLE, STRIMMER
grooving tool	ROUTER
hammers etc	BALL-PANE HAMMER
	BALL-PEIN HAMMER
	BEETLE, CLAW HAMMER
	CROSS-PEIN HAMMER
	KNAPPING HAMMER
	LUMP HAMMER, MADGE
	MALLET, SCABBLING HAMMER
	SLEDGE HAMMER, TACK HAMMER
	WALLER'S HAMMER
harvesting	BALE FORK, BINDER
	(COMBINE) HARVESTER
	FLAIL, HAY-FORK
	HAY-KNIFE, PITCHFORK, RAKE
	TEDDER, THRESHING MACHINE
hedge-cutting	AXE, BILLHOOK
	HATCHET, SLASHER
hide scraper	SLATER
locksmith	OUSTITI, OUTSIDERS
	SKELETON KEY
mason	CHISEL, DRAG COMB
	MALLET, SCABBLING HAMMER
	WALLER'S HAMMER
metal-working	CALLIPERS, DIE, DRILL
	FILE, HAMMER, HAMMER DRILL
	MOLE GRIP, PINC(H)ERS
	PLIERS, PUNCH, REAMER
	RIMER, RASP, SHEARS, SPANNER
	SWAGE, TAP, TIN SNIPS, WRENCH
narrow spade	LOY
painter and glazier	BUCKET
	DISTEMPER BRUSH
	PAINT BRUSH
	PAPERHANGER'S BRUSH
	PASTE TABLE, PLUMB BOB
	PUTTY KNIFE, SCISSORS
	SCRAPER, SPIRIT LEVEL
	STRAIGHT-EDGE, TACK HAMMER

planes	BADGER PLANE	animals	ZOOTHERAPY
	BENCH PLANE, BLOCK PLANE	antigens	IMMUNOTHERAPY
	FILLISTER(PLANE)	association with	
	GROOVING PLANE, JACK PLANE	unpleasant thoughts	AVERSION THERAPY
	MOULDING PLANE, RABBIT PLANE	auto-suggestion	COUEISM
	REBATE PLANE, SMOOTHING PLANE	balanced diet	MACROBIOTICS
	TONGUING PLANE	bladder diseases	UROLOGY
plasterer's tools	HAWK, LARRY	blood	
	MOULDING TOOL, PLUMB-LINE	—disorders	HAEMATOLOGY
	SIEVE, SPIRIT-LEVEL, TROWEL	—serum	SEROTHERAPY
printer's tool	SHOOTING-STICK	bodily reflexes	REFLEXOLOGY
pulverising tool	MULLER	body-energy radiated	
saws	BACK SAW, BAND SAW, BOW SAW	as colours	COLOUR THERAPY
	CHAIN SAW, CIRCULAR SAW	bone and muscle disorders	ORTHOPAEDICS
	COMPASS SAW, COPING SAW	burning herbs	MOXIBUSTION
	CROSSCUT SAW, FLOORING SAW	chemicals	CHEMOTHERAPY
	FRET SAW, HACK SAW, HAND SAW	children's diseases	PAEDIATRICS
	JIG SAW, KEYHOLE SAW	climatic environment	CLIMATOTHERAPY
	PANEL SAW, PIT SAW, RIP SAW	combining chemicals	CHELATION THERAPY
	SCROLL SAW, TENON SAW	control by electronic	
sculptor's tools	BOASTER, BOLSTER	monitoring	BIOFEEDBACK
	BOUCHARDE, CHISEL	crafts or hobbies	OCCUPATIONAL THERAPY
	FILE, MALLET, RIFFLER	crystals	CRYSTAL THERAPY
shipwright's tool	CAULKING IRON	deafness in babies	NATURAL AURALISM
shovel	MAIN	deep	
slater's tools	RIPPER, SAX, ZAX	—massage	ROLFING
spade		—X-rays etc	DEEP THERAPY
—narrow	LOY	defective eyesight	ORTHOPTICS
—Scottish	CAS CROM, CASCHROM	deformities in children	ORTHOP(A)EDICS
—turf-cutting	SLANE		ORTHOP(A)EDY
spanners etc	ADJUSTABLE SPANNER		ORTHOP(A)EDIA)
	ALLENBY TOOL, BOX SPANNER	diet	
	MOLE GRIP, RING SPANNER	—exercise, etc	POLAR THERAPY
	SOCKET SPANNER	—meditation, etc	AYURVEDA
	STILLSON (WRENCH)	diseases	THERAPEUTICS
	STRAP WRENCH, TORQUE WRENCH	—or injury of bones	ORTHOP(A)EDICS
thatching	EAVES HOOK, EAVES KNIFE		ORTHOP(A)EDY
	REED KNIFE, REED LEGGETT		ORTHOP(A)EDIA
	SHEARING HOOK, SPAR HOOK	disturbed children	ORTHOGENICS
	STRAW RAKE, YOKE	drawing metal bars over	
watchmaker's tool	FRAISE	affected parts	TRACTORATION
wheelwright's tools	AUGER	drug-induced sleep	NARCOTHERAPY
	BOXING ENGINE, BRUZZ	drugs	
	JARVIS, SAMSON, SPOKESHAVE	— having opposite	
	TRAVELLER	effects to symptoms	ALLOPATHY
woodturner's chisel	BRUZZE		HOM(O)EOPATHY
trade		—in small doses	HOM(O)EOPTAHY
trademark	TM	electric shocks	AVERSION THERAPY, ECT
trade name	TN		ELECTRO-CONVULSIVE THERAPY
Trade Union	TU		SHOCK THERAPY
Trade Union Congress	TUC	electricity	ELECTROLOGY
treatment			ELECTRO-THERAPEUTICS
by/of/with:			ELECTRO-THERAPY
acting out one's problems	PSYCHODRAMA	essential oils	AROMATHERAPY
acupressure	SHIATSU	exercise	PHYSIOTHERAPY
acupuncture	STYLOSTIXIS	exposing subconscious	PSYCHOANALYSIS

extracts from animal	
organs	OPOTHERAPY
	ORGANOTHERAPY
extreme cold	CRYOTHERAPY
eye muscles	ORTHOPTICS
faulty position of	
teeth	ORTHODONTICS
feet	CHIROPODY, PEDICURE
	PODIATRY
finger pressure	ACUPRESSURE, SHIATSU
foot massage	REFLEXOLOGY
	ZONE THERAPY
hands and nails	MANICURE
heat from electric	
currents	DIATHERMY
herbs	HERBALISM
high	
—body temperature	PYRETOTHERAPY
—pressure	HYPERBARIC TREATMENT
Hindu	AYURVEDA
homeopathy treating	
chemical imbalance	BIOCHEMICS
hypnosis etc	HYPNOTHERAPY
	PSYCHOTHERAPEUTICS
	PSYCHOTHERAPY
illumination in	
colour	COLOUR THERAPY
Indian (yoga)	AYURVEDIC MEDICINE
	STRUCTURAL INTEGRATION
induced current	FARADISM
ionised air	NEGATIVE ION THERAPY
interferon	CYTOKINE TREATMENT
light	PHOTOTHERAPEUTICS
	PHOTOTHERAPY
low temperatures	CRYOTHERAPY
manipulation	CHIROPRACTIC
	OSTEOPATHY
many different drugs	POLYPHARMACY
massage	OSTEOPATHY
	PHYSIOTHERAPEUTICS
	PHYSIOTHERAPY, ROLFING
medicines introduced	
by electricity	CATAPHORESIS
	ELECTROPHORESIS
meditation	TM
	TRANSCENDENTAL MEDITATION
mental illness	ORTHOPSYCHIATRY
	PSYCHODRAMA
	PSYCHOTHERAPEUTICS
	PSYCHOTHERAPY
monitoring responses	BIOFEEDBACK
Moslem	UNANI
movement	KINESIPATHY
	KINESITHERAPY
mud baths	PELOTHERAPY
natural processes	NATUROPATHY

needles	ACUPUNCTURE
	STYLOSTIXIS
nervous system	NEUROLOGY
neurosis	BEHAVIOUR THERAPY
own blood	
cells	ADOPTIVE IMMUNOTHERAPY
pendulums	RADIESTHESIA
plant extracts	HERBALISM
pleasant mental images	IMAGING
posture	ALEXANDER TECHNIQUE
psyche	RADIONICS, PSIONICS
psychosomatic	
disorders	DIANETICS
radiation	RADIOTHERAPEUTICS
	RADIOTHERAPY
radium	CURIETHERAPY
'reliving' early years	PRIMAL THERAPY
rhythmic	
exercise	CURATIVE EUR(H)YTHMICS
salts of gold	CHRYSOTHERAPY
skin	DERMATOLOGY
small doses of drugs	HOM(O)EOPATHY
spinal manipulation	CHIROPRACTIC
spiritual	CHANNELLING
	FAITH HEALING
stylostixis	ACUPUNCTURE
Sun	HELIOTHERAPY
sweet-smelling oils	AROMATHERAPY
tree chemicals	FORESTRY THERAPY
ultra-violet rays	ACTINOTHERAPY
unpleasant stimuli	AVERSION THERAPY
vitamins	MEGAVITAMIN TREATMENT
water	HYDROPATHY
	HYDROTHERAPEUTICS
	HYDROTHERAPY
women's diseases	GYNAECOLOGY
X-rays	RADIOTHERAPEUTICS
	RADIOTHERAPY
treaty	ASSIENTO
America/England	ASHBURTON, JAY
anti-nuclear	RORATONGA
anti Warsaw Pact	ATLANTIC TREATY
	BAGHDAD PACT
	BRUSSELS TREATY
Austria/England	VIENNA
/France	ARRAS, LUNEVILLE
	VERSAILLES
/France/England	VERSAILLES
/France/Prussia	DRESDEN
/Prussia	BRESLAU
/Turkey	PASSAROWITZ
	ZSITVA TOROK
Britain/Austria	ST GERMAIN
/France	AIX-LA-CHAPELLE
/Germany	NEVILLY, VERSAILLES
/Hungary	TRIANON

/Italy	LONDON TREATY
	ST JEAN DE MAURIENNE
/Malaya	YANDABU
/Maoris	WAITANGI
/Russia	NYSTAD
/South Africa	COLENSO
	VEREENIGING
/Turkey	SEVRES
	(see also England below)
Burgundy/France	ARRAS
	CENTO, BAGHDAD PACT
Communist bloc	WARSAW PACT
Denmark/England	WEDMORE
England/China	NANKING
/France	AMIENS, BASSEIN, CALAIS
	CHATEAU CAMBRESIS
	CHAUMONT, DOVER, GHENT
	LOCARNO, PARIS
	TROYES, UTRECHT
/France/Holland	BARRIER
/France/Russia	HANOVER
/France/Spain	SEVILLE
/Ireland	KILMAINHAM
/Russia	PARIS
/Scotland	EDINBURGH
France/Holland	NIMWEGEN
/Prussia	BASEL
/Russia	TILSIT
/Spain	CAMBRAI, PYRENNEES
Germany/Romania	BUCHAREST
/Russia	BREST-LITOVSK
Greece/Rome	PHOENICE
Italy/Spain	BARCELONA
	NATO, ATLANTIC TREATY
Rome/Syria	APAMEA
Russia/Turkey	ADRIANOPLE
slave treaty	ASSIENTO
trees[1]	
including: species	
Abele	ASPEN, POPLAR
Abies	FIR
acacia	WATTLE
acajou	CASHEW-TREE
Adansonia	BAOBAB
alder	ALNUS
almond	AMYGDALUS
Aesculus	HORSE-CHESTNUT
amboyna	WALAN
Amelanchier	JUNE-BERRY, SHADBUSH
	SNOWY MESPILUS
American	
—larch	BLACK LARCH, TAMARACK
—willow	PUSSY WILLOW
Amur cork tree	PHELLODENDRON
Antarctic beech	NOTHOFAGUS
Antiar	UPAS

apple	PYRUS
Araucaria	CHILE(AN) PINE
	MONKEY-PUZZLE
arbor vitae	THUJA, THUYA, TREE OF LIFE
Arbutus	STRAWBERRY-TREE
Aria	WHITEBEAM
Arundinaria	BAMBOO
ash	FRAXINUS
—sapling	GROUND-ASH
aspen	ABELE, POPULUS
	TREMBLING POPLAR
Aucuba	JAPANESE LAUREL
Aucuparia	MOUNTAIN ASH
balsam poplar	TACAMAHAC
bamboo	ARUNDINARIA
baobab	ADANSONIA
Barbados cedar	JUNIPER
bastard cedar	CEDRELA
bay	LAUREL
beech	FAGUS
Betula	BIRCH
birch	BETULA, BIRK
bird-cherry	HACKBERRY, HAGBERRY
bitter oak	CERRIS
black	
—larch	AMERICAN LARCH, TAMARACK
—mulberry	MORUS
—thorn	SLOE
box	BUXUS
Buxus	BOX
Brazil-wood	SAP(P)IAN
buckthorn	JUJUBE
Carpinus	HORNBEAM
cashew-tree	ACAJOU
Castanea	CHESTNUT
Casuarina	SWAMP-OAK
cedar	CEDRUS, DEODAR
—gum	EUCALYPTUS
Cedrela	RED CEDAR
Celtis	NETTLE-TREE
Cercis	JUDAS TREE, REDBUD
Cerris	BITTER OAK
chestnut	CASTANEA
Chile(an) pine	ARAUCARIA
	MONKEY-PUZZLE
Chinese Dove tree	DAVIDIA
classification	
—alder	BETULACEAE
—ash	OLEACEAE
—Austrian pine	PINACEAE
—bay	LAURACEAE
—beech	FAGACEAE
—birch	BETULACEAE
—bird cherry	ROSACEAE
—blackthorn	ROSACEAE
—box	BUXACEAE

—buckthorn	RHAMNACEAE	Conium	HEMLOCK
—bullace	ROSACEAE	conker-tree	HORSE CHESTNUT
—cedar of Lebanon	PINACEAE	cornelian cherry	CORNEL, CORNUS
—Chile(an) pine	PINACEAE	Corylus	HAZEL
—cornel	CORNACEAE	cottonwood	POPULUS
—crab	ROSACEAE	cowrie pine	COWDIE, KAURI
—deodar	PINACEAE	crab	MALUS
—dogwood	CORNACEAE	Crataegus	HAWTHORN
—Douglas fir	PINACEAE	Cydonia	QUINCE
—elder	CAPRIFOLIACEAE	cypress	CUPRESSUS
—elm	ULMACEAE	damson	DAMASK-PLUM
—gean	ROSACEAE	Davidia	CHINESE DOVE TREE
—guelder rose	CAPRIFOLIACEAE		GHOST TREE
—hawthorn	ROSACEAE		HANDKERCHIEF TREE
—hazel	BETULACEAE	deodar	HIMALAYAN CEDAR
—holly	AQUIFOLIACEAE	dogwood	CORNEL(IAN), CORNUS
—hornbeam	BETULACEAE		PRICKWOOD
—horse chestnut	HIPPOCASTANACEAE	Douglas fir	PSEUDOTSUGA
—Indian cedar	PINACEAE	dragon-tree	DRACAENA
—juniper	PINACEAE	dwarfed	BONSAI
—laburnum	LEGUMINOSAE	elm	ULMUS
—larch	PINACEAE	—rock	WAHOO
—Lawson's cypress	PINACEAE	—winged	WAHOO
—lime	TILIACLEAE	Eucalyptus	CIDER GUM
—locust tree	LEGUMINOSAE	evergreen oak	HOLM-OAK
—magnolia	MAGNOLIACEAE	exudes	
—maple	ACERACEAE	—latex	MILKWOOD
—medlar	ROSACEAE	—sugar	ALHAGI, MANNA-ASH
—monkey-puzzle tree	PINACEAE		MANNA-LARCH, TAMARISK
—mountain ash	ROSACEAE	false acacia	LOCUST-TREE, ROBINIA
—oak	FAGACEAE	fir	ABIES
—plane	PLATANACEAE	—with white marked	
—poplar	SALICACEAE	needles	SILVER-FIR
—rowan	ROSACEAE	forest tree	DRYAD
—Scots pine	PINACEAE	fustet	YOUNG FUSTIC
—service tree	ROSACEAE	ghost tree	DAVIDIA
—silver fir	PINACEAE	golden rain	LABURNUM
—sloe	ROSACEAE	great sallow	GOAT-SALLOW, GOAT-WILLOW
—spindle-tree	CELASTRACEAE	gum	SAPOTA
—spruce fir	PINACEAE	handkerchief tree	DAVIDIA
—stone pine	PINACEAE	horse-chestnut	AESCULUS, CONKER TREE
—strawberry tree	ERICACEAE		HIPPOCANASTACEAE
—sweet chestnut	FAGACEAE	hawthorn	CRATAEGUS, THORN-TREE
—sycamore	ACERACEAE		WHITETHORN
—tulip tree	MAGNOLIACEAE	hazel	CORYLUS
—walnut	JUGLANDACEAE	hemlock	CONIUM
—wayfaring tree	CAPRIFOLIACEAE	Himalayan cedar	DEODAR
—whitebeam	ROSACEAE	holly	ILEX
—wild		holm-oak	HOLLY-OAK, ILEX
apple	ROSACEAE	hop hornbeam	OSTRYA
cherry	ROSACEAE	hornbeam	BETULA, CARPINUS,
pear	ROSACEAE		WITCH-HAZEL
plum	ROSACEAE	incense cedar	LIBOCEDRUS
—willow	SALICACEAE	Japanese laurel	AUCUBA
—yew	TAXACEAE	Judas tree	CERCIS, REDBUD
cluster-pine	PINASTER	jujube-tree	ZIZYPHUS

June-berry	AMELANCHIER, SHADBUSH	plane	BUTTONWOOD, MAPLE
juniper	BARBADOS CEDAR, JUNIPERUS		PLATAN(E), PLATANUS
	PENCIL-CEDAR, SAVIN(E)	poplar	ABELE, ASP(EN), POPULUS
Kauri pine	COWDIE, COWRIE	Populus	ASPEN, COTTONWOOD, POPLAR
laburnum	GOLDEN RAIN	prickly ash	TOOTHACHE TREE
larch	LARIX	prickwood	DOGWOOD
Larix	LARCH	Pseudotsuga	DOUGLAS FIR
lentisk	MASTIC(H)	Pterocarya	WING NUT
Librocedrus	INCENSE CEDAR	Pyrus	APPLE, PEAR, WHITEBEAM
lilac	SYRINGA	Quercus	OAK
lime	LIND(EN), TEIL, TILIA	quince	CYDONIA
linden	LIME, TEIL, TILIA	red	
liquidambar	SWEET GUM	—cedar	CEDRELA, VIRGINIAN JUNIPER
Liriodendron	TULIP-TREE	—gum	EUCALYPTUS
locust	ALGAR(R)OBA, ALGARROBO	—pine	NORWAY PINE
	CAROB, ROBINIA	—wood	SEQUOIA, WELLINGTONIA
magnolia	UMBRELLA-TREE	Rhus	SMOKE-BUSH, SMOKE-TREE
maidenhair	GINGKO, GINKGO		SUMACH
Malus	CRAB	Robinia	LOCUST-TREE, FALSE ACACIA
maple	ACER, MASTEL	rock elm	WAHOO
mastic(h)	LENTISK	rowan	SORBUS, MOUNTAIN-ASH
medlar	MESPILUS	—like	SERVICE
Mespilus	MEDLAR	Sabal	PALMETTO
mesquite	ALGAR(R)OBA, ALGARROBO	sacred	BO(DHI)
miniature	BONSAI	Salix	SALLOW, WILLOW
monkey-puzzle	ARAUCARIA	sallow	SALIX, WILLOW
	CHILE(AN) PINE	sambuca	ELDER
Morus	BLACK MULBERRY	Sapota	GUM
mountain-ash	QUICKEN (TREE)	savin(e)	JUNIPER
	QUICK-BEAM, RODDIN, ROWAN	screw-pine	PANDANUS
	SORB(IN), SORBUS, WICKEN	Sequoia	MAMMOTH-TREE, REDWOOD
	WICKY, WITCHEN		WASHINGTONIA, WELLINGTONIA
mulberry	SYCAMINE	service tree	SORB
—fig	SYCAMORE, SYCOMORE	shadbush	AMELANCHIER, JUNE-BERRY
nettle-tree	CELTIS, HOOP-ASH	Siberian cedar	AROLLA
Nothofagus	ANTARCTIC BEECH	silk-cotton tree	ERIODENDRON
nut-pine	STONE-PINE	sloe	BLACKTHORN
oak	DURMAST, QUERCUS	smoke-tree	RHUS, SUMACH
—sapling	GROUND-OAK	Snowy Mespilus	AMELANCHIER
oil-palm	ELAEIS	Sophora	PAGODA-TREE
oldest species	BRISTLE CONE PINE	sorbus	MOUNTAIN-ASH, WHITEBEAM
osier	SALIX, SALLOW, WILLOW	Spanish oak	ROBLE
	WIDDY, WITHE, WITHY	spindle-tree	EUONYMUS, PRICKWOOD
Ostrya	HOP HORNBEAM	spruce	PICEA
pagoda-tree	SOPHORA	—fir	PICEA
palm	(see separate entry)	stone-pine	NUT-PINE
palmetto	SABAL	strawberry-tree	ARBUTUS
Pandanus	SCREW-PINE	sumach	RHUS, SMOKE-BUSH
papaw	CARICA, PAPAYA		SMOKE-TREE
pear	PYRUS	swamp	
Phellodendron	AMUR CORK TREE	—cypress	TAXODIUM
Picea	FIR, (NORWAY) SPRUCE	—oak	CASUARINA
pinaster	CLUSTER-PINE	sweet gum	LIQUIDAMBAR
Pinus	(SCOTS) PINE	Swiss stone pine	AROLLA, CEMBRA
pitch-tree	AMBOINA, KAURI PINE	sycamine	MULBERRY-TREE
	SILVER FIR, SPRUCE	sycamore	ACER, PLANE, MULBERRY-FIG

Syringa	LILAC
tacamahac	BALSAM POPLAR
tallow-tree	ALEURITES, PENTADESMA
	SAPIUM
tamarack	BLACK LARCH
	AMERICAN LARCH
Taxodium	SWAMP-CYPRESS
Taxus	YEW
teil	LIME, LINDEN
terebinth	TURPENTINE-TREE
thorntree	HAWTHORN
Thuja	ARBOR VITAE, THUYA
	TREE OF LIFE
Tilia	LIME, LINDEN
toothache tree	PRICKLY-ASH
tree of	
—heaven	AILANTO
—life	ARBOR VITAE, THUJA, THUYA
trembling poplar	ASPEN
tulip-tree	LIRIODENDRON
Turkey oak	CERRIS
turpentine-tree	TEREBINTH
Ulmus	ELM
umbrella-tree	ELKWOOD, MAGNOLIA
upas	ANTIAR
Venetian sumach	FUSTET
Viburnum	WAYFARING-TREE
Virginian juniper	RED CEDAR
Vitex	AGNUS CASTUS
walan	AMBOYNA
walnut	JUGLANS
Washingtonia	REDWOOD, SEQUIOA
wattle	ACACIA
wax-tree	JAPANESE SUMAC
	WAX-MYRTLE
wayfaring tree	MEAL-TREE, VIBURNUM
Wellingtonia	REDWOOD, SEQUIOA
whitebeam	ARIA, SORBUS, PYRUS
whitethorn	HAWTHORN
wild	
—apple	CRAB
—cherry	GEAN
willow	OSIER, SALIX, SALLOW
	WIDDY, WITHE, WITHY
wing nut	PTEROCARYA
winged elm	WAHOO
witch-hazel	HORNBEAM, WYCH-ELM
with crown cut off	POLLARD
wych-elm	SCOTCH ELM, WITCH-ELM
	WITCHEN, WITCH-HAZEL
yew	TAXUS
Zizyphus	JUJUBE-TREE
trees[2]	ARBOR
including: relating to	
terms	
stem of tree	CAUDEX, TRUNK

tree-carving	DENDROGLYPH
tree cultivation	ARBORICULTURE
	SILVICULTURE
tree-dweller	SILVAN
tree dwelling	ARBOREAL
tree garden	ARBORETUM
tree growth of region	SILVA
tree-like growth	ARBORESCENCE
tree-measuring instrument	DENDROMETER
tree-planting day	ARBOR DAY
tree-worship	DENDROLATRY
Trinidad and Tobago	TT
capital	PORT OF SPAIN
coin	CENT, DOLLAR
trophy	
acting	(*see* theatre *below*)
agricultural machinery	BURKE TROPHY
air	
—race	KING'S CUP
—speed record	SCHNEIDER TROPHY
American football	LOMBARDI TROPHY
	SUPERBOWL TROPHY
athletics	
JESSE OWENS INTERNATIONAL TROPHY	
Atlantic crossing	BLUE RIBAND
	HALE TROPHY
VIRGIN ATLANTIC CHALLENGE TROPHY	
arts	PRAEMIUM IMPERIALE
Australian football	PREMIERSHIP CUP
badminton	
—ladies	UBER CUP
—men	THOMAS CUP
baseball	CY YOUNG AWARD
bowls	MIDDLETON CUP, WALKER CUP
	WATERLOO CUP
boxing	LONSDALE BELT
broomball	TAITTINGER TROPHY
chemistry	NOBEL PRIZE
college football	HEISMAN TROPHY
cookery	GLENFIDDITCH AWARD
coursing	WATERLOO CUP
cricket	
—Australia	GILLETTE CUP
	MCDONALD'S CUP
	SHEFFIELD SHIELD
	SHELL TROPHY
v West Indies	FRANK WORRELL TROPHY
—England	
v Australia	ASHES
v West Indies	WISDEN TROPHY
—county matches	GILLETTE CUP
	NATWEST TROPHY
—fastest century	LAWRENCE TROPHY
—India	DEODHAR TROPHY
	DULEEP TROPHY
MOIN-UD-DOWLAH GOLD CUP	

	NEHRU TROPHY, RANJI TROPHY
	WILLS TROPHY
v Sri Lanka	GOPLANAN TROPHY
—New Zealand	PLUNKET SHIELD
—Pakistan	QUAID-E-AZAM TROPHY
	WILLS CUP
—South Africa	CASTLE BOWL, CURRIE CUP
	NISSAN SHIELD
—West Indies	SHELL SHIELD
croquet	MACROBERTSON SHIELD
	PRESIDENT'S CUP
curling	STRATHCONA CUP
cycling	BIDLAKE PLAQUE
	SAUNDERS TROPHY
darts	BRITISH GOLD CUP
	NATIONS CUP
debating	SILVER QUAICH
fashion design	GOLDEN THIMBLE
films	
—American	OSCAR
—British	BAFTA AWARD
—European	FELIX
—French	CAESAR
—international	PALME D'OR
—TV and cinema	GOLDEN GLOBE AWARD
—Venice	GOLDEN LION
football	
—Footballer of the Year	BALLON D'OR
—highest scorer	GOLDEN BOOT AWARD
—World Cup	JULES RIMET TROPHY
golf	CANADA CUP, CURTIS CUP
	HARRY VARDON TROPHY
	HOPMAN CUP, MURPHY'S CUP
	RYDER CUP, VAGLIANO TROPHY
	WALKER CUP, WORLD CUP
greyhound racing	SCURRY GOLD CUP
hockey	INTERCONTINENTAL CUP
horse-racing	
—Australia	MELBOURNE CUP
—England	ASCOT GOLD CUP
	CHELTENHAM GOLD CUP
	CORONATION CUP, GOODWOOD CUP
	ONE THOUSAND GUINEAS
	TWO THOUSAND GUINEAS
—France	CHALLENGE D'OR PIAGET
	GRAND PRIX DE DEAUVILLE
	PRIX JACQUES LE MAROIS
	PRIX KERGORLAY
	PRIX MAURICE GHEEST
	PRIX MORNY
	PRIX STAVROS NIARCHOS
—Ireland	GALLOWAY PLATE
ice hockey	CANADA CUP, HART TROPHY
	JAMES NORRIS TROPHY
	ROSS TROPHY, STANLEY CUP
jazz	BIRD PRIZE

jargon	GOLDEN BULL AWARD
literature	BOOKER PRIZE
	WHITBREAD PRIZE
—Britain	BRITISH BOOK AWARD, NIBBIE
—crime stories	DIAMOND DAGGER AWARD
	GOLD DAGGER AWARD
—economics	FISHER PRIZE
—fiction	HIGHAM AWARD
	PULITZER PRIZE
—first novel	BETTY TRASK AWARD
over 40	MCKITTRICK PRIZE
over 60	SAGITTARIUS PRIZE
—international	NOBEL PRIZE
—non-fiction	SILVER PEN AWARD
—science-fiction	HUGO AWARD
	NEBULA AWARD
—USA	NATIONAL BOOK AWARD
	PULITZER PRIZE, TURNER AWARD
medicine and	
psychology	NOBEL PRIZE
moto-cross	COUPE DES NATIONS
motor-cycle racing	TOURIST TROPHY
	EUROLANTIC TROPHY
motor racing	BRITISH EMPIRE TROPHY
	GORDON BENNETT TROPHY
	ULSTER TROPHY
	VANDERBILT CUP
musical composition	BRITTEN TROPHY
newspaper reporting	PULITZER
officialese	GOLDEN BULL AWARD
painting	TURNER PRIZE
peace	NOBEL PRIZE
physics	NOBEL PRIZE
play	SAMUEL BECKETT AWARD
polo	ABERA TROPHY, CARTIER GOLD CUP
	CHAMPION CUP, CHELTENHAM CUP
	CICERO CUP, COWDRAY PAR
	GOLD CUP, CUP OF THE AMERICAS
	DAVIDOFF GOLD CUP, DOLLAR CUP
	DUKE OF SUTHERLAND'S CUP
	HORSE AND HOUND CUP
	PRINCE OF WALES TROPHY
	POLO TROPHY, QUEEN'S CUP
	RALPH LAUREN TROPHY
	ROYAL WINDSOR CUP
	TEXACO TROPHY
	WESTCHESTER CUP
pop music	DIAMOND AWARD
powerboat racing	CETREK NEEDLES TROPHY
	HARMSWORTH TROPHY
recording	
—American	GRAMMY
—British	BRITS AWARD
rock music	ELVIS
rowing	BRITANNIA CUP
	DIAMOND SCULLS

	DOUBLE SCULLS CHALLENGE CUP
	GRAND CHALLENGE CUP, LADIES' PLATE
	NICKALL'S CUP, PRINCE PHILIP CUP
	PRINCESS ELIZABETH CUP
	QUEEN MOTHER CUP, SILVER GOBLETS
	STEWARD'S CUP, THAMES CUP
	VISITOR'S CUP, WYFOLD CUP
Rugby League	CHALLENGE CUP
	HARRY SUNDERLAND TROPHY
	JOHN PLAYER SPECIAL TROPHY
	LANCE TOOD AWARD
	PREMIERSHIP TROPHY
	REGAL TROPHY
—Australia	WINFIELD CUP
Rugby Union	WORLD CUP
—Australia/New Zealand	BLEDISLOE CUP
—England/Scotland	CALCUTTA CUP
—New Zealand	RANFURLY SHIELD
—South Africa	CURRIE CUP
science	NOBEL PRIZE
shinty	CAMANCHD CUP
	KEYLINE MACAULAY CUP
	MACDONALD CUP
shooting	ALEXANDRA CUP, BISLEY CUP
	CONNAUGHT CUP
	DUKE OF CAMBRIDGE TROPHY
	EYRE MEMORIAL CUP
	GENERAL'S CUP, GOLDFIELD CUP
	HUTTON TANKARD
	KING GEORGE V CUP
	QUEEEN'S CUP, QUEEN'S PRIZE
	RAVEN CUP, SIMBANG CUP
	TIMES CHALLENGE CUP, TURNER CUP
	VIZIANAGRAM TROPHY
	WINAN'S CUP, WOOD CUP
	WHITGIFT CUP, WYNESS CUP
show jumping	DUBAI CUP
	KING GEORGE V GOLD CUP
	NATIONS CUP, PRESIDENT'S CUP
	QUEEN ELIZABTH II CUP
	WORLD CUP
snooker	EMBASSY CUP, POT BLACK CUP
soccer	CHARITY SHIELD
	FOOTBALL ASSOCIATION CUP
	FOOTBALL LEAGUE CUP
	FREIGHT ROVER CUP
	UEFA CUP, WORLD CUP
—amateur	FOOTBALL ASSOCIATION VASE
—South America	LIBERATORES CUP
song writing	IVOR NOVELLO AWARD
speedway racing	GOLDEN HELMET AWARD
stage	
—American	TONY
surfing	TRIPLE CROWN, WORLD CUP
table tennis	CORBILLON CUP
	SWAYTHLING CUP

tennis	DAVIS CUP, FEDERATION CUP
	NATIONS CUP, WORLD CUP
—Germany	LUFTHANSA CUP
—ladies	MAUD WATSON TROPHY
	WIGHTMAN CUP
television	BAFTA AWARD
—acting, programme,	
etc	EMMY
—advertising	GOLDEN BREAK AWARD
—science programme	SCI-TECH AWARD
theatre	IAN CHARLESON AWARD
	LARRY OLIVIER AWARD
transport	
(air, land or water)	SEGRAVE TROPHY
writing	(*see* literature *above*)
yachting	ADMIRAL'S CUP, AMERICA CUP
	ASTRID CUP, BATHSHEBA TROPHY
	BIRKETT CUP, BONES TROPHY
	BRABAZON TROPHY, BRITANNIA CUP
	CAMROSE MEMORIAL TROPHY
	CARRITT CUP, CAYLEY CUP
	CELLINE VASE
	CHAMPAGNE MUMM TROPHY
	CHISHOLM CUP
	CORONATION CHALLENGE BOWL
	CORUM TROPHY, COURTNEY TROPHY
	CREIGHTON TROPHY, DE MAAS CUP
	DOWSON TROPHY, DUNELM TROPHY
	FITZPATRICK-ROBERTSON CUP
	FREEMANTLE SALVER, GRENFELL TROPHY
	GRETTON CUP, HAYLES BOWL
	HAYLING HULL TROPHY
	HEWITT TROPHY, HYLAND TROPHY
	PAMELA SNAGGE TROPHY
	PRESTON CUP, PURDY CUP
	QUARTER-TON CUP, RATSEY CUP
	RAYMOND TROPHY, REDWING CUP
	RYS TROPHY, SOUTHERN CROSS CUP
	SUNBEAM SALVER, TOMAHAWK TROPHY
	WHITBREAD CUP

tropical

American	(*see* **South America**)
bean	COW(HAGE), COWITCH
	LABLAB
bird	BARBET, DRONGO(-SHRIKE)
	HONEY-EATER, HUMMING-BIRD
	JACANA, KING-CROW
	KING-VULTURE, SALAGANE
	SUN-BIRD, SWIFTLET
	TROCHILUS, TROGON
cashew-nut tree	LENTISK
climber	COCCOLUS, COW(H)AGE
	COWITCH, LIANA
dal	PIGEON-PEA
dish	DA(H)L, DHOLL
fern	DICKSONIA, ELKHORN-FERN

—genus	SCHIZAE
fever	(*see* **disease**)
fish	CHAETODON, CORAL FISH
	DANIO, SEA-SURGEON
	TRIGGERFISH
flower	ANTHURIUM
fruit	ANANA, CHINESE GOOSEBERRY
	MANGO(STAN), MANGOSTEEN
	TAMARIND
gourd	LOOFA(H), LUFFA
grass	SORGHUM
gum	KINO
herb	ZINGIBER
humming-bird	RUBY-THROAT, SABRE-WING
	SAPPHIRE-WING
	SWALLOW-TAILED BIRD
leaf-climbers	GLORIOSA
mallow	GOSSYPIUM, URENA
narcotic fruit	INDIAN BERRY
nut	BEN(-NUT)
orchid	DENDROBIUM
papyrus	CYPERUS
pigeon-pea	DA(H)L, DHOLL
plant	BATATA, BIGNONIA, CROTON
	DERRIS, HIBISCUS, FALSE PAREIRA
	LAPORTEA, SWEET-POTATO
	VELVET-LEAF, YAM
potato	YAM
resin	ELEMI
seabird	PHAETON, TROPIC-BIRD
sedge	CYPERUS
shrub	CAPSICUM
tree	CARAPA, GNETUM, MACACO
	RAUWOLFIA, TAMARIND
—anchovy-pear	LECYTHIS
—Brazil-nut	LECYTHIS
—cannon-ball tree	LECYTHIS
—dragon-tree	CORDYLINE
—erythrina	CORAL-TREE
—flamboyant	POINCIANA
—flowering	COMBRETUM
—Kigelia	SAUSAGE-TREE
—mangosteen	GARCINIA
—mahogany	CARAPA, CEDRELA
—monkey-pot	LECYTHIS
—Moringa	HORSE-RADISH TREE
—Poinciana	FLAMBOYANTE, FLAME-LEAF
	PEACOCK-FLOWER
Tunisia	TN
capital	TUNIS
coin	DINAR, MILLIME
governor	BEY
Turkey	TR
administrative official	VAIVODE
	VOIVODE, WAIVODE
admiral	CAPITAN

ambassador	ELCHEE, EL(T)CHI
armed attendant	CAVASS, KAVASS
army officer	BIMBASHI, BINBASHI
band	METHER
bath	HAMMAN, HUMM(A)UM
bay	KORFEZI
boat	PERMAGY
brazier	MANGAL
cap	MARTAGAN
cape (headland)	BUR-UN, BUR-NU
capital	ANGORA, ANKARA
carpet	CADANE
cart	AR(A)BA
castle	HISAR
cavalryman	SPAHEE, SPAHI
clotted cream	KAYMAK
coin	
—unit	KURUSH
—100 kurush	LIRA
—$^1/_{40}$ piastre	PARA
—silver	PIASTRE
obsolete	ASPER
commander	AG(H)A
—in-chief	SERASKIER
cymbal	CROTALO
dagger	ATAGHAN, YATAG(H)AN
dam	BARAJ
dancer	CENGHI
decree	FIRMAN, HATTI-SHERIF
	IRADE
division	SANJAK
dog	ANATOLIAN
drink	AIRAN, BOZA, MASTIC(H)
dulcimer	SANTIR, SANT(O)UR
dynasty	OSMANLI, OTTOMAN, SELJUK
emblem	CRESCENT
execution	GANCH
felt cap	CALPA(C)K, KALPAK
female slave	ODALISK, ODALI(S)QUE
fermented milk	YAOURT, YOGH(O)URT
feudal militiaman	TIMARIOT
filo pastry	YUFKA
flag	CRESCENT
forest	ORMANI
governor	BASHAW, BEGLERBEG
	BEY, CAIMAC(AM), KAIMAKAM
	PASHA, PACHA, VALI, WALI
grape-juice syrup	PEKMEZ
guard house	DERBEND
gulf	KORFEZI
harbour	LIMAN
harem	SERAGLIO, SERAI(L)
head of division	MUTESSARIF
headgear	FEZ
hors d'oeuvres	HUMMUS, MEZE
hot drink	SALEP

ice cream	KAYMAK, SALEP	porter	HAM(M)AL
imperial government	PORTE	power	CRESCENT
infidel	GIAOUR	prime minister	GRAND VIZIER
inn	CAFENET, (CARAVAN)SERAI	property dedicated to God	WAQ'F
	KHAN	province	EYALET, VILAYET
instrument	SAZ	ravioli	MANTI
irregular soldier	BASHI-BAZOUK	reform bill	TANZIMAT
island	ADASI	river	IRMAK, NEHRI
javelin	JEREED, JERID	robe	CAFTAN, DOL(L)MAN
jurisdiction of pasha	PACHALIC		KAFTAN
	PASHALIK	rug	KHILIM, KONIA
land division	SANJAK	ruler	ATABEG, ATABEK, CALIPH
lake	GOL(U)		KHAN, PADISHAH, SULTAN
language	OSMANLI, OTTOMAN	sailor	GALIONGEE
law	MULTOCA	savoury pie	BOREK
manna	TREHALA	sea	DENIZI
measures		seed paste	HUMMUS, HOUM(O)US
—25"	ENDAZE		TAHINA, TAHINI
—30"	ARSHEEN, ARSHIN(E)	servant	HAM(M)AL
—2½ acres	DJERIB	ship	CAIC, CAIQUE, PATAMAR
—1 bushel	KILEH		SAIC(K), SAIQUE
meat		smoking (hookah)	CHILLUM
—dish	CABOB, KABAB, KABOB	soldier	JANISSARY, JANIZAR(Y)
	KEBAB, KEBOB		NIZAM
—on skewer	SHISH KEBAB	standard	CRESCENT, HORSETAIL
—pizza	LAHMACUN	strait	BOGAZI
men's quarters	SELAMLIK	stream	CAYI
military		street	CADDESI
—chief	BASHAW, PACHA	stuffed	
	PASHA, ZAIM	—aubergines	IMAM BAYILDI
—district	ZIAMET	—vineleaves	DOLMA(DE
—music	JANIZARY MUSIC	sultan	GRAND SIGNIOR
milk pudding	TAVUK GOGSU	sweetmeat	BULBUL, HAL(A)VA(H)
minced lamb	CIG KOFTE		LOKUM, LOUKOUM
minister	WAZIR, WESIER	sword-bearer	SELICTAR
	VESIR, VISIER, VIZI(E)R	theologian	ULEMA
Moslem	SALAR	title	AG(H)A, BASHAW, BEG, BEY
—sect	BEKTASHI, KARMATHIAN		DEY, GHAZI, PACHA, PASHA
	MEVLEVI, (WHIRLING) DERVISH	—of respect	EFFENDI
mountain	DAG		HODJA, KHO(D)JA
—range	SILSILESI	Turk	OSMANLI, OTTAMITE
non-Moslem	RAYAH		OTTOMITE, SELJUK
officer	AG(H)A	vest	YELEK
order of knighthood	MEDJIDIE	village	KOY
orchid root drink	SALEP	vine	SOMA
palace	SERAGLIO	wagon	AR(A)BA, AROBA
—guard	BOSTANGI	walnut salad	MUHAMARRA
pass	GEDIGI	war minister	SERASKIER
pastry	KADAYIF	water-pipe	CHILLIM, HOOKA(H)
—with nuts, etc	BACLAVA, BAKLAVA		NARG(H)ILE, NARGILEH
pavilion	KIOSK		NARG(H)IL(L)Y
pipe	CHIBOUK, CHIBOUQUE	weight	
plain	OVASI	—1½ drams	MUSCAL
policeman	CAVASS, KAVASS	—2¼lb	OKE
	ZABTIEH, ZAPTIAH, ZAPTIEH	—17lb	BATMAN
port	LIMAN	—125lb	CANTAR, KANTAR, QUANTAR

—509lb	CHEKI
women's quarters	SERAGLIO, SERAIL
yoghurt soup	YAYLA CORBASI
twelve	DOZ(EN), XII
12½ cents	BIT
Apostles	ANDREW, BARTHOLEMEW, JAMES
	JAMES (brother of John), JOHN
	JUDAS, MATTHEW, PETER, PHILIP
	SIMON, THADDEUS, THOMAS
base	DUODECIMAL
Christmas presents	DRUMMERS
combining form	DODECA-
having 12	
—columns	DODECASTYLE
—faces	DODECAHEDRON
—leaves per sheet	DUODECIMO
—sides	DODECAGON
—stamens	DODECANDRIAN
	DODECANDROUS
—styles	DODECAGYNIAN
	DODECAGYNOUS
—syllables	DODECASYLLABIC
—tones	DODECAPHONIC
—yearly intervals	DUODECENNIAL
E(E)C members	BELGIUM, DENMARK
	FRANCE, GREAT BRITAIN
	GREECE, IRELAND, ITALY
	LUXEMBURG, NETHERLANDS
	PORTUGAL, SPAIN
	WEST GERMANY
fold	DUODENARY
Glorious Twelfth	AUGUST
hours	AM, PM
hundred	MCC
in Norse mythology	GODS
inches	FOOT
jobs	LABOURS OF HERCULES
men	JURY
peers of Charlemagne	DOUZEPERS, PALADIN
signs of Zodiac	(*see* **Zodiac**)
tables	ROMAN LAW
tribes	ISRAELITES
twelfth	DUODECIMAL, DUODENARY
twenty	SCORE, XX
combining form	ICOS(A)-
having	
—20	
faces	ICOSAHEDRONAL
stamens	ICOSANDRIAN, ICOSANDROUS
—24 faces	ICOSITETRAHEDRONAL
Twentieth Century	
Dictionary	TCD
twenty-five pounds sterling	PONY
twenty-six in Norse	
mythology	GODDESSES
twenty-seven Books	NEW TESTAMENT, NT

twenty-twenty	VISION
twenty thousand	K
two	COMPANY, PAIR, PR, TWAIN
a penny	CHEAP, TRIVIAL
alternative courses	DILEMMA
choices	DILEMMA
Christmas presents	TURTLE DOVES
cleft	BIFID, BIPARTITE
combining form	BI-, DI-
companies monopolising trade	DUOPOLY
eyed steak	KIPPER
faced	HYPOCRITICAL
—god	JANUS
fold	BINAL, DOUBLE, DUAL, DUPLEX
	DUPLICATE, TWIFOLD
for his heels	JACK, KNAVE
grooved tablet	DIGLYPH
groups	BIS, BRACE, COMPANY
	COUPLE, DOUBLE, DUAD
	DUAL, DUO, PAIR
	TWAIN, TWOSOME
having two	
—adductor muscles	DIMYARIAN
—amyl groups	DIAMYL
—ancestral groups	DIPHYLETIC
—at one birth	DITOKOUS
—atoms	DIATOMIC
—axes	DIAXIAL, DIAXON(IC)
—beats	DICROTIC
per bar	DUPLE
—branches	BIFURCATE(D), BISULCATE
	DICHOTOMOUS, DIVARICATE
	TWIFORKED, TWYFORKED
—breeding seasons p.a.	DIGONEUTIC
—bundles of stamens	DIDELPHOUS
—butyl groups	DIBUTYL
—carpels	DICARPELLARY
—cells	BICAMERAL, BILOCULAR
—chromium atoms	BICHROMATE
	DICHROMATE
—claws	DIDACTYL
—colours	DICHROM(AT)IC
—cotyledons	DICOTYLEDONOUS
—cusps	BICUSPID
—double	
refractive power	BIREFRINGENT
serrations	BISERRATE
—ears	BINAURAL
—electrodes	DIODE
—ethyl groups	DIETHYL
—eyes	BINOCULAR
—faces	BIFACIAL, DIHEDRAL
—feet	BIPED(AL)
—fibres	BINERVATE
—fingers	DIDACTYLOUS
—focal lengths	BIFOCAL

—forms	DIMORPHIC, TWIFORMED	—sets of teeth	DIPHYODONT
	TWYFORMED	—sexes	BISEXUAL
—furrows	BISULCATE	—sides	BILATERAL
—gills	DIBRANCHIATE	—sheaths	DITHECAL
—gods	DITHEISTIC	—spore cases	DITHECAL
—halves	DIMIDIATE	—stable states	BISTABLE
—hands	BIMANAL, BIMANOUS	—stamens	DIANDROUS
—heads	BICEPS, BICIPITAL	—stomachs	DIGASTRIC
	DICEPHALOUS	—styles	DIGYNIAN, DIGYNOUS
—husbands	BIGAMOUS, DIANDROUS	—sulphur atoms	BISULPHIDE, DISULPHIDE
	DIGAMOUS	—syllables	DISYLLABLE, DISYLLABIC
—hydrogen atoms	DIACID, DIBASIC	—terms	BINOMIAL
—hydroxyl groups	DIHYDRIC	—thecae	DITHECAL
—independently heritable		—threads	BIFILAR
characters	DIHYBRID	—toes	DIDACTYLOUS
—keys	BITONAL	before and two	
—languages	BIGLOT, BILINGUAL	behind	ZYGODACTYL(IC)
	DIGLOT	—types of spore	HETEROSPOROUS
—legs	BIPOD(AL)	—use of two	
—letters	BILITERAL	elements	AMPHIBIAN, AMPHIBIOUS
—lips	BILABIAL	hands	AMBIDEXT(E)ROUS
—leaflets	BIFOLIOLATE	—valencies	BIVALENT, DIATOMIC
—leaves	BIFOLIATE		DIVALENT
—lobes	BILOBAR, BILOBATE	—valves	BIVALVE, DIVALVULAR
	BILOBED, BILOBULAR	—variants	BIVARIATE, DIVARIATE
	DITHECAL	—ways	BIVIOUS
—lines	DIGRAM	—wheels	BICYCLE
—loculi	BILOCULAR, DITHECAL	—whorls	DICYCLIC
—marriages	BIGAMOUS, DIGAMOUS	of stamens	(OB)DIPLOSTEMONOUS
—measures	DIMETER	—wings	BIPLANE, DIPTERAL
—metals	BIMETALLIC		DIPTEROUS
—methyl radicals	DIMETHYL	—wives	BIGAMOUS, DIGAMOUS
—months' duration	BIMESTRIAL		DIGYNIAN, DIGYNOUS
—oxygen atoms	DIOXIDE	—wombs	DIDELPHIC
—pairs of stamens	DIDYNAMIAN	—words	BINOMIAL
	DIDYNAMOUS	—xylem strands	DIARCH
—parts	BIPARTITE, DIMEROUS	—yearly occurrences	BIANNUAL
	DIDYMOUS	—zones	BIZONAL
—perianth whorls	DI(PLO)CHLAMYDEOUS	hulled boat	CATAMARAN
—petals	BIPETALOUS	hundred	CC, H, S, SIGMA
	DIPETALOUS	—and fifty	E, K
—phenyl groups	DIPHENYL	thousand	E
—pistils	DIGYNIAN, DIGYNOUS	—thousand	H, S, SIGMA
—planes	DIHEDRAL	—years	BICENTARY, BICENTENNIAL
—points	BICUSPID(ATE)	in song	LILLYWHITE BOYS
—poles	BIPOLAR, DIPOLAR	letter word	BILITERAL
—prongs	BIDENTAL, BIDENTATE(D)	letters, one sound	DIGRAPH
	BIFURCATE(D)	men in office	DUUMVIR(RATE)
—rays	DIACT(INAL), DIACTINE	month period	BIMESTER
—rings	DICYCLIC	notes	DUPLET
—rows	BIFARIOUS, BISERIAL	one of two at a birth	TWIN
	DISTICHOUS	penny	CHEAP, WORTHLESS
—sacs	DITHECAL	performers	DUET(T), DUETTO, DUO
—sepals	DISEPALOUS	persons	COMPANY, DUO
—separate sexes	DIOECIOUS		TWOSOME
—series	BISERIAL	—ruling	DIARCHY

Scottish	TWA(E), TWAY	time	CROSS, DECEIVE
speaking	DIALOGUE	times	DUPL(ICAT)E
	DUALOGUE	under par	EAGLE
spots	DEUCE	vowels sounded as one	DIPHTHONG
stars	GEMINI	winged plane	BIPLANE
thousand	Z	type	(*see* **printing**)

U

Uganda	EAU
capital	KAMPALA
coin	CENT, SHILLING
Ulster	NI
Defence Association	UDA
Defence Regiment	UDR
Freedom Fighters	UFF
Unionists	UU
Volunteer Force	UVF
united	
United Arab Emirates	UAE
—capital	DUBAI
—coin	FILS, DIRHAM
United Arab Republic	ET, UAR
United Dominions Trust	UDT
United Free Church	UF
United Kingdom	UK
United Nations	
—Association	UNA
—(Organisation)	UNO
United Presbyterian	UP
United Press	UP
United States	US, USA
—Army	USA
—(Army) Air Force	US(A)AF
—Navy	USN
—Ship	USS
universal	
Universal Decimal Classification	UDC
universal organisation	UN
Universal Postal Union	UPU
universal set	E
Universal Time	UT
university	U, UNIV
academic dress	GOWN, MORTARBOARD
—Oxford	SUBFUSC, SUBFUSK
accounts for food	BATTELS
administrator	VICE-CHANCELLOR
	RECTOR
American	CALTECH, HARVARD, YALE
annual feast	GAUDY, RAG
at university	UP
basic degree	BACCALAUREATE
body of senior members	CONGREGATION
brochure	PROSPECTUS
built in recent years	REDBRICK
business representative	SYNDIC
class	SEMINAR, TUTORIAL
course (half-year)	SEMESTER
degree ceremony (Amer.)	COMMENCEMENT
department	FACULTY
entrance examination	MATRICULATION
expel from university	RUSTICATE
	SEND DOWN
fellow	DON
first-year student	FRESHER, FRESHMAN
food shop	BUTTERY
former student	ALUMNA, ALUMNUS
four branches of mathematics	QUADRIVIUM
fraternity (Amer.)	PHI BETA KAPPA
governing body	SENATE
—Scotland	SENATUS ACADEMICUS
governor (Amer.)	REGENT
graduate	ALUMNA, ALUMNUS
	BA, BSC
graduates' conference	CONVOCATION
Grants Committee	UGC
grounds	CAMPUS
higher degree	MASTER, DOCTOR
—Europe	LICENTIATE
honours examination	
—Cambridge	TRIPOS
—Oxford	GREATS, MODS
instructor	LECTURER, TUTOR
liberal arts	TRIVIUM
member	BA, DON, F, FELLOW
	MA, PROF(ESSOR)
men's club (Amer.)	FRATERNITY
non-resident student	EXTRAMURAL
official responsible for	
—ceremonies	BEADLE
—discipline	PROCTOR
—financial matters	BURSAR
—records	REGISTRAR
old American universities	IVY LEAGUE
one	
—awarded a degree	GRADUATE
first-class honours in mathematics (Camb.)	WRANGLER
—holding professorship created by royal grant	REGIUS PROFESSOR
—representing university at sport	BLUE
—studying for degree	UNDERGRADUATE
—waiting to receive degree	GRADUAND
paid leave for research or travel	SABBATICAL
place of those who pass without honours	GULF
press	CUP, OUP
principal	VICE-CHANCELLOR, RECTOR
—German	RECTOR MAGNIFICUS

proctor's assistant (Oxford and Cambridge)	BULLDOG
second-year student (Amer.)	SOPHOMORE
Senate committee —member (Camb.)	SYNDIC
senior lecturer	READER, PROFESSOR
servant	BEDDER, FAG, GYP SCOUT, SKIP
steward	MANCIPLE
student (Cambridge and Dublin)	(SUB-)SIZAR, (SUB-)SIZER
teacher	DON, LECTURER PROFESSOR, READER TUTOR
teachers' union	UAT
term	SEMESTER
the university that one attended	ALMA MATER
titular head of university	CHANCELLOR
universities	
—America	CALTECH, COLUMBIA DUKE, HARVARD PRINCETON, STANFORD, YALE
—England	ASTON, BATH, BIRMINGHAM BRADFORD, BRISTOL BRUNEL, BUCKINGHAM CAMBRIDGE, CITY, DURHAM EAST ANGLIA, ESSEX, EXETER HULL, KEELE, KENT, LANCASTER LEEDS, LEICESTER, LIVERPOOL LONDON, LOUGHBOROUGH
	MANCHESTER, NEWCASTLE NOTTINGHAM, OPEN, OXFORD READING, SALFORD, SHEFFIELD SOUTHAMPTON, SURREY, SUSSEX WARWICK, YORK
—France	SORBONNE
—Ireland	DUBLIN
—Japan	KOKUGAKUIN
—Northern Ireland	BELFAST
—Scotland	ABERDEEN, DUNDEE EDINBURGH GLASGOW, HERIOT-WATT ST ANDREWS, STIRLING STRATHCLYDE
—Wales	WALES
vice-chancellor's mace bearer	BEADLE
—(Oxford and Cambridge)	BEDELL
women's club (Amer.)	SORORITY
Uruguay	ROU, U, URU
capital	MONTE VIDEO
coin	CENTESIMO, PESO
US(A)	(*see* **America, states**)
USSR	(*see also* **Russia**)
republics of the former USSR	
—now in CIS	AZERBAIJAN, BELARUS GEORGIA, KAZAKHSTAN MOLDOVA, RUSSIA(N FEDERATION) TADJIKISTAN, TURKMENISTAN UKRAINE, UZBEKISTAN
—not in CIS	ARMENIA, ESTONIA LATVIA, LITHUANIA

V

Vanuatu

capital	PORT VILA
coin	CENTIME, FRANC, VATU
old name	NEW HEBRIDES

vegetable

beans	(*see* **pulses**)
Belgian endive	CHICORY
black salsify	SCORZONERA
Brassica	CABBAGES
bulb	GARLIC
cabbages, etc	BRASSICA
chard	LEAF BEET
chicory	BELGIAN ENDIVE
Chinese cabbage	PAKCHOI
corn etc	(*see* **cereals**)
courgette	ZUCCHINI
edible seaweed	LAVER, SEA LETTUCE
endive	ESCAROLE
flowers, leaves	ARTICHOKE, ASPARAGUS
	BORECOLE, BROCCOLI, CABBAGE
	CALABRESE, CARDOON, CAULIFLOWER
	CELERY, CHARD, CHICON, CHIC(C)ORY
	CHINESE CABBAGE, CHINESE LEAVES
	COLE(WORT), COLLARD, CORN SALAD
	COS, CURLY KALE, DWARF FENNEL
	ENDIVE, FENNEL, FINNOCHIO
	FINOC(C)HIO, FLORENCE FENNEL
	FRENCH FENNEL, FRISE(E), GLASSWORT
	GLOBE ARTICHOKE, GOOD KING HENRY
	GOOSEFOOT, KALE, KAIL, KOHLRABI
	, LAMB'S LETTUCE, LEAF BEET
	LEEK, LETTUCE, MARSH SAMPHIRE
	MUNG BEANSHOOTS, ORACH(E)
	OYSTER PLANT, POKEWEED
	RADICCHIO, RAMSON, RAPE, ROMAINE
	SALAD BURNET, SALSAFY, SALSIFY
	SAMPHIRE, SAVOY, SAXIFRAGE
	SCORZONERA, SEAKALE(BEET)
	SILVER BEET, SORREL
	SPINACH(BEET), SPROUTING BROCCOLI
	SUCCORY, SWEET FENNEL
	SWISS CHARD
fresh fruit and vegetables	CRUDITES
fruit pod	AUBERGINE, BRINJAL
	BREADFRUIT, BREADNUT
	CAPSICUM, CHAYOTE, CHOWCHOW
	CUCUMBER, CUSTARD MARROW, DOODY

	EGG-PLANT, GOURD, KARELA
	LADIES' FINGERS, MANGETOUT
	OKRA, PIMIENTO, PEPPER
	PUMPKIN, SQUASH, SUGAR PEA
	TOMATO, ZUCCHINI
	(*see also* **fruit, pulses**)
Good King Henry	GOOSEFOOT
ladies's fingers	OKRA
leaf beet	CHARD
leafy vegetables	GREENS, POTHERB
—America	POKEWEED
leek	ROCAMBOLE, SCALLION
mushroom	(*see* **fungus**)
okra	LADIES' FINGERS
oyster plant	SALSIFY
	VEGETABLE OYSTER
peas	(*see* **pulses**)
potatoes	ARRAN PILOT, ASPERGES
	BELLE DE FONTENAY, BRODICK
	BINTJE, CARA, CARLINGFORD, CATRIONA
	CHARLOTTE, CORNICHON, DESIREE
	DUKE OF YORK, ELVIRA, EPICURE
	ESTIMA, FOREMOST, FRENCH CHARLOTTE
	HOMEGUARD, JERSEY MIDS
	KING EDWARD, LA RATTE, MAJESTIC
	MARFONA, MARIS PEER, MARIS PIPER
	PENTA, PENTLAND DELL
	PENTLAND JAVELIN
	PENTLAND SQUIRE, PINK FIR APPLE
	RECORD, ROMANO, SHARPES EXPRESS
	ULSTER CHIEFTAIN, WILJA
—American	RUSSET BURBANK
—Irish	MURPHY, PRATIE
—Scottish	TATTIE, TATTY
—slang	SPUD
pulses	(*see separate entry*)
rocambole	LEEK
root	AHIPA, ARTICHOKE, BEETROOT
	CARROT, CASSAVA, CELERIAC
	CHINESE WATER-CHESTNUT
	COCOYAM, DASHEEN, EARTHNUT
	EDDO, FINNOCHIO, FLORENCE FENNEL
	JERUSALEM ARTICHOKE
	MANDIOC(C)(A), MANI(H)OC
	MANIHOT, MOOLI, OCA, ONION
	SALEP, SALOOP, SCALLION
	SHALLOT, PARSNIP
	PIGNUT, POTATO, RUTABAGA
	SUGAR BEET, SWEDE, SWEET POTATO
	TARO, TURNIP, YAM
salad	ALEXANDERS, CABBAGE LETTUCE
	CELERY
	CHICORY, CHINESE LETTUCE
	CHIVE, COS LETTUCE, CRESS
	CUCUMBER, ENDIVE, ESCAROLE
	ONION, RADISH, RAMPION, PEPPER

	SPRING ONION, TOMATO
	WATERCRESS, YARROW
salsify	OYSTER PLANT
	VEGETABLE OYSTER
scallion	LEEK, SPRING ONION
scorzonera	BLACK SALSIFY
sedge tuber	WATER CHESTNUT
spring onion	SCALLION
squashes	ACORN, BUTTERBALL
	BUTTERCUP, BUTTERNUT, CALABAZA
	CHRISTOPHINE, COURGETTE
	CUSTARD, DELICATA
	GEL REUZIN, GOLDEN DELICIOUS
	GOLDEN NUGGET, GREEN DELICA
	HOKAIDO, KARELA, KOBOCHE
	LITTLE APPLE, LITTLE GEM
	ONION, PATTYPAN, PUMPKIN
	RED KURI, SCALLOP, SPAGHETTI
	SWEET DUMPLING, SWEET POTATO
	TABLE QUEEN, TURBAN
	(VEGETABLE) MARROW, ZAPALLO
sweet	
—potato	YAM
New Zealand	KUMARA
—turnip	RUTABAGA, SWEDE
turnip	
—Scottish	NEEP
—Swedish	RUTABAGA, SWEDE
vegetable oyster	OYSTER PLANT
	SALSIFY
young	
—cabbage	SPRING GREENS
—onion	GREEN ONION
—turnip tops	RAPPINI
zucchini	COURGETTE
vegetable dishes	
beans	BAKED BEANS
cabbage	BUBBLE AND SQUEAK
	CAULIFLOWER AU GRATIN
	COLESLAW
candied	SUCCADE
carrot	CARROT CAKE
chick-peas and spices	FALAFEL, FELAFEL
diced vegetables	
—battered and fried (Ind.)	PAKORA
—salad	MACEDOINE
French	PISSALADIERE
	RATATOUILLE, TIAN
—fries	POTATO CHIPS
garnish of vegetable	
strips	JARDINIERE
	JULIENNE
German	
—cabbage	ROTKOHL, SAUERKRAUT
—potatoes	KARTOFFELKNODEL
	KARTOFFELPUFFER

Greek	DOLMA(DE), FASIOLA
	TSATSIKI, TZATZIKA
in	
—syrup	SUCCADE
—thin pancake	SPRING ROLL
Indian	RAITA
Indonesian	GADO-GADO
Irish	CHAMP, COLCANNON
Italian	GNOCCHI, PEPERONATA
Jewish	FALAFEL, FELEFEL, LATKE
lentil cake	CHILLADA
mashed potatoes	
—and cabbage	BUBBLE AND SQUEAK
Irish	COLCANNON
—piped and browned	DUCHESSE
maize dish (US)	SUCCOTASH
Mexican	CAESAR SALAD
	GUACAMOLE
Middle Eastern	BABA GOUNASH
	DOLMA(DE)
	FALAFEL, FELAFEL
	HUMM(O)US
mixed, diced	MACEDOINE, MIREPOIS
	MIREPOIX
peas	A LA FRANCAIS
	MUSHY PEAS
	PEASE PUDDING
pickled cabbage	SAUERKRAUT
potato	ANNA, BOULANGERE, CHIPS
	CRISPS, CROQUETTE
	DAUPHINOIS, DUCHESSE
	FONDANT, HASH BROWN
	HUNTER'S PIE, LYONNAISE
	MASHED, PARISIENNE, SCALLOPS
	SHEPHERD'S PIE, TORTILLA
—cake	GALETTE
—chips	FRENCH FRIES
—sliced and fried	GAME CHIP
—stewed (Scot.)	STOVIES
salad	CALIFORNIAN SALAD
	COLESLAW, EGG MAYONNAISE
	LOBSTER MAYONNAISE
	PATIO SALAD, ROMA SALAD
	RUSSIAN SALAD, SALADE NICOISE
	TAHITIAN SALAD, WALDORF SALAD
salad dressing	(*see* **sauces**)
Scottish	STOVIES
Singapore	GADO-GADO
small green peas	PETIT POIS
Swiss	RO(E)STI
Turkish	IMAM BAYILDI
vehicle	
amphibious	DUCK, DUKW, WEASEL
—tracked	AMTRACK
amusement vehicle	DODGEM (CAR)
	DUNE BUGGY

articulated	
—bus	BENDIBUS
—vehicle	RIG
cab	CABRIOLET
car	(*see* **motor-car**)
carriage	(*see separate entry*)
cross-country	
vehicle	ALL-TERRAIN VEHICLE, ATV
	SCRAMBLER
delivery vehicle	
—American	PANEL TRUCK
—milk	FLOAT
flat-bottomed	FLOAT
general-purpose	
vehicle	LORRY, PICK-UP
	TRUCK, UTILITY, VAN
hired vehicle	MINICAB, (TAXI)CAB
	TAXI
horse-drawn vehicle	(*see* **carriage**)
large box-van	PANTECHNICON
lunar	MOON BUGGY
man-powered vehicle	BICYCLE
	HOBBY-HORSE, JAMPAN
	JINRICKSHA(W), JINRIKISHA
	LITTER, MONOCYCLE, PALANQUIN
	PEDICAB, PENNY-FARTHING
	RICKSHA(W), SCOOTER, SEDAN CHAIR
	TRICYCLE, TRISHAW, UNICYCLE
	VELOCIPEDE
military	(BREN-GUN)CARRIER
	HALF-TRACK, JEEP
	PERSONNEL CARRIER
	SCOUT CAR, TANK
motor-car	(*see separate entry*)
motorised pedal-	
cycle	MOPED
one-wheeled	MONOCYCLE, UNICYCLE
open coach	CHARABANC
public transport	
vehicle	COACH, MINBUS, (OMNI)BUS
	TRAM, TROLLEY-BUS
—American	GREYHOUND, STREET-CAR
police vehicle	BLACK MARIA, HOOLIVAN
	PATROL CAR
railway vehicle	BOGIE TRUCK, CABOOSE
	DANDY CART, (FLY-)COACH
	FREIGHTLINER, LOCOMOTIVE
	PONY ENGINE, PULLMAN
	SLEEPER, (TANK-)ENGINE
	TENDER, WAGON-LIT
small	
—bus	MINIBUS
—car	MINI(CAR)
—taxi	MINICAB
snow vehicle	(BOB)SLEIGH, DRAG, LUGE
	KIBITKA, SKIBOB, SKIDOO

	SKIMOBILE, SLED(GE), SNOCAT
	SNOWMOBILE, TOBOGGAN
	WEASEL
three-wheeled	TRICYCLE, TRISHAW
touring coach	CHARABANC
tractor	CRAWLER
two-wheeled	BICYCLE, JINRICKSHA(W)
	JINRIKISHA, MOTOR-CYCLE
	(MOTOR-)SCOOTER, RICKSHA(W)
very large	JUGGERNAUT
with	
—removable top	CONVERTIBLE
	RAGTOP, SOFT-TOP
—two doors	COUPE
veins	(*see* **circulation**)
Venetian	
boat	GONDOLA
boatman	GONDOLIER
bridge	RIALTO
coin	BETSO, DUCATOON, SEQUIN
	ZECCHINE, ZECCHINO
	ZECHIN, ZEQUIN
dance	FORLANA, FURLANA
magistrate	DOGE, PODESTA
merchant	ANTONIO, POLO
mosaic	TERRAZZO
noble	DOGE, MAGNIFICO
prosecutor	AVVOCADORE
resort	LIDO
rose	SIEN(N)A
ship	ARGOSY, FRIGATOON
state barge	BUCENTAUR
sumach	FUSTET
sword	SCHIAVONE
Venezuela	YV
capital	SANTIAGO
coin	BOLIVAR, CENTIMO
	LOCHO, MEDIO
verse	V
additional syllable	HYPERCATALEXIS
ancient Phrygian metre	GALLIAMBIC
answering	
—alternately	AMOEBAEAN
—stanza	ANTISTROPHE
anthology	FLORILEGIUM
apparent rhyme	EYE-RHYME
Arabic	G(H)AZAL, GHAZEL
burlesque poem	DOGGEREL, MACARONIC
Byzantine verse	POLITICAL VERSE
canto	DUAN
choliamb	SCAZON
classic hexameters	HEROIC VERSE
closed rhyme	RIMA CHIUSA
collection of poems	ANTHOLOGY, DIVAN
combining	
—dactyls with trochees	LOGAOEDIC

—parallel sentences	REPORTED VERSES
competition in verse	TENSON, TENZON
concise poem	EPIGRAM
concluding lines	EPILOGUE
continuation of sense	
beyond end of line	ENJAMB(E)MENT
continuity of verses	SYNAPHE(I)A
corresponding in	
arrangement of syllables	TAUTOMETRIC
couplet	DISTICH
—burlesque	HUDIBRASTIC
—heroic	RIDING-RHYME
—with 12 and 14	
syllables	POULTER'S MEASURE
dactyl and	
—spondee	ADONIC
—three trochees	GLYCONIC VERSE
—trochee	ADONIC
dactylic hexameter	DOLICHURUS
	PYTHIAN VERSE
division of	
—foot	SEMEION
—line	HEMISTIC
—poem	DUAN
double	
—foot	DIPODY
—limerick	TWINER
—spondee	DISPONDEE
downbeat	THESIS
duration of	
—half of long syllable	MORA
—short syllable	MORA
eight strophes	OCTASTROPHIC
emphasising	
—sound of words	PHONETIC POETRY
—the word itself	HERMETIC POETRY
	POESIA ERMETICA
—verbal imagery	IMAGISM
—visual effect of	
words	CONCRETE POETRY
feet	
—½ foot	SEMIPED
—1 foot	MONOMETER
—1½ feet	SESQUIPEDAL(IAN)
—2 feet	DIMETER, DIPODY
combined	SYZYGY
—2½ feet	PENTHEMIMER
iambi	DIAMB
—3 feet	TRIMETER, TRIPODY
—4 feet	GLYCONIC, TETRAMETER
	TETRAPODY
—5 feet	PENTAMETER, PENTAPODY
—6 feet	HEXAMETER, HEXAPODY
	SENARIUS, SENARY
—7 feet	HEPTAMETER, HEPTAPODY
	SEPTENARIUS, SEPTENARY

—7 half-feet	HEPHTHEMIMER
—8 feet	OCTAMETER, OCTAPODY
	OCTONARION
final	
—letters of lines	
spell word	TELESTICH
—stanza	ENVOI
foot of	
—1 syllable	MONOSYLLABLE
—2 syllables	DISYLLABLE
long:short	CHOREE, CHOREUS
	TROCHEE
long:long	SPONDEE
short:long	IAMB(US)
short:short	PYRRHIC
—3 syllables	TRISYLLABLE
long:long:long	MOLOSSUS
long:long:short	ANTIBACCHIUS
long:short:long	AMPHIMACER, CRETIC
long:short:short	DACTYL
short:long:long	BACCHIUS
short:long:short	AMPHIBRACH
short:short:long	ANAP(A)EST, IONIC
short:short:short	TRIBRACH
	TRISEME
—4 syllables	QUADRISYLLABLE
	TETRASYLLABLE
long:long:long:short	EPITRITE
long:long:short:short	IONIC
long:short:short:long	CHORIAMB
long:short:short:short	PAEON
short:long:long:short	ANTISPAST
short:short:long:long	IONIC
short:short:	
short:short	PROCELEUSMATIC
	TETRASEME
—5 syllables	PENTASYLLABLE
dactyl and spondee	ADONIC
short:long:long:	
short:long	DOCHMIUS
—6 syllables	SEXISYLLABLE
—7 syllables	HEPTASYLLABLE
	SEPTASYLLABLE
—8 syllables	OCTASYLLABLE
—10 syllables	DECASYLLABLE
—11 syllables	HENDECASYLLABLE
—12 syllables	DODECASYLLABLE
6 iambs	ALEXANDRINE
—14 syllables	FOURTEENER
—15 syllables	FIFTEENER
—16 syllables	SIXTEENER
free verse	VERS LIBRE
French	
—alexandrine	HEROIC VERSE
—epic	CHANSON DE GESTE
—lyrical poem	RONDEAU, RONDEL

—medieval poem	PASTOURELLE
funeral	
—ode	EPICEDE, EPICEDIUM
—oration	ELOGE, ELOGIUM, ELOGY
—song	ELEGY
Greek style	ALCAIC, ADONIC
group of	
—Greek verses	SYSTEM
—lines	STANZA
half	
—a line	HEMISTICH
—foot	SEMIPED
—of long syllable	MORA
having	
—additional syllable	HYPERMETRICAL
—different rhythms	ASYNARTETE
—each word a syllable longer	
than the one before	RHOPALIC
—eight	
feet	OCTAPODAL
strophes	OCTASTROPHIC
—equal number of	
time-units	ISORHYTHMIC
—full number of syllables	ACATALECTIC
—same	
stanza structure	
throughout	MONOSTROPHIC
syllable	
arrangement	TAUTOMETRIC(AL)
heavily accented verse	SPRUNG RHYTHM
heroic	
—couplet	RIDING-RHYME
—poem	EPIC, ODE
humorous poem	
—4 lines	CLERIHEW
—5 lines	LIMERICK
—in jumbled language	MACARONIC VERSE
iambic trimeter	CHOLIAMB, SCAZON
in form of a letter	EPISTLE
initial letters	
—forming word	ACROSTIC
—reproducing first verse	PARACROSTIC
introduction	PROLOGUE
introductory syllable	ANACRUSIS
irregular verse	DOGGEREL
irregularly divided	ALLOIOSTROPHOS
Italian	
—stanza	OTTAVA RIMA
—triplet	TERZA RIMA
Japanese verse	HAIKAI, HAIKU, HOKKU
	LINKED VERSE, RENGA
	TANKA
lacking one syllable	CATALECTIC
laisse	TIRADE
last	
—part of ode	EPODE

—six lines of sonnet	SESTET(T), SESTETTE
Latin verse	LEONINE
light verse	VERS DE SOCIETE
line	STICH
—½ line	HEMISTICH
—1 line	MONOSTICH
—2 lines	COUPLET, DISTICH
—2 couplets	CLERIHEW
—3 lines	TERCET, TERZETTA
	TRIAD, TRISTICH
—4 lines	CLERIHEW, QUATRAIN
	SAPPHIC, TETRASTICH
Welsh	ENGLYN
—5 lines	CINQUAIN, LIMERICK
	PENTASTICH
—6 lines	HEXASTICH, SIXAINE
—7 lines	RHYME-ROYAL
—8 lines	HUITAIN, OCTASTICH
	OCTAVE, SPENSERIAN
—10 lines	DECASTICH, DIZAIN
—13 lines	RONDEAU, RONDEL
—14 lines	RONDEL, SONNET
	PYTHIAN VERSE
—19 lines	VILLANELLE
lines	
—beginning and ending	
with same word	SERPENTINE VERSE
—ending with same word	KYRIELLE
—repeated at intervals	REFRAIN
long	
—narrative	EPIC, SAGA
—treated as short	IRRATIONAL
longer verse followed by	
shorter one	EPODE
love poem	AMORET
lyrical poem	IDYLL
Malay verse	PANT(O)UM
mark of division	SEMEION
metrical	
—pattern	SCANSION
—stress	ICTUS
—tale	FABLIAU
mixed with prose	MENIPPEAN
modern Greek verse	POLITICAL VERSE
monologue in verse	MONOPOEM
mournful ode	MONODY
mourning song	ELEGY
narrative poem	BALLAD
natural metre	SPRUNG RHYTHM
nonsense verse	AMPHIGORY
occasional verse	VERS D'OCCASION
ode	
—of lamentation	THRENE, THRENODY
—to victory	EPINICION, EPINIKION
old	
—Latin verse	SATURNIAN

—lyrical poem	SONNET
—six-lined six-stanza poem	SESTINA
—two-rhyme poem	VILLANELLE
part of ode	STROPHE
pastoral poem	BUCOLIC, ECLOGUE
	GEORGIC, IDYL(L)
patchwork of verses	CENTO
patterned by syllables	SYLLABICS
	SYLLABLE VERSE
pause	
—in line	C(A)ESURA
—of one mora	LIMMA
pensive verse	ELEGY
Persian	G(H)AZAL, GHAZEL
Phrygian metre	GALLIAMBIC
pithy and sententious saying	GNOME
poem	
—about returning	NOSTOS
—celebrating wedding	EPITHALAMION
	EPITHALAMIUM
	PROTHALAMION
—honouring victory	EPINICION
	EPINIKION
—in triplets	BALLADE
Italian	TERZA-RIMA
—lamenting death	ELEGY
—made up from unconnected	
fragments of poems	CENTO
—of retraction	PALINODE
—on	
husbandry	BUCOLIC, GEORGIC
rural life	IDYLL
—without metre	
or rhyme	BLANK VERSE
	FREE VERSE, VERS LIBRE
poet	RHYMESTER, VERSIFIER
poetic dialogue	AMOEBEUM
poets	(see separate entry)
printed in specific	
shape	CALLIGRAM(ME)
prose into verse	METAPHRASE
quatrain	COMMON METRE
	SERVICE METRE
	SHORT METRE
quatrains of eight-	
syllable lines	LONG-MEASURE
redundant word	CHEVILLE
reversed dactyl	ANAP(A)EST
rhyme of	
—final syllables	MALE RHYMES
—two or more syllables	FEMININE RHYME
sandwich rhyme	RIMA CHIUSA
scazon	CHOLIAMB
section of long poem	CANTO, STANZA
series of	
—rhyming lines	MONORHYME

—stanzas (Italian)	CANZONE
short	
—clause in Latin prose	CLAUSULA
—epic	EPYLLION
—form (Italian)	STORNELLO
—hymn	CATHISMA, TROPARION
—lines ending with	
same word	KYRIELLE
—narrative	LAY
—pastoral poem	ECLOGUE, IDYL(L)
—poem	DITHYRAMB
—simple verses	JINGLE
—syllable	MORA
song of victory	EPINICION, EPINIKION
spondee, choriamb,	
iambus	ASCLEPIAD
stanza	STROPHE, TROPARION
stress	ICTUS
string of verses	
on one rhyme	LAISSE, TIRADE
stringing together	
of poems	RHAPSODY
syllable(s) introductory	
to rhythm of line	ANACRUSIS
test for one claiming	
benefit of clergy	NECK VERSE
tetrameter in tonics	SOTADEAN, SOTADIC
three stanzas	TRIAD
tribrach, iamb, trochee	TRISEME
triple rhyme	SDRUCCIOLA
trochaic dipody	DITROCHEE
two-rhymed	
—French verse	VIRELAY
—ten-syllable lines	HEROIC COUPLET
typographic	CONCRETE POETRY
unequal strophes	HETEROSTROPHIC
unit of	
—metre	FOOT
—time	SEMEION
unrhymed poem	BLANK VERSE
	FREE VERSE, VERS LIBRE
upbeat	ARSIS
use of gods in poetry	THEOTECHNY
using	
—letter-juggling	EMERGENT POETRY
—symbols	SEMIOTIC POETRY
verse into prose	METAPHRASE
visual	CONCRETE POETRY
wedding ode	EPITHALAMION
	EPITHALAMIUM
	PROTHALAMION
Welsh improvised verse	PENNILL(ION)
with extra syllables	ROVE-OVER
work omitting words	
containing a particular	
letter	LIPOGRAM

worthless	DOGGEREL
would-be rhyme	EYE-RHYME
vestments	(*see* church—garments)
Victoria	
Victoria Cross	VC
Victoria Medal of Honour	VMH
video	
video cassette recorder	VCR
video frequency	VF
video tape recorder	VTD
Vietnam	VN
bay	DAM, VINH, VUNG
cape (headland)	MUI
capital	HANOI
coin	
—10 xu	HAO
—10 hao	DONG
gulf	VUNG
hill	DEO
island	CU LAO, DO, HON
mountain	BONOM, DEO, NGOC
	NUI, PHU
New Year	TET
river	DA, IA, NAM, SONG
virtues	
Christian	CHARITY, FAITH, HOPE
	HUMILITY
	FORTITUDE, JUSTICE
	PRUDENCE, TEMPERANCE
violin	AMATI, CREMONA
	STRAD(IVARIUS)
—strings	A, D, E, G
vitamin	
A	AXEROPHTHOL, BIOTIN
	CAROTENE, ERGOSIA, RETINOL
B	ADERMIN, ANEURIN, BIOTIN
	COBALAMINE, CYANOCOBALAMIN(E)
	FOLIC ACID, INOSITOL
	LACTOFLAVIN, NIACIN
	NICOTINAMIDE, NICOTINIC ACID
	OROTIC ACID, PANTHENOL
	PANTOTHENIC ACID, PTEROIC ACID
	PTEROYLGLUTAMIC ACID
	PYRIDOXIN(E), RIBOFLAVIN
	THIAMIN(E)
C	ASCORBIC ACID
	CEVITAMIC ACID
D	CALCIFEROL, CHOLECALCIFEROL
E	TOCOPHEROL
F	LINOLE(N)IC ACID
G (now B)	LACTOFLAVIN, RIBOFLAVIN
H	BIOTIN
K	MENADIONE, PHYLLOQUINONE
	PHYTONADIONE
M (now B)	FOLIC ACID
	PTEROYLGLUTAMIC ACID

P	CITRIN
PP	NICOTINIC ACID
X (now P)	(*see* P above)
in yeast	TORULIN
volcano	
apex	CONE
cavity in lava	AMYGDULE
cloud of hot gas etc	NUEE ARDENTE
crater outside lava cone	MAAR
cylindrical channel	PIPE
extinct (France)	PUY
formed from fragments by	
volcanic action	PYROCLASTIC
goddess	PELE
lake in extinct volcano	CRATER LAKE
large crater	CALDERA
lava flow	COULEE
liquid lava	PYROCLASTIC ROCK
mineral-filled cavity	AMYGDULE
mud volcano	PAINT POT, SALSE
natural phenomena	VOLCANISM
	VOLCANICITY, VULCANISM
pertaining to	VOLCANIC, VULCANIAN
pillar of solidifed	
lava	VOLCANIC NECK
rocks, etc	EJECTA, TEPHRA
—angular rocks	AGGLOMERATE, BLOCKS
—banded	EUTAXITE
—basalt lava	TOADSTONE
—black and shiny	OBSIDIAN, PITCHSTONE
—broken by volcanic	
action	PYROCLASTIC
—compacted mixture	TUFF
—coarse material	CINDER
—cooled magma	IGNEOUS RAOCK
—dust	POZZ(U)OLANA
	PUZZOLANA
—earthy tuff	TRASS
—ejected by Vesuvius	IDOCRASO
	VESUVIANITE
—fine	
grained ash	HORNSTONE
material	ASH
textured rock	PUMICE, RHYOLITE
—fragments	TUFF
—fused	GLASS
—glass	PE(A)RLITE, PITCHSTONE
—lava fragments	SCORIA, SLAG
—molten material	LAVA, MAGMA
—mud	MOYA
—porous	PUMICE, TUFA, TUFF
—ropy lava	PAHOEHOE
—rough	
cindery lava	SLAG
lava	AA, SCORIA
—rounded rocks	BOMBS, PILLOW LAVA

—small rocks	LAPILLI		MAUNA KEA, MAUNA LOA
—smooth lava	PAHOEHOE	—Iceland	EDFELL, GJASTYKKI
—soil (India)	BLACK COTTON EARTH		GRIMSVOTEN, HAIMAEY
—split lava	PILLOW		HELGAFELL, HEKLA
—stopping vent	NECK, PLUG		MOUNT LAKI, SURTSEY
—tuff	TARRAS, TERRAS, TRASS	—Indonesia	ANAK KRAKATAU, KELI MUTU
—vitreous	OBSIDIAN, PALAGONITE		KELUT, KRAKATOA
—with			MOUNT LAMINGTON
plagioclase	ANDESITE		MOUNT MERAPI, MOUNT RIN(D)JANI
steam holes	SCORIA		RAOENG, SEMERU, SLAMAT
steam or gas hole	FUMAROLE, HORNITO		TAMBORA, TOBA
	MOFETTE, SOLFATARA	—Italy	SALSA, STROMBOLI
	SUFFIONE		VESUVIUS, VULCANO
stream of lava	COULEE	—Japan	FUJIYAMA, SAKURAJIMA, USU
study	VOLCANOLOGY	—Java	RAOENG
	VULCANOLOGY	—Lipari Islands	VULCANO
subordinate cone	MONTIC(U)LE	—Martinique	MONT PELEE
	MONTICULUS	—Mexico	EL CHICHON
volcanic rock	EXTRUSIVE ROCK		NEVADA DEL RUIZ
—glassy	VOLCANIC GLASS		PARICUTIN, POPOCATEPETL
volcanoes		—New Zealand	RUAPEHU
—Aegean	SANTORINI, THERA	—Nicaragua	CONCEPCION
—Alaska	MOUNT KATMAI, REDOUBT	—Réunion	
—America	CRATER LAKE, GLACIER PEAK	Island	PITON DE LA FOURNESSE
	LASSEN, MOUNT ADAMS	—Russia	KLYUCHEVSKAYA SOPKA
	MOUNT BAKER, MOUNT HOOD		KORYAKSKAYA
	MOUNT JEFFERSON, MOUNT MAZAMA		MOUNT TOLBACHIK
	MOUNT MCLOUGHLIN, MOUNT RANIER	—Sicily	ETNA
	MOUNT ST HELENS, MOUNT SHASTA	—Solomon Islands	TINAKULA
	MOUNT SPUR, NEWBERRY CRATER	—Spain	PICO DE TEIDE
	SUNSET CRATER	—Tristan da Cunha	THE PEAK
—Antarctic	EREBUS	—Virgin Islands	GROS PITON
—Argentina	MOUNT SIDLEY		HODDER'S VOLCANO
	OJOS DEL SALADO		KICK-'EM-JENNY, MORNE AU DIABLE
—Azores	FAIAL		MORNE DIABOLOTIN, MORNE PATATES
—Cameroon	MOUNT CAMEROON		MOUNT MISERY, MOUNT ST CATHERINE
—Chile	GUALLATIRI, LASCAR		NEVIS PEAK, PETIT PITON
	TUPUNGATITO		QUALIBOU(LA), SOUFRIERE
—Colombia	PURACE		THE MOUNTAIN, THE QUILL
—Costa Rica	IRAZU, MOUNT ARENAL	—with wide base	SHIELD VOLCANO
—Ecuador	CHIMBORAZO, COTOPAXI	—Zaire	NYIRAGONGO
	SANGAY	**volunteer**	
—enclosing Pacific		Voluntary Aid Detachment	VAD
Ocean	RING OF FIRE	Voluntary Defence Corps	VDC
—Greece	SANTORINI, THIRA	Voluntary Service Overseas	VOS
—Guatemala	TACANA, TAJUMULCO	Volunteer (Officers') Decoration	VD
—Hawaii	AIRI, HALEMAUMAU	Volunteer Reserve Decoration	VRD
	HUALALAI, KILAUEA (IKI)		

Wales	CYMRU
waterfall	CATARACT, CHUTE
	FORCE, LIN(N), RAPID
Africa	VICTORIA
Argentina	DEL IGUAZU
Austria	KRIMMLER FALLE
Brazil	GUIARA, GLASS, IGUAZA
	PATOS-MARIBONDO
	PAULO ALFONSO, SEVEN FALLS
	URUBU-PUNGA
Canada	CHRUCHILL, GRAND
	HORSESHOE, NIAGARA
	TAKKAKAW
cascade pool	LIN(N)
England	CA(U)LDRON SNOUT
	SCALE FORCE, STANLEY FORCE
	SCALEBER FORCE, THE STRID
France	GARVARNIE
Guyana	KAIETEUR, KING GEORGE VI
	KOITUOK, RORAIMA
highest	ANGEL
Ireland	POWERSCOURT
New Zealand	CLEVE-GARTH, SUTHERLAND
North America	NIAGARA, RIBBON
	SILVER STRAND, YOSEMITE
Norway	ITIGARD, KILE, KVELLFOSSEN
	MONGEFOSSEN
	OSTRE MARDOLA FOSS
	TYSSESTRENGANE
Paraguay	GUAIRA, SEVEN FALLS
Scotland	CROMACH, FALLS OF BRUAR
	FALLS OF CLYDE, FOYERS
	EAS-COUL-AULIN
	GREY MARE'S TAIL
South Africa	TUGELA, VICTORIA
steep	CATARACT
Tanzania	KALAMBO
Uganda	OWEN FALLS
Venezuela	ANGEL, CUQUENAN
	KUKENAAM
Wales	PISTYLL RHAIADR
	PISTYLL-Y-LLYN
	SWALLOW FALLS
where water atomises	BRIDAL VEIL
Zaire	STANLEY
Zambia	RAINBOW, VICTORIA
weapon	
African spear	ASSAGAI, ASSEGA(A)I,

anti	
—submarine	DEPTH-CHARGE, MINE
	TORPEDO
—tank	BEEHIVE, (LAND)MINE
	STICKY BOMB
axe	
—2-edged	TWIBILL
—Bronze Age	PALSTAFF, PALSTAVE
—long-handled	BROWNBILL, GISARME
	GLAIVE, HALBERD, HALBERT
	LOCHABER AXE, PARTISAN
	SPARTH(E), SPONTOON
	VOU(L)GE, WELSH HOOK
—long-headed	JETHART STAFF
—Red Indian	TOMAHAWK
blowpipe	SARBACANE
buried	LANDMINE
burning	FLAMETHROWER
	INCENDIARY BOMB, NAPALM
bow	FOOTBOW, CROSSBOW, LONG-BOW
—crossbow	ARB(A)LAST, ARBALEST
	AR(CU)BALIST
catapult	(E)SPRINGAL(D)
cavalry	LANCE, SABRE
club	(*see* **club**)
dagger	(*see* **knife**)
device for	
—cocking crossbow	CRANEQUIN
	GOAT'S FOOT, MOULINET
	WINDAS, WINDLASS
—testing gunpowder	EPROUVETTE
dropped from aircraft	BOMB, TORPEDO
engines of war	
—boring	TEREBRA
—cutting	SIEGE SCYTHE
—large crossbow	BAL(L)ISTA
—moveable tower	BELFRY, SIEGE TOWER
Roman	MUSCULUS
—stone-throwing	BAL(L)ISTA, BRICOLE
	CATAPULT, MANGONEL
	ONAGER, PERRIER, PETRARY
	SCORPION, STONEBOW
	TORMENTUM, TREBUCHET
fired from	
—aircraft	MISSILE
—air-pistol/rifle	DART, PELLET
—blowpipe	DART
—bow	ARROW
—crossbow	BOLT, QUARREL
—gun	BULLET, SHELL
—launcher	MISSILE
—ship	BAR-SHOT, CASE-SHOT
	CHAIN-SHOT, DEPTH-CHARGE
	GRAPE(-SHOT), LANGRAGE
	LANGREL, LANGRIDGE
	MISSILE, TORPEDO

—shotgun	CARTRIDGE, PELLET, SHOT
—silo	MISSILE
fixed to	
—fingers	KNUCKLEDUSTER
—rifle	BAYONET
floating	MINE
for killing	
—fish	PRIEST
—salmon	LEISTER
—whales	HARPOON
fragment of shell, etc	SHRAPNEL
gavelock	JAVELIN
grenade	MILLS BOMB, PINEAPPLE
gun	(see separate entry)
halberd	BROWNBILL
harpoon	(GRAIN)STAFF
Indian	LATHI, PATA
iron-tipped staff	QUARTER-STAFF
javelin	GAVELOCK
—Oriental	JEREED, JERID
—Roman	PILE, PILUM
—Turkish	JEREED, JERID
knife	(see separate entry)
mortar	
—British	STOKES, TOC EMMA
—German	MINENWERFER
	MOANING MINNIE
mine	ACOUSTIC, CONTACT
	MAGNETIC
officer's halberd	SPONTOON
rocket-propelled	MISSILE
Roman javelin	PILE, PILUM
Scottish salmon spear	WASTER
Siva's trident	TRISUL(A)
spear	
—3-pronged	TRIDENT
—African	ASSAGAI, ASSEGA(A)I
—cavalry	LANCE
—infantry	PIKE
—old	GADE, GALING, GAID
	GLAIVE, LA(U)NCEGAY(E)
—Roman	PILE, PILUM
—salmon	LEISTER
Scottish	WASTER
—throwing	GAVELOCK, JAVELIN
—whales	HARPOON
spear-thrower (Australian)	WOOOMERA
spiked	
—ball	CALTRAP, CALTHROP
—club	MACE
—shaft	PIKE, LANCE, SPEAR
swinging bar	FLAIL
sword	(see separate entry)
Turkish javelin	JEREED, JERID
undersea	DEPTH CHARGE, MINE
	TORPEDO

war-hammer	MARTEL
weather	(see meteorology)
weight	
0.06 grams	GRAIN
3 scruples	DRACHM
8 drachms	OUNCE TROY
$^1/_{16}$ ounce	DRAM, DRACHM
1.1 ounce	OUNCE TROY
16 drams	OUNCE
20 grains	SCRUPLE
24 grains	DWT, PENNYWEIGHT
480 grains	OUNCE
8 ounces (gold, silver)	MARK
12 ounces Troy	POUND
16 ounces	POUND
4lb	
—(loaf)	QUARTERN
—on 104lb allowance	TRET
7-10lb (wool or cheese)	CLOVE
14lb	STONE
16lb (cheese)	STONE
22lb (hay)	STONE
24lb (wool)	STONE
25lb (US)	QUARTER
28lb	QUARTER
—(wool)	TOD
32lb	SLUG
36lb (straw)	TRUSS
56lb	
—(butter)	FIRKIN
—(old hay)	TRUSS
60lb (new hay)	TRUSS
100lb	CENTAL, QUINTAL
112lb	CWT, HUNDREDWEIGHT
120lb (glass)	SEAM
140lb (flour)	BOLL
240lb	PACK
—(wool)	WOOL-PACK
750-1200lb (tobacco)	HOGSHEAD
4000lb	LAST
13 stone	WEY
2 weys	SACK
½cwt (hops)	HOP-POCKET
cwt (old)	QUINTAL
19½cwts (lead)	FOTHER
25½cwts (coal)	CHALDRON
atomic weight of element	GRAM-ATOM
litre of hydrogen	CRITH
nylon, rayon, silk	DENIER
silver and gold	TROY
	(for metric weights see French)
Welsh	CAMBRIAN, CYMRIC
bards' assembly	GORSEDD
beloved	BACH
boat	CORACLE
burial chamber	CISTVAEN, KISTVAEN

Welsh

capital	CARDIFF
char	TORGOCH
congress of bards	EISTEDDFOD
dish	LAVER BREAD
divine inspiration	HYWL
dog	CORGI
druids' meeting	GORSEDD
emblem	LEEK
fervour	HYWL
fiddler	CROWDER
fish (Lake Bala)	GWINIAD, GWYNIAD
four-line stanza	ENGLIN
giant	IDRIS
hill	DUN
hollow in hillside	CWM
improvised verse	PENNILL(ION)
lament	PLANXTY
liquor	METHEGLIN
mountain	MYNNYDD
Nationalist Party	PLAID CYMRU, WNP
patron saint	DAVID
payment to new king	MISE
porch	GALILEE
riots	REBECCA
sea	MOR
stanza	PENNILL
the Welsh	CYMRY
tribe	SILURES
valley	CWM
violin	CROUD, CROUTH
	CROWD, CRWTH

West Indian

allspice	JAMAICAN PEPPER
ball of dough	FLOAT
Barbados cherry	MALPHIGIA
bark	CARIBBEE-BARK
	CASCARILLA
belief in snake deity	ZOMBIISM
birch	SAMYDA
bird	GREEN SPARROW
	SOLITAIRE
	TODY, TREMBLER
bobolink	BUTTER-BIRD
bread	COO-COO
cake	BAMMIE
Canna	TOUS-LES-MOIS
capsicum	CHERRY-PEPPER, PIM(I)ENTO
cassava	MANIOC, TAPIOCA
—juice	CASSAREEP, CASSARIPE
chief	CACIQUE, CAZIQUE
clay	BARBADOS EARTH
climbing plant	SCOTCH ATTORNEY
compressed dika seed	DIKA-BREAD
dance	BEGUINE, CHA-CHA(-CHA)
	LIMBO, MAMBO, R(H)UMBA

West Indian

demoiselle fish	COW-PILOT
dish	PEPPER-POT
drink	CURACAO, CURACOA
	EAU DE CREOLES, MOBBIE
	MOBBY, RUM, SANGAREE
	SANGRIA, TAFIA
drum	BONGO
durra	NEGRO-CORN
edible	
—frog	CRAPAUD
—starch	TOUS-LES-MOIS
—tuber	YAM
extinct tribe	TAINO
farm	PEN
fibre	ABACA, MANIL(L)A-HEMP
fish	BARRACOUTA, BARRACUDA
	COBIA, CRAB-EATER, GUPPY
	MILLIONS, SERGEANT-FISH
—dish	ACCRA
flea	CHIGGER, CHIGOE, CHIGRE
	JIGGER
flycatcher	SOLITAIRE
folk-song	CALYPSO
freshwater tortoise	HIC(C)ATEE
fruit	A(C)KEE, ANANA(S)
	ANCHOVY-PEAR, BARBADOS CHERRY
	BARBADOS GOOSEBERRY, BULLOCK'S
	HEART, COCO PLUM, CUSTARD-APPLE
	GENIPAP, GRANADILLA, GRENADILLA
	MAMMEE(-APPLE), NASEBERRY
	PASSION FRUIT, PENGUIN
	PINGUIN, SAPODILLA-PLUM
	STAR-APPLE
ghost	DUPPY, JUMBIE, JUMBY
groundnut	PINDA
gum	ANIME, COURBARIL
hog-rat	HUTIA, MUSK-CAVY
insectivore	AGOUTA
Jamaican	
—birthwort	CONTRAYERVA
—pepper	ALLSPICE
language	CARIB, TAINO
lizard	GALLIWASP
locust tree	COURBARIL
magic	MYALISM, OBEAH, OBI(A)
	OBY, VAUDOO, VAUDOUX
	VOODOO, VOUDOU
manioc	CASSAVA, TAPIOCA
marmalade-tree	MAMMEE-SAPOTA
mesquite	CASHAW
mulberry	RAMOON
music	CALYPSO, REGGAE
Negro	QUASHEE, QUASHIE
oil from dika	DIKA-BUTTER
orange dye	AN(N)ATTA
	AN(N)ATTO, ARNOTTO

passion-flower	BULL-HOOF	**whale**	GRAMPUS
	LOVE-IN-A-MIST	baleen whales	MYSTACOCETI
peanut	PINDA	finback	RORQUAL
pepper	PIM(I)ENTO	group	POD, SCHOOL
pineapple	KARATAS	order	CETACEA
pirate	BUCCANEER, BUCCANIER	rorqual	FINBACK SEI
	FILIBUSTER	types	BLUE, BOTTLENOSE, BOWHEAD
plant	BIKA, SAVANNA FLOWER		BRYDE'S, FIN, GREY, HUMPBACK
plantation	PEN		KILLER, MINKE, RIGHT, SEI, SPERM
poinciana	PEACOCK-FLOWER		SULPHUR BOTTOM
potatoes	EDDOES	toothed	ODONTOCETI
prickly-pear	TUNA	whale food	KRILL, PLANKTON
pumpkin	CALABAZA	**which**	
race	CARIB	which	
resin	ANIME	—is	QE
rock music	REGGAE	—see	QV
rodent	HOG-RAT, HUTIA	—was to be	
rum	TAF(F)IA	done	QEF
ship	DROG(H)ER	found	QEI
shrub	BARBADOS-PRIDE	proved	QED
spice	PIMENTO	**wind**	
spiny cactus	DILDO	Aegean	ETESIAN
spurge	MANIHOT, MANIOC	Africa	BERG WIND, CHILI
squash	CHRISTOPHINE		HARMATTAN, LESTE
stew	PEPPERPOT	anticlockwise round low	
superstition	VAUDOO, VAUDOUX	pressure (North)	CYCLONE
	VOODOO, VOUDOU	Argentina	ZONDA
sweet potato	BATATA	Asia	KARABURAN
tapioca	CASSAVA,MANIOC	Australia	
taro	DASHEEN	—cyclone	WILLY-WILLY
thrush	SOLITAIRE	—north-easter	BRICKFIELDER (WIND)
thunderstorm	HOUVARI	—south wind	SOUTHERLY BU(R)STER
timber	(*see separate entry*)	—stormy	BUSTER
tortoise	HIC(C)ATEE	autumn winds	EQUINOCTIAL GALES
tree	A(C)KEE, BARBADOS CHERRY	Beaufort scale	
	BLACKBULLY, BOLLETRIE, BULLY-TREE	No. mph.	
	BULLET-TREE, BULLETRIE, CANELLA	0 <1	CALM
	COCO-PLUM, COCUS-WOOD, GAUZE-TREE	1 1-3	LIGHT AIR
	GENIPAP, GRANADILLA, GRENADILLA	2 4-7	LIGHT BREEZE
	HERCULES CLUB, HOG-PLUM, MALPHIGIA	3 8-12	GENTLE BREEZE
	LACE-TREE, LOCUST-TREE, MAMMEE	4 13-18	MODERATE BREEE
	PIMENTO, PRICKLY ASH, QUASSIA	5 19-24	FRESH BREEZE
	SAPODILLA, SWEETWOOD	6 25-31	STRONG BREEZE
	TOOTHACHE-TREE, XANTHOXYLUM	7 32-38	NEAR GALE
	YACCA	8 39-46	GALE
tree-nesting termite	DUCK-ANT	9 47-54	STRONG GALE
voodoo priestess	MAMBO	10 55-65	STORM
white man	BUCKRA	11 66-75	VIOLENT STORM
wild mango	DIKA	12 >75	HURRICANE
witchcraft	OBEAH, OBI(A), OBY	brief	FLURRY, GUST
	MYALISM	California	NORTHER, SANTA ANNA
Western Samoa	WS	Cape Horn	WILLIWAW SQUALL
capital	APIA	carrying particles	DUST-STORM
coin			SAND-STORM
—unit	SENE	caused by	
—100 sene	TALA	—avalanche	AVALANCHE WIND

—convection currents	THERMAL	—Egypt	K(H)AMSIN
downwards	KATABATIC	—Iran	SAMOON, SAMUN
on slopes	MOUNTAIN WIND	—Italy	S(C)IROC(C)O
upwards	ANABATIC	—Java	KOEMBANG
—insolation	PLANETARY	—Kurdistan	RESHABAR
Central America	NORTE, TEMPORALES	—mountain	FO(E)HN
change direction		—North Africa	GIBLI
—anticlockwise	BACK	—Rockies	CHINOOK
—clockwise	VEER	—South America	NEVADOS, ZONDA
China Sea	TYPHOON	—Sudan	HABOOB
clockwise round low		—Sumatra	BOHOROK
pressure (North)	ANTICYCLONE	hurricane	BAGUIO
cold		increase in strength	FRESHEN
—Andes	NEVADOS, PUNA	indicator	WEATHER VANE
—Australia	SOUTHERLY BUR(S)TER		WIND SOCK, WIND VANE
—down glacier	GLACIER BREEZE	Iran	SAMOON, SAMUN, SEISTAN
—France	BISE, MISTRAL	Iraq	SHAMAL
—from Arctic or Antarctic	POLAR WIND	Italy	S(C)IROC(CO), TRAMONTANA
—Italy	BISE	Java	KOEMBANG
—off mountains to sea	WILLIWAW	land breeze (Peru)	TERRAL
—Switzerland	BISE	law governing wind	
—with snow	BLIZZARD	direction	BUYS BALLOT'S LAW
consistent winds		light breeze	CAT'S-PAW
at sea	ANTITRADES		MACKEREL-BREEZE
	TRADE WINDS, WESTERLIES	localised whirl of dust	DUST DEVIL
convection wind	ANABATIC, KATABATIC		WIND DEVIL
	VALLEY WIND	Madeira	LESTE
cool sea breeze	DOCTOR	measuring instrument	ANEMOMETER
Cuba - squall	BAYAMO	Mediterranean	ETESIAN, GREGALE
desert wind	DUST STORM, SAND STORM		LEVANTER, MAESTRO
	S(C)IROC(CO)		PONENTE, SOLANO
diagram of wind direction		Mexico	NORTE, PAPAGAYO
and speed	WIND ROSE	most frequent from a	
direction		particular direction	PREVAILING WIND
—from which wind is		New Zealand	NOR'-WESTER
blowing	UPWIND, WINDWARD	north	AQUILO(N), BOREAS
—of wind	SET	—Asia	SEISTAN
—towards which wind		—Central America	NORTE
is blowing	DOWNWIND, LEEWARD	—France	BISE
east	EURUS	—Iran	SEISTAN
—Mediterranean	LEVANT(ER), SOLANO	—Italy	BISE, TRAMONTANA
—Spain	SOLANO	—Mediterranean	ETESIAN
European	HELM	—Mexico	PAPAGAYO
force measurement	BEAUFORT SCALE	—North America	NORTHER
frequently changing		—South America	ZONDA
direction	BAFFLING WIND	—Switzerland	BISE
gentle breeze	ZEPHYR	—Turkey	MELTEMI
high altitude	JET STREAM	North Africa	CHILI, GIBLI
hot			S(C)IROC(CO)
—Africa	BERG WIND, CHILI, HARMATTAN	North America	NORTHER
—Andes	ZONDA	north-east	IMBAT, TRADE
—Arabia	HABOOB, SAMIEL, SHAMAL	—Adriatic	BORA
	SIMOOM, SIMOON	—Aegean	ETESIAN
—Argentina	ZONDA	—Africa	HARMATTAN
—Asia	TEBBAD	—Asia	KARABURAN, PURGA
—Australia	BRICKFIELDER	—Australia	BRICKFIELDER

—Central Asia/Siberia	BURAN
—Europe	HELM
—Indian Ocean	MONSOON
—Mediterranean	GREGALE
—Switzerland	BISE
north-west	
—Iraq	SHAMAL
—Mediterranean	MAESTRO
—Milton	ARGESTES
off shore	LAND BREEZE
on shore	SEA BREEZE
Peru	TERRAL, VIRAZON
Philippines - hurricane	BAGUIO
planetary winds	
—north and south of horse	
latitudes	WESTERLIES
—towards Equator	TRADE WINDS
region of light winds	CALMS OF CANCER
	CALMS OF CAPRICORN
	DOLDRUMS
	HORSE LATITUDES
Rocky Mountains	CHINOOK
rotating	ANTICYLONE, CYCLONE
	HURRICANE, TORNADO
	TYPHOON, WHIRLWIND
Russia - windstorm	BURAN
sand-storm	HABOOB, TEBBAD
sea breeze	
—Arabian Sea	BAT FURAN
—Peru	VIRAZON
seasonally reversing	
system	MONSOON
short violent storm	(LINE)SQUALL
Sicily	S(C)IROC(CO)
side	
—away from wind	LEEWARD
—facing wind	WINDWARD
slight breeze	MACKEREL-BREEZE
south	AUSTER, NOTUS
—Africa	LESTE
—Australia	SOUTHERLY BUSTER
—Egypt	K(H)AMSIN
—Italy	S(C)IROC(CO)
—North Africa	CHILI, GIBLI, S(C)IROC(CO)
—Sicily	S(C)IROC(CO)
south-east	EURUS, TRADE
—Africa	CAPE DOCTOR
—Indian Ocean	MONSOON
—Spain	SOLANO
south-west	AFER, LIBECC(H)IO
—Central America	TEMPORALES
—Indian Ocean	MONSOON
—South America	PAMPERO
—Spain	LEVECHE, VENDEVALES
Spain	LEVECHE, SOLANO
	VENDEVALES

speed	
—scale	BEAUFORT SCALE
—measuring instrument	ANEMOMETER
—record	ANEMOGRAM
—recording instrument	ANEMOGRAPH
spring winds	EQUINOCTIAL GALES
squall	BLIRT, BLORE
—Cuba	BAYAMO
—East Indies	SUMATRA
—India	NOR'-WESTER
—Magellan Strait	WILLIWAW
—Scotland	DROW
storm	GALE, HURRICANE
	TEMPEST
Sumatra	BOHOROK
tempest	BOURASQUE
tempestuous	EUROCLYDON
	EURAQUILA
through mountain passes	STOWED WIND
tornado	
—America	TWISTER
—at sea	WATERSPOUT
transitory breeze	SLANT
tropical thunderstorm	TORNADO
violent gust	BLORE
west	FAVONIUS, TRADE(S)
	ZEPHYR
—Mediterranean	PONENTE
—southern	
hemisphere	BRAVE WEST WINDS
ocean	ROARING FORTIES
West Indies -	
thunderstorm	HOUVARI
whirlwind	TORNADO, TOURBILLION
	TYPHON, TWISTER
	WHITE SQUALL
wind	
—of 120 days	SEISTAN
—scale	(*see* Beaufort Scale *above*)
wine	
add sugar to grape	
juice	CHAPTALIZE, GALLIZE
	GALLISE
at room temperature	CHAMBRE
champagne and	
—orange juice	BUCK'S FIZZ
—stout	BLACK VELVET
claret	
—India	LOLL-SHRAUB
	LOLL-SHROB
—with soda-water, etc	BADMINTON
classification	
—Corsican	
guaranteed	
standard	APPELLATION CONTROLEE
ordinary standard	VIN DE CORSE

—French	
excellent	(GRAND) CRU (CLASSE)
	LES GRANDS VINS
good	CRU BOURGEOIS
	CRU EXCEPTIONEL
	PREMIER(GRAND) CRU (CLASSE)
	VDQS
guaranteed	
standard	APPELLATION CONTROLEE
ordinary	VIN DE PAYS
	VIN DE TABLE
	VIN ORDINAIRE
—German	
excellent	AUSLESE, BEERENAUSLESE
	EISWEIN, KABINETT
	QUALITATSWEIN MIT PRADICAT
	QUALITATSWEIN MP, SPATLESE
	TROCKENBEERENAUSLESE
good	QUALITATSWEIN BA
ordinary	TAFELWEIN
superior table wine	LANDWEIN
—Greek	
ordinary	EPITRAPEZIO
mature	ENDIKOS DIATIRIMENON
—Hungarian	
best wine	MINOSEGI BOR
ordinary wine	KIMERT BOR
table wine	ASZTALI BOR
—Italian	
aged for 3 years	RISERVA
good	VINO TIPICO
guaranteed standard	DOC, DOCG
	GARANTITA
ordinary	VINO DA BANCO
	VINO DA PASTA
	VINO DA TAVOLA
	VINO ORDINARIO
—Portuguese	
best quality	GARRAFEIRA
good	RESERVA
guaranteed	
quality	DENOMINACAO DE ORIGEN
ordinary	VINHO DE CONSUMO
	VINHO DE MESA
—Romanian	
light wine	VIN USOR
ordinary	VIN DE MASA
superior	VIN SUPERIOR
—Russian	
dessert wine	DESERTNOE VINO
Georgian wine	GRUZINSKOE VINO
ordinary wine	STOLOVOE VINO
—Spanish	
aged	
—3 years	RESERVA
—5 years	GRAN RESERVA
guaranteed	
standard	DENOMINACION DE ORIGEN
ordinary	VINO CORRIENTE
	VINO DE MESA
	VINO DE PASTO
sherry types	
—dry	FINO
—dry, light	MANZANILLA
—medium	AMONTILLADO
—pale, rich	CORTADOR, PALO
—sweet	OLOROSO
—Yugoslav	
dessert wine	DESERTNO VINO
selected wine	CUVENO VINO
table wine	STOLNO VINO
crust on port	BEESWING, FLOR
divination from wine	OENOMANCY
draw off, leaving sediment	DECANT
fragrance	BOUQUET
freezing before	
pressing	CRYOEXTRACTION
general terms	
—Austrian	
estate	WEINGARTEN, WEINGUT
estate-bottled	ORIGINALABFULLUNG
group of vineyards	EINZELLAGE
semi-sparkling	SCHLUCK
small vineyard area	REID
wine bar	HEURIGE
without added sugar	NATURWEIN
—Bulgarian	
dry	SUHO
red	CHERVENO
sparkling	ISKRIASHTO
sweet	SLADKO
vineyards	LOZIA
white	BJALO
wine	VINO
—French	
at room temperature	CHAMBRE
blend	CUVEE
cellar	CAVE
cool	FRAIS
crop	RECOLTE
dry	SEC
early	PRIMEUR
field in vineyard	CLIMAT
from white grapes	BLANC DE BLANC
group of vineyards	COMMUNE, CRU
half-dry (sweet)	DEMI-SEC
hillside	COTE(AU)
house-name	
—Bordeaux	CHATEAU
—Burgundy	DOMAINE
manager	RECOLTANT
merchant	NEGOCIANT

method of making sparkling wine	METHODE CHAMPENOISE
noble rot	POURRITURE NOBLE
owner	PROPRIETAIRE
parish	COMMUNE, FINAGE
pink	ROSE
pinkish	PELURE D'OIGNON
red	ROUGE
slightly sparkling	CREMANT, PERLANT
still	NATUREL
storage building	CHAI
sweet	DOUX
very dry	BRUT
vat	CUVE
vineyard(s)	CLIMAT, CRU VIGNOBLE
—under one owner	MONOPOLE
—walled	CLOS
vintage	RECOLTE
white	BLANC
wine	VIN
—grower	VITICULTEUR
—growing areas	ALSACE, BORDEAUX BURGUNDY CHAMPAGNE LOIRE, RHONE
—German	
bottle (Franconia)	BOCKSBEUTEL
bottler	ABFULLER
cafe wine	SCHOFFENWEIN
carbonated	PERLWEIN
cellar	KELLER
commune	GEMEINDE
cooperative	WINZERVEREIN
dry	TROCKEN
estate-bottled	ERZEUGER ABFULLUNG
Franconian	STEINWEIN
from frozen grapes	EISWEIN
group of vineyards	GROSSLAGE
half-dry	HALBTROCKEN
parish	GEMEINDE
pink wine	ROSEWEIN, SCHILLERWEIN WEISSHERBST
red wine	ROTWEIN
rural district	KREIS
semi-sparkling	PERLWEIN
sparkling	SCHAUMWEIN, SEKT SPRITZIG
unfermented juice	SUSS RESERVE
vineyard	EINZELLAGE
white wine	WEISSWEIN
wine	WEIN
winery	WEINKELLEREI
wine-producing	
—area	GEBEIT, LANDE

—areas	FRANCONIA MOSEL-SAAR-RUWER, NAHE RHEINGAU, RHEINPFALZ
—district	BEREICH
winery	WEINKELLEREI
—Greek	
dry	XIROS
factory	OINOPOIEION
old wine	PALAION
pink	KOKKINELI, ROSE
producer	OINOPARAGOGAS
red	ERYTHROS, MAVROS
resin flavoured	RETSINA
sparkling wine	AFROTHES
white	LEFKOS
wine	OINOS
—Hungarian	
bottled	PALACKOZOTT
dry	SZARAZ
from very ripe grapes	ASZU
natural Tokay	SZAMORODNI
red	VOROS
sweet	EDES
white	FEHER
—Italian	
aged in cask	RISERVA
association of growers	CONSORZIO
bar	CANTINA
bitter	AMARO
company making wine	CASA VINICOLA
concentrated	COTTO
cooked	COTTO
co-operative	CANTINA SOCIALE CONSORZIO
dark red	NERO
dry	AMARO, SECCO
estate	TENEMENTI
firm	CASA
flask	FIASCO
fortified	VINO LIQUOROSO
from	
—dried grapes	PASSITO VIN(O) SANTO
—finest area	CLASSICO
holding	TENEMENTI
house	CASA
light red	CHIARETTO
medium sweet	ABBOCCATO, AMABILE
mellow	STRAVECCHIO
pink	ROSATO
red	ROSSO
ripe	STRAVECCHIO
slightly sparkling	FRIZZANTE
sparkling	SPUMANTE
sweet	DOLCE
very dry	AMARO

vintage	VENDEMMIA	red	KRASNOE
white	BIANCO	white	BELOE
wine	VINO	wine	VINO
—cellar	CANTINA	—Spanish	
winery	CANTINA	aged	CON CRIANZA
—Portuguese		bar	BODEGA
dry	BRUTO, SECO	cask	BOTA
estate	QUINTA	controlling body	CONSEJO REGULADOR
—bottled	ENGARRAFADO NA ORIGEM	crop	COSECHA
farm	QUINTA	dry	SECO
legally-defined		good	FINO
area	REGIAO DEMARCADA	light red	CLARETE
light red	CLARETE	not aged	SIN CRIANZA
matured	MADURO	pink	ROSADO
pink	ROSADO	range of sherry casks	SOLERA
port terms		red	TINTO
—dark port	RUBY	sparkling	ESPUMOSO
—from		sweet	ABOCADO, DULCE
one good year	VINTAGE	very dry (sherry)	FINO
white grapes	WHITE PORT	vineyard	VINA, VINEDO
—good non-vintage	CRUSTED	vintage	COSECHA, VENDIMIA
	VINTAGE CHARACTER	warehouse	BODEGA
—pale from ageing	TAWNY	white	BLANCO
—trough for crushing		wine	VINO
grapes	LAGAR	—cellar	BODEGA
—warehouse	LODGE	young wine	VINO VERDE
red	TINTO	—Swiss	
sparkling	ESPUMANTE	from maker's own	
sweet	ADAMADO, DOCE	vineyards	PREMIER CRU
vineyard	VINHA	pink wine	OEIL DE PERDRIX
vintage	COLHEITA	—Yugoslav	
white	BRANCO	dry	SUHO
wine	VINHO	medium dry	POLSUHO
—cellar	ADEGA	natural	PRIRODNO
young wine	VINHO VERDE	pink	RUZICA
—Romanian		red	CRNO
bottled	IMBUTELIAT	sparkling	BISER
dry	SEC	sweet	SLATKO
grape	STRUGURE	white	BIJELO
pink	ROSE	inferior wine	PLONK
red	ROSU	kept too long	MADERISED
sparkling	SPUMOS	make sparkling wine	CHAMPENISE
state farming		—method	METHODE CHAMPENOISE
organisation	GAS, IAS	peach-flavoured	PECHER
sweet	DULCE	science of wine	OENOLOGY
vine	VIE	sediment	LEES
vineyard	VILE	sequence at tasting	FLIGHT
vintage	RECOLTA	slightly sparkling	PETILLANT
white	ALB	sweet wine from partially	
wine	VIN	dried grapes	STRAW-WINE
—cellar	PIVNITA	types	
—Russian		—Algerian	PINARD
champagne	SHAMPANSKOE	—American	
dry	SUKHOE	California	AHLGREN, BARBERA
factory	VINOZAVOD		BEAULIEU, BRANDER
pink	ROSOVOE		BUENA VISTA

CALLOWAY, CHAPPELLET
CHATEAU ST JEAN, CLOS DU BOIS
CRESTA BLANCA, CRIBARI, ESSENSIA
GALLO, HEITZ, INGLENOOK, FETZER
FELTON-EMPIRE, FIRESTONE, MARTINI
MASSON, MONDAVI, MONTICELLO
MOUNT PALOMAR, PARDUCCI, RIDGE
ROUDON-SMITH, SANFORD
SIERRA VISTA, SONOMA, ZACA MESA

East   CATAWBA
CHATEAU GRAND TRAVERS
HENRI MARCHANT, HERON HILL
LABRUSCA, LAKE COUNTRY
SCUPPERNONG

North-west   HAVILAND, QUAIL RUN
SALISHAN, ST CHAPELLE

—Australian   BLEASDALE, BUNDARRA
CHATEAU REMY, GRAND HERMITAGE
LAKE'S FOLLY, MOUNT BARKER
ORLANDO, PORPHYRY, ROTHBURY
ROXBURGH, RUTHERGLEN
QUELLTALER, SEPPELT
VASSE FELIX

—Austrian   GUMPOLDSKIRCHEN
HEURIGE, SCHLUCK

—Bulgarian   GAMZA, HEMUS, MELNIK
MISKET

—Corsican   MUSCATELLU, PATRIMONIO

—Cypriot   AFAMES, BELLAPAIS
COMMANDARIA
DOMAINE D'AHERA
NEGRO, OTHELLO
SEMELI, SHERRY

—Egyptian   CRU DES PTOLEMEES
OMAR KHAYYAM
REINE CLEOPATRE

—French   ANJOU, BARSAC, BEAUJOLAIS
BEAUNE, BORDEAUX, BURGUNDY
CHABLIS, CHAMBERTIN, CHAMPAGNE
CHATEAUNEUF-DU-PAPE, CHENAS
CHINON, FLEURIE, GIGONDAS, GRAVES
HERMITAGE, JULIENAS, LIRAC
MACON, MARGAUX, MEDOC, MERSAULT
MUSCADET, NUIT ST GEORGES
POMEROL, POMMARD, POUILLY-FUISSE
POUILLY-FUME, SANCERRE, SAUTERNES
ST EMILION, ST ESTEPHE, ST JULIEN
TAVEL, VOLNAY, VOUVRAY

—German   BACHARACH, BADEN
BERNKASTELER, FRANKEN
HOCK, JOHANNISBERGER
LIEBFRAUMILCH, MOSELBLUMCHEN
MOSEL(LE), MARCOBRUNNER
NIERSTEINER, PIESPORTER
RHEIN-WINE, RHINE(-WINE)
RUDESHEIMER, STEINBERGER

—Greek   AMINTAION, CHATEAU CARRAS
DEMESTICA, KOUTAKIS, KRASSI
LINDOS, MALVASIA, MALVASIE
MANTINIA, MAVRODAPHNE, METAXIS
NAOUSSA, RETSINA, RHODITIS
RO(M)BOLA, VERDEA

—Hungarian   BIKAVER, BULL'S BLOOD
ESSENCIA, HARSLEVELU
KEKFRANKOS, TOKAY

—Italian   ASTI (SPUMANTE), BARBERA
BARDOLINI, BAROLA, CHIANTI
FALERNIAN, FRASCATI, FRIULI
LACHRYMA CHRISTI, LAMBRUSCO
ORVIETO, SOAVE, TRENTINO
VALPOLICELLA, VERDICCHIO

—Lebanese   CHATEAU MUSAR

—Madeira   BUAL, MADEIRA
MALMSEY, SERCIAL, VERDELHO

—new wine   MUST

—New Zealand   BABICH, MONTANA
NOBILO

—North African   CHANTEBLED
CHATEAU FERIANI
CHATEAU MORNAG
CHATEAU THIBAR, CHELLAH
COTEAUX DE CARTHAGE
CUVEE DU PRESIDENT, GHARB
GRIS DE BOULAOUANE, MAGON
MUSCAT DE KELIBIA, RENAULT
SIDI SELEM, TARIK
ZAER, ZEMMOUR

—pink wine   BLUSH WINE, ROSE

—Portuguese   BUCELLAS, DAO, DOURO
LISBON, MADEIRA
MATEUS ROSE, PORT, SANTOS

—Romanian   BABEASCA, COTNARI, PERLA
SEGARCEA, SADOVA

—rosé   BLUSH WINE

—Russian   CHUMAI, GRATIESTI
GURDZHAANI, NAPAREVIL
NEGRU DE PURKAR, ROMANESTI
TETRA, TRIFESTI

—Sicilian   MARSALA, SETTESOLI

—South African   CONSTANTIA
FLEUR DU CAP
MEERLUST, ZANDVLEIT

—Spanish   ALICANT(E), JEREZ, MALAGA
MONTILLA, PETER-SEE-ME, RIOJA
SACK, SHERRY, TARRAGONA, TORO
VALENCIA, XERES

—sparkling wine   ASTI SPUMANTE
CHAMPAGNE, LAMBRUSCO
MOUSSEC, POMAGNE
VALPOLICELLA

—Swiss   DOLE, DORIN, ERMITAGE
FENDANT, GORON, HUMAGNE

	MALVOISIE, NOSTRANO	defect of vision	ASTIGMATISM
	PERLAN, SALVAGNIN	defective vision	ANOPIA
	SCHAFISER, TWANNER, VITI	deficiency	
—Turkish	BUZBAG, DIKMEN	—in oxygen	ANOXIA
	KOROGLU, TRAKYA	—of CO_2	ACAPNIA
—Yugoslav	BOGDANUSA, GRK, DINGAC	disinclined to read	ALITERATE
	MALVASIA, MARASTINA, OPOL	dwarfism without	
	PLAVAC, PLAVINA, POSIP	disproportion	ATELEIOSIS
	POSTUP, PROSEK, VUGAVA	failure to	
	VRANAC, ZILAVKA	—menstruate	AMENORRHOEA
unfortified wine	TABLE WINE	—secrete	
warm wine drink	BISHOP, MULL	milk	AGALACTIA
wine		urine	ANURIA
—waiter	SOMMELIER	having short stem	ACAULESCENT
—with		hopelessness	ANOMIE, ANOMY
blackcurrants	KIR	illiterate	ANALPHABEIC
eggs, etc	FLIP, FUSTIAN, NOG	imperfect development	AGENESIS
honey	OENOMEL	—of organ or part	APLASIA
juniper berries	GENEVRETTE	impermeability to	
lemon, etc	COBBLER	radiant heat	ATHERMANCY
milk	POSSET	inability	
spices	AQUA MIRABILIS	—of heart to empty itself	ASYSTOLE
	BISHOP, HIPPOCRAS, SANGAREE	—to	
	SANGRAI, WASSAIL	co-ordinate	
—Scott	PIGMENT	movements	ATAXIA, ATAXY
spirit, eggs, etc	EGG-FLIP	express thought in	
spirits added	FORTIFIED WINE	words	APHASIA
sugar and soda-water	BADMINTON	speak	ALOGIA
unpleasant taste	CORKED	swallow	APHAGIA, APHAGY
wormwood	VERMOUTH	understand spoken	
Wise Men	MAGI, BALTHAZAR,	or written words	APHASIA
	GASPAR(CASPAR), MELCHIOR	intermission of fever	APYREXIA
without		lack of	
meaning: absence of		—blood	ANAEMIA
deficiency of		—co-ordination	ASYNERGIA
failure of		in walking	ABASIA
lack of		—nervous energy	ANEURIA
lacking		—power	ADYNAMIA
loss of		—sense of	
minus		smell	ANOSMIA
want of, etc		touch	ANAPHIA
absence of		—strength	ADYNAMIA
—brain	ANCEPHALY	—syntactical sequence	ANACOLUTHIA
—emotion	APATHY	—understanding	ANOESIS
—feeling	ANAESTHESIA	—vitamins	AVITAMINOSIS
—law	ANARCHY	lawlessness	ANOMIA
—oxygen	ANAEROBIC	little or no change	AMETABOLOUS
—pain	ANALGESIA	loss of	
—passage in body	ATRESIA	—ability to manipulate	
—pulsation	ACROTISM	objects	APRAXIA
—thyroid gland	ATHYRIA	—appetite	ANOREXIA, ANOREXY
abstinence from food	ABROSIA	—feeling	ANAESTHESIA
absolute silence	ANACOUSTIC	—hair	ALOPECIA
calmness	ATARAXIA, ATARAXY	—honour	ATIMY
cessation of breathing	APNOEA	—memory	AMNESIA
deathlessness	ATHANASY	—power	

of		—animation	INANIMATE
—voluntary movement	AKINESIA	—astigmatism	ANASTIGMATIC
	AKINESIS	—awns	MUTICIOUS
—writing	AGRAPHIA	—beak	EROSTRATE
to read	ALEXIA	—being an image	ANICONIC
—sense of smell	ANOSMIA	—belief in God	ATHEISM
—speech	ALALIA, APHEMIA	—blame	INCULPABLE
—taste	AGEUSIA	—blood	EXSANGUINOUS
—voice	APHONIA, APHONY	—body	INCORPOREAL
making no angle	AGONIC	opening	ATRESIA
mental defectiveness	AMENTIA	—bracteoles	EBRACTEOLATE
never meeting	ASYMPTOTE	—bracts	EBRACTEATE
non-moral	AMORAL	—care(sloth)	ACEDIA
not		—cause	ACAUSAL
—arranged in belts	AZONAL	—central cylinder	ASTELY
—conforming to type	ATYPICAL	—change	INVARIABLE
—connected	ASYNARTETE	—children	ISSUELESS
—cyclic	ACYCLIC		SINE PROLE, SP
—divided into cells	ACELLULAR	—chromatic aberration	ACHROMATIC
—in rows	ASTICHOUS	—coelom	ACOELOMATE
—joined	AZYGOUS	—colour	ACHROMATIC
—liable to decay	ASEPTIC	—columns	ASTYLAR
—local	AZONIC	—congruousness	INCONCINNOUS
—periodic	APERIODIC	—conjunctions	ASYNDETON
—political	APOLITICAL	—consideration (law)	NUDE
—social	ASOCIAL	—date	SA
—standing in a		—defective vision	ANASTIGMATIC
fixed position	ASTATIC	—desire	INAPPETENT
—typical	ATYPICAL	—distinct	
—yoked	AZYGOUS	joints	ANARTHROUS
opposed to theology	ATHEOLOGY	margin	IMMARGINATE
reducing sexual desire	ANAPHRODISIAC	—disturbance	ATARAXIA, ATARAXY
rejection as spurious	ATHETESIS	—doubt	SINE DUBIO
sexless	ASEXUAL	—echo	ANECHOIC
stoppage of pulse	ASPHYXIA, ASPHYXY	—effect	INSIGNIFICANT, INVALID
straight	ATROPOUS	—end	ETERNAL, INFINITE
ungrammatical	ASYNTACTIC	—energy	ATONY
unknowableness	ACATALEPSY	—equality	IMPARITY
unleavened	AZYMOUS	—faith	NULLIFIDIAN
want of		—fault	IMPECCABLE
—power	ADYNAMY	—fear	IMPAVID
—strength	ADYNAMY	—feeling	INSENSATE
wasting away	ATROPHY	—feet	APODOUS
weakness of digestion	APEPSIA, APEPSY	—fever	APYREXIA, APYREXY
without		—fingers	ADACTYL
—a		—flavour	INSIPID
day fixed	SD, SINE DIE	—flowers	ANANTHOUS
head	ACEPHALOUS	—foresight	IMPROVIDENT
placenta	APLACENTAL	—form or shape	INFORM
septum	ASEPTATE	—free oxygen	ANAEROBI(OTI)C
skin	APELLOUS	—fruit	ACARPOUS
tail	AN(O)UROUS	—gills	ABRANCHIATE
—accent	ATONIC	—gravity	AGRAVIC
—albumen	EXALBUMINOUS	—hands	AMANOUS
—alteration	INVARIABLE	—harmony	ANHARMONIC
—anthers	ADESPOTA	—hinges	ECARDINATE

—hope	ANOMIE, ANOMY		—reverberation	ANECHOIC
—horns	ACEROUS, MOOLY		—ribs	ECOSTATE
	MUL(L)EY		—sap	EXSUCCOUS
—importance	INDIFFERENT		—sensation	INSENSATE
—inclination	ACLINIC		—sepals	ASEPALOUS
—indication	INDESIGNATE		—settled dwelling	NOMADIC, VAGRANT
—infection	ASEPTIC		—sex	ASEXUAL
—interest	INSIPID		—sexual desire	ANAPHRODISIAC
—irises	ANIRIDIA		—shadow	ASCIAN
—issue	SP, SINE PROLE		—shame	IMPRUDENT
—knowledge	NESCIENT		—smell	INODOROUS, ANOSMIC
—leaves	APHYLLOUS		—sound	ANACOUSTIC
—lens (eye)	APHACIA		—speech	OBMUTESCENT
—lid	INOPERCULATE		—spherical	
—life	AZOIC, EXANIMATE		aberration	APLANATIC
	INANIMATE		—spine	MUTICIOUS
—light	APHOTIC		—spirit	EXANIMATE, INANIMATE
—limbs	AMELIA			INSIPID
—liquid	ANEROID		—stalk	SESSILE
—logic	ALOGICAL		—stamens	ANANDROUS
—male issue	SMP		—stipules	EXSTIPULATE
—means of			—stomach	AGASTRIC
communication	INCOMMUNICADO		—strength	ASTHENIA
—method	IMMETHODICAL		—surviving issue	SPS
—milk	AGALAXY		—symmetry	ASYMMETRY
—mitosis	AMITOSIS		—synchronism	ASYNCHRONOUS
—modesty	IMPRUDENT		—tail	ECAUDATE
—money	BROKE, IMPECUNIOUS		—taste	INSIPID
—morals	IMMORAL		—teeth	EDENTATE, EDENTULOUS
—mouth	ASTOM(AT)OUS		—the article	ANARTHROUS
—movement	IMMOBILE		—thematic vowel	ATHEMATIC
—name	INNOMINATE		—thought	IMPROVIDENT
—nerves	ANEURIN		—tone	ATONIC
—nodes	ENODAL		—tongue	AGLOSSAL
—nucleus	ENUCLEATE		—transparency	OPAQUE
—offspring	ATOCIA		—turning	ATROPOUS
—operculum	INOPERCULATE		—understanding of	
—opposition	NEM CON		numbers	INNUMERATE
—pain	ANODYNE		words	ILLITERATE
—parasites	AXENIC		—validity	INVALID
—perception	AGNOSIA		—voice	ANAUDIA
—perianth	ACHLAMYDEOUS		—water	ANHYDROUS, NEAT
—permanence	IMPERMANENT		—weight	IMPONDERABLE
—personality	IMPERSONAL		—will	INTESTATE
—petals	APETALOUS		power	AB(O)ULIA
or sepals	ACHLAMYDEOUS		—willingness	NOLITION
—placenta	IMPLACENTAL		—wings	APTERAL, APTEROUS
—point	ASTIGMATIC, MUTICIOUS		—wisdom	INSIPIENT
—polarity	ASTATIC		**woman**	
—power	IMPOTENT		Australian woman	ADELAIDE, SHEILA
—probity	IMPROBITY		Dutch woman	FROW, VROUW
—proportion	INCONCINNOUS		Egyptian woman	BINT
—qualification	LAY		French woman	FEMME
—rays	ABACTINAL		German woman	FRAU
—religion	IRRELIGIOUS		Italian woman	DONNA
—restraint	IMMODEST		Spanish woman	MUJER

Women's		sun	HELIOLATRY
—Institute	WI	symbols	SYMBOLOLATRY
—Land Army	WLA	trees	DENDROLATRY
—Liberal Federation	WLF	Virgin Mary	MARIOLATRY
—Rural Institute	WRI	wealth	PLUTOLATRY
—Voluntary Service	WVS	wonders	THAUMATOLATRY
	(*see also* **girls**)	words	EPEOLATRY, LOGOLATRY
word		world	COSMOLATRY
word of four letters	QUADRILITERAL		(*see also* **belief**)
	TETRAGRAM	**write**	
word processor/processing	WP	including: description of	
words per minute	WPM	engraving	
	(*see also* **language**)	drawing (of)	
world		photograph (of)	
world bank	BIS	record (of)	
World Boxing Association	WBA	writing (about)	
World Boxing Council	WBC	3-D image	HOLOGRAPHY
World Championship Tennis	WCT	accidental omission	
World Council of Churches	WCC	of letter(s)	LIPOGRAPHY
World Health Organisation	WHO	adages	PAROEMIOGRAPHY
World Meteorological Organisation	WMO	ancient inscriptions	EPIGRAPHY
World Wildlife Fund	WWF	atmospheric conditions	AEROGRAPHY
worldwide	MONDIAL		METEOROGRAPHY
worship		bad	
including: reverence for		—spelling	PSEUDOGRAPHY
worship of		—writing	CACOGRAPHY
animal/human forms	THERIANTHROPISM	biography	PROSOPOGRAPHY
animals	THERIOLATRY	blood pressure	KYMOGRAPH
	ZOOLATRY	bones	OSTEOGRAPHY
angels	ANGELOLATRY	books	BIBLIOGRAPHY
books	BIBLIOLATRY	burnt-in photograph	PYROPHOTOGRAPH
Christ	CHRISTOLATRY	calculation chart	ABAC, NOMOGRAM
church forms and			NOMOGRAPH
traditions	ECCLESIOLATRY	ceramics	CERAMOGRAPHY
dead	NECROLATRY	cervix	CERVICOGRAPHY
devil	SATANISM	character representing	
Earth	GEOLATRY	sound	PHONOGRAPH
fetishes	FETICHISM, FETISHISM	chemical anaylsis by	
fire	PYROLATRY	electrolysis	POLAROGRAPHY
fish	ICHTHYOLATRY	ciphers	STEGANOGRAPHY
heavenly host	SABAISM	colour	
horses	HIPPOLATRY	—analysis	CHROMATOGRAPHY
idols	IDOLATRY, IDOLISM	—frequencies	SPECTROGRAPH
images	ICONOLATRY	—printing	CHROMOLITHOGRAPHY
Luther	LUTHEROLATRY		CHROMOTYPOGRAPHY
man	ANTHROPOLATRY		CHROMOXYLOGRAPHY
nature	PHYSIOLATRY	contour feathers	PTERYLOGRAPHY
nobility	LORDOLATRY	copying	MIMEOGRAPH
one god	MONOLATRY		PANTOGRAPHY
sacred things	HIEROLATRY	—drawings	EIDOGRAPHY
saints	HAGIOLATRY, HIEROLATRY	correct writing	ORTHOGRAPHY
self	AUTOLATRY	dancing	CHORE(O)GRAPHY
Shakespeare	BARDOLATRY	death	THANATOGRAPHY
snakes	OPHIOLATRY	description of	
stars	ASTROLATRY	—nature	PHYSIOGRAHPY
stone	LITHOLATRY	—skin	DERMATOGRAPHY

descriptive		image using radio-isotope	
—astronomy	URANOGRAPHY	in specimen	AUTORADIOGRAPH
—biography	PROSOPOGRAPHY	inscriptions	EPIGRAPHY
dictionaries	LEXICOGRAPHY	interwoven letters	MONOGRAM
diseases	NOSOGRAPHY	laws	NOMOGRAPHY
	PATHOGRAPHY	life	
distant thunderstorms	KERAUNOGRAPHY	—and writings	BIOBIBLIOGRAPHY
document wholly		—of individual	BIOGRAPHY, BIOSCOPE
written by author	NOMOGRAPH		PROSOPOGRAPHY
drawing spirals	HELICOGRAPHY	light image	PHOTOGRAPHY
Earth	CHOROGRAPHY	lithography in	
	GEOGRAPHY	colour	CHROMOLITHOGRAPHY
	TOPOGRAPHY	magnetic variations	MAGNETOGRAPH
electrically-charged		magnified photograph	MICROPHOTOGRAPH
powder	XEROGRAPHY	many copies	POLYGRAPH
electrolytic		map-making	CARTOGRAPHY
determination of		—from aerial	
ion concentration	POLAROGRAPHY	photographs	PHOTOGRAMMETRY
electrotype copying	GLYPHOGRAPHY	meteorological records	AEROGRAPHY
elevation drawing	ORTHOGRAPHY		METEOROGAPHY
ellipses	ELLIPSOGRAPH	mimes	MIMOGRAPHY
engraving		minerals	ORYCTOGRAPHY
—from stone	LITHOGRAPHY	Moon	SELENOGRAPHY
—on		motion pictures	CINEMATOGRAPHY
brass	CHALCOGRAPHY		KINEMATOGRAPHY
copper	CHALCOGRAPHY	—through	
gemstones	GLYPTOGRAPHY	microscope	CINEMICROGRAPHY
stones, etc	EPIGRAPHY	mountains	OR(E)OGRAPHY
	LITHOGRAPHY	movement	
wood	XYLOGRAPHY	—or duration	CHRONOGRAPHY
—photographically	HELIOGRAPHY	—of heart	CARDIOGRAPHY
	HELIOGRAVURE	muscular contractions	MYOGRAPHY
enlarged photograph	PHOTOMICROGRAPHY	myths in art	MYTHOGRAPHY
exact copy	APOGRAPH	natural wonders	THAUMATOGRAPHY
false writing	PSEUDOGRAPH	nature	PHYSIOGRAPHY
features of Mars	AREOGRAPHY	notation for dances	ORCHESOGRAPHY
fine writing	CALLIGRAPHY	obituaries	NECROGRAPHY
fishes	ICTHYOGRAPHY	old manuscripts	PALAEOGRAPHY
fluid pressure	KYMOGRAPH	oil paint on stone	LITHOCHROMATICS
fossils	ORYCTOGRAPHY	omission of letters	LIPOGRAPHY
gamma-ray photography	SCINTIGRAPHY	one subject	MONOGRAPH
geography	CHOROGRAPHY	opinions of	
—of living things	BIOGEOGRAPHY	philosophers	DOXOGRAPHY
ground plans	ICHNOGRAPHY	organs of plants	
handwriting	CH(E)IROGRAPHY	or animals	ORGANOGRAPHY
heart movements	CARDIOGRAPHY	original manuscript	AUTOGRAPH
heat	THERMOGRAPHY	perspective drawing	SCENOGRAPHY
height of land	HYPSOGRAPHY	phonetic typewriting	STENOTYPY
	TOPOGRAPHY	photograph of sun by	
—and depth of water	BATHYOROGRAPHY	monochromatic light	SPECTROHELIOGRAPH
human		photographic	
—population	DEMOGRAPHY	—engraving	HELIOGRAPH
—races	ETHNOGRAPHY		HELIOGRAVURE
hymns	HYMNOGRAPHY	—impression on	
ideography	PASIGRAPHY	wood block	PHOTOXYLOGRAPHY
illustration	ICONOGRAPHY	zinc plate	PHOTOZINCOGRAPHY

photography	
—by	
gamma rays	SCINTIGRAPHY
short wave	RADIOGRAPHY
split laser	HOLOGRAPHY
—of	
cyclic	
movement	CHRONOCYCLOGRAPHY
manuscripts	ROTOGRAPHY
moving objects	CHRONOPHOTOGRAPHY
	(see also separate entry)
physical geography	PHYSIOGRAPHY
picture-writing	HYPERGRAPHY
	IDEOGRAPHY, PICTOGRAPHY
planet Mars	AREOGRAPHY
poker work	PYROGRAPHY
population	DEMOGRAPHY
pottery	CERAMOGRAPHY
printing	TYPOGRAPHY
—from	
photograph	PHOTOLITHOGRAPHY
stone	LITHOGRAPHY
—with whole words	
cast in type	LOGOGRAPHY
private mark	IDIOGRAPH
proverbs	PAROEMIOGRAPHY
quick writing	STENOGRAPHY
radiography	ROENTGENOGRAPHY
reproduction of	
transmitted drawings	TELAUTOGRAPHY
reversed image	ROTOGRAPH
rocks	ORYCTOGRAPHY
	PETROGRAPHY
relationship between	
members of a group	SOCIOGRAM
sacred symbols	HIEROGRAM
	HIEROGRAPH
scene painting	SCENOGRAPHY
seas	OCEANOGRAPHY
secret writing	CRYPTOGRAPHY
	STEGANOGRAPHY
sexual perversion	PORNOGRAPHY
shape of mouldings	CYMOGRAPH
shorthand	BRACHYGRAPHY
	STENOGRAPHY
	TACHYGRAPHY
showing	
—resemblances of	
individuals in group	DENDOGRAM
—wear in machinery	FERROGRAM
sign for whole phrase	PHRASEOGRAPH
signature	AUTOGRAPH
signed by all parties	SYNGRAPH
silk-screen printing	SERIGRAPHY
skin	DERMATOGRAPHY
sound vibration	PHONOAUTOGRAPH

spirit-writing	PSYCHOGRAPHY
spoken sound	PHONOGRAPHY
stars and galaxies	URANOGRAPHY
still-life pictures	RHYPAROGRAPHY
Sun	CORONAGRAPHY
	CORONOGRAPHY
symbol representing	
thing itself	IDEOGRAM, IDEOGRAPH
symbolic writing	IDEOGRAPHY
	SYMBOLOGRAPHY
teeth	ODONTOGRAPHY
three	
—dimensional picture	STEREOGRAPH
	VECTOGRAPH
—letters, one sound	TRIGRAPH
tides	MARIGRAPHY
topography	CHOROGRAPHY
trade mark	IDIOGRAPH
transmission of	
—drawings etc, by	
telegraphy	PHOTOTELEGRAPHY
—messages by electric	
impulses	TELEGRAPHY
two letters, one sound	DIGRAPH
unintentional repetition	
in copying	DITTOGRAPHY
using oil-film	EVAPOROGRAPH
vibrations	VIBROGRAPH
voluminous writing	POLYGRAPHY
wind pressure and speed	ANEMOGRAPHY
world	COSMOGRAPHY
woven in coloured silk	STEVENGRAPH
writing	
—on	
both sides	OPISTHOGRAPHY
one subject	MONOGRAPH
wax	CEROGRAPHY
—with stylus	STYLOGRAPHY
written	
—character	IDEOGRAM, IDEOGRAPH
—cyphers	CRYPTOGRAPHY
wrong words	PARAGRAPHIA
X-rays	(see separate entry)

writers

American (m)   ARDREY, ASIMOV, BALDWIN
BELLOW, BRODSKY, BRZEZINSKI
BURROUGHS, CAPOTE, CHANDLER, COHN
CREELEY, DE VRIES, DICK, DOS PASSOS
FAULKNER, FIEDLER, FITZGERALD
GARLAND, GINSBERG, GOODMAN
HAMMETT, HAWTHORNE, HEMINGWAY
HIGGINS, HOWELLS, JAMES, KENEALLY
KEROUAC, KNIGHT, KRISTOL
LONDON, MACDONALD
MAILER, MELVILLE, MENCKEN, MILLER
NORRIS, O'HARA, POE, POHL, POIRIER

ROBBINS, ROSENBERG, ROTH, RUMAKER
RUNYON, SANTAYANA, SAROYAN
SILVERBERG, SINCLAIR, SINGER
SONTAG, SPILLANE, STEINBECK, STOW
THOREAU, TOFFLER, TRILLING
TWAIN, UPDIKE, VIDAL, WATTS, WHITMAN
WILLIAMSON, WILSON, WOLFE

(f)	GARNER, HANRAHAN
	JOLLEY, STEIN
Argentinian	BORGES, TORRE
Australian (m)	CLARKE, FURPHY

LAWSON, PATTERSON
RICHARDSON, WHITE

(f)	ASTLEY, FRANKLIN

MCCULLOUGH, STEAD

Austrian	ARTMANN, BAYER, FRIED, KAFKA

RUHM, WERFEL

Belgian	MAETERLINCK, SIMENON
British (m)	ADDISON, ALDINGTON, ALDISS

AMIS, ARCHER, ARNOLD, BALLARD
BARSTOW, BENNETT, BIRRELL, BLAIR
BRADBURY, BRAINE, BROPHY, BUCHAN
BURGESS, BURNS, CALDER, CARLYLE
CHAUCER, CHESTERTON, CHURCHILL
CHUTE, CLARKE, COLLINS, CONGREVE
CONNOLLY, CONRAD, CREASEY, DAHL
DEFOE, DENNIS, DICKENS, DRYDEN
DURRELL, FIELDING, FLEMING, FORD
FORSTER, FORSYTHE, FOWLES
GALSWORTHY, GARNETT, GISSING
GOLDING, GOLDSMITH, GRAY
GREEN, GREENE, HAGGARD, HARDY
HAZLITT, HEPPENSTALL, HIGGINS
HOPKINS, HUXLEY, INNES, ISHERWOOD
JOHNSON, KENT, KINGSLEY, KIPLING
KOESTLER, LAMB, LANG, LAWRENCE
LE CARRE, LEE, LEHMANN, LEWIS
LODGE, LUDLUM, MAUGHAM, MACLEAN
MEREDITH, MILNE, MILTON, MOORE, NAIRN
NORMAN, ORWELL, PAUL, PEACOCK
PEAKE, PEPYS, POWELL, PRIESTLEY
READE, RUSKIN, RUSSELL, SANSOM
SCOTT, SHAKESPEARE, SILLITOE
SMOLLETT, SNOW, SPENSER, STERNE
STEVENSON, STOREY, STRACHEY
STRONG, SWIFT, THACKERAY, THWAITE
TOLKIEN, TROLLOPE, VERNE, WAIN
WALLACE, WALPOLE, WARNER, WAUGH
WELLS, WILSON, WODEHOUSE

(f)	ALLINGHAM, AUSTEN

BAINBRIDGE, BOWEN, BRONTE
CARTLAND, CHRISTIE, CROMPTON
DU MAURIER, ELLIOT, GASKELL
HEYER, HIGHSMITH, INNES, JAMES
LEHMANN, LESSING, MURDOCH
POTTER, RENDELL, RICHARDSON

SAYERS, SPARK, TAYLOR, WELDON
WEST, WOOLF

Bulgarian	CANETTI
Chilean	NARUDA
Cuban	RODRIGUEZ
Czech	CAPEK, HASEK, HAVEL, SEIFERT
Danish	ANDERSON
dramatists	(see separate entry)
Egyptian	MAHFOUZ
Finnish	SILLANPAA
French (m)	ARAGON, ARRABAL, BALZAC

BAUDELAIRE, BENDA, BERNANOS
BRETON, BUTOR
CAMUS, CHAMFLEURY, CHAMSON
COCTEAU, CORNEILLE, DAUDET
DE MAISTRE, DE SADE
DU JARDIN, DUGARD, DUHAMEL
DUMAS, D'URFE, FLAUBERT
FONTANELLE, FRANCE
GAUTIER, GENET, GIDE, GIRAUDOUX
GONCOURT, HUGO, HUYSMANS, LARBAUD
LAUGIER, MALRAUX, MARTIN
MAUPASSANT, MAURIAC, PERSE, PICABIA
PONGE, PROUST, RABELAIS, RACINE
RIMBAUD, ROBBE-GRILLET, ROLLAND
ROMAINS, ROUSSEL, SARTRE
SIMON, SOLLERS, SOREL, STENDAHL
VOLTAIRE, ZOLA

(f)	COLETTE, SAND, SAGAN

SARRAUTE

German	BALL, BENJAMIN, BENN

BOBROWSKI, BOLL, DOBLIN
FALLADA, FONTANE
GOETHE, GRASS, HARDENBERG
HERDER, HESSE, HOFFMANN, JENS
JOHNSON, JUNGER, LEWIN, KAFKA
KASTNER, KIPPHARDT, KISCH
LESSING, MANN
NOVALIS, PAQUET, PFEMFERT
RAABE, RENN, RICHTER, SCHILLER
SCHREYER, SPENGLER, SUDERMANN
TIECK, WALDEN, WEISS, WILLE

Ghanaian	ARMAH
Greek	AESCHYLUS, ARISTOPHANES

ELYTIS, EURIPIDES
SEFERIS, SOPHOCLES

Guatemalan	ASTURIAS
Hungarian	KOESTLER, NORDAU
Icelandic	LAXNESS
Irish (m)	BEHAN, JOYCE, MOORE
(f)	O'BRIEN
Israeli	AGNON
Italian	CALVINO, CAPUNANA

D'ANNUNZIO, LAMPEDUSA
MACHIAVELLI, MONTALE
MORAVIA, QUASIMODO, SILONE

	TRANQUILLI, VERGA
Japanese	KAWABATA, MISHIMA
Kenyan	THIONG'O
Martinician	CESAIRE
Mexican	FUENTES, MARQUEZ, RULFO
New Zealand (m)	CURNOW, DAVIN, GEE
	HULME, HYDE, IHIMAERA
	SARGESON, SHADBOLT
	(f) FRAME, MANSFIELD, MARSH
Nigerian	ACHEBE, EKWENSI
	OKIGBO, SAYINKA, TUTUOLA
poets	*(see separate entry)*
Polish	BRZEZINSKI, MILOSZ
Puerto Rican	JIMINEZ
Russian (m)	ANDREYEV, BELY, BUGAKOV
	CHEKHOV, DOSTOEVSKY
	EHRENBURG
	FEDIN, GASTEV, GOGOL, GORKY
	GRUZDEV, IVANOV, KAVERIN
	LUNACHARSKY, LUNTS, NABOKOV
	NIKITIN, OSTROVSKY, PASTERNAK
	POZNER, PUSHKIN
	SELYUNIN, SHKLOVSKY, SHOLOKHOV

	SLONIMSKY, SOLZHENITSYN
	TIKHONOV, TOLSTOY, TURGENEV
	ZAMYATIN, ZOSHCHENKO
	(f) POLONSHAYA
Somali	FARAH
South African (m)	COETZEE, FUGARD
	PATON, SMITH
	(f) GORDIMER, HEAD
Spanish	ALEXANDRE, CARRERE, CELA
	CERVANTES, GOYTISOLO, LORCA
	PARMENO, PINILLOS, TORRE
Swedish	IBSEN, JOHNSON, LAGERQUIST
	MARTINSON, STRINDBERG
	WEISS, ZACHS
Swiss	CENDRARS, SISMONDI
West Indian (m)	DE BOISSIERE, HARRIS
	HEARNE, JAMES, LAMMING
	LOVELACE, MAIS, MCKAY, MENDES
	MITTELHOLZER, REID, SELVEN
	STOMER
	(f) BENNETT
Yugoslav	ANDIC

X-ray	RADIOGRAM, SKIAGRAPH
of	
—bile ducts	CHOLANGIOGRAPHY
—blood vessels	ANGIOGRAPHY
	ARTERIOGRAPHY
—bones	OSTEOGRAPHY
—brain	ENCEPALOGRAPHY
	VENTRICULOGRAPHY
—breast	MAMMOGRAPHY
—gall bladder	CHOLANGIOGRAPHY
—kidneys	PYELOGRAPHY
—layer of body	TOMOGRAPHY
—lymph glands	LYMPHOGRAPHY
—salivary duct	SIALOGRAPHY
—spinal cord	MYELOGRAPHY
—urinary tract	UROGRAPHY
photography	ROENTGENOGRAPHY
xerography	XERORADIOGRAPHY
xanthium	BURDOCK, BUR-MARIGOLD
	CLOTBUR, CLOTE
Xantippe	SHREW
Xeres	SHERRY

yachting

classes	CENTAUR, CHS, CONTESSA
	DARING, DRAGON
	ETCHELL'S, FLYING DUTCHMAN
	FLYING FIFTEEN, FOLKBOAT, FOURTEEN
	HALF-TONNER, IOR, J-CLASS
	LIGHTWAVE, MERMAID, MINI-TWELVE
	OYSTER, REDWING, SEVEN
	SIGMA, SIX-METRE
	SOLING, SONATA, SPRING, SQUIB
	SUNBEAM, SUNBIRD, SWALLOW, TOPPER
	TORNADO, TWELVE-METRE
	TYPHOON, ULTRA
	VICTORY, XOD
races	AMERICA'S CUP, FASTNET
	RORC CHANNEL RACE
	WHITBREAD ROUND THE WORLD
	WHITBREAD TRANSATLANTIC
round-the-world	
sailors	BLYTH, CHICHESTER
	EDWARDS(f), JAMES(f), FRANCIS(f)
	KNOX-JOHNSTON, SLOCUM
venues	
—Australia	SYDNEY
—England	COWES, HAYLING ISLAND
	LYMINGTON, POOLE, SWANSEA
—Ireland	COUNTY DOWN, DUBLIN
	DUNLOGHAIRE
—Italy	PONTECERVO
—Mediterranean	SARDINIA
—Netherlands	HOORH
—Pacific	HAWAII
—Sweden	MARSTRAND
yacht-club president	COMMODORE

Yemen	ADEN
capital	SANA'A
coin	DINAR, FILS, RI(Y)AL
Yiddish	(*see* **Hebrew**)
Yugoslavia	YU
capitals	BELGRADE, BEOGRAD
	LJUBLJANA, SARAJEVO
	SKOPJE, ZAGREB
coins	DINAR, DNR, PARA
countries (former republics)	BOSNIA(-HERZEGOVINA)
	CROATIA, MACEDONIA
	SLOVENIA
republics	KOSSOVO, MONTENEGRO
	SERBIA, VOIVODINA
federation of villages	ZUPA
governor	ZUPAN
kebabs	CEVAPCICI
newsagency	TANJUG
parliament	SKUPSHTINA
province	BANAT

Z

Zaire	ZR	crab	CANCER
capital	KINSHASHA, LEOPOLDVILLE	fishes	PISCES
coins	LIKUTA, SENGI, ZAIRE	goat	CAPRICORN(US)
Zambia	Z	lion	LEO
capital	LUSAKA	ram	ARIES
coins	KWA(T)CHA, NGWEE	scorpion	SCORPIO
Zamenhof's language	ESPERANTO	twins	GEMINI
Zantippe (Zentippe)	SHREW	virgin	VIRGO
Zanzibar	EAZ	water-carrier	AQUARIUS
Zimbabwe	ZW	**zoological regions**	
capital	HARARE, SALISBURY	Arctic region	ARCTOGAEA
coins	CENT, DOLLAR	Australasian region	NOTOGAEA
Zodiac (signs)		Neotropical region	NEOGAEA
archer	SAGITTARIUS	region of the bear	ARCTOGAEA
balance	LIBRA	southern region	NOTOGAEA
bull	TAURUS	tropical America	NEOGAEA

Other Crossword books

Sunday Express Complete Guide to Cryptic Crosswords
J. A. Coleman

The ideal book for the crossword puzzler, from the novice who knows in theory what cryptic puzzles are all about to more expert practitioners. It covers the whole subject of cryptic crosswords in detail with the different types of cryptic clue and shows how to interpret and solve them.
£12.99

Sunday Express Crossword Dictionary
Gillian Clark

Designed to allow you to compete with compilers on equal terms, this dictionary is a valuable aid to solving all types of crossword: cryptic, definitional and general knowledge. It contains approximately 70,000 words organised in 125 major thematic categories.
£4.99

Eric Dobby Reference Books